AN INTRODUCTION TO CLASSICAL ECONOMETRIC THEORY

Paul A. Ruud
University of California, Berkeley

New York • Oxford
OXFORD UNIVERSITY PRESS
2000

Oxford University Press

Oxford New York
Athens Auckland Bangkok Bogotá Buenos Aires Calcutta
Cape Town Chennai Dar es Salaam Delhi Florence Hong Kong Istanbul
Karachi Kuala Lumpur Madrid Melbourne Mexico City Mumbai
Nairobi Paris São Paulo Singapore Taipei Tokyo Toronto Warsaw

and associated companies in
Berlin Ibadan

Published by Oxford University Press, Inc.,
198 Madison Avenue, New York, New York, 10016
http://www.oup-usa.org

Library of Congress Cataloging-in-Publication Data

Ruud, Paul Arthur.
An introduction to classical econometric theory / Paul A. Ruud.
p. cm.
Includes bibliographical references and index.
ISBN 0-19-511164-8
1. Econometrics. I. Title.
HB139.R88 2000
330'.01'5195—dc21 99-089456

Printing (last digit): 9 8 7 6 5 4 3

Printed in the United States of America
on acid-free paper

CONTENTS

LIST OF FIGURES

LIST OF TABLES

PREFACE

My purpose in writing this textbook is to provide graduate students with an introduction to classical econometric theory. Econometric theory is the collection of mathematical ideas and principles that motivates much of the empirical analysis by economists. The term *classical* refers to analyzing data as the outcome of repeatable experiments. To introduce this material to graduate students, I have followed a particular pedagogical approach.

I have striven to develop the material in a natural order for the *introduction* of ideas and their foundations. After we have mastered a theory, our internalization of that theory often follows its logic. Certain lemmas come before a principal proposition because the lemmas hold intermediate results. When I began teaching econometrics as a professor at Berkeley, I used such an ordering in my lectures. My experience has taught me to introduce and motivate the principal proposition first. The chapters of this book use this same approach. Hence, intuition and motivation appear at the outset. Empirical illustrations often open a chapter, whereas technical arguments and proofs tend to appear in closing sections.

To provide reference points for students, I have organized this textbook around a few unifying principles. *Mathematical projection* is the primary theoretical principle. The familiar geometry of the ordinary least-squares fit introduces this principle. It reappears in partitioned regression, restricted regression, the conditional expectation, the population projection, generalized least squares, instrumental variables, and the relative efficiency of estimators. The *latent variable model* is the primary econometric modeling pinciple. One moves from such statistical concepts as the conditional expectation to such economic concepts as the demand function through the conceptual framework of latent variables.

This textbook focuses on econometrics, treating introductory linear algebra, calculus, probability, and statistics as prerequisites. Nevertheless, several appendices contain summaries of this foundational material. These appendices are handy references but introductory texts are my recommended source for learning.

To explore this book superficially I invite the reader to leaf through the text, reading the prefaces and overviews of each of the four parts and the chapter overviews. The overviews appear at the end of each part or chapter and provide numbered lists of the important points.

I am grateful to many people for invaluable help with writing this textbook. Most directly, I have benefitted from the support of my wife Valerie, my office assistants, Grace Katagiri and Michelle Mains, my graduate student assistant Petra Geraats, and my editor Ken MacLeod. David Romer, James Stock, and Mark Watson all generously contributed to several of the empirical examples. Prinicipal among those who reviewed portions of manuscripts were Eva Balslev, David Belsley, Axel Boersch-Supan, Steven Bond, Richard Carson, John Chipman, Bronwyn Hall, Erik Heitfield, David Hendry, Kris Lybecker, Bent Nielsen, Dale Poirier, James Powell, Thomas Rothenberg, and Douglas Steigerwald. Nuffield College kindly provided the ideal home away from home for much of my writing.

Berkeley, California

To obtain data sets, computer programs, copies of figures, errata, and answers to frequent questions visit the internet site at *http://elsa.berkeley.edu/users/ruud/cet/_*. Professors will also be able to retrieve suggested answers to the exercises.

PART I

ORDINARY LEAST SQUARES

Econometrics concerns the analysis of data describing economic phenomena. Economic data come almost exclusively from nonexperimental sources. Social scientists generally must accept the conditions under which their subjects act and the responses occur. These researchers cannot specify or choose the level of a stimulus and then record the outcome. They can just observe the natural experiments that take place.

For example, many economists have studied the influence of monetary policy on macroeconomic conditions, yet the effects of actions by central banks continue to be widely debated. If a central bank could experiment with monetary policy over repeated trials under identical conditions, economists might be able to isolate the effects of policy more accurately. This would remove some of the controversies.

However, no one can turn back the clock to try various policies under essentially the same conditions. Each time a central bank contemplates an action, it faces a new set of conditions. The actors and technologies have all changed. The social, economic, and political orders are different. To learn about one aspect of the economic world, one must take into account many others. To apply past experience effectively, one must take into account similarities and differences between the past, present, and future.

In the simplest experimental setting, a researcher can repeat an experiment under two predetermined settings of a single stimulus to measure the effect of the change in stimulus. By holding everything else constant, one isolates a particular effect of interest. Consider the situation of an economist who wants to measure the effect of gender or race on earnings. It is ludicrous to imagine the economist changing the race or sex of a large group of otherwise identical individuals in order to observe the change in their earnings. Instead, one must examine the variation in earnings observable across a heterogeneous mixture of working adults with different levels of education, different native abilities, and different levels of work experience, as well as different genders and races. Untangling race or gender variation in earnings is a difficult research goal.

In the next four chapters we introduce the method of ordinary least-squares linear regression. This is the primary way economists try to isolate such variation as the variation in earnings associated with gender and the variation in prices associated with the discount rate of the central bank.

Our introduction will focus on the properties of ordinary least-squares regression that hold no matter what data are studied with this tool. Hence, researchers can rely upon these properties in every setting. In addition, these properties have analogues in the statistical analysis that follows in Part II. We will use the analogies to organize concepts and to emphasize differences between statistical properties and those we are about to discuss in Part I.

We will use several concepts from linear algebra that the reader should have encountered before: linear vector space, linear dependence, basis, dimension, inner product, length, and orthogonality.[1] This list will look technical and threatening to some eyes. Those who have found linear algebra difficult may discover that the material in these chapters helps to make these concepts easier. We will use these concepts and the associated matrix notation, including matrix multiplication, transposes, and inverses, to express solutions to systems of linear equations.

[1] For reference, see Appendix C.

CHAPTER 1

THE LEAST-SQUARES LINEAR FIT

Actual examples frequently introduce new ideas better than abstract descriptions and so we launch our study of econometrics with an analysis of the earnings of individuals. This analysis illustrates one of the basic methods economists use to decompose the variation in a variable, in this case earnings, into covariation with such other variables as years of education, years of experience, gender, or race. The decomposition is a useful way to summarize observable patterns among a set of variables, comparable to using the sample average to describe the central value of a single variable. In data describing economic phenomena, one often seeks such decomposition to account for coincidental variation in factors that ideally would be constant over the observations.

1.1 EARNINGS AND ATTRIBUTES OF WORKERS

Labor economists frequently study the determinants of earnings or wages. Discrimination by employers, the effectiveness of unions, and the path of wages over time are examples of the influences that motivate such study. We will examine a data set provided by the U. S. Bureau of the Census to motivate the use of a common tool in these investigations, a method called *ordinary least squares*. Economists use this basic method to explore multivariate relationships and we use ordinary least squares to introduce econometrics.

We extracted our data from the Current Population Survey (CPS) of March 1995, restricting the sample to people in the employed labor force, aged 18 to 65.[1] We excluded those people employed by the Armed Forces, self-employed, or working without payment. The summary statistics in Table 1.1 give a casual description of the variables in this data set of 1289 observations. The variable called "Wage" measures average hourly earnings. For employees who are not paid by the hour, the wage is computed as the ratio of weekly earnings to the usual hours worked per week. This definition explains the extremely low minimum of $0.84 per hour. The variable "Education" is the years of school attended by the individual. We see that most people in this

[1] We give a detailed explanation in Section 1.6.

Table 1.1
Summary Statistics

Variable	Average	Standard Deviation	Minimum	Maximum
Wage	12.37	7.90	0.84	64.08
Education	13.15	2.81	0.00	20.00
Experience	18.79	11.66	0.00	56.00
Age	37.93	11.49	18.00	65.00
Female	0.50	0.50	0.00	1.00
Nonwhite	0.15	0.36	0.00	1.00
Union member	0.16	0.37	0.00	1.00

data set finished high school, but that there is considerable variation in education as well. The minimum level of education was zero years in school and 20 is the highest recorded level of education. This variable is "top coded" so that the value 20 actually represents 20 *or more* years of schooling.[2] There is also much variation in age and work experience, which ranges from zero to 55 years. The last three variables in the table deserve special comment: Female, Nonwhite, and Union Member. These are *indicator* variables that equal either zero or one.[3] These variables *indicate* whether an individual possesses a particular characteristic. Conveniently, the average of such variables is the fraction of observations with the characteristic. For example, 50% of the people in the sample are female.

On first inspection of a set of data, it is natural to ask whether this sample appears to be representative of a population of workers. Are as many as 16% unionized and as few as 15% nonwhite? Is a minimum observed average wage of only $0.84 reasonable? We can find information easily on some factors. According to the *Economic Report of the President 1996*, in 1995 15% of the civilian workers were nonwhite and 46% were female.[4] Average hourly earnings in private nonagricultural industries was $11.46.[5] An approximate average age for the general population between 20 and 64 years old is 39.83 years.[6] Although average hourly earnings appear to be a bit high in the sample, we find general agreement.

A starting point for studying wage discrimination and union effects is to compare the sample means of different groups. In Table1.2, we list the differences in sample means for men and women, whites and nonwhites, and union members and others. The differences are all large and statistically significant, assuming a normal distribution for wages. The last column of Table 1.2 gives the standard t-statistic for testing the null hypothesis of equal means, assuming unequal

[2] We coded the education variable from responses to a question with categorical answers. For those students who enter doctorate programs immediately after receiving their B.A. degree, we specified 4 years to complete a Ph.D. degree. See Section 1.6. Obviously, many programs take longer. Perhaps the reader is familiar with such a program.

[3] "Dummy" variable is also a common name for indicator variables. One can only speculate as to why.

[4] Table B-33, *Civilian employment by demographic characteristic, 1954–95* and Table B-32, *Civilian employment and unemployment by sex and age, 1947–95.*

[5] Table B-43, *Hours and earnings in private nonagricultural industries, 1959–95.*

[6] This is a weighted average based on the figures in Table B-30, *Population by age group, 1929–95*. There are several reasons we expect this average to be higher than the sample average. First, the age range is older, omitting 18 and 19 year olds. Second, the age groups are 20–24, 25–44, and 45–64 and we took midpoints of these intervals to compute the average. Third, the working adult population is probably younger than the general population.

Table 1.2
Average Wage by Group

Group	Average	Standard Deviation	Difference	Sample Size	Test Statistic
Men	14.119	8.415		648	
Women	10.594	6.902	3.525	641	8.227
White	12.794	8.141		1092	
Nonwhite	9.990	5.842	2.804	197	5.798
Union	14.222	5.901		205	
Nonunion	12.015	8.174	−2.207	1084	4.586

variances. In this sample, men receive wages that are \$3.53 per hour higher than women, whites receive \$2.80 more than nonwhites, and union members receive \$2.21 more than those who do not belong to unions.

Simple differences in averages are somewhat misleading about the levels associated with each contrast. There is systematic variation in the characteristics of each group that confound the divergence in wages. Consider, for example, the contrast in union membership rates among men and women: 19% of the men in the sample are members of unions whereas only 13% of the women are. The racial composition of men and women is also quite distinct: 86% of the men are white but 83% of the women are white. These percentages come from the figures in Table 1.3. The average difference in wage between men and women almost certainly reflects union membership and racial differences, as well as gender. And union and racial differences in wages surely reflect gender differences also.

In addition, the groups differ in educational levels attained and years of job experience. Setting aside wage variation associated with gender, race, and union membership, we expect wages to vary with education and experience. Both higher education and higher experience generally coincide with higher wages. Table 1.4 summarizes education and experience by group. In this sample, women are less educated and less experienced than men; whites are more educated and more experienced than nonwhites; and nonunion workers have about the same education but are much less experienced than union members.

Ignoring the other characteristics of individuals, we can look at the association between wages and education or experience. Figure 1.1 shows a scatter plot of observed wage versus education level. The figure also displays average wage, for each year of education. There is a clear pattern of rising average wage with education, although there is also a lot of variation around

Table 1.3
Composition of Sample

Gender	Race	Nonunion	Union
Men	White	461	98
	Nonwhite	63	26
Women	White	471	62
	Nonwhite	89	19

Table 1.4
Education and Experience by Group

Group	Average Education	Average Experience
Men	13.233	19.052
Women	13.056	18.524
White	13.249	18.983
Nonwhite	12.569	17.716
Union	13.171	22.927
Nonunion	13.140	18.007

the averages. In Figure 1.2 we plot wage versus experience, for both the individual data points and for the average within groups spanning 6 years of experience. On average wages rise and then fall with experience. This pattern is plausible. Therefore, we conclude that wages apparently vary systematically with education and experience in these data as well.

In Table 1.5 we give another description of the covariation among the variables in the data set, the correlation coefficients for pairs of variables. The first column shows what we have already seen: wage is positively correlated with education, experience, and union membership and negatively correlated with being female and nonwhite. In addition, we also observe an extremely high correlation between age and experience. It is not surprising to find that education and experience are negatively correlated: those who leave school sooner will tend to have more work experience. Although the correlations are small, several other features among the variables noted earlier are borne out by the signs of the correlations. For example, union membership and experience are positively correlated and we saw that on average union members have more experience than nonmembers.

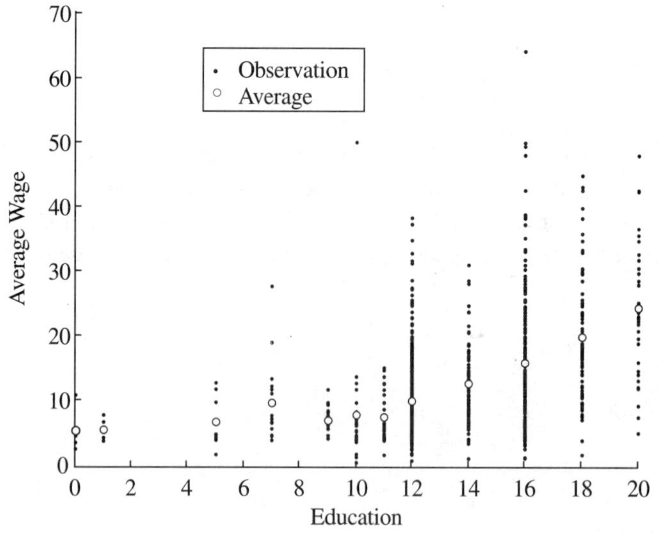

Figure 1.1 Wage versus education.

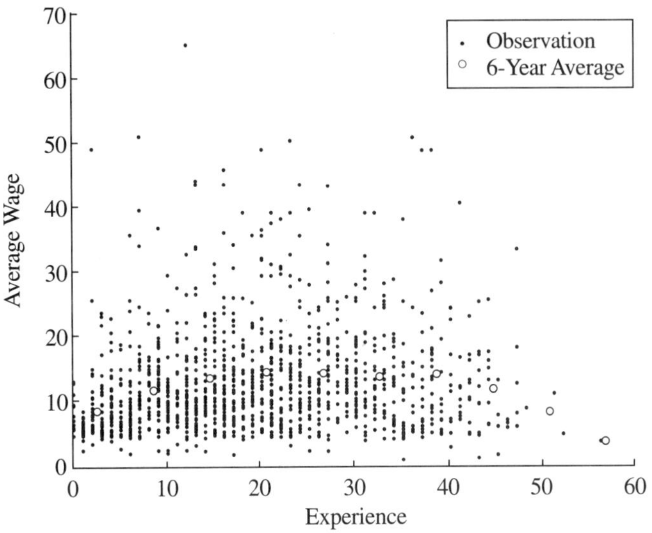

Figure 1.2 Wage versus experience.

Table 1.5
Correlation Coefficients

	Wage	Education	Experience	Age	Female	Nonwhite	Union
Wage	1.000						
Education	0.457	1.000					
Experience	0.173	−0.180	1.000				
Age	0.288	0.062	0.971	1.000			
Female	−0.223	−0.031	−0.023	−0.031	1.000		
Nonwhite	−0.128	−0.087	−0.039	−0.061	0.043	1.000	
Union	0.102	0.004	0.154	0.158	−0.089	0.081	1.000

1.2 GENERALIZING THE SAMPLE AVERAGE

With so many attributes varying simultaneously across individuals, we would like to have a way of separating the wage variation associated with one attribute, say gender, from another attribute, such as education. *Ordinary least squares* (OLS) is one method for decomposing the differences in wages among many characteristics. Because in this sample nonwhites earn less than whites, union members earn more than nonmembers, and experienced workers earn more than inexperienced workers, part of the average difference in the wages between women and men is related to distinctions in the composition of the female and male labor forces. Researchers use the ordinary least-squares technique to sort out such simultaneous variation in several variables.

A simple way to describe the multivariate relationship among wages and the attributes of workers is to fit a function of the additive form

$$y = x_1\beta_1 + x_2\beta_2 + \cdots + x_K\beta_K + \varepsilon \tag{1.1}$$

where y represents the wage and the xs represent the other variables. In general settings, we will call y the left-hand side (LHS) variable and the xs the right-hand side (RHS) variables. The βs are *coefficients* that we choose to make the RHS of the equation reproduce the behavior of the LHS variable. The term ε is a residual term that balances the equation; it is necessary because no weighted sum of the xs can reproduce the observations of the wage exactly, observation after observation. Nevertheless, by studying the fitted values of $\beta_1, \ldots, \beta_K$, one may be able to infer patterns in the data. With this simple functional form, we can associate higher wages with two or more coincident differences in gender, race, education, or other attributes.

The method of ordinary least squares is a widely used method for fitting the βs. They are chosen to solve the optimization problem

$$\min_{\beta_1,\ldots,\beta_K} \sum_{n=1}^{N} [y_n - (x_{n1}\beta_1 + x_{n2}\beta_2 + \cdots + x_{nK}\beta_K)]^2 \tag{1.2}$$

where n indexes the observations in a data set. The term "least squares" refers to *minimizing* the sum of *squared* differences $y_n - (x_{n1}\beta_1 + \cdots + x_{nK}\beta_K)$. We will call these differences *residuals* and the objective function

$$f(\beta_1, \ldots, \beta_K) = \sum_{n=1}^{N} [y_n - (x_{n1}\beta_1 + x_{n2}\beta_2 + \cdots + x_{nK}\beta_K)]^2$$

the *sum of squared residuals*. When the residuals are evaluated at their least-squares values, the residuals are called the *fitted residuals*.

In the simplest case, OLS yields the sample average as the fitted coefficient. Consider the case in which $K = 1$ and $x_{n1} = 1$ for all n. OLS finds the value of β_1 that is closest to all of the y_n in the sum of squared residuals sense:

$$\min_{\beta_1} \sum_{n=1}^{N} (y_n - \beta_1)^2$$

Then OLS reduces to minimizing a univariate quadratic function over β_1 and the result is the average:

$$\hat{\beta}_1 \equiv \operatorname*{argmin}_{\beta_1} \sum_{n=1}^{N} (y_n - \beta_1)^2 = \frac{\sum_{n=1}^{N} y_n}{N}$$

In subsequent chapters, we will describe how this special case illustrates general properties of OLS.

Using the simple average, we can generalize a step further. Consider the case in which $K = 2$ and x_{n2} is the indicator variable that equals one when the individual is female and zero when the individual is male. Let us retain $x_{n1} = 1$ from the previous case. In this new case, OLS will fit a function of the form

$$x_{n1}\beta_1 + x_{n2}\beta_2 = \begin{cases} \beta_1 & \text{if the } n\text{th individual is male } (x_{n2} = 0) \\ \beta_1 + \beta_2 & \text{if the } n\text{th individual is female } (x_{n2} = 1) \end{cases} \tag{1.3}$$

to the wage data. We will interpret the fitted value of β_1 as the overall level of the wage for men and β_2 as the sample differential between women and men. In this case, the average also appears as an explanation of the OLS fit. We can restate (1.2) as

$$\begin{aligned}
&\min_{\beta_1,\beta_2} \sum_{n=1}^{N} (y_n - \beta_1 - x_{n2}\beta_2)^2 \\
&\quad = \min_{\beta_1,\beta_2} \left[\sum_{\{n \mid x_{n2}=0\}} (y_n - \beta_1)^2 + \sum_{\{n \mid x_{n2}=1\}} (y_n - \beta_1 - \beta_2)^2 \right] \\
&\quad = \left[\min_{\beta_1} \sum_{\{n \mid x_{n2}=0\}} (y_n - \beta_1)^2 \right] + \left[\min_{\gamma} \sum_{\{n \mid x_{n2}=1\}} (y_n - \gamma)^2 \right]
\end{aligned} \tag{1.4}$$

so that the fitted value of β_1 is the average of wage for males only, the fitted value of $\beta_1 + \beta_2 \equiv \gamma$ is the average of wage for females, and, therefore, the fitted value of β_2 is the *difference* in the average for females and the average for males. We have already calculated this value to be approximately \$3.53. Because y is the wage, we interpret this number as a measure of the difference in wages between men and women.

Of course, the average does not always appear in such obvious ways in the OLS solution to (1.2). Suppose that we extend the list of characteristics to include indicator variables for nonwhites and union members. That is, let $K = 4$, retain x_{n1} and x_{n2} as before, and additionally let

$$x_{n3} = \begin{cases} 1 & \text{if the } n\text{th individual is nonwhite} \\ 0 & \text{if otherwise} \end{cases}$$

$$x_{n4} = \begin{cases} 1 & \text{if the } n\text{th individual is a union member} \\ 0 & \text{if otherwise} \end{cases}$$

According to Table 1.3, the observations cannot be divided into four mutually exclusive groups based on these RHS variables, which correspond to four functions of $\beta_1, \ldots, \beta_4$. Therefore, we cannot use the solution strategy exhibited in (1.4). Instead, we simply provide the numerical solution calculated with an electronic computer using special software. For our data set, the fitted equation is (approximately)

$$\hat{\mu} = 14.112 - 3.307 \cdot x_2 - 2.771 \cdot x_3 + 2.025 \cdot x_4 \tag{1.5}$$

where we introduce the symbol $\hat{\mu}$ to distinguish *fitted* values from *observed* values of wages. This is our first description of the variation in wages in terms of several characteristics. These fitted coefficient values are interpreted as average differences in wages associated exclusively with the respective characteristic. All of these values are somewhat smaller in magnitude than the differences in averages in Table 1.2. For example, the average gap associated with union membership has fallen from \$2.21 to \$2.03. In some sense, these new numbers account for possible "double counting" in the differences in crude sample averages. We will explain the sense in the coming chapters.

The three characteristics in (1.5) (gender, race, and union membership) identify eight subsamples of individuals within the data set. Table 1.6 contains a box for each subsample and compares the subsample average (denoted $\bar{y}$) with the fitted value given by (1.5). Although the overall

Table 1.6
Average and Fitted Wage

		Union Membership	
Gender	Race	Nonunion	Union
Men	White	$\bar{y} = 14.405$	$\bar{y} = 15.367$
		$\hat{\beta}_1 = 14.112$	$\hat{\beta}_1 + \hat{\beta}_4 = 16.137$
	Nonwhite	$\bar{y} = 10.298$	$\bar{y} = 13.605$
		$\hat{\beta}_1 + \hat{\beta}_3 = 11.341$	$\hat{\beta}_1 + \hat{\beta}_3 + \hat{\beta}_4 = 13.366$
Women	White	$\bar{y} = 10.575$	$\bar{y} = 13.615$
		$\hat{\beta}_1 + \hat{\beta}_2 = 10.805$	$\hat{\beta}_1 + \hat{\beta}_2 + \hat{\beta}_4 = 12.829$
	Nonwhite	$\bar{y} = 8.471$	$\bar{y} = 11.139$
		$\hat{\beta}_1 + \hat{\beta}_2 + \hat{\beta}_3 = 8.034$	$\hat{\beta}_1 + \hat{\beta}_2 + \hat{\beta}_3 + \hat{\beta}_4 = 10.058$

patterns are the same, many of the cells contain large differences. For example, nonwhite nonunion men receive much less on average ($10.30) than the OLS fitted value ($11.34) and nonwhite union women receive much more on average ($11.14) than the OLS fitted value ($10.06).

Additively separable differences in wages are not the best description of these data. We can make the differences multiplicatively separable by placing the natural logarithm of wages into y. If

$$\log w_n = y_n = \beta_1 + x_{n2}\beta_2 + x_{n3}\beta_3 + x_{n4}\beta_4 + \varepsilon_n \tag{1.6}$$

then

$$\begin{aligned} w_n &= \exp(\beta_1 + x_{n2}\beta_2 + x_{n3}\beta_3 + x_{n4}\beta_4 + \varepsilon_n) \\ &= e^{\beta_1} \times \left(e^{\beta_2}\right)^{x_{n2}} \times \left(e^{\beta_3}\right)^{x_{n3}} \times \left(e^{\beta_4}\right)^{x_{n4}} \times e^{\varepsilon_n} \end{aligned}$$

Furthermore, for $|\beta_k| \leq 0.3$, the approximation $e^{\beta_k} \approx 1 + \beta_k$ has an error smaller than 4% so that

$$w_n \approx e^{\beta_1} \times (1 + \beta_2)^{x_{n2}} \times (1 + \beta_3)^{x_{n3}} \times (1 + \beta_4)^{x_{n4}} \times e^{\varepsilon_n}$$

and we can interpret the slopes as approximate percentage differences. The OLS fitted equation for (1.6) is

$$\hat{\mu} = 2.469 - 0.266 \cdot x_2 - 0.222 \cdot x_3 + 0.251 \cdot x_4$$

assigning women 26.6% lower wages than men, nonwhites 22.2% lower wages than whites, and union members 25.1% higher wages than others.

In Table 1.7, we produce the average and fitted values of log-wages for the eight subsamples. By and large, these numbers are much closer than those in Table 1.6. The greatest deviation occurs for nonunion, nonwhite men. Thus, in studies of wages economists commonly examine the (natural) logarithm of wages instead of their level in this way. We will describe several additional reasons later in this book. For the present, this transformation of wages illustrates a useful feature of the least-squares fitted line: although it is linear in y and the xs, the function need not be linear in the variables of interest. Through transformations, we can also fit nonlinear relationships.

Table 1.7
Average and Fitted Log-Wage

Gender	Race	Union Membership: Nonunion	Union Membership: Union
Men	White	$\bar{y} = 2.494$	$\bar{y} = 2.658$
		$\hat{\beta}_1 = 2.469$	$\hat{\beta}_1 + \hat{\beta}_4 = 2.720$
	Nonwhite	$\bar{y} = 2.140$	$\bar{y} = 2.546$
		$\hat{\beta}_1 + \hat{\beta}_3 = 2.246$	$\hat{\beta}_1 + \hat{\beta}_3 + \hat{\beta}_4 = 2.497$
Women	White	$\bar{y} = 2.183$	$\bar{y} = 2.513$
		$\hat{\beta}_1 + \hat{\beta}_2 = 2.203$	$\hat{\beta}_1 + \hat{\beta}_2 + \hat{\beta}_4 = 2.454$
	Nonwhite	$\bar{y} = 2.029$	$\bar{y} = 2.289$
		$\hat{\beta}_1 + \hat{\beta}_2 + \hat{\beta}_3 = 1.980$	$\hat{\beta}_1 + \hat{\beta}_2 + \hat{\beta}_3 + \hat{\beta}_4 = 2.231$

A collection of fitted functions for the log-wage is described in Table 1.8. The first three "runs" correspond to the three fitted functions that we have just described in terms of averages.[7] The remaining runs add education and experience variables to the RHS. In the second to the last line, we list the value of the sum of squared residuals (SSR) for each function. Note that this number falls in moving across the table, adding to the list of RHS variables. This is a natural consequence of OLS:

$$\min_{\beta_1,\ldots,\beta_K} \sum_{n=1}^{N} \left[y_n - \left(\sum_{k=1}^{K} x_{nk}\beta_k \right) \right]^2 \geq \min_{\beta_1,\ldots,\beta_{K+1}} \sum_{n=1}^{N} \left[y_n - \left(\sum_{k=1}^{K+1} x_{nk}\beta_k \right) \right]^2$$

because the first term implicitly constrains $\beta_{K+1} = 0$ whereas the second term minimizes over the same parameters as the first *and* β_{K+1}.

Note also that *all* of the coefficients change as the list of RHS variables changes in Table 1.8. This phenomenon is also a consequence of minimizing the SSR over the coefficients. As additional RHS variables are included, the extra coefficients make it possible to reduce the SSR further. And furthermore, as new coefficients are added, the old coefficients will change their optimal values as the new overall minimum is determined.

The last line of Table 1.8 reports an additional calculation, labeled R^2.[8] The R^2 is a measure of the percentage of the variation in the log-wage variable that is captured by the RHS variables besides the constant term. The R^2 equals the squared value of the sample correlation between the LHS variable y and the RHS *fitted value* $\hat{\mu}$, where[9]

$$\hat{\mu}_n \equiv \sum_{k=1}^{K} x_{nk}\hat{\beta}_k \tag{1.7}$$

[7] One "runs a regression" in the same sense that one "runs" any computer program, because "regression" is generally used.

[8] The symbol R^2 is pronounced the way it looks: "R squared."

[9] Algebraically,

$$R^2 = \frac{\left[\sum_n y_n\hat{\mu}_n - \left(\sum_n y_n\right)\left(\sum_n \hat{\mu}_n\right)/N\right]^2}{\left[\sum_n {y_n}^2 - \left(\sum_n y_n\right)^2/N\right]\left[\sum_n {\hat{\mu}_n}^2 - \left(\sum_n \hat{\mu}_n\right)^2/N\right]}$$

Table 1.8
OLS Fits for Log-Wage

RHS Variable ($x_{\cdot k}$)	Estimated Coefficient ($\hat{\beta}_k$) Run 1	Run 2	Run 3	Run 4	Run 5
Constant (one)	2.342	2.486	2.469	0.906	0.779
Female		−0.289	−0.266	−0.249	−0.242
Nonwhite			−0.222	−0.134	−0.131
Union member			0.251	0.180	0.173
Education				0.100	0.095
Experience				0.0128	0.039
(Experience)^2					−0.00063
SSR	442.831	415.837	398.418	289.766	278.753
R^2	NA[a]	0.061	0.100	0.346	0.371

[a] NA, not applicable.

When the constant (one) is the only RHS variable, the sum of squared residuals is 442.831. In the second OLS run, we can interpret the R^2 value as saying that gender accounts for a 6.1% decline in the SSR from 442.831 to 415.837 ($\frac{442.831-415.837}{442.831} \approx 0.061$). After adding the remaining RHS variables, the RHS variables capture roughly 37.1% of the sample variation in log-wage. This interpretation of the R^2 measure of fit is explained in Chapter 3.

Now let us examine the additional entries in the table, Runs 4 and 5. As almost anyone would predict, higher wages are associated with higher levels of education and higher levels of experience. According to the fourth run, in this data set every additional year of education corresponds roughly to a 10.0% increase in observed wages and every additional year of experience to 1.28% higher wages.[10] The fitted coefficient for gender falls a bit, but race and union effects change dramatically. The coefficient of nonwhite almost halves while the coefficient of union falls by about two-thirds.

In the fifth run, we add the square of experience as an additional RHS variable. We have already noted in Figure 1.2 a humped shape in sample averages for various levels of experience. Several economic theories also predict that wage growth declines with experience, so we have reasons to expect a nonlinear association between wages and experience. Including a transformation of a RHS variable is another way to generalize the functional form of the fitted relationship among the variables of interest.

When we include the square of experience, the fitted coefficients resemble those in the previous run except for the experience coefficient, which more than doubles from 1.28 to 3.90%. This larger effect applies, however, only to the percentage for individuals with no experience. The negative coefficient for squared experience indicates that the increase in wages associated with greater experience declines as experience increases. Wages appear to reach a maximum at

[10] This interpretation of the coefficients follows from the logrithmic derivative $d \log y/dx = (1/y) \cdot dy/dx$ so that if $\log y = \beta x$ then $\beta = (1/y) \cdot dy/dx$, the *percentage change* in y for a change in x.

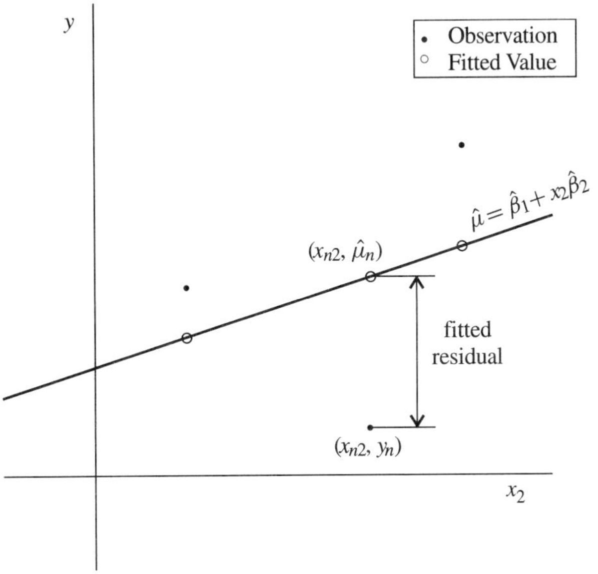

Figure 1.3 Simple OLS fit.

roughly 31 years of experience ($\frac{0.039}{2\times 0.00063} \approx 31$) and to decline thereafter. This is consistent with the profile of wages suggested in Figure 1.2.

It is helpful to see a graphic description of the OLS fitting procedure to become comfortable with the fits including education and experience as RHS variables. Let us consider a simple example in which there are two RHS variables, x_{n1} and x_{n2}, and $x_{n1} = 1$. In Figure 1.3, we show a hypothetical scatter plot of x_{n2} and the LHS variable y_n, and the OLS fitted line $\hat{\mu} = \hat{\beta}_1 + x_{n2}\hat{\beta}_2$. In this example, because it is constant, we do not need to graph x_{n1} also. The fitted residuals $y_n - \hat{\mu}_n$ are the vertical distances between the data points and the fitted line, where data points above the line correspond to positive fitted residuals and data points below the line to negative fitted residuals. OLS minimizes the sum of the squared values of these distances.

One can construct other ways to measure the distance between the data points and the fitted line. For example, one could choose residuals perpendicular to the fitted line and minimize their sum of squares instead or, alternatively, one might minimize the sum of the absolute value of the residuals. We will reconsider the OLS criterion in the second half of this book. For now, keep in mind that it is the vertical residual that enters the OLS minimization problem. This reflects our goal to fit the values of the LHS variable as closely as possible with a linear combination of RHS variables.

The fitted relationships for log-wages illustrate the potential usefulness of OLS. This example may also evoke questions and concerns about the interpretation of these fitted functions. Much of this book addresses such questions. In the last section of this introductory chapter, we summarize the basic statistical structure that econometricians (and many others) have used to analyze the properties of OLS. This basic, or *classical*, structure is the starting point for many generalizations that are responses to its weaknesses.

1.3 OLS REGRESSION

In the first two parts of this book, we will motivate multivariate OLS further as a generalization of the crude average. The average is a direct and intuitive measure of a central tendency. In addition, classical statistical theory about averages is relatively simple and widely applied.

In place of summarizing the central tendency of y with a scalar, the sample average, OLS generalizes the central value to

$$\sum_{k=1}^{K} x_{nk}\hat{\beta}_k = [x_{n1} \quad \cdots \quad x_{nK}] \begin{bmatrix} \hat{\beta}_1 \\ \vdots \\ \hat{\beta}_K \end{bmatrix} = \underset{1\times K}{\mathbf{x}_n'} \; \underset{K\times 1}{\hat{\boldsymbol{\beta}}} \equiv \hat{\mu}_n \tag{1.8}$$

($n = 1, \ldots, N$), where $\mathbf{x}_n$ is a column vector of K observable RHS variables and $\hat{\boldsymbol{\beta}}$ is a column vector of K fitted coefficients.[11] In the analysis ahead, it will be essential that this *multiple regression function* $\mathbf{x}_n'\hat{\boldsymbol{\beta}}$ has a linear functional form in the $\hat{\beta}_k$.[12] This is less restrictive than it may appear at first, because we are relatively free to choose the elements of $\mathbf{x}_n$. Thus, various transformations of a basic RHS variable can be included in the same spirit as adding experience squared to the log-wage equation.

Because the fitted function is linear in the coefficients, OLS yields fitted values of the coefficients that are weighted sums of the $\{y_n\}$; in other words, the OLS coefficients are linear functions of the LHS variable. Our first goal will be to explain the nature of this linear function. Subsequently, we will show how this linearity in the LHS variable provides a structure that makes the statistical analysis of the ordinary least-squares fit relatively straightforward. Under comparable assumptions to the simple location model, we will derive comparable sampling properties of the OLS fitted coefficients.

We will also focus our attention on the interpretation of the OLS fit. NOTE: do not necessarily assume that there is a causal relationship running from $\mathbf{x}$ to y. In empirical research where the values of x can be fixed before the experiment that yields y is conducted, such causal interpretations are reasonable. But in economics such predetermination of $\mathbf{x}$ is rare. Experimental work in game theory is an example in which the stimuli are predetermined. One might also suppose that the behavior of a price-taking firm in a competitive market could be treated as causally determined by prices. But this would not be strictly correct. Because price is the equilibrium outcome of the actions of every firm, price and quantity are simultaneously determined.

Given the linear structure, you may not be surprised to learn that matrix algebra plays a role in the analysis of ordinary least squares and the linear regression function. Table 1.9 summarizes the important objects.[13] We have already introduced the parameter vector $\boldsymbol{\beta}$ of K slope coefficients. All of the other objects have a row for each observation in the data set, N rows in all. The vector $\mathbf{y}$ collects together all of the observations on the LHS variable. The matrix $\mathbf{X}$ does the same for the RHS variables, allocating a column to each RHS variable. Together, $\mathbf{X}$ and $\mathbf{y}$ form a virtual

[11] We will use boldface in mathematical expressions to denote a column vector or a matrix.

[12] The term "multiple" refers to *several* RHS variables.

[13] The notation $\mathbf{X} = [\mathbf{x}_n]'$ is somewhat unfortunate given that this means to stack the $\mathbf{x}_n'$ one upon another. Such expressions occur frequently because matrix linear algebra tends to be organized around column vectors whereas text is horizontal, encouraging the use of such row vectors as $[a_1, a_2, \ldots, a_N]$. As a result, in econometric writing transposes in text are required to stack rows into a matrix.

spreadsheet of observations such that rows correspond to the same observations. We will write (1.8) stacked over observations

$$\begin{bmatrix} \mathbf{x}_1'\boldsymbol{\beta} \\ \mathbf{x}_2'\boldsymbol{\beta} \\ \vdots \\ \mathbf{x}_N'\boldsymbol{\beta} \end{bmatrix} = \underset{N\times K}{\mathbf{X}}\ \underset{K\times 1}{\boldsymbol{\beta}}$$

where

$$\mathbf{X} \equiv \begin{bmatrix} \mathbf{x}_1' \\ \mathbf{x}_2' \\ \vdots \\ \mathbf{x}_N' \end{bmatrix} = \begin{bmatrix} x_{11} & x_{12} & \cdots & x_{1K} \\ x_{21} & x_{22} & \cdots & x_{2K} \\ \vdots & \vdots & & \vdots \\ x_{N1} & x_{N2} & \cdots & x_{NK} \end{bmatrix} = [x_{nk}]$$

The symbol $\boldsymbol{\iota}_N$ (the Greek letter *iota*) denotes a column vector of N ones; $\mathbf{I}_N$ is the usual matrix notation for an $N \times N$ identity matrix. We will drop the subscript N on these two objects when there is no ambiguity about their dimensions.

With this notation, we can deliver an algebraic generalization of the sample average. The sample average is

$$\bar{y} = \frac{\boldsymbol{\iota}'\mathbf{y}}{\boldsymbol{\iota}'\boldsymbol{\iota}}$$

More generally, the OLS fitted coefficients are

$$\hat{\boldsymbol{\beta}} = (\mathbf{X}'\mathbf{X})^{-1}\mathbf{X}'\mathbf{y}$$

Note especially that the fitted vector for $\boldsymbol{\beta}$, $\hat{\boldsymbol{\beta}}$, is a linear function of $\mathbf{y}$. The subject of the next chapter is the derivation and geometry of this special function.

Table 1.9
Summary of Basic Notation

$\boldsymbol{\iota}_N$	$N \times 1$ vector of ones
$\mathbf{I}_N$	$N \times N$ identity matrix
$\mathbf{y}$	$N \times 1$ vector $[y_1, \ldots, y_N]' = [y_n]'$
$\mathbf{X}$	$N \times K$ matrix $[\mathbf{x}_1, \ldots, \mathbf{x}_N]' = [\mathbf{x}_n]'$
$\boldsymbol{\beta}$	$K \times 1$ vector $[\beta_1, \ldots, \beta_K]' = [\beta_k]'$

1.4 OVERVIEW

1. Economists rarely run experiments in which the researcher hold some variables constant while varying others to observe the effects. As a result, empirical research relies on variation that occurs spontaneously in historical observations and methods to isolate covariance between variables given contemporaneous changes in other variables.
2. For example, any effort to measure the differences in wages between men and women must account for coincidental differences in race, education, work experience, and union membership among men and women.

3. The difference in sample averages of a variable is a common measure of the overall difference in the levels of two samples. The sample average is the number closest to all of the observations in a sample in the SSR sense:

$$\bar{y} \equiv \frac{\sum_{n=1}^{N} y_n}{N} = \underset{\beta_1}{\operatorname{argmin}} \sum_{n=1}^{N} (y_n - \beta_1)^2$$

4. The OLS fitted regression line

$$\hat{\beta}_1 + x_{n2}\hat{\beta}_2 + \cdots + x_{nK}\hat{\beta}_K = \underset{\beta_1,\beta_2,\ldots,\beta_K}{\operatorname{argmin}} \sum_{n=1}^{N} (y_n - \beta_1 - x_{n2}\beta_2 - \cdots - x_{nK}\beta_K)^2$$

is a generalization of the sample average that assigns slope coefficients to each RHS variable x_{nk} so that the fitted line is closest to the y_n, $n = 1, \ldots, N$, in the SSR sense.

5. Every additional RHS variable lowers the minimized SSR.

6. By making y_n and x_{nk} transformations of variables, relationships that are nonlinear can be fitted in the variables of interest. The natural logarithm and power transformations are examples. Power transformations of RHS variables create polynomial regression functions.

7. All of the observations and variables are collected in the matrix terms $\mathbf{y}$ and $\mathbf{X}\boldsymbol{\beta}$ where $\mathbf{y} \equiv [y_n]'$, $\mathbf{X} \equiv [\mathbf{x}_n]'$, $\mathbf{x}_n \equiv [x_{nk}]'$, and $\boldsymbol{\beta} \equiv [\beta_k]'$.

1.5 EXERCISES

1.1 Show that $\iota'\iota = N$ and $\iota\iota'$ is an $N \times N$ matrix of ones. Also show that

$$\left(\frac{1}{\iota'\iota} \cdot \iota\iota'\right)\left(\frac{1}{\iota'\iota} \cdot \iota\iota'\right) = \frac{1}{\iota'\iota} \cdot \iota\iota',$$

$$\left(\mathbf{I}_N - \frac{1}{\iota'\iota} \cdot \iota\iota'\right)\left(\mathbf{I}_N - \frac{1}{\iota'\iota} \cdot \iota\iota'\right) = \mathbf{I}_N - \frac{1}{\iota'\iota} \cdot \iota\iota'$$

1.2 Using the results of Exercise 1.1, confirm the equivalence of the statistics in the first column of Table 5.2 with the corresponding entries in Table 5.1:

$$\hat{\beta} = \bar{y} = \frac{\sum_{n=1}^{N} y_n}{N} = \frac{\iota'\mathbf{y}}{\iota'\iota}$$

$$s^2 = \frac{\sum_{n=1}^{N} (y_n - \bar{y})^2}{N-1} = \frac{\mathbf{y}'(\mathbf{I} - \frac{1}{\iota'\iota} \cdot \iota\iota')\mathbf{y}}{N-1}$$

1.3 Show that equation (1.3) has the equivalent parameterization

$$z_{n1}\beta_1 + z_{n2}\gamma$$

where $\gamma = \beta_1 + \beta_2$, z_{n1} is an indicator variable for men, and $z_{n2} = x_{n2}$ is an indicator variable for women. What are the OLS fitted values for β_1 and γ?

1.4 Note that in Table 1.6 some subsample averages are closer to the corresponding fitted regression values than others.

1. Explain why this is reasonable in light of the number of observations in each cell.
2. Describe a set of RHS variables that would provide OLS fitted values equal to the subsample averages.

1.6 APPENDIX: DATA COLLECTION

In this section, we give a brief description of our collection of the wage data. Additional details appear in the files on the internet. We extracted the data from the March CPS 1995, using the Data Extraction System (DES) available on an internet site of the Census Bureau (http://www.census.gov/DES/www/welcome.html). We used both the person and the household data files. The criteria for the extract from the CPS person data file are summarized in Table 1.10. We also extracted household data containing all the households of the so-called "outgoing" rotation groups for which wage data were available: whenever the variable labeled HMIS (month in sample) equaled 4 or 8.

We merged the extracts of the household and person data files to obtain all the people in the outgoing rotation groups. There were many observations for which earnings data were completely missing. We dropped these observations and in addition those that are not in the universe for the basic CPS earnings items (AHRLYWK=0), leaving 13,258 observations. From these, we drew a random (unweighted) subsample in which each observation had a 10% probability of inclusion. This resulted in 1314 observations.

We drew 9 variables from the CPS. These variables appear first in Table 1.11. This table also lists several new variables we created using the information in the extract. These variables include indicator variables FEMALE (1 if female, 0 if male), NONWHITE (0 if white, 1 if not), UNION (1 if union member, 0 if not), and WKPAY (0 if pad by the hour, 1 if not). We also created the variable YRSSCH (years of schooling) from the variable AHGA (educational attainment) as in Table 1.12. The variable EXP (potential work experience) equals AAGE (age) minus YRSSCH (years of schooling) minus 6.

Among the people who were not paid by the hour (WKPAY=1), 14 had top coded weekly earnings. The variable WAGE equals hourly pay (AHRSPAY) in dollars for those paid by the hour, and gross earnings last week (AGRSWK) divided by usual hours worked per week (AUSLHRS) for all others. This produced missing values for 23 observations. In addition, there are two observations with WAGE = 0. We treated these observations as missing earnings as well and they were dropped from the sample. The final data set contained 1289 observations that are stored in the final ASCII data set *wage.dat*.

Table 1.10
CPS Person Data Selection Criteria

Variable	Name	Selection Criteria
Age	AAGE	18–65
Labor force status	ALFSR	1 (working, excluding Armed Forces)
Class of worker	ACLSWRK	1,2,3,4 (excluding self-employed and those working without pay)

Table 1.11
Variables in Wage Data Set

Variable	Description	CPS
AAGE	Age	√
ACLSWKR	Class of worker	√
AHERNTF	Indicator for hourly wage top coded at $99.99	√
AHGA	Educational attainment	√
AHRS1	Total hours worked last week	√
AHRSPAY	Hourly pay in cents	√
AGRSWK	Weekly salary in dollars	√
AUSLHRS	Usual weekly hours	√
AWERNTF	Indicator for weekly earnings top coded at $1923	√
EXP	Years of potential labor force experience	
FEMALE	Indicator for female	
NONWHITE	Indicator for nonwhite	
UNION	Indicator for union member	
WAGE	Earnings per hour (in dollars)	
WKPAY	Indicator for "not paid by the hour"	
YRSSCH	Years of schooling	

Table 1.12
Definition of YRSSCH

YRSSCH	CPS Description (AHGA)
0	Less than first grade
1	First, second, third, or fourth grade
5	Fifth or sixth grade
7	Seventh and eighth grade
9	Ninth grade
10	Tenth grade
11	Eleventh grade
12	Twelfth grade no diploma
12	High school graduate
12	Some college but no degree
14	Associates degree-occupational/vocational
14	Associates degree-academic program
16	Bachelors degree (B.A., A.B., B.S.)
18	Masters degree (M.A., M.S., M.Eng., M.Ed., M.S.W., M.B.A.)
20	Professional school degree (M.D., D.D.S., D.V.M., L.L.B., J.D.)
20	Doctorate degree (Ph.D., Ed.D.)

CHAPTER 2

THE GEOMETRY OF LEAST SQUARES

2.1 INTRODUCTORY EXAMPLE

Our ultimate goal is to interpret the fitted results of OLS regression. In this chapter, we begin by describing the geometric nature of the OLS fitting procedure. In particular, we show how the OLS fitted values capture all of the sample correlation between the RHS variables and the LHS variable. To illustrate, we take the residuals from the third fitted regression and calculate the sample average, which is 4.06819×10^{-10}, and the correlations with each of the RHS variables, obtaining the values in Table 2.1. All of the entries have the magnitude 10^{-9}, which is effectively zero given the numerical accuracy of the calculations.[1] A comparison with the correlations between the log-wage and these same variables emphasizes that before the fitted values are subtracted from log-wages there is substantial correlation. These correlations of zero are one sense in which we can understand the OLS regression fit. They are a property of choosing the fitted coefficients as the minimizers of the SSR.

We illustrate the second feature explained below by running an additional regression. We add the age of the individual as an additional RHS variable to the third run. The fitted coefficients are exactly the same as those in Table 1.8 with the exception that an entry for age appears with a fitted coefficient equal to zero. In addition, our regression software prints out the following message:

```
*** WARNING: At least one coefficient in the table above could not be esti-
mated due to singularity of the data.
```

The "singularity" to which the output refers turns out to be caused by an artifact of this data set. The measure of experience in the data set is actually calculated as the age of the individual less their

[1] Note that these numbers should be interpreted as "numerical" zeros. Except in special circumstances computer software produces round-off errors that introduce small discrepancies such as these. Note also that different computers and different software programs will typically produce correlations slightly different from those that we report.

Table 2.1
Sample Correlations for the Fitted Residual

RHS Variable	Correlation with Fitted Residuals $(y - X\hat{\beta})$	Correlation with Log-Wage (y)
Education	-0.073×10^{-9}	0.448
Experience	-0.655×10^{-9}	0.193
$(\text{Experience})^2$	-0.526×10^{-9}	0.115
Female	-0.252×10^{-9}	−0.247
Nonwhite	-0.316×10^{-9}	−0.134
Union member	-0.670×10^{-9}	0.166

education less six years. The original survey data do not include an explicit measure of experience. Economists occasionally call this artificial measure "potential" experience to acknowledge this difference. When we regress age on a constant, education, experience, and the other RHS variables, we get the results in Table 2.2. This regression clearly corroborates the exact linear relationship among these variables: not only are the coefficients the appropriate values, but the SSR is zero and the R^2 equals one. All of the variation in age is captured by this OLS fit because there is an exact linear relationship among the variables.

In this chapter, we will also explain this "singularity" issue. In brief, because of this exact linear relationship among the RHS variables, there is no unique set of values for the coefficients that minimizes the SSR. Regression software typically responds by pointing out the occurrence of this situation and choosing a particular set of values from among the many that give the same minimum SSR. In our example, the software chose to set the coefficient of the age variable to zero and, as a result, reproduced the coefficients from a previous regression. To illustrate this nonuniqueness further, we also fit the regression with the education variable replaced by the age variable. The results are in Table 2.3. Only three coefficients differ compared to Run 3 of Table 1.8: the new coefficient for age, the intercept, and the coefficient for experience, which has changed sign. Not only is the minimized sum of squared residuals the same, but so are the fitted

Table 2.2
Age Regression

RHS Variable	Coefficient
Constant (one)	6.000
Education	1.000
Experience	1.000
$(\text{Experience})^2$	-0.158×10^{-16}
Female	-0.152×10^{-15}
Nonwhite	-0.141×10^{-15}
Union member	-0.204×10^{-15}
SSR	0.000
R^2	1.000

Table 2.3
Log-Wage Regression

Variable (X_k)	Coefficient ($\hat{\beta}_k$)
Constant (one)	0.209
Age	0.095
Experience	−0.056
(Experience)^2	−0.00063
Female	−0.242
Nonwhite	−0.131
Union member	0.173
SSR	278.753
R^2	0.371

coefficients of all the other RHS variables. In every one of the previous runs, *all* of the coefficients changed somewhat when we changed the list of RHS variables. Our discussion will resolve this paradox as well.

2.2 ORDINARY LEAST SQUARES

To explain the fitting procedure, we are going to explore the geometric nature of the ordinary least-squares (OLS) method for fitting a regression line $\mathbf{X}\boldsymbol{\beta}$ to the vector $\mathbf{y}$. This leads us to depict the data in y and $\mathbf{X}$ in a way that is different from how such data are often seen graphed. Given several variables, we often graph variables in pairs to see how they vary together. For example, Figure 1.1 is a graph of wages and education. Each point in this graph is a different observation in the data set.

Instead of this kind of graph, we are going to graph points, or vectors, for different variables. That is, each vector will represent all the observations for one variable. The axes of our alternative graph will correspond to the *observations*, instead of the variables. In Figure 2.1, we display a vector of three observations of an LHS variable labeled $\mathbf{y}$.

The basic geometric ideas are illustrated in Figures 2.2–2.4. Figure 2.2 shows how we will think of the data in $\mathbf{y}$ and $\mathbf{X}$ as vectors. Each column of $\mathbf{X}$ is a vector and two columns are represented by the vectors $\mathbf{X}_1$ and $\mathbf{X}_2$. In the figures, the plane that contains all of the vectors in $\mathbf{X}$ is important and is labeled Col($\mathbf{X}$).

Figure 2.3 illustrates the importance of Col($\mathbf{X}$), pictured as a plane in three dimensions. The OLS fitting procedure finds the vector in Col($\mathbf{X}$), labeled $\hat{\boldsymbol{\mu}}$, that is as close to $\mathbf{y}$ as one can get. Because it is like a shadow or projected image, $\hat{\boldsymbol{\mu}}$ is called a *projection* of $\mathbf{y}$. Figure 2.4 illustrates the second aspect of OLS that we discuss: how $\hat{\boldsymbol{\mu}}$ is decomposed into the fitted components $\hat{\boldsymbol{\mu}}_1$ and $\hat{\boldsymbol{\mu}}_2$ that equal the column vectors in $\mathbf{X}$ multiplied by the OLS fitted values of the coefficients, $\hat{\boldsymbol{\mu}}_1 = \mathbf{X}_1\hat{\boldsymbol{\beta}}_1$ and $\hat{\boldsymbol{\mu}}_2 = \mathbf{X}_2\hat{\boldsymbol{\beta}}_2$.

The method of OLS solves

$$\hat{\boldsymbol{\beta}} \equiv \underset{\boldsymbol{\beta}}{\operatorname{argmin}}(\mathbf{y} - \mathbf{X}\boldsymbol{\beta})'(\mathbf{y} - \mathbf{X}\boldsymbol{\beta}) \tag{2.1}$$

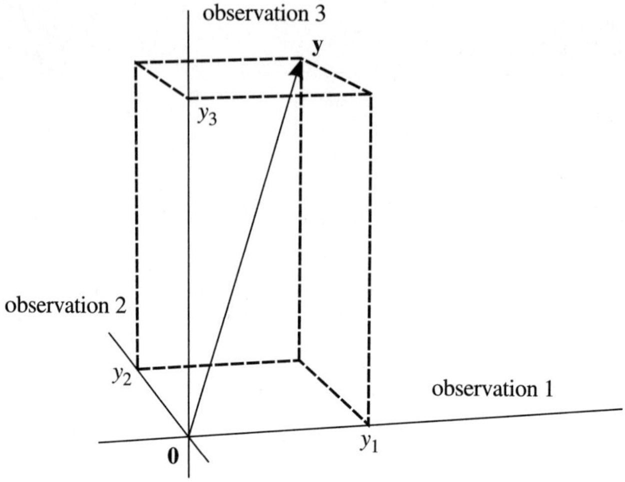

Figure 2.1 Three observations of y.

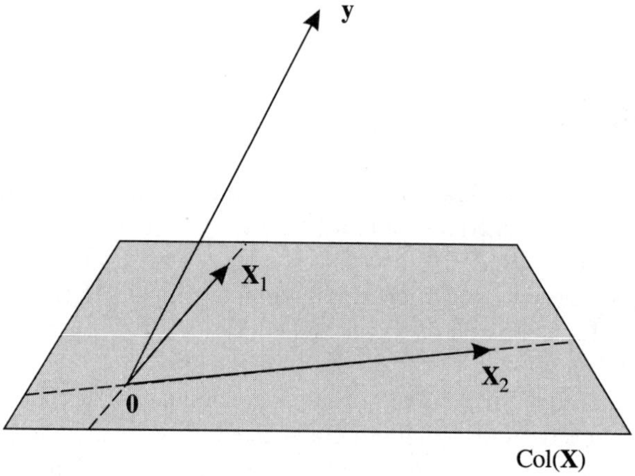

Figure 2.2 Vector representation of data.

In words, $\hat{\boldsymbol{\beta}}$ is the value of $\boldsymbol{\beta}$ that minimizes the squared distance between $\mathbf{y}$ and possible $\mathbf{X}\boldsymbol{\beta}$. The sum of squared deviations between elements of $\mathbf{y}$ and $\mathbf{X}\boldsymbol{\beta}$ is the squared *Euclidean* distance between $\mathbf{y}$ and $\mathbf{X}\boldsymbol{\beta}$:[2]

$$(\mathbf{y}-\mathbf{X}\boldsymbol{\beta})'(\mathbf{y}-\mathbf{X}\boldsymbol{\beta}) = \sum_{n=1}^{N}(y_n - \mathbf{x}_n'\boldsymbol{\beta})^2 \equiv \|\mathbf{y}-\mathbf{X}\boldsymbol{\beta}\|^2$$

We will explain the solution to (2.1) as a two-step process. The first step finds the point on a subspace that is closest to a given point not in that subspace. The subspace is the set of possible

[2] See Section C.4 for a summary of distance, or vector length.

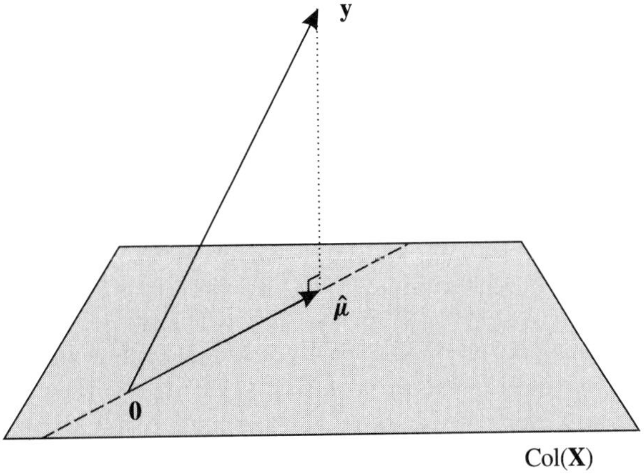

Figure 2.3 Orthogonal projection.

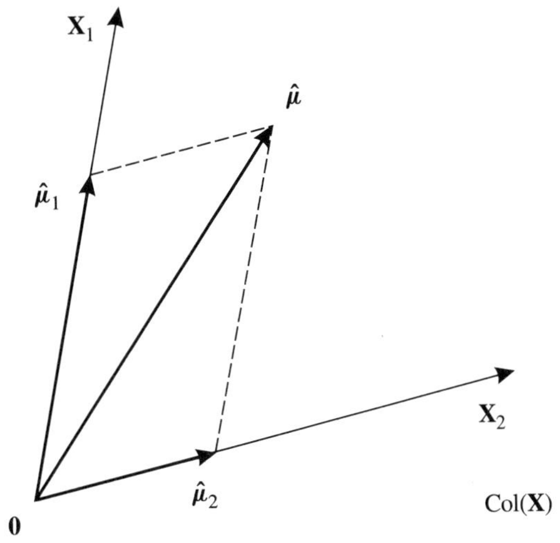

Figure 2.4 Vector decomposition.

N-dimensional real-valued vectors $\mathbf{X}\boldsymbol{\beta}$ that can be created by changing $\boldsymbol{\beta}$ and this subspace is called the *column space* of $\mathbf{X}$.

Definition 1 (Column Space) *The* column space of $\mathbf{X}$, *denoted by* Col($\mathbf{X}$), *is the linear subspace of* $\mathbb{R}^N$ *spanned by linear combinations of the column vectors of* $\mathbf{X}$:[3]

$$\mathrm{Col}(\mathbf{X}) \equiv \{\mathbf{z} \in \mathbb{R}^N \mid \mathbf{z} = \mathbf{X}\boldsymbol{\alpha},\ \boldsymbol{\alpha} \in \mathbb{R}^K\}$$

[3] $\mathbb{R}$ denotes the set of real numbers and $\mathbb{R}^N$ denotes the Cartesian product $\mathbb{R} \times \cdots \times \mathbb{R}$ of N such sets.

Given this definition, we describe the first step of the solution to (2.1) as finding

$$\hat{\boldsymbol{\mu}} \equiv \underset{\boldsymbol{\mu} \in \mathrm{Col}(\mathbf{X})}{\operatorname{argmin}} \|\mathbf{y} - \boldsymbol{\mu}\|^2 \tag{2.2}$$

The second step finds a $\hat{\boldsymbol{\beta}}$ by finding a solution to

$$\hat{\boldsymbol{\mu}} = \mathbf{X}\hat{\boldsymbol{\beta}} \tag{2.3}$$

We use this decomposition because the solution to the first step is unique, whereas there may be many solutions to the second step. The two steps also involve very different operations: optimization versus solving linear equations. Each of these operations plays a fundamental and distinct role in econometric analysis and we want to keep them distinct.

The geometric nature of the OLS solution is summarized in the following proposition.

PROPOSITION 1 (ORDINARY LEAST-SQUARES FIT) *Let $\hat{\boldsymbol{\beta}}$ be any solution to (2.1) and let $\hat{\boldsymbol{\mu}} = \mathbf{X}\hat{\boldsymbol{\beta}}$.*

1. *The vector of fitted values $\hat{\boldsymbol{\mu}}$ is the unique* orthogonal projection *of $\mathbf{y}$ onto* $\mathrm{Col}(\mathbf{X})$.
2. *The vector of* fitted residuals $\mathbf{y} - \hat{\boldsymbol{\mu}}$ *is orthogonal to* $\mathrm{Col}(\mathbf{X})$.
3. *If* $\dim[\mathrm{Col}(\mathbf{X})] = K$, *then (2.1) has the unique solution*[4]

$$\hat{\boldsymbol{\beta}} = (\mathbf{X}'\mathbf{X})^{-1}\mathbf{X}'\mathbf{y} = (\mathbf{X}'\mathbf{X})^{-1}\mathbf{X}'\hat{\boldsymbol{\mu}}$$

This proposition contains three basic ideas that we will explain below.[5]

1. The OLS regression problem involves minimizing the squared distance, or simply the distance itself, between the observed vector $\mathbf{y}$ and a regression vector $\mathbf{X}\boldsymbol{\beta}$ that belongs to $\mathrm{Col}(\mathbf{X})$.
2. The fitted vector $\hat{\boldsymbol{\mu}} = \mathbf{X}\hat{\boldsymbol{\beta}}$ has a special geometric relationship to the observed vector $\mathbf{y}$: it is the *orthogonal projection* onto $\mathrm{Col}(\mathbf{X})$. The residual vector $\mathbf{y} - \hat{\boldsymbol{\mu}}$ is *perpendicular* to $\hat{\boldsymbol{\mu}}$ and any other vector in $\mathrm{Col}(\mathbf{X})$. This is the reason the residual sample correlations in Table 2.2 are all (approximately) zero.
3. If the dimension of $\mathrm{Col}(\mathbf{X})$ equals the number of columns in $\mathbf{X}$, then $\hat{\boldsymbol{\beta}}$ is unique. Furthermore, $\hat{\boldsymbol{\beta}}$ is a linear function of $\mathbf{y}$. Nothing is lost in the formula for $\hat{\boldsymbol{\beta}}$ if we replace $\mathbf{y}$ with $\hat{\boldsymbol{\mu}}$; the fitted vector $\hat{\boldsymbol{\mu}}$ contains all the information in $\mathbf{y}$ about $\hat{\boldsymbol{\beta}}$. We can describe $\hat{\boldsymbol{\beta}}$ as a two-step process, finding $\hat{\boldsymbol{\mu}}$ in the first step and finding $\hat{\boldsymbol{\beta}}$ from $\hat{\boldsymbol{\mu}}$ in the second step. When there are many possible values for $\hat{\boldsymbol{\beta}}$, we can still describe the set of $\hat{\boldsymbol{\beta}}$ consistent with $\hat{\boldsymbol{\mu}}$.

---

[4] We will denote the dimension of a linear vector space $\mathbb{S}$ by $\dim(\mathbb{S})$. To review dimension, see Proposition C.3 and the surrounding material in Appendix C.

[5] The proof of this proposition is on p. 33.

The geometry of orthogonal projections provides an intuitive way to picture these characteristics of OLS regression. Later, when we consider the statistical properties of OLS, this geometric picture will also be helpful.

2.3 EXAMPLES OF OLS

EXAMPLE 2.1

Consider the simplest case in which there are two observations and a single RHS variable ($N = 2$, $K = 1$) and

$$\mathbf{X} = \begin{bmatrix} 1 \\ 1 \end{bmatrix} \equiv \iota$$

In this case, $\text{Col}(\mathbf{X}) = \{\mathbf{z} \in \mathbb{R}^2 \mid z_1 = z_2\}$ and, as discussed on p. 8, $\hat{\beta} = \bar{y}$, the average of the two realized values of y:

$$\bar{y} \equiv \frac{y_1 + y_2}{2} = \underset{\beta}{\text{argmin}} \left[(y_1 - \beta)^2 + (y_2 - \beta)^2\right]$$

In a two-dimensional graph, Col($\mathbf{X}$) is the 45° line through the origin into the positive orthant and $\hat{\boldsymbol{\beta}}$ is the distance along this line to the fitted value $\mathbf{X}\hat{\boldsymbol{\beta}} = \hat{\boldsymbol{\mu}} = \iota\mathbf{y}$. See Figure 2.5. If a line segment is drawn between the points (y_1, y_2) and (y_2, y_1), it will intersect Col($\mathbf{X}$) at the end of the vector $\hat{\boldsymbol{\mu}}$, the midpoint of the segment: the two points, (y_1, y_2) and its reflection in the 45° line (y_2, y_1), have the same average that lies at this midpoint. The vector $\hat{\boldsymbol{\mu}}$ is the closest point in Col($\mathbf{X}$) to $\mathbf{y}$ and $\hat{\boldsymbol{\mu}}$ forms a right angle with the vector $\mathbf{y} - \hat{\boldsymbol{\mu}}$.

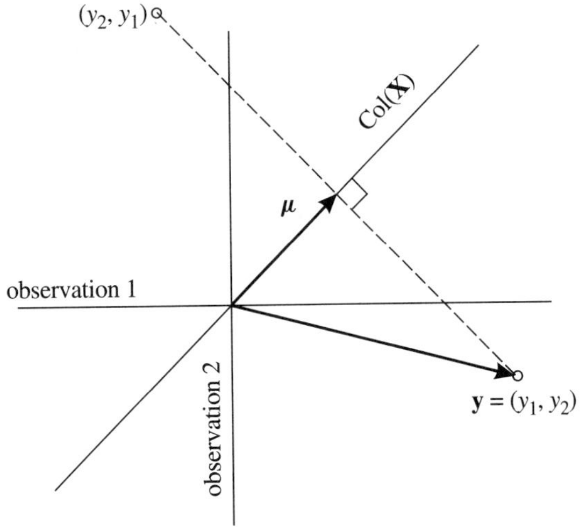

Figure 2.5 Ordinary least-squares projection in two dimensions.

The right angle between the *fitted* vector $\hat{\mu}$ and the *residual* vector $\mathbf{y} - \hat{\mu}$ in this example illustrates the general character of an *orthogonal projection*. We will give a more rigorous definition of orthogonal projections shortly. They generally solve the OLS problem, which seeks the closest point to $\mathbf{y}$ in the linear subspace Col($\mathbf{X}$). This result is also consistent with our intuition about the smallest distance between a point and a plane in three dimensions.

EXAMPLE 2.2

Consider the case with three observations and two RHS variables ($N = 3$, $K = 2$),

$$\mathbf{X} = [\,\mathbf{X}_1 \quad \mathbf{X}_2\,] = \begin{bmatrix} 1 & x_{12} \\ 1 & x_{22} \\ 1 & x_{32} \end{bmatrix}$$

In this case, Col($\mathbf{X}$) is a plane containing three points: the origin, $\mathbf{X}_1 = \iota \equiv [1, 1, 1]'$, and $\mathbf{X}_2 \equiv [x_{12}, x_{22}, x_{32}]'$. See Figure 2.6. We can picture $\mathbf{y}$ as a vector off the plane. The fitted vector $\hat{\mu}$ is the vector lying in Col($\mathbf{X}$) below $\mathbf{y}$ that is closest to $\mathbf{y}$. Thus, intuition (correctly) suggests that $\mathbf{y} - \hat{\mu}$ is perpendicular to the plane Col($\mathbf{X}$) and to the vector $\hat{\mu}$. The fitted regression coefficient vector $\hat{\beta}$ gives the unique linear combination of ι and $\mathbf{X}_2$ that equals $\hat{\mu}$. Let

$$\hat{\mu}_1 \equiv \iota\hat{\beta}_1 \quad \text{and} \quad \hat{\mu}_2 \equiv \mathbf{X}_2\hat{\beta}_2$$

so that $\hat{\mu} = \hat{\mu}_1 + \hat{\mu}_2$. The $\hat{\mu}_k$ ($k = 1, 2$) can be determined graphically by constructing a parallelogram around $\hat{\mu}$ with sides that are parallel to the two column vectors in $\mathbf{X}$ and with $\hat{\mu}$ on a diagonal. See Figure 2.7, where $\hat{\mu}_1$ points in the direction of $\mathbf{X}_1$, $\hat{\mu}_2$ points in the direction of $\mathbf{X}_2$, and $\hat{\mu}$ is the vector sum of $\hat{\mu}_1$ and $\hat{\mu}_2$.[6] The coefficients are determined by the proportion of the RHS vector in the fitted component:

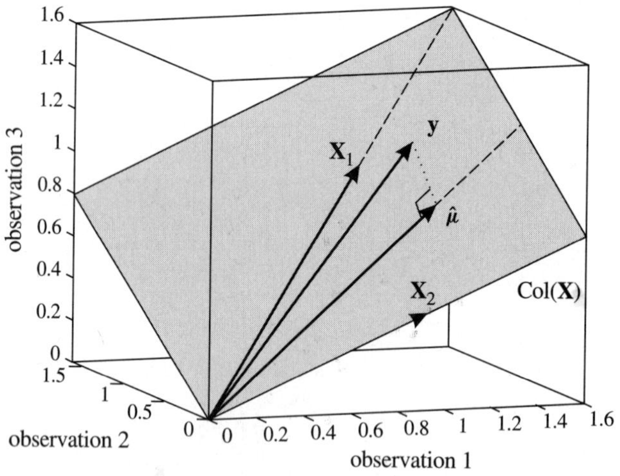

Figure 2.6 Ordinary least-squares projection in three dimensions.

[6] See also Figure C.2 and the accompanying text that reviews vector addition.

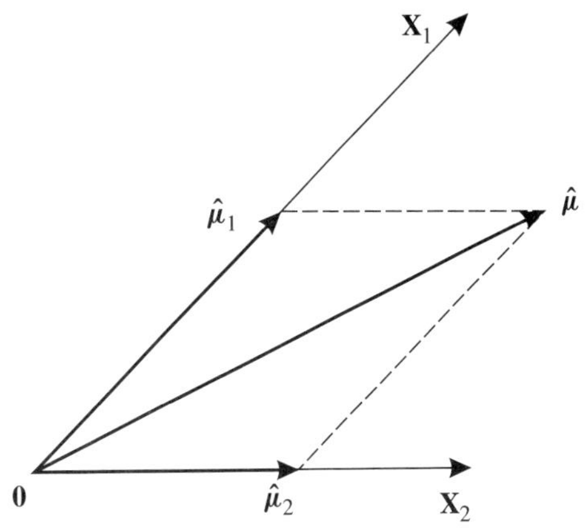

Figure 2.7 Decomposing $\hat{\mu}$ to get $\hat{\beta}$.

$$\hat{\beta}_1 = \frac{\iota'(\iota\hat{\beta}_1)}{\iota'\iota} = \frac{\iota'\hat{\boldsymbol{\mu}}_1}{\iota'\iota} \quad \text{and} \quad \hat{\beta}_2 = \frac{\mathbf{X}_2'(\mathbf{X}_2\hat{\beta}_2)}{\mathbf{X}_2'\mathbf{X}_2} = \frac{\mathbf{X}_2'\hat{\boldsymbol{\mu}}_2}{\mathbf{X}_2'\mathbf{X}_2}$$

In this way, $\hat{\boldsymbol{\mu}}$ determines $\hat{\boldsymbol{\beta}}$.

In Example 2.2, $\dim[\text{Col}(\mathbf{X})] = K$ so that part 3 of Proposition 1 applies and OLS has a unique solution. Suppose that we violate this requirement by adding a third column to $\mathbf{X}$ such that the dimension of Col($\mathbf{X}$) is still only 2 (even though $K = 3$). To do this, we add a vector that is linearly dependent on the first two. In Figure 2.6, the new vector must lie in the original plane Col($\mathbf{X}$); in Figure 2.7, the new vector could point in any direction on the page from the origin. This does not change the location of $\hat{\boldsymbol{\mu}}$, because Col($\mathbf{X}$) is unchanged. But finding $\hat{\boldsymbol{\beta}}$ has changed. There are many ways, instead of only one, to express $\hat{\boldsymbol{\mu}}$ as a linear combination of the column vectors in the expanded $\mathbf{X}$.

EXAMPLE 2.3

For example, suppose we choose the third column of $\mathbf{X}$ to be $\mathbf{X}_3 = \mathbf{X}_1 - 2\mathbf{X}_2$. If $\hat{\boldsymbol{\mu}} = \mathbf{X}_1\hat{\beta}_1 + \mathbf{X}_2\hat{\beta}_2$, then we can also express $\hat{\boldsymbol{\mu}}$ in terms of the additional $\mathbf{X}_3$ as

$$\begin{aligned}\hat{\boldsymbol{\mu}} &= \mathbf{X}_1\hat{\beta}_1 + \frac{1}{2}(\mathbf{X}_1 - \mathbf{X}_3)\hat{\beta}_2 \\ &= \mathbf{X}_1\left(\hat{\beta}_1 + \frac{1}{2}\hat{\beta}_2\right) + \mathbf{X}_3\left(-\frac{1}{2}\hat{\beta}_2\right) \\ &= \mathbf{X}_1\tilde{\beta}_1 + \mathbf{X}_3\tilde{\beta}_3\end{aligned}$$

where $\tilde{\beta}_1 \equiv \hat{\beta}_1 + \frac{1}{2}\hat{\beta}_2$ and $\tilde{\beta}_3 \equiv -\frac{1}{2}\hat{\beta}_2$. See Figure 2.8, where $\tilde{\mathbf{y}}_1 \equiv \mathbf{X}_1\tilde{\beta}_1$ and $\tilde{\mathbf{y}}_3 \equiv \mathbf{X}_3\tilde{\beta}_3$. This is only one of an infinite number of possibilities.

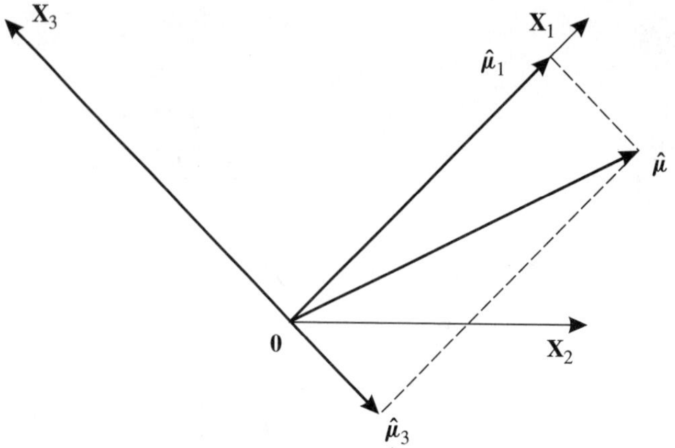

Figure 2.8 Decomposing $\hat{\mu}$ with collinear RHS variables.

2.4 ORTHOGONAL PROJECTION

In this section, we derive the geometric role of $\hat{\boldsymbol{\mu}}$ as the orthogonal projection of $\mathbf{y}$. Orthogonal projection is a powerful mathematical concept that appears in many applications of mathematics in addition to OLS regression. One sees applications of projection repeatedly in econometric theory and projection will be one of the themes of this book.

For the moment, the possibility of linear dependence among the RHS variables motivates our two-step interpretation of OLS. Such linear dependence does not affect the computation of $\hat{\boldsymbol{\mu}}$. The difficulties caused by linear dependence are isolated to converting $\hat{\boldsymbol{\mu}}$ into $\hat{\boldsymbol{\beta}}$. In this sense, linear dependence among the RHS variables has no fundamental bearing on how well a linear regression fits $\mathbf{y}$, the distance to the fitted vector depending only on $\hat{\boldsymbol{\mu}}$.

We begin by studying a special case for which we can construct a solution directly. We will show now that $\hat{\boldsymbol{\mu}} = \mathbf{X}\hat{\boldsymbol{\beta}} = \mathbf{X}(\mathbf{X}'\mathbf{X})^{-1}\mathbf{X}'\mathbf{y}$ only when the column vectors of $\mathbf{X}$ are linearly independent. For *any* two vectors $\boldsymbol{\mu}$ and $\hat{\boldsymbol{\mu}}$,

$$\begin{aligned}\|\mathbf{y} - \boldsymbol{\mu}\|^2 &= \left\|\mathbf{y} - \hat{\boldsymbol{\mu}} + \hat{\boldsymbol{\mu}} - \boldsymbol{\mu}\right\|^2 \\ &= \left\|\mathbf{y} - \hat{\boldsymbol{\mu}}\right\|^2 + \left\|\hat{\boldsymbol{\mu}} - \boldsymbol{\mu}\right\|^2 + 2\left(\mathbf{y} - \hat{\boldsymbol{\mu}}\right)'\left(\hat{\boldsymbol{\mu}} - \boldsymbol{\mu}\right)\end{aligned}$$

If $\hat{\boldsymbol{\mu}} - \boldsymbol{\mu}$ is orthogonal to $\mathbf{y} - \hat{\boldsymbol{\mu}}$ (denoted $\hat{\boldsymbol{\mu}} - \boldsymbol{\mu} \perp \mathbf{y} - \hat{\boldsymbol{\mu}}$), so that the inner product of these two vectors is zero, we have the Pythagorean theorem.[7]

THEOREM 1 (PYTHAGORAS) *If* $\mathbf{z}_1, \mathbf{z}_2 \in \mathbf{R}^N$ *and* $\mathbf{z}_1 \perp \mathbf{z}_2$ *then*

$$\|\mathbf{z}_1 + \mathbf{z}_2\|^2 = \|\mathbf{z}_1\|^2 + \|\mathbf{z}_2\|^2$$

[7] See Appendix C for a summary of orthogonality in a Euclidean vector space.

Proof. By hypothesis, $\mathbf{z}_1'\mathbf{z}_2 = 0$. Therefore,

$$\begin{aligned}\|\mathbf{z}_1 + \mathbf{z}_2\|^2 &= (\mathbf{z}_1 + \mathbf{z}_2)'(\mathbf{z}_1 + \mathbf{z}_2) \\ &= \mathbf{z}_1'\mathbf{z}_1 + \mathbf{z}_1'\mathbf{z}_2 + \mathbf{z}_2'\mathbf{z}_1 + \mathbf{z}_2'\mathbf{z}_2 \\ &= \|\mathbf{z}_1\|^2 + \|\mathbf{z}_2\|^2\end{aligned}$$

□[8]

We can use the Pythagorean theorem to identify an important property of orthogonality. If there is a $\hat{\boldsymbol{\mu}} \in \text{Col}(\mathbf{X})$ such that[9]

$$\mathbf{X}'(\mathbf{y} - \hat{\boldsymbol{\mu}}) = \mathbf{0} \tag{2.4}$$

then for all other $\boldsymbol{\mu} \in \text{Col}(\mathbf{X})$,

$$\boldsymbol{\mu}'(\mathbf{y} - \hat{\boldsymbol{\mu}}) = 0$$
$$(\boldsymbol{\mu} - \hat{\boldsymbol{\mu}})'(\mathbf{y} - \hat{\boldsymbol{\mu}}) = 0$$

and

$$\|\mathbf{y} - \boldsymbol{\mu}\|^2 = \|\mathbf{y} - \hat{\boldsymbol{\mu}}\|^2 + \|\hat{\boldsymbol{\mu}} - \boldsymbol{\mu}\|^2 \tag{2.5}$$

$$\geq \|\mathbf{y} - \hat{\boldsymbol{\mu}}\|^2$$

In words, because $\mathbf{y} - \hat{\boldsymbol{\mu}}$ is orthogonal to $\text{Col}(\mathbf{X})$, $\hat{\boldsymbol{\mu}}$ is at least as close to $\mathbf{y}$ as any other $\boldsymbol{\mu}$ in $\text{Col}(\mathbf{X})$ to $\mathbf{y}$. Therefore $\hat{\boldsymbol{\mu}}$ is one solution to the OLS (minimum distance) problem (repeated here for convenience)

$$\hat{\boldsymbol{\mu}} = \underset{\boldsymbol{\mu} \in \text{Col}(\mathbf{X})}{\text{argmin}} \|\mathbf{y} - \boldsymbol{\mu}\|^2 \tag{2.2}$$

Furthermore, this $\hat{\boldsymbol{\mu}}$ is the *unique* solution. To see this, note that for every other possible solution $\tilde{\mu}$ it must be that $\|\mathbf{y} - \tilde{\mu}\|^2 = \|\mathbf{y} - \hat{\boldsymbol{\mu}}\|^2$ because no other $\boldsymbol{\mu}$ is closer than $\hat{\boldsymbol{\mu}}$. But then (2.5) implies that $\|\hat{\boldsymbol{\mu}} - \tilde{\boldsymbol{\mu}}\|^2 = 0$ and $\tilde{\boldsymbol{\mu}}$ must be equal to $\hat{\boldsymbol{\mu}}$. Therefore, we have established that the orthogonality condition (2.4) completely characterizes the OLS fitted vector $\hat{\boldsymbol{\mu}}$.

Now we will construct $\hat{\boldsymbol{\mu}}$ for a special case and show that the unique solution to (2.4), and therefore to (2.2), actually exists. This will provide preparation for proving the existence of the unique solution in the general case in the next section. According to (2.4),[10]

$$\mathbf{X}'(\mathbf{y} - \mathbf{X}\hat{\boldsymbol{\beta}}) = \mathbf{0}$$

We can solve these K linear equations for $\hat{\boldsymbol{\beta}}$,

$$\mathbf{X}'\mathbf{X}\hat{\boldsymbol{\beta}} - \mathbf{X}'\mathbf{y} = \mathbf{0} \quad \Leftrightarrow \quad \hat{\boldsymbol{\beta}} = (\mathbf{X}'\mathbf{X})^{-1}\mathbf{X}'\mathbf{y} \tag{2.6}$$

provided that $\mathbf{X}'\mathbf{X}$ is *nonsingular* .[11] The solution for $\hat{\boldsymbol{\mu}}$ follows immediately as

---

[8] We will use the symbol □ to signal the end of a proof.

[9] The bold zero, $\mathbf{0}$, denotes a vector or matrix of zeros. Usually the dimensions will be clear from the context. In (2.4), $\mathbf{0}$ is a column vector of K zeros.

[10] These K linear equations are called *normal equations* because they characterize the *normal vector* to $\text{Col}(\mathbf{X})$.

[11] See Definition C.15 (Nonsingular, p. 850).

$$\hat{\mu} = \mathbf{X}\hat{\beta} = \mathbf{X}(\mathbf{X}'\mathbf{X})^{-1}\mathbf{X}'\mathbf{y} \tag{2.7}$$

Note that $\hat{\beta}$ and $\hat{\mu}$ have a one-to-one relationship. We can also obtain $\hat{\beta}$ from $\hat{\mu}$: premultiplying (2.7) by $(\mathbf{X}'\mathbf{X})^{-1}\mathbf{X}'$ gives

$$(\mathbf{X}'\mathbf{X})^{-1}\mathbf{X}'\hat{\mu} = (\mathbf{X}'\mathbf{X})^{-1}\mathbf{X}'\mathbf{X}\hat{\beta} = \hat{\beta} \tag{2.8}$$

So when is $\mathbf{X}'\mathbf{X}$ nonsingular? The examples and figures illustrate a general point about $\hat{\mu}$ that answers this question: $\hat{\mu}$ is a unique linear combination of the columns of $\mathbf{X}$ only if those columns are linearly independent. In formal terms, if $\dim[\mathrm{Col}(\mathbf{X})] = K$, so that the columns of $\mathbf{X}$ form a *basis* for $\mathrm{Col}(\mathbf{X})$, then $\hat{\mu}$ is a unique linear combination of that basis.[12] Now we will show that the algebraic significance of $\dim[\mathrm{Col}(\mathbf{X})] = K$ is that $\mathbf{X}'\mathbf{X}$ is nonsingular and, therefore, the matrix inverse $(\mathbf{X}'\mathbf{X})^{-1}$ and the solution vector $\hat{\mu} = \mathbf{X}(\mathbf{X}'\mathbf{X})^{-1}\mathbf{X}'\mathbf{y}$ are well defined.

Lemma 2.1 $\dim[\mathrm{Col}(\mathbf{X})] \equiv \mathrm{rank}(\mathbf{X}) = K$ *if and only if* $\mathbf{X}'\mathbf{X}$ *is nonsingular.*

Proof. If $\dim[\mathrm{Col}(\mathbf{X})] < K$, then there is an $\boldsymbol{\alpha} \in \mathbb{R}^K$, $\boldsymbol{\alpha} \neq \mathbf{0}$ such that $\mathbf{X}\boldsymbol{\alpha} = \mathbf{0}$. But then $\mathbf{X}'\mathbf{X}\boldsymbol{\alpha} = \mathbf{0}$, so that $\mathbf{X}'\mathbf{X}$ is singular. The converse is also true: if $\mathbf{X}\boldsymbol{\alpha} \neq \mathbf{0}$ for all $\boldsymbol{\alpha} \neq \mathbf{0}$, then

$$\boldsymbol{\alpha}'\mathbf{X}'\mathbf{X}\boldsymbol{\alpha} = \|\mathbf{X}\boldsymbol{\alpha}\|^2 > 0$$

and $\mathbf{X}'\mathbf{X}\boldsymbol{\alpha} \neq 0$ so that $\mathbf{X}'\mathbf{X}$ is nonsingular. □

Because $\dim[\mathrm{Col}(\mathbf{X})] \equiv \mathrm{rank}(\mathbf{X})$, if $\dim[\mathrm{Col}(\mathbf{X})] = K$ then $\mathbf{X}$ is said to be *full (column) rank*.[13] If $\dim[\mathrm{Col}(\mathbf{X})] < K$ then $\mathbf{X}$ is called *rank deficient*.[14] The following example contains one of the simplest cases of rank deficiency.

EXAMPLE 2.4

When $K = 2$, $\mathbf{X} = [\mathbf{X}_1, \mathbf{X}_2]$, and $\mathbf{X}_1 = \boldsymbol{\iota}$, as in Example 2.2, we can easily solve the first-order conditions for (2.1) to get the recursive solution

$$\hat{\beta}_2 = \frac{\sum_{n=1}^{N}(x_{n2} - \bar{x}_2)y_n}{\sum_{n=1}^{N}(x_{n2} - \bar{x}_2)^2}$$

$$\hat{\beta}_1 = \bar{y} - \bar{x}_2\hat{\beta}_2$$

where $\bar{x}_2$ is the sample average $\sum_{n=1}^{N} x_{n2}/N$. But this solution is well defined only if x_{n2} is not a constant like x_{n1} so that $\sum_{n=1}^{N}(x_{n2} - \bar{x}_2)^2 \neq 0$. Otherwise, $\mathrm{rank}(\mathbf{X}) < K$ and there is linear dependence between $\mathbf{X}_1$ and $\mathbf{X}_2$, as in $x_{n2} = c \Leftrightarrow \mathbf{X}_2 - c \cdot \boldsymbol{\iota} = \mathbf{0}$.

---

[12] See Definition C.9 (p. 847) for the *basis* of a linear vector space.

[13] See Definition C.14 (Matrix Rank, p. 855).

[14] See Definitions C.14 (p. 850) and C.20 (p. 850).

So far in this chapter, for the special case where $\mathbf{X}$ is full-column rank, we have already proved points 2 and 3 of Proposition 1. It remains to explain orthogonal projection and thereby to establish point 1. To introduce orthogonal projection formally, we begin with the projection theorem.

2.4.1 The Projection Theorem

There is an important general geometric principle at work in the problem that we have just solved. There are many more situations in which we will apply this principle and so we introduce it here.

THEOREM 2 (PROJECTION) *Let* $\mathbf{y} \in \mathbb{R}^N$ *and let* $\mathbb{S} \subseteq \mathbb{R}^N$ *be a linear subspace. Then* $\hat{\boldsymbol{\mu}} \in \mathbb{S}$ *is a solution to the program*

$$\min_{\boldsymbol{\mu} \in \mathbb{S}} \|\mathbf{y} - \boldsymbol{\mu}\|^2$$

if and only if $\mathbf{y} - \hat{\boldsymbol{\mu}} \perp \mathbb{S}$. *Furthermore,* $\hat{\boldsymbol{\mu}}$ *is the unique solution and exists.*

A proof appears in Section 2.6.3. Much of the argument already appears in the development of (2.4)–(2.5) and the discussion immediately following these equations. Additional work proves that $\mathbf{y} - \hat{\boldsymbol{\mu}} \perp \mathbb{S}$ is not only a *sufficient* but also a *necessary* condition for the optimality of $\hat{\boldsymbol{\mu}}$, and that the optimal $\hat{\boldsymbol{\mu}}$ exists even though we may not know an expression for it.

The projection theorem is a general foundation for understanding the structure of the OLS problem, for which the subspace $\mathbb{S}$ is $\text{Col}(\mathbf{X})$. First, the theorem identifies the mechanism of minimization, which is finding a $\hat{\boldsymbol{\mu}} \in \text{Col}(\mathbf{X})$ such that $\mathbf{y} - \hat{\boldsymbol{\mu}} \perp \text{Col}(\mathbf{X})$. Second, the projection theorem clarifies that $\text{Col}(\mathbf{X})$, and not $\mathbf{X}$ itself, determines the optimal $\hat{\boldsymbol{\mu}}$. Now we will focus on $\hat{\boldsymbol{\mu}}$ itself.

2.4.2 Orthogonal Projectors

We may view $\hat{\boldsymbol{\mu}}$ as a function of $\mathbf{y}$. For every $\mathbf{y}$, there is a unique

$$\hat{\boldsymbol{\mu}} = \underset{\boldsymbol{\mu} \in \mathbb{S}}{\text{argmin}} \|\mathbf{y} - \boldsymbol{\mu}\|^2$$

This transformation $\hat{\boldsymbol{\mu}}$ is called the *orthogonal projection* of $\mathbf{y}$, hence the name of Theorem 2. We will now show that the orthogonal projection $\hat{\boldsymbol{\mu}}$ is always a linear transformation of $\mathbf{y}$. Given this, we will find the matrix $\mathbf{P}$ so that $\hat{\boldsymbol{\mu}} = \mathbf{P}\mathbf{y}$. Such matrices as $\mathbf{P}$ are called *orthogonal projectors.*

In the special case that $\mathbb{S} = \text{Col}(\mathbf{X})$ and $\mathbf{X}$ is full-column rank, the matrix

$$\mathbf{P}_\mathbf{X} \equiv \mathbf{X}(\mathbf{X}'\mathbf{X})^{-1}\mathbf{X}' \tag{2.9}$$

in (2.7) is the linear transformation of $\mathbf{y}$ onto $\text{Col}(\mathbf{X})$ that produces $\hat{\boldsymbol{\mu}}$. Note that $\mathbf{P}_\mathbf{X}$ has two properties as a linear transformation of vectors in $\mathbb{R}^N$: it leaves all vectors in $\text{Col}(\mathbf{X})$ unchanged and it transforms vectors orthogonal to $\text{Col}(\mathbf{X})$ to the zero vector:

$$\mathbf{z} \in \mathrm{Col}(\mathbf{X}) \quad \Rightarrow \quad \mathbf{P_X z} = \mathbf{z} \tag{2.10}$$

and

$$\mathbf{z} \perp \mathrm{Col}(\mathbf{X}) \quad \Rightarrow \quad \mathbf{P_X z} = \mathbf{0} \tag{2.11}$$

It is easy to verify (2.10) directly. For every $\mathbf{z} \in \mathrm{Col}(\mathbf{X})$ there is an $\boldsymbol{\alpha}$ such that $\mathbf{z} = \mathbf{X}\boldsymbol{\alpha}$. Now observe that $\mathbf{P_X z} = \mathbf{P_X X}\boldsymbol{\alpha} = \mathbf{X}(\mathbf{X}'\mathbf{X})^{-1}\mathbf{X}'\mathbf{X}\boldsymbol{\alpha} = \mathbf{X}\boldsymbol{\alpha} = \mathbf{z}$. We can also verify (2.11) directly. If $\mathbf{z} \perp \mathrm{Col}(\mathbf{X})$ then $\mathbf{z}'\mathbf{x} = 0\ \forall \mathbf{x} \in \mathrm{Col}(\mathbf{X})$ so that $\mathbf{X}'\mathbf{z} = \mathbf{0}$ and $\mathbf{P_X z} = \mathbf{X}(\mathbf{X}'\mathbf{X})^{-1}\mathbf{X}'\mathbf{z} = \mathbf{X}(\mathbf{X}'\mathbf{X})^{-1} \cdot \mathbf{0} = \mathbf{0}$.

Given the projection theorem, we can deduce that there is also such a matrix for rank-deficient $\mathbf{X}$. To see this, note first that the projection theorem supports the following basic result.

LEMMA 2.2 (ORTHOGONAL DECOMPOSITION) *For every $\mathbf{z} \in \mathbb{R}^N$, we can decompose $\mathbf{z}$ uniquely into the vector sum $\mathbf{z}_1 + \mathbf{z}_2$ where $\mathbf{z}_1 \in \mathrm{Col}(\mathbf{X})$ and $\mathbf{z}_2 \in \mathrm{Col}^{\perp}(\mathbf{X}) \equiv \{\mathbf{z} \in \mathbb{R}^N \mid \mathbf{X}'\mathbf{z} = \mathbf{0}\}$.*[15]

This lemma is straightforward and also has familiar examples. One is that any vector in a Cartesian plane can always be decomposed uniquely into its "x" and "y" coordinates, each representing mutually orthogonal components of the vector (x, y). We give a proof of Lemma 2.2 in Section 2.6.3 (p. 40).[16]

The significance of this orthogonal decomposition lemma is that it identifies the orthogonal projection mapping.

DEFINITION 2 (ORTHOGONAL PROJECTION) *Let $\mathbb{S}$ be a K-dimensional linear subspace of $\mathbb{R}^N$ so that for every $\mathbf{z} \in \mathbb{R}^N$ there is a unique $\mathbf{z}_1 \in \mathbb{S}$ and a unique $\mathbf{z}_2 \in \mathbb{S}^{\perp}$ such that $\mathbf{z} = \mathbf{z}_1 + \mathbf{z}_2$. Then the mapping of $\mathbb{R}^N$ into $\mathbb{S}^{\perp}$ that associates each $\mathbf{z}$ with its corresponding $\mathbf{z}_1$ is an* orthogonal projection.

In the Cartesian plane, one may tend to view the vector (x, y) as a construction of the x and y coordinates. This definition reverses this direction of thought. Given any point (x, y) in the Cartesian plane, it is always possible to find such orthogonal projections as the "x" component $(x, 0)$.

Thus, (2.10) and (2.11) state that when $\mathbb{S} = \mathrm{Col}(\mathbf{X})$ then $\mathbf{P_X z} = \mathbf{z}_1$ is the orthogonal projection of $\mathbf{z}$ onto $\mathrm{Col}(\mathbf{X})$. Only the component of $\mathbf{z}$ in $\mathrm{Col}(\mathbf{X})$ survives premultiplication by $\mathbf{P_X}$. The complementary component of $\mathbf{z}$ in $\mathrm{Col}^{\perp}(\mathbf{X})$ is annihilated. The linear property of orthogonal projection follows immediately.

[15] The subspace $\mathrm{Col}^{\perp}(\mathbf{X})$ is the *orthogonal complement* of $\mathrm{Col}(\mathbf{X})$. See Definition C.19 (Orthogonal Complement, p. 854).

[16] Alternatively, this lemma is a consequence of Theorems C.2 (Direct Sum, p. 845) and C.11 (Orthogonal Complement, p. 854).

Lemma 2.3 *The orthogonal projection from $\mathbb{R}^N$ onto a subspace $\mathbb{S}$ is a linear transformation.*[17]

As a result, every orthogonal projection from $\mathbb{R}^N$ into a subspace $\mathbb{S}$ can be represented by a matrix $\mathbf{P}$, called an *orthogonal projector.*

Definition 3 (Orthogonal Projector) *Let $\mathbb{S}$ be a K-dimensional linear subspace of $\mathbb{R}^N$ so that for every $\mathbf{z} \in \mathbb{R}^N$ there is a unique $\mathbf{z}_1 \in \mathbb{S}$ and a unique $\mathbf{z}_2 \in \mathbb{S}^\perp$ such that $\mathbf{z} = \mathbf{z}_1 + \mathbf{z}_2$. Then an $N \times N$ matrix $\mathbf{P}$ such that $\mathbf{Pz} = \mathbf{z}_1$ is an* orthogonal projector *onto $\mathbb{S}$.*

In general, an orthogonal projector preserves the component of a vector in a subspace $\mathbb{S}$ and annihilates the component in the complementary orthogonal subspace $\mathbb{S}^\perp$. These properties define an orthogonal projection and $\mathbf{P_X}$ exhibits them in (2.10) and (2.11).

Another useful property of orthogonal projectors follows immediately from this definition.

Lemma 2.4 (Projector Uniqueness) *If $\mathbf{P}$ is an orthogonal projector onto a subspace $\mathbb{S}$* of *$\mathbb{R}^N$, then $\mathbf{P}$ is unique.*

Proof. Let $\mathbf{P}_1$ and $\mathbf{P}_2$ be two orthogonal projectors onto $\mathbb{S}$. By Definition 2, the orthogonal projection is unique: $\mathbf{P}_1\mathbf{z} = \mathbf{P}_2\mathbf{z}$ for all $\mathbf{z} \in \mathbb{R}^N$. Setting $\mathbf{z}$ equal to each of the natural basis vectors in $\mathbf{I}_N$, we have the matrix equality $\mathbf{P}_1\mathbf{I}_N = \mathbf{P}_2\mathbf{I}_N$ or $\mathbf{P}_1 = \mathbf{P}_2$. □

Having described the essential features of orthogonal projection, we conclude this section by collecting together the results that constitute a proof of our main result, Proposition 1.

Proof of Proposition 1. The first point of the proposition follows from the projection theorem (Theorem 2) and Definition 2. Also according to the projection theorem, $\mathbf{y} - \hat{\boldsymbol{\mu}} \perp \text{Col}(\mathbf{X})$, which proves the second element of the proposition. Based on this orthogonality, (2.6) proves the third and final element of the proposition: we solve the orthogonality conditions for $\hat{\boldsymbol{\beta}}$. □

[17] See Definition C.10 (Linear Transformation, p. 847). The proof of this lemma is straightforward. Consider $\mathbf{w}, \mathbf{z} \in \mathbb{R}^N$ and their unique orthogonal decompositions $\mathbf{w} = \mathbf{w}_1 + \mathbf{w}_2$ and $\mathbf{z} = \mathbf{z}_1 + \mathbf{z}_2$ where $\mathbf{w}_1, \mathbf{z}_1 \in \mathbb{S}$. Then,

$$a \cdot \mathbf{w} + b \cdot \mathbf{z} = (a \cdot \mathbf{w}_1 + b \cdot \mathbf{z}_1) + (a \cdot \mathbf{w}_2 + b \cdot \mathbf{z}_2)$$

is the unique orthogonal decomposition of $a \cdot \mathbf{w} + b \cdot \mathbf{z}$. Therefore, its orthogonal projection onto $\mathbb{S}$ is $a \cdot \mathbf{w}_1 + b \cdot \mathbf{z}_1$. That is, the orthogonal projection of a linear combination of vectors equals the linear combination of the individual orthogonal projections of the vectors.

The projection theorem supports our claim above that $\hat{\mu}$ is not changed by the introduction of a linearly dependent column to $\mathbf{X}$. The vector $\hat{\mu}$ is determined by $\text{Col}(\mathbf{X})$ and not $\mathbf{X}$ itself; $\hat{\mu}$ is defined to be the closest point in $\text{Col}(\mathbf{X})$ to $\mathbf{y}$. When we introduce a linearly dependent column to $\mathbf{X}$, we leave $\text{Col}(\mathbf{X})$ unchanged by definition and we leave $\hat{\mu}$ unchanged by the theorem. However, if we begin with an $\mathbf{X}$ that is rank deficient then $\mathbf{X}'\mathbf{X}$ is singular and its inverse does not exist. As a result, we cannot solve for $\hat{\boldsymbol{\beta}}$ and $\hat{\mu}$ as in (2.6)–(2.7). Nevertheless, the tools that we have developed for full-column rank $\mathbf{X}$ also enable us to construct $\hat{\mu}$ for rank-deficient $\mathbf{X}$.

2.5 EXACT MULTICOLLINEARITY

Now we extend our analysis of the solution to OLS to the case of deficient rank. Orthogonal projectors also provide a simple solution for this case, generally called *exact multicollinearity.*

DEFINITION 4 (MULTICOLLINEARITY) *If there is a nonzero vector* $\boldsymbol{\alpha} \in \mathbb{R}^K$ *such that* $\mathbf{X}\boldsymbol{\alpha} = \mathbf{0}$, *then the RHS variables, the column vectors of* $\mathbf{X}$, *are linearly dependent. This situation is called* exact multicollinearity.

Note that neither the definition of an orthogonal projector nor the projection theorem relates to the rank of such a matrix as $\mathbf{X}$. A fundamental concept to these constructions is the linear vector subspace and $\text{Col}(\mathbf{X})$ is well defined regardless of the rank of $\mathbf{X}$. We can conclude, therefore, that a unique $\hat{\mu}$ exists even when $\mathbf{X}$ is rank deficient.

We have just seen that orthogonal projectors have the property that they are unique. Let us denote *the* orthogonal projector onto $\text{Col}(\mathbf{X})$ generally by $\mathbf{P_X}$, rather than referring specifically to the formula given by (2.9). Now *any* orthogonal projector onto $\text{Col}(\mathbf{X})$ that we may find is *the* orthogonal projector $\mathbf{P_X}$. When $\mathbf{X}$ and, therefore, $\mathbf{X}'\mathbf{X}$ are singular, we cannot use (2.9) to find $\mathbf{P_X}$ in general. But we can use this formula indirectly. When $\dim[\text{Col}(\mathbf{X})] < K$, we can find $\mathbf{P_X}$ by applying our formula to *any linearly independent subset* of the columns of $\mathbf{X}$ that is a basis for $\text{Col}(\mathbf{X})$.

LEMMA 2.5 *Let* $\mathbf{P_X}$ *denote the orthogonal projector onto* $\text{Col}(\mathbf{X})$ *and let* $\mathbf{X}_1$ *be any matrix composed of a linearly independent subset of the columns of* $\mathbf{X}$ *such that* $\text{Col}(\mathbf{X}_1) = \text{Col}(\mathbf{X})$. *Then* $\mathbf{P_X} = \mathbf{X}_1(\mathbf{X}_1'\mathbf{X}_1)^{-1}\mathbf{X}_1'$.

We leave a formal proof as Exercise 2.9.

For illustration, let us return to Examples 2.2 and 2.3: Before we add an additional column such as $\mathbf{X}_3$ to $\mathbf{X}$, the formula $\mathbf{P_X} = \mathbf{X}(\mathbf{X}'\mathbf{X})^{-1}\mathbf{X}'$ provides the unique orthogonal projector. Given the additional column, we could also compute $\mathbf{P_X} = \mathbf{W}(\mathbf{W}'\mathbf{W})^{-1}\mathbf{W}'$ by setting $\mathbf{W} = [\iota, \mathbf{X}_3]$. Yet another procedure would be to set $\mathbf{P_X} = \mathbf{Z}(\mathbf{Z}'\mathbf{Z})^{-1}\mathbf{Z}'$ where $\mathbf{Z} = [\mathbf{X}_2, \mathbf{X}_3]$. All yield the same projection matrix $\mathbf{P_X}$, and, by premultiplication of $\mathbf{y}$, the same $\hat{\mu}$. In each instance, we can compute the orthogonal projector from the general formula by reducing the matrix of RHS variables to columns that form a linearly independent basis for its column space.

This is exactly what many regression programs do when they encounter multicollinearity in **X**. Each time a linear relationship is discovered among the columns of **X**, one of the offending columns is dropped from the remaining calculations. This is equivalent to assigning a zero to the coefficient for the associated RHS variable instead of some fitted value, so the action is often flagged for the researcher by setting the coefficient to zero exactly. This action is clearly arbitrary; if the RHS variables are entered in a different order, then different coefficients may be set to zero. But this does not affect the goodness of fit, as we have just seen. What *is* affected is the interpretation of the fitted coefficients. In most cases in applied economics, the researcher knows about, or discovers, the multicollinearity and chooses the RHS variables to omit.

On the other hand, some respecification of the RHS variables is clearly warranted if they are multicollinear. We should not expect to find a unique set of coefficients from the OLS fit. In practice, we choose particular values for the coefficients from a set of values that produces the same fit. Setting some coefficients to zero is one such choice.

EXAMPLE 2.5 (Multicollinearity)

In the introductory example of this chapter, the variables age, education, experience, and the constant 1 have an exact linear relationship:

$$0 = 6 - age + education + experience$$

By restricting the RHS variables to contain no more than three of these variables, we can find one solution to the OLS regression problem. But no matter which variable we exclude we obtain the same $\hat{\boldsymbol{\mu}}$ and the same SSR. Furthermore, we can find many other solutions. If $x_{n1} = 1$, $x_{n2} = age$, $x_{n3} = education$, and $x_{n4} = experience$, and $\boldsymbol{\alpha}' = [6, -1, 1, 1, 0, \ldots, 0]$, then $x_n\boldsymbol{\alpha} = 0$ so that for all scalars c,

$$\hat{\boldsymbol{\beta}} = \tilde{\boldsymbol{\beta}} + c \cdot \boldsymbol{\alpha} \quad \Rightarrow \quad \hat{\boldsymbol{\mu}} = \mathbf{X}\tilde{\boldsymbol{\beta}} = \mathbf{X}\hat{\boldsymbol{\beta}}$$

If we compare the fitted coefficients in Run 5 of Table 1.8 with those in Table 2.3, we see that this relationship holds numerically:

$$\begin{bmatrix} 0.779 \\ 0.000 \\ 0.095 \\ 0.039 \end{bmatrix} \approx \begin{bmatrix} 0.209 \\ 0.095 \\ 0.000 \\ -0.056 \end{bmatrix} + 0.095 \cdot \begin{bmatrix} 6 \\ -1 \\ 1 \\ 1 \end{bmatrix}$$

where $\hat{\boldsymbol{\beta}}$ contains the coefficients from Run 5 and $\tilde{\boldsymbol{\beta}}$ contains the coefficients in Table 2.3.

How can we identify a linearly independent subset of the columns of **X** that spans Col(**X**)? Orthogonal projection itself provides a method built on the following observation. We can determine constructively whether a vector $\mathbf{z}_k$ lies in the space spanned by a set of linearly independent vectors $\{\mathbf{z}_1, \ldots, \mathbf{z}_{k-1}\}$ by forming a matrix **W** with columns that are the vectors $\mathbf{z}_1, \ldots, \mathbf{z}_{k-1}$. This matrix is full-column rank so that the orthogonal projector onto Col(**W**) is $\mathbf{P_W} = \mathbf{W}\left(\mathbf{W}'\mathbf{W}\right)^{-1}\mathbf{W}'$. If $\mathbf{P_W}\mathbf{z}_k = \mathbf{z}_k$ then $\mathbf{z}_k \in \text{Col}(\mathbf{W})$ and vice versa.

To construct a subset of linearly independent columns of $\mathbf{X} = [\mathbf{X}_1, \ldots, \mathbf{X}_K]$, we apply this test iteratively to each of the K column vectors $\mathbf{X}_k$ $(k = 1, \ldots, K)$ of $\mathbf{X}$. We can begin by placing $\mathbf{X}_1$ in this subset.[18] Our rule for admission of each of the additional columns will be that the candidate vector must not be linearly dependent on those already in the subset. We apply the rule by examining the orthogonal projection of the candidate vector onto the column space of the admitted subset. If this projection equals the candidate, then the candidate is linearly dependent, denied admission, and dropped from further consideration. After we go through all of the columns of $\mathbf{X}$, we will obtain a basis for $\mathrm{Col}(\mathbf{X})$ to which we can apply Lemma 2.5 for $\mathbf{P_X}$.

2.6 MATHEMATICAL NOTES

In this section, we give a more formal description of the process of finding a basis for $\mathrm{Col}(\mathbf{X})$ just described. There are no new concepts. But a simple change in this process yields a new expression for orthogonal projectors that will prove useful later in this book. The altered process is an important mathematical algorithm in its own right, called *Gram-Schmidt orthonormalization*.

We also show several additional properties of orthogonal projectors and provide the proofs for several results given earlier in the chapter.

2.6.1 Gram–Schmidt Orthonormalization

Let the iterations be indexed by $k = 1, \ldots, K$, so that there is an iteration for each column of $\mathbf{X}$. Let $\mathbf{Z}_k$ be the matrix whose columns are the linearly independent columns of $\mathbf{X}$ admitted after the kth iteration and set $\mathbf{Z}_1 = \mathbf{X}_1$, the first column of $\mathbf{X}$. At the beginning of the kth iteration $(k \geq 2)$, we check whether

$$\|\mathbf{X}_k - \mathbf{P}_{k-1}\mathbf{X}_k\| = 0 \tag{2.12}$$

where

$$\mathbf{P}_{k-1} \equiv \mathbf{Z}_{k-1}\left(\mathbf{Z}_{k-1}'\mathbf{Z}_{k-1}\right)^{-1}\mathbf{Z}_{k-1}' \equiv \mathbf{P}_{\mathbf{Z}_{k-1}} \tag{2.13}$$

to see whether the kth column of $\mathbf{X}$, $\mathbf{X}_k$, is linearly dependent on the previous $k-1$ columns of $\mathbf{X}$. Because we have chosen $\mathbf{Z}_k$ to contain linearly independent vectors, every projector $\mathbf{P}_k$ is well defined. If (2.12) is satisfied, then we drop $\mathbf{X}_k$ and set $\mathbf{Z}_k = \mathbf{Z}_{k-1}$; otherwise, we add $\mathbf{X}_k$ as an additional basis vector to $\mathbf{Z}_k$:

$$\mathbf{Z}_k = \begin{cases} \mathbf{Z}_{k-1} & \text{if } \|\mathbf{X}_k - \mathbf{P}_{k-1}\mathbf{X}_k\| = 0 \\ [\mathbf{Z}_{k-1}, \mathbf{X}_k] & \text{if } \|\mathbf{X}_k - \mathbf{P}_{k-1}\mathbf{X}_k\| > 0 \end{cases} \tag{2.14}$$

When we reach the final iteration, $\mathrm{Col}(\mathbf{Z}_K) = \mathrm{Col}(\mathbf{X})$ and $\mathbf{P}_K \equiv \mathbf{P}_{\mathbf{Z}_K} = \mathbf{P_X}$.

Recall that in the introductory example we discovered the linear dependence among the constant, age, experience, and schooling variables through an OLS fit. In effect, we are carrying out this procedure repeatedly to uncover all linear dependence among the RHS variables, and beginning with a subset of RHS variables to ensure linear independence at every step.

[18] We will suppose that none of the $\mathbf{X}_k$ $(k = 1, \ldots, K)$ is a vector of zeros.

We have just developed a method for finding a basis for Col($\mathbf{X}$). It will be analytically helpful to be able to express $\hat{\boldsymbol{\mu}}$ in terms of an *orthonormal* basis: a set of mutually orthogonal, unit-length vectors that spans Col($\mathbf{X}$). To find an orthonormal basis, we alter our method for finding a basis slightly in two ways. First, each admitted member of the basis is normalized to unit length and second, rather than placing an $\mathbf{X}_k$ into the basis, we insert the residual $\mathbf{X}_k - \mathbf{P}_{k-1}\mathbf{X}_k$. This residual is orthogonal to all of the basis vectors in the $\mathbf{Z}_{k-1}$ that have preceded. Thus, we produce an orthonormal basis by starting with

$$\mathbf{Z}_1 = \frac{1}{\|\mathbf{X}_1\|} \cdot \mathbf{X}_1$$

instead of $\mathbf{X}_1$. At the kth iteration ($k = 2, \ldots, K$), we continue to set $\mathbf{P}_{k-1} = \mathbf{P}_{\mathbf{Z}_{k-1}}$ but alter (2.14) to

$$\mathbf{Z}_k = \begin{cases} \mathbf{Z}_{k-1} & \text{if } \|\mathbf{w}_k\| = 0 \\ [\mathbf{Z}_{k-1}, \frac{1}{\|\mathbf{w}_k\|} \cdot \mathbf{w}_k] & \text{if } \|\mathbf{w}_k\| > 0 \end{cases} \tag{2.15}$$

where

$$\mathbf{w}_k = \mathbf{X}_k - \mathbf{P}_{k-1}\mathbf{X}_k = (\mathbf{I} - \mathbf{P}_{k-1})\,\mathbf{X}_k$$

This process is called *Gram-Schmidt orthonormalization.*[19]

Note that the orthonormalization of $\mathbf{Z}_k$ simplifies the expression for the projector. Now, every $\mathbf{Z}_k'\mathbf{Z}_k$ is an identity matrix so that

$$\mathbf{P}_k = \mathbf{Z}_k \left(\mathbf{Z}_k'\mathbf{Z}_k\right)^{-1} \mathbf{Z}_k' = \mathbf{Z}_k\mathbf{Z}_k', \quad k = 1, \ldots, K$$

This simplification of an orthogonal projector will be an analytical boon and so we give it the dignity of a lemma:

> **Lemma 2.6** *Let* $\mathbf{P}$ *be an orthogonal projector onto a* K*-dimensional subspace of* $\mathbb{R}^N$. *There are* $N \times K$ *matrices* $\mathbf{Z}$ *such that the column vectors of* $\mathbf{Z}$ *are orthonormal* ($\mathbf{Z}'\mathbf{Z} = \mathbf{I}_K$) *and* $\mathbf{P} = \mathbf{Z}\mathbf{Z}'$.

This form for orthogonal projectors gives them the analytical appearance of the most familiar orthogonal projection: taking a vector $(x_1, x_2) \in \mathbb{R}^2$ to $(x_1, 0)$ or to $(0, x_2)$. For an amplification of this idea, see Exercise 2.15.

2.6.2 Properties of Orthogonal Projectors

Here we collect four more properties of orthogonal projectors. We have already noted, and exploited, that orthogonal projectors are unique. Orthogonal projectors have four other properties that will prove useful to us. As a special case, the matrix $\mathbf{P}_{\mathbf{X}} = \mathbf{X}(\mathbf{X}'\mathbf{X})^{-1}\mathbf{X}'$ exhibits all of these properties. First, it is symmetric,

$$\mathbf{P}_{\mathbf{X}} = \mathbf{X}(\mathbf{X}'\mathbf{X})^{-1}\mathbf{X}' = \left(\mathbf{X}(\mathbf{X}'\mathbf{X})^{-1}\mathbf{X}'\right)' = \mathbf{P}_{\mathbf{X}}'$$

[19] See also C.10 (p. 853).

Second,

$$\mathbf{P_X P_X} = \left[\mathbf{X(X'X)^{-1}X'}\right]\left[\mathbf{X(X'X)^{-1}X'}\right] = \mathbf{X(X'X)^{-1}X'} = \mathbf{P_X}$$

This property has a special name.

DEFINITION 5 (IDEMPOTENT) *The matrix* $\mathbf{A}$ *is* idempotent *if* $\mathbf{A}$ *is square and* $\mathbf{AA} = \mathbf{A}$.

Third, a quadratic form in $\mathbf{P_X}$ is always nonnegative: for any $\mathbf{w} \in \mathbb{R}^N$,

$$\mathbf{w'P_X w} = \mathbf{w'P_X P_X w} = \mathbf{w'P_X' P_X w} = (\mathbf{P_X w})' \, \mathbf{P_X w} = \|\mathbf{P_X w}\|^2 \geq 0 \tag{2.16}$$

This property also has a name.

DEFINITION 6 (POSITIVE SEMIDEFINITE) *The matrix* $\mathbf{A}$ *is* positive semidefinite *if* $\mathbf{A}$ *is square and* $\mathbf{w'Aw} \geq 0$ *for all conformable* $\mathbf{w}$.

Fourth,

$$\mathbf{z} \in \mathrm{Col}^{\perp}(\mathbf{X}) \Rightarrow (\mathbf{I} - \mathbf{P_X})\,\mathbf{z} = \mathbf{z}$$
$$\mathbf{z} \in \mathrm{Col}(\mathbf{X}) \Rightarrow (\mathbf{I} - \mathbf{P_X})\,\mathbf{z} = \mathbf{0}$$

so that $\mathbf{I} - \mathbf{P_X}$ is also an orthogonal projector, but onto $\mathrm{Col}^{\perp}(\mathbf{X})$, the orthogonal complement of $\mathrm{Col}(\mathbf{X})$.

We gather these four properties into one lemma for future reference.

LEMMA 2.7 (ORTHOGONAL PROJECTORS) *If* $\mathbf{P}$ *is an orthogonal projector onto the subspace* $\mathbb{S}$ *of* $\mathbb{R}^N$, *then* $\mathbf{P}$ *is symmetric, idempotent, and positive semidefinite and* $\mathbf{I} - \mathbf{P}$ *is an orthogonal projector onto* $\mathbb{S}^{\perp}$.

Proof. **Symmetric:** By definition, $\mathbf{Pz} \perp (\mathbf{I} - \mathbf{P})\,\mathbf{z}$ for all $\mathbf{z} \in \mathbb{R}^N$. That is,

$$0 = [(\mathbf{I} - \mathbf{P})\,\mathbf{z}]'\,\mathbf{Pz} = \mathbf{z}'\left(\mathbf{P} - \mathbf{P'P}\right)\mathbf{z}$$

Because this is true for *all* $\mathbf{z}$, $\mathbf{P} - \mathbf{P'P} = \mathbf{0}$ or $\mathbf{P} = \mathbf{P'P}$. Because $\mathbf{P'P}$ is symmetric, so is $\mathbf{P}$. **Idempotent:** By definition, $\mathbf{Pz} \in \mathbb{S}$ for all $\mathbf{z} \in \mathbb{R}^N$. Also by definition, $\mathbf{P}\,(\mathbf{Pz}) = \mathbf{Pz}$ for all $\mathbf{z}$. Therefore, $\mathbf{PP} = \mathbf{P}$. **Positive semidefinite:** This follows immediately from the previous two properties. See (2.16). **Duality:** Let $\mathbf{z} = \mathbf{z}_1 + \mathbf{z}_2$ where $\mathbf{z}_1 \in \mathbb{S}$ and $\mathbf{z}_2 \in \mathbb{S}^{\perp}$, as in Definition 3. Then $(\mathbf{I} - \mathbf{P})\,\mathbf{z} = \mathbf{z} - \mathbf{z}_1 = \mathbf{z}_2 \in \mathbb{S}^{\perp}$ so that $\mathbf{I} - \mathbf{P}$ is the orthogonal projector onto $\mathbb{S}^{\perp}$. □

2.6.3 Proofs

The proof of the projection theorem rests largely on the Pythagorean theorem.

Proof of Theorem 2. **Sufficiency:** If $\hat{\boldsymbol{\mu}} \in \mathbb{S}$ and $\mathbf{y} - \hat{\boldsymbol{\mu}} \in \mathbb{S}^{\perp}$, then $\boldsymbol{\mu} \in \mathbb{S}$ implies $\hat{\boldsymbol{\mu}} - \boldsymbol{\mu} \in \mathbb{S}$ implies $\boldsymbol{\mu} - \hat{\boldsymbol{\mu}} \perp \mathbf{y} - \hat{\boldsymbol{\mu}}$ and

$$\begin{aligned} \|\mathbf{y} - \boldsymbol{\mu}\|^2 &= \|\mathbf{y} - \hat{\boldsymbol{\mu}} + \hat{\boldsymbol{\mu}} - \boldsymbol{\mu}\|^2 \\ &= \|\mathbf{y} - \hat{\boldsymbol{\mu}}\|^2 + \|\hat{\boldsymbol{\mu}} - \boldsymbol{\mu}\|^2 \\ &\geq \|\mathbf{y} - \hat{\boldsymbol{\mu}}\|^2 \end{aligned} \tag{2.17}$$

by the Pythagorean theorem (1). **Necessity:** Suppose that

$$\hat{\boldsymbol{\mu}} = \underset{\boldsymbol{\mu} \in \mathbb{S}}{\operatorname{argmin}} \|\mathbf{y} - \boldsymbol{\mu}\|^2 \tag{2.18}$$

but that there is a $\boldsymbol{\delta} \in \mathbb{S}$ such that $\boldsymbol{\delta}'\left(\mathbf{y} - \hat{\boldsymbol{\mu}}\right) \neq 0$. If we set

$$\boldsymbol{\mu} = \hat{\boldsymbol{\mu}} + \frac{\boldsymbol{\delta}'\left(\mathbf{y} - \hat{\boldsymbol{\mu}}\right)}{\boldsymbol{\delta}'\boldsymbol{\delta}}\boldsymbol{\delta}$$

which is a member of $\mathbb{S}$, then

$$\begin{aligned} \left(\boldsymbol{\mu} - \hat{\boldsymbol{\mu}}\right)'\left(\mathbf{y} - \boldsymbol{\mu}\right) &= \left[\frac{\boldsymbol{\delta}'\left(\mathbf{y} - \hat{\boldsymbol{\mu}}\right)}{\boldsymbol{\delta}'\boldsymbol{\delta}}\boldsymbol{\delta}\right]'\left[\mathbf{y} - \hat{\boldsymbol{\mu}} - \frac{\boldsymbol{\delta}'\left(\mathbf{y} - \hat{\boldsymbol{\mu}}\right)}{\boldsymbol{\delta}'\boldsymbol{\delta}}\boldsymbol{\delta}\right] \\ &= \frac{\left[\boldsymbol{\delta}'\left(\mathbf{y} - \hat{\boldsymbol{\mu}}\right)\right]^2}{\boldsymbol{\delta}'\boldsymbol{\delta}} - \frac{\boldsymbol{\delta}'\left(\mathbf{y} - \hat{\boldsymbol{\mu}}\right)}{\boldsymbol{\delta}'\boldsymbol{\delta}}\boldsymbol{\delta}'\boldsymbol{\delta}\frac{\boldsymbol{\delta}'\left(\mathbf{y} - \hat{\boldsymbol{\mu}}\right)}{\boldsymbol{\delta}'\boldsymbol{\delta}} \\ &= 0 \end{aligned}$$

That is, $\boldsymbol{\mu} - \hat{\boldsymbol{\mu}} \perp \mathbf{y} - \boldsymbol{\mu}$ and, applying the Pythagorean theorem,

$$\begin{aligned} \left\|\mathbf{y} - \hat{\boldsymbol{\mu}}\right\|^2 &= \|\mathbf{y} - \boldsymbol{\mu}\|^2 + \left\|\boldsymbol{\mu} - \hat{\boldsymbol{\mu}}\right\|^2 \\ &> \|\mathbf{y} - \boldsymbol{\mu}\|^2 \end{aligned}$$

contradicting (2.18). Therefore, $\mathbf{y} - \hat{\boldsymbol{\mu}} \in \mathbb{S}^{\perp}$. **Uniqueness:** According to (2.17),

$$\|\mathbf{y} - \boldsymbol{\mu}\|^2 = \left\|\mathbf{y} - \hat{\boldsymbol{\mu}}\right\|^2 \Leftrightarrow \left\|\hat{\boldsymbol{\mu}} - \boldsymbol{\mu}\right\|^2 = 0$$

so that if $\boldsymbol{\mu}$ is optimal, then $\boldsymbol{\mu} = \hat{\boldsymbol{\mu}}$. **Existence:** If $\mathbf{y} \in \mathbb{S}$ then $\hat{\boldsymbol{\mu}} = \mathbf{y}$. If $\mathbf{y} \notin \mathbb{S}$, then let

$$\mathbb{B} = \left\{\boldsymbol{\mu} \in \operatorname{Col}(\mathbf{X}) \mid \|\mathbf{y} - \boldsymbol{\mu}\|^2 \leq \|\mathbf{y}\|^2\right\}$$

Because $\mathbf{0} \in \mathbb{B}$, this set is not empty. Because (2.17) implies that $\left\|\mathbf{y} - \hat{\boldsymbol{\mu}}\right\|^2 \leq \|\mathbf{y}\|^2$, $\hat{\boldsymbol{\mu}} \in \mathbb{B}$ if it exists. Furthermore, $\mathbb{B}$ is closed and bounded. Because it is a continuous function of $\boldsymbol{\mu}$, $\|\mathbf{y} - \boldsymbol{\mu}\|^2$ has a minimum on $\mathbb{B}$.[20] Therefore, $\hat{\boldsymbol{\mu}}$ exists. □

The next proof also relies on the Pythagorean theorem.

[20] According to Weierstrass theorem, a continuous function on a closed and bounded interval attains both a maximum and a minimum on the interval. For one introduction, see Simon and Blume (1994, Ch. 30).

Proof of Lemma 2.2. By the projection theorem, there is a unique $\mathbf{z}_1 \in \text{Col}(\mathbf{X})$ such that $\|\mathbf{z} - \mathbf{z}_1\| \leq \|\mathbf{z} - \mathbf{w}\|$ for all $\mathbf{w} \in \text{Col}(\mathbf{X})$ and $\mathbf{z}_2 \equiv \mathbf{z} - \mathbf{z}_1 \in \text{Col}^{\perp}(\mathbf{X})$. To show that there are no other $\mathbf{w}_1 \in \text{Col}(\mathbf{X})$, $\mathbf{w}_2 \in \text{Col}^{\perp}(\mathbf{X})$ such that $\mathbf{z} = \mathbf{w}_1 + \mathbf{w}_2$ suppose otherwise. Then $(\mathbf{z}_1 - \mathbf{w}_1) + (\mathbf{z}_2 - \mathbf{w}_2) = \mathbf{0}$ and $(\mathbf{z}_1 - \mathbf{w}_1) \perp (\mathbf{z}_2 - \mathbf{w}_2)$. The Pythagorean theorem implies that $0 = \|\mathbf{z}_1 - \mathbf{w}_1\|^2 + \|\mathbf{z}_2 - \mathbf{w}_2\|^2$ but this implies that $\mathbf{z}_1 = \mathbf{w}_1$ and $\mathbf{z}_2 = \mathbf{w}_2$. □

2.7 OVERVIEW

1. The OLS fitting problem can be written

$$\hat{\boldsymbol{\beta}} \equiv \underset{\boldsymbol{\beta}}{\text{argmin}} \, (\mathbf{y} - \mathbf{X}\boldsymbol{\beta})' \, (\mathbf{y} - \mathbf{X}\boldsymbol{\beta})$$

which can be decomposed into first finding the fitted vector

$$\hat{\boldsymbol{\mu}} \equiv \underset{\boldsymbol{\mu} \in \text{Col}(\mathbf{X})}{\text{argmin}} \, \|\mathbf{y} - \boldsymbol{\mu}\|^2$$

and the fitted coefficients such that

$$\mathbf{X}\hat{\boldsymbol{\beta}} = \hat{\boldsymbol{\mu}}$$

2. The orthogonal projector $\mathbf{P}_{\mathbf{X}}$ onto $\text{Col}(\mathbf{X})$ has the defining properties

$$\boldsymbol{\mu} \in \text{Col}(\mathbf{X}) \Rightarrow \mathbf{P}_{\mathbf{X}}\boldsymbol{\mu} = \boldsymbol{\mu}$$
$$\boldsymbol{\mu} \in \text{Col}^{\perp}(\mathbf{X}) \Rightarrow \mathbf{P}_{\mathbf{X}}\boldsymbol{\mu} = \mathbf{0}$$

$\mathbf{P}_{\mathbf{X}}$ is unique and produces a unique orthogonal decomposition of any vector $\mathbf{z} \in \mathbb{R}^N$: $\mathbf{z} = \mathbf{P}_{\mathbf{X}}\mathbf{z} + (\mathbf{I} - \mathbf{P}_{\mathbf{X}})\,\mathbf{z}$ where $\mathbf{P}_{\mathbf{X}}\mathbf{z} \in \text{Col}(\mathbf{X})$ and $(\mathbf{I} - \mathbf{P}_{\mathbf{X}})\,\mathbf{z} \in \text{Col}^{\perp}(\mathbf{X})$. As a result,

$$\|\mathbf{y} - \boldsymbol{\mu}\|^2 = \|\mathbf{y} - \mathbf{P}_{\mathbf{X}}\mathbf{y}\|^2 + \|\mathbf{P}_{\mathbf{X}}\mathbf{y} - \boldsymbol{\mu}\|^2$$

for all $\boldsymbol{\mu} \in \text{Col}(\mathbf{X})$.

3. Therefore, the fitted vector $\hat{\boldsymbol{\mu}} = \mathbf{P}_{\mathbf{X}}\mathbf{y}$ is the unique orthogonal projection of $\mathbf{y}$ onto $\text{Col}(\mathbf{X})$ and $\mathbf{y} - \hat{\boldsymbol{\mu}} \in \text{Col}^{\perp}(\mathbf{X})$.

4. If $\text{rank}(\mathbf{X}) = K$ then $\mathbf{X}'\mathbf{X}$ is nonsingular and the orthogonality condition $\mathbf{y} - \hat{\boldsymbol{\mu}} \in \text{Col}^{\perp}(\mathbf{X}) \Leftrightarrow \mathbf{X}'\left(\mathbf{y} - \hat{\boldsymbol{\mu}}\right) = \mathbf{0}$ can be solved to yield

$$\hat{\boldsymbol{\beta}} = \left(\mathbf{X}'\mathbf{X}\right)^{-1}\mathbf{X}'\mathbf{y}$$
$$\mathbf{P}_{\mathbf{X}} = \mathbf{X}\left(\mathbf{X}'\mathbf{X}\right)^{-1}\mathbf{X}'$$

5. When $\mathbf{X}$ is not full-column rank, this orthogonal projector formula also provides a method to construct a basis for $\text{Col}(\mathbf{X})$ from the columns of $\mathbf{X}$. This is closely related to Gram-Schmidt orthonormalization, a construction of an orthonormal basis for $\text{Col}(\mathbf{X})$: $\mathbf{Z}$ such that $\text{Col}(\mathbf{Z}) = \text{Col}(\mathbf{X})$ and $\mathbf{Z}'\mathbf{Z} = \mathbf{I}_{\text{rank}(\mathbf{X})}$. Given such a $\mathbf{Z}$, $\mathbf{P}_{\mathbf{X}} = \mathbf{Z}\mathbf{Z}'$.

6. Thus, the orthogonal projector is a *geometric* concept: It is "coordinate free" in the sense that projectors are invariant to the basis with which we choose to express the vectors of a subspace. In contrast, $\hat{\boldsymbol{\beta}}$ is "coordinate specific" because it is tied to the basis provided by the columns of $\mathbf{X}$.

In this chapter, we have explained the geometric character of the solution to the OLS fitting problem. The central idea is orthogonality. When they are orthogonal, two vectors and their sum form the right-angled triangle associated with the Pythagorean theorem. This theorem is the foundation of OLS solution, which is described in the projection theorem: The closest point to $\mathbf{y}$ in Col($\mathbf{X}$) is the vector $\hat{\boldsymbol{\mu}}$ that forms a right-angled triangle when combined with $\mathbf{y} - \hat{\boldsymbol{\mu}}$.

The consequences of this geometric relationship are that the OLS fitted values are unique and the OLS fitted residuals are orthogonal to the explanatory variables, but the OLS fitted coefficients may not be unique. Only if the RHS variables are linearly independent is the solution to OLS in β well defined. Chapter 3 describes in more detail the way OLS fits $\boldsymbol{\beta}$ in that case.

2.8 EXERCISES

2.8.1 Review

2.1 Repeat the calculations in the introductory example for a data set.

2.2 Write and execute a computer program to compute $\hat{\boldsymbol{\mu}}$ and $\hat{\boldsymbol{\beta}}$. Include a procedure to assign fitted coefficients equal to zero to columns of $\mathbf{X}$ that are linearly dependent on the columns that precede them.

2.3 Define the following terms:
(a) column space of $\mathbf{X}$;
(b) multicollinearity;
(c) orthogonality;
(d) orthogonal projection;
(e) fitted vector;
(f) fitted residual vector.

2.4 Consider a case such as Example 2.1 in which there are two observations and a single RHS variable ($N = 2$, $K = 1$) and

$$\mathbf{X} = \begin{bmatrix} 1 \\ 2 \end{bmatrix}$$

(a) What is Col($\mathbf{X}$)?
(b) What is $\hat{\boldsymbol{\beta}}$?
(c) Draw a figure for this problem analogous to Figure 2.5.

***2.5** (a) Show that the linear transformation in $\mathbb{R}^2$ that takes every point (a_1, a_2) to $(a_1, 0)$ is an orthogonal projection. Draw an illustration of this orthogonal projection.
(b) Generalize this example to $\mathbb{R}^N$ and zeroing out an arbitrary selection of elements.

---

*A starred exercise is referenced later in the text.

2.6 Write a general expression for all of the ways $\hat{\boldsymbol{\mu}}$ can be written in terms of $\mathbf{X}_1, \mathbf{X}_2, \mathbf{X}_3$ in Example 2.3.

***2.7** Let ι denote a vector of N ones. Show that $\mathbf{P}_\iota \mathbf{y} = \mathrm{E}_N[y_n] \cdot \iota$ and $N^{-1}\|(\mathbf{I}-\mathbf{P}_\iota)\mathbf{y}\|^2 = \mathrm{Var}_N[y_n]$ where

$$\mathrm{E}_N[y_n] \equiv \sum_{n=1}^{N} y_n \frac{1}{N}$$

is the first empirical moment of y_n and

$$\mathrm{Var}_N[y_n] \equiv \sum_{n=1}^{N} (y_n - \mathrm{E}_N[y_n])^2 \frac{1}{N}$$

is the empirical variance of y_n.[21]

2.8 One can replace $\mathbf{y}$ with $\hat{\boldsymbol{\mu}}$ in $\hat{\boldsymbol{\beta}} = (\mathbf{X}'\mathbf{X})^{-1}\mathbf{X}'\mathbf{y}$ and obtain the same OLS fitted coefficients. Show this *without* using the algebraic solution for $\hat{\boldsymbol{\beta}}$ by demonstrating the more general result that

$$\left\{\hat{\boldsymbol{\beta}} \mid \hat{\boldsymbol{\beta}} = \operatorname*{argmin}_{\boldsymbol{\beta}} \|\mathbf{y}-\mathbf{X}\boldsymbol{\beta}\|^2\right\} = \left\{\hat{\boldsymbol{\beta}} \mid \hat{\boldsymbol{\beta}} = \operatorname*{argmin}_{\boldsymbol{\beta}} \left\|\hat{\boldsymbol{\mu}}-\mathbf{X}\boldsymbol{\beta}\right\|^2\right\}$$

In your demonstration, justify each of the following equalities:

$$\min_{\boldsymbol{\beta}} \|\mathbf{y}-\mathbf{X}\boldsymbol{\beta}\|^2 = \min_{\boldsymbol{\mu}\in\mathrm{Col}(\mathbf{X})} \|\mathbf{y}-\boldsymbol{\mu}\|^2 \tag{2.19}$$

$$= \min_{\boldsymbol{\mu}\in\mathrm{Col}(\mathbf{X})} \left(\left\|\mathbf{y}-\hat{\boldsymbol{\mu}}\right\|^2 + \left\|\hat{\boldsymbol{\mu}}-\boldsymbol{\mu}\right\|^2\right) \tag{2.20}$$

$$= \left\|\mathbf{y}-\hat{\boldsymbol{\mu}}\right\|^2 + \min_{\boldsymbol{\mu}\in\mathrm{Col}(\mathbf{X})} \left\|\hat{\boldsymbol{\mu}}-\boldsymbol{\mu}\right\|^2 \tag{2.21}$$

$$= \left\|\mathbf{y}-\hat{\boldsymbol{\mu}}\right\|^2 + \min_{\boldsymbol{\beta}} \left\|\hat{\boldsymbol{\mu}}-\mathbf{X}\boldsymbol{\beta}\right\|^2 \tag{2.22}$$

Does the argument rest on whether $\mathbf{X}$ is full-column rank?

2.9 (Projector Uniqueness) Prove Lemma 2.5.

2.10 (Projector Uniqueness) Show that the OLS fitted values $\hat{\boldsymbol{\mu}}$ are invariant to nonsingular linear transformations of the columns of $\mathbf{X}$. That is, $\mathbf{P}_{\mathbf{X}} = \mathbf{P}_{\mathbf{XA}}$ if $\mathbf{A}$ is a nonsingular $K \times K$ matrix. Also argue that this is based on an invariance of minimization (you know what I mean).

***2.11** Show that the OLS SSR satisfy

$$\left\|\mathbf{y}-\hat{\boldsymbol{\mu}}\right\|^2 = \mathbf{y}'(\mathbf{I}-\mathbf{P}_{\mathbf{X}})\mathbf{y}$$

2.12 Show that the first-order conditions for (2.1) are

$$\left.\frac{\partial(\mathbf{y}-\mathbf{X}\boldsymbol{\beta})'(\mathbf{y}-\mathbf{X}\boldsymbol{\beta})}{\partial\boldsymbol{\beta}}\right\|_{\boldsymbol{\beta}=\hat{\boldsymbol{\beta}}} = -2\cdot\mathbf{X}'\left(\mathbf{y}-\mathbf{X}\hat{\boldsymbol{\beta}}\right) = \mathbf{0}$$

[21] See Definition E.3 (Empirical Distribution, p. 902) and Definition E.4 (Sample Moments, p. 903).

which is equivalent to equation (2.4). Thus, calculus provides another way to construct the orthogonality conditions. (HINT: You may find the summary of matrix differentiation in Appendix G helpful.)

***2.13** **(Orthonormal Basis)** Suppose that $\mathbf{X}$ is full-column rank.

(a) Show that an orthonormal basis for $\text{Col}(\mathbf{X})$ can be constructed recursively by

$$\mathbf{w}_k = \left[\mathbf{I} - \mathbf{Z}_{k-1}\mathbf{Z}_{k-1}'\right]\mathbf{X}_k$$

$$\mathbf{z}_k = \frac{1}{\|\mathbf{w}_k\|} \cdot \mathbf{w}_k$$

$(k = 2, \ldots, K)$ where $\mathbf{X}_k$ is the kth column of $\mathbf{X}$, $\mathbf{Z}_k = [\mathbf{z}_1, \mathbf{z}_2, \ldots, \mathbf{z}_k]$ and $\mathbf{w}_1 = \frac{1}{\|\mathbf{X}_1\|} \cdot \mathbf{X}_1$.

(b) What happens to this process if $\dim[\text{Col}(\mathbf{X})] < K$? What adjustment remedies this problem?

(c) Given $\dim[\text{Col}(\mathbf{X})] = K$, show that

i. $\mathbf{Z} = \mathbf{XC}$ where $\mathbf{C}$ is an upper-right triangular and nonsingular matrix and $\mathbf{Z} \equiv \mathbf{Z}_K$,

ii. $\mathbf{X} = \mathbf{ZA}$ where $\mathbf{A}$ is a nonsingular matrix,

iii. $\mathbf{Z}'\mathbf{Z} = \mathbf{I}$ and $\mathbf{P}_\mathbf{X} = \mathbf{ZZ}'$,

iv. $\mathbf{A} = \mathbf{Z}'\mathbf{X}$.[22]

2.14 Show that for any $N \times K$ matrix $\mathbf{X}$ where $K \leq N, \mathbf{P}_k \equiv \mathbf{P}_{\mathbf{Z}_k}$ $(k = 1, \ldots, K)$ is unchanged by replacing (2.14) with (2.15) in the construction of a full-column rank matrix $\mathbf{Z}_K$ such that $\text{Col}(\mathbf{Z}_K) = \text{Col}(\mathbf{X})$.

***2.15** **(Orthogonal Projectors)** This exercise generalizes the idea expressed in Exercise 2.5. An orthogonal projector can be thought of as simply cancelling the contributions to a vector of some elements of an orthonormal basis. That is, if $\{\mathbf{b}_1, \ldots, \mathbf{b}_N\}$ is an orthonormal basis of $\mathbb{R}^N$ (so that $\|\mathbf{b}_n\| = 1$ and $\mathbf{b}_n'\mathbf{b}_m = 0$ for all $n, m = 1, \ldots, N,\ n \neq m$) the orthogonal projection of a vector $\mathbf{z} = \sum_{n=1}^{N} \alpha_n \mathbf{b}_n$ onto the subspace spanned by $\{\mathbf{b}_1, \ldots, \mathbf{b}_M\},\ M < N$, is simply $\sum_{n=1}^{M} \alpha_n \mathbf{b}_n$.

Let $\mathbf{P}$ be an orthogonal projector onto a K-dimensional subspace of $\mathbb{R}^N$.

(a) Given only $\mathbf{P}$, how can a matrix $\mathbf{B}_1$ be found that

i. is full-column rank,

ii. $\mathbf{B}_1'\mathbf{B}_1 = \mathbf{I}_K$, and

iii. $\mathbf{P} = \mathbf{B}_1\mathbf{B}_1'$?

(HINT: Exercise 2.13.)

(b) Show how to find a second matrix $\mathbf{B}_2$ that

i. is full-column rank,

ii. $\mathbf{B}_2'\mathbf{B}_2 = \mathbf{I}_{N-K}$,

iii. $\mathbf{B}_2'\mathbf{B}_1$ is an $(N - K) \times K$ matrix of zeros, and

iv. $\mathbf{B} = [\mathbf{B}_1, \mathbf{B}_2]$ is nonsingular.

(HINT: Consider the orthogonal projector $\mathbf{I} - \mathbf{P}$.)

(c) Show that for every $\mathbf{z} \in \mathbb{R}^N$, $\mathbf{z} = \mathbf{B}\boldsymbol{\alpha} = \mathbf{B}_1\boldsymbol{\alpha}_1 + \mathbf{B}_2\boldsymbol{\alpha}_2$ for some $\boldsymbol{\alpha} \in \mathbb{R}^N$.

(d) Show that $\mathbf{Pz} = \mathbf{B}_1\boldsymbol{\alpha}_1$, confirming the interpretation of orthogonal projectors given above.

2.16 **(Multicollinearity)** Suppose that $\mathbf{X}$ is not full-column rank and consider two different submatrices of $\mathbf{X}$, $\mathbf{Z}_1$ and $\mathbf{Z}_2$, where (1) $\mathbf{Z}_1 \neq \mathbf{Z}_2$, (2) $\text{Col}(\mathbf{X}) = \text{Col}(\mathbf{Z}_1) = \text{Col}(\mathbf{Z}_2)$, and (3) both $\mathbf{Z}_1$ and $\mathbf{Z}_2$ are full-column rank. Suppose, however, that $\mathbf{Z}_1$ and $\mathbf{Z}_2$ both contain $\mathbf{X}_k$, the kth column of $\mathbf{X}$. Will the fitted coefficient for $\mathbf{X}_k$ be the same in the OLS fit of $\mathbf{y}$ to $\mathbf{Z}_1$ and the OLS fit of $\mathbf{y}$ to $\mathbf{Z}_2$? Explain your answer.

2.17 Interpret the term

---

[22] The matrix $\mathbf{A}$ is also upper-right triangular. This decomposition of $\mathbf{X}$ into $\mathbf{ZA}$ where $\mathbf{Z}'\mathbf{Z} = \mathbf{I}$ and $\mathbf{A}$ is upper-right triangular is a member of a general family called *QR decompositions*. See Rao (1973, p. 21).

$$\frac{\delta'(\mathbf{y}-\hat{\boldsymbol{\mu}})}{\delta'\delta}\delta$$

in terms of orthogonal projection and explain its role in the proof of Theorem 2 (Projection).

***2.18 (Orthogonal Projectors)**

(a) Show directly that $\mathbf{I}-\mathbf{X}(\mathbf{X}'\mathbf{X})^{-1}\mathbf{X}'$ is also an orthogonal projection matrix: it orthogonally projects $\mathbb{R}^N$ onto $\mathrm{Col}^{\perp}(\mathbf{X})$.

(b) Show, therefore, that the residual vector is orthogonal to the fitted vector: $\hat{\boldsymbol{\mu}}'(\mathbf{y}-\hat{\boldsymbol{\mu}})=0$.

(c) Show that if $\mathbf{P}$ is any orthogonal projector, then $\mathbf{I}-\mathbf{P}$ is symmetric and idempotent.

(d) Show that $\mathbf{Pz}$ and $(\mathbf{I}-\mathbf{P})\mathbf{z}$ are orthogonal.

***2.19 (Quadratic Forms)** Show that if $\mathbf{P}$ is an orthogonal projector then

(a) the quadratic form $\mathbf{z}'\mathbf{Pz}$ is positive and

(b) $\mathbf{z}'\mathbf{z}\geq\mathbf{z}'\mathbf{Pz}$.

2.8.2 Extensions

2.20 (Algebra Review) Extend the argument supporting Lemma 2.1 to show that $\mathrm{rank}(\mathbf{X})=\mathrm{rank}(\mathbf{X}'\mathbf{X})$. Use the following steps.

(a) Show that for all $\boldsymbol{\alpha}\in\mathbb{R}^K$, $\mathbf{X}'\mathbf{X}\boldsymbol{\alpha}=0$ implies that $\mathbf{X}\boldsymbol{\alpha}=\mathbf{0}$. (HINT: $\mathbf{X}\boldsymbol{\alpha}=\mathbf{0}$ if and only if $\|\mathbf{X}\boldsymbol{\alpha}\|=0$.)

(b) Because $\mathbf{X}\boldsymbol{\alpha}=\mathbf{0}$ also implies $\mathbf{X}'\mathbf{X}\boldsymbol{\alpha}=\mathbf{0}$, argue that $\mathrm{Col}^{\perp}(\mathbf{X}')=\mathrm{Col}^{\perp}(\mathbf{X}'\mathbf{X})$.

(c) Use Theorem C.11, which states that

$$N=\dim[\mathrm{Col}(\mathbf{X})]+\dim[\mathrm{Col}^{\perp}(\mathbf{X})]$$

and Theorem C.12, which states that

$$\mathrm{rank}(\mathbf{X})=\dim[\mathrm{Col}(\mathbf{X})]=\dim[\mathrm{Col}(\mathbf{X}')]=\mathrm{rank}(\mathbf{X}')$$

to show that $\mathrm{rank}(\mathbf{X})=\mathrm{rank}(\mathbf{X}'\mathbf{X})$. (HINT: Apply Theorem C.11 to $\mathbf{X}'$ and $\mathbf{X}'\mathbf{X}$.)

2.21 (Cauchy–Schwarz Inequality) Show that $|\mathbf{x}'\mathbf{y}|\leq\|\mathbf{x}\|\,\|\mathbf{y}\|$. (HINT: Consider the squared Euclidean length of the orthogonal projection $\left[\mathbf{I}-\mathbf{x}(\mathbf{x}'\mathbf{x})^{-1}\mathbf{x}'\right]\mathbf{y}$.)

***2.22 (Matrix Square Root)** Let $\mathbf{X}$ be a full-column rank $N\times K$ matrix. Show that there is a *nonsingular* $K\times K$ matrix $\mathbf{A}$ such that $\mathbf{X}'\mathbf{X}=\mathbf{A}'\mathbf{A}$. (HINT: Exercise 2.13.)

***2.23 (Orthogonal Matrices)** An *orthogonal* matrix is any square matrix $\mathbf{B}$ such that $\mathbf{B}'\mathbf{B}=\mathbf{I}$. This means that $\mathbf{B}^{-1}=\mathbf{B}'$. A two-dimensional geometric example of an orthogonal matrix as a transformation is one that rotates all vectors an equal amount around the origin. Another two-dimensional example is a reflection of all vectors in a line. Confirm these examples by showing that $\|\mathbf{x}\|=\|\mathbf{Bx}\|$ and $\mathbf{x}'\mathbf{y}=(\mathbf{Bx})'(\mathbf{By})$ and interpreting these facts appropriately.

***2.24 (Generalized Inverses)** Let $\mathbf{X}^{-}=(\mathbf{X}'\mathbf{X})^{-1}\mathbf{X}'$. Multiplied on the left, the matrix $\mathbf{X}^{-}$ acts as an inverse matrix on $\mathbf{X}$, providing a solution to the N equations

$$\hat{\boldsymbol{\mu}}=\mathbf{X}\hat{\boldsymbol{\beta}}\quad\Leftrightarrow\quad(\mathbf{X}'\mathbf{X})^{-1}\mathbf{X}'\hat{\boldsymbol{\mu}}=(\mathbf{X}'\mathbf{X})^{-1}\mathbf{X}'\mathbf{X}\hat{\boldsymbol{\beta}}=\hat{\boldsymbol{\beta}}$$

(a) What matrix do you get when you multiply $\mathbf{X}$ by $\mathbf{X}^{-}$ on the right?

(b) Show that $\mathbf{X}^- = (\mathbf{X}'\mathbf{X})^{-1}\mathbf{X}'$ has the defining property of a *generalized inverse* of a matrix: $\mathbf{X}\mathbf{X}^-\mathbf{X} = \mathbf{X}$.
(c) Given an $N \times K$ matrix $\mathbf{Z}$ such that $\mathbf{Z}'\mathbf{X} = 0$, construct another generalized inverse for $\mathbf{X}$ using $\mathbf{X}^-$.
(d) Show that in addition $\mathbf{X}^-\mathbf{X}\mathbf{X}^- = \mathbf{X}^-$.
(e) Does your second generalized inverse have this additional property?
(f) Show that $\mathbf{X}(\mathbf{X}'\mathbf{X})^{-2}\mathbf{X}'$ is a generalized inverse of $\mathbf{X}\mathbf{X}'$. Does it also possess the property described in Part d?
(g) Find a generalized inverse for $\mathbf{P}_\mathbf{X}$.

***2.25 (Goodness of Fit)** There is a natural way to measure the goodness of fit between $\mathbf{y}$ and $\hat{\boldsymbol{\mu}}$, given that $\hat{\boldsymbol{\mu}}$ is the orthogonal projection of $\mathbf{y}$ onto $\text{Col}(\mathbf{X})$. This measure describes in an intuitively appealing way the fraction of the variation in $\mathbf{y}$ exhibited by the linear regression fit. It equals

$$r^2 \equiv 1 - \frac{\sum_{n=1}^N (y_n - \hat{\mu}_n)^2}{\sum_{n=1}^N y_n^2}$$

When $\mathbf{y} = \hat{\boldsymbol{\mu}}$ so that the fit is "perfect," r^2 equals one. When $\hat{\boldsymbol{\beta}} = \mathbf{0}$ and $\hat{\boldsymbol{\mu}} = \mathbf{0}$, r^2 equals zero. Otherwise, r^2 lies between zero and one. The r^2 measure is unit free. In this question, you derive these properties.

(a) Show that

$$\|\mathbf{y}\|^2 = \|\hat{\boldsymbol{\mu}}\|^2 + \|\mathbf{y} - \hat{\boldsymbol{\mu}}\|^2$$

(b) Why is this an example of the Pythagorean theorem, which states that the square of the length of the hypotenuse of a right-angled triangle equals the sum of the squares of the lengths of the other two sides?
(c) Show that $0 \le r^2 \le 1$.

2.26 (Least Absolute Deviations) Consider the *least absolute deviations* (LAD) fitting procedure:

$$\hat{\boldsymbol{\beta}}_{\text{LAD}} = \underset{\boldsymbol{\beta}}{\operatorname{argmin}} \sum_{n=1}^{N} |y_n - \mathbf{x}_n'\boldsymbol{\beta}|$$

(a) Show that this estimator equals the median in the location model ($K = 1, x_n = 1$).
(b) Show that the fitting procedure is equivalent to a linear programming problem, which has the general form

$$\min_{\mathbf{x}} \mathbf{a}'\mathbf{x} \quad \text{subject to} \quad \mathbf{A}\mathbf{x} \ge \mathbf{b}$$

(c) Show that the LAD fit has the property

$$\boldsymbol{\delta}'\mathbf{X}' \,\text{sgn}\Big[\mathbf{y} - \mathbf{X}(\hat{\boldsymbol{\beta}}_{\text{LAD}} + \lambda \cdot \boldsymbol{\delta})\Big] \le \mathbf{0}$$

for all $\lambda > 0$ and $\boldsymbol{\delta} \in \mathbb{R}^K$. NOTE: The sgn (or signum) function is defined as

$$\text{sgn}(x) \equiv \begin{cases} -1 & \text{if } x < 0 \\ 0 & \text{if } x = 0 \\ 1 & \text{if } x > 0 \end{cases}$$

(d) Is the LAD fit a linear one?
(e) Is the LAD fit unique?
(f) Show that the LAD objective function treats an increase in the absolute value of a residual as equivalent to an increase in the absolute value of a smaller residual. Contrast this with the objective function used by OLS.

(g) For what sort of data would you prefer the LAD fit to the OLS fit?

***2.27 (Duality)** Prove the dual result to Proposition 1 that

$$(\mathbf{I} - \mathbf{P}_{\mathbf{X}})\mathbf{y} = \underset{\mathbf{z} \in \mathrm{Col}^{\perp}(\mathbf{X})}{\operatorname{argmin}} \|\mathbf{y} - \mathbf{z}\|^2$$

[HINT: $\mathrm{Col}^{\perp}(\mathbf{X})$ is a linear vector subspace like $\mathrm{Col}(\mathbf{X})$.]

2.28 Dropping an RHS variable from the OLS fit is equivalent to constraining its coefficient to be zero. This is one way to select unique fitted coefficients when there is multicollinearity such that $\mathrm{rank}(\mathbf{X}) = K-1$. Explain how constraining two fitted coefficients to have the same value can also select unique fitted coefficients.

CHAPTER 3

PARTITIONED FIT

3.1 INTRODUCTORY EXAMPLE

In this chapter, we investigate the way OLS breaks the fitted values into the individual coefficients fitted for each RHS variable. To that end, we describe a simple example involving the seasonal adjustment of economic time series. Consider the time series data U. S. national unemployment rates, recorded monthly. For the time period January 1970 to November 1993 this rate is pictured in Figure 3.1. The series shows pronounced seasonality within the years, as well as some evidence of cycles with longer periodicity.

The series graphed as "fitted" in this figure is the fitted values from an OLS fit of the unemployment series on 12 indicator variables signaling the 12 months of the year:

$$\mathbf{x}_t'\boldsymbol{\beta} = \sum_{k=1}^{12} x_{tk}\beta_k$$

where

$$x_{tk} = \begin{cases} 1 & \text{if } k\text{th month} \\ 0 & \text{if otherwise} \end{cases} \tag{3.1}$$

($k = 1, \ldots, 12$). An intercept term would lead to exact multicollinearity among the RHS variables: $1 - \sum_{k=1}^{12} x_{tk} = 0$.[1] These OLS fitted values are simply the averages of all the observations for a particular month of the year. We illustrated such fits in Chapter 1 [see equation (1.4) and the preceding discussion].

Figure 3.2 shows a "seasonally adjusted" unemployment series, the difference between the actual unemployment rate and the seasonal (monthly) component of the OLS fit plus the sample average,

$$y_t^s \equiv y_t - \sum_{k=1}^{12} x_{tk}\hat{\beta}_k + \bar{y} \tag{3.2}$$

[1] Such multicollinearity is often called the *dummy variable trap*.

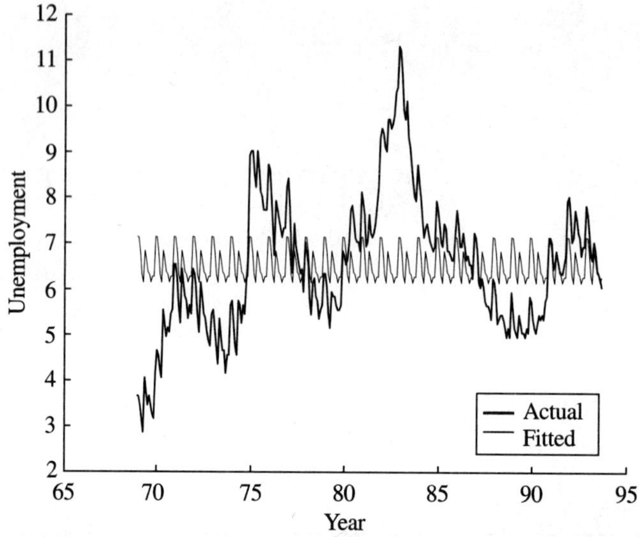

Figure 3.1 U. S. national unemployment rate and fitted seasonal pattern.

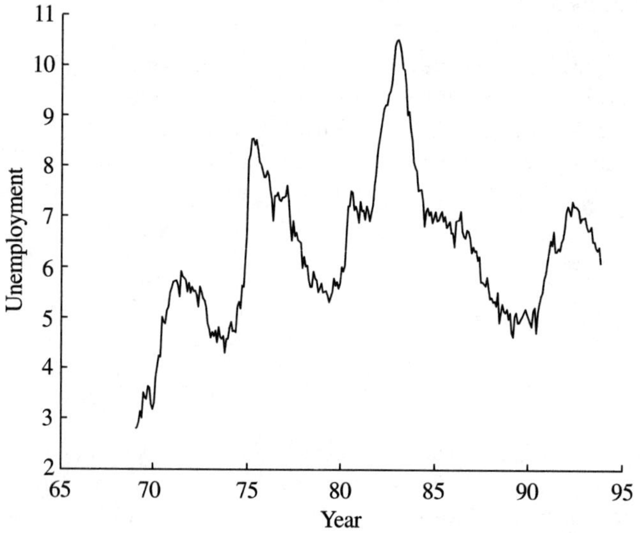

Figure 3.2 Seasonally adjusted U. S. national unemployment rate.

where y_t is the unemployment rate. There is an overall level of unemployment that persists through all the months that is added back in as $\bar{y}$. Although it still exhibits some chatter, this series is smoother, suggesting some success in removing seasonal patterns while retaining longer term trends.

Our data on the unemployment rate include another 12 months after November 1993 and we will try a little forecasting of this series with our OLS fitting procedure. As Figure 3.1 shows, the seasonal OLS fit agrees closely with the end of this series, compared to rather wide fluctuations earlier. So a forecast based on the seasonal trends alone may not perform too badly. Figure 3.3 shows the extra 12 months of data that were not included in the seasonal fit and the continuation of the seasonal fit. The overall pattern is clearly the same, but a secular trend down in unemployment is clearly being missed.

As an alternative approach, we also fit a model in which we predict the unemployment rate time series with its own past values. To be precise, we specified

$$\mathbf{x}_t'\boldsymbol{\beta} = \beta_1 + \sum_{k=2}^{13} z_{t,k-1}\beta_k \tag{3.3}$$

where

$$z_{tk} \equiv y_{t-k}, \qquad k = 1, \ldots, 12$$

so that a constant and the unemployment rate in each of the previous 12 months of an observation are the RHS variables. The y_{t-k} variables are often called *lags* of y_t. We also have data for the 12 months of 1969 to fill in the RHS variable values for the first year, 1970. We will call this the "dynamic" model. The unemployment rate and the fitted values from the OLS fit are pictured in Figure 3.4. The fit follows the series quite closely, apparently capturing both seasonal and secular trends. We also forecast the next 12 months with this model, using the forecasts themselves to fill in for the months that follow the estimation period. Those forecasts are shown

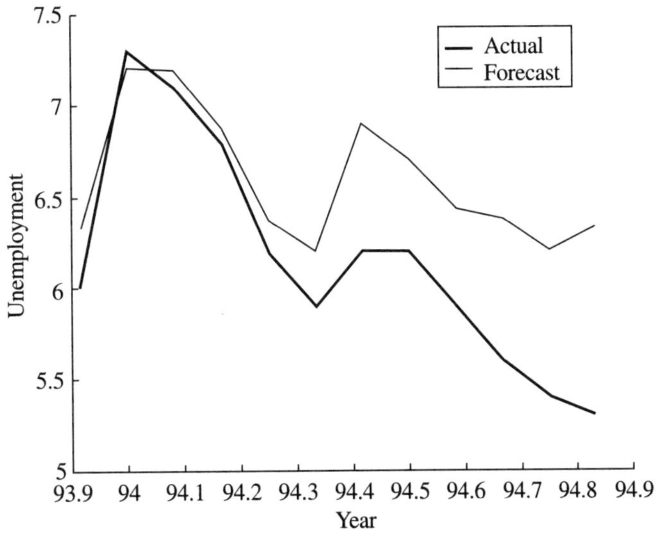

Figure 3.3 Unemployment rate: actual and seasonal forecast, 1993:12–1994:11.

in Figure 3.5. Although the initial months are not forecast as well, the overall performance seems much better.

Finally, we put the two specifications together, specifying

$$\mathbf{x}_t'\boldsymbol{\beta} = \sum_{k=1}^{12} z_{tk}\beta_k + \sum_{k=13}^{24} x_{t,k-13}\beta_k \tag{3.4}$$

giving the OLS fits in Figure 3.6. Note that the 12 monthly indicators replace the single constant RHS variable. In effect, we have 12 intercepts, one for each month, where we had one before. As expected, the fit is even closer to the actual data. The seasonal component of the fit has relatively more variation in it compared to the original seasonal model. The forecasts from this hybrid model are also better, as Figure 3.7 shows.

In Table 3.1, we give the OLS fitted coefficients for (3.3) and (3.4). Both include the terms in (3.3) and these are the only coefficients shown. The first column gives the coefficients $\hat{\boldsymbol{\beta}}_{\mathrm{D}}$ for the pure dynamic model (3.3), pictured in Figure 3.4. The second column gives the coefficients $\hat{\boldsymbol{\beta}}_{\mathrm{H}}$ for the hybrid model (3.3), shown in Figure 3.6. Both fits have coefficients near one for the previous month's unemployment rate, while the remaining coefficients are relatively small. However, the pattern of the remaining coefficients is quite different: the purely dynamic fit exhibits much more dependence on the more distant past than the hybrid model with monthly coefficients. Roughly speaking, the inclusion of the seasonal component appears to shorten the importance of the past to the two preceding months. In both of these months, higher unemployment contributes to a higher forecast of current unemployment.

Now we will illustrate a surprising feature of the OLS fitting procedure with these data. We fit the pure dynamic model a second time with different data. In place of the LHS variable unemployment, we used the seasonally adjusted unemployment series $\{y_t^{\mathrm{s}}\}$ described in (3.2).

Table 3.1
OLS Fitted Coefficients for Lagged Unemployment

	Model		
RHS Variable	Dynamic ($\hat{\beta}_{\mathrm{D}}$)	Hybrid ($\hat{\beta}_{\mathrm{H}}$)	Two-Step ($\hat{\beta}_{\mathrm{S}}$)
y_{t-1}	1.0348	0.9772	0.9772
y_{t-2}	−0.1409	0.1595	0.1595
y_{t-3}	−0.1616	−0.0524	−0.0524
y_{t-4}	0.2810	−0.0352	−0.0352
y_{t-5}	0.2506	0.0161	0.0161
y_{t-6}	−0.5489	−0.0869	−0.0869
y_{t-7}	0.5266	0.0699	0.0699
y_{t-8}	−0.2848	−0.0777	−0.0777
y_{t-9}	−0.2676	0.0378	0.0378
y_{t-10}	0.1279	−0.0625	−0.0625
y_{t-11}	0.1638	−0.0386	−0.0386
y_{t-12}	−0.0250	0.0599	0.0599

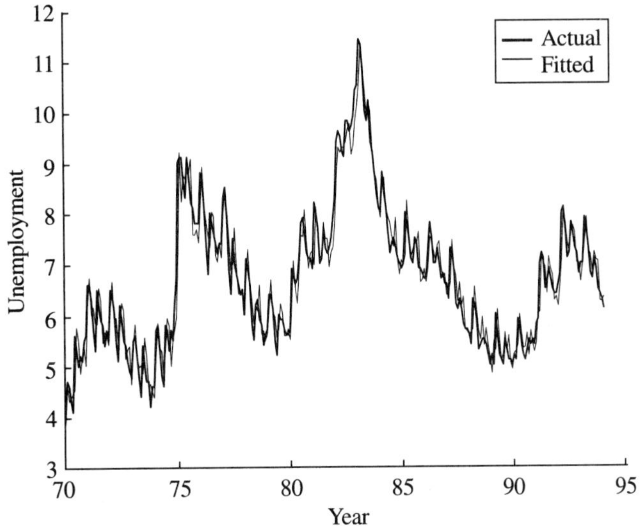

Figure 3.4 U. S. national unemployment rate and dynamic fit.

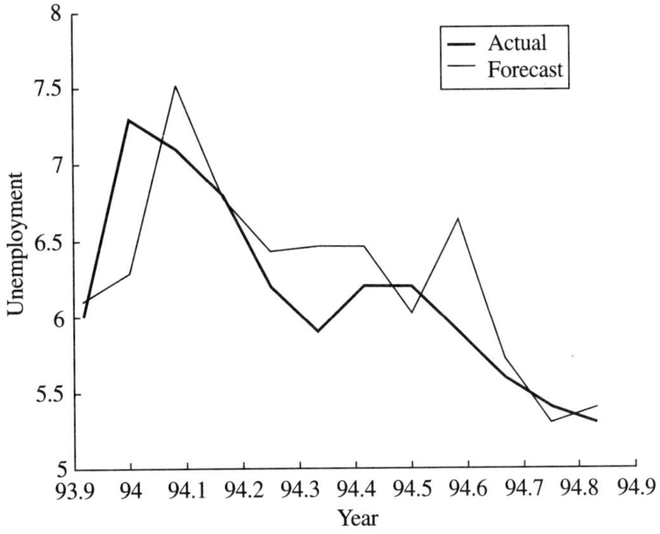

Figure 3.5 Unemployment: actual data and dynamic forecast, 1993:12–1994:11.

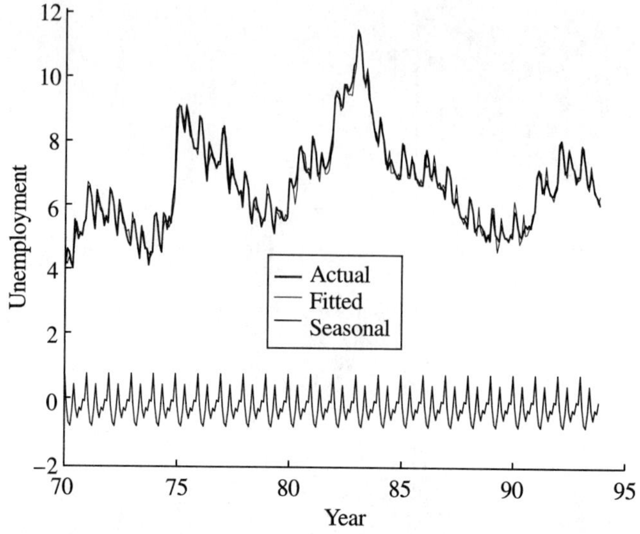

Figure 3.6 Unemployment, fitted values, and seasonal component.

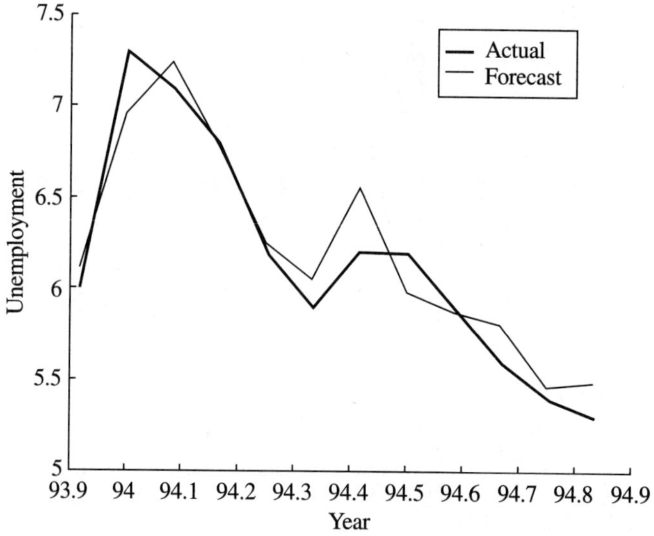

Figure 3.7 Unemployment: actual data and hybrid forecast, 1993:12–1994:11.

For each of the RHS lagged unemployment variables, we substituted series seasonally adjusted in the same way. We denote these $\{z^{s}_{tk}\}$ $(k = 2, \ldots, 13)$. The two-step fit of the pure dynamic model to the seasonally adjusted data, $\hat{\boldsymbol{\beta}}_{\mathrm{S}}$, delivers the same dynamic coefficients as the second column of the table, even though no monthly indicator variables were included on the RHS: for $k = 2, \ldots, 13$, $\hat{\beta}_{\mathrm{H}k} = \hat{\beta}_{\mathrm{S}k}$ in the two fitted functions

$$\sum_{k=1}^{12} z_{tk} \underbrace{\hat{\beta}_{\mathrm{H}k}}_{\text{equal}} + \sum_{k=13}^{24} x_{t,k-13}\hat{\beta}_{\mathrm{H}k}$$

$$\hat{\beta}_{\mathrm{S}1} + \sum_{k=2}^{13} z^{s}_{tk} \overbrace{\hat{\beta}_{\mathrm{S}k}}$$

Furthermore, the fitted value of the intercept $\hat{\beta}_{\mathrm{S}1}$ is exactly zero.

This is an illustration of a general feature of OLS fits that helps our interpretation of the fitted coefficients. The general idea is that each OLS fitted coefficient captures the covariation of its RHS variable with the LHS variable that cannot be captured by the other RHS variables. Intuitively speaking, our seasonal adjustment removes from the LHS and RHS variables the variation that monthly indicator variables can capture through the OLS fit: the seasonally adjusted variables are the fitted *residuals* (plus a constant) from the OLS fit to the monthly indicator variables alone. The second-round OLS fit of the residual for unemployment on the residuals for the lagged unemployment variables will capture variation in the unemployment rate that only the lagged unemployment variables can fit. And their fitted coefficients are *identically* equal to the fitted OLS coefficients of the original RHS lagged unemployment variables when the monthly indicators are also RHS variables.

Furthermore, the seasonal variables capture the overall level of the unemployment series. As a result, there is nothing for the intercept term to fit and its fitted value is zero. This chapter explains this feature of the OLS fitting procedure.

In this chapter, we will generalize the notion of an orthogonal projection. The generalization arises in two important situations: partitioned fit and restricted least squares. In terms of the previous chapter, we are going to explain the decomposition of $\hat{\boldsymbol{\mu}}$ into its K components $\mathbf{X}_k\hat{\beta}_k$, $k = 1, \ldots, K$, as in Figure 2.7, and hence, the nature of the elements of $\hat{\boldsymbol{\beta}}$. From this point on, we will tend to focus on problems in which $\hat{\boldsymbol{\beta}}$ is unique. Therefore, we will often assume the following:

ASSUMPTION 3.1 (FULL RANK) *The $N \times K$ matrix $\mathbf{X}$ is full-column rank:* $\mathrm{rank}(\mathbf{X}) = K$ *and* $N > K$.

The number of observations is greater than the number of RHS variables. They could be equal, but that is rare and we will eventually need more observations.

3.2 PARTITIONED FIT

We have already discussed the formula for the OLS fitted value of $\boldsymbol{\beta}$: $\hat{\boldsymbol{\beta}} = (\mathbf{X}'\mathbf{X})^{-1}\mathbf{X}'\mathbf{y}$. We are about to look inside this formula at an expression for a subvector of $\hat{\boldsymbol{\beta}}$: $\hat{\boldsymbol{\beta}}_1$ in the decomposition $\mathbf{X}\hat{\boldsymbol{\beta}} = \mathbf{X}_1\hat{\boldsymbol{\beta}}_1 + \mathbf{X}_2\hat{\boldsymbol{\beta}}_2$. This expression for $\hat{\boldsymbol{\beta}}_1$ has two basic uses, one conceptual and the other practical. First, the expression aids in understanding the OLS fit. We can interpret $\hat{\boldsymbol{\beta}}_1$ as the least-squares coefficients in a fit of $\mathbf{y}$ on $\mathbf{X}_1$ alone, after the component of $\mathbf{X}_1$ that is collinear with $\mathbf{X}_2$ has been removed from $\mathbf{X}_1$. Second, we can apply this formula to reduce the dimensionality of a fitting problem. Such reductions are useful when computing capabilities are limiting. We will explain these uses below.

How does OLS sort out the coefficient for one RHS variable from the coefficient for another? In most data sets, this is complicated by the simultaneous variation of all the RHS variables from observation to observation. Consider the data graphed in Figure 3.8. It appears that higher values of y are associated with higher values of x_1. But this is actually not so if we take into account another variable x_2. Figures 3.9 and 3.10 graph y_n against both x_{n1} and x_{n2}. Inspection of the graphs reveals that y is increasing with x_{n2} and actually decreasing with x_{n1}. We have chosen the data to lie exactly on the plane $y = -x_1/4 + x_2/2$. But this was not apparent from the graph of y_n versus x_{n1} because it ignored the simultaneous changes in x_{n2} that occur in the data as x_{n1} changes. The marvel of OLS is that it would reveal exactly the relationship among the three variables.

If we could predetermine the values of $\mathbf{X}$, we might alter the values of the RHS variables one at a time in order to actually see the change in $\mathbf{y}$ in *ceteris paribus* fashion. Figure 3.11 depicts such a situation. Given such a design of $\mathbf{X}$, it is much easier to infer the relationship between y_n and x_{n1} from their graph, Figure 3.12. This would enable us to fit the elements of $\boldsymbol{\beta}$ directly. But economic data sets rarely yield such straightforward comparisons. In addition, data

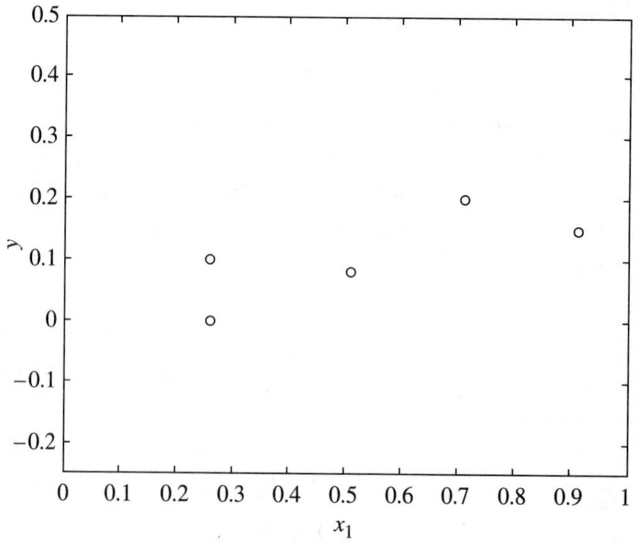

Figure 3.8 The association between two variables.

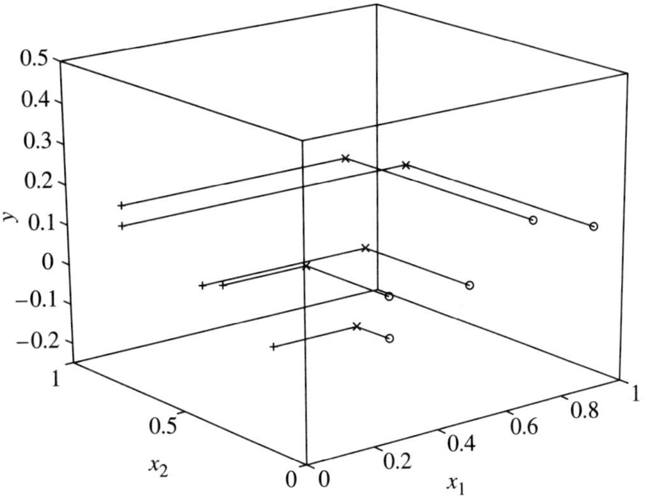

Figure 3.9 The association between three variables.

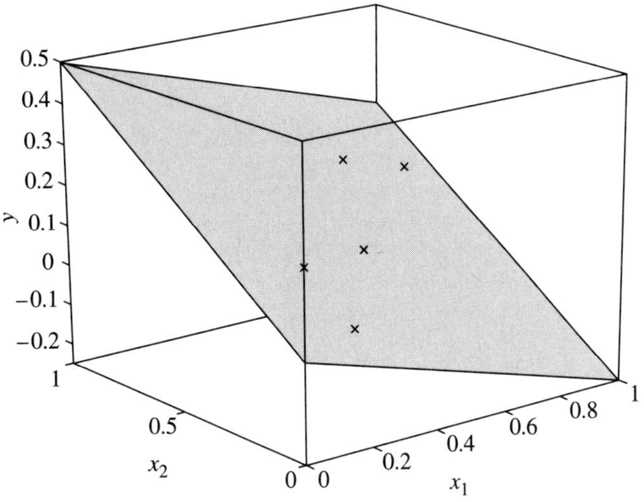

Figure 3.10 The association between three variables.

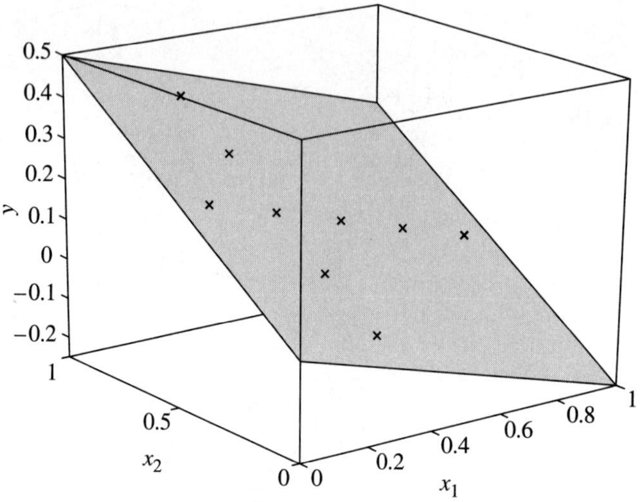

Figure 3.11 The association between three variables.

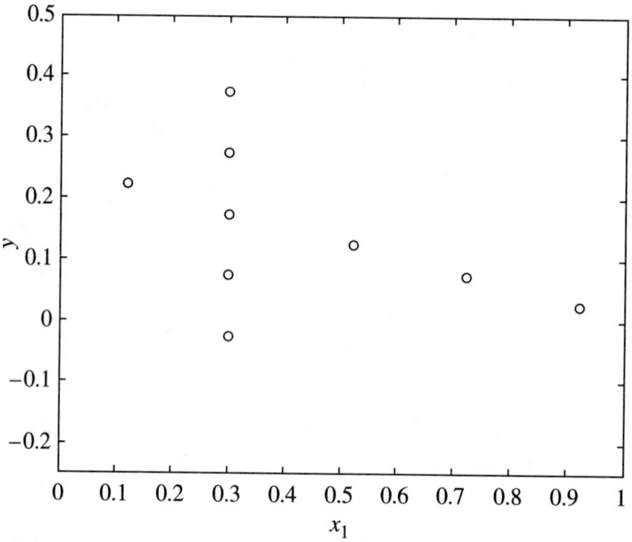

Figure 3.12 The association between two variables.

never exhibit such perfect collinearity. There are always nonzero residuals in OLS fits. Given these considerations, how does OLS allocate the variation in y among the RHS variables and the residual?

It is possible to describe simply how OLS assigns values to the elements of $\boldsymbol{\beta}$ when all of the RHS variables change from observation to observation. To do so we will examine the vector $\boldsymbol{\mu} \equiv \mathbf{X}\boldsymbol{\beta}$ in terms of two components $\boldsymbol{\mu}_1 \equiv \mathbf{X}_1\boldsymbol{\beta}_1$ and $\boldsymbol{\mu}_2 \equiv \mathbf{X}_2\boldsymbol{\beta}_2$. This is often called a *partition* because this is exactly what we are doing to the matrices

$$
\begin{aligned}
\boldsymbol{\mu} &\equiv \underset{N\times K}{\mathbf{X}} \; \underset{K\times 1}{\boldsymbol{\beta}} \\
&= [\mathbf{X}_1 \quad \mathbf{X}_2] \begin{bmatrix} \boldsymbol{\beta}_1 \\ \boldsymbol{\beta}_2 \end{bmatrix} \\
&= \underset{N\times K_1}{\mathbf{X}_1} \; \underset{K_1\times 1}{\boldsymbol{\beta}_1} + \underset{N\times K_2}{\mathbf{X}_2} \; \underset{K_2\times 1}{\boldsymbol{\beta}_2} \\
&= \boldsymbol{\mu}_1 + \boldsymbol{\mu}_2
\end{aligned}
$$

where $K = K_1 + K_2$. We generalize $\mathbf{X}_1$ to denote the first K_1 columns of $\mathbf{X}$ and $\mathbf{X}_2$ to denote the last $K_2 = K - K_1$ columns of $\mathbf{X}$. Here is the mathematical result, due to Lovell (1963).

PROPOSITION 2 (PARTITIONED FIT) *If Assumption 3.1 holds, and*

$$
\begin{aligned}
\mathbf{X}_{1\perp 2} &\equiv \left(\mathbf{I} - \mathbf{P}_{\mathbf{X}_2}\right)\mathbf{X}_1 \\
\mathbf{y}_{\perp 2} &\equiv \left(\mathbf{I} - \mathbf{P}_{\mathbf{X}_2}\right)\mathbf{y} \\
\mathbf{P}_{\mathbf{X}_2} &\equiv \mathbf{X}_2(\mathbf{X}_2'\mathbf{X}_2)^{-1}\mathbf{X}_2'
\end{aligned}
$$

then[2]

1. *The OLS fitted vector* $\hat{\boldsymbol{\mu}}_1 \equiv \mathbf{X}_1\hat{\boldsymbol{\beta}}_1$ *is the unique projection of* $\mathbf{y}$ *(or* $\hat{\boldsymbol{\mu}}$*) onto* $\text{Col}(\mathbf{X}_1)$ *such that elements of* $\text{Col}(\mathbf{X}_2)$ *and* $\text{Col}^{\perp}(\mathbf{X})$ *are annihilated. Furthermore,* $\hat{\boldsymbol{\mu}}_1 = \mathbf{P}_{12}\mathbf{y} = \mathbf{P}_{12}\hat{\boldsymbol{\mu}}$*, where the unique projector is*

$$
\mathbf{P}_{12} = \mathbf{X}_1\left(\mathbf{X}_{1\perp 2}'\mathbf{X}_1\right)^{-1}\mathbf{X}_{1\perp 2}' \tag{3.5}
$$

2. *The OLS fitted coefficients* $\hat{\boldsymbol{\beta}}_1$ *are*

$$
\hat{\boldsymbol{\beta}}_1 = \left(\mathbf{X}_{1\perp 2}'\mathbf{X}_{1\perp 2}\right)^{-1}\mathbf{X}_{1\perp 2}'\mathbf{y}_{\perp 2} \tag{3.6}
$$

The first element of this proposition states that $\hat{\boldsymbol{\mu}}_1$ is generally a *nonorthogonal* projection of $\mathbf{y}$.[3] We will explain this generalization of orthogonal projection below. We will focus first on the interpretation of $\hat{\boldsymbol{\beta}}_1$ given by this proposition. We can interpret (3.6) in an interesting way, in terms of two OLS fitting steps.

[2] The suffix "$\perp 2$" in the subscripts describes the fact that these transformations are orthogonal to $\mathbf{X}_2$. For example $\mathbf{X}_2'\mathbf{y}_{\perp 2} = 0$.

[3] The proof of this proposition is on p. 61 and p. 64.

Step 1: Using $\mathbf{X}_2$ as the RHS variable matrix, calculate the OLS fitted residuals for $\mathbf{y}$ and for each of the variables in $\mathbf{X}_1$ as LHS variables. Denote these residuals by $\mathbf{y}_{\perp 2}$ and $\mathbf{X}_{1\perp 2}$, respectively.

Step 2: Calculate $\hat{\boldsymbol{\beta}}_1$ as the OLS fitted coefficients from $\mathbf{y}_{\perp 2}$ as the LHS variable and $\mathbf{X}_{1\perp 2}$ as the RHS variable matrix.

EXAMPLE 3.1

We have implicitly seen these two steps in Example 2.4. In a slight change of notation, let $K = 2$, $\mathbf{X} = [\mathbf{X}_1, \mathbf{X}_2]$, $\mathbf{X}_2 = \iota$, so that

$$\hat{\beta}_1 = \frac{\sum_{n=1}^{N}(x_{n1} - \bar{x}_1)y_n}{\sum_{n=1}^{N}(x_{n1} - \bar{x}_1)^2}$$

Because

$$\sum_{n=1}^{N}(x_{n1} - \bar{x}_1)\bar{y} = 0$$

we can also write

$$\begin{aligned}\hat{\beta}_1 &= \frac{\sum_{n=1}^{N}(x_{n1} - \bar{x}_1)(y_n - \bar{y})}{\sum_{n=1}^{N}(x_{n1} - \bar{x}_1)^2} \\ &= (\mathbf{X}'_{1\perp 2}\mathbf{X}_{1\perp 2})^{-1}\mathbf{X}'_{1\perp 2}\mathbf{y}_{\perp 2}\end{aligned}$$

where

$$\begin{aligned}\mathbf{X}_{1\perp 2} &\equiv (\mathbf{I} - \mathbf{P}_\iota)\mathbf{X}_1 = [x_{n1} - \bar{x}_1]' \\ \mathbf{y}_{\perp 2} &\equiv (\mathbf{I} - \mathbf{P}_\iota)\mathbf{y} = [y_n - \bar{y}]'\end{aligned}$$

Because $\mathbf{X}_2$ is a column of ones, the OLS fits in the first step just calculate the sample averages $\bar{x}_1$ and $\bar{y}$. The residuals from the first step are deviations from sample averages: $x_{n1} - \bar{x}_1$ and $y_n - \bar{y}$. Then the second step yields $\hat{\beta}_1$ from the one-dimensional OLS fit of $y_n - \bar{y}$ to $x_{n1} - \bar{x}_1$ $(n = 1, \ldots, N)$.

The general expression $\mathbf{P}_{\mathbf{X}_2}\mathbf{X}_1$ is the fitted values of the columns of $\mathbf{X}_1$ obtained from individual fits on $\mathbf{X}_2$:

$$\mathbf{P}_{\mathbf{X}_2}\mathbf{X}_1 = \begin{bmatrix}\mathbf{P}_{\mathbf{X}_2}\mathbf{X}_{11} & \mathbf{P}_{\mathbf{X}_2}\mathbf{X}_{12} & \ldots & \mathbf{P}_{\mathbf{X}_2}\mathbf{X}_{1K_1}\end{bmatrix}$$

where $\mathbf{X}_{1k}$ is the kth column of $\mathbf{X}_1$. The expression $\mathbf{X}_{1\perp 2} \equiv (\mathbf{I} - \mathbf{P}_{\mathbf{X}_2})\mathbf{X}_1 = \mathbf{X}_1 - \mathbf{P}_{\mathbf{X}_2}\mathbf{X}_1$ holds the corresponding fitted residuals. Computing these fitted residuals, and comparable residuals for $\mathbf{y}$, $\mathbf{y}_{\perp 2}$, comprises the first step. In the second step, we compute the OLS fitted coefficients with $\mathbf{y}_{\perp 2}$ as the LHS variable and $\mathbf{X}_{1\perp 2}$ as the RHS variables. The new RHS variables $\mathbf{X}_{1\perp 2}$ have the common linear component between $\mathbf{X}_1$ and $\mathbf{X}_2$ removed from $\mathbf{X}_1$:

$$\mathbf{X}'_{1\perp 2}\mathbf{X}_2 = \mathbf{X}'_1(\mathbf{I} - \mathbf{P}_{\mathbf{X}_2})'\mathbf{X}_2 = \mathbf{X}'_1(\mathbf{I} - \mathbf{P}_{\mathbf{X}_2})\mathbf{X}_2 = \mathbf{0} \tag{3.7}$$

because $\mathbf{I} - \mathbf{P}_{\mathbf{X}_2}$ is a symmetric orthogonal projector [Lemma 2.7 (Orthogonal Projectors, p. 38)]. The new RHS variable $\mathbf{y}_{\perp 2}$ is also orthogonal to the variables in $\mathbf{X}_2$. Therefore, we can view $\hat{\boldsymbol{\beta}}_1$ as capturing the component of $\mathbf{y}$ collinear with $\mathbf{X}_1$ *that cannot be fitted with* $\mathbf{X}_2$.

Indeed, if we included $\mathbf{X}_2$ along with $\mathbf{X}_{1\perp 2}$ on the RHS, the additional coefficients would all be zero. That is, if we fit $\mathbf{y}_{\perp 2}$ to $[\mathbf{X}_{1\perp 2}, \mathbf{X}_2]\,\gamma$ we obtain the OLS fitted coefficients

$$\begin{aligned}
\hat{\gamma} &= \begin{bmatrix} \mathbf{X}'_{1\perp 2}\mathbf{X}_{1\perp 2} & \mathbf{X}'_{1\perp 2}\mathbf{X}_2 \\ \mathbf{X}'_2\mathbf{X}_{1\perp 2} & \mathbf{X}'_2\mathbf{X}_2 \end{bmatrix}^{-1} \begin{bmatrix} \mathbf{X}'_{1\perp 2}\mathbf{y}_{\perp 2} \\ \mathbf{X}'_2\mathbf{y}_{\perp 2} \end{bmatrix} \\
&= \begin{bmatrix} \mathbf{X}'_{1\perp 2}\mathbf{X}_{1\perp 2} & \mathbf{0} \\ \mathbf{0} & \mathbf{X}'_2\mathbf{X}_2 \end{bmatrix}^{-1} \begin{bmatrix} \mathbf{X}'_{1\perp 2}\mathbf{y}_{\perp 2} \\ \mathbf{0} \end{bmatrix} \\
&= \begin{bmatrix} \left(\mathbf{X}'_{1\perp 2}\mathbf{X}_{1\perp 2}\right)^{-1} & \mathbf{0} \\ \mathbf{0} & \left(\mathbf{X}'_2\mathbf{X}_2\right)^{-1} \end{bmatrix} \begin{bmatrix} \mathbf{X}'_{1\perp 2}\mathbf{y}_{\perp 2} \\ \mathbf{0} \end{bmatrix} \\
&= \begin{bmatrix} \left(\mathbf{X}'_{1\perp 2}\mathbf{X}_{1\perp 2}\right)^{-1}\mathbf{X}'_{1\perp 2}\mathbf{y}_{\perp 2} \\ \left(\mathbf{X}'_2\mathbf{X}_2\right)^{-1}\mathbf{0} \end{bmatrix} \\
&= \begin{bmatrix} \hat{\boldsymbol{\beta}}_1 \\ \mathbf{0} \end{bmatrix}
\end{aligned} \tag{3.8}$$

The fitted coefficient for $\boldsymbol{\beta}_2$ is exactly zero. The transformed $\mathbf{y}$ and $\mathbf{X}_1$, $\mathbf{y}_{\perp 2}$ and $\mathbf{X}_{1\perp 2}$, have had all the original linear association with $\mathbf{X}_2$ removed and we interpret $\mathbf{X}_1\hat{\boldsymbol{\beta}}_1$ as the component of $\mathbf{y}$ that can only be fit by $\mathbf{X}_1$. This characteristic describes how OLS is decomposing $\hat{\boldsymbol{\mu}}$ into $\hat{\boldsymbol{\mu}}_1$ and $\hat{\boldsymbol{\mu}}_2$.

To obtain geometric insight, we examine the fitted vector $\hat{\boldsymbol{\mu}}_1$. Proposition 2 states that like $\hat{\boldsymbol{\mu}}$, $\hat{\boldsymbol{\mu}}_1$ is a linear transformation of $\mathbf{y}$. Indeed, the matrix $\mathbf{P}_{12}$ is formally similar to the orthogonal projector $\mathbf{P}_{\mathbf{X}_1}$.

$$\mathbf{P}_1 \equiv \mathbf{X}_1(\underbrace{\mathbf{X}'_1}\,\mathbf{X}_1)^{-1}\underbrace{\mathbf{X}'_1}$$

$$\mathbf{P}_{12} = \mathbf{X}_1(\mathbf{X}'_{1\perp 2}\mathbf{X}_1)^{-1}\mathbf{X}'_{1\perp 2}$$

Compared to $\mathbf{P}_{\mathbf{X}_1}$, $\mathbf{X}_{1\perp 2}$ has replaced $\mathbf{X}_1$ twice in $\mathbf{P}_{12}$. An immediate consequence of this replacement is that $\mathbf{P}_{12}$ preserves $\mathrm{Col}(\mathbf{X}_1)$,

$$\mathbf{P}_{12}\mathbf{X}_1 = \mathbf{X}_1\left(\mathbf{X}'_{1\perp 2}\mathbf{X}_1\right)^{-1}\mathbf{X}'_{1\perp 2}\mathbf{X}_1 = \mathbf{X}_1 \tag{3.9}$$

but $\mathbf{P}_{12}$ annihilates $\mathrm{Col}(\mathbf{X}_2)$,

$$\mathbf{P}_{12}\mathbf{X}_2 = \mathbf{X}_1\left(\mathbf{X}'_{1\perp 2}\mathbf{X}_1\right)^{-1}\mathbf{X}'_{1\perp 2}\mathbf{X}_2 = \mathbf{0} \tag{3.10}$$

using (3.7). In particular, $\mathbf{P}_{12}$ preserves $\hat{\boldsymbol{\mu}}_1 \equiv \mathbf{X}_1\hat{\boldsymbol{\beta}}_1 \in \mathrm{Col}(\mathbf{X}_1)$ and annihilates $\hat{\boldsymbol{\mu}}_2 \equiv \mathbf{X}_2\hat{\boldsymbol{\beta}}_2 \in \mathrm{Col}(\mathbf{X}_2)$. In other words, $\mathbf{P}_{12}$ transforms $\hat{\boldsymbol{\mu}}$ into $\hat{\boldsymbol{\mu}}_1$: $\mathbf{P}_{12}\hat{\boldsymbol{\mu}} = \mathbf{P}_{12}\left(\hat{\boldsymbol{\mu}}_1 + \hat{\boldsymbol{\mu}}_2\right) = \hat{\boldsymbol{\mu}}_1$.

A graphic illustration of $\mathbf{P}_{12}\hat{\boldsymbol{\mu}}$ is insightful. Recall our graphic representation of $\hat{\boldsymbol{\mu}}_1$ as a linear transformation of $\hat{\boldsymbol{\mu}}$ in Figure 2.7. We reproduce that graph in Figure 3.13, where $\hat{\boldsymbol{\mu}}_1$ is found by sliding from $\hat{\boldsymbol{\mu}}$ to $\mathrm{Col}(\mathbf{X}_1)$ along the direction of $\mathrm{Col}(\mathbf{X}_2)$. Look at the structure of $\mathbf{P}_{12}$: expanding $\mathbf{X}_{1\perp 2} = \left(\mathbf{I} - \mathbf{P}_{\mathbf{X}_2}\right)\mathbf{X}_1$ gives

$$\mathbf{P}_{12} = \underbrace{\mathbf{X}_1}_{\text{trailing term}}\left[\mathbf{X}'_1(\mathbf{I} - \mathbf{P}_{\mathbf{X}_2})\mathbf{X}_1\right]^{-1}\underbrace{\mathbf{X}'_1(\mathbf{I} - \mathbf{P}_{\mathbf{X}_2})}_{\text{leading term}}$$

The $\mathbf{I} - \mathbf{P}_{\mathbf{X}_2}$ in the leading term annihilates any vector in $\mathrm{Col}(\mathbf{X}_2)$ so that $\mathbf{P}_{12}\hat{\boldsymbol{\mu}}_2 = \mathbf{0}$ in particular. The leading term sends $\hat{\boldsymbol{\mu}}$ on an orthogonal projection toward $\mathrm{Col}^{\perp}(\mathbf{X}_2)$. Figure 3.13 illustrates

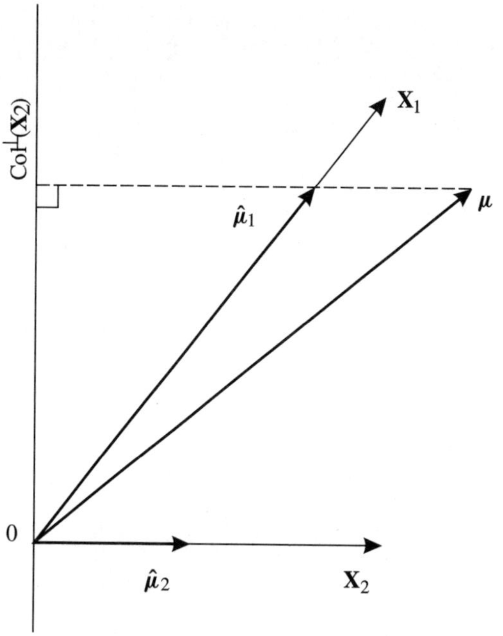

Figure 3.13 Nonorthogonal projection.

how $\mathbf{P}_{12}$ thus moves along Col($\mathbf{X}_2$). But the trailing $\mathbf{X}_1$ ensures that the final result will lie in Col($\mathbf{X}_1$). The rest of the expression for $\mathbf{P}_{12}$ ensures that $\mathbf{X}_1$ is preserved under the transformation: $\mathbf{P}_{12}\mathbf{X}_1 = \mathbf{X}_1$.

Our final comment about Proposition 2 reconciles the expressions for $\hat{\boldsymbol{\mu}}_1 = \mathbf{P}_{12}\mathbf{y}$ and $\hat{\boldsymbol{\beta}}_1$. First note that because it is an orthogonal projector, $\mathbf{I} - \mathbf{P}_{\mathbf{X}_2}$ is symmetric and idempotent [Lemma 2.7 (Orthogonal Projectors, p. 38)] so that

$$(\mathbf{I} - \mathbf{P}_{\mathbf{X}_2})'(\mathbf{I} - \mathbf{P}_{\mathbf{X}_2}) = (\mathbf{I} - \mathbf{P}_{\mathbf{X}_2})(\mathbf{I} - \mathbf{P}_{\mathbf{X}_2}) = \mathbf{I} - \mathbf{P}_{\mathbf{X}_2} \tag{3.11}$$

Equation (3.6) implies that

$$\begin{aligned}
\hat{\boldsymbol{\mu}}_1 &\equiv \mathbf{X}_1\hat{\boldsymbol{\beta}}_1 && (3.12)\\
&= \mathbf{X}_1\left(\mathbf{X}'_{1\perp 2}\mathbf{X}_{1\perp 2}\right)^{-1}\mathbf{X}'_{1\perp 2}\mathbf{y}_{\perp 2}\\
&= \mathbf{X}_1\left[\mathbf{X}'_1(\mathbf{I} - \mathbf{P}_{\mathbf{X}_2})'(\mathbf{I} - \mathbf{P}_{\mathbf{X}_2})\mathbf{X}_1\right]^{-1}\mathbf{X}'_1(\mathbf{I} - \mathbf{P}_{\mathbf{X}_2})'(\mathbf{I} - \mathbf{P}_{\mathbf{X}_2})\mathbf{y}\\
&= \mathbf{X}_1\left[\mathbf{X}'_1(\mathbf{I} - \mathbf{P}_{\mathbf{X}_2})\mathbf{X}_1\right]^{-1}\mathbf{X}'_1(\mathbf{I} - \mathbf{P}_{\mathbf{X}_2})\mathbf{y} && (3.13)\\
&= \mathbf{P}_{12}\mathbf{y}
\end{aligned}$$

Thus, $\hat{\boldsymbol{\mu}}_1 = \mathbf{P}_{12}\mathbf{y}$ follows from the expression for $\hat{\boldsymbol{\beta}}_1$. To prove the proposition, it remains only to derive $\hat{\boldsymbol{\beta}}_1$ and show the additional equality $\mathbf{P}_{12}\mathbf{y} = \mathbf{P}_{12}\hat{\boldsymbol{\mu}}$.

The news of Proposition 2 is the particular expressions for $\hat{\boldsymbol{\beta}}_1$ and $\hat{\boldsymbol{\mu}}_1$. We have already seen that $\hat{\boldsymbol{\beta}}$ is a function of $\hat{\boldsymbol{\mu}}$. So it comes as no surprise that we can recover $\hat{\boldsymbol{\mu}}_1$ from $\hat{\boldsymbol{\mu}}$ as well as from $\mathbf{y}$. To prove the new proposition, we will return to the theory of projection, developing the generalization of orthogonal projection.

3.3 PROJECTION

We can always relate projection to minimizing length. We shall prove the second part of Proposition 2 first, using an orthogonal decomposition of the residual sum of squares fitting criterion used by OLS.[4]

Proof of Proposition 2, Part 2. The orthogonal decomposition

$$\mathbf{y} - \boldsymbol{\mu} = \left(\mathbf{I} - \mathbf{P}_{\mathbf{X}_2}\right)(\mathbf{y} - \boldsymbol{\mu}) + \mathbf{P}_{\mathbf{X}_2}(\mathbf{y} - \boldsymbol{\mu})$$

gives the Pythagorean relationship

$$\|\mathbf{y} - \boldsymbol{\mu}\|^2 = \left\|\left(\mathbf{I} - \mathbf{P}_{\mathbf{X}_2}\right)(\mathbf{y} - \boldsymbol{\mu})\right\|^2 + \left\|\mathbf{P}_{\mathbf{X}_2}(\mathbf{y} - \boldsymbol{\mu})\right\|^2$$

Now note that

$$\begin{aligned}\left(\mathbf{I} - \mathbf{P}_{\mathbf{X}_2}\right)(\mathbf{y} - \boldsymbol{\mu}) &= \left(\mathbf{I} - \mathbf{P}_{\mathbf{X}_2}\right)\mathbf{y} - \left(\mathbf{I} - \mathbf{P}_{\mathbf{X}_2}\right)\mathbf{X}_1\boldsymbol{\beta}_1 + \left(\mathbf{I} - \mathbf{P}_{\mathbf{X}_2}\right)\mathbf{X}_2\boldsymbol{\beta}_2 \\ &= \mathbf{y}_{\perp 2} - \mathbf{X}_{1\perp 2}\boldsymbol{\beta}_1\end{aligned}$$

so that

$$\|\mathbf{y} - \boldsymbol{\mu}\|^2 = \|\mathbf{y}_{\perp 2} - \mathbf{X}_{1\perp 2}\boldsymbol{\beta}_1\|^2 + \left\|\mathbf{P}_{\mathbf{X}_2}(\mathbf{y} - \mathbf{X}_1\boldsymbol{\beta}_1) - \mathbf{X}_2\boldsymbol{\beta}_2\right\|^2 \tag{3.14}$$

decomposing the squared length of any residual into a squared length that depends only on $\boldsymbol{\beta}_1$ and another squared length that depends on both components of $\boldsymbol{\beta}$. The second term has a surprising property: for *any value* of $\boldsymbol{\beta}_1$, this term can be minimized over $\boldsymbol{\beta}_2$ to zero. Because $\mathbf{P}_{\mathbf{X}_2}(\mathbf{y} - \mathbf{X}_1\boldsymbol{\beta}_1)$ is a member of Col($\mathbf{X}_2$), $\mathbf{X}_2\boldsymbol{\beta}_2$ can always fit it exactly. This means that $\hat{\boldsymbol{\beta}}_1$ minimizes the first term alone and the OLS solution is the expression for $\hat{\boldsymbol{\beta}}_1$ given in the proposition. Expressed formally,

$$\begin{aligned}\min_{\boldsymbol{\beta}} \|\mathbf{y} - \boldsymbol{\mu}\|^2 &= \min_{\boldsymbol{\beta}_1}\left\{\|\mathbf{y}_{\perp 2} - \mathbf{X}_{1\perp 2}\boldsymbol{\beta}_1\|^2 + \min_{\boldsymbol{\beta}_2}\left\|\mathbf{P}_{\mathbf{X}_2}(\mathbf{y} - \mathbf{X}_1\boldsymbol{\beta}_1) - \mathbf{X}_2\boldsymbol{\beta}_2\right\|^2\right\} \\ &= \min_{\boldsymbol{\beta}_1}\|\mathbf{y}_{\perp 2} - \mathbf{X}_{1\perp 2}\boldsymbol{\beta}_1\|^2\end{aligned}$$

We can use Proposition 1 (OLS Fit, p. 24) to find the solution provided that $\mathbf{X}_{1\perp 2}$ is full rank. To see that it is consider

$$\mathbf{X} = \left(\mathbf{I} - \mathbf{P}_{\mathbf{X}_2} + \mathbf{P}_{\mathbf{X}_2}\right)\mathbf{X} = \left[\mathbf{X}_{1\perp 2} + \mathbf{P}_{\mathbf{X}_2}\mathbf{X}_1 \quad \mathbf{X}_2\right]$$

The columns of $\mathbf{P}_{\mathbf{X}_2}\mathbf{X}_1$ are linearly dependent on $\mathbf{X}_2$. But $\mathbf{X}$ is full-column rank, so that $\mathbf{X}_{1\perp 2}$ must also be full-column rank. Therefore, Proposition 1 implies that $\hat{\boldsymbol{\beta}}_1 = \left(\mathbf{X}'_{1\perp 2}\mathbf{X}_{1\perp 2}\right)^{-1}\mathbf{X}'_{1\perp 2}\mathbf{y}_{\perp 2}$. □

To gain further insight into the linear transformation $\mathbf{P}_{12}$, we shall rewrite the minimum distance problem for $\boldsymbol{\beta}_1$ in terms of the original data:

[4] A constructive proof of Proposition 2 is described in Exercises 3.10 and 3.11.

$$
\begin{aligned}
\|\mathbf{y}_{\perp 2} - \mathbf{X}_{1\perp 2}\boldsymbol{\beta}_1\|^2 &= \left\|\left(\mathbf{I} - \mathbf{P}_{\mathbf{X}_2}\right)(\mathbf{y} - \mathbf{X}_1\boldsymbol{\beta}_1)\right\|^2 \\
&= (\mathbf{y} - \mathbf{X}_1\boldsymbol{\beta}_1)'\left(\mathbf{I} - \mathbf{P}_{\mathbf{X}_2}\right)'\left(\mathbf{I} - \mathbf{P}_{\mathbf{X}_2}\right)(\mathbf{y} - \mathbf{X}_1\boldsymbol{\beta}_1) \\
&= (\mathbf{y} - \mathbf{X}_1\boldsymbol{\beta}_1)'\left(\mathbf{I} - \mathbf{P}_{\mathbf{X}_2}\right)(\mathbf{y} - \mathbf{X}_1\boldsymbol{\beta}_1) \qquad (3.15)
\end{aligned}
$$

In this form, the program for $\boldsymbol{\beta}_1$ is a generalization of the OLS problem where squared distance is not simply the sum of squared elements. The matrix $\mathbf{I} - \mathbf{P}_{\mathbf{X}_2}$ has been inserted into the middle of the quadratic expression where (implicitly) an identity matrix once sat, creating a *generalized distance* measure. In the expressions (3.13) and (3.15), we have come upon the solution

$$
\mathbf{X}_1\left(\mathbf{X}_1'\mathbf{A}\mathbf{X}_1\right)^{-1}\mathbf{X}_1'\mathbf{A}\mathbf{y} = \underset{\mathbf{z}\in\mathrm{Col}(\mathbf{X}_1)}{\operatorname{argmin}}\ (\mathbf{y} - \mathbf{z})'\mathbf{A}(\mathbf{y} - \mathbf{z}) \qquad (3.16)
$$

where $\mathbf{A} = \mathbf{I} - \mathbf{P}_{\mathbf{X}_2}$ (provided that $\mathbf{X}_1'\mathbf{A}\mathbf{X}_1$ is nonsingular).

In this chapter, we will concentrate on linear transformations of the form $\mathbf{X}\left(\mathbf{X}'\mathbf{A}\mathbf{X}\right)^{-1}\mathbf{X}'\mathbf{A}$, explaining that they are a generalization of orthogonal projectors. Our present emphasis is the mechanism that isolates $\mathbf{X}_1$ in the OLS analysis. In the next chapter, where we encounter this mathematical structure in another setting, we will clarify the nature of this generalized distance measure.

In a discussion of projection, it is natural to write

$$
\mathbf{X}\left(\mathbf{X}'\mathbf{A}\mathbf{X}\right)^{-1}\mathbf{X}'\mathbf{A} = \mathbf{X}\left(\mathbf{Z}'\mathbf{X}\right)^{-1}\mathbf{Z}' \qquad (3.17)
$$

where $\mathbf{Z} \equiv \mathbf{A}'\mathbf{X}$. This form makes two properties plain: (1) the preservation of $\mathrm{Col}(\mathbf{X})$, because

$$
\begin{aligned}
\mathbf{w} \in \mathrm{Col}(\mathbf{X}) &\Leftrightarrow \mathbf{w} = \mathbf{X}\boldsymbol{\alpha} \qquad (3.18) \\
&\Rightarrow \left[\mathbf{X}\left(\mathbf{Z}'\mathbf{X}\right)^{-1}\mathbf{Z}'\right]\mathbf{w} = \left[\mathbf{X}\left(\mathbf{Z}'\mathbf{X}\right)^{-1}\mathbf{Z}'\right]\mathbf{X}\boldsymbol{\alpha} \\
&= \mathbf{X}\left[\left(\mathbf{Z}'\mathbf{X}\right)^{-1}\mathbf{Z}'\mathbf{X}\right]\boldsymbol{\alpha} = \mathbf{X}\boldsymbol{\alpha} = \mathbf{w}
\end{aligned}
$$

and (2) the annihilation of $\mathrm{Col}^{\perp}(\mathbf{Z})$, because

$$
\begin{aligned}
\mathbf{w} \perp \mathrm{Col}(\mathbf{Z}) &\Leftrightarrow \mathbf{Z}'\mathbf{w} = \mathbf{0} \qquad (3.19) \\
&\Rightarrow \left[\mathbf{X}\left(\mathbf{Z}'\mathbf{X}\right)^{-1}\mathbf{Z}'\right]\mathbf{w} = \mathbf{X}\left(\mathbf{Z}'\mathbf{X}\right)^{-1}\left(\mathbf{Z}'\mathbf{w}\right) = \mathbf{0}
\end{aligned}
$$

If every element of $\mathbb{R}^N$ can be expressed as a linear combination of vectors from $\mathrm{Col}(\mathbf{X})$ and $\mathrm{Col}^{\perp}(\mathbf{Z})$, then these two characteristics, (3.18) and (3.19), completely describe the linear transformation (3.17).[5] For this reason, it is convenient to be able to refer to the concept of vector spaces called a *direct sum*.[6]

DEFINITION 7 (DIRECT SUM) *Let $\mathbb{S}_1$ and $\mathbb{S}_2$ be two disjoint vector subspaces of $\mathbb{R}^N$ so that $\mathbb{S}_1 \cap \mathbb{S}_2 = \{\mathbf{0}\}$. The vector space*

$$
\mathbb{V} = \left\{\mathbf{z} \in \mathbb{R}^N \mid \mathbf{z} = \mathbf{z}_1 + \mathbf{z}_2,\ \mathbf{z}_1 \in \mathbb{S}_1,\ \mathbf{z}_2 \in \mathbb{S}_2\right\}
$$

is called the direct sum *of $\mathbb{S}_1$ and $\mathbb{S}_2$ and it is denoted by $\mathbb{V} = \mathbb{S}_1 \oplus \mathbb{S}_2$.*

[5] Compare these equations with (2.10) and (2.11) starting on p. 32 and the accompanying discussion of orthogonal projectors.

[6] Also see the discussion surrounding Definition C.5 (Direct Sum, p. 845).

Restating our argument, if $\mathbb{R}^N = \text{Col}(\mathbf{X}) \oplus \text{Col}^{\perp}(\mathbf{Z})$ then (3.18) and (3.19) describe the linear transformation (3.17). We have already used such decomposition in $\mathbb{R}^N = \text{Col}(\mathbf{X}) \oplus \text{Col}^{\perp}(\mathbf{X})$. If $\mathbf{Z} = \mathbf{X}$, then $\mathbf{X}\left(\mathbf{Z}'\mathbf{X}\right)^{-1}\mathbf{Z}'$ is the familiar orthogonal projector $\mathbf{P_X} = \mathbf{X}\left(\mathbf{X}'\mathbf{X}\right)^{-1}\mathbf{X}'$. But as you know, the basis of a linear vector space does not necessarily consist of orthogonal vectors. And so vector spaces can also be broken into direct sums of nonorthogonal subspaces. In general, projectors are transformations into components of such nonorthogonal subspaces.

Definition 8 (Projector) *Let $\mathbb{R}^N$ be the direct sum of two linear subspaces $\mathbb{S}_1$ and $\mathbb{S}_2$: $\mathbb{R}^N = \mathbb{S}_1 \oplus \mathbb{S}_2$. Let $\mathbf{z} \in \mathbb{R}^N$ so that $\mathbf{z} = \mathbf{z}_1 + \mathbf{z}_2$ for unique $\mathbf{z}_i \in \mathbb{S}_i$ $(i = 1, 2)$. Then $\mathbf{P}$ is a* projector onto $\mathbb{S}_1$ along $\mathbb{S}_2$ *if $\mathbf{Pz} = \mathbf{z}_1$ for all $\mathbf{z}$.*

It follows from this definition that $\mathbf{P}$ is unique. The proof of this uniqueness is identical to the proof for the uniqueness of orthogonal projectors.[7]

Lemma 3.1 *Let $\mathbb{R}^N = \mathbb{S}_1 \oplus \mathbb{S}_2$. The projector $\mathbf{P}$ onto $\mathbb{S}_1$ along $\mathbb{S}_2$ is unique.*

Because it is a useful generalization of the orthogonal projector, we introduce the supplementary notation $\mathbf{P}_{\mathbf{X}\perp\mathbf{Z}}$ for the projector onto $\text{Col}(\mathbf{X})$ along $\text{Col}^{\perp}(\mathbf{Z})$, when $\mathbb{R}^N = \text{Col}(\mathbf{X}) \oplus \text{Col}^{\perp}(\mathbf{Z})$. We prove formally in Section 3.4 that

$$\mathbf{P}_{\mathbf{X}\perp\mathbf{Z}} = \mathbf{X}\left(\mathbf{Z}'\mathbf{X}\right)^{-1}\mathbf{Z}' \tag{3.20}$$

when $\mathbf{X}$ and $\mathbf{Z}$ are $N \times K$ matrices and $\mathbf{Z}'\mathbf{X}$ is nonsingular. For orthogonal projectors, $\mathbf{P_X} \equiv \mathbf{P}_{\mathbf{X}\perp\mathbf{X}}$. Returning to the particular case of $\mathbf{P}_{12}$, we now interpret that matrix as a projector.[8]

Lemma 3.2 *Given Assumption 3.1, the matrix $\mathbf{P}_{12} = \mathbf{X}_1\left(\mathbf{X}_{1\perp 2}'\mathbf{X}_1\right)^{-1}\mathbf{X}_{1\perp 2}'$ is the unique projector onto* $\text{Col}(\mathbf{X}_1)$ *along* $\text{Col}(\mathbf{X}_2) \oplus \text{Col}^{\perp}(\mathbf{X})$.

Proof. Because $\mathbf{X}$ is full rank,

$$\begin{aligned}\mathbb{R}^N &= \text{Col}(\mathbf{X}) \oplus \text{Col}^{\perp}(\mathbf{X}) \\ &= \text{Col}(\mathbf{X}_1) \oplus \left[\text{Col}(\mathbf{X}_2) \oplus \text{Col}^{\perp}(\mathbf{X})\right]\end{aligned}$$

---

[7] See Lemma 2.4 (p. 33).

[8] In this notation,

$$\mathbf{P}_{12} = \mathbf{P}_{\mathbf{X}_1\perp\mathbf{X}_{1\perp 2}}$$

which we deem too rich in subscripts and "perps" for a regular diet. We will continue with $\mathbf{P}_{12}$.

We have already shown that $\mathbf{P}_{12}$ preserves Col($\mathbf{X}_1$) and annihilates Col($\mathbf{X}_2$) [see (3.9) and (3.10)]. Therefore, to prove the lemma we need only show that Col$^{\perp}$($\mathbf{X}$) is also annihilated by $\mathbf{P}_{12}$. To see this, note that for all $\mathbf{z} \in$ Col$^{\perp}$($\mathbf{X}$), $\mathbf{P}_{\mathbf{X}_2}\mathbf{z} = \mathbf{0}$ and $\mathbf{X}_1'\mathbf{z} = \mathbf{0}$. Therefore,

$$\mathbf{X}_{1\perp 2}'\mathbf{z} = \mathbf{X}_1'\left(\mathbf{I} - \mathbf{P}_{\mathbf{X}_2}\right)'\mathbf{z} = \mathbf{X}_1'\left(\mathbf{I} - \mathbf{P}_{\mathbf{X}_2}\right)\mathbf{z} = \mathbf{X}_1'\mathbf{z} = \mathbf{0}$$

These properties characterize $\mathbf{P}_{12}$ as a projector onto Col($\mathbf{X}_1$) along Col($\mathbf{X}_2$) $\oplus$ Col$^{\perp}$($\mathbf{X}$). Its uniqueness follows from Lemma 3.1. □

The projector $\mathbf{P}_{12}$ annihilates the component of $\mathbf{y}$ that lives in Col$^{\perp}$($\mathbf{X}$), the OLS fitted residual $\mathbf{y} - \hat{\boldsymbol{\mu}}$, just as $\mathbf{P}_{\mathbf{X}}$ does. In addition, the partitioned fit extracts $\hat{\boldsymbol{\mu}}_1$ from $\hat{\boldsymbol{\mu}}$. Thus, we can continue to think of OLS as a two-step process, from $\mathbf{y}$ to $\hat{\boldsymbol{\mu}}$, and then a decomposition of $\hat{\boldsymbol{\mu}}$ into the components of $\mathbf{X}\hat{\boldsymbol{\beta}}$ by such projectors as $\mathbf{P}_{12}$. The element $\hat{\boldsymbol{\beta}}_1$ is calculated from $\hat{\boldsymbol{\mu}}_1 \equiv \mathbf{X}_1\hat{\boldsymbol{\beta}}_1$ exactly the same way $\hat{\boldsymbol{\beta}}$ is calculated from $\hat{\boldsymbol{\mu}}$:

$$\hat{\boldsymbol{\beta}}_1 = (\mathbf{X}_1'\mathbf{X}_1)^{-1}\mathbf{X}_1'\hat{\boldsymbol{\mu}}_1$$

An extension of Figure 2.7 to three dimensions is shown in Figure 3.14, where the transformation of $\mathbf{y}$ by $\mathbf{P}_{12}$ also appears. Note that one of the sides of the three-dimensional box is parallel to $\mathbf{X}_2$ and another is perpendicular to Col($\mathbf{X}$). As a result, movement from $\mathbf{y}$ along Col($\mathbf{X}_2$) $\oplus$ Col$^{\perp}$($\mathbf{X}$) corresponds to movement parallel to the back panel of the box in this figure. Traveling onto Col($\mathbf{X}_1$) from $\mathbf{y}$ within that panel, we arrive at $\hat{\boldsymbol{\mu}}_1$.

Now we will complete our proof of Proposition 2.

Proof of Proposition 2, Part 1. We showed that $\hat{\boldsymbol{\mu}}_1 = \mathbf{P}_{12}\mathbf{y}$ from the expression $\hat{\boldsymbol{\beta}}_1 = \left(\mathbf{X}_{1\perp 2}'\mathbf{X}_{1\perp 2}\right)^{-1}\mathbf{X}_{1\perp 2}'\mathbf{y}_{\perp 2}$ [see (3.12)–(3.13)]. Lemma 3.2 states that $\mathbf{P}_{12}\mathbf{y}$ is the unique projection onto Col($\mathbf{X}_1$) along (annihilating) Col($\mathbf{X}_2$) $\oplus$ Col$^{\perp}$($\mathbf{X}$). Thus, $\mathbf{P}_{12}\mathbf{y} = \mathbf{P}_{12}\left(\mathbf{y} - \hat{\boldsymbol{\mu}} + \hat{\boldsymbol{\mu}}\right) = \mathbf{P}_{12}\hat{\boldsymbol{\mu}}$. □

EXAMPLE 3.2 **(Seasonal Effects)**

Let us return to the introductory example of this chapter. Recall that we obtained OLS fitted residuals for the unemployment rate and each lag of the unemployment rate from initial regressions on the monthly indicator variables. We found that the OLS fitted coefficients for the LHS unemployment residual on the RHS unemployment lags residuals produced the same coefficients as an original OLS fit for the LHS unemployment rate on the RHS unemployment rate lags *and* the monthly indicators. This corresponds to the second claim of Proposition 2 concerning $\hat{\boldsymbol{\beta}}_1$.

We also found that the fitted intercept in the OLS fit for residuals was zero. This corresponds to (3.8), where we showed that $\mathbf{X}_2$ has no explanatory power. The monthly indicator variables comprise the columns of $\mathbf{X}_2$ in this example. Therefore, if they were included as RHS variables in the OLS fit for residuals, their fitted coefficients would be zero. As a result, the fitted coefficient of any variable that is a linear combination of the indicator variables will also be zero. The constant RHS variable 1 is the simple sum of the monthly indicator variables. Thus, its fitted coefficient is exactly zero.

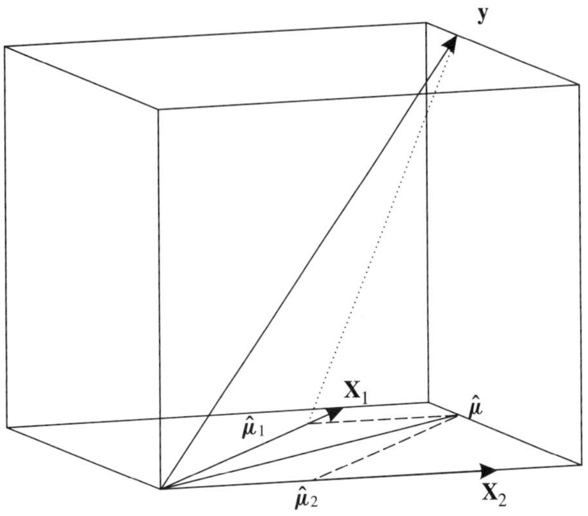

Figure 3.14 Projection by P_{12}.

EXAMPLE 3.3 **(Multiple Intercepts)**

We also comment on another feature of the introductory example that is related to Proposition 2: the fact that the fitted values of the first-step calculations are monthly averages. We saw this phenomenon previously in Chapter 1 in a similar situation. In the present case, the OLS fit to the 12 monthly indicator variables decomposes into 12 separate OLS problems, each with its own intercept parameter:

$$\min_{\beta} \sum_{t=1}^{T} \left(y_t - \sum_{k=1}^{12} x_{tk}\hat{\beta}_k \right)^2 = \sum_{k=1}^{12} \min_{\beta_k} \sum_{\{t|x_{tk}=1\}} (y_t - \beta_k)^2$$

where we have an OLS fit equal to the average for the data of each month. The x_{tk} variables are defined in (3.1).

Note that the monthly indicator variables are all mutually orthogonal: whenever one of these variables is one, all others are zero so that

$$\sum_{t=1}^{T} x_{tk}x_{tm} = 0 \quad \text{if } k \neq m$$

We can use this orthogonality to explain the decomposition above geometrically and to illustrate a special case of partitioned regression.

In general, if $\mathbf{X}_1'\mathbf{X}_2 = 0$ so that $\text{Col}(\mathbf{X}_1) \perp \text{Col}(\mathbf{X}_2)$, then $\mathbf{X}_{1\perp 2} = \left(\mathbf{I} - \mathbf{P}_{\mathbf{X}_2}\right)\mathbf{X}_1 = \mathbf{X}_1$ and $\hat{\boldsymbol{\beta}}_1 = \left(\mathbf{X}_1'\mathbf{X}_1\right)^{-1}\mathbf{X}_1'\mathbf{y}$. In words, the OLS fitted coefficients for the RHS $\mathbf{X}_1$ are the same for the LHS variable $\mathbf{y}$, whether $\mathbf{X}_2$ is on the RHS or not. In terms of projection, orthogonal projection onto $\text{Col}(\mathbf{X}_1)$ is along $\text{Col}(\mathbf{X}_2)$ by virtue of the orthogonality of these subspaces.

Therefore, we can view any one of the indicator variables as $\mathbf{X}_1$ and the rest as $\mathbf{X}_2$. The OLS fit of the unemployment rate to any one of the monthly indicator variables is the average for that month and so the OLS fit of the unemployment rate to all of the monthly indicators simultaneously is a sequence of monthly averages.

EXAMPLE 3.4 (Panel Data)

Suppose you are given data on the earnings of ten thousand individuals observed through time at five annual intervals. Such data are often called *panel data*, because the data can be arrayed in a panel, or rectangular table. For individual n in time period t, you choose the RHS to be

$$\mathbf{x}'_{nt}\boldsymbol{\beta} = \sum_{k=1}^{K_1} x_{ntk}\beta_{1k} + \sum_{k=1}^{10{,}000} d_{ntk}\beta_{2k}$$

where

$$d_{ntk} = \begin{cases} 0 & \text{if } n \neq k \\ 1 & \text{if } n = k \end{cases}$$

is the kth dummy (indicator) variable. The kth dummy variable equals one for the kth individual (in every time period) and zero otherwise. As a result, the coefficient β_{2k} appears only in the RHS function for the kth individual, and every individual's RHS has a unique intercept. Such a specification can reflect individual specific characteristics that the x_{ntk} do not measure.

Using partitioned regression, the OLS fitted coefficients can be computed for the regression of the natural logarithm of earnings on K_1 RHS variables such as schooling, experience, IQ, and *ten thousand* dummy variables, one for each individual, without actually creating over ten thousand columns in $\mathbf{X}$. Imagine the output from regression software, after requesting an OLS fit to so many RHS variables!

We first partition the regression function so that the coefficients for the ten thousand intercepts are separated from the other RHS variables. In the first step, one places the dummy variables in $\mathbf{X}_2 = [d_{ntk}]$ where k indexes the columns and both n and t index the rows. As in the case of monthly dummy variables, the OLS fitted values for $\mathbf{X}_1$ fitted to $\mathbf{X}_2$ are averages. In this case, each average applies to a single individual over time because each indicator variable groups the observations this way. Thus, each element of the matrix of OLS fitted *residuals* $\mathbf{X}_{1\perp 2}$ is a difference of the form $x_{ntk} - \bar{x}_{nk}$, where

$$\bar{x}_{nk} \equiv \frac{1}{5}\sum_{t=1}^{5} x_{ntk}$$

is the average over the 5 years of the kth RHS variable for the nth individual. Similarly, $\mathbf{y}_{\perp 2} = [y_{nt} - \bar{y}_n]'$ where $\bar{y}_n = \sum_t y_{nt}/5$ is the average over the 5 years of y_{nt} for the nth individual. Although it may take a while, the computer memory requirements for these calculations are quite modest.

In the second step, one computes the OLS fitted coefficients for the K_1 RHS variables in $\mathbf{X}_1$ using $\hat{\boldsymbol{\beta}}_1 = \left(\mathbf{X}'_{1\perp 2}\mathbf{X}_{1\perp 2}\right)^{-1}\mathbf{X}'_{1\perp 2}\mathbf{y}_{\perp 2}$. This calculation is no more onerous than an OLS fit without all ten thousand intercepts. If desired, one can also compute $\hat{\beta}_{2n} = \bar{y}_n - \sum_{k=1}^{K_1} \bar{x}_{nk}\hat{\beta}_{1k}$ $(n = 1, \ldots, 10{,}000)$. This follows from Exercise 3.4.

3.4 PROJECTORS

In this section, we tie up a few loose ends about projectors. Several properties of orthogonal projectors hold for projectors generally. We have already noted that projectors are unique in

Lemma 3.1. We have also repeatedly used the fact that orthogonal projectors are idempotent. See (3.13) and (3.15).

LEMMA 3.3 *Projectors are idempotent.*

The proof of this lemma is identical to the proof of this property for orthogonal projectors. See the proof of Lemma 2.7 (p. 38).

The geometric essence of a projector $\mathbf{P}$ onto a subspace $\mathbb{S}$ is that after projection, a second transformation by a projector onto $\mathbb{S}$ has no effect. Thus, because $\mathbf{Pz} \in \mathbb{S}$ for all $\mathbf{z}$ then $\mathbf{P}(\mathbf{Pz}) = \mathbf{Pz}$. Indeed, every idempotent matrix is a projector (Exercise 3.9).

As we have expressed projectors in (3.17), $\mathbf{X}(\mathbf{Z}'\mathbf{X})^{-1}\mathbf{Z}'$ is a projector onto $\text{Col}(\mathbf{X})$ along $\text{Col}^{\perp}(\mathbf{Z})$. Definition 8 requires, however, that $\mathbb{R}^N = \text{Col}(\mathbf{X}) \oplus \text{Col}^{\perp}(\mathbf{Z})$. This condition and the condition that $\mathbf{X}$ and $\mathbf{Z}$ be full-column rank are necessary and sufficient conditions for the matrix $\mathbf{Z}'\mathbf{X}$ to be nonsingular.

LEMMA 3.4 *Let $\mathbf{X}$ and $\mathbf{Z}$ be two $N \times K$ matrices. The matrix $\mathbf{Z}'\mathbf{X}$ is nonsingular if and only if* $\text{rank}(\mathbf{X}) = \text{rank}(\mathbf{Z}) = K$ *and* $\mathbb{R}^N = \text{Col}(\mathbf{X}) \oplus \text{Col}^{\perp}(\mathbf{Z})$.

Proof. **Sufficiency:** If $\mathbb{R}^N = \text{Col}(\mathbf{X}) \oplus \text{Col}^{\perp}(\mathbf{Z})$, then by Definition 7 $\text{Col}(\mathbf{X}) \cap \text{Col}^{\perp}(\mathbf{Z}) = \{\mathbf{0}\}$. That is, $\mathbf{Z}'\mathbf{Xa} = \mathbf{0}$ if and only if $\mathbf{Xa} = \mathbf{0}$. Because $\mathbf{X}$ is full-column rank, $\mathbf{Xa} = \mathbf{0}$ if and only if $\mathbf{a} = \mathbf{0}$. In other words, $\mathbf{Z}'\mathbf{X}$ is full-column rank. Because it is square, $\mathbf{Z}'\mathbf{X}$ is nonsingular.[9] **Necessity:** If $\mathbf{Z}'\mathbf{X}$ is nonsingular, then for every $\mathbf{w} \in \mathbb{R}^N$

$$\mathbf{w} = \mathbf{X}(\mathbf{Z}'\mathbf{X})^{-1}\mathbf{Z}'\mathbf{w} + \left(\mathbf{I} - \mathbf{X}(\mathbf{Z}'\mathbf{X})^{-1}\mathbf{Z}'\right)\mathbf{w} \tag{3.21}$$

where $\mathbf{X}(\mathbf{Z}'\mathbf{X})^{-1}\mathbf{Z}'\mathbf{w} \in \text{Col}(\mathbf{X})$ and $\left(\mathbf{I} - \mathbf{X}(\mathbf{Z}'\mathbf{X})^{-1}\mathbf{Z}'\right)\mathbf{w} \in \text{Col}^{\perp}(\mathbf{Z})$. Now we show that this decomposition is unique. For any other $\mathbf{w}_1 \in \text{Col}(\mathbf{X})$ and $\mathbf{w}_2 \in \text{Col}^{\perp}(\mathbf{Z})$ such that $\mathbf{w} = \mathbf{w}_1 + \mathbf{w}_2$, it follows that $\mathbf{w}_1 = \mathbf{X}\boldsymbol{\alpha}$ for some $\boldsymbol{\alpha}$ and $\mathbf{Z}'\mathbf{w}_2 = \mathbf{0}$ so that

$$\begin{aligned}
\mathbf{X}(\mathbf{Z}'\mathbf{X})^{-1}\mathbf{Z}'\mathbf{w} &= \mathbf{X}(\mathbf{Z}'\mathbf{X})^{-1}\mathbf{Z}'(\mathbf{w}_1 + \mathbf{w}_2) \\
&= \mathbf{X}(\mathbf{Z}'\mathbf{X})^{-1}\mathbf{Z}'\mathbf{X}\boldsymbol{\alpha} \\
&= \mathbf{w}_1
\end{aligned}$$

returning the original decomposition. Therefore, (3.21) is a unique decomposition so that $\mathbb{R}^N$ is the direct sum of $\text{Col}(\mathbf{X})$ and $\text{Col}^{\perp}(\mathbf{Z})$. Also, if $\mathbf{Z}'\mathbf{X}$ is nonsingular then $\mathbf{Z}'\mathbf{Xa} = \mathbf{0}$ if and only if $\mathbf{a} = \mathbf{0}$. As reasoned above, because $\mathbb{R}^N = \text{Col}(\mathbf{X}) \oplus \text{Col}^{\perp}(\mathbf{Z})$, it follows that $\mathbf{Z}'\mathbf{Xa} = \mathbf{0}$ if and only if $\mathbf{Xa} = \mathbf{0}$. Therefore, $\mathbf{X}$ is full-column rank. Finally, because

[9] See Definition C.15 and Theorem C.12 for a summary of nonsingularity and rank.

$$\begin{aligned} N = \dim \mathbb{R}^N &= \dim \operatorname{Col}(\mathbf{X}) + \dim \operatorname{Col}^{\perp}(\mathbf{Z}) \\ &= \operatorname{rank}(\mathbf{X}) + N - \operatorname{rank}(\mathbf{Z}) \\ &= K + N - \operatorname{rank}(\mathbf{Z}) \quad \Leftrightarrow \quad \operatorname{rank}(\mathbf{Z}) = K \end{aligned}$$

Z is full-column rank. □

This lemma establishes our expression for a general projector.

LEMMA 3.5 *Let* $\mathbf{X}$ *and* $\mathbf{Z}$ *be two* $N \times K$ *real matrices, where* $K \leq N$. *If* $\mathbf{Z}'\mathbf{X}$ *is nonsingular so that* $\mathbf{X}\left(\mathbf{Z}'\mathbf{X}\right)^{-1}\mathbf{Z}'$ *is well defined. Then* $\mathbf{X}\left(\mathbf{Z}'\mathbf{X}\right)^{-1}\mathbf{Z}' = \mathbf{P}_{\mathbf{X}\perp\mathbf{Z}}$ *is the projector onto* $\operatorname{Col}(\mathbf{X})$ *along* $\operatorname{Col}^{\perp}(\mathbf{Z})$.

Proof. Equations (3.18) and (3.19) demonstrate that $\mathbf{X}\left(\mathbf{Z}'\mathbf{X}\right)^{-1}\mathbf{Z}'$ preserves $\operatorname{Col}(\mathbf{X})$ and annihilates $\operatorname{Col}^{\perp}(\mathbf{Z})$. In addition, because $\mathbf{Z}'\mathbf{X}$ is nonsingular, Lemma 3.4 states that $\mathbb{R}^N = \operatorname{Col}(\mathbf{X}) \oplus \operatorname{Col}^{\perp}(\mathbf{Z})$. Therefore, by Definition 8, $\mathbf{X}\left(\mathbf{Z}'\mathbf{X}\right)^{-1}\mathbf{Z}'$ is the projector onto $\operatorname{Col}(\mathbf{X})$ along $\operatorname{Col}^{\perp}(\mathbf{Z})$, denoted $\mathbf{P}_{\mathbf{X}\perp\mathbf{Z}}$. □

3.5 OVERVIEW

1. The decomposition of $\mathbf{X}\boldsymbol{\beta}$ into $\mathbf{X}_1\boldsymbol{\beta}_1 + \mathbf{X}_2\boldsymbol{\beta}_2$ corresponds to a conformable partition of

$$\mathbf{X} = [\mathbf{X}_1 \quad \mathbf{X}_2] \qquad \text{and} \qquad \boldsymbol{\beta} = \begin{bmatrix} \boldsymbol{\beta}_1 \\ \boldsymbol{\beta}_2 \end{bmatrix}$$

2. Projection in $\mathbb{R}^N$ is generally defined as a movement along one subspace onto another, where the direct sum of the two subspaces is the entire vector space. Thus, given that $\operatorname{Col}(\mathbf{X}) \oplus \operatorname{Col}^{\perp}(\mathbf{Z}) = \mathbb{R}^N$ the projector in $\mathbb{R}^N$ along $\operatorname{Col}(\mathbf{Z})$ onto $\operatorname{Col}(\mathbf{X})$ is $\mathbf{P}_{\mathbf{X}\perp\mathbf{Z}} = \mathbf{X}(\mathbf{Z}'\mathbf{X})^{-1}\mathbf{Z}'$. This projector is unique.

3. The component $\hat{\boldsymbol{\mu}}_1 = \mathbf{X}_1\hat{\boldsymbol{\beta}}_1$ of the OLS fitted vector $\hat{\boldsymbol{\mu}} = \mathbf{X}_1\hat{\boldsymbol{\beta}}_1 + \mathbf{X}_2\hat{\boldsymbol{\beta}}_2$ is a projection of $\mathbf{y}$ onto $\operatorname{Col}(\mathbf{X}_1)$, but not an orthogonal one; $\hat{\boldsymbol{\mu}}_1$ is also the projection of $\hat{\boldsymbol{\mu}}$ onto $\operatorname{Col}(\mathbf{X}_1)$ along $\operatorname{Col}(\mathbf{X}_2)$. If $\mathbf{X}$ is full-column rank, then the projector for $\hat{\boldsymbol{\mu}}_1 = \mathbf{P}_{12}\mathbf{y}$ is

$$\begin{aligned} \mathbf{P}_{12} &\equiv \mathbf{X}_1\left[\mathbf{X}_1'(\mathbf{I} - \mathbf{P}_{\mathbf{X}_2})\mathbf{X}_1\right]^{-1}\mathbf{X}_1'(\mathbf{I} - \mathbf{P}_{\mathbf{X}_2}) \\ &= \mathbf{X}_1(\mathbf{X}_{1\perp 2}'\mathbf{X}_1)^{-1}\mathbf{X}_{1\perp 2}' \end{aligned}$$

where $\mathbf{P}_{\mathbf{X}_2} \equiv \mathbf{X}_2(\mathbf{X}_2'\mathbf{X}_2)^{-1}\mathbf{X}_2'$ is the orthogonal projector onto $\operatorname{Col}(\mathbf{X}_2)$ and $\mathbf{X}_{1\perp 2} \equiv \left(\mathbf{I} - \mathbf{P}_{\mathbf{X}_2}\right)\mathbf{X}_1$ is the matrix of OLS fitted residuals from regressions of the column vectors of $\mathbf{X}_1$ onto $\operatorname{Col}(\mathbf{X}_2)$. This projection is along $\operatorname{Col}(\mathbf{X}_2) \oplus \operatorname{Col}^{\perp}(\mathbf{X})$ onto $\operatorname{Col}(\mathbf{X}_1)$. The projector $\mathbf{P}_{12}$ also applies to $\hat{\boldsymbol{\mu}}$: $\hat{\boldsymbol{\mu}}_1 = \mathbf{P}_{12}\hat{\boldsymbol{\mu}}$.

4. Also, a subvector of the OLS coefficient vector can be written explicitly as

$$\begin{aligned} \hat{\boldsymbol{\beta}}_1 &= \left[\mathbf{X}_1'(\mathbf{I} - \mathbf{P}_{\mathbf{X}_2})\mathbf{X}_1\right]^{-1}\mathbf{X}_1'(\mathbf{I} - \mathbf{P}_{\mathbf{X}_2})\mathbf{y} \\ &= \left(\mathbf{X}_{1\perp 2}'\mathbf{X}_1\right)^{-1}\mathbf{X}_{1\perp 2}'\mathbf{y} \end{aligned}$$

or

$$\hat{\beta}_1 = \left(\mathbf{X}'_{1\perp 2}\mathbf{X}_{1\perp 2}\right)^{-1}\mathbf{X}'_{1\perp 2}\mathbf{y}_{\perp 2}$$

where $\mathbf{y}_{\perp 2} \equiv (\mathbf{I} - \mathbf{P}_{\mathbf{X}_2})\mathbf{y}$. This can be interpreted as a two-step fit: first, obtain the fitted residuals $\mathbf{X}_{1\perp 2} \equiv (\mathbf{I} - \mathbf{P}_{\mathbf{X}_2})\mathbf{X}_1$ and $\mathbf{y}_{\perp 2} \equiv \left(\mathbf{I} - \mathbf{P}_{\mathbf{X}_2}\right)\mathbf{y}$ from the OLS fit of each column vector in $\mathbf{X}_1$ and $\mathbf{y}$ on the matrix $\mathbf{X}_2$; and second, regress $\left(\mathbf{I} - \mathbf{P}_{\mathbf{X}_2}\right)\mathbf{y}$ on $(\mathbf{I} - \mathbf{P}_{\mathbf{X}_2})\mathbf{X}_1$.

3.6 EXERCISES

3.6.1 Review

3.1 **(Projectors)** Show that $\mathbf{P}_{12}$ in (3.5) is an idempotent matrix. Compare $\mathbf{P}_{12}$ with $(\mathbf{I} - \mathbf{P}_{\mathbf{X}_2})\mathbf{P}_{12}$ as projectors.

3.2 Consider a partitioned regression function $\mathbf{X}\boldsymbol{\beta} = \mathbf{X}_1\boldsymbol{\beta}_1 + \mathbf{X}_2\boldsymbol{\beta}_2$ where $\mathbf{X}_2$ contains one RHS variable, an indicator (dummy) variable that equals one for a particular observation and zero for all other observations. What special properties does the OLS fit possess?

3.3 **(Average Analogy)** Find the OLS fit for each of the following dummy variable specifications. Let $N = 100$.

(a) $x_{n1} = \mathbf{1}\{n \leq 50\}, x_{n2} = \mathbf{1}\{n > 50\}$;
(b) $x_{n1} = 1, x_{n2} = \mathbf{1}\{n > 50\}$;
(c) $x_{n1} = \mathbf{1}\{n \leq 33\}, x_{n2} = \mathbf{1}\{n \leq 66\} - \mathbf{1}\{n \leq 33\}, x_{n3} = \mathbf{1}\{n > 66\}$;
(d) $x_{n1} = 1, x_{n2} = \mathbf{1}\{n \leq 33\}, x_{n3} = \mathbf{1}\{n \leq 66\}$;
(e) $x_{n1} = 1, x_{n2} = \mathbf{1}\{n \leq 50\}, x_{n3} = \mathbf{1}\{n > 33\}$.

***3.4** **(Deviations from Averages)** Let $\mathbf{X}$ be full-column rank and $x_{nK} = 1$ for all n.

(a) Show that the OLS fit of $y_n - \bar{y}$ on $x_{nk} - \bar{x}_k$ $(k = 1, \ldots, K-1)$ gives the same fitted coefficients for these explanatory variables as the OLS fit of y_n on x_{nk} $(k = 1, \ldots, K)$ gives for coefficients β_k $(k = 1, \ldots, K-1)$.
(b) Given the $\hat{\beta}_k$ $(k < K)$, show that

$$\hat{\beta}_K = \bar{y} - \sum_{k=1}^{K-1} \bar{x}_k \hat{\beta}_k$$

***3.5** **(Projector Properties)** Prove that all projectors $\mathbf{P}$, not just orthogonal ones, are

(a) unique and
(b) idempotent ($\mathbf{PP} = \mathbf{P}$).

3.6 Explain the consequences for $\mathbf{P}_{12}$ if $\mathbf{X}$ is not full-column rank. Interpret this situation.

3.7 Answer Exercise 2.16 using the partitioned fit formula. Note that $\mathbf{X}_1$ and $\mathbf{X}_2$ may *not* be a partition of $\mathbf{X}$ in this case. (HINT: Consider $\mathbf{X}_1$ and $\mathbf{X}_2$ when both have the kth column of $\mathbf{X}$ in the first column.)

3.8 Review the proof of Proposition 2.

(a) Show that

$$\hat{\beta}_2 = (\mathbf{X}_2'\mathbf{X}_2)^{-1}\mathbf{X}_2'\left(\mathbf{y} - \mathbf{X}_1\hat{\beta}_1\right) \tag{3.22}$$
$$= (\mathbf{X}_2'\mathbf{X}_2)^{-1}\mathbf{X}_2'\mathbf{y} - (\mathbf{X}_2'\mathbf{X}_2)^{-1}\mathbf{X}_2'\mathbf{X}_1\hat{\beta}_1$$

in the partitioned OLS fit.

(b) The total derivative of differentiable function, $f(x_1, x_2)$, with respect to one of its arguments, x_2, is

$$\frac{df(x_1,x_2)}{dx_2} = \frac{\partial f(x_1,x_2)}{\partial x_2} + \frac{dx_1}{dx_2}\cdot\frac{\partial f(x_1,x_2)}{\partial x_1}$$

Draw an analogy between this formula and (3.22). [HINT: Think of $(\mathbf{X}'\mathbf{X})^{-1}\mathbf{X}'\mathbf{y}$ as analogous to df/dx, the total change in f associated with a change in x.]

***3.9 (Projectors/Orthogonal Projectors)** Let $\mathbf{A}$ be an idempotent matrix so that $\mathbf{A}^2 = \mathbf{A}$.

(a) Show that $\mathbf{A}$ is a projector.[10]

(b) Show that if $\mathbf{A}$ is symmetric then $\mathbf{A}$ is an orthogonal projector.

***3.10 (Partitioned Inverse)** Let $\mathbf{A}$ be a nonsingular matrix. Derive the partitioned inverse formula

$$\begin{bmatrix} \mathbf{A}_{11} & \mathbf{A}_{12} \\ \mathbf{A}_{21} & \mathbf{A}_{22} \end{bmatrix}^{-1} = \begin{bmatrix} \mathbf{W}^{-1} & -\mathbf{W}_{12}^{-1}\mathbf{A}_{12}\mathbf{A}_{22}^{-1} \\ -\mathbf{A}_{22}^{-1}\mathbf{A}_{21}\mathbf{W}^{-1} & \mathbf{A}_{22}^{-1} + \mathbf{A}_{22}^{-1}\mathbf{A}_{21}\mathbf{W}^{-1}\mathbf{A}_{12}\mathbf{A}_{22}^{-1} \end{bmatrix} \tag{3.23}$$

where

$$\mathbf{W} = \mathbf{A}_{11} - \mathbf{A}_{12}\mathbf{A}_{22}^{-1}\mathbf{A}_{21}$$

(HINT: Solve for the partitioned elements of $\mathbf{B}$ from the formula $\mathbf{AB} = \mathbf{I}$.)

***3.11 (Partitioned Fit)** Use (3.23) to derive (3.6) constructively from the fitting formula

$$\hat{\beta} = (\mathbf{X}'\mathbf{X})^{-1}\mathbf{X}'\mathbf{y} \tag{3.24}$$
$$= \begin{bmatrix} \mathbf{X}_1'\mathbf{X}_1 & \mathbf{X}_1'\mathbf{X}_2 \\ \mathbf{X}_2'\mathbf{X}_1 & \mathbf{X}_2'\mathbf{X}_2 \end{bmatrix}^{-1} \begin{bmatrix} \mathbf{X}_1'\mathbf{y} \\ \mathbf{X}_2'\mathbf{y} \end{bmatrix}$$

3.12 Show that $\mathbf{y}_{\perp 2}$ can be replaced by $\mathbf{y}$ in (3.6) so that

$$\hat{\beta}_1 = (\mathbf{X}_{1\perp 2}'\mathbf{X}_{1\perp 2})^{-1}\mathbf{X}_{1\perp 2}'\mathbf{y}$$

3.13 (Orthogonal RHS Variables) If the RHS variables in $\mathbf{X}_1$ are orthogonal to the RHS variables in $\mathbf{X}_2$, then $\mathbf{X}_1'\mathbf{X}_2 = \mathbf{0}$. Show that the OLS coefficients from a fit of $\mathbf{y}$ on $\mathbf{X}_1$ and $\mathbf{X}_2$ are the same as the OLS coefficients from separate fits of $\mathbf{y}$ on $\mathbf{X}_1$ alone and $\mathbf{y}$ on $\mathbf{X}_2$ alone. Explain this result in three dimensions with the rectangle in Figure 3.15.

3.14 Suppose that the RHS variables in $\mathbf{X}_1$ are orthogonal to the LHS variable $\mathbf{y}$ so that $\mathbf{X}_1'\mathbf{y} = \mathbf{0}$. Does this mean that $\hat{\beta}_1 = \mathbf{0}$ in the partitioned OLS fit $\mathbf{X}_1\hat{\beta}_1 + \mathbf{X}_2\hat{\beta}_2$? Explain.

3.15 Consider a *panel* data set with N individuals observed in each of T time periods. Define N dummy variables associated with each of the individuals:

[10] In some algebra texts, projections are *defined* as those linear transformations represented by idempotent matrices.

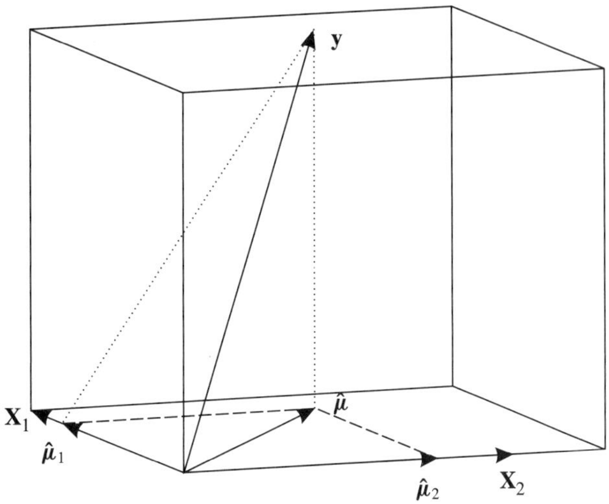

Figure 3.15 Orthogonal RHS variables.

$$d_{ntk} = \begin{cases} 0 & \text{if } n \neq k \\ 1 & \text{if } n = k \end{cases}$$

and let $\mathbf{D}_k$ be the column vector $[d_{ntk};\ n = 1, \ldots, N,\ t = 1, \ldots, T]'$.

(a) Show that the dummy variables for individuals in a panel data set are mutually orthogonal; that is, $\mathbf{D}_k'\mathbf{D}_j = 0\ (k, j = 1, \ldots, N,\ k \neq j)$.

(b) Show that $\mathbf{D}_k'\mathbf{D}_k = T\ (k = 1, \ldots, N)$.

(c) Show that fitting a vector $\mathbf{z} = [z_{nt};\ n = 1, \ldots, N,\ t = 1, \ldots, T]'$ to all the dummy variables by OLS gives N coefficients that are the sample averages

$$\bar{z}_n \equiv \frac{1}{T}\sum_{t=1}^{T} z_{nt}, \qquad n = 1, \ldots, N$$

(HINT: Use Exercise 3.13.)

(d) Show that the OLS fitted residuals are the differences $z_{nt} - \bar{z}_n\ (n = 1, \ldots, N,\ t = 1, \ldots, T)$.

3.16 (Partitioned Projection) Suppose that $\mathbf{X} = [\mathbf{X}_1, \mathbf{X}_2]$ is full-column rank. Show

$$\mathbf{P}_{\mathbf{X}} \equiv \mathbf{X}(\mathbf{X}'\mathbf{X})^{-1}\mathbf{X}' = \mathbf{P}_{\mathbf{X}_2} + (\mathbf{I} - \mathbf{P}_{\mathbf{X}_2})\mathbf{P}_{12} \tag{3.25}$$

by showing that

$$\left[\mathbf{P}_{\mathbf{X}_2} + (\mathbf{I} - \mathbf{P}_{\mathbf{X}_2})\mathbf{P}_{12}\right]\mathbf{X}_1 = \mathbf{X}_1$$
$$\left[\mathbf{P}_{\mathbf{X}_2} + (\mathbf{I} - \mathbf{P}_{\mathbf{X}_2})\mathbf{P}_{12}\right]\mathbf{X}_2 = \mathbf{X}_2$$

$$\mathbf{z}'\mathbf{x} = 0\ \forall \mathbf{x} \in \text{Col}(\mathbf{X}) \quad \Rightarrow \quad \left[\mathbf{P}_{\mathbf{X}_2} + (\mathbf{I} - \mathbf{P}_{\mathbf{X}_2})\mathbf{P}_{12}\right]\mathbf{z} = \mathbf{0}$$

where $\mathbf{X} = [\mathbf{X}_1, \mathbf{X}_2]$, $\mathbf{P}_{\mathbf{X}_2} = \mathbf{X}_2\left(\mathbf{X}_2'\mathbf{X}_2\right)^{-1}\mathbf{X}_2'$, and $\mathbf{P}_{12}$ is given in (3.13). Draw $\mathbf{P}_{\mathbf{X}}\mathbf{y}$, $\mathbf{P}_{\mathbf{X}_2}\mathbf{y}$, and $(\mathbf{I} - \mathbf{P}_{\mathbf{X}_2})\mathbf{P}_{12}\mathbf{y}$ in a figure like Figure 3.13.

3.17 (Partitioned Projection) Here is an alternative approach to the preceding exercise. Again, suppose that $\mathbf{X}$ is full-column rank.

(a) Show that

$$\mathbf{P_X} = \mathbf{P_{X_1}} + \mathbf{P_{X_2}}$$

if $\mathbf{X}_1 \perp \mathbf{X}_2$.

(b) Use the facts that $(\mathbf{I} - \mathbf{P_{X_2}})\mathbf{X}_1 \equiv \mathbf{X}_{1\perp 2}$ and $\mathbf{X}_{1\perp 2} \perp \mathbf{X}_2$ to show (3.25).

(c) Show that the OLS fitted residuals from fitting $\mathbf{y}$ to $\mathbf{X}$ are equal to the OLS fitted residuals from fitting $\left(\mathbf{I} - \mathbf{P_{X_2}}\right)\mathbf{y}$ to $\left(\mathbf{I} - \mathbf{P_{X_2}}\right)\mathbf{X}_1$.

3.18 **(Law of Iterated Projections)** Let $\mathbf{X} = [\mathbf{X}_1, \mathbf{X}_2]$ consist of two submatrices $\mathbf{X}_1$ and $\mathbf{X}_2$. Prove the *law of iterated projections* that

$$\mathbf{P_{X_1}y} = \mathbf{P_{X_1}P_Xy}$$

(HINT: Use Exercise 3.16.)

3.19 **(Goodness of Fit)** If $\iota \in \mathrm{Col}(\mathbf{X})$, show that

$$\|\mathbf{y} - \iota\bar{y}\|^2 = \left\|\hat{\boldsymbol{\mu}} - \iota\bar{y}\right\|^2 + \left\|\mathbf{y} - \hat{\boldsymbol{\mu}}\right\|^2$$

where $\bar{y}$ is the sample average of the y_n. The R^2 measure of fit that most computer programs print is a slight modification of r^2 in Exercise (2.25):[11]

$$R^2 = \frac{\left\|\hat{\boldsymbol{\mu}} - \iota\bar{y}\right\|^2}{\|\mathbf{y} - \iota\bar{y}\|^2}$$

Show that this measure of goodness of fit has the same properties as r^2, if the constant one is an RHS variable. Explain why R^2 measures the improvement in fit of the multivariate model over the simple location model. State a more general condition than including a constant on the RHS that yields these same properties for R^2.

NOTE: The expression in the numerator of R^2 is usually called the *explained (or regression) sum of squares*.

3.20 Exercise 3.16 implies that

$$\mathbf{y'P_Xy} = \mathbf{y'P_{X_2}y} + \mathbf{y'(I - P_{X_2})P_{12}y}$$

(a) Show that $\mathbf{y'(I - P_{X_2})P_{12}y} = \mathbf{y'P_{X_{1\perp 2}}y}$.

(b) How could you interpret the terms in this decomposition in terms of $\hat{\boldsymbol{\mu}} = \mathbf{P_Xy}$, $\mathbf{P_{X_2}y}$, and $\mathbf{P_{X_{1\perp 2}}y}$?

(c) Interpret the goodness-of-fit measure

$$\frac{\mathbf{y'P_{X_{1\perp 2}}y}}{\mathbf{y'P_Xy}}$$

3.6.2 Extensions

3.21 Let $\mathbf{A}^-$ be the generalized inverse of $\mathbf{A}$ so that $\mathbf{AA^-A} = \mathbf{A}$. Show that $\mathbf{AA}^-$ is a projector onto $\mathrm{Col}(\mathbf{A})$.[12]

***3.22** Show that

---

[11] The R^2 is also called the *coefficient of determination.*

[12] For the introduction to generalized inverses, see Exercise 2.24.

$$(\mathbf{A}_{11} - \mathbf{A}_{12}\mathbf{A}_{22}^{-1}\mathbf{A}_{21})^{-1} = \mathbf{A}_{11}^{-1} + \mathbf{A}_{11}^{-1}\mathbf{A}_{12}\mathbf{W}^{-1}\mathbf{A}_{21}\mathbf{A}_{11}^{-1}$$

where

$$\mathbf{W} = \mathbf{A}_{22} - \mathbf{A}_{21}\mathbf{A}_{11}^{-1}\mathbf{A}_{12}$$

provided that $\mathbf{A}_{11}$, $\mathbf{A}_{22}$, and $\mathbf{W}$ are nonsingular. (HINT: Use the result of Exercise 3.10.)

3.23 Let $\mathbf{X}$ and $\mathbf{Z}$ be two $N \times K$ real matrices, $K \leq N$. Show that if $\mathbf{Z}'\mathbf{X}$ is nonsingular then we can always find a matrix $\mathbf{A}$ so that

$$\mathbf{X}\left(\mathbf{Z}'\mathbf{X}\right)^{-1}\mathbf{Z}' = \mathbf{X}\left(\mathbf{X}'\mathbf{A}\mathbf{X}\right)^{-1}\mathbf{X}'\mathbf{A}$$

Hence, these two forms of a projector are always formally equivalent.

CHAPTER 4

RESTRICTED LEAST SQUARES

4.1 INTRODUCTION

Once one begins to analyze a data set, questions often suggest new specifications for the RHS. For example, in the study of earnings data one immediately encounters two kinds of earnings, hourly and salaried. Although the first OLS fit pools these observations together without discrimination, one wonders whether the effective hourly earnings of salaried employees have quite different coefficients in an OLS fit for those observations alone.

Separate OLS fits for hourly and salaried employees appear in Table 4.1 and there are some interesting differences in the coefficients. It appears that the overall wage level of salaried employees is 10% lower than hourly employees, as seen in the difference in intercept coefficients. On the other hand, salaried employees receive a higher rate of return to education. Nonwhites appear to earn proportionately less in salaried jobs. The most striking difference appears in the coefficients for union membership; union membership is associated with a much higher wage for hourly employees (28.4% higher) than for salaried employees (4.5% higher). The coefficients for the female indicator variable and the experience variables are virtually identical.

Empirical research investigates such questions and observations more thoroughly. We use them to motivate our interest in a general OLS technique called *restricted least squares* (RLS). Note that the two OLS fits for hourly and salaried employees are more flexible fits over the entire sample than the single uniform OLS fit that we have used in previous chapters. The earlier OLS fit for log-wages is a restricted version of the OLS fit in Table 4.1 because the latter permits hourly and salaried earnings to have different fitted coefficients. We formalize this by writing the latter specification as the partitioned RHS

$$\mu_n = (1 - d_n) \cdot \mathbf{x}_n' \boldsymbol{\beta}_1 + d_n \cdot \mathbf{x}_n' \boldsymbol{\beta}_2$$

where d_n is an indicator variable for observations with salaried earnings,

$$d_n \equiv \begin{cases} 0 & \text{if individual } n \text{ earns hourly wages} \\ 1 & \text{if individual } n \text{ earns a salary} \end{cases}$$

Table 4.1
Wage Equations for Hourly and Salaried Employees

RHS	Hourly	Salaried	Difference
Constant (one)	1.057	0.964	0.093
Female	−0.213	−0.220	0.007
Nonwhite	−0.115	−0.141	0.026
Union member	0.284	0.045	0.239
Education	0.067	0.094	−0.027
Experience	0.0351	0.0356	−0.0005
(Experience)^2	−0.00057	−0.00059	0.00002
SSR	121.671	140.492	
R^2	0.327	0.299	
Observations	764	525	

In this way the coefficient vector is $\boldsymbol{\beta}_1$ for hourly employees and $\boldsymbol{\beta}_2$ for salaried employees. The restricted RHS constrains $\boldsymbol{\beta}_1 = \boldsymbol{\beta}_2$, so that the coefficient vectors are identical. This was our specification in earlier chapters.

We calculated the entries in Table 4.1 by fitting with OLS to separate subsamples. We can just as well create $\mathbf{X} = [(1 - d_n) \cdot \mathbf{x}_n', \ d_n \cdot \mathbf{x}_n'; n = 1, \ldots, N]$ and fit the unrestricted RHS to the *entire* sample. Then we obtain the fitted coefficients in the "Hourly" column of Table 4.1 for $\boldsymbol{\beta}_1$ and the fitted coefficients in the "Salaried" column for $\boldsymbol{\beta}_2$. The sum of squared residuals (SSR) for this combined OLS fit is 262.163, which is the sum of the two SSR entries in the table.[1] The R^2 of the unrestricted OLS fit is 0.408.

The differences between the two sets of fitted coefficients suggest several patterns. Most prominent is that the union membership appears to be associated with relatively high wages in hourly wages and not nearly so in other earnings. On the other hand, the higher schooling levels coincide with greater earnings more strongly in nonhourly wages. The fitted coefficients also suggest that wages of women and nonwhites are relatively lower in nonhourly wages. Despite these differences, the profile of earnings over experience levels appears to be similar in the two kinds of wages.[2]

We have already shown other examples of RLS fits in Chapter 1. In Table 1.8 (OLS Fits for Log-Wage, p. 12), the first four columns of coefficients are RLS fits relative to the last column. Some of the coefficients are constrained to be zero in each of these columns.

As a third example of RLS, we return to the dynamic model for the unemployment data. The part of the RHS that depends on lagged values of the LHS variable is often called a *distributed lag*. Many researchers feel that the pattern of the coefficients in a distributed lag should be smooth, arguing that the effects of a particular lag, say y_{t-k}, should not be dramatically different from the adjacent lags, y_{t-k-1} and y_{t-k+1}. Inspection of our previous fit of the

[1] A simpler example of fitting separate regressions for subsamples appears on page 75.

[2] It is natural to wonder whether the differences in fitted coefficients occur "by chance" in our sample or whether the differences reflect patterns that we could expect to see in additional data. The next part of this book develops the tools of statistical inference that researchers use to answer such questions. Exercise 11.1 (p. 227) addresses this particular question.

coefficients of the 12-month distributed lag in unemployment shows that this is roughly true: the first lag coefficient has the largest value and the remaining coefficients quickly diminish in moving down the entries in Table 3.1 (p. 50). The longer lags have coefficients that fluctuate nearer zero.

Researchers have occasionally imposed smoothness in distributed lag specifications by constraining the coefficients to follow a low-order polynomial pattern. This yields a rather interesting set of linear restrictions on the coefficients, which we will explain in the next section. When we compute the RLS fit for a quartic polynomial on the distributed lag in unemployment, we get the results pictured in Figure 4.1 and listed in Table 4.2. We also display the original OLS fitted coefficients.

The restrictions have substantially smoothed the pattern of the distributed lag. The coefficients of the first and second lags change substantially, with the fall in the first offset by an almost equivalent rise in the second. Many researchers would say that the RLS fit has oversmoothed the distributed lag. Note that the agreement at the thirteenth lag arises from the restrictions: both specifications maintain that the coefficient of y_{t-13} be zero. At this point, we have no formal basis for choosing between the two fits.

In this chapter, we describe RLS generally, as yet another application of projection. As in the previous chapter, the projection is not necessarily orthogonal. However, we will also draw a close connection between orthogonal projection as minimization of distance and general projection as minimization of generalized distance. The concepts introduced for OLS in Chapter 2 recur in RLS. As a result, we also show a direct relationship between the RLS fit and the OLS fit.

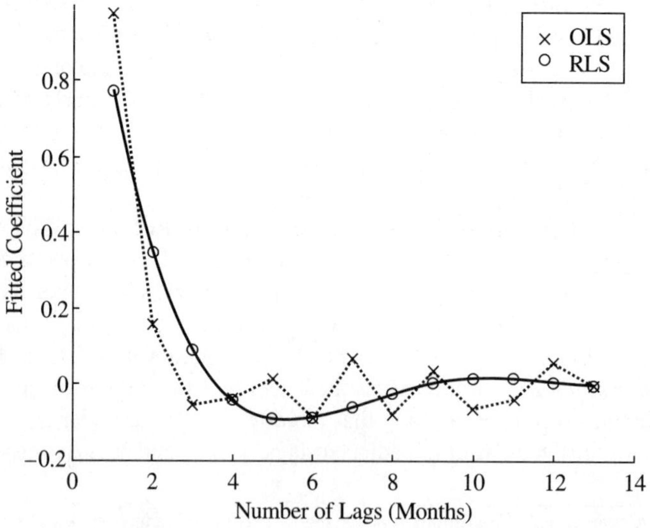

Figure 4.1 Unrestricted and restricted polynomial distributed lag coefficients.

Table 4.2
OLS Fitted and RLS Coefficients for Lagged Unemployment

RHS Variable	Model	
	OLS	RLS
y_{t-1}	0.9772	0.7741
y_{t-2}	0.1595	0.3494
y_{t-3}	−0.0524	0.0928
y_{t-4}	−0.0352	−0.0406
y_{t-5}	0.0161	−0.0897
y_{t-6}	−0.0869	−0.0868
y_{t-7}	0.0699	−0.0580
y_{t-8}	−0.0777	−0.0231
y_{t-9}	0.0378	0.0047
y_{t-10}	−0.0625	0.0184
y_{t-11}	−0.0386	0.0173
y_{t-12}	0.0599	0.0071

4.2 LINEAR RESTRICTIONS

Occasionally, we are interested in the values of the fitted coefficients when constraints are added to the permissible values of the slope coefficients. Sometimes these constraints are inequalities that sign several coefficients. Linear equalities are a simpler form of constraints. We may want to fit a model subject to equality among several coefficients, requiring that the fitted effects of several variables be the same value. Such restrictions can always be written in the form

$$\boldsymbol{\beta} = \mathbf{S}\boldsymbol{\gamma} + \mathbf{s} \tag{4.1}$$

where $\mathbf{S}$ is a $K \times M$ matrix of known constants, $\mathbf{s}$ is a $K \times 1$ vector of known constants, and $\boldsymbol{\gamma}$ is an $M \times 1$ vector of unknown parameters. There are fewer parameters in $\boldsymbol{\gamma}$ than in $\boldsymbol{\beta}$; $M < K$; $K - M$ restrictions constrain the original K coefficients to depend on M unconstrained parameters.

EXAMPLE 4.1 (Exclusion Restrictions)

The simplest linear restrictions are *exclusion*, or "zero," restrictions. In this case, $\mathbf{s} = \mathbf{0}$. If we restrict the coefficient of a RHS variable to be zero, then we are excluding it from the OLS fit. Suppose $K = 5$ and $\mathbf{X} = [\mathbf{X}_1, \ldots, \mathbf{X}_K]$ so that

$$\mathbf{X}\boldsymbol{\beta} \equiv \beta_1 + \mathbf{X}_2\beta_2 + \mathbf{X}_3\beta_3 + \mathbf{X}_4\beta_4 + \mathbf{X}_5\beta_5$$

the restrictions

$$\beta_2 = 0$$

$$\beta_4 = 0$$

simplify the RHS to

$$\begin{aligned}\mathbf{X}\boldsymbol{\beta} &= \beta_1 + 0 \cdot \mathbf{X}_2 + \mathbf{X}_3\beta_3 + 0 \cdot \mathbf{X}_4 + \mathbf{X}_5\beta_5 \\ &= \beta_1 + \mathbf{X}_3\beta_3 + \mathbf{X}_5\beta_5\end{aligned}$$

thereby excluding x_2 and x_4. We can write

$$\boldsymbol{\beta} = \begin{bmatrix}\beta_1 \\ 0 \\ \beta_3 \\ 0 \\ \beta_5\end{bmatrix} = \begin{bmatrix}1 & 0 & 0 \\ 0 & 0 & 0 \\ 0 & 1 & 0 \\ 0 & 0 & 0 \\ 0 & 0 & 1\end{bmatrix}\begin{bmatrix}\beta_1 \\ \beta_3 \\ \beta_5\end{bmatrix}$$

so that two restrictions make five parameters a linear function of only three. In our notation,

$$\boldsymbol{\gamma} \equiv \begin{bmatrix}\gamma_1 \\ \gamma_2 \\ \gamma_3\end{bmatrix} = \begin{bmatrix}\beta_1 \\ \beta_3 \\ \beta_5\end{bmatrix}$$

Exclusion restrictions appear in Table 1.8.

EXAMPLE 4.2 (Equality Restrictions)

Another common linear restriction requires some of the fitted coefficients to be equal. One might require several sources of income (labor, transfer, and rental) to have the same coefficients in an OLS fit with the LHS variable household consumption. Such equality constraints as these two

$$\begin{aligned}\beta_2 &= \beta_3 \\ \beta_3 &= \beta_4\end{aligned}$$

also reduce the five-parameter RHS

$$\begin{aligned}\mathbf{X}\boldsymbol{\beta} &= \beta_1 + \mathbf{X}_2\beta_2 + \mathbf{X}_3\beta_3 + \mathbf{X}_4\beta_4 + \mathbf{X}_5\beta_5 \\ &= \beta_1 + \mathbf{X}_2\beta_4 + \mathbf{X}_3\beta_4 + \mathbf{X}_4\beta_4 + \mathbf{X}_5\beta_5\end{aligned}$$

to a two-parameter RHS. Note that we do not include the redundant restriction $\beta_2 = \beta_4$ in our list of restrictions. In this case, we write (4.1) as

$$\boldsymbol{\beta} = \begin{bmatrix}\beta_1 \\ \beta_4 \\ \beta_4 \\ \beta_4 \\ \beta_5\end{bmatrix} = \begin{bmatrix}1 & 0 & 0 \\ 0 & 1 & 0 \\ 0 & 1 & 0 \\ 0 & 1 & 0 \\ 0 & 0 & 1\end{bmatrix}\begin{bmatrix}\beta_1 \\ \beta_4 \\ \beta_5\end{bmatrix}$$

so that

$$\boldsymbol{\gamma} \equiv \begin{bmatrix}\gamma_1 \\ \gamma_2 \\ \gamma_3\end{bmatrix} = \begin{bmatrix}\beta_1 \\ \beta_4 \\ \beta_5\end{bmatrix}$$

Our introductory example illustrated equality restrictions with two subsamples, hourly and salaried employees.

EXAMPLE 4.3 (Simple Linear Restriction)
As a final example, consider the single linear restriction

$$\beta_3 + \beta_4 + \beta_5 = 1$$

This restriction occurs in the Cobb–Douglas cost function

$$c = aq^{\beta_2} p_1^{\beta_3} p_2^{\beta_4} p_3^{\beta_5} \Leftrightarrow$$
$$\log c = \beta_1 + \beta_2 \log q + \beta_3 \log p_1 + \beta_4 \log p_2 + \beta_5 \log p_3$$

where c is total costs, q is output level, and p_1, p_2, and p_3 are the prices of the input factors. We can substitute this restriction into $\mathbf{X}\boldsymbol{\beta}$ to obtain

$$\begin{aligned} \mathbf{X}\boldsymbol{\beta} &= \beta_1 + \mathbf{X}_2\beta_2 + \mathbf{X}_3\beta_3 + \mathbf{X}_4\beta_4 + \mathbf{X}_5\beta_5 \\ &= \beta_1 + \mathbf{X}_2\beta_2 + \mathbf{X}_3(1 - \beta_4 - \beta_5) + \mathbf{X}_4\beta_4 + \mathbf{X}_5\beta_5 \end{aligned}$$

One restriction reduces five coefficients to four unrestricted ones:

$$\boldsymbol{\beta} = \begin{bmatrix} \beta_1 \\ \beta_2 \\ \beta_4 \\ \beta_4 \\ \beta_5 \end{bmatrix} = \begin{bmatrix} 1 & 0 & 0 & 0 \\ 0 & 1 & 0 & 0 \\ 0 & 0 & -1 & -1 \\ 0 & 0 & 1 & 0 \\ 0 & 0 & 0 & 1 \end{bmatrix} \begin{bmatrix} \beta_1 \\ \beta_2 \\ \beta_4 \\ \beta_5 \end{bmatrix} + \begin{bmatrix} 0 \\ 0 \\ 1 \\ 0 \\ 0 \end{bmatrix}$$

The restrictions for the dynamic unemployment model included simple linear restrictions like this one.

4.3 RESTRICTED LEAST SQUARES

Generally, we compute the RLS fit in a simple and direct way.

PROPOSITION 3 (RESTRICTED LEAST SQUARES) *Given the restrictions $\boldsymbol{\beta} = \mathbf{S}\boldsymbol{\gamma} + \mathbf{s}$, where $\mathbf{S}$ is a $K \times M$ matrix of known constants, $\mathbf{s}$ is a $K \times 1$ vector of known constants, and $\boldsymbol{\gamma}$ is an $M \times 1$ vector of unknown parameters, if $\mathbf{XS}$ is full-column rank then*

1. *The RLS fitted vector is the orthogonal projection of $\mathbf{y}$ plus the translation given in*

$$\hat{\boldsymbol{\mu}}_{\mathrm{R}} = \mathbf{P}_{\mathbf{XS}}\mathbf{y} + (\mathbf{I} - \mathbf{P}_{\mathbf{XS}})\,\mathbf{Xs}$$

where $\mathbf{P}_{\mathbf{XS}} = \mathbf{XS}\left[(\mathbf{XS})'\mathbf{XS}\right]^{-1}(\mathbf{XS})'$.

2. *The RLS coefficient vector is*

$$\hat{\boldsymbol{\beta}}_{\mathrm{R}} \equiv \underset{\{\beta \mid \beta = \mathbf{S}\gamma + \mathbf{s}\}}{\operatorname{argmin}} \|\mathbf{y} - \mathbf{X}\beta\|^2 \tag{4.2}$$

$$= \mathbf{S}\left[(\mathbf{XS})'\mathbf{XS}\right]^{-1}(\mathbf{XS})'(\mathbf{y} - \mathbf{Xs}) + \mathbf{s} \tag{4.3}$$

Proof. We prove this proposition by substituting the restrictions directly into the objective function and deriving an unconstrained minimum in $\boldsymbol{\gamma}$. The restrictions imply that

$$\mathbf{X}\boldsymbol{\beta} = \mathbf{X}(\mathbf{S}\boldsymbol{\gamma} + \mathbf{s}) = \mathbf{X}\mathbf{S}\boldsymbol{\gamma} + \mathbf{X}\mathbf{s}$$

yielding the unconstrained minimization

$$\hat{\boldsymbol{\gamma}} = \underset{\boldsymbol{\gamma}}{\operatorname{argmin}} \left\| (\mathbf{y} - \mathbf{X}\mathbf{s}) - (\mathbf{X}\mathbf{S})\,\boldsymbol{\gamma} \right\|^2 \tag{4.4}$$

By choosing a new matrix of RHS variables $\mathbf{X}_{\mathrm{R}} = \mathbf{X}\mathbf{S}$ and a new LHS vector $\mathbf{y}_{\mathrm{R}} = \mathbf{y} - \mathbf{X}\mathbf{s}$, we can find the solution with two equations: the OLS fit of $\mathbf{y}_{\mathrm{R}}$ to $\mathbf{X}_{\mathrm{R}}$,

$$\begin{aligned} \hat{\boldsymbol{\gamma}} &= \left(\mathbf{X}_{\mathrm{R}}'\mathbf{X}_{\mathrm{R}}\right)^{-1}\mathbf{X}_{\mathrm{R}}'\mathbf{y}_{\mathrm{R}} \\ &= (\mathbf{S}'\mathbf{X}'\mathbf{X}\mathbf{S})^{-1}\mathbf{S}'\mathbf{X}'(\mathbf{y} - \mathbf{X}\mathbf{s}) \end{aligned} \tag{4.5}$$

and the restrictions expressing $\boldsymbol{\beta}$ as a function of $\boldsymbol{\gamma}$,

$$\begin{aligned} \hat{\boldsymbol{\beta}}_{\mathrm{R}} &= \mathbf{S}\hat{\boldsymbol{\gamma}} + \mathbf{s} \\ &= \mathbf{S}(\mathbf{S}'\mathbf{X}'\mathbf{X}\mathbf{S})^{-1}\mathbf{S}'\mathbf{X}'(\mathbf{y} - \mathbf{X}\mathbf{s}) + \mathbf{s} \end{aligned} \tag{4.6}$$

which is (4.3). The expression for fitted vector $\hat{\boldsymbol{\mu}}_{\mathrm{R}}$ follows after substituting these solutions into $\mathbf{X}\hat{\boldsymbol{\beta}}_{\mathrm{R}}$:

$$\begin{aligned} \hat{\boldsymbol{\mu}}_R \equiv \mathbf{X}\hat{\boldsymbol{\beta}}_{\mathrm{R}} &= \mathbf{X}\left[\mathbf{S}(\mathbf{S}'\mathbf{X}'\mathbf{X}\mathbf{S})^{-1}\mathbf{S}'\mathbf{X}'(\mathbf{y} - \mathbf{X}\mathbf{s}) + \mathbf{s}\right] \\ &= \mathbf{P}_{\mathbf{XS}}\,(\mathbf{y} - \mathbf{X}\mathbf{s}) + \mathbf{X}\mathbf{s} \\ &= \mathbf{P}_{\mathbf{XS}}\mathbf{y} + (\mathbf{I} - \mathbf{P}_{\mathbf{XS}})\,\mathbf{X}\mathbf{s} \end{aligned}$$

□

EXAMPLE 4.4 (Continuation)

Reconsider Examples 4.1–4.3 to see how RLS is implemented. The exclusion restrictions in Example 4.1 leave the LHS variable unchanged and they simply reduce the list of RHS variables from $\mathbf{X} = [\boldsymbol{\iota}, \mathbf{X}_2, \mathbf{X}_3, \mathbf{X}_4, \mathbf{X}_5]$ to $\mathbf{X}_{\mathrm{R}} = [\boldsymbol{\iota}, \mathbf{X}_3, \mathbf{X}_5]$. The equality restrictions in Example 4.2 also leave the LHS variable unchanged but we write

$$\beta_1 + \mathbf{X}_2\beta_2 + \mathbf{X}_3\beta_3 + \mathbf{X}_4\beta_4 + \mathbf{X}_5\beta_5 = \beta_1 + (\mathbf{X}_2 + \mathbf{X}_3 + \mathbf{X}_4)\,\beta_4 + \mathbf{X}_5\beta_5$$

so that

$$\mathbf{X}_{\mathrm{R}} = [\boldsymbol{\iota} \quad \mathbf{X}_2 + \mathbf{X}_3 + \mathbf{X}_4 \quad \mathbf{X}_5]$$

Finally, $\mathbf{s} \neq 0$ in Example 4.3 so the LHS variable changes. If we write

$$\begin{aligned} \beta_1 + \mathbf{X}_2\beta_2 + \mathbf{X}_3\,(1 - \beta_4 - \beta_5) + \mathbf{X}_4\beta_4 + \mathbf{X}_5\beta_5 = \mathbf{X}_3 + \beta_1 + \mathbf{X}_2\beta_2 \\ + (\mathbf{X}_4 - \mathbf{X}_3)\,\beta_4 + (\mathbf{X}_5 - \mathbf{X}_3)\,\beta_5 \end{aligned}$$

then

$$\mathbf{y}_{\mathrm{R}} = \mathbf{y} - \mathbf{X}_3$$

and

$$\mathbf{X}_\mathrm{R} = [\boldsymbol{\iota} \quad \mathbf{X}_2 \quad \mathbf{X}_4 - \mathbf{X}_3 \quad \mathbf{X}_5 - \mathbf{X}_3]$$

Note that Proposition 3 does not require $\mathbf{X}$ to be full-column rank, only $\mathbf{XS}$. One of the ways in which empirical researchers overcome multicollinearity in $\mathbf{X}$ is to impose restrictions on $\boldsymbol{\beta}$, thereby reducing the dimensionality of the OLS fitting problem. However, only certain kinds of restrictions deliver a full-column rank $\mathbf{XS}$ when $\mathbf{X}$ is rank deficient.

EXAMPLE 4.5

In the earnings data, the variables age, education, experience, and the constant 1 have an exact linear relationship:

$$0 = 6 - age + education + experience$$

If $x_{n1} = 1$, $x_{n2} = age$, $x_{n3} = education$, and $x_{n4} = experience$, then $\mathbf{X}\alpha = 0$ for

$$\boldsymbol{\alpha} = [6 \quad -1 \quad 1 \quad 1 \quad 0 \quad \cdots \quad 0]'$$

For $\mathbf{XS}$ to be full-column rank, $\mathbf{S}$ effectively must remove this singularity in $\mathbf{X}$. We saw in Chapter 2 that constraining $\beta_2 = 0$ or $\beta_3 = 0$ accomplishes this.

In Example 2.5, we noted that if $\mathbf{X}\boldsymbol{\alpha} = \mathbf{0}$ then for any $\hat{\boldsymbol{\beta}}$ such that $\mathbf{X}\hat{\boldsymbol{\beta}} = \hat{\boldsymbol{\mu}}$, there are many $\tilde{\boldsymbol{\beta}} = \hat{\boldsymbol{\beta}} + c \cdot \boldsymbol{\alpha} \neq \hat{\boldsymbol{\beta}}$ so that $\mathbf{X}\tilde{\boldsymbol{\beta}} = \hat{\boldsymbol{\mu}}$. Thus, for a restriction to overcome multicollinearity, the restriction must choose a unique $\boldsymbol{\beta}$ from the set of such $\tilde{\boldsymbol{\beta}}$. That is, the system of equations

$$\tilde{\boldsymbol{\beta}} = \hat{\boldsymbol{\beta}} + c \cdot \boldsymbol{\alpha}$$
$$\tilde{\boldsymbol{\beta}} = \mathbf{S}\boldsymbol{\gamma} + \mathbf{s}$$

must have a unique solution in $\tilde{\boldsymbol{\beta}}$, c, and $\boldsymbol{\gamma}$. Substituting $\tilde{\boldsymbol{\beta}}$ out and rewriting,

$$[\mathbf{S} \quad -\boldsymbol{\alpha}]\begin{bmatrix}\boldsymbol{\gamma} \\ c\end{bmatrix} = \mathbf{s} - \hat{\boldsymbol{\beta}}$$

has a unique solution if and only if $[\mathbf{S}, -\boldsymbol{\alpha}]$ is nonsingular. We conclude that Col($\mathbf{S}$) must not contain $\boldsymbol{\alpha}$.

If $\mathbf{X}$ is already full rank, then $\mathbf{XS}$ will also be full rank provided that the restrictions $\boldsymbol{\beta} = \mathbf{S}\boldsymbol{\gamma} + \mathbf{s}$ do not contain any redundant, or linearly dependent, restrictions. In other words, $\mathbf{S}$ must be full-column rank. Remember that there are fewer parameters in $\boldsymbol{\gamma}$ than in $\boldsymbol{\beta}$. As a result, if $\mathbf{X}$ and $\mathbf{S}$ are both full-column rank, then $\mathbf{XS}$ is also full-column rank.[3]

EXAMPLE 4.6

Here is how we fit a quartic polynomial distributed lag for unemployment. If we denote the distributed lag by

[3] This follows from the fundamental result of linear algebra that the rank of a matrix equals the rank of its product with a nonsingular matrix. See Theorem C.13 (p. 855).

$$\sum_{k=1}^{12} y_{t-k}\beta_k$$

then our restrictions take the form

$$\beta_k = \gamma_1 + k\gamma_2 + k^2\gamma_3 + k^3\gamma_4 + k^4\gamma_5, \qquad k = 1, \ldots, 12 \tag{4.7}$$

That is,

$$\begin{aligned}
\beta_1 &= \gamma_1 + \gamma_2 + \gamma_3 + \gamma_4 + \gamma_5 \\
\beta_2 &= \gamma_1 + 2\cdot\gamma_2 + 4\cdot\gamma_3 + 8\cdot\gamma_4 + 16\cdot\gamma_5 \\
&\vdots \\
\beta_{12} &= \gamma_1 + 12\cdot\gamma_2 + 144\cdot\gamma_3 + 1728\cdot\gamma_4 + 20736\cdot\gamma_5
\end{aligned}$$

We are replacing 12 β coefficients with linear functions of five γ coefficients. In matrix form, we have

$$\begin{bmatrix} \beta_1 \\ \beta_2 \\ \vdots \\ \beta_{12} \end{bmatrix} = \begin{bmatrix} 1 & 1 & 1 & 1 & 1 \\ 1 & 2 & 2^2 & 2^3 & 2^4 \\ \vdots & \vdots & \vdots & \vdots & \vdots \\ 1 & 12 & 12^2 & 12^3 & 12^4 \end{bmatrix} \begin{bmatrix} \gamma_1 \\ \gamma_2 \\ \gamma_3 \\ \gamma_4 \\ \gamma_5 \end{bmatrix} \tag{4.8}$$

We will also impose two constraints on the polynomial in (4.7): that it be equal to zero when $k = 13$ and that its first derivative is zero when $k = 13$. Inspection of Figure 4.1 displays the evidence of this. The coefficients die out smoothly at the thirteenth lag. The restrictions are linear equations in γs:

$$\begin{aligned}
0 &= \gamma_1 + 13\cdot\gamma_2 + 13^2\cdot\gamma_3 + 13^3\cdot\gamma_4 + 13^4\cdot\gamma_5 \\
0 &= \gamma_2 + 2\cdot 13\cdot\gamma_3 + 3\cdot 13^2\cdot\gamma_4 + 4\cdot 13^3\cdot\gamma_5
\end{aligned} \tag{4.9}$$

Substituting (4.9) for γ_1 and γ_2 into (4.8) reduces the free parameters to γ_3, γ_4, and γ_5: some of the elements of **S** are

$$\begin{bmatrix} \beta_1 \\ \beta_2 \\ \vdots \\ \beta_{12} \end{bmatrix} = \begin{bmatrix} 144 & 3888 & 76896 \\ 121 & 3388 & 68123 \\ \vdots & \vdots & \vdots \\ 1 & 38 & 963 \end{bmatrix} \begin{bmatrix} \gamma_3 \\ \gamma_4 \\ \gamma_5 \end{bmatrix}$$

As a result, we fit these γs by replacing the y_{t-k} $(k = 1, \ldots, 12)$ with three RHS variables in $\mathbf{W} = \mathbf{XS}$:

$$\begin{aligned}
w_{t1} &= 144\cdot y_{t-1} + 121\cdot y_{t-2} + \cdots + y_{t-12} \\
w_{t2} &= 3888\cdot y_{t-1} + 3388\cdot y_{t-2} + \cdots + 38\cdot y_{t-12} \\
w_{t3} &= 76896\cdot y_{t-1} + 68123\cdot y_{t-2} + \cdots + 963\cdot y_{t-12}
\end{aligned}$$

We substitute the fitted coefficients for these RHS variables into the equation above to obtain the RLS coefficients for $\boldsymbol{\beta}$.

It is often helpful to see how the location model illustrates a new concept. With linear restrictions, we can actually work out both $\hat{\boldsymbol{\beta}}$ and $\hat{\boldsymbol{\beta}}_{\mathrm{R}}$ analytically.

EXAMPLE 4.7 (Location Model)

Let us generalize the simple location model into a two-location model for illustration. Let $N = N_1 + N_2$ and let $\mathbf{X}$ be the $N \times 2$ matrix of zeros and ones

$$\mathbf{X} = \begin{bmatrix} \boldsymbol{\iota}_{N_1} & 0 \\ 0 & \boldsymbol{\iota}_{N_2} \end{bmatrix}$$

so that the unrestricted model specifies

$$\mathbf{x}_n'\boldsymbol{\beta} = \begin{cases} \beta_1 & \text{if } n \le N_1 \\ \beta_2 & \text{otherwise} \end{cases}$$

Let the restriction be that the two subsamples have the same mean:

$$\begin{bmatrix} \beta_1 \\ \beta_2 \end{bmatrix} = \begin{bmatrix} 1 \\ 1 \end{bmatrix} \gamma_1$$

Then the unrestricted fitted coefficients are simply subsample means:

$$\hat{\boldsymbol{\beta}} = \begin{bmatrix} N_1 & 0 \\ 0 & N_2 \end{bmatrix}^{-1} \begin{bmatrix} \boldsymbol{\iota}_{N_1}'\mathbf{y}_1 \\ \boldsymbol{\iota}_{N_2}'\mathbf{y}_2 \end{bmatrix} = \begin{bmatrix} \bar{y}_1 \\ \bar{y}_2 \end{bmatrix}$$

where $\mathbf{y}_1 \equiv [y_n;\ n = 1, \ldots, N_1]'$, $\mathbf{y}_2 \equiv [y_n;\ n = N_1 + 1, \ldots, N]'$,

$$\bar{y}_1 \equiv \frac{1}{N_1}\sum_{n=1}^{N_1} y_n \qquad \text{and} \qquad \bar{y}_2 \equiv \frac{1}{N_2}\sum_{n=N_1+1}^{N} y_n$$

The restricted fitted coefficient is the overall sample mean:

$$\mathbf{XS} = \begin{bmatrix} \boldsymbol{\iota}_{N_1} & 0 \\ 0 & \boldsymbol{\iota}_{N_2} \end{bmatrix} \begin{bmatrix} 1 \\ 1 \end{bmatrix} = \begin{bmatrix} \boldsymbol{\iota}_{N_1} \\ \boldsymbol{\iota}_{N_2} \end{bmatrix} = \boldsymbol{\iota}_N$$

and

$$\hat{\boldsymbol{\beta}}_{\mathrm{R}} = \begin{bmatrix} 1 \\ 1 \end{bmatrix} N^{-1}\boldsymbol{\iota}_N'\mathbf{y} = \begin{bmatrix} \bar{y} \\ \bar{y} \end{bmatrix}$$

where

$$\bar{y} \equiv \frac{1}{N}\sum_{n=1}^{N} y_n$$

More generally, there is a simple relationship between the restricted and unrestricted estimators. We know from the projection theorem (p. 31) that for *any* $\boldsymbol{\beta}$,

$$\|\mathbf{y} - \mathbf{X}\boldsymbol{\beta}\|^2 = \|\mathbf{y} - \hat{\boldsymbol{\mu}}\|^2 + \|\hat{\boldsymbol{\mu}} - \mathbf{X}\boldsymbol{\beta}\|^2 \tag{4.10}$$

The first term $\|\mathbf{y} - \hat{\boldsymbol{\mu}}\|^2$ does not depend on the arbitrary $\boldsymbol{\beta}$, so that the RLS problem (4.2) is equivalent to restricted minimization of the second term in (4.10):

$$\hat{\boldsymbol{\beta}}_{\mathrm{R}} = \underset{\{\boldsymbol{\beta}|\boldsymbol{\beta}=\mathbf{S}\boldsymbol{\gamma}+\mathbf{s}\}}{\operatorname{argmin}} \left\| \hat{\boldsymbol{\mu}} - \mathbf{X}\boldsymbol{\beta} \right\|^2 \tag{4.11}$$

As a result, we could just as well replace $\mathbf{y}$ with $\hat{\boldsymbol{\mu}}$ in (4.5)–(4.6) and write

$$\hat{\boldsymbol{\gamma}} = (\mathbf{S}'\mathbf{X}'\mathbf{X}\mathbf{S})^{-1}\mathbf{S}'\mathbf{X}'\left(\hat{\boldsymbol{\mu}} - \mathbf{X}\mathbf{s}\right) \tag{4.12}$$

This yields a projection expression for $\hat{\boldsymbol{\beta}}_{\mathrm{R}}$ in terms of $\hat{\boldsymbol{\beta}}$:

$$\begin{aligned} \hat{\boldsymbol{\beta}}_{\mathrm{R}} = \mathbf{S}\hat{\boldsymbol{\gamma}} + \mathbf{s} &= \mathbf{S}(\mathbf{S}'\mathbf{X}'\mathbf{X}\mathbf{S})^{-1}\mathbf{S}'\mathbf{X}'\left(\hat{\boldsymbol{\mu}} - \mathbf{X}\mathbf{s}\right) + \mathbf{s} \\ &= \mathbf{S}(\mathbf{S}'\mathbf{X}'\mathbf{X}\mathbf{S})^{-1}\mathbf{S}'\mathbf{X}'\mathbf{X}\left(\hat{\boldsymbol{\beta}} - \mathbf{s}\right) + \mathbf{s} \\ &= \mathbf{P}_{\mathbf{S}\perp\mathbf{X}'\mathbf{X}\mathbf{S}}\hat{\boldsymbol{\beta}} + (\mathbf{I} - \mathbf{P}_{\mathbf{S}\perp\mathbf{X}'\mathbf{X}\mathbf{S}})\,\mathbf{s} \end{aligned} \tag{4.13}$$

where $\mathbf{P}_{\mathbf{S}\perp\mathbf{X}'\mathbf{X}\mathbf{S}} = \mathbf{S}(\mathbf{S}'\mathbf{X}'\mathbf{X}\mathbf{S})^{-1}\mathbf{S}'\mathbf{X}'\mathbf{X}$.[4] The RLS vector of fitted values can also be reexpressed in terms of projection of $\hat{\boldsymbol{\mu}}$:

$$\begin{aligned} \hat{\boldsymbol{\mu}}_{\mathrm{R}} \equiv \mathbf{X}\hat{\boldsymbol{\beta}}_{\mathrm{R}} &= \mathbf{X}\left[\mathbf{S}(\mathbf{S}'\mathbf{X}'\mathbf{X}\mathbf{S})^{-1}\mathbf{S}'\mathbf{X}'\left(\hat{\boldsymbol{\mu}} - \mathbf{X}\mathbf{s}\right) + \mathbf{s}\right] \\ &= \mathbf{P}_{\mathbf{X}\mathbf{S}}\hat{\boldsymbol{\mu}} + (\mathbf{I} - \mathbf{P}_{\mathbf{X}\mathbf{S}})\,\mathbf{X}\mathbf{s} \end{aligned} \tag{4.14}$$

In the previous chapter, we described such matrices as $\mathbf{P}_{\mathbf{S}\perp\mathbf{X}'\mathbf{X}\mathbf{S}}$ in terms of projection. In the next section, we give the geometric interpretation of (4.13) in terms of generalized distance.

4.4 GENERALIZED DISTANCE

According to (4.13), the linear transformation of $\hat{\boldsymbol{\beta}}$ to $\hat{\boldsymbol{\beta}}_{\mathrm{R}}$ is a projection of $\hat{\boldsymbol{\beta}}$, the term $\mathbf{P}_{\mathbf{S}\perp\mathbf{X}'\mathbf{X}\mathbf{S}}\hat{\boldsymbol{\beta}}$, followed by a translation, the term $(\mathbf{I} - \mathbf{P}_{\mathbf{S}\perp\mathbf{X}'\mathbf{X}\mathbf{S}})\,\mathbf{s}$. The fitted RLS vector $\hat{\boldsymbol{\mu}}_{\mathrm{R}}$ has a similar interpretation in both Proposition 3 and equation (4.14). Let us consider the projection term first and return to the translation term below. In effect, we will consider first the special case in which $\mathbf{s} = \mathbf{0}$, eliminating the translation term altogether.

When $\mathbf{s} = \mathbf{0}$, the interpretation of $\hat{\boldsymbol{\mu}}_{\mathrm{R}}$ as a projection of $\mathbf{y}$, or of $\hat{\boldsymbol{\mu}}$, is familiar. Using (4.10)–(4.11), we find either projection via OLS:

$$\begin{aligned} \mathbf{P}_{\mathbf{X}\mathbf{S}}\mathbf{y} &= \underset{\boldsymbol{\mu}\in\mathrm{Col}(\mathbf{X}\mathbf{S})}{\operatorname{argmin}} \; (\mathbf{y} - \boldsymbol{\mu})'\,(\mathbf{y} - \boldsymbol{\mu}) \\ &= \underset{\boldsymbol{\mu}\in\mathrm{Col}(\mathbf{X}\mathbf{S})}{\operatorname{argmin}} \; \left(\hat{\boldsymbol{\mu}} - \boldsymbol{\mu}\right)'\left(\hat{\boldsymbol{\mu}} - \boldsymbol{\mu}\right) \\ &= \mathbf{P}_{\mathbf{X}\mathbf{S}}\hat{\boldsymbol{\mu}} \end{aligned}$$

Recall that the corresponding fitted coefficients are a one-to-one function of this fitted vector: for example, $\hat{\boldsymbol{\beta}}_{\mathrm{R}} = \left(\mathbf{X}'\mathbf{X}\right)^{-1}\mathbf{X}'\mathbf{P}_{\mathbf{X}\mathbf{S}}\hat{\boldsymbol{\mu}}$.[5] This one-to-one linear relationship explains the projection term in $\hat{\boldsymbol{\beta}}_{\mathrm{R}}$: the (nonorthogonal) projection of $\hat{\boldsymbol{\beta}}$ to get $\hat{\boldsymbol{\beta}}_{\mathrm{R}}$ is the transformation of the orthogonal projection of $\hat{\boldsymbol{\mu}}$ under this one-to-one function.

---

[4] This projector form was introduced in (3.20) on p. 63.

[5] See equations (2.7)–(2.8).

Casual inspection shows how similar the programs for $\hat{\boldsymbol{\beta}}_{\mathrm{R}}$ and $\hat{\boldsymbol{\mu}}_{\mathrm{R}}$ are. According to (4.11) and (4.13), when $\mathbf{s} = \mathbf{0}$, we may also write the restricted coefficient vector as

$$\mathbf{P}_{\mathbf{S}\perp\mathbf{X}'\mathbf{X}\mathbf{S}}\hat{\boldsymbol{\beta}} = \underset{\boldsymbol{\beta}\in\mathrm{Col}(\mathbf{S})}{\operatorname{argmin}} \left(\hat{\boldsymbol{\beta}} - \boldsymbol{\beta}\right)' \mathbf{X}'\mathbf{X} \left(\hat{\boldsymbol{\beta}} - \boldsymbol{\beta}\right) \tag{4.15}$$

If $\mathbf{X}'\mathbf{X}$ were equal to $\mathbf{I}_K$ then the problems, and their solutions, would be completely analogous. For $\hat{\boldsymbol{\mu}}_{\mathrm{R}}$, we seek a vector $\boldsymbol{\mu}$ in Col($\mathbf{XS}$) that is close to $\hat{\boldsymbol{\mu}}$ and for $\hat{\boldsymbol{\beta}}_{\mathrm{R}}$ a vector $\boldsymbol{\beta}$ in Col($\mathbf{S}$) that is close to $\hat{\boldsymbol{\beta}}$. The substantive difference is the central $\mathbf{X}'\mathbf{X}$ term in the quadratic form of (4.15), and the change in projector that results.

The presence of $\mathbf{X}'\mathbf{X}$ reflects the transformation of an ordinary minimum-distance problem (in $\boldsymbol{\mu}$) to a *generalized minimum-distance* problem (in $\boldsymbol{\beta}$). We can interpret $\boldsymbol{\alpha}'\mathbf{X}'\mathbf{X}\boldsymbol{\alpha}$ as a new measure of the squared length of any $\boldsymbol{\alpha} \in \mathbb{R}^K$ because this function of $\boldsymbol{\alpha}$ inherits all the necessary properties of squared length through its form $\boldsymbol{\alpha}'\mathbf{X}'\mathbf{X}\boldsymbol{\alpha} = \|\mathbf{X}\boldsymbol{\alpha}\|^2$ as the *Euclidean* squared length of $\mathbf{X}\boldsymbol{\alpha}$.[6] Scalar multiplication of a vector multiplies its squared length by the square of the scalar:

$$(c \cdot \boldsymbol{\alpha})' \mathbf{X}'\mathbf{X} (c \cdot \boldsymbol{\alpha}) = c^2 \boldsymbol{\alpha}'\mathbf{X}'\mathbf{X}\boldsymbol{\alpha}$$

This squared length is positive, for

$$\boldsymbol{\alpha}'\mathbf{X}'\mathbf{X}\boldsymbol{\alpha} = \|\mathbf{X}\boldsymbol{\alpha}\|^2 \geq 0$$

yet zero if and only if $\boldsymbol{\alpha}$ is the zero vector:

$$\boldsymbol{\alpha}'\mathbf{X}'\mathbf{X}\boldsymbol{\alpha} = \|\mathbf{X}\boldsymbol{\alpha}\|^2 = 0 \Leftrightarrow \mathbf{X}\boldsymbol{\alpha} = \mathbf{0} \Leftrightarrow \boldsymbol{\alpha} = \mathbf{0}$$

Finally, the *triangle inequality* holds for the length itself:

$$\begin{aligned}\sqrt{(\boldsymbol{\alpha} + \boldsymbol{\beta})' \mathbf{X}'\mathbf{X} (\boldsymbol{\alpha} + \boldsymbol{\beta})} &= \|\mathbf{X}(\boldsymbol{\alpha} + \boldsymbol{\beta})\| \\ &\leq \|\mathbf{X}\boldsymbol{\alpha}\| + \|\mathbf{X}\boldsymbol{\beta}\| \\ &\leq \sqrt{\boldsymbol{\alpha}'\mathbf{X}'\mathbf{X}\boldsymbol{\alpha}} + \sqrt{\boldsymbol{\beta}'\mathbf{X}'\mathbf{X}\boldsymbol{\beta}}\end{aligned}$$

Geometrically, the difference between distance and generalized distance is the difference between spheres and their generalization, ellipses. An example is a useful starting point for comparison.

EXAMPLE 4.8

Consider the restricted case where $N = 2$, $K = 1$, and

$$\mathbf{X}\boldsymbol{\beta} = \begin{bmatrix} 1 & 0 \\ 0 & 2 \end{bmatrix} \begin{bmatrix} \beta_1 \\ \beta_2 \end{bmatrix}$$

Let the restrictions state that $\beta_1 = \gamma_1$, $\beta_2 = \gamma_1$:

$$\mathbf{XS}\gamma = \begin{bmatrix} 1 \\ 2 \end{bmatrix} \gamma_1$$

so that observation 2 has twice the fitted value of observation 1.

[6] See Section C.4 for a summary of vector length.

The unrestricted estimator for this problem is somewhat contrived: given $\mathbf{y}$, $\hat{\beta}_1 = y_1$ and $\hat{\beta}_2 = y_2/2$, delivering a perfect fit. The restricted estimator is

$$\hat{\gamma}_1 = \frac{y_1 + 2y_2}{5} = \hat{\beta}_{R1} = \hat{\beta}_{R2}.$$

The OLS minimization is depicted in the left panel of Figure 4.2. This is analogous to Figure 2.5 (p. 25). If we transform this minimization to the parameter space (β_1, β_2), everything looks slightly different, as in the second panel. Because the scale of β_2 is one-half that of y_2, distance from $\hat{\boldsymbol{\beta}}$ to the restricted parameter space where $\beta_1 = \beta_2$ gets measured in elliptical contours rather than circular ones.

Using (4.15), we can explicitly express these ellipses as

$$\left(\hat{\boldsymbol{\beta}} - \boldsymbol{\beta}\right)' \mathbf{X}'\mathbf{X} \left(\hat{\boldsymbol{\beta}} - \boldsymbol{\beta}\right) = \left(\hat{\beta}_1 - \beta_1\right)^2 + 4\left(\hat{\beta}_2 - \beta_2\right)^2 = \delta^2$$

for various values of δ. The closest restricted value is not found with an orthogonal projection, as it is in the space of observations. Instead, the transformation of $\hat{\boldsymbol{\beta}}$ is a general projection:

$$\hat{\boldsymbol{\beta}}_R = \begin{bmatrix} 1 \\ 1 \end{bmatrix} (5)^{-1} \begin{bmatrix} 1 & 4 \end{bmatrix} \begin{bmatrix} \hat{\beta}_1 \\ \hat{\beta}_2 \end{bmatrix} = \begin{bmatrix} \left(\hat{\beta}_1 + 4\hat{\beta}_2\right)/5 \\ \left(\hat{\beta}_1 + 4\hat{\beta}_2\right)/5 \end{bmatrix}$$

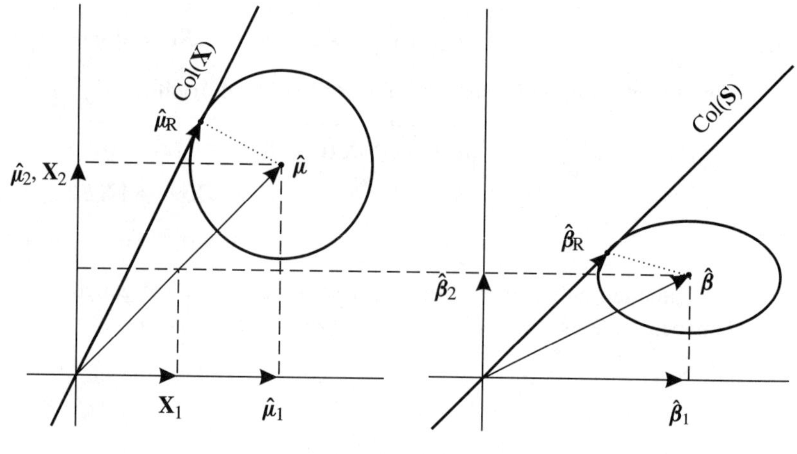

Figure 4.2 RLS as a projection of OLS.

We formalize our discussion with the following definition.

Definition 9 (Generalized Length) *Let* $\mathbf{A}$ *be a nonsingular* $N \times N$ *matrix such that* $\mathbf{w}'\mathbf{A}\mathbf{w} \geq 0$ *for all* $\mathbf{w} \in \mathbb{R}^N$. *Then the* generalized length *of* w with respect to $\mathbf{A}$ *is* $\sqrt{\mathbf{w}'\mathbf{A}\mathbf{w}}$. *We will denote* $\sqrt{\mathbf{w}'\mathbf{A}\mathbf{w}} \equiv \|\mathbf{w}\|_{\mathbf{A}}$ *to generalize our notation.*[7]

[7] Statisticians often call this Mahalanobis length, after P. C. Mahalanobis, who first suggested its use in statistics.

We make two comments, both about the matrix $\mathbf{A}$, before we use this definition. The metric $\mathbf{A}$ must have the property $\mathbf{w}'\mathbf{A}\mathbf{w} \geq 0$ for all $\mathbf{w}$, otherwise generalized length is not well defined. We will return to the characterization of matrices with this property in Chapter 7. For the moment, we note that we have an example in the matrix $\mathbf{X}'\mathbf{X}$. According to Assumption 3.1, $\mathbf{X}'\mathbf{X}$ is nonsingular so that, for all $\mathbf{w} \in \mathbb{R}^K$, $\mathbf{w} \neq \mathbf{0}$,

$$\|\mathbf{w}\|^2_{\mathbf{X}'\mathbf{X}} = \mathbf{w}'\left(\mathbf{X}'\mathbf{X}\right)\mathbf{w} = (\mathbf{X}\mathbf{w})'\,\mathbf{X}\mathbf{w} = \|\mathbf{X}\mathbf{w}\|^2 > 0$$

Indeed, the generalized distance is the standard Euclidean distance of a linear transformation. As we will see, this is always true for generalized distance.

Note also that our example $\mathbf{A} = \mathbf{X}'\mathbf{X}$ is symmetric, which we may also take as a general property of $\mathbf{A}$. Because it is a scalar, $\mathbf{w}'\mathbf{A}\mathbf{w}$ equals its matrix transpose,

$$\mathbf{w}'\mathbf{A}\mathbf{w} = \left(\mathbf{w}'\mathbf{A}\mathbf{w}\right)' = \mathbf{w}'\mathbf{A}'\mathbf{w}$$

so that

$$\mathbf{w}'\mathbf{A}\mathbf{w} = \frac{\mathbf{w}'\mathbf{A}\mathbf{w} + \mathbf{w}'\mathbf{A}'\mathbf{w}}{2} = \mathbf{w}'\left(\frac{\mathbf{A} + \mathbf{A}'}{2}\right)\mathbf{w}$$

Therefore, we can always replace $\mathbf{A}$ with $\frac{1}{2}\left(\mathbf{A} + \mathbf{A}'\right)$, which is symmetric. In this sense, the matrix $\mathbf{A}$ in the expression $\mathbf{w}'\mathbf{A}\mathbf{w}$ can always be treated as symmetric.

Now we will write (4.15) as

$$\mathbf{P}_{\mathbf{S}\perp\mathbf{X}'\mathbf{X}\mathbf{S}}\hat{\boldsymbol{\beta}} = \underset{\boldsymbol{\beta}\in\mathrm{Col}(\mathbf{S})}{\operatorname{argmin}} \left\|\hat{\boldsymbol{\beta}} - \boldsymbol{\beta}\right\|^2_{\mathbf{X}'\mathbf{X}} \tag{4.16}$$

formally connecting generalized minimum distance to projection. The projector $\mathbf{P}_{\mathbf{S}\perp\mathbf{X}'\mathbf{X}\mathbf{S}}$ maps $\hat{\boldsymbol{\beta}}$ to $\mathrm{Col}(\mathbf{S})$, but not orthogonally because distance is measured elliptically rather than spherically.

4.4.1 Translation

The second term of $\hat{\boldsymbol{\beta}}_{\mathrm{R}}$ in (4.13) translates the projection of $\hat{\boldsymbol{\beta}}$ by $(\mathbf{I} - \mathbf{P}_{\mathbf{S}\perp\mathbf{X}'\mathbf{X}\mathbf{S}})\,\mathbf{s}$. This translation arises from a translation that appears in the RLS program itself, which we can now write as

$$\hat{\boldsymbol{\beta}}_{\mathrm{R}} = \underset{\boldsymbol{\beta}\in\mathrm{Col}(\mathbf{S})+\mathbf{s}}{\operatorname{argmin}} \left\|\hat{\boldsymbol{\beta}} - \boldsymbol{\beta}\right\|^2_{\mathbf{X}'\mathbf{X}} \tag{4.17}$$

It is $\boldsymbol{\beta} - \mathbf{s}$, rather than simply $\boldsymbol{\beta}$, that must lie in $\mathrm{Col}(\mathbf{S})$, according to the restrictions $\boldsymbol{\beta} = \mathbf{S}\boldsymbol{\gamma} + \mathbf{s}$. To take advantage of our projection technique, we reparameterize the problem in terms of $\mathbf{b} \equiv \boldsymbol{\beta} - \mathbf{s}$. Setting $\boldsymbol{\beta} = \mathbf{b} + \mathbf{s}$ everywhere gives

$$\begin{aligned}
\hat{\boldsymbol{\beta}}_{\mathrm{R}} &= \left(\underset{\mathbf{b}\in\mathrm{Col}(\mathbf{S})}{\operatorname{argmin}} \left\|\hat{\boldsymbol{\beta}} - \mathbf{b} - \mathbf{s}\right\|^2_{\mathbf{X}'\mathbf{X}}\right) + \mathbf{s} \\
&= \mathbf{P}_{\mathbf{S}\perp\mathbf{X}'\mathbf{X}\mathbf{S}}(\hat{\boldsymbol{\beta}} - \mathbf{s}) + \mathbf{s} \\
&= \mathbf{P}_{\mathbf{S}\perp\mathbf{X}'\mathbf{X}\mathbf{S}}\hat{\boldsymbol{\beta}} + (\mathbf{I} - \mathbf{P}_{\mathbf{S}\perp\mathbf{X}'\mathbf{X}\mathbf{S}})\,\mathbf{s}
\end{aligned}$$

just as before. The additional **s** on the RHS of the first equation arises because the argument of the minimization changes from $\boldsymbol{\beta}$ to $\mathbf{b}$ yet we are solving for $\hat{\boldsymbol{\beta}}_R = \hat{\mathbf{b}} + \mathbf{s}$.

EXAMPLE 4.9

We picture this minimization as an extension to our previous example and figure. In this case,

$$\mathbf{s} = \begin{bmatrix} 0 \\ 1 \end{bmatrix}$$

In Figure 4.3, we show the translation of Col(**S**) to Col(**S**) + **s**. The minimum generalized distance ellipses appear for both sets, showing that an additional term is necessary to reach Col(**S**) + **s** from Col(**S**). The figure also shows that this term is $(\mathbf{I} - \mathbf{P}_{\mathbf{S}\perp\mathbf{X}'\mathbf{X}\mathbf{S}})\mathbf{s}$. For simplicity, we label the vector $\mathbf{P}_{\mathbf{S}\perp\mathbf{X}'\mathbf{X}\mathbf{S}}\mathbf{s}$ with the point **Ps**. The vector $(\mathbf{I} - \mathbf{P}_{\mathbf{S}\perp\mathbf{X}'\mathbf{X}\mathbf{S}})\mathbf{s}$ is the difference between **s** and **Ps**.

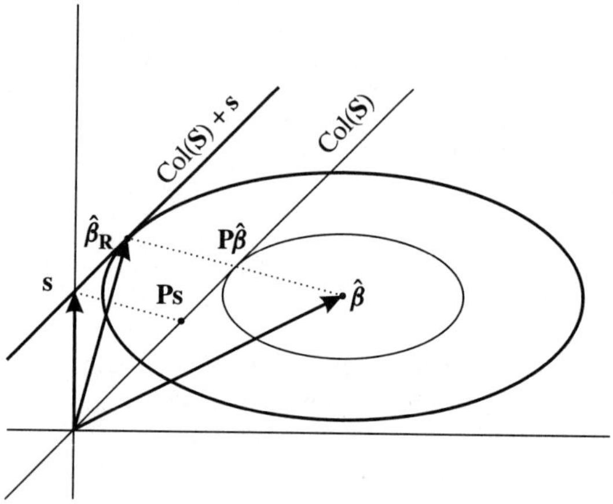

Figure 4.3 RLS as a projection and translation of OLS.

We have been following a path parallel to the one we took with ordinary minimum distance and orthogonal projection in Chapter 2. First, we have found the solution to a specific generalized minimum distance problem (RLS). Second, we have interpreted the particular solution in terms of projection. Now we turn to a broader interpretation, revisiting the projection theorem.

4.5 GENERALIZED PROJECTION

Although generalized distance may appear to complicate matters, we can actually keep our discussion within the boundaries of the projection theorem and realize some conceptual economy. To do this we will exploit more fully the concepts of a linear vector space and a measure of vector length. Thus far, we have discussed only Euclidean vector spaces, denoted $\mathbb{E}^N$.[8] In this section, we review *vector spaces* with *inner products* and generalize $\mathbb{E}^N$.[9]

Roughly speaking, vector spaces are sets of elements (vectors) that can be combined by the elementary operations of vector addition and scalar multiplication to yield other elements of the same set. The real vector space $\mathbb{R}^N$ is the most familiar example. The *Euclidean* vector space $\mathbb{E}^N$ has two additional important features: an *inner product* and a measure of *length*. The inner product of two Euclidean vectors $\mathbf{z}_1$ and $\mathbf{z}_2$ is $\mathbf{z}_1'\mathbf{z}_2$ and the length, or *norm*, of a Euclidean vector z_1 is the square root of the inner product of the vector with itself, $\sqrt{\mathbf{z}_1'\mathbf{z}_1}$. The inner product of Euclidean vectors has an abstract counterpart and there are other interesting examples of vector spaces with inner products and their associated norms. In this book, we describe several and in this chapter we encounter our first example.[10]

As we have explained above, we will view $\sqrt{\mathbf{z}_1'\mathbf{A}\mathbf{z}_1}$ as a vector length, provided that $\mathbf{z}_1'\mathbf{A}\mathbf{z}_1$ is positive for all $\mathbf{z}_1 \in \mathbb{R}^N$. This, of course, is the Euclidean measure of length when $\mathbf{A} = \mathbf{I}_N$, the identity matrix. For the discussion in this chapter, the analogue to the Euclidean inner product of two vectors is the *generalized inner product*

$$\langle \mathbf{z}_1, \mathbf{z}_2 \rangle_{\mathbf{A}} \equiv \mathbf{z}_1'\mathbf{A}\mathbf{z}_2 \tag{4.18}$$

This generalized inner product also reduces to the Euclidean inner product in the special case $\mathbf{A} = \mathbf{I}_N$. Thus, the generalized vector length is also the square root of the inner product of a vector with itself:

$$\|\mathbf{z}\|_{\mathbf{A}} = \sqrt{\langle \mathbf{z}, \mathbf{z} \rangle_{\mathbf{A}}}$$

Two vectors are *orthogonal* in a vector space if their inner product equals zero. Given the inner product and its associated length, the Pythagorean theorem holds in generalized Euclidean spaces: let

$$\langle \mathbf{z}_1, \mathbf{z}_2 \rangle_{\mathbf{A}} = 0 \quad \Leftrightarrow \quad \mathbf{z}_1 \perp_{\mathbf{A}} \mathbf{z}_2$$

so that

$$\begin{aligned} \mathbf{z}_1 \perp_{\mathbf{A}} \mathbf{z}_2 \quad \Rightarrow \quad \|\mathbf{z}_1 + \mathbf{z}_2\|_{\mathbf{A}}^2 &= \|\mathbf{z}_1\|_{\mathbf{A}}^2 + 2\,\langle \mathbf{z}_1, \mathbf{z}_2 \rangle_{\mathbf{A}} + \|\mathbf{z}_2\|_{\mathbf{A}}^2 \\ &= \|\mathbf{z}_1\|_{\mathbf{A}}^2 + \|\mathbf{z}_2\|_{\mathbf{A}}^2 \end{aligned}$$

The Pythagorean theorem is the basis for the projection theorem as we explained it for $\mathbb{E}^N$, and it is so for inner product spaces more generally.

---

8 Although the distinction may seem like a fine one, it is useful to distinguish between $\mathbb{R}^N$ and $\mathbb{E}^N$ in the same way as it is useful to distinguish between a linear vector space and a linear vector space with a norm. We can associate other norms than the Euclidean with $\mathbb{R}^N$. For example, $\|\mathbf{z}\| = \max_n |z_n|$ is also a norm.

9 We give formal definitions of a vector space (Definition C.1, p. 841), an inner product (Definition C.16, p. 852), and a norm (Definition C.21, p. 855) in Appendix C.

10 All of the vector spaces that we examine are examples of *Hilbert* spaces. Here is a brief family tree of related vector spaces. A vector space with an inner product is called a *pre-Hilbert* space and a vector space with a norm is called a *normed* space. A normed vector space in which every Cauchy sequence has a limit in the space is called *complete*. Such spaces are called *Banach* spaces. A pre-Hilbert space can always be assigned the norm $\|\cdot\| = \sqrt{\langle \cdot, \cdot \rangle}$ (see Section C.4). If a pre-Hilbert space is complete, it is called a *Hilbert* space. Luenberger (1969) is an excellent reference for these concepts.

THEOREM 3 (PROJECTION) *Let* $\mathbf{y} \in \mathbb{R}^N$ *and let* $\mathbb{S} \subset \mathbb{R}^N$ *be a linear subspace. Let* $\mathbf{A}$ *be a nonsingular* $N \times N$ *matrix such that* $\mathbf{z}'\mathbf{A}\mathbf{z} > 0$ *for all* $\mathbf{z} \in \mathbb{R}^N$, $\mathbf{z} \neq 0$. *Then* $\hat{\boldsymbol{\mu}} \in \mathbb{S}$ *is the unique solution to the program*

$$\min_{\boldsymbol{\mu} \in \mathbb{S}} \|\mathbf{y} - \boldsymbol{\mu}\|_{\mathbf{A}}^2$$

if and only if $\mathbf{y} - \hat{\boldsymbol{\mu}} \perp_{\mathbf{A}} \mathbb{S}$ *(that is,* $\mathbf{y} - \hat{\boldsymbol{\mu}} \in \{\mathbf{v} \in \mathbb{R}^N \mid \mathbf{v} \perp_{\mathbf{A}} \mathbf{z}\ \forall \mathbf{z} \in \mathbb{S}\}$*).*

Proof. The proof is identical to the proof of Theorem 2 (Projection, p. 31), except that we replace Euclidean inner products and norms with their generalized counterparts. Note that the orthogonal complement in this theorem has a generalized definition also. □

THEOREM 4 *Let* $\mathbf{X}$ *be full-column rank and let the conditions of Theorem 3 hold. Then*

$$\mathbf{P}_{\mathbf{X}\perp\mathbf{A}\mathbf{X}}\mathbf{y} = \underset{\boldsymbol{\mu} \in \text{Col}(\mathbf{X})}{\text{argmin}} \|\mathbf{y} - \boldsymbol{\mu}\|_{\mathbf{A}}^2$$

uniquely.

Proof. Because $\mathbf{A}$ is nonsingular and $\mathbf{X}$ is full-column rank,

$$\boldsymbol{\alpha}' \left(\mathbf{X}'\mathbf{A}\mathbf{X}\right) \boldsymbol{\alpha} = (\mathbf{X}\boldsymbol{\alpha})' \mathbf{A} (\mathbf{X}\boldsymbol{\alpha}) = 0 \Leftrightarrow \mathbf{X}\boldsymbol{\alpha} = \mathbf{0} \Leftrightarrow \boldsymbol{\alpha} = \mathbf{0}$$

so that $\mathbf{X}'\mathbf{A}\mathbf{X}$ is nonsingular and, according to Lemma 3.5 (p. 68), $\mathbf{P}_{\mathbf{X}\perp\mathbf{A}\mathbf{X}}$ is the unique projector onto $\text{Col}(\mathbf{X})$ along $\text{Col}^{\perp}(\mathbf{A}\mathbf{X})$. Therefore,

$$\mathbf{P}_{\mathbf{X}\perp\mathbf{A}\mathbf{X}}\mathbf{y} \in \text{Col}(\mathbf{X})$$

$$\mathbf{y} - \mathbf{P}_{\mathbf{X}\perp\mathbf{A}\mathbf{X}}\mathbf{y} = (\mathbf{I} - \mathbf{P}_{\mathbf{X}\perp\mathbf{A}\mathbf{X}})\,\mathbf{y} \in \text{Col}^{\perp}(\mathbf{A}\mathbf{X})$$

and

$$\boldsymbol{\mu} \in \text{Col}(\mathbf{X}) \quad \Rightarrow \quad \boldsymbol{\mu}'\mathbf{A}\,(\mathbf{y} - \mathbf{P}_{\mathbf{X}\perp\mathbf{A}\mathbf{X}}\mathbf{y}) = 0$$

Therefore, $\mathbf{P}_{\mathbf{X}\perp\mathbf{A}\mathbf{X}}\mathbf{y}$ satisfies all the conditions in Theorem 3 characterizing the unique, optimal, $\hat{\boldsymbol{\mu}}$. □

Note that the projector $\mathbf{P}_{\mathbf{X}\perp\mathbf{A}\mathbf{X}}$ is the *orthogonal* projector onto $\text{Col}(\mathbf{X})$ in this generalization of $\mathbb{E}^N$:

$$z \in \text{Col}(\mathbf{X}) \quad \Rightarrow \quad \mathbf{P}_{\mathbf{X}\perp\mathbf{A}\mathbf{X}}z = z$$

$$z \perp_{\mathbf{A}} \text{Col}(\mathbf{X}) \quad \Rightarrow \quad \mathbf{P}_{\mathbf{X}\perp\mathbf{A}\mathbf{X}}z = \mathbf{0}$$

We will often continue to work within $\mathbb{E}^N$ in this book and the nonorthogonal projector will be a useful idea. Nevertheless, it is helpful to recognize that a single concept, orthogonal projection is at the core of many of the econometric topics that we consider.

In this chapter, such projection appears in the first (projection) term of the RLS fitted coefficients (4.13): $\hat{\boldsymbol{\beta}}_{\mathrm{R}} = \mathbf{P}_{\mathbf{S}\perp\mathbf{X}'\mathbf{X}\mathbf{S}}\hat{\boldsymbol{\beta}} + (\mathbf{I} - \mathbf{P}_{\mathbf{S}\perp\mathbf{X}'\mathbf{X}\mathbf{S}})\,\mathbf{s}$. This projection is the outcome of a generalized minimum-distance problem. In the first chapter of Part II, we will introduce a further generalization of these ideas in the setting of random variables.

4.6 OVERVIEW

1. Linear restrictions on $\boldsymbol{\beta}$ can always be written in the form $\boldsymbol{\beta} = \mathbf{S}\boldsymbol{\gamma} + \mathbf{s}$, where $\mathbf{S}$ and $\mathbf{s}$ contain known constants. Restricted least squares (RLS) finds

$$\hat{\boldsymbol{\beta}}_{\mathrm{R}} = \underset{\{\boldsymbol{\beta}|\boldsymbol{\beta}=\mathbf{S}\boldsymbol{\gamma}+\mathbf{s}\}}{\operatorname{argmin}} \|\mathbf{y} - \mathbf{X}\boldsymbol{\beta}\|^2$$

2. RLS can be solved by OLS:

$$\mathbf{y} - \mathbf{X}\boldsymbol{\beta} = \mathbf{y} - \mathbf{X}\,(\mathbf{S}\gamma + \mathbf{s}) = (\mathbf{y} - \mathbf{X}\mathbf{s}) - (\mathbf{X}\mathbf{S})\,\boldsymbol{\gamma}$$

so that

$$\begin{aligned}\hat{\boldsymbol{\gamma}} &= \left[(\mathbf{X}\mathbf{S})'\,(\mathbf{X}\mathbf{S})\right]^{-1}(\mathbf{X}\mathbf{S})'\,(\mathbf{y} - \mathbf{X}\mathbf{s})\\ \hat{\boldsymbol{\beta}}_{\mathrm{R}} &= \mathbf{S}\hat{\boldsymbol{\gamma}} + \mathbf{s}\\ \hat{\boldsymbol{\mu}}_{\mathrm{R}} &= \mathbf{P}_{\mathbf{X}\mathbf{S}}\mathbf{y} + (\mathbf{I} - \mathbf{P}_{\mathbf{X}\mathbf{S}})\,\mathbf{X}\mathbf{s}\end{aligned}$$

3. There is also an interesting relationship between RLS and OLS based on the Pythagorean decomposition

$$\|\mathbf{y} - \mathbf{X}\boldsymbol{\beta}\|^2 = \left\|\mathbf{y} - \mathbf{X}\hat{\boldsymbol{\beta}}\right\|^2 + \left\|\mathbf{X}\hat{\boldsymbol{\beta}} - \mathbf{X}\boldsymbol{\beta}\right\|^2$$

Thus,

$$\hat{\boldsymbol{\beta}}_{\mathrm{R}} = \underset{\boldsymbol{\beta}\in\mathrm{Col}(\mathbf{S})+\mathbf{s}}{\operatorname{argmin}} \left\|\mathbf{X}\hat{\boldsymbol{\beta}} - \mathbf{X}\boldsymbol{\beta}\right\|^2$$

This relationship introduces generalized distance:

$$\begin{aligned}\left\|\mathbf{X}\hat{\boldsymbol{\beta}} - \mathbf{X}\boldsymbol{\beta}\right\|^2 &= \left(\hat{\boldsymbol{\beta}} - \boldsymbol{\beta}\right)'(\mathbf{X}'\mathbf{X})\left(\hat{\boldsymbol{\beta}} - \boldsymbol{\beta}\right)\\ &= \left\|\hat{\boldsymbol{\beta}} - \boldsymbol{\beta}\right\|^2_{\mathbf{X}'\mathbf{X}}\end{aligned}$$

The generalization reflects the one-to-one transformation of $\boldsymbol{\mu} = \mathbf{X}\boldsymbol{\beta}$ to $\boldsymbol{\beta}$: $\boldsymbol{\beta} = (\mathbf{X}'\mathbf{X})^{-1}\mathbf{X}'\boldsymbol{\mu}$.

4. General projection minimizes generalized distance:

$$\mathbf{P}_{\mathbf{S}\perp\mathbf{X}'\mathbf{X}\mathbf{S}}\hat{\boldsymbol{\beta}} = \underset{\boldsymbol{\beta}\in\mathrm{Col}(\mathbf{S})}{\operatorname{argmin}} \left\|\hat{\boldsymbol{\beta}} - \boldsymbol{\beta}\right\|^2_{\mathbf{X}'\mathbf{X}}$$

5. General projection can be interpreted as orthogonal projection when we generalize the inner product and change our concept of orthogonality accordingly:

Concept	Vector Space: Euclidean, $\mathbb{E}^N$	Vector Space: Generalization
Vectors	$\mathbf{z}_1, \mathbf{z}_2 \in \mathbb{R}^N$	
Zero vector	$[0; n = 1, \ldots, N]'$	
Vector addition	$\mathbf{z}_1 + \mathbf{z}_2 = [z_{1n} + z_{2n}; n = 1, \ldots, N]'$	
Scalar multiplication	$\alpha \cdot \mathbf{z}_1 = [\alpha \mathbf{z}_{1n}]', \ \alpha \in \mathbb{R}$	
Inner product	$\mathbf{z}_1'\mathbf{z}_2$	$\mathbf{z}_1'\mathbf{A}\mathbf{z}_2$
Length	$\sqrt{\mathbf{z}_1'\mathbf{z}_1}$	$\sqrt{\mathbf{z}_1'\mathbf{A}\mathbf{z}_1}$
Orthogonal projector onto Col($\mathbf{X}$)	$\mathbf{P}_\mathbf{X} = \mathbf{X}\left(\mathbf{X}'\mathbf{X}\right)^{-1}\mathbf{X}'$	$\mathbf{P}_{\mathbf{X}\perp\mathbf{A}\mathbf{X}} = \mathbf{X}\left(\mathbf{X}'\mathbf{A}\mathbf{X}\right)^{-1}\mathbf{X}'\mathbf{A}$

4.7 EXERCISES

4.7.1 Review

4.1 Show that $\hat{\boldsymbol{\beta}}_\mathrm{R}$ in Proposition 3 lies in a vector subspace of $\mathbb{R}^K$ of dimension M when $\mathbf{s} = \mathbf{0}$.

4.2 Show the equivalence of three ways to write the fitted RLS coefficients (for $\mathbf{s} = \mathbf{0}$):

$$\begin{aligned}\hat{\boldsymbol{\beta}}_\mathrm{R} &= \underset{\boldsymbol{\beta}\in\mathrm{Col}(\mathbf{S})}{\operatorname{argmin}} \|\mathbf{y} - \mathbf{X}\boldsymbol{\beta}\|^2 \\ &= \underset{\boldsymbol{\beta}\in\mathrm{Col}(\mathbf{S})}{\operatorname{argmin}} \left\|\hat{\boldsymbol{\mu}} - \mathbf{X}\boldsymbol{\beta}\right\|^2 \\ &= \underset{\boldsymbol{\beta}\in\mathrm{Col}(\mathbf{S})}{\operatorname{argmin}} \left(\hat{\boldsymbol{\beta}} - \boldsymbol{\beta}\right)'\mathbf{X}'\mathbf{X}\left(\hat{\boldsymbol{\beta}} - \boldsymbol{\beta}\right)\end{aligned}$$

4.3 **(Generalized Inner Product)** Given $\mathbf{A} = \mathbf{C}'\mathbf{C}$, where $\mathbf{C}$ is a nonsingular, real $N \times N$ matrix, show that for $\mathbf{x}, \mathbf{y} \in \mathbb{R}^N$

(a) $\mathbf{x}'\mathbf{A}\mathbf{y}$ has the properties of an inner product, and

(b) $\sqrt{\mathbf{x}'\mathbf{A}\mathbf{x}}$ has the properties of a norm.[11]

4.4 Suppose that $\mathbf{X}$ is column rank deficient, but $\mathbf{X}_1$ is full-column rank and $\mathrm{Col}(\mathbf{X}) = \mathrm{Col}(\mathbf{X}_1)$. Given that $\mathbf{A}$ is nonsingular, find an expression for $\mathbf{P}_{\mathbf{X}\perp\mathbf{A}\mathbf{X}}$.

4.5 **(Generalized Pythagorean Theorem)** Let $\mathbf{A}$ be a nonsingular symmetric matrix such that $\mathbf{z}'\mathbf{A}\mathbf{z} > 0$ for all $\mathbf{z} \in \mathbb{R}^N$, $\mathbf{z} \neq \mathbf{0}$. Confirm that $\mathbf{X}'\mathbf{A}\mathbf{X}$ is nonsingular and that

$$\begin{aligned}(\mathbf{y} - \boldsymbol{\mu})'\mathbf{A}(\mathbf{y} - \boldsymbol{\mu}) =& \mathbf{y}'\left(\mathbf{I} - \mathbf{P}_{\mathbf{X}\perp\mathbf{A}\mathbf{X}}\right)\mathbf{A}\left(\mathbf{I} - \mathbf{P}_{\mathbf{X}\perp\mathbf{A}\mathbf{X}}\right)\mathbf{y} \\ &+ \left[\mathbf{P}_{\mathbf{X}\perp\mathbf{A}\mathbf{X}}(\mathbf{y} - \boldsymbol{\mu})\right]'\mathbf{A}\left[\mathbf{P}_{\mathbf{X}\perp\mathbf{A}\mathbf{X}}(\mathbf{y} - \boldsymbol{\mu})\right]\end{aligned} \tag{4.19}$$

if $\boldsymbol{\mu} \in \mathrm{Col}(\mathbf{X})$.

[11] For review of these concepts of linear algebra, see Definitions C.16 (p. 852) and Definition C.21 (p. 855).

4.6 (Generalized Projection) Using the conditions and result of Exercise 4.5, show that

$$\mathbf{P}_{\mathbf{X}\perp\mathbf{AX}}\mathbf{y} = \underset{\boldsymbol{\mu}\in\text{Col}(\mathbf{X})}{\text{argmin}}\,(\mathbf{y}-\boldsymbol{\mu})'\mathbf{A}(\mathbf{y}-\boldsymbol{\mu})$$

where

$$\mathbf{P}_{\mathbf{X}\perp\mathbf{AX}} = \mathbf{X}(\mathbf{X}'\mathbf{AX})^{-1}\mathbf{X}'\mathbf{A}$$

Show furthermore that $\hat{\boldsymbol{\mu}} \equiv \mathbf{P}_{\mathbf{X}\perp\mathbf{AX}}\mathbf{y} = \mathbf{X}\hat{\boldsymbol{\beta}}$ implies that

$$\hat{\boldsymbol{\beta}} = (\mathbf{X}'\mathbf{AX})^{-1}\mathbf{X}'\mathbf{Ay}$$

4.7 (Partitioned Fit) In the previous chapter, we note in (3.16) that

$$\hat{\boldsymbol{\beta}}_1 = \left[\mathbf{X}_1'\left(\mathbf{I}-\mathbf{P}_{\mathbf{X}_2}\right)\mathbf{X}_1\right]^{-1}\mathbf{X}_1'\left(\mathbf{I}-\mathbf{P}_{\mathbf{X}_2}\right)\mathbf{y}$$

is the solution to

$$\min_{\boldsymbol{\beta}_1}\,(\mathbf{y}-\mathbf{X}_1\boldsymbol{\beta}_1)'\left(\mathbf{I}-\mathbf{P}_{\mathbf{X}_2}\right)(\mathbf{y}-\mathbf{X}_1\boldsymbol{\beta}_1)$$

if $\mathbf{X}$ is full-(column) rank.

(a) Exercise 4.6 does not imply this. Why not?

(b) Show that it is true nevertheless. (HINT: Recall that $\mathbf{I}-\mathbf{P}_{\mathbf{X}_2}$ is symmetric and idempotent.)

4.8 Compare the argument showing that $\hat{\boldsymbol{\beta}}_{\text{R}} = \text{argmin}_{\{\boldsymbol{\beta}|\boldsymbol{\beta}=\mathbf{S}\boldsymbol{\gamma}+\mathbf{s}\}}\left\|\hat{\boldsymbol{\mu}}-\mathbf{X}\boldsymbol{\beta}\right\|^2$ with equation (4.10) with the derivation of $\hat{\boldsymbol{\beta}}_1 = \text{argmin}_{\boldsymbol{\beta}_1}\|\mathbf{y}_{\perp 2}-\mathbf{X}_{1\perp 2}\boldsymbol{\beta}_1\|^2$ starting on page 61.

4.9 Reconsider the restricted OLS program

$$\min_{\boldsymbol{\mu}\in\text{Col}(\mathbf{XS})}\|\mathbf{y}-\boldsymbol{\mu}\|^2$$

Show that for $\boldsymbol{\mu}\in\text{Col}(\mathbf{X})$

$$\|\mathbf{y}-\boldsymbol{\mu}\|^2 = \left\|\mathbf{y}-\hat{\boldsymbol{\mu}}\right\|^2 + \left\|\hat{\boldsymbol{\mu}}-\boldsymbol{\mu}\right\|^2$$

For $\mathbf{s}=\mathbf{0}$, use this result to show that

$$\begin{aligned}\hat{\boldsymbol{\mu}}_{\text{R}} &= \underset{\boldsymbol{\mu}\in\text{Col}(\mathbf{XS})}{\text{argmin}}\left\|\hat{\boldsymbol{\mu}}-\boldsymbol{\mu}\right\|^2\\ &= \mathbf{P}_{\mathbf{XS}}\hat{\boldsymbol{\mu}}\end{aligned}$$

4.10 Consider restricted OLS where $N=2$, $K=1$, as in Example 4.8, but

$$\mathbf{X} = \begin{bmatrix}1 & 2\\ 2 & 1\end{bmatrix}$$

and the restrictions state that $\beta_1=\beta_2$.

(a) Find the restricted RHS $\mathbf{XS}\boldsymbol{\gamma}$.

(b) Find the restricted and unrestricted OLS fitted coefficients.

(c) Derive and graph an ellipse representing a level set for the squared generalized distance

$$\left\|\boldsymbol{\beta}-\hat{\boldsymbol{\beta}}\right\|^2_{\mathbf{X}'\mathbf{X}} = \left(\hat{\boldsymbol{\beta}}-\boldsymbol{\beta}\right)'\mathbf{X}'\mathbf{X}\left(\hat{\boldsymbol{\beta}}-\boldsymbol{\beta}\right)$$

similar to Figure 4.2.

(d) Also find and graph the projection from $\hat{\boldsymbol{\beta}}$ to $\hat{\boldsymbol{\beta}}_{\text{R}}$.

4.11 (RLS) Show each equality for the RLS program that follows:

$$\begin{aligned}\hat{\boldsymbol{\mu}}_{\mathrm{R}} &= \underset{\boldsymbol{\mu}\in\mathrm{Col}(\mathbf{XS})+\mathbf{Xs}}{\operatorname{argmin}} \|\mathbf{y}-\boldsymbol{\mu}\|^2 \\ &= \left(\underset{\mathbf{m}\in\mathrm{Col}(\mathbf{XS})}{\operatorname{argmin}} \|\mathbf{y}-\mathbf{Xs}-\mathbf{m}\|^2\right)+\mathbf{Xs} \\ &= \mathbf{P}_{\mathbf{XS}}(\mathbf{y}-\mathbf{Xs})+\mathbf{Xs} \\ &= \mathbf{P}_{\mathbf{XS}}\mathbf{y}+(\mathbf{I}-\mathbf{P}_{\mathbf{XS}})\,\mathbf{Xs}\end{aligned}$$

4.12 Explain why Assumption 3.1 (Full Rank, p. 53) is not necessary for Proposition 3 (Restricted Least Squares). Explain that constraining $\boldsymbol{\beta} = \mathbf{S}\boldsymbol{\gamma} + \mathbf{s}$ can be a method of selecting unique fitted coefficients when $\mathbf{X}$ is not full rank.

4.7.2 Extensions

4.13 (Generalized Duality) The dual problem to the generalized minimum-distance program

$$\min_{\mathbf{z}\in\mathrm{Col}(\mathbf{X})} \|\mathbf{y}-\mathbf{z}\|_{\mathbf{A}}^2$$

is

$$\min_{\mathbf{z}\in\mathrm{Col}^{\perp}(\mathbf{X})} \|\mathbf{y}-\mathbf{z}\|_{\mathbf{A}}^2$$

Prove that the solution to the generalized dual problem is

$$(\mathbf{I}-\mathbf{P}_{\mathbf{A}^{-1}\mathbf{X}\perp\mathbf{X}})\,\mathbf{y} = \underset{\mathbf{z}\in\mathrm{Col}^{\perp}(\mathbf{X})}{\operatorname{argmin}} \|\mathbf{y}-\mathbf{z}\|_{\mathbf{A}}^2$$

where $\mathbf{A}$ is a nonsingular symmetric matrix such that $\mathbf{z}'\mathbf{A}\mathbf{z} \geq 0$ for all conformable $\mathbf{z}$. Compare this solution with the Euclidean dual in Exercise 2.27.

4.14 (Dual to RLS) In this exercise, one shows that the RLS solution (4.2) also has the general form

$$\hat{\boldsymbol{\beta}}_{\mathrm{R}} = \underset{\mathbf{R}\boldsymbol{\beta}=\mathbf{r}}{\operatorname{argmin}} \|\mathbf{y}-\mathbf{X}\boldsymbol{\beta}\|^2 \tag{4.20}$$

where $\mathbf{R}$ is a $(K-M)\times K$ matrix, $\mathbf{r}$ is a $(K-M)\times 1$ vector of known constants, and $\mathrm{rank}(\mathbf{R}) = K-M$ so that there are no redundant or mutually exclusive restrictions.

(a) Show that $\mathbf{R}\boldsymbol{\beta} = \mathbf{r}$ can always be written in the form $\boldsymbol{\beta} = \mathbf{S}\boldsymbol{\gamma} + \mathbf{s}$. (HINT: Show that we can always order and partition the elements of $\boldsymbol{\beta}$ and $\mathbf{R}$ so that

$$\mathbf{R}\boldsymbol{\beta} = \mathbf{R}_1\boldsymbol{\beta}_1 + \mathbf{R}_2\boldsymbol{\beta}_2 = \mathbf{r}$$

$\mathbf{R}_1$ is nonsingular, and $\boldsymbol{\beta}_2$ has M elements.)

(b) Show also that the regression problem can always be rewritten so that we may take $\mathbf{s} = \mathbf{0}$ and $\mathbf{r} = \mathbf{0}$.

(c) Let $\mathbf{r} = \mathbf{0}$ and show that (4.20) can also be written as

$$\begin{aligned}\hat{\boldsymbol{\beta}}_{\mathrm{R}} &= \underset{\boldsymbol{\beta}\in\mathrm{Col}^{\perp}(\mathbf{R}')}{\operatorname{argmin}} \left\|\hat{\boldsymbol{\mu}}-\mathbf{X}\boldsymbol{\beta}\right\|^2 \\ &= \underset{\boldsymbol{\beta}\in\mathrm{Col}^{\perp}(\mathbf{R}')}{\operatorname{argmin}} \left\|\hat{\boldsymbol{\beta}}-\boldsymbol{\beta}\right\|_{\mathbf{X}'\mathbf{X}}^2\end{aligned}$$

Use the result of Exercise 4.13 to show that when $\mathbf{r} = \mathbf{0}$,

$$\hat{\boldsymbol{\beta}}_{\text{R}} = \hat{\boldsymbol{\beta}} - (\mathbf{X}'\mathbf{X})^{-1}\mathbf{R}'\left[\mathbf{R}(\mathbf{X}'\mathbf{X})^{-1}\mathbf{R}'\right]^{-1}\mathbf{R}\hat{\boldsymbol{\beta}}$$

(d) Show that when $\mathbf{r} \neq \mathbf{0}$, the solution for $\hat{\boldsymbol{\beta}}_{\text{R}}$ is

$$\begin{aligned}\hat{\boldsymbol{\beta}}_{\text{R}} &= \underset{\boldsymbol{\beta}\in\text{Col}^{\perp}(\mathbf{R}')+\mathbf{R}'(\mathbf{R}\mathbf{R}')^{-1}\mathbf{r}}{\operatorname{argmin}} \left\|\hat{\boldsymbol{\beta}} - \boldsymbol{\beta}\right\|^2_{\mathbf{X}'\mathbf{X}} \\ &= \left(\mathbf{I} - \mathbf{P}_{(\mathbf{X}'\mathbf{X})^{-1}\mathbf{R}'\perp\mathbf{R}'}\right)\hat{\boldsymbol{\beta}} + \mathbf{P}_{(\mathbf{X}'\mathbf{X})^{-1}\mathbf{R}'\perp\mathbf{R}'}\mathbf{R}'(\mathbf{R}\mathbf{R}')^{-1}\mathbf{r} \\ &= \hat{\boldsymbol{\beta}} - (\mathbf{X}'\mathbf{X})^{-1}\mathbf{R}'\left[\mathbf{R}(\mathbf{X}'\mathbf{X})^{-1}\mathbf{R}'\right]^{-1}\left(\mathbf{R}\hat{\boldsymbol{\beta}} - \mathbf{r}\right)\end{aligned} \tag{4.21}$$

4.15 (Lagrangian Derivation of RLS) The solution (4.20) can also be derived by the method of Lagrange.[12] Let $\boldsymbol{\lambda}$ be a vector of M Lagrange multipliers for the M restrictions. The Lagrangian is

$$\mathfrak{L} = \frac{1}{2}(\mathbf{y} - \mathbf{X}\boldsymbol{\beta})'(\mathbf{y} - \mathbf{X}\boldsymbol{\beta}) + \boldsymbol{\lambda}'(\mathbf{R}\boldsymbol{\beta} - \mathbf{r})$$

(a) Show that the first-order conditions are

$$\mathbf{0} = -\mathbf{X}'\left(\mathbf{y} - \mathbf{X}\hat{\boldsymbol{\beta}}_{\text{R}}\right) + \mathbf{R}'\hat{\boldsymbol{\lambda}}_{\text{R}} \tag{4.22}$$

$$\mathbf{0} = \mathbf{R}\hat{\boldsymbol{\beta}}_{\text{R}} - \mathbf{r} \tag{4.23}$$

(b) Show that

$$\hat{\boldsymbol{\lambda}}_{\text{R}} = \left[\mathbf{R}(\mathbf{X}'\mathbf{X})^{-1}\mathbf{R}'\right]^{-1}(\mathbf{R}\hat{\boldsymbol{\beta}} - \mathbf{r}) \tag{4.24}$$

and solve for $\hat{\boldsymbol{\beta}}_{\text{R}}$.

(c) Economists are particularly fond of the method of Lagrange because Lagrange multipliers can be interpreted as "shadow prices" of constraints. Show that the shadow price of a constraint that is satisfied by $\hat{\boldsymbol{\beta}}$ is zero.

***4.16 (Recursive Updating)** Given $\mathbf{X} = [\mathbf{x}_1, \ldots, \mathbf{x}_N]'$ and $\mathbf{y} = [y_1, \ldots, y_N]'$ [$N \geq \text{rank}(\mathbf{X})$], suppose that one receives a new observation $(\mathbf{x}_{N+1}, y_{N+1})$. Show that the OLS fitted coefficients can be updated by the formula

$$\hat{\boldsymbol{\beta}}_{[N+1]} = \hat{\boldsymbol{\beta}}_{[N]} + (\mathbf{X}'\mathbf{X})^{-1}\mathbf{x}_{N+1}\frac{y_{N+1} - \mathbf{x}'_{N+1}\hat{\boldsymbol{\beta}}_{[N]}}{1 + \mathbf{x}'_{N+1}(\mathbf{X}'\mathbf{X})^{-1}\mathbf{x}_{N+1}}$$

where $\hat{\boldsymbol{\beta}}_{[N]} \equiv (\mathbf{X}'\mathbf{X})^{-1}\mathbf{X}'\mathbf{y}$. [HINT: Consider updating as restricted OLS applied to the unrestricted OLS fit for the RHS

$$\begin{bmatrix}\mathbf{X} & 0 \\ 0 & \mathbf{x}'_{N+1}\end{bmatrix}\begin{bmatrix}\boldsymbol{\beta}_1 \\ \boldsymbol{\beta}_2\end{bmatrix}$$

which permits the $(N+1)$th observation to have different coefficients from the previous N observations and use the matrix inverse identity in Exercise 3.22.]

[12] For an introduction to Lagrangians, see Simon and Blume (1994, Theorem 18.2).

4.17 It is tempting to view

$$(\mathbf{y}-\mathbf{X}_1\boldsymbol{\beta}_1)'\left(\mathbf{I}-\mathbf{P}_{\mathbf{X}_2}\right)(\mathbf{y}-\mathbf{X}_1\boldsymbol{\beta}_1)$$

as a generalized distance [see (3.15) on p. 62). Although it is true that

$$\mathbf{z}'\left(\mathbf{I}-\mathbf{P}_{\mathbf{X}_2}\right)\mathbf{z}=\mathbf{z}'\left(\mathbf{I}-\mathbf{P}_{\mathbf{X}_2}\right)'\left(\mathbf{I}-\mathbf{P}_{\mathbf{X}_2}\right)\mathbf{z}=\left\|\left(\mathbf{I}-\mathbf{P}_{\mathbf{X}_2}\right)\mathbf{z}\right\|^2\geq 0$$

note that $\mathbf{I}-\mathbf{P}_{\mathbf{X}_2}$ is singular.

(a) Show that $\sqrt{\mathbf{w}'\left(\mathbf{I}-\mathbf{P}_{\mathbf{X}_2}\right)\mathbf{w}}$ is not a norm on $\mathbb{R}^N$ by describing a $\mathbf{w}\neq\mathbf{0}$ in $\mathbb{R}^N$ such that $\mathbf{w}'\left(\mathbf{I}-\mathbf{P}_{\mathbf{X}_2}\right)\mathbf{w}=0$.

(b) More generally, consider an orthogonal projector $\mathbf{P}$ onto a subspace of $\mathbb{R}^N$. Argue that $\|\cdot\|_{\mathbf{P}}$ is a norm on Col($\mathbf{P}$), but not on $\mathbb{R}^N$ unless $\mathbf{P}=\mathbf{I}_N$.

(c) Show that if rank($\mathbf{X}$) = rank($\mathbf{PX}$) then

$$\underset{\boldsymbol{\mu}\in\text{Col}(\mathbf{X})}{\text{argmin}}\,(\mathbf{y}-\boldsymbol{\mu})'\mathbf{P}(\mathbf{y}-\boldsymbol{\mu})$$

is one to one with

$$\underset{\boldsymbol{\mu}_*\in\text{Col}(\mathbf{X}_*)}{\text{argmin}}\,(\mathbf{y}_*-\boldsymbol{\mu}_*)'(\mathbf{y}_*-\boldsymbol{\mu}_*)$$

where $\mathbf{y}_*=\mathbf{Py}$, $\boldsymbol{\mu}_*=\mathbf{P}\boldsymbol{\mu}$, and $\mathbf{X}_*=\mathbf{PX}$.

(d) Show that

$$\mathbf{P}_{\mathbf{X}_*}\mathbf{y}_*=\underset{\boldsymbol{\mu}_*\in\text{Col}(\mathbf{X}_*)}{\text{argmin}}\,(\mathbf{y}_*-\boldsymbol{\mu}_*)'(\mathbf{y}_*-\boldsymbol{\mu}_*)$$

and

$$\mathbf{P}_{\mathbf{X}\perp\mathbf{PX}}\mathbf{y}=\underset{\boldsymbol{\mu}\in\text{Col}(\mathbf{X})}{\text{argmin}}\,(\mathbf{y}-\boldsymbol{\mu})'\mathbf{P}(\mathbf{y}-\boldsymbol{\mu})$$

4.18 Show that

$$\begin{aligned}\left\|\hat{\boldsymbol{\mu}}-\hat{\boldsymbol{\mu}}_{\text{R}}\right\|^2&=\left\|\hat{\boldsymbol{\beta}}-\hat{\boldsymbol{\beta}}_{\text{R}}\right\|^2_{\mathbf{X}'\mathbf{X}}\\&=\left(\mathbf{R}\hat{\boldsymbol{\beta}}-\mathbf{r}\right)'\left[\mathbf{R}\left(\mathbf{X}'\mathbf{X}\right)^{-1}\mathbf{R}'\right]^{-1}\left(\mathbf{R}\hat{\boldsymbol{\beta}}-\mathbf{r}\right)\end{aligned}$$

using (4.21) in Exercise 4.14. Give an interpretation of the final right-hand side expression in terms of the generalization of Euclidean length described in Section 4.5.

CHAPTER 5

Overview of Ordinary Least Squares

5.1 GEOMETRIC THEORY

Starting with the concepts of

1. a vector space,
2. linear dependence, a basis, dimension of a vector space,
3. an inner product, length of a vector, and orthogonality,

we have developed the idea of a projection as the solution to a minimum-distance problem. The OLS problem

$$\min_{\boldsymbol{\beta}} \|\mathbf{y} - \mathbf{X}\boldsymbol{\beta}\|^2$$

is a minimum-distance problem in which we seek the element of the subspace $\mathrm{Col}(\mathbf{X})$ that is closest to the vector $\mathbf{y}$. The dimension of this subspace determines the uniqueness of the solution in $\boldsymbol{\beta}$. The optimal fitted values of $\mathbf{X}\boldsymbol{\beta}$, however, are always unique. They are given by

$$\hat{\boldsymbol{\mu}} = \mathbf{P_X y} = \underset{\boldsymbol{\mu} \in \mathrm{Col}(\mathbf{X})}{\mathrm{argmin}} \|\mathbf{y} - \boldsymbol{\mu}\|^2$$

where $\mathbf{P_X}$ is the orthogonal projector onto $\mathrm{Col}(\mathbf{X})$, so that $\mathbf{y} - \hat{\boldsymbol{\mu}} \in \mathrm{Col}^{\perp}(\mathbf{X})$.

The orthogonal projector $\mathbf{P_X}$ is a geometric concept; it is a one-to-one function of the *subspace* $\mathrm{Col}(\mathbf{X})$, not the *matrix* $\mathbf{X}$. If $\mathbf{X}$ is full-column rank, then *one* functional form for $\mathbf{P_X}$ is

$$\mathbf{P_X} = \mathbf{X}\left(\mathbf{X}'\mathbf{X}\right)^{-1}\mathbf{X}' \tag{5.1}$$

Thus we can interpret OLS as a two-step procedure. In the first step, one obtains the orthogonal projection $\mathbf{P_X y}$ of $\mathbf{y}$ onto $\mathrm{Col}(\mathbf{X})$. In the second step, if $\mathbf{X}$ is full rank, one decomposes this vector into the components determined by the basis in $\mathbf{X}$: $\hat{\boldsymbol{\beta}} = (\mathbf{X}'\mathbf{X})^{-1}\mathbf{X}'\mathbf{P}_{\mathbf{X}}\mathbf{y}$. The two steps combine to yield $\hat{\boldsymbol{\beta}} = (\mathbf{X}'\mathbf{X})^{-1}\mathbf{X}'\mathbf{y}$.

But if there is multicollinearity among the column vectors in $\mathbf{X}$, then given a basis for $\mathrm{Col}(\mathbf{X})$, say the column vectors of $\mathbf{X}_1$, we alter (5.1) to

$$\mathbf{P}_{\mathbf{X}} = \mathbf{X}_1\left(\mathbf{X}_1'\mathbf{X}_1\right)^{-1}\mathbf{X}_1$$

No matter what basis we use, we obtain the same projector because it is unique. Indeed, we can even derive such a basis using the orthogonal projector, by recursively applying the projector to identify linearly independent vectors in $\mathrm{Col}(\mathbf{X})$. Furthermore, we can even make this basis orthonormal. Then we obtain

$$\mathbf{P}_{\mathbf{X}} = \mathbf{P}_{\mathbf{R}} = \mathbf{R}\mathbf{R}'$$

where the column vectors of $\mathbf{R}$ comprise the orthonormal basis.

We generalized orthogonal projection for the partitioned model, where $\mathbf{X}\boldsymbol{\beta} = \mathbf{X}_1\boldsymbol{\beta}_1 + \mathbf{X}_2\boldsymbol{\beta}_2$. We saw that

$$\hat{\boldsymbol{\mu}}_1 \equiv \mathbf{X}_1\hat{\boldsymbol{\beta}}_1 = \mathbf{X}_1\left(\mathbf{X}_{1\perp 2}'\mathbf{X}_1\right)^{-1}\mathbf{X}_{1\perp 2}'\mathbf{y}$$

where

$$\mathbf{X}_{1\perp 2} \equiv \left(\mathbf{I} - \mathbf{P}_{\mathbf{X}_2}\right)\mathbf{X}_1$$
$$\mathbf{P}_{\mathbf{X}_2} \equiv \mathbf{X}_2\left(\mathbf{X}_2'\mathbf{X}_2\right)^{-1}\mathbf{X}_2'$$

The projector

$$\mathbf{P}_{12} = \mathbf{X}_1\left(\mathbf{X}_{1\perp 2}'\mathbf{X}_1\right)^{-1}\mathbf{X}_{1\perp 2}'$$

preserves elements of $\mathrm{Col}(\mathbf{X}_1)$ and annihilates $\mathrm{Col}^{\perp}(\mathbf{X}_{1\perp 2}) = \mathrm{Col}(\mathbf{X}_2) \oplus \mathrm{Col}^{\perp}(\mathbf{X})$, thereby isolating $\hat{\boldsymbol{\mu}}_1$. We can also write

$$\hat{\boldsymbol{\mu}}_1 = \mathbf{X}_1\left(\mathbf{X}_{1\perp 2}'\mathbf{X}_1\right)^{-1}\mathbf{X}_{1\perp 2}'\hat{\boldsymbol{\mu}}$$

because $\mathbf{y} - \hat{\boldsymbol{\mu}} \in \mathrm{Col}^{\perp}(\mathbf{X})$ so that $\mathbf{P}_{12}\left(\mathbf{y} - \hat{\boldsymbol{\mu}}\right) = 0$. In this case, the annihilation of $\hat{\boldsymbol{\mu}}_2$ corresponds to a movement onto $\mathrm{Col}(\mathbf{X}_1)$ along $\mathrm{Col}(\mathbf{X}_2)$. A general form for the projector onto $\mathrm{Col}(\mathbf{X})$ along $\mathrm{Col}^{\perp}(\mathbf{Z})$, denoted $\mathbf{P}_{\mathbf{X}\perp Z}$, is

$$\mathbf{P}_{\mathbf{X}\perp Z} = \mathbf{X}\left(\mathbf{Z}'\mathbf{X}\right)^{-1}\mathbf{Z}' \tag{5.2}$$

if $\mathbf{Z}'\mathbf{X}$ is nonsingular. The orthogonal projector $\mathbf{P}_{\mathbf{X}} \equiv \mathbf{P}_{\mathbf{X}\perp\mathbf{X}}$ is a special case.

Such projectors also arise in the restricted least-squares problem:

$$\hat{\boldsymbol{\beta}}_{\mathrm{R}} \equiv \underset{\boldsymbol{\beta}=\mathbf{S}\boldsymbol{\gamma}+\mathbf{s}}{\mathrm{argmin}}\, \|\mathbf{y} - \mathbf{X}\boldsymbol{\beta}\|^2 = \mathbf{P}_{\mathbf{S}\perp\mathbf{X}'\mathbf{X}\mathbf{S}}\left(\hat{\boldsymbol{\beta}} - \mathbf{s}\right) + \mathbf{s}$$

In this case, $\mathbf{XS}$ must be full rank. The general projector provides the unique solution to the generalized minimum-distance problem

$$\hat{\boldsymbol{\beta}}_{\mathrm{R}} = \underset{\boldsymbol{\beta}\in\mathrm{Col}(\mathbf{S})+\mathbf{s}}{\mathrm{argmin}} \left\|\hat{\boldsymbol{\beta}} - \boldsymbol{\beta}\right\|_{\mathbf{X}'\mathbf{X}}^2$$

where

$$\left\|\hat{\beta}-\beta\right\|_{\mathbf{X}'\mathbf{X}}^2 \equiv \left(\hat{\beta}-\beta\right)'\mathbf{X}'\mathbf{X}\left(\hat{\beta}-\beta\right)$$

This is one example of a general solution that we can write as

$$\mathbf{P}_{\mathbf{X}\perp\mathbf{A}\mathbf{X}}\mathbf{y} = \underset{\mu\in\mathrm{Col}(\mathbf{X})}{\operatorname{argmin}} \|\mathbf{y}-\mu\|_{\mathbf{A}}^2$$

for any nonsingular matrix $\mathbf{A}$ such that $\mathbf{z}'\mathbf{A}\mathbf{z} > 0$ for all $\mathbf{z} \neq \mathbf{0}$, $\mathbf{z} \in \mathbb{R}^N$.

We will encounter the projector (5.2) in several new ways in later parts of this book. As we noted, if a generalization of $\mathbb{E}^N$ is constructed, then such projectors are the orthogonal projectors in that space. In the next part of this book, we will introduce yet another vector space, one consisting of vectors that are random variables, and projections in that vector space.

5.2 ECONOMETRIC SPECIFICATIONS

We also introduced, through our examples, several common, useful specifications for linear models.

1. **Indicators:** Indicator, or "dummy," RHS variables capture such discrete characteristics as the gender, race, or union status of an earner. We also used indicator variables to fit monthly seasonal variations in the national unemployment rate.

2. **Polynomial RHS variables:** Although the RHS function is linear in the coefficients and variables in $\mathbf{X}$, the RHS need not be linear in such a variable as experience in the labor force. One of the simplest ways to introduce nonlinearity is to include polynomial functions of such variables as RHS variables. For example, economists frequently include the square of experience as an RHS variable for the study of earnings. So-called "interactions" also introduce nonlinearity.

   Interactions with indicator variables also provide a method to provide differences in the RHS function for subsamples. We interacted (multiplied) an indicator for salaried earners with all of the RHS variables of the earnings function to permit changes in the coefficients for salaried earners and hourly-wage earners.

3. **Lagged dependent LHS variables:** In the study of such time series as the unemployment rate, so-called "lagged" values of the LHS variable serve as RHS variables to capture dynamics. Such specifications comprise a complex set of functions and we return to them in Chapter 20.

4. **Transformed LHS variables:** Just as one is not restricted to linear functions on the RHS, one can transform the LHS variable to obtain a new, nonlinear relationship with the RHS variables. Economists usually transform earnings with the natural logarithmic function. There are several reasons for this, and one is that the fitted coefficients can be interpreted as elasticities.

5.3 ECONOMETRIC METHOD

In this part, we have illustrated several informal uses for OLS fitted equations.

1. **Decomposition of variation:** Each OLS fitted coefficient provides a measure of the change in the LHS variable as the RHS variable changes among the observations, supposing that the values of the other RHS variables do not change. Generally, of course, the other RHS variables do change over a sequence of observations in a data set. In this sense, OLS offers a method of decomposing the overall changes in the LHS variable as several RHS variables change simultaneously from observation to observation.

   For example, we noted that men and women obtain different average levels of education and we used the OLS fit of log-earnings on an indicator for gender and a schooling variable (among other RHS variables) to describe the change in wages with schooling separately from changes in wages with gender.

2. **Exploring conjectures:** Besides summarizing patterns among observations, one may want to compare those patterns with conjectures about what one would find in the sample. Does the return in additional earnings to experience fall over a profile of earners of various ages, as some theories predict? Do unions raise earnings or do the characteristics of union members account for wage differentials?

3. **Forecasting:** OLS can be used as a naive forecasting tool.

All of these uses were informal in the sense that we left the goals of the data analysis vague and we gave the motivation for using OLS as convenience and intelligibility. If we have a more refined purpose, then we will want our method of analysis to serve that purpose. Any attempt to choose our method leads inevitably to making assumptions about the data we observe and the relationship of the data to our purpose. What does an OLS fit imply about gender discrimination? We begin to present formalizations of purposes and assumptions in the next part of this book.

PART II

LINEAR REGRESSION

This part of the book weds statistical methodology to the OLS technique. The fundamental difference between what has gone before and what is to come is that we build our analysis on probabilistic assumptions about the way the data are generated.

All of our previous analysis of OLS focused on geometric properties of the procedure. Such properties describe the nature of the fit and help us understand how OLS summarizes an entire data set. But these properties do not answer another set of questions encountered by those who collect and analyze data: what do the data "say" about the process that generated them? What can be inferred about the world in general from particular observations? Under what conditions is OLS useful for such inference? The rest of this book describes some of the ways statisticians and econometricians have narrowed these questions so that answers could be obtained. This part of the book focuses on generalizing the OLS analysis to such questions.

We assume that the reader is familiar with such concepts from probability as mean and variance and such basic statistical theory as estimation of a population mean and hypothesis testing for equality of the population means of two sampling experiments.

Let us summarize the simple location model in which the average is the central statistic. We intend this summary to be a brief review of material that is already familiar to the reader and to establish a common point of departure for the rest of this part of the book. Many of the concepts and results that one meets in this model have counterparts in the linear regression model and an increased understanding of linear regression will result from keeping the analysis of the location model in mind.

In the simple location model, interest focuses on the marginal mean of a random variable Y. Inference follows from a random sample of observations of Y, denoted $\{y_1, \ldots, y_N\}$. All statistical inference rests on assumptions or beliefs about the process that generates the sample data set. The classical assumptions are listed in Table II.1. The entries of the table follow the order in which the assumptions are often considered. The consequences in the second column follow from all the assumptions listed in the corresponding row in the table and the rows above.

Table II.1
Summary of Assumptions and Results for the Location Model

Assumptions	Results
$\mathrm{E}[y_n] = \beta_0$	• $\mathrm{E}[\hat{\beta}] = \beta_0$ for $\hat{\beta} = N^{-1}\sum_{n=1}^{N} y_n \equiv \bar{y}$
$\mathrm{Var}[y_n] = \sigma_0^2$, $\mathrm{Cov}[y_n, y_m] = 0$, $n \neq m$	• $\mathrm{Var}[\hat{\beta}] = \sigma_0^2/N$ • $\mathrm{E}[s^2] = \sigma_0^2$, where $s^2 = \sum_{n=1}^{N}(y_n - \bar{y})^2/(N-1)$ • $\hat{\beta}$ is a minimum variance linear unbiased estimator
$y_n \sim \mathfrak{N}(\beta_0, \sigma_0^2)$	• $\sqrt{N}(\hat{\beta} - \beta_0)/\sigma_0 \xrightarrow{d} \mathfrak{N}(0, 1)$ • $\hat{\beta} \sim \mathfrak{N}(\beta_0, \sigma_0^2/N)$ • $s^2 \sim \chi_{N-1}^2 \sigma_0^2/(N-1)$ • $\hat{\beta}$ and s^2 are independent • $[\hat{\beta}, (N-1)s^2/N]$ is the maximum likelihood estimator

Note especially that this analysis rests largely on the simple mathematical structure of the statistic $\hat{\beta}$, which is the average of the $\{y_n\}$. In mathematical terms, $\bar{y}$ is a *linear* function of the $\{y_n\}$. Because $\hat{\beta}$ is a sum of random variables, its mean and its variance are relatively easy to derive. This linearity is also fundamental to the normality of $\hat{\beta}$ under the assumption of normally distributed $\{y_n\}$: sums of normal random variables are also normally distributed.

The results involving s^2 are somewhat paradoxical. This statistic is the sum of squared, normally distributed, random variables—just as one would expect for a chi-square random variable. However, there are N, not $N-1$, elements in the sum; one might expect the degrees of freedom to be N instead of $N-1$. Furthermore, the normal random variables $\{y_n - \hat{\beta}\}$ are not independently distributed, as the standard motivation of a chi-square distribution requires. In fact, the resolution of the paradox lies in accounting for this dependence. The independence of s^2 and $\hat{\beta}$ is a second surprise. One might casually predict that these statistics are dependently distributed because they both depend on $\{y_n; n = 1, \ldots, N\}$. But, of course, this turns out to be incorrect.

It may be convenient to remember the connections between assumptions and consequences in terms of the nature of each assumption. The first is an assumption about the *first moment* of the data, and from it follow first-moment consequences: we have an unbiased estimator of the first moment. The second assumption is about the second moments of the data, and from it (and the first assumption) follow second-moment consequences: we obtain the second moment of our estimator, a second-moment optimality result, and an estimator of a second moment. Finally, the third assumption is about the distribution of the data, and from it (and the previous assumptions) follow distributional consequences: we obtain the actual distributions of our statistics.

Now let us compare the simple location model with ordinary least squares and the linear regression model in matrix notation. Compare the first column of Table II.2 with the entries in Table II.1 and see that the entries below are simply restatements in a new notation. Then compare the two columns of Table II.2 and see how similar the entries are. Matrix products replace scalar sums and a matrix inverse replaces a scalar reciprocal. In this table, we have not emphasized the relationships between assumptions and consequences, nor have we given a complete list of consequences. Our purpose is simply to introduce the linear regression model as a multivariate generalization of the location model and to provide an indication of coming results.

Table II.2
Analogues in the Location and Regression Models

Location Model	Linear Regression
Model Assumptions	
$\mathrm{E}\left[\mathbf{y}\right] = \iota\beta_0$	$\mathrm{E}\left[\mathbf{y} \mid \mathbf{X}\right] = X\boldsymbol{\beta}_0$
$\mathrm{Var}\left[\mathbf{y}\right] = \sigma_0^2 \cdot \mathbf{I}$	$\mathrm{Var}\left[\mathbf{y} \mid \mathbf{X}\right] = \sigma_0^2 \cdot \mathbf{I}$
$\mathbf{y} \sim \mathfrak{N}(\beta_0, \sigma_0^2 \cdot \mathbf{I})$	$\mathbf{y} \mid \mathbf{X} \sim \mathfrak{N}(\mathbf{X}\boldsymbol{\beta}_0, \sigma_0^2 \cdot \mathbf{I})$
Analysis	
$\hat{\beta} = \dfrac{\iota' y}{\iota'\iota} = \bar{y}$	$\hat{\boldsymbol{\beta}} = (\mathbf{X}'\mathbf{X})^{-1}\mathbf{X}'\mathbf{y}$
$\mathrm{E}\left[\hat{\beta}\right] = \beta_0$	$\mathrm{E}\left[\hat{\boldsymbol{\beta}} \mid \mathbf{X}\right] = \boldsymbol{\beta}_0$
$\mathrm{Var}\left[\hat{\beta}\right] = \dfrac{\sigma_0^2}{\iota'\iota}$	$\mathrm{Var}\left[\hat{\boldsymbol{\beta}} \mid \mathbf{X}\right] = \sigma_0^2 \cdot (\mathbf{X}'\mathbf{X})^{-1}$
$\hat{\beta} \sim \mathfrak{N}[\beta_0, \sigma_0^2/(\iota'\iota)]$	$\hat{\boldsymbol{\beta}} \mid \mathbf{X} \sim \mathfrak{N}[\boldsymbol{\beta}_0, \sigma_0^2 \cdot (\mathbf{X}'\mathbf{X})^{-1}]$
$s^2 = \dfrac{\mathbf{y}'\left[\mathbf{I} - (\iota\iota'/\iota'\iota)\right] y}{N-1}$	$s^2 = \dfrac{\mathbf{y}'[\mathbf{I} - \mathbf{X}(\mathbf{X}'\mathbf{X})^{-1}\mathbf{X}']\mathbf{y}}{N-K}$
$s^2 \sim \dfrac{\chi_{N-1}^2 \sigma_0^2}{N-1}$	$s^2 \sim \dfrac{\chi_{N-K}^2 \sigma_0^2}{N-K}$

CHAPTER 6

Linear Unbiased Estimation

One popular criterion for estimators is *unbiasedness*. Because they are random variables, estimators are not exact procedures. But in some cases estimators can be exact "on average." That is, if the estimation procedure is repeated by drawing a new sample of observations and calculating the same statistic, then the expected value of the statistic equals the population value to be estimated.

In this chapter, we describe circumstances in which the OLS fitted coefficients are unbiased estimators of population coefficients in the conditional mean of the LHS, or *dependent*, variable given the RHS, or *explanatory*, variables. Under these circumstances, an unbiased estimate of the expected difference in the log-wage between a white and a nonwhite individual with the same years of schooling, the same years of experience, the same sex, and the same union membership status is 0.131, the fitted OLS coefficient of the dummy variable for race from Run 5 of Table 1.8. And if we collected another sample of individuals from the Current Population Survey (CPS) with the same criteria and fit another OLS regression, we would expect a similar fitted value.

6.1 EXPERIMENTAL EXAMPLE

For any inference, one begins with the assumption that there is a stable process that generates the data. We are interested in estimating certain features of this *data-generating process*. Because we do not know the features of the process generating our CPS data, we use an artificial data-generating process to further illustrate the ideas in this chapter and the ones that follow.

To simplify, we will focus on the variables log-wage (y) and experience (x) alone. We will treat both as random variables and make the joint distribution of (x, y) a continuous distribution that could have generated the actual data set that we have been analyzing. In Figure 6.1, we show a frequency plot of experience for the 1995 CPS data and the marginal probability density function (p.d.f.) that we have chosen to represent the population. Figure 6.2 depicts such plots for the log-wage variable. The observed frequencies for these variables could easily have been generated by these distributions. These marginal density functions come from the joint p.d.f.

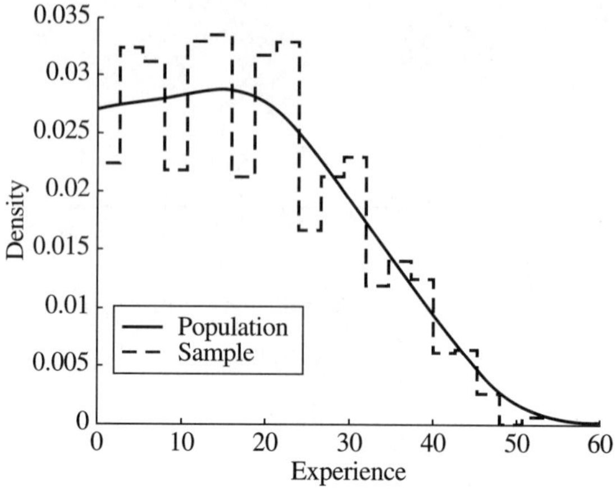

Figure 6.1 Marginal distribution of experience.

shown in Figure 6.3. The joint distribution has two modes, one with less experience and lower wages than the other. The first mode appears around 1 year of experience and a log-wage of about 1.8 whereas the second mode sits at about 12 years of experience and a log-wage of 2.25.

Figure 6.4 is a plot of the conditional probability density functions of log-wage given different experience levels. Therefore, this figure is derived from the joint density in Figure 6.3 by scaling the surface at each level of experience so that the area under the function integrates to one. The ridge in Figure 6.4 locates the modes of the conditional distributions. For low experience levels, the conditional mode of log-wage increases with experience, but it appears to decline at the highest levels of experience.

The conditional mean is a more popular measure of central tendency than the mode. The conditional mean given experience is graphed in Figure 6.5. Overall, the conditional mean tells the same story as the mode. In this chapter, we will show that the OLS fit can be used to investigate such relationships. The quadratic specification in experience for our previous OLS fit is an approximation to this function and we can relate the statistical properties of the OLS fit to such population properties when a sampling procedure is specified.

To illustrate this, we drew random samples of 1289 observations from this joint distribution of experience and log-wage as though we were repeating the experiment that yielded our original data set. For each new sample that we drew, we computed the OLS fitted coefficients for the quadratic specification: $\log w = \beta_1 + \beta_2 x + \beta_3 x^2 + u$. After computing 1000 fits, we had obtained 1000 draws from the distribution of OLS coefficients for this experiment.

Figure 6.6 is a frequency distribution of the observed fitted values of β_3. All of the coefficients have qualitatively similar distributions: symmetric and bell shaped. The average values of the coefficients were 2.000, 0.033, and -0.000568 for β_1, β_2, and β_3, respectively. In Figure 6.7, we compare the average quadratic fit and the conditional mean function. The two functions bear some similarity. Although the figure demonstrates the nonquadratic character of the conditional mean function, note that the maximum absolute percentage difference between these two functions is less than 2%. In classical statistical inference, we treat our estimates from a particular sample as though it were one of the 1000 draws we computed. In this chapter we focus on the central tendency of the draws. In the next chapter we focus on the variation.

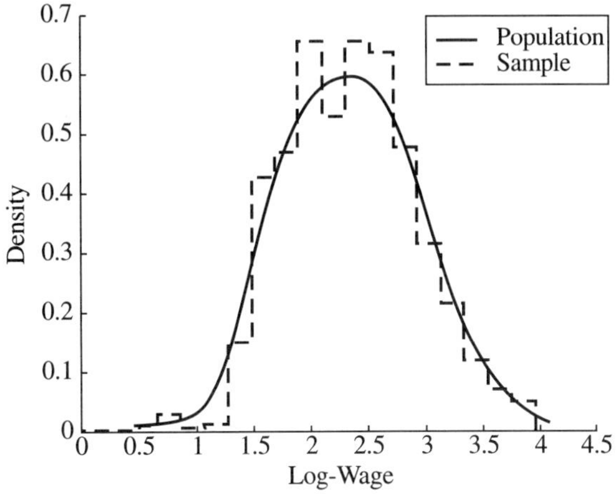

Figure 6.2 Marginal distribution of log-wage.

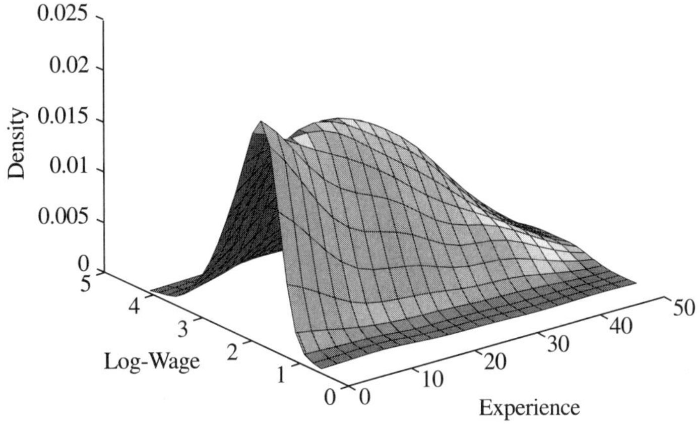

Figure 6.3 Joint distribution of experience and log-wage.

Econometricians often specify one more element of the hypothetical data-generating process, an assumption about the set of functions to which the conditional mean belongs. Suppose, for example, that the conditional mean were actually quadratic. In practice, one does not know the conditional mean or its functional form. But we will show that such an assumption is a useful starting point for analysis. To illustrate, we repeat the previous experiment, but adjust each observation of log-wage by subtracting the original conditional mean given experience and adding $2.0+0.033 \cdot x - 0.000568 \cdot x^2$. This produces a data set in which the conditional mean of log-wage is exactly quadratic. Because this quadratic function is close to the original conditional mean, the adjustment leaves the p.d.f.s shown in Figures 6.3 and 6.4 essentially unchanged. One thousand draws on the estimated coefficients had average values of 1.9985, 0.0331, and -0.000570 for β_1, β_2, and β_3, respectively. Under these conditions, the OLS procedure provides a useful estimator

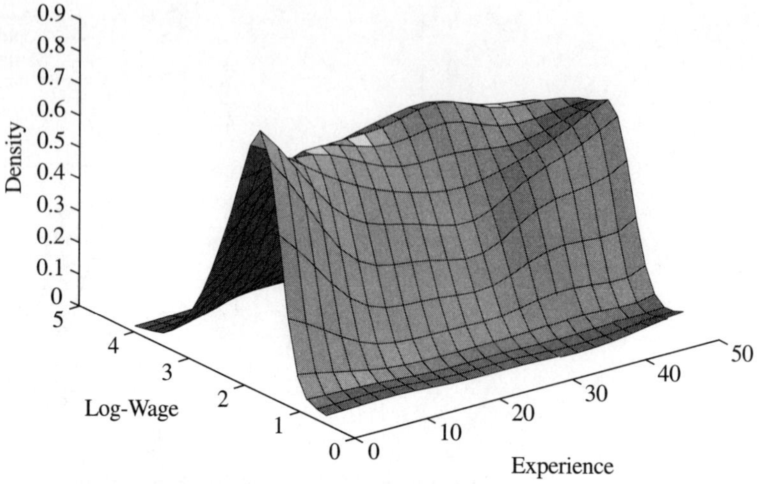

Figure 6.4 Conditional wage distributions.

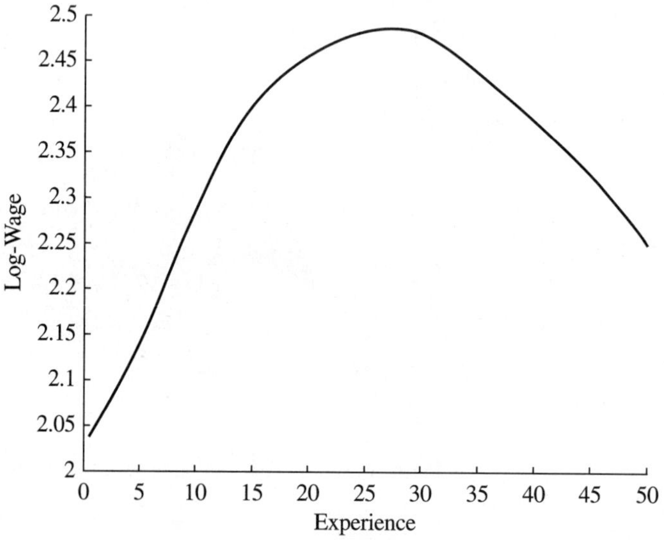

Figure 6.5 Conditional mean given experience.

of the population parameter values. The sampling property that these average values illustrate is the first subject of this chapter.

The second subject is the conditional mean. Generally, economists have related the predictions of their theories to the conditional mean. Loosely speaking, their hope is that a theory may be right (or wrong) on average, recognizing that a simplification will not explain every instance exactly. Several theories in labor economics, for example, yield predictions about the distribution of wages conditional on experience. Generally, these theories predict that wages will tend to increase as experience increases. Some theories make the more refined prediction that the return

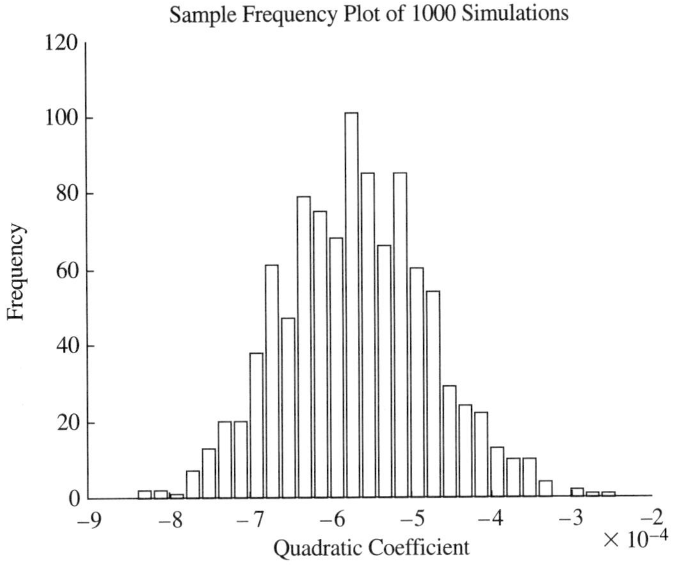

Figure 6.6 Frequency distribution of fitted coefficients.

to experience will fall, and even become negative, as experience increases. Labor economists have estimated the mean of wages conditional on experience (and other characteristics) to compare theory with reality.

It is important to be able to interpret the conditional mean accurately. In particular, remember that the conditional mean does not necessarily describe a *causal* relationship running from the

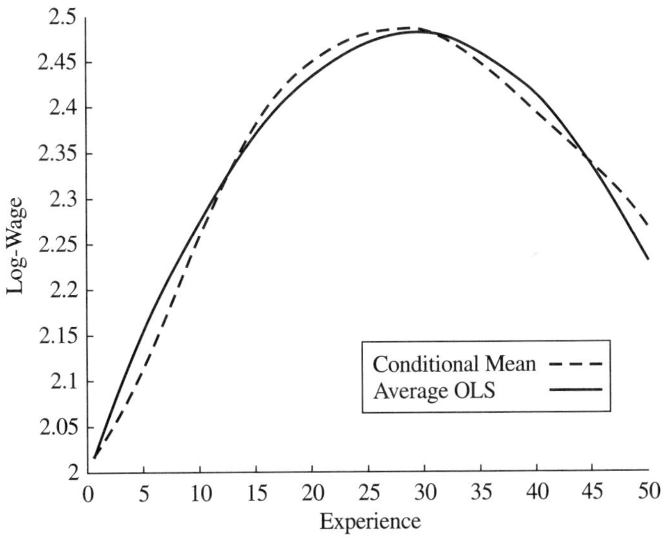

Figure 6.7 Average OLS quadratic versus conditional mean.

conditioning variables to the variable under expectation. The conditional mean is merely a function of a joint probability distribution. Furthermore, one should use the probability distribution to interpret the conditional mean. If, in our earnings example, the theory describes the profile of wages over a population of workers with different levels of experience, then we have been studying the appropriate conditional mean. If, however, the theory concerns the wage profile of an individual worker over a lifetime, then we may have the wrong conditional mean under analysis. Additional assumptions or inquiries must establish that we will average across individuals at a point in time to study individuals over time.

Statistical properties of the OLS estimator rest on assumptions about the process that actually generates the data. This dependence of statistical properties on assumptions contrasts with the geometric properties described in the previous chapters that do not require any assumptions. The geometric properties describe the OLS fit itself. On the other hand, the statistical assumptions that we maintain from this point on, and the properties that depend on them, may fail to hold. Nevertheless, analysts regularly make these assumptions because they have found them reliable, and therefore useful, in many settings. In addition, one can often make diagnostic checks for evidence against the assumptions. Given an empirical question, the practice of classical statistical analysis generally involves a balance between making assumptions and checking them.

We have already discussed our first assumption (made at the beginning of Chapter 3), based on the geometry of OLS. We are studying the properties of $\hat{\boldsymbol{\beta}}$ when it is uniquely defined because $\text{rank}(\mathbf{X}) = K$. This is a property that can be checked because $\mathbf{X}$ is observable. As far as assumptions go, this one does not require much faith. The assumptions that appear in the following chapters impose restrictions on the data-generating process that cannot be unequivocally confirmed or refuted in practice. These assumptions form the basis for statistical inference.

6.2 FIRST MOMENTS

From this point on, we will treat the elements of both $\mathbf{y}$ and $\mathbf{X}$ as random variables with a joint probability distribution. The fundamental assumption underlying the classical statistical use of OLS estimators places a restriction on the conditional mean, or first moment, of $\mathbf{y}$ given $\mathbf{X}$.[1]

> **Assumption 6.1 (First Moments)** *Conditional on* $\mathbf{X}$, *the mean of* $\mathbf{y}$ *is a linear combination of the columns of* $\mathbf{X}$: $\text{E}[y_n \mid \mathbf{X}] = \mathbf{x}_n'\boldsymbol{\beta}_0$ *where* $\boldsymbol{\beta}_0$ *is an unknown vector of K constants.*

To distinguish a representative value of the parameter vector from the particular value that corresponds to the conditional mean of $\mathbf{y}$, we use the subscript 0 to denote the so-called *population value* of $\boldsymbol{\beta}$.[2] The linear functional form of this conditional mean function is expressed conveniently

[1] The expectation of a random variable is often called the *first moment*. The term "moment" comes from a physical interpretation of this integral. For example, the first moment is the balance point of an object. In probability, the rth moment of the random variable Z is $\text{E}[Z^r]$. See also the section on expectations in Section D.2.

[2] The term $\boldsymbol{\beta}_0$ is usually pronounced "beta not," not "beta zero." Not! No, really. Trust me. (Editor's note: naught or nought.)

for the entire data set as $\mathrm{E}[\mathbf{y} \mid \mathbf{X}] = \mathbf{X}\boldsymbol{\beta}_0 \equiv \boldsymbol{\mu}_0$, based on the following definition of the notation for expectations.[3]

Definition 10 (Matrix Expectation) *Let* $\mathbf{Z} = [z_{ij}]$ *be a matrix containing elements that are random variables. The expectation of the matrix, denoted* $\mathrm{E}[\mathbf{Z}]$*, is the matrix containing the expectations of the individual elements,* $\left[\mathrm{E}[z_{ij}]\right]$.

We have already seen that the linearity of $\mathbf{X}\boldsymbol{\beta}_0$ in $\mathbf{X}$ does not restrict this function to be linear in such basic variables as years of experience in the labor force. These variables can enter the columns of $\mathbf{X}$ transformed in various ways and thereby influence $\mathbf{X}\boldsymbol{\beta}_0$ in nonlinear ways. Indeed, it is generally suspected that the conditional mean of one random variable given others is a nonlinear function of the latter. So this flexibility is desirable.

On the other hand, the linearity of $\mathbf{X}\boldsymbol{\beta}_0$ in the elements of $\boldsymbol{\beta}_0$ is fundamental to this analysis. One can also imagine conditional mean functions that are nonlinear functions of unknown parameters. We study such cases in Chapter 21. Nevertheless, given the flexibility in specifying $\mathbf{X}$, linearity in $\boldsymbol{\beta}_0$ is less restrictive than it may at first appear.

Given Assumptions 3.1 and 6.1, we are able to find the mean of $\hat{\boldsymbol{\beta}}$ as described in our first statistical result:

Proposition 4 (Unbiased Estimation) *If Assumption 6.1 (First Moments) holds,*

1. $\mathrm{E}[\hat{\boldsymbol{\mu}} \mid \mathbf{X}] = \mathbf{X}\boldsymbol{\beta}_0 \equiv \boldsymbol{\mu}_0$,
2. $\mathrm{E}[\mathbf{y} - \hat{\boldsymbol{\mu}} \mid \mathbf{X}] = \mathbf{0}$, *and*
3. $\mathrm{E}[\hat{\boldsymbol{\beta}} \mid \mathbf{X}] = \boldsymbol{\beta}_0$, *if Assumption 3.1 (Full Rank, p. 53) also holds.*

We call $\hat{\boldsymbol{\beta}}$ an *unbiased* estimator of $\boldsymbol{\beta}_0$.[4] In the introduction, we created a sampling experiment that satisfied the assumptions of this proposition and illustrated this sampling property. When the conditional mean of log-wage given experience was a quadratic function with coefficients 1.5, 0.02, and 0.0003, the average of 1000 realizations of $\hat{\boldsymbol{\beta}}$ gave close values of 1.494689, 0.0200864, and −0.00029474, respectively. If we increased the number of replications from 1000 toward infinity, we would observe these sample means converge toward their corresponding population mean values as their sampling variances fell with the number of replications.[5]

Note that a direct consequence of this result is that the marginal expectation of $\hat{\boldsymbol{\beta}}$ is also $\boldsymbol{\beta}_0$.

An immediate algebraic consequence of our definition of the expectation of matrices and the linearity of expectations is

---

[3] The regression function is often narrowly defined to be the conditional mean function.

[4] We prove this proposition on p. 112.

[5] See Section E.2.4 for a summary of this idea.

Lemma 6.1 (Linearity of Expectations) *Let* $\mathbf{A}$ *and* $\mathbf{B}$ *be matrices of constants and* $\mathbf{Z}$ *a matrix of random variables such that* $\mathbf{A}$ *is conformable with* $\mathbf{Z}$ *on the left and* $\mathbf{B}$ *is conformable on the right. Then* $\mathrm{E}[\mathbf{AZ}] = \mathbf{A}\,\mathrm{E}[\mathbf{Z}]$ *and* $\mathrm{E}[\mathbf{ZB}] = \mathrm{E}[\mathbf{Z}]\mathbf{B}$.

Proof. Starting with the definition of the expectation of a matrix,

$$\begin{aligned}\mathrm{E}[\mathbf{AZ}] &= \mathrm{E}\left[\sum_k a_{ik} z_{kj}\right] = \sum_k \mathrm{E}[a_{ik} z_{kj}] \\ &= \sum_k a_{ik}\,\mathrm{E}[z_{kj}] = \mathbf{A}\,\mathrm{E}[\mathbf{Z}]\end{aligned}$$

Furthermore, $\mathrm{E}[\mathbf{B}'\mathbf{Z}'] = \mathbf{B}'\,\mathrm{E}[\mathbf{Z}']$ so that $\mathrm{E}[\mathbf{ZB}] = \mathrm{E}[\mathbf{Z}]\mathbf{B}$. □

Proof of Proposition 4. The linearity of $\hat{\boldsymbol{\beta}}$ in $\mathbf{y}$ plays a key role. Applying Lemma 6.1 to $\hat{\boldsymbol{\mu}}$, where $\mathbf{A} = \mathbf{P_X}$,

$$\begin{aligned}\mathrm{E}[\hat{\boldsymbol{\mu}} \mid \mathbf{X}] &= \mathrm{E}[\mathbf{P_X y} \mid \mathbf{X}] = \mathbf{P_X}\,\mathrm{E}[\mathbf{y} \mid \mathbf{X}] \\ &= \mathbf{P_X X}\boldsymbol{\beta}_0 = \mathbf{X}\boldsymbol{\beta}_0\end{aligned}$$

so that the mean of $\hat{\boldsymbol{\mu}}$ is the population mean vector $\mathbf{X}\boldsymbol{\beta}_0$. Now,

$$\mathrm{E}[\mathbf{y} - \hat{\boldsymbol{\mu}} \mid \mathbf{X}] = \mathrm{E}[\mathbf{y} \mid \mathbf{X}] - \mathrm{E}[\hat{\boldsymbol{\mu}} \mid \mathbf{X}] = \mathbf{X}\boldsymbol{\beta}_0 - \mathbf{X}\boldsymbol{\beta}_0 = \mathbf{0}$$

If $\mathbf{X}$ is full rank, then $\hat{\boldsymbol{\beta}}$ is well defined and receives a similar treatment to $\hat{\boldsymbol{\mu}}$:

$$\begin{aligned}\mathrm{E}[\hat{\boldsymbol{\beta}} \mid \mathbf{X}] &= \mathrm{E}[(\mathbf{X}'\mathbf{X})^{-1}\mathbf{X}'\mathbf{y} \mid \mathbf{X}] = (\mathbf{X}'\mathbf{X})^{-1}\mathbf{X}'\,\mathrm{E}[\mathbf{y} \mid \mathbf{X}] \\ &= (\mathbf{X}'\mathbf{X})^{-1}\mathbf{X}'\mathbf{X}\boldsymbol{\beta}_0 = \boldsymbol{\beta}_0\end{aligned}$$

□

The linear dependence of the OLS statistics $\hat{\boldsymbol{\mu}}$ and $\hat{\boldsymbol{\beta}}$ on $\mathbf{y}$ is critical to this proof. Without linearity in $\mathbf{y}$, it would not be possible to move the expectation operator through to $\mathbf{y}$. Because the elements of $\hat{\boldsymbol{\beta}}$ are weighted sums of the elements of $\mathbf{y}$, where the weights can be treated conditionally as constants, the conditional mean of $\hat{\boldsymbol{\beta}}$ is the weighted sum of the conditional means of the elements of $\mathbf{y}$. Assumption 6.1 applies to these elements.

Note an important feature of Assumption 6.1 that is essential to the proposition: the mean of each element of $\mathbf{y}$ is conditional on *all* the elements of $\mathbf{X}$. This is easy to miss or forget. After all, the conditional mean of y_n depends only on $\mathbf{x}_n$, not the entire matrix $\mathbf{X}$. However, the proof of the proposition requires conditioning on $\mathbf{X}$. Without this, the expectation cannot be moved past $(\mathbf{X}'\mathbf{X})^{-1}$, a nonlinear function of $\mathbf{X}$ that depends on all of its elements.

This feature of Assumption 6.1 rules out some interesting specifications. For example, it is awkward to apply this assumption to the dynamic specification for the unemployment rate in Chapter 3. The lagged unemployment rate appears on the RHS so that elements of $\mathbf{y}$ are also in $\mathbf{X}$. If we condition on all of $\mathbf{X}$, then we condition on $\{y_1, \ldots, y_{T-1}\}$ and the only observation of unemployment that would *not* be treated as predetermined is the last one. Studying the conditional mean of one observation generally produces vague conclusions. On the other hand, Proposition 4 will generally fail without such conditioning. When elements of $\mathbf{y}$ also appear in $\mathbf{X}$, the statistics $\hat{\boldsymbol{\beta}}$ and $\hat{\boldsymbol{\mu}}$ are not linear functions of the elements of $\mathbf{y}$. Thus, we cannot determine the means of these statistics unless we specify more about the distribution of $\mathbf{y}$ than just its conditional first moment.

For the time being, we will set aside such specifications. We will return to their analysis in Chapter 13, where we will weaken Assumption 6.1 to $\mathrm{E}[y_n \mid \mathbf{x}_n] = \mathbf{x}_n' \boldsymbol{\beta}_0$ $(n = 1, \ldots, N)$.

6.3 CONDITIONAL MEANS

Given the first moment assumption, the analysis of the first moments of the OLS statistics $\hat{\boldsymbol{\mu}}$ and $\hat{\boldsymbol{\beta}}$ is straightforward. It is the justification of the first moment assumption that is most challenging. Why make an assumption about the *conditional mean* of $\mathbf{y}$ given $\mathbf{X}$? The leading reason is that when it exists, the conditional mean is, in a restricted sense, an optimal function for prediction. If we seek to predict $\mathbf{y}$ based on prior knowledge of $\mathbf{X}$, then we may choose to focus our attention on functions of $\mathbf{X}$ that predict $\mathbf{y}$ well.

One measure of prediction accuracy is called *mean squared error* (MSE). Let $m(\mathbf{X})$ be a prediction of y_n conditional on $\mathbf{X}$.

Definition 11 (Mean Squared Error) *The* mean squared error *of* $m(\mathbf{X})$ *for* y_n *is the mean (or expectation) of the squared (prediction) error,* $\mathrm{E}\left[\left(y_n - m(\mathbf{X})\right)^2\right]$.

It follows immediately from this definition that the conditional mean is an optimal prediction function relative to *all* other functions of the conditioning variables.

Lemma 6.2 (Minimum MSE Predictor) *Suppose that the first two conditional moments of* y_n *given* $\mathbf{X}$ *exist. The conditional mean of the random variable* y_n *given the random variables in* $\mathbf{X}$, $\mathrm{E}[y_n \mid \mathbf{X}]$, *is a* minimum MSE *(MMSE)* prediction *function of* y_n *conditional on* $\mathbf{X}$.

Proof. The *conditional* MSE has a simple decomposition into two terms, a variance term and a squared bias term. Denoting $\mu_n(\mathbf{X}) \equiv \mathrm{E}[y_n \mid \mathbf{X}]$,[6]

$$
\begin{aligned}
&\mathrm{E}\left[\left(y_n - m_n(\mathbf{X})\right)^2 \mid \mathbf{X}\right] \\
&\quad = \mathrm{E}\left[\left(y_n - \mu_n(\mathbf{X}) + \mu_n(\mathbf{X}) - m_n(\mathbf{X})\right)^2 \mid \mathbf{X}\right] \\
&\quad = \mathrm{Var}[y_n \mid \mathbf{X}] + \left(\mu_n(\mathbf{X}) - m_n(\mathbf{X})\right)^2
\end{aligned} \tag{6.1}
$$

because

$$
\begin{aligned}
&\mathrm{E}\left[\left(\mu_n(\mathbf{X}) - m_n(\mathbf{X})\right)\left(y_n - \mu_n(\mathbf{X})\right) \mid \mathbf{X}\right] \\
&\quad = \left(\mu(\mathbf{X}) - m_n(\mathbf{X})\right) \mathrm{E}[y_n - \mu_n(\mathbf{X}) \mid \mathbf{X}] \\
&\quad = \left(\mu_n(\mathbf{X}) - m_n(\mathbf{X})\right) \cdot 0 \\
&\quad = 0
\end{aligned} \tag{6.2}
$$

Therefore,

$$\mathrm{E}\left[(y_n - m_n(\mathbf{X}))^2\right] = \mathrm{E}\left[\mathrm{Var}[y_n \mid \mathbf{X}]\right] + \mathrm{E}\left[\left(\mu_n(\mathbf{X}) - m_n(\mathbf{X})\right)^2\right]$$

and the (marginal) MSE is minimized to the expected conditional variance of y_n given $\mathbf{X}$ when $m_n(\mathbf{X})$ equals $\mu_n(\mathbf{X}) \equiv \mathrm{E}[y_n \mid \mathbf{X}]$. □

Note that unlike the OLS fitting procedure this lemma does not restrict attention to *linear* functions of $\mathbf{X}$. The conditional mean is not necessarily a linear function, nor are the prediction functions that it dominates in MSE. That is to say, Assumption 6.1 is a substantive restriction on the conditional mean.

6.4 PROJECTION OF RANDOM VARIABLES

This discussion of the conditional mean may be familiar. In this section, we show that this property of the conditional mean is another application of minimizing a measure of distance with projection. Minimizing MSE and OLS are parallel concepts. Understanding this correspondence makes the conceptual content of this material compact and explains the convenient way in which these two structures fit together. In addition, we will use the projection structure of minimizing MSE in later chapters for the study of estimation and relative efficiency.

Looking over the previous section, one may note some superficial commonalities between the mean squared error and the sum of squared residuals: both objective functions involve squared deviations that can be decomposed into two terms, one of which yields the optimum by inspection. Compare (6.1) with

$$\boldsymbol{\mu} \in \mathrm{Col}(\mathbf{X}) \Rightarrow \|\mathbf{y} - \boldsymbol{\mu}\|^2 = \|\mathbf{y} - \mathbf{P_X y}\|^2 + \|\mathbf{P_X y} - \boldsymbol{\mu}\|^2$$

Both decompositions rest on a cross-product term reducing to zero: compare (6.2) with

$$(\mathbf{y} - \mathbf{P_X y})' \left(\mathbf{P_X y} - \boldsymbol{\mu}\right) = 0, \quad \boldsymbol{\mu} \in \mathrm{Col}(\mathbf{X})$$

On the other hand, there are also substantial differences: the minimization of MSE occurs over *functions* of all the elements in $\mathbf{X}$, not a finite dimensional subspace such as $\mathrm{Col}(\mathbf{X})$. Also, MSE is a measure of distance to a *scalar* random variable y_n, not an N-dimensional vector like $\mathbf{y}$.

To explain the analogies and the differences, we will describe the relevant vector space, just as we described a generalization of $\mathbb{E}^N$ in Chapter 4. How can we interpret y_n and the elements of x_n as vectors and what is their inner product? The answers indicate what constitutes orthogonality, length, and projection. In addition, to focus attention properly, we will discuss only the *random variables* y_n and x_{nk} $(k = 1, \ldots, K)$ for a particular n, and not an observed sample in $\mathbf{y}$ and $\mathbf{X}$. A preliminary example may help obtain the appropriate perspective.

EXAMPLE 6.1

Suppose that $K = 1$ and that (x_n, y_n) is a pair of discrete random variables. Let us take the support of (x_n, y_n) to be the J pairs of real numbers $\mathbb{S} = \left\{(a_j, b_j)\,;\ j = 1, \ldots, J\right\}$ and denote

[6] Because the notation may suggest otherwise, keep in mind that $\mathrm{E}[y_n \mid \mathbf{X}]$ is only a function of $\mathbf{X}$.

$$\Pr\{(x_n, y_n) = (a_j, b_j)\} \equiv p_j, \quad (j = 1, \ldots, J)$$

By definition, all $p_j > 0$ and $\sum_{j=1}^{J} p_j = 1$. We can draw a sample of N *independent and identically distributed* (i.i.d.) replications (or observations) indexed by $n = 1, \ldots, N$ from this discrete distribution. But we do not focus on that dimension, though we have in previous analysis. Instead, we focus on the joint distribution of the random variables (x_n, y_n). We will show that for a *fixed n*, both y_n and x_n are vectors in a space with J dimensions. Each outcome (a_j, b_j) corresponds to another dimension in this vector space. Although it is unnecessary (because n is fixed), we will retain the subscript n to remind the reader that there are two kinds of dimension: replications indexed by n and discrete outcomes indexed by j.

In general, we will interpret y_n, the elements of $\mathbf{x}_n$, and functions $f(\mathbf{x}_n, y_n)$ of $\mathbf{x}_n$ and y_n as vectors in a vector space of real-valued random variables.[7] We construct this vector space by specifying a zero vector, scalar multiplication, and vector addition. In this space, the zero vector is the scalar constant zero. Scalar multiplication and vector addition correspond to ordinary real transformations of random variables. If α is a real number then the scalar multiple of a random variable w is simply the random variable αw. If z_n and w_n are two random variables then their vector sum is just the random variable $z_n + w_n$. Finally, we will interpret equality of two random variables to mean the probability that they are equal is one: $z_n = w_n$ if and only if $\Pr\{z_n = w_n\} = 1$.[8]

EXAMPLE 6.2 (Continuation)

Let us continue our previous example. The zero vector of our vector space is a random variable that is zero in every one of the J outcomes so that we may consider the 3-tuple of random variables $(x_n, y_n, 0)$ with the support $\{(a_j, b_j, 0);\ j = 1, \ldots, J\}$. Thus, $x_n + 0 = x_n$ or $\Pr\{x_n + 0 = x_n\} = 1$. Scalar multiplication corresponds to transforming a random variable into another random variable by multiplying it by a real number. For example, $z_n = \alpha y_n$ is a random variable with the support $\{\alpha b_j;\ j = 1, \ldots, J\}$ and

$$\Pr\{z_n = c\} = \sum_{\{j|\alpha b_j = c\}} p_j, \quad j = 1, \ldots, J$$

Also, the joint distribution of the 4-tuple $(x_n, y_n, z_n, 0)$ is well specified. Vector addition corresponds to combining two random variables into a third by adding them together. For example, $w_n = x_n + z_n$ is a random variable with the support $\{a_j + \alpha b_j;\ j = 1, \ldots, J\}$ and

$$\Pr\{w_n = c\} = \sum_{\{j|a_j + \alpha b_j = c\}} p_j, \quad j = 1, \ldots, J$$

Again, the joint distribution of $(w_n, x_n, y_n, z_n, 0)$ is well specified.

If a set is a vector space, then that set is closed under linear transformation. The set of all real-valued functions of x_n and y_n is such a set. If $f_1(x_n, y_n)$ and $f_2(x_n, y_n)$ are two such

[7] See Definition C.1 (p. 841) and the discussion in Appendix C for a summary of the linear algebra of vector spaces.

[8] This notion of equality is necessary because random variables may differ only on a set of outcomes with no probability. See the discussion after Definition D.5 for further comment.

functions and α_1 and α_2 are two real scalars, then $\alpha_1 f_1(x_n, y_n) + \alpha_2 f_2(x_n, y_n)$ is also a real-valued function and, therefore, a member of this set. This property, along with certain associative, commutative, and distributative properties, makes the set of all real-valued functions of x_n and y_n a vector space.

This vector space containing random variables has subspaces, as all vector spaces do. For example, given a vector space spanned by functions $f(x_n, y_n)$ of x_n and y_n, we can generate a vector subspace spanned by functions $g(x_n)$ of x_n alone. If y_n is an element of this subspace, then $y_n = g(x_n)$ for some function $g(\cdot)$ and in algebraic terms the vector y_n is linearly dependent on the functions of x_n. In terms of probability, y_n and x_n have a *singular distribution*. That is, the distribution of y_n conditional on x_n is degenerate, with $\Pr\{y_n = g(x_n)\} = 1$.

EXAMPLE 6.3 (Continuation)

The vector space in these examples is, in fact, just a new interpretation of $\mathbb{R}^J$. That is, there is a one-to-one correspondence between every random variable and an element of $\mathbb{R}^J$. The simplest correspondence assigns each random variable to the J-tuple of its values in the J possible outcomes. The random variable x_n, for instance, corresponds to $\mathbf{a} \equiv [a_1, \ldots, a_J]'$. Similarly, y_n corresponds to $\mathbf{b} \equiv [b_1, \ldots, b_J]'$. Furthermore, αy_n corresponds to $[\alpha b_1, \ldots, \alpha b_J]' = \alpha \cdot \mathbf{b}$ and $x_n + \alpha y_n$ to $[a_1 + \alpha b_1, \ldots, a_J + \alpha b_J]' = \mathbf{a} + \alpha \cdot \mathbf{b}$.

The jth dimension corresponds to the jth outcome, which occurs with probability p_j. Given these probabilities, every (random variable) vector is uniquely and completely described by its support, a set of J real outcomes. In effect, we showed in Example 6.2 that the addition and scalar multiplication of these (random variable) vectors corresponds to the addition and scalar multiplication of these vectors in $\mathbb{R}^J$.

Now random variables are not always discrete with finite support, so the vector spaces we have in mind may be *infinite dimensional*.[9] In general, one cannot express all possible random variables $f(x, y)$ as linear combinations of a finite collection of such random variables. For example, the functions f that we may allow include all polynomial functions. Given any finite collection of random variables $\{f_1(x, y), \ldots, f_M(x, y)\}$, we can always find an $f_{M+1}(x, y)$ that is not linearly dependent on the elements of the set if x and y are continuously distributed.

For this vector space, we define the inner product of vectors to be the expectation of the multiplication of the two random variables z_{n1} and z_{n2}:[10]

$$\langle z_{n1}, z_{n2} \rangle \equiv \mathrm{E}[z_{n1} z_{n2}] \tag{6.3}$$

EXAMPLE 6.4 (Continuation)

Returning to our example of a discrete, finite-dimensional vector space, we see that the inner product of two random variable vectors $z_{n1} = f_1(x_n, y_n)$ and $z_{2n} = f_2(x_n, y_n)$ is

[9] Infinite-dimensional vector spaces tend to make many people feel dizzy. The delicate reader is assured that we will not go deeply into such spaces with our analytical spaceship. We shall just casually peek out the portal for a moment and then stay within the safety of merely large-dimensional space inside our craft. See Luenberger (1969) for reference.

[10] Discrete and continuous random variables are reviewed in Section D.2 (p. 868).

$$\mathrm{E}[z_{n1}z_{n2}] = \sum_{j=1}^{J} f_1(a_j, b_j)\, f_2(a_j, b_j)\, p_j$$

This implies that the inner product defined in (6.3) is equivalent to the generalized Euclidean inner product encountered in (4.18). If we form the vectors in $\mathbb{R}^J$ that correspond to these random variables,

$$\underset{J\times 1}{\mathbf{d}_i} \equiv \left[f_i(a_j, b_j);\ j = 1, \ldots, J\right]', \qquad i = 1, 2$$

and we create a diagonal matrix with the corresponding probabilities,

$$\underset{J\times J}{\mathbf{A}} = \begin{bmatrix} p_1 & 0 & 0 & \cdots & 0 \\ 0 & p_2 & 0 & \cdots & 0 \\ 0 & 0 & p_3 & \ddots & \vdots \\ \vdots & \vdots & \ddots & \ddots & 0 \\ 0 & 0 & \cdots & 0 & p_J \end{bmatrix} \equiv \mathrm{diag}(p_j;\ j = 1, \ldots, J)$$

then we can write the inner product with the same matrix notation:

$$\mathrm{E}[z_{n1}z_{n2}] = \mathbf{d}_1'\mathbf{A}\mathbf{d}_2$$

If $\mathrm{E}[z_{n1}z_{n2}]$ equals zero, then z_{n1} and z_{n2} are said to be *orthogonal*. Thus, two uncorrelated random variables are orthogonal if one has a mean equal to zero and econometricians often use the term "orthogonal" to describe such random variables. With the vector inner product defined in (6.3), the residual vector $y_n - \mu(x_n) \equiv y - \mathrm{E}[y_n \mid x_n]$ is orthogonal to all functions of x_n alone: following (6.2) and using iterated expectations,[11]

$$\begin{aligned} \mathrm{E}\big[m(x_n)\,(y_n - \mu(x_n))\big] &= \mathrm{E}\big[m(x_n)\,\mathrm{E}[y_n - \mu(x_n) \mid x_n]\big] \\ &= 0 \end{aligned}$$

Length in this vector space is measured as the square root of the inner product of a vector with itself, $\mathrm{E}[z_n^2]$. With this distance measure, no other function of x is closer to y than $\mu(x)$: if we take the expectation of (6.1) over x_n, then

$$\begin{aligned} \mathrm{E}\big[(y_n - m(x_n))^2\big] &= \mathrm{E}\big[(y_n - \mu(x_n))^2\big] + \mathrm{E}\big[(\mu(x_n) - m(x_n))^2\big] \\ &\geq \mathrm{E}\big[(y_n - \mu(x_n))^2\big] \end{aligned}$$

In this sense, the OLS fitted vector $\hat{\boldsymbol{\mu}}$ and the conditional mean $\mu(x_n)$ are parallel concepts. The conditional mean is also an orthogonal projection.[12] This parallel is at the center of a close association of OLS with the estimation of the linear conditional mean specified in Assumption 6.1 (First Moment, p. 110).

Keep in mind that the conditional mean as orthogonal projection may be a *nonlinear* function of x_n, because it minimizes the MSE over *all* functions of x_n.

---

11 Regarding *iterated expectations*, see the discussion on p. 881.

12 The analogue to the (matrix) orthogonal projector of $\mathbb{E}^N$ is the conditional expectation *operator* $\mathrm{E}[\cdot \mid \mathbf{X}]$.

EXAMPLE 6.5 (Continuation)
The marginal mean of y_n is

$$\mathrm{E}[y_n] = \sum_{j=1}^{J} b_j\, p_j$$

The conditional distribution of y_n given $x_n = a_0 \in \{a_j;\ j = 1, \ldots, J\}$ is

$$\Pr\{y_n = b_0 \mid x_n = a_0\} = \frac{\sum_{j=1}^{J} \mathbf{1}\{a_j = a_0\}\, \mathbf{1}\{b_j = b_0\}\, p_j}{\sum_{j=1}^{J} \mathbf{1}\{a_j = a_0\}\, p_j}$$

and the conditional mean is

$$\mathrm{E}[y_n \mid x_n = a_0] = \frac{\sum_{j=1}^{J} \mathbf{1}\{a_j = a_0\}\, b_j\, p_j}{\sum_{j=1}^{J} \mathbf{1}\{a_j = a_0\}\, p_j}$$

Given that b_j $(j = 1, \ldots, J)$ can be anything, this conditional mean is generally a *nonlinear* function of a_0.

Not only can the conditional mean be a nonlinear function, in general a conditional mean depends on every variable in the conditioning set. Thus, we can extend our discussion of the conditional mean beyond these examples to the multivariate case $\mathrm{E}[y_n \mid \mathbf{x}_n]$ where $\mathbf{x}_n$ is a vector of K variables. Our assumption, that $\mathrm{E}[y_n \mid \mathbf{X}] = \mathbf{x}_n' \boldsymbol{\beta}_0$, makes two kinds of restrictions about the conditional mean (orthogonal projection). Besides linearity in $\mathbf{x}_n$, the assumption excludes from $\mathrm{E}[y_n \mid \mathbf{X}]$ elements of $\mathbf{X}$ that are not in the nth row of the matrix. That is, the conditional mean of y_n depends only on the elements of $\mathbf{x}_n$, despite the fact that all the other $\mathbf{x}_m$, $m \neq n$, are in the conditioning set. These restrictions make the assumption about first moments substantive because, as we will see, these restrictions are testable.

6.5 MATHEMATICAL NOTES

For completeness, we restate the Pythagorean (Theorem 1, p. 28) and projection (Theorem 2, p. 119) theorems for general real vector spaces.[13] We will be using these theorems for random variables as well as for vectors in Euclidean spaces. Having already seen the versions particular to Euclidean spaces, one can appreciate the mathematical elegance of the general theorems. Two fundamental concepts, the inner product and the norm, support these results.

Let $\mathbb{V}$ be a real linear vector space as defined in Definition C.1 (p. 841). We suppose that $\mathbb{V}$ can be associated with an inner product as in Definition C.16 (p. 852). The inner product of $\mathbf{v}_1, \mathbf{v}_2 \in \mathbb{V}$ is denoted by $\langle \mathbf{v}_1, \mathbf{v}_2 \rangle$. Then the Cauchy–Schwarz inequality (Lemma C.1, p. 852) holds and the function $\|\mathbf{v}_1\| \equiv \sqrt{\langle \mathbf{v}_1, \mathbf{v}_1 \rangle}$ is a norm (Definition C.21, p. 855).[14] In addition, if $\langle \mathbf{v}_1, \mathbf{v}_2 \rangle = 0$ then $\mathbf{v}_1$ and $\mathbf{v}_2$ are orthogonal ($\mathbf{v}_1 \perp \mathbf{v}_2$).

We can obtain two theorems within this framework:

[13] See Luenberger (1969) for a complete treatment.

[14] See the discussion starting on p. 856.

Theorem 5 (Pythagoras) *If* $\mathbf{v}_1, \mathbf{v}_2 \in \mathbb{V}$ *and* $\mathbf{v}_1 \perp \mathbf{v}_2$ *then* $\|\mathbf{v}_1 + \mathbf{v}_2\|^2 = \|\mathbf{v}_1\|^2 + \|\mathbf{v}_2\|^2$.

Proof. The proof is identical to the one given previously. Only the notation for an inner product has changed. Using the properties of an inner product,

$$\begin{aligned}\|\mathbf{v}_1 + \mathbf{v}_2\|^2 &= \langle \mathbf{v}_1 + \mathbf{v}_2, \mathbf{v}_1 + \mathbf{v}_2\rangle \\ &= \langle \mathbf{v}_1, \mathbf{v}_1\rangle + \langle \mathbf{v}_1, \mathbf{v}_2\rangle + \langle \mathbf{v}_2, \mathbf{v}_1\rangle + \langle \mathbf{v}_2, \mathbf{v}_2\rangle \\ &= \|\mathbf{v}_1\|^2 + \|\mathbf{v}_2\|^2\end{aligned}$$

□

Theorem 6 (Projection) *Let* $y \in \mathbb{V}$ *and let* $\mathbb{S} \subseteq \mathbb{V}$ *be a linear subspace of* $\mathbb{V}$. *Then*

$$\hat{\boldsymbol{\mu}} = \underset{\boldsymbol{\mu} \in \mathbb{S}}{\text{argmin}} \, \|y - \boldsymbol{\mu}\|^2$$

if and only if $y - \hat{\boldsymbol{\mu}} \perp \mathbb{S}$. *In addition, if* $\hat{\boldsymbol{\mu}}$ *exists then* $\hat{\boldsymbol{\mu}}$ *is unique.*

Again, the proof is a repetition of the one that we gave on p. 39. There is one omission however: this theorem does not establish the *existence* of the optimal $\hat{\boldsymbol{\mu}}$. Additional structure is required to obtain existence as a general result.[15] In the econometric applications in this book, the existence of $\hat{\boldsymbol{\mu}}$ will almost always be an assumption. For example, Lemma 6.2 assumes that the conditional mean of y_n given $\mathbf{X}$ exists. Given that, the orthogonality in (6.2) establishes $\mathrm{E}[y_n \,|\, \mathbf{X}]$ as an optimal orthogonal projection of y_n onto functions of $\mathbf{X}$.

Note, however, that $\mathrm{E}[y_n \,|\, \mathbf{X}]$ is not the *unique* orthogonal projection. In general, random variables may be *equal with probability one*, yet not equal. They may differ only on a set of outcomes with probability zero.[16] These differences do not show up in such expected values as (6.1) and (6.2). Therefore, strictly speaking $\mathrm{E}[y_n \,|\, \mathbf{X}]$ is not generally unique as an MMSE prediction function. However, any other minimizer of the conditional MSE equals $\mathrm{E}[y_n \,|\, \mathbf{X}]$ with probability one because the expected value of their squared difference equals zero.[17] In other words, the distance between them is zero. Hence, $\mathrm{E}[y_n \,|\, \mathbf{X}]$ is a representative of a class of functions *equal in*

15 Every sequence $\{\mathbf{z}_1, \mathbf{z}_2, \ldots\}$ in $\mathbb{V}$ that satisfies

$$\lim_{i,j \to \infty} \|\mathbf{z}_i - \mathbf{z}_j\| = 0$$

must have a limit in $\mathbb{V}$ to establish the existence of the projection. Such sequences are called *Cauchy sequences*. If $\mathbb{V}$ has this property then $\mathbb{V}$ is called *complete*. In a normed vector space, every convergent sequence is a Cauchy sequence but the converse does not hold.

16 See the comments on p. 870.

17 According to Chebychev's inequality (D.3, p. 875), if Y has a finite second moment then

$$\Pr\{|Y - b| > a\} \leq \frac{\mathrm{E}[(Y - b)^2]}{a^2}$$

for any b and any $a > 0$. It follows that if $\mathrm{E}[(Y - b)^2] = 0$ also, then $\Pr\{|Y - b| > a\} = 0$ for any $a > 0$. That is, $\Pr\{Y = b\} = 1$.

MSE. This equivalence class is unique and, for most practical purposes, $E[y_n \mid \mathbf{X}]$ is *the* MMSE prediction function.

In addition to the Pythagorean and projection theorems, all of the projection structure in Section 2.4.2 applies to a general linear vector space as well as the N-dimensional Euclidean space $\mathbb{E}^N$ (denoted $\mathbb{R}^N$ at that point). For every $\mathbf{v} \in \mathbb{V}$, we can decompose $\mathbf{v}$ uniquely into the vector sum $\mathbf{v}_1 + \mathbf{v}_2$ where $\mathbf{v}_1 \in \mathbb{S}$ and $\mathbf{v}_2 \in \mathbb{S}^{\perp}$ (Lemma 2.2, p. 32). The mapping of $\mathbb{V}$ onto $\mathbb{S}$ that associates each $\mathbf{v}$ with its corresponding $\mathbf{v}_1$ is called an orthogonal projection (Definition 2, p. 32) and the orthogonal projection is a linear transformation (Lemma 2.3, p. 33).

Once again, for a vector space of random variables uniqueness must refer to an equivalence class of random variables that are equal with probability one.

6.6 METHODOLOGICAL NOTES

Before concluding this chapter, let us step back from the technical material and consider the methodological significance of this analysis. How does one apply it? In the next several chapters of this book, we will maintain Assumption 6.1, thereby basing our analysis on several key ideas. First, we suppose that our sampling procedure is repeatable. Second, we accept that the conditional mean defined by the repeatable sampling procedure holds our primary interest. Third, we suppose that the linear functional form is correct. Every one of these ideas can be challenged.

The repeated sampling paradigm is challengeable because in economics (at least) one can never actually average over an infinite number of observations the way an expectation does. As a result, the stability, existence (finiteness), and linearity that one asserts for the conditional mean under repeated sampling cannot be factual. A degree of belief is required to live by it.

Some statistical applications of OLS cannot offer repeated sampling even as an approximate possibility. The empirical study of macroeconomics with time series data is a leading example. It is obvious that one cannot resample the outcome of the economy of a particular country in a previous time period. For aggregate time series, one may view different time periods, or different countries, as replications. Which seems appropriate will depend on the conditional mean one wishes to study. Note that in making a choice, it is only the conditional mean that must be held to be invariant across the sampling units. Other aspects of the economies may differ within Assumption 6.1.

An alternative approach is to view repeated sampling as a hypothetical possibility. This may have been suggested first by Koopmans (1937):

> The observations . . . constituting one sample, a repeated sample consists of a set of values which the variables would have assumed if in these years the systematic components had been the same and the erratic components had been other independent random drawings from the distribution they are supposed to have.[18]

Some researchers adopt yet another position: they embrace the uniqueness of each observation as a realization from a distribution that may not be sampled again. This viewpoint has been formalized in Bayesian analysis, but not within the classical statistical framework. If we choose

[18] This quote is taken from Hendry and Morgan (1995, p. 287).

to imagine replication of an actually unique experiment, to put a classical framework on the situation, then statistical analysis becomes speculative. Such speculation is often useful, but there is a risk of confusing it with classical statistical inference.

Even granting repeated sampling, a focus on the conditional mean can be questioned. There are other measures of central tendency, such as the conditional median. The conditional median has the additional advantage that it always exists, whereas the conditional mean may not (at least in theory). But there are larger issues still: why focus on the central tendency of a distribution at all? Is prediction necessarily the objective? Bayesians, for example, argue that data analysis should be developed within a formal framework for making decisions under uncertainty, with a specified loss function over actions and outcomes and a distribution function for all the unknowns in the decision. Minimizing the MSE criterion to select a prediction function and deriving an unbiased estimator of that function generally fail to satisfy these requirements.

Finally, if repeated sampling and estimation of a conditional mean are granted, who can assert that the linearity of the conditional mean is a fact? For the usual reason, no one can. Indeed, most individuals will readily accept that the conditional mean almost certainly is not *exactly* linear. We can also respond to such concerns. It is certainly possible to generalize the class of functions to which conditional means may belong. We can also point out that linearity of the conditional mean function is a property that repeated sampling can investigate, when repeated sampling is possible.

The debate surrounding Assumption 6.1 and related issues began early in this century and continues to this day.[19] This will not prevent us from proceeding. All assumptions are arguable and every formal method of inference makes assumptions. We will make Assumption 6.1 and similar assumptions on two grounds, both pragmatic: first, the classical assumptions, of which this is one, form the core of a significant share of econometric thought. Second, we feel that the classical theory provides a pedagogically attractive introduction to econometric thought. The simplicity of the theory and the intelligibility of its weaknesses and strengths make it so.

6.7 OVERVIEW

1. For a matrix $\mathbf{Z}$ of random variables, and constant, conformable, matrices $\mathbf{A}$ and $\mathbf{B}$, $\mathrm{E}[\mathbf{AZ}] = \mathbf{A}\,\mathrm{E}[\mathbf{Z}]$ and $\mathrm{E}[\mathbf{ZB}] = \mathrm{E}[\mathbf{Z}]\mathbf{B}$.
2. The conditional mean function $\mu(\mathbf{x}_n) \equiv \mathrm{E}[y_n \mid \mathbf{x}_n]$ is the MMSE prediction function for y_n given $\mathbf{x}_n$.
3. Our first statistical assumption is that $\mathrm{E}[y_n \mid \mathbf{X}] = \mathbf{x}_n'\boldsymbol{\beta}_0$. This is a restriction on the process that generates the data, specifying a linear functional form in the elements of the nth row of $\mathbf{X}$.
4. Under this assumption, the OLS fitted coefficients are an unbiased estimator of $\boldsymbol{\beta}_0$.
5. Within the vector space spanned by functions of the random variables in y_n and $\mathbf{x}_n$, the conditional mean function $\mathrm{E}[y_n \mid \mathbf{x}_n]$ is an orthogonal projection, analogous to the OLS fitted vector $\hat{\boldsymbol{\mu}}$. This interpretation rests on constructing a vector space in which random variables are vectors. Assumption 6.1 assigns the same functional form to $\mathrm{E}[\mathbf{y} \mid \mathbf{X}]$ as $\hat{\boldsymbol{\mu}}$, making the analogy between these projections even closer. Table 6.1 lists the elements of the analogy.

[19] For collections of important writing about related debates, see Poirier (1994) and Hendry and Morgan (1995).

Table 6.1
Comparison of Normed Vector Spaces

	Vector Space	
Concept	Generalization of Euclidean	Random Variable
Vectors	$\mathbf{x}, \mathbf{y} \in \mathbb{R}^N$	$x, y \in \mathbb{R}$ jointly distributed random variables
Zero vector	$[0; n = 1, \ldots, N]'$	0, constant over all outcomes
Vector addition	$\mathbf{x} + \mathbf{y} = [x_n + y_n]'$	$x + y$
Scalar multiplication	$\alpha \cdot \mathbf{x} = [\alpha x_n]', \alpha \in \mathbb{R}$	$\alpha\, x, \alpha \in \mathbb{R}$
Inner product	$\mathbf{x}'\mathbf{A}\mathbf{y} = \sum_{m,n} x_m y_n a_{mn}$	$\mathrm{E}[x\, y]$
Length	$\sqrt{\mathbf{x}'\mathbf{A}\mathbf{x}}$	$\sqrt{\mathrm{E}[x^2]}$
Orthogonal projection	$\mathbf{X}\left(\mathbf{X}'\mathbf{A}\mathbf{X}\right)^{-1}\mathbf{X}'\mathbf{A}\mathbf{y}$	$\mathrm{E}[y\vert x]$

6.8 EXERCISES

6.8.1 Review

6.1 (Monte Carlo) Carry out the following Monte Carlo experiment:

(a) Compute 100 draws of a pseudorandom variable x_n from a uniform distribution on [1, 10].

(b) Compute 100 conditional draws of a pseudorandom variable y_n $(n = 1, \ldots, N)$ from a normal distribution with conditional mean equal to $10 - x_n - (25/x_n)$ and conditional variance equal to 25.

(c) Compute the OLS fitted coefficients of the regression function $\mathrm{E}[y_n \mid x_n] = \beta_{01} + \beta_{02}x_n + \beta_{03}x_n^{-1}$.

Repeat steps (b) and (c) of this experiment 1000 times holding the x_n constant and compute the sample means of the three fitted coefficients. How do they compare with the population coefficients? Also graph a frequency plot of each set of fitted coefficients.

6.2 (Expectation) Use the linearity of expectations (Lemma 6.1, p. 112) to show that the the expected value of the sample mean, $\bar{y} = \iota'\mathbf{y}/(\iota'\iota)$, equals $\mu = \mathrm{E}[y_n], n = 1, \ldots, N$, where $\mathbf{y} = [y_n]'$.

6.3 (Means) Suppose that the pair of discrete random variables (x, y) has a joint distribution described by the probability function

$$\Pr\{x = i, y = j\} = \begin{cases} \frac{i+j}{18} & \text{if } i, j \in \{0, 1, 2\} \\ 0 & \text{if otherwise} \end{cases}$$

Find numerical values for $\mathrm{E}[y]$ and $\mathrm{E}[y \mid x]$. Also find the numerical values of the β_1 and β_2 in $\beta_1 + \beta_2 x$ that minimize

$$\mathrm{E}[(y - \beta_1 - \beta_2 x)^2]$$

Compare $\mathrm{E}[y \mid x]$ and $\beta_1 + x\beta_2$.

6.4 (Vector Space of Random Variables) To draw a parallel between the Euclidean vector space $\mathbb{E}^J$ and a vector space of random variables, consider a discrete random variable y with J possible outcomes and the set of random variables $f(y)$ that can be generated as real functions $f(\cdot)$ of y.

(a) Show that the set of random variables $\{f(y) \mid f : \mathbb{R} \to \mathbb{R}\}$ is a vector space.
(b) Show that this vector space has a dimension equal to J.
(c) Show that the expectation $\mathrm{E}[f_1(y)\, f_2(y)]$ is an inner product on this vector space. Give a matrix representation of this inner product.
(d) Describe the norm corresponding to this inner product.

6.5 (Projection Analogue) Suppose that Assumption 6.1 (First Moments, p. 110) applies to the random variables $y \in \mathbb{R}$ and $\mathbf{x} \in \mathbb{R}^K$.

(a) Show that $\boldsymbol{\beta}_0 = \left(\mathrm{E}[\mathbf{x}\mathbf{x}']\right)^{-1} \mathrm{E}[\mathbf{x}y]$, provided these expectations exist and the second moment matrix of $\mathbf{x}$ is nonsingular.
(b) Suppose that the joint distribution of $\mathbf{x}$ and y is discrete. Let there be J possible outcomes and denote

$$\Pr\{(\mathbf{x}, y) = (\mathbf{x}_j, y_j)\} = p_j,\ j = 1, \ldots, J$$

Show that $\boldsymbol{\beta}_0 = \left(\mathbf{X}'\mathbf{A}\mathbf{X}\right)^{-1} \mathbf{X}'\mathbf{A}\mathbf{y}$ where $\mathbf{X} = [x_{jk}]$, $\mathbf{y} = [y_j]$, and $\mathbf{A}$ is a diagonal matrix with p_j as the jth diagonal element:

$$a_{ij} = \begin{cases} p_j & \text{if } i = j, \\ 0 & \text{if } i \neq j, \end{cases} \quad \text{so that} \quad \mathbf{A} = \left[a_{ij}\right] = \mathrm{diag}(p_j)$$

(c) What is $\boldsymbol{\beta}_0$ if all the p_j are equal?

6.6 (Variance Decomposition) Show that for any two jointly distributed random variables U and V such that $\mathrm{Var}[U]$ exists,

$$\mathrm{Var}[U] = \mathrm{E}\Big[\mathrm{Var}[U \mid V]\Big] + \mathrm{Var}\Big[\mathrm{E}[U \mid V]\Big]$$

Interpret this variance decomposition as an example of the Pythagorean theorem.

6.8.2 Extensions

6.7 (Method of Moments) This exercise describes a statistical motivation of the OLS estimator based on Assumption 6.1 (First Moments).

(a) Show that this assumption implies orthogonality between the random variables in $\mathbf{x}_n$ and the random variable $y_n - \mathbf{x}_n'\boldsymbol{\beta}_0$: that is,

$$\mathrm{E}[\mathbf{x}_n \left(y_n - \mathbf{x}_n'\boldsymbol{\beta}_0\right)] = \mathbf{0}$$

Give additional conditions on the joint distribution of $\mathbf{x}_n$ and y_n that make $\boldsymbol{\beta}_0$ the unique solution to

$$\boldsymbol{\beta} : \mathrm{E}[\mathbf{x}_n \left(y_n - \mathbf{x}_n'\boldsymbol{\beta}\right)] = \mathbf{0}$$

(b) Show that the OLS estimator $\hat{\boldsymbol{\beta}}$ is analogous to $\boldsymbol{\beta}_0$ in the sense that it is the unique solution to

$$\boldsymbol{\beta} : \mathrm{E}_N[\mathbf{x}_n \left(y_n - \mathbf{x}_n'\boldsymbol{\beta}\right)] = \mathbf{0}$$

where sample moments have replaced population moments. This is an example of a *method-of-moments estimator*, which constructs parameter estimators that equate empirical moments with population counterparts.

6.8 (Minimum Mean Absolute Error) Consider *mean absolute error* (MAE), $\mathrm{E}[|y - \mu|]$, as a measure of prediction accuracy.

(a) Show that the median is the solution to

$$\min_{\mu} \mathrm{E}[|y - \mu|]$$

(b) Show that $\mathrm{E}[|\cdot|]$ is a norm for a vector space, where the vector space consists of random variables that are real functions of y.

(c) Show that the median is not a linear operator in general; a linear operator f has the property that $f(\alpha \cdot x + y) = \alpha \cdot f(x) + f(y)$ for all $\alpha \in \mathbb{R}$, x, and y.

(d) Is the median a projection?

(e) Compare the median and mean in terms of existence.

(f) What is the minimum MAE predictor conditional on a vector of random variables x?

CHAPTER 7

VARIANCES AND COVARIANCES

7.1 INTRODUCTION

Variance and covariance are ways to describe the dispersion of data. In Figure 7.1, we plot the scatter for the age and experience variables in the 1995 CPS data. As expected, these two variables exhibit a high positive correlation, which is captured by the thin and positively sloped shape of the scatter. Figure 7.2 shows the scatter plot for the schooling and log-wage variables in the same data set. The discrete character of the schooling variable is obvious in the striated pattern of the scatter. We can also see that the correlation between these two variables, though positive, is much weaker. The scatter is much fatter. Given the scales that we have chosen for the schooling and log-wage axes, we also see that the log-wage has relatively less variation because the scatter is wider than it is high.

Figures 7.1 and 7.2 also show the *variance–covariance ellipse* for each pair of variables, centered at the means. The variance ellipse is a geometric representation of the variance and covariance of the data. The horizontal and vertical dimensions of the area occupied by the ellipse show the relative variation in the two variables. We have chosen the scale of one sample standard deviation for each variable. The thinness of the ellipse along a slope of relative standard deviations shows the degree of correlation and the direction of the slope shows the sign of the correlation. If the axes of the ellipse were horizontal and vertical, there would be no correlation. Because age and experience are relatively highly correlated, their variance ellipse is quite thin relative to the variance ellipse of schooling and log-wage. These two ellipses summarize much of the information in the scatter plot.[1]

We will use the variance ellipse to provide intuition about the second-moment properties of the OLS estimator, given second-moment assumptions described in Section 7.2. To prepare for this, let us first describe the variance ellipse for the two-dimensional cases just plotted. We give a general treatment of variance ellipses in Section 7.4.

[1] Note that the scale of the ellipse is arbitrary: we chose a standard deviation scale for simplicity. We did not choose the scale to capture a certain percentage of the data, or any other similar criterion.

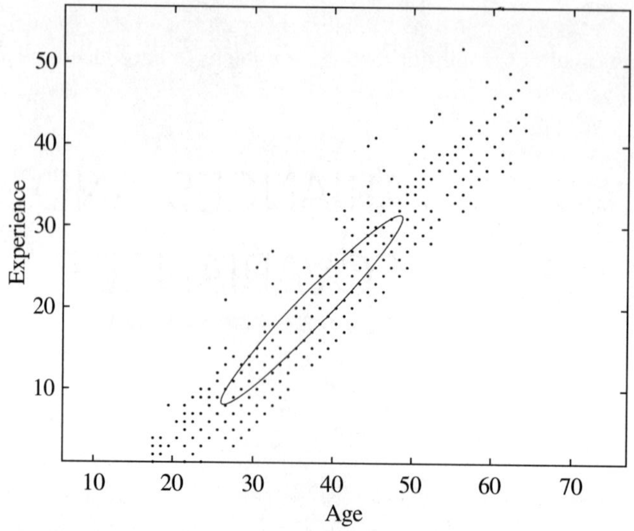

Figure 7.1 The scatter plot and variance ellipse of age and experience.

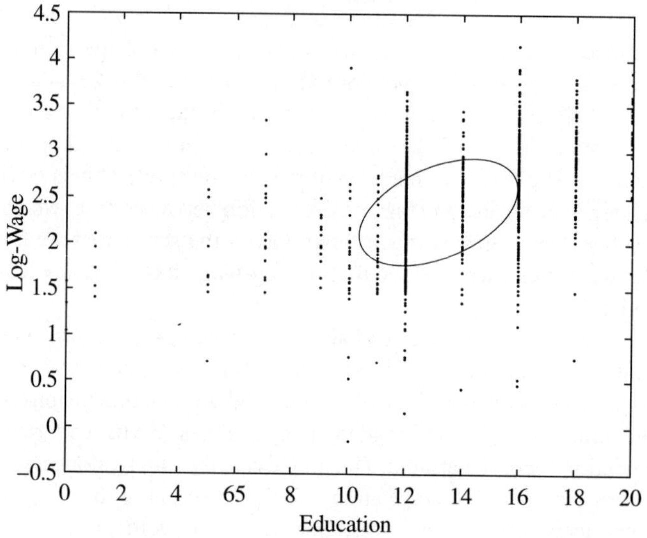

Figure 7.2 The scatter plot and variance ellipse of education and log-wage.

In the two-dimensional case, consider first a random variable $\mathbf{y}$ containing elements with equal variance, $\mathrm{Var}(y_1) = \mathrm{Var}(y_2) = \sigma^2$, and with no covariance, $\mathrm{Cov}(y_1, y_2) = 0$. The mathematical expression for the variance ellipse of y (the ellipse and its interior) is

$$\mathbb{V}_{\mathbf{y}} = \left\{ \mathbf{w} \in \mathbb{R}^2 \,\middle|\, \frac{w_1^2 + w_2^2}{\sigma^2} \leq 1 \right\} = \left\{ \mathbf{w} \mid \|\mathbf{w}\|^2 \leq \sigma^2 \right\}$$

This set is a sphere with its center located at the origin and with a radius equal to $\sigma = \sqrt{\mathrm{Var}(y_i)}$, the measure of length for random variables we introduced in Chapter 6. The symmetrical shape of the sphere captures the constant variance of *all* linear combinations $\mathbf{a}'\mathbf{y}$ of $\mathbf{y}$ that have the same length $\|\mathbf{a}\|$:

$$\mathrm{Var}(\mathbf{a}'\mathbf{y}) = \sigma^2 \left(a_1^2 + a_2^2\right) = \sigma^2 \|\mathbf{a}\|^2$$

If we introduce an increase in the variance of one element relative to the other, then we modify our expression for the variance ellipse. Suppose now that $\mathrm{Var}(y_1) = \sigma_1^2 > \mathrm{Var}(y_2) = \sigma_2^2$. We want the circle to stretch in the direction of the larger variance, turning the sphere into an ellipse. The generalization

$$\mathbb{V}_{\mathbf{y}} = \left\{ \mathbf{w} \in \mathbb{R}^2 \left| \left(\frac{w_1}{\sigma_1}\right)^2 + \left(\frac{w_2}{\sigma_2}\right)^2 \le 1 \right. \right\}$$

accomplishes this. See Figure 7.3. Within this ellipse, w_1 reaches its largest absolute value of σ_1 when $w_2 = 0$, and w_2 reaches its largest absolute value of σ_2 when $w_1 = 0$. Thus, the ellipse shows the relative magnitudes of the two random variables y_1 and y_2.

If in addition we introduce covariance, so that

$$\mathrm{Cov}(y_1, y_2) = \rho\sigma_1\sigma_2 > 0$$

then the ellipse should thin out along the direction of covariance, reflecting the association between the random variables. This generalization appears in

$$\mathbb{V}_{\mathbf{y}} = \left\{ \mathbf{w} \in \mathbb{R}^2 \left| \left(\frac{w_1}{\sigma_1}\right)^2 - 2\rho\left(\frac{w_1}{\sigma_1}\right)\left(\frac{w_2}{\sigma_2}\right) + \left(\frac{w_2}{\sigma_2}\right)^2 \le 1 - \rho^2 \right. \right\} \tag{7.1}$$

and we plot it in Figure 7.4. This third ellipse still shows the relative magnitudes of the elements of $\mathbf{y}$. For example, the largest value of w_1 occurs when

$$\frac{dw_1}{dw_2} = -\left(\frac{w_1}{\sigma_1^2} - \frac{\rho}{\sigma_1}\frac{w_2}{\sigma_2}\right)^{-1}\left(\frac{w_2}{\sigma_2^2} - \frac{\rho}{\sigma_2}\frac{w_1}{\sigma_1}\right) = 0$$

or $w_2 = \rho\sigma_2 w_1/\sigma_1$. Solving for the intersection of this line with the boundary, we find that

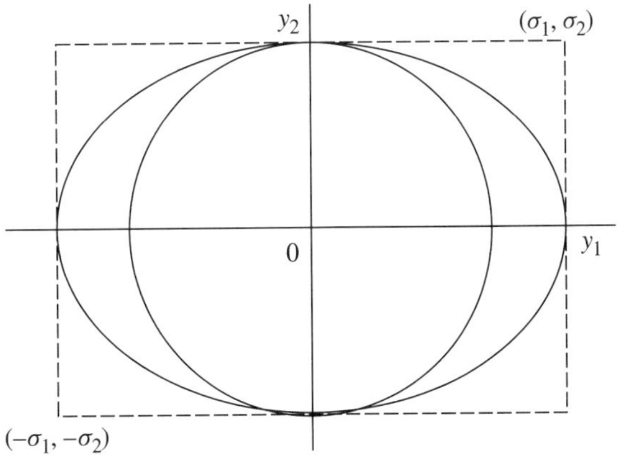

Figure 7.3 Variance ellipse: equal versus unequal variances.

$$\left(\frac{w_1}{\sigma_1}\right)^2 - 2\rho\left(\frac{w_1}{\sigma_1}\right)\left(\frac{\rho\sigma_2 w_1/\sigma_1}{\sigma_2}\right) + \left(\frac{\rho\sigma_2 w_1/\sigma_1}{\sigma_2}\right)^2 = 1 - \rho^2$$

which simplifies to $w_1^2 = \sigma_1^2 \Leftrightarrow |w_1| = \sigma_1$.

Finally, note what happens as y_1 and y_2 become perfectly correlated. As ρ approaches one, the variance ellipse narrows along the line

$$\left(\frac{w_1}{\sigma_1} - \frac{w_2}{\sigma_2}\right)^2 = 0 \Leftrightarrow w_2 = \frac{\sigma_2}{\sigma_1} w_1$$

until it collapses to a line segment in the limit. See Figure 7.5. Distributions that are degenerate in this way are called *singular* distributions.

The variance ellipses for (age, experience) and (schooling, log-wage) correspond to (7.1) with sample moments in place of σ_1, σ_2, and ρ. Through these examples, an understanding may be developed of the descriptive character of the variance ellipse and, in turn, the variances and covariances of multivariate random variables. These parameters are the focus of this chapter and the next two chapters.

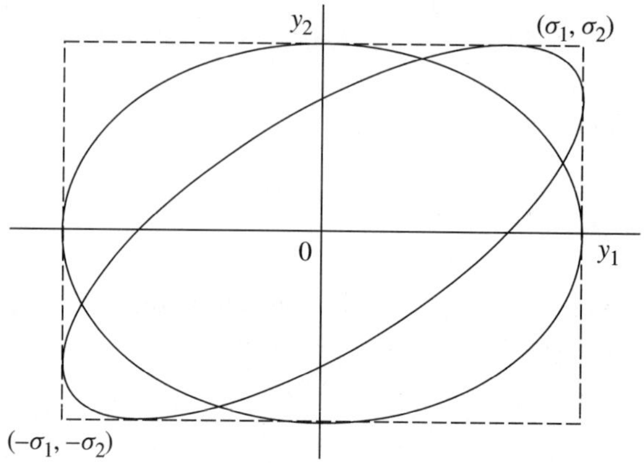

Figure 7.4 Variance ellipse: noncovariance versus covariance.

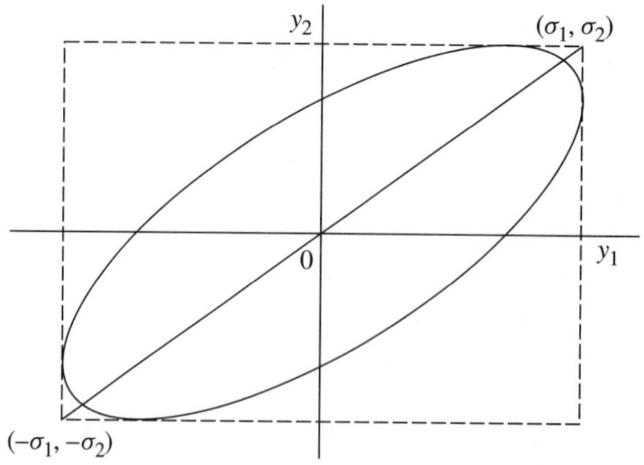

Figure 7.5 Variance ellipse: singular covariance.

7.2 SECOND MOMENTS

The assumption about the first moments of the data led to a result about the first moments of the OLS estimator. To obtain the second-moment properties of the estimator, we must make additional assumptions about the second moments of $\mathbf{y}$ conditional on $\mathbf{X}$. Before introducing these assumptions, we will provide some new notation. This notation, which uses matrices, substantially simplifies the mathematical form of the material.

The second moments of a random vector are usually collected in a *variance-covariance matrix* laid out like the entries of Table 7.1, which contains the sample variances and covariances of the data from the CPS summarized previously in Table 1.1 (p. 4). Such tables are often simplified by removing redundant terms above (or below) the main diagonal. Review, for example, the table of correlations for these same variables (Table 1.5, p. 7). The layout of the table is a matrix form that we now define.

DEFINITION 12 (COVARIANCE MATRIX) *The* covariance matrix *of the random vectors* $\mathbf{y} = [y_m; m = 1, \ldots, M]'$ *and* $\mathbf{z} = [z_n; n = 1, \ldots, N]'$, *denoted* $\text{Cov}[\mathbf{y}, \mathbf{z}]$, *is the matrix*

$$\begin{aligned}\text{Cov}[\mathbf{y}, \mathbf{z}] &\equiv [\text{Cov}[y_m, z_n]; \quad m = 1, \ldots, M,\ n = 1, \ldots, N] \\ &= \Big[\text{E}[y_m - \text{E}[y_m]][z_n - \text{E}[z_n]]; \quad m = 1, \ldots, M,\ n = 1, \ldots, N\Big] \\ &= \text{E}\big[(\mathbf{y} - \text{E}[\mathbf{y}])\,(\mathbf{z} - \text{E}[\mathbf{z}])'\big]\end{aligned}$$

There is an important special case of the covariance matrix.

DEFINITION 13 (VARIANCE–COVARIANCE MATRIX) *The covariance matrix specializes to the* variance–covariance *(or simply,* variance*) matrix, when* $\mathbf{y} = \mathbf{z}$. *The variance matrix is denoted* $\text{Var}[\mathbf{y}] \equiv \text{Cov}[\mathbf{y}, \mathbf{y}]$ *and is a square, symmetric matrix with variances* $(\text{Cov}[y_m, y_m] = \text{Var}[y_m])$ *arrayed along the main diagonal and covariances everywhere else. The covariance between the* mth *and* nth *elements of y are in positions* (m, n) *and* (n, m) *of the variance matrix.*[2]

Because we are dealing with linear transformations of random variables in OLS, we will frequently use the following lemma. It is a matrix version of the simple quadratic expansion

$$(aY + bZ)^2 = a^2Y^2 + 2abYZ + b^2Z^2$$

and the basic probability result that

$$\text{Var}[aY + bZ] = a^2\,\text{Var}[Y] + 2ab\,\text{Cov}[Y, Z] + b^2\,\text{Var}[Z]$$

[2]Many writers abbreviate $\text{Var}[\mathbf{y}]$ to $\text{V}[\mathbf{y}]$. Less common is the abbreviation of $\text{Cov}[\mathbf{y}, \mathbf{z}]$ to $\text{C}[\mathbf{y}, \mathbf{z}]$. $\text{Var}[\mathbf{y}]$ is often called the *covariance* matrix, as an abbreviation of *variance–covariance*. We will use the abbreviation *variance* matrix to be consistent with the notation. *Covariance* matrix will be reserved for $\text{Cov}[\mathbf{y}, \mathbf{z}]$, which is, of course, a generalization of the variance matrix.

Table 7.1
Sample Covariances

	Wage	Education	Experience	Age	Female	Nonwhite	Union
Wage	62.352	10.143	15.948	26.092	−0.882	−0.363	0.295
Education	10.143	7.918	−5.911	2.007	−0.044	−0.088	0.004
Experience	15.948	−5.911	136.022	130.111	−0.132	−0.164	0.659
Age	26.092	2.007	130.111	132.118	−0.176	−0.253	0.663
Female	−0.882	−0.044	−0.132	−0.176	0.250	0.008	−0.016
Nonwhite	−0.363	−0.088	−0.164	−0.253	0.008	0.130	0.011
Union	0.295	0.004	0.659	0.663	−0.016	0.011	0.134

LEMMA 7.1 (BILINEARITY OF COVARIANCES) $\mathrm{Cov}[\mathbf{Ay}, \mathbf{Bz}] = \mathbf{A}\,\mathrm{Cov}[\mathbf{y}, \mathbf{z}]\mathbf{B}'$ *and* $\mathrm{Var}[\mathbf{Ay}] = \mathbf{A}\,\mathrm{Var}[\mathbf{y}]\mathbf{A}'$.

Proof. In the following sequence of equalities, we apply Lemma 6.1 (p. 112) repeatedly:

$$\begin{aligned}
\mathrm{Cov}[\mathbf{Ay}, \mathbf{Bz}] &\equiv \mathrm{E}\big[(\mathbf{Ay} - \mathrm{E}[\mathbf{Ay}])\,(\mathbf{Bz} - \mathrm{E}[\mathbf{Bz}])'\big] \\
&= \mathrm{E}\big[(\mathbf{Ay} - \mathbf{A}\,\mathrm{E}[\mathbf{y}])\,(\mathbf{Bz} - \mathbf{B}\,\mathrm{E}[\mathbf{z}])'\big] \\
&= \mathrm{E}\big[\mathbf{A}\,(\mathbf{y} - \mathrm{E}[\mathbf{y}])\,(\mathbf{z} - \mathrm{E}[\mathbf{z}])'\,\mathbf{B}'\big] \\
&= \mathbf{A}\,\mathrm{E}\big[(\mathbf{y} - \mathrm{E}[\mathbf{y}])\,(\mathbf{z} - \mathrm{E}[\mathbf{z}])'\big]\mathbf{B}' \\
&= \mathbf{A}\,\mathrm{Cov}[\mathbf{y}, \mathbf{z}]\mathbf{B}'
\end{aligned}$$

It immediately follows that $\mathrm{Cov}[\mathbf{Ay}, \mathbf{Ay}] \equiv \mathrm{Var}[\mathbf{Ay}] = \mathbf{A}\,\mathrm{Var}[\mathbf{y}]\mathbf{A}'$. □

Now we state our second-moment, or variance–covariance, assumption. This assumption will lead to several second moment properties for OLS fitted coefficients.

ASSUMPTION 7.1 (SECOND MOMENTS) *Conditional on* **X**, *the variance matrix of* y *is a* scalar *matrix:* $\mathrm{Var}[\mathbf{y} \mid \mathbf{X}] = \sigma_0^2 \cdot \mathbf{I}_N$.

This assumption restricts the conditional second moments of **y**: it states that the elements of **y** have equal variances and are mutually uncorrelated, conditional on all of the elements of **X**. Independent sampling produces such variance matrices, but recall that zero covariances do not imply independence. Assumption 7.1 is a weaker assumption than assuming that the elements of **y** are independent and identically distributed, conditional on **X**.

This assumption also introduces a new, unknown population parameter into our analysis, σ_0^2. This parameter is the variance of each of the elements of **y** conditional on **X**. Eventually, we will find an unbiased estimator for σ_0^2. In this chapter, we restrict our discussion to Assumption 7.1.

We refer to $\text{Var}[\mathbf{y} \mid \mathbf{X}]$ as a *scalar* matrix. Scalar matrices get their name from their properties as linear transformations. If we premultiply $\mathbf{z} \in \mathbb{R}^N$ by $\alpha \cdot \mathbf{I}_N$, $\alpha \in \mathbb{R}$, then the result is $\alpha \cdot \mathbf{z}$, so that the transformed vector is a *scalar multiple* of the original vector.

7.3 SPHERICAL DISTRIBUTIONS

Scalar variance matrices are special, and a useful way to characterize this is to observe that the variance ellipse associated with a scalar variance matrix is a sphere. We described this for the two-dimensional case briefly in the introductory section of this chapter. Now we explain why multivariate distributions with scalar variance matrices are generally called *spherical*.[3] This will lead to our general discussion of variance ellipses in the next section.

Consider the special class of matrix transformations called *orthogonal*.[4] This class comprises a group of linear transformations that preserves scalar variance matrices. If $\mathbf{R}$ is an $N \times N$ orthogonal matrix and if $\text{Var}[\mathbf{y}] = \sigma^2 \cdot \mathbf{I}_N$, then

$$\text{Var}[\mathbf{R}'\mathbf{y}] = \mathbf{R}'(\sigma^2 \cdot \mathbf{I}_N)\mathbf{R} = \sigma^2 \cdot \mathbf{R}'\mathbf{R} = \sigma^2 \cdot \mathbf{I}_N \tag{7.2}$$

As linear transformations, orthogonal matrices are represented geometrically in two dimensions as *rotations* and *reflections* of a vector space. Given any two vectors $\mathbf{z}_1$ and $\mathbf{z}_2$ from $\mathbb{R}^N$ and an orthogonal matrix $\mathbf{R}$,

$$\begin{aligned} \mathbf{z}_1'\mathbf{z}_2 &= \mathbf{z}_1'\mathbf{R}\mathbf{R}'\mathbf{z}_2 = (\mathbf{R}'\mathbf{z}_1)'(\mathbf{R}'\mathbf{z}_2) \quad \Rightarrow \\ \|\mathbf{z}_1\|^2 &= \mathbf{z}_1'\mathbf{R}\mathbf{R}'\mathbf{z}_1 = (\mathbf{R}'\mathbf{z}_1)'(\mathbf{R}'\mathbf{z}_1) = \left\|\mathbf{R}'\mathbf{z}_1\right\|^2 \end{aligned}$$

Therefore, angles and distances between vectors are preserved under transformation by $\mathbf{R}'$. We can interpret (7.2) as indicating that scalar variance matrices are preserved under rotation of a random vector. Given data from a multivariate distribution with a scalar variance matrix, there would be no way to determine from the sample variance matrix whether the data points had undergone rotation before delivery.

EXAMPLE 7.1

A family of two-dimensional orthogonal matrices is[5]

$$\mathbf{R} = \begin{bmatrix} \sqrt{1-\theta^2} & -\theta \\ \theta & \sqrt{1-\theta^2} \end{bmatrix}$$

[3] The term "spherical" has other uses in probability. Spherical distributions can also be distributions on the *surface of a sphere*. Distributions with *spherically symmetric* probability density functions are a refinement of the spherical distributions that we describe in this chapter. See footnote 2 on p. 196 and the discussion of the multivariate normal probability density function.

[4] See Definition C.22 (Orthogonal Matrix, p. 856). Briefly described, R is called orthogonal if $R'R = I$. The columns (or the rows) of R can also be viewed as an orthonormal basis.

[5] This family of orthogonal matrices excludes some possibilities. A larger family of orthogonal matrices for $\mathbb{R}^2$ is described by

$$R = \begin{bmatrix} \sin\theta & -\cos\theta \\ \cos\theta & \sin\theta \end{bmatrix}$$

where θ can be interpreted as the angle of rotation.

Letting $\text{Var}[\mathbf{y}] = \sigma^2 \cdot \mathbf{I}_2$ and $\mathbf{z} = \mathbf{R}'\mathbf{y}$,

$$\text{Var}[z_1] = (1 - \theta^2)\,\text{Var}[y_1] + \theta^2\,\text{Var}[y_2] = \sigma^2$$
$$\text{Var}[z_2] = (-\theta)^2\,\text{Var}[y_1] + (1 - \theta^2)\,\text{Var}[y_2] = \sigma^2$$
$$\text{Cov}[z_1, z_2] = \sqrt{1 - \theta^2}\,(-\theta)\,\text{Var}[y_1] + \theta\sqrt{1 - \theta^2}\,\text{Var}[y_2] = 0$$

Thus, $\mathbf{z}$ has the same scalar variance matrix as $\mathbf{y}$.

The preservation (invariance?) of scalar variance matrices after orthogonal transformation of the random vector has a useful geometric representation. Spheres are the geometric shape that is invariant to rotation and reflection. The elements of a sphere in $\mathbb{R}^N$ are the set of vectors $\mathbf{y}$ with a bounded length, say r^2:

$$\left\{\mathbf{a} \in \mathbb{R}^N \mid \mathbf{a}'\mathbf{a} \leq r^2\right\}$$

If we rotate this set of points, by applying an orthogonal linear transformation $\mathbf{R}$, we obtain the same set of points:

$$\left\{\mathbf{w} = \mathbf{R}'\mathbf{a} \mid \mathbf{a} \in \mathbb{R}^N,\ \mathbf{a}'\mathbf{a} \leq r^2\right\} = \left\{\mathbf{w} \in \mathbb{R}^N \mid \mathbf{w}'\mathbf{R}'\mathbf{R}\mathbf{w} \leq r^2\right\}$$
$$= \left\{\mathbf{w} \in \mathbb{R}^N \mid \mathbf{w}'\mathbf{w} \leq r^2\right\}$$

Thus, analysts have associated scalar covariance matrices geometrically with spheres and frequently call multivariate distributions with scalar variance matrices spherical distributions.

Because Assumption 7.1 (Second Moments) assigns a scalar variance matrix to $\mathbf{y}$ conditional on $\mathbf{X}$, econometricians often restate this assumption as "$\mathbf{y}$ has a spherical distribution conditional on $\mathbf{X}$." From now on, we will depict the conditional variance of $\mathbf{y}$ geometrically as a sphere. Figure 7.6 shows the geometry for two observations. The circle centered at $\boldsymbol{\mu}_0$ and labeled $\mathbb{V}_\mathbf{y}$ represents the variance of $\mathbf{y}$ about its mean. Note that a realization of $\mathbf{y}$ can occur anywhere in the two-dimensional plane. Figure 7.7 shows the version for three observations. In this case, realizations of $\mathbf{y}$ occur anywhere in three-space. In previous figures (Figures 2.5 and 2.6), we have

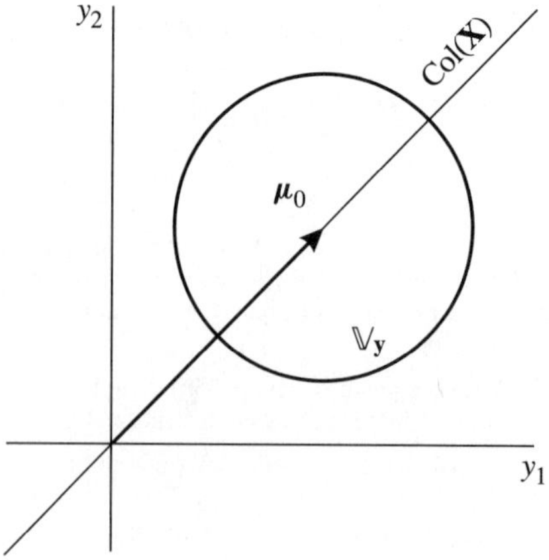

Figure 7.6 The variance sphere of $\mathbf{y}$ for two observations.

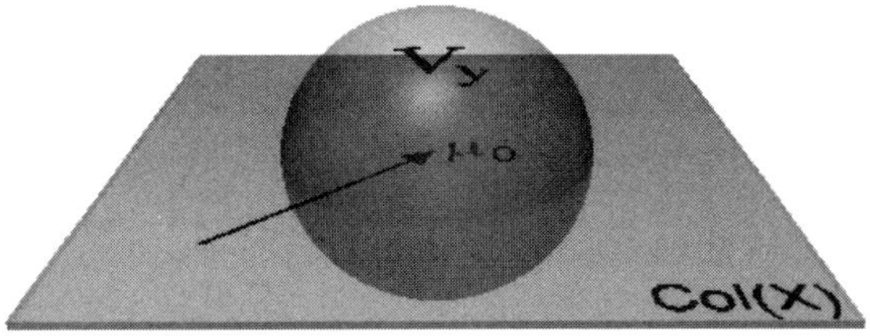

Figure 7.7 The variance sphere of **y** for three observations.

placed a *particular realization* of **y** in the figure as a vector. For convenience, we placed **y** above Col(**X**), but generally **y** could appear anywhere. Now in the current figures, we have removed **y** and in its stead picture the *distribution* of **y** in terms of its first two *moments*.

7.4 THE VARIANCE ELLIPSE

Ellipses can represent all of the information in general variance matrices. In this section, we explain variance matrices and ellipses more extensively. We have been focusing on the *spherical* character of *scalar* variance matrices. Now we generalize to the *elliptical* character of *all* variance matrices.

The variance matrix describes the distribution of a random variable in two important ways. One way is that the column space of the variance matrix is the linear subspace that contains the random variable centered by its mean.

> **LEMMA 7.2 (VARIANCE COLUMN SPACE)** *If* $\mathbf{y}$ *is a random vector with finite* $\mathrm{E}[\mathbf{y}] = \boldsymbol{\mu}$ *and* $\mathrm{Var}[\mathbf{y}] = \boldsymbol{\Omega}$, *then* $\Pr\{\mathbf{y} - \boldsymbol{\mu} \in \mathrm{Col}(\boldsymbol{\Omega})\} = 1$.

Proof. If $\boldsymbol{\Omega}$ is full rank, then $\mathrm{Col}(\boldsymbol{\Omega})$ places no restrictions on $\mathbf{y}$ or $\boldsymbol{\mu}$. Suppose, therefore, that $\mathrm{rank}(\boldsymbol{\Omega}) < N$ where $\mathbf{y}$ has N elements. Now consider any nonzero vector $\mathbf{a} \in \mathrm{Col}^{\perp}(\boldsymbol{\Omega})$. Then $\mathrm{E}[\mathbf{a}'(\mathbf{y} - \boldsymbol{\mu})] = 0$ and

$$\mathrm{Var}[\mathbf{a}'(\mathbf{y} - \boldsymbol{\mu})] = \mathbf{a}'\boldsymbol{\Omega}\mathbf{a} = 0$$

so that, by Jensen's inequality (Lemma D.1, p. 874), $\mathbf{a}'(\mathbf{y} - \boldsymbol{\mu})$ is a constant equal to 0 with probability one. In other words, $\Pr\{\mathbf{a} \perp \mathbf{y} - \boldsymbol{\mu}\} = 1$ and, therefore according to Theorem C.8 (p. 850), $\Pr\{\mathbf{y} - \boldsymbol{\mu} \in \mathrm{Col}(\boldsymbol{\Omega})\} = 1$. □

We see, then, that variance matrices can be singular. Generally, random variables can have *singular distributions* and one of the common ways in which this occurs formally is when random variables are linearly dependent.[6] In that case, there is a linear combination of the random variables that equals a constant and has no variance.

The variance matrix also describes the pattern of dispersion among the elements of a random vector. These patterns have a geometric interpretation called the variance ellipse. This ellipse

[6] See Definition D.17 (Singular Distribution, p. 881).

depends only on the variance matrix $\mathbf{\Omega}$ and yields a multivariate interval that reflects variance and covariance.[7]

Definition 14 (Variance Ellipse) *Given the random variable* $\mathbf{y} \in \mathbb{R}^N$ *with the variance matrix* $\mathbf{\Omega}$*, the* variance ellipse $\mathbb{V}_{\mathbf{y}}$ *of* $\mathbf{y}$ *is the set*

$$\mathbb{V}_{\mathbf{y}} = \left\{ \mathbf{w} = \mathbf{\Omega a} \mid \mathbf{a} \in \mathbb{R}^N,\ \mathbf{a}'\mathbf{\Omega a} \leq 1 \right\}$$

The definition reflects Lemma 7.2 in constructing elements of the ellipse so that they are members of the subspace Col($\mathbf{\Omega}$). Note that the *quadratic form* $\mathbf{a}'\mathbf{\Omega a}$ equals Var[$\mathbf{a}'\mathbf{y}$], which is always positive. The upper bound of 1 is chosen for convenience. Any constant would serve the same purpose. It is the shape and relative size of a variance ellipse that interests us. This constant delivers an ellipse tangent to a box with dimensions that coincide with the lengths (standard deviations) of the random variables.

Because $\mathbf{a}'\mathbf{\Omega a} = \text{Var}[\mathbf{a}'\mathbf{y}] \geq 0$, we see that variance matrices are positive semi-definite (Definition 6, p. 38), like orthogonal projectors. If $\mathbf{\Omega}$ is nonsingular then the inequality is strict for any $\mathbf{a} \neq 0$ and $\mathbf{\Omega}$ is called *positive definite*.

Definition 15 (Positive Definite) *The matrix* $\mathbf{A}$ *is* positive definite *if* $\mathbf{A}$ *is square and* $\mathbf{w}'\mathbf{A}\mathbf{w} > 0$ *for all conformable* $\mathbf{w} \neq \mathbf{0}$.

If $\mathbf{\Omega}$ is nonsingular, then $\mathbf{w} = \mathbf{\Omega a}$ implies that $\mathbf{a} = \mathbf{\Omega}^{-1}\mathbf{w}$ and the variance ellipse can also be written as

$$\mathbb{V}_{\mathbf{y}} = \left\{ \mathbf{w} \in \mathbb{R}^N \mid \mathbf{w}'\mathbf{\Omega}^{-1}\mathbf{w} \leq 1 \right\} \tag{7.3}$$

Note that $\mathbf{\Omega}^{-1}$ is also positive definite because $\mathbf{w}'\mathbf{\Omega}^{-1}\mathbf{w} = \mathbf{a}'\mathbf{\Omega a} \geq 0$. Therefore, the variance ellipse is the set of points with a generalized Euclidean length (with respect to $\mathbf{\Omega}^{-1}$) less than or equal to one.[8]

In the one-dimensional case,

$$\mathbb{V}_{\mathbf{y}} = \left\{ w \in \mathbb{R} \mid w^2/\sigma^2 \leq 1 \right\} = \{ w \mid -\sigma \leq w \leq \sigma \}$$

where σ is the standard deviation of y. Thus, the univariate interval has the width of two standard deviations. We have already described two-dimensional examples in the introduction of this chapter. There we showed two-dimensional ellipses bounded by rectangles two standard deviations on each side. In addition, we depicted increasing covariance as the ellipse collapsing toward a diagonal. The reader can check that (7.3) corresponds to (7.1) in the two-dimensional case.

A central characteristic of variance ellipses is that they are transformed in a natural way by linear transformations.

---

[7] Malinvaud (1970, pp. 160–165) gives a derivation of our definition. According to Malinvaud, Darmois (1945) originally defined the variance ellipse, but he called it the *concentration ellipsoid*.

[8] For the discussion of generalized length, see Sections 4.4–4.5.

Lemma 7.3 *Let* $\mathbf{y} \in \mathbb{R}^N$ *be a vector of random variables and* $\mathbf{z} = \mathbf{A}\mathbf{y} \in \mathbb{R}^K$ *for a constant matrix* $\mathbf{A}$. *If we denote* $\operatorname{Var}[\mathbf{y}] = \mathbf{\Omega}$, *then the variance ellipse of* $\mathbf{z}$ *is the image of the variance ellipse of* $\mathbf{y}$ *under the linear transformation* $\mathbf{A}$:

$$\begin{aligned}\mathbb{V}_{\mathbf{z}} &\equiv \left\{\mathbf{w} = \mathbf{A\Omega A'a} \mid \mathbf{a} \in \mathbb{R}^K,\ \mathbf{a'A\Omega A'a} \leq 1\right\} \\ &= \left\{\mathbf{w} = \mathbf{Av} \mid \mathbf{v} \in \mathbb{V}_{\mathbf{y}}\right\}\end{aligned}$$

We prove this lemma on p. 144 in Section 7.6.3, *Linear Transformation of Variance Ellipses*.

Most of the OLS statistics that we study in the next chapter are linear functions of $\mathbf{y}$. This makes their variance matrices analytically tractable, because we can apply Lemma 7.1. This linearity also makes their associated variance ellipses linear transformations of the spherical variance ellipse of $\mathbf{y}$. When the linear transformation is a projection, as in the cases of $\hat{\boldsymbol{\mu}}$ and $\mathbf{y}-\hat{\boldsymbol{\mu}}$, the resultant variance ellipse is easy to visualize and has a character that would otherwise be obscured. For this reason, we will make use of Lemma 7.3 to develop an intuitive understanding of the mathematical material in the next two chapters.

7.5 MINIMUM MSE LINEAR PREDICTION

The fundamental significance of covariance is that it can be exploited for prediction. If two random variables vary together, then one can help predict the other in the sense that the mean squared error of prediction can be reduced. This is such a natural result that people engage in conditional forecasting all the time. We saw in Chapter 3 how lagged values of the unemployment rate improved our forecasts. This improvement rests on the serial correlation in unemployment that common sense and experience anticipate. If we compare prediction functions with the MSE criterion, then we can derive a minimum MSE (MMSE) prediction function. The conditional mean $\mathrm{E}[y_n \mid \mathbf{x}_n]$ is optimal, as we saw in Lemma 6.2 (Minimum MSE Predictor, p. 113), when we optimize over all functions of x_n. It is interesting to restrict our search to linear functions of $\mathbf{x}_n$. In that case, we obtain an optimal prediction function analogous the OLS fitted vector.

Lemma 7.4 (MMSE Linear Predictor) *Suppose that the second moments of* y_n *and* $\mathbf{x}_n$ *are finite and that* $\mathrm{E}[\mathbf{x}_n\mathbf{x}_n']$ *is nonsingular. The linear predictor* $\mathbf{x}_n'\boldsymbol{\gamma}_0$ *is the unique MMSE linear predictor of* y_n *if and only if* $\mathrm{E}[(y_n - \mathbf{x}_n'\boldsymbol{\gamma}_0)\,\mathbf{x}_n'\boldsymbol{\gamma}] = 0$ *for all constant* $\boldsymbol{\gamma} \in \mathbb{R}^K$. *Furthermore, if the elements of* $\mathbf{x}_n$ *are linearly independent, then*[9]

$$\boldsymbol{\gamma}_0 = \left(\mathrm{E}[\mathbf{x}_n\mathbf{x}_n']\right)^{-1}\mathrm{E}[\mathbf{x}_n y_n] \tag{7.4}$$

and

$$\mathrm{E}[y_n^2] - \mathrm{E}[y_n\mathbf{x}_n']\left(\mathrm{E}[\mathbf{x}_n\mathbf{x}_n']\right)^{-1}\mathrm{E}[\mathbf{x}_n y_n] = \min_{\boldsymbol{\gamma}\in\mathbb{R}^K} \mathrm{E}[(y_n - \mathbf{x}_n'\boldsymbol{\gamma})^2] \tag{7.5}$$

[9] To be more precise, we should say that the elements of $\mathbf{x}_n$ must be linearly independent with probability greater than zero; that is, for all $\mathbf{a} \in \mathbb{R}^K$, $\Pr\{\mathbf{a}'\mathbf{x}_n = 0\} < 1$.

Proof. This lemma is another version of the projection theorem (Theorem 6, p. 119). Noting that

$$\begin{aligned}\mathrm{E}[(y_n - \mathbf{x}_n'\boldsymbol{\gamma}_0)\,\mathbf{x}_n'\boldsymbol{\gamma}] &= \mathrm{E}[(\mathbf{x}_n'\boldsymbol{\gamma})'(y_n - \mathbf{x}_n'\boldsymbol{\gamma}_0)]\\ &= \boldsymbol{\gamma}'\,\mathrm{E}[\mathbf{x}_n(y_n - \mathbf{x}_n'\boldsymbol{\gamma}_0)]\end{aligned}$$

we find that $\mathrm{E}[(y_n - \mathbf{x}_n'\boldsymbol{\gamma}_0)\,\mathbf{x}_n'\boldsymbol{\gamma}] = 0$ for all $\boldsymbol{\gamma}$ if and only if $y_n - \mathbf{x}_n'\boldsymbol{\gamma}_0$ and every element of $\mathbf{x}_n$ are orthogonal, that is $\mathrm{E}[\mathbf{x}_n(y_n - \mathbf{x}_n'\boldsymbol{\gamma}_0)] = 0$. It follows from the projection theorem (Theorem 6, p. 119) that $\mathbf{x}_n'\boldsymbol{\gamma}_0$ is the unique solution to

$$\min_{\mu \in \mathbb{S}} \mathrm{E}[(y_n - \mu_n)^2]$$

where $\mathbb{S} = \left\{z_n = \mathbf{x}_n'\boldsymbol{\gamma} \mid \boldsymbol{\gamma} \in \mathbb{R}^K\right\}$.

Solving

$$\mathrm{E}[\mathbf{x}_n(y_n - \mathbf{x}_n'\boldsymbol{\gamma}_0)] = \mathbf{0} \quad \Leftrightarrow \quad \mathrm{E}[\mathbf{x}_n y_n] = \mathrm{E}[\mathbf{x}_n\mathbf{x}_n']\boldsymbol{\gamma}_0 \tag{7.6}$$

yields (7.4) for $\boldsymbol{\gamma}_0$. Substituting (7.4) into the MSE function $\mathrm{E}[(y_n - \mathbf{x}_n'\boldsymbol{\gamma}_0)^2]$ gives (7.5). □

Lemma 7.4 is closely related to Lemma 6.2 (Minimum MSE Predictor, p. 113), the only difference being that the prediction function is restricted to be *linear* in $\mathbf{x}_n$ in the present case. The conditions of Lemma 7.4 still permit the conditional mean to be *nonlinear*. If the conditional mean is linear, as we assume it to be in the classical linear regression model, then the conditional mean and the MMSE linear predictor are identical.

Also note the formal similarities with OLS that follow from the restriction to linear predictors: in effect we have replaced summation over observations with expectation over the sample space, so that population moments appear instead of sample moments. Using the expectation with respect to the *empirical distribution* makes this particularly clear:[10]

$$\begin{aligned}\hat{\boldsymbol{\beta}} &= \left(\mathbf{X}'\mathbf{X}\right)^{-1}\mathbf{X}'\mathbf{y}\\ &= \left(\sum_{n=1}^{N}\mathbf{x}_n\mathbf{x}_n'\frac{1}{N}\right)^{-1}\sum_{n=1}^{N}\mathbf{x}_n y_n\frac{1}{N}\\ &= \left(\mathrm{E}_N[\mathbf{x}_n\mathbf{x}_n']\right)^{-1}\mathrm{E}_N[\mathbf{x}_n y_n]\end{aligned}$$

The analogy between the population moments in the MMSE linear predictor and the sample moments in the OLS fit works neatly in partitioned forms as well. The partitioned form is useful, because it permits us to isolate the additional contribution of $\mathbf{x}_n$ to the prediction of y_n beyond the marginal mean $\mathrm{E}[y_n]$.

EXAMPLE 7.2

As an example, reconsider Example 3.1 (p. 58), where $K = 2$ and $x_{n2} = 1$, so that

[10] See Definition E.3 (Empirical Distribution, p. 902) and Definition E.4 (Sample Moment, p. 903).

$$\hat{\beta}_1 = \frac{\sum_{n=1}^{N}(x_{n1} - \bar{x}_1)(y_n - \bar{y})}{\sum_{n=1}^{N}(x_{n1} - \bar{x}_1)^2}$$
$$\hat{\beta}_2 = \bar{y} - \bar{x}_1\hat{\beta}_1$$

We can also write

$$\hat{\beta}_1 = \frac{\mathrm{Cov}_N[x_{n1}, y_n]}{\mathrm{Var}_N[x_{n1}]}$$
$$\hat{\beta}_2 = \mathrm{E}_N[y_n] - \mathrm{E}_N[x_{n1}]\hat{\beta}_1$$

where Var_N, and Cov_N denote centered second moments with respect to the empirical distribution. We can easily solve the first-order conditions of

$$\min_{\gamma_1, \gamma_2} \mathrm{E}[(y_n - \gamma_1 x_{n1} - \gamma_2)^2]$$

to find that

$$\gamma_{01} = \frac{\mathrm{Cov}[x_{n1}, y_n]}{\mathrm{Var}[x_{n1}]}$$
$$\gamma_{02} = \mathrm{E}[y_n] - \mathrm{E}[x_{n1}]\gamma_{01}$$

Thus, γ_{01} and γ_{02} are exact analogues to $\hat{\beta}_1$ and $\hat{\beta}_2$.

The partitioned form in this example emphasizes that *covariance* between y_n and its prediction variable x_{n1} is the foundation of the MMSE linear prediction function. More generally, recall the partitioned OLS formulas[11]

$$\hat{\boldsymbol{\beta}}_1 = \left(\mathbf{X}'_{1\perp 2}\mathbf{X}_{1\perp 2}\right)^{-1}\mathbf{X}'_{1\perp 2}\mathbf{y}_{\perp 2}$$
$$\hat{\boldsymbol{\beta}}_2 = \left(\mathbf{X}'_2\mathbf{X}_2\right)^{-1}\mathbf{X}'_2(\mathbf{y} - \mathbf{X}_1\hat{\boldsymbol{\beta}}_1)$$

When $\mathbf{X}_2$ is a column vector of ones, $\boldsymbol{\iota}$, every element of $\mathbf{X}_{1\perp 2}$ and $\mathbf{y}_{\perp 2}$ is a deviation from a sample mean.[12] As a result, when $\mathbf{x}_n = \left[\mathbf{x}'_{1n}, 1\right]'$ these expressions can be rewritten

$$\hat{\boldsymbol{\beta}}_1 = (\mathrm{Var}_N[\mathbf{x}_{1n}])^{-1}\,\mathrm{Cov}_N[\mathbf{x}_{1n}, y_n]$$
$$\hat{\beta}_2 = \mathrm{E}_N[y_n] - \mathrm{E}_N[\mathbf{x}'_{1n}]\hat{\boldsymbol{\beta}}_1$$

Similarly, we can rewrite the optimal $\boldsymbol{\gamma}_0$ of Lemma 7.4 in a partitioned form:

$$\boldsymbol{\gamma}_{01} = (\mathrm{Var}[\mathbf{x}_{1n}])^{-1}\,\mathrm{Cov}[\mathbf{x}_{1n}, y_n] \tag{7.7}$$
$$\gamma_{02} = \mathrm{E}[y_n] - \mathrm{E}[\mathbf{x}'_{1n}]\boldsymbol{\gamma}_{01} \tag{7.8}$$

The formula in (7.7) emphasizes the central importance of covariance in prediction. If there is no covariance between y_n and $\mathbf{x}_n$, then knowledge of $\mathbf{x}_n$ cannot lower the MSE in predicting y_n through a linear function. In that case, the MMSE linear predictor of y_n is simply its marginal mean, $\mathrm{E}[y_n]$. But in general the MMSE linear predictor is

---

[11] The derivation of the expression for $\hat{\boldsymbol{\beta}}_2$ is part of Exercise 3.8.

[12] See also Exercises 2.7 (p. 41) and 3.4 (p. 69).

$$\mathbf{x}_n'\gamma_0 = \mathrm{E}[y_n] + (\mathbf{x}_{1n} - \mathrm{E}[\mathbf{x}_{1n}])' (\mathrm{Var}[\mathbf{x}_{1n}])^{-1} \mathrm{Cov}[\mathbf{x}_{1n}, y_n]$$

which adjusts the marginal mean by a linear function of $\mathbf{x}_{1n}$ with coefficients that depend on second moments. If $\mathrm{Cov}[\mathbf{x}_{1n}, y_n]$ were zero, then $\mathbf{x}_{1n}$ could not help predict y_n. This function is so important that it is often given its own notation:[13]

$$\mathrm{E}^*[y_n \mid \mathbf{x}_{1n}] \equiv \mathrm{E}[y_n] + (\mathbf{x}_{1n} - \mathrm{E}[\mathbf{x}_{1n}])' (\mathrm{Var}[\mathbf{x}_{1n}])^{-1} \mathrm{Cov}[\mathbf{x}_{1n}, y_n] \tag{7.9}$$

In this light, we can interpret our second-moment assumption, that $\mathrm{Var}[\mathbf{y} \mid \mathbf{X}] = \sigma_0^2 \cdot \mathbf{I}_N$, to state that $y_n - \mathbf{x}_n'\boldsymbol{\beta}_0$ cannot help in predicting $y_m - \mathbf{x}_m'\boldsymbol{\beta}_0$ when $m \neq n$ through a *linear* function. To this limited extent, one may treat these residuals as unrelated. It is still possible within these assumptions that nonlinear functions of such residuals may provide useful predictors. By ruling out covariance among the $y_m - \mathbf{x}_m'\boldsymbol{\beta}_0$, one effectively assumes that $\mathbf{x}_n'\boldsymbol{\beta}_0$ captures all of the predictable linear variation in y_n. The distributed lag model for unemployment in Chapter 3 is an example in which such an assumption may be dubious. Unusually high unemployment in one month may very well augur unusually high unemployment in the next. For the earnings data, however, this assumption seems much more plausible. In a random sample of U.S. residents, we do not expect to find covariance among the differences between the observed wages and their MMSE linear predictors.

The variance ellipsoid and the MMSE linear predictor are both functions of the variance matrix and there is a geometric relationship between them. The MMSE linear predictor is the y-component of the point of tangency of an ellipsoid proportional to the variance ellipsoid of (y_n, x_n) to the "conditioning set"

$$\mathbb{C}(\mathbf{x}_n) \equiv \left\{ \begin{bmatrix} y \\ \mathbf{x} \end{bmatrix} \in \mathbb{R} \times \mathbb{R}^K \mid \mathbf{x} = \mathbf{x}_n \right\}$$

Figure 7.8 depicts this relationship when $K = 1$ and $\mathrm{E}[y_n] = \mathrm{E}[x_n] = 0$. One can see that the tangent point will move in proportion as the tangent ellipse expands or contracts with x_n.

This tangency property corresponds to minimizing a generalized length function.

Lemma 7.5 (Partitioned Quadratic) *Let* $\mathbf{y} \in \mathbb{R}^N$ *be a random variable with* $\mathrm{E}[\mathbf{y}] = 0$ *and* $\mathrm{Var}[\mathbf{y}] = \boldsymbol{\Omega}$, *a nonsingular matrix. Partition* $\mathbf{z} \in \mathbb{R}^N$ *into* $\mathbf{z}=[\mathbf{z}_1', \mathbf{z}_2']'$. *Then*

$$\mathbf{z}'\boldsymbol{\Omega}^{-1}\mathbf{z} = \left(\mathbf{z}_1 - \boldsymbol{\Omega}_{12}\boldsymbol{\Omega}_{22}^{-1}\mathbf{z}_2\right)' \left(\boldsymbol{\Omega}_{11} - \boldsymbol{\Omega}_{12}\boldsymbol{\Omega}_{22}^{-1}\boldsymbol{\Omega}_{21}\right)^{-1} \left(\mathbf{z}_1 - \boldsymbol{\Omega}_{12}\boldsymbol{\Omega}_{22}^{-1}\mathbf{z}_2\right) + \mathbf{z}_2'\boldsymbol{\Omega}_{22}^{-1}\mathbf{z}_2 \tag{7.10}$$

$$\boldsymbol{\Omega}_{12}\boldsymbol{\Omega}_{22}^{-1}\mathbf{z}_2 = \operatorname*{argmin}_{\mathbf{z}_1} \mathbf{z}'\boldsymbol{\Omega}^{-1}\mathbf{z} \tag{7.11}$$

and

$$\mathbf{z}_2'\boldsymbol{\Omega}_{22}^{-1}\mathbf{z}_2 = \min_{\mathbf{z}_1} \mathbf{z}'\boldsymbol{\Omega}^{-1}\mathbf{z}$$

[13] This MMSE linear predictor is variously called the *wide-sense regression* of y_n given $\mathbf{x}_{1n}$, the *population linear projection* of y_n on $\mathbf{x}_{1n}$, and other, similar terms.

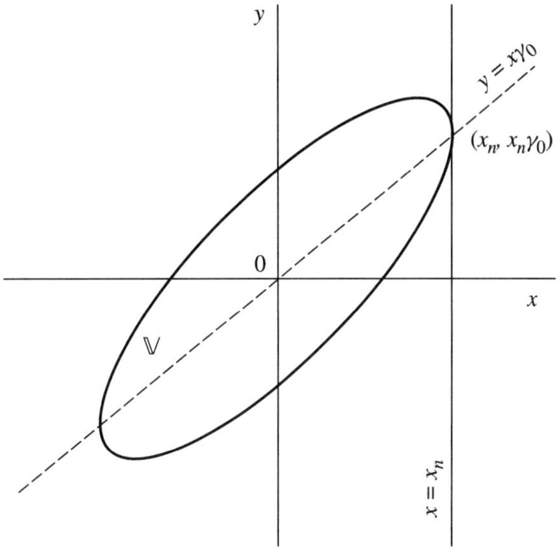

Figure 7.8 The MMSE predictor.

The linear combination $\boldsymbol{\Omega}_{12}\boldsymbol{\Omega}_{22}^{-1}\mathbf{z}_2$ is the MMSE linear predictor of $\mathbf{y}_1$ given $\mathbf{y}_2 = \mathbf{z}_2$, even when $\mathbf{y}_1$ is not scalar. In addition, it is the location of the lowest possible elliptical level set of the generalized distance function along the subset of $\mathbf{z}$ such that $\mathbf{z}_2$ is constant. This optimality property (7.11) follows from the quadratic decomposition (7.10). We prove the decomposition in Section 7.6.4.

It follows from Lemma 7.5 that

$$\mathbf{x}_n'\boldsymbol{\gamma}_0 = \underset{y}{\operatorname{argmin}}\, \mathbf{w}(y, \mathbf{x})'\boldsymbol{\Omega}^{-1}\mathbf{w}(y, \mathbf{x})$$

where the objective function on the RHS is the criterion function in the variance ellipsoid (7.3) with

$$\mathbf{w}(y, \mathbf{x}) = \begin{bmatrix} y - \mathrm{E}[y_n] \\ \mathbf{x}_1 - \mathrm{E}[\mathbf{x}_{1n}] \end{bmatrix}$$

and $\mathbf{x}_n'\boldsymbol{\gamma}_0$ given in (7.9). This is the relationship depicted in Figure 7.8. Note the graphic similarity between this minimization and OLS. In the two-dimensional case of Figure 7.8, the minimization of the generalized distance along the vertical direction is analogous to the minimization of the squared "vertical" residuals as described in Figure 1.3.

This relationship between the MMSE linear predictor and the quadratic function that determines the variance ellipsoid gives the quadratic function additional significance. Furthermore, the relationship suggests that a more general principle is at work. Indeed, we will explore *estimators* and *test statistics* constructed from an analogous minimization problem in Chapters 21 and 22.

7.6 MATHEMATICAL NOTES

These notes cover two results given above: first, that "the linear transformation of a variance ellipsoid is the variance ellipsoid of the linear transformation" (Lemma 7.3) and second, that the MMSE linear predictor is an element of a tangent point on a multiple of the variance ellipse. We also derive two intermediate results that hold independent interest. We apply the Gram–Schmidt orthonormalization process to a set of random variables and find a matrix "square root" for variance matrices. We also extend the Cauchy–Schwarz inequality to generalized inner products.

7.6.1 A Square Root of the Variance Matrix

Having found the MMSE linear predictor, we can also derive a convenient analytical tool: a square root for variance matrices. We construct this square root by building up an orthonormal basis for the elements of a vector $\mathbf{y}$ with mean $\mathrm{E}[\mathbf{y}] = 0$ and finite variance $\mathrm{Var}[\mathbf{y}] = \mathbf{\Omega}$. To do this, we combine the MMSE linear predictor with Gram–Schmidt orthonormalization. The result is a random vector $\mathbf{z}$ with two properties: (1) its elements are orthonormal and (2) $\mathbf{y}$ is linearly dependent on $\mathbf{z}$. Therefore, $\mathbf{y} = \mathbf{Cz}$ for a constant matrix $\mathbf{C}$ and

$$\mathbf{\Omega} = \mathrm{Var}[\mathbf{y}] = \mathrm{Var}[\mathbf{Cz}] = \mathbf{C}\,\mathrm{Var}[\mathbf{z}]\mathbf{C}' = \mathbf{CC}'$$

Lemma 7.6 (Cholesky Decomposition) *Every $K \times K$ nonsingular variance matrix $\mathbf{\Omega}$ can be factored into the matrix product $\mathbf{CC}'$, where $\mathbf{C}$ is lower-left triangular.*

Proof. Let $\mathbf{y} = [y_k]$ be a vector of K random variables such that $\mathrm{E}[\mathbf{y}] = \mathbf{0}$ and $\mathrm{Var}[\mathbf{y}] = \mathbf{\Omega}$. In this proof we construct the matrix $\mathbf{C}$ from the coefficients of a sequence of MMSE linear predictors. We apply Gram–Schmidt orthonormalization to the elements of $\mathbf{y}$ using the same steps that we used for a set of Euclidean vectors in Chapter 2.[14] This delivers an orthonormal basis for all random variables $\{\boldsymbol{\alpha}'\mathbf{y} \mid \boldsymbol{\alpha} \in \mathbb{R}^K\}$.

Let

$$z_1 = \frac{y_1}{\sqrt{\mathrm{E}[y_1^2]}} \tag{7.12}$$

be the first basis vector. The normalization gives z_1 unit length. Because $\mathbf{\Omega}$ is nonsingular, we iteratively compute the normalized linear projection residuals z_k according to

$$w_k = y_k - \overset{*}{\mathrm{E}}[y_k \mid \mathbf{z}_{k-1}] \tag{7.13}$$

$$z_k = \frac{w_k}{\sqrt{\mathrm{E}[w_k^2]}} \tag{7.14}$$

14 For the earlier discussion of Gram–Schmidt orthonormalization, see pp. 35–37 and Exercise 2.13.

for $k = 2, \ldots, K$, where we accumulate them in the column vectors $\mathbf{z}_k = \left[\mathbf{z}'_{k-1}, z_k\right]'$. Nonsingularity guarantees that no (nonzero) linear combination of the elements of $\mathbf{y}$ has a variance of zero so that $\mathrm{E}[w_k^2] > 0$ for every $k = 1, \ldots, K$.

Note incidentally that by construction

$$\mathrm{E}[\mathbf{z}_k \mathbf{z}'_k] = \mathbf{I}_k \tag{7.15}$$

and by definition (7.9)

$$\overset{*}{\mathrm{E}}[y_k \mid \mathbf{z}_{k-1}] = \mathbf{z}'_{k-1} \boldsymbol{\gamma}_k$$

where

$$\begin{aligned}\boldsymbol{\gamma}_k &= \left(\mathrm{E}[\mathbf{z}_{k-1}\mathbf{z}'_{k-1}]\right)^{-1} \mathrm{E}[\mathbf{z}_{k-1} y_k] \\ &= \mathrm{E}[\mathbf{z}_{k-1} y_k]\end{aligned} \tag{7.16}$$

It follows that

$$\begin{aligned}\mathrm{E}[w_k^2] &= \mathrm{E}[y_k^2] - \mathrm{E}[y_k \mathbf{z}'_{k-1}] \left(\mathrm{E}[\mathbf{z}_{k-1}\mathbf{z}'_{k-1}]\right)^{-1} \mathrm{E}[\mathbf{z}_{k-1} y_k] \\ &= \mathrm{E}[y_k^2] - \boldsymbol{\gamma}'_k \boldsymbol{\gamma}_k\end{aligned} \tag{7.17}$$

as in Lemma 7.5.

The resultant vector of random variables $\mathbf{z} \equiv \mathbf{z}_K$ is a recursive linear transformation of $\mathbf{y}$: z_1 depends only on y_1, z_2 depends on y_2 and z_1, and z_k depends on y_k and $z_1, \ldots, z_{k-1}$ (that is $\mathbf{z}_{k-1}$). We may write

$$\mathbf{C}\mathbf{z} = \mathbf{y}$$

where $\mathbf{C}$ is a lower-left triangular square matrix. According to (7.13)–(7.17), the kth row of $\mathbf{C}$ is

$$\begin{bmatrix}\boldsymbol{\gamma}'_k & \sqrt{\mathrm{E}[y_k^2] - \boldsymbol{\gamma}'_k\boldsymbol{\gamma}_k} & \underset{1\times(K-k)}{\mathbf{0}}\end{bmatrix}$$

Therefore,

$$\boldsymbol{\Omega} = \mathrm{E}[\mathbf{y}\mathbf{y}'] = \mathrm{E}[\mathbf{C}\mathbf{z}\mathbf{z}'\mathbf{C}] = \mathbf{C}\,\mathrm{E}[\mathbf{z}\mathbf{z}']\mathbf{C}' = \mathbf{C}\mathbf{C}' \qquad \square$$

Nonsingular variance matrices can always be decomposed in this way. Indeed, any nonsingular positive-definite matrix has this decomposition.[15] This particular decomposition is called a *Cholesky decomposition*. There are actually other ways to find matrices that satisfy $\mathbf{C}\mathbf{C}' = \boldsymbol{\Omega}$, but we will not need them.[16] Often, the matrix $\mathbf{C}$ is called a matrix *square root* of $\boldsymbol{\Omega}$.

---

[15] See Exercise 7.18.

[16] In econometrics, another popular matrix decomposition is the eigenvalue decomposition. It is possible to find an orthogonal matrix $\mathbf{R}$ and a diagonal matrix $\boldsymbol{\Lambda}$ such that $\boldsymbol{\Omega} = \mathbf{R}'\boldsymbol{\Lambda}\mathbf{R}$. The columns of $\mathbf{R}$ are called eigenvectors and the diagonal elements of $\boldsymbol{\Lambda}$ are called eigenvalues. Then $\mathbf{A} = \mathbf{R}'\boldsymbol{\Lambda}^{1/2}$ where $\boldsymbol{\Lambda}^{1/2}$ denotes another diagonal matrix whose diagonal elements are the square roots of the corresponding elements of $\boldsymbol{\Lambda}$. See also Theorem C.16 (Eigenvalue Decomposition, p. 866).

Yet another possibility is $\mathbf{A} = \mathbf{R}'\boldsymbol{\Lambda}^{1/2}\mathbf{R}$ because $\mathbf{R}\mathbf{R}' = \mathbf{I}$. In this case, $\boldsymbol{\Omega} = \mathbf{A}\mathbf{A}$ where $\mathbf{A}$ is symmetric.

A useful corollary that follows from this proof is

LEMMA 7.7 *The variance matrix* $\boldsymbol{\Omega} = [\omega_{ij}]$ *is nonsingular if and only if*

$$\omega_{11} > 0,$$
$$\omega_{kk} - \boldsymbol{\Omega}_{k,k-1}\boldsymbol{\Omega}_{k-1,k-1}^{-1}\boldsymbol{\Omega}_{k-1,k} > 0, \qquad k = 2, \ldots, K$$

where

$$\boldsymbol{\Omega}_{k,k-1} \equiv [\omega_{k1}, \ldots, \omega_{k,k-1}]$$
$$\boldsymbol{\Omega}_{k-1,k} \equiv \boldsymbol{\Omega}'_{k,k-1}$$

and

$$\boldsymbol{\Omega}_{k-1,k-1} \equiv [\omega_{ij}; i, j = 1, \ldots, k-1]$$

Proof. Returning to the proof of Lemma 7.6, let $\mathbf{y} \in \mathbb{R}^K$ be a vector of random variables with $\mathrm{E}[\mathbf{y}] = \mathbf{0}$ and $\mathrm{Var}[\mathbf{y}] = \boldsymbol{\Omega}$. According to Lemma 7.4,

$$\begin{aligned}\omega_{kk} - \boldsymbol{\Omega}_{k,k-1}\boldsymbol{\Omega}_{k-1,k-1}^{-1}\boldsymbol{\Omega}_{k-1,k} &= \min_{\boldsymbol{\gamma}\in\mathbb{R}^{k-1}} \mathrm{E}\big[\big(y_k - [y_1, \ldots, y_{k-1}]\boldsymbol{\gamma}\big)^2\big] \\ &= \mathrm{E}\big[\big(y_k - \mathrm{E}^*[y_k \mid y_1, \ldots, y_{k-1}]\big)^2\big]\end{aligned}$$

Note that because $\mathbf{z}_{k-1}$ is a linear transformation of $[y_1, \ldots, y_{k-1}]$,

$$\mathrm{E}^*[y_k \mid y_1, \ldots, y_{k-1}] = \mathrm{E}^*[y_k \mid \mathbf{z}_{k-1}]$$

Therefore,

$$\mathrm{Var}\big[y_k - \mathrm{E}^*[y_k \mid y_1, \ldots, y_{k-1}]\big] = \mathrm{E}[w_k^2]$$

where w_k is defined in (7.13). As mentioned above, if $\boldsymbol{\Omega}$ is nonsingular then $\mathrm{E}[w_k^2] > 0$ for $k = 1, \ldots, K$. On the other hand, if $\mathrm{E}[w_k^2] > 0$ then $\boldsymbol{\Omega}$ has a nonsingular Cholesky factor $\mathbf{C}$ so that $\boldsymbol{\Omega}$ is nonsingular. □

If $\boldsymbol{\Omega}$ is singular, then the Cholesky decomposition can be modified to create a full-column rank $\mathbf{C}$ such that $\boldsymbol{\Omega} = \mathbf{C}\mathbf{C}'$. If $\boldsymbol{\Omega}$ is singular, then some iterations will produce a MSE of zero:

$$\mathrm{E}[w_k^2] = \mathrm{E}[y_k^2] - \mathrm{E}[y_k\,\mathbf{z}'_{k-1}]\,\mathrm{E}[\mathbf{z}_{k-1}\,y_k] = 0$$

When this occurs

$$y_k = \mathrm{E}^*[y_k \mid \mathbf{z}_{k-1}] = \mathbf{z}'_{k-1}\,\mathrm{E}[\mathbf{z}_{k-1}\,y_k]$$

with probability one and we set $\mathbf{z}_k = \mathbf{z}_{k-1}$. Because the Gram–Schmidt process produces a basis for linear combinations $\boldsymbol{\alpha}'\mathbf{y}$, the number of such iterations will be $K - \text{rank}(\boldsymbol{\Omega})$ and the columns of the resultant $\mathbf{C}$ will be $\text{rank}(\boldsymbol{\Omega})$ instead of K.

7.6.2 The Cauchy–Schwarz Inequality

A proof below is simplified if we use the Cauchy–Schwarz inequality. The basic Cauchy–Schwarz inequality for Euclidean vectors states that[17]

$$\left(\mathbf{a}'\mathbf{b}\right)^2 \leq \mathbf{a}'\mathbf{a} \cdot \mathbf{b}'\mathbf{b} \tag{7.18}$$

for $\mathbf{a}, \mathbf{b} \in \mathbb{R}^N$. This can be rewritten as

$$\mathbf{a}'\mathbf{a} - \mathbf{a}'\mathbf{P}_\mathbf{b}\mathbf{a} = \mathbf{a}'\left(\mathbf{I} - \mathbf{P}_\mathbf{b}\right)\mathbf{a} = \|(\mathbf{I} - \mathbf{P}_\mathbf{b})\mathbf{a}\|^2 \geq 0$$

or $\mathbf{a}'\mathbf{a} \geq \mathbf{a}'\mathbf{P}_\mathbf{b}\mathbf{a}$. In words, the inequality states that the Euclidean length of a vector is greater than or equal to the Euclidean length of its orthogonal projection. If we understand how orthogonal projection minimizes length, this inequality has a simple geometric interpretation in Euclidean spaces.

The following "generalized" Cauchy–Schwarz inequality can be justified in the same way using an orthogonal projection of random variables

LEMMA 7.8 (CAUCHY–SCHWARZ INEQUALITY) *Let $\boldsymbol{\Omega}$ be an $N \times N$ variance matrix. Then for $\mathbf{a}, \mathbf{b} \in \mathbb{R}^N$,*

$$\left(\mathbf{a}'\boldsymbol{\Omega}\mathbf{b}\right)^2 \leq \mathbf{a}'\boldsymbol{\Omega}\mathbf{a} \cdot \mathbf{b}'\boldsymbol{\Omega}\mathbf{b}$$

Proof. Let $\mathbf{y}$ be a random variable such that $\text{E}[\mathbf{y}] = 0$ and $\text{Var}[\mathbf{y}] = \boldsymbol{\Omega}$. Then

$$\text{Var}\left[\begin{bmatrix} \mathbf{a}'\mathbf{y} \\ \mathbf{b}'\mathbf{y} \end{bmatrix}\right] = \begin{bmatrix} \mathbf{a}'\boldsymbol{\Omega}\mathbf{a} & \mathbf{a}'\boldsymbol{\Omega}\mathbf{b} \\ \mathbf{b}'\boldsymbol{\Omega}\mathbf{a} & \mathbf{b}'\boldsymbol{\Omega}\mathbf{b} \end{bmatrix}$$

Now find the MSE of the MMSE linear predictor of $\mathbf{a}'\mathbf{y}$ given $\mathbf{b}'\mathbf{y}$:

$$\text{E}\left[\left(\mathbf{a}'\mathbf{y} - \frac{\mathbf{a}'\boldsymbol{\Omega}\mathbf{b}}{\mathbf{b}'\boldsymbol{\Omega}\mathbf{b}}\mathbf{b}'\mathbf{y}\right)^2\right] = \mathbf{a}'\boldsymbol{\Omega}\mathbf{a} - \frac{\left(\mathbf{a}'\boldsymbol{\Omega}\mathbf{b}\right)^2}{\mathbf{b}'\boldsymbol{\Omega}\mathbf{b}} \geq 0$$

□

The Cauchy–Schwarz inequality therefore states that

$$\left(\text{Cov}[\mathbf{a}'\mathbf{y}, \mathbf{b}'\mathbf{y}]\right)^2 \leq \text{Var}[\mathbf{a}'\mathbf{y}]\ \text{Var}[\mathbf{b}'\mathbf{y}]$$

or that the correlation between $a'y$ and $b'y$ must be less than one in absolute value.

Here is an alternative proof that uses the Cholesky square root of $\boldsymbol{\Omega}$. Let $\boldsymbol{\Omega} = \mathbf{C}\mathbf{C}'$. Then

$$\mathbf{a}'\boldsymbol{\Omega}\mathbf{b} = \mathbf{a}'\mathbf{C}\mathbf{C}'\mathbf{b} = \left(\mathbf{C}'\mathbf{a}\right)'\mathbf{C}'\mathbf{b}$$

17 See Lemma C.1 (Cauchy–Schwarz Inequality, p. 852).

Applying the Cauchy–Schwarz inequality for Euclidean inner products,

$$\begin{aligned}(\mathbf{a}'\boldsymbol{\Omega}\mathbf{b})^2 &= \left[(\mathbf{C}'\mathbf{a})'\,\mathbf{C}'\mathbf{b}\right]^2 \\ &\le (\mathbf{C}'\mathbf{a})'\,\mathbf{C}'\mathbf{a}\cdot(\mathbf{C}'\mathbf{b})\,\mathbf{C}'\mathbf{b} \\ &= \mathbf{a}'\boldsymbol{\Omega}\mathbf{a}\cdot\mathbf{b}'\boldsymbol{\Omega}\mathbf{b}\end{aligned}$$

which is the desired result. In this way, Lemma 7.8 is simply a transformation of (7.18).

7.6.3 Linear Transformation of Variance Ellipses

In these notes, we also prove Lemma 7.3, which states that the variance ellipse of $\mathbf{z} = \mathbf{A}\mathbf{y}$ is the image of the variance ellipse of $\mathbf{y}$ under the linear transformation $\mathbf{A}$. We will use the following intermediate result below, in conjunction with the variance matrix square root and Cauchy–Schwarz inequality just described.

Lemma 7.9 *Let* $\mathbf{A}$ *be a matrix. Then* $\mathrm{Col}(\mathbf{A}) = \mathrm{Col}(\mathbf{A}\mathbf{A}')$.

Proof. Theorem C.12 (Matrix Rank, p. 854) states that $\mathrm{rank}(\mathbf{A}) = \mathrm{rank}(\mathbf{A}')$. Exercise 2.20 states that $\mathrm{rank}(\mathbf{A}') = \mathrm{rank}(\mathbf{A}\mathbf{A}')$, so that $\mathrm{rank}(\mathbf{A}) = \mathrm{rank}(\mathbf{A}\mathbf{A}')$. Furthermore, $\mathrm{Col}(\mathbf{A}\mathbf{A}') \subseteq \mathrm{Col}(\mathbf{A})$. Because these vector spaces have the same dimension, $\mathrm{Col}(\mathbf{A}\mathbf{A}') = \mathrm{Col}(\mathbf{A})$. □

Proof of Lemma 7.3. The proof rests in part on the Cauchy–Schwarz inequality. To highlight this feature, we consider a special case first. Suppose that $\boldsymbol{\Omega} = \mathbf{I}_N$ so that $\mathrm{Var}[\mathbf{z}] = \mathbf{A}\mathbf{A}'$ according to Lemma 7.1 (Bilinearity of Covariance). By Definition 14,

$$\begin{aligned}\mathbb{V}_{\mathbf{y}} &\equiv \{\mathbf{w} = \mathbf{a} \mid \mathbf{a} \in \mathbb{R}^N,\ \mathbf{a}'\mathbf{a} \le 1\} \\ \mathbb{V}_{\mathbf{z}} &\equiv \{\mathbf{w} = \mathbf{A}\mathbf{A}'\mathbf{b} \mid \mathbf{b} \in \mathbb{R}^K,\ \mathbf{b}'\mathbf{A}\mathbf{A}'\mathbf{b} \le 1\}\end{aligned}$$

The image of $\mathbb{V}_{\mathbf{y}}$ under the linear transformation $\mathbf{A}$ is

$$\mathbf{A}\mathbb{V}_y \equiv \left\{\mathbf{w} = \mathbf{A}\mathbf{x} \mid \mathbf{x} \in \mathbb{V}_{\mathbf{y}}\right\}$$

We will demonstrate that $\mathbb{V}_{\mathbf{z}} \subseteq \mathbf{A}\mathbb{V}_{\mathbf{y}}$ and that $\mathbf{A}\mathbb{V}_{\mathbf{y}} \subseteq \mathbb{V}_{\mathbf{z}}$ so that $\mathbb{V}_{\mathbf{z}} = \mathbf{A}\mathbb{V}_{\mathbf{y}}$.[18]
$\mathbb{V}_{\mathbf{z}}$ is contained in the image of $\mathbb{V}_{\mathbf{y}}$: The definition of $\mathbb{V}_{\mathbf{z}}$ states that for any $\mathbf{z}_0 \in \mathbb{V}_{\mathbf{z}}$, there is a $\mathbf{b} \in \mathbb{R}^K$ so that $\mathbf{z}_0 = \mathbf{A}\mathbf{A}'\mathbf{b}$ and $\mathbf{b}'\mathbf{A}\mathbf{A}'\mathbf{b} \le 1$. Let $\mathbf{y}_0 = \mathbf{A}'\mathbf{b}$. Clearly, $\mathbf{z}_0 = \mathbf{A}\mathbf{y}_0$, $\mathbf{y}_0 \in \mathbb{R}^N$, and

$$\mathbf{y}_0'\mathbf{y}_0 = \mathbf{b}'\mathbf{A}\mathbf{A}'\mathbf{b} \le 1$$

so that $\mathbf{y}_0 \in \mathbb{V}_{\mathbf{y}}$.

[18] We found this proof method in Malinvaud (1970, pp. 162–165).

The image of $\mathbb{V}_{\mathbf{y}}$ is contained in $\mathbb{V}_{\mathbf{z}}$: Given any $\mathbf{y}_0 \in \mathbb{V}_{\mathbf{y}}$, let $\mathbf{z}_0 = \mathbf{A}\mathbf{y}_0$ denote the image of $\mathbf{y}_0$ under the linear transformation $\mathbf{A}$. Lemma 7.9 implies that there is always a $\mathbf{b} \in \mathbb{R}^K$ such that $\mathbf{z}_0 = \mathbf{A}\mathbf{y}_0 = \mathbf{A}\mathbf{A}'\mathbf{b}$. It does not follow that $\mathbf{y}_0$ equals $\mathbf{A}'\mathbf{b}$. Nevertheless, if we denote $\mathbf{y}_1 \equiv \mathbf{A}'\mathbf{b}$ then $\mathbf{A}\mathbf{y}_0 = \mathbf{A}\mathbf{y}_1$ and

$$\mathbf{y}_1'\mathbf{y}_0 = \mathbf{b}'\mathbf{A}\mathbf{y}_0 = \mathbf{b}'\mathbf{A}\mathbf{y}_1 = \mathbf{y}_1'\mathbf{y}_1$$

This equality and the Cauchy–Schwarz inequality (7.18) imply that

$$\mathbf{b}'\mathbf{A}\mathbf{A}'\mathbf{b} = \mathbf{y}_1'\mathbf{y}_1 = \frac{(\mathbf{y}_0'\mathbf{y}_1)^2}{\mathbf{y}_1'\mathbf{y}_1} \leq \mathbf{y}_0'\mathbf{y}_0$$

Finally, $\mathbf{y}_0 \in \mathbb{V}_{\mathbf{y}}$ gives

$$\mathbf{b}'\mathbf{A}\mathbf{A}'\mathbf{b} \leq \mathbf{y}_0'\mathbf{y}_0 \leq 1$$

In other words, $\mathbf{z}_0 = \mathbf{A}\mathbf{A}'\mathbf{b} \in \mathbb{V}_{\mathbf{z}}$. This completes the proof of Lemma 7.3 for the special case $\mathbf{\Omega} = \mathbf{I}_N$.

Now we generalize this proof to an arbitrary variance matrix $\mathbf{\Omega}$ so that

$$\mathbb{V}_{\mathbf{y}} = \{\mathbf{w} = \mathbf{\Omega}\mathbf{a} \mid \mathbf{a}'\mathbf{\Omega}\mathbf{a} \leq 1\}$$
$$\mathbb{V}_{\mathbf{z}} = \{\mathbf{w} = \mathbf{A}\mathbf{\Omega}\mathbf{A}'\mathbf{b} \mid \mathbf{b}'\mathbf{A}\mathbf{\Omega}\mathbf{A}'\mathbf{b} \leq 1\}$$

The first part is essentially unchanged.

$\mathbb{V}_{\mathbf{z}}$ is contained in the image of $\mathbb{V}_{\mathbf{y}}$: The definition of $\mathbb{V}_{\mathbf{z}}$ states that for any $\mathbf{z}_0 \in \mathbb{V}_{\mathbf{z}}$, then there is a $\mathbf{b} \in \mathbb{R}^K$ so that $\mathbf{z}_0 = \mathbf{A}\mathbf{\Omega}\mathbf{A}'\mathbf{b}$ and $\mathbf{b}'\mathbf{A}\mathbf{\Omega}\mathbf{A}'\mathbf{b} \leq 1$. If we let $\mathbf{a} = \mathbf{A}'\mathbf{b}$ and $\mathbf{y}_0 = \mathbf{\Omega}\mathbf{a}$, then $\mathbf{z}_0 = \mathbf{A}\mathbf{y}_0$, $\mathbf{y}_0 \in \mathrm{Col}(\mathbf{\Omega})$, and

$$\mathbf{a}'\mathbf{\Omega}\mathbf{a} = \mathbf{b}'\mathbf{A}\mathbf{\Omega}\mathbf{A}'\mathbf{b} \leq 1$$

so that $\mathbf{y}_0 \in \mathbb{V}_{\mathbf{y}}$.

The second part of the proof uses the square root of $\mathbf{\Omega}$ to reproduce the previous argument.

The image of $\mathbb{V}_{\mathbf{y}}$ is contained in $\mathbb{V}_{\mathbf{z}}$: Let $\mathbf{y}_0 \doteq \mathbf{\Omega}\mathbf{a}$ be any member of $\mathbb{V}_{\mathbf{y}}$ and let $\mathbf{z}_0 = \mathbf{A}\mathbf{y}_0 = \mathbf{A}\mathbf{\Omega}\mathbf{a}$. Note that Lemma 7.6 states that there is always a matrix $\mathbf{C}$ such that $\mathbf{\Omega} = \mathbf{C}\mathbf{C}'$. If we also let $\mathbf{B} = \mathbf{A}\mathbf{C}$, then Lemma 7.9 states that $\mathrm{Col}(\mathbf{B}) = \mathrm{Col}(\mathbf{B}\mathbf{B}')$. Therefore, there is always a $\mathbf{b}$ such that $\mathbf{B}\left(\mathbf{C}'\mathbf{a}\right) = \mathbf{B}\mathbf{B}'\mathbf{b}$ and

$$\mathbf{z}_0 = \mathbf{A}\mathbf{\Omega}\mathbf{a} = \mathbf{A}\mathbf{C}\mathbf{C}'\mathbf{a} = \mathbf{B}\left(\mathbf{C}'\mathbf{a}\right) = \mathbf{B}\mathbf{B}'\mathbf{b} = \mathbf{A}\mathbf{\Omega}\mathbf{A}'\mathbf{b}$$

$$\mathbf{b}'\mathbf{A}\mathbf{\Omega}\mathbf{a} = \mathbf{b}'\mathbf{A}\mathbf{\Omega}\mathbf{A}'\mathbf{b} \tag{7.19}$$

If we apply the Cauchy–Schwarz inequality (Lemma 7.8) to $\mathbf{a}$ and $\mathbf{A}'\mathbf{b}$ we obtain

$$\frac{(\mathbf{b}'\mathbf{A}\mathbf{\Omega}\mathbf{a})^2}{\mathbf{b}'\mathbf{A}\mathbf{\Omega}\mathbf{A}\mathbf{b}} \leq \mathbf{a}'\mathbf{\Omega}\mathbf{a}$$

and (7.19) simplifies this inequality to

$$\mathbf{b}'\mathbf{A}\mathbf{\Omega}\mathbf{A}\mathbf{b} \leq \mathbf{a}'\mathbf{\Omega}\mathbf{a}$$

Because $\mathbf{y}_0 \in \mathbb{V}_\mathbf{y}$,

$$\mathbf{b}'\mathbf{A}\boldsymbol{\Omega}\mathbf{A}\mathbf{b} \leq \mathbf{a}'\boldsymbol{\Omega}\mathbf{a} \leq 1$$

This implies that $\mathbf{z}_0 = \mathbf{A}\mathbf{y}_0 \in \mathbb{V}_\mathbf{z}$ as required. □

7.6.4 A Quadratic Decomposition

In this section, we confirm the relationship between the MMSE linear predictor and the quadratic form of a variance ellipsoid in (7.11). This equation rests on the orthogonality between the prediction error and the predictor variables that is established by Lemma 7.4 (MMSE Linear Predictor).

Proof of Lemma 7.5. Given the random variable $\mathbf{y}$ with $\mathrm{E}[\mathbf{y}] = \mathbf{0}$ and

$$\mathrm{Var}[\mathbf{y}] = \mathrm{Var}\left[\begin{bmatrix} \mathbf{y}_1 \\ \mathbf{y}_2 \end{bmatrix}\right] = \begin{bmatrix} \boldsymbol{\Omega}_{11} & \boldsymbol{\Omega}_{12} \\ \boldsymbol{\Omega}_{21} & \boldsymbol{\Omega}_{22} \end{bmatrix}$$

the optimal linear predictor of $\mathbf{y}_1$ given $\mathbf{y}_2$ is $\boldsymbol{\Omega}_{12}\boldsymbol{\Omega}_{22}^{-1}\mathbf{y}_2$.

The orthogonality between $\mathbf{y}_1 - \boldsymbol{\Omega}_{12}\boldsymbol{\Omega}_{22}^{-1}\mathbf{y}_2$ and $\mathbf{y}_2$ implies that

$$\mathrm{Var}\left[\begin{bmatrix} \mathbf{y}_1 - \boldsymbol{\Omega}_{12}\boldsymbol{\Omega}_{22}^{-1}\mathbf{y}_2 \\ \mathbf{y}_2 \end{bmatrix}\right] = \begin{bmatrix} \boldsymbol{\Omega}_{11} - \boldsymbol{\Omega}_{12}\boldsymbol{\Omega}_{22}^{-1}\boldsymbol{\Omega}_{21} & \mathbf{0} \\ \mathbf{0} & \boldsymbol{\Omega}_{22} \end{bmatrix} \tag{7.20}$$

The variance of $\mathbf{y}_1 - \boldsymbol{\Omega}_{12}\boldsymbol{\Omega}_{22}^{-1}\mathbf{y}_2$ in the upper left-hand corner comes from

$$\begin{aligned}
\mathrm{Var}[\mathbf{y}_1 - \boldsymbol{\Omega}_{12}\boldsymbol{\Omega}_{22}^{-1}\mathbf{y}_2] &= \mathrm{Var}[\mathbf{y}_1] - \mathrm{Cov}[\mathbf{y}_1, \boldsymbol{\Omega}_{12}\boldsymbol{\Omega}_{22}^{-1}\mathbf{y}_2] - \mathrm{Cov}[\boldsymbol{\Omega}_{12}\boldsymbol{\Omega}_{22}^{-1}\mathbf{y}_2, \mathbf{y}_1] \\
&\quad + \mathrm{Var}[\boldsymbol{\Omega}_{12}\boldsymbol{\Omega}_{22}^{-1}\mathbf{y}_2] \\
&= \mathrm{Var}[\mathbf{y}_1] - \mathrm{Cov}[\mathbf{y}_1, \mathbf{y}_2]\left(\boldsymbol{\Omega}_{12}\boldsymbol{\Omega}_{22}^{-1}\right)' - \boldsymbol{\Omega}_{12}\boldsymbol{\Omega}_{22}^{-1}\,\mathrm{Cov}[\mathbf{y}_2, \mathbf{y}_1] \\
&\quad + \boldsymbol{\Omega}_{12}\boldsymbol{\Omega}_{22}^{-1}\,\mathrm{Var}[\mathbf{y}_2]\left(\boldsymbol{\Omega}_{12}\boldsymbol{\Omega}_{22}^{-1}\right)' \\
&= \boldsymbol{\Omega}_{11} - \boldsymbol{\Omega}_{12}\boldsymbol{\Omega}_{22}^{-1}\boldsymbol{\Omega}_{21} - \boldsymbol{\Omega}_{12}\boldsymbol{\Omega}_{22}^{-1}\boldsymbol{\Omega}_{21} \\
&\quad + \boldsymbol{\Omega}_{12}\boldsymbol{\Omega}_{22}^{-1}\boldsymbol{\Omega}_{22}\boldsymbol{\Omega}_{22}^{-1}\boldsymbol{\Omega}_{21} \\
&= \boldsymbol{\Omega}_{11} - \boldsymbol{\Omega}_{12}\boldsymbol{\Omega}_{22}^{-1}\boldsymbol{\Omega}_{21}
\end{aligned}$$

which uses Lemma 7.1 (Bilinearity of Covariances, p. 130).

We can also write

$$\mathrm{Var}\left[\begin{bmatrix} \mathbf{y}_1 - \boldsymbol{\Omega}_{12}\boldsymbol{\Omega}_{22}^{-1}\mathbf{y}_2 \\ \mathbf{y}_2 \end{bmatrix}\right] = \mathrm{Var}[\mathbf{A}\mathbf{y}]$$

where

$$\mathbf{A} = \begin{bmatrix} \mathbf{I} & -\boldsymbol{\Omega}_{12}\boldsymbol{\Omega}_{22}^{-1} \\ \mathbf{0} & \mathbf{I} \end{bmatrix}$$

and $\mathbf{A}$ is nonsingular.[19] Therefore,

[19] This is comparable to the Gram–Schmidt orthogonalization that appears in the Cholesky decomposition.

$$\mathbf{z}'\boldsymbol{\Omega}^{-1}\mathbf{z} = \mathbf{z}'\mathbf{A}'(\mathbf{A}\boldsymbol{\Omega}\mathbf{A}')^{-1}\mathbf{A}\mathbf{z} \tag{7.21}$$

Because $\mathbf{A}\boldsymbol{\Omega}\mathbf{A}'$ is the block-diagonal variance matrix in (7.20) and

$$\mathbf{A}\mathbf{z} = \begin{bmatrix} \mathbf{z}_1 - \boldsymbol{\Omega}_{12}\boldsymbol{\Omega}_{22}^{-1}\mathbf{z}_2 \\ \mathbf{z}_2 \end{bmatrix}$$

(7.21) expands to

$$\begin{aligned} \mathbf{z}'\boldsymbol{\Omega}^{-1}\mathbf{z} &= \left(\mathbf{z}_1 - \boldsymbol{\Omega}_{12}\boldsymbol{\Omega}_{22}^{-1}\mathbf{z}_2\right)' \left(\boldsymbol{\Omega}_{11} - \boldsymbol{\Omega}_{12}\boldsymbol{\Omega}_{22}^{-1}\boldsymbol{\Omega}_{21}\right)^{-1} \left(\mathbf{z}_1 - \boldsymbol{\Omega}_{12}\boldsymbol{\Omega}_{22}^{-1}\mathbf{z}_2\right) \\ &\quad + \mathbf{z}_2'\boldsymbol{\Omega}_{22}^{-1}\mathbf{z}_2 \end{aligned}$$

which is (7.10).[20] Given this decomposition, the first term is minimized to be zero for any $\mathbf{z}_2$ by setting $\mathbf{z}_1 = \boldsymbol{\Omega}_{12}\boldsymbol{\Omega}_{22}^{-1}\mathbf{z}_2$. Therefore

$$\boldsymbol{\Omega}_{12}\boldsymbol{\Omega}_{22}^{-1}\mathbf{z}_2 = \underset{\mathbf{z}_1}{\operatorname{argmin}}\, \mathbf{z}'\boldsymbol{\Omega}^{-1}\mathbf{z}$$

and

$$\mathbf{z}_2'\boldsymbol{\Omega}_{22}^{-1}\mathbf{z}_2 = \min_{\mathbf{z}_1} \mathbf{z}'\boldsymbol{\Omega}^{-1}\mathbf{z}$$

confirming (7.11). □

For later use, we also give the following, closely related, result:

LEMMA 7.10 (PARTITIONED QUADRATIC II) *Let* $\mathbf{z}$ *be a partitioned vector* $[\mathbf{z}_1', \mathbf{z}_2']'$ *and let* $\mathbf{A} = \left[\mathbf{A}_{ij};\ i, j = 1, 2\right]$ *be a conformably partitioned symmetric nonsingular matrix. Then*

$$\begin{aligned} \mathbf{z}'\mathbf{A}\mathbf{z} &= \left(\mathbf{z}_1 + \mathbf{A}_{11}^{-1}\mathbf{A}_{12}\mathbf{z}_2\right)' \mathbf{A}_{11} \left(\mathbf{z}_1 + \mathbf{A}_{11}^{-1}\mathbf{A}_{12}\mathbf{z}_2\right) \\ &\quad + \mathbf{z}_2' \left(\mathbf{A}_{22} - \mathbf{A}_{21}\mathbf{A}_{11}^{-1}\mathbf{A}_{12}\right) \mathbf{z}_2 \end{aligned}$$

Proof. Lemma 7.5 (Partitioned Quadratic) and partitioned matrix inversion could be applied to prove this lemma. It is more direct to expand all terms:

$$\begin{aligned} \mathbf{z}'\mathbf{A}\mathbf{z} &= \begin{bmatrix} \mathbf{z}_1' & \mathbf{z}_2' \end{bmatrix} \begin{bmatrix} \mathbf{A}_{11} & \mathbf{A}_{12} \\ \mathbf{A}_{21} & \mathbf{A}_{22} \end{bmatrix} \begin{bmatrix} \mathbf{z}_1 \\ \mathbf{z}_1 \end{bmatrix} \\ &= \mathbf{z}_1'\mathbf{A}_{11}\mathbf{z}_1 + 2\mathbf{z}_1'\mathbf{A}_{12}\mathbf{z}_2 + \mathbf{z}_2'\mathbf{A}_{22}\mathbf{z}_2 \end{aligned} \tag{7.22}$$

and on the RHS

$$\begin{aligned} &\left(\mathbf{z}_1 + \mathbf{A}_{11}^{-1}\mathbf{A}_{12}\mathbf{z}_2\right)' \mathbf{A}_{11} \left(\mathbf{z}_1 + \mathbf{A}_{11}^{-1}\mathbf{A}_{12}\mathbf{z}_2\right) \\ &\quad = \left(\mathbf{z}_1 + \mathbf{A}_{11}^{-1}\mathbf{A}_{12}\mathbf{z}_2\right)' \left(\mathbf{A}_{11}\mathbf{z}_1 + \mathbf{A}_{12}\mathbf{z}_2\right) \\ &\quad = \mathbf{z}_1'\mathbf{A}_{11}\mathbf{z}_1 + 2\mathbf{z}_1'\mathbf{A}_{12}\mathbf{z}_2 + \mathbf{z}_2'\mathbf{A}_{21}\mathbf{A}_{11}^{-1}\mathbf{A}_{12}\mathbf{z}_2 \end{aligned} \tag{7.23}$$

[20] This equality can also be derived algebraically using the partitioned inverse formula [equation (3.23), p. 70].

$$\mathbf{z}_2'\left(\mathbf{A}_{22} - \mathbf{A}_{21}\mathbf{A}_{11}^{-1}\mathbf{A}_{12}\right)\mathbf{z}_2 = \mathbf{z}_2'\mathbf{A}_{22}\mathbf{z}_2 - \mathbf{z}_2'\mathbf{A}_{21}\mathbf{A}_{11}^{-1}\mathbf{A}_{12}\mathbf{z}_2 \tag{7.24}$$

The RHS of (7.22) equals the sum of the RHS of (7.23) and (7.24). □

7.7 OVERVIEW

1. Covariance matrices

$$\text{Cov}[\mathbf{z}_1, \mathbf{z}_2] \equiv \text{E}[(\mathbf{z}_1 - \text{E}[\mathbf{z}_1])(\mathbf{z}_2 - \text{E}[\mathbf{z}_2])']$$

are a notation for second moments of vectors of random variables. Variance–covariance matrices,

$$\text{Var}[\mathbf{z}_1] \equiv \text{Cov}[\mathbf{z}_1, \mathbf{z}_1]$$

are a special symmetric case.

2. For vectors $\mathbf{y}$ and $\mathbf{z}$ of random variables, and constant, conformable matrices $\mathbf{A}$ and $\mathbf{B}$, $\text{Cov}[\mathbf{Ay}, \mathbf{Bz}] = \mathbf{A}\,\text{Cov}[\mathbf{y}, \mathbf{z}]\mathbf{B}'$ and $\text{Var}[\mathbf{Ay}] = \mathbf{A}\,\text{Var}[\mathbf{y}]\mathbf{A}'$.
3. Our second statistical assumption is $\text{Var}[\mathbf{y} \mid \mathbf{X}] = \sigma_0^2 \cdot \mathbf{I}_N$. This restricts the conditional variance of every y_n $(n = 1, \ldots, N)$ to be constant and the conditional covariance between y_n and every other y_m $(m \neq n, m = 1, \ldots, N)$ to be zero.
4. A geometric representation of a scalar variance–covariance matrix is a sphere. Thus, one often restates this assumption as asserting that, conditional on $\mathbf{X}$, $\mathbf{y}$ has a spherical distribution.
5. In the general case, this geometric representation is formalized as the variance ellipse. The variance ellipse of a vector of K real random variables $\mathbf{z}$ with finite variance–covariance matrix $\boldsymbol{\Omega}$ is the set

$$\mathbb{V}_{\mathbf{z}} = \left\{\mathbf{w} = \boldsymbol{\Omega}\mathbf{a} \mid \mathbf{a} \in \mathbb{R}^K,\ \mathbf{a}'\boldsymbol{\Omega}\mathbf{a} \leq 1\right\}$$

When $\boldsymbol{\Omega}$ is nonsingular,

$$\mathbb{V}_{\mathbf{z}} = \left\{\mathbf{w} \mid \mathbf{w}'\boldsymbol{\Omega}^{-1}\mathbf{w} \leq 1\right\}$$

6. Covariance is exploited by the MMSE linear predictor for y_n given a row vector x_n:

$$\text{E}^*[y_n \mid \mathbf{x}_n] \equiv \text{E}[y_n] + (\mathbf{x}_n - \text{E}[\mathbf{x}_n])'\,\gamma_0$$

where

$$\gamma_0 = (\text{Var}[\mathbf{x}_n])^{-1}\,\text{Cov}[\mathbf{x}_n, y_n]$$

provided that $\text{Var}(\mathbf{x}_n)$ is nonsingular. The MMSE linear predictor is a projection of y_n onto the subspace of linear functions of $\mathbf{x}_n$. Even though the conditional expectation $\text{E}[y_n \mid \mathbf{x}_n]$ may be nonlinear, the MMSE linear predictor is a linear function of $\mathbf{x}_n$ by construction. Thus, $\text{E}^*[y_n \mid \mathbf{x}_n]$ is a closer analogue to the OLS fitted vector $\hat{\boldsymbol{\mu}} \equiv \mathbf{P_X y}$ than the conditional expectation $\text{E}[y_n \mid \mathbf{x}_n]$ unless $\text{E}^*[y_n \mid \mathbf{x}_n] = \text{E}[y_n \mid \mathbf{x}_n]$ because the latter is linear.

7. Variance matrices possess "square roots": for every $\boldsymbol{\Omega} = \text{Var}[\mathbf{z}]$ there is a full-column rank matrix $\mathbf{C}$ such that $\boldsymbol{\Omega} = \mathbf{CC}'$. One method for finding such $\mathbf{C}$ corresponds to Gram–Schmidt orthonormalization of the vector space spanned by linear combinations of the elements of $\mathbf{z}$. The orthonormalization is a sequence of MMSE linear predictions.

7.8 EXERCISES

7.8.1 Review

7.1 The logarithmic transformation of wages not only improves the functional form of the regression model, it also stabilizes conditional variances. Use the 1995 CPS data to compare the variances of wages and log-wages for men versus women, whites versus nonwhites, and highschool graduates versus others.

7.2 **(Correlation)** Correlation is equivalent to covariance, except that correlations are normalized covariances. Correlation coefficients are frequently denoted by the Greek letter ρ. If $\text{Var}[\mathbf{z}] = [\sigma_{ij}]$ then the correlation between z_i and z_j is

$$\rho_{ij} \equiv \frac{\sigma_{ij}}{\sqrt{\sigma_{ii}\sigma_{jj}}} = \frac{\sigma_{ij}}{\sigma_i \sigma_j}$$

where standard deviations are $\sigma_i \equiv \sqrt{\sigma_{ii}}$.

(a) Show that $|\rho_{ij}| \leq 1$. [HINT: Consider the Cauchy–Schwarz inequality (Lemma 7.8).]

(b) Show that the MMSE linear predictor of z_i using z_j is given by

$$\text{E}^*[z_i \mid z_j] = \text{E}[z_i] + \sigma_i \rho_{ij} \frac{z_j - \text{E}[z_j]}{\sigma_j}$$

Interpret the terms in this expression.

(c) The *partial correlation coefficient* between z_i and z_j given z_k is defined to be the correlation coefficient between the residuals

$$z_i - \text{E}^*[z_i \mid z_j] = \text{E}[z_i] + \sigma_i \rho_{ik} \frac{z_k - \text{E}[z_k]}{\sigma_k}$$

and

$$z_j - \text{E}^*[z_j \mid z_k] = z_j - \text{E}[z_j] + \sigma_j \rho_{jk} \frac{z_k - \text{E}[z_k]}{\sigma_k}$$

Find this partial correlation coefficient in terms of the correlation coefficients ρ_{ij}, ρ_{ik}, and ρ_{jk} and the standard deviations σ_i, σ_j, and σ_k.

7.3 Let $\text{Var}[\mathbf{y}] = \mathbf{I}$ and $\mathbf{z}_1 = \mathbf{Ay}$ and $\mathbf{z}_2 = \mathbf{By}$ be linear transformations of $\mathbf{y}$.

(a) Show that $\text{Var}[\mathbf{z}_1] = \mathbf{AA}'$ and $\text{Cov}[\mathbf{z}_1, \mathbf{z}_2] = \mathbf{AB}'$.

(b) Why, for general $\mathbf{A}$, are the elements of $\mathbf{z}_1$ correlated although the elements of $\mathbf{y}$ are not?

(c) Under what conditions is $\text{Var}[\mathbf{z}_1]$ singular?

7.4 Consider the two-dimensional case in which the variance matrix is diagonal but not scalar,

$$\text{Var}[\mathbf{z}] = \begin{bmatrix} \sigma_1^2 & 0 \\ 0 & \sigma_2^2 \end{bmatrix}$$

A family of orthogonal (rotation) matrices for two dimensions,

$$\mathbf{R}(\theta) = \begin{bmatrix} \sqrt{1-\theta^2} & -\theta \\ \theta & \sqrt{1-\theta^2} \end{bmatrix}, \qquad \theta^2 \leq 1$$

was described in Example 7.1. Show that the elements of $\mathbf{w} = \mathbf{R}(\theta)\mathbf{z}$ are uncorrelated for all θ if and only if $\sigma_1^2 = \sigma_2^2$. Draw a figure of the variance ellipses that illustrates how unequal variances lead to correlation after rotation. Given this example, comment on the sufficiency of orthogonal projection for zero correlation.

7.5 If Assumption 6.1 (First Moments, p. 110) fails to hold but Assumptions 3.1 (Full Rank, p. 53) and 7.1 (Second Moments, p. 130) do hold, what does the OLS estimator estimate?

***7.6** Let $\mathbf{\Omega}$ be a $K \times K$ variance matrix.
(a) Show that $\mathbf{\Omega}$ is positive semidefinite for all $\mathbf{w} \in \mathbb{R}^K$, $\mathbf{w}'\mathbf{\Omega}\mathbf{w} \geq 0$.
(b) Show that $\mathbf{\Omega}$ is nonsingular if and only if $\mathbf{\Omega}$ is positive definite.
(c) Show that $\mathbf{\Omega}^{-1}$ is positive definite if $\mathbf{\Omega}$ is nonsingular.

7.7 **(Minimizing Variance)** Correlation can be exploited to reduce the variance of a linear combination of random variables. Let $\mathbf{z} = [z_1, z_2]'$ be a two-dimensional random variable with a mean equal to the zero vector and the nonsingular variance matrix $\mathbf{\Omega}$. Solve

$$\alpha^* = \underset{\alpha}{\operatorname{argmin}} \operatorname{Var}[z_1 + \alpha z_2]$$

What determines the sign of α^*?

***7.8** **(MMSE Linear Predictor)** Let $\mathbf{z}$ be a vector of random variables with $\mathrm{E}[\mathbf{z}] = \mathbf{0}$ and $\operatorname{Var}[\mathbf{z}] = \mathbf{\Omega}$ finite. Partition $\mathbf{z}$ into the first element z_1 and the rest of the vector $\mathbf{z}_2$ and partition $\mathbf{\Omega}$ conformably:

$$\operatorname{Var}[\mathbf{z}] = \operatorname{Var}\left[\begin{bmatrix} z_1 \\ \mathbf{z}_2 \end{bmatrix}\right] = \begin{bmatrix} \Omega_{11} & \mathbf{\Omega}_{12} \\ \mathbf{\Omega}_{21} & \mathbf{\Omega}_{22} \end{bmatrix}$$

(a) Show that the MMSE predictor of z_1 that is a linear function of $\mathbf{z}_2$ is $\mathrm{E}^*[z_1 \mid \mathbf{z}_2] = \mathbf{z}_2'\boldsymbol{\beta}$ where $\boldsymbol{\beta} = \mathbf{\Omega}_{22}^{-1}\mathbf{\Omega}_{21}$.
(b) Show that the forecast error $z_1 - \mathbf{z}_2'\boldsymbol{\beta}$ is uncorrelated with every element of $\mathbf{z}_2$.
(c) Show that z_1 is linearly dependent (with probability equal to one) on $\mathbf{z}_2$ if the variance of the forecast error is zero.
(d) Draw an analogy between these results and those of OLS regression.

***7.9** **(Law of Iterated Projections)** Let the conditions of Lemma 7.4 (MMSE Linear Predictor, 135) hold. Consider the MMSE linear predictor of y given $\mathbf{x} = [\mathbf{x}_1', \mathbf{x}_2']'$,

$$\mathrm{E}^*[y \mid \mathbf{x}_1, \mathbf{x}_2] = \alpha_0 + \mathbf{x}_1'\boldsymbol{\gamma}_{01} + \mathbf{x}_2'\boldsymbol{\gamma}_{02}$$

(a) Confirm the Pythagorean relationship

$$\mathrm{E}[(y - \alpha - \mathbf{x}_1'\boldsymbol{\gamma}_1 - \mathbf{x}_2'\boldsymbol{\gamma}_2)^2] = \mathrm{E}\left[\left(y - \mathrm{E}^*[y \mid \mathbf{x}_1, \mathbf{x}_2]\right)^2\right] + \mathrm{E}\left[\left(\mathrm{E}^*[y \mid \mathbf{x}_1, \mathbf{x}_2] - \alpha - \mathbf{x}_1'\boldsymbol{\gamma}_1 - \mathbf{x}_2'\boldsymbol{\gamma}_2\right)^2\right]$$

Is the nonsingularity of $\mathrm{E}[\mathbf{x}\mathbf{x}']$ necessary for this relationship?
(b) Use this decomposition to show that $\mathrm{E}^*[y \mid \mathbf{x}_1] = \alpha_0 + \mathbf{x}_1'\boldsymbol{\gamma}_{01} + \mathrm{E}^*[\mathbf{x}_2 \mid \mathbf{x}_1]'\boldsymbol{\gamma}_{02}$.
(c) If $\operatorname{Cov}[y, \mathbf{x}_1] = 0$, does this imply that $\boldsymbol{\gamma}_{01} = \mathbf{0}$? Explain.

***7.10** Confirm the partitioned MSE relationship in (7.7). (HINT: Follow the proof method (p. 61) of Proposition 2 (Partitioned Regression, p. 57).)
In addition, consider the MMSE linear predictor of y given $\mathbf{x}_1$ and $\mathbf{x}_2$,

$$\mathrm{E}^*[y \mid \mathbf{x}_1, \mathbf{x}_2] = \alpha_0 + \mathbf{x}_1'\boldsymbol{\gamma}_{01} + \mathbf{x}_2'\boldsymbol{\gamma}_{02}$$

and generalize (7.7) to

$$\boldsymbol{\gamma}_{01} = \left(\mathrm{E}\left[(\mathbf{x}_1 - \mathrm{E}^*[\mathbf{x}_1 \mid \mathbf{x}_2])(\mathbf{x}_1 - \mathrm{E}^*[\mathbf{x}_1 \mid \mathbf{x}_2])'\right]\right)^{-1} \mathrm{E}\left[(\mathbf{x}_1 - \mathrm{E}^*[\mathbf{x}_1 \mid \mathbf{x}_2])y\right] \qquad (7.25)$$

Compare this expression with the partitioned regression formula (3.6).

7.11 Explain the following statement: "The relationship between the conditional mean $\mathrm{E}[y_n \mid \mathbf{x}_n]$ and $\mathbf{x}_n'\boldsymbol{\gamma}_0$ (the MMSE linear predictor) is analogous to the relationship between the fitted OLS $\hat{\boldsymbol{\mu}}$ and the fitted RLS $\hat{\boldsymbol{\mu}}_{\mathrm{R}}$."

7.12 **(Variance Column Space)** Let $\mathrm{Col}(\mathbf{X}) = \mathrm{Col}(\boldsymbol{\Omega})$ where $\mathbf{X}$ is a full-column rank matrix and $\boldsymbol{\Omega} = \mathrm{Var}[\mathbf{z}]$. Show that

$$\Pr\{\mathbf{z} = \mathbf{P}_{\mathbf{X}}\mathbf{z}\} = 1$$

7.13 **(Symmetric Positive Definite)** Show that if $\mathbf{A}$ is symmetric and positive definite then $\mathbf{A}^{-1}$ is also symmetric and positive definite.

7.14 **(Quadratic Forms)** Let $\boldsymbol{\Omega} = \mathbf{A}'\mathbf{A}$ be a $K \times K$ matrix. Show that $\mathbf{a}'\boldsymbol{\Omega}\mathbf{a} \geq 0$ for all $\mathbf{a} \in \mathbb{R}^K$.

7.15 **(Matrix Square Root)** Let $\boldsymbol{\Omega} = \mathbf{C}\mathbf{C}'$ be a factorization of the nonsingular variance matrix $\boldsymbol{\Omega}$. One example is the Cholesky decomposition (Lemma 7.6, p. 140). Show that $\mathbf{C}$ is not unique by constructing another distinct matrix square root for $\boldsymbol{\Omega}$ from $\mathbf{C}$. (HINT: Consider orthogonal matrices.)

7.16 **(Spherical Distributions)** Let $\mathbf{y}$ be a vector of N random variables with a spherical joint distribution. Show that if we rewrite $\mathbf{y} = \mathbf{R}\mathbf{z}$, where the columns of $\mathbf{R}$ are an orthogonal basis for $\mathbb{R}^N$, then the elements of the vector $\mathbf{z}$ are uncorrelated.

7.17 **(Partitioned Quadratic)** Use the partitioned inverse formula (Exercise 3.10) to show that

$$\begin{aligned}\mathbf{z}'\boldsymbol{\Omega}^{-1}\mathbf{z} = &\left(\mathbf{z}_1 - \boldsymbol{\Omega}_{12}\boldsymbol{\Omega}_{22}^{-1}\mathbf{z}_2\right)'\left(\boldsymbol{\Omega}_{11} - \boldsymbol{\Omega}_{12}\boldsymbol{\Omega}_{22}^{-1}\boldsymbol{\Omega}_{21}\right)^{-1}\left(\mathbf{z}_1 - \boldsymbol{\Omega}_{12}\boldsymbol{\Omega}_{22}^{-1}\mathbf{z}_2\right)\\ &+ \mathbf{z}_2'\boldsymbol{\Omega}_{22}^{-1}\mathbf{z}_2\end{aligned}$$

***7.18** **(Cholesky Decomposition)** This exercise provides an algebraic derivation of the Cholesky decomposition. Let $\mathbf{A} \equiv \left[a_{ij}\right]$ be a $K \times K$ real, symmetric, positive-definite matrix. Find an upper-right triangular matrix $\mathbf{C}$ so that $\mathbf{A} = \mathbf{C}'\mathbf{C}$ using the following steps.

(a) First, show that if $\mathbf{A}$ is positive definite, then every submatrix $\mathbf{B}_i \equiv \left[a_{jk};\ j, k = 1, \ldots, i < K\right]$ is also positive definite.

(b) The procedure is iterative. Now consider the ith iteration. Set $\mathbf{B}_i$ equal to the upper left-hand $i \times i$ corner of $\mathbf{A}$ and partition

$$\mathbf{B}_i = \begin{bmatrix} \mathbf{B}_{i-1} & \mathbf{d}_i \\ \mathbf{d}_i' & \mathbf{f}_i \end{bmatrix}$$

where $\mathbf{f}_i \equiv a_{ii}$ is 1×1. Suppose that we have already found (in the previous iteration) a Cholesky decomposition for the upper left-hand corner of this partition: $\mathbf{B}_{i-1} = \mathbf{C}_{i-1}'\mathbf{C}_{i-1}$ where $\mathbf{C}_{i-1}$ is nonsingular and known. Find $\mathbf{g}_i$ and $\mathbf{h}_i$ as functions of $\mathbf{C}_{i-1}$, $\mathbf{d}_i$, and $\mathbf{f}_i$ such that

$$\mathbf{C}_i = \begin{bmatrix} \mathbf{C}_{i-1} & \mathbf{g}_i \\ 0 & \mathbf{h}_i \end{bmatrix}$$

is nonsingular and $\mathbf{B}_i = \mathbf{C}_i'\mathbf{C}_i$.

(c) There is a direct way to initialize the iterations. In the first iteration, consider the 2×2 upper left-hand corner of matrix $\mathbf{A}$ by setting

$$\mathbf{B}_2 = \begin{bmatrix} a_{11} & a_{12} \\ a_{21} & a_{22} \end{bmatrix}$$

What is $\mathbf{B}_1$? Find $\mathbf{C}_1$.

(d) How can this algorithm be modified to factor an $\mathbf{A}$ that is positive semidefinite?

(e) Show that this factorization implies that all symmetric, positive semidefinite matrices are valid variance matrices.

7.8.2 Extensions

***7.19** Consider the two-dimensional random variable $\mathbf{z}$ where the variance matrix is not scalar:

$$\text{Var}[\mathbf{z}] = \sigma^2 \cdot \begin{bmatrix} 1 & \rho \\ \rho & 1 \end{bmatrix}$$

Let a family of orthogonal matrices be denoted by

$$\mathbf{R}(\theta) = \begin{bmatrix} \sqrt{1-\theta^2} & \theta \\ -\theta & \sqrt{1-\theta^2} \end{bmatrix}, \qquad \theta^2 \leq 1$$

Find θ so that the elements of $\mathbf{w} = \mathbf{R}(\theta)\mathbf{z}$ are uncorrelated. Draw a figure of the covariance ellipses illustrating the rotation.

7.20 Let $\mathbf{z}$ be a K-dimensional random vector where $\text{E}[\mathbf{z}] = \mathbf{0}$ and $\text{Var}[\mathbf{z}] = \mathbf{\Omega}$. Show that $\text{E}[\mathbf{z}'\mathbf{\Omega}^{-1}\mathbf{z}] = K$ if $\mathbf{\Omega}$ is nonsingular.

7.21 Let $\text{Var}[\mathbf{z}] = \sigma_0^2 \cdot \mathbf{I}$. Show that if $\mathbf{P}$ and $\mathbf{Q}$ are orthogonal projectors such that $\text{Col}(\mathbf{P}) \perp \text{Col}(\mathbf{Q})$, then $\text{Cov}[\mathbf{Pz}, \mathbf{Qz}] = \mathbf{0}$.

7.22 Under Assumptions 3.1 (Full Rank, p. 53), 6.1 (First Moments, p. 110), and 7.1 (Second Moments, p. 130), show that

(a) $\text{Var}[\mathbf{y} - \hat{\boldsymbol{\mu}} \mid \mathbf{X}] = \sigma_0^2 \cdot (\mathbf{I} - \mathbf{P_X})$,
(b) $\text{Cov}[\hat{\boldsymbol{\mu}}, \mathbf{y} - \hat{\boldsymbol{\mu}} \mid \mathbf{X}] = \mathbf{0}$, and
(c) $\text{Var}[\hat{\boldsymbol{\beta}} \mid \mathbf{X}] = \sigma_0^2 \cdot (\mathbf{X}'\mathbf{X})^{-1}$.

7.23 Under Assumptions 6.1 (First Moments, p. 110) and 7.1 (Second Moments, p. 130), find $\text{Var}[\hat{\boldsymbol{\mu}} \mid \mathbf{X}]$

(a) when $\mathbf{X}$ is full-column rank and
(b) when $\mathbf{X}$ is rank deficient (not full-column rank).

7.24 **(Restricted Least Squares)** Given that the second moments of y_n and $\mathbf{x}_n$ exist, show that

$$\underset{\boldsymbol{\beta}}{\text{argmin}}\, \text{E}[(y_n - \mathbf{x}_n'\boldsymbol{\beta})^2] = \underset{\boldsymbol{\beta}}{\text{argmin}}\, \text{E}\Big[\big(\text{E}[y_n \mid \mathbf{x}_n] - \mathbf{x}_n'\boldsymbol{\beta}\big)^2\Big]$$

Draw an analogy with (4.2) and (4.11), which states that

$$\underset{\{\boldsymbol{\beta} \mid \boldsymbol{\beta} = \mathbf{S}\gamma + \mathbf{s}\}}{\text{argmin}} \|\mathbf{y} - \mathbf{X}\boldsymbol{\beta}\|^2 = \underset{\{\boldsymbol{\beta} \mid \boldsymbol{\beta} = \mathbf{S}\gamma + \mathbf{s}\}}{\text{argmin}} \left\|\hat{\boldsymbol{\mu}} - \mathbf{X}\boldsymbol{\beta}\right\|^2$$

7.25 Consider $\text{Col}(\mathbf{\Omega})$ where $\mathbf{\Omega}$ is a variance matrix. Let $\mathbf{a}, \mathbf{b} \in \text{Col}(\mathbf{\Omega})$.

(a) Show that $\langle \mathbf{a}, \mathbf{b} \rangle_{\mathbf{\Omega}} \equiv \mathbf{a}'\mathbf{\Omega}\mathbf{b}$ is an inner product on $\text{Col}(\mathbf{\Omega})$.
(b) Show that $\|\mathbf{a}\|_{\mathbf{\Omega}} \equiv \sqrt{\mathbf{a}'\mathbf{\Omega}\mathbf{a}}$ is a norm on $\text{Col}(\mathbf{\Omega})$.
(c) Show that the variance ellipse can be written for all $\mathbf{\Omega}$, nonsingular and singular,

$$\begin{aligned} \mathbb{V}_{\mathbf{y}} &= \left\{\mathbf{w} = \mathbf{\Omega}\mathbf{a} \mid \mathbf{a} \in \mathbb{R}^N,\ \mathbf{a}'\mathbf{\Omega}\mathbf{a} \leq 1\right\} \\ &= \left\{\mathbf{w} = \mathbf{\Omega}\mathbf{a} \mid \mathbf{a} \in \text{Col}(\mathbf{\Omega}),\ \|\mathbf{a}\|_{\mathbf{\Omega}}^2 \leq 1\right\} \end{aligned}$$

7.26 Show that the only positive-definite orthogonal projection matrix is the identity matrix.

7.27 **(Singular Value Decomposition)** Let $\mathbf{A}$ be a real symmetric matrix. Let $\mathbf{B}$ be a full-column rank matrix such that $\text{Col}(\mathbf{B}) = \text{Col}(\mathbf{A})$ so that the columns of $\mathbf{B}$ are a basis for the columns of $\mathbf{A}$.

(a) Given $\mathbf{A}$, how could you find such a $\mathbf{B}$?

(b) Show that $\mathbf{A} = \mathbf{BC}'$ where $\mathbf{C}$ has the same dimensions as $\mathbf{B}$.

(c) Show that there is a nonsingular matrix $\mathbf{D}$ so that $\mathbf{C} = \mathbf{BD}$. [HINT: Show that $\text{Col}(\mathbf{B}) = \text{Col}(\mathbf{C})$.]

(d) Hence, show that $\mathbf{A}$ can always be decomposed into $\mathbf{A} = \mathbf{BHB}'$ where $\mathbf{H}$ is nonsingular and symmetric and $\mathbf{B}$ is full-column rank. Such decompositions are called *singular value decompositions*.

(e) Use this result to propose a matrix square root for $\mathbf{A}$ if it is also positive semidefinite.

7.28 **(Eigenvalue Decomposition)** In econometrics, another popular decomposition for symmetric matrices is the *eigenvalue decomposition*. It is always possible to find an orthogonal matrix $\mathbf{R}$ and a diagonal matrix $\mathbf{\Lambda}$ such that $\mathbf{\Omega} = \mathbf{R\Lambda R}'$. The columns of $\mathbf{R}$ are called eigenvectors and the diagonal elements of $\mathbf{\Lambda}$ are called eigenvalues. See also Theorem C.16 (Eigenvalue Decomposition, p. 866).

(a) Show that one matrix square root of $\mathbf{\Omega}$ is $\mathbf{A} = \mathbf{R}'\mathbf{\Lambda}^{1/2}$ where $\mathbf{\Lambda}^{1/2}$ denotes another diagonal matrix whose diagonal elements are the square roots of the corresponding elements of $\mathbf{\Lambda}$.

(b) Construct a second matrix square root with the additional property that it is symmetric.

7.29 Show that one can always view the generalized Euclidean inner product $\mathbf{x}'\mathbf{\Omega}\mathbf{y}$ of two vectors $\mathbf{x}$ and $\mathbf{y}$ with a nonsingular variance matrix $\mathbf{\Omega}$ as the ordinary Euclidean inner product of a linear transformation of the vectors.

CHAPTER 8

VARIANCES AND COVARIANCES OF ORDINARY LEAST SQUARES

Estimation, prediction, and testing are basic statistical goals and for each a primary concern is accuracy. The accuracy of OLS rests in part on the sampling variances of its statistics. In this chapter we describe these variances and their estimation. Estimation of variances permits us, for example, to assess the precision of the estimated coefficient -0.242 of the dummy variable for females in the log-wage equation in Run 5 of Table 1.8. Provided that certain assumptions hold, an unbiased estimate of the sampling variance of the OLS estimator for this coefficient is 0.0261. This is evidence that we can interpret the value -0.242 as close enough to the population coefficient to infer that the latter is a substantial negative percentage. If the estimated variance were much larger, say 0.25, we might well infer that a positive population coefficient is also reasonably consistent with the sample evidence.

Alternatively, we might wish to predict the log-wage of a surveyed individual who did not provide responses to questions about income. Under certain conditions the value of the OLS fitted regression is an unbiased prediction. Furthermore, we can estimate the variance in the prediction method in order to measure the uncertainty surrounding the prediction itself. Its variance is a simple function of the variance matrix of the OLS fitted coefficients.

8.1 EXPERIMENTAL EXAMPLE

To illustrate some of the variance and covariance properties of OLS statistics, let us return to the artificial experiment described in Chapter 6. We make several adjustments to our data-generating process for experience and log-wages. The first adjustment is one that we have made before: we will make the conditional mean of the log-wage conditional on experience *exactly* equal to the quadratic function $2.0 + 0.033 \cdot x - 0.000568 \cdot x^2$. Our second adjustment creates a constant conditional variance for all levels of experience.

The conditional variance function of log-wage given experience for the original joint distribution of experience and log-wage appears in Figure 8.1. This is the variance for the conditional p.d.f.'s shown in Figure 6.4. The conditional variance is obviously changing and has an overall tendency to rise with experience levels. In our adjustment to the data-generating process, we scale

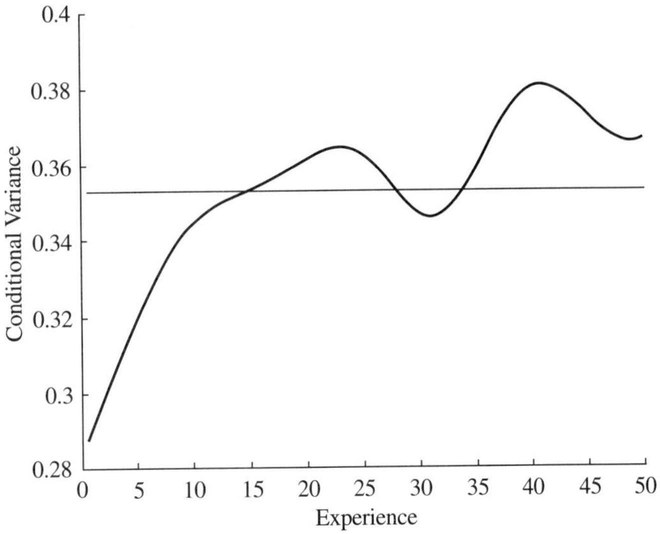

Figure 8.1 Conditional variance of log-wage given experience.

the conditional distribution for each experience level so that the variance is constant and equals 0.3531. As a result the joint p.d.f. has the same general appearance as before (see Figure 6.3) with somewhat more spread at the lowest levels of experience. The difference is so subtle, however, that we do not graph the new joint p.d.f.[1]

We use a much smaller sample size in this experiment, setting the number of observations to only five. This gives us enough observations to satisfy Assumption 3.1 but not so few that the fitted residuals are all equal to zero. To make our samples conditional on **X**, we set the experience variable equal to the 10th, 30th, 50th, 70th, and 90th percentiles of the marginal p.d.f. of experience and held the elements of x constant at these five values for all experiments. We draw each of the five observations independently from the adjusted conditional p.d.f. of the log-wage given the respective experience level. In this way, our data-generating process satisfies Assumptions 3.1, 6.1, and 7.1.

Given this method for drawing a single sample of five observations, we drew 10, 000 such samples and calculated the OLS fit for the quadratic function in experience. As before, the OLS estimators of the coefficients average to values quite close to the values that we chose: 2.003, 0.0325, and −0.000558, respectively. This is another empirical corroboration that these estimators are unbiased. The sample variance matrix of these 10, 000 OLS coefficients was

$$\begin{bmatrix} 7.394 \times 10^{-1} & -7.803 \times 10^{-2} & 1.670 \times 10^{-3} \\ -7.803 \times 10^{-2} & 1.026 \times 10^{-2} & -2.401 \times 10^{-4} \\ 1.670 \times 10^{-3} & -2.401 \times 10^{-4} & 5.947 \times 10^{-6} \end{bmatrix}$$

and the corresponding correlations were

[1] This reflects that the figures are graphed in the units of standard deviations, not variances. The smallest standard deviation, 0.5360, rises only 10% to 0.5942.

$$\begin{bmatrix} 1.000 & -0.896 & 0.796 \\ -0.896 & 1.000 & -0.972 \\ 0.796 & -0.972 & 1.000 \end{bmatrix}$$

One can see immediately that the coefficient estimators exhibit strong covariance and have quite different variances. Figure 8.2 shows the empirical variance ellipse of $\hat{\beta}_2$ and $\hat{\beta}_3$ (in white) centered on the population values and a scatter plot of the realizations of these fitted coefficients. In this chapter and in Chapter 9 we will explain the nonspherical character of the joint distribution of the OLS fitted coefficients illustrated by this example.

By design, the population residuals $y_n - \mathbf{x}_n'\beta_0$ have constant variance $\sigma_0^2 = 0.3531$ and no covariance. It is instructive to examine the sampling behavior of the OLS fitted residuals $y_n - \mathbf{x}_n'\hat{\boldsymbol{\beta}}$. These are sample analogues of the population residuals and hold information about the population variance σ_0^2.

The sample averages of the OLS fitted residuals were of the order 10^{-3}. The sample variance matrix was

$$\begin{bmatrix} 0.0513 & -0.1028 & 0.0172 & 0.0621 & -0.0277 \\ -0.1028 & 0.2333 & -0.1048 & -0.0655 & 0.0399 \\ 0.0172 & -0.1048 & 0.1890 & -0.1331 & 0.0318 \\ 0.0621 & -0.0655 & -0.1331 & 0.2046 & -0.0681 \\ -0.0277 & 0.0399 & 0.0318 & -0.0681 & 0.0242 \end{bmatrix}$$

and the correlation coefficients were

$$\begin{bmatrix} 1.000 & -0.940 & 0.174 & 0.607 & -0.787 \\ -0.940 & 1.000 & -0.499 & -0.300 & 0.531 \\ 0.174 & -0.499 & 1.000 & -0.677 & 0.470 \\ 0.607 & -0.300 & -0.677 & 1.000 & -0.968 \\ -0.787 & 0.531 & 0.470 & -0.968 & 1.000 \end{bmatrix}$$

Therefore, relative to their standard errors, the averages are near zero. This is what Proposition 4 (Unbiased Estimation, p. 111) tells us we should find. Note that unlike the population residuals, these OLS fitted residuals have variances that differ by a factor of 10 and every variance is smaller than σ_0^2. In addition, the fitted residuals are highly correlated among themselves.

Therefore it appears that the fitted residuals are misleading about the variance matrix of the population residuals. However it is possible to construct a simple unbiased estimator of σ_0^2 with the fitted residuals. The sample average of the squared fitted residuals from a single sample has an average value of 0.14048 over the 10, 000 experiments.[2] The percent that this statistic underestimates σ_0^2 is $0.14048/0.3531 = 0.3978$, almost exactly 2/5. This is not a coincidence. As shown below, the numerator 2 is the number of observations (5 in our example) less the number of RHS variables (3 in our example) and the denominator is the number of observations. Knowing this, we can construct an unbiased estimator of σ_0^2 from the sum of the squared fitted

[2] This value is equal to the average of the diagonal elements in the sample variance matrix.

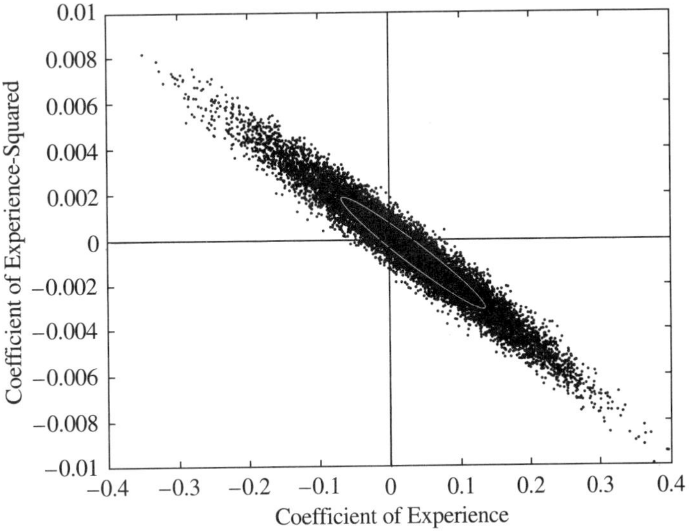

Figure 8.2 Scatter plot and variance ellipse of experience coefficients.

residuals by dividing it by $N - K$ instead of N. Although this statistic clearly overstates the sample variation in the *fitted* residuals, this estimator is, in fact, unbiased for σ_0^2, the variance of the *population* residuals. The average of this estimator across the 10, 000 samples was 0.3514, which is reasonably close to $\sigma_0^2 = 0.3531$.

In this chapter, we give analytical results that characterize these phenomena and yield the basic method for estimating the variance of OLS fitted coefficients. To explain the results, we combine the concepts about variance and covariance in Chapter 7 with the OLS statistics.

8.2 SECOND-MOMENT PROPERTIES

We will explain the consequences of Assumption 7.1 in the same way we studied OLS regression, by following the OLS transformations of $\mathbf{y}$ to $\hat{\boldsymbol{\mu}}$ followed by $\hat{\boldsymbol{\mu}}$ to $\hat{\boldsymbol{\beta}}$. The basic results are contained in the following proposition:

Proposition 5 (Variances of OLS) *Under Assumption 7.1 (Second Moments, p. 130),*

1. $\mathrm{Var}[\hat{\boldsymbol{\mu}} \mid \mathbf{X}] = \sigma_0^2 \cdot \mathbf{P_X}$,
2. $\mathrm{Var}[\mathbf{y} - \hat{\boldsymbol{\mu}} \mid \mathbf{X}] = \sigma_0^2 \cdot (\mathbf{I} - \mathbf{P_X})$,
3. $\mathrm{Cov}[\hat{\boldsymbol{\mu}}, \mathbf{y} - \hat{\boldsymbol{\mu}} \mid \mathbf{X}] = \mathbf{0}$, *and*
4. $\mathrm{Var}[\hat{\boldsymbol{\beta}} \mid \mathbf{X}] = \sigma_0^2 \cdot (\mathbf{X}'\mathbf{X})^{-1}$, *adding Assumption 3.1 (Full Rank, p. 53).*

Thus, given the conditional variance matrix for $\mathbf{y}$, we can derive the conditional variance matrices for $\hat{\boldsymbol{\mu}}$, $\mathbf{y} - \hat{\boldsymbol{\mu}}$, and $\hat{\boldsymbol{\beta}}$.[3] Note that none of the variance matrices for the statistics possesses the scalar matrix form of the $\mathrm{Var}[\mathbf{y} \mid \mathbf{X}]$. The first two variance matrices turn out to be proportional to familiar orthogonal projection matrices. In general, the diagonals of these variance matrices are not constant and the off-diagonal covariance elements are not zero. That the covariance of $\hat{\boldsymbol{\mu}}$ and $\mathbf{y} - \hat{\boldsymbol{\mu}}$ is zero is a surprising result, but one that follows in part from the geometric orthogonality of these two vectors.

In this chapter we will also derive an unbiased estimator of σ_0^2, the new parameter introduced by Assumption 7.1. This estimator is a generalization of the variance estimator of the simple location model, the sample variance of the differences between y and its estimated mean. The superficial differences are that $\boldsymbol{\iota}\bar{y}$ is replaced by its generalization $\hat{\boldsymbol{\mu}}$, and that the denominator is $N - K$ instead of $N - 1$ (see Table 5.2, p. 103).

Proposition 6 (Estimation of the Variance) *Under Assumptions 3.1 (p. 53), 6.1 (p. 110), and 7.1 (p. 130), the variance estimator*

$$s^2 \equiv \frac{(\mathbf{y} - \hat{\boldsymbol{\mu}})'(\mathbf{y} - \hat{\boldsymbol{\mu}})}{N - K}$$

is conditionally unbiased: $\mathrm{E}[s^2 \mid \mathbf{X}] = \sigma_0^2$.

It follows immediately that the marginal expectation of s^2 is also σ_0^2.[4] These results give Proposition 5 (Variances of OLS) practical, as well as theoretical, significance. Given this unbiased estimator of σ_0^2, the sampling variances of $\hat{\boldsymbol{\mu}}$ and $\hat{\boldsymbol{\beta}}$ can actually be estimated. For example, $s^2 \cdot (\mathbf{X}'\mathbf{X})^{-1}$ is an unbiased estimator of $\mathrm{Var}[\hat{\boldsymbol{\beta}} \mid \mathbf{X}]$. The standard errors reported in the introductory example are the square roots of the diagonal elements of this matrix.

Using the fitted residuals to estimate the conditional variance of the y_n seems intuitive to many students, as indeed it is. But setting the denominator equal to the sample size minus the number of RHS variables is often puzzling. After all, there are N squared residuals in the sum. There are other puzzles, too. Although the $y_n - \mu_n$ $(n = 1, \ldots, N)$ all have the same conditional variance σ_0^2, note that Proposition 5 states that the fitted residuals $y_n - \hat{\mu}_n$ have different variances for each n: the diagonal elements of $\mathbf{I} - \mathbf{P}_\mathbf{X}$ are *not* equal and depend on $\mathbf{X}$ in a complicated way. We will explain intuitively how the sum of the squared fitted residuals yields an unbiased estimator of σ_0^2 in spite of these complications.

In this chapter, we extend the geometric treatment of OLS to these two propositions. The algebraic proofs of these propositions are short, but they provide limited insight. The geometry gives a helpful image describing how the propositions hold, as we follow the transformations of $\mathbf{y}$ to $\hat{\boldsymbol{\mu}}$ and $\hat{\boldsymbol{\mu}}$ to $\hat{\boldsymbol{\beta}}$.

We have seen previously that within this geometry, the scalar variance matrix of $\mathbf{y}$ is equivalent to an N-dimensional sphere. For this reason, the distributions of random variables with scalar

[3] We prove this proposition on p. 160.

[4] We prove this proposition on p. 165.

variance matrices are called *spherical* distributions. But scalar variance matrices are not the only variance matrices that yield spherical distributions: the variance ellipse of $\hat{\mu}$ is also a sphere. Because $\hat{\mu}$ is the orthogonal projection of $\mathbf{y}$ onto $\mathrm{Col}(\mathbf{X})$, the variance ellipse of $\hat{\mu}$ is the same orthogonal projection of the variance ellipse of $\mathbf{y}$.

This relationship is illustrated graphically in Figure 8.3. The three-dimensional sphere represents the variance of $\mathbf{y}$ around its mean μ_0 and the intersection of this sphere with the plane $\mathrm{Col}(\mathbf{X})$ represents the variance of $\hat{\mu}$ centered at its mean, the same μ_0. The figure shows that every point inside the variance sphere of $\mathbf{y}$ projects orthogonally into a point inside a region of $\mathrm{Col}(\mathbf{X})$ that is also spherical, with the same radius, but in a lower dimension. Thus the conditional distribution of $\hat{\mu}$ is also spherical, despite its nonscalar variance matrix.

The variance matrix of $\mathbf{y} - \hat{\mu}$ has a similar interpretation. The variance matrix of $\mathbf{y} - \hat{\mu}$ is the orthogonal projection of $\mathbf{y}$'s variance sphere onto $\mathrm{Col}^{\perp}(\mathbf{X})$. This projection is also a sphere, with the same radius as the original sphere of $\mathbf{y}$, but in a vector subspace of $\mathbb{R}^N$ with dimension $N - K$. Thus, we can attach simple interpretations to the complex expressions for $\mathrm{Var}[\hat{\mu} \mid \mathbf{X}]$ and $\mathrm{Var}[\mathbf{y} - \hat{\mu} \mid \mathbf{X}]$ in Results 1 and 2 of Proposition 5.

The spherical representation of the variance matrices of $\mathbf{y}$, $\hat{\mu}$, and $\mathbf{y} - \hat{\mu}$ reflects a fundamental symmetry that helps to explain the zero correlation between $\hat{\mu}$ and $\mathbf{y} - \hat{\mu}$ described in Result 3 of Proposition 5 and the variance estimator of Proposition 6. For example, we will show that the projection $\mathbf{I} - \mathbf{P_X}$ is analogous to replacing K elements of $\mathbf{y} - \mathbf{X}\beta$ with zeros and that s^2 is analogous to an average of the squares of the remaining $N - K$ nonzero elements. Viewed this way, s^2 is unbiased in the same way as a sample average for a population mean.

Generally, the distribution of $\hat{\beta}$ is not spherical. Instead, the variance matrix has an elliptical representation. The elliptical shape displays the covariance among the elements of $\hat{\beta}$ and the unequal variances. The linear, nonsingular, transformation from $\hat{\mu}$ to $\hat{\beta}$ induces this elliptical shape. Whereas the transformation of $\mathbf{y}$ into $\hat{\mu}$ is an orthogonal one, the transformation from $\hat{\mu}$ to $\hat{\beta}$ is not and the symmetry of spheres is lost. The nature of the elliptical result can be seen to rest on the character of $\mathbf{X}$, just as it determines how $\hat{\mu}$ turns into $\hat{\beta}$.

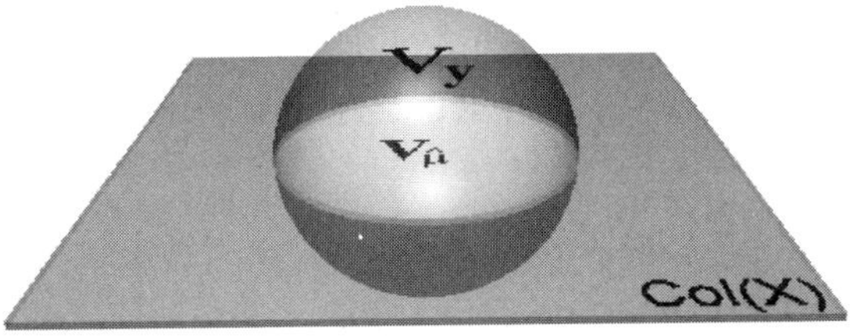

Figure 8.3 Projection of variance sphere of $\mathbf{y}$ onto $\mathrm{Col}(\mathbf{X})$.

8.3 VARIANCE AND COVARIANCE MATRICES

The proof of Proposition 5 consists of repeated applications of Lemma 7.1. Notice again the importance of linearity in $\mathbf{y}$ for analyzing the moments of the OLS statistics.

Proof of Proposition 5. Applying Lemma 7.1 to $\text{Var}[\hat{\boldsymbol{\mu}} \mid \mathbf{X}]$, and using the symmetry and idempotency of $\mathbf{P_X}$,

$$\begin{aligned}\text{Var}[\hat{\boldsymbol{\mu}} \mid \mathbf{X}] &= \text{Var}[\mathbf{P_X y} \mid \mathbf{X}] \\ &= \mathbf{P_X}\,\text{Var}[\mathbf{y} \mid \mathbf{X}]\mathbf{P_X} \\ &= \mathbf{P_X}(\sigma_0^2 \cdot \mathbf{I})\mathbf{P_X} \\ &= \sigma_0^2 \cdot \mathbf{P_X} \end{aligned} \tag{8.1}$$

The covariance case is a slight generalization of the algebraic argument:

$$\begin{aligned}\text{Cov}[\hat{\boldsymbol{\mu}}, \mathbf{y} - \hat{\boldsymbol{\mu}} \mid \mathbf{X}] &= \text{Cov}[\mathbf{P_X y}, (\mathbf{I} - \mathbf{P_X})\mathbf{y} \mid \mathbf{X}] \\ &= \mathbf{P_X}\,\text{Var}[\mathbf{y} \mid \mathbf{X}](\mathbf{I} - \mathbf{P_X}) \\ &= \mathbf{P_X}(\sigma_0^2 \cdot \mathbf{I})(\mathbf{I} - \mathbf{P_X}) \\ &= \mathbf{0} \end{aligned} \tag{8.2}$$

We leave the analogous derivations for $\text{Var}[\mathbf{y} - \hat{\boldsymbol{\mu}} \mid \mathbf{X}]$ and $\text{Var}[\hat{\boldsymbol{\beta}} \mid \mathbf{X}]$ as exercises. □

The most obvious feature of the variance matrices of OLS statistics is that they are not scalar. Within each of the vectors $\hat{\boldsymbol{\mu}}$, $\mathbf{y} - \hat{\boldsymbol{\mu}}$, and $\hat{\boldsymbol{\beta}}$, the elements are mutually correlated and their variances are not equal. One should expect this for $\hat{\boldsymbol{\mu}}$ and $\mathbf{y} - \hat{\boldsymbol{\mu}}$ because every element of these vectors is a linear combination of *all* the elements of $\mathbf{y}$. For the elements of $\hat{\boldsymbol{\mu}}$, we can simplify the correlation structure further because every element is a linear combination of the elements of $\hat{\boldsymbol{\beta}}$. Thus

$$\begin{aligned}\text{Cov}[\hat{\mu}_m, \hat{\mu}_n \mid \mathbf{X}] &= \text{Cov}[\mathbf{x}_m'\hat{\boldsymbol{\beta}}, \mathbf{x}_n'\hat{\boldsymbol{\beta}} \mid \mathbf{X}] \\ &= \sum_{k=1}^{K}\sum_{j=1}^{K} x_{mk}x_{nj}\,\text{Cov}[\hat{\beta}_k, \hat{\beta}_j \mid \mathbf{X}]\end{aligned}$$

and as a result, we expect $\text{Cov}[\hat{\mu}_m, \hat{\mu}_n \mid \mathbf{X}]$ to be nonzero and to vary with the observation indices m and n. Such a source of covariance is common in statistical analysis and, as we will show in later chapters, in statistical models. In the current statistical analysis, every element of $\hat{\boldsymbol{\mu}}$ is a linear combination of all the elements of y. As a result, even though the elements of $\mathbf{y}$ are uncorrelated, the elements of $\hat{\boldsymbol{\mu}}$ are correlated. The same logic applies to the elements of $\mathbf{y} - \hat{\boldsymbol{\mu}}$ and to the elements of $\hat{\boldsymbol{\beta}}$.

On the other hand, we cannot take such intuition as conclusive because equation (8.2) shows that *all* of the elements of $\hat{\boldsymbol{\mu}}$ are uncorrelated with *all* of the elements of $\mathbf{y} - \hat{\boldsymbol{\mu}}$. This is surprising because $\hat{\boldsymbol{\mu}}$ and $\mathbf{y} - \hat{\boldsymbol{\mu}}$ are both linear functions of $\mathbf{y}$. Here is the sample covariance matrix between the five elements of $\mathbf{y}$ and $\mathbf{y} - \hat{\boldsymbol{\mu}}$ from our introductory example:

$$\begin{bmatrix} 0.0006 & 0.0001 & -0.0033 & 0.0038 & -0.0011 \\ 0.0003 & 0.0001 & -0.0017 & 0.0018 & -0.0006 \\ 0.0003 & -0.0004 & -0.0002 & 0.0006 & -0.0002 \\ 0.0006 & -0.0015 & 0.0011 & 0.0000 & -0.0001 \\ 0.0016 & -0.0039 & 0.0023 & 0.0005 & -0.0005 \end{bmatrix}$$

The largest correlation turns out to be -0.0151. Perhaps this result seems analogous to the geometric orthogonality between these two vectors, but the analogy is not immediate. In general,

$$\mathbf{y}'\mathbf{z} = 0 \quad \not\Rightarrow \quad \text{Cov}[\mathbf{y}, \mathbf{z}] = \mathbf{0}$$

because the matrix of covariances describes the expectation of an *outer product*, not an *inner product*. Actually, the lack of correlation between $\hat{\boldsymbol{\mu}}$ and $\mathbf{y} - \hat{\boldsymbol{\mu}}$ reflects *both* the orthogonality of $\text{Col}(\mathbf{X})$ and $\text{Col}^{\perp}(\mathbf{X})$ *and* the scalar variance matrix of $\mathbf{y}$. Without both conditions, the last equality in (8.2) would not follow.

EXAMPLE 8.1

To illustrate, consider the orthogonal linear transformation on $\mathbb{R}^2$, $\mathbf{z} = \mathbf{R}'\mathbf{u}$, where

$$\mathbf{R} = \begin{bmatrix} 1 & -\theta \\ \theta & 1 \end{bmatrix}$$

so that

$$\begin{bmatrix} z_1 \\ z_2 \end{bmatrix} = \begin{bmatrix} u_1 + \theta u_2 \\ -\theta u_1 + u_2 \end{bmatrix} \tag{8.3}$$

Let $\mathbf{u} = [u_1, u_2]'$ have a scalar variance matrix $\sigma^2 \cdot \mathbf{I}_2$ so that u_1 and u_2 are uncorrelated and have equal variance $\sigma^2 = \text{Var}[u_1] = \text{Var}[u_2]$. No matter what θ is chosen, the zs have a covariance of zero:

$$\text{Cov}[z_1, z_2] = -\theta \, \text{Var}[u_1] + \theta \, \text{Var}[u_2] = 0$$

This example shows that it is possible to find collections of linear combinations that have zero covariance. It also shows the combined effect of orthogonality and a scalar variance matrix. If the columns of $\mathbf{R}$ were not orthogonal but the variance matrix remained scalar, the covariance would be nonzero. If the variances were not equal but the columns of $\mathbf{R}$ were orthogonal, the covariance would also be nonzero.

The geometry of these variance matrices gives further insight into their nature. In the linear regression model, the variance ellipse of $\mathbf{y}$ is a sphere in $\mathbb{R}^N$ with center at the origin and radius σ_0: using (7.3),

$$\mathbb{V}_{\mathbf{y}} = \left\{\mathbf{z} \in \mathbb{R}^N \mid \mathbf{z}'\mathbf{z} \le \sigma_0^2\right\} \tag{8.4}$$

The variance ellipse of $\hat{\boldsymbol{\mu}}$ is

$$\begin{aligned} \mathbb{V}_{\hat{\boldsymbol{\mu}}} &\equiv \left\{\mathbf{z} = \sigma_0^2 \cdot \mathbf{P_X}\boldsymbol{\alpha} \mid \boldsymbol{\alpha} \in \mathbb{R}^N,\ \sigma_0^2 \cdot \boldsymbol{\alpha}'\mathbf{P_X}\boldsymbol{\alpha} \le 1\right\} \\ &= \left\{\mathbf{z} = \mathbf{P_X}\boldsymbol{\gamma} \mid \boldsymbol{\gamma} \in \mathbb{R}^N,\ (\mathbf{P_X}\boldsymbol{\gamma})'\mathbf{P_X}\boldsymbol{\gamma} \le \sigma_0^2\right\} \\ &= \left\{\mathbf{z} \in \text{Col}(\mathbf{X}) \mid \mathbf{z}'\mathbf{z} \le \sigma_0^2\right\} \end{aligned} \tag{8.5}$$

This is the expression for a sphere in the subspace $\text{Col}(\mathbf{X})$, just as geometric intuition promises. Despite the apparent algebraic complexity of the expression for $\text{Var}[\hat{\boldsymbol{\mu}} \mid \mathbf{X}]$, the variance of $\hat{\boldsymbol{\mu}}$ actually has a structure analogous to the variance of $\mathbf{y}$.

The variance ellipse of $\hat{\boldsymbol{\beta}}$

$$\mathbb{V}_{\hat{\beta}} = \left\{ \mathbf{z} \in \mathbb{R}^K \mid \mathbf{z}'\mathbf{X}'\mathbf{X}\mathbf{z} \leq \sigma_0^2 \right\} \tag{8.6}$$

is the image of the variance ellipse of $\hat{\boldsymbol{\mu}}$ under the linear transformation $\hat{\boldsymbol{\beta}} = (\mathbf{X}'\mathbf{X})^{-1}\mathbf{X}'\hat{\boldsymbol{\mu}}$. Because $\hat{\boldsymbol{\mu}}$ and $\hat{\boldsymbol{\beta}}$ have a one-to-one relationship, their variance ellipses are one to one. For every $\boldsymbol{\mu} \in \mathrm{Col}(\mathbf{X})$, there is a $\mathbf{z}$ such that $\boldsymbol{\mu} = \mathbf{X}\mathbf{z}$ and

$$\frac{\boldsymbol{\mu}'\boldsymbol{\mu}}{\sigma_0^2} \leq 1 \quad \Leftrightarrow \quad \frac{\mathbf{z}'\mathbf{X}'\mathbf{X}\mathbf{z}}{\sigma_0^2} = \mathbf{z}'\left(\mathrm{Var}[\hat{\boldsymbol{\beta}} \mid \mathbf{X}]\right)^{-1}\mathbf{z} \leq 1$$

The variance ellipse of $\hat{\boldsymbol{\mu}}$ is spherical because it is the orthogonal projection of the spherical variance ellipse of $\mathbf{y}$. The variance ellipse of $\hat{\boldsymbol{\beta}}$ is generally nonspherical because $\hat{\boldsymbol{\beta}}$ is not merely an orthogonal transformation of $\hat{\boldsymbol{\mu}}$. Later in this chapter, we will examine the variance matrix of $\hat{\boldsymbol{\beta}}$ more closely.

EXAMPLE 8.2

In Figure 8.4, we give a two-dimensional illustration of the relationship between $\mathbb{V}_{\hat{\mu}}$ and $\mathbb{V}_{\hat{\beta}}$ for the special case $K = 2$, $\mathbf{X} = [\mathbf{X}_1, \mathbf{X}_2]$, and $\beta_{01} = \beta_{02} = 1$, so that $\boldsymbol{\mu}_0 = \mathbf{X}_1 + \mathbf{X}_2$. We have chosen the lengths of $\mathbf{X}_1$ and $\mathbf{X}_2$ specially so that the scales of the two ellipses align. For each of four points on the boundary of $\mathbb{V}_{\hat{\mu}}$, we display their destination in $\mathbb{V}_{\hat{\beta}}$. The four points correspond to locations where the slope of the boundary equals the direction of either $\mathbf{X}_1$ or $\mathbf{X}_2$. The image of these points in (β_1, β_2) is the pair of coefficients on $\mathbf{X}_1$ and $\mathbf{X}_2$ that reproduces them as vectors. The oblique angle between $\mathbf{X}_1$ and $\mathbf{X}_2$ corresponds to a positive sample correlation between these two RHS variables. This induces a negative correlation between $\hat{\boldsymbol{\beta}}_1$ and $\hat{\boldsymbol{\beta}}_2$, which is captured by the negative slope of their variance ellipse.

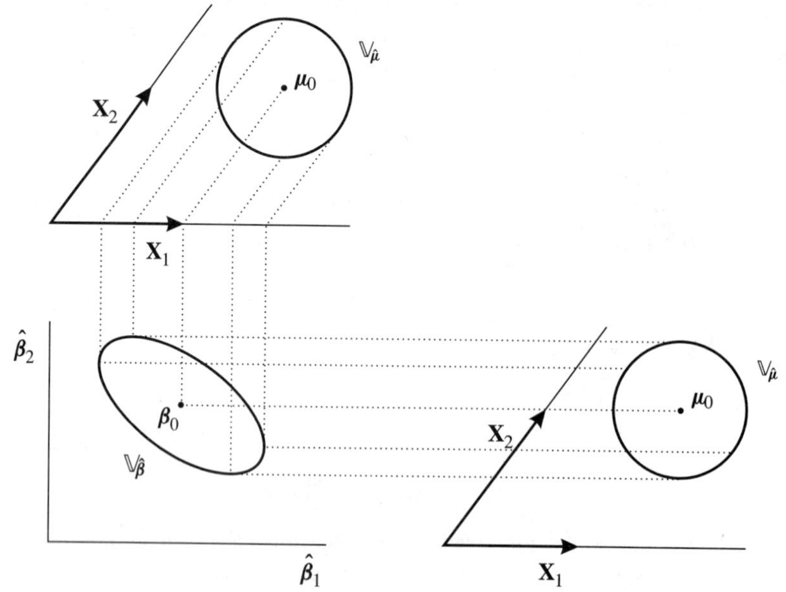

Figure 8.4 Relationship between $\mathbb{V}_{\hat{\mu}}$ and $\mathbb{V}_{\hat{\beta}}$.

We will now explain that the spherical variance ellipse of $\mathbf{y}$ also accounts for $\text{Cov}[\hat{\boldsymbol{\mu}}, \mathbf{y} - \hat{\boldsymbol{\mu}} \mid \mathbf{X}] = \mathbf{0}$. In Chapter 7 (Section 7.3), we motivated the variance sphere for $\mathbf{y}$ by noting that orthogonal transformations of $\mathbf{y}$ have the same scalar variance matrix. Thus, any two elements of an orthogonal transformation of $\mathbf{y}$ are uncorrelated, just as every y_n $(n = 1, \ldots, N)$ is uncorrelated with every y_m $(m \neq n)$. Now we will show that $\hat{\boldsymbol{\mu}}$ and $\mathbf{y} - \hat{\boldsymbol{\mu}}$ are composed of two disjoint sets of such uncorrelated elements, and that this is why they are uncorrelated.

To see this, let the columns of $\mathbf{R}_1$ be an orthonormal basis for $\text{Col}(\mathbf{X})$ and the columns of $\mathbf{R}_2$ be an orthonormal basis for $\text{Col}^{\perp}(\mathbf{X})$.[5] The matrix $\mathbf{R} = [\mathbf{R}_1, \mathbf{R}_2]$ is an orthogonal matrix so that $\mathbf{RR}' = \mathbf{R}'\mathbf{R} = \mathbf{I}_N$. Let

$$\mathbf{z} = \begin{bmatrix} \mathbf{z}_1 \\ \mathbf{z}_2 \end{bmatrix} \equiv \mathbf{R}'\mathbf{y} = \begin{bmatrix} \mathbf{R}_1'\mathbf{y} \\ \mathbf{R}_2'\mathbf{y} \end{bmatrix} \tag{8.7}$$

and note that $\mathbf{y} = \mathbf{RR}'\mathbf{y} = \mathbf{Rz}$. The vector $\mathbf{z}$ is an orthogonal transformation of $\mathbf{y}$ and $\text{Var}[\mathbf{z} \mid \mathbf{X}] = \sigma_0^2 \cdot \mathbf{I}$. Therefore, $\text{Cov}[\mathbf{z}_1, \mathbf{z}_2 \mid \mathbf{X}] = \mathbf{0}$. Furthermore, Lemma 2.6 states that

$$\begin{aligned} \mathbf{P}_\mathbf{X} &= \mathbf{R}_1\mathbf{R}_1' \\ \mathbf{I} - \mathbf{P}_\mathbf{X} &= \mathbf{R}_2\mathbf{R}_2' \end{aligned}$$

so that

$$\begin{aligned} \hat{\boldsymbol{\mu}} &= \mathbf{R}_1\mathbf{z}_1 \\ \mathbf{y} - \hat{\boldsymbol{\mu}} &= \mathbf{R}_2\mathbf{z}_2 \end{aligned}$$

Applying the bilinearity of covariance matrices (Lemma 7.1, p. 130),

$$\begin{aligned} \text{Cov}[\hat{\boldsymbol{\mu}}, \mathbf{y} - \hat{\boldsymbol{\mu}} \mid \mathbf{X}] &= \text{Cov}[\mathbf{R}_1\mathbf{z}_1, \mathbf{R}_2\mathbf{z}_2 \mid \mathbf{X}] \\ &= \mathbf{R}_1 \text{Cov}[\mathbf{z}_1, \mathbf{z}_2 \mid \mathbf{X}]\mathbf{R}_2' \\ &= \mathbf{0} \end{aligned}$$

Thus, the spherical distribution of $\mathbf{y}$ implies the spherical distribution of $\mathbf{z}$, which in turn implies the covariance of zero between $\hat{\boldsymbol{\mu}}$ and $\mathbf{y} - \hat{\boldsymbol{\mu}}$.

We have just seen that orthogonal projections are closely related to orthogonal transformations. The geometry of orthogonal transformations just examined is applied in the next section to explain the unbiased variance estimator s^2.

8.4 ESTIMATION OF THE VARIANCE PARAMETER

The second moment assumption yields another kind of second moment result, as described in Proposition 6. In addition to the variance matrices of the OLS vectors, we can also estimate the second moment parameter σ_0^2. This is useful for estimating the variance of $\mathbf{y}$ conditional on $\mathbf{X}$ and for estimating the variance matrices of $\hat{\boldsymbol{\mu}}$, $\mathbf{y} - \hat{\boldsymbol{\mu}}$, and $\hat{\boldsymbol{\beta}}$. Other than the scalar parameter σ_0^2, these matrices are functions of the observable $\mathbf{X}$. Therefore, an estimator of σ_0^2 is sufficient to estimate them.

[5] See Lemma 2.6 (p. 37) and Exercise 2.15.

It is natural to think of the OLS fitted residuals as analogous to the deviations $\mathbf{y} - \boldsymbol{\mu}_0$, and to try to use the fitted residuals to estimate σ_0^2. If we could observe $\mathbf{y} - \boldsymbol{\mu}_0$, then the squared length of $\mathbf{y} - \boldsymbol{\mu}_0$ divided by sample size would be an unbiased estimator of σ_0^2: because

$$\begin{aligned}
\mathrm{E}[(\mathbf{y} - \boldsymbol{\mu}_0)'(\mathbf{y} - \boldsymbol{\mu}_0) \mid \mathbf{X}] &= \mathrm{E}\left[\sum_{n=1}^{N} (y_n - \mu_0)^2 \mid \mathbf{X}\right] \\
&= \sum_{n=1}^{N} \mathrm{Var}[y_n \mid \mathbf{X}] \\
&= \sigma_0^2 N
\end{aligned}$$

the expectation of $(\mathbf{y} - \boldsymbol{\mu}_0)'(\mathbf{y} - \boldsymbol{\mu}_0)/N$ is σ_0^2. In effect, we are replacing the unobservable $\mathbf{y} - \boldsymbol{\mu}_0$ with the observable $\mathbf{y} - \hat{\boldsymbol{\mu}}$ to produce the feasible estimator

$$s^2 \equiv \frac{(\mathbf{y} - \hat{\boldsymbol{\mu}})'(\mathbf{y} - \hat{\boldsymbol{\mu}})}{N - K} \tag{8.8}$$

The analogy is more apt than might at first be thought. Whereas the variance matrix of $\mathbf{y}$ (and $\mathbf{y} - \boldsymbol{\mu}_0$) is a scalar matrix, the variance matrix of $\mathbf{y} - \hat{\boldsymbol{\mu}}$ is not. Note particularly the changing variances: using Proposition 5, we can take a diagonal element of $\mathrm{Var}[\mathbf{y} - \hat{\boldsymbol{\mu}} \mid \mathbf{X}]$ to see that

$$\mathrm{Var}[y_n - \hat{\mu}_n \mid \mathbf{X}] = \sigma_0^2 \left[1 - \mathbf{x}_n'(\mathbf{X}'\mathbf{X})^{-1}\mathbf{x}_n\right] \tag{8.9}$$

That a variance estimator based on the fitted residuals has such a simple form is actually somewhat surprising when we look at this expression. The expectation of the numerator of s^2 is the sum of these terms.

That the *simple* average of the squared fitted residuals will underestimate σ_0^2 is plain to see. As we have just seen, the average of the squared $y_n - \mu_{0n}$ is an unbiased estimator of σ_0^2. The expectation of the average of the squared fitted residuals must be less than this, because $\hat{\boldsymbol{\mu}}$ minimizes this statistic:

$$(\mathbf{y} - \hat{\boldsymbol{\mu}})'(\mathbf{y} - \hat{\boldsymbol{\mu}}) = \min_{\boldsymbol{\mu} \in \mathrm{Col}(\mathbf{X})} (\mathbf{y} - \boldsymbol{\mu})'(\mathbf{y} - \boldsymbol{\mu}) \le (\mathbf{y} - \boldsymbol{\mu}_0)'(\mathbf{y} - \boldsymbol{\mu}_0)$$

so that

$$\mathrm{E}\left[\frac{(\mathbf{y} - \hat{\boldsymbol{\mu}})'(\mathbf{y} - \hat{\boldsymbol{\mu}})}{N} \middle| \mathbf{X}\right] \le \sigma_0^2$$

Therefore, the variation of the fitted residuals will surely understate the true variation of $\mathbf{y}$ around $\boldsymbol{\mu}_0 = \mathbf{X}\boldsymbol{\beta}_0$. Remarkably, the inflation factor that yields an unbiased estimator is simply $N/(N-K)$, a function of the sample size and the number of explanatory variables alone.

That s^2 is an unbiased estimator of σ_0^2 can be viewed as resting on two geometric observations. First, the distribution of $\mathbf{y} - \hat{\boldsymbol{\mu}}$ is spherical, just as the distribution of $\mathbf{y}$, and has the same scale σ_0. Because $\mathbf{I} - \mathbf{P}_\mathbf{X}$ is also an orthogonal projector, we can use the same logic as (8.5) to find

$$\mathbb{V}_{\mathbf{y}-\hat{\boldsymbol{\mu}}} = \left\{\mathbf{z} \in \mathrm{Col}^{\perp}(\mathbf{X}) \mid \mathbf{z}'\mathbf{z} \le \sigma_0^2\right\}$$

Second, the $\mathbf{y} - \hat{\boldsymbol{\mu}}$ lies in a vector subspace of dimension $N - K$ whereas $\mathbf{y}$ is N-dimensional. The expected squared length of $\mathbf{y} - \boldsymbol{\mu}_0$ equals $\sigma_0^2 N$ and the expected squared length of $\mathbf{y} - \hat{\boldsymbol{\mu}}$ is shorter in proportion to the loss of dimension: $\mathrm{E}[(\mathbf{y} - \hat{\boldsymbol{\mu}})'(\mathbf{y} - \hat{\boldsymbol{\mu}}) \mid \mathbf{X}] = \sigma_0^2 (N - K)$. Here is the formal proof.

Proof of Proposition 6. Let us return to the orthogonal decomposition (8.7) in the previous section, where the columns of $\mathbf{R}_2$ form an orthonormal basis for $\mathrm{Col}^{\perp}(\mathbf{X})$ and $\mathbf{y} - \hat{\boldsymbol{\mu}} = \mathbf{R}_2\mathbf{R}_2'\mathbf{y} = \mathbf{R}_2\mathbf{z}_2$. Now observe that the vector $\mathbf{z}_2$ contains $N - K$ elements with mean zero and a scalar variance matrix. Because $\mathrm{Col}(\mathbf{R}_2) \perp \mathrm{Col}(\mathbf{X})$ and $\mathbf{z}_2 \equiv \mathbf{R}_2'\mathbf{y}$,

$$\mathrm{E}[\mathbf{z}_2 \mid \mathbf{X}] = \mathbf{R}_2'\mathbf{X}\boldsymbol{\beta}_0 = \mathbf{0}$$

Because $\mathbf{R}_2$ is an orthonormal basis [of $\mathrm{Col}^{\perp}(\mathbf{X})$],

$$\begin{aligned} \mathrm{Var}[\mathbf{z}_2 \mid \mathbf{X}] &= \mathbf{R}_2' \left(\sigma_0^2 \cdot \mathbf{I}_N\right) \mathbf{R}_2 \\ &= \sigma_0^2 \cdot \mathbf{R}_2'\mathbf{R}_2 \\ &= \sigma_0^2 \cdot \mathbf{I}_{N-K} \end{aligned}$$

We can now show that the squared length of $\mathbf{y} - \hat{\boldsymbol{\mu}}$ equals the squared length of $\mathbf{z}_2$,

$$(\mathbf{y} - \hat{\boldsymbol{\mu}})'(\mathbf{y} - \hat{\boldsymbol{\mu}}) = (\mathbf{R}_2\mathbf{z}_2)'\mathbf{R}_2\mathbf{z}_2 = \mathbf{z}_2'\mathbf{R}_2'\mathbf{R}_2\mathbf{z}_2 = \mathbf{z}_2'\mathbf{z}_2 \tag{8.10}$$

After taking expectations,

$$\begin{aligned} \mathrm{E}[(\mathbf{y} - \hat{\boldsymbol{\mu}})'(\mathbf{y} - \hat{\boldsymbol{\mu}}) \mid \mathbf{X}] &= \mathrm{E}[\mathbf{z}_2'\mathbf{z}_2 \mid \mathbf{X}] \\ &= \sum_{j=1}^{N-K} \mathrm{Var}[z_{2j} \mid \mathbf{X}] \\ &= \sigma_0^2 (N - K) \end{aligned}$$

Therefore, after dividing both sides by $N - K$, we have $\mathrm{E}[s^2 \mid \mathbf{X}] = \sigma_0^2$. □

This proof hinges on the spherical distribution of $\mathbf{y} - \hat{\boldsymbol{\mu}}$. In effect, the transformation $\mathbf{z}_2$ makes this explicit.

EXAMPLE 8.3

It may be helpful to see these manipulations in a more concrete setting. Let us construct a three-dimensional case. Suppose that $\mathbf{z} \in \mathbb{R}^3$ has the variance matrix

$$\mathrm{Var}[\mathbf{z}] = \begin{bmatrix} 1 & 0 & 0 \\ 0 & 1 & 0 \\ 0 & 0 & 0 \end{bmatrix}$$

so that $\mathbf{z}$ has a spherical distribution in a two-dimensional subspace. Now if we rotate $\mathbf{z}$, we will obtain a transformed random variable with a variance matrix that has different variances on the diagonal and nonzero covariances off the diagonal. We have already seen that a simple form of orthogonal (rotation) matrix in two dimensions is given by

$$\begin{bmatrix} \sqrt{1-\theta^2} & \theta \\ -\theta & \sqrt{1-\theta^2} \end{bmatrix}$$

We can use this matrix to generate an interesting orthogonal transformation in three dimensions:

$$\begin{aligned} \mathbf{R} &= \begin{bmatrix} \sqrt{1-\theta^2} & \theta & 0 \\ -\theta & \sqrt{1-\theta^2} & 0 \\ 0 & 0 & 1 \end{bmatrix} \begin{bmatrix} 1 & 0 & 0 \\ 0 & \sqrt{1-\theta^2} & \theta \\ 0 & -\theta & \sqrt{1-\theta^2} \end{bmatrix} \\ &= \begin{bmatrix} \sqrt{1-\theta^2} & \theta\sqrt{1-\theta^2} & \theta^2 \\ -\theta & 1-\theta^2 & \theta\sqrt{1-\theta^2} \\ 0 & -\theta & \sqrt{1-\theta^2} \end{bmatrix} \end{aligned}$$

We can confirm that $\mathbf{RR}' = \mathbf{I}_3$. When we apply $\mathbf{R}$ to $\mathbf{z}$ we obtain the variance matrix

$$\begin{aligned} \mathrm{Var}[\mathbf{Rz}] &= \mathbf{R}\,\mathrm{Var}[\mathbf{z}]\mathbf{R}' \\ &= \begin{bmatrix} 1-\theta^4 & -\gamma\theta^3 & -\gamma\theta^2 \\ -\gamma\theta^3 & 1-\theta^2+\theta^4 & (\theta^2-1)\,\theta \\ -\gamma\theta^2 & (\theta^2-1)\,\theta & \theta^2 \end{bmatrix} \end{aligned}$$

where $\gamma \equiv \sqrt{1-\theta^2}$. As promised, the variance matrix of $\mathbf{Rz}$ is not scalar.

The rotation disguises the spherical character of $\mathbf{Rz}$, just as the nonscalar variance of $\mathbf{y} - \hat{\boldsymbol{\mu}}$ conceals its spherical character.

If we explicitly restrict the third element of $\mathbf{z}$ to be zero, we see $\mathbf{Rz}$ to be

$$\mathbf{R}\begin{bmatrix} z_1 \\ z_2 \\ 0 \end{bmatrix} = \begin{bmatrix} \sqrt{1-\theta^2}z_1 + \theta\sqrt{1-\theta^2}z_2 \\ -\theta z_1 + \left(1-\theta^2\right) z_2 \\ -\theta z_2 \end{bmatrix}$$

and the source of the covariances: every element depends on z_2 and the first and second elements both depend on z_1.

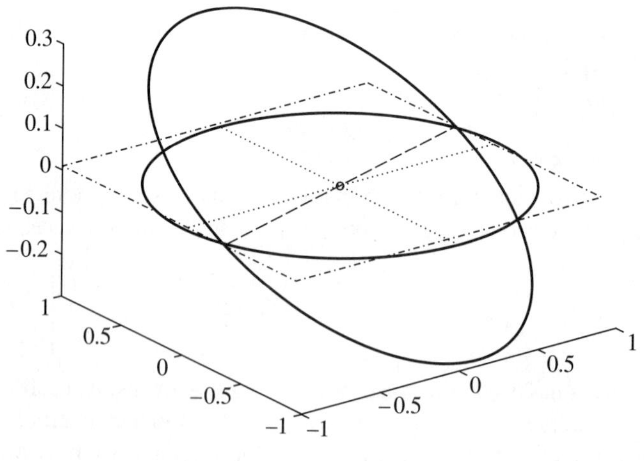

Figure 8.5 Sphere and rotated sphere.

This rotation is pictured in Figure 8.5 for $\theta = -0.3$, applied to the variance sphere of $\mathbf{z}$. Both variance ellipses are shown in $\mathbb{R}^3$. Although it appears to make a two-dimensional random variable into a three-dimensional one, the transformation $\mathbf{R}$ merely changes the two-dimensional subspace in which the random variable and its variance ellipse rest.

Finally, remember that no matter how we rotate a vector, its *Euclidean* length is preserved. As a result, the expectation of its Euclidean length is also preserved:

$$\begin{aligned}\mathbf{R}^{-1} = \mathbf{R}' \quad &\Rightarrow \quad \mathbf{z}'\mathbf{z} = \mathbf{z}'\mathbf{R}'\mathbf{R}\mathbf{z}\\ &\Rightarrow \quad \mathrm{E}[\mathbf{z}'\mathbf{z}] = \mathrm{E}[\mathbf{z}'\mathbf{R}'\mathbf{R}\mathbf{z}]\\ &\Rightarrow \quad \sum_{n=1}^{N} \mathrm{Var}[z_n] = \sum_{n=1}^{N} \mathrm{Var}\big[[\mathbf{R}\mathbf{z}]_n\big]\end{aligned}$$

In this example, we see this in the fact that the diagonals of both variance matrices sum to 2.

In this example, we have used rotations to disguise a spherical distribution. In the preceding theoretical argument, we implicitly use orthogonal transformations to uncover a spherical distribution. If we examined an orthogonal transformation of $\mathbf{y} - \hat{\boldsymbol{\mu}}$,

$$\mathbf{R}'\left(\mathbf{y} - \hat{\boldsymbol{\mu}}\right) = \begin{bmatrix}\mathbf{R}_1'\mathbf{R}_2\mathbf{z}_2\\ \mathbf{R}_2'\mathbf{R}_2\mathbf{z}_2\end{bmatrix} = \begin{bmatrix}\mathbf{0}\\ \mathbf{z}_2\end{bmatrix}$$

we would see the spherical character of $\mathbf{y} - \hat{\boldsymbol{\mu}}$ directly.

8.5 METHODOLOGICAL NOTE

The notion of repeated sampling takes on additional significance when one interprets $\mathrm{Var}[\hat{\boldsymbol{\beta}} \mid \mathbf{X}]$ as the sampling variance of the estimator $\hat{\boldsymbol{\beta}}$. The experiment that one must repeat holds $\mathbf{X}$ fixed in every sample. Even in situations in which repeated sampling of $(y_n, \mathbf{x}_n)$ seems like a sensible description of the data-generating process, it may not be credible to resample $\mathbf{y}$ for the same $\mathbf{X}$. In the CPS data, for example, it is impractical to draw another 1289 individuals with the same configuration of characteristics. We can certainly find individuals with the same $\mathbf{x}_n$ as *some* of the individuals in our sample, but we cannot match all 1289 cases. In situations in which $(y_n, \mathbf{x}_n)$ are sampled jointly, the *marginal* variance,

$$\begin{aligned}\mathrm{Var}[\hat{\boldsymbol{\beta}}] &= \mathrm{E}[(\hat{\boldsymbol{\beta}} - \boldsymbol{\beta}_0)(\hat{\boldsymbol{\beta}} - \boldsymbol{\beta}_0)']\\ &= \mathrm{E}\big[\mathrm{E}[(\hat{\boldsymbol{\beta}} - \boldsymbol{\beta}_0)(\hat{\boldsymbol{\beta}} - \boldsymbol{\beta}_0)' \mid \mathbf{X}]\big]\\ &= \mathrm{E}\big[\mathrm{Var}[(\hat{\boldsymbol{\beta}} \mid \mathbf{X}]\big]\end{aligned}$$

is the sampling variance of the estimator.

An important consequence of Propositions 5 and 6 is that we have an unbiased estimator of the conditional variance matrix of $\hat{\boldsymbol{\beta}}$ in $s^2 \cdot (\mathbf{X}'\mathbf{X})^{-1}$. Although the conditional and marginal variances differ conceptually, we can estimate the marginal variance with the same estimator: using the law of iterated expectations,

$$
\begin{aligned}
\mathrm{E}[s^2 \cdot (\mathbf{X}'\mathbf{X})^{-1}] &= \mathrm{E}\big[\mathrm{E}[s^2 \mid \mathbf{X}] \cdot (\mathbf{X}'\mathbf{X})^{-1}\big] \\
&= \mathrm{E}[\sigma_0^2 \cdot (\mathbf{X}'\mathbf{X})^{-1}] \\
&= \mathrm{E}\big[\mathrm{Var}[\hat{\boldsymbol{\beta}} \mid \mathbf{X}]\big] \\
&= \mathrm{Var}[\hat{\boldsymbol{\beta}}]
\end{aligned}
$$

This would not be possible if s^2 were a biased estimator conditional on $\mathbf{X}$.

8.6 OVERVIEW

1. The second-moment assumption, $\mathrm{Var}[\mathbf{y} \mid \mathbf{X}] = \sigma_0^2 \cdot \mathbf{I}_N$, implies second-moment statistical properties for OLS statistics.
2. Because the conditional distribution of $\mathbf{y}$ is spherical, the conditional distributions of $\hat{\boldsymbol{\mu}}$ and $\mathbf{y} - \hat{\boldsymbol{\mu}}$ are also spherical. In detail, the variance matrices of these orthogonal projections of $\mathbf{y}$ are proportional to their corresponding projection matrices,

$$
\begin{aligned}
\mathrm{Var}[\hat{\boldsymbol{\mu}} \mid \mathbf{X}] &= \sigma_0^2 \cdot \mathbf{P}_\mathbf{X} \\
\mathrm{Var}[\mathbf{y} - \hat{\boldsymbol{\mu}} \mid \mathbf{X}] &= \sigma_0^2 \cdot (\mathbf{I} - \mathbf{P}_\mathbf{X})
\end{aligned}
$$

   where the factor of proportionality σ_0^2 is the same factor that appears in $\mathrm{Var}[\mathbf{y} \mid \mathbf{X}]$. In contrast to the scalar variance matrix of $\mathbf{y}$, the elements of both $\hat{\boldsymbol{\mu}}$ and $\mathbf{y} - \hat{\boldsymbol{\mu}}$ generally have nonzero covariances and unequal variances. These nonscalar variance matrices reflect that $\hat{\boldsymbol{\mu}} \in \mathrm{Col}(\mathbf{X})$ and $\mathbf{y} - \hat{\boldsymbol{\mu}} \in \mathrm{Col}^\perp(\mathbf{X})$.
3. The spherical variance ellipses of $\hat{\boldsymbol{\mu}}$ and $\mathbf{y} - \hat{\boldsymbol{\mu}}$ are orthogonal projections of the spherical variance ellipse of $\mathbf{y}$ onto $\mathrm{Col}(\mathbf{X})$ and $\mathrm{Col}^\perp(\mathbf{X})$, respectively.
4. The spherical distribution of $\mathbf{y} - \hat{\boldsymbol{\mu}}$ leads directly to an unbiased estimator of σ_0^2, through

$$
\mathrm{E}[(\mathbf{y} - \hat{\boldsymbol{\mu}})'(\mathbf{y} - \hat{\boldsymbol{\mu}}) \mid \mathbf{X}] = \sigma_0^2\,(N - K)
$$

   where $N - K$ is the dimension of $\mathrm{Col}^\perp(\mathbf{X})$. Thus,

$$
s^2 \equiv \frac{(\mathbf{y} - \hat{\boldsymbol{\mu}})'\,(\mathbf{y} - \hat{\boldsymbol{\mu}})}{N - K}
$$

   is an unbiased estimator of σ_0^2, given Assumptions 3.1, 6.1, and 7.1.
5. The conditional distribution of $\hat{\boldsymbol{\beta}}$ is not spherical. Its conditional variance ellipse is the image of the variance sphere of $\hat{\boldsymbol{\mu}}$ under a one-to-one linear transformation.

8.7 EXERCISES

8.7.1 Review

8.1 (Monte Carlo) Repeat the Monte Carlo experiment in Exercise 6.1 with the following changes.

(a) In addition to sample means, compute the sample variances and covariances of the three OLS fitted coefficients. Compare these values with their population counterparts.

(b) Also compute the average value of s^2 for each OLS fit and check whether this estimator appears to be unbiased for the conditional variance of y_n given x_n.

8.2 (Monte Carlo) Repeat the Monte Carlo experiment in Exercise 6.1, making each of the following adjustments separately.

(a) Instead of y_n, fit $y_n + x_n$ to the explanatory variables 1, x_n, and x_n^{-1}.

(b) Instead of y_n, fit $y_n + x_n$ to the explanatory variables 1 and x_n^{-1}.

(c) Generate x_n from a uniform distribution on the interval [9, 10], instead of [1, 10].

Compare the sample means and variances of the fitted coefficients with those from the Monte Carlo experiment in Exercise 8.1. Try to explain your findings.

8.3 (Exact Multicollinearity) Consider a situation in which Assumptions 6.1 (First Moments, p. 110) and 7.1 (Second Moments, p. 130) hold but Assumption 3.1 (Full Rank, p. 53) is violated so that $\mathbf{X}$ is rank deficient.

(a) What can we infer about the variance matrix of $\hat{\boldsymbol{\beta}}$ under such conditions?

(b) How does exact multicollinearity affect $\text{Var}[\hat{\boldsymbol{\mu}} \,|\, \mathbf{X}]$?

(c) Show that $\text{E}[(\hat{\boldsymbol{\mu}} - \boldsymbol{\mu}_0)'(\hat{\boldsymbol{\mu}} - \boldsymbol{\mu}_0)/\operatorname{rank}(\mathbf{X}) \,|\, \mathbf{X}] = \sigma_0^2$. Find an unbiased estimator for σ_0^2 allowing for exact multicollinearity.

8.4 Explain why Proposition 6 (Estimation of the Variance, p. 158) requires Assumption 6.1 whereas Proposition 5 (Variances of OLS, p. 157) does not.

8.5 (OLS Fitted Residuals) Show that

$$\text{Var}[y_n - \hat{\mu}_n \,|\, \mathbf{X}] = \sigma_0^2 \left[1 - \mathbf{x}_n'(\mathbf{X}'\mathbf{X})^{-1}\mathbf{x}_n\right]$$

Also prove that this variance is less than or equal to σ_0^2. What transformation of the OLS fitted residuals would result in constant variances equal to σ_0^2?

8.6 (Forecast Variance) Suppose that you have sample data on a pair of variables: $\{(x_n, y_n);\ n = 1, \ldots, N\}$. Under the assumptions of Proposition 5 (Variances of OLS, p. 157), find the conditional variance of the forecast error of the OLS forecast $\hat{\beta}_1 + \hat{\beta}_2 x_{N+1}$ for y_{N+1} given $\{x_n;\ n = 1, \ldots, N+1\}$ using the simple regression model $\text{E}[y_n \,|\, x_n] = \beta_{01} + \beta_{02} x_n$.

8.7 (Restricted Least Squares) Show that the restricted least-squares program (4.2) is equivalent to

$$\min_{\boldsymbol{\beta}} (\hat{\boldsymbol{\beta}} - \boldsymbol{\beta})' \text{Var}[\hat{\boldsymbol{\beta}} \,|\, \mathbf{X}]^{-1} (\hat{\boldsymbol{\beta}} - \boldsymbol{\beta}) \qquad \text{subject to} \qquad \mathbf{R}\boldsymbol{\beta} = \mathbf{r}$$

when $\operatorname{rank}(\mathbf{X}) = K$ and Assumption 7.1 (Second Moments, p. 130) holds.

8.8 (Variance Estimator) The *trace* of a square matrix $\mathbf{A}$, denoted $\operatorname{tr}(\mathbf{A})$, is the sum of its diagonal elements. That is, $\operatorname{tr}(\mathbf{A}) = \sum_{j=1}^{J} a_{jj}$ where $\mathbf{A} = [a_{ij};\ i, j = 1, \ldots, J]$. Prove the following properties of matrix traces:

(a) If $\mathbf{A}$ is a square matrix and c is a scalar, then $\operatorname{tr}(c \cdot \mathbf{A}) = c \cdot \operatorname{tr}(\mathbf{A})$.

(b) If $\mathbf{A}$ and $\mathbf{B}$ are square, conformable matrices under addition, then $\operatorname{tr}(\mathbf{A} + \mathbf{B}) = \operatorname{tr}(\mathbf{A}) + \operatorname{tr}(\mathbf{B})$.

(c) If $\mathbf{A}$ and $\mathbf{B}$ are conformable matrices under multiplication and $\mathbf{AB}$ is square, then $\operatorname{tr}(\mathbf{AB}) = \operatorname{tr}(\mathbf{BA})$.

(d) Use these properties of the matrix trace function to show that $\text{E}[s^2 \,|\, \mathbf{X}] = \sigma_0^2$ under the assumptions of Proposition 6. [HINT: $s^2 = \operatorname{tr}(s^2) = \operatorname{tr}[\mathbf{y}'(\mathbf{I} - \mathbf{P}_\mathbf{X})\mathbf{y}]$.]

8.9 (Subsample Variance) Suppose that you want to estimate the variance σ_0^2 with a subsample of the observations $n = 1, \ldots, N_1 < N$. Show that

$$s_1^2 \equiv \frac{(\mathbf{y}_1 - \hat{\boldsymbol{\mu}}_1)'(\mathbf{y}_1 - \hat{\boldsymbol{\mu}}_1)}{N_1 - \operatorname{tr}\left[(\mathbf{X}'\mathbf{X})^{-1}\mathbf{X}_1'\mathbf{X}_1\right]}$$

where $\mathbf{y}_1 \equiv [y_1, \ldots, y_{N_1}]'$ and $\hat{\boldsymbol{\mu}}_1 \equiv [\hat{\mu}_1, \ldots, \hat{\mu}_{N_1}]' = \mathbf{X}_1\hat{\boldsymbol{\beta}}$, is an unbiased estimator under the assumptions of Proposition 6. (HINT: Use the results of Exercise 8.8.)

8.10 In Proposition 5 the covariance between the fitted residuals $y_n - \mathbf{x}_n'\hat{\boldsymbol{\beta}}$ and $y_m - \mathbf{x}_m'\hat{\boldsymbol{\beta}}$ is given (correctly) as

$$\operatorname{Cov}[\hat{u}_n,\ \hat{u}_m \mid \mathbf{X}] = -\sigma_0^2 \cdot \mathbf{x}_n'(\mathbf{X}'\mathbf{X})^{-1}\mathbf{x}_m$$

while

$$\begin{aligned}\operatorname{Cov}[-\mathbf{x}_n'\hat{\boldsymbol{\beta}},\ -\mathbf{x}_m'\hat{\boldsymbol{\beta}} \mid \mathbf{X}] &= \mathbf{x}_n' \operatorname{Var}[\hat{\boldsymbol{\beta}} \mid \mathbf{X}]\mathbf{x}_m' \\ &= \sigma_0^2 \cdot \mathbf{x}_n'(\mathbf{X}'\mathbf{X})^{-1}\mathbf{x}_m\end{aligned}$$

has the opposite sign. Resolve this paradox.

8.11 **(RLS Variance)** Under the assumptions of Proposition 5 (Variances of OLS, p. 157), find the variance matrix of the restricted OLS estimator (Proposition 3, p. 79) in the special case in which we can partition $\mathbf{X}\boldsymbol{\beta} = \mathbf{X}_1\boldsymbol{\beta}_1 + \mathbf{X}_2\boldsymbol{\beta}_2$ and the restrictions take the form $\boldsymbol{\beta}_1 = \mathbf{0}$.

8.12 **(Image of a Variance Ellipse)** Show that the ellipse $\mathbb{V}_{\hat{\mu}}$ is identically the image of $\mathbb{V}_{\mathbf{y}}$ under orthogonal projection on Col($\mathbf{X}$) using the following steps.

(a) Using (8.4) and (8.5), show that $\mathbb{V}_{\hat{\mu}} \subseteq \mathbb{V}_{\mathbf{y}}$ and $\mathbb{V}_{\hat{\mu}} = \mathbf{P}_{\mathbf{X}}\mathbb{V}_{\hat{\mu}} \subseteq \mathbf{P}_{\mathbf{X}}\mathbb{V}_{\mathbf{y}}$.

(b) Use the fact that $\boldsymbol{\gamma}'\boldsymbol{\gamma} \geq \boldsymbol{\gamma}'\mathbf{P}_{\mathbf{X}}\boldsymbol{\gamma}$ for all $\boldsymbol{\gamma}$ to show that $\mathbf{P}_{\mathbf{X}}\mathbb{V}_{\mathbf{y}} \subseteq \mathbb{V}_{\hat{\mu}}$.[6]

8.7.2 Extensions

8.13 **(Forecast Variance)** Suppose that you are forecasting a realization of y_{N+1} with $\mathbf{x}_{N+1}'\hat{\boldsymbol{\beta}}$, conditional on the RHS vector $\mathbf{x}_{N+1}$. Take the assumptions of Proposition 5 (Variances of OLS, p. 157) as given.

(a) Show that the variance of the prediction is

$$\operatorname{Var}[\mathbf{x}_{N+1}'\hat{\boldsymbol{\beta}} \mid \mathbf{X}] = \sigma_0^2 \cdot \mathbf{x}_{N+1}'(\mathbf{X}'\mathbf{X})^{-1}\mathbf{x}_{N+1}$$

and that the variance of the forecast error is

$$\operatorname{Var}[y_{N+1} - \mathbf{x}_{N+1}'\hat{\boldsymbol{\beta}} \mid \mathbf{X}] = \sigma_0^2 \left(1 + \mathbf{x}_{N+1}'(\mathbf{X}'\mathbf{X})^{-1}\mathbf{x}_{N+1}\right)$$

(b) Given that the first element of every $\mathbf{x}_n$ is the constant one, show that the value of $\mathbf{x}_{N+1}$ that minimizes the variance of the forecast error is the sample average of the columns of $\mathbf{X}$.

8.14 **(Forecast Variance)** Consider the OLS fit of

$$\begin{bmatrix} \mathbf{y} \\ \underset{M\times 1}{\mathbf{0}} \end{bmatrix}$$

to

$$\begin{bmatrix} \mathbf{X} & \underset{N\times M}{\mathbf{0}} \\ \mathbf{X}_f & -\mathbf{I}_M \end{bmatrix} \begin{bmatrix} \boldsymbol{\beta} \\ \boldsymbol{\gamma} \end{bmatrix}$$

[6] See Exercise 2.19 regarding $\boldsymbol{\gamma}'\boldsymbol{\gamma} \geq \boldsymbol{\gamma}'\mathbf{P}_{\mathbf{X}}\boldsymbol{\gamma}$.

where $\mathbf{X}_f$ is an $M \times K$ matrix containing M explanatory variable values.[7]

(a) Show that the OLS fitted coefficients for $\boldsymbol{\beta}$ are identically equal to the OLS fitted coefficients from a regression of $\mathbf{y}$ on $\mathbf{X}$.

(b) Show that the OLS fitted coefficients for $\boldsymbol{\gamma}$ are the forecasts $\mathbf{X}_f \hat{\boldsymbol{\beta}}$.

(c) Show that the estimated variance matrix for $\hat{\boldsymbol{\beta}}$ equals the estimated variance matrix from an OLS regression of $\mathbf{y}$ on $\mathbf{X}$.

(d) Show that the estimated variance matrix for $\hat{\boldsymbol{\gamma}}$ is the estimated variance matrix of the forecasts $\mathbf{X}_f \hat{\boldsymbol{\beta}}$ under the assumptions of Proposition 5 (Variances of OLS, p. 157).

***8.15 (Recursive Residuals)** The OLS fitted residuals possess a spherical variance ellipse. *Recursive residuals* are an important example of a linear transformation of these fitted residuals that possesses a scalar variance matrix under the assumptions of Proposition 5 (Variances of OLS, p. 157).

Suppose that the first K observations in a data set of N observations possess linearly independent RHS variables, so that we can fit OLS coefficients with these observations alone. Let $\mathbf{X}_{[M]} \equiv [\mathbf{x}_n;\ n = 1, \ldots, M]'$ and $\mathbf{y}_{[M]} \equiv [y_n;\ n = 1, \ldots, M]'$ denote counterparts to $\mathbf{X}$ and $\mathbf{y}$ that possess only the first M observations (rows). Then the initial estimator of $\boldsymbol{\beta}_0$ is $\hat{\boldsymbol{\beta}}_{[K]} \equiv \mathbf{X}_{[K]}^{-1}\mathbf{y}_{[K]}$. Now consider the forecast error in the prediction $\mathbf{x}'_{K+1}\hat{\boldsymbol{\beta}}_{[K]}$ for the next observation y_{K+1}. Because $\mathrm{Var}[\hat{\boldsymbol{\beta}}_{[K]} \,|\, \mathbf{X}] = \sigma_0^2 \cdot \left(\mathbf{X}'_{[K]}\mathbf{X}_{[K]}\right)^{-1}$, the forecast error has a conditional variance equal to

$$\mathrm{Var}[y_{K+1} - \mathbf{x}'_{K+1}\hat{\boldsymbol{\beta}}_{[K]} \,|\, \mathbf{X}] = \sigma_0^2 \left(1 + \mathbf{x}'_{K+1}(\mathbf{X}'_{[K]}\mathbf{X}_{[K]})^{-1}\mathbf{x}_{K+1}\right)$$

We can repeat this process, adding observations one at time, and obtain the sequence of fitted coefficients $\hat{\boldsymbol{\beta}}_{[n]} \equiv (\mathbf{X}'_{[n]}\mathbf{X}_{[n]})^{-1}\mathbf{X}'_{[n]}\mathbf{y}_{[n]}$ and the sequence of "one-step-ahead" forecast errors $y_{n+1} - \mathbf{x}'_{n+1}\hat{\boldsymbol{\beta}}_{[n]}$ for $n = K, \ldots, N-1$. Each forecast error has a variance analogous to the one above. By standardizing each forecast error according to

$$\hat{v}_n = \frac{y_n - \mathbf{x}'_n\hat{\boldsymbol{\beta}}_{[n-1]}}{\sqrt{1 + \mathbf{x}'_n(\mathbf{X}'_{[n-1]}\mathbf{X}_{[n-1]})^{-1}\mathbf{x}_n}}$$

($n = K+1, \ldots, N$), we obtain a sequence of random variables $\{\hat{v}_n\}$ with constant variance σ_0^2.

In this exercise, you must show that these recursive residuals are also uncorrelated.

(a) There are only $N - K$ recursive residuals. Why does the formula for $\hat{v}_n$ fail for $n = 1, \ldots, K$?

(b) Show that $\mathrm{Cov}[y_n, \hat{\boldsymbol{\beta}}_{[m]} \,|\, \mathbf{X}] = \mathbf{0}$, $K \le m < n$ $(n = K+1, \ldots, N)$.

(c) Exercise 4.16 states that

$$\hat{\boldsymbol{\beta}}_{[n]} = \hat{\boldsymbol{\beta}}_{[n-1]} + \left(\mathbf{X}'_{[n-1]}\mathbf{X}_{[n-1]}\right)^{-1}\mathbf{x}_n \frac{y_n - \mathbf{x}'_n\hat{\boldsymbol{\beta}}_{[n-1]}}{1 + \mathbf{x}'_n\left(\mathbf{X}'_{[n-1]}\mathbf{X}_{[n-1]}\right)^{-1}\mathbf{x}_n}$$

Use this result to show algebraically that

i. $\mathrm{Cov}[\hat{\boldsymbol{\beta}}_{[n]}, \hat{\boldsymbol{\beta}}_{[n]} - \hat{\boldsymbol{\beta}}_{[n-1]} \,|\, \mathbf{X}] = \mathbf{0}$, and

ii. $\mathrm{Cov}[\hat{v}_n, \hat{v}_{n-1} \,|\, \mathbf{X}] = 0$.

(d) Explain why these steps imply that $\mathrm{Var}[\hat{\mathbf{v}} \,|\, \mathbf{X}] = \sigma_0^2 \cdot \mathbf{I}_{N-K}$ where $\hat{\mathbf{v}} \equiv [\hat{v}_n;\ n = K+1, \ldots, N]'$.

8.16 (Recursive Residuals) Using the steps below, confirm that the OLS fitted residuals are a linear transformation of the recursive residuals in Exercise 8.15: $\mathbf{y} - \hat{\boldsymbol{\mu}} = \mathbf{R}_2\hat{\mathbf{v}}$ where the columns of $\mathbf{R}_2$ form an orthonormal basis for $\mathrm{Col}^{\perp}(\mathbf{X})$.

(a) Rewrite the numerator of the recursive residuals as linear combinations of $\mathbf{y}$:

---

[7] See Greene (1997, p. 370).

$$y_n - \mathbf{x}_n'\hat{\boldsymbol{\beta}}_{[n-1]} = \mathbf{e}_n'\left(\mathbf{I}_N - \mathbf{P}_{\mathbf{X}\perp\mathbf{X}_{[n-1]}}\right)\mathbf{y} = \mathbf{w}_n'\mathbf{y},\ n = K+1, \ldots, N$$

where $\mathbf{e}_n$ is the nth natural basis vector of $\mathbb{R}^N$ and $\mathbf{X}_{[n]}$ is the matrix $\mathbf{X}$ with its last $N-n$ rows filled with zeros. Let $\mathbf{w}_n = \left(\mathbf{I}_N - \mathbf{P}_{\mathbf{X}_{[n-1]}\perp\mathbf{X}}\right)\mathbf{e}_n$ denote the coefficients of $\mathbf{y}$ in $\hat{v}_n$.

(b) Confirm the following properties of the $\mathbf{w}_n$:

i. every $\mathbf{w}_n \in \mathrm{Col}^{\perp}(\mathbf{X})$;

ii. the $\mathbf{w}_n$ are mutually orthogonal: $\mathbf{w}_n'\mathbf{w}_m = 0$ if $n \neq m$;

iii. the $\mathbf{w}_n$ $(n = K+1, \ldots, N)$ comprise a basis for $\mathrm{Col}^{\perp}(\mathbf{X})$;

iv. the Euclidean length of $\mathbf{w}_n$ is

$$\|\mathbf{w}_n\| = \sqrt{1 + \mathbf{x}_n'\left(\mathbf{X}_{[n-1]}'\mathbf{X}_{[n-1]}\right)^{-1}\mathbf{x}_n}$$

(c) Use the fact that

$$\hat{v}_n = \frac{\mathbf{w}_n'\mathbf{y}}{\|\mathbf{w}_n\|}$$

to find $\mathbf{R}_2$ so that $\mathbf{y} - \hat{\boldsymbol{\mu}} = \mathbf{R}_2\hat{\mathbf{v}}$. (HINT: Recall that $\mathbf{R}_2'\mathbf{R}_2 = \mathbf{I}_{N-K}$ and $\mathbf{R}_2\mathbf{R}_2' = \mathbf{I} - \mathbf{P}_{\mathbf{X}}$.)

(d) Confirm that the OLS fitted residuals are one to one with the recursive residuals:

$$\hat{v}_n = \frac{\mathbf{w}_n'\left(\mathbf{y} - \hat{\boldsymbol{\mu}}\right)}{\|\mathbf{w}_n\|}$$

(e) According to Part d of Exercise 8.15,

$$\hat{s}^2 \equiv \sum_{n=K+1}^{N} \frac{\left(y_n - \mathbf{x}_n'\hat{\boldsymbol{\beta}}_{[n-1]}\right)^2}{\|\mathbf{w}_n\|^2 (N-K)}$$

is an unbiased variance estimator. Find the relationship between s^2 and $\hat{s}^2$.

***8.17 (Generalized Inverse Invariance)** The generalized inverse (Exercise 2.24) of a matrix $\boldsymbol{\Omega}$ is any $\boldsymbol{\Omega}^-$ that satisfies $\boldsymbol{\Omega}\boldsymbol{\Omega}^-\boldsymbol{\Omega} = \boldsymbol{\Omega}$. Show that the quadratic form $\mathbf{z}'\boldsymbol{\Omega}^-\mathbf{z}$ is invariant to the choice of generalized inverse $\boldsymbol{\Omega}^-$ provided that $\mathbf{z} \in \mathrm{Col}(\boldsymbol{\Omega})$. Also show that variance ellipses can be written generally as

$$\mathbb{V}_{\mathbf{y}} = \left\{\mathbf{z} \in \mathrm{Col}(\boldsymbol{\Omega}) \mid \mathbf{z}'\boldsymbol{\Omega}^-\mathbf{z} \leq 1\right\}$$

Apply this result to writing out the variance ellipses of $\hat{\boldsymbol{\mu}}$ and $\mathbf{y} - \hat{\boldsymbol{\mu}}$.

8.18 (Generalized Inverse) Using the singular-value decomposition (Exercise 7.27) of a positive semidefinite matrix $\boldsymbol{\Omega} = \mathbf{BHB}'$, where $\mathbf{H}$ is nonsingular and symmetric and $\mathbf{B}$ is full-column rank, construct a generalized inverse for $\boldsymbol{\Omega}$.

8.19 (Generalized Inverse) Another generalized inverse of variance matrices follows from the *eigenvalue decomposition* (Exercise 7.28). Let $\mathrm{Var}[\mathbf{z}] = \boldsymbol{\Omega} = \mathbf{R}\boldsymbol{\Lambda}\mathbf{R}'$ be an eigenvalue decomposition of $\boldsymbol{\Omega}$. Show that a generalized inverse of $\boldsymbol{\Omega}$ is $\mathbf{R}\boldsymbol{\Lambda}^*\mathbf{R}'$ where $\boldsymbol{\Lambda}^*$ is a diagonal matrix whose diagonal elements equal the reciprocals of the nonzero eigenvalues and zero otherwise. Also interpret the quadratic form $\mathbf{z}'\mathbf{R}\boldsymbol{\Lambda}^*\mathbf{R}'\mathbf{z}$.

CHAPTER 9

EFFICIENT ESTIMATION

9.1 INTRODUCTION

The OLS estimator $\hat{\boldsymbol{\beta}}$ has several desirable properties. First, this estimator is linear in the random variable $\mathbf{y}$. As a result, the computation of $\hat{\boldsymbol{\beta}}$ is relatively simple and the conditional moments of $\hat{\boldsymbol{\beta}}$ are simple functions of the conditional moments of $\mathbf{y}$. In particular, we can derive the first and second moments of the OLS estimator from the first and second moments of $\mathbf{y}$, conditional on $\mathbf{X}$. Second, if the mean of $\mathbf{y}$ conditional on $\mathbf{X}$ is $\mathbf{X}\boldsymbol{\beta}_0$, the OLS estimator is unbiased: $\mathrm{E}[\hat{\boldsymbol{\beta}} \mid \mathbf{X}] = \boldsymbol{\beta}_0$. Third, the conditional variance matrix of the OLS estimator is $\sigma_0^2 \cdot (\mathbf{X}'\mathbf{X})^{-1}$ if the variance matrix of $\mathbf{y}$ is the scalar matrix $\sigma_0^2 \cdot \mathbf{I}$. In this chapter, we study the $\mathrm{Var}[\hat{\boldsymbol{\beta}} \mid \mathbf{X}]$ itself.

From this variance matrix, we will show that the sampling distribution of the OLS estimator behaves in a natural way. As the variance of $\mathbf{y}$ around its mean decreases, the sample size increases, or the dispersion of the explanatory variables increases, the variance of the OLS estimator falls.

Given the variance matrix of the OLS estimator $\hat{\boldsymbol{\beta}}$, we can also compare this variance matrix with alternative estimators for $\boldsymbol{\beta}_0$. The OLS estimator is only one of many estimators that can be constructed. One alternative estimator is the restricted least-squares (RLS) estimator. This estimator is a linear, unbiased estimator for $\boldsymbol{\beta}_0$, provided that our assumptions hold under the restrictions. This estimator is superior to the OLS estimator in an obvious way: $\hat{\boldsymbol{\beta}}$ fails to exploit all the information available and implicitly estimates some unnecessary parameters. One might expect this failure to lead to some kind of statistical inferiority, and indeed it does.

Having imposed all available parametric restrictions, the OLS/RLS estimator has a remarkable statistical property relative to all linear and unbiased estimators. According to the Gauss–Markov theorem, the sampling variance of any linear combination of the OLS estimator is less than or equal to the sampling variance of the same linear combination of any other linear, unbiased estimator. This property is called *relative efficiency*.

DEFINITION 16 (RELATIVE EFFICIENCY) *Let $\boldsymbol{\theta}_0 \in \mathbb{R}^K$ be an unknown parameter vector and $\hat{\boldsymbol{\theta}}_A$ and $\hat{\boldsymbol{\theta}}_B$ be unbiased estimators: $\mathrm{E}[\hat{\boldsymbol{\theta}}_A] = \mathrm{E}[\hat{\boldsymbol{\theta}}_B] = \boldsymbol{\theta}_0$. The estimator $\hat{\boldsymbol{\theta}}_A$ is* efficient relative to *the estimator $\hat{\boldsymbol{\theta}}_B$ if $\mathrm{Var}[\mathbf{c}'\hat{\boldsymbol{\theta}}_A] \le \mathrm{Var}[\mathbf{c}'\hat{\boldsymbol{\theta}}_B]$ for all $\mathbf{c} \in \mathbb{R}^K$.*

Relative efficiency requires that whatever linear combination of the parameters we consider, the variance must be smaller for the relatively efficient estimator.[1] In particular, this means that $\text{Var}[\hat{\theta}_{Ak}] \leq \text{Var}[\hat{\theta}_{Bk}]$ for each $k = 1, \ldots, K$. But for relative efficiency, the variance inequality must hold for all other linear combinations as well. Because, for example,

$$\text{Var}[\mathbf{c}'\hat{\boldsymbol{\theta}}_A] = \mathbf{c}' \text{Var}[\hat{\boldsymbol{\theta}}_A]\mathbf{c} = \sum_{i,j} c_i c_j \text{Cov}[\hat{\theta}_{Ai}, \hat{\theta}_{Aj}]$$

relative efficiency concerns the covariances as well. The linear combinations provide a way to reduce a multidimensional comparison of the many elements of variance matrices to a set of scalar comparisons.

Relative efficiency implies that the variance ellipse of the relatively "larger" variance matrix contains the variance ellipse of the "smaller" one. We state this formally as a lemma, and leave its proof to the *Mathematical Notes*, p. 190 of this chapter.

LEMMA 9.1 *Let* $\text{Var}[\hat{\boldsymbol{\theta}}_A] = \boldsymbol{\Omega}_A$ *and* $\text{Var}[\hat{\boldsymbol{\theta}}_B] = \boldsymbol{\Omega}_B$ *be two* $K \times K$ *variance matrices. Then* $\mathbf{c}'\boldsymbol{\Omega}_A\mathbf{c} \leq \mathbf{c}'\boldsymbol{\Omega}_B\mathbf{c}$ *for all* $\mathbf{c} \in \mathbb{R}^K$ *if and only if* $\mathbb{V}_{\hat{\boldsymbol{\theta}}_A} \subseteq \mathbb{V}_{\hat{\boldsymbol{\theta}}_B}$.

The LHS of Figure 9.1 illustrates relative efficiency as described by Lemma 9.1. To emphasize that both estimators are unbiased, we have centered the ellipses on $\boldsymbol{\theta}_0$, rather than the origin. On the RHS, Figure 9.1 shows a situation in which neither variance matrix dominates the other in the sense of relative efficiency.

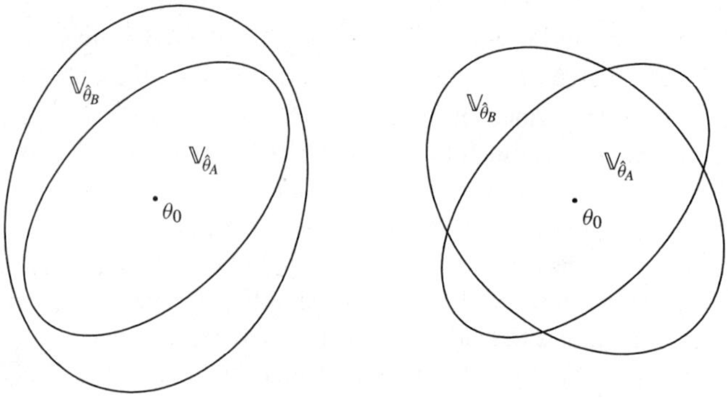

Figure 9.1 Relative efficiency.

[1] Definition 16 implies that the difference between the variance matrices of an estimator and a relatively efficient estimator is a positive semidefinite matrix:

$$\begin{aligned} 0 &\leq \text{Var}[\mathbf{c}'\hat{\boldsymbol{\theta}}_B] - \text{Var}[\mathbf{c}'\hat{\boldsymbol{\theta}}_A] \\ &= \mathbf{c}' \text{Var}[\hat{\boldsymbol{\theta}}_B]\mathbf{c} - \mathbf{c}' \text{Var}[\hat{\boldsymbol{\theta}}_A]\mathbf{c} \\ &= \mathbf{c}' \left(\text{Var}[\hat{\boldsymbol{\theta}}_B] - \text{Var}[\hat{\boldsymbol{\theta}}_A]\right) \mathbf{c} \end{aligned}$$

The term "positive semidefinite" is popular in econometric writing, but rather formal as a description of relative efficiency.

In every instance in this chapter, we will make relative efficiency comparisons. Each statement about how $\text{Var}[\hat{\boldsymbol{\beta}} \mid \mathbf{X}]$ changes with the characteristics of the data-generating process is a comparison of two estimators and the comparison of RLS and OLS variances obviously has this character also.

9.2 DESIGN AND PRECISION

In the previous chapter, we focused our attention on $\hat{\boldsymbol{\mu}}$ and $\mathbf{y} - \hat{\boldsymbol{\mu}}$. Now we examine the variance matrix of $\hat{\boldsymbol{\beta}}$ more closely. Although this matrix does not yield a spherical distribution, several observations help us interpret the second moments of the OLS estimator of $\boldsymbol{\beta}_0$. First, and most obviously, the variance of $\hat{\boldsymbol{\beta}}$ grows proportionately with σ_0^2. Second, the variance matrix depends on the matrix of RHS variables $\mathbf{X}$. In experimental settings, the researcher may be able to choose the elements of $\mathbf{X}$ prior to observing the outcomes in $\mathbf{y}$. For this reason, $\mathbf{X}$ is often called the *design* matrix. The inverse of the matrix $\mathbf{X}'\mathbf{X}$ is proportional to the variance and it is occasionally called the *precision* matrix. We will explain the ways in which the experiment can be "designed" to yield small sampling variance in the OLS estimator.

EXAMPLE 9.1

In the special case of two explanatory variables in which the first is the constant one, we get the formulas:

$$\hat{\beta}_2 = \frac{\sum_{n=1}^{N}(x_{n2} - \bar{x}_2)y_n}{\sum_{n=1}^{N}(x_{n2} - \bar{x}_2)^2}$$

$$\hat{\beta}_1 = \bar{y} - \bar{x}_2\hat{\beta}_2$$

The variance of $\hat{\beta}_2$ follows directly as

$$\text{Var}[\hat{\beta}_2 \mid \mathbf{X}] = \frac{\sigma_0^2}{\sum_{n=1}^{N}(x_{n2} - \bar{x}_2)^2} = \frac{\sigma_0^2}{N \cdot \text{Var}_N[x_{n2}]}$$

In this special case, we see clearly that

1. As σ_0^2 grows, so does the variance of $\hat{\beta}_2$.
2. Holding the sample variation in x_2 constant, $\text{Var}[\hat{\beta}_2 \mid \mathbf{X}] \to 0$ as $N \to \infty$.
3. As the empirical variance of x_2, $\text{Var}_N[x_{n2}]$, diminishes, $\text{Var}[\hat{\beta}_2 \mid \mathbf{X}]$ grows.

The second property is analogous to the behavior of the variance of the sample mean as the sample size grows. That property is general for OLS coefficient estimators. The third property is specific to the multiple linear regression model. As we shall see, this property is closely linked to the issue of multicollinearity.

Figures 9.2, 9.3, and 9.4 illustrate these situations. In Figure 9.2, a smaller value of σ_0^2 leads to observations that are much closer to the regression line on average. As a result, the estimated slope coefficient has smaller sampling variance. In Figure 9.3, a larger number of observations makes the central location of the regression line much clearer. And in Figure 9.4, the data with a narrower range of x_2 values provide much less information about the slope than data in which the values are spread out.

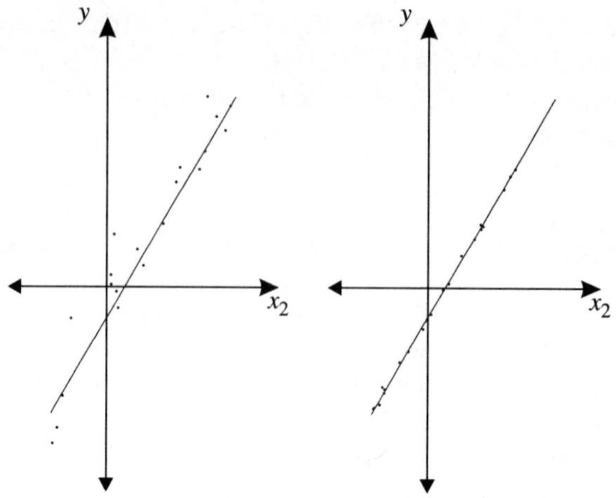

Figure 9.2 Scatter plots for large and small variances.

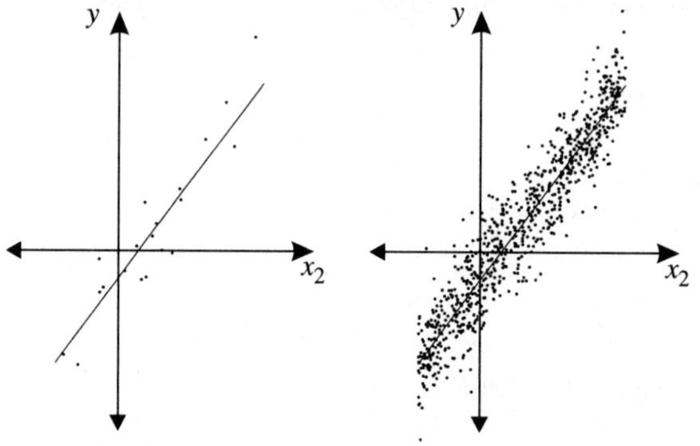

Figure 9.3 Scatter plots for two sample sizes.

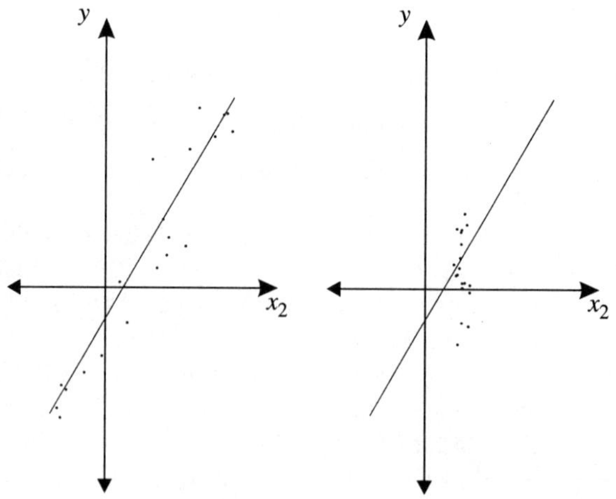

Figure 9.4 Scatter plots for two sample variances of x_2.

Now we will generalize our observations to the K-dimensional case. This is trivial for the relationship between σ_0^2 and $\text{Var}[\hat{\boldsymbol{\beta}} \mid \mathbf{X}]$. Nevertheless, we belabor the point to initiate a pattern of comparisons: if we consider two data-generating processes that differ only in the variance parameter, say $\sigma_A^2 < \sigma_B^2$, then obviously the difference in $\text{Var}[\mathbf{c}'\hat{\boldsymbol{\beta}} \mid \mathbf{X}]$,

$$\mathbf{c}'\left[\sigma_B^2 \cdot (\mathbf{X}'\mathbf{X})^{-1}\right]\mathbf{c} - \mathbf{c}'\left[\sigma_A^2 \cdot (\mathbf{X}'\mathbf{X})^{-1}\right]\mathbf{c} = (\sigma_B^2 - \sigma_A^2)\,\mathbf{c}'(\mathbf{X}'\mathbf{X})^{-1}\mathbf{c} > 0$$

is positive for all $\mathbf{c} \neq \mathbf{0}$. We conclude that a smaller sampling variance for $\mathbf{y}$ yields a relative efficiency improvement.

In the following sections, we will focus on understanding ways in which we may think of $(\mathbf{X}'\mathbf{X})^{-1}$ improving the efficiency of $\hat{\boldsymbol{\beta}}$, not because we can necessarily make it so, but because it helps us to understand our empirical results: why is it that some estimated coefficients have small sampling variances relative to their estimated coefficients and others have large ones? In many actual applications, $\mathbf{X}$ is given and so there is no changing $\mathbf{X}'\mathbf{X}$, but it is still helpful to understand how our estimation is affected by its characteristics.

9.2.1 Dispersion

Increasing the dispersion of $\mathbf{X}$ may be the simplest way to imagine an efficiency improvement through $\mathbf{X}'\mathbf{X}$. As a basic example, consider the choice between the design matrix $\mathbf{X}$ and another design $a \cdot \mathbf{X}$, where $a > 1$. The latter design has the same mathematical effect on efficiency as decreasing the variance of $\mathbf{y}$ by the factor a^{-2}. The choice is between the conditional variances $\sigma_0^2 \cdot (\mathbf{X}'\mathbf{X})^{-1}$ and $\sigma_0^2 \cdot (a^2 \cdot \mathbf{X}'\mathbf{X})^{-1} = (\sigma_0^2/a^2) \cdot (\mathbf{X}'\mathbf{X})^{-1}$.

As simple as this method is, practical concerns often constrain its exploitation. As the dispersion in the elements of $\mathbf{X}$ grows, the credibility of Assumption 6.1 may diminish. For example, we could add dispersion to $\mathbf{X}$ for our wage equation if we included people who are self-employed. But it seems unlikely that the conditional mean of hourly earnings for the self-employed is the same as the conditional mean of hourly earnings for others. Pursuing dispersion in $\mathbf{X}$ without regard for the constancy of $\text{E}[\mathbf{y} \mid \mathbf{X}]$ could fail to yield improvements in efficiency if it leads to violations in Assumption 6.1.

9.2.2 Sample Size

Another way to imagine gaining efficiency is the addition of another observation. Let[2]

$$\mathbf{X}_{[N+1]} \equiv [\mathbf{x}_n;\ n = 1, \ldots, N+1]' = \begin{bmatrix} \mathbf{X} \\ \mathbf{x}'_{N+1} \end{bmatrix}$$

Then,

$$\mathbf{X}'_{[N+1]}\mathbf{X}_{[N+1]} = \mathbf{X}'\mathbf{X} + \mathbf{x}_{N+1}\mathbf{x}'_{N+1}$$

The variance matrix of the OLS estimator becomes[3]

---

2 We also considered this situation in Exercise 4.16.

3 We use the matrix inverse formula in Exercise 3.22,

$$\begin{aligned}\text{Var}[\hat{\boldsymbol\beta}_{[N+1]} \mid \mathbf{X}_{[N+1]}] &= \sigma_0^2 \cdot (\mathbf{X}'_{[N+1]}\mathbf{X}_{[N+1]})^{-1} \\ &= \sigma_0^2 \cdot \left[(\mathbf{X}'\mathbf{X})^{-1} - \frac{1}{m} \cdot (\mathbf{X}'\mathbf{X})^{-1}\mathbf{x}'_{N+1}\mathbf{x}_{N+1}(\mathbf{X}'\mathbf{X})^{-1}\right] \\ &= \text{Var}[\hat{\boldsymbol\beta} \mid \mathbf{X}] - \frac{\sigma_0^2}{m} \cdot (\mathbf{X}'\mathbf{X})^{-1}\mathbf{x}'_{N+1}\mathbf{x}_{N+1}(\mathbf{X}'\mathbf{X})^{-1}\end{aligned} \tag{9.1}$$

where

$$\begin{aligned}m &= 1 + \mathbf{x}'_{N+1}(\mathbf{X}'\mathbf{X})^{-1}\mathbf{x}_{N+1} \\ &= 1 + \frac{\text{Var}[\mathbf{x}'_{N+1}\hat{\boldsymbol\beta} \mid \mathbf{X}_{[N+1]}]}{\sigma_0^2} \\ &\geq 0\end{aligned}$$

For all $\mathbf{c} \in \mathbb{R}^K$

$$\mathbf{c}'(\mathbf{X}'\mathbf{X})^{-1}\mathbf{x}'_{N+1}\mathbf{x}_{N+1}(\mathbf{X}'\mathbf{X})^{-1}\mathbf{c} = \left[\mathbf{x}'_{N+1}(\mathbf{X}'\mathbf{X})^{-1}\mathbf{c}\right]^2 \geq 0$$

Therefore,

$$\text{Var}[\mathbf{c}'\hat{\boldsymbol\beta}_{[N+1]} \mid \mathbf{X}_{[N+1]}] \leq \text{Var}[\mathbf{c}'\hat{\boldsymbol\beta} \mid \mathbf{X}]$$

We conclude that the additional observation makes $\hat{\boldsymbol\beta}_{[N+1]}$ efficient relative to $\hat{\boldsymbol\beta}$. If this were not so, it would be a disturbing outcome. We expect to confirm that more information about $\boldsymbol\beta_0$, in the form of more observations from the data-generating process, leads to more accuracy in our estimator. Otherwise, we would question the value of the estimator.

9.2.3 Near Multicollinearity

Near multicollinearity refers to situations in which the explanatory variables are "almost" linearly dependent. In this situation, the separate effects of the RHS variables cannot be estimated "precisely." We discussed exact multicollinearity in our introduction to OLS. If the RHS are exactly multicollinear (linearly dependent), then the OLS fitted coefficients are not well defined because they are not unique. No discussion of the variance matrix is possible under these conditions.

Unlike sample size, there is no uniquely compelling measure of near multicollinearity. Nor is there a unique pair of experiments to compare. The rank of $\mathbf{X}$ is K and remains K unless we have exact multicollinearity, in which case the rank of $\mathbf{X}$ is less than or equal to $K-1$. Near multicollinearity concerns full rank $\mathbf{X}$ only.

Fortunately, the fundamental issue appears within the partitioned OLS formulas previously described in Chapter 3. If we partition $\mathbf{X} = [\mathbf{X}_1, \mathbf{X}_2]$, we can find the variance matrix of $\hat{\boldsymbol\beta}_1$ in the same way we found the variance of the entire $\hat{\boldsymbol\beta}$ vector in Section 8.3:

$$\begin{aligned}\text{Var}[\hat{\boldsymbol\beta}_1 \mid \mathbf{X}] &= \text{Var}\left[\left[\mathbf{X}_1'\left(\mathbf{I} - \mathbf{P}_{\mathbf{X}_2}\right)\mathbf{X}_1\right]^{-1}\mathbf{X}_1'\left(\mathbf{I} - \mathbf{P}_{\mathbf{X}_2}\right)y \mid \mathbf{X}\right] \\ &= \sigma_0^2 \cdot \left[\mathbf{X}_1'\left(\mathbf{I} - \mathbf{P}_{\mathbf{X}_2}\right)\mathbf{X}_1\right]^{-1}\end{aligned} \tag{9.2}$$

$$\left(\mathbf{A}_{11} - \mathbf{A}_{12}\mathbf{A}_{22}^{-1}\mathbf{A}_{21}\right)^{-1} = \mathbf{A}_{11}^{-1} + \mathbf{A}_{11}^{-1}\mathbf{A}_{12}\mathbf{W}\mathbf{A}_{21}\mathbf{A}_{11}^{-1}$$

$$\mathbf{W} = \left(\mathbf{A}_{22} - \mathbf{A}_{21}\mathbf{A}_{11}^{-1}\mathbf{A}_{12}\right)^{-1}$$

setting $\mathbf{A}_{11} = \mathbf{X}'\mathbf{X}$, $\mathbf{A}_{22} = \mathbf{I}$, and $\mathbf{A}_{12} = \mathbf{A}_{21}' = \mathbf{x}'_{N+1}$.

We will use this equation to study the variance of (any) one element of $\hat{\boldsymbol{\beta}}$ as we change $\mathbf{X}$.

So let $\mathbf{X}_1$ be the first column of $\mathbf{X}$ and recall that $\mathbf{X}_1'\left(\mathbf{I}-\mathbf{P}_{\mathbf{X}_2}\right)\mathbf{X}_1 = \mathbf{X}_{1\perp 2}'\mathbf{X}_{1\perp 2}$ where $\mathbf{X}_{1\perp 2} \equiv \left(\mathbf{I}-\mathbf{P}_{\mathbf{X}_2}\right)\mathbf{X}_1$.[4] In the present case, $\mathbf{X}_{1\perp 2}$ is the fitted residual vector from the OLS fit of the variable in $\mathbf{X}_1$ on all of the other RHS variables in $\mathbf{X}_2$. As a result, $\mathbf{X}_1'\left(\mathbf{I}-\mathbf{P}_{\mathbf{X}_2}\right)\mathbf{X}_1$ is scalar and equals the OLS SSR. If $\mathbf{X}_1$ were linearly dependent on the columns of $\mathbf{X}_2$, then $\mathbf{X}$ would be rank deficient and this SSR would equal zero. We will characterize near multicollinearity as designs with an $\mathbf{X}_1'\left(\mathbf{I}-\mathbf{P}_{\mathbf{X}_2}\right)\mathbf{X}_1$ near zero. As the squared residuals become smaller, the relationship between $\mathbf{X}_1$ and $\mathbf{X}_2$ approaches a linear one.

We consider a choice between two designs that differ in $\mathbf{X}_1'\left(\mathbf{I}-\mathbf{P}_{\mathbf{X}_2}\right)\mathbf{X}_1$. Because we have already seen that dispersion affects efficiency, suppose that $\mathbf{X}_1'\mathbf{X}_1$ and $\mathbf{X}_2'\mathbf{X}_2$ are equal in both designs. Inspection of (9.2) reveals that the design with a smaller $\mathbf{X}_1'\left(\mathbf{I}-\mathbf{P}_{\mathbf{X}_2}\right)\mathbf{X}_1$ will have a larger $\mathrm{Var}[\hat{\boldsymbol{\beta}}_1 \mid \mathbf{X}]$. In this sense, more "near multicollinearity" decreases the efficiency of the OLS estimator.

Note how this relates to the discussion of dispersion above. If $\mathbf{X}$ were not full rank, then neither would $a \cdot \mathbf{X}$ be and increasing scale would have no benefits for the estimation of the elements of $\boldsymbol{\beta}_0$. On the other hand, we can now imagine different designs with the same dispersion in the individual columns of $\mathbf{X}$ that yield different precision.

EXAMPLE 9.2

In Figure 9.5, we construct a graphic representation of increasing collinearity among two explanatory variables for $K = 2$ and $\mathbf{X} = [\mathbf{X}_1, \mathbf{X}_2]$. The two panels show $\mathrm{Col}(\mathbf{X})$ and $\mathbb{V}_{\hat{\mu}}$ for two designs with the same $\mathbf{X}_1'\mathbf{X}_1$ and $\mathbf{X}_2'\mathbf{X}_2$ and $\boldsymbol{\mu}_0 = \mathbf{X}_1 + \mathbf{X}_2$. In the left panel, $\mathbf{X}_1'\mathbf{X}_2 = \mathbf{0}$ and in the right panel $\mathbf{X}_2$ has rotated clockwise so that $\mathbf{X}_1'\mathbf{X}_2 > 0$. As a result, the minimum distance between $\mathbf{X}_1$ and $\mathrm{Col}(\mathbf{X}_2)$ is lower in the right panel. The projections of $\mathbb{V}_{\hat{\mu}}$ show $\mathbb{V}_{\hat{\beta}_1} = \mathbb{V}_{\hat{\mu}_1}$ and $\mathbb{V}_{\hat{\beta}_2} = \mathbb{V}_{\hat{\mu}_2}$ as thick lines in $\mathrm{Col}(\mathbf{X}_1)$ and $\mathrm{Col}(\mathbf{X}_2)$. $\mathbb{V}_{\hat{\beta}_1}$ is centered on the same point in both panels so that it is apparent that the nonorthogonality of $\mathbf{X}_1$ and $\mathbf{X}_2$ leads to a wider interval. For the same reason, $\mathbb{V}_{\hat{\beta}_2}$ is also wider. Further rotation of $\mathbf{X}_2$ toward $\mathbf{X}_1$ will lead to an expansion of both intervals.

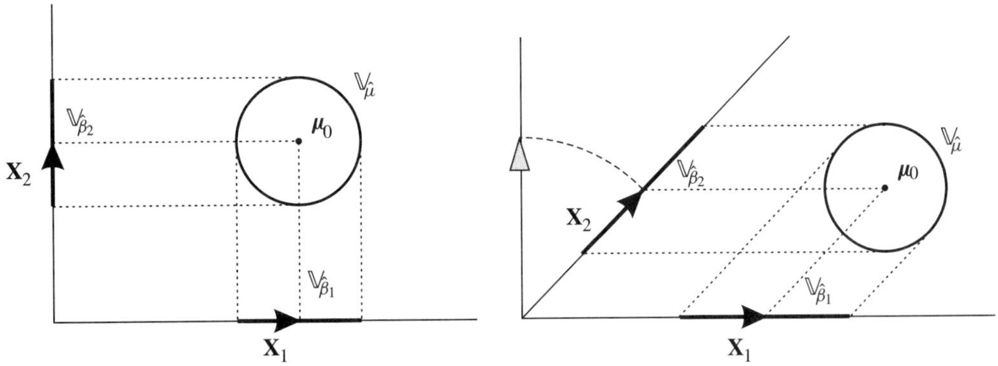

Figure 9.5 Increasing collinearity.

[4] See Proposition 2 (Partitioned Fit, p. 57).

Although $\text{Var}[\hat{\boldsymbol{\beta}} \mid \mathbf{X}]$ is undefined when there is exact multicollinearity, it is natural to consider the variance to be infinite. In our example, rotation of $\mathbf{X}_2$ further clockwise toward $\mathbf{X}_1$ brings ever widening $\mathbb{V}_{\hat{\beta}_1}$ and $\mathbb{V}_{\hat{\beta}_2}$. Rank deficiency in $\mathbf{X}$ makes estimation of $\boldsymbol{\beta}$ impossible so that, in effect, $\hat{\boldsymbol{\beta}}$ has no likely bounds on its values, element by element. This is manifest in an infinite variance.

On the other hand, note that multicollinearity, exact or near, does not make the data uninformative about $\boldsymbol{\beta}_0$. To take the extreme, suppose that $\mathbf{X}_1 = \mathbf{X}_2\mathbf{A}$ so that $\mathbf{X}_1$ is linearly dependent on $\mathbf{X}_2$. Then

$$\mathbf{X}\boldsymbol{\beta} = \mathbf{X}_1\boldsymbol{\beta}_1 + \mathbf{X}_2\boldsymbol{\beta}_2 = \mathbf{X}_2\left(\mathbf{A}\boldsymbol{\beta}_1 + \boldsymbol{\beta}_2\right)$$

If $\mathbf{X}_2$ is full-column rank, then the linear combination $\mathbf{A}\boldsymbol{\beta}_1 + \boldsymbol{\beta}_2$ of the elements of $\boldsymbol{\beta}$ can still be estimated. When there is merely *near* multicollinearity, then certain linear combinations of $\boldsymbol{\beta}$ may be precisely estimated even though individual elements of $\hat{\boldsymbol{\beta}}$ have relatively large sampling variance.

Recognizing this, one can also see that near multicollinearity is just low dispersion in certain *transformations* of the explanatory variables. Consider the linear combination $\mathbf{c}'\hat{\boldsymbol{\beta}}$ such that $c_1 = 1$.[5] Taking $\mathbf{X}_1$ as the first column of $\mathbf{X}$, we can always isolate $\mathbf{c}'\boldsymbol{\beta}$ through the regression partition

$$\mathbf{X}\boldsymbol{\beta} = \beta_1 \cdot \mathbf{X}_1 + \mathbf{X}_2\boldsymbol{\beta}_2 = \left(\mathbf{c}'\boldsymbol{\beta}\right) \cdot \mathbf{X}_1 + \left(\mathbf{X}_2 - \mathbf{X}_1\mathbf{c}_2'\right)\boldsymbol{\beta}_2$$

so that $\mathbf{c}'\boldsymbol{\beta}$ is the coefficient of the first explanatory variable when the remaining explanatory variables are $\mathbf{Z} \equiv \mathbf{X}_2 - \mathbf{X}_1\mathbf{c}_2'$. Then, using (9.2),

$$\text{Var}[\mathbf{c}'\hat{\boldsymbol{\beta}} \mid \mathbf{X}] = \frac{\sigma_0^2}{\mathbf{X}_1'\left(\mathbf{I} - \mathbf{P}_{\mathbf{Z}}\right)\mathbf{X}_1} \tag{9.3}$$

Therefore, a relatively large variance in $\mathbf{c}'\hat{\boldsymbol{\beta}}$ corresponds to relatively low dispersion in $\left(\mathbf{I} - \mathbf{P}_{\mathbf{Z}}\right)\mathbf{X}_1$.

9.2.4 Forecast Variance

An insightful application of (9.3) occurs in the context of forecasting new values of the dependent variable. Conditional on the explanatory variables $\mathbf{x}_{N+1}$, an unbiased forecast of y_{N+1} is $\mathbf{x}_{N+1}'\hat{\boldsymbol{\beta}}$. The conditional variance of this prediction is

$$\text{Var}[\mathbf{x}_{N+1}'\hat{\boldsymbol{\beta}} \mid \mathbf{X}, \mathbf{x}_{N+1}] = \sigma_0^2 \cdot \mathbf{x}_{N+1}'(\mathbf{X}'\mathbf{X})^{-1}\mathbf{x}_{N+1}$$

This, of course, is just a new notation for the variance just considered in (9.3). The conditional variance of the forecast error $y_{N+1} - \mathbf{x}_{N+1}'\hat{\boldsymbol{\beta}}$ is larger owing to the presence of the random variable y_{N+1}:

$$\begin{aligned}\text{Var}[y_{N+1} - \mathbf{x}_{N+1}'\hat{\boldsymbol{\beta}} \mid \mathbf{X}, \mathbf{x}_{N+1}] &= \text{Var}[y_{N+1} \mid \mathbf{X}, \mathbf{x}_{N+1}] + \text{Var}[\mathbf{x}_{N+1}'\hat{\boldsymbol{\beta}} \mid \mathbf{X}, \mathbf{x}_{N+1}] \\ &= \sigma_0^2\left[1 + \mathbf{x}_{N+1}'(\mathbf{X}'\mathbf{X})^{-1}\mathbf{x}_{N+1}\right] \end{aligned} \tag{9.4}$$

When the regression function includes an intercept, there is a value for $\mathbf{x}_{N+1}$ that minimizes these variances.

[5] Because we can always reorder the elements of $\boldsymbol{\beta}$ and rescale $\mathbf{c}$, there is no loss of generality in taking $c_1 = 1$.

Lemma 9.2 (Forecast Variance) *Let the assumptions of Proposition 5 (OLS Variances, p. 157) hold. If $\mathbf{x}_n$ contains a constant element, the value of $\mathbf{x}_{N+1}$ that minimizes the variance of the forecast error (9.4) is the sample average of the columns of* $\mathbf{X}$,

$$\bar{\mathbf{x}} \equiv \left(\iota'\iota\right)^{-1}\iota'\mathbf{X}$$

Proof. Let $\mathbf{c}' = \mathbf{x}'_{N+1}$ and the first element of $\mathbf{x}_n$ be the constant one. Then according to (9.3),

$$\text{Var}[\mathbf{x}'_{N+1}\hat{\boldsymbol{\beta}} \mid \mathbf{X}, \mathbf{x}_{N+1}] = \frac{\sigma_0^2}{\iota'\left(\mathbf{I}-\mathbf{P}_\mathbf{Z}\right)\iota}$$

where $\mathbf{Z} \equiv \mathbf{X}_2 - \iota\mathbf{x}'_{2,N+1}$. The denominator is largest when ι is orthogonal to Col($\mathbf{Z}$).[6] In that case,

$$\iota'\left(\mathbf{X}_2 - \iota\mathbf{x}'_{2,N+1}\right) = 0 \qquad \Leftrightarrow \qquad \mathbf{x}'_{2,N+1} = \left(\iota'\iota\right)^{-1}\iota'\mathbf{X}_2$$

Because $1 = \left(\iota'\iota\right)^{-1}\iota'\iota$, the variance is minimized at

$$\mathbf{x}'_{N+1} = \begin{bmatrix}1 & \left(\iota'\iota\right)^{-1}\iota'\mathbf{X}_2\end{bmatrix} = \left(\iota'\iota\right)^{-1}\iota'\mathbf{X}$$

Note incidentally that the minimum variance equals σ_0^2/N, the sampling variance of the simple average of i.i.d. random variables. □

Lemma 9.2 states that the fitted value with the smallest sampling variance occurs in the middle of the constellation of explanatory variable observations where $(\mathbf{I}-\mathbf{P}_\mathbf{Z})\,\iota$ is longest. Figure 9.6 depicts the the conditional variance ellipse of the fitted value around its conditional mean in the case of two explanatory variables. Note that the boundaries of the variance ellipse are equidistant from the expected value, although a casual glance suggests otherwise. The shortest ellipse is marked at $\bar{x}_2$.

The forecast standard deviation continues to grow as we move away from the sample mean of the explanatory variables and, eventually, beyond the range of the observed values of the explanatory variables. Practically, researchers often regard this forecast interval as an understatement of the actual uncertainty surrounding a forecast for such values. Prediction outside the range where one actually fits the regression function is qualitatively different and is distinguished by the label *out-of-sample forecasting*. Of course, such forecasting often holds special interest precisely because it concerns potential outcomes beyond previous experience. All the same, out-of-sample forecasting involves a heavier reliance on the statistical assumptions.

Dispersion, sample size, and near multicollinearity are all ways to understand the impact of $\mathbf{X}$ on $\text{Var}[\hat{\boldsymbol{\beta}} \mid \mathbf{X}]$. They explain how data are informative about $\hat{\boldsymbol{\beta}}$. Our discussion does not offer insight

[6] Recall the Pythagorean relationship for any orthogonal projector $\mathbf{P}$ and conformable vector $\mathbf{z}$

$$\mathbf{z}'\mathbf{z} = \mathbf{z}'\left(\mathbf{P}+\mathbf{I}-\mathbf{P}\right)\mathbf{z} = \mathbf{z}'\mathbf{P}\mathbf{z} + \mathbf{z}'\left(\mathbf{I}-\mathbf{P}\right)\mathbf{z} \geq \mathbf{z}'\left(\mathbf{I}-\mathbf{P}\right)\mathbf{z}$$

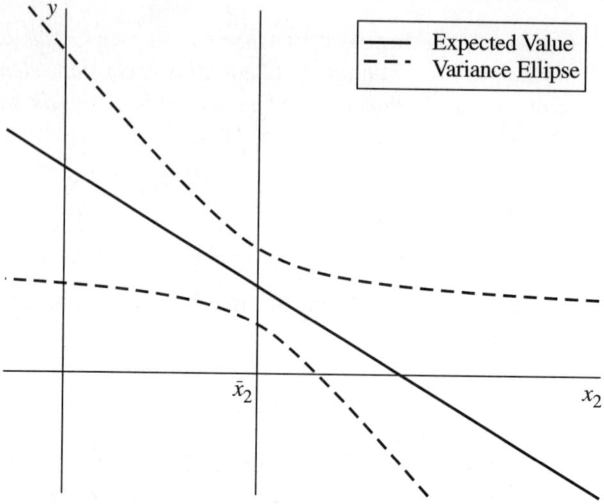

Figure 9.6 Forecast variance in simple regression.

into *remedies* for large sampling variances. Given $\mathbf{X}$, conditional sampling variances are fixed and one must live with them. Is there another unbiased estimator for $\boldsymbol{\beta}_0$ in addition to OLS that has smaller sampling variance? The answer to such a question is a qualified yes. If there is additional information about $\boldsymbol{\beta}_0$ that the OLS estimator is not exploiting then there is usually a route to a more efficient estimator. We consider such a situation in the next section.

9.3 RESTRICTED ESTIMATION

We can also apply the concept of relative efficiency to a comparison of two estimators, OLS and RLS. Having found the variance matrix of the OLS estimator, we can similarly find the variance of the *restricted* OLS estimator when restrictions are available. Because the estimators generally differ, it is natural to ask whether their variances differ in a systematic way. In particular, one might suspect that the restricted estimator has less variance than the unrestricted estimator. A simple example suggests why this might be so.

EXAMPLE 9.3

The relative efficiency of a restricted estimator versus an unrestricted one is illustrated by extending Example 4.7. We let

$$\mathbf{X} = \begin{bmatrix} \iota_{N_1} & 0 \\ 0 & \iota_{N_2} \end{bmatrix} \quad \text{and} \quad \boldsymbol{\beta}_0 = \begin{bmatrix} \beta_{01} \\ \beta_{02} \end{bmatrix}$$

so that the unrestricted model specifies unequal means but equal variances for two subsamples of observations in $\mathbf{y}$. The unrestricted OLS estimators of β_{01} and β_{02} are the subsample means

$$\hat{\beta}_1 = \bar{y}_1 = \frac{1}{N_1}\sum_{n=1}^{N_1} y_n, \qquad \hat{\beta}_2 = \bar{y}_2 = \frac{1}{N_2}\sum_{n=N_1+1}^{N_1+N_2} y_n$$

and the variances of these estimators are inversely proportional to the subsample sizes,

$$\text{Var}[\hat{\beta}_1] = \frac{\sigma_0^2}{N_1}, \qquad \text{Var}[\hat{\beta}_2] = \frac{\sigma_0^2}{N_2}$$

Under the restriction that the subsample means are equal, $\beta_1 = \beta_2$, the restricted OLS estimators are the mean of the entire sample,

$$\hat{\beta}_{1R} = \hat{\beta}_{2R} = \bar{y} = \frac{1}{N_1 + N_2}\sum_{n=1}^{N_1+N_2} y_n$$

which have smaller variances

$$\text{Var}[\hat{\beta}_{1R}] = \text{Var}[\hat{\beta}_{2R}] = \frac{\sigma_0^2}{N_1 + N_2} < \frac{\sigma_0^2}{N_1}, \frac{\sigma_0^2}{N_2}$$

Grouping the two samples together to estimate a single mean clearly reduces the sampling variance by applying more observations to the estimation of the unknown parameters.

This example does illustrate a general phenomenon. If we impose linear restrictions on our estimator of $\boldsymbol{\beta}_0$, then the restricted least-squares estimator has smaller variance than the unrestricted estimator.

PROPOSITION 7 (RESTRICTED LEAST-SQUARES EFFICIENCY) *Let Assumptions 3.1 (Full Rank, p. 53), 6.1 (First Moments, p. 110), and 7.1 (Second Moments, p. 130) hold and also the linearly independent restrictions* $\boldsymbol{\beta}_0 = \mathbf{S}\boldsymbol{\gamma}_0 + \mathbf{s}$ *for given* $\mathbf{S}$ *and* $\mathbf{s}$. *Then the variance of any linear combination of the elements of the OLS* $\hat{\boldsymbol{\beta}}$ *is greater than the variance of the same linear combination of the RLS* $\hat{\boldsymbol{\beta}}_{\text{R}}$. *That is, for any* $\mathbf{c} \in \mathbb{R}^K$

$$\text{Var}[\mathbf{c}'\hat{\boldsymbol{\beta}} \mid \mathbf{X}] \geq \text{Var}[\mathbf{c}'\hat{\boldsymbol{\beta}}_{\text{R}} \mid \mathbf{X}]$$

Proof. We established that $\hat{\boldsymbol{\mu}}_{\text{R}} = \mathbf{P}_{\mathbf{XS}}\hat{\boldsymbol{\mu}} + (\mathbf{I} - \mathbf{P}_{\mathbf{XS}})\,\mathbf{X}s$ where the restrictions are $\boldsymbol{\beta} = \mathbf{S}\boldsymbol{\gamma} + \mathbf{s}$.[7] This enables us to derive the variance matrix of $\hat{\boldsymbol{\mu}}_{\text{R}}$ from the variance of $\hat{\boldsymbol{\mu}}$. Using the bilinearity of covariances (Lemma 7.1, p. 130) and the variance of $\hat{\boldsymbol{\mu}}$ (Proposition 5, p. 157),

$$\begin{aligned}\text{Var}[\hat{\boldsymbol{\mu}}_R \mid \mathbf{X}] &= \text{Var}[\mathbf{P}_{\mathbf{XS}}\hat{\boldsymbol{\mu}} \mid \mathbf{X}] \\ &= \sigma_0^2 \cdot \mathbf{P}_{\mathbf{XS}}\mathbf{P}_{\mathbf{X}}\mathbf{P}_{\mathbf{XS}} \\ &= \sigma_0^2 \cdot \mathbf{P}_{\mathbf{XS}}\end{aligned}$$

[7]See equation 4.14 (p. 84).

because $\text{Col}(\mathbf{XS}) \subseteq \text{Col}(\mathbf{X})$ implies that $\mathbf{P_X P_{XS}} = \mathbf{P_{XS}}$. The covariance between $\hat{\boldsymbol{\mu}}$ and $\hat{\boldsymbol{\mu}}_\text{R}$ turns out to be exactly the same expression:

$$\begin{aligned}\text{Cov}[\hat{\boldsymbol{\mu}}, \hat{\boldsymbol{\mu}}_\text{R} \mid \mathbf{X}] &= \text{Var}[\hat{\boldsymbol{\mu}} \mid \mathbf{X}]\mathbf{P_{XS}} \\ &= \sigma_0^2 \cdot \mathbf{P_X P_{XS}} \\ &= \text{Var}[\hat{\boldsymbol{\mu}}_\text{R} \mid \mathbf{X}]\end{aligned} \tag{9.5}$$

As a result,

$$\begin{aligned}\text{Var}[\hat{\boldsymbol{\mu}} \mid \mathbf{X}] &= \text{Var}[(\hat{\boldsymbol{\mu}} - \hat{\boldsymbol{\mu}}_\text{R}) + \hat{\boldsymbol{\mu}}_\text{R} \mid \mathbf{X}] \\ &= \text{Var}[\hat{\boldsymbol{\mu}}_\text{R} \mid \mathbf{X}] + \text{Var}[\hat{\boldsymbol{\mu}} - \hat{\boldsymbol{\mu}}_\text{R} \mid \mathbf{X}] \\ &\quad + \text{Cov}[\hat{\boldsymbol{\mu}} - \hat{\boldsymbol{\mu}}_\text{R}, \hat{\boldsymbol{\mu}}_\text{R} \mid \mathbf{X}] \\ &\quad + \text{Cov}[\hat{\boldsymbol{\mu}}_\text{R}, \hat{\boldsymbol{\mu}} - \hat{\boldsymbol{\mu}}_\text{R} \mid \mathbf{X}] \\ &= \text{Var}[\hat{\boldsymbol{\mu}}_\text{R} \mid \mathbf{X}] + \text{Var}[\hat{\boldsymbol{\mu}} - \hat{\boldsymbol{\mu}}_\text{R} \mid \mathbf{X}]\end{aligned} \tag{9.6}$$

because

$$\text{Cov}[\hat{\boldsymbol{\mu}} - \hat{\boldsymbol{\mu}}_\text{R}, \hat{\boldsymbol{\mu}}_\text{R} \mid \mathbf{X}] = \text{Cov}[\hat{\boldsymbol{\mu}}, \hat{\boldsymbol{\mu}}_\text{R} \mid \mathbf{X}] - \text{Var}[\hat{\boldsymbol{\mu}}_\text{R} \mid \mathbf{X}] = \mathbf{0}$$

We can conclude that $\hat{\boldsymbol{\mu}}_\text{R}$ is efficient relative to $\hat{\boldsymbol{\mu}}$ using Definition 16: for any $\mathbf{c} \in \mathbb{R}^N$,

$$\text{Var}[\mathbf{c}'\hat{\boldsymbol{\mu}} \mid \mathbf{X}] = \text{Var}[\mathbf{c}'\hat{\boldsymbol{\mu}}_\text{R} \mid \mathbf{X}] + \text{Var}[\mathbf{c}'(\hat{\boldsymbol{\mu}} - \hat{\boldsymbol{\mu}}_\text{R}) \mid \mathbf{X}] \geq \text{Var}[\mathbf{c}'\hat{\boldsymbol{\mu}}_\text{R} \mid \mathbf{X}]$$

Finally, note that any linear combination $\mathbf{c}'\hat{\boldsymbol{\mu}}$ can be written as a linear combination of $\hat{\boldsymbol{\beta}}$,

$$\mathbf{c}'\hat{\boldsymbol{\mu}} = \mathbf{c}'\mathbf{X}\hat{\boldsymbol{\beta}}$$

and vice versa

$$\mathbf{d}'\hat{\boldsymbol{\beta}} = \mathbf{d}'\left(\mathbf{X}'\mathbf{X}\right)^{-1}\mathbf{X}'\hat{\boldsymbol{\mu}}$$

because $\hat{\boldsymbol{\mu}}$ and $\hat{\boldsymbol{\beta}}$ are one to one. It follows immediately that $\hat{\boldsymbol{\beta}}_\text{R}$ and $\hat{\boldsymbol{\mu}}_\text{R}$ share the relative efficiency property, compared to $\hat{\boldsymbol{\beta}}$ and $\hat{\boldsymbol{\mu}}$, respectively. Also, the fact that we can consider any linear combination of $\boldsymbol{\mu}$ implies that this result is invariant to the parameterization of the regression equation. We can transform $\mathbf{X}\boldsymbol{\beta} = \mathbf{XAA}^{-1}\boldsymbol{\beta} = \mathbf{Z}\boldsymbol{\gamma}$ where $\mathbf{Z} = \mathbf{XA}$ and $\boldsymbol{\gamma} = \mathbf{A}^{-1}\boldsymbol{\beta}$ and obtain the same results for $\boldsymbol{\gamma}$. □

Such variance inequalities are important in estimation theory. They give us a criterion for choosing among competing estimators. Clearly, we prefer to use the RLS estimator over the OLS estimator when the restrictions are correct because the former has an unambiguously smaller variance matrix. In the next section, we will describe another important variance inequality called the Gauss–Markov theorem.

These variance inequalities rest on a fundamental characteristic generally possessed by estimators that are efficient relative to a set of alternative estimators: the covariance between a relatively efficient estimator $\hat{\boldsymbol{\theta}}$ and its difference with an alternative estimator $\tilde{\boldsymbol{\theta}} - \hat{\boldsymbol{\theta}}$ is always zero. It is generally true that an efficient estimator is uncorrelated with diff[illegible] with inefficient estimators because otherwise another estimator exists that is a linear com[illegible]on of the efficient estimator and the difference that is even more efficient. This, of course, is a contradiction. A similar logic supports the lack of correlation between rational forecasts and forecast errors in economic models.[8] If such a nonzero correlation exists then a better forecast can be constructed by exploiting this correlation.

Of course, the reader has encountered this logic before in various incarnations of the projection theorem.[9] In this case, we are dealing with a special situation in which the orthogonal projection is the zero vector.[10]

Proposition 8 (Orthogonality of Efficient Estimators) *Let $\hat{\boldsymbol{\theta}}$ and $\tilde{\boldsymbol{\theta}}$ be jointly distributed, unbiased, finite variance, estimators of the K-dimensional real parameter vector $\boldsymbol{\theta}_0$. Then $\hat{\boldsymbol{\theta}}$ is efficient relative to the set of unbiased estimators $\hat{\boldsymbol{\theta}}+\mathbf{A}(\tilde{\boldsymbol{\theta}}-\hat{\boldsymbol{\theta}})$ indexed by real $K \times K$ matrices $\mathbf{A}$ if and only if* $\mathrm{Cov}[\tilde{\boldsymbol{\theta}} - \hat{\boldsymbol{\theta}}, \hat{\boldsymbol{\theta}}] = \mathbf{0}$.

Proof. This proposition is a corollary of the projection theorem (Theorem 6, p. 119). Given any $\mathbf{c} \in \mathbb{R}^K$, consider the estimators of the scalar $\mathbf{c}'\boldsymbol{\theta}_0$ given by

$$\mathbf{c}'\left[\hat{\boldsymbol{\theta}} + \mathbf{A}(\tilde{\boldsymbol{\theta}} - \hat{\boldsymbol{\theta}})\right] = \mathbf{c}'\hat{\boldsymbol{\theta}} - z$$

where $z \equiv \mathbf{c}'\mathbf{A}\left(\hat{\boldsymbol{\theta}} - \tilde{\boldsymbol{\theta}}\right)$. Think of z as an element of the subspace $\mathbb{S}$ that is the vector space of random variables that are linear combinations of the elements of $\tilde{\boldsymbol{\theta}} - \hat{\boldsymbol{\theta}}$. The estimator $\hat{\boldsymbol{\theta}}$ is relatively efficient if and only if the minimum distance problem

$$\min_{z \in \mathbb{S}} \left\| \mathbf{c}'\hat{\boldsymbol{\theta}} - z - \mathbf{c}'\boldsymbol{\theta}_0 \right\|^2 = \min_{z \in \mathbb{S}} \mathrm{Var}[\mathbf{c}'(\hat{\boldsymbol{\theta}} - \boldsymbol{\theta}_0) - z]$$

has a solution at $z = 0$ for all $\mathbf{c}$. According to the projection theorem, the origin, 0, is closest to $\mathbf{c}'\left(\hat{\boldsymbol{\theta}} - \boldsymbol{\theta}_0\right)$ among vectors in $\mathbb{S}$ if and only if $\mathbf{c}'\left(\hat{\boldsymbol{\theta}} - \boldsymbol{\theta}_0\right)$ and the elements of $\mathbb{S}$ are orthogonal. See Figure 9.7 for an illustration of this orthogonality. That is,

$$\begin{aligned} 0 &= \mathrm{E}[\mathbf{c}'(\hat{\boldsymbol{\theta}} - \boldsymbol{\theta}_0) \cdot (\tilde{\boldsymbol{\theta}} - \hat{\boldsymbol{\theta}})] \\ &= \mathrm{E}[(\tilde{\boldsymbol{\theta}} - \hat{\boldsymbol{\theta}})(\hat{\boldsymbol{\theta}} - \boldsymbol{\theta}_0)'\mathbf{c}] \\ &= \mathrm{E}[(\tilde{\boldsymbol{\theta}} - \hat{\boldsymbol{\theta}})(\hat{\boldsymbol{\theta}} - \boldsymbol{\theta}_0)']\mathbf{c} \\ &= \mathrm{Cov}[\tilde{\boldsymbol{\theta}} - \hat{\boldsymbol{\theta}}, \hat{\boldsymbol{\theta}}]\mathbf{c} \end{aligned}$$

---

8 See Sargent (1979, Chapter X).

9 For example, see the discussion of the MMSE linear predictor following Example 7.2.

10 The following proposition was popularized in a slightly different form by Hausman (1978). See also Lehmann (1983, Theorem 2.1.1) and Rao [1973, Theorem 51.2.(i), p. 317] for a similar result. Lehmann cites Barankin (1949), Stein (1950), and Bahadur (1957) as early references.

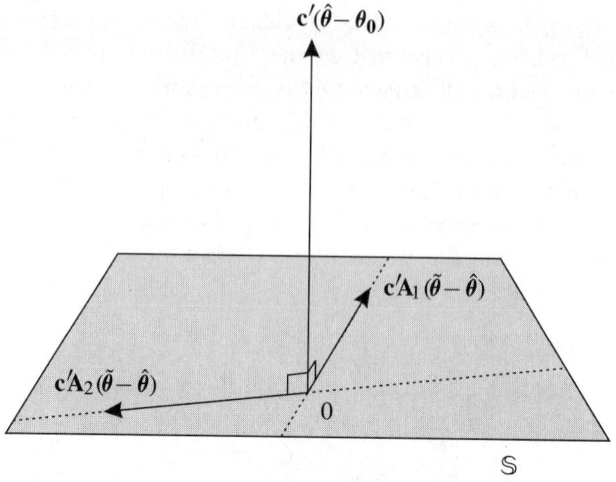

Figure 9.7 Illustration of relative efficiency.

This orthogonality holds for all $\mathbf{c}$ if and only if $\text{Cov}[\tilde{\boldsymbol{\theta}} - \hat{\boldsymbol{\theta}}, \hat{\boldsymbol{\theta}}] = \mathbf{0}$.[11] □

Note that two equivalent forms of $\text{Cov}[\tilde{\boldsymbol{\theta}} - \hat{\boldsymbol{\theta}}, \hat{\boldsymbol{\theta}}] = \mathbf{0}$ are

$$\text{Cov}[\tilde{\boldsymbol{\theta}}, \hat{\boldsymbol{\theta}}] = \text{Var}[\hat{\boldsymbol{\theta}}] \tag{9.7}$$

$$\text{Var}[\tilde{\boldsymbol{\theta}} - \hat{\boldsymbol{\theta}}] = \text{Var}[\tilde{\boldsymbol{\theta}}] - \text{Var}[\hat{\boldsymbol{\theta}}] \tag{9.8}$$

In the next section, we apply this proposition to the concrete case in which we compare the variance of the OLS estimator with the family of linear unbiased estimators.

9.4 THE GAUSS–MARKOV THEOREM

We have just seen an example of relative efficiency in that RLS is better than OLS. Suppose we have imposed all known linear restrictions so that the OLS estimator before us is implicitly the RLS estimator. This OLS estimator has a further efficiency property. We can compare the variance matrix of OLS not just with a single competing estimator, but with a whole set of competing estimators.

[11] Note that the projection theorem also states that the set of relatively efficient unbiased estimators contains all $\hat{\boldsymbol{\theta}} + \mathbf{A}\left(\tilde{\boldsymbol{\theta}} - \hat{\boldsymbol{\theta}}\right)$ such that its distance from $\hat{\boldsymbol{\theta}}$ is zero:

$$\begin{aligned} &\text{Var}[\hat{\boldsymbol{\theta}}] = \text{Var}[\hat{\boldsymbol{\theta}} + \mathbf{A}(\tilde{\boldsymbol{\theta}} - \hat{\boldsymbol{\theta}})] \\ \Leftrightarrow \quad &\text{Var}[\mathbf{A}(\tilde{\boldsymbol{\theta}} - \hat{\boldsymbol{\theta}})] = \mathbf{0} \end{aligned}$$

Because estimators are random variables, this set may contain more than just $\hat{\boldsymbol{\theta}}$. Otherwise, $\hat{\boldsymbol{\theta}}$ would be the *unique* relatively efficient unbiased estimator. See the related discussion of the projection theorem on p. 119.

THEOREM 7 (GAUSS-MARKOV) *Let Assumptions 3.1 (Full Rank, p. 53), 6.1 (First Moments, p. 110), and 7.1 (Second Moments, p. 130) hold. Among all linear, unbiased, estimators for* $\boldsymbol{\beta}_0$*, the OLS estimator is the only relatively efficient estimator. That is, if* $\tilde{\boldsymbol{\beta}} = \mathbf{A}\mathbf{y}$ *and* $\mathrm{E}[\tilde{\boldsymbol{\beta}} \mid \mathbf{X}] = \boldsymbol{\beta}_0$*, then* $\mathrm{Var}[\mathbf{c}'\tilde{\boldsymbol{\beta}}] \geq \mathrm{Var}[\mathbf{c}'\hat{\boldsymbol{\beta}}]$ *for all* $\mathbf{c} \in \mathbb{R}^K$.

9.4.1 Geometry of the Gauss–Markov Theorem

We can draw a simple geometric picture of the Gauss–Markov theorem, justified formally below by Lemmas 9.1 and 7.3. In the two-dimensional Figure 9.8, we depict the variation in $\mathbf{y}$ by the circle around $\iota\beta_0 = \boldsymbol{\mu}_0$. The symmetry of the circle $\mathbb{V}_\mathbf{y}$ reflects the constancy of the variance of $\boldsymbol{\alpha}'\mathbf{y}$ for all directions $\boldsymbol{\alpha} \in \mathbb{R}^2 : \|\boldsymbol{\alpha}\| = 1$. The corresponding variation of $\iota\hat{\beta} = \hat{\boldsymbol{\mu}}$ is the orthogonal projection of all the points in this circle onto $\mathrm{Col}(\mathbf{X})$; this projection is the interval $[A, B]$ given by the intersection of $\mathbb{V}_\mathbf{y}$ and $\mathrm{Col}(\mathbf{X})$. This interval is also centered at $\iota\beta_0$. The variation of a nonorthogonal projection $\iota\tilde{\beta} = \tilde{\mu}$ is also the corresponding projection of the interior of the $\mathbb{V}_\mathbf{y}$ onto $\mathrm{Col}(\mathbf{X})$. The interval $[A', B']$ in Figure 9.8 is an example. The nonorthogonal projection along the direction $(1, 0)$ yields a larger interval, also centered at $\iota\beta_0$, that contains the interval of variation of $\hat{\boldsymbol{\mu}}$. This is a graphic demonstration of the Gauss–Markov theorem in two dimensions.

The three-dimensional Figure 9.9 demonstrates more dramatically the general spherical nature of the variation in $\hat{\boldsymbol{\mu}}$. As before, the sphere labeled $\mathbb{V}_\mathbf{y}$ depicts the variation in $\mathbf{y}$, just as the circle does in two dimensions. Although it is not shown, the center of this sphere is $\boldsymbol{\mu}_0$. The variation in $\hat{\boldsymbol{\mu}}$ implied by $\mathbb{V}_\mathbf{y}$ is the circle formed by the intersection of $\mathbb{V}_\mathbf{y}$ with $\mathrm{Col}(\mathbf{X})$. That circle is also the orthogonal projection of the points in the sphere $\mathbb{V}_\mathbf{y}$ onto $\mathrm{Col}(\mathbf{X})$. A

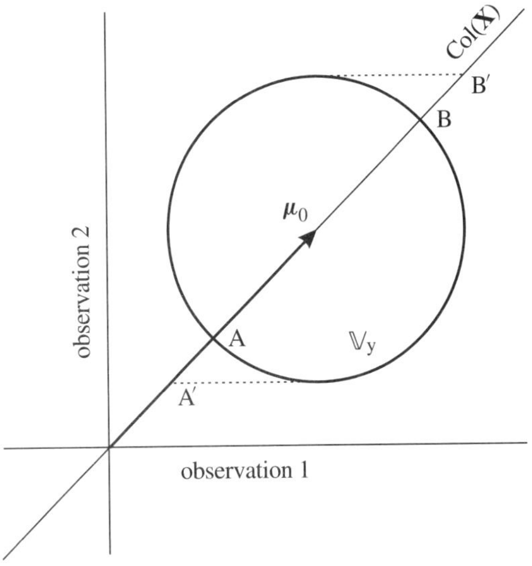

Figure 9.8 Projection of $\mathbb{V}_y$ in two dimensions.

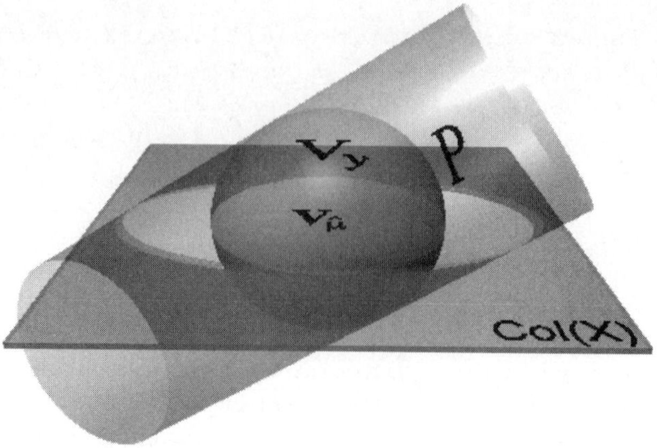

Figure 9.9 Projection of $\mathbb{V}_y$ in three dimensions.

nonorthogonal projection of $\mathbb{V}_{\mathbf{y}}$ onto Col($\mathbf{X}$) is depicted by the intersection of the cylinder marked P with Col($\mathbf{X}$). This cylinder has the same radius as $\mathbb{V}_{\mathbf{y}}$. One sees the larger, elliptical shape of all nonorthogonal projections of $\mathbb{V}_{\mathbf{y}}$ by this example. These ellipses always contain the disk $\mathbb{V}_{\hat{\boldsymbol{\mu}}}$ representing the variation in $\hat{\boldsymbol{\mu}}$, anticipating the optimality of OLS described by the Gauss–Markov theorem.

These pictures for variation of fitted vectors translate into parallel results for coefficient estimators because their variation follows directly from the variation in the fitted vectors. In all cases, linear projections of $\mathbf{y}$ onto Col($\mathbf{X}$) exhibit elliptical variation. This is because their variation is the image of the sphere $\mathbb{V}_{\mathbf{y}}$ under projection. The smallest image of $\mathbb{V}_{\mathbf{y}}$ under linear projections onto Col($\mathbf{X}$) is obviously the image under orthogonal projection. The variation in linear estimators of coefficient vectors is, in turn, the image of the variation in fitted vectors. The smallest ellipse for fitted vectors has the smallest image corresponding to variation in coefficient estimators, yielding the efficiency of the Gauss–Markov theorem.

9.4.2 Proof of the Gauss–Markov Theorem

Proof. We prove the Gauss–Markov theorem using fitted vectors $\mathbf{X}\boldsymbol{\beta}$, in sympathy with the geometry. That is, we will compare $\hat{\boldsymbol{\mu}} \equiv \mathbf{X}\hat{\boldsymbol{\beta}} = \mathbf{P_X y}$ with $\tilde{\boldsymbol{\mu}} \equiv \mathbf{X}\tilde{\boldsymbol{\beta}} = \mathbf{XAy}$. First note that the property of unbiasedness restricts the possible $\mathbf{A}$ matrices. Using Assumption 6.1,

$$\mathbf{X}\boldsymbol{\beta}_0 = \mathrm{E}[\mathbf{X}\tilde{\boldsymbol{\beta}} \mid \mathbf{X}] = \mathrm{E}[\mathbf{XAy} \mid \mathbf{X}] = \mathbf{XA}\,\mathrm{E}[\mathbf{y} \mid \mathbf{X}] = \mathbf{XAX}\boldsymbol{\beta}_0$$

for all possible $\boldsymbol{\beta}_0$, so that

$$\mathbf{XAX} = \mathbf{X} \tag{9.9}$$

In words, $\mathbf{XA}$ must be a projector onto Col($\mathbf{X}$), just as $\mathbf{P_X}$. This restriction places a restriction in turn on $\mathrm{Cov}[\tilde{\boldsymbol{\mu}}, \hat{\boldsymbol{\mu}} \mid \mathbf{X}]$:

$$\begin{aligned}\operatorname{Cov}[\tilde{\boldsymbol{\mu}}, \hat{\boldsymbol{\mu}} \mid \mathbf{X}] &= \operatorname{Cov}[\mathbf{XAy}, \mathbf{P_X y} \mid \mathbf{X}] \\ &= \mathbf{XA} \operatorname{Var}[\mathbf{y} \mid \mathbf{X}]\mathbf{P_X} \\ &= \mathbf{XA}(\sigma_0^2 \cdot \mathbf{I})\mathbf{P_X} \\ &= \sigma_0^2 \cdot \mathbf{XAP_X} \\ &= \sigma_0^2 \cdot \mathbf{P_X} \\ &= \operatorname{Var}[\hat{\boldsymbol{\mu}} \mid \mathbf{X}]\end{aligned} \tag{9.10}$$

using Assumption 7.1 and $\mathbf{XAP_X} = \mathbf{P_X}$. This restriction on the covariance has the form of (9.7). Applying Proposition 8, we conclude that $\hat{\boldsymbol{\mu}}$ is efficient relative to all other linear, unbiased estimators of $\boldsymbol{\mu}_0$. Under Assumption 3.1, this strict relative efficiency also applies to $\hat{\boldsymbol{\beta}}$. □

The Gauss–Markov theorem assures us that among all linear and unbiased estimators, the OLS estimator possesses the smallest variance. Therefore, if the conditional variances are larger than we wish, then we will have to search among either nonlinear or biased estimators to obtain smaller variances. Within the theoretical framework of Assumptions 3.1, 6.1, and 7.1, nonlinear estimation is intractable. First and second moments do not imply sharp results for nonlinear functions of $\mathbf{y}$, and so nonlinear alternatives to OLS must await additional (or alternative) assumptions. Biased estimators are problematic for two reasons. First of all, biased estimators have unknown biases (otherwise we could remove them). Secondly, we must choose an alternative objective function in place of variance. Any constant K-dimensional vector is a linear, biased, zero-variance estimator for $\boldsymbol{\beta}_0$. Mean squared error is an obvious generalization, but this objective function does not yield feasible optimal estimators. Thus, the Gauss–Markov theorem is an interesting result.

9.5 MATHEMATICAL NOTES

These notes tie up a few loose ends in this chapter. We prove Lemma 9.1 and we comment on two distinct applications of the concept of relative efficiency.

We will use the following lemma to prove Lemma 9.1.

LEMMA 9.3 *Let $\boldsymbol{\Omega}_A$, $\boldsymbol{\Omega}_B$ be two $K \times K$ variance (symmetric and positive semidefinite) matrices. If $\boldsymbol{\Omega}_B - \boldsymbol{\Omega}_A$ is positive semi-definite, then* $\operatorname{Col}(\boldsymbol{\Omega}_A) \subseteq \operatorname{Col}(\boldsymbol{\Omega}_B)$.

Proof. This is a proof by contradiction. That $\operatorname{Col}(\boldsymbol{\Omega}_A) \subseteq \operatorname{Col}(\boldsymbol{\Omega}_B)$ is equivalent to $\boldsymbol{\Omega}_B\mathbf{a} = 0 \Rightarrow \boldsymbol{\Omega}_A\mathbf{a} = 0$. Suppose that $\boldsymbol{\Omega}_B - \boldsymbol{\Omega}_A$ is positive semidefinite but there is also an $\mathbf{a}$ such that $\boldsymbol{\Omega}_A\mathbf{a} \neq 0$, $\boldsymbol{\Omega}_B\mathbf{a} = 0$. Then $\mathbf{a}'(\boldsymbol{\Omega}_B - \boldsymbol{\Omega}_A)\mathbf{a} = -\mathbf{a}'\boldsymbol{\Omega}_A\mathbf{a} < 0$. But $\boldsymbol{\Omega}_A$ is a variance matrix and must be positive semidefinite. This is a contradiction so that $\operatorname{Col}(\boldsymbol{\Omega}_A)$ must be a subspace of $\operatorname{Col}(\boldsymbol{\Omega}_B)$. □

Proof of Lemma 9.1. According to Definition 14 (Variance Ellipse, p. 134),

$$\mathbb{V}_{\hat{\theta}_A} = \{\mathbf{z} = \boldsymbol{\Omega}_A\mathbf{a} \mid \mathbf{a} \in \mathbb{R}^K,\ \mathbf{a}'\boldsymbol{\Omega}_A\mathbf{a} \le 1\}$$

$$\mathbb{V}_{\hat{\theta}_B} = \{\mathbf{z} = \boldsymbol{\Omega}_B\mathbf{b} \mid \mathbf{b} \in \mathbb{R}^K,\ \mathbf{b}'\boldsymbol{\Omega}_B\mathbf{b} \le 1\}$$

The zero vector is an element of every variance ellipse, so that we will consider only $\mathbf{a} \neq 0$, $\mathbf{a} \in \mathrm{Col}(\boldsymbol{\Omega}_A)$. For all such $\mathbf{a}$,

$$\frac{1}{\sqrt{\mathbf{a}'\boldsymbol{\Omega}_A\mathbf{a}}} \cdot \boldsymbol{\Omega}_A\mathbf{a} \in \mathbb{V}_{\hat{\theta}_A}$$

Necessity: If $\mathbb{V}_{\hat{\theta}_A} \subseteq \mathbb{V}_{\hat{\theta}_B}$ then for every $\mathbf{a}$ there is a $\mathbf{b}$ such that

$$\frac{1}{\sqrt{\mathbf{a}'\boldsymbol{\Omega}_A\mathbf{a}}} \cdot \boldsymbol{\Omega}_A\mathbf{a} = \boldsymbol{\Omega}_B\mathbf{b}, \qquad \mathbf{b}'\boldsymbol{\Omega}_B\mathbf{b} \le 1$$

For all $\mathbf{a} \neq \mathbf{0}$, $\mathbf{a} \in \mathrm{Col}(\boldsymbol{\Omega}_A)$,

$$\begin{aligned}
\mathbf{a}'\left(\boldsymbol{\Omega}_B - \boldsymbol{\Omega}_A\right)\mathbf{a} &= \mathbf{a}'\boldsymbol{\Omega}_B\mathbf{a} - \left(\mathbf{a}'\boldsymbol{\Omega}_B\mathbf{b}\right)^2 \\
&\ge \mathbf{a}'\boldsymbol{\Omega}_B\mathbf{a} - \frac{\left(\mathbf{a}'\boldsymbol{\Omega}_B\mathbf{b}\right)^2}{\mathbf{b}'\boldsymbol{\Omega}_B\mathbf{b}} \\
&\ge 0
\end{aligned}$$

using the Cauchy–Schwarz inequality (Lemma 7.8, p. 143). Thus, $\boldsymbol{\Omega}_B - \boldsymbol{\Omega}_A \ge 0$.

Sufficiency: If $\boldsymbol{\Omega}_B - \boldsymbol{\Omega}_A \ge 0$, then Lemma 9.3 implies that $\mathrm{Col}(\boldsymbol{\Omega}_A) \subseteq \mathrm{Col}(\boldsymbol{\Omega}_B)$. Given $\mathbf{a} \neq \mathbf{0}$, $\mathbf{a} \in \mathrm{Col}(\boldsymbol{\Omega}_A)$, where $\mathbf{a}'\boldsymbol{\Omega}_A\mathbf{a} \le 1$, we can find a $\mathbf{b}$ such that $\mathbf{z} = \boldsymbol{\Omega}_B\mathbf{b} = \boldsymbol{\Omega}_A\mathbf{a}$. For all such $\mathbf{a} \neq \mathbf{0}$,

$$\left(\mathbf{b}'\boldsymbol{\Omega}_B\mathbf{b}\right)^2 = \left(\mathbf{b}'\boldsymbol{\Omega}_A\mathbf{a}\right)^2 \le \frac{\left(\mathbf{b}'\boldsymbol{\Omega}_A\mathbf{a}\right)^2}{\mathbf{a}'\boldsymbol{\Omega}_A\mathbf{a}} \le \mathbf{b}'\boldsymbol{\Omega}_A\mathbf{b} \le \mathbf{b}'\boldsymbol{\Omega}_B\mathbf{b} \le 1$$

where the second inequality is the Cauchy–Schwarz inequality. Thus, $\mathbf{b}'\boldsymbol{\Omega}_B\mathbf{b} \le 1$ and every $\mathbf{z} \in \mathbb{V}_{\hat{\theta}_A}$ is also an element of $\mathbb{V}_{\hat{\theta}_B}$.

Note that we have used the concept of relative efficiency in two distinct ways in this chapter. In the first way, we compared the efficiency of different experimental designs. We were imagining a choice between *experiments*, not between *estimators*. In contrast, the rest of the chapter compared the efficiency of different estimators, given an experiment. The concept of relative efficiency rests only on a comparison of variances and does not require that the estimators have a well-defined joint distribution. However, in econometric theory, experimental design has received relatively little attention and most discussions of relative efficiency are about choices between estimators defined over the same experiment.

9.6 OVERVIEW

1. Relative efficiency is one criterion for comparing unbiased estimators. If $\mathrm{E}[\hat{\boldsymbol{\theta}}_A] = \mathrm{E}[\hat{\boldsymbol{\theta}}_B] = \boldsymbol{\theta}_0 \in \mathbb{R}^K$, then the estimator $\hat{\boldsymbol{\theta}}_A$ is *efficient relative to* the estimator $\hat{\boldsymbol{\theta}}_B$ if $\mathrm{Var}[\mathbf{c}'\hat{\boldsymbol{\theta}}_A] \le \mathrm{Var}[\mathbf{c}'\hat{\boldsymbol{\theta}}_B]$ for all $\mathbf{c} \in \mathbb{R}^K$. A geometric interpretation of relative efficiency is that the variance ellipse of $\hat{\boldsymbol{\theta}}_A$ is a subset of the variance ellipse of $\hat{\boldsymbol{\theta}}_B$.

2. The conditional variance of $\hat{\boldsymbol{\beta}}$ depends on the conditional variance of $\mathbf{y}$ and $\mathbf{X}'\mathbf{X}$: compared to an initial conditional distribution for which $\mathrm{E}[\mathbf{y}\,|\,\mathbf{X}] = \mathbf{X}\boldsymbol{\beta}_0$ and $\mathrm{Var}[\mathbf{y}\,|\,\mathbf{X}] = \sigma_0^2 \cdot \mathbf{I}_N$, one obtains a relatively efficient OLS estimator of $\boldsymbol{\beta}_0$ by
   (a) increasing the overall scale of explanatory variables $\mathbf{X}$,
   (b) increasing the sample size N, or
   (c) reducing the collinearity between explanatory variables.
3. Also, the RLS estimator is efficient relative to the unrestricted OLS estimator. This is an example of a general result: imposing correct restrictions generally yields sharper inferences.
4. According to the projection theorem, an unbiased estimator $\hat{\boldsymbol{\theta}}$ is relatively efficient within a set of unbiased estimators $\mathbb{U}$ that includes all linear combinations $\hat{\boldsymbol{\theta}} + \mathbf{A}\left(\tilde{\boldsymbol{\theta}} - \hat{\boldsymbol{\theta}}\right), \tilde{\boldsymbol{\theta}} \in \mathbb{U}$, if and only if the orthogonality $\mathrm{Cov}[\hat{\boldsymbol{\theta}}, \tilde{\boldsymbol{\theta}} - \hat{\boldsymbol{\theta}}] = \mathbf{0}$ holds.
5. Assumption 7.1 (Second Moments) yields another second-moment result, the relative efficiency of OLS estimators $\hat{\boldsymbol{\mu}}$ and $\hat{\boldsymbol{\beta}}$ among all linear and unbiased estimators for $\boldsymbol{\mu}_0$ and $\boldsymbol{\beta}_0$ respectively.
   (a) The spherical nature of the distribution of $\hat{\boldsymbol{\mu}}$ is characteristic of the efficiency of the OLS estimator: all other projections of the variance sphere of $\mathbf{y}$ onto $\mathrm{Col}(\mathbf{X})$ are ellipses that contain the variance ellipse of $\hat{\boldsymbol{\mu}}$.
   (b) Because $\hat{\boldsymbol{\mu}}$ and $\hat{\boldsymbol{\beta}}$ have a linear one-to-one relationship, $\hat{\boldsymbol{\beta}}$ shares the relative efficiency property with $\hat{\boldsymbol{\mu}}$.

9.7 EXERCISES

9.7.1 Review

9.1 Graph the variance ellipse $\mathbb{V}_{\hat{\boldsymbol{\beta}}}$ for the two cases discussed in Example 9.2. Interpret the differences in terms of the effects of increasing multicollinearity on the conditional sampling variance of $\hat{\boldsymbol{\beta}}$. (HINT: Review Figure 8.4.)

9.2 **(Monte Carlo)** Using a computer, generate an artificial data set of 21 observations as follows:
   (a) Set $w_n = \frac{1}{20}(n-1)$ for $n = 1, \ldots, 21$.
   (b) Set $y_n = w_n^2 + \varepsilon_n$ where $\varepsilon_n \sim \mathfrak{N}(0, \frac{1}{100})$.
   Using this data set, compute OLS fitted values for each of the following specifications:

$$\mathrm{E}[y_n \,|\, w_n] = \beta_1 + \beta_2 w_n$$
$$\mathrm{E}[y_n \,|\, w_n] = \beta_1 + \beta_2 w_n^2$$
$$\mathrm{E}[y_n \,|\, w_n] = \beta_1 + \beta_2 e^{w_n}$$
$$\mathrm{E}[y_n \,|\, w_n] = \beta_1 + \beta_2 \cos(w_n)$$

Compare the fitted values. Also compute and compare out-of-sample forecasts for $\mathbf{y}$ for values of w from -2 to 3.

9.3 **(RLS)** Show that $\mathrm{Cov}[\hat{\boldsymbol{\beta}}, \hat{\boldsymbol{\beta}}_{\mathrm{R}} \,|\, \mathbf{X}] = \mathrm{Var}[\hat{\boldsymbol{\beta}}_{\mathrm{R}} \,|\, \mathbf{X}]$ under the assumptions of Proposition 5 (Variances of OLS, p. 157). What does this imply?

9.4 Let $\mathrm{E}[\mathbf{y}\,|\,\mathbf{X}] = \mathbf{X}_1\boldsymbol{\beta}_{01} + \mathbf{X}_2\boldsymbol{\beta}_{02}$ and $\mathrm{Var}[\mathbf{y}\,|\,\mathbf{X}] = \sigma_0^2 \cdot \mathbf{I}$. Draw a geometric representation in two dimensions of an increase in the scale of $\mathbf{X}_1$ and $\mathbf{X}_2$ leading to a decrease in the sampling variances of the coefficients. Show that if $\mathbf{X}_1$ and $\mathbf{X}_2$ are not orthogonal, an increase in the scale of $\mathbf{X}_1$ will decrease the sampling variance of the estimators of *both* the coefficients.

9.5 Let $K = 2$ and $\mathbf{X}\boldsymbol{\beta} = \mathbf{X}_1 + \mathbf{X}_2$. Suppose $\mathbf{X}_1'\mathbf{X}_1 = \mathbf{X}_2'\mathbf{X}_2$ and compare $\text{Var}[\hat{\beta}_1 \mid \mathbf{X}]$, $\text{Var}[\hat{\beta}_1 + \hat{\beta}_2 \mid \mathbf{X}]$, and $\text{Var}[\hat{\beta}_1 - \hat{\beta}_2 \mid \mathbf{X}]$ as $\mathbf{X}_1'\mathbf{X}_2 \to \mathbf{X}_1'\mathbf{X}_1$. Construct a graphic illustration along the lines of Figure 9.5.

9.6 (Partitioned Regression) Let $\mathbf{X}_2'\mathbf{X}_1 = \mathbf{0}$. We have already seen that such orthogonality implies that algebraically $\hat{\boldsymbol{\beta}}_1$ is not affected by the presence of $\mathbf{X}_2$ in the OLS regression (Example 3.3, Exercise 3.13). Show that in addition $\text{Cov}[\hat{\boldsymbol{\beta}}_1, \hat{\boldsymbol{\beta}}_2 \mid \mathbf{X}] = \mathbf{0}$, as might be expected.

9.7 Use Exercise 3.22 to confirm equation (9.1):

$$\sigma_0^2 \cdot (\mathbf{X}'\mathbf{X} + \mathbf{x}_{N+1}\mathbf{x}_{N+1}')^{-1} = \sigma_0^2 \cdot (\mathbf{X}'\mathbf{X})^{-1} - \frac{\sigma_0^2}{1 + \mathbf{x}_{N+1}'(\mathbf{X}'\mathbf{X})^{-1}\mathbf{x}_{N+1}} \cdot (\mathbf{X}'\mathbf{X})^{-1}\mathbf{x}_{N+1}\mathbf{x}_{N+1}'(\mathbf{X}'\mathbf{X})^{-1}$$

9.8 Under what circumstances does the distribution of $\hat{\boldsymbol{\beta}}$ *marginal* of $\mathbf{X}$ hold interest? Describe the *marginal* variance matrix of $\hat{\boldsymbol{\beta}}$ under the assumptions of Proposition 5 (Variances of OLS, p. 157). Do the elements of this matrix always exist? If they are finite, how can one estimate the marginal variance matrix, $\text{Var}[\hat{\boldsymbol{\beta}}]$?

***9.9** Consider the following alternative approach to Exercise 8.15, in which we constructed a vector of $N - K$ recursive residuals

$$\hat{v}_n = \frac{y_n - \mathbf{x}_n'\hat{\boldsymbol{\beta}}_{[n-1]}}{1 + \mathbf{x}_n'\left(\mathbf{X}_{[n-1]}'\mathbf{X}_{[n-1]}\right)^{-1}\mathbf{x}_n}, \quad n > K$$

possessing a scalar variance matrix $\sigma_0^2 \cdot \mathbf{I}_{N-K}$. In this expression for $\hat{v}_n$,

$$\mathbf{X}_{[m]} \equiv [\mathbf{x}_n;\ n = 1, \ldots, m]'$$
$$\mathbf{y}_{[m]} \equiv [y_n;\ n = 1, \ldots, m]'$$

and

$$\hat{\boldsymbol{\beta}}_{[m]} \equiv \left(\mathbf{X}_{[m]}'\mathbf{X}_{[m]}\right)^{-1}\mathbf{X}_{[m]}'\mathbf{y}_{[m]}$$

$\hat{\boldsymbol{\beta}}_{[m]}$ is the vector of OLS fitted coefficients based only on the "first" m observations. Use the concept of relative efficiency to argue that the key intermediate result,

$$\text{Cov}\left[\hat{\boldsymbol{\beta}}_{[n]}, \hat{\boldsymbol{\beta}}_{[n]} - \hat{\boldsymbol{\beta}}_{[n-1]} \mid \mathbf{X}\right] = \mathbf{0}, \quad n > K$$

holds.

9.10 Although increasing the scale of $\mathbf{X}$ improves the efficiency of the OLS estimator, increasing the scale of a subset of the columns of $\mathbf{X}$ does not necessarily improve efficiency.

(a) Let $\mathbf{X} = [\mathbf{X}_1, \mathbf{X}_2]$ and suppose that one may replace $\mathbf{X}_1$ with $a \cdot \mathbf{X}_1$, where $a > 1$, before drawing observations on $\mathbf{y}$. Show that this will decrease $\text{Var}[\mathbf{c}_1'\hat{\boldsymbol{\beta}}_1 \mid \mathbf{X}]$, but it may increase or decrease the variance of $\text{Var}[\mathbf{c}'\hat{\boldsymbol{\beta}} \mid \mathbf{X}]$.

(b) In contrast, show that increasing the scale of a subset of *rows* (observations) of $\mathbf{X}$ always improves efficiency.

9.11 If $\boldsymbol{\Omega}_A$ and $\boldsymbol{\Omega}_B$ are symmetric, positive-definite matrices, and $\boldsymbol{\Omega}_B - \boldsymbol{\Omega}_A$ is positive semidefinite, then $\boldsymbol{\Omega}_A^{-1} - \boldsymbol{\Omega}_B^{-1}$ is positive semidefinite.
Prove this lemma with the following steps:
(a) Show that when $\boldsymbol{\Omega}_B - \boldsymbol{\Omega}_A$ is positive semidefinite,

$$\boldsymbol{\Omega} = \begin{bmatrix} \boldsymbol{\Omega}_B & \boldsymbol{\Omega}_A \\ \boldsymbol{\Omega}_A & \boldsymbol{\Omega}_A \end{bmatrix}$$

is a positive semidefinite matrix. [HINT: Use Proposition 8 (Orthogonality of Efficient Estimators, p. 185).]
(b) Now consider $\mathbf{c}'\boldsymbol{\Omega}\mathbf{c}$ where

$$\mathbf{c}' = \mathbf{a}' \begin{bmatrix} \boldsymbol{\Omega}_B^{-1} & -\boldsymbol{\Omega}_A^{-1} \end{bmatrix}$$

and show that $\boldsymbol{\Omega}_A^{-1} - \boldsymbol{\Omega}_B^{-1}$ is positive semidefinite.
(c) What connection does this result have to Lemma 9.1?

9.12 **(RLS)** In the proof of Proposition 7 (Restricted Least-Squares Efficiency, p. 183), we show the variance inequality $\mathrm{Var}[\mathbf{c}'\hat{\boldsymbol{\mu}}_{\mathrm{R}} \,|\, \mathbf{X}] \leq \mathrm{Var}[\mathbf{c}'\hat{\boldsymbol{\mu}} \,|\, \mathbf{X}]$ for any $\mathbf{c} \in \mathbb{R}^N$. Show that this relative efficiency of $\hat{\boldsymbol{\mu}}_{\mathrm{R}}$ to $\hat{\boldsymbol{\mu}}$ does not require Assumption 3.1 (Full Rank, p. 53), but that the relative efficiency of $\hat{\boldsymbol{\beta}}_{\mathrm{R}}$ to $\hat{\boldsymbol{\beta}}$ does.

9.13 **(Gauss–Markov Theorem)** Prove the Gauss–Markov theorem (Theorem 7, p. 187) again with the following steps.
(a) Show that symmetric, idempotent, matrices are positive semidefinite. (HINT: See Exercises 2.19 and 3.9.)
(b) Show that if $\mathrm{E}[\mathbf{A}\mathbf{y} \,|\, \mathbf{X}] = \boldsymbol{\beta}_0$ for all $\boldsymbol{\beta}_0$ then $\mathbf{A}\mathbf{X} = \mathbf{I}_K$ and

$$\begin{aligned} \mathrm{Var}[\mathbf{A}\mathbf{y} \,|\, \mathbf{X}] &= \sigma_0^2 \cdot \mathbf{A}\mathbf{A}' \\ &= \mathrm{Var}[\hat{\boldsymbol{\beta}} \,|\, \mathbf{X}] + \sigma_0^2 \cdot \mathbf{A}\,(\mathbf{I} - \mathbf{P}_{\mathbf{X}})\,\mathbf{A}' \end{aligned}$$

(c) Show furthermore that if $\mathrm{E}[\mathbf{A}\mathbf{y} \,|\, \mathbf{X}] = \boldsymbol{\beta}_0$ for all $\boldsymbol{\beta}_0$ then $\mathrm{Var}[\mathbf{c}'\mathbf{A}\mathbf{y} \,|\, \mathbf{X}] \geq \mathrm{Var}[\mathbf{c}'\hat{\boldsymbol{\beta}} \,|\, \mathbf{X}]$ for all $\mathbf{c} \in \mathbb{R}^K$.

9.14 **(Gauss–Markov Theorem)** Resolve the following paradox: the Gauss–Markov theorem (Theorem 7, p. 187) states that $\hat{\boldsymbol{\beta}}$ is the minimum-variance linear unbiased estimator, whereas the restricted least-squares estimator $\hat{\boldsymbol{\beta}}_{\mathrm{R}}$ is clearly a more efficient linear unbiased estimator when $\mathbf{R}\boldsymbol{\beta}_0 = \mathbf{r}$.

9.15 **(Gauss–Markov Theorem)** Prove that $\mathbf{XAX} = \mathbf{X}$ implies that $\mathbf{XA}$ is a projector onto $\mathrm{Col}(\mathbf{X})$, as we claimed in our proof of the Gauss–Markov theorem (Theorem 7, p. 187) in Section 9.4.2.

9.7.2 Extensions

9.16 Consider two full-column rank design matrices, $\mathbf{X}_A$ and $\mathbf{X}_B$, for the estimation of $\mathrm{E}[\mathbf{y} \,|\, \mathbf{X}] = \mathbf{X}\boldsymbol{\beta}_0$. Show that if $\mathbf{X}_B'\mathbf{X}_B - \mathbf{X}_A'\mathbf{X}_A$ is a positive semidefinite matrix, then design B is efficient relative to design A for the OLS estimator of $\boldsymbol{\beta}_0$. [HINT: Use Lemma 9.1 and the definition of variance ellipses (Definition 14, p. 134).]

9.17 Let $\mathbf{A}$ and $\mathbf{B}$ be two symmetric, positive-definite matrices. Show $\mathbf{B}-\mathbf{A}$ is positive semidefinite if and only if $\mathbf{A}^{-1}-\mathbf{B}^{-1}$ is also positive semidefinite. [HINT: Use Lemma 9.1 and consider $\mathbf{w} = \left(1/\sqrt{\mathbf{z}'\mathbf{A}^{-1}\mathbf{z}}\right)\cdot \mathbf{z}$ for any $\mathbf{z} \in \{\boldsymbol{\alpha} \mid \boldsymbol{\alpha}'\mathbf{A}^{-1}\boldsymbol{\alpha} \leq 1\}$.]

9.18 **(MMSE)** Show that the MMSE linear estimator $\mathbf{d}'\mathbf{y}$ of $\mathbf{c}'\boldsymbol{\beta}_0$,

$$\mathbf{d} = \operatorname*{argmin}_{\mathbf{a}\in\mathbb{R}^N} \mathrm{E}[(\mathbf{a}'\mathbf{y} - \mathbf{c}'\boldsymbol{\beta}_0)^2]$$

is a function of unknown parameters, as well as $\mathbf{c}$. Compare this outcome with the MMSE linear *unbiased* estimator.

9.19 Under random sampling, the variance of the sample average falls inversely with the size of the sample (Table 5.1). However, this may not be so for OLS. The variation in x_n affects the rate of decline for each coefficient individually. Show what happens to $\mathrm{Var}[\mathbf{c}'\hat{\boldsymbol{\beta}}_N]$, $\mathbf{c} \in \mathbb{R}^K$, as $N \to \infty$ in each of the following cases.

(a) Suppose $\mathrm{E}_N[\mathbf{x}_n\mathbf{x}_n']$ approaches a constant, nonsingular matrix as $N \to \infty$.

(b) Suppose that $\mathbf{x}_n$ approaches a fixed point $\boldsymbol{\xi}$ uniformly as n grows.

(c) Also consider a case in which elements of $\mathbf{x}_n$ have increasing sample variation. Let $K = 2$ and let $x_{n1} = 1$, $x_{n2} = n$, as for time series data with a time trend on the RHS. Show that

$$(\mathbf{X}'\mathbf{X})^{-1} = \frac{2}{N(N-1)} \cdot \begin{bmatrix} 2N+1 & -3 \\ -3 & \frac{6}{N+1} \end{bmatrix}$$

so that the variance of the intercept is $O(N^{-1})$ but the variance of the coefficient on time is $O(N^{-3})$.

9.20 **(Information Loss)** Consider the partitioned regression $\mathrm{E}[\mathbf{y} \mid \mathbf{X}] = \mathbf{X}_1\boldsymbol{\beta}_{01} + \mathbf{X}_2\boldsymbol{\beta}_{02}$ when the conditional expectation of $\mathbf{X}_2$ given $\mathbf{X}_1$ is known:

$$\mathbf{Z}(\mathbf{X}_1) = \mathrm{E}[\mathbf{X}_2 \mid \mathbf{X}_1]$$

Provided that $\mathbf{Z}(\mathbf{X}_1)$ is not a linear function of $\mathbf{X}_1$ so that $\mathrm{rank}([\mathbf{X}_1, \mathbf{Z}(\mathbf{X}_1)]) = K$, one can estimate $\boldsymbol{\beta}_0$ with an OLS fit of $\mathbf{y}$ to $[\mathbf{X}_1, \mathbf{Z}(\mathbf{X}_1)]$ instead of $\mathbf{X} = [\mathbf{X}_1, \mathbf{X}_2]$. Show that this estimator is inefficient relative to the usual OLS estimator $\hat{\boldsymbol{\beta}} \equiv (\mathbf{X}'\mathbf{X})^{-1}\mathbf{X}'\mathbf{y}$ when $\mathrm{Var}[\mathbf{y} \mid \mathbf{X}] = \sigma_0^2 \cdot \mathbf{I}$. Explain.

9.21 **(Relative Efficiency)** Proposition 8 (Orthogonality of Efficient Estimators, p. 185) contains a *matrix* of orthogonality conditions, $\mathrm{Cov}[\tilde{\boldsymbol{\theta}} - \hat{\boldsymbol{\theta}}, \hat{\boldsymbol{\theta}}] = \mathbf{0}$. The orthogonal projection theorem for $\mathbb{R}^N$ (Theorem 2, p. 31) implicitly contains only a *vector* of orthogonality conditions: if the columns of $\mathbf{X}$ are a basis for the subspace $\mathbb{S}$ then $\mathbf{y} - \hat{\boldsymbol{\mu}} \perp \mathbb{S} \Leftrightarrow \mathbf{X}'(\mathbf{y} - \hat{\boldsymbol{\mu}}) = \mathbf{0}$. Explain this difference in orthogonality conditions.

9.22 **(Relative Efficiency)** Let $\tilde{\boldsymbol{\theta}}$ be an unbiased estimator of $\boldsymbol{\theta}_0$ and suppose that $\mathrm{Var}[\tilde{\boldsymbol{\theta}}] = \boldsymbol{\Omega}$ is a finite, nonsingular matrix. If $\mathbf{R}\boldsymbol{\theta}_0 = \mathbf{r}$ show that the restricted estimator

$$\hat{\boldsymbol{\theta}} = \operatorname*{argmin}_{\{\boldsymbol{\theta} \mid \mathbf{R}\boldsymbol{\theta} = \mathbf{r}\}} (\tilde{\boldsymbol{\theta}} - \boldsymbol{\theta})'\boldsymbol{\Omega}^{-1}(\tilde{\boldsymbol{\theta}} - \boldsymbol{\theta})$$

is efficient relative to $\tilde{\boldsymbol{\theta}}$.

CHAPTER 10

NORMAL DISTRIBUTION THEORY

10.1 INTRODUCTION

Having found the first and second moments of the OLS estimator under assumptions about the first and second moments of the data, we proceed one step further to the complete distribution of the estimator under an additional assumption about the distribution of the data. This step is also our last in the development of the classical linear regression model. In subsequent chapters of this book, we will consider various departures from this classical framework.

There are two primary motives for making stronger assumptions about the distribution of the data and, consequently, the estimators: (1) the desire to make probability statements about the population data-generating process and (2) interest in finding estimators with efficiency properties stronger than the Gauss–Markov theorem provides for the OLS estimator. When combined with our earlier assumptions, the following assumption enables us to address both motives.

ASSUMPTION 10.1 (NORMAL DISTRIBUTION) *The dependent variable* $\mathbf{y}$ *is distributed as a multivariate normal random variable, conditional on* $\mathbf{X}$.[1]

To illustrate the ability to make probability statements under this assumption, let us return to the CPS earnings data. Under the moment assumptions, we have already estimated coefficients for the returns to experience in hourly earnings. The quadratic fit yields a linear coefficient of 0.0391 and a quadratic coefficient of −0.000632. The unbiased estimator of the sampling variance matrix of these estimates is

$$\begin{bmatrix} 1.502 \times 10^{-5} & -3.284 \times 10^{-7} \\ -3.284 \times 10^{-7} & 7.875 \times 10^{-9} \end{bmatrix}$$

Figure 10.1 shows an *interval estimator* for this pair of coefficients: under the additional assumption of a multivariate normal distribution, there is a 95% probability in repeated samples that this interval contains the population values of these coefficients. The interval estimator looks like

[1] For a review of the univariate normal distribution, see Section D.4.

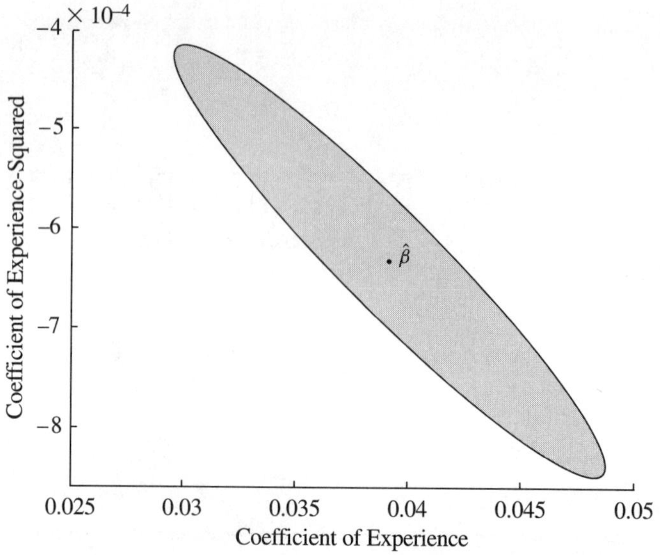

Figure 10.1 Ninety-five percent confidence interval for experience coefficients.

the variance ellipses discussed previously. Indeed, the interval estimators are scaled versions of variance ellipses, where the distribution theory determines the radius. Whereas we chose the value one for convenience in variance ellipses, the distribution of the OLS estimators and the coverage probability (95% in our example) determine the size of the elliptical interval estimator.

In this chapter, we are adding a distributional assumption to our previous moment assumptions. In effect, we are specifying *all* of the conditional moments of $\mathbf{y}$ given $\mathbf{X}$. When we combine Assumptions 6.1, 7.1, and 10.1, we will write

$$\mathbf{y} \mid \mathbf{X} \sim \mathfrak{N}(\mathbf{X}\boldsymbol{\beta}_0, \sigma_0^2 \cdot \mathbf{I}_N)$$

to mean "Conditional on $\mathbf{X}$, $\mathbf{y}$ has a multivariate normal distribution with mean $\mathbf{X}\boldsymbol{\beta}_0$ and variance matrix $\sigma_0^2 \cdot \mathbf{I}_N$." Mathematically, this means that the conditional probability density function (p.d.f.) of $\mathbf{y}$ is

$$\phi(\mathbf{y} - \mathbf{X}\boldsymbol{\beta}_0, \sigma_0^2 \cdot \mathbf{I}_N) \equiv \left(2\pi\sigma_0^2\right)^{-N/2} \exp\left[-\frac{(\mathbf{y} - \mathbf{X}\boldsymbol{\beta}_0)'(\mathbf{y} - \mathbf{X}\boldsymbol{\beta}_0)}{2\sigma_0^2}\right] \tag{10.1}$$

We cover the theory of the multivariate normal distribution in Sections 10.5.1 and 10.5.4. For now it is enough to note that this p.d.f. involves the data only through a familiar quadratic form: the squared Euclidean length of $\mathbf{y} - \mathbf{X}\boldsymbol{\beta}_0$. There are several properties of the multivariate normal distribution that follow:

1. The p.d.f. for $\mathbf{y}$ is *spherically symmetric* about $\mathbf{X}\boldsymbol{\beta}_0$ where it attains its maximum.[2] This distribution is bell shaped, as Figure 10.2 shows for the two-dimensional ($N = 2$) case.
2. The first two moments of $\mathbf{y}$ completely determine its p.d.f. This property holds generally for the multivariate normal distribution.

[2] Spherically symmetric p.d.f.s have the general form $f(\|\mathbf{z} - \boldsymbol{\mu}\|^2)$. Elliptically symmetric p.d.f.s take the form $f[(\mathbf{z} - \boldsymbol{\mu})'\mathbf{A}(\mathbf{z} - \boldsymbol{\mu})]$.

3. Linear combinations of $\mathbf{y}$ also possess a multivariate normal distribution.
4. If they are uncorrelated, then multivariate normal random variables are also independently distributed.

The last two of these properties are not obvious consequences of the p.d.f. But the properties themselves are transparent and applicable. So we proceed, leaving their proof to Section 10.5, *Basic Distribution Theory*.

The final property, that uncorrelated multivariate normal random variables are independent, implies that this distributional assumption implicitly strengthens Assumption 7.1. Without normality, the zero covariances left open the possibility that $y_n - \mathbf{x}_n' \boldsymbol{\beta}_0$ might help predict $y_m - \mathbf{x}_m' \boldsymbol{\beta}_0$ $(m \neq n)$ through some nonlinear function. With normality comes conditional independence for these random variables, so that no such relationship exists. As always, additional assumptions narrow the range of possible data generating processes.

The presence of the squared Euclidean length of $\mathbf{y} - \mathbf{X}\boldsymbol{\beta}_0$ in the normal p.d.f. also relates this distribution to the chi-square distribution.[3] A common motivation of the chi-square distribution is that it is the distribution of independently distributed $\mathfrak{N}(0, 1)$ random variables, squared and summed. That is the squared length of $\mathbf{z} \sim \mathfrak{N}(\mathbf{0}, \mathbf{I})$. We will use a generalization of this description:

Lemma 10.1 (Minimum Chi-Square) *Let* $\mathbf{z} \sim \mathfrak{N}(\mathbf{0}, \mathbf{I}_N)$ *and* $\mathbb{S}$ *be an* M*-dimensional subspace of* $\mathbb{R}^N$*. Then*

$$\min_{\boldsymbol{\mu} \in \mathbb{S}} \|\mathbf{z} - \boldsymbol{\mu}\|^2 \sim \chi^2_{N-M}$$

$$\min_{\boldsymbol{\mu} \in \mathbb{S}^\perp} \|\mathbf{z} - \boldsymbol{\mu}\|^2 \sim \chi^2_{M}$$

and these two random variables are independently distributed.[4]

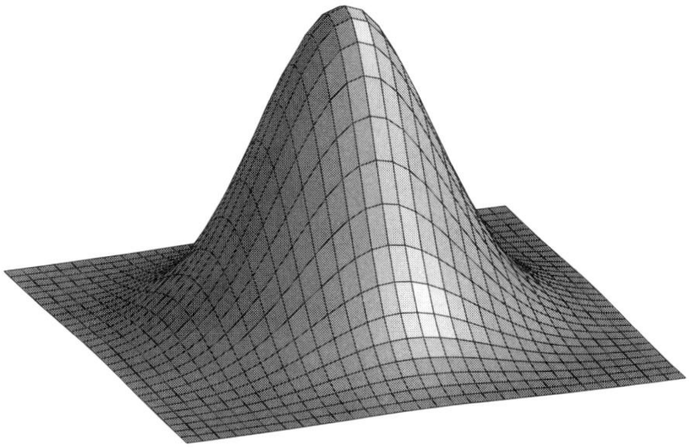

Figure 10.2 Bivariate normal p.d.f.

[3] See Definition D.30 (Chi-Square Distribution, p. 888).

[4] We take a chi-square distribution with zero degrees of freedom to be the distribution of a constant equal to zero.

This lemma is a sort of "probabilistic-Pythagorean-projection" theorem. We form right-angled triangles out of **z** and its orthogonal projections. Orthogonality of two sides implies their independence and the squared length of each side is distributed as chi-square so that $\chi^2_N = \chi^2_{N-M} + \chi^2_M$. The degrees of freedom for each of "the other two sides" is a reduction from an original N degrees of freedom by the dimension of the minimization. We also prove this result toward the end of this chapter. In the next section, we apply these relationships to the OLS estimators.

10.2 DISTRIBUTION THEORY FOR OLS ESTIMATORS

The distribution theory of $\hat{\boldsymbol{\mu}}$, $\mathbf{y} - \hat{\boldsymbol{\mu}}$, and $\hat{\boldsymbol{\beta}}$ is relatively straightforward under the assumption of normally distributed **y**. All three statistics are *linear* functions of **y** and so Property 3 yields normal distributions for all three. According to Property 2, the normal distribution is completely determined by the first two moments. Therefore, the following proposition is an extension of Propositions 4 (Expectations of OLS) and 5 (Variances of OLS) under Assumption 10.1. The independence of $\hat{\boldsymbol{\mu}}$ and $\mathbf{y} - \hat{\boldsymbol{\mu}}$ also rests on Property 4. We prove this proposition formally in the *Mathematical Notes* section (p. 209).

Proposition 9 (Normality of OLS) *Under Assumptions 3.1 (First Moments, p. 110), 7.1 (Second Moments, p. 130), and 10.1 (Normal Distribution, p. 195),*

1. $\hat{\boldsymbol{\mu}} \,|\, \mathbf{X} \sim \mathfrak{N}(\mathbf{X}\boldsymbol{\beta}_0, \sigma_0^2 \cdot \mathbf{P_X})$,
2. $\mathbf{y} - \hat{\boldsymbol{\mu}} \,|\, \mathbf{X} \sim \mathfrak{N}\big(\mathbf{0}, \sigma_0^2 \cdot (\mathbf{I} - \mathbf{P_X})\big)$,
3. $\hat{\boldsymbol{\mu}}$ *and* $\mathbf{y} - \hat{\boldsymbol{\mu}}$ *are independent, and*
4. $\hat{\boldsymbol{\beta}} \,|\, \mathbf{X} \sim \mathfrak{N}\big(\boldsymbol{\beta}_0, \sigma_0^2 \cdot (\mathbf{X}'\mathbf{X})^{-1}\big)$, *if Assumption 3.1 (Full Rank, p. 53) holds.*

This proposition implicitly states several interesting facts. First, normality has turned the covariance orthogonality of $\hat{\boldsymbol{\mu}}$ and $\mathbf{y} - \hat{\boldsymbol{\mu}}$ into distributional independence. Thus, knowledge of $\hat{\boldsymbol{\mu}}$ indicates *nothing* about $\mathbf{y} - \hat{\boldsymbol{\mu}}$ and vice versa. This independence helps to make the joint distribution of $\hat{\boldsymbol{\beta}}$ and s^2 analytically tractable, as discussed below.

Second, note that the distribution of $\mathbf{y} - \hat{\boldsymbol{\mu}}$ does not depend on $\boldsymbol{\beta}_0$. The multivariate normal distribution is completely characterized by its mean vector and variance matrix; we have already derived these for $\mathbf{y} - \hat{\boldsymbol{\mu}}$ under weaker conditions and neither the first nor the second moments of $\mathbf{y} - \hat{\boldsymbol{\mu}}$ are functions of $\boldsymbol{\beta}_0$. The implication of this observation is that the OLS fitted residuals are completely uninformative about the regression slope parameters $\boldsymbol{\beta}_0$. The residuals can contribute only to the estimation of the variance parameter σ_0^2 and, as it happens, our OLS estimator s^2 of σ_0^2 is only a function of the OLS fitted residuals.

We can also find the distribution of s^2 from the distribution of **y**. Because it is not a linear function of **y**, s^2 does not have a normal distribution. Instead, its distribution is proportional to that of a chi-square random variable (Definition D.30, p. 888).

Proposition 10 (Distribution of Variance Estimator) *Under Assumptions 3.1 (Full Rank, p. 53), 6.1 (First Moments, p. 110), 7.1 (Second Moments, p. 130), and 10.1 (Normal Distribution, p. 195), $s^2 \sim \sigma_0^2\, \chi_{N-K}^2/(N-K)$ and independent of $\hat{\boldsymbol{\mu}}$ and $\hat{\boldsymbol{\beta}}$, where χ_{N-K}^2 denotes a random variable distributed as chi-square with $N-K$ degrees of freedom.*

We prove this proposition formally on p. 210. We can see immediately that the independence of s^2 and $\hat{\boldsymbol{\mu}}$ follows from the independence of $\mathbf{y}-\hat{\boldsymbol{\mu}}$ and $\hat{\boldsymbol{\mu}}$ and the fact that s^2 is a function of $\mathbf{y}-\hat{\boldsymbol{\mu}}$ only. As for the chi-square distribution, we will give a geometric explanation for this result that rests on our previous study of $\mathbf{y}-\hat{\boldsymbol{\mu}}$.

We have already shown that $\mathbf{y}-\hat{\boldsymbol{\mu}}$ has a spherical distribution within $\mathrm{Col}^{\perp}(\mathbf{X})$ under Assumption 7.1. With the addition of Assumption 10.1, we have found that this distribution is multivariate normal. As a result, we will be able think of $\mathbf{y}-\hat{\boldsymbol{\mu}}$ as though it were drawn from the $\mathfrak{N}(\mathbf{0}, \sigma_0^2 \cdot \mathbf{I}_{N-K})$, the multivariate normal distribution of a spherically distributed (about $\mathbf{0}$), $(N-K)$-dimensional, random variable. This view is obscured by looking at this vector in a higher dimensional vector space; recall the discussion in Section 8.4. Now the squared Euclidean length of a $\mathfrak{N}(\mathbf{0}, \sigma_0^2 \cdot \mathbf{I}_{N-K})$ random variable is equivalent to the sum of $N-K$ independent standard normal random variables squared, multiplied by σ_0^2:

$$(\mathbf{y}-\hat{\boldsymbol{\mu}})'(\mathbf{y}-\hat{\boldsymbol{\mu}}) \sim \sigma_0^2 \sum_{m=1}^{N-K} z_m^2 \sim \sigma_0^2\, \chi_{N-K}^2$$

where $z_m \overset{i.i.d.}{\sim} \mathfrak{N}(0,1)$, $m = 1, \ldots, N-K$. This random variable is distributed, according to a popular motivation of the chi-square distribution, as a chi-square random variable with $N-K$ degrees of freedom multiplied by σ_0^2. Because s^2 is the squared length of $\mathbf{y}-\hat{\boldsymbol{\mu}}$ divided by $N-K$, the proposition follows.

Lemma 10.1 summarizes this process. Because $(1/\sigma_0)\cdot(\mathbf{y}-\boldsymbol{\mu}_0) \sim \mathfrak{N}(\mathbf{0}, \mathbf{I}_N)$, its squared length is a chi-square random variable

$$\frac{\|\mathbf{y}-\boldsymbol{\mu}_0\|^2}{\sigma_0^2} \sim \chi_N^2 \tag{10.2}$$

The minimization of the distance between $\mathbf{y}-\boldsymbol{\mu}_0$ and $\mathrm{Col}(\mathbf{X})$ produces

$$\frac{\|\mathbf{y}-\hat{\boldsymbol{\mu}}\|^2}{\sigma_0^2} = \min_{\boldsymbol{\mu}\in\mathrm{Col}(\mathbf{X})} \frac{\|\mathbf{y}-\boldsymbol{\mu}_0-\boldsymbol{\mu}\|^2}{\sigma_0^2} \sim \chi_{N-K}^2 \tag{10.3}$$

where the reduction in the degrees of freedom from N to $N-K$ reflects the number of parameters in the minimization. Therefore

$$s^2 = \frac{\|\mathbf{y}-\hat{\boldsymbol{\mu}}\|^2}{N-K} \sim \frac{\sigma_0^2}{N-K}\chi_{N-K}^2$$

Proposition 10 also has a remarkable feature that we have not encountered before: it states that the conditional distribution of s^2 given $\mathbf{X}$ does not actually depend on $\mathbf{X}$. Therefore, the marginal and conditional distributions of s^2 are identical and s^2 is independent of $\mathbf{X}$. This is not true of $\hat{\boldsymbol{\mu}}$, $\mathbf{y}-\hat{\boldsymbol{\mu}}$, or $\hat{\boldsymbol{\beta}}$. We will see more examples of this below.

In the next two sections, we describe the application of these distributional results for OLS statistics. Propositions 9 and 10 describe the joint distribution of the OLS estimators $\hat{\boldsymbol{\beta}}$ and s^2 completely. In the next section, we construct interval estimators for $\boldsymbol{\beta}_0$ and σ_0^2 from this joint distribution. These interval estimators are a natural extension of the point estimators $\hat{\boldsymbol{\beta}}$ and s^2, giving a region of likely values that reflects statistical precision and covariance. In particular, we show how the variance ellipse plays a role in the interval estimator for $\boldsymbol{\beta}_0$.

10.3 INTERVAL ESTIMATORS

We will approach interval estimation with several steps. Although econometric analysis tends to focus on $\boldsymbol{\beta}_0$, we will begin with the variance parameter σ_0^2. This interval estimator is simpler in several ways: it is univariate and it is a direct application of Proposition 10. Thus, we use this case as an introduction to interval estimation. In our second and third steps, we construct interval estimators for $\boldsymbol{\beta}_0$, supposing that σ_0^2 is known and then supposing that it is unknown. In both cases, the variance ellipse of $\hat{\boldsymbol{\beta}}$ provides the basic shape of the interval estimator. The distribution theory determines the radius of the ellipse. We discuss linear functions of $\boldsymbol{\beta}_0$ in our fourth, and final, step. Important special cases include interval estimators for individual elements of $\boldsymbol{\beta}_0$ and interval estimators for predictions of the LHS variable at particular values of the RHS variables.

10.3.1 Variance

Let us begin with finding an interval estimator for σ_0^2. The distribution of s^2 depends only on σ_0^2 and this statistic is independently distributed with $\hat{\boldsymbol{\beta}}$, so a univariate, marginal analysis is appropriate. In general, one constructs an interval estimator from a probability statement about a *pivotal statistic*. In this case, we use the statistic $(N-K)s^2/\sigma_0^2$. As stated in Proposition 10, the distribution of this statistic is the chi-square distribution with $N-K$ degrees of freedom. This statistic is called *pivotal* because its distribution does not depend on unknown parameters.

Thus, we can always compute the probability of an event for the pivotal statistic. In particular, we can compute the probability that the pivotal statistic will fall in a specified interval $[c_0, c_1]$ in the next sample:

$$\Pr\{(N-K)\,s^2/\sigma_0^2 \in [c_0, c_1]\} = \Pr\{\chi^2_{N-K} \in [c_0, c_1]\}$$

Also, we can reverse the process and, given a probability $1-\alpha$, we can find an interval $[c_0(\alpha), c_1(\alpha)]$ with that level of probability:

$$\Pr\{\chi^2_{N-K} \in [c_0(\alpha), c_1(\alpha)]\} \equiv 1-\alpha \tag{10.4}$$

This enables us to convert the abstract probability statement into an interval estimator for the unknown σ_0^2. Given α and $[c_0(\alpha), c_1(\alpha)]$,

$$\begin{aligned} 1-\alpha &= \Pr\left\{c_0(\alpha) \le \frac{(N-K)\,s^2}{\sigma_0^2} \le c_1(\alpha)\right\} \\ &= \Pr\left\{\frac{(N-K)\,s^2}{c_1(\alpha)} \le \sigma_0^2 \le \frac{(N-K)\,s^2}{c_0(\alpha)}\right\} \end{aligned}$$

With probability $1-\alpha$, the interval

$$\left[\frac{N-K}{c_1(\alpha)}s^2, \frac{N-K}{c_0(\alpha)}s^2\right]$$

will contain σ_0^2.

This interval is an interval estimator for σ_0^2. Like the point estimator s^2, it is random in the sense that new samples will yield different intervals. What is systematic about these intervals is that under repeated sampling we expect these intervals to contain σ_0^2 $100(1-\alpha)\%$ of the time. For this reason, such intervals are often called $100(1-\alpha)\%$ *confidence intervals*.

This interval estimator is not unique, even given α. The most convenient choices for the cs are the *quantile values*, $\chi^2_{N-K;\alpha/2}$ and $\chi^2_{N-K;1-\alpha/2}$, where

$$q \equiv \Pr\left\{\chi_\nu^2 \le \chi^2_{\nu;q}\right\}, \qquad 0 < q < 1$$

defines the qth quantile of the χ_ν^2 distribution. Mathematical and statistical software frequently provides functions for such calculations. The resultant interval estimator is

$$\left[s^2\frac{N-K}{\chi^2_{N-K;1-\alpha/2}}, s^2\frac{N-K}{\chi^2_{N-K;\alpha/2}}\right]$$

which contains σ_0^2 with probability $1-\alpha$ in repeated sampling.[5] Another method for choosing these endpoint parameters is to minimize the expected length of the interval. For this case, one must use special tables or computational methods to find[6]

$$\min_{c_0,c_1|1-\alpha=\Pr\{c_0\le\chi^2_{N-K}\le c_1\}} \frac{1}{c_0}-\frac{1}{c_1} \quad \Leftrightarrow \quad \begin{cases} 1-\alpha = \Pr\{c_0 \le \chi^2_{N-K} \le c_1\} \\ c_0^{N-K+2}e^{-c_0} = c_1^{N-K+2}e^{-c_1} \end{cases}$$

This interval differs from the previous one because the p.d.f. of the chi-square distribution is asymmetric.

10.3.2 Coefficient Vector with Known Variance

To obtain an interval estimator for $\boldsymbol{\beta}_0$, we use a pivotal statistic similar to the one that yields an interval estimator for σ_0^2. There is a chi-square distribution associated with $\hat{\boldsymbol{\mu}}$ and $\hat{\boldsymbol{\beta}}$ that is analogous to that for s^2 in Proposition 10. According to Lemma 10.1,

$$\frac{\left\|\hat{\boldsymbol{\mu}}-\boldsymbol{\mu}_0\right\|^2}{\sigma_0^2} = \min_{\boldsymbol{\mu}\in\text{Col}^\perp(\mathbf{X})} \frac{\|\mathbf{y}-\boldsymbol{\mu}_0-\boldsymbol{\mu}\|^2}{\sigma_0^2} \sim \chi_K^2 \tag{10.5}$$

The degrees of freedom equal K, which is N minus the $N-K$ degrees of freedom in the choice of the minimizing $\boldsymbol{\mu}$. Equivalently, K is the dimension of $\text{Col}(\mathbf{X})$, the subspace to which $\hat{\boldsymbol{\mu}}$ belongs. And like the sum of squared fitted residuals, the squared length of $\hat{\boldsymbol{\mu}}-\boldsymbol{\mu}_0$ is independent of $\mathbf{X}$.

[5] This is a generalization of an interval estimator familiar to those who have studied the normal location model [see equation (E.6), p. 906].

[6] One can easily derive this characterization using the p.d.f. for the chi-square distribution given in Definition D.30 (p. 888).

When σ_0^2 is known, $\left\|\hat{\boldsymbol{\mu}}-\boldsymbol{\mu}_0\right\|^2/\sigma_0^2$ is a pivotal statistic for constructing an interval estimator for $\boldsymbol{\mu}_0$ or $\boldsymbol{\beta}_0$. We will construct the interval estimator for $\boldsymbol{\mu}_0$ first, following our usual pattern. Because $\boldsymbol{\mu}_0$ and $\boldsymbol{\beta}_0$ are one to one, the interval estimator for $\boldsymbol{\beta}_0$ follows directly. For $\boldsymbol{\mu}_0$ we consider probability intervals of the form

$$1-\alpha=\Pr\left\{\chi_K^2 \leq c_1(\alpha)\right\}$$

which lead to

$$1-\alpha=\Pr\left\{\left\|\hat{\boldsymbol{\mu}}-\boldsymbol{\mu}_0\right\|^2 \leq \sigma_0^2\ \chi_{K;1-\alpha}^2\right\}$$

and the $100\,(1-\alpha)\%$ interval estimator for $\boldsymbol{\mu}_0$

$$\left\{\boldsymbol{\mu} \in \operatorname{Col}(\mathbf{X}) \mid \left\|\boldsymbol{\mu}-\hat{\boldsymbol{\mu}}\right\|^2 \leq \sigma_0^2\ \chi_{K;1-\alpha}^2\right\}$$

Note that this interval is closely related to the variance ellipsoid of $\hat{\boldsymbol{\mu}}$,

$$\mathbb{V}_{\hat{\mu}}=\left\{\mathbf{z} \in \operatorname{Col}(\mathbf{X}) \mid \mathbf{z}'\mathbf{z} \leq \sigma_0^2\right\}$$

described in (8.5) on p. 161. There are two differences. The interval estimator is centered on $\hat{\boldsymbol{\mu}}$, rather than the origin, and its squared radius is $\sigma_0^2\ \chi_{K;1-\alpha}^2$, rather than σ_0^2. Hence, the variance matrix determines the shape and baseline volume of the interval estimator for $\boldsymbol{\mu}_0$. But the point estimator $\hat{\boldsymbol{\mu}}$ determines the location of the interval estimator and the confidence level $1-\alpha$ scales the volume of the interval estimator.

We place no lower bound comparable to the c_0 in (10.4) in the interval estimator for $\boldsymbol{\mu}_0$. If we had used such an interval, then the confidence interval for $\boldsymbol{\mu}_0$ would have a hole at the center, excluding the point estimator $\hat{\boldsymbol{\mu}}$ from the interval estimator. This paradoxical situation does not arise without the lower bound. It can be ruled out formally by seeking the confidence interval for $\boldsymbol{\mu}_0$ with the smallest Euclidean volume.

These observations also apply to the interval estimator for $\boldsymbol{\beta}_0$. Using the one-to-one relationship $\hat{\boldsymbol{\mu}}=\mathbf{X}\hat{\boldsymbol{\beta}}$, we find the pivotal statistic

$$\frac{\left(\boldsymbol{\beta}_0-\hat{\boldsymbol{\beta}}\right)'\mathbf{X}'\mathbf{X}\left(\boldsymbol{\beta}_0-\hat{\boldsymbol{\beta}}\right)}{\sigma_0^2}=\frac{\left\|\hat{\boldsymbol{\mu}}-\boldsymbol{\mu}_0\right\|^2}{\sigma_0^2} \sim \chi_K^2 \tag{10.6}$$

and the corresponding interval estimator for $\boldsymbol{\beta}_0$,

$$\left\{\boldsymbol{\beta} \in \mathbb{R}^K \,\middle|\, \left(\boldsymbol{\beta}-\hat{\boldsymbol{\beta}}\right)'\mathbf{X}'\mathbf{X}\left(\boldsymbol{\beta}-\hat{\boldsymbol{\beta}}\right) \leq \sigma_0^2\ \chi_{K;1-\alpha}^2\right\} \tag{10.7}$$

Naturally, this interval estimator is also a simple transformation of the variance ellipse of $\hat{\boldsymbol{\beta}}$,[7]

$$\mathbb{V}_{\hat{\beta}} \equiv \left\{\mathbf{z} \in \mathbb{R}^K \mid \mathbf{z}'\mathbf{X}'\mathbf{X}\mathbf{z} \leq \sigma_0^2\right\}$$

The center of $\mathbb{V}_{\hat{\beta}}$ has been translated from the origin to the point estimator $\hat{\boldsymbol{\beta}}$ and the squared radius has been changed from σ_0^2 to $\sigma_0^2\ \chi_{K;1-\alpha}^2$. This relationship between the interval estimator and the variance ellipsoid seems natural. One expects the region of high probability to reflect the

[7] See equation (8.6).

variance and covariance of the elements of $\hat{\boldsymbol{\beta}}$. Under Assumption 10.1, we find a direct influence of the variance matrix on the estimation interval through the variance ellipse.

10.3.3 Coefficient Vector with Unknown Variance

Such confidence intervals as (10.7) largely hold pedagogical interest. Because σ_0^2 is generally unknown, the boundaries of the interval actually cannot be calculated. However, we can construct a feasible alternative by noticing that we have found two statistics, the squared lengths of $\hat{\boldsymbol{\mu}} - \boldsymbol{\mu}_0$ and $\mathbf{y} - \hat{\boldsymbol{\mu}}$, that are proportional to chi-square random variables, where σ_0^2 is the common factor of the proportionality. We can combine these two statistics in a ratio to create a pivotal statistic with a distribution that does not depend on σ_0^2:

$$\frac{\left\|\hat{\boldsymbol{\mu}} - \boldsymbol{\mu}_0\right\|^2 / \sigma_0^2}{\left\|\mathbf{y} - \hat{\boldsymbol{\mu}}\right\|^2 / \sigma_0^2} = \frac{\left(\hat{\boldsymbol{\beta}} - \boldsymbol{\beta}_0\right)' \mathbf{X}'\mathbf{X} \left(\hat{\boldsymbol{\beta}} - \boldsymbol{\beta}_0\right)}{s^2 (N - K)} \sim \frac{\chi_K^2}{\chi_{N-K}^2} \tag{10.8}$$

Because the two statistics are independently distributed (Proposition 9, point 3, or Lemma 10.1), we can be sure that σ_0^2 does not enter the distribution in any way. We could just as well use the reciprocal of this statistic, but placing terms involving $\boldsymbol{\beta}_0$ in the numerator is convenient for deriving elliptical sets comparable to (10.7).

Given the ability to compute critical values from the distribution of the ratio (10.8), our confidence interval will be analogous to the one we derived for a known variance. Precedent dictates that we create a slightly different ratio, by dividing each chi-square random variable with its degrees of freedom parameter:

$$\frac{\left(\boldsymbol{\beta}_0 - \hat{\boldsymbol{\beta}}\right)' \mathbf{X}'\mathbf{X} \left(\boldsymbol{\beta}_0 - \hat{\boldsymbol{\beta}}\right) / K}{s^2} \sim \frac{\chi_K^2 / K}{\chi_{N-K}^2 / (N - K)} \tag{10.9}$$

These normalizations give both numerator and denominator expectations equal to 1. The ratio on the RHS has the *Snedecor* $F_{K,N-K}$ *distribution* (Definition D.32, p. 890).[8] This leads to our next proposition.

PROPOSITION 11 (*F* STATISTIC) *Under Assumptions 3.1, 6.1, 7.1, and 10.1,*

$$\frac{\left(\boldsymbol{\beta}_0 - \hat{\boldsymbol{\beta}}\right)' \mathbf{X}'\mathbf{X} \left(\boldsymbol{\beta}_0 - \hat{\boldsymbol{\beta}}\right) / K}{s^2} \sim F_{K,N-K}$$

In effect, a feasible interval estimator for $\boldsymbol{\beta}_0$ replaces σ_0^2 with s^2 and the chi-square critical value with a critical value for the F distribution: denoting the qth quantile of the $F_{K,N-K}$ distribution by

[8] See Theorem D.15 on p. 891.

$$q \equiv \Pr\{F_{K,N-K} \leq F_{K,N-K;q}\}$$

then

$$1-\alpha = \Pr\left\{\frac{\left(\boldsymbol{\beta}_0 - \hat{\boldsymbol{\beta}}\right)' \mathbf{X}'\mathbf{X}\left(\boldsymbol{\beta}_0 - \hat{\boldsymbol{\beta}}\right)/K}{s^2} \leq F_{K,N-K;1-\alpha}\right\}$$
$$= \Pr\left\{\left(\boldsymbol{\beta}_0 - \hat{\boldsymbol{\beta}}\right)' \mathbf{X}'\mathbf{X}\left(\boldsymbol{\beta}_0 - \hat{\boldsymbol{\beta}}\right) \leq s^2\, K\, F_{K,N-K;1-\alpha}\right\}$$

and

$$\left\{\boldsymbol{\beta} \in \mathbb{R}^K \,\middle|\, \left(\boldsymbol{\beta} - \hat{\boldsymbol{\beta}}\right)' \mathbf{X}'\mathbf{X}\left(\boldsymbol{\beta} - \hat{\boldsymbol{\beta}}\right) \leq s^2\, K\, F_{K,N-K;1-\alpha}\right\} \tag{10.10}$$

is the feasible counterpart to (10.7). Note that the basic shape of the interval estimator remains proportional to the variance ellipsoid. On average, however, this feasible interval has a larger radius than the infeasible one, owing to the "substitution" of the constant σ_0^2 with the "noisy" alternative s^2.

10.3.4 Linear Functions of Coefficients

To complete our study of OLS interval estimators, we consider interval estimation of linear combinations $\mathbf{R}\boldsymbol{\beta}_0$ of $\boldsymbol{\beta}_0$. An important special case is a single element of $\boldsymbol{\beta}_0$: the matrix $\mathbf{R}$ can be a row vector that selects one coefficient. Another important special case is a vector of predictions for the LHS variable. Each row of $\mathbf{R}$ can be a vector of values for the RHS variables $\mathbf{x}$. Whatever the specification of $\mathbf{R}$, we proceed in essentially the same way as in the previous sections.

Let $\mathbf{R}$ be $(K-M) \times K$ and full row rank. As another linear transformation of $\mathbf{y}$, the mean of $\mathbf{R}\hat{\boldsymbol{\beta}}$ is $\mathbf{R}\boldsymbol{\beta}_0$, its conditional variance is $\mathbf{R}\,\mathrm{Var}[\hat{\boldsymbol{\beta}} \mid \mathbf{X}]\mathbf{R}' = \sigma_0^2 \cdot \mathbf{R}\left(\mathbf{X}'\mathbf{X}\right)^{-1}\mathbf{R}'$, and its conditional distribution is multivariate normal:

$$\mathbf{R}\hat{\boldsymbol{\beta}} \mid \mathbf{X} \sim \mathfrak{N}\left[\mathbf{R}\boldsymbol{\beta}_0,\ \sigma_0^2 \cdot \mathbf{R}(\mathbf{X}'\mathbf{X})^{-1}\mathbf{R}'\right]$$

It follows from the following lemma that the squared generalized distance

$$\frac{(\mathbf{R}\boldsymbol{\beta} - \mathbf{R}\boldsymbol{\beta}_0)'\left[\mathbf{R}\left(\mathbf{X}'\mathbf{X}\right)^{-1}\mathbf{R}'\right]^{-1}(\mathbf{R}\boldsymbol{\beta} - \mathbf{R}\boldsymbol{\beta}_0)}{\sigma_0^2} \sim \chi^2_{K-M} \tag{10.11}$$

also has a chi-square distribution.

> **Lemma 10.2 (Chi-Square Quadratic Forms)** *Let $\mathbf{z} \in \mathbb{R}^M$ possess the $\mathfrak{N}(\boldsymbol{\mu}, \boldsymbol{\Omega})$ distribution where $\boldsymbol{\Omega}$ is nonsingular. Then $(\mathbf{z}-\boldsymbol{\mu})'\,\boldsymbol{\Omega}^{-1}\,(\mathbf{z}-\boldsymbol{\mu}) \sim \chi^2_M$.*

We prove this lemma in Section 10.5.2. For the moment, note the similarity to (10.6). Both are quadratic forms like those in variance ellipsoids (7.3): the central matrix $[\sigma_0^2 \cdot \mathbf{R}(\mathbf{X}'\mathbf{X})^{-1}\mathbf{R}']^{-1}$

is the inverse of the variance matrix of the "wings" $\mathbf{R}\boldsymbol{\beta} - \mathbf{R}\boldsymbol{\beta}_0$. The degrees of freedom equal the number of elements in the wing terms.

To form a confidence interval, we use the pivotal statistic

$$\frac{(\mathbf{R}\boldsymbol{\beta}_0 - \mathbf{R}\hat{\boldsymbol{\beta}})'\left(\mathbf{R}(\mathbf{X}'\mathbf{X})^{-1}\mathbf{R}'\right)^{-1}(\mathbf{R}\boldsymbol{\beta}_0 - \mathbf{R}\hat{\boldsymbol{\beta}})/(K-M)}{s^2} \sim F_{K-M,N-K}, \tag{10.12}$$

the analogue to (10.9). The resultant interval estimator is

$$\left\{\boldsymbol{\gamma} \in \text{Col}(\mathbf{R}) \mid (\boldsymbol{\gamma} - \mathbf{R}\hat{\boldsymbol{\beta}})'\left[\mathbf{R}(\mathbf{X}'\mathbf{X})^{-1}\mathbf{R}'\right]^{-1}(\boldsymbol{\gamma} - \mathbf{R}\hat{\boldsymbol{\beta}}) \le s^2\ (K-M)\ F_{K-M,N-K;1-\alpha}\right\}$$

the analogue to (10.10).

10.4 EFFICIENCY OF OLS

The final implication of Assumption 10.1 (Normal Distribution) concerns the relative efficiency of the OLS estimators. Under the additional assumption of normally distributed data, we have a stronger property for the OLS coefficients than Theorem 7 (Gauss–Markov, p. 187). We also obtain a form of relative efficiency for s^2, the estimator of the variance. Just as Assumption 7.1 (Second Moments), we find that the normality assumption delivers both distributional and efficiency properties for OLS estimators.

Proposition 12 (Efficiency of OLS) *Given Assumptions 3.1, 6.1, 7.1, and 10.1, $(\hat{\boldsymbol{\beta}}, s^2)$ is efficient relative to all unbiased estimators of $(\boldsymbol{\beta}_0, \sigma_0^2)$.*

This proposition relates closely to another property of the OLS estimators: $\hat{\boldsymbol{\beta}}$ is the maximum likelihood estimator of $\boldsymbol{\beta}_0$ and s^2 is proportional to the MLE of σ_0^2.[9] We will defer our study of maximum likelihood estimators to Chapter 14, having already covered a good deal of ground in this chapter. In Chapter 14, we prove this proposition on pp. 309–310.

In terms of the conceptual organization of the material, however, the efficiency of OLS estimators belongs at this point. As we have developed the classical statistical theory of OLS, we introduce assumptions and deduce their consequences. We find that there is an overall pattern to the theory. The second-moment assumption delivers second-moment results of two kinds: the second moments of the *distribution* of our estimators and the *relative efficiency* of our estimators. The normality assumption has parallel results: the complete *distribution* of our estimators and stronger *relative efficiency*.

10.5 BASIC DISTRIBUTION THEORY

The fundamental distribution theory for the propositions of this chapter begins with the multivariate normal distribution. We establish its key properties, listed on pp. 196 and 197, first.

[9] The impatient reader may find the proof of this proposition for $\hat{\boldsymbol{\beta}}$ on p. 309. Part of the proof for s^2 is sketched in Exercise 14.16.

Mathematical notes for this chapter cover the formal details of the multivariate normal distribution and its relationship to the chi-square and F distributions. We use the results to prove the propositions of this chapter.

10.5.1 The Multivariate Normal Distribution

In this section, we establish several results for the multivariate normal distribution. It is simplest to begin with the multivariate normal distribution with a nonsingular variance matrix. For this case, we will explain one of the most important properties of the multivariate normal distribution: linear combinations of multivariate normal random variables also possess a multivariate normal distribution. Because we are studying *linear* statistics, this property will make our analysis relatively tidy.

Second, we will derive conditional and marginal distributions for subvectors of multivariate normal random variables. As luck (and mathematics) would have it, both of these distributions also belong to the multivariate normal family. A closely related, and equally important, property follows: multivariate normal random variables are independent if and only if they are uncorrelated. For random variables in general, independence implies zero covariance but not the reverse. The multivariate normal distribution presents a notable exception.

Finally, we will generalize to the case of singular variance matrices. The singularity of the variances of $\hat{\boldsymbol{\mu}}$ and $\mathbf{y} - \hat{\boldsymbol{\mu}}$ has already played an important role in our explanation of the Gauss–Markov theorem and the variance estimator s^2. This role will be extended under the assumption of normality.[10]

DEFINITION 17 (MULTIVARIATE NORMAL DISTRIBUTION) *The vector of random variables* $\mathbf{y}$ *has a* multivariate normal distribution *[denoted* $\mathfrak{N}(\boldsymbol{\mu}, \boldsymbol{\Omega})$*] with mean vector* $\boldsymbol{\mu}$ *and nonsingular variance matrix* $\boldsymbol{\Omega}$ *if the p.d.f. of* $\mathbf{y}$*, denoted* $f_y(\cdot)$*, is*

$$\begin{aligned} f_{\mathbf{y}}(\mathbf{w}) &= \phi(\mathbf{w} - \boldsymbol{\mu}, \boldsymbol{\Omega}) \\ &\equiv \det(2\pi \cdot \boldsymbol{\Omega})^{-1/2} \exp\left[-\frac{1}{2}(\mathbf{w} - \boldsymbol{\mu})'\boldsymbol{\Omega}^{-1}(\mathbf{w} - \boldsymbol{\mu})\right] \end{aligned}$$

Note that the multivariate normal p.d.f. is completely determined by the first two moments of this distribution (Property 2, p. 196). As a result, when presented with a multivariate normal random variable, one only need determine its mean and its variance to obtain its complete distribution.

Also note that the quadratic form defining a variance ellipse is a fundamental term in the multivariate normal p.d.f. Contour sets of the p.d.f. are proportional to the boundary of the variance ellipse (7.3) (Property 1, p. 196). The consequence of this elliptical symmetry is that convenient multivariate probability intervals for the multivariate normal distribution are variance ellipses.

Now we present a quintessential property of the multivariate normal distribution (Property 3, p. 197), that linear transformations of multivariate normal random variables are also normally distributed.

[10] The univariate normal distribution is reviewed in Appendix D.4.

Lemma 10.3 *Let* $\boldsymbol{\mu} \in \mathbb{R}^N$ *be a vector of* N *constants, let* $\boldsymbol{\Omega}$ *be a nonsingular* $N \times N$, *and let* $\mathbf{z} \sim \mathfrak{N}(\boldsymbol{\mu}, \boldsymbol{\Omega})$. *For every* $\boldsymbol{\alpha} \in \mathbb{R}^N$ *and nonsingular* $N \times N$ *matrix* $\mathbf{B}$, $\mathbf{y} = \boldsymbol{\alpha} + \mathbf{Bz}$ *has the nonsingular multivariate normal distribution* $\mathfrak{N}(\boldsymbol{\alpha} + \mathbf{B}\boldsymbol{\mu}, \mathbf{B}\boldsymbol{\Omega}\mathbf{B}')$.

Proof. If $\mathbf{y} = \boldsymbol{\alpha} + \mathbf{Bz}$ where $\mathbf{B}$ is nonsingular, then $\mathbf{z} = \mathbf{B}^{-1}(\mathbf{y} - \boldsymbol{\alpha})$ and $\partial\mathbf{z}/\partial\mathbf{y}' = \mathbf{B}^{-1}$. According to Definition 17 and Theorem D.6 (Transformation of Variables, p. 882), the p.d.f. of $\mathbf{y}$ is

$$f_{\mathbf{y}}(\mathbf{w}) = \left|\det(\mathbf{B}^{-1})\right| \cdot \phi\left[\mathbf{B}^{-1}(\mathbf{w} - \boldsymbol{\alpha}) - \boldsymbol{\mu},\ \boldsymbol{\Omega}\right]$$

Noting that

$$\begin{aligned}
&\left[\mathbf{B}^{-1}(\mathbf{w} - \boldsymbol{\alpha}) - \boldsymbol{\mu}\right]' \boldsymbol{\Omega}^{-1} \left[\mathbf{B}^{-1}(\mathbf{w} - \boldsymbol{\alpha}) - \boldsymbol{\mu}\right] \\
&\quad = (\mathbf{w} - \boldsymbol{\alpha} - \mathbf{B}\boldsymbol{\mu})' \left(\mathbf{B}^{-1}\right)' \boldsymbol{\Omega}^{-1}\mathbf{B}^{-1} (\mathbf{w} - \boldsymbol{\alpha} - \mathbf{B}\boldsymbol{\mu}) \\
&\quad = (\mathbf{w} - \boldsymbol{\alpha} - \mathbf{B}\boldsymbol{\mu})' \left(\mathbf{B}\boldsymbol{\Omega}\mathbf{B}'\right)^{-1} (\mathbf{w} - \boldsymbol{\alpha} - \mathbf{B}\boldsymbol{\mu})
\end{aligned}$$

and[11]

$$\begin{aligned}
|\det(\mathbf{B})| \sqrt{\det(2\pi\boldsymbol{\Omega})} &= \sqrt{[\det(\mathbf{B})]^2 \det(2\pi\boldsymbol{\Omega})} \\
&= \sqrt{\det(\mathbf{B}) \det(2\pi\boldsymbol{\Omega}) \det(\mathbf{B}')} \\
&= \sqrt{\det(2\pi\mathbf{B}\boldsymbol{\Omega}\mathbf{B}')}
\end{aligned}$$

gives

$$f_{\mathbf{y}}(\mathbf{w}) = \phi(\mathbf{w} - \boldsymbol{\alpha} - \mathbf{B}\boldsymbol{\mu},\ \mathbf{B}\boldsymbol{\Omega}\mathbf{B}')$$

which is the $\mathfrak{N}(\boldsymbol{\alpha} + \mathbf{B}\boldsymbol{\mu}, \mathbf{B}\boldsymbol{\Omega}\mathbf{B}')$ p.d.f. □

The multivariate normal p.d.f. is often motivated as the p.d.f. of a nonsingular linear transformation of a vector of *independent and identically distributed* (i.i.d.) standard normal random variables. If $\mathbf{z} \sim \mathfrak{N}(\mathbf{0}, \mathbf{I})$, then $\boldsymbol{\mu} + \mathbf{A}z \sim \mathfrak{N}(\boldsymbol{\mu}, \boldsymbol{\Omega})$ where $\boldsymbol{\Omega} = \mathbf{AA}'$. A corollary to Lemma 10.3 is that an $\mathfrak{N}(\boldsymbol{\mu}, \boldsymbol{\Omega})$ random variable can always be transformed into a vector of i.i.d. standard normal random variables. Given the variance matrix $\boldsymbol{\Omega}$, we can always find a nonsingular matrix $\mathbf{A}$ such that $\boldsymbol{\Omega} = \mathbf{AA}'$. A leading example of such an $\mathbf{A}$ is the Cholesky matrix described in Section 7.6.1. Then Lemma 10.3 states that if $\mathbf{y} \sim \mathfrak{N}(\boldsymbol{\mu}, \boldsymbol{\Omega})$ then $\mathbf{A}^{-1}(\mathbf{y} - \boldsymbol{\mu}) \sim \mathfrak{N}(\mathbf{0}, \mathbf{I})$. This ability to linearly transform a vector of correlated normal random variables into a vector of uncorrelated normal random variables is heavily exploited in statistics. The proof of the next lemma is one example.

The linear property of the multivariate normal distribution is intimately associated with another property: that marginal and conditional distributions are also multivariate normal.

[11] These manipulations use Lemma C.4.

Lemma 10.4 (Multivariate Normal Factorization) *Let* $\mathbf{y} \sim \mathfrak{N}(\boldsymbol{\mu}, \boldsymbol{\Omega})$ *and partition*

$$\mathbf{y} = \begin{bmatrix} \mathbf{y}_1 \\ \mathbf{y}_2 \end{bmatrix}, \qquad \boldsymbol{\mu} = \begin{bmatrix} \boldsymbol{\mu}_1 \\ \boldsymbol{\mu}_2 \end{bmatrix}, \qquad \boldsymbol{\Omega} = \begin{bmatrix} \boldsymbol{\Omega}_{11} & \boldsymbol{\Omega}_{12} \\ \boldsymbol{\Omega}'_{12} & \boldsymbol{\Omega}_{22} \end{bmatrix}$$

Then the marginal distribution of $\mathbf{y}_2$ *is* $\mathfrak{N}(\boldsymbol{\mu}_2, \boldsymbol{\Omega}_{22})$ *and the conditional distribution of* $\mathbf{y}_1$ *given* $\mathbf{y}_2$ *is*

$$\mathbf{y}_1 \mid \mathbf{y}_2 \sim \mathfrak{N}\left[\boldsymbol{\mu}_1 + \boldsymbol{\Omega}_{12}\boldsymbol{\Omega}_{22}^{-1}(\mathbf{y}_2 - \boldsymbol{\mu}_2)\,,\ \boldsymbol{\Omega}_{11} - \boldsymbol{\Omega}_{12}\boldsymbol{\Omega}_{22}^{-1}\boldsymbol{\Omega}'_{12}\right]$$

Proof. According to Lemma 7.5 (Partitioned Quadratic, p. 138),

$$\begin{aligned}\mathbf{z}'\boldsymbol{\Omega}^{-1}\mathbf{z} &= \left(\mathbf{z}_1 - \boldsymbol{\Omega}_{12}\boldsymbol{\Omega}_{22}^{-1}\mathbf{z}_2\right)'\left(\boldsymbol{\Omega}_{11} - \boldsymbol{\Omega}_{12}\boldsymbol{\Omega}_{22}^{-1}\boldsymbol{\Omega}'_{12}\right)^{-1}\left(\mathbf{z}_1 - \boldsymbol{\Omega}_{12}\boldsymbol{\Omega}_{22}^{-1}\mathbf{z}_2\right)\\ &\quad + \mathbf{z}_2'\boldsymbol{\Omega}_{22}^{-1}\mathbf{z}_2\end{aligned}$$

Exercise 10.6 states that

$$\det \boldsymbol{\Omega} = \det\left(\boldsymbol{\Omega}_{11} - \boldsymbol{\Omega}_{12}\boldsymbol{\Omega}_{22}^{-1}\boldsymbol{\Omega}'_{12}\right) \cdot \det \boldsymbol{\Omega}_{22}$$

For brevity, let $\boldsymbol{\gamma} \equiv \boldsymbol{\Omega}_{22}^{-1}\boldsymbol{\Omega}_{21}$ and $\boldsymbol{\Omega}_{1|2} \equiv \boldsymbol{\Omega}_{11} - \boldsymbol{\Omega}_{12}\boldsymbol{\Omega}_{22}^{-1}\boldsymbol{\Omega}'_{12}$. After setting $\mathbf{z} = \mathbf{y} - \boldsymbol{\mu}$, we can write the joint p.d.f. of $\mathbf{y}$ as

$$\begin{aligned}\phi(\mathbf{y} - \boldsymbol{\mu}, \boldsymbol{\Omega}) &= \det(2\pi\boldsymbol{\Omega})^{-1/2}\exp\left(-\frac{1}{2}\mathbf{z}'\boldsymbol{\Omega}^{-1}\mathbf{z}\right)\\ &= \det(2\pi\boldsymbol{\Omega}_{1|2})^{-1/2}\cdot\det(2\pi\boldsymbol{\Omega}_{22})^{-1/2}\\ &\quad \cdot\exp\left[-\frac{1}{2}\left(\mathbf{z}_1 - \boldsymbol{\gamma}'\mathbf{z}_2\right)'\boldsymbol{\Omega}_{1|2}^{-1}\left(\mathbf{z}_1 - \boldsymbol{\gamma}'\mathbf{z}_2\right)\right]\\ &\quad \cdot\exp\left(-\frac{1}{2}\mathbf{z}_2'\boldsymbol{\Omega}_{22}^{-1}\mathbf{z}_2\right)\\ &= \phi(\mathbf{z}_1 - \boldsymbol{\gamma}'\mathbf{z}_2,\ \boldsymbol{\Omega}_{1|2})\cdot\phi(\mathbf{z}_2,\ \boldsymbol{\Omega}_{22})\\ &= \phi(\mathbf{y}_1 - \boldsymbol{\mu}_1 - \boldsymbol{\gamma}'(\mathbf{y}_2 - \boldsymbol{\mu}_2),\ \boldsymbol{\Omega}_{1|2})\cdot\phi(\mathbf{y}_2 - \boldsymbol{\mu}_2,\ \boldsymbol{\Omega}_{22})\end{aligned}$$

This is the product of two normal p.d.f.s. Conditional on $\mathbf{y}_2$, the first factor integrates over $\mathbf{y}_1$ to 1 so that the second factor is the marginal p.d.f. of $\mathbf{y}_2$. Dividing the joint p.d.f. by this marginal, we obtain the conditional p.d.f. for $\mathbf{y}_1$ given $\mathbf{y}_2$ as the first factor. The distributions have the moments specified in the lemma. □

Not only is the conditional p.d.f. multivariate normal. Note that the normal distribution delivers a linear conditional mean and a constant conditional variance. Therefore, for this distribution, the MMSE predictor and the MMSE *linear* predictor coincide; in our notation, $\mathrm{E}[\mathbf{y}_1 \mid \mathbf{y}_2] = \mathrm{E}^*[\mathbf{y}_1 \mid \mathbf{y}_2]$.

A third, and very important, property of the multivariate normal distribution concerns covariances. In general, two random variables may be uncorrelated and dependently distributed.

But if two multivariate normal random variables are uncorrelated, then they are independently distributed (Property 4, p. 197). The normality of the conditional p.d.f. is responsible for this.

Lemma 10.5 *Let* $\mathbf{y} \sim \mathfrak{N}(\boldsymbol{\mu}, \boldsymbol{\Omega})$ *and partition*

$$\mathbf{y} = \begin{bmatrix} \mathbf{y}_1 \\ \mathbf{y}_2 \end{bmatrix}, \qquad \mu = \begin{bmatrix} \mu_1 \\ \mu_2 \end{bmatrix}, \qquad \boldsymbol{\Omega} = \begin{bmatrix} \boldsymbol{\Omega}_{11} & \boldsymbol{\Omega}_{12} \\ \boldsymbol{\Omega}'_{12} & \boldsymbol{\Omega}_{22} \end{bmatrix}$$

Then $\mathbf{y}_1 \sim \mathfrak{N}(\boldsymbol{\mu}_1, \boldsymbol{\Omega}_{11})$ *independently of* $\mathbf{y}_2 \sim \mathfrak{N}(\boldsymbol{\mu}_2, \boldsymbol{\Omega}_{22})$ *if and only if* $\boldsymbol{\Omega}_{12} = \mathbf{0}$.

Proof. Using Lemma 10.4, $\boldsymbol{\Omega}_{12} = \mathbf{0}$ if and only if $\boldsymbol{\Omega}_{12}\boldsymbol{\Omega}_{22}^{-1} = \mathbf{0}$ if and only if

$$\phi(\mathbf{y}_1 - \boldsymbol{\mu}_1, \boldsymbol{\Omega}_{11}) \cdot \phi(\mathbf{y}_2 - \boldsymbol{\mu}_2, \boldsymbol{\Omega}_{22}) = \phi(\mathbf{y} - \boldsymbol{\mu}, \boldsymbol{\Omega})$$

so that the joint p.d.f. is the product of two marginal p.d.f.s and $\mathbf{y}_1$ and $\mathbf{y}_2$ are independently distributed. □

Finally, we must define the multivariate normal distribution for such random vectors as $\mathbf{y} - \hat{\boldsymbol{\mu}}$ that possess singular variance matrices. Because $\mathbf{y} - \hat{\boldsymbol{\mu}}$ is a singular transformation of a multivariate normal random variable with a nonsingular variance matrix, we use the following.

Definition 18 (Singular Multivariate Normal) *Let* $\mathbf{y}$ *be a random variable with* $\mathrm{E}[\mathbf{y}] = \boldsymbol{\mu}$ *and singular* $\mathrm{Var}[\mathbf{y}] = \boldsymbol{\Omega}$ *and let* $\mathbf{A}$ *be* any *full-column rank matrix such that* $\mathbf{AA}' = \boldsymbol{\Omega}$. *If* $\mathbf{A}'\mathbf{y}$ *has a nonsingular multivariate normal distribution, then* $\mathbf{y}$ *has a singular normal distribution, also denoted by* $\mathfrak{N}(\boldsymbol{\mu}, \boldsymbol{\Omega})$.

Gram–Schmidt orthonormalization (see Lemma 7.6, p. 140) establishes the existence of $\mathbf{A}$ for any variance matrix, although the matrix $\mathbf{A}$ is not unique. Nevertheless, if $\mathbf{B}$ is a full-column rank matrix such that $\mathbf{B} \neq \mathbf{A}$ and $\mathbf{BB}' = \boldsymbol{\Omega}$, then $\mathbf{B}$ is a nonsingular linear transformation of $\mathbf{A}$ and $\mathbf{B}'\mathbf{y}$ is a nonsingular linear transformation of $\mathbf{A}'\mathbf{y}$. Thus, $\mathbf{B}'\mathbf{y}$ also has a nonsingular multivariate normal distribution. So any $\mathbf{A}$ or $\mathbf{B}$ will do, just as the definition states. In all events, we see that $\mathbf{y}$ has a nonsingular multivariate normal distribution within the subspace $\mathrm{Col}(\boldsymbol{\Omega})$.

For $\hat{\boldsymbol{\mu}}$ and $\mathbf{y} - \hat{\boldsymbol{\mu}}$, we have already found that it is convenient to express $\mathrm{Var}[\hat{\boldsymbol{\mu}} \mid \mathbf{X}] = \mathbf{R}_1\mathbf{R}_1'$ and $\mathrm{Var}[\mathbf{y} - \hat{\boldsymbol{\mu}} \mid \mathbf{X}] = \mathbf{R}_2\mathbf{R}_2'$ where the columns of $\mathbf{R}_1$ are an orthonormal basis of $\mathrm{Col}(\mathbf{X})$ and the columns of $\mathbf{R}_2$ are an orthonormal basis of $\mathrm{Col}^{\perp}(\mathbf{X})$.[12] We use these decompositions once again in our proof of Proposition 9.

Proof of Proposition 9. Because we established the conditional means and variances of $\hat{\boldsymbol{\mu}}$, $\mathbf{y} - \hat{\boldsymbol{\mu}}$, and $\hat{\boldsymbol{\beta}}$ under weaker assumptions, we take these as given. To establish the singular normal distributions of $\hat{\boldsymbol{\mu}}$ and $\mathbf{y} - \hat{\boldsymbol{\mu}}$, recall that

[12] See Sections 8.3 and 8.4 and particularly the discussion that begins on p. 163.

$$\mathbf{z}_1 = \mathbf{R}_1'\hat{\boldsymbol{\mu}} = \mathbf{R}_1'\mathbf{R}_1\mathbf{R}_1'\mathbf{y} = \mathbf{R}_1'\mathbf{y},$$
$$\mathbf{z}_2 = \mathbf{R}_2'\left(\mathbf{y} - \hat{\boldsymbol{\mu}}\right) = \mathbf{R}_2'\mathbf{R}_2\mathbf{R}_2'\mathbf{y} = \mathbf{R}_2'\mathbf{y}$$

Because $\mathbf{R} = [\mathbf{R}_1, \mathbf{R}_2]$ is nonsingular, Lemma 10.3 implies that $\mathbf{R}'\mathbf{y}$ has a nonsingular multivariate normal distribution:

$$\mathbf{R}'\mathbf{y} \,|\, \mathbf{X} \sim \mathfrak{N}\left(\begin{bmatrix}\mathbf{R}_1'\boldsymbol{\mu} \\ \mathbf{0}\end{bmatrix}, \sigma_0^2 \cdot \begin{bmatrix}\mathbf{I}_K & \mathbf{0} \\ \mathbf{0} & \mathbf{I}_{N-K}\end{bmatrix}\right)$$

According to Lemma 10.5, $\mathbf{z}_1$ and $\mathbf{z}_2$ are independently distributed nonsingular multivariate normal vectors. Therefore, by Definition 18, $\hat{\boldsymbol{\mu}}$ and $\mathbf{y} - \hat{\boldsymbol{\mu}}$ have singular multivariate normal distributions conditional on $\mathbf{X}$. The independence of $\mathbf{z}_1$ and $\mathbf{z}_2$ also implies the conditional independence of $\hat{\boldsymbol{\mu}}$ and $\mathbf{y} - \hat{\boldsymbol{\mu}}$. That $\hat{\boldsymbol{\beta}} = \left(\mathbf{X}'\mathbf{X}\right)^{-1}\mathbf{X}'\mathbf{R}_1\mathbf{z}_1$ is also conditionally normally distributed follows from Lemma 10.3 because $\left(\mathbf{X}'\mathbf{X}\right)^{-1}\mathbf{X}'\mathbf{R}_1$ is nonsingular. □

10.5.2 The Chi-Square and F Distributions

We return to proving Proposition 10: under Assumptions 3.1, 6.1, 7.1, and 10.1,

$$s^2 \,|\, \mathbf{X} \sim \sigma_0^2 \chi_{N-K}^2/(N-K)$$

and independent of $\hat{\boldsymbol{\mu}}$ and $\hat{\boldsymbol{\beta}}$.

We have already explained that the independence of $\mathbf{y} - \hat{\boldsymbol{\mu}}$ and $\hat{\boldsymbol{\mu}}$ in Proposition 9 implies the indepence of s^2 and $\hat{\boldsymbol{\mu}}$ (and $\hat{\boldsymbol{\beta}}$). All that remains is to prove Lemma 10.1: if $\mathbf{z} \sim \mathfrak{N}(\mathbf{0}, \mathbf{I}_N)$ and $\mathbb{S}$ is an M-dimensional subspace of $\mathbb{R}^N$, then

$$\min_{\boldsymbol{\mu}\in\mathbb{S}} \|\mathbf{z} - \boldsymbol{\mu}\|^2 \sim \chi_{N-M}^2$$

$$\min_{\boldsymbol{\mu}\in\mathbb{S}^\perp} \|\mathbf{z} - \boldsymbol{\mu}\|^2 \sim \chi_M^2$$

and these two random variables are independently distributed.

Proof of Lemma 10.1. Let $\mathbf{B}$ be a matrix whose columns are an orthonormal basis for the subspace $\mathbb{S}$. Then $\mathbf{B}'\mathbf{B} = \mathbf{I}_M$ and $\mathbf{B}\mathbf{B}' = \mathbf{P}_\mathbf{B}$ is the orthogonal projector onto $\mathbb{S}$. Applying Lemma 2.7 (Orthogonal Projectors, p. 38), $\mathbf{I} - \mathbf{P}_\mathbf{B}$ is the orthogonal projector onto $\mathbb{S}^\perp$ so that

$$\mathbf{z}'\mathbf{B}\mathbf{B}'\mathbf{z} = \min_{\boldsymbol{\mu}\in\mathbb{S}^\perp} \|\mathbf{z} - \boldsymbol{\mu}\|^2$$

Because $\mathbf{z} \sim \mathfrak{N}(\mathbf{0}, \mathbf{I}_N)$, Lemma 10.3 implies that $\mathbf{B}'\mathbf{z} \sim \mathfrak{N}(\mathbf{0}, \mathbf{I}_M)$ and Theorem D.11 (Sums of Squared Standard Normals, p. 889) further implies that $\mathbf{z}'\mathbf{B}\mathbf{B}'\mathbf{z} \sim \chi_M^2$.

The same argument demonstrates the dual result

$$\mathbf{z}'\mathbf{C}\mathbf{C}'\mathbf{z} = \min_{\boldsymbol{\mu}\in\mathbb{S}} \|\mathbf{z} - \boldsymbol{\mu}\|^2 \sim \chi_{N-M}^2$$

for $\mathbf{C}$ with columns forming an orthonormal basis for $\mathbb{S}^{\perp}$. In addition $\mathbf{B}'\mathbf{C} = \mathbf{0}$ by construction so that $\text{Cov}[\mathbf{B}'\mathbf{z}, \mathbf{C}'\mathbf{z}] = \mathbf{0}$. Therefore, by Lemma 10.5, $\mathbf{B}'\mathbf{z}$ and $\mathbf{C}'\mathbf{z}$ are independently distributed. The independence of $\mathbf{z}'\mathbf{B}\mathbf{B}'\mathbf{z}$ and $\mathbf{z}'\mathbf{C}\mathbf{C}'\mathbf{z}$ follows immediately. □

Taking $\mathbb{S} = \text{Col}(\mathbf{X})$, this result tells us that

$$\frac{\|\mathbf{y} - \hat{\boldsymbol{\mu}}\|^2}{\sigma_0^2} = \min_{\boldsymbol{\mu} \in \text{Col}(\mathbf{X})} \frac{\|\mathbf{y} - \boldsymbol{\mu}_0 - \boldsymbol{\mu}\|^2}{\sigma_0^2} \sim \chi^2_{N-K}$$

The distribution of s^2 follows.

In Section 10.3.4 we used another relationship between the multivariate normal and the chi-square distributions. Here is the proof of that lemma.

Proof of Lemma 10.2. Let $\mathbf{A}$ be an $N \times N$ nonsingular matrix such that $\boldsymbol{\Omega} = \mathbf{A}\mathbf{A}'$ (Lemma 7.6, p. 140). Then $\mathbf{w} \equiv \mathbf{A}^{-1}(\mathbf{z} - \boldsymbol{\mu}) \sim \mathfrak{N}(\mathbf{0}, \mathbf{I}_N)$ and, using Theorem D.11 (Sums of Squared Standard Normals, p. 889),

$$(\mathbf{z} - \boldsymbol{\mu})' \, \boldsymbol{\Omega}^{-1} \, (\mathbf{z} - \boldsymbol{\mu}) = \left[\mathbf{A}^{-1}(\mathbf{z} - \boldsymbol{\mu})\right]' \mathbf{A}^{-1}(\mathbf{z} - \boldsymbol{\mu}) = \mathbf{w}'\mathbf{w} \sim \chi^2_N$$ □

It follows that

$$\left(\mathbf{R}\boldsymbol{\beta}_0 - \mathbf{R}\hat{\boldsymbol{\beta}}\right)' \left(\text{Var}[\mathbf{R}\boldsymbol{\beta}_0 - \mathbf{R}\hat{\boldsymbol{\beta}}]\right)^{-1} \left(\mathbf{R}\boldsymbol{\beta}_0 - \mathbf{R}\hat{\boldsymbol{\beta}}\right) \sim \chi^2_{K-M}$$

and this is equivalent to (10.11). Combining these results with Theorem D.15 (Snedecor F Ratio, p. 891) proves Proposition 11.

Such quadratic forms are prevalent in econometrics because they are pivotal and possess a convenient distribution. Their pivotal character follows from the way in which the vector of statistics is standardized. The vector in the "wings" of the quadratic form has a mean equal to the zero vector because it is the difference between the vector of statistics and its mean. In addition, this vector is normalized by a "square root" of its variance matrix, as we see in the proof of the lemma. As a result, the "nonstandard" first and second moments are not present in the distribution of the transformed statistic.

Viewed geometrically, these quadratic forms are a generalized Euclidean length, measuring the distance between a statistic and its mean relative to sampling variance. This interpretation is central to our intuitive understanding of confidence intervals for $\boldsymbol{\beta}_0$.

10.5.3 Singular Variances and Generalized Inverses

In the preceding, we have employed two distinct relationships between the multivariate normal and the chi-square distributions, Lemmas 10.1 (Minimum Chi-Square) and 10.2 (Chi-Square Quadratic Forms). In the following we combine these into a single result with the *generalized inverse* of variance matrices. These provide a standard treatment for such singular variance matrices as $\text{Var}[\hat{\boldsymbol{\mu}} \mid \mathbf{X}]$ and $\text{Var}[\mathbf{y} - \hat{\boldsymbol{\mu}} \mid \mathbf{X}]$.

To begin, we review the generalized inverse of a matrix, a concept that does not introduce any fundamentally new ideas. Indeed, we have already exploited an important example in the relationship between $\hat{\boldsymbol{\mu}}$ and $\hat{\boldsymbol{\beta}}$. Although we cannot invert the matrix $\mathbf{X}$ to solve $\hat{\boldsymbol{\mu}} = \mathbf{X}\hat{\boldsymbol{\beta}}$ for $\hat{\boldsymbol{\beta}}$, we found that $\hat{\boldsymbol{\beta}}$ has the unique solution $(\mathbf{X}'\mathbf{X})^{-1}\mathbf{X}'\hat{\boldsymbol{\mu}}$ when $\mathbf{X}$ is full rank. In effect, we can think of $(\mathbf{X}'\mathbf{X})^{-1}\mathbf{X}'$ as analogous to the inverse of a nonsingular matrix. It is, in fact, a generalized inverse of $\mathbf{X}$. The generalized inverse helps to summarize neatly several relationships previously encountered.

DEFINITION 19 (GENERALIZED INVERSE) *The* generalized inverse *of a matrix* $\mathbf{A}$ *is any matrix, denoted* $\mathbf{A}^-$, *such that* $\mathbf{A}\mathbf{A}^-\mathbf{A} = \mathbf{A}$.

In exercises of previous chapters, we developed the following points that we hope are now readily accessible to the reader.

- *The matrix* $\mathbf{A}$ *does not have to be a square matrix.* A very important example of a generalized inverse is $(\mathbf{X}'\mathbf{X})^{-1}\mathbf{X}'$, which is a generalized inverse of $\mathbf{X}$ when $\mathbf{X}$ is full-column rank.
- *Generalized inverses are not unique.* Another important example of a generalized inverse for $\mathbf{X}$ is $(\mathbf{Z}'\mathbf{X})^{-1}\mathbf{Z}'$, provided $\mathbf{Z}'\mathbf{X}$ is nonsingular.
- *Generalized inverses are intimately associated with projectors.* The matrix $\mathbf{A}\mathbf{A}^-$ is a projector onto $\text{Col}(\mathbf{A})$ and projectors are their own generalized inverses.
- *Generalized inverses of nonsingular matrices are ordinary inverses.*

We will use generalized inverses of singular variance matrices throughout the rest of this book. The generalized inverse $(\mathbf{A}'\mathbf{A})^{-1}\mathbf{A}'$ of a full-column rank matrix $\mathbf{A}$ is so prevalent that it deserves its own designation. From this point on we will denote[13]

$$\mathbf{A}^+ \equiv (\mathbf{A}'\mathbf{A})^{-1}\mathbf{A}' \tag{10.13}$$

This generalized inverse has the special property that $\mathbf{A}^+\mathbf{A} = \mathbf{I}$, the identity matrix.

LEMMA 10.6 (VARIANCE GENERALIZED INVERSE) *Given a singular variance matrix* $\boldsymbol{\Omega}$, *a generalized inverse of* $\boldsymbol{\Omega}$ *is*

$$\boldsymbol{\Omega}^- = (\mathbf{A}\mathbf{A}')^- = (\mathbf{A}^+)'\mathbf{A}^+ \tag{10.14}$$

where $\mathbf{A}$ *is a full-column rank matrix such that* $\boldsymbol{\Omega} = \mathbf{A}\mathbf{A}'$.

[13] The notation $\mathbf{A}^+$ is often reserved for the *Moore–Penrose generalized inverse*, of which (10.13) is an example. This generalized inverse has the additional properties

$$\mathbf{A}^+\mathbf{A}\mathbf{A}^+ = \mathbf{A}^+$$
$$(\mathbf{A}\mathbf{A}^+)' = \mathbf{A}\mathbf{A}^+$$
$$(\mathbf{A}^+\mathbf{A})' = \mathbf{A}^+\mathbf{A}$$

These properties define a unique $\mathbf{A}^+$ [see Rao (1973, p. 26)]. If $\mathbf{A}$ is full-column rank, then $\mathbf{A}^+ = (\mathbf{A}'\mathbf{A})^{-1}\mathbf{A}'$.

Proof. Given $\mathbf{A}$,

$$\begin{aligned}\boldsymbol{\Omega}\left(\mathbf{A}^{+}\right)'\mathbf{A}^{+}\boldsymbol{\Omega} &= \boldsymbol{\Omega}\mathbf{A}\left(\mathbf{A}'\mathbf{A}\right)^{-2}\mathbf{A}'\boldsymbol{\Omega} \\ &= \mathbf{A}\mathbf{A}'\mathbf{A}\left(\mathbf{A}'\mathbf{A}\right)^{-2}\mathbf{A}'\mathbf{A}\mathbf{A}' \\ &= \mathbf{A}\mathbf{A}' \\ &= \boldsymbol{\Omega}\end{aligned}$$

so that $\boldsymbol{\Omega}^{-}$ satisfies Definition 19. □

This expression for the generalized inverse of a variance matrix allows us to derive standardized quadratic forms for random vectors with singular variance matrices:

LEMMA 10.7 *Let* $\mathbf{z} \sim \mathfrak{N}(\boldsymbol{\mu}, \boldsymbol{\Omega})$ *be a random vector in* $\mathbb{R}^N$ *and* $\operatorname{rank}(\boldsymbol{\Omega}) = M \leq N$. *Then*

$$q \equiv (\mathbf{z} - \boldsymbol{\mu})'\,\boldsymbol{\Omega}^{-}\,(\mathbf{z} - \boldsymbol{\mu})$$

is invariant to the choice of $\boldsymbol{\Omega}^{-}$ *and* $q \sim \chi^2_M$.

Proof. Let $\mathbf{A}$ be a full-column rank matrix such that $\boldsymbol{\Omega} = \mathbf{A}\mathbf{A}'$. Therefore,

$$\mathbf{A} = \boldsymbol{\Omega}\mathbf{A}\left(\mathbf{A}'\mathbf{A}\right)^{-1} = \boldsymbol{\Omega}\mathbf{A}^{+\prime}$$

Now first we show that $\boldsymbol{\Omega}^{-}$ can be *any* generalized inverse of $\boldsymbol{\Omega}$. Using Lemma 7.2 (Variance Column Space, p. 133) $\mathbf{z} - \boldsymbol{\mu} \in \operatorname{Col}(\boldsymbol{\Omega}) = \operatorname{Col}(\mathbf{A})$ so that for each $\mathbf{z}$ there is a unique vector $\mathbf{w} \in \mathbb{R}^N$ such that

$$\mathbf{z} - \boldsymbol{\mu} = \mathbf{A}\mathbf{w} = \boldsymbol{\Omega}\mathbf{A}^{+\prime}\mathbf{w}$$

with probability one. For all $\boldsymbol{\Omega}^{-}$,

$$(\mathbf{z} - \boldsymbol{\mu})'\,\boldsymbol{\Omega}^{-}\,(\mathbf{z} - \boldsymbol{\mu}) = \mathbf{w}'\mathbf{A}^{+}\boldsymbol{\Omega}\boldsymbol{\Omega}^{-}\boldsymbol{\Omega}\mathbf{A}^{+\prime}\mathbf{w} = \mathbf{w}'\mathbf{A}^{+}\boldsymbol{\Omega}\mathbf{A}^{+\prime}\mathbf{w}$$

Therefore, $(\mathbf{z} - \boldsymbol{\mu})'\,\boldsymbol{\Omega}^{-}\,(\mathbf{z} - \boldsymbol{\mu})$ is invariant to the choice of generalized inverse $\boldsymbol{\Omega}^{-}$.

Now, using Definition 18 (Singular Multivariate Normal), $\mathbf{w} = \mathbf{A}^{+}(\mathbf{z} - \boldsymbol{\mu})$ has a nonsingular multivariate normal distribution. The moments of $\mathbf{w}$ are

$$\begin{aligned}\mathrm{E}[\mathbf{w}] &= \mathbf{A}^{+}\left[\mathrm{E}[\mathbf{z}] - \boldsymbol{\mu}\right] = \mathbf{0}, \\ \mathrm{Var}[\mathbf{w}] &= \mathbf{A}^{+}\,\mathrm{Var}[\mathbf{z}]\mathbf{A}^{+\prime} = \mathbf{A}^{+}\mathbf{A}\left(\mathbf{A}^{+}\mathbf{A}\right)' = \mathbf{I}_M\end{aligned}$$

because $\mathbf{A}^{+}\mathbf{A} = \mathbf{I}_M$. Using (10.14) and Theorem D.11 (Sums of Squared Standard Normals, p. 889),

$$(\mathbf{z} - \boldsymbol{\mu})'\,\boldsymbol{\Omega}^{-}\,(\mathbf{z} - \boldsymbol{\mu}) = (\mathbf{z} - \boldsymbol{\mu})'\left(\mathbf{A}^{+}\right)'\mathbf{A}^{+}\,(\mathbf{z} - \boldsymbol{\mu}) = \mathbf{w}'\mathbf{w} \sim \chi^2_M$$ □

Thus, we have a generalization of Lemma 10.2 in which we have only replaced a nonsingular matrix inverse with a generalized inverse and adjusted the degrees of freedom in the chi-square distribution to equal the rank of the variance matrix. Viewed geometrically, these quadratic forms remain generalized Euclidean lengths as well. Within the subspace $\text{Col}(\boldsymbol{\Omega})$, which is where $\mathbf{z}-\boldsymbol{\mu}$ lies, the function $f(\mathbf{x}) = \sqrt{\mathbf{x}'\boldsymbol{\Omega}^{-}\mathbf{x}}$ is a norm.[14] We lose none of the structure of these quadratic forms in passing from nonsingular to singular variance matrices.

With generalized inverses, we can streamline the structure of our theory in two ways. First, the result

$$\frac{(\mathbf{y}-\hat{\boldsymbol{\mu}})'(\mathbf{y}-\hat{\boldsymbol{\mu}})}{\sigma_0^2} \sim \chi^2_{N-K}$$

may appear anomalous, because no generalized inverse appears in the quadratic form. But this is not so, because the identity matrix is a generalized inverse for any projector. In this particular case, we use this fact as follows:

$$\left[\sigma_0^2 \cdot (\mathbf{I}-\mathbf{P_X})\right]\left[\frac{1}{\sigma_0^2}\mathbf{I}\right]\left[\sigma_0^2 \cdot (\mathbf{I}-\mathbf{P_X})\right] = \sigma_0^2 \cdot (\mathbf{I}-\mathbf{P_X})$$

so that $1/\sigma_0^2 \cdot \mathbf{I}$ appears as the normalizing matrix in the quadratic form for $\mathbf{y}-\hat{\boldsymbol{\mu}}$.

Second, and closely related, note that we may now write variance ellipses generally as

$$\mathbb{V}_z = \left\{\mathbf{w} \in \text{Col}(\boldsymbol{\Omega}) \mid \|\mathbf{w}\|^2_{\boldsymbol{\Omega}^-} \le 1\right\}$$

where $\boldsymbol{\Omega} = \text{Var}[\mathbf{z}]$, not just those for nonsingular variance matrices. The generalized inverse appears in the generalized Euclidean norm for every case.

10.5.4 Singular Multivariate Normal Distributions

In this section, we briefly discuss the cumulative distribution function (c.d.f.) and p.d.f. of singular multivariate normal distributions. Let $\mathbf{y} \sim \mathfrak{N}(\boldsymbol{\mu}, \boldsymbol{\Omega})$ be a singular multivariate normal random variable. In effect, $\mathbf{y}$ has a nonsingular multivariate normal distribution within the subspace $\text{Col}(\boldsymbol{\Omega})$. Let $\mathbf{AA}' = \boldsymbol{\Omega}$, where $\mathbf{A}$ is an $N \times K$ full-column rank matrix, $K < N$. Then $\mathbf{z} \equiv \mathbf{A}^+(\mathbf{y}-\boldsymbol{\mu}) \sim \mathfrak{N}[\mathbf{0}, (\mathbf{A}'\mathbf{A})^{-1}]$ has a nonsingular multivariate normal distribution and $\mathbf{y} = \boldsymbol{\mu} + \mathbf{Az}$ so that the c.d.f. of $\mathbf{y}$ is

$$\begin{aligned} F(\mathbf{x}) &= \Pr\{\boldsymbol{\mu} + \mathbf{Az} \le \mathbf{x}\} \\ &= \int \mathbf{1}\{\boldsymbol{\mu} + \mathbf{Az} \le \mathbf{x}\}\, \phi[\mathbf{z}, (\mathbf{A}'\mathbf{A})^{-1}]\, d\mathbf{z} \end{aligned}$$

As previously mentioned, such c.d.f.s do not have closed forms. Nor is there a function $f(y)$ such that

$$F(\mathbf{x}) = \int_{-\infty}^{\mathbf{x}} f(\mathbf{y})\, d\mathbf{y}$$

Because not all N constraints can bind simultaneously on K variables, one can see by inspection that

[14] Outside of $\text{Col}(\boldsymbol{\Omega})$, $\sqrt{\mathbf{x}'\boldsymbol{\Omega}^{-}\mathbf{x}}$ is not a norm because it can be zero for nonzero vectors. Consider, for example, $\mathbf{x} \in \text{Col}^{\perp}(\mathbf{A})$ and $\mathbf{x} \ne \mathbf{0}$ when the columns of $\mathbf{A}$ are a basis for $\text{Col}(\boldsymbol{\Omega})$. Then $\mathbf{A}'\mathbf{x} = \mathbf{0}$ and $\mathbf{x}'\boldsymbol{\Omega}^{-}\mathbf{x} = \mathbf{x}'\mathbf{A}(\mathbf{A}'\mathbf{A})^{-2}\mathbf{A}'\mathbf{x} = 0$.

$$\frac{\partial^N F(\mathbf{x})}{\partial x_1 \cdots \partial x_N} = 0$$

except on boundaries in which this derivative is not well defined. See Figure 10.3 for a surface plot of the singular bivariate normal c.d.f. At every point at which the cross-partial derivative exists, the surface is flat along one axis. In effect, the K-dimensional distribution has no "volume" in $\mathbb{R}^N$ the same way that a singular matrix has a determinant equal to zero. To overcome this lacuna in the distribution theory, one must define p.d.f.s for *mixed* multivariate distributions. We will cover this topic in Chapter 28.

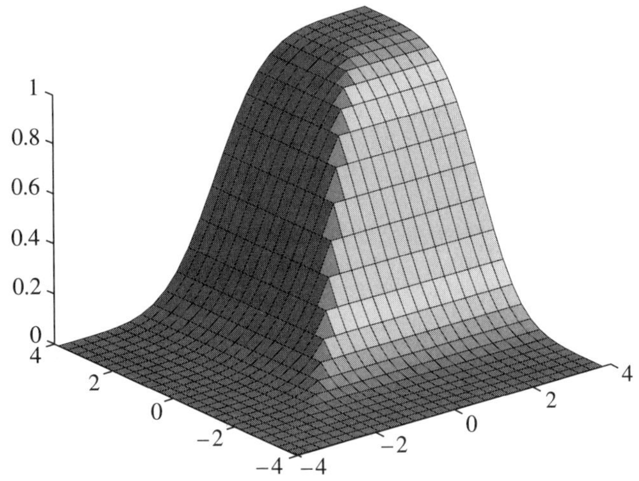

Figure 10.3 Singular bivariate normal c.d.f.

10.6 METHODOLOGICAL NOTES

The elliptical interval estimator for $\mathbf{R}\boldsymbol{\beta}_0$ presented above is *ad hoc* from a theoretical point of view. It is certainly *convenient* to use the chi-square and F distributions to construct these intervals. The generalization of variance ellipses is also aesthetically pleasing. But from a theoretical standpoint, the researcher may choose other shapes if so desired. For example, in choosing a confidence interval for two coefficients, the researcher may prefer to narrow the interval for one parameter at the expense of increasing the interval in the other dimension.

The variance-elliptical intervals possess another geometric property that may give them additional appeal: for a given level of probability, the F ellipses have the smallest Euclidean volume. Although we will not show this formally, one can understand why informally. The contours of the multivariate p.d.f. of $\hat{\boldsymbol{\beta}}$ correspond to the boundaries of these ellipses. Therefore, at every boundary point the rate of change of the probability of the interval with respect to moving the boundary is the same. These are the marginal conditions required to find an interval with minimum volume subject to an overall probability constraint.

If we are somehow indifferent about the various directions in the parameter space, then this geometric property may settle the issue. Also, the practical difficulties of computing intervals with the desired shape are significant deterrents. In contrast, the variance-elliptical intervals are standard fare for today's computer software. Occasionally, researchers use the *simultaneous confidence intervals* proposed by Scheffé (1959) (see Exercise 10.22). These intervals are rectangular, but their probabilities are only known to exceed $1 - \alpha$.

10.7 OVERVIEW

1. Our third statistical assumption specifies that the distribution of $\mathbf{y}$ conditional on $\mathbf{X}$ is multivariate normal.
2. The multivariate normal distribution $\mathfrak{N}(\boldsymbol{\mu}, \boldsymbol{\Omega})$ possesses several analytical properties that make the distribution theory of OLS statistics tractable under the normality assumption:
   (a) The mean $\boldsymbol{\mu}$ and the variance matrix $\boldsymbol{\Omega}$ characterize the distribution.
   (b) Linear combinations of multivariate normal random variables also possess a multivariate normal distribution.
   (c) The variance matrix $\boldsymbol{\Omega}$ may be singular, in which case the random variable is multivariate normal in the subspace $\mathrm{Col}(\boldsymbol{\Omega})$.
   (d) If they are uncorrelated, then multivariate normal random variables are also independently distributed.
   (e) The p.d.f. of nonsingular multivariate normal distributions,

$$\phi(\mathbf{z} - \boldsymbol{\mu}, \boldsymbol{\Omega}) \equiv [\det(2\pi\boldsymbol{\Omega})]^{-1/2} \exp\left[-\frac{1}{2}(\mathbf{z} - \boldsymbol{\mu})'\boldsymbol{\Omega}^{-1}(\mathbf{z} - \boldsymbol{\mu})\right]$$

   is *elliptically symmetric* about $\boldsymbol{\mu}$ where it attains its maximum. The boundary of the variance ellipse is proportional to the level sets of the p.d.f. when $\boldsymbol{\mu} = \mathbf{0}$.
3. The following are corresponding consequences of adding the conditional normality assumption that follow from these analytical properties of the multivariate distribution:
   (a) In combination with Assumptions 6.1 and 7.1, Assumption 10.1 specifies the complete distribution of $\mathbf{y}$ given $\mathbf{X}$.
   (b) The conditional distribution of $\hat{\boldsymbol{\beta}}$ given $\mathbf{X}$ is multivariate normal.
   (c) The conditional distributions of $\hat{\boldsymbol{\mu}}$ and $\mathbf{y} - \hat{\boldsymbol{\mu}}$ are multivariate normal.
   (d) Conditional on $\mathbf{X}$, $\hat{\boldsymbol{\mu}}$ and $\mathbf{y} - \hat{\boldsymbol{\mu}}$ are independently distributed. Therefore, conditional on $\mathbf{X}$, $\hat{\boldsymbol{\beta}}$ and s^2 are also independently distributed.
   (e) Probability intervals for $\hat{\boldsymbol{\beta}}$ (and $\hat{\boldsymbol{\mu}}$ and $\mathbf{y} - \hat{\boldsymbol{\mu}}$) that are proportional to variance ellipses centered on the mean have minimum Euclidean volume among all intervals with the same probability.
4. If $\mathbf{z} \sim \mathfrak{N}(\boldsymbol{\mu}, \boldsymbol{\Omega})$ then the standardized quadratic form $(\mathbf{z} - \boldsymbol{\mu})'\boldsymbol{\Omega}^{-}(\mathbf{z} - \boldsymbol{\mu})$, where $\boldsymbol{\Omega}^{-}$ denotes the *generalized inverse* of $\boldsymbol{\Omega}$, has a chi-square distribution with degrees of freedom equal to the rank of $\boldsymbol{\Omega}$. If $\mathbf{z}_1 \sim \mathfrak{N}(\boldsymbol{\mu}_1, \boldsymbol{\Omega}_{11})$ and $\mathbf{z}_2 \sim \mathfrak{N}(\boldsymbol{\mu}_2, \boldsymbol{\Omega}_{22})$ are independently distributed then

$$\frac{\mathrm{rank}(\boldsymbol{\Omega}_{22})\ (\mathbf{z}_1 - \boldsymbol{\mu}_1)'\boldsymbol{\Omega}_{11}^{-}(\mathbf{z}_1 - \boldsymbol{\mu}_1)}{\mathrm{rank}(\boldsymbol{\Omega}_{11})\ (\mathbf{z}_2 - \boldsymbol{\mu}_2)'\boldsymbol{\Omega}_{22}^{-}(\mathbf{z}_2 - \boldsymbol{\mu}_2)}$$

   has an F distribution with $\mathrm{rank}(\boldsymbol{\Omega}_{11})$ and $\mathrm{rank}(\boldsymbol{\Omega}_{22})$ degrees of freedom.
5. Hence, under Assumptions 3.1, 6.1, 7.1, and 10.1, we have the pivotal statistics
   (a) $(\mathbf{y} - \hat{\boldsymbol{\mu}})'(\mathbf{y} - \hat{\boldsymbol{\mu}})/\sigma_0^2 = (N - K)s^2/\sigma_0^2 \sim \chi^2_{N-K}$,
   (b) $(\mathbf{R}\boldsymbol{\beta} - \mathbf{R}\boldsymbol{\beta}_0)'[\mathbf{R}(\mathbf{X}'\mathbf{X})^{-1}\mathbf{R}']^{-1}(\mathbf{R}\boldsymbol{\beta} - \mathbf{R}\boldsymbol{\beta}_0)/\sigma_0^2 \sim \chi^2_{K-M}$ where $K - M = \mathrm{rank}(\mathbf{R})$,
   (c) $\hat{F} \equiv [(\mathbf{R}\boldsymbol{\beta} - \mathbf{R}\boldsymbol{\beta}_0)'[\mathbf{R}(\mathbf{X}'\mathbf{X})^{-1}\mathbf{R}']^{-1}(\mathbf{R}\boldsymbol{\beta} - \mathbf{R}\boldsymbol{\beta}_0)/M]/s^2 \sim F_{K-M,N-K}$.
   Feasible $100(1 - \alpha)\%$ confidence intervals are

$$\left[s^2 \frac{N-K}{\chi^2_{N-K;1-\alpha/2}},\ s^2 \frac{N-K}{\chi^2_{N-K;\alpha/2}} \right]$$

for σ_0^2 and

$$\left\{ \gamma \in \text{Col}(\mathbf{R}) \mid (\gamma - \mathbf{R}\hat{\boldsymbol{\beta}})' \left(\mathbf{R}(\mathbf{X}'\mathbf{X})^{-1}\mathbf{R}' \right)^{-1} (\gamma - \mathbf{R}\hat{\boldsymbol{\beta}}) \leq s^2\ (K - M)\ F_{K-M,N-K;1-\alpha} \right\}$$

for $\mathbf{R}\boldsymbol{\beta}_0$.

6. We will soon show that $\hat{\boldsymbol{\beta}}$ is efficient relative to all unbiased estimators of $\boldsymbol{\beta}_0$, including *nonlinear* ones, under normality. In addition, s^2 is efficient relative to all unbiased estimators of σ_0^2.

10.8 EXERCISES

10.8.1 Review

10.1 **(Log-Normal)** In addition to functional form and homoskedasticity, the logarithmic transformation of wages makes the marginal distribution of wages more symmetric, and hence closer to normal.
(a) Use the 1995 CPS data to confirm this claim.
(b) Find the the log-normal p.d.f. That is, find the p.d.f. of the e^y where $y \sim \mathfrak{N}(\mu, \sigma^2)$.

10.2 Let $y \sim \mathfrak{N}(0, 1)$ and show that y and y^2 are uncorrelated but dependently distributed. Find $\text{E}[y \mid y^2]$ and $\text{E}[y^2 \mid y]$. Using computer software for three-dimensional plotting, graph the joint c.d.f. of y and y^2.

10.3 Confirm that the $\mathfrak{N}(\mathbf{0}, \mathbf{I}_N)$ distribution is the product of N univariate standard normal p.d.f.s.

10.4 For the univariate $\mathfrak{N}(\mu, \sigma^2)$ distribution, show that
(a) the p.d.f. integrates to 1,[15]
(b) the mean is finite and equals μ,
(c) all odd moments about μ are 0,
(d) the second moment about μ (the variance) is σ^2, and
(e) the fourth moment about μ is $3\sigma^4$.

10.5 Let $\mathbf{y} \in \mathbb{R}^2$ possess a bivariate normal distribution with mean vector $\boldsymbol{\mu} \in \mathbb{R}^2$ and variance matrix $\boldsymbol{\Omega} = \left[\omega_{ij};\, i, j = 1, 2\right]$. Find the mean and variance of y_1 conditional on y_2. Compare this conditional mean with the MMSE linear predictor of y_1 given y_2. Also compare the conditional variance with the minimized MSE of the optimal linear predictor.

***10.6** **(Partitioned Determinant)** Just as there is a useful formula for the inverse of a partitioned matrix, there is a partitioned-matrix determinant formula. Let the square matrix $\mathbf{A}$ be partitioned according to

$$\mathbf{A} = \begin{bmatrix} \mathbf{A}_{11} & \mathbf{A}_{12} \\ \mathbf{A}_{21} & \mathbf{A}_{22} \end{bmatrix}$$

[15] HINT: Consider the joint p.d.f. of two independently distributed standard normal random variables and a change of variables to polar coordinates.

Show that

$$\det(\mathbf{A}) = \det(\mathbf{A}_{11})\,\det(\mathbf{A}_{22} - \mathbf{A}_{21}\mathbf{A}_{11}^{-1}\mathbf{A}_{12})$$

[HINT: Note that

$$\mathbf{A} = \begin{bmatrix} \mathbf{I} & \mathbf{0} \\ \mathbf{A}_{21}\mathbf{A}_{11}^{-1} & \mathbf{A}_{22} - \mathbf{A}_{21}\mathbf{A}_{11}^{-1}\mathbf{A}_{12} \end{bmatrix} \begin{bmatrix} \mathbf{A}_{11} & \mathbf{A}_{12} \\ \mathbf{0} & \mathbf{I} \end{bmatrix}$$

and use the co-factor expansion (Lemma C.14) to find

$$\det\left(\begin{bmatrix} \mathbf{B} & \mathbf{C} \\ \mathbf{0} & \mathbf{I} \end{bmatrix}\right) = \det\left(\begin{bmatrix} \mathbf{I} & 0 \\ \mathbf{C} & \mathbf{B} \end{bmatrix}\right)]$$

10.7 (Normal Factorization) Use the partitioned quadratic formula (Lemma 7.5, p. 138) and the partitioned determininant formula in Exercise 10.6 to prove Lemma 10.4.

10.8 (Normal Factorization) Let $\mathbf{y} \sim \mathfrak{N}(\boldsymbol{\mu}, \boldsymbol{\Omega})$ and partition

$$\mathbf{y} = \begin{bmatrix} \mathbf{y}_1 \\ \mathbf{y}_2 \end{bmatrix}, \qquad \boldsymbol{\mu} = \begin{bmatrix} \boldsymbol{\mu}_1 \\ \boldsymbol{\mu}_2 \end{bmatrix}, \qquad \boldsymbol{\Omega} = \begin{bmatrix} \boldsymbol{\Omega}_{11} & \boldsymbol{\Omega}_{12} \\ \boldsymbol{\Omega}_{12}' & \boldsymbol{\Omega}_{22} \end{bmatrix}$$

(a) Find $\mathrm{E}^*[\mathbf{y}_1 \mid \mathbf{y}_2]$.

(b) What is the joint distribution of

$$\mathbf{z}_1 = \mathbf{y}_1 - \mathrm{E}^*[\mathbf{y}_1 \mid \mathbf{y}_2] \qquad \text{and} \qquad \mathbf{z}_2 = \mathbf{y}_2 - \boldsymbol{\mu}_2 \tag{10.15}$$

Write out the their joint p.d.f.

(c) Invert the linear transformation of the **y**s and apply the transformation-of-variables formula (Theorem D.6, p. 882) to recover the p.d.f. of **y** in the form of a product of conditional and marginal p.d.f.s.

10.9 (Recursive Residuals) As in Exercises 8.15 and 9.9, let $\hat{\boldsymbol{\beta}}_{[m]}$ be the OLS estimator for $\boldsymbol{\beta}_0$ using the first m observations ($m \geq K$). Under the conditions of Proposition 9 (Normality of OLS, p. 198), show that the $N - K$ recursive residuals $y_n - \mathbf{x}_n'\hat{\boldsymbol{\beta}}_{[n-1]}$, $n = K+1, \ldots, N$, are independent but not identically distributed (i.n.i.d.) $\mathfrak{N}(0, \sigma^2 f_n)$ where $f_n = 1 + \mathbf{x}_n'(\mathbf{X}_{n-1}'\mathbf{X}_{n-1})\mathbf{x}_n$.

10.10 (Confidence Intervals) Using $\alpha = 0.95$ and values for K and N that you choose, confirm that the critical values $\chi^2_{K;1-\alpha}$ in the infeasible confidence interval (10.7) are smaller than the values $K\,F_{K,N-K;1-\alpha}$ in the feasible confidence interval (10.10). What can you conclude about the expected squared radius of the feasible confidence interval relative to the infeasible confidence interval?

10.11 (Minimum Chi-Square) Confirm Lemma 10.1 (Minimum Chi-Square) for the case in which the subspace $\mathbb{S}$ of $\mathbb{R}^N$ is the set of vectors $[z_n;\ n = 1, \ldots, N]' \in \mathbb{R}^N$ with $z_n = 0$ for $n = 1, \ldots, M < N$.

10.12 (Generalized Inverse) Under the conditions of Proposition 9 (Normality of OLS, p. 198), interpret

$$\frac{(\hat{\boldsymbol{\mu}} - \boldsymbol{\mu}_0)'(\hat{\boldsymbol{\mu}} - \boldsymbol{\mu}_0)}{\sigma_0^2} \sim \chi^2_K$$

as an application of Lemma 10.7.

10.13 (Exact Multicollinearity) Given **X**, what is the joint conditional distribution of s^2 and $\hat{\boldsymbol{\mu}}$ if one drops Assumption 3.1 (Full Rank, p. 53) from Proposition 10 (Distribution of Variance Estimator, p. 199)?

***10.14 (RLS)** Recall that $\hat{\boldsymbol{\beta}}_{\mathrm{R}} - \hat{\boldsymbol{\beta}}$ is a projection [see equation (4.17), p. 87].

(a) Show that $\hat{\boldsymbol{\beta}}_{\mathrm{R}} - \hat{\boldsymbol{\beta}}$ has a singular normal distribution.

(b) Show that

$$\mathrm{Var}[\hat{\boldsymbol{\beta}}_{\mathrm{R}} - \hat{\boldsymbol{\beta}} \mid \mathbf{X}] = \sigma_0^2 \cdot (\mathbf{X}'\mathbf{X})^{-1}\mathbf{R}' \left[\mathbf{R}(\mathbf{X}'\mathbf{X})^{-1}\mathbf{R}'\right]^{-1} \mathbf{R}(\mathbf{X}'\mathbf{X})^{-1}$$

(c) Show that

$$\left(\mathrm{Var}[\hat{\boldsymbol{\beta}}_{\mathrm{R}} - \hat{\boldsymbol{\beta}} \mid \mathbf{X}]\right)^{-} = \frac{1}{\sigma_0^2} \cdot \mathbf{X}'\mathbf{X} = \left(\mathrm{Var}[\hat{\boldsymbol{\beta}} \mid \mathbf{X}]\right)^{-1}$$

so that the quadratic form (10.6) can be interpreted as

$$\frac{(\hat{\boldsymbol{\beta}}_{\mathrm{R}} - \hat{\boldsymbol{\beta}})'\mathbf{X}'\mathbf{X}(\hat{\boldsymbol{\beta}}_{\mathrm{R}} - \hat{\boldsymbol{\beta}})}{\sigma_0^2} = (\hat{\boldsymbol{\beta}}_{\mathrm{R}} - \hat{\boldsymbol{\beta}})' \left(\mathrm{Var}[\hat{\boldsymbol{\beta}} \mid \mathbf{X}]\right)^{-1} (\hat{\boldsymbol{\beta}}_{\mathrm{R}} - \hat{\boldsymbol{\beta}}) \tag{10.16}$$

$$= (\hat{\boldsymbol{\beta}}_{\mathrm{R}} - \hat{\boldsymbol{\beta}})' \left(\mathrm{Var}[\hat{\boldsymbol{\beta}}_{\mathrm{R}} - \hat{\boldsymbol{\beta}} \mid \mathbf{X}]\right)^{-} (\hat{\boldsymbol{\beta}}_{\mathrm{R}} - \hat{\boldsymbol{\beta}}) \tag{10.17}$$

(d) Show how to apply Lemma 10.1 (Minimum Chi-Square) to obtain the distribution of the quadratic form in (10.16). [HINT: See (4.15) and Exercise 4.14.]

10.15 (Minimum Chi-Square) Let $\mathbf{y} \sim \mathfrak{N}(\mathbf{0}, \mathbf{I}_N)$ and $\mathbf{P}$ be an orthogonal projector from $\mathbb{R}^N$ onto a J-dimensional subspace $\mathbb{S}$. Show that $\mathbf{y}'\mathbf{P}\mathbf{y} \sim \chi^2_J$.

10.8.2 Extensions

10.16 (i.i.d.) Show that if the $y_n - \mathbf{x}_n'\boldsymbol{\beta}_0$ are i.i.d. conditional on $\mathbf{X}$, then the marginal distribution of s^2 is invariant to $\boldsymbol{\beta}_0$ and the marginal distribution of the OLS fitted coefficient vector $\hat{\boldsymbol{\beta}}_1$ is invariant to $\boldsymbol{\beta}_{02}$ for partitioned regression $\mathbf{X}\boldsymbol{\beta}_0 = \mathbf{X}_1\boldsymbol{\beta}_{01} + \mathbf{X}_2\boldsymbol{\beta}_{02}$.

10.17 (Quadratic Forms) Let $\boldsymbol{\Omega}$ be a variance matrix and $\mathbf{W}$ a full-column rank matrix such that $\mathbf{W}\mathbf{W}' = \boldsymbol{\Omega}$. Let $\mathbf{W}^+ \equiv (\mathbf{W}'\mathbf{W})^{-1}\mathbf{W}'$ be the Moore–Penrose generalized inverse of $\mathbf{W}$. Show

(a) $\mathbf{P}_{\mathbf{W}} = \mathbf{W}\mathbf{W}^+$ and $\mathbf{W}^+\mathbf{y}$ is the coefficient vector of $\mathbf{W}$ for the orthogonal projection of $\mathbf{y}$ onto $\mathrm{Col}(\mathbf{W})$,

(b) the quadratic form $\mathbf{y}'\boldsymbol{\Omega}^-\mathbf{y} = (\mathbf{W}^+\mathbf{y})'\mathbf{W}^+\mathbf{y}$ is the squared length of the coefficient vector of $\mathbf{W}$ for the orthogonal projection of $\mathbf{y}$ onto $\mathrm{Col}(\mathbf{W})$,

(c) $\mathbf{W}^+\boldsymbol{\Omega}(\mathbf{W}')^+ = \mathbf{I}$, and

(d) $\mathbf{W}'\boldsymbol{\Omega}^-\mathbf{W} = \mathbf{I}$ for *all* generalized inverses $\boldsymbol{\Omega}^-$.

10.18 (Norm) Let $\boldsymbol{\Omega}$ be a variance matrix. Show that $\|\mathbf{v}\|^2_{\boldsymbol{\Omega}^-} \equiv \mathbf{v}'\boldsymbol{\Omega}^-\mathbf{v}$ is a norm on the vector subspace $\mathrm{Col}(\boldsymbol{\Omega})$.

10.19 Show that the variance ellipse of $\hat{\boldsymbol{\beta}}$ yields the interval estimator with the smallest volume.

10.20 (RLS Misspecification) Show that *all* of the elements of the RLS estimator $\hat{\boldsymbol{\beta}}_{\mathrm{R}}$ (Proposition 3, p. 79) may be biased when $\mathbf{R}\boldsymbol{\beta}_0 \neq \mathbf{r}$, regardless of whether the elements appear in the restrictions.

10.21 (Ratio of Normals) In the analysis of earnings, we estimated a quadratic function in experience. The ratio of the linear coefficient over twice the quadratic coefficient is the peak of the earnings–experience profile. Find the p.d.f. of the corresponding ratio using the two OLS estimators of these coefficients. Can you construct a pivotal statistic for the peak of the earnings–experience profile?

10.22 **(Scheffé Simultaneous Confidence Intervals)** Let $\hat{\sigma}_k^2$ denote the kth diagonal element of $s^2 \cdot (\mathbf{X}'\mathbf{X})^{-1}$, the unbiased estimator of $\text{Var}[\hat{\boldsymbol{\beta}} \mid \mathbf{X}]$. Under the assumptions of Proposition 9 (Normality of OLS, p. 198) confirm the *simultaneous confidence intervals* (Scheffé, 1959)

$$\Pr\left\{ \left| \beta_{0k} - \hat{\beta}_k \right| \le \hat{\sigma}_k \sqrt{K\, F_{K,N-K;1-\alpha}};\ k = 1, \ldots, K \,\middle|\, \mathbf{X} \right\} \ge 1 - \alpha$$

using the following steps.

(a) Show that

$$\left(\boldsymbol{\beta}_0 - \hat{\boldsymbol{\beta}}\right)' \mathbf{X}'\mathbf{X} \left(\boldsymbol{\beta}_0 - \hat{\boldsymbol{\beta}}\right) = \max_{\mathbf{c} \in \mathbb{R}^K} \frac{\left[\mathbf{c}'(\boldsymbol{\beta}_0 - \hat{\boldsymbol{\beta}})\right]^2}{\mathbf{c}'(\mathbf{X}'\mathbf{X})^{-1}\mathbf{c}}.$$

[HINT: This looks very much like the Cauchy–Schwarz inequality (Lemma 7.8, p. 143).]

(b) Show that

$$\Pr\left\{ \max_{\mathbf{c} \in \mathbb{R}^K} \frac{\left[\mathbf{c}'(\boldsymbol{\beta}_0 - \hat{\boldsymbol{\beta}})\right]^2}{\mathbf{c}'(\mathbf{X}'\mathbf{X})^{-1}\mathbf{c}} \le s^2\, K\, F_{K,N-K;1-\alpha} \,\middle|\, \mathbf{X} \right\} = 1 - \alpha$$

(c) Show that

$$\Pr\left\{ \forall \mathbf{c} \in \mathbb{R}^K,\ \left| \mathbf{c}'(\boldsymbol{\beta}_0 - \hat{\boldsymbol{\beta}}) \right| \le \sqrt{s^2\, K\, F_{K,N-K;1-\alpha}\, \mathbf{c}'(\mathbf{X}'\mathbf{X})^{-1}\mathbf{c}} \,\middle|\, \mathbf{X} \right\} = 1 - \alpha$$

and use this result to establish the lower bound on the probability of the simultaneous confidence intervals given above.

10.23 **(Minimum Chi-Square)** Let $\tilde{\boldsymbol{\theta}}$ be an unbiased estimator of $\boldsymbol{\theta}_0$ and suppose that $\text{Var}[\tilde{\boldsymbol{\theta}}] = \boldsymbol{\Omega}$ is a finite, nonsingular matrix. Also let $\mathbf{R}\boldsymbol{\theta}_0 = \mathbf{r}$ and

$$\hat{\boldsymbol{\theta}} = \underset{\{\boldsymbol{\theta} \mid \mathbf{R}\boldsymbol{\theta} = \mathbf{r}\}}{\text{argmin}} (\tilde{\boldsymbol{\theta}} - \boldsymbol{\theta})'\boldsymbol{\Omega}^{-1}(\tilde{\boldsymbol{\theta}} - \boldsymbol{\theta})$$

(a) Show that a generalized inverse of $\text{Var}[\tilde{\boldsymbol{\theta}} - \hat{\boldsymbol{\theta}}]$ is $(\text{Var}[\tilde{\boldsymbol{\theta}}])^{-1}$.

(b) Suppose that $\tilde{\boldsymbol{\theta}} \sim \mathfrak{N}(\boldsymbol{\theta}_0, \boldsymbol{\Omega})$. What is the distribution of $(\tilde{\boldsymbol{\theta}} - \hat{\boldsymbol{\theta}})'\boldsymbol{\Omega}^{-1}(\tilde{\boldsymbol{\theta}} - \hat{\boldsymbol{\theta}})$? Discuss the differences between Lemmas 10.1 and 10.7 for this case.

***10.24** **(Minimum Chi-Square)** Let $\mathbf{z} \sim \mathfrak{N}(\mathbf{0}, \mathbf{I}_N)$ and $\mathbb{S}_j$ $(j = 1, \ldots, J)$ be a sequence of nested subspaces of $\mathbb{R}^N$, $\mathbb{S}_J \subset \mathbb{S}_{J-1} \subset \cdots \subset \mathbb{S}_2 \subset \mathbb{S}_1 \subset \mathbb{S}_0 = \mathbb{R}^N$. Show that

$$m_j = \min_{\boldsymbol{\mu} \in \mathbb{S}_{j+1}} \|\mathbf{z} - \boldsymbol{\mu}\|^2 - \min_{\boldsymbol{\mu} \in \mathbb{S}_j} \|\mathbf{z} - \boldsymbol{\mu}\|^2$$

forms a sequence $\{m_j;\ j = 0, \ldots, J\}$ of independently distributed, chi-square, random variables. Use the following steps.

(a) Show that

$$\min_{\boldsymbol{\mu} \in \mathbb{S}_{j+1}} \|\mathbf{z} - \boldsymbol{\mu}\|^2 = \min_{\boldsymbol{\mu} \in \mathbb{S}_j} \|\mathbf{z} - \boldsymbol{\mu}\|^2 + \min_{\boldsymbol{\mu} \in \mathbb{S}_{j+1}} \left\|\mathbf{z}_j - \boldsymbol{\mu}\right\|^2$$

is equivalent to

$$\mathbf{z}'(\mathbf{I} - \mathbf{P}_{j+1})\mathbf{z} = \mathbf{z}'(\mathbf{I} - \mathbf{P}_j)\mathbf{z} + \mathbf{z}'(\mathbf{P}_j - \mathbf{P}_{j+1})\mathbf{z}$$

(b) Show that

$$\mathbf{z}'(\mathbf{I} - \mathbf{P}_{j+1})\mathbf{z} \sim \chi^2_{N-M_{j+1}}$$
$$\mathbf{z}'(\mathbf{I} - \mathbf{P}_{j})\mathbf{z} \sim \chi^2_{N-M_{j}}$$
$$\mathbf{z}'(\mathbf{P}_j - \mathbf{P}_{j+1})\mathbf{z} \sim \chi^2_{M_j-M_{j+1}}$$

and $\mathbf{z}'(\mathbf{I} - \mathbf{P}_j)\mathbf{z}$ is independent of $\mathbf{z}'(\mathbf{P}_j - \mathbf{P}_{j+1})\mathbf{z}$.

(c) Show that $m_j = \mathbf{z}'(\mathbf{P}_j - \mathbf{P}_{j+1})\mathbf{z}$ is independent of m_k for all $k < j$.

***10.25 (Minimum Chi-Square)** Show that the results of Exercise 10.24 are a generalization of Lemma 10.1 (Minimum Chi-Square, p. 197): Let $\mathbf{z} \sim \mathfrak{N}(\mathbf{0}, \mathbf{I}_N)$ and $\mathbb{S}_j$ $(j = 1, \ldots, J)$ be a sequence of nested subspaces of $\mathbb{R}^N$, $\mathbb{S}_J \subset \mathbb{S}_{J-1} \subset \cdots \subset \mathbb{S}_2 \subset \mathbb{S}_1 \subset \mathbb{S}_0 = \mathbb{R}^N$. Denote the dimension of $\mathbb{S}_j$ by M_j. Show that

$$\min_{\boldsymbol{\mu}\in\mathbb{S}_{j+1}} \|\mathbf{z} - \boldsymbol{\mu}\|^2 = \min_{\boldsymbol{\mu}\in\mathbb{S}_j} \|\mathbf{z} - \boldsymbol{\mu}\|^2 + \min_{\boldsymbol{\mu}\in\mathbb{S}_{j+1}} \left\|\mathbf{z}_j - \boldsymbol{\mu}\right\|^2$$

is equivalent to

$$\left\|\mathbf{z} - \mathbf{z}_{j+1}\right\|^2 = \min_{\boldsymbol{\mu}\in\mathbb{S}_{j+1}^{\perp}\cap\mathbb{S}_j} \left\|\mathbf{z} - \mathbf{z}_{j+1} - \boldsymbol{\mu}\right\|^2 + \min_{\boldsymbol{\mu}\in\mathbb{S}_j^{\perp}} \left\|\mathbf{z} - \mathbf{z}_{j+1} - \boldsymbol{\mu}\right\|^2$$

where $\mathbb{S}_{j+1}^{\perp} \cap \mathbb{S}_j$ is the orthogonal complement of $\mathbb{S}_j^{\perp}$ within $\mathbb{S}_{j+1}^{\perp}$.

CHAPTER 11

HYPOTHESIS TESTING

11.1 INTRODUCTION

We can also apply the distribution theory of the previous chapter to testing hypotheses. There is a close relationship between the interval estimators that we have already derived and the hypothesis tests that we present in this chapter.

For example, we estimated coefficients for female and nonwhite indicator variables in the log-wage equation. These are the differences in observed wages while taking into account the coincident effects of other variables such as education and experience. A classical test of the hypothesis that the population coefficients are actually zero looks for evidence that contradicts the hypothesis beyond a reasonable doubt. In Figure 11.1, we display the 95% confidence interval for the coefficients, showing that the point (0, 0) does not fall within this interval.

This is the kind of evidence that leads to a rejection of the hypothesis. If we are willing to entertain a 5% chance of mistakenly rejecting the hypothesis when it is valid, then the failure of the hypothesized value to fall within the 95% confidence interval is sufficiently contradictory to convict the hypothesis of falsehood.

In Chapter 4, we also examined the possibility that the coefficients for earnings paid on an hourly basis differed from the coefficients for other types of earnings. Some of the estimates differed substantially in economic terms. Union membership increases the conditional mean of log-wages an estimated 28.4% for earnings paid hourly, but its effect is only 4.5% for other jobs. On the other hand, coefficients such as those for experience were virtually unchanged. Knowing that differences will occur between estimators simply because there is sampling variation, we use hypothesis tests to judge whether the differences are greater than sampling variation would cause.

For the earnings example, we calculated a statistic with a known distribution under the hypothesis that the coefficients for all earnings are the same. The value of the statistic, called an F statistic, was 11.52. The p.d.f. for this statistic, *given that the hypothesis is correct*, appears in Figure 11.2. The observed value of 11.52 is in the extreme right-hand tail of the distribution. The probability of observing this value, or a higher one, is only 2.941×10^{-14}. Given such an unusual outcome, it is hard to believe that the hypothesis is true. We conclude that the coefficients for earnings paid hourly are significantly different from the coefficients for other earnings in *statistical* terms as well as in *economic* ones.

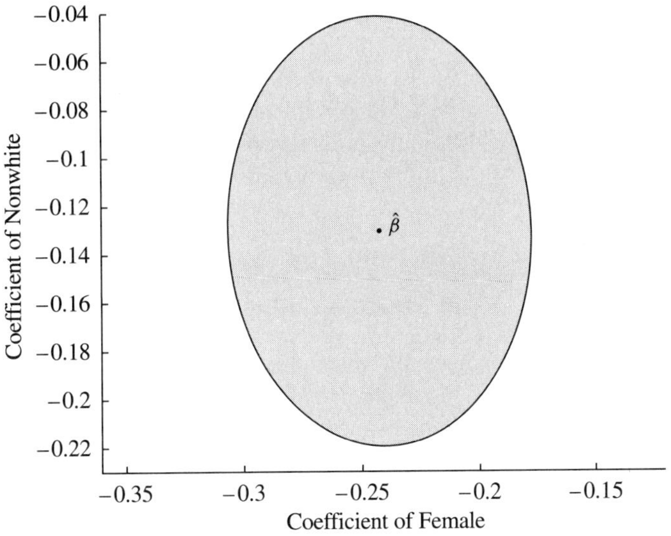

Figure 11.1 Ninety-five percent confidence interval for female and nonwhite coefficients.

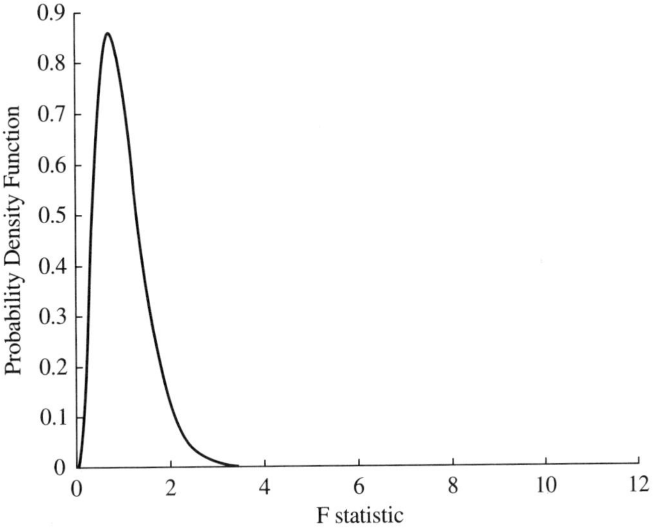

Figure 11.2 Distribution of hypothesis test statistic.

Much of our discussion of the estimation theory for OLS statistics concerns the relative efficiency of estimators. We can study this topic without a distributional assumption such as multivariate normality, because relative efficiency depends on second moments, not probabilities. Under the normality assumption, we can make probability statements that lead to interval estimators and hypothesis tests. The analysis of distribution theory in Chapter 10 focused on cases in which restrictions $\mathbf{R}\boldsymbol{\beta}_0 = \mathbf{r}$ were true. In this chapter, we entertain the alternative hypothesis that $\mathbf{R}\boldsymbol{\beta}_0 \neq \mathbf{r}$ and study the sampling properties of the classical test statistics.

In the next section, we describe hypothesis tests. The classical hypothesis tests are closely related to the interval estimators and rest on the same distributional results. In effect, the evidence in favor of a hypothesis is that it is consistent with a corresponding interval estimator. Subsequently, we examine the ability of hypothesis tests to reveal false hypotheses.

11.2 HYPOTHESIS TESTING

Interval estimation is a convenient precursor to the classical hypothesis tests that we describe in this section. Given a distribution theory for our estimators, we have found interval estimators that correspond directly to the hypothesis tests. A general method for testing whether the hypothesis $H_0 : \mathbf{R}\boldsymbol{\beta}_0 = \mathbf{r}$ is supported at the $100\alpha\%$ level of significance is to check whether r is an element of the $100(1-\alpha)\%$ confidence interval for $\mathbf{R}\boldsymbol{\beta}_0$ given in (10.10).

Recall that classical hypothesis tests consist of several components:

1. two competing hypotheses, a favored "null" hypothesis and an alternative hypothesis;
2. a test statistic, with a distribution known under the null hypothesis;
3. a significance level, the tolerable probability of mistakenly rejecting the null hypothesis when it is correct; and
4. a critical region, the values of the test statistic deemed adverse to the null hypothesis.

The test statistic falls into the critical region with probability equal to the significance level under the null hypothesis.[1]

In the present case, the null hypothesis is a linear restriction on the coefficient vector $\boldsymbol{\beta}_0$, $H_0 : \mathbf{R}\boldsymbol{\beta}_0 = \mathbf{r}$ and the alternative hypothesis is the complementary $H_1 : \mathbf{R}\boldsymbol{\beta}_0 \neq \mathbf{r}$. We suppose that $\mathbf{R}$ is a full-rank $(K-M) \times K$ matrix in which $M \leq K$ and $\mathbf{r}$ is a column vector of $K-M$ elements. The test statistic is the so-called F statistic

$$\hat{F} \equiv \frac{(\mathbf{R}\hat{\boldsymbol{\beta}} - \mathbf{r})'[\mathbf{R}(\mathbf{X}'\mathbf{X})^{-1}\mathbf{R}']^{-1}(\mathbf{R}\hat{\boldsymbol{\beta}} - \mathbf{r})/\,(K-M)}{s^2} \tag{11.1}$$

which has the $F_{K-M,N-K}$ distribution under H_0. For the significance level α, the critical region is $\{F \mid F > F_{K-M,N-K;1-\alpha}\}$. If $\hat{F}$ is unusually large in the sense that it falls into this critical region, then one "rejects" H_0 in favor of the alternative $H_1 : \mathbf{R}\boldsymbol{\beta}_0 \neq \mathbf{r}$ at the $100\alpha\%$ level of significance. Otherwise, one "accepts" the null hypothesis $\mathbf{R}\boldsymbol{\beta}_0 = \mathbf{r}$. This is the conventional way to test linear hypotheses in the normal classical regression model.

Note that this critical region for $\hat{F}$, written in terms of r, translates into the complement of the interval estimator for $\mathbf{R}\boldsymbol{\beta}_0$:

$$\left\{\gamma \in \text{Col}(\mathbf{R}) \,\middle|\, \left(\gamma - \mathbf{R}\hat{\boldsymbol{\beta}}\right)' \left[\mathbf{R}\left(\mathbf{X}'\mathbf{X}\right)^{-1}\mathbf{R}'\right]^{-1} \left(\gamma - \mathbf{R}\hat{\boldsymbol{\beta}}\right) \leq s^2\,(K-M)\,F_{K-M,N-K;1-\alpha}\right\}$$

[1] The significance level is also called the *size* of the test.

Whenever $\hat{F}$ falls *within* the critical region of the hypothesis test, the hypothesized value $\mathbf{r}$ is *outside* the estimation interval for $\mathbf{R}\boldsymbol{\beta}_0$ and vice versa. This duality between interval estimation and hypothesis testing is natural, because both rest on the same distributional result, (10.12). It emphasizes a general hypothesis testing principle, the comparison of an unrestricted estimator with its hypothesized value.

Testing a single restriction on $\boldsymbol{\beta}_0$ is an important special case of the F test. Perhaps this occurs most commonly in a hypothesis that one element of $\boldsymbol{\beta}_0$ is zero. For notational ease, let β_{01} be that element of $\boldsymbol{\beta}_0$. Partitioning $\mathbf{X}$ conformably, $\mathbf{X}_1$ is the first column of $\mathbf{X}$. Recalling that[2]

$$\operatorname{Var}[\hat{\beta}_1 \mid \mathbf{X}] = \sigma_0^2 \left[\mathbf{X}_1' \left(\mathbf{I} - \mathbf{P}_{\mathbf{X}_2}\right) \mathbf{X}_1\right]^{-1}$$

the interval estimator simplifies to

$$\left\{ \beta_1 \in \mathbb{R} \left| \frac{\left(\beta_1 - \hat{\beta}_1\right)^2 \mathbf{X}_1' \left(\mathbf{I} - \mathbf{P}_{\mathbf{X}_2}\right) \mathbf{X}_1}{s^2} \le F_{1,N-K;1-\alpha} \right. \right\}$$

$$= \left\{ \beta_1 \in \mathbb{R} \left| \left| \frac{\beta_1 - \hat{\beta}_1}{\hat{\sigma}_1} \right| \le t_{N-K;1-\alpha/2} \right. \right\}$$

$$= \left\{ \beta_1 \in \mathbb{R} \left| \left| \beta_1 - \hat{\beta}_1 \right| \le \hat{\sigma}_1 \, t_{N-K;1-\alpha/2} \right. \right\}$$

where

$$\hat{\sigma}_1^2 = \frac{s^2}{\mathbf{X}_1' \left(\mathbf{I} - \mathbf{P}_{\mathbf{X}_2}\right) \mathbf{X}_1}$$

is a scalar and $(t_\nu)^2 \sim F_{1,\nu}$ (Theorems D.13 and D.15).[3] This interval estimator has a dual test statistic, the t statistic

$$\hat{t} = \frac{\hat{\beta}_1 - r}{\hat{\sigma}_1}$$

used to test $H_0 : \beta_{01} = r$ against $H_1 : \beta_{01} \neq r$. This t statistic is the ratio of the difference between the estimated coefficient and its hypothesized value over the estimated standard error of the coefficient, a formula that is reminiscent of the t statistic for a hypothesis test about the population mean of a normal distribution (see section E.2.2).

Unlike the F test, one can also consider such one-sided alternative hypotheses as $H_1 : \beta_{01} > r$. In this case, one focuses on unusually large values of $\hat{t}$ and the acceptance interval is

$$\left\{\hat{t} \in \mathbb{R} \mid \hat{t} \le t_{N-K;1-\alpha}\right\}$$

Note the change in the critical value from the t distribution: $t_{N-K;1-\alpha} < t_{N-K;1-\alpha/2}$ to maintain the significance level equal to α. As a result, the one-sided test is more likely to reject the null hypothesis under the alternative hypothesis than the two-sided test. One therefore prefers the one-sided test when the one-sided alternative is appropriate.[4]

---

[2] See equation (9.2) on p. 178.

[3] The first diagonal element of $s^2 \cdot (\mathbf{X}'\mathbf{X})^{-1}$ is also equal to $\hat{\sigma}_1^2$.

[4] See Judge et al. (1980) for a brief introduction to hypothesis tests for multivariate inequalities.

There are several insightful ways to interpret the quadratic form in the numerator of the $\hat{F}$ test statistic. All of them rest on the RLS estimator $\hat{\boldsymbol{\beta}}_{\mathrm{R}}$ that satisfies the restrictions $\mathbf{R}\boldsymbol{\beta} = \mathbf{r}$. Originally, in Chapter 4, we presented RLS for linear restrictions of the form $\boldsymbol{\beta} = \mathbf{S}\boldsymbol{\gamma} + \mathbf{s}$, because this is a natural way to implement RLS. In hypothesis testing, the restrictions often take the form $\mathbf{R}\boldsymbol{\beta} = \mathbf{r}$, because it is natural to compare the restricted value r with the unrestricted estimator $\mathbf{R}\hat{\boldsymbol{\beta}}$. The two forms of restrictions are equivalent and one can always be derived from the other.[5]

Because $\mathbf{R}\boldsymbol{\beta} = \mathbf{r}$ is convenient for hypothesis testing, we also derive $\hat{\boldsymbol{\beta}}_{\mathrm{R}}$ in the terms of these restrictions and find the alternative expressions for the F statistic. In Exercises 4.14 and 4.15, we provide two derivations of

$$\hat{\boldsymbol{\beta}}_{\mathrm{R}} = \hat{\boldsymbol{\beta}} - \left(\mathbf{X}'\mathbf{X}\right)^{-1}\mathbf{R}'\left[\mathbf{R}\left(\mathbf{X}'\mathbf{X}\right)^{-1}\mathbf{R}'\right]^{-1}\left(\mathbf{R}\hat{\boldsymbol{\beta}} - \mathbf{r}\right)$$

As a result, the numerator of $\hat{F}$ can be written

$$\begin{aligned}(\mathbf{R}\hat{\boldsymbol{\beta}} - r)'[\mathbf{R}(\mathbf{X}'\mathbf{X})^{-1}\mathbf{R}']^{-1}(\mathbf{R}\hat{\boldsymbol{\beta}} - r) &= (\hat{\boldsymbol{\beta}}_{\mathrm{R}} - \hat{\boldsymbol{\beta}})'\mathbf{X}'\mathbf{X}(\hat{\boldsymbol{\beta}}_{\mathrm{R}} - \hat{\boldsymbol{\beta}}) \\ &= \left\|\hat{\boldsymbol{\beta}}_{\mathrm{R}} - \hat{\boldsymbol{\beta}}\right\|^2_{\mathbf{X}'\mathbf{X}}\end{aligned} \tag{11.2}$$

In this form, the test statistic is measuring a generalized distance between *all* the elements of the restricted and unrestricted estimators.[6] When the two estimators differ substantially, this is evidence against the restrictions. The distribution theory of the F statistic formalizes the measurement of the distance between $\hat{\boldsymbol{\beta}}_{\mathrm{R}}$ and $\hat{\boldsymbol{\beta}}$ by describing a doubtful outcome if H_0 is assumed to be true.

Repeating (4.11), we can always relate $\hat{\boldsymbol{\mu}}_{\mathrm{R}}$ to $\hat{\boldsymbol{\mu}}$ through

$$\begin{aligned}\hat{\boldsymbol{\mu}}_{\mathrm{R}} = \underset{\{z=\mathbf{X}\boldsymbol{\beta}|\mathbf{R}\boldsymbol{\beta}=\mathbf{r}\}}{\operatorname{argmin}} \left\|\hat{\boldsymbol{\mu}} - \mathbf{z}\right\|^2 \quad &\Rightarrow \quad \hat{\boldsymbol{\mu}}_{\mathrm{R}} \perp (\hat{\boldsymbol{\mu}} - \hat{\boldsymbol{\mu}}_{\mathrm{R}}) \\ &\Leftrightarrow \quad \hat{\boldsymbol{\mu}}_{\mathrm{R}}'\hat{\boldsymbol{\mu}} = \hat{\boldsymbol{\mu}}_{\mathrm{R}}'\hat{\boldsymbol{\mu}}_{\mathrm{R}}\end{aligned}$$

so that

$$\left\|\hat{\boldsymbol{\mu}}\right\|^2 + \left\|\mathbf{y} - \hat{\boldsymbol{\mu}}\right\|^2 = \|\mathbf{y}\|^2 = \left\|\hat{\boldsymbol{\mu}}_{\mathrm{R}}\right\|^2 + \left\|\mathbf{y} - \hat{\boldsymbol{\mu}}_{\mathrm{R}}\right\|^2$$

Therefore, we can also write (11.2) as

$$\begin{aligned}\left\|\hat{\boldsymbol{\beta}}_{\mathrm{R}} - \hat{\boldsymbol{\beta}}\right\|^2_{\mathbf{X}'\mathbf{X}} &= \left\|\hat{\boldsymbol{\mu}}_{\mathrm{R}} - \hat{\boldsymbol{\mu}}\right\|^2 \\ &= \left\|\hat{\boldsymbol{\mu}}\right\|^2 - \left\|\hat{\boldsymbol{\mu}}_{\mathrm{R}}\right\|^2 \\ &= \left\|\mathbf{y} - \hat{\boldsymbol{\mu}}_{\mathrm{R}}\right\|^2 - \left\|\mathbf{y} - \hat{\boldsymbol{\mu}}\right\|^2\end{aligned} \tag{11.3}$$

---

[5] For example, given $\mathbf{R}\boldsymbol{\beta} = \mathbf{r}$ we can order and partition $\mathbf{R}$ and $\boldsymbol{\beta}$ so that $\mathbf{R}\boldsymbol{\beta} = \mathbf{R}_1\boldsymbol{\beta}_1 + \mathbf{R}_2\boldsymbol{\beta}_2$ where $\mathbf{R}_1$ is nonsingular. Then

$$\boldsymbol{\beta} = \begin{bmatrix}\boldsymbol{\beta}_1 \\ \boldsymbol{\beta}_2\end{bmatrix} = \begin{bmatrix}\mathbf{R}_1^{-1}\mathbf{r} - \mathbf{R}_1^{-1}\mathbf{R}_2\boldsymbol{\beta}_2 \\ \boldsymbol{\beta}_2\end{bmatrix} = \begin{bmatrix}-\mathbf{R}_1^{-1}\mathbf{R}_2 \\ \mathbf{I}_{K-M}\end{bmatrix}\boldsymbol{\beta}_2 + \begin{bmatrix}\mathbf{R}_1^{-1}\mathbf{r} \\ \mathbf{0}\end{bmatrix}$$

is $\boldsymbol{\beta} = \mathbf{S}\boldsymbol{\gamma} + \mathbf{s}$ where

$$\mathbf{S} = \begin{bmatrix}-\mathbf{R}_1^{-1}\mathbf{R}_2 \\ \mathbf{I}_{K-M}\end{bmatrix} \quad \text{and} \quad \mathbf{s} = \begin{bmatrix}\mathbf{R}_1^{-1}\mathbf{r} \\ \mathbf{0}\end{bmatrix}$$

Thus, RLS subject to either expression of the restrictions is the same program.

[6] See also Exercise 10.14.

The numerator of the $\hat{F}$ statistic is also a standardized difference in the restricted and unrestricted minimum sum of squared residuals. In this sense, the $\hat{F}$ statistic is measuring how much the goodness of fit improves when the restrictions are removed: a large increase suggests that the restrictions are false.

EXAMPLE 11.1

In Chapter 4, we estimated two wage equations, one for those who work for hourly wages and one for those who do not. Given the information in Table 4.1 (p. 75) and the original (restricted) regression for the entire data set in Table 1.8 (p. 12), we can compute an $\hat{F}$ statistic for the null hypothesis that the coefficients are all the same for both types of workers. The sum of squared residuals for the restricted regression is 278.753. The sum of squared residuals for the unrestricted regression is the sum of the residual sum of squares for the hourly and nonhourly wage regressions: $121.671 + 140.492 = 262.163$.[7] Therefore, $\hat{F} = 11.525$. The probability that an $F_{7,1275}$ random variable exceeds this $\hat{F}$ statistic is so small that it is effectively zero. Therefore, we find strong evidence against the equality of the coefficients. At the 1% level of significance we reject the null hypothesis.

This sort of split-sample test is called a Chow test, after Chow (1960). It is one of the most popular applications of the F test.

EXAMPLE 11.2

OLS regression software commonly prints out an F statistic for the null hypothesis that all of the coefficients except the intercept are equal to zero. This statistic is often described in terms of various *sums of squares*. Let $\mathbf{X}_2 = \boldsymbol{\iota}$ in the partition $\mathbf{X} = [\mathbf{X}_1, \mathbf{X}_2]$ and recall the orthogonal projector decomposition $\mathbf{P}_\mathbf{X} = \mathbf{P}_{\mathbf{X}_2} + \mathbf{P}_{\mathbf{X}_{1\perp 2}}$.[8] Then $\left\|\mathbf{y} - \hat{\boldsymbol{\mu}}_\mathrm{R}\right\|^2$ is the *total sum of squares*

$$\left\|\mathbf{y} - \hat{\boldsymbol{\mu}}_\mathrm{R}\right\|^2 = \|\mathbf{y} - \boldsymbol{\iota}\bar{y}\|^2 = \mathbf{y}'\left(\mathbf{I} - \mathbf{P}_{\mathbf{X}_2}\right)\mathbf{y}$$

$\left\|\mathbf{y} - \hat{\boldsymbol{\mu}}\right\|^2$ is the *residual (or error) sum of squares*

$$\left\|\mathbf{y} - \hat{\boldsymbol{\mu}}\right\|^2 = \mathbf{y}'\left(\mathbf{I} - \mathbf{P}_\mathbf{X}\right)\mathbf{y}$$

and the difference

$$\left\|\mathbf{y} - \hat{\boldsymbol{\mu}}_\mathrm{R}\right\|^2 - \left\|\mathbf{y} - \hat{\boldsymbol{\mu}}\right\|^2 = \mathbf{y}'\left(\mathbf{P}_\mathbf{X} - \mathbf{P}_{\mathbf{X}_2}\right)y = \mathbf{y}'\mathbf{P}_{\mathbf{X}_{1\perp 2}}\mathbf{y}$$

is the *regression (or explained) sum of squares*. We can write the F statistic for $H_0 : \boldsymbol{\beta}_{01} = 0$ as a function of the sums of squares

$$\hat{F} = \frac{\mathbf{y}'\mathbf{P}_{\mathbf{X}_{1\perp 2}}\mathbf{y}/(K-1)}{\mathbf{y}'\left(\mathbf{I} - \mathbf{P}_\mathbf{X}\right)\mathbf{y}/(N-K)} \tag{11.4}$$

The software often prints the sums of squares as well.

[7] See the comment on p. 76 to see why one sums the residual sum of squares for the two regressions.

[8] See Exercise 3.17.

Alternatively, recall the R^2 goodness-of-fit measure

$$R^2 = \frac{\mathbf{y}'\mathbf{P}_{\mathbf{X}_{1\perp 2}}\mathbf{y}}{\mathbf{y}'\left(\mathbf{I} - \mathbf{P}_{\mathbf{X}_2}\right)\mathbf{y}}$$

that is the ratio of the regression and total sum of squares. The F statistic is also given by

$$\hat{F} = \frac{N-K}{K-1}\frac{R^2}{1-R^2}$$

Unlike R^2, the F statistic takes into account the number of explanatory variables. A value of R^2 near one that corresponds to a large number of explanatory variables may have a small, statistically insignificant F statistic.[9]

Each of the alternative interpretations of the numerator of the F statistic illustrates general hypothesis testing methods. In the present analysis, the methods are all equivalent. But we will apply these methods in other situations and obtain alternative test statistics. In Exercise 11.5, we introduce yet another method.

11.3 STATISTICAL POWER

Now we turn to the behavior of the F statistic under the alternative hypothesis $H_1 : \mathbf{R}\boldsymbol{\beta}_0 \neq \mathbf{r}$. Researchers usually describe these properties with the concept of *statistical power.*

DEFINITION 20 (POWER OF A HYPOTHESIS TEST) *The power of a hypothesis test at the $100\alpha\%$ level of significance is the probability of rejecting the null hypothesis when a member of the alternative hypothesis actually holds.*

Statistical power is, in a sense, the counterpart in hypothesis testing to relative efficiency in estimation. Given a hypothesis, we may seek a most powerful test among a family of tests, just as we may seek a relatively efficient estimator among a family of estimators. In Section 11.3.1 we explain the power characteristics of the F test. In Section 11.3.2 we discuss the specialization to the t test. Finally, we discuss optimality and the F test.

---

[9] Incidentally, this weakness in the R^2 measure has led to the widespread use of an alternative goodness-of-fit measure called *adjusted* R^2, or $\bar{R}^2$:

$$\bar{R}^2 = 1 - \frac{RSS/(N-K)}{TSS/(N-1)} = 1 - \frac{RSS}{TSS}\frac{N-1}{N-K}$$

In this notation, the plain R^2 measure is just (see Exercise 3.19)

$$R^2 = 1 - \frac{RSS}{TSS}$$

so the adjustment corresponds to dividing each sum of squares by its "degrees of freedom," the rank of the projection matrix associated with the sum of squares. Although it penalizes the goodness of fit for adding explanatory variables, this adjustment also removes the interpretation possesed by R^2: the fraction of the variation in $\mathbf{y}$ exhibited by the linear regression fit.

11.3.1 Power Comparisons for Tests

We collect the properties of the power of the F test in the following proposition.

PROPOSITION 13 (POWER OF THE F TEST) *Under Assumptions 3.1, 6.1, 7.1, and 10.1, the power function* $\Pr\{\hat{F} \geq F_{K-M,N-K;1-\alpha} \mid \mathbf{R}\boldsymbol{\beta}_0\}$

1. *strictly increases with c in* $\mathbf{r} - \mathbf{R}\boldsymbol{\beta}_0 = c \cdot \boldsymbol{\gamma}$ *for every* $\boldsymbol{\gamma} \in \mathbb{R}^{K-M}$, $\boldsymbol{\gamma} \neq 0$,
2. *strictly increases with the relative efficiency of* $\mathbf{R}\hat{\boldsymbol{\beta}}$,
3. *strictly decreases with the sampling variance of* s^2, *and*
4. *strictly increases as valid restrictions are removed from* $\mathbf{R}\boldsymbol{\beta}_0 = \mathbf{r}$.

We discuss the justification of this proposition in Section 11.4, *Basic Distribution Theory*. Here we discuss its implications.

First, we see that as $\mathbf{r} - \mathbf{R}\boldsymbol{\beta}_0$ grows out from the origin in any direction within $\mathbb{R}^N$, the power of the F test becomes higher. Obviously, this is a desirable property for a hypothesis test to have. But not all tests necessarily possess it, so it is worth checking.

Second, we see that the power of the F test improves with the efficiency with which we estimate $\mathbf{R}\hat{\boldsymbol{\beta}}$ or s^2. These are also desirable properties. It would be odd to find that as our knowledge of the population parameters improved, our test did not also improve. Perhaps the improvement in power associated with the sampling variance of s^2 is not expected. After all, s^2 is independent of $\mathbf{R}\hat{\boldsymbol{\beta}}$. Nevertheless, better knowledge of σ_0^2 tightens our interval estimator for $\mathbf{R}\hat{\boldsymbol{\beta}}_0$ and, similarly, increases the power of the F test.

The final property of the test is the most interesting, and deserves the most explanation. If one could know that some of the restrictions in $\mathbf{R}\boldsymbol{\beta}_0 = \mathbf{r}$ are true, it seems sensible not to test those restrictions and to conduct an F test on the subset of restrictions that may be false. The final property of an F test states that this action improves the power of the test. In a sense, this property is analogous to the relative efficiency of the RLS estimator over the OLS estimator. In that case, it is better not to unnecessarily estimate parameters. In the current hypothesis testing case, it is better not to unnecessarily test restrictions.

Tests of a single linear restriction are, therefore, the most powerful tests of that one restriction. Researchers often conduct such tests using the $\hat{t}$ statistic described in Chapter 10. In using several t tests, one may neglect that the $\hat{t}$ statistics have a dependent distribution, the topic of our next section.

11.3.2 t Statistics

It is common in descriptions of estimation results to see tables of estimated coefficients $\hat{\beta}_k$ $(k = 1, \ldots, K)$ and the t statistics that would be used to test $\beta_k = 0$ for each coefficient. In practice, the coefficients with t statistics larger in absolute value than $t_{0.975,N-K}$ (which is usually approximately 2) are often labeled "significant." Inevitably, one makes comparisons across the entries in these tables. Careful interpretation of such comparisons must acknowledge several statistical properties that we have already explained.

First, these statistics are dependently distributed. The coefficients vary together according to the variance matrix $\sigma_0^2 \cdot (\mathbf{X}'\mathbf{X})^{-1}$. Among t statistics the presence of s in all the denominators introduces another source of probabilistic dependence. As a result of dependence, the t statistics are giving related information. For example, if one of the t statistics is "significant," conditional on that outcome another may also be "significant" with high probability even though the associated population coefficient is zero. This situation can arise with dependence. For this reason, and human frailty, comparisons of t statistics within tables of estimated coefficients have limited value for statistical inference.

A useful way to illustrate this point is to observe that a table of statistically insignificant t statistics for $\beta_k = 0$ $(k = 1, \ldots, K)$ can coincide with a statistically significant F statistic for $H_0 : \boldsymbol{\beta}_0 = \mathbf{0}$. This occurs when the interval estimator for $\boldsymbol{\beta}_0$ does not contain the origin but the estimates of the marginal variances of the $\hat{\boldsymbol{\beta}}_k$ are large enough to make the marginal interval estimators for the β_{0k} all contain zero. Figure 11.3 gives a two-dimensional illustration. The interior ellipse has a radius proportional to $F_{1,30;0.95}$, which is the critical value for a one-dimensional test, whereas the exterior ellipse has a radius proportional to $2 \cdot F_{2,30;0.95}$, the comparable number for a two-dimensional test. The box shows where the acceptance regions fall on the axes for the one-dimensional t statistics and the exterior ellipse shows the acceptance region for the two-dimensional F test. In this case, the covariance between the estimators causes the t statistics to suggest a different outcome than the F statistic: both acceptance regions for the t statistics include zero, but the elliptical acceptance region of the F test statistic excludes the origin.

The converse can also occur: a table of statistically significant t statistics for $\beta_k = 0$ $(k = 1, \ldots, K)$ can coincide with a statistically insignificant F statistic for $H_0 : \boldsymbol{\beta} = \mathbf{0}$. Figure 11.4 illustrates this case. In this case, however, a small change in the level of significance will lead to similar conclusions. If one reports the probability, or *p value*, for the test statistics, then this will be clear. In this illustration, the p values for the t statistics are 0.9774 for β_1 and 0.9714 for

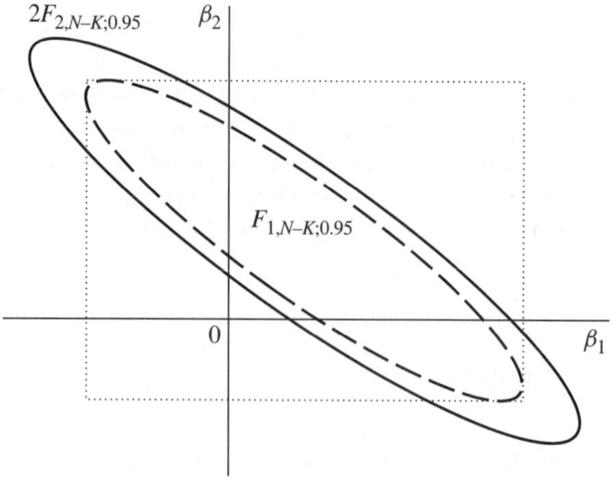

Figure 11.3 Joint versus marginal statistical significance.

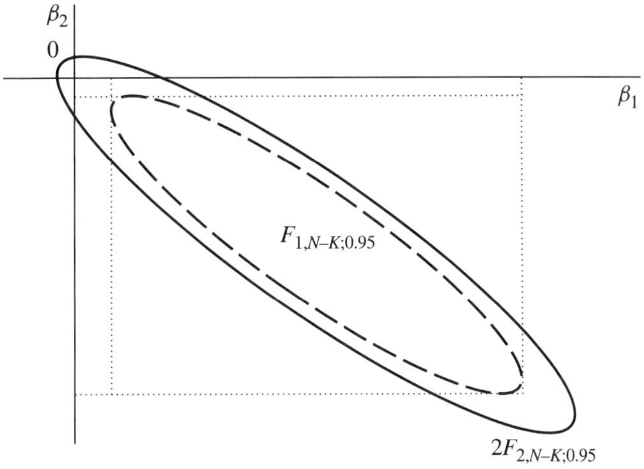

Figure 11.4 Joint versus marginal statistical significance.

β_2 whereas the p value of the F statistic is 0.9317. At the 5% level of significance, the t statistics are statistically significant and the F statistic is not, but practically speaking this distinction is too sharp.

Second, the sound bite "significant estimated coefficient" is often heard as "fairly large effect," rather than "the interval estimator does not contain zero." The phrase "insignificant estimated coefficient" may sound like "negligible effect." But the fact that the interval estimator contains zero says nothing about whether the interval estimator contains large coefficient values as well. We might ascribe such failures in communication to confusion of hypothesis testing with interval estimation.[10] The *statistical* significance of t statistics concerns particular values of the coefficients. One evaluates the *qualitative* significance of the estimated coefficients using interval estimation, evaluating the entire range of likely values.

Put another way, an "insignificant" t statistic can occur for two reasons: the estimated coefficient may be qualitatively close to zero *or* the estimated standard error may be very large. In the latter case, a statistically imprecise estimate supports both a small and a large effect in the population; it is uninformative.

11.3.3 Optimal Power and the F Test

The F test does not possess an optimal power function. One might expect a result analogous to earlier results on the efficiency of OLS estimators, especially in light of those results. Nevertheless, just as two estimators may not be ordered by relative efficiency, two hypothesis tests may have power functions that cross in the parameter space of the alternative hypothesis. Hence, the very existence of a most powerful test would be an interesting result and such tests do occur in special cases. However, testing $\mathbf{R}\boldsymbol{\beta}_0 = \mathbf{r}$ in the normal regression model is not one of those cases. The

[10] We also recognize that there may be other explanations for this usage.

reason is analogous to the fact that this statistical theory does not provide an optimal interval estimator for $\mathbf{R}\boldsymbol{\beta}_0$.

To see an example of crossing power functions, compare the F test of $\mathbf{R}\boldsymbol{\beta}_0 = \mathbf{r}$ and the F test of the subset $\mathbf{R}_1\boldsymbol{\beta}_{01} = \mathbf{r}_1$. The latter is more powerful than the former when $\mathbf{R}_1\boldsymbol{\beta}_{01} \neq \mathbf{r}_1$ and $\mathbf{R}_2\boldsymbol{\beta}_{02} = \mathbf{r}_2$. Now consider the opposite case, $\mathbf{R}_1\boldsymbol{\beta}_{01} = \mathbf{r}_1$ and $\mathbf{R}_2\boldsymbol{\beta}_{02} \neq \mathbf{r}_2$. The latter test has power equal to the significance level. On the other hand, the F test of $\mathbf{R}\boldsymbol{\beta}_0 = \mathbf{r}$ still has power that exceeds α. Thus, the power functions cross.

In hypothesis testing in several directions, this phenomenon is ubiquitous. Ultimately, we can always choose to construct a test that concentrates power in particular directions at the expense of power in other directions. This is what we do when we drop restrictions from a set $\mathbf{R}\boldsymbol{\beta}_0 = \mathbf{r}$: we set the power in the omitted directions to zero and gain power in the directions of the restrictions we retain.

The simplest example of this phenomenon occurs with the two-sided t test. We may choose an asymmetric acceptance interval for the $\hat{t}$ statistic, provided the probability of the interval is α under the null hypothesis. This will place more power on the side of the interval that is closer to zero, thereby improving the power on that side relative to the usual symmetric two-sided test. This may be desirable, but the decision belongs to the researcher applying the test.

11.4 BASIC DISTRIBUTION THEORY

The formal analysis of statistical power involves two distributions that generalize distributions we have already used.

DEFINITION 21 (NONCENTRAL CHI-SQUARE DISTRIBUTION) *If $\mathbf{z} \sim \mathfrak{N}(\boldsymbol{\mu}, \mathbf{I}_\nu)$ $(\nu \in \mathbb{N})$ then the distribution of $w = \mathbf{z}'\mathbf{z}$ is the noncentral chi-square distribution with degrees of freedom parameter ν and noncentrality parameter $\lambda = \boldsymbol{\mu}'\boldsymbol{\mu}$.*[11] *This is denoted by $w \sim \chi^2_\nu(\lambda)$.*

Notice that the noncentral chi-square distribution depends on $\boldsymbol{\mu}$ only through its squared length $\lambda = \boldsymbol{\mu}'\boldsymbol{\mu}$.[12] The parameter λ is called the *noncentrality parameter*. When the scalar $\lambda = 0$, the noncentral chi-square distribution specializes to the chi-square distribution, sometimes called the *central chi-square* distribution for this reason.

The noncentral chi-square distribution arises in our distribution theory because under the alternative hypothesis the statistic $\mathbf{R}\hat{\boldsymbol{\beta}} - \mathbf{r}$ has a multivariate normal distribution with a *nonzero* mean. When the parameter σ_0^2 is known and we use the chi-square distribution for interval estimation hypothesis testing, the noncentral chi-square is useful for studying power. Typically, of course, we do not know σ_0^2 and we employ the F distribution. For this case, the second distribution that we need follows predictably from the noncentral chi-square.

---

[11] Some authors prefer to define the noncentrality parameter as $\frac{1}{2}\boldsymbol{\mu}'\boldsymbol{\mu}$ and others use $\sqrt{\boldsymbol{\mu}'\boldsymbol{\mu}} = \|\boldsymbol{\mu}\|$.

[12] See Appendix F for a discussion of the noncentral distributions.

DEFINITION 22 (NONCENTRAL F DISTRIBUTION) *Let $\chi^2_{\nu_1}(\lambda)$ and $\chi^2_{\nu_2}$ be independently distributed. Then the distribution of*

$$F_{\nu_1,\nu_2}(\lambda) = \frac{\chi^2_{\nu_1}(\lambda)/\nu_1}{\chi^2_{\nu_2}/\nu_2}$$

is called the noncentral F *distribution with ν_1 and ν_2 degrees of freedom and noncentrality parameter λ.*

In the classical hypothesis test of $H_0 : \mathbf{R}\boldsymbol{\beta}_0 = \mathbf{r}$, the test statistic $\hat{F}$ has a noncentral F distribution under the alternative hypothesis $\mathbf{R}\boldsymbol{\beta}_0 \neq \mathbf{r}$. The noncentrality parameter of the distribution of $\hat{F}$ is

$$\lambda = (\mathbf{r} - \mathbf{R}\boldsymbol{\beta}_0)' \left[\sigma_0^2 \cdot \mathbf{R}\left(\mathbf{X}'\mathbf{X}\right)^{-1}\mathbf{R}'\right]^{-1} (\mathbf{r} - \mathbf{R}\boldsymbol{\beta}_0)$$

It arises in the distribution of the chi-square numerator of the $\hat{F}$ statistic,

$$\begin{aligned}&\left(\mathbf{r} - \mathbf{R}\hat{\boldsymbol{\beta}}\right)' \left[\sigma_0^2 \cdot \mathbf{R}\left(\mathbf{X}'\mathbf{X}\right)^{-1}\mathbf{R}'\right]^{-1} \left(\mathbf{r} - \mathbf{R}\hat{\boldsymbol{\beta}}\right)\\ &= \left[\mathbf{r} - \mathbf{R}\boldsymbol{\beta}_0 - \mathbf{R}\left(\hat{\boldsymbol{\beta}} - \boldsymbol{\beta}_0\right)\right]' \left[\sigma_0^2 \cdot \mathbf{R}\left(\mathbf{X}'\mathbf{X}\right)^{-1}\mathbf{R}'\right]^{-1} \left[\mathbf{r} - \mathbf{R}\boldsymbol{\beta}_0 - \mathbf{R}\left(\hat{\boldsymbol{\beta}} - \boldsymbol{\beta}_0\right)\right]\end{aligned}$$

Following the proof technique of Lemma 10.2 (Chi-Square Quadratic Forms, p. 204), this is a quadratic form $\mathbf{z}'\mathbf{z}$ in a $\mathbf{z} \sim \mathfrak{N}(\boldsymbol{\mu}, \mathbf{I}_{K-M})$ random variable where

$$\boldsymbol{\mu} \equiv \mathbf{A}^{-1}(\mathbf{r} - \mathbf{R}\boldsymbol{\beta}_0) \tag{11.5}$$

and

$$\mathbf{A}\mathbf{A}' \equiv \sigma_0^2 \cdot \mathbf{R}\left(\mathbf{X}'\mathbf{X}\right)^{-1}\mathbf{R}' \tag{11.6}$$

If $\boldsymbol{\mu}$ were the zero vector, then this quadratic form would have a chi-square distribution with $K-M$ degrees of freedom. In general, this quadratic form has a noncentral chi-square distribution.

In Figure 11.5, we replot Figure 11.2, the p.d.f. of the F test statistic for different values of the noncentrality parameter λ. This illustrates how probability moves to the right as the noncentrality parameter grows, causing the probability of rejection to grow. The observed value of 11.52 for $\hat{F}$ suggests that the noncentrality parameter was higher than any of the values we chose.

Proposition 13 rests on the noncentral F distribution of $\hat{F}$ under $\mathbf{R}\boldsymbol{\beta}_0 \neq \mathbf{r}$ and the following lemma.

LEMMA 11.1 *For every α between 0 and 1, the function* $\Pr\{F_{\nu_1,\nu_2}(\lambda) \geq F_{\nu_1,\nu_2;1-\alpha}\}$ *is*

1. *an increasing function of λ,*
2. *a decreasing function of ν_1, and*
3. *an increasing function of ν_2.*

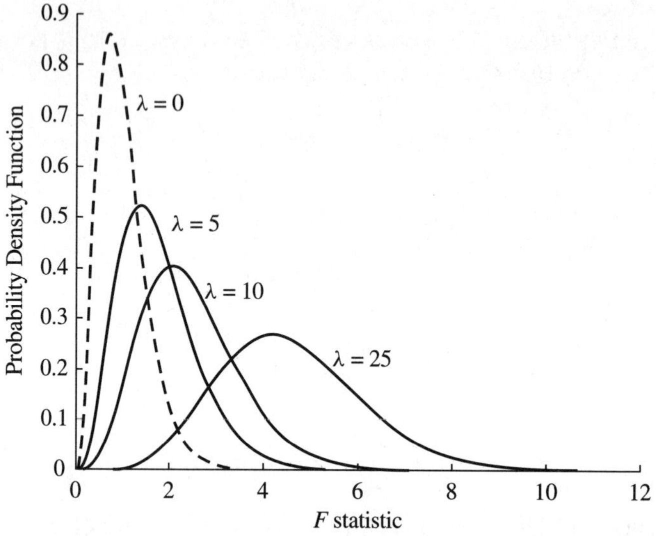

Figure 11.5 Distribution of hypothesis test statistic under alternatives.

We discuss the proof of this lemma in Appendix F and we comment here on the relationship between this lemma and Proposition 13.

Properties 1 and 2 of the F test derive from the noncentrality parameter, which is the squared generalized Euclidean distance between $\mathbf{r}$ and $\mathbf{R}\boldsymbol{\beta}_0$ with respect to the inverse of $\mathrm{Var}[\mathbf{R}\hat{\boldsymbol{\beta}} \mid \mathbf{X}]$. That the distribution of our test statistic under the alternative hypothesis depends on this one scalar greatly simplifies the study of its power function. The first property simply recognizes that the noncentrality parameter is a measure of distance: setting $\mathbf{r} - \mathbf{R}\boldsymbol{\beta}_0 = c \cdot \boldsymbol{\gamma}$ we have

$$\lambda = c^2 \boldsymbol{\gamma}' \left[\sigma_0^2 \cdot \mathbf{R}\left(\mathbf{X}'\mathbf{X}\right)^{-1}\mathbf{R}'\right]^{-1} \boldsymbol{\gamma}$$

which is an increasing function of the scale parameter c.

Note that the distance between $\mathbf{r}$ and $\mathbf{R}\boldsymbol{\beta}_0$ also grows as our ability to estimate $\mathbf{R}\hat{\boldsymbol{\beta}}$ improves. The variance ellipse of $\mathbf{R}\hat{\boldsymbol{\beta}}$ is

$$\left\{\boldsymbol{\gamma} \in \mathrm{Col}(\mathbf{R}) \mid (\boldsymbol{\gamma} - \mathbf{R}\boldsymbol{\beta}_0)' \left[\sigma_0^2 \cdot \mathbf{R}\left(\mathbf{X}'\mathbf{X}\right)^{-1}\mathbf{R}'\right]^{-1} (\boldsymbol{\gamma} - \mathbf{R}\boldsymbol{\beta}_0) \leq 1\right\}$$

and when this interval shrinks (as $\mathbf{R}\hat{\boldsymbol{\beta}}$ becomes relatively more efficient), this corresponds to the quadratic form

$$(\boldsymbol{\gamma} - \mathbf{R}\boldsymbol{\beta}_0)' \left[\sigma_0^2 \cdot \mathbf{R}\left(\mathbf{X}'\mathbf{X}\right)^{-1}\mathbf{R}'\right]^{-1} (\boldsymbol{\gamma} - \mathbf{R}\boldsymbol{\beta}_0)$$

getting larger for any $\boldsymbol{\gamma}$. That is, the noncentrality parameter grows and so does the power of the test, giving us Property 2 of the F test.

Property 3 holds for two reasons. The first is also related to the noncentrality parameter and the second concerns the denominator degrees of freedom. To explain either reason, we must first note that the sampling variance of s^2 is $2\sigma_0^4/(N - K)$. This follows from the facts that

$s^2 \sim \sigma_0^2 \chi^2_{N-K}/(N-K)$ and $\mathrm{Var}[\chi^2_\nu] = 2\nu$.[13] Thus, the sampling variance of s^2 decreases as σ_0^2 decreases and as $N-K$ increases. Now the parameter σ_0^2 appears in the noncentrality parameter, increasing λ as σ_0^2 falls. This is the first way in which decreasing the sampling variance of s^2 improves power.

Second, as the denominator degrees of freedom, $\nu_2 = N-K$, grows, the sampling variance of σ_0^2 falls and the power of the F test also increases. Thus, adding observations (increasing N) and placing correct linear restrictions on $\hat{\boldsymbol{\beta}}$ (thereby decreasing K) improve the power of the F test. These effects reflect improvements in the estimation of σ_0^2. Incidentally, placing correct linear restrictions on $\hat{\boldsymbol{\beta}}$ will also increase power through an improvement in the efficiency of $\mathbf{R}\hat{\boldsymbol{\beta}}$.

A subtler property of the F test is that the power of the test increases as valid restrictions are removed from the null hypothesis. Formally, this follows because the degrees of freedom $\nu_1 = K - M$ fall, without affecting the noncentrality parameter λ or the degrees of freedom $\nu_2 = N-K$. To see this, consider a test of $H_0 : \mathbf{R}_1\boldsymbol{\beta}_0 = \mathbf{r}_1$ where we have partitioned

$$\mathbf{R} = \begin{bmatrix} \mathbf{R}_1 \\ \mathbf{R}_2 \end{bmatrix} \quad \text{and} \quad r = \begin{bmatrix} \mathbf{r}_1 \\ \mathbf{r}_2 \end{bmatrix}$$

The matrix $\mathbf{R}_1$ has $K - M_1 < K - M$ rows and the corresponding F test has fewer degrees of freedom in the denominator than the test we have just been considering. If $\mathbf{R}_2\boldsymbol{\beta}_0 = \mathbf{r}_2$, then we can show that the noncentrality parameters of the two F statistics are equal, essentially because the last $M_1 - M$ elements of $\mathbf{r} - \mathbf{R}\boldsymbol{\beta}_0$ are zero.

Let us choose $\mathbf{A}$ in (11.6) to be the Cholesky factor so that we may partition $\mathbf{A}$ conformably with $\mathbf{R}$ as

$$\mathbf{A} = \begin{bmatrix} \mathbf{A}_{11} & \mathbf{0} \\ \mathbf{A}_{21} & \mathbf{A}_{22} \end{bmatrix}$$

It follows from the partitioned inverse formula (Exercise 3.10) that $\mathbf{A}^{-1}$ has the same block lower-left triangular form: let

$$\mathbf{A}^{-1} = \begin{bmatrix} \mathbf{B}_{11} & 0 \\ \mathbf{B}_{12} & \mathbf{B}_{22} \end{bmatrix}$$

noting that $\mathbf{B}_{11}^{-1} = \mathbf{A}'_{11}$. Then

$$\begin{aligned} \lambda &= (\mathbf{r} - \mathbf{R}\boldsymbol{\beta}_0)' \left[\sigma_0^2 \cdot \mathbf{R}\left(\mathbf{X}'\mathbf{X}\right)^{-1}\mathbf{R}'\right]^{-1} (\mathbf{r} - \mathbf{R}\boldsymbol{\beta}_0) \\ &= \left(\mathbf{r}_1 - \mathbf{R}_1\boldsymbol{\beta}_0\right)\mathbf{B}_{11}\mathbf{B}'_{11}\left(\mathbf{r}_1 - \mathbf{R}_1\boldsymbol{\beta}_0\right) \\ &= (r_1 - \mathbf{R}_1\beta_0)' \left[\sigma_0^2 \cdot \mathbf{R}_1\left(\mathbf{X}'\mathbf{X}\right)^{-1}\mathbf{R}'_1\right]^{-1} (\mathbf{r} - \mathbf{R}_1\boldsymbol{\beta}_0) \end{aligned}$$

so that the noncentrality parameters are equal.

The practical significance of this result is that an F test that includes restrictions in the null hypothesis that are true is less powerful than an F test that excludes the true restrictions from the null. As we just saw, the noncentrality parameter of an F test is unchanged by such exclusions. The diminution of the numerator degrees of freedom increases the power.

---

[13] See Proposition 10 (p. 199) and Theorem D.10 (p. 889).

11.5 METHODOLOGICAL NOTES

In practice, researchers often use hypothesis tests to specify the elements of $\mathbf{X}$, the matrix of explanatory variables, based on statistical criteria. However, these applications are not covered by the statistical theory that we have presented. That is not to say that such *specification searches* are inappropriate, only that they are not justified by this formal framework.

So-called *pretest estimators* are a leading example of a way in which practitioners sometimes apply test statistics in informal ways. A simple, yet common, version of a pretest estimator is the following procedure:

1. Choose a significance level α.
2. Compute $\hat{\boldsymbol{\beta}}$.
3. Compute the $\hat{F}$ test statistic for $H_0 : \mathbf{R}\boldsymbol{\beta}_0 = \mathbf{r}$.
4. Estimate $\boldsymbol{\beta}$ with

$$\hat{\boldsymbol{\beta}}_\alpha = \begin{cases} \hat{\boldsymbol{\beta}} & \text{if } \hat{F} > F_{K-M,N-K;1-\alpha} \\ \hat{\boldsymbol{\beta}}_{\mathrm{R}} & \text{if } \hat{F} \leq F_{K-M,N-K;1-\alpha} \end{cases} \tag{11.7}$$

$$= \hat{\boldsymbol{\beta}}_{\mathrm{R}} + \mathbf{1}\{\hat{F} > F_{K-M,N-K;1-\alpha}\} \left(\hat{\boldsymbol{\beta}} - \hat{\boldsymbol{\beta}}_{\mathrm{R}}\right)$$

That is, choose the unrestricted estimator if it does not pass the hypothesis test for $H_0 : \mathbf{R}\boldsymbol{\beta}_0 = \mathbf{r}$. Otherwise, choose the restricted estimator, imposing $\mathbf{R}\hat{\boldsymbol{\beta}}_{\mathrm{R}} = \mathbf{r}$.

Equation (11.7) states that the pretest estimator is not a linear estimator of $\mathbf{y}$. Indeed, the estimator is no longer a continuous function of $\mathbf{y}$, because there is a sudden jump between $\hat{\boldsymbol{\beta}}$ and $\hat{\boldsymbol{\beta}}_{\mathrm{R}}$ wherever $\hat{F} = F_{K-M,N-K;1-\alpha}$. As a result, the distribution theory of the pretest estimator is analytically difficult. In general the pretest estimator is biased, its variance matrix is misestimated, and its distribution is not normal. Although the application of pretest estimation is certainly widespread, these properties are rarely taken into account formally. It is common practice to report estimates as though no pretesting occurred, but to acknowledge the pretesting in some way.[14]

Still more informal and more elaborate are a wide range of *sequential fitting* procedures. In their most casual form, the procedure is to compute initial OLS fits and to examine various statistics, including the R^2 goodness of fit, the t statistics, and the signs and magnitudes of the fitted coefficients. Researchers discard the fits that they consider unsatisfactory because the R^2 is too low, some t statistics are too small, or the sign or magnitude of some fitted coefficients is implausible. New fits are then tried, with such new explanatory variables as nonlinear transformations of the original ones, seeking results that are more pleasing than those already found.

A family of sequential fitting procedures called *stepwise* regressions are available in statistical software. Broadly speaking, stepwise regressions are a sequence of pretest estimators in which variables are added (or removed) from the RHS depending on the value of their t statistics when the variables are included. There are various criteria and algorithms.

Given our discussion of pretest estimators, it is obvious that the statistical properties of stepwise regression are intractable, let alone the more complex informal procedures. Without

[14] Judge et al. (1980, Section 3.3) give an introduction to pretest estimators.

such analysis, there is ample cause for concern about their application, especially when the researcher presents the usual array of statistics for the final fit without reference to their method of calculation. Clearly, the statistics are not what they appear to be. After a sequence of regressions that searches for RHS specifications with t statistics over 2, the probability that a t statistic is "statistically significant at the 5% level of significance" is *one*.

The basic peril is that sequential procedures rest on features of the sample that will not recur on average under repeated sampling. For example, one may find a regression with a very high R^2 that forecasts quite poorly out of the sample. The fitting procedure is too sensitive to the data at hand, chasing the observations and overlooking the conditional mean. Because some sequential fitting seems inevitable in empirical work, we advise researchers always to report such analysis along with the final statistics. Goldberger (1991, p. 261) puts this succinctly: "As a writer, it is a good idea to put yourself in the position of a prospective reader: provide the information that you would want to have if you were the reader."

Before closing the chapter on hypothesis testing, we also remind the reader that strong statistical evidence against the null hypothesis is generally evidence against every aspect of the null hypothesis. The formal analysis tends to focus the student's attention on the parameter restrictions, but assumptions 6.1, 7.1, and 10.1 are all part of the hypothesis that fixes the distribution of the test statistic. As we encounter new hypothesis tests in the remainder of this book, keep in mind that the tests will have power against alternatives to the null hypothesis that may be easily overlooked in application.

11.6 OVERVIEW

1. A hypothesis test for $H_0 : \mathbf{R}\boldsymbol{\beta}_0 = \mathbf{r}$ accepts this null hypothesis at the $100\alpha\%$ level of significance if r is a member of the $100(1-\alpha)\%$ confidence interval for $\mathbf{R}\boldsymbol{\beta}_0$.
2. Thus, classical hypothesis testing and interval estimation are dual to one another. Both require a pivotal statistic, a statistic with a known distribution under the null hypothesis. In the normal regression model, the F statistic

$$\hat{F} \equiv \frac{(\mathbf{R}\hat{\boldsymbol{\beta}} - \mathbf{r})'[\mathbf{R}(\mathbf{X}'\mathbf{X})^{-1}\mathbf{R}']^{-1}(\mathbf{R}\hat{\boldsymbol{\beta}} - \mathbf{r})/(K-M)}{s^2}$$

is pivotal with an $F_{K-M,N-K}$ distribution if $\mathbf{R}\boldsymbol{\beta}_0 = \mathbf{r}$. Also, the t statistic

$$\hat{t} \equiv \frac{\mathbf{c}'\hat{\boldsymbol{\beta}} - r}{\sqrt{s^2 \cdot \mathbf{c}'(\mathbf{X}'\mathbf{X})^{-1}\mathbf{c}}}$$

is pivotal with a t_{N-K} distribution if $\mathbf{c}'\boldsymbol{\beta}_0 = r$.
3. The test statistics explicitly compare a hypothesized value with an unrestricted estimator of this value. In an F statistic, the squared distance between these is standardized by the estimated variance matrix of their difference. The t statistic is the ratio of the (scalar) difference to the estimated standard deviation.
4. Thus, the test statistics are unit free. Furthermore, a statistically significant test statistic does not imply a qualitatively large difference between the hypothesized value and the unrestricted estimator. Nor does a statistically insignificant test statistic imply a qualitatively small difference.
5. There are other interpretations of the F statistic:
   (a) as a comparison of the complete vectors of restricted and unrestricted estimators and
   (b) as a comparison of the restricted and unrestricted goodness of fits.

6. The power of a hypothesis test at the $100\alpha\%$ level of significance is the probability of rejecting the null hypothesis when a member of the alternative hypothesis actually holds.
7. The power of an F test strictly increases
   (a) with the length of $\mathbf{r} - \mathbf{R}\boldsymbol{\beta}_0 = c \cdot \boldsymbol{\gamma}$ along every $\boldsymbol{\gamma} \in \mathbb{R}^{K-M}$, $\boldsymbol{\gamma} \neq \mathbf{0}$,
   (b) with the relative efficiency of $\mathbf{R}\hat{\boldsymbol{\beta}}$,
   (c) with the reciprocal of the sampling variance of s^2, and
   (d) as valid restrictions are removed from $\mathbf{R}\boldsymbol{\beta}_0 = \mathbf{r}$.
8. The relationship between t statistics and F statistics is not a simple one. Individual restrictions may possess statistically significant or insignificant t statistics while the F statistic for the combined restrictions is statistically significant or insignificant.
9. In practice, researchers often apply the simple hypothesis test within more general specification searches. Often, these methods do not possess formal justification.

11.7 EXERCISES

11.7.1 Review

11.1 **(Chow Test)** Consider a Chow test when one of the subsamples has too few observations to estimate the entire coefficient vector. Under the null hypothesis,

$$H_0 : y_n \,|\, \mathbf{X} \sim \mathfrak{N}(\mathbf{x}_n'\boldsymbol{\beta}_0, \sigma_0^2), \qquad n = 1, \ldots, N$$

Under the alternative hypothesis, the first $M < K$ observations have different regression coefficients than the rest of the sample:

$$H_1 : y_n \,|\, \mathbf{X} \sim \begin{cases} \mathfrak{N}\left(\mathbf{x}_n'\boldsymbol{\beta}_1, \sigma_0^2\right) & \text{if } n = 1, \ldots, M, \\ \mathfrak{N}\left(\mathbf{x}_n'\boldsymbol{\beta}_0, \sigma_0^2\right) & \text{if } n = M+1, \ldots, N \end{cases}$$

In this case, explain why one cannot implement the F-test statistics described by (11.1) and (11.2). On the other hand, the statistic implied by (11.3) is feasible:

$$\hat{F} = \frac{\left(\|\mathbf{y} - \hat{\boldsymbol{\mu}}_R\|^2 - \|\mathbf{y} - \hat{\boldsymbol{\mu}}\|^2\right)/M}{\|\mathbf{y} - \hat{\boldsymbol{\mu}}\|^2 / (N - K - M)}$$

Show that $\hat{F} \sim F_{M,N-K-M}$ under H_0.

11.2 Show that $\hat{F}$ for $\mathbf{R}\boldsymbol{\beta}_0 - \mathbf{r} = \mathbf{0}$ equals the largest t statistic among all one-dimensional tests for restrictions of the form $\mathbf{c}'(\mathbf{R}\boldsymbol{\beta}_0 - \mathbf{r}) = \mathbf{0}$. In other words,

$$\left(\boldsymbol{\beta}_0 - \hat{\boldsymbol{\beta}}\right)' \mathbf{R}' \left[\mathbf{R}\left(\mathbf{X}'\mathbf{X}\right)^{-1}\mathbf{R}'\right]^{-1} \mathbf{R}\left(\boldsymbol{\beta}_0 - \hat{\boldsymbol{\beta}}\right) = \max_{\mathbf{c} \in \mathbb{R}^K} \frac{\left[\mathbf{c}'\mathbf{R}(\boldsymbol{\beta}_0 - \hat{\boldsymbol{\beta}})\right]^2}{\mathbf{c}'\mathbf{R}'\left[\mathbf{R}\left(\mathbf{X}'\mathbf{X}\right)^{-1}\mathbf{R}'\right]^{-1}\mathbf{R}\mathbf{c}}$$

[Hint: Use the Cauchy–Schwarz inequality (Lemma 7.8, p. 143).] Does this overcome the lack of a most powerful test in multidimensional problems? Why or why not?

11.7.2 Extensions

11.3 (Relative Efficiency) For the classical normal regression model, show that the feasible probability interval for $\mathbf{R}\boldsymbol{\beta}_0$

$$\left\{\boldsymbol{\gamma} \in \text{Col}(\mathbf{R}) \,\middle|\, \left(\boldsymbol{\gamma} - \mathbf{R}\hat{\boldsymbol{\beta}}\right)' \left[\mathbf{R}\left(\mathbf{X}'\mathbf{X}\right)^{-1}\mathbf{R}'\right]^{-1} \left(\boldsymbol{\gamma} - \mathbf{R}\hat{\boldsymbol{\beta}}\right) \leq s^2\ (K-M)\ F_{K-M,N-K;1-\alpha}\right\}$$

has a larger expected squared radius $\text{E}[s^2\ (K-M)\ F_{K-M,N-K;1-\alpha}]$ than the squared radius of the infeasible interval

$$\left\{\boldsymbol{\gamma} \in \text{Col}(\mathbf{R}) \,\middle|\, \left(\boldsymbol{\gamma} - \mathbf{R}\hat{\boldsymbol{\beta}}\right)' \left[\mathbf{R}\left(\mathbf{X}'\mathbf{X}\right)^{-1}\mathbf{R}'\right]^{-1} \left(\boldsymbol{\gamma} - \mathbf{R}\hat{\boldsymbol{\beta}}\right) \leq \sigma_0^2\ \chi^2_{K-M;1-\alpha}\right\}$$

based on knowledge of σ_0^2.

11.4 (Sequential Testing) Consider the set of $K-M$ linear restrictions $H_0 : \mathbf{R}\boldsymbol{\beta}_0 = \mathbf{r}$ for $\text{E}[\mathbf{y} \mid \mathbf{X}] = \mathbf{X}\boldsymbol{\beta}_0$ and $\text{Var}[\mathbf{y} \mid \mathbf{X}] = \sigma_0^2 \cdot \mathbf{I}$. Let the rows of $\mathbf{R}$ be the vectors $\mathbf{R}_j'$, $j = 1, \ldots, K-M$ and $\mathbf{r} = [r_1, \ldots, r_{K-M}]'$. Consider a sequence of hypothesis tests for $H_{0j} : \mathbf{R}_j'\boldsymbol{\beta}_0 = r_j$, $j = 1, \ldots, K-M$. The first test in the sequence examines $H_{01} : \mathbf{R}_1'\boldsymbol{\beta}_0 = r_1$. If this hypothesis is accepted, H_{01} is *imposed* and the second test examines H_{02}. In general, if hypotheses $H_{01}, \ldots, H_{0,j}$ are sequentially accepted, then the $(j+1)$th test maintains $H_{01}, \ldots, H_{0j}$ and tests only whether $\mathbf{R}_{j+1}'\boldsymbol{\beta}_0 = r_{j+1}$. The sequence stops when a hypothesis is rejected. Many researchers use this sequential testing method for model selection.

(a) Show that there is no loss in generality assuming that $\mathbf{R}_j'\boldsymbol{\beta}_0 = \beta_{0j}$ and $r_j = 0$.

(b) Now consider a sequence of hypothesis tests for $H_{0j} : \beta_{0j} = 0$, $j = 1, \ldots, K-M$. Let the columns of $\mathbf{X}$ be denoted $\mathbf{X}_k$, $k = 1, \ldots, K$. Show that the numerators of the corresponding sequence of F statistics,

$$\min_{\boldsymbol{\mu} \in \text{Col}(\mathbf{W}_{j+1})} \|\mathbf{y} - \boldsymbol{\mu}\|^2 - \min_{\boldsymbol{\mu} \in \text{Col}(\mathbf{W}_j)} \|\mathbf{y} - \boldsymbol{\mu}\|^2$$

where $\mathbf{W}_j = [\mathbf{X}_j, \ldots, \mathbf{X}_K]$, are independently distributed $\sigma_0^2\chi_1^2$ random variables under $H_0 : \boldsymbol{\beta}_{01} = \mathbf{0}$, where $\boldsymbol{\beta}_{01} = [\beta_{01}, \ldots, \beta_{0,K-M}]'$. (HINT: Use Exercise 10.24.)

(c) Suppose σ_0^2 were known. How could one replace the F tests with chi-square tests? What would be the advantage in doing this? If each chi-square test in the sequence uses the significance level α, then what is the significance level of the sequential procedure as a test of H_0?

11.5 (F Test) Show that the numerator of the statistic $\hat{F}$ in (11.1) can also be expressed as

$$\begin{aligned}(\mathbf{R}\hat{\boldsymbol{\beta}} - \mathbf{r})'[\mathbf{R}(\mathbf{X}'\mathbf{X})^{-1}\mathbf{R}']^{-1}(\mathbf{R}\hat{\boldsymbol{\beta}} - \mathbf{r}) &= \mathbf{g}(\hat{\boldsymbol{\beta}}_{\text{R}})' \left(\mathbf{X}'\mathbf{X}\right)^{-1} \mathbf{g}(\hat{\boldsymbol{\beta}}_{\text{R}}) \\ &= \left\|\mathbf{g}(\hat{\boldsymbol{\beta}}_{\text{R}})\right\|^2_{(\mathbf{X}'\mathbf{X})^{-1}}\end{aligned}$$

where $\mathbf{g}(\hat{\boldsymbol{\beta}}_{\text{R}})$ is the gradient

$$\mathbf{g}(\hat{\boldsymbol{\beta}}_{\text{R}}) \equiv \frac{1}{2}\left.\frac{\partial \|\mathbf{y} - \mathbf{X}\boldsymbol{\beta}\|^2}{\partial \boldsymbol{\beta}}\right|_{\boldsymbol{\beta} = \hat{\boldsymbol{\beta}}_{\text{R}}} = -\mathbf{X}'\left(\mathbf{y} - \mathbf{X}\hat{\boldsymbol{\beta}}_{\text{R}}\right)$$

Give a new interpretation of the F statistic.

11.6 (Lagrange Multipliers) Show that the numerator of the $\hat{F}$ statistic is also a quadratic form in the vector of Lagrange multipliers $\hat{\boldsymbol{\lambda}}_{\text{R}}$ for the restrictions $\mathbf{R}\boldsymbol{\beta} = \mathbf{r}$ (Exercise 4.15) and the inverse of the variance matrix of the Lagrange multipliers.

CHAPTER 12

Overview of Linear Regression

Part II contains the statistical theory of the OLS estimation. This theory rests on three basic assumptions about the sampling distribution from which one observes the data in the LHS variable $\mathbf{y}$ and the RHS variables $\mathbf{X}$. As we accumulate the assumptions, we build an increasingly detailed model of the population and develop more sophisticated properties for OLS. Our primary goal is to provide order to the classical statistical theory by emphasizing the progressive character of these assumptions and their associated results.

This part of the book also extends the application of projection to random variables. The geometry of the OLS fit also appears in the conditional mean and in the relative efficiency of estimators. This geometry and the mathematics of the multivariate normal distribution comprise the probability distribution theory that undergirds the OLS statistical theory.

12.1 STATISTICAL THEORY

Part I explains the fit of a linear relationship by OLS. For the OLS fitted coefficients $\hat{\boldsymbol{\beta}}$ to be well defined, we assume that the matrix $\mathbf{X}$ of explanatory variables is full-column rank. In *Part II*, we add the distributional assumptions listed in Table 12.1. The assumptions map to results in three categories: first moment, second moment, and distribution.

That the first moment of $\mathbf{y}$ conditional on $\mathbf{X}$ is $\mathbf{X}\boldsymbol{\beta}_0$ implies two first-moment results. In particular, the OLS fitted coefficients $\hat{\boldsymbol{\beta}}$ are unbiased estimators of the population coefficients in $\boldsymbol{\beta}_0$. The linearity of $\hat{\boldsymbol{\beta}}$ in $\mathbf{y}$ is the key property of the OLS fit that supports these results: a linear combination of expected values equals the expected value of the linear combination.

That the second moment of $\mathbf{y}$ conditional on $\mathbf{X}$ is $\sigma_0^2 \cdot \mathbf{I}_N$ implies three second-moment results. First, because $\hat{\boldsymbol{\beta}}$ is linear in $\mathbf{y}$, the conditional variance matrix of $\hat{\boldsymbol{\beta}}$ follows easily from the conditional variance matrix of $\mathbf{y}$. Second, the variance parameter σ_0^2 possesses an unbiased estimator s^2, which is the sample variance of the OLS fitted residuals adjusted for overfitting relative to $\mathbf{X}\boldsymbol{\beta}_0$. Third, the variance matrix of the OLS fitted coefficients yields the smallest variances for linear unbiased estimators of linear combinations of the elements of $\boldsymbol{\beta}_0$.

Finally, that the conditional distribution of $\mathbf{y}$ is multivariate normal implies the conditional distribution of the OLS estimators. This stronger assumption also strengthens the relative efficiency of these estimators. The distributional properties lead to pivotal statistics that make interval estimators and hypothesis tests feasible.

12.2 PROBABILITY DISTRIBUTION THEORY

1. The conditional mean $\mathrm{E}[\mathbf{y}_n|\mathbf{x}_n]$ and the MMSE linear predictor $\mathrm{E}^*[\mathbf{y}_n|\mathbf{x}_n]$ are orthogonal projections, analogous to the OLS fitted vector $\hat{\boldsymbol{\mu}}$. By construction $\mathrm{E}^*[\mathbf{y}_n|\mathbf{x}_n]$ is also linear in $\mathbf{x}_n$, like the elements of $\hat{\boldsymbol{\mu}}$.[1]

   If $\mathrm{E}[\mathbf{y}|\mathbf{X}] = \mathbf{X}\boldsymbol{\beta}_0$, then $\mathrm{E}[\hat{\boldsymbol{\mu}}|\mathbf{X}] = \mathbf{X}\boldsymbol{\beta}_0$. If $\mathbf{X}$ is full-column rank also, then $\mathrm{E}[\hat{\boldsymbol{\beta}}|\mathbf{X}] = \boldsymbol{\beta}_0$.
2. The conditional variance matrix $\mathrm{Var}[\mathbf{y}|\mathbf{X}] = \sigma_0^2 \cdot \mathbf{I}_N$ has a geometric representation as an ellipse. The variance ellipse of a projection of $\mathbf{y}$, $\mathbf{Py}$, equals the projection of the variance ellipse of $\mathbf{y}$.

   The variance ellipse of a scalar variance matrix is a sphere. Thus, if $\mathrm{Var}[\mathbf{y}|\mathbf{X}] = \sigma_0^2 \cdot \mathbf{I}_N$, then $\mathbf{y}$, $\hat{\boldsymbol{\mu}} \equiv \mathbf{P_X y}$, and $\mathbf{y} - \hat{\boldsymbol{\mu}}$ are also spherically distributed, despite the apparent heteroskedasticity and covariance among their elements. Furthermore, the random variables in $\hat{\boldsymbol{\mu}}$ are orthogonal (uncorrelated) to those in $\mathbf{y} - \hat{\boldsymbol{\mu}}$.

   On the other hand, $\hat{\boldsymbol{\beta}}$ is not spherically distributed. Its elliptical character depends on $\mathbf{X}$.
3. Covariance is the source of predictive power (in MSE) in one random variable for another:

$$\mathrm{Cov}[z_1, z_2] \neq 0 \quad \Leftrightarrow \quad \min_{\alpha,\beta} \mathrm{E}[(z_1 - \alpha - \beta z_2)^2] < \mathrm{E}[(z_1 - \mathrm{E}[z_1])^2]$$

Table 12.1.
Summary of Assumptions and Results for the Classical Regression Model

Assumptions	Results
First moment: $\mathrm{E}[\mathbf{y}|\mathbf{X}] = \mathbf{X}\boldsymbol{\beta}_0$	• $\mathrm{E}(\hat{\boldsymbol{\mu}}|\mathbf{X}) = \mathbf{X}\boldsymbol{\beta}_0$, $\mathrm{E}[\hat{\boldsymbol{\beta}}|\mathbf{X}] = \boldsymbol{\beta}_0$, where $\hat{\boldsymbol{\mu}} = \mathbf{P_X y}$ and $\hat{\boldsymbol{\beta}} = (\mathbf{X}'\mathbf{X})^{-1}\mathbf{X}'\mathbf{y}$
Second moment: $\mathrm{Var}[\mathbf{y}|\mathbf{X}] = \sigma_0^2 \cdot \mathbf{I}_N$	• $\mathrm{Var}[\hat{\boldsymbol{\beta}}|\mathbf{X}] = \sigma_0^2 \cdot (\mathbf{X}'\mathbf{X})^{-1}$ • $\mathrm{E}(s^2|\mathbf{X}) = \sigma_0^2$, where $s^2 = (\mathbf{y} - \hat{\boldsymbol{\mu}})'(\mathbf{y} - \hat{\boldsymbol{\mu}})/(N-K)$ • $\hat{\boldsymbol{\beta}}$ is efficient relative to other linear unbiased estimators
Distribution: $\mathbf{y}|\mathbf{X} \sim \mathfrak{N}(\mathbf{X}\boldsymbol{\beta}_0, \sigma_0^2 \cdot \mathbf{I}_N)$	• $\hat{\boldsymbol{\beta}}|\mathbf{X} \sim \mathfrak{N}[\boldsymbol{\beta}_0, \sigma_0^2 \cdot (\mathbf{X}'\mathbf{X})^{-1}]$ and independent of s^2 • $s^2 \sim \sigma_0^2\, \chi^2_{N-K}/(N-K)$ • $\hat{\boldsymbol{\beta}}$ and s^2 are efficient relative to other unbiased estimators

[1] Thus, $\mathrm{E}^*[\mathbf{y}_n|\mathbf{x}_n]$ is a restricted projection relative to $\mathrm{E}[\mathbf{y}_n|\mathbf{x}_n]$ and its MMSE linear predictor as well.

This is one of several examples of the projection theorem at work. In addition,

(a) the Gram–Schmidt orthonormalization of a set of random variables through a sequence of orthogonal projections provides the Choleski factorization $\mathbf{CC}'$ of a variance matrix $\boldsymbol{\Omega}$ and

(b) the orthogonality condition $\mathrm{E}[(\tilde{\boldsymbol{\theta}} - \hat{\boldsymbol{\theta}})\hat{\boldsymbol{\theta}}'] = \mathbf{0}$ coincides with the efficiency of an unbiased estimator $\hat{\boldsymbol{\theta}}$ relative to another unbiased estimator $\tilde{\boldsymbol{\theta}}$ and the set of unbiased estimators $\hat{\boldsymbol{\theta}} + \mathbf{A}(\tilde{\boldsymbol{\theta}} - \hat{\boldsymbol{\theta}})$ indexed by a matrix $\mathbf{A}$.

4. The multivariate normal distribution has the following properties:

(a) the distribution is characterized by its first two moments;

(b) linear combinations of multivariate normal random variables also possess a multivariate normal distribution;

(c) if they are uncorrelated, then multivariate normal random variables are also independently distributed;

(d) the conditional mean and MMSE linear predictor are identical; and

(e) variance ellipses coincide with isodensity contours.

5. The chi-square and F distributions arise as the distributions of transformations of multivariate normal random variables. These are distributions for pivotal test statistics and corresponding interval estimators. In their noncentral generalizations, they determine the power functions of the test statistics.

PART III

GENERALIZATIONS OF THE LINEAR MODEL

Having built up the regression edifice affectionately known as the classical model, we turn to critical reconsideration of the elements of the theory. Every assumption represents a restriction on the data-generating process and every data set presents opportunities for unclassical behavior. Exceptions to our restrictions will generally result in exceptions to the statistical properties that we have derived and in possibilities for misguided inferences.

There is a clear hierarchy among the assumptions. The specification of the regression function is foundational. Without it, we would never have proceeded to take up the others. The most recent assumption, the specification of the distribution function as a member of the family of normal distributions, is the most narrow and most dispensible. In the remainder of this book, we will reconsider each of the assumptions in the reverse of the order in which we introduced them, working our way back to the most fundamental components of the theory.

Our analysis will follow a pattern. We begin the review of each assumption with the typical reasons for questioning it. These doubts provide alternative specifications of our model, which often generalize the classical model in some way. Given such generalizations, we then reconsider the properties of the classical methods, checking whether they continue to work and, if not, how they may fail. Failures naturally lead to a search for diagnostic tests to detect each deviation from classical conditions and for alternative estimation methods that do not share the weaknesses of OLS.

As you probably expect, the analysis continues to grow in its complexity. The fundamental departure from the previous material is that we must work with *nonlinear* estimators. Linearity, or sometimes quadraticity, in the dependent variable **y** has been a critical characteristic of the statistics that we have studied up to this point. We will frequently encounter statistics that do not possess such convenient analytical forms hereafter. The variety and complexity of these forms are some of the most intimidating characteristics of this new material.

We will cope with this variety and complexity in two basic ways:

1. interpreting many new methods as an approximate application of the OLS method that we have already studied in detail; and
2. showing how the approximate distribution theory is essentially analogous to the exact distribution theory of the classical model.

In fact, such exact results as those that we have been able to provide so far generally elude the analyst in the problems to come. Exact moments and distributions for our statistics are simply not available, except perhaps as numerical calculations for particular experiments. Thus, analysts have sought approximate results and, fortunately, many situations provide a delightfully familiar theory. This theory reproduces, in effect, results that have clear counterparts in the theory of the classical regression model.

CHAPTER 13

Nonnormal Distribution Theory

13.1 INTRODUCTION

The first assumption that we reconsider is our most recent one: that the distribution of $\mathbf{y}$ conditional on $\mathbf{X}$ is multivariate normal. We begin by introducing several distributions that one might substitute for the normal distribution, yet maintain that the $y_n - \mathbf{x}_n'\boldsymbol{\beta}_0$ are distributed independently and identically with mean zero and constant, finite variance. Although there are countless ways to differ from the normal distribution, we focus on a set of parametric distributions that have "fatter tails" than the normal distribution. Such deviations from normality are among the most studied because of their empirical, as well as theoretical, significance.

Outside normal distribution theory, the OLS estimator is not relatively efficient among unbiased estimators. For fat-tailed distributions, we expect OLS to be overly sensitive to relatively large deviations $y_n - \mathbf{x}_n'\boldsymbol{\beta}_0$ because these occur more frequently than in normal distributions. Therefore, we turn to alternative estimation methods next, describing the leading alternative, *least absolute deviations* (LAD), in Section 13.3. The LAD estimator is not a linear estimator in $\mathbf{y}$ so that its distribution is difficult to analyze. Nevertheless LAD is also unbiased when the conditional distribution of $\mathbf{y}$ given $\mathbf{X}$ is symmetric around $\boldsymbol{\mu}_0 = \mathbf{X}\boldsymbol{\beta}_0$. The particular nonlinearity of LAD makes it less sensitive to relatively large deviations $y_n - \mathbf{x}_n'\boldsymbol{\beta}_0$ than OLS. In addition, the LAD fit is reasonably easy to compute, making LAD a practical alternative to OLS as well.

Finally, we explain an alternative approach to nonnormal distributions. Because OLS remains an unbiased estimator, we reassess the *distribution* of the OLS estimator in the absence of a normal distribution theory. The leading approach is an approximate method, called *asymptotic distribution theory*. In asymptotic distribution theory, the specification of the possible distributions is less specific than parametric distributions. In this chapter, we state only bounds on certain moments of the distribution. Given these bounds, we can derive an approximate distribution theory for OLS that rests on a remarkable regularity in the behavior of sample averages as the sample size approaches infinity. The approximation parallels the exact theory that we have described under the normality assumption and is, therefore, very convenient.

Table 13.1
OLS and LAD Fits for Log-Wage[a]

	Estimated Coefficient	
RHS Variable	OLS	LAD
Constant (one)	(0.779) (0.075)	(0.639) (0.077)
Female	−0.242 (0.026)	−0.273 (0.027)
Nonwhite	−0.131 (0.036)	−0.095 (0.037)
Union member	0.173 (0.036)	0.157 (0.037)
Education	0.095 (0.0048)	0.106 (0.0050)
Experience	0.039 (0.0039)	0.039 (0.0040)
(Experience)^2	−0.00063 (0.000089)	−0.00061 (0.000091)
SSR	278.753	280.464
SAR	453.591	451.771

[a] The numbers in parentheses are estimates of standard errors. SSR, sum of squared residuals; SAR, sum of the absolute value of the fitted residuals.

To illustrate some of the ideas that follow, we have reestimated the log-wage equation using the LAD estimator. Our original OLS fitted coefficients and the LAD fitted coefficients appear together in Table 13.1. The fitted coefficients are quite similar, except perhaps for the coefficients of nonwhite and union, which both diminish in magnitude by substantive amounts. The estimated standard errors are large enough to suggest, however, that the differences are not statistically significant.[1] The estimates of the standard errors for the two estimators are also similar. Asymptotic approximation yields the estimates of the standard errors for the LAD estimator and implies that we treat the LAD fitted coefficients as approximately normally distributed. These approximations and these statistics suggest that nonnormality is not an important issue in the estimation of this log-earnings equation with this data set.

13.2 NONNORMAL PARAMETRIC DISTRIBUTIONS

As elegant and familiar as it may be, the normal distribution is not "normal," as in occurring "usually" or "generally."[2] This distribution does arise in many natural settings and it can be

[1] For a formal test of whether the estimated coefficients differ significantly statistically, see Section 22.3.

[2] Indeed, some authors have complained about the descriptor "normal," eschewing it in favor of "Gaussian." This label, obviously, acknowledges the contributions of Karl Friedrich Gauss (1777–1855) to the early study and application of this distribution.

generated mathematically in an elegant way (described in Section 13.4.3, *Central Limit Theorem*). But a convincing case cannot be made for its universal appropriateness as the distribution for modeling economic data. Nevertheless the normal distribution is "standard" in the sense that this distribution is clearly a reference point for a great deal of statistical distribution theory.[3]

Indeed, economists have identified many important counterexamples: the distributions of income and wealth are (positively) skewed toward the upper tail. The distribution of earned income across individuals (as opposed to households) is notably nonnormal in that many individuals have exactly no earnings, something that does not happen for a continuously distributed random variable. The distribution of stock returns clearly has "fatter" tails than the normal distribution.

Statisticians and econometricians have focused attention on the kurtosis of the conditional distribution of **y** given **X**, while often restricting this distribution to be symmetric. This restriction reflects several related factors. Symmetry is appealing when one has no idea which direction the distribution might be skewed or no particular concern about positive or negative deviations about the conditional mean. Parametric p.d.f.s that are symmetric tend to be more tractable. In addition, there is no controversy about the center of the distribution when it is symmetric. Under symmetry, the mean and the median, for example, coincide.

13.2.1 The Student *t* Distribution

Although it first arose in OLS sampling theory, the t distribution is a handy alternative to the normal distribution for the conditional distribution of **y** given **X**.[4] In addition, the t distribution has an appealing motivation as a *mixture* of normal distributions.

One of the simplest examples of a mixture arises this way. Consider mixing together random samples from two different distributions, say $\mathfrak{N}(0, \sigma_1^2)$ and $\mathfrak{N}(0, \sigma_2^2)$, so that one does not know which distribution generated a particular observation. If the fraction α of the sample came from the $\mathfrak{N}(0, \sigma_1^2)$ distribution, then the p.d.f. of each observation in the mixture would be

$$f_U(u) = \alpha\, \phi(u, \sigma_1^2) + (1 - \alpha)\, \phi(u, \sigma_2^2)$$

The second and fourth moments of this mixture are[5]

$$\begin{aligned} \mathrm{E}[U^2] &= \alpha\sigma_1^2 + (1 - \alpha)\, \sigma_2^2 \\ \mathrm{E}[U^4] &= 3\alpha\sigma_1^4 + 3\,(1 - \alpha)\, \sigma_2^4 \end{aligned}$$

It turns out that the p.d.f. of the mixture has a larger kurtosis than the normal p.d.f. (unless $\alpha = 0, 1$ or $\sigma_1^2 = \sigma_2^2$): the kurtosis is[6]

$$\gamma_2 = \frac{3\alpha\sigma_1^4 + 3\,(1 - \alpha)\, \sigma_2^4}{\left[\alpha\sigma_1^2 + (1 - \alpha)\, \sigma_2^2\right]^2} - 3$$

---

3 The label "normal" is subtly normative, especially outside professional circles. Ambitious students should take note how powerful such labels can be.

4 For review, see Definition D.31 (Student t Distribution, p. 889) and the following material.

5 See Theorem D.12 (p. 889).

6 See Definition D.9 (Moments, p. 871) and the following discussion.

$$= 3\frac{\alpha(1-\alpha)\left(\sigma_1^2 - \sigma_2^2\right)^2}{\left[\alpha\sigma_1^2 + (1-\alpha)\sigma_2^2\right]^2}$$
$$\geq 0$$

This simple mixture implicitly treats the variance parameter as a Bernoulli random variable with a probability of α that it is σ_1^2 and a probability $1-\alpha$ that it is σ_2^2. To obtain the t distribution, consider a continuous mixture of normal distributions over the variance parameter. If the variance σ^2 is proportional to the reciprocal of a chi-square random variable with ν degrees of freedom

$$\sigma^2 = \gamma^2 \frac{\nu}{\chi_\nu^2} \tag{13.1}$$

then the product of its square root with a standard normal random variable z,

$$U \equiv \sigma \cdot z = \gamma \frac{z}{\sqrt{\chi_\nu^2/\nu}} \sim \gamma \cdot t_\nu \tag{13.2}$$

is proportional to a t_ν random variable. The p.d.f. of this mixture is

$$f_U(u) = \frac{\Gamma[(\nu+1)/2]}{\Gamma(1/2)\,\Gamma(\nu/2)} \frac{1}{\sqrt{\nu\gamma^2}} \left(1 + \frac{u^2}{\nu\gamma^2}\right)^{-(\nu+1)/2} \tag{13.3}$$

where $\Gamma(\cdot)$ is the *gamma function*.[7]

The t distribution is well known for its fatter-than-normal tails, with the degree of "obesity" depending on the parameter ν. When $\nu = 1$, the distribution is so fat that it has another special name, *Cauchy*.[8] The Cauchy distribution does not possess a mean, let alone a variance. When $\nu = 2$, the mean exists, but the variance is still infinite. Both first and second moments exist for $\nu > 2$. As ν approaches infinity the t_ν distribution approaches the standard normal distribution because

$$\begin{aligned}
\lim_{\nu\to\infty}\left(1 + \frac{u^2}{\nu}\right)^{-(\nu+1)/2} &= \lim_{\nu\to\infty} \exp\left[-\frac{\nu+1}{2}\log\left(1 + \frac{u^2}{\nu}\right)\right] \\
&= \exp\left[\lim_{\nu\to\infty} -\frac{\nu+1}{2}\log\left(1 + \frac{u^2}{\nu}\right)\right] \\
&= \exp\left(-\frac{u^2}{2}\right)
\end{aligned}$$

which is proportional to the standard normal p.d.f.[9]

The existence of moments is an important issue and subtle phenomenon. It is important because it is nonsensical to estimate a mean that does not exist. It is subtle because two distributions that have virtually identical p.d.f.s can differ markedly in moments. For example, consider the mixture of an $\mathfrak{N}(0, 1/2)$ distribution and a Cauchy distribution:

$$f_Y(y) = \alpha\,\phi(y, 1/2) + \frac{(1-\alpha)}{\pi(1+y^2)}, \qquad 0 \leq \alpha \leq 1$$

[7] See Definition D.28 (Gamma Function, p. 888).

[8] This distribution is named after the Baron Augustin Louis Cauchy (1789–1857). We do not know whether the Baron was obese, but we are confident that it is irrelevant to the association of his name with this distribution.

[9] The last equality follows from l'Hôpital's rule.

The largest absolute difference between this p.d.f. and $\phi(y, 1/2)$ occurs at $y = 0$ and equals $(1 - \alpha)(\sqrt{\pi} - 1)/\pi$. By choosing $1 - \alpha$ to be a small positive number, we can make this difference as small as we like. But the moments of the mixture will not exist so long as $\alpha < 1$.

13.2.2 Laplace (Double Exponential) Distribution

The *Laplace*, or *double exponential*, *distribution* may be the leading nonnormal distribution for analysis.[10] Its canonical p.d.f. and c.d.f. are

$$f_U(u) = \frac{1}{2}e^{-|u|}$$

$$F_U(u) = \begin{cases} \frac{1}{2}e^{u} & \text{if } u \le 0 \\ 1 - \frac{1}{2}e^{-u} & \text{if } u \ge 0 \end{cases}$$

This p.d.f. has tails that approach zero much more slowly than the normal p.d.f. The limit of the normal p.d.f. divided by the double exponential p.d.f. is zero,

$$\lim_{u \to \infty} \sqrt{\frac{2}{\pi}}e^{-\frac{1}{2}u^2 + |u|} = 0 \tag{13.4}$$

because the quadratic term dominates the linear (absolute value) term. The center of the distribution has an idiosyncratic cusp where the p.d.f. is not differentiable. See Figure 13.1.

The first two moments of the Laplace distribution are $\mathrm{E}[U] = 0$ and $\mathrm{Var}[U] = 2$. Therefore, the Laplace p.d.f. associated with a mean equal to μ and a variance equal to σ^2 is

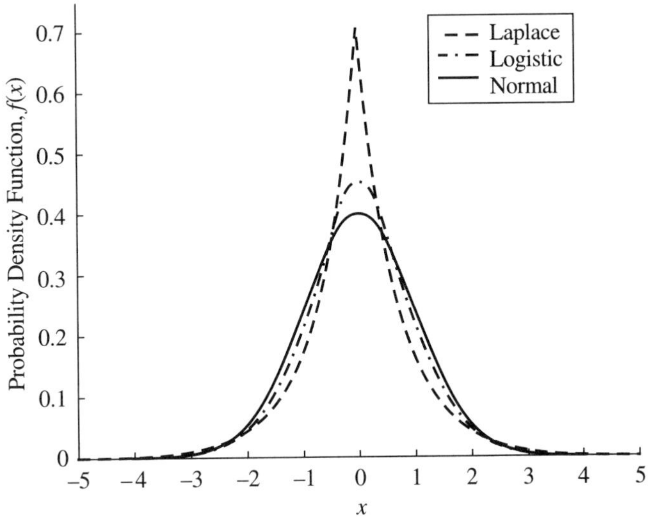

Figure 13.1 The Laplace, logistic, and normal distributions.

[10] The Marquis Pierre Simon de Laplace (1749–1827) also contributed significantly to the early study of the normal distribution, generalizing a 1718 tract of Abraham de Moivre (1667–1754).

$$f_Y(y) = \frac{1}{\sqrt{2\sigma^2}} e^{-\sqrt{2}\,|y-\mu|/\sigma}$$

where $Y = \mu + \sigma U/\sqrt{2}$. Besides its fat p.d.f. tails, the Laplace distribution is important because the maximum likelihood estimator for the mean μ minimizes the sum of the absolute value of the fitted residuals—a primary alternative to OLS. In the i.i.d. case, the maximum likelihood estimator for μ is the sample median. We will return to LAD estimation in the next section. We will introduce maximum likelihood estimators in Chapter 14.

13.2.3 Logistic Distribution

Another distribution with exponential tails is the *logistic distribution*, which has the canonical p.d.f. and c.d.f.

$$f_U(u) = \frac{1}{2 + e^{-u} + e^{u}} \tag{13.5}$$

$$F_U(u) = \frac{1}{1 + e^{-u}} \tag{13.6}$$

The first moment of this distribution is zero, and the second moment is $\frac{1}{3}\pi^2$ so that the p.d.f. with mean μ variance σ^2 is

$$f_Y(y) = \frac{\pi}{\sigma\sqrt{3}} \left[\exp\left(\frac{\pi}{\sqrt{3}} \frac{y-\mu}{\sigma} \right) + 2 + \exp\left(-\frac{\pi}{\sqrt{3}} \frac{y-\mu}{\sigma} \right) \right]^{-1}$$

Unlike the Laplace distribution, the logistic has a continuously differentiable p.d.f. Both p.d.f.s appear in Figures 13.1 and 13.2 along with the normal p.d.f., all standardized so that their first moments are zero and their second moments are one. Linear regression models with this distribution instead of the normal have been studied relatively little.

13.2.4 Power Exponential Distribution

Poirier et al. (1986) proposed the *power exponential distribution* as another family of distributions that contains the normal as a member. In this case, a natural form for the p.d.f. is

$$f_U(u) = \frac{\nu}{2^{(1/\nu)+1}\Gamma(1/\nu)} \exp\left(-\frac{1}{2} |u|^{\nu} \right)$$

for $\nu \geq 0$. The standard normal p.d.f. is the special case in which $\nu = 2$ and fatter tails occur for $\nu < 2$. The Laplace distribution is also a special case: $\nu = 1$. The mean of this p.d.f. is zero and the variance is $2^{2/\nu}[\Gamma(3/\nu)/\Gamma(1/\nu)]$. Therefore the standardized form of the p.d.f. for mean μ and variance σ^2 is

$$f_Y(y) = \frac{\nu}{2^{(1/\nu)+1}\,\Gamma(1/\nu)\,\gamma} \exp\left(-\frac{1}{2} \left| \frac{y-\mu}{\gamma} \right|^{\nu} \right)$$

where $\gamma^2 = [\Gamma(1/\nu)/2^{2/\nu}\Gamma(3/\nu)]\sigma^2$.

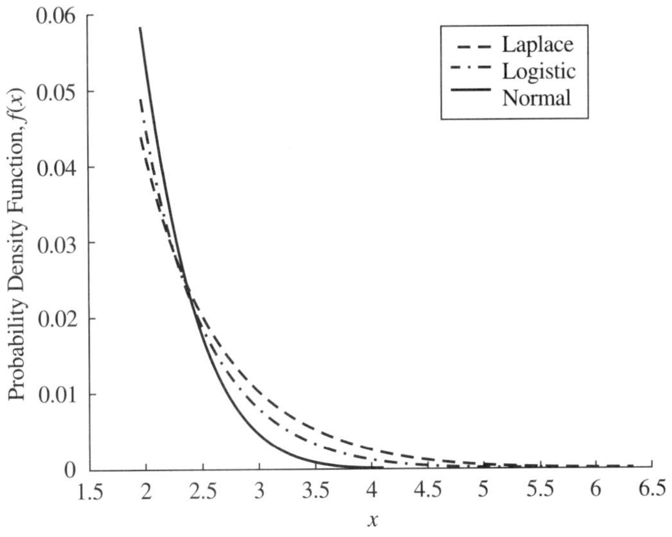

Figure 13.2 Comparison of tail behavior.

It would be natural to address hypothesis tests for the null hypothesis that the conditional distribution of $\mathbf{y}$ is normal at this point, but we will pass over this and go on to an alternative to OLS estimators. The theory for the standard tests of normality in conditional regression models builds on the asymptotic distribution theory of Section 13.4 and the likelihood theory of the next chapter. We will explain such tests in Chapter 17.

13.3 LAD ESTIMATION

The concern with fat-tailed p.d.f.s arises commonly from viewing the data as a mixture of observations from at least two populations. As we showed in Section 13.2.1, the mixture of normally distributed data always has larger kurtosis or "fat tails." The OLS estimator can be a poor choice for such data-generating processes.

How does our estimation theory change? Drastically, if we entertain any of the distributions described above as alternative specifications to normality. Unfortunately none of these distributions possesses the property that *sums* of such random variables have simple distributions, let alone normal ones. As a result, the distribution of the OLS estimator is analytically intractable. In addition, although OLS is the most efficient *linear* unbiased estimator, there are *nonlinear* unbiased estimators that will be efficient relative to OLS.

We will use the LAD estimator to illustrate these points. LAD is the primary alternative estimation method for regression models. In the special case of the location model, the LAD estimator is the sample median.

13.3.1 The Sample Median

The sample median is defined as the observation with half the sample above it and half below. Suppose that we have a random sample of N (odd) independent observations $\{v_1, \ldots, v_N\}$ on the random variable V.[11] If we reorder the observations so that

$$v_{(1)} \leq v_{(2)} \leq \cdots \leq v_{(N)}$$

then the sample median is $v_{(r)}$ where $r = (N+1)/2$. This is the solution to the LAD problem

$$\min_{\beta} \sum_{n=1}^{N} |y_n - \beta|$$

To see this, note that for all $\beta \neq y_n, n = 1, \ldots, N$, the derivative of the objective function,

$$\frac{d}{d\beta} \sum_{n=1}^{N} |y_n - \beta| = \sum_{n=1}^{N} (\mathbf{1}\{y_n - \beta < 0\} - \mathbf{1}\{y_n - \beta > 0\}) \tag{13.7}$$

is the number of observations below β minus the number of observations above β. At the sample median, increases and decreases in β increase the sum of absolute deviations (residuals). Furthermore, the sample median is the only value of β with this property so that it is also the unique LAD solution.

A comparison with OLS is instructive because it shows how OLS is relatively more sensitive to the largest and smallest observations in the sample. Consider first what would happen to the sample median and mean if any observation above the median had been larger. The sample median would be the same, whereas the sample mean would increase. Indeed, as we artificially increase such an observation more and more the sample mean increases proportionately while the sample median remains constant. On the other hand, decreasing an observation strictly above the sample median will decrease the sample mean. The sample median remains unaffected by such decreases until the observation falls below the median observation. At that point, the observation that we are varying becomes the median observation and further decreases lower the median one for one until a third observation becomes the median. Thus the median has a bounded response to changes in one observation. Inefficiency in the sample mean comes in part from its excessive sensitivity to the outlying observations that are more common in fat-tailed distributions than in the normal.

The distribution theory for the sample median is workable for continuous distributions. Let the p.d.f. $f_V(v)$ of V be symmetric around β_0 so that β_0 is both the mean and median of the distribution. We denote the c.d.f. with $F_V(v)$. The probability that the rth order statistic $V_{(r)}$ is below v is the probability that *at least* r of the observations are below v:[12]

$$F_{V_{(r)}}(v) = \sum_{n=r}^{N} \binom{N}{n} F_V(v)^n [1 - F_V(v)]^{N-n} \tag{13.8}$$

a sum of the binomial probabilities that at least n observations out of N fall below v. Differentiating with respect to v and summing, we obtain the p.d.f.[13]

---

[11] We have specified an odd number of observations because the definition of the sample median is clear. The case for even numbers of observations introduces unnecessary complications.

[12] See Definition E.2 (Order Statistics, p. 902).

[13] See Section 13.5.1 for the derivation.

$$f_{V_{(r)}}(v) = \frac{N!}{(r-1)!\,(N-r)!} f_V(v) F(v)^{r-1} [1 - F(v)]^{N-r} \tag{13.9}$$

If $N - r = r - 1$, then we obtain the p.d.f. of the sample median for odd $N = 2r - 1$:

$$f_{V_{[(N+1)/2]}}(v) = \left\{ N! \Big/ \left[\left(\frac{N-1}{2} \right)! \right]^2 \right\} f_V(v) \left\{ F_V(v) \left[1 - F_V(v) \right] \right\}^{(N-1)/2} \tag{13.10}$$

If f_V is symmetric about the mean β_0 of V, so that

$$\begin{aligned} F_V(v) &= \Pr\{V - \beta_0 \leq v - \beta_0\} \\ &= \Pr\{V - \beta_0 \geq -(v - \beta_0)\} \\ &= 1 - F_V(2\beta_0 - v) \end{aligned}$$

then the p.d.f. of the sample median is also symmetric about β_0.

For particular distributions, we can compare the sampling behavior of the sample mean with that for the sample median. We expect the median to be more efficient when the tails of the distribution are fat, so that we approach situations in which the variance of the sample mean does not exist. Comparisons for different t distributions are interesting because the t approaches the normal as the degrees of freedom grow and because we know the p.d.f.s for both. For the special case in which the degrees of freedom equal two, the variance of the t distribution does not exist so that the variance of the sample mean is also infinite. An analytical result can actually be found in this case: the variance of the sample median equals exactly $2/(N+1)$. Even though the variance for a single observation does not exist, the variance of the median exists even for a sample size $N = 3$.

For degrees of freedom larger than 2, the variance of the t distribution is $\nu/(\nu - 2)$ so that the variance of the sample average is $\nu/[N(\nu - 2)]$. We compare these variances with those of the sample median for various values of ν and N in Figure 13.3. The plots in this figure show the ratio of the variance of the mean to the variance of the median. Therefore, larger values occur as the efficiency of the median improves relative to the average. For values greater than one, the median is relatively more efficient. At the lowest degrees of freedom, the t_ν p.d.f. has its fattest tails and the median is relatively efficient. This relative efficiency does not necessarily diminish with the sample size. But as the degrees of freedom grow, the relative efficiency of the sample average grows and dominates the median for all sample sizes once we reach five degrees of freedom. This dominance persists for sample sizes even larger than those we have depicted.

13.3.2 LAD Linear Regression

The LAD estimator generalizes the median to multiple linear regression.[14] Formally,

$$\begin{aligned} \hat{\mu}_{\text{LAD}} &= \underset{\mu \in \text{Col}(\mathbf{X})}{\text{argmin}} \sum_{n=1}^{N} |y_n - \mu_n| \\ \hat{\beta}_{\text{LAD}} &= (\mathbf{X}'\mathbf{X})^{-1}\mathbf{X}'\hat{\mu}_{\text{LAD}} \end{aligned}$$

[14] Symmetry suggests that least squared deviations (LSD) would be a good alternative to the term OLS, but for some reason this has not caught on.

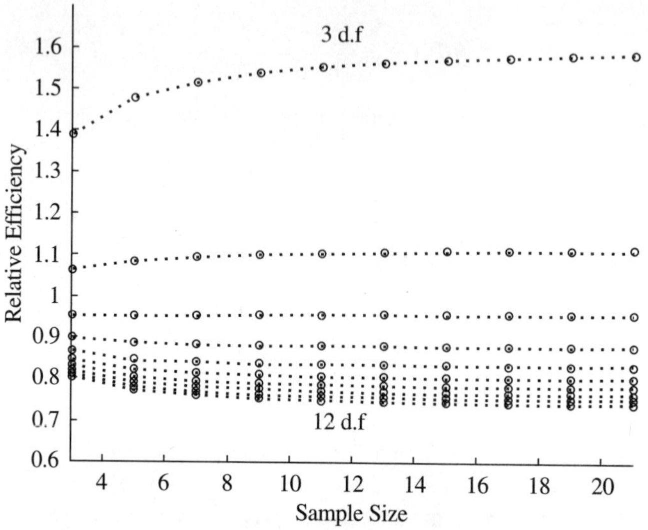

Figure 13.3 Relative efficiency of median versus mean for t distribution.

Note that while the regression function is linear in $\boldsymbol{\beta}$, the LAD estimator is nonlinear in $\mathbf{y}$. Although no "closed form" solution for $\hat{\boldsymbol{\mu}}_{\text{LAD}}$ exists, we can still readily find some useful properties that have recognizable simplifications for the case of the sample median.[15,16] In most data sets, $\hat{\boldsymbol{\beta}}_{\text{LAD}}$ is unique and it is the solution to setting K of the N fitted residuals equal to zero. The computational problem is discovering which K residuals these are. Most statistical software computes the solution, and so rapidly for moderate sample sizes that the difference with OLS calculations is negligible.

For some data sets, several sets of K residuals yield the same minimum value for the sum of absolute deviations function. In such cases, $\hat{\boldsymbol{\beta}}_{\text{LAD}}$ is not unique. Rather, it is a closed convex set of values. In fitting the location model for an even number of observations N, this often happens for the sample median because $v_{(r)}$ and $v_{(r+1)}$, where $r = N/2$, and all the values in between them yield the same goodness of fit. We will ignore such cases for ease of exposition, assuming that $\hat{\boldsymbol{\beta}}_{\text{LAD}}$ is unique.

One way to understand the difference between OLS and LAD is to compare their "first-order" conditions. If we rewrite the LAD objective function as

$$\sum_{n=1}^{N} |y_n - \mu_n| = \sum_{n=1}^{N} (y_n - \mu_n)\,\text{sgn}(y_n - \mu_n)$$

where sgn$(\cdot)$ denotes the "sign" (signum) function

[15] For the development of these properties, see Section 13.5.2.

[16] Students often ask what the term "closed form" means. This is an informal phrase describing an algebraic expression involving only elementary mathematical functions into which actual numbers can be substituted, or "plugged in." What constitutes an elementary mathematical function is a matter of taste.

$$\operatorname{sgn}(z) \equiv \begin{cases} -1, & \text{if } z < 0 \\ 0, & \text{if } z = 0 \\ 1, & \text{if } z > 0 \end{cases} \tag{13.11}$$

then when $\hat{\boldsymbol{\beta}}_{\text{LAD}}$ is unique[17]

$$\mathbf{0} = \sum_{n=1}^{N} \mathbf{x}_n (y_n - \mathbf{x}_n' \hat{\boldsymbol{\beta}}_{\text{OLS}}) \tag{13.12}$$

$$\mathbf{0} = \sum_{n=1}^{N} \mathbf{x}_n \operatorname{sgn}(y_n - \mathbf{x}_n' \hat{\boldsymbol{\beta}}_{\text{LAD}}) \tag{13.13}$$

We can see by inspection that a local change in y_n always changes $\hat{\boldsymbol{\beta}}_{\text{OLS}}$ but that $\hat{\boldsymbol{\beta}}_{\text{LAD}}$ is *unchanged* unless the sign of a fitted LAD residual changes.

This local insensitivity also means that the LAD estimator is not a linear function of y_n. The nonlinear nature of the LAD regression estimator complicates its distribution theory. Nevertheless, under symmetry of the conditional p.d.f. the LAD estimator is unbiased.

Proposition 14 (Unbiased LAD) *Let the p.d.f. of* $\mathbf{y}$ *conditional on* $\mathbf{X}$ *be symmetric about* $\mathbf{X}\boldsymbol{\beta}_0$. *When it exists,* $\mathrm{E}[\hat{\boldsymbol{\beta}}_{\text{LAD}} \mid \mathbf{X}] = \boldsymbol{\beta}_0$.

The proof of this result appears in Section 13.5.2. This proof stands on the symmetry of the absolute value function around the origin. This feature does not help us with other moments of $\hat{\boldsymbol{\beta}}_{\text{LAD}}$ and in particular we do not know its conditional variance. Thus, we are limited to the knowledge that both OLS and LAD are unbiased estimators under many symmetric distributions. We cannot compare them analytically in terms of efficiency.

Nevertheless, the demonstrable insensitivity of LAD to the relative magnitude of the fitted residuals may be a desirable property if the tails of the conditional p.d.f. of $\mathbf{y}$ are fatter than normal. We have already illustrated this possibility in the previous section with the sample median, the special case in which $x_n = 1$. We cannot establish additional properties without more detailed distribution theory.

Because exact distributions are analytically complex, analysts generally use simpler approximation methods. Asymptotic distribution theory is the leading method for deriving such approximations. In fact, the LAD standard errors in Table 13.1 are asymptotic approximations. An approximate distribution for a fixed sample size is the asymptotic distribution of statistics as the sample size approaches infinity. The appeal of this method of approximation is the simplicity of its results: the linearity and normality of statistics of the classical regression model are effectively reproduced in these approximations. Indeed, asymptotic theory also applies to the OLS estimator, enabling us to view our exact, normal distribution theory as approximately correct even when the conditional distribution of $\mathbf{y}$ given $\mathbf{X}$ is not normal.

---

[17] Technically, the LAD objective function is not differentiable anywhere there is an n such that $y_n - \mathbf{x}_n' \boldsymbol{\beta} = 0$. The "first-order" condition for LAD is not strictly correct. See Section 13.5.2.

13.4 ASYMPTOTIC DISTRIBUTION THEORY

Asymptotic distribution theory generally studies the distributions of statistics in the limit as the sample size approaches infinity. Such study produces useful results because such statistics as sample averages smooth out idiosyncracies in individual observations in powerful and systematic ways. To see this, we will apply two notions of convergence in the limit for sequences of random variables. Let $\{U_N\} = \{U_1, U_2, U_3, \ldots\}$ denote an infinite sequence of random variables indexed by N. This could be a sequence of OLS or LAD estimators as the sample size increases.

1. **Convergence in Distribution.** The most general kind of convergence that we consider occurs when the sequence of distribution functions of the U_N converges in the limit. That is, the sequence of c.d.f.s $\{F_{U_N}(u)\}$ converges to a limit c.d.f. $F_U(u)$. Such convergence is called *convergence in distribution* (or "in law") and denoted by $U_N \xrightarrow{d} U$.
2. **Convergence in Probability.** An important special case of convergence in distribution occurs when the limiting c.d.f. is that of a constant, say θ_0. This is called *convergence in probability* because it is a probabilistic version of ordinary deterministic convergence: for convergence in probability, the probability that U_N converges to θ_0 as N approaches infinity is virtually one. We denote convergence in probability by $U_N \xrightarrow{p} \theta_0$, although this is equivalent to $U_N \xrightarrow{d} \theta_0$.

Two fundamental theoretical results are the foundation for applying these ideas of convergence to sampling distributions of estimators. Their application to OLS estimators rests on the property that the OLS estimators are functions of sample averages.

1. **Law of Large Numbers.** *Laws of large numbers* basically state that as the sample size approaches infinity, a sample average converges in probability to its mean. There are several ways of thinking about this. One is to view the sample average as the finite sample counterpart to the population mean and that one is reproducing the population experiment as the sample size grows. Laws of large numbers are at the root of a classical understanding of probability: the limit of the sample frequency of an outcome, as an experiment is repeated over and over, is *defined* to be the probability of the outcome.
2. **Central Limit Theorem.** *Central limit theorems* play a major role in the application of convergence in distribution to estimators. They state conditions under which a standardized sample average will converge in distribution so that the asymptotic distribution is normal.

Now we will use an alternative to the distributional assumption that $\mathbf{y}$ is conditionally multivariate normal (Assumption 10.1). In its place, we introduce assumptions about the behavior of $\mathbf{x}_n$ as well as y_n. This is because we must cover the asymptotic behavior of every component of $\hat{\boldsymbol{\beta}}$ as N changes. In particular, we introduce independent sampling for both y_n and $\mathbf{x}_n$. In place of the normal distribution, we assume that the fourth moments of all the data exist.

> **Assumption 13.1 (I.I.D.)** *The observations* $\{(y_n, \mathbf{x}_n)\,;\ n = 1, \ldots, N\}$ *are i.i.d. across n and their fourth moments exist.*

Under this assumption, y_n and $\mathbf{x}_n$ are jointly distributed and each pair $(y_n, \mathbf{x}_n)$ is drawn independently from the same distribution. When we combine Assumption 13.1 with Assumption 6.1

(First Moment, p. 110), it will not be necessary to condition the mean of y_n on the entire matrix $\mathbf{X}$. Given independence among the observations, $\mathrm{E}[y_n \mid \mathbf{X}] = \mathrm{E}[y_n \mid \mathbf{x}_n]$.[18]

We will also require a population version of Assumption 3.1.

ASSUMPTION 13.2 (POPULATION FULL RANK) *The second moment matrix of the explanatory variables, $\mathbf{D} \equiv \mathrm{E}[\mathbf{x}_n \mathbf{x}_n']$, is a nonsingular matrix.*

These assumptions about the behavior of $\mathbf{x}_n$ and y_n rule out some forms of behavior that one expects in economic data. For example, elements of $\mathbf{x}_n$ that are deterministic but not constant are not i.i.d. In quarterly time series, dummy variables for the quarter (winter, spring, summer, and fall) are deterministic, nonconstant explanatory variables. Our goal is not to present the most general theory at this point,[19] but to describe the important elements of such theory in an accessible way. These assumptions permit us to prove the following (representative) proposition about OLS estimators (in Sections 13.4.2 and 13.4.3).

PROPOSITION 15 (ASYMPTOTIC DISTRIBUTION OF OLS) *Let Assumptions 6.1 (First Moment, p. 110), 7.1 (Second Moment, p. 130), 13.1 (I. I. D.), and 13.2 (Population Full Rank) hold for all sample sizes N. Then as $N \to \infty$*

$$\hat{\boldsymbol{\beta}} \equiv (\mathbf{X}'\mathbf{X})^{-1}\mathbf{X}'\mathbf{y} \xrightarrow{p} \boldsymbol{\beta}_0 \tag{13.14}$$

$$s^2 \equiv \frac{\mathbf{y}'(\mathbf{I} - \mathbf{P}_{\mathbf{X}})\mathbf{y}}{N-K} \xrightarrow{p} \sigma_0^2 \tag{13.15}$$

and

$$\left[s^2 \cdot \mathbf{R}\,(\mathbf{X}'\mathbf{X})^{-1}\,\mathbf{R}'\right]^{-1/2} \mathbf{R}\left(\hat{\boldsymbol{\beta}} - \boldsymbol{\beta}_0\right) \xrightarrow{d} \mathfrak{N}(\mathbf{0}, \mathbf{I}_M) \tag{13.16}$$

$$\left(\hat{\boldsymbol{\beta}} - \boldsymbol{\beta}_0\right)' \mathbf{R}' \left[s^2 \cdot \mathbf{R}(\mathbf{X}'\mathbf{X})^{-1}\mathbf{R}'\right]^{-1} \mathbf{R}\left(\hat{\boldsymbol{\beta}} - \boldsymbol{\beta}_0\right) \xrightarrow{d} \chi_M^2 \tag{13.17}$$

for all full rank $M \times K$ matrices $\mathbf{R}$.

There is a special term, "consistent," that is used to describe the convergence in probability of an estimator to a population value.

DEFINITION 23 (CONSISTENT ESTIMATOR) *If $\hat{\theta}_N \xrightarrow{p} \theta_0$ for all possible θ_0 then $\hat{\theta}_N$ is* a consistent *estimator of θ_0.*

Therefore, one usually describes equations (13.14) and (13.15) in words as stating that $\hat{\boldsymbol{\beta}}$ and s^2 are consistent estimators.

---

[18] This moves us a step closer to coping with a dynamic regression model such as the one fitted for unemployment in Chapter 3. We still cannot accommodate that situation, however, with our current assumption of independence.

[19] For deterministic explanatory variables, see the Chebychev law of large numbers (Theorem 13, p. 449) and Liapounov central limit theorem (Theorem 14, p. 449) and Exercise 18.15.

We have stated equations (13.16) and (13.17) of this proposition in what may seem, at first, an awkward way. While unadorned $\hat{\boldsymbol{\beta}}$ and s^2 converge in probability to the population parameters that they estimate, the asymptotic normality of $\mathbf{R}\hat{\boldsymbol{\beta}}$ has an elaborate expression in which a matrix square root premultiplies $\hat{\boldsymbol{\beta}}$ after subtracting off $\boldsymbol{\beta}_0$. Why not simply write that $\mathbf{R}\hat{\boldsymbol{\beta}}$ converges in distribution to $\mathfrak{N}[\mathbf{R}\boldsymbol{\beta}_0, \sigma_0^2 \cdot \mathbf{R}(\mathbf{X}'\mathbf{X})^{-1}\mathbf{R}']$?

The answer is that the elements of $\mathbf{X}'\mathbf{X}$ are exploding as N approaches infinity. To have $\mathbf{R}\hat{\boldsymbol{\beta}}$ converge in distribution to something other than $\mathbf{R}\boldsymbol{\beta}_0$, $\mathbf{R}\hat{\boldsymbol{\beta}}$ must be standardized so that its first two moments are well behaved in the limit. Subtracting $\mathbf{R}\boldsymbol{\beta}_0$ delivers a statistic with the same zero mean for all N. Premultiplying the difference by $[\mathbf{R}(\mathbf{X}'\mathbf{X})^{-1}\mathbf{R}']^{-1/2}$ stabilizes the variance at $\sigma_0^2 \cdot \mathbf{I}_M$: the matrix $[\mathbf{R}(\mathbf{X}'\mathbf{X})^{-1}\mathbf{R}']^{-1/2}$ is proportional to the matrix square root of the inverse of $\text{Var}[\mathbf{R}\hat{\boldsymbol{\beta}} \mid \mathbf{X}] = \sigma_0^2 \cdot \mathbf{R}(\mathbf{X}'\mathbf{X})^{-1}\mathbf{R}'$. These two transformations stabilize the sampling behavior of $\mathbf{R}\hat{\boldsymbol{\beta}}$ so that the sequence of distributions has constant mean and variance. Given these two moments, the distribution of the standardized $\mathbf{R}\hat{\boldsymbol{\beta}}$ converges to the multivariate normal.

Researchers use these asymptotic distributional results as follows. Because it converges in probability to $\mathbf{R}\boldsymbol{\beta}_0$ as N approaches infinity, econometricians accept $\mathbf{R}\hat{\boldsymbol{\beta}}$ as a passable estimator. Because $[s^2 \cdot \mathbf{R}(\mathbf{X}'\mathbf{X})^{-1}\mathbf{R}']^{-1/2}\mathbf{R}(\hat{\boldsymbol{\beta}} - \boldsymbol{\beta}_0)$ is approximately distributed as $\mathfrak{N}(\mathbf{0}, \mathbf{I}_M)$, econometricians frequently treat $\mathbf{R}\hat{\boldsymbol{\beta}}$ as approximately distributed $\mathfrak{N}[\mathbf{R}\boldsymbol{\beta}_0, s^2 \cdot \mathbf{R}\left(\mathbf{X}'\mathbf{X}\right)^{-1}\mathbf{R}']$ and treat s^2 as a constant. Confidence intervals and hypothesis tests derive from the pivotal quadratic statistic in (13.17), which has a limit chi-square distribution that is consistent with the limit normal distribution associated with $\hat{\boldsymbol{\beta}}$.

By comparison with the results of normal distribution theory, we find that the inference procedures are essentially unchanged. In effect, we substitute the χ^2_M/M distribution for the $F_{M,N-K}$ distribution. For example, the $100(1-\alpha)\%$ confidence interval for $\mathbf{R}\boldsymbol{\beta}_0$ based on the normality assumption is

$$\left\{\gamma \in \text{Col}(\mathbf{R}) \,\middle|\, \left(\gamma - \mathbf{R}\hat{\boldsymbol{\beta}}\right)' \left[\mathbf{R}\left(\mathbf{X}'\mathbf{X}\right)^{-1}\mathbf{R}'\right]^{-1} \left(\gamma - \mathbf{R}\hat{\boldsymbol{\beta}}\right) \le s^2 M\, F_{M,N-K;1-\alpha}\right\}$$

whereas the asymptotic approximation without the normality assumption is

$$\left\{\gamma \in \text{Col}(\mathbf{R}) \,\middle|\, \left(\gamma - \mathbf{R}\hat{\boldsymbol{\beta}}\right)' \left[\mathbf{R}(\mathbf{X}'\mathbf{X})^{-1}\mathbf{R}'\right]^{-1} \left(\gamma - \mathbf{R}\hat{\boldsymbol{\beta}}\right) \le s^2\, \chi^2_{M;1-\alpha}\right\} \tag{13.18}$$

In fact, as the denominator degrees of freedom $(N-K)$ get larger, the values $M\, F_{M,N-K;1-\alpha}$ grow closer to $\chi^2_{M;1-\alpha}$.

This is a consequence of Proposition 15, but we can also confirm it directly. Recall that the ratio

$$\frac{\chi^2_M/M}{\chi^2_{N-K}/(N-K)}$$

of independently distributed chi-square random variables has the $F_{M,N-K}$ distribution. As $N-K$ gets larger, the $\chi^2_{N-K}/(N-K)$ term converges in distribution to the constant 1. To see this, note that

$$\text{E}\left[\frac{\chi^2_{N-K}}{N-K}\right] = \frac{1}{N-K}\,\text{E}[\chi^2_{N-K}] = \frac{1}{N-K}\,(N-K) = 1,$$

$$\text{Var}\left[\frac{\chi^2_{N-K}}{N-K}\right] = \frac{1}{(N-K)^2}\,\text{Var}[\chi^2_{N-K}] = \frac{1}{(N-K)^2} 2\,(N-K) = \frac{2}{N-K}$$

The variance approaches zero as $N-K$ approaches infinity so that the distribution of $\chi^2_{N-K}/(N-K)$ degenerates to that of a constant, where the constant is its mean. The distribution of the F ratio, in turn, converges to the distribution of the numerator χ^2_M/M. Although this explanation is somewhat informal, it gives the essential outline of the equivalence of the normal and asymptotic results for large enough N.

In Figure 13.4, we plot the c.d.f.s for the $\chi^2_3/3$ and $F_{3,N-K}$ distributions. The critical values for the confidence intervals above come from these functions. In this case, we can see how the c.d.f.s of the F distribution approach those of the corresponding chi-square divided by its degrees of freedom. Also note, however, that the convergence of the corresponding critical values is slower than this figure suggests. In the flattest part of the c.d.f.s the horizontal difference in the functions is much larger than the vertical distance. And it is the horizontal distance that measures the difference in critical values.

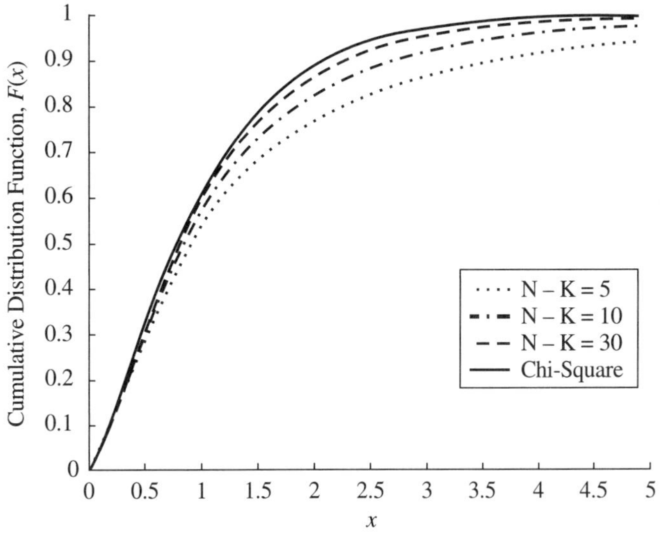

Figure 13.4 $F_{3,N-K}$ distribution versus $\chi^2_3/3$ distribution.

13.4.1 Convergence in Distribution

Figure 13.4 depicts the phenomenon that we have been calling convergence in distribution.

Definition 24 (Convergence in Distribution) *If the c.d.f.s F_{U_N} of the sequence of random variables $\{U_N\}$ converge to the c.d.f. F_U as $N \to \infty$ at all points z where $F_U(z)$ is continuous, then $\{U_N\}$* converges in distribution *to U. This will be denoted $U_N \xrightarrow{d} U$.*

The conventional notation that "$U_N \xrightarrow{d} U$" often misleads students. It looks as though there is some random variable out there to which the U_N are getting closer. This is after all the familiar understanding of the limit of a sequence. But this is not what is meant. Convergence in distribution refers only to the sequence of c.d.f.s, $\{F_{U_N}\}$, which is a *deterministic* sequence. The random variable U is simply a symbol for the limit c.d.f. A notation sometimes seen that symbolizes this relationship better for many students is $U_N \overset{a}{\sim} U$, read as "$\{U_N\}$ is distributed *asymptotically* as U."

As mentioned above, the case in which F_U is the c.d.f. of a constant receives special attention in asymptotic distribution theory.

DEFINITION 25 (CONVERGENCE IN PROBABILITY) *If $\{U_N\}$ converges in distribution to a constant U, then $\{U_N\}$* converges in probability *to U. The value U is often called the* probability limit, *or* plim, *of $\{U_N\}$. There are two common notations: $U_N \xrightarrow{p} U$ and $\operatorname{plim}_{N\to\infty} U_N = U$.*[20]

Because convergent deterministic sequences also have constant limits, we can make a useful comparison between "ordinary" convergence and convergence in probability. Here, for convenience, is a definition of deterministic convergence.

DEFINITION 26 (CONVERGENCE) *The sequence $\{U_N\}$ converges to the limit U if for every $\epsilon > 0$ there exists an $N^*(\epsilon)$ such that if $N > N^*(\epsilon)$ then $|U_N - U| < \epsilon$.*

For a comparison with convergence in probability, consider this lemma (proven in Section 13.5.3):

LEMMA 13.1 *The sequence of random variables $\{U_N\}$ converges in probability to the constant U if and only if for every $\epsilon, \delta > 0$ there exists an $N^*(\epsilon, \delta)$ such that*

$$N > N^*(\epsilon, \delta) \quad \Rightarrow \quad Pr\{|U_N - U| < \epsilon\} > 1 - \delta \tag{13.19}$$

In words, this lemma states that the probability limit of the sequence is U if for every neighborhood of U the probability that U_N falls in the neighborhood is eventually arbitrarily high. To think about this concept in terms of conventional limits we can fix ϵ and see that the definition implies that

$$\lim_{N\to\infty} \Pr\{|U_N - U| < \epsilon\} = 1$$

On the other hand, for a fixed δ we have only that every *marginal* probability that a particular $|U_N - U|$ is arbitrarily small exceeds $1 - \delta$ for all N bigger than some threshold. This does not imply that

$$\Pr\{\lim_{N\to\infty} U_N = U\} = 1$$

which concerns the *joint* probability

[20]The term *plim* is usually pronounced **pē′lĭm**, although some prefer **plĭm**.

$$\Pr\{\exists N^*(\varepsilon) \Rightarrow \forall N > N^*(\varepsilon), \ |U_N - U| < \varepsilon\}$$

about the entire sequence $\{|U_1 - U|, |U_2 - U|, \ldots\}$. This latter statement is stronger, and is a different notion of stochastic convergence to a constant called *almost sure convergence*.[21] However, the distinction will not be important in this book and we will restrict our attention to convergence in probability.

Convergence in distribution and its refinement, convergence in probability, follow several predictable rules. Here is a summary of the convergence rules that we use frequently.

Lemma 13.2 (Probability Limit Continuity) *Given a continuous function* $g(u)$, *if* $U_N \xrightarrow{p} U$ *then* $g(U_N) \xrightarrow{p} g(U)$.

Lemma 13.3 (Slutsky) *If* $U_N \xrightarrow{d} U$ *and* $W_N \xrightarrow{p} W$ *then* $W_N + U_N \xrightarrow{d} W + U$ *and* $W_N U_N \xrightarrow{d} W U$.

A generalization of the Slutsky lemma is

Lemma 13.4 (Convergence in Distribution Continuity) *Given a continuous function* $g(u)$, *if* $U_N \xrightarrow{d} U$ *then* $g(U_N) \xrightarrow{d} g(U)$.

Proofs of these lemmas appear in Section 13.5.3. Note that all of these results apply to W_N and U_N that are matrices.

We will apply these lemmas to the OLS estimator. Here is a sketch of the proof of Proposition 15. First, we will argue that

$$\frac{1}{N} \cdot \mathbf{X}'\mathbf{X} \xrightarrow{p} \mathbf{D} \equiv \mathrm{E}[\mathbf{x}_n \mathbf{x}_n']$$

$$\frac{1}{N} \cdot \mathbf{X}'\mathbf{y} \xrightarrow{p} \mathbf{D}\boldsymbol{\beta}_0$$

by a law of large numbers. Then we will apply Lemma 13.2 (Probability Limit Continuity) to obtain

$$\left[\frac{1}{N} \cdot \mathbf{X}'\mathbf{X}\right]^{-1} \xrightarrow{p} \mathbf{D}^{-1}$$

and

$$\hat{\boldsymbol{\beta}} = \left(\frac{1}{N} \cdot \mathbf{X}'\mathbf{X}\right)^{-1} \frac{1}{N} \cdot \mathbf{X}'\mathbf{y}$$

[21] For discussions of almost sure convergence, and other forms of convergence, see Rao (1973, p. 110) or White (1984, ch. 2). Statisticians and econometricians frequently refer to the distinction between convergence in probability and almost sure convergence as *weak* versus *strong* convergence.

$$\begin{aligned}&\xrightarrow{p} \mathbf{D}^{-1}\mathbf{D}\boldsymbol{\beta}_0\\&= \boldsymbol{\beta}_0\end{aligned}$$

Second, a central limit theorem will imply that

$$\frac{1}{\sqrt{N}} \cdot \mathbf{X}'\left(\mathbf{y} - \mathbf{X}\boldsymbol{\beta}_0\right) \xrightarrow{d} \mathfrak{N}(\mathbf{0}, \sigma_0^2 \cdot \mathbf{D})$$

We can combine this result with the probability limit of $(1/N) \cdot \mathbf{X}'\mathbf{X}$ using the Slutsky lemma (Lemma 13.3) to argue that

$$\begin{aligned}\sqrt{N}\left(\hat{\boldsymbol{\beta}} - \boldsymbol{\beta}_0\right) &= \left(\frac{1}{N} \cdot \mathbf{X}'\mathbf{X}\right)^{-1} \frac{1}{\sqrt{N}} \cdot \mathbf{X}'\left(\mathbf{y} - \mathbf{X}\boldsymbol{\beta}_0\right)\\&\xrightarrow{d} \mathbf{D}^{-1}\mathfrak{N}(\mathbf{0}, \sigma_0^2 \cdot \mathbf{D})\\&\sim \mathfrak{N}(\mathbf{0}, \sigma_0^2 \cdot \mathbf{D}^{-1})\end{aligned}$$

Additional work delivers the results of Proposition 15, but these steps give an indication of the use of these convergence lemmas and outline several central arguments.

To complete the arguments, we need a law of large numbers and a central limit theorem. These are the subjects of the next two sections. Within these sections we also prove Proposition 15.

13.4.2 Law of Large Numbers

Our first link between convergence in distribution and estimation is the law of large numbers. Roughly speaking, a law of large numbers (LLN) states conditions such that a sample average converges in probability to its mean. There is a fundamental analogy in this result. The sample average is the mean of the *empirical* distribution and its limit is the mean of the *population* distribution. One way to connect the abstract notion of probability with actual experience is to conceptualize a (population) probability as the limit of an empirical probability (or frequency) as the sample size approaches infinity. An LLN extends such convergent behavior to the first moments of these probability distributions. We will use one of the most transparent of such laws:

THEOREM 8 (CHEBYCHEV'S LLN) *Let $\{U_n\}$ be a sequence of i.i.d. random variables such that* $\mathrm{E}[U_n]$ *and* $\mathrm{Var}[U_n]$ *exist ($n = 1, 2, 3, \ldots$). Denote*

$$\mathrm{E}_N[U] \equiv \frac{1}{N}\sum_{n=1}^{N} U_n$$

then $\mathrm{E}_N[U] \xrightarrow{p} \mathrm{E}[U]$ *as $N \to \infty$.*

We prove this theorem in Section 13.5.3. The behavior of the variance of $\mathrm{E}_N[U]$ is the key element in this LLN. Independence implies that all covariances among the U_n are zero, so that the variance of $\mathrm{E}_N[U]$ simplifies to the sum of the variances of the U_n divided by N^2. Then the key mechanism is that the variance of $\mathrm{E}_N[U]$ converges to zero because the variances of the U_n ($n = 1, \ldots, N$) are all equal:[22]

$$\lim_{N\to\infty} \mathrm{Var}\big[\mathrm{E}_N[U]\big] = \lim_{N\to\infty} \frac{1}{N^2}\sum_{n=1}^{N} \mathrm{Var}[U] = \lim_{N\to\infty} \frac{\mathrm{Var}[U]}{N} = 0$$

As a result, $\mathrm{E}_N[U]$ converges in distribution to the constant equal to its mean.

EXAMPLE 13.1 [Bernoulli Distribution]

Let the random variable U have the Bernoulli distribution with $\Pr\{U = 1\} = \theta_0$. Then $\mathrm{E}[U] = \theta_0$ and $\mathrm{Var}[U] = \theta_0(1 - \theta_0)$. Therefore, the sample average of an i.i.d. sequence of outcomes $\{U_n\}$ converges in probability to θ_0. The sample average is, of course, the sample *frequency* of the outcome $U_n = 1$ and this is an example of the convergence of the empirical distribution to the population distribution.

The application of this LLN to the asymptotic behavior of $\hat{\boldsymbol{\beta}}$ and s^2 works through their functional dependence on sums of variables. We transform these sums into sample averages:[23]

$$\begin{aligned}\hat{\boldsymbol{\beta}} &= \left(\frac{1}{N}\cdot \mathbf{X}'\mathbf{X}\right)^{-1} \frac{1}{N}\cdot \mathbf{X}'\mathbf{y} \\ &= \left(\mathrm{E}_N[\mathbf{x}_n\mathbf{x}_n']\right)^{-1} \mathrm{E}_N[\mathbf{x}_n y_n] \end{aligned} \tag{13.20}$$

and

$$\begin{aligned} s^2 &= \frac{N}{N-K}\left[\frac{\mathbf{y}'\mathbf{y}}{N} - \hat{\boldsymbol{\beta}}'\left(\frac{1}{N}\cdot \mathbf{X}'\mathbf{X}\right)\hat{\boldsymbol{\beta}}\right] \\ &= \frac{N}{N-K}\left(\mathrm{E}_N[y_n^2] - \hat{\boldsymbol{\beta}}'\,\mathrm{E}_N[\mathbf{x}_n\mathbf{x}_n']\hat{\boldsymbol{\beta}}\right) \end{aligned} \tag{13.21}$$

Note that the presence of K in the formula for s^2 will be irrelevant because we consider $N \to \infty$. For our purposes $N/(N-K)$ is essentially 1 for such limits. Because all of the averages are second-order sample moments, the U_n of the lemma have the forms $x_{nk}x_{nj}$, $x_{nk}y_n$, and y_n^2. The second-order moments of these random variables are functions of the fourth-order moments of $(y_n, \mathbf{x}_n)$. This is why Assumption 13.1 (I.I.D.) states that fourth moments exist. The following proof formalizes these arguments.

---

22 In fact, references usually state Chebychev's LLN with less restrictive assumptions that imply this condition. For example, see Exercise 13.5.

23 We make a slight abuse of our notation here. We cannot use the symbol y in the place of y_n the way that we distinguish the generic random variable U from its nth replication U_n in Theorem 8 (Chebychev's LLN). There should be no confusion, however, if it is understood that

$$\mathrm{E}_N[x_n y_n] \equiv \frac{1}{N}\sum_{n=1}^{N} x_n y_n$$

denotes the empirical expectation while $\mathrm{E}[x_n y_n]$ is the population mean. We hope that the advantage of a parallel notation outweighs the formal lapse.

Proof of Proposition 15, (13.14) and (13.15). First, let us determine the asymptotic behavior of each of the averages in the expressions for $\hat{\boldsymbol{\beta}}$ and s^2 [equations (13.20) and (13.21)]. We can show that $\mathrm{E}_N[\mathbf{x}_n\mathbf{x}_n']$, $\mathrm{E}_N[\mathbf{x}_n y_n]$, and $\mathrm{E}_N[y_n^2]$ all contain averages that satisfy Chebychev's LLN (Theorem 8). First, Assumption 13.1 states that $(y_n, \mathbf{x}_n)$ are independently distributed, which implies that the elements of these averages are all uncorrelated. Second, this assumption states that all of their fourth moments are bounded. As we just pointed out, this implies that the first and second moments of the elements of these averages are all bounded. Therefore, we can apply Chebychev's LLN. Now let us find the probability limits of these averages.

1. Assumption 13.2 (Population Full Rank) and Chebychev's LLN imply that

$$\frac{1}{N}\cdot\mathbf{X}'\mathbf{X} = \mathrm{E}_N[\mathbf{x}_n\mathbf{x}_n'] \xrightarrow{p} \mathrm{E}[\mathbf{x}_n\mathbf{x}_n'] = \mathbf{D} \tag{13.22}$$

a nonsingular matrix.

2. Rather than $\mathrm{E}_N[\mathbf{x}_n y_n]$, it is more convenient to analyze $\mathrm{E}_N[\mathbf{x}_n(y_n - \mathbf{x}_n'\boldsymbol{\beta}_0)]$. Assumption 6.1 (First Moment) implies that $\mathrm{E}[\mathbf{x}_n(y_n - \mathbf{x}_n'\boldsymbol{\beta}_0)\,|\,\mathbf{X}] = \mathbf{0}$ so that $\mathrm{E}[\mathbf{x}_n(y_n - \mathbf{x}_n'\boldsymbol{\beta}_0)] = \mathbf{0}$, using iterated expectations. Therefore, Chebychev's LLN implies that

$$\begin{aligned}\frac{1}{N}\cdot\mathbf{X}'(\mathbf{y}-\mathbf{X}\boldsymbol{\beta}_0) &= \mathrm{E}_N[\mathbf{x}_n(y_n - \mathbf{x}_n'\boldsymbol{\beta}_0)]\\ &\xrightarrow{p} \mathrm{E}[\mathbf{x}_n(y_n - \mathbf{x}_n'\boldsymbol{\beta}_0)]\\ &= \mathbf{0}\end{aligned}$$

Because $\mathrm{E}_N[\mathbf{x}_n\mathbf{x}_n'] \xrightarrow{p} \mathbf{D}$, Lemma 13.2 (Probability Limit Continuity) implies that

$$\begin{aligned}\mathrm{E}_N[\mathbf{x}_n y_n] &= \mathrm{E}_N[\mathbf{x}_n(y_n - \mathbf{x}_n'\boldsymbol{\beta}_0)] + \mathrm{E}_N[\mathbf{x}_n\mathbf{x}_n']\boldsymbol{\beta}_0\\ &\xrightarrow{p} \mathrm{E}[\mathbf{x}_n\mathbf{x}_n']\boldsymbol{\beta}_0\\ &= \mathbf{D}\boldsymbol{\beta}_0\end{aligned} \tag{13.23}$$

3. Rather than $\mathrm{E}_N[y_n^2]$, consider $\mathrm{E}_N[(y_n - \mathbf{x}_n'\boldsymbol{\beta}_0)^2]$. Using Assumptions 6.1 (First Moment) and 7.1 (Second Moment) and the law of iterated expectations,

$$\mathrm{E}[(y_n - \mathbf{x}_n'\boldsymbol{\beta}_0)^2] = \sigma_0^2$$

so that

$$\mathrm{E}_N[(y_n - \mathbf{x}_n'\boldsymbol{\beta}_0)^2] \xrightarrow{p} \sigma_0^2$$

by Chebychev's LLN. Because $\mathrm{E}_N[\mathbf{x}_n\mathbf{x}_n'] \xrightarrow{p} \mathbf{D}$ and $\mathrm{E}_N[\mathbf{x}_n y_n] \xrightarrow{p} \mathbf{D}\boldsymbol{\beta}_0$, probability limit continuity implies that

$$\begin{aligned}\mathrm{E}_N[y_n^2] &= \mathrm{E}_N[(y_n - \mathbf{x}_n'\boldsymbol{\beta}_0)^2] + 2\,\mathrm{E}_N[\mathbf{x}_n'\boldsymbol{\beta}_0(y_n - \mathbf{x}_n'\boldsymbol{\beta}_0)]\\ &\quad + \mathrm{E}_N[(\mathbf{x}_n'\boldsymbol{\beta}_0)^2]\\ &= \mathrm{E}_N[(y_n - \mathbf{x}_n'\boldsymbol{\beta}_0)^2] + 2\boldsymbol{\beta}_0'\,\mathrm{E}_N[\mathbf{x}_n y_n]\\ &\quad - \boldsymbol{\beta}_0'\,\mathrm{E}_N[\mathbf{x}_n\mathbf{x}_n']\boldsymbol{\beta}_0\\ &\xrightarrow{p} \sigma_0^2 + \boldsymbol{\beta}_0'\mathbf{D}\boldsymbol{\beta}_0\end{aligned} \tag{13.24}$$

Finally, we put these results together using the rules described at the end of the previous section. Because a matrix inverse is a continuous function of the elements of a nonsingular matrix, probability limit continuity and (13.22) imply that

$$(\mathrm{E}_N[\mathbf{x}_n\mathbf{x}_n'])^{-1} \xrightarrow{p} \mathbf{D}^{-1} \tag{13.25}$$

Combining this with (13.23), we find that

$$\hat{\boldsymbol{\beta}} = \left(\mathrm{E}_N[\mathbf{x}_n\mathbf{x}_n']\right)^{-1} \mathrm{E}_N[\mathbf{x}_n y_n] \xrightarrow{p} \mathbf{D}^{-1}\mathbf{D}\boldsymbol{\beta}_0 = \boldsymbol{\beta}_0$$

again using probability limit continuity. Combining this in turn with (13.24),

$$\begin{aligned} s^2 &= \frac{N}{N-K}\left[\mathrm{E}_N[y_n^2] - \hat{\boldsymbol{\beta}}'\,\mathrm{E}_N[\mathbf{x}_n\mathbf{x}_n']\hat{\boldsymbol{\beta}}\right] \\ &\xrightarrow{p} 1 \cdot \left[(\sigma_0^2 + \boldsymbol{\beta}_0'\mathbf{D}\boldsymbol{\beta}_0) - \boldsymbol{\beta}_0'\mathbf{D}\boldsymbol{\beta}_0\right] \\ &= \sigma_0^2 \end{aligned}$$

so that both $\hat{\boldsymbol{\beta}}$ and s^2 converge to their respective population values. □

13.4.3 Central Limit Theorem

Our second link between convergence in distribution and estimation is a set of results called central limit theorems. Each central limit theorem (CLT) states conditions that imply that a standardized sample average converges in distribution to a normally distributed random variable.

Theorem 9 (Lindberg–Levy CLT) *Let $\{U_n\}$ be a sequence of i.i.d. random variables. If $\mathrm{Var}[U_n]$ is strictly positive and finite, then the distribution of*

$$W_N \equiv \frac{\mathrm{E}_N[U] - \mathrm{E}[U]}{\sqrt{\mathrm{Var}[U]/N}} = \sqrt{N}\,\mathrm{E}_N\left[\frac{U - \mathrm{E}[U]}{\sqrt{\mathrm{Var}[U]}}\right]$$

converges to the $\mathfrak{N}(0, 1)$ distribution as N approaches infinity. That is, $W_N \xrightarrow{d} W \sim \mathfrak{N}(0, 1)$.

We prove this lemma in Section D.5.3. We discuss such central limit results extensively in Section D.5 and the reader may wish to read that material before tackling the proof.

There is an inconvenient technicality in the application of the CLT to such multivariate statistics as OLS fitted coefficients: the theorem applies to scalar random variables, not vectors such as the ones we face. To overcome this, we will use the *Cramér–Wold device*.[24]

[24] See Billingsley (1968, p. 48) or Rao (1973, p. 123).

LEMMA 13.5 (CRAMÉR–WOLD DEVICE) *Let* $\{\mathbf{W}_N\}$ *be a sequence of random* $K \times 1$ *vectors. If* $\mathbf{c}'\mathbf{W}_N \xrightarrow{d} \mathbf{c}'\mathbf{W}$ *for every finite* $\mathbf{c} \in \mathbb{R}^K$, *then* $\mathbf{W}_N \xrightarrow{d} \mathbf{W}$.

This lemma permits us to look at linear combinations of vectors and to apply the CLT to them. This works directly because any linear combination of sample averages is also a sample average. It also combines nicely with the asymptotic normal distribution because linear combinations of multivariate normal random variables are also normally distributed. Now we can complete the proof of Proposition 15.

Proof of Proposition 15, (13.16) and (13.17). Consider a linear combination $N^{-1}\mathbf{c}'\mathbf{X}'(\mathbf{y} - \mathbf{X}\boldsymbol{\beta}_0) = \mathrm{E}_N[U]$, where $U \equiv \mathbf{c}'\mathbf{x}_n(y_n - \mathbf{x}_n'\boldsymbol{\beta}_0)$ and $\mathbf{c} \in \mathbb{R}^K$, $\mathbf{c} \neq \mathbf{0}$. The elements in this sum are i.i.d. by Assumption 13.1 (I.I.D.). Assumptions 6.1 and 7.1 (First and Second Moment) imply that

$$\mathrm{E}[U \mid \mathbf{x}_n] = 0,$$
$$\mathrm{Var}[U \mid \mathbf{x}_n] = \sigma_0^2 \cdot \mathbf{c}'\mathbf{x}_n\mathbf{x}_n'\mathbf{c}$$

Adding Assumption 13.2 (Population Full Rank) to this, we have[25]

$$\begin{aligned}\mathrm{Var}[U] &= \mathrm{E}\big[\mathrm{Var}[U \mid \mathbf{x}_n]\big] + \mathrm{Var}\big[\mathrm{E}[U \mid \mathbf{x}_n]\big] \\ &= \sigma_0^2 \cdot \mathbf{c}'\mathbf{D}\mathbf{c} \\ &> 0\end{aligned}$$

Therefore,

$$W_N \equiv \sqrt{N}\,\mathrm{E}_N\left[\frac{U - \mathrm{E}[U]}{\sqrt{\mathrm{Var}[U]}}\right] = \sqrt{N}\frac{\mathrm{E}_N[\mathbf{c}'\mathbf{x}_n(y_n - \mathbf{x}_n'\boldsymbol{\beta}_0)]}{\sigma_0\sqrt{\mathbf{c}'\mathbf{D}\mathbf{c}}} \xrightarrow{d} \mathfrak{N}(0, 1)$$

by the Lindberg–Levy CLT. Equivalently, because this is true for all $\mathbf{c} \in \mathbb{R}^K$, the Cramér–Wold device (Lemma 13.5) implies that

$$\sqrt{N}\frac{\mathrm{E}_N[\mathbf{x}_n(y_n - \mathbf{x}_n'\boldsymbol{\beta}_0)]}{\sigma_0} = \frac{\mathbf{X}'(\mathbf{y} - \mathbf{X}\boldsymbol{\beta}_0)}{\sigma_0\sqrt{N}} \xrightarrow{d} \mathfrak{N}(\mathbf{0}, \mathbf{D}) \tag{13.26}$$

Using (13.25) and the Slutsky lemma (Lemma 13.3),

$$\begin{aligned}\frac{\sqrt{N}}{\sigma_0}\left(\hat{\boldsymbol{\beta}} - \boldsymbol{\beta}_0\right) &= \left(\frac{\mathbf{X}'\mathbf{X}}{N}\right)^{-1}\frac{\mathbf{X}'(\mathbf{y} - \mathbf{X}\boldsymbol{\beta}_0)}{\sigma_0\sqrt{N}} \\ &\xrightarrow{d} \mathbf{D}^{-1}\mathfrak{N}(\mathbf{0}, \mathbf{D}) \\ &\sim \mathfrak{N}(\mathbf{0}, \mathbf{D}^{-1})\end{aligned} \tag{13.27}$$

and, using convergence in distribution continuity (Lemma 13.4),

$$\frac{\sqrt{N}}{\sigma_0}\mathbf{R}\left(\hat{\boldsymbol{\beta}} - \boldsymbol{\beta}_0\right) \xrightarrow{d} \mathfrak{N}(\mathbf{0}, \mathbf{R}\mathbf{D}^{-1}\mathbf{R}')$$

[25] We use the result of Exercise 6.6 (p. 123).

for any $M \times K$ matrix $\mathbf{R}$. Because we have already shown that $s^2 \xrightarrow{p} \sigma_0^2$, the Slutsky lemma allows the substitution of s^2 for σ_0^2:

$$\begin{aligned}
&\left[s^2 \cdot \mathbf{R}\left(\mathbf{X}'\mathbf{X}\right)^{-1}\mathbf{R}'\right]^{-1/2}\mathbf{R}\left(\hat{\boldsymbol{\beta}} - \boldsymbol{\beta}_0\right) \\
&= \sqrt{\frac{\sigma_0^2}{s^2}} \cdot \left[\mathbf{R}\left(\frac{1}{N}\cdot\mathbf{X}'\mathbf{X}\right)^{-1}\mathbf{R}'\right]^{-1/2}\frac{\sqrt{N}}{\sigma_0}\mathbf{R}\left(\hat{\boldsymbol{\beta}} - \boldsymbol{\beta}_0\right) \\
&\xrightarrow{d} 1 \cdot \left(\mathbf{R}\mathbf{D}^{-1}\mathbf{R}'\right)^{-1/2}\mathfrak{N}(\mathbf{0}, \mathbf{R}\mathbf{D}^{-1}\mathbf{R}') \\
&\sim \mathfrak{N}(\mathbf{0}, \mathbf{I}_M)
\end{aligned}$$

Finally, the continuity of convergence in distribution (Lemma 13.4) and Lemma 10.2 (Chi-Square Quadratic Forms, p. 204) also imply that

$$\left(\hat{\boldsymbol{\beta}} - \boldsymbol{\beta}_0\right)'\mathbf{R}'\left[s^2 \cdot \mathbf{R}\left(\mathbf{X}'\mathbf{X}\right)^{-1}\mathbf{R}'\right]^{-1}\mathbf{R}\left(\hat{\boldsymbol{\beta}} - \boldsymbol{\beta}_0\right) \xrightarrow{d} \chi_M^2$$

because the sum of squares is a continuous function of its arguments. □

13.4.4 Sample Size

Inevitably one asks the question, "How many observations are required for asymptotic distributions to yield a reliable approximation?" The simplest truthful answer is that no one knows, at least not without additional information about the data-generating process. There are formal theorems that refine central limit theorems with additional moment restrictions, bounding the distance between F_{U_N} and its normal limit or increasing the rate of convergence of F_{U_N}.[26]

Alternatively, one can employ Monte Carlo calculations for evidence that the sample size is too small to rely on an asymptotic approximation. For example, we took the OLS fitted coefficients $\hat{\boldsymbol{\beta}}_{\text{OLS}}$ in Table 13.1 and OLS fitted variance s^2 and the design matrix $\mathbf{X}$ of the log-earnings data and generated one hundred thousand artificial data sets with a conditional Laplace distribution with variance s^2 around $\mathbf{X}\hat{\boldsymbol{\beta}}_{\text{OLS}}$. For the estimated intercept parameters, we plot the empirical c.d.f. of the Monte Carlo simulations and the normal c.d.f. predicted by the asymptotic approximation in Figures 13.5 and 13.6. These figures show how close the agreement is for that experiment. There are enough simulations to obtain an extremely accurate assessment. Although the empirical c.d.f. agrees closely with the asymptotic approximation, a statistical test rejects the null hypothesis that the two distributions are identical. For example, the t test statistic for whether 1% of the true probability lies above the ninety-ninth percentile of the normal approximation is 125.8, rejecting the hypothesis resoundly.[27]

When we use only the first 10 observations for the same experiment, we obtain Figures 13.7 and 13.8. The tail probabilities are distinctly different between the asymptotic approximation

26 For example, see Phillips (1983) and Rothenberg (1984b).

27 The sample frequency that the Monte Carlo simulations exceeded the ninety-ninth percentile of the normal approximation was 0.0101 but the estimated standard error of this sample frequency as an estimator of the population probability was only 8.0286×10^{-5}.

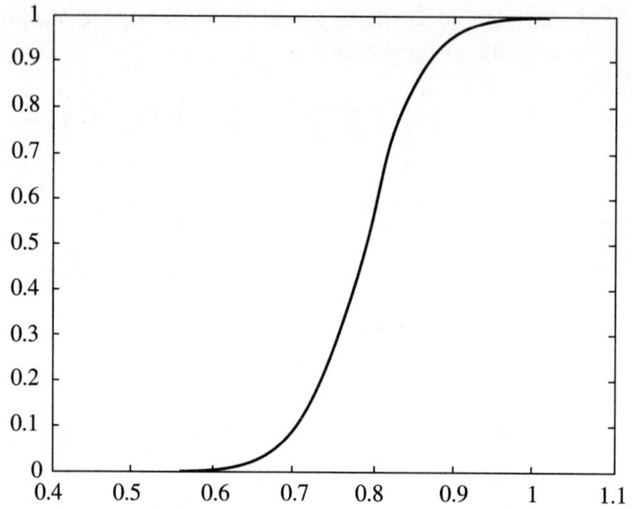

Figure 13.5 Approximate and empirical c.d.f.s.

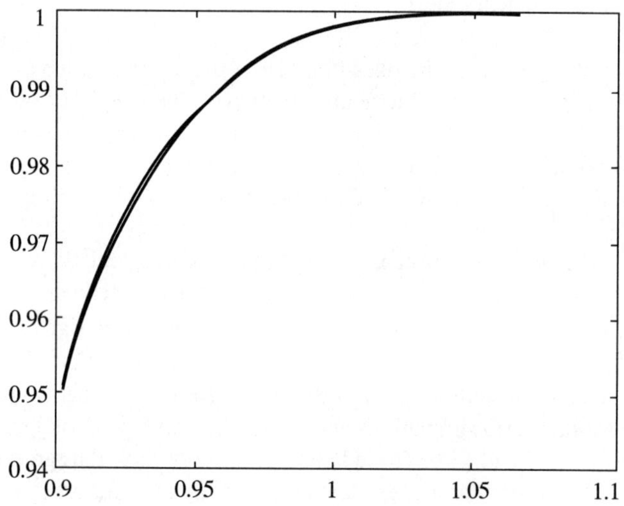

Figure 13.6 Approximate and empirical c.d.f.s.

and the estimate of the actual. Such Monte Carlo evidence can reveal potential weakness in the asymptotic approximation. It is limited, but readily available, information about whether the sample size smooths away specific kinds of nonnormality.

Note that in general one must make additional assumptions to those of a central limit theorem to assess the quality of its asymptotic approximation. Our Monte Carlo experiment specifies the complete sampling distribution of the data. The theorems mentioned above add assumptions about moments higher than the second. Thus, refinements of a central limit theorem require refinements of the assumptions.

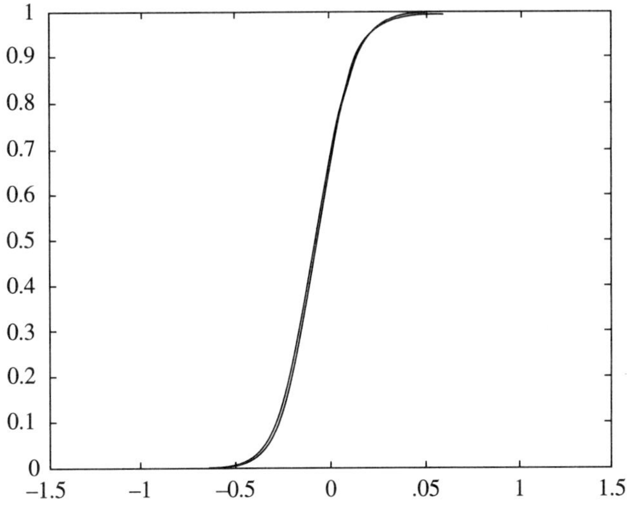

Figure 13.7 Approximate and empirical c.d.f.s.

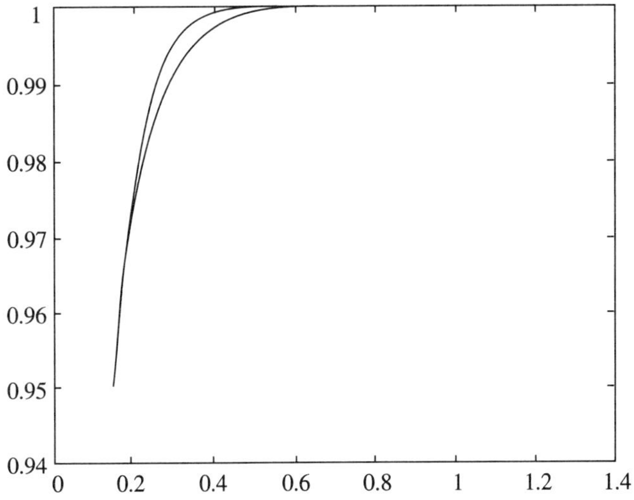

Figure 13.8 Approximate and empirical c.d.f.s.

Also note that the feasibility of increasing the sample size is not a prerequisite for applying asymptotic approximations. One might think that contemplation of the asymptotic behavior of statistics makes sense only in the context of such repeatable experiments as observing coin flips. But this misses the point of the statistical theory: approximating distributions for small samples with those for infinite samples. The quality of such approximation is affected by the number of observations, but not by whether that number can be increased.

13.5 MATHEMATICAL NOTES

In these mathematical notes, we cover a variety of details. First, we derive for completeness a special binomial identity that simplifies the p.d.f. of order statistics described in Section 13.3.1. Second, we support the claims about the LAD fit in Section 13.3.2. Finally, we give formal proofs of the convergence results that we described in Section 13.4.

13.5.1 The Density of an Order Statistic

The p.d.f. of an order statistic that we give in (13.9) rests on the following binomial identity:

$$\frac{d}{dp}\sum_{n=r}^{N}\binom{N}{n}p^n(1-p)^{N-n}=\frac{N!}{(r-1)!\,(N-r)!}p^{r-1}(1-p)^{N-r} \tag{13.28}$$

Here is its derivation:

$$\begin{aligned}
&\frac{d}{dp}\sum_{n=r}^{N}\binom{N}{n}p^n(1-p)^{N-n}\\
&=\sum_{n=r}^{N}\left[\binom{N}{n}np^{n-1}(1-p)^{N-n}-\binom{N}{n}p^n(N-n)(1-p)^{N-n-1}\right]\\
&=\frac{N!}{(r-1)!\,(N-r)!}p^{r-1}(1-p)^{N-r}\\
&\quad+\sum_{n=r+1}^{N}\frac{N!}{(n-1)!\,(N-n)!}p^{n-1}(1-p)^{N-n}-\sum_{n=r}^{N-1}\binom{N}{n}p^n(1-p)^{N-n-1}(N-n)\\
&=\frac{N!}{(r-1)!\,(N-r)!}p^{r-1}(1-p)^{N-r}\\
&\quad+\sum_{m=r}^{N-1}\frac{N!}{m!\,(N-m-1)!}p^m(1-p)^{N-m-1}-\sum_{n=r}^{N-1}\frac{N!}{n!\,(N-n-1)!}p^n(1-p)^{N-n-1}\\
&=\frac{N!}{(r-1)!\,(N-r)!}p^{r-1}(1-p)^{N-r}
\end{aligned}$$

We use (13.28) when we differentiate the c.d.f. (13.8) to obtain the p.d.f. The c.d.f. of the rth order statistic is the LHS of (13.28) when we substitute $p = F_V(v)$. Then (13.9) is equivalent to a slight change to (13.28): using the chain rule of differentiation,

$$\frac{d}{dv}\sum_{n=r}^{N}\binom{N}{n}p^n(1-p)^{N-n}=\frac{N!}{(r-1)!\,(N-r)!}\frac{dp}{dv}p^{r-1}(1-p)^{N-r}$$

where $dp/dv = f_V(v)$.

13.5.2 Properties of LAD Fit

To gain insight into the LAD fitting procedure, we study the objective function. Two examples that illustrate the basic features appear in Figure 13.9. They show convexity, piecewise linearity, the existence of a global minimum, and its possible uniqueness.

The LAD objective function

$$g(\boldsymbol{\beta}) \equiv \sum_{n=1}^{N} \left| y_n - \mathbf{x}_n' \boldsymbol{\beta} \right|$$

is a continuous convex function because it is the sum of absolute value functions, which are continuous and convex. From this we can conclude that the global minimum over $\mathbb{R}^K$, if it exists, will be found on a closed and convex set.[28]

Even though it may seem obvious, we will confirm that a global minimum exists. Note that if we go far enough in any direction then $g(\boldsymbol{\beta})$ will eventually approach infinity. For each direction $\boldsymbol{\delta} \in \mathbb{R}^K$, consider the univariate function of a distance parameter $\alpha > 0$,

$$\begin{aligned} g(\alpha \cdot \boldsymbol{\delta}) &= \sum_{n=1}^{N} \left| y_n - \alpha \cdot \mathbf{x}_n' \boldsymbol{\delta} \right| \\ &= \sum_{n=1}^{N} \operatorname{sgn}(y_n - \alpha \cdot \mathbf{x}_n' \boldsymbol{\delta}) \left(y_n - \alpha \cdot \mathbf{x}_n' \boldsymbol{\delta} \right) \end{aligned}$$

There is an $\alpha(\boldsymbol{\delta})$ such that $\mathbf{s} \equiv [\operatorname{sgn}(y_n - \alpha \cdot \mathbf{x}_n' \boldsymbol{\delta}),\, n = 1, \ldots, N]'$ is constant for all $\alpha > \alpha(\boldsymbol{\delta})$ so that

$$g(\alpha \cdot \boldsymbol{\delta}) = \mathbf{s}'\mathbf{y} - \alpha \cdot \mathbf{s}'\mathbf{X}\boldsymbol{\delta}, \ \alpha > \alpha(\boldsymbol{\delta})$$

is a linear function. Every $\left| y_n - \alpha \left(\mathbf{x}_n' \boldsymbol{\delta} \right) \right|$ increases beyond this point and we conclude that $g(\alpha \cdot \boldsymbol{\delta}) \to \infty$ as $\alpha \to \infty$. Because this is true for every direction $\boldsymbol{\delta}$, the global minimum exists.

When we write

$$g(\boldsymbol{\beta}) = \sum_{n=1}^{N} \left(y_n - \mathbf{x}_n' \boldsymbol{\beta} \right) \operatorname{sgn} \left(y_n - \mathbf{x}_n' \boldsymbol{\beta} \right)$$

we see that the objective function is piecewise linear, such that kinks appear wherever a $\operatorname{sgn}(y_n - \mathbf{x}_n' \boldsymbol{\beta})$ changes. For all values of $\boldsymbol{\beta}$ such that $y_n - \mathbf{x}_n' \boldsymbol{\beta} \neq 0$ for every $n = 1, \ldots, N$, the gradient of $g(\boldsymbol{\beta})$ is

$$\frac{\partial g(\boldsymbol{\beta})}{\partial \boldsymbol{\beta}} = - \sum_{n=1}^{N} \mathbf{x}_n \operatorname{sgn}(y_n - \mathbf{x}_n' \boldsymbol{\beta})$$

---

[28] For a review of convex functions and their minima, see Simon and Blume (1994, Ch. 21). Also, be sure to distinguish between convex *functions* and convex *sets*. A function $g(z)$ defined on $\mathbb{R}^K$ is convex if

$$g[\alpha z_1 + (1 - \alpha) z_2] \leq \alpha g(z_1) + (1 - \alpha) g(z_2)$$

for all $\alpha \in [0, 1]$. A subset $\mathbb{A} \subseteq \mathbb{R}^K$ is convex if

$$z_1, z_2 \in \mathbb{A} \quad \Rightarrow \quad \alpha z_1 + (1 - \alpha) z_2 \in \mathbb{A}$$

for all $\alpha \in [0, 1]$.

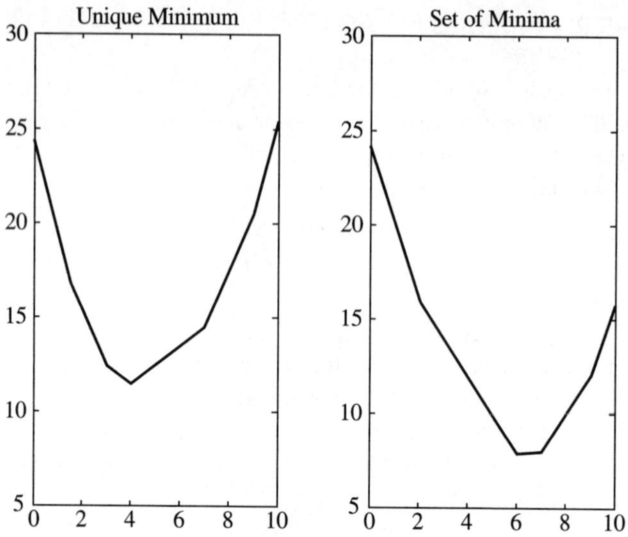

Figure 13.9 Sum of absolute residuals function.

But we know that a global minimum will occur at a kink where the gradient is undefined. Nevertheless, at a global minimum $\hat{\boldsymbol{\beta}}_{\text{LAD}}$, for each direction $\boldsymbol{\delta} \in \mathbb{R}^K$,

$$\lim_{\alpha \to 0^+} \boldsymbol{\delta}' \frac{\partial g(\boldsymbol{\beta})}{\partial \boldsymbol{\beta}}\bigg|_{\boldsymbol{\beta}=\hat{\boldsymbol{\beta}}_{\text{LAD}}+\alpha\cdot\boldsymbol{\delta}} \geq 0$$

$$\lim_{\alpha \to 0^-} \boldsymbol{\delta}' \frac{\partial g(\boldsymbol{\beta})}{\partial \boldsymbol{\beta}}\bigg|_{\boldsymbol{\beta}=\hat{\boldsymbol{\beta}}_{\text{LAD}}+\alpha\cdot\boldsymbol{\delta}} \leq 0$$

so that $g(\boldsymbol{\beta})$ is increasing no matter which direction we move away from $\hat{\boldsymbol{\beta}}_{\text{LAD}}$. Furthermore, if there is a unique global minimum, it must occur at a point in $\mathbb{R}^K$ determined by K linearly independent equations $y_n - \mathbf{x}_n'\boldsymbol{\beta} = 0$.[29] Therefore, we loosely write

$$\sum_{n=1}^{N} \mathbf{x}_n \operatorname{sgn}(y_n - \mathbf{x}_n'\hat{\boldsymbol{\beta}}_{\text{LAD}}) = \mathbf{0}$$

taking advantage of the sgn function, which equals zero at the argument value zero.

A global minimum $\hat{\boldsymbol{\beta}}_{\text{LAD}}$ is not unique if the derivative of a facet of $g(\boldsymbol{\beta})$ at $\hat{\boldsymbol{\beta}}_{\text{LAD}}$ happens to be zero. A simple example of this occurs when fitting the location model with an even number of observations N. As we saw in Section 13.3.1, the derivative of the objective function with respect to the location parameter $\boldsymbol{\beta}$ given in (13.7) equals the number of observations below $\boldsymbol{\beta}$ minus the number of observations above $\boldsymbol{\beta}$. This is constant and zero for $v_{(r)} \leq \boldsymbol{\beta} \leq v_{(r+1)}$ when N is even and $r = N/2$.

[29] More than K fitted residuals may be zero at a unique global minimum, but there must be at least K.

Proof of Proposition 14. To prove that $\hat{\boldsymbol{\beta}}_{\text{LAD}}$ is unbiased, consider the LAD program

$$\hat{\boldsymbol{\mu}}_{\text{LAD}} = \underset{\boldsymbol{\mu} \in \text{Col}(\mathbf{X})}{\text{argmin}} \sum_{n=1}^{N} |y_n - \mu_n|$$

If $\mathbf{y}$ is distributed symmetrically around $\boldsymbol{\mu}_0$, then $\boldsymbol{\varepsilon} \equiv \mathbf{y} - \boldsymbol{\mu}_0$ is symmetrically distributed around the zero vector. That is, the distribution of $\boldsymbol{\varepsilon}$ is the same as the distribution of $-\boldsymbol{\varepsilon}$, conditional on $\mathbf{X}$. Consider the LAD objective function as a function of $\boldsymbol{\varepsilon}$ and denote

$$\hat{\boldsymbol{\mu}}_{\text{LAD}}(\boldsymbol{\varepsilon}) \equiv \underset{\boldsymbol{\mu} \in \text{Col}(\mathbf{X})}{\text{argmin}} \sum_{n=1}^{N} |\mu_{0n} + \varepsilon_n - \mu_n|$$

The absolute value function permits us to write

$$\begin{aligned}
\sum_{n=1}^{N} |\mu_{0n} + \varepsilon_n - \mu_n| &= \sum_{n=1}^{N} |-\mu_{0n} - \varepsilon_n + \mu_n| \\
&= \sum_{n=1}^{N} |\mu_{0n} - \varepsilon_n - (2\mu_{0n} - \mu_n)|
\end{aligned}$$

As a result,

$$\begin{aligned}
\hat{\boldsymbol{\mu}}_{\text{LAD}}(-\boldsymbol{\varepsilon}) &\equiv \underset{\boldsymbol{\mu} \in \text{Col}(\mathbf{X})}{\text{argmin}} \sum_{n=1}^{N} |\mu_{0n} - \varepsilon_n - \mu_n| \\
&= 2\boldsymbol{\mu}_0 - \hat{\boldsymbol{\mu}}_{\text{LAD}}(\boldsymbol{\varepsilon})
\end{aligned}$$

Put another way,

$$-\left[\boldsymbol{\mu}_0 - \hat{\boldsymbol{\mu}}_{\text{LAD}}(-\boldsymbol{\varepsilon})\right] = \boldsymbol{\mu}_0 - \hat{\boldsymbol{\mu}}_{\text{LAD}}(\boldsymbol{\varepsilon})$$

so that $\hat{\boldsymbol{\mu}}_{\text{LAD}}$ is symmetrically distributed around $\boldsymbol{\mu}_0$, conditional on $\mathbf{X}$. Therefore, if its expectation exists, the conditional expectation of $\hat{\boldsymbol{\mu}}_{\text{LAD}}$ is $\boldsymbol{\mu}_0$, and $\hat{\boldsymbol{\beta}}_{\text{LAD}} = (\mathbf{X}'\mathbf{X})^{-1}\mathbf{X}'\hat{\boldsymbol{\mu}}_{\text{LAD}}$ is an unbiased estimator of $\boldsymbol{\beta}_0$. □

13.5.3 Convergence Proofs

In this section, we prove various convergence results. The "epsilon–delta" proofs that follow are like dotting your *i*s and crossing your *t*s: both are necessary for precise communication, but neither is sufficient for teaching ideas. Nevertheless, these proofs are instructive. None of them uses difficult mathematical arguments, but it is a challenge to come up with some of the arguments on your own. It is also a challenge to work through such proofs when they seem tedious or laborious. As you work through this material, try to outline each proof in your own words in terms of general strategy, ignoring the simplest steps and highlighting the cleverest ones.

Proof of Lemma 13.1. **Sufficiency:** First note that for $\epsilon > 0$,

$$\begin{aligned}\Pr\{|U_N - U| \le \epsilon\} &= \Pr\{U - \epsilon \le U_N \le U + \epsilon\} \\ &\ge \Pr\{U - \epsilon < U_N \le U + \epsilon\} \\ &= F_{U_N}(U + \epsilon) - F_{U_N}(U - \epsilon) \end{aligned} \tag{13.29}$$

If $U_N \overset{d}{\to} U$, then for all $u \neq U$ (U is a point of discontinuity in F_U),

$$F_{U_N}(u) \to F_U(u) = \mathbf{1}\{U \le u\}$$

where $\mathbf{1}\{U \le u\}$ is the c.d.f. of the constant U. That is, for every $u \neq U$ and $\eta > 0$ there is an $N^{**}(u, \eta)$ such that

$$N > N^{**}(u, \eta) \qquad \Rightarrow \qquad \left|F_{U_N}(u) - F_U(u)\right| < \eta$$

Note in particular that

$$\begin{aligned}\left|F_{U_N}(U - \epsilon) - F_U(U - \epsilon)\right| &= F_{U_N}(U - \epsilon) \\ \left|F_{U_N}(U + \epsilon) - F_U(U + \epsilon)\right| &= 1 - F_{U_N}(U + \epsilon)\end{aligned}$$

If we choose $\eta = \delta/2$, then there is an

$$N^*(\epsilon, \delta) \ge \max\{N^{**}(U - \epsilon, \delta/2),\ N^{**}(U + \epsilon, \delta/2)\}$$

so that

$$N > N^*(\epsilon, \delta) \qquad \Rightarrow \qquad F_{U_N}(U - \epsilon),\ 1 - F_{U_N}(U + \epsilon) < \delta/2$$

Combining this with (13.29), for every $\epsilon, \delta > 0$ there is an $N^* = N^*(\epsilon, \delta)$ such that for all $N > N^*$

$$\begin{aligned}\Pr\{|U_N - U| \le \epsilon\} &\ge F_{U_N}(U + \epsilon) - F_{U_N}(U - \epsilon) \\ &= 1 - \left[1 - F_{U_N}(U + \epsilon) + F_{U_N}(U - \epsilon)\right] \\ &> 1 - \delta\end{aligned}$$

Because ϵ and δ are arbitrary, we can strengthen this to

$$\Pr\{|U_N - U| < \epsilon\} > 1 - \delta$$

by choosing $N^*(\epsilon - 0, \delta)$, thereby proving sufficiency.

Necessity: Note that because $F_{U_N}(u)$ is nondecreasing,[30]

$$\begin{aligned}\sup_{u:|u-U|\ge\epsilon} \left|F_{U_N}(u) - \mathbf{1}\{U \le u\}\right| &= \max\left\{F_{U_N}(U - \epsilon),\ 1 - F_{U_N}(U + \epsilon)\right\} \\ &\le 1 - \Pr\{|U_N - U| < \epsilon\}\end{aligned}$$

[30] The term $\sup_{a \in \mathbb{A}} g(a)$ denotes the *supremum* or *least upper bound* over the set $\mathbb{A}$. It is the smallest value that is greater than or equal to $g(a)$ for all $a \in \mathbb{A}$. The distinction between the supremum and the maximum is that the latter may not be well defined. For example, $\sup_{x<0} = 0$, whereas there is no maximum over the open set $\{x \mid x < 0\}$. See Simon and Blume (1994, p. 804) for further discussion.

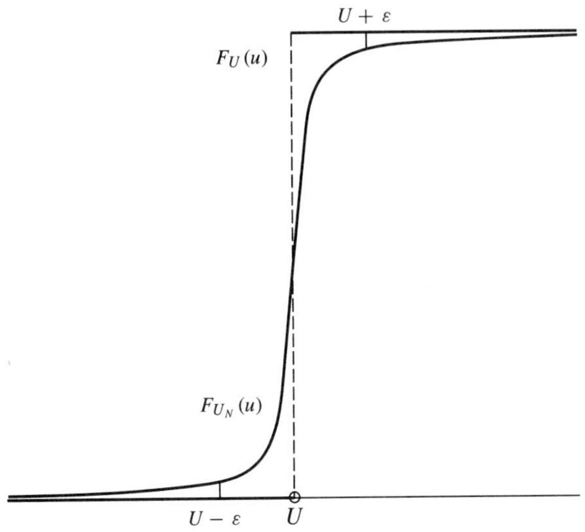

Figure 13.10 $F_{U_N}(z)$ versus $F_U(z)$.

See Figure 13.10. The biggest differences between $F_{U_N}(u)$ and $\mathbf{1}\{U \leq u\}$ occur in the boundary set $\{u \mid |u - U| = \epsilon\}$. There the differences are probabilities of regions that always omit part of $\{u \mid |u - U| \geq \epsilon\}$ so that $\Pr\{|U_N - U| \geq \epsilon\} = 1 - \Pr\{|U_N - U| < \epsilon\}$ always exceeds the biggest difference.

Therefore, for a particular $u \neq U$ we can choose an $\epsilon > 0$ such that $\epsilon < |U - u|$ so that for any $\delta > 0$ there is an N^* such that (13.19) reduces to

$$N > N^* \qquad \Rightarrow \qquad \left|F_{U_N}(u) - \mathbf{1}\{U \leq u\}\right| < \delta$$

That is, $F_{U_N}(u)$ converges to $\mathbf{1}\{U \leq u\}$, the c.d.f. of the constant U. □

Proof of Lemma 13.2. Let $\Pr\{|U_N - U| < \epsilon\} > 1 - \delta$ for all $N > N^*$. Because g is continuous at U, for every $\eta > 0$ there is an $\epsilon(\eta, U) > 0$ such that

$$\forall U : |U_N - U| < \epsilon(\eta, U) \qquad \Rightarrow \qquad |g(U_N) - g(U)| < \eta$$

Therefore,

$$\Pr\{|g(U_N) - g(U)| < \eta\} \geq \Pr\{|U_N - U| < \epsilon(\eta, U)\} > 1 - \delta$$

for all $N > N^*$. □

The proof of the analogous result for deterministic convergence has the same structure, but no probabilistic statements are required. The key additional element of the argument is that because $|U_N - U| < \epsilon(\eta, U)$ implies $|g(U_N) - g(U)| < \eta$ then $\Pr\{|g(U_N) - g(U)| < \eta\} \geq \Pr\{|U_N - U| < \epsilon(\eta, U)\}$. The logic here is that if the occurrence of event A implies the occurrence of event B then $\Pr\{B\} \geq \Pr\{A\}$.

We use the following two lemmas to prove Lemma 13.3.

Lemma 13.6 If $U_N \xrightarrow{d} U$ and $U_N - W_N \xrightarrow{p} 0$, then $W_N \xrightarrow{d} U$.

Proof. We follow Rao (1973, p. 122). Let u be a continuity point of $F_U(u)$. First, we bound $F_{W_N}(u)$ above:

$$\begin{aligned} F_{W_N}(u) &\equiv \Pr\{W_N < u\} \\ &= \Pr\{U_N < u + U_N - W_N\} \\ &= \Pr\{U_N < u + U_N - W_N,\ U_N - W_N < \epsilon\} \\ &\quad + \Pr\{U_N < u + U_N - W_N,\ U_N - W_N \geq \epsilon\} \\ &\leq \Pr\{U_N < u + \epsilon\} + \Pr\{U_N - W_N \geq \epsilon\} \\ &= F_{U_N}(u+\epsilon) + \Pr\{U_N - W_N \geq \epsilon\} \end{aligned}$$

for any $\epsilon > 0$. The last inequality follows from the facts that

$$\begin{aligned} &\{(U_N, W_N) \mid U_N < u + U_N - W_N,\ U_N - W_N < \epsilon\} \subseteq \{(U_N, W_N) \mid U_N < u + \epsilon\} \\ &\{(U_N, W_N) \mid U_N < u + U_N - W_N,\ U_N - W_N \geq \epsilon\} \subseteq \{(U_N, W_N) \mid U_N - W_N \geq \epsilon\} \end{aligned}$$

It follows from $U_N - W_N \xrightarrow{p} 0$ and from u being a continuity point of F_U that for sufficiently small ϵ

$$\limsup_{N\to\infty} F_{W_N}(u) \leq F_U(u+\epsilon)$$

Using a similar approach, we bound $F_{U_N}(u)$ from below:

$$\begin{aligned} F_{U_N}(u-\epsilon) &= \Pr\{W_N < u - \epsilon + W_N - U_N,\ W_N - U_N < \epsilon\} \\ &\quad + \Pr\{W_N < u - \epsilon + W_N - U_N,\ W_N - U_N \geq \epsilon\} \\ &\leq \Pr\{W_N < u\} + \Pr\{W_N - U_N \geq \epsilon\} \end{aligned}$$

so that

$$\liminf_{N\to\infty} F_{W_N}(u) \geq F_U(u-\epsilon)$$

for sufficiently small ϵ. By letting $\epsilon \to 0$,

$$\lim_{N\to\infty} F_{W_N}(u) = F_U(u)$$

which proves the lemma. □

LEMMA 13.7 If $U_N \xrightarrow{d} U$ and $W_N \xrightarrow{p} 0$, then $W_N U_N \xrightarrow{p} 0$.

Proof. The proof involves the same approach as the proof of the previous lemma. Once again, we bound the critical probability: for $\delta > 0$

$$\begin{aligned}\Pr\{|U_N W_N| > \epsilon\} &= \Pr\{|U_N W_N| > \epsilon,\ |W_N| \le \frac{\epsilon}{\delta}\}\\ &\quad + \Pr\{|U_N W_N| > \epsilon,\ |W_N| > \frac{\epsilon}{\delta}\}\\ &\le \Pr\{|U_N| > \delta\} + \Pr\{|W_N| > \frac{\epsilon}{\delta}\}\end{aligned}$$

But this time we need only an upper bound, because we are going to show that the limit of this probability is zero. Because $W_N \xrightarrow{p} 0$,

$$\limsup_{N\to\infty} \Pr\{|W_N U_N| > \epsilon\} \le 1 - F_U(\delta) - F_U(-\delta)$$

By letting $\delta \to \infty$,

$$\lim_{N\to\infty} \Pr\{|W_N U_N| > \epsilon\} = 0$$

which proves that $W_N U_N \xrightarrow{p} 0$. □

Proof of Lemma 13.3. Because $U_N \xrightarrow{d} U$ and W is a constant, $W + U_N \xrightarrow{d} W + U$. In addition, because $W_N \xrightarrow{p} W$,

$$(W_N + U_N) - (W + U_N) = W_N - W \xrightarrow{p} 0$$

Therefore, using Lemma 13.6, $W_N + U_N \xrightarrow{d} W + U$. Now $WU_N \xrightarrow{d} WU$ also. In addition, using Lemma 13.7,

$$W_N U_N - WU_N = (W_N - W)U_N \xrightarrow{p} 0$$

Therefore, using Lemma 13.6, $W_N U_N \xrightarrow{d} WU$. □

Proof of Lemma 13.4. See Rao (1973, p. 124). □

Proof of Theorem 8 (Chebychev's LLN). Because the U_n are i.i.d., the first sample moment has the expectation

$$\mathrm{E}\big[\mathrm{E}_N[U]\big] = \frac{1}{N}\sum_{n=1}^{N} \mathrm{E}[U_n] = \mathrm{E}[U]$$

and the variance

$$\mathrm{Var}\big[\mathrm{E}_N[U]\big] = \frac{1}{N^2}\sum_{n=1}^{N} \mathrm{Var}[U] = \frac{\mathrm{Var}[U]}{N}$$

According to Chebychev's inequality (Lemma D.3, p. 875), for any $\epsilon > 0$,

$$\Pr\{|\mathrm{E}_N[U] - \mathrm{E}[U]| > \epsilon\} < \frac{\mathrm{Var}\left[\mathrm{E}_N[U]\right]}{\epsilon^2} = \frac{\mathrm{Var}[U]}{N\epsilon^2}$$

which approaches zero as N approaches infinity. Therefore, $\mathrm{E}_N[U] \xrightarrow{p} \mu$. □

13.6 OVERVIEW

1. The conditional distribution of $\mathbf{y}$ given $\mathbf{X}$ may not be normal. Primarily, researchers are concerned that the distribution may have fatter tails than the normal distribution.
2. There are several parametric distributions that might serve in place of the normal specification. The Student t distribution and the power exponential both generalize the normal distribution to larger families that include distributions with fatter tails. The Laplace and logistic distributions are alternative distributions that have simpler parametric forms and fatter tails.
3. None of these distributions delivers tractable distributions for the OLS estimator. Nevertheless we know that the OLS estimator is not the most efficient unbiased estimator if any of these distributions are the conditional distribution of $\mathbf{y}$. Without the normality assumption, the OLS estimator remains the most efficient *linear* unbiased estimator, but we cannot say much else about its distribution beyond estimating its variance matrix.
4. Nonlinear unbiased estimators may be efficient relative to the OLS estimator. The LAD estimator is a leading nonlinear alternative to OLS. In the special case of the simple location model, the LAD estimator corresponds to the sample median, which illustrates many of the properties of the LAD regression fit. In particular, the LAD estimator is less sensitive to outlying observations so that it may be efficient relative to the OLS estimator for some fat-tailed distributions. In addition to the problems of nonnormal distribution theory, the nonlinear character of LAD prevents us from making more precise statements about the distribution of the LAD estimator or its relative efficiency.
5. Asymptotic distribution theory provides an approximation to the distribution of the OLS estimator that does not depend on the normality assumption. The approximation does rely on a sufficiently large sample size for the approximation error to be negligible.
6. The asymptotic distribution theory has three conceptual components:
   (a) convergence in probability to a constant and its generalization convergence in distribution,
   (b) laws of large numbers and central limit theorems that apply these concepts of convergence to sums of random variables,
   (c) the functional dependence of OLS estimators on sums of random variables.
7. Convergence in distribution refers to the limit of a sequence of c.d.f.s associated with a sequence of random variables $\{U_N\}$ as $N \to \infty$. Convergence in probability is a special case in which the limiting c.d.f. is the c.d.f. of a constant.
8. Laws of large numbers provide conditions under which the empirical mean of a random sample converges in probability to the population mean.
9. Central limit theorems provide conditions under which the standardized empirical mean of a random sample converges in distribution to a standard normal random variable. The standardization makes the mean zero and variance one for all sample sizes, thereby preventing the distribution from collapsing to that of a constant or from becoming unstable.
10. The asymptotic distribution theory of the OLS estimator is practically identical to the exact distribution theory under the normality assumption. The principal difference is that the asymptotic approximation

effectively treats the OLS estimator s^2 of the variance as though it were the population variance σ_0^2 for inferences about $\boldsymbol{\beta}_0$ using the distribution of $\hat{\boldsymbol{\beta}}$.

13.7 EXERCISES

13.7.1 Review

13.1 (Logistic Distribution) A distribution that is quite similar to the normal is based on the simple c.d.f.

$$F(x) = \frac{1}{1+e^{-x}}$$

called the *logistic*.

(a) Show that $F(x)$ has the properties of a c.d.f.
(b) Find the p.d.f. and confirm that it is symmetric about 0.
(c) Find the mean and the variance of this distribution.
(d) Graph the standard normal and a standardized logistic p.d.f. Which has fatter tails?

13.2 (Mixture of Normals) A *mixture* of normal p.d.f.s is one way to generalize the normal distribution. As a simple case, consider the univariate p.d.f.

$$f(y;\mu,\sigma_0^2,\sigma_1^2,\gamma) = \gamma\cdot\phi(y-\mu;\sigma_0^2) + (1-\gamma)\cdot\phi(y-\mu;\sigma_1^2)$$

where γ is an additional parameter between 0 and 1.

(a) Show that a random variable with this p.d.f. can be generated as a randomized selection of a random variable from either an $\mathfrak{N}(\mu,\sigma_0^2)$ distribution or an $\mathfrak{N}(\mu,\sigma_1^2)$ distribution.
(b) Graph this p.d.f. for the case $\mu = 0$, $\sigma_0^2 = 2\sigma_1^2 = 2$, and $\gamma = 1/2$.
(c) Show that the mean and variance of this mixture distribution are μ and $\gamma\,\sigma_0^2 + (1-\gamma)\,\sigma_1^2$, respectively.
(d) Show that the third (centered) moment about μ of this p.d.f. is 0, like the normal distribution, but that the fourth centered moment is not three times the second moment squared, unlike the normal, unless $\sigma_0^2 = \sigma_1^2$ or $\gamma \in \{0,1\}$. In addition, show that this mixture distribution is platykurtic (fat tailed) relative to the normal distribution. [HINT: Show that the difference between the fourth moment and three times the second moment squared is $3(\sigma_0^2-\sigma_1^2)^2\gamma\,(1-\gamma)$.]

13.3 (Mixtures of Normals) Suppose that, conditional on $\mathbf{X}$, each y_n is independently and identically distributed as a mixture of normals (Exercise 13.2) with mean $\mathbf{x}_n'\boldsymbol{\beta}_0$ and constant variance.

(a) Argue that $\hat{\boldsymbol{\mu}}$, $\mathbf{y}-\hat{\boldsymbol{\mu}}$, and $\hat{\boldsymbol{\beta}}$ also have conditional p.d.f.s that are also mixtures of normals.
(b) Argue that $\hat{\boldsymbol{\mu}}$ and $\mathbf{y}-\hat{\boldsymbol{\mu}}$ are generally dependently distributed conditional on $\mathbf{X}$.

13.4 (Fat Tails) The normal p.d.f. has the thinnest tails of the distributions described in this chapter.

(a) Confirm that the ratio of a standard normal p.d.f. over a logistic p.d.f. converges to zero in the tails, as in (13.4).
(b) Show that the Laplace and logistic p.d.f.s have tails of comparable order.
(c) Show that the tails of the Student t p.d.f. are heavier than those of the logistic p.d.f for any finite, positive degrees of freedom parameter ν.

13.5 (Chebychev's LLN) Show that Chebychev's LLN (Theorem 8) need not require independence or identical distributions using the following exceptions to the conditions of the theorem. In each case, use the logic of the theorem's proof to show that $\text{E}_N[U] \xrightarrow{p} \text{E}[U]$ as $N \to \infty$.

(a) Let $\text{E}[U_n] = \mu_n$ and $\text{Var}[U_n] = \sigma_n^2$ so that $\{U_n\}$ is a sequence of i.n.i.d. random variables. Also let

$$\bar{\mu}_N \equiv \frac{1}{N}\sum_{n=1}^{N} \mu_n \qquad \text{and} \qquad \bar{\sigma}_N^2 \equiv \frac{1}{N}\sum_{n=1}^{N} \sigma_n^2$$

and suppose that

$$\lim_{N\to\infty} \bar{\mu}_N = \mu \qquad \text{and} \qquad \lim_{N\to\infty} \frac{\bar{\sigma}_N^2}{N} = 0.$$

(b) Let $\text{E}[U_n] = \mu$ and $\text{Var}[U_n] = \sigma^2$ but instead of independence suppose that $\text{Cov}[U_n, U_m] = 0$ for all $n \neq m$.

(c) Let $\text{E}[U_n] = \mu$ and $\text{Var}[U_n] = \sigma^2$ but instead of independence suppose that $\text{Cov}[U_n, U_m] = \sigma^2 \rho^{|n-m|}$ where $|\rho| < 1$.

13.6 (Convergence of Moments) Let $Z_N \xrightarrow{d} Z$. Construct an example to show that the limit of $\text{E}[Z_N]$ may not equal $\text{E}[Z]$. (HINT: Try constructing a distribution for Z_N from the mixture of two distributions with weights that depend on N.)

13.7 (Almost Sure Convergence) Consider the stochastic sequence $\{U_N\}$ where

$$\Pr\{U_N = U\} = \begin{cases} 1 - \frac{1}{N} & \text{if U = 0} \\ \frac{1}{N} & \text{if U = 1} \end{cases}$$

Show that $\{U_N\}$ converges *in probability* to zero but that $\{U_N\}$ does not converge *almost surely* to zero.

13.8 Let the conditions of Proposition 15 hold. Show that $\sqrt{N}(s^2 - \sigma_0^2) \xrightarrow{d} \mathfrak{N}(0, \mu_4 - \sigma_0^4)$, where $\mu_4 \equiv \text{E}[(y_n - \mathbf{x}_n'\boldsymbol{\beta}_0)^4]$, using the following steps.

(a) Show that

$$\sqrt{N}\left(s^2 - \sigma_0^2\right) = \sigma_0^2 \frac{K}{N-K} + \frac{N}{N-K}\Big[\sqrt{N}\,\text{E}_N[(y_n - \mathbf{x}_n'\boldsymbol{\beta}_0)^2 - \sigma_0^2] - \sqrt{N}\left(\hat{\boldsymbol{\beta}} - \boldsymbol{\beta}_0\right)'\text{E}_N[\mathbf{x}_n\mathbf{x}_n']\left(\hat{\boldsymbol{\beta}} - \boldsymbol{\beta}_0\right)\Big]$$

(b) Show that

$$\sqrt{N}\left(s^2 - \sigma_0^2\right) - \sqrt{N}\,\text{E}_N[(y_n - \mathbf{x}_n'\boldsymbol{\beta}_0)^2 - \sigma_0^2] \xrightarrow{p} 0$$

(c) Show that

$$\sqrt{N}\frac{\text{E}_N[(y_n - \mathbf{x}_n'\boldsymbol{\beta}_0)^2 - \sigma_0^2]}{\sqrt{\mu_4 - \sigma_0^4}} \xrightarrow{d} \mathfrak{N}(0, 1)$$

(d) How could you estimate the variance of this asymptotic distribution?

13.9 Resolve the following paradox: the asymptotic approximation of the distribution of $\hat{\boldsymbol{\beta}}$ and s^2 implies that we treat s^2 as a constant when we draw inferences about $\boldsymbol{\beta}_0$ but we treat s^2 as a normally distributed random variable when we draw inferences about σ_0^2.

13.10 Consider the simple regression with a time trend:

$$\mathrm{E}[y_t] = \beta_1 + \beta_2 t, \qquad t = 1, \ldots, T$$

Show that the elements of $\hat{\boldsymbol{\beta}}_N$ are approximately normal, but that they converge at different rates as $T \to \infty$. (HINT: See Exercise 9.19.)

13.11 **(Consistency)** Using Definition 23 (Consistent Estimator, p. 257), explain why it is possible for a consistent estimator to be biased and for an unbiased estimator to be inconsistent.

If an estimator is *asymptotically unbiased*, then its expectation approaches the population parameter as the sample size approaches infinity. Can an asymptotically unbiased estimator be inconsistent?

13.12 **(Consistency)** Show that if $\sqrt{N}U_N \xrightarrow{d} \mathfrak{N}(0, \sigma_0^2)$ then $U_N \xrightarrow{p} 0$.

13.7.2 Extensions

***13.13** **(Skewness)** An alternative p.d.f. to the normal that exhibits skewness arises from the transformation from $\mathbb{R}$ to $\mathbb{R}$

$$\tau(y, \boldsymbol{\alpha}) = \frac{1}{2}\left((\alpha_1 + 1/\alpha_1)y + (\alpha_1 - 1/\alpha_1)\sqrt{y^2 + 4\alpha_2}\right)$$

for $\alpha_1, \alpha_2 > 0$.

(a) Confirm that the transformation is monotonically strictly increasing over $\mathbb{R}$ and find its inverse.
(b) Explain how the transformation induces skewness in the distribution of y given that $\tau(y, \boldsymbol{\alpha})$ is normally distributed.
(c) Derive the p.d.f. of $\tau(y, \alpha)$.
(d) Show that when $\alpha_1 = 1$, then α_2 may take any value without affecting the p.d.f. of y. What potential problem does this suggest?

***13.14** **(Skewness)** Azzalini (1985, 1986) suggests a skewed version of the normal p.d.f. induced by latent (unobserved) sample selection. Suppose that (y, z) are jointly distributed bivariate normal random variables,

$$\begin{bmatrix} y \\ z \end{bmatrix} \sim \mathfrak{N}\left(\begin{bmatrix} \mu_y \\ \mu_z \end{bmatrix}, \begin{bmatrix} \sigma_y^2 & \sigma_{yz} \\ \sigma_{yz} & \sigma_z^2 \end{bmatrix}\right)$$

Suppose that z is not observed. Moreover, y is not observed unless $z \geq 0$.

(a) Show that the p.d.f. of y is

$$\phi(y - \mu_y, \sigma_y^2)\frac{\Phi\left(\mu_z + \sigma_{yz}(y - \mu_y)/\sigma_y^2,\ \sigma_z^2 - \sigma_{yz}^2/\sigma_y^2\right)}{\Phi\left(\mu_z, \sigma_z^2\right)}$$

where

$$\Phi(\mu, \sigma^2) \equiv \int_0^\infty \phi(y - \mu, \sigma^2)\, dy$$

is one minus the c.d.f. of the $\mathfrak{N}(\mu, \sigma^2)$ distribution.

(b) Show that this p.d.f. is skewed.

13.15 **(Median)** Let $\{Y_n\}$ be i.i.d. draws from a distribution with p.d.f. f_Y. Using the following steps, show that the asymptotic approximation for the distribution of the sample median is normal with mean equal to the median of Y_n, β_0, and variance $4 f_Y(\beta_0)^2$.

(a) Denote standardized sample median $W_N = \sqrt{N}\left(V_{[(N+1)/2]} - \beta_0\right)$. Suppose that $f_Y(y)$ is continuous, admitting the first-order approximation

$$f_Y(y+\varepsilon) = f_Y(y) + o(\varepsilon)$$

Use (13.10) to argue that

$$f_{W_N}(w) = \frac{N!\left[f_Y(\beta_0) + o(N^{-\frac{1}{2}})\right]}{2^{N-1}\sqrt{N}\left\{\left[\frac{1}{2}(N-1)\right]!\right\}^2} \cdot \left[1 + \frac{2f_Y(\beta_0)w}{\sqrt{N}} + o(N^{-\frac{1}{2}})\right]^{\frac{1}{2}(N-1)} \cdot \left[1 - \frac{2f_Y(\beta_0)w}{\sqrt{N}} + o(N^{-\frac{1}{2}})\right]^{\frac{1}{2}(N-1)}$$

(b) Show that

$$\lim_{n\to\infty}\left[1 \pm \frac{2f_Y(\beta_0)w}{\sqrt{N}} + o(N^{-\frac{1}{2}})\right]^{\frac{1}{2}(N-1)} = \exp\left(-\frac{1}{4}\left[2f_Y(\beta_0)w\right]^2\right)$$

(c) Use Stirling's approximation (Lemma D.5, p. 899) to show that as $N \to \infty$

$$\frac{N!}{2^{N-1}\sqrt{N}\left[\left(\frac{1}{2}(N-1)\right)!\right]^2} \to \frac{2}{\sqrt{2\pi}}$$

(d) Combine these results to show that the normalized sample median is asymptotically normally distributed.

(e) Compare the asymptotic relative efficiency of the sample mean and the sample median for several distributions with the same mean and variance: normal, double exponential, and logistic.

13.16 (Order Statistics) Let

$$Z_N = \sqrt{N}\left(Y_{(r)} - \mu_p\right)$$

where $r = Np$, $0 < p < 1$, for some fixed p, and

$$\mu_p \equiv F_Y^{-1}(p)$$

Show that Z_N is asymptotically normally distributed with mean zero and variance

$$\frac{p(1-p)}{f_Y(\mu_p)^2}$$

using the method described in Exercise 13.15.

13.17 (Extreme Values) Let $Y_1, \ldots, Y_N$ be i.i.d. draws from a continuous distribution with p.d.f. $f(y)$ and c.d.f. $F(y)$. The *order statistics* are these same values ranked in increasing order, denoted $Y_{(1)} \leq Y_{(2)} \leq \cdots \leq Y_{(N)}$.

(a) Consider the maximum value $Y_{(N)}$ of an i.i.d. sample of N observations. Suppose that the support of Y has no upper bound, that $1 - F(y)$ tends to zero exponentially fast as $y \to \infty$ and that

$$\frac{d}{dy}\left[\frac{1-F(y)}{f(y)}\right] \to 0$$

Show that when

$$Z_N = \frac{Y_{(N)} - a_N}{b_N}$$

then

$$\Pr\{Z_N < z\} = \left(1 - \exp\{\log[1 - F(a_N + b_N z)]\}\right)^N$$

(HINT: See Exercise 13.16.)

(b) Consider large values of $Y_{(N)}$ in the neighborhood of

$$a_N = F^{-1}(1 - N^{-1})$$

Use a Taylor series expansion to show that

$$\Pr\{Z_N < z\} - \left\{1 - N^{-1}\exp[-b_N\, z\, f(a_N)]\right\}^N \to 0$$

(c) Now set

$$b_N = \frac{1}{N\, f(a_N)}$$

to show that

$$\Pr\{Z_N < z\} - \exp\left(-e^{-z}\right) \to 0$$

This limiting distribution is called the *extreme value* or *Weibull* distribution.

CHAPTER 14

Maximum Likelihood Estimation

14.1 INTRODUCTION

Once we depart from the normality assumption, our interest in nonlinear estimators such as the LAD regression estimator grows. In this chapter, we describe a general procedure for developing such estimators based on alternative specifications of the conditional distribution of $\mathbf{y}$ given $\mathbf{X}$. This procedure is called *maximum likelihood estimation.*

Although the *maximum likelihood estimator* (MLE) is generally a nonlinear function of $\mathbf{y}$, often defined only implicitly, researchers have constructed a distribution theory for the MLE using asymptotic approximation methods similar to those introduced in Chapter 13. According to the asymptotic approximations permitted under the assumptions of this chapter, MLEs are linear transformations of normally distributed random variables *in the limit* as the sample size approaches infinity. This result expands into a distribution theory that resembles the distribution theory for OLS estimators of Part II in many ways. We will use this resemblance to organize our presentation of the MLE.

In likelihood theory, inference about unknown parameters begins with the specification of the *probability function* (p.f.), either *probability mass function* (p.m.f.) or *probability density function* (p.d.f.), of the observations in a sample of random variables. This function fully characterizes the behavior of any potential data that one will use to learn about the parameters of the data-generating process. Given a sample of observations from a distribution with the specified p.f., the MLE is the value of the parameters that maximizes this probability, or *likelihood*, function. This approach has intuitive appeal, in that one is choosing parameter values that make what one has actually observed more likely to occur than any other parameter values do. In this sense, the MLE is more consistent with the facts than any other explanation (that is, any other parameter values).

This chapter introduces the basic concepts and relationships that motivate the MLE. Chapter 15 combines these elements with asymptotic approximations to investigate the distribution of the MLE and to apply that distribution to statistical inference. In both chapters, three items are central:

1. the logarithm of the likelihood function (or p.f.),
2. its gradient or vector of first partial derivatives, and
3. its Hessian or matrix of second partial derivatives.

We will show that the centrality of these particular things reflects the essentially quadratic character of maximum likelihood theory and its resemblance to ordinary least squares with normally distributed data.

After presenting the basic probability model in the next section, we introduce the *log-likelihood function* and a fundamental property of this function, the *expected log-likelihood inequality*. This inequality states that the expected value of the log-likelihood function is maximized at the population parameter values. The MLE is the sample counterpart: it is the value of the parameters that maximizes the empirical expectation of the log-likelihood function. Because maximization characterizes the estimator, the gradient of the log-likelihood function, called the *score function*, plays a key role in the theory. Although the sampling distribution of the MLE is generally intractable, we can study the sampling behavior of the score function evaluated at the population parameter values: its expectation is zero and its variance matrix, called the *information matrix*, can be derived. This information matrix is actually proportional to the expectation of the Hessian of the log-likelihood function. As a result, the inverse of the information matrix also provides a lower bound on the variance matrix of all unbiased estimators, as described in the *Cramér–Rao inequality*. In some special cases, we find that the MLE is efficient relative to all unbiased estimators.

14.2 PROBABILITY MODEL SPECIFICATION

We began our study of OLS with a convenient, understandable way to fit a line to data. In the first two parts of this book, we developed a probabilistic model for the data that culminated in the specification of a normal p.d.f. for $\mathbf{y}$ conditional on $\mathbf{X}$. In contrast, formal likelihood theory begins with the specification of the p.f. of the data given several unknown parameters. The following assumption effectively subsumes Assumptions 6.1, 7.1, and 10.1.

> **Assumption 14.1 (Distribution)** *The pair (U, V) is a random variable and the N variables $\{(U_1, V_1)\dots, (U_N, V_N)\}$ are an i.i.d. random sample of (U, V). But for $\boldsymbol{\theta}_0$, the conditional distribution of U given V is known. That is, the functional form of $F_{U|V}(u \mid v; \boldsymbol{\theta}_0)$ is completely known but the value of the real-valued parameter vector $\boldsymbol{\theta}_0$ is unknown. The parameter vector $\boldsymbol{\theta}_0$ is finite dimensional: $\boldsymbol{\theta}_0$ has K elements so that $\boldsymbol{\theta}_0 \in \mathbb{R}^K$.*

We will treat the case in which the joint distribution of (U, V) is known as the special case in which V is a constant. All of the results that we present apply to this case as well. Because empirical economic research usually studies the behavior of one or more variables conditional on several explanatory variables, the conditional specification is more common in econometrics. For this reason, we take such specifications as our starting point. Hence, for notational simplicity, we will drop the subscript of c.d.f.s and simply denote $F_{U|V}$ by F. In addition, when V is a constant the c.d.f. of U will simply be $F(u; \boldsymbol{\theta}_0)$. We will refer to this as the *unconditional* case and $F(u \mid v; \boldsymbol{\theta}_0)$ as the *conditional* case.

We will denote the support of F by $\mathbb{S}(\boldsymbol{\theta}_0)$ so that[1]

$$\int_{\mathbb{S}(\boldsymbol{\theta}_0)} dF(u \mid v; \boldsymbol{\theta}_0) = 1$$

We will denote the p.f. (p.m.f. or p.d.f.) corresponding to F by f. Thus,

$$\int_{\mathbb{S}(\boldsymbol{\theta}_0)} dF(u \mid v; \boldsymbol{\theta}_0) = \begin{cases} \sum_{u \in \mathbb{S}(\boldsymbol{\theta}_0)} f(u \mid v; \boldsymbol{\theta}_0) & \text{if } U \text{ is discrete} \\ \int_{\mathbb{S}(\boldsymbol{\theta}_0)} f(u \mid v; \boldsymbol{\theta}_0)\, du & \text{if } U \text{ is continuous} \end{cases}$$

Assumption 14.1 implies that the conditional p.f. for $\{U_1, \ldots, U_N\}$ given $\{V_1, \ldots, V_N\}$ is

$$\prod_{n=1}^{N} f(u_n \mid v_n; \boldsymbol{\theta}_0) \tag{14.1}$$

EXAMPLE 14.1 (Normal Location Scale)[2]

A popular specification for i.i.d. data is the normal p.d.f.

$$\begin{aligned} f(u; \boldsymbol{\theta}_0) &= \frac{1}{\sqrt{2\pi\sigma_0^2}} \exp\left[-\frac{(u - \beta_0)^2}{2\sigma_0^2}\right] \\ &\equiv \phi(u - \beta_0,\ \sigma_0^2) \end{aligned}$$

The support of this distribution is $\mathbb{S}(\boldsymbol{\theta}_0) = \mathbb{R}$, the entire real line. The parameter vector is $\boldsymbol{\theta}_0 = (\beta_0, \sigma_0^2)$. Because observations are independently distributed, the p.d.f. of the sample is the product

$$\prod_{n=1}^{N} f(u_n; \boldsymbol{\theta}_0) = \left(2\pi\sigma_0^2\right)^{-N/2} \exp\left[-\frac{1}{2\sigma_0^2} \sum_{n=1}^{N} (u_n - \beta_0)^2\right]$$

Usually we will specify a *conditional* distribution.

EXAMPLE 14.2 (Normal Linear Regression)

We described $(y_n, \mathbf{x}_n)$ as a jointly distributed random variable in Chapter 13.[3] In the fashion of that chapter, we can specify $U = y_n$, $V = \mathbf{x}_n$, and the conditional p.d.f.

[1] This is the Stieltjes form of the probability integral. See Definition D.13 (Stieltjes Integral, p. 875).

[2] A *location model* for y_n parameterizes the (conditional) expectation of y_n. A *location-scale model* also parameterizes its (conditional) standard deviation. The normal distribution is completely determined by its location and scale parameters, μ and σ, respectively. One can generate various alternative conditional regression models by the location-scale transformation

$$y = \mu + \sigma\varepsilon$$

where ε has a distribution other than the normal.

[3] In particular, see Assumption 13.1 (I.I.D., p. 256).

$$f(u_n \mid v_n; \boldsymbol{\theta}_0) = \frac{1}{\sqrt{2\pi\sigma_0^2}} \exp\left[-\frac{(y_n - \mathbf{x}_n'\boldsymbol{\beta}_0)^2}{2\sigma_0^2}\right]$$
$$\equiv \phi(y_n - \mathbf{x}_n'\boldsymbol{\beta}_0, \ \sigma_0^2)$$

without specifying the marginal distribution of $\mathbf{x}_n$. The support of this distribution is the real line, the parameter vector is $\boldsymbol{\theta}_0 = [\boldsymbol{\beta}_0', \sigma_0^2]'$. Because observations are independently distributed, the conditional p.d.f. of the sample is the product

$$\prod_{n=1}^{N} f(u_n \mid v_n; \boldsymbol{\theta}_0) = \left[2\pi\sigma_0^2\right]^{-N/2} \exp\left[-\frac{(\mathbf{y} - \mathbf{X}\boldsymbol{\beta}_0)'(\mathbf{y} - \mathbf{X}\boldsymbol{\beta}_0)}{2\sigma_0^2}\right]$$
$$\equiv \phi(\mathbf{y} - \mathbf{X}\boldsymbol{\beta}_0, \ \sigma_0^2 \cdot \mathbf{I}_N)$$

In Chapter 13, we left the marginal distribution of $\mathbf{x}_n$ largely unspecified, except for restrictions on certain moments. Here, we will also assume that the marginal distribution of $\mathbf{x}_n$ does not depend on $\boldsymbol{\theta}_0$.

Comparing Examples 14.1 and 14.2 indicates that a conditional p.f. can encompass an unconditional p.f. as a special case. If $\mathbf{x}_n = 1$ $(n = 1, \ldots, N)$, then these examples coincide.

EXAMPLE 14.3 (Student *t* Linear Regression)

In Chapter 13, we also discussed the t distribution as an alternative to the normal with p.d.f.s that exhibit fatter tails. If we assume that the random variable $(y_n - \mathbf{x}_n'\boldsymbol{\beta}_0)/\sigma_0$ has a t_{ν_0} distribution conditional on $\mathbf{x}_n$ then the conditional p.d.f. of $U = y_n$ given $V = \mathbf{x}_n$ is

$$f(u_n \mid v_n; \boldsymbol{\theta}_0) = \frac{\Gamma[(\nu_0 + 1)/2]}{\Gamma(\nu_0/2)} \frac{1}{\sqrt{\pi\nu_0\sigma_0^2}} \left[1 + \frac{(y_n - \mathbf{x}_n'\boldsymbol{\beta}_0)^2}{\nu_0\sigma_0^2}\right]^{-(\nu_0+1)/2}$$

The support of this distribution is also $\mathbb{S}(\boldsymbol{\theta}_0) = \mathbb{R}$ and the parameter vector is $\boldsymbol{\theta}_0 = [\boldsymbol{\beta}_0', \sigma_0^2, \nu_0]'$. Because this distribution approaches the normal as the degrees of freedom parameter approaches infinity, ν_0 might be estimated, along with $\boldsymbol{\beta}_0$ and σ_0^2, to allow the data to choose the degree that the distribution is fatter than normal. Again, we leave the marginal distribution of $\mathbf{x}_n$ unspecified, except that it does not depend on $\boldsymbol{\theta}_0$.

EXAMPLE 14.4 (Laplace Linear Regression)

The Laplace distribution with mean $\mathbf{x}_n'\boldsymbol{\beta}_0$ and variance σ_0^2 leads to the conditional p.d.f.

$$f(u_n \mid v_n; \boldsymbol{\theta}_0) = \frac{1}{\sqrt{2\sigma_0^2}} e^{-\sqrt{2}\frac{|y_n - \mathbf{x}_n'\boldsymbol{\beta}_0|}{\sigma_0}}$$

for $U = y_n$ and $V = \mathbf{x}_n$, with support $\mathbb{S}(\boldsymbol{\theta}_0) = \mathbb{R}$. The parameter vector is $\boldsymbol{\theta}_0 = [\boldsymbol{\beta}_0', \sigma_0^2]$.

Specifying the distribution of the observable data as a function of the unknown parameter vector $\boldsymbol{\theta}_0$ implicitly specifies the expected value (as a function of $\boldsymbol{\theta}_0$) of any transformation of these random variables. That is, given a function $g(\cdot)$, one can always obtain the expected value *function*

$$h(\boldsymbol{\theta}_0) \equiv \mathrm{E}[g(U)] = \int g(u)\, dF(u; \boldsymbol{\theta}_0)$$

for an unconditional specification, or

$$h(v; \boldsymbol{\theta}_0) \equiv \mathrm{E}[g(U, V) \mid V = v] = \int g(u, v)\, dF(u \mid v; \boldsymbol{\theta}_0)$$

for a conditional specification (provided that the expected value exists). This will be a key property of the statistical theory built on Assumption 14.1 (Distribution). Note that because $\boldsymbol{\theta}_0$ is unknown, it is the function $h(\cdot)$ that follows from the assumption. As a concrete example, note that the specification of the conditional normal distribution in Example 14.2 implies that

$$\mathrm{E}[e^{ty_n} \mid \mathbf{x}_n] = \exp\left(\mathbf{x}_n' \boldsymbol{\beta}_0\, t + \frac{\sigma_0^2}{2} t^2\right)$$

giving the moment-generating function for the distribution of y_n with arguments t and $\boldsymbol{\theta}_0 = [\boldsymbol{\beta}_0', \sigma_0^2]'$.[4] A more fundamental application of this principle appears in the next section.

14.3 THE LIKELIHOOD FUNCTION

For the unconditional specification, the p.f. $f(u; \boldsymbol{\theta}_0)$ describes the likely values of every random variable U_n $(n = 1, \ldots, N)$ for a specific value of the parameter vector $\boldsymbol{\theta}_0$. In practice, we observe a realization of the random sample $\{U_1, \ldots, U_N\}$ but we do not know $\boldsymbol{\theta}_0$. The sample *likelihood function* describes this situation by treating the u argument of f as given and treating the $\boldsymbol{\theta}_0$ argument as variable. In this reversal of roles, the p.f. becomes the likelihood function, which describes the likely values of the unknown parameter vector $\boldsymbol{\theta}_0$ given realizations of the random variable U.

DEFINITION 27 (LIKELIHOOD FUNCTION) *The* likelihood function *of $\boldsymbol{\theta}$ for a random variable U with p.f. $f(u; \boldsymbol{\theta}_0)$ is defined to be*

$$\ell(\boldsymbol{\theta}; U) \equiv f(U; \boldsymbol{\theta})$$

We will denote the logarithm of the likelihood function, the log-likelihood function, *by*

$$L(\boldsymbol{\theta}; U) = \log\, \ell(\boldsymbol{\theta}; U)$$

The algebraic relationship in this definition is not merely a change in notation. The p.f. describes potential outcomes of a random variable U given V and a parameter vector fixed at $\boldsymbol{\theta}_0$. For the likelihood function, we evaluate the p.f. at a random variable and consider the result as a function of the variable parameter $\boldsymbol{\theta}$. Shortly, we will explain how the likelihood, or log-likelihood, function of $\boldsymbol{\theta}$ is informative about $\boldsymbol{\theta}_0$ based on a random sample $\{U_1, \ldots, U_N\}$. For

[4] See Definition D.10 (Moment-Generating Function, p. 872).

the moment, note that we may treat the entire random sample as a single multivariate random variable and apply Definition 27 to derive the *sample* log-likelihood function under Assumption 14.1 (Distribution). Using (14.1), the sample log-likelihood function is

$$L(\boldsymbol{\theta}; U_1, \ldots, U_N) = \log \prod_{n=1}^{N} f(U_n; \boldsymbol{\theta}) \tag{14.2}$$

$$= \sum_{n=1}^{N} L(\boldsymbol{\theta}; U_n)$$

These ideas extend to conditional specifications as well.

DEFINITION 28 (CONDITIONAL LIKELIHOOD FUNCTION) *The* conditional likelihood function *of* $\boldsymbol{\theta}$ *for a random variable* U *with conditional p.f.* $f(u \mid v; \boldsymbol{\theta}_0)$ *given the random variable* V *is*

$$\ell(\boldsymbol{\theta}; U \mid V) \equiv f(U \mid V; \boldsymbol{\theta})$$

We will denote the logarithm of the likelihood function, the conditional log-likelihood function, *by*

$$L(\boldsymbol{\theta}; U \mid V) = \log \ell(\boldsymbol{\theta}; U \mid V)$$

In general, the p.f., conditional or not, may not be defined over all possible values of the real parameter vector $\boldsymbol{\theta}$. For example, the variance parameter of a normal distribution must be positive. In any use of the log-likelihood function, we must respect such restrictions. We will denote by $\boldsymbol{\Theta}$ the set of parameter values of $\boldsymbol{\theta}$ permitted by the probability model. This set is called the *parameter space*. From this point on, $\boldsymbol{\theta}$ will always be a member of $\boldsymbol{\Theta}$. Obviously, $\boldsymbol{\theta}_0 \in \boldsymbol{\Theta}$.

EXAMPLE 14.5 (Normal Linear Regression)

Continuing Example 14.2, the sample conditional log-likelihood function of the normal linear regression model with N observations is

$$\sum_{n=1}^{N} L(\boldsymbol{\theta}; y_n \mid \mathbf{x}_n) = \sum_{n=1}^{N} \left[-\frac{1}{2} \log(2\pi\sigma^2) - \frac{(y_n - \mathbf{x}_n'\boldsymbol{\beta})^2}{2\sigma^2} \right] \tag{14.3}$$

$$= -\frac{N}{2} \log(2\pi\sigma^2) - \frac{(\mathbf{y} - \mathbf{X}\boldsymbol{\beta})'(\mathbf{y} - \mathbf{X}\boldsymbol{\beta})}{2\sigma^2}$$

The parameter space is $\boldsymbol{\Theta} = \mathbb{R}^K \times \mathbb{R}_+$, which excludes negative variances.

In the special i.i.d. case where $\mathbf{x}_n = 1$,

$$\sum_{n=1}^{N} L(\boldsymbol{\theta}; y_n) = -\frac{N}{2} \log(2\pi\sigma^2) - \frac{1}{2\sigma^2} \sum_{n=1}^{N} (y_n - \beta)^2$$

EXAMPLE 14.6 (Student t Linear Regression)

The corresponding sample conditional log-likelihood function for the Student t linear regression model in Example 14.3 is

$$\sum_{n=1}^{N} L(\boldsymbol{\theta}; y_n \mid \mathbf{x}_n) = -\frac{N}{2}\log(\pi\nu\sigma^2) + N\log\Gamma\left(\frac{\nu+1}{2}\right) - N\log\Gamma\left(\frac{\nu}{2}\right) - \frac{\nu+1}{2}\sum_{n=1}^{N}\log\left[1+\frac{(y_n-\mathbf{x}_n'\boldsymbol{\beta})^2}{\nu\sigma^2}\right] \tag{14.4}$$

This log-likelihood function shares some of the features of the normal one, but the sum of the logarithms is a significant analytical complication. The parameter space for $\boldsymbol{\theta} = [\boldsymbol{\beta}', \sigma^2, \nu]'$ is $\boldsymbol{\Theta} = \mathbb{R}^K \times \mathbb{R}_+ \times \mathbb{R}_+$, because both the variance and the degrees of freedom parameters must be positive.

EXAMPLE 14.7 (Laplace Linear Regression)

The sample log-likelihood function of a conditional Laplace distribution is

$$\sum_{n=1}^{N} L(\boldsymbol{\theta}; y_n \mid \mathbf{x}_n) = -\frac{N}{2}\log(2\sigma^2) - \frac{\sqrt{2}}{\sigma}\sum_{n=1}^{N}\left|y_n - \mathbf{x}_n'\boldsymbol{\beta}\right|$$

Our interest in the log-likelihood function derives from its relationship to the unknown $\boldsymbol{\theta}_0$. A special feature of the log-likelihood function is that its *expectation* is maximized at the parameter value $\boldsymbol{\theta}_0$, when the expectation exists.[5] We will assume something stronger, in anticipation of later requirements.

ASSUMPTION 14.2 (DOMINANCE I) $\mathrm{E}[\sup_{\boldsymbol{\theta}\in\boldsymbol{\Theta}} |L(\boldsymbol{\theta}; U \mid V)|]$ *exists.*[6]

LEMMA 14.1 (EXPECTED LOG-LIKELIHOOD INEQUALITY) *If $L(\boldsymbol{\theta}; U \mid V)$ is the conditional log-likelihood function for $\boldsymbol{\theta}$ and Assumption 14.2 holds, then*

$$\mathrm{E}[L(\boldsymbol{\theta}; U \mid V) \mid V] \le \mathrm{E}[L(\boldsymbol{\theta}_0; U \mid V) \mid V] \tag{14.5}$$

[5] Some authors call this inequality the "information inequality." We do not use this term for several reasons. First, many (other) authors call Theorem 10 (Cramér–Rao Inequality, p. 306) the information inequality. Second, the expected log-likelihood inequality is really a special case of an inequality from information theory. We refer to that inequality as the information *theory* inequality (Lemma D.2, p. 875). Third, we think the term "expected log-likelihood inequality" is more apt for our discussion.

[6] Such assumptions are called *dominance conditions* because this assumption effectively asserts that $|L(\boldsymbol{\theta}; U \mid V)|$ is "dominated" by a function of (U, V) alone. In particular, the function $h(U, V) \equiv \sup_{\boldsymbol{\theta}\in\boldsymbol{\Theta}} |L(\boldsymbol{\theta}; U \mid V)|$ does not depend on $\boldsymbol{\theta}$ and it is always bigger than (dominates) $|L(\boldsymbol{\theta}; U \mid V)|$. The existence of $\mathrm{E}[h(U)]$ implies the existence of $\mathrm{E}[L(\boldsymbol{\theta}; U \mid V)]$ for all $\boldsymbol{\theta} \in \boldsymbol{\Theta}$.

We prove this lemma in Section 14.9.

It may be helpful to discuss this lemma first for the unconditional case in which

$$\mathrm{E}[L(\boldsymbol{\theta}; U)] \leq \mathrm{E}[L(\boldsymbol{\theta}_0; U)]$$

Note that this inequality depends on the principle that we emphasized at the end of the previous section: the specification of the p.f. of U determines expected values of functions of U. Therefore Assumption 14.1 (Distribution) implicitly determines the function

$$Q(\boldsymbol{\theta}, \boldsymbol{\theta}_0) \equiv \mathrm{E}[L(\boldsymbol{\theta}; U)]$$

which depends on $\boldsymbol{\theta}$ because the log-likelihood function L does and depends on $\boldsymbol{\theta}_0$ because Q is the expected value of a function of U. The expected log-likelihood inequality states that

$$Q(\boldsymbol{\theta}_0, \boldsymbol{\theta}_0) = \max_{\boldsymbol{\theta} \in \boldsymbol{\Theta}} Q(\boldsymbol{\theta}, \boldsymbol{\theta}_0)$$

This property of the expected log-likelihood function is the cornerstone of the maximum likelihood method of estimation. We introduce that method in the next section. Now we give several examples of the conditional case.

EXAMPLE 14.8 (Normal Linear Regression)

The conditional expectation of the conditional log-likelihood function of $y_n \mid \mathbf{x}_n \sim \mathfrak{N}(\mathbf{x}_n'\boldsymbol{\beta}_0, \sigma_0^2)$ is

$$\begin{aligned}\mathrm{E}[L(\boldsymbol{\theta}; y_n \mid \mathbf{x}_n) \mid \mathbf{x}_n] &= -\frac{1}{2}\log(2\pi\sigma^2) - \frac{\mathrm{E}[(y_n - \mathbf{x}_n'\boldsymbol{\beta})^2]}{2\sigma^2} \\ &= -\frac{1}{2}\left[\log(2\pi\sigma^2) + \frac{\sigma_0^2 + (\mathbf{x}_n'\boldsymbol{\beta} - \mathbf{x}_n'\boldsymbol{\beta}_0)^2}{\sigma^2}\right]\end{aligned} \tag{14.6}$$

which is uniquely maximized at $\mathbf{x}_n'\boldsymbol{\beta} = \mathbf{x}_n'\boldsymbol{\beta}_0$ and $\sigma^2 = \sigma_0^2$.[7] The conditional expectation of the conditional log-likelihood of the entire sample is the sum of such terms

$$\mathrm{E}[L(\boldsymbol{\theta}; \mathbf{y} \mid \mathbf{X}) \mid \mathbf{X}] = -\frac{N}{2}\log(2\pi\sigma^2) - \frac{N\sigma_0^2 + (\boldsymbol{\beta} - \boldsymbol{\beta}_0)'\mathbf{X}'\mathbf{X}(\boldsymbol{\beta} - \boldsymbol{\beta}_0)}{2\sigma^2} \tag{14.7}$$

which is uniquely maximized at $\boldsymbol{\beta} = \boldsymbol{\beta}_0$ ($\mathbf{X}\boldsymbol{\beta} = \mathbf{X}\boldsymbol{\beta}_0$) and $\sigma^2 = \sigma_0^2$ if $\mathbf{X}$ is full-column rank.

EXAMPLE 14.9 (Student *t* Linear Regression)

In the case of Student t linear regression, the expected log-likelihood function is analytically intractable. This illustrates the analytical power of the expected log-likelihood inequality. But we must confirm that $\mathrm{E}[L(\boldsymbol{\theta}; U \mid V)]$ exists. This is easy to show for $\nu_0 > 2$, because the concavity of the logarithmic function implies that

[7] Recall that

$$\begin{aligned}\mathrm{E}[(U-\mu)^2] &= \mathrm{E}[(U - \mathrm{E}[U] + \mathrm{E}[U] - \mu)^2] \\ &= \mathrm{Var}[U] + (\mathrm{E}[U] - \mu)^2\end{aligned}$$

See, for example, the proof of Lemma 6.2 (Minimum MSE Predictor, p. 113).

$$\log(1+z^2) \le z^2$$

and the second conditional moment of y_n exists (Theorem D.12, p. 889), and then

$$\mathrm{E}\left[\log\left[1+\frac{(y_n-\mathbf{x}_n'\boldsymbol{\beta})^2}{\nu\sigma^2}\right]\middle|\,\mathbf{x}_n\right] \le \mathrm{E}\left[\frac{(y_n-\mathbf{x}_n'\boldsymbol{\beta})^2}{\nu\sigma^2}\middle|\,\mathbf{x}_n\right]$$

$$= \frac{\nu_0\sigma_0^2+\left(\mathbf{x}_n'\boldsymbol{\beta}_0-\mathbf{x}_n'\boldsymbol{\beta}\right)^2}{\nu\sigma^2\,(\nu_0-2)}$$

Provided therefore that $\mathbf{x}_n$ has finite second moments, the expected log-likelihood exists.

EXAMPLE 14.10 (LAD Linear Regression)

The conditional expectation of the conditional log-likelihood function for the Laplace specification is

$$\begin{aligned}\mathrm{E}[L(\boldsymbol{\theta};\,y_n\,|\,\mathbf{x}_n)\,|\,\mathbf{x}_n] &= -\frac{1}{2}\log(2\sigma^2) - \frac{\sqrt{2}}{\sigma}\mathrm{E}[|y_n-\mathbf{x}_n'\boldsymbol{\beta}|\,|\,\mathbf{x}_n]\\ &= -\frac{1}{2}\log(2\sigma^2)\\ &\quad -\sqrt{2}\frac{\sigma_0}{\sigma}\left(\frac{|\mathbf{x}_n'\boldsymbol{\beta}_0-\mathbf{x}_n'\boldsymbol{\beta}|}{\sigma_0}+\frac{1}{\sqrt{2}}e^{-\sqrt{2}\frac{|\mathbf{x}_n'\boldsymbol{\beta}_0-\mathbf{x}_n'\boldsymbol{\beta}|}{\sigma_0}}\right)\end{aligned}$$

Therefore, Assumption 14.2 is satisfied when the first moment of $\mathbf{x}_n$ exists. Despite the individual absolute value terms, the sum

$$g(z) = \frac{|z|}{\sigma_0}+\frac{1}{\sqrt{2}}e^{-\sqrt{2}\frac{|z|}{\sigma_0}}$$

is a continuously differentiable function and

$$\frac{dg(z)}{dx} = \frac{\mathrm{sgn}(z)}{\sigma_0}\left(1-e^{-\sqrt{2}\frac{|z|}{\sigma_0}}\right)$$

Because the sign of this derivative equals the sign of its argument, g is minimized at the origin and[8]

$$\mathrm{E}[L(\boldsymbol{\theta};\,y_n\,|\,\mathbf{x}_n)\,|\,\mathbf{x}_n] \le -\frac{1}{2}\log 2\sigma^2 - \frac{\sigma_0}{\sigma} \le \mathrm{E}[L(\boldsymbol{\theta}_0;\,y_n\,|\,\mathbf{x}_n)\,|\,\mathbf{x}_n]$$

Note that the expected log-likelihood inequality implies the *unconditional* inequality

[8] To obtain the second inequality, note that

$$\begin{aligned}&\log\frac{\sigma_0}{\sigma} \le \frac{\sigma_0}{\sigma}-1 \quad\Leftrightarrow\\ &\frac{1}{2}\log\frac{2\sigma_0^2}{2\sigma^2}-\frac{\sigma_0}{\sigma} \le -1 \quad\Leftrightarrow\\ &-\frac{1}{2}\log 2\sigma^2-\frac{\sigma_0}{\sigma} \le -\frac{1}{2}\log 2\sigma_0^2-1.\end{aligned}$$

$$\mathrm{E}[L(\boldsymbol{\theta}; U \mid V)] \le \mathrm{E}[L(\boldsymbol{\theta}_0; U \mid V)]$$

The law of iterated expectations establishes this inequality as a general principle: we can take expectations over V on both sides of (14.5) so that

$$\begin{aligned}\mathrm{E}[L(\boldsymbol{\theta}; U \mid V)] &= \mathrm{E}\big[\mathrm{E}[L(\boldsymbol{\theta}; U \mid V) \mid V]\big] \\ &\le \mathrm{E}[L(\boldsymbol{\theta}_0; U \mid V) \mid V] \\ &= \mathrm{E}[L(\boldsymbol{\theta}_0; U \mid V)]\end{aligned}$$

Therefore, we will eventually rely on the inequality in this form because our *sampling* is not conditional on V although our specification is *conditional*.

14.4 THE MAXIMUM LIKELIHOOD ESTIMATOR

Because the true parameter value $\boldsymbol{\theta}_0$ maximizes the expectation of the log-likelihood function, it is natural to construct an estimator of $\boldsymbol{\theta}_0$ from the value of $\boldsymbol{\theta}$ that maximizes the sample, or empirical, counterpart: the average log-likelihood functions of the N observations.[9] We will denote this function by

$$\mathrm{E}_N[L(\boldsymbol{\theta}; U \mid V)] \equiv \sum_{n=1}^{N} L(\boldsymbol{\theta}; U_n \mid V_n)\frac{1}{N}$$

where $\mathrm{E}_N[\cdot]$ refers to the empirical expectation (or sample average). This notation reinforces an analogy between the average log-likelihood function and the expectation of the log-likelihood function

$$\mathrm{E}[L(\boldsymbol{\theta}; U \mid V)] \equiv \int L(\boldsymbol{\theta}; u \mid v)\, dF(u \mid v; \boldsymbol{\theta}_0)$$

where $F(u \mid v; \boldsymbol{\theta}_0)$ is the joint c.d.f. of (U, V). From this point on, we will often abbreviate $\mathrm{E}_N[L(\boldsymbol{\theta}; U \mid V)] = \mathrm{E}_N[L(\boldsymbol{\theta})]$ and $\mathrm{E}[L(\boldsymbol{\theta}; U \mid V)] = \mathrm{E}[L(\boldsymbol{\theta})]$. Implicitly, the latter function also depends on $\boldsymbol{\theta}_0$ of course.

DEFINITION 29 (MAXIMUM LIKELIHOOD ESTIMATOR) *The MLE is a value of the parameter vector that maximizes the sample average log-likelihood function. We will denote this estimator by* $\hat{\boldsymbol{\theta}}_N$:

$$\hat{\boldsymbol{\theta}}_N \equiv \operatorname*{argmax}_{\boldsymbol{\theta} \in \Theta} \mathrm{E}_N[L(\boldsymbol{\theta})]$$

In the unconditional case, one may think intuitively of this method as finding a value for $\boldsymbol{\theta}$ that is "most likely" to yield the random sample $(U_1, \ldots U_N)$. In other words, the MLE is the best "rationalization" of what is observed. One may think of the sample log-likelihood function as a

[9] Fisher (1922, 1925) proposed the method of maximum likelihood.

measure of fit, with the best fit possessing the largest log-likelihood value. Compared to OLS, the log-likelihood function serves the same role as the negative of the sum of squared residuals (SSR).

EXAMPLE 14.11 (Normal Linear Regression)

The empirical expectation of the conditional log-likelihood function is analogous to (14.6):

$$\begin{aligned} \mathrm{E}_N[L(\boldsymbol{\theta})] &= -\frac{1}{2}\log(2\pi\sigma^2) - \frac{\mathrm{E}_N[(y_n - \mathbf{x}_n'\boldsymbol{\beta})^2]}{2\sigma^2} \\ &= -\frac{1}{2}\log(2\pi\sigma^2) - \frac{(\mathbf{y}-\mathbf{X}\boldsymbol{\beta})'(\mathbf{y}-\mathbf{X}\boldsymbol{\beta})/N}{2\sigma^2} \end{aligned}$$

The log-likelihood function of a normally distributed sample is differentiable. In fact, the only term involving $\boldsymbol{\beta}$ is proportional to the SSR. As a result, the OLS fitted coefficients and the MLE are identical. But not all log-likelihood functions have such a simple structure. In this example, we follow a more generic approach.

Applying the calculus,[10] we obtain the partial derivatives

$$\begin{aligned} \mathrm{E}_N[L_{\boldsymbol{\beta}}(\boldsymbol{\theta})] &= \frac{1}{\sigma^2}\cdot \mathrm{E}_N[\mathbf{x}_n(y_n - \mathbf{x}_n'\boldsymbol{\beta})] \\ &= \frac{1}{\sigma^2 N}\cdot \mathbf{X}'(\mathbf{y}-\mathbf{X}\boldsymbol{\beta}) \end{aligned} \tag{14.8}$$

$$\begin{aligned} \mathrm{E}_N[L_{\sigma^2}(\boldsymbol{\theta})] &= -\frac{1}{2\sigma^4}\left\{\sigma^2 - \mathrm{E}_N[(y_n - \mathbf{x}_n'\boldsymbol{\beta})^2]\right\} \\ &= -\frac{1}{2\sigma^4}\left[\sigma^2 - \frac{1}{N}(\mathbf{y}-\mathbf{X}\boldsymbol{\beta})'(\mathbf{y}-\mathbf{X}\boldsymbol{\beta})\right] \end{aligned} \tag{14.9}$$

where $L_{\boldsymbol{\theta}} \equiv \partial L(\boldsymbol{\theta})/\partial\boldsymbol{\theta}$. Setting these vector derivatives to zero and solving, we obtain the unique solution

$$\begin{aligned} \hat{\boldsymbol{\beta}}_N &= \left(\mathrm{E}_N[\mathbf{x}_n\mathbf{x}_n']\right)^{-1}\mathrm{E}_N[\mathbf{x}_n\mathbf{y}_n] \\ &= \left(\mathbf{X}'\mathbf{X}\right)^{-1}\mathbf{X}'\mathbf{y} \end{aligned} \tag{14.10}$$

$$\begin{aligned} \hat{\sigma}_N^2 &= \mathrm{E}_N[(y_n - \mathbf{x}_n'\hat{\boldsymbol{\beta}}_N)]^2 \\ &= \frac{(\mathbf{y}-\mathbf{X}\hat{\boldsymbol{\beta}}_N)'(\mathbf{y}-\mathbf{X}\hat{\boldsymbol{\beta}}_N)}{N} \end{aligned} \tag{14.11}$$

The Hessian matrix confirms that this point is a local maximum of $L(\boldsymbol{\theta};\, y\,|\,\mathbf{X})$.[11] By further differentiation, we have

$$\begin{aligned} \mathrm{E}_N[L_{\boldsymbol{\theta}\boldsymbol{\theta}}(\boldsymbol{\theta})] &= \begin{bmatrix} -\frac{1}{\sigma^2}\cdot \mathrm{E}_N[\mathbf{x}_n\mathbf{x}_n'] & -\frac{1}{\sigma^4}\cdot \mathrm{E}_N[\mathbf{x}_n(y_n - \mathbf{x}_n'\boldsymbol{\beta})] \\ -\frac{1}{\sigma^4}\cdot \mathrm{E}_N[(y_n - \mathbf{x}_n'\boldsymbol{\beta})\mathbf{x}_n'] & \frac{1}{2\sigma^4} - \frac{1}{\sigma^6}\mathrm{E}_N[(y_n - \mathbf{x}_n'\boldsymbol{\beta})^2] \end{bmatrix} \\ &= \begin{bmatrix} -\frac{1}{\sigma^2 N}\cdot \mathbf{X}'\mathbf{X} & -\frac{1}{\sigma^4 N}\cdot \mathbf{X}'(\mathbf{y}-\mathbf{X}\boldsymbol{\beta}) \\ -\frac{1}{\sigma^4 N}\cdot(\mathbf{y}-\mathbf{X}\boldsymbol{\beta})'\mathbf{X} & \frac{1}{2\sigma^4} - \frac{1}{\sigma^6 N}(\mathbf{y}-\mathbf{X}\boldsymbol{\beta})'(\mathbf{y}-\mathbf{X}\boldsymbol{\beta}) \end{bmatrix} \end{aligned}$$

---

[10] See Appendix G for an introduction to differentiation of functions with respect to arguments that are vectors. To obtain $L_\beta(\theta)$, apply (G.5) and (G.6) to differentiate $(y_n - \mathbf{x}_n'\boldsymbol{\beta})'(y_n - \mathbf{x}_n'\boldsymbol{\beta}) = y_n'y_n + 2\boldsymbol{\beta}'\mathbf{x}_n y_n + \boldsymbol{\beta}'\mathbf{x}_n\mathbf{x}_n'\boldsymbol{\beta}$ with respect to $\boldsymbol{\beta}$.

[11] The second-order necessary condition for a point to be the local maximum of a twice continuously differentiable function is that the Hessian be negative semidefinite at the point. See Simon and Blume (1994, Theorem 17.6).

so that

$$\mathrm{E}_N[L_{\theta\theta}(\hat{\theta}_N)] = \begin{bmatrix} -\frac{1}{\hat{\sigma}_N^2} \cdot \mathrm{E}_N[\mathbf{x}_n\mathbf{x}_n'] & \mathbf{0} \\ \mathbf{0} & -\frac{1}{2\hat{\sigma}_N^4} \end{bmatrix}$$
$$= \begin{bmatrix} -\frac{1}{\hat{\sigma}_N^2 N} \cdot \mathbf{X}'\mathbf{X} & \mathbf{0} \\ \mathbf{0} & -\frac{1}{2\hat{\sigma}_N^4} \end{bmatrix} \qquad (14.12)$$

which is negative definite. Thus, the MLE for $\boldsymbol{\beta}_0$ is the OLS estimator that we have denoted by $\hat{\boldsymbol{\beta}}$. But the MLE for σ_0^2 is not the OLS estimator s^2. The MLE differs by a multiplicative factor: $s^2 = \hat{\sigma}_N^2 N/(N-K)$.

EXAMPLE 14.12 (Student *t* Linear Regression)

The first-order derivatives for maximizing the log-likelihood function of the Student t linear regression are fairly complicated. These derivatives do not yield analytical solutions for the MLE $[\hat{\boldsymbol{\beta}}_N', \hat{\sigma}_N^2, \hat{\nu}_N]'$. This is actually the general rule with the MLE and its application typically requires numerical optimization on a computer. We discuss methods of numerical optimization in Chapter 16.

EXAMPLE 14.13 (LAD Linear Regression)

Inspection of Example 14.7 shows that the LAD fitted regression coefficients correspond to the MLE for $\boldsymbol{\beta}_0$ in the Laplace specification. The Laplace log-likelihood is not differentiable everywhere because the absolute value function is not differentiable at the origin. However, because the objective function is globally concave, it has only one, possibly set-valued, local maximum. The MLE is computed using linear programming (LP) algorithms. To understand this, note that one can write the LAD optimization problem in the standard LP form as

$$\min_{\boldsymbol{\varepsilon}_1, \boldsymbol{\varepsilon}_2} \boldsymbol{\iota}'\boldsymbol{\varepsilon}_1 + \boldsymbol{\iota}'\boldsymbol{\varepsilon}_2 \qquad \text{s.t.} \qquad \boldsymbol{\varepsilon}_1, \boldsymbol{\varepsilon}_2 \geq 0,$$
$$\boldsymbol{\varepsilon}_1 \geq \mathbf{y} - \mathbf{X}\boldsymbol{\beta},$$
$$\boldsymbol{\varepsilon}_2 \geq -(\mathbf{y} - \mathbf{X}\boldsymbol{\beta})$$

Typically, programmers make transformations to this setup in actual software.[12]

14.5 IDENTIFICATION

Before attempting to employ the MLE, it is necessary to ask whether the data-generating process is sufficiently informative about the parameters of the model. This check is analogous to our initial analysis of the OLS fit, in which we examined the circumstances that $\hat{\boldsymbol{\beta}}$ is not unique. We found that $\mathbf{X}$ must be full-column rank, or else there is an infinite number of values for $\hat{\boldsymbol{\beta}}$ that provide the same OLS fit. More than this, *every* value of $\boldsymbol{\beta}$ is equivalent to a set of coefficient

[12] For a discussion of LAD computing, see Bloomfield and Steiger (1983).

values that produces the same linear fit. Because if there is an $\boldsymbol{\alpha} \in \mathbb{R}^K$, $\boldsymbol{\alpha} \neq \mathbf{0}$, such that $\mathbf{X}\boldsymbol{\alpha} = \mathbf{0}$, then $\boldsymbol{\beta} + c \cdot \boldsymbol{\alpha}$ gives the same RHS fit no matter what value c takes:

$$\mathbf{X}(\boldsymbol{\beta} + c \cdot \boldsymbol{\alpha}) = \mathbf{X}\boldsymbol{\beta} + c \cdot \mathbf{X}\boldsymbol{\alpha} = \mathbf{X}\boldsymbol{\beta}$$

As a result, no matter what values $\mathbf{y}$ takes, the SSR will be equal for all c:

$$\|\mathbf{y} - \mathbf{X}(\boldsymbol{\beta} + c \cdot \boldsymbol{\alpha})\|^2 = \|\mathbf{y} - \mathbf{X}\boldsymbol{\beta}\|^2$$

The SSR will certainly change with $\mathbf{y}$, but this equality will persist for all $\mathbf{y}$.

Consider a parallel situation in which the log-likelihood function evaluated at any $\boldsymbol{\theta}_0$ in the parameter space is always equal to the log-likelihood function evaluated at some $\boldsymbol{\theta}_1 \in \boldsymbol{\Theta}, \boldsymbol{\theta}_1, \neq \boldsymbol{\theta}_0$, no matter what values (u, v) takes in $\mathbb{S}(\boldsymbol{\theta}_0)$. Then the conditional p.f.s are identical for $\boldsymbol{\theta}_0$ and $\boldsymbol{\theta}_1$,

$$f(u \mid v; \boldsymbol{\theta}_0) = f(u \mid v; \boldsymbol{\theta}_1)$$

and data drawn from these two distributions will have the same sampling properties. Given a choice between them, there is no way to distinguish whether $\boldsymbol{\theta}$ equals $\boldsymbol{\theta}_0$ or $\boldsymbol{\theta}_1$. If every element of the parameter space has such counterparts, then efforts to estimate $\boldsymbol{\theta}_0$ are futile. Here is a characterization of the opposite situation:

DEFINITION 30 (GLOBAL IDENTIFICATION) *The parameter vector $\boldsymbol{\theta}_0$ is* globally identified *in $\boldsymbol{\Theta}$ if, for every $\boldsymbol{\theta}_1 \in \boldsymbol{\Theta}$, $\boldsymbol{\theta}_0 \neq \boldsymbol{\theta}_1$ implies that*

$$\Pr\{f(U \mid V; \boldsymbol{\theta}_0) \neq f(U \mid V; \boldsymbol{\theta}_1)\} > 0$$

We rule out many infeasible estimation problems using an additional assumption, which generalizes Assumption 3.1 (Full Rank, p. 53) for linear regression. Not knowing the population parameter vector, we will assume that no matter what value it takes in $\boldsymbol{\Theta}$, $\boldsymbol{\theta}_0$ is globally identified.

ASSUMPTION 14.3 (GLOBAL IDENTIFICATION) *Every parameter vector $\boldsymbol{\theta}_0 \in \boldsymbol{\Theta}$ is globally identified.*

With this assumption, the expected log-likelihood inequality is strengthened.

LEMMA 14.2 (STRICT EXPECTED LOG-LIKELIHOOD INEQUALITY) *Under Assumptions 14.1 (Distribution), 14.2 (Dominance I), and 14.3 (Global Identification), $\boldsymbol{\theta} \neq \boldsymbol{\theta}_0$ implies* $\mathrm{E}[L(\boldsymbol{\theta})] < \mathrm{E}[L(\boldsymbol{\theta}_0)]$.

See Section 14.9 for the proof.

EXAMPLE 14.14 (Linear Regression)

Exact multicollinearity among explanatory variables in a linear regression $E[\mathbf{y} \mid \mathbf{X}] = \mathbf{X}\boldsymbol{\beta}_0$ is a failure of global identification in the classical regression model. Both the conditional normal and Student t regression models fail to identify $\boldsymbol{\beta}_0$ if $\mathbf{X}$ is not full-column rank and sampling is conditional on $\mathbf{X}$. Note that if $\mathbf{X}$ is rank deficient, then the expected log-likelihood inequality $E[L(\boldsymbol{\theta})] \leq E[L(\boldsymbol{\theta}_0)]$ still holds. For example, the normal log-likelihood still attains its maximum in $\boldsymbol{\beta}$ at $\boldsymbol{\beta}_0$ because

$$-(\boldsymbol{\beta} - \boldsymbol{\beta}_0)' \mathbf{X}'\mathbf{X} (\boldsymbol{\beta} - \boldsymbol{\beta}_0) \leq 0$$

But the inequality is not strict for all $\boldsymbol{\beta} \neq \boldsymbol{\beta}_0$. If, on the other hand, $\mathbf{X}$ is full-column rank then $\boldsymbol{\beta}_0$ is the location of the unique maximum of $E[L(\boldsymbol{\theta})]$.

Identification concerns the *expected value* of the log-likelihood and not the sample log-likelihood function. Nevertheless, one can discover failures of identification in the sample log-likelihood function. For example, this can occur for conditional linear regression when $\mathbf{X}$ is fixed in repeated samples. But if a sample log-likelihood function fails to have a unique global maximum, this does not always imply a failure of global identification.

EXAMPLE 14.15 (Linear Regression)

Perhaps the simplest example of this distinction occurs when the sample size is less than the dimension of $\boldsymbol{\theta}$. Suppose that a linear regression model has $N + 1$ explanatory variables. Then $\mathbf{X}'\mathbf{X}$ will be singular and the MLE will not be unique. However, if the explanatory variables have a nonsingular marginal distribution then additional observations will overcome this problem.

EXAMPLE 14.16 (Linear Regression)

We can run into such difficulties even when the sample size exceeds the number of parameters. Suppose that $E[y_n \mid \mathbf{x}_n] = \mathbf{x}_n'\boldsymbol{\beta}_0$ and one is sampling $(y_n, \mathbf{x}_n)$ jointly. Let the $\mathbf{x}_n$ possess a multinomial marginal distribution. In a sample of $N < \infty$ observations, there may be a nonzero probability that the matrix $\mathbf{X}$ is rank deficient while there is also a nonzero probability that $\mathbf{X}$ is not rank deficient. The former implies that the log-likelihood may fail to have a unique global maximum and the latter implies that $\boldsymbol{\beta}_0$ is globally identified.

To be more specific, suppose that $K = 2$, $x_{n1} = 1$, and x_{n2} is a binomial random variable with probability mass function (p.m.f.)

$$f_{x_{n2}}(x) = \begin{cases} \alpha & \text{if } x = 1 \\ 1 - \alpha & \text{if } x = 0 \end{cases} \qquad 0 < \alpha < 1$$

In a sample of N observations, the probability that all of the x_{n2} are equal is $\alpha^N + (1 - \alpha)^N$, the probability that all zeros or all ones are observed. This is the probability that $\mathbf{X}$ will be rank deficient and the log-likelihood function will have many global maxima in $\boldsymbol{\beta}$. On the other hand, the probability that $\mathbf{X}$ is not rank deficient is $1 - \alpha^N - (1 - \alpha)^N > 0$ so that $\boldsymbol{\beta}_0$ is globally identified. As $N \to \infty$, this probability approaches 1 in the limit, directly confirming global identification.

A special kind of global identification occurs when the support of the distribution $\mathbb{S}(\boldsymbol{\theta}_0)$ depends on $\boldsymbol{\theta}_0$. A single observation can rule out certain values of $\boldsymbol{\theta}$.

EXAMPLE 14.17 (Uniform Distribution)

If U has the *uniform* (or *rectangular*) distribution then its support is an interval $\mathbb{S}(\theta_0) = [0, \theta_0]$ that depends on the parameter θ and its p.d.f. is

$$f(u; \theta_0) = \begin{Bmatrix} 1/\theta_0 & \text{if } u \in \mathbb{S}(\theta_0) \\ 0 & \text{if } u \notin \mathbb{S}(\theta_0) \end{Bmatrix} = \frac{\mathbf{1}\{u \in [0, \theta_0]\}}{\theta_0}$$

The parameter space is the positive real line excluding the boundaries 0 and ∞: $\boldsymbol{\Theta} = (0, \infty)$. Given a random sample $(U_1, \ldots, U_N)$, the MLE is the largest observed value, $\max_n U_n \equiv U_{(N)}$.[13] If we consider $\theta_0 < \theta_1$, then we see that $\Pr\{\theta_0 < U \leq \theta_1\} = 0$ when $\theta = \theta_0$ but this probability equals $(\theta_1 - \theta_0)/\theta_1 > 0$ if $\theta = \theta_1$. The reverse occurs if $\theta_1 < \theta_0$. Because one cannot observe realizations of U above the population value of θ, θ_0 is globally identified. In terms of Definition 30, we see that in this example,

$$\begin{aligned} &\Pr\{f(U; \theta_0) \neq f(U; \theta_1)\} \\ &\quad = \Pr\left\{\frac{\mathbf{1}\{U \in [0, \theta_0]\}}{\theta_0} \neq \frac{\mathbf{1}\{U \in [0, \theta_1]\}}{\theta_1}\right\} \\ &\quad = \Pr\left\{\frac{\theta_1}{\theta_0} \neq \mathbf{1}\{U \in [0, \theta_1]\}\right\} \\ &\quad = 1 \end{aligned}$$

confirming our conclusion.

This example of the uniform distribution also illustrates that the maximum likelihood estimator cannot necessarily be found with simple calculus when the support of the distribution depends on the unknown parameter values. In such cases, the sample log-likelihood function may not be differentiable everywhere in the parameter space and standard optimization methods break down. Fortunately, many interesting problems, like the normal regression model, do not have this feature and much theory for the MLE has been built on the next assumption.

ASSUMPTION 14.4 (DIFFERENTIABILITY) *The p.f. $f(u \mid v; \boldsymbol{\theta})$ is twice continuously differentiable in $\boldsymbol{\theta}$ for all $\boldsymbol{\theta} \in \boldsymbol{\Theta}$. Furthermore, the support $\mathbb{S}(\boldsymbol{\theta})$ of $f(u \mid v; \boldsymbol{\theta})$ does not depend on $\boldsymbol{\theta}$, and differentiation and integration are interchangeable in the sense that*

$$\frac{\partial}{\partial \boldsymbol{\theta}} \int_{\mathbb{S}} dF(u \mid v; \boldsymbol{\theta}) = \int_{\mathbb{S}} \frac{\partial}{\partial \boldsymbol{\theta}} dF(u \mid v; \boldsymbol{\theta}),$$

$$\frac{\partial^2}{\partial \boldsymbol{\theta}\, \partial \boldsymbol{\theta}'} \int_{\mathbb{S}} dF(u \mid v; \boldsymbol{\theta}) = \int_{\mathbb{S}} \frac{\partial^2}{\partial \boldsymbol{\theta}\, \partial \boldsymbol{\theta}'} dF(u \mid v; \boldsymbol{\theta})$$

[13] See Examples E.5, E.8, and E.11.

and

$$\frac{\partial \, \mathrm{E}[L(\boldsymbol{\theta}) \mid V = v]}{\partial \boldsymbol{\theta}} = \mathrm{E}\left[\frac{\partial L(\boldsymbol{\theta})}{\partial \boldsymbol{\theta}} \mid V = v\right] \tag{14.13}$$

$$\frac{\partial^2 \, \mathrm{E}[L(\boldsymbol{\theta}) \mid V = v]}{\partial \boldsymbol{\theta} \, \partial \boldsymbol{\theta}'} = \mathrm{E}\left[\frac{\partial^2 L(\boldsymbol{\theta})}{\partial \boldsymbol{\theta} \, \partial \boldsymbol{\theta}'} \mid V = v\right] \tag{14.14}$$

where all terms exist. In this case, we denote the support of $F(u)$ simply by $\mathbb{S}$.

Thus, we are avoiding such specifications as the Laplace distribution. This does not mean that the theory cannot be extended to such cases. In fact, it can.[14] But the lack of differentiability adds technical difficulty that obscures the most important ideas. The interchange of differentiation and integration, also commonly referred to as "differentiation under the integral," is ensured in part by requiring $\mathbb{S}(\boldsymbol{\theta}) = \mathbb{S}$. If the support of U depends on $\boldsymbol{\theta}_0$, then the region of integration changes with $\boldsymbol{\theta}$ and our derivatives would have more complicated expressions: we would differentiate the limits of integration as well as the integrand.[15] The uniform support assumption rules this out.[16]

With these additional assumptions, ordinary calculus usually helps to locate the MLE. The maximum of the log-likelihood function may fall on the boundary of the parameter space $\boldsymbol{\Theta}$, however, and there may also be several local maxima and minima in the interior of $\boldsymbol{\Theta}$. We will have to watch for these possibilities, though we have not encountered them yet in linear regression.

Though it may seem straightforward, the differentiability of the log-likelihood function is a powerful assumption for the distribution theory of the MLE. Because of this assumption, the quadratic structure of the OLS criterion and the linear structure of the OLS estimator will reappear in the asymptotic analysis of the MLE.[17] Whereas the OLS criterion is exactly quadratic in $\boldsymbol{\beta}$, we will be able to treat the log-likelihood function $L(\boldsymbol{\theta}; u)$ as approximately quadratic in $\boldsymbol{\theta}$. Similarly, we will be able to approximate the derivatives of the log-likelihood function as linear functions of $\boldsymbol{\theta}$ and the MLE as a linear function of approximately multivariate normal statistics.

With this quadratic analogy in mind, we introduce three concepts that play prominent roles in the analysis of the MLE: the *score vector*, the *information matrix*, and the *Cramér–Rao inequality*. The first two concepts relate to the remaining key elements of a quadratic function, its first and second derivatives. The Cramér–Rao inequality is a result about relative efficiency similar to the Gauss–Markov theorem. We will show how

$$\boldsymbol{\theta}_0 = \underset{\boldsymbol{\theta} \in \boldsymbol{\Theta}}{\operatorname{argmax}} \, \mathrm{E}[L(\boldsymbol{\theta})]$$

[14] For LAD specifically, see Koenker and Bassett (1978, 1982).

[15] According to Leibniz's rule, if $a(x)$, $b(x)$, and $g(x, y)$ are differentiable functions then

$$\frac{d}{dx} \int_{a(x)}^{b(x)} g(x, y) \, dy = b'(x) \, g[x, b(x)] - a'(x) \, g[x, a(x)] + \int_{a(x)}^{b(x)} \frac{\partial g(x, y)}{\partial x} \, dy$$

[16] Dominance conditions similar in form to Assumption 14.2 give primitive sufficient conditions for differentiation under the integral. See, for example, Amemiya (1985, Theorem 1.3.2) and Newey and McFadden (1994, Lemma 3.6).

[17] Differentiability is not a necessary condition for the quadratic approximation to hold. As previously mentioned, the LAD problem can also be sufficiently smooth for such approximation.

translates into the first-order conditions

$$\left.\frac{\partial \, \mathrm{E}[L(\boldsymbol{\theta})]}{\partial \boldsymbol{\theta}}\right|_{\boldsymbol{\theta}=\boldsymbol{\theta}_0} = \mathbf{0}$$

and the second-order conditions that the Hessian matrix

$$\left.\frac{\partial^2 \, \mathrm{E}[L(\boldsymbol{\theta})]}{\partial \boldsymbol{\theta}\, \partial \boldsymbol{\theta}'}\right|_{\boldsymbol{\theta}=\boldsymbol{\theta}_0}$$

is a negative definite matrix. In addition, we will demonstrate that the variance matrix of every unbiased estimator of $\boldsymbol{\theta}_0$ is greater than or equal to the inverse of the negative of this Hessian matrix. Thus, the significance of differentiation under the integral is that what holds for the MLE with a finite sample will also hold for $\boldsymbol{\theta}_0$ with the population, or with an "infinite sample."

14.6 THE SCORE FUNCTION

In all of the cases we will consider, the MLE $\hat{\boldsymbol{\theta}}_N$ is an implicit function of the data u characterized by

$$\hat{\boldsymbol{\theta}}_N = \underset{\boldsymbol{\theta}\in\Theta}{\operatorname{argmax}}\, \mathrm{E}_N[L(\boldsymbol{\theta})] \in \underset{\boldsymbol{\theta}\in\Theta}{\operatorname{argzero}}\, \mathrm{E}_N[L_{\boldsymbol{\theta}}(\boldsymbol{\theta})]$$

The first-order conditions

$$\mathbf{0} = \mathrm{E}_N[L_{\boldsymbol{\theta}}(\hat{\boldsymbol{\theta}}_N)] \quad \Leftrightarrow \quad \hat{\boldsymbol{\theta}}_N \in \underset{\boldsymbol{\theta}\in\Theta}{\operatorname{argzero}}\, \mathrm{E}_N[L_{\boldsymbol{\theta}}(\boldsymbol{\theta})] \tag{14.15}$$

are often called the *normal equations* or *likelihood equations*. Typically we do not have a closed form expression for $\hat{\boldsymbol{\theta}}_N$ and it must be expressed as an implicit function of the data in this way. In practice, $\hat{\boldsymbol{\theta}}_N$ must be calculated on a computer by numerical methods for maximizing differentiable functions. We describe such methods in Chapter16.

DEFINITION 31 (SCORE FUNCTION) *The* score *function is defined as the vector of first partial derivatives of the log-likelihood function with respect to the parameter vector* $\boldsymbol{\theta}$*:*

$$L_{\boldsymbol{\theta}}(\boldsymbol{\theta}) \equiv \frac{\partial L(\boldsymbol{\theta})}{\partial \boldsymbol{\theta}}$$

Given that the population parameter value $\boldsymbol{\theta}_0$ maximizes $\mathrm{E}[L(\boldsymbol{\theta})]$, we expect an analogy to the normal equations to hold for the derivatives: that is, $\mathrm{E}[L_{\boldsymbol{\theta}}(\boldsymbol{\theta}_0)] = \mathbf{0}$. Such an analogy does hold under certain conditions.

LEMMA 14.3 (SCORE IDENTITY) *Under Assumptions 14.1 (Distribution) and 14.4 (Differentiability),*

$$\mathrm{E}[L_{\boldsymbol{\theta}}(\boldsymbol{\theta}_0) \mid V = v] = \mathbf{0}$$

Proof. First, we derive an integral property of p.f.s. Because Assumption 14.1 states that $F(u \mid v; \boldsymbol{\theta})$ is a proper c.d.f.,

$$1 = \int_{\mathbb{S}} dF(u \mid v; \boldsymbol{\theta}) = \begin{cases} \sum_{u \in \mathbb{S}} f(u \mid v; \boldsymbol{\theta}) & \text{if } U \text{ is discrete} \\ \int_{\mathbb{S}} f(u \mid v; \boldsymbol{\theta})\, du & \text{if } U \text{ is continuous} \end{cases} \tag{14.16}$$

for *all* $\boldsymbol{\theta} \in \boldsymbol{\Theta}$.[18] Given Assumption 14.4 we can differentiate both sides of this equality with respect to $\boldsymbol{\theta}$, obtaining

$$\mathbf{0} = \begin{cases} \sum_{u \in \mathbb{S}} \frac{\partial}{\partial \boldsymbol{\theta}} f(u \mid v; \boldsymbol{\theta}) & \text{if } U \text{ is discrete} \\ \int_{\mathbb{S}} \frac{\partial}{\partial \boldsymbol{\theta}} f(u \mid v; \boldsymbol{\theta})\, du & \text{if } U \text{ is continuous} \end{cases} \tag{14.17}$$

This equation states how changes in $f(u \mid v; \boldsymbol{\theta})$ resulting from changes in $\boldsymbol{\theta}$ are restricted by (14.16). We can rewrite (14.17) as

$$\mathbf{0} = \begin{cases} \sum_{u \in \mathbb{S}} \frac{1}{f} \cdot f_{\boldsymbol{\theta}}\, f & \text{if } U \text{ is discrete} \\ \int_{\mathbb{S}} \frac{1}{f} \cdot f_{\boldsymbol{\theta}}\, f\, du & \text{if } U \text{ is continuous} \end{cases} = \int_{\mathbb{S}} \frac{1}{f(u \mid v; \boldsymbol{\theta})} \cdot f_{\boldsymbol{\theta}}(u \mid v; \boldsymbol{\theta})\, dF(u \mid v; \boldsymbol{\theta}) \tag{14.18}$$

where $f \equiv f(u \mid v; \boldsymbol{\theta})$ and $f_{\boldsymbol{\theta}} \equiv f_{\boldsymbol{\theta}}(u \mid v; \boldsymbol{\theta})$.

Now we interpret this integral equation as an expectation. Consider the random variable

$$L_{\boldsymbol{\theta}}(\boldsymbol{\theta}; U \mid V) = \frac{1}{f(U \mid V; \boldsymbol{\theta})} \cdot f_{\boldsymbol{\theta}}(U \mid V; \boldsymbol{\theta}) \tag{14.19}$$

In general, under Assumption 14.1 (Distribution),

$$\mathrm{E}[L_{\boldsymbol{\theta}}(\boldsymbol{\theta}; U \mid V) \mid V = v] \equiv \int_{\mathbb{S}} \frac{1}{f(u \mid v; \boldsymbol{\theta})} \cdot f_{\boldsymbol{\theta}}(u \mid v; \boldsymbol{\theta}) \underbrace{dF(u \mid v; \boldsymbol{\theta}_0)}_{\text{evaluated at } \boldsymbol{\theta}_0,\ \text{not } \boldsymbol{\theta}}$$

because $\boldsymbol{\theta}_0$ is the value of $\boldsymbol{\theta}$ for the conditional distribution of U. Note that for arbitrary $\boldsymbol{\theta}$ this expected value is not zero. Not all terms in this expression are evaluated at the same parameter values. However, if we set $\boldsymbol{\theta} = \boldsymbol{\theta}_0$ then we have an expression such as (14.18). Therefore, we interpret (14.18) as the required result by setting $\boldsymbol{\theta}$ equal to $\boldsymbol{\theta}_0$ in $L_{\boldsymbol{\theta}}(\boldsymbol{\theta}; U \mid v)$ and abbreviating $L_{\boldsymbol{\theta}}(\boldsymbol{\theta}_0; U \mid v) \equiv L_{\boldsymbol{\theta}}(\boldsymbol{\theta}_0)$. □

The conditional normal regression model provides a convenient example of this result.

EXAMPLE 14.18 (Normal Linear Regression)

The sample average score is displayed in equations (14.8) and (14.9). From these we see that

$$\mathrm{E}[L_{\boldsymbol{\beta}}(\boldsymbol{\theta})] = \frac{1}{\sigma^2} \cdot \mathrm{E}[\mathbf{x}_n \mathbf{x}_n'] \, (\boldsymbol{\beta}_0 - \boldsymbol{\beta})$$

[18] See Section D2.1 for a summary of such integrals.

$$\mathrm{E}[L_{\sigma^2}(\boldsymbol{\theta})] = -\frac{1}{2\sigma^4}\left(\sigma^2 - \left\{\sigma_0^2 + \mathrm{E}\left[\left(\mathbf{x}_n'\boldsymbol{\beta}_0 - \mathbf{x}_n'\boldsymbol{\beta}\right)^2\right]\right\}\right)$$

which equal zero at $\boldsymbol{\beta} = \boldsymbol{\beta}_0$ and $\sigma^2 = \sigma_0^2$. Note that these equations also give the derivatives of $\mathrm{E}[L(\boldsymbol{\theta})]$ in Example 14.8, showing that (14.13) is satisfied.

14.7 THE INFORMATION MATRIX

Finding the MLE involves more than finding a solution to the normal equations (14.15). If we find a $\tilde{\theta}_N$ such that

$$\mathbf{0} = \mathrm{E}_N[L_{\boldsymbol{\theta}}(\tilde{\boldsymbol{\theta}}_N)]$$

we must check that we have a global maximum. Otherwise our solution cannot be the MLE $\hat{\boldsymbol{\theta}}_N$. A sufficient condition for $\tilde{\boldsymbol{\theta}}_N$ to be a local maximum is that the *Hessian matrix*

$$\mathrm{E}_N[L_{\boldsymbol{\theta}\boldsymbol{\theta}}(\boldsymbol{\theta})] \equiv \frac{\partial^2 \mathrm{E}_N[L(\boldsymbol{\theta})]}{\partial\boldsymbol{\theta}\,\partial\boldsymbol{\theta}'}$$

evaluated at $\tilde{\boldsymbol{\theta}}_N$ is negative definite: for all $\mathbf{c} \in \mathbb{R}^K$, $\mathbf{c} \neq 0$,

$$\mathbf{c}'\,\mathrm{E}_N[L_{\boldsymbol{\theta}\boldsymbol{\theta}}(\tilde{\boldsymbol{\theta}}_N)]\mathbf{c} < 0$$

This condition arises from a local quadratic approximation of $\mathrm{E}_N[L(\boldsymbol{\theta})]$ and it guarantees that $\mathrm{E}_N[L(\boldsymbol{\theta})]$ is strictly concave in a neighborhood of $\tilde{\boldsymbol{\theta}}_N$.[19]

In the population, we already know that $\mathrm{E}[L(\boldsymbol{\theta})]$ is maximized at $\boldsymbol{\theta}_0$ under Assumption 14.3 (Likelihood Identification) and we have just confirmed that the first-order conditions are satisfied. Now we will consider the second-order conditions. To do so we must make another assumption.

ASSUMPTION 14.5 (FINITE INFORMATION) $\mathrm{Var}[L_{\boldsymbol{\theta}}(\boldsymbol{\theta}_0)]$ *exists.*

This assumption is comparable to Assumption 13.1 (p. 256), which bounded $\mathrm{Var}[\mathbf{x}_n(y_n - \mathbf{x}_n'\boldsymbol{\beta}_0)]$ (along with some other moments). But this assumption serves an additional purpose. This variance matrix is intimately related to the second-order conditions: the variance of the score vector, evaluated at $\boldsymbol{\theta}_0$, is the negative of the Hessian of the expectation of the log-likelihood function.

LEMMA 14.4 (INFORMATION IDENTITY) *Under Assumptions 14.1 (Distribution), 14.4 (Differentiability), and 14.5 (Finite Information),*

$$\mathrm{E}[L_{\boldsymbol{\theta}\boldsymbol{\theta}}(\boldsymbol{\theta}_0) \mid V = v] = -\,\mathrm{Var}[L_{\boldsymbol{\theta}}(\boldsymbol{\theta}_0) \mid V = v] \tag{14.20}$$

and this matrix is negative semidefinite.

19 See Simon and Blume (1994, Ch. 21).

Proof. The proof of this equality is similar to the proof of Lemma 14.3. Given Assumptions 14.1 (Distribution) and 14.4 (Differentiability), Lemma 14.3 yields (14.18)

$$\mathbf{0} = \int_{\mathbb{S}} L_{\boldsymbol{\theta}}(\boldsymbol{\theta}; u \mid v)\, dF(u \mid v; \boldsymbol{\theta})$$

Applying Assumption 14.4 (Differentiability) again, we differentiate both sides with respect to $\boldsymbol{\theta}$ to get

$$\mathbf{0} = \int_{\mathbb{S}} \left[L_{\boldsymbol{\theta\theta}}(\boldsymbol{\theta}; u \mid v) + L_{\boldsymbol{\theta}}(\boldsymbol{\theta}; u \mid v) L_{\boldsymbol{\theta}}(\boldsymbol{\theta}; u \mid v)' \right] dF(u \mid v; \boldsymbol{\theta}) \tag{14.21}$$

using (14.19) to obtain

$$\begin{aligned} \frac{\partial (L_{\boldsymbol{\theta}}\, f)}{\partial \boldsymbol{\theta}'} &= \frac{\partial L_{\boldsymbol{\theta}}}{\partial \boldsymbol{\theta}'} f + L_{\boldsymbol{\theta}} \frac{\partial f}{\partial \boldsymbol{\theta}'} \\ &= L_{\boldsymbol{\theta\theta}}\, f + L_{\boldsymbol{\theta}}\, (f_{\boldsymbol{\theta}})' \\ &= \left(L_{\boldsymbol{\theta\theta}} + L_{\boldsymbol{\theta}} L_{\boldsymbol{\theta}}' \right) f \end{aligned}$$

where $f \equiv f(u \mid v; \boldsymbol{\theta})$ and $L_{\boldsymbol{\theta}} \equiv L_{\boldsymbol{\theta}}(\boldsymbol{\theta}; u \mid v)$.[20] Setting $\boldsymbol{\theta}$ equal to $\boldsymbol{\theta}_0$, we rewrite (14.21) as

$$\begin{aligned} \mathrm{E}[L_{\boldsymbol{\theta\theta}}(\boldsymbol{\theta}_0; U \mid V) \mid V = v] &= -\,\mathrm{E}[L_{\boldsymbol{\theta}}(\boldsymbol{\theta}_0; U \mid V) L_{\boldsymbol{\theta}}(\boldsymbol{\theta}_0; U \mid V)' \mid V = v] \\ &= -\,\mathrm{Var}[L_{\boldsymbol{\theta}}(\boldsymbol{\theta}_0; U \mid V) \mid V = v] \end{aligned} \tag{14.22}$$

because $\mathrm{E}[L_{\boldsymbol{\theta}}(\boldsymbol{\theta}_0; U \mid v)] = \mathbf{0}$ by the score identity (Lemma 14.3, p. 300). Both sides of this equation exist according to Assumptions 14.4 (Differentiability) and 14.5 (Finite Information). This confirms (14.20).

That this Hessian is *negative* semidefinite is clear from the fact that it is the negative of a variance matrix, which is positive semidefinite. □

The normal location model provides an important and simple example.

EXAMPLE 14.19 (Normal Location)

Using the score in equations (14.8) and (14.9), we can derive these matrices for the normal location model, $U \sim \mathfrak{N}(\beta_0, \sigma_0^2)$, by setting $x_n = 1$. The variance matrix for one observation is

$$\mathrm{Var}[L_{\boldsymbol{\theta}}(\boldsymbol{\theta}_0)] = \begin{bmatrix} \frac{1}{\sigma_0^2} & 0 \\ 0 & \frac{1}{2\sigma_0^4} \end{bmatrix} \tag{14.23}$$

The upper left-hand corner is the variance of $L_{\boldsymbol{\beta}}(\boldsymbol{\theta}_0)$. The covariance of $L_{\beta}(\boldsymbol{\theta}_0)$ and $L_{\sigma^2}(\boldsymbol{\theta}_0)$ is zero because odd central moments of the normal distribution are zero. The lower right-hand corner is proportional to the variance of a χ_1^2 random variable:

[20] See Appendix G for a description of matrices of second-order cross-partial derivatives.

$$\mathrm{Var}[L_\sigma(\boldsymbol{\theta}_0)] = \left(\frac{1}{2\sigma_0^2}\right)^2 \mathrm{Var}\left[\frac{(U-\beta_0)^2}{\sigma_0^2}\right] = \frac{1}{2\sigma_0^4}$$

We can also use the information identity (Lemma 14.4) to derive the expression in (14.23). The Hessian of the normal log-likelihood function is

$$L_{\boldsymbol{\theta}\boldsymbol{\theta}}(\boldsymbol{\theta}) = \begin{bmatrix} -\frac{1}{\sigma^2} & -\frac{1}{\sigma^4}(U-\beta) \\ -\frac{1}{\sigma^4}(U-\beta) & \frac{1}{2\sigma^4} - \frac{1}{\sigma^6}(U-\beta)^2 \end{bmatrix}$$

which has an expectation that agrees with (14.23) when the Hessian is evaluated at $\boldsymbol{\theta}_0$ and multiplied by -1.

The variance matrix of the score vector $L_{\boldsymbol{\theta}}(\boldsymbol{\theta}_0; U \mid V)$ plays such an important role in the theory of the MLE that the matrix has a special name.

Definition 32 (Conditional Information) *The conditional variance matrix of the score vector $L_{\boldsymbol{\theta}}(\boldsymbol{\theta}; U \mid V)$ given $V = v$ and evaluated at $\boldsymbol{\theta}_0$,*

$$\Im(\boldsymbol{\theta}_0 \mid v) \equiv \mathrm{E}[L_{\boldsymbol{\theta}}(\boldsymbol{\theta}_0)\, L_{\boldsymbol{\theta}}(\boldsymbol{\theta}_0)' \mid V = v] = \mathrm{Var}[L_{\boldsymbol{\theta}}(\boldsymbol{\theta}_0) \mid V = v]$$

is the conditional information matrix.[21]

Even though we do not know $\boldsymbol{\theta}_0$, we can always find the conditional information matrix *function*

$$\Im(\boldsymbol{\theta} \mid v) \equiv \int_{\mathbb{S}} L_{\boldsymbol{\theta}}(\boldsymbol{\theta}; u \mid v)\, L_{\boldsymbol{\theta}}(\boldsymbol{\theta}; u \mid v)'\, dF(u \mid v; \boldsymbol{\theta})$$

because we have specified $F(u \mid v; \boldsymbol{\theta})$ for all $\boldsymbol{\theta} \in \boldsymbol{\Theta}$. For example, see (14.23). However, if our specification is conditional for U given V, then we are limited to deriving this conditional version.

Definition 33 (Population Information) *The marginal expectation*

$$\Im(\boldsymbol{\theta}_0) \equiv \mathrm{E}[L_{\boldsymbol{\theta}}(\boldsymbol{\theta}_0; U \mid V)\, L_{\boldsymbol{\theta}}(\boldsymbol{\theta}_0; U \mid V)']$$

is the population information matrix.

Without knowledge of the marginal distribution of V, it is not possible to take the additional expectation step to obtain a parametric expression for $\Im(\boldsymbol{\theta}_0)$. Nevertheless the *population* information matrix is still the *unconditional* variance matrix of the *conditional* score vector: because $\mathrm{E}[L_{\boldsymbol{\theta}}(\boldsymbol{\theta}_0; U \mid V) \mid V] = \mathbf{0}$,

[21] Sir R. A. Fisher, regarded by many as the father of modern statistics, chose the term "information" to describe this matrix.

$$\begin{aligned}\mathrm{Var}[L_{\boldsymbol{\theta}}(\boldsymbol{\theta}_0; U \mid V)] &= \mathrm{E}\big[\mathrm{Var}[L_{\boldsymbol{\theta}}(\boldsymbol{\theta}_0; U \mid V) \mid V]\big] + \mathrm{Var}\big[\mathrm{E}[L_{\boldsymbol{\theta}}(\boldsymbol{\theta}_0; U \mid V) \mid V]\big] \\ &= \mathrm{E}[\Im(\boldsymbol{\theta}_0 \mid V)] \\ &= \Im(\boldsymbol{\theta}_0) \qquad (14.24)\end{aligned}$$

EXAMPLE 14.20 (Normal Linear Regression)

Again using the score in equations (14.8) and (14.9), we can derive the conditional information matrix for the normal linear regression model:

$$\Im(\boldsymbol{\theta}_0 \mid \mathbf{x}_n) = \begin{bmatrix} \frac{1}{\sigma_0^2} \cdot \mathbf{x}_n \mathbf{x}_n' & \mathbf{0} \\ \mathbf{0} & \frac{1}{2\sigma_0^4} \end{bmatrix} \qquad (14.25)$$

Its derivation follows Example 14.19 exactly. The Hessian of the conditional normal regression log-likelihood function is

$$L_{\boldsymbol{\theta\theta}}(\boldsymbol{\theta}; y_n \mid \mathbf{x}_n) = \begin{bmatrix} -\frac{1}{\sigma^2} \cdot \mathbf{x}_n \mathbf{x}_n' & -\frac{1}{\sigma^4} \cdot \mathbf{x}_n (y_n - \mathbf{x}_n' \boldsymbol{\beta}) \\ -\frac{1}{\sigma^4} \cdot (y_n - \mathbf{x}_n' \boldsymbol{\beta}) \mathbf{x}_n' & N/(2\sigma^4) - (y_n - \mathbf{x}_n' \boldsymbol{\beta})^2/\sigma^6 \end{bmatrix}$$

which has a conditional expectation that agrees with (14.25) when the Hessian is evaluated at $\boldsymbol{\theta}_0$ and multiplied by -1. Without specifying a distribution for $\mathbf{x}_n$, we can say only that

$$\Im(\boldsymbol{\theta}_0) = \begin{bmatrix} \frac{1}{\sigma_0^2} \cdot \mathrm{E}[\mathbf{x}_n \mathbf{x}_n'] & \mathbf{0} \\ \mathbf{0} & \frac{1}{2\sigma_0^4} \end{bmatrix}$$

It is possible for the information matrix to be singular even when $\boldsymbol{\theta}_0$ is globally identifiable and the expected log-likelihood function is uniquely maximized at $\boldsymbol{\theta}_0$. The second-order condition that the Hessian be negative definite is sufficient but not necessary for a local maximum. Hence, we must assume this condition explicitly. Because the information identity (Lemma 14.4) states that the information matrix is negative semidefinite, we require only the following assumption.

ASSUMPTION 14.6 (NONSINGULAR INFORMATION) *The information matrix* $\Im(\boldsymbol{\theta}_0)$ *is nonsingular for all possible* $\boldsymbol{\theta}_0 \in \boldsymbol{\Theta}$.

As the previous example shows, this assumption is comparable to the assumption that $\mathbf{X}$ has full rank (Assumption 3.1, p. 53) in the linear regression model. In the probability models that we will consider, this assumption is met whenever Assumption 14.3 (Global Identification, p. 296) is satisfied.

14.8 THE CRAMÉR–RAO LOWER BOUND

The information matrix earned its name as a measure of how much we can learn about $\boldsymbol{\theta}_0$ from the random sample $\{(U_1, V_1), \ldots, (U_N, V_N)\}$. This property is described in the following theorem.[22]

[22] Fisher (1925) is generally credited with this result, although Cramer (1946) and Rao (1945) provided the present form.

THEOREM 10 (CRAMÉR–RAO INEQUALITY) *Let $\tilde{\boldsymbol{\theta}}$ be an unbiased estimator of $\boldsymbol{\theta}_0$ with finite variance matrix and let differentiation and integration be interchangeable so that*

$$\frac{\partial\, \mathrm{E}[\tilde{\boldsymbol{\theta}} \mid v_1, \ldots, v_N]}{\partial \boldsymbol{\theta}_0} = \frac{\partial}{\partial \boldsymbol{\theta}_0} \int_{\mathbb{S}} \tilde{\boldsymbol{\theta}} \prod_{n=1}^{N} dF(u_n \mid v_n; \boldsymbol{\theta}_0)$$

$$= \int_{\mathbb{S}} \tilde{\boldsymbol{\theta}} \frac{\partial}{\partial \boldsymbol{\theta}_0} \prod_{n=1}^{N} dF(u_n \mid v_n; \boldsymbol{\theta}_0)$$

If Assumptions 14.1 (Distribution), 14.4 (Differentiability), 14.5 (Finite Information), and 14.6 (Nonsingular Information) also hold, then the conditional sampling variance of an unbiased estimator is greater than or equal (in the positive semidefinite matrix sense) to $\left(N \cdot \mathrm{E}_N[\Im(\boldsymbol{\theta}_0 \mid v)]\right)^{-1}$ given $V_n = v_n$, $n = 1, \ldots, N$.

In some cases we can find estimators with variances equal to the Cramér–Rao lower bound. Before we prove this theorem, we will walk through such a special case. We observed in Proposition 12 (Efficiency of OLS, p. 205) that the OLS/MLE estimator of $\boldsymbol{\beta}_0$ in the conditional normal linear regression model is efficient relative to all other unbiased estimators. We begin with the simplest case of this.

EXAMPLE 14.21 (Normal Location)

Let us return to the i.i.d. normal probability model of Example 14.1. Suppose that the variance parameter σ_0^2 is known so that

$$\mathrm{E}_N[L(\boldsymbol{\theta})] = -\frac{1}{2} \log 2\pi\sigma_0^2 - \frac{1}{2\sigma_0^2} \mathrm{E}_N[(U - \boldsymbol{\theta})^2]$$

and $\hat{\boldsymbol{\theta}}_N = \sum_{n=1}^{N} U_n/N = \mathrm{E}_N[U]$. This MLE is unbiased and $\mathrm{Var}[\hat{\boldsymbol{\theta}}_N] = \sigma_0^2/N$. Let $\tilde{\boldsymbol{\theta}} = \tilde{\boldsymbol{\theta}}(U_1, \ldots, U_N)$ denote another unbiased estimator. Then

$$\begin{aligned}
\boldsymbol{\theta}_0 &= \mathrm{E}[\tilde{\boldsymbol{\theta}}] \\
&= \int_{-\infty}^{\infty} \tilde{\boldsymbol{\theta}} \prod_{n=1}^{N} f(u_n; \boldsymbol{\theta}_0)\, du_n \\
&= \int_{-\infty}^{\infty} \tilde{\boldsymbol{\theta}} \left(2\pi\sigma_0^2\right)^{-N/2} \exp\left[-\frac{1}{2\sigma_0^2} \sum_{n=1}^{N} (u_n - \boldsymbol{\theta}_0)^2\right] du_1 \cdots du_N
\end{aligned} \tag{14.26}$$

Because this is true for all possible $\boldsymbol{\theta}_0$, we can apply the differentiation technique that we used to derive the score and information identities (Lemmas 14.3 and 14.4): taking the partial derivative of both sides with respect to $\boldsymbol{\theta}_0$,

$$1 = \int_{-\infty}^{\infty} \tilde{\boldsymbol{\theta}} \left[\frac{1}{\sigma_0^2} \sum_{n=1}^{N} (u_n - \boldsymbol{\theta}_0)\right] \prod_{n=1}^{N} f(u_n; \boldsymbol{\theta}_0)\, du_n \tag{14.27}$$

Multiplying both sides by σ_0^2/N, this equation becomes

$$\frac{\sigma_0^2}{N} = \int_{-\infty}^{\infty} \tilde{\boldsymbol{\theta}}\ (\bar{u} - \boldsymbol{\theta}_0) \prod_{n=1}^{N} f(u_n; \boldsymbol{\theta}_0)\ du_n \tag{14.28}$$

where $\bar{u} \equiv \sum_{n=1}^{N} u_n/N$. Put another way,

$$\mathrm{Var}[\hat{\boldsymbol{\theta}}_N] = \mathrm{Cov}[\tilde{\boldsymbol{\theta}}, \hat{\boldsymbol{\theta}}_N]$$

But this is a condition for relative efficiency [Proposition 8 (Orthogonality of Efficient Estimators, p. 185) and equation (9.7)] showing that the sample average is the minimum variance unbiased estimator of the mean of a normal distribution. Furthermore, the variance of $\hat{\boldsymbol{\theta}}_N$ equals the inverse of the information, $1/\sigma_0^2$ in (14.19), multiplied by the sample size:

$$\frac{1}{N\,\Im(\boldsymbol{\theta}_0)} = \frac{1}{N/\sigma_0^2} = \frac{\sigma_0^2}{N}$$

Now, reexamine this proof and note how it turns on a special relationship among the MLE $\hat{\boldsymbol{\theta}}_N$, the population parameter value $\boldsymbol{\theta}_0$, the score $\mathrm{E}_N[L_{\boldsymbol{\theta}}(\boldsymbol{\theta}_0)]$, and the information matrix $\Im(\boldsymbol{\theta}_0)$. That relationship is

$$\begin{aligned}
\hat{\boldsymbol{\theta}}_N &= \mathrm{E}_N[U] \\
&= \boldsymbol{\theta}_0 + \sigma_0^2 \left(\frac{1}{\sigma_0^2} \mathrm{E}_N[U - \boldsymbol{\theta}_0] \right) \\
&= \boldsymbol{\theta}_0 + \Im(\boldsymbol{\theta}_0)^{-1}\, \mathrm{E}_N[L_{\boldsymbol{\theta}}(\boldsymbol{\theta}_0)]
\end{aligned} \tag{14.29}$$

in which we have replaced summation with empirical expectation. The score appears when we differentiate (14.26) and the information matrix enters when we multiply (14.27). The final step of the proof substitutes this relationship into the integral as in (14.28). We can trace this relationship to the quadratic log-likelihood function for $\boldsymbol{\theta}$ in the conditional normal linear regression model: treating σ_0^2 as known so that $\boldsymbol{\theta} = \boldsymbol{\beta}$ alone,

$$\begin{aligned}
\mathrm{E}_N[L(\boldsymbol{\theta})] &= -\frac{1}{2\sigma_0^2} \mathrm{E}_N[(U - \boldsymbol{\theta})^2] + c_0 \\
&= -\frac{1}{2\sigma_0^2} \left(\boldsymbol{\theta} - \hat{\boldsymbol{\theta}}_N \right)^2 - \frac{1}{2\sigma_0^2} \mathrm{E}_N[(U - \hat{\boldsymbol{\theta}}_N)^2] + c_0 \\
&= -\frac{1}{2} \Im(\boldsymbol{\theta}_0) \left(\boldsymbol{\theta} - \hat{\boldsymbol{\theta}}_N \right)^2 + c_1
\end{aligned}$$

where c_0 and d_0 are constant with respect to $\boldsymbol{\theta}$.[23]

Although log-likelihood functions are not generally quadratic, there are several ways in which this quadratic expression has general significance and the first of these is the Cramér–

[23] The constants are $c_0 = \log 2\pi\sigma_0^2$ and

$$d_0 = -\frac{1}{2\sigma_0^2} \mathrm{E}_N[U - \hat{\theta}_N]^2 + c_0$$

The second equality follows from equation (4.10) for the case $x_n = 1$.

Rao inequality. Consider the quadratic approximation to the average conditional log-likelihood function for $\boldsymbol{\theta} \in \mathbb{R}^K$ given by

$$\begin{aligned} \mathrm{E}_N[L(\boldsymbol{\theta})] &\approx \mathrm{E}_N[L(\boldsymbol{\theta}_0)] + \mathrm{E}_N[L_{\boldsymbol{\theta}}(\boldsymbol{\theta}_0)]'(\boldsymbol{\theta} - \boldsymbol{\theta}_0) \\ &\quad - \frac{1}{2}(\boldsymbol{\theta} - \boldsymbol{\theta}_0)' \mathrm{E}_N[\Im(\boldsymbol{\theta}_0 \mid v)](\boldsymbol{\theta} - \boldsymbol{\theta}_0) \\ &= -\frac{1}{2}\left(\boldsymbol{\theta} - \boldsymbol{\theta}^*\right)' \mathrm{E}_N[\Im(\boldsymbol{\theta}_0 \mid v)]\left(\boldsymbol{\theta} - \boldsymbol{\theta}^*\right) + c_2 \end{aligned} \tag{14.30}$$

where

$$\boldsymbol{\theta}^* \equiv \boldsymbol{\theta}_0 + \left(\mathrm{E}_N[\Im(\boldsymbol{\theta}_0 \mid v)]\right)^{-1} \mathrm{E}_N[L_{\boldsymbol{\theta}}(\boldsymbol{\theta}_0)] \tag{14.31}$$

and

$$c_2 \equiv \mathrm{E}_N[L(\boldsymbol{\theta}_0)] + \frac{1}{2}\left(\boldsymbol{\theta}_0 - \boldsymbol{\theta}^*\right)' \mathrm{E}_N[\Im(\boldsymbol{\theta}_0 \mid v)]\left(\boldsymbol{\theta}_0 - \boldsymbol{\theta}^*\right)$$

does not depend on $\boldsymbol{\theta}$. This quadratic function has the same value and the same gradient as $\mathrm{E}_N[L(\boldsymbol{\theta})]$ at $\boldsymbol{\theta}_0$ and has a Hessian equal to the conditional expectation of the Hessian of $L(\boldsymbol{\theta})$ at $\boldsymbol{\theta}_0$.

The maximum of this quadratic is the (generally infeasible, but still well defined) estimator $\boldsymbol{\theta}^*$. This estimator is unbiased, because the score identity (Lemma 14.3) holds, and this estimator has a conditional variance matrix equal to the Cramér–Rao lower bound,

$$\begin{aligned} \mathrm{Var}[\boldsymbol{\theta}^* \mid v_1, \ldots, v_N] &= \left(\mathrm{E}_N[\Im(\boldsymbol{\theta}_0 \mid v)]\right)^{-1} \mathrm{Var}\big[\mathrm{E}_N[L_{\boldsymbol{\theta}}(\boldsymbol{\theta}_0)]\big]\left(\mathrm{E}_N[\Im(\boldsymbol{\theta}_0 \mid v)]\right)^{-1} \\ &= \left(N \cdot \mathrm{E}_N[\Im(\boldsymbol{\theta}_0 \mid v)]\right)^{-1}, \end{aligned} \tag{14.32}$$

because Lemma 14.4 (Information Identity) holds. We will use this estimator in our proof of the Cramér–Rao inequality.

Proof of Theorem 10. The proof of this proposition is reminiscent of our proof of the Gauss-Markov theorem.[24] One derives a covariance restriction on estimators from the property of unbiasedness and then one applies this restriction to derive the characterization of efficiency and variance inequality. Let $\tilde{\boldsymbol{\theta}}$ be a conditionally unbiased estimator for $\boldsymbol{\theta}_0$ so that given $V_n = v_n$

$$\boldsymbol{\theta}_0 = \int_{\mathbb{S}} \tilde{\boldsymbol{\theta}} \prod_{n=1}^{N} dF(u_n \mid v_n; \boldsymbol{\theta}_0) \tag{14.33}$$

for any $\boldsymbol{\theta}_0$. Using the same approach as (14.17)–(14.19), we differentiate (14.33) with respect to $\boldsymbol{\theta}_0$ and obtain a restriction on the covariance between $\tilde{\boldsymbol{\theta}}$ and the score evaluated at $\boldsymbol{\theta}_0$:

$$\begin{aligned} \mathbf{I}_K &= \int_{\mathbb{S}} \tilde{\boldsymbol{\theta}} \left[\sum_{n=1}^{N} L_{\boldsymbol{\theta}}(\boldsymbol{\theta}_0; u_n \mid v_n)'\right] \prod_{n=1}^{N} dF(u_n \mid v_n; \boldsymbol{\theta}_0) \\ &= N \cdot \mathrm{E}\big[\tilde{\boldsymbol{\theta}}\ \mathrm{E}_N[L_{\boldsymbol{\theta}}(\boldsymbol{\theta}_0)'] \mid v_1, \ldots, v_N\big] \\ &= N \cdot \mathrm{Cov}\big[\tilde{\boldsymbol{\theta}}, \mathrm{E}_N[L_{\boldsymbol{\theta}}(\boldsymbol{\theta}_0)] \mid v_1, \ldots, v_N\big] \end{aligned} \tag{14.34}$$

[24] See Section 9.4.2.

We can show that this restriction implies the relative efficiency condition (Proposition 8, p. 185).[25] Postmultiplying both sides of (14.34) by $\left(N \cdot \mathrm{E}_N[\Im(\boldsymbol{\theta}_0)]\right)^{-1}$ gives

$$\begin{aligned}\left(N \cdot \mathrm{E}_N[\Im(\boldsymbol{\theta}_0)]\right)^{-1} &= \mathrm{Cov}\left[\tilde{\boldsymbol{\theta}},\, \mathrm{E}_N[L_{\boldsymbol{\theta}}(\boldsymbol{\theta}_0)]\left(\mathrm{E}_N[\Im(\boldsymbol{\theta}_0)]\right)^{-1} \mid v_1, \ldots, v_N\right] \\ &= \mathrm{Cov}\left[\tilde{\boldsymbol{\theta}},\, \boldsymbol{\theta}^* \mid v_1, \ldots, v_N\right]\end{aligned}$$

using (14.31). Moreover, using (14.32)

$$\mathrm{Var}[\boldsymbol{\theta}^* \mid v_1, \ldots, v_N] = \mathrm{Cov}[\tilde{\boldsymbol{\theta}},\, \boldsymbol{\theta}^* \mid v_1, \ldots, v_N]$$

Therefore, $\boldsymbol{\theta}^*$ is efficient relative to the set of all unbiased estimators and no unbiased estimator has a smaller variance matrix than $\mathrm{Var}[\boldsymbol{\theta}^* \mid v_1, \ldots, v_N] = \left(N \cdot \mathrm{E}_N[\Im(\boldsymbol{\theta}_0 \mid v)]\right)^{-1}$. □

A special case of this proposition is a result that we described in the distribution theory for the OLS estimator when the data are conditionally normally distributed.

Proposition 12 (Efficiency of OLS, p. 205) *Given Assumptions 3.1, 6.1, 7.1, and 10.1, conditional on* $\mathbf{X}$, $\hat{\boldsymbol{\beta}}$ *is efficient relative to all unbiased estimators of* $\boldsymbol{\beta}_0$.

Proof. Using (14.25),

$$\left(N \cdot \mathrm{E}_N[\Im(\boldsymbol{\theta}_0 \mid v)]\right)^{-1} = \begin{bmatrix} \frac{1}{\sigma_0^2} \cdot \mathbf{X}'\mathbf{X} & \mathbf{0} \\ \mathbf{0} & \frac{N}{2\sigma_0^4} \end{bmatrix}^{-1} = \begin{bmatrix} \sigma_0^2 \cdot (\mathbf{X}'\mathbf{X})^{-1} & \mathbf{0} \\ \mathbf{0} & 2\sigma_0^4/N \end{bmatrix}$$

Because

$$\mathrm{Var}[\hat{\boldsymbol{\beta}} \mid \mathbf{X}] = \sigma_0^2 \cdot \left(\mathbf{X}'\mathbf{X}\right)^{-1}$$

the OLS/ML estimator for $\boldsymbol{\beta}_0$ attains the Cramér–Rao lower bound. Applying Theorem 10, the proposition is proved. □

Although it provides insight into the Cramér–Rao lower bound, the quadratic log-likelihood function is not necessary for constructing relatively efficient unbiased estimators from $\boldsymbol{\theta}^*$.

[25] Our proof of the Gauss-Markov theorem also makes this step. Given that $\mathrm{E}[\mathbf{y} \mid \mathbf{X}] = \mathbf{X}\boldsymbol{\beta}_0$ and $\tilde{\boldsymbol{\beta}} = \mathbf{A}\mathbf{y}$ is unbiased, we begin with the equality

$$\boldsymbol{\beta}_0 = \mathrm{E}[\mathbf{X}\tilde{\boldsymbol{\beta}} \mid \mathbf{X}] = \mathbf{A}\mathbf{X}\boldsymbol{\beta}_0$$

Differentiating both sides with respect to $\boldsymbol{\beta}_0$, we obtain

$$\mathbf{I}_K = \mathbf{A}\mathbf{X}$$

which leads to the necessary covariance restriction in (9.10).

EXAMPLE 14.22 (Normal Linear Regression)

Let us treat $\boldsymbol{\beta}_0$ as known and consider the estimation of σ_0^2. The log-likelihood function is not a quadratic function of σ^2. Using (14.9) and (14.25), we find that (14.31) delivers

$$\begin{aligned}\boldsymbol{\theta}^* &= \sigma_0^2 + \frac{2\sigma_0^4}{N}\left[-\frac{\sigma_0^2 - (\mathbf{y}-\mathbf{X}\boldsymbol{\beta}_0)'(\mathbf{y}-\mathbf{X}\boldsymbol{\beta}_0)}{2\sigma_0^4}\right] \\ &= \frac{(\mathbf{y}-\mathbf{X}\boldsymbol{\beta}_0)'(\mathbf{y}-\mathbf{X}\boldsymbol{\beta}_0)}{N} \end{aligned} \tag{14.35}$$

which is the sample variance of the (population) residual $\mathbf{y}-\mathbf{X}\boldsymbol{\beta}_0$. This estimator is also the MLE for this problem. Because the numerator is distributed as $\sigma_0^2\chi_N^2$, the variance of this unbiased estimator is

$$\mathrm{Var}[\boldsymbol{\theta}^*] = \mathrm{Var}[\sigma_0^2\chi_N^2/N] = \frac{\sigma_0^4}{N^2}\mathrm{Var}[\chi_N^2] = \frac{2\sigma_0^4}{N}$$

which is the Cramér–Rao lower bound.

Although our examples of $\boldsymbol{\theta}^*$ are MLEs, $\boldsymbol{\theta}^*$ is generally an infeasible estimator.

EXAMPLE 14.23 (Normal Linear Regression)

Now let us consider the case in which *both* $\boldsymbol{\beta}_0$ and σ_0^2 are unknown and $\boldsymbol{\theta}_0 = [\boldsymbol{\beta}_0', \sigma_0^2]'$. The block-diagonality of the information matrix (14.25) leads to the same expressions for $\boldsymbol{\theta}^*$ that we obtained for $\boldsymbol{\beta}$ and σ^2 separately: using the expressions in that matrix, (14.8), and (14.9),

$$\begin{aligned}\boldsymbol{\theta}^* &= \begin{bmatrix}\boldsymbol{\beta}_0\\ \sigma_0^2\end{bmatrix} + \begin{bmatrix}\sigma_0^2\cdot(\mathbf{X}'\mathbf{X})^{-1} & \mathbf{0}\\ \mathbf{0} & 2\sigma_0^4/N\end{bmatrix}\begin{bmatrix}\frac{1}{\sigma_0^2}\cdot\mathbf{X}'(\mathbf{y}-\mathbf{X}\boldsymbol{\beta}_0)\\ -\frac{\sigma_0^2-(\mathbf{y}-\mathbf{X}\boldsymbol{\beta}_0)'(\mathbf{y}-\mathbf{X}\boldsymbol{\beta}_0)}{2\sigma_0^4}\end{bmatrix}\\ &= \begin{bmatrix}\hat{\boldsymbol{\beta}}\\ (\mathbf{y}-\mathbf{X}\boldsymbol{\beta}_0)'(\mathbf{y}-\mathbf{X}\boldsymbol{\beta}_0)/N\end{bmatrix}\end{aligned}$$

The σ^2 component of this estimator is infeasible because it depends on the unknown $\boldsymbol{\beta}_0$. The MLE for σ_0^2 is given in (14.11) as

$$\hat{\sigma}^2 = \frac{(\mathbf{y}-\mathbf{X}\hat{\boldsymbol{\beta}})'(\mathbf{y}-\mathbf{X}\hat{\boldsymbol{\beta}})}{N} = \frac{N-K}{N}s^2$$

which is similar but biased.

The relative efficiency of s^2 among unbiased estimators of σ_0^2 is a less tractable result than that of $\hat{\boldsymbol{\beta}}$ as an estimator of $\boldsymbol{\beta}_0$. A proof is beyond our scope because we do not explain *sufficient statistics*.[26] Instead we refer the reader to Lehmann (1983, Corollary 1.1, Section 2.1) and Exercises 14.15 and 14.16.

[26] A statistic $T(Y)$ is sufficient for the population parameter $\boldsymbol{\theta}_0$ that indexes the d.f. of the random variable Y if the distribution of Y conditional on $T(Y)$ does not depend on $\boldsymbol{\theta}_0$.

EXAMPLE 14.24 (Symmetric Densities)

Suppose that the elements of $\mathbf{y} - \mathbf{X}\boldsymbol{\beta}_0$ are i.i.d. with the p.d.f. $f(\mathbf{z}, \boldsymbol{\gamma}_0)$ given deterministic explanatory variables $\mathbf{X}$ and the parameters $\boldsymbol{\theta}_0 = [\boldsymbol{\beta}_0', \boldsymbol{\gamma}_0']'$. The $\boldsymbol{\gamma}_0$ are "nuisance parameters" in the sense that they are not directly interesting. In addition, let $f(\mathbf{z}, \boldsymbol{\gamma})$ be symmetric in $\mathbf{z}$ for all $\boldsymbol{\gamma}$:

$$f(\mathbf{z}, \boldsymbol{\gamma}) = f(-\mathbf{z}, \boldsymbol{\gamma})$$

The Student t and logistic p.d.f.s are special cases. Symmetry implies that

$$\frac{\partial f(\mathbf{z}, \boldsymbol{\gamma})}{\partial z} = -\frac{\partial f(-\mathbf{z}, \boldsymbol{\gamma})}{\partial \mathbf{z}}$$

$$\frac{\partial f(\mathbf{z}, \boldsymbol{\gamma})}{\partial \boldsymbol{\gamma}} = \frac{\partial f(-\mathbf{z}, \boldsymbol{\gamma})}{\partial \boldsymbol{\gamma}}$$

so that

$$L_{\boldsymbol{\beta}}(\boldsymbol{\theta}_0; y_n \mid \mathbf{x}_n)\, L_{\boldsymbol{\gamma}}(\boldsymbol{\theta}_0; y_n \mid \mathbf{x}_n)' = -\frac{1}{\left[f(z_n, \boldsymbol{\gamma})\right]^2} \cdot \mathbf{x}_n \frac{\partial f(z_n, \boldsymbol{\gamma})}{\partial z_n} \frac{\partial f(z_n, \boldsymbol{\gamma})}{\partial \boldsymbol{\gamma}'}$$

is an *odd* function of $z_n = y_n - \mathbf{x}_n \boldsymbol{\beta}_0$.[27] Therefore, if the information matrix exists, the off-diagonal block of the information matrix for the partition in $\boldsymbol{\beta}$ and $\boldsymbol{\gamma}$ is zero:

$$\mathrm{E}[L_{\boldsymbol{\beta}}(\boldsymbol{\theta}_0; z_n)\, L_{\boldsymbol{\gamma}}(\boldsymbol{\theta}_0; z_n)'] = \mathbf{0}$$

Furthermore, the conditional Cramér–Rao lower bound for unbiased estimators of $\boldsymbol{\beta}_0$ given $\mathbf{X}$ is simply

$$\mathrm{E}[L_{\boldsymbol{\beta}}(\boldsymbol{\theta}_0; \mathbf{z})\, L_{\boldsymbol{\beta}}(\boldsymbol{\theta}_0; \mathbf{z})' \mid \mathbf{X}]^{-1} = \frac{1}{\mathrm{Var}[f'(z_n)/f(z_n)]} \cdot (\mathbf{X}'\mathbf{X})^{-1}$$

where $\mathbf{z} \equiv [z_n]'$. Thus, these models generally lead to a lower bound proportional to $(\mathbf{X}'\mathbf{X})^{-1}$.

14.9 MATHEMATICAL NOTES

Proof of Lemma 14.1. This lemma is a special case of the information theory inequality (Lemma D.2, p. 875), which is a special case of Jensen's inequality (Lemma D.1, p. 874). Jensen's inequality states that if $h(\cdot)$ is a strictly concave function and $\mathrm{E}[Z]$ exists, then[28]

$$\mathrm{E}[h(Z)] \leq h(\mathrm{E}[Z])$$

The inequality is strict if Z is not a constant. We will take this result as given.[29]

27 The function $f(\mathbf{z})$ is *odd* if $f(-\mathbf{z}) = -f(\mathbf{z})$. Functions that are symmetric around zero are called *even*.

28 It is convenient here to state the result in terms of concave $h(\cdot)$, rather than convex. This is easy because if $h(\cdot)$ is convex, then by definition $-h(\cdot)$ is concave.

29 For the proof of Jensen's inequality, see p. 878.

Consider two random variables W and U and their p.f.s $f_W(w)$ and $f_U(u)$. The expectation of the random variable $Z = f_W(U)/f_U(U)$ is

$$\begin{aligned}
\mathrm{E}[Z] &= \int_{\mathbb{S}_U} \frac{f_W(u)}{f_U(u)}\, dF_U(u) \\
&= \begin{cases} \sum_{u\in\mathbb{S}_U} f_W(u) & \text{if } U \text{ is discrete} \\ \int_{\mathbb{S}_U} f_W(u)\, du & \text{if } U \text{ is continuous} \end{cases} \\
&\leq 1
\end{aligned}$$

where $\mathbb{S}_U$ is the support of $f_U(u)$. Therefore, $\mathrm{E}[Z]$ exists. We can set $h(\cdot)$ equal to $\log(\cdot)$, which is a strictly concave function. If we apply Jensen's inequality (Lemma D.1, p. 874) to this $h(\cdot)$ and Z,

$$\mathrm{E}\big[\log[f_W(U)/f_U(U)]\big] = \mathrm{E}[h(Z)] \leq h(\mathrm{E}[Z]) \leq \log(1) = 0$$

If $\Pr\{f_W(U)/f_U(U) \neq 1\} > 0$, then the inequality is strict. This proves the information theory inequality.

In addition, if we denote $\log f_W(U) = L(\boldsymbol{\theta}; U)$ and $\log f_U(U) = L(\boldsymbol{\theta}_0; U)$, then

$$\mathrm{E}[L(\boldsymbol{\theta}; U)] - \mathrm{E}[L(\boldsymbol{\theta}_0; U)] = \mathrm{E}\big[\log[f_W(U)/f_U(U)]\big] \leq 0$$

which is equivalent to the expected log-likelihood inequality because $\mathrm{E}[L(\boldsymbol{\theta}; U)]$ exists under Assumption 14.2 (Dominance I). □

Proof of Lemma 14.2. Continuing the proof of Lemma 14.1, we find that the information theory inequality

$$\mathrm{E}\big[\log[f_W(U)/f_U(U)]\big] = \int \log\left[\frac{f_W(u)}{f_U(u)}\right] dF_U(u) \leq 0$$

is strict if $\Pr\{f_W(U)/f_U(U) \neq 1\} > 0$. This condition is equivalent to global identification when $\log f_W(U) = L(\boldsymbol{\theta}; U)$ and $\log f_U(U) = L(\boldsymbol{\theta}_0; U)$. Therefore, if $\boldsymbol{\theta}_0$ is globally identified, the expected log-likelihood inequality is strict. □

14.10 OVERVIEW

1. Given a random sample $\{(U_1, V_1), \ldots, (U_N, V_N)\}$ of the random variable (U, V) and given $f(u \mid v; \boldsymbol{\theta}_0)$, the conditional p.f. of U conditional on V, the sample average conditional log-likelihood function is

$$\mathrm{E}_N[L(\boldsymbol{\theta})] \equiv \frac{1}{N}\sum_{n=1}^{N} \log f(U_n \mid V_n; \boldsymbol{\theta})$$

2. If the expectations exist and $\boldsymbol{\theta}_0$ is globally identified, then the population counterpart

$$\mathrm{E}[L(\boldsymbol{\theta})] \equiv \mathrm{E}[\log f(U \mid V; \boldsymbol{\theta})]$$

obeys the expected log-likelihood inequality

$$\mathrm{E}[L(\boldsymbol{\theta})] < \mathrm{E}[L(\boldsymbol{\theta}_0)]$$

for all $\boldsymbol{\theta} \neq \boldsymbol{\theta}_0$. Put another way,

$$\boldsymbol{\theta}_0 = \underset{\boldsymbol{\theta} \in \boldsymbol{\Theta}}{\operatorname{argmax}}\, \mathrm{E}[L(\boldsymbol{\theta})]$$

where $\boldsymbol{\Theta}$ is the parameter space of values $\boldsymbol{\theta}_0$ may take.

3. This population property motivates the maximum likelihood estimator (MLE) by analogy with the random sample:

$$\hat{\boldsymbol{\theta}} \equiv \underset{\boldsymbol{\theta} \in \boldsymbol{\Theta}}{\operatorname{argmax}}\, \mathrm{E}_N[L(\boldsymbol{\theta})]$$

4. Under certain conditions, a closely related analogy occurs between the population and sample behaviors of the score

$$L_{\boldsymbol{\theta}}(\boldsymbol{\theta}) \equiv \frac{\partial \log f(U \mid V; \boldsymbol{\theta})}{\partial \boldsymbol{\theta}}$$

In the population $\mathrm{E}[L_{\boldsymbol{\theta}}(\boldsymbol{\theta}_0)] = \mathbf{0}$ and in the sample $\mathrm{E}_N[L_{\boldsymbol{\theta}}(\hat{\boldsymbol{\theta}})] = \mathbf{0}$. The latter comprises the first-order conditions (normal equations) for the MLE.

5. The second-order conditions for a local maximum also yield an analogy. Generally $\mathrm{E}_N[L_{\boldsymbol{\theta}\boldsymbol{\theta}}(\hat{\boldsymbol{\theta}})]$ will be negative definite. Because

$$\mathrm{E}[L_{\boldsymbol{\theta}\boldsymbol{\theta}}(\boldsymbol{\theta}_0) \mid V = v] = -\operatorname{Var}[L_{\boldsymbol{\theta}}(\boldsymbol{\theta}_0) \mid V = v]$$

the expected Hessian is negative definite at $\boldsymbol{\theta}_0$ whenever the variance of the score (the information matrix) is nonsingular. We denote the information matrix by $\Im(\boldsymbol{\theta}_0) \equiv \operatorname{Var}[L_{\boldsymbol{\theta}}(\boldsymbol{\theta}_0)]$.

6. The variance matrix of every unbiased estimator of $\boldsymbol{\theta}_0$ is constrained by the Cramér–Rao lower bound: if $\tilde{\boldsymbol{\theta}}$ is an unbiased estimator then for all $\mathbf{c} \in \mathbb{R}^K$

$$\operatorname{Var}[c'\tilde{\boldsymbol{\theta}} \mid v_1, \ldots, v_N] \geq \frac{1}{N}\mathbf{c}' E_N[\Im(\boldsymbol{\theta}_0 \mid v_1]^{-1}\mathbf{c}$$

given $V_n = v_n$, $n = 1, \ldots, N$. In other words, $\operatorname{Var}[\tilde{\boldsymbol{\theta}} \mid v_1, \ldots, v_N] - \left(N \cdot \mathrm{E}_N[\Im(\boldsymbol{\theta}_0 \mid v)]\right)^{-1}$ is positive semidefinite.

7. In particular, the variance of OLS estimator $\hat{\boldsymbol{\beta}}$ conditional on $\mathbf{X}$ equals the information matrix, implying that $\hat{\boldsymbol{\beta}}$ is efficient relative to all unbiased estimators of $\boldsymbol{\beta}_0$ in the normal linear regression model. Also, s^2 is efficient relative to all unbiased estimators of σ_0^2.

We might hope for a general procedure to produce unbiased, relatively efficient estimators. The MLE is generally biased and cannot, therefore, be relatively efficient. In Chapter 15, we show how asymptotic distribution theory leads to the conclusion that the MLE has these properties approximately. This rests on the basic result that the log-likelihood function is approximately quadratic with a normally distributed gradient, just as in the normal linear regression model, as the sample size approaches infinity.

14.11 EXERCISES

14.11.1 Review

14.1 (Likelihood Identities) Suppose that U is a continuous random variable with the p.d.f. $f(u;\boldsymbol{\theta}_0)$, which is twice continuously differentiable in $\boldsymbol{\theta}_0$. Let $\{U_1,\ldots,U_N\}$ be a random sample of U.

(a) Prove that $\mathrm{E}[L_{\boldsymbol{\theta}}(\boldsymbol{\theta}_0)]=0$.

(b) Suppose also that $\mathrm{Var}[L_{\boldsymbol{\theta}}(\boldsymbol{\theta}_0)]$ exists. Prove that $\mathrm{E}[L_{\boldsymbol{\theta\theta}}(\boldsymbol{\theta}_0)]=-\mathrm{Var}[L_{\boldsymbol{\theta}}(\boldsymbol{\theta}_0)]$.

14.2 (Score Identity) The score identity (Lemma 14.3, p. 300) still holds if the score function is continuously differentiable except on a set of outcomes that has a probability equal to zero. The Laplace linear regression model described in Examples 14.7, 14.10, and 14.13 is a case in point. For this model,

(a) find the score function $L_{\boldsymbol{\theta}}(\boldsymbol{\theta})$ and show that the set of outcomes in which the score is undefined occurs with a probability of zero,

(b) find the gradient of the expected value of the log-likelihood function, $\partial\,\mathrm{E}[L(\boldsymbol{\theta})]/\partial\boldsymbol{\theta}$,

(c) show that $\mathrm{E}[L_{\boldsymbol{\theta}}(\boldsymbol{\theta})]=\partial\,\mathrm{E}[L(\boldsymbol{\theta})]/\partial\boldsymbol{\theta}$, and

(d) show that $\mathrm{E}[L_{\boldsymbol{\theta}}(\boldsymbol{\theta}_0)]=\mathbf{0}$.

14.3 (Score Identity) Use the log-likelihood inequality (Lemma 14.1, p. 290) to give an alternative proof of the score identity (Lemma 14.3, p. 300).

14.4 (MLE) Find the MLE for θ_0 in the exponential model:

$$F(u;\theta_0)=\begin{cases}0 & \text{if } u<0\\ 1-e^{-u/\theta_0} & \text{if } u\ge 0\end{cases}$$

Is the MLE unbiased? Find the information matrix and the variance of the MLE. Is the MLE efficient relative to other unbiased estimators?

14.5 (MLE) Under Assumption 14.1, show that the computation of MLE does not require the specification of the marginal distribution of V when the p.f. of V is invariant to $\boldsymbol{\theta}_0$.

14.6 (Cramér–Rao) Does Theorem 10 (Cramér–Rao Lower Bound, p. 306) imply that the variance bound can be achieved by a feasible estimator? Explain.

14.7 (Cramér–Rao) Let $\{U_1,\ldots,U_N\}$ be a random sample from the distribution with c.d.f. $F(u;\boldsymbol{\theta}_0)$, $\boldsymbol{\theta}_0\in\mathbb{R}^K$. Suppose that $F(u;\boldsymbol{\theta}_0)$ satisfies conditions that admit the existence of the information matrix. Suppose also that there is an unbiased estimator $\tilde{\boldsymbol{\theta}}=\tilde{\boldsymbol{\theta}}(U_1,\ldots,U_N)$ for $\boldsymbol{\theta}_0$ whose variance matrix attains the Cramér–Rao lower bound.

(a) Show that $\mathrm{E}[\tilde{\boldsymbol{\theta}}-\boldsymbol{\theta}^*]=\mathbf{0}$ and $\mathrm{Var}[\tilde{\boldsymbol{\theta}}-\boldsymbol{\theta}^*]$ is a matrix of zeros, where $\boldsymbol{\theta}^*$ is the Cramér–Rao estimator defined in (14.31).

(b) Show that $\tilde{\boldsymbol{\theta}}$ exists if and only if the average score can be expressed as

$$\mathrm{E}_N[L(\boldsymbol{\theta}_0)]=\Im(\boldsymbol{\theta}_0)\left(\tilde{\boldsymbol{\theta}}-\boldsymbol{\theta}_0\right)$$

except perhaps for a set of outcomes of probability zero.

(c) Give two examples in which such a $\tilde{\boldsymbol{\theta}}$ exists and confirm that the average score satisfies the restriction above.

***14.8 (OLS)** In Example 14.11, we showed that the OLS estimator $\hat{\boldsymbol{\beta}}$ is one component of a local maximum of the normal log-likelihood. Prove that this point is a global maximum using the following steps.

(a) Reparameterize the log-likelihood function

$$\mathrm{E}_N[L(\boldsymbol{\theta})] = -\frac{1}{2}\log(2\pi\sigma^2) - \frac{\mathrm{E}_N[(y_n - \mathbf{x}_n'\boldsymbol{\beta})^2]}{2\sigma^2}$$

in terms of $\gamma = \sigma^{-1}$ and $\delta = \sigma^{-1} \cdot \boldsymbol{\beta}$.

(b) Show that the Hessian of the reparameterized log-likelihood function is

$$\frac{\partial^2 \mathrm{E}_N[L(\boldsymbol{\theta})]}{\partial\boldsymbol{\theta}\,\partial\boldsymbol{\theta}'} = \begin{bmatrix} -\gamma^{-2} & \underset{1\times K}{\mathbf{0}} \\ \underset{K\times 1}{\mathbf{0}} & \underset{K\times K}{\mathbf{0}} \end{bmatrix} - \mathrm{E}_N[\mathbf{z}_n\mathbf{z}_n'] \tag{14.36}$$

where $\mathbf{z}_n = \left[y_n, -\mathbf{x}_n'\right]'$ and $\boldsymbol{\theta} = \left[\gamma,\ \delta'\right]'$.

(c) Prove that this Hessian is negative definite for all parameter values so that this log-likelihood is globally concave.

(d) Find the unique maximum in $(\boldsymbol{\delta}, \gamma)$ of the log-likelihood function. Why does this show that the OLS estimator is a component of the global maximum of the normal log-likelihood function?

14.9 (Logistic Distribution) Suppose that y_n has the logistic p.d.f.

$$f(z - \mathbf{x}_n'\boldsymbol{\beta}_0, \sigma_0) = \frac{1}{\sigma_0}\left(2 + e^{-(z-\mathbf{x}_n'\boldsymbol{\beta}_0)/\sigma_0} + e^{(z-\mathbf{x}_n'\boldsymbol{\beta}_0)/\sigma_0}\right)^{-1}$$

conditional on $\mathbf{x}_n$ and that $(\mathbf{x}_n, y_n)$ are i.i.d.

(a) Find the log-likelihood, score, and Hessian functions for the unknown parameters $\boldsymbol{\theta}_0 = \left[\boldsymbol{\beta}_0', \sigma_0\right]'$.

(b) Use the score function to show that this MLE and the LAD estimator treat large fitted residuals similarly. Explain why this is so.

14.11.2 Extensions

14.10 (Identification) Discuss identification of the parameters $\mu_y, \mu_z, \sigma_y^2, \sigma_z^2$, and σ_{yz} of the skewed p.d.f. in Exercise 13.14.

***14.11 (Exponential Family)** The *exponential family of distributions* possess p.f.s of the form

$$f(u;\boldsymbol{\theta}) = \begin{cases} \exp[a(c) + b(\boldsymbol{\theta}) + c(\boldsymbol{\theta})g(u)] & \text{if } u \in \mathbb{S} \\ 0 & \text{if } u \notin \mathbb{S} \end{cases}$$

where $g(u) \in \mathbb{R}^K$ is a vector of K real-valued transformations of u and $\boldsymbol{\theta} \in \boldsymbol{\Theta} \subseteq \mathbb{R}^K$ is a vector of parameters. The functions $a(c)$ and $b(\boldsymbol{\theta})$ are real scalars and the function $c(\boldsymbol{\theta})$ is a row vector of K transformations of $\boldsymbol{\theta}$.

(a) Show that the binomial, negative binomial, Poisson, normal, and chi-square distributions are members of the exponential family.

(b) Consider continuous distributions from the exponential family and suppose that

$$\int_{\mathbb{S}} f(u;\boldsymbol{\theta})\,du = 1$$

and that $\partial c(\boldsymbol{\theta})/\partial\boldsymbol{\theta}$ is nonsingular for all $\boldsymbol{\theta} \in \boldsymbol{\Theta}$. Find the expectation of $g(U)$, where U is a random draw from the p.d.f. $f(u;\boldsymbol{\theta}_0)$. [Hint: Use the score identity (Lemma 14.3, p. 300).]

(c) Also find the variance of $g(U)$.

(d) How do your answers to Parts (b) and (c) change if $f(u;\boldsymbol{\theta})$ is a *discrete* member of the exponential family? Assume that

$$\sum_{u \in \mathbb{S}} f(u; \boldsymbol{\theta}) = 1$$

and that $\partial c(\boldsymbol{\theta})/\partial \boldsymbol{\theta}$ is nonsingular for all $\boldsymbol{\theta} \in \boldsymbol{\Theta}$.

(e) Show that $\boldsymbol{\theta}$ is identified if $\mathrm{Var}[g(U)]$ is nonsingular.

14.12 **[Conditional ML]** Show that the Cramér–Rao lower bound for a conditional probability model $f_{W|Z}(w; \boldsymbol{\theta}_0 \mid z)$ is always greater (in the positive semidefinite sense) than the same bound for the complete joint probability model $f_U(u; \boldsymbol{\theta}_0) = f_{W|Z}(w; \boldsymbol{\theta}_0 \mid z)\, f_Z(z; \boldsymbol{\theta}_0)$.

***14.13** **(Restricted ML)** Suppose that $\boldsymbol{\theta}_0 = [\boldsymbol{\theta}_{01}', \boldsymbol{\theta}_{02}']'$ where $\boldsymbol{\theta}_{02}$ is an M-dimensional subvector of $\boldsymbol{\theta}_0 \in \mathbb{R}^K$. If $\boldsymbol{\theta}_{02}$ is known, then this knowledge can be imposed in estimation and the Cramér–Rao lower bound reduced. Prove this with the following steps.

(a) Show that the Cramér-Rao lower bound for unbiased estimators of $\boldsymbol{\theta}_0$ is

$$\frac{1}{N} \cdot \begin{bmatrix} \mathfrak{I}_{11}(\boldsymbol{\theta}_0)^{-1} & \mathbf{0} \\ \mathbf{0} & \mathbf{0} \end{bmatrix}$$

when we partition the information matrix conformably with $\boldsymbol{\theta}$ into

$$\mathfrak{I}(\boldsymbol{\theta}_0) = \begin{bmatrix} \mathfrak{I}_{11}(\boldsymbol{\theta}_0) & \mathfrak{I}_{12}(\boldsymbol{\theta}_0) \\ \mathfrak{I}_{12}(\boldsymbol{\theta}_0) & \mathfrak{I}_{22}(\boldsymbol{\theta}_0) \end{bmatrix}$$

(b) Show that this bound is lower (in the positive semidefinite sense) than the Cramér–Rao lower bound for unrestricted unbiased estimators.

14.14 **(MLE)** Suppose that U is continuously distributed. Suppose also that $N = K$ and that $\hat{\boldsymbol{\theta}}_N = \hat{\boldsymbol{\theta}}(U_1, \ldots, U_N)$ is one to one and continuously differentiable. Using the inverse of the MLE as a function of $(U_1, \ldots, U_N)$, find an expression for the p.d.f. of the MLE under the assumptions of this chapter. Try to generalize this expression to cases in which $N > K$.

14.15 **(Sufficient Statistics)** Show that $(\hat{\boldsymbol{\beta}}, s^2)$ are sufficient statistics for $(\boldsymbol{\beta}_0, \sigma_0^2)$ conditional on $\mathbf{X}$, in the conditional normal model $\mathbf{y} \mid \mathbf{X} \sim \mathfrak{N}(\mathbf{X}\boldsymbol{\beta}_0, \sigma_0^2 \cdot \mathbf{I}_N)$, for $\mathbf{X}$ full-column rank. That is, show that the distribution of $\mathbf{y}$ conditional on $\mathbf{X}$, $\hat{\boldsymbol{\beta}}$, and s^2 does not depend on the population parameters $\boldsymbol{\beta}_0$ and σ_0^2.

14.16 **(Efficiency of s^2)** In this exercise, we go through some of the steps supporting the relative efficiency of s^2 among all unbiased estimators of σ_0^2 in the conditional normal model $\mathbf{y} \mid \mathbf{X} \sim \mathfrak{N}(\mathbf{X}\boldsymbol{\beta}_0, \sigma_0^2 \cdot \mathbf{I}_N)$, for $\mathbf{X}$ full column rank.

(a) Using Jensen's inequality (Lemma D.1), show that if $\hat{\gamma}(\mathbf{y}, \mathbf{X})$ is an unbiased estimator of σ_0^2 with a finite variance then $\mathrm{E}[\hat{\gamma} \mid \mathbf{X}, \hat{\boldsymbol{\beta}}, s^2]$ has a smaller variance.

(b) Take as given that if $\mathrm{E}[f(\hat{\boldsymbol{\beta}}, s^2) \mid \mathbf{X}] = 0$ for every possible value of $[\boldsymbol{\beta}_0', \sigma_0^2]$, then $f(\hat{\boldsymbol{\beta}}, s^2) = 0$ with probability one. Show that (with probability one) there is only one unbiased estimator of σ_0^2 that is a function of $[\hat{\boldsymbol{\beta}}', s^2]$ alone.

(c) Use the previous two results to show that s^2 is efficient relative to all other unbiased estimators of σ_0^2.

14.17 **(Unconditional ML)** Suppose that the joint p.f. of (U, V) is $F_{U|V}(u, v; \boldsymbol{\theta}_0) f_V(v; \boldsymbol{\alpha}_0)$ for unknown parameter vectors $\boldsymbol{\theta}_0$ and $\boldsymbol{\gamma}_0$. Consider the unconditional alternative to the conditional MLE $\hat{\boldsymbol{\theta}}$ defined in Definition 28:

$$\tilde{\boldsymbol{\theta}} \equiv \operatorname*{argmax}_{\boldsymbol{\theta}\in\boldsymbol{\Theta}} \mathrm{E}_N[\log f_U(\boldsymbol{\theta}, \boldsymbol{\alpha}; U)]$$

where $f_U(\boldsymbol{\theta}_0, \boldsymbol{\alpha}_0; U)$ is the marginal p.f. of U. Show that the information matrix of this marginal log-likelihood is smaller (in the "positive semidefinite matrix" sense) than the conditional information matrix. What does this imply about the Cramér–Rao lower bound for unbiased estimators that do not depend on V?

CHAPTER 15

MAXIMUM LIKELIHOOD ASYMPTOTIC DISTRIBUTION THEORY

15.1 INTRODUCTION

In general the maximum likelihood estimator (MLE) that we introduced in the previous chapter does not possess a distribution theory comparable to the special case of the normal linear regression model. The primary reason is that the MLE is an *implicit* function of the random sample: we have only the optimization problem $\hat{\boldsymbol{\theta}}_N = \text{argmax}_{\boldsymbol{\theta}\in\boldsymbol{\Theta}} \text{E}_N[L_{\boldsymbol{\theta}}(\boldsymbol{\theta})]$ to describe the MLE as a function of the random sample. Although the distribution of $\hat{\boldsymbol{\theta}}_N$ is well defined, practically speaking this distribution must be approximated, either numerically or by some analytical method. This chapter covers the principal analytical approximation method, the asymptotic distribution theory that we introduced in Chapter 13.

As an implicit function, the MLE is generally not even a function of sample averages of the data. As a result, it is not immediately apparent how one can apply asymptotic distribution theory to this estimator. The fundamental insight that overcomes the implicit character of the MLE is that the *sample log-likelihood function* is a sum of i.i.d. random variables. Because the (U_n, V_n) are i.i.d. so are any such transformations as the $L(\boldsymbol{\theta}) \equiv L(\theta; U_n \mid V_n)(n = 1, \ldots, N)$. As a result, the law of large numbers (LLN) can apply to the sample average log-likelihood function itself so that

$$\text{E}_N[L(\boldsymbol{\theta})] \xrightarrow{p} \text{E}[L(\boldsymbol{\theta})]$$

for any fixed parameter value $\boldsymbol{\theta}$. Under conditions described in this chapter, it then follows that

$$\begin{aligned}\hat{\boldsymbol{\theta}}_N &= \underset{\boldsymbol{\theta}\in\boldsymbol{\Theta}}{\text{argmax}}\, \text{E}_N[L(\boldsymbol{\theta})] \\ &\xrightarrow{p} \underset{\boldsymbol{\theta}\in\boldsymbol{\Theta}}{\text{argmax}}\, \text{E}[L(\boldsymbol{\theta})] \\ &= \boldsymbol{\theta}_0\end{aligned}$$

In this way, the MLE proves to be consistent without possessing a convenient analytical expression.

A second insight provides a limiting normal distribution for $\sqrt{N}(\hat{\boldsymbol{\theta}}_N - \boldsymbol{\theta}_0)$ as the sample size approaches infinity. Given the consistency of the MLE, the behavior of the score function matters only within an arbitrarily small neighborhood of $\boldsymbol{\theta}_0$. After all, $\hat{\boldsymbol{\theta}}_N$ will fall within such neighborhoods with arbitrarily high probability for a large enough sample size N. And within such neighborhoods, the score function is essentially *linear*. That is, the Taylor series approximation

$$\mathrm{E}_N[L_{\boldsymbol{\theta}}(\boldsymbol{\theta})] \approx \mathrm{E}_N[L_{\boldsymbol{\theta}}(\boldsymbol{\theta}_0)] + \mathrm{E}_N[L_{\boldsymbol{\theta\theta}}(\boldsymbol{\theta}_0)]\,(\boldsymbol{\theta} - \boldsymbol{\theta}_0)$$

has a negligible error for $\boldsymbol{\theta}$ near $\boldsymbol{\theta}_0$. In particular, provided that the MLE solves the first-order conditions $\mathbf{0} = \mathrm{E}_N[L_{\boldsymbol{\theta}}(\hat{\boldsymbol{\theta}}_N)]$, then

$$\mathbf{0} = \mathrm{E}_N[L_{\boldsymbol{\theta}}(\hat{\boldsymbol{\theta}}_N)] \approx \mathrm{E}_N[L_{\boldsymbol{\theta}}(\boldsymbol{\theta}_0)] + \mathrm{E}_N[L_{\boldsymbol{\theta\theta}}(\boldsymbol{\theta}_0)]\left(\hat{\boldsymbol{\theta}}_N - \boldsymbol{\theta}_0\right)$$

so that the implicit MLE becomes explicit: solving this approximation for $\hat{\boldsymbol{\theta}}_N$ gives

$$\hat{\boldsymbol{\theta}}_N \approx \boldsymbol{\theta}_0 + \{-\mathrm{E}_N[L_{\boldsymbol{\theta\theta}}(\boldsymbol{\theta}_0)]\}^{-1}\,\mathrm{E}_N[L_{\boldsymbol{\theta}}(\boldsymbol{\theta}_0)] \tag{15.1}$$

This approximation is analogous to the OLS coefficient estimator

$$\hat{\boldsymbol{\beta}}_N = \boldsymbol{\beta}_0 + \{\mathrm{E}_N[\mathbf{x}_n\mathbf{x}_n']\}^{-1}\,\mathrm{E}_N[\mathbf{x}_n(y_n - \mathbf{x}_n'\beta_0)]$$

and the normal asymptotic distribution for $\sqrt{N}(\hat{\boldsymbol{\theta}}_N - \boldsymbol{\theta}_0)$ has a derivation similar to that for $\sqrt{N}(\hat{\boldsymbol{\beta}}_N - \boldsymbol{\beta}_0)$ in Section 13.4.3. Based on the original insight that the $L(\boldsymbol{\theta}; U_n \mid V_n)(n = 1, \ldots, N)$ are i.i.d., one sees that both $\mathrm{E}_N[L_{\boldsymbol{\theta}}(\boldsymbol{\theta}_0)]$ and $\mathrm{E}_N[L_{\boldsymbol{\theta\theta}}(\boldsymbol{\theta}_0)]$ are also averages of i.i.d. random variables. Because the score terms have expectation zero and variance $\Im(\boldsymbol{\theta}_0)$, the central limit theorem (CLT) can indicate that

$$\sqrt{N}\,\mathrm{E}_N[L_{\boldsymbol{\theta}}(\boldsymbol{\theta}_0)] \xrightarrow{d} \mathfrak{N}[\mathbf{0}, \Im(\boldsymbol{\theta}_0)]$$

Because the Hessian terms have expectation $-\Im(\boldsymbol{\theta}_0)$, the law of large numbers (LLN) can imply that

$$-\mathrm{E}_N[L_{\boldsymbol{\theta\theta}}(\boldsymbol{\theta}_0)] \xrightarrow{p} \Im(\boldsymbol{\theta}_0)$$

Thus, one can show that

$$\begin{aligned}\sqrt{N}\left(\hat{\boldsymbol{\theta}}_N - \boldsymbol{\theta}_0\right) &\approx \{-\mathrm{E}_N[L_{\boldsymbol{\theta\theta}}(\boldsymbol{\theta}_0)]\}^{-1}\sqrt{N}\,\mathrm{E}_N[L_{\boldsymbol{\theta}}(\boldsymbol{\theta}_0)]\\ &\xrightarrow{d} \mathfrak{N}[\mathbf{0}, \Im(\boldsymbol{\theta}_0)^{-1}]\end{aligned}$$

where the approximation error is negligible.

In this way, using averages of log-likelihood terms, one can overcome the actual complexity of the MLE with asymptotic distribution theory. Having done so, it is easy to establish the asymptotic efficiency of the MLE, as well as its consistency and asymptotic normality. The approximant (15.1) differs from the Cramér–Rao "estimator"

$$\boldsymbol{\theta}^* \equiv \boldsymbol{\theta}_0 + [\Im(\boldsymbol{\theta}_0)]^{-1}\,\mathrm{E}_N[L_{\boldsymbol{\theta}}(\boldsymbol{\theta}_0)] \tag{15.2}$$

only in the Hessian term.[1] This difference is also negligible asymptotically so that the MLE is asymptotically equivalent to the relatively efficient unbiased estimator.

[1] See equation (14.31) and Section 14.8 more generally, especially the proof of the Cramér–Rao inequality starting on p. 308.

In this chapter, we will combine the likelihood ingredients of Chapter 14 with the asymptotic distribution theory of Chapter 13 to refine and substantiate this heuristic introduction. We will describe the asymptotic distribution theory in two components. In the first component, we introduce conditions that ensure that the MLE converges in probability to the parameter values it estimates. In the second component, we extend the conditions so that the standardized MLE converges in distribution to a multivariate normal random variable. Then, almost as a bonus, we find that the MLE is an efficient estimator under our conditions.

PROPOSITION 16 (ML ASYMPTOTICS) *Under Assumptions 14.1 (Distribution, p. 285), 14.2 (Dominance I, p. 290), 14.3 (Global Identification, p. 296), and 15.1 (Compactness, p. 323), the MLE $\hat{\boldsymbol{\theta}}_N$ is consistent, that is*

$$\hat{\boldsymbol{\theta}}_N \xrightarrow{p} \boldsymbol{\theta}_0$$

Under the additional Assumptions 14.4 (Differentiability, p. 298), 14.5 (Finite Information, p. 302), 14.6 (Nonsingular Information, p. 305), 15.2 (Interior, p. 324), and 15.3 (Dominance II, p. 327), the MLE is also asymptotically normal so that

$$\{-\mathrm{E}_N[L_{\boldsymbol{\theta\theta}}(\hat{\boldsymbol{\theta}}_N)]\}^{1/2}\sqrt{N}(\hat{\boldsymbol{\theta}}_N - \boldsymbol{\theta}_0) \xrightarrow{d} \mathfrak{N}(\mathbf{0}, \mathbf{I}_K)$$

Finally, the MLE is asymptotically efficient relative to all other consistent and uniformly asymptotically normal (CUAN) estimators.[2]

The practical application of this proposition is to treat $\hat{\boldsymbol{\theta}}_N$ as approximately normally distributed with mean $\boldsymbol{\theta}_0$ and variance $\{N \cdot \mathrm{E}_N[L_{\boldsymbol{\theta\theta}}(\hat{\boldsymbol{\theta}}_N)]\}^{-1}$. Therefore, the MLE is approximately unbiased for $\boldsymbol{\theta}_0$ and we can compute confidence intervals and hypothesis test statistics comparable to those applied to the normal linear regression model.

We will refer to $\boldsymbol{\theta}_0$ as the *approximate* mean of $\hat{\boldsymbol{\theta}}_N$ and $\{N \cdot \mathrm{E}_N[L_{\boldsymbol{\theta\theta}}(\hat{\boldsymbol{\theta}}_N)]\}^{-1}$ as an *approximate* variance of $\hat{\boldsymbol{\theta}}$. It turns out that there are several common approximations to the variance matrix, as we will explain in Section 15.4.

This chapter is organized around the three basic results of this proposition. Their proofs, and several of the assumptions, appear in the sections below. Note as the theory unfolds that asymptotic normality requires more assumptions than consistency. We have chosen, however, not to emphasize the relationships between assumptions and results in asymptotic distribution theory. Indeed, we often use assumptions stronger than necessary to simplify the presentation.[3]

15.2 CONSISTENCY

For the OLS estimator, we showed consistency by applying the LLN (Theorem 8, p. 262) directly to elements of the estimator. Such direct methods of proof are generally unavailable for the MLE because closed form solutions for finite sample estimators do not exist. Almost all that is known

[2] CUAN estimators are described in Section 15.5.

[3] For more advanced treatments, see Amemiya (1985) and Newey and McFadden (1994).

analytically about the MLE is that it maximizes the sample log-likelihood function. A general mechanism for demonstrating the consistency of the MLE rests on two observations:

1. The sample average log-likelihood function converges to the expected log-likelihood for any value of $\boldsymbol{\theta}$:
$$\mathrm{E}_N[L(\boldsymbol{\theta})] \xrightarrow{p} \mathrm{E}[L(\boldsymbol{\theta})]$$
For each $\boldsymbol{\theta}$, this convergence follows generally from the LLN.
2. $\hat{\boldsymbol{\theta}}_N$ maximizes $\mathrm{E}_N[L(\boldsymbol{\theta})]$ by construction (Definition 29), $\boldsymbol{\theta}_0$ uniquely maximizes $\mathrm{E}[L(\boldsymbol{\theta})]$ according to the strict log-likelihood inequality (Lemma 14.2):
$$\hat{\boldsymbol{\theta}}_N \equiv \operatorname*{argmax}_{\boldsymbol{\theta}\in\boldsymbol{\Theta}} \mathrm{E}_N[L(\boldsymbol{\theta})]$$
$$\boldsymbol{\theta}_0 = \operatorname*{argmax}_{\boldsymbol{\theta}\in\boldsymbol{\Theta}} \mathrm{E}[L(\boldsymbol{\theta})]$$

As a result, $\hat{\boldsymbol{\theta}}_N$ converges to $\boldsymbol{\theta}_0$, provided that the relationships are continuous.

In effect, the mechanism is analogous to Lemma 13.2: given a continuous function $g(\cdot)$, if $U_N \xrightarrow{p} U$ then $g(U_N) \xrightarrow{p} g(U)$. We may think of $\mathrm{E}_N[L(\boldsymbol{\theta})]$ as the analogue of U_N and $\operatorname{argmax}_{\boldsymbol{\theta}\in\boldsymbol{\Theta}}(\cdot)$ as the analogue of the function $g(\cdot)$. But there are important differences. The argument of the $\operatorname{argmax}_{\boldsymbol{\theta}\in\boldsymbol{\Theta}}(\cdot)$ is a *function* (of $\boldsymbol{\theta}$), not a real vector. For the analogy to work, $\operatorname{argmax}_{\boldsymbol{\theta}\in\boldsymbol{\Theta}}(\cdot)$ must be a *continuous* function of its functional argument and we must define what we mean by the probability limit of a sequence of random *functions*, as opposed to a sequence of random variables.

How is the distance between two functions over a set containing an infinite number of possible comparisons at different values of $\boldsymbol{\theta}$ measured? To reduce the infinite dimensional character of a function to a one-dimensional concept of convergence, we take the supremum of the absolute difference of the function values over all $\boldsymbol{\theta}$ in $\boldsymbol{\Theta}$.

Definition 34 (Uniform Convergence in Probability) *The sequence of real-valued functions* $\{g_N(\boldsymbol{\theta})\}$ converges uniformly in probability *to the limit function* $g_0(\boldsymbol{\theta})$ *if* $\sup_{\boldsymbol{\theta}\in\boldsymbol{\Theta}} |g_N(\boldsymbol{\theta}) - g_0(\boldsymbol{\theta})| \xrightarrow{p} 0$. *We will say that* $g_N(\boldsymbol{\theta}) \xrightarrow{p} g_0(\boldsymbol{\theta})$ *uniformly.*

When we were studying the asymptotic behavior of the OLS estimator, and we could analyze its closed form expression, we used Chebychev's LLN to show when averages of random variables would converge. Now that we are studying sequences of random functions, we will use a *uniform* LLN corresponding to the uniform convergence in probability we have just defined.

Lemma 15.1 (Uniform LLN) *Suppose that* $g(\boldsymbol{\theta}; U)$ *is a continuous function over* $\boldsymbol{\theta} \in \boldsymbol{\Theta}$, *a closed and bounded subset of* $\mathbb{E}^K$, *and that* $\{U_n\}$ *is a sequence of i.i.d. random variables with c.d.f.* $F_U(u)$. *If* $\mathrm{E}[\sup_{\boldsymbol{\theta}\in\boldsymbol{\Theta}} \|g(\boldsymbol{\theta}; U)\|]$ *exists, then*

1. $\mathrm{E}[g(\boldsymbol{\theta}; U)]$ *is continuous over* $\boldsymbol{\theta} \in \boldsymbol{\Theta}$ *and*
2. $\mathrm{E}_N[g(\boldsymbol{\theta}; U)] \xrightarrow{p} \mathrm{E}[g(\boldsymbol{\theta}; U)]$ *uniformly.*

See Amemiya (1985, Ch. 4) and Newey and McFadden (1994, Section 2) and the references cited there for proofs and further discussion of this result. We will apply the uniform LLN to the sample average log-likelihood. The following lemma (Amemiya, 1973) makes the key connection between the uniform convergence of $\mathrm{E}_N[L(\boldsymbol{\theta})]$ to $\mathrm{E}[L(\boldsymbol{\theta})]$ and the convergence of $\hat{\boldsymbol{\theta}}_N$ to $\boldsymbol{\theta}_0$.

Lemma 15.2 (Consistency of Maxima) *If there is a sequence of functions $Q_N(\boldsymbol{\theta})$ that converges in probability uniformly to a function $Q_0(\boldsymbol{\theta})$ on the closed and bounded parameter space $\boldsymbol{\Theta}$ and if $Q_0(\boldsymbol{\theta})$ is continuous and uniquely maximized at $\boldsymbol{\theta}_0$, then $\hat{\boldsymbol{\theta}}_N \equiv \operatorname{argmax}_{\boldsymbol{\theta}\in\boldsymbol{\Theta}} Q_N(\boldsymbol{\theta})$ converges in probability to $\boldsymbol{\theta}_0$.*

The proof appears in Section 15.8. The lemma itself is fairly intuitive. If a sequence of functions Q_N converges to a function Q_0 in the limit, then one expects characteristics of the Q_N to converge to those of Q_0. Now, this will not be true for all characteristics. For example, Q_0 may be concave although none of the Q_N are. But the lemma states that for the global maximum we have asymptotic agreement. This provides the foundation for consistency of the MLE.

That convergence of $Q_N(\boldsymbol{\theta})$ is uniform is a key element. Consider, for example,

$$Q_N(\theta) = Q_{0N}(\theta) + Q_{1N}(\theta)$$

where

$$\begin{aligned} Q_{0N}(\theta) &= \frac{N}{2N - (1/2)} g_0(\theta - \theta_0) \\ Q_{1N}(\theta) &= g_0[4\log(N\theta/2)] \end{aligned}$$

and

$$g_0(x) = \exp(-x^2)$$

We show $Q_N(\theta)$ for several values of N in Figure 15.1. Because

$$\lim_{N\to\infty} Q_{1N}(\theta) = 0$$

for every $\theta \geq 0$,

$$Q_0 = \lim_{N\to\infty} Q_N(\theta) = \lim_{N\to\infty} Q_{0N}(\theta) = \frac{1}{2} g_0(\theta - \theta_0)$$

But for large enough N, the maximum of $Q_{0N}(\theta)$ will be approximately one-half the maximum of $Q_{1N}(\theta)$, both $Q_{0N}(2/N)$, $Q_{1N}(\theta_0) \approx 0$, and

$$\begin{aligned} \hat{\theta}_N &= \operatorname*{argmax}_{\theta\geq 0} Q_N(\theta) \\ &\approx \operatorname*{argmax}_{\theta\geq 0} Q_{1N}(\theta) \\ &= \frac{2}{N} \end{aligned}$$

As a result,

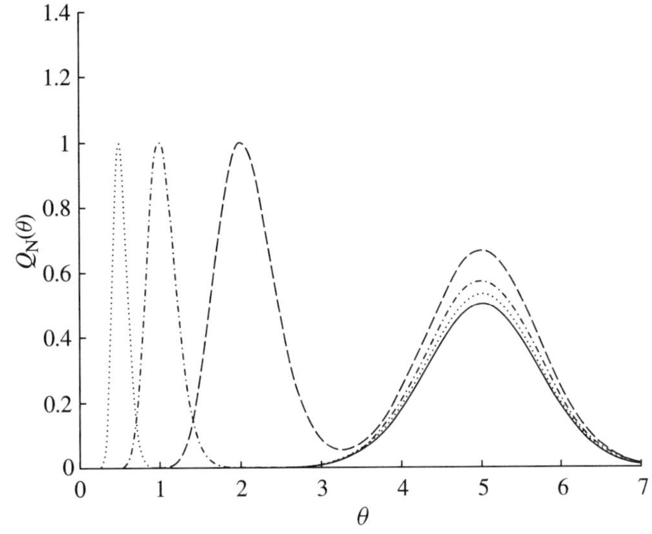

Figure 15.1 Nonuniform convergence.

$$\lim_{N\to\infty} \hat{\theta}_N = 0$$

whereas

$$\begin{aligned}\operatorname*{argmax}_{\theta\geq 0} \lim_{N\to\infty} Q_N(\theta) &= \operatorname*{argmax}_{\theta\geq 0} Q_{0N}(\theta) \\ &= \theta_0\end{aligned}$$

If the convergence of $Q_N(\theta)$ were uniform this would not occur. But there is always a $\theta > 0$ (for example, $\theta = 2/N$) such that

$$Q_N(\theta) - Q_0(\theta) > \tfrac{1}{2}$$

no matter how large N gets.[4]

To apply these ideas to the MLE we must narrow the range of problems that we consider. We will restrict $\boldsymbol{\Theta}$, the set of parameter values permitted in $L(\boldsymbol{\theta})$.

> **Assumption 15.1 (Compactness)** *The parameter space $\boldsymbol{\Theta}$ is a closed and bounded subset of $\mathbb{E}^K$, K-dimensional Euclidean space.*

This assumption, when it is combined with the differentiability of $E_N[L(\boldsymbol{\theta})]$, will help to guarantee that $E_N[L(\boldsymbol{\theta})]$ is "well behaved." In particular, we can apply one of the basic results

[4] You may be able to see from this example that uniform convergence is stronger than necessary. But such convergence is often available, so we will not consider other possibilities.

of multivariate calculus (Weierstrass' theorem) that a continuous function has a maximum (and a minimum) on a closed and bounded subset of $\mathbb{R}^K$.[5]

These assumptions and the appropriate definition of convergence for a sequence of random *functions* enable us to implement the mechanism for proving consistency of the MLE.

Given Lemma 15.2, we can prove the first part of our main proposition.

Proof of Proposition 16, Part 1. We let the $g(\boldsymbol{\theta}; U)$ in Lemma 15.1 equal $L(\boldsymbol{\theta}; U \mid V)$, the conditional log-likelihood function for $\boldsymbol{\theta}$ evaluated at the random variable (U, V). Now we verify that the conditions of the lemma are met: in the order of the conditions,

- Assumption 14.4 (Differentiability, p. 298) implies that g is continuous,[6]
- Assumption 15.1 (Compactncss) statcs that $\boldsymbol{\Theta}$ is a closed and bounded subset of $\mathbb{E}^K$,
- Assumption 14.1 (Distribution, p. 285) states that the (U_n, V_n) are i.i.d. with conditional c.d.f. $F_{U|V}(u \mid v; \boldsymbol{\theta}_0)$, and
- Assumption 14.2 (Dominance I) states that $\mathrm{E}[\sup_{\boldsymbol{\theta}\in\boldsymbol{\Theta}} |g(\boldsymbol{\theta}; U)|]$ exists.

Therefore, $\mathrm{E}[L(\boldsymbol{\theta})]$ is continuous and

$$\mathrm{E}_N[L(\boldsymbol{\theta})] \xrightarrow{p} \mathrm{E}[L(\boldsymbol{\theta})] \tag{15.3}$$

uniformly.

To apply Lemma 15.2 (Consistency of Maxima), we let $Q_N(\boldsymbol{\theta}) = \mathrm{E}_N[L(\boldsymbol{\theta})]$ and $Q_0(\boldsymbol{\theta}) = \mathrm{E}[L(\boldsymbol{\theta})]$. Under the additional Assumption 14.3 (Likelihood Identification, p. 296), we can invoke the strict expected log-likelihood inequality (Lemma 14.2, p. 296): $\boldsymbol{\theta} \neq \boldsymbol{\theta}_0$ implies $\mathrm{E}[L(\boldsymbol{\theta})] < \mathrm{E}[L(\boldsymbol{\theta}_0)]$. That is, $Q_0(\boldsymbol{\theta})$ is uniquely maximized at $\boldsymbol{\theta}_0$. Therefore,

$$\hat{\boldsymbol{\theta}}_N = \underset{\boldsymbol{\theta}\in\boldsymbol{\Theta}}{\operatorname{argmax}}\, Q_N(\boldsymbol{\theta}) \xrightarrow{p} \boldsymbol{\theta}_0$$

□

15.3 ASYMPTOTIC NORMALITY

Establishing consistency of an estimator is often the hardest part. Nevertheless, to demonstrate the asymptotic normality of the MLE, we need to narrow our assumptions further. Our analytical goal is to obtain approximating statistics that are functions of averages to which a law of large numbers or a central limit theorem can be applied. We can do this using Taylor series approximations as long as the MLE is the solution to the normal equations. To ensure this is almost certainly so, we also assume that $\boldsymbol{\theta}_0$ is not on the boundary of the parameters space.

[5] See, for example, Simon and Blume (1994, p. 823).

[6] Note that we can relax Assumption 14.4 (Differentiability, p. 298) and still use this result.

> **Assumption 15.2 (Interior)** *There is an open subset of $\boldsymbol{\Theta}$ that contains the population parameter value $\boldsymbol{\theta}_0$.*

From this point forward, we will take it for granted that the MLE solves the normal equations.[7] Proceeding from the normal equations, a first-order Taylor series expansion gives[8]

$$\mathrm{E}_N[L_{\boldsymbol{\theta}}(\hat{\boldsymbol{\theta}}_N)] = \mathbf{0} = \mathrm{E}_N[L_{\boldsymbol{\theta}}(\boldsymbol{\theta}_0)] + \mathrm{E}_N[L_{\boldsymbol{\theta\theta}}(\bar{\boldsymbol{\theta}}_N)]\,(\hat{\boldsymbol{\theta}}_N - \boldsymbol{\theta}_0) \tag{15.4}$$

where $\bar{\boldsymbol{\theta}}_N = \alpha_N \hat{\boldsymbol{\theta}}_N + (1 - \alpha_N)\boldsymbol{\theta}_0$, $\alpha_N \in [0, 1]$.[9] This permits us to write

$$\sqrt{N}(\hat{\boldsymbol{\theta}}_N - \boldsymbol{\theta}_0) = \{-\mathrm{E}_N[L_{\boldsymbol{\theta\theta}}(\bar{\boldsymbol{\theta}}_N)]\}^{-1}\sqrt{N}\,\mathrm{E}_N[L_{\boldsymbol{\theta}}(\boldsymbol{\theta}_0)]$$

which is still not an explicit function for $\hat{\boldsymbol{\theta}}_N$. But asymptotically, this is the "solution" for $\hat{\boldsymbol{\theta}}_N$.

We will use the same approach for the general MLE that we used for the special case of normal linear regression. Because $\mathrm{E}_N[L(\boldsymbol{\theta})]$ is a sample average of i.i.d. terms, so are its derivatives. Given the consistency of the MLE and Assumption 15.2 (Interior), we will argue

1. **(Score)** that $\sqrt{N}\,\mathrm{E}_N[L_{\boldsymbol{\theta}}(\boldsymbol{\theta}_0)]$ obeys the Lindberg–Levy CLT (Theorem 9, p. 265) for sample averages and
2. **(Information)** that $\mathrm{E}_N[L_{\boldsymbol{\theta\theta}}(\bar{\boldsymbol{\theta}}_N)]$ obeys an LLN, converging in probability to $-\mathfrak{I}(\boldsymbol{\theta}_0)$.
3. **(Asymptotic Distribution)** Taken together, these two results imply that $\sqrt{N}(\hat{\boldsymbol{\theta}}_N - \boldsymbol{\theta}_0)$ converges in distribution to $\mathfrak{N}[\mathbf{0}, \mathfrak{I}(\boldsymbol{\theta}_0)^{-1}]$.

We give each step of this part of the proof for Proposition 16 its own section.

15.3.1 Score

Let us begin with the score term, which ultimately gives the MLE its asymptotic normality.

> **Lemma 15.3** *Under Assumptions 14.1 (Distribution, p. 285), 14.4 (Differentiability, p. 298), and 14.5 (Finite Information, p. 302),*
>
> $$\sqrt{N}\,\mathrm{E}_N[L_{\boldsymbol{\theta}}(\boldsymbol{\theta}_0)] \xrightarrow{d} \mathfrak{N}[\mathbf{0}, \mathfrak{I}(\boldsymbol{\theta}_0)]$$

[7] Although the MLE may fail to solve the normal equations in a finite sample, we can show that such events do not occur (with probability one) in the asymptotic theory under Assumption 15.2. Because the MLE is consistent, the probability that $\hat{\boldsymbol{\theta}}_N$ is inside the open neighborhood of $\boldsymbol{\Theta}$ containing $\boldsymbol{\theta}_0$ approaches one. This means that the probability that $\hat{\boldsymbol{\theta}}_N$ is an interior maximum and $L_{\boldsymbol{\theta}}(\hat{\boldsymbol{\theta}}) = \mathbf{0}$ approaches one also.

[8] Regarding this Taylor's approximation, see equation (G.7) (p. 924) and the surrounding discussion.

[9] Alternatively, this is an application of the mean value theorem (e.g., Simon and Blume 1994, p. 825). Strictly speaking, (15.4) should be written

$$\mathbf{0} = \mathrm{E}_N[L_{\boldsymbol{\theta}}(\boldsymbol{\theta}_0)] + \left[\mathrm{E}_N[L_{\boldsymbol{\theta}_k\boldsymbol{\theta}}(\bar{\boldsymbol{\theta}}^k_N)];\, k = 1, \ldots, K\right]\,(\hat{\boldsymbol{\theta}}_N - \boldsymbol{\theta}_0)$$

because we must expand each element of the score with its own mean value $\bar{\boldsymbol{\theta}}^k_N$. But our arguments are not affected by our "white lie" and we gain valuable notational simplicity.

Proof. Because the (U_n, V_n) are i.i.d. (Assumption 14.1),

$$\sqrt{N}\,\mathrm{E}_N[L_{\boldsymbol{\theta}}(\boldsymbol{\theta}_0)] = \frac{1}{\sqrt{N}}\sum_{n=1}^{N} L_{\boldsymbol{\theta}}(\boldsymbol{\theta}_0; U_n \mid V_n)$$

is the sum of i.i.d. random variables $L_{\boldsymbol{\theta}}(\boldsymbol{\theta}_0; U_n \mid V_n)$. Given Assumptions 14.1 and 14.4, the score identity (Lemma 14.3, p. 300) holds so that $\mathrm{E}[\mathbf{c}'L_{\boldsymbol{\theta}}(\boldsymbol{\theta}_0)] = \mathbf{0}$. Given also Assumption 14.5, $\mathrm{Var}[\mathbf{c}'L_{\boldsymbol{\theta}}(\boldsymbol{\theta}_0)] = \mathbf{c}'\Im(\boldsymbol{\theta}_0)\mathbf{c}$ exists for all $\mathbf{c} \in \mathbb{R}^K$. The Lindberg–Levy CLT (Theorem 9, p. 265) therefore implies that

$$\sqrt{N}\,\mathrm{E}_N[\mathbf{c}'L_{\boldsymbol{\theta}}(\boldsymbol{\theta}_0)] \xrightarrow{d} \mathfrak{N}[\mathbf{0}, \mathbf{c}'\Im(\boldsymbol{\theta}_0)\mathbf{c}]$$

and the lemma follows by the Cramér–Wold device (Lemma 13.5, p. 266). □

We did not use several assumptions listed in the proposition for this intermediate result. The assumptions sufficient for consistency of the MLE do not play a role because the population parameter value $\boldsymbol{\theta}_0$ is given for this part. When we prove the asymptotic normality of $\hat{\boldsymbol{\theta}}_N$, these assumptions reenter the analysis.

15.3.2 Information

The Hessian term $\mathrm{E}_N[L_{\boldsymbol{\theta\theta}}(\bar{\boldsymbol{\theta}}_N)]$ poses a new problem: this matrix depends on the unknown vector $\bar{\boldsymbol{\theta}}_N$. This is an important difference from OLS where the Hessian $\mathbf{X}'\mathbf{X}$ is observed. Fortunately, $\bar{\boldsymbol{\theta}}_N$ is well behaved asymptotically.

Lemma 15.4 *Under Assumptions 14.1 (Distribution, p. 285), 14.2 (Dominance I, p. 290), 14.3 (Global Identification, p. 296), and 15.1 (Compactness, p. 323),* $\bar{\boldsymbol{\theta}}_N \xrightarrow{p} \boldsymbol{\theta}_0$.

Proof. Because $\bar{\boldsymbol{\theta}}_N$ always lies between $\hat{\boldsymbol{\theta}}_N$ and $\boldsymbol{\theta}_0$, $\bar{\boldsymbol{\theta}}_N$ is always closer to $\boldsymbol{\theta}_0$ than is $\hat{\boldsymbol{\theta}}_N$. Because we showed that $\hat{\boldsymbol{\theta}}_N \xrightarrow{p} \boldsymbol{\theta}_0$ under these assumptions in Section 15.2, it follows that $\bar{\boldsymbol{\theta}}_N \xrightarrow{p} \boldsymbol{\theta}_0$. □

One final technical obstacle remains: while $\bar{\boldsymbol{\theta}}_N \xrightarrow{p} \boldsymbol{\theta}_0$ implies $g(\bar{\boldsymbol{\theta}}_N) \xrightarrow{p} g(\boldsymbol{\theta}_0)$ for continuous g (Lemma 13.2, p. 261), we have a situation in which g is a function of the random sample, and therefore *random*. Uniform convergence in probability grants us passage here as well as in the consistency of maxima (Lemma 15.2) above.

Lemma 15.5 *If*

1. $g_N(\boldsymbol{\theta}) \xrightarrow{p} g_0(\boldsymbol{\theta})$ *uniformly for all* $\boldsymbol{\theta} \in \boldsymbol{\Theta}$, *a closed and bounded subset of* $\mathbb{E}^K$,
2. $g_0(\boldsymbol{\theta})$ *is continuous, and*
3. $\boldsymbol{\theta}_N \xrightarrow{p} \boldsymbol{\theta}_0 \in \boldsymbol{\Theta}$,

then $g_N(\boldsymbol{\theta}_N) \xrightarrow{p} g_0(\boldsymbol{\theta}_0)$.

See Section 14.9, *Mathematical Notes*, for the proof. Application of this lemma to the Hessian term will require uniform convergence in probability and so we add another assumption.

Assumption 15.3 (Dominance II) $\mathrm{E}\left[\sup_{\theta\in\Theta} |L_{\theta\theta}(\theta)|\right]$ *exists.*

Now we can state and prove our second intermediate result.

Lemma 15.6 *Under the assumptions of Lemma 15.4 and Assumptions 14.4 (Differentiability, p. 298), 14.5 (Finite Information, p. 302), 15.1 (Compactness, p. 323), and 15.3 (Dominance II),* $\mathrm{E}_N[-L_{\theta\theta}(\bar{\theta}_N)] \xrightarrow{p} \Im(\theta_0)$.

Proof. First we establish the uniform convergence in probability of $\mathrm{E}_N[L_{\theta\theta}(\theta)]$ to $\mathrm{E}[L_{\theta\theta}(\theta)]$. To do this we use the argument in Section 15.2 for $\mathrm{E}_N[L(\theta)]$. Assumption 14.4 implies that $L_{\theta\theta}(\theta)$ is continuous. Assumption 15.1 states that Θ is compact. Assumption 14.1 states that the (U_n, V_n) are i.i.d. Finally, Assumption 15.3 states that $\mathrm{E}[\sup_{\theta\in\Theta} |L_{\theta\theta}(\theta)|]$ also exists. Therefore, the uniform LLN (Lemma 15.1) implies that $\mathrm{E}_N[L_{\theta\theta}(\theta)] \xrightarrow{p} \mathrm{E}[L_{\theta\theta}(\theta)]$ uniformly in $\theta \in \Theta$.

Now we use the continuity lemma above. Lemma 15.4 states that $\bar{\theta}_N \xrightarrow{p} \theta_0$. Applying Lemma 15.5, $\mathrm{E}_N[L_{\theta\theta}(\bar{\theta}_N)] \xrightarrow{p} \mathrm{E}[L_{\theta\theta}(\theta_0)]$. Finally, the assumptions of Lemma 14.4 (Information Identity) are met so that $\mathrm{E}[L_{\theta\theta}(\theta_0)] = -\Im(\theta_0)$, giving the result. □

15.3.3 Asymptotic Distribution

With these results, we can argue that the MLE is asymptotically normal in the same way that we did for the OLS estimator: the normalized score evaluated at the population parameter value converges in distribution to a normal random variable and the Hessian converges to a constant population Hessian matrix. Hence, the score vector is linear in the unknown parameters and normally distributed. As a result, the normalized MLE converges in distribution to a multivariate normal random variable. Coincidentally, the variance of the score equals the population Hessian so that the approximate variance matrix of the MLE equals the inverse of the Hessian.

Proof of Proposition 16, Part 2. We have just shown (Lemmmas 15.3 and 15.6) that

$$\sqrt{N}\,\mathrm{E}_N[L_\theta(\theta_0)] \xrightarrow{d} \mathfrak{N}[\mathbf{0}, \Im(\theta_0)]$$
$$\mathrm{E}_N[-L_{\theta\theta}(\bar{\theta}_N)] \xrightarrow{p} \Im(\theta_0) \tag{15.5}$$

Using Lemma 13.2 (Probability Limit Continuity, p. 261) and Assumption 14.6 (Nonsingular Information, p. 305),

$$\{\mathrm{E}_N[-L_{\theta\theta}(\bar{\theta}_N)]\}^{-1} \xrightarrow{p} \Im(\theta_0)^{-1}$$

because the inverse of a *nonsingular* matrix is a continuous function. Using the Taylor series approximation (15.4) and Lemma 13.3 (Slutsky, p. 261), we have

$$\begin{aligned}\sqrt{N}(\hat{\boldsymbol{\theta}}_N - \boldsymbol{\theta}_0) &= \{-\mathrm{E}_N[L_{\boldsymbol{\theta\theta}}(\bar{\boldsymbol{\theta}}_N)]\}^{-1}\sqrt{N}\,\mathrm{E}_N[L_{\boldsymbol{\theta}}(\boldsymbol{\theta}_0)] \\ &\xrightarrow{d} \Im(\boldsymbol{\theta}_0)^{-1}\mathfrak{N}[\mathbf{0}, \Im(\boldsymbol{\theta}_0)] \\ &\sim \mathfrak{N}[\mathbf{0}, \Im(\boldsymbol{\theta}_0)^{-1}]\end{aligned} \tag{15.6}$$

Replacing $\bar{\boldsymbol{\theta}}_N$ with $\hat{\boldsymbol{\theta}}_N$, we also have

$$\mathrm{E}_N[-L_{\boldsymbol{\theta\theta}}(\hat{\boldsymbol{\theta}}_N)] \xrightarrow{p} \Im(\boldsymbol{\theta}_0)$$

Because square roots of nonsingular matrices are continuous functions of the elements of the matrix, Lemma 13.2 states that

$$\{-\mathrm{E}_N[L_{\boldsymbol{\theta\theta}}(\hat{\boldsymbol{\theta}}_N)]\}^{1/2} \xrightarrow{p} \Im(\boldsymbol{\theta}_0)^{1/2}$$

so that combined with (15.6) by Lemma 13.3 (Slutsky, 261),

$$\begin{aligned}\{-\mathrm{E}_N[L_{\boldsymbol{\theta\theta}}(\hat{\boldsymbol{\theta}}_N)]\}^{1/2}\sqrt{N}(\hat{\boldsymbol{\theta}}_N - \boldsymbol{\theta}_0) &\xrightarrow{d} \Im(\boldsymbol{\theta}_0)^{1/2}\mathfrak{N}[\mathbf{0}, \Im(\boldsymbol{\theta}_0)^{-1}] \\ &\sim \mathfrak{N}(\mathbf{0}, \mathbf{I}_K)\end{aligned}$$

This proves Part 2. □

First, let us show how this result applies to a familiar setting.

EXAMPLE 15.1 (Normal Linear Regression)

In normal linear regression,[10]

$$\begin{aligned}\mathrm{E}_N[-L_{\boldsymbol{\theta\theta}}(\hat{\boldsymbol{\theta}}_N)] &= \begin{bmatrix}\frac{1}{\hat{\sigma}_N^2}\mathrm{E}_N[\mathbf{x}_n\mathbf{x}_n'] & 0 \\ 0 & \frac{1}{2\hat{\sigma}_N^4}\end{bmatrix} \\ &= \begin{bmatrix}\frac{1}{\hat{\sigma}_N^2}\left(\frac{1}{N}\cdot\mathbf{X}'\mathbf{X}\right) & 0 \\ 0 & \frac{1}{2\hat{\sigma}_N^4}\end{bmatrix} \\ &= \mathrm{E}_N[\Im(\hat{\boldsymbol{\theta}}_N \mid \mathbf{x}_n)]\end{aligned}$$

Applying Proposition 16 (ML Asymptotics, p. 320), we find that

$$\begin{bmatrix}\frac{1}{\hat{\sigma}_N}\left(\frac{1}{N}\cdot\mathbf{X}'\mathbf{X}\right)^{1/2}\sqrt{N}\left(\hat{\boldsymbol{\beta}}_N - \boldsymbol{\beta}_0\right) \\ \frac{1}{\sqrt{2\hat{\sigma}_N^4}}\sqrt{N}\left(\hat{\sigma}_N^2 - \sigma_0^2\right)\end{bmatrix} \xrightarrow{d} \mathfrak{N}(\mathbf{0}, \mathbf{I}_{K+1})$$

Therefore, $\sqrt{N}(\hat{\boldsymbol{\beta}}_N - \boldsymbol{\beta}_0)$ converges in distribution to an $\mathfrak{N}(\mathbf{0}, \sigma_0^2\cdot\mathbf{D}^{-1})$ random variable, where

[10] See (14.12) in Example 14.11.

$\mathbf{D} \equiv \mathrm{E}[\mathbf{x}_n \mathbf{x}_n']$. We have derived this asymptotic result previously for $\hat{\beta}_N$ under weaker conditions.[11] We also find that

$$\sqrt{N}\left(\hat{\sigma}_N^2 - \sigma_0^2\right) \xrightarrow{d} \mathfrak{N}(\mathbf{0}, 2\sigma_0^4)$$

This approximation differs, of course, with the exact $\sigma_0^2\, \chi_{N-K}^2 / N$ distribution of $\hat{\sigma}^2$. But one can show that the exact distribution implies the asymptotic one directly.[12]

Before leaving this result, we wish to note that the moments of the asymptotic distribution of a (standardized) estimator may not equal the limits, if they exist, of the moments of the (standardized) estimator. This situation reflects the result that moments do not generally characterize distributions. In particular, it is possible for two p.d.f.s to be extremely close, yet their moments can be quite far apart.[13] As a result, there is ambiguity in referring to the asymptotic moments of such a sequence of random variables as $\sqrt{N}(\hat{\boldsymbol{\theta}}_N - \boldsymbol{\theta}_0)$. We will refer to $\Im(\boldsymbol{\theta}_0)^{-1}$ as the *asymptotic* (or *limiting*) variance of $\sqrt{N}(\hat{\boldsymbol{\theta}}_N - \boldsymbol{\theta}_0)$, based on (15.6). We even lapse into calling $\Im(\boldsymbol{\theta}_0)^{-1}$ the asymptotic variance of $\hat{\boldsymbol{\theta}}_N$, even though this is formally misleading, because this usage is common.

15.4 VARIANCE ESTIMATION

Following Proposition 16, we approximate the variance matrix of the MLE with the matrix $\{N \cdot \mathrm{E}_N[-L_{\boldsymbol{\theta\theta}}(\hat{\boldsymbol{\theta}}_N)]\}^{-1}$. In fact, we can approximate the variance several ways. According to the theory in Section 15.3.3, we can replace $\mathrm{E}_N[-L_{\boldsymbol{\theta\theta}}(\hat{\boldsymbol{\theta}}_N)]$ with any estimator that converges in probability to the information matrix $\Im(\boldsymbol{\theta}_0)$. The asymptotic distribution theory of the MLE delivers three consistent estimators of the information matrix $\Im(\boldsymbol{\theta}_0)$:

the empirical mean of minus the Hessian,	$\mathrm{E}_N[-L_{\boldsymbol{\theta\theta}}(\hat{\boldsymbol{\theta}}_N)]$;
the empirical variance of the score,	$\mathrm{Var}_N[L_{\boldsymbol{\theta}}(\hat{\boldsymbol{\theta}}_N)]$;
the empirical information,	$\mathrm{E}_N[\Im(\hat{\boldsymbol{\theta}}_N)]$.

Each of these estimators has a population analogue, in which the MLE $\hat{\boldsymbol{\theta}}_N$ is replaced by $\boldsymbol{\theta}_0$ and the empirical expectation is replaced by the population expectation. The estimators are two-step estimators in the sense that in the first step we estimate $\boldsymbol{\theta}_0$ consistently with $\hat{\boldsymbol{\theta}}_N$ and in the second step we "plug in" $\hat{\boldsymbol{\theta}}_N$ for $\boldsymbol{\theta}_0$ in an estimator for another population parameter, the information matrix in this case.

To use the empirical information estimator, remember that the population information function $\Im(\boldsymbol{\theta})$ is known only when the log-likelihood $L(\boldsymbol{\theta})$ is unconditional. This estimator is an empirical expectation like the other two when the log-likelihood is a conditional one. When the log-likelihood is conditional, as in $L_{\boldsymbol{\theta}}(\boldsymbol{\theta}; u \mid v)$, then only the conditional information function, given by

$$\Im(\boldsymbol{\theta}_0 \mid V) = \mathrm{E}[L_{\boldsymbol{\theta}}(\boldsymbol{\theta}_0; U \mid V) L_{\boldsymbol{\theta}}(\boldsymbol{\theta}_0; U \mid V)' \mid V]$$

---

[11] See (13.27) where the assumption of conditionally normally distributed data was dropped.

[12] See Exercise 15.6.

[13] For an example, see the mixture of a normal and a Cauchy distribution in the discussion of the existence of moments on p. 248.

is known. Because the marginal distribution of V is unspecified, $\Im(\boldsymbol{\theta})$ is unknown.[14] However, using the law of iterated expectations, we can also write

$$\Im(\boldsymbol{\theta}_0) = \mathrm{E}[\Im(\boldsymbol{\theta}_0 \mid V)]$$

Therefore, the empirical information matrix estimator must be $\mathrm{E}_N[\Im(\hat{\boldsymbol{\theta}}_N \mid V)]$ for conditional log-likelihood specifications. Just as we abbreviate the expectations of the log-likelihood function and its derivatives, we will typically abbreviate $\mathrm{E}_N[\Im(\hat{\boldsymbol{\theta}}_N \mid V)]$ with $\mathrm{E}_N[\Im(\hat{\boldsymbol{\theta}}_N)]$ as in the list above.

EXAMPLE 15.2 (Normal Linear Regression)

We have already compared $\mathrm{E}_N[-L_{\boldsymbol{\theta}\boldsymbol{\theta}}(\hat{\boldsymbol{\theta}}_N)]$ and $\mathrm{E}_N[\Im(\hat{\boldsymbol{\theta}}_N)]$ for the normal linear regression model (see Example 15.1) and found that they are equal. The empirical variance of the score has a different form:

$$\mathrm{Var}_N[L_{\boldsymbol{\theta}}(\hat{\boldsymbol{\theta}}_N)] = \begin{bmatrix} \frac{1}{\hat{\sigma}_N^4}\,\mathrm{E}_N[\mathbf{x}_n(y_n - \mathbf{x}_n'\hat{\boldsymbol{\beta}}_N)^2\mathbf{x}_n'] & \frac{1}{2\hat{\sigma}_N^6}\cdot \mathrm{E}_N[\mathbf{x}_n(y_n - \mathbf{x}_n'\hat{\boldsymbol{\beta}}_N)^3] \\ \bullet & \frac{1}{4\hat{\sigma}_N^8}\left\{\mathrm{E}_N[(y_n - \mathbf{x}_n'\hat{\boldsymbol{\beta}}_N)^4] - \hat{\sigma}_N^4\right\} \end{bmatrix}$$

This estimator uses fourth moments of the empirical distribution of the explanatory variables and the OLS fitted residuals that do not appear in the other estimators.

Proving the consistency of any of the three variance matrix estimators follows the lines of the proof of Lemma 15.6. Evaluated at a $\boldsymbol{\theta} \in \boldsymbol{\Theta}$, each estimator converges in probability uniformly to its expectation. Because $\hat{\boldsymbol{\theta}}_N \xrightarrow{p} \boldsymbol{\theta}_0$, evaluated at $\hat{\boldsymbol{\theta}}_N$ each estimator converges in probability to $\Im(\boldsymbol{\theta}_0)$. Because matrix inversion is a continuous transformation, the inverse of each matrix is also a consistent estimator for the variance matrix of the asymptotic distribution of $\sqrt{N}(\hat{\boldsymbol{\theta}}_N - \boldsymbol{\theta}_0)$.

A corollary to Proposition 16 follows from these information matrix estimators. Close examination of the proof on p. 327 reveals that we can substitute for $\mathrm{E}_N[-L_{\boldsymbol{\theta}\boldsymbol{\theta}}(\hat{\boldsymbol{\theta}}_N)]$ any matrix that converges in probability to the information matrix. As a result,

$$\mathrm{E}_N[-L_{\boldsymbol{\theta}\boldsymbol{\theta}}(\hat{\boldsymbol{\theta}}_N)]^{1/2}\sqrt{N}(\hat{\boldsymbol{\theta}}_N - \boldsymbol{\theta}_0)$$
$$\mathrm{Var}_N[L_{\boldsymbol{\theta}}(\hat{\boldsymbol{\theta}}_N)]^{1/2}\sqrt{N}(\hat{\boldsymbol{\theta}}_N - \boldsymbol{\theta}_0)$$

and

$$\mathrm{E}_N[\Im(\hat{\boldsymbol{\theta}}_N)]^{1/2}\sqrt{N}(\hat{\boldsymbol{\theta}}_N - \boldsymbol{\theta}_0)$$

are all asymptotically equivalent pivotal statistics and any of the three variance estimators is appropriate.

Using this corollary, we find that some of the properties of the normal distribution example carry over to general symmetric p.d.f.s.

[14] See Definition 31 (Conditional Information, p. 304) and the accompanying discussion.

EXAMPLE 15.3 (Symmetric Densities)

As in Example 14.24, let the conditional p.d.f. of y_n given $\mathbf{x}_n$ be $f(y_n - \mathbf{x}_n'\boldsymbol{\beta}_0, \boldsymbol{\gamma}_0)$ where $f(z, \boldsymbol{\gamma})$ is a symmetric function of z for all $\boldsymbol{\gamma}$. Example 14.24 showed that if it exists, the information matrix is block-diagonal in the terms for $\boldsymbol{\beta}$ and $\boldsymbol{\gamma}$. Because the population residuals, $y_n - \mathbf{x}_n'\boldsymbol{\beta}_0$, are i.i.d.,

$$L_{\boldsymbol{\beta}}(\boldsymbol{\theta}) = \mathbf{x}_n \frac{f'(y_n - \mathbf{x}_n'\boldsymbol{\beta}, \boldsymbol{\gamma})}{f(y_n - \mathbf{x}_n'\boldsymbol{\beta}, \boldsymbol{\gamma})} \quad \Rightarrow \quad \mathrm{Var}[L_{\boldsymbol{\beta}}(\boldsymbol{\theta}_0) \mid \mathbf{x}_n] = \omega_0^2 \cdot \mathbf{x}_n\mathbf{x}_n' \tag{15.7}$$

where

$$\omega_0^2 \equiv \omega^2(\boldsymbol{\gamma}_0) = \mathrm{Var}\left[\frac{f'(y_n - \mathbf{x}_n'\boldsymbol{\beta}_0, \boldsymbol{\gamma}_0)}{f(y_n - \mathbf{x}_n'\boldsymbol{\beta}_0, \boldsymbol{\gamma}_0)}\right]$$

Therefore we obtain the information matrix estimator

$$\mathrm{E}_N[\Im(\hat{\boldsymbol{\theta}}_N \mid \mathbf{x}_n)] = \begin{bmatrix} \omega^2(\hat{\gamma}_N) \cdot \mathrm{E}_N[\mathbf{x}_n\mathbf{x}_n'] & \mathbf{0} \\ \mathbf{0} & \Im_{\gamma\gamma}(\hat{\boldsymbol{\theta}}_N \mid \mathbf{x}_n) \end{bmatrix}$$

We discover that the nonlinear MLE for $\boldsymbol{\beta}_0$ still possesses an approximate variance matrix that is proportional to $(\mathbf{X}'\mathbf{X})^{-1}$. Furthermore, we can study the asymptotic relative efficiency loss of OLS versus ML by comparing only the variance of $y_n - \mathbf{x}_n'\boldsymbol{\beta}_0$ with $1/\omega_0^2$.

15.5 EFFICIENCY

Although many MLEs are biased, and therefore cannot be efficient, the approximate asymptotic distribution of the MLE exhibits no bias and the variance matrix of its asymptotic distribution equals the Cramér–Rao lower bound for unbiased estimators. Moreover, one can show that the MLE and the efficient (but infeasible) Cramér–Rao estimator are the same estimator asymptotically. Formally, this means that

$$\sqrt{N}(\hat{\boldsymbol{\theta}}_N - \boldsymbol{\theta}_0) - \sqrt{N}(\boldsymbol{\theta}^* - \boldsymbol{\theta}_0) = \sqrt{N}\left(\hat{\boldsymbol{\theta}}_N - \boldsymbol{\theta}^*\right) \xrightarrow{p} \mathbf{0}$$

so that the difference in the estimators converges to zero in probability. This is called *asymptotic equivalence*.

DEFINITION 35 (ASYMPTOTIC EQUIVALENCE) *Two estimators $\hat{\boldsymbol{\theta}}_{AN}$ and $\hat{\boldsymbol{\theta}}_{BN}$ are* asymptotically equivalent *if $\sqrt{N}\left(\hat{\boldsymbol{\theta}}_{AN} - \hat{\boldsymbol{\theta}}_{BN}\right) \xrightarrow{p} \mathbf{0}$.*

To see that $\hat{\boldsymbol{\theta}}_N$ and $\boldsymbol{\theta}^*$ are asymptotically equivalent, note that because

$$-\{\mathrm{E}_N[L_{\boldsymbol{\theta\theta}}(\bar{\boldsymbol{\theta}}_N)]\}^{-1} \xrightarrow{p} \Im(\boldsymbol{\theta}_0)^{-1}$$

and $\sqrt{N}\,\mathrm{E}_N[L_{\boldsymbol{\theta}}(\boldsymbol{\theta}_0)]$ converges in distribution,

$$\begin{aligned}\sqrt{N}(\hat{\boldsymbol{\theta}}_N - \boldsymbol{\theta}_0) - \sqrt{N}(\boldsymbol{\theta}^* - \boldsymbol{\theta}_0) &= \sqrt{N}(\hat{\boldsymbol{\theta}}_N - \boldsymbol{\theta}^*) \\ &= \left[-\{\mathrm{E}_N[L_{\boldsymbol{\theta\theta}}(\bar{\boldsymbol{\theta}}_N)]\}^{-1} - \Im(\boldsymbol{\theta}_0)^{-1}\right]\sqrt{N}\,\mathrm{E}_N[L_{\boldsymbol{\theta}}(\boldsymbol{\theta}_0)] \\ &\xrightarrow{p} \mathbf{0}\end{aligned}$$

using (14.31), (15.5) and the Slutsky lemma (Lemma 13.3, p. 261), and the equivalence of convergence in distribution to a constant and convergence in probability. Therefore, using the asymptotic approximation of its distribution that we derived above, the MLE is approximately efficient.

This sort of asymptotic equality, in which the difference between two statistics vanishes in the (probability) limit, occurs frequently in the asymptotic analysis of estimation. Here it enables us to find a feasible alternative to the Cramér–Rao estimator $\boldsymbol{\theta}^*$. In the next section, we will introduce additional estimators that are also asymptotically equal to $\boldsymbol{\theta}^*$. In fact, there is an infinite number of ways to reproduce $\boldsymbol{\theta}^*$ asymptotically and some of them create a technical ambiguity in the approximate relative efficiency of the MLE. For example, consider a modification to the MLE $\hat{\boldsymbol{\theta}}_N$ given by

$$\tilde{\boldsymbol{\theta}}_N = \begin{cases}\hat{\boldsymbol{\theta}}_N & \text{if} \quad N^{1/4}\left\|\hat{\boldsymbol{\theta}}_N - \boldsymbol{\theta}_1\right\| > 1 \\ \boldsymbol{\theta}_1 & \text{if} \quad N^{1/4}\left\|\hat{\boldsymbol{\theta}}_N - \boldsymbol{\theta}_1\right\| \leq 1\end{cases}$$

This estimator is like a "black hole," pulling $\tilde{\boldsymbol{\theta}}_N$ into the constant value $\boldsymbol{\theta}_1$ whenever $\hat{\boldsymbol{\theta}}_N$ is within an $N^{-1/4}$ neighborhood of $\boldsymbol{\theta}_1$. This perturbation of $\hat{\boldsymbol{\theta}}_N$ is negligible asymptotically if $\boldsymbol{\theta}_0 \neq \boldsymbol{\theta}_1$. The probability that $\hat{\boldsymbol{\theta}}_N$ falls into the black hole approaches zero as the probability that $\hat{\boldsymbol{\theta}}_N$ falls within a $N^{-1/2}$ neighborhood of $\boldsymbol{\theta}_0$ approaches one.

But if $\boldsymbol{\theta}_0 = \boldsymbol{\theta}_1$ then

$$\sqrt{N}\left(\tilde{\boldsymbol{\theta}}_N - \boldsymbol{\theta}_0\right) \xrightarrow{p} \mathbf{0}$$

essentially because the probability of falling inside the $N^{-1/4}$ neighborhood of $\boldsymbol{\theta}_1 = \boldsymbol{\theta}_0$ approaches one. The black hole occurs almost certainly so that $\tilde{\boldsymbol{\theta}}_N$ becomes the constant $\boldsymbol{\theta}_1 = \boldsymbol{\theta}_0$. Such an estimator is called *superefficient*. It is just as efficient as $\boldsymbol{\theta}^*$ if $\boldsymbol{\theta}_0 \neq \boldsymbol{\theta}_1$ and more efficient if $\boldsymbol{\theta}_0 = \boldsymbol{\theta}_1$.

Now $\tilde{\boldsymbol{\theta}}_N$ has no practical importance but one must take it into account to make a correct statement about the asymptotic relative efficiency of the MLE.[15] We must restrict the class of competing estimators to exclude the superefficient. One such class is the consistent and *uniformly* asymptotically normal (CUAN) estimators.

Definition 36 (CUAN Estimators) *An estimator $\hat{\boldsymbol{\theta}}$ for $\boldsymbol{\theta}_0$ is CUAN if $\hat{\boldsymbol{\theta}} \xrightarrow{p} \boldsymbol{\theta}_0$ and if $\sqrt{N}\left(\hat{\boldsymbol{\theta}} - \boldsymbol{\theta}_0\right)$ converges in distribution to a normal distribution uniformly over compact (closed and bounded) intervals of $\boldsymbol{\theta}$.*

[15] LeCam (1953) proves that the points of superefficiency must be countable.

The superefficient estimator $\tilde{\boldsymbol{\theta}}_N$ converges too rapidly at $\boldsymbol{\theta}_1 = \boldsymbol{\theta}_0$ to be CUAN. Rao (1963) proves that within the class of CUAN estimators, the MLE is efficient. His proof completes the proof of Part 3 of Proposition 16.

15.6 LINEARIZED MLE

There are also feasible, two-step versions of the Cramér–Rao estimator,

$$\boldsymbol{\theta}^* \equiv \boldsymbol{\theta}_0 + [\Im(\boldsymbol{\theta}_0)]^{-1}\,\mathrm{E}_N[L_{\boldsymbol{\theta}}(\boldsymbol{\theta}_0)] \tag{15.8}$$

Let $\check{\boldsymbol{\theta}}_N$ be an initial CUAN estimator and consider the empirical analogue

$$\hat{\boldsymbol{\theta}}_N^* = \check{\boldsymbol{\theta}}_N + \mathrm{E}_N[\Im(\check{\boldsymbol{\theta}}_N)]^{-1}\,\mathrm{E}_N[L_{\boldsymbol{\theta}}(\check{\boldsymbol{\theta}}_N)] \tag{15.9}$$

Such estimators are called *linearized maximum likelihood estimators* (LMLE).[16] They are also asymptotically efficient.

> **Lemma 15.7 (LMLE)** *Given the assumptions of Proposition 16 and a CUAN estimator $\check{\boldsymbol{\theta}}_N$ for $\boldsymbol{\theta}_0$, the LMLE in (15.9) is asymptotically equivalent to the Cramér–Rao estimator in the sense that*
>
> $$\sqrt{N}\left(\hat{\boldsymbol{\theta}}_N^* - \boldsymbol{\theta}^*\right) \xrightarrow{p} \mathbf{0}$$

See Section 15.8 for a proof. The linear approximation of the score in a neighborhood of $\boldsymbol{\theta}_0$ continues to play a central role in this asymptotic distribution theory. The restriction to CUAN estimators provides starting values close enough to $\boldsymbol{\theta}_0$ to make the linear approximation valid. Also note that the asymptotic theory permits us to substitute either of the other consistent information matrix estimators into (15.9), the empirical mean of the Hessian or the empirical variance of the score.[17]

In cases in which the information matrix is block-diagonal, the LMLE gives insight into the significance of the block-diagonality.

EXAMPLE 15.4 (Symmetric Densities)

As in Examples 14.24 and 15.3, suppose that the conditional p.d.f. of y_n given $\mathbf{x}_n$ is $f(y_n - \mathbf{x}_n'\boldsymbol{\beta}_0, \boldsymbol{\gamma}_0)$ where $f(z, \boldsymbol{\gamma})$ is a symmetric function of z for all $\boldsymbol{\gamma}$. The t distribution is a special case. Based on Example 15.3, a consistent information matrix estimator is

$$\mathrm{E}_N[\Im(\check{\boldsymbol{\theta}}_N \mid \mathbf{x}_n)] = \begin{bmatrix} \omega^2(\check{\boldsymbol{\gamma}}_N)\cdot \mathrm{E}_N[\mathbf{x}_n\mathbf{x}_n'] & \mathbf{0} \\ \mathbf{0} & \mathrm{E}_N[\Im_{\gamma\gamma}(\check{\boldsymbol{\theta}}_N \mid \mathbf{x}_n)] \end{bmatrix}$$

where

---

[16] Rothenberg and Leenders (1964) introduced this method to the econometrics literature.

[17] See Section 15.4.

$$\omega_0^2 \equiv \omega^2(\gamma_0) = \mathrm{Var}\left[\frac{f'(y_n - \mathbf{x}_n'\boldsymbol{\beta}_0, \gamma_0)}{f(y_n - \mathbf{x}_n'\boldsymbol{\beta}_0, \gamma_0)}\right]$$

and $\check{\boldsymbol{\theta}}_N$ is a CUAN estimator of $\boldsymbol{\theta}_0$. Using the score for $\boldsymbol{\beta}$ in (15.7), an LMLE for $\boldsymbol{\theta}_0$ is

$$\begin{bmatrix}\hat{\boldsymbol{\beta}}_N^* \\ \hat{\gamma}_N^*\end{bmatrix} = \begin{bmatrix}\check{\boldsymbol{\beta}}_N \\ \check{\gamma}_N\end{bmatrix} + \begin{bmatrix}\omega^{-2}(\check{\gamma}_N)\cdot(\mathrm{E}_N[\mathbf{x}_n\mathbf{x}_n'])^{-1}\,\mathrm{E}_N\left[\mathbf{x}_n\frac{f'(y_n-\mathbf{x}_n'\check{\boldsymbol{\beta}}_N,\check{\gamma}_N)}{f(y_n-\mathbf{x}_n'\check{\boldsymbol{\beta}}_N,\check{\gamma}_N)}\right] \\ \mathrm{E}_N[\Im_{\gamma\gamma}(\check{\boldsymbol{\theta}}_N\,|\,\mathbf{x}_n)]^{-1}\,\mathrm{E}_N[L_\gamma(\check{\boldsymbol{\theta}}_N\,|\,\mathbf{x}_n)]\end{bmatrix}$$

The block-diagonal information matrix prevents the score for γ from entering the LMLE for $\boldsymbol{\beta}_0$ (and vice versa).

As a result, we can simplify the LMLE for $\boldsymbol{\beta}_0$ to an OLS calculation:

$$\hat{\boldsymbol{\beta}}_N^* = (\mathbf{X}'\mathbf{X})^{-1}\mathbf{X}'\check{\mathbf{y}}_N$$

where

$$\check{\mathbf{y}}_N = \left[\mathbf{x}_n'\check{\boldsymbol{\beta}}_N + \frac{f'(y_n - \mathbf{x}_n'\check{\boldsymbol{\beta}}_N, \check{\gamma}_N)}{\omega^2(\check{\gamma}_N)\, f(y_n - \mathbf{x}_n'\check{\boldsymbol{\beta}}_N, \check{\gamma}_N)};\; n = 1, \ldots, N\right]'$$

Even if we use $\hat{\boldsymbol{\beta}}_{\text{OLS}}$ for $\check{\boldsymbol{\beta}}_N$, this formula shows the nonlinearity in $\mathbf{y}$ that nonnormal distributions introduce into an efficient estimator of the linear regression coefficients.

We can interpret the LMLE for $\boldsymbol{\beta}_0$ as the LMLE we would obtain if we knew γ_0 were equal to $\check{\gamma}_N$. Only the score and information terms associated with $\boldsymbol{\beta}$ appear in the estimator. The block-diagonality of the information matrix also implies that the asymptotic variance of the estimator is $\omega_0^{-2}\cdot(\mathrm{E}[\mathbf{x}_n\mathbf{x}_n'])^{-1}$. This is the asymptotic variance that we would obtain if we knew γ_0 and imposed the constraint $\gamma = \gamma_0$ in our MLE for $\boldsymbol{\beta}_0$. It is as though γ_0 and $\check{\gamma}_N$ were freely substitutable in the estimation of $\boldsymbol{\beta}_0$.

This is unexpected. In general, adding information about unknown parameters enables one to improve estimator efficiency for the parameters that remain unknown. Recall the comparison of the restricted and unrestricted estimators for $\boldsymbol{\beta}_0$ given the linear restrictions in the normal linear model: the restricted estimator is relatively efficient (Proposition 7, p. 183). These are examples of something much more general.

The ability to estimate parameters of interest such as $\boldsymbol{\beta}_0$ efficiently, with or without knowledge of other (nuisance) parameters such as γ_0, is an important statistical idea called *adaptive estimation*. Although adaptive estimation is not always possible, there are interesting cases in which it is. Adaptive estimation of $\boldsymbol{\beta}_0$ in the linear regression model with nonnormal symmetric p.d.f.s is an important example.

15.7 RESTRICTED ESTIMATION

In this section, we show that fewer parameters can generally be estimated more efficiently, when the restrictions imposed to reduce the number of parameters are correct. To see this as a general result, compare the restricted MLE with the unrestricted MLE in the special case in which $\boldsymbol{\theta} = [\boldsymbol{\theta}_1', \boldsymbol{\theta}_2']'$, $\boldsymbol{\Theta} = \boldsymbol{\Theta}_1 \times \boldsymbol{\Theta}_2$, and the parameter restrictions are $\boldsymbol{\theta}_2 = \mathbf{0}$. Note that the restricted MLE

$$\hat{\boldsymbol{\theta}}_R = \begin{bmatrix} \hat{\boldsymbol{\theta}}_{1\mathrm{R}} \\ \hat{\boldsymbol{\theta}}_{2\mathrm{R}} \end{bmatrix} = \begin{bmatrix} \operatorname{argmax}_{\boldsymbol{\theta}\in\boldsymbol{\Theta}:\boldsymbol{\theta}_2=\mathbf{0}} \mathrm{E}_N[L(\boldsymbol{\theta})] \\ \mathbf{0} \end{bmatrix}$$

has the asymptotic variance matrix

$$\mathbf{V}_{\mathrm{R}} = \begin{bmatrix} \Im_{11}(\boldsymbol{\theta}_0)^{-1} & \mathbf{0} \\ \mathbf{0} & \mathbf{0} \end{bmatrix}$$

Compared to the asymptotic variance of the unrestricted MLE, $\Im(\boldsymbol{\theta}_0)^{-1}$, the matrix $\mathbf{V}_{\mathrm{R}}$ is smaller in the positive semidefinite sense: this is demonstrated by

$$\Im(\boldsymbol{\theta}_0)\left[\Im(\boldsymbol{\theta}_0)^{-1} - \mathbf{V}_{\mathrm{R}}\right]\Im(\boldsymbol{\theta}_0) = \begin{bmatrix} \mathbf{0} & \mathbf{0} \\ \mathbf{0} & \Im_{22}(\boldsymbol{\theta}_0) - \Im_{21}(\boldsymbol{\theta}_0)\Im_{11}(\boldsymbol{\theta}_0)^{-1}\Im_{12}(\boldsymbol{\theta}_0) \end{bmatrix}$$

and the observation that the lower right-hand term is a conditional variance matrix. Thus, the most efficient restricted estimator is efficient relative to the most efficient unrestricted estimator.[18]

However, there are cases in which this efficiency ranking is not strict and the unrestricted estimator is also efficient relative to the restricted estimator. Consider the OLS $\hat{\boldsymbol{\beta}}_{\mathrm{R}}$ versus $\hat{\boldsymbol{\beta}}$ more closely:

EXAMPLE 15.5 (RLS)

Let $\mathrm{E}[\mathbf{y} \mid \mathbf{X}] = \mathbf{X}_1\boldsymbol{\beta}_{01} + \mathbf{X}_2\boldsymbol{\beta}_{02}$ and $\mathrm{Var}[\mathbf{y} \mid \mathbf{X}] = \sigma_0^2\cdot\mathbf{I}$ and let $\check{\boldsymbol{\beta}}_2 = \mathbf{Ay}$ be an initial unbiased estimator of $\boldsymbol{\beta}_{02}$. If $\boldsymbol{\beta}_{02}$ were known, then we would estimate $\boldsymbol{\beta}_{01}$ efficiently by using the RLS estimator

$$\hat{\boldsymbol{\beta}}_{\mathrm{R}1} = (\mathbf{X}_1'\mathbf{X}_1)^{-1}\mathbf{X}_1'(\mathbf{y} - \mathbf{X}_2\boldsymbol{\beta}_{02})$$

This estimator would have a conditional $\mathfrak{N}[\boldsymbol{\beta}_1, \sigma^2 \cdot (\mathbf{X}_1'\mathbf{X}_1)^{-1}]$ distribution. On the other hand, if we were to simply substitute our estimator for $\boldsymbol{\beta}_{02}$ into this estimator for $\boldsymbol{\beta}_{01}$, as in

$$\tilde{\boldsymbol{\beta}}_1 = (\mathbf{X}_1'\mathbf{X}_1)^{-1}\mathbf{X}_1'(\mathbf{y} - \mathbf{X}_2\check{\boldsymbol{\beta}}_2)$$

we would obtain a less efficient estimator. Because $\check{\boldsymbol{\beta}}_2$ is unbiased, this estimator would be unbiased and $\mathbf{AX}_1 = \mathbf{0}$. Its variance matrix is

$$\mathrm{Var}[\tilde{\boldsymbol{\beta}}_1 \mid \mathbf{X}] = \sigma_0^2 \cdot (\mathbf{X}_1'\mathbf{X}_1)^{-1} + \sigma_0^2 \cdot (\mathbf{X}_1'\mathbf{X}_1)^{-1}\mathbf{X}_1'\mathbf{X}_2\mathbf{AA}'\mathbf{X}_2'\mathbf{X}_1(\mathbf{X}_1'\mathbf{X}_1)^{-1}$$

which is larger than $\mathrm{Var}[\hat{\boldsymbol{\beta}}_{\mathrm{R}1}]$.

However, the two estimators are equivalent when the columns of $\mathbf{X}_1$ and $\mathbf{X}_2$ are orthogonal so that $\mathbf{X}_1'\mathbf{X}_2 = \mathbf{0}$. Then $\hat{\boldsymbol{\beta}}_{\mathrm{R}1}$ and $\tilde{\boldsymbol{\beta}}_1$ are identical. Any knowledge about $\boldsymbol{\beta}_{02}$ is irrelevant because it is unnecessary for estimation. A key sign of this is that the OLS fitting problem decomposes into two separate orthogonality conditions:

$$\mathbf{0} = \mathbf{X}'(\mathbf{y} - \mathbf{X}\hat{\boldsymbol{\beta}}) = \mathbf{X}'\mathbf{y} - \mathbf{X}'\mathbf{X}\hat{\boldsymbol{\beta}} = \begin{bmatrix} \mathbf{X}_1'\mathbf{y} - \mathbf{X}_1'\mathbf{X}_1\hat{\boldsymbol{\beta}}_1 \\ \mathbf{X}_2'\mathbf{y} - \mathbf{X}_2'\mathbf{X}_2\hat{\boldsymbol{\beta}}_2 \end{bmatrix}$$

Equivalently, the partial derivative matrix of the score is block-diagonal.

[18] See also Exercises 14.13 and 15.14.

The block-diagonality of the information matrix between parameters for the expectation vector and the nuisance parameters of a symmetric distribution (Example 15.4) is analogous to the orthogonality of $\mathbf{X}_1$ and $\mathbf{X}_2$ in this example. We also see this in one of the simplest cases: the log-likelihood for i.i.d. $\mathfrak{N}(\beta_0, \sigma_0^2)$ data.

EXAMPLE 15.6 (Normal Location)

The MLE for $\boldsymbol{\theta}_0 = (\beta_0, \sigma_0^2)$ given N observations in $\mathbf{y} \sim \mathfrak{N}(\beta_0 \cdot \boldsymbol{\iota},\ \sigma_0^2 \cdot \mathbf{I})$ is

$$\hat{\mu} = \bar{y} = \frac{\boldsymbol{\iota}'\mathbf{y}}{N}, \qquad \hat{\sigma}^2 = \frac{\mathbf{y}'(\mathbf{I} - \mathbf{P}_\iota)\mathbf{y}}{N-1}$$

We proved in Chapter 10 that these statistics are independently distributed for every sample size N. This independence appears in the information matrix. The score is

$$L_\mu(\boldsymbol{\theta}_0) = \frac{\boldsymbol{\iota}'\boldsymbol{\varepsilon}_0}{\sigma_0^2} \tag{15.10}$$

$$L_{\sigma^2}(\boldsymbol{\theta}_0) = -\frac{1}{2}\left(\frac{1}{\sigma_0^2} - \frac{\boldsymbol{\varepsilon}_0'\boldsymbol{\varepsilon}_0}{\sigma_0^4}\right) \tag{15.11}$$

where we denote $\boldsymbol{\varepsilon}_0 \equiv \mathbf{y} - \beta_0 \cdot \boldsymbol{\iota} \sim \mathfrak{N}(\mathbf{0},\ \sigma_0^2 \cdot \mathbf{I})$.[19] These two terms are uncorrelated because the first and third moments of a normal random variable with a zero expectation equal zero.[20]

The analogy with orthogonal $\mathbf{X}_1$ and $\mathbf{X}_2$ is not exact for a finite sample size N. Although the estimator of β_0 does not change with knowledge of σ_0^2, the MLE of σ_0^2 does change if we know β_0. Nevertheless, the analogy holds asymptotically. Knowledge of μ_0 does not change the asymptotic distribution of the MLE $\hat{\sigma}^2$. In the asymptotic limit, the score is a multivariate linear function within a shrinking neighborhood of $\boldsymbol{\theta}_0$. The partial derivative matrix of this linear function is minus the information matrix and when it is block-diagonal, solving the normal equations becomes two separate subproblems. Thus, the estimation of μ_0 and σ_0^2 become separate subproblems just as the estimation of β_{01} and β_{02} become separate in Example 15.5.

15.8 MATHEMATICAL NOTES

In these notes, we give two of the more technical proofs. First, we discuss the proof of Lemma 15.2. We illustrate the basic method of the proof in Figure 15.2 where we plot $Q_0(\boldsymbol{\theta})$ over a closed interval representing $\boldsymbol{\Theta}$ and a uniform δ-neighborhood of this function. The probability that $Q_N(\boldsymbol{\theta})$ is completely contained within this neighborhood approaches 1. Therefore, because $Q_N(\boldsymbol{\theta}_0)$ must exceed $Q_0(\boldsymbol{\theta}_0) - \delta$, the probability that $\hat{\boldsymbol{\theta}}_N$ is contained in the interval

$$(a(\delta), d(\delta)) \equiv \{\boldsymbol{\theta} \mid Q_0(\boldsymbol{\theta}_0) - \delta < Q_0(\boldsymbol{\theta}) + \delta\}$$

also approaches 1. Our intuition tells us that we can make these intervals around $\boldsymbol{\theta}_0$ as small as we like by choosing small enough δ, thereby establishing that $\hat{\boldsymbol{\theta}}_N$ is consistent.

---

19 These are simplifications of the equations in Example 14.11 (p. 294).

20 See Theorem D.8 (p. 887).

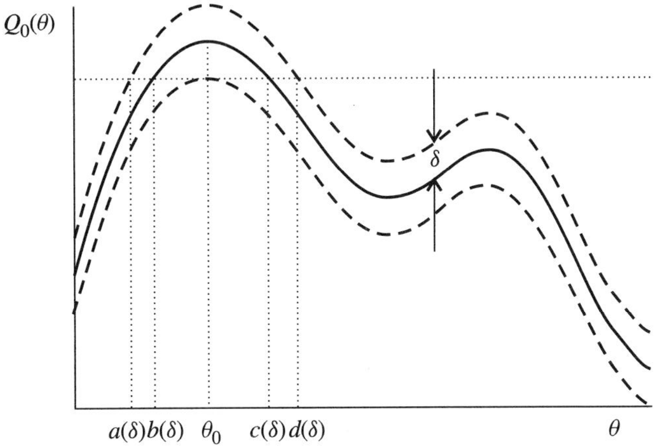

Figure 15.2 Convergence of the MLE.

To formalize this intuition, the proof actually considers narrower intervals:

$$\begin{aligned}(a(\delta/2), d(\delta/2)) &= \{\boldsymbol{\theta} \mid Q_0(\boldsymbol{\theta}_0) - \delta/2 < Q_0(\boldsymbol{\theta}) + \delta/2\} \\ &= \{\boldsymbol{\theta} \mid Q_0(\boldsymbol{\theta}_0) - \delta < Q_0(\boldsymbol{\theta})\} \\ &\equiv [b(\delta), c(\delta)]\end{aligned}$$

The probability that $\hat{\boldsymbol{\theta}}_N$ is within this interval also approaches 1 as N approaches infinity. Furthermore, if we set

$$\delta = \delta(\epsilon) \equiv Q(\boldsymbol{\theta}_0) - \max_{\|\boldsymbol{\theta}-\boldsymbol{\theta}_0\| \geq \epsilon} Q_0(\boldsymbol{\theta})$$

then

$$\begin{aligned}(b[\delta(\epsilon)], c[\delta(\epsilon)]) &= \{\boldsymbol{\theta} \mid Q_0(\boldsymbol{\theta}_0) - \delta(\epsilon) < Q_0(\boldsymbol{\theta})\} \\ &= \left\{\boldsymbol{\theta} \mid \max_{\|\boldsymbol{\theta}-\boldsymbol{\theta}_0\| \geq \epsilon} Q_0(\boldsymbol{\theta}) < Q_0(\boldsymbol{\theta})\right\} \\ &\subseteq \{\boldsymbol{\theta} \mid \|\boldsymbol{\theta} - \boldsymbol{\theta}_0\| < \epsilon\}\end{aligned}$$

By definition, $(b[\delta(\epsilon)], c[\delta(\epsilon)])$ excludes all elements of $\{\boldsymbol{\theta} \mid \|\boldsymbol{\theta} - \boldsymbol{\theta}_0\| \geq \epsilon\}$. Therefore,

$$\Pr\left\{\hat{\boldsymbol{\theta}}_N \in (b[\delta(\epsilon)], c[\delta(\epsilon)])\right\} \leq \Pr\left\{\left\|\hat{\boldsymbol{\theta}}_N - \boldsymbol{\theta}_0\right\| < \epsilon\right\}$$

and it follows that $\hat{\boldsymbol{\theta}}_N \xrightarrow{p} \boldsymbol{\theta}_0$.

Proof of Lemma 15.2 (Consistency of Maxima). We use essentially the same argument as Amemiya (1985) and Newey and McFadden (1994). According to Definition 33 (Uniform Convergence in Probability), if

$$\mathbb{A}_N \equiv \left\{Q_N(\boldsymbol{\theta}) \,\middle|\, \sup_{\boldsymbol{\theta}\in\Theta} |Q_N(\boldsymbol{\theta}) - Q_0(\boldsymbol{\theta})| < \delta/2\right\}$$

for any $\delta > 0$, then $\lim_{N\to\infty} \Pr\{\mathbb{A}_N\} = 1$. For all elements of $\mathbb{A}_N$,

$$Q_N(\hat{\boldsymbol{\theta}}_N) < Q_0(\hat{\boldsymbol{\theta}}_N) + \delta/2$$
$$Q_0(\boldsymbol{\theta}_0) - \delta/2 < Q_N(\boldsymbol{\theta}_0)$$

Putting these inequalities together with $Q_N(\boldsymbol{\theta}_0) \leq Q_N(\hat{\boldsymbol{\theta}}_N)$ (by definition of $\hat{\boldsymbol{\theta}}_N$),

$$Q_0(\boldsymbol{\theta}_0) - \delta/2 < Q_N(\hat{\boldsymbol{\theta}}_N) < Q_0(\hat{\boldsymbol{\theta}}_N) + \delta/2$$

so that

$$\lim_{N\to\infty} \Pr\{Q_0(\boldsymbol{\theta}_0) - \delta < Q_0(\hat{\boldsymbol{\theta}}_N)\} = 1 \tag{15.12}$$

Now we complete the argument by showing that this bound on function values translates into a bound on the distance between $\hat{\boldsymbol{\theta}}_N$ and $\boldsymbol{\theta}_0$. Let

$$\mathbb{B}(\boldsymbol{\theta}_0, \epsilon) \equiv \{\boldsymbol{\theta} \in \boldsymbol{\Theta} \mid \|\boldsymbol{\theta} - \boldsymbol{\theta}_0\| < \epsilon\}$$

be an open neighborhood of $\boldsymbol{\theta}_0$ for some $\epsilon > 0$. The complement of $\mathbb{B}(\boldsymbol{\theta}_0, \epsilon)$ in $\boldsymbol{\Theta}$, $\boldsymbol{\Theta} - \mathbb{B}(\boldsymbol{\theta}_0, \epsilon)$ is closed and bounded and $Q_0(\boldsymbol{\theta})$ is continuous on $\boldsymbol{\Theta}$ so that $\max_{\boldsymbol{\theta}\in\boldsymbol{\Theta}-\mathbf{B}(\boldsymbol{\theta}_0,\epsilon)} Q_0(\boldsymbol{\theta})$ exists. If

$$\delta(\epsilon) \equiv Q_0(\boldsymbol{\theta}_0) - \max_{\boldsymbol{\theta}\in\boldsymbol{\Theta}-\mathbb{B}(\boldsymbol{\theta}_0,\epsilon)} Q_0(\boldsymbol{\theta})$$

then the definition of $\boldsymbol{\theta}_0$ implies that $\delta(\epsilon) > 0$. Furthermore,

$$Q_0(\boldsymbol{\theta}_0) - \delta(\epsilon) < Q_0(\boldsymbol{\theta}) \qquad \Rightarrow \qquad \boldsymbol{\theta} \in \mathbb{B}(\boldsymbol{\theta}_0, \epsilon)$$

Therefore,

$$\Pr\{Q_0(\boldsymbol{\theta}_0) - \delta(\epsilon) < Q_0(\hat{\boldsymbol{\theta}}_N)\} \leq \Pr\{\hat{\boldsymbol{\theta}}_N \in \mathbb{B}(\boldsymbol{\theta}_0, \epsilon)\}$$

and, in the face of (15.12),

$$\lim_{N\to\infty} \Pr\{\hat{\boldsymbol{\theta}}_N \in \mathbb{B}(\boldsymbol{\theta}_0, \epsilon)\} = 1$$

Because this is true for any $\epsilon > 0$, $\hat{\boldsymbol{\theta}}_N \xrightarrow{p} \boldsymbol{\theta}_0$. □

It is tempting to say that we can make this interval arbitrarily small through the continuity of $Q_0(\boldsymbol{\theta})$ by decreasing δ, thereby proving that $\hat{\boldsymbol{\theta}}_N$ converges in probability to $\boldsymbol{\theta}_0$. But unfortunately, continuity implies bounds on $Q_0(\boldsymbol{\theta})$ from bounds on $\boldsymbol{\theta}$, not the reverse.[21]

The next proof shares some elements of the last one. In this case, the continuity of the limiting function g_0 does play a central role. But in this case the *convergence* of the arguments of the functions is an *hypothesis* of the lemma, not a *result*.

Proof of Lemma 15.5. According to the definition of continuity, for any $\epsilon > 0$ there is a δ such that

$$\|\boldsymbol{\theta}_N - \boldsymbol{\theta}_0\| < \delta \qquad \Rightarrow \qquad |g_0(\boldsymbol{\theta}_N) - g_0(\boldsymbol{\theta}_0)| < \epsilon/2$$

[21] Recall that a function $f(\cdot)$ is continuous at x_0 if $\lim_{\epsilon\to 0} f(x_0+\epsilon) = f(x_0)$: that is, if for every $\epsilon > 0$ there is a $\delta > 0$ such that $\|x - x_0\| < \delta$ *implies* $|f(x_0+\epsilon) - f(x_0)| < \epsilon$.

because g_0 is continuous. According to the definition of probability limits, the probability of the set

$$\mathbb{A}_N = \{(\boldsymbol{\theta}_N, g_N) \mid \|\boldsymbol{\theta}_N - \boldsymbol{\theta}_0\| < \delta\}$$

approaches 1 as $N \to \infty$ for any $\delta > 0$ because $\boldsymbol{\theta}_N \xrightarrow{p} \boldsymbol{\theta}_0$. Therefore, we can get $g_0(\boldsymbol{\theta}_0)$ as close to $g_0(\boldsymbol{\theta}_N)$ as we wish (in probability) for a large enough N.

The definition of uniform convergence in probability in (15.3) states that if

$$\mathbb{B}_N \equiv \left\{ (\boldsymbol{\theta}_N, g_N) \;\middle|\; \sup_{\boldsymbol{\theta} \in \boldsymbol{\Theta}} |g_N(\boldsymbol{\theta}) - g_0(\boldsymbol{\theta})| < \epsilon/2 \right\}$$

for any $\epsilon > 0$, then $\lim_{N\to\infty} \Pr\{\mathbb{B}_N\} = 1$. In particular, we can set $\boldsymbol{\theta} = \boldsymbol{\theta}_N \in \boldsymbol{\Theta}$ so that

$$|g_N(\boldsymbol{\theta}_N) - g_0(\boldsymbol{\theta}_N)| < \epsilon/2$$

for all $(\boldsymbol{\theta}_N, g_N) \in \mathbb{B}_N$. In words, the uniform convergence of g_N enables us to get $g_0(\boldsymbol{\theta}_N)$ arbitrarily close to $g_N(\boldsymbol{\theta}_N)$.

Because both $\boldsymbol{\theta}_N \xrightarrow{p} \boldsymbol{\theta}_0$ and $g_N \xrightarrow{p} g_0$ uniformly and

$$\lim_{N\to\infty} \Pr\{\mathbb{A}_N \cup \mathbb{B}_N\} \geq \lim_{N\to\infty} \Pr\{\mathbb{B}_N\} = 1$$

it follows that

$$\begin{aligned}\lim_{N\to\infty} \Pr\{\mathbb{A}_N \cap \mathbb{B}_N\} &= \lim_{N\to\infty} \Pr\{\mathbb{A}_N\} + \Pr\{\mathbb{B}_N\} - \Pr\{\mathbb{A}_N \cup \mathbb{B}_N\} \\ &= 1\end{aligned}$$

so that $\mathbb{A}_N \cap \mathbb{B}_N$ occurs asymptotically with a probability equal to one. Now we have already shown that for all $(\boldsymbol{\theta}_N, g_N) \in \mathbb{A}_N \cap \mathbb{B}_N$,

$$|g_0(\boldsymbol{\theta}_N) - g_0(\boldsymbol{\theta}_0)| < \epsilon/2, \;\; |g_N(\boldsymbol{\theta}_N) - g_0(\boldsymbol{\theta}_N)| < \epsilon/2$$

Applying the triangle inequality to these two inequalities,

$$|g_N(\boldsymbol{\theta}_N) - g_0(\boldsymbol{\theta}_0)| < \epsilon$$

for all $(\boldsymbol{\theta}_N, g_N) \in \mathbb{A}_N \cap \mathbb{B}_N$.[22] Therefore,

$$\lim_{N\to\infty} \Pr\{|g_N(\boldsymbol{\theta}_N) - g_0(\boldsymbol{\theta}_0)| < \epsilon\} = 1$$

and we have shown that $g_N(\boldsymbol{\theta}_N) \xrightarrow{p} g_0(\boldsymbol{\theta}_0)$. □

The proof of Lemma 15.7 is similar to the demonstration that the MLE $\hat{\boldsymbol{\theta}}_N$ and the Cramér–Rao estimator $\boldsymbol{\theta}^*$ are asymptotically equivalent in Section 15.5.

Proof of Lemma 15.7. A linear expansion of the score around $\boldsymbol{\theta}_0$ gives

$$\{\mathrm{E}_N[\Im(\check{\boldsymbol{\theta}}_N)]\}^{-1}\, \mathrm{E}_N[L_{\boldsymbol{\theta}}(\check{\boldsymbol{\theta}}_N)] = \{\mathrm{E}_N[\Im(\check{\boldsymbol{\theta}}_N)]\}^{-1} \big\{ \mathrm{E}_N[L_{\boldsymbol{\theta}}(\boldsymbol{\theta}_0)]$$

[22] See equation (C.6) (p. 856) regarding the triangle inequality.

$$+ \mathrm{E}_N[L_{\theta\theta}(\bar{\theta}_N)](\check{\theta}_N - \theta_0)\}$$

where $\bar{\theta}_N \xrightarrow{p} \theta_0$ also. Using the argument in Section 15.3.2,

$$\mathrm{E}_N[\Im(\check{\theta}_N)] \xrightarrow{p} \Im(\theta_0) \tag{15.13}$$

$$\mathrm{E}_N[L_{\theta\theta}(\bar{\theta}_N)] \xrightarrow{p} -\Im(\theta_0) \tag{15.14}$$

so that

$$\{\mathrm{E}_N[\Im(\check{\theta}_N)]\}^{-1}\,\mathrm{E}_N[L_{\theta\theta}(\bar{\theta}_N)] \xrightarrow{p} -\mathbf{I}_K \tag{15.15}$$

according to Lemma 13.2 (p. 261).

Therefore,

$$\begin{aligned}
\sqrt{N}\left(\hat{\theta}^*_N - \theta^*\right) &= \sqrt{N}\Big[\check{\theta}_N - \theta_0 - (\theta^* - \theta_0) \\
&\quad + \{\mathrm{E}_N[\Im(\check{\theta}_N)]\}^{-1}\Big\{\mathrm{E}_N[L_\theta(\theta_0)] + \mathrm{E}_N[L_{\theta\theta}(\bar{\theta}_N)]\left(\check{\theta}_N - \theta_0\right)\Big\}\Big] \\
&= \Big[I_K + \{\mathrm{E}_N[\Im(\check{\theta}_N)]\}^{-1}\,\mathrm{E}_N[L_{\theta\theta}(\bar{\theta}_N)]\Big]\sqrt{N}\left(\check{\theta}_N - \theta_0\right) \\
&\quad - \Big\{\sqrt{N}\,(\theta^* - \theta_0) - \{\mathrm{E}_N[\Im(\check{\theta}_N)]\}^{-1}\sqrt{N}\,\mathrm{E}_N[L_\theta(\theta_0)]\Big\} \\
&\xrightarrow{p} \mathbf{0}
\end{aligned}$$

where θ^* is the Cramér–Rao estimator. To see this, apply (15.15) and the Slutsky lemma (Lemma 13.3, p. 261) to the first term. For the second term, apply (15.8), (15.3), and the Slutsky lemma. Because both terms converge in distribution to zero, the lemma is proved. □

15.9 OVERVIEW

1. The MLE $\hat{\theta}_N$ is an implicit function of the data. One analyzes this estimator indirectly through the sample average log-likelihood function $\mathrm{E}_N[L(\theta)]$ and its derivatives $\mathrm{E}_N[L_\theta(\theta)]$ and $\mathrm{E}_N[L_{\theta\theta}(\theta)]$. For a fixed value of θ, all of these functions are averages of i.i.d. random variables when the data are i.i.d. As a result, such asymptotic laws as the LLN and the CLT can be applied to these functions, as opposed to $\hat{\theta}_N$ itself.
2. If

$$\mathrm{E}_N[L(\theta)] \xrightarrow{p} \mathrm{E}[L(\theta)] \quad \text{uniformly in } \theta$$

then

$$\hat{\theta}_N \equiv \operatorname*{argmax}_{\theta\in\Theta} \mathrm{E}_N[L(\theta)] \xrightarrow{p} \operatorname*{argmax}_{\theta\in\Theta} \mathrm{E}[L(\theta)] = \theta_0$$

so that $\hat{\theta}_N$ is a consistent estimator of θ_0. This result is analogous to the continuity of probability limits: if $g(\cdot)$ is continuous at U and $U_N \xrightarrow{p} U$ then $g(U_N) \xrightarrow{p} g(U)$.

3. Given the normal equations and the consistency of $\hat{\theta}$, the first-order approximation of the score

$$\begin{aligned}\mathbf{0} &= \sqrt{N}\,\mathrm{E}_N[L_{\boldsymbol\theta}(\hat{\boldsymbol\theta}_N)]\\ &\approx \sqrt{N}\,\mathrm{E}_N[L_{\boldsymbol\theta}(\boldsymbol\theta_0)] + \mathrm{E}_N[L_{\boldsymbol{\theta\theta}}(\boldsymbol\theta_0)]\,\sqrt{N}\left(\hat{\boldsymbol\theta}_N - \boldsymbol\theta_0\right)\end{aligned}$$

is accurate for large sample sizes N so that $\hat{\boldsymbol\theta}_N$ and

$$\boldsymbol\theta_0 + \mathrm{E}_N[-L_{\boldsymbol{\theta\theta}}(\boldsymbol\theta_0)]^{-1}\,\mathrm{E}_N[L_{\boldsymbol\theta}(\boldsymbol\theta_0)]$$

are asymptotically equivalent estimators of $\boldsymbol\theta_0$. We prove this using the exact (mean value) relationship

$$\mathbf{0} = \sqrt{N}\,\mathrm{E}_N[L_{\boldsymbol\theta}(\boldsymbol\theta_0)] + \mathrm{E}_N[L_{\boldsymbol{\theta\theta}}(\bar{\boldsymbol\theta}_N)]\,\sqrt{N}\left(\hat{\boldsymbol\theta}_N - \boldsymbol\theta_0\right)$$

where $\bar{\boldsymbol\theta}_N$ is intermediate to $\boldsymbol\theta_0$ and $\hat{\boldsymbol\theta}_N$.
   (a) $\sqrt{N}\,\mathrm{E}_N[L_{\boldsymbol\theta}(\boldsymbol\theta_0)]$ converges in distribution to the $\mathfrak{N}[\mathbf{0}, \mathfrak{I}(\boldsymbol\theta_0)]$ distribution according to a central limit theorem.
   (b) $\mathrm{E}_N[-L_{\boldsymbol{\theta\theta}}(\bar{\boldsymbol\theta}_N)]$ converges in probability to $\mathfrak{I}(\boldsymbol\theta_0)$ according to a law of large numbers.
   (c) As a result, as $N \to \infty$, $\sqrt{N}(\hat{\boldsymbol\theta} - \boldsymbol\theta_0) \xrightarrow{d} \mathfrak{I}(\boldsymbol\theta_0)^{-1}\mathfrak{N}[\mathbf{0}, \mathfrak{I}(\boldsymbol\theta_0)] \sim \mathfrak{N}[\mathbf{0}, \mathfrak{I}(\boldsymbol\theta_0)^{-1}]$.

4. In application, we treat the $\hat{\boldsymbol\theta}_N$ as normally distributed with an expected value equal to $\boldsymbol\theta_0$ and a variance matrix equal to the inverse of an estimator of the information matrix. Three popular information estimators are the Hessian of the sample log-likelihood function $N \cdot \mathrm{E}_N[-L_{\boldsymbol{\theta\theta}}(\hat{\boldsymbol\theta}_N)]$, the sample variance of the score $N \cdot \mathrm{Var}_N[L_{\boldsymbol\theta}(\hat{\boldsymbol\theta}_N)]$, and the sample information $N \cdot \mathrm{E}_N[\mathfrak{I}(\hat{\boldsymbol\theta}_N)]$, each evaluated at the estimator $\hat{\boldsymbol\theta}_N$.
5. The MLE $\hat{\boldsymbol\theta}_N$ is also asymptotically efficient because its asymptotic variance matrix equals the Cramér–Rao lower bound. More than this, the MLE and the efficient, but infeasible, Cramér–Rao estimator

$$\boldsymbol\theta^* = \boldsymbol\theta_0 + \mathfrak{I}(\boldsymbol\theta_0)^{-1}\,\mathrm{E}_N[L_{\boldsymbol\theta}(\boldsymbol\theta_0)]$$

   are asymptotically equivalent: $\sqrt{N}(\hat{\boldsymbol\theta}_N - \boldsymbol\theta^*) \xrightarrow{p} \mathbf{0}$.
6. The LMLE, which is a feasible version of the Cramér–Rao estimator

$$\hat{\boldsymbol\theta}^*_N = \check{\boldsymbol\theta}_N + \mathrm{E}_N[\mathfrak{I}(\check{\boldsymbol\theta}_N)]^{-1}\,\mathrm{E}_N[L_{\boldsymbol\theta}(\check{\boldsymbol\theta}_N)]$$

   is also asymptotically equivalent to the Cramér–Rao estimator provided that $\check{\boldsymbol\theta}_N$ is a CUAN estimator of $\boldsymbol\theta_0$. We can also substitute $\mathrm{E}_N[-L_{\boldsymbol{\theta\theta}}(\hat{\boldsymbol\theta}_N)]$ or $\mathrm{Var}_N[L_{\boldsymbol\theta}(\hat{\boldsymbol\theta}_N)]$ into the LMLE for the empirical information term.
7. Fewer parameters can generally be estimated more efficiently, when the restrictions imposed to reduce the number of parameters are correct. If, however, the information matrix is block-diagonal in restricted versus unrestricted parameters then the restricted and unrestricted MLEs for the unrestricted parameters will be asymptotically equivalent.

It is unfortunate that this asymptotic theory rests on the assumption that the parameter space is compact. Researchers who use the approximations must know the boundaries of the parameter space before they can proceed. In practice, this requirement is generally ignored. In special cases, the assumption can be dropped. For example, if the log-likelihood function is globally concave, then the same results are obtained without compactness of $\boldsymbol\Theta$.[23] On the other hand, the boundaries can be arbitrarily large. When researchers find that their computations of the MLE lead to unexpected parameter estimates with large absolute values, this usually suggests some misspecification of the model. We take up computation of the MLE in Chapter 16.

---

23 For example, see Newey and McFadden (1994, Theorem 2.7, p. 2133).

15.10 EXERCISES

15.10.1 Review

15.1 (Dominance) Show that Assumption 14.2 (Dominance I) is satisfied by the log-likelihood function for the $\mathfrak{N}(\mu, \sigma^2)$ distribution if the parameter space $\boldsymbol{\Theta}$ is bounded and closed, provided that the parameter space bounds σ^2 below by a strictly positive number.

15.2 (Normality) The MLE for (μ, σ^2) in the $\mathfrak{N}(\mu, \sigma^2)$ probability model is

$$\hat{\mu}_N = \mathrm{E}_N[U] \qquad \text{and} \qquad \hat{\sigma}_N^2 = \mathrm{E}_N[(U - \hat{\mu}_N)^2]$$

Show how the asymptotic distribution of $\sqrt{N}(\hat{\sigma}_N^2 - \sigma_0^2)$ differs with and without the normality assumption. Suppose that sampling is always i.i.d. and that all the moments of U exist.

15.3 Use the results of this chapter to state conditions such that the LAD estimator is a consistent MLE for Example 14.10.

15.4 (Symmetric Densities) In such specifications as Example 15.3, we may not know the functional form of

$$\omega^2(\boldsymbol{\gamma}_0) \equiv \omega_0 = \mathrm{Var}\left[\frac{f'(y_n - \mathbf{x}_n'\boldsymbol{\beta}_0, \boldsymbol{\gamma}_0)}{f(y_n - \mathbf{x}_n'\boldsymbol{\beta}_0, \boldsymbol{\gamma}_0)}\right]$$

Describe conditions such that

$$\hat{\omega}_N^2 = \mathrm{Var}_N\left[\frac{f'(y_n - \mathbf{x}_n'\hat{\boldsymbol{\beta}}_N, \hat{\boldsymbol{\gamma}}_N)}{f(y_n - \mathbf{x}_n'\hat{\boldsymbol{\beta}}_N, \hat{\boldsymbol{\gamma}}_N)}\right]$$

is a consistent estimator of ω_0^2. How would one use this estimator for inference about $\boldsymbol{\beta}_0$?

15.5 (Information Estimation) Confirm the expression given for the information matrix estimator $\mathrm{Var}_N[L_{\boldsymbol{\theta}}(\hat{\boldsymbol{\theta}}_N)]$ in Example 15.2. [HINT: Use the normal equations in (14.8) and (14.9) to simplify.]

15.6 (CLT) Show that the p.d.f. of a chi-square random variable with ν degrees of freedom, standardized by its mean and standard deviation, converges to the p.d.f. of the standard normal distribution. Also show how this result relates to the asymptotic distribution of the MLE of the variance in the $\mathfrak{N}(\mu, \sigma^2)$ distribution.

15.7 (MLE for Uniform) If the random variable U has the uniform distribution with parameter θ_0, then its p.d.f. is $\mathbf{1}\{0 \le U \le \theta_0\}$. Given a sample of N realizations $\{U_1, \ldots, U_N\}$, the MLE for θ_0 is the largest observed value $\hat{\theta}_N = U_{(N)}$.

(a) Find the p.d.f. of $\hat{\theta}_N$. [HINT: Use (13.9).]

(b) Show that the mean and variance of $\hat{\theta}_N$ are $N/(N+1)\theta_0$ and $\{N/[(2+N)(N+1)^2]\}\theta_0^2$.

(c) Is $\hat{\theta}_N$ consistent? How could you correct the bias in $\hat{\theta}_N$?

(d) How would you standardize $\hat{\theta}_N$ to find an asymptotic approximation to its distribution?

(e) Show that the limiting distribution of your standardized statistic is an exponential distribution.

15.8 (LMLE) Suggest some explanations for large differences (relative to the estimated sampling variances) between the MLE and some LMLE.

15.10.2 Extensions

15.9 (Identification) Explain why Assumption 14.3 (Likelihood Identification, p. 296) does not imply that the information matrix is positive definite, provided that the information matrix exists. (HINT: Is a negative definite Hessian a necessary condition for a local optimum?)

15.10 (Consistency) Suppose that $Q_N(\boldsymbol{\theta}) \xrightarrow{p} Q_0(\boldsymbol{\theta})$ for all $\boldsymbol{\theta} \in \mathbb{R}^K$ and that $Q_0(\boldsymbol{\theta})$ is uniquely maximized at $\boldsymbol{\theta}_0$. Also suppose that $Q_N(\boldsymbol{\theta})$ is strictly concave. Using the following steps, show that compactness of the parameter space can be dropped as an assumption if the objective function is concave.

(a) Show that $Q_N(\boldsymbol{\theta})$ is continuous.

(b) Show that $Q_0(\boldsymbol{\theta})$ is also concave (and therefore continuous).

(c) Because $Q_N(\boldsymbol{\theta})$ is concave and $Q_N(\boldsymbol{\theta}) \xrightarrow{p} Q_0(\boldsymbol{\theta})$, it follows that $Q_N(\boldsymbol{\theta}) \xrightarrow{p} Q_0(\boldsymbol{\theta})$ uniformly on any compact subset of $\mathbb{R}^K$.[24] Use this result to show that

$$\hat{\boldsymbol{\theta}}_N \equiv \underset{\theta}{\operatorname{argmax}}\, Q_N(\boldsymbol{\theta})$$

exists with probability one and converges in probability to $\boldsymbol{\theta}_0$:[25]

i. for $\delta > 0$ and $\mathbb{C} \equiv \{\boldsymbol{\theta} \in \mathbb{R}^K \mid \|\boldsymbol{\theta} - \boldsymbol{\theta}_0\| \le \delta\}$,

$$\tilde{\boldsymbol{\theta}}_N \equiv \underset{\boldsymbol{\theta}\in\mathbb{C}}{\operatorname{argmax}}\, Q_N(\boldsymbol{\theta}) \xrightarrow{p} \boldsymbol{\theta}_0$$

ii. and for the boundary $\mathbb{B}$ of $\mathbb{C}$,

$$\lim_{N\to\infty} \Pr\left\{Q_N(\tilde{\boldsymbol{\theta}}_N) > \max_{\boldsymbol{\theta}\in\mathbb{B}} Q_N(\boldsymbol{\theta})\right\} = 1$$

iii. so that the concavity of $Q_N(\boldsymbol{\theta})$ implies that

$$\lim_{N\to\infty} \Pr\left\{Q_N(\tilde{\boldsymbol{\theta}}_N) > Q_N(\boldsymbol{\theta})\right\} = 1$$

for any $\theta \notin \mathbb{C}$.

iv. Now apply Lemma 15.2 to a compact set containing $\boldsymbol{\theta}_0$ to complete the proof.

15.11 (LAD) Let $(y_n, \mathbf{x}_n)$ satisfy Assumptions 13.1 and 13.2 (p. 257) and suppose that the *conditional median* of y_n given $\mathbf{x}_n$ is $\mathbf{x}_n'\boldsymbol{\beta}_0$. Prove that the LAD estimator is a consistent estimator of $\boldsymbol{\beta}_0$ using the following steps.

(a) Show that if the median μ_0 of the random variable Z is unique, then

$$\mathrm{E}[|Z - \mu|] = \mathrm{E}[|Z - \mu_0|] + (\mu_0 - \mu)\,[1 - 2\Pr\{Z \le \mu\}]$$

and

$$\mu_0 = \underset{\mu}{\operatorname{argmin}}\, \mathrm{E}[|Z - \mu|]$$

(b) Use this result to show that $\boldsymbol{\beta}_0$ is the unique solution to

$$\min_{\boldsymbol{\beta}} \mathrm{E}\left[\left|y_n - \mathbf{x}_n'\boldsymbol{\beta}\right|\right]$$

---

24 See Andersen and Gill (1982).

25 This development follows Newey and Powell (1987, Lemma A) and Newey and McFadden (1994, pp. 2133–2134).

(c) Combine this with Exercise 15.10 to prove that

$$\hat{\boldsymbol{\beta}}_{\text{LAD}} \equiv \underset{\boldsymbol{\beta}}{\operatorname{argmin}} \sum_{n=1}^{N} \left| y_n - \mathbf{x}_n' \boldsymbol{\beta} \right| \xrightarrow{p} \boldsymbol{\beta}_0$$

15.12 (Superefficiency) Suppose the $\sqrt{N}(\hat{\boldsymbol{\theta}}_N - \boldsymbol{\theta}_0) \xrightarrow{d} \mathfrak{N}(\mathbf{0}, \mathbf{V})$ where $\mathbf{V}$ is a nonsingular variance matrix. Now consider another estimator

$$\tilde{\boldsymbol{\theta}}_N \equiv \begin{cases} \hat{\boldsymbol{\theta}}_N & \text{if } N^{\delta} \left\| \hat{\boldsymbol{\theta}}_N - \boldsymbol{\theta}_1 \right\| > 1 \\ \boldsymbol{\theta}_1 & \text{if } N^{\delta} \left\| \hat{\boldsymbol{\theta}}_N - \boldsymbol{\theta}_1 \right\| \leq 1 \end{cases}$$

for some $\delta \in (0, \frac{1}{2})$. The estimator $\tilde{\boldsymbol{\theta}}_N$ is an example of a *superefficient* estimator: show that $\sqrt{N}(\tilde{\boldsymbol{\theta}}_N - \hat{\boldsymbol{\theta}}_N) \xrightarrow{p} 0$ if $\boldsymbol{\theta}_0 \neq \boldsymbol{\theta}_1$ but that $\sqrt{N}(\tilde{\boldsymbol{\theta}}_N - \boldsymbol{\theta}_0) \xrightarrow{p} \mathbf{0}$ if $\boldsymbol{\theta}_0 = \boldsymbol{\theta}_1$.

15.13 (Superefficiency) Let $\hat{\theta}_N$ be the sample mean of realizations from an $\mathfrak{N}(\mu_0, 1)$ population and let

$$\tilde{\theta}_N \equiv \begin{cases} \hat{\theta}_N & \text{if } \left|\hat{\theta}_N\right| > N^{-\delta} \\ 0 & \text{if } \left|\hat{\theta}_N\right| \leq N^{-\delta} \end{cases}$$

where $0 < \delta < 1/2$ so that $\tilde{\theta}_N$ is superefficient when $\mu_0 = 0$ (Exercise 15.12). Show that the reduction in MSE for μ_0 near zero is balanced by an increase in MSE at points a moderate distance away by studying the case in which $\mu_0 = N^{-\delta}$.

***15.14 (Restricted ML)** Compare the MLE

$$\hat{\boldsymbol{\theta}} \equiv \underset{\boldsymbol{\theta} \in \boldsymbol{\Theta}}{\operatorname{argmax}}\, \mathrm{E}_N[L(\boldsymbol{\theta})]$$

with the restricted MLE

$$\hat{\boldsymbol{\theta}}_R \equiv \underset{\boldsymbol{\theta} \in \boldsymbol{\Theta}: \boldsymbol{\theta}_2 = \boldsymbol{\theta}_{02}}{\operatorname{argmax}}\, \mathrm{E}_N[L(\boldsymbol{\theta})]$$

when $\boldsymbol{\theta}_0 = (\boldsymbol{\theta}_{01}, \boldsymbol{\theta}_{02})$ where $\boldsymbol{\theta}_{02}$ is an M-dimensional subvector of $\boldsymbol{\theta} \in \mathbb{R}^K$ and $\boldsymbol{\theta}_{02}$ is known.

(a) Show that $\hat{\boldsymbol{\theta}}_{\text{R}}$ is efficient relative to $\hat{\boldsymbol{\theta}}$ asymptotically. In other words, $\sqrt{N}(\hat{\boldsymbol{\theta}}_{\text{R}} - \boldsymbol{\theta}_0) \xrightarrow{d} \mathfrak{N}(\mathbf{0}, \mathbf{V}_{\text{R}})$ and $\sqrt{N}(\hat{\boldsymbol{\theta}} - \boldsymbol{\theta}_0) \xrightarrow{d} \mathfrak{N}(\mathbf{0}, \mathbf{V})$ and $\mathbf{V} - \mathbf{V}_{\text{R}}$ is positive semidefinite. (HINT: Use Exercise 14.13.)

(b) Show the stronger result that the joint asymptotic distribution of $\hat{\boldsymbol{\theta}}_{\text{R}}$ and $\hat{\boldsymbol{\theta}}$ is

$$\sqrt{N}\begin{bmatrix} \hat{\boldsymbol{\theta}}_{\text{R}} - \boldsymbol{\theta}_0 \\ \hat{\boldsymbol{\theta}} - \boldsymbol{\theta}_0 \end{bmatrix} \xrightarrow{d} \mathfrak{N}\left(\begin{bmatrix} \mathbf{0} \\ \mathbf{0} \end{bmatrix}, \begin{bmatrix} \mathbf{V}_{\text{R}} & \mathbf{V}_{\text{R}} \\ \mathbf{V}_{\text{R}} & \mathbf{V} \end{bmatrix} \right)$$

15.15 (Quadratic Approximation) Consider the approximation of the log-likelihood function $\mathrm{E}_N[L(\boldsymbol{\theta})]$ within a shrinking neighborhood of the population parameter vector $\boldsymbol{\theta}_0$: let $\boldsymbol{\theta} = \boldsymbol{\theta}_0 + \boldsymbol{\delta}/\sqrt{N}$. Suppose that the data are i.i.d., $\boldsymbol{\theta}_0$ is identified, $L(\boldsymbol{\theta})$ is twice continuously differentiable, the information matrix $\mathfrak{I}(\boldsymbol{\theta}_0)$ exists and is nonsingular, and $\mathrm{E}_N[L_{\boldsymbol{\theta}\boldsymbol{\theta}}(\boldsymbol{\theta})]$ converges uniformly in $\boldsymbol{\theta}$ to its expectation.

(a) Show that

$$\mathrm{E}_N[L(\boldsymbol{\theta}) - L(\boldsymbol{\theta}_0)] - \left(\left[\sqrt{N}\,\mathrm{E}_N[L_{\boldsymbol{\theta}}(\boldsymbol{\theta}_0)]\right]'\boldsymbol{\delta} - \frac{1}{2}\boldsymbol{\delta}'\Im(\boldsymbol{\theta}_0)\boldsymbol{\delta}\right) \xrightarrow{p} 0$$

so that

$$\mathrm{E}_N[L(\boldsymbol{\theta})] \approx \mathrm{E}_N[L(\boldsymbol{\theta}_0)] + \left[\sqrt{N}\,\mathrm{E}_N[L_{\boldsymbol{\theta}}(\boldsymbol{\theta}_0)]\right]'\boldsymbol{\delta} - \frac{1}{2}\boldsymbol{\delta}'\Im(\boldsymbol{\theta}_0)\boldsymbol{\delta} \tag{15.16}$$

(b) Show that the maximum of the RHS of (15.16) is

$$\boldsymbol{\delta}^* = \Im(\boldsymbol{\theta}_0)^{-1}\sqrt{N}\,\mathrm{E}_N[L_{\boldsymbol{\theta}}(\boldsymbol{\theta}_0)]$$

or

$$\boldsymbol{\theta}^* = \boldsymbol{\theta}_0 + \Im(\boldsymbol{\theta}_0)^{-1}\,\mathrm{E}_N[L_{\boldsymbol{\theta}}(\boldsymbol{\theta}_0)]$$

15.16 (Restricted LMLE) Let the conditions of Proposition 15.7 (LMLE, p. 333) hold. Partition the parameter vector $\boldsymbol{\theta} = [\boldsymbol{\theta}_1', \boldsymbol{\theta}_2']'$.

(a) What is the LMLE subject to the restrictions $\boldsymbol{\theta}_2 = \mathbf{0}$?

(b) Generalize your estimator to nonlinear restrictions of the form $\boldsymbol{\theta}_2 = \mathbf{s}(\boldsymbol{\theta}_1)$.

(c) Consider general restrictions $\mathbf{r}(\boldsymbol{\theta}) = \mathbf{0}$. Working by analogy to the RLS coefficients

$$\hat{\boldsymbol{\beta}}_{\mathrm{R}} = \hat{\boldsymbol{\beta}} - (\mathbf{X}'\mathbf{X})^{-1}\mathbf{R}'\left[\mathbf{R}(\mathbf{X}'\mathbf{X})^{-1}\mathbf{R}'\right]^{-1}\left(\mathbf{R}\hat{\boldsymbol{\beta}} - \mathbf{r}\right)$$

from (4.21), consider

$$\hat{\boldsymbol{\theta}}_{\mathrm{R}}^* = \hat{\boldsymbol{\theta}} - \Im(\hat{\boldsymbol{\theta}})^{-1}\mathbf{r}_\theta(\hat{\boldsymbol{\theta}})'\left[\mathbf{r}_\theta(\hat{\boldsymbol{\theta}})\Im(\hat{\boldsymbol{\theta}})^{-1}\mathbf{r}_\theta(\hat{\boldsymbol{\theta}})'\right]^{-1}\mathbf{r}(\hat{\boldsymbol{\theta}}) \tag{15.17}$$

where $\hat{\boldsymbol{\theta}}$ is the unrestricted MLE. Show that $\hat{\boldsymbol{\theta}}_{\mathrm{R}}^*$ is asymptotically equivalent to $\hat{\boldsymbol{\theta}}_{\mathrm{R}}$ using an asymptotic argument parallel to the one in Exercise 4.15. Does $\hat{\boldsymbol{\theta}}_{\mathrm{R}}^*$ satisfy the restrictions exactly?

(d) Suppose the restrictions take the form $\boldsymbol{\theta} = \mathbf{s}(\boldsymbol{\gamma})$ where $\mathbf{s} : \mathbb{R}^M \to \mathbb{R}^K$ gives a lower dimensional $(M < K)$ parameterization of the likelihood function. What LMLE could you use in this case?

***15.17 (Restricted LMLE)** Suppose that $\check{\boldsymbol{\theta}}$ is a $\sqrt{N}$-consistent estimator of $\boldsymbol{\theta}_0$. Derive a restricted LMLE for $\boldsymbol{\theta}_2 = \mathbf{0}$ based on a quadratic approximation to the *unrestricted* log-likelihood function.

(a) That is, let

$$Q(\boldsymbol{\theta}) \equiv \mathrm{E}_N[L(\check{\boldsymbol{\theta}})] + \mathrm{E}_N[L_{\boldsymbol{\theta}}(\check{\boldsymbol{\theta}})]'\left(\boldsymbol{\theta} - \check{\boldsymbol{\theta}}\right) - \frac{1}{2}\left(\boldsymbol{\theta} - \check{\boldsymbol{\theta}}\right)'\mathrm{E}_N[\Im(\check{\boldsymbol{\theta}})]\left(\boldsymbol{\theta} - \check{\boldsymbol{\theta}}\right)$$

and show that

$$\check{\boldsymbol{\theta}}_1 - \mathrm{E}_N[\Im_{11}(\check{\boldsymbol{\theta}})]^{-1}\left(\mathrm{E}_N[L_1(\check{\boldsymbol{\theta}})] - \mathrm{E}_N[\Im_{12}(\check{\boldsymbol{\theta}})]\check{\boldsymbol{\theta}}_2\right) = \underset{\boldsymbol{\theta}\in\boldsymbol{\Theta}}{\operatorname{argmax}}\, Q(\boldsymbol{\theta})$$

[HINT: Use Lemma 7.10 (Partitioned Quadratic II, p. 147).]

(b) What differences exist between this restricted LMLE and the conventional one?

(c) Show that this estimator is asymptotically equivalent to $\hat{\boldsymbol{\theta}}_{\mathrm{R}}$ under the usual assumptions. [HINT: Use a linear approximation to $\mathrm{E}_N[L_1(\check{\boldsymbol{\theta}})]$ around $\boldsymbol{\theta}_0$.]

(d) How does this LMLE simplify when $\check{\boldsymbol{\theta}} = \hat{\boldsymbol{\theta}}$, the unrestricted MLE?

***15.18 (Parameter Space Boundary)** The normal distribution is a special case of the Student t distribution, approached in the limit as the degrees of freedom approach infinity.[26] Let us reparameterize the distribution in Example 14.3 in terms of the reciprocal of the degrees of freedom parameter $\alpha = \nu^{-1}$,

$$f(y \mid \mu, \alpha, \sigma) \equiv \frac{\Gamma[(\nu+1)/2]}{\Gamma(\nu/2)} \frac{1}{\sqrt{\pi \nu \sigma^2}} \left[1 + \frac{(y-\mu)^2}{\nu \sigma^2}\right]^{-(\nu+1)/2}$$

and define

$$\begin{aligned} f(y \mid \mu, 0, \sigma) &\equiv \lim_{\alpha \to 0} f(y \mid \mu, \alpha, \sigma) \\ &= \frac{1}{\sqrt{2\pi\sigma^2}} \exp\left[-\frac{(y-\mu)^2}{2\sigma^2}\right] \end{aligned}$$

We require $\sigma \geq 0$ and $\alpha \geq 0$. Therefore the normal distribution occurs on a boundary of the parameter space.

(a) Use[27]

$$\begin{aligned} \left.\frac{\partial \log f(y \mid \mu, \alpha, \sigma)}{\partial \alpha}\right|_{\alpha=0} &= \lim_{\alpha \to 0} \frac{\partial \log f(y \mid \mu, \alpha, \sigma)}{\partial \alpha} \\ &= -\frac{1}{4} + \frac{(y-\mu)^2}{4\sigma^4}\left[(y-\mu)^2 - 2\sigma^2\right] \end{aligned}$$

to show that the restricted ($\alpha = 0$) and the unrestricted MLEs of the population parameter vector $\boldsymbol{\theta}_0 = \left[\beta_0', \sigma_0, \alpha_0\right]'$ will coincide with positive probability if $\alpha_0 = 0$.

(b) Use this phenomenon to argue that the unrestricted MLE cannot be approximately normally distributed.

[26] Viewed as a chi-square mixture of normal distributions (p. 248), the mixing distribution of $\sigma^2 = \gamma^2(\nu/\chi_\nu^2)$ approaches the constant γ^2 because $\chi_\nu^2/\nu \xrightarrow{p} 1$ as $\nu \to \infty$. To confirm this, note that $\mathrm{E}[\chi_\nu^2] = \nu$ and $\mathrm{Var}[\chi_\nu^2] = 2\nu$ so that $\mathrm{E}[\chi_\nu^2/\nu] = 1$ and $\mathrm{Var}[\chi_\nu^2/\nu] = 2/\nu \to 0$ as $\nu \to \infty$.

[27] You are also welcome to confirm this limit.

CHAPTER 16

MAXIMUM LIKELIHOOD COMPUTATION

16.1 INTRODUCTION

Often, direct computation of the MLE is not possible. General numerical methods for computing of maximum likelihood estimators are necessary. This chapter gives an overview of such methods, all of which are iterative algorithms that search for the maximum of a function of several arguments.

At the outset of this discussion it should be understood that the mathematical program of maximizing an arbitrary function numerically on a computer does not have a solution that is both reliable and feasible. Such phenomena as multiple local maxima, discontinuities, numerical instability, and large dimension are common practical problems. Computers and computer programs are finite machines with limits of speed, reliability, and accuracy. Thus, experience remains useful in the implementation of any method.

We reestimated the log-wage regression, specifying that the distribution of the log-wage conditional on the RHS variables possessed the Student t_ν p.d.f. with the usual linear mean.[1] The sample log-likelihood function is

$$L(\boldsymbol{\theta}; \mathbf{y} \mid \mathbf{X}) = -\frac{N}{2}\log(\pi\nu\sigma^2) - \frac{\nu+1}{2}\sum_{n=1}^{N}\log\left[1 + \frac{(y_n - \mathbf{x}_n'\boldsymbol{\beta})^2}{\nu\sigma^2}\right] + N\left[\log\Gamma\left(\frac{\nu+1}{2}\right) - \log\Gamma\left(\frac{\nu}{2}\right)\right] \quad (16.1)$$

We reparameterized $\gamma = \nu\sigma^2$ for analytical simplicity and we used the Newton–Raphson algorithm described below to compute the values of $(\boldsymbol{\beta}, \gamma, \nu)$ that numerically maximize this log-likelihood function. The values are reported in Table 16.1, along with the OLS and LAD estimates that we calculated earlier. The regression slope coefficients continue to be qualitatively the same. The estimated degrees of freedom parameter $\hat{\nu}$ is quite small (6.331 with an estimated

[1] Lange et al. (1989) explore such statistical regression models. See their references for earlier uses of the Student t_ν distribution. Geweke (1993) applies this model with Bayesian techniques to some well-known macroeconomic time series. He finds evidence in favor of the Student t_ν distribution with degrees of freedom in the range of 3 to 7.

Table 16.1
OLS, Student *t*, and LAD Fits for Log-Wage

RHS Variable	Estimated Coefficient[a] OLS	Student *t*	LAD
Constant (one)	0.779 (0.075)	0.711 (0.072)	0.639 (0.077)
Female	−0.242 (0.026)	−0.256 (0.024)	−0.273 (0.027)
Nonwhite	−0.131 (0.036)	−0.116 (0.034)	−0.095 (0.037)
Union member	0.173 (0.036)	0.161 (0.038)	0.157 (0.037)
Education	0.095 (0.0048)	0.100 (0.0043)	0.106 (0.0050)
Experience	0.039 (0.0039)	0.040 (0.0037)	0.039 (0.0040)
(Experience)^2	−0.00063 (0.000089)	−0.00064 (0.000080)	−0.00061 (0.000091)
$\gamma = \nu\sigma^2$	n.a.	0.934 (0.198)	n.a.
ν	n.a.	6.330 (1.015)	n.a.

[a]The numbers in parentheses are estimates of standard errors. n.a., not applicable.

standard error of 1.015) compared to what might be expected for near normal data (say, greater than 30). The estimated standard errors were computed using the sample variance matrix of the scores, $\mathrm{Var}_N[L_{\boldsymbol{\theta}}(\hat{\boldsymbol{\theta}}_N)]$. Although the estimated standard errors are close to those estimated for OLS, those for the Student *t* specification are almost all lower than the OLS standard errors. This is consistent with a small gain in estimation efficiency derived from accounting for fat tails.

To introduce computational issues, we will begin with the simplest and crudest method: calculating the values of a function over a grid of values and searching for local maxima over those values. This introduces two basic issues, that computing a maximum requires iterative search and that searching in high-dimensional spaces is difficult.

To cope with many dimensions, we explain *search directions* and *line searches* along them. Typical search directions depend on the derivatives, or *gradient*, of the objective function to be maximized. The first search direction that we introduce, called *steepest ascent*, is the direction in which the objective function is increasing most rapidly.

Although steepest ascent is appealing, search directions based on the Hessian, as well as the gradient, of the objective function tend to work better. We cover many of the search directions based on both under the general framework of quadratic approximations to the objective function. In this framework, there are many points of contact with the asymptotic distribution theory of the maximum likelihood estimator. In particular, the linearized maximum likelihood estimator (LMLE) is closely related to widely used search directions.

Besides choosing a search direction, computation of the MLE involves several other decisions. In Section 16.5, *Convergence Criteria*, we discuss numerical rules for stopping the iterative calculations. We describe the role that transformations of the parameters can play in Section 16.6. This also motivates our coverage of the asymptotic distribution theory for transformations of the

MLE. Finally, we explain two useful techniques that can be combined with quadratic optimization methods: *concentrating* the likelihood function and the *Gauss–Seidel algorithm*.

16.2 GRID SEARCH

A simple and reliable method for finding roots of nonlinear equations and maxima of functions over closed intervals is a grid search. This method provides a quick illustration of the kinds of problems that arise. In a one-dimensional maximization problem

$$\max_{\theta \in [a,b]} Q(\theta)$$

the interval $[a, b]$ can be divided into a number of subintervals,

$$\{[a, \theta_1], [\theta_1, \theta_2], \ldots, [\theta_n, b]\}$$

and, after computing the function value at each boundary, infer that the maximum lies in one of the intervals with a boundary that includes the highest function value:

$$\{[\theta_i, \theta_{i+1}] \mid \max_j Q(\theta_j) = \max[Q(\theta_i), Q(\theta_{i+1})]\}$$

One then repeats the process in each of the chosen subintervals, as though they were the original interval. Such repetition is called *iteration*. The process will yield smaller and smaller intervals that contain local maxima so that arbitrary precision can be obtained for the critical value.

But for some problems this method is woefully inadequate for finding the global maximum. We can mistakenly drop the interval that contains the global maximum if the grid is insufficiently fine, even though the function is continuous. On the other hand, if we choose many, short subintervals at each iteration, then each iteration becomes more costly in computational time because so many more function evaluations and comparisons are necessary. An exhaustive search is infeasible because that requires an infinite amount of calculation. In a multidimensional setting, these two problems are compounded by a third: the grid search must cover every dimension so that calculations increase exponentially with the dimension of the parameter vector. If one chooses n intervals on each of k dimensions, one has on the order of n^k function calculations per iteration.

However, if more is known about the function Q, one can make adjustments. For example, if Q is differentiable and its first derivative is bounded $\|Q_\theta\| < M$, then the subintervals can be chosen in such a way that no local maxima are missed. Clearly, such information about the function will be very helpful to the econometrician searching for the MLE as well.

16.3 POLYNOMIAL APPROXIMATION

One popular way to exploit differentiability of the maximand Q is approximation with a polynomial. The optimum of the polynomial approximant is an approximation to the optimum of Q. The simplest such approximation is a quadratic function

$$Q(\theta) \approx a + b(\theta - \theta_0) + \frac{1}{2}c\,(\theta - \theta_0)^2$$

where a, b, and c are chosen to fit Q well in a neighborhood of the starting value θ_0. Given values for a, b, and c, the approximant to the location of the optimum of Q is $-b/c$, $c < 0$. There are several ways to choose such parameters. When Q is differentiable, a second-order Taylor series yields a quadratic approximation based on Q and its first two derivatives:[2]

$$Q(\theta) \approx Q(\theta_0) + Q_\theta(\theta_0)(\theta - \theta_0) + \frac{1}{2} Q_{\theta\theta}(\theta_0)\,(\theta - \theta_0)^2$$

Another approach is to choose a, b, and c to fit three points where Q has already been computed:

$$Q(\theta_0) = a + b\theta_0 + \frac{1}{2}c\theta_0^2$$

$$Q(\theta_1) = a + b\theta_1 + \frac{1}{2}c\theta_1^2$$

$$Q(\theta_2) = a + b\theta_2 + \frac{1}{2}c\theta_2^2$$

EXAMPLE 16.1

To illustrate with a simple analytical and graphic example, suppose we use the second-order Taylor series to approximate the local optimum of a sine function with a quadratic. At θ_0,

$$Q(\theta_0) = \sin\,\theta_0$$

$$Q_\theta(\theta_0) = \cos\,\theta_0$$

$$Q_{\theta\theta}(\theta_0) = -\sin\,\theta_0$$

yielding the approximation

$$Q(\theta) \approx \sin\,\theta_0 + (\theta - \theta_0)\cos\,\theta_0 - \frac{1}{2}(\theta - \theta_0)^2 \sin\,\theta_0$$

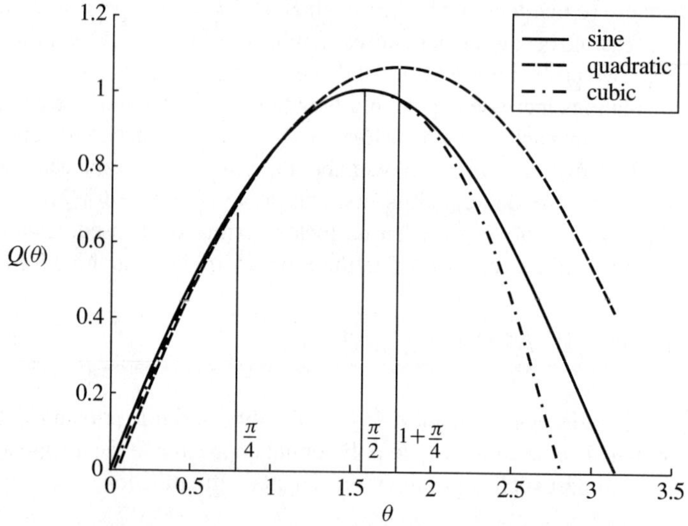

Figure 16.1 Approximation of sine by quadratic and cubic polynomials.

[2] See Taylor's approximation (Theorem D.18, p. 898).

At $\theta_0 = \pi/4$, $\sin\theta_0 = \cos\theta_0 = 1/\sqrt{2}$ so that the optimum of the quadratic approximation occurs at $\theta = 1 + \pi/4$, which overshoots the exact optimum at $\pi/2$. Nevertheless, $\sin(1 + \pi/4) \approx 0.977$, which exceeds the starting value $1/\sqrt{2} \approx 0.707$. The sine function and this quadratic approximation are shown in Figure 16.1.

EXAMPLE 16.2

Although the sine function does increase at the approximate optimum $1+\pi/4$, we can refine the approximation using the new information that $Q(1+\pi/4) = 0.977$ by approximating Q with a cubic polynomial

$$Q(\theta) \approx a + b(\theta - \theta_0) + \frac{1}{2}c\,(\theta - \theta_0)^2 + \frac{1}{6}d(\theta - \theta_0)^3$$

If we retain the requirements that this approximant and its first two derivatives coincide with Q and its first two derivatives at $\theta_0 = \pi/4$, then the quadratic terms retain their values in the previous example: $a = b = -c = 1/\sqrt{2}$. The parameter d is chosen to equate the cubic approximant and Q at $\theta = 1 + \pi/4$: $d = 6 \cdot [\sin(1+\pi/4) - (a + b + c/2)]$. Using ordinary calculus, we find the maximum of this approximant at θ equal to

$$\theta_0 - \frac{c + \sqrt{c^2 - 2db}}{d} \approx 1.5681$$

which is quite close to the true optimum at $\pi/2 \approx 1.5708$. This cubic approximant is also shown in Figure 16.1.

16.4 LINE SEARCHES

A general approach to overcoming the high dimension of maximization problems is the *line search*, a grid search in one dimension through a parameter space with several dimensions. Given a starting point $\boldsymbol{\theta}_1$ and a *search direction* (or "line") $\boldsymbol{\delta}$, an iteration attempts to solve the *one-dimensional* problem

$$\lambda^* = \underset{\lambda}{\operatorname{argmax}}\; Q(\boldsymbol{\theta}_1 + \lambda \cdot \boldsymbol{\delta}) \tag{16.2}$$

The scalar parameter λ is called the *step length*. The starting point for the next iteration becomes

$$\boldsymbol{\theta}_2 = \boldsymbol{\theta}_1 + \lambda^* \cdot \boldsymbol{\delta} \tag{16.3}$$

the optimal value of $\boldsymbol{\theta}$ along the search direction $\boldsymbol{\delta}$ starting at $\boldsymbol{\theta}_1$. Methods that employ line searches differ according to the choice of $\boldsymbol{\delta}$ and the method of approximating λ^*. We will describe several methods for choosing $\boldsymbol{\delta}$.

By convention, we will restrict $\lambda \geq 0$. Because the *directional derivative* of Q is

$$\frac{\partial Q(\boldsymbol{\theta}_1 + \lambda \cdot \boldsymbol{\delta})}{\partial \lambda} = Q_{\boldsymbol{\theta}}(\boldsymbol{\theta}_1 + \lambda \cdot \boldsymbol{\delta})'\boldsymbol{\delta}$$

all line search methods require

$$\left.\frac{\partial Q(\boldsymbol{\theta}_1 + \lambda \cdot \boldsymbol{\delta})}{\partial \lambda}\right|_{\lambda=0} = Q_{\boldsymbol{\theta}}(\boldsymbol{\theta}_1)'\boldsymbol{\delta} > 0 \tag{16.4}$$

so that Q is increasing with respect to the step length λ in a neighborhood of the starting value $\boldsymbol{\theta}_1$. Thus, a positive value of λ that increases Q will always exist.

Figures 16.2 and 16.3 illustrate a line search reducing a two-dimensional problem to a one-dimensional problem. The white line in Figure 16.2 traces the surface of the function along a line in the parameter space. The induced function of λ, $Q(\boldsymbol{\theta}_1 + \lambda \cdot \boldsymbol{\delta})$, is pictured in Figure 16.3. The point marked by 0 on the λ-axis represents the starting point $\boldsymbol{\theta}_1$ and a vector running from this point to the point marked by 1 on the λ-axis is the direction $\boldsymbol{\delta}$ in the parameter space.

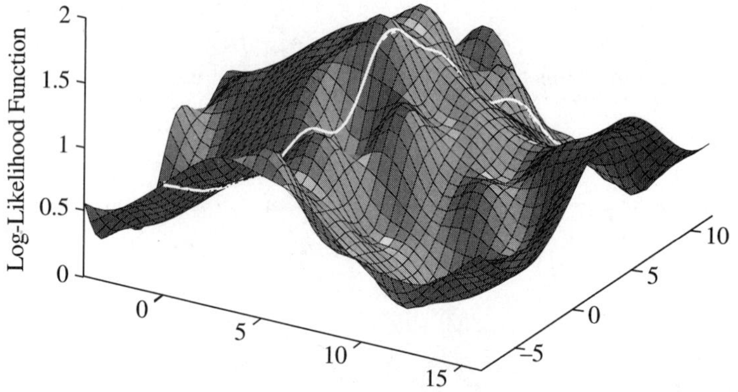

Figure 16.2 Line search in a two-dimensional parameter space.

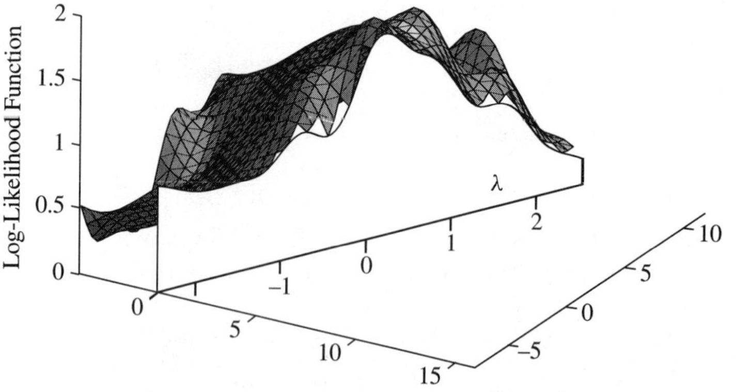

Figure 16.3 Log-likelihood function in step length.

16.4.1 The Method of Steepest Ascent

Perhaps the most obvious direction to search for a local maximum of any function is to follow the *gradient*, or vector of first partial derivatives, of the function. To do this, set $\boldsymbol{\delta} = Q_{\boldsymbol{\theta}}(\boldsymbol{\theta}_1)$. By definition, the elements of the gradient are the rates of change in the function for a small *ceteris paribus* change in each element of $\boldsymbol{\theta}$. As a vector, this search direction guarantees that the function value will improve if the entire vector $\boldsymbol{\theta}$ is moved in that direction (at least locally):

$$\left.\frac{\partial Q[\boldsymbol{\theta}_1 + \lambda \cdot Q_{\boldsymbol{\theta}}(\boldsymbol{\theta}_1)]}{\partial \lambda}\right|_{\lambda=0} = Q_{\boldsymbol{\theta}}(\boldsymbol{\theta}_1)' Q_{\boldsymbol{\theta}}(\boldsymbol{\theta}_1) > 0$$

unless $\boldsymbol{\theta}_1$ is a critical value of Q.

The gradient also has a local optimality property. Among all directions with the same length, setting $\boldsymbol{\delta} = Q_{\boldsymbol{\theta}}(\boldsymbol{\theta}_1)$ gives the fastest rate of increase of $Q(\boldsymbol{\theta}_1 + \lambda \cdot \boldsymbol{\delta})$ with respect to λ:

$$Q_{\boldsymbol{\theta}}(\boldsymbol{\theta}_1) = \underset{\{\boldsymbol{\delta}:\|\boldsymbol{\delta}\| = \|Q_{\boldsymbol{\theta}}(\boldsymbol{\theta}_1)\|\}}{\operatorname{argmax}} \frac{\partial Q(\boldsymbol{\theta}_1 + \lambda \cdot \boldsymbol{\delta})}{\partial \lambda}$$

This is a fundamental property of the gradient.[3] A related property is that the gradient is the normal vector to all the directions of $\boldsymbol{\theta}$ that leave Q constant: given any search direction $\boldsymbol{\delta}$ so that Q is locally constant,

$$\begin{aligned} Q(\boldsymbol{\theta}_1 + \lambda \cdot \boldsymbol{\delta}) = c \qquad \Leftrightarrow \qquad 0 &= \left.\frac{\partial Q(\boldsymbol{\theta}_1 + \lambda \cdot \boldsymbol{\delta})}{\partial \lambda}\right|_{\lambda=0} \\ &= \boldsymbol{\delta}' Q_{\boldsymbol{\theta}}(\boldsymbol{\theta}_1) \end{aligned}$$

In words, the gradient $Q_{\boldsymbol{\theta}}(\boldsymbol{\theta}_1)$ is orthogonal to the direction $\boldsymbol{\delta}$ of the level set of the function as pictured in a contour plot. In a local sense, this orthogonality is an optimum distance condition.

The method of steepest ascent implicitly approximates the maximand $Q(\boldsymbol{\theta})$ as a *linear* function in the neighborhood of $\boldsymbol{\theta}_1$:

$$Q(\boldsymbol{\theta}) \approx Q(\boldsymbol{\theta}_1) + Q_{\boldsymbol{\theta}}(\boldsymbol{\theta}_1)'(\boldsymbol{\theta} - \boldsymbol{\theta}_1)$$

As a result, the method provides a search direction $\boldsymbol{\delta}$, but no guidance for the step length λ. Linear functions do not have local maxima and they are more appropriate for approximating such systems of equations as first-order conditions. Maximization involves the curvature of a function. But steepest ascent does not exploit curvature, making it a relatively slow algorithm for many practical problems.

---

[3] A direct proof uses the Cauchy–Schwarz inequality (Lemma C.1, p. 852). According to (16.4),

$$\left.\frac{\partial Q(\boldsymbol{\theta}_1 + \lambda \cdot \boldsymbol{\delta})}{\partial \lambda}\right|_{\lambda=0} = \boldsymbol{\delta}' Q_{\boldsymbol{\theta}}(\boldsymbol{\theta}_1) \le \|\boldsymbol{\delta}\| \cdot \|Q_{\boldsymbol{\theta}}(\boldsymbol{\theta}_1)\|$$

This upperbound is attained only if $\boldsymbol{\delta} = a \cdot Q_{\boldsymbol{\theta}}(\boldsymbol{\theta}_1)$, $a > 0$: in that case,

$$\boldsymbol{\delta}' Q_{\boldsymbol{\theta}}(\boldsymbol{\theta}_1) = a \, \|Q_{\boldsymbol{\theta}}(\boldsymbol{\theta}_1)\|^2$$

The constraint $\|\boldsymbol{\delta}\| = \|Q_{\boldsymbol{\theta}}(\boldsymbol{\theta}_1)\|$ implies that $a = \pm 1$. Therefore the largest value of $\boldsymbol{\delta}' Q_{\boldsymbol{\theta}}(\boldsymbol{\theta}_1)$ occurs at $a = 1$ so that the optimal $\boldsymbol{\delta}$ equals $Q_{\boldsymbol{\theta}}(\boldsymbol{\theta}_1)$.

EXAMPLE 16.3 (OLS)

Let us apply steepest ascent to the OLS problem

$$\max_{\boldsymbol{\beta}} -\frac{1}{2}(\mathbf{y}-\mathbf{X}\boldsymbol{\beta})'(\mathbf{y}-\mathbf{X}\boldsymbol{\beta})$$

where $\boldsymbol{\theta} = \boldsymbol{\beta}$ and $Q(\boldsymbol{\beta}) = -\frac{1}{2}(\mathbf{y}-\mathbf{X}\boldsymbol{\beta})'(\mathbf{y}-\mathbf{X}\boldsymbol{\beta})$. On the ith iteration, let the starting point be denoted $\boldsymbol{\beta}_i$ so that $\boldsymbol{\delta}_i = \mathbf{X}'(\mathbf{y}-\mathbf{X}\boldsymbol{\beta}_i)$ and each line search solves

$$\begin{aligned}
\lambda_i &= \operatorname*{argmax}_{\lambda} -\frac{1}{2}[\mathbf{y}-\mathbf{X}(\boldsymbol{\beta}_i+\lambda\cdot\boldsymbol{\delta}_i)]'[\mathbf{y}-\mathbf{X}(\boldsymbol{\beta}_i+\lambda\cdot\boldsymbol{\delta}_i)] \\
&= \operatorname*{argmax}_{\lambda} \left[\boldsymbol{\delta}_i'\mathbf{X}'(\mathbf{y}-\mathbf{X}\boldsymbol{\beta}_i)\right]\lambda - \frac{1}{2}\left[\boldsymbol{\delta}_i'\mathbf{X}'\mathbf{X}\boldsymbol{\delta}_i\right]\lambda^2 \\
&= \frac{\boldsymbol{\delta}_i'\mathbf{X}'(\mathbf{y}-\mathbf{X}\boldsymbol{\beta}_i)}{\boldsymbol{\delta}_i'\mathbf{X}'\mathbf{X}\boldsymbol{\delta}_i} \\
&= \frac{\boldsymbol{\delta}_i'\boldsymbol{\delta}_i}{\boldsymbol{\delta}_i'\mathbf{X}'\mathbf{X}\boldsymbol{\delta}_i}
\end{aligned}$$

and the best step yields

$$\boldsymbol{\beta}_{i+1} = \boldsymbol{\beta}_i + \lambda_i\cdot\boldsymbol{\delta}_i = \boldsymbol{\beta}_i + \frac{(\mathbf{y}-\mathbf{X}\boldsymbol{\beta}_i)'\mathbf{X}\mathbf{X}'(\mathbf{y}-\mathbf{X}\boldsymbol{\beta}_i)}{(\mathbf{y}-\mathbf{X}\boldsymbol{\beta}_i)'\mathbf{X}\mathbf{X}'\mathbf{X}\mathbf{X}'(\mathbf{y}-\mathbf{X}\boldsymbol{\beta}_i)}\cdot\mathbf{X}'(\mathbf{y}-\mathbf{X}\boldsymbol{\beta}_i)$$

Figure 16.4 illustrates what this path looks like in a two-dimensional case. Each $\boldsymbol{\delta}_i$ is orthogonal to an elliptical level set and $\boldsymbol{\beta}_{i+1}$ occurs at a tangency between the ray $\boldsymbol{\beta} = \boldsymbol{\beta}_i + \lambda\cdot\boldsymbol{\delta}_i$ and a higher elliptical level set.

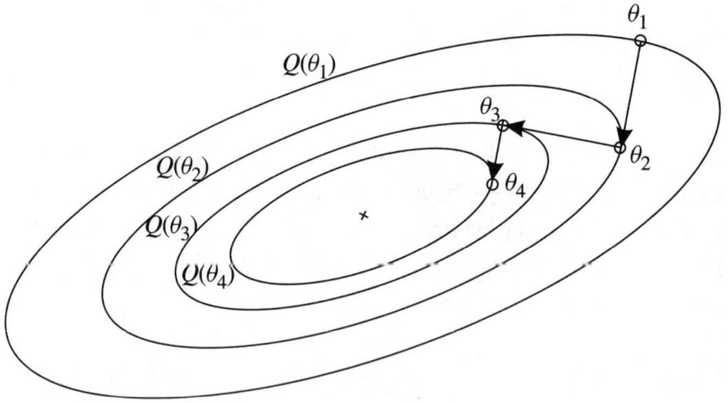

Figure 16.4 Optimization by steepest ascent: path on a quadratic function.

All of the remaining methods for choosing $\boldsymbol{\delta}$ that we will consider rest on quadratic approximations to Q, a more natural family of approximants because concave quadratic functions have simple maxima.

16.4.2 Quadratic Methods

Let us begin our discussion of quadratic optimization methods with a review of functions that are exactly quadratic. First, recall that if Q is a quadratic function then Q has the functional form

$$Q(\boldsymbol{\theta}) = a + \mathbf{b}'\boldsymbol{\theta} + \frac{1}{2}\boldsymbol{\theta}'\mathbf{C}\boldsymbol{\theta} \tag{16.5}$$

Because the first and second partial derivatives are

$$Q_{\boldsymbol{\theta}}(\boldsymbol{\theta}) = \mathbf{b} + \mathbf{C}\boldsymbol{\theta} \tag{16.6}$$

$$Q_{\boldsymbol{\theta}\boldsymbol{\theta}}(\boldsymbol{\theta}) = \mathbf{C} \tag{16.7}$$

the matrix $\mathbf{C}$ is the Hessian. The Hessian $\mathbf{C}$ is negative definite if Q is strictly concave. In that case, Q attains its maximum at

$$\boldsymbol{\theta}^* = -\mathbf{C}^{-1}\mathbf{b}$$

the value of $\boldsymbol{\theta}$ that uniquely solves the first-order conditions $Q_{\boldsymbol{\theta}}(\boldsymbol{\theta}^*) = \mathbf{0}$. It is always possible to rewrite (16.5) as

$$\begin{aligned} Q(\boldsymbol{\theta}) &= a + b'\boldsymbol{\theta} + \frac{1}{2}\boldsymbol{\theta}'C\boldsymbol{\theta} \\ &= a + \boldsymbol{\theta}^{*\prime}\mathbf{C}\boldsymbol{\theta} + \frac{1}{2}\boldsymbol{\theta}'\mathbf{C}\boldsymbol{\theta} + \frac{1}{2}\boldsymbol{\theta}^{*\prime}\mathbf{C}\boldsymbol{\theta}^* - \frac{1}{2}\boldsymbol{\theta}^{*\prime}\mathbf{C}\boldsymbol{\theta}^* \\ &= a - \frac{1}{2}\boldsymbol{\theta}^{*\prime}\mathbf{C}\boldsymbol{\theta}^* + \frac{1}{2}(\boldsymbol{\theta} - \boldsymbol{\theta}^*)'\mathbf{C}(\boldsymbol{\theta} - \boldsymbol{\theta}^*) \end{aligned}$$

to display the optimality of $\boldsymbol{\theta}^*$.

We have just seen that strictly concave quadratic functions are relatively easy to maximize. In addition, we can characterize $\boldsymbol{\theta}^*$ in terms of the first and second partial derivatives of Q at any parameter value $\boldsymbol{\theta}_1$:

$$\begin{aligned} \boldsymbol{\theta}^* &= -\mathbf{C}^{-1}\mathbf{b} \\ &= \boldsymbol{\theta}_1 - \mathbf{C}^{-1}(\mathbf{b} + \mathbf{C}\boldsymbol{\theta}_1) \\ &= \boldsymbol{\theta}_1 - Q_{\boldsymbol{\theta}\boldsymbol{\theta}}(\boldsymbol{\theta}_1)^{-1}Q_{\boldsymbol{\theta}}(\boldsymbol{\theta}_1) \end{aligned} \tag{16.8}$$

Thus, $\boldsymbol{\theta}^*$ depends on the function only through its first and second derivatives at any point $\boldsymbol{\theta}_1$. The expression in (16.8) suggests a modification to the search direction of steepest ascent. For quadratic functions, if we were to set $\delta = -Q_{\boldsymbol{\theta}\boldsymbol{\theta}}(\boldsymbol{\theta}_1)^{-1}Q_{\boldsymbol{\theta}}(\boldsymbol{\theta}_1)$, then a single line search would yield the optimal value of $\boldsymbol{\theta}$ at the step length equal to one, no matter what the starting value. In contrast to steepest ascent, the gradient is premultiplied by the inverse of the negative Hessian, producing a search direction that makes an optimal adjustment to the starting value in both direction and length.

EXAMPLE 16.4 **(Ordinary Least Squares)**

Although we already know the outcome, let us apply our general results for quadratic functions to the OLS problem. Starting at the trial value $\boldsymbol{\beta}_1$,

$$Q_{\beta}(\beta_1) = \mathbf{X}'(\mathbf{y} - \mathbf{X}\beta_1)$$
$$Q_{\beta\beta}(\beta_1) = -\mathbf{X}'\mathbf{X}$$

According to (16.8),

$$\begin{aligned}\beta^* &= \beta_1 - \left(-\mathbf{X}'\mathbf{X}\right)^{-1}\mathbf{X}'(\mathbf{y} - \mathbf{X}\beta_1)\\ &= (\mathbf{X}'\mathbf{X})^{-1}\mathbf{X}'\mathbf{y}\end{aligned}$$

as we expect.

EXAMPLE 16.5 (Cramér–Rao Inequality)

We have already used these relationships to describe the Cramér–Rao estimator. The quadratic function [equation (14.30), p. 308]

$$Q(\theta) = \mathrm{E}_N[L\,(\theta_0)] + \mathrm{E}_N[L_\theta\,(\theta_0)]'\,(\theta - \theta_0) - \frac{1}{2}\,(\theta - \theta_0)'\,\Im\,(\theta_0)\,(\theta - \theta_0)$$

has the partial derivatives

$$Q_\theta(\theta_0) = \mathrm{E}_N[L_\theta(\theta_0)]$$
$$Q_{\theta\theta}(\theta_0) = -\Im(\theta_0)$$

The maximum

$$\theta^* = \theta_0 + \Im(\theta_0)^{-1}\,\mathrm{E}_N[L_\theta(\theta_0)]$$

is the Cramér–Rao estimator in (14.31).

As in one dimension, quadratic optimization methods approximate general functions with quadratic functions, for example, the Taylor series approximation[4]

$$Q(\theta) \approx Q(\theta_1) + Q_\theta(\theta_1)'(\theta - \theta_1) + \frac{1}{2}\,(\theta - \theta_1)'\,Q_{\theta\theta}(\theta_1)\,(\theta - \theta_1)$$

These optimization methods use the maximum of the quadratic approximation as a further approximation of the maximum of the original function. A line search in the neighborhood of $\lambda = 1$ helps to refine the quadratic approximation of the optimum. For the Taylor series approximation above, the search direction is

$$\delta = -Q_{\theta\theta}(\theta_1)^{-1}Q_\theta(\theta_1)$$

In the line search (16.2), a concave quadratic function will yield the optimal $\lambda^* = 1$, as in (16.8). One hopes that the particular Q to be maximized yields values nearby.

[4] See equation (G.8) (p. 924) and the surrounding text.

16.4.3 Quadratic Methods and the MLE

Now we will describe how these ideas combine with the log-likelihood function in the computation of the MLE. Throughout our discussion, we continue with the i.i.d. sampling framework of Chapter 14, so that

$$L(\boldsymbol{\theta}; u) = \sum_{n=1}^{N} L(\boldsymbol{\theta}; u_n)$$

We drop the data argument for notational simplicity. For example, we will continue to denote empirical moments by

$$\mathrm{E}_N[L(\boldsymbol{\theta})] \equiv \mathrm{E}_N[L(\boldsymbol{\theta}; U)] = \frac{1}{N}\sum_{n=1}^{N} L(\boldsymbol{\theta}; U_n)$$

In the methods that we introduce below for maximizing $\mathrm{E}_N[L(\boldsymbol{\theta})]$, all use $\mathrm{E}_N[L_{\boldsymbol{\theta}}(\boldsymbol{\theta}_1)]$ for the first-order term in the quadratic approximation. The methods differ according to their Hessian terms.

NEWTON–RAPHSON

Among the oldest and most popular is the method of Newton–Raphson (NR). The NR method is based on the obvious choice for the Hessian term: the exact Hessian of the log-likelihood function at $\boldsymbol{\theta}_1$. The search direction of NR is

$$\boldsymbol{\delta}_{\mathrm{NR}}(\boldsymbol{\theta}_1) = \{-\,\mathrm{E}_N[L_{\boldsymbol{\theta\theta}}(\boldsymbol{\theta}_1)]\}^{-1}\,\mathrm{E}_N[L_{\boldsymbol{\theta}}(\boldsymbol{\theta}_1)] \tag{16.9}$$

In other words, the NR method is based on the second-order Taylor series approximation of $\mathrm{E}_N[L(\boldsymbol{\theta})]$ at $\boldsymbol{\theta}_1$.

Problems may arise with the NR method when the log-likelihood function is not strictly concave so that the Hessian fails to be negative definite. It is helpful to distinguish two phenomena. First, the Hessian may be only negative semidefinite, so that the problem is merely singularity of the Hessian. Second, the function may not be concave at $\boldsymbol{\theta}_1$ so that the Hessian fails to be negative semidefinite.

If the Hessian is singular and negative semidefinite, the search direction cannot be calculated according to (16.9). We can generalize (16.9) by changing the inverse to a generalized inverse. Indeed, a generalized inverse is a practical way to try to cope with the numerical hazards of *nearly* singular Hessian matrices. Even though the Hessian is singular, the search direction will still point in a direction that increases the log-likelihood function locally:

$$\begin{aligned}
\left.\frac{\partial\,\mathrm{E}_N[L(\boldsymbol{\theta}_1 + \lambda\cdot\boldsymbol{\delta})]}{\partial\lambda}\right|_{\lambda=0} &= \boldsymbol{\delta}'\,\mathrm{E}_N[L_{\boldsymbol{\theta}}(\boldsymbol{\theta}_1)] \\
&= -\,\mathrm{E}_N[L_{\boldsymbol{\theta}}(\boldsymbol{\theta}_1)]'\,\{\mathrm{E}_N[L_{\boldsymbol{\theta\theta}}(\boldsymbol{\theta}_1)]\}^{-}\,\mathrm{E}_N[L_{\boldsymbol{\theta}}(\boldsymbol{\theta}_1)] \\
&\geq 0
\end{aligned}$$

Note, however, that we must choose among generalized inverses.

When the Hessian is nonsingular but fails to be negative semidefinite, the search direction *may* point toward decreases in the log-likelihood function. This is simple enough to check and one response is to search in the opposite direction by simply changing the sign of the search direction. Goldfeld, Quandt, and Trotter (GQT) (1966) suggest the search direction

$$\boldsymbol{\delta}_{\mathrm{GQT}}(\boldsymbol{\theta}_1) = \{-\mathrm{E}_N[L_{\boldsymbol{\theta}\boldsymbol{\theta}}(\boldsymbol{\theta}_1)] + \alpha \cdot \mathbf{I}_K\}^{-1}\,\mathrm{E}_N[L_{\boldsymbol{\theta}}(\boldsymbol{\theta}_1)]$$

where α is chosen so that the modified Hessian is negative definite. Choosing a large value of α makes this search direction similar to that of steepest ascent. Greenstadt (1967) suggests replacing the Hessian with a modification to its eigenvalue decomposition. If

$$\mathrm{E}_N[L_{\boldsymbol{\theta}\boldsymbol{\theta}}(\boldsymbol{\theta}_1)] = \mathbf{X}\boldsymbol{\Lambda}\mathbf{X}'$$

where $\boldsymbol{\Lambda} = \mathrm{diag}(\lambda_i)$ is a diagonal matrix composed of eigenvalues and the columns of $\mathbf{X}$ are the associated eigenvectors, then $\mathbf{X}\,\mathrm{diag}(-|\lambda_i|)\mathbf{X}'$ is Greenstadt's substitute. By construction, this matrix is negative definite if the Hessian is nonsingular.

Two other methods have more appeal from a statistical point of view. They replace the Hessian with negative definite matrices with the same probability limit: the empirical information matrix and the empirical variance of the score.

MODIFIED SCORING

Any search direction that is in the half space $\{\mathbf{v} \in \mathbb{R}^K \mid \mathbf{v}' Q_{\boldsymbol{\theta}}(\boldsymbol{\theta}_1) \geq 0\}$ will lead to an increase:[5]

$$\boldsymbol{\delta}' Q_{\boldsymbol{\theta}}(\boldsymbol{\theta}_1) \geq 0 \qquad \Rightarrow \qquad \left.\frac{\partial Q(\boldsymbol{\theta}_1 + \lambda \cdot \boldsymbol{\delta})}{\partial \lambda}\right|_{\lambda=0} = \boldsymbol{\delta}' Q_{\boldsymbol{\theta}}(\boldsymbol{\theta}_1) \geq 0$$

As a result, premultiplying the score by any positive semidefinite matrix will yield a direction of increase. The classical method of scoring avoids Hessians that fail to be negative definite by replacing the negative of the average Hessian matrix with the empirical information matrix:

$$\boldsymbol{\delta}_{\mathrm{S}}(\boldsymbol{\theta}_1) = \mathrm{E}_N[\Im(\boldsymbol{\theta}_1)]^{-1}\,\mathrm{E}_N[L_{\boldsymbol{\theta}}(\boldsymbol{\theta}_1)] \tag{16.10}$$

Because the information is positive semidefinite, $\boldsymbol{\delta}_S$ will always point in a direction of increase. Rao (1973) called iteration of $\boldsymbol{\theta}_i = \boldsymbol{\theta}_{i-1} + \boldsymbol{\delta}_{\mathrm{S}}(\boldsymbol{\theta}_{i-1})$ the *method of scoring*. Combined with a line search, this quadratic method may be called the *modified method of scoring*.

BHHH ALGORITHM

The connection between the Hessian and the information matrices is a special feature of log-likelihood functions. Just as there are three common ways to estimate the information matrix, there are three common choices for the approximation to the negative of the Hessian. The third alternative, called *BHHH* or "B-H-cubed" after the four authors, Berndt, Hall, Hall, and Hausman (1974), is to use the empirical second moments of the score:

$$\boldsymbol{\delta}_{\mathrm{BH}^3}(\boldsymbol{\theta}_1) = \{\mathrm{E}_N[L_{\boldsymbol{\theta}}(\boldsymbol{\theta}_1)L_{\boldsymbol{\theta}}(\boldsymbol{\theta}_1)']\}^{-1}\,\mathrm{E}_N[L_{\boldsymbol{\theta}}(\boldsymbol{\theta}_1)] \tag{16.11}$$

This third matrix has the advantage, shared with the information matrix, that it is positive semidefinite so that the search direction is always a direction of local increase. This search direction

[5] Let $\mathbf{v}$ be a vector belonging to a vector space $\mathbb{V}$. The subset $\{\mathbf{u} \in \mathbb{V} \mid \langle \mathbf{u}, \mathbf{v}\rangle \geq 0\}$ is called a *half space*. Geometrically speaking, this is the set of vectors that form angles with v less than or equal to right angles.

is simply the OLS fitted coefficient vector from a regression of the constant one on the score vector for each observation. If we let the $N \times K$ matrix of scores be $\mathbf{G} = [L_{\boldsymbol{\theta}}(\boldsymbol{\theta}_1; u_n);\ n = 1, \ldots, N]'$ and $\boldsymbol{\iota}_N$ be a vector of N ones, then $\boldsymbol{\delta}_{\mathrm{BH}^3} = (\mathbf{G}'\mathbf{G})^{-1}\mathbf{G}'\boldsymbol{\iota}_N$.

An attractive characteristic of the BHHH search direction is that it requires the computation of the score only. This is a significant advantage in programming time. Computational time is an issue in search algorithms and BHHH saves a considerable amount of computation for the search direction. Only the first derivatives need to be computed analytically, whereas the modified method of scoring and NR both require additional analytical calculations for the Hessian approximant. These extra calculations can be very worthwhile in the neighborhood of the MLE $\hat{\boldsymbol{\theta}}_N$, however, and no choice of Hessian approximant uniformly dominates the others. We used the BHHH algorithm in our computations for the Student t regression models and found a numerical maximum quite quickly.

GAUSS–NEWTON REGRESSION

The *Gauss–Newton regression* (GNR) for *nonlinear least squares* (NLS) is closely related to the NR and BHHH algorithms. Suppose, for example, that we have independent observations where $y_n \mid \mathbf{x}_n \sim \mathfrak{N}[\mu(\boldsymbol{\beta}_0; \mathbf{x}_n), \sigma_0^2]$, where $\mu : \mathbb{R}^K \times \mathbb{R}^K \to \mathbb{R}$ is continuously differentiable in $\boldsymbol{\beta}$. Then the log-likelihood function for $\boldsymbol{\beta}_0$ and σ_0^2 is

$$\begin{aligned}
\mathrm{E}_N[L(\boldsymbol{\theta})] &= -\frac{1}{2N}\sum_{n=1}^{N}\left\{\log(2\pi\sigma^2) + \frac{[y_n - \mu(\boldsymbol{\beta}; \mathbf{x}_n)]^2}{\sigma^2}\right\} \\
&= -\frac{1}{2}\log(2\pi\sigma^2) - \frac{[\mathbf{y} - \boldsymbol{\mu}(\boldsymbol{\beta})]'[\mathbf{y} - \boldsymbol{\mu}(\boldsymbol{\beta})]}{2\sigma^2 N}
\end{aligned}$$

where $\boldsymbol{\mu}(\boldsymbol{\beta}) \equiv [\mu(\boldsymbol{\beta}; \mathbf{x}_n)]'$. The computation of the MLE for $\boldsymbol{\beta}_0$ corresponds to calculating the least-squares fit for a nonlinear function. As in OLS, we can compute the MLE for σ_0^2 after computing $\boldsymbol{\beta}$.

The score for $\boldsymbol{\beta}$ is

$$\begin{aligned}
\mathrm{E}_N[L_{\boldsymbol{\beta}}(\boldsymbol{\theta})] &= \frac{1}{\sigma^2 N}\sum_{n=1}^{N}\mu_{\boldsymbol{\beta}}(\boldsymbol{\beta}; \mathbf{x}_n)[y_n - \mu(\boldsymbol{\beta}; \mathbf{x}_n)] \\
&= \frac{1}{\sigma^2 N}\mathbf{W}(\boldsymbol{\beta})'[\mathbf{y} - \boldsymbol{\mu}(\boldsymbol{\beta})] \qquad (16.12)
\end{aligned}$$

where

$$\mathbf{W}(\boldsymbol{\beta}) \equiv \frac{\partial \boldsymbol{\mu}(\boldsymbol{\beta})}{\partial \boldsymbol{\beta}'}$$

is an $N \times K$ matrix of partial derivatives. The Hessian for $\boldsymbol{\beta}$ is

$$\begin{aligned}
\mathrm{E}_N[L_{\boldsymbol{\beta\beta}}(\boldsymbol{\theta})] &= -\frac{1}{\sigma^2 N}\sum_{n=1}^{N}\left\{\mu_{\boldsymbol{\beta}}(\boldsymbol{\beta}; \mathbf{x}_n)\mu_{\boldsymbol{\beta}}(\boldsymbol{\beta}; \mathbf{x}_n)' - [y_n - \mu(\boldsymbol{\beta}; \mathbf{x}_n)] \cdot \mu_{\boldsymbol{\beta\beta}}(\boldsymbol{\beta}; \mathbf{x}_n)\right\} \\
&= -\frac{1}{\sigma^2 N}\mathbf{W}(\boldsymbol{\beta})'\mathbf{W}(\boldsymbol{\beta}) + \frac{1}{\sigma^2 N}\sum_{n=1}^{N}[y_n - \mu(\boldsymbol{\beta}; \mathbf{x}_n)] \cdot \mu_{\boldsymbol{\beta\beta}}(\boldsymbol{\beta}; \mathbf{x}_n)
\end{aligned}$$

The second term of the Hessian has a mean equal to zero at the population parameter values. If we drop this term as an approximation to the Hessian, the quadratic search direction is

$$\delta_{\mathrm{GNR}}(\boldsymbol{\beta}) = [\mathbf{W}(\boldsymbol{\beta})'\mathbf{W}(\boldsymbol{\beta})]^{-1}\mathbf{W}(\boldsymbol{\beta})'[\mathbf{y} - \boldsymbol{\mu}(\boldsymbol{\beta})] \tag{16.13}$$

So the direction is the OLS fitted coefficients from a regression of the current fitted residual on the partial derivatives of the nonlinear regression function.

Often the step size λ is restricted to 1 in GNR, just as in the method of scoring. Then the updating formula is

$$\boldsymbol{\beta}_{i+1} = \boldsymbol{\beta}_i + [\mathbf{W}(\boldsymbol{\beta}_i)'\mathbf{W}(\boldsymbol{\beta}_i)]^{-1}\mathbf{W}(\boldsymbol{\beta}_i)'[\mathbf{y} - \boldsymbol{\mu}(\boldsymbol{\beta}_i)]$$

This formula also arises from a linear approximation of the regression function:

$$\boldsymbol{\mu}(\boldsymbol{\beta}) \approx \boldsymbol{\mu}(\boldsymbol{\beta}_i) + \mathbf{W}(\boldsymbol{\beta}_i)(\boldsymbol{\beta} - \boldsymbol{\beta}_i)$$

If we substitute this approximation into the NLS problem, we can write

$$\begin{aligned}\boldsymbol{\beta}_{i+1} &= \left(\mathbf{X}_*'\mathbf{X}_*\right)^{-1}\mathbf{X}_*'\mathbf{y}_* \\ &= \underset{\boldsymbol{\beta}}{\operatorname{argmin}}(\mathbf{y}_* - \mathbf{X}_*\boldsymbol{\beta})'(\mathbf{y}_* - \mathbf{X}_*\boldsymbol{\beta})\end{aligned} \tag{16.14}$$

where

$$\mathbf{y}_* \equiv \mathbf{y} - \boldsymbol{\mu}(\boldsymbol{\beta}_i) + \mathbf{W}(\boldsymbol{\beta}_i)\boldsymbol{\beta}_i \tag{16.15}$$

$$\mathbf{X}_* \equiv \mathbf{W}(\boldsymbol{\beta}_i) \tag{16.16}$$

EXAMPLE 16.6 (Exponential Regression)

Rather than fit a linear regression function $\mathbf{x}_n'\boldsymbol{\beta}$ to the logarithm of wages, we might decide to fit a nonlinear regression function $\mu_n = \exp(\mathbf{x}_n'\boldsymbol{\beta})$ to wages themselves. The GNR is a convenient approach to this because

$$\mathbf{W}(\boldsymbol{\beta}) = [\mu_n \cdot \mathbf{x}_n;\, n = 1, \ldots, N]'$$

Table 16.2
Log-Wage OLS versus Wage NLS

RHS Variable	Estimated Coefficient OLS	Estimated Coefficient NLS
Constant (one)	0.779	0.815
Female	−0.242	−0.237
Nonwhite	−0.131	−0.140
Union member	0.173	0.060
Education	0.095	0.104
Experience	0.039	0.036
(Experience)^2	−0.00063	−0.00056

We did this for our wage data set and the algorithm converged after four iterations. The OLS log-wage coefficients appear with the NLS wage coefficients in Table 16.2. Although most coefficients are similar, there is substantial disagreement between the two coefficients for the Union indicator variable. It is not necessary for the coefficients to be similar. We will discuss this further in Chapter 21.

These four quadratic methods, NR, modified scoring, BHHH, and GNR, comprise the numerical optimization algorithms most closely related to statistical theory. Because of this relationship, all of these procedures provide convenient estimators of the variance–covariance matrix of the MLE on convergence to the MLE $\hat{\boldsymbol{\theta}}$. This is the inverse of the matrix used for the Hessian of the quadratic approximation. This matrix must be calculated to find the search direction. We have presented these estimators earlier in Section 15.4.

These methods are by no means the only ones in common use. For additional numerical methods, we refer the reader to Greene (1990) and Quandt (1983).

16.4.4 LMLE

By now it may be plain that the calculation of the LMLE corresponds to a single iteration of one of the quadratic optimization methods we have just described, constraining the step length to equal one. In other words, we simply add the search direction onto the initial estimator. Implicitly the LMLE corresponds to the maximum of a quadratic approximation of the log-likelihood function. The ability to use any initial $\check{\boldsymbol{\theta}}_N$ that is CUAN is a property of quadratic functions: the maximum of a quadratic function can be found from any starting value given the first and second derivatives at that point.

EXAMPLE 16.7 **(Student *t* Linear Regression)**

The OLS fitted coefficients $\check{\boldsymbol{\beta}} = \hat{\boldsymbol{\beta}}_{\text{OLS}}$ are initial consistent estimators of $\boldsymbol{\beta}_0$ in the Student t regression model, provided that the variance of the t distribution exists. We can compute consistent estimators of ν_0 and $\gamma_0 = \nu_0 \sigma_0^2$ by maximizing the log-likelihood function over ν and γ, holding $\boldsymbol{\beta} = \hat{\boldsymbol{\beta}}_{\text{OLS}}$.[6] These initial values are $\check{\nu} = 6.59$ and $\check{\gamma} = 0.99$. From a computational standpoint, it is often sensible to begin MLE calculations with such restricted maximization anyway. We then computed the LMLE using (16.11) and obtained the values in Table 16.3.

As can be seen, the LMLE parameter values are very close to the MLE. The LMLE based on the NR search direction appears to be closer, reflecting a better quadratic approximation based on the Hessian. Nevertheless, the differences are not qualitatively important. Of course, this sort of agreement does not occur in every case.

[6] Given the parameterization of the Student t log-likelihood function (16.1), it seems natural to fit ν and $\nu\sigma^2$ rather than ν and σ^2.

Table 16.3
ML versus LMLE Parameters for Log-Wage

RHS Variable	Estimated Coefficient MLE	LMLE[a]	LMLE[b]
Constant (one)	0.7113241	0.7107734	0.7207741
Female	−0.2558971	−0.2560619	−0.2536299
Nonwhite	−0.1162087	−0.1161001	−0.1190193
Union member	0.1607215	0.1605870	0.1671523
Education	0.1002407	0.1002809	0.0990366
Experience	0.0401985	0.0402138	0.0405282
$(\text{Experience})^2$	−0.0006397	−0.0006399	−0.0006487
ν	6.3300582	6.3207907	6.4719586
$\nu\sigma^2$	0.9343316	0.9304342	0.9702322
Log-likelihood	−806.6988	−806.7002	−806.8016

[a]Newton–Raphson.
[b]BHHH.

16.5 CONVERGENCE CRITERIA

Convergence of the iterated procedures should be judged on the basis of standard criteria for a maximum: the first and second derivatives. It is unwise, but common in statistical software, to claim that an algorithm has converged to a critical value of the log-likelihood function on the ith iteration because the differences $\boldsymbol{\theta}_i - \boldsymbol{\theta}_{i-1}$ are small. Such circumstances also arise when an algorithm is moving very slowly in the parameter space because its search direction is poor or the function is poorly approximated by a quadratic. Convergence should be determined by how close the score is to zero and whether the Hessian is negative definite.

In terms of our sequence of maximization problems in one dimension (16.2), we have found a critical value of the function when the derivative of the function with respect to its argument is zero at the current values for $\boldsymbol{\theta}$:

$$\left.\frac{\partial\,\mathrm{E}_N[L(\boldsymbol{\theta}_i + \lambda \cdot \boldsymbol{\delta}_i)]}{\partial\lambda}\right|_{\lambda=0} = 0$$

For such quadratic methods as the modified method of scoring, the left-hand derivative has a simple, intuitive, expression

$$\frac{\partial\,\mathrm{E}_N[L(\boldsymbol{\theta}_i + \lambda \cdot \boldsymbol{\delta}_i)]}{\partial\lambda} = \mathrm{E}_N[L_{\boldsymbol{\theta}}(\boldsymbol{\theta}_i; u)]'\{\mathrm{E}_N[L_{\boldsymbol{\theta\theta}}(\boldsymbol{\theta}_i)]\}^{-1}\,\mathrm{E}_N[L_{\boldsymbol{\theta}}(\boldsymbol{\theta}_i)] \tag{16.17}$$

This expression will be zero when a maximum has been reached, for then the optimal step size is zero and the derivative with respect to the step size is zero. Numerical convergence can be judged by whether this expression is numerically small, say 10^{-5}.

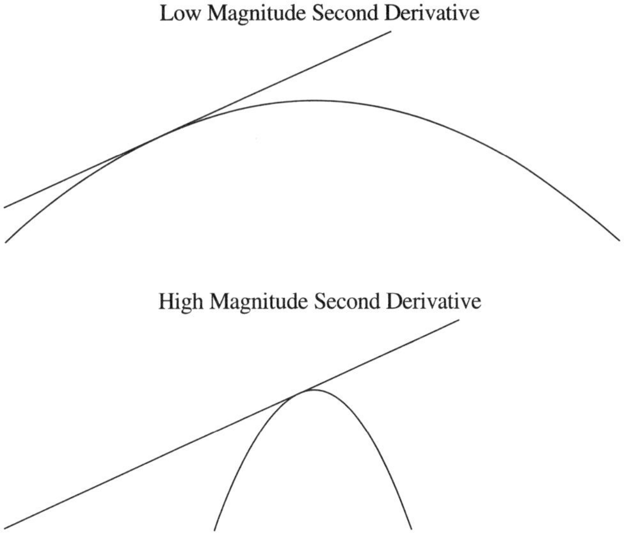

Figure 16.5 Illustration of convergence criterion.

Convergence is judged by the size of the quadratic form (16.17) in the score vector. From a geometric viewpoint, this is a sensible criterion. When the second derivative is large, we can tolerate relatively large first derivatives because we are still confident that we are close to the critical value. A small second derivative, however, indicates that the first derivative is changing slowly so that setting the first derivative to zero may require substantial movement in the parameter space. See Figure 16.5.

One must also confirm that the Hessian is negative definite before claiming convergence to a local maximum. It is possible for quadratic maximization methods to appear to converge based on (16.17) when in fact they have not. Much statistical software does not provide this check and it remains the responsibility of the researcher to calculate the Hessian, perhaps numerically, and confirm that the log-likelihood function is locally strictly concave.

Remember that convergence to a local maximum does not imply that the global maximum has been discovered. In many applications, one must try lots of starting values for numerical optimization to gain some confidence that the global maximum has been located. In some cases, one can show that there is only one local maximum so that convergence to the unique local maximum implies convergence to the global maximum. This uniqueness usually rests on the global concavity of the log-likelihood function, a rather special feature.

EXAMPLE 16.8 (Student t Linear Regression)

The log-likelihood function for Student t linear regression can have many local maxima, particularly for values of ν between 0 and 1.[7] To compute the estimates in Table 16.1, we followed one of the suggestions of Lange et al. (1989), computing the restricted MLE for a grid of values for the degrees of freedom parameter ν. The grid consisted of the integers from 1 to 30. We used the

[7] For example, see Lange et al. (1989) and Gabrielsen (1982).

NR search direction and accepted convergence if the Hessian was negative definite and (16.17) was between 0 and 10^{-5}. Convergence always occurred within four iterations.

Figure 16.6 shows the values obtained for the log-likelihood for each value of ν.[8] These identify a local maximum near $\nu = 6$. They also show that the log-likelihood function is not globally concave in ν.

We then used the parameter values obtained at $\nu = 6$ as starting values for unrestricted estimation, achieving convergence after three iterations of NR. Thus, despite the potential for difficulty, maximizing this log-likelihood was straightforward.

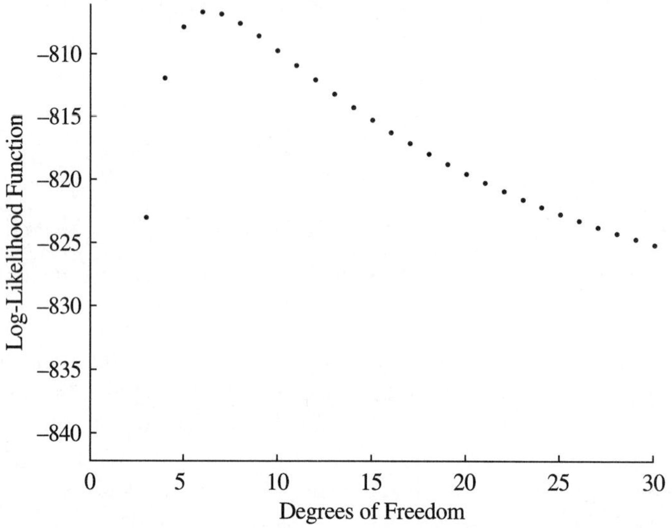

Figure 16.6 Grid of maximized log-likelihood values in ν.

16.6 TRANSFORMATIONS OF PARAMETERS

A special topic worthy of note is the role of parameter transformation in the computation of maximum likelihood estimators. Parameter transformations are used in two important ways: (1) to impose restrictions on parameter estimates and (2) to improve quadratic approximations. These two purposes often are achieved by a single transformation.

EXAMPLE 16.9 (Normal Variance)

The variance parameter of the normal distribution must be positive. Estimating this parameter for an i.i.d. sample of N observations from the $\mathfrak{N}(0, \sigma^2)$ distribution, we would maximize the log-likelihood function

$$\mathrm{E}_N[L(\sigma^2)] = -\frac{N}{2}\log\sigma^2 - \frac{\sum_{n=1}^{N} U_n^2}{2\sigma^2}$$

[8] We do not show the values for $\nu = 1, 2$. These were -854.4704 and -977.1121, respectively. The horizontal axis of the figure is drawn roughly at the level of the maximum of the log-likelihood function for the normal linear regression model.

A simple reparameterization of this function in terms of the parameter $\gamma = \log \sigma^2$ permits parameter values to be unrestricted and improves the quality of quadratic approximations. The alternative function becomes

$$\mathrm{E}_N[L(\gamma)] = -\frac{N}{2}\gamma - \frac{\sum_{n=1}^{N} U_n^2}{2\exp(\gamma)}$$

See Figures 16.7 and 16.8 for examples of this function and its quadratic approximations, where $N = 2$ and $\sum_{n=1}^{N} y_n^2 = 2$. Figure 16.8 shows the quadratic approximation in γ, transformed by replacing $\gamma = \log \sigma^2$ for comparability with Figure 16.7. The maximum of the log-likelihood function is at $\sigma^2 = 1.0$ and the approximations were made around $\sigma^2 = 1.6$.

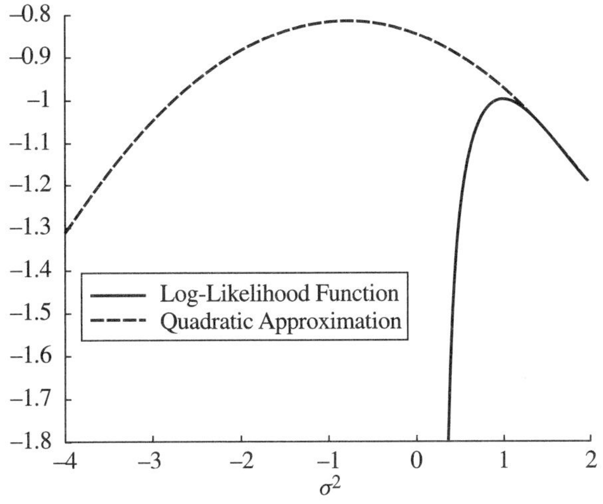

Figure 16.7 Quadratic approximation of $L(\sigma^2)$.

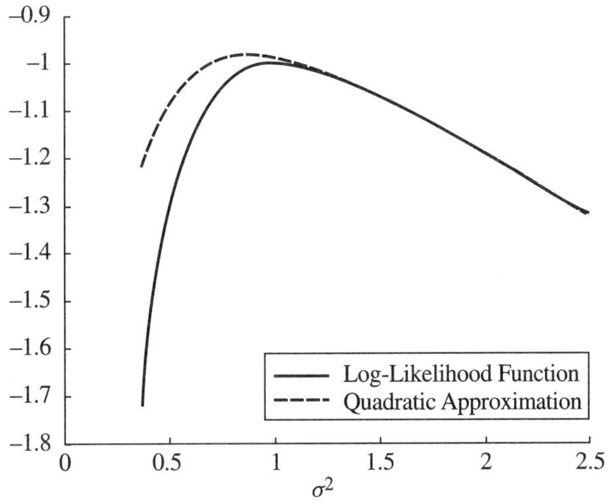

Figure 16.8 Quadratic approximation of $L(\log \sigma^2)$.

EXAMPLE 16.10 (Variance Matrix)

Correlation coefficients must lie within the interval $(-1, 1)$. The transformation $\rho = 2\arctan(\gamma)/\pi$ enforces this restriction. More generally, variance matrices must be positive semidefinite, if not positive definite. These are often reparameterized in terms of a Cholesky factorization: $\mathbf{\Omega} = \mathbf{CC}'$ where $\mathbf{C}$ is lower-left triangular. In this case, $\mathbf{C}$ and $-\mathbf{C}$ are observationally equivalent so that global identification fails. Restricting the parameter space so that diagonal elements of $\mathbf{C}$ must be positive reestablishes global identification. This is also a good computational practice in many situations, because it prevents an algorithm from taking some nonlocal steps that can lead to inefficient cycling between $\mathbf{C}$ and $-\mathbf{C}$. If one encounters such steps, then one should reconsider the parameterization because the quadratic approximation is failing or the MLE is on the boundary of the parameter space.

Note that ML estimation is *invariant* to nonsingular transformations of thc paramctcrs. If $\boldsymbol{\gamma} = \mathbf{g}(\boldsymbol{\theta})$ is a one-to-one reparameterization, then the MLE for $\boldsymbol{\gamma}$ is

$$\hat{\boldsymbol{\gamma}}_N = \operatorname*{argmax}_{\boldsymbol{\gamma}\in\boldsymbol{\Gamma}} \mathrm{E}_N\{L\left[\mathbf{g}^{-1}(\boldsymbol{\gamma})\right]\}$$

where $\boldsymbol{\Gamma}$ is the parameter space $\{\boldsymbol{\gamma} = \mathbf{g}(\boldsymbol{\theta}) \mid \boldsymbol{\theta} \in \boldsymbol{\Theta}\}$. Because the reparameterization is one to one,

$$\max_{\boldsymbol{\gamma}\in\boldsymbol{\Gamma}} \mathrm{E}_N\left\{L\left[\mathbf{g}^{-1}(\boldsymbol{\gamma})\right]\right\} = \max_{\boldsymbol{\theta}\in\boldsymbol{\Theta}} \mathrm{E}_N[L(\boldsymbol{\theta})]$$

and $\hat{\boldsymbol{\gamma}}_N = \mathbf{g}(\hat{\boldsymbol{\theta}}_N)$. This is called *invariance*: reparameterization does not alter the location of the MLE.

Given this reciprocal relationship between $\hat{\boldsymbol{\gamma}}_N$ and $\hat{\boldsymbol{\theta}}_N$, we can infer that the general asymptotic properties of the MLE $\hat{\boldsymbol{\theta}}_N$ are also possessed by $\hat{\boldsymbol{\gamma}}_N$. Thus, $\hat{\boldsymbol{\gamma}}_N$ is a consistent estimator of $\boldsymbol{\gamma}_0 = \mathbf{g}(\boldsymbol{\theta}_0)$ and $\sqrt{N}(\hat{\boldsymbol{\gamma}}_N - \boldsymbol{\gamma}_0)$ converges in distribution to a normal random variable. We can express this limit distribution in terms of $\boldsymbol{\theta}$. Because the score for $\boldsymbol{\gamma}$ is

$$\begin{aligned}\frac{\partial L\left[\mathbf{g}^{-1}(\boldsymbol{\gamma})\right]}{\partial \boldsymbol{\gamma}} &= \frac{\partial \mathbf{g}^{-1}(\boldsymbol{\gamma})}{\partial \boldsymbol{\gamma}} L_{\theta}[\mathbf{g}^{-1}(\boldsymbol{\gamma})] \\ &= \left[\mathbf{g}_{\theta}(\boldsymbol{\theta})\right]^{-1} L_{\theta}(\boldsymbol{\theta})\end{aligned}$$

the information matrix for $\boldsymbol{\gamma}$ is

$$\mathrm{Var}\left[\left(\mathbf{g}_{\theta}(\boldsymbol{\theta}_0)\right)^{-1} L_{\theta}(\boldsymbol{\theta}_0)\right] = \left[\mathbf{g}_{\theta}(\boldsymbol{\theta}_0)\right]^{-1} \Im(\boldsymbol{\theta}_0) \left[\mathbf{g}_{\theta}(\boldsymbol{\theta}_0)'\right]^{\;1}$$

Applying Proposition 16 (ML Asymptotics, p. 320), we find that

$$\left[\mathbf{g}_{\theta}(\hat{\boldsymbol{\theta}}_N)\right]^{-1} \mathrm{E}_N[\Im(\hat{\boldsymbol{\theta}}_N)]^{1/2} \sqrt{N}(\hat{\boldsymbol{\gamma}}_N - \boldsymbol{\gamma}_0) \xrightarrow{d} \mathfrak{N}(\mathbf{0}, \mathbf{I})$$

Therefore we treat $\hat{\boldsymbol{\gamma}}_N$ as approximately normally distributed with mean $\boldsymbol{\gamma}_0$ and variance matrix $\mathbf{g}_{\theta}(\hat{\boldsymbol{\theta}}_N)\Im(\hat{\boldsymbol{\theta}}_N)^{-1}\mathbf{g}_{\theta}(\hat{\boldsymbol{\theta}}_N)'$.

This an example of a general and useful result widely known as the *delta method* for finding the asymptotic distribution of a transformation $\mathbf{g}(\hat{\boldsymbol{\theta}}_N)$. Given a consistent estimator of the approximate variance of $\sqrt{N}(\hat{\boldsymbol{\theta}}_N - \boldsymbol{\theta}_0)$, say $\hat{\mathbf{\Omega}}$, the approximate variance of $\sqrt{N}[\mathbf{g}(\hat{\boldsymbol{\theta}}_N) - \mathbf{g}(\boldsymbol{\theta}_0)]$ is $\mathbf{g}_{\theta}(\hat{\boldsymbol{\theta}}_N)\hat{\mathbf{\Omega}}\,\mathbf{g}_{\theta}(\hat{\boldsymbol{\theta}}_N)'$. This approximation is justified by the following lemma.

LEMMA 16.1 (DELTA METHOD) *If* $\sqrt{N}(\hat{\boldsymbol{\theta}}_N - \boldsymbol{\theta}_0) \xrightarrow{d} \mathfrak{N}(\mathbf{0}, \boldsymbol{\Omega})$ *and* $\mathbf{g}(\boldsymbol{\theta})$ *is continuous at* $\boldsymbol{\theta}_0$*, then* $\sqrt{N}[\mathbf{g}(\hat{\boldsymbol{\theta}}_N) - \mathbf{g}(\boldsymbol{\theta}_0)] \xrightarrow{d} \mathfrak{N}(\mathbf{0}, \mathbf{J}_0\boldsymbol{\Omega}\mathbf{J}_0')$ *where* $\mathbf{J}(\boldsymbol{\theta}) \equiv \partial\mathbf{g}(\boldsymbol{\theta})/\partial\boldsymbol{\theta}'$ *is a matrix of partial derivatives and* $\mathbf{J}_0 \equiv \mathbf{J}(\boldsymbol{\theta}_0)$.

Proof. This proof follows the familiar path of first-order Taylor approximations: expanding $\mathbf{g}(\hat{\boldsymbol{\theta}}_N)$ around $\boldsymbol{\theta}_0$, we obtain

$$\sqrt{N}\left[\mathbf{g}(\hat{\boldsymbol{\theta}}_N) - \mathbf{g}(\boldsymbol{\theta}_0)\right] = \mathbf{J}(\bar{\boldsymbol{\theta}}_N)\sqrt{N}(\hat{\boldsymbol{\theta}}_N - \boldsymbol{\theta}_0)$$

for some $\bar{\boldsymbol{\theta}}_N = \alpha_N\hat{\boldsymbol{\theta}}_N + (1-\alpha_N)\boldsymbol{\theta}_0, \alpha_N \in [0, 1]$. Therefore, $\bar{\boldsymbol{\theta}}_N \xrightarrow{p} \boldsymbol{\theta}_0$ and $\mathbf{J}(\bar{\boldsymbol{\theta}}_N) \xrightarrow{p} \mathbf{J}_0$, using Lemma 13.2 (p. 261). Lemma 13.3 implies that

$$\sqrt{N}\left[\mathbf{g}(\hat{\boldsymbol{\theta}}_N) - \mathbf{g}(\boldsymbol{\theta}_0)\right] \xrightarrow{d} \mathbf{J}_0\,\mathfrak{N}(\mathbf{0}, \boldsymbol{\Omega}) \sim \mathfrak{N}(\mathbf{0}, \mathbf{J}_0\boldsymbol{\Omega}\mathbf{J}_0')$$

proving the lemma. □

In general, it would be nonsensical to treat both $\hat{\boldsymbol{\gamma}}_N$ and $\hat{\boldsymbol{\theta}}_N$ as normally distributed when there is a nonlinear relationship between them. But asymptotically, because they vary in a small neighborhood, there is a linear relationship between them and normal distributions for both makes sense. Therefore, sensible application of the delta method is limited to situations in which this approximate linearity holds for all likely values of the random variables.

EXAMPLE 16.11 (Distribution of a Ratio)

When we maximized the log-likelihood function of the Student t log-wage regression, we chose to fit the parameters $(\boldsymbol{\beta}, \gamma, \nu)$ instead of $(\boldsymbol{\beta}, \sigma^2, \nu)$ because the functional form of the log-likelihood suggests the former: the parameter σ^2 always appears with ν and the product appears in a similar way to the variance parameter of the normal log-likelihood. To estimate the conditional variance of log-wage, we need only compute $\hat{\gamma}/\left(\hat{\nu} - 2\right)$, which is 0.216. This is quite close to the OLS estimator for the variance, which is 0.218. To estimate the sampling standard deviation of $\hat{\gamma}/\left(\hat{\nu} - 2\right)$, we used the delta method. This seems reasonable in light of the estimated standard error for $\hat{\nu}$, which is 0.253. The ratio is quite linear in the range of probable values of $\hat{\nu}$.

The matrix of partial derivatives is

$$\mathbf{J}(\boldsymbol{\theta}) = \begin{bmatrix} \dfrac{1}{\nu - 2} & -\dfrac{\gamma}{(\nu - 2)^2} \end{bmatrix}$$

and we estimate $\mathbf{J}_0$ with

$$\hat{\mathbf{J}} = \mathbf{J}(\hat{\boldsymbol{\theta}}_N) = \begin{bmatrix} \dfrac{1}{\hat{\nu} - 2} & -\dfrac{\hat{\gamma}}{\left(\hat{\nu} - 2\right)^2} \end{bmatrix}$$

Multiplying this in a quadratic form with the estimated variance matrix of $(\hat{\gamma}, \hat{\nu})$, say $\hat{\boldsymbol{\Omega}} = \left[\hat{\omega}_{ij}\right]$, gives the variance estimator

$$\frac{\hat{\omega}_{\gamma\gamma}\left(\hat{\nu} - 2\right)^2 - 2\hat{\omega}_{\gamma\nu}\hat{\gamma}\left(\hat{\nu} - 2\right) + \hat{\omega}_{\nu\nu}\hat{\gamma}^2}{\left(\hat{\nu} - 2\right)^4}$$

and a variance estimate of 0.0011, which corresponds to a standard error of 0.0336.

16.7 CONCENTRATING THE LIKELIHOOD FUNCTION

There is an analytical tool called *concentrating* the likelihood function that is also quite useful in numerical maximization. As we have seen, a key difficulty in these maximization problems is the high dimension of $\boldsymbol{\theta}$. One can reduce the number of dimensions if a subset of the normal equations can be solved and if the solution can be substituted back into the likelihood function.

Let the parameter vector be partitioned into $\boldsymbol{\theta} = [\boldsymbol{\theta}_1', \boldsymbol{\theta}_2']'$. Given any $\boldsymbol{\theta}_2$, one can find the optimal value of $\boldsymbol{\theta}_1$ as a function of $\boldsymbol{\theta}_2$ by solving the first-order conditions

$$\left.\frac{\partial \, \mathrm{E}_N[L(\boldsymbol{\theta})]}{\partial \boldsymbol{\theta}_1}\right|_{\boldsymbol{\theta}_1=\hat{\boldsymbol{\theta}}_1} \equiv \mathrm{E}_N[L_1(\hat{\boldsymbol{\theta}}_1, \boldsymbol{\theta}_2)] = \mathbf{0} \qquad \Leftrightarrow \qquad \boldsymbol{\theta}_1 = \hat{\boldsymbol{\theta}}_1(\boldsymbol{\theta}_2) \tag{16.18}$$

Substituting this function into the original log-likelihood yields the concentrated average log-likelihood function

$$\mathrm{E}_N[L^c(\boldsymbol{\theta}_2)] \equiv \mathrm{E}_N\left[L\big(\hat{\boldsymbol{\theta}}_1(\boldsymbol{\theta}_2), \boldsymbol{\theta}_2\big)\right] \tag{16.19}$$

which yields the MLE for $\hat{\boldsymbol{\theta}}_2$ as its maximum

$$\hat{\boldsymbol{\theta}}_2 = \underset{\boldsymbol{\theta}_2}{\operatorname{argmax}} \, \mathrm{E}_N[L^c(\boldsymbol{\theta}_2)]$$

In two dimensions, concentrating the log-likelihood in one parameter is like taking the profile of the log-likelihood in the other parameter as the new log-likelihood function. Figure 16.9 shows a surface with two local maxima located at different values of $\boldsymbol{\theta}_1$. Figure 16.10 illustrates the nature of the concentrated function as the highest value of the function over $\boldsymbol{\theta}_1$ for each $\boldsymbol{\theta}_2$. This also shows why the concentrated likelihood function is also called the *profile likelihood.*

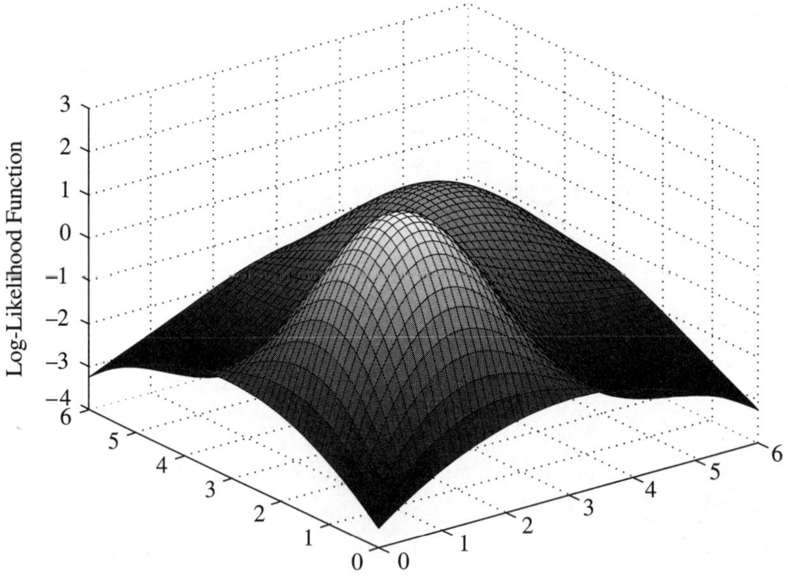

Figure 16.9 A multimodal log-likelihood function.

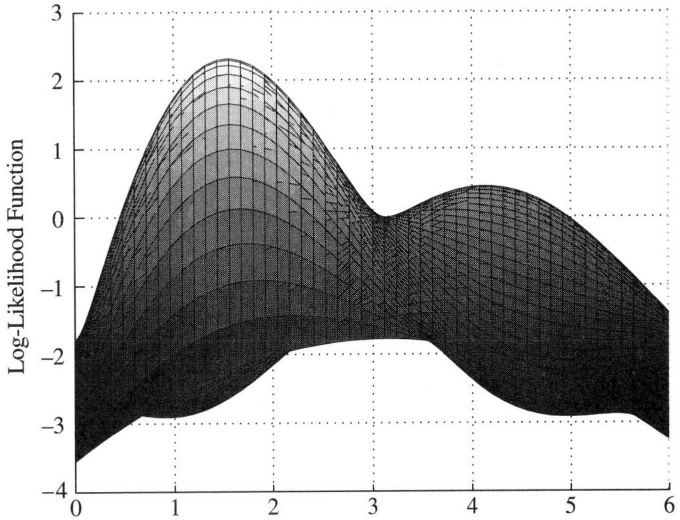

Figure 16.10 View of concentrated log-likelihood.

EXAMPLE 16.12 **(Normal Linear Regression)**

Consider the linear model for which the MLE for the variance parameter can be expressed as a function of the MLE for the slopes in $\boldsymbol{\beta}$:

$$
\begin{aligned}
0 &= \mathrm{E}_N[L_{\sigma^2}(\hat{\boldsymbol{\theta}};\, y_n \,|\, \mathbf{x}_n)] \\
&= -\frac{1}{2[\hat{\sigma}^2(\boldsymbol{\beta})]^2}\left[\hat{\sigma}^2(\boldsymbol{\beta}) - \frac{(\mathbf{y}-\mathbf{X}\boldsymbol{\beta})'(\mathbf{y}-\mathbf{X}\boldsymbol{\beta})}{N}\right]
\end{aligned}
$$

so that

$$
\hat{\sigma}^2(\boldsymbol{\beta}) = \frac{(\mathbf{y}-\mathbf{X}\boldsymbol{\beta})'(\mathbf{y}-\mathbf{X}\boldsymbol{\beta})}{N}
$$

Substituting this relationship into the log-likelihood function, we obtain the concentrated log-likelihood function

$$
\mathrm{E}_N[L^c(\boldsymbol{\beta};\, y_n \,|\, \mathbf{x}_n)] = -\frac{1}{2}\left\{\log\left[2\pi\,\frac{(\mathbf{y}-\mathbf{X}\boldsymbol{\beta})'(\mathbf{y}-\mathbf{X}\boldsymbol{\beta})}{N}\right] + 1\right\}
$$

In this way, the dimension of the maximization problem has been reduced by one, and the maximization of the log-likelihood function has become much simpler for the algorithms mentioned above. The concentrated log-likelihood is a monotonic transformation of a quadratic problem.

Asymptotically, the concentrated log-likelihood function has properties similar to an ordinary log-likelihood. If we replace expectations with the probability limits of empirical moments, then we obtain identities comparable to the score identity (Lemma 14.3, p. 300) and the information identity (Lemma 14.4, p. 302). For notational clarity, let us denote $L^c(\boldsymbol{\theta}_2; u) \equiv L(\boldsymbol{\theta}_c; u)$ where $\boldsymbol{\theta}_c \equiv [\hat{\boldsymbol{\theta}}_1(\boldsymbol{\theta}_2)', \boldsymbol{\theta}_2']'$.

Lemma 16.2 (Concentrated LLF) *Given the assumptions of Proposition 16 (ML Asymptotics, p. 320) and the existence of*

$$\mathrm{E}\left[\sup_{\boldsymbol{\theta}\in\Theta} |L_{\boldsymbol{\theta}}(\boldsymbol{\theta}; U)|\right] \tag{16.20}$$

then

$$\mathrm{E}_N[L^c_{\boldsymbol{\theta}_2}(\boldsymbol{\theta}_{02})] \xrightarrow{p} \mathbf{0} \tag{16.21}$$

$$\mathrm{E}_N[L^c_{\boldsymbol{\theta}_2}(\boldsymbol{\theta}_{02})L^c_{\boldsymbol{\theta}_2}(\boldsymbol{\theta}_{02})'] + \mathrm{E}_N[L^c_{\boldsymbol{\theta}_2\boldsymbol{\theta}_2}(\boldsymbol{\theta}_{02})] \xrightarrow{p} \mathbf{0} \tag{16.22}$$

and

$$\sqrt{N}(\hat{\boldsymbol{\theta}}_2 - \boldsymbol{\theta}_{02}) \xrightarrow{d} \mathfrak{N}[0, \Im_{2|1}(\boldsymbol{\theta}_0)^{-1}] \tag{16.23}$$

where

$$\begin{aligned} \mathrm{E}_N\left[L^c_{\boldsymbol{\theta}_2}(\boldsymbol{\theta}_{02})L^c_{\boldsymbol{\theta}_2}(\boldsymbol{\theta}_{02})'\right] &\xrightarrow{p} \Im_{2|1}(\boldsymbol{\theta}_0) \\ &\equiv \Im_{22}(\boldsymbol{\theta}_0) - \Im_{21}(\boldsymbol{\theta}_0)\Im_{11}(\boldsymbol{\theta}_0)^{-1}\Im_{12}(\boldsymbol{\theta}_0) \end{aligned} \tag{16.24}$$

The proof appears below in the *Mathematical Notes* section.

For practical purposes then, we may treat the concentrated log-likelihood function as though it were an ordinary log-likelihood for all of our calculations. The asymptotic distribution theory is the same in these general relationships. There is a difference, however, in the expression for the variance matrix, $\Im_{2|1}(\boldsymbol{\theta}_0)$, but it has an intuitive explanation.

Note first that we may interpret $\Im_{2|1}(\boldsymbol{\theta}_0)$ as the asymptotic conditional variance of $\sqrt{N}\,\mathrm{E}_N[L_2(\boldsymbol{\theta}_0)]$ given $\sqrt{N}\,\mathrm{E}_N[L_1(\boldsymbol{\theta}_0)]$. This variance matrix has the functional form of the conditional variance of one normal random vector conditional on another, given that they have a joint multivariate normal distribution (Lemma 10.4, p. 208). Because (16.18) states that $\mathrm{E}_N[L_1(\boldsymbol{\theta}_c)] \equiv \mathbf{0}$,

$$\begin{aligned} \frac{\partial}{\partial\boldsymbol{\theta}_2}L^c(\boldsymbol{\theta}_2; u) &\equiv \frac{\partial}{\partial\boldsymbol{\theta}_2}L(\boldsymbol{\theta}_c; u) \\ &= L_2(\boldsymbol{\theta}_c; u_n) + \left[\frac{\partial}{\partial\boldsymbol{\theta}_2}\hat{\boldsymbol{\theta}}_1(\boldsymbol{\theta}_2)'\right] L_1(\boldsymbol{\theta}_c; u) \\ &= L_2(\boldsymbol{\theta}_c; u_n) \end{aligned} \tag{16.25}$$

the score of the concentrated log-likelihood is L_2 evaluated at a point for which $L_1 \equiv \mathbf{0}$. The asymptotic distribution theory reflects this conditional fact, reducing the marginal variance of L_2 according to conditioning on L_1.

Alternatively, one can see that the inverse of this matrix is indeed the asymptotic marginal variance matrix of $\sqrt{N}(\hat{\boldsymbol{\theta}}_{2N} - \boldsymbol{\theta}_{02})$. Given that the asymptotic variance of the entire parameter vector $\sqrt{N}(\hat{\boldsymbol{\theta}}_N - \boldsymbol{\theta}_0)$ is $\Im(\boldsymbol{\theta}_0)^{-1}$, if we partition $\Im(\boldsymbol{\theta}_0)$ conformably with $(\boldsymbol{\theta}_1, \boldsymbol{\theta}_2)$ and apply the formula of a partitioned inverse (Exercise 3.10, p. 70), then we find that $\Im_{2|1}(\boldsymbol{\theta}_0)^{-1}$ is the (2, 2) element.

EXAMPLE 16.13 (Normal Linear Regression)

The score and the Hessian of the average concentrated log-likelihood function are

$$\mathrm{E}_N[L^c_{\boldsymbol{\beta}}(\boldsymbol{\beta}; y_n \mid \mathbf{x}_n)] = \frac{2}{\hat{\sigma}^2(\boldsymbol{\beta})} \cdot \mathrm{E}_N[\mathbf{x}_n(y_n - \mathbf{x}_n'\boldsymbol{\beta})]$$

$$\mathrm{E}_N[L^c_{\boldsymbol{\beta}\boldsymbol{\beta}}(\boldsymbol{\beta}; y_n \mid \mathbf{x}_n)] = -\frac{2}{\hat{\sigma}^2(\boldsymbol{\beta})} \cdot \mathrm{E}_N[\mathbf{x}_n\mathbf{x}_n'] + \frac{1}{[\hat{\sigma}^2(\boldsymbol{\beta})]^2} \cdot \mathrm{E}_N[\mathbf{x}_n(y_n - \mathbf{x}_n'\boldsymbol{\beta})^2\mathbf{x}_n']$$

If we replace expectations with probability limits, then we obtain an analogy to the score identity. To see this, note that $\hat{\sigma}^2(\boldsymbol{\beta}_0) \xrightarrow{p} \sigma_0^2$ and

$$\mathrm{E}_N[L^c_{\boldsymbol{\beta}}(\boldsymbol{\beta}_0; y_n \mid \mathbf{x}_n)] = \frac{1}{\hat{\sigma}^2(\boldsymbol{\beta}_0)} \cdot \mathrm{E}_N[\mathbf{x}_n(y_n - \mathbf{x}_n'\boldsymbol{\beta}_0)] \xrightarrow{p} \mathbf{0}$$

An analogy to the information matrix is

$$\mathrm{Var}_N[L^c_{\boldsymbol{\beta}}(\boldsymbol{\beta}_0; y_n \mid \mathbf{x}_n)] \xrightarrow{p} \frac{1}{\sigma_0^2} \cdot \mathrm{E}[\mathbf{x}_n\mathbf{x}_n']$$

which is the inverse of the matrix of the asymptotic distribution of $\sqrt{N}(\hat{\boldsymbol{\beta}}_N - \boldsymbol{\beta}_0)$. Furthermore, we have the analogy

$$\mathrm{E}_N[L^c_{\boldsymbol{\beta}\boldsymbol{\beta}}(\boldsymbol{\beta}; y_n \mid \mathbf{x}_n)] \xrightarrow{p} -\frac{1}{\sigma_0^2} \cdot \mathrm{E}[\mathbf{x}_n\mathbf{x}_n']$$

to the information identity. As expected, $\sqrt{N}(\hat{\boldsymbol{\beta}}_N - \boldsymbol{\beta}_0)$ has an asymptotic variance matrix equal to $\sigma_0^2 \cdot \mathrm{E}[\mathbf{x}_n\mathbf{x}_n']^{-1}$.

The concentrated log-likelihood function is not only an analytical device. Grid search is a numerical form of concentrating the log-likelihood function. Figure 16.6 and Example 16.8 illustrate this.

16.8 THE GAUSS–SEIDEL ALGORITHM

It is not always possible to concentrate the likelihood function analytically. Concentration of the likelihood requires the ability to solve analytically for a subset of the parameters using the normal equations. An alternative numerical procedure is the Gauss–Seidel algorithm, which maximizes the function iteratively over subsets of the parameter vector. This approach is most useful when quadratic approximations are poor. It is also a way to overcome extremely large dimensions in the parameter space.

This algorithm works best when the Hessian matrix is block-diagonal, because in that case the quadratic approximation breaks up into the two quadratic functions that each step of Gauss–Seidel maximizes. Otherwise, Gauss–Seidel can be very slow, particularly as the Hessian approaches singularity.

EXAMPLE 16.14 (Gauss–Seidel)

Suppose that we applied the Gauss–Seidel algorithm to the simple OLS problem

$$\min_{\boldsymbol{\beta}} \sum_{n=1}^{N} (y_n - \beta_1 - \beta_2 x_{2n})^2$$

The algorithm would iterate between

$$\beta_{1i} = \bar{y} - \beta_{2,i-1}\bar{x}_2$$

and

$$\beta_{2i} = \frac{\sum_{n=1}^{N} x_{2n}(y_n - \beta_{1,i})}{\sum_{n=1}^{N} x_{2n}^2}$$

Therefore,

$$\begin{aligned}\beta_{2i} &= \hat{\beta}_2 a + \beta_{2,i-1}(1-a) \\ &= \hat{\beta}_2 \left(1 - (1-a)^i\right) + (1-a)^i \beta_{20}\end{aligned}$$

where

$$a \equiv \frac{\sum_{n=1}^{N} (x_{2n} - \bar{x}_2)^2}{\sum_{n=1}^{N} x_{2n}^2}$$

As x_{2n} approaches collinearity with a constant, a approaches zero and the speed with which β_{2i} approaches $\hat{\beta}_2$ slows to a standstill.

16.9 MATHEMATICAL NOTES

The mathematical notes contain the proofs of several results and a description of *stochastic order*.

16.9.1 Proofs

Proof of Lemma 16.2. Let $\boldsymbol{\theta}_c(\boldsymbol{\theta}_2) \equiv [\hat{\boldsymbol{\theta}}_1(\boldsymbol{\theta}_2)', \boldsymbol{\theta}_2']'$ and $\boldsymbol{\theta}_{0c} \equiv [\hat{\boldsymbol{\theta}}_1(\boldsymbol{\theta}_{02})', \boldsymbol{\theta}_{02}']$. Using (16.18) and the implicit function theorem,

$$\begin{aligned}\mathbf{0} = L_{11}(\boldsymbol{\theta}_c; U)\frac{\partial \hat{\boldsymbol{\theta}}_1(\boldsymbol{\theta}_2)}{\partial \boldsymbol{\theta}_2'} + L_{12}(\boldsymbol{\theta}_c; U) \quad &\Rightarrow \\ \frac{\partial \hat{\boldsymbol{\theta}}_1(\boldsymbol{\theta}_2)'}{\partial \boldsymbol{\theta}_2} = -\,\mathrm{E}_N[L_{21}(\boldsymbol{\theta}_c)]\; \mathrm{E}_N[L_{11}(\boldsymbol{\theta}_c)]^{-1}& \\ = -\bar{L}_{21}\,\bar{L}_{11}^{-1}&\end{aligned}$$

where we denote $\bar{L}_{21} \equiv \mathrm{E}_N[L_{21}(\boldsymbol{\theta}_c)]$ and $\bar{L}_{22} \equiv \mathrm{E}_N[L_{22}(\boldsymbol{\theta}_c)]$.[9] Therefore,

[9] See, for example, Simon and Blume (1994, p. 341).

$$L^c_{\boldsymbol{\theta}_2}(\boldsymbol{\theta}_2; U) = L_2(\boldsymbol{\theta}_c; U) - \bar{L}_{21}\, \bar{L}_{11}^{-1}\, L_1(\boldsymbol{\theta}_c; U) \tag{16.26}$$

$$\mathrm{E}_N[L^c_{\boldsymbol{\theta}_2}(\boldsymbol{\theta}_2)] = \mathrm{E}_N[L_2(\boldsymbol{\theta}_c)] \tag{16.27}$$

where the second equality follows from the first and (16.18). The second equality is an example of the envelope theorem.[10]

Because $\hat{\boldsymbol{\theta}}_1(\boldsymbol{\theta}_{02})$ is the restricted MLE for $\boldsymbol{\theta}_1$ given $\boldsymbol{\theta}_2 = \boldsymbol{\theta}_{02}$, Proposition 16 (ML Asymptotics, p. 320) implies that $\hat{\boldsymbol{\theta}}_1(\boldsymbol{\theta}_{02}) \xrightarrow{p} \boldsymbol{\theta}_{01}$ and $\boldsymbol{\theta}_c(\boldsymbol{\theta}_{02}) \xrightarrow{p} \boldsymbol{\theta}_0$. Under the dominance hypothesis (16.20) of the lemma and the other assumptions, the uniform LLN (Lemma 15.1, p. 321) implies that $\mathrm{E}_N[L_2(\boldsymbol{\theta})] \xrightarrow{p} \mathrm{E}[L_2(\boldsymbol{\theta})]$ uniformly. Therefore, using (16.27),

$$\mathrm{E}_N\big[L^c_{\boldsymbol{\theta}_2}(\boldsymbol{\theta}_{02})\big] = \mathrm{E}_N\big[L_2[\boldsymbol{\theta}_c(\boldsymbol{\theta}_{02})]\big] \xrightarrow{p} \mathrm{E}[L_2(\boldsymbol{\theta}_0)] = \mathbf{0}$$

This confirms (16.21).

Proposition 16 also implies (16.23). This is an immediate consequence of $\sqrt{N}(\hat{\boldsymbol{\theta}} - \boldsymbol{\theta}_0) \xrightarrow{d} \mathfrak{N}[\mathbf{0}, \mathfrak{I}(\boldsymbol{\theta}_0)^{-1}]$ and the partitioned inverse formula [equation (3.23), p. 70].

Now expand

$$\begin{aligned}\mathrm{E}_N\big[L^c_{\boldsymbol{\theta}_2}(\boldsymbol{\theta}_{02})L^c_{\boldsymbol{\theta}_2}(\boldsymbol{\theta}_{02})'\big] = {} & \mathrm{E}_N[L_2(\boldsymbol{\theta}_{0c})L_2(\boldsymbol{\theta}_{0c})'] \\ & + \bar{L}_{21}\, \bar{L}_{11}^{-1}\, \mathrm{E}_N[L_1(\boldsymbol{\theta}_{0c})L_1(\boldsymbol{\theta}_{0c})']\, \bar{L}_{11}^{-1}\, \bar{L}'_{21} \\ & + \mathrm{E}_N[L_2(\boldsymbol{\theta}_{0c})\, L_1(\boldsymbol{\theta}_{0c})']\, \bar{L}_{11}^{-1}\, \bar{L}'_{21} \\ & + \bar{L}_{21}\, \bar{L}_{11}^{-1}\, \mathrm{E}_N[L_1(\boldsymbol{\theta}_{0c})\, L_2(\boldsymbol{\theta}_{0c})']\end{aligned}$$

where $\bar{L}_{21}$ and $\bar{L}_{22}$ are also evaluated at $\boldsymbol{\theta}_{0c} \equiv \boldsymbol{\theta}_c(\boldsymbol{\theta}_{02})$. Because $\boldsymbol{\theta}_{0c} \xrightarrow{p} \boldsymbol{\theta}_0$ and

$$\mathrm{E}_N[L_{kj}(\boldsymbol{\theta}_0)] \xrightarrow{p} \mathrm{E}[L_{kj}(\boldsymbol{\theta}_0)] = -\mathfrak{I}_{kj}(\boldsymbol{\theta}_0)$$

$$\mathrm{E}_N[L_k(\boldsymbol{\theta}_0)\, L_j(\boldsymbol{\theta}_0)'] \xrightarrow{p} \mathrm{E}[L_k(\boldsymbol{\theta}_0)\, L_j(\boldsymbol{\theta}_0)'] = \mathfrak{I}_{kj}(\boldsymbol{\theta}_0)$$

uniformly for $k, j = 1, 2$, then

$$\begin{aligned}\mathrm{E}_N\big[L^c_{\boldsymbol{\theta}_2}(\boldsymbol{\theta}_{02})L^c_{\boldsymbol{\theta}_2}(\boldsymbol{\theta}_{02})'\big] & \xrightarrow{p} \mathfrak{I}_{22} + \mathfrak{I}_{21}\mathfrak{I}_{11}^{-1}\mathfrak{I}_{12} \\ & \qquad - \mathfrak{I}_{21}\mathfrak{I}_{11}^{-1}\mathfrak{I}_{12} - \mathfrak{I}_{21}\mathfrak{I}_{11}^{-1}\mathfrak{I}_{12} \\ & = \mathfrak{I}_{22} - \mathfrak{I}_{21}\mathfrak{I}_{11}^{-1}\mathfrak{I}_{12}\end{aligned}$$

where $\mathfrak{I}_{kj} \equiv \mathfrak{I}_{kj}(\boldsymbol{\theta}_0)$, confirming (16.24).

Finally, differentiating (16.25) we get

$$\begin{aligned}\mathrm{E}_N[L^c_{\boldsymbol{\theta}_2\boldsymbol{\theta}_2}(\boldsymbol{\theta}_2)] & = \frac{\partial}{\partial \boldsymbol{\theta}'_2}\, \mathrm{E}_N[L_2(\boldsymbol{\theta}_c)] \\ & = \mathrm{E}_N[L_{22}(\boldsymbol{\theta}_c)] + \mathrm{E}_N[L_{21}(\boldsymbol{\theta}_c)]\frac{\partial \hat{\boldsymbol{\theta}}_1(\boldsymbol{\theta}_2)}{\partial \boldsymbol{\theta}'_2} \\ & = \mathrm{E}_N[L_{22}(\boldsymbol{\theta}_c)] - \mathrm{E}_N[L_{21}(\boldsymbol{\theta}_c)]\, \bar{L}_{11}^{-1}\, \bar{L}_{12}\end{aligned}$$

[10] See Simon and Blume (1994, Section 19.2) concerning envelope theorems.

Rewriting this equation in terms of sample moments and evaluating at $\boldsymbol{\theta}_{02}$,

$$\mathrm{E}_N\big[L^c_{\boldsymbol{\theta}_2\boldsymbol{\theta}_2}(\boldsymbol{\theta}_{02})\big] = \bar{L}_{22}[\boldsymbol{\theta}_c(\boldsymbol{\theta}_{02})] - \bar{L}_{21}[\boldsymbol{\theta}_c(\boldsymbol{\theta}_{02})]\,\bar{L}_{11}[\boldsymbol{\theta}_c(\boldsymbol{\theta}_{02})]^{-1}\,\bar{L}_{12}[\boldsymbol{\theta}_c(\boldsymbol{\theta}_{02})]$$

$$\xrightarrow{p} \mathfrak{I}_{22} - \mathfrak{I}_{21}\mathfrak{I}_{11}^{-1}\mathfrak{I}_{12}$$

which confirms (16.22). □

16.9.2 Stochastic Order

The concept of *asymptotic equivalence* (Definition 34, p. 331) is one example of an asymptotic relationship that can be described in the terms of *stochastic order*. We do not use the notation associated with stochastic order (except in a few exercises), but it is useful and is encountered frequently in econometric and statistical writing, so we explain it here. It generalizes the notation for the order of deterministic sequences given in Section B.1, *Limits*.

Given what we have already discussed, the simplest is the "little-'o'-'p'" notation:

DEFINITION 37 (STOCHASTICALLY NEGLIGIBLE) *If $U_N \xrightarrow{p} 0$, then $U_N = o_p(1)$. If $U_N = N^r\, o_p(1)$, then $U_N = o_p(N^r)$.*

According to this notation, the asymptotic equivalence of the MLE and the LMLE means that $\sqrt{N}(\hat{\boldsymbol{\theta}}_N - \hat{\boldsymbol{\theta}}^*_N) = o_p(1)$. This is a probabilistic generalization of $V_N = o(1)$ meaning that $\lim_{N\to\infty} V_N = 0$.

The generalization of $O(1)$ parallels the description of probability limits in Lemma 13.1 (p. 260):

DEFINITION 38 (STOCHASTICALLY BOUNDED) *If U_N is a stochastic sequence such that for every $\delta > 0$ there is a constant $M(\delta)$ and an $N^*(\delta)$ so that*

$$N > N^*(\delta) \quad\Rightarrow\quad \Pr\{|U_N| < M(\delta)\} > 1 - \delta$$

then $U_N = O_p(1)$. If $U_N = N^r\, O_p(1)$, then $U_N = O_p(N^r)$.

One of the most common uses of this concept of stochastic order is "root-n" ($\sqrt{N}$) consistency.

DEFINITION 39 ($\sqrt{N}$-CONSISTENT) *If $\sqrt{N}(\boldsymbol{\theta}_N - \boldsymbol{\theta}_0) = O_p(1)$, then $\boldsymbol{\theta}_N$ is $\sqrt{N}$ consistent for $\boldsymbol{\theta}_0$.*

The class of $\sqrt{N}$-consistent estimators is a generalization of the class of CUAN estimators.

16.9.3 Uniqueness of the MLE

When the MLE is the unique local maximum of the log-likelihood function within the parameter space, computation is greatly simplified because a local maximum is the global maximum and the unique solution to the normal equations. Hence, a researcher needs to carry out only one numerical optimization. The cases in which the MLE possesses this uniqueness property often rest on the global concavity of the log-likelihood function.

LEMMA 16.3 (GLOBAL CONCAVITY) *Let $L(\boldsymbol{\theta})$ be a twice continuously differentiable log-likelihood function with $\boldsymbol{\theta}$ varying in a connected open subset $\boldsymbol{\Theta} \subset \mathbb{R}^K$. Suppose that*

1. *there is a $\boldsymbol{\theta}_1$ in the interior of $\boldsymbol{\Theta}$ such that $L_{\boldsymbol{\theta}}(\boldsymbol{\theta}_1) = \mathbf{0}$ and*
2. *the Hessian matrix $L_{\boldsymbol{\theta\theta}}(\boldsymbol{\theta})$ is negative definite for all $\boldsymbol{\theta} \in \boldsymbol{\Theta}$.*

Then

1. *$L(\boldsymbol{\theta})$ is strictly concave in $\boldsymbol{\theta}$,*
2. *there is a unique local (and therefore global) maximum $\hat{\boldsymbol{\theta}} \in \boldsymbol{\Theta}$, and*
3. *$L(\boldsymbol{\theta})$ has no other critical points in $\boldsymbol{\Theta}$.*

This is a basic result of multivariate calculus.[11] This result is intuitive, but it applies only to such cases as the normal linear regression model where one can demonstrate analytically that the Hessian is negative definite for all parameter values.

EXAMPLE 16.15 (Normal Linear Regression)
We may reparameterize the log-likelihood function of the normal linear regression model (14.3) as

$$L(\boldsymbol{\theta}) = \frac{N}{2}\log(2\pi\gamma) - \frac{1}{2}(\gamma\mathbf{y} - \mathbf{X}\boldsymbol{\delta})'(\gamma\mathbf{y} - \mathbf{X}\boldsymbol{\delta})$$

where $\gamma = 1/\sigma$ and $\boldsymbol{\delta} = \gamma \cdot \boldsymbol{\beta}$. The Hessian is

$$L_{\boldsymbol{\theta\theta}}(\boldsymbol{\theta}) = \begin{bmatrix} -\mathbf{X}'\mathbf{X} & \mathbf{X}'\mathbf{y} \\ \mathbf{y}'\mathbf{X} & -\mathbf{y}'\mathbf{y} - \frac{N}{\gamma^2} \end{bmatrix}$$

which is negative definite if $\mathbf{X}$ is full-column rank.

Note that this lemma stipulates that the log-likelihood function possesses an interior local maximum. If we find an interior local maximum numerically, we can apply the result. But before we even start to maximize the log-likelihood function, we would like to know that such a maximum

[11] See Simon and Blume (1994, Theorems 21.3 and 21.6).

actually exists. Such existence is usually established by showing that the log-likelihood function "turns down" eventually no matter what direction we venture in the parameter space. If the log-likelihood function has this property, then sufficient second-order conditions for a unique local optimum can be much weaker than global concavity as Mäkeläinen et al. (1981, Corollary 2.5) and Gabrielsen (1982) show.

Lemma 16.4 (Local Concavity at Critical Points) *Let $L(\boldsymbol{\theta})$ be a twice continuously differentiable log-likelihood function with $\boldsymbol{\theta}$ varying in a connected open subset $\boldsymbol{\Theta} \subset \mathbb{R}^K$. Suppose that*

1. $\lim_{j\to\infty} L(\boldsymbol{\theta}^{(j)}) = c$ *for every sequence* $\{\boldsymbol{\theta}^{(j)}; j = 1, 2, \ldots\}$ *in* $\boldsymbol{\Theta}$ *converging to the boundary of* $\boldsymbol{\Theta}$, *where c is a real number or* $-\infty$,[12] *and*
2. *the Hessian matrix* $L_{\boldsymbol{\theta\theta}}(\boldsymbol{\theta})$ *is negative definite for all* $\boldsymbol{\theta} \in \boldsymbol{\Theta}$ *such that* $L_{\boldsymbol{\theta}}(\boldsymbol{\theta}) = \mathbf{0}$.

Then

1. *there is a unique local (and therefore global) maximum* $\hat{\boldsymbol{\theta}} \in \boldsymbol{\Theta}$, *and*
2. $L(\boldsymbol{\theta})$ *has no other critical points in* $\boldsymbol{\Theta}$.

In this result, the existence of a root of the normal equations is a result instead of a condition. We will apply this result in later chapters.

EXAMPLE 16.16 (Student *t*)

Copas (1975) shows that the Hessian of the Cauchy location-scale log-likelihood function satisfies the condition of this lemma. Mäkeläinen et al. (1981, Corollary 2.5) and Gabrielsen (1982) note that this result extends to the Student *t* distribution for all degrees of freedom greater than or equal to one and that the first condition is also met with probability one. Therefore,

$$L(\mu, \sigma) = \mathrm{E}_N\left[-\frac{1}{2}\log\left(\frac{\Gamma[(\nu+1)/2]}{\sqrt{\nu}\Gamma(1/2)\,\Gamma(\nu/2)}\right) - \log\sigma - \frac{\nu+1}{2}\log\left(1 + \frac{(y_n-\mu)^2}{\nu\sigma^2}\right)\right]$$

has a unique finite maximum for all $\nu \geq 1$. Although this result does not carry over to the linear regression model, we have seen that this generalization can be practically similar in Example 16.8.

16.10 OVERVIEW

1. Local quadratic approximation of the log-likelihood function produces a convenient approximation to the maximum likelihood estimator (MLE).

[12] A sequence $\{\boldsymbol{\theta}^{(j)}; j = 1, 2, \ldots\}$ in $\boldsymbol{\Theta}$ converges to the boundary of $\boldsymbol{\Theta}$ if for every compact set $\mathbb{S} \subset \boldsymbol{\Theta}$ there exists an integer $n \geq 1$ such that $\boldsymbol{\theta}^{(j)} \notin \boldsymbol{\Theta}$ for every $j \geq n$ (Mäkeläinen et al., 1981, p. 759).

2. Iterative computational methods for the MLE refine this approximation repeatedly until they reach a local maximum of the log-likelihood function.
3. Such methods turn high-dimensional searches into a sequence of one-dimensional searches.
4. The various information matrix estimators provide different approximations to the Hessian and, therefore, different search directions.
5. The linearized MLE (LMLE) is a single iteration of these computational algorithms when the step size equals one and the starting value is a consistent estimator.
6. A a sensible numerical convergence criterion measures the length of the gradient against the curvature of the log-likelihood function.
7. Parameter transformations can improve the quality of the quadratic approximation. Transformations can also impose constraints on parameter values.
8. In some cases, concentrating the log-likelihood function is possible. This also reduces the dimensionality of the optimization problem.
9. The Gauss–Seidel method is a numerical optimization technique that effectively concentrates the log-likelihood function numerically by maximizing the log-likelihood function over subsets of the parameters.

16.11 EXERCISES

16.11.1 Review

16.1 (GNR) Consider the nonlinear conditional regression model $y_n \mid \mathbf{x}_n \sim \mathfrak{N}\left(\mu(\boldsymbol{\beta}_0; \mathbf{x}_n), \sigma_0^2\right)$ where ML estimation of $\boldsymbol{\beta}_0$ corresponds to NLS. What is the difference between the Gauss–Newton and the BHHH search directions?

16.2 (BHHH) A search direction closely related to $\boldsymbol{\delta}_{\text{BH}^3}$ is

$$\boldsymbol{\delta} = \text{Var}_N[L_{\boldsymbol{\theta}}(\boldsymbol{\theta}_i, U)]^{-1} \, \text{E}_N[L_{\boldsymbol{\theta}}(\boldsymbol{\theta}_i, U)]$$

Show that the length of this search direction is always longer than the length of $\boldsymbol{\delta}_{\text{BH}^3}$.

16.3 (BHHH) Consider the optimization of the multivariate normal log-likelihood function

$$\text{E}_N[L(\boldsymbol{\mu}, \boldsymbol{\Omega}; \mathbf{y})] = -\frac{1}{2} \log \det \boldsymbol{\Omega} - \frac{1}{2} \text{E}_N[(\mathbf{y} - \boldsymbol{\mu})' \, \boldsymbol{\Omega}^{-1} \, (\mathbf{y} - \boldsymbol{\mu})]$$

(a) How can this log-likelihood be maximized over $\boldsymbol{\mu}$ and $\boldsymbol{\Omega}$ without numerical optimization algorithms?
(b) Will a single iteration of such quadratic algorithms as BHHH yield the optimum?
(c) Suppose that the number of observations N is less than the number of parameters in $\boldsymbol{\mu}$ and $\boldsymbol{\Omega}$. Show that the BHHH algorithm will break down because its approximation to the Hessian is singular, whereas the other quadratic approximations will generally work. Can you suggest a way to help overcome this problem with BHHH?

16.4 (Parameter Transformations) Consider the product of two averages:

$$\bar{y}_{1N}\,\bar{y}_{2N} = \left(\sum_{n=1}^{N} \frac{y_{1n}}{N}\right)\left(\sum_{n=1}^{N} \frac{y_{2n}}{N}\right)$$

where the y_{jn} are i.i.d. with $\mathrm{E}[y_{jn}] = \mu_j$ and $\mathrm{Var}[y_{jn}] = \sigma_j^2$, $j = 1, 2$. Find an asymptotic approximation of the distribution of this product under the assumptions that the y_ns are drawn independently and identically from a bivariate distribution with finite second moments.

16.5 (Parameter Transformations) On p. 13, we computed an estimate of the peak of the wage profile. Using the CPS data, reestimate this peak and compute an asymptotic approximation of its standard error.

16.6 (Reparameterization) Example 16.9 notes that transforming the variance parameter in the log-likelihood function of the normal distribution improves the quadratic approximation of the function. Consider the normal linear regression model for which the variance estimator s^2 possesses a $\left[\sigma_0^2/(N-K)\right]\chi^2_{N-K}$ distribution. Asymptotically,

$$\sqrt{\frac{N-K}{2}}\left(\frac{s^2}{\sigma_0^2} - 1\right) \xrightarrow{d} \mathfrak{N}(0, 1)$$

(a) Give an asymptotic approximation for the distribution of $\log s^2/\sigma_0^2$.
(b) Standardize $\log s^2/\sigma_0^2$ so that it is approximately an $\mathfrak{N}(0, 1)$ random variable and graph its p.d.f., the p.d.f. for $\sqrt{(N-K)/2}\left[(s^2/\sigma_0^2) - 1\right]$, and the standard normal p.d.f. $N - K = 5$, 10, and 20. Which transformation of s^2 appears to have the p.d.f. closest to the normal p.d.f.?

16.7 (Order) Show that if the stochastic sequence U_N converges in distribution, then $U_N = O_p(1)$.

16.8 (Concavity) Globally concave log-likelihood functions are often easier to maximize numerically than other log-likelihood functions. One reason is that the MLE is the unique local maximum, if it exists. Another reason is that most of the quadratic approximations described in this chapter are globally concave functions. Such quadratic functions have unique maxima.

(a) Show that the normal log-likelihood function

$$L(\mu, \sigma) = -\log\sigma - \frac{(y-\mu)^2}{2\sigma^2}$$

is not globally concave in the parameters μ and σ^2.

(b) Show that the reparameterized function

$$L(\delta, \gamma) = \log\gamma - (\gamma y - \delta)^2$$

where $\delta = \mu/\sigma$ and $\gamma = 1/\sigma$ is globally concave.

(c) Show that the reparameterized logistic log-likelihood function

$$\log\gamma - \log\left(2 + e^{-(\gamma y - \delta)} + e^{\gamma y - \delta}\right)$$

is also globally concave.

16.9 (Initial Estimator) Find an initial consistent estimator of the degrees of freedom parameter for the Student t linear regression model based on (1) the second and fourth moments of the Student t distribution,

$$m_2 = \frac{\nu\sigma}{\nu - 2} \quad \text{and} \quad m_4 = \frac{3\nu^2\sigma^2}{(\nu-4)(\nu-2)}$$

and (2) the second and fourth sample moments of the OLS fitted residuals,

$$\hat{\mu}_2 = 0.2163 \qquad \text{and} \qquad \hat{\mu}_4 = 0.2388$$

This estimator could be used in Table 16.1 as the missing entry for ν for the OLS estimator. How would you compute an estimated standard error of this estimator for ν?

16.11.2 Extensions

16.10 **(LMLE)** Suppose that the third derivatives of the log-likelihood function satisfy the uniform LLN (Lemma 15.1, p. 321) so that

$$\mathrm{E}_N\left[\frac{\partial^3 L(\boldsymbol{\theta})}{\partial\theta_i\,\partial\theta_j\,\partial\theta_k}\right] \xrightarrow{p} \mathrm{E}\left[\frac{\partial^3 L(\boldsymbol{\theta})}{\partial\theta_i\,\partial\theta_j\,\partial\theta_k}\right]$$

uniformly in $\boldsymbol{\theta} \in \boldsymbol{\Theta}$. Show that the initial consistent estimator in the LMLE can be merely N^{δ}-consistent for $\delta > \frac{1}{4}$, that is $N^{\delta}(\check{\boldsymbol{\theta}}_N - \boldsymbol{\theta}_0) = O_p(1)$.

***16.11** **(LMLE)** Under the conditions of Lemma 15.7 (LMLE, p. 333), show that an optimal step length for the given search direction also produces an estimator that is asymptotically equivalent to the MLE.[13] (Such step lengths may improve the small sample performance of the LMLE.)

16.12 **(LMLE)** Show that the LMLE will work with any initial estimator that is $\sqrt{N}$ consistent under the conditions of Lemma 15.7 (LMLE, p. 333).

***16.13** Suppose that $\{(\mathbf{x}_n, y_n),\ n = 1, \ldots, N\}$ are i.i.d. random variables and that the conditional distribution of y_n given $\mathbf{x}_n$ is $\mathfrak{N}[\mu(\boldsymbol{\beta}_0; \mathbf{x}_n),\ \sigma_0^2]$ where $\mu(\boldsymbol{\beta}_0; \mathbf{x}_n)$ is a twice continuously differentiable function.

(a) Give sufficient conditions so that the NLS estimator $\hat{\boldsymbol{\beta}}_{\text{NLS}}$ for $\boldsymbol{\beta}_0$ is consistent.

(b) Give sufficient conditions so that

$$\sqrt{N}(\hat{\boldsymbol{\beta}}_{\text{NLS}} - \boldsymbol{\beta}_0) \xrightarrow{d} \mathfrak{N}(\mathbf{0}, \mathbf{V})$$

where

$$\mathbf{V} = \sigma_0^2 \cdot \left\{\operatorname*{plim}_{N\to\infty} \mathrm{E}_N[\mu_{\boldsymbol{\beta}}(\boldsymbol{\beta}_0; \mathbf{x}_n)\mu_{\boldsymbol{\beta}}(\boldsymbol{\beta}_0; \mathbf{x}_n)']\right\}^{-1}$$

Explain how OLS is a special case.

(c) Give an estimator of the asymptotic variance of $\hat{\boldsymbol{\beta}}_{\text{NLS}}$.

(d) Show that the asymptotic distribution of the NLS estimator is not changed by removing the normality assumption while retaining $\mathrm{E}[y_n \mid \mathbf{x}_n] = \mu(\boldsymbol{\beta}_0; \mathbf{x}_n)$ and $\mathrm{Var}[y_n \mid \mathbf{x}_n] = \sigma_0^2 < \infty$.

---

[13] See Newey (1987a).

CHAPTER 17

Maximum Likelihood Statistical Inference

17.1 INTRODUCTION

Interval estimation has a familiar form in the asymptotic distribution theory for MLEs. The asymptotic normal distribution and consistent variance estimates play right into the elliptical probability regions based on quadratic forms.[1] Suppose that we have obtained the MLE and $\sqrt{N}(\hat{\boldsymbol{\theta}} - \boldsymbol{\theta}_0) \xrightarrow{d} \mathfrak{N}[\mathbf{0}, \Im(\boldsymbol{\theta}_0)]$ and we are interested in an interval estimator for $\boldsymbol{\gamma}_0 = \boldsymbol{\gamma}(\boldsymbol{\theta}_0)$. Let $\boldsymbol{\gamma} : \mathbb{R}^K \to \mathbb{R}^{K-M}$ be continuous and rank $\boldsymbol{\gamma}_\theta(\boldsymbol{\theta}) = K - M \leq K$. According to the delta method (Lemma 16.1, p. 367) and the continuity of quadratic forms,

$$N \cdot (\hat{\boldsymbol{\gamma}} - \boldsymbol{\gamma}_0)' \left(\hat{\mathbf{J}}\hat{\Im}^{-1}\hat{\mathbf{J}}'\right)^{-1} (\hat{\boldsymbol{\gamma}} - \boldsymbol{\gamma}_0) \xrightarrow{d} \chi^2_{K-M}$$

where $\hat{\boldsymbol{\gamma}} \equiv \boldsymbol{\gamma}(\hat{\boldsymbol{\theta}})$, $\hat{\mathbf{J}} \equiv \boldsymbol{\gamma}_\theta(\hat{\boldsymbol{\theta}})$, and $\hat{\Im} \equiv \mathrm{E}_N[\Im(\hat{\boldsymbol{\theta}})]$. Therefore,

$$\left\{\boldsymbol{\gamma} \in \mathbb{R}^{K-M} \mid N \cdot (\hat{\boldsymbol{\gamma}} - \boldsymbol{\gamma})' \left(\hat{\mathbf{J}}\hat{\Im}^{-1}\hat{\mathbf{J}}'\right)^{-1} (\hat{\boldsymbol{\gamma}} - \boldsymbol{\gamma}) \leq \chi^2_{K-M;1-\alpha}\right\} \tag{17.1}$$

is a $100(1 - \alpha)\%$ approximate confidence interval for $\boldsymbol{\gamma}(\boldsymbol{\theta}_0)$. This is the most direct method of interval estimation, given our overall approach.

In Figure 17.1, we draw such a confidence interval for estimates of the Student t model for log-wages in Table 16.1 (p. 348). Along the horizontal axis, we measure the coefficient of the linear experience term. This measures the return in wages to experience in the labor force for those with no experience. Along the vertical axis is the location in years of the fitted peak of the earnings profile.[2] The ellipse drawn with a heavy solid line is the approximate joint 95% confidence interval of these two parameters based on (17.1).

[1] For review, see Section 10.3.

[2] The peak of the earnings profile equals minus the ratio of the linear coefficient to twice the coefficient of the quadratic experience term.

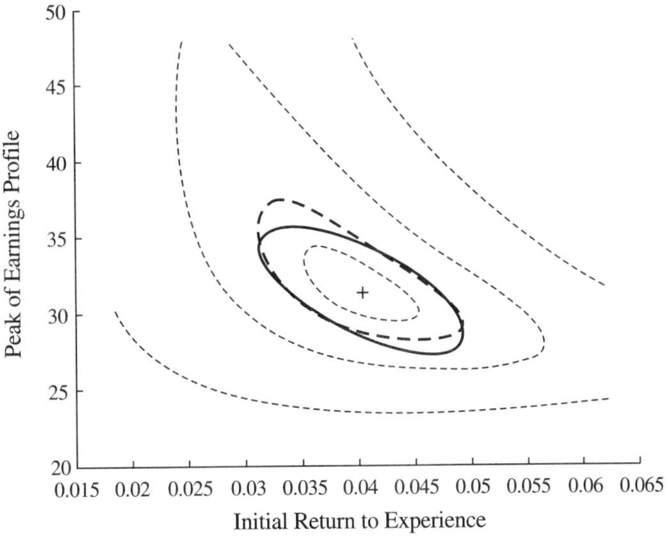

Figure 17.1 Contours of the concentrated log-likelihood function.

In Figure 17.1, we also illustrate a second method for approximating this 95% confidence interval. As is usual with asymptotic approximations, there are several alternative interval estimators that are asymptotically equivalent when the model is correctly specified. The dashed lines in Figure 17.1 are contours of the concentrated log-likelihood function in the initial return to experience and the peak of the earnings profile. The contour with the heavy dashed line corresponds to another 95% confidence interval estimator for the two parameters. As one can see, the elliptical interval is similar to the nonelliptical one except in the northwest direction.

This deviation is almost entirely due to the nonlinear transformation of the regression coefficients to get peak years. In Figure 17.2 we plot these confidence intervals for the experience coefficients themselves. In this case, there is scant deviation between the delta method and the log-likelihood contour approximations. This difference could be reduced further by choosing a different estimator of the information matrix in the Wald version. We have used the sample variance matrix of the elements of the score. If we replace this with minus the average Hessian matrix, then the confidence intervals are indistinguishable because the local quadratic approximation of the Student t log-likelihood function is so accurate at this distance from the MLE.

Given the general duality between confidence intervals and hypothesis tests, there are also several asymptotically equivalent methods for testing such restrictions as $H_0 : \mathbf{r}(\boldsymbol{\theta}_0) = \mathbf{0}$ [or $\boldsymbol{\gamma}(\boldsymbol{\theta}_0) = \boldsymbol{\gamma}_0$]. Econometricians have tended to focus on the differences among these hypothesis testing methods and in this chapter so will we. But our basic theme is the same. All of the methods rest implicitly on a quadratic approximation of the log-likelihood function and their differences grow out of alternative approximations.

There are three popular methods for computing hypothesis test statistics in the likelihood framework: the Wald (W), the likelihood ratio (LR), and the score (S) statistics. Under general conditions, all three statistics are asymptotically equivalent under the null hypothesis. The Wald statistic follows the familiar lines of the F test statistic for the normal linear regression

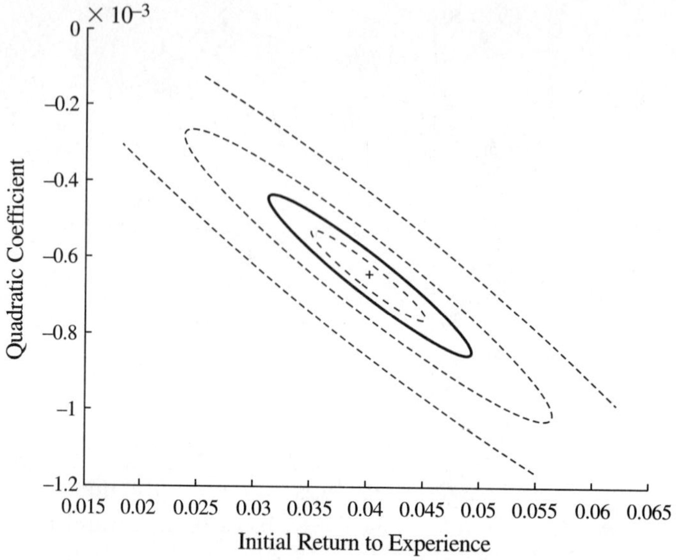

Figure 17.2 Contours of the concentrated log-likelihood function.

model. The Wald test statistic is a statistical measure of the differences between estimated and hypothesized parameter values. The LR test statistic is closely associated with likelihood theory itself. Given that the log-likelihood function is the basic goodness-of-fit measure, the LR statistic measures the difference in fit of the two sets of parameter values, estimated with and without the restrictions of the hypothesis. The S test statistic is a statistical measure of the difference between the score of the restricted parameters and zero. If the restrictions of the null hypothesis are true, then the restricted MLE should be close to the unrestricted MLE and the derivatives of the log-likelihood function with respect to the constrained parameters should be almost zero.

Operationally the tests have important differences. The Wald test requires estimation only of the unrestricted model. The score test, on the other hand, requires estimation only of the restricted model. The likelihood ratio test requires both restricted and unrestricted estimators, but given these its calculation is simpler than the other two.

We have already implicitly touched on these three test statistics in the linear regression model, where they turn out to be exactly equal.

EXAMPLE 17.1 (Restricted Least Squares)

Recall testing the linear restrictions $H_0 : \mathbf{R}\boldsymbol{\beta}_0 = \mathbf{r}$ in the normal regression model $\mathbf{y} \mid \mathbf{X} \sim \mathfrak{N}(\mathbf{X}\boldsymbol{\beta}_0, \sigma_0^2 \cdot \mathbf{I})$. Let $\mathbf{R}$ be full rank and $K - M = \text{rank}(\mathbf{R})$. Because $\hat{\boldsymbol{\beta}} \mid \mathbf{X} \sim \mathfrak{N}[\boldsymbol{\beta}_0, \sigma_0^2 \cdot (\mathbf{X}'\mathbf{X})^{-1}]$, under H_0 $\mathbf{R}\hat{\boldsymbol{\beta}} \sim \mathfrak{N}[\mathbf{r}, \sigma^2 \cdot \mathbf{R}(\mathbf{X}'\mathbf{X})^{-1}\mathbf{R}']$. When σ_0^2 is known, we compute the test statistic

$$\mathcal{W} = (\mathbf{R}\hat{\boldsymbol{\beta}} - \mathbf{r})'[\sigma_0^2 \cdot \mathbf{R}(\mathbf{X}'\mathbf{X})^{-1}\mathbf{R}']^{-1}(\mathbf{R}\hat{\boldsymbol{\beta}} - \mathbf{r}) \tag{17.2}$$

which has a χ^2_{K-M} distribution when H_0 is true. Roughly speaking, $\mathcal{W}$ is a simplified form of the regression test statistic (11.1),

$$\hat{F} \equiv \frac{(\mathbf{R}\hat{\boldsymbol{\beta}} - \mathbf{r})'[\mathbf{R}(\mathbf{X}'\mathbf{X})^{-1}\mathbf{R}']^{-1}(\mathbf{R}\hat{\boldsymbol{\beta}} - \mathbf{r})/(K - M)}{s^2}$$

The estimator of the variance in $\hat{F}$ is replaced by the (known) population variance and the numerator is no longer normalized by its degrees of freedom.

The statistic (17.2) illustrates the basic form of a Wald test statistic: $\mathcal{W}$ is a quadratic form in a normally distributed vector and the inverse of its variance matrix. This statistic has two other interpretations.

This $\mathcal{W}$ statistic has another form. Recall also that the restricted estimator can be written[3]

$$\hat{\boldsymbol{\beta}}_{\mathrm{R}} = \hat{\boldsymbol{\beta}} - (\mathbf{X}'\mathbf{X})^{-1}\mathbf{R}'\left[\mathbf{R}(\mathbf{X}'\mathbf{X})^{-1}\mathbf{R}'\right]^{-1}(\mathbf{R}\hat{\boldsymbol{\beta}} - \mathbf{r}) \tag{17.3}$$

We used (17.3) to show that[4]

$$\begin{aligned}(\mathbf{R}\hat{\boldsymbol{\beta}} - \mathbf{r})'[\mathbf{R}(\mathbf{X}'\mathbf{X})^{-1}\mathbf{R}']^{-1}(\mathbf{R}\hat{\boldsymbol{\beta}} - \mathbf{r}) &= (\hat{\boldsymbol{\beta}}_{\mathrm{R}} - \hat{\boldsymbol{\beta}})'\mathbf{X}'\mathbf{X}(\hat{\boldsymbol{\beta}}_{\mathrm{R}} - \hat{\boldsymbol{\beta}}) \\ &= \left\|\hat{\boldsymbol{\beta}}_{\mathrm{R}} - \hat{\boldsymbol{\beta}}\right\|^2_{\mathbf{X}'\mathbf{X}} \\ &= \left\|\mathbf{y} - \hat{\boldsymbol{\mu}}_{\mathrm{R}}\right\|^2 - \left\|\mathbf{y} - \hat{\boldsymbol{\mu}}\right\|^2\end{aligned}$$

Therefore,

$$\begin{aligned}\mathcal{W} &= -\frac{1}{\sigma_0^2}\cdot\{(\mathbf{y} - \mathbf{X}\hat{\boldsymbol{\beta}})'(\mathbf{y} - \mathbf{X}\hat{\boldsymbol{\beta}}) - (\mathbf{y} - \mathbf{X}\hat{\boldsymbol{\beta}}_{\mathrm{R}})'(\mathbf{y} - \mathbf{X}\hat{\boldsymbol{\beta}}_{\mathrm{R}})\} \\ &= 2\left[L(\hat{\boldsymbol{\beta}}, \sigma_0^2; \mathbf{y} \mid \mathbf{X}) - L(\hat{\boldsymbol{\beta}}_{\mathrm{R}}, \sigma_0^2; \mathbf{y} \mid \mathbf{X})\right] \\ &= \mathcal{LR}\end{aligned} \tag{17.4}$$

The difference in the log-likelihood functions is also the log of the *ratio* of the likelihood functions, hence the name *likelihood ratio* (LR) for this statistic. Its equivalence with $\mathcal{W}$ rests on the equivalence of the distance between restricted and unrestricted estimators, $\|\hat{\boldsymbol{\beta}}_{\mathrm{R}} - \hat{\boldsymbol{\beta}}\|^2_{\mathbf{X}'\mathbf{X}}$, and the change in the quadratic criterion function, $-\|\mathbf{y} - \mathbf{X}\hat{\boldsymbol{\beta}}\|^2 + \|\mathbf{y} - \mathbf{X}\hat{\boldsymbol{\beta}}_{\mathrm{R}}\|^2$.

A third interpretation of the test statistic involves the score evaluated at the restricted estimator:

$$\begin{aligned}L_{\boldsymbol{\beta}}(\hat{\boldsymbol{\beta}}_{\mathrm{R}}, \sigma_0^2; \mathbf{y} \mid \mathbf{X}) &= \frac{1}{\sigma_0^2}\cdot\mathbf{X}'(\mathbf{y} - \mathbf{X}\hat{\boldsymbol{\beta}}_{\mathrm{R}}) \\ &= \frac{1}{\sigma_0^2}\cdot\mathbf{X}'\mathbf{X}(\hat{\boldsymbol{\beta}} - \hat{\boldsymbol{\beta}}_{\mathrm{R}}) \\ &= \frac{1}{\sigma_0^2}\cdot\mathbf{R}'\left[\mathbf{R}(\mathbf{X}'\mathbf{X})^{-1}\mathbf{R}'\right]^{-1}(\mathbf{R}\hat{\boldsymbol{\beta}} - \mathbf{r})\end{aligned} \tag{17.5}$$

The Wald test for whether $\mathbf{R}\hat{\boldsymbol{\beta}} - \mathbf{r}$ is significantly different from zero is equivalent to a test for whether the score $L_{\boldsymbol{\beta}}(\hat{\boldsymbol{\beta}}_{\mathrm{R}}, \sigma_0^2; \mathbf{y} \mid \mathbf{X})$ is significantly different from zero. Under H_0 [using (17.3)],

---

[3] See Exercises 4.14 and 4.15.

[4] See (11.2) and (11.3) on p. 226.

$$L_\beta(\hat{\boldsymbol{\beta}}_R, \sigma^2; \mathbf{y}) \sim \mathfrak{N}\left(\mathbf{0}, \frac{1}{\sigma_0^2} \cdot \mathbf{A}\right)$$

where

$$\mathbf{A} = \mathbf{R}'\left[\mathbf{R}(\mathbf{X}'\mathbf{X})^{-1}\mathbf{R}'\right]^{-1}\mathbf{R}$$

The variance matrix $\sigma_0^2 \cdot \mathbf{A}$ is $K \times K$ but only has a rank of $K - M$. It is easy to verify that a generalized inverse of $\mathbf{A}$ is $(\mathbf{X}'\mathbf{X})^{-1}$. If we construct a quadratic form in the score and a generalized inverse of its variance matrix we obtain (Lemma 10.7, p. 213)

$$\begin{aligned} S &= L_\beta(\hat{\boldsymbol{\beta}}_R, \sigma_0^2; \mathbf{y} \mid \mathbf{X})' \left[\sigma_0^2 \cdot (\mathbf{X}'\mathbf{X})^{-1}\right] L_\beta(\hat{\boldsymbol{\beta}}_R, \sigma_0^2; \mathbf{y} \mid \mathbf{X}) \\ &= \mathcal{W} \end{aligned}$$

In this model all three test statistics are equal.

We will show that this equality reflects the quadratic character of the log-likelihood function in this example.

17.2 THE CLASSICAL HYPOTHESIS TEST STATISTICS

We begin our discussion of the classical hypothesis tests by describing each. For this introduction, we will write the null hypothesis as a restriction on a subset of the parameter vector $\boldsymbol{\theta} = [\boldsymbol{\theta}_1', \boldsymbol{\theta}_2']'$: specifically, $H_0 : \boldsymbol{\theta}_{02} = \mathbf{0}$. Let the dimension of $\boldsymbol{\theta}_2$ be $K - M < K$ so that under H_0 there are M unknown parameters.[5] For simplicity, we will suppose that the data-generating process is i.i.d. so that the information matrix is constant for all observations. To generalize for conditional likelihood specifications, replace $\Im(\boldsymbol{\theta})$ with $\mathrm{E}_N[\Im(\boldsymbol{\theta})]$ in the formulas that follow. Otherwise, we maintain the assumptions of Proposition 16 (ML Asymptotics, p. 320) that support the asymptotic distribution theory for the MLE.

17.2.1 The Wald Test

The Wald test is a familiar test procedure. It compares the unrestricted estimator with the values specified by the null hypothesis in a quadratic form normalized with the inverse of the variance matrix of the estimator. In general, to compute the Wald test statistic for $H_0 : \boldsymbol{\theta}_{02} = \mathbf{0}$,

1. compute the *unrestricted* MLE

$$\hat{\boldsymbol{\theta}} = \underset{\boldsymbol{\theta} \in \boldsymbol{\Theta}}{\operatorname{argmax}}\, \mathrm{E}_N[L(\boldsymbol{\theta})]$$

2. compute an estimator of the variance matrix of the asymptotic distribution of $\sqrt{N}(\hat{\boldsymbol{\theta}} - \boldsymbol{\theta}_0)$, for example, the information matrix estimator $\Im(\hat{\boldsymbol{\theta}})^{-1}$,

[5] Although it may seem restrictive, this is a general formulation because we can always reparameterize the parameter vector so that the restrictions of the null hypothesis take this form. In particular, if the null hypothesis were $H_0 : \boldsymbol{\theta}_{02} = \mathbf{t}_2$ for a known $\mathbf{t}_2$ then one reparameterizes $\boldsymbol{\theta}$ to $[\boldsymbol{\theta}_1', \boldsymbol{\theta}_2' - \mathbf{t}_2']'$. We discuss general restrictions further in Section 17.4.

3. and finally compute the quadratic form[6]

$$\mathcal{W} = N \cdot \hat{\boldsymbol{\theta}}_2' \hat{\mathbf{V}}_{\mathrm{W}}^{-1} \hat{\boldsymbol{\theta}}_2 \tag{17.6}$$

where $\hat{\mathbf{V}}_{\mathrm{W}}$ is the (2, 2) block of $[\Im(\hat{\boldsymbol{\theta}})]^{-1}$ partitioned conformably with $\boldsymbol{\theta}$: that is,

$$\hat{\mathbf{V}}_{\mathrm{W}} = \left\{ \Im_{22}(\hat{\boldsymbol{\theta}}) - \Im_{21}(\hat{\boldsymbol{\theta}}) \left[\Im_{11}(\hat{\boldsymbol{\theta}}) \right]^{-1} \Im_{12}(\hat{\boldsymbol{\theta}}) \right\}^{-1} \tag{17.7}$$

which is a consistent estimator of the asymptotic variance of $\hat{\boldsymbol{\theta}}_2$.

4. Compare $\mathcal{W}$ with the critical value of a chi-square distribution with $K-M$ degrees of freedom.

17.2.2 The Score Test

The score test statistic examines how much $\mathrm{E}_N[L_2(\hat{\boldsymbol{\theta}}_{\mathrm{R}})]$ deviates from the zero vector.[7] An intuition for this check is that $\mathrm{E}[L_{\boldsymbol{\theta}}(\boldsymbol{\theta}_0)] = \mathbf{0}$ so that if $\hat{\boldsymbol{\theta}}_{\mathrm{R}}$ is in the neighborhood of $\boldsymbol{\theta}_0$, as it should be under $H_0 : \boldsymbol{\theta}_{02} = \mathbf{0}$, then $\mathrm{E}_N[L_2(\hat{\boldsymbol{\theta}}_{\mathrm{R}})]$ should not deviate significantly from zero. Given this observation, the score test has the form of a Wald test, a quadratic form in a random vector and the inverse of its variance matrix. One can compute the score test statistic for H_0 as follows:

1. compute the *restricted* MLE

$$\begin{aligned} \hat{\boldsymbol{\theta}}_{\mathrm{R}} &\equiv \underset{\{\boldsymbol{\theta} \in \Theta : \boldsymbol{\theta}_2 = \mathbf{0}\}}{\operatorname{argmax}} \ \mathrm{E}_N[L(\boldsymbol{\theta})] \\ &= \begin{bmatrix} \underset{\boldsymbol{\theta}_1}{\operatorname{argmax}} \, \mathrm{E}_N[L(\boldsymbol{\theta}_1, \mathbf{0})] \\ \mathbf{0} \end{bmatrix} \end{aligned} \tag{17.8}$$

and the score for the restricted parameters $\mathrm{E}_N[L_2(\hat{\boldsymbol{\theta}}_{\mathrm{R}})]$,

2. compute a consistent estimator of the variance matrix of the asymptotic distribution of $\sqrt{N}\,\mathrm{E}_N[L_{\theta}(\boldsymbol{\theta}_0)]$, for example, the information matrix estimator $\Im(\hat{\boldsymbol{\theta}}_{\mathrm{R}})$,

3. and finally compute the quadratic form

$$S = N \cdot \mathrm{E}_{\mathrm{N}}[L_2(\hat{\boldsymbol{\theta}}_{\mathrm{R}})]' \hat{\mathbf{V}}_{\mathrm{S}}^{-1} \mathrm{E}_{\mathrm{N}}[L_2(\hat{\boldsymbol{\theta}}_{\mathrm{R}})] \tag{17.9}$$

where $\hat{\mathbf{V}}_{\mathrm{S}}$ is a consistent estimator of the *conditional* variance matrix of $\sqrt{N}\,\mathrm{E}_N[L_2(\boldsymbol{\theta}_0)]$ given $\sqrt{N}\,\mathrm{E}_N[L_1(\boldsymbol{\theta}_0)]$, according to their joint asymptotically normal distribution. For example,

$$\hat{\mathbf{V}}_{\mathrm{S}} = \Im_{22}(\hat{\boldsymbol{\theta}}_{\mathrm{R}}) - \Im_{21}(\hat{\boldsymbol{\theta}}_{\mathrm{R}}) \left[\Im_{11}(\hat{\boldsymbol{\theta}}_{\mathrm{R}}) \right]^{-1} \Im_{12}(\hat{\boldsymbol{\theta}}_{\mathrm{R}}) \tag{17.10}$$

4. Compare S with the critical value of a chi-square distribution with $K - M$ degrees of freedom.

Remember that Step 3 uses the *conditional* variance of $\sqrt{N}\,\mathrm{E}_N[L_2(\boldsymbol{\theta}_0)]$ given $\sqrt{N}\,\mathrm{E}_N[L_1(\boldsymbol{\theta}_0)]$ by noting that $\mathrm{E}_N[L_1(\hat{\boldsymbol{\theta}}_{\mathrm{R}})] = \mathbf{0}$. This equality holds for every N because $\hat{\boldsymbol{\theta}}_{\mathrm{R}}$ is the restricted

---

6 The expression for the variance matrix comes from the partitioned inverse formula (Exercise 3.10, p. 70).

7 Rao (1947) proposed the score test statistic. Another form, called the *Lagrange multiplier test*, was proposed by Aitchison and Silvey (1958) and Silvey (1959).

maximum of $\mathrm{E}_N[L(\boldsymbol{\theta})]$ over $\boldsymbol{\theta}_1$. In this intuitive sense, we should condition on $\sqrt{N}\,\mathrm{E}_N[L_1(\boldsymbol{\theta}_0)]$ asymptotically.

There are two particularly convenient ways to compute the score test statistic with most econometrics software packages. The first is

$$S = N \cdot \mathrm{E}_N[L_{\theta}(\hat{\boldsymbol{\theta}}_{\mathrm{R}})]' \left[\Im(\hat{\boldsymbol{\theta}}_{\mathrm{R}})\right]^{-1} \mathrm{E}_N[L_{\theta}(\hat{\boldsymbol{\theta}}_{\mathrm{R}})] \tag{17.11}$$

This is identical with (17.9)–(17.10) because $\mathrm{E}_N[L_1(\hat{\boldsymbol{\theta}}_{\mathrm{R}})] \equiv \mathbf{0}$ and $\hat{\mathbf{V}}_{\mathrm{S}}^{-1}$ is the (2, 2) block of the partitioned $[\Im(\hat{\boldsymbol{\theta}}_{\mathrm{R}})]^{-1}$. In this form, the score test is the quadratic convergence criterion for *unrestricted* MLE computation evaluated at the starting point $\hat{\boldsymbol{\theta}}_{\mathrm{R}}$.[8] One can compute the test statistic in this manner with many software packages: after computing the unrestricted MLE, compute a single iteration of MLE calculations for the unrestricted model using $\hat{\boldsymbol{\theta}}_{\mathrm{R}}$ as the starting value and take the value of the convergence criterion as S.

The second convenient method for computing the score statistic uses the outer-product estimator for the variance matrix estimator. If we denote the $N \times K$ matrix of derivatives by

$$\hat{\mathbf{G}} \equiv [L_{\theta}(\hat{\boldsymbol{\theta}}_{\mathrm{R}}; U_n)]'$$

then

$$\mathrm{E}_N[L_{\theta}(\hat{\boldsymbol{\theta}}_{\mathrm{R}})] = N^{-1} \cdot \hat{\mathbf{G}}'\boldsymbol{\iota}$$
$$\mathrm{Var}_N[L_{\theta}(\hat{\boldsymbol{\theta}}_{\mathrm{R}})] = N^{-1} \cdot \hat{\mathbf{G}}'\hat{\mathbf{G}}$$

and a score test statistic is

$$\begin{aligned} S_{\mathrm{OLS}} &= N \cdot \mathrm{E}_N[L_{\theta}(\hat{\boldsymbol{\theta}}_{\mathrm{R}})]' \left\{\mathrm{Var}_N[L_{\theta}(\hat{\boldsymbol{\theta}}_{\mathrm{R}})]\right\}^{-1} \mathrm{E}_N[L_{\theta}(\hat{\boldsymbol{\theta}}_{\mathrm{R}})] \\ &= \boldsymbol{\iota}'\hat{\mathbf{G}}(\hat{\mathbf{G}}'\hat{\mathbf{G}})^{-1}\hat{\mathbf{G}}'\boldsymbol{\iota} \end{aligned} \tag{17.12}$$

This statistic is the regression sum of squares, or the squared length of the OLS fitted vector, from the regression of $\boldsymbol{\iota}$ (a vector of ones) on the columns of $\hat{\mathbf{G}}$. This statistic is *not* identical to S in practice, but the statistics are asymptotically equivalent under the null hypothesis because they differ only in the estimation of the variance matrix.

The appeal of the score test in applied research is the ease with which it can be used as a diagnostic tool. If one prefers the parametric model at hand, but feels compelled to support some of its restrictions, then one can use a score test without reestimating a more complicated specification. Because it is novel, we will give two examples of the score test.

EXAMPLE 17.2 (Linear Regression)

Consider first the familiar situation of testing $H_0 : \boldsymbol{\beta}_2 = \mathbf{0}$ in a partitioned regression $\mathbf{X}\boldsymbol{\beta} = \mathbf{X}_1\boldsymbol{\beta}_1 + \mathbf{X}_2\boldsymbol{\beta}_2$ for a conditionally normally distributed dependent variable $\mathbf{y}$. In contrast to Example 17.1, let the variance σ_0^2 be unknown. The restricted MLE is

$$\hat{\boldsymbol{\beta}}_{\mathrm{R}} = \begin{bmatrix} (\mathbf{X}_1'\mathbf{X}_1)^{-1}\mathbf{X}_1'\mathbf{y} \\ \mathbf{0} \end{bmatrix}$$

---

[8] See equation (16.17) on p. 362.

$$\hat{\sigma}_{\mathrm{R}}^2 = \frac{(\mathbf{y} - \mathbf{X}\hat{\boldsymbol{\beta}}_{\mathrm{R}})'(\mathbf{y} - \mathbf{X}\hat{\boldsymbol{\beta}}_{\mathrm{R}})}{N}$$

The score for $\boldsymbol{\beta}_2$ is

$$\begin{aligned} \mathrm{E}_N[L_2(\hat{\boldsymbol{\theta}}_{\mathrm{R}})] &= \frac{1}{\hat{\sigma}_{\mathrm{R}}^2} \cdot \mathbf{X}_2'(\mathbf{y} - \mathbf{X}\hat{\boldsymbol{\beta}}_{\mathrm{R}}) \\ &= \frac{1}{\hat{\sigma}_{\mathrm{R}}^2} \cdot \mathbf{X}_2'(\mathbf{I} - \mathbf{P}_{\mathbf{X}_1})\mathbf{y} \end{aligned}$$

and, given the block-diagonality of the information matrix in $\boldsymbol{\beta}$ and σ^2,

$$\hat{\mathbf{V}}_{\mathrm{S}} = \frac{1}{\hat{\sigma}_{\mathrm{R}}^2} \cdot \mathbf{X}_2'(\mathbf{I} - \mathbf{P}_{\mathbf{X}_1})\mathbf{X}_2$$

Therefore, denoting $\mathbf{X}_{2\perp 1} \equiv (\mathbf{I} - \mathbf{P}_{\mathbf{X}_1})\mathbf{X}_2$,

$$\begin{aligned} S &= \frac{1}{\hat{\sigma}_{\mathrm{R}}^2} \cdot (\mathbf{y} - \mathbf{X}\hat{\boldsymbol{\beta}}_{\mathrm{R}})'\mathbf{X}_{2\perp 1}\left(\mathbf{X}_{2\perp 1}'\mathbf{X}_{2\perp 1}\right)^{-1}\mathbf{X}_{2\perp 1}'(\mathbf{y} - \mathbf{X}\hat{\boldsymbol{\beta}}_{\mathrm{R}}) \\ &= \frac{1}{\hat{\sigma}_{\mathrm{R}}^2} \cdot (\mathbf{y} - \mathbf{X}\hat{\boldsymbol{\beta}}_{\mathrm{R}})'\mathbf{X}\left(\mathbf{X}'\mathbf{X}\right)^{-1}\mathbf{X}'(\mathbf{y} - \mathbf{X}\hat{\boldsymbol{\beta}}_{\mathrm{R}}) \end{aligned}$$

where we have exploited the orthogonality of $\mathbf{X}_1$ and the $\mathbf{y} - \mathbf{X}\hat{\boldsymbol{\beta}}_{\mathrm{R}}$. We could calculate this statistic as the regression sum of squares from an OLS fit of the standardized fitted residuals $(\mathbf{y} - \mathbf{X}\hat{\boldsymbol{\beta}}_{\mathrm{R}})/\hat{\sigma}_{\mathrm{R}}$ on all of the explanatory variables.

The next example illustrates more dramatically the convenience of requiring only estimation under the null hypothesis.

EXAMPLE 17.3 (Box–Cox Transformation)

We can generalize the log-wage model to make the logarithmic transformation of the wage a special case. Box and Cox (1964) suggested the so-called *Box–Cox transformation*

$$\tau(w, \lambda) \equiv \frac{w^\lambda - 1}{\lambda}, \qquad w \geq 0$$

where λ is another unknown parameter to be estimated. In the special case that $\lambda = 1$, we obtain a linear transformation: $\tau(w, 1) = w - 1$. Applied to the dependent variable, the constant -1 merely adjusts the intercept parameter of the model.

If $\lambda = 0$, then we get a logarithmic transformation. To see this, we must recognize that

$$\tau(w, 0) \equiv \lim_{\lambda \to 0} \tau(w, \lambda) = \lim_{\lambda \to 0} \frac{\partial w^\lambda / \partial \lambda}{\partial \lambda / \partial \lambda} = \lim_{\lambda \to 0} w^\lambda \log w = \log w$$

These two cases, $\lambda = 0, 1$, are familiar specifications that make the Box–Cox transformation an attractive way to generalize the linear regression model. By estimating λ, the data can choose the transformation.

Instead, we will compute a score test statistic for the null hypothesis that $\lambda = 0$ in our log Student *t* regression model for wages. Given that we have already had to program the score vector for this model to compute our estimates, the additional term for the Box–Cox parameter is readily at hand. Using the change-of-variables formula, the p.d.f. of the Box–Cox Student t distribution is

$$\frac{1}{\sigma}\left|\frac{\partial\tau(w,\lambda)}{\partial w}\right| f_t\left[\frac{\tau(w,\lambda)-\mu}{\sigma}\right] = \frac{w^{\lambda-1}}{\sigma} f_t\left[\frac{\tau(w,\lambda)-\mu}{\sigma}\right]$$

where $f_t(\cdot)$ denotes a Student t p.d.f. Therefore, the score for λ is

$$L_\lambda = \log w + \frac{1}{\sigma}\frac{\partial\tau(w,\lambda)}{\partial\lambda}\left[\left.\frac{d\log f_t(\varepsilon)}{d\varepsilon}\right|_{\varepsilon=\frac{\tau(w,\lambda)-\mu}{\sigma}}\right]$$

and we simply take the score already calculated for the intercept parameter, multiply it by

$$\lim_{\lambda\to 0}\frac{\partial\tau(w,\lambda)}{\partial\lambda} = \lim_{\lambda\to 0}\frac{\lambda w^\lambda\log w - w^\lambda + 1}{\lambda^2} = \frac{1}{2}(\log w)^2$$

and add $\log w$ for each observation.

The value of the score statistic (17.12) is $S = 2.322$. Under the null hypothesis, the distribution from which this must come is χ_1^2 and the p value of the statistic is 0.13. So our assumption that $\lambda = 0$ is supported by the test at conventional levels of significance.

17.2.3 The Likelihood Ratio Test

Ostensibly, the likelihood ratio is fundamentally different from the score and the Wald tests. Estimation under both the null and alternative hypotheses is necessary and neither a quadratic form nor a matrix inverse is calculated: after estimation, we compute two times a difference in log-likelihood function values. The LR test compares the goodness of fit of the unrestricted and restricted models using the likelihood function as the goodness-of-fit criterion.[9] Given that our estimation method rests entirely on maximizing the likelihood function, it is natural to look for evidence against the null hypothesis in a large difference between the unrestricted and restricted maxima of the log-likelihood function.

To compute the test statistic $\mathcal{LR}$,

1. compute the restricted MLE $\hat{\boldsymbol{\theta}}_\mathrm{R}$ and record the value of the log-likelihood function at convergence,

$$L(\hat{\boldsymbol{\theta}}_\mathrm{R}; U_1, \ldots, U_N) = N\,\mathrm{E}_N[L(\hat{\boldsymbol{\theta}}_\mathrm{R})]$$

2. compute the unrestricted MLE $\hat{\boldsymbol{\theta}}$ and record the value of the log-likelihood function at convergence,

$$L(\hat{\boldsymbol{\theta}}; U_1, \ldots, U_N) = N\,\mathrm{E}_N[L(\boldsymbol{\theta})]$$

3. and compute

$$\mathcal{LR} = 2\left[L(\hat{\boldsymbol{\theta}}; U_1, \ldots, U_N) - L(\hat{\boldsymbol{\theta}}_\mathrm{R}; U_1, \ldots, U_N)\right] \tag{17.13}$$

[9] Neyman and Pearson (1928) formulated the LR test.

$$= 2N\left\{\mathrm{E}_N[L(\hat{\boldsymbol{\theta}})] - \mathrm{E}_N[L(\hat{\boldsymbol{\theta}}_\mathrm{R})]\right\}$$

This statistic is always positive because the unrestricted maximum value always exceeds the restricted one.

4. Compare $\mathcal{LR}$ with the critical value of a chi-square distribution with $K - M$ degrees of freedom.

For comparison, let us return to the two preceding examples.

EXAMPLE 17.4 (Linear Regression)

Consider first the familiar situation of testing $H_0 : \boldsymbol{\beta}_2 = \mathbf{0}$ in a partitioned regression $\mathbf{X}\boldsymbol{\beta} = \mathbf{X}_1\boldsymbol{\beta}_1 + \mathbf{X}_2\boldsymbol{\beta}_2$ for a conditionally normally distributed dependent variable $\mathbf{y}$. Then,

$$\mathcal{LR} = 2N\left\{-\frac{1}{2}\log\frac{\left\|\mathbf{y} - \mathbf{X}\hat{\boldsymbol{\beta}}\right\|^2}{N} + \frac{1}{2}\log\frac{\left\|\mathbf{y} - \mathbf{X}\hat{\boldsymbol{\beta}}_\mathrm{R}\right\|^2}{N}\right\}$$

$$= N\log\frac{\left\|\mathbf{y} - \mathbf{X}\hat{\boldsymbol{\beta}}_\mathrm{R}\right\|^2}{\left\|\mathbf{y} - \mathbf{X}\hat{\boldsymbol{\beta}}\right\|^2}$$

EXAMPLE 17.5 (Box–Cox Transformation)

The maximized log-likelihood of the Student t probability model for log-wages is -3826.072. By generalizing the dependent variable to the Box–Cox transformation of wages and maximizing the log-likelihood function over λ as well, the log-likelihood function increases to -3825.093.[10] Therefore, the LR test for the log-wage specification gives $\mathcal{LR} = 1.957$, which is qualitatively similar to the score statistic. The probability value for this test is a little higher at 0.16.

Both of these examples show that the test statistics can differ for the same null hypothesis. In the next section, we explain why.

17.2.4 A Graphic Description of the Test Statistics

The Wald, score, and LR tests are exactly the same test in Example 17.1, but in general these test statistics differ for a finite sample size. Figure 17.3 describes the difference between the three test statistics. To simplify the figure, we plot only the dimension of a parameter that does *not* enter the null hypothesis. The profile of the sample average log-likelihood function $\mathrm{E}_N[L(\boldsymbol{\theta})]$ is drawn as a solid line with its maximum at $\hat{\boldsymbol{\theta}}$, the unrestricted MLE for $\boldsymbol{\theta}_0$. The restricted MLE is shown as $\hat{\boldsymbol{\theta}}_\mathrm{R}$. It is convenient to take the LR test as a reference point for the other two tests. The $\mathcal{LR}$ is marked as the change in height between $\mathrm{E}_N[L(\hat{\boldsymbol{\theta}})]$ and $\mathrm{E}_N[L(\hat{\boldsymbol{\theta}}_\mathrm{R})]$, ignoring the factor of proportionality $2N$.

10 This required 13 iterations of the BHHH algorithm starting from the log Student t estimates.

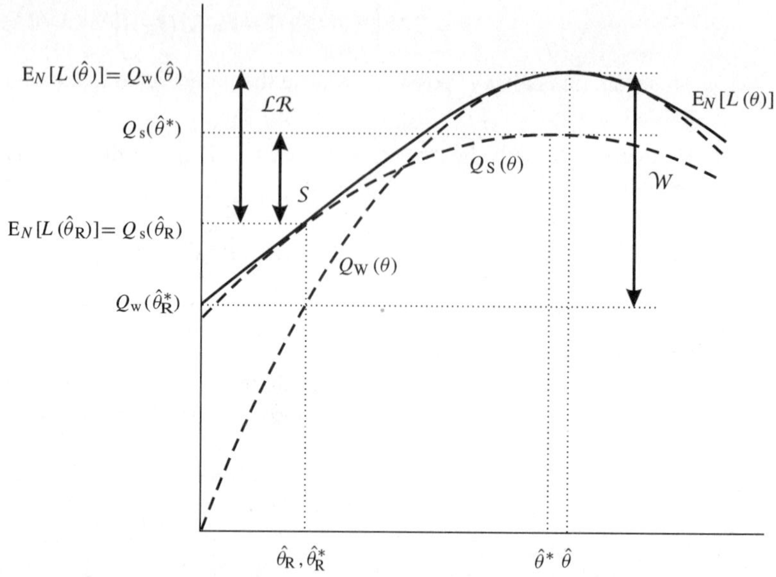

Figure 17.3 The relationship among the Wald, LR, and score tests.

The test statistic S is an approximation of the test statistic $\mathcal{LR}$ based on a quadratic approximation $Q_S(\boldsymbol{\theta})$ of $E_N[L(\boldsymbol{\theta})]$ at $\boldsymbol{\theta} = \hat{\boldsymbol{\theta}}_R$. In Figure 17.3, the profile of $Q_S(\boldsymbol{\theta})$ is the parabola tangent to $E_N[L(\boldsymbol{\theta})]$ at $\hat{\boldsymbol{\theta}}_R$, $\hat{\boldsymbol{\theta}}^*$ is the maximum of this parabola, and the value of S is proportional to the difference $Q_S(\hat{\boldsymbol{\theta}}^*) - Q_S(\hat{\boldsymbol{\theta}}_R)$. To confirm this, note that we approximate $E_N[L(\hat{\boldsymbol{\theta}})]$ with the quadratic function

$$Q_S(\boldsymbol{\theta}) \equiv E_N[L(\hat{\boldsymbol{\theta}}_R)] + E_N[L_{\boldsymbol{\theta}}(\hat{\boldsymbol{\theta}}_R)]'\left(\boldsymbol{\theta} - \hat{\boldsymbol{\theta}}_R\right) - \frac{1}{2}\left(\boldsymbol{\theta} - \hat{\boldsymbol{\theta}}_R\right)'\Im(\hat{\boldsymbol{\theta}}_R)\left(\boldsymbol{\theta} - \hat{\boldsymbol{\theta}}_R\right)$$

as in modified scoring (Section 16.4.3). We can also compute an approximation to $\hat{\boldsymbol{\theta}}$ using the LMLE

$$\hat{\boldsymbol{\theta}}^* = \operatorname*{argmax}_{\boldsymbol{\theta}\in\Theta} Q_S(\boldsymbol{\theta}) = \hat{\boldsymbol{\theta}}_R + \Im(\hat{\boldsymbol{\theta}}_R)^{-1} E_N[L_{\boldsymbol{\theta}}(\hat{\boldsymbol{\theta}}_R)]$$

If the score test uses the same estimator of the information matrix, $\Im(\hat{\boldsymbol{\theta}}_R)$, then

$$\begin{aligned} S &= N \cdot E_N[L_{\boldsymbol{\theta}}(\hat{\boldsymbol{\theta}}_R)]'\Im(\hat{\boldsymbol{\theta}}_R)^{-1} E_N[L_{\boldsymbol{\theta}}(\hat{\boldsymbol{\theta}}_R)] \\ &= 2N\left[Q_S(\hat{\boldsymbol{\theta}}^*) - E_N[L(\hat{\boldsymbol{\theta}}_R)]\right] \qquad (17.14) \\ &= 2N\left[Q_S(\hat{\boldsymbol{\theta}}^*) - Q_S(\hat{\boldsymbol{\theta}}_R)\right] \end{aligned}$$

In words, the score test statistic is an LR test with $\mathrm{E}_N[L(\hat{\boldsymbol{\theta}})]$ replaced by an approximation $Q_{\mathrm{S}}(\boldsymbol{\theta})$ that depends only on the restricted MLE $\hat{\boldsymbol{\theta}}_{\mathrm{R}}$.

Similarly, we can interpret the $\mathcal{W}$ test statistic as an approximation of $\mathcal{LR}$ based on a quadratic approximation of $\mathrm{E}_N[L(\boldsymbol{\theta})]$ at $\boldsymbol{\theta} = \hat{\boldsymbol{\theta}}$. That quadratic approximation is

$$\begin{aligned} Q_{\mathrm{W}}(\boldsymbol{\theta}) &\equiv \mathrm{E}_N[L(\hat{\boldsymbol{\theta}})] + \mathrm{E}_N[L_{\boldsymbol{\theta}}(\hat{\boldsymbol{\theta}})]' \left(\boldsymbol{\theta} - \hat{\boldsymbol{\theta}}\right) \\ &\quad - \frac{1}{2}\left(\boldsymbol{\theta} - \hat{\boldsymbol{\theta}}\right)' \Im(\hat{\boldsymbol{\theta}}) \left(\boldsymbol{\theta} - \hat{\boldsymbol{\theta}}\right) \\ &= \mathrm{E}_N[L(\hat{\boldsymbol{\theta}})] - \frac{1}{2}\left(\boldsymbol{\theta} - \hat{\boldsymbol{\theta}}\right)' \Im(\hat{\boldsymbol{\theta}}) \left(\boldsymbol{\theta} - \hat{\boldsymbol{\theta}}\right) \end{aligned} \tag{17.15}$$

which is simpler than $Q_{\mathrm{S}}(\boldsymbol{\theta})$ because $\mathrm{E}_N[L_{\boldsymbol{\theta}}(\hat{\boldsymbol{\theta}})] = \mathbf{0}$. The profile of this function is the parabola tangent to $\mathrm{E}_N[L(\boldsymbol{\theta})]$ at $\hat{\boldsymbol{\theta}}$ in Figure 17.3.

Deriving the restricted maximum of $Q_{\mathrm{W}}(\boldsymbol{\theta})$ involves an unfamiliar step. It is convenient to expand[11]

$$\begin{aligned} -\frac{1}{2}\left(\boldsymbol{\theta} - \hat{\boldsymbol{\theta}}\right)' \Im(\hat{\boldsymbol{\theta}}) \left(\boldsymbol{\theta} - \hat{\boldsymbol{\theta}}\right) &= -\frac{1}{2}\left[\boldsymbol{\theta}_1 - \hat{\boldsymbol{\theta}}^*_{\mathrm{R}1}(\boldsymbol{\theta}_2)\right]' \hat{\Im}_{11} \left[\boldsymbol{\theta}_1 - \hat{\boldsymbol{\theta}}^*_{\mathrm{R}1}(\boldsymbol{\theta}_2)\right] \\ &\quad - \frac{1}{2}\left(\boldsymbol{\theta}_2 - \hat{\boldsymbol{\theta}}_2\right)' \left(\hat{\Im}_{22} - \hat{\Im}_{21}\hat{\Im}_{11}^{-1}\hat{\Im}_{12}\right) \left(\boldsymbol{\theta}_2 - \hat{\boldsymbol{\theta}}_2\right) \end{aligned} \tag{17.16}$$

where

$$\begin{aligned} \hat{\boldsymbol{\theta}}^*_{\mathrm{R}1}(\boldsymbol{\theta}_2) &\equiv \underset{\boldsymbol{\theta}_1}{\operatorname{argmax}}\; Q_{\mathrm{W}}(\boldsymbol{\theta}) \\ &= \hat{\boldsymbol{\theta}}_1 - \hat{\Im}_{11}^{-1}\hat{\Im}_{12}\left(\boldsymbol{\theta}_2 - \hat{\boldsymbol{\theta}}_2\right) \end{aligned} \tag{17.17}$$

and $\hat{\Im} \equiv \Im(\hat{\boldsymbol{\theta}})$. Clearly, $\hat{\boldsymbol{\theta}}^*_{\mathrm{R}1}(\boldsymbol{\theta}_2)$ maximizes (17.16), and hence $Q_{\mathrm{W}}(\boldsymbol{\theta})$, over $\boldsymbol{\theta}_1$ for a given $\boldsymbol{\theta}_2$ by setting the second quadratic in (17.16) to zero. In effect, we have found a sort of *restricted* LMLE.

Given $\hat{\boldsymbol{\theta}}^*_{\mathrm{R}1}(\boldsymbol{\theta}_2)$, the quadratic interpretation of $\mathcal{W}$ follows directly. Setting $\boldsymbol{\theta}_2$ equal to its restricted value, $\mathbf{0}$, we compute an approximation to $\hat{\boldsymbol{\theta}}_{\mathrm{R}}$ with

$$\hat{\boldsymbol{\theta}}^*_{\mathrm{R}} = \begin{bmatrix} \hat{\boldsymbol{\theta}}^*_{\mathrm{R}1}(\mathbf{0}) \\ \mathbf{0} \end{bmatrix} \tag{17.18}$$

and by combining (17.15)–(17.17),

$$\begin{aligned} \mathcal{W} &= N \cdot \hat{\boldsymbol{\theta}}_2' \left(\hat{\Im}_{22} - \hat{\Im}_{21}\hat{\Im}_{11}^{-1}\hat{\Im}_{12}\right)\hat{\boldsymbol{\theta}}_2 \\ &= 2N\left[\mathrm{E}_N[L(\hat{\boldsymbol{\theta}})] - Q_{\mathrm{W}}(\hat{\boldsymbol{\theta}}^*_{\mathrm{R}})\right] \\ &= 2N\left[Q_{\mathrm{W}}(\hat{\boldsymbol{\theta}}) - Q_{\mathrm{W}}(\hat{\boldsymbol{\theta}}^*_{\mathrm{R}})\right] \end{aligned} \tag{17.19}$$

[11] This expansion uses Lemma 7.10 (Partitioned Quadratic II, p. 147).

Therefore, the Wald test statistic is an LR test statistic with $\mathrm{E}_N[L(\hat{\boldsymbol{\theta}}_\mathrm{R})]$ replaced by an approximation $Q_\mathrm{W}(\boldsymbol{\theta})$ that depends only on the unrestricted MLE $\hat{\boldsymbol{\theta}}$. In Figure 17.3, the difference $Q_\mathrm{W}(\hat{\boldsymbol{\theta}}) - Q_\mathrm{W}(\hat{\boldsymbol{\theta}}_\mathrm{R}^*)$ represents $\mathcal{W}$.

EXAMPLE 17.6 (Restricted Least Squares)

When the variance parameter is unknown and must be estimated, then the log-likelihood function of the conditional normal linear regression model is not a quadratic function of the parameters. If the null hypothesis to test is $H_0 : \boldsymbol{\beta}_{02} = \mathbf{0}$ in the partitioned regression $\mathbf{X}\boldsymbol{\beta} = \mathbf{X}_1\boldsymbol{\beta}_1 + \mathbf{X}_2\boldsymbol{\beta}_2$, let us rederive the Wald, likelihood ratio, and score test statistics. To compute the Wald test statistic (17.6) we require

$$\begin{aligned}\hat{\mathbf{V}}_\mathrm{W} &= \left(\hat{\Im}_{22} - \hat{\Im}_{21}\hat{\Im}_{11}^{-1}\hat{\Im}_{12}\right)^{-1}\\ &= \left(\frac{1}{\hat{\sigma}^2}\cdot\left\{\mathrm{E}_N[\mathbf{x}_{2n}\mathbf{x}_{2n}'] - \mathrm{E}_N[\mathbf{x}_{2n}\mathbf{x}_{1n}']\left(\mathrm{E}_N[\mathbf{x}_{1n}\mathbf{x}_{1n}']\right)^{-1}\mathrm{E}_N[\mathbf{x}_{1n}\mathbf{x}_{2n}']\right\}\right)^{-1}\\ &= N\hat{\sigma}^2\cdot\left[\mathbf{X}_2'\mathbf{X}_2 - \mathbf{X}_2'\mathbf{X}_1\left(\mathbf{X}_1'\mathbf{X}_1\right)^{-1}\mathbf{X}_1'\mathbf{X}_2\right]^{-1}\\ &= N\hat{\sigma}^2\cdot\left(\mathbf{X}_{2\perp1}'\mathbf{X}_{2\perp1}\right)^{-1}\end{aligned}$$

which follows from the conditional information matrix given in Example 15.1 and $\mathbf{X}_{2\perp1} \equiv \left(\mathbf{I} - \mathbf{P}_{\mathbf{X}_1}\right)\mathbf{X}_2$.[12] Therefore,

$$\begin{aligned}\mathcal{W} &= N\cdot\hat{\boldsymbol{\beta}}_2'[N\hat{\sigma}^2\cdot(\mathbf{X}_{2\perp1}'\mathbf{X}_{2\perp1})^{-1}]^{-1}\hat{\boldsymbol{\beta}}_2\\ &= \frac{\hat{\boldsymbol{\beta}}_2'\mathbf{X}_{2\perp1}'\mathbf{X}_{2\perp1}\hat{\boldsymbol{\beta}}_2}{\hat{\sigma}^2}\\ &= N\frac{\mathbf{y}'\mathbf{P}_{\mathbf{X}_{2\perp1}}\mathbf{y}}{\mathbf{y}'\left(\mathbf{I} - \mathbf{P}_\mathbf{X}\right)\mathbf{y}}\end{aligned}$$

This is proportional to the F statistic from normal distribution theory.[13] For this case, this Wald statistic differs from the one in Example 17.1 only in that σ_0^2 is replaced by the MLE $\hat{\sigma}^2$. Nevertheless, the two Wald statistics are asymptotically equivalent because $\hat{\sigma}^2 \xrightarrow{p} \sigma_0^2$.

The likelihood ratio test has a simple form based on the concentrated log-likelihood function in Example 16.12:

$$\begin{aligned}\mathcal{LR} &= -N\left\{\log\left[\frac{2\pi(\mathbf{y} - \mathbf{X}\hat{\boldsymbol{\beta}})'(\mathbf{y} - \mathbf{X}\hat{\boldsymbol{\beta}})}{N}\right] + 1\right\}\\ &\quad + N\left\{\log\left[\frac{2\pi(\mathbf{y} - \mathbf{X}\hat{\boldsymbol{\beta}}_\mathrm{R})'(\mathbf{y} - \mathbf{X}\hat{\boldsymbol{\beta}}_\mathrm{R})}{N}\right] + 1\right\}\\ &= N\log\left[\frac{\mathbf{y}'\left(\mathbf{I} - \mathbf{P}_{\mathbf{X}_1}\right)\mathbf{y}}{\mathbf{y}'\left(\mathbf{I} - \mathbf{P}_\mathbf{X}\right)\mathbf{y}}\right]\end{aligned}$$

12 We introduced the notation $\mathbf{X}_{2\perp1}$ in Proposition 2 (Partitioned Fit, p. 57).

13 Compare the expression in equation (11.4) (p. 227).

This is the logarithm of the ratio of the restricted and unrestricted residual sum of squares. This nonquadratic form follows from the estimation of σ_0^2.

Finally, the score test statistic is a function of the score evaluated at $\hat{\boldsymbol{\theta}}_{\mathrm{R}}$,

$$\begin{aligned}\mathrm{E}_N[L_2(\hat{\boldsymbol{\theta}}_{\mathrm{R}})] &= \frac{1}{\hat{\sigma}_{\mathrm{R}}^2} \cdot \mathrm{E}_N[\mathbf{x}_{2n}(y_n - \mathbf{x}_{1n}'\hat{\boldsymbol{\beta}}_{\mathrm{R}1})] \\ &= \frac{1}{N\hat{\sigma}_{\mathrm{R}}^2} \cdot \mathbf{X}_{2\perp 1}'\mathbf{y}\end{aligned}$$

and its estimated variance matrix

$$\hat{\mathbf{V}}_{\mathrm{S}} = \frac{1}{N\hat{\sigma}_{\mathrm{R}}^2} \cdot \mathbf{X}_{2\perp 1}'\mathbf{X}_{2\perp 1}$$

where $\hat{\sigma}_{\mathrm{R}}^2 = \mathbf{y}'\left(\mathbf{I} - \mathbf{P}_{\mathbf{X}_1}\right)\mathbf{y}/N$. Therefore,

$$S = N\frac{\mathbf{y}'\mathbf{P}_{\mathbf{X}_{2\perp 1}}\mathbf{y}}{\mathbf{y}'\left(\mathbf{I} - \mathbf{P}_{\mathbf{X}_1}\right)\mathbf{y}}$$

This differs from the Wald test only in the denominator, which equals the restricted, not the unrestricted, residual sum of squares.

17.3 ASYMPTOTIC DISTRIBUTION THEORY

Although they are not exactly equal, under the null hypothesis the three test statistics are asymptotically equivalent. This equivalence rests on the accuracy of quadratic approximations of the log-likelihood function within $N^{-1/2}$ neighborhoods of $\boldsymbol{\theta}_0$. We have just seen that the Wald and score test statistics are quadratic approximations evaluated at estimators that fall within these neighborhoods. Because these estimators are all near $\boldsymbol{\theta}_0$ for large N if the null hypothesis is true, we can expect the quadratic approximations to work.

It will be helpful to introduce a notation for "asymptotically equal in probability." When $A_N - B_N \xrightarrow{p} 0$, A_N and B_N are asymptotically equal in probability. Rather than write out the convergence of the difference, we will write $A_N \overset{p}{=} B_N$.[14] This makes many mathematical arguments more readable.

Consider any two CUAN estimators $\hat{\boldsymbol{\theta}}_A$ and $\hat{\boldsymbol{\theta}}_B$ that possess a joint asymptotic normal distribution

$$\begin{bmatrix}\sqrt{N}\left(\hat{\boldsymbol{\theta}}_A - \boldsymbol{\theta}_0\right) \\ \sqrt{N}\left(\hat{\boldsymbol{\theta}}_B - \boldsymbol{\theta}_0\right)\end{bmatrix} \xrightarrow{d} \mathfrak{N}(\mathbf{0}, \mathbf{V})$$

Then

$$\begin{aligned}\mathrm{E}_N[L(\hat{\boldsymbol{\theta}}_B)] = &\ \mathrm{E}_N[L(\hat{\boldsymbol{\theta}}_A)] + \mathrm{E}_N[L_{\boldsymbol{\theta}}(\hat{\boldsymbol{\theta}}_A)]'\left(\hat{\boldsymbol{\theta}}_B - \hat{\boldsymbol{\theta}}_A\right) \\ &+ \frac{1}{2}\left(\hat{\boldsymbol{\theta}}_B - \hat{\boldsymbol{\theta}}_A\right)'\mathrm{E}_N[L_{\boldsymbol{\theta\theta}}(\bar{\boldsymbol{\theta}})]\left(\hat{\boldsymbol{\theta}}_B - \hat{\boldsymbol{\theta}}_A\right)\end{aligned} \tag{17.20}$$

[14] Some authors write $A_N = B_N + o_p(1)$. See Definition 37 (Stochastically Negligible, p. 374).

where $\bar{\boldsymbol{\theta}}$ is between $\hat{\boldsymbol{\theta}}_A$ and $\hat{\boldsymbol{\theta}}_B$. Therefore, given that $\mathrm{E}_N[L_{\boldsymbol{\theta\theta}}(\bar{\boldsymbol{\theta}})] \overset{p}{=} -\Im(\boldsymbol{\theta}_0)$ [or $\mathrm{E}_N[L_{\boldsymbol{\theta\theta}}(\bar{\boldsymbol{\theta}})] \overset{p}{\to} -\Im(\boldsymbol{\theta}_0)$],

$$N\,\mathrm{E}_N[L(\hat{\boldsymbol{\theta}}_B)] \overset{p}{=} N\,\mathrm{E}_N[L(\hat{\boldsymbol{\theta}}_A)] + N\,\mathrm{E}_N[L_{\boldsymbol{\theta}}(\hat{\boldsymbol{\theta}}_A)]'\left(\hat{\boldsymbol{\theta}}_B - \hat{\boldsymbol{\theta}}_A\right) - \frac{N}{2}\left(\hat{\boldsymbol{\theta}}_B - \hat{\boldsymbol{\theta}}_A\right)'\Im(\boldsymbol{\theta}_0)\left(\hat{\boldsymbol{\theta}}_B - \hat{\boldsymbol{\theta}}_A\right) \tag{17.21}$$

According to this the difference in log-likelihood function values behaves asymptotically the same as the difference in quadratic function values. When $L(\boldsymbol{\theta})$ is quadratic in θ, its Hessian is a constant matrix and, therefore, equals $-\Im(\boldsymbol{\theta}_0)$. In that case (17.21) holds exactly in (17.20). More generally, this quadratic behavior occurs asymptotically. As a result, the three test statistics are equivalent asymptotically under the null hypothesis.

17.3.1 The Likelihood Ratio Test

To derive the asymptotic distribution of $\mathcal{LR}$ under the null hypothesis, we apply (17.21) with $\hat{\boldsymbol{\theta}}_A = \hat{\boldsymbol{\theta}}$ and $\hat{\boldsymbol{\theta}}_B = \hat{\boldsymbol{\theta}}_{\mathrm{R}}$. Both estimators are asymptotically linear in the same score $\mathrm{E}_N[L_{\boldsymbol{\theta}}(\boldsymbol{\theta}_0)]$, making their joint asymptotic distribution follow from previous principles. Using (15.6) and the proof of Part 2 of Proposition 16 on p. 327,

$$\begin{bmatrix} \sqrt{N}\left(\hat{\boldsymbol{\theta}} - \boldsymbol{\theta}_0\right) \\ \sqrt{N}\left(\hat{\boldsymbol{\theta}}_{\mathrm{R}} - \boldsymbol{\theta}_0\right) \end{bmatrix} = \begin{bmatrix} -\{\mathrm{E}_N[L_{\boldsymbol{\theta\theta}}(\bar{\boldsymbol{\theta}})]\}^{-1} \\ \begin{bmatrix} -\{\mathrm{E}_N[L_{11}(\bar{\boldsymbol{\theta}})]\}^{-1} & \mathbf{0} \\ \mathbf{0} & \mathbf{0} \end{bmatrix} \end{bmatrix} \sqrt{N}\,\mathrm{E}_N[L_{\boldsymbol{\theta}}(\boldsymbol{\theta}_0)] \overset{d}{\to} \mathfrak{N}(\mathbf{0}, \mathbf{V}) \tag{17.22}$$

where $\bar{\boldsymbol{\theta}}$ lies between $\hat{\boldsymbol{\theta}}$ and $\boldsymbol{\theta}_0$ and

$$\mathbf{V} = \begin{bmatrix} \Im(\boldsymbol{\theta}_0)^{-1} & \begin{bmatrix} \Im_{11}(\boldsymbol{\theta}_0)^{-1} & \mathbf{0} \\ \mathbf{0} & \mathbf{0} \end{bmatrix} \\ \begin{bmatrix} \Im_{11}(\boldsymbol{\theta}_0)^{-1} & \mathbf{0} \\ \mathbf{0} & \mathbf{0} \end{bmatrix} & \begin{bmatrix} \Im_{11}(\boldsymbol{\theta}_0)^{-1} & \mathbf{0} \\ \mathbf{0} & \mathbf{0} \end{bmatrix} \end{bmatrix}$$

Therefore, (17.21) implies that

$$\begin{aligned} \mathcal{LR} &= 2N\left\{\mathrm{E}_N[L(\hat{\boldsymbol{\theta}})] - \mathrm{E}_N[L(\hat{\boldsymbol{\theta}}_{\mathrm{R}})]\right\} \\ &\overset{p}{=} \mathrm{E}_N\left[N \cdot (\hat{\boldsymbol{\theta}} - \hat{\boldsymbol{\theta}}_{\mathrm{R}})'\Im(\boldsymbol{\theta}_0)\,(\hat{\boldsymbol{\theta}} - \hat{\boldsymbol{\theta}}_{\mathrm{R}})\right] \\ &\equiv \mathcal{MC} \end{aligned} \tag{17.23}$$

because $\mathrm{E}_N[L_{\boldsymbol{\theta}}(\hat{\boldsymbol{\theta}})] = \mathbf{0}$.[15] This quadratic form in (17.23) is a key asymptotic representation of $\mathcal{LR}$. The *minimum chi-square* statistic $\mathcal{MC}$ measures a generalized distance between the unrestricted and restricted MLEs of the *entire* parameter vector.[16] This generalized distance is measured with respect to the information matrix. We can just as well describe the $\mathcal{W}$ and $\mathcal{S}$ statistics as similar approximations to $\mathcal{MC}$ and show their asymptotic equivalence with $\mathcal{LR}$.

---

[15] Wilks (1938) and Wald (1943) first derived the asymptotic distribution of $\mathcal{LR}$ under assumptions like ours.

[16] This is a generalization of the comparison of OLS with RLS in (11.2). We explain the "minimum chi-square" label in Section 22.1.4. Also see Exercise 17.13.

17.3.2 The Score Test

Demonstrating the asymptotic equivalence of S to $\mathcal{MC}$ begins with the LMLE forecast of the unrestricted MLE in terms of the restricted MLE:

$$\hat{\boldsymbol{\theta}}^* = \hat{\boldsymbol{\theta}}_\mathrm{R} + \Im(\hat{\boldsymbol{\theta}}_\mathrm{R})^{-1}\,\mathrm{E}_N[L_\theta(\hat{\boldsymbol{\theta}}_\mathrm{R})]$$

Using this forecast,

$$\begin{aligned} S &= N \cdot \mathrm{E}_N[L_\theta(\hat{\boldsymbol{\theta}}_\mathrm{R})]'\Im(\hat{\boldsymbol{\theta}}_\mathrm{R})^{-1}\,\mathrm{E}_N[L_\theta(\hat{\boldsymbol{\theta}}_\mathrm{R})] \\ &= N \cdot (\hat{\boldsymbol{\theta}}^* - \hat{\boldsymbol{\theta}}_\mathrm{R})'\Im(\hat{\boldsymbol{\theta}}_\mathrm{R})\,(\hat{\boldsymbol{\theta}}^* - \hat{\boldsymbol{\theta}}_\mathrm{R}) \end{aligned}$$

which is another way to write the analogy between $\mathcal{LR}$ and S already given in (17.14).

Under the null hypothesis, Lemma 15.7 (LMLE, p. 333) implies that

$$\sqrt{N}(\hat{\boldsymbol{\theta}}^* - \hat{\boldsymbol{\theta}}) \xrightarrow{p} \mathbf{0} \tag{17.24}$$

because $\hat{\boldsymbol{\theta}}_\mathrm{R}$ is CUAN. This asymptotic equivalence leads to the one that we seek to show. Starting from (17.23),

$$\begin{aligned} \mathcal{MC} &\equiv N \cdot (\hat{\boldsymbol{\theta}} - \hat{\boldsymbol{\theta}}_\mathrm{R})'\Im(\boldsymbol{\theta}_0)\,(\hat{\boldsymbol{\theta}} - \hat{\boldsymbol{\theta}}_\mathrm{R}) \\ &\overset{p}{=} N \cdot (\hat{\boldsymbol{\theta}}^* - \hat{\boldsymbol{\theta}}_\mathrm{R})'\Im(\boldsymbol{\theta}_0)\,(\hat{\boldsymbol{\theta}}^* - \hat{\boldsymbol{\theta}}_\mathrm{R}) \\ &\overset{p}{=} S \end{aligned}$$

where the second equality uses (17.24) and the third uses $\Im(\hat{\boldsymbol{\theta}}_\mathrm{R}) \xrightarrow{p} \Im(\boldsymbol{\theta}_0)$. This proves the asymptotic equivalence of $\mathcal{MC}$ (and $\mathcal{LR}$) and S under the null hypothesis.

17.3.3 The Wald Test

We also establish the asymptotic distribution of $\mathcal{W}$ under the null hypothesis by showing that it is asymptotically equivalent to $\mathcal{MC}$.[17] At $\hat{\boldsymbol{\theta}}$, the forecast of $\hat{\boldsymbol{\theta}}_\mathrm{R}$ is given by (17.18) as

$$\hat{\boldsymbol{\theta}}_\mathrm{R}^* = \begin{bmatrix} \hat{\boldsymbol{\theta}}_1 + \Im_{11}(\hat{\boldsymbol{\theta}})^{-1}\Im_{12}(\hat{\boldsymbol{\theta}})\,\hat{\boldsymbol{\theta}}_2 \\ \mathbf{0} \end{bmatrix}$$

Using this forecast, we can also write (17.19) as

$$\begin{aligned} \mathcal{W} &= N \cdot \hat{\boldsymbol{\theta}}_2' \begin{bmatrix} -\Im_{21}(\hat{\boldsymbol{\theta}})\,\Im_{11}(\hat{\boldsymbol{\theta}})^{-1} & \mathbf{I}_{K-M} \end{bmatrix} \Im(\hat{\boldsymbol{\theta}}) \begin{bmatrix} -\Im_{11}(\hat{\boldsymbol{\theta}})^{-1}\Im_{12}(\hat{\boldsymbol{\theta}}) \\ \mathbf{I}_{K-M} \end{bmatrix} \hat{\boldsymbol{\theta}}_2 \\ &= N \cdot (\hat{\boldsymbol{\theta}} - \hat{\boldsymbol{\theta}}_\mathrm{R}^*)'\Im(\hat{\boldsymbol{\theta}})\,(\hat{\boldsymbol{\theta}} - \hat{\boldsymbol{\theta}}_\mathrm{R}^*) \end{aligned}$$

Under the null hypothesis,[18]

---

[17] Wald (1943) demonstrated the asymptotic equivalence of the likelihood ratio and Wald statistics.

[18] This is a special case of Exercise 15.17, using the linear approximation to $\mathrm{E}_N[L_1(\hat{\boldsymbol{\theta}})]$:

$$\mathbf{0} = \operatorname*{plim}_{N\to\infty} \sqrt{N}\left\{\mathrm{E}_N[L_1(\boldsymbol{\theta}_0)] - \Im_{11}(\boldsymbol{\theta}_0)\left(\hat{\boldsymbol{\theta}}_1 - \boldsymbol{\theta}_{01}\right) - \Im_{12}(\boldsymbol{\theta}_0)\left(\hat{\boldsymbol{\theta}}_2 - \boldsymbol{\theta}_{02}\right)\right\}$$

$$\sqrt{N}(\hat{\boldsymbol{\theta}}_{\mathrm{R}}^{*} - \hat{\boldsymbol{\theta}}_{\mathrm{R}}) \xrightarrow{p} \mathbf{0} \tag{17.25}$$

With this equivalence, we can rewrite (17.23) as

$$\begin{aligned} \mathcal{MC} &\equiv N \cdot (\hat{\boldsymbol{\theta}} - \hat{\boldsymbol{\theta}}_{\mathrm{R}})' \Im(\boldsymbol{\theta}_0)\,(\hat{\boldsymbol{\theta}} - \hat{\boldsymbol{\theta}}_{\mathrm{R}}) \\ &\overset{p}{=} N \cdot (\hat{\boldsymbol{\theta}} - \hat{\boldsymbol{\theta}}_{\mathrm{R}}^{*})' \Im(\boldsymbol{\theta}_0)\,(\hat{\boldsymbol{\theta}} - \hat{\boldsymbol{\theta}}_{\mathrm{R}}^{*}) \\ &\overset{p}{=} \mathcal{W} \end{aligned}$$

where the second equality uses (17.25) and the third uses $\Im(\hat{\boldsymbol{\theta}}_{\mathrm{R}}) \xrightarrow{p} \Im(\boldsymbol{\theta}_0)$. Therefore we have established the asymptotic equivalence of $\mathcal{MC}$ (and $\mathcal{LR}$) and $\mathcal{W}$ under the null hypothesis.

17.3.4 The $C(\alpha)$ Test

We can, of course, forecast *both* the restricted and unrestricted maximum log-likelihoods from an initial CUAN estimator $\check{\boldsymbol{\theta}} = [\check{\boldsymbol{\theta}}_1', \mathbf{0}]'$. This is the essence of the $C(\alpha)$ test proposed by Neyman (1959), completing the family of classical hypothesis tests by requiring neither $\hat{\boldsymbol{\theta}}$ nor $\hat{\boldsymbol{\theta}}_{\mathrm{R}}$. Using the LMLE, we can forecast $\hat{\boldsymbol{\theta}}$ and $\hat{\boldsymbol{\theta}}_{\mathrm{R}}$ with the statistics $\hat{\boldsymbol{\theta}}^{*}$ and $\hat{\boldsymbol{\theta}}_{\mathrm{R}}^{*}$ in

$$\begin{aligned} \hat{\boldsymbol{\theta}}^{*} &= \check{\boldsymbol{\theta}} + \Im(\check{\boldsymbol{\theta}})^{-1}\, \mathrm{E}_N[\check{L}_{\boldsymbol{\theta}}] \\ \hat{\boldsymbol{\theta}}_{\mathrm{R1}}^{*} &= \check{\boldsymbol{\theta}}_1 + \Im_{11}(\check{\boldsymbol{\theta}})^{-1}\, \mathrm{E}_N[\check{L}_1] \\ \hat{\boldsymbol{\theta}}_{\mathrm{R2}}^{*} &= \mathbf{0} \end{aligned}$$

Predicting $\mathcal{MC}$ as a comparison of the entire parameter vector gives

$$\begin{aligned} C(\alpha) &\equiv N \cdot (\hat{\boldsymbol{\theta}}^{*} - \hat{\boldsymbol{\theta}}_{\mathrm{R}}^{*})' \Im(\check{\boldsymbol{\theta}})\,(\hat{\boldsymbol{\theta}}^{*} - \hat{\boldsymbol{\theta}}_{\mathrm{R}}^{*}) \\ &= N \cdot \left[\mathrm{E}_N[\check{L}_{\boldsymbol{\theta}}]' \Im(\check{\boldsymbol{\theta}})^{-1}\, \mathrm{E}_N[\check{L}_{\boldsymbol{\theta}}] - \mathrm{E}_N[\check{L}_1]' \Im_{11}(\check{\boldsymbol{\theta}})^{-1}\, \mathrm{E}_N[\check{L}_1]\right] \end{aligned} \tag{17.26}$$

This test statistic looks like S with an adjustment term. The second quadratic function reduces the first, taking into account that $\check{L}_{\boldsymbol{\theta}} \equiv L_{\boldsymbol{\theta}}(\check{\boldsymbol{\theta}})$ will generally be longer than $L_{\boldsymbol{\theta}}(\hat{\boldsymbol{\theta}}_{\mathrm{R}})$ because only $L_1(\hat{\boldsymbol{\theta}}_{\mathrm{R}}) \equiv \mathbf{0}$. This statistic is asymptotically equivalent to $\mathcal{W}$, $\mathcal{LR}$, and S if $\boldsymbol{\theta}_{02} = \mathbf{0}$ using a familiar argument:

$$\begin{aligned} \mathcal{MC} &\equiv N \cdot (\hat{\boldsymbol{\theta}} - \hat{\boldsymbol{\theta}}_{\mathrm{R}})' \Im(\boldsymbol{\theta}_0)\,(\hat{\boldsymbol{\theta}} - \hat{\boldsymbol{\theta}}_{\mathrm{R}}) \\ &\overset{p}{=} N \cdot (\hat{\boldsymbol{\theta}}^{*} - \hat{\boldsymbol{\theta}}_{\mathrm{R}}^{*})' \Im(\check{\boldsymbol{\theta}})\,(\hat{\boldsymbol{\theta}}^{*} - \hat{\boldsymbol{\theta}}_{\mathrm{R}}^{*}) \\ &\overset{p}{=} C(\alpha) \end{aligned}$$

Researchers use the so-called "trinity" of test statistics, $\mathcal{W}$, $\mathcal{LR}$, and S, more frequently than the $C(\alpha)$ test. Presumably, this reflects the popularity and feasibility of the MLEs $\hat{\boldsymbol{\theta}}$ and $\hat{\boldsymbol{\theta}}_{\mathrm{R}}$ and the degree of arbitrariness in the $C(\alpha)$ test afforded by the choice of $\check{\boldsymbol{\theta}}$. However, on the basis of asymptotic distribution theory the $C(\alpha)$ test is on an equal footing and completes the collection of tests.

17.3.5 Limiting Distribution

Under the null hypothesis, the four tests have an asymptotic chi-square distribution with degrees of freedom equal to the number of restrictions in the null hypothesis. There are several ways to derive this distribution. A direct method analyzes the $\mathcal{W}$ statistic, which is a quadratic form in $\hat{\boldsymbol{\theta}}_2$ with the inverse of its estimated asymptotic variance matrix. According to Proposition 16 (ML Asymptotics, p. 320) and the partitioned matrix inverse (3.23),

$$\hat{\mathbf{V}}_{\mathrm{W}}^{-1/2}\sqrt{N}\hat{\boldsymbol{\theta}}_2 \xrightarrow{d} \mathfrak{N}(\mathbf{0}, \mathbf{I}_{K-M})$$

under $H_0 : \boldsymbol{\theta}_{02} = \mathbf{0}$.[19] Therefore,

$$\mathcal{W} = \left(\hat{\mathbf{V}}_{\mathrm{W}}^{-1/2}\sqrt{N}\hat{\boldsymbol{\theta}}_2\right)'\hat{\mathbf{V}}_{\mathrm{W}}^{-1/2}\sqrt{N}\hat{\boldsymbol{\theta}}_2 = N\cdot\hat{\boldsymbol{\theta}}_2'\hat{\mathbf{V}}_{\mathrm{W}}^{-1}\hat{\boldsymbol{\theta}}_2 \xrightarrow{d} \chi^2_{K-M}$$

using Theorem D.11 (Sums of Squared Standard Normals, p. 889) and Lemma 13.4 (Convergence in Distribution Continuity, p. 261). The asymptotic equivalence of the other test statistics establishes their (identical) asymptotic behavior.

Incidentally, we have also proved that

$$\mathcal{MC} \equiv \mathrm{E}_N\left[N\cdot(\hat{\boldsymbol{\theta}} - \hat{\boldsymbol{\theta}}_{\mathrm{R}})'\Im(\boldsymbol{\theta}_0)\,(\hat{\boldsymbol{\theta}} - \hat{\boldsymbol{\theta}}_{\mathrm{R}})\right] \xrightarrow{d} \chi^2_{K-M}$$

This result is an analogue to the numerator of an F test statistic for $K - M$ linear restrictions on the coefficients in a normal linear regression model:[20]

$$(\hat{\boldsymbol{\beta}} - \hat{\boldsymbol{\beta}}_{\mathrm{R}})'\left[\sigma_0^2\cdot(\mathbf{X}'\mathbf{X})^{-1}\right]^{-1}(\hat{\boldsymbol{\beta}} - \hat{\boldsymbol{\beta}}_{\mathrm{R}}) \sim \chi^2_{K-M}$$

In both cases, the difference in estimators is normalized by the inverse of the variance of the unrestricted estimator. And both can be understood as examples of Lemma 10.1 (Minimum Chi-Square, p. 197).[21] We will discuss test statistics of this form further in Chapter 22.

17.4 PARAMETER TRANSFORMATIONS AND INVARIANCE

The test statistics have all been derived for the simplest form of a null hypothesis, zero restrictions on a subvector of parameters. Parametric hypotheses do not always present themselves in this form, although parameter transformations can generally cast them this way. It is not necessary, however, to recast every hypothesis. We can deal directly with any hypothesis $H_0 : \mathbf{r}(\boldsymbol{\theta}_0) = \mathbf{0}$ provided that the function $\mathbf{r}$ satisfies the following conditions.

ASSUMPTION 17.1 (REGULAR RESTRICTIONS) *The parameters $\boldsymbol{\theta}_0$ satisfy the restrictions $\mathbf{r}(\boldsymbol{\theta}_0) = \mathbf{0}$ where $\mathbf{r} : \mathbb{R}^K \to \mathbb{R}^{K-M}$ is a twice continuously differentiable function and its partial derivative matrix $\mathbf{r}_\theta(\boldsymbol{\theta})$ has rank $K - M$ for $\boldsymbol{\theta} \in \boldsymbol{\Theta}$.*

We require the rank condition to prevent redundancy (or degeneracy) among the restrictions. In effect, a partition of $\boldsymbol{\theta} = [\boldsymbol{\theta}_1', \boldsymbol{\theta}_2']'$ exists so that $\boldsymbol{\theta}_1$ contains M elements and $\mathbf{r}(\boldsymbol{\theta}) = \boldsymbol{\alpha}$ defines

[19] The matrix $\hat{\mathbf{V}}_{\mathrm{W}}$ appears in (17.7). Proposition 16 uses minus the empirical Hessian as the information estimator, whereas we have substituted the empirical information matrix here. Section 15.4 explains the asymptotic equivalence of these information estimators.

[20] See (10.11) and (11.2) and note that $\mathbf{R}\boldsymbol{\beta}_0 = \mathbf{r}$ under the null hypothesis.

[21] See Exercise 17.13. For test statistics based on $\mathcal{MC}$, see Exercise 17.18.

an implicit function $\boldsymbol{\theta}_2 = \mathbf{h}(\boldsymbol{\theta}_1, \boldsymbol{\alpha})$.[22] Although the function $\mathbf{h}$ may not be tractable, we may think of $\mathbf{r}(\boldsymbol{\theta}) = \mathbf{0}$ as the restriction $\boldsymbol{\alpha} = \mathbf{0}$ in the alternative parameterization:

$$\boldsymbol{\theta} = \begin{bmatrix} \boldsymbol{\theta}_1 \\ \mathbf{h}(\boldsymbol{\theta}_1, \boldsymbol{\alpha}) \end{bmatrix}$$

If such an $\mathbf{h}(\boldsymbol{\theta}_1, \boldsymbol{\alpha})$ is tractable, then we can also explicitly parameterize the restricted model in terms of the M parameters in $\boldsymbol{\gamma} = \boldsymbol{\theta}_1$ alone:[23]

$$\boldsymbol{\theta} = \mathbf{s}(\boldsymbol{\gamma}) \equiv \begin{bmatrix} \boldsymbol{\gamma} \\ \mathbf{h}(\boldsymbol{\gamma}, \mathbf{0}) \end{bmatrix}$$

Such restricted parameterizations are computationally attractive because they reduce the dimensionality of the maximization required to compute the MLE. To compute all of the test statistics, it is merely necessary to compute the restricted MLE with an algorithm for constrained optimization:[24]

$$\hat{\boldsymbol{\theta}}_{\mathrm{R}} \equiv \underset{\boldsymbol{\theta} \in \boldsymbol{\Theta}:\mathbf{r}(\boldsymbol{\theta})=\mathbf{0}}{\operatorname{argmax}} \; \mathrm{E}_N[L(\boldsymbol{\theta})]$$

Under Assumption 17.1, the asymptotic distribution theory of the restricted MLE is the same as that for the MLE.[25]

After computing $\hat{\boldsymbol{\theta}}_{\mathrm{R}}$, and the unconstrained estimator $\hat{\boldsymbol{\theta}}$, we compute the LR test statistic as

$$\begin{aligned} \mathcal{LR} &\equiv 2N \left\{ \max_{\boldsymbol{\theta} \in \boldsymbol{\Theta}} \mathrm{E}_N[L(\boldsymbol{\theta})] - \max_{\boldsymbol{\theta} \in \boldsymbol{\Theta}:\mathbf{r}(\boldsymbol{\theta})=\mathbf{0}} \mathrm{E}_N[L(\boldsymbol{\theta})] \right\} \\ &= 2N \left\{ \mathrm{E}_N[L(\hat{\boldsymbol{\theta}})] - \mathrm{E}_N[L(\hat{\boldsymbol{\theta}}_{\mathrm{R}})] \right\} \end{aligned} \tag{17.27}$$

The Wald test examines $\mathbf{r}(\hat{\boldsymbol{\theta}})$, which is the unrestricted estimator of $\mathbf{r}(\boldsymbol{\theta}_0)$, forming the usual quadratic form in the inverse of an estimator of its asymptotic variance matrix:[26]

$$\mathcal{W} \equiv N \cdot \mathbf{r}(\hat{\boldsymbol{\theta}})' \left[\mathbf{r}_{\boldsymbol{\theta}}(\hat{\boldsymbol{\theta}})' \Im(\hat{\boldsymbol{\theta}})^{-1} \mathbf{r}_{\boldsymbol{\theta}}(\hat{\boldsymbol{\theta}}) \right]^{-1} \mathbf{r}(\hat{\boldsymbol{\theta}}) \tag{17.28}$$

The score test rests upon the restricted estimator alone:

$$S \equiv N \cdot \mathrm{E}_N[L_{\boldsymbol{\theta}}(\hat{\boldsymbol{\theta}}_{\mathrm{R}})]' \Im(\hat{\boldsymbol{\theta}}_{\mathrm{R}})^{-1} \mathrm{E}_N[L_{\boldsymbol{\theta}}(\hat{\boldsymbol{\theta}}_{\mathrm{R}})] \tag{17.29}$$

The matrix $\Im(\boldsymbol{\theta}_0)^{-1}$ is a generalized inverse for the singular asymptotic variance matrix of $\sqrt{N}\,\mathrm{E}_N[L_{\boldsymbol{\theta}}(\hat{\boldsymbol{\theta}}_{\mathrm{R}})]$.

---

22 See Simon and Blume (1994, p. 341) regarding the implicit function theorem.

23 See Exercise 4.14 for an example of linear $r(\theta)$.

24 We do not describe such methods here. In practice, reparameterization is usually possible. For an introduction to constrained optimization, see Simon and Blume (1994, Chapters 18–19).

25 We may write a restricted version of log-likelihood function $L(\boldsymbol{\theta})$ as $L[\mathbf{s}(\boldsymbol{\theta}_1)]$. Because $\boldsymbol{\Theta}$ is compact so is the parameter space $\{\boldsymbol{\theta}_1 \mid [\boldsymbol{\theta}_1', \boldsymbol{\theta}_2'] \in \boldsymbol{\Theta}\}$. Because $\mathbf{s}$ is twice continuously differentiable, $L[\mathbf{s}(\boldsymbol{\theta}_1)]$ remains twice continuously differentiable. Hence, $L[\mathbf{s}(\boldsymbol{\theta}_1)]$ will satisfy the assumptions applied to $L(\boldsymbol{\theta})$ for Proposition 16 (ML Asymptotics, p. 320) to apply.

26 For the asymptotic distribution of a function of $\hat{\boldsymbol{\theta}}$, review the delta method (Lemma 16.1, p. 367).

The approximate distribution of these test statistics remains χ^2_{K-M} under H_0 and the supporting asymptotic theory is substantially unchanged by the presence of the implicit restrictions. The theory effectively treats the restrictions as linear. To see this, we need only examine the restricted maximization term. Let us choose a partition of $\boldsymbol{\theta}$ so that the restrictions deliver an implicit function for $\boldsymbol{\theta}_2$ given $\boldsymbol{\theta}_1$. According to the rank condition, rank $\mathbf{r}_{\boldsymbol{\theta}}(\boldsymbol{\theta}) = K - M$, the vector $\boldsymbol{\theta}_2$ contains $K - M$ elements. The implicit function theorem states that

$$\frac{\partial \boldsymbol{\theta}_2}{\partial \boldsymbol{\theta}_1'} = -\mathbf{r}_2(\boldsymbol{\theta})[\mathbf{r}_1(\boldsymbol{\theta})]^{-1} \equiv \mathbf{S}(\boldsymbol{\theta})$$

and, therefore, the score and Hessian of the restricted log-likelihood function are

$$\begin{aligned}\frac{\partial L(\boldsymbol{\theta}_1, \mathbf{h}(\boldsymbol{\theta}_1); u)}{\partial \boldsymbol{\theta}_1} &= L_1(\boldsymbol{\theta}; u) + \mathbf{S}(\boldsymbol{\theta})' L_2(\boldsymbol{\theta}; u) \\ &= \mathbf{J}(\boldsymbol{\theta}) L_{\boldsymbol{\theta}}(\boldsymbol{\theta}; u) \end{aligned} \tag{17.30}$$

$$\begin{aligned}\frac{\partial^2 L(\boldsymbol{\theta}_1, \mathbf{h}(\boldsymbol{\theta}_1); u)}{\partial \boldsymbol{\theta}_1 \, \partial \boldsymbol{\theta}_1'} &= \mathbf{J}(\boldsymbol{\theta}) L_{\boldsymbol{\theta\theta}}(\boldsymbol{\theta}; u) \mathbf{J}(\boldsymbol{\theta})' \\ &\quad + \left[L_2(\boldsymbol{\theta}; u)' \frac{\partial}{\partial \boldsymbol{\theta}_1'} \mathbf{S}_k(\boldsymbol{\theta}) \right] \end{aligned} \tag{17.31}$$

where $\mathbf{J}(\boldsymbol{\theta}) \equiv [\mathbf{I}_M, \ \mathbf{S}(\boldsymbol{\theta})']$, $\mathbf{S}_k(\boldsymbol{\theta})$ denotes the kth column of $\mathbf{S}(\boldsymbol{\theta})$, and $\boldsymbol{\theta}_2 = \mathbf{h}(\boldsymbol{\theta}_1)$ denotes the implicit function for $\boldsymbol{\theta}_2$ given $\boldsymbol{\theta}_1$.[27]

Now both the score vector and Hessian matrix are still sums of i.i.d. terms, so that our previous techniques apply. The information matrix is

$$\mathrm{Var}[\mathbf{J}(\boldsymbol{\theta}_0) \, L_{\boldsymbol{\theta}}(\boldsymbol{\theta}_0; U)] = \mathbf{J}(\boldsymbol{\theta}_0) \, \Im(\boldsymbol{\theta}_0) \, \mathbf{J}(\boldsymbol{\theta}_0)'$$

The expectation of the Hessian equals the negative of this information matrix because the final term is a linear function of an element of the score, which has expectation zero. Finally, the standardized score converges in distribution to a multivariate normal with the appropriate variance matrix:

$$\sqrt{N} \, \mathrm{E}_N[\mathbf{J}(\boldsymbol{\theta}_0) L_{\boldsymbol{\theta}}(\boldsymbol{\theta}_0; U)] \xrightarrow{d} \mathfrak{N}[\mathbf{0}, \mathbf{J}(\boldsymbol{\theta}_0) \, \Im(\boldsymbol{\theta}_0) \, \mathbf{J}(\boldsymbol{\theta}_0)']$$

These expressions are identical to those we obtain if the restrictions were the linear equations $\boldsymbol{\theta}_2 = \mathbf{S}(\boldsymbol{\theta}_0) \, \boldsymbol{\theta}_1$. Just as in many previous situations, the asymptotic distribution theory of transformations is intrinsically linear.

Therefore, if we artificially reparameterize the log-likelihood linearly in terms of $\boldsymbol{\gamma}_1 = \boldsymbol{\theta}_1$ and $\boldsymbol{\gamma}_2 = \boldsymbol{\theta}_2 - \mathbf{S}(\boldsymbol{\theta}_0) \, \boldsymbol{\theta}_1$, then the restrictions take the form $\boldsymbol{\gamma}_2 = \mathbf{0}$. That is, suppose we write

$$L(\boldsymbol{\theta}; u) = L\left[\boldsymbol{\gamma}_1, \boldsymbol{\gamma}_2 + \mathbf{S}(\boldsymbol{\theta}_0) \, \boldsymbol{\gamma}_1; u\right] \tag{17.32}$$

Expressed in this way, all of our previous equations apply to the nonlinear restrictions that we are considering. In particular, we can conclude that under the null hypothesis all the test statistics converge in distribution to a χ^2_{K-M} random variable.

---

[27] In the last term, the contents within the brackets are row vectors of $K - M$ elements that are stacked, resulting in a $(K - M) \times (K - M)$ matrix. We obtain the expression by noting that each scalar element of the vector

$$\mathbf{S}(\boldsymbol{\theta}) L_2(\boldsymbol{\theta}) = \left[\mathbf{S}_k(\boldsymbol{\theta})' L_2(\boldsymbol{\theta}; u)\right] = \left[L_2(\boldsymbol{\theta}; u)' \mathbf{S}_k(\boldsymbol{\theta})\right]$$

can be transposed without changing the vector.

The likelihood ratio test statistic also has a "small sample" property relative to parameter transformations: the test is *invariant* to reparameterizations of the parameter vector $\boldsymbol{\theta}$ or the restriction function $\mathbf{s}(\boldsymbol{\theta})$. Maximization is invariant to one-to-one transformations of the parameters: for example, if $\mathbf{h} : \mathbb{R}^K \to \mathbb{R}^K$ is a one-to-one transformation and $\boldsymbol{\Theta}$ is the image of $\boldsymbol{\Gamma}$ under $\mathbf{h}$ then, for example,

$$\max_{\boldsymbol{\theta}\in\boldsymbol{\Theta}} \mathrm{E}_N[L(\boldsymbol{\theta})] = \max_{\boldsymbol{\gamma}\in\boldsymbol{\Gamma}} \mathrm{E}_N\{L[\mathbf{h}(\boldsymbol{\gamma})]\}$$

and

$$\hat{\boldsymbol{\gamma}} = \operatorname*{argmax}_{\boldsymbol{\gamma}\in\boldsymbol{\Gamma}} \mathrm{E}_N\{L[\mathbf{h}(\boldsymbol{\gamma})]\}$$

$$\mathbf{h}(\hat{\boldsymbol{\gamma}}) = \hat{\boldsymbol{\theta}} = \operatorname*{argmax}_{\boldsymbol{\theta}\subset\boldsymbol{\Theta}} \mathrm{E}_N[L(\boldsymbol{\theta})]$$

Alternatively, if $\mathbf{g} : \mathbb{R}^{K-M} \to \mathbb{R}^{K-M}$ and one to one then $\mathbf{g}[\mathbf{r}(\boldsymbol{\theta})] - \mathbf{g}(\mathbf{0}) \equiv \mathbf{s}(\boldsymbol{\theta}) = \mathbf{0}$ is an equivalent set of restrictions and

$$\max_{\boldsymbol{\theta}\in\boldsymbol{\Theta}:\mathbf{r}(\boldsymbol{\theta})=\mathbf{0}} \mathrm{E}_N[L(\boldsymbol{\theta})] = \max_{\boldsymbol{\theta}\in\boldsymbol{\Theta}:\mathbf{s}(\boldsymbol{\theta})=\mathbf{0}} \mathrm{E}_N[L(\boldsymbol{\theta})]$$

Therefore, no matter what equivalent way we calculate $\mathcal{LR}$, we always get the same outcome.

This invariance property is particularly significant because the $\mathcal{W}$ and S tests are not always invariant. Given the fundamental character of the likelihood function, these failures of invariance may be regarded as failures in the approximations to $\mathcal{LR}$ that these statistics represent. Their linear approximations of $\hat{\boldsymbol{\theta}}$, $\hat{\boldsymbol{\theta}}_{\mathrm{R}}$, and $\mathbf{r}(\boldsymbol{\theta})$, and quadratic approximations of $L(\boldsymbol{\theta})$ can vary with the parameterization. In fact, the potential variation can be so great that it is possible to manipulate the value of a test statistic to any positive value.

EXAMPLE 17.7 (Wald Test)

Consider a test of the linear restriction $\theta_1 = \theta_2$ rewritten as

$$\frac{\theta_1 - \alpha}{\theta_2 - \alpha} = 1$$

where we can choose any $\alpha \neq \hat{\boldsymbol{\theta}}_2$. The Wald test of this restriction begins with a derivation of the asymptotic distribution of

$$\sqrt{N}\left(\frac{\hat{\boldsymbol{\theta}}_1 - \alpha}{\hat{\boldsymbol{\theta}}_2 - \alpha} - 1\right)$$

using the delta method.[28] The matrix of partial derivatives is

$$\mathbf{J}(\boldsymbol{\theta}_0) = \begin{bmatrix} \dfrac{1}{\theta_{02} - \alpha} & -\dfrac{\theta_{01} - \alpha}{(\theta_{02} - \alpha)^2} \end{bmatrix}$$

giving the approximate variance

[28] We examined a similar problem in Example 16.11 (p. 367).

$$\left(\hat{\theta}_2-\alpha\right)^{-2}\hat{\Im}^{11}-2\left(\hat{\theta}_1-\alpha\right)\left(\hat{\theta}_2-\alpha\right)^{-3}\hat{\Im}^{12}+\left(\hat{\theta}_2-\alpha\right)^{-4}\hat{\Im}^{22}$$

where

$$\Im(\hat{\theta})^{-1}\equiv\begin{bmatrix}\hat{\Im}^{11} & \hat{\Im}^{12}\\ \hat{\Im}^{12} & \hat{\Im}^{22}\end{bmatrix}$$

The Wald statistic is the ratio of the squared restriction residual divided by an estimator of ω^2:

$$\mathcal{W}=\frac{N\left(\hat{\theta}_1-\hat{\theta}_2\right)^2}{\hat{\Im}^{11}-2\hat{\Im}^{12}\left(\hat{\theta}_1-\alpha\right)\left(\hat{\theta}_2-\alpha\right)^{-1}+\hat{\Im}^{22}\left(\hat{\theta}_2-\alpha\right)^{-2}}$$

By choosing α close to $\hat{\theta}_2$, we can make $\mathcal{W}$ as close to zero as we please. By choosing $\alpha = \hat{\theta}_2 - \hat{\Im}^{12}/\hat{\Im}^{11}$, we obtain the largest possible $\mathcal{W}$ in this family, equal to $N(\hat{\theta}_1-\hat{\theta}_2)^2/[\hat{\Im}^{22}-(\hat{\Im}^{12})^2/\hat{\Im}^{11}]$. So there is a limit, in this case, to how far our machination can take us.[29]

For the general Wald test, we create a quadratic form in $\mathbf{r}(\hat{\theta})$. First, using the delta method (Lemma 16.1, p. 367),

$$\sqrt{N}[\mathbf{r}(\hat{\theta})-\mathbf{r}(\theta_0)]\xrightarrow{d}\mathbf{r}_\theta(\theta_0)\,\mathfrak{N}\left[0,\Im(\theta_0)^{-1}\right]$$

The Wald statistic accounts for the switch to $\mathbf{r}$ in the variance matrix estimator: according to the linear approximation,

$$\sqrt{N}[\mathbf{r}(\hat{\theta})-\mathbf{r}(\theta_0)]\xrightarrow{d}\mathfrak{N}[0,\mathbf{r}_\theta(\theta_0)\Im(\theta_0)^{-1}\mathbf{r}_\theta(\theta_0)']$$

leading to the quadratic form of the Wald statistic:

$$\mathcal{W}=\mathcal{N}\cdot\mathbf{r}(\hat{\theta})'[\mathbf{r}_\theta(\hat{\theta})\Im(\hat{\theta})^{-1}\mathbf{r}_\theta(\hat{\theta})']^{-1}\mathbf{r}(\hat{\theta})$$

This statistic is invariant to reparameterizations of θ, but not of the restrictions in $\mathbf{r}(\theta)$. For example, given any equivalent set of restrictions, $\mathbf{g}[\mathbf{r}(\theta)]-\mathbf{g}(\mathbf{0})\equiv\mathbf{s}(\theta)=\mathbf{0}$, the alternative Wald statistic is

$$\mathcal{W}'=N\cdot\mathbf{s}(\hat{\theta})[\mathbf{s}_\theta(\hat{\theta})\Im(\hat{\theta})^{-1}\mathbf{s}_\theta(\hat{\theta})']^{-1}\mathbf{s}(\hat{\theta})$$

Because

$$\mathbf{s}_\theta(\theta)=\mathbf{g}_\mathbf{r}[\mathbf{r}(\theta)]\,\mathbf{r}_\theta(\theta)$$

we can write

$$\mathcal{W}'=N\cdot\left\{\mathbf{g}_\mathbf{r}[\mathbf{r}(\hat{\theta})]^{-1}\mathbf{s}(\hat{\theta})\right\}'[\mathbf{r}_\theta(\hat{\theta})\Im(\hat{\theta})^{-1}\mathbf{r}_\theta(\hat{\theta})']^{-1}\left\{\mathbf{g}_\mathbf{r}[\mathbf{r}(\hat{\theta})]^{-1}\mathbf{s}(\hat{\theta})\right\}$$

which equals $\mathcal{W}$ only if $\mathbf{g}$ is exactly linear.

The score test statistic is

$$\mathcal{S}=N\cdot\mathrm{E}_N[L_\theta(\hat{\theta}_\mathrm{R})]'\Im(\hat{\theta}_\mathrm{R})^{-1}\mathrm{E}_N[L_\theta(\hat{\theta}_\mathrm{R})]$$

29 For more deviousness, see Gregory and Veall (1985).

where

$$\hat{\boldsymbol{\theta}}_{\mathrm{R}} \equiv \operatorname*{argmax}_{\boldsymbol{\theta}\in\boldsymbol{\Theta}:\mathbf{r}(\boldsymbol{\theta})=\mathbf{0}} \mathrm{E}_N[L(\boldsymbol{\theta})]$$

In this version, this statistic is invariant. An exception occurs when the information matrix is estimated with the Hessian matrix. In that case, the additional nonlinear term that appears in (17.31) causes the failure of invariance. Asymptotically, this term is negligible because its population expectation is $\mathbf{0}$ at $\boldsymbol{\theta}_0$. But in small samples, its contribution could be large. Alternatively, the asymptotically negligible terms can be dropped from the Hessian, thereby recreating invariance.[30]

Lack of invariance is troublesome. Without invariance, one's inference may be ambiguous as a test statistic varies with different parameterizations. This leaves open the possibility of searching for a parameterization for which asymptotic approximation of the distribution works best. There are special cases in which transformations are used to improve asymptotic approximation.[31] But general methods of this sort are not available.

17.5 POWER

Two conditions combine to yield the equivalence of the test statistics in this chapter: (1) the truth of the null hypothesis and (2) asymptotic limits. Both are necessary for the quadratic approximation to be accurate in a region of the parameter space that includes both the unrestricted and the restricted estimator. If the null hypothesis is false, then the estimators $\hat{\boldsymbol{\theta}}$ and $\hat{\boldsymbol{\theta}}_{\mathrm{R}}$ will not converge to the same point, $\boldsymbol{\theta}_0$, around which the approximation occurs. We study the power of these tests when this occurs in this section.

The first result about power is that asymptotically the tests are extremely powerful. There is a particular term for this kind of power.

DEFINITION 40 (CONSISTENT TEST) *If the probability of rejecting the null hypothesis when it is false approaches one as the sample size approaches infinity, then the test is* consistent.

We use this definition in the following proposition.

PROPOSITION 17 (CLASSICAL TEST CONSISTENCY) *The Wald, likelihood ratio, score, and $C(\alpha)$ tests are consistent.*

For example, consider the Wald test of $H_0 : \boldsymbol{\theta}_{02} = \mathbf{0}$ at the $100(1-\alpha)\%$ level of significance. We reject H_0 if

[30] For an example, see Exercise 17.9.

[31] For example, see Rothenberg (1984b, Section 6.2).

$$\mathcal{W} = N \cdot \hat{\boldsymbol{\theta}}_2'(\hat{\Im}_{22} - \hat{\Im}_{21}\hat{\Im}_{11}^{-1}\hat{\Im}_{12})\hat{\boldsymbol{\theta}}_2 > \chi^2_{K-M;1-\alpha}$$

If $\boldsymbol{\theta}_{02} \neq \mathbf{0}$, then

$$\hat{\boldsymbol{\theta}}_2 \xrightarrow{p} \boldsymbol{\theta}_{02} \neq \mathbf{0}$$

$$\hat{\Im}_{22} - \hat{\Im}_{21}\hat{\Im}_{11}^{-1}\hat{\Im}_{12} \xrightarrow{p} \Im_{22}(\boldsymbol{\theta}_0) - \Im_{21}(\boldsymbol{\theta}_0)\Im_{11}(\boldsymbol{\theta}_0)^{-1}\Im_{12}(\boldsymbol{\theta}_0)$$

so that

$$\frac{\mathcal{W}}{N} = \hat{\boldsymbol{\theta}}_2'(\hat{\Im}_{22} - \hat{\Im}_{21}\hat{\Im}_{11}^{-1}\hat{\Im}_{12})\hat{\boldsymbol{\theta}}_2 \xrightarrow{p} \lambda \tag{17.33}$$

where

$$\lambda \equiv \boldsymbol{\theta}_{02}'\left[\Im_{22} - \Im_{21}\Im_{11}^{-1}\Im_{12}\right]\boldsymbol{\theta}_{02} > 0$$

As a result, we expect $\mathcal{W}$ to grow without bound as $N \to \infty$, surely exceeding the critical value $\chi^2_{K-M;1-\alpha}$.

To show this formally, note that for all $\epsilon > 0$

$$\lim_{N\to\infty} \Pr\left\{\left|\frac{W}{N} - \lambda\right| < \epsilon\right\} = 1 \tag{17.34}$$

according to (17.33). Now we can always find $\epsilon > 0$ such that $0 < \epsilon < \lambda$. Therefore, for all $N > \chi^2_{K-M;1-\alpha}/(\lambda - \epsilon)$ we have

$$\begin{aligned}\Pr\{\mathcal{W} > \chi^2_{\mathcal{K}-\mathcal{M};1-\alpha}\} &= \Pr\left\{\frac{W}{N} > \frac{\chi^2_{K-M;1-\alpha}}{N}\right\} \\ &\geq \Pr\left\{\frac{W}{N} > \lambda - \epsilon\right\} \\ &\geq \Pr\left\{\left|\frac{W}{N} - \lambda\right| < \epsilon\right\} \\ &\xrightarrow[N\to\infty]{} 1\end{aligned}$$

using (17.34) in the last line. In words, $\mathcal{W}$ is a consistent test. Similar arguments apply to the other test statistics.

17.5.1 Local Power

One can make more refined comparisons of the tests by considering artificial violations of the null hypothesis called *local alternatives* or *Pitman drift*.[32] We have already emphasized that the log-likelihood function is essentially quadratic within neighborhoods that shrink at the rate $N^{-1/2}$. Local alternatives are precisely elements of such shrinking neighborhoods. For example, instead of a fixed $\boldsymbol{\theta}_{02} \neq \mathbf{0}$, consider a sequence of alternative models for which $\boldsymbol{\theta}_{02}$ is changing with N:

---

[32] See Pitman (1949).

$$\boldsymbol{\theta}_{02}(N) = \frac{1}{\sqrt{N}} \cdot \boldsymbol{\delta}$$

This keeps the data-generating process $\boldsymbol{\theta}_{02}(N)$ with an $N^{-1/2}$ neighborhood of $\mathbf{0}$, but never equal to $\mathbf{0}$. As a result, this sequence of alternatives leads to an approximation of the power of the test statistics in regions of modest power.

The direct effect of Pitman drift appears in the asymptotic behavior of the various estimators. All still converge in probability to $\boldsymbol{\theta}_0$ because $\boldsymbol{\theta}_{02}(N) \to \mathbf{0}$ and estimators that were asymptotically equivalent above remain so under this sequence of alternative models. The asymptotic distribution of $\sqrt{N}(\hat{\boldsymbol{\theta}}_R - \boldsymbol{\theta}_0)$ and its cousins, however, exhibits bias:[33]

$$\sqrt{N}\left[\hat{\boldsymbol{\theta}}_R - \boldsymbol{\theta}_0(N)\right] \xrightarrow{d} \mathfrak{N}\left(\begin{bmatrix} \mathfrak{I}_{11}^{-1}\mathfrak{I}_{12} \\ -\mathbf{I}_{K-M} \end{bmatrix}\boldsymbol{\delta}, \begin{bmatrix} \mathfrak{I}_{11}^{-1} & \mathbf{0} \\ \mathbf{0} & \mathbf{0} \end{bmatrix}\right) \tag{17.35}$$

As a result, we find analogous results slightly different from those under the null hypothesis. All test statistics remain asymptotically equivalent for such local alternatives; however, their common asymptotic distribution is the *noncentral* chi-square with $K - M$ degrees of freedom.[34] Using the $\mathcal{MC}$ statistic and (17.35), the noncentrality parameter is

$$\begin{aligned}\lambda &= \boldsymbol{\delta}'\left[\mathfrak{I}_{21}\mathfrak{I}_{11}^{-1} \quad -\mathbf{I}_{K-M}\right]\mathfrak{I}\begin{bmatrix} \mathfrak{I}_{11}^{-1}\mathfrak{I}_{12} \\ -\mathbf{I}_{K-M} \end{bmatrix}\boldsymbol{\delta} \\ &= \boldsymbol{\delta}'\left(\mathfrak{I}_{22} - \mathfrak{I}_{21}\mathfrak{I}_{11}^{-1}\mathfrak{I}_{12}\right)\boldsymbol{\delta}\end{aligned}$$

This is a special case of the noncentral F distribution that we covered in Chapter 11. Here the degrees of freedom in the denominator have reached infinity so that only the numerator of the ratio of chi-squares is random. As a result, three of the properties described in Proposition 13 (p. 229) carry over. Local power increases with λ so that greater efficiency (through larger information) or stronger hypothesis violations (through larger $\boldsymbol{\delta}$) improve power. Furthermore, removing restrictions from the null hypothesis that are true also increases the local power of the tests because it decreases the degrees of freedom while preserving the magnitude of the noncentrality parameter.[35]

Among the three tests, the score test is the only one that is constructed local to the null hypothesis. This unique property leads to a special operational property as well: the score test statistic is identical for all alternative hypotheses with the same restrictions *local* to the null hypothesis.

---

[33] We are skipping over a technical detail here. That is, we will take for granted that

$$\sqrt{N}\,\mathrm{E}_N\{L_{\boldsymbol{\theta}}[\boldsymbol{\theta}_0(N)]\} \xrightarrow{d} \mathfrak{N}[0, \mathfrak{I}(\boldsymbol{\theta}_0)]$$

See Engle (1984) for a discussion. Given this asymptotic behavior, the asymptotic distribution for $\hat{\boldsymbol{\theta}}_R$ follows from

$$\mathbf{0} = \sqrt{N}\,\mathrm{E}_N[L_1(\boldsymbol{\theta}_0(N))] + \mathfrak{I}_{11}(\bar{\boldsymbol{\theta}})\sqrt{N}\left(\hat{\boldsymbol{\theta}}_{R1} - \boldsymbol{\theta}_{01}\right) + \mathfrak{I}_{12}(\bar{\theta})\sqrt{N}\,[-\theta_{02}(N)]$$

where $\bar{\boldsymbol{\theta}}$ lies on the line segment between $\boldsymbol{\theta}_0(N)$ and $\hat{\boldsymbol{\theta}}_R$.

[34] See Definition 21 (Noncentral Chi-Square Distribution, p. 232).

[35] Concerning these power properties, also see Lemma F.4 (p. 919).

EXAMPLE 17.8 (Box–Cox Transformation)

The first-order approximation of the Box–Cox transformation around $\lambda = 0$ is

$$\tau(y, \lambda) \approx \log y + \frac{1}{2} (\log y)^2 \lambda$$

and any transformation with this first-order approximation will yield the same score test for the logarithmic transformation of the dependent variable of a regression model. The simplest example is the RHS quadratic function itself. If we posed the alternative transformation to $\log y$ to be $\log y + \frac{1}{2}(\log y)^2\lambda$ and found the score test for the null hypothesis $\lambda = 0$, we would compute the same score test as in Example 17.3. The first-order approximation around $\lambda = 1$ is

$$\frac{y^\lambda - 1}{\lambda} \approx y - 1 + (y \log y - y + 1)(\lambda - 1)$$

Therefore, the Box–Cox transformation does not yield the same score test as do such simple transformations as the quadratic $y + \frac{1}{2}y^2\lambda$ for the linear null hypothesis.

It may be tempting to view this feature of the score test as a distinct advantage over the other tests. Implicit in whatever alternative hypothesis one chooses to construct a score test, there is a family of alternative hypotheses that leads to the same score test. We seem to obtain a test that has power to reject more alternative hypotheses than just the particular one specified. This is true, but it is also true for the Wald and LR tests. As we have just seen, all three tests are asymptotically equivalent for local alternatives. It is just that the score test statistic is the only test that is determined solely by the local alternatives. As a result, in application it may be helpful to describe a score test in terms of its local alternatives, as well as the particular alternative hypothesis that initially motivates the test.

EXAMPLE 17.9 (Normality Test)

Now we can describe a score test for normality to fill a gap in Chapter 13. This test was originally proposed by Jarque and Bera (1980), who postulated the *Pearson (1895) family distributions* as generalizations of the normal distribution.[36] The p.d.f.s of these distributions are characterized by the differential equation

$$\frac{\partial f_{\mathrm{P}}(z)}{\partial z} = -\frac{a_1 + z}{a_2 + a_3 z + a_4 z^2} f_{\mathrm{P}}(z)$$

where the a_j $(j = 1, \ldots, 4)$ are population parameters.[37] As one can check, the $\mathfrak{N}(\mu, \sigma^2)$ p.d.f. is the case $a_1 = -\mu$, $a_2 = \sigma^2$, and $a_3 = a_4 = 0$. Jarque and Bera (1980) test these last two restrictions with a score test.

Evaluated at the MLE and summed over observations, the two score elements for a_3 and a_4 are functions of the sample only through[38]

$$\mathrm{E}_N[(y_n - \mathbf{x}_n'\hat{\boldsymbol{\beta}}_{\mathrm{ML}})^3] \quad \text{and} \quad \mathrm{E}_N[(y_n - \mathbf{x}_n'\hat{\boldsymbol{\beta}}_{\mathrm{ML}})^4] - 3\hat{\sigma}^4_{\mathrm{ML}}$$

[36] See also Bowman and Shenton (n.d.).

[37] See Johnson and Kotz (1970a, pp. 9–15) for an introduction to the Pearson family of distributions.

[38] See Exercise 17.20.

Therefore, this score test simply checks whether the ML/OLS fitted residuals satisfy the third- and fourth-moment restrictions of the normal distribution. The actual score test statistic is

$$S = \frac{N}{6}\left\{\frac{\mathrm{E}_N[(y_n - \hat{\mu}_{\mathrm{ML},n})^3]}{\hat{\sigma}^3_{\mathrm{ML}}}\right\}^2 + \frac{N}{24}\left\{\frac{\mathrm{E}_N[(y - \hat{\mu}_{\mathrm{ML},n})^4] - 3\hat{\sigma}^4_{\mathrm{ML}}}{\hat{\sigma}^4_{\mathrm{ML}}}\right\}^2$$

based on the empirical information matrix. Under the null hypothesis, $S \xrightarrow{d} \chi^2_2$.

From our derivation of the score, we can see that the same local alternatives are generated by a score test based on the generalized exponential distribution

$$f_Y(y) = c(\mu, \sigma^2, a_3, a_4) \exp\left[-\frac{1}{2}\left(\frac{y-\mu}{\sigma}\right)^2 + \frac{a_3}{3}\left(\frac{y-\mu}{\sigma}\right)^3 - \frac{a_4}{4}\left(\frac{y-\mu}{\sigma}\right)^4\right]$$

where $c(\mu, \sigma^2, a_3, a_4)$ is the normalizing constant that makes this p.d.f. integrate to one (and the scores integrate to zero).[39] The Pearson distributions have a score that is a linear transformation of the score of this generalized exponential.

17.5.2 Neyman–Pearson Lemma

Up to this point, we have taken the testing methods for granted, implicitly motivating them as analogues of the statistics developed for the normal linear regression model. The central optimality result of likelihood theory states that the LR test is the most powerful test of one hypothesis against another, provided that all parameters are known in both hypotheses. Suppose there are two completely specified p.d.f.s, $H_0 : f_0(y)$ and $H_1 : f_1(y)$. Let $\mathbb{C}_\alpha$ and $\mathbb{C}'_\alpha$ be two critical regions corresponding to the significance level α:

$$\Pr\{Y \in \mathbb{C}_\alpha \mid H_0\} = \Pr\{Y \in \mathbb{C}'_\alpha \mid H_0\} = \alpha$$

The *most powerful* critical region of level α, $\mathbb{C}_\alpha$, satisfies

$$\Pr\{Y \in \mathbb{C}_\alpha \mid H_1\} \geq \Pr\{Y \in \mathbb{C}'_\alpha \mid H_1\}$$

for all other $\mathbb{C}'_\alpha$. The LR critical region is defined by the scalar c_α such that

$$\Pr\{Y \mid f_1(Y)/f_0(Y) \geq c_\alpha\} = \alpha$$

THEOREM 11 (NEYMAN–PEARSON LEMMA) *For any significance level α, the LR critical region is the most powerful critical region.*

Proof. Let $\mathbb{C}_\alpha$ denote the likelihood ratio critical region. By definition,

[39] Generally both this generalized exponential and the Pearson must have constraints on the support of the distribution to ensure that these are proper distributions. Alternatively, the parameters may be restricted. For example, for the p.d.f. of this generalized exponential to have tails that approach zero, $a_4 \geq 0$ and $a_3 \neq 0$ implies $a_4 > 0$. The distributions are unimodal if and only if $a_3^2 < 4a_4$.

$$\alpha = \int_{\mathbb{C}_\alpha} f_0(y)\,dy = \int_{\mathbb{C}'_\alpha} f_0(y)\,dy$$

so that

$$\int_{\mathbb{C}_\alpha \setminus \mathbb{C}'_\alpha} f_0(y)\,dy = \int_{\mathbb{C}'_\alpha \setminus \mathbb{C}_\alpha} f_0(y)\,dy$$

Now for all $Y \in \mathbb{C}_\alpha$, and hence all $Y \in \mathbb{C}_\alpha \setminus \mathbb{C}'_\alpha$, we have $f_1(Y) \geq c_\alpha\, f_0(Y)$. On the other hand, if $Y \in \mathbb{C}'_\alpha \setminus \mathbb{C}_\alpha$, we have $f_1(Y) < c_\alpha\, f_0(Y)$. Therefore,

$$\int_{\mathbb{C}_\alpha - \mathbb{C}'_\alpha} f_1(y)\,dy \geq \int_{\mathbb{C}'_\alpha - \mathbb{C}_\alpha} f_1(y)\,dy$$

which implies

$$\int_{\mathbb{C}_\alpha} f_1(y)\,dy \geq \int_{\mathbb{C}'_\alpha} f_1(y)\,dy$$

or $\Pr\{Y \in \mathbb{C}_\alpha \mid H_1\} \geq \Pr\{Y \in \mathbb{C}'_\alpha \mid H_1\}$, as required. □

In situations with analytically tractable likelihood functions, one may be able to extend the Neyman–Pearson lemma to something stronger.

EXAMPLE 17.10 (Chi-Square Degrees of Freedom)

Consider the case of $Y \sim \chi^2_{\nu_0}$ and testing

$$H_0 : \nu_0 = a \qquad \text{versus} \qquad H_1 : \nu_0 = b$$

where $a < b$. The likelihoods are

$$f_0(y) = \frac{1}{2^{a/2}\Gamma(a/2)} y^{a/2-1} e^{-\frac{1}{2}y}$$

$$f_1(y) = \frac{1}{2^{b/2}\Gamma(b/2)} y^{b/2-1} e^{-\frac{1}{2}y}$$

and the LR is

$$\frac{f_1(y)}{f_0(y)} = \frac{\Gamma(a/2)}{\Gamma(b/2)} \left(\frac{y}{2}\right)^{\frac{1}{2}(b-a)}$$

which is strictly increasing in y. Therefore, the LR critical region is equivalent to $\mathbb{C}_\alpha = \{Y \mid Y \geq \chi^2_{a;1-\alpha}\}$. This region is most powerful against *all* alternative hypotheses $\nu_0 > a$.

In this case, the alternative hypothesis can be a set of models so that the LR test is *uniformly most powerful* over the whole set. The key analytical feature of the LR is that it is *monotone*. The LR is also monotone for the normal distribution with unknown mean.

EXAMPLE 17.11 (Quadratic Log-Likelihood)

Suppose that $Y \sim \mathfrak{N}(\mu_0, \sigma_0^2)$ and $H_0 : \mu_0 = a$ versus $H_1 : \mu_0 = b$ where $a < b$. The LR is

$$\frac{f_1(y)}{f_0(y)} = \exp\left\{\frac{1}{2\sigma_0^2}[(y-a)^2 - (y-b)^2]\right\}$$

$$= \exp\left\{\frac{1}{2\sigma_0^2}[2y(b-a) + a^2 - b^2]\right\}$$

which is strictly increasing in y. Therefore, $\mathbb{C}_\alpha = \{Y \mid Y > a + \sigma_0 Z_{1-\alpha}\}$, where $Z_{1-\alpha}$ is the $100(1-\alpha)$ percentile of the $\mathfrak{N}(0, 1)$ distribution. This is the uniformly most powerful critical region for all $\mu_0 = b > a$.

This example uses a familiar "one-sided" situation and prepares us to note that there is no most powerful critical region for two-sided alternatives. Given any two-sided critical region, we can always find another with more power either above or below a. We need go no further to conclude that the W, LR, and S test statistics that we have presented above are not uniformly most powerful tests. There are special classes of tests within which these classical tests are most powerful, but we will not pursue those classes here.[40] In any case, within classical hypothesis testing it remains the responsibility of the researcher to choose the directions in the parameter space from the null hypothesis in which to concentrate statistical power.

17.6 INTERVAL ESTIMATION

Interval estimators are dual to hypothesis tests and all of the test statistics described above have counterparts in interval estimation. Perhaps the most natural and widely used interval estimator is the elliptical interval corresponding to the Wald test statistic:

$$\hat{\mathbf{\Gamma}}_{\mathrm{W}} \equiv \left\{\boldsymbol{\gamma} \in \mathbb{R}^{K-M} \mid N \cdot (\hat{\boldsymbol{\gamma}} - \boldsymbol{\gamma})' \left(\hat{\boldsymbol{\gamma}}_\theta \hat{\mathfrak{I}}^{-1} \hat{\boldsymbol{\gamma}}_\theta'\right)^{-1} (\hat{\boldsymbol{\gamma}} - \boldsymbol{\gamma}) \le \chi^2_{K-M;1-\alpha}\right\} \tag{17.36}$$

where $\boldsymbol{\gamma} : \mathbb{R}^K \rightarrow \mathbb{R}^{K-M}$ is a continuous function with rank $\boldsymbol{\gamma}_\theta(\boldsymbol{\theta}) = K - M \le K$, $\hat{\boldsymbol{\gamma}} \equiv \boldsymbol{\gamma}(\hat{\boldsymbol{\theta}})$, $\boldsymbol{\gamma}_0 \equiv \boldsymbol{\gamma}(\boldsymbol{\theta}_0)$, $\hat{\boldsymbol{\theta}}$ is the MLE such that $\sqrt{N}(\hat{\boldsymbol{\theta}} - \boldsymbol{\theta}_0) \xrightarrow{d} \mathfrak{N}[\mathbf{0}, \mathfrak{I}(\boldsymbol{\theta}_0)]$. The LR counterpart is

$$\hat{\mathbf{\Gamma}}_{\mathrm{LR}} \equiv \{\boldsymbol{\gamma} \in \mathbb{R}^{K-M} \mid 2N\{\mathrm{E}_N[L^c(\hat{\boldsymbol{\gamma}})] - \mathrm{E}_N[L^c(\boldsymbol{\gamma})]\} \le \chi^2_{K-M;1-\alpha}\} \tag{17.37}$$

where $\hat{\boldsymbol{\gamma}} \equiv \boldsymbol{\gamma}(\hat{\boldsymbol{\theta}})$ and

$$\mathrm{E}_N[L^c(\mathbf{c})] \equiv \max_{\boldsymbol{\theta} \in \boldsymbol{\Theta} : \boldsymbol{\gamma}(\boldsymbol{\theta}) = \mathbf{c}} \mathrm{E}_N[L(\boldsymbol{\theta})]$$

is a concentrated log-likelihood function. The score counterpart is

$$\hat{\mathbf{\Gamma}}_{\mathrm{S}} \equiv \left\{\boldsymbol{\gamma} \in \mathbb{R}^{K-M} \mid N \cdot \mathrm{E}_N\left[L_\theta[\hat{\boldsymbol{\theta}}_{\mathrm{R}}(\boldsymbol{\gamma})]\right]' \mathfrak{I}[\hat{\boldsymbol{\theta}}_{\mathrm{R}}(\boldsymbol{\gamma})]^{-1} \mathrm{E}_N\left[L_\theta[\hat{\boldsymbol{\theta}}_{\mathrm{R}}(\boldsymbol{\gamma})]\right] \le \chi^2_{K-M;1-\alpha}\right\} \tag{17.38}$$

where

[40] See Cox and Hinkley (1974), Lehmann (1986), and Poirier (1995) for discussions of most powerful tests.

$$\hat{\boldsymbol{\theta}}_{\mathrm{R}}(\mathbf{c}) \equiv \underset{\boldsymbol{\theta}\in\boldsymbol{\Theta}:\boldsymbol{\gamma}(\boldsymbol{\theta})=\mathbf{c}}{\operatorname{argmax}} \ \mathrm{E}_N[L(\boldsymbol{\theta})]$$

One can also derive an interval estimator based on the $C(\alpha)$ test statistic, but we have never seen this applied and do not pursue it here.

The discussion of parameter transformations and invariance of test statistics applies directly to these interval estimators: all three intervals are usually invariant to transformations of $\boldsymbol{\theta}$. The leading exception occurs with the score interval when one estimates the information matrix with the Hessian matrix.

The LR and score intervals require much more computation than the Wald version and, consequently, are used much less frequently in practice. We made a comparison between $\hat{\boldsymbol{\Gamma}}_{\mathrm{W}}$ and $\hat{\boldsymbol{\Gamma}}_{\mathrm{LR}}$ in Section 17.1. We calculated the latter interval numerically by calculating a grid of values for the concentrated log-likelihood function and interpolating the level sets with cubic polynomials. Such numerical computer packages as Matlab provide this capability. Our calculations show that these interval estimators may differ and illustrate the effects of the invariance property possessed by the LR test statistic.

17.7 OVERVIEW

1. The likelihood ratio (LR) test provides a general method for testing restrictions on the population parameters in the likelihood framework. This test examines the difference in the maximum of log-likelihood function over the unrestricted and restricted parameter sets.
2. We interpret three other test statistics as approximations to the LR test based on local quadratic approximations of the log-likelihood function.
   (a) The score [or Lagrange multiplier (LM)] test statistic approximation is local to the restricted maximum likelihood estimator (MLE).
   (b) The Wald test statistic approximation is local to the unrestricted MLE.
   (c) The $C(\alpha)$ test statistic approximation is local to a consistent estimator.
3. These test statistics are also comparisons of the difference between unrestricted and restricted MLEs, $\hat{\boldsymbol{\theta}}$ and $\hat{\boldsymbol{\theta}}_{\mathrm{R}}$ respectively. Under the null hypothesis, the test statistics are all asymptotically equivalent to

$$\mathcal{MC} = \mathrm{E}_N\left[(\hat{\boldsymbol{\theta}} - \hat{\boldsymbol{\theta}}_{\mathrm{R}})' \left[N \cdot \Im(\boldsymbol{\theta}_0)\right] (\hat{\boldsymbol{\theta}} - \hat{\boldsymbol{\theta}}_{\mathrm{R}})\right]$$

   which is a quadratic form in the difference $\hat{\boldsymbol{\theta}} - \hat{\boldsymbol{\theta}}_{\mathrm{R}}$ standardized by the information matrix multiplied by the sample size, $N \cdot \Im(\boldsymbol{\theta}_0)$. The information matrix is a generalized inverse for the asymptotic variance of $\hat{\boldsymbol{\theta}} - \hat{\boldsymbol{\theta}}_{\mathrm{R}}$, endowing the quadratic form with a χ^2 distribution asymptotically. The degrees of freedom equal the number of restrictions in the hypothesis.
4. The Wald test statistic for $H_0 : \boldsymbol{\theta}_{02} = \mathbf{0}$ reduces to

$$\mathcal{W} = N \cdot \hat{\boldsymbol{\theta}}_2' \hat{\mathbf{V}}_{\mathrm{W}}^{-1} \hat{\boldsymbol{\theta}}_2$$

   where $\hat{\mathbf{V}}_{\mathrm{W}}$ is a consistent estimator of the asymptotic variance of $\hat{\boldsymbol{\theta}}_2$.
5. The score test statistic for $H_0 : \boldsymbol{\theta}_{02} = \mathbf{0}$ reduces to

$$\mathcal{S} = N \cdot \mathrm{E}_N[L_2(\hat{\boldsymbol{\theta}}_{\mathrm{R}})]' \hat{\mathbf{V}}_{\mathrm{S}}^{-1} \mathrm{E}_N[L_2(\hat{\boldsymbol{\theta}}_{\mathrm{R}})]$$

   where $\hat{\mathbf{V}}_{\mathrm{S}}$ is a consistent estimator of the asymptotic variance of $\mathrm{E}_N[L_2(\hat{\boldsymbol{\theta}}_{\mathrm{R}})]$.

6. The LR test and some versions of the score test are invariant to reparameterizations of the parameter vector. The Wald test is not invariant to reparameterizations of the restrictions in the null hypothesis and can be quite sensitive to such changes.

7. The score test is invariant within a class of alternative hypotheses with the same restrictions local to the null hypothesis.

8. The various test statistics are also asymptotically equivalent against local alternative hypotheses. For fixed alternative hypotheses, the statistics generally differ.

9. Hypothesis tests and interval estimators are dual so that various interval estimators follow from these test statistics. The Wald version of an interval estimator is most convenient. But owing to its lack of invariance, this interval estimator will not be as reliable in some settings.

17.8 EXERCISES

17.8.1 Review

17.1 Let the assumptions of Proposition 16 (ML Asymptotics, p. 320) hold. Also, partition the parameter vector $\boldsymbol{\theta}$ into $[\boldsymbol{\theta}_1', \boldsymbol{\theta}_2']'$ and suppose that $\boldsymbol{\theta}_1$ and $\boldsymbol{\theta}_2$ have the same dimensions. Write out the $\mathcal{LR}$, $\mathcal{S}$, and $\mathcal{W}$ test statistics for each of the following null hypotheses:

(a) $H_0 : \boldsymbol{\theta}_{02} = \mathbf{t}_2$ for known $\mathbf{t}_2$,
(b) $H_0 : \boldsymbol{\theta}_{01} = \boldsymbol{\theta}_{02}$, and
(c) $H_0 : \boldsymbol{\theta}_{01} = \alpha \cdot \boldsymbol{\theta}_{02}$ where α is an unknown scalar.

17.2 (*F* **Test**) Show that W for $H_0 : \mathbf{R}\boldsymbol{\beta}_0 = \mathbf{r}$ in the normal linear regression model when the variance σ_0^2 is unknown is

$$\mathcal{W} = (K - M)\, N\hat{F} = \frac{(\mathbf{R}\hat{\boldsymbol{\beta}} - \mathbf{r})'[\mathbf{R}(\mathbf{X}'\mathbf{X})^{-1}\mathbf{R}']^{-1}(\mathbf{R}\hat{\boldsymbol{\beta}} - \mathbf{r})}{\hat{\sigma}^2}$$

where $\hat{F}$ is the F statistic in (11.1).

17.3 **[$C(\alpha)$ Test]** Add a representation of the $C(\alpha)$ test to Figure 17.3.

17.4 **(Convergence Criterion)** Provide an interpretation of the computational convergence criterion (16.17) discussed in Section 16.5 in terms of hypothesis testing.

17.5 **(Quadratic Approximation)** Confirm the quadratic approximation in (17.21) using the following steps.

(a) Write out a second-order Taylor series expansion for $\mathrm{E}_N[L(\hat{\boldsymbol{\theta}}_B)]$ around $\boldsymbol{\theta} = \hat{\boldsymbol{\theta}}_B$.
(b) Use the argument in Section 15.3.2 to show that the Hessian in the expansion converges in probability to the information matrix $\Im(\boldsymbol{\theta}_0)$.
(c) Use a relationship such as (15.4) to show that $\sqrt{N}\,\mathrm{E}_N[L(\hat{\boldsymbol{\theta}}_A)]$ converges in distribution.
(d) Finally, combine these results with $\sqrt{N}\left(\hat{\boldsymbol{\theta}}_A - \boldsymbol{\theta}_0\right) \xrightarrow{d} \mathfrak{N}(0, \mathbf{V}_A)$ and $\sqrt{N}\left(\hat{\boldsymbol{\theta}}_B - \boldsymbol{\theta}_0\right) \xrightarrow{d} \mathfrak{N}(0, \mathbf{V}_B)$ to obtain (17.21).

17.6 (Ordering Test Statistics) Using the following steps, show that $S \leq \mathcal{LR} \leq \mathcal{W}$ for linear restrictions on the normal linear regression model.[41] That is, suppose $\mathbf{y}\,|\,\mathbf{X} \sim \mathfrak{N}(\mathbf{X}\boldsymbol{\beta}_0, \sigma_0^2 \cdot \mathbf{I})$ and consider $H_0 : \mathbf{R}\boldsymbol{\beta}_0 = \mathbf{0}$.

(a) Show that

$$\left\|\mathbf{y} - \hat{\boldsymbol{\mu}}_{\mathrm{R}}\right\|^2 - \left\|\mathbf{y} - \hat{\boldsymbol{\mu}}\right\|^2 \geq 0$$

and

$$S = N \frac{\left\|\mathbf{y} - \hat{\boldsymbol{\mu}}_{\mathrm{R}}\right\|^2 - \left\|\mathbf{y} - \hat{\boldsymbol{\mu}}\right\|^2}{\left\|\mathbf{y} - \hat{\boldsymbol{\mu}}_{\mathrm{R}}\right\|^2}$$

$$\mathcal{LR} = N \log \frac{\left\|\mathbf{y} - \hat{\boldsymbol{\mu}}_{\mathrm{R}}\right\|^2}{\left\|\mathbf{y} - \hat{\boldsymbol{\mu}}\right\|^2}$$

$$\mathcal{W} = N \frac{\left\|\mathbf{y} - \hat{\boldsymbol{\mu}}_{\mathrm{R}}\right\|^2 - \left\|\mathbf{y} - \hat{\boldsymbol{\mu}}\right\|^2}{\left\|\mathbf{y} - \hat{\boldsymbol{\mu}}\right\|^2}$$

where $\hat{\boldsymbol{\mu}} = \mathbf{P_X y}$ is the OLS unrestricted fitted vector and $\hat{\boldsymbol{\mu}}_{\mathrm{R}} = \left(\mathbf{P_X} - \mathbf{P}_{\mathbf{X}(\mathbf{X}'\mathbf{X})^{-1}\mathbf{R}'}\right)\mathbf{y}$ is the restricted counterpart.

(b) The concavity of the logarithmic function implies that

$$\log x \leq x - 1$$

Show that this inequality implies that $S \leq \mathcal{LR} \leq \mathcal{W}$.

17.7 (Test Consistency) Following Proposition 17 (Classical Test Consistency, p. 402), we show that the Wald test is consistent. Prove that the LR, score, and $C(\alpha)$ tests are also consistent under the same conditions.

17.8 Using an example, show that the four classical test statistics are not necessarily asymptotically equivalent when the null hypothesis is false.

17.9 (Invariance) Suppose that $\boldsymbol{\theta} \in \mathbb{R}^2$ and consider testing the restriction $\theta_1 = \theta_2$ in the form $\theta_1/\theta_2 = 1$.

(a) Reparameterize the likelihood function in terms of θ_1 and $\gamma \equiv \theta_1/\theta_2$.

(b) Find the score, Hessian, and information matrix for the reparameterization in terms of the original score, Hessian, and information matrix.

(c) Show that the score test is invariant to the reparameterization if the information matrix is used to estimate the variance of the score.

(d) Show that the score test is not invariant if the Hessian matrix is used to estimate the variance of the score. What term can be dropped from the Hessian to make the test invariant? Is this score test statistic always positive?

17.10 [$C(\alpha)$ Test] Explain the $C(\alpha)$ test for the restrictions $\boldsymbol{\theta}_2 = \mathbf{0}$ on $\boldsymbol{\theta} = [\boldsymbol{\theta}_1', \boldsymbol{\theta}_2']'$.

(a) Construct a generalization of $C(\alpha)$ for restrictions $\mathbf{r}(\boldsymbol{\theta}) = \mathbf{0}$.

(b) Show that $C(\alpha) \geq 0$ in (17.26). Is this true for your generalization of this test statistic?

17.11 (Score Test) In (17.11), the score test statistic is

$$S = N \cdot \mathrm{E}_N[L_{\boldsymbol{\theta}}(\hat{\boldsymbol{\theta}}_{\mathrm{R}})]' \Im(\hat{\boldsymbol{\theta}}_{\mathrm{R}})^{-1} \mathrm{E}_N[L_{\boldsymbol{\theta}}(\hat{\boldsymbol{\theta}}_{\mathrm{R}})]$$

---

41 Berndt and Savin (1977) inspired this question. See also Breusch (1979).

which is a quadratic form in the score $\mathrm{E}_N[L_{\boldsymbol{\theta}}(\hat{\boldsymbol{\theta}}_{\mathrm{R}})]$ and the inverse of an estimator of the asymptotic variance of $\mathrm{E}_N[L_{\boldsymbol{\theta}}(\boldsymbol{\theta}_0)]$.

(a) Show that $\sqrt{N}\,\mathrm{E}_N[L_{\boldsymbol{\theta}}(\hat{\boldsymbol{\theta}}_{\mathrm{R}})]$ and $\sqrt{N}\,\mathrm{E}_N[L_{\boldsymbol{\theta}}(\boldsymbol{\theta}_0)]$ are not asymptotically equivalent.

(b) The normalizing matrix $\Im(\hat{\boldsymbol{\theta}}_{\mathrm{R}})$ seems to treat $\hat{\boldsymbol{\theta}}_{\mathrm{R}}$ as though it were equal to $\boldsymbol{\theta}_0$. Explain this paradox.

17.12 (Pivotal Statistics) As in (17.36), a popular confidence interval for $\boldsymbol{\theta}_0$ rests on the asymptotically pivotal statistic

$$N(\hat{\boldsymbol{\theta}}_N-\boldsymbol{\theta}_0)'\Im(\hat{\boldsymbol{\theta}}_N)(\hat{\boldsymbol{\theta}}_N-\boldsymbol{\theta}_0)\xrightarrow{d}\chi^2_K$$

It is also true that

$$N(\hat{\boldsymbol{\theta}}_N-\boldsymbol{\theta}_0)'\Im(\boldsymbol{\theta}_0)(\hat{\boldsymbol{\theta}}_N-\boldsymbol{\theta}_0)\xrightarrow{d}\chi^2_K$$

is an asymptotically pivotal statistic. What difficulties does this version present for confidence intervals and hypothesis tests?

17.8.2 Extensions

17.13 (Minimum Chi-Square) Under the assumptions of Proposition 16 (ML Asymptotics, p. 320), prove that $\mathrm{E}_N[N\cdot(\hat{\boldsymbol{\theta}}-\hat{\boldsymbol{\theta}}_{\mathrm{R}})'\Im(\boldsymbol{\theta}_0)\,(\hat{\boldsymbol{\theta}}-\hat{\boldsymbol{\theta}}_{\mathrm{R}})]\xrightarrow{d}\chi^2_{K-M}$ by means of Lemma 10.1 (Minimum Chi-Square, p. 197). [HINT: Note that $\mathrm{E}_N[N\cdot(\hat{\boldsymbol{\theta}}-\boldsymbol{\theta}_0)'\Im(\boldsymbol{\theta}_0)\,(\hat{\boldsymbol{\theta}}-\boldsymbol{\theta}_0)]\xrightarrow{d}\chi^2_K$.]

17.14 (Score Test) In contrast to Example 17.9, follow Poirier et al. (1986) and use the power exponential family of distributions with p.d.f.

$$f_U(u)=\frac{\nu}{2^{(1/\nu)+1}\Gamma(1/\nu)\,\sigma}\exp\left(-\frac{1}{2}\left|\frac{u-\mu}{\sigma}\right|^{\nu}\right)$$

to derive a score test of normality in the normal regression model. Does this test share any local alternatives with the score test of Jarque and Bera (1980)?

17.15 (Generalized Inverse) Let the assumptions of Proposition 16 (ML Asymptotics, p. 320) hold. For restrictions $\mathbf{r}(\boldsymbol{\theta}_0)=\mathbf{0}$ such that $\mathbf{r}_{\boldsymbol{\theta}}(\boldsymbol{\theta}_0)$ is full-row rank, show that

(a) $\Im(\boldsymbol{\theta}_0)$ is a generalized inverse for the asymptotic variance of $\hat{\boldsymbol{\theta}}-\hat{\boldsymbol{\theta}}_{\mathrm{R}}$ and

(b) $\Im(\boldsymbol{\theta}_0)^{-1}$ is a generalized inverse for the asymptotic variance of $\mathrm{E}_N[L_{\theta}(\hat{\boldsymbol{\theta}}_{\mathrm{R}})]$.

(c) Use Lemma 10.7 to argue directly that $\mathcal{MC}$ and S have χ^2 distributions asymptotically under $\mathbf{r}(\boldsymbol{\theta}_0)=\mathbf{0}$.

17.16 (Score Test) Consider a score test for skewness based on the transformation in Exercise 13.13. What problem arises when the parameter α_2 is unknown? Why does this problem disappear when one restricts $\alpha_2=1/\alpha_1$?

17.17 (Lagrange Multiplier Test) Consider restricted ML estimation under the conditions of Proposition 16 (ML Asymptotics, p. 320). Use the following steps to show the equivalence of the Lagrange multiplier (LM) and score tests. Let the restrictions be $\mathbf{r}(\boldsymbol{\theta}_0)=\mathbf{0}$ such that $\mathbf{r}_{\boldsymbol{\theta}}(\boldsymbol{\theta}_0)$ is full-row rank. Denote the number of rows $K-M$.

(a) Given the restricted MLE, $\hat{\boldsymbol{\theta}}_{\mathrm{R}}$, in (17.8), show that the Lagrange multipliers $\hat{\boldsymbol{\lambda}}$ of the restrictions and the score $\mathrm{E}_N[L_{\boldsymbol{\theta}}(\hat{\boldsymbol{\theta}}_{\mathrm{R}})]$ are linearly dependent:

$$\mathrm{E}_N[L_{\boldsymbol{\theta}}(\hat{\boldsymbol{\theta}}_{\mathrm{R}})]-\mathbf{r}_{\boldsymbol{\theta}}(\hat{\boldsymbol{\theta}}_{\mathrm{R}})'\hat{\boldsymbol{\lambda}}=\mathbf{0}$$

(b) Show that $\mathbf{r}_{\theta}(\hat{\boldsymbol{\theta}}_{\mathrm{R}})\Im(\hat{\boldsymbol{\theta}}_{\mathrm{R}})^{-1}\mathbf{r}_{\theta}(\hat{\boldsymbol{\theta}}_{\mathrm{R}})'$ is positive definite and use this fact to show that asymptotically, under $\mathbf{r}(\boldsymbol{\theta}_0) = \mathbf{0}$, the Lagrange multipliers are a linear transformation of the score $\mathrm{E}_N[L_{\theta}(\hat{\boldsymbol{\theta}}_{\mathrm{R}})]$:

$$\sqrt{N}\hat{\boldsymbol{\lambda}} \overset{p}{=} \left[\mathbf{r}_{\theta}(\boldsymbol{\theta}_0)\Im(\boldsymbol{\theta}_0)^{-1}\mathbf{r}_{\theta}(\boldsymbol{\theta}_0)'\right]^{-1} \mathbf{r}_{\theta}(\boldsymbol{\theta}_0)\Im(\boldsymbol{\theta}_0)^{-1}\sqrt{N}\,\mathrm{E}_N[L_{\theta}(\hat{\boldsymbol{\theta}}_{\mathrm{R}})]$$

(c) Using the previous result and the Wald testing principle, justify the LM test statistic

$$\mathcal{LM} = N \cdot \hat{\boldsymbol{\lambda}}'\mathbf{r}_{\theta}(\hat{\boldsymbol{\theta}}_{\mathrm{R}})\Im(\hat{\boldsymbol{\theta}}_{\mathrm{R}})^{-1}\mathbf{r}_{\theta}(\hat{\boldsymbol{\theta}}_{\mathrm{R}})'\hat{\boldsymbol{\lambda}} \xrightarrow{d} \chi^2_{K-M}$$

under $\mathbf{r}(\boldsymbol{\theta}_0) = \mathbf{0}$.

(d) Show that $\mathcal{LM} = S$, where S is given by (17.29).

***17.18 (Minimum Chi-Square)** We showed that the Wald, LR, and score test statistics were asymptotically equivalent to

$$N \cdot \left(\hat{\boldsymbol{\theta}} - \hat{\boldsymbol{\theta}}_{\mathrm{R}}\right)' \Im(\boldsymbol{\theta}_0) \left(\hat{\boldsymbol{\theta}} - \hat{\boldsymbol{\theta}}_{\mathrm{R}}\right)$$

(a) Show that the minimum chi-square (MC) statistics

$$\mathcal{MC}_1 \equiv N \cdot \left(\hat{\boldsymbol{\theta}} - \hat{\boldsymbol{\theta}}_{\mathrm{R}}\right)' \Im(\hat{\boldsymbol{\theta}}) \left(\hat{\boldsymbol{\theta}} - \hat{\boldsymbol{\theta}}_{\mathrm{R}}\right)$$

and

$$\mathcal{MC}_2 \equiv N \cdot \left(\hat{\boldsymbol{\theta}} - \hat{\boldsymbol{\theta}}_{\mathrm{R}}\right)' \Im(\hat{\boldsymbol{\theta}}_{\mathrm{R}}) \left(\hat{\boldsymbol{\theta}} - \hat{\boldsymbol{\theta}}_{\mathrm{R}}\right)$$

are also asymptotically equivalent test statistics. These are LR like in that they require estimation with and without the restrictions of the null hypothesis.

(b) For $H_0 : \boldsymbol{\theta}_{02} = \mathbf{0}$, show that we can obtain the Wald test statistic by replacing $\Im(\hat{\boldsymbol{\theta}})$ in $\mathcal{MC}_1$ with

$$\begin{bmatrix} \mathbf{0} & \mathbf{0} \\ \mathbf{0} & \Im_{22}(\hat{\boldsymbol{\theta}}) - \Im_{21}(\hat{\boldsymbol{\theta}})\Im_{11}(\hat{\boldsymbol{\theta}})^{-1}\Im_{12}(\hat{\boldsymbol{\theta}}) \end{bmatrix}$$

(c) Show that when we replace $\hat{\boldsymbol{\theta}}$ with $\boldsymbol{\theta}_0$ in this matrix, it is a generalized inverse for the asymptotic variance of $\sqrt{N}\left(\hat{\boldsymbol{\theta}} - \hat{\boldsymbol{\theta}}_{\mathrm{R}}\right)$.

(d) Relate these MC statistics to the $C(\alpha)$ statistic.

17.19 (LMLE) An alternative use of LMLEs in testing is to place them into the log-likelihood function itself. Let $\hat{\boldsymbol{\theta}}$ and $\hat{\boldsymbol{\theta}}_{\mathrm{R}}$ denote the unrestricted and restricted MLEs, respectively, and let $\breve{\boldsymbol{\theta}}$ denote any $\sqrt{N}$-consistent estimator.

(a) Show that

$$\mathcal{LR}_{\mathrm{W}} = 2\left[L(\hat{\boldsymbol{\theta}}; U_1, \ldots, U_N) - L(\hat{\boldsymbol{\theta}}^*_{\mathrm{R}}; U_1, \ldots, U_N)\right]$$

where

$$\hat{\boldsymbol{\theta}}^*_{\mathrm{R}} = \begin{bmatrix} \hat{\boldsymbol{\theta}}_1 + \Im_{11}(\hat{\boldsymbol{\theta}})^{-1}\Im_{12}(\hat{\boldsymbol{\theta}})\,\hat{\boldsymbol{\theta}}_2 \\ 0 \end{bmatrix}$$

$$\mathcal{LR}_{\mathrm{S}} = 2\left[L(\hat{\boldsymbol{\theta}}^*; U_1, \ldots, U_N) - L(\hat{\boldsymbol{\theta}}_{\mathrm{R}}; U_1, \ldots, U_N)\right]$$

where

$$\hat{\boldsymbol{\theta}}^* = \hat{\boldsymbol{\theta}}_{\mathrm{R}} + \Im(\hat{\boldsymbol{\theta}}_{\mathrm{R}})^{-1}\,\mathrm{E}_N[L_{\theta}(\hat{\boldsymbol{\theta}}_{\mathrm{R}})]$$

and

$$\mathcal{LR}_{C(\alpha)} = 2\left[L(\hat{\boldsymbol{\theta}}^*; U_1, \ldots, U_N) - L(\hat{\boldsymbol{\theta}}^*_{\mathrm{R}}; U_1, \ldots, U_N)\right]$$

where

$$\hat{\boldsymbol{\theta}}^* = \check{\boldsymbol{\theta}} + \check{\mathfrak{I}}_N^{-1} \mathrm{E}_N[\check{L}_{\boldsymbol{\theta}}]$$

$$\hat{\boldsymbol{\theta}}^*_{\mathrm{R}} = \begin{bmatrix} \check{\boldsymbol{\theta}}_1 + \check{\mathfrak{I}}_{11}^{-1} \mathrm{E}_N[\check{L}_1] \\ \mathbf{0} \end{bmatrix}$$

are all asymptotically equivalent to the LR test statistic under the null hypothesis $H_0 : \boldsymbol{\theta}_{02} = \mathbf{0}$.

(b) Explain why these three statistics are not necessarily positive. Suggest alternative statistics based on Newey's modified LMLE (Exercise 16.11).

(c) Evaluate the following claim: "The LMLE is not the MLE. Because of this, the LMLE should not be used as the basis for likelihood ratio tests."

17.20 (Jarque–Bera Test of Normality) Jarque and Bera (1980) propose a score test of normality based on the more general Pearson family of p.d.f.s. These satisfy a differential equation,

$$\frac{df_{\mathrm{P}}(z; a)}{dz} = \frac{a_1 + z}{a_2 + a_3 z + a_4 z^2}$$

the constraints

$$f_{\mathrm{P}}(z; a) \geq 0 \qquad \text{and} \qquad \int f_{\mathrm{P}}(z; a)\, dz = 1$$

and are parameterized by $a_1, \ldots, a_4$. The normal distribution is the special case in which $a_3 = a_4 = 0$.

One does not need to solve the differential equation to implement the score test of normality. One needs only the score with respect to a_3 and a_4 evaluated at $a_3 = a_4 = 0$, which can be found using

$$\left.\frac{\partial \log f_{\mathrm{P}}(z; a)}{\partial a_j}\right|_{a_3=a_4=0} = \int \left.\frac{\partial^2 \log f_{\mathrm{P}}(z; a)}{\partial a_j\, \partial z}\right|_{a_3=a_4=0} dz$$

$$= -\int \left(\left.\frac{\partial}{\partial a_j} \frac{a_1 + z}{a_2 + a_3 z + a_4 z^2}\right|_{a_3=a_4=0} \right) dz$$

Constants of integration depend on the restriction that the expectation of the score is zero:

$$\int \left.\frac{\partial \log f_{\mathrm{P}}(z; a)}{\partial a_j}\right|_{a_3=a_4=0} f_{\mathrm{P}}(z; a)\, dz = 0$$

(a) Show that the required scores are

$$\left.\frac{\partial \log f_{\mathrm{P}}(z; a)}{\partial a_3}\right|_{a_3=a_4=0} = \frac{1}{3\sigma^4}(z-\mu)^3 + \frac{\mu}{2\sigma^4}\left[(z-\mu)^2 - \sigma^2\right]$$

$$\left.\frac{\partial \log f_{\mathrm{P}}(z; a)}{\partial a_4}\right|_{a_3=a_4=0} = \frac{1}{4\sigma^4}\left[(z-\mu)^4 - 3\sigma^4\right] + \frac{2\mu}{3\sigma^4}(z-\mu)^3 - \frac{\mu^2}{2\sigma^4}\left[(z-\mu)^2 - \sigma^2\right]$$

(b) How could you construct a test statistic for normality from these functions?

17.21 Argue that the test essentially examines whether the third- and fourth-moment restrictions of the normal distribution are satisfied.

17.22 **(Testing on the Boundary)** The Student t distribution contains the normal as a special case, suggesting that one can construct hypothesis test statistics for normality with this generalization. Suppose that $\{(\mathbf{x}_n, y_n);\ n = 1, \ldots, N\}$ are i.i.d. Using the information in Exercise 15.18,

(a) create a score test for

$$H_0 : \frac{y_n - \mathbf{x}_n' \boldsymbol{\beta}_0}{\sigma_0} \sim \mathfrak{N}(0, 1) \sim t_\infty$$

against the alternative hypothesis that

$$H_1 : \frac{y_n - \mathbf{x}_n' \boldsymbol{\beta}_0}{\sigma_0} \sim t_{1/\alpha_0},\ \alpha_0 > 0$$

(b) argue that the Wald and LR tests do not possess approximately chi-square distributions under H_0, and

(c) explain why the score test does not suffer from this difficulty.

CHAPTER 18

Heteroskedasticity

In this chapter and in Chapter 19, we reconsider the assumption that the conditional variance matrix of **y** is a scalar matrix (Assumption 7.1, p. 130). We return to maintaining the conditional normality assumption (Assumption 10.1, p. 195) and derive estimators and hypothesis tests using the ML method described in Chapters 14–17. We will remove the normality assumption as well when we discuss estimation by the method of moments in Chapter 21.

In data sets describing economic phenomena, the assumptions of no covariance and constant variance across observations are sometimes unreasonable. For example, macroeconomic series of data through time surely involve dependence, and firms within an industry vary so much in their observed characteristics that treating their unobserved characteristics as though they were drawn from an identical distribution seems naive. Generally, dependence among the observations coincides with nonzero covariance and nonidentical distributions have different variances. Faced with such prevalent exceptions, we study estimation and inference when

$$\mathrm{Var}[\mathbf{y} \mid \mathbf{X}] \equiv \boldsymbol{\Omega}_0 \neq \sigma_0^2 \cdot \mathbf{I} \tag{18.1}$$

where $\boldsymbol{\Omega}_0$ is symmetric and positive definite. Its off-diagonal elements may not be zero and its diagonal elements may not be equal. Because the conditional variance ellipse of **y** is no longer a sphere, the distribution of **y** is often called *nonspherical* in this case.

Four basic questions arise in our analytical framework, faced with a potentially nonscalar $\boldsymbol{\Omega}_0$:

1. What are the effects on the properties of OLS statistics?

2. How can we test for a nonscalar $\boldsymbol{\Omega}_0$?

3. What corrections can we make to our OLS procedures?

4. What is the ML alternative to OLS if we decide that $\boldsymbol{\Omega}_0$ is not scalar?

We can begin to answer the first question immediately. Several properties of the OLS estimation procedure for the coefficient vector $\boldsymbol{\beta}_0$ remain unchanged for general $\boldsymbol{\Omega}_0$:

- unbiasedness (Proposition 4, p. 111),
- consistency (Proposition 15, p. 257),
- normality (Proposition 9, p. 198), and
- asymptotic normality (Proposition 15, p. 257).

None of these properties relies on the assumption of a scalar variance matrix. Because the OLS estimator $\hat{\boldsymbol{\beta}}_{\text{OLS}} = (\mathbf{X}'\mathbf{X})^{-1}\mathbf{X}'\mathbf{y}$ is linear in $\mathbf{y}$, these properties are preserved. However, several properties are affected:

- the variance matrix $\text{Var}[\hat{\boldsymbol{\beta}}_{\text{OLS}} \mid \mathbf{X}]$ (Proposition 5, p. 157),
- the estimation of this matrix (Propositions 6, p. 158, and 10, p. 199),
- the distribution of pivotal statistics (Proposition 11, p. 203), and
- the relative efficiency of the estimator (Propositions 7, p. 187, and 12, p. 205).

All of these are *second-moment* properties that rest on the *second-moment* assumption of a scalar variance matrix. So even though $\hat{\boldsymbol{\beta}}_{\text{OLS}}$ may be unbiased and normally distributed, its variance matrix changes. To say anything more informative we must be more specific about the form of $\boldsymbol{\Omega}_0$.

Instead of Assumption 3 (Second Moment, p. 130), we will permit different conditional variances, $\text{Var}[y_n \mid \mathbf{x}_n] = \sigma_{0n}^2$. This is called conditional *heteroskedasticity*. The conditional variance matrix $\text{Var}[\mathbf{y} \mid \mathbf{X}]$ will be merely *diagonal*:

$$\boldsymbol{\Omega}_0 = \begin{bmatrix} \sigma_1^2 & 0 & 0 & \cdots & 0 \\ 0 & \sigma_2^2 & 0 & \cdots & 0 \\ 0 & 0 & \sigma_3^2 & \ddots & \vdots \\ \vdots & \vdots & \ddots & \ddots & 0 \\ 0 & 0 & \cdots & 0 & \sigma_N^2 \end{bmatrix} = \text{diag}(\sigma_n^2;\, n = 1, \ldots, N) \tag{18.2}$$

In Chapter 19, we describe *serial correlation*, in which the off-diagonal elements of $\boldsymbol{\Omega}_0$ may be nonzero.

Otherwise, we will continue to maintain that Assumptions 3.1 (Full Rank, p. 53), 6.1 (First Moment, p. 110), and 10.1 (Normality, p. 195) hold. Because we will use asymptotic approximations, we also adopt Assumptions 13.1 (I.I.D., p. 256) and 13.2 (Population Full Rank, p. 257). Before analyzing the implications of these assumptions formally, we revisit the analysis of individual earnings.

18.1 HETEROSKEDASTICITY IN WAGES

Up to this point, we have assumed that the conditional variance of the log-wage is the same for all observations. But there are good reasons to suspect that the conditional variance changes with some of the variables that appear in the conditional mean. For example, Mincer (1974) argues that the variance of wages conditional on education should increase with education. Those with higher educations have wider choices in jobs and greater scope for trading such nonpecuniary rewards as independence or status against earnings. Conditional on experience, wage variance may also increase as uncertainty about worker productivity decreases and earnings approach productivity. Such heterogeneous conditional variances are a particular exception to a scalar conditional variance matrix (Assumption 7.1) called *heteroskedasticity*.

Actually, we already have some statistical evidence that heteroskedasticity may be present. In Chapter 16, we estimated the log-wage regression given a conditional Student t distribution and obtained a point estimate near six for the degrees of freedom. This is a substantial departure from conditional normality and it is consistent with underlying heteroskedasticity. In Section 13.2.1, (13.1)–(13.3) we describe the Student t distribution as a mixture of *normal* distributions, where the variance *differs* across random draws. A variance is drawn as $\sigma^2 \sim \nu/\chi^2_\nu$. Conditional on this variance, an $\mathfrak{N}(0, \sigma^2)$ draw yields a random variable that is t_ν marginal of σ^2. Therefore, the low estimated degrees of freedom parameter is consistent with different variances among normal distributions.

Popular methods for exploring heteroskedasticity examine the behavior of the OLS fitted residuals. Ideally, one would investigate heteroskedasticity using observations on $(y_n - \mathbf{x}'_n\boldsymbol{\beta}_0)^2$ because it is the conditional mean of this random variable that may vary with variables $\mathbf{z}_n$:

$$\mathrm{Var}[y_n \mid \mathbf{x}_n, \mathbf{z}_n] = \mathrm{E}[(y_n - \mathbf{x}'_n\boldsymbol{\beta}_0)^2 \mid \mathbf{x}_n, \mathbf{z}_n]$$

But this residual is not observable. Using the tools at hand, a practical alternative approach is to study the squared OLS fitted residual to see whether there is evidence that this observable variable varies systematically with $\mathbf{z}_n$. Intuitively, heteroskedasticity in $\varepsilon_n \equiv y_n - \mathbf{x}'_n\boldsymbol{\beta}_0$ will show up as heteroskedasticity in $\hat{\varepsilon}_n \equiv y_n - \mathbf{x}'_n\hat{\boldsymbol{\beta}}_{\mathrm{OLS}}$.

Figure 18.1 shows a box-and-whisker plot of the OLS fitted residuals from the hourly wage regression in Table 4.1.[1] This graph suggests an increase in the range of the residuals as schooling increases. The analogous plot for different levels of experience in Figure 18.2 seems far less clear. But we also need to be cautious about reading too much into such graphs. Even when the y_n are conditionally *homoskedastic* (constant variance), we know that the OLS fitted residuals are heteroskedastic conditional on the explanatory variables.[2]

We can also quantify such graphic patterns using OLS. Table 18.1 contains OLS statistics from a regression of the squared OLS log-wage fitted residual divided by s^2 on the constant, schooling, experience, female indicator, nonwhite indicator, and union indicator variables. Taken at face value, there appears to be empirical support for the hypotheses that the conditional variance of log-earnings increases with both education and experience. In addition, the distribution of hourly wages for union members seems to be more compressed than for nonunion members.

We must also exercise caution, however, in interpreting these OLS statistics. Although it is true that underlying heteroskedasticity in the y_n will contribute to heteroskedasticity in $\hat{\varepsilon}_n$, the OLS fitted residuals are heteroskedastic even when the conditional variance of y_n is constant. Put another way, the dependent variable in this regression is not the one we desire, but an estimated substitute, and our interpretation of all the statistics should take this substitution into account.

One of the results of this chapter is that one can carry out a score test for heteroskedasticity with this simple regression. Such a test does take into account the first-step estimation of the coefficients in the log-wage regression. In this case, the score test statistic equals one-half the explained sum of squares from the second-step OLS fit of the standardized squared OLS fitted residuals to variables that may explain conditional heteroskedasticity. This statistic equals 29.50 for the OLS fit reported in Table 18.1. Under the null hypothesis of conditional homoskedasticity, this is a draw from a distribution that is approximately chi-square with 5 degrees of freedom. But such a value is so rare for that distribution that the evidence does not support homoskedasticity.

---

[1] In a box-and-whisker plot, the ends of the box show the first and third quartiles of the data. The line through the middle of the box is the median and the "whiskers" extend to the minimum and maximum of the data. In our figures, we restrict these plots to cases with at least 10 observations.

[2] Proposition 5 (Variances of OLS, p. 157) states that $\mathrm{Var}[\mathbf{y} - \hat{\boldsymbol{\mu}} \mid X] = \sigma_0^2 \cdot (\mathbf{I} - \mathbf{P_X})$.

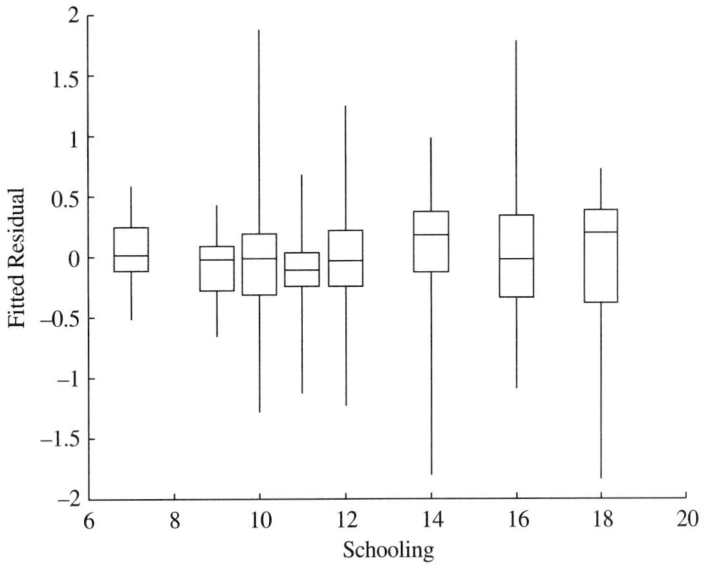

Figure 18.1 Box plots of OLS fitted residuals by schooling level.

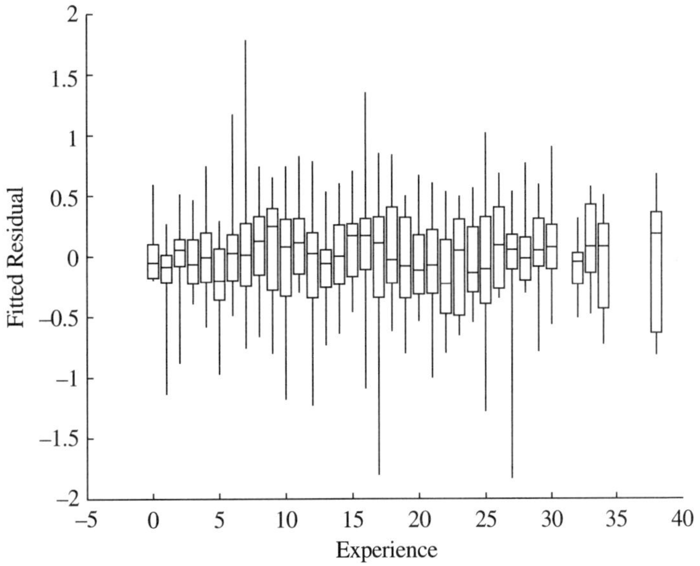

Figure 18.2 Box plots of OLS fitted residuals by experience level.

Table 18.1
OLS Fit for Squared OLS Fitted Residuals

Variable	Coefficient	Standard Error
Constant	−0.897	0.419
Female	0.174	0.143
Nonwhite	−0.279	0.186
Union	−0.376	0.190
Schooling	0.119	0.030
Experience	0.025	0.006

We also describe two methods for taking heteroskedasticity into account in the estimation of β_0: (1) a correction to the estimates of the standard errors of the OLS estimators and (2) relatively efficient *weighted least squares* (WLS) estimators. Table 18.2 gives the standard OLS statistics and two sets of alternatives for the log-wage regression for hourly wages. The estimated standard errors for OLS in the corrected OLS column take into account possible heteroskedasticity. These estimates are sometimes higher and sometimes lower than those in the first column. Heteroskedasticity does not bias estimates of the standard errors in a particular direction. Both the estimated coefficients and the standard errors change in the weighted LS column. Asymptotically, the feasible WLS estimator is efficient relative to the OLS estimator and, indeed, its estimated standard errors are often smaller than those estimated for OLS under corrected OLS.

In the following sections, we will explain why these alternative estimators are used and how they are derived.

Table 18.2
Reestimation with Heteroskedasticity

Explanatory Variable	OLS	Corrected[a] OLS	Weighted[b] LS
Constant	1.057	1.057	1.136
	(0.089)	(0.100)	(0.071)
Female	−0.213	−0.213	−0.213
	(0.030)	(0.029)	(0.027)
Nonwhite	−0.115	−0.115	−0.110
	(0.038)	(0.034)	(0.034)
Union	0.284	0.284	0.280
	(0.039)	(0.035)	(0.035)
Schooling	0.067	0.067	0.058
	(0.006)	(0.007)	(0.005)
Experience	0.035	0.035	0.038
	(0.004)	(0.004)	(0.004)
$(\text{Experience})^2$	−0.00057	−0.00057	−0.00061
	(0.00010)	(0.00011)	(0.00009)

[a]The numbers in parentheses are estimated standard errors, computed with the Eicker–White estimator (p. 429).

[b]See the description of the feasible WLS estimator (p. 435) with multiplicative heteroskedasticity and the explanatory variables in Table 18.1.

18.2 HETEROSKEDASTICITY AND OLS

We begin with answers to the first question listed at the beginning of this chapter: what are the effects on the properties of OLS statistics? The first results that we derived from the scalar variance matrix assumption were the variance matrices of OLS statistics given in Proposition 5 (Variances of OLS, p. 157). These matrix expressions no longer apply for general $\boldsymbol{\Omega}_0$. An immediate consequence is that the OLS estimator for $\mathrm{Var}[\hat{\boldsymbol{\beta}}_{\mathrm{OLS}} \mid \mathbf{X}]$ is biased. One can examine the particular effect of heteroskedasticity in simple cases.

EXAMPLE 18.1 (Simple OLS)

Consider the simple ($K = 1$) conditional normal linear regression model $y_n \mid x_n \sim \mathfrak{N}(\beta_0 x_n, \sigma_{0n}^2)$ ($n = 1, \ldots, N$) so that the variance can differ across observations. The OLS estimator for β_0 is

$$\hat{\beta}_{\mathrm{OLS}} = \frac{\sum_{n=1}^N x_n y_n}{\sum_{n=1}^N x_n^2} = \beta_0 + \frac{\sum_{n=1}^N x_n (y_n - \beta_0 x_n)}{\sum_{n=1}^N x_n^2}$$

which is still an unbiased estimator, but its conditional sampling variance is

$$\begin{aligned} \mathrm{Var}[\hat{\beta}_{\mathrm{OLS}} \mid \mathbf{X}] &= \frac{\sum_{n=1}^N \mathrm{Var}[x_n (y_n - \beta_0 x_n) \mid x_n]}{\left(\sum_{n=1}^N x_n^2\right)^2} \\ &= \frac{\sum_{n=1}^N x_n^2 \sigma_{0n}^2}{\left(\sum_{n=1}^N x_n^2\right)^2} \end{aligned} \tag{18.3}$$

under independent sampling. This simplifies to the usual OLS variance when the σ_{0n}^2 are all equal.

The OLS estimator s^2 has a conditional expectation equal to

$$\begin{aligned} \mathrm{E}[s^2 \mid \mathbf{X}] &= \frac{1}{N-1} \mathrm{E}\left[(\mathbf{y} - \mathbf{X}\beta_0)' (\mathbf{I} - \mathbf{P_X}) (\mathbf{y} - \mathbf{X}\beta_0)\right] \\ &= \frac{1}{N-1} \mathrm{E}\left[\sum_{n=1}^N (y_n - x_n \beta_0)^2 - \frac{\left[\sum_{n=1}^N x_n (y_n - x_n \beta_0)\right]^2}{\sum_{n=1}^N x_n^2} \right] \\ &= \frac{\sum_{n=1}^N \sigma_{0n}^2 \left[\left(\sum_{j=1}^N x_j^2\right) - x_n^2\right]}{(N-1) \sum_{n=1}^N x_n^2} \end{aligned}$$

Therefore, the OLS estimated sampling variance of $\hat{\beta}_{\mathrm{OLS}}$ has the expected value

$$\mathrm{E}[s^2 (\mathbf{X}'\mathbf{X})^{-1} \mid \mathbf{X}] = \frac{\sum_{n=1}^N \sigma_{0n}^2 \left[\left(\sum_{j=1}^N x_j^2\right) - x_n^2\right]}{(N-1) \left(\sum_{n=1}^N x_n^2\right)^2}$$

which does not equal $\mathrm{Var}[\hat{\beta}_{\mathrm{OLS}} \mid \mathbf{X}]$ as given in (18.3). The bias in the estimator is negative if

$$N\sum_{n=1}^{N} x_n^2\sigma_{0n}^2 - \left(\sum_{n=1}^{N} x_n^2\right)\left(\sum_{n=1}^{N} \sigma_{0n}^2\right) = N^2 \operatorname{Cov}_N[x_n, \sigma_{0n}^2] > 0$$

and positive otherwise. The bias depends, therefore, on the sample covariance between σ_{0n}^2 and x_n^2. Remarkably, there is no bias in this estimator for the simple location model where $x_n = 1$.

In broad terms, the general situation is similar to this example. When $\operatorname{Var}[\mathbf{y} \mid \mathbf{X}]$ is not scalar, the OLS estimator has a conditional variance matrix given by

$$\begin{aligned}\operatorname{Var}[\hat{\boldsymbol{\beta}}_{\text{OLS}} \mid \mathbf{X}] &= \operatorname{Var}[(\mathbf{X}'\mathbf{X})^{-1}\mathbf{X}'\mathbf{y} \mid \mathbf{X}] \\ &= (\mathbf{X}'\mathbf{X})^{-1}\mathbf{X}' \operatorname{Var}[\mathbf{y} \mid \mathbf{X}]\mathbf{X}(\mathbf{X}'\mathbf{X})^{-1} \\ &= (\mathbf{X}'\mathbf{X})^{-1}\mathbf{X}'\boldsymbol{\Omega}_0\mathbf{X}(\mathbf{X}'\mathbf{X})^{-1} \qquad (18.4)\end{aligned}$$

for which the OLS estimator $s^2(\mathbf{X}'\mathbf{X})^{-1}$ is biased. In general, the bias of any element can be positive or negative. We cannot offer analytical results to explain the directions of the biases as specific as those in Example 18.1.

Along with this bias, s^2 also possesses a less tractable distribution under general $\boldsymbol{\Omega}_0$. The variance of the OLS fitted residual vector $\mathbf{y} - \hat{\boldsymbol{\mu}}_{\text{OLS}}$ is now

$$\begin{aligned}\operatorname{Var}[\mathbf{y} - \hat{\boldsymbol{\mu}}_{\text{OLS}} \mid \mathbf{X}] &= \operatorname{Var}[(\mathbf{I} - \mathbf{P}_{\mathbf{X}})\,\mathbf{y} \mid \mathbf{X}] \\ &= (\mathbf{I} - \mathbf{P}_{\mathbf{X}})\,\boldsymbol{\Omega}_0\,(\mathbf{I} - \mathbf{P}_{\mathbf{X}}) \qquad (18.5)\end{aligned}$$

an expression comparable to (18.4). This means that s^2 is not a quadratic form in $\mathbf{y} - \hat{\boldsymbol{\mu}}_{\text{OLS}}$ normalized by its variance matrix and, therefore, s^2 is not proportional to a random variable with a chi-square distribution.[3] In a simple sense, the collapse of the OLS distribution theory for s^2 is expected. Given that the conditional variance matrix of $\mathbf{y}$ no longer depends on a single variance parameter, we lose the meaning of s^2 as an estimator.

Test statistics do not possess the distributions previously derived under the assumption of a scalar variance matrix either. For example, the simple t statistic no longer contains a chi-square random variable in its denominator so that its distribution theory fails. Furthermore, just as there are no general statements about the bias of the OLS estimator for $\operatorname{Var}[\hat{\boldsymbol{\beta}}_{\text{OLS}} \mid \mathbf{X}]$, no general characterization of the problems with the inference procedures can be derived. One can say only that the *nominal* significance level of a hypothesis test about $\boldsymbol{\beta}_0$ does not equal the actual probability of rejecting the hypothesis when it is true.

In addition to problems with inference, the OLS estimator is generally an inefficient estimator under more general variance structures. A basic counterexample illustrates the reasons.

EXAMPLE 18.2 (Simple OLS)

Returning to the heteroskedastic normal linear regression model in Example 18.1, suppose that the first N_1 observations have a smaller variance than the remaining $N - N_1$ observations. For additional simplicity, we will keep $x_n = 1$ for all observations. Let us denote

[3] Recall Lemma 10.7 (p. 213). Also see the discussion following Proposition 10 (Distribution of Variance Estimator, p. 199).

$$\mathrm{Var}[y_n] = \begin{cases} \sigma_{01}^2 & \text{if } 1 \le n \le N_1 \\ \sigma_{02}^2 & \text{if } N_1 < n \le N \end{cases}$$

where $\sigma_{01}^2 < \sigma_{02}^2$.

Now consider an estimator of β_0 that uses only the first N_1 observations

$$\tilde{\beta} = \frac{\sum_{n=1}^{N_1} y_n}{N_1}, \qquad \mathrm{Var}[\tilde{\beta}] = \frac{\sigma_{01}^2}{N_1}$$

and compare its variance with that of the OLS estimator,

$$\mathrm{Var}[\hat{\beta}_{\mathrm{OLS}} \mid \mathbf{X}] = \frac{\sigma_{01}^2 N_1 + \sigma_{02}^2 (N - N_1)}{N^2}$$

If σ_{01}^2 is small enough, that is

$$\sigma_{01}^2 < \frac{N_1}{N + N_1} \sigma_{02}^2$$

then $\tilde{\beta}$ is efficient relative to $\hat{\beta}_{\mathrm{OLS}}$. Apparently the OLS estimator relies too heavily on the relatively noisy observations ($n = N_1 + 1, \ldots, N$).

Using heteroskedasticity, we have shown how the "second-moment" properties of OLS may be altered by dropping the "second-moment" assumption that $\mathrm{Var}[\mathbf{y} \mid \mathbf{X}]$ is a scalar matrix. In the next section, we begin to discuss a response to the difficulties these changes raise. A recurring theme in this chapter and in Chapter 19 is that OLS fitted residuals can play a key role in both testing and estimation in these new circumstances. This happens because $\hat{\boldsymbol{\beta}}_{\mathrm{OLS}}$ has two properties. First, it is the restricted MLE when there is homoskedasticity and no covariance among the y_n (conditional on $\mathbf{x}_n$) so that $\hat{\boldsymbol{\beta}}_{\mathrm{OLS}}$ can be used in a diagnostic score test of heteroskedasticity. Second, $\hat{\boldsymbol{\beta}}_{\mathrm{OLS}}$ remains unbiased and consistent even when there is conditional heteroskedasticity. As a consequence, the OLS estimator is a valid "first-step" estimator that one can plug into a relatively efficient LML estimator.

18.3 TESTING FOR HETEROSKEDASTICITY

Given the problems that nonscalar variance matrices cause, it is sensible to test for heteroskedasticity when it is plausible as a caution against mistaken inference. The OLS fitted residuals play an important role in such hypothesis tests. There is information about $\boldsymbol{\Omega}_0$ in the sampling distribution of $\mathbf{y} - \hat{\boldsymbol{\mu}}_{\mathrm{OLS}}$, but these OLS fitted residuals must be used with care. Equation (18.5) shows that the fitted residuals are heteroskedastic and autocorrelated even when $\boldsymbol{\Omega}_0$ is a scalar variance matrix. Because they depend on a common $\hat{\boldsymbol{\beta}}_{\mathrm{OLS}}$, the fitted residuals are correlated; and because each $\hat{\boldsymbol{\beta}}_{\mathrm{OLS}}$ is multiplied by a different vector of explanatory variable values for each observation, these residuals are heteroskedastic.

Nevertheless we have already seen that these residuals yield a simple variance estimator in the homoskedastic case. This estimator is the basis for testing heteroskedasticity in the simplest case.

EXAMPLE 18.3 (OLS)

Let us return to Example 18.2, where the variance differs only across two subsamples. Books on introductory statistics often discuss this case.[4] If we partition the data set into $y_1 \equiv [y_n; n \leq N_1]'$, $y_2 \equiv [y_n; n > N_1]'$, then independent estimators of these variances are the OLS variance estimators within the subsamples:

$$s_1^2 = \frac{(y_1 - \hat{\mu}_1)'(y_1 - \hat{\mu}_1)}{N_1 - 1}$$

$$s_2^2 = \frac{(y_2 - \hat{\mu}_2)'(y_2 - \hat{\mu}_2)}{N - N_1 - 1}$$

where $\hat{\mu}_j$ contains the sample average of the elements of y_j $(j = 1, 2)$. The ratio of the variance estimators has an F distribution under the null hypothesis of homoskedasticity and normality: because $\sigma_{01}^2 = \sigma_{02}^2$,

$$\frac{s_1^2}{s_2^2} \sim \frac{\sigma_{01}^2[\chi_{N_1-1}^2/(N_1 - 1)]}{\sigma_{02}^2[\chi_{N-N_1-1}^2/(N - N_1 - 1)]} = \frac{\chi_{N_1-1}^2/(N_1 - 1)}{[\chi_{N-N_1-1}^2/N - N_1 - 1)]} \sim F_{N_1-1,N-N_1-1}$$

One-sided and two-sided tests can be constructed from this pivotal statistic.

This test statistic generalizes directly to multiple regression. All that changes are the degrees of freedom because the number of explanatory variables exceeds one. As long as the sample splits into two constant-variance subsamples, separate OLS fits yield independent estimators of the variances that plug right in.

18.3.1 The Goldfeld–Quandt F Test

Goldfeld and Quandt (1965) suggested a generalization of this test when the variance changes monotonically with a single explanatory variable z_n. In the *Goldfeld–Quandt test* for heteroskedasticity, one ranks the observations by z_n, forming the subsamples from observations with the highest and lowest values of z_n. It is possible to improve the power of the test by removing some fraction of observations with values of z_n around its median value. This may increase the separation across subsamples of the values of σ_{0n}^2 sufficiently to offset the loss of observations. If one drops observations $N_1 + 1$ through N_2 say, so that we partition the data set into $\mathbf{y}_1 \equiv [y_n; n \leq N_1]'$, $\mathbf{y}_2 \equiv [y_n; n > N_2]'$, $\mathbf{X}_1 \equiv [\mathbf{x}_n; n \leq N_1]'$, and $\mathbf{X}_2 \equiv [\mathbf{x}_n; n > N_2]'$, then $s_1^2/s_2^2 \sim F_{N_1-K,N-N_2-K}$ under the null hypothesis of homoskedasticity. Again, one can construct one- or two-sided tests. A one-sided test is appropriate if, for example, σ_{0n}^2 increases with z_n.

The choice of N_1 and N_2 is not a formal part of the test. To implement this test, one must make a choice and many practitioners choose $N_1 \approx N/3$ and $N_2 \approx 2N/3$.

18.3.2 The Breusch–Pagan Score Test

Although we can construct Goldfeld–Quandt tests when $\mathbf{z}_n$ is a vector of explanatory variables, the *Breusch–Pagan test* based on the score test method offers a convenient alternative (Breusch and Pagan, 1979; Godfrey, 1978c). To derive this test, we specify the alternative hypothesis

[4] For example, see Larsen and Marx (1986, pp. 373–375).

$$y_n \mid (\mathbf{x}_n, \mathbf{z}_n) \sim \mathfrak{N}(\mathbf{x}_n'\boldsymbol{\beta}_0, \gamma_{01} + \mathbf{z}_{2n}'\boldsymbol{\gamma}_{02})$$

independently over n, where $\mathbf{z}_{2n}$ is a row vector of M explanatory variables and $\boldsymbol{\gamma}_{02}$ is a column vector of M parameters. We have partitioned the explanatory variables of the conditional variance for exposition: the null hypothesis of homoskedasticity corresponds to $H_0 : \boldsymbol{\gamma}_{02} = \mathbf{0}$.

The vectors $\mathbf{x}_n$ and $\mathbf{z}_n$ may share variables or be the same vector.[5] Note that this specification simply applies the regression idea to the second moment of y_n, giving a simple, flexible relationship between σ_{0n}^2 and $\mathbf{z}_n$.

The Breusch–Pagan score test requires two OLS calculations.

1. Compute the restricted MLE, $\hat{\boldsymbol{\theta}}_R = [\hat{\boldsymbol{\beta}}_{OLS}', \hat{\gamma}_{R1}, \mathbf{0}']'$, which contains the OLS fitted coefficients $\hat{\boldsymbol{\beta}}_{OLS} = (\mathbf{X}'\mathbf{X})^{-1}\mathbf{X}'\mathbf{y}$ and the ML variance estimator $\hat{\gamma}_{R1} = \hat{\sigma}^2 = (\mathbf{y} - \hat{\boldsymbol{\mu}}_{OLS})'(\mathbf{y} - \hat{\boldsymbol{\mu}}_{OLS})/N$.
2. In the second calculation, we regress the squared values of the OLS fitted residuals,

$$w_n(\hat{\boldsymbol{\beta}}_{OLS}) \equiv (y_n - \hat{\mu}_{OLS,n})^2, \qquad n = 1, \ldots, N$$

divided by $\hat{\sigma}^2$, on a constant 1 and $\mathbf{z}_{2n}$ using OLS.

The score test statistic equals one-half the regression (explained) sum of squares from this OLS fit:

$$S = \frac{1}{2} \cdot \left[\frac{1}{\hat{\sigma}^2} \cdot \mathbf{w}(\hat{\boldsymbol{\beta}}_{OLS})\right]' \mathbf{P}_{\mathbf{Z}_{2\perp 1}} \left[\frac{1}{\hat{\sigma}^2} \cdot \mathbf{w}(\hat{\boldsymbol{\beta}}_{OLS})\right] \tag{18.6}$$

$$= \frac{\mathbf{w}(\hat{\boldsymbol{\beta}}_{OLS})'\mathbf{P}_{\mathbf{Z}_{2\perp 1}}\mathbf{w}(\hat{\boldsymbol{\beta}}_{OLS})}{2\hat{\sigma}^4}$$

where $\mathbf{w}(\hat{\boldsymbol{\beta}}_{OLS}) \equiv [w_n(\hat{\boldsymbol{\beta}}_{OLS})]'$, $\mathbf{Z}_1 = \boldsymbol{\iota}_N$ is a vector of N ones, and $\mathbf{Z}_2 \equiv [\mathbf{z}_{2n}]'$.[6] We derive S completely in Section 18.7.3. Under the null hypothesis of homoskedasticity, S converges in distribution to a χ_M^2 random variable and one rejects the null at the $100\alpha\%$ level of significance if S exceeds $\chi_{M;1-\alpha}^2$.

Quite apart from being a score test statistic, this test has intuitive appeal. Loosely speaking, the squared OLS fitted residuals are estimators of the σ_{0n}^2 and the second OLS regression checks whether the variables $\mathbf{z}_n$ capture variation in σ_{0n}^2.[7] Let us pursue this intuition by considering what we might do if $\boldsymbol{\beta}_0$ were observable, so that we also observe $w_n(\boldsymbol{\beta}_0) \equiv (y_n - \mathbf{x}_n'\boldsymbol{\beta}_0)^2$. Each $w_n(\boldsymbol{\beta}_0)$ is distributed as an independent $\sigma_{0n}^2\, \chi_1^2$ random variable under the normality assumption. Thus, the model states that[8]

$$\mathrm{E}[\mathbf{w}(\boldsymbol{\beta}_0) \mid \mathbf{X}, \mathbf{Z}] = \left[\sigma_{0n}^2\right]' = \mathbf{Z}\boldsymbol{\gamma}_0$$

$$\mathrm{Var}[\mathbf{w}(\boldsymbol{\beta}_0) \mid \mathbf{X}, \mathbf{Z}] = 2\,\mathrm{diag}[(\sigma_{0n}^2)^2] = 2\,\mathrm{diag}[(\mathbf{z}_n'\boldsymbol{\gamma}_0)^2]$$

and we could test H_0 directly with an OLS regression test for $H_0 : \boldsymbol{\gamma}_{02} = \mathbf{0}$. Setting

---

[5] For this new notation, Assumptions 13.1 and 13.2 cover all the nonredundant elements of $\mathbf{x}_n$ and $\mathbf{z}_n$.

[6] See also the generalizations in Example 22.1.

[7] Remember that in general the conditional expectation of a squared OLS fitted residual does not equal the conditional variance σ_{0n}^2 (Proposition 5, p. 157).

[8] Recall that the mean and variance of a χ_ν^2 distribution are ν and 2ν, respectively (Theorem D.10, p. 889).

$$\hat{\boldsymbol{\gamma}} = (\mathbf{Z}'\mathbf{Z})^{-1}\mathbf{Z}'\mathbf{w}(\boldsymbol{\beta}_0)$$
$$\hat{\omega}^2 = \frac{\mathbf{w}(\boldsymbol{\beta}_0)'\,(\mathbf{I} - \mathbf{P}_{\mathbf{Z}})\,\mathbf{w}(\boldsymbol{\beta}_0)}{N - M - 1}$$

the Wald statistic would be[9, 10]

$$\mathcal{W} = \frac{\hat{\boldsymbol{\gamma}}_2'(\mathbf{Z}_{1\perp 2}'\mathbf{Z}_{1\perp 2})\hat{\boldsymbol{\gamma}}_2}{\hat{\omega}^2} = \frac{\mathbf{w}(\boldsymbol{\beta}_0)'\mathbf{P}_{\mathbf{Z}_{2\perp 1}}\mathbf{w}(\boldsymbol{\beta}_0)}{\hat{\omega}^2} \tag{18.7}$$

This is virtually the same test statistic as (18.6); only the variance estimators in the denominators differ.

In fact, S and $\mathcal{W}$ have the same asymptotic distribution under H_0 and local alternatives. More than this, $S \overset{p}{=} \mathcal{W}$ so that they are *equivalent* tests asymptotically. This means that the score test is asymptotically equivalent to a test based on a *known* $\boldsymbol{\beta}_0$. We will explain this paradox in Section 18.5.2.

Note that the Breusch–Pagan score test is not altered by posing the heteroskedasticity in the more general form $h(\gamma_1, \gamma_{21}z_{2n1}, \ldots, \gamma_{2M}z_{2nM})$ where $h : \mathbb{R}^{M+1} \to \mathbb{R}^1$ is continuously differentiable.[11] This is symptomatic of the general property of score tests described in Section 17.5 on local power. Because score tests rest on derivatives of the log-likelihood function evaluated at restricted parameter values, score tests explicitly rely only on local information about the alternative hypothesis. In a local neighborhood of the null hypothesis, the heteroskedasticity function $h(\gamma_1, \gamma_{21}z_{2n1}, \ldots, \gamma_{2M}z_{2nM})$ is effectively linear: using a Taylor series approximation,

$$\begin{aligned}
h(\gamma_1, \gamma_{21}z_{2n1}, \ldots, \gamma_{2M}z_{2nM}) &= h(\gamma_1, 0, \ldots, 0) \\
&\quad + \sum_{m=1}^{M} h_{m+1}(\gamma_1, 0, \ldots, 0)\, \gamma_{2m}z_{2nm} \\
&\quad + o(\|\boldsymbol{\gamma}_2\|) \\
&\approx \delta_1 + \mathbf{z}_{2n}'\boldsymbol{\delta}_2
\end{aligned}$$

where $\delta_{2m} \equiv h_{m+1}(\gamma_1, 0, \ldots, 0)\,\gamma_{2m}$ $(m = 1, \ldots, M)$. As a result, the particular h is irrelevant to the functional form of the test statistic, provided that it is differentiable at H_0. This invariance does not hold for the Wald or likelihood ratio versions of this test.

Rather than rely on the asymptotic approximation of the χ_M^2 distribution, one can compute the exact probability value conditional on $(\mathbf{X}, \mathbf{Z})$ of the Breusch–Pagan score test statistic by numerical integration. The test statistic is pivotal if the variances are constant. Its distribution does not depend on $\boldsymbol{\beta}_0$ because the distribution of the OLS fitted residuals does not. Furthermore, the statistic is unchanged if we multiply $\mathbf{y} - \hat{\boldsymbol{\mu}}_{\text{OLS}}$ by a scalar, therefore the distribution of the test

[9] Here we are using the partitioned regression formula $\hat{\boldsymbol{\gamma}}_2 = (\mathbf{Z}_{2\perp 1}'\mathbf{Z}_{2\perp 1})^{-1}\mathbf{Z}_{2\perp 1}'\mathbf{w}(\boldsymbol{\beta}_0)$ and its associated variance matrix $\text{Var}[\hat{\boldsymbol{\gamma}}_2 \mid \mathbf{Z}] = \text{Var}[w_{0n} \mid \mathbf{Z}] \cdot (\mathbf{Z}_{2\perp 1}'\mathbf{Z}_{2\perp 1})^{-1}$ under homoskedasticity. For review, see the discussion surrounding equation (9.2) (p. 178).

[10] We discussed such Wald tests for linear restrictions in Example 17.1 (p. 382), although we assumed that the variance parameter was known. For the related F statistic, see equation (11.4) (p. 227).

[11] Some authors restrict

$$h(\gamma_1, \gamma_{21}z_{2n1}, \ldots, \gamma_{2M}z_{2nM}) = g(\gamma_1 + \mathbf{z}_{2n}'\boldsymbol{\gamma}_2)$$

but this is unnecessary for the score test equivalence. Such specifications are convenient for estimation, however.

statistic does not depend on σ_0^2. Monte Carlo integration is a conceptually simple and computationally intensive procedure for making the calculation. If $\boldsymbol{\xi}_1 \sim \mathfrak{N}(\mathbf{0}, \mathbf{I}_N)$, $\boldsymbol{\xi}_2 \equiv (\mathbf{I} - \mathbf{P_X})\,\boldsymbol{\xi}_1$, and $\boldsymbol{\xi}_3 \equiv [\xi_{2n}^2]'$, then

$$S(\boldsymbol{\xi}_1) \equiv \frac{N}{2} \cdot \frac{\boldsymbol{\xi}_3' \mathbf{P}_{\mathbf{Z}_{2\perp 1}} \boldsymbol{\xi}_3}{\boldsymbol{\xi}_3' \mathbf{P}_{\mathbf{Z}_1} \boldsymbol{\xi}_3} \tag{18.8}$$

has the distribution of S under the null hypothesis. Simulating $\boldsymbol{\xi}_1$ and $S(\boldsymbol{\xi}_1)$ repeatedly on the computer permits us to observe the frequency with which $S(\boldsymbol{\xi}_1)$ exceeds the value of S, thereby calculating a numerical estimate of the probability value. This numerical calculation can be made as accurate as desired by adjusting the number of repetitions.

EXAMPLE 18.4

As described earlier in Section 18.1, the Breusch–Pagan score test for conditional heteroskedasticity in the log-wage regression equals 29.50 when $\mathbf{z}_n$ includes the indicator variables for female, nonwhite, and union and the additional variables schooling and experience. Under the null hypothesis of homoskedasticity this is a draw from an approximately chi-square distribution with 5 degrees of freedom. In 1000 simulations of $S(\boldsymbol{\xi}_1)$ none exceeded 29.50. The estimate of the probability of exceeding $11.705 \approx \chi^2_{5;0.95}$ was 0.042 with a standard error of 0.0063. Therefore, the exact distribution of the score test statistic is close enough to the asymptotic approximation to conclude that there is strong evidence of conditional heteroskedasticity.

If one is convinced that heteroskedasticity is present, then alternative inference procedures to those associated with OLS are required. In the next two sections, we discuss corrections to OLS and an alternative approach called weighted least squares (WLS).

18.4 ADJUSTMENTS TO OLS

Because OLS still yields an estimator of $\boldsymbol{\beta}_0$, one might seek to overcome the primary impediment to its statistical employment: misestimation of its variance matrix. It may be possible to recover an estimator of $\mathrm{Var}[\hat{\boldsymbol{\beta}}_{\mathrm{OLS}} \,|\, \mathbf{X}]$ from $(\mathbf{y} - \hat{\boldsymbol{\mu}}_{\mathrm{OLS}})(\mathbf{y} - \hat{\boldsymbol{\mu}}_{\mathrm{OLS}})'$. Example 18.1 illustrates this possibility, where $s^2/(N-1)$ is an unbiased estimator of the sampling variance of the sample mean even in the presence of heteroskedasticity. In that case, the average of the squared OLS fitted residuals is an unbiased estimator for the average of the underlying variances. Indeed, this special case has a more general counterpart.

EXAMPLE 18.5 (Simple OLS)

Returning to the heteroskedastic normal linear regression example, suppose that x_n is not constant. Note that $\mathrm{E}[(\mathbf{y} - \hat{\boldsymbol{\mu}}_{\mathrm{OLS}})(\mathbf{y} - \hat{\boldsymbol{\mu}}_{\mathrm{OLS}})' \,|\, \mathbf{X}]$ is a linear function of the σ_{0n}^2 parameters. In particular, observe that we can write out the diagonal elements of (18.5) as

$$\mathrm{E}[(y_n - \hat{\mu}_{\mathrm{OLS},n})^2 \,|\, \mathbf{X}] = \frac{\mathbf{X}'\mathbf{X} - 2x_n^2}{\mathbf{X}'\mathbf{X}} \sigma_{0n}^2 + \sum_{j=1}^{N} \frac{x_n^2 x_j^2}{(\mathbf{X}'\mathbf{X})^2} \sigma_{0j}^2$$

This is a system of linear equations

$$E[\mathbf{w}(\hat{\beta}_{\text{OLS}}) \mid \mathbf{X}] = \mathbf{A}\boldsymbol{\omega}_0 \tag{18.9}$$

where $\boldsymbol{\omega}_0 \equiv [\sigma_{01}^2, \ldots, \sigma_{0N}^2]'$, and

$$\mathbf{A} \equiv \text{diag}\left(\frac{\mathbf{X}'\mathbf{X} - 2x_n^2}{\mathbf{X}'\mathbf{X}}\right) + \mathbf{a}\mathbf{a}'$$

$$\mathbf{a} \equiv \left[\frac{x_n^2}{\mathbf{X}'\mathbf{X}};\ n = 1, \ldots, N\right]'$$

From the expectation (18.9), we can construct an estimator for $\boldsymbol{\omega}_0$ if the matrix $\mathbf{A}$ is nonsingular: $\hat{\boldsymbol{\omega}} = \mathbf{A}^{-1}\mathbf{w}(\hat{\beta}_{\text{OLS}})$. Clearly, this estimator is unbiased:

$$E[\hat{\boldsymbol{\omega}} \mid \mathbf{X}] = \mathbf{A}^{-1}\,E[\mathbf{w}(\hat{\beta}_{\text{OLS}}) \mid \mathbf{X}] = \mathbf{A}^{-1}\mathbf{A}\boldsymbol{\omega}_0 = \boldsymbol{\omega}_0$$

Using the matrix inverse

$$\left(\mathbf{B} + \mathbf{a}\mathbf{a}'\right)^{-1} = \mathbf{B}^{-1} - \frac{1}{1 + \mathbf{a}'\mathbf{B}^{-1}\mathbf{a}} \cdot \mathbf{B}^{-1}\mathbf{a}\mathbf{a}'\mathbf{B}^{-1}$$

we can solve this system analytically.[12] This $\hat{\boldsymbol{\omega}} = \mathbf{A}^{-1}\mathbf{w}(\hat{\beta}_{\text{OLS}})$ in turn allows us to estimate $\text{Var}[\hat{\beta}_{\text{OLS}} \mid \mathbf{X}]$ without bias:

$$(\mathbf{X}'\mathbf{X})^{-1}\mathbf{X}'\,\text{diag}(\hat{\omega}_n)X\,(\mathbf{X}'\mathbf{X})^{-1} = \frac{\sum_{n=1}^{N} \alpha_n x_n^2 (y_n - \hat{\mu}_{\text{OLS},n})^2}{(\mathbf{X}'\mathbf{X})^2 + \sum_{n=1}^{N} \alpha_n x_n^4}$$

where

$$\alpha_n \equiv \frac{\mathbf{X}'\mathbf{X}}{\mathbf{X}'\mathbf{X} - 2x_n^2}$$

This example illustrates three points that also arose in testing for heteroskedasticity. First, the second moments of the OLS fitted residuals contain information about the second moments of $\mathbf{y}$ conditional on $\mathbf{X}$. Second, one must exercise care in using the fitted residuals, because they are heteroskedastic and correlated even if the variance matrix of $\mathbf{y}$ is scalar. Nevertheless, there is a simple and attractive interpretation: it appears that sometimes we can virtually replace the unknown σ_{0n}^2 with the $(y_n - \hat{\mu}_{\text{OLS},n})^2$. Indeed, as the sample size approaches infinity, each of the α_n approaches 1 and

$$\frac{\frac{1}{N}\sum_{n=1}^{N} \alpha_n x_n^2 (y_n - \hat{\mu}_{\text{OLS},n})^2}{\left[\left(\frac{1}{N}\mathbf{X}'\mathbf{X}\right)^2 + \frac{1}{N^2}\sum_{n=1}^{N} \alpha_n x_n^4\right]} \overset{p}{=} \frac{\frac{1}{N}\sum_{n=1}^{N} x_n^2 (y_n - \hat{\mu}_{\text{OLS},n})^2}{\left(\frac{1}{N}\mathbf{X}'\mathbf{X}\right)^2}$$

provided that $\mathbf{X}'\mathbf{X} = \sum_{n=1}^{N} x_n^2$ and $\sum_{n=1}^{N} x_n^4$ are both $O(N)$ and $N^{-1} \cdot \mathbf{X}'\mathbf{X}$ does not approach zero in the limit. Third, this estimator works because we are not really estimating all of the σ_{0n}^2. Rather, we are estimating only a function of these variances. In the example, that function is the sampling variance of a scalar $\hat{\beta}_{\text{OLS}}$.

---

12 See Exercise 3.22.

White (1980) proposed an asymptotic generalization of Example 18.5 by showing under quite general conditions that

$$\frac{1}{N} \cdot \mathbf{X}' \operatorname{diag}[(y_n - \hat{\mu}_{\mathrm{OLS},n})^2]\mathbf{X} \overset{p}{=} \frac{1}{N} \cdot \mathbf{X}'\boldsymbol{\Omega}_0\mathbf{X} \tag{18.10}$$

As a result, an approximate variance matrix for the OLS estimator $\hat{\boldsymbol{\beta}}_{\mathrm{OLS}}$ simply replaces the σ_{0n}^2 with $(y_n - \hat{\mu}_{\mathrm{OLS},n})^2$ in (18.4):

$$\widehat{\operatorname{Var}[\hat{\boldsymbol{\beta}}_{\mathrm{OLS}} \mid \mathbf{X}]} = (\mathbf{X}'\mathbf{X})^{-1}\mathbf{X}' \operatorname{diag}[(y_n - \hat{\mu}_{\mathrm{OLS},n})^2]\mathbf{X}(\mathbf{X}'\mathbf{X})^{-1} \tag{18.11}$$

This is often called the *Eicker–White* variance estimator.[13]

The key insight into constructing such consistent estimators is that this variance matrix is a function of sample averages to which laws of large numbers apply. If it were evaluated at $\boldsymbol{\beta}_0$, this matrix would be a consistent estimator. If instead it is evaluated at such a consistent estimator as $\hat{\boldsymbol{\beta}}_{\mathrm{OLS}}$, and if

$$\mathbf{g}_N(\boldsymbol{\beta}) = \frac{1}{N} \cdot \mathbf{X}' \operatorname{diag}[(y_n - \mathbf{x}_n'\boldsymbol{\beta})^2]\mathbf{X}$$

converges in probability *uniformly* in $\boldsymbol{\beta}$ by the uniform LLN (Lemma 15.1, p. 321), then Lemma 15.5 (p. 326) implies (18.10).

The great attraction of this estimator is that it does not require a parametric specification for the heteroskedasticity. Unlike the diagnostic tests for heteroskedasticity just discussed, there is no need for variables to explain the heteroskedasticity. Thus the method is quite general.

Davidson and MacKinnon (1993) caution that this estimator is "somewhat unreliable in small samples," with a tendency to underestimate $\operatorname{Var}[\hat{\boldsymbol{\beta}}_{\mathrm{OLS}} \mid \mathbf{X}]$. We already know that in the homoskedastic case, for which this estimator applies,

$$\mathrm{E}[\boldsymbol{\iota}' \operatorname{diag}[(y_n - \hat{\mu}_{\mathrm{OLS},n})^2]\boldsymbol{\iota} \mid \mathbf{X}] = \mathrm{E}[(\mathbf{y} - \hat{\boldsymbol{\mu}}_{\mathrm{OLS}})'(\mathbf{y} - \hat{\boldsymbol{\mu}}_{\mathrm{OLS}}) \mid \mathbf{X}] = (N-K)\sigma_0^2$$

which underestimates $\boldsymbol{\iota}'\boldsymbol{\Omega}_0\boldsymbol{\iota}$ by the factor of $(N-K)/N$. For this reason, a simple correction multiplies the Eicker–White estimator by $N/(N-K)$. Davidson and MacKinnon (1993) recommend dividing each squared fitted residual by $1 - \mathbf{x}_n'(\mathbf{X}'\mathbf{X})^{-1}\mathbf{x}_n$ because this inflates the expectation of the squared residual correctly in the homoskedastic case.[14] We followed this advice in our calculations in the corrected OLS column of Table 18.2.

18.5 HETEROSKEDASTICITY AND WLS/GLS

We have seen how to adjust the estimation of the variance matrix of the OLS estimator $\hat{\boldsymbol{\beta}}_{\mathrm{OLS}}$ for heteroskedasticity. Now we turn to correcting another deficiency of the OLS estimator, that it is no longer efficient relative to all unbiased estimators of $\boldsymbol{\beta}_0$. Example 18.2 proves this and also suggests where efficiency gains lie. Observations with smaller conditional variances will receive relatively more weight in a relatively efficient estimation method.

[13] Eicker (1967) also proposed this estimator.

[14] See equation (8.9).

EXAMPLE 18.6 (Normal Location)

Reconsider the simplest OLS problem where $N = 2$, $K = 1$, and $\mathbf{X} = \iota_2$ so that $\mathrm{E}[y_n] = \beta_0$, $n = 1, 2$. Suppose that $\mathbf{y}$ is bivariate normal with variance matrix

$$\mathrm{Var}[\mathbf{y}] \equiv \mathbf{\Omega}_0 = \begin{bmatrix} \sigma_{01}^2 & 0 \\ 0 & \sigma_{02}^2 \end{bmatrix}$$

so that y_1 and y_2 are uncorrelated and their variances differ. If we know σ_{01}^2 and σ_{02}^2, then we can normalize the elements of $\mathbf{y}$ so that they are homoskedastic:

$$\mathrm{Var}\left[\frac{y_n}{\sigma_{0n}}\right] = \frac{1}{\sigma_{0n}^2}\,\mathrm{Var}[y_n] = 1$$

Although it delivers constant variance, this normalization also affects the first moments:

$$\mathrm{E}\left[\frac{y_n}{\sigma_{0n}}\right] = \frac{1}{\sigma_{0n}}\,\mathrm{E}[y_n] = \frac{\beta_0}{\sigma_{0n}}$$

In effect, the normalized location model becomes a simple regression model with the dependent variable y_n/σ_{0n} and the explanatory variable $1/\sigma_{0n}$.

We can apply the OLS/ML estimator to this simple regression model to obtain the efficient unbiased estimator:

$$\hat{\beta} = \frac{\sum_{n=1}^{2}(1/\sigma_{0n})(y_n/\sigma_{0n})}{\sum_{n=1}^{2}(1/\sigma_{0n})^2} = \frac{\sigma_{02}^2 y_1 + \sigma_{01}^2 y_2}{\sigma_{02}^2 + \sigma_{01}^2} \tag{18.12}$$

This linear estimator is a *weighted average*, rather than a simple average, of y_1 and y_2. The weights place more weight on the observation with the smaller variance.

The weighted average uses weights so that observations with smaller variances are more influential in the estimator. If one observation is expected to be closer to β_0 than the other, then presumably our estimator of the conditional mean should be closer to the first observation than to the second.

EXAMPLE 18.7 (Normal Location)

Continuing with the preceding example, note that the variance ellipse of $\mathbf{y} = [y_n; n = 1, 2]'$ is the set

$$\begin{aligned}\mathbb{V}_{\mathbf{y}} &= \left\{\mathbf{w} \in \mathbb{R}^2 \mid \mathbf{w}'\mathbf{\Omega}_0^{-1}\mathbf{w} \le 1\right\} \\ &= \left\{\mathbf{w} \in \mathbb{R}^2 \mid w_1^2/\sigma_{01}^2 + w_2^2/\sigma_{02}^2 \le 1\right\}\end{aligned}$$

Such an ellipse is displayed in Figure 18.3, centered on the mean of $\mathbf{y}$, for the case $\sigma_{01}^2 > \sigma_{02}^2$. The weighted average (18.12) is the projection onto

$$\mathrm{Col}(\mathbf{X}) = \{\mathbf{w} = \iota_2\beta,\ \beta \in \mathbb{R}\}$$

given by the slope of the boundary of the ellipsoid $\mathbb{V}_{\mathbf{y}}$ where it intersects $\mathrm{Col}(\mathbf{X})$. This yields the shortest variance ellipse for a linear unbiased estimator of β_0.

To confirm this, observe that the slope of this boundary is given by the implicit function theorem as

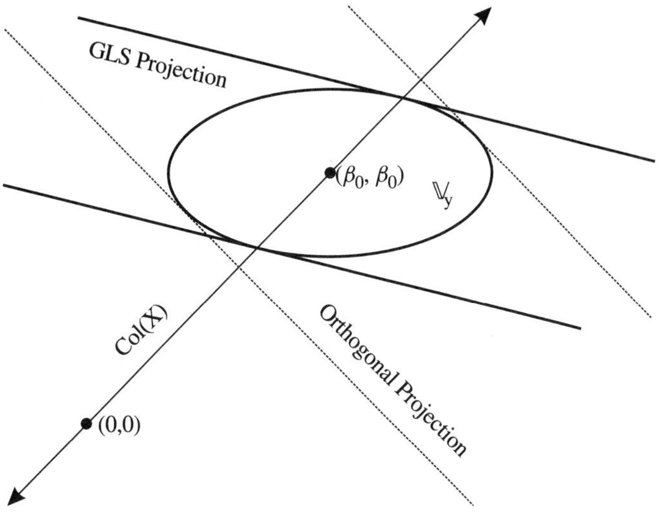

Figure 18.3 Heteroskedastic variance ellipsoid.

$$0 = 2\frac{w_1}{\sigma_{01}^2} + 2\frac{w_2}{\sigma_{02}^2}\frac{dw_2}{dw_1} \quad \Leftrightarrow \quad \frac{dw_2}{dw_1} = -\frac{\sigma_{02}^2}{\sigma_{01}^2}\frac{w_1}{w_2}$$

The intersection of this boundary with Col(**X**) occurs at $w_1 = w_2$ where

$$\left.\frac{dw_2}{dw_1}\right|_{w_2=w_1} = -\frac{\sigma_{02}^2}{\sigma_{01}^2}$$

and the slope of the line joining $(\hat{\beta}, \hat{\beta})$ [from (18.12)] and (y_1, y_2) equals the same ratio of variances:

$$\frac{y_2 - \hat{\beta}}{y_1 - \hat{\beta}} = \frac{(\sigma_{02}^2 + \sigma_{01}^2)y_2 - (\sigma_{02}^2 y_1 + \sigma_{01}^2 y_2)}{(\sigma_{02}^2 + \sigma_{01}^2)y_1 - (\sigma_{02}^2 y_1 + \sigma_{01}^2 y_2)} = -\frac{\sigma_{02}^2}{\sigma_{01}^2}$$

What is the optimal projection for multiple regression? We can find the answer by transforming the regression problem in the same way as Example 18.6. By dividing each y_n by its standard deviation σ_{0n}, we obtain the homoskedastic specification

$$\mathrm{E}\left[\frac{y_n}{\sigma_{0n}}\,\middle|\,\mathbf{x}_n, \sigma_{0n}\right] = \frac{1}{\sigma_{0n}} \cdot \mathbf{x}_n'\boldsymbol{\beta}_0$$

$$\mathrm{Var}\left[\frac{y_n}{\sigma_{0n}}\,\middle|\,\mathbf{x}_n, \sigma_{0n}\right] = 1$$

where the explanatory variables are x_{nk}/σ_{0n} $(k = 1, \ldots, K)$. The OLS estimator provides the MLE for this case, as inspection of the average conditional log-likelihood function shows

$$\begin{aligned}\mathrm{E}_N[L(\boldsymbol{\beta}; y_n \mid \mathbf{x}_n, \sigma_{0n})] &= -\frac{1}{2}\log 2\pi - \frac{1}{2N}\sum_{n=1}^{N}\left[\log\sigma_{0n}^2 + \frac{(y_n - \mathbf{x}_n'\boldsymbol{\beta})^2}{\sigma_{0n}^2}\right] \\ &= -\frac{1}{2}\log 2\pi - \frac{1}{2N}\sum_{n=1}^{N}\left[\log\sigma_{0n}^2 + \left(\frac{y_n}{\sigma_{0n}} - \frac{1}{\sigma_{0n}}\cdot\mathbf{x}_n'\boldsymbol{\beta}\right)^2\right]\end{aligned}$$

Given σ_{0n}^2, the MLE for β_0 is called the *weighted least squares* (WLS) estimator because the ordinary SSR has been replaced by the weighted sum of squares in this objective function. The weights are equal to $1/\sigma_{0n}$. If we transform

$$y_{*n} = \frac{y_n}{\sigma_{0n}}, \qquad \mathbf{x}_{*n} = \frac{1}{\sigma_{0n}} \cdot \mathbf{x}_n$$

and denote $\mathbf{y}_* \equiv [y_{*n}]'$ and $\mathbf{X}_* \equiv [\mathbf{x}_{*n}]'$, then

$$\hat{\boldsymbol{\beta}}_{\text{WLS}} = (\mathbf{X}_*'\mathbf{X}_*)^{-1}\mathbf{X}_*'\mathbf{y}_*$$

In the actual application of this formula in computer programs, it is easy to overlook that this transformation must be applied to the constant explanatory variable 1 corresponding to the intercept. *Every* element of $\mathbf{x}_n$ must be divided by σ_{0n} and this often means that no constant explanatory variable appears in $\mathbf{x}_{*n}$.

Without much additional work, we can extend this analysis to a more general case that we will apply frequently. If $\mathbf{y} \,|\, \mathbf{X} \sim \mathfrak{N}(\mathbf{X}\boldsymbol{\beta}_0, \boldsymbol{\Omega}_0)$ and $\boldsymbol{\Omega}_0$ is any known nonsingular variance matrix, then the sample average conditional log-likelihood function for $\boldsymbol{\beta}_0$ is

$$\mathrm{E}_N[L(\boldsymbol{\beta})] = -\frac{1}{2N}\log\det(2\pi\boldsymbol{\Omega}_0) - \frac{1}{2N}\underbrace{(\mathbf{y}-\mathbf{X}\boldsymbol{\beta})'\boldsymbol{\Omega}_0^{-1}(\mathbf{y}-\mathbf{X}\boldsymbol{\beta})}_{\text{generalized distance}} \tag{18.13}$$

using the p.d.f. of the multivariate normal distribution.[15] Therefore, ML estimation of $\boldsymbol{\beta}_0$ given $\boldsymbol{\Omega}_0$ corresponds to minimizing a generalized distance between $\mathbf{y}$ and Col($\mathbf{X}$). This method is called *generalized least squares* (GLS). The projection onto Col($\mathbf{X}$)

$$\hat{\boldsymbol{\mu}}_{\text{GLS}} = \mathbf{P}_{\mathbf{X}\perp\boldsymbol{\Omega}_0^{-1}\mathbf{X}}\mathbf{y} = \mathbf{X}(\mathbf{X}'\boldsymbol{\Omega}_0^{-1}\mathbf{X})^{-1}\mathbf{X}'\boldsymbol{\Omega}_0^{-1}\mathbf{y} \tag{18.14}$$

minimizes this distance [maximizes $L(\boldsymbol{\beta})$] and the corresponding GLS fitted coefficients,

$$\hat{\boldsymbol{\beta}}_{\text{GLS}} = (\mathbf{X}'\mathbf{X})^{-1}\mathbf{X}'\hat{\boldsymbol{\mu}}_{\text{GLS}} = (\mathbf{X}'\boldsymbol{\Omega}_0^{-1}\mathbf{X})^{-1}\mathbf{X}'\boldsymbol{\Omega}_0^{-1}\mathbf{y} \tag{18.15}$$

are MLEs.[16]

The GLS estimator is also called Aitken's estimator, following Aitken's (1935) generalization of the Gauss–Markov theorem (Theorem 7, p. 187) to the general linear regression model.

Theorem 12 (Aitken) *Let* $\mathbf{X}$ *be an* $N \times K$ *matrix of full-column rank and* $\mathbf{y}$ *be a random variable such that* $\mathrm{E}[\mathbf{y} \,|\, \mathbf{X}] = \mathbf{X}\boldsymbol{\beta}_0$ *and* $\mathrm{Var}[\mathbf{y} \,|\, \mathbf{X}] = \boldsymbol{\Omega}_0$, *a positive definite matrix. The GLS estimator*

$$\hat{\boldsymbol{\beta}}_{\text{GLS}} = \left(\mathbf{X}'\boldsymbol{\Omega}_0^{-1}\mathbf{X}\right)^{-1}\mathbf{X}'\boldsymbol{\Omega}_0^{-1}\mathbf{y}$$

is efficient relative to all other linear unbiased estimators for $\boldsymbol{\beta}_0$.

Proof. Let $\boldsymbol{\Omega}_0 = \mathbf{C}_0\mathbf{C}_0'$ be the Cholesky factorization of $\boldsymbol{\Omega}_0$ and note that

[15] See Definition 17 (Multivariate Normal Distribution, p. 206).

[16] Recall Theorem 4 (p. 90).

$$\mathrm{E}[\mathbf{C}_0^{-1}\mathbf{y}\,|\,\mathbf{X}] = \mathbf{C}_0^{-1}\mathbf{X}\boldsymbol{\beta}_0$$
$$\mathrm{Var}[\mathbf{C}_0^{-1}\mathbf{y}\,|\,\mathbf{X}] = \mathbf{C}_0^{-1}\boldsymbol{\Omega}_0\left(\mathbf{C}_0^{-1}\right)' = \mathbf{I}_N$$

Applying the Gauss–Markov theorem to this linear transformation of $\mathbf{y}$, the relatively efficient linear unbiased estimator of $\boldsymbol{\beta}_0$ is

$$\left[\left(\mathbf{C}_0^{-1}\mathbf{X}\right)'\mathbf{C}_0^{-1}\mathbf{X}\right]^{-1}\left(\mathbf{C}_0^{-1}\mathbf{X}\right)'\mathbf{C}_0^{-1}\mathbf{y} = \left(\mathbf{X}'\boldsymbol{\Omega}_0^{-1}\mathbf{X}\right)^{-1}\mathbf{X}'\boldsymbol{\Omega}_0^{-1}\mathbf{y}$$
$$= \hat{\boldsymbol{\beta}}_{\mathrm{GLS}}$$

proving the theorem. □

Aitken's theorem is interesting in its own right because it establishes the GLS estimators that we just derived as MLEs for normal distributions as optimal linear unbiased estimators without the normality assumption. As for the scalar variance matrix, the normal MLE implicitly reproduces the Gauss–Markov estimator. The proof of this theorem also suggests a way to compute the GLS/Aitken estimator with OLS software: first, transform the data and second, fit the transformed LHS variable to the transformed RHS variables.

The GLS estimator simplifies to WLS when we face heteroskedasticity only because we can easily find the matrix square root $\mathbf{C}_0 = \boldsymbol{\Omega}_0^{1/2} = \mathrm{diag}[\sigma_{0n}]$. That permits us to write $\mathbf{y}_* = \boldsymbol{\Omega}_0^{-1/2}\mathbf{y}$ and $\mathbf{X}_* = \boldsymbol{\Omega}_0^{-1/2}\mathbf{X}$ and

$$\hat{\boldsymbol{\beta}}_{\mathrm{WLS}} = (\mathbf{X}_*'\mathbf{X}_*)^{-1}\mathbf{X}_*'\mathbf{y}_*$$
$$= \left[\left(\boldsymbol{\Omega}_0^{-1/2}\mathbf{X}\right)'\boldsymbol{\Omega}_0^{-1/2}\mathbf{X}\right]^{-1}\left(\boldsymbol{\Omega}_0^{-1/2}\mathbf{X}\right)'\boldsymbol{\Omega}_0^{-1/2}\mathbf{y}$$
$$= (\mathbf{X}'\boldsymbol{\Omega}_0^{-1}\mathbf{X})^{-1}\mathbf{X}'\boldsymbol{\Omega}_0^{-1}\mathbf{y}$$

The WLS estimator is generally infeasible because σ_{0n} is not known. We have introduced WLS (and GLS) as a stepping stone to the feasible MLE that we are about to describe. However, there is one special case in which WLS is practical. That occurs when $\sigma_{0n}^2 = \gamma_0^2 z_n^2$ so that the unknown variances are proportional to a single observable variable z_n^2. In this case the unknown parameter γ_0 cancels out of the WLS formula and one can standardize y_n and $\mathbf{x}_n$ by z_n alone. To see why this should be so, note that

$$\mathrm{Var}[y_n\,|\,\mathbf{x}_n] = \gamma_0^2 z_n^2 \quad\Leftrightarrow\quad \mathrm{Var}[y_n/z_n\,|\,z_n^{-1}\cdot\mathbf{x}_n] = \gamma_0^2$$

so that the transformed regression model is homoskedastic. No further corrections are necessary.

18.5.1 Maximum Likelihood

Now let us consider estimation when we do not observe σ_{0n}^2 but we can specify a parametric model $\sigma_{0n}^2 = h(\mathbf{z}_n'\boldsymbol{\gamma}_0)$ $(n = 1, \ldots, N)$ where z_{nm} $(m = 1, \ldots, M+1)$ are observed variables and $\boldsymbol{\gamma}_0 \in \mathbb{R}^{M+1}$. Because we will not be considering homoskedasticity specially, we will incorporate the constant term into the linear index $\mathbf{z}_n'\boldsymbol{\gamma}_0$ from this point on. The function h must be specified, and there are several convenient choices. Given the linearity of the mean

$\mathbf{x}_n$, one candidate is the linear form $h(\mathbf{z}_n'\boldsymbol{\gamma}) = \mathbf{z}_n'\boldsymbol{\gamma}$ that we initially posed for the Breusch–Pagan score test. This function has the drawback, however, that negative values of the variance are possible and we must take care to ensure that such values are ruled out. A more popular specification is the *multiplicative heteroskedasticity* form $h(\mathbf{z}_n'\boldsymbol{\gamma}) = \exp(\mathbf{z}_n'\boldsymbol{\gamma})$, because the exponential transformation constrains the variances to be positive. Another is the quadratic $h(\mathbf{z}_n'\boldsymbol{\gamma}) = (\mathbf{z}_n'\boldsymbol{\gamma})^2$.

The particular choice of h, whether the exponential, the square, or some other function, is not central, so we will retain the general form with the understanding that one must specify h. The conditional log-likelihood function for $\boldsymbol{\theta}_0 = [\boldsymbol{\beta}_0', \boldsymbol{\gamma}_0']'$ under the assumption of normally distributed data is

$$\mathrm{E}_N[L(\boldsymbol{\theta})] = -\frac{1}{2}\log 2\pi - \frac{1}{2N}\sum_{n=1}^{N}\left[\log\sigma_n^2 + \frac{(y_n-\mu_n)^2}{\sigma_n^2}\right]$$

We derive the score, Hessian, and information matrix in Section 18.7. It is not possible to solve analytically for the MLE from the normal equations. But the implicit function has an interesting structure. The MLE $\hat{\boldsymbol{\beta}}_{\mathrm{ML}}$, given $\hat{\boldsymbol{\gamma}}_{\mathrm{ML}}$, has the expression

$$\hat{\boldsymbol{\beta}}_{\mathrm{ML}} = (\mathbf{X}'\hat{\boldsymbol{\Omega}}_{\mathrm{ML}}^{-1}\mathbf{X})^{-1}\mathbf{X}'\hat{\boldsymbol{\Omega}}_{\mathrm{ML}}^{-1}\mathbf{y} \tag{18.16}$$

where

$$\hat{\boldsymbol{\Omega}}_{\mathrm{ML}} \equiv \mathrm{diag}[h(\mathbf{z}_n'\hat{\boldsymbol{\gamma}}_{\mathrm{ML}})]$$

This, obviously, is the ML counterpart to $\hat{\boldsymbol{\beta}}_{\mathrm{GLS}}$ in which the MLE $\hat{\boldsymbol{\Omega}}_{\mathrm{ML}}$ replaces the population matrix $\boldsymbol{\Omega}_0$.

Solving for $\hat{\boldsymbol{\gamma}}_{\mathrm{ML}}$ as a function of $\hat{\boldsymbol{\beta}}_{\mathrm{ML}}$ is not analytically possible. In the special case that $h(\mathbf{Z}\boldsymbol{\gamma}) = \mathbf{Z}\boldsymbol{\gamma}$, we have the implicit function

$$\hat{\boldsymbol{\gamma}}_{\mathrm{ML}} = (\mathbf{Z}'\hat{\boldsymbol{\Lambda}}_{\mathrm{ML}}^{-1}\mathbf{Z})^{-1}\mathbf{Z}'\hat{\boldsymbol{\Lambda}}_{\mathrm{ML}}^{-1}\hat{\mathbf{w}}_{\mathrm{ML}} \tag{18.17}$$

where

$$\hat{\boldsymbol{\Lambda}}_{\mathrm{ML}} \equiv \hat{\boldsymbol{\Omega}}_{\mathrm{ML}}^{2} \tag{18.18}$$

and

$$\hat{\mathbf{w}}_{\mathrm{ML}} \equiv \left[w_n(\hat{\boldsymbol{\beta}}_{\mathrm{ML}})\right]'$$

In form, (18.17) resembles the GLS expression for $\hat{\boldsymbol{\beta}}_{\mathrm{ML}}$. This is because the conditional heteroskedasticity in y_n implies conditional heteroskedasticity in $w_n(\beta_0) \equiv (y_n - \mu_{0n})^2$ as well. But keep in mind that the variance matrix $\hat{\boldsymbol{\Lambda}}_{\mathrm{ML}}$ depends on $\hat{\boldsymbol{\gamma}}_{\mathrm{ML}}$ so that this is still an implicit function for $\hat{\boldsymbol{\gamma}}_{\mathrm{ML}}$. Also note that this regression for $\hat{\boldsymbol{\gamma}}_{\mathrm{ML}}$ is equivalent to the Breusch–Pagan score test regression when $\hat{\boldsymbol{\theta}}_{\mathrm{ML}}$ is replaced by $\hat{\boldsymbol{\theta}}_{\mathrm{R}}$ (the OLS estimator) on the RHS.[17]

For general h, the conditional information matrix is

$$\Im(\boldsymbol{\theta}_0) = \begin{bmatrix} \mathrm{E}_N\left[\frac{1}{\sigma_{0n}^2}\cdot\mathbf{x}_n\mathbf{x}_n'\right] & \mathbf{0} \\ \mathbf{0} & \mathrm{E}_N\left[\frac{1}{2}\left(\frac{h^{(1)}(\mathbf{z}_n'\boldsymbol{\gamma}_0)}{\sigma_{0n}^2}\right)^2\cdot\mathbf{z}_n\mathbf{z}_n'\right]\end{bmatrix}$$

[17] The additional constant in $\mathbf{Z}$ does not affect the regression sum of squares.

which bears some similarity to the homoskedastic version.[18] In particular, note that the covariances between the scores of first-moment and second-moment parameters are all zero. The score for $\boldsymbol{\beta}_0$ is a linear function of $y_n - \mathbf{x}_n'\boldsymbol{\beta}_0$ whereas the score for $\boldsymbol{\gamma}$ is a linear function of $(y_n - \mathbf{x}_n'\boldsymbol{\beta}_0)^2$. The covariance between the scores for $\boldsymbol{\beta}_0$ and $\boldsymbol{\gamma}_0$ are zero because the first and third centered moments of normal random variables are zero (Theorem D.8, p. 887).

Asymptotic approximation of the distribution of the MLE (Proposition 16, p. 320) assigns the variance $\left[N \cdot \Im(\boldsymbol{\theta}_0)\right]^{-1}$.[19] Because the information matrix is block-diagonal, $\hat{\boldsymbol{\beta}}_{\text{ML}}$ has an approximate variance matrix equal to $\left(\mathbf{X}'\boldsymbol{\Omega}_0^{-1}\mathbf{X}\right)^{-1}$, the inverse of the upper left-hand corner of the information matrix. Note that this is identical to the conditional sampling variance of the GLS estimator:

$$\begin{aligned}\text{Var}[\hat{\boldsymbol{\beta}}_{\text{GLS}} \mid \mathbf{X}] &= (\mathbf{X}'\boldsymbol{\Omega}_0^{-1}\mathbf{X})^{-1}\mathbf{X}'\boldsymbol{\Omega}_0^{-1}\,\text{Var}[\mathbf{y} \mid \mathbf{X}]\boldsymbol{\Omega}_0^{-1}\mathbf{X}(\mathbf{X}'\boldsymbol{\Omega}_0^{-1}\mathbf{X})^{-1} \\ &= (\mathbf{X}'\boldsymbol{\Omega}_0^{-1}\mathbf{X})^{-1}\end{aligned}$$

This means that there is (asymptotically) no loss of efficiency from the estimation of both $\boldsymbol{\beta}_0$ and $\boldsymbol{\gamma}_0$. We can do as well without knowing $\boldsymbol{\gamma}_0$ as knowing it. In other words, $\hat{\boldsymbol{\beta}}_{\text{ML}}$ is adaptive in the presence of heteroskedasticity. This is surprising given the obvious dependence of $\hat{\boldsymbol{\beta}}_{\text{GLS}}$ on $\boldsymbol{\gamma}_0$ and the general gain in efficiency that restricted estimation delivers. It is analogous, at least, to the homoskedastic case in which efficient estimation of $\boldsymbol{\beta}_0$ does not depend on any variance parameters.

18.5.2 FGLS

The MLE is somewhat difficult to compute because iterative calculations are required to solve (18.16) and (18.17) simultaneously. In this section, we will analyze alternative estimators that plug in a consistent estimator $\check{\boldsymbol{\gamma}}$ for $\boldsymbol{\gamma}_0$ in $\hat{\boldsymbol{\beta}}_{\text{GLS}}$ (18.15). Such estimators are called *feasible generalized least squares* (FGLS) estimators, because lack of knowledge of $\boldsymbol{\gamma}_0$ makes the GLS estimator infeasible.

Strictly speaking, the MLE above is a member of this family of estimators, but not a convenient one. For linear heteroskedasticity, a computationally simpler alternative takes these steps:

Step 1: Fit an OLS regression of $w_n(\hat{\boldsymbol{\beta}}_{\text{OLS}}) \equiv \left(y_n - \mathbf{x}_n'\hat{\boldsymbol{\beta}}_{\text{OLS}}\right)^2$ on $\mathbf{z}_n$ and denote the fitted coefficients by $\check{\boldsymbol{\gamma}}$.

Step 2: Plug in $\check{\boldsymbol{\gamma}}$ for $\boldsymbol{\gamma}_0$ in the GLS estimator to compute the FGLS estimator $\hat{\boldsymbol{\beta}}_{\text{FGLS}} = (\mathbf{X}'\check{\boldsymbol{\Omega}}^{-1}\mathbf{X})^{-1}\mathbf{X}'\check{\boldsymbol{\Omega}}^{-1}\mathbf{y}$.

Similarly convenient first steps are available for the multiplicative and quadratic models of heteroskedasticity. If $h(\mathbf{z}_n'\boldsymbol{\gamma}) = \exp(\mathbf{z}_n'\boldsymbol{\gamma})$, then the LHS variable should be $\log w_n(\hat{\boldsymbol{\beta}}_{\text{OLS}})$ instead. If $h(\mathbf{z}_n'\boldsymbol{\gamma}) = (\mathbf{z}_n'\boldsymbol{\gamma})^2$, then fit $|w_n(\hat{\boldsymbol{\beta}}_{\text{OLS}})|$ to $\mathbf{z}_n$ with OLS in Step 1.

---

[18] See Example 14.20 (p. 305).

[19] Proposition 16 actually puts the MLE $\hat{\boldsymbol{\theta}}_N$ into this expression for the variance, not $\boldsymbol{\theta}_0$. But asymptotically it makes no difference because $\hat{\boldsymbol{\theta}}_N \xrightarrow{p} \boldsymbol{\theta}_0$.

The ease of replacing $\hat{\boldsymbol{\gamma}}_{\text{ML}}$ with an inefficient estimator for $\boldsymbol{\gamma}_0$ might incur a cost in relative efficiency, but this also is not so. The FGLS estimator is also an adaptive estimator for $\boldsymbol{\beta}_0$.

EXAMPLE 18.8 (Location)

Reconsider Example 18.6 but suppose that we have N pairs of observations:

$$\mathbf{y}_n = \begin{bmatrix} y_{1n} \\ y_{2n} \end{bmatrix} \sim \mathfrak{N}\left(\begin{bmatrix} 1 \\ 1 \end{bmatrix}\beta_0, \begin{bmatrix} \sigma_{01}^2 & 0 \\ 0 & \sigma_{02}^2 \end{bmatrix}\right)$$

$(n = 1, \ldots, N)$ where $\sigma_{01}^2 > \sigma_{02}^2$. An FGLS estimator is

$$\hat{\beta}_{\text{FGLS}} = \frac{s_2^2\,\hat{\beta}_{\text{OLS},1} + s_1^2\,\hat{\beta}_{\text{OLS},2}}{s_1^2 + s_2^2}$$

where

$$\hat{\beta}_{\text{OLS},j} \equiv \sum_{n=1}^{N} \frac{y_{jn}}{N}, \qquad s_j^2 \equiv \sum_{n=1}^{N} \frac{(y_{jn} - \hat{\beta}_{\text{OLS},j})^2}{N-1}$$

$(j = 1, 2)$. The distribution of $\hat{\beta}_{\text{FGLS}}$ conditional on s_1^2 and s_2^2 is

$$\hat{\beta}_{\text{FGLS}} \sim \mathfrak{N}\left[\beta_0, \frac{s_2^4\,\sigma_1^2 + s_1^4\,\sigma_2^2}{N\left(s_1^2 + s_2^2\right)^2}\right]$$

Now as $N \to \infty$, consider the joint distribution of $\sqrt{N}(\hat{\beta}_{\text{FGLS}} - \beta_0)$ and $\left(s_1^2, s_2^2\right)$. The $s_j^2 \xrightarrow{d} \sigma_j^2$ (constants) and

$$\sqrt{N}\left(\hat{\beta}_{\text{FGLS}} - \beta_0\right) \xrightarrow{d} \mathfrak{N}\left[0, \frac{\sigma_2^4\sigma_1^2 + \sigma_1^4\sigma_2^2}{\left(\sigma_1^2 + \sigma_2^2\right)^2}\right]$$

where

$$\frac{\sigma_2^4\,\sigma_1^2 + \sigma_1^4\,\sigma_2^2}{\left(\sigma_1^2 + \sigma_2^2\right)^2} = \frac{\sigma_2^2\,\sigma_1^2}{\sigma_1^2 + \sigma_2^2} = \text{Var}[\hat{\beta}_{\text{GLS}}]$$

We find, therefore, that $\hat{\beta}_{\text{FGLS}}$ is an adaptive estimator just like the MLE.

FGLS is a leading example of a general approach to estimation of complicated econometric models called *two-step* estimation.The estimator of $\boldsymbol{\beta}_0$ depends on preliminary (first-step) estimation of the parameters in $\boldsymbol{\gamma}_0$. Another example of a general two-step estimator is the LMLE.[20] The LMLE also has the property that the second-step estimator is efficient relative to the MLE. Indeed, the two estimators are asymptotically equivalent. As it happens, the FGLS estimator is actually a particular example of the LMLE.

To derive the LMLE, we require the information matrix and the score vector, developed in Section 18.7. Substituting these into the LMLE formula, we obtain

[20] See Lemma 15.7 (p. 333).

$$\begin{aligned}
\hat{\boldsymbol{\theta}}_{\mathrm{LML}} &= \check{\boldsymbol{\theta}} + \{\mathrm{E}_N[\Im(\check{\boldsymbol{\theta}} \mid \mathbf{x}_n, \mathbf{z}_n)]\}^{-1}\, \mathrm{E}_N[L_{\boldsymbol{\theta}}(\check{\boldsymbol{\theta}})] \\
&= \begin{bmatrix} \check{\beta} \\ \check{\gamma} \end{bmatrix} + \begin{bmatrix} \mathbf{X}'\check{\boldsymbol{\Omega}}^{-1}\mathbf{X} & \mathbf{0} \\ \mathbf{0} & \frac{1}{2}\check{\mathbf{Z}}_*'\check{\boldsymbol{\Omega}}^{-2}\check{\mathbf{Z}}_* \end{bmatrix}^{-1} \begin{bmatrix} \mathbf{X}'\check{\boldsymbol{\Omega}}^{-1}(\mathbf{y} - \mathbf{X}\check{\beta}) \\ \frac{1}{2}\check{\mathbf{Z}}_*'\check{\boldsymbol{\Omega}}^{-2}[\check{\mathbf{w}} - \mathbf{h}(\mathbf{Z}\check{\gamma})] \end{bmatrix} \\
&= \begin{bmatrix} (\mathbf{X}'\check{\boldsymbol{\Omega}}^{-1}\mathbf{X})^{-1}\mathbf{X}'\check{\boldsymbol{\Omega}}^{-1}\mathbf{y} \\ (\check{\mathbf{Z}}_*'\check{\boldsymbol{\Omega}}^{-2}\check{\mathbf{Z}}_*)^{-1}\check{\mathbf{Z}}_*'\check{\boldsymbol{\Omega}}^{-2}\check{\mathbf{w}}_* \end{bmatrix}
\end{aligned} \tag{18.19}$$

where

$$\check{\mathbf{w}}_* \equiv \check{\mathbf{w}} - \mathbf{h}(\mathbf{Z}\check{\gamma}) + \check{\mathbf{Z}}_*\check{\gamma}$$

$$\check{\mathbf{Z}}_* \equiv \left.\frac{\partial \mathbf{h}(\mathbf{Z}\boldsymbol{\gamma})}{\partial \boldsymbol{\gamma}}\right|_{\boldsymbol{\gamma}=\check{\gamma}}$$

and all terms are evaluated at $\boldsymbol{\theta} = \check{\boldsymbol{\theta}}$. Although taking matrix derivatives is not effortless, one can verify these expressions easily for scalar $\boldsymbol{\beta}$ and $\boldsymbol{\gamma}$. The reader can also check that these expressions simplify to their OLS counterparts when $\boldsymbol{\Omega} = \sigma^2 \cdot \mathbf{I}$.

The expression in (18.19) yields the FGLS estimator for the $\boldsymbol{\beta}$ component of the LMLE. The block-diagonality of the information matrix zeros out the contribution to this component that the score with respect $\boldsymbol{\gamma}$ would otherwise make. The direct effect is to make the functional form of the LMLE for $\boldsymbol{\beta}_0$ the same, whether we treat $\boldsymbol{\gamma}_0$ as known or unknown. Because the LMLE is generally asymptotically equivalent to the MLE, the implication is that FGLS is asymptotically equivalent to GLS for parametric models of heteroskedasticity.

The LMLE also yields an asymptotically efficient estimator of $\boldsymbol{\gamma}_0$. The estimator is computed as one iteration of (weighted) Gauss–Newton regression (GNR).[21] This expression is the generalization of (18.17) for arbitrary h. As expected, the LMLE for $\boldsymbol{\gamma}_0$ treats $\check{\boldsymbol{\beta}}$ as though it were $\boldsymbol{\beta}_0$ and this estimator is also adaptive.

The same basic phenomenon underlies the Breusch–Pagan test for heteroskedasticity. The asymptotic distribution of that score test statistic is also unaffected by the presence of $\hat{\boldsymbol{\beta}}_{\mathrm{OLS}}$ in place of $\boldsymbol{\beta}_0$. It is this block-diagonality of the information matrix that removes the asymptotic effect of estimating $\boldsymbol{\beta}_0$. Recall that generally the score test is exactly a measure of the distance between the resticted MLE and the unrestricted LMLE computed with the restricted MLE as the starting point.[22] In the present case, both estimators for $\boldsymbol{\gamma}_0$ behave (asymptotically) as though $\boldsymbol{\beta}_0$ were given. In this way, the score test statistic is invariant asymptotically to knowledge of $\boldsymbol{\beta}_0$.

FIRST-STEP ESTIMATION OF $\boldsymbol{\gamma}_0$

To motivate the first-step OLS estimator of $\boldsymbol{\gamma}_0$, consider how we could estimate $\boldsymbol{\gamma}_0$ if $\mathbf{w}(\boldsymbol{\beta}_0)$ were observable and $h(\mathbf{z}_n'\boldsymbol{\gamma}) = \mathbf{z}_n'\boldsymbol{\gamma}$. We would face a linear regression problem because

$$\mathrm{E}[w_n(\boldsymbol{\beta}_0) \mid \mathbf{x}_n, \mathbf{z}_n] = \mathbf{z}_n'\boldsymbol{\gamma}_0$$

---

21 Compare $\hat{\boldsymbol{\gamma}}_{\mathrm{LML}}$ with (16.14)–(16.16) in Section 16.4.3.

22 See equation (17.14) and Section 17.3.2.

The LHS variable $\mathbf{w}(\boldsymbol{\beta}_0)$ would also be heteroskedastic:[23]

$$\text{Var}[w_n(\boldsymbol{\beta}_0) \mid \mathbf{x}_n, \mathbf{z}_n] = 2[h(\mathbf{z}_n'\boldsymbol{\gamma}_0)]^2$$

But because efficiency is not the primary concern, we could simplify our method by ignoring this heteroskedasticity in $\mathbf{w}(\boldsymbol{\beta}_0)$ and estimating $\boldsymbol{\gamma}_0$ inefficiently by OLS:

$$\check{\boldsymbol{\gamma}}(\boldsymbol{\beta}_0) = (\mathbf{Z}'\mathbf{Z})^{-1}\mathbf{Z}'\mathbf{w}(\boldsymbol{\beta}_0)$$

We obtain a feasible estimator by plugging in $\hat{\boldsymbol{\beta}}_{\text{OLS}}$ for $\boldsymbol{\beta}_0$ in $\check{\boldsymbol{\gamma}}(\boldsymbol{\beta}_0)$. This feasible estimator for $\boldsymbol{\gamma}_0$ will be consistent if the function $\check{\boldsymbol{\gamma}}(\boldsymbol{\beta})$ converges in probability uniformly in $\boldsymbol{\beta}$.[24] In addition, $\check{\boldsymbol{\gamma}}(\hat{\boldsymbol{\beta}}_{\text{OLS}})$ is the fitted coefficient vector from the OLS regression for squared OLS fitted residuals in the Breusch–Pagan score test.

Now consider the multiplicative model in which $h(\mathbf{z}_n'\boldsymbol{\gamma}) = \exp(\mathbf{z}_n'\boldsymbol{\gamma})$. Although the OLS regression of $\log w_n(\hat{\boldsymbol{\beta}}_{\text{OLS}})$ on $\mathbf{z}_n$ may seem natural, there is a little sleight of hand in this version of Step 1 above. In fact,

$$\text{E}[w_n(\boldsymbol{\beta}_0) \mid \mathbf{x}_n, \mathbf{z}_n] = \exp(\mathbf{z}_n'\boldsymbol{\gamma}_0) \quad \not\Rightarrow \quad \text{E}[\log w_n(\boldsymbol{\beta}_0)] = \mathbf{z}_n'\boldsymbol{\gamma}_0$$

so the recommendation to regress $\log w(\hat{\boldsymbol{\beta}}_{\text{OLS}})$ on $\mathbf{z}_n$ may be paradoxical. The resolution lies in explaining that only estimation of the intercept is biased by the log transformation and that this bias does not affect the WLS estimator. Because $w_n(\boldsymbol{\beta}_0)/\exp(\mathbf{z}_n'\boldsymbol{\gamma}_0) \sim \chi_1^2$,

$$\text{E}\left[\log\left(\frac{w_n(\boldsymbol{\beta}_0)}{\exp(\mathbf{z}_n'\boldsymbol{\gamma}_0)}\right) \mid \mathbf{x}_n, \mathbf{z}_n\right] = \text{E}[\log \chi_1^2] \approx -1.2704$$

Therefore,

$$\text{E}[\log w_n(\boldsymbol{\beta}_0) \mid \mathbf{x}_n, \mathbf{z}_n] = \text{E}[\log \chi_1^2] + \mathbf{z}_n'\boldsymbol{\gamma}_0$$

and the OLS fitted coefficient for the intercept will be biased in the regression of $\log w_n(\boldsymbol{\beta}_0)$ on $\mathbf{z}_n$. Consequently, the regression estimates a function that yields expressions proportionate to the variances:

$$\exp\big[\text{E}[\log \chi_1^2] + \mathbf{z}_n'\boldsymbol{\gamma}_0\big] = \alpha \exp(\mathbf{z}_n'\boldsymbol{\gamma}_0) = \alpha\sigma_{0n}^2$$

But this does not affect the second stage estimation asymptotically because multiplication of the variance matrix by a constant does not change the WLS estimator:

$$\hat{\boldsymbol{\beta}}_{\text{GLS}} = (\mathbf{X}'\boldsymbol{\Omega}_0^{-1}\mathbf{X})^{-1}\mathbf{X}'\boldsymbol{\Omega}_0^{-1}\mathbf{y} = \left[\mathbf{X}'(\alpha \cdot \boldsymbol{\Omega}_0)^{-1}\mathbf{X}\right]^{-1}\mathbf{X}'(\alpha \cdot \boldsymbol{\Omega}_0)^{-1}\mathbf{y}$$

Similar reasoning works for the squared specification of heteroskedasticity. In both cases, one should exercise care in the estimation of the variance $(\mathbf{X}'\boldsymbol{\Omega}_0^{-1}\mathbf{X})^{-1}$ because $(\mathbf{X}'\boldsymbol{\Omega}^{-1}\mathbf{X})^{-1}$ actually estimates $[\mathbf{X}'(\alpha \cdot \boldsymbol{\Omega}_0)^{-1}\mathbf{X}]^{-1}$. One can correct $(\mathbf{X}'\check{\boldsymbol{\Omega}}^{-1}\mathbf{X})^{-1}$ by dividing by α. Alternatively, if one computes the FGLS estimator by reweighting the data and applying OLS, then OLS will

---

[23] Recall that the variance of a χ_1^2 random variable is 2 (Theorem D.10, p. 889) and note that $\mathbf{w}(\boldsymbol{\beta}_0)$ is distributed as a χ_1^2 random variable multiplied by the constant $h(\mathbf{z}_n'\boldsymbol{\gamma}_0)$.

[24] See Lemma 15.5 (p. 326).

estimate the sampling variance consistently because s^2 will implicitly estimate the appropriate factor of proportionality and make the correction.[25]

Applied researchers generally use the FGLS estimator, not the MLE. It is computationally convenient and the asymptotic distribution theory suggests no advantage in computing the MLE. Often, researchers will iterate the FGLS procedure, by alternating between (1) fitting $\boldsymbol{\gamma}$ as a function of the latest FGLS estimator for $\boldsymbol{\beta}_0$ and (2) fitting a new FGLS for $\boldsymbol{\beta}_0$ with the latest $\boldsymbol{\gamma}$. This amounts to a Gauss–Seidel algorithm for the MLE if (1) we replace the unweighted NLS calculation of Step 1 with a solution to the normal equations for $\boldsymbol{\gamma}$ and (2) check that the log-likelihood function increases with each parameter change within the iterations.

EXAMPLE 18.9

The estimates in Table 18.2 under the column weighted LS are FGLS estimates of the log-wage regression with the multiplicative specification of heteroskedasticity. We computed these estimates as follows. First, we computed the natural logarithm of the squared values of the OLS fitted residuals corresponding to the estimates under OLS in Table 18.2. Second, we regressed this new variable on the explanatory variables listed in Table 18.1. The reciprocal of the exponential of the OLS fitted values from this regression became the weights in a WLS fit of the log-wage to its explanatory variables. The estimates are repeated under FWLS in Table 18.3 along with the fitted heteroskedasticity coefficients.

For comparison, we also computed the MLE using the feasible weighted least squares (FWLS) estimator as a starting value for the numerical optimization. The Newton–Raphson algorithm proved to be extremely slow so we switched to the BHHH algorithm for the heteroskedasticity coefficients alone initially. After this converged, we used the Newton–Raphson algorithm on the complete parameter vector. The table shows the final estimates and the enormous change in the log-likelihood from the starting values. Because the log-wage coefficients and their estimated standard errors change very little, it appears that most of our efforts were expended in improving the estimates of the variance parameters. There, the biggest change is a larger decrease in variance for nonwhites. On the other hand, the FWLS and ML estimates of the mean coefficients appear to behave as the asymptotic theory predicts, being virtually equivalent.

Table 18.3
Log-Wage Regression with Heteroskedasticity

Explanatory Variable	FWLS	MLE
Mean		
Constant	1.136 (0.071)	1.131 (0.072)
Female	−0.213 (0.02)	−0.210 (0.027)
Nonwhite	−0.110 (0.034)	0.110 (0.031)
Union	0.280 (0.035)	0.283 (0.034)

(continued)

[25] See Harvey (1976).

Table 18.3 *(Continued)*

Explanatory Variable	FWLS	MLE
Schooling	0.058 (0.005)	0.059 (0.005)
Experience	0.038 (0.004)	0.037 (0.004)
(Experience)^2	−0.00061 (0.00009)	−0.00060 (0.00009)
Variance		
Constant	−5.409 (n.a.)[a]	−3.871 (0.071)
Female	0.223 (n.a.)	0.172 (0.027)
Nonwhite	−0.078 (n.a.)	−0.356 (0.034)
Union	−0.278 (n.a.)	−0.332 (0.035)
Schooling	0.127 (n.a.)	0.118 (0.005)
Experience	0.031 (n.a.)	0.029 (0.004)
Log-likelihood	−4005.623	−347.482

[a] n.a., not available.

18.5.3 Adaptive Estimation

The FGLS estimator and the MLE are asymptotically equivalent to the GLS estimator. In other words, replacing the unknown covariance parameters with consistent but inefficient estimators does not affect the asymptotic distribution of the GLS estimator. Researchers can act as though they knew the true covariance parameters when they do not. This is not possible generally, but such delusional behavior often works for problems involving GLS.

This particular lack of an efficiency gain is analogous to the asymptotic equivalence of the ML and GLS estimators. There is no covariance between estimators of the slope and variance parameters. Estimators of the parameters in $\boldsymbol{\Omega}_0$ are functions of fitted residuals, whereas the GLS estimator of $\boldsymbol{\beta}_0$ is a function of fitted values. In OLS, these statistics are uncorrelated when the variance matrix of $\mathbf{y}$ is scalar. In GLS, an analogous lack of correlation holds asymptotically as the sample size approaches infinity.

First, let us show with an OLS example how the substitution of an estimator for a population parameter usually affects efficiency. Then we will discuss the special features of the normal general linear model.

Now consider the general normal model $\mathbf{y} \mid \mathbf{X}, \mathbf{Z} \sim \mathfrak{N}[\boldsymbol{\mu}(\boldsymbol{\beta}_0, \mathbf{X}),\ \boldsymbol{\Omega}(\boldsymbol{\gamma}_0, \mathbf{Z})]$, where $\mathbf{y}$ contains N observations, $\boldsymbol{\beta}_0 \in \mathbb{R}^{K_\beta}$ and $\boldsymbol{\gamma}_0 \in \mathbb{R}^{K_\gamma}$. We allow the functional dependence of both the mean vector and the variance matrix on the unknown parameters to be nonlinear. If we denote $\boldsymbol{\mu}_0 \equiv \boldsymbol{\mu}(\boldsymbol{\beta}_0, \mathbf{X})$, $\boldsymbol{\Omega}_0 \equiv \boldsymbol{\Omega}(\boldsymbol{\gamma}_0, \mathbf{Z})$, and $\boldsymbol{\varepsilon}_0 \equiv \mathbf{y} - \boldsymbol{\mu}_0$, then the generalizations of (15.10) and (15.11) are

$$L_{\beta}(\boldsymbol{\theta}_0) = \left.\frac{\partial \mu(\boldsymbol{\beta}, \mathbf{X})'}{\partial \boldsymbol{\beta}}\right|_{\boldsymbol{\beta}=\boldsymbol{\beta}_0} \boldsymbol{\Omega}_0^{-1}\boldsymbol{\varepsilon}_0 \tag{18.20}$$

$$L_{\gamma}(\boldsymbol{\theta}_0) = -\frac{1}{2} \cdot \left.\frac{\partial[\text{vec}\,\boldsymbol{\Omega}(\boldsymbol{\gamma}, \mathbf{Z})]'}{\partial \boldsymbol{\gamma}}\right|_{\boldsymbol{\gamma}=\boldsymbol{\gamma}_0} \text{vec}(\boldsymbol{\Omega}_0^{-1} - \boldsymbol{\Omega}_0^{-1}\boldsymbol{\varepsilon}_0\boldsymbol{\varepsilon}_0'\boldsymbol{\Omega}_0^{-1}) \tag{18.21}$$

These expressions have familiar elements, but they deserve some explanation before we use them to demonstrate block-diagonality of the information matrix.

We explain the fundamentals of vector derivatives in Appendix G. We derive these particular derivatives in Section G.5 (p. 928). The leading partial derivative in (18.20) is $\mathbf{X}'$ when $\boldsymbol{\mu}_0 = \mathbf{X}\boldsymbol{\beta}_0$ and generally a $K_\beta \times N$ matrix of partial derivatives. The trailing term $\boldsymbol{\Omega}_0^{-1}\boldsymbol{\varepsilon}_0$ is the $N \times 1$ vector of partial derivatives of L with respect to the N elements of $\boldsymbol{\mu}$. The leading partial derivative in (18.21) is analogous to $\partial\boldsymbol{\mu}'/\partial\boldsymbol{\beta}$, except that we must turn $\boldsymbol{\Omega}$ into a vector like $\boldsymbol{\mu}$ to construct a matrix of partial derivatives. This is what the vec operator does: it constructs a single column vector out of the column vectors within its argument by stacking them sequentially. Thus, the leading matrix of partial derivatives in (18.21) is $K_\gamma \times N^2$. The second vec expression contains the partial derivatives of L with respect to the elements of $\boldsymbol{\Omega}$ and is $N^2 \times 1$. We derive versions of these derivatives for the heteroskedastic case in detail in Section 18.7.1.

Now if we focus on the terms $\boldsymbol{\Omega}_0^{-1}\boldsymbol{\varepsilon}_0$ and $\text{vec}(\boldsymbol{\Omega}_0^{-1} - \boldsymbol{\Omega}_0^{-1}\boldsymbol{\varepsilon}_0\boldsymbol{\varepsilon}_0'\boldsymbol{\Omega}_0^{-1})$, we can confirm that the covariance of all their elements equals zero. The product of two elements will always have the form $a\varepsilon_{0n} + b\varepsilon_{0n}\varepsilon_{0m}\varepsilon_{0p}$ $(m, n, p = 1, \ldots, N)$. Because the distribution of $\boldsymbol{\varepsilon}_0$ is symmetric around its mean $\mathbf{0}$ and all moments of the distribution exist, the expectations of these products are all zero. We conclude that the information matrix is block-diagonal in the partition of $\boldsymbol{\theta} = [\boldsymbol{\beta}', \boldsymbol{\gamma}']'$. Note that the functional forms of $\boldsymbol{\mu}(\boldsymbol{\beta}_0, \mathbf{X})$ and $\boldsymbol{\Omega}(\boldsymbol{\gamma}_0, \mathbf{Z})$ are immaterial to this result. The critical elements are multivariate normality and the partition of the parameters between those that enter $\boldsymbol{\mu}$ and those that enter $\boldsymbol{\Omega}$.

The equivalence of FGLS and linearized maximum likelihood (LML) for $\boldsymbol{\beta}$ follows directly from this block-diagonality: using the definition of the linearized maximum likelihood estimator (LMLE)[26]

$$\begin{aligned}
\begin{bmatrix} \hat{\boldsymbol{\beta}}_{\text{LML}} \\ \hat{\boldsymbol{\gamma}}_{\text{LML}} \end{bmatrix} &= \begin{bmatrix} \check{\boldsymbol{\beta}} \\ \check{\boldsymbol{\gamma}} \end{bmatrix} + \begin{bmatrix} \check{\Im}_{\beta\beta} & \check{\Im}_{\beta\gamma} \\ \check{\Im}_{\gamma\beta} & \check{\Im}_{\gamma\gamma} \end{bmatrix}^{-1} \begin{bmatrix} \check{L}_\beta \\ \check{L}_\gamma \end{bmatrix} \\
&= \begin{bmatrix} \check{\boldsymbol{\beta}} + \check{\Im}_{\beta\beta}^{-1}\check{L}_\beta \\ \check{\boldsymbol{\gamma}} + \check{\Im}_{\gamma\gamma}^{-1}\check{L}_\gamma \end{bmatrix}
\end{aligned} \tag{18.22}$$

where $\check{L}_\theta \equiv L_\theta(\check{\boldsymbol{\theta}})$ and $\check{\Im} \equiv \Im(\check{\boldsymbol{\theta}})$. In the linear models that we have been studying $\boldsymbol{\mu} = \mathbf{X}\boldsymbol{\beta}$, $L_\beta = \mathbf{X}'\boldsymbol{\Omega}^{-1}(\mathbf{y} - \mathbf{X}\boldsymbol{\beta})$, and $\Im_{\beta\beta} = \mathbf{X}'\boldsymbol{\Omega}^{-1}\mathbf{X}$. Substituting these into the expression for $\hat{\boldsymbol{\beta}}_{\text{LML}}$, we obtain the FGLS estimator:

$$\begin{aligned}
\hat{\boldsymbol{\beta}}_{\text{LML}} &= \check{\boldsymbol{\beta}} + \check{\Im}_{\beta\beta}^{-1}\check{L}_\beta \\
&= \check{\boldsymbol{\beta}} + (\mathbf{X}'\check{\boldsymbol{\Omega}}^{-1}\mathbf{X})^{-1}\mathbf{X}'\check{\boldsymbol{\Omega}}^{-1}(\mathbf{y} - \mathbf{X}\check{\boldsymbol{\beta}}) \\
&= (\mathbf{X}'\check{\boldsymbol{\Omega}}^{-1}\mathbf{X})^{-1}\mathbf{X}'\check{\boldsymbol{\Omega}}^{-1}\mathbf{y}
\end{aligned}$$

[26] See the definition of the LMLE in equation (15.9).

$$= \hat{\boldsymbol{\beta}}_{\text{FGLS}}$$

In Section 18.7.1, we show that $L_\gamma = \frac{1}{2} \cdot \mathbf{Z}_*' \boldsymbol{\Omega}^{-2} \left[\mathbf{w}(\boldsymbol{\beta}) - \mathbf{h}(\mathbf{Z}\boldsymbol{\gamma})\right]$ and $\Im_{\gamma\gamma} = \frac{1}{2}\mathbf{Z}_*'\boldsymbol{\Omega}^{-2}\mathbf{Z}_*$ where $\mathbf{Z}_* \equiv [h^{(1)}(\mathbf{z}_n'\boldsymbol{\gamma}) \cdot \mathbf{z}_n]'$ and $h^{(1)}(\cdot)$ is the first derivative of $h(\cdot)$.[27] These yield the LMLE for $\boldsymbol{\gamma}$

$$\begin{aligned} \hat{\boldsymbol{\gamma}}_{\text{LML}} &= \check{\boldsymbol{\gamma}} + \check{\Im}_{\gamma\gamma}^{-1} \check{L}_\gamma \\ &= \check{\boldsymbol{\gamma}} + (\check{\mathbf{Z}}_*' \check{\boldsymbol{\Omega}}^{-2} \check{\mathbf{Z}}_*)^{-1} \check{\mathbf{Z}}_*' \check{\boldsymbol{\Omega}}^{-2} \left[\mathbf{w}(\check{\boldsymbol{\beta}}) - \mathbf{h}(\mathbf{Z}\check{\boldsymbol{\gamma}})\right] \end{aligned}$$

In the special case of linear heteroskedasticity, $\mathbf{h}(\mathbf{Z}\boldsymbol{\gamma}) = \mathbf{Z}\boldsymbol{\gamma}$, $\mathbf{Z}_* = \mathbf{Z}$, and this LMLE simplifies to the FGLS form

$$\hat{\boldsymbol{\gamma}}_{\text{LML}} = (\check{\mathbf{Z}}_*' \check{\boldsymbol{\Omega}}^{-2} \check{\mathbf{Z}}_*)^{-1} \check{\mathbf{Z}}_*' \check{\boldsymbol{\Omega}}^{-2} \mathbf{w}(\check{\boldsymbol{\beta}})$$

18.6 METHODOLOGICAL NOTES

The OLS estimator can be more efficient than the FWLS estimator in small samples. The simplest conditions are when $\text{Var}[\mathbf{y} \mid \mathbf{X}] = \sigma_0^2 \cdot \mathbf{I}$. In general, the estimated weights in the FWLS estimator will not be constant, introducing inefficiency. Of course, as the sample size gets very large this variation becomes negligible in the asymptotic distribution of the estimator and FWLS is asymptotically equivalent to OLS. But in small samples, the variation in the weights is influential. This effect persists when $\text{Var}[\mathbf{y} \mid \mathbf{X}]$ is nonscalar.

EXAMPLE 18.10 (OLS versus WLS)

Consider estimation of the mean μ for a heteroskedastic data-generating process where half the observations are $\mathfrak{N}(\mu, \sigma_1^2)$ and half are $\mathfrak{N}(\mu, \sigma_2^2)$. We will compare the sampling variances of the simple sample average, $\hat{\mu}_{\text{OLS}} = N^{-1} \sum_{n=1}^{N} y_n$, and the FWLS estimator,

$$\hat{\mu}_{\text{FWLS}} = \frac{s_2^2 \bar{y}_1 + s_1^2 \bar{y}_2}{s_1^2 + s_2^2}$$

where $\bar{y}_1$ and $\bar{y}_2$ are averages within the homoskedastic subsamples and s_1^2 and s_2^2 are the corresponding subsample estimators of the variances σ_1^2 and σ_2^2, respectively. Both estimators are unbiased so that this comparison of second moments is also comparison of MSEs.

Figure 18.4 plots the ratio $\text{Var}[\hat{\mu}_{\text{FWLS}}]/\,\text{Var}[\hat{\mu}_{\text{OLS}}]$ against σ_1/σ_2 for the case $N = 4$. By choosing a small sample size we have made the relative efficiency of OLS over FWLS particularly pronounced for σ_1/σ_2 near one. The sampling variances are inversely proportional to the sample size so we can interpret the results as follows. When there is no heteroskedasticity ($\sigma_1/\sigma_2 = 1$), we can obtain the same sampling variance from FWLS as from OLS if we give FWLS 50% more observations than OLS. The two estimators possess comparable sampling variances when

[27] See particularly (18.24) and (18.25).

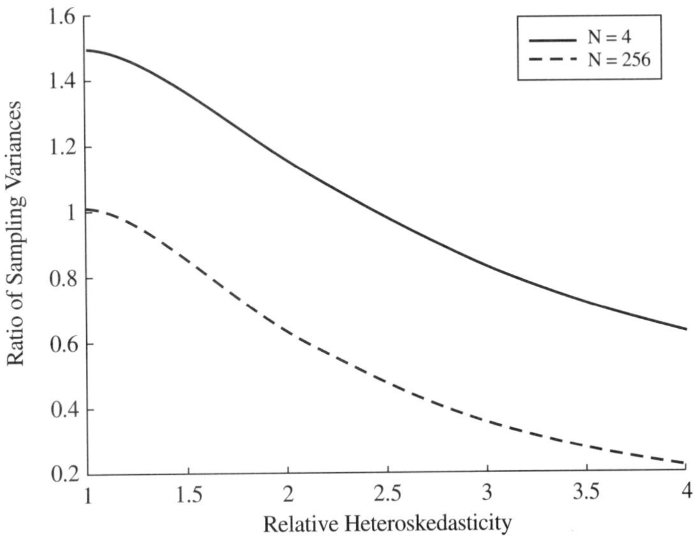

Figure 18.4 Relative Efficiency of OLS and FWLS

$\sigma_1/\sigma_2 \approx 2.5$. In other words, the σ_1^2 must be over six times greater than σ_2^2. For even more pronounced heteroskedasticity, the FWLS estimator is relatively efficient.

The effect of a large sample size also appears in Figure 18.4, where we plot the same relationship for $N = 256$. The overall shape of the function is the same but the region in which OLS dominates FWLS is considerably smaller. In this case, FWLS has a smaller sampling variance once σ_1^2 and σ_2^2 differ by approximately 20% or more. This is still a nontrivial amount of heteroskedasticity and suggests that the scope for preferring OLS in practice is appreciable.

Thus, corrections for heteroskedasticity can introduce more sampling variance than they remove, particularly when the heteroskedasticity is mild. See Rothenberg (1984a) for approximations to the distribution of the FGLS estimator that capture such effects.[28] Reseachers frequently apply FWLS when such a test as the Breusch–Pagan yields evidence against homoskedasticity. This is an informal estimation procedure and formal methods require research into the distributions of such estimators in small samples.

18.7 MATHEMATICAL NOTES

In these notes, we work out the necessary score, Hessian, and information terms to produce the normal equations, the LMLE and the Breusch–Pagan score test. We also discuss changes to the asymptotic distribution theory that accommodate heteroskedasticity.

[28] Rothenberg shows that, to a second order of approximation, the distribution of the FGLS estimator remains normally distributed such that the variance is the only affected aspect of the approximate distribution. See his article for the regularity conditions.

18.7.1 Score and Information

The normal equations are simplest when we build them up using the chain rule of differentiation and expanding terms only as needed. Let us abbreviate $\mu_n \equiv \mathbf{x}_n'\boldsymbol{\beta}$ and $\sigma_n^2 \equiv \mathbf{z}_n'\boldsymbol{\gamma}$. Then the log-likelihood of one observation is

$$L(\theta;\, y_n \,|\, \mathbf{x}_n, \mathbf{z}_n) = -\frac{1}{2}\left[\log(2\pi\sigma_n^2) + \frac{(y_n - \mu_n)^2}{\sigma_n^2}\right]$$

We have previously written the score vector elements,

$$L_{\mu_n}(\theta;\, y_n \,|\, \mathbf{x}_n, \mathbf{z}_n) = \frac{y_n - \mu_n}{\sigma_n^2}$$

$$L_{\sigma_n^2}(\theta;\, y_n \,|\, \mathbf{x}_n, \mathbf{z}_n) = -\frac{1}{2}\left[\frac{1}{\sigma_n^2} - \frac{(y_n - \mu_n)^2}{\sigma_n^4}\right]$$

and Hessian matrix elements,[29]

$$L_{\mu_n\mu_n}(\theta;\, y_n \,|\, \mathbf{x}_n, \mathbf{z}_n) = -\frac{1}{\sigma_n^2}$$

$$L_{\mu_n\sigma_n^2}(\theta;\, y_n \,|\, \mathbf{x}_n, \mathbf{z}_n) = -\frac{y_n - \mu_n}{\sigma_n^4}$$

$$L_{\sigma_n^2\sigma_n^2}(\theta;\, y_n \,|\, \mathbf{x}_n, \mathbf{z}_n) = \frac{1}{2}\left[\frac{1}{\sigma_n^4} - \frac{2(y_n - \mu_n)^2}{\sigma_n^6}\right]$$

For the conditional information matrix, we need the conditional expected values

$$\mathfrak{H}_{\mu_n\mu_n}(\theta_0 \,|\, \mu_{0n}, \sigma_{0n}) \equiv -\mathrm{E}[L_{\mu_n\mu_n}(\theta_0;\, y_n \,|\, \mathbf{x}_n, \mathbf{z}_n) \,|\, \mu_{0n}, \sigma_{0n}] = \frac{1}{\sigma_{0n}^2}$$

$$\mathfrak{H}_{\mu_n\sigma_n^2}(\theta_0 \,|\, \mu_{0n}, \sigma_{0n}) \equiv -\mathrm{E}[L_{\mu_n\sigma_n^2}(\theta_0;\, y_n \,|\, \mathbf{x}_n, \mathbf{z}_n) \,|\, \mu_{0n}, \sigma_{0n}] = 0$$

$$\mathfrak{H}_{\sigma_n^2\sigma_n^2}(\theta_0 \,|\, \mu_{0n}, \sigma_{0n}) \equiv -\mathrm{E}[L_{\sigma_n^2\sigma_n^2}(\theta_0;\, y_n \,|\, \mathbf{x}_n, \mathbf{z}_n) \,|\, \mu_{0n}, \sigma_{0n}] = \frac{1}{2\sigma_{0n}^4}$$

18.7.2 The Maximum Likelihood Estimator

Using[30]

$$\frac{\partial(\mu_n, \sigma_n^2)}{\partial\boldsymbol{\theta}} = \begin{bmatrix} \frac{\partial\mu_n}{\partial\boldsymbol{\beta}} & \frac{\partial\sigma_n^2}{\partial\boldsymbol{\beta}} \\ \frac{\partial\mu_n}{\partial\boldsymbol{\gamma}} & \frac{\partial\sigma_n^2}{\partial\boldsymbol{\gamma}} \end{bmatrix} = \begin{bmatrix} \mathbf{x}_n & \mathbf{0} \\ \mathbf{0} & h^{(1)}(\mathbf{z}_n'\boldsymbol{\gamma}) \cdot \mathbf{z}_n \end{bmatrix}$$

the normal equations are

---

[29] Example 14.20 (p. 305).

[30] We use the derivative notation $h^{(n)}(x) \equiv d^n h(x)/dx^n$ to distinguish derivatives from matrix transposes.

$$
\begin{aligned}
\mathbf{0} &= \mathrm{E}_N[L_{\boldsymbol{\beta}}(\boldsymbol{\theta})] \\
&= \frac{1}{N} \cdot \sum_{n=1}^{N} \mathbf{x}_n \frac{y_n - \hat{\mu}_{\mathrm{ML},n}}{\hat{\sigma}_n^2} \\
&= \frac{1}{N} \cdot \mathbf{X}' \hat{\boldsymbol{\Omega}}_{\mathrm{ML}}^{-1} (\mathbf{y} - \mathbf{X}\hat{\boldsymbol{\beta}}_{\mathrm{ML}})
\end{aligned}
\tag{18.23}
$$

and

$$
\begin{aligned}
\mathbf{0} &= \mathrm{E}_N[L_{\boldsymbol{\gamma}}(\boldsymbol{\theta})] \\
&= -\frac{1}{2N} \cdot \sum_{n=1}^{N} h^{(1)}(\mathbf{z}_n' \hat{\boldsymbol{\gamma}}_{\mathrm{ML}}) \cdot \mathbf{z}_n \left[\frac{1}{\hat{\sigma}_n^2} - \frac{(y_n - \hat{\mu}_{\mathrm{ML},n})^2}{\hat{\sigma}_n^4} \right] \\
&= \frac{1}{2N} \cdot \hat{\mathbf{Z}}_{*\mathrm{ML}}' \hat{\boldsymbol{\Lambda}}_{\mathrm{ML}}^{-1} \left[\hat{\mathbf{w}}_{\mathrm{ML}} - \mathbf{h}(\mathbf{Z}\hat{\boldsymbol{\gamma}}_{\mathrm{ML}}) \right]
\end{aligned}
\tag{18.24}
$$

where $\hat{\mathbf{Z}}_{*\mathrm{ML}} \equiv \left[h^{(1)}(\mathbf{z}_n'\hat{\boldsymbol{\gamma}}_{\mathrm{ML}}) \cdot \mathbf{z}_n\right]'$ and $\hat{\boldsymbol{\Lambda}}_{\mathrm{ML}}$, and $\hat{\mathbf{w}}_{\mathrm{ML}}$ are defined in (18.18). Equation (18.23) is equivalent to (18.16). In the special case in which $h(\mathbf{z}_n'\boldsymbol{\gamma}) = \mathbf{z}_n'\boldsymbol{\gamma}$, then $h^{(1)}(\mathbf{z}_n'\hat{\boldsymbol{\gamma}}_{\mathrm{ML}}) = 1$ and $\hat{\mathbf{Z}}_{*\mathrm{ML}} = \mathbf{Z}$ so that (18.24) yields (18.17).

We estimate the information matrix with the average conditional information:[31]

$$
\begin{aligned}
\mathrm{E}_N[\Im(\theta \mid \mathbf{x}_n, \mathbf{z}_n)] &= \mathrm{E}_N\left[\frac{\partial(\mu_n, \sigma_n^2)}{\partial \boldsymbol{\theta}} \mathfrak{H}(\boldsymbol{\theta} \mid \mu_{0n}, \sigma_{0n}) \left(\frac{\partial(\mu_n, \sigma_n^2)}{\partial \boldsymbol{\theta}} \right)' \right] \\
&= \begin{bmatrix} \mathrm{E}_N[\mathbf{x}_n \frac{1}{\sigma_n^2} \mathbf{x}_n'] & \mathbf{0} \\ \mathbf{0} & \mathrm{E}_N\left[\mathbf{z}_n \frac{\left(h^{(1)}(\mathbf{z}_n'\boldsymbol{\gamma})\right)^2}{2\sigma_n^4} \mathbf{z}_n' \right] \end{bmatrix} \\
&= \frac{1}{N} \begin{bmatrix} \mathbf{X}'\boldsymbol{\Omega}^{-1}\mathbf{X} & \mathbf{0} \\ \mathbf{0} & \frac{1}{2}\mathbf{Z}_*'\boldsymbol{\Omega}^{-2}\mathbf{Z}_* \end{bmatrix}
\end{aligned}
\tag{18.25}
$$

where $\mathbf{Z}_* \equiv [h^{(1)}(\mathbf{z}_n'\boldsymbol{\gamma}) \cdot \mathbf{z}_n]'$. By comparison with Example 14.20, we can see a couple of changes from the homoskedastic case. The quadratic form in $\mathbf{X}$ is now weighted by the $\boldsymbol{\Omega}^{-1}$ term and there is diagonal block for variance parameters with a similar quadratic form. The weighting matrix $\frac{1}{2}\boldsymbol{\Omega}^{-2}$ replaces $\boldsymbol{\Omega}^{-1}$ because this term involves fourth moments of the normal distribution.

Using this information matrix, we estimate the variance of $\hat{\boldsymbol{\beta}}_{\mathrm{ML}}$ with $(\mathbf{X}'\hat{\boldsymbol{\Omega}}_{\mathrm{ML}}^{-1}\mathbf{X})^{-1}$ and the variance of $\hat{\boldsymbol{\gamma}}_{\mathrm{ML}}$ with $2(\hat{\mathbf{Z}}_{*\mathrm{ML}}'\hat{\boldsymbol{\Omega}}_{\mathrm{ML}}^{-2}\hat{\mathbf{Z}}_{*\mathrm{ML}})^{-1}$, where $\hat{\boldsymbol{\theta}}_{\mathrm{ML}}$ replaces $\boldsymbol{\theta}$. We also find that the Cramér-Rao lower bound for the variance of $\boldsymbol{\beta}_0$ is $\mathrm{E}[\sigma_{0n}^{-2} \cdot \mathbf{x}_n\mathbf{x}_n']^{-1}$ and for the variance of $\boldsymbol{\gamma}_0$ is $2 \cdot \left\{\mathrm{E}\left[\left(h^{(1)}(\mathbf{z}_n'\boldsymbol{\gamma}_0)\right)^2 \sigma_{0n}^{-4} \cdot \mathbf{z}_n\mathbf{z}_n'\right]\right\}^{-1}$. Both variance matrices imply that estimation of one parameter vector is incidental to the limiting variance of the estimator of the other parameter vector. That is, the MLE for each parameter vector is adaptive.

31 See Section 15.4.

18.7.3 The Breusch–Pagan Score Test

Finally, we derive the Breusch–Pagan score test. Because $\mathbf{0} = \mathrm{E}_N[L_\beta(\hat{\boldsymbol{\theta}}_{\mathrm{R}})]$ and $\Im_{\boldsymbol{\beta\gamma}} = \mathbf{0}$ the score test statistic does not depend on $\hat{L}_\beta$ or $\hat{\Im}_{\boldsymbol{\beta\beta}}$ in the same way as the LMLE for $\boldsymbol{\gamma}_0$:

$$S = N \cdot \mathrm{E}_N[L_{\boldsymbol{\theta}}(\hat{\boldsymbol{\theta}}_{\mathrm{R}})]'\Im(\hat{\boldsymbol{\theta}}_{\mathrm{R}})^{-1}\,\mathrm{E}_N[L_{\boldsymbol{\theta}}(\hat{\boldsymbol{\theta}}_{\mathrm{R}})]$$
$$= N \cdot \mathrm{E}_N[L_{\boldsymbol{\gamma}}(\hat{\boldsymbol{\theta}}_{\mathrm{R}})]'\Im_{\boldsymbol{\gamma\gamma}}(\hat{\boldsymbol{\theta}}_{\mathrm{R}})^{-1}\,\mathrm{E}_N[L_{\boldsymbol{\gamma}}(\hat{\boldsymbol{\theta}}_{\mathrm{R}})]$$

If we impose the restrictions of the null hypothesis that $\boldsymbol{\gamma}_2 = \mathbf{0}$, then

$$h(\mathbf{z}_n'\boldsymbol{\gamma}) = h(\gamma_1) = \sigma^2$$

and

$$h^{(1)}(\mathbf{z}_n'\boldsymbol{\gamma}) = h^{(1)}(\gamma_1)$$
$$\mathbf{Z}_* = h^{(1)}(\gamma_1)\cdot\mathbf{Z}$$

Simplifying $\mathrm{E}_N[L_{\boldsymbol{\gamma}}(\boldsymbol{\theta})]$ in (18.24), we get

$$\mathrm{E}_N[L_{\boldsymbol{\gamma}}(\boldsymbol{\theta})] = \frac{h^{(1)}(\gamma_1)}{2\sigma^4 N}\cdot\mathbf{Z}'[\mathbf{w}(\boldsymbol{\beta}) - \iota\sigma^2]$$

where $\mathbf{w}(\boldsymbol{\beta}) \equiv [(y_n - \mathbf{x}_n'\boldsymbol{\beta})^2]'$. Because $\mathrm{Var}[(y_n - \mathbf{x}_n'\boldsymbol{\beta}_0)^2 \,|\, \mathbf{x}_n] = 2\sigma_0^4$ under homoskedasticity,

$$\mathrm{E}_N[\Im_{\boldsymbol{\gamma\gamma}}(\theta_0)] = \frac{\left[h^{(1)}(\gamma_{01})\right]^2}{2\sigma_0^4 N}\cdot\mathbf{Z}'\mathbf{Z}$$

Substituting these into S along with the restricted ML/OLS estimates $(\hat{\boldsymbol{\beta}}_{\mathrm{OLS}}, \hat{\sigma}^2)$ gives

$$S = \frac{1}{2\hat{\sigma}^4}\cdot[\mathbf{w}(\hat{\boldsymbol{\beta}}_{\mathrm{OLS}}) - \iota\hat{\sigma}^2]'\mathbf{P}_{\mathbf{Z}}[\mathbf{w}(\hat{\boldsymbol{\beta}}_{\mathrm{OLS}}) - \iota\hat{\sigma}^2]$$
$$= \frac{1}{2}\cdot\left[\frac{1}{\hat{\sigma}^2}\cdot\mathbf{w}(\hat{\boldsymbol{\beta}}_{\mathrm{OLS}})\right]'\mathbf{P}_{\mathbf{Z}_{2\perp1}}\left[\frac{1}{\hat{\sigma}^2}\cdot\mathbf{w}(\hat{\boldsymbol{\beta}}_{\mathrm{OLS}})\right]$$

because $\mathbf{Z}_1 = \iota$ and

$$0 = \mathrm{E}_N[L_{\gamma_1}(\hat{\theta}_{\mathrm{R}})]$$
$$= \mathbf{Z}_1'(\mathbf{w}(\hat{\boldsymbol{\beta}}_{\mathrm{OLS}}) - \iota\hat{\sigma}^2) \qquad \Leftrightarrow \qquad \hat{\sigma}^2 = (\mathbf{Z}_1'\mathbf{Z}_1)^{-1}\mathbf{Z}_1'\mathbf{w}(\hat{\boldsymbol{\beta}}_{\mathrm{OLS}})$$
$$= \mathbf{Z}_1'(\mathbf{w}(\hat{\boldsymbol{\beta}}_{\mathrm{OLS}}) - \mathbf{Z}_1\hat{\sigma}^2)$$

imply that

$$\mathbf{Z}_2'\left[\mathbf{w}(\hat{\boldsymbol{\beta}}_{\mathrm{OLS}}) - \mathbf{Z}_1\hat{\gamma}_{\mathrm{R}1}\right] = \mathbf{Z}_2'(\mathbf{I} - \mathbf{P}_{\mathbf{Z}_1})\mathbf{w}(\hat{\boldsymbol{\beta}}_{\mathrm{OLS}}) = \mathbf{Z}_{2\perp1}'\mathbf{w}(\hat{\boldsymbol{\beta}}_{\mathrm{OLS}})$$

Note that the scalar $h^{(1)}(\hat{\gamma}_{\mathrm{R}1})$ cancels out of $\mathbf{P}_{\mathbf{Z}_{2\perp1}}$ so that the score test does not depend on h and the linear heteroskedasticity specification captures the local alternatives for nonlinear h.

18.7.4 Regularity

In order to apply the asymptotic theory of the MLE as we have done, our model must satisfy the assumptions in Chapter 14. There are no difficulties adopting the i.i.d. distributional assumption (Assumption 14.1, p. 285) for $(y_n, \mathbf{x}_n, \mathbf{z}_n)$. We have specified a conditional likelihood for y_n given $(\mathbf{x}_n, \mathbf{z}_n)$, so that even though y_n is conditionally heteroskedastic, marginally it is homoskedastic if its variance exists. Thus, y_n may appear to have a p.d.f. with tails fatter than normal.

Our normal heteroskedastic linear regression model is also identified provided that $\mathbf{x}_n$ and $\mathbf{z}_n$ possess no linear dependence among their elements. Therefore, as in Chapter 13, we must be able to assume that the second-moment matrices $\mathrm{E}[\mathbf{x}_n\mathbf{x}_n']$ and $\mathrm{E}[\mathbf{z}_n\mathbf{z}_n']$ are both finite, nonsingular matrices. With these conditions, we can satisfy Assumption 14.3 (Likelihood Identification, p. 296). The support of normal distribution is $\mathbb{R}$ and the normal p.d.f. is infinitely continuously differentiable so that Assumption 14.4 (Differentiability, p. 298) is also met.

In addition, we have already seen that the normal distribution satisfies Assumptions 15.2 (Interior, p. 324) and 14.5 (Finite Information, p. 302) in Examples 14.18 (p. 301) and 14.20 (p. 305).

The conditions in Assumptions 14.2 (Dominance I, p. 290) and 15.3 (Dominance II, p. 327) remain. These can also fail in general, as the following example shows.

EXAMPLE 18.11 (Linear Heteroskedasticity)

Suppose that the $y_n \sim \mathfrak{N}(\mu, \gamma_1 + \gamma_2 z_n)$ are independently distributed conditional on z_n, so that the conditional log-likelihood function is

$$L(\mu, \mathbf{\Omega}) = -\frac{1}{2}\sum_{n=1}^{N}\left[\log[2\pi(\gamma_1 + \gamma_2 z_n)] + \frac{(y_n - \mu)^2}{\gamma_1 + \gamma_2 z_n}\right]$$

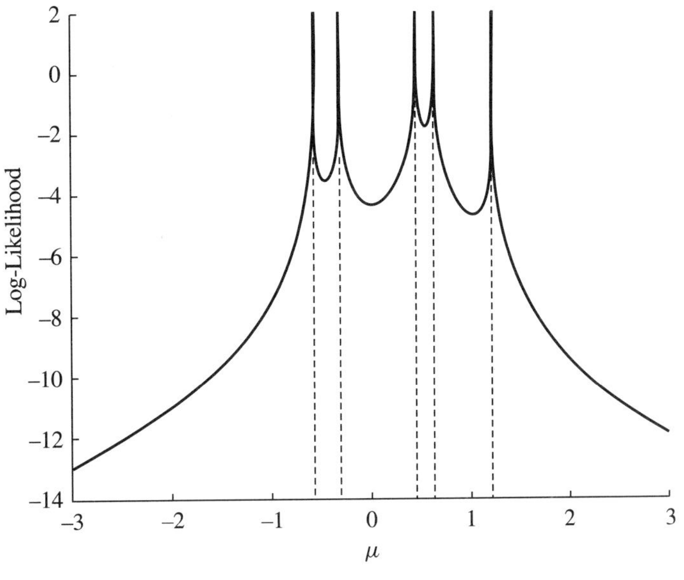

Figure 18.5 Unbounded log-likelihood function allowing linear heteroskedasticity.

We will now show that there are maxima of $L(\mu, \mathbf{\Omega})$ that yield infinite values of L. Take any initial values of $\boldsymbol{\gamma}$, say γ_{11} and γ_{12}, such that $\sigma_n^2 \equiv \gamma_1 + \gamma_2 z_n > 0$ for all observations and

$$j = \underset{n:1 \leq n \leq N}{\text{argmin}}\ \gamma_{11} + \gamma_{12} z_n$$

is unique. If we set $\mu = y_j$ so that the jth residual is exactly zero then, as we lower the initial value of γ_{11} toward $-\gamma_{12} z_j$, the log-likelihood function grows without bound. This occurs because the $\log[2\pi(\gamma_{11} + \gamma_{12} z_j)]$ is exploding while $(y_j - \mu)^2/(\gamma_{11} + \gamma_{12} z_j) = 0$ for all γ_{11}. All the other σ_n^2 are also getting smaller, but they are not approaching zero so that the rest of the log-likelihood function remains finite.

Figure 18.5 depicts an example of such a log-likelihood function. This function has the variance parameters γ_1 and γ_2 concentrated out, leaving poles in the function for various values of μ.

This is a general failure of linear models of heteroskedasticity.[32] We would like to rule out such phenomena on the grounds that a variance is approaching zero, the lower bound for variances and not a credible value. Unless we can bound $\sigma_n^2 = \gamma_1 + \gamma_2 z_n$, such maxima will always occur. To do that in this example requires not only bounds on $\boldsymbol{\gamma}$ but also on z_n.

For the model of this chapter, these comments are conditional on $(\mathbf{x}_n, \mathbf{z}_n)$, but we must also find that the expected values of the log-likelihood function and its derivatives over $(\mathbf{x}_n, \mathbf{z}_n)$ are dominated. There is an additional issue here because the $h(\mathbf{z}_n'\boldsymbol{\gamma})$ terms in the log-likelihood, score, Hessian, and conditional information present the possibility that their expectations may not exist even though the moments of $\mathbf{z}_n$ are finite and $\mathbf{\Theta}$ is closed and bounded.

The simplest approach is to be able to assume that $h(\mathbf{z}_n'\boldsymbol{\gamma})$ is uniformly bounded below by a strictly positive number. This is analogous to the bound that would be placed on the variance under i.i.d. normal sampling.[33] This along with uniform bounds on the expectations of various functions of $\mathbf{x}_n$ and $\mathbf{z}_n$ will do the job. To write these out would merely restate the assumptions of Chapter 14 in their particular form for the conditional normal model that we are studying. We will not give general primitive conditions here to guarantee that these expectations exist because that is beyond our scope. In practice, researchers often adopt the general assumptions of Chapter 14 directly without considering the implied constraints on the data-generating process.

18.7.5 Asymptotic Theory for Heteroskedasticity

We have discussed the asymptotic distribution of the MLE for i.i.d. sampling of $(y_n, \mathbf{x}_n, \mathbf{z}_n)$, allowing only *conditional* heteroskedasticity. It is possible and desirable to permit more heterogeneity in the data-generating process than this. Both the law of large numbers (LLN) and the central limit theorem (CLT) generalize to sums of independently *not* identically distributed (i.n.i.d.) random variables. Provided that the distributions are not *too* different, similar results hold.

---

[32] Such failures also arise with the multiplicative model of heteroskedasticity. See Crisp and Burridge (1994).

[33] See Exercise 15.1.

Theorem 13 (Chebychev's LLN) *Let $\{U_n\}$ be a sequence of independent random variables such that* $E[U_n] = \mu_n$, $\text{Var}[U_n] \equiv \sigma_n^2$ *exist* $(n = 1, 2, 3, \ldots)$. *Denote*

$$E_N[\mu] \equiv \frac{1}{N}\sum_{n=1}^{N}\mu_n$$

$$E_N[\sigma^2] \equiv \frac{1}{N}\sum_{n=1}^{N}\sigma_n^2$$

If

$$\lim_{N\to\infty}\frac{1}{N}E_N[\sigma^2] = 0 \tag{18.26}$$

then $E_N[U] - E_N[\mu] \xrightarrow{p} 0$ *as* $N \to \infty$.

The proof of this lemma is identical to the previous, simpler version (Theorem 8, p. 262). The condition (18.26) limits the heterogeneity of the second moments. It is equivalent to requiring that the variance of $E_N[U]$ converges to zero asymptotically, which is the key to the LLN. Note that if the σ_n^2 are uniformly bounded, then this condition is satisfied. With this lemma, we can extend our asymptotic theory for the OLS estimator and the WLS estimator to situations in which the conditioning variables **x** and **z** are fixed or sampling distributions are not identical for some reason. The CLT has i.n.i.d. forms also:

Theorem 14 (Liapounov CLT) *Let $\{U_n\}$ be a sequence of i.n.i.d. random variables where* $E[U_n] = \mu_n$, $\text{Var}[U_n] = \sigma_n^2 > \epsilon > 0$, *and* $E[|U_n - \mu_n|^3] = \gamma_n$ *all exist. If*

$$\lim_{N\to\infty}\frac{\left(\sum_{n=1}^{N}\gamma_n\right)^{1/3}}{\left(\sum_{n=1}^{N}\sigma_n^2\right)^{1/2}} = 0$$

then

$$\sqrt{N}\frac{E_N[U-\mu]}{\sqrt{E_N[\sigma^2]}} \xrightarrow{d} \mathfrak{N}(0,1)$$

We will not prove this CLT, but note that one proof method is similar to the one we give in Section D.5.3 for Theorem 9 (Lindberg–Levy CLT, p. 265).[34] Note once again that this CLT allows for heterogeneity within certain bounds. The third absolute moments of the distribution cannot be too large relative to the second (absolute) moments. This has the effect of preventing the tails of the p.d.f.s from being too fat and preventing a few observations from dominating the distribution of the sum.

[34] Chung (1974) provides a proof of the Liapounov CLT.

We will illustrate the application of these results with the OLS estimator in the presence of heteroskedasticity. Suppose that the $\mathbf{x}_n$ are not random variables, but that $\lim_{N\to\infty} N^{-1}\cdot\mathbf{X}'\mathbf{X} = \mathbf{D}_1$ and

$$\lim_{N\to\infty} \frac{1}{N} \sum_{n=1}^{N} h(\mathbf{z}_n'\boldsymbol{\gamma}) \cdot \mathbf{x}_n\mathbf{x}_n' = \mathbf{D}_2(\boldsymbol{\gamma})$$

where $\mathbf{D}_1$ and $\mathbf{D}_2(\boldsymbol{\gamma})$ are finite positive definite matrices. Then

$$\frac{1}{N} \cdot \mathbf{X}'(\mathbf{y} - \mathbf{X}\boldsymbol{\beta}_0) = \mathrm{E}_N[\mathbf{x}_n(y_n - \mathbf{x}_n'\boldsymbol{\beta}_0)] \xrightarrow{p} \mathbf{0}$$

by Chebychev's LLN, so that

$$\hat{\boldsymbol{\beta}}_{\text{OLS}} - \boldsymbol{\beta}_0 = \left(\frac{1}{N} \cdot \mathbf{X}'\mathbf{X}\right)^{-1} \frac{1}{N} \cdot \mathbf{X}'(\mathbf{y} - \mathbf{X}\boldsymbol{\beta}_0) \xrightarrow{p} \mathbf{0}$$

and $\hat{\boldsymbol{\beta}}_{\text{OLS}}$ is a consistent estimator of $\boldsymbol{\beta}_0$.

To obtain asymptotic normality for $\hat{\boldsymbol{\beta}}_{\text{OLS}}$, we will require additional moment restrictions. The third absolute moment of the $\mathfrak{N}(0, \sigma^2)$ distribution is $\sigma^3\sqrt{8/\pi}$. Therefore, if

$$\lim_{N\to\infty} \frac{1}{N} \sum_{n=1}^{N} h(\mathbf{z}_n'\boldsymbol{\gamma})^{3/2} \left|x_{ni}x_{nj}x_{nk}\right| = D_{3,ijk}(\boldsymbol{\gamma})$$

exists for all i, j, k, then

$$\frac{\left[\sum_{n=1}^{N} (\mathbf{c}'\mathbf{x}_n)^3 \sigma_{0n}^3\right]^{1/3}}{\left[\sum_{n=1}^{N} (\mathbf{c}'\mathbf{x}_n)^2 \sigma_{0n}^2\right]^{1/2}} = \frac{O(N^{1/3})}{O(N^{1/2})} = O(N^{-1/6})$$

Applying Liapounov's CLT for a $\mathbf{c} \in \mathbb{R}^K$,

$$\sqrt{N}\frac{\mathbf{c}'\,\mathrm{E}_N[\mathbf{x}_n(y_n - \mathbf{x}_n'\boldsymbol{\beta}_0)]}{\sqrt{\mathbf{c}'\,\mathrm{E}_N[\mathbf{x}_n\sigma_{n0}^2\mathbf{x}_n']\mathbf{c}}} \xrightarrow{d} \mathfrak{N}(0, 1)$$

so that

$$(\mathbf{X}'\boldsymbol{\Omega}_0\mathbf{X})^{-1/2}\mathbf{X}'(\mathbf{y} - \mathbf{X}\boldsymbol{\beta}_0) \xrightarrow{d} \mathfrak{N}(\mathbf{0}, \mathbf{I})$$

If

$$\frac{1}{N} \cdot \mathbf{X}'\hat{\boldsymbol{\Omega}}X \xrightarrow{p} \mathbf{D}_2(\boldsymbol{\gamma}_0)$$

for some estimator $\mathbf{X}'\hat{\boldsymbol{\Omega}}\,\mathbf{X}$ of $\mathbf{X}'\boldsymbol{\Omega}_0\mathbf{X}$, then

$$(\mathbf{X}'\hat{\boldsymbol{\Omega}}X)^{-1/2}\mathbf{X}'\mathbf{X}(\hat{\boldsymbol{\beta}}_{\text{OLS}} - \boldsymbol{\beta}_0) - (\mathbf{X}'\boldsymbol{\Omega}_0\mathbf{X})^{-1/2}\mathbf{X}'(\mathbf{y} - \mathbf{X}\boldsymbol{\beta}_0) \xrightarrow{p} \mathbf{0}$$

and we treat $\hat{\boldsymbol{\beta}}_{\text{OLS}}$ as approximately $\mathfrak{N}[\boldsymbol{\beta}_0, (\mathbf{X}'\mathbf{X})^{-1}\mathbf{X}'\hat{\boldsymbol{\Omega}}X(\mathbf{X}'\mathbf{X})^{-1}]$.

Similar arguments apply to the FGLS and ML estimators. Note also that this argument does not rest on the assumption that y_n is conditionally normally distributed. All of these estimators may be consistent and asymptotically normal, even when the normal distributional assumption does not hold. For the moment, we are motivating our estimators as MLEs based on the normal distribution. But in Chapter 21 we will drop the normality assumption entirely, taking advantage of this observation.

18.8 OVERVIEW

1. Heteroskedasticity occurs when the variances of y_n conditional on $\mathbf{X}$ are not constant. This is an exception to the second-moment property that $\boldsymbol{\Omega}_0 \equiv \text{Var}[\mathbf{y} \mid \mathbf{X}]$ is a scalar matrix. Heteroskedasticity is a common concern in cross-sectional data, but it can arise in time-series data as well. One often models heteroskedasticity in terms of observable variables, denoted by $\mathbf{z}_n$, which are functions of $\mathbf{x}_n$.
2. As an exception to the classical second-moments assumption, heteroskedasticity generally removes second-moment properties of ordinary least squares (OLS) and properties that rest on them. The variance of the OLS estimator $\hat{\boldsymbol{\beta}}_{\text{OLS}}$ is misestimated, $\hat{\boldsymbol{\beta}}_{\text{OLS}}$ is not efficient relative to other linear and unbiased estimators, and test statistics are no longer pivotal.
3. Nevertheless, some important OLS properties are preserved by heteroskedasticity. The $\hat{\boldsymbol{\beta}}_{\text{OLS}}$ remains unbiased because this behavior rests on the first-moment assumption. Similarly, consistency of the estimator is preserved. This estimator remains conditionally normally distributed also, because $\hat{\boldsymbol{\beta}}_{\text{OLS}}$ is still a linear function of normally distributed random variables.
4. There are tests for heteroskedasticity constructed from the OLS fitted residuals. The Goldfeld–Quandt test is a generalization of the classical test for different variances in two independently distributed samples. The Breusch–Pagan test is a score test computed by OLS regression of the squared OLS fitted residuals on the $\mathbf{z}_n$ variables hypothesized to explain the heteroskedasticity.
5. The Eicker–White variance estimator is consistent for the asymptotic variance matrix of $\hat{\boldsymbol{\beta}}_{\text{OLS}}$ even when the heteroskedasticity has an unspecified form. This variance estimator is constructed by replacing the unknown variances in the correct formula for the conditional variance with squared OLS fitted residuals. In part, the estimator works because implicitly it is a function only of the unknown slope coefficients, which are estimated consistently by OLS.
6. The relatively efficient linear unbiased estimator is a weighted least squares (WLS) procedure in which each observation $(y_n, \mathbf{x}_n, \mathbf{z}_n)$ is weighted (divided) by the conditional standard deviation σ_{0n} of y_n given $\mathbf{x}_n$ and $\mathbf{z}_n$: $[(1/\sigma_{0n})y_n, (1/\sigma_{0n}) \cdot \mathbf{x}_n]$. This is actually just OLS applied to a regression equation transformed to satisfy the assumptions of the classical linear model.
7. The WLS estimator is a special case of the generalized least squares (GLS), or Aitken, estimator

$$\hat{\boldsymbol{\beta}}_{\text{GLS}} \equiv \left(\mathbf{X}'\boldsymbol{\Omega}_0^{-1}\mathbf{X}\right)^{-1} \mathbf{X}'\boldsymbol{\Omega}_0^{-1}\mathbf{y}$$

8. When $\boldsymbol{\Omega}_0$ is unknown, but one specifies a parametric heteroskedasticity model

$$\text{Var}[y_n \mid \mathbf{x}_n, \mathbf{z}_n] = h(\mathbf{z}_n, \boldsymbol{\gamma}_0)$$

   the maximum likelihood estimator (MLE) is a feasible version of $\hat{\boldsymbol{\beta}}_{\text{WLS}}$:

$$\hat{\boldsymbol{\beta}}_{\text{ML}} \equiv \left(\mathbf{X}'\hat{\boldsymbol{\Omega}}_{\text{ML}}^{-1}\mathbf{X}\right)^{-1} \mathbf{X}'\hat{\boldsymbol{\Omega}}_{\text{ML}}^{-1}\mathbf{y}$$

   where $\hat{\boldsymbol{\Omega}}_{\text{ML}}$ contains the fitted variances $h(\mathbf{z}_n, \hat{\boldsymbol{\gamma}}_{\text{ML}})$ for the MLE $\hat{\boldsymbol{\gamma}}_{\text{ML}}$.
9. The linearized MLE (LMLE) that is asymptotically equivalent to the MLE is also a feasible GLS (FGLS) estimator:

$$\hat{\boldsymbol{\beta}}_{\text{LML}} = \left(\mathbf{X}'\check{\boldsymbol{\Omega}}^{-1}\mathbf{X}\right)^{-1}\mathbf{X}'\check{\boldsymbol{\Omega}}^{-1}\mathbf{y}$$

Both the MLE and the LMLE are asymptotically equivalent to the GLS estimator because the information matrix is block-diagonal in the $\boldsymbol{\beta}$ and $\boldsymbol{\gamma}$ parameter vectors. Asymptotically, the estimation of these parameters breaks up into separate problems (given an initial consistent estimator).

10. In several popular specifications for the heteroskedasticity, a consistent estimator of $\boldsymbol{\gamma}_0$ is an OLS regression analogous to the Breusch–Pagan score test regression.

18.9 EXERCISES

18.9.1 Review

18.1 (WLS) Weighted least squares puts more weight on observations with less conditional variance, thereby decreasing the sampling variance of the OLS estimator.

(a) Confirm this for the case of simple regression using two observations: let $\mathrm{E}[y_n \mid x_n] = \beta_0 x_n$, $\mathrm{Var}[y_n \mid x_n] = \sigma_{0n}^2$, $n = 1, 2$. Show, using calculus, that among estimators

$$\hat{\beta} = \frac{\sum_{n=1}^{2} w_n^2 x_n y_n}{\sum_{n=1}^{2} w_n^2 x_n^2} = \underset{\beta}{\text{argmin}} \sum_{n=1}^{2} w_n \left(y_n - \beta x_n\right)^2$$

a $\hat{\beta}$ with the smallest conditional variance sets $w_n = 1/\sigma_{0n}$.

(b) However, merely putting *relatively more* weight on the observation with smaller σ_{0n}^2 does not necessarily decrease the variance of a $\hat{\beta}$ relative to OLS. Suppose that $\sigma_{01}^2 < \sigma_{02}^2$. Find a ratio w_1/w_2 that yields the same sampling variance for $\hat{\beta}$ as OLS.

(c) Given σ_{01}/σ_{02}, show that the ratio w_1/w_2 is increasing in x_1/x_2. Try to explain why this is so.

18.2 (OLS) Let $\mathrm{E}[\mathbf{y} \mid \mathbf{X}] = \mathbf{X}\boldsymbol{\beta}_0$ and $\mathrm{Var}[\mathbf{y} \mid \mathbf{X}] = \boldsymbol{\Omega}_0$ where $\boldsymbol{\beta}_0 \in \mathbb{R}^K$ and $\mathbf{X}$ is full-row rank.

(a) Find the conditional variance matrix of $\hat{\boldsymbol{\mu}}_{\text{OLS}} \equiv \mathbf{P}_{\mathbf{X}}\mathbf{y}$ given $\mathbf{X}$.

(b) Also find $\mathrm{Var}[\mathbf{y} - \hat{\boldsymbol{\mu}}_{\text{OLS}} \mid \mathbf{X}]$.

(c) Show that $\mathbf{y} - \hat{\boldsymbol{\mu}}_{\text{OLS}}$ and $\hat{\boldsymbol{\mu}}_{\text{OLS}}$ are generally correlated.

18.3 (OLS) Let $\mathrm{E}[\mathbf{y} \mid \mathbf{X}] = \mathbf{X}\boldsymbol{\beta}_0$ and $\mathrm{Var}[\mathbf{y} \mid \mathbf{X}] = \boldsymbol{\Omega}_0$ where $\boldsymbol{\beta}_0 \in \mathbb{R}^K$, $\mathbf{X}$ is full-row rank, and $\boldsymbol{\Omega}_0$ is nonsingular. Show that for all $\mathbf{c} \in \mathbb{R}^K$,

$$\begin{aligned}&\mathrm{Var}[\mathbf{c}'\hat{\boldsymbol{\beta}}_{\text{OLS}} \mid \mathbf{X}] - \mathrm{Var}[\mathbf{c}'\hat{\boldsymbol{\beta}}_{\text{GLS}} \mid \mathbf{X}]\\ &= \mathbf{c}'\left[(\mathbf{X}'\mathbf{X})^{-1}\mathbf{X}'\boldsymbol{\Omega}_0\mathbf{X}(\mathbf{X}'\mathbf{X})^{-1} - (\mathbf{X}'\boldsymbol{\Omega}_0^{-1}\mathbf{X})^{-1}\right]\mathbf{c} \geq 0\end{aligned}$$

directly from these expressions for the variance matrices. (HINT: Use the Cholesky decomposition of $\boldsymbol{\Omega}_0$ to express this difference in terms of an orthogonal projection matrix.)

18.4 (Eicker–White Variance Estimator) Explain why the presence of conditional heteroskedasticity in log-wages suggested by the score test (p. 418 and Example 18.4) implies that our test for equal coefficients in Example 11.1 may be faulty. Formulate and execute an alternative test based on the same unrestricted OLS estimators of the coefficients as in Table 4.1 and the Eicker–White estimator for their variance matrices.

18.5 (Partitioned Fit) Find the generalized partitioned regression formula for the GLS estimator of $\mathrm{E}[\mathbf{y}\,|\,\mathbf{X}] = \mathbf{X}_1\boldsymbol{\beta}_1 + \mathbf{X}_2\boldsymbol{\beta}_2$ where $\mathrm{Var}[\mathbf{y}\,|\,\mathbf{X}] = \boldsymbol{\Omega}_0$.

18.6 (Restricted GLS) Show that the restricted GLS estimator, subject to the restriction $\mathbf{R}\boldsymbol{\beta}_0 = \mathbf{r}$, is

$$\hat{\boldsymbol{\beta}}_{\mathrm{RGLS}} = \hat{\boldsymbol{\beta}}_{\mathrm{GLS}} - (\mathbf{X}'\boldsymbol{\Omega}_0^{-1}\mathbf{X})^{-1}\mathbf{R}'[\mathbf{R}(\mathbf{X}'\boldsymbol{\Omega}_0^{-1}\mathbf{X})^{-1}\mathbf{R}']^{-1}(\mathbf{R}\hat{\boldsymbol{\beta}}_{\mathrm{GLS}} - \mathbf{r})$$

18.7 Let $\mathrm{E}[\mathbf{y}\,|\,\mathbf{X}] = \mathbf{X}\boldsymbol{\beta}_0$ and $\mathrm{Var}[\mathbf{y}\,|\,\mathbf{X}] = \boldsymbol{\Omega}_0$. Show that

$$\mathrm{E}[s^2\,|\,\mathbf{X}] = \frac{\mathrm{tr}[(\mathbf{I} - \mathbf{P}_{\mathbf{X}})\boldsymbol{\Omega}_0]}{N - K}$$

(HINT: Use the approach in Exercise 8.8.)

18.8 (Projection) According to (18.14), the GLS projector is

$$\mathbf{P}_{\mathbf{X}\perp\boldsymbol{\Omega}_0^{-1}\mathbf{X}} = \mathbf{X}\left(\mathbf{X}'\boldsymbol{\Omega}_0^{-1}\mathbf{X}\right)^{-1}\mathbf{X}'\boldsymbol{\Omega}_0^{-1}$$

Show that for any matrix $\boldsymbol{\Lambda}$ such that $\mathrm{Col}(\boldsymbol{\Lambda}\mathbf{X}) = \mathrm{Col}(\boldsymbol{\Omega}_0^{-1}\mathbf{X})$ it follows that $\mathbf{P}_{\mathbf{X}\perp\boldsymbol{\Lambda}\mathbf{X}} = \mathbf{P}_{\mathbf{X}\perp\boldsymbol{\Omega}_0^{-1}\mathbf{X}}$ so that in general other weight matrices besides $\boldsymbol{\Omega}_0^{-1}$ yield the GLS projector.

18.9 (Relative Efficiency) Let $\mathrm{E}[\mathbf{y}\,|\,\mathbf{X}] = \mathbf{X}\boldsymbol{\beta}_0$ and $\mathrm{Var}[\mathbf{y}\,|\,\mathbf{X}] = \boldsymbol{\Omega}_0$ where $\boldsymbol{\beta}_0 \in \mathbb{R}^K$, $\mathbf{X}$ is full-row rank, and $\boldsymbol{\Omega}_0$ is nonsingular. Show that the RLS estimator $\hat{\boldsymbol{\beta}}_{\mathrm{R}}$ is not generally efficient relative to the OLS estimator $\hat{\boldsymbol{\beta}}$.

18.9.2 Extensions

18.10 (Recursive Residuals) How could one use the recursive residuals described in Exercises 8.15, 8.16, 9.9, and 10.9 to test the null hypothesis of homoskedasticity against the alternative in Example 18.3? Is your test equivalent to the one in the example?

18.11 (Singular Variance) Suppose that the variance matrix $\boldsymbol{\Omega}_0$ is singular. Show that the GLS estimator is

$$(\mathbf{X}'\boldsymbol{\Omega}_0^{-}\mathbf{X})^{-1}\mathbf{X}'\boldsymbol{\Omega}_0^{-}\mathbf{y} = \underset{\boldsymbol{\beta}}{\mathrm{argmin}}(\mathbf{y} - \mathbf{X}\boldsymbol{\beta})'\boldsymbol{\Omega}_0^{-}(\mathbf{y} - \mathbf{X}\boldsymbol{\beta})$$

provided that $\mathbf{X}'\boldsymbol{\Omega}_0^{-}\mathbf{X}$ is nonsingular.

18.12 (FGLS) Suppose that $\mathrm{E}[y_n\,|\,\mathbf{x}_n] = \mathbf{x}_n'\boldsymbol{\beta}_0$ and $\mathrm{Var}[y_n\,|\,\mathbf{x}_n] = \left(\mathbf{z}_n'\boldsymbol{\gamma}_0\right)^2$ where $\left|\mathbf{z}_n'\boldsymbol{\gamma}_0\right| > a > 0$ for all possible $\mathbf{z}_n$ $(n = 1, \ldots, N)$. Also suppose that conditional on $\{[\mathbf{x}_n', \mathbf{z}_n']'\}$ the $\{y_n\}$ are independent and normally distributed. Let $w_n(\boldsymbol{\beta}) \equiv (y_n - \mathbf{x}_n'\boldsymbol{\beta})^2$. Consider the two-step FGLS estimator that regresses $\left|w_n(\hat{\boldsymbol{\beta}}_{\mathrm{OLS}})\right|$ on $\mathbf{z}_n$ in the first step to fit $\check{\boldsymbol{\gamma}}$ and replaces $\boldsymbol{\gamma}_0$ with $\check{\boldsymbol{\gamma}}$ in $\hat{\boldsymbol{\beta}}_{\mathrm{WLS}}$ in the second step.[35]

(a) Show that

$$\mathrm{E}[|w_n(\boldsymbol{\beta}_0)|\,|\,\mathbf{x}_n, \mathbf{z}_n] = \alpha \cdot \mathbf{z}_n'\boldsymbol{\gamma}_0$$

and find α.

(b) Argue that the OLS regression of $|w_n(\boldsymbol{\beta}_0)|$ on $\mathbf{z}_n$ will estimate $\boldsymbol{\gamma}_0$ up to a scalar factor of proportionality. Give conditions so that this is also true for $\check{\boldsymbol{\gamma}}$.

[35] See Harvey (1976).

(c) In general, $\check{\gamma}$ is an inconsistent estimator of γ_0. How does this affect the asymptotic relative efficiency of the FGLS estimator described above?

(d) Suggest a consistent estimator of the asymptotic variance of this FGLS estimator that uses OLS software output.

***18.13 (Two-Step Estimation)** Suppose that $\mathrm{E}[y_n \mid \mathbf{x}_n] = \mathbf{x}_n'\boldsymbol{\beta}_0$ and $\mathrm{Var}[y_n \mid \mathbf{x}_n] = \sigma_0^2 \left(\mathbf{x}_n'\boldsymbol{\beta}_0\right)^2$ so that the conditional variance of y_n increases with the magnitude of its conditional mean. Also suppose that conditional on $\{\mathbf{x}_n\}$ the $\{y_n\}$ are independent and normally distributed. Describe an efficient two-step estimator of $\boldsymbol{\beta}_0$ and show thereby that FGLS is relatively inefficient. Explain the source of inefficiency.

18.14 (Nonlinear Least Squares) Reconsider the NLS estimator of Exercise 16.13. Suppose that $\{(y_n, \mathbf{x}_n, \mathbf{z}_n)\,,\ n = 1, \ldots, N\}$ are i.i.d. random variables and that the conditional distribution of y_n given $\mathbf{x}_n$ and $\mathbf{z}_n$ is $\mathfrak{N}[\mu(\boldsymbol{\beta}_0; \mathbf{x}_n),\ h(\mathbf{z}_n'\boldsymbol{\gamma}_0)]$.

(a) Give sufficient conditions so that the NLS estimator $\hat{\boldsymbol{\beta}}_{\mathrm{NLS}}$ for $\boldsymbol{\beta}_0$ is still consistent.

(b) How might you estimate the asymptotic variance of $\hat{\boldsymbol{\beta}}_{\mathrm{NLS}}$ without specifying $h(\cdot)$?

(c) Write out the log-likelihood and show that the MLE for $\boldsymbol{\beta}_0$ is a weighted NLS estimator.

(d) What is the asymptotic variance of $\hat{\boldsymbol{\beta}}_{\mathrm{ML}}$?

18.15 (Liapounov CLT) Proposition 15 (Asymptotic Distribution of OLS, p. 257) assumes that the $\mathbf{x}_n$ $(n = 1, \ldots, N)$ are i.i.d. Suppose instead that the $\mathbf{x}_n$ are deterministic such that

$$\lim_{N\to\infty} \frac{1}{N} \cdot \mathbf{X}'\mathbf{X} = \mathbf{D},$$

where $\mathbf{D}$ is a finite, nonsingular matrix. Let the $y_n - \mathbf{x}_n'\boldsymbol{\beta}_0$ be i.i.d. random variables with mean zero and variance σ_0^2. Use the Liapounov CLT (Theorem 14) to show that $\sqrt{N}\left(\hat{\boldsymbol{\beta}}_{\mathrm{OLS}} - \boldsymbol{\beta}_0\right)$ is asymptotically normal. State any additional assumptions that you require.

CHAPTER 19

SERIAL CORRELATION

Another way in which the conditional variance matrix of **y** may not be a scalar matrix (Assumption 7.1) is for the off-diagonal elements to be nonzero. These are the conditional covariances among the elements of **y** given **X**. One of the principal contexts in which nonzero covariances seem likely is time series data. This is by no means the only setting in which econometricians model covariances, but it is a natural one to introduce.

We have already emphasized the importance of covariance in linear prediction. The MMSE linear predictor of one random variable given a set of other random variables is a function of the covariance parameters. For multiviarate normal random variables, the MMSE linear predictor is the conditional mean, the MMSE predictor. We will show how this function plays a central role in the regression analysis of a time series that is serially correlated.

In broad terms, the questions that we answer in this chapter are identical to those of the previous one:

1. What effects does serial correlation have on OLS statistics?
2. How can we detect serial correlation?
3. What corrections can we make to our OLS procedures?
4. What is the ML alternative to OLS if we decide that serial correlation is present?

And in broad terms, the answers are essentially the same: the second-moment properties of OLS, and those that rest on them, all fail. Following a description of estimation of the Phillips curve, we answer these questions in detail.

19.1 THE PHILLIPS CURVE

In empirical macroeconomic research, the relationship between inflation and unemployment is one of the most studied. This relationship played a key role in theory and policy during the early 1960s after Phillips (1958) demonstrated a stable negative association between unemployment and inflation of wages in the United Kingdom over almost 100 years. Following Phillips, other researchers found a similar relationship between unemployment and general price inflation, which came to be called the *Phillips curve*.[1]

However, the apparent trade-off between unemployment and inflation failed abruptly in the United States in the early 1970s when both inflation and unemployment climbed together.[2] Friedman (1968) and Phelps (1968) predicted this sort of failure, arguing that in the long run the unemployment rate will return to its equilibrium, or *natural*, rate—a rate that does not depend on such nominal variables as inflation. This reasoning led to the *expectations-augmented Phillips curve*. In the short run, this specification allows a trade-off between inflation and unemployment because expectations about inflation may fail to anticipate supply shocks to the economy. But in the long run, unemployment is fixed at the natural rate.

To estimate the natural rate of unemployment, we will follow the general approach described in Staiger et al. (1996, 1997). We parameterize the expectations-augmented Phillips curve as

$$\mathrm{E}[\dot{p}_t \,|\, t-1] = \dot{p}_t^{\mathrm{e}} + \gamma_{01}\,(n_{t-1} - \bar{n}_0) + \mathbf{w}_t'\boldsymbol{\gamma}_{02}$$

where $\dot{p}_t$ is inflation, $\dot{p}_t^{\mathrm{e}}$ is the rate of inflation expected in time period $t-1$ for period t, n_{t-1} is the unemployment rate in the previous time period, and $\mathbf{w}_t$ is a vector of additional variables that measures supply shocks. The $\mathrm{E}[\cdot\,|\,t-1]$ notation refers to the expected value conditional on all variables realized in or before period $t-1$. The natural rate of unemployment is $\bar{n}_0$: in long-run equilibrium, there are no supply shocks ($\mathbf{w}_t = \mathbf{0}$) and $\mathrm{E}[\dot{p}_t \,|\, t-1] = \dot{p}_t^{\mathrm{e}}$ so that

$$0 = \gamma_{01}\,(n_{t-1} - \bar{n}_0) \qquad \Leftrightarrow \qquad n_{t-1} = \bar{n}_0$$

for all periods. Interest focuses on the value of $\bar{n}_0$ and the speed of adjustment γ_{01}.

One must provide an empirical specification for $\dot{p}_t^{\mathrm{e}}$, the expectations about inflation. A simple and reasonable starting place is to specify that $\dot{p}_t^{\mathrm{e}} = \dot{p}_{t-1}$; that is, expected future inflation is today's inflation. Using this model, one can apply OLS to the estimation of

$$\mathrm{E}[\dot{p}_t - \dot{p}_{t-1} \,|\, t-1] = -\gamma_{01}\bar{n}_0 + \gamma_{01}n_{t-1} + \mathbf{w}_t'\boldsymbol{\gamma}_{02} = \mathbf{x}_t'\boldsymbol{\beta}_0 \tag{19.1}$$

where $\mathbf{x}_t = [1, n_{t-1}, \mathbf{w}_t']'$ and $\boldsymbol{\beta}_0 = [-\gamma_{01}\bar{n}_0, \gamma_{01}, \boldsymbol{\gamma}_{02}']'$.

To estimate the slope coefficients, we use U.S. data from the Bureau of Labor Statistics (BLS).[3] Following Staiger et al. (1996), the sample period for the estimates is 1955:1 (January 1955) to 1994:12 (December 1994) and the supply shock variables are an indicator variable for Nixon-era price controls (*nixon*) and a lagged index of the producer price indexes for food and energy (*pfe*). The OLS estimation results are

$$\dot{p}_t - \dot{p}_{t-1} = \underset{(0.650)}{0.185} - \underset{(0.105)}{0.030}\, n_{t-1} + \underset{(0.0057)}{0.0057}\, pfe_t + \underset{(0.979)}{0.294}\, nixon_t + \hat{\varepsilon}_t \tag{19.2}$$

The precision of the parameter estimates is quite low. Indeed, an F test for the null hypothesis that the slope coefficients are all zero has a probability value equal to 0.723, suggesting that there is no evidence to reject that hypothesis.

The ratio $-\beta_{01}/\beta_{02} \equiv \bar{n}_0$ is the natural rate of unemployment. The corresponding ratio of estimated slope coefficients, which equals 6.174, is a consistent estimator. The estimated standard

[1] For example, see Samuelson and Solow (1960), Lipsey and Parkin (1970), and Gordon (1990).

[2] Okun (1980, p. 166) commented, "Since 1970 the Phillips curve has become an unidentifed flying object and has eluded all econometric efforts to nail it down."

[3] James Stock and Mark Watson kindly provided the data set, as well as advice about estimating the NAIRU. For further information about the data, see Staiger et al. (1997).

error based on the delta method is a whopping 42.966, but, because a confidence interval for β_{02} contains zero, this asymptotic approximation is doubtful.[4] Indeed, a 95% confidence interval for $\bar{n}_0$ based on the LR does not exist in this case.[5]

But more fundamentally, the classical regression assumptions are also doubtful. In particular, it is likely that the changes in inflation are correlated over the monthly observations, even when their distribution is conditional on these explanatory variables. The estimated Phillips curve has left much unexplained: the R^2 goodness-of-fit statistic is only 0.3%. Surely economic conditions over a period of several months are similar enough that their effects will persist over that time period. We have already seen in Chapter 3 that the unemployment rate follows short-run trends.

To investigate the possibility that changes in inflation are correlated conditional on the explanatory variables, we turn again to the OLS fitted residuals $\hat{\varepsilon}_t \equiv y_t - \mathbf{x}_t'\hat{\boldsymbol{\beta}}$. Ideally, we would use the population residuals $y_t - \mathbf{x}_t'\boldsymbol{\beta}_0$, but these are not observable. Taking the OLS fitted residuals as substitutes, we find the sample correlations -0.498 for $\hat{\varepsilon}_t$ and $\hat{\varepsilon}_{t-1}$, 0.093 for $\hat{\varepsilon}_t$ and $\hat{\varepsilon}_{t-2}$, and -0.093 for $\hat{\varepsilon}_t$ and $\hat{\varepsilon}_{t-3}$. Although one should expect some correlation among OLS fitted residuals, we will show in this chapter that these correlations are strong evidence against the hypothesis that the analogous correlations among the population residuals are zero.

Supposing that there is correlation among the observations over time, then the OLS estimates have misleading estimated standard errors and a relatively efficient feasible estimator may be available. Correcting the standard errors or using another estimator may improve the apparent precision of the OLS estimates above. To do this, we must specify a model for the correlation. One of the most convenient specifications, which we explain shortly as *first-order autocorrelation*, leads us to estimate a linear regression of the OLS fitted residuals $\hat{\varepsilon}_t$ on its lagged value $\hat{\varepsilon}_{t-1}$. In the current case, that fitted regression is

$$\hat{\varepsilon}_t = -\underset{(0.0397)}{0.498}\,\hat{\varepsilon}_{t-1} + \hat{v}_t \tag{19.3}$$

where the OLS estimate of the standard error appears in parentheses below the OLS fitted coefficient. This regression is analogous to the squared OLS fitted residual regression introduced to investigate heteroskedasticity. The standard t test for whether the population coefficient is zero is a score test for nonzero first-order autocorrelation. This score test clearly rejects that null hypothesis.

In a further analogy with the steps for coping with potential heteroskedasticity, we use the estimated autocorrelation coefficient in this regression for OLS fitted residuals to correct for first-order autocorrelation. Rather than reweighting the observations, the appropriate transformation of the original regression equation is the *quasi first difference*

$$y_{*t} \equiv y_t - \hat{\phi} y_{t-1} = \left(\mathbf{x}_t - \hat{\phi}\cdot\mathbf{x}_{t-1}\right)'\boldsymbol{\beta} + \varepsilon_t - \hat{\phi}\varepsilon_{t-1} = \mathbf{x}_{*t}'\boldsymbol{\beta} + \varepsilon_{*t}$$

where $\hat{\phi} = -0.498$. The OLS estimates of this equation are

$$y_{*t} = \underset{(0.376)}{0.214}\left(1 - \hat{\phi}\right) - \underset{(0.061)}{0.035}\,n_{*t-1} + \underset{(0.0044)}{0.0147}\,pfe_{*t} + \underset{(0.575)}{0.136}\,nixon_{*t} + \hat{\varepsilon}_{*t} \tag{19.4}$$

The precision of the parameter estimates remains low, but it has improved substantially, although the F test for the null hypothesis that the slope coefficients are all zero now has a probability

[4] This interval corresponds to the Wald test statistic interval in equation (17.36) (p. 408).

[5] See equation (17.37) for the confidence interval constructed with the concentrated likelihood ratio test statistic. In this case, the concentrated log-likelihood ratio function reaches a maximum of 0.0833 over the interval $[-200, 200]$ for $\bar{n}_0$.

value equal to 0.006. Relative to their estimated standard errors, the estimated coefficients are qualitatively the same as before. The new point estimate of the natural rate of employment equals 6.153%, which is also quite similar. The delta method standard error has fallen to 21.395, but one should still be concerned about the reliablity of the asymptotic approximation.

We will return to this empirical example in Chapter 25 where we will present some of the analysis by Staiger et al. (1996). In this chapter, we explain the rationale behind the quasi first differencing procedure just applied.

19.2 THE BASIC AUTOREGRESSIVE MODEL

After the conditional mean, the primary feature of time series data for the conditional normal linear regression model is conditional covariance among the observations. Intuition about many time series suggests that observations closest in time will possess the largest positive correlation. This may not be true for all time series, but probably will be true for such macroeconomic series as national income, consumption, investment, and the unemployment rate, which all move smoothly from month to month. If the unemployment rate is unusually high this month, taking such predetermined factors as seasonality into account, then it is a good bet that the unemployment rate will exceed its conditional mean next month. On the other hand, casual thought also predicts that the correlation between two observations of a time series should diminish as the time period between them grows. Hence, the unemployment rate this month is probably less correlated with the unemployment rate a year ago, and even less so with the rate 2 years ago.

In contrast to the example of heteroskedasticity, we will suppose that changes in the conditional distribution of y_t over time are captured completely by the conditional mean $\mathbf{x}_t'\boldsymbol{\beta}_0$ so that the $y_t - \mathbf{x}_t'\boldsymbol{\beta}_0$ are identically distributed. Conditional on $\mathbf{X}\boldsymbol{\beta}_0$, we will continue to treat $\mathbf{y}$ as multivariate normal, but we will focus on the implications of $\boldsymbol{\Omega}_0 \equiv \mathrm{Var}[\mathbf{y} \mid \mathbf{X}]$ being nondiagonal.

19.2.1 The Autocorrelation Function

We just described the crudest intuition about the likely correlations among the elements of the time series $\{y_t - \mu_t\}$. This intuition can be formalized as a description of the *autocorrelation function.* As a first approximation, we will suppose that

$$\mathrm{Cov}[y_t, y_{t+n} \mid \mathbf{X}] = \mathrm{Cov}[y_s, y_{s+n} \mid \mathbf{X}] < \infty$$

for all integers t, s, and n. Under this restriction the sequence $y_t - \mathrm{E}[y_t \mid \mathbf{X}]$ is called *covariance (or weakly) stationary.*[6] When a time series is covariance stationary, then the autocorrelation function ρ_n describes the correlation among its elements:

$$\rho_n \equiv \frac{\mathrm{Cov}[y_t, y_{t+n} \mid \mathbf{X}]}{\sqrt{\mathrm{Var}[y_t \mid \mathbf{X}]\,\mathrm{Var}[y_{t+n} \mid \mathbf{X}]}} = \frac{\mathrm{Cov}[y_t, y_{t+n} \mid \mathbf{X}]}{\mathrm{Var}[y_t \mid \mathbf{X}]} \tag{19.5}$$

[6] A covariance stationary process has constant mean as well as constant autocovariance function.

This function depends only on the number n of time periods between two elements of the time series. Because every value is a correlation, all ρ_n are less than or equal to one in absolute value. By definition, $\rho_0 = 1$. Random variables are perfectly correlated with themselves.

Perhaps the simplest way to parameterize an autocorrelation function that is largest when n is small and that dies out as n grows is

$$\rho_n = \phi_0^{|n|} \tag{19.6}$$

where ϕ_0 is a parameter between -1 and 1.[7] When $n = 0$, $\rho_0 = 1$ as required. If $0 < \phi_0 < 1$, then the correlations are all positive and they decline geometrically as the distance n grows, vanishing in the limit as n approaches infinity. If $-1 < \phi_0 < 0$, then the correlations alternate in sign as in our empirical example of the Phillips curve ($\hat{\rho}_1 = -0.498$, $\hat{\rho}_2 = 0.093$, and $\hat{\rho}_3 - 0.093$). If we adopt this autocorrelation function, then we write the conditional variance matrix as

$$\mathbf{\Omega}_0 = \sigma_0^2 \cdot \begin{bmatrix} 1 & \phi_0 & \phi_0^2 & \cdots & \phi_0^{T-1} \\ \phi_0 & 1 & \phi_0 & \cdots & \phi_0^{T-2} \\ \phi_0^2 & \phi_0 & 1 & \ddots & \vdots \\ \vdots & \vdots & \ddots & \ddots & \phi_0 \\ \phi_0^{T-1} & \phi_0^{T-2} & \cdots & \phi_0 & 1 \end{bmatrix} \tag{19.7}$$

where σ_0^2 is still $\text{Var}[y_t \,|\, \mathbf{X}]$. We have specified a variance matrix that captures covariance among the observations in a simple but credible way with the additional parameter ϕ_0.

To complete our specification, we must check that this matrix, which is certainly symmetric, is also positive definite. Otherwise we will have to reconsider the autocorrelation function (19.6). A direct verification method is the calculation of the Cholesky decomposition.[8] If the factors are real nonsingular matrices, then $\mathbf{\Omega}_0$ is positive definite. The special structure of $\mathbf{\Omega}_0$ gives a tractable answer: denoting $\mathbf{\Omega}_0 = \mathbf{C}_0\mathbf{C}_0'$,

$$\mathbf{C}_0 = \sigma_0\sqrt{1-\phi_0^2} \cdot \begin{bmatrix} 1/\sqrt{1-\phi_0^2} & 0 & 0 & 0 & \cdots & 0 \\ \phi_0/\sqrt{1-\phi_0^2} & 1 & 0 & 0 & \cdots & 0 \\ \phi_0^2/\sqrt{1-\phi_0^2} & \phi_0 & 1 & 0 & \cdots & 0 \\ \phi_0^3/\sqrt{1-\phi_0^2} & \phi_0^2 & \phi_0 & 1 & \ddots & \vdots \\ \vdots & \vdots & \vdots & \ddots & \ddots & 0 \\ \phi_0^{T-1}/\sqrt{1-\phi_0^2} & \phi_0^{T-2} & \phi_0^{T-3} & \cdots & \phi_0 & 1 \end{bmatrix} \tag{19.8}$$

or

$$c_{0mn} = \begin{Bmatrix} \sigma_0\phi_0^{m-n} & \text{if} & n = 1 \\ \sigma_0\phi_0^{m-n}\sqrt{1-\phi_0^2} & \text{if} & 1 < n \le m \\ 0 & \text{if} & m < n \end{Bmatrix}$$

---

[7] We have used the symbol ϕ previously for the multivariate normal p.d.f. Its current alternative use as a parameter of covariance is also quite common and will reappear in Chapter 25.

[8] See the Cholesky decomposition (Lemma 7.6, p. 140).

One can confirm this solution by matrix multiplication.

We conclude that $\mathbf{C}_0$ is real and $\mathbf{\Omega}_0$ qualifies as a variance matrix if and only if $\phi_0^2 \leq 1$. Furthermore, $\mathbf{\Omega}_0$ is nonsingular if and only if ϕ_0^2 is strictly less than 1. But ϕ_0 is a coefficient of correlation, so we expect this bound. From this point on, we will assume that $\phi_0^2 < 1$.

19.2.2 The Log-Likelihood Function

Combined with Assumptions 6.1 (First Moments) and 10.1 (Normal Distribution), (19.7) specifies the conditional distribution of $\mathbf{y}$ completely. Every step of our analysis depends on understanding the nature of this conditional distribution and so we will derive the log-likelihood function at the outset.

The Cholesky factor of $\mathbf{\Omega}_0$ in (19.8) simplifies the derivation of the log-likelihood function. As noted in (18.13), the form of thc log-likelihood function for general $\mathbf{\Omega}$ is

$$\mathrm{E}_T[L(\boldsymbol{\beta}, \mathbf{\Omega} \,|\, \mathbf{X})] = -\frac{1}{2T} \log \det(2\pi \cdot \mathbf{\Omega}) - \frac{1}{2T}(\mathbf{y} - \mathbf{X}\boldsymbol{\beta})'\mathbf{\Omega}^{-1}(\mathbf{y} - \mathbf{X}\boldsymbol{\beta})$$

Given $\mathbf{\Omega} = \mathbf{C}\mathbf{C}'$, we can write

$$\begin{aligned} \log\, \det(2\pi \cdot \mathbf{\Omega}) &= T \log 2\pi + 2 \log \det \mathbf{C} \\ &= T \log 2\pi + T \log \sigma^2 + (T-1) \log(1 - \phi^2) \end{aligned} \tag{19.9}$$

using the fact that the determinant of $\mathbf{C}$ is just the product of its diagonal elements.[9] The matrix $\mathbf{C}^{-1}$ is

$$\mathbf{C}^{-1} = \frac{1}{\sigma\sqrt{1-\phi^2}} \cdot \begin{bmatrix} \sqrt{1-\phi^2} & 0 & 0 & 0 & \cdots & 0 \\ -\phi & 1 & 0 & 0 & \cdots & 0 \\ 0 & -\phi & 1 & 0 & \cdots & 0 \\ 0 & 0 & -\phi & 1 & \ddots & \vdots \\ \vdots & \vdots & \vdots & \ddots & \ddots & 0 \\ 0 & 0 & 0 & \cdots & -\phi & 1 \end{bmatrix}$$

which one can confirm by multiplication of $\mathbf{C}$ by $\mathbf{C}^{-1}$. This gives the transformation

$$\mathbf{C}^{-1}(\mathbf{y} - \mathbf{X}\boldsymbol{\beta}) = \begin{bmatrix} \varepsilon_1(\boldsymbol{\beta})/\sigma \\ \frac{\varepsilon_2(\boldsymbol{\beta}) - \phi\varepsilon_1(\boldsymbol{\beta})}{\sigma\sqrt{1-\phi^2}} \\ \vdots \\ \frac{\varepsilon_T(\boldsymbol{\beta}) - \phi\varepsilon_{T-1}(\boldsymbol{\beta})}{\sigma\sqrt{1-\phi^2}} \end{bmatrix} \tag{19.10}$$

where we denote $\varepsilon_t(\boldsymbol{\beta}) \equiv y_t - \mathbf{x}_t'\boldsymbol{\beta}$. Putting together (19.9) and (19.10), we obtain

$$\begin{aligned} &\mathrm{E}_T[L(\boldsymbol{\theta} \,|\, \mathbf{X})] \\ &= -\frac{1}{2} \log 2\pi\sigma^2 - \frac{T-1}{T} \log(1-\phi^2) - \frac{\varepsilon_1^2}{2\sigma^2 T} - \frac{1}{2T} \sum_{t=2}^{T} \frac{(\varepsilon_t - \phi\varepsilon_{t-1})^2}{\sigma^2(1-\phi^2)} \end{aligned}$$

---

[9] See Lemma C.3 (Triangular Matrix Volume, p. 860) on the determinant of a triangular matrix.

$$
\begin{aligned}
&= \frac{1}{T}\left[-\frac{1}{2}\log\frac{2\pi\sigma_v^2}{(1-\phi^2)} - \frac{1}{2}\frac{\varepsilon_1^2}{\sigma_v^2/(1-\phi^2)}\right] \\
&\quad + \frac{T-1}{T}\,\mathrm{E}_{T|1}\left[-\frac{1}{2}\log 2\pi\sigma_v^2 - \frac{1}{2}\frac{(\varepsilon_t-\phi\varepsilon_{t-1})^2}{\sigma_v^2}\right] \qquad (19.11)\\
&= \frac{1}{T}L(\boldsymbol{\theta};\, y_1\,|\,\mathbf{X}) + \frac{T-1}{T}\,\mathrm{E}_{T|1}[L(\boldsymbol{\theta}\,|\,\mathbf{X})]
\end{aligned}
$$

where $\sigma_v^2 \equiv \sigma^2(1-\phi^2)$ and $\boldsymbol{\theta} \equiv [\boldsymbol{\beta}', \sigma_v^2, \phi]'$.[10] For clarity, we have further abbreviated $\varepsilon_t \equiv \varepsilon_t(\boldsymbol{\beta})$. Also, we denote the empirical expectation over $t = 2, \ldots, T$ conditional on the first observation by $\mathrm{E}_{T|1}[\cdot]$.

We have broken the log-likelihood function into two terms. The first term of the log-likelihood function, $L(\boldsymbol{\theta};\, y_1\,|\,\mathbf{X})$, is the marginal log-likelihood function of the first observation y_1. $L(\boldsymbol{\theta};\, y_1\,|\,\mathbf{X})$ is the log-likelihood of the $\mathfrak{N}(\mathbf{x}_1'\boldsymbol{\beta}, \sigma_v^2/(1-\phi^2))$ distribution. The second term, which we denote by $\mathrm{E}_{T|1}[L(\boldsymbol{\theta}\,|\,\mathbf{X})]$, is the average log-likelihood of the rest of the data conditional on y_1. This specifies $\varepsilon_t - \phi\varepsilon_{t-1}$ as i.i.d. $\mathfrak{N}(0, \sigma_v^2)$. In effect, we have taken advantage of the general result that if $\mathbf{z} \sim \mathfrak{N}(\mathbf{0}, \boldsymbol{\Omega})$ then $\mathbf{C}^{-1}\mathbf{z} \sim \mathfrak{N}(\mathbf{0}, \mathbf{I})$ for any $\mathbf{CC}' = \boldsymbol{\Omega}$.[11] Often, we will drop the $L(\boldsymbol{\theta};\, y_1\,|\,\mathbf{X})$ term because it simplifies the mathematics. This omission makes no difference asymptotically because it is the contribution of a single observation.

This model of autocorrelation is called *autoregressive* (AR) because the i.i.d. $\mathfrak{N}(0, \sigma_{0v}^2)$ elements in

$$
[v_{0t};\, t = 1, \ldots, T]' \equiv \sigma_{0v}\cdot \mathbf{C}_0^{-1}\boldsymbol{\varepsilon}(\boldsymbol{\beta}_0) \qquad (19.12)
$$

allow us to write

$$
\varepsilon_{0t} = \phi_0\varepsilon_{0,t-1} + v_{0t} \quad (t = 2, \ldots, T) \qquad (19.13)
$$

where $\varepsilon_{0t} \equiv \varepsilon_t(\boldsymbol{\beta}_0)$. Equation (19.13) is a regression equation with the elements of $\boldsymbol{\varepsilon}_0$ on both the LHS and RHS. One may usefully think of the ε_{0t} as actually generated by such a process, where each i.i.d. v_{0t} is realized after $\varepsilon_{0,t-1}$ and these two random variables are combined in (19.13) to yield a new ε_{0t}. Because

$$
\begin{aligned}
\mathrm{E}[\varepsilon_{0,t-1}v_{0t}\,|\,\mathbf{X}] &= \mathrm{E}[\varepsilon_{0,t-1}(\varepsilon_{0t} - \phi_0\varepsilon_{0,t-1})\,|\,\mathbf{X}] \\
&= \mathrm{Cov}[\varepsilon_{0,t-1}\varepsilon_{0,t}\,|\,\mathbf{X}] - \phi_0\,\mathrm{Var}[\varepsilon_{0,t-1}\,|\,\mathbf{X}] \qquad (19.14)\\
&= 0
\end{aligned}
$$

the v_{0t} are independent of $\varepsilon_{01}, \ldots, \varepsilon_{0,t-1}$ and the MMSE forecast of ε_{0t} at time $t-1$ is

$$
\mathrm{E}[\varepsilon_{0t}\,|\,\varepsilon_{01}, \ldots, \varepsilon_{0,t-1}, \mathbf{X}] = \phi_0\varepsilon_{0,t-1} \qquad (19.15)
$$

Its MSE is

$$
\mathrm{Var}[\varepsilon_{0t}\,|\,\varepsilon_{01}, \ldots, \varepsilon_{0,t-1}, \mathbf{X}] = \sigma_{0v}^2 \qquad (19.16)
$$

This AR form is insightful because we see that

---

[10] This one-to-one reparameterization will not affect the analysis. See Section 17.4.

[11] We used such transformations to prove that if $\mathbf{z} \sim \mathfrak{N}(\boldsymbol{\mu}, \boldsymbol{\Omega})$ and $\boldsymbol{\Omega}$ is nonsingular then $(\mathbf{z}-\boldsymbol{\mu})'\boldsymbol{\Omega}^{-1}(\mathbf{z}-\boldsymbol{\mu}) \sim \chi_\nu^2$, where $\mathbf{z} \in \mathbb{R}^\nu$ (Lemma 10.2, p. 204).

$$\mathrm{E}_{T|1}[L(\boldsymbol{\theta}\,|\,\mathbf{X})] = \frac{1}{T-1}\sum_{t=2}^{T} L(\boldsymbol{\theta};\, y_t\,|\,y_1, \ldots, y_{t-1},\, \mathbf{X}) \tag{19.17}$$

$$= \frac{1}{T-1}\sum_{t=2}^{T} L(\theta;\, y_t\,|\,y_{t-1},\, \mathbf{X}) \tag{19.18}$$

$$= -\frac{1}{2}\left[\log 2\pi\sigma_\upsilon^2 + \frac{\mathrm{E}_{T|1}[(\varepsilon_t - \phi\varepsilon_{t-1})^2]}{\sigma_\upsilon^2}\right] \tag{19.19}$$

consists of conditional log-likelihood functions for y_t given all the previous values. Generally, we can rewrite a log-likelihood function as the sum of conditional log-likelihood functions as in (19.17). In this AR model, we find that there is a refinement to the required conditioning: only y_{t-1} is needed in (19.18) to condition completely on the past. More specifically, the log-likelihood function depends only on the prediction (or forecast) error $\varepsilon_t - \phi\varepsilon_{t-1}$ in (19.19). This special form of the log-likelihood is called the *prediction-error decomposition*.

We also discover that our assumptions imply certain conditional moments for y_t: using (19.15),

$$\begin{aligned}\mathrm{E}[y_t\,|\,t-1] &\equiv \mathrm{E}[y_t\,|\,\mathbf{X},\, y_1, \ldots, y_{t-1}]\\ &= \mathrm{E}[\mathbf{x}_t'\boldsymbol{\beta}_0 + \phi_0\varepsilon_{0,t-1}\,|\,\mathbf{X},\, y_1, \ldots, y_{t-1}]\\ &= \mathbf{x}_t'\boldsymbol{\beta}_0 + \phi_0(y_{t-1} + \mathbf{x}_{t-1}'\boldsymbol{\beta}_0)\end{aligned} \tag{19.20}$$

and, using (19.16),

$$\mathrm{Var}[y_t\,|\,t-1] = \mathrm{Var}[\upsilon_{0t}\,|\,t-1] = \sigma_{0\upsilon}^2 \tag{19.21}$$

for $t = 2, \ldots, T$. The first observation cannot be conditioned on the past so that its moments remain in the form

$$\mathrm{E}[y_1\,|\,\mathbf{X}] = \mathbf{x}_1'\boldsymbol{\beta}_0 \tag{19.22}$$

$$\mathrm{Var}[y_1\,|\,\mathbf{X}] \equiv \sigma_0^2 = \frac{\sigma_{0\upsilon}^2}{1-\phi_0^2} \tag{19.23}$$

The conditional normality assumption and these conditional moments for the observable y_t are equivalent to conditional normality, $\mathrm{E}[\mathbf{y}\,|\,\mathbf{X}] = \mathbf{X}\boldsymbol{\beta}_0$ and the $\mathrm{Var}[\mathbf{y}\,|\,\mathbf{X}] = \boldsymbol{\Omega}_0$ specification in (19.7). The conditional moments are the primary conceptual basis for procedures described below.

Note that this normal model of autocorrelation imposes a more restrictive structure than covariance stationarity. The normal distribution causes the distribution of any sequence $\{\varepsilon_{0t}, \varepsilon_{0,t+1}, \ldots, \varepsilon_{0,t+m}\}$ to have the same joint distribution as $\{\varepsilon_{0,t+n}, \varepsilon_{0,t+n+1}, \ldots, \varepsilon_{0,t+n+m}\}$. Such sequences are called *strictly stationary*.

19.3 AUTOCORRELATION AND OLS

In the presence of autocorrelation, OLS retains all of the properties that it keeps when there is heteroskedasticity: $\hat{\boldsymbol{\beta}}_{\mathrm{OLS}}$ is unbiased, consistent, normally distributed, and asymptotically normally distributed.[12] Autocorrelation also takes away from OLS what it loses with heteroskedasticity: unbiased estimation of its variance matrix, its pivotal statistics, and its relative efficiency. These similarities rest on the failure of the same assumption, that the conditional variance matrix of **y** is a scalar matrix (Assumption 7.1).

EXAMPLE 19.1

Consider the simple ($K = 1$) normal linear regression model $\mathbf{y} \sim \mathfrak{N}(\beta_0 \cdot \mathbf{X}, \mathbf{\Omega}_0)$. The sampling variance of the OLS fitted coefficient is

$$\text{Var}[\hat{\beta}_{\text{OLS}} \,|\, \mathbf{X}] = \frac{\mathbf{X}'\mathbf{\Omega}_0\mathbf{X}}{(\mathbf{X}'\mathbf{X})^2} = \sigma_0^2 \frac{\sum_{t=1}^{T}\sum_{n=1}^{T} x_t x_n \phi_0^{|t-n|}}{(\mathbf{X}'\mathbf{X})^2}$$

The OLS estimator for the variance parameter has a mean equal to

$$\text{E}[s^2 \,|\, \mathbf{X}] = \sigma_0^2 \frac{\sum_{t=1}^{T}\left[T x_t^2 - \sum_{n=1}^{T} x_t x_n \phi_0^{|t-n|}\right]}{(T-1)\ \mathbf{X}'\mathbf{X}}$$

Therefore, the OLS estimated sampling variance of $\hat{\beta}$ has expectation

$$\text{E}[s^2(\mathbf{X}'\mathbf{X})^{-1} \,|\, \mathbf{X}] = \sigma_0^2 \frac{\sum_{t=1}^{T}\left[T x_t^2 - \sum_{n=1}^{T} x_t x_n \phi_0^{|t-n|}\right]}{(T-1)\ (\mathbf{X}'\mathbf{X})^2}$$

which is less than $\text{Var}[\hat{\beta} \,|\, \mathbf{X}]$ for large T if

$$0 \le \sum_{t=1}^{T} \sum_{n \ne t} x_t x_n \phi_0^{|t-n|}$$

This will occur if, for example, $\phi_0 > 0$ and $x_t > 0$ for all t. But in general, the OLS estimator of the conditional variance can be biased in either direction.

Because the basic variance formula fails, the distribution of such pivotal statistics as the F statistic changes so that they are no longer pivotal. As the example shows, the distribution of the variance estimator depends on the unknown parameter ϕ_0. We can demonstrate the failure of $\hat{\boldsymbol{\beta}}_{\text{OLS}}$ to be relatively efficient with the following (extreme) example.

EXAMPLE 19.2

Again, consider the simple normal linear regression model $\mathbf{y} \,|\, \mathbf{X} \sim \mathfrak{N}(\beta_0 \cdot \mathbf{X}, \mathbf{\Omega}_0)$ ($t = 1, \ldots, T$). In this case, suppose that the disturbances are perfectly autocorrelated: $\text{Cov}[y_t, y_s \,|\, \mathbf{X}] = \sigma_0^2$ so that $\mathbf{\Omega}_0 = \sigma_0^2 \cdot \iota\iota'$. OLS will fail to take this correlation into account at the cost of estimator efficiency. Note that this variance matrix implies

$$\text{Var}[(y_t - \beta_0 x_t) - (y_s - \beta_0 x_s) \,|\, \mathbf{X}] = 0$$

so that $y_t - \beta_0 x_t = y_s - \beta_0 x_s$. As a result, the estimator

[12] The asymptotic properties require new results for dependently distributed random variables. We cover these topics in Section 19.9.

$$\tilde{\beta} = \frac{y_t - y_s}{x_t - x_s} = \beta_0$$

for any t, s such that $x_t \neq x_s$ has a variance of zero whereas

$$\text{Var}[\hat{\beta}_{\text{OLS}} \mid \mathbf{X}] = \sigma_0^2 \frac{\sum_{t=1}^{T} \sum_{s=1}^{T} x_t x_s}{\left(\sum_{t=1}^{T} x_t^2\right)^2} > 0$$

So the (linear) estimator $\tilde{\beta}$ is efficient relative to $\hat{\beta}_{\text{OLS}}$.

Therefore, by exploiting the covariance among the observations we can generally construct an estimator that is efficient relative to the OLS estimator. In light of these failures of OLS properties, we now turn to testing for the presence of autocorrelation using the OLS estimator.

19.4 TESTING FOR AUTOCORRELATION

19.4.1 Breusch–Godfrey Score Test

Following Breusch (1978) and Godfrey (1978a, 1978b), we can use the same general strategy to test for autocorrelation that we adopted for testing heteroskedasticity. Given OLS estimates, we will examine the behavior of the OLS fitted residuals $\hat{\varepsilon}_t$ for evidence of autocorrelation. The formal test is a score test, exploiting the fact that the OLS estimator is the restricted MLE under the hypothesis that $\phi_0 = 0$. The test statistic is the OLS F test (or t test) statistic for the hypothesis that $\phi_0 = 0$ in the *artificial* specification $\text{E}[\hat{\varepsilon}_t \mid \hat{\varepsilon}_{t-1}] = \phi_0 \hat{\varepsilon}_{t-1}$ $(t = 2, \ldots, T)$. One may think of this artificial model as an approximation to (19.15), where we replace the unobservable ε_{0t} with OLS fitted residuals $\hat{\varepsilon}_t$. Asymptotic distribution theory formally justifies this simple approximation.

To carry out the test,

1. compute the OLS fitted residuals $\hat{\varepsilon}_t \equiv y_t - \mathbf{x}_t' \hat{\boldsymbol{\beta}}_{\text{OLS}}$ from the regression of y_t on $\mathbf{x}_t$ and then
2. fit the OLS regression of $\hat{\varepsilon}_t$ on $\hat{\varepsilon}_{t-1}$ $(t = 2, \ldots, T)$ alone (i.e., without an intercept).

The F test (or t test) for whether the coefficient for $\hat{\varepsilon}_{t-1}$ is equal to zero is the score test of $H_0 : \phi_0 = 0$.

To formally derive this test procedure, one first finds the score by differentiating (19.19) with respect to ϕ and evaluating the result at the OLS estimators for $\hat{\beta}_{\text{OLS}}$ and $\hat{\sigma}_v^2 = \hat{\sigma}^2 = \sum_{t=1}^{T} \hat{\varepsilon}_t^2 / T$ and at $\phi = 0$:

$$\text{E}_{T|1}[L_\phi(\boldsymbol{\theta} \mid \mathbf{X})] = \frac{1}{\sigma_v^2} \text{E}_{T|1}[\varepsilon_{t-1}(\varepsilon_t - \phi \varepsilon_{t-1})] \quad \Rightarrow$$

$$\text{E}_{T|1}[L_\phi(\hat{\boldsymbol{\theta}}_{\text{R}} \mid \mathbf{X})] = \frac{\text{E}_{T|1}[\hat{\varepsilon}_{t-1} \hat{\varepsilon}_t]}{\hat{\sigma}^2} \tag{19.24}$$

In addition, one obtains the information matrix, either as the variance of the score terms or as the expectation of the Hessian. We derive both the complete score vector and the information matrix in Section 19.9.1. A key feature of the information matrix is that it is block-diagonal in each of the parameters $\boldsymbol{\beta}$, σ_v^2, and ϕ. Therefore, the only information term required is

$$\mathrm{E}_{T|1}[\Im_{\phi\phi}(\boldsymbol{\theta}_0 \,|\, \mathbf{X})] = \frac{1}{1-\phi_0^2} \qquad \Rightarrow$$

$$\mathrm{E}_{T|1}[\Im_{\phi\phi}(\hat{\boldsymbol{\theta}}_{\mathrm{R}} \,|\, \mathbf{X})] = 1$$

and the score test of $\phi = 0$ simplifies to the ratio

$$S = (T-1)\frac{\{\mathrm{E}_{T|1}[L_\phi(\hat{\boldsymbol{\theta}}_{\mathrm{R}} \,|\, \mathbf{X})]\}^2}{\mathrm{E}_{T|1}[\Im_{\phi\phi}(\hat{\boldsymbol{\theta}}_{\mathrm{R}} \,|\, \mathbf{X})]} = (T-1)\frac{\left(\mathrm{E}_{T|1}[\hat{\varepsilon}_{t-1}\hat{\varepsilon}_t]\right)^2}{\hat{\sigma}^4} \tag{19.25}$$

The asymptotic distribution of S is χ_1^2 if $\phi = 0$. A two-sided critical region at the $100\alpha\%$ level of significance is $S \geq \chi^2_{1;1-\alpha}$.

Strictly speaking, S is not the F test statistic that we introduced above. The two statistics are approximately equal and asymptotically equivalent. To see this, let $\hat{\boldsymbol{\varepsilon}} \equiv [\hat{\varepsilon}_t;\, t = 2, \ldots, T]'$ and $\hat{\boldsymbol{\varepsilon}}_{-1} \equiv [\hat{\varepsilon}_{t-1};\, t = 2, \ldots, T]'$ so that the F test statistic from Step 2 above is[13]

$$F = \frac{\hat{\boldsymbol{\varepsilon}}'\mathbf{P}_{\hat{\boldsymbol{\varepsilon}}_{-1}}\hat{\boldsymbol{\varepsilon}}}{\hat{\boldsymbol{\varepsilon}}'(\mathbf{I}-\mathbf{P}_{\hat{\boldsymbol{\varepsilon}}_{-1}})\hat{\boldsymbol{\varepsilon}}/(T-2)} = \frac{\left(\hat{\boldsymbol{\varepsilon}}'_{-1}\hat{\boldsymbol{\varepsilon}}\right)^2}{[\hat{\boldsymbol{\varepsilon}}'_{-1}\hat{\boldsymbol{\varepsilon}}_{-1}\cdot\hat{\boldsymbol{\varepsilon}}'\hat{\boldsymbol{\varepsilon}} - \left(\hat{\boldsymbol{\varepsilon}}'_{-1}\hat{\boldsymbol{\varepsilon}}\right)^2]/(T-2)}$$

where $\mathbf{P}_{\hat{\boldsymbol{\varepsilon}}_{-1}} \equiv \hat{\boldsymbol{\varepsilon}}_{-1}\left(\hat{\boldsymbol{\varepsilon}}'_{-1}\hat{\boldsymbol{\varepsilon}}_{-1}\right)^{-1}\hat{\boldsymbol{\varepsilon}}'_{-1}$. Because

$$\hat{\boldsymbol{\varepsilon}}'_{-1}\hat{\boldsymbol{\varepsilon}}_{-1} \approx \hat{\boldsymbol{\varepsilon}}'\hat{\boldsymbol{\varepsilon}} \approx \sum_{t=1}^{T}\hat{\varepsilon}_t^2 = T\hat{\sigma}^2$$

it follows that

$$F \approx \frac{\left(\hat{\boldsymbol{\varepsilon}}'_{-1}\hat{\boldsymbol{\varepsilon}}\right)^2}{(T-1)\,\hat{\sigma}^4 - \left(\hat{\boldsymbol{\varepsilon}}'_{-1}\hat{\boldsymbol{\varepsilon}}\right)^2/(T-2)}$$

$$= S\left(1 - \frac{S}{T-2}\right)^{-1}$$

For T large relative to the score test statistic, F is approximately S. The F version of the test is intuitive and convenient with OLS regression software. Also, to test against a one-sided alternative rather than the two-sided one, the corresponding t test will serve that purpose. For example, based on (19.3), the score test rejects the hypothesis of no serial correlation for the Phillips curve where the t test statistic equals $-0.498/0.0397 = -12.544$.

Alternatively, we can compute the score test for autocorrelation as the squared length of the OLS fitted vector from regressing the standardized fitted residual $\hat{\sigma}^{-1}\cdot\hat{\varepsilon}_t$ on its lagged value $\hat{\sigma}^{-1}\cdot\hat{\varepsilon}_{t-1}$:

$$S \approx \left(\hat{\sigma}^{-1}\cdot\hat{\boldsymbol{\varepsilon}}\right)'\mathbf{P}_{\hat{\sigma}^{-1}\cdot\hat{\boldsymbol{\varepsilon}}_{-1}}\left(\hat{\sigma}^{-1}\cdot\hat{\boldsymbol{\varepsilon}}\right)$$

This regression form of the score test is shared with such other score test statistics as the Breusch–

[13] Recall equation (11.3) (p. 226) and note that the restricted fitted vector is $\mathbf{0}$.

Pagan heteroskedasticity test.[14] Yet another simple form is

$$S \approx (T-1)\hat{\phi}_1^2$$

where

$$\hat{\phi}_1 \equiv \frac{\mathrm{E}_{T|1}[\hat{\varepsilon}_{t-1}\hat{\varepsilon}_t]}{\mathrm{E}_{T|1}[\hat{\varepsilon}_t^2]} \tag{19.26}$$

is the OLS fitted coefficient.

19.4.2 The Durbin–Watson Test

OLS regression software commonly provides a diagnostic test for autocorrelation called the *Durbin–Watson (DW) test*, proposed by Durbin and Watson (1950, 1951). The score test statistic is closely related to this statistic:

$$DW = \frac{\sum_{t=2}^{T}\left(\hat{\varepsilon}_t - \hat{\varepsilon}_{t-1}\right)^2}{\sum_{t=1}^{T}\hat{\varepsilon}_t^2} \approx 2\left[1 - \sqrt{\frac{S}{T-1}}\right]$$

Texts often provide special tables of critical values for DW values: a range is given that depends on the sample size and the number of explanatory variables. This table accounts for features of the exact distribution of the test statistic. Such tables are obsolete given the relative ease with which we can simulate the draws from the exact distribution just as we did for the Breusch–Pagan score test of heteroskedasticity. Alternatively, some software packages calculate exact probability values with the Imhof (1980) algorithm.[15]

There is no compelling reason to prefer the score test to the Durbin–Watson or vice versa in practice. The former is conceptually neater because it fits within the general likelihood framework that we are using. The prevalence of the Durbin–Watson test reflects, in part, its appearance before score tests were widely appreciated.

19.5 VARIANCE ESTIMATION FOR OLS

Consistent estimation of the asymptotic variance of the OLS estimator is possible without specifying functional forms for serial covariance like (19.7). Researchers have extended the Eicker–White variance matrix estimator for heteroskedastic problems to serially correlated cases as well. If nonzero covariances are only pth-order, so that for $j > p$

$$\mathrm{Cov}[y_t, y_{t-j} \mid \mathbf{X}] = 0$$

then we can simply extend the White–Eicker principle to the nonzero terms. Instead of just $\hat{\varepsilon}_t^2$ in place of ω_{tt} in $\mathbf{X}'\mathbf{\Omega}_0\mathbf{X}$, include $\hat{\varepsilon}_t\hat{\varepsilon}_{t-j}$ in place of $\omega_{t,t-j}$ for $j = 0, \pm 1, \pm 2, \ldots, \pm p$. If we let

[14] Compare this statistic with (18.6).

[15] The Imhof algorithm computes c.d.f. of a quadratic form $\mathbf{z}'\mathbf{A}\mathbf{z}$ for $\mathbf{z} \sim \mathfrak{N}(\mathbf{0}, \mathbf{I})$. Clint Cummins kindly provided the following additional references. For source code for the Imhof algorithm, see Farebrother (1990). Farebrother (1980) provides a faster algorithm for fewer than 90 observations.

$$\mathbf{\Lambda}_{Tj} \equiv \mathrm{E}_{T|j}[\mathbf{x}_t\hat{\varepsilon}_t\hat{\varepsilon}_{t-j}\mathbf{x}'_{t-j}], \qquad j = 0, 1, \ldots, p$$

then

$$\hat{\mathbf{\Lambda}}_T = \hat{\mathbf{\Lambda}}_{T0} + \sum_{j=1}^{p} \left(\hat{\mathbf{\Lambda}}_{Tj} + \hat{\mathbf{\Lambda}}'_{Tj}\right) \stackrel{p}{=} \frac{1}{T} \cdot \mathbf{X}'\mathbf{\Omega}_0\mathbf{X}$$

Therefore,

$$\widehat{\mathrm{Var}[\hat{\boldsymbol{\beta}}_{\mathrm{OLS}} \mid \mathbf{X}]} = (\mathbf{X}'\mathbf{X})^{-1}\hat{\mathbf{\Lambda}}_T(\mathbf{X}'\mathbf{X})^{-1} \tag{19.27}$$

is an estimator of $\mathrm{Var}[\hat{\boldsymbol{\beta}}_{\mathrm{OLS}} \mid \mathbf{X}]$.

There is a limit to how far one can carry out this approach. One might try setting $p = T$ so that all possible covariances are included. In that case,

$$\hat{\mathbf{\Lambda}}_T = \mathbf{X}'\hat{\boldsymbol{\varepsilon}}\hat{\boldsymbol{\varepsilon}}'\mathbf{X} = \left(\mathbf{X}'\hat{\boldsymbol{\varepsilon}}\right)\left(\mathbf{X}'\hat{\boldsymbol{\varepsilon}}\right)'$$

which is a matrix with a rank equal to one. Because $\mathbf{X}'\mathbf{\Omega}_0\mathbf{X}$ is nonsingular, this cannot be sensible. The consistency of the White–Eicker procedure relies on p being small relative to the number of observations T.

Nevertheless, it is also possible to account for nonzero covariances of all orders if the covariances $\omega_{t,t-j}$ diminish fast enough as j grows. Such covariances appear in the particular model for covariance that we are considering in this chapter [see (19.7)]. One can allow p to grow with the sample size T so that asymptotically all covariances are eventually included. This estimator was suggested by Hansen (1982).

Unfortunately, Hansen's estimator often fails to be positive semidefinite. Newey and West (1987b) suggested a popular alternative estimator that overcomes this weakness:

$$\hat{\mathbf{\Lambda}}_T = \hat{\mathbf{\Lambda}}_{T0} + \sum_{j=1}^{p} \left(1 - \frac{j}{p+1}\right)\left(\hat{\mathbf{\Lambda}}_{Tj} + \hat{\mathbf{\Lambda}}'_{Tj}\right)$$

They reweight Hansen's estimator so that higher order covariance terms receive less weight. Covariances must diminish anyway for the asymptotic distribution theory to work and this reweighting does not destroy the consistency of the variance matrix estimator.

The implementation of either estimator depends on the selection of p. Andrews (1991) offers a method for doing this, but it is beyond the scope of our treatment. Simply setting $p = 12$ for the example of the Phillips curve, we amend the OLS estimates in (19.2) to

$$\dot{p}_t - \dot{p}_{t-1} = \underset{(0.230)}{0.185} - \underset{(0.040)}{0.030}\, n_{t-1} + \underset{(0.0172)}{0.0057}\, pfe_t + \underset{(0.479)}{0.294}\, nixon_t + \hat{\varepsilon}_t \tag{19.28}$$

Except for the slope of pfe_t, the estimated standard errors decrease so that OLS appears to be more precise than its uncorrected estimator suggests. These variance estimators remain a topic of ongoing research and, although their use is widespread, Andrews (1991) (among others) documents their unreliability in some circumstances.

19.6 SERIAL CORRELATION AND GLS

In the previous chapter, we showed that in general the GLS estimator for $\boldsymbol{\beta}_0$ is[16]

$$\hat{\boldsymbol{\beta}}_{\mathrm{GLS}} = (\mathbf{X}'\boldsymbol{\Omega}_0^{-1}\mathbf{X})^{-1}\mathbf{X}'\boldsymbol{\Omega}_0^{-1}\mathbf{y}$$

For conditional heteroskedasticity, there is a simple reweighting of the data that provides a convenient, equivalent OLS fitted coefficient. There is also a handy transformation for AR models to compute $\hat{\boldsymbol{\beta}}_{\mathrm{GLS}}$ by OLS. We can rewrite the conditional moments in (19.20)–(19.23) as

$$\mathrm{E}[y_{*t} \,|\, \mathbf{X}_*] = \mathbf{x}'_{*t}\boldsymbol{\beta}_0$$
$$\mathrm{Var}[y_{*t} \,|\, \mathbf{X}_*] = \sigma_{0v}^2$$

where

$$y_{*t} \equiv \begin{cases} \sqrt{1-\phi_0^2}\, y_t & \text{if} \quad t = 1 \\ y_t - \phi_0 y_{t-1} & \text{if} \quad t > 1 \end{cases}$$

$$\mathbf{x}_{*t} \equiv \begin{cases} \sqrt{1-\phi_0^2} \cdot \mathbf{x}_t & \text{if} \quad t = 1 \\ \mathbf{x}_t - \phi_0 \cdot \mathbf{x}_{t-1} & \text{if} \quad t > 1 \end{cases}$$

In addition,

$$\mathrm{Cov}[y_{*t}, y_{*t-1} \,|\, \mathbf{X}_*] = \mathrm{Cov}[v_{0t}, v_{0,t-1} \,|\, \mathbf{X}_*] = 0$$

so that the entire transformed data set has the linear mean vector and scalar variance matrix specification

$$\mathrm{E}[\mathbf{y}_* \,|\, \mathbf{X}_*] = \mathbf{X}_*\boldsymbol{\beta}_0$$
$$\mathrm{Var}[\mathbf{y}_* \,|\, \mathbf{X}_*] = \sigma_{0v}^2 \cdot \mathbf{I}$$

If ϕ_0 is known, we obtain the GLS estimator with OLS as

$$\hat{\boldsymbol{\beta}}_{\mathrm{GLS}} = (\mathbf{X}'_*\mathbf{X}_*)^{-1}\mathbf{X}'_*\mathbf{y}_* \tag{19.29}$$

The two expressions for $\hat{\boldsymbol{\beta}}_{\mathrm{GLS}}$ are equivalent. Note that

$$\mathbf{y}_* = \sigma_0\sqrt{1-\phi_0^2} \cdot \mathbf{C}_0^{-1}\mathbf{y}$$
$$\mathbf{X}_* = \sigma_0\sqrt{1-\phi_0^2} \cdot \mathbf{C}_0^{-1}\mathbf{X}$$

which leads to

$$\begin{aligned} \hat{\boldsymbol{\beta}}_{\mathrm{GLS}} &= (\mathbf{X}'\mathbf{C}_0^{-1\prime}\mathbf{C}_0^{-1}\mathbf{X})^{-1}\mathbf{X}'\mathbf{C}_0^{-1\prime}\mathbf{C}_0^{-1}\mathbf{y} \\ &= (\mathbf{X}'\boldsymbol{\Omega}_0^{-1}\mathbf{X})^{-1}\mathbf{X}'\boldsymbol{\Omega}_0^{-1}\mathbf{y} \end{aligned}$$

This is an example of a general strategy for turning GLS estimation problems into OLS problems. If we find any variance decomposition $\boldsymbol{\Omega}_0 = \mathbf{C}_0\mathbf{C}_0'$, then the transformed $\mathbf{y}_* \equiv \mathbf{C}_0^{-1}\mathbf{y}$ satisfies

---

16 See equation (18.15) and the surrounding discussion on p. 432.

the assumptions of the classical normal linear regression model and we can apply OLS inference procedures.

19.6.1 Maximum Likelihood Estimation

Feasible estimation requires that we estimate ϕ_0 as well as $\boldsymbol{\beta}_0$. We discuss the MLE first, describing approaches to its computation and the effects of serial correlation on its distribution theory.

COMPUTATION

Econometricians have studied the MLE for the AR model of correlation frequently. People have suggested various iterative schemes for approximating the MLE using OLS software. The methods (named after their authors) are frequently encountered in software packages as estimation commands so that it is not necessary to program the algorithms oneself. An account of the methods gives the flavor of the development of econometrics in this area:

- Durbin (1960) suggested several initial estimators for ϕ. One is based on the Durbin–Watson statistic and is essentially (19.26). Another initial estimator is the fitted coefficient $\hat{\phi}$ in the OLS fit

$$y_t = \hat{\phi} y_{t-1} + \mathbf{x}_t'\hat{\boldsymbol{\beta}} - \mathbf{x}_{t-1}'(\widehat{\phi \cdot \boldsymbol{\beta}}) + \hat{u}_t$$

  of (19.20).
- Cochrane and Orcutt (1949) proposed iterating between the computation of $\boldsymbol{\beta}$ given ϕ and the computation of ϕ given $\boldsymbol{\beta}$, maximizing $L(\boldsymbol{\theta} \mid y_1)$. On the iteration $i+1$, given $\hat{\phi}_{(i)}$ one solves the normal equation $L_{\boldsymbol{\beta}}(\boldsymbol{\theta} \mid y_1) = \mathbf{0}$ [see equation (19.30)] for $\hat{\boldsymbol{\beta}}_{(i+1)}$ by fitting the OLS regression of $\hat{y}_{*t} \equiv y_t - \hat{\phi}_{(i)} y_{t-1}$ on $\hat{\mathbf{x}}_{*t} \equiv \mathbf{x}_t - \hat{\phi}_{(i)} \cdot \mathbf{x}_{t-1}$. Then $L_{\phi}(\boldsymbol{\theta} \mid y_1) = 0$ (19.32) is solved for $\hat{\phi}_{(i+1)}$ with the regression of $\hat{\varepsilon}_t$ on $\hat{\varepsilon}_{t-1}$. This method ignores the contribution of the first observation to the log-likelihood function. This method is a Gauss–Seidel algorithm and every step improves $L(\boldsymbol{\theta} \mid y_1)$ until a critical value is reached. But like all iterative methods, it may converge to a local, rather than global, optimum.
- Prais and Winsten (1954) introduced the first observation into the calculation of $\hat{\boldsymbol{\beta}}$ by adding $\sqrt{1-\hat{\phi}_{(i)}^2}\, y_1$ and $\sqrt{1-\hat{\phi}_{(i)}^2} \cdot \mathbf{x}_1$ to the Cochrane–Orcutt regression for $\boldsymbol{\beta}$ given ϕ. Therefore, their method corresponds to FGLS. They did not suggest any change to the Cochrane–Orcutt calculation for $\hat{\phi}_{(i)}$.
- Hildreth and Lu (1960) suggested substituting a grid search over the interval $[-1, 1]$ in place of the Cochrane–Orcutt iteration. For each value of ϕ on the grid, one can maximize the full $L(\boldsymbol{\theta})$ function using Prais–Winsten/GLS for $\hat{\boldsymbol{\beta}}(\phi)$ and setting

$$\hat{\sigma}_{\upsilon}^2(\phi) = \frac{1}{T}\left\{ \frac{[\hat{\varepsilon}_1(\phi)]^2}{1-\phi^2} + \sum_{t=2}^{T} [\hat{\varepsilon}_t(\phi) - \phi\, \hat{\varepsilon}_{t-1}(\phi)]^2 \right\}$$

  where $\hat{\varepsilon}_t(\phi) \equiv y_t - \mathbf{x}_t'\hat{\boldsymbol{\beta}}(\phi)$. This function for the variance parameter solves the normal equation $L_{\sigma_{\upsilon}^2}(\boldsymbol{\theta}) = 0$ given $\boldsymbol{\beta} = \hat{\boldsymbol{\beta}}(\phi)$ and ϕ. The method corresponds to maximizing the concentrated log-likelihood function

$$L^c(\phi) = \max_{\beta,\sigma_v^2} L(\boldsymbol{\theta})$$

- Beach and MacKinnon (1978) showed how to replace the Cochrane–Orcutt calculation for ϕ with the maximization of the complete log-likelihood $L(\boldsymbol{\theta})$ over ϕ. They rewrite the normal equation $L_\phi(\boldsymbol{\theta}) = 0$ as a cubic equation in ϕ and identify the unique root that maximizes $L(\boldsymbol{\theta})$ given $\boldsymbol{\beta}$ and σ_v^2. Combining this calculation with Prais–Winsten/GLS for $\boldsymbol{\beta}$ yields a Gauss–Seidel maximization algorithm for the log-likelihood function of the entire data set.
- Alternatively, conditioning on y_1, we can simply treat the computation as an NLS problem. That is, the LS fit of (19.20) is computed restricting the scalar coefficient of y_{t-1} multiplied by the coefficient vector of $\mathbf{x}_t$ to equal the coefficient vector of $\mathbf{x}_{t-1}$.

When computational costs were more important, econometricians were concerned about the differences in sampling behavior among the various estimators. The general consensus now is that there is no compelling reason to prefer another estimator to the MLE for the complete data set.[17] The first observation is not a liability and it can be an asset in certain situations. Also, the presence of the variance term $\log(1-\phi^2)$ in $L(\boldsymbol{\theta}; y_1)$ constrains the MLE for ϕ to take values such that the autocorrelations die out. Of course, in large samples the first observation hardly matters and asymptotically the estimators are all equivalent.

DISTRIBUTION THEORY

The asymptotic distribution theory for the MLE poses a new problem: dependence within averages. The LLN and the CLT that we have been using stipulate that the individual observations are independently distributed. These results can be generalized to the not independently (but still) identically distributed case. We describe this generalization in Section 19.9. The basic approach rests on the prediction-error decomposition of the average log-likelihood function and, broadly speaking, the arguments in Chapter 14. The consistency of the MLE for AR autocorrelation follows from the Chebychev LLN by showing that the variance of the sample average log-likelihood still converges to zero despite the autocorrelation. The asymptotic normality requires an alternative CLT that allows dependence among the elements of the sample average score. Under the conditions described below,

$$\sqrt{T}\,\mathrm{E}_{T|1}[L_{\boldsymbol{\theta}}(\boldsymbol{\theta}_0)] \xrightarrow{d} \mathfrak{N}[\mathbf{0}, \mathfrak{I}(\boldsymbol{\theta}_0)]$$

where the information matrix is

$$\mathfrak{I}(\boldsymbol{\theta}_0) = \lim_{T\to\infty} \mathrm{E}\Big[\mathrm{E}_{T|1}\big[\mathrm{Var}[L_{\boldsymbol{\theta}}(\boldsymbol{\theta}_0) \mid y_{t-1}, \mathbf{x}_1, \ldots, \mathbf{x}_t]\big]\Big]$$

We derive this matrix in Section 19.9.1.[18] It follows that we estimate the information matrix with

$$\mathrm{E}_{T|1}[\mathfrak{I}(\boldsymbol{\theta}_0 \mid y_{t-1}, \mathbf{x}_1, \ldots, \mathbf{x}_t)] = \begin{bmatrix} \frac{1}{T-1}\cdot \mathbf{X}'\hat{\boldsymbol{\Omega}}_{\mathrm{ML}}\mathbf{X} & \mathbf{0} & \mathbf{0} \\ \mathbf{0} & 1/(2\hat{\sigma}_{v,\mathrm{ML}}^4) & 0 \\ \mathbf{0} & 0 & 1/(1-\hat{\phi}_{\mathrm{ML}}^2) \end{bmatrix}$$

where $\hat{\boldsymbol{\Omega}}_{\mathrm{ML}}$ is (19.7) evaluated at the MLE.

---

[17] See the discussions in Davidson and MacKinnon (1993), Greene (1990), and Judge et al. (1980).

[18] See equation (19.39).

Given these asymptotic results, the MLE has the usual approximate distribution. By inverting the estimated information matrix above, we find an estimator of the asymptotic variance of $\sqrt{T}(\hat{\boldsymbol{\beta}}_{\text{ML}} - \boldsymbol{\beta}_0)$ to be $(T-1)\cdot(\mathbf{X}'\hat{\boldsymbol{\Omega}}_{\text{ML}}\mathbf{X})^{-1}$. In other words, $\hat{\boldsymbol{\beta}}_{\text{ML}}$ is approximately normal with mean value $\boldsymbol{\beta}_0$ and variance matrix $(\mathbf{X}'\hat{\boldsymbol{\Omega}}_{\text{ML}}\mathbf{X})^{-1}$. Once again the MLE for $\boldsymbol{\beta}_0$ is asymptotically equivalent to GLS.

19.6.2 FGLS

The similarities with the heteroskedasticity model continue with the FGLS estimator derived as a linearized MLE. Given such an initial consistent estimator $\check{\boldsymbol{\beta}}$ for $\boldsymbol{\beta}_0$ as OLS, convenient estimators for ϕ_0 and $\sigma_{0\upsilon}^2$ are

$$\check{\phi} \equiv \mathrm{E}_{T|1}[\check{\varepsilon}_{t-1}\check{\varepsilon}_t] / \mathrm{E}_{T|1}[\check{\varepsilon}_{t-1}^2]$$

and

$$\check{\sigma}_\upsilon^2 \equiv \mathrm{Var}_{T|1}[\check{\upsilon}_t]$$

where $\check{\varepsilon}_t \equiv y_t - \mathbf{x}_t'\check{\boldsymbol{\beta}}$ and $\check{\upsilon}_t \equiv \check{\varepsilon}_t - \check{\phi}\check{\varepsilon}_{t-1}$. These are the MLEs given $\boldsymbol{\beta} = \check{\boldsymbol{\beta}}$ and the statistics from OLS regression of $\check{\varepsilon}_t$ on its lagged value. Plugging these initial estimators into the LML equation (15.9), we obtain

$$
\begin{aligned}
\hat{\boldsymbol{\theta}}_{\text{LML}} &= \check{\boldsymbol{\theta}} + \{\mathrm{E}_{T|1}[\Im(\check{\boldsymbol{\theta}})]\}^{-1}\,\mathrm{E}_{T|1}[L_{\boldsymbol{\theta}}(\check{\boldsymbol{\theta}})] \\
&= \begin{bmatrix} \check{\boldsymbol{\beta}} \\ \check{\sigma}_\upsilon^2 \\ \check{\phi} \end{bmatrix} + \begin{bmatrix} \mathbf{X}'\check{\boldsymbol{\Omega}}\mathbf{X} & \mathbf{0} & \mathbf{0} \\ \mathbf{0} & T/(2\check{\sigma}_\upsilon^4) & 0 \\ \mathbf{0} & 0 & T/(1-\check{\phi}^2) \end{bmatrix}^{-1} \begin{bmatrix} \mathbf{X}'\check{\boldsymbol{\Omega}}^{-1}(\mathbf{y} - \mathbf{X}\check{\boldsymbol{\beta}}) \\ 0 \\ 0 \end{bmatrix} \\
&= \begin{bmatrix} (\mathbf{X}'\check{\boldsymbol{\Omega}}^{-1}\mathbf{X})^{-1}\mathbf{X}'\check{\boldsymbol{\Omega}}^{-1}\mathbf{y} \\ \check{\sigma}_\upsilon^2 \\ \check{\phi} \end{bmatrix}
\end{aligned}
$$

This yields the FGLS estimator for $\boldsymbol{\beta}_0$ as an asymptotically efficient estimator and as asymptotically equivalent to the GLS estimator. It also shows us that our *initial* estimators of ϕ_0 and $\sigma_{0\upsilon}^2$ ($\check{\phi}$ and $\check{\sigma}_\upsilon^2$) are asymptotically equivalent to the MLEs. Asymptotically, the block-diagonality of the information matrix makes further updating of these parameters unnecessary for efficiency. Thus, the estimates of the Phillips curve we gave in (19.3)–(19.4) are equal to these LMLEs for the AR model of serial correlation.

19.7 PREDICTION

One of the most entertaining aspects of time series analysis is forecasting future realizations. There is no doubt that accurate forecasts are valuable information, giving a forceful, if base, motive for our interest. But predicting the future also holds a virtually mystical fascination for us that transcends dismal economics. One remedy for fatigue in students of econometrics is an opportunity to predict an interesting time series.

Conditional on the data set and the true parameter values, the conditional mean is the MMSE forecasting function. In the AR model we have derived this function:

$$\begin{aligned}\mathrm{E}[y_{T+1} \mid T] &= \mathbf{x}'_{T+1}\boldsymbol{\beta}_0 + \phi_0 \varepsilon_{0T} \\ &= (\mathbf{x}_{T+1} - \phi_0 \cdot \mathbf{x}_T)'\boldsymbol{\beta}_0 + \phi_0 y_T\end{aligned}$$

For a prediction one period further, the conditional mean is a linear function of the previous prediction:

$$\begin{aligned}\mathrm{E}[y_{T+2} \mid T] &= \mathrm{E}[\mathbf{x}'_{T+2}\boldsymbol{\beta}_0 + \phi_0 \varepsilon_{0,T+1} \mid T] \\ &= (\mathrm{E}[\mathbf{x}_{T+2} \mid T] - \phi_0 \cdot \mathrm{E}[\mathbf{x}_{T+1} \mid T])'\,\boldsymbol{\beta}_0 + \phi_0\, \mathrm{E}[y_{T+1} \mid T]\end{aligned}$$

Note that if y_{t-1} is an element of $\mathbf{x}_t$, then $\mathrm{E}[y_{T+1} \mid T]$ appears not only in the final term but also in

$$\mathrm{E}[\mathbf{x}_{T+2} \mid T] = \begin{bmatrix}\mathbf{x}'_{1,T+2} & \mathrm{E}[y_{T+1} \mid T]\end{bmatrix}'$$

Additional steps into the future proceed with the same recursion:

$$\begin{aligned}\mathrm{E}[\mathbf{x}_{T+n} \mid T] &= \begin{bmatrix}\mathbf{x}'_{1,T+n} & \mathrm{E}[y_{T+n-1} \mid T]\end{bmatrix}' \\ \mathrm{E}[y_{T+n} \mid T] &= (\mathrm{E}[\mathbf{x}_{T+n} \mid T] - \phi_0 \cdot \mathrm{E}[\mathbf{x}_{T+n-1} \mid T])'\,\boldsymbol{\beta}_0 + \phi_0\, \mathrm{E}[y_{T+n-1} \mid T]\end{aligned}$$

$(n = 3, 4, \ldots)$.

In practice, one replaces the unknown population parameters with estimators. The first point forecast will be

$$\hat{\mu}_{T+1} = (\mathbf{x}_{T+1} - \hat{\phi} \cdot \mathbf{x}_T)'\hat{\boldsymbol{\beta}} + \hat{\phi} y_T$$

and additional point forecasts iterate on

$$\begin{aligned}\hat{\mathbf{x}}_{T+n} &= \begin{bmatrix}\mathbf{x}'_{1,T+n} & \hat{\mu}_{T+n-1}\end{bmatrix}' \\ \hat{\mu}_{T+n} &= (\hat{\mathbf{x}}_{T+n} - \hat{\phi} \cdot \hat{\mathbf{x}}_{T+n-1})'\hat{\boldsymbol{\beta}} + \hat{\phi}\hat{\mu}_{T+n-1}\end{aligned}$$

$(n = 2, 3, 4, \ldots)$. Interval forecasts require estimators of the variance matrix of these forecasts and one derives asymptotic approximations with the delta method. In samples that are too small for asymptotic approximations, there are no general analytical results because the estimators $\hat{\boldsymbol{\beta}}$ and $\hat{\phi}$ are generally nonlinear and the forecasts are also nonlinear in these parameter estimators. It is possible that simpler methods yield smaller MSE forecasts. The leading competitor to these forecasts is simple OLS fitted values using regressions that ignore autocorrelation in disturbance terms and remove y_{t-1} from the RHS.

19.8 METHODOLOGICAL NOTES

In this chapter and in Chapter 18, we have introduced nonscalar variance matrices with first-order AR serial correlation and conditional heteroskedasticity. In these methodological notes, we caution against casual or routine application of the methods of inference that we have described.

First, a significant test statistic may indicate deviations from any aspect of the null hypothesis. Although the Breusch–Godfrey and Durbin–Watson tests are designed to detect first-order AR serial correlation, these tests are also sensitive to misspecification of the conditional mean.

Therefore, researchers often consider this possibility when a significant test statistic pops up on some computer output.

To illustrate this possiblity, suppose that

$$\mathrm{E}[y_n \mid \mathbf{X}_n] = \beta_{01} + \beta_{02}x_n + \beta_{03}x_n^2, \qquad n = 1, \ldots, N$$

and the variance matrix of y_n is scalar. If the data are entered into the computer regression program in the order of increasing x_n, and if one fits a regression excluding the squared term, then it would not be surprising to find evidence of serial correlation.

Figure 19.1 illustrates the problem. Where the best straight line lies above the quadratic mean, the fitted residuals are more likely to be negative. Similarly where this line lies below the quadratic mean there is a series of fitted residuals that tend to be positive. This is exactly the sort of behavior that the tests of serial correlation detect. So one may see "evidence" of serial correlation when actually an explanatory variable has been omitted.

Such concerns arise with all hypothesis test statistics. In general, the null hypothesis includes more restrictions on the data-generating process than the restrictions relaxed under the explicit alternative hypothesis. As a result, the associated test statistic generally has power to detect several restrictions. The Breusch–Pagan score test for heteroskedasticity has the same potential sensitivity to errors in functional form as the tests for serial correlation. In regions in which the best straight line is furthest from the quadratic mean the fitted residuals tend to be largest. This could be detected as heteroskedasticity related to the value of x_n even though the data-generating process is homoskedastic around its mean.

Such interpretation of significant hypothesis test statistics emphasizes the roles that the null and alternative hypotheses play in classical statistical inference. The null hypothesis embodies everything thought to be true. Its alternative includes all aspects of the model that the researcher will reconsider if there is strong empirical evidence against them. One may legitimately decide to include in the alternative hypothesis aspects of the model that a particular test statistic does not explicitly, or originally, address. In that case, however, we should also consider whether there is a better test statistic for the concerns at hand.

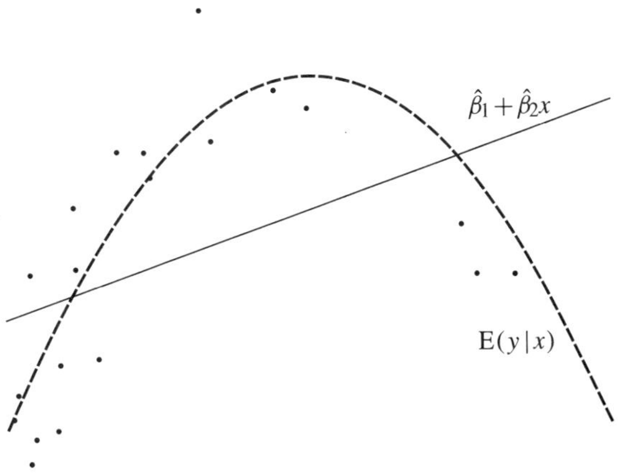

Figure 19.1 Serial correlation versus omitted explanatory variables.

We also wish to remind the student that the FGLS estimator may be inefficient relative to the OLS estimator in small samples. Although the FGLS estimator is asymptotically equivalent to the GLS estimator, in small samples the estimation of the variance matrix $\mathbf{\Omega}$ may actually increase the variance of the FGLS estimator relative to GLS and even OLS. The asymptotic approximation of the distribution of FGLS treats the estimated $\mathbf{\Omega}$ as though it contained no sampling variation whereas $\hat{\mathbf{\Omega}}$ clearly does.

We noted in our discussion of heteroskedasticity that OLS dominates FGLS when $\mathbf{\Omega}$ is near scalar. Here we wish to add that substantial correlation can be present and yet OLS may dominate FGLS. This occurs because some combinations of explanatory variables and serial correlation leave the GLS and OLS estimators exactly equal.

EXAMPLE 19.3

Suppose that we observe two *correlated* random variables with the same means and variances: $E[y_1] = E[y_2] = \mu$, $\text{Var}[y_i] = \sigma_0^2$, and $\text{Cov}[y_1, y_2] = \phi_0\sigma_0^2 \neq 0$. The only change from Example 18.7 is in the variance matrix,

$$\mathbf{\Omega}_0 = \begin{bmatrix} \sigma_0^2 & \phi_0\sigma_0^2 \\ \phi_0\sigma_0^2 & \sigma_0^2 \end{bmatrix}$$

The variance ellipsoid of $\mathbf{y} = [y_n; n = 1, 2]'$ is displayed in Figure 19.2. Note that $\mathbf{X} = [1, 1]'$. Looking at the figure, we can see that the unbiased, minimum variance projection of $\mathbf{y}$ onto $\text{Col}(\mathbf{X})$ is the orthogonal projection. In other words, OLS and GLS appear to be identical.

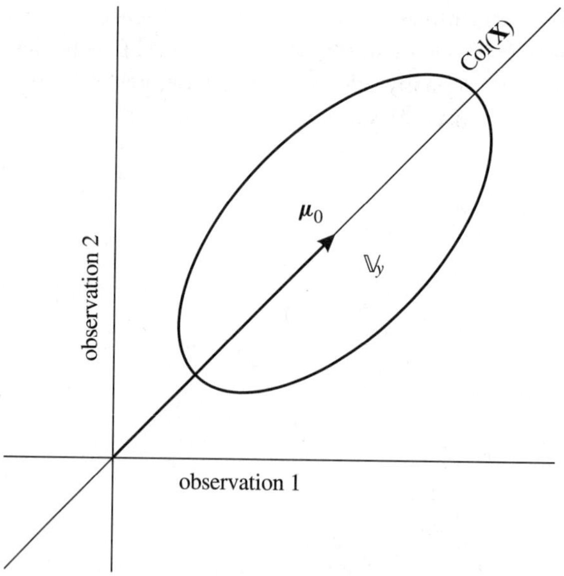

Figure 19.2 Correlated variance ellipsoid.

This is a simple example of a more general result (Miliken and Albohali, 1984).

> **LEMMA 19.1 (OLS/GLS IDENTITY)** *Let* $\mathbf{X}$ *be full-column rank. The OLS and GLS estimators are identical if and only if* $\mathrm{Col}(\mathbf{\Omega}_0^{-1}\mathbf{X}) = \mathrm{Col}(\mathbf{X})$ *or, equivalently,* $\mathrm{Col}(\mathbf{\Omega}_0\mathbf{X}) = \mathrm{Col}(\mathbf{X})$.

This lemma follows directly as a property of projectors. A proof appears in Section 19.9.4. Additional examples appear in Exercises 19.4 and 24.7.

When OLS and GLS are equal, the FGLS estimator may or may not equal the OLS estimator. In many cases, $\mathrm{Col}(\hat{\mathbf{\Omega}}^{-1}\mathbf{X}) = \mathrm{Col}(\mathbf{X})$ also holds and establishes an equality. Thus, FGLS need not entail a loss in efficiency relative to OLS. On the other hand, Lemma 19.1 shows that $\mathbf{\Omega}_0$ need not be approximately scalar for OLS to dominate the FGLS estimator in sampling variances. More generally, there are situations in which $\mathbf{X}'\mathbf{\Omega}_0^{-1}\mathbf{X}$ is roughly proportional to $\mathbf{X}'\mathbf{X}$ and these also confer an advantage on the OLS estimator.

19.9 MATHEMATICAL NOTES

These notes present the details of the log-likelihood and its associated terms and discuss changes to the asymptotic distribution theory necessitated by the model of serial correlation.

19.9.1 Score and Information

Without changing the asymptotic analysis, we use only the term

$$\mathrm{E}_{T|1}[L(\boldsymbol{\theta}\,|\,\mathbf{X})] \equiv \mathrm{E}_{T|1}\left[-\frac{1}{2}\log 2\pi\sigma_v^2 - \frac{1}{2}\frac{(\varepsilon_t - \phi\varepsilon_{t-1})^2}{\sigma_v^2}\right]$$

of the complete log-likelihood function given in (19.19). Differentiating this with respect to each of the parameters, we obtain the scores[19]

$$\mathrm{E}_{T|1}[L_{\boldsymbol{\beta}}(\boldsymbol{\theta}\,|\,\mathbf{X})] = \frac{1}{\sigma_v^2}\,\mathrm{E}_{T|1}[(\mathbf{x}_t - \phi\cdot\mathbf{x}_{t-1})(\varepsilon_t - \phi\varepsilon_{t-1})] \tag{19.30}$$

$$\mathrm{E}_{T|1}[L_{\sigma_v^2}(\boldsymbol{\theta}\,|\,\mathbf{X})] = -\frac{1}{2\sigma_v^4}\left\{\sigma_v^2 - \mathrm{E}_{T|1}[(\varepsilon_t - \phi\varepsilon_{t-1})^2]\right\} \tag{19.31}$$

$$\mathrm{E}_{T|1}[L_{\phi}(\boldsymbol{\theta}\,|\,\mathbf{X})] = \frac{1}{\sigma_v^2}\,\mathrm{E}_{T|1}[\varepsilon_{t-1}(\varepsilon_t - \phi\varepsilon_{t-1})] \tag{19.32}$$

The scores for $\boldsymbol{\beta}$ and σ_v^2 have the functional form of the uncorrelated case except that *quasi-differences* $\varepsilon_t - \phi\varepsilon_{t-1}$ and $\mathbf{x}_t - \phi\cdot\mathbf{x}_{t-1}$ replace ε_t and $\mathbf{x}_t$.[20] The score for ϕ has the form of the score for an OLS regression of ε_t on ε_{t-1}.

---

[19] Remember that $\varepsilon_t = y_t - \mathbf{x}_t'\boldsymbol{\beta}$ is a function of $\boldsymbol{\beta}$.

[20] One may compare these expressions with those in Example 14.11 (p. 294).

To derive the information matrix, we will find the variance matrix of the first two scores evaluated at $\boldsymbol{\theta}_0 = [\boldsymbol{\beta}_0', \sigma_{0\upsilon}^2, \phi_0]'$. It is convenient to rewrite these elements in terms of the quasidifferences

$$\upsilon_{0t} \equiv \varepsilon_{0t} - \phi_0 \varepsilon_{0,t-1} \tag{19.33}$$

$$\mathbf{x}_{*t} \equiv \mathbf{x}_t - \phi_0 \cdot \mathbf{x}_{t-1} \tag{19.34}$$

We know that the υ_{0t} are i.i.d. $\mathfrak{N}(0, \sigma_\upsilon^2)$ from (19.10) and that $\varepsilon_{0,t-1}$ and υ_{0t} are independent normal random variables from (19.14). Therefore, using the score in (19.30)–(19.32), typical score elements for $t > 1$ are

$$L_{\boldsymbol{\beta}}(\boldsymbol{\theta}_0) = \frac{1}{\sigma_{0\upsilon}^2} \mathbf{x}_{*t} \upsilon_{0t} \tag{19.35}$$

$$L_{\sigma_\upsilon^2}(\boldsymbol{\theta}_0) = -\frac{1}{2\sigma_{0\upsilon}^4} \left(\sigma_{0\upsilon}^2 - \upsilon_{0t}^2\right) \tag{19.36}$$

$$L_{\phi}(\boldsymbol{\theta}_0) = \frac{1}{\sigma_{0\upsilon}^2} \varepsilon_{0,t-1} \upsilon_{0t} \tag{19.37}$$

The variances of $L_{\boldsymbol{\beta}}(\boldsymbol{\theta}_0)$ and $L_{\sigma_\upsilon^2}(\boldsymbol{\theta}_0)$ also have the same functional form as their counterparts in the serially uncorrelated case, (14.25). In addition,

$$\begin{array}{lclcrcl} \mathrm{E}[\varepsilon_{0,t-1}\upsilon_{0t}^2 \mid \mathbf{X}] & = & 0 & \Rightarrow & \mathrm{E}[L_\phi(\boldsymbol{\theta}_0)\, L_{\boldsymbol{\beta}}(\boldsymbol{\theta}_0)\,] & = & \mathbf{0} \\ \mathrm{E}[\varepsilon_{0,t-1}\upsilon_{0t}^3 \mid \mathbf{X}] & = & 0 & \Rightarrow & \mathrm{E}[L_\phi(\boldsymbol{\theta}_0)\, L_{\sigma_\upsilon^2}(\boldsymbol{\theta}_0)] & = & 0 \end{array} \tag{19.38}$$

showing block-diagonality in the information matrix between $\mathfrak{I}_{\phi\phi}(\boldsymbol{\theta}_0)$ and the rest of the matrix.

Finally, differentiating (19.32) again, and taking the expectation, yields the information matrix element

$$\mathfrak{I}_{\phi\phi}(\theta_0 \mid X) = \frac{1}{\sigma_{0\upsilon}^2} \mathrm{E}[\varepsilon_{0,t-1}^2] = \frac{1}{1 - \phi_0^2}$$

Gathering these results together, the complete conditional information matrix is

$$\begin{aligned} \mathrm{Var}[L_{\boldsymbol{\theta}}(\boldsymbol{\theta}_0) \mid y_{t-1}, x_1, \ldots, x_t] &= \mathfrak{I}(\theta_0 \mid y_{t-1}, x_1, \ldots, x_t) \\ &= \begin{bmatrix} \frac{1}{\sigma_{0\upsilon}^2} \cdot \mathbf{x}_{*t}\mathbf{x}_{*t}' & \mathbf{0} & \mathbf{0} \\ \mathbf{0} & 1/(2\sigma_{0\upsilon}^4) & 0 \\ \mathbf{0} & 0 & 1/(1-\phi_0^2) \end{bmatrix} \end{aligned} \tag{19.39}$$

19.9.2 Breusch–Godfrey Score Test

Like the Breusch–Pagan score test for heteroskedasticity, this score test is pivotal. If the exact significance level of a statistic is required, one can simply simulate the value by Monte Carlo. Recall that $\hat{\boldsymbol{\varepsilon}} = \mathbf{P_X}\boldsymbol{\varepsilon}_0$ where $\mathbf{P_X} \equiv \mathbf{X}(\mathbf{X}'\mathbf{X})^{-1}\mathbf{X}'$ and $\boldsymbol{\varepsilon}_0 \equiv \left[y_t - \mathbf{x}_t'\boldsymbol{\beta}_0\right]'$. Under the null hypothesis, we can therefore write

$$S = (T-1)\frac{\boldsymbol{\varepsilon}_0'\mathbf{Q}_1\boldsymbol{\varepsilon}_0}{\boldsymbol{\varepsilon}_0'\mathbf{Q}_2\boldsymbol{\varepsilon}_0} \sim (T-1)\frac{\mathbf{z}'\mathbf{Q}_1\mathbf{z}}{\mathbf{z}'\mathbf{Q}_2\mathbf{z}}$$

where $\mathbf{Q}_1$ and $\mathbf{Q}_2$ are submatrices of $\mathbf{P_X}$,

$$\mathbf{Q}_1 \equiv \mathbf{P_X}\begin{bmatrix}\mathbf{0}\\ \mathbf{I}_{T-1}\end{bmatrix}\begin{bmatrix}\mathbf{I}_{T-1} & \mathbf{0}\end{bmatrix}\mathbf{P_X}$$

$$\mathbf{Q}_2 \equiv \mathbf{P_X}\begin{bmatrix}\mathbf{I}_{T-1}\\ \mathbf{0}\end{bmatrix}\begin{bmatrix}\mathbf{I}_{T-1} & \mathbf{0}\end{bmatrix}\mathbf{P_X}$$

and $\mathbf{z} \sim \mathfrak{N}(\mathbf{0}, \mathbf{I}_T)$. By replicating draws of $\mathbf{z}$ we can replicate the statistic S under the null hypothesis and calculate any property of its distribution to any desired precision. In particular, one could compute the frequency with which the simulated statistics exceeded the value of the score test statistic for the sample at hand, thereby computing the exact probability value.

19.9.3 Asymptotic Distribution Theory

For clarity, we will abstract initially from the estimation of $\boldsymbol{\beta}_0$ and consider

$$\mathrm{E}_{T|1}[L(\boldsymbol{\theta})] = -\frac{1}{2}\log 2\pi\sigma_v^2 - \frac{1}{2}\frac{\mathrm{E}_{T|1}[(\varepsilon_{0t} - \phi\varepsilon_{0,t-1})^2]}{\sigma_v^2}$$

as a function of ϕ and σ_v^2 only. The argument for unknown $\boldsymbol{\beta}_0$ is the same in spirit, but not in simplicity.

To demonstrate consistency, we will show that this average sample log-likelihood still converges in probability uniformly to its expectation. And we will apply the logic of the Chebychev LLN once again to do so. Provided that the variance of an average converges to zero, the Chebychev inequality will deliver convergence in probability to the expectation.

The variance of the sum of squares in $\mathrm{E}_{T|1}[L(\boldsymbol{\theta})]$ requires fourth-order moments of the multivariate normal distribution. In general, if $\mathbf{z} \sim \mathfrak{N}(\mathbf{0}, [\sigma_{ij}; i, j = 1, 2, 3, 4])$ then

$$\mathrm{E}[z_1 z_2 z_3 z_4] = \sigma_{12}\sigma_{34} + \sigma_{13}\sigma_{24} + \sigma_{14}\sigma_{23}$$

so that

$$\begin{aligned}\mathrm{Cov}\left[\varepsilon_{0t}^2, \varepsilon_{0,t-n}^2\right] &= 2\sigma_0^4\phi_0^{2n}\\ &= \mathrm{Cov}[\varepsilon_{0t}\varepsilon_{0,t-1}, \varepsilon_{0,t-n}\varepsilon_{0,t-n-1}]\end{aligned}$$

for $n \geq 0$.[21] Now after some manipulation,

$$\begin{aligned}\mathrm{Var}\left[\sum_{t=2}^{T}\frac{\varepsilon_{0t}^2}{T-1}\right] &= \frac{1}{(T-1)^2}\sum_{t=2}^{T}\sum_{n=2}^{T}\mathrm{Cov}[\varepsilon_{0t}^2, \varepsilon_{0n}^2]\\ &= \frac{2\sigma_0^4}{(T-1)^2}\left(\sum_{t=2}^{T}\sum_{n=2}^{T}\phi_0^{2|t-n|}\right)\\ &= \frac{2\sigma_0^2}{(T-1)^2}\frac{(T-1) - 2\phi_0^2 - (T-1)\,\phi_0^4 + 2\phi_0^{2T}}{\left(1-\phi_0^2\right)^2}\end{aligned} \tag{19.40}$$

[21] We must work through some algebra to show these results. One approach is to use the multivariate normal moment-generating function (m.g.f.) $M_{\mathbf{Z}}(\mathbf{t}) = \exp(\mathbf{t}'\boldsymbol{\mu} + \frac{1}{2}\mathbf{t}'\boldsymbol{\Omega}\mathbf{t})$ for $\mathbf{Z} \sim \mathfrak{N}(\boldsymbol{\mu}, \boldsymbol{\Omega})$.

which approaches 0 as $T \to \infty$.[22] The variance of $\sum_{t=2}^{T} \varepsilon_{0,t}\varepsilon_{0,t-1}$ behaves identically. Therefore, the sample average log-likelihood converges in probability to its expectation,

$$\mathrm{E}\{\mathrm{E}_{T|1}[L(\theta)]\} = -\frac{1}{2}\log 2\pi\sigma_v^2 - \frac{1}{2}\frac{\mathrm{E}[\varepsilon_{0t}^2 - 2\phi\varepsilon_{0t}\varepsilon_{0,t-1} + \phi^2\varepsilon_{0,t-1}^2]}{\sigma_v^2}$$
$$= -\frac{1}{2}\log 2\pi\sigma_v^2 - \frac{1}{2}\frac{\sigma_0^2 - 2\phi_0\sigma_0^2\phi + \sigma_0^2\phi^2}{\sigma_v^2} \qquad (19.41)$$

This convergence is uniform on a closed and bounded parameter space that satisfies $|\phi| < 1$.

The consistency of the MLE follows from the arguments in Section 15.2. The expected log-likelihood function (19.41) is maximized at $\phi = \phi_0$ and $\sigma_v^2 = \sigma_0^2(1-\phi_0^2)$, the population values that the MLE estimates. Because the sample average log-likelihood function converges in probability to its expectation uniformly in the parameters ϕ and σ_v^2, the MLE converges in probability to ϕ_0 and σ_v^2.

If we now consider adding $\boldsymbol{\beta}$ into the problem, we must analyze

$$\mathrm{E}_{T|1}[L(\boldsymbol{\theta})] = -\frac{1}{2}\log 2\pi\sigma_v^2 - \frac{1}{2}\frac{\mathrm{E}_{T|1}[(\mathbf{x}_t - \phi\cdot\mathbf{x}_{t-1})'(\boldsymbol{\beta}-\boldsymbol{\beta}_0) + \varepsilon_{0t} - \phi\varepsilon_{0,t-1})]^2}{\sigma_v^2}$$

which implies two additional terms,

$$\mathrm{E}_{T|1}[(\mathbf{x}_t - \phi\cdot\mathbf{x}_{t-1})(\boldsymbol{\beta}-\boldsymbol{\beta}_0)]^2$$

and

$$\mathrm{E}_{T|1}[(\varepsilon_{0t} - \phi\varepsilon_{0,t-1})(\mathbf{x}_t - \phi\cdot\mathbf{x}_{t-1})'(\boldsymbol{\beta}-\boldsymbol{\beta}_0)]$$

that must converge in probability to their expectations. If, for example, the $\mathbf{x}_t$ are also AR time series, then the same arguments apply to these sums and the MLE for $\boldsymbol{\theta}_0 = [\boldsymbol{\beta}_0', \sigma_{0v}^2, \phi_0]'$ is consistent.

Once we have established consistency, we must also make adjustments to our previous arguments for asymptotic normality. The parameter ϕ presents the basic difficulty, so we will focus our attention there first, assuming $\boldsymbol{\beta}_0$ and σ_{0v}^2 known. Using the usual linear expansion of the score,

$$\sqrt{T}(\hat{\phi}_{\mathrm{ML}} - \phi_0) = \left\{-\mathrm{E}_{T|1}[L_{\phi\phi}(\bar{\phi})]\right\}^{-1}\sqrt{T}\,\mathrm{E}_{T|1}[L_\phi(\phi_0)]$$

The L_ϕ score is given in (19.32) so that

$$\sqrt{T}\,\mathrm{E}_{T|1}[L_\phi(\phi_0)] = \frac{1}{\sigma_{0v}^2}\sqrt{T}\,\mathrm{E}_{T|1}[\varepsilon_{0,t-1}v_{0t}]$$

which does not contain a sum of i.n.i.d. terms. So we cannot apply the Liapounov CLT.

One way to overcome the dependence uses the following properties of the elements of the sum:

---

[22] The key algebraic identity is

$$\sum_{t=1}^{T}\sum_{v=1}^{T}\alpha^{|t-v|} = \frac{T - 2\alpha - T\alpha^2 + 2\alpha^{T+1}}{(1-\alpha)^2}$$

which can be confirmed by multiplying both sides by $(1-\alpha)^2$.

$$\mathrm{E}[\varepsilon_{0,t-1}\upsilon_{0t} \mid \varepsilon_{01}, \ldots, \varepsilon_{0,t-1}] = 0 \tag{19.42}$$

$$\frac{1}{T}\sum_{t=2}^{T}(\varepsilon_{0,t-1}\upsilon_{0t})^2 \xrightarrow{p} \mathrm{Var}[\varepsilon_{0,t-1}\upsilon_{0t}] \tag{19.43}$$

The first property (19.42) characterizes $\{\varepsilon_{0,t-1}\upsilon_{0t}\}$ as a *martingale difference sequence*. The conditional expectation of an element of a martingale difference sequence given all preceding elements of the sequence is zero.[23] We proved the second property (19.43) above using (19.40). It establishes that the sample variance of the elements of the sequence is a consistent estimator for the average variance, in this case the same for all elements. These properties enable us to use the following CLT (White, 1984).

THEOREM 15 (MARTINGALE DIFFERENCE CLT) *Let $\{U_t\}$ be a sequence such that $\mathrm{E}[U_t \mid U_n, n \le t] = 0$, $\mathrm{Var}[U_t] \equiv \sigma_t^2 > \epsilon > 0$, and $\mathrm{E}[|U_t|^3]$ is uniformly bounded. If*

$$\bar{\sigma}^2 \equiv \lim_{T\to\infty} \mathrm{E}_T[\sigma_t^2]$$

exists and

$$\mathrm{E}_T[U_t^2] \xrightarrow{p} \bar{\sigma}^2$$

then

$$\sqrt{T}\frac{\mathrm{E}_T[U]}{\bar{\sigma}} \xrightarrow{d} \mathfrak{N}(0, 1)$$

We have stated this result in a stronger form than White (1984). As he points out, this CLT is similar to the Liapounov CLT in the bounded third-moment condition. In addition, the martingale difference property has weakened the independence requirement, but in exchange the sample variance of the sequence must consistently estimate the average variance. This condition is implied by the third-moment bound if the $\{U_t\}$ are independent.

Returning to the AR model and the additional parameters $\boldsymbol{\beta}$ and σ_υ^2, we find that their scores also contain martingale difference sequences:

$$L_{\boldsymbol{\beta}}(\theta_0) = \frac{1}{\sigma_{0\upsilon}^2}\sum_{t=2}^{T}(\mathbf{x}_t - \phi_0 \cdot \mathbf{x}_{t-1})\upsilon_{0t}$$

$$L_{\sigma_\upsilon^2}(\theta_0) = -\frac{1}{2\sigma_{0\upsilon}^4}\sum_{t=2}^{T}\left(\sigma_{0\upsilon}^2 - \upsilon_{0t}^2\right)$$

If the absolute third moments of these elements are also uniformly bounded (which constrains the behavior of $\mathbf{x}_t$) and the sample variance of these scores consistently estimates the information matrix, then the Cramér–Wold device and the martingale difference CLT imply that

[23] See White (1984, Section III.5, V.5) for an introduction to martingale difference sequences.

$$\sqrt{T-1}\,\mathrm{E}_{T|1}[L_{\theta}(\theta_0)] \xrightarrow{d} \mathfrak{N}[\mathbf{0}, \mathfrak{I}(\theta_0)]$$

Levine (1983) points out that these asymptotic forces have a different, general application to the marginal log-likelihood function of elements of stationary stochastic processes. Suppose that $L(\theta; y_t)$ is the marginal log-likelihood for every y_t in the sequence $\{y_t;\ t = 1, \ldots, T\}$. If the population parameter value θ_0 is identified, then θ_0 is the unique maximum in θ of $\mathrm{E}[L(\theta; y_t)]$. Therefore, one can often construct a consistent estimator for θ_0 from the maximum $\hat{\theta}$ of the sample average log-likelihood function, $\mathrm{E}_T[L(\theta; y_t)]$, provided that this function converges in probability uniformly to its expectation. Typically, one proves this with a uniform LLN for dependent sequences.

Furthermore, this $\hat{\theta}$ will be asymptotically normal when such a CLT as Theorem 15 applies to $\sqrt{T}\,\mathrm{E}_T[L_{\theta}(\theta_0; y_t)]$ and a uniform LLN applies to $\mathrm{E}_T[L_{\theta\theta}(\theta; y_t)]$ in a neighborhood of θ_0. Then the analysis of the MLE in Section 15.3.3 applies to this estimator, so that

$$\sqrt{T}\left(\hat{\theta} - \theta_0\right) \stackrel{p}{=} \{\mathrm{E}_T[L_{\theta\theta}(\theta; y_t)]\}^{-1}\sqrt{T}\mathrm{E}_T[L_{\theta}(\theta_0; y_t)]$$

Although $\mathrm{E}_T[L(\theta; y_t)]$ is an average of log-likelihood functions, this objective function is not the average log-likelihood function of the *sample* if $\{y_t\}$ is a dependent sequence. The log-likelihood function for first-order AR serial correlation illustrates this. Thus, it is inappropriate to call the $\hat{\theta}$ that maximizes $\mathrm{E}_T[L(\theta; y_t)]$ an MLE. Instead, researchers often refer to such estimators as a *quasi maximum likelihood estimator* (QMLE) or a *pseudo maximum likelihood estimator*. These estimators play an important role in providing convenient initial estimators for some of the parameters in the process generating a dependent stochastic sequence.

19.9.4 OLS versus GLS

The following proof of the necessary and sufficient conditions for OLS to equal GLS is a direct application of the properties of projections.

Proof of Lemma 19.1. The OLS and GLS estimators are equal if and only if their fitted values are equal. The fitted values are equal if and only if the projectors are equal. As we have seen, the GLS estimator uses the projection

$$\begin{aligned}\hat{\mu}_{\mathrm{GLS}} &= \mathbf{X}(\mathbf{X}'\mathbf{\Omega}_0^{-1}\mathbf{X})^{-1}\mathbf{X}'\mathbf{\Omega}_0^{-1}\mathbf{y} \\ &= \mathbf{P}_{\mathbf{X}\perp\mathbf{Z}}\mathbf{y}\end{aligned}$$

where $\mathbf{Z} = \mathbf{\Omega}_0^{-1}\mathbf{X}$. According to Lemma 3.4 (p. 67) this projector is well defined if and only if $\mathbb{R}^N = \mathrm{Col}^{\perp}(\mathbf{Z}) \oplus \mathrm{Col}(\mathbf{X})$. According to Lemmas 3.1 (p. 63) and 3.5 (p. 68), this projector is the orthogonal projector onto $\mathrm{Col}(\mathbf{X})$ if and only if $\mathrm{Col}^{\perp}(\mathbf{Z}) = \mathrm{Col}^{\perp}(\mathbf{X})$. But then $\mathrm{Col}(\mathbf{\Omega}_0^{-1}\mathbf{X}) = \mathrm{Col}(\mathbf{Z}) = \mathrm{Col}(\mathbf{X})$. This proves the first part.

Now $\mathrm{Col}(\mathbf{\Omega}_0^{-1}\mathbf{X}) = \mathrm{Col}(\mathbf{X})$ and $\mathbf{X}$ is full-column rank if and only if the equation $\mathbf{\Omega}_0^{-1}\mathbf{X}\boldsymbol{\alpha} = \mathbf{X}\boldsymbol{\beta}$ determines a one-to-one relationship between $\boldsymbol{\alpha}, \boldsymbol{\beta} \in \mathbb{R}^K$.[24] Equiva-

[24] In particular,

$$\boldsymbol{\alpha} = \left(\mathbf{X}'\mathbf{\Omega}_0^{-1}\mathbf{X}\right)^{-1}\mathbf{X}'\mathbf{X}\boldsymbol{\beta}$$

lently, $\mathbf{X}\boldsymbol{\alpha} = \boldsymbol{\Omega}_0\mathbf{X}\boldsymbol{\beta}$ determines a one-to-one relationship between $\boldsymbol{\alpha}, \boldsymbol{\beta} \in \mathbb{R}^K$ and this implies that $\mathrm{Col}(\mathbf{X}) = \mathrm{Col}(\boldsymbol{\Omega}_0\mathbf{X})$. □

19.10 OVERVIEW

1. Serial correlation occurs when the covariances of the y_n conditional on $\mathbf{X}$ are not zero. This is another exception to the second-moment property that $\boldsymbol{\Omega}_0 \equiv \mathrm{Var}[\mathbf{y} \mid \mathbf{X}]$ is a scalar matrix. Serial correlation arises in time-series data where the observations have a specific serial order. A simple model of serial correlation is first-order autoregressive (AR) for which the correlations die out geometrically as the distance between observations grows.
2. As an exception to the classical second-moments assumption, serial correlation has the same general effects as heteroskedasticity. The variance of the ordinary least squares (OLS) estimator $\hat{\boldsymbol{\beta}}_{\mathrm{OLS}}$ is misestimated, $\hat{\boldsymbol{\beta}}_{\mathrm{OLS}}$ is not efficient relative to other linear and unbiased estimators, and test statistics are no longer pivotal. On the other hand, $\hat{\boldsymbol{\beta}}_{\mathrm{OLS}}$ remains unbiased, consistent, and conditionally normally distributed.
3. OLS-based tests for serial correlation can also be constructed from the OLS fitted residuals. The Breusch–Godfrey test is a another score test computed by OLS regression of the OLS fitted residuals on their lagged values. This test is closely related to the original Durbin–Watson test for serial correlation.
4. The Eicker–White variance estimator for the asymptotic variance matrix of $\hat{\boldsymbol{\beta}}_{\mathrm{OLS}}$ does not extend directly to the serially correlated case. The Newey–West variance estimator includes analogous covariance terms that are products of OLS fitted residuals, but downweights these covariances as the lag length grows, thereby preserving the consistency of the estimator.
5. The relatively efficient linear unbiased estimator is a generalized least squares (GLS) procedure in which adjacent observations, $(y_t, \mathbf{x}_t)$ and $(y_{t-1}, \mathbf{x}_{t-1})$, are quasidifferenced with the correlation parameter ϕ_0:

   $$(y_t - \phi_0 y_{t-1}, \mathbf{x}_t - \phi_0 \cdot \mathbf{x}_{t-1})$$

   This GLS is OLS applied to a regression equation transformed to satisfy the assumptions of the classical linear model by removing the serial correlation.
6. The maximum likelihood estimator (MLE) is a feasible version of $\hat{\boldsymbol{\beta}}_{\mathrm{GLS}}$:

   $$\hat{\boldsymbol{\beta}}_{\mathrm{ML}} \equiv \left(\mathbf{X}'\hat{\boldsymbol{\Omega}}_{\mathrm{ML}}^{-1}\mathbf{X}\right)^{-1}\mathbf{X}'\hat{\boldsymbol{\Omega}}_{\mathrm{ML}}^{-1}\mathbf{y}$$

   where $\hat{\boldsymbol{\Omega}}_{\mathrm{ML}}$ contains the fitted correlations $\hat{\phi}_{\mathrm{ML}}^{|n|}$. The linearized MLE (LMLE) that is asymptotically equivalent to the MLE is also a feasible GLS (FGLS) estimator:

   $$\hat{\boldsymbol{\beta}}_{\mathrm{LML}} = \left(\mathbf{X}'\check{\boldsymbol{\Omega}}^{-1}\mathbf{X}\right)^{-1}\mathbf{X}'\check{\boldsymbol{\Omega}}^{-1}\mathbf{y}$$

   Both the MLE and the LMLE are asymptotically equivalent to the GLS estimator because the information matrix is block-diagonal in the $\boldsymbol{\beta}$, σ^2, and ϕ parameter vectors.
7. A consistent estimator of ϕ_0 is the OLS fitted coefficient from the Breusch–Godfrey score test regression.
8. Prediction of future values of the dependent variable can exploit the serial correlation using a recursive procedure based on the quasidifferencing transformation.

---

and

$$\boldsymbol{\beta} = \left(\mathbf{X}'\mathbf{X}\right)^{-1}\mathbf{X}'\boldsymbol{\Omega}_0^{-1}\mathbf{X}\boldsymbol{\alpha}$$

19.11 EXERCISES

19.11.1 Review

19.1 [AR Restrictions] According to (19.20), the AR model for serial correlation places nonlinear restrictions on the coefficients of $\mathrm{E}[y_t \mid t-1]$. Describe a test of these restrictions. Suggest some alternative hypotheses this test possesses power to detect.

19.2 (Score Test) Let the conditional log-likelihood of $\mathbf{y}$ given $\mathbf{X}$ be (19.11). Noting that

$$\mathrm{E}[y_t \mid t-1] = \mathbf{x}_t'\boldsymbol{\beta}_0 + \phi_0(y_{t-1} + \mathbf{x}_{t-1}'\boldsymbol{\beta}_0)$$

(a) show that the OLS F test for $\phi_0 = 0$ in the artificial specification

$$\mathrm{E}[y_t \mid t-1] = \mathbf{x}_t'\boldsymbol{\beta}_0 + \phi_0\hat{\varepsilon}_{t-1}$$

is asymptotically equivalent to the Breusch–Pagan test and

(b) show that the fitted coefficient $\hat{\phi}$ from this regression is a consistent estimator of ϕ_0.

(c) What is the asymptotic distribution of the vector of fitted coefficients for $\boldsymbol{\beta}_0$?

19.3 (Autocorrelation Function) Compute an estimate of the autocorrelation function up to 7 lags for the AR model for serial correlation using the estimate $\hat{\phi} = -0.498$ reported in (19.3) and compare these values with those given on p. 457.

19.4 (OLS versus GLS) Using the following steps, show that the OLS and GLS estimators are approximately equal if $\boldsymbol{\Omega}_0$ equals (19.7) and the explanatory variables are a constant and a time trend: $K = 2$ and $x_{tk} = t^{k-1}$ for $k = 1, 2$.

(a) Show that

$$\boldsymbol{\Omega}_0^{-1} = \frac{1}{\sigma_0^2\left(1-\phi_0^2\right)} \cdot \begin{bmatrix} 1-\phi_0^2 & -\phi_0\sqrt{1-\phi_0^2} & 0 & 0 & \cdots & 0 \\ -\phi_0\sqrt{1-\phi_0^2} & 1+\phi_0^2 & -\phi_0 & 0 & \cdots & 0 \\ 0 & -\phi_0 & 1+\phi_0^2 & -\phi_0 & \cdots & 0 \\ 0 & 0 & -\phi_0 & 1+\phi_0^2 & \ddots & \vdots \\ \vdots & \vdots & \vdots & \ddots & \ddots & -\phi_0 \\ 0 & 0 & 0 & \cdots & -\phi_0 & 1+\phi_0^2 \end{bmatrix}$$

(b) Let $\mathbf{Z} = \boldsymbol{\Omega}_0^{-1}\mathbf{X}$ and show that

$$z_{tk} = \frac{1}{\sigma_0^2}t^{k-1} \qquad k = 1, 2 \qquad t = 3, \ldots, T-1$$

Therefore, $\mathbf{Z} \approx (1/\sigma_0^2) \cdot \mathbf{X}$.

(c) Show that the discrepancies in rows 1, 2, and T are asymptotically negligible. Hint:

$$\begin{aligned}\hat{\boldsymbol{\beta}}_{\mathrm{GLS}} - \hat{\boldsymbol{\beta}}_{\mathrm{OLS}} &= \left[\left(\mathbf{X}'\boldsymbol{\Omega}_0^{-1}\mathbf{X}\right)^{-1}\mathbf{X}'\boldsymbol{\Omega}_0^{-1} - (\mathbf{X}'\mathbf{X})^{-1}\mathbf{X}'\right]\mathbf{y} \\ &= \left(\mathbf{X}'\boldsymbol{\Omega}_0^{-1}\mathbf{X}\right)^{-1}\left[\mathbf{X}'\boldsymbol{\Omega}_0^{-1} - \mathbf{X}'\boldsymbol{\Omega}_0^{-1}\mathbf{X}\left(\mathbf{X}'\mathbf{X}\right)^{-1}\mathbf{X}'\right]\mathbf{y} \\ &= \left(\mathbf{X}'\boldsymbol{\Omega}_0^{-1}\mathbf{X}\right)^{-1}\mathbf{X}'\boldsymbol{\Omega}_0^{-1}\left[\mathbf{I} - \mathbf{X}\left(\mathbf{X}'\mathbf{X}\right)^{-1}\mathbf{X}'\right]\mathbf{y}\end{aligned}$$

19.5 (OLS versus GLS) If the OLS and GLS coefficient estimators are identical, can one use the estimated sampling variance matrix from OLS software for inferences about the population values of the regression coefficients? Explain your answer.

19.6 Derive an asymptotic approximation to the distribution of the first-order sample correlation among the OLS fitted residuals under the AR model for serial correlation.

19.7 (LMLE) Section 19.6.1 reviews several methods for computing estimators that are asymptotically equivalent to the MLE for normal linear regression with AR autocorrelation. Propose a two-step estimator of $\boldsymbol{\beta}_0$ based on the LMLE. Which of the listed estimators is most similar to your LMLE?

19.8 (GNR) Section 19.6.1 notes that NLS can be used to compute an estimator that is asymptotically equivalent to the MLE for normal linear regression with AR autocorrelation. Describe the application of Gauss–Newton regression (p. 359) to this problem.

19.11.2 Extensions

19.9 (Concentrated Likelihood) The sample mean log-likelihood function for the AR autocorrelated normal regression model appears in (19.11).[25]

(a) Show that concentrating σ_v^2 out of the log-likelihood yields

$$\begin{aligned} \mathrm{E}_T[L^{\mathrm{c}}(\boldsymbol{\beta}, \phi \mid \mathbf{X})] = & -\frac{1}{2}\log 2\pi + \frac{1}{2T}\log(1-\phi^2) \\ & -\frac{1}{2}\log\left[\frac{1}{T}(1-\phi^2)\varepsilon_1^2 + \frac{T-1}{T}\,\mathrm{E}_{T|1}(\varepsilon_t - \phi\varepsilon_{t-1})^2\right] \end{aligned}$$

(b) Show that the first-order condition for maximizing this concentrated log-likelihood function with respect to ϕ corresponds to equating a cubic polynomial in ϕ with zero

$$\phi^3 + a\phi^2 + b\phi + c = 0$$

Find the coefficients a, b, and c of this polynomial. Anderson (1971, pp. 354–355) shows that this polynomial has a unique real root in the interval $[-1, 1]$. Beach and MacKinnon (1978, p. 53) give a closed-form expression for this root:

$$\phi = -2\sqrt{\frac{q}{3}}\cos\left(\frac{\tau}{3} + \frac{\pi}{3}\right) - \frac{a}{3}$$

where

$$\tau = \cos^{-1}\left(\frac{-r\sqrt{27}}{2q\sqrt{q}}\right) \in [0, \pi]$$

$$q = \frac{a^2}{3} - b$$

$$r = \frac{2a^3}{27} - \frac{ab}{3} + c$$

(c) Beach and MacKinnon (1978) suggest maximizing $\mathrm{E}_T[L^{\mathrm{c}}(\boldsymbol{\beta}, \phi \mid \mathbf{X})]$ by iteratively maximizing with respect to $\boldsymbol{\beta}$, ϕ held fixed, and maximizing with respect to ϕ, $\boldsymbol{\beta}$ held fixed.

---

[25] This exercise follows the work in Beach and MacKinnon (1978).

Alternatively, one could concentrate ϕ out of $\mathrm{E}_T[L^c(\boldsymbol{\beta}, \phi \mid \mathbf{X})]$ and maximize the resulting concentrated log-likelihood function over $\boldsymbol{\beta}$ only. Discuss the merits of these two approaches.

19.10 Do Exercise 19.3 and then suggest a test for whether the estimated autocorrelation function differs from estimates based on the autocorrelation function of the OLS fitted residuals.

19.11 (Information) If $\mathbf{y} \mid \mathbf{X} \sim \mathfrak{N}\left[\mathbf{X}\boldsymbol{\beta}_0, \boldsymbol{\Omega}(\boldsymbol{\gamma}_0)\right]$, then

$$L(\boldsymbol{\beta}, \boldsymbol{\gamma}; \mathbf{y} \mid \mathbf{X}) = -\frac{1}{2} \log \det[2\pi \cdot \boldsymbol{\Omega}(\boldsymbol{\gamma})] - \frac{1}{2}\boldsymbol{\varepsilon}(\boldsymbol{\beta})'\boldsymbol{\Omega}(\boldsymbol{\gamma})^{-1}\boldsymbol{\varepsilon}(\boldsymbol{\beta})$$

where $\boldsymbol{\varepsilon}(\boldsymbol{\beta}) \equiv \mathbf{y} - \mathbf{X}\boldsymbol{\beta}$, is the log-likelihood function.[26] Given that

$$\frac{\partial L}{\partial \boldsymbol{\beta}} = \mathbf{X}'\boldsymbol{\Omega}(\boldsymbol{\gamma})^{-1}\boldsymbol{\varepsilon}(\boldsymbol{\beta})$$

$$\frac{\partial L}{\partial \boldsymbol{\gamma}} = -\frac{1}{2}\frac{\partial\left[\operatorname{vec}\boldsymbol{\Omega}(\boldsymbol{\gamma})\right]'}{\partial \boldsymbol{\gamma}} \operatorname{vec}\left[\boldsymbol{\Omega}(\boldsymbol{\gamma})^{-1} - \boldsymbol{\Omega}(\boldsymbol{\gamma})^{-1}\boldsymbol{\varepsilon}(\boldsymbol{\beta})\boldsymbol{\varepsilon}(\boldsymbol{\beta})'\boldsymbol{\Omega}(\boldsymbol{\gamma})^{-1}\right]$$

where $\boldsymbol{\gamma} = [\gamma_1, \ldots, \gamma_J]'$, show that the information matrix is block-diagonal in $\boldsymbol{\beta}$ and $\boldsymbol{\gamma}$.

19.12 [AR(2)] Consider the following generalization of the AR normal linear regression model: let $\mathrm{E}[y_t \mid \mathbf{x}_t] = \mathbf{x}_t'\boldsymbol{\beta}_0$ and denote $\varepsilon_t \equiv y_t - \mathbf{x}_t'\boldsymbol{\beta}_0$. Suppose that

$$\varepsilon_t = \phi_{01}\varepsilon_{t-1} + \phi_{02}\varepsilon_{t-2} + u_t$$

where $\{u_t\}$ is a sequence of i.i.d. $\mathfrak{N}(0, \sigma_{0u}^2)$ random variables. Suppose that $\{\varepsilon_t\}$ is covariance stationary for $t = 1, \ldots, T$.

(a) Given ϕ_{01} and ϕ_{02}, find a simple transformation for y_t and $\mathbf{x}_t$ $(t = 3, \ldots, T)$ that will yield GLS from OLS.

(b) Show that

$$\mathrm{E}[\varepsilon_t \mid t-1] = \phi_{01}\varepsilon_{t-1} + \phi_{02}\varepsilon_{t-2}$$

and suggest a consistent estimator for ϕ_{01} and ϕ_{02} based on OLS fitted residuals, $\hat{\varepsilon}_t \equiv y_t - \mathbf{x}_t'\boldsymbol{\beta}_{\mathrm{OLS}}$.

19.13 (Quasi-MLE) The consistency of the OLS estimator in the face of residual serial correlation is an example of a consistent quasi maximum likelihood estimator.[27] Consider a stationary dependent process $\{y_t\}$ with marginal log-likelihood function $L(\boldsymbol{\theta}_0; y_t)$. Suppose that $\boldsymbol{\theta}_0$ belongs to the interior of a K-dimensional, compact, convex parameter space $\boldsymbol{\Theta}$.

(a) Using an example, show that the sample mean log-likelihood function $\mathrm{E}_T[L(\boldsymbol{\theta}; y_t)]$ is generally not proportional to the log-likelihood function based on the sample.

(b) Suppose that $\boldsymbol{\theta}$ is globally identified by the marginal distribution of y_t. Confirm that

$$\boldsymbol{\theta}_0 = \operatorname*{argmax}_{\boldsymbol{\theta} \in \boldsymbol{\Theta}} \mathrm{E}[L(\boldsymbol{\theta}; y_t)]$$

despite the dependence among the y_t.

---

26 See equation (18.13).

27 See Levine (1983).

(c) In addition, suppose that the dependence among the y_t satisfies the restriction

$$|\text{Cov}[L(\boldsymbol{\theta};\, y_t),\, L(\boldsymbol{\theta};\, y_{t-s})]| \leq \rho^s \, \text{Var}[L(\boldsymbol{\theta};\, y_t)], \quad s \geq s^*$$

for some ρ, $0 \leq \rho < 1$, some $s^* > 0$, and all $\boldsymbol{\theta} \in \boldsymbol{\Theta}$. Show that the quasi-MLE

$$\hat{\boldsymbol{\theta}} = \underset{\boldsymbol{\theta} \in \boldsymbol{\Theta}}{\text{argmax}} \, \text{E}_T[L(\boldsymbol{\theta};\, y_t)]$$

which ignores the dependence, is consistent. State any additional assumptions that you require.

CHAPTER 20

INSTRUMENTAL VARIABLES ESTIMATION

This chapter begins our reconsideration of the first and fundamental assumption of the classical linear model, that $E[y_n \mid \mathbf{x}_n] = \mathbf{x}_n'\boldsymbol{\beta}_0$.[1] This assumption is fundamental: it is the property that the term "linear regression" describes and without it OLS loses its significance as an estimator for parameters of the conditional mean of y_n. Failures of this assumption lead to failures of the results that rest on it, that the OLS estimator is unbiased or consistent.

We will analyze two distinct failures of the linear regression assumption. One failure, discussed in Chapter 21, concerns situations in which the conditional mean of y_n given $\mathbf{x}_n$ is a *nonlinear* parametric function of $\boldsymbol{\beta}_0$. For example, we have introduced the possibility that

$$E[y_n \mid \mathbf{x}_n] = \exp(\mathbf{x}_n'\boldsymbol{\beta}_0)$$

in Example 16.6 (Exponential Regression, p. 360). In general, no simple transformation will deliver a linear regression form for such a specification.

The failure that we discuss in this chapter arises when $E[y_n \mid \mathbf{x}_n]$ is not the conditional mean that one wishes to estimate. Instead, interest focuses on the coefficients of a linear regression $E[y_n \mid \mathbf{x}_n^*] = \mathbf{x}_n^{*\prime}\boldsymbol{\beta}_0$ where $\mathbf{x}_n^*$ contains (at least in part) random variables that are not observed. We will call such unobservables *latent variables*. Econometricians use latent variables widely in their models to describe phenomena underlying the data that they analyze. This chapter introduces latent variable models.

Examples of this admittedly abstract description help in understanding it. In the next section, we give our first example, reconsidering the econometric model of the Phillips curve and its estimation. A key feature of this example is that we cannot estimate $\boldsymbol{\beta}_0$ directly with OLS but we can with GLS. The GLS estimator is a special case of a larger family of estimators called *instrumental variables* (IV) estimators, the other principal subject of this chapter.

We will describe several additional latent variable models after the Phillips curve. These models culminate in the general problem of omitting explanatory variables from a conditional mean to be estimated by OLS. Looking closely at the asymptotic behavior of OLS, we will

[1] We first introduced this specification, in a stronger form, in Assumption 6.1 (First Moments, p. 110). We later relaxed the specification to the one described here with the addition of Assumption 13.1 (I.I.D., p. 256).

interpret its inconsistency as a natural compensation for the omitted explanatory variables. Finally, we explain how IV estimation overcomes potential inconsistency, explore the possible relative efficiency of different IV estimators, and discuss the methodological requirements of this approach to estimation.

20.1 THE PHILLIPS CURVE REVISITED

We can describe our earlier model of the Phillips curve in terms of several latent variables. First, observed inflation ($\dot{p}_t^{\mathrm{o}}$) and unemployment (n_t^{o}) variables are both sums of latent nonseasonal and seasonal components:

$$\dot{p}_t^{\mathrm{o}} = \dot{p}_t^* + \dot{p}_t^{\mathrm{s}}$$
$$n_t^{\mathrm{o}} = n_t^* + n_t^{\mathrm{s}}$$

Neither seasonal ($\dot{p}_t^{\mathrm{s}}$) nor nonseasonal ($\dot{p}_t^*$) components are directly observable. The seasonally adjusted series published by the Bureau of Labor Statistics (BLS) are actually fitted time series from a particular statistical method. We treated $\dot{p}_t^*$ as though it were equal to the BLS variable ($\dot{p}_t$).

In addition, the Phillips curve contains the expected inflation variable $\dot{p}_t^{\mathrm{e}}$. Although there are surveys that collect peoples' expectations about prices, $\dot{p}_t^{\mathrm{e}}$ is not observable because it has no actual counterpart. There is no unique expectation about inflation for the U.S. economy, as these very surveys show. Nevertheless, macroeconomic models often include a price expectation variable as an important element of the actual economy that economists seek to describe and predict. To make these models tractable, it is necessary to specify such simplifications. We will think of $\dot{p}_t^{\mathrm{e}}$ loosely as an index of the expectations of all the participants in the economy.

To these latent variables we add a sixth: the residual term ε_t in the (nonseasonal) Phillips curve equation

$$\dot{p}_t^* = \dot{p}_t^{\mathrm{e}} + \gamma_{01}\left(n_{t-1}^* - \bar{n}_0\right) + w_t\gamma_{02} + \varepsilon_t$$

This residual is not merely the difference between actual inflation and its conditional mean at the end of the previous time period. Instead, ε_t follows a first-order linear autoregression

$$\varepsilon_t = \phi_0\varepsilon_{t-1} + \upsilon_t \qquad (t = 2, \ldots, T) \tag{20.1}$$

as in (19.13), where υ_t is the seventh (and last) latent variable.[2] This autoregression reflects the general dependence in time series variables that are not included explicitly as explanatory variables, but influence inflation just the same. For every $\upsilon_t = \varepsilon_t - \phi_0\varepsilon_{t-1}$, we assume in keeping with (19.11) that

$$\upsilon_t \sim \mathfrak{N}(0, \sigma_{0\upsilon}^2) \qquad (t = 2, \ldots, T) \tag{20.2}$$

i.i.d. conditional on the n_t, w_t, and ε_1. Also, in keeping with (19.22)–(19.23), we assert that

$$\varepsilon_1 \sim \mathfrak{N}[0, \sigma_{0\upsilon}^2/(1 - \phi_0^2)] \tag{20.3}$$

[2] We change our notation from the ε_{0t} and υ_{0t} in Chapter 19 to the ε_t and υ_t here to reflect the perspective that the distributions of these latent variables are invariant with respect to the population parameters $\boldsymbol{\beta}_0$. Think of the latent variables υ_t as determined outside of, or prior to, the Phillips curve relationship.

Finally, for this model of latent variables to be complete, we must specify the behavior of $\dot{p}_t^{\mathrm{e}}$. In Chapter 19, we assume that $\dot{p}_t^{\mathrm{e}}$ equals $\dot{p}_{t-1}^*$. This leads to the linear model

$$y_t = \mathbf{x}_t' \boldsymbol{\beta}_0 + \varepsilon_t \tag{20.4}$$

for $y_t \equiv \dot{p}_t - \dot{p}_{t-1}$ and $\mathbf{x}_t$ as described by (19.1). OLS delivers an unbiased estimator of $\boldsymbol{\beta}_0$ in this model, but GLS delivers an asymptotically efficient estimator. The GLS estimator corresponds (approximately) to OLS applied to

$$y_t - \phi_0 y_{t-1} = (\mathbf{x}_t - \phi_0 \cdot \mathbf{x}_{t-1})' \boldsymbol{\beta}_0 + \upsilon_t \quad (t = 2, \ldots, T) \tag{20.5}$$

to estimate $\boldsymbol{\beta}_0$ given ϕ_0.

Now let us generalize the model for $\dot{p}_t^{\mathrm{e}}$ slightly. Suppose instead that

$$\dot{p}_t^{\mathrm{e}} = \dot{p}_{t-1}^* + \alpha_0 \left(\dot{p}_{t-1}^* - \dot{p}_{t-2}^*\right) \tag{20.6}$$

where $|\alpha_0| < 1$. This equation permits recent changes in the rate of inflation to affect expected inflation also. Ambitious economic actors might well use prediction functions such as this because they can have a mean squared prediction error smaller than the prediction $\dot{p}_{t-1}$.

This new specification for expected inflation alters the original linear model (19.1) so that

$$\begin{aligned} \mathbf{x}_t &= \begin{bmatrix} 1 & n_{t-1} & \mathbf{w}_t & y_{t-1} \end{bmatrix}' \qquad (t = 1, \ldots, T) \\ \boldsymbol{\beta}_0 &= \begin{bmatrix} -\gamma_{01}\bar{n}_0 & \gamma_{01} & \boldsymbol{\gamma}_{02} & \alpha_0 \end{bmatrix}' \end{aligned} \tag{20.7}$$

In effect, the lagged dependent variable y_{t-1} appears as an additional explanatory variable. We will write this new model in partitioned form as

$$y_t = \mathbf{x}_{1t}' \boldsymbol{\beta}_{01} + \beta_{02} y_{t-1} + \varepsilon_t \quad (t = 1, \ldots, T) \tag{20.8}$$

where we partition $\mathbf{x}_t = \left[\mathbf{x}_{1t}', x_{2t}\right]'$ and $\boldsymbol{\beta}_0 = \left[\boldsymbol{\beta}_{01}', \beta_{02}\right]'$ conformably and set $x_{2t} = y_{t-1}$.

To complete our new specification, we should also describe the distribution of an additional latent variable, y_0. Together, y_0 and ε_1 are the initial conditions of the dynamic regression specification (20.8) for y_t. The initial distribution can establish the conditional covariance stationarity of $\{y_t\}$ given $\mathbf{X}_1 \equiv [\mathbf{x}_{1t}]'$ that our previous model possessed. The specification is comparable to (20.3) for that model. For the moment, we forgo deriving these conditions.[3] We will simply treat $\{y_t\}$ as conditionally covariance stationary from this point on.

Our primary reason for introducing this model is that the regression function

$$\mathrm{E}[y_t \,|\, \mathbf{x}_t] = \mathbf{x}_t' \boldsymbol{\beta}_0 + \mathrm{E}[\varepsilon_t \,|\, \mathbf{x}_t] \tag{20.9}$$

has an unusual characteristic relative to situations that we have already studied. Because the random variable y_{t-1} appears in the last column of $\mathbf{x}_t$, we cannot assume that $\mathrm{E}[\varepsilon_t \,|\, \mathbf{x}_t]$ is zero. Certainly $\mathrm{E}[\varepsilon_1] = 0$ and $\mathrm{E}[\upsilon_t] = 0$ $(t = 2, \ldots, T)$ by assumption so that

$$\mathrm{E}[\varepsilon_t] = \mathrm{E}[\phi_0 \varepsilon_{t-1} + \upsilon_t] = \phi_0 \,\mathrm{E}[\varepsilon_{t-1}] + \mathrm{E}[\upsilon_t] = 0 \qquad (t = 2, \ldots, T)$$

by (20.1) and recursive substitution. But these are all *marginal* expectations.

For the regression function, we must consider the *conditional* mean. Intuition suggests that this is not zero because y_{t-1} depends on ε_{t-1}, which is correlated with ε_t. It would be surprising

[3] A derivation appears in Section 20.10.1.

to find that y_{t-1} is not correlated with ε_t or that y_{t-1} does not influence $\mathrm{E}[\varepsilon_t \mid \mathbf{x}_t]$. Indeed, using the conditional covariance stationarity of $\{y_t\}$, we can confirm this intuition. First, note that the disturbance ε_t in (20.4) is generally not orthogonal to the RHS variable y_{t-1}:[4]

$$\mathrm{E}[y_{t-1}\varepsilon_t] = \mathrm{E}\Big[\mathrm{E}\big[y_{t-1}\,\mathrm{E}[\varepsilon_t \mid \varepsilon_1, \ldots, \varepsilon_{t-1}, \mathbf{X}_1] \mid \mathbf{X}_1\big]\Big] \tag{20.10}$$

$$= \phi_0\,\mathrm{E}\big[\mathrm{E}[y_{t-1}\varepsilon_{t-1} \mid \mathbf{X}_1]\big] \tag{20.11}$$

$$= \phi_0\,\mathrm{E}\big[\mathrm{E}[\beta_{02}y_{t-2}\varepsilon_{t-1} + \varepsilon_{t-1}^2 \mid \mathbf{X}_1]\big] \tag{20.12}$$

$$= \phi_0\beta_{02}\,\mathrm{E}[y_{t-1}\varepsilon_t] + \phi_0\,\mathrm{Var}[\varepsilon_t] \tag{20.13}$$

$$= \frac{\phi_0}{1-\phi_0\beta_{02}}\,\mathrm{Var}[\varepsilon_t] \tag{20.14}$$

Therefore, $\mathrm{E}[\varepsilon_t \mid \mathbf{x}_t] \neq 0$ and $\mathrm{E}[y_t \mid \mathbf{x}_t] \neq \mathbf{x}_t'\boldsymbol{\beta}_0$ unless $\phi_0 = 0$.[5] In other words, $\mathbf{x}_t'\boldsymbol{\beta}_0$ is not the regression function unless the ε_t are serially uncorrelated.

Furthermore, the OLS fitted coefficients are inconsistent estimators of $\boldsymbol{\beta}_0$. One can simply view this as a result of the failure of the first moment assumption. But it is also instructive to write out the defect in OLS itself:

$$\begin{aligned}\hat{\boldsymbol{\beta}}_{\mathrm{OLS}} &= \left(\mathbf{X}'\mathbf{X}\right)^{-1}\mathbf{X}'\mathbf{y}\\ &= \left(\mathbf{X}'\mathbf{X}\right)^{-1}\mathbf{X}'\left(\mathbf{X}\boldsymbol{\beta}_0 + \boldsymbol{\varepsilon}\right)\\ &= \boldsymbol{\beta}_0 + \left(\mathbf{X}'\mathbf{X}\right)^{-1}\mathbf{X}'\boldsymbol{\varepsilon}\\ &= \boldsymbol{\beta}_0 + \left(\mathrm{E}_T[\mathbf{x}_t\mathbf{x}_t']\right)^{-1}\mathrm{E}_T[\mathbf{x}_t\varepsilon_t]\end{aligned}$$

The critical term is the empirical moment $\mathrm{E}_T[\mathbf{x}_t\varepsilon_t]$. Because $\mathbf{x}_t$ and ε_t are not orthogonal, $\mathrm{E}_T[\mathbf{x}_t\varepsilon_t]$ will not converge in probability to zero. That implies in turn the inconsistency of every element of $\hat{\boldsymbol{\beta}}$. Even if only one element of $\mathrm{E}[\mathbf{x}_t\varepsilon_t]$ is nonzero, the leading $(\mathrm{E}_T[\mathbf{x}_t\mathbf{x}_t'])^{-1}$ matrix will generally spread this defect to other elements of the estimator.

However, we can show that the GLS fitted coefficients *are* consistent estimators of $\boldsymbol{\beta}_0$. The GLS estimator corresponds (approximately) to OLS applied to the quasidifferenced relationship

$$\begin{aligned}y_t - \phi_0 y_{t-1} &= (\mathbf{x}_t - \phi_0 \cdot \mathbf{x}_{t-1})'\,\boldsymbol{\beta}_0 + \upsilon_t\\ &= \left(\mathbf{x}_{1t} - \phi_0 \cdot \mathbf{x}_{1,t-1}\right)'\boldsymbol{\beta}_{01} + \beta_{02}\,(y_{t-1} - \phi_0 y_{t-2}) + \upsilon_t\end{aligned} \tag{20.15}$$

$(t = 3, \ldots, T)$ to estimate $\boldsymbol{\beta}_0$ given ϕ_0. This relationship is an exact analogue to (20.5) for the simpler model without a lagged dependent explanatory variable. The transformed explanatory variable $y_{*t-1} \equiv y_{t-1} - \phi_0 y_{t-2}$ is uncorrelated with the residual υ_t because the former depends only

[4] Equation (20.10) uses the law of iterated expectations, (20.11) uses (20.1) and the assumption that the υ_t are conditionally i.i.d. with mean zero, (20.12) uses $\mathrm{E}[\varepsilon_{t-1} \mid \mathbf{X}_1] = 0$ and (20.8) for $t-1$ in place of t, (20.13) uses the conditional covariance stationarity of $\{\varepsilon_t\}$, and (20.14) rests on the equating the RHS of (20.10) with (20.13) and solving for $\mathrm{E}[y_{t-1}\varepsilon_t]$.

[5] Lemma 7.4 (MMSE Linear Predictor, p. 135) implies that the MMSE *linear* predictor of ε_t given y_{t-1} will depend on y_{t-1}. Moreover, $\mathrm{E}[\varepsilon_t \mid y_{t-1}]$ is the MMSE predictor of ε_t given y_{t-1} and must yield at least as small an MSE (Lemma 6.2, p. 113). Therefore,

$$\mathrm{E}[\varepsilon_t \mid y_{t-1}] = \mathrm{E}\left[\mathrm{E}[\varepsilon_t \mid y_{t-1}] \mid \mathbf{x}_t\right] = \mathrm{E}[\varepsilon_t \mid \mathbf{x}_t]$$

must also be nonzero.

on $v_1, \ldots, v_{t-1}$, all of which are conditionally independent of v_t. In other words, $\mathbf{x}_{*t} \equiv \mathbf{x}_t - \phi_0 \cdot \mathbf{x}_{t-1}$ is orthogonal to v_t and, as a result, the GLS estimator

$$\begin{aligned} \hat{\boldsymbol{\beta}}_{\text{GLS}} &= \left(\mathbf{X}_*'\mathbf{X}_*\right)^{-1}\mathbf{X}_*'\mathbf{y}_* && (20.16)\\ &= \left(\mathbf{X}_*'\mathbf{X}_*\right)^{-1}\mathbf{X}_*'\left(\mathbf{X}_*\boldsymbol{\beta}_0 + \boldsymbol{v}\right) \\ &= \boldsymbol{\beta}_0 + \left(\mathbf{X}_*'\mathbf{X}_*\right)^{-1}\mathbf{X}_*'\boldsymbol{v} \\ &= \boldsymbol{\beta}_0 + \left(\mathrm{E}_{T|2}[\mathbf{x}_{*t}\mathbf{x}_{*t}']\right)^{-1}\mathrm{E}_{T|2}[\mathbf{x}_{*t}v_t] && (20.17) \end{aligned}$$

is consistent.[6]

Up to this point, we have described GLS as a method for deriving an estimator that is efficient relative to OLS. The current example illustrates that GLS can overcome the inconsistency of OLS in some cases as well.

Although it is rather specific, there are general principles present in this example that one can readily appreciate. First, the possibility of correlation between the explanatory variables and the residual term in (20.4) is not special. Researchers are often concerned about the omission from $\mathbf{x}_t$ of explanatory variables that are correlated with those that do appear in $\mathbf{x}_t$. Broadly speaking, such omissions are the general cause of correlation between the included explanatory variables and the residual term. For example, we may rewrite either (20.8) or (20.15) as

$$y_t = \mathbf{x}_{1t}'\boldsymbol{\beta}_{01} + \beta_{02}y_{t-1} + \underbrace{\phi_0 y_{t-1} - \phi_0 \cdot \mathbf{x}_{1,t-1}'\boldsymbol{\beta}_{01} + \phi_0\beta_{02}y_{t-2} + v_t}_{\varepsilon_t} \qquad (20.18)$$

so that

$$\varepsilon_t = \phi_0 y_{t-1} - \phi_0 \cdot \mathbf{x}_{1,t-1}'\boldsymbol{\beta}_{01} + \phi_0\beta_{02}y_{t-2} + v_t$$

The residual, in this case, contains y_{t-1} and the "omitted" explanatory variables $\left(\mathbf{x}_{1,t-1}, y_{t-2}\right)$, all of which are correlated with y_{t-1}. We will present several other important examples of correlation between explanatory variables and the residual term in the next section.

In addition, the consistent GLS estimator for this example illustrates a natural approach to overcoming this problem in estimation. Note that

$$\begin{aligned} \hat{\boldsymbol{\beta}}_{\text{GLS}} &= \left(\mathbf{X}_*'\mathbf{X}_*\right)^{-1}\mathbf{X}_*'\mathbf{y}_* \\ &= \left(\mathbf{X}'\boldsymbol{\Omega}_0^{-1}\mathbf{X}\right)^{-1}\mathbf{X}'\boldsymbol{\Omega}_0^{-1}\mathbf{y} && (20.19)\\ &= \boldsymbol{\beta}_0 + \left(\mathbf{X}'\boldsymbol{\Omega}_0^{-1}\mathbf{X}\right)^{-1}\mathbf{X}'\boldsymbol{\Omega}_0^{-1}\boldsymbol{\varepsilon} \end{aligned}$$

Just as $\mathbf{x}_{*t}$ is orthogonal to v_t, the transformed explanatory variables in $\boldsymbol{\Omega}_0^{-1}\mathbf{X}$ are orthogonal to the ε_t. Let $[z_{tk}] = \mathbf{Z} \equiv \boldsymbol{\Omega}_0^{-1}\mathbf{X}$ denote these variables. Written in terms of $\mathbf{Z}$, we have a member of the general family of estimators called instrumental variables (IV) estimators:[7]

---

[6] Here we denote the empirical expectation over observations $t = 3, \ldots, T$ conditional on the first two observations by $\mathrm{E}_{T|2}[w_t] \equiv \sum_{t=3}^{T} w_t/(T-2)$.

[7] The instrumental variables estimation method is generally attributed to Reiersøl (1941).

$$\begin{aligned}\hat{\boldsymbol{\beta}}_{\mathrm{IV}} &= \left(\mathbf{Z}'\mathbf{X}\right)^{-1}\mathbf{Z}'\mathbf{y} \\ &= \boldsymbol{\beta}_0 + \left(\mathbf{Z}'\mathbf{X}\right)^{-1}\mathbf{Z}'\boldsymbol{\varepsilon} \\ &= \boldsymbol{\beta}_0 + \left(\mathrm{E}_{T|2}[\mathbf{z}_t\mathbf{x}_t']\right)^{-1}\mathrm{E}_{T|2}[\mathbf{z}_t\varepsilon_t]\end{aligned} \tag{20.20}$$

The z_{tk} ($k = 1, \ldots, K$) are so-called instrumental variables (or *instruments*). By inspection we see that this IV estimator is consistent if the instrumental variables z_{tk} exhibit two characteristics: (1) $(\mathrm{E}_{T|2}[\mathbf{z}_t\mathbf{x}_t'])^{-1}$ converges in probability and (2) the z_{tk} are orthogonal to ε_t so that $\mathrm{E}_{T|2}[\mathbf{z}_t\varepsilon_t]$ converges in probability to a vector of zeros. In this chapter we describe how such instrumental variables arise in several models with latent variables.

20.2 LATENT VARIABLE MODELS

Econometrics is filled with latent variable models such as the one we have just studied. In this section we introduce several other important examples. All lead to the linear specification

$$y_n = \mathbf{x}_n'\boldsymbol{\beta}_0 + \varepsilon_n \qquad (n = 1, \ldots, N) \tag{20.21}$$

where ε_n is an unobserved, or latent, random variable. It is not merely the residual $y_n - \mathrm{E}[y_n \mid \mathbf{x}_n]$ defined by the choice of conditioning variables in $\mathbf{x}_n$.[8] In each model that we describe, at least one of the explanatory variables in $\mathbf{x}_n$ is correlated with ε_n so that $\mathrm{E}[\varepsilon_n \mid \mathbf{x}_n]$ is a function of $\mathbf{x}_n$ and, therefore, not zero. This in turn implies that $\mathrm{E}[y_n \mid \mathbf{x}_n] \neq \mathbf{x}_n'\boldsymbol{\beta}_0$ and that the OLS fit of y_n to $\mathbf{x}_n$ will yield inconsistent estimators of $\boldsymbol{\beta}_0$.

Researchers often call ε_n a *disturbance* or *error term*. This seems appropriate when assumptions are made directly about the behavior of the latent ε_n, rather than about the observable variables y_n and $\mathbf{x}_n$ only. The next example, measurement errors in the explanatory variables, contains such assumptions and describes simply a fundamental problem in actual empirical work.

EXAMPLE 20.1 (Errors in Variables)

Suppose that we are interested in the regression function

$$\mathrm{E}[y_n \mid \mathbf{x}_n^*] = \mathbf{x}_n^{*\prime}\boldsymbol{\beta}_0$$

but some of the explanatory variables in $\mathbf{x}_n^*$ are not observable. Such economic variables as expected price inflation, transaction costs, ability or productivity of an employee, and supply or demand shocks are examples of such latent variables. But we may observe *proxy variables*: actual inflation might take the place of price expectations or an individual's IQ might serve as an imperfect measure of cognitive ability. We denote these proxy variables with $\mathbf{x}_n$ and let

$$\mathbf{x}_n = \mathbf{x}_n^* + \boldsymbol{v}_n$$

where $\boldsymbol{v}_n$ denotes the measurement errors in the proxy variables. It is simplest to suppose that $\mathrm{E}[\boldsymbol{v}_n] = \mathbf{0}$ so that the proxy variables exhibit no systematic bias. We also assume that the $\boldsymbol{v}_n$ are

[8] The term "latent" has a narrower meaning for some writers. They require that latent variables are not implicit functions of observable variables. Within this definition, $\varepsilon_n = y_n - \mathbf{x}_n'\boldsymbol{\beta}_0$ is not latent. Instead, ε_n would be called "unmeasured." See Aigner et al. (1984, p. 1323) and the reference they cite, Bentler (1982).

uncorrelated with both the x^*_{nk} $(k = 1, \ldots, K)$ and $u_n \equiv y_n - \mathbf{x}^{*\prime}_n \boldsymbol{\beta}_0$. Then the feasible regression relationship is given by

$$\begin{aligned} y_n &= (\mathbf{x}_n - \boldsymbol{v}_n)' \boldsymbol{\beta}_0 + u_n \\ &= \mathbf{x}'_n \boldsymbol{\beta}_0 + \varepsilon_n \end{aligned}$$

where the latent disturbance $\varepsilon_n \equiv u_n - \boldsymbol{v}'_n \boldsymbol{\beta}_0$ is correlated with $\mathbf{x}_n$ because v_n is a latent component of $\mathbf{x}_n$.

Another explanation for correlation between the explanatory variables and the residual term is a *system of simultaneous equations*. Such models are common in econometrics, in part because multivariate optimization and equilibrium are prevalent features of economic models.

EXAMPLE 20.2 **(Simultaneous Equations)**

Consider the simple market model in which there is a supply function

$$q_{sn} = \mathbf{x}'_{s1n} \boldsymbol{\beta}_{0s1} + \beta_{0s2} p_n + \varepsilon_{sn} \tag{20.22}$$

for the aggregate supply of a good q_{sn} available at market price p_n and a demand function

$$q_{dn} = \mathbf{x}'_{d1n} \boldsymbol{\beta}_{0d1} + \beta_{0d2} p_n + \varepsilon_{dn} \tag{20.23}$$

for the aggregate demand q_{dn} at market price p_n. The ε_{sn} and ε_{dn} are latent random disturbance terms. We partition the observable explanatory variables $\mathbf{x}_{sn} \equiv \left[\mathbf{x}'_{s1n}, p_n\right]'$ and $\mathbf{x}_{dn} \equiv \left[\mathbf{x}'_{d1n}, p_n\right]'$ to distinguish the market price from $\mathbf{x}_{s1n}$ and $\mathbf{x}_{d1n}$. These are assumed to be predetermined, capturing exogenous shifts in the supply and demand functions. Let $\mathbf{x}_n \equiv \left[\mathbf{x}'_{s1n}, \mathbf{x}'_{d1n}\right]'$ and $(\varepsilon_{sn}, \varepsilon_{dn})$ be i.i.d. random variables with finite fourth moments and $\mathrm{E}[\varepsilon_{sn} \mid \mathbf{x}_n] = \mathrm{E}[\varepsilon_{dn} \mid \mathbf{x}_n] = 0$.

In equilibrium, the market price will clear the market so that the observed quantity transacted, y_n, equals both the desired supply and the desired demand:

$$y_n = q_{sn} = q_{dn}$$

Therefore,

$$y_n = \mathbf{x}'_{s1n} \boldsymbol{\beta}_{0s1} + \beta_{0s2} p_n + \varepsilon_{sn} = \mathbf{x}'_{d1n} \boldsymbol{\beta}_{0d1} + \beta_{0d2} p_n + \varepsilon_{dn}$$

and we can solve this system of simultaneous equations for the equilibrium price

$$p_n = \frac{1}{\beta_{0s2} - \beta_{0d2}} \left(\mathbf{x}'_{d1n} \boldsymbol{\beta}_{0d1} - \mathbf{x}'_{s1n} \boldsymbol{\beta}_{0s1} + \varepsilon_{dn} - \varepsilon_{sn}\right) \tag{20.24}$$

given that $\beta_{0d2} < 0 < \beta_{0s2}$.[9] It follows that the explanatory variable p_n in both demand and supply equations will be correlated with both ε_{sn} and ε_{dn}. Because p_n and y_n are jointly determined by the interaction of supply and demand, p_n is a function of the latent disturbance terms in both supply and demand functions. OLS estimation of either (20.22) or (20.23) will yield biased and inconsistent estimates.

Our final example is the most direct. For discussions of estimation, we will also use this example to describe all of the previous examples as well.

---

[9] We give a detailed description of simultaneous equations models in Chapter 26.

EXAMPLE 20.3 (Omitted Variables)

Often, some of the desired explanatory variables are simply not available in a particular data set. We can represent this as a partitioned regression,

$$\mathrm{E}[y_n \mid \mathbf{x}_n] = \mathbf{x}'_{1n}\boldsymbol{\beta}_{01} + \mathbf{x}'_{2n}\boldsymbol{\beta}_{02}$$

in which $\mathbf{x}_{2n}$ is latent. Conditioning on what is observable, we find that

$$\mathrm{E}[y_n \mid \mathbf{x}_{1n}] = \mathbf{x}'_{1n}\boldsymbol{\beta}_{01} + \mathrm{E}[\mathbf{x}'_{2n} \mid \mathbf{x}_{1n}]\boldsymbol{\beta}_{02} \tag{20.25}$$

which does not equal $\mathbf{x}'_{1n}\boldsymbol{\beta}_{01}$ when $\mathbf{x}_{1n}$ and $\mathbf{x}_{2n}$ are not orthogonal. In effect, $\mathbf{x}'_{2n}\boldsymbol{\beta}_{02}$ is a component of a disturbance term so that $\mathbf{x}_{1n}$ is correlated with the disturbance term.

As simple as it is, this example can capture the essence of the estimation problem in all of our examples and so we devote a section of this chapter to the omission of explanatory variables.

20.3 OMITTED EXPLANATORY VARIABLES

Given that omitting explanatory variables makes OLS inconsistent, what else can be said about OLS? In this section, we explain first that the OLS estimator is generally a consistent estimator of the MMSE linear prediction function for y_n given $\mathbf{x}_n$. We then show how to interpret the probability limit of the OLS estimator as the sum of two terms in MMSE linear prediction. The first term measures the change in the prediction of y_n with respect to the $\mathbf{x}_n$ holding omitted explanatory variables constant. The second term is indirect, capturing the change in the prediction of y_n related to predictable changes in the omitted explanatory variables.

It is the first of these two effects that we seek to estimate in our examples. If we could include the omitted explanatory variables, then the two effects would not be confounded in the OLS estimator. The effects are confounded, however, because OLS fits the best possible prediction (in the MSE sense) with the available explanatory variables. The following lemma gives the initial formal result.

Lemma 20.1 *If the second moments of y_n and $\mathbf{x}_n$ are finite,* $\mathrm{E}[\mathbf{x}_n\mathbf{x}'_n]$ *is nonsingular, and*

$$\mathrm{E}_N[\mathbf{x}_n\mathbf{x}'_n] \xrightarrow{p} \mathrm{E}[\mathbf{x}_n\mathbf{x}'_n]$$

$$\mathrm{E}_N[\mathbf{x}_n y_n] \xrightarrow{p} \mathrm{E}[\mathbf{x}_n y_n]$$

then the OLS estimator $\hat{\boldsymbol{\beta}}_{\mathrm{OLS}} = \left(\mathbf{X}'\mathbf{X}\right)^{-1}\mathbf{X}'\mathbf{y}$ *is consistent for the coefficients of the MMSE linear predictor of both y_n and its conditional mean* $\mathrm{E}[y_n \mid \mathbf{x}_n]$.

Proof. This lemma stands directly on the shoulders of Lemma 7.4 (MMSE Linear Predictor, p. 135). This states that $\mathbf{x}'_n\boldsymbol{\gamma}_0$, where

$$\boldsymbol{\gamma}_0 = \left(\mathrm{E}[\mathbf{x}_n\mathbf{x}'_n]\right)^{-1}\mathrm{E}[\mathbf{x}_n y_n]$$

is the MMSE linear predictor of y_n. That this is also the MMSE linear predictor of $\mathrm{E}[y_n \mid \mathbf{x}_n]$ follows from the underlying Pythagorean relationship

$$\mathrm{E}[(y_n - \mathbf{x}_n'\boldsymbol{\gamma})^2] = \mathrm{E}\big[(y_n - \mathrm{E}[y_n \mid \mathbf{x}_n])^2\big] + \mathrm{E}\big[(\mathrm{E}[y_n \mid \mathbf{x}_n] - \mathbf{x}_n'\boldsymbol{\gamma})^2\big]$$

that goes along with the optimality of $\mathrm{E}[y_n \mid \mathbf{x}_n]$. That $\hat{\boldsymbol{\beta}}_{\mathrm{OLS}}$ converges in probability to $\boldsymbol{\gamma}_0$ is an application of the continuity of probability limits (Lemma 13.2, p. 261).[10] □

We interpret the probability limit of OLS as the population counterpart to the estimator itself. For a fixed N, OLS delivers the closest fit as measured by the sum of squared residuals. In the limit as $N \to \infty$, the OLS estimator approaches the closest fit as measured by MSE. Note that this is true regardless of the actual data-generating process. In particular, OLS possesses this property even when there are omitted explanatory variables. Now we will use this property to interpret the OLS estimator in that instance.

To do this, we need only find the MMSE linear predictor of a y_n given $\mathbf{x}_{1n}$ alone in terms of the MMSE linear predictor given $\mathbf{x}_n \equiv \big[\mathbf{x}_{1n}', \mathbf{x}_{2n}'\big]'$.[11]

Lemma 20.2 (Law of Iterated Projections) *If the second moments of y_n and $\mathbf{x}_n$ are finite, then*

$$\mathrm{E}^*[y_n \mid \mathbf{x}_{1n}] = \mathrm{E}^*\big[\mathrm{E}^*[y_n \mid \mathbf{x}_n] \mid \mathbf{x}_{1n}\big]$$

Proof. By Lemma 7.4 (MMSE Linear Predictor, p. 135),

$$\mathrm{E}[(y_n - \alpha - \mathbf{x}_n'\boldsymbol{\gamma})^2] = \mathrm{E}\big[(y_n - \mathrm{E}^*[y_n \mid \mathbf{x}_n])^2\big] + \mathrm{E}\big[(\mathrm{E}^*[y_n \mid \mathbf{x}_n] - \alpha - \mathbf{x}_n'\boldsymbol{\gamma})^2\big]$$

It is the second term that the MMSE linear predictor $\mathrm{E}^*[y_n \mid \mathbf{x}_n]$ minimizes. If we constrain $\boldsymbol{\gamma}_2$ in $\boldsymbol{\gamma} \equiv \big[\boldsymbol{\gamma}_1', \boldsymbol{\gamma}_2'\big]'$ to equal zero and minimize this term over $\boldsymbol{\gamma}_1$, then we obtain $\mathrm{E}^*[y_n \mid \mathbf{x}_{1n}]$. Hence

$$\mathrm{E}^*[y_n \mid \mathbf{x}_{1n}] = \mathrm{E}^*\big[\mathrm{E}^*[y_n \mid \mathbf{x}_n] \mid \mathbf{x}_{1n}\big] = \alpha_0 + \mathbf{x}_{1n}'\boldsymbol{\gamma}_{01} + \mathrm{E}^*[\mathbf{x}_{2n}' \mid \mathbf{x}_{1n}]\boldsymbol{\gamma}_{02}$$ □

This lemma implies that we may describe the coefficients of $\mathbf{x}_{1n}$ in $\mathrm{E}^*[y_n \mid \mathbf{x}_{1n}]$ as the sum of two terms because

$$\begin{aligned}\mathrm{E}^*[y_n \mid \mathbf{x}_{1n}] &= \alpha_0 + \mathbf{x}_{1n}'\boldsymbol{\gamma}_{01} + \mathrm{E}^*[\mathbf{x}_{2n}' \mid \mathbf{x}_{1n}]\boldsymbol{\gamma}_{02} \\ &= \alpha_0 + \boldsymbol{\tau}_0'\boldsymbol{\gamma}_{02} + \mathbf{x}_{1n}'(\boldsymbol{\gamma}_{01} + \boldsymbol{\Pi}_0\boldsymbol{\gamma}_{02})\end{aligned} \tag{20.26}$$

where we denote

$$\begin{aligned}\mathrm{E}^*[y_n \mid \mathbf{x}_n] &= \alpha_0 + \mathbf{x}_n'\boldsymbol{\gamma}_0 \\ \mathrm{E}^*[\mathbf{x}_{2nk} \mid \mathbf{x}_{1n}] &= \tau_{0k} + \mathbf{x}_{1n}'\boldsymbol{\pi}_{0k} \qquad k = K_1 + 1, \ldots, K\end{aligned}$$

[10] Proposition 15 (Asymptotic Distribution of OLS, p. 257) is one example of such convergence based on more primitive assumptions.

[11] See also Exercises 3.18 and 7.9.

$\boldsymbol{\tau}_0 \equiv [\tau_{0k}]'$, $\mathbf{\Pi}_0$ is the $K_1 \times (K - K_1)$ matrix of coefficients $[\boldsymbol{\pi}_{0k};\ k = K_1 + 1, \ldots, K]$, and we partition the K elements of $\mathbf{x}_n$ into K_1 and $K - K_1$ elements $[\mathbf{x}'_{1n}, \mathbf{x}'_{2n}]'$, respectively. The first term in the coefficient vector of $\mathbf{x}_{1n}$ in (20.26) is $\boldsymbol{\gamma}_{01}$, the coefficient vector of $\mathbf{x}_{1n}$ in $\mathrm{E}^*[y_n \mid \mathbf{x}_n]$. The second term is the product of the coefficients of $\mathbf{x}_{1n}$ in $\mathrm{E}^*[\mathbf{x}_{2n} \mid \mathbf{x}_{1n}]$ and the coefficient vector of $\mathbf{x}_{2n}$ in $\mathrm{E}^*[y_n \mid \mathbf{x}_n]$. This term is an adjustment to $\boldsymbol{\gamma}_{01}$ that takes into account predictable differences in y_n that are associated with $\mathbf{x}_{2n}$ and that $\mathbf{x}_{1n}$ can also capture through its power to predict $\mathbf{x}_{2n}$.

These two components are analogous to the components of the total derivative of a function of two variables $f(x_1, x_2)$ with respect to the first variable:

$$\frac{df(x_1, x_2)}{dx_1} = \frac{\partial f(x_1, x_2)}{\partial x_1} + \frac{dx_2}{dx_1}\frac{\partial f(x_1, x_2)}{\partial x_2}$$

The first term is the *ceteris paribus* change in f for a change in x_1 and the second term is the product of the *ceteris paribus* change in f for a change in x_2 and the change in x_2 accompanying a change in x_1.[12] In this analogy, we interpret the function f as $\mathrm{E}^*[y \mid \mathbf{x}_{1n}, \mathbf{x}_{2n}]$. The derivative dx_2/dx_1 corresponds to $\mathbf{\Pi}_0$.

Suppose now that $\mathrm{E}[y_n \mid \mathbf{x}_n] = \mathbf{x}'_{1n}\boldsymbol{\beta}_{01} + \beta_{02}x_{2n}$ but that we do not include one variable, x_{2n}, in the OLS estimation of $\boldsymbol{\beta}_{01}$. Lemmas 20.1 and 20.2 indicate that when we regress y_n on $\mathbf{x}_{1n}$ alone, the OLS fitted coefficients $\hat{\boldsymbol{\beta}}_{\mathrm{R}1}$ will generally converge in probability to

$$\boldsymbol{\gamma}_{01} = \boldsymbol{\beta}_{01} + \mathbf{\Pi}_0\beta_{02} \tag{20.27}$$

Therefore, we can interpret the probability limit of the elements of $\hat{\boldsymbol{\beta}}_{1\mathrm{R}}$ as the sum of two terms: the direct change in the expected value of y_n associated with a change in $\mathbf{x}_{1nk}$, $\boldsymbol{\beta}_{01k}$, plus an indirect change in the expected value of y_n associated with changes in x_{2n}, $\pi_{0k}\beta_{02}$, for each k.

If there were no correlation between x_{2n} and $\mathbf{x}_{1n}$, then the latter would have no (linear) predictive power for x_{2n} and there would be no indirect effect because $\mathbf{\Pi}_0 = \mathbf{0}$. We would estimate only $\boldsymbol{\beta}_{01}$. This also occurs, of course, if $\beta_{02} = 0$. Otherwise, to the extent that linear prediction allows, the OLS procedure fits the variation in y_n with $\mathbf{x}_{1n}$ as well as possible, leading to the addition of the indirect effects to the direct ones in the probability limit of $\hat{\boldsymbol{\beta}}_{\mathrm{R}1}$.

Note that in general *all* of the estimated coefficients may be affected by the omission of an explanatory variable. The bias and inconsistency are not limited only to the coefficients of those explanatory variables that are correlated with the omitted variable. One can see this algebraically in $\mathbf{\Pi}_0 = (\mathrm{Var}[\mathbf{x}_{1n}])^{-1}\,\mathrm{Cov}[\mathbf{x}_{1n}, x_{2n}]$. The covariance term is premultiplied by the inverse of a variance matrix, which potentially spreads any nonzero covariance across all elements of the matrix product. This phenomenon represents the effects of MSE optimization: as one coefficient adjusts to account for a missing explanatory variable, the other coefficients adjust in turn to account for this. As a result, the effects of an omitted explanatory variable generally vitiate estimates of every coefficient.

In special cases, it is possible to predict the effects of the omitted explanatory variable.

EXAMPLE 20.4 (Errors in Variables)

The model of errors in explanatory variables predicts a definite direction for inconsistency in simple regression. Researchers commonly use this prediction to interpret their estimates of multivariate regressions. Specializing the model described in Example 20.1 to simple regression, we have

12 Recall Exercise 3.8.

$$y_n = \beta_0 x_n - \beta_0 \upsilon_n + u_n$$

so that an OLS fit of y_n to x_n implicitly omits υ_n. Because

$$\mathrm{Cov}[u_n, \upsilon_n] = \mathrm{Cov}[x_n^*, u_n] = \mathrm{Cov}[x_n^*, \upsilon_n] = 0 \tag{20.28}$$

it follows that

$$\mathrm{E}[x_n \upsilon_n] = \mathrm{Cov}[x_n, \upsilon_n] = \mathrm{Var}[\upsilon_n] > 0 \tag{20.29}$$

In words, the observable proxy variable x_n and its measurement error υ_n are positively correlated. Therefore

$$\pi_0 = \frac{\mathrm{Cov}[x_n, \upsilon_n]}{\mathrm{E}[x_n^2]} = \frac{\mathrm{Var}[\upsilon_n]}{\mathrm{E}[x_n^2]} > 0$$

in $\mathrm{E}^*[\upsilon_n \mid x_n] = x_n \pi_0$ and the inconsistency in $\hat{\boldsymbol{\beta}}_{\mathrm{OLS}}$, which is $-\pi_0 \beta_0$, will have the opposite sign of β_0.

We can also show that the inconsistency is not so large that the *sign* of plim $\hat{\beta}_{\mathrm{OLS}}$ differs from that of β_0: using (20.28),

$$\mathrm{E}[x_n^2] = \mathrm{E}[x_n^{*2}] + \mathrm{Var}[\upsilon_n] \qquad \Rightarrow \qquad 0 < \pi_0 < 1 \tag{20.30}$$

Therefore, errors in an explanatory variables shrink the probability limit toward zero relative to the coefficient:

$$\operatorname{plim} \hat{\beta}_{\mathrm{OLS}} = \beta_0 (1 - \pi_0) \tag{20.31}$$

In other words, it diminishes the apparent influence of a latent explanatory variable. This is exactly what common sense suggests measurement error should do.

Figure 20.1 gives a graphic description of this example for the case in which $\mathrm{E}[x_n^*] = 0$. The variance ellipsoid for (x_n^*, y_n) is labeled $\mathbb{V}^*$. It is framed by a dashed box two standard deviations

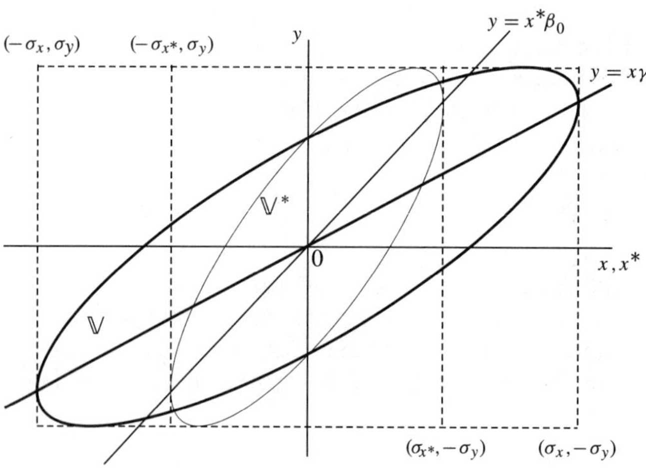

Figure 20.1 Errors in variables.

on each side, as in Figures 7.3–7.5. The MMSE linear prediction line $y = x^*\beta_0$ for this ellipsoid appears as a solid line. As in Figure 7.8, this line intersects the vertical tangents to the variance ellipsoid. The variance ellipsoid for (x_n, y_n) is thicker and is labeled $\mathbb{V}$. It is framed by a box that is the same height as that for $\mathbb{V}^*$ because the standard deviation of y_n is constant. The box framing $\mathbb{V}$ is wider than that for $\mathbb{V}^*$ because the variance of x_n is larger than the variance of x_n^* by $\text{Var}[\upsilon_n]$, as in (20.30). As a result, the line of vertical tangent points to $\mathbb{V}$ must have a smaller slope, yet the slope will not change sign; and that thick line is the MMSE linear prediction line $y = x\gamma_0$.

We cannot offer such simple descriptions of the inconsistency of OLS in the dynamic regression or simultaneous equations examples. Instead, we characterize the explanatory variables that have been omitted by finding MMSE linear predictors for each case. In all of our examples, a latent variable model describes the cause of $\text{E}[\varepsilon_n \mid \mathbf{x}_n] \neq 0$ despite the general structure in which $y_n = \mathbf{x}_n'\boldsymbol{\beta}_0 + \varepsilon_n$ and $\text{E}[\varepsilon_n] = 0$. In each case, interest focuses on $\mathbf{x}_n'\boldsymbol{\beta}_0$ but this is not the conditional mean of y_n given $\mathbf{x}_n$. We will reformulate every cause as an inability to condition the mean of y_n on all of the necessary explanatory variables. A critical explanatory variable is latent and, for this reason, omitted.

For errors in explanatory variables (Example 20.1), this point is trivial. If one could include in the conditioning set the measurement error $\boldsymbol{\upsilon}_n$, then

$$\text{E}[y_n \mid \mathbf{x}_n, \boldsymbol{\upsilon}_n] = \mathbf{x}_n'\boldsymbol{\beta}_0 - \boldsymbol{\upsilon}_n'\boldsymbol{\beta}_0$$

would be specified well enough to estimate $\boldsymbol{\beta}_0$ with OLS. But that is simply stating that if $\mathbf{x}_n^*$ were observable we could regress y_n on $\mathbf{x}_n^*$. For the dynamic regression in the previous section, this point is not trivial.

EXAMPLE 20.5 (Dynamic Regression)

We saw in (20.15) and (20.18) that the success of GLS estimation implicitly rests on the inclusion of additional variables in the regression equation. That is, if we expand the conditioning set to include $\mathbf{x}_{t-1} \equiv [\mathbf{x}_{1,t-1}', y_{t-2}]'$ then we obtain

$$\text{E}[y_t \mid \mathbf{x}_t, \mathbf{x}_{t-1}] = \mathbf{x}_t'\boldsymbol{\beta}_0 + \phi_0(y_{t-1} - \mathbf{x}_{t-1}'\boldsymbol{\beta}_0) \tag{20.32}$$

Aternatively, this conditional mean corrects $\mathbf{x}_t'\boldsymbol{\beta}_0$ for the missing latent explanatory variable $\varepsilon_{t-1} = y_{t-1} - \mathbf{x}_{t-1}'\boldsymbol{\beta}_0$:

$$\text{E}[y_t \mid \mathbf{x}_t, \mathbf{x}_{t-1}] = \mathbf{x}_t'\boldsymbol{\beta}_0 + \phi_0\varepsilon_{t-1} = \text{E}[y_t \mid \mathbf{x}_t, \varepsilon_{t-1}] \tag{20.33}$$

This conditional mean also suggests a consistent estimator of $\boldsymbol{\beta}_0$. If we expand (20.32), then

$$\begin{aligned}\text{E}[y_t \mid \mathbf{x}_t, \mathbf{x}_{t-1}] = {} & \mathbf{x}_{1t}'\boldsymbol{\beta}_{01} + (\beta_{02} + \phi_0)\, y_{t-1} \\ & + \mathbf{x}_{1,t-1}'(-\phi_0 \cdot \boldsymbol{\beta}_{01}) + (\phi_0\beta_{02})\, y_{t-2}\end{aligned} \tag{20.34}$$

can be estimated with OLS. The fitted coefficients of $\mathbf{x}_{1t}$ are consistent estimators of $\boldsymbol{\beta}_{01}$ and the coefficients of $\mathbf{x}_{1,t-1}$ are consistent estimators of $\phi_0 \cdot \boldsymbol{\beta}_{01}$. Hence, ϕ_0 is consistently estimated by the ratios of these coefficients. This in turn implies that we may estimate β_{02} with the fitted coefficient of y_{t-1} minus the estimator of ϕ_0 or the fitted coefficient of y_{t-2} divided by the estimator of ϕ_0.[13]

[13] This ratio will not be a reliable estimator if $\phi_0 = 0$. For this reason, the difference estimator is preferred. The same issue arises in the estimation of ϕ_0. Consistent estimation requires that the element of $\boldsymbol{\beta}_{01}$ be nonzero.

We can find an analogous regression function for the simultaneous equations example. This function is also linear in the explanatory variables so that OLS provides consistent estimators of its coefficients. In this case, however, the OLS estimator does not enable us to estimate the coefficients of the supply function.

EXAMPLE 20.6 (Simultaneous Equations)

Reconsider the simultaneous demand and supply functions in Example 20.2. Our goal is to find the MMSE linear prediction of the supply q_{sn} in (20.22) given p_n and the predetermined variables $\mathbf{x}_n \equiv [\mathbf{x}'_{s1n}, \mathbf{x}'_{d1n}]'$.

To do this, we note first that p_n, $\mathbf{x}_n$, and $\varepsilon_{dn} - \varepsilon_{sn}$ are linearly dependent according to (20.24). This dependence implies that

$$\begin{aligned} \mathrm{E}^*[y_n \mid p_n, \mathbf{x}_n] &= \mathbf{x}'_{s1n}\boldsymbol{\beta}_{0s1} + \beta_{0s2} p_n + \mathrm{E}^*[\varepsilon_{sn} \mid p_n, \mathbf{x}_n] \\ &= \mathbf{x}'_{s1n}\boldsymbol{\beta}_{0s1} + \beta_{0s2} p_n + \mathrm{E}^*[\varepsilon_{sn} \mid \varepsilon_{dn} - \varepsilon_{sn}, \mathbf{x}_n] \end{aligned} \tag{20.35}$$

Assuming that $\mathrm{E}[\varepsilon_{sn} \mid \mathbf{x}_n] = \mathrm{E}[\varepsilon_{dn} \mid \mathbf{x}_n] = 0$ and that $[\varepsilon_{sn}, \varepsilon_{dn}]'$ has finite conditional second moments,

$$\begin{aligned} \mathrm{E}^*[\varepsilon_{sn} \mid \varepsilon_{dn} - \varepsilon_{sn}, \mathbf{x}_n] &= \gamma_{0s} (\varepsilon_{dn} - \varepsilon_{sn}) \\ &= \gamma_{0s} \left[(\beta_{0s2} - \beta_{0d2})\, p_n - \left(\mathbf{x}'_{d1n}\boldsymbol{\beta}_{0d1} - \mathbf{x}'_{s1n}\boldsymbol{\beta}_{0s1} \right) \right] \end{aligned} \tag{20.36}$$

Combining this with (20.35), we obtain

$$\begin{aligned} \mathrm{E}^*[y_n \mid p_n, \mathbf{x}_n] &= \mathbf{x}'_{s1n}\boldsymbol{\beta}_{0s1} + \beta_{0s2} p_n + \gamma_{0s} (\varepsilon_{dn} - \varepsilon_{sn}) \\ &= \mathbf{x}'_{s1n} \left[(1 + \gamma_{0s}) \cdot \boldsymbol{\beta}_{0s1} \right] + \left[\beta_{0s2} + \gamma_{0s} (\beta_{0s2} - \beta_{0d2}) \right] p_n \\ &\quad + \mathbf{x}'_{d1n} (-\gamma_{0s} \cdot \boldsymbol{\beta}_{0d1}) \end{aligned} \tag{20.37}$$

Therefore, if we regress y_n on $\mathbf{x}_n$ and p_n then we will estimate these coefficients. The coefficients of the explanatory variables in the supply equation, $\mathbf{x}_{s1n}$ and p_n, will not be the coefficient vector of the supply equation, $\boldsymbol{\beta}_{0s}$. In addition, the $\mathbf{x}_{d1n}$ will possess nonzero coefficients. We cannot estimate the supply equation with OLS.

Unfortunately, we cannot recover an estimator for $\boldsymbol{\beta}_{0s}$ in this example the way we can estimate $\boldsymbol{\beta}_0$ from (20.34). The presence of the unknown γ_{0s} in all of these expressions for the coefficients prevents this. On the other hand, if $\varepsilon_{dn} - \varepsilon_{sn}$ were observable then applying OLS to (20.37) would yield estimates of the parameters in the supply function. We will exploit this observation below to motivate an IV estimator for the supply function. Before this, we broach IV estimation as a general method.

The study of omitting and including explanatory variables anticipates IV estimation because including the additional explanatory variables in OLS is a special case of IV. Using partitioned regression (Proposition 2, p. 57), we have seen that when $\mathbf{x}_{2n}$ is included in the OLS fit then the fitted coefficient vector for $\mathbf{x}_{1n}$ is

$$\begin{aligned} \hat{\boldsymbol{\beta}}_{\mathrm{OLS},1} &= \left[\mathbf{X}'_1 (\mathbf{I} - \mathbf{P}_2) \mathbf{X}_1 \right]^{-1} \mathbf{X}'_1 (\mathbf{I} - \mathbf{P}_2)\, \mathbf{y} \\ &= \left(\mathbf{X}'_{1\perp 2} \mathbf{X}_1 \right)^{-1} \mathbf{X}'_{1\perp 2} \mathbf{y} \end{aligned} \tag{20.38}$$

where $\mathbf{P}_2 \equiv \mathbf{X}_2(\mathbf{X}_2'\mathbf{X}_2)^{-1}\mathbf{X}_2'$ is the orthogonal projector onto $\mathrm{Col}(\mathbf{X}_2)$ and $\mathbf{X}_{1\perp 2} \equiv (\mathbf{I} - \mathbf{P}_2)\,\mathbf{X}_1$.[14] These are coefficients obtained from a general projection of y onto $\mathrm{Col}(\mathbf{X}_1)$ along $\mathrm{Col}^{\perp}(\mathbf{X}_2)$. By moving along $\mathrm{Col}^{\perp}(\mathbf{X}_2)$, the $\mathbf{X}_2\hat{\boldsymbol{\beta}}_{\mathrm{OLS},2}$ term that might otherwise be confounded with $\mathbf{X}_1\hat{\boldsymbol{\beta}}_{\mathrm{OLS},1}$ is annihilated. By moving onto $\mathrm{Col}(\mathbf{X}_1)$, the $\mathbf{X}_1\hat{\boldsymbol{\beta}}_{\mathrm{OLS},1}$ is isolated. The essence of IV estimation is such generalized projection. Whenever there are variables $\mathbf{z}_n$ like $\mathbf{X}_{1\perp 2}$ that identify a subspace orthogonal to the omitted explanatory variables, then IV estimation may be possible. If in addition the $\mathbf{z}_n$ are not orthogonal to *any* linear combination of the explanatory variables, then projection along the subspace spanned by $\mathbf{z}_n$ will not annihilate $\mathbf{x}_n'\boldsymbol{\beta}_0$ and one can estimate $\boldsymbol{\beta}_0$ with IV.[15]

20.4 CONSISTENT ESTIMATION

Given identification of the parameters, we offer the following asymptotic distribution theory for IV estimators. This theory is a direct generalization of that for OLS estimators in Section 13.4. First, we state several assumptions beginning with a summary of the latent model that is the focus of the discussion so far.

Assumption 20.1 (Latent Variable Model) *The random variables* $\{(y_n, \mathbf{x}_n, \varepsilon_n)\,;\, n = 1, \ldots, N\}$ *are i.i.d. such that* $y_n = \mathbf{x}_n'\boldsymbol{\beta}_0 + \varepsilon_n$ *for a coefficient vector* $\boldsymbol{\beta}_0 \in \mathbb{R}^K$ *and the moment restriction* $\mathrm{E}[\varepsilon_n] = 0$ *for all n. The pair* $(y_n, \mathbf{x}_n)$ *is observable but the* ε_n *is a latent disturbance term.*

This is a loose specification that contains $\mathrm{E}[y_n \mid \mathbf{x}_n] = \mathbf{x}_n'\boldsymbol{\beta}_0$ as a special case. If it were not for the restriction that $\mathrm{E}[\varepsilon_n] = 0$, the assumption would be vacuous. The residual ε_n could be merely *defined* to be $y_n - \mathbf{x}_n'\boldsymbol{\beta}_0$ for any $\boldsymbol{\beta}_0$ that we might choose. Instead, $\mathrm{E}[y_n] = \mathrm{E}[\mathbf{x}_n']\boldsymbol{\beta}_0$, which rules out some values for $\mathrm{E}[y_n]$, $\mathrm{E}[\mathbf{x}_n]$, and $\boldsymbol{\beta}_0$ jointly.

In addition, we state conditions that help us to establish that $\boldsymbol{\beta}_0$ is identified.

Assumption 20.2 (Instruments) *The vector* $\mathbf{z}_n$ *is an observable vector with K elements* z_{nk} $(k = 1, \ldots, K)$. *The* $\{(y_n, \mathbf{x}_n, \varepsilon_n, \mathbf{z}_n)\,;\, n = 1, \ldots, N\}$ *are i.i.d. such that* $\mathrm{E}[\varepsilon_n \mid \mathbf{z}_n] = 0$ *for all n and as* $N \to \infty$ *the second-order empirical moments converge in probability to*

$$\mathrm{E}_N[\mathbf{z}_n\varepsilon_n] \xrightarrow{p} \mathbf{0}, \tag{20.39}$$

$$\mathrm{E}_N[\mathbf{z}_n\mathbf{x}_n'] \xrightarrow{p} \mathrm{E}[\mathbf{z}_n\mathbf{x}_n'] \equiv \mathbf{D}_{zx} \tag{20.40}$$

where $\mathbf{D}_{zx}$ *is a finite nonsingular matrix.*

---

14 Actually, this particular formula is only implicit in Proposition 2 where we wrote $\hat{\boldsymbol{\beta}}_1 = (\mathbf{X}_{1\perp 2}'\mathbf{X}_{1\perp 2})^{-1}\mathbf{X}_{1\perp 2}'\mathbf{y}_{\perp 2}$. The difference lies in whether the orthogonal projector $\mathbf{I} - \mathbf{P}_2$ appears once or twice in each matrix product. It does not matter which, because $\mathbf{I} - \mathbf{P}_2$ is idempotent.

15 Lemma 3.4 (p. 67) states the analogous requirements for a fixed sample size N: for $\mathbf{Z}'\mathbf{X}$ to be nonsingular and $\mathbf{P}_{\mathbf{X}\perp\mathbf{Z}} \equiv \mathbf{X}\left(\mathbf{Z}'\mathbf{X}\right)^{-1}\mathbf{Z}'$ to be well defined, $\mathbf{Z}$ must have the same number of variables (columns) as $\mathbf{X}$, must be full-(column) rank, and no $\mathbf{Z}\boldsymbol{\alpha}$, except the zero vector, can be orthogonal to any $\mathbf{X}\boldsymbol{\gamma}$ $(\boldsymbol{\alpha}, \boldsymbol{\gamma} \in \mathbb{R}^K)$. Otherwise, $\mathrm{Col}(\mathbf{X}) \cap \mathrm{Col}^{\perp}(\mathbf{Z}) \neq \{\mathbf{0}\}$ and we cannot take the direct sum of these two subspaces.

Here we have the generalizations of assumptions from the classical linear model. First,

$$\mathrm{E}[y_n \mid \mathbf{z}_n] = \mathrm{E}[\mathbf{x}_n' \mid \mathbf{z}_n]\boldsymbol{\beta}_0$$

replaces first moments that were conditional on $\mathbf{x}_n$.[16] This conditional mean offers the possibility that $\boldsymbol{\beta}_0$ is identified if the variation in $\mathbf{z}_n$ is adequate. Second, the nonsingularity of $\mathbf{D}_{zx}$ replaces the nonsingularity of the second moment matrix of $\mathbf{x}_n$.[17] We do not give specific details about the data-generating process that imply such convergence.[18] In previous chapters, we have provided leading examples for which a law of large numbers delivers this behavior. Here, we will skip over such justification in order to simplify. Our final assumption has a similar flavor.

Assumption 20.3 (Convergence) *The random variables* $\{(y_n, \mathbf{x}_n, \varepsilon_n, \mathbf{z}_n);\ n = 1, \ldots, N\}$ *are i.i.d. such that* $\mathrm{Var}[y_n \mid \mathbf{z}_n] = \sigma_0^2$ *for all n and as* $N \to \infty$ *the sequence*

$$\sqrt{N}\,\mathrm{E}_N[\mathbf{z}_n\varepsilon_n] \xrightarrow{d} \mathfrak{N}(0, \sigma_0^2 \cdot \mathbf{D}_{zz}) \tag{20.41}$$

where

$$\mathrm{E}_N[\mathbf{z}_n\mathbf{z}_n'] \xrightarrow{p} \mathrm{E}[\mathbf{z}_n\mathbf{z}_n'] \equiv \mathbf{D}_{zz} \tag{20.42}$$

and $\mathbf{D}_{zz}$ *is a finite nonsingular matrix.*

These assumptions parallel elements of the proof sketched on p. 261 for the asymptotic distribution of the OLS estimator (Proposition 15, p. 257). The major difference is that we have two nonsingular matrices, $\mathbf{D}_{zx}$ and $\mathbf{D}_{zz}$, in place of the probability limit of $\mathrm{E}_N[\mathbf{x}_n\mathbf{x}_n']$. A similar argument to that proof supports the following proposition.

Proposition 18 (Asymptotic Distribution of IV) *Let Assumptions 20.1–20.3 hold. Then as* $N \to \infty$,

$$\hat{\boldsymbol{\beta}}_{\mathrm{IV}} \equiv (\mathbf{Z}'\mathbf{X})^{-1}\mathbf{Z}'\mathbf{y} \xrightarrow{p} \boldsymbol{\beta}_0 \tag{20.43}$$

$$\hat{\sigma}_{\mathrm{IV}}^2 \equiv \frac{\mathbf{y}'(\mathbf{I} - \mathbf{P}_{\mathbf{X}\perp\mathbf{Z}})'(\mathbf{I} - \mathbf{P}_{\mathbf{X}\perp\mathbf{Z}})\mathbf{y}}{N} \xrightarrow{p} \sigma_0^2 \tag{20.44}$$

and

$$\mathbf{Z}'\mathbf{X}\left(\hat{\sigma}_{\mathrm{IV}}^2 \cdot \mathbf{Z}'\mathbf{Z}\right)^{-1/2}\left(\hat{\boldsymbol{\beta}}_{\mathrm{IV}} - \boldsymbol{\beta}_0\right) \xrightarrow{d} \mathfrak{N}(\mathbf{0}, \mathbf{I}_K) \tag{20.45}$$

16 See Assumption 6.1 (First Moments, p. 110).

17 See Assumption 13.2 (Population Full Rank, p. 257).

18 Note that Assumptions 20.1 and 20.2 are redundant. We will require only (20.39). That $\mathrm{E}[\varepsilon_n \mid \mathbf{z}_n] = 0$ is consistent with this probability limit, but not necessary for it. That $\mathrm{E}[\varepsilon_n] = 0$ follows from the conditional mean $\mathrm{E}[\varepsilon_n \mid \mathbf{z}_n] = 0$.

The variance parameter estimator equals the empirical variance of the IV fitted residuals. Because it is not an orthogonal projector, $\mathbf{P}_{\mathbf{X}\perp\mathbf{Z}} \equiv \mathbf{X}\left(\mathbf{Z}'\mathbf{X}\right)^{-1}\mathbf{Z}'$ is asymmetric. As a result, the sum of squared residuals in the numerator includes both $\mathbf{I} - \mathbf{P}_{\mathbf{X}\perp\mathbf{Z}}$ and its transpose.

With this result in hand, we can conduct the usual methods of inference concerning $\boldsymbol{\beta}_0$ with an IV estimator. Both confidence intervals and hypothesis tests follow familiar lines using the asymptotically pivotal statistic in (20.45). These approximate procedures treat $\hat{\boldsymbol{\beta}}_{\text{IV}}$ as though, conditional on $\mathbf{X}$, $\mathbf{Z}$, and $\hat{\sigma}^2_{\text{IV}}$,

$$\hat{\boldsymbol{\beta}}_{\text{IV}} \mid \left\{\mathbf{X}, \mathbf{Z}, \hat{\sigma}^2_{\text{IV}}\right\} \sim \mathfrak{N}[\boldsymbol{\beta}_0,\ \hat{\sigma}^2_{\text{IV}} \cdot \left(\mathbf{Z}'\mathbf{X}\right)^{-1}\mathbf{Z}'\mathbf{Z}\left(\mathbf{X}'\mathbf{Z}\right)^{-1}] \tag{20.46}$$

To actually implement the method of IV for a particular regression equation, the starting point is the specification of the instrumental variables themselves. Latent variable models often suggest instrumental variables. We look for variables, or functions of variables, that are both (1) uncorrelated with the residual term and (2) correlated with the explanatory variables of interest. More than this, the instrumental variable matrix $\mathbf{Z} \equiv \left[\mathbf{z}_n'\right]'$ must combine with the explanatory variable matrix $\mathbf{X} \equiv [\mathbf{x}_n]'$ so that $\mathbf{Z}'\mathbf{X}$ is nonsingular (with probability one). Two of our examples provide such variables.

EXAMPLE 20.7 **(Dynamic Regression)**

In the dynamic regression model, $\mathbf{X} = \left[\left[\mathbf{x}_{1t}', y_{t-1}\right]'\right]'$ and we can immediately include in $\mathbf{z}_t$ all the variables in $\mathbf{x}_{1t}$. By assumption, $\text{E}[\varepsilon_t \mid \mathbf{X}_1] = 0$ and this implies that $\text{E}[\varepsilon_t \mid \mathbf{x}_{1t}] = 0$. Furthermore, because $\mathbf{X}_1$ is full rank, these variables do not violate any of the additional rank requirements. The $\mathbf{x}_{1,t-1,k}$ $(k = 1, \ldots, K)$ are also potential instrumental variables because $\text{E}[\varepsilon_t \mid \mathbf{x}_{1,t-1}] = 0$. In addition,

$$y_{t-1} = \mathbf{x}_{1,t-1}'\boldsymbol{\beta}_{01} + \beta_{02}y_{t-1} + \varepsilon_{t-1}$$

so that y_{t-1} is correlated with all the variables in $\mathbf{x}_{1,t-1}$. But we must take care to select one that is not collinear with the variables in $\mathbf{x}_{1t}$. This rules out, for example, the constant 1 that typically appears in both $\mathbf{x}_{1t}$ and $\mathbf{x}_{1,t-1}$. It would also rule out seasonal dummy variables. However, the variation over time in the unemployment rate would presumably make that variable acceptable. In summary, any $\mathbf{Z} = \left[[\mathbf{x}_{1t}', \mathbf{x}_{1,t-1,k}']'\right]'$ making $\mathbf{Z}'\mathbf{X}$ nonsingular delivers an IV estimator for this model.

It seems that without any knowledge of GLS, but equipped with the IV estimator, we can easily construct consistent estimators of the dynamic regression with AR(1) serial correlation. A similar logic works for the simultaneous equations example.

EXAMPLE 20.8 **(Simultaneous Equations)**

Consider IV estimation of the supply equation (20.22). Once again, the elements of $\mathbf{x}_{s1n}$ are obvious candidate instrumental variables. In addition, because the price variable is determined in equilibrium by both supply and demand factors, all of the variables in $\mathbf{x}_{d1n}$ are potential instrumental variables. Note that we have no structure that allows us to include p_n in the list of instrumental variables. We can never rule out that a function of p_n is correlated with ε_{sn}. Therefore we are restricted to using functions of $\mathbf{x}_n \equiv [\mathbf{x}_{s1n}', \mathbf{x}_{d1n}']'$. For example, we can specify any x_{dnk}

(except p_n) and $\mathbf{z}_n = \left[\mathbf{x}'_{s1n}, x_{dnk}\right]'$ such that $\mathrm{E}[\mathbf{z}_n\mathbf{x}'_n]$ is nonsingular to construct an IV estimator for $\boldsymbol{\beta}_{0s} = \left[\boldsymbol{\beta}'_{0s1}, \boldsymbol{\beta}_{0s2}\right]'$.

In both of these examples, there is generally an infinite number of IV estimators. We can also consider general functions of the valid instrumental variables. For example, the family $\mathbf{Z} = \left\{\left[\mathbf{x}'_{s1n}, f(\mathbf{x}_{s1n}, \mathbf{x}_{d1n})\right]'\right\}'$ for various functions f contains potential instrument matrices for the supply equation of the simultaneous market system. The necessary orthogonality will still hold, so that we are constrained only by the requirement that $\mathbf{Z}'\mathbf{X}$ be nonsingular. This is critical for the errors in explanatory variables example.

EXAMPLE 20.9 (Errors in Variables)
Example 20.1 with errors in the explanatory variables comes with no "extra" variables comparable to $\mathbf{x}_{1,t-1}$ or $\mathbf{x}_{d1n}$ in the previous two examples. However, nonlinear functions of the observed explanatory variables may still provide a valid instrument matrix $\mathbf{Z}$ under well-specified circumstances. To illustrate, consider a case with three explanatory variables, one of which is measured with error. Let

$$\mathrm{E}[y_n \mid x_{2n}, x^*_{n3}] = \beta_{01} + \beta_{02}x_{2n} + \beta_{03}x^*_{n3}$$

and $x_{n3} = x^*_{n3} + \upsilon_n$ be the variable measured with error. Suppose that both x_{2n} and x^2_{2n} are correlated with x^*_{n3}. Because x^2_{2n} is uncorrelated with υ_n, $\mathbf{z}_n = \left[1, x_{2n}, x^2_{2n}\right]$ would generally be a valid list of instrumental variables.

However, most researchers would not accept such an estimator for empirical use. The reason is that there is another, plausible interpretation of the estimated coefficients. Because we do not know that the conditional mean is a linear function of x_{2n} in actual applications, we might consider the possibility that x^2_{2n} should also be included as an RHS explanatory variable. But if it is, then we will need a third instrumental variable and we are back to looking for another function of x_{2n} to serve as an instrumental variable. Because such an argument can be made for any function of x_{2n}, the use of nonlinear functions as instrumental variables for the errors-in-variables problem is widely viewed with suspicion.

Thus, we must recognize that not all problems have IV solutions. There are situations in which the parameters of the model cannot be estimated. In this characteristic, these situations are similar to exact multicollinearity among the explanatory variables. When there is exact multicollinearity, the matrix $\mathbf{X}'\mathbf{X}$ is singular. When there is no consistent IV estimator, one cannot construct a nonsingular $\mathbf{Z}'\mathbf{X}$ from the available information. In both cases, the parameters of the model are not identified.

20.5 TWO-STAGE LEAST SQUARES

The IV estimators that latent models suggest are often more specific than a list of possible instrumental variables. The models may also offer insight into the particular functions of the available variables that provide appealing estimators. In this section, we delve more deeply into the the example of simultaneous equations. In such linear systems, an intuitively attractive instrumental variable for p_n is $\mathbf{x}'_n\check{\boldsymbol{\pi}}_p$, the OLS fitted value from the regression of p_n on *all* of the possible instrumental variables $\mathbf{x}_n$. Rather than a single variable as Example 20.8 suggests, this instrument conveniently combines all of the available variables into the linear combination that is most highly correlated with p_n. We will motivate the resultant IV estimator, known as *two-stage least squares* (2SLS), from the latent character of the simultaneous equations model itself.[19]

For this model, we have already found in (20.37) that

$$\mathrm{E}^*[y_n \mid p_n, \mathbf{x}_n] = \mathbf{x}_{s1n}'\boldsymbol{\beta}_{0s1} + \beta_{0s2}p_n + \gamma_{0s}(\varepsilon_{dn} - \varepsilon_{sn}) \tag{20.47}$$

where

$$\varepsilon_{dn} - \varepsilon_{sn} = (\beta_{0s2} - \beta_{0d2})\, p_n - \mathbf{x}_{d1n}'\boldsymbol{\beta}_{0d1} + \mathbf{x}_{s1n}'\boldsymbol{\beta}_{0s1} \tag{20.48}$$

according to (20.24). If we observed the latent variable $\varepsilon_{dn} - \varepsilon_{sn}$, then we could simply include $\varepsilon_{dn} - \varepsilon_{sn}$ as an additional explanatory variable with $\mathbf{x}_{s1n}$ and p_n to estimate $\boldsymbol{\beta}_{0s}$ with OLS. An intuitive approach to estimation is to seek an estimated proxy for this latent variable.

Such a variable is indeed available. If we rewrite (20.48) as

$$\begin{aligned}\varepsilon_{dn} - \varepsilon_{sn} &= (\beta_{0s2} - \beta_{0d2})\left(p_n - \frac{\mathbf{x}_{d1n}'\boldsymbol{\beta}_{0d1} - \mathbf{x}_{s1n}'\boldsymbol{\beta}_{0s1}}{\beta_{0s2} - \beta_{0d2}}\right)\\ &= (\beta_{0s2} - \beta_{0d2})\left(p_n - \mathbf{w}_n'\boldsymbol{\pi}_{0p}\right)\end{aligned}$$

where the elements of $\mathbf{w}_n$ are a basis for the elements of $\mathbf{x}_n \equiv \left[\mathbf{x}_{d1n}', \mathbf{x}_{s1n}'\right]'$ and $\boldsymbol{\pi}_{0p}$ contains the appropriate functions of $[1/(\beta_{0s2} - \beta_{0d2})] \cdot \boldsymbol{\beta}_{0d1}$ and $[1/(\beta_{0s2} - \beta_{0d2})] \cdot \boldsymbol{\beta}_{0s1}$, then

$$\mathrm{E}^*[y_n \mid p_n, \mathbf{x}_n] = \mathbf{x}_{s1n}'\boldsymbol{\beta}_{0s1} + \beta_{0s2}p_n + \gamma_{0s}(\beta_{0s2} - \beta_{0d2})\left(p_n - \mathbf{w}_n'\boldsymbol{\pi}_{0p}\right) \tag{20.49}$$

Because

$$\mathrm{E}[p_n \mid \mathbf{x}_n] = \mathbf{w}_n'\boldsymbol{\pi}_{0p}$$

the parameter vector $\boldsymbol{\pi}_{0p}$ is estimated consistently by the OLS fitted coefficients $\breve{\boldsymbol{\pi}}_p$ from a regression of p_n on $\mathbf{w}_n$. Thus, the OLS fitted residual $p_n - \mathbf{w}_n'\breve{\boldsymbol{\pi}}_p$ may serve as an estimated proxy variable for the latent $p_n - \mathbf{w}_n'\boldsymbol{\pi}_{0p}$, or equivalently for $\varepsilon_{dn} - \varepsilon_{sn}$. Provided that multicollinearity does not arise, we may consider the OLS regression of y_n on $\mathbf{x}_{sn} \equiv \left[\mathbf{x}_{s1n}', p_n\right]'$ and $p_n - \mathbf{w}_n'\breve{\boldsymbol{\pi}}_p$ as a possible estimation method for β_{0s} and $\gamma_{0s}(\beta_{0s2} - \beta_{0d2})$.

A formal rationalization for this method describes it as a two-step estimator. In the first step we compute an estimator $\breve{\boldsymbol{\pi}}_p$ of $\boldsymbol{\pi}_{0p}$ and in the second step we estimate $\boldsymbol{\beta}_{0s}$ as a function $\hat{\boldsymbol{\beta}}_s(\breve{\boldsymbol{\pi}}_p)$ of $\breve{\boldsymbol{\pi}}_p$, treating $\breve{\boldsymbol{\pi}}_p$ as though it were $\boldsymbol{\pi}_{0p}$. Such estimators are consistent given that (1) the first-step estimator $\breve{\boldsymbol{\pi}}_p$ is consistent, (2) $\boldsymbol{\beta}_{0s}$ is identified, and (3) the second-step estimator $\hat{\boldsymbol{\beta}}_s(\boldsymbol{\pi}_p)$ converges in probability uniformly to $\boldsymbol{\beta}_s(\boldsymbol{\pi}_p)$ where $\boldsymbol{\beta}_s(\boldsymbol{\pi}_{0p}) = \boldsymbol{\beta}_{0s}$.[20] We have used these conditions before for variance matrix estimators and LMLEs.[21] Given (1), we consider (2) and (3).

The identification of $\boldsymbol{\beta}_{0s}$ is not assured in general, but we can give a simple, reasonable condition that implies identification. Because $\boldsymbol{\pi}_{0p}$ is identified by our choice of $\mathbf{w}_n$, look at estimation of $\boldsymbol{\beta}_{0s}$ if $\boldsymbol{\pi}_{0p}$ were known. We could regress y_n on $\mathbf{x}_{sn}$ and $p_n - \mathbf{w}_n'\boldsymbol{\pi}_{0p}$ to estimate $\boldsymbol{\beta}_{0s}$ provided that these explanatory variables are linearly independent. However $\mathbf{x}_{sn} \equiv \left[\mathbf{x}_{s1n}', p_n\right]'$ is

19 Theil (1953) and Basmann (1957) independently proposed the 2SLS method.

20 See Lemma 15.5 (p. 326).

21 See the consistent estimators of the information matrix in Section 15.4.

linearly dependent on $[\mathbf{w}_n', p_n]'$ so that exact multicollinearity among the explanatory variables is possible. We can rule this out if $p_n - \mathbf{w}_n'\boldsymbol{\pi}_{0p}$ includes a contribution from an element of $\mathbf{x}_{d1n}$ that is linearly independent of $\mathbf{x}_{s1n}$. Therefore $\boldsymbol{\beta}_{0s}$ is identified if there is an element $\mathbf{x}_{dnk}$ of $\mathbf{x}_{d1n}$ in $\mathbf{w}_n$ with a nonzero coefficient in $\boldsymbol{\pi}_{0p}$.[22]

Note that this is equivalent to requiring the existence of an instrumental variable as in Example 20.8. Because x_{dnk} is *not* collinear with $\mathbf{x}_{s1n}$ and *is* correlated with p_n, the instrument vector $\mathbf{z}_n = [\mathbf{x}_{s1n}', x_{dnk}]'$ yields a nonsingular $\mathrm{E}[\mathbf{z}_n\mathbf{x}_n']$. As a result, IV estimation is feasible and $\boldsymbol{\beta}_{0s}$ is identified.

Given the identification of $\boldsymbol{\beta}_{0s}$, let us study the asymptotic behavior of the two-step estimator. This estimator has a tractable functional form that makes a direct analysis workable. Let us denote the first-step estimator by

$$\check{\boldsymbol{\pi}}_p = (\mathbf{W}'\mathbf{W})^{-1}\mathbf{W}'\mathbf{p}$$

where $\mathbf{W} \equiv [\mathbf{w}_n']'$ and $\mathbf{p} \equiv [p_n]'$. Then the OLS fitted residual is $\check{\boldsymbol{\upsilon}}_p \equiv (\mathbf{I} - \mathbf{P_W})\,\mathbf{p}$. Using the formula (20.38) for the partitioned OLS fit, we obtain the two-stage least-squares IV estimator

$$\begin{aligned}\hat{\boldsymbol{\beta}}_{s,2\mathrm{SLS}} &= \left[\mathbf{X}_s'\left(\mathbf{I} - \mathbf{P}_{\check{\upsilon}_p}\right)\mathbf{X}_s\right]^{-1}\mathbf{X}_s'\left(\mathbf{I} - \mathbf{P}_{\check{\upsilon}_p}\right)\mathbf{y}\\ &= \left(\mathbf{X}_s'\mathbf{P_W}\mathbf{X}_s\right)^{-1}\mathbf{X}_s'\mathbf{P_W}\mathbf{y}\end{aligned} \tag{20.50}$$

where $\mathbf{X}_s \equiv [\mathbf{x}_{sn}]'$, $\mathbf{y} \equiv [y_n]'$, and[23]

$$\mathbf{Z} \equiv \left(\mathbf{I} - \mathbf{P}_{\check{\upsilon}_p}\right)\mathbf{X}_s = \mathbf{P_W}\mathbf{X}_s = \left[\left[\mathbf{x}_{s1n}', \mathbf{w}_n'\check{\boldsymbol{\pi}}_p\right]'\right]$$

Therefore, the instrumental variables are the fitted values from OLS regressions of the explanatory variables on $\mathbf{w}_n$. Such regressions fit the elements of $\mathbf{x}_{s1n}$ perfectly so that these explanatory variables are also instrumental variables. However, p_n is replaced by its OLS fitted value $\mathbf{w}_n'\check{\boldsymbol{\pi}}_p$.

This functional form makes confirming the consistency of this IV estimator direct. We have

$$\begin{aligned}\hat{\boldsymbol{\beta}}_{s,2\mathrm{SLS}} &= \left(\mathbf{X}_s'\mathbf{P_W}\mathbf{X}_s\right)^{-1}\mathbf{X}_s'\mathbf{P_W}\mathbf{y}\\ &= \boldsymbol{\beta}_{0s} + \left(\mathbf{X}_s'\mathbf{P_W}\mathbf{X}_s\right)^{-1}\mathbf{X}_s'\mathbf{P_W}\boldsymbol{\varepsilon}_s\\ &= \boldsymbol{\beta}_{0s} + \left\{\mathrm{E}_N[\mathbf{x}_{sn}\mathbf{w}_n']\left(\mathrm{E}_N[\mathbf{w}_n\mathbf{w}_n']\right)^{-1}\mathrm{E}_N[\mathbf{w}_n\mathbf{x}_{sn}']\right\}^{-1}\\ &\quad \mathrm{E}_N[\mathbf{x}_{sn}\mathbf{w}_n']\left(\mathrm{E}_N[\mathbf{w}_n\mathbf{w}_n']\right)^{-1}\mathrm{E}_N[\mathbf{w}_n\varepsilon_{sn}]\end{aligned}$$

---

[22] In Chapter 26 we will look into this requirement more closely.

[23] This remarkably simple result rests on the partitioned regression equation (20.38) and the properties of orthogonal projection. Because we chose $\mathbf{W}$ so that $\mathrm{Col}([\mathbf{x}_{s1n}]') \subseteq \mathrm{Col}(\mathbf{W})$ and because $\check{\boldsymbol{\upsilon}}_p \perp \mathrm{Col}(\mathbf{W})$ by construction, then

$$\left(\mathbf{I} - \mathbf{P}_{\check{\upsilon}_p}\right)[\mathbf{x}_{s1n}]' = [\mathbf{x}_{s1n}]' = \mathbf{P_W}[\mathbf{x}_{s1n}]'$$

Because

$$\check{\boldsymbol{\upsilon}}_p'\mathbf{p} = \mathbf{p}'(\mathbf{I} - \mathbf{P_W})\,\mathbf{p} = \check{\boldsymbol{\upsilon}}_p'\check{\boldsymbol{\upsilon}}_p$$

then

$$\left(\mathbf{I} - \mathbf{P}_{\check{\upsilon}_p}\right)\mathbf{p} = \mathbf{p} - \check{\boldsymbol{\upsilon}}_p = \mathbf{Z}\check{\boldsymbol{\pi}}_p = \mathbf{P_W}\mathbf{p}$$

Therefore, $\left(\mathbf{I} - \mathbf{P}_{\check{\upsilon}_p}\right)\mathbf{X}_s = \mathbf{P_W}\mathbf{X}_s$.

where $\boldsymbol{\varepsilon}_s \equiv [\varepsilon_{sn}]'$. Assuming that every sample mean converges to a population counterpart, the critical term for consistency of the estimator is the $\mathrm{E}_N[\mathbf{w}_n\varepsilon_{sn}]$. By assumption, $\mathrm{E}[\varepsilon_{sn} \mid \mathbf{w}_n] = 0$ so that $\mathrm{E}[\mathbf{w}_n\varepsilon_{sn}] = \mathbf{0}$ and $\mathrm{E}_N[\mathbf{w}_n\varepsilon_{sn}]$ converges in probability to zero. Therefore, $\hat{\beta}_{s,2SLS}$ is a consistent IV estimator.

The projection term $\mathbf{P_W}$ in this estimator has two other analytical consequences. First, the projection term simplifies the asymptotic variance of the 2SLS estimator. Because the instrument matrix is $\mathbf{Z} \equiv \mathbf{P_W X}_s$ in this IV estimator,

$$\mathbf{Z'Z} = (\mathbf{P_W X}_s)' \mathbf{P_W X}_s = \mathbf{X}_s' \mathbf{P_W X}_s = (\mathbf{P_W X}_s)' \mathbf{X}_s = \mathbf{Z' X}_s$$

so that the approximate variance of $\hat{\boldsymbol{\beta}}_{s,2SLS}$ is $\hat{\sigma}^2_{IV} \cdot (\mathbf{Z'Z})^{-1}$, using (20.46).

Second, the projection term also gives the 2SLS estimator of the supply equation a useful interpretation: the instrumental variables $\mathbf{P_W X}_s$ are estimators of the MMSE linear predictions of $\mathbf{X}_s$ given the $\mathbf{W}$. The actual MMSE linear predictions are as highly correlated with the explanatory variables of the supply equation as linear functions of $\mathbf{w}_n$ can be. Yet, as functions of $\mathbf{w}_n$ alone, these predictions are also orthogonal to ε_{sn}. Viewed loosely as estimates, the instruments in $\mathbf{P_W X}_s$ are feasible approximations of these predictions.

The 2SLS estimator has wide applicability outside our simple simultaneous equations model. For instance, we can apply 2SLS to Example 20.7, substituting the OLS fitted value from the regression of y_{t-1} on $\mathbf{x}_{1,t-1}$ as an instrumental variable instead of a single $x_{1,t-1,k}$. In the remainder of this chapter and in the next chapter also, we will return to studying 2SLS.

Having established the basic distribution theory for IV estimation and illustrated the selection of instrumental variables, there remain several topics to complete our treatment. First, many IV estimators are two-step estimators such as FGLS and 2SLS where the instrument matrix is actually a function of a preliminary estimator. In some cases, this first-step estimation affects the asymptotic approximation of the variance of the IV estimator. We discuss the necessary correction in the next section. Second, we have noted that the IV procedure offers a potentially enormous menu of estimators where each item differs according to the instrumental variable ingredients. How do we choose from among all the delicious choices? One answer to this question is to select the IV estimator that is efficient relative to all those available. We discuss two cases in which this is possible in the following section. Third, we briefly describe in Section 20.8 circumstances in which the asymptotic approximation to the distribution of the IV estimator is poor. Finally, we emphasize the importance of latent variable models in IV estimation under *Methodological Notes*.

20.6 TWO-STEP VARIANCE ESTIMATION

Given that there may be several ways to compute such IV estimators as 2SLS, we must be alert to hazards in estimating the variance-covariance matrix of two-step estimators. It is tempting to accept the variance estimates that OLS, GLS, or IV software prints out automatically with the parameter estimates. But such variance estimates generally ignore the fact that parameters were estimated in the first step. These parameters are treated as constants, not random variables, and this may cause misestimation of the sampling variance in the second step. A reliable rule, suggested by Newey, is that the variance estimator of a two-step estimator can ignore the variance in the initial estimator if the two-step estimator is consistent when the first-step estimator is replaced with arbitrary parameter values. If the two-step estimator is consistent only with the population parameter value (or consistent estimators), then the variance estimator must be adjusted.

Let us illustrate the potential problem with the 2SLS estimator.

EXAMPLE 20.10 (Simultaneous Equations)

If we compute the 2SLS estimator of the supply equation by fitting y_n to the explanatory variables $\check{\mathbf{W}} \equiv \left[\mathbf{X}_s, \check{\upsilon}_p\right]$ with OLS software, then we will obtain an estimator of the variance matrix of the fitted coefficients based on the OLS equations: $s^2_{\text{OLS}} \cdot \left(\check{\mathbf{W}}'\check{\mathbf{W}}\right)^{-1}$ where

$$s^2 = \frac{\left\|\mathbf{y} - \mathbf{X}_s\hat{\boldsymbol{\beta}}_{\text{2SLS}} - \hat{\delta}\check{\upsilon}_p\right\|^2}{N - K - 1}$$

$\hat{\delta}$ is the fitted coefficient of $\check{\upsilon}$ and K is the number of variables in $\mathbf{x}_{sn}$. Using a partitioned inverse, the estimator of the variance matrix for $\hat{\boldsymbol{\beta}}_{\text{2SLS}}$ will be

$$\mathbf{V}_{\text{OLS}} \equiv s^2 \cdot \left[\mathbf{X}_s' \left(\mathbf{I} - \mathbf{P}_{\check{\upsilon}_p}\right) \mathbf{X}_s\right]^{-1} = s^2 \cdot \left(\mathbf{X}_s'\mathbf{P}_{\mathbf{W}}\mathbf{X}_s\right)^{-1}$$

On the other hand, IV software will compute the estimator with the equations in Proposition 18 as in

$$\mathbf{V}_{\text{IV}} \equiv \hat{\sigma}^2_{\text{IV}} \cdot \left(\mathbf{Z}'\mathbf{X}_s\right)^{-1} \mathbf{Z}'\mathbf{Z} \left(\mathbf{X}_s'\mathbf{Z}\right)^{-1} = \hat{\sigma}^2_{\text{IV}} \cdot \left(\mathbf{X}_s'\mathbf{P}_{\mathbf{W}}\mathbf{X}_s\right)^{-1}$$

where

$$\hat{\sigma}^2_{\text{IV}} = \frac{\left\|\mathbf{y} - \mathbf{X}_s\hat{\boldsymbol{\beta}}_{\text{2SLS}}\right\|^2}{N}$$

In this case, the matrix components are equal but the scalar multipliers for the residual variance are not. Asymptotically, we can ignore the difference in denominators, but not the difference in numerators. One can see that s^2 will be strictly less than $\hat{\sigma}^2_{\text{IV}}$ because the former is using the minimized sum of squared residuals. As a result, $\mathbf{V}_{\text{OLS}}$ will underestimate the approximate sampling variance of the 2SLS estimator.

Essentially, the OLS estimator fails to take into account that one of its explanatory variables is a function of an estimator. Quite naturally, the OLS estimator treats all of the explanatory variables as observed without error because that is an assumption stipulated by its estimation theory. In this example this treatment leads unambiguously to underestimation of the sampling variance.

Notice that the rule applies to Example 20.10. The IV version of 2SLS uses the instrument matrix $\mathbf{W} \equiv \left\{[\mathbf{x}_{s1n}', \mathbf{w}_n'\check{\boldsymbol{\pi}}_p]'\right\}'$. Even if we put some $\boldsymbol{\pi}_{1p}$ in place of $\check{\boldsymbol{\pi}}_p$ in these instruments the IV estimator will remain consistent because $\mathbf{w}_n'\boldsymbol{\pi}_{1p}$ will also be orthogonal to ε_{sn}. The only restriction on $\boldsymbol{\pi}_{1p}$ is that $\mathbf{Z}'\mathbf{X}$ remain nonsingular. On the other hand, the OLS version of 2SLS will be inconsistent using $\boldsymbol{\pi}_{1p}$. The conditional mean specifies that the latent explanatory variable is $\upsilon_n = y_n - \mathbf{w}_n'\boldsymbol{\pi}_{0p}$ and replacing this with $y_n - \mathbf{w}_n'\boldsymbol{\pi}_{1p}$ would incur an error-in-variables problem. The rule says that the IV estimation method produces a consistent estimator of the asymptotic variance of the 2SLS estimator whereas the OLS estimation does not.

In general, one works out the proper sampling variance of such two-step estimators using the following result, a generalization of the delta method (Lemma 16.1, p. 367):[24]

PROPOSITION 19 (TWO-STEP ASYMPTOTIC VARIANCE) *Suppose that the two-step estimator $\hat{\boldsymbol{\theta}}_N(\check{\boldsymbol{\gamma}}_N)$ is a consistent, asymptotically normal estimator of $\boldsymbol{\theta}_0$. In particular, let $\check{\boldsymbol{\gamma}}_N \xrightarrow{p} \boldsymbol{\gamma}_0$, $\hat{\boldsymbol{\theta}}_N(\boldsymbol{\gamma}) \xrightarrow{p} \boldsymbol{\theta}(\boldsymbol{\gamma})$ uniformly, $\boldsymbol{\theta}(\boldsymbol{\gamma}_0) = \boldsymbol{\theta}_0$, and*

$$\sqrt{N}\begin{bmatrix} \hat{\boldsymbol{\theta}}_N(\boldsymbol{\gamma}_0) - \boldsymbol{\theta}_0 \\ \check{\boldsymbol{\gamma}}_N - \boldsymbol{\gamma}_0 \end{bmatrix} \xrightarrow{d} \mathfrak{N}\left(\mathbf{0}, \begin{bmatrix} \boldsymbol{\Omega}_{\theta\theta} & \boldsymbol{\Omega}_{\theta\gamma} \\ \boldsymbol{\Omega}_{\gamma\theta} & \boldsymbol{\Omega}_{\gamma\gamma} \end{bmatrix}\right)$$

If $\boldsymbol{\theta}(\boldsymbol{\gamma})$ is continuously differentiable and

$$\frac{\partial \hat{\boldsymbol{\theta}}_N(\boldsymbol{\gamma})}{\partial \boldsymbol{\gamma}'} \xrightarrow{p} \frac{\partial \boldsymbol{\theta}(\boldsymbol{\gamma})}{\partial \boldsymbol{\gamma}'} \equiv \mathbf{J}(\boldsymbol{\gamma})$$

uniformly then

$$\sqrt{N}\left[\hat{\boldsymbol{\theta}}_N(\check{\boldsymbol{\gamma}}_N) - \boldsymbol{\theta}_0\right] \xrightarrow{d} \mathfrak{N}(\mathbf{0}, \mathbf{V})$$

where

$$\mathbf{V} \equiv \boldsymbol{\Omega}_{\theta\theta} + \mathbf{J}_0\boldsymbol{\Omega}_{\theta\gamma} + \boldsymbol{\Omega}_{\gamma\theta}\mathbf{J}_0' + \mathbf{J}_0\boldsymbol{\Omega}_{\gamma\gamma}\mathbf{J}_0'$$
$$\mathbf{J}_0 \equiv \mathbf{J}(\boldsymbol{\gamma}_0)$$

In general, the asymptotic variance of the two-step estimator will not be $\boldsymbol{\Omega}_{\theta\theta}$, the asymptotic variance of the infeasible estimator $\hat{\boldsymbol{\theta}}(\boldsymbol{\gamma}_0)$. The actual variance will depend on the asymptotic variance of the initial estimator, $\boldsymbol{\Omega}_{\gamma\gamma}$, and the first-order influence of the initial estimator on the final estimator, $\mathbf{J}_0$. We expect, for example, that as either $\boldsymbol{\Omega}_{\gamma\gamma}$ or $\mathbf{J}_0$ grows the variance of the two-step estimator grows and the formula for $\mathbf{V}$ bears this out. There is an additional factor, however, that influences this relationship and that is the covariance between $\check{\boldsymbol{\gamma}}$ and $\hat{\boldsymbol{\theta}}(\boldsymbol{\gamma}_0)$, $\boldsymbol{\Omega}_{\gamma\theta}$. It is possible that this covariance makes the asymptotic variance of the two-step estimator smaller than that of the infeasible one. We cannot say in general that the asymptotic variance of the two-step estimator is larger than $\boldsymbol{\Omega}_{\theta\theta}$.

To apply this proposition, we generally estimate each of the terms in the variance with empirical counterparts evaluated at the estimators $\check{\boldsymbol{\gamma}}$ and $\hat{\boldsymbol{\theta}}(\check{\boldsymbol{\gamma}})$.

EXAMPLE 20.11 (Dynamic Regression)

The GLS estimator (20.16) will become inconsistent if we replace ϕ_0 with $\phi_1 \neq \phi_0$ because this causes an errors-in-variables problem in (20.15). In particular, if $\phi_1 = 0$ then the GLS estimator simplifies to OLS, which is inconsistent. It is uniquely $y_{t-1} - \phi_0 y_{t-2}$ that is orthogonal to the latent residual υ_t. Therefore the FGLS estimator $\hat{\boldsymbol{\beta}}_{\text{FGLS}}$ *is* consistent by virtue of the consistency of $\check{\phi}$. The rule tells us that the FGLS/OLS procedure will produce an inconsistent

[24] See, for example, Murphy and Topel (1985).

estimator of the asymptotic variance of $\hat{\boldsymbol{\beta}}_{\text{FGLS}} = \left(\mathbf{X}'\check{\boldsymbol{\Omega}}^{-1}\mathbf{X}\right)^{-1}\mathbf{X}'\check{\boldsymbol{\Omega}}^{-1}\mathbf{y}$. That procedures uses the expression $\hat{\sigma}_\upsilon^2 \cdot \left(\mathbf{X}'\check{\boldsymbol{\Omega}}^{-1}\mathbf{X}\right)^{-1}$ where $\check{\boldsymbol{\Omega}}$ is evaluated at a consistent estimator $\check{\phi}$ and $\hat{\sigma}_\upsilon^2$ is the empirical variance of the fitted residuals

$$\begin{aligned}\hat{\upsilon}_t &\equiv y_t - \check{\phi} y_{t-1} - \left(\mathbf{x}_t - \check{\phi}\cdot\mathbf{x}_{t-1}\right)'\hat{\boldsymbol{\beta}}_{\text{FGLS}} \\ &= \check{y}_{*t} - \check{\mathbf{x}}_{*t}'\hat{\boldsymbol{\beta}}_{\text{FGLS}}\end{aligned}$$

Working out the necessary terms to correct the variance estimator is a bit tedious. We can save some effort by noting that as in (20.17)

$$\begin{aligned}\sqrt{T}\left(\hat{\boldsymbol{\beta}}_{\text{FGLS}} - \boldsymbol{\beta}_0\right) &= \left(\mathrm{E}_{T|2}[\check{\mathbf{x}}_{*t}\check{\mathbf{x}}_{*t}']\right)^{-1}\sqrt{T}\,\mathrm{E}_{T|2}[\check{\mathbf{x}}_{*t}(\varepsilon_t - \check{\phi}\varepsilon_{t-1})] \\ &\overset{p}{=} \left(\mathrm{E}[\mathbf{x}_{*t}\mathbf{x}_{*t}']\right)^{-1}\sqrt{T}\,\mathrm{E}_{T|2}[\check{\mathbf{x}}_{*t}(\varepsilon_t - \check{\phi}\varepsilon_{t-1})]\end{aligned}$$

Therefore, we can ignore the presence of $\check{\phi}$ in the most awkward term. What remains is to work out the derivative of $\mathrm{E}_{T|2}[\check{\mathbf{x}}_{*t}(\varepsilon_t - \check{\phi}\varepsilon_{t-1})]$ with respect to $\check{\phi}$ and a consistent estimator of the joint asymptotic variance matrix of $\sqrt{T}\,\mathrm{E}_{T|2}[\mathbf{x}_{*t}\upsilon_t]$ and $\sqrt{T}\left(\check{\phi} - \phi_0\right)$.

We estimate $\mathbf{J}_0$ with

$$\hat{\mathbf{J}} = \left(\mathrm{E}_{T|2}[\check{\mathbf{x}}_{*t}\check{\mathbf{x}}_{*t}']\right)^{-1}\mathrm{E}_{T|2}[-\mathbf{x}_{t-1}(\hat{\varepsilon}_t - \check{\phi}\hat{\varepsilon}_{t-1}) - \check{\mathbf{x}}_{*t}\hat{\varepsilon}_{t-1}]$$

where $\hat{\varepsilon}_t \equiv y_t - \mathbf{x}_t'\hat{\boldsymbol{\beta}}_{\text{FGLS}}$. We can estimate the $\boldsymbol{\Omega}_{\theta\theta}$ term several ways and one of the most convenient is $\hat{\sigma}_\upsilon^2 \cdot \left(\mathbf{X}'\check{\boldsymbol{\Omega}}^{-1}\mathbf{X}\right)^{-1}$. The other terms depend on the estimator $\check{\phi}$.

Newey's rule is formalized by the following result.[25]

Lemma 20.3 *Suppose that the conditions of Proposition 19 hold.*

1. *If $\hat{\boldsymbol{\theta}}(\boldsymbol{\gamma}) \xrightarrow{p} \boldsymbol{\theta}_0$ for $\boldsymbol{\gamma} \neq \boldsymbol{\gamma}_0$ within an open neighborhood of $\boldsymbol{\gamma}_0$, then $\mathbf{J}_0 = \mathbf{0}$.*
2. *Suppose also that $\mathbf{J}(\boldsymbol{\gamma})$ has constant rank within an open neighborhood of $\boldsymbol{\gamma}_0$. If every neighborhood of $\boldsymbol{\gamma}_0$ also contains a $\boldsymbol{\gamma} \neq \boldsymbol{\gamma}_0$ such that $\hat{\boldsymbol{\theta}}(\boldsymbol{\gamma})$ does not converge in probability to $\boldsymbol{\theta}_0$, then $\mathbf{J}_0 \neq \mathbf{0}$.*

Through uniform convergence, this result reduces the issue of estimator consistency to a consideration of the function $\boldsymbol{\theta}(\boldsymbol{\gamma})$ and its matrix of partial derivatives. In a sense, the lemma indicates nothing more than that if $\boldsymbol{\theta}(\boldsymbol{\gamma})$ changes with $\boldsymbol{\gamma}$ in the neighborhood of $\boldsymbol{\gamma}_0$ then its derivative is nonzero and otherwise the derivative is zero. The implication is the rule that the asymptotic variance of a two-step estimator $\hat{\boldsymbol{\theta}}(\check{\boldsymbol{\gamma}})$ treats the initial consistent estimator $\check{\boldsymbol{\gamma}}$ as

[25] This lemma is a special case of a more general one given by Newey and McFadden (1994, Theorem 6.2). They consider $\hat{\boldsymbol{\theta}}_N(\check{\boldsymbol{\gamma}}_N)$ for $\check{\boldsymbol{\gamma}}_N \xrightarrow{p} \boldsymbol{\gamma} \neq \boldsymbol{\gamma}_0$. This complicates the proof, but the general ideas are the same.

though it were $\boldsymbol{\gamma}_0$ whenever the consistency of the second-step estimator is robust to replacing $\check{\boldsymbol{\gamma}}$ with a value other than $\boldsymbol{\gamma}_0$.

20.7 EFFICIENCY

With many latent variable models comes a large menu of IV estimators. One approach to selecting a particular estimator is to take the one that is efficient relative to all those available. It is not always possible to find such treasure, but there are instructive cases in which one can and our previous examples of latent variable models include two. One case is the dynamic regression model with AR(1) serial correlation for which the GLS estimator is the best IV estimator. The other case is the simultaneous equations model of market supply and demand.

20.7.1 Simultaneous Equations

Under conditions such as those of the simultaneous equations model, the 2SLS IV estimator is asymptotically efficient relative to other IV estimators. This is a welcome bonus that does not follow automatically from our motivation through latent variables. In proving this property, we will develop a useful intuition about instruments that yield asymptotically relatively efficient estimators.

Speaking intuitively, the best instruments provide the best predictions of all the explanatory variables. An instrument vector $\mathbf{z}_n$ makes consistent estimation possible by factoring the total variation in $y_n = \mathbf{x}_n'\boldsymbol{\beta}_0 + \varepsilon_n$ into two pieces,

$$\mathrm{E}_N[\mathbf{z}_n y_n] = \mathrm{E}_N[\mathbf{z}_n\mathbf{x}_n']\boldsymbol{\beta}_0 + \mathrm{E}_N[\mathbf{z}_n\varepsilon_n]$$

The first RHS expression captures the variation in y_n that covaries with $\mathbf{z}_n$ through $\mathbf{x}_n$ while the second RHS term converges in probability to zero, because ε_n is orthogonal to $\mathbf{z}_n$. The IV estimator is the solution to

$$\mathrm{E}_N[\mathbf{z}_n y_n] = \mathrm{E}_N[\mathbf{z}_n\mathbf{x}_n']\hat{\boldsymbol{\beta}}_{\mathrm{IV}}$$

which replaces $\mathrm{E}_N[\mathbf{z}_n\varepsilon_n]$ with $\mathbf{0}$. An ideal situation would be for $\mathrm{E}_N[\mathbf{z}_n\varepsilon_n]$ to be exactly zero for then we would obtain an equation in observables determining $\boldsymbol{\beta}_0$ exactly. Short of this, the larger the $\mathrm{E}_N[\mathbf{z}_n\mathbf{x}_n']\boldsymbol{\beta}_0$ part, the smaller the $\mathrm{E}_N[\mathbf{z}_n\varepsilon_n]$ part will be. The best instruments maximize the magnitude of $\mathrm{E}_N[\mathbf{z}_n\mathbf{x}_n']\boldsymbol{\beta}_0$ in some sense.

A simple sense would be that the instruments are good predictors of the explanatory variables. An example of this occurs with OLS when $\mathrm{E}[\mathbf{y}\,|\,\mathbf{X}] = \mathbf{X}\boldsymbol{\beta}_0$ and OLS is the minimum variance estimator conditional on $\mathbf{X}$. Any full-rank matrix $\mathbf{Z}$ such that $\mathrm{Col}(\mathbf{Z}) = \mathrm{Col}(\mathbf{X})$ gives perfect linear predictions of $\mathbf{X}$. Such a $\mathbf{Z}$ also gives the OLS estimator as the IV estimator because $\mathbf{P}_{\mathbf{X}\perp\mathbf{Z}} = \mathbf{P}_{\mathbf{X}}$. Projecting along $\mathrm{Col}^{\perp}(\mathbf{Z})$ is the same as projecting along $\mathrm{Col}^{\perp}(\mathbf{X})$.

The 2SLS estimator appears to be another example of instrumental variables that predict explanatory variables optimally. 2SLS uses the instrumental variables $[\mathbf{x}_{s1n}', \mathbf{w}_n'\check{\boldsymbol{\pi}}_p]'$ that are OLS fitted values from regressions of each explanatory variable x_{snk} on $\mathbf{w}_n$, all of the variables in the system that are orthogonal to the latent residuals. Roughly speaking, these instrumental variables are orthogonal to the latent residuals because the instrumental variables are linear combinations of $\mathbf{w}_n$. At the same time, these instrumental variables are closest to the explanatory variables $\mathbf{x}_{sn}$ as measured by the sum of squared residuals.

We can formalize a characterization of optimal instrumental variables for the general case that corroborates these examples.

LEMMA 20.4 (EFFICIENT INSTRUMENTAL VARIABLES) *Suppose that the assumptions of Proposition 18 hold for every element of a set of instrument vector sequences $\mathbb{Z}$. If there is a relatively efficient instrument vector sequence $\{\mathbf{z}_n^*\} \in \mathbb{Z}$, then the MMSE linear prediction of every $\mathbf{x}_n'\boldsymbol{\alpha}$, $\boldsymbol{\alpha} \in \mathbb{R}^K$, given $\mathbf{z}_n^*$ has the smallest MSE among all members of $\mathbb{Z}$.*

Proof. Let $\{\mathbf{z}_n\}$ denote an element of $\mathbb{Z}$ and $\hat{\boldsymbol{\beta}}_{\mathrm{IV}} = (\mathbf{Z}'\mathbf{X})^{-1}\mathbf{Z}'\mathbf{y}$ the corresponding IV estimator using $\mathbf{Z} \equiv [\mathbf{z}_n']'$ as the instrument matrix. Proposition 18 implies that the asymptotic variance of the standardized IV estimator $\sqrt{N}\left(\hat{\boldsymbol{\beta}}_{\mathrm{IV}} - \boldsymbol{\beta}_0\right)$ is

$$\left(\mathrm{E}[\mathbf{z}_n\mathbf{x}_n']\right)^{-1}\mathrm{E}[\sigma_0^2 \cdot \mathbf{z}_n\mathbf{z}_n']\left(\mathrm{E}[\mathbf{x}_n\mathbf{z}_n']\right)^{-1} = \sigma_0^2 \cdot \mathbf{D}_{zx}^{-1}\mathbf{D}_{zz}\mathbf{D}_{zx}^{-1\prime}$$

Hence, minimizing the asymptotic variance of any linear combination $\sqrt{N}\boldsymbol{\alpha}'(\hat{\boldsymbol{\beta}}_{\mathrm{IV}} - \boldsymbol{\beta}_0)$ amounts to minimizing $\boldsymbol{\alpha}'\mathbf{D}_{zx}^{-1}\mathbf{D}_{zz}\mathbf{D}_{zx}^{-1\prime}\boldsymbol{\alpha}$ with respect to the choice of the instruments $\mathbf{z}_n$. We can rewrite this optimization problem as follows:

$$\begin{aligned}
\operatorname*{argmin}_{\{\mathbf{z}_n\}\in\mathbb{Z}} \boldsymbol{\alpha}'\mathbf{D}_{zx}^{-1}\mathbf{D}_{zz}\mathbf{D}_{zx}^{-1\prime}\boldsymbol{\alpha} &= \operatorname*{argmax}_{\{\mathbf{z}_n\}\in\mathbb{Z}} \boldsymbol{\alpha}'\left(\mathbf{D}_{zx}^{-1}\mathbf{D}_{zz}\mathbf{D}_{zx}^{-1\prime}\right)^{-1}\boldsymbol{\alpha} \\
&= \operatorname*{argmin}_{\{\mathbf{z}_n\}\in\mathbb{Z}} -\boldsymbol{\alpha}'\mathbf{D}_{zx}'\mathbf{D}_{zz}^{-1}\mathbf{D}_{zx}\boldsymbol{\alpha} \\
&= \operatorname*{argmin}_{\{\mathbf{z}_n\}\in\mathbb{Z}} \boldsymbol{\alpha}'\left(\mathbf{D}_{xx} - \mathbf{D}_{xz}\mathbf{D}_{zz}^{-1}\mathbf{D}_{xz}'\right)\boldsymbol{\alpha} \\
&= \operatorname*{argmin}_{\{\mathbf{z}_n\}\in\mathbb{Z}} \min_{\boldsymbol{\gamma}} \mathrm{E}[(\mathbf{x}_n'\boldsymbol{\alpha} - \mathbf{z}_n'\boldsymbol{\gamma})^2]
\end{aligned} \tag{20.51}$$

The first equality follows from Exercise 9.11, which states that if $\mathbf{A}$ and $\mathbf{B}$ are symmetric positive definite matrices, then $\mathbf{B} - \mathbf{A}$ is positive semidefinite if and only if $\mathbf{A}^{-1} - \mathbf{B}^{-1}$ is positive semidefinite.[26] The last equality rests on Lemma 7.4 (MMSE Linear Predictor, p. 135).[27]

---

[26] In other words,

$$\mathbf{x}'\mathbf{B}\mathbf{x} \geq \mathbf{x}'\mathbf{A}\mathbf{x} \quad \Leftrightarrow \quad \mathbf{x}'\mathbf{A}^{-1}\mathbf{x} \geq \mathbf{x}'\mathbf{B}^{-1}\mathbf{x}$$

Now

$$\min_{\mathbf{C}\in\mathbb{M}} \mathbf{x}'\mathbf{C}\mathbf{x} = \mathbf{x}'\mathbf{A}\mathbf{x} \quad \Leftrightarrow \quad \mathbf{x}'\mathbf{B}\mathbf{x} \geq \mathbf{x}'\mathbf{A}\mathbf{x},\ \forall \mathbf{B} \in \mathbb{M}$$

for a set $\mathbb{M}$ of positive definite matrices. Therefore,

$$\max_{\mathbf{C}\in\mathbb{M}} \mathbf{x}'\mathbf{C}^{-1}\mathbf{x} = \mathbf{x}'\mathbf{A}^{-1}\mathbf{x}$$

[27] Entering the optimal prediction coefficients $\mathbf{D}_{zz}^{-1}\mathbf{D}_{zx}\boldsymbol{\alpha}$ into the MSE function for $\mathbf{x}_n'\boldsymbol{\alpha}$ gives

$$\mathrm{E}[(\mathbf{x}_n'\boldsymbol{\alpha} - \mathbf{z}_n'\mathbf{D}_{zz}^{-1}\mathbf{D}_{zx}\boldsymbol{\alpha})^2] = \boldsymbol{\alpha}'\left(\mathbf{D}_{xx} - \mathbf{D}_{zx}'\mathbf{D}_{zz}^{-1}\mathbf{D}_{zx}\right)\boldsymbol{\alpha}$$

Previously, we have interpreted relative efficiency in terms of the orthogonality of efficient estimators (Proposition 8, p. 185). Lemma 20.4 is a weaker result, establishing a necessary and sufficient condition for, but not the existence of, an optimal instrument vector. An optimal choice for all $\boldsymbol{\alpha}$ may not exist for an arbitrary $\mathbb{Z}$. The orthogonality of efficient estimators rests on additional structure: that the competing estimators form a linear vector space that makes an orthogonal projection optimal. When the choice set $\mathbb{Z}$ for instruments is a vector space then we may have a comparable structure.

We can often see how to construct the optimal instruments from this characterization. Obviously, if the set $\mathbb{Z}$ includes $\mathbf{x}_n$ then $\mathbf{x}_n$ is the optimal choice, setting the MSE criterion function to its lowest possible value of zero. Two more interesting cases spring from vector spaces that we have discussed before. If $\mathbb{Z}$ is the vector space of all functions of a particular vector $\mathbf{z}_n$ then we can set $\mathbf{z}_n^* = \mathrm{E}[\mathbf{x}_n \mid \mathbf{z}_n]$ following Lemma 6.2 (MMSE Predictor, p. 113). Alternatively Lemma 7.4 (MMSE Linear Predictor, p. 135) states that if $\mathbb{Z}$ consists only of all linear combinations of a $\mathbf{z}_n$ then the MMSE linear predictors of $\mathbf{x}_n$ given $\mathbf{z}_n$ will be optimal.

We can apply this property to understanding the 2SLS estimator of the simultaneous equations model. The notation of the market model is slightly different from the general IV notation. The explanatory variables are $\mathbf{x}_{sn}$ (instead of $\mathbf{x}_n$) and the set of possible instruments are functions of $\mathbf{w}_n$ (see Example 20.8). Now $\mathbf{x}_{s1n}$ obviously provides the best predictions of itself. Our last instrumental variable must give us, in combination with $\mathbf{x}_{s1n}$, the smallest MSE predictor of p_n. That is the conditional mean $\mathbf{w}_n'\boldsymbol{\pi}_{0p}$ but it is not observable. Fortunately, any other instrumental variable that gives the same probability limits for $\mathrm{E}_N[\mathbf{z}_n\mathbf{x}_n']$ and $\mathrm{E}_N[\mathbf{z}_n\mathbf{z}_n']$ will work as well asymptotically. Thus, the 2SLS estimator achieves asymptotic efficiency by substituting the feasible $\mathbf{w}_n'\check{\boldsymbol{\pi}}_p$, an empirical analogue for $\mathbf{w}_n'\boldsymbol{\pi}_{0p}$: for example,

$$\begin{aligned}
\operatorname*{plim}_{N\to\infty} \mathrm{E}_N[(\mathbf{w}_n'\check{\boldsymbol{\pi}}_p)\mathbf{x}_n'] &= \left(\operatorname*{plim}_{N\to\infty} \check{\boldsymbol{\pi}}_p'\right)\left(\operatorname*{plim}_{N\to\infty} \mathrm{E}_N[\mathbf{w}_n\mathbf{x}_n']\right) \\
&= \boldsymbol{\pi}_{0p}' \operatorname*{plim}_{N\to\infty} \mathrm{E}_N[\mathbf{w}_n\mathbf{x}_n'] \\
&= \operatorname*{plim}_{N\to\infty} \mathrm{E}_N[(\mathbf{w}_n'\boldsymbol{\pi}_{0p})\mathbf{x}_n']
\end{aligned}$$

This feasible substitution works very much the way that FGLS is asymptotically equivalent to GLS in Chapters 18 and 19.

20.7.2 Dynamic Regression

As one might anticipate, the GLS estimator of the dynamic regression model is asymptotically efficient relative to any IV estimator that we can construct with the observable variables. In this case, the efficiency of the GLS estimator among IV estimators is confirmed by showing that this estimator is also the MLE.[28] To write out the log-likelihood function, we use the prediction-error decomposition, as for the simpler regression model in (19.17)–(19.19). As we show in Section 20.10.2, the conditional log-likelihood function given y_1 and y_2 is essentially the same:

$$L(\theta \mid y_1, y_2) = -\frac{T-2}{2}\log 2\pi\sigma_\upsilon^2 - \frac{\mathrm{E}_{T|2}\left[\left(y_t - \phi y_{t-1} - (\mathbf{x}_t - \phi\cdot\mathbf{x}_{t-1})'\boldsymbol{\beta}\right)^2\right]}{2\sigma_\upsilon^2} \tag{20.52}$$

[28] The 2SLS estimator of the market model is not, in general, the MLE. We defer our discussion of the MLE until Chapter 26.

Because it maximizes the second term of this function, the GLS estimator given in (20.16) is the (approximate) MLE for $\phi = \phi_0$. We can therefore apply Proposition 16 (ML Asymptotics, p. 320) to deduce its relative efficiency.

It is important to add that the linearized MLE is not as simple as *feasible* GLS. Substituting an initial consistent estimator for ϕ_0 into the GLS estimator produces an *inefficient* estimator (Example 20.11). Hatanaka (1974) derived an asymptotically efficient estimator that is implemented as follows.

1. Estimate $\boldsymbol{\beta}_0$ initially using IV. We might use 2SLS with the instruments $\mathbf{z}_t = [\mathbf{x}'_{1t}, \mathbf{x}'_{1,t-1}]'$, for example. Let us denote this initial consistent estimator by $\check{\beta}$.
2. Estimate ϕ_0 from the simple regression of the IV fitted residuals $\check{\varepsilon}_t = y_t - \mathbf{x}'_t\check{\beta}$ on their lagged values $\check{\varepsilon}_{t-1}$ $(t = 2, \ldots, T)$. Denote this initial consistent estimator as $\check{\phi}$.
3. In the second step, regress $\check{y}_{*t} \equiv y_t - \check{\phi} y_{t-1}$ on $\check{\mathbf{x}}_{*t} \equiv \mathbf{x}_t - \check{\phi} \cdot \mathbf{x}_{t-1}$ and $\check{\varepsilon}_{t-1} \equiv y_{t-1} - \mathbf{x}'_{t-1}\check{\boldsymbol{\beta}}$ with OLS. The estimator of $\boldsymbol{\beta}_0$ is the estimated coefficient vector for $\check{\mathbf{x}}_{*t}$ and the estimator for ϕ_0 is the estimated coefficient on $\check{\varepsilon}_{t-1}$ plus $\check{\phi}$.

So, in addition to the feasible GLS transformation that one expects to compute, we include the IV residual as an additional explanatory variable. We derive this estimator (and its approximate variance) as an LMLE in Section 20.10.3.

The presence of the explanatory variable $\check{\varepsilon}_{t-1}$ is reminiscent of the 2SLS estimator that inserts the fitted residual $\check{v}_n$ as an explanatory variable in the OLS regression for the supply equation. But these two procedures are only superficially analogous. Note that ε_{t-1} is not required as a latent explanatory variable in the mean of y_t conditional on y_{t-1}, $\mathbf{x}_t$, and $\mathbf{x}_{t-1}$. The $\check{\varepsilon}_{t-1}$ appear because the information matrix is not block-diagonal in the regression coefficients $\boldsymbol{\beta}_0$ and the variance-covariance parameter ϕ_0. It is because of this non-block-diagonality that the FGLS estimator is not the LMLE.[29]

Speaking intuitively, the loss of block-diagonality relative to the FGLS estimator in (18.22) stems from the need to sort out how the observed autocorrelation in $\{y_t\}$ is assigned to β_{02} versus ϕ_0. Note that these coefficients enter symmetrically into the regression equation (20.18): the coefficient of y_{t-1} is $\beta_{02} + \phi_0$ and the coefficient of y_{t-2} is $\beta_{02}\phi_0$. It is only by virtue of variation in the explanatory variables $\mathbf{x}_{1t}$ and $\mathbf{x}_{1,t-1}$ that it is possible to identify these two parameters. The coefficients of $\mathbf{x}_{1t}$ are $\boldsymbol{\beta}_{01}$ and the coefficients of $\mathbf{x}_{1,t-1}$ are $\phi_0 \cdot \boldsymbol{\beta}_{01}$ in (20.18). Because both of these are estimated consistently by OLS, ϕ_0 is identified in their ratios. This in turn implies that β_{02} is identified. This intimate relationship between ϕ_0 and β_{02} is reflected in the covariance of their MLEs (non-block-diagonality of the information matrix).

20.7.3 IV and GLS

We have examined IV and GLS separately, but the two methods combine in a natural way in many cases. If for example

$$\mathrm{E}[\mathbf{y} \mid \mathbf{Z}] = \mathrm{E}[\mathbf{X} \mid \mathbf{Z}]\boldsymbol{\beta}_0$$

[29] Recall that this was a key feature in the cases of heteroskedasticity [equation (18.19)] and AR(1) serial correlation [equation (18.22)].

$$\text{Var}[\mathbf{y} \mid \mathbf{Z}] = \boldsymbol{\Omega}_0$$

then one might expect the efficient IV estimator to be

$$\hat{\boldsymbol{\beta}}_{\text{IV}} = \left[\boldsymbol{\mu}_{\mathbf{X}}(\mathbf{Z})'\boldsymbol{\Omega}_0^{-1}\mathbf{X}\right]^{-1} \boldsymbol{\mu}_{\mathbf{X}}(\mathbf{Z})'\boldsymbol{\Omega}_0^{-1}\mathbf{y} \tag{20.53}$$

where

$$\boldsymbol{\mu}_{\mathbf{X}}(\mathbf{Z}) \equiv \text{E}[\mathbf{X} \mid \mathbf{Z}]$$

Given Lemma 20.4 (Efficient Instrumental Variables), the relative efficiency of such estimators follows from conditions that make the choice set of instrumental variables a linear vector space.

EXAMPLE 20.12 (Heteroskedasticity and IV)
Suppose that $(y_n, \mathbf{x}_n, \mathbf{w}_n)$ are i.i.d. such that

$$\text{E}[y_n \mid \mathbf{w}_n] = \text{E}[\mathbf{x}_n' \mid \mathbf{w}_n]\boldsymbol{\beta}_0$$
$$\text{Var}[y_n \mid \mathbf{w}_n] = \sigma_0^2(\mathbf{w}_n) \equiv \sigma_{0n}^2$$

$n = 1, \ldots, N$. Let J be the number of instrumental variables in $\mathbf{w}_n$ and K the number of explanatory variables in $\mathbf{x}_n$ and suppose $J \geq K$. Consider the set of sequences of instrument vectors

$$\begin{aligned}\mathbb{Z} = \Big\{\{\mathbf{z}_n\} \mid \mathbf{z}_n = f(\mathbf{w}_n),\ f : \mathbb{R}^J \to \mathbb{R}^K,\\ \text{E}[\mathbf{z}_n\mathbf{x}_n'] \text{ is nonsingular, and}\\ \text{E}_N[\mathbf{z}_n\sigma_{0n}^2\mathbf{z}_n'],\ \text{E}_N[\mathbf{z}_n\mathbf{x}_n'] \text{ converge in probability}\Big\}\end{aligned}$$

This is a linear vector space. Suppose that it contains more than the zero vector.

For all $\{\mathbf{z}_n\} \in \mathbb{Z}$, the asymptotic variance of the IV estimator $\hat{\boldsymbol{\beta}}_{\text{IV}} = \left(\mathbf{Z}'\mathbf{X}\right)^{-1}\mathbf{Z}'\mathbf{y}$ is

$$\left(\text{E}[\mathbf{z}_n\mathbf{x}_n']\right)^{-1}\text{E}[\mathbf{z}_n\sigma_{0n}^2\mathbf{z}_n']\left(\text{E}[\mathbf{x}_n\mathbf{z}_n']\right)^{-1}$$

transforming the criterion for efficient instruments (20.15) into[30]

$$\underset{\{\mathbf{z}_n\}\in\mathbb{Z}}{\text{argmin}}\ \min_{\boldsymbol{\gamma}} \text{E}\left[\left(\sigma_{0n}^{-1} \cdot \mathbf{x}_n'\boldsymbol{\alpha} - \sigma_{0n} \cdot \mathbf{z}_n'\boldsymbol{\gamma}\right)^2\right] \tag{20.54}$$

By inspection, we find that an optimal instrument vector equals the conditional mean of $\sigma_{0n}^{-1} \cdot \mathbf{x}_n$ given $\mathbf{w}_n$, that is $\{\mathbf{z}_n^*\} = \{\sigma_{0n}^{-2} \cdot \text{E}[\mathbf{x}_n \mid \mathbf{w}_n]\}$, provided that it is a member of $\mathbb{Z}$. Therefore, (20.53) is the optimal IV estimator in this case.

Analogous extensions to models with conditional autoregressive serial correlation are also possible.[31]

---

[30] By writing $\text{E}[\mathbf{z}_n\mathbf{x}_n'] = \text{E}[(\sigma_{0n} \cdot \mathbf{z}_n)(\sigma_{0n}^{-1} \cdot \mathbf{x}_n')]$ and $\text{E}[\mathbf{z}_n\sigma_{0n}^2\mathbf{z}_n'] = \text{E}[(\sigma_{0n} \cdot \mathbf{z}_n)(\sigma_{0n} \cdot \mathbf{z}_n)']$, we have the same objective function as in the lemma after replacing $\mathbf{z}_n$ with $\sigma_{0n} \cdot \mathbf{z}_n$ and $\mathbf{x}_n$ with $\sigma_{0n}^{-1} \cdot \mathbf{x}_n$.

[31] See, for example, Exercise 20.30.

20.8 ISSUES IN SMALL SAMPLES

There are additional concerns facing users of IV estimators that do not possess simple practical answers. In small samples, the instrumental variables estimators "explain" the explanatory variables better than in the population. As a result, the small sample properties of IV estimation can differ substantially from the asymptotic ones.

Note first that it is possible to compute the IV estimator even though the slope coefficients are not estimable with the selected instrumental variables.

EXAMPLE 20.13

Consider i.i.d. sampling and a simple regression equation

$$y_n = \beta_0 x_n + \varepsilon_n$$

where ε_n is correlated with x_n. Suppose that there is another variable z_n such that $\mathrm{E}[z_n x_n] = \mathrm{E}[z_n \varepsilon_n] = 0$. Thus, β_0 cannot be estimated using z_n as an instrumental variable. Yet, if x_n and z_n are continuously distributed, the probability that $\mathrm{E}_N[z_n x_n]$ equals its expected value is zero. As a result, the IV fitted coefficient

$$\hat{\beta}_{\mathrm{IV}} = \frac{\mathrm{E}_N[z_n y_n]}{\mathrm{E}_N[z_n x_n]}$$

and the estimator of its sampling variance can be computed for any given sample $\{(x_n, y_n, z_n)\ ;\ n = 1, \ldots, N\}$ even though $\hat{\beta}_{\mathrm{IV}}$ fails to estimate β_0 in any meaningful way.

The probability limit of an IV estimator does not exist when $\left(\mathrm{plim}\, \mathrm{E}_N[\mathbf{z}_n \mathbf{x}_n']\right)^{-1}$ is not well defined, yet in small samples $\mathrm{E}_N[\mathbf{z}_n \mathbf{x}_n']$ may be nonsingular generally. Thus, the instruments $\mathbf{z}_n$ appear to be predictors, albeit poor ones, of the explanatory variables $\mathbf{x}_n$. In this extreme situation the estimated variance of the IV estimator seriously underestimates the asymptotic variance, which is effectively infinite.

It is generally unrealistic to suppose that instrumental variables are exactly orthogonal. But their correlation with the explanatory variables can be weak. Bound et al. (1995) note that the IV estimator has a bias that approaches that of the OLS estimator as the R^2 between the instrumental variables and a single explanatory variable approaches zero.[32] As a result, many empirical researchers are wary of IV estimates based on instrumental variables that yield low R^2s for linear fits to the explanatory variables. Bound et al. suggest routine reporting of the R^2 and F statistics from regressions of explanatory variables on instrumental variables to guide interpretation of IV estimates.

Paradoxically, the small sample bias in the 2SLS estimator is reduced by *dropping* instrumental variables. But we can interpet this result as another example of the effects of overfitting the explanatory variables in small samples.

---

[32] See also Staiger and Stock (1997), among others.

EXAMPLE 20.14

Consider again i.i.d. sampling for $\{(w_n, x_n, y_n, \varepsilon_n)\,;\ n = 1, \ldots, N\}$ and a simple regression equation

$$y_n = \beta_0 x_n + \varepsilon_n$$

where $\mathrm{E}[\varepsilon_n] = 0$, ε_n is correlated with x_n and w_n is correlated with x_n but not ε_n. If we restrict our instrumental variables to linear functions $z(w_n, x_n, \varepsilon_n)$, the best instrumental variable for x_n is

$$z_n^* = x_n - \frac{\mathrm{Cov}[x_n, \varepsilon_n]}{\mathrm{Var}[\varepsilon_n]}\varepsilon_n$$

the prediction residual of the MMSE predictor of x_n proportional to ε_n. By construction, this variable is uncorrelated with ε_n and its prediction MSE for x_n is

$$\mathrm{E}\Big[\big(x_n - z_n^*\big)^2\Big] = \frac{\mathrm{Cov}^2[x_n, \varepsilon_n]}{\mathrm{Var}[\varepsilon_n]}$$

No instrumental variable can have a lower prediction MSE. However, if N is small enough then the OLS fitted value of x_n to a constant and w_n can be closer on average. In that case, we see that the 2SLS instrumental variable must be correlated with ε_n as well.

More generally, the 2SLS does not eliminate correlation between the instrumental variables and the explanatory variables in small samples. It may be preferable to drop some RHS variables from the first "stage" even though this *reduces* the goodness of fit.[33] The risk of overfitting the explanatory variables increases as the number of first-stage RHS variables increases.

Thus, in small samples the IV estimator is biased in the same direction as the OLS estimator. When the instrumental variables are weakly correlated with the explanatory variables, this effect is particularly severe. However, these qualitative findings do not provide clear guidelines for empirical research and their implementation is currently a matter of judgment.

20.9 METHODOLOGICAL NOTES

The interpretation of IV estimators deserves careful thought. IV estimators include the OLS estimator as a special case and are more complex.

One can always interpret OLS as an estimator of the coefficients of the MMSE linear prediction function of one variable conditional on several others. If this prediction function coincides with the conditional mean, then OLS estimates parameters of the conditional mean. Neither of these interpretations requires a latent model. The MMSE predictor of one variable conditional on a set of other variables is always well defined if the necessary moments exist.

In the econometric literature, motivation for IV estimation has generally come out of interest in the conditional mean of a latent model. The projection implicit in a particular IV estimation is not given independent significance. Of course, the probability limit of IV fitted coefficients is also well defined for any sets of instrumental and explanatory variables if certain moments exist. But those population parameters are usually sought in so far as they are *invariant* to particular

[33] For introductions to more refined approximations of the distribution of the 2SLS estimator see Phillips (1983) and Rothenberg (1984b), particularly pp. 918–924.

instrumental variables that identify the parameters. They are not sought because they correspond to solutions to an MMSE prediction problem.[34] The instruments are merely a means to an end.

In this vein, we argue that the latent model is crucial to the interpretation of IV estimators. Although we can fit coefficients with various sets of instrumental variables without any latent variable model in mind, what would be the point? The set of latent variable models that can motivate a particular IV estimator is so large that such exploration is uninformative. Furthermore, examining an array of IV estimators and finding that they are not (statistically) significantly different is not conclusive evidence for claiming that they all estimate a parameter vector of interest. It is consistent with such a claim to be sure, but it is not necessarily so. In our opinion, researchers must support that claim with a convincing latent model.

Many researchers feel that justifying instrumental variables is *the* problem in empirical economic science. Particular recognition of this appears in searches for so-called *natural experiments*, data sets containing exogenous differences in factors that influence the variable of interest that occur naturally, not by the design of the researcher. In effect, the researcher exploits these exogenous differences to create instrumental variables. Examples of this approach are Angrist and Krueger (1992), Card (1992), and Eissa (1995). In such cases the latent model can be quite simple, asserting only the exogeneity of one discrete dissimiliarity among the observations.

Such natural experiments can be compelling, but they share the property of all latent models that the required exogeneity is a maintained assumption. If we commit to a latent variable model, then we necessarily maintain some assumptions that cannot be tested. This is the essence of what cannot be observed. We might hope that IV offers an opportunity to relax assumptions and provides a more robust estimation strategy. Such hope is fulfilled, but only within the context of the latent variable model.

Finally, in our discussion of the failure of OLS as an estimator, it is important to recognize that as we have considered alternative assumptions to $\mathrm{E}[y_n \mid \mathbf{x}_n] = \mathbf{x}_n' \boldsymbol{\beta}_0$, the alternatives do not necessarily rule out that $\mathrm{E}[y_n \mid \mathbf{x}_n]$ is a linear function of $\mathbf{x}_n$.[35] Such alternative models as linear simultaneous equations and errors in variables merely stipulate that $\mathrm{E}[y_n \mid \mathbf{x}_n]$ does not hold primary interest, whether it is linear in $\mathbf{x}_n$ or not. Instead, interest focuses on the parameters of a different (linear) conditional mean, one that conditions on additional, latent, variables. Again, though it may be that $\mathrm{E}[y_n \mid \mathbf{x}_n] = \mathbf{x}_n' \boldsymbol{\delta}_0$, the alternative models simply assert that estimates of $\boldsymbol{\delta}_0$ are not the goal. OLS will estimate such a $\boldsymbol{\delta}_0$ without bias and its failure will be only that $\boldsymbol{\delta}_0$ does not equal $\boldsymbol{\beta}_0$, the parameter vector of interest. Goldberger (1991, Ch. 31) makes this point forcefully.

20.10 MATHEMATICAL NOTES

The first section of these notes derives explicit conditions for the covariance stationarity that we assumed for the dynamic regression model on p. 488. These conditions are quite simple: both β_{02} and ϕ_0 must be less than one in absolute value. The second section derives the log-likelihood function for the dynamic regression model and the third uses this function to show that Hatanaka's estimator is relatively efficient because it is an LMLE.

The next to last section gives a proof of Proposition 19 (Two-Step Asymptotic Variance, p. 507). The proof follows predictable lines, using a linearization of the two-step estimator that is

---

[34] See Exercise 20.18 for a description of the MMSE problem that the probability limit of the IV estimator solves.

[35] We will also consider nonlinear models in this chapter.

analogous to the delta method. The last section connects the characterization of optimal instrument vectors (Lemma 20.4, p. 510) with the orthogonality of efficient estimators (Proposition 8, p. 185).

20.10.1 Covariance Stationarity

To derive the conditions under which the dynamic regression model (20.8) is conditionally covariance stationary, we rewrite it as a second-order difference equation:

$$
\begin{aligned}
y_t - \beta_{02} y_{t-1} &= \mathbf{x}'_{1t} \boldsymbol{\beta}_{01} + \varepsilon_t \qquad \Leftrightarrow \qquad (20.55)\\
y_t - \phi_0 y_{t-1} - \beta_{02}\left(y_{t-1} - \phi_0 y_{t-2}\right) &= \left(\mathbf{x}_{1t} - \phi_0 \mathbf{x}_{1,t-1}\right)' \boldsymbol{\beta}_{01} + \upsilon_t \qquad \Leftrightarrow\\
y_t - \left(\phi_0 + \beta_{02}\right) y_{t-1} + \phi_0 \beta_{02} y_{t-2} &= \left(\mathbf{x}_{1t} - \phi_0 \mathbf{x}_{1,t-1}\right)' \boldsymbol{\beta}_{01} + \upsilon_t \qquad (20.56)
\end{aligned}
$$

Multiplying (20.56) by $y_t - \mathrm{E}[y_t \,|\, \mathbf{X}_1]$, $y_{t-1} - \mathrm{E}[y_{t-1} \,|\, \mathbf{X}_1]$, and $y_{t-2} - \mathrm{E}[y_{t-2} \,|\, \mathbf{X}_1]$, respectively, and taking expected values, we obtain

$$
\begin{aligned}
\mathrm{Var}[y_t \,|\, \mathbf{X}_1] - (\phi_0 + \beta_{02})\,\mathrm{Cov}[y_t, y_{t-1} \,|\, \mathbf{X}_1] + \phi_0\beta_{02}\,\mathrm{Cov}[y_t, y_{t-2} \,|\, \mathbf{X}_1] &= \sigma^2_{0\upsilon}\\
\mathrm{Cov}[y_{t-1}, y_t \,|\, \mathbf{X}_1] - (\phi_0 + \beta_{02})\,\mathrm{Var}[y_{t-1} \,|\, \mathbf{X}_1] + \phi_0\beta_{02}\,\mathrm{Cov}[y_{t-1}, y_{t-2} \,|\, \mathbf{X}_1] &= 0\\
\mathrm{Cov}[y_{t-2}, y_t \,|\, \mathbf{X}_1] - (\phi_0 + \beta_{02})\,\mathrm{Cov}[y_{t-2}, y_{t-1} \,|\, \mathbf{X}_1] + \phi_0\beta_{02}\,\mathrm{Var}[y_{t-2} \,|\, \mathbf{X}_1] &= 0
\end{aligned}
$$

Conditional covariance stationarity means that

$$
\begin{aligned}
\mathrm{Var}[y_t \,|\, \mathbf{X}_1] &= \mathrm{Var}[y_{t-1} \,|\, \mathbf{X}_1] = \mathrm{Var}[y_{t-2} \,|\, \mathbf{X}_1]\\
\mathrm{Cov}[y_t, y_{t-1} \,|\, \mathbf{X}_1] &= \mathrm{Cov}[y_{t-1}, y_{t-2} \,|\, \mathbf{X}_1]
\end{aligned}
$$

leaving three equations in three unknowns. We solve these to find

$$
\begin{aligned}
\mathrm{Var}[y_t \,|\, \mathbf{X}_1] &= \sigma^2_{0\upsilon} \frac{1 + \phi_0\beta_{02}}{\left(1 - \phi_0^2\right)\left(1 - \beta_{02}^2\right)\left(1 - \phi_0\beta_{02}\right)}\\
\mathrm{Cov}[y_t, y_{t-1} \,|\, \mathbf{X}_1] &= \sigma^2_{0\upsilon} \frac{\phi_0 + \beta_{02}}{\left(1 - \phi_0^2\right)\left(1 - \beta_{02}^2\right)\left(1 - \phi_0\beta_{02}\right)}
\end{aligned}
$$

For the first expression to be a variance it must be positive and finite. This constraint requires only that both ϕ_0 and β_{02} be less than one in absolute value. These are necessary and sufficient conditions for conditional covariance stationarity. In addition, $|\phi_0|, |\beta_{02}| < 1$ also make the covariance term satisfy the Cauchy–Schwarz inequality (Lemma 7.8, p. 143)

$$
\left(\mathrm{Cov}[y_t, y_{t-1} \,|\, \mathbf{X}_1]\right)^2 < \left(\mathrm{Var}[y_t \,|\, \mathbf{X}_1]\right)^2
$$

The appropriate initial conditions are that

$$
\mathrm{Var}[y_0 \,|\, \mathbf{X}_1] = \sigma^2_{0\upsilon} \frac{1 + \phi_0\beta_{02}}{\left(1 - \phi_0^2\right)\left(1 - \beta_{02}^2\right)\left(1 - \phi_0\beta_{02}\right)}
$$

and, using (20.55),

$$
\begin{aligned}
\mathrm{Cov}[y_0, \varepsilon_1 \,|\, \mathbf{X}_1] &= \mathrm{Cov}[y_0, y_1 \,|\, \mathbf{X}_1] - \beta_{02}\,\mathrm{Var}[y_0 \,|\, \mathbf{X}_1]\\
&= \sigma^2_{0\upsilon} \frac{\phi_0}{\left(1 - \phi_0\beta_{02}\right)\left(1 - \phi_0^2\right)}
\end{aligned}
$$

20.10.2 Dynamic Regression Log-Likelihood

To find the log-likelihood function for the dynamic regression model, we put down the log-density function for the latent variables specified in (20.2) and (20.3). Given the plain character of their joint distribution, this is straightforward:

$$\begin{aligned}\log f_{\upsilon,\varepsilon_1,y_0} &= -\frac{T-2}{2}\log 2\pi\sigma_{0\upsilon}^2 - \frac{\mathrm{E}_{T|2}[\upsilon_t^2]}{2\sigma_{0\upsilon}^2} \\ &\quad -\frac{1}{2}\log[2\pi\sigma_{0\upsilon}^2/(1-\phi_0^2)] - \frac{\varepsilon_1^2}{2\sigma_{0\upsilon}^2/(1-\phi_0^2)} \\ &\quad -\frac{1}{2}\log 2\pi\sigma_{0y}^2 - \frac{(y_0-\mu_0)^2}{2\sigma_{0y}^2}\end{aligned}$$

As in previous discussions of this model, we will skip over the details concerning the marginal distribution of the latent y_0.[36] With this log-density we make the change of variables from ε_1 and υ_t $(t = 2, \ldots, T)$ to the observable y_t $(t = 1, \ldots, T)$ based on (20.1) and (20.8):

$$\varepsilon_1 = y_1 - \mathbf{x}_{11}'\boldsymbol{\beta}_{01} - \beta_{02}y_0$$

and

$$\begin{aligned}\upsilon_t &= \varepsilon_t - \phi_0\varepsilon_{t-1} \\ &= y_t - \phi_0 y_{t-1} - (\mathbf{x}_t - \phi_0\cdot\mathbf{x}_{t-1})'\boldsymbol{\beta}_0 \end{aligned} \tag{20.57}$$

$(t = 2, \ldots, T)$. Because this transformation is recursive, the matrix of partial derivatives is triangular with ones on the main diagonal. As a result the Jacobian is 1 and the log-density function for y_t $(t = 0, 1, \ldots, T)$ is

$$\begin{aligned}\log f_y &= -\frac{T-2}{2}\log 2\pi\sigma_{0\upsilon}^2 - \frac{\mathrm{E}_{T|2}\left[\left(y_t - \phi_0 y_{t-1} - (\mathbf{x}_t - \phi_0\cdot\mathbf{x}_{t-1})'\boldsymbol{\beta}_0\right)^2\right]}{2\sigma_\upsilon^2} \\ &\quad -\frac{1}{2}\log\frac{2\pi\sigma_{0\upsilon}^2}{1-\phi_0^2} - \frac{\left(y_1 - \mathbf{x}_{1t}'\boldsymbol{\beta}_{01} - \beta_{02}y_0\right)^2}{2\sigma_{0\upsilon}^2/(1-\phi_0^2)} \\ &\quad -\frac{1}{2}\log 2\pi\sigma_{0y}^2 - \frac{(y_0-\mu_0)^2}{2\sigma_{0y}^2}\end{aligned}$$

By integrating out y_0 to get the marginal p.d.f., we obtain the unconditional log-likelihood function. In our analysis, we approximate this function with the log-likelihood conditional on y_1 and y_2. The functional form of this approximation is identical to the conditional log-likelihood function (19.19) of the comparable static regression model.

20.10.3 Hatanaka's Estimator

We will show that Hatanaka's (1974) estimator (p. 512) is an LMLE and therefore asymptotically efficient.[37] Because of the similarity of the log-likelihoods, the scores for $\boldsymbol{\beta}$ and ϕ are essentially those found in (19.30) and (19.32):

---

36 See the comment on p. 488 and Section 20.10.1.

37 See Lemma 15.7 (LMLE, p. 333).

$$\begin{bmatrix} L_\beta(\boldsymbol{\theta}) \\ L_\phi(\boldsymbol{\theta}) \end{bmatrix} = \frac{1}{\sigma_v^2}\mathbf{W}'\boldsymbol{v}$$

where

$$\mathbf{W} \equiv \left[\left[\mathbf{x}_t' - \phi\cdot\mathbf{x}_{t-1}' \quad \varepsilon_{t-1}\right]'; t = 3, \ldots, T\right]'$$
$$\boldsymbol{v} \equiv \left[\varepsilon_t - \phi\varepsilon_{t-1}; t = 3, \ldots, T\right]'$$

We can treat σ_v^2 as a known constant because the information matrix is block-diagonal relative to σ_v^2, just as in (19.38). If we use the Gauss–Newton search direction (16.13) and the initial consistent estimator $\left[\check{\boldsymbol{\beta}}', \check{\phi}\right]'$, we obtain the LMLE

$$\begin{aligned} \begin{bmatrix} \hat{\boldsymbol{\beta}} \\ \hat{\phi} \end{bmatrix} &= \begin{bmatrix} \check{\boldsymbol{\beta}} \\ \check{\phi} \end{bmatrix} + (\check{\mathbf{W}}'\check{\mathbf{W}})^{-1}\check{\mathbf{W}}'\check{\boldsymbol{v}} \\ &= \begin{bmatrix} \mathbf{0} \\ \check{\phi} \end{bmatrix} + (\check{\mathbf{W}}'\check{\mathbf{W}})^{-1}\check{\mathbf{W}}'\check{\mathbf{y}}_* \end{aligned} \tag{20.58}$$

because

$$\begin{aligned} \check{v}_t &= \check{\varepsilon}_t - \check{\phi}\check{\varepsilon}_{t-1} \\ &= y_t - \check{\phi}\cdot y_{t-1} - \left(\mathbf{x}_t - \check{\phi}\,\mathbf{x}_{t-1}\right)'\check{\boldsymbol{\beta}} \\ &= \check{y}_{*t} - \check{\mathbf{w}}_t' \begin{bmatrix} \check{\boldsymbol{\beta}} \\ 0 \end{bmatrix} \end{aligned}$$

The term $(\check{\mathbf{W}}'\check{\mathbf{W}})^{-1}\check{\mathbf{W}}'\check{\mathbf{y}}_*$ is the OLS fitted coefficients in Step 3 of Hatanaka's procedure. To obtain $\hat{\phi}$, we add the slope estimated for the explanatory variable $\check{\varepsilon}_{t-1}$ to the initial estimator $\check{\phi}$.

An estimator of the asymptotic variance of this estimator is the inverse information matrix estimator $\hat{\sigma}_v^2\cdot(\check{\mathbf{W}}'\check{\mathbf{W}})^{-1}$ where $\hat{\sigma}_v^2 = \mathrm{E}_{T|2}[\hat{v}_t^2]$. This is the output of OLS software so in this case we can rely on the variance estimator that ignores the estimation in the first step.

20.10.4 Two-Step Estimation

The proof of Proposition 19 is straight application of asymptotic linearization. It is instructive to compare the following argument with the proof of the delta method (Lemma 16.1, p. 367).

Proof of Proposition 19. We expand $\hat{\boldsymbol{\theta}}_N(\check{\boldsymbol{\gamma}})$ around $\boldsymbol{\gamma}_0$ to obtain

$$\sqrt{N}\left[\hat{\boldsymbol{\theta}}_N(\check{\boldsymbol{\gamma}}_N) - \boldsymbol{\theta}_0\right] = \sqrt{N}\left[\hat{\boldsymbol{\theta}}_N(\boldsymbol{\gamma}_0) - \boldsymbol{\theta}_0\right] + \left.\frac{\partial\hat{\boldsymbol{\theta}}_N(\boldsymbol{\gamma})}{\partial\boldsymbol{\gamma}'}\right|_{\boldsymbol{\gamma}=\bar{\boldsymbol{\gamma}}_N} \sqrt{N}\left(\check{\boldsymbol{\gamma}}_N - \boldsymbol{\gamma}_0\right)$$

where $\bar{\boldsymbol{\gamma}}_N$ lies on the line segment running between $\check{\boldsymbol{\gamma}}_N$ and $\boldsymbol{\gamma}_0$. The consistency of $\check{\boldsymbol{\gamma}}_N$ implies the consistency of $\bar{\boldsymbol{\gamma}}_N$ and, hence,

$$\frac{\partial\hat{\boldsymbol{\theta}}_N(\bar{\boldsymbol{\gamma}}_N)}{\partial\boldsymbol{\gamma}'} \xrightarrow{p} \mathbf{J}(\boldsymbol{\gamma}_0) \equiv \mathbf{J}_0$$

following Lemma 15.5. Applying the Slutsky lemma (Lemma 13.3, p. 261),

$$\sqrt{N}\left[\hat{\boldsymbol{\theta}}_N(\check{\boldsymbol{\gamma}}_N)-\boldsymbol{\theta}_0\right]\overset{p}{=}\sqrt{N}\left[\hat{\boldsymbol{\theta}}_N(\boldsymbol{\gamma}_0)-\boldsymbol{\theta}_0\right]+\mathbf{J}_0\sqrt{N}\left(\check{\boldsymbol{\gamma}}_N-\boldsymbol{\gamma}_0\right)$$

$$\xrightarrow{d}\mathfrak{N}(\mathbf{0},\,\boldsymbol{\Omega}_{\theta\theta}+\mathbf{J}_0\boldsymbol{\Omega}_{\theta\gamma}+\boldsymbol{\Omega}_{\gamma\theta}\mathbf{J}_0'+\mathbf{J}_0\boldsymbol{\Omega}_{\gamma\gamma}\mathbf{J}_0')$$

which is the result. □

The formula for the asymptotic variance suggests the critical role that the matrix of partial derivatives $\partial\hat{\boldsymbol{\theta}}(\gamma)/\partial\gamma'$ plays in adjusting the variance matrix of a two-step estimator. Here is the proof of Lemma 20.3, which motivates Newey's rule that adjustment is necessary only when the consistency of the two-step estimator $\hat{\boldsymbol{\theta}}_N(\check{\boldsymbol{\gamma}})$ hinges on the consistency of the initial (first-step) estimator $\check{\boldsymbol{\gamma}}$.

Proof of Lemma 20.3. (1) If $\hat{\boldsymbol{\theta}}(\boldsymbol{\gamma})\xrightarrow{p}\boldsymbol{\theta}_0$ for every $\boldsymbol{\gamma}$ in an open neighborhood of $\boldsymbol{\gamma}_0$ then by hypothesis $\boldsymbol{\theta}(\boldsymbol{\gamma})=\boldsymbol{\theta}_0$ and $\mathbf{J}_0=\mathbf{0}$. (2) On the other hand, suppose that $\mathbf{J}(\boldsymbol{\gamma})$ has constant rank within an open neighborhood of $\boldsymbol{\gamma}_0$. Within this neighborhood, there is a $\boldsymbol{\gamma}_1\neq\boldsymbol{\gamma}_0$ such $\boldsymbol{\theta}(\boldsymbol{\gamma}_1)\neq\boldsymbol{\theta}_0$ by hypothesis. By the mean value theorem, there is also a $\bar{\boldsymbol{\gamma}}$ on the line segment joining $\boldsymbol{\gamma}_0$ and $\boldsymbol{\gamma}_1$ such that

$$\boldsymbol{\theta}(\boldsymbol{\gamma}_1)-\boldsymbol{\theta}(\boldsymbol{\gamma}_0)=\mathbf{J}(\bar{\boldsymbol{\gamma}})\;(\boldsymbol{\gamma}_1-\boldsymbol{\gamma}_0)\neq\mathbf{0}$$

Therefore, $\mathbf{J}(\bar{\boldsymbol{\gamma}})\neq\mathbf{0}$. Because the rank of $\mathbf{J}(\boldsymbol{\gamma})$ is constant, $\mathbf{J}(\boldsymbol{\gamma}_0)\equiv\mathbf{J}_0\neq\mathbf{0}$. □

20.10.5 Optimal Instruments

In Section 20.7 (Efficiency), we characterized the optimal instrument vectors from a set $\mathbb{Z}\equiv\{\{\mathbf{z}_n;\,n=1,\ldots,N\}\}$ as those with the smallest MSE for predicting the explanatory variables with a linear transformation (Lemma 20.4, p. 510). Here we explicitly connect this characterization to the orthogonality of efficient estimators (Proposition 8, p. 185).

If $\mathbb{Z}$ is a linear vector space then so is $\left\{\{\mathbf{z}_n'\boldsymbol{\gamma}\}\mid\{\mathbf{z}_n\}\in\mathbb{Z},\ \boldsymbol{\gamma}\in\mathbb{R}^K\right\}$ and

$$\min_{\mathbf{z}_n\in\mathbb{Z}}\min_{\gamma}\mathrm{E}[(\mathbf{x}_n'\boldsymbol{\alpha}-\mathbf{z}_n'\boldsymbol{\gamma})^2]=\min_{\mu\in\{\mathbf{z}_n'\boldsymbol{\gamma}\mid\mathbf{z}_n\in\mathbb{Z}\}}\mathrm{E}[(\mathbf{x}_n'\boldsymbol{\alpha}-\mu)^2]$$

is a standard projection program on the vector space

$$\left\{\{\mathbf{z}_n'\boldsymbol{\gamma}\}\mid\{\mathbf{z}_n\}\in\mathbb{Z},\ \boldsymbol{\gamma}\in\mathbb{R}^K\right\}+\left\{\mathbf{x}_n'\boldsymbol{\alpha}\mid\boldsymbol{\alpha}\in\mathbb{R}^K\right\}$$

The projection theorem (Theorem 6, p. 119) tells us that if there is a $\{\mathbf{z}_n^*\}$ that solves (20.51) then it satisfies the orthogonality condition

$$\mathrm{E}[(\mathbf{x}_n'\boldsymbol{\alpha}-\mathbf{z}_n^{*\prime}\boldsymbol{\alpha})\mathbf{z}_n'\boldsymbol{\gamma}]=\boldsymbol{\alpha}'\,\mathrm{E}[(\mathbf{x}_n-\mathbf{z}_n^*)\mathbf{z}_n']\boldsymbol{\gamma}=0 \tag{20.59}$$

for all $\boldsymbol{\alpha},\gamma\in\mathbb{R}^K$ and $\mathbf{z}_n\in\mathbb{Z}$.[38] Therefore, Lemma 20.4 implies that

$$\mathrm{E}[\mathbf{x}_n\mathbf{z}_n']=\mathrm{E}[\mathbf{z}_n^*\mathbf{z}_n'] \tag{20.60}$$

---

[38] There is no loss of generality in setting $\boldsymbol{\gamma}=\boldsymbol{\alpha}$. In general, there will be a whole subspace of solutions to (20.51).

for all $\mathbf{z}_n \in \mathbb{Z}$.

Now if we examine the asymptotic covariance between IV estimators using $\mathbf{z}_n^*$ and $\mathbf{z}_n$, we find that this covariance equals the asymptotic variance of the IV estimator using $\mathbf{z}_n^*$. To see this, let $\hat{\boldsymbol{\beta}}_{\text{IV}}^* \equiv \left(\mathbf{Z}^{*\prime}\mathbf{X}\right)^{-1}\mathbf{Z}^{*\prime}\mathbf{y}$ and $\hat{\boldsymbol{\beta}}_{\text{IV}} \equiv \left(\mathbf{Z}'\mathbf{X}\right)^{-1}\mathbf{Z}'\mathbf{y}$ be the corresponding IV estimators and note that for every $\alpha \in \mathbb{R}^K$

$$
\begin{aligned}
&\operatorname*{plim}_{N\to\infty} N \cdot \left(\mathbf{Z}'\mathbf{X}\right)^{-1}\mathbf{Z}'\left(\mathbf{y}-\mathbf{X}\boldsymbol{\beta}_0\right)\left(\mathbf{y}-\mathbf{X}\boldsymbol{\beta}_0\right)'\mathbf{Z}^*\left(\mathbf{X}'\mathbf{Z}^*\right)^{-1} \\
&\quad = \operatorname*{plim}_{N\to\infty} \sigma_0^2 \cdot \left(\mathrm{E}_N[\mathbf{z}_n\mathbf{x}_n']\right)^{-1}\mathrm{E}_N[\mathbf{z}_n\mathbf{z}_n^{*\prime}]\left(\mathrm{E}_N[\mathbf{x}_n\mathbf{z}_n^{*\prime}]\right)^{-1} \\
&\quad = \operatorname*{plim}_{N\to\infty} \sigma_0^2 \cdot \left(\mathrm{E}_N[\mathbf{z}_n^*\mathbf{x}_n']\right)^{-1}\mathrm{E}_N[\mathbf{z}_n^*\mathbf{z}_n^{*\prime}]\left(\mathrm{E}_N[\mathbf{x}_n\mathbf{z}_n^{*\prime}]\right)^{-1}
\end{aligned}
$$

using (20.60). In other words, $\hat{\boldsymbol{\beta}}_{\text{IV}}^* \equiv \left(\mathbf{Z}^{*\prime}\mathbf{X}\right)^{-1}\mathbf{Z}^{*\prime}\mathbf{y}$ is orthogonal to the difference $\hat{\boldsymbol{\beta}}_{\text{IV}} - \hat{\boldsymbol{\beta}}_{\text{IV}}^* \equiv \left(\mathbf{Z}'\mathbf{X}\right)^{-1}\mathbf{Z}'\mathbf{y} - \hat{\boldsymbol{\beta}}_{\text{IV}}^*$. This confirms explicitly through Proposition 8 (Orthogonality of Efficient Estimators, p. 185) what Lemma 20.4 already states: that a relatively efficient instrument vector $\{\mathbf{z}_n^*\} \in \mathbb{Z}$ produces the best MMSE linear prediction of $\mathbf{x}_n'\boldsymbol{\alpha}$ among all members of $\mathbb{Z}$.

Note in addition that (20.60) implies $\mathrm{E}[\mathbf{x}_n\mathbf{z}_n^{*\prime}] = \mathrm{E}[\mathbf{z}_n^*\mathbf{z}_n^{*\prime}]$ so that the asymptotic variance of $\hat{\boldsymbol{\beta}}_{\text{IV}}$ simplifies to $\operatorname{plim}_{N\to\infty}\sigma_0^2 \cdot \left(\mathrm{E}_N[\mathbf{z}_n^*\mathbf{z}_n^{*\prime}]\right)^{-1}$.

20.11 OVERVIEW

1. The equation

$$y_n = \mathbf{x}_n'\boldsymbol{\beta}_0 + \varepsilon_n$$

represents a latent variable model for which we make assumptions about the latent residual term ε_n. This term generally represents explanatory variables omitted from the regression function $\mathbf{x}_n'\boldsymbol{\beta}_0$ with K explanatory variables. We assume that $\mathrm{E}[\varepsilon_n] = 0$.

2. Several examples motivate this model:
   (a) dynamic regression,
   (b) errors-in-variables,
   (c) simultaneous equations,
   (d) omitted explanatory variables.

3. An instrumental variables (IV) estimator of $\boldsymbol{\beta}_0$ requires K instrumental variables z_{nk} $(k = 1, \ldots, K)$ with two properties:

$$
\begin{aligned}
&\mathrm{E}_N[\mathbf{z}_n\varepsilon_n] \xrightarrow{p} \mathrm{E}[\mathbf{z}_n\varepsilon_n] = \mathbf{0} \\
&\mathrm{E}_N[\mathbf{z}_n\mathbf{x}_n'] \xrightarrow{p} \mathrm{E}[\mathbf{z}_n\mathbf{x}_n'], \qquad \text{a nonsingular matrix}
\end{aligned}
$$

The first property, which states that $\mathbf{z}_n$ and ε_n are orthogonal in the population, often follows from the assumption that

$$\mathrm{E}[y_n \mid \mathbf{z}_n] = \mathrm{E}[\mathbf{x}_n \mid \mathbf{z}_n]'\boldsymbol{\beta}_0 \qquad \Leftrightarrow \qquad \mathrm{E}[\varepsilon_n \mid \mathbf{z}_n] = 0$$

where $\boldsymbol{\beta}_0$ are the parameters of interest. The IV estimator exploits the orthogonality property by requiring the IV fitted residuals to be orthogonal in the sample to the instrumental variables:

$$\mathrm{E}_N[\mathbf{z}_n(y_n - \mathbf{x}_n'\hat{\boldsymbol{\beta}}_{\mathrm{IV}})] = \mathbf{0} \quad \Rightarrow \quad \hat{\boldsymbol{\beta}}_{\mathrm{IV}} \equiv \left(\mathrm{E}_N[\mathbf{z}_n\mathbf{x}_n']\right)^{-1}\mathrm{E}_N[\mathbf{z}_n y_n] = \left(\mathbf{Z}'\mathbf{X}\right)^{-1}\mathbf{Z}'\mathbf{y}$$

4. Under i.i.d. sampling, ordinary least squares (OLS) estimates consistently the parameters of the linear regression $\mathbf{x}_n'(\boldsymbol{\beta}_0 + \boldsymbol{\pi}_0)$ where

$$\boldsymbol{\pi}_0 \equiv \left(\mathrm{E}[\mathbf{x}_n\mathbf{x}_n']\right)^{-1}\mathrm{E}[\mathbf{x}_n\varepsilon_n]$$

are the coefficients of the MMSE linear predictor of ε_n given $\mathbf{x}_n$. Therefore, OLS is inconsistent if there is covariance between $\mathbf{x}_n$ and ε_n, as one would generally expect if ε_n contains omitted explanatory variables. The nonorthogonality of $\mathbf{x}_n$ and ε_n in the population causes the inconsistency of OLS because it produces a consistent estimator of the coefficients of the MMSE linear predictor of y_n given $\mathbf{x}_n$.

5. For the errors-in-variables model, the probability limit of the OLS estimator has a smaller length than $\boldsymbol{\beta}_0$.

6. Under certain assumptions, the IV estimator is consistent and approximately normally distributed with mean $\boldsymbol{\beta}_0$ and variance $\sigma_0^2 \cdot \left(\mathbf{Z}'\mathbf{X}\right)^{-1}\mathbf{Z}'\mathbf{Z}\left(\mathbf{X}'\mathbf{Z}\right)^{-1}$ where $\mathrm{Var}[\mathbf{y} \mid \mathbf{Z}] = \sigma_0^2 \cdot \mathbf{I}_N$. A consistent estimator of σ_0^2 is the empirical variance of the IV fitted residuals:

$$\hat{\sigma}_{\mathrm{IV}}^2 = \mathrm{E}_N\left[\left(y_n - \mathbf{x}_n'\hat{\boldsymbol{\beta}}_{\mathrm{IV}}\right)^2\right]$$

7. Latent variable models may suggest instrumental variables:
   (a) The dynamic regression with autoregressive serial correlation implies that some lagged explanatory variables are correlated with y_{t-1} but not ε_t.
   (b) Some explanatory variables from another equation in the simultaneous system are uncorrelated with the disturbance term but correlated with an endogenous explanatory variable.

8. These models may also yield relatively efficient choices of instrumental variables. These choices are always (linear transformations of) optimal MMSE predictors of the explanatory variables:
   (a) The two-stage least-squares (2SLS) estimator

$$\hat{\boldsymbol{\beta}}_{\mathrm{2SLS}} \equiv \left(\mathbf{X}'\mathbf{P}_{\mathbf{W}}\mathbf{X}\right)^{-1}\mathbf{X}'\mathbf{P}_{\mathbf{W}}\mathbf{y}$$

   employs instruments $\mathbf{P}_{\mathbf{W}}\mathbf{X}$ that are MMSE linear predictors of the explanatory variables given all the predetermined variables $\mathbf{W}$ in the simultaneous system.
   (b) The GLS estimator is an IV estimator because the elements of $\mathbf{Z} = \boldsymbol{\Omega}_0^{-1}\mathbf{X}$ are uncorrelated with ε_t even though an element of $\mathbf{x}_t$ is. These instrumental variables are one-to-one linear transformations of the explanatory variables.

9. In small samples, the IV estimator is biased towards the OLS estimator when the instrumental variables are weakly correlated with the explanatory variables.

20.12 EXERCISES

20.12.1 Review

20.1 Reestimate the Phillips curve for the model described in Section 20.1. Is the hypothesis $\alpha_0 = 0$ supported by the estimates?

20.2 Give counterexamples to the following claims:

(a) "Although errors in the explanatory variables cause inconsistency in the OLS estimator, errors in the dependent variable do not."

(b) "Including an unnecessary explanatory variable in an OLS regression does not lead to inconsistency of the OLS estimator."

20.3 We occasionally hear the remark that excluding an explanatory variable from a linear regression may result in misestimation of the slope coefficients whereas including an "irrelevant" explanatory variable will lead only to estimator inefficiency. Hence, it is argued, we should err on the side of including explanatory variables that are probably unnecessary. Describe a latent model in which this is true and another in which it is false.

20.4 (Projection and IV) Let us denote the IV estimator by $\hat{\boldsymbol{\beta}}_{\text{IV}} = (\mathbf{W}'\mathbf{X})^{-1}\mathbf{W}'\mathbf{y}$.

(a) Describe the IV fitted vector $\mathbf{X}\hat{\boldsymbol{\beta}}_{\text{IV}}$ in terms of projection.

(b) Compare the IV projection with the partitioned regression projection (Section 3.3).

(c) Sometimes researchers associate an instrumental variable w_{nk} with a particular explanatory variable, say x_{nk}, in multiple regression models. Explain why such an association is mistaken in general.

20.5 (OLS) Consider the partitioned regression $\text{E}[y_n \mid \mathbf{x}_n] = \mathbf{x}_{n1}'\boldsymbol{\beta}_{01} + \mathbf{x}_{n2}'\boldsymbol{\beta}_{02}$. Let $\hat{\boldsymbol{\beta}} = [\hat{\boldsymbol{\beta}}_1', \hat{\boldsymbol{\beta}}_2']'$ be the OLS fitted coefficient vector.

(a) Show that the OLS estimator $\hat{\boldsymbol{\beta}}_1$ for $\boldsymbol{\beta}_{01}$ has the IV form

$$\hat{\boldsymbol{\beta}}_1 = \left(\mathbf{X}_{1\perp 2}'\mathbf{X}_1\right)^{-1}\mathbf{X}_{1\perp 2}'\mathbf{y}$$

where

$$\mathbf{X}_{2\perp 1} = \left(\mathbf{I} - \mathbf{P}_{\mathbf{X}_1}\right)\mathbf{X}_2$$

$$\mathbf{P}_{\mathbf{X}_1} = \mathbf{X}_1\left(\mathbf{X}_1'\mathbf{X}_1\right)^{-1}\mathbf{X}_1'$$

(b) The OLS fitted coefficient vector

$$\hat{\boldsymbol{\beta}}_{\text{R}1} = \left(\mathbf{X}_1'\mathbf{X}_1\right)\mathbf{X}_1'\mathbf{y}$$

from the regression that omits $\mathbf{x}_{n2}$ is generally biased and inconsistent as an estimator for $\boldsymbol{\beta}_{01}$. Show that we can also write[39]

$$\hat{\boldsymbol{\beta}}_1 = \hat{\boldsymbol{\beta}}_{\text{R}1} - \left(\mathbf{X}_1'\mathbf{X}_1\right)^{-1}\mathbf{X}_1'\mathbf{X}_2\hat{\boldsymbol{\beta}}_2$$

and interpret this equation as an analogue to (20.27).

20.6 (Partitioned 2SLS) Consider the partitioned regression function $\mathbf{x}_n'\boldsymbol{\beta} = \mathbf{x}_{1n}'\boldsymbol{\beta}_1 + \mathbf{x}_{2n}'\boldsymbol{\beta}_2$ and show that

$$\mathbf{P}_{\mathbf{X}\perp\bar{\mathbf{X}}} = \mathbf{P}_{\mathbf{X}_1\perp\bar{\mathbf{X}}_1} + \left(\mathbf{I} - \mathbf{P}_{\mathbf{X}_1\perp\bar{\mathbf{X}}_1}\right)\mathbf{P}_{\mathbf{X}_2\perp\check{\mathbf{X}}_2}$$

where $\bar{\mathbf{X}} \equiv \mathbf{P}_{\mathbf{W}}\mathbf{X}$ and $\check{\mathbf{X}}_2 \equiv \left(\mathbf{I} - \mathbf{P}_{\bar{\mathbf{X}}_1}\right)\bar{\mathbf{X}}_2$.

20.7 (Errors in Variables) Reconsider the simple errors-in-variables model in Example 20.4 and argue that we could just as well view the LHS variable as x_n and the RHS variable as y_n.

---

[39] Showing this result was Exercise 3.8.

(a) Show that the reciprocal of the OLS fitted slope from such a "reverse" regression and the OLS fitted slope from fitting y_n to x_n have probability limits that bound β_0.
(b) Extend the model to include an intercept,

$$y_n = \beta_{01} + \beta_{02}x_n - \beta_{02}v_n + u_n$$

and show that the OLS fitted slope coefficient from fitting y to x and a constant still converges to an underestimate of β_{02} while the OLS fitted slope coefficient from fitting x to y and a constant also converges to an overestimate of β_{02}.

***20.8 (Errors in Variables)** As in Example 20.1, suppose that

$$\mathrm{E}[y_n \mid \mathbf{x}_n^*] = \mathbf{x}_n^{*\prime}\boldsymbol{\beta}_0, \qquad n = 1, \ldots, N$$

but some of the explanatory variables in $\mathbf{x}_n^*$ are not observable. Let $\mathbf{x}_{jn}$ $(j = 1, 2)$ denote two sets of proxy variables where

$$\mathbf{x}_{jn} = \mathbf{x}_n^* + \boldsymbol{v}_{jn}$$

and v_{jn} denotes measurement errors with $\mathrm{E}[\boldsymbol{v}_{jn}] = 0$. Assume that $\boldsymbol{v}_{1n}$ and $\boldsymbol{v}_{2n}$ are uncorrelated with both x_{nk}^* $(k = 1, \ldots, K)$ and $u_n \equiv y_n - \mathbf{x}_n^{*\prime}\boldsymbol{\beta}_0$. Assume also that $\boldsymbol{v}_{1n}$ is uncorrelated with $\boldsymbol{v}_{2n}$. Propose an IV estimator for $\boldsymbol{\beta}_0$.

20.9 (Lagged Dependent Variable) Suppose

$$y_t = \mathbf{x}_{1t}'\boldsymbol{\beta}_{01} + \beta_{02}y_{t-1} + \varepsilon_t, \qquad t = 1, \ldots, T$$

where $\{\varepsilon_t\}$ is a sequence of i.i.d. $\mathfrak{N}(0, \sigma_0^2)$ random disturbances.
(a) Using (essentially) the transformation (19.12), apply the change-of-variables procedure to derive the log-likelihood function from the distribution of $\boldsymbol{\varepsilon}_t$ for observations $t = 2, \ldots, T$ conditional on y_1. Show that OLS is still the (approximate) MLE for the regression slopes.
(b) What distinguishes this model from one without y_{t-1} as an explanatory variable but with autoregressive ε_t: $\varepsilon_t = \phi_0\varepsilon_{t-1} + v_t$ where $\{v_t\}$ is a sequence of i.i.d. $\mathfrak{N}(0, \sigma_v^2)$ random disturbances?

20.10 (Lagged Dependent Variable) How can we use Hatanaka's (1974) estimation procedure with OLS estimates to compute a score test for no autocorrelation ($\phi_0 = 0$) in the log-likelihood function (20.52)?

In addition, consider the dynamic specification

$$y_t = \mathbf{x}_{1t}'\boldsymbol{\beta}_{01} + \beta_{02}y_{t-1} + \cdots + \beta_{0,p+1}y_{t-p} + \varepsilon_t, \qquad t = 1, \ldots, T$$

where $\varepsilon_1 \sim \mathfrak{N}\left[0, \sigma_{0v}^2/(1 - \phi_0^2)\right]$

$$\varepsilon_t = \phi_0\varepsilon_{t-1} + v_t, \qquad t = 2, \ldots, T$$

and $\{v_t\}$ is a sequence of i.i.d. $\mathfrak{N}(0, \sigma_{0v}^2)$ random variables.
(a) How is Hatanaka's (1974) FGLS procedure changed?
(b) How is the score test for autocorrelation changed?

20.11 (MMSE Prediction) Conditional on the data set and the true parameter values, the conditional mean is the MMSE forecasting function. In Section 19.7, we noted that if

$$y_t = \mathbf{x}_t'\boldsymbol{\beta}_0 + \varepsilon_t, \qquad t = 1, \ldots, T$$

where $\varepsilon_1 \sim \mathfrak{N}\left[0, \sigma_{0v}^2/(1 - \phi_0^2)\right]$,

$$\varepsilon_t = \phi_0 \varepsilon_{t-1} + \upsilon_t, \qquad t = 2, \ldots, T$$

and $\{\upsilon_t\}$ is a sequence of i.i.d. $\mathfrak{N}(0, \sigma_{0\upsilon}^2)$ random variables, then

$$\begin{aligned} \mathrm{E}[y_{T+1} \mid T] &= \mathbf{x}'_{T+1}\boldsymbol{\beta}_0 + \phi_0 \varepsilon_T \\ &= (\mathbf{x}_{T+1} - \phi_0 \cdot \mathbf{x}_T)'\boldsymbol{\beta}_0 + \phi_0 y_T \end{aligned}$$

when $\mathbf{x}_t$ contains no lagged dependent variable. Find the corresponding MMSE forecasting function for the dynamic regression model in which one element of $\mathbf{x}_t$ is y_{t-1} and the rest are nonstochastic.

20.12 (MMSE Prediction) Suppose that the MMSE linear predictor of y_n is $\mathbf{x}'_n\boldsymbol{\gamma}_0$. What is the MMSE linear predictor of the conditional mean $\mathrm{E}[y_n \mid \mathbf{x}_n]$ given $\mathbf{x}_n$? Prove your claim.

20.13 (GLS and IV) The variance matrix of the disturbance terms in the dynamic regression model of Section 20.1 is $\boldsymbol{\Omega}_0 = \sigma_{0\upsilon}^2 \cdot \left[\phi_0^{|i-j|}\right]$.

(a) Show that

$$\boldsymbol{\Omega}_0^{-1} = \frac{1}{\sigma_{0\upsilon}^2\left(1-\phi_0^2\right)} \cdot \begin{bmatrix} 1 & -\phi_0 & 0 & 0 & \cdots & 0 \\ -\phi_0 & 1+\phi_0^2 & -\phi_0 & 0 & \cdots & 0 \\ 0 & -\phi_0 & 1+\phi_0^2 & -\phi_0 & \cdots & 0 \\ 0 & 0 & -\phi_0 & 1 & \ddots & \vdots \\ \vdots & \vdots & \vdots & \ddots & \ddots & -\phi_0 \\ 0 & 0 & 0 & \cdots & -\phi_0 & 1 \end{bmatrix}$$

(b) Show that the instrument matrix in (20.20) can be written as

$$\mathbf{z}_t = \begin{cases} \mathbf{x}_t - \phi_0 \cdot \mathbf{x}_{t+1} & \text{if } t = 1 \\ \mathbf{x}_t - \phi_0 \cdot \mathbf{x}_{t-1} - \phi_0 \cdot (\mathbf{x}_{t+1} - \phi_0 \mathbf{x}_t) & \text{if } t = 2, \ldots, T-1 \\ \mathbf{x}_t - \phi_0 \cdot \mathbf{x}_{t-1} & \text{if } t = T \end{cases}$$

so that the optimal GLS instruments are functions of future, as well as past, values of each explanatory variable.

(c) Confirm that the instrumental variable constructed with the lagged dependent explanatory variable is orthogonal to the latent disturbance ε_t:

$$\mathrm{E}\Big[\Big(y_{t-1} - \phi_0 y_{t-2} - \phi_0(y_t - \phi_0 y_{t-1})\Big)\varepsilon_t\Big] = 0, \quad t = 2, \ldots, T-1$$

(HINT: The autocovariances $\mathrm{Cov}[y_t, y_{t-s} \mid \mathbf{X}]$ depend only on s.)

(d) Does this orthogonality condition hold if we replace ϕ_0 with some other value? What does this imply about estimating the sampling variance of the corresponding feasible IV estimator?

20.14 (2SLS) Both the dynamic regression model and the simultaneous equations model have straightforward conditional mean functions when conditioning on latent variables. The supply function possesses the conditional mean

$$\mathrm{E}[y_n \mid \mathbf{x}_{s1n}, p_n, \upsilon_n] = \mathbf{x}'_{sn}\boldsymbol{\beta}_{0s} + \gamma_{0s}\left(\beta_{0s2} - \beta_{0d2}\right)\left(p_n - \mathbf{w}'_n\boldsymbol{\pi}_{0p}\right)$$

given in (20.49) where $p_n - \mathbf{w}'_n\boldsymbol{\pi}_{0p}$ is a residual term that is linear in p_n and $\mathbf{w}_n$. Similarly, the dynamic regression possesses the conditional mean

$$\mathrm{E}[y_t \mid \mathbf{x}_t, \mathbf{x}_{t-1}] = \mathbf{x}'_t\boldsymbol{\beta}_0 + \phi_0\varepsilon_{t-1} = \mathrm{E}[y_t \mid \mathbf{x}_t, \varepsilon_{t-1}]$$

given in (20.33) where ε_{t-1} is a linear combination of y_{t-1} and $\mathbf{x}_{t-1}$. The 2SLS estimator for $\boldsymbol{\beta}_{0s}$ regresses p_n on $\mathbf{w}_n$ and uses the OLS fitted values as an instrumental variable. An analogous procedure for the dynamic regression would be to regress y_{t-1} on $\mathbf{x}_{t-1}$ and use the OLS fitted values as an instrumental variable. Explain why such a 2SLS estimator would be inconsistent.

20.15 **(2SLS)** Show that we can compute the 2SLS estimator of the supply equation (20.50) by replacing p_n with its OLS fitted value $\mathbf{w}_n' \check{\boldsymbol{\pi}}_p$ and running OLS. Will the OLS estimator of the sampling variance of the IV estimator be consistent?

20.16 **(2SLS)** Describe the 2SLS estimator for the demand equation (20.23) in Example 20.2. Be sure to include any additional assumptions that you require.

20.17 **(2SLS)** Suppose that the number of variables (columns) in $\mathbf{W}$ equals the number of explanatory variables (columns) in $\mathbf{X}_s$ in (20.50) for $\hat{\boldsymbol{\beta}}_{2\text{SLS}}$.

(a) Under what circumstances would this occur?

(b) Show that in this case the 2SLS estimator simplifies to a simple IV estimator:

$$\hat{\boldsymbol{\beta}}_{2\text{SLS}} = \left(\mathbf{X}_s' \mathbf{P}_{\mathbf{W}} \mathbf{X}_s\right)^{-1} \mathbf{X}_s' \mathbf{P}_{\mathbf{W}} y = \left(\mathbf{Z}' \mathbf{X}_s\right)^{-1} \mathbf{Z}' \mathbf{y}$$

where $\mathbf{W} = \mathbf{Z}$.

20.18 **(MMSE and IV)** Under the conditions of Proposition 18, show that the probability limit of the IV estimator is the solution to the MMSE linear prediction problem

$$\min_{\boldsymbol{\gamma}} \mathrm{E}\left[\left(\mu_y(\mathbf{z}_n) - \mu_x(\mathbf{z}_n)\boldsymbol{\gamma}\right)^2\right]$$

where $\mu_y(\mathbf{z}_n)$ and $\mu_x(\mathbf{z}_n)$ are the MMSE linear predictors given $\mathbf{z}_n$ of y_n and $\mathbf{x}_n$, respectively. Explain the relationship between this result and Exercise 20.17 Part b. Are the elements of $\boldsymbol{\gamma}$ invariant to a nonsingular transformation of the $\mathbf{z}_n$? Can you provide a similar interpretation of the 2SLS estimator?

20.19 **(Heteroskedasticity and IV)** Suppose that $(y_n, \mathbf{x}_n, \mathbf{z}_n)$ are i.i.d. such that

$$\mathrm{E}[y_n \,|\, \mathbf{z}_n] = \mathrm{E}[\mathbf{x}_n' \,|\, \mathbf{z}_n]\boldsymbol{\beta}_0$$
$$\mathrm{Var}[y_n \,|\, \mathbf{z}_n] = \sigma_0^2(\mathbf{z}_n) \equiv \sigma_{0n}^2$$

$n = 1, \ldots, N$. Let the number of instrumental variables in $\mathbf{z}_n$ equal the number of explanatory variables in $\mathbf{x}_n$. How would you estimate the asymptotic variance matrix of the IV estimator? Give sufficient conditions for your variance estimator to be consistent.

20.20 **(Two-Step Estimation)** Consider two-step estimation of the partitioned regression $\mathrm{E}(y_n \,|\, \mathbf{X}) = \mathbf{x}_{1n}'\boldsymbol{\beta}_{01} + \mathbf{x}_{2n}'\boldsymbol{\beta}_{02}$, $n = 1, \ldots, N$. Suppose that you have a preliminary estimator of $\boldsymbol{\beta}_{01}$, $\check{\boldsymbol{\beta}}_1 \,|\, \mathbf{X} \sim \mathfrak{N}(\boldsymbol{\beta}_{01}, \mathbf{V}_1)$ and you estimate $\boldsymbol{\beta}_{02}$ from the OLS fit of $\mathbf{y} - \mathbf{X}_1\check{\boldsymbol{\beta}}_1$ to $\mathbf{X}_2$. Let $\boldsymbol{\Sigma}_0 = \mathrm{Var}[\mathbf{y} \,|\, \mathbf{X}]$ and $\mathbf{C}_0 = \mathrm{Cov}[\mathbf{y}, \check{\boldsymbol{\beta}}_1 \,|\, \mathbf{X}]$ and find the variance of this two-step estimator. Compare your answer with Lemma 19. Confirm that your answer gives the correct variance when $\check{\boldsymbol{\beta}}_1 = \hat{\boldsymbol{\beta}}_{\text{OLS},1}$ is the $\boldsymbol{\beta}_1$ component of $\hat{\boldsymbol{\beta}}_{\text{OLS}} = (\mathbf{X}'\mathbf{X})^{-1}\mathbf{X}'\mathbf{y}$.

20.12.2 Extensions

20.21 **(IV)** For the consistency of the IV estimator in Proposition 18 (Asymptotic Distribution of IV, p. 500) it is sufficient in Assumption 20.2 (Instruments, p. 499) that $\mathrm{E}_N[\mathbf{z}_n\varepsilon_n] \xrightarrow{p} 0$. We also assume the stronger condition that $\mathrm{E}[\varepsilon_n \mid \mathbf{z}_n] = 0$. This exercise develops another rationale for the stronger condition.

(a) Suppose that the economic argument for $\mathrm{E}[\mathbf{z}_n \varepsilon_n] = \mathbf{0}$ implies more generally that if $\mathrm{E}[g(\mathbf{z}_n)\varepsilon_n]$ exists for some continuous transformation $g : \mathbb{R}^K \to \mathbb{R}$ then $\mathrm{E}[g(\mathbf{z}_n)\varepsilon_n] = 0$. Consider functions that are indicators for closed and bounded intervals of $\mathbb{R}^K$:

$$g(\mathbf{z}_n) = \mathbf{1}\{a_{nk} \le z_{nk} \le b_{nk}; \quad k = 1, \ldots, K\}$$

Interpret $\mathrm{E}[g(\mathbf{z}_n)\varepsilon_n] = 0$ as a restriction on a conditional expectation of ε_n.

(b) Use this interpretation to argue that $\mathrm{E}[\varepsilon_n \mid \mathbf{z}_n] = 0$. What does this restriction imply about IV estimators based on functions of $\mathbf{z}_n$?

(c) A stronger restriction is that if $\mathrm{Cov}[g(\mathbf{z}_n), h(\varepsilon_n)]$ exists for some continuous transformations $g : \mathbb{R}^K \to \mathbb{R}$ and $h : \mathbb{R} \to \mathbb{R}$ then $\mathrm{Cov}[g(\mathbf{z}_n), h(\varepsilon_n)] = 0$. Use a similar argument to show that this restriction implies that $\mathbf{z}_n$ and ε_n are independently distributed.[40]

20.22 (GLS and IV) Suppose that $\{\mathbf{x}_n, y_n, \mathbf{z}_n\}$ is an i.i.d. sequence such that

$$\mathrm{E}[y_n \mid \mathbf{z}_n] = \mathrm{E}[\mathbf{x}_n' \mid \mathbf{z}_n]\boldsymbol{\beta}_0$$
$$\mathrm{Var}[y_n \mid \mathbf{z}_n] = \sigma_{0n}^2$$

Take the conditions of Assumptions 20.1–20.3 as given.

(a) Show that $(1/\sigma_{0n}^2) \cdot \mathbf{z}_n$ are relatively efficient instrumental variables among the set of instrumental variables

$$\left\{\alpha_n \cdot \mathbf{z}_n \mid \mathrm{E}_N[\mathbf{z}_n \alpha_n^2 \mathbf{z}_n'] \text{ converges in probability}\right\}$$

if $\mathrm{E}[\mathbf{x}_n' \mid \mathbf{z}_n] = \mathbf{z}_n' \boldsymbol{\Psi}_0$ for a nonsingular matrix $\boldsymbol{\Psi}_0$.

(b) What are relatively efficient instrumental variables if $\boldsymbol{\Psi}_0$ were not square, but still full-column rank? If $\boldsymbol{\Psi}_0$ were unknown, but σ_{0n}^2 were known, what would be feasible, asymptotically equivalent, instrumental variables?

(c) Suggest an asymptotically relatively efficient feasible IV estimator for $\boldsymbol{\beta}_0$ given that $\sigma_{0n}^2 = \exp(\mathbf{z}_n' \boldsymbol{\gamma}_0)$ where $\boldsymbol{\gamma}_0$ is unknown.

20.23 (GLS and IV) Suppose that $\{\mathbf{x}_n, y_n, \mathbf{z}_n\}$ is a covariance stationary sequence such that

$$\mathrm{E}[y_n \mid \mathbf{z}_n] = \mathrm{E}[\mathbf{x}_n' \mid \mathbf{z}_n]\boldsymbol{\beta}_0$$
$$\mathrm{Var}[y_n \mid \mathbf{z}_n] = \sigma_0^2$$
$$\mathrm{Cov}[y_n y_{n-j} \mid \mathbf{z}_n] = \phi_0^{|j|}\sigma_0^2$$

(a) Show that $\left(1 + \phi_0^2\right)\mathbf{z}_t - \phi_0 \mathbf{z}_{t-1} - \phi_0 \mathbf{z}_{t+1}$ are relatively efficient instrumental variables if $\mathrm{E}[\mathbf{x}_n' \mid \mathbf{z}_n] = \mathbf{z}_n' \boldsymbol{\Psi}_0$ and $\boldsymbol{\Psi}_0$ is a nonsingular matrix.

(b) What are relatively efficient instrumental variables if $\boldsymbol{\Psi}_0$ is not square, but still full-column rank? If $\boldsymbol{\Psi}_0$ were unknown, but ϕ_0 were known, what would be feasible, asymptotically equivalent, instrumental variables?

(c) Suggest an asymptotically relatively efficient, feasible, IV estimator for $\boldsymbol{\beta}_0$ given that ϕ_0 is unknown.

20.24 (Nonlinear IV) Replace the linear function $\mathbf{x}_n' \boldsymbol{\beta}_0$ with a more general nonlinear function $\mu(\boldsymbol{\beta}_0; \mathbf{x}_n)$ in Assumption 20.1 (Latent Variable Model, p. 499). Alter the other assumptions of Proposition 18 (Asymptotic Distribution of IV, p. 500) so that the nonlinear IV (NIV) estimator,

[40] See, for example, Feller (1971, p. 136).

$$\hat{\boldsymbol{\beta}}_{\text{NIV}} = \underset{\boldsymbol{\beta}}{\text{argzero}}\, \text{E}_N\left[\mathbf{z}_n'\left(y_n - \mu(\boldsymbol{\beta}; \mathbf{x}_n)\right)\right]$$

is consistent and asymptotically normal.

20.25 (Orthogonality) The covariance matrix between $\mathbf{x}_n$ and $\mathbf{z}_n$ is

$$\text{Cov}[\mathbf{x}_n, \mathbf{z}_n] = \text{E}\left[\left(\mathbf{x}_n - \text{E}(\mathbf{x}_n)\right)\left(\mathbf{z}_n - \text{E}(\mathbf{z}_n)\right)'\right]$$

but orthogonality concerns whether $\text{E}[\mathbf{x}_n\mathbf{z}_n']$ equals zero. Explain why "correlation" is an appropriate term for discussing possible orthogonality between potential instrumental variables and explanatory variables, when there is a constant among the explanatory variables. (HINT: Find a partitioned IV formula when one partitions both $\mathbf{x}_n$ and $\mathbf{z}_n$ between the constant and the other variables.)

***20.26 (Score Test for Serial Correlation)** In the dynamic regression (20.8) with autoregressive disturbances (20.1), if there is no autocorrelation in $\{\varepsilon_t\}$ ($\phi_0 = 0$), then the OLS estimator remains consistent and asymptotically efficient. Testing for autocorrelation has more importance than when $\mathbf{x}_t$ contains no lagged values of y_t, because the OLS estimator is inconsistent when autocorrelation is present.

Again following Breusch (1978) and Godfrey (1978a, 1978b), the score test method still works for the null hypothesis $\phi_0 = 0$, but the test itself is no longer based simply on the OLS regression of the OLS fitted residual $\hat{\varepsilon}_t$ on its lagged value $\hat{\varepsilon}_{t-1}$, as described in Section 19.4.1.[41] Show that the score test augments the explanatory variables of the auxiliary regression of $\hat{\varepsilon}_t$ on $\hat{\varepsilon}_{t-1}$ with all of the explanatory variables $\mathbf{x}_t$ in the conditional mean of y_t. We then test the statistical significance of the coefficient of $\hat{\varepsilon}_{t-1}$. Comment on the need for these additional explanatory variables.

***20.27 (Two-Step Estimation)** In Example 20.5, we noted that OLS with the LHS variable y_t and the RHS variables $\mathbf{x}_t$ and $\mathbf{x}_{t-1}$ will deliver consistent estimators of $\boldsymbol{\beta}_{01}$, $\beta_{02} + \phi_0$, $\phi_0 \cdot \boldsymbol{\beta}_{01}$, and $\phi_0\beta_{02}$.

(a) Compare this estimator to Durbin's initial estimator (p. 469) for the static regression model with AR serial correlation.

(b) Given the initial consistent estimator for $\boldsymbol{\beta}_{01}$ describe a second step OLS estimator for β_{02} and ϕ_0 based on the partitioning

$$y_t - \mathbf{x}_{1t}'\boldsymbol{\beta}_{01} = \beta_{02}y_{t-1} + \phi_0\left(y_{t-1} - \mathbf{x}_{1,t-1}'\boldsymbol{\beta}_{01}\right) - \phi_0\beta_{02}y_{t-2} + \upsilon_t$$

(c) What sources of asymptotic inefficiency are present in this estimator for β_{02}?

20.28 (Omitted Variables) The first-step estimator of $\boldsymbol{\beta}_{01}$ in Exercise 20.27 has the partitioned/IV form

$$\hat{\boldsymbol{\beta}}_{01} = \left[\mathbf{X}_1'\left(\mathbf{I} - \mathbf{P}\right)\mathbf{X}_1\right]^{-1}\mathbf{X}_1\left(\mathbf{I} - \mathbf{P}\right)\mathbf{y}$$

where $\mathbf{X}_1 \equiv [\mathbf{x}_{1t}']'$ and $\mathbf{P}$ is the orthogonal projector onto $\text{Col}\left(\left[[y_{t-1}, \mathbf{x}_{t-1}']'\right]\right)$. This estimator is based on expanding the conditional mean

$$\text{E}[y_t \mid \mathbf{x}_t, \mathbf{x}_{t-1}] = \mathbf{x}_t'\boldsymbol{\beta}_0 + \phi_0\varepsilon_{t-1}$$

[41] Durbin (1970) also suggested an alternative to the Durbin–Watson test for y_{t-1} among the explanatory variables called the h test. It can be calculated easily from OLS regression software output as

$$\left(1 - \frac{DW}{2}\right)\sqrt{\frac{T}{1 - Ts_y^2}}$$

where s_y^2 is the estimated variance of the OLS fitted coefficient for y_{t-1}. Software packages frequently calculate Durbin's h statistic automatically, except in cases in which $1 - Ts_y^2 \leq 0$. Asymptotically this does not occur. Its asymptotic distribution is normal under the null hypothesis that $\phi_0 = 0$.

using $\varepsilon_{t-1} = y_{t-1} - \mathbf{x}_{t-1}'\boldsymbol{\beta}_0$. Apply the same approach to the supply function in the simultaneous equations model, using the conditional mean

$$\mathrm{E}[y_n \mid \mathbf{w}_n, p_n] = \mathbf{x}_{sn}'\boldsymbol{\beta}_{0s} + \gamma_{0s}(\beta_{0s2} - \beta_{0d2})\left(p_n - \mathbf{w}_n'\boldsymbol{\pi}_{0p}\right)$$

given in (20.49), and comment on any difficulties that you encounter.

20.29 (LMLE) The LMLE is a two-step estimator that does not require adjustment of the asymptotic variance matrix estimator as in Proposition 19 (Two-Step Asymptotic Variance, p. 507). Yet the LMLE is inconsistent if we substitute a value other than the population parameter value for the initial consistent estimator. Explain why this is not a contradiction to Proposition 19. What is the implication for asymptotic variance estimation for Hatanaka's (1974) estimator?

20.30 (Serial Correlation and IV) Suppose that the sequence $\{y_t, \mathbf{x}_t, \mathbf{w}_t;\quad t = 1, \ldots, T\}$ is strictly stationary such that

$$\mathrm{E}[y_t \mid \{\mathbf{w}_t\}] = \mathrm{E}[\mathbf{x}_t' \mid \mathbf{w}_t]\boldsymbol{\beta}_0$$

$$\mathrm{Var}[y_t, y_{t-j} \mid \{\mathbf{w}_t\}] = \sigma_0^2\phi_0^{|j|}$$

for $t = 1, \ldots, T$ and $j = 0, \pm 1, \pm 2, \ldots$. Let J be the number of instrumental variables in $\mathbf{w}_n$ and K the number of explanatory variables in $\mathbf{x}_n$ and suppose $J \geq K$. Consider the set of sequences of instrument vectors

$$\mathbb{Z} = \Big\{\{\mathbf{z}_t\} \mid \mathbf{z}_t = f(\mathbf{w}_{t+j};\ j = 0, \pm 1, \pm 2),\ f: \mathbb{R}^{5J} \to \mathbb{R}^K,$$
$$\mathrm{E}[\mathbf{z}_t\mathbf{x}_t'] \text{ is nonsingular, and}$$
$$\mathrm{E}_N[\mathbf{z}_t\mathbf{z}_t'],\ \mathrm{E}_N[\mathbf{z}_t\mathbf{x}_t'] \text{ converge in probability}\Big\}$$

Show that if it belongs to $\mathbb{Z}$ then

$$\mathbf{z}_t^* = \mathrm{E}[\mathbf{x}_t \mid \mathbf{w}_t] - \phi_0 \cdot \mathrm{E}[\mathbf{x}_{t-1} \mid \mathbf{w}_{t-1}] - \phi_0 \cdot (\mathrm{E}[\mathbf{x}_{t+1} \mid \mathbf{w}_{t+1}] - \phi_0 \cdot \mathrm{E}[\mathbf{x}_t \mid \mathbf{w}_t])$$

is an optimal instrument vector for almost all t. (HINT: Consider $y_t - \phi_0 y_{t-1}$.)

20.31 (Heteroskedasticity and IV) Suppose that $(y_n, \mathbf{x}_n, \mathbf{w}_n)$ are i.i.d. such that

$$\mathrm{E}[y_n \mid \mathbf{w}_n] = \mathrm{E}[\mathbf{x}_n' \mid \mathbf{w}_n]\boldsymbol{\beta}_0$$

$$\mathrm{Var}[y_n \mid \mathbf{w}_n] = \sigma_0^2(\mathbf{w}_n) \equiv \sigma_{0n}^2$$

$n = 1, \ldots, N$. Let J be the number of instrumental variables in $\mathbf{w}_n$ and K the number of explanatory variables in $\mathbf{x}_n$ and suppose $J \geq K$. In addition, suppose that

$$\mathrm{E}_N[\mathbf{w}_n\mathbf{x}_n'] \xrightarrow{p} \mathrm{E}[\mathbf{w}_n\mathbf{x}_n']$$

$$\mathrm{E}_N[\mathbf{w}_n\mathbf{w}_n'] \xrightarrow{p} \mathrm{E}[\mathbf{w}_n\mathbf{w}_n']$$

where $\mathrm{E}[\mathbf{w}_n\mathbf{x}_n']$ is full-column rank. Consider the set of sequences of instrument vectors

$$\mathbb{Z} = \left\{\{\mathbf{z}_n\} \mid \mathbf{z}_n' = \mathbf{w}_n'\boldsymbol{\Pi},\quad \boldsymbol{\Pi} \text{ is a } J \times K \text{ real matrix}\right\}$$

(a) Show that

$$\mathbf{z}_n^{*\prime} = \mathbf{w}_n'\left(\mathrm{E}[\mathbf{w}_n\sigma_{0n}^2\mathbf{w}_n']\right)^{-1}\mathrm{E}[\mathbf{w}_n\mathbf{x}_n']$$

is the optimal instrument vector in $\mathbb{Z}$.

(b) What is a feasible substitute for $\mathbf{z}_n^*$ that yields an asymptotically equivalent estimator?[42] (HINT: Review the Eicker–White heteroskedasticity-consistent variance estimator for OLS.)

20.32 (Errors in Variables) Consider the multivariate case of errors in variables where

$$y_n = \mathbf{x}_n^{*\prime}\boldsymbol{\beta}_0 + u_n$$
$$\mathbf{x}_n = \mathbf{x}_n^* + \boldsymbol{v}_n$$

Suppose that $\mathrm{E}[\mathbf{x}_n^*\mathbf{x}_n^{*\prime}]$ and $\mathrm{Var}[\boldsymbol{v}_n]$ are finite and nonsingular and that

$$\mathrm{E}[u_n] = 0, \qquad \mathrm{Cov}[\mathbf{x}_n^*, u_n] = \mathbf{0}, \qquad \mathrm{Cov}[\mathbf{x}_n^*, \boldsymbol{v}_n] = \mathbf{0}$$
$$\mathrm{E}[\boldsymbol{v}_n] = \mathbf{0}, \qquad \mathrm{Cov}[\boldsymbol{v}_n, u_n] = \mathbf{0}$$

Let $\boldsymbol{\delta}_0 \equiv \mathrm{plim}\hat{\boldsymbol{\beta}}_{\mathrm{OLS}}$ and show that $\|\boldsymbol{\delta}_0\| \leq \|\boldsymbol{\beta}_0\|$.

20.33 (IV Efficiency Bound) Let

$$y_n = \mathbf{x}_n'\boldsymbol{\beta}_0 + \varepsilon_n, \qquad n = 1, \ldots, N$$

where $\{(\mathbf{x}_n, \varepsilon_n)\}$ is an i.i.d. sequence with finite second moments. Show that the asymptotic variance of CUAN IV estimators of $\boldsymbol{\beta}_0$ is bounded below by

$$\mathrm{Var}[\varepsilon_n]\left\{\mathrm{E}\left[\left(\mathbf{x}_n - \mathrm{Cov}[\mathbf{x}_n, \varepsilon_n]\frac{\varepsilon_n}{\mathrm{Var}[\varepsilon_n]}\right)\left(\mathbf{x}_n - \mathrm{Cov}[\mathbf{x}_n, \varepsilon_n]\frac{\varepsilon_n}{\mathrm{Var}[\varepsilon_n]}\right)'\right]\right\}^{-1}$$

Can you give an example of a model and estimator in which this bound is achieved asymptotically? Can you suggest a tighter bound?

[42] See Cragg (1983).

CHAPTER 21

THE GENERALIZED METHOD OF MOMENTS

In this chapter, we complete our survey of violations of the classical first moment assumption that $E[y_n \mid \mathbf{x}_n]$ is the linear function $\mathbf{x}_n'\boldsymbol{\beta}_0$. In addition to situations in which $\boldsymbol{\beta}_0$ is not the coefficient vector of this conditional mean, the first moment assumption is also violated when $E[y_n \mid \mathbf{x}_n] = \mu(\boldsymbol{\beta}_0; \mathbf{x}_n)$ is a nonlinear function of $\boldsymbol{\beta}_0$. Estimation of $\boldsymbol{\beta}_0$ generally cannot exploit the OLS method when this occurs. However, such straightforward alternatives as nonlinear least squares (NLS) are available.

We also extend our previous study of IV estimation to an estimation method called the *generalized method of moments* (GMM). This method contains both IV and NLS as special cases. Two insights are the keys to the GMM.

1. Moment equations are fundamental building blocks in all the estimation techniques that we have examined. In principle, we can construct estimators directly from moment equations, thereby using a "method of moments." Moreover, such equations need not be linear in the unknown parameters or the dependent variable y_n. It is necessary only that the moment equations define implicit functions of the data for the parameters.
2. The GLS technique that we explored with linear regression models carries over to the method of moments framework. According to an asymptotic distribution theory, the moment equations are effectively linear in both unknown parameters and dependent data as the sample size approaches infinity. Thereby, GLS plays its usual role providing a relatively efficient weighting of the data in estimation.

One can view the OLS estimator as a GMM estimator that exploits the orthogonality conditions, or moment equations,

$$E[\mathbf{x}_n(y_n - \mathbf{x}_n'\boldsymbol{\beta}_0)] = \mathbf{0}$$

These follow from the linear conditional mean of the classical linear model. The family of GMM estimators that we will describe generalizes the moment equations, replacing $\mathbf{x}_n(y_n - \mathbf{x}_n'\boldsymbol{\beta}_0)$ with a nonlinear function $\mathbf{g}(y_n, \mathbf{x}_n, \boldsymbol{\theta}_0)$ such that

$$\mathrm{E}[\mathbf{g}(y_n, \mathbf{x}_n, \boldsymbol{\theta}_0)] = \mathbf{0}$$

defines an implicit function for $\boldsymbol{\theta}_0$. In addition, rather than equating the number of moments to the number of parameters as in OLS, the GMM permits the number of moments to exceed the number of parameters. It combines the moments by weighting them in a fashion analogous to GLS.

We will illustrate the source of such generalizations with classic macroeconomic theory and econometrics based on the assumption of rational expectations.[1]

21.1 A RANDOM WALK

Hall (1978) deduced an implication of the life-cycle/permanent-income hypothesis: that the marginal utility of consumption is a first-order autoregressive process and that lagged values of such variables as disposable income and consumption do not have additional predictive power for the marginal utility of consumption. Written formally, Hall's model states that

$$\mathrm{E}[U'(C_t) \mid t-1] = \frac{1+\delta}{1+r} U'(C_{t-1}) \tag{21.1}$$

($t = 1, \ldots, N$) where $U'(\cdot)$ is marginal utility, C_t is consumption by a "representative" consumer in period t, δ is the subjective discount rate, and r is the constant real interest rate for borrowing and lending.[2] This hypothesis is commonly called "the random walk of consumption" hypothesis.

To test the hypothesis, Hall specified a quadratic utility function, thereby parameterizing (21.1) as[3]

$$\mathrm{E}[C_t \mid t-1] = \gamma_{01} + \gamma_{02} C_{t-1}$$

He fit a linear regression with consumption as the dependent variable and four lagged values of consumption as explanatory variables. He used quarterly seasonally adjusted data from 1948:I to 1977:I where C_t was real consumption per capita of nondurables and services measured in 1972 dollars and obtained the OLS fit[4,5]

$$C_t = \underset{(8.3)}{8.2} + \underset{(0.092)}{1.130}\, C_{t-1} - \underset{(0.142)}{0.040}\, C_{t-2} + \underset{(0.142)}{0.030}\, C_{t-3} - \underset{(0.093)}{0.113}\, C_{t-4} + \hat{\varepsilon}_t$$

The F statistic for the null hypothesis that the coefficients of C_{t-2}, C_{t-3}, and C_{t-4} are all equal to zero equaled 1.7, which has a probability value of 0.171. Thus, Hall found little evidence against the random walk theory.

He also fit a linear regression that included lagged values of real disposable income per capita (Y_t) as additional explanatory variables, obtaining[6]

---

[1] Romer (1996, Ch. 7) inspired this introductory example.

[2] Sargent (1987) is a good reference for such dynamic macroeconomic theory.

[3] This specification is not really a random walk. A pure random walk is the special case in which $\gamma_{01} = 0$ and $\gamma_{02} = 1$. In the model, this occurs when $\delta = r$.

[4] See Hall (1978, p. 983). The OLS estimated standard errors appear below the estimated coefficients in parentheses.

[5] The notation 1948:I refers to the first quarter of the year 1948. Roman numerals after the colon (I, II, III, IV) refer to quarters of the year.

[6] Hall (1978, p. 983).

$$C_t = \underset{(11)}{-\ 23} + \underset{(0.047)}{1.076}\, C_{t-1} + \underset{(0.043)}{0.049}\, Y_{t-1} - \underset{(0.052)}{0.051}\, Y_{t-2}$$
$$- \underset{(0.051)}{0.023}\, Y_{t-3} - \underset{(0.037)}{0.024}\, Y_{t-4} + \hat{\eta}_t$$

In this case, the F statistic for zero coefficients on the disposable income variables was 2.0 with a probability value equal to 0.100, providing weak evidence against the theory.[7]

Hall's work has been influential and has sparked many responses. For example, Campbell and Mankiw (1989) noted that lagged income may not help predict consumption simply because lagged values of income do not predict changes in *income*. If a traditional Keynesian consumption function were appropriate, then one might specify that

$$\mathrm{E}[C_t - C_{t-1} \mid Y_t - Y_{t-1}] = \gamma_0 (Y_t - Y_{t-1})$$

where γ_0 is the marginal propensity to consume out of disposable income. If lagged values of income are uncorrelated with changes in income, then failures to predict consumption with the former do not necessarily support the life-cycle/permanent-income hypothesis. Indeed, Campbell and Mankiw find that lagged changes in income have little predictive power for changes in income.

Campbell and Mankiw (1989) took another approach, testing the random walk hypothesis against a particular generalization of Hall's model. They suggested that a fraction of consumers β_{02} simply spends its current income (so that $\gamma_0 = 1$), while the remainder follows Hall's model. If this is true, then

$$C_t - C_{t-1} = \beta_{01} + \beta_{02} (Y_t - Y_{t-1}) + \varepsilon_t \tag{21.2}$$

where ε_t is the unpredictable change in the consumption of the fraction of consumers behaving according to Hall's random walk theory.[8] Note that in this specification, Campbell and Mankiw restricted the coefficient of C_{t-1} to equal one. This restriction is not rejected by hypothesis tests and does not change other inferences qualitatively.

Furthermore, Campbell and Mankiw argued, OLS estimation of β_{02} is inappropriate to test Hall's model as a special case, $H_0 : \beta_{02} = 0$. Changes in income and changes in permanent income will be correlated so that

$$\mathrm{E}[\varepsilon_t \mid Y_t - Y_{t-1}] \neq 0$$

and

$$\begin{aligned}\mathrm{E}[C_t - C_{t-1} \mid Y_t - Y_{t-1}] &= \beta_{01} + \beta_{02} (Y_t - Y_{t-1}) + \mathrm{E}[\varepsilon_t \mid Y_t - Y_{t-1}] \\ &\neq \beta_{01} + \beta_{02} (Y_t - Y_{t-1})\end{aligned}$$

This is a violation of the fundamental assumption (First Moment, p. 110) supporting the property that the OLS estimator is unbiased for $\boldsymbol{\beta}_0$.

To estimate β_{02}, Campbell and Mankiw use 2SLS, which is a special case of a *generalized method of moments* (GMM) estimator that we discuss in this chapter. They motivate the estimator

[7] Hall also found a statistically significant relationship with an index of stock prices. Our account is necessarily much abbreviated.

[8] One can also think of β_{02} more generally as the product of the marginal propensity to consume out of income (γ_0) and the fraction of consumers who adhere to a Keynesian consumption function.

with the theoretical prediction of Hall's model that no variable realized before period t will be correlated with ε_t. In particular, for every positive integer j

$$\mathrm{E}\big[(C_{t-j} - C_{t-j-1})\,\varepsilon_t \,|\, t-1\big] = 0$$

and, by the law of iterated expectations,

$$\mathrm{E}[(C_{t-j} - C_{t-j-1})\varepsilon_t] = \mathrm{Cov}[C_{t-j} - C_{t-j-1}, \varepsilon_t] = 0 \tag{21.3}$$

Such *moment equations* are restrictions on the data-generating process that yield information about the unknown β_{02}: substituting (21.2) into (21.3) gives the orthogonality restriction

$$\mathrm{E}\big[(C_{t-j} - C_{t-j-1})\big(C_t - C_{t-1} - \beta_{01} - \beta_{02}(Y_t - Y_{t-1})\big)\big] = 0$$

or

$$\begin{aligned}\mathrm{E}[(C_{t-j} - C_{t-j-1})(C_t - C_{t-1})] =& \beta_{01}\,\mathrm{E}[C_{t-j} - C_{t-j-1}] \\ &+ \beta_{02}\,\mathrm{E}[(C_{t-j} - C_{t-j-1})(Y_t - Y_{t-1})]\end{aligned} \tag{21.4}$$

$j = 1, 2, 3, \ldots$.

The 2SLS estimator exploits these moment equations. In Chapter 20, we produced this estimator as a solution to estimating a system of linear simultaneous equations. In this chapter, we will interpret 2SLS as a GMM procedure. Note particularly that there are more moment equations than unknown parameters. The GMM is a method for combining an overabundance of moment equations. We will show how 2SLS is an example below.

Campbell and Mankiw compute the 2SLS estimator for (21.1) after making several adjustments. First, they replace the levels of consumption and income with logs of these variables.[9] Second, they use a different sample than Hall did: quarterly data from 1953:3 to 1986:4. Third, they discard the moment condition for $j = 1$.[10] Instead of reporting their results, we reproduce them using quarterly data from the sample period 1953:3 to 1986:4 denominated in chained 1992 dollars.[11]

The 2SLS estimator can be computed in two OLS steps (or stages) and it is useful to report the results of both steps. In the first step, we regress the explanatory variables on instrumental variables. Campbell and Mankiw regress the first difference in the log of disposable income (x_t) on lags 2 through 5 of the first difference in the log of consumption (y_t):

$$\begin{aligned}\hat{x}_t =& -\underset{(0.0020)}{0.0066} + \underset{(0.162)}{0.102}\, y_{t-2} + \underset{(0.168)}{0.301}\, y_{t-3} \\ &+ \underset{(0.168)}{0.374}\, y_{t-4} - \underset{(0.159)}{0.506}\, y_{t-5}\end{aligned} \tag{21.5}$$

The R^2 for this fit is 0.123 so that the fit is a loose one; however, the F test for the null hypothesis that the coefficients of the zs are all zero has a probability value of 0.01.[12] Therefore, lagged changes in consumption do help predict changes in income. In contrast, the lagged values of income changes give the OLS fit

---

9 Campbell and Mankiw (1989, p. 190) argue that aggregate consumption series exhibit increases in the mean and variance of first differences over time. The logarithmic transformation helps to stabilize both. In addition, the linear specification is justified by a particularly restrictive form for preferences.

10 We discuss their reason in Chapter 25.

11 See appendix.

12 The OLS R^2 is the squared length of $\hat{\mu} - \iota\bar{y}$ divided by the squared length of $\mathbf{y} - \iota\bar{y}$. See Exercise 3.19.

$$\hat{x}_t = \underset{(0.0016)}{0.0097} + \underset{(0.087)}{0.027}\, x_{t-2} + \underset{(0.086)}{0.171}\, x_{t-3} - \underset{(0.086)}{0.089}\, x_{t-4} - \underset{(0.086)}{0.201}\, x_{t-5}$$

with an R^2 equal to 0.077 and an F test with probability value 0.035.

This confirms qualitatively the concern about the power of Hall's test expressed by Campbell and Mankiw. It appears that lagged income changes are relatively weak predictors of income changes. Moreover, lagged consumption is a somewhat better predictor of income changes than lagged income itself. These are important statistics for such IV estimators as 2SLS because it is essential that the covariance on the RHS of (21.4) is not zero. Otherwise, β_{02} does not actually enter into this equation and it cannot be used to help estimate this parameter.

In the second step of the 2SLS estimator, we use the fitted values from the first step regression (21.5) in place of income change itself as the explanatory variable in the OLS estimation (21.2). Intuitively, this explanatory variable is a component of income change that is uncorrelated with ε_t because it is the part predictable with lagged changes in consumption. The fitted equation is

$$y_t = \underset{(0.0011)}{0.0045} + \underset{(0.114)}{0.435}\, \hat{x}_t + \hat{\varepsilon}_t \tag{21.6}$$

where y_t is the first difference in log consumption and $\hat{x}_t$ is the fitted value in (21.5).[13] One can see from the standard error 0.114 that the estimated coefficient 0.435 is (statistically) significantly different from zero. This number is also significant for the theory that Campbell and Mankiw propose: taken literally, it implies that approximately 40% of the U. S. population consumes out of total, not permanent, income.[14]

Campbell and Mankiw make an *ad hoc* adjustment to Hall's model when they take logarithmic transformations of the consumption and income variables. Strictly speaking, the marginal utility of consumption cannot be proportional to the logarithm of consumption. Nor for that matter is the linear specification employed by Hall very satisfactory.[15] Thus, Hall also suggests (but does not estimate) the constant-relative-risk-aversion utility, $U(C) = C^{\gamma_0}/\gamma_0$. Hansen and Singleton (1982) implemented essentially this form in one of the earliest applications of GMM.[16] They also permitted the interest rate r to vary over time.[17] This utility function turns (21.1) into

$$\mathrm{E}[C_t^{\gamma_0 - 1} \mid t-1] = \frac{1+\delta_0}{1+r_t} C_{t-1}^{\gamma_0 - 1}$$

---

13 The standard errors in this equation are not those from the OLS fit. They are adjusted to take into account that the explanatory variable $\hat{x}_t$ has been estimated and therefore contributes an additional source of variation into the OLS estimator.

14 This rejection of the random walk hypothesis does not rest solely on the IV estimation technique. If we repeat Hall's original test within the framework of Campbell and Mankiw, we also reject the random walk hypothesis. For this sample, which differs from Hall's,

$$\log C_t = \underset{(0.010)}{-0.011} \underset{(0.090)}{+1.278} \log C_{t-1} \underset{(0.146)}{-0.239} \log C_{t-2} \underset{(0.146)}{+0.110} \log C_{t-3} \underset{(0.090)}{-0.148} \log C_{t-4}$$

and the F test for whether the last three coefficients equal zero has a probability value of 0.001.

15 Linear marginal utility implies a consumption level of satiation or "bliss." Also, it does not allow risk aversion in preferences.

16 Strictly speaking, they apply generalized IV, which is a special case of GMM.

17 Campbell and Mankiw (1989) also analyze the case of a variable interest rate.

To accommodate this functional form, Hansen and Singleton write the moment equations analogous to (21.3) as

$$\mathrm{E}\left\{ z_{tj} \left[\frac{1+r_t}{1+\delta_0} \left(\frac{C_t}{C_{t-1}} \right)^{\gamma_0 - 1} - 1 \right] \middle| t-1 \right\} = 0 \tag{21.7}$$

for instrumental variables z_{tj}, $j = 1, 2, 3, \ldots$.[18]

Given the nonlinear-in-parameters form of these moments, we will show how it is natural to consider instrumental variables such as

$$(1 + r_{t-j}) \left(\frac{C_{t-j}}{C_{t-j-1}} \right)^{\gamma_0 - 1} \quad \text{and} \quad (1 + r_{t-j}) \left(\frac{C_{t-j}}{C_{t-j-1}} \right)^{\gamma_0 - 1} \log \frac{C_{t-j}}{C_{t-j-1}}$$

These are partial derivatives of the moment in (21.7) with respect to the parameters $(1 + \delta_0)^{-1}$ and γ_0, but they have been evaluated at lagged values of the variables to preserve orthogonality. The resulting moments are nonlinear in both variables and parameters. Yet these equations still provide the necessary information about a population to estimate its parameters with a random sample.

21.2 DEFINITION OF GMM

In this section we will describe the *generalized method of moments* (GMM) estimator in broad terms.[19] Following a general definition, we will relate the GMM to three special cases. Two of these cases, ML and 2SLS, have already been discussed extensively. The other case, nonlinear least squares, we have touched on only in the context of numerical optimization methods.[20]

First, we will note how the MLE implicitly exploits moment equations. Such moment equations are the basis of all the GMM estimators that we will discuss. We also articulate the (ordinary) *method of moments* (MM) and interpret IV as an example: the IV fitted coefficients equate sample moments to analogous population moments.

Second, we focus on a nonlinear aspect of GMM with a discussion of *nonlinear least squares* (NLS). Here our purpose is to highlight the nature of optimal instrumental variables for a particular nonlinear estimation problem. The key property is that such instruments are related to the gradient of the regression function with respect to the parameters. This is a generalization of $\mathbf{x}_n = \partial \left(\mathbf{x}_n' \boldsymbol{\beta} \right) / \partial \boldsymbol{\beta}$ as the optimal instrumental variables for the classical linear regression model.

Third, we reinterpret the 2SLS estimator as an outcome of having more moment equations than unknown parameters. Instead of fitting sample moments to population moments, 2SLS minimizes a generalized distance between sample and population moments. Two elements, moments and generalized distance, comprise the core of GMM.

Generally speaking, the approach of GMM estimation rests on probability model specifications that imply that there is a sequence of vector-valued empirical moment functions $\mathbf{g}_N(\boldsymbol{\theta})$ with the property that

[18] Through a series of examples, Newey and McFadden (1994) give a thorough analysis of these moment equations and GMM.

[19] Burguete et al. (1982) and Hansen (1982) proposed the GMM formulation.

[20] See Section 16.4.3 (Gauss–Newton Regression).

$$\mathbf{g}_N(\boldsymbol{\theta}_0) \xrightarrow{p} \mathbf{0} \quad \text{and} \quad \mathbf{g}_N(\boldsymbol{\theta}_1) \stackrel{p}{\nrightarrow} \mathbf{0} \text{ if } \boldsymbol{\theta}_1 \neq \boldsymbol{\theta}_0 \tag{21.8}$$

Given $\mathbf{g}_N(\boldsymbol{\theta})$, one also chooses a symmetric positive semidefinite matrix $\mathbf{C}_N$ and thereby specifies an estimator that minimizes the (generalized) length of the empirical vector $\mathbf{g}_N(\boldsymbol{\theta})$:

$$\begin{aligned} \hat{\boldsymbol{\theta}}_{\text{GMM}} &\equiv \operatorname*{argmin}_{\boldsymbol{\theta}\in\boldsymbol{\Theta}} \|\mathbf{g}_N(\boldsymbol{\theta})\|_{\mathbf{C}_N} \\ &= \operatorname*{argmin}_{\boldsymbol{\theta}\in\boldsymbol{\Theta}} \mathbf{g}_N(\boldsymbol{\theta})'\mathbf{C}_N\,\mathbf{g}_N(\boldsymbol{\theta}) \end{aligned} \tag{21.9}$$

Thus, $\hat{\boldsymbol{\theta}}_{\text{GMM}}$ possesses a sample property that is analogous to the asymptotic (or population) property of $\boldsymbol{\theta}_0$ given by (21.8). The choice of $\mathbf{C}_N$ is, of course, important.

Typically, $\mathbf{g}_N(\boldsymbol{\theta})$ is derived as a set of moment conditions

$$\mathrm{E}[\mathbf{g}_j(U;\boldsymbol{\theta}_0)] = 0$$

for functions $\mathbf{g}_j(\cdot)$ ($j = 1, \ldots, J$) of the observable random variable U and the unknown parameter vector $\boldsymbol{\theta}_0$. It is convenient to stack these $\mathbf{g}_j(\cdot)$ into the vector-valued function $\mathbf{g}(\cdot) \equiv \left[\mathbf{g}_j(\cdot);\ j = 1, \ldots, J\right]'$ so that we denote

$$\mathbf{g}_N(\boldsymbol{\theta}) \equiv \mathrm{E}_N[\mathbf{g}(U;\boldsymbol{\theta})]$$

One can motivate all of the estimators that we have discussed to this point within this framework.

21.2.1 Turning Moments into Estimators

As a familiar example of GMM, reconsider the MLE corresponding to the average log-likelihood function $\mathrm{E}_N[L(\boldsymbol{\theta})]$. Under the assumptions of Lemma 14.3 (Score Identity, p. 300),

$$\mathrm{E}[L_{\boldsymbol{\theta}}(\boldsymbol{\theta}_0)] = \mathbf{0}$$

and, provided that a law of large numbers also applies,

$$\mathrm{E}_N[L_{\boldsymbol{\theta}}(\boldsymbol{\theta}_0)] \xrightarrow{p} \mathbf{0}$$

We have considered MLEs that solve the normal equations:

$$\mathrm{E}_N[L_{\boldsymbol{\theta}}(\hat{\boldsymbol{\theta}})] = \mathbf{0}$$

This is equivalent to solving the minimum distance problem

$$\hat{\boldsymbol{\theta}} = \operatorname*{argmin}_{\boldsymbol{\theta}} \mathrm{E}_N[L_{\boldsymbol{\theta}}(\boldsymbol{\theta})]'\mathbf{C}_N\,\mathrm{E}_N[L_{\boldsymbol{\theta}}(\boldsymbol{\theta})]$$

for any $\mathbf{C}_N$ that is positive definite. Therefore, the MLE is a special case of the GMM estimator in which $\mathbf{g}(U;\boldsymbol{\theta})$ is the score of a log-likelihood function $L_{\boldsymbol{\theta}}(\boldsymbol{\theta};U)$.

Note also that the MLE includes problems in which the score function may be a nonlinear function of both data and parameters. There is nothing inherent in likelihood functions that would cause them to produce linear score functions in general. Nevertheless, the score identity is a fairly general property and this places ML within the GMM framework.

The unrestricted MLE is also a special GMM estimator because it succeeds in setting the length of the moment functions to zero. Thus, evaluated at the MLE, the sample expectation of the score vector equals the population expectation exactly. There is a direct analogy between the score identity and the normal equations.

One can also find other GMM estimators that equate the sample moments to the population moments. This typically occurs in situations in which the number of moment equations equals the number of unknown parameters ($J = K$). Then the number of equations equals the number of unknowns and $\mathbf{g}_N(\hat{\boldsymbol{\theta}}_{\text{GMM}}) = \mathbf{0}$ may define an implicit function for $\hat{\boldsymbol{\theta}}_{\text{GMM}}$. If it does, then the implicit function theorem tells us that the matrix of partial derivatives $\partial \mathbf{g}_N(\boldsymbol{\theta})/\partial \boldsymbol{\theta}'$ must be nonsingular at $\hat{\boldsymbol{\theta}}_{\text{GMM}}$ and

$$\mathbf{g}_N(\hat{\boldsymbol{\theta}}_{\text{GMM}}) = \mathbf{0} \qquad \Leftrightarrow \qquad \left\| \mathbf{g}_N(\hat{\boldsymbol{\theta}}) \right\|_{\mathbf{C}_N} = 0$$

provided only that $\mathbf{C}_N$ is positive definite. A simple choice for $\mathbf{C}_N$ would be the identity matrix $\mathbf{I}_J$.

Method of moments (MM) estimators are a leading example. In MM, the sample moments and the functions of parameters are additively separable:

$$g_{Nj}(\boldsymbol{\theta}) = \mathrm{E}_N[U^j] - \mu_j(\boldsymbol{\theta})$$

where $\mu_j(\boldsymbol{\theta}_0) \equiv \mathrm{E}[U^j]$ is the jth moment of U. The function $\boldsymbol{\mu}(\boldsymbol{\theta}) \equiv \left[\mu_j(\boldsymbol{\theta})\right]'$ must be invertible so that the MM estimator is

$$\hat{\boldsymbol{\theta}}_{\text{MOM}} = \boldsymbol{\mu}^{-1}\left(\mathrm{E}_N[U^j]\right)$$

IV is an MM estimator, using all moments up to second order. Given the IV model described in Assumptions 20.1 and 20.2 (p. 499), these moments are

$$\begin{aligned}
\mathrm{E}[\mathbf{x}_n\mathbf{x}_n'] &= \mathbf{D}_{xx} \\
\mathrm{E}[\mathbf{x}_n y_n] &= \mathbf{D}_{xx}\boldsymbol{\beta}_0 + \boldsymbol{\rho}_0 \\
\mathrm{E}[\mathbf{z}_n\mathbf{x}_n'] &= \mathbf{D}_{zx} \\
\mathrm{E}[\mathbf{z}_n y_n] &= \mathbf{D}_{zx}\boldsymbol{\beta}_0 \\
\mathrm{E}[y_n^2] &= \sigma_0^2 + 2\cdot\boldsymbol{\beta}_0'\boldsymbol{\rho}_0 + \boldsymbol{\beta}_0'\mathbf{D}_{xx}\boldsymbol{\beta}_0
\end{aligned}$$

assuming that one element in both $\mathbf{x}_n$ and $\mathbf{z}_n$ is the constant 1.[21] Choosing values of the unknown parameters so that the corresponding sample moments equal these population moments we obtain an implicit function for the MM estimator:

$$\mathrm{E}_N[\mathbf{x}_n\mathbf{x}_n'] = \hat{\mathbf{D}}_{xx} \tag{21.10}$$

$$\mathrm{E}_N[\mathbf{x}_n y_n] = \hat{\mathbf{D}}_{xx}\hat{\boldsymbol{\beta}} + \hat{\boldsymbol{\rho}} \tag{21.11}$$

$$\mathrm{E}_N[\mathbf{z}_n\mathbf{x}_n'] = \hat{\mathbf{D}}_{zx} \tag{21.12}$$

$$\mathrm{E}_N[\mathbf{z}_n y_n] = \hat{\mathbf{D}}_{zx}\hat{\boldsymbol{\beta}} \tag{21.13}$$

$$\mathrm{E}_N[y_n^2] = \hat{\sigma}^2 + 2\cdot\hat{\boldsymbol{\beta}}'\hat{\boldsymbol{\rho}} + \hat{\boldsymbol{\beta}}'\hat{\mathbf{D}}_{xx}\hat{\boldsymbol{\beta}} \tag{21.14}$$

This system has a direct solution. Combining (21.12) with (21.13) gives

[21] If $\mathbf{x}_n$ and $\mathbf{z}_n$ both contain the constant 1, then the first moments of all the other elements of $\mathbf{x}_n$ and $\mathbf{z}_n$ appear in the matrices $\mathrm{E}[\mathbf{x}_n\mathbf{x}_n']$ and $\mathrm{E}[\mathbf{z}_n\mathbf{z}_n']$ and the first moment of y_n appears in both $\mathrm{E}[\mathbf{x}_n y_n]$ and $\mathrm{E}[\mathbf{z}_n y_n]$.

$$\hat{\boldsymbol{\beta}} = \hat{\mathbf{D}}_{zx}^{-1} \mathrm{E}_N[\mathbf{z}_n y_n] = \left(\mathbf{Z}'\mathbf{X}\right)^{-1} \mathbf{Z}'\mathbf{y} = \hat{\boldsymbol{\beta}}_{\mathrm{IV}}$$

Substituting this result and (21.10) into (21.11), we obtain

$$\hat{\rho} = \mathrm{E}_N[\mathbf{x}_n y_n] - \hat{\mathbf{D}}_{xx}\hat{\boldsymbol{\beta}} = \frac{1}{N} \cdot \mathbf{X}'(\mathbf{y} - \mathbf{X}\hat{\boldsymbol{\beta}}_{\mathrm{IV}})$$

so that the covariance between the explanatory variables and the latent ε_n is estimated with the sample covariance between the explanatory variables and the IV fitted residuals. Finally, substituting our expressions for $\hat{\boldsymbol{\beta}}$ and $\hat{\rho}$ into (21.14) gives

$$\begin{aligned}
\hat{\sigma}^2 &= \mathrm{E}_N[y_n^2] - 2 \cdot \hat{\rho}'\hat{\boldsymbol{\beta}} - \hat{\boldsymbol{\beta}}'\hat{\mathbf{D}}_{xx}\hat{\boldsymbol{\beta}} \\
&= \frac{1}{N} \cdot \left[\mathbf{y}'\mathbf{y} - 2 \cdot \hat{\boldsymbol{\beta}}_{\mathrm{IV}}\mathbf{X}'(\mathbf{y} - \mathbf{X}\hat{\boldsymbol{\beta}}_{\mathrm{IV}}) - \hat{\boldsymbol{\beta}}_{\mathrm{IV}}'\mathbf{X}'\mathbf{X}\hat{\boldsymbol{\beta}}_{\mathrm{IV}}\right] \\
&= \frac{1}{N} \cdot \left[\mathbf{y}'\mathbf{y} - 2 \cdot \hat{\boldsymbol{\beta}}_{\mathrm{IV}}\mathbf{X}'\mathbf{y} + \hat{\boldsymbol{\beta}}_{\mathrm{IV}}'\mathbf{X}'\mathbf{X}\hat{\boldsymbol{\beta}}_{\mathrm{IV}}\right] \\
&= \frac{1}{N} \cdot \left(\mathbf{y} - \mathbf{X}\hat{\boldsymbol{\beta}}_{\mathrm{IV}}\right)'\left(\mathbf{y} - \mathbf{X}\hat{\boldsymbol{\beta}}_{\mathrm{IV}}\right)
\end{aligned}$$

which equals the sample variance of the IV fitted residuals. Thus, we arrive at the IV estimators described in Proposition 18 (Asymptotic Distribution of IV, p. 500) through the MM.

In retrospect, this interpretation of IV implies that we could have *derived* the OLS estimator from such moments in Chapter 6.[22] There we began our statistical assumptions with $\mathrm{E}[\mathbf{y} \,|\, \mathbf{X}] = \mathbf{X}\boldsymbol{\beta}_0$. Given this, we also have the marginal mean

$$\mathrm{E}[\mathbf{x}_n(y_n - \mathbf{x}_n'\boldsymbol{\beta}_0)] = \mathbf{0}$$

and we can obtain the OLS estimator as the GMM/IV counterpart.

The OLS estimator is, of course, also the MLE when $\mathbf{y}$ is normally distributed conditional on $\mathbf{X}$. But as we have already seen, the normality assumption is not necessary to many of the properties of the OLS estimator. Based only on the moment condition $\mathrm{E}[\mathbf{y} \,|\, \mathbf{X}] = \mathbf{X}\beta_0$, we found that $\hat{\boldsymbol{\beta}}_{\mathrm{OLS}}$ is unbiased. Now one sees that we can also motivate the OLS estimator itself with this moment condition. We have shown in addition that the normality assumption is not necessary for an approximate distribution theory for $\hat{\boldsymbol{\beta}}_{\mathrm{OLS}}$ based on its asymptotic behavior as $N \to \infty$.[23] It is feasible, therefore, to loosen the normality assumption to moment assumptions and retain many statistical properties.

Two ingredients make such relaxation feasible, moments that obey a law of large numbers and a central limit theorem. These ingredients generally appear in the recipes for GMM estimation methods (that do not rest on distributional assumptions) and the method of ML (that do).

21.2.2 Nonlinear Least Squares

We have just described the MLE as an estimator that rests on nonlinear moment conditions. It is useful to explore a particular MLE more closely in order to see a more detailed example

22 We chose not to motivate the OLS estimator by the MM in order to accelerate the exposition of the entire classical linear regression model. Using an MM approach is a sensible alternative to our choice.

23 Proposition 15 (Asymptotic Distribution of OLS, p. 257).

of nonlinear moment conditions. The nonlinear normal regression model is well suited to this purpose. Consider a situation in which

$$y_n \sim \mathfrak{N}[\mu(\boldsymbol{\beta}_0; \mathbf{x}_n),\ \sigma_0^2]$$

independently for each $n = 1, \ldots, N$. The conditional mean of y_n given $\mathbf{x}_n$,

$$\mathrm{E}[y_n \,|\, \mathbf{x}_n] = \mu(\boldsymbol{\beta}_0; \mathbf{x}_n) \tag{21.15}$$

is a nonlinear function. This example contains another specific way in which the first moment assumption (Assumption 2, p. 110) of the classical linear model might be violated.

The conditional log-likelihood function of this model has the same general functional form as described in Example 14.11:

$$\mathrm{E}_N[L(\boldsymbol{\theta})] = -\frac{1}{2}\log(2\pi\sigma^2) - \frac{\mathrm{E}_N\left[\left(y_n - \mu(\boldsymbol{\beta}; \mathbf{x}_n)\right)^2\right]}{2\sigma^2}$$

and we see that the MLE for $\boldsymbol{\beta}$ amounts to minimizing the sum of squared fitted residuals over the nonlinear functions $\mu(\boldsymbol{\beta}; \mathbf{x}_n)$ $(n = 1, \ldots, N)$. As in the linear regression case, the estimation of σ_0^2 is irrelevant to that of $\boldsymbol{\beta}_0$ so that the MLE corresponds to NLS.

The score for $\boldsymbol{\beta}$ is

$$\mathrm{E}_N[L_{\boldsymbol{\beta}}(\boldsymbol{\theta})] = \frac{1}{\sigma^2} \cdot \mathrm{E}_N\left[\mu_{\boldsymbol{\beta}}(\boldsymbol{\beta}; \mathbf{x}_n)\left(y_n - \mu(\boldsymbol{\beta}; \mathbf{x}_n)\right)\right]$$

where

$$\mu_{\boldsymbol{\beta}}(\boldsymbol{\beta}; \mathbf{x}_n) \equiv \frac{\partial \mu(\boldsymbol{\beta}; \mathbf{x}_n)}{\partial \boldsymbol{\beta}}$$

and

$$\mathrm{E}_N\left[\mu_{\boldsymbol{\beta}}(\hat{\boldsymbol{\beta}}_{\mathrm{NLS}}; \mathbf{x}_n)\left(y_n - \mu(\hat{\boldsymbol{\beta}}_{\mathrm{NLS}}; \mathbf{x}_n)\right)\right] = \mathbf{0} \tag{21.16}$$

defines an implicit function for the estimator $\hat{\boldsymbol{\beta}}_{\mathrm{NLS}}$ in terms of the data. Using the law of iterated expectations, we can confirm directly that these normal equations correspond to the population moments

$$\mathrm{E}\left[\mu_{\boldsymbol{\beta}}(\boldsymbol{\beta}_0; \mathbf{x}_n)\left(y_n - \mu(\boldsymbol{\beta}_0; \mathbf{x}_n)\right)\right] = \mathbf{0}$$

Because it is sufficient that $\mathrm{E}[y_n \,|\, \mathbf{x}_n] = \mu(\boldsymbol{\beta}_0; \mathbf{x}_n)$ for these population moments to hold, one may infer that under reasonable conditions the NLS estimator will be a consistent estimator for nonnormal conditional distributions as well.

Note also that when y_n is conditionally normally distributed, one may view the partial derivatives $\partial\mu(\boldsymbol{\beta}; \mathbf{x}_n)/\partial\boldsymbol{\beta}$ as efficient instrumental variables. Relative to OLS, NLS requires orthogonality between the fitted residuals and these derivatives, instead of just $\mathbf{x}_n$. The relative efficiency of these derivatives as instrumental variables carries over to nonnormal distributions as we will show in Section 21.4.4.

21.2.3 Two-Stage Least Squares

The MLE is a special GMM estimator in the sense that the number of moments equals the number of unknown parameters. In our introductory example concerning the random walk hypothesis, there are *more* moment conditions than parameters.[24] As a result, the J sample moment equations may comprise too many equations for any one K-dimensional $\boldsymbol{\theta}$ to satisfy simultaneously.

Campbell and Mankiw (1989) use *two-stage least squares* (2SLS) in this situation. The 2SLS procedure is an example of another aspect of the GMM, its combination of all of the chosen moments. Like IV, there are moment conditions

$$\begin{aligned}
\mathrm{E}_N[\mathbf{z}_n\varepsilon_n] &\xrightarrow{p} \mathbf{0} \\
\mathrm{E}_N[\mathbf{z}_n\mathbf{x}_n'] &\xrightarrow{p} \mathrm{E}[\mathbf{z}_n\mathbf{x}_n'] \equiv \mathbf{D}_{zx} \\
\mathrm{E}_N[\mathbf{z}_n\mathbf{z}_n'] &\xrightarrow{p} \mathrm{E}[\mathbf{z}_n\mathbf{z}_n'] \equiv \mathbf{D}_{zz}
\end{aligned}$$

relating the latent disturbance $\varepsilon_n = y_n - \mathbf{x}_n'\boldsymbol{\beta}_0$, the explanatory variables $\mathbf{x}_n$, and the instrumental variables $\mathbf{z}_n$. One assumes that the matrices $\mathbf{D}_{zx}$ and $\mathbf{D}_{zz}$ are finite nonsingular matrices. Unlike IV, the number of instrumental variables J exceeds the number of explanatory variables K. Focusing on the relationship among the moments, we have

$$\mathrm{E}_N[\mathbf{z}_n y_n] = \mathrm{E}_N[\mathbf{z}_n\mathbf{x}_n']\boldsymbol{\beta}_0 + \mathrm{E}_N[\mathbf{z}_n\varepsilon_n] \tag{21.17}$$

When $J = K$, we convert this into an estimation equation by replacing $\mathrm{E}_N[\mathbf{z}_n\varepsilon_n]$ with its probability limit and $\boldsymbol{\beta}_0$ with $\hat{\boldsymbol{\beta}}_{\mathrm{IV}}$.

When $J > K$, the estimation problem is similar to that of GLS because we also assume that

$$\sqrt{N}\,\mathrm{E}_N[\mathbf{z}_n\varepsilon_n] \xrightarrow{d} \mathfrak{N}(\mathbf{0}, \sigma_0^2 \cdot \mathbf{D}_{zz}) \tag{21.18}$$

In (21.17), the moment vector $\mathrm{E}_N[\mathbf{z}_n y_n]$ is comparable to a vector of dependent variables and the $J \times K$ moment matrix $\mathrm{E}_N[\mathbf{z}_n\mathbf{x}_n']$ is comparable to a full-column rank matrix of explanatory variables. According to (21.18), the "residuals" $\mathrm{E}_N[\mathbf{z}_n\varepsilon_n]$ are (approximately) normally distributed with mean zero and variance matrix $\sigma_0^2 \cdot \mathbf{D}_{zz}$. A "feasible GLS" procedure is to estimate $\boldsymbol{\beta}_0$ as the minimizer of the generalized distance between $\mathrm{E}_N[\mathbf{z}_n y_n]$ and $\mathrm{E}_N[\mathbf{z}_n\mathbf{x}_n']\boldsymbol{\beta}$ with respect to the inverse of an estimated variance matrix. Indeed, the 2SLS estimator solves[25]

$$\begin{aligned}
\hat{\boldsymbol{\beta}}_{2\mathrm{SLS}} &= \underset{\boldsymbol{\beta}}{\operatorname{argmin}} \left\| \mathrm{E}_N[\mathbf{z}_n y_n] - \mathrm{E}_N[\mathbf{z}_n\mathbf{x}_n']\boldsymbol{\beta} \right\|^2_{(\mathrm{E}_N[\mathbf{z}_n\mathbf{z}_n'])^{-1}} \\
&= \underset{\boldsymbol{\beta}}{\operatorname{argmin}}\, (\mathbf{y} - \mathbf{X}\boldsymbol{\beta})'\,\mathbf{Z}\left(\mathbf{Z}'\mathbf{Z}\right)^{-1}\mathbf{Z}'\,(\mathbf{y} - \mathbf{X}\boldsymbol{\beta}) \\
&= \left(\mathbf{X}'\mathbf{P}_{\mathbf{Z}}\mathbf{X}\right)^{-1}\mathbf{X}'\mathbf{P}_{\mathbf{Z}}\mathbf{y}
\end{aligned}$$

The combination of "extra" moment equations through generalized minimum distance is a way in which GMM generalizes the MM. Because there is no exact solution to all the moment equations, GMM finds an approximate one. It balances the extent to which each moment equation

[24] See equation (21.4).

[25] The scalar σ_0^2 in the variance matrix does not affect the minimization and we omit it.

is satisfied according to the weight matrix $\mathbf{C}_N$. Setting $\mathbf{C}_N$ to equal the inverse of an estimator of the variance of the sample moments is a familiar choice, akin to GLS. We explain in Section 21.4 that GLS and GMM are entirely analogous in this respect.

GMM estimation offers a new interpretation of all the estimators that we have studied. For example, the method of moments motivates the OLS estimator, a procedure that we proposed in Part I as simply a practical method to fit multivariate relationships. With a normality assumption, OLS is the MLE. But without such an assumption, OLS is still a relatively efficient linear unbiased estimator given certain moment conditions. These moment conditions are a basis for constructing the estimator itself.

The GMM also expands the kinds of probability models that one can propose and estimate. It is not necessary to specify a p.f. and, therefore, all the moments of a random variable. One can predicate statistical inference on a limited set of moments. Thus, we are considering an approach that diminishes the specificity of the assumptions.

Moment equations and minimum generalized distance are the essential components of GMM. The IV estimator anticipates estimation based on moments. In GMM, the nature of moments is generalized in two ways. First, the moments can be nonlinear functions of the unknown parameters. Second, there may be more moments than parameters. The GLS estimator illustrates estimation based on minimizing a generalized distance in an inverse variance matrix. In GMM, these two concepts come together in a single estimation strategy. To describe the theory, we begin with identification.

21.3 IDENTIFICATION

Before setting out to construct an estimator of the parameter vector, one must first confirm that the parameter vector is identified. The definition of identification of $\boldsymbol{\theta}_0$ that we used for the MLE is inapplicable.[26] It requires the specification of the distribution of the observed random variable U. Therefore, we give a definition appropriate for the current setting. The following assumption describes the setting for identification.

Assumption 21.1 (Moments) *The $\{U_n\}$ is a sequence of M-variate random variables, $\boldsymbol{\theta}_0$ is a K-dimensional parameter vector, and $\mathbf{g}(U, \boldsymbol{\theta})$ is a continuously differentiable function $\mathbf{g} : \mathbb{R}^M \times \mathbb{R}^K \to \mathbb{R}^J$ $(J \geq K)$ such that $\mathrm{E}[\mathbf{g}(U_n; \boldsymbol{\theta}_0)] = \mathbf{0}$. Furthermore,*

$$\mathbf{g}_N(\boldsymbol{\theta}) \equiv \mathrm{E}_N[\mathbf{g}(U; \boldsymbol{\theta})] \xrightarrow{p} \mathrm{E}[\mathbf{g}(U; \boldsymbol{\theta})] \equiv \mathbf{g}_0(\boldsymbol{\theta})$$

uniformly and the limiting function $\mathbf{g}_0(\boldsymbol{\theta})$ is continuously differentiable.

Basically, we require the sequence of functions $\mathbf{g}_N(\boldsymbol{\theta})$ to be sample moments that satisfy a uniform law of large numbers. As we have seen, such theorems exist for U_n that are both

[26] See Definition 30 (Global Identification, p. 296).

dependently and heterogeneously distributed. In addition, the moment function $\mathbf{g}$ is differentiable so that we can apply calculus to solving the minimization problem in (21.9). Identification of $\boldsymbol{\theta}_0$ depends on $\mathbf{g}$ in a straightforward way.

Definition 41 (Moment Identification) *The parameter vector $\boldsymbol{\theta}_0$ is* globally identified *in the parameter space $\boldsymbol{\Theta}$ by the moment function $\mathbf{g}$ if*

$$\mathrm{E}[\mathbf{g}(U;\boldsymbol{\theta})] = \mathbf{g}_0(\boldsymbol{\theta}) = \mathbf{0} \quad \Leftrightarrow \quad \boldsymbol{\theta} = \boldsymbol{\theta}_0$$

For clarity, one should apply this definition with the understanding that the moment restrictions $\mathrm{E}[\mathbf{g}(U;\boldsymbol{\theta}_0)] = \mathbf{0}$ comprise everything that is known about the distribution of U. Identification is a property of the probability model. It is not possible for the researcher to *make* parameters identified and it is critical for researchers to recognize situations in which identification fails. We will assume that identification holds below.

On the other hand, the moment restrictions are assumptions after all. As such, the researcher has complete freedom to specify a set of moment conditions for which $\boldsymbol{\theta}_0$ is identified. In practice then, the study of identification yields an understanding of the foundations of an inference method and what one must maintain is true in order to make a particular statistical inference. A simple example is the *order condition* for identification:

Lemma 21.1 (Order Condition) *If $\boldsymbol{\theta}_0$ is globally identified then the number of moment conditions J is at least as large as the number of unknown parameters K.*

This lemma contains a relatively straightforward condition for researchers to maintain. Essentially, they must specify at least K moment conditions so that the number of (population) equations is greater than or equal to the number of unknown (population) parameters.

When there are exactly K moment conditions, the parameters are *exactly identified.* When there are more than K moment conditions, the parameters are overidentified. The implicit function theorem allows us to strengthen the order condition to a sufficient, but generally less tractable, *rank condition* for local identification.[27,28]

Definition 42 (Local Identification) *Let U be a random variable with p.f. $f_U(u;\boldsymbol{\theta}_0)$ and let $\boldsymbol{\Theta} \subset \mathbb{R}^K$ be the parameter space that contains $\boldsymbol{\theta}_0$. The parameter vector $\boldsymbol{\theta}_0$ is* locally identified *if there is a neighborhood of $\boldsymbol{\theta}_0$, $\mathbf{B}(\boldsymbol{\theta}_0) \subseteq \boldsymbol{\Theta}$ such that $\boldsymbol{\theta}_1 \in \mathbf{B}(\boldsymbol{\theta}_0)$, $\boldsymbol{\theta}_0 \neq \boldsymbol{\theta}_1$ implies that* $\Pr\{f_U(U;\boldsymbol{\theta}_0) \neq f_U(U;\boldsymbol{\theta}_1)\} > 0$.

---

27 We are following Rothenberg's (1971, Theorem 1, p. 579) analysis.

28 Simon and Blume (1994, p. 341) explain the implicit function theorem.

LEMMA 21.2 (RANK CONDITION) *If* $\mathbf{g}$ *is differentiable in* $\boldsymbol{\theta}$,

$$\mathrm{E}[\mathbf{g}_{\boldsymbol{\theta}}(U;\boldsymbol{\theta}_0)] = \left.\frac{\partial\,\mathrm{E}[\mathbf{g}(U;\boldsymbol{\theta})]}{\partial\boldsymbol{\theta}'}\right|_{\boldsymbol{\theta}=\boldsymbol{\theta}_0}$$

$\mathrm{E}[\mathbf{g}_{\boldsymbol{\theta}}(U;\boldsymbol{\theta}_0)]$ *has constant rank in a neighborhood of* $\boldsymbol{\theta}_0$, *and* $\mathrm{E}[\mathbf{g}_{\boldsymbol{\theta}}(U;\boldsymbol{\theta}_0)]$ *has full-column rank, then* $\boldsymbol{\theta}_0$ *is locally identified.*

We have used the rank condition before. We obtained identification in the IV setting by assuming that $\mathrm{E}[\mathbf{z}_n\mathbf{x}_n'] \equiv \mathbf{D}_{zx}$ is nonsingular.[29] This condition satisfies the rank condition (Lemma 21.2) because for IV

$$\mathbf{g}(U;\boldsymbol{\theta}) = \mathbf{z}_n\left(y_n - \mathbf{x}_n'\boldsymbol{\beta}\right) \qquad \Rightarrow \qquad \mathbf{g}_{\boldsymbol{\theta}}(U;\boldsymbol{\theta}_0) = \mathbf{z}_n\mathbf{x}_n'$$

Actually, the rank condition is necessary and sufficient for global identification in this case. Because the moment equations

$$\mathrm{E}[\mathbf{g}(U;\boldsymbol{\theta}_0)] = \mathrm{E}[\mathbf{z}_n y_n] - \mathrm{E}[\mathbf{z}_n\mathbf{x}_n']\boldsymbol{\beta}_0 = \mathbf{0}$$

are linear in $\boldsymbol{\beta}_0$, the nonsingularity of $\mathrm{E}[\mathbf{z}_n\mathbf{x}_n']$ is necessary and sufficient for $\boldsymbol{\beta}_0$ to be the unique solution.

Indeed, whenever $\mathbf{g}(U;\boldsymbol{\theta})$ is linear in $\boldsymbol{\theta}$, the rank condition is necessary and sufficient for global identification. Suppose that

$$\mathbf{g}(U;\boldsymbol{\theta}) = h(U) + \mathbf{G}(U)\boldsymbol{\theta}$$

as in IV orthogonality conditions. Then

$$\mathrm{E}[\mathbf{g}_{\boldsymbol{\theta}}(U;\boldsymbol{\theta})] = \mathrm{E}[\mathbf{G}(U)]$$

and the rank condition is simply that the expected value of $\mathbf{G}(U)$ be full-column rank. When $\mathbf{z}_n = \mathbf{x}_n$ as in OLS, this condition is Assumption 13.2 (Population Full Rank, p. 257), which we used in our treatment of the asymptotic distribution theory for OLS.

Like all identification, the rank condition is a property of the population, not the sample. Also, identification is a discrete property: it either holds or it does not. An implication is that the sample moment matrix $\mathrm{E}_N[\mathbf{z}_n\mathbf{x}_n']$ may be full-column rank even though $\mathbf{D}_{zx}$ fails the rank condition for identification. To give a simple example, two random variables may be uncorrelated yet an *estimate* of their correlation will generally be nonzero. As a result, the empirical distribution produces pseudoidentification. Identification ultimately is an assumption. Nevertheless one may look for sample evidence that the rank condition fails to hold. The rank condition is useful because it suggests where that evidence is.

GMM applies to nonlinear as well as linear moment conditions. In general practice, researchers often simply *assume* identification because more basic conditions are hard to formulate for nonlinear models. This contrasts sharply with the identification of the parameters of a likelihood function where the expected log-likelihood inequality (Lemma 14.1, p. 290) provides additional information about the population parameters. Remember that specification of the likelihood function implies specification of all moments of all functions of U. This is the source of the extra identification power possessed by ML over GMM.

[29] See Assumption 20.2 (Instruments, p. 499).

Our second assumption provides for the identification of $\boldsymbol{\theta}_0$ with GMM:

Assumption 21.2 (Identification) *The parameter vector $\boldsymbol{\theta}_0$ is globally identified by the moment function $\mathbf{g}$ in $\boldsymbol{\Theta}$, a compact subset of $\mathbb{R}^K$. Furthermore, $\mathbf{C}_N \xrightarrow{p} \mathbf{C}_0$, a symmetric positive semidefinite matrix such that*

$$\mathbf{g}_0(\boldsymbol{\theta}) \notin \mathrm{Col}^{\perp}(\mathbf{C}_0)$$

for all $\boldsymbol{\theta} \in \boldsymbol{\Theta}$, $\boldsymbol{\theta} \neq \boldsymbol{\theta}_0$.

This assumption also guarantees that the GMM criterion function is a nonnegative function so that within some subspace of $\mathbb{R}^J$ this function is a measure of vector length. It also prevents the identification provided by $\mathbf{g}_0(\boldsymbol{\theta})$ from being lost in the GMM criterion function. If $\mathbf{C}_0\mathbf{g}_0(\boldsymbol{\theta}) = \mathbf{0}$ for some $\boldsymbol{\theta} \neq \boldsymbol{\theta}_0$, then the limiting objective function will not have a *unique* minimum at $\boldsymbol{\theta}_0$.

21.4 DISTRIBUTION THEORY

Overall, the asymptotic distribution theory of GMM estimators parallels that for MLEs described in Chapter 15. Rather than work through similar detail, we will make less primitive, generic, assumptions that many probability models satisfy.

Assumption 21.3 (Asymptotic Limits)

1. *The empirical matrix of partial derivatives converge in probability:*

$$\mathbf{G}_N(\boldsymbol{\theta}) \equiv \mathrm{E}_N[\mathbf{g}_{\boldsymbol{\theta}}(U;\boldsymbol{\theta})] \xrightarrow{p} \mathrm{E}[\mathbf{g}_{\boldsymbol{\theta}}(U;\boldsymbol{\theta})] \equiv \mathbf{G}_0(\boldsymbol{\theta}) \tag{21.19}$$

uniformly in $\boldsymbol{\theta} \in \boldsymbol{\Theta}$ where
(a) $\mathbf{G}_0(\boldsymbol{\theta})$ exists,
(b) $\mathbf{G}_0(\boldsymbol{\theta})$ is continuous,
(c) differentiation under the integral sign is allowed so that

$$\frac{\partial \mathbf{g}_0(\boldsymbol{\theta})}{\partial \boldsymbol{\theta}'} = \frac{\partial\, \mathrm{E}[\mathbf{g}(U;\boldsymbol{\theta})]}{\partial \boldsymbol{\theta}'} = \mathbf{G}_0(\boldsymbol{\theta})$$

and
(d) $\mathbf{G}_0(\boldsymbol{\theta})$ is constant rank in a neighborhood of $\boldsymbol{\theta}_0$.

2. *The empirical second moments of $\mathbf{g}(U;\boldsymbol{\theta})$ converge in probability:*

$$\boldsymbol{\Lambda}_N(\boldsymbol{\theta}) \equiv \mathrm{E}_N[\mathbf{g}(U;\boldsymbol{\theta})\mathbf{g}(U;\boldsymbol{\theta})'] \xrightarrow{p} \boldsymbol{\Lambda}_0(\boldsymbol{\theta}) \tag{21.20}$$

uniformly in $\boldsymbol{\theta} \in \boldsymbol{\Theta}$ where $\boldsymbol{\Lambda}_0(\boldsymbol{\theta})$ is positive definite.

3. *The normalized sample moments evaluated at $\boldsymbol{\theta}_0$ converge in distribution:*

$$\sqrt{N}\mathbf{g}_N(\boldsymbol{\theta}_0) \xrightarrow{d} \mathfrak{N}[0, \boldsymbol{\Lambda}_0(\boldsymbol{\theta}_0)] \tag{21.21}$$

The matrix $\mathbf{G}_0(\boldsymbol{\theta}_0)$ is comparable to the information matrix. Note, however, that $\mathbf{G}_0(\boldsymbol{\theta}_0)$ is generally asymmetric and not square ($K \leq J$). Because differentiation under the integral sign is allowed, the identification condition in Assumption 21.2 implies that $\text{rank}(\mathbf{G}_0) = K$, or that $\mathbf{G}_0$ is full-column rank.

Note once again that the probability limit and distribution limit of Assumption 21.3 may hold for both dependently and heterogeneously distributed data.[30] If the data are dependent, then $\boldsymbol{\Lambda}_0$ may have a complicated form because it includes covariance terms among the different observations.

Rolling these assumptions up together, we obtain:

Proposition 20 (GMM Asymptotics) *Under Assumptions 21.1–21.3,*

$$\sqrt{N}\left(\hat{\boldsymbol{\theta}}_{\text{GMM}} - \boldsymbol{\theta}_0\right) \xrightarrow{d} \mathfrak{N}(\mathbf{0}, \mathbf{V}_0)$$

where $\hat{\boldsymbol{\theta}}_{\text{GMM}}$ *is defined in (21.9),*

$$\mathbf{V}_0 \equiv \left(\mathbf{G}_0'\mathbf{C}_0\mathbf{G}_0\right)^{-1} \mathbf{G}_0'\mathbf{C}_0\boldsymbol{\Lambda}_0\mathbf{C}_0\mathbf{G}_0 \left(\mathbf{G}_0'\mathbf{C}_0\mathbf{G}_0\right)^{-1} \tag{21.22}$$

$\mathbf{G}_0 \equiv \mathbf{G}_0(\boldsymbol{\theta}_0)$, *and* $\boldsymbol{\Lambda}_0 \equiv \boldsymbol{\Lambda}_0(\boldsymbol{\theta}_0)$.

In the following sections, we highlight the differences and similarities in the asymptotic distribution theory for GMM versus ML. The overall strategy is the same: first, we establish the consistency of the GMM estimator and second, based on its consistency, we prove that the GMM estimator is asymptotically normally distributed using a linear approximation to the moment equations.

21.4.1 Proof of Consistency

To prove the consistency of the GMM estimator, one follows the same general argument as for the MLE. Both estimators are *extremum estimators* in that an optimization defines each. For comparability, let

$$\hat{\boldsymbol{\theta}}_{\text{GMM}} = \operatorname*{argmax}_{\boldsymbol{\theta}\in\boldsymbol{\Theta}} Q_N(\boldsymbol{\theta})$$

where

$$Q_N(\boldsymbol{\theta}) \equiv -\mathbf{g}_N(\boldsymbol{\theta})'\mathbf{C}_N\,\mathbf{g}_N(\boldsymbol{\theta})$$

Hence, application of Lemma 15.2 (Consistency of Maxima, p. 322) is the basic approach.

To use this lemma, we must show first that

$$Q_N(\boldsymbol{\theta}) \equiv -\mathbf{g}_N(\boldsymbol{\theta})'\mathbf{C}_N\,\mathbf{g}_N(\boldsymbol{\theta}) \xrightarrow{p} -\mathbf{g}_0(\boldsymbol{\theta})'\mathbf{C}_0\,\mathbf{g}_0(\boldsymbol{\theta}) \equiv Q_0(\boldsymbol{\theta}) \tag{21.23}$$

uniformly in $\boldsymbol{\theta} \in \boldsymbol{\Theta}$. We defer some of the details of the demonstration to Section 21.6.1 in the *Mathematical Notes* of this chapter. The foundation of (21.23) is the uniform convergence of $\mathbf{g}_N(\boldsymbol{\theta}) \equiv \text{E}_N[\mathbf{g}(U;\boldsymbol{\theta})]$ to $\mathbf{g}_0(\boldsymbol{\theta}) \equiv \text{E}[\mathbf{g}(U;\boldsymbol{\theta})]$ and $\mathbf{C}_N$ to $\mathbf{C}_0$. The former convergence

[30] White (1984) gives an extensive treatment of this topic.

is Assumption 21.1. Because $\mathbf{C}_N$ is not a function of $\boldsymbol{\theta}$, Assumption 21.2 covers its uniform convergence to $\mathbf{C}_0$.

Second, $Q_0(\boldsymbol{\theta})$ must be uniquely minimized at $\boldsymbol{\theta}_0$. We can show that this is guaranteed by Assumption 21.2 (Identification). If $\boldsymbol{\theta}_1 \neq \boldsymbol{\theta}_0$, then this assumption asserts that $\mathbf{g}_0(\boldsymbol{\theta}_1) \notin \text{Col}^{\perp}(\mathbf{C}_0)$. Also, we can let $\mathbf{AA}' = \mathbf{C}_0$ be the Cholesky decomposition of $\mathbf{C}_0$ and know that (1) $\mathbf{A}$ is nonsingular and (2) $\text{Col}(\mathbf{A}) = \text{Col}(\mathbf{C}_0)$. Therefore, $\mathbf{g}_0(\boldsymbol{\theta}_1) \notin \text{Col}^{\perp}(\mathbf{A})$, or $\mathbf{A}'\mathbf{g}_0(\boldsymbol{\theta}_1) \neq 0$, and

$$Q_0(\boldsymbol{\theta}_1) = -\left\| A'\mathbf{g}_0(\boldsymbol{\theta}_1)\right\|^2 < 0$$

Therefore, $Q_0(\boldsymbol{\theta}) = 0$ uniquely at $\boldsymbol{\theta} = \boldsymbol{\theta}_0$.

Thus, Lemma 15.2 implies that $\hat{\boldsymbol{\theta}}_{\text{GMM}} \xrightarrow{p} \boldsymbol{\theta}_0$. □

21.4.2 Proof of Asymptotic Normality

Given the consistency of the GMM estimator, we can derive its asymptotic normality from a linearization comparable to the linearization of the ML score function. The quadratic character of the GMM criterion function $Q_N(\boldsymbol{\theta})$ leads to a slightly different development. Unlike ML, the second derivatives of the GMM objective function play no explicit part. Only the first derivatives of the *moment* function matter.

The first-order conditions that define $\hat{\boldsymbol{\theta}}_{\text{GMM}}$ as an implicit function are

$$0 = \mathbf{G}_N(\hat{\boldsymbol{\theta}}_{\text{GMM}})'\mathbf{C}_N\, \mathbf{g}_N(\hat{\boldsymbol{\theta}}_{\text{GMM}})$$

These are satisfied asymptotically with probability one, using the same argument as for the MLE.[31] Now we expand only $\mathbf{g}_N(\hat{\boldsymbol{\theta}}_{\text{GMM}})$:

$$\mathbf{g}_N(\hat{\boldsymbol{\theta}}_{\text{GMM}}) = \mathbf{g}_N(\boldsymbol{\theta}_0) + \mathbf{G}_N(\bar{\boldsymbol{\theta}})\left(\hat{\boldsymbol{\theta}}_{\text{GMM}} - \boldsymbol{\theta}_0\right) \tag{21.24}$$

where $\bar{\boldsymbol{\theta}}$ is the mean value between $\hat{\boldsymbol{\theta}}_{\text{GMM}}$ and $\boldsymbol{\theta}_0$. As a result, we have the linear representation

$$\sqrt{N}\left(\hat{\boldsymbol{\theta}}_{\text{GMM}} - \boldsymbol{\theta}_0\right) = -\left[\mathbf{G}_N(\hat{\boldsymbol{\theta}}_{\text{GMM}})'\mathbf{C}_N\mathbf{G}_N(\bar{\theta})\right]^{-1}\mathbf{G}_N(\hat{\boldsymbol{\theta}}_{\text{GMM}})'\mathbf{C}_N\,\sqrt{N}\cdot\mathbf{g}_N(\theta_0) \tag{21.25}$$

provided that the Hessian-like term

$$\mathbf{G}_N(\hat{\boldsymbol{\theta}}_{\text{GMM}})'\mathbf{C}_N\mathbf{G}_N(\bar{\theta}) \tag{21.26}$$

is nonsingular.

The consistency of $\hat{\boldsymbol{\theta}}_{\text{GMM}}$ and $\bar{\boldsymbol{\theta}}$, Assumptions 21.2 and 21.3, and Lemma 15.1 (Uniform LLN, p. 321) imply that

$$\mathbf{G}_N(\hat{\boldsymbol{\theta}}_{\text{GMM}}),\ \mathbf{G}_N(\bar{\boldsymbol{\theta}}) \xrightarrow{p} \mathbf{G}_0 \tag{21.27}$$

$$\mathbf{G}_N(\hat{\boldsymbol{\theta}}_{\text{GMM}})'\mathbf{C}_N \xrightarrow{p} \mathbf{G}_0'\mathbf{C}_0 \tag{21.28}$$

and

$$\mathbf{G}_N(\hat{\boldsymbol{\theta}}_{\text{GMM}})'\mathbf{C}_N\mathbf{G}_N(\bar{\boldsymbol{\theta}}) \xrightarrow{p} \mathbf{G}_0'\mathbf{C}_0\mathbf{G}_0 \tag{21.29}$$

31 See footnote 7 on p. 325.

In Section 21.6.2 of the *Mathematical Notes*, we show that $\mathbf{G}_0'\mathbf{C}_0\mathbf{G}_0$ is nonsingular. It follows from this and Assumption 21.3 (p. 545) that (21.26) is also nonsingular with probability one as $N \to \infty$. The continuity of matrix inverses for nonsingular matrices and Lemma 13.2 (Probability Limit Continuity, p. 261) further imply that

$$\left[\mathbf{G}_N(\hat{\boldsymbol{\theta}}_{\text{GMM}})'\mathbf{C}_N\mathbf{G}_N(\bar{\boldsymbol{\theta}})\right]^{-1} \xrightarrow{p} \left(\mathbf{G}_0'\mathbf{C}_0\mathbf{G}_0\right)^{-1}$$

Therefore, by the Cramér–Wold device (Lemma 13.5, p. 266) and the Slutsky lemma (Lemma 13.3, p. 261),

$$\begin{aligned}\sqrt{N}\left(\hat{\boldsymbol{\theta}}_{\text{GMM}} - \boldsymbol{\theta}_0\right) &\overset{p}{=} -\left(\mathbf{G}_0'\mathbf{C}_0\mathbf{G}_0\right)^{-1}\mathbf{G}_0'\mathbf{C}_0\sqrt{N}\mathbf{g}_N(\boldsymbol{\theta}_0)\\ &\xrightarrow{d} \mathfrak{N}\left[\mathbf{0}, \left(\mathbf{G}_0'\mathbf{C}_0\mathbf{G}_0\right)^{-1}\mathbf{G}_0'\mathbf{C}_0\boldsymbol{\Lambda}_0\mathbf{C}_0\mathbf{G}_0\left(\mathbf{G}_0'\mathbf{C}_0\mathbf{G}_0\right)^{-1}\right]\end{aligned} \tag{21.30}$$

This completes the proof of Proposition 20. □

A corollary of this proof is that an asymptotically equivalent estimator is the linearized form

$$\hat{\boldsymbol{\theta}}^*_{\text{GMM}} = \check{\boldsymbol{\theta}} - \left[\mathbf{G}_N(\check{\boldsymbol{\theta}})'\mathbf{C}_N\mathbf{G}_N(\check{\boldsymbol{\theta}})\right]^{-1}\mathbf{G}_N(\check{\boldsymbol{\theta}})'\mathbf{C}_N\mathbf{g}_N(\check{\boldsymbol{\theta}}) \tag{21.31}$$

where $\check{\boldsymbol{\theta}}$ is an initial, $\sqrt{N}$-consistent estimator of $\boldsymbol{\theta}_0$.[32] The primary difference between this linearized estimator and the LMLE appears in the matrix inverse term, where a Hessian or its approximant would appear in the LMLE.[33] The GMM theory does not require second partial derivatives of the moment functions and this feature appears in this linearized GMM estimator.

21.4.3 Variance Matrix Estimation

Consistent estimation of the aysmptotic variance matrix $\mathbf{V}_0$ in Proposition 20 follows familiar lines. We simply plug $\hat{\boldsymbol{\theta}}_{\text{GMM}}$ into the sample counterparts of the components of $\mathbf{V}_0$, as in

$$\hat{\mathbf{V}}_N \equiv \left(\hat{\mathbf{G}}_N'\mathbf{C}_N\hat{\mathbf{G}}_N\right)^{-1}\hat{\mathbf{G}}_N'\mathbf{C}_N\hat{\boldsymbol{\Lambda}}_N\mathbf{C}_N\hat{\mathbf{G}}_N\left(\hat{\mathbf{G}}_N'\mathbf{C}_N\hat{\mathbf{G}}_N\right)^{-1} \tag{21.32}$$

where

$$\begin{aligned}\hat{\mathbf{G}}_N &\equiv \mathbf{G}_N(\hat{\boldsymbol{\theta}}_{\text{GMM}})\\ \hat{\boldsymbol{\Lambda}}_N &\equiv \boldsymbol{\Lambda}_N(\hat{\boldsymbol{\theta}}_{\text{GMM}})\\ &= \mathrm{E}_N[\mathbf{g}(U;\hat{\boldsymbol{\theta}}_{\text{GMM}})\,\mathbf{g}(U;\hat{\boldsymbol{\theta}}_{\text{GMM}})']\\ &= \mathrm{Var}_N[\mathbf{g}(U;\hat{\boldsymbol{\theta}}_{\text{GMM}})]\end{aligned}$$

---

32 A first-order expansion gives

$$\sqrt{N}\cdot\mathbf{g}_N(\check{\boldsymbol{\theta}}) \overset{p}{=} \sqrt{N}\cdot\mathbf{g}_N(\boldsymbol{\theta}_0) + \mathbf{G}_N(\bar{\boldsymbol{\theta}})\sqrt{N}\cdot\left(\check{\boldsymbol{\theta}} - \boldsymbol{\theta}_0\right)$$

where $\mathbf{G}_N(\bar{\boldsymbol{\theta}}) \overset{p}{=} \mathbf{G}_N(\check{\boldsymbol{\theta}}) \overset{p}{=} \mathbf{G}_0$. Therefore, by substituting this into $\hat{\boldsymbol{\theta}}^*$ we obtain

$$\begin{aligned}\sqrt{N}\left(\hat{\boldsymbol{\theta}}^* - \boldsymbol{\theta}_0\right) &\overset{p}{=} \left[\mathbf{G}_0'\mathbf{C}_0\mathbf{G}_0\right]^{-1}\mathbf{G}_0'\mathbf{C}_0\sqrt{N}\cdot\mathbf{g}_N(\boldsymbol{\theta}_0)\\ &\overset{p}{=} \sqrt{N}\left(\hat{\boldsymbol{\theta}} - \boldsymbol{\theta}_0\right)\end{aligned}$$

as in equation (21.30).

33 See Lemma 15.7 (LMLE, p. 333).

The empirical matrix of partial derivatives $\mathbf{G}_N$ is comparable to the empirical Hessian in ML estimation. The empirical variance matrix $\mathbf{\Lambda}_N$ is comparable to the empirical variance of the score. Each is a consistent estimator for its population counterpart by the same arguments: $\hat{\boldsymbol{\theta}}_{\mathrm{GMM}}$ is consistent and

$$\mathbf{G}_N(\boldsymbol{\theta}) \xrightarrow{p} \mathbf{G}_0(\boldsymbol{\theta}),$$
$$\mathbf{\Lambda}_N(\boldsymbol{\theta}) \xrightarrow{p} \mathrm{E}[\mathbf{g}(U;\boldsymbol{\theta})\,\mathbf{g}(U;\boldsymbol{\theta})']$$

uniformly in $\boldsymbol{\theta}$ according to (21.19) and (21.20). Under these conditions and Assumption 21.2, Lemma 15.5 (p. 326) states that $\hat{\mathbf{V}}_N$ converges in probability to $\mathbf{V}_0$ (21.22).

The convergence of $\mathbf{G}_N(\boldsymbol{\theta})$ and $\mathbf{\Lambda}_N(\boldsymbol{\theta})$ can hold under sampling that is independent but not necessarily identical. Recall that Chebychev's LLN (Theorem 13, p. 449) applies to these functions provided that their elements have variances that converge to zero.

The asymptotic variance estimator in (21.32) is often called the *sandwich* estimator. This name describes the way that the $\hat{\mathbf{G}}_N'\mathbf{C}_N\hat{\mathbf{\Lambda}}_N\mathbf{C}_N\hat{\mathbf{G}}_N$ term rests between two $(\hat{\mathbf{G}}_N'\mathbf{C}_N\hat{\mathbf{G}}_N)^{-1}$ terms like the contents of a sandwich between two slices of bread.

Huber (1967) and White (1982) applied these arguments to the asymptotic variance of the MLE. Among the situations they considered were cases in which the log-likelihood function is misspecified yet the MLE is still consistent because the score identity (Lemma 14.3, p. 300) holds. Such an estimator is called a *quasi-* (or *psuedo*)-MLE. Leading examples are the OLS estimator for $\boldsymbol{\beta}_0$ in $\mathrm{E}[y_n \mid \mathbf{x}_n]$ when y_n is not normally or not spherically distributed. In such cases, the information identity (Lemma 14.4, p. 302) generally fails and the various estimators of the information matrix converge to different limits. Nevertheless, the quasi-MLE is a GMM estimator and we can apply (21.32) to obtain the Huber–White estimator of the asymptotic variance

$$\hat{\mathbf{V}}_N = \left\{\mathrm{E}_N[-L_{\boldsymbol{\theta}\boldsymbol{\theta}}(\hat{\boldsymbol{\theta}}_N)]\right\}^{-1} \mathrm{Var}_N[L_{\boldsymbol{\theta}}(\hat{\boldsymbol{\theta}}_N)] \left\{\mathrm{E}_N[-L_{\boldsymbol{\theta}\boldsymbol{\theta}}(\hat{\boldsymbol{\theta}}_N)]\right\}^{-1}$$

Rather than use the empirical variance of the score or the negative empirical Hessian, these two information matrix estimators appear together in an estimator that consistently estimates the asymptotic variance of the quasi-MLE.

EXAMPLE 21.1

One may view the Eicker–White variance estimator for OLS in the presence of heteroskedasticity as a special case of the Huber–White estimator. The OLS estimator is the GMM estimator given by

$$\mathbf{g}(y_n;\mathbf{x}_n,\boldsymbol{\beta}) = \mathbf{x}_n(y_n - \mathbf{x}_n'\boldsymbol{\beta}),$$
$$\mathbf{C}_N = \mathbf{I}_K$$

so that

$$\mathbf{G}_N(\boldsymbol{\theta}) = \mathrm{E}_N[\mathbf{x}_n\mathbf{x}_n'] = \frac{1}{N}\cdot\mathbf{X}'\mathbf{X}$$
$$\mathbf{\Lambda}_N(\boldsymbol{\theta}) = \mathrm{E}_N[\mathbf{x}_n\left(y_n - \mathbf{x}_n'\boldsymbol{\beta}\right)^2\mathbf{x}_n']$$

Substituting the GMM/OLS estimator $\hat{\boldsymbol{\beta}} = \left(\mathbf{X}'\mathbf{X}\right)^{-1}\mathbf{X}'\mathbf{y}$ for $\boldsymbol{\theta}$, the resultant estimator of the variance matrix of OLS is the Eicker–White heteroskedasticity-consistent variance estimator (18.11).

Researchers have adapted the GMM variance matrix estimator to serially dependent cases as well. If nonzero covariances were only pth order, so that for $j > p$

$$\mathrm{Cov}[\mathbf{g}(U_t;\boldsymbol{\theta}_0), \mathbf{g}(U_{t-j};\boldsymbol{\theta}_0)] = \mathrm{E}[\mathbf{g}(U_t;\boldsymbol{\theta}_0)\mathbf{g}(U_{t-j};\boldsymbol{\theta}_0)'] = \mathbf{0}$$

then a consistent estimator of the asymptotic variance matrix $\boldsymbol{\Lambda}_0$ is

$$\hat{\boldsymbol{\Lambda}}_N = \hat{\boldsymbol{\Lambda}}_{N0} + \sum_{j-1}^{p} \left(\hat{\boldsymbol{\Lambda}}_{Nj} + \hat{\boldsymbol{\Lambda}}'_{Nj}\right) \tag{21.33}$$

where

$$\hat{\boldsymbol{\Lambda}}_{Nj} \equiv \frac{1}{N-j} \sum_{t=j+1}^{N} \mathbf{g}(U_t;\hat{\boldsymbol{\theta}}_{\mathrm{GMM}})\, \mathbf{g}(U_{t-j};\hat{\boldsymbol{\theta}}_{\mathrm{GMM}})'$$

$(j = 0, 1, \ldots, p)$.

The extensions and cautions described in Section 19.5 also apply here. Hansen (1982) noted that one must allow p to grow with the sample size to control for covariances that die out slowly. The Newey and West (1987b) estimator

$$\hat{\boldsymbol{\Lambda}}_N = \hat{\boldsymbol{\Lambda}}_{N0} + \sum_{j=1}^{p} \left(1 - \frac{j}{p+1}\right) \left(\hat{\boldsymbol{\Lambda}}_{Nj} + \hat{\boldsymbol{\Lambda}}'_{Nj}\right) \tag{21.34}$$

is a popular alternative to (21.33) because (21.34) is positive definite. The selection of p and the small sample behavior of these estimators remain open topics of research.

21.4.4 Efficiency

Having found the asymptotic distribution of the GMM estimator and an estimator for its variance matrix, we finally consider the choice of the weighting matrix $\mathbf{C}_N$. Because this matrix affects the variance matrix, and hence relative efficiency of the GMM estimator, it is natural to seek an optimal choice. We have already suggested that an analogy between GLS for the linear regression model and GMM is apt.[34] The GLS estimator is a member of the family of estimators indexed by the positive definite weighting matrix $\mathbf{C}$:

$$\begin{aligned} \hat{\mu}(\mathbf{C}) &= \mathbf{X}\left(\mathbf{X}'\mathbf{C}\mathbf{X}\right)^{-1}\mathbf{X}'\mathbf{C}'\mathbf{y} \\ &= \underset{\boldsymbol{\mu}\in\mathrm{Col}(\mathbf{X})}{\operatorname{argmin}}\, (\mathbf{y}-\boldsymbol{\mu})'\,\mathbf{C}\,(\mathbf{y}-\boldsymbol{\mu}) \end{aligned} \tag{21.35}$$

Aitken's theorem (Theorem 12, p. 432) states that a relatively efficient estimator in this family is the GLS/Aitken estimator $\hat{\mu}_{\mathrm{GLS}}$, which sets

$$\mathbf{C} = \boldsymbol{\Omega}_0^{-1} = (\mathrm{Var}[\mathbf{y} \mid \mathbf{X}])^{-1}$$

Now to make the analogy, think of each sample moment as though it were an observation in a sample of J observations. For any $\sqrt{N}$-consistent estimator $\boldsymbol{\theta}_N$, (21.24) and (21.27) imply that

[34] See the discussion of 2SLS following equation (21.18).

$$\begin{aligned}\sqrt{N}\mathbf{g}_N(\boldsymbol{\theta}_N) &= \sqrt{N}\mathbf{g}_N(\boldsymbol{\theta}_0) + \mathbf{G}_N(\bar{\boldsymbol{\theta}})\sqrt{N}\,(\boldsymbol{\theta}_N - \boldsymbol{\theta}_0) \\ &\stackrel{p}{=} \sqrt{N}\mathbf{g}_N(\boldsymbol{\theta}_0) + \mathbf{G}_0\sqrt{N}\,(\boldsymbol{\theta}_N - \boldsymbol{\theta}_0)\end{aligned} \tag{21.36}$$

so that the moment function $\sqrt{N}\mathbf{g}_N(\boldsymbol{\theta}_N)$ is linear in $\sqrt{N}\,(\boldsymbol{\theta}_N - \boldsymbol{\theta}_0)$, just as the residual $\mathbf{y} - \mathbf{X}\boldsymbol{\beta}$ is linear in $\boldsymbol{\beta}$. In that analogy, $\mathbf{y}$ is analogous to $\sqrt{N}\mathbf{g}_N(\boldsymbol{\theta}_0)$ and the matrix $\mathbf{X}$ is analogous to $\mathbf{G}_0$.

This analogy extends to the GMM criterion function:

$$\begin{aligned}&N \cdot \mathbf{g}_N(\boldsymbol{\theta}_N)'\mathbf{C}_N\mathbf{g}_N(\boldsymbol{\theta}_N) \stackrel{p}{=} \\ &\quad N \cdot \left[\mathbf{g}_N(\boldsymbol{\theta}_0) + \mathbf{G}_0\,(\boldsymbol{\theta}_N - \boldsymbol{\theta}_0)\right]' \mathbf{C}_N \left[\mathbf{g}_N(\boldsymbol{\theta}_0) + \mathbf{G}_0\,(\boldsymbol{\theta}_N - \boldsymbol{\theta}_0)\right]\end{aligned} \tag{21.37}$$

using (21.36). Comparison with the GLS criterion function in (21.35) suggests that an optimal weight matrix is

$$\mathbf{C}_0 = \boldsymbol{\Lambda}_0^{-1}$$

because

$$\sqrt{N}\mathbf{g}_N(\boldsymbol{\theta}_0) \xrightarrow{d} \mathfrak{N}(0, \boldsymbol{\Lambda}_0)$$

This conjecture is correct. However $\boldsymbol{\Lambda}_0^{-1}$ is not the only optimal weight matrix. Hansen (1982) provides the following result.

Proposition 21 (GMM Efficiency) *Under the assumptions of Proposition 20, a CUAN GMM estimator $\hat{\boldsymbol{\theta}}_{\text{GMM}}$ defined by (21.9) is asymptotically efficient relative to all others if and only if*

$$\text{Col}(\mathbf{C}_0\mathbf{G}_0) = \text{Col}(\boldsymbol{\Lambda}_0^{-1}\mathbf{G}_0) \tag{21.38}$$

so that $\mathbf{V}_0 = \left(\mathbf{G}_0'\boldsymbol{\Lambda}_0^{-1}\mathbf{G}_0\right)^{-1}$.

For a proof, see Section 21.6.3. Thus, $\mathbf{C}_0$ need not equal $\boldsymbol{\Lambda}_0^{-1}$ for relative efficiency. This is also a property of GLS estimators. If one notes that the projector for GLS given in (21.35) corresponds to a projection onto $\text{Col}(\mathbf{X})$ along $\text{Col}(\boldsymbol{\Omega}_0^{-1}\mathbf{X})$, then it is apparent that any $\mathbf{C}_0$ that satisfies (21.38) will provide the same unique projector. This condition is necessary and sufficient because projections are unique in general.

EXAMPLE 21.2 (Nonlinear Weighted IV)

Suppose that

$$\begin{aligned}\text{E}[y_n - \mu(\boldsymbol{\beta}_0; \mathbf{x}_n) \mid \mathbf{w}_n] &= 0, \\ \text{Var}[y_n - \mu(\boldsymbol{\beta}_0; \mathbf{x}_n) \mid \mathbf{w}_n] &= \sigma_0^2(\mathbf{w}_n) \equiv \sigma_{0n}^2\end{aligned}$$

for $(y_n, \mathbf{x}_n, \mathbf{w}_n)$ independently distributed over $n = 1, \ldots, N$, where μ is a known function, $\boldsymbol{\beta}_0$ is a vector of K unknown parameters, $\mathbf{x}_n$ is a vector of K explanatory variables, and $\mathbf{w}_n$ is a vector of J instrumental variables. Consider a GMM estimator based on the moment/orthogonality equations

$$\mathrm{E}\big[z_j(\mathbf{w}_n)\left(y_n - \mu(\boldsymbol{\beta}_0; \mathbf{x}_n)\right)\big] = \mathbf{0}, \qquad j = 1, \ldots, J$$

for instrument functions $z_j(\cdot)$. Then

$$\mathbf{G}_N(\boldsymbol{\theta}) = -\,\mathrm{E}_N[\mathbf{z}_n \mu_{\boldsymbol{\beta}}(\boldsymbol{\beta}; \mathbf{x}_n)'],$$
$$\boldsymbol{\Lambda}_N(\boldsymbol{\theta}) = \mathrm{E}_N\big[\mathbf{z}_n \left(y_n - \mu(\boldsymbol{\beta}_0; \mathbf{x}_n)\right)^2 \mathbf{z}_n'\big]$$

and

$$\mathbf{G}_0 = -\,\mathrm{E}[\mathbf{z}_n \mu_{\boldsymbol{\beta}}(\boldsymbol{\beta}_0; \mathbf{x}_n)']$$
$$\boldsymbol{\Lambda}_0 = \mathrm{E}[\mathbf{z}_n \sigma_{0n}^2\, \mathbf{z}_n']$$

for given instrument vector $\mathbf{z}_n \equiv \left[z_j(\mathbf{w}_n);\ j = 1, \ldots, J\right]'$.

Given such an initial consistent estimator as NLS, $\hat{\boldsymbol{\beta}}_{\mathrm{NLS}}$ in (21.16), an asymptotically relatively efficient GMM estimator (21.9) among all choices for the weight matrix $\mathbf{C}_N$ is the one corresponding to

$$\mathbf{C}_N = \left(\frac{1}{N} \cdot \mathbf{Z}'\hat{\mathbf{D}}\mathbf{Z}\right)^{-1} = \left[\boldsymbol{\Lambda}_N(\hat{\boldsymbol{\beta}}_{\mathrm{NLS}})\right]^{-1}$$

where $\mathbf{Z} \equiv [\mathbf{z}_n]'$ is an $N \times J$ matrix of instrumental variables and $\hat{\mathbf{D}} = \mathrm{diag}\{[y_n - \mu(\hat{\boldsymbol{\beta}}_{\mathrm{NLS}}; \mathbf{x}_n)]^2\}$.

Given $\hat{\boldsymbol{\beta}}_{\mathrm{NLS}}$, an asymptotically equivalent linearized GMM estimator is

$$\hat{\boldsymbol{\beta}}_{\mathrm{GMM}} = \hat{\boldsymbol{\beta}}_{\mathrm{NLS}} + \left[\hat{\mathbf{M}}'\mathbf{Z}\left(\mathbf{Z}'\hat{\mathbf{D}}\mathbf{Z}\right)^{-1}\mathbf{Z}'\hat{\mathbf{M}}\right]^{-1} \hat{\mathbf{M}}'\mathbf{Z}\left(\mathbf{Z}'\hat{\mathbf{D}}\mathbf{Z}\right)^{-1}\mathbf{Z}'\left(\mathbf{y} - \hat{\boldsymbol{\mu}}\right)$$
$$= \left[\hat{\mathbf{M}}'\mathbf{Z}\left(\mathbf{Z}'\hat{\mathbf{D}}\mathbf{Z}\right)^{-1}\mathbf{Z}'\hat{\mathbf{M}}\right]^{-1} \hat{\mathbf{M}}'\mathbf{Z}\left(\mathbf{Z}'\hat{\mathbf{D}}\mathbf{Z}\right)^{-1}\mathbf{Z}'\left(\mathbf{y} - \hat{\boldsymbol{\mu}} + \hat{\mathbf{M}}\hat{\boldsymbol{\beta}}_{\mathrm{NLS}}\right) \qquad (21.39)$$

where

$$\hat{\boldsymbol{\mu}} \equiv \left[\mu(\hat{\boldsymbol{\beta}}_{\mathrm{NLS}}; \mathbf{x}_n)\right]'$$
$$\hat{\mathbf{M}} \equiv \left[\mu_{\boldsymbol{\beta}}(\hat{\boldsymbol{\beta}}_{\mathrm{NLS}}; \mathbf{x}_n)\right]'$$
$$\mathbf{Z}'\hat{\mathbf{M}} = -N \cdot \mathbf{G}_N(\hat{\boldsymbol{\beta}}_{\mathrm{NLS}})$$

This estimator is exactly analogous to the LMLE (15.9) and the GNR (16.14).[35] It is very much like the 2SLS estimator, except that $\hat{\mathbf{D}}$ appears to account for the heteroskedasticity and $\hat{\mathbf{M}}$ generalizes the linear term $\mathbf{X}$.

Note that this optimal GMM estimator takes the instrumental variables as given. This example illustrates that Proposition 21 is silent on the selection of instrumental variables. The moments

[35] Cragg (1983) and Cumby et al. (1983) are early examples of such estimators.

that support GMM estimation are primitives, not a set of choices. In general, one should use all available moments or suffer inefficiency asymptotically. The proposition describes the optimal use of all the moments that the researcher provides.

However, because the example specifies *conditional* moments there is an infinite set of possible instruments that can be constructed as functions of $\mathbf{w}_n$. Our analysis of NLS in Section 21.2.2 suggests that asymptotically optimal instruments might be functions of $\mu_{\beta}(\boldsymbol{\beta}_0; \mathbf{x}_n)$. Our study of heteroskedasticity in Section 18.5 and Example 20.12 suggests in addition that these variables should be weighted by σ_{0n}^{-2}. We confirm these two conjectures with a generalization of the preceding example.

EXAMPLE 21.3 (Nonlinear Weighted IV)

Continuing from Example 21.2, the asymptotic variance of the efficient GMM estimator is

$$\left\{\mathrm{E}[\mu_{\beta}(\boldsymbol{\beta}_0; \mathbf{x}_n)\mathbf{z}_n'] \left(\mathrm{E}[\mathbf{z}_n \sigma_{0n}^2 \mathbf{z}_n']\right)^{-1} \mathrm{E}[\mathbf{z}_n \mu_{\beta}(\boldsymbol{\beta}_0; \mathbf{x}_n)']\right\}^{-1} \tag{21.40}$$

for a given instrument vector $\mathbf{z}_n \equiv \left[z_j(\mathbf{w}_n);\ j = 1, \ldots, J\right]$. Following the proof for Lemma 20.4, the optimal $\{\mathbf{z}_n\}$ from a set of choices $\mathbb{Z}$ must satisfy

$$\mathbf{z}_n^* = \underset{\{\mathbf{z}_n\}\in\mathbb{Z}}{\operatorname{argmin}} \min_{\gamma} \mathrm{E}\left[\left(\frac{1}{\sigma_{0n}} \cdot \mu_{\beta}(\boldsymbol{\beta}_0; \mathbf{x}_n)'\boldsymbol{\alpha} - \sigma_{0n} \cdot \mathbf{z}_n'\boldsymbol{\gamma}\right)^2\right]$$

This is the same program as in Example 20.12 except that $\mathbf{x}_n$ has been replaced with the more general term $\mu_{\beta}(\boldsymbol{\beta}_0; \mathbf{x}_n)$. If

$$\begin{aligned} \mathbb{Z} = \Big\{\{\mathbf{z}_n\} \mid \mathbf{z}_n = f(\mathbf{w}_n),\ f : \mathbb{R}^J \to \mathbb{R}^K, \\ \mathrm{E}[\mathbf{z}_n \mathbf{x}_n'] \text{ is nonsingular, and} \\ \mathrm{E}_N[\mathbf{z}_n \sigma_{0n}^2 \mathbf{z}_n'],\ \mathrm{E}_N[\mathbf{z}_n \mathbf{x}_n'] \text{ converge in probability}\Big\} \end{aligned}$$

and $\left\{\sigma_{0n}^{-2} \cdot \mathrm{E}[\mu_{\beta}(\boldsymbol{\beta}_0; \mathbf{x}_n) \mid \mathbf{w}_n]\right\} \in \mathbb{Z}$, then the latter is an efficient instrument vector.[36]

To capitalize on this result easily, both $\sigma_0^2(\mathbf{w}_n)$ and $\mathrm{E}[\mu_{\beta}(\boldsymbol{\beta}_0; \mathbf{x}_n) \mid \mathbf{w}_n]$ must be known, parametric, functions of $\mathbf{w}_n$.[37] One might, for example, specify that $\sigma_0^2(\mathbf{w}_n) = \exp(\mathbf{w}_n'\boldsymbol{\gamma}_0)$. The conditional expectation of a matrix of partial derivatives presents new problems because the conditional moment restriction $\mathrm{E}[y_n - \mu(\boldsymbol{\beta}_0; \mathbf{x}_n) \mid \mathbf{w}_n] = 0$ generally provides no clues about $\mathrm{E}[\mu_{\beta}(\boldsymbol{\beta}_0; \mathbf{x}_n) \mid \mathbf{w}_n]$. This shows how special the linear models are. If $\mu(\boldsymbol{\beta}_0; \mathbf{x}_n)$ is linear in $\mathbf{x}_n$ and $\mathrm{E}[\mathbf{x}_n \mid \mathbf{w}_n]$ is linear in $\mathbf{w}_n$, then $\mathrm{E}[\mu_{\beta}(\boldsymbol{\beta}_0; \mathbf{x}_n) \mid \mathbf{w}_n]$ is also linear in $\mathbf{w}_n$ and a weighted 2SLS estimator is a feasible, asymptotically efficient IV estimator. Otherwise, one must be content to choose a reasonable parametric specification for $\mathrm{E}[\mu_{\beta}(\boldsymbol{\beta}_0; \mathbf{x}_n) \mid \mathbf{w}_n]$ and fit it with NLS in the first step of a two-step feasible estimator.

---

36 Chamberlain (1987) derives this general form of optimal instruments. Also see Newey and McFadden (1994, Theorem 5.3).

37 Chamberlain (1987) shows how to approximate the efficient estimator nonparametrically under certain conditions. Newey (1990) provides an efficient nonparametric estimator for the homoskedastic case.

If these parametric specifications are correct, then the feasible efficient-GMM efficient-IV estimator simplifies from (21.39) to

$$\hat{\boldsymbol{\beta}}_{\text{GMM}} = \left(\hat{\mathbf{M}}'\hat{\mathbf{D}}^{-1}\hat{\mathbf{M}}\right)^{-1}\hat{\mathbf{M}}'\hat{\mathbf{D}}^{-1}\left(\mathbf{y} - \hat{\boldsymbol{\mu}} + \hat{\boldsymbol{M}}\hat{\boldsymbol{\beta}}_{\text{NLS}}\right) \tag{21.41}$$

where now $\hat{\mathbf{M}}$ contains the first-step NLS fitted values for $\mathrm{E}[\mu_{\boldsymbol{\beta}}(\boldsymbol{\beta}_0; \mathbf{x}_n) \mid \mathbf{w}_n]$ and $\hat{\mathbf{D}}$ contains (on its diagonal) the first-step fitted values for σ_{0n}^2. Thus, the 2SLS flavor of the previous GMM estimator disappears with the introduction of efficient instrumental variables and a purely GLS/IV statistic remains.

On the other hand, if $\mathbf{x}_n$ appears in $\mathbb{Z}$ then $\mathrm{E}[\mu_{\boldsymbol{\beta}}(\boldsymbol{\beta}_0; \mathbf{x}_n) \mid \mathbf{w}_n]$ is simply $\mu_{\boldsymbol{\beta}}(\boldsymbol{\beta}_0; \mathbf{x}_n)$. No further specification is required. The weighted NLS estimator suggested above the example is indeed the efficient IV estimator in this case and (21.41) sets $\hat{\mathbf{M}} = [\mu_{\boldsymbol{\beta}}(\hat{\boldsymbol{\beta}}_{\text{NLS}}; \mathbf{x}_n)]'$. The feasibility of this estimator depends only on a specification for σ_{0n}^2.

If one is not forthcoming, there is an alternative to directly approximating $\sigma_0^2(\mathbf{w}_n)$ proposed by Cragg (1983). He noted that because the presence of heteroskedasticity makes $\mu_{\boldsymbol{\beta}}(\boldsymbol{\beta}_0; \mathbf{x}_n)$ an inefficient instrument vector, one can improve the asymptotic efficiency of the GMM estimator based on the NLS orthogonality conditions

$$\mathrm{E}\left[\mu_{\boldsymbol{\beta}}(\boldsymbol{\beta}_0; \mathbf{x}_n)\left(y_n - \mu(\boldsymbol{\beta}_0; \mathbf{x}_n)\right)\right] = \mathbf{0}$$

by adding instrumental variables and increasing the number of moments.[38] Cragg also noted that one can do this efficiently without specifying $\sigma_0^2(\mathbf{w}_n)$ explicitly by using the Eicker–White variance estimator. Because

$$\begin{aligned}\boldsymbol{\Lambda}_N &= \mathrm{E}_N[\mathbf{g}(U; \hat{\boldsymbol{\theta}})\,\mathbf{g}(U; \hat{\boldsymbol{\theta}})'] \\ &= \mathrm{E}_N\left[\mu_{\boldsymbol{\beta}}(\hat{\boldsymbol{\beta}}; \mathbf{x}_n)\left(y_n - \mu(\hat{\boldsymbol{\beta}}; \mathbf{x}_n)\right)^2 \mu_{\boldsymbol{\beta}}(\hat{\boldsymbol{\beta}}; \mathbf{x}_n)'\right]\end{aligned}$$

is a consistent estimator of $\boldsymbol{\Lambda}_0$ given any consistent $\hat{\boldsymbol{\beta}}$, the linearized GMM estimator (for example)

$$\hat{\boldsymbol{\beta}}_{\text{GMM}} = \left[\hat{\mathbf{M}}'\mathbf{Z}\left(\mathbf{Z}'\hat{\mathbf{D}}\mathbf{Z}\right)^{-1}\mathbf{Z}'\hat{\mathbf{M}}\right]^{-1}\hat{\mathbf{M}}'\mathbf{Z}\left(\mathbf{Z}'\hat{\mathbf{D}}\mathbf{Z}\right)^{-1}\mathbf{Z}'\left(\mathbf{y} - \hat{\boldsymbol{\mu}} + \hat{\mathbf{M}}\hat{\boldsymbol{\beta}}_{\text{NLS}}\right)$$

accomplishes this. In addition, our knowledge of efficient instruments implies that we want an instrument matrix $[\mathbf{z}_n]$ with variables whose MMSE linear predictors of $\left[\sigma_0^2(\mathbf{w}_n)\right]^{-1} \cdot \mu_{\boldsymbol{\beta}}(\boldsymbol{\beta}_0; \mathbf{x}_n)$ are as small as possible. Thus, rather than approximating $\sigma_0^2(\mathbf{x}_n)$ one attempts to approximate $\left[\sigma_{0n}^2(\mathbf{w}_n)\right]^{-1} \cdot \mu_{\boldsymbol{\beta}}(\boldsymbol{\beta}_0; \mathbf{x}_n)$.

This same approach applies to the instrumental variables case. Rather than approximating $\sigma_0^2(\mathbf{w}_n)$ and $\mathrm{E}[\mu_{\boldsymbol{\beta}}(\boldsymbol{\beta}_0; \mathbf{x}_n) \mid \mathbf{w}_n]$ separately, one can just as well specify functions of $\mathbf{w}_n$ that may provide good linear predictors of the scalar product $\left[\sigma_0^2(\mathbf{w}_n)\right]^{-1} \cdot \mathrm{E}[\mu_{\boldsymbol{\beta}}(\boldsymbol{\beta}_0; \mathbf{x}_n) \mid \mathbf{w}_n]$. Extensions to cases with serial correlation are also possible. An early example is the work by Cumby et al. (1983).

Finally, Greene (1997) notes that the two approximation methods are not mutually exclusive. It seems reasonable that preliminary attempts to fit $\sigma_0^2(\mathbf{w}_n)$ with a parametric function may lead to instrumental variables that approximate $\left[\sigma_0^2(\mathbf{w}_n)\right]^{-1} \cdot \mathrm{E}[\mu_{\boldsymbol{\beta}}(\boldsymbol{\beta}_0; \mathbf{x}_n) \mid \mathbf{w}_n]$ better with fewer variables. The savings in moment functions may provide better behaved estimators in small samples.

[38] Cragg (1983) actually restricted his attention to a linear regression model.

21.5 METHODOLOGICAL NOTES

GMM is an attractive alternative to ML estimation because it rests on weaker assumptions. Rather than requiring specification of a conditional distribution, GMM uses only moment functions. When they are uncomfortable asserting distributional assumptions, researchers find extra confidence in GMM estimators that are not sensitive to such specific claims. On the other hand, this confidence generally comes at a cost in the efficiency of the estimators employed. As so often happens, unrestricted estimation is less efficient than restricted estimation.

In special cases, the score function of a log-likelihood function corresponds to a natural set of moment functions. One obtains the properties of an MLE when the likelihood specification is correct. If it is not, then properties of GMM estimators are nevertheless maintained. The normal regression model is a leading example. Gourieroux et al. (1984) provide an analysis of more general examples.

GMM also affords flexibility in the selection of moments that does not arise in ML estimation. The likelihood function specifies all moments and the score gives the most efficient moment functions. Often, the researcher applying GMM has many moment functions from which to choose. The selection of instrumental variables is one example. Another is the selection of the orders of the moments. How should one choose?

The asymptotic distribution theory suggests that one should include every available moment function. Proposition 21 provides the optimal combinations of the moment functions and $\hat{\mathbf{\Lambda}}_N$ makes such combinations asymptotically feasible. But the sample may not be large enough to rely on the asymptotic approximation. In our description of FGLS (pp. 442, 474), we noted that sampling variance in the weighting matrix can overwhelm the benefits of GLS. In GMM, the sampling variance of $\hat{\mathbf{\Lambda}}_N$ can have the same effect. Recall also the potential to overfit with instrumental variables (p. 514). As a generalization of IV estimation, GMM can suffer the same ills.

Thus, one has reasons to restrain an inclusion of every moment function in GMM estimation. Newey (1988) provides an asymptotic theory that demonstrates the feasibility of adaptive estimation of regression models by adding moments at a certain rate as the sample size grows. But small sample guidelines remain a question for current research. In practice, researchers often use the same approach as Hansen and Singleton (1982, p. 1284, footnotes 12 and 15), who experiment with various moment restrictions and note where variances and point estimates seem unstable.

21.6 MATHEMATICAL NOTES

21.6.1 Uniform Convergence of the GMM Criterion Function

Here we prove that $Q_N(\boldsymbol{\theta}) \xrightarrow{p} Q_0(\boldsymbol{\theta})$ uniformly in $\boldsymbol{\theta} \in \boldsymbol{\Theta}$ to complete the proof of GMM consistency in Section 21.4.1. The triangle inequality implies that

$$\begin{aligned}
|Q_N(\boldsymbol{\theta}) - Q_0(\boldsymbol{\theta})| &= \left|\mathbf{g}_N(\boldsymbol{\theta})'\mathbf{C}_N\,\mathbf{g}_N(\boldsymbol{\theta}) - \mathrm{E}[\mathbf{g}(U;\boldsymbol{\theta})]'\mathbf{C}_0\,\mathrm{E}[\mathbf{g}(U;\boldsymbol{\theta})]\right| \\
&\leq \left|\{\mathbf{g}_N(\boldsymbol{\theta}) - \mathrm{E}[\mathbf{g}(U;\boldsymbol{\theta})]\}'\,\mathbf{C}_N\,\{\mathbf{g}_N(\boldsymbol{\theta}) - \mathrm{E}[\mathbf{g}(U;\boldsymbol{\theta})]\}\right| \\
&\quad + 2\left|\mathrm{E}[\mathbf{g}(U;\boldsymbol{\theta})]'\mathbf{C}_N\,\{\mathbf{g}_N(\boldsymbol{\theta}) - \mathrm{E}[\mathbf{g}(U;\boldsymbol{\theta})]\}\right| \\
&\quad + \left|\mathrm{E}[\mathbf{g}(U;\boldsymbol{\theta})]'\,(\mathbf{C}_N - \mathbf{C}_0)\,\mathrm{E}[\mathbf{g}(U;\boldsymbol{\theta})]\right|
\end{aligned}$$

Applying the Cauchy–Schwarz inequality to the right-hand side gives[39]

$$\begin{aligned}|Q_N(\boldsymbol{\theta}) - Q_0(\boldsymbol{\theta})| \le &\|\mathbf{g}_N(\boldsymbol{\theta}) - \mathrm{E}[\mathbf{g}(U;\boldsymbol{\theta})]\| \, \|\mathbf{C}_N\| \\ &+ 2\,\|\mathrm{E}[\mathbf{g}(U;\boldsymbol{\theta})]\| \, \|\mathbf{g}_N(\boldsymbol{\theta}) - \mathrm{E}[\mathbf{g}(U;\boldsymbol{\theta})]\| \, \|\mathbf{C}_N\| \\ &+ \|\mathrm{E}[\mathbf{g}(U;\boldsymbol{\theta})]\| \, \|\mathbf{C}_N - \mathbf{C}_0\|\end{aligned}$$

where the magnitude of a matrix is $\left\|[a_{ij}]\right\| \equiv \sqrt{\sum_{i,j} a_{ij}^2}$. By Assumption 21.1,

$$\|\mathbf{g}_N(\boldsymbol{\theta}) - \mathrm{E}[\mathbf{g}(U;\boldsymbol{\theta})]\| \xrightarrow{p} 0$$

uniformly in $\boldsymbol{\theta} \in \boldsymbol{\Theta}$ and $\mathrm{E}[\mathbf{g}(U;\boldsymbol{\theta})]$ is continuous. Assumption 21.2 states that $\boldsymbol{\Theta}$ is compact and therefore $\|\mathrm{E}[\mathbf{g}(U;\boldsymbol{\theta})]\|$ is bounded for $\boldsymbol{\theta} \in \boldsymbol{\Theta}$. This assumption also implies that

$$\|\mathbf{C}_N - \mathbf{C}_0\| \xrightarrow{p} 0$$

which is also uniform in $\boldsymbol{\theta}$. Therefore $Q_N(\boldsymbol{\theta})$ converges in probability uniformly to $Q_0(\boldsymbol{\theta})$ on $\boldsymbol{\Theta}$. Note additionally that the continuity of $\mathrm{E}[\mathbf{g}(U;\boldsymbol{\theta})]$ implies that $Q_0(\boldsymbol{\theta})$ is continuous.

21.6.2 Nonsingularity of the GMM Hessian

Lemma 21.3 *Under Assumptions 21.2–21.3, $\mathbf{G}_0'\mathbf{C}_0\mathbf{G}_0$ is nonsingular.*

Proof. Let

$$\mathbf{g}_0(\boldsymbol{\theta}_1) = \mathbf{g}_0(\boldsymbol{\theta}_0) + \mathbf{G}_0(\bar{\boldsymbol{\theta}})\,(\boldsymbol{\theta}_1 - \boldsymbol{\theta}_0)$$

so that

$$\begin{aligned}\left[\mathbf{g}_0(\boldsymbol{\theta}_1) - \mathbf{g}_0(\boldsymbol{\theta}_0)\right]' \mathbf{C}_0 \left[\mathbf{g}_0(\boldsymbol{\theta}_1) - \mathbf{g}_0(\boldsymbol{\theta}_0)\right] &= \mathbf{g}_0(\boldsymbol{\theta}_1)'\mathbf{C}_0\mathbf{g}_0(\boldsymbol{\theta}_1) \\ &= (\boldsymbol{\theta}_1 - \boldsymbol{\theta}_0)'\,\mathbf{G}_0(\bar{\boldsymbol{\theta}})'\mathbf{C}_0\mathbf{G}_0(\bar{\boldsymbol{\theta}})\,(\boldsymbol{\theta}_1 - \boldsymbol{\theta}_0)\end{aligned}$$

where $\bar{\boldsymbol{\theta}}$ is the mean value. Because $\mathbf{g}_0(\boldsymbol{\theta}_1)'\mathbf{C}_0\mathbf{g}_0(\boldsymbol{\theta}_1) > 0$ for all $\boldsymbol{\theta}_1 \neq \boldsymbol{\theta}_0$ (Assumption 21.2), $\mathbf{G}_0(\bar{\boldsymbol{\theta}})'\mathbf{C}_0\mathbf{G}_0(\bar{\boldsymbol{\theta}})$ is positive definite and therefore nonsingular. Assumption 21.3 implies that $\mathbf{G}_0(\boldsymbol{\theta}_0)'\mathbf{C}_0\mathbf{G}_0(\boldsymbol{\theta}_0)$ is also nonsingular, because $\bar{\boldsymbol{\theta}}$ approaches $\boldsymbol{\theta}_0$ as $\boldsymbol{\theta}_1$ approaches $\boldsymbol{\theta}_0$. □

---

[39] The application of the Cauchy–Schwarz inequality works as follows: using (G.15), write

$$\mathbf{a}'\boldsymbol{\Omega}\mathbf{b} = \left(\mathbf{a}' \otimes \mathbf{b}'\right) \operatorname{vec} \boldsymbol{\Omega}$$

so that the Cauchy–Schwarz inequality implies that

$$\begin{aligned}\left|\mathbf{a}'\boldsymbol{\Omega}\mathbf{b}\right| &= \left|\left(\mathbf{a}' \otimes \mathbf{b}'\right) \operatorname{vec} \boldsymbol{\Omega}\right| \\ &\le \|\mathbf{a} \otimes \mathbf{b}\| \, \|\operatorname{vec} \boldsymbol{\Omega}\| \\ &= \sqrt{\mathbf{a}'\mathbf{a} \otimes \mathbf{b}'\mathbf{b}}\, \|\boldsymbol{\Omega}\| \\ &= \|\mathbf{a}\| \, \|\mathbf{b}\| \, \|\boldsymbol{\Omega}\|\end{aligned}$$

21.6.3 GMM Efficiency

Proof of Proposition 21. Let us index the elements of the set of GMM estimators with $\mathbf{C}_0$, the probability limit of $\mathbf{C}_N$. According to (21.37), these estimators are asymptotically one to one with the solutions of the generalized minimum distance problem

$$\mathbf{P}_{\mathbf{X}\perp\mathbf{C}_0\mathbf{X}}\mathbf{y} = \underset{\boldsymbol{\mu}\in\mathrm{Col}(\mathbf{X})}{\operatorname{argmin}} (\mathbf{y}-\boldsymbol{\mu})'\,\mathbf{C}_0\,(\mathbf{y}-\boldsymbol{\mu})$$

where

$$\mathbf{y} \sim \mathfrak{N}(0, \boldsymbol{\Lambda}_0) \overset{p}{=} \sqrt{N}\cdot\mathbf{g}_N(\boldsymbol{\theta}_0)$$
$$\mathbf{X} \equiv \mathbf{G}_0$$

Aitken's theorem (Theorem 12, p. 432) states that $\mathbf{P}_{\mathbf{X}\perp\boldsymbol{\Lambda}_0^{-1}\mathbf{X}}\mathbf{y}$ is efficient relative to all linear unbiased estimators $\mathbf{P}_{\mathbf{X}\perp\mathbf{C}_0\mathbf{X}}\mathbf{y}$ for E[$\mathbf{y}$]. Therefore, if $\mathbf{C}_0 = \boldsymbol{\Lambda}_0^{-1}$ then $\hat{\boldsymbol{\theta}}_{\mathrm{GMM}}$ is relatively efficient with asymptotic variance $\mathbf{V}_0 = \left(\mathbf{G}_0'\boldsymbol{\Lambda}_0^{-1}\mathbf{G}_0\right)^{-1}$.

If (21.38) holds, $\mathbf{P}_{\mathbf{X}\perp\mathbf{C}_0\mathbf{X}}$ equals $\mathbf{P}_{\mathbf{X}\perp\boldsymbol{\Lambda}_0^{-1}\mathbf{X}}$, the unique projector onto Col($\mathbf{X}$) along Col($\boldsymbol{\Lambda}_0^{-1}\mathbf{X}$).[40] Therefore (21.38) is sufficient for the relative efficiency of $\hat{\boldsymbol{\theta}}_{\mathrm{GMM}}$.

The necessity of (21.38) is subtler and reflects the uniqueness of orthogonal projections. According to the Proposition 8 (Orthogonality of Efficient Estimators, p. 185) undergirding Aitken's theorem, all relatively efficient $\mathbf{P}_{\mathbf{X}\perp\mathbf{C}_0\mathbf{X}}\mathbf{y}$ must be equal to $\mathbf{P}_{\mathbf{X}\perp\boldsymbol{\Lambda}_0^{-1}\mathbf{X}}\mathbf{y}$ with probability one.[41] That is,

$$\begin{aligned}&\mathrm{Var}[\mathbf{P}_{\mathbf{X}\perp\mathbf{C}_0\mathbf{X}}\mathbf{y} - \mathbf{P}_{\mathbf{X}\perp\boldsymbol{\Lambda}_0^{-1}\mathbf{X}}\mathbf{y}]\\ &= \left(\mathbf{P}_{\mathbf{X}\perp\mathbf{C}_0\mathbf{X}} - \mathbf{P}_{\mathbf{X}\perp\boldsymbol{\Lambda}_0^{-1}\mathbf{X}}\right)\boldsymbol{\Lambda}_0\left(\mathbf{P}_{\mathbf{X}\perp\mathbf{C}_0\mathbf{X}} - \mathbf{P}_{\mathbf{X}\perp\boldsymbol{\Lambda}_0^{-1}\mathbf{X}}\right)\\ &= \mathbf{0}\end{aligned}$$

It follows that $\mathbf{P}_{\mathbf{X}\perp\mathbf{C}_0\mathbf{X}} = \mathbf{P}_{\mathbf{X}\perp\boldsymbol{\Lambda}_0^{-1}\mathbf{X}}$, which implies (21.38), again according to the uniqueness of projectors onto Col($\mathbf{X}$) along Col($\boldsymbol{\Lambda}_0^{-1}\mathbf{X}$). □

21.7 OVERVIEW

1. Generalized method of moments (GMM) is an alternative method to maximum likelihood (ML).[42] GMM is based on the specification of a few moments rather than an entire distribution function. The (ordinary) method of moments (MM) and linear instrumental variables (IV) are special cases.

---

[40] This statement rests on Lemmas 3.1, 3.4, and 3.5.

[41] See especially footnote 11 on p. 186.

[42] The method of moments was proposed by Karl Pearson, long after maximum likelihood was first discussed by Gauss and Bernoulli (1777). GMM has many closely related predecessors. Examples include Berkson's minimum chi-square and Rothenberg's use of classical minimum distance.

2. All estimators discussed previously have GMM interpretations, including ML. Such interpretations show that some distributional assumptions are unnecessary to motivate an estimator. In particular, the normal distribution is not necessary to motivate the GLS estimator.
3. Identification with a finite number of moment equations is fundamentally different from identification with a likelihood function. The basic issue is whether the population parameters are the unique solution to the moment equations.
   (a) There must be at least as many moment equations as parameters to estimate.
   (b) The rank condition is necessary and sufficient for local identification.
4. In many respects, the asymptotic distribution theories of GMM and ML are similar. The salient difference is that the second derivatives of the GMM objective function play no explicit role. Only the first derivatives of the moment function matter because the objective function is quadratic in the moment function.
5. Estimation of the variance matrix of the GMM estimator rests conveniently on empirical second moments and the "sandwich" estimator. When the GMM variance estimator is applied to the MLE, one obtains a variance estimator that is robust to misspecifications of the likelihood function that do not make the quasi-MLE inconsistent.
6. When there are more moments than parameters, the relatively efficient GMM estimator weights various moments in the same way that GLS weights various observations with the inverse of a variance matrix. When there are more instrumental variables than explanatory variables, the 2SLS estimator is an example of a relatively efficient GMM estimator.
7. GMM takes the moment equations as given. Thus, the choice of moments, or instrumental variables, is a separate issue. In large samples, one should use all available moments (assuming there is a finite number), optimally weighted. In small samples, fewer moments may provide better estimators.

21.8 EXERCISES

21.8.1 Review

21.1 Hall (1978) also suggests (but does not estimate) a model with the constant-relative-risk-aversion utility function $U(C) = C^{\gamma_0}/\gamma_0$.
   (a) What is the Euler equation for such a model?
   (b) Consider the parameter value $\gamma = 0$ in this Euler equation.
   (c) What problems does this pose for this model?

21.2 Campbell and Mankiw (1989) considered lagged first differences in income and in consumption *separately* as instrumental variables. Comment.

21.3 Researchers use (20.31) to anticipate the direction of bias or inconsistency in OLS.
   (a) What would Campbell and Mankiw (1989) expect the bias to be in the OLS estimator of β_{02} in (21.2),

$$C_t - C_{t-1} = \beta_{01} + \beta_{02}\,(Y_t - Y_{t-1}) + \varepsilon_t$$

   (b) In fact, the OLS fit is

$$y_t = \underset{(0.0004)}{0.0039} + \underset{(0.031)}{0.209}\,x_t + \hat{\varepsilon}_t$$

   Compare the fitted value for β_{02} with the 2SLS estimator and comment.

21.4 (IV and GMM) Describe how the assumptions supporting the IV estimator,

- Assumption 20.1 (Latent Variable Model, p. 499),
- Assumption 20.2 (Instruments, p. 499), and
- Assumption 20.3, (Convergence, p. 500)

fit within the assumptions of the GMM estimator in this chapter.

21.5 (Errors in Variables) Reconsider the model of errors in explanatory variables in Example 20.1. Assume that the variables $\mathbf{x}_n^*$, $\boldsymbol{v}_n$, and u_n are i.i.d. from a joint distribution with finite first and second moments.

(a) Show that the parameters in $\boldsymbol{\beta}_0$ are not identified.
(b) Give an interpretation of the inconsistency of OLS in terms of your analysis of identification.
(c) Extend your analysis to the model in Exercise 20.8.
(d) Suppose that necessary fourth moments exist and derive a GMM estimator for this model.

21.6 (IV) Consider a regression model

$$y_n = \mathbf{x}_n'\boldsymbol{\beta}_0 + \varepsilon_n, \qquad n = 1, \ldots, N$$

in which ε_n is a latent random variable that is correlated with the explanatory variables in $\mathbf{x}_n$. Let the elements of $\mathbf{x}_n$ include the constant 1.

Assume i.i.d. sampling and that

$$\mathrm{E}[\varepsilon_n] = 0 \tag{21.42}$$

$$\mathrm{Var}[\varepsilon_n] = \sigma_0^2 \tag{21.43}$$

and

$$\mathrm{E}[\mathbf{x}_n\mathbf{x}_n'] = \mathbf{D}_{xx} \tag{21.44}$$

where $\mathbf{D}_{xx}$ is a positive-definite matrix. In addition, let

$$\mathrm{Cov}[\mathbf{x}_n, \varepsilon_n] = \rho_0 \tag{21.45}$$

(a) Consider the first and second sample moments of $(\mathbf{x}_n, y_n)$: $\bar{\boldsymbol{x}} \equiv (1/N)\sum_{n=1}^N \mathbf{x}_n$, $\bar{y} \equiv (1/N)\sum_{n=1}^N y_n$, $(1/N) \cdot \mathbf{X}'\mathbf{X}$, $(1/N) \cdot \mathbf{y}'\mathbf{y}$, and $(1/N) \cdot \mathbf{X}'\mathbf{y}$. Find their expected values in terms of the unknown parameters.
(b) Show that the moments in (21.42)–(21.45) are insufficient to construct an estimator for $\boldsymbol{\beta}_0$.
(c) Suppose that there are K *instrumental variables*, z_{nk} $(k = 1, \ldots, K)$ that are uncorrelated with ε_n,

$$\mathrm{Cov}[\mathbf{z}_n, \varepsilon_n] = \mathbf{0} \tag{21.46}$$

yet correlated with $\mathbf{x}_n$,

$$\mathrm{E}[\mathbf{z}_n\mathbf{x}_n'] = \mathbf{D}_{zx} \tag{21.47}$$

where $\mathbf{D}_{zx}$ is also nonsingular. Find the expected values of the additional first and second moments $\mathrm{E}_N[\mathbf{z}_n] = (1/N)\sum_{n=1}^N \mathbf{z}_n$, $\mathrm{E}_N[\mathbf{z}_n\mathbf{z}_n'] = (1/N)\cdot\mathbf{Z}'\mathbf{Z}$, and $\mathrm{E}_N[\mathbf{z}_n\mathbf{x}_n'] = (1/N)\cdot\mathbf{Z}'\mathbf{X}$ in terms of the unknown parameters.
(d) By equating all the first and second sample moments above to their population values, find a method-of-moments estimator for all of the unknown parameters. Show in particular that the estimator of $\boldsymbol{\beta}_0$ is the IV estimator $(\mathbf{Z}'\mathbf{X})^{-1}\mathbf{Z}'\mathbf{y}$.

21.7 (Weighted 2SLS) On p. 553, we say "If $\mu(\boldsymbol{\beta}_0; \mathbf{x}_n)$ is linear in $\mathbf{x}_n$ and $\mathrm{E}[\mathbf{x}_n \mid \mathbf{w}_n]$ is linear in $\mathbf{w}_n$, then $\mathrm{E}[\mu_{\boldsymbol{\beta}}(\boldsymbol{\beta}_0; \mathbf{x}_n) \mid \mathbf{w}_n]$ is also linear in $\mathbf{w}_n$ and a weighted 2SLS estimator is a feasible, asymptotically efficient IV estimator." Taking $\sigma_{0n}^2 = \exp(\mathbf{w}_n' \boldsymbol{\gamma}_0)$, propose such a feasible estimator for Example 21.3.

21.8 (Efficiency of ML) Demonstrate the efficiency of ML relative to GMM using the following steps. Let the likelihood function be $L(\boldsymbol{\theta}; U)$ and the population value of $\boldsymbol{\theta}$ be $\boldsymbol{\theta}_0$. Suppose that $\{U_1, \ldots, U_N\}$ is a random sample of the random variable U.

(a) Let $\mathbf{g}(U; \boldsymbol{\theta})$ be a vector of moment functions that satisfy the restrictions $\mathrm{E}[\mathbf{g}(U; \boldsymbol{\theta}_0)] = \mathbf{0}$. Prove the *generalized information identity*

$$\mathrm{E}[\mathbf{g}_{\boldsymbol{\theta}}(U; \boldsymbol{\theta}_0)] = -\,\mathrm{Cov}[\mathbf{g}(U; \boldsymbol{\theta}_0),\ L_{\boldsymbol{\theta}}(\boldsymbol{\theta}_0; U)]$$

(b) Let

$$\sqrt{N}\,\mathrm{E}_N[\mathbf{g}(U; \boldsymbol{\theta}_0)] \xrightarrow{d} \mathfrak{N}(\mathbf{0}, \boldsymbol{\Lambda}_0), \qquad \mathrm{E}_N[\mathbf{g}_{\boldsymbol{\theta}}(U; \boldsymbol{\theta}_0)] \xrightarrow{p} \mathbf{G}_0$$

$$\sqrt{N}\,\mathrm{E}_N[L_{\boldsymbol{\theta}}(\boldsymbol{\theta}_0; U)] \xrightarrow{d} \mathfrak{N}(\mathbf{0}, \mathfrak{I}_0), \qquad \mathrm{E}_N[L_{\boldsymbol{\theta}\boldsymbol{\theta}}(\boldsymbol{\theta}_0; U)] \xrightarrow{p} \mathfrak{I}_0$$

$$\mathrm{E}_N[\mathbf{g}(U; \boldsymbol{\theta}_0)\, L_{\boldsymbol{\theta}}(\boldsymbol{\theta}_0; U)'] \xrightarrow{p} \mathrm{Cov}[\mathbf{g}(U; \boldsymbol{\theta}_0),\ L_{\boldsymbol{\theta}}(\boldsymbol{\theta}_0; U)]$$

and

$$\sqrt{N}\left(\hat{\boldsymbol{\theta}}_{\mathrm{GMM}} - \boldsymbol{\theta}_0\right) \stackrel{p}{=} -\left(\mathbf{G}_0'\mathbf{C}_0\mathbf{G}_0\right)^{-1} \mathbf{G}_0'\mathbf{C}_0 \sqrt{N}\,\mathrm{E}_N[\mathbf{g}(U; \boldsymbol{\theta}_0)]$$

as in (21.30) and

$$\sqrt{N}(\hat{\boldsymbol{\theta}}_{\mathrm{ML}} - \boldsymbol{\theta}_0) \stackrel{p}{=} \mathfrak{I}_0^{-1} \sqrt{N}\,\mathrm{E}_N[L_{\boldsymbol{\theta}}(\boldsymbol{\theta}_0; U)]$$

as in (15.6). Using the generalized information identity, show that the asymptotic variance of $\hat{\boldsymbol{\theta}}_{\mathrm{ML}}$ equals the asymptotic covariance of $\hat{\boldsymbol{\theta}}_{\mathrm{ML}}$ and $\hat{\boldsymbol{\theta}}_{\mathrm{GMM}}$.

(c) Use this relationship among second moments to show that ML is asymptotically efficient relative to GMM.

21.9 (Identification and NLS) Consider NLS where

$$Q_N = \mathrm{E}_N\left[\left(y_n - \mu(\boldsymbol{\beta}; \mathbf{x}_n)\right)^2\right] \xrightarrow{p} \mathrm{E}\left[\left(y_n - \mu(\boldsymbol{\beta}; \mathbf{x}_n)\right)^2\right] = Q_0(\boldsymbol{\beta})$$

uniformly.[43] Then $\boldsymbol{\beta}_0$ is identified if $Q_0(\boldsymbol{\beta})$ is uniquely minimized at $\boldsymbol{\beta} = \boldsymbol{\beta}_0$.

(a) Argue that the MSE function is minimized at the conditional mean of y_n given $\mathbf{x}_n$, $\mathrm{E}[y_n \mid \mathbf{x}_n] \equiv \mu(\boldsymbol{\beta}_0; \mathbf{x}_n)$.

(b) Argue that any other minimizer of the MSE is equal to this conditional mean with probability one so that identification of $\boldsymbol{\beta}_0$ rests on the behavior of $\mu(\boldsymbol{\beta}; \mathbf{x}_n)$ as a function of $\boldsymbol{\beta}$.

(c) As an example, consider $\mu(\boldsymbol{\beta}; \mathbf{x}) = \beta_1 + \beta_2 x^{\beta_3}$. Show that $\mu(\boldsymbol{\beta}; x)$ intersects $\mu(\boldsymbol{\beta}_0; x)$ at no more than three values of $x > 0$. Use this fact to give a sufficient condition for variation in x_n over n to identify $\boldsymbol{\beta}_0$.

21.10 (Restricted GMM) Show that

$$\hat{\boldsymbol{\theta}}_{\mathrm{R}}^{*} \equiv \hat{\boldsymbol{\theta}} - \hat{\mathbf{V}}_N \mathbf{r}_{\boldsymbol{\theta}}(\hat{\boldsymbol{\theta}})' \left[\mathbf{r}_{\boldsymbol{\theta}}(\hat{\boldsymbol{\theta}})' \hat{\mathbf{V}}_N \mathbf{r}_{\boldsymbol{\theta}}(\hat{\boldsymbol{\theta}})\right]^{-1} \mathbf{r}(\hat{\boldsymbol{\theta}}) \tag{21.48}$$

is a linearized restricted GMM estimator for

[43] See Newey and McFadden (1994, Section 2.2.2).

$$\hat{\boldsymbol{\theta}}_{\mathrm{R}} \equiv \underset{\{\boldsymbol{\theta}|\mathbf{r}(\boldsymbol{\theta})=\mathbf{0}\}}{\operatorname{argmin}} \ \mathbf{g}_N(\boldsymbol{\theta})'\mathbf{C}_N\mathbf{g}_N(\boldsymbol{\theta})$$

in the sense that $\sqrt{N}\left(\hat{\boldsymbol{\theta}}^*_{\mathrm{R}} - \hat{\boldsymbol{\theta}}_{\mathrm{R}}\right) \overset{p}{=} \mathbf{0}$.

21.8.2 Extensions

21.11 (Two-Step Estimators) Let the assumptions of Proposition 20 (GMM Asymptotics, p. 546) hold. Suppose that the moments and parameters partition into

$$\mathbf{g}_N(\boldsymbol{\theta}) = \begin{bmatrix} \mathbf{g}_{1N}(\boldsymbol{\theta}_1) \\ \mathbf{g}_{2N}(\boldsymbol{\theta}_1, \boldsymbol{\theta}_2) \end{bmatrix}$$

(a) Under what conditions can one construct a two-step estimator for $\boldsymbol{\theta}_{02}$ based on

$$\check{\boldsymbol{\theta}}_1 = \underset{\boldsymbol{\theta}_1}{\operatorname{argmin}} \ \mathbf{g}_{1N}(\boldsymbol{\theta}_1)'\mathbf{C}_{1N}\mathbf{g}_{1N}(\boldsymbol{\theta}_1)$$

as the first step and

$$\check{\boldsymbol{\theta}}_2 = \underset{\boldsymbol{\theta}_2}{\operatorname{argmin}} \ \mathbf{g}_{2N}(\check{\boldsymbol{\theta}}_1, \boldsymbol{\theta}_2)'\mathbf{C}_{2N}\mathbf{g}_{2N}(\check{\boldsymbol{\theta}}_1, \boldsymbol{\theta}_2)$$

as the second?

(b) Under what conditions is such a two-step estimator efficient relative to other GMM estimators?

21.12 (Pseudo-ML) Not all estimation based on moment restrictions is motivated as GMM. Gourieroux et al. (1984) describe a class of pseudo-MLEs based on the multivariate *linear exponential family of distributions* with the p.f.s

$$f(\mathbf{z};\boldsymbol{\theta}) = \begin{cases} \exp[a(\mathbf{z}) + b(\boldsymbol{\theta}) + \mathbf{c}(\boldsymbol{\theta})'\mathbf{z}] & \text{if} \quad \mathbf{z} \in \mathbb{S} \\ 0 & \text{if} \quad \mathbf{z} \notin \mathbb{S} \end{cases}$$

The support $\mathbb{S} \subseteq \mathbb{R}^J$ does not depend on $\boldsymbol{\theta}$, $a(\mathbf{z})$ and $b(\boldsymbol{\theta})$ are real-valued scalars, and $\mathbf{c}(\boldsymbol{\theta})$ is a vector of J transformations of $\boldsymbol{\theta} \in \boldsymbol{\Theta} \subset \mathbb{R}^K$. Suppose that

$$\int_{\mathbb{S}} f(\mathbf{z};\boldsymbol{\theta})\, d\mathbf{z} = 1$$

if the distribution is continuous and that

$$\sum_{\mathbf{z}\in\mathbb{S}} f(\mathbf{z};\boldsymbol{\theta}) = 1$$

if the distribution is discrete. Also suppose that $b(\boldsymbol{\theta})$ and $\mathbf{c}(\boldsymbol{\theta})$ are twice continuously differentiable and the Jacobian matrix of $\mathbf{c}(\boldsymbol{\theta})$, $\partial\mathbf{c}(\boldsymbol{\theta})'/\partial\boldsymbol{\theta}$, is full-row rank for $\boldsymbol{\theta} \in \boldsymbol{\Theta}$. Let $F(\mathbf{z};\boldsymbol{\theta})$ denote the c.d.f. corresponding to $f(\mathbf{z};\boldsymbol{\theta})$.

(a) Suppose that $J = K$ and

$$\int_{\mathbb{S}} \mathbf{z}\, dF(\mathbf{z};\boldsymbol{\theta}) = \boldsymbol{\theta}$$

Show that for all $\boldsymbol{\theta} \in \boldsymbol{\Theta}$, $\boldsymbol{\theta} \neq \boldsymbol{\theta}_0$,

$$b(\boldsymbol{\theta}) + \mathbf{c}(\boldsymbol{\theta})'\boldsymbol{\theta}_0 < b(\boldsymbol{\theta}_0) + \mathbf{c}(\boldsymbol{\theta}_0)'\boldsymbol{\theta}_0$$

[Hint: Review the log-likelihood inequality (Lemma 14.1, p. 290).]

(b) Suppose that $\{(\mathbf{x}_n, y_n)\,;\ n = 1, \ldots, N\}$ is an i.i.d. sample from a distribution with the property that $\mathrm{E}[y_n \mid \mathbf{x}_n] = \mu(\boldsymbol{\beta}_0; \mathbf{x}_n)$. Using the previous inequality and $J = 1$, show that, even though $f\Big[y; \mu(\boldsymbol{\beta}_0; \mathbf{x}_n)\Big]$ may not be the conditional p.f. of y_n given $\mathbf{x}_n$, the pseudo-MLE

$$\hat{\boldsymbol{\beta}} = \underset{\boldsymbol{\beta}}{\operatorname{argmax}}\, \mathrm{E}_N\Big[\log f\Big(y_n; \mu(\boldsymbol{\beta}; \mathbf{x}_n)\Big)\Big]$$

is a consistent estimator of $\boldsymbol{\beta}_0$.

(c) Show that

$$0 = \frac{\partial b(\boldsymbol{\theta})}{\partial \boldsymbol{\theta}} + \frac{\partial \mathbf{c}(\boldsymbol{\theta})'}{\partial \boldsymbol{\theta}}\boldsymbol{\theta}$$

(HINT: See Exercise 14.11.)

(d) Although the pseudo-MLE is not based on GMM, show that the GMM efficiency bound also applies to the pseudo-MLE and derive the bound.

(e) Show how to modify the pseudo-MLE so that this efficiency bound is obtained asymptotically.

21.9 APPENDIX: DATA COLLECTION

The Bureau of Economic Analysis (BEA) of the U.S. Department of Commerce (http://www.bea.doc.gov) collects and distributes the national income and product accounts (NIPA) data for the United States. A convenient internet source of these (and many other) macroeconomic data is the website of the Federal Reserve Board of St. Louis (http://www.stls.frb.org/fred), which maintains the database FRED (Federal Reserve Economic Data). We originally obtained our data from FRED, but recently many of the series changed from quarterly to monthly frequencies. At the time of writing, our data appeared on the website of Economic Information Systems, Inc. in the NIPA quarterly tables file http://www.econ-line.com/data/NQ.zip. This file was compressed with the zip format. Once decompressed (unzipped) the file loads conveniently into spreadsheet software. This source is particularly straightforward because the series are recorded from to 1947 to the present.

The BEA reports real (as opposed to nominal) measures of consumption and income in *chained (1992) dollars*. These measures rest on Fisher indexes. Landefeld and Parker (1997) describe their advantages and disadvantages. They note a principal limitation, that the chained (1992) dollars are not additive over components of the national accounts. For example, in chained (1992) dollars total personal consumption expenditures do not equal the sum of its three components, expenditures on durable goods, nondurable goods, and services. The differences tend to grow as the time period is further from the base year 1992.

The empirical work reported in Section 21.1 uses the sum of personal consumption expenditures on nondurable goods and services. To compensate for the additivity problem, we computed the change in the (natural) logarithm of the sum of real consumption of nondurables and services from period $t-1$ to t in chained period t dollars instead of chained 1992 dollars. The nominal value in period t equals the real value in chained period t dollars. We took the price index for chained period t dollars of a particular consumption series to be the ratio of the nominal period t value over the chained 1992 dollar value. To compute the chained period t value of each consumption series in period $t-1$, we multiplied its value in chained 1992 dollars by this price index. Finally, we computed the difference in the logarithms of the *real* value of consumption of nondurable goods and services as the logarithm of the nominal sum of period t consumption less the logarithm of the chained period t dollar sum of period $t - 1$ consumption.

The specific data series in the data from Economic Information Systems, Inc. have labels. Nominal personal consumption in nondurable goods and in services are series NQ101_04 and NQ101_05. The chained 1992 dollar values of these two series are NQ102_04 and NQ102_05. Disposable personal income in chained 1992 dollars is series NQ201_32. In our file, all of the series ran from 1947:I to 1998:IV. We restricted our estimation sample to the period Campbell and Mankiw (1989) used.

CHAPTER 22

Generalized Method of Moments Hypothesis Tests

Hypothesis testing in the GMM framework is similar to that in the likelihood framework. The general principle of comparing an estimator with an hypothesized value works essentially the same way. In Chapter 21 we presented the GMM estimator and an estimator of its variance matrix. Given a parametric hypothesis, these estimators combine in a Wald test statistic for example. Under the null hypothesis, the Wald test statistic has the usual asymptotic chi-square distribution with degrees of freedom equal to the number of restrictions in the hypothesis.

In the first section of this chapter, we briefly describe this Wald test and its asymptotically equivalent alternatives, the GMM analogues to the score and likelihood ratio tests. The second section introduces tests of moment restrictions, as opposed to parameter restrictions. The foundation of the GMM framework is a set of moment restrictions that identifies the parameters to be estimated and the GMM estimation method provides a way to combine moment restrictions when there are more moments than parameters. Tests of moment restrictions are natural and possible in this setting.

For example, Campbell and Mankiw (1989) exclude the first lag of the first difference in the log of consumption as an instrumental variable in their two-stage least squares (2SLS) estimation of a consumption equation. Their concern is that this variable is not a valid instrumental variable. We will show that a test of the null hypothesis that this first lag of consumption growth is a valid instrumental variable is the change in the 2SLS distance function with and without this instrumental variable divided by an estimator of the residual variance. The actual value of this statistic for the data that we examined in Chapter 21 is 0.326 and under the null hypothesis this is a realization of a χ_1^2 random variable. Because this is not an unusual value for such a random variable, the test does not provide evidence against the validity of this instrumental variable.

One can also test, as Campbell and Mankiw do, whether the maintained instrumental variables are valid instruments. The test is called a test of over identifying restrictions, and the test statistic is simply the 2SLS distance function divided by the estimated residual variance. For our data this statistic equals 3.539 and its comparison distribution is χ_3^2. Once again there is little evidence against the validity of the higher lags in consumption growth as instrumental variables. The probability value of 3.539 is 32%.

In the third section, we discuss Hausman specification tests. These tests focus on whether estimators of parameters of interest are consistent in the face of possible failures in the restrictions of the model. In the consumption growth equation of Campbell and Mankiw, for example, the coefficient of income growth is the central parameter because it measures the percentage of consumers who consume their current income in violation of the permanent income hypothesis. Given the earlier concern with the first lag of consumption growth as a valid instrument, we use a Hausman specification test to learn whether the 2SLS estimate of this one central parameter changes significantly after dropping the second through fourth lags of consumption growth as valid instrumental variables. For this hypothesis, the Hausman specification test is more powerful than the overidentifying restrictions test.

To compute the test statistic, we first compute the 2SLS estimator that uses only the fifth lag in consumption growth as an instrumental variable:

$$y_t = \underset{(0.0023)}{0.0034} + \underset{(0.260)}{0.557}\,\hat{x}_t + \hat{\varepsilon}_t \tag{22.1}$$

We reported the 2SLS estimator using lags two through five in Chapter 21 as

$$y_t = \underset{(0.0011)}{0.0045} + \underset{(0.114)}{0.435}\,\hat{x}_t + \hat{\varepsilon}_t \tag{22.2}$$

The point estimate of the percentage of current income consumers changes. The loss of instrumental variables also increases the sampling variance of the estimator, as one expects.

Are the slope estimates in agreement? Because 2SLS is relatively efficient, an estimator for the variance of the difference in estimators is the difference in variances. Thus, a formal test statistic for whether the estimates have the same probability limit is the ratio

$$\frac{(0.557 - 0.435)^2}{(0.260)^2 - (0.114)^2} \approx 0.10$$

which is drawn (asymptotically) from a χ_1^2 distribution under the null hypothesis. At all conventional levels of significance, this outcome supports the validity of the instrumental variables.

The last half of this chapter contains the supporting arguments for the test statistics that we describe. We return there to the minimum chi-square lemma that played a key role in the distribution of OLS pivotal statistics and introduce two new statistical methods: sequential hypothesis testing and minimum distance estimation.

22.1 TESTS OF PARAMETER RESTRICTIONS

Consider testing a set of parameter restrictions given the estimation framework of GMM described in Chapter 21. Let the null hypothesis consist of $K - M$ restrictions $\mathbf{r}(\boldsymbol{\theta}_0) = \mathbf{0}$ and suppose that the restrictions satisfy Assumption 17.1 (Regular Restrictions, p. 397), which we repeat here for convenience.

ASSUMPTION 22.1 (REGULAR RESTRICTIONS) *The parameters $\boldsymbol{\theta}_0$ satisfy the restrictions $\mathbf{r}(\boldsymbol{\theta}_0) = \mathbf{0}$ where $\mathbf{r} : \mathbb{R}^K \to \mathbb{R}^{K-M}$ is a twice continuously differentiable function and its partial derivative matrix $\mathbf{R}(\boldsymbol{\theta}) \equiv \mathbf{r}_{\boldsymbol{\theta}}(\boldsymbol{\theta})$ has rank $K - M$ for $\boldsymbol{\theta} \in \boldsymbol{\Theta}$.*

Thus, it is possible to write the parameter vector in the restricted form $\boldsymbol{\theta} = \mathbf{s}(\boldsymbol{\gamma}),\ \boldsymbol{\gamma} \in \mathbb{R}^M$.

22.1.1 Wald Test

It is natural to begin with the Wald test, because its statistic is least specific to the likelihood framework. Under the conditions of Proposition 20, we have the unrestricted GMM estimator

$$\hat{\boldsymbol{\theta}}_N \equiv \underset{\boldsymbol{\theta}}{\operatorname{argmin}}\ Q_N(\boldsymbol{\theta}) \tag{22.3}$$

where

$$Q_N(\boldsymbol{\theta}) \equiv \mathbf{g}_N(\boldsymbol{\theta})' \hat{\boldsymbol{\Lambda}}_N^{-1} \mathbf{g}_N(\boldsymbol{\theta}) \tag{22.4}$$

and $\hat{\boldsymbol{\Lambda}}_N$ is any consistent estimator of the asymptotic variance of $\sqrt{N} \cdot \mathbf{g}_N(\boldsymbol{\theta}_0)$.[1,2] The estimator $\hat{\boldsymbol{\theta}}_N$ is consistent and asymptotically normal,

$$\sqrt{N}\left(\hat{\boldsymbol{\theta}}_N - \boldsymbol{\theta}_0\right) \xrightarrow{d} \mathfrak{N}(\mathbf{0}, \mathbf{V}_0) \tag{22.5}$$

From this estimator, we can construct a consistent estimator of $\mathbf{r}(\boldsymbol{\theta}_0)$ in the statistic $\hat{\mathbf{r}}_N \equiv \mathbf{r}(\hat{\boldsymbol{\theta}}_N)$. According to the delta method (Lemma 16.1, p. 367),

$$\sqrt{N}\left[\hat{\mathbf{r}}_N - \mathbf{r}(\boldsymbol{\theta}_0)\right] \xrightarrow{d} \mathfrak{N}(\mathbf{0}, \mathbf{R}_0\mathbf{V}_0\mathbf{R}_0')$$

where $\mathbf{R}_0 = \mathbf{R}(\boldsymbol{\theta}_0)$. We can also estimate the asymptotic variance $\mathbf{R}_0\mathbf{V}_0\mathbf{R}_0'$ consistently with $\hat{\mathbf{R}}_N\hat{\mathbf{V}}_N\hat{\mathbf{R}}_N'$ where $\hat{\mathbf{R}}_N \equiv \mathbf{R}(\hat{\boldsymbol{\theta}}_N)$ and (21.32) defines $\hat{\mathbf{V}}_N$, an estimator of the asymptotic variance of $\hat{\boldsymbol{\theta}}_N$.

With these elements, one can compute the Wald test statistic

$$\mathcal{W} \equiv N \cdot \hat{\mathbf{r}}_N' \left[\hat{\mathbf{R}}_N\hat{\mathbf{V}}_N\hat{\mathbf{R}}_N'\right]^{-1} \hat{\mathbf{r}}_N \tag{22.6}$$

to test $\mathbf{r}(\boldsymbol{\theta}_0) = \mathbf{0}$. Compared to the likelihood-based Wald statistic (17.28), the matrix $\hat{\mathbf{V}}_N$ replaces the inverse information matrix estimator for the asymptotic variance of the MLE. Otherwise the Wald statistics are identical. Both are a quadratic form in the difference of an unrestricted estimator $\mathbf{r}(\hat{\boldsymbol{\theta}}_N)$ and its hypothesized value $\mathbf{r}(\boldsymbol{\theta}_0) = \mathbf{0}$ normalized by an estimator, $\hat{\mathbf{R}}_N\hat{\mathbf{V}}_N\hat{\mathbf{R}}_N'$, of the asymptotic variance matrix of the difference. Therefore, under the null hypothesis $\mathcal{W}$ converges in distribution to a χ^2_{K-M} random variable. Under alternative hypotheses, the test has statistical power to detect that $\mathbf{r}(\boldsymbol{\theta}_0) \neq \mathbf{0}$. Given the significance level α, one rejects the null hypothesis in favor of the alternative when $\mathcal{W}$ exceeds $\chi^2_{K-M;1-\alpha}$, the 100 $(1-\alpha)$ percentile of the χ^2_{K-M} distribution.

The Wald test statistic generally changes when the restrictions $\mathbf{r}(\boldsymbol{\theta}_0) = \mathbf{0}$ are transformed nonlinearly into an equivalent expression of the restrictions. The presence of the matrix of partial derivatives $\hat{\mathbf{R}}_N = \mathbf{R}(\hat{\boldsymbol{\theta}}_N)$ signals the linear approximation behind the test statistic that creates this sensitivity.[3] The remaining three test statistics do not share this property with the Wald statistic; they are all invariant to reparameterization of the restrictions.

---

[1] See Section 21.4.3.

[2] Initially, we will consider only relatively efficient GMM estimators. See Section 21.4.4.

[3] See Example 17.7 and the surrounding discussion.

22.1.2 Gradient Test

One can always construct an asymptotically equivalent test that is based on the restricted GMM estimator

$$\hat{\boldsymbol{\theta}}_{\mathrm{R}N} \equiv \underset{\{\boldsymbol{\theta}|\mathbf{r}(\boldsymbol{\theta})=\mathbf{0}\}}{\operatorname{argmin}}\ Q_N(\boldsymbol{\theta}) \tag{22.7}$$

and the gradient of the GMM criterion function

$$\frac{\partial Q_N(\boldsymbol{\theta})}{\partial \boldsymbol{\theta}} = 2 \cdot \mathbf{G}_N(\boldsymbol{\theta})' \hat{\boldsymbol{\Lambda}}_N^{-1} \mathbf{g}_N(\boldsymbol{\theta}) \tag{22.8}$$

where

$$\mathbf{G}_N(\boldsymbol{\theta}) \equiv \frac{\partial \mathbf{g}_N(\boldsymbol{\theta})}{\partial \boldsymbol{\theta}'}$$

If $\mathbf{r}(\boldsymbol{\theta}_0) = \mathbf{0}$, then the gradient for unconstrained estimation evaluated at the restricted estimator will be within reasonable sampling variation of zero. To measure the distance, one uses the statistic

$$\mathcal{G} \equiv N \cdot \mathbf{g}_N(\hat{\boldsymbol{\theta}}_{\mathrm{R}N})' \hat{\boldsymbol{\Lambda}}_N^{-1} \hat{\mathbf{G}}_N \left(\hat{\mathbf{G}}_N' \hat{\boldsymbol{\Lambda}}_N^{-1} \hat{\mathbf{G}}_N \right)^{-1} \hat{\mathbf{G}}_N' \hat{\boldsymbol{\Lambda}}_N^{-1} \mathbf{g}_N(\hat{\boldsymbol{\theta}}_{\mathrm{R}N}) \tag{22.9}$$

$$= N \cdot \mathbf{g}_N(\hat{\boldsymbol{\theta}}_{\mathrm{R}N})' \hat{\boldsymbol{\Lambda}}_N^{-1} \hat{\mathbf{G}}_N \hat{\mathbf{V}}_N \hat{\mathbf{G}}_N' \hat{\boldsymbol{\Lambda}}_N^{-1} \mathbf{g}_N(\hat{\boldsymbol{\theta}}_{\mathrm{R}N}) \tag{22.10}$$

where (21.32) defines $\hat{\mathbf{G}}_N$ and $\hat{\boldsymbol{\Lambda}}_N$ when evaluated at $\hat{\boldsymbol{\theta}}_{\mathrm{R}N}$.

Like the score test in (17.11) or (17.29), the gradient test statistic $\mathcal{G}$ equals a quadratic form in the gradient of the estimation criterion function and the variance matrix of the unrestricted estimator. The scalar factor 2 that appears in (22.8) cancels out with a corresponding scalar in the normalizing variance term. Other than this, (22.10) is analogous to the score statistic. Because the term "score" refers specifically to the gradient of a log-likelihood function, we will call this GMM counterpart a *gradient* or Lagrange multiplier (LM) test.

22.1.3 Distance Difference Test

One can also use another equivalent test statistic comparable to the likelihood ratio (LR) statistic in (17.27):

$$\mathcal{DD} \equiv N \left[Q_N(\hat{\boldsymbol{\theta}}_{\mathrm{R}N}) - Q_N(\hat{\boldsymbol{\theta}}_N) \right] \tag{22.11}$$

$$= N \left[\min_{\{\boldsymbol{\theta} \in \boldsymbol{\Theta}|\mathbf{r}(\boldsymbol{\theta})=\mathbf{0}\}} Q_N(\boldsymbol{\theta}) - \min_{\boldsymbol{\theta} \in \boldsymbol{\Theta}} Q_N(\boldsymbol{\theta}) \right] \tag{22.12}$$

This *distance difference* (DD) test statistic equals the difference in the minimized GMM distance function values, restricted and unrestricted, multiplied by the number of observations.[4]

The superficial differences with the LR statistic are a missing scalar factor of 2 and a difference in minima in place of a difference in maxima. We could recast the GMM estimation program as

[4] The name for this test statistic is an awkward business. Newey and West (1987a) call this the "difference" test statistic whereas Newey and McFadden (1994) label it the "distance metric" test statistic. After careful thought, we use the compromise "distance difference." After all, the likelihood ratio test statistic is really a log-likelihood difference. Because the GMM objective function is a generalized distance function, our compromise seems apt, if not widely used.

$$\hat{\boldsymbol{\theta}}_N = \underset{\boldsymbol{\theta}\in\boldsymbol{\Theta}}{\operatorname{argmax}}\, Q_N^*(\boldsymbol{\theta})$$

by defining

$$Q_N^*(\boldsymbol{\theta}) \equiv -\frac{1}{2} Q_N(\boldsymbol{\theta})$$

and then $\mathcal{DD}$ would appear more familiar: $2N\left[Q_N^*(\hat{\boldsymbol{\theta}}_N) - Q_N^*(\hat{\boldsymbol{\theta}}_{\mathrm{R}N})\right]$. This recasting would also remove the factor 2 in the gradient (22.8) above.

The advantages and disadvantages of the DD statistic parallel those of the likelihood ratio. Neither requires estimation of variance matrices or matrix inversion and both require restricted and unrestricted estimation.

22.1.4 Minimum Chi-Square Test

Finally, the *minimum chi-square* (MC) statistic is a GMM test statistic.[5] It is given by the quadratic form

$$\begin{aligned}\mathcal{MC} &\equiv N \cdot \left(\hat{\boldsymbol{\theta}}_N - \hat{\boldsymbol{\theta}}_{\mathrm{R}N}\right)' \hat{\mathbf{G}}_N' \hat{\boldsymbol{\Lambda}}_N^{-1} \hat{\mathbf{G}}_N \left(\hat{\boldsymbol{\theta}}_N - \hat{\boldsymbol{\theta}}_{\mathrm{R}N}\right)\\ &= N \cdot \left(\hat{\boldsymbol{\theta}}_N - \hat{\boldsymbol{\theta}}_{\mathrm{R}N}\right)' \hat{\mathbf{V}}_N^{-1} \left(\hat{\boldsymbol{\theta}}_N - \hat{\boldsymbol{\theta}}_{\mathrm{R}N}\right)\end{aligned} \tag{22.13}$$

It is a feasible counterpart to (17.23) in likelihood testing where an estimator of the asymptotic variance of the *unrestricted* estimator appears inverted in the center of the quadratic form.[6] This corresponds to normalizing $\hat{\boldsymbol{\theta}}_N - \hat{\boldsymbol{\theta}}_{\mathrm{R}N}$ by a generalized inverse of its (estimated) asymptotic variance matrix: the inverse of the variance of the unrestricted estimator alone. For likelihood models, this would be the information matrix.

We encountered an example of the MC statistic in the test statistic for linear restrictions $\mathbf{R}\boldsymbol{\beta}_0 = \mathbf{r}$ on the regression coefficients in the normal linear model with $\mathrm{E}(\mathbf{y}\,|\,\mathbf{X}) = \mathbf{X}\boldsymbol{\beta}_0$. The statistic in the numerator of the F test statistic (11.1) can be rewritten in terms of the change in the sum of squared residuals or a generalized distance between the restricted and unrestricted estimators:[7]

$$\frac{\left\|\mathbf{y} - \mathbf{X}\hat{\boldsymbol{\beta}}_{\mathrm{R}}\right\|^2 - \left\|\mathbf{y} - \mathbf{X}\hat{\boldsymbol{\beta}}\right\|^2}{\sigma_0^2} = \frac{(\hat{\boldsymbol{\beta}} - \hat{\boldsymbol{\beta}}_{\mathrm{R}})'\mathbf{X}'\mathbf{X}(\hat{\boldsymbol{\beta}} - \hat{\boldsymbol{\beta}}_{\mathrm{R}})}{\sigma_0^2} \tag{22.14}$$

The central matrix $(1/\sigma_0^2)\cdot\mathbf{X}'\mathbf{X} = \left[\mathrm{Var}(\hat{\boldsymbol{\beta}}\,|\,\mathbf{X})\right]^{-1}$ is a generalized inverse of the singular variance matrix of $\hat{\boldsymbol{\beta}}$ and $\hat{\boldsymbol{\beta}}_{\mathrm{R}}$. The connection between these two expressions is the Pythagorean relationship previously given in (4.10):

$$\|\mathbf{y} - \mathbf{X}\boldsymbol{\beta}\|^2 = \left\|\mathbf{y} - \mathbf{X}\hat{\boldsymbol{\beta}}\right\|^2 + \left(\hat{\boldsymbol{\beta}} - \boldsymbol{\beta}\right)'\mathbf{X}'\mathbf{X}\left(\hat{\boldsymbol{\beta}} - \boldsymbol{\beta}\right) \tag{22.15}$$

[5] We follow the terminology of Newey and West (1987a).

[6] See also Exercise 17.18, where we give a feasible MC test statistic.

[7] See (11.3).

In GMM testing, the MC statistic is closely related to the DD statistic because asymptotically the GMM distance function also partitions through a Pythagorean relationship such as (22.15).

> **Lemma 22.1** *Let the assumptions of Proposition 20 (GMM Asymptotics, p. 546) hold. Let $\hat{\boldsymbol{\theta}}_N$ be the GMM estimator in (22.3) and $\check{\boldsymbol{\theta}}_N$ be a jointly distributed $\sqrt{N}$-consistent estimator of $\boldsymbol{\theta}_0$, then*
>
> $$N Q_N(\check{\boldsymbol{\theta}}_N) \overset{p}{=} N Q_N(\hat{\boldsymbol{\theta}}_N) + N \cdot \left(\hat{\boldsymbol{\theta}}_N - \check{\boldsymbol{\theta}}_N\right)' \hat{\mathbf{G}}_N' \hat{\boldsymbol{\Lambda}}_N^{-1} \hat{\mathbf{G}}_N \left(\hat{\boldsymbol{\theta}}_N - \check{\boldsymbol{\theta}}_N\right)$$

A proof, which appears on page 598, replicates the projection argument in ordinary least squares. To apply the lemma, we set $\check{\boldsymbol{\theta}}_N = \hat{\boldsymbol{\theta}}_{\mathrm{R}N}$. The asymptotic equivalence of $\mathcal{DD}$ and $\mathcal{MC}$ is immediate.

"Minimum chi-square" describes a view of $\mathcal{MC}$ as the χ^2_{K-M} outcome of minimizing a function that has an asymptotic χ^2_K distribution at an initial value. Recall the minimum chi-square lemma (Lemma 10.1, p. 197) that supports the distribution theory for OLS test statistics. This lemma states (in part) that if $\mathbf{z} \sim \mathfrak{N}(\mathbf{0}, \mathbf{I}_K)$ and $\mathbb{S}$ is an M-dimensional subspace of $\mathbb{R}^K$ then

$$\min_{\boldsymbol{\mu} \in \mathbb{S}} \|\mathbf{z} - \boldsymbol{\mu}\|^2 \sim \chi^2_{K-M} \tag{22.16}$$

Now $\hat{\mathbf{V}}_N^{-1/2} \sqrt{N} \cdot \left(\hat{\boldsymbol{\theta}}_N - \boldsymbol{\theta}_0\right) \xrightarrow{d} z \sim \mathfrak{N}(\mathbf{0}, \mathbf{I}_K)$.[8] Hence

$$N \cdot \left(\hat{\boldsymbol{\theta}}_N - \boldsymbol{\theta}_0\right)' \hat{\mathbf{V}}_N^{-1} \left(\hat{\boldsymbol{\theta}}_N - \boldsymbol{\theta}_0\right) \xrightarrow{d} \chi^2_K$$

and, under $\mathbf{r}(\boldsymbol{\theta}_0) = \mathbf{0}$,

$$\mathcal{MC} = \min_{\{\boldsymbol{\theta} | \mathbf{r}(\boldsymbol{\theta}) = \mathbf{0}\}} N \cdot \left(\hat{\boldsymbol{\theta}}_N - \boldsymbol{\theta}\right)' \hat{\mathbf{V}}_N^{-1} \left(\hat{\boldsymbol{\theta}}_N - \boldsymbol{\theta}\right) \xrightarrow{d} \chi^2_{K-M} \tag{22.17}$$

according to the distribution theory provided in Section 22.4.2. Thus $\mathcal{MC}$ is the *minimum chi-square*.

22.1.5 Special Identities

Newey and West (1987a) note several special identities among these test statistics. These require that the same $\hat{\boldsymbol{\Lambda}}_N$ appear in every statistic. First, when $\boldsymbol{\theta}_0$ is exactly identified $(J = K)$ then

$$\mathcal{DD} = N Q_N(\hat{\boldsymbol{\theta}}_{\mathrm{R}N}) = \mathcal{G} \tag{22.18}$$

Exact identification of the complete parameter vector implies that all of the empirical moments will be set to zero.[9] Therefore, $Q_N(\hat{\boldsymbol{\theta}}_N) = 0$ and the first equality follows from (22.12). Exact

[8] This holds by (22.5) and the consistency of $\hat{\mathbf{V}}_N$ as an estimator of $\mathbf{V}_0$.

[9] Actually, in finite samples it may not be possible to equate all of the empirical moments to zero when the parameters are exactly identified. However, asymptotically this will not occur with probability equal to one. Therefore, asymptotic approximations may ignore this possibility.

identification also implies that $\hat{\mathbf{G}}_N$ is a nonsingular matrix. As a result, this matrix cancels out of (22.9) and the second equality follows.

A pair of identities arises when the moment equations are linear in $\boldsymbol{\theta}$. Then the unrestricted GMM distance function is quadratic in $\boldsymbol{\theta}$ and

$$\mathcal{DD} = \mathcal{G} = \mathcal{MC}$$

We prove this (p. 589) as a corollary to the general asymptotic equivalence of all the test statistics. For the moment, note that only the Wald test depends on the matrix $\hat{\mathbf{R}}_N$ of partial derivatives of the restrictions. This distinction is at the root of its omission from this set of equalities.

If, in addition to linear moment functions, we face linear parameter restrictions then the Wald test statistic is no longer the odd one out and all four statistics are identically equal. This equality is essentially the equality that we described in Section 17.2.4, which explains the approximate equality of the likelihood-based test statistics. When the restricted and unrestricted log-likelihood functions are quadratic, then the approximations are exact and the LR, Wald, score, and $C(\alpha)$ tests are all equal. Similarly, when the unrestricted *and the restricted* GMM distance functions are quadratic, then the DD, Wald, gradient, and MC tests are all equal.

22.1.6 Generalizing Likelihood-Based Diagnostics

To illustrate GMM tests of parametric restrictions, we reconsider the Breusch–Pagan test for conditional heteroskedasticity in the linear regression model. In so doing, we also show how one can generally rework likelihood-based tests within the GMM framework. The motivation for doing this is to remove from the testing procedure artifacts arising out of the likelihood function that are tangential to the central hypothesis.

EXAMPLE 22.1 (Heteroskedasticity)

Koenker (1981) notes that the Breusch–Pagan test for heteroskedasticity (p. 424) does not require normality, but the form of the Breusch–Pagan score test does contain elements of the normality assumption. One can restrict the model specification to the conditional moments

$$\mathrm{E}[y_n \mid \mathbf{x}_n, \mathbf{z}_n] = \mathbf{x}_n'\boldsymbol{\beta}_0$$
$$\mathrm{Var}[y_n \mid \mathbf{x}_n, \mathbf{z}_n] = \mathbf{z}_n'\boldsymbol{\gamma}_0 = \gamma_{01} + \mathbf{z}_{2n}'\boldsymbol{\gamma}_{02}$$

and derive a GMM gradient test based on the moments in the score function of the Breusch–Pagan test,[10]

$$\mathbf{g}(U;\boldsymbol{\theta}_0) = \begin{bmatrix} \mathbf{x}_n(y_n - \mathbf{x}_n'\boldsymbol{\beta}_0) \\ \mathbf{z}_n\left[(y_n - \mathbf{x}_n'\boldsymbol{\beta}_0)^2 - \gamma_{01}\right] \end{bmatrix}$$

Note that we impose the restrictions of homoskedasticity on these moments, leaving unspecified their functional form under heteroskedasticity.

Under the null hypothesis of homoskedasticity, the expectation of the moment vector is the zero vector. If $\boldsymbol{\gamma}_{02} \neq \mathbf{0}$, however, then

$$\mathrm{E}\left[\mathbf{z}_{2n}\left((y_n - \mathbf{x}_n'\boldsymbol{\beta}_0)^2 - \gamma_{01}\right)\right] = \mathrm{E}[\mathbf{z}_{2n}\mathbf{z}_{2n}']\boldsymbol{\gamma}_{02} \neq \mathbf{0}$$

[10] See (18.23) and (18.24).

If the third and fourth conditional moments of y_n are also constant under the null hypothesis, the variance matrix of the moment vector is

$$\boldsymbol{\Lambda}_0 = \begin{bmatrix} \gamma_{01} \cdot \mathrm{E}[\mathbf{x}_n \mathbf{x}_n'] & \delta_{01} \cdot \mathrm{E}[\mathbf{x}_n \mathbf{z}_n'] \\ \delta_{01} \cdot \mathrm{E}[\mathbf{z}_n \mathbf{x}_n'] & (\delta_{02} - \gamma_{01}^2) \cdot \mathrm{E}[\mathbf{z}_n \mathbf{z}_n'] \end{bmatrix}$$

where

$$\delta_{01} \equiv \mathrm{E}[(y_n - \mathbf{x}_n' \boldsymbol{\beta}_0)^3 \mid \mathbf{x}_n, \mathbf{z}_n]$$

and

$$\delta_{02} \equiv \mathrm{E}[(y_n - \mathbf{x}_n' \boldsymbol{\beta}_0)^4 \mid \mathbf{x}_n, \mathbf{z}_n]$$

There are several possible test statistics for $\mathrm{E}(\mathbf{g}_2) = \mathbf{0}$ depending on assumptions about the third and fourth moments. The Breusch–Pagan test imposes two restrictions on $\boldsymbol{\Lambda}_0$ arising from the normality assumption:[11]

$$\delta_{01} = 0 \qquad \text{and} \qquad \delta_{02} = 3\gamma_{01}^2$$

The symmetry of the normal distribution appears in a zero third moment and the kurtosis in the relationship between the fourth and second moments.

The third-moment restriction makes $\boldsymbol{\Lambda}_0$ block-diagonal. This has two effects on the GMM gradient test. First, OLS delivers the restricted GMM estimator. If δ_{01} were not equal to zero, then estimation of $\boldsymbol{\beta}_0$ and $\boldsymbol{\gamma}_0$ would be intertwined so that estimation of $\boldsymbol{\beta}_0$ would be nonlinear. Second, the gradient test depends only on the moments containing $(y_n - \mathbf{x}_n'\boldsymbol{\beta})^2$. This effect appeared earlier in the Breusch–Pagan score test (Section 18.7.3).

To derive the GMM gradient test statistic, we will first confirm that the restricted GMM estimator can be calculated with OLS.[12] We will require

$$\mathbf{G}_N(\boldsymbol{\theta}) = \begin{bmatrix} \mathrm{E}_N[\mathbf{x}_n \mathbf{x}_n'] & \underset{K\times 1}{\mathbf{0}} \\ -2\,\mathrm{E}_N\left[\mathbf{z}_n (y_n - \mathbf{x}_n'\boldsymbol{\beta})\mathbf{x}_n'\right] & -\mathrm{E}_N[\mathbf{z}_n] \end{bmatrix}$$

where K is the dimension of $\boldsymbol{\beta}_0$ and M is the dimension of $\boldsymbol{\gamma}_{02}$. Because

$$\mathrm{E}\left[\mathbf{z}_n (y_n - \mathbf{x}_n'\boldsymbol{\beta}_0)\mathbf{x}_n'\right] = \underset{(M+1)\times K}{\mathbf{0}}$$

we simplify $\mathbf{G}_N(\boldsymbol{\theta})$ without asymptotic consequences by replacing the lower right-hand block with a matrix of zeros. Then the GMM first-order conditions are[13]

$$\begin{aligned} \mathbf{0} &= \mathrm{E}_N[\mathbf{x}_n \mathbf{x}_n'] \left[\mathrm{E}_N(\mathbf{x}_n \mathbf{x}_n')\right]^{-1} \mathrm{E}_N[\mathbf{x}_n (y_n - \mathbf{x}_n' \hat{\boldsymbol{\beta}}_{\mathrm{R}N})] \\ &= \mathbf{X}' \left(\mathbf{y} - \mathbf{X}\hat{\boldsymbol{\beta}}_{\mathrm{R}N}\right) \\ \mathbf{0} &= \mathrm{E}_N[\mathbf{z}_n'] \left[\mathrm{E}(\mathbf{z}_n \mathbf{z}_n')\right]^{-1} \mathrm{E}_N\left[\mathbf{z}_n \left((y_n - \mathbf{x}_n' \hat{\boldsymbol{\beta}}_{\mathrm{R}N})^2 - \hat{\gamma}_{1\mathrm{R}N}\right)\right] \\ &= \boldsymbol{\iota}' \mathbf{P}_{\mathbf{Z}} \left(\hat{\mathbf{w}} - \boldsymbol{\iota}\hat{\gamma}_{1\mathrm{R}N}\right) \\ &= \boldsymbol{\iota}' \left(\hat{\mathbf{w}} - \boldsymbol{\iota}\hat{\gamma}_{1\mathrm{R}N}\right) \end{aligned}$$

---

[11] See Theorem D.8 (Normal Moments, p. 887).

[12] This is not immediate because the moments involving z_{2n} could enter into the estimation of γ_{01}.

[13] We have removed the irrelevant scalar factors from the Hessian terms.

where ι is a column vector of N ones and where $\hat{\mathbf{w}} \equiv [\hat{w}_n]'$ and $\hat{w}_n \equiv (y_n - \mathbf{x}_n'\hat{\boldsymbol{\beta}}_{RN})^2$.[14] Therefore, $\hat{\boldsymbol{\theta}}_{RN} = (\hat{\boldsymbol{\beta}}_{RN}, \hat{\gamma}_{1RN})$ where

$$\hat{\boldsymbol{\beta}}_{RN} = (\mathbf{X}'\mathbf{X})^{-1}\mathbf{X}'\mathbf{y} = \hat{\boldsymbol{\beta}}_{OLS}$$

and

$$\hat{\gamma}_{1RN} = \frac{\iota'\hat{\mathbf{w}}}{N} = \mathrm{E}_N[(y_n - \mathbf{x}_n'\hat{\boldsymbol{\beta}}_{OLS})^2] = \hat{\sigma}^2_{OLS}$$

The fourth-moment restriction of normality leads to estimating δ_{02} with the sample variance of the fitted OLS residuals: $\hat{\boldsymbol{\delta}}_2 = 3\hat{\gamma}^2_{1RN}$. The resulting score/gradient test statistic is[15]

$$\begin{aligned}\mathcal{G}_1 &= \left(\hat{\mathbf{w}} - \iota\hat{\gamma}_{1RN}\right)'\mathbf{Z}\left[2\hat{\gamma}^2_{1RN}\cdot\mathbf{Z}'\mathbf{Z}\right]^{-1}\mathbf{Z}'\left(\hat{\mathbf{w}} - \iota\hat{\gamma}_{1RN}\right)\\ &= N\frac{\hat{\mathbf{w}}'\mathbf{P}_{(\mathbf{I}-\mathbf{P}_\iota)\mathbf{Z}_2}\hat{\mathbf{w}}}{2\hat{\mathbf{w}}'\iota}\end{aligned}$$

This equals one-half the explained sum of squares from an OLS fit of $\hat{w}_n/\hat{\sigma}^2_{OLS}$ on $\mathbf{z}_n$, the Breusch–Pagan score test statistic.

Alternatively, one could abandon the normality assumption and maintain only that $y_n - \mathbf{x}_n'\boldsymbol{\beta}_0$ is symmetrically distributed so that $\delta_{01} = 0$ but $\delta_{02} \neq 3\gamma^2_{01}$ in general. In that case, one replaces the estimator of δ_{02} with $\hat{\delta}_2 = \mathrm{E}_N[(y_n - \mathbf{x}_n'\hat{\boldsymbol{\beta}}_{OLS})^4] = \hat{\mathbf{w}}'\hat{\mathbf{w}}/N$, the fourth empirical moment of the OLS fitted residuals. This changes the denominator of the previous statistic:

$$\mathcal{G}_2 = N\frac{\hat{\mathbf{w}}'\mathbf{P}_{(\mathbf{I}-\mathbf{P}_\iota)\mathbf{Z}_2}\hat{\mathbf{w}}}{\hat{\mathbf{w}}'\left(\mathbf{I}-\mathbf{P}_\iota\right)\hat{\mathbf{w}}}$$

which equals the sample size times the centered R^2 from an OLS fit of $\hat{w}_n$ to $\mathbf{z}_n$. This is the Studentized test statistic suggested by Koenker (1981). In cases with nonnormally distributed residuals, he argues that the nominal significance level of $\mathcal{G}_2$ will typically be closer to its actual value than for $\mathcal{G}_1$. Under normality, $\mathcal{G}_2$ has the same asymptotic distribution as $\mathcal{G}_1$ because both statistics use consistent estimators of the variance matrix $\boldsymbol{\Lambda}_0$. Thus, one prefers $\mathcal{G}_2$ as a test statistic when asymptotic approximations are accurate.

Finally, one might drop the third-moment restriction as well. This is Exercise 22.6.

With this example, we end our presentation of tests of parameter restrictions for GMM estimators. In the next section, we extend the use of these test statistics to tests of moment restrictions.

22.2 TESTS OF MOMENT RESTRICTIONS

A key feature of GMM is its combination of moment restrictions when there are more moments than parameters. Because estimation may proceed with fewer moments, the possibility arises for testing whether some of the moment restrictions fail to hold. The extra moment restrictions are often called *overidentifying* restrictions.

[14] Because $\mathbf{z}_n = [1,\ \mathbf{z}_{2n}']'$, $\iota \in \mathrm{Col}(\mathbf{Z})$ and $\mathbf{P}_{\mathbf{Z}}\iota = \iota$.

[15] Note that in the unrestricted model, the parameter vectors $\boldsymbol{\beta}_0$ and $\boldsymbol{\gamma}_0$ are exactly identified. Therefore, the DD and gradient statistics are equal.

EXAMPLE 22.2 (2SLS)

Consider estimation under the conditions of Proposition 18 (Asymptotic Distribution of IV, p. 500). However, let the number of instrumental variables J in $\mathbf{z}_n$ exceed the number of explanatory variables K in $\mathbf{x}_n$ so that one estimates $\boldsymbol{\beta}_0$ in $\mathrm{E}[y_n \mid \mathbf{z}_n] = \mathrm{E}[\mathbf{x}_n' \mid \mathbf{z}_n]\boldsymbol{\beta}_0$ with 2SLS. Suppose that only the first $M \geq K$ instrumental variables z_{nj}, $j = 1, \ldots, M$, are reliable, so that the moment restrictions

$$\mathrm{E}[z_{nj}(y_n - \mathbf{x}_n'\boldsymbol{\beta}_0)] = 0, \qquad j = 1, \ldots, M \tag{22.19}$$

identify $\boldsymbol{\beta}_0$. One can test whether

$$\mathrm{E}[z_{nj}(y_n - \mathbf{x}_n'\boldsymbol{\beta}_0)] = 0, \qquad j = M+1, \ldots, J \tag{22.20}$$

For example, after estimating $\boldsymbol{\beta}_0$ consistently using 2SLS with the first M instrumental variables,

$$\hat{\boldsymbol{\beta}}_N = \left(\mathbf{X}'\mathbf{P}_{\mathbf{Z}_1}\mathbf{X}\right)^{-1}\mathbf{X}'\mathbf{P}_{\mathbf{Z}_1}\mathbf{y}$$

where

$$\mathbf{X} \equiv [\mathbf{x}_n]'$$
$$\mathbf{Z}_1 \equiv \left[[z_{nk};\ k = 1, \ldots, M]'\right]'$$

one can test whether

$$\mathrm{E}_N[\mathbf{z}_{2n}(y_n - \mathbf{x}_n'\boldsymbol{\beta}_0)] \xrightarrow{p} \mathbf{0}$$

where

$$\mathbf{z}_{2n} \equiv \left[z_{nj};\ j = M+1, \ldots, J\right]'$$

with

$$\mathcal{W} \equiv \left(\mathbf{y} - \mathbf{X}\hat{\boldsymbol{\beta}}_N\right)'\mathbf{Z}_2\hat{\mathbf{V}}_{\mathcal{W}}^{-1}\mathbf{Z}_2'\left(\mathbf{y} - \mathbf{X}\hat{\boldsymbol{\beta}}_N\right) \tag{22.21}$$

where

$$\mathbf{Z}_2 \equiv [\mathbf{z}_{2n}]'$$
$$\hat{\mathbf{V}}_{\mathcal{W}} = \hat{\sigma}^2 \cdot \mathbf{Z}_2'\left(\mathbf{I} - \mathbf{P}_{\mathbf{X}\perp\mathbf{P}_{\mathbf{Z}_1}\mathbf{X}}\right)\left(\mathbf{I} - \mathbf{P}_{\mathbf{X}\perp\mathbf{P}_{\mathbf{Z}_1}\mathbf{X}}\right)'\mathbf{Z}_2$$

and

$$\hat{\sigma}^2 = \left(\mathbf{y} - \mathbf{X}\hat{\boldsymbol{\beta}}_N\right)'\left(\mathbf{y} - \mathbf{X}\hat{\boldsymbol{\beta}}_N\right)/N$$

Under (22.19) and the additional moment restrictions (22.20), $\mathcal{W}$ converges in distribution to a χ^2_{J-M} random variable. One rejects the orthogonality in (22.20) at the $100\alpha\%$ level of significance whenever m exceeds the critical value $\chi^2_{J-M;1-\alpha}$.

This example constructs a pivotal test statistic using the Wald test principle: the initial estimator does not impose the (moment) restrictions of the null hypothesis and we plug the unconstrained estimator into the restrictions to test whether they seem to be satisfied. Not surprisingly, there are several asymptotically equivalent statistics. Let us present them all in the GMM framework.

We begin by partitioning the moment restrictions into a set of M reliable moment conditions that identifies $\boldsymbol{\theta}_0$,

$$\mathrm{E}\left[\mathbf{g}_1(U;\boldsymbol{\theta}_0)\right] = \mathbf{0}$$

where

$$\mathbf{g}_1(U;\boldsymbol{\theta}) \equiv \left[g_j(U;\boldsymbol{\theta});\quad j=1,\ldots,M\right]'$$

and a set of remaining questionable moment restrictions that comprises the null hypothesis under scrutiny,

$$\mathrm{E}[\mathbf{g}_2(U;\boldsymbol{\theta}_0)] = \mathbf{0}$$

where

$$\mathbf{g}_2(U;\boldsymbol{\theta}) \equiv \left[g_j(U;\boldsymbol{\theta}_0);\quad j=M+1,\ldots,J\right]'$$

Now we exploit the theory for parametric restrictions by artificially recasting the tests of overidentifying moment restrictions as tests of parametric restrictions.[16]

Consider the augmented moment functions

$$\mathbf{g}^{\mathrm{a}}(U;\boldsymbol{\theta},\boldsymbol{\psi}) = \begin{bmatrix} \mathbf{g}_1(U;\boldsymbol{\theta}) \\ \mathbf{g}_2(U;\boldsymbol{\theta}) - \boldsymbol{\psi} \end{bmatrix} \tag{22.22}$$

the augmented GMM distance function

$$Q^{\mathrm{a}}_{\mathrm{N}}(\boldsymbol{\theta};\boldsymbol{\psi}) = -\frac{1}{2}\mathbf{g}^{\mathrm{a}}_N(\boldsymbol{\theta},\boldsymbol{\psi})'\hat{\boldsymbol{\Lambda}}_N^{-1}\mathbf{g}^{\mathrm{a}}_N(\boldsymbol{\theta},\boldsymbol{\psi})$$

and the parametric null hypothesis $\boldsymbol{\psi}_0 \equiv \mathrm{E}[\mathbf{g}_2(U;\boldsymbol{\theta})] = \mathbf{0}$, where $\boldsymbol{\psi}$ is a vector of $J-M$ additional parameters. By construction $Q^{\mathrm{a}}_N(\boldsymbol{\theta},\mathbf{0}) = Q_N(\boldsymbol{\theta})$ and restricted GMM estimation corresponds to estimating $\boldsymbol{\theta}_0$ with all of the moment restrictions:[17]

$$\begin{bmatrix} \hat{\boldsymbol{\theta}}^{\mathrm{a}}_{\mathrm{R}N} \\ \underset{(J-M)\times 1}{\mathbf{0}} \end{bmatrix} = \underset{\{(\boldsymbol{\theta},\boldsymbol{\psi})|\boldsymbol{\psi}=\mathbf{0}\}}{\operatorname{argmin}}\; Q^{\mathrm{a}}_N(\boldsymbol{\theta};\boldsymbol{\psi}) = \underset{\boldsymbol{\theta}}{\operatorname{argmin}}\; Q_N(\boldsymbol{\theta}) = \begin{bmatrix} \hat{\boldsymbol{\theta}}_N \\ \underset{(J-M)\times 1}{\mathbf{0}} \end{bmatrix}$$

Hence, we can apply all of the previous test statistics for parametric restrictions directly to $Q^{\mathrm{a}}_N(\boldsymbol{\theta};\boldsymbol{\psi})$ to test the moment restrictions.

Before doing so, we examine the unrestricted estimator of the augmented parameter vector. One expects the unrestricted estimator,

$$\begin{bmatrix} \hat{\boldsymbol{\theta}}^{\mathrm{a}}_N \\ \hat{\boldsymbol{\psi}}_N \end{bmatrix} = \underset{\{(\boldsymbol{\theta},\boldsymbol{\psi})|\boldsymbol{\psi}=\mathbf{0}\}}{\operatorname{argmin}}\; Q^{\mathrm{a}}_N(\boldsymbol{\theta};\boldsymbol{\psi})$$

to omit the moments in $\mathbf{g}_2$ from the estimation of $\boldsymbol{\theta}_0$. To confirm this, partition the estimation criterion function (Lemma 7.5, p. 138) into

$$\begin{aligned} Q^{\mathrm{a}}_N(\boldsymbol{\theta},\boldsymbol{\psi}) &= \mathbf{g}^{\mathrm{a}}_N(\boldsymbol{\theta},\boldsymbol{\psi})'\hat{\boldsymbol{\Lambda}}_N^{-1}\mathbf{g}^{\mathrm{a}}_N(\boldsymbol{\theta},\boldsymbol{\psi}) \\ &= \mathbf{g}_{1N}(\boldsymbol{\theta})'\hat{\boldsymbol{\Lambda}}_{11}^{-1}\mathbf{g}_{1N}(\boldsymbol{\theta}) \\ &\quad + \mathbf{h}_N(\boldsymbol{\theta},\boldsymbol{\psi})'\left(\hat{\boldsymbol{\Lambda}}_{22} - \hat{\boldsymbol{\Lambda}}_{21}\hat{\boldsymbol{\Lambda}}_{11}^{-1}\hat{\boldsymbol{\Lambda}}_{12}\right)^{-1}\mathbf{h}_N(\boldsymbol{\theta},\boldsymbol{\psi}) \end{aligned}$$

[16] Newey and McFadden (1994, pp. 2232–2233), for example, use this approach.

[17] We will place the dimensions of a submatrix of zeros beneath each entry with a zero.

where

$$\mathbf{h}_N(\boldsymbol{\theta}, \boldsymbol{\psi}) \equiv \mathbf{g}_{2N}(\boldsymbol{\theta}) - \boldsymbol{\psi} - \hat{\boldsymbol{\Lambda}}_{21}\hat{\boldsymbol{\Lambda}}_{11}^{-1}\mathbf{g}_{1N}(\boldsymbol{\theta})$$

We have placed the $\boldsymbol{\psi}$ parameters, which are exactly identified, in the second "conditional" quadratic form. Whatever value $\hat{\boldsymbol{\theta}}_N^{\mathrm{a}}$ takes, minimization of $Q_N^{\mathrm{a}}(\boldsymbol{\theta}, \boldsymbol{\psi})$ over $\boldsymbol{\psi}$ will reduce this second term to zero by setting

$$\hat{\boldsymbol{\psi}}_N = \mathbf{g}_{2N}(\hat{\boldsymbol{\theta}}_N^{\mathrm{a}}) - \hat{\boldsymbol{\Lambda}}_{21}\hat{\boldsymbol{\Lambda}}_{11}^{-1}\mathbf{g}_{1N}(\hat{\boldsymbol{\theta}}_N^{\mathrm{a}}) \tag{22.23}$$

Thus, the unrestricted estimator $\hat{\boldsymbol{\theta}}_N^{\mathrm{a}}$ minimizes the first quadratic form in $\mathbf{g}_{1N}(\boldsymbol{\theta})$ alone:

$$\mathbf{0} = \hat{\mathbf{G}}_1'\hat{\boldsymbol{\Lambda}}_{11}^{-1}\mathbf{g}_{1N}(\hat{\boldsymbol{\theta}}_N^{\mathrm{a}})$$

In general, overidentification of $\boldsymbol{\theta}_0$ under the alternative hypothesis $(M > K)$ manifests itself in the unrestricted estimator (22.23) of the auxiliary $\boldsymbol{\psi}_0$ parameters as well as the estimator of $\boldsymbol{\theta}_0$. Although it may seem natural to estimate $\boldsymbol{\psi}_0$ with $\mathbf{g}_{2N}(\hat{\boldsymbol{\theta}}_N^{\mathrm{a}})$ alone, this would be inefficient. The statistic $\mathbf{g}_{1N}(\hat{\boldsymbol{\theta}}_N^{\mathrm{a}})$ is an estimator of zero that is correlated with $\mathbf{g}_{2N}(\hat{\boldsymbol{\theta}}_N^{\mathrm{a}})$. Consequently, (22.23) is relatively efficient because it exploits this correlation to reduce variance.

One obtains an estimator of the asymptotic variance of the unrestricted estimator with the standard formula in (21.32). The variance matrix estimator of the unrestricted estimator $\hat{\boldsymbol{\theta}}_N^{\mathrm{a}}$ is

$$\hat{\mathbf{V}}_N^{\mathrm{a}} = \left[\left(\hat{\mathbf{G}}_N^{\mathrm{a}}\right)'\hat{\boldsymbol{\Lambda}}_N^{-1}\hat{\mathbf{G}}_N^{\mathrm{a}}\right]^{-1}$$

where

$$\hat{\mathbf{G}}_N^{\mathrm{a}} \equiv \left[\hat{\mathbf{G}}_N \left[\begin{matrix}\mathbf{0}\\ -\mathbf{I}_{J-M}\end{matrix}\right]\right]$$

Now, given the augmented parameterization and its estimators, one can apply the various test statistics in the previous section to testing the moment restrictions in $\mathrm{E}[\mathbf{g}_2(U; \boldsymbol{\theta}_0)] = \boldsymbol{\psi}_0 = \mathbf{0}$. This is largely a matter of replacing statistics with their augmented versions. For the Wald test statistic, replace $\hat{\mathbf{V}}_N$ with $\hat{\mathbf{V}}_N^{\mathrm{a}}$ and set

$$\hat{\mathbf{r}}_N = \hat{\boldsymbol{\psi}}_N$$

and

$$\hat{\mathbf{R}}_N = \left[\underset{(J-M)\times K}{\mathbf{0}} \quad \mathbf{I}_{J-M}\right]$$

in (22.6) to obtain[18]

$$\mathcal{W} = N \cdot \hat{\mathbf{r}}_N'\left[\hat{\mathbf{R}}_N\hat{\mathbf{V}}_N^{\mathrm{a}}\hat{\mathbf{R}}_N'\right]^{-1}\hat{\mathbf{r}}_N$$

The previous gradient statistic in (22.10) becomes

[18] The appropriate estimator of the variance matrix for the Wald test works out to

$$\hat{\mathbf{R}}_N\hat{\mathbf{V}}_N^{\mathrm{a}}\hat{\mathbf{R}}_N' = \hat{\boldsymbol{\Lambda}}_{22} - \hat{\boldsymbol{\Lambda}}_{21}\hat{\boldsymbol{\Lambda}}_{11}^{-1}\hat{\boldsymbol{\Lambda}}_{12}$$
$$+ \left(\hat{\mathbf{G}}_{2N} - \hat{\boldsymbol{\Lambda}}_{21}\hat{\boldsymbol{\Lambda}}_{11}^{-1}\hat{\mathbf{G}}_{1N}\right)\left(\hat{\mathbf{G}}_N'\hat{\boldsymbol{\Lambda}}_N^{-1}\hat{\mathbf{G}}_N\right)^{-1}\left(\hat{\mathbf{G}}_{2N} - \hat{\boldsymbol{\Lambda}}_{21}\hat{\boldsymbol{\Lambda}}_{11}^{-1}\hat{\mathbf{G}}_{1N}\right)'$$

$$\mathcal{G} = N \cdot \mathbf{g}_N^{\text{a}}(\hat{\boldsymbol{\theta}}_{\text{R}N}^{\text{a}})' \hat{\boldsymbol{\Lambda}}_N^{-1} \hat{\mathbf{G}}_N^{\text{a}} \hat{\mathbf{V}}_N^{\text{a}} \hat{\mathbf{G}}_N^{\text{a}\prime} \hat{\boldsymbol{\Lambda}}_N^{-1} \mathbf{g}_N^{\text{a}}(\hat{\boldsymbol{\theta}}_{\text{R}N}^{\text{a}})$$

and requires only $\hat{\mathbf{R}}_N \hat{\mathbf{V}}_N^{\text{a}} \hat{\mathbf{R}}_N'$ because the other elements are multiplied by zeros. The MC statistic is

$$\mathcal{MC} = N \cdot \left(\hat{\boldsymbol{\theta}}_N^{\text{a}} - \hat{\boldsymbol{\theta}}_N\right)' \left(\hat{\mathbf{V}}_N^{\text{a}}\right)^{-1} \left(\hat{\boldsymbol{\theta}}_N^{\text{a}} - \hat{\boldsymbol{\theta}}_N\right)$$

Because the null hypothesis is a linear function of $\boldsymbol{\psi}_0$ and the GMM distance function is a quadratic function of $\boldsymbol{\psi}$, we can refine our description of the statistics in several respects. The GMM distance difference statistic (22.12) is

$$\begin{aligned}
\mathcal{DD} &= N\left[\mathcal{Q}_N^{\text{a}}(\hat{\boldsymbol{\theta}}_{\text{R}N}^{\text{a}}, \mathbf{0}) - \mathcal{Q}_N^{\text{a}}(\hat{\boldsymbol{\theta}}_N^{\text{a}}, \hat{\boldsymbol{\psi}}_N)\right] \\
&= N\left[\mathcal{Q}_N(\hat{\boldsymbol{\theta}}_N) - \mathcal{Q}_N^{\text{a}}(\hat{\boldsymbol{\theta}}_N^{\text{a}}, \hat{\boldsymbol{\psi}}_N)\right] \\
&= N \cdot \mathbf{g}_N(\hat{\boldsymbol{\theta}}_N)' \hat{\boldsymbol{\Lambda}}^{-1} \mathbf{g}_N(\hat{\boldsymbol{\theta}}_N) - N \cdot \mathbf{g}_{1N}(\hat{\boldsymbol{\theta}}_N^{\text{a}})' \hat{\boldsymbol{\Lambda}}_{11}^{-1} \mathbf{g}_{1N}(\hat{\boldsymbol{\theta}}_N^{\text{a}})
\end{aligned}$$

In words, the test statistic becomes the difference in the estimation criterion functions for ordinary GMM estimation with and without the questionable moments.

EXAMPLE 22.3 (Instrumental Variables)

Let us apply the DD test statistic to the previous example. The alternative estimators are the IV estimators without and with the questionable instrumental variables:

$$\hat{\boldsymbol{\beta}}_N^{\text{a}} = \left(\mathbf{X}'\mathbf{P}_{\mathbf{Z}_1}\mathbf{X}\right)^{-1} \mathbf{X}'\mathbf{P}_{\mathbf{Z}_1}\mathbf{y}$$

and

$$\hat{\boldsymbol{\beta}}_{\text{R}N}^{\text{a}} = \left(\mathbf{X}'\mathbf{P}_{\mathbf{Z}}\mathbf{X}\right)^{-1} \mathbf{X}'\mathbf{P}_{\mathbf{Z}}\mathbf{y}$$

Thus

$$\mathcal{DD} = \frac{\left(\mathbf{y} - \mathbf{X}\hat{\boldsymbol{\beta}}_{\text{R}N}^{\text{a}}\right)' \mathbf{P}_{\mathbf{Z}} \left(\mathbf{y} - \mathbf{X}\hat{\boldsymbol{\beta}}_{\text{R}N}^{\text{a}}\right) - \left(\mathbf{y} - \mathbf{X}\hat{\boldsymbol{\beta}}_N^{\text{a}}\right)' \mathbf{P}_{\mathbf{Z}_1} \left(\mathbf{y} - \mathbf{X}\hat{\boldsymbol{\beta}}_N^{\text{a}}\right)}{\hat{\sigma}^2} \tag{22.24}$$

The estimated variance $\hat{\sigma}^2$ can be the estimated variance from either IV estimation. Under the null hypothesis, this statistic converges in distribution to a χ^2_{J-M} random variable. This is the test statistic that we used to examine the validity of each lagged value of consumption growth as an instrumental variable at the outset of this chapter.

Because the GMM distance function is exactly quadratic in all of the parameters, this $\mathcal{DD}$ statistic must be exactly equal to the $\mathcal{W}$ statistic in (22.21), provided that both use the same $\hat{\sigma}^2$. We leave the confirmation of this claim as an exercise.

22.2.1 Overidentifying Restrictions Tests

When the parameter vector $\boldsymbol{\theta}_0$ is exactly identified under the alternative hypothesis, GMM moment tests are called *tests of overidentifying restrictions* and are a special case of the moments tests above where $M = K$ and $J > K$. As in (22.18), the effect is equality of the DD and gradient statistics to the sample size times the minimum GMM distance function:

$$\mathcal{DD} = NQ_N(\hat{\boldsymbol{\theta}}_N) = \mathcal{G}$$

This particular test statistic is often called Hansen's (1982) J test statistic.

This simplification of the test statistic has additional significance. Note that the test statistic is invariant to which $J - K$ moment restrictions are deemed to be the restrictions of the null hypothesis. For this reason, one may choose to use this test of overidentifying moment restrictions as an omnibus test for failures in *any* moment restrictions when the designation of maintained moment restrictions is artificial. Of course, such a test leaves open which moments are invalid should the test statistic appear statistically significant.

Neither the MC nor the Wald statistic generally shares this invariance property because these statistics depend on the unrestricted estimator. Different choices of overidentifying restrictions are like nonlinear transformations of parametric restrictions. The unrestricted estimator is simpler, however. With the exact identification of $\boldsymbol{\theta}_0$, $\mathbf{g}_{1N}(\hat{\boldsymbol{\theta}}^{\mathrm{a}}_N) = \mathbf{0}$ and (22.23) becomes $\hat{\boldsymbol{\psi}}_N = \mathbf{g}_{2N}(\hat{\boldsymbol{\theta}}^{\mathrm{a}}_N)$.[19]

EXAMPLE 22.4 (Instrumental Variables)

Returning to Example 22.2, let $M = K$. The GMM estimation criterion function is

$$Q_N(\boldsymbol{\theta}) = \frac{(\mathbf{y} - \mathbf{X}\boldsymbol{\beta})' \mathbf{P_Z} (\mathbf{y} - \mathbf{X}\boldsymbol{\beta})}{N\breve{\sigma}^2}$$

where $\breve{\sigma}^2$ is a consistent estimator of σ_0^2. This variance estimator happens to be irrelevant to the feasible GMM estimator

$$\begin{aligned}\hat{\boldsymbol{\beta}}_{\mathrm{2SLS}} &= \left(\mathbf{X}'\mathbf{P_Z}\mathbf{X}\right)^{-1}\mathbf{X}'\mathbf{P_Z}\mathbf{y} \\ &= \underset{\boldsymbol{\beta}}{\operatorname{argmin}}\, (\mathbf{y} - \mathbf{X}\boldsymbol{\beta})' \mathbf{P_Z} (\mathbf{y} - \mathbf{X}\boldsymbol{\beta})\end{aligned}$$

Therefore, we can use $\hat{\boldsymbol{\beta}}_{\mathrm{2SLS}}$ to estimate σ_0^2:

$$\hat{\sigma}^2 = \frac{\hat{\boldsymbol{\varepsilon}}'_{\mathrm{2SLS}}\hat{\boldsymbol{\varepsilon}}_{\mathrm{2SLS}}}{N}$$

where $\hat{\boldsymbol{\varepsilon}}_{\mathrm{2SLS}} \equiv \mathbf{y} - \mathbf{X}\hat{\boldsymbol{\beta}}_{\mathrm{2SLS}}$ is the 2SLS fitted residual vector. Then the DD test for overidentifying restrictions is

$$\mathcal{DD} = N\frac{\hat{\boldsymbol{\varepsilon}}'_{\mathrm{2SLS}}\mathbf{P_Z}\hat{\boldsymbol{\varepsilon}}_{\mathrm{2SLS}}}{\hat{\boldsymbol{\varepsilon}}'_{\mathrm{2SLS}}\hat{\boldsymbol{\varepsilon}}_{\mathrm{2SLS}}}$$

which equals the sample size times the uncentered R^2 from an OLS fit of $\hat{\varepsilon}_{\mathrm{2SLS}}$ to $\mathbf{Z}$.[20] The test

[19] The normalizing variance matrix of the Wald test statistic also simplifies to

$$\begin{aligned}\hat{\mathbf{R}}_N\hat{\mathbf{V}}^{\mathrm{a}}_N\hat{\mathbf{R}}'_N &= \left[\hat{\mathbf{G}}_{2N}\hat{\mathbf{G}}_{1N}^{-1} - \mathbf{I}_{J-K}\right]\hat{\boldsymbol{\Lambda}}_N\left[\hat{\mathbf{G}}_{2N}\hat{\mathbf{G}}_{1N}^{-1} - \mathbf{I}_{J-K}\right]' \\ &= \hat{\boldsymbol{\Lambda}}_{22} - \hat{\mathbf{G}}_{2N}\hat{\mathbf{G}}_{1N}^{-1}\hat{\boldsymbol{\Lambda}}_{12} - \hat{\boldsymbol{\Lambda}}_{21}\left(\hat{\mathbf{G}}_{2N}\hat{\mathbf{G}}_{1N}^{-1}\right)' \\ &\quad + \hat{\mathbf{G}}_{2N}\hat{\mathbf{G}}_{1N}^{-1}\hat{\boldsymbol{\Lambda}}_{11}\left(\hat{\mathbf{G}}_{2N}\hat{\mathbf{G}}_{1N}^{-1}\right)'\end{aligned}$$

[20] This is the test statistic for overidentifying restrictions that we report for the Campbell–Mankiw consumption function in the opening of this chapter.

looks like a test for covariance between these fitted residuals and any of the instrumental variables. Except possibly for the estimator of the variance parameter σ_0^2, $\mathcal{DD}$ is actually identical to all of the other test statistics because the GMM estimation criterion function is exactly quadratic.

Higher order moments are an obvious place to look for testing distributional assumptions. These are generally available in likelihood settings where the parametric distribution of the data implies many moment restrictions on the parameters. Here is one example.

EXAMPLE 22.5 (Normality)

The OLS estimator is the GMM estimator corresponding to the moment functions

$$\mathbf{g}_1(U;\boldsymbol{\theta}_0) = \begin{bmatrix} \mathbf{x}_n(y_n - \mathbf{x}_n'\boldsymbol{\beta}_0) \\ (y_n - \mathbf{x}_n'\boldsymbol{\beta}_0)^2 - \sigma_0^2 \end{bmatrix}$$

The conditional normal distribution $y_n \mid \mathbf{x}_n \sim \mathfrak{N}(\mathbf{x}_n'\boldsymbol{\beta}_0, \sigma_0^2)$ also specifies third- and fourth-moment functions:

$$\mathbf{g}_2(U;\boldsymbol{\theta}_0) = \begin{bmatrix} (y_n - \mathbf{x}_n'\boldsymbol{\beta}_0)^3 \\ (y_n - \mathbf{x}_n'\boldsymbol{\beta}_0)^4 - 3\sigma_0^4 \end{bmatrix}$$

Applying the gradient statistic with the OLS estimator $(\hat{\boldsymbol{\beta}}_{\text{OLS}}, \hat{\sigma}^2_{\text{OLS}})$, one obtains the Jarque and Bera (1980) test statistic for normality,

$$\frac{\left\{\mathrm{E}_N[(y_n - \mathbf{x}_n'\hat{\boldsymbol{\beta}}_{\text{OLS}})^3]\right\}^2}{6\hat{\sigma}^6_{\text{OLS}}} + \frac{\left\{\mathrm{E}_N[(y_n - \mathbf{x}_n'\hat{\boldsymbol{\beta}}_{\text{OLS}})^4] - 3\hat{\sigma}^4_{\text{OLS}}\right\}^2}{24\hat{\sigma}^8_{\text{OLS}}}$$

which they originally based on the parametric alternative hypothesis of the Pearson family of p.d.f.s.[21] Under the null hypothesis, this statistic is asymptotically χ_2^2.

To obtain this particular statistic, one imposes restrictions on the estimator of the variance matrix $\boldsymbol{\Lambda}_0$ that are implied by the normality hypothesis. Because normality is the hypothesis under scrutiny, these seem sensible. We expect such restrictions to improve the precision of the variance estimator and, hence, the asymptotic approximation of the distribution of the test statistic under the null hypothesis. Note that this contrasts with the heteroskedasticity test in Example 22.1 where normality is considered to be incidental.

Testing moment restrictions often holds the researcher's direct interest. In the next section, we describe an indirect motivation for such interest, focusing on the difference between two estimators for $\boldsymbol{\theta}_0$. This leads naturally to GMM tests of particular linear combinations of the moment restrictions.

22.3 HAUSMAN SPECIFICATION TESTS

Hausman (1978) suggested a general class of diagnostic tests based on the comparison of two estimators, say $\tilde{\boldsymbol{\theta}}_N$ and $\hat{\boldsymbol{\theta}}_N$, for the same parameter vector $\boldsymbol{\theta}_0$. By this device, a researcher may

[21] See Exercises 17.20 and 22.13.

specify deviations to a working model in terms of the sampling behavior of parameter estimators, rather than population moments or parameters. Under the null hypothesis both of the estimators are $\sqrt{N}$ consistent so that $\sqrt{N}(\tilde{\boldsymbol{\theta}}_N - \hat{\boldsymbol{\theta}}_N) \xrightarrow{d} \mathfrak{N}(\mathbf{0}, \mathbf{V}_{\mathrm{D}})$. Under departures from this model the estimators diverge in probability: $\operatorname{plim} \tilde{\boldsymbol{\theta}}_N - \hat{\boldsymbol{\theta}}_N \neq \mathbf{0}$. A statistical comparison of the estimators then has power to detect such departures.

The Hausman specification test statistic takes the familiar quadratic form

$$\mathcal{HS} = N \cdot \left(\tilde{\boldsymbol{\theta}}_N - \hat{\boldsymbol{\theta}}_N\right)' \hat{\mathbf{V}}_{\mathrm{D}}^{-} \left(\tilde{\boldsymbol{\theta}}_N - \hat{\boldsymbol{\theta}}_N\right) \qquad (22.25)$$

where $\hat{\mathbf{V}}_{\mathrm{D}}^{-}$ is a consistent estimator of a generalized inverse of $\mathbf{V}_{\mathrm{D}}$. It is necessary in general to account for the possibility that $\mathbf{V}_{\mathrm{D}}$ is singular. In this respect, this statistic is like the MC statistic in (22.13).

Hausman also pointed out that the statistical comparison is particularly convenient when one of the two estimators, say $\hat{\boldsymbol{\theta}}_N$, is asymptotically efficient relative to any linear combination of both estimators that is consistent under the null hypothesis. In that case, the asymptotic variance of the difference $\sqrt{N} \cdot (\tilde{\boldsymbol{\theta}}_N - \hat{\boldsymbol{\theta}}_N)$ equals the difference in the asymptotic variances of $\sqrt{N} \cdot (\tilde{\boldsymbol{\theta}}_N - \boldsymbol{\theta}_0)$ and $\sqrt{N} \cdot (\hat{\boldsymbol{\theta}}_N - \boldsymbol{\theta}_0)$.[22] As a result, consistent estimation of $\mathbf{V}_{\mathrm{D}}$ is usually quite simple. Computation of the individual estimators typically produces consistent estimators of their individual asymptotic variance matrices. The researcher estimates $\mathbf{V}_{\mathrm{D}}$ by subtracting the estimated variance matrix of the relatively efficient estimator $\hat{\boldsymbol{\theta}}_N$ from the estimated variance matrix of $\tilde{\boldsymbol{\theta}}_N$. This is how we compared estimates of the income growth coefficient in our introduction.

The relative efficiency of $\hat{\boldsymbol{\theta}}_N$ occurs at the expense of its inconsistency under deviations from the null hypothesis. In most applications of the Hausman specification test, one chooses the inefficient estimator so that under such deviations $\tilde{\boldsymbol{\theta}}_N$ remains consistent for $\boldsymbol{\theta}_0$ and the two estimators necessarily diverge. The following is a leading example.

EXAMPLE 22.6 (Hausman-Wu Exogeneity Test)[23]

Consider a special case of Example 22.2 where $z_{nj} = x_{nj}$ for $j = 1, \ldots, K_1 < K$ and for $j = M+1, \ldots, J$ where $M = J - (K - K_1)$. That is, the first $K_1 < K$ explanatory variables in $\mathbf{x}_n$ are considered to be valid instrumental variables, but the last $K - K_1$ explanatory variables are suspect. Put another way, we partition the instrument matrix $\mathbf{Z}$ into $[\mathbf{Z}_1, \mathbf{Z}_2] = [\mathbf{Z}_1, \mathbf{X}_2]$ and the submatrix of instruments $\mathbf{Z}_1$ into $[\mathbf{X}_1, \mathbf{W}]$. Furthermore, we suppose that there are enough additional instrumental variables z_{nj} $(j = K_1 + 1, \ldots, M)$ in $\mathcal{W}$ so that $\boldsymbol{\beta}_0$ is identifiable in any case: $M \geq K$.

If the null hypothesis is true, then the OLS estimator

$$\hat{\boldsymbol{\beta}}_{\mathrm{OLS}} = \left(\mathbf{X}'\mathbf{X}\right)^{-1} \mathbf{X}'\mathbf{y}$$

is the relatively efficient 2SLS/GMM estimator of $\boldsymbol{\beta}_0$. On the other hand, if the null hypothesis is false, then $\hat{\boldsymbol{\beta}}_{\mathrm{OLS}}$ is inconsistent. Nevertheless, the 2SLS estimator that uses the remaining instrumental variables,

$$\hat{\boldsymbol{\beta}}_{2\mathrm{SLS}} = \left(\mathbf{X}'\mathbf{P}_{\mathbf{Z}_1}\mathbf{X}\right)^{-1} \mathbf{X}'\mathbf{P}_{\mathbf{Z}_1}\mathbf{y}$$

22 Recall Proposition 8 (Orthogonality of Efficient Estimators, p. 185).

23 See Wu (1973) and Hausman (1978). Durbin (1954) makes an early reference to this test.

is a consistent estimator of $\boldsymbol{\beta}_0$.

Hausman suggested a test statistic based on the contrast $\hat{\boldsymbol{\beta}}_{2SLS} - \hat{\boldsymbol{\beta}}_{OLS}$. Because $\hat{\boldsymbol{\beta}}_{OLS}$ is efficient relative to $\hat{\boldsymbol{\beta}}_{2SLS}$,

$$\text{Var}(\hat{\boldsymbol{\beta}}_{2SLS} - \hat{\boldsymbol{\beta}}_{OLS}) = \text{Var}(\hat{\boldsymbol{\beta}}_{2SLS}) - \text{Var}(\hat{\boldsymbol{\beta}}_{OLS}) \tag{22.26}$$

and a consistent estimator of the contrast is immediately available in the estimated variances of each estimator. Therefore, it is conceptually easy to construct an MC test statistic,

$$\mathcal{HS} = \frac{\left(\hat{\boldsymbol{\beta}}_{2SLS} - \hat{\boldsymbol{\beta}}_{OLS}\right)' \left[(\mathbf{X}'\mathbf{P}_{\mathbf{Z}_1}\mathbf{X})^{-1} - (\mathbf{X}'\mathbf{X})^{-1}\right]^{-} \left(\hat{\boldsymbol{\beta}}_{2SLS} - \hat{\boldsymbol{\beta}}_{OLS}\right)}{\hat{\sigma}^2}$$

As usual, $\hat{\sigma}^2$ may be the estimator of the variance parameter from either OLS or 2SLS.

In this example, it remains to find a generalized inverse and the rank of the difference in variance matrices and, hence, to find the degrees of freedom of the limiting chi-square distribution of the test statistic under the null hypothesis. This is a general issue for Hausman specification tests. It is preferable to derive analytical results for these objects than to leave their calculation to the computer. In some cases, statistical or numerical error leads to mistaken calculations. In linear models, it is usually possible to find analytical expressions.

For example, Hausman (1978) also showed how to implement the exogeneity test statistic as an OLS test of linear restrictions. If we rewrite

$$\begin{aligned}\mathbf{X}\boldsymbol{\beta} &= \mathbf{X}_1\boldsymbol{\beta}_1 + \mathbf{X}_2\boldsymbol{\beta}_2 \\ &= \mathbf{X}_1\boldsymbol{\beta}_1 + \mathbf{P}_{\mathbf{Z}_1}\mathbf{X}_2\boldsymbol{\beta}_2 + \left(\mathbf{I} - \mathbf{P}_{\mathbf{Z}_1}\right)\mathbf{X}_2\boldsymbol{\beta}_2\end{aligned}$$

then under the null hypothesis an OLS regression of $\mathbf{y}$ on $\mathbf{X}_1$, $\mathbf{P}_{\mathbf{Z}_1}\mathbf{X}_2\boldsymbol{\beta}_2$, and $(\mathbf{I} - \mathbf{P}_{\mathbf{Z}_1})\mathbf{X}_2$ will yield two consistent estimators of $\boldsymbol{\beta}_2$. We can test their equality with the common F test for zero restrictions by introducing $\boldsymbol{\gamma} = \mathbf{0}$ into

$$\begin{aligned}&\mathbf{X}_1\boldsymbol{\beta}_1 + \mathbf{P}_{\mathbf{Z}_1}\mathbf{X}_2\boldsymbol{\beta}_2 + \left(\mathbf{I} - \mathbf{P}_{\mathbf{Z}_1}\right)\mathbf{X}_2\boldsymbol{\beta}_2 \\ &\quad = \mathbf{X}_1\boldsymbol{\beta}_1 + \mathbf{P}_{\mathbf{Z}_1}\mathbf{X}_2\left(\boldsymbol{\beta}_2 + \boldsymbol{\gamma}\right) + \left(\mathbf{I} - \mathbf{P}_{\mathbf{Z}_1}\right)\mathbf{X}_2\boldsymbol{\beta}_2 \\ &\quad = \mathbf{X}_1\boldsymbol{\beta}_1 + \mathbf{X}_2\boldsymbol{\beta}_2 + \mathbf{P}_{\mathbf{Z}_1}\mathbf{X}_2\boldsymbol{\gamma}\end{aligned}$$

The F test of $\boldsymbol{\gamma} = \mathbf{0}$ in an OLS fit of $\mathbf{y}$ to $\mathbf{X}\boldsymbol{\beta} + \mathbf{P}_{\mathbf{Z}_1}\mathbf{X}_2\boldsymbol{\gamma}$ is asymptotically equivalent to $\mathcal{HS}$. Therefore, the statistic can be interpreted as measuring whether a potentially damaging component of $\mathbf{X}_2$ has predictive power beyond what the null hypothesis predicts. We also find that the appropriate degrees of freedom equal the number of variables in $\mathbf{X}_2$.

To confirm the equivalence of these tests, note that the partitioned regression formula for the fitted $\hat{\boldsymbol{\gamma}}$ gives

$$\hat{\boldsymbol{\gamma}} = \left[\mathbf{X}_2'\mathbf{P}_{\mathbf{Z}_1}\left(\mathbf{I} - \mathbf{P}_{\mathbf{X}}\right)\mathbf{P}_{\mathbf{Z}_1}\mathbf{X}_2\right]^{-1}\mathbf{X}_2'\mathbf{P}_{\mathbf{Z}_1}\left(\mathbf{I} - \mathbf{P}_{\mathbf{X}}\right)\mathbf{y}$$

Because $\mathbf{X}_1$ is in $\mathbf{Z}_1$, $\mathbf{P}_{\mathbf{Z}_1}\mathbf{X}_1 = \mathbf{X}_1$ and $\left(\mathbf{I} - \mathbf{P}_{\mathbf{X}}\right)\mathbf{P}_{\mathbf{Z}_1}\mathbf{X}_1 = \mathbf{0}$ and

$$\mathbf{X}'\mathbf{P}_{\mathbf{Z}_1}\left(\mathbf{I} - \mathbf{P}_{\mathbf{X}}\right)\mathbf{y} = \begin{bmatrix}\mathbf{0} \\ \left[\mathbf{X}_2'\mathbf{P}_{\mathbf{Z}_1}\left(\mathbf{I} - \mathbf{P}_{\mathbf{X}}\right)\mathbf{P}_{\mathbf{Z}_1}\mathbf{X}_2\right]\hat{\boldsymbol{\gamma}}\end{bmatrix}$$

Therefore,

$$\begin{aligned}\hat{\boldsymbol{\beta}}_{2SLS} - \hat{\boldsymbol{\beta}}_{OLS} &= \left[(\mathbf{X}'\mathbf{P}_{\mathbf{Z}_1}\mathbf{X})^{-1}\mathbf{X}'\mathbf{P}_{\mathbf{Z}_1} - (\mathbf{X}'\mathbf{X})^{-1}\mathbf{X}' \right]\mathbf{y} \\ &= (\mathbf{X}'\mathbf{P}_{\mathbf{Z}_1}\mathbf{X})^{-1}\left[\mathbf{X}'\mathbf{P}_{\mathbf{Z}_1} - \mathbf{X}'\mathbf{P}_{\mathbf{Z}_1}\mathbf{X}(\mathbf{X}'\mathbf{X})^{-1}\mathbf{X}' \right]\mathbf{y} \\ &= (\mathbf{X}'\mathbf{P}_{\mathbf{Z}_1}\mathbf{X})^{-1}\mathbf{X}'\mathbf{P}_{\mathbf{Z}_1}(\mathbf{I} - \mathbf{P}_{\mathbf{X}})\mathbf{y} \\ &= (\mathbf{X}'\mathbf{P}_{\mathbf{Z}_1}\mathbf{X})^{-1}\begin{bmatrix} \mathbf{0} \\ \left[\mathbf{X}_2'\mathbf{P}_{\mathbf{Z}_1}(\mathbf{I} - \mathbf{P}_{\mathbf{X}})\mathbf{P}_{\mathbf{Z}_1}\mathbf{X}_2\right]\hat{\boldsymbol{\gamma}} \end{bmatrix} \end{aligned} \tag{22.27}$$

so that the estimator contrast $\hat{\boldsymbol{\beta}}_{2SLS} - \hat{\boldsymbol{\beta}}_{OLS}$ is a linear, nonsingular function of $\hat{\boldsymbol{\gamma}}$.[24] This implies the equivalence of the tests.[25]

It is insightful to interpret the general Hausman specification test within the GMM testing framework. Provided that the two estimators, $\tilde{\boldsymbol{\theta}}_N$ and $\hat{\boldsymbol{\theta}}_N$, are GMM estimators, one can always do this. Often, a Hausman specification test is equivalent to a GMM test of a set of moment restrictions. The Hausman–Wu exogeneity test is one example.

EXAMPLE 22.7 (Hausman–Wu Exogeneity Test)

Reconsider Example 22.6 to find the DD test for the moment restrictions $E[\mathbf{x}_{2n}(y_n - \mathbf{x}_n'\boldsymbol{\beta}_0)] = \mathbf{0}$. By substituting in the expressions for $\hat{\boldsymbol{\beta}}^{a}_N$ and $\hat{\boldsymbol{\beta}}^{a}_{RN}$, the DD test statistic (22.24) can be rewritten in terms of orthogonal projectors as

$$\mathcal{DD} = \frac{\mathbf{y}'\left[\mathbf{P}_{\mathbf{Z}} - \mathbf{P}_{\mathbf{P}_{\mathbf{Z}}\mathbf{X}} - \left(\mathbf{P}_{\mathbf{Z}_1} - \mathbf{P}_{\mathbf{P}_{\mathbf{Z}_1}\mathbf{X}}\right)\right]\mathbf{y}}{\hat{\sigma}^2}$$

We can simplify the linear combination of orthogonal projectors substantially. Note first that $\mathbf{P}_{\mathbf{P}_{\mathbf{Z}}\mathbf{X}} = \mathbf{P}_{\mathbf{X}}$ because $\text{Col}(\mathbf{X}) \subset \text{Col}(\mathbf{Z})$. Now consider the remaining terms, $\mathbf{P}_{\mathbf{Z}} - \mathbf{P}_{\mathbf{Z}_1}$ and $\mathbf{P}_{\mathbf{P}_{\mathbf{Z}_1}\mathbf{X}}$, and observe (1) that they are mutually orthogonal,

$$\begin{aligned}(\mathbf{P}_{\mathbf{Z}} - \mathbf{P}_{\mathbf{Z}_1})\mathbf{P}_{\mathbf{P}_{\mathbf{Z}_1}\mathbf{X}} &= (\mathbf{P}_{\mathbf{Z}} - \mathbf{P}_{\mathbf{Z}_1})\mathbf{P}_{\mathbf{Z}_1}\mathbf{X}(\mathbf{X}'\mathbf{P}_{\mathbf{Z}_1}\mathbf{X})^{-1}\mathbf{X}'\mathbf{P}_{\mathbf{Z}_1} \\ &= (\mathbf{P}_{\mathbf{Z}_1} - \mathbf{P}_{\mathbf{Z}_1})\mathbf{X}(\mathbf{X}'\mathbf{P}_{\mathbf{Z}_1}\mathbf{X})^{-1}\mathbf{X}'\mathbf{P}_{\mathbf{Z}_1} \\ &= \mathbf{0}\end{aligned}$$

because $\mathbf{P}_{\mathbf{Z}}\mathbf{P}_{\mathbf{Z}_1} = \mathbf{P}_{\mathbf{Z}_1}$, and (2) that

$$\mathbf{P}_{\mathbf{Z}} - \mathbf{P}_{\mathbf{Z}_1} = \mathbf{P}_{(\mathbf{I} - \mathbf{P}_{\mathbf{Z}_1})\mathbf{X}_2}$$

using $\mathbf{Z} = [\mathbf{Z}_1, \mathbf{X}_2]$ and (3.25) in Exercise 3.16.[26] Therefore,

---

[24] The inverse function is

$$\hat{\boldsymbol{\gamma}} = \left[0 \quad \left[\mathbf{X}_2'\mathbf{P}_{\mathbf{Z}_1}(\mathbf{I} - \mathbf{P}_{\mathbf{X}})\mathbf{P}_{\mathbf{Z}_1}\mathbf{X}_2\right]^{-1} \right](\mathbf{X}'\mathbf{P}_{\mathbf{Z}_1}\mathbf{X})\left(\hat{\boldsymbol{\beta}}_{2SLS} - \hat{\boldsymbol{\beta}}_{OLS}\right)$$

[25] Such equivalence appeared in hypothesis testing for the linear regression model in (22.14), which equates the normalized length of $\hat{\boldsymbol{\beta}} - \hat{\boldsymbol{\beta}}_R$ with the normalized length of $\mathbf{R}\hat{\boldsymbol{\beta}} - \mathbf{r}$.

[26] For the partitioned matrix $\mathbf{X} = [\mathbf{X}_1, \mathbf{X}_2]$, Exercise 3.17 explains the orthogonal projector $\mathbf{P}_{\mathbf{X}}$ decomposition

$$\mathbf{P}_{\mathbf{X}} = \mathbf{P}_{\mathbf{X}_2} + \mathbf{P}_{\mathbf{X}_{1\perp 2}}$$

where

$$\mathbf{X}_{1\perp 2} \equiv (\mathbf{I} - \mathbf{P}_{\mathbf{X}_2})\mathbf{X}_1$$

$$\begin{aligned}\mathbf{P_Z} - \mathbf{P_{P_Z X}} - \left(\mathbf{P_{Z_1}} - \mathbf{P_{P_{Z_1} X}}\right) &= \left[(\mathbf{P_Z} - \mathbf{P_{Z_1}}) + \mathbf{P_{P_{Z_1} X}}\right] - \mathbf{P_X} \\ &= \left[\mathbf{P}_{(\mathbf{I}-\mathbf{P_{Z_1}})\mathbf{X}_2} + \mathbf{P_{P_{Z_1} X}}\right] - \mathbf{P_X} \\ &= \mathbf{P_A} - \mathbf{P_X}\end{aligned}$$

where $\mathbf{A} \equiv \left[\mathbf{P_{Z_1} X}, \left(\mathbf{I} - \mathbf{P_{Z_1}}\right)\mathbf{X}_2\right]$.[27]

Returning to the GMM test statistic, we have that

$$\mathcal{DD} = \frac{\mathbf{y}'\left[\mathbf{P_A} - \mathbf{P_X}\right]\mathbf{y}}{\hat{\sigma}^2} = \frac{\mathbf{y}'\left[(\mathbf{I} - \mathbf{P_X}) - (\mathbf{I} - \mathbf{P_A})\right]\mathbf{y}}{\hat{\sigma}^2}$$

contains the change in the OLS sum of squared residuals from regressions on **X** and **A**, respectively, like the numerator of an F test statistic.[28] Furthermore,

$$\begin{aligned}\mathrm{Col}(\mathbf{A}) &= \mathrm{Col}(\left[\mathbf{X}_1, \mathbf{P_{Z_1}}\mathbf{X}_2, \left(\mathbf{I} - \mathbf{P_{Z_1}}\right)\mathbf{X}_2\right]) \\ &= \mathrm{Col}([\mathbf{X}_1, \mathbf{X}_2, \mathbf{P_{Z_1}}\mathbf{X}_2]) \\ &= \mathrm{Col}([\mathbf{X}, \mathbf{P_{Z_1}}\mathbf{X}_2])\end{aligned}$$

So we can just as well take $\mathbf{A} = \left[\mathbf{X}, \mathbf{P_{Z_1}}\mathbf{X}_2\right]$. In other words, the Hausman–Wu exogeneity test is equivalent to a test of the moment conditions $\mathrm{E}[\mathbf{x}_{2n}(y_n - \mathbf{x}_n'\boldsymbol{\beta}_0)] = \mathbf{0}$.

More generally, Hausman specification tests are equivalent to a GMM test of *linear combinations* of moment restrictions. We illustrate this with a generalization of the Hausman–Wu exogeneity test.

EXAMPLE 22.8 **(Instrumental Variables Test)**

Instead of testing explanatory variables as instrumental variables as in Example 22.6, suppose that one wishes to test the validity of a set of instrumental variables for $\mathbf{x}_{2n}$ given that the x_{2nk} cannot serve as instrumental variables. That is, $\mathbf{Z}_2$ contains additional instrumental variables for $\mathbf{X}_2$. The primary difference with the analysis in Example 22.7 is that $\mathrm{Col}(\mathbf{X}) \not\subset \mathrm{Col}(\mathbf{Z})$ so that $\mathbf{P_{P_Z X}} \neq \mathbf{P_X}$ and

$$\mathbf{P_Z} - \mathbf{P_{P_Z X}} - \left(\mathbf{P_{Z_1}} - \mathbf{P_{P_{Z_1} X}}\right) = \mathbf{P_A} - \mathbf{P_{P_Z X}}$$

where $\mathbf{A} \equiv \left[\mathbf{P_{Z_1} X}, \left(\mathbf{I} - \mathbf{P_{Z_1}}\right)\mathbf{Z}_2\right]$.

We can still view the GMM DD test as comparable to an F test:

$$\begin{aligned}\mathrm{Col}(\mathbf{A}) &= \mathrm{Col}([\mathbf{P_{Z_1} X}, (\mathbf{I} - \mathbf{P_{Z_1}})\mathbf{Z}_2]) \\ &= \mathrm{Col}([\mathbf{X}_1, \mathbf{P_{Z_1}}\mathbf{X}_2, (\mathbf{I} - \mathbf{P_{Z_1}})\mathbf{Z}_2, (\mathbf{P_Z} - \mathbf{P_{Z_1}})\mathbf{X}_2]) \\ &= \mathrm{Col}([\mathbf{X}_1, \mathbf{P_Z}\mathbf{X}_2, (\mathbf{I} - \mathbf{P_{Z_1}})\mathbf{Z}_2, (\mathbf{P_Z} - \mathbf{P_{Z_1}})\mathbf{X}_2]) \\ &= \mathrm{Col}([\mathbf{P_Z X}, (\mathbf{I} - \mathbf{P_{Z_1}})\mathbf{Z}_2])\end{aligned}$$

---

[27] The composition of $\mathbf{P}_{(\mathbf{I}-\mathbf{P_{Z_1}})\mathbf{X}_2} + \mathbf{P_{P_{Z_1} X}}$ into $\mathbf{P_A}$ also uses the decomposition in Exercises 3.16 and 3.17.

[28] See (11.3).

because

$$\begin{aligned}(\mathbf{P_Z} - \mathbf{P_{Z_1}})\,\mathbf{X}_2 &= (\mathbf{I} - \mathbf{P_{Z_1}})\,\mathbf{Z}_2\left[\mathbf{Z}_2'\,(\mathbf{I} - \mathbf{P_{Z_1}})\,\mathbf{Z}_2\right]\mathbf{Z}_2'\,(\mathbf{I} - \mathbf{P_{Z_1}})\,\mathbf{X}_2 \\ &= (\mathbf{I} - \mathbf{P_{Z_1}})\,\mathbf{Z}_2\mathbf{S}\end{aligned} \tag{22.28}$$

where $\mathbf{S} = \left[\mathbf{Z}_2'\,(\mathbf{I} - \mathbf{P_{Z_1}})\,\mathbf{Z}_2\right]\mathbf{Z}_2'\,(\mathbf{I} - \mathbf{P_{Z_1}})\,\mathbf{X}_2$. As a result, the GMM test of the moment conditions $\mathrm{E}[\mathbf{z}_{2n}(y_n - \mathbf{x}_n'\boldsymbol{\beta}_0)] = \mathbf{0}$ corresponds to an F test for whether the coefficients of $(\mathbf{I} - \mathbf{P_{Z_1}})\,\mathbf{Z}_2$ are zero in the regression of $\mathbf{y}$ on $\mathbf{P_Z X}$ and $(\mathbf{I} - \mathbf{P_{Z_1}})\,\mathbf{Z}_2$. The degrees of freedom for this test equals the number of variables in $\mathbf{Z}_2$, which is also the number of moments under test.

On the other hand, the Hausman specification test for this situation, proposed by Spencer and Berk (1981), compares the two 2SLS estimators

$$\hat{\boldsymbol{\beta}}^{\mathrm{a}}_N = \left(\mathbf{X}'\mathbf{P_{Z_1}X}\right)^{-1}\mathbf{X}'\mathbf{P_{Z_1}y} \tag{22.29}$$

and

$$\hat{\boldsymbol{\beta}}^{\mathrm{a}}_{\mathrm{R}N} = \left(\mathbf{X}'\mathbf{P_Z X}\right)^{-1}\mathbf{X}'\mathbf{P_Z y} \tag{22.30}$$

through the contrast

$$\begin{aligned}\hat{\boldsymbol{\beta}}^{\mathrm{a}}_N - \hat{\boldsymbol{\beta}}^{\mathrm{a}}_{\mathrm{R}N} &= \left[\left(\mathbf{X}'\mathbf{P_{Z_1}X}\right)^{-1}\mathbf{X}'\mathbf{P_{Z_1}} - \left(\mathbf{X}'\mathbf{P_Z X}\right)^{-1}\mathbf{X}'\mathbf{P_Z}\right]\mathbf{y} \\ &= \left(\mathbf{X}'\mathbf{P_{Z_1}X}\right)^{-1}\left[\mathbf{X}'\mathbf{P_{Z_1}} - \mathbf{X}'\mathbf{P_{Z_1}X}\left(\mathbf{X}'\mathbf{P_Z X}\right)^{-1}\mathbf{X}'\mathbf{P_Z}\right]\mathbf{y} \\ &= \left(\mathbf{X}'\mathbf{P_{Z_1}X}\right)^{-1}\mathbf{X}'\mathbf{P_{Z_1}}\left[\mathbf{I} - \mathbf{P_Z X}\left(\mathbf{X}'\mathbf{P_Z X}\right)^{-1}\mathbf{X}'\mathbf{P_Z}\right]\mathbf{y} \\ &= \left(\mathbf{X}'\mathbf{P_{Z_1}X}\right)^{-1}\mathbf{X}'\mathbf{P_{Z_1}}\left(\mathbf{I} - \mathbf{P_{P_Z X}}\right)\mathbf{y} \\ &= \left(\mathbf{X}'\mathbf{P_{Z_1}X}\right)^{-1}\begin{bmatrix}\mathbf{0} \\ \mathbf{X}_2'\mathbf{P_{Z_1}}\left(\mathbf{I} - \mathbf{P_{P_Z X}}\right)\mathbf{y}\end{bmatrix}\end{aligned}$$

Therefore, by analogy with (22.27), one can execute the Hausman test as an F test for whether the coefficients of $\mathbf{P_{Z_1}X}_2$ are zero in the regression of $\mathbf{y}$ on $\mathbf{P_Z X}$ and $\mathbf{P_{Z_1}X}_2$. This test has fewer degrees of freedom than the GMM test when the number of variables (columns) in $\mathbf{X}_2$ is smaller than the number of variables in $\mathbf{Z}_2$.

More than this, the Hausman specification test is testing a linear combination of the moment restrictions. If we write the regression function of the GMM F test as

$$\mathbf{X}_1\boldsymbol{\beta}_1 + \mathbf{P_Z X}_2\boldsymbol{\beta}_2 + (\mathbf{I} - \mathbf{P_{Z_1}})\,\mathbf{Z}_2\boldsymbol{\gamma}$$

then, using (22.28), the regression function of the Hausman F test is

$$\mathbf{X}_1\boldsymbol{\beta}_1 + \mathbf{P_Z X}_2\boldsymbol{\beta}_2 + (\mathbf{I} - \mathbf{P_{Z_1}})\,\mathbf{Z}_2\mathbf{S}\boldsymbol{\delta}$$

One uses the former to test $\boldsymbol{\gamma} = \mathbf{0}$ and the latter to test $\boldsymbol{\delta} = \mathbf{0}$. Because $\boldsymbol{\delta} = \mathbf{R}\boldsymbol{\gamma}$, where $\mathbf{R} = (\mathbf{S}'\mathbf{S})^{-1}\mathbf{S}'$, the Hausman specification test is generally a test of a linear combination of the restrictions tested by the GMM test constructed from the same moment restrictions.

The relationship between Hausman specification tests and GMM tests of moment restrictions in settings more general than these examples exhibits the same feature, but not with the same detail. If one considers efficient ($\mathbf{C}_N = \Lambda_N^{-1}$) GMM estimators based on $\mathbf{g}_1$ and $\mathbf{g}$, $\hat{\boldsymbol{\theta}}^{\mathrm{a}}_N$ and $\hat{\boldsymbol{\theta}}^{\mathrm{a}}_{\mathrm{R}N}$, respectively, then

$$\sqrt{N}\left(\hat{\boldsymbol{\theta}}^{\mathrm{a}}_{N} - \hat{\boldsymbol{\theta}}^{\mathrm{a}}_{\mathrm{R}N}\right) \overset{p}{=} \sqrt{N}\left(\hat{\boldsymbol{\theta}}^{\mathrm{a}}_{N} - \hat{\boldsymbol{\theta}}^{a*}_{\mathrm{R}N}\right)$$
$$= \left(\hat{\mathbf{G}}'_N \hat{\boldsymbol{\Lambda}}_N^{-1} \hat{\mathbf{G}}_N\right)^{-1} \hat{\mathbf{G}}'_N \hat{\boldsymbol{\Lambda}}_N^{-1} \begin{bmatrix} \underset{M\times 1}{\mathbf{0}} \\ \sqrt{N}\cdot\hat{\boldsymbol{\psi}}_N \end{bmatrix} \tag{22.31}$$

where $\hat{\boldsymbol{\theta}}^{\mathrm{a}*}_{\mathrm{R}N}$ is the linearized GMM estimator that uses $\hat{\boldsymbol{\theta}}^{\mathrm{a}}_{N}$ for the initial $\sqrt{N}$-consistent estimator and $\hat{\boldsymbol{\psi}}_N$ appears in (22.23).[29] Thus, the estimator contrast $\hat{\boldsymbol{\theta}}^{\mathrm{a}}_{N} - \hat{\boldsymbol{\theta}}^{\mathrm{a}}_{\mathrm{R}N}$ is asymptotically linearly dependent on $\hat{\boldsymbol{\psi}}_N$, the unrestricted estimator of the suspicious moments. If these are nonzero, (22.31) shows how this leads to inconsistency in the restricted estimator for $\boldsymbol{\theta}_0$ through the transformation $(\hat{\mathbf{G}}'_N \hat{\boldsymbol{\Lambda}}_N^{-1} \hat{\mathbf{G}}_N)^{-1}\hat{\mathbf{G}}'_N \hat{\boldsymbol{\Lambda}}_N^{-1}$.

The asymptotic equivalence in (22.31) also shows that the Hausman specification test has power to detect only certain departures from the hypothesis that $\boldsymbol{\psi}_0 \equiv \mathrm{E}[\mathbf{g}_2(U;\boldsymbol{\theta}_0)] = \mathbf{0}$. Whenever $\boldsymbol{\psi}_0 \neq \mathbf{0}$ but $\mathbf{G}'_0\left[\boldsymbol{\Lambda}_0^{21}, \boldsymbol{\Lambda}_0^{22}\right]' \boldsymbol{\psi}_0 = \mathbf{0}$, $\hat{\boldsymbol{\theta}}^{\mathrm{a}}_{\mathrm{R}N}$ remains $\sqrt{N}$ consistent and the asymptotic size of the specification test will equal its power.[30] This can occur because $\mathbf{G}_0$ is merely full-column rank and not nonsingular. Because of this, the Hausman specification test will generally have power to detect nonzero values only for the linear combinations of the moments in $\mathbf{G}'_0[\boldsymbol{\Lambda}_0^{21}, \boldsymbol{\Lambda}_0^{22}]'\boldsymbol{\psi}_0$. This property of the specification test holds by its design as a test to detect when the GMM estimator $\hat{\boldsymbol{\theta}}_N = \hat{\boldsymbol{\theta}}^{\mathrm{a}}_{\mathrm{R}N}$ is inconsistent.

EXAMPLE 22.9 (Instrumental Variables Test)

For the previous example, (22.31) becomes[31]

$$\hat{\boldsymbol{\beta}}^{\mathrm{a}}_{N} - \hat{\boldsymbol{\beta}}^{\mathrm{a}}_{\mathrm{R}N} = -\left(\mathbf{X}'\mathbf{P}_{\mathbf{Z}}\mathbf{X}\right)^{-1}\mathbf{X}'\mathbf{P}_{\mathbf{Z}}\left(\mathbf{y} - \mathbf{X}\hat{\boldsymbol{\beta}}^{\mathrm{a}}_{N}\right) \tag{22.32}$$

---

[29] The unrestricted estimator sets

$$\mathbf{0} = \mathbf{G}^{\mathrm{a}}_N(\hat{\boldsymbol{\theta}}^{\mathrm{a}}_{N}, \hat{\boldsymbol{\psi}}_N)'\hat{\boldsymbol{\Lambda}}_N^{-1}\mathbf{g}^{\mathrm{a}}_N(\hat{\boldsymbol{\theta}}^{\mathrm{a}}_{N}, \hat{\boldsymbol{\psi}}_N)$$

Taking the $\boldsymbol{\theta}$ rows,

$$\mathbf{0} = \mathbf{G}_N(\hat{\boldsymbol{\theta}}^{\mathrm{a}}_{N})'\hat{\boldsymbol{\Lambda}}_N^{-1}\left[\mathbf{g}_N(\hat{\boldsymbol{\theta}}^{\mathrm{a}}_{N}) - \begin{bmatrix} \underset{M\times 1}{\mathbf{0}} \\ \sqrt{N}\cdot\hat{\boldsymbol{\psi}}_N \end{bmatrix}\right]$$

so that

$$\mathbf{G}_N(\hat{\boldsymbol{\theta}}^{\mathrm{a}}_{N})'\hat{\boldsymbol{\Lambda}}_N^{-1}\mathbf{g}_N(\hat{\boldsymbol{\theta}}^{\mathrm{a}}_{N}) = \mathbf{G}_N(\hat{\boldsymbol{\theta}}^{\mathrm{a}}_{N})'\hat{\boldsymbol{\Lambda}}_N^{-1}\begin{bmatrix} \underset{M\times 1}{\mathbf{0}} \\ \sqrt{N}\cdot\hat{\boldsymbol{\psi}}_N \end{bmatrix}$$

[30] Here we are using the notation $[\boldsymbol{\Lambda}_0^{ij}] \equiv \boldsymbol{\Lambda}_0^{-1}$.

[31] The second equality (22.33) follows from

$$\mathbf{X}'\mathbf{P}_{\mathbf{Z}}\left(\mathbf{y} - \mathbf{X}\hat{\boldsymbol{\beta}}^{\mathrm{a}}_{N}\right) = \mathbf{X}'\mathbf{P}_{\mathbf{Z}}\left[\mathbf{P}_{\mathbf{Z}_1} + (\mathbf{I} - \mathbf{P}_{\mathbf{Z}_1})\right]\left(\mathbf{y} - \mathbf{X}\hat{\boldsymbol{\beta}}^{\mathrm{a}}_{N}\right)$$
$$= \mathbf{X}'\mathbf{P}_{\mathbf{Z}}\left(\mathbf{I} - \mathbf{P}_{\mathbf{Z}_1}\right)\left(\mathbf{y} - \mathbf{X}\hat{\boldsymbol{\beta}}^{\mathrm{a}}_{N}\right)$$

and $\mathbf{Z}'_1(\mathbf{I} - \mathbf{P}_{\mathbf{Z}_1}) = \mathbf{0}$. The third equality (22.34) follows from the presence of $\mathbf{X}_1$ in both $\mathbf{Z}_1$ and $\mathbf{Z}$ and (22.29) so that

$$\mathbf{X}'\mathbf{P}_{\mathbf{Z}_1}\left(\mathbf{y} - \mathbf{X}\hat{\boldsymbol{\beta}}^{\mathrm{a}}_{N}\right) = \mathbf{0}$$

$$= -\left(\mathbf{X}'\mathbf{P_Z X}\right)^{-1}\mathbf{X}'\mathbf{Z}\left(\mathbf{Z}'\mathbf{Z}\right)^{-1}\begin{bmatrix}\mathbf{0}\\ \mathbf{Z}_2'\left(\mathbf{I}-\mathbf{P}_{\mathbf{Z}_1}\right)\left(\mathbf{y}-\mathbf{X}\hat{\boldsymbol{\beta}}_N^{\text{a}}\right)\end{bmatrix} \tag{22.33}$$

$$= -\left(\mathbf{X}'\mathbf{P_Z X}\right)^{-1}\begin{bmatrix}\mathbf{0}\\ \mathbf{X}_2'\mathbf{P_Z}\left(\mathbf{y}-\mathbf{X}\hat{\boldsymbol{\beta}}_N^{\text{a}}\right)\end{bmatrix} \tag{22.34}$$

Even though the $\hat{\boldsymbol{\psi}}_N$ term in (22.33) has as many elements as $\mathbf{Z}_2$ has columns, after transformation by $\mathbf{X}'\mathbf{Z}(\mathbf{Z}'\mathbf{Z})^{-1}$ the number of nonzero elements equals the number of columns in $\mathbf{X}_2$. If $\mathbf{X}_2$ has fewer columns than $\mathbf{Z}_2$, then the Hausman specification test does not detect some patterns of covariance between $\mathbf{z}_{2n}$ and $y_n - \mathbf{x}_n'\boldsymbol{\beta}_0$.

The Hausman specification test is a more powerful test than the GMM test of $\boldsymbol{\psi}_0 = \mathbf{0}$ for violations of the restrictions on particular linear combination of the moments, $\mathbf{G}_0'[\boldsymbol{\Lambda}_0^{21}, \boldsymbol{\Lambda}_0^{22}]'\boldsymbol{\psi}_0 = \mathbf{0}$. As the GMM test of that hypothesis, there are no other GMM tests that dominate the Hausman test. If it were not for its determination of the consistency of the GMM estimator $\hat{\boldsymbol{\theta}}_N$, this linear combination of moments might not attract interest. However, this interpretation has made the Hausman test a popular diagnostic tool among GMM tests in general.

To this point, we have focused on describing various hypothesis tests within the GMM estimation framework. We began with tests of restrictions on parameters, which bear strong similarities to their likelihood-based counterparts. We followed with tests of restrictions on moments, casting these tests as restrictions on artificial parameters associated with overidentifying moments. Such tests do not arise as automatically for ML estimation because the normal equations yield the same number of moments as parameters. However, even there one can easily find additional moments because the distributional assumptions implicitly specify an infinite set of moment restrictions. Example 22.5 and Exercise 22.24 are cases in point.

Finally, we presented Hausman specification tests as a generalization of tests of moment restrictions to linear combinations of moment restrictions. These linear combinations arise naturally in statistical comparisons of parameters of interest with and without subsets of moment restrictions.

Hereafter we give formal justifications for the properties that we have claimed for the various test statistics, primarily asymptotic equivalence. In addition, we relax the restriction that $\mathbf{C}_N = \hat{\boldsymbol{\Lambda}}_N^{-1}$ generalizing the class of test statistics considered so far. Within this more general class, we show that the statistics for $\mathbf{C}_N = \hat{\boldsymbol{\Lambda}}_N^{-1}$ are more powerful than others, justifying (in part) limiting our discussion to these statistics.

The minimum chi-square lemma receives particular attention, not only in relating the MC test statistic to the others, but also in motivating two new statistical methods. The first is sequential hypothesis testing, in which one tests a sequence of successively more restrictive models. The second is the minimum distance method of estimation, which is similar to GMM estimation except that moment equations are replaced by parameter restrictions.

22.4 EQUIVALENCE AMONG TEST STATISTICS

This section justifies the various asymptotic equivalences among the test statistics that we have described. The approach mimics the one given in 17.3. We will describe GMM tests of parametric restrictions in terms of the contrast $\hat{\boldsymbol{\theta}}_N - \hat{\boldsymbol{\theta}}_{\mathrm{R}N}$. The tests differ according to the estimators that are approximated with a linear forecast based on local behavior of the empirical moment functions.

We will derive the GMM test statistics for a general weighting matrix $\mathbf{C}_N$ in the GMM distance function, replacing (22.4) with

$$Q_N(\boldsymbol{\theta}) = \mathbf{g}_N(\boldsymbol{\theta})'\mathbf{C}_N\,\mathbf{g}_N(\boldsymbol{\theta})$$

All of the tests given above take $\mathbf{C}_N = \hat{\boldsymbol{\Lambda}}_N^{-1}$. Although this is the leading case, by making it a special case below we are able to point out the effects of this restriction on the statistical testing theory. The leading outcome is the distance difference test statistic. As we explain in the second section, without the proper normalization by $\hat{\boldsymbol{\Lambda}}_N^{-1}$ the GMM distance function will not possess a limiting chi-square distribution.

22.4.1 A Trinity of GMM Test Statistics

For general $\mathbf{C}_N$ the Wald, gradient, and minimum chi-square statistics make up a trinity of GMM test statistics. There is no statistic comparable to the likelihood ratio (LR).[32] We derive the Wald and gradient test statistics and relate both of them to a minimum chi-square (MC) statistic.

The Wald test examines $\sqrt{N}\cdot\mathbf{r}(\hat{\boldsymbol{\theta}}_N)$ for statistically significant departures from the zero vector. This unrestricted estimator is equivalent to $\hat{\mathbf{R}}_N\sqrt{N}\cdot\left(\hat{\boldsymbol{\theta}}_N - \hat{\boldsymbol{\theta}}_{\mathrm{R}N}\right)$ as linear approximation shows[33]

$$\begin{aligned}\sqrt{N}\cdot\mathbf{r}(\hat{\boldsymbol{\theta}}_N) &\overset{p}{=} \sqrt{N}\cdot\mathbf{r}(\hat{\boldsymbol{\theta}}_{\mathrm{R}N}) + \hat{\mathbf{R}}_N\sqrt{N}\cdot\left(\hat{\boldsymbol{\theta}}_N - \hat{\boldsymbol{\theta}}_{\mathrm{R}N}\right)\\ &= \hat{\mathbf{R}}_N\sqrt{N}\cdot\left(\hat{\boldsymbol{\theta}}_N - \hat{\boldsymbol{\theta}}_{\mathrm{R}N}\right)\end{aligned}$$

where $\hat{\mathbf{R}}_N \equiv \mathbf{R}(\hat{\boldsymbol{\theta}}_N)$. Therefore, the Wald test statistic is equivalent to a squared generalized distance between the restricted and unrestricted estimators:

$$\begin{aligned}\mathcal{W} &= N\cdot\hat{\mathbf{r}}_N'\left[\hat{\mathbf{R}}_N\hat{\mathbf{V}}_N\hat{\mathbf{R}}_N'\right]^{-1}\hat{\mathbf{r}}_N\\ &\overset{p}{=} N\cdot\left(\hat{\boldsymbol{\theta}}_N - \hat{\boldsymbol{\theta}}_{\mathrm{R}N}\right)'\hat{\mathbf{R}}_N'\left[\hat{\mathbf{R}}_N\hat{\mathbf{V}}_N\hat{\mathbf{R}}_N'\right]^{-1}\hat{\mathbf{R}}_N\left(\hat{\boldsymbol{\theta}}_N - \hat{\boldsymbol{\theta}}_{\mathrm{R}N}\right)\end{aligned} \tag{22.35}$$

where $\hat{\mathbf{r}}_N \equiv \mathbf{r}(\hat{\boldsymbol{\theta}}_N)$ and $\hat{\mathbf{V}}_N$ is the GMM variance matrix estimator in (21.32).

The gradient test examines the gradient $\hat{\mathbf{G}}_N'\mathbf{C}_N\,\mathbf{g}(\hat{\boldsymbol{\theta}}_{\mathrm{R}N})$ for statistically significant departures from the zero vector. The asymptotic equivalence of $\hat{\boldsymbol{\theta}}_N$ and the linearized GMM estimator (21.31) implies that

$$\begin{aligned}\left(\hat{\mathbf{G}}_N'\mathbf{C}_N\hat{\mathbf{G}}_N\right)^{-1}\hat{\mathbf{G}}_N'\mathbf{C}_N\sqrt{N}\cdot\mathbf{g}(\hat{\boldsymbol{\theta}}_{\mathrm{R}N}) &= \sqrt{N}\cdot\left(\hat{\boldsymbol{\theta}}_N^{*} - \hat{\boldsymbol{\theta}}_{\mathrm{R}N}\right)\\ &\overset{p}{=} \sqrt{N}\cdot\left(\hat{\boldsymbol{\theta}}_N - \hat{\boldsymbol{\theta}}_{\mathrm{R}N}\right)\end{aligned}$$

32 More precisely, the distance difference statistic is not asymptotically pivotal for general $\mathbf{C}_N$ so that it cannot be the basis of a hypothesis test.

33 One can derive a forecast for $\hat{\boldsymbol{\theta}}_{\mathrm{R}N}$ itself, if desired. See Exercise 22.19.

Therefore,

$$\hat{\mathbf{R}}_N \left(\hat{\mathbf{G}}_N' \mathbf{C}_N \hat{\mathbf{G}}_N\right)^{-1} \hat{\mathbf{G}}_N' \mathbf{C}_N \sqrt{N} \cdot \mathbf{g}(\hat{\boldsymbol{\theta}}_{\mathrm{R}N}) \stackrel{p}{=} \hat{\mathbf{R}}_N \sqrt{N} \cdot \left(\hat{\boldsymbol{\theta}}_N - \hat{\boldsymbol{\theta}}_{\mathrm{R}N}\right)$$

and

$$\begin{aligned} \mathcal{G} &= N \cdot \mathbf{g}_N(\hat{\boldsymbol{\theta}}_{\mathrm{R}N})' \hat{\mathbf{H}}_N \left(\hat{\mathbf{H}}_N' \hat{\boldsymbol{\Lambda}}_N \hat{\mathbf{H}}_N\right)^{-1} \hat{\mathbf{H}}_N' \mathbf{g}_N(\hat{\boldsymbol{\theta}}_{\mathrm{R}N}) \\ &\stackrel{p}{=} N \cdot \left(\hat{\boldsymbol{\theta}}_N - \hat{\boldsymbol{\theta}}_{\mathrm{R}N}\right)' \hat{\mathbf{R}}_N' \left[\hat{\mathbf{R}}_N \hat{\mathbf{V}}_N \hat{\mathbf{R}}_N'\right]^{-1} \hat{\mathbf{R}}_N \left(\hat{\boldsymbol{\theta}}_N - \hat{\boldsymbol{\theta}}_{\mathrm{R}N}\right) \end{aligned} \tag{22.36}$$

where

$$\hat{\mathbf{H}}_N \equiv \mathbf{C}_N \hat{\mathbf{G}}_N \left(\hat{\mathbf{G}}_N' \mathbf{C}_N \hat{\mathbf{G}}_N\right)^{-1} \hat{\mathbf{R}}_N$$

The normalizing matrix $\hat{\mathbf{H}}_N \left(\hat{\mathbf{H}}_N' \hat{\boldsymbol{\Lambda}}_N \hat{\mathbf{H}}_N\right)^{-1} \hat{\mathbf{H}}_N'$ is more complicated than its likelihood counterpart in (17.9) and (17.10). This occurs because the GMM estimator is not necessarily efficient.

The third member of the trinity is the MC test statistic itself:

$$\mathcal{MC} = N \cdot \left(\hat{\boldsymbol{\theta}}_N - \hat{\boldsymbol{\theta}}_{\mathrm{R}N}\right)' \hat{\mathbf{R}}_N' \left(\hat{\mathbf{R}}_N \hat{\mathbf{V}}_N \hat{\mathbf{R}}_N'\right)^{-1} \hat{\mathbf{R}}_N \left(\hat{\boldsymbol{\theta}}_N - \hat{\boldsymbol{\theta}}_{\mathrm{R}N}\right) \tag{22.37}$$

In this case, $\hat{\mathbf{R}}_N$ can be evaluated at either estimator. As in the gradient statistic, the generalized inverse of the variance matrix that appears in this quadratic form is more complex than its likelihood cousin where no $\hat{\mathbf{R}}_N$ terms appear.

The three test statistics in this section are applicable for any $\mathbf{C}_N$ in the estimation criterion function. They can be used for preliminary diagnostic checks before computing an efficient GMM estimator or with an efficient GMM estimator. However, with an efficient GMM estimator further simplification of the gradient and generalized test statistics is possible. In addition, we can obtain a GMM analogue to the LR test statistic, expanding this GMM trinity to a quartet.

22.4.2 Minimum Chi-Square

When we normalize by $\mathbf{C}_N = \hat{\boldsymbol{\Lambda}}_N^{-1}$, the GMM distance function itself has a convenient limiting distribution when it is evaluated at $\boldsymbol{\theta}_0$:

$$N \cdot Q_N(\boldsymbol{\theta}_0) = N \cdot \mathbf{g}_N(\boldsymbol{\theta}_0)' \hat{\boldsymbol{\Lambda}}_N^{-1} \mathbf{g}_N(\boldsymbol{\theta}_0) \stackrel{d}{\rightarrow} \chi_J^2$$

Because $\sqrt{N}\mathbf{g}_N(\boldsymbol{\theta}_0) \stackrel{d}{\rightarrow} \mathfrak{N}(\mathbf{0}, \boldsymbol{\Lambda}_0)$ and $\hat{\boldsymbol{\Lambda}}_N^{-1} \stackrel{p}{\rightarrow} \boldsymbol{\Lambda}_0$, Lemma 13.4 (Convergence in Distribution Continuity, p. 261) implies this property. In this section we will discuss how minimizing $N \cdot Q_N(\boldsymbol{\theta})$ over restricted and unrestricted values of $\boldsymbol{\theta}$ leads to additional statistics that possess limiting chi-square distributions with fewer than J degrees of freedom.

Let us review such relationships in the classical normal linear model. Recall that we applied Lemma 10.1 (Minimum Chi-Square, p. 197) to $(1/\sigma_0) \cdot (\mathbf{y} - \mathbf{X}\boldsymbol{\beta}_0) \sim \mathfrak{N}(\mathbf{0}, \mathbf{I}_N)$ and $\mathrm{Col}(\mathbf{X})$. The Pythagorean triangle between $\mathbf{y} - \mathbf{X}\boldsymbol{\beta}_0$, $\mathbf{y} - \mathbf{X}\hat{\boldsymbol{\beta}}$, and $\mathbf{X}\hat{\boldsymbol{\beta}} - \mathbf{X}\boldsymbol{\beta}_0$ that is described by (22.47)–(22.49) is echoed in the joint distribution of their squared Euclidean lengths:

$$\frac{\|\mathbf{y} - \mathbf{X}\boldsymbol{\beta}_0\|^2}{\sigma_0^2} \sim \chi^2_N, \quad \frac{\left\|\mathbf{y} - \mathbf{X}\hat{\boldsymbol{\beta}}\right\|^2}{\sigma_0^2} \sim \chi^2_{N-K}, \quad \frac{\left\|\mathbf{X}\hat{\boldsymbol{\beta}} - \mathbf{X}\boldsymbol{\beta}_0\right\|^2}{\sigma_0^2} \sim \chi^2_K \tag{22.38}$$

where the squared lengths of the orthogonal sides, $\|\mathbf{y} - \mathbf{X}\hat{\boldsymbol{\beta}}\|^2/\sigma_0^2$ and $\|\mathbf{X}\hat{\boldsymbol{\beta}} - \mathbf{X}\boldsymbol{\beta}_0\|^2/\sigma_0^2$, are independently distributed.[34]

Lemma 10.1 (Minimum Chi-Square, p. 197) also applies to an asymptotic result for the GMM distance function.[35]

Lemma 22.2 (Minimum Chi-Square II) *Let the assumptions of Proposition 20 hold. If* $\mathbf{C}_N = \hat{\boldsymbol{\Lambda}}_N^{-1}$ *in the GMM distance function* $Q_N(\boldsymbol{\theta})$ *then*

$$N \cdot Q_N(\boldsymbol{\theta}_0) \xrightarrow{d} \chi^2_J$$

If $\hat{\boldsymbol{\theta}}_N$ *is the corresponding GMM estimator, then*

$$\min_{\boldsymbol{\theta}} N \cdot Q_N(\boldsymbol{\theta}) = N \cdot Q_N(\hat{\boldsymbol{\theta}}_N) \xrightarrow{d} \chi^2_{J-K} \tag{22.39}$$

$$N \cdot Q_N(\boldsymbol{\theta}_0) - N \cdot Q_N(\hat{\boldsymbol{\theta}}) \xrightarrow{d} \chi^2_K \tag{22.40}$$

and these two statistics are asymptotically independent.

A proof appears on p. 598. The lemma gives the analogues to the elements of (22.38). The minimized value of the GMM distance function (22.39) corresponds to $\|\mathbf{y} - \mathbf{X}\hat{\boldsymbol{\beta}}\|^2/\sigma_0^2$ and the generalized distance (22.40) corresponds to $\|\mathbf{X}\hat{\boldsymbol{\beta}} - \mathbf{X}\boldsymbol{\beta}_0\|^2/\sigma_0^2$. Perhaps the most salient difference is that the least squares statistics depend on the unknown variance parameter σ_0^2 whereas the GMM statistics use the estimated variance matrix $\hat{\boldsymbol{\Lambda}}_N$. This reflects the use of empirical moments, not individual observations, in GMM. The empirical moments come with empirical variances, but individual observations do not.

Lemma 22.2 also delivers the asymptotic distribution of the test statistic of overidentifying restrictions. Besides its asymptotic chi-square distribution, note that the test statistic is independently distributed with the quadratic form we associate with MD estimation. Minimization of the chi-square $N \cdot Q_N(\boldsymbol{\theta}_0)$ over $\boldsymbol{\theta}_0$ partitions the sampling variation in the empirical moments into two orthogonal pieces. This has a practical use that we describe in the next section.

The parametric restrictions of a null hypothesis $\mathbf{r}(\boldsymbol{\theta}_0) = \mathbf{0}$ lead to a second round application of the minimum chi-square lemma. Taking

$$N \cdot \left[Q_N(\boldsymbol{\theta}_0) - Q_N(\hat{\boldsymbol{\theta}}_N)\right] \xrightarrow{d} \chi^2_K$$

as the initial GMM distance function, and substituting $\boldsymbol{\theta}_0 = \mathbf{s}(\boldsymbol{\gamma}_0)$ for the restrictions of the null hypothesis, Lemma 22.2 implies that

[34] We proved Proposition 11 (F Statistic, p. 203) with these results.

[35] See Chamberlain (1982, Proposition 8′).

$$\min_{\gamma} N \cdot \left\{ Q_N[\mathbf{s}(\boldsymbol{\gamma})] - Q_N(\hat{\boldsymbol{\theta}}_N) \right\} = N \cdot \left[Q_N(\hat{\boldsymbol{\theta}}_{\mathrm{R}N}) - Q_N(\hat{\boldsymbol{\theta}}_N) \right]$$
$$= \mathcal{DD}$$
$$\xrightarrow{d} \chi^2_{K-M} \tag{22.41}$$

and

$$N \cdot \left[Q_N(\boldsymbol{\theta}_0) - Q_N(\hat{\boldsymbol{\theta}}_N) \right] - N \cdot \left[Q_N(\hat{\boldsymbol{\theta}}_{\mathrm{R}N}) - Q_N(\hat{\boldsymbol{\theta}}_N) \right] = N \cdot \left[Q_N(\boldsymbol{\theta}_0) - Q_N(\hat{\boldsymbol{\theta}}_{\mathrm{R}N}) \right]$$
$$\xrightarrow{d} \chi^2_M \tag{22.42}$$

where these two statistics are asymptotically independently distributed. Thus, we have derived the asymptotic distribution of the DD test statistic. In addition, we have shown that it is independently distributed with the test statistic for overidentifying moment restrictions.

We have already explained the asymptotic equivalence of the DD and MC test statistics (p. 569). We will use the MC statistic to draw the asymptotic equivalence of these two statistics with the Wald and gradient statistics when $\mathbf{C}_N = \hat{\boldsymbol{\Lambda}}_N^{-1}$. A similar argument relates the Wald, score, and LR statistics in Section 17.3. The gradient test forecasts the unrestricted estimator from the restricted one with the linearized GMM estimator (21.31)

$$\hat{\boldsymbol{\theta}}_N^* = \hat{\boldsymbol{\theta}}_{\mathrm{R}N} - \left(\hat{\mathbf{G}}_N' \hat{\boldsymbol{\Lambda}}_N^{-1} \hat{\mathbf{G}}_N \right)^{-1} \hat{\mathbf{G}}_N' \hat{\boldsymbol{\Lambda}}_N^{-1} \mathbf{g}_N(\hat{\boldsymbol{\theta}}_{\mathrm{R}N})$$

yielding

$$\mathcal{MC} \stackrel{p}{=} N \cdot \left(\hat{\boldsymbol{\theta}}_N^* - \hat{\boldsymbol{\theta}}_{\mathrm{R}N} \right)' \hat{\mathbf{G}}_N' \hat{\boldsymbol{\Lambda}}_N^{-1} \hat{\mathbf{G}}_N \left(\hat{\boldsymbol{\theta}}_N^* - \hat{\boldsymbol{\theta}}_{\mathrm{R}N} \right)$$
$$= N \cdot \mathbf{g}_N(\hat{\boldsymbol{\theta}}_{\mathrm{R}N})' \hat{\boldsymbol{\Lambda}}_N^{-1} \hat{\mathbf{G}}_N \left(\hat{\mathbf{G}}_N' \hat{\boldsymbol{\Lambda}}_N^{-1} \hat{\mathbf{G}}_N \right)^{-1} \hat{\mathbf{G}}_N' \hat{\boldsymbol{\Lambda}}_N^{-1} \mathbf{g}_N(\hat{\boldsymbol{\theta}}_{\mathrm{R}N})$$
$$= \mathcal{G}$$

Similarly, the Wald test forecasts the restricted estimator from the unrestricted estimator:

$$\hat{\boldsymbol{\theta}}_{\mathrm{R}N}^* \equiv \hat{\boldsymbol{\theta}}_N - \left(\hat{\mathbf{G}}_N' \hat{\boldsymbol{\Lambda}}_N^{-1} \hat{\mathbf{G}}_N \right)^{-1} \hat{\mathbf{R}}_N' \left[\hat{\mathbf{R}}_N \left(\hat{\mathbf{G}}_N' \hat{\boldsymbol{\Lambda}}_N^{-1} \hat{\mathbf{G}}_N \right)^{-1} \hat{\mathbf{R}}_N' \right]^{-1} \hat{\mathbf{r}}_N$$

is asymptotically equivalent to $\hat{\boldsymbol{\theta}}_{\mathrm{R}N}$ so that[36]

$$\mathcal{MC} \stackrel{p}{=} N \cdot \left(\hat{\boldsymbol{\theta}}_N - \hat{\boldsymbol{\theta}}_{\mathrm{R}N}^* \right)' \hat{\mathbf{G}}_N' \hat{\boldsymbol{\Lambda}}_N^{-1} \hat{\mathbf{G}}_N \left(\hat{\boldsymbol{\theta}}_N - \hat{\boldsymbol{\theta}}_{\mathrm{R}N}^* \right)$$
$$= N \cdot \hat{\mathbf{r}}_N' \left[\hat{\mathbf{R}}_N \left(\hat{\mathbf{G}}_N' \hat{\boldsymbol{\Lambda}}_N^{-1} \hat{\mathbf{G}}_N \right)^{-1} \hat{\mathbf{R}}_N' \right]^{-1} \hat{\mathbf{r}}_N$$
$$= \mathcal{W}$$

These asymptotic equivalences become identities under conditions that make quadratic approximations exact. In particular, if the moment functions are linear in $\boldsymbol{\theta}$,

[36] See Exercise 22.19.

$$\mathbf{g}_N(\boldsymbol{\theta}) = \mathbf{g}_N + \mathbf{G}_N\boldsymbol{\theta}$$

then the GMM distance function is quadratic, as in

$$\begin{aligned} Q_N(\boldsymbol{\theta}) &= (\mathbf{g}_N + \mathbf{G}_N\boldsymbol{\theta})' \hat{\boldsymbol{\Lambda}}_N^{-1} (\mathbf{g}_N + \mathbf{G}_N\boldsymbol{\theta}) \\ &= \left(\mathbf{g}_N + \mathbf{G}_N\hat{\boldsymbol{\theta}}_N\right)' \hat{\boldsymbol{\Lambda}}_N^{-1} \left(\mathbf{g}_N + \mathbf{G}_N\hat{\boldsymbol{\theta}}_N\right) + \left(\hat{\boldsymbol{\theta}}_N - \boldsymbol{\theta}\right)' \mathbf{G}_N'\hat{\boldsymbol{\Lambda}}_N^{-1}\mathbf{G}_N \left(\hat{\boldsymbol{\theta}}_N - \boldsymbol{\theta}\right) \end{aligned}$$

where

$$\hat{\boldsymbol{\theta}}_N = \left(\mathbf{G}_N'\hat{\boldsymbol{\Lambda}}_N^{-1}\mathbf{G}_N\right)^{-1} \mathbf{G}_N'\hat{\boldsymbol{\Lambda}}_N^{-1}\mathbf{g}_N$$

In words, the asymptotic equivalence in Lemma 22.1 is an equality. It follows that the linearized GMM estimator is also exact. Therefore, $\mathcal{DD} \equiv \mathcal{MC} \equiv \mathcal{G}$.

The Wald statistic uses an approximation to the restricted GMM estimator for general restrictions. As a result, $\mathcal{W}$ is excluded from the preceding identities. However, if the restrictions are linear in $\boldsymbol{\theta}$,

$$\mathbf{r}(\boldsymbol{\theta}) = R\boldsymbol{\theta} + \mathbf{r} \qquad \Leftrightarrow \qquad \boldsymbol{\theta} = \mathbf{S}\boldsymbol{\gamma}$$

in addition to linear moment functions, then the restricted GMM distance function is also quadratic and the Wald forecast of the restricted estimator is also exact. Therefore, $\mathcal{DD} \equiv \mathcal{MC} \equiv \mathcal{G} \equiv \mathcal{W}$.

22.5 STATISTICAL POWER

In the previous section, we described GMM test statistics for a general weighting matrix $\mathbf{C}_N$ in the GMM distance function and then noted an effect of setting $\mathbf{C}_N = \hat{\boldsymbol{\Lambda}}_N^{-1}$. That effect is the relationship between the test statistics and the GMM distance function. There is also an effect on the power of the test statistics. Test statistics with $\mathbf{C}_N = \hat{\boldsymbol{\Lambda}}_N^{-1}$ are locally most powerful relative to other choices of $\mathbf{C}_N$. This gives a methodological reason to prefer such test statistics.

This statistical power is essentially a corollary to relatively efficient estimation when $\mathbf{C}_N = \hat{\boldsymbol{\Lambda}}_N^{-1}$. The more precise the estimator, the better one can detect exceptions to null hypotheses. To confirm this intuition for GMM testing, we consider local alternatives to the parametric null hypothesis $H_0 : \mathbf{r}(\boldsymbol{\theta}_0) = \mathbf{0}$ of the form $H_1 : \mathbf{r}[\boldsymbol{\theta}_0(N)] = (1/\sqrt{N}) \cdot \boldsymbol{\delta}$ for some $\boldsymbol{\delta} \in \mathbb{R}^{K-M}$.[37] For any $\mathbf{C}_N$, the unrestricted estimator will (correctly) capture $\boldsymbol{\delta}$ in its limiting distribution:

$$\begin{aligned} \sqrt{N}\left\{\mathbf{r}(\hat{\boldsymbol{\theta}}_N) - \mathbf{r}[\boldsymbol{\theta}_0(N)]\right\} &= \sqrt{N}\mathbf{r}(\hat{\boldsymbol{\theta}}_N) - \boldsymbol{\delta} \\ &\xrightarrow{d} \mathfrak{N}(\mathbf{0}, \mathbf{R}_0\mathbf{V}_0\mathbf{R}_0') \end{aligned}$$

where $\mathbf{R}_0 \equiv \mathbf{R}(\boldsymbol{\theta}_0)$ and $\sqrt{N}[\hat{\boldsymbol{\theta}}_N - \boldsymbol{\theta}_0(N)] \xrightarrow{d} \mathfrak{N}(\mathbf{0}, \mathbf{V}_0)$. That is, $\sqrt{N}\mathbf{r}(\hat{\boldsymbol{\theta}}_N) \xrightarrow{d} \mathfrak{N}(\boldsymbol{\delta}, \mathbf{R}_0\mathbf{V}_0\mathbf{R}_0')$ and, as a result, the Wald test statistic converges in distribution to a noncentral chi-square random variable with $K - M$ degrees of freedom and noncentrality parameter

[37] We introduced local alternative hypotheses in Section 17.5.1.

$$\lambda = \boldsymbol{\delta}' \left(\mathbf{R}_0\mathbf{V}_0\mathbf{R}_0'\right)^{-1} \boldsymbol{\delta}'$$

All of the test statistics that are asymptotically equivalent under the null hypothesis are also asymptotically equivalent under the sequence of local alternative hypotheses.

We can compare the statistical power of various GMM test statistics with this noncentrality parameter. The larger the noncentrality parameter is, the more powerful a test statistic is.[38] We will show that a relatively efficient estimator yields the largest noncentrality parameter for every $\boldsymbol{\delta}$. If $\mathbf{C}_N = \hat{\boldsymbol{\Lambda}}_N^{-1} \xrightarrow{p} \boldsymbol{\Lambda}_0^{-1}$, then the corresponding GMM estimator is efficient relative to GMM estimators indexed by $\mathbf{C}_N$.[39] Let $\mathbf{V}_0^* \equiv \left(\mathbf{G}_0'\boldsymbol{\Lambda}_0^{-1}\mathbf{G}_0\right)^{-1}$ denote the asymptotic variance of the relatively efficient estimator and note that

$$\mathbf{a}'\mathbf{V}_0^*\mathbf{a} \leq \mathbf{a}'\mathbf{V}_0\mathbf{a}, \qquad \forall \mathbf{a} \in \mathbb{R}^K$$

This implies that

$$\mathbf{b}'\mathbf{R}_0\mathbf{V}_0^*\mathbf{R}_0'\mathbf{b} \leq \mathbf{b}'\mathbf{R}_0\mathbf{V}_0\mathbf{R}_0'\mathbf{b}, \qquad \forall \mathbf{b} \in \mathbb{R}^{K-M}$$

because $\mathbf{R}_0'\mathbf{b} \in \mathbb{R}^K$. Furthermore,[40]

$$\mathbf{c}' \left(\mathbf{R}_0\mathbf{V}_0\mathbf{R}_0'\right)^{-1} \mathbf{c} \leq \mathbf{c}' \left(\mathbf{R}_0\mathbf{V}_0^*\mathbf{R}_0'\right)^{-1} \mathbf{c}, \qquad \forall \mathbf{c} \in \mathbb{R}^{K-M}$$

This proves that the relatively efficient estimator yields (locally) most powerful test statistics.

Using such test statistics requires relatively efficient estimation, at least implicitly. However, the asymptotic distribution theory permits one to use linearized GMM estimators in place of the GMM estimators themselves as in the $C(\alpha)$ test statistic (17.26). Thus, given $\sqrt{N}$-consistent GMM estimator $\check{\boldsymbol{\theta}}_N$, the unrestricted estimator

$$\hat{\boldsymbol{\theta}}_N^* = \check{\boldsymbol{\theta}}_N - \left(\check{\mathbf{G}}_N'\check{\boldsymbol{\Lambda}}_N^{-1}\check{\mathbf{G}}_N\right)^{-1} \check{\mathbf{G}}_N'\check{\boldsymbol{\Lambda}}_N^{-1}\mathbf{g}_N(\check{\boldsymbol{\theta}}_N)$$

and the approximately restricted estimator[41]

$$\hat{\boldsymbol{\theta}}_{RN}^* = \hat{\boldsymbol{\theta}}_N^* - \left(\check{\mathbf{G}}_N'\check{\boldsymbol{\Lambda}}_N^{-1}\check{\mathbf{G}}_N\right)^{-1} \check{\mathbf{R}}_N' \left[\check{\mathbf{R}}_N \left(\check{\mathbf{G}}_N'\check{\boldsymbol{\Lambda}}_N^{-1}\check{\mathbf{G}}_N\right)^{-1} \check{\mathbf{R}}_N'\right]^{-1} \mathbf{r}(\hat{\boldsymbol{\theta}}_N^*)$$

can be plugged into the MC test statistic, as in

$$\mathcal{MC} \stackrel{p}{=} N \cdot \left(\hat{\boldsymbol{\theta}}_N^* - \hat{\boldsymbol{\theta}}_{RN}^*\right)' \check{\mathbf{G}}_N'\check{\boldsymbol{\Lambda}}_N^{-1}\check{\mathbf{G}}_N \left(\hat{\boldsymbol{\theta}}_N^* - \hat{\boldsymbol{\theta}}_{RN}^*\right)$$

to conduct an asymptotically equivalent test.[42]

---

38 Lemma F.4 (p. 919).

39 Proposition 21 (GMM Efficiency, p. 551).

40 Exercise 9.11 states that if $\mathbf{A}$ and $\mathbf{B}$ are symmetric positive definite matrices, then $\mathbf{B} - \mathbf{A}$ is positive semidefinite if and only if $\mathbf{A}^{-1} - \mathbf{B}^{-1}$ is positive semidefinite.

41 See Exercise 22.19.

42 Alternatively, one can set

$$\hat{\boldsymbol{\theta}}_{RN}^* = \hat{\boldsymbol{\theta}}_N^* - \left(\check{\mathbf{G}}_N'\check{\boldsymbol{\Lambda}}_N^{-1}\check{\mathbf{G}}_N\right)^{-1} \check{\mathbf{R}}_N' \left[\check{\mathbf{R}}_N \left(\check{\mathbf{G}}_N'\check{\boldsymbol{\Lambda}}_N^{-1}\check{\mathbf{G}}_N\right)^{-1} \check{\mathbf{R}}_N'\right]^{-1} \left[\check{\mathbf{r}}_N + \check{\mathbf{R}}_N \left(\hat{\boldsymbol{\theta}}_N^* - \check{\boldsymbol{\theta}}_N\right)\right]$$

22.6 SEQUENTIAL TESTING

The minimum chi-square decomposition of the (optimal) GMM distance function into independent chi-square random variables (Lemma 22.2) has an extended use in testing a sequence of successively more restrictive hypotheses. Under the null hypothesis that all of the restrictions are correct, the successive GMM test statistics are independently distributed. As a result, one can analyze the statistical properties of the testing sequence relatively easily.

EXAMPLE 22.10

At the beginning of this chapter, we reported the test statistic for overidentifying instrumental variables applied to the consumption growth equation of Campbell and Mankiw. One might have greatest confidence in the fifth lag of consumption growth as an instrumental variable and successively less confidence in the fourth, third, and second lag of consumption growth. Rather than testing whether all of the instrumental variables are valid, as in a test of overidentifying restrictions, one might test sequentially the fourth through second lags assuming that the fifth lag is a valid instrument. This is a natural procedure when, for example, evidence against the fourth lag will also be taken as evidence against the third and second.

Using the DD statistic, we computed test statistics for

1. the fourth lag given that the fifth lag is an instrument,
2. the third lag given that the fourth and fifth lags are instruments, and
3. the second lag given that the third, fourth, and fifth lags are instruments.

Under the null hypothesis that all are valid instrumental variables, asymptotically the test statistics are independently distributed χ_1^2 random variables.[43] The test statistics (and their probability values) are 1.14 (28%), 1.36 (24%), and 1.74 (19%), respectively. At the 5% level of significance, each variable is an acceptable instrument conditional on higher lags being valid instrumental variables. In the end, we accept all three just as in the test of overidentifying restrictions.[44]

Such sequential hypothesis testing is often called "top-down" or "general-to-specific" testing.[45] When this method applies, there is a sequence of hypotheses, $H_1, \ldots, H_{K-M}$, such that H_1 is a special case of H_2 and so on until H_{K-M} is the most general case. Using our previous notation for parametric restrictions $\mathbf{r}(\boldsymbol{\theta}) = \mathbf{0}$, we can describe such a sequence formally with

$$H_k : r_j(\boldsymbol{\theta}) = 0, \qquad j = k, \ldots, K - M$$

[43] For all of the test statistics, we used the estimate of the variance parameter from 2SLS using only the fifth lag of consumption growth as an instrumental variable. Under the null hypothesis, it does not matter which estimate we use. Under the alternative hypothesis, only our choice is a consistent estimator.

[44] Note that the sum of the three test statistics approximately equals the overidentifying restrictions test statistic, just as it should. The former is 3.532 and the latter is 3.539, the discrepancy coming from different estimates of the variance parameter. The overidentifying restrictions statistic naturally uses the variance estimate for 2SLS using all the instrumental variables.

[45] See Hendry (1995) for a general discussion of general-to-specific testing, including a case for a reductionist approach to econometric model selection.

where $r_j(\boldsymbol{\theta})$ is the jth element of $\mathbf{r}(\boldsymbol{\theta})$ and $k = 1, \ldots, K-M$. The last hypothesis, H_{K-M}, imposes only one restriction on $\boldsymbol{\theta}$ and the first imposes the entire vector of restrictions. The sequence of test statistics is the GMM statistics for

$$H_k' : r_k(\boldsymbol{\theta}) = 0$$

given that

$$r_{k+1}(\boldsymbol{\theta}) = \cdots = r_{K-M}(\boldsymbol{\theta}) = 0$$

The independence of the test statistics under H_1 is an iterative application of the minimum chi-square lemma (Lemma 22.2). If we denote

$$\hat{\boldsymbol{\theta}}_{\mathrm{R}k} \equiv \begin{cases} \min\limits_{\{\boldsymbol{\theta} | r_j(\boldsymbol{\theta})=0, j=k,\ldots,K-M\}} \mathcal{Q}_N(\boldsymbol{\theta}) & \text{if } k = 1, \ldots, K-M \\ \hat{\boldsymbol{\theta}}_N & \text{if } k = K-M+1 \end{cases}$$

and the DD test statistic for the kth test by

$$\begin{aligned} \mathcal{DD}_k &\equiv \min_{\{\boldsymbol{\theta} | r_j(\boldsymbol{\theta})=0, j=k,\ldots,K-M\}} N \cdot \left[\mathcal{Q}_N(\boldsymbol{\theta}) - \mathcal{Q}_N(\hat{\boldsymbol{\theta}}_{\mathrm{R},k+1}) \right] \\ &= N \cdot \left[\mathcal{Q}_N(\hat{\boldsymbol{\theta}}_{\mathrm{R}k}) - \mathcal{Q}_N(\hat{\boldsymbol{\theta}}_{\mathrm{R},k+1}) \right] \end{aligned}$$

then

$$N \cdot \left[\mathcal{Q}_N(\boldsymbol{\theta}_0) - \mathcal{Q}_N(\hat{\boldsymbol{\theta}}_{\mathrm{R},k+1}) \right] = N \cdot \left[\mathcal{Q}_N(\boldsymbol{\theta}_0) - \mathcal{Q}_N(\hat{\boldsymbol{\theta}}_{\mathrm{R}k}) \right] + \mathcal{DD}_k$$

and just as in (22.41) and (22.42),

$$\begin{aligned} \mathcal{DD}_k &\xrightarrow{d} \chi_1^2 \\ N \cdot \left[\mathcal{Q}_N(\boldsymbol{\theta}_0) - \mathcal{Q}_N(\hat{\boldsymbol{\theta}}_{\mathrm{R}k}) \right] &\xrightarrow{d} \chi_{K-M+1-k}^2 \end{aligned}$$

where the χ_1^2 and $\chi_{K-M+1-k}^2$ are independent. As we proceed backward, from $k = K - M$ to $k = 1$, each $\mathcal{DD}_k$ is carved out of the preceding $N \cdot \left[\mathcal{Q}_N(\boldsymbol{\theta}_0) - \mathcal{Q}_N(\hat{\boldsymbol{\theta}}_{\mathrm{R},k+1}) \right]$ so that $\mathcal{DD}_k$ is independent of every $\mathcal{DD}_{k+1}, \ldots, \mathcal{DD}_{K-M}$ under H_k.

In applications, researchers often test each additional restriction with the Wald statistic, not the DD. The Wald statistic is more convenient because the testing sequence stops at any iteration where a restriction is rejected by a test. Thus, one potentially avoids unnecessary computation of an estimator that is rejected.

The independence in the sequence of test statistics has the direct consequence of permitting the researcher to specify the overall significance level (or size) of the testing sequence. If α_j is the nominal significance level of the jth test, then the significance level of the sequence of tests from H'_{K-M} down to H'_k is

$$1 - \prod_{j=k}^{K-M} (1 - \alpha_j)$$

the probability that none of the test statistics falls into its critical region. Thus, if the overall sequence is to be $\bar{\alpha}$ and each test has the same significance level α then

$$1 - (1-\alpha)^{K-M} = \bar{\alpha} \qquad \Leftrightarrow \qquad \alpha = 1 - (1-\bar{\alpha})^{1/(K-M)}$$

In the example above, an overall significance level of 5% implies that the significance level for each of the individual tests should be $1 - 0.95^{1/3} \approx 0.017$.[46] In general, the individual tests in the sequence have a lower significance level than the significance level of the sequence.

Note that these results apply equally to such a sequence of likelihood ratio tests. Both the GMM test statistics and the likelihood ratio statistic are asymptotically equivalent to MC test statistics. Therefore, the minimum chi-square lemma also applies to the likelihood ratio statistic and its Wald and score counterparts. Furthermore, Anderson (1971) has shown that in certain cases the general-to-specific testing method using the likelihood ratio has the most power among a general class of tests.

One obvious alternative test method is the specific-to-general testing sequence. The statistics in such sequences are not independently distributed so that control over the significance level of the procedure is problematic. In addition, one faces the possibility that under an alternative hypothesis a test early in the sequence may have little or no power to detect misspecification at a higher level. On the other hand, it is often convenient to test from the most restrictive model toward the most general because restricted estimation is easier and the gradient test is simple.

22.7 MINIMUM DISTANCE ESTIMATION

The MC test statistic is dual to an estimation procedure called *minimum distance* (MD).[47] Because the MC statistic is asymptotically equivalent to the DD statistic, as in

$$\begin{aligned}\mathcal{MC} &= N \cdot \left(\hat{\boldsymbol{\theta}} - \hat{\boldsymbol{\theta}}_{RN}\right)' \hat{\mathbf{G}}_N' \hat{\boldsymbol{\Lambda}}_N^{-1} \hat{\mathbf{G}}_N \left(\hat{\boldsymbol{\theta}} - \hat{\boldsymbol{\theta}}_{RN}\right) \\ &\overset{p}{=} N \left[Q_N(\hat{\boldsymbol{\theta}}_{RN}) - Q_N(\hat{\boldsymbol{\theta}}_N) \right] \\ &= \min_{\{\boldsymbol{\theta} | \mathbf{r}(\boldsymbol{\theta}) = \mathbf{0}\}} N \left[Q_N(\boldsymbol{\theta}) - Q_N(\hat{\boldsymbol{\theta}}_N) \right]\end{aligned}$$

one might anticipate that

$$\hat{\boldsymbol{\theta}}_{RN}^{+} \equiv \underset{\{\boldsymbol{\theta} | \mathbf{r}(\boldsymbol{\theta}) = \mathbf{0}\}}{\operatorname{argmin}} N \cdot \left(\hat{\boldsymbol{\theta}}_N - \boldsymbol{\theta}\right)' \hat{\mathbf{G}}_N' \hat{\boldsymbol{\Lambda}}_N^{-1} \hat{\mathbf{G}}_N \left(\hat{\boldsymbol{\theta}}_N - \boldsymbol{\theta}\right) \tag{22.43}$$

is an asymptotically equivalent estimator to

$$\hat{\boldsymbol{\theta}}_{RN} \equiv \underset{\{\boldsymbol{\theta} | \mathbf{r}(\boldsymbol{\theta}) = \mathbf{0}\}}{\operatorname{argmin}} \mathbf{g}_N(\boldsymbol{\theta})' \hat{\boldsymbol{\Lambda}}_N^{-1} \mathbf{g}_N(\boldsymbol{\theta})$$

when $\mathbf{r}(\boldsymbol{\theta}_0) = \mathbf{0}$. In this section, we show that this is correct.

The $\hat{\boldsymbol{\theta}}_{RN}^{+}$ is an example of a minimum distance estimator, a class of estimators interesting in its own right, independent of the MC test statistic. MD estimation begins with an initial, unrestricted, estimator $\hat{\boldsymbol{\theta}}_N$ of the parameter vector $\boldsymbol{\theta}_0$, a symmetric positive semidefinite weighting matrix $\mathbf{A}_N$, and a vector of parameter restrictions $\mathbf{r}(\boldsymbol{\theta}_0) = \mathbf{0}$. It is conceptually convenient to write the restrictions in terms of a parameterization $\boldsymbol{\theta}_0 = \mathbf{s}(\boldsymbol{\gamma}_0)$.[48] That way we can view the vector of functions $\hat{\boldsymbol{\theta}}_N - \mathbf{s}(\boldsymbol{\gamma})$ as comparable to the moment function $\mathbf{g}_N(\boldsymbol{\theta})$. Both vectors have a probability

46 In some cases, one might increase the level of significance at the more restrictive levels in acknowledgment that the most restricted models seem less likely to hold. Less convincing evidence will confirm one's suspicions.

47 This section draws particularly on Chamberlain (1982). See the references cited there for earlier work.

48 For a discussion of such reparameterizations, review the comments at the start of Section 17.4.

limit equal to zero when they are evaluated at the population values of their parameter arguments. With this interpretation, MD and GMM are similar procedures. The MD method finds the value of the parameters that minimizes the squared generalized length of $\hat{\boldsymbol{\theta}}_N - \mathbf{s}(\boldsymbol{\gamma})$ with respect to $\mathbf{A}_N$:

$$\hat{\boldsymbol{\gamma}}_{\text{MD}} \equiv \underset{\boldsymbol{\gamma}}{\text{argmin}} \left[\hat{\boldsymbol{\theta}}_N - \mathbf{s}(\boldsymbol{\gamma})\right]' \mathbf{A}_N \left[\hat{\boldsymbol{\theta}}_N - \mathbf{s}(\boldsymbol{\gamma})\right]$$

$$\begin{aligned} \hat{\boldsymbol{\theta}}_{\text{MD}} &\equiv \mathbf{s}(\hat{\boldsymbol{\gamma}}_{\text{MD}}) \\ &= \underset{\{\boldsymbol{\theta}|\mathbf{r}(\boldsymbol{\theta})=\mathbf{0}\}}{\text{argmin}} \left(\hat{\boldsymbol{\theta}}_N - \boldsymbol{\theta}\right)' \mathbf{A}_N \left(\hat{\boldsymbol{\theta}}_N - \boldsymbol{\theta}\right) \end{aligned} \tag{22.44}$$

We will support the MD estimation method with the following assumptions.

Assumption 22.2 (Regular Restrictions) *The set $\boldsymbol{\Gamma} \equiv \{\boldsymbol{\gamma} \mid \boldsymbol{\theta} = \mathbf{s}(\boldsymbol{\gamma}) \in \boldsymbol{\Theta}\}$ is a compact subset of $\mathbb{R}^M$, $\mathbf{s}(\boldsymbol{\gamma})$ is continuously differentiable, the matrix of partial derivatives $\mathbf{S}(\boldsymbol{\gamma}) \equiv \partial \mathbf{s}(\boldsymbol{\gamma})/\partial \boldsymbol{\gamma}$ has rank equal to M on $\boldsymbol{\Gamma}$, $\boldsymbol{\theta}_0 \in \{\boldsymbol{\theta} \mid \boldsymbol{\theta} = \mathbf{s}(\boldsymbol{\gamma}),\ \boldsymbol{\gamma} \in \boldsymbol{\Gamma}\}$, and $\boldsymbol{\gamma}_0 \in \boldsymbol{\Gamma}$ such that $\boldsymbol{\theta}_0 = \mathbf{s}(\boldsymbol{\gamma}_0)$ is unique.*

This assumption is implied by Assumption 22.1.[49] The next assumption is similar to GMM Assumption 21.2 (Identification, p. 545).

Assumption 22.3 (Asymptotic Limits) *The weighting matrix $\mathbf{A}_N$ converges in probability to $\mathbf{A}_0$ where $\mathbf{A}_0$ is symmetric and positive definite and $\sqrt{N} \cdot (\hat{\boldsymbol{\theta}}_N - \boldsymbol{\theta}_0) \xrightarrow{d} \mathfrak{N}(\mathbf{0}, \mathbf{V}_0)$ where $\mathbf{V}_0$ is a symmetric positive definite matrix.*

Combined with the previous assumption, the identification of $\boldsymbol{\gamma}_0$ is assured.

These assumptions are sufficient for the following description of the asymptotic behavior of the MD estimator.

Proposition 22 (Minimum Distance Estimation) *If Assumptions 22.2 and 22.3 hold then*

$$\hat{\boldsymbol{\gamma}}_{\text{MD}} \xrightarrow{p} \boldsymbol{\gamma}_0$$

and

$$\sqrt{N} \cdot (\hat{\boldsymbol{\gamma}}_{\text{MD}} - \boldsymbol{\gamma}_0) \xrightarrow{d} \mathfrak{N}(\mathbf{0}, \mathbf{W}_0)$$

where

$$\mathbf{W}_0 = \left(\mathbf{S}_0'\mathbf{A}_0\mathbf{S}_0\right)^{-1} \mathbf{S}_0'\mathbf{A}_0\mathbf{V}_0\mathbf{A}_0\mathbf{S}_0 \left(\mathbf{S}_0'\mathbf{A}_0\mathbf{S}_0\right)^{-1}$$

and $\mathbf{S}_0 \equiv \mathbf{S}(\boldsymbol{\gamma}_0)$.

---

[49] For amplification, see the discussion at the beginning of Section 17.4.

For a proof, see p. 599. The parallels with GMM estimation immediately suggest that an efficient choice for $\mathbf{A}_N$ in the MD estimator is a consistent estimator $\hat{\mathbf{V}}_N^{-1}$ of the inverse of the asymptotic variance $\mathbf{V}_0$ of $\hat{\boldsymbol{\theta}}_N$. This is correct and the usual argument proves it. The asymptotic covariance between an MD estimator and one for which $\mathbf{A}_0 = \mathbf{V}_0^{-1}$ equals

$$\left[(\mathbf{S}_0'\mathbf{A}_0\mathbf{S}_0)^{-1}\mathbf{S}_0'\mathbf{A}_0\right]\mathbf{V}_0\left[\mathbf{V}_0^{-1}\mathbf{S}_0(\mathbf{S}_0'\mathbf{V}_0^{-1}\mathbf{S}_0)^{-1}\right] = (\mathbf{S}_0'\mathbf{V}_0^{-1}\mathbf{S}_0)^{-1}$$

which is the asymptotic variance of the latter estimator, so it is relatively efficient.

We have already encountered an example of MD estimation in the restricted least squares (RLS) estimator for the classical linear regression model. In that instance[50]

$$\mathrm{E}(\mathbf{y}\,|\,\mathbf{X}) = \mathbf{X}\boldsymbol{\beta}_0 \tag{22.45}$$

$$\boldsymbol{\beta}_0 = \mathbf{S}\boldsymbol{\gamma}_0 \tag{22.46}$$

Given only the OLS estimator $\hat{\boldsymbol{\beta}}_{\mathrm{OLS}} \equiv (\mathbf{X}'\mathbf{X})^{-1}\mathbf{X}'\mathbf{y}$ one can compute the RLS estimator for the restricted parameterization. Because the sum of squared residuals factors according to[51]

$$\mathbf{y} - \mathbf{X}\boldsymbol{\beta} = \mathbf{y} - \mathbf{X}\hat{\boldsymbol{\beta}}_{\mathrm{OLS}} + \mathbf{X}\hat{\boldsymbol{\beta}}_{\mathrm{OLS}} - \mathbf{X}\boldsymbol{\beta} \tag{22.47}$$

$$\mathbf{y} - \mathbf{X}\hat{\boldsymbol{\beta}}_{\mathrm{OLS}} \perp \mathbf{X}\hat{\boldsymbol{\beta}}_{\mathrm{OLS}} - \mathbf{X}\boldsymbol{\beta} \tag{22.48}$$

$$\begin{aligned}\|\mathbf{y} - \mathbf{X}\boldsymbol{\beta}\|^2 &= \left\|\mathbf{y} - \mathbf{X}\hat{\boldsymbol{\beta}}_{\mathrm{OLS}}\right\|^2 + \left\|\mathbf{X}\hat{\boldsymbol{\beta}} - \mathbf{X}\boldsymbol{\beta}\right\|^2 \\ &= \left\|\mathbf{y} - \mathbf{X}\hat{\boldsymbol{\beta}}_{\mathrm{OLS}}\right\|^2 + \left(\hat{\beta} - \beta\right)'\mathbf{X}'\mathbf{X}\left(\hat{\beta} - \beta\right)\end{aligned} \tag{22.49}$$

as[52]

$$\hat{\boldsymbol{\beta}}_{\mathrm{RLS}} = \underset{\boldsymbol{\beta}\in\mathrm{Col}(\mathbf{S})}{\mathrm{argmin}}\,(\mathbf{y} - \mathbf{X}\boldsymbol{\beta})'(\mathbf{y} - \mathbf{X}\boldsymbol{\beta}) \tag{22.50}$$

$$= \underset{\boldsymbol{\beta}\in\mathrm{Col}(\mathbf{S})}{\mathrm{argmin}}\left(\hat{\boldsymbol{\beta}}_{\mathrm{OLS}} - \boldsymbol{\beta}\right)'\mathbf{X}'\mathbf{X}\left(\hat{\boldsymbol{\beta}}_{\mathrm{OLS}} - \boldsymbol{\beta}\right) \tag{22.51}$$

$$= \mathbf{S}\left(\mathbf{S}'\mathbf{X}'\mathbf{X}\mathbf{S}\right)^{-1}\mathbf{S}'\mathbf{X}'\mathbf{X}\hat{\boldsymbol{\beta}}_{\mathrm{OLS}} \tag{22.52}$$

Note that (22.50) and (22.51) state that the RLS and MD estimators are identical. Given Proposition 22 (Minimum Distance Estimation), a general asymptotic equivalence of the restricted GMM estimator and a MD estimator follows.[53]

Proposition 23 (MD and GMM) *Let Assumption 22.2 and the conditions of Proposition 20 (GMM Asymptotics, p. 546) hold where* $\mathbf{A}_N = \hat{\mathbf{G}}_N'\mathbf{C}_N\hat{\mathbf{G}}_N$. *Then the restricted GMM estimator*

---

50 See Chapter 4 (Restricted Least Squares) and Section 9.3 (Restricted Estimation).

51 See equation (4.10).

52 See equations (4.11)–(4.13) and the conditions of Proposition 3 (Restricted Least Squares, p. 79).

53 See Chamberlain (1982, Proposition 9).

$$\hat{\boldsymbol{\theta}}_N \equiv \underset{\{\boldsymbol{\theta}|\boldsymbol{\theta}=\mathbf{s}(\boldsymbol{\gamma})\}}{\operatorname{argmin}} N \cdot \mathbf{g}_N(\boldsymbol{\theta})'\mathbf{C}_N \mathbf{g}_N(\boldsymbol{\theta}) \tag{22.53}$$

is asymptotically equivalent to

$$\hat{\boldsymbol{\theta}}^+_{\mathrm{R}N} \equiv \underset{\{\boldsymbol{\theta}|\mathbf{r}(\boldsymbol{\theta})=\mathbf{0}\}}{\operatorname{argmin}} N \cdot \left(\hat{\boldsymbol{\theta}}_N - \boldsymbol{\theta}\right)' \hat{\mathbf{G}}_N' \mathbf{C}_N \hat{\mathbf{G}}_N \left(\hat{\boldsymbol{\theta}}_N - \boldsymbol{\theta}\right)$$

in the sense that $\sqrt{N}\left(\hat{\boldsymbol{\theta}}_{\mathrm{R}N} - \hat{\boldsymbol{\theta}}^+_{\mathrm{R}N}\right) \stackrel{p}{=} 0$.

This proposition states that as far as restricted GMM is concerned the unrestricted estimator $\hat{\boldsymbol{\theta}}_N$ contains all of the information in the moments that the restricted GMM estimator $\hat{\boldsymbol{\theta}}_{\mathrm{R}N}$ exploits.[54] It is as though one could replace the GMM distance function with

$$NQ_N(\check{\boldsymbol{\theta}}_N) \stackrel{p}{=} NQ_N(\hat{\boldsymbol{\theta}}_N) + N \cdot \left(\hat{\boldsymbol{\theta}}_N - \check{\boldsymbol{\theta}}_N\right)' \hat{\mathbf{G}}_N' \mathbf{C}_N \hat{\mathbf{G}}_N \left(\hat{\boldsymbol{\theta}}_N - \check{\boldsymbol{\theta}}_N\right)$$

(Lemma 22.1) and minimize over all $\sqrt{N}$-consistent $\check{\boldsymbol{\theta}}_N$. We give a proof of the proposition on p. 600.

The equivalence of the two estimators that we mentioned at the outset of this section is a special case of this result where $\mathbf{C}_N = \hat{\boldsymbol{\Lambda}}_N^{-1}$. We can also write

$$\begin{aligned} \mathcal{MC} &\equiv N \cdot \left(\hat{\boldsymbol{\theta}}_N - \hat{\boldsymbol{\theta}}_{\mathrm{R}N}\right)' \hat{\mathbf{V}}_N^{-1} \left(\hat{\boldsymbol{\theta}}_N - \hat{\boldsymbol{\theta}}_{\mathrm{R}N}\right) \\ &\stackrel{p}{=} N \cdot \left(\hat{\boldsymbol{\theta}}_N - \hat{\boldsymbol{\theta}}^+_{\mathrm{R}N}\right)' \hat{\mathbf{V}}_N^{-1} \left(\hat{\boldsymbol{\theta}}_N - \hat{\boldsymbol{\theta}}^+_{\mathrm{R}N}\right) \\ &= \min_{\{\boldsymbol{\theta}|\mathbf{r}(\boldsymbol{\theta})=\mathbf{0}\}} N \cdot \left(\hat{\boldsymbol{\theta}}_N - \boldsymbol{\theta}\right)' \hat{\mathbf{V}}_N^{-1} \left(\hat{\boldsymbol{\theta}}_N - \boldsymbol{\theta}\right) \end{aligned}$$

It is this relationship that motivates the "minimum chi-square" name of this test statistic.

22.8 MATHEMATICAL NOTES

These mathematical notes contain the proofs of four basic results that appear above. The first two concern the MC test statistic, establishing a link to the DD test statistic and then extending this link to the Pythagorean relationship described by the minimum chi-square lemma. The second two proofs cover the properties of the minimum distance estimation method. The first of these proves the consistency and asymptotic normality of the estimator along the lines of previous proofs of this kind. The final proof establishes the link between the restricted GMM estimator and a particular MD estimator.

In this first proof, we will construct an asymptotic analogue to the partition of the sum of squared residuals into the Pythagorean relationship

$$\|\mathbf{y} - \boldsymbol{\mu}\|^2 = \left\|\mathbf{y} - \hat{\boldsymbol{\mu}}\right\|^2 + \left\|\hat{\boldsymbol{\mu}} - \boldsymbol{\mu}\right\|^2$$

[54] This is not to say that there is no more information to be gained from the moments. If there is additional information, then $\hat{\boldsymbol{\theta}}_{\mathrm{R}N}$ fails to use it. Worse than that, perhaps, is that $\hat{\boldsymbol{\theta}}_{\mathrm{R}N}$ fails to use the information in $\hat{\boldsymbol{\theta}}_N$ efficiently. See Exercise 22.21.

or

$$(\mathbf{y}-\boldsymbol{\mu})'(\mathbf{y}-\boldsymbol{\mu}) = (\mathbf{y}-\boldsymbol{\mu})'(\mathbf{I}-\mathbf{P}_{\mathbf{X}})(\mathbf{y}-\boldsymbol{\mu}) + (\mathbf{y}-\boldsymbol{\mu})'\mathbf{P}_{\mathbf{X}}(\mathbf{y}-\boldsymbol{\mu})$$

for $\boldsymbol{\mu} \in \text{Col}(\mathbf{X})$ and $\hat{\boldsymbol{\mu}} \equiv \mathbf{P}_{\mathbf{X}}\mathbf{y}$. This partition is a link between MD and its RLS interpretation.

Proof of Lemma 22.1. We will prove this result for the more general weighting matrix $\mathbf{C}_N$ specified in Proposition 20, rather than the special case $\mathbf{C}_N = \hat{\boldsymbol{\Lambda}}_N^{-1}$. First, we introduce $\mathbf{P}_{\mathbf{C}_N^{1/2}\hat{\mathbf{G}}_N}$ as the counterpart to the orthogonal projector $\mathbf{P}_{\mathbf{X}}$. Using linear approximations, we find

$$\begin{aligned}-\mathbf{C}_N^{1/2}\hat{\mathbf{G}}_N\sqrt{N}\cdot\left(\hat{\boldsymbol{\theta}}_N-\check{\boldsymbol{\theta}}_N\right) &\overset{p}{=} \mathbf{C}_N^{1/2}\hat{\mathbf{G}}_N\left(\hat{\mathbf{G}}_N'\mathbf{C}_N\hat{\mathbf{G}}_N\right)^{-1}\hat{\mathbf{G}}_N'\mathbf{C}_N\sqrt{N}\cdot\mathbf{g}_N(\check{\boldsymbol{\theta}}_N)\\ &= \mathbf{P}_{\mathbf{C}_N^{1/2}\hat{\mathbf{G}}_N}\sqrt{N}\cdot\mathbf{g}_N(\check{\boldsymbol{\theta}}_N)\end{aligned} \tag{22.54}$$

and

$$\begin{aligned}\sqrt{N}\cdot\mathbf{C}_N^{1/2}\sqrt{N}\cdot\mathbf{g}(\hat{\boldsymbol{\theta}}_N) &\overset{p}{=} \mathbf{C}_N^{1/2}\sqrt{N}\cdot\mathbf{g}_N(\check{\boldsymbol{\theta}}_N) + \mathbf{C}_N^{1/2}\hat{\mathbf{G}}_N\left(\hat{\boldsymbol{\theta}}_N-\check{\boldsymbol{\theta}}_N\right)\\ &= \left(\mathbf{I}-\mathbf{P}_{\mathbf{C}_N^{1/2}\hat{\mathbf{G}}_N}\right)\mathbf{C}_N^{1/2}\sqrt{N}\cdot\mathbf{g}_N(\check{\boldsymbol{\theta}}_N)\end{aligned} \tag{22.55}$$

These admit the partition of the GMM distance function into

$$\begin{aligned}N\cdot\mathbf{g}_N(\check{\boldsymbol{\theta}}_N)'\mathbf{C}_N\,\mathbf{g}_N(\check{\boldsymbol{\theta}}_N) &= N\cdot\mathbf{g}_N(\check{\boldsymbol{\theta}}_N)'\mathbf{C}_N^{1/2\prime}\left(\mathbf{I}-\mathbf{P}_{\mathbf{C}_N^{1/2}\hat{\mathbf{G}}_N}\right)\mathbf{C}_N^{1/2}\mathbf{g}_N(\check{\boldsymbol{\theta}}_N)\\ &\quad + N\cdot\mathbf{g}_N(\check{\boldsymbol{\theta}}_N)'\mathbf{C}_N^{1/2\prime}\mathbf{P}_{\mathbf{C}_N^{1/2}\hat{\mathbf{G}}_N}\mathbf{C}_N^{1/2}\mathbf{g}_N(\check{\boldsymbol{\theta}}_N)\\ &\overset{p}{=} N\cdot\mathbf{g}_N(\hat{\boldsymbol{\theta}}_N)'\mathbf{C}_N\,\mathbf{g}_N(\hat{\boldsymbol{\theta}}_N)\\ &\quad + N\cdot\left(\hat{\boldsymbol{\theta}}_N-\check{\boldsymbol{\theta}}_N\right)'\hat{\mathbf{G}}_N'\mathbf{C}_N\hat{\mathbf{G}}_N\left(\hat{\boldsymbol{\theta}}_N-\check{\boldsymbol{\theta}}_N\right)\end{aligned}$$

or

$$N\cdot Q_N(\check{\boldsymbol{\theta}}_N) \overset{p}{=} N\cdot Q_N(\hat{\boldsymbol{\theta}}_N) + N\cdot\left(\hat{\boldsymbol{\theta}}_N-\check{\boldsymbol{\theta}}_N\right)'\hat{\mathbf{G}}_N'\mathbf{C}_N\hat{\mathbf{G}}_N\left(\hat{\boldsymbol{\theta}}_N-\check{\boldsymbol{\theta}}_N\right)$$

□

The next proof is an extension of the proof of Lemma 22.1, setting the generic $\sqrt{N}$-consistent estimator of that result equal to $\boldsymbol{\theta}_0$.

Proof of Lemma 22.2. Assumption 21.3 (Asymptotic Limits, p. 545) and $\mathbf{C}_N = \hat{\boldsymbol{\Lambda}}_N^{-1}$ imply by the Slutsky lemma (Lemma 13.3, p. 261) that

$$\mathbf{C}_N^{1/2}\sqrt{N}\cdot\mathbf{g}_N(\boldsymbol{\theta}_0) \xrightarrow{d} \mathbf{z} \sim \mathfrak{N}(\mathbf{0}, \mathbf{I}_J)$$

and

$$N\cdot Q_N(\boldsymbol{\theta}_0) \xrightarrow{d} \mathbf{z}'\mathbf{z} \sim \chi_J^2$$

The OLS projection theorem (Theorem 2, p. 31) and (2.9) imply that

$$\mathbf{z}'\left(\mathbf{I}-\mathbf{P_X}\right)\mathbf{z}=\min_{\boldsymbol{\mu}\in\mathrm{Col}(\mathbf{X})}\|\mathbf{z}-\boldsymbol{\mu}\|^2$$

where $\mathbf{X}\equiv\mathbf{C}_0^{1/2}\mathbf{G}_0$. Because

$$\mathbf{P}_{\mathbf{C}_N^{1/2}\hat{\mathbf{G}}_N}\mathbf{C}_N^{1/2}\sqrt{N}\cdot\mathbf{g}_N(\boldsymbol{\theta}_0)\xrightarrow{d}\mathbf{P_X}\mathbf{z}$$

we may use (22.54)–(22.55) to write

$$\begin{aligned}N\cdot Q_N(\hat{\boldsymbol{\theta}}_N)&\overset{p}{=}N\cdot\mathbf{g}_N(\boldsymbol{\theta}_0)'\mathbf{C}_N^{1/2\prime}\left(\mathbf{I}-\mathbf{P}_{\mathbf{C}_N^{1/2}\hat{\mathbf{G}}_N}\right)\mathbf{C}_N^{1/2}\mathbf{g}_N(\boldsymbol{\theta}_0)\\&\xrightarrow{d}\mathbf{z}'\left(\mathbf{I}-\mathbf{P_X}\right)\mathbf{z}\end{aligned}$$

and

$$N\cdot\left[Q_N(\boldsymbol{\theta}_0)-Q_N(\hat{\boldsymbol{\theta}}_N)\right]\xrightarrow{d}\mathbf{z}'\mathbf{P_X}\mathbf{z}$$

The proposition is, therefore, an application of Lemma 10.1 (Minimum Chi-Square, p. 197) to these limiting distributions. □

The next two proofs cover properties of the MD estimator. First, we establish its consistency and asymptotic normality along familiar lines. Second, we show that there is an MD estimator based on the unrestricted GMM estimator that is asymptotically equivalent to the restricted GMM estimator.

Proof of Proposition 22. We will prove consistency and then confirm the asymptotic distribution of the MD estimator, following the same general argument as for GMM estimators.

Consistency: Because $\sqrt{N}\left(\hat{\boldsymbol{\theta}}_N-\boldsymbol{\theta}_0\right)\xrightarrow{d}\mathfrak{N}(\mathbf{0},\mathbf{V}_0)$ and $\mathbf{A}_N\xrightarrow{p}\mathbf{A}_0$,

$$\begin{aligned}D_N(\boldsymbol{\gamma})&\equiv-\left[\hat{\boldsymbol{\theta}}_N-\mathbf{s}(\boldsymbol{\gamma})\right]'\mathbf{A}_N\left[\hat{\boldsymbol{\theta}}_N-\mathbf{s}(\boldsymbol{\gamma})\right]\\&\xrightarrow{p}-\left[\boldsymbol{\theta}_0-\mathbf{s}(\boldsymbol{\gamma})\right]'\mathbf{A}_0\left[\boldsymbol{\theta}_0-\mathbf{s}(\boldsymbol{\gamma})\right]\\&\equiv D_0(\boldsymbol{\gamma})\end{aligned}$$

Because $\boldsymbol{\Gamma}$ is compact, this convergence is uniform in $\boldsymbol{\gamma}\in\boldsymbol{\Gamma}$. Because $\mathbf{s}(\boldsymbol{\gamma})$ is continuously differentiable, $D_0(\boldsymbol{\gamma})$ is continuous. Because $\boldsymbol{\gamma}_0\in\boldsymbol{\Gamma}$ such that $\boldsymbol{\theta}_0=\mathbf{s}(\boldsymbol{\gamma}_0)$ is unique and $\mathbf{A}_0$ is positive definite, the $D_0(\boldsymbol{\gamma})$ is maximized uniquely over $\boldsymbol{\gamma}\in\boldsymbol{\Gamma}$ at $\boldsymbol{\gamma}=\boldsymbol{\gamma}_0$. Therefore, by Lemma 15.2 (Consistency of Maxima, p. 322), $\hat{\boldsymbol{\gamma}}_{\mathrm{MD}}\xrightarrow{p}\boldsymbol{\gamma}_0$.

Asymptotic Normality: Proceeding from the first-order conditions for the MD estimator, the consistency of $\hat{\boldsymbol{\gamma}}_{\mathrm{MD}}$ and a first-order Taylor series expansion gives[55]

$$\begin{aligned}\mathbf{0}&=\sqrt{N}\cdot\mathbf{S}(\hat{\boldsymbol{\gamma}}_{\mathrm{MD}})'\mathbf{A}_N\left[\hat{\boldsymbol{\theta}}_N-\mathbf{s}(\hat{\boldsymbol{\gamma}}_{\mathrm{MD}})\right]\\&\overset{p}{=}\mathbf{S}_0'\mathbf{A}_0\sqrt{N}\cdot\left[\hat{\boldsymbol{\theta}}_N-\mathbf{s}(\boldsymbol{\gamma}_0)\right]-\mathbf{S}_0'\mathbf{A}_0\mathbf{S}_0\sqrt{N}\cdot\left(\hat{\boldsymbol{\gamma}}_{\mathrm{MD}}-\boldsymbol{\gamma}_0\right)\end{aligned}$$

Therefore,

55 This step rests on the same logic as in Section 21.4.2 for the GMM estimator.

$$\sqrt{N} \cdot (\hat{\boldsymbol{\gamma}}_{\mathrm{MD}} - \boldsymbol{\gamma}_0) \stackrel{p}{=} (\mathbf{S}_0' \mathbf{A}_0 \mathbf{S}_0)^{-1} \mathbf{S}_0' \mathbf{A}_0 \sqrt{N} \cdot \left(\hat{\boldsymbol{\theta}}_N - \boldsymbol{\theta}_0\right)$$
$$\xrightarrow{d} \mathfrak{N}(\mathbf{0}, \mathbf{W}_0)$$

□

The following proof shows that two estimators, $\hat{\boldsymbol{\gamma}}_N$ and $\hat{\boldsymbol{\gamma}}_N^+$, are asymptotically equivalent: $\sqrt{N}\,(\hat{\boldsymbol{\gamma}}_N - \hat{\boldsymbol{\gamma}}_N^+) \stackrel{p}{=} \mathbf{0}$. The strategy of the proof is to expand by linear approximation the first-order conditions that define $\hat{\boldsymbol{\gamma}}_N$ around the value of $\hat{\boldsymbol{\gamma}}_N^+$. This gives a term depending on $\sqrt{N}\,(\hat{\boldsymbol{\gamma}}_N - \hat{\boldsymbol{\gamma}}_N^+)$ and another term such that their sum equals zero. By showing that the latter term converges in probability to zero, the equivalence is proved.

Proof of Proposition 23. The assumptions of Proposition 20 (GMM Asymptotics, p. 546) imply that Assumption 22.3 holds. Note that $\hat{\boldsymbol{\theta}}_{N,\mathrm{R}} = \mathbf{s}(\hat{\boldsymbol{\gamma}}_N)$ and $\hat{\boldsymbol{\theta}}_{N,\mathrm{R}}^+ = \mathbf{s}(\hat{\boldsymbol{\gamma}}_N^+)$ where

$$\hat{\boldsymbol{\gamma}}_N \equiv \operatorname*{argmin}_{\boldsymbol{\gamma}\in\boldsymbol{\Gamma}} N \cdot \mathbf{g}_N[\mathbf{s}(\boldsymbol{\gamma})]' \mathbf{C}_N\, \mathbf{g}_N[\mathbf{s}(\boldsymbol{\gamma})]$$

$$\hat{\boldsymbol{\gamma}}_N^+ \equiv \operatorname*{argmin}_{\boldsymbol{\gamma}\in\boldsymbol{\Gamma}} N \cdot \left[\hat{\boldsymbol{\theta}}_N - \mathbf{s}(\boldsymbol{\gamma})\right]' \hat{\mathbf{G}}_N' \mathbf{C}_N \hat{\mathbf{G}}_N \left[\hat{\boldsymbol{\theta}}_N - \mathbf{s}(\boldsymbol{\gamma})\right]$$

Now according to the chain rule

$$\frac{\partial Q_N(\boldsymbol{\theta})}{\partial \boldsymbol{\gamma}} = \mathbf{S}(\boldsymbol{\gamma})' \frac{\partial Q_N(\boldsymbol{\theta})}{\partial \boldsymbol{\theta}}$$

Therefore, when we expand $\mathbf{g}_N(\hat{\boldsymbol{\theta}}_{\mathrm{R}N})$ around $\hat{\boldsymbol{\theta}}_N$, we obtain

$$\begin{aligned}
\mathbf{0} &= \sqrt{N} \cdot \left.\frac{\partial Q_N(\boldsymbol{\theta})}{\partial \boldsymbol{\gamma}}\right|_{\boldsymbol{\gamma}=\hat{\boldsymbol{\gamma}}_N} \\
&= \sqrt{N} \cdot \mathbf{S}(\hat{\boldsymbol{\gamma}}_N)' \mathbf{G}_N(\hat{\boldsymbol{\theta}}_{\mathrm{R}N})' \mathbf{C}_N \left[\mathbf{g}_N(\hat{\boldsymbol{\theta}}_N) + \mathbf{G}(\bar{\boldsymbol{\theta}}_N)\left(\hat{\boldsymbol{\theta}}_{\mathrm{R}N} - \hat{\boldsymbol{\theta}}_N\right)\right] \\
&\stackrel{p}{=} \sqrt{N} \cdot \mathbf{S}_0' \mathbf{G}_0' \mathbf{C}_0 \mathbf{g}_N(\hat{\boldsymbol{\theta}}_N) + \sqrt{N} \cdot \mathbf{S}_0' \mathbf{G}_0' \mathbf{C}_0 \mathbf{G}_0 \left(\hat{\boldsymbol{\theta}}_{\mathrm{R}N}^+ - \hat{\boldsymbol{\theta}}_N\right) \\
&\quad + \mathbf{S}_0' \mathbf{G}_0' \mathbf{C}_0 \mathbf{G}_0 \sqrt{N} \cdot \left(\hat{\boldsymbol{\theta}}_{\mathrm{R}N} - \hat{\boldsymbol{\theta}}_{\mathrm{R}N}^+\right)
\end{aligned}$$

Now the first two RHS terms converge in probability to zero because they are asymptotically equivalent to the LHS gradients in

$$\sqrt{N} \cdot \left.\frac{\partial Q_N(\boldsymbol{\theta})}{\partial \boldsymbol{\theta}}\right|_{\boldsymbol{\theta}=\hat{\boldsymbol{\theta}}_N} = \mathbf{0}$$

and

$$\sqrt{N} \left.\frac{\partial \left(\hat{\boldsymbol{\theta}}_N - \boldsymbol{\theta}\right)' \hat{\mathbf{G}}_N' \mathbf{C}_N \hat{\mathbf{G}}_N \left(\hat{\boldsymbol{\theta}}_N - \boldsymbol{\theta}\right)}{\partial \boldsymbol{\gamma}}\right|_{\boldsymbol{\gamma}=\hat{\boldsymbol{\gamma}}_N^+} = \mathbf{0}$$

respectively. Using

$$\sqrt{N} \cdot \left(\hat{\boldsymbol{\theta}}_{RN} - \hat{\boldsymbol{\theta}}^{+}_{RN}\right) \overset{p}{=} \mathbf{S}_0 \sqrt{N} \cdot (\hat{\boldsymbol{\gamma}}_N - \hat{\boldsymbol{\gamma}}^{+}_N)$$

the remaining expression is equivalent to

$$\mathbf{0} \overset{p}{=} \mathbf{S}_0 \mathbf{G}_0' \mathbf{C}_0 \mathbf{G}_0 \mathbf{S}_0 \sqrt{N} \cdot (\hat{\boldsymbol{\gamma}}_N - \hat{\boldsymbol{\gamma}}^{+}_N)$$

Because $\mathbf{S}_0 \mathbf{G}_0' \mathbf{C}_0 \mathbf{G}_0 \mathbf{S}_0$ is nonsingular, it follows that $\sqrt{N} \cdot (\hat{\boldsymbol{\gamma}}_N - \hat{\boldsymbol{\gamma}}^{+}_N)$, making the two restricted estimators asymptotically equivalent. □

22.9 METHODOLOGICAL NOTES

All of the tests in this chapter examine whether specific linear combinations of moment restrictions hold in the population. For the most part, these linear combinations simplify to subsets of moment restrictions. Hausman specification tests alone motivate more general linear combinations by focusing on comparisons of estimators of the parameter vector. Such comparisons generalize directly to subvectors of the parameter vector and multiple estimators of the parameter vector. In addition, one of the estimators need not be relatively efficient.[56]

Factorization of a log-likelihood function or a GMM objective function frequently underlies the parameter comparison in a Hausman test. We have seen this in the factorization (or partitioning) of the GMM objective function for testing a subset of moment restrictions. Similarly, a log-likelihood function factors into conditional and marginal components. One may feel that one of these components is correctly specified although the complete likelihood may be misspecified. Under the hypothesis of correct specification, the MLE corresponding to either component is an inefficient estimator that can be compared with the complete likelihood MLE. Ruud (1984) interprets such Hausman specification tests as generalizations of the Chow test (Example 11.2).

Occasionally, researchers apply Hausman specification tests to choose among two alternative estimators. Such estimation methods yield pretest estimators. As explained in Chapter 11, pretest estimators do not possess the sampling distributions of the original estimators and should be interpreted carefully.

All of the tests that we have described fall within the classical approach to statistical inference. The foundation of this approach is the specification of a general model that is correct. Tests of restrictions to this general model follow. We have not covered *nonnested hypothesis tests*, a leading way in which researchers have extended classical inference. In these tests, no model is a restricted version of another. For an introduction to such tests, see Davidson and MacKinnon (1993, Section 11.3).

22.10 OVERVIEW

1. There are generalized method of moments (GMM) hypothesis test statistics that are analogous to the likelihood test statistics. This analogy occurs because both the generalized distance and the log-likelihood function are quadratic functions of the parameter vector asymptotically under hypotheses local to the

[56] See, for example, Ruud (1984).

null hypothesis. All the GMM test statistics are quadratic forms in the difference between restricted and unrestricted estimators and a generalized inverse of the variance matrix.

2. Likelihood score tests rederived in the GMM framework are insensitive to violations of the distributional assumption while retaining power against the parametric null hypothesis.
3. In addition, one can test whether some of the moment restrictions are not satisfied. These are called tests of overidentifying restrictions, although it is not necessarily clear which restrictions those are.
4. Specification tests reduce the parameter differences to a subset of the complete parameter vector. The appeal of these tests is that they focus attention on the parameters of interest. Compared to the classical test of restrictions, the specification test increases power in some directions of the parameter space, while reducing the power to zero in others. These tests apply to both GMM and likelihood settings.
5. Minimum distance estimation is an alternative restricted estimation method based on the quadratic form of test statistics.

22.11 EXERCISES

22.11.1 Review

22.1 Produce an illustration like Figure 17.3 for the GMM test statistics, including a representation of the MC test statistic.

22.2 Explain the absence of the multiplicative factor 2 in the DD when one compares this test statistic with the LR test statistic.

22.3 What are the consequences for the GMM hypothesis test if one uses a $\mathbf{C}_N$ that does not produce a relatively efficient GMM estimator?

22.4 Use a simple example to illustrate that the DD test fails to have a limiting chi-square distribution if $\mathbf{C}_0 \neq \boldsymbol{\Lambda}_0^{-1}$ even though $\mathrm{Col}(\mathbf{C}_0\mathbf{G}_0) = \mathrm{Col}(\boldsymbol{\Lambda}_0^{-1}\mathbf{G}_0)$ so that estimation is relatively efficient.

22.5 **[Breusch–Godfrey AR Test]** Consider the moment functions of the regression model with AR disturbances:

$$\mathbf{g}(U;\boldsymbol{\theta}) = \begin{bmatrix} (\mathbf{x}_t - \rho \cdot \mathbf{x}_{t-1})\, v_t \\ v_t^2 - \sigma^2 \\ \varepsilon_{t-1} v_t \end{bmatrix}$$

where $v_t = \varepsilon_t - \rho\varepsilon_{t-1}$ and $\varepsilon_t = y_t - \mathbf{x}_t'\boldsymbol{\beta}$. Suppose that conditional on $\{\mathbf{x}_t\}$, the $v_t, t = 1, \ldots, T$, are i.i.d. and that the ε_t are stationary. Also suppose that the first four conditional moments of v_t,

$$\mathrm{E}(v_t \,|\, \mathbf{X}) = 0, \quad \mathrm{E}(v_t^2 \,|\, \mathbf{X}) = \sigma^2$$
$$\mathrm{E}(v_t^3 \,|\, \mathbf{X}) = \delta_1, \quad \mathrm{E}(v_t^4 \,|\, \mathbf{X}) = \delta_2$$

are finite. Show that the GMM gradient test for $\rho = 0$ corresponds to the Breusch–Godfrey score test (Section 19.4.1) based on the additional assumption that the v_t are normally distributed.

22.6 (Heteroskedasticity Test) In Example 22.1, we discussed testing for conditional heteroskedasticity without assuming a conditional normal distribution, as in the Breusch–Pagan score test (Section 18.7.3). In this exercise, consider the case in which the third moment δ_1 is nonzero. Suppose that one can estimate the third moment parameter consistently with $\hat{\delta}_1 = \mathrm{E}_N[(y_n - \mathbf{x}_n'\hat{\boldsymbol{\beta}}_{\mathrm{OLS}})^3]$. Find a GMM test for heteroskedasticity using the following steps.

(a) The variance matrix of the moment equations $\boldsymbol{\Lambda}_0$ is not block-diagonal in this case. What does this imply about the OLS estimator of $\boldsymbol{\beta}_0$ and γ_{01}?

(b) Work out the linearized restricted GMM estimator (21.31) for $\boldsymbol{\beta}_0$ and γ_{01} under the restrictions of homoskedasticity. Use the OLS estimator as an initial estimator.

(c) Find an expression for the gradient test statistic $\mathcal{G}_3(\boldsymbol{\theta})$ that could be evaluated at this restricted GMM estimator. Also show $\mathcal{G}_3(\boldsymbol{\theta}) \geq \mathcal{G}_2(\boldsymbol{\theta})$ where

$$\mathcal{G}_2(\boldsymbol{\theta}) \equiv N \frac{\mathbf{w}(\boldsymbol{\theta})'\mathbf{P}_{(\mathbf{I}-\mathbf{P}_\iota)\mathbf{Z}_2}\mathbf{w}(\boldsymbol{\theta})}{\mathbf{w}(\boldsymbol{\theta})'(\mathbf{I}-\mathbf{P}_\iota)\mathbf{w}(\boldsymbol{\theta})}$$

is the GMM gradient test function when one assumes that δ_{01} equals zero. What does this suggest about testing for conditional heteroskedasticity when $\delta_{01} \neq 0$?

22.7 (Instrumental Variables) Find a way to compute the GMM test in Example 22.3 as the difference in OLS sums of squared residuals.

22.8 (Simultaneous Equations) Reconsider the market model of Example 20.2 (Simultaneous Equations, p. 492). GMM and the moment equations

$$\mathrm{E}_N[\mathbf{z}_n \varepsilon_{sn}] = \mathbf{0}$$

where the elements of $\mathbf{z}_n$ are a basis for $[\mathbf{x}_{s1n}', \mathbf{x}_{d1n}']'$ and

$$\varepsilon_{sn} = q_{sn} - \mathbf{x}_{s1n}'\boldsymbol{\beta}_{0s1} - \beta_{0s2}p_n$$

yield the 2SLS estimator.[57]

(a) Given that the 2SLS estimator is consistent and asymptotically normal, explain how to test the overidentifying restrictions.

(b) Suppose in addition that some of the variables in $\mathbf{x}_{d1n}$ have coefficients equal to zero. In other words, these particular instrumental variables are uncorrelated with q_{sn}. Show that the exclusion of the corresponding moment equations increases the power of the test of overidentifying restrictions.

22.9 (Pretest Estimation) One might use the Hausman specification test to choose between two estimators based on different sets of moment restrictions. Describe the properties of such an estimation procedure.

22.10 (Moment Tests) In GMM tests of a subset of $J - M < J - K$ moment restrictions, substantial simplification occurs when $\mathbf{C}_N = \hat{\boldsymbol{\Lambda}}^{-1}$.

(a) Show that the gradient is

$$\begin{bmatrix} \mathbf{G}(\boldsymbol{\theta})' \\ \mathbf{S}' \end{bmatrix} \hat{\boldsymbol{\Lambda}}^{-1} \mathbf{g}^{\mathrm{a}}(U; \boldsymbol{\theta}, \boldsymbol{\psi})$$

where

$$\mathbf{S}' = \begin{bmatrix} \mathbf{0} & \mathbf{I}_{J-M} \end{bmatrix}$$

[57] See Sections 20.5 and 21.2.3.

(b) Show that the unrestricted GMM estimator is defined by

$$\mathbf{0} = \mathbf{G}_1(\hat{\boldsymbol{\theta}}_U)'\hat{\boldsymbol{\Lambda}}_{11}^{-1}\mathbf{g}_{1N}(\hat{\boldsymbol{\theta}}_U)$$

and

$$\hat{\boldsymbol{\psi}}_U = \mathbf{g}_{2N}(\hat{\boldsymbol{\theta}}_U) - \hat{\boldsymbol{\Lambda}}_{21}\hat{\boldsymbol{\Lambda}}_{11}^{-1}\mathbf{g}_{1N}(\hat{\boldsymbol{\theta}}_U)$$

(c) Show that the Wald statistic is

$$\mathcal{W} = N \cdot \mathbf{g}_2(\hat{\boldsymbol{\theta}}_U)'\hat{\mathbf{V}}_{\mathcal{W}}^{-1}\mathbf{g}_2(\hat{\boldsymbol{\theta}}_U)$$

where

$$\mathbf{0} = \mathbf{G}_{1N}(\hat{\boldsymbol{\theta}}_U)'\hat{\boldsymbol{\Lambda}}_{11}^{-1}\mathbf{g}_{1N}(\hat{\boldsymbol{\theta}}_U)$$

$$\hat{\boldsymbol{\psi}}_U = \mathbf{g}_{2N}(\hat{\boldsymbol{\theta}}_U) - \hat{\boldsymbol{\Lambda}}_{21}\hat{\boldsymbol{\Lambda}}_{11}^{-1}\mathbf{g}_{1N}(\hat{\boldsymbol{\theta}}_U)$$

and

$$\hat{\mathbf{V}}_{\mathcal{W}} = \left[\mathbf{S}'\hat{\boldsymbol{\Lambda}}^{-1}\mathbf{S} - \mathbf{S}'\hat{\boldsymbol{\Lambda}}^{-1}\hat{\mathbf{G}}\left(\hat{\mathbf{G}}'\hat{\boldsymbol{\Lambda}}^{-1}\hat{\mathbf{G}}\right)^{-1}\hat{\mathbf{G}}'\hat{\boldsymbol{\Lambda}}^{-1}\mathbf{S}\right]^{-1}$$

(d) Also show that the gradient test is

$$\mathcal{G} = \mathbf{g}(\hat{\boldsymbol{\theta}})'\hat{\boldsymbol{\Lambda}}^{-1}\mathbf{S}\hat{\mathbf{V}}_{\mathcal{W}}\mathbf{S}'\hat{\boldsymbol{\Lambda}}^{-1}\mathbf{g}(\hat{\boldsymbol{\theta}})$$

22.11 (Hausman Test) Show that the coefficients in the Hausman specification test regression on p. 580 are identical to the unrestricted estimates.

22.12 (Minimum Chi-Square) Find analogous relationships to (22.47)–(22.49) between the OLS and RLS estimators. Also find the analogue to (22.38).

22.13 (Normality Test) Use Theorem D.8 (Normal Distribution, p. 887) to show that the variance matrix of the moments in Example 22.5 is

$$\boldsymbol{\Lambda}_0 = \begin{bmatrix} \sigma_0^2 \cdot \mathrm{E}[\mathbf{x}_n\mathbf{x}_n'] & \mathbf{0} & 3\sigma_0^4 \cdot \mathrm{E}[\mathbf{x}_n] & \mathbf{0} \\ \mathbf{0} & 2\sigma_0^4 & 0 & 12\sigma_0^6 \\ 3\sigma_0^4 \cdot \mathrm{E}[\mathbf{x}_n'] & 0 & 15\sigma_0^6 & 0 \\ \mathbf{0} & 12\sigma_0^6 & 0 & 96\sigma_0^8 \end{bmatrix}$$

Show further that the conditional variance of $\mathbf{g}_2$ given $\mathbf{g}_1$ is

$$\begin{bmatrix} 6\sigma_0^6 & 0 \\ 0 & 24\sigma_0^8 \end{bmatrix}$$

Hence, a test statistic for skewness is

$$\frac{\left(\mathrm{E}_N[y_n - \mathbf{x}_n'\hat{\boldsymbol{\beta}}_{\mathrm{OLS}}]^3\right)^2}{6\hat{\sigma}^6}$$

and an independently distributed test statistic for kurtosis is

$$\frac{\left\{\mathrm{E}_N[(y_n - \mathbf{x}_n'\boldsymbol{\beta}_0)^4 - 3\hat{\sigma}^4]\right\}^2}{24\hat{\sigma}^8}$$

22.14 **(MD)** Consider estimation of the coefficients of the MMSE linear predictor of y_n given (x_{n2}, x_{n3}),

$$[\pi_{01}, \pi_{02}, \pi_{03}]' = \underset{\pi}{\operatorname{argmin}}\, \mathrm{E}[[y_n - (\pi_1 + \pi_2 x_{n2} + \pi_3 x_{n3})]^2]$$

Suppose that $\mathrm{E}[y_n \mid \mathbf{x}_n]$ is not linear and $\mathrm{Var}[y_n \mid \mathbf{x}_n]$ is not constant but that $(y_n, \mathbf{x}_n)$ are i.i.d. with finite fourth moments.[58]

(a) Using the unrestricted OLS estimator $\hat{\pi} = (\mathbf{X}'\mathbf{X})^{-1}\mathbf{X}'\mathbf{y}$ where $\mathbf{X} = [[1, x_{n2}, x_{n3}]';\ n = 1, \ldots, N]'$, find the MD estimator under the restriction that $\pi_{03} = 0$.

(b) Show that the MD estimator is efficient relative to the RLS estimator for π_{01} and π_{02}.

(c) Show that if $\mathrm{E}[y_n \mid \mathbf{x}_n]$ is linear and $\mathrm{Var}[y_n \mid \mathbf{x}_n]$ is constant, then the MD estimator is asymptotically equivalent to the RLS estimator.

22.15 **(MD)** Describe a relatively efficient MD estimator based on the two-step estimator of the dynamic regression model given in Exercise 20.27.

22.16 **(Hausman Test)** The variance matrix difference (22.26) excited many people when it was first published by Hausman because it made the computation of the variance estimator for a difference in estimators a convenient by-product of the calculations of the two estimators.

(a) What problems can you anticipate with this variance estimator?

(b) Confirm the variance formula $\mathrm{Var}[\hat{\boldsymbol{\delta}}_1 - \hat{\boldsymbol{\delta}}_2] = \mathrm{Var}[\hat{\boldsymbol{\delta}}_2] - \mathrm{Var}[\hat{\boldsymbol{\delta}}_1]$ in the following cases:

i. $\hat{\boldsymbol{\delta}}_1 = \hat{\boldsymbol{\beta}}_{\mathrm{R}}$ and $\hat{\boldsymbol{\delta}}_2 = \hat{\boldsymbol{\beta}}$,

ii. $\hat{\boldsymbol{\delta}}_1 = \hat{\boldsymbol{\delta}}_{\mathrm{OLS}}$ and $\hat{\boldsymbol{\delta}}_2 = \hat{\boldsymbol{\delta}}_{IV}$,

iii. $\hat{\boldsymbol{\delta}}_1 = \hat{\boldsymbol{\beta}}_{\mathrm{GLS}}$ and $\hat{\boldsymbol{\delta}}_2 = \hat{\boldsymbol{\beta}}_{\mathrm{OLS}}$.

(c) Show that the exogeneity test can also be interpreted as a test of whether the IV residuals are correlated with the residuals of the questionable explanatory variables after they have been regressed on the valid instruments.

22.11.2 Extensions

22.17 **(Hausman Test)** Often researchers compare informally IV estimators based on different sets of instrumental variables. Construct a Hausman specification test that formalizes such a comparison. Can you figure out a way to compute this statistic with a regression? What problems do you face determining the degrees of freedom of the test?

22.18 Describe a $C(\alpha)$-like (Section 17.3.4) GMM test statistic.

22.19 **(Restricted GMM)** Recall that when the restrictions are expressed in the form $\mathbf{R}\boldsymbol{\beta}_0 = \mathbf{0}$, the restricted least-squares estimator can be written as[59]

$$\begin{aligned}\hat{\boldsymbol{\beta}}_{\mathrm{RLS}} &= \underset{\{\boldsymbol{\beta} \mid \boldsymbol{\beta} \in \mathrm{Col}^{\perp}(\mathbf{R}')\}}{\operatorname{argmin}} \left(\hat{\boldsymbol{\beta}}_{\mathrm{OLS}} - \boldsymbol{\beta}\right)' \mathbf{X}'\mathbf{X}\left(\hat{\boldsymbol{\beta}}_{\mathrm{OLS}} - \boldsymbol{\beta}\right) \\ &= \hat{\boldsymbol{\beta}} - (\mathbf{X}'\mathbf{X})^{-1}\mathbf{R}'\left(\mathbf{R}(\mathbf{X}'\mathbf{X})^{-1}\mathbf{R}'\right)\mathbf{R}\hat{\boldsymbol{\beta}} \end{aligned} \tag{22.56}$$

Such a representation occurs for the general MD estimator as well.

Show that the restricted GMM estimator $\hat{\boldsymbol{\theta}}_{\mathrm{R}N}$ in (22.53) is asymptotically equivalent to

58 See Chamberlain (1982).

59 See Exercise 4.14.

$$\hat{\boldsymbol{\theta}}^*_{RN} \equiv \hat{\boldsymbol{\theta}}_N - (\hat{\mathbf{G}}'_N \mathbf{C}_N \hat{\mathbf{G}}_N)^{-1} \hat{\mathbf{R}}'_N \left[\hat{\mathbf{R}}_N (\hat{\mathbf{G}}'_N \mathbf{C}_N \hat{\mathbf{G}}_N)^{-1} \hat{\mathbf{R}}'_N \right]^{-1} \hat{\mathbf{r}}_N \tag{22.57}$$

where

$$\hat{\mathbf{r}}_N \equiv \mathbf{r}(\hat{\boldsymbol{\theta}}_N), \qquad \hat{\mathbf{R}}_N \equiv \left. \frac{\partial \mathbf{r}(\boldsymbol{\theta})}{\partial \boldsymbol{\theta}'} \right|_{\boldsymbol{\theta}=\hat{\boldsymbol{\theta}}_N}$$

(HINT: Use the approach of Exercise 4.15.)

22.20 **(Linearized MD)** Find a linearized MD estimator given restrictions of the form $\boldsymbol{\theta}_0 = \mathbf{s}(\boldsymbol{\gamma}_0)$.

22.21 Using MD, find a more efficient restricted estimator than $\hat{\boldsymbol{\theta}}^*_{RN}$ in (22.57) when $\mathbf{C}_N \neq \hat{\boldsymbol{\Lambda}}_N^{-1}$. Show that a test statistic based on the squared generalized distance between $\hat{\boldsymbol{\theta}}_N$ and your estimator is identical to the Wald test statistic based on the inefficient estimator.

22.22 **(Two-Step and MD)** One can apply the minimum distance method to the two-step estimation framework described in Proposition 19 (Two-Step Asymptotic Variance, p. 507). Consider the two-step estimator $\hat{\boldsymbol{\theta}}_N(\check{\boldsymbol{\gamma}}_N)$ for a parametetr vector $\boldsymbol{\theta}_0$ based on the initial estimator $\check{\boldsymbol{\gamma}}_N$ for the nuisance parameter vector $\boldsymbol{\gamma}_0$. Among other conditions, we supposed that

$$\sqrt{N} \begin{bmatrix} \hat{\boldsymbol{\theta}}_N(\boldsymbol{\gamma}_0) - \boldsymbol{\theta}_0 \\ \check{\boldsymbol{\gamma}}_N - \boldsymbol{\gamma}_0 \end{bmatrix} \xrightarrow{d} \mathfrak{N}\left(\mathbf{0}, \begin{bmatrix} \boldsymbol{\Omega}_{\theta\theta} & \boldsymbol{\Omega}_{\theta\gamma} \\ \boldsymbol{\Omega}_{\gamma\theta} & \boldsymbol{\Omega}_{\gamma\gamma} \end{bmatrix} \right)$$

Thus, given a consistent estimator $\hat{\boldsymbol{\Omega}}$ of the variance matrix $\boldsymbol{\Omega}$, a minimum distance estimator is

$$\begin{bmatrix} \hat{\boldsymbol{\theta}}_{MD} \\ \hat{\boldsymbol{\gamma}}_{MD} \end{bmatrix} = \underset{\boldsymbol{\theta},\boldsymbol{\gamma}}{\operatorname{argmin}} \begin{bmatrix} \hat{\boldsymbol{\theta}}_N(\boldsymbol{\gamma}) - \boldsymbol{\theta} \\ \check{\boldsymbol{\gamma}}_N - \boldsymbol{\gamma} \end{bmatrix}' \begin{bmatrix} \hat{\boldsymbol{\Omega}}_{\theta\theta} & \hat{\boldsymbol{\Omega}}_{\theta\gamma} \\ \hat{\boldsymbol{\Omega}}_{\gamma\theta} & \hat{\boldsymbol{\Omega}}_{\gamma\gamma} \end{bmatrix}^{-1} \begin{bmatrix} \hat{\boldsymbol{\theta}}_N(\boldsymbol{\gamma}) - \boldsymbol{\theta} \\ \check{\boldsymbol{\gamma}}_N - \boldsymbol{\gamma} \end{bmatrix}$$

Compare the asymptotic properties of the two estimators.

22.23 **(Hausman test)** Suggest a gradient version of the Hausman specification test.[60]

22.24 **(White–Chesher Information Matrix Test)** White (1982) proposed a specification test for likelihood specifications $L(\boldsymbol{\theta}; y)$ based on examining the information identity

$$\mathrm{E}[L_{\boldsymbol{\theta}\boldsymbol{\theta}}(\boldsymbol{\theta}_0; y) + L_{\boldsymbol{\theta}}(\boldsymbol{\theta}_0; y) L_{\boldsymbol{\theta}}(\boldsymbol{\theta}_0; y)'] = \mathbf{0}$$

The test is generally called the *information matrix test.* This exercise reproduces Chesher's (1984) interpretation of such tests as a test for heterogeneity.

Let the p.f. of the random variable Y be $f_{Y|\boldsymbol{\theta}}(y \mid \boldsymbol{\theta})$ given the parameter vector $\boldsymbol{\theta} \in \mathbb{R}^K$ and suppose that $f_Y(\cdot)$ satisfies the assumptions of Proposition 16 (MLE Asymptotics, p. 320). The null hypothesis is that $\boldsymbol{\theta}$ is a constant parameter vector $\mu_{\boldsymbol{\theta}}$ and the alternative hypothesis is that $\boldsymbol{\theta}$ is continuously distributed with p.d.f. $f_{\boldsymbol{\theta}}(t)$ on the compact support $\boldsymbol{\Theta}$. In other words, the p.f. of Y is a mixture. Under i.i.d. sampling for Y and (possibly) $\boldsymbol{\theta}$, derive a score test for the null hypothesis using the following steps.

(a) Suppose that $\boldsymbol{\theta}$ has an elliptically symmetric distribution with mean vector $\bar{\boldsymbol{\theta}}$ and variance matrix $a \cdot \mathbf{CC}'$ where $\mathbf{C}$ is a lower triangular matrix. Parameterize the alternative hypothesis as $a = 0$ and show that the score function is

$$L_a(\bar{\boldsymbol{\theta}}, a, \mathbf{C}; y) = -\frac{1}{f_Y(y)} \int \frac{1}{2\sqrt{a}} \cdot \mathbf{z}'\mathbf{C}' \frac{\partial f_{Y|\boldsymbol{\theta}}(y \mid \boldsymbol{\theta})}{\partial \boldsymbol{\theta}} f_{\mathbf{Z}}(\mathbf{z})\, d\mathbf{z}$$

[60] See White (1982) and Ruud (1984).

where $\boldsymbol{\theta} = \bar{\boldsymbol{\theta}} + \sqrt{a} \cdot \mathbf{Cz}$ and $f_Z(\mathbf{z}) = \mathbf{g}(\mathbf{z}'\mathbf{z})$ is spherically symmetric.[61] (Assume that differentiation under the integral sign is permissible.)

(b) Use l'Hôpital's rule to define the score L_a at $a = 0$:

$$\lim_{\alpha \to 0} L_a(\bar{\boldsymbol{\theta}}, a, \mathbf{C}; y) = \frac{1}{2} \operatorname{tr}\left\{\mathbf{C}' \left[L_{\boldsymbol{\theta}\boldsymbol{\theta}}(\bar{\boldsymbol{\theta}}, 0, \mathbf{C}) + L_{\boldsymbol{\theta}}(\bar{\boldsymbol{\theta}}, 0, \mathbf{C}) L_{\boldsymbol{\theta}}(\bar{\boldsymbol{\theta}}, 0, \mathbf{C})'\right] \mathbf{C}\right\}$$

61 Provided that the first two moments exist, $\mathrm{E}(\mathbf{z}) = \mathbf{0}$ and $\mathrm{E}(\mathbf{zz}') = \mathbf{I}_K$ according to the symmetry of $f_Z(\mathbf{z})$.

CHAPTER 23

OVERVIEW

In Part III, we have extended the classical linear regression model to data-generating processes that are nonnormal, nonspherical, and nonlinear. The chapters work progressively through these new situations.

1. If y_n is not normally distributed conditional on $\mathbf{x}_n$, then the distribution theory of the OLS estimator becomes intractable. Such nonlinear estimators as LAD may be relatively efficient, but their distributions are no more tractable. Asymptotic distribution theory provides an approximate, normal distribution for these estimators. Such approximations require fairly modest restrictions on the distribution of $\{(y_n, \mathbf{x}_n), n = 1, \ldots, N\}$ and sample sizes N that are sufficiently large.
2. Given a specification of the conditional p.f. $f(y_n; \boldsymbol{\theta}_0 \mid \mathbf{x}_n)$, one can derive alternative, nonlinear estimators of the regression parameters for nonnormal distributions with the maximum likelihood estimator (MLE)

$$\hat{\boldsymbol{\theta}}_{\mathrm{ML}} \equiv \underset{\boldsymbol{\theta} \in \boldsymbol{\Theta}}{\operatorname{argmax}} \, \mathrm{E}_N[L(\boldsymbol{\theta})]$$

where

$$L(\boldsymbol{\theta}) \equiv \log f(y_n; \boldsymbol{\theta} \mid \mathbf{x}_n)$$

is the conditional log-likelihood function. According to the Cramér–Rao lower bound, the variance of unbiased estimators for the parameter vector $\boldsymbol{\theta}_0$ is bounded below by $\left[N \cdot \Im(\boldsymbol{\theta}_0)\right]^{-1}$ where

$$\Im(\boldsymbol{\theta}_0) \equiv \mathrm{Var}[L_{\boldsymbol{\theta}}(\boldsymbol{\theta}_0; y_n \mid \mathbf{x}_n)]$$

is the information matrix and

$$L_{\boldsymbol{\theta}}(\boldsymbol{\theta}) \equiv \frac{\partial L(\boldsymbol{\theta})}{\partial \boldsymbol{\theta}}$$

is the score vector.
3. In some cases, the MLE is unbiased and achieves this variance bound. More generally, the MLE is approximated by

$$\sqrt{N}\left(\hat{\boldsymbol{\theta}}_{\text{ML}} - \boldsymbol{\theta}_0\right) \overset{p}{=} \Im(\boldsymbol{\theta}_0)^{-1}\sqrt{N}\,\text{E}_N[L_{\boldsymbol{\theta}}(\boldsymbol{\theta}_0)] \tag{23.1}$$

so that the relative efficency of the MLE is asymptotic.

4. The method of maximum likelihood (ML) applies equally well to nonspherical distributions when one loosens the second moment assumptions of the classical model. Conditional heteroskedasticity and autoregressive serial correlation are leading examples of situations in which $\text{Var}[\mathbf{y} \mid \mathbf{X}] = \boldsymbol{\Omega}_0$ is not a scalar matrix. The MLE has a convenient interpretation as generalized least squares (GLS),

$$\hat{\boldsymbol{\beta}}_{\text{GLS}} \equiv \left(\mathbf{X}'\boldsymbol{\Omega}_0^{-1}\mathbf{X}\right)^{-1}\mathbf{X}'\boldsymbol{\Omega}_0^{-1}\mathbf{y}$$

5. Many exceptions to the classical first moment assumption arise as latent variable models. In these models, $\text{E}(y_n \mid \mathbf{x}_n)$ is no longer the simple linear function $\mathbf{x}_n'\boldsymbol{\beta}_0$ where $\boldsymbol{\beta}_0$ is the parameter vector of interest. When there is a vector of instrumental variables $\mathbf{z}_n$ having the same dimension as $\mathbf{x}_n$ and possessing the properties that

$$\text{E}[y_n \mid \mathbf{z}_n] = \text{E}(\mathbf{x}_n \mid \mathbf{z}_n)\boldsymbol{\beta}_0$$
$$\text{E}[\mathbf{z}_n\mathbf{x}_n'] \text{ is nonsingular}$$

then $\boldsymbol{\beta}_0$ is identified. The moment equations (or orthogonality conditions)

$$\text{E}[\mathbf{z}_n(y_n - \mathbf{x}_n'\boldsymbol{\beta}_0)] = \mathbf{0}$$

suggest the instrumental variables (IV) estimator

$$\hat{\boldsymbol{\beta}}_{\text{IV}} \equiv \left(\mathbf{Z}'\mathbf{X}\right)^{-1}\mathbf{Z}'\mathbf{y}$$

Relative efficiency may be achieved among IV estimators if there are functions of $\mathbf{z}_n$ that are MMSE predictors of $\mathbf{x}_n$.

6. Alternatively, the conditional first moment restriction may be explicitly nonlinear in $\boldsymbol{\beta}_0$, as in

$$\text{E}[y_n - \mu(\boldsymbol{\beta}_0; \mathbf{x}_n) \mid \mathbf{z}_n] = 0$$

or yet more generally,

$$\text{E}[\mathbf{g}(\boldsymbol{\beta}_0; y_n, \mathbf{x}_n) \mid \mathbf{z}_n] = 0$$

One can estimate $\boldsymbol{\beta}_0$ with the generalized method of moments (GMM), a method that contains elements of nonlinear least squares (NLS), GLS, and IV. Specifically,

$$\hat{\boldsymbol{\beta}}_{\text{GMM}} \equiv \underset{\boldsymbol{\beta}}{\text{argmin}}\,\text{E}_N[\mathbf{g}(\boldsymbol{\beta})]'\mathbf{C}_N\,\text{E}_N[\mathbf{g}(\boldsymbol{\beta})]$$

where $\mathbf{C}_N$ is usually a consistent estimator of $\text{Var}[\mathbf{g}(\boldsymbol{\beta}_0)]^{-1}$.

Running through this epic of generalizations of the classical linear model are several themes.

1. In every case, the estimators are *asymptotically linear*. That is,

$$\sqrt{N}\left(\hat{\boldsymbol{\theta}} - \boldsymbol{\theta}_0\right) \overset{p}{=} \sqrt{N}\,\text{E}_N[\boldsymbol{\psi}(U_n)]$$

where $\mathrm{E}[\boldsymbol{\psi}(U_n)] = \mathbf{0}$ and $\mathrm{Var}[\boldsymbol{\psi}(U_n)]$ exists. Because of this property and a central limit theorem, the estimators are asymptotically normally distributed with an asymptotic variance equal to $\mathrm{Var}[\boldsymbol{\psi}(U_n)]$.

2. The asymptotic linearity of the estimators coincides with interpreting all of the estimation procedures as minimization of generalized distance. In this way, the estimators generalize OLS and their statistical theory is analogous.
   (a) GLS is the most direct generalization:

$$\hat{\boldsymbol{\beta}}_{\mathrm{GLS}} = \operatorname*{argmin}_{\boldsymbol{\beta}} (\mathbf{y} - \mathbf{X}\boldsymbol{\beta})' \, \boldsymbol{\Omega}_0^{-1} \, (\mathbf{y} - \mathbf{X}\boldsymbol{\beta})$$

   This is equivalent to the minimum distance problem

$$\hat{\boldsymbol{\mu}}_{\mathrm{GLS}} = \operatorname*{argmin}_{\boldsymbol{\mu} \in \mathrm{Col}(\mathbf{X})} (\mathbf{y} - \boldsymbol{\mu})' \, \boldsymbol{\Omega}_0^{-1} \, (\mathbf{y} - \boldsymbol{\mu})$$

   Alternatively, GLS is OLS after a linear transformation of the data by $\boldsymbol{\Omega}_0^{-1/2}$.
   (b) According to (23.1), the log-likelihood function is approximated by

$$N \, \mathrm{E}_N[L(\boldsymbol{\theta}_N) - L(\boldsymbol{\theta}_0)] \stackrel{p}{=} -\frac{1}{2} (\boldsymbol{\psi}_N - \boldsymbol{\beta}_N)' \, \Im(\boldsymbol{\theta}_0) \, (\boldsymbol{\psi}_N - \boldsymbol{\beta}_N) + \frac{1}{2} \boldsymbol{\psi}_N' \Im(\boldsymbol{\theta}_0) \boldsymbol{\psi}_N \qquad (23.2)$$

   where

$$\boldsymbol{\beta}_N \equiv \sqrt{N} \, (\boldsymbol{\theta}_N - \boldsymbol{\theta}_0)$$
$$\boldsymbol{\psi}_N \equiv \Im(\boldsymbol{\theta}_0)^{-1} \sqrt{N} \, \mathrm{E}_N \, L_{\boldsymbol{\theta}}(\boldsymbol{\theta}_0)$$

   and $\boldsymbol{\beta}_N$ is bounded. Maximizing $L(\boldsymbol{\theta}_N)$ over $\boldsymbol{\theta}_N$ is asymptotically equivalent to minimizing the leading generalized distance in $\boldsymbol{\beta}_N$.
   (c) GMM has a similar underlying approximation. Given

$$\sqrt{N} \, \mathrm{E}_N[\mathbf{g}(\boldsymbol{\theta}_N)] \stackrel{p}{=} \sqrt{N} \, \mathrm{E}_N[\mathbf{g}(\boldsymbol{\theta}_0)] + \mathrm{E}[\mathbf{g}_{\boldsymbol{\theta}}(\boldsymbol{\theta}_0)] \sqrt{N} (\boldsymbol{\theta}_N - \boldsymbol{\theta}_0)$$

   and a weighting matrix $\mathbf{C}_N$ we obtain

$$N \cdot \mathrm{E}_N[\mathbf{g}(\boldsymbol{\theta}_N)]' \mathbf{C}_N \, \mathrm{E}_N[\mathbf{g}(\boldsymbol{\theta}_N)] \stackrel{p}{=} (\mathbf{y}_N - \mathbf{X}\boldsymbol{\beta}_N)' \, \mathbf{C}_N \, (\mathbf{y}_N - \mathbf{X}\boldsymbol{\beta}_N) \qquad (23.3)$$

   where

$$\mathbf{y}_N \equiv \sqrt{N} \, \mathrm{E}_N[\mathbf{g}(\boldsymbol{\theta}_0)]$$
$$\mathbf{X} \equiv -\mathrm{E}[\mathbf{g}_{\boldsymbol{\theta}}(\boldsymbol{\theta}_0)]$$

   Asymptotic approximations make this general simplification possible. They also endow the vector to be fitted with a multivariate normal distribution, making the approximate, asymptotic distribution theory analogous to the exact theory for OLS and a conditionally normally distributed dependent variable.

3. Moment conditions underlie the distance measures and projection characterizes their minimization.
   (a) The GLS fitted vector

$$\mathbf{y} - \hat{\boldsymbol{\mu}}_{\mathrm{GLS}} \perp \mathrm{Col}(\boldsymbol{\Omega}_0^{-1}\mathbf{X}) \qquad \Leftrightarrow \qquad \hat{\boldsymbol{\mu}}_{\mathrm{GLS}} = \mathbf{P}_{\mathbf{X} \perp \boldsymbol{\Omega}_0^{-1}\mathbf{X}} \mathbf{y}$$

is a nonorthogonal projection onto Col(**X**) that takes into account differences in variances and nonzero covariances in an optimal way for minimum variance estimation.

(b) Like GLS, the IV fitted vector

$$\mathbf{y} - \hat{\boldsymbol{\mu}}_{\mathrm{IV}} \perp \mathrm{Col}(\mathbf{Z}) \qquad \Leftrightarrow \qquad \hat{\boldsymbol{\mu}}_{\mathrm{IV}} = \mathbf{P}_{\mathbf{X}\perp\mathbf{Z}}\mathbf{y}$$

is a nonorthogonal projection onto Col(**X**). Unlike GLS, the direction of the projection may be critical to the consistency of the resultant estimator.

(c) Given identification and consistency, ML distribution theory rests on the score identity

$$\mathrm{E}[L_{\boldsymbol{\theta}}(\boldsymbol{\theta}_0)] = \mathbf{0}$$

and the variance of the score, the information matrix. Projection is trivial in the unrestricted case because the optimal $\boldsymbol{\beta}_N$ in (23.2) is actually equal to $\boldsymbol{\psi}_N$, giving (23.1). If restrictions apply to $\boldsymbol{\beta}_N$, then nonorthogonal projection is optimal as in restricted least squares (RLS).

(d) GMM is analogous to GLS, as (23.3) shows.

4. Hypothesis tests also rest on generalized distance, measuring the distance between different estimators of the parameters.

5. The approximate quadratic structure of these econometric problems is exploited in many numerical optimization methods as well.

Not all of the estimation theory is captured by a method of moments, however. There are important differences among the estimation methods that arise primarily with respect to parameter identification and estimator consistency. Identification of parameters and consistency of the MLE rests on properties of the likelihood function, not primarily the score function. In contrast, GMM identification and consistency fall upon properties of the moment functions.

At the end, we have highlighted the role of latent models in econometrics. Our models of nonnormal and nonspherical distributions are largely specifications for capturing observable phenomena, whereas the models motivating IV involve unobservable variables. There are, of course, latent models for nonnormal and nonspherical behavior as well. Such models are an essential tool in economics and econometrics. In Part IV we will describe several important examples.

PART IV

LATENT VARIABLE MODELS

There is nothing like a latent variable to stimulate the imagination
—ARTHUR GOLDBERGER.[1]

Equipped with the ML and GMM estimation methods, we will analyze several prominent econometric models in this final part. The models grow out of a wide variety of empirical settings, yet they share basic building blocks. Ultimately, these models provide restricted conditional moments that identify parameters of interest.

We can group the empirical settings into four broad categories. Chapter 24 introduces panel data, which replicate observations in two ways, typically across individuals and time periods. Chapter 25 returns to pure time series data such as those discussed in Chapter 19, *Serial Correlation*, while Chapter 26 considers multivariate dependent data such as simultaneous observations of price and quantity in a market. Finally, in the last two chapters of this part, we analyze limited dependent variables: for example, discrete variables that are limited to integer values or continuous variables that are strictly positive.

Despite the variety of sampling schemes, the associated econometric models possess common, fundamental, features. Primarily, each econometric model for the observed data rests upon a latent-variable model. That is, researchers view the observable variables as functions of unobserved, underlying, variables. This approach assists in the marriage of theoretical and empirical modeling because abstract, idealized, theoretical concepts often have no direct real-world counterpart. The latent-variable model adapts conveniently to such concepts and one can build an empirical model on a specification of the relationships between the theoretical and the actual.

In this way, latent-variable models play a key role in the economist's search for structure. As Goldberger describes it,

> The search for structural parameters is a search for invariant features of the mechanisms that generate observable variables. Invariant features are those that remain stable—or vary individually—over the set of populations in which we are interested.[2]

Ultimately, it is the invariant features that make prediction and much of policy analysis possible.

In addition, latent variables offer a way to build parsimonious models with natural methods of estimation. Latent variables can generate covariance among observations and heterogeneity

[1] Chamberlain (1990, p. 126).

[2] Chamberlain (1990, p. 128).

across observations. By nature, such covariance and heterogeneity always satisfy the restrictions that probability distributions place on these functions. Frequently, estimation would be straightforward, even trivial, if the latent variables were known. By extension, estimation with observable variables mimics the latent approach.

Finally, a side benefit of latent-variable models is that their features combine easily. Just as one may model covariance and heterogeneity separately, one may simply mix covariance and heterogeneity into a single model.

We have provided examples of these features in heteroskedasticity, serial correlation, and instrumental variables. Unobserved heterogeneity in the variance of a normal linear regression model leads to Student t linear regression.[3] Although we initiated our analysis of serial correlation with a simple parametric form for the autocorrelation structure, much of the convenience and appeal of this specification derives from its latent variable interpretation.[4] For IV techniques, the latent variable structure is the basis of interpretation.[5]

As another example, let us motivate quadratic conditional heteroskedasticity with a latent variable model.[6] Suppose

$$y_n \mid \mathbf{x}_n, \boldsymbol{\beta}_n \sim \mathfrak{N}(\mathbf{x}_n' \boldsymbol{\beta}_n, \sigma_0^2)$$

conditional on $\mathbf{x}_n$ and $\boldsymbol{\beta}_n$, where $\boldsymbol{\beta}_n$ is a latent vector of regression coefficients. We could specify such a latent model to capture unobserved variations in taste across individual consumers. If we additionally assume that

$$\boldsymbol{\beta}_n \mid \mathbf{x}_n \sim \mathfrak{N}(\boldsymbol{\beta}_0, \boldsymbol{\Omega}_0)$$

then the conditional distribution of y_n given $\mathbf{x}_n$ alone is $\mathfrak{N}(\mathbf{x}_n' \boldsymbol{\beta}_0, \sigma_0^2 + \mathbf{x}_n' \boldsymbol{\Omega}_0 \mathbf{x}_n)$.[7] As a result, this specification identifies variance and covariance in unobserved marginal effects of $\mathbf{x}_n$ on y_n. Moreover, the functional form of the derived heteroskedasticity produces positive variances provided only that σ_0^2 and $\boldsymbol{\Omega}_0$ behave as variances.

Look for each of these as you read the following chapters:

1. the empirical modeling issue,
2. the latent-variable model that this issue motivates, and
3. the econometric estimators and test statistics that the model produces.

These items provide the motivation and structure of the material. Keeping them in mind as you work through details will help you to see both the forest and its trees.

---

[3] See Section 13.2.1.

[4] See Sections 19.2.2 and 20.1 and Example 20.5 (Dynamic Regression, p. 497).

[5] See Sections 20.2 and 20.3.

[6] We mention quadratic heteroskedasticity in Section 18.5.1.

[7] Hildreth and Houck (1968).

CHAPTER 24

Panel Data Models

24.1 INTRODUCTION

Researchers often have several ways to observe a general economic phenomenon. Labor economists collect employment data from different individuals at a given time and from particular individuals at different times. Macroeconomists have similar opportunities, collecting aggregate data for different countries and different time periods. If both kinds of observations are viewed as replications of a single underlying process, then the researcher will analyze them together in a single data set. Such data sets, with at least two modes (or dimensions) of replication, are called *panel data sets*. These examples contain the most common structure, a cross section of individuals or countries at several moments in time.

Such data offer opportunities to examine aspects of a general phenomenon that one can address in no other way. For example, although one may observe the number of years of schooling an individual receives, one does not observe the quality of the schools. If school quality is also a determinant of individuals' wages, then one may wish to condition on school quality in attempts to estimate returns to personal investments in education, returns to work experience, and black-white wage differentials.[1] Panel data in which school quality varies across individuals but is constant over time for each individual make this possible.

Alternatively, consider a study of gross national product (GNP) per capita. Individual nations have many unique characteristics that are difficult to quantify, yet we wish to include them in the set of conditioning variables. These characteristics include aspects of geography, history, and culture that are predetermined and, therefore, constant over the years in which we observe a cross section of nations. In a cross-sectional data set for one year, we cannot condition on such characteristics without quantifying them. But a panel data set in which we repeatedly observe each nation's GNP offers an alternative approach.

[1] See, for example, Card and Krueger (1992a, 1992b).

In this chapter, we will focus on this issue of unobserved, time-invariant characteristics of individual observations. We begin by introducing two approaches that frame most thinking about estimation in this setting. One approach treats the overall effect of these characteristics as an additional unknown parameter. This *fixed-effects* approach uses the variation in explanatory variables over time to identify regression coefficients. OLS produces unbiased, consistent estimators. The second approach makes assumptions about the distribution of the latent individual-specific effect. These assumptions make a GLS estimator appropriate. Because it reduces the number of parameters to be estimated, this *random-effects* approach offers potentially large improvements in statistical precision.

The random-effects model also identifies the coefficients of time-invariant explanatory variables. Otherwise, these coefficients are confounded with the individual-specific effects. Following the introduction to basic models and methods, we discuss generalizations and tests of the random-effects approach that exploit this feature. The generalizations involve time-invariant explanatory variables, individual-invariant explanatory variables, and lagged dependent explanatory variables. The tests are Hausman specification tests that compare estimators that require variation over time with those that do not. These tests are designed to detect failures of a fundamental assumption of the basic random-effects model: that the individual-specific random effect is uncorrelated with the explanatory variables.

In the last sections of this chapter, we review a random-effects specification that relaxes this critical assumption. A key element of this specification is that the MMSE linear predictor of the latent effect is the same for all individuals. This allows correlation of the individual-specific random effect with explanatory variables, but the correlation must be constant across individuals. Given this, it is still possible to estimate regression coefficients for time-invariant explanatory variables.

24.2 FIXED INDIVIDUAL EFFECTS

To begin, we will consider the classical linear regression model in which we partition the conditional expectation into time-variant and time-invariant components, $\mathbf{x}'_{nt}\boldsymbol{\beta}_0$ and $\mathbf{z}_n^{*\prime}\boldsymbol{\eta}_0$, respectively:

$$\mathrm{E}[y_{nt}\,|\,\mathbf{X}, \mathbf{Z}^*] = \mathbf{x}'_{nt}\boldsymbol{\beta}_0 + \mathbf{z}_n^{*\prime}\boldsymbol{\eta}_0, \qquad n = 1, \ldots, N \quad t = 1, \ldots, T \tag{24.1}$$

where n indexes the individuals of the cross section and t indexes the time period of observation. The matrix $\mathbf{X}$ contains the $\mathbf{x}_{nt}$s and the matrix $\mathbf{Z}^*$ contains the $\mathbf{z}_n^*$s. The vector $\mathbf{z}_n^*$ represents unobserved characteristics of the individuals that are constant from time period to time period.

Whether or not $\mathbf{z}_n^*$ is observed, $\boldsymbol{\beta}_0$ is identified by the conditional expectation of the differences $y_{nt} - y_{n,t-1}$:

$$\mathrm{E}[y_{nt} - y_{n,t-1}\,|\,\mathbf{X}] = \left(\mathbf{x}_{nt} - \mathbf{x}_{n,t-1}\right)'\boldsymbol{\beta}_0$$

so that one OLS estimator of $\boldsymbol{\beta}_0$ projects $y_{nt} - y_{n,t-1}$ onto $\mathbf{x}_{nt} - \mathbf{x}_{n,t-1}$. Thus, *changes* in y_{nt} and $\mathbf{x}_{nt}$ isolate the coefficients of the time-variant explanatory variables. By watching the growth in individuals' wages, one can identify the effect of work experience, which changes over time, without simultaneously controlling for school quality and race, which are fixed for each individual.

As natural as it may seem, this approach is *ad hoc*. If $\mathbf{z}_n^*$ is not observed, why should we use first differences and not second differences (if $T \geq 3$)? After all, the conditional expectation of the acceleration in wages has the same property that it is invariant to $\mathbf{z}_n^*$. Or we could examine $y_{nt} + y_{n,t-1} - 2y_{n,t-2}$.

The usual formal motivation for a particular estimator rests on second-moment restrictions on the data-generating process. The simplest starting point is to assume that

$$\text{Var}[\mathbf{y} \mid \mathbf{X}, \mathbf{Z}^*] = \sigma_{0\varepsilon}^2 \cdot \mathbf{I}_{NT} \tag{24.2}$$

where $\mathbf{y}$ is an $NT \times 1$ vector of all y_{nt}. In addition, because the $\mathbf{z}_n^*$ are unobserved (latent) variables, we must treat the $\alpha_n \equiv \mathbf{z}_n^{*\prime}\boldsymbol{\eta}_0$ as additional unknown parameters. As such, the α_n are usually called *fixed effects*. Each is a distinct intercept for the regression function of an individual in the cross section.

The optimal GMM estimator of $\boldsymbol{\beta}_0$ is then OLS regression of y_{nt} on $\mathbf{x}_{nt}$ and N dummy variables indicating each of the N individuals. We can use partitioned regression to isolate the OLS estimator of $\boldsymbol{\beta}_0$ as in Example 3.4. First we define the dummy variables (DV)

$$d_{ntk} \equiv \begin{cases} 0 & \text{if } n \neq k \\ 1 & \text{if } n = k \end{cases}$$

and $\mathbf{d}_{nt} \equiv [d_{nt1}, \ldots, d_{ntN}]'$ that indicate when observation (n, t) corresponds to the kth individual. Then the α_n are the coefficients of these dummy variables:

$$\alpha_n = \underset{1\times N}{\mathbf{d}'_{nt}} \; \underset{N\times 1}{\boldsymbol{\alpha}} \tag{24.3}$$

where $\boldsymbol{\alpha} \equiv [\alpha_1, \ldots, \alpha_N]'$. We apply partitioned regression to

$$\text{E}[y_{nt} \mid \mathbf{X}, \mathbf{Z}^*] = \mathbf{x}'_{nt}\boldsymbol{\beta}_0 + \mathbf{d}'_{nt}\boldsymbol{\alpha}$$

to find the OLS fitted coefficient vector for $\boldsymbol{\beta}_0$ alone to be

$$\hat{\boldsymbol{\beta}}_{\text{DV}} \equiv \left(\mathbf{X}'_{\text{DV}}\mathbf{X}_{\text{DV}}\right)^{-1} \mathbf{X}'_{\text{DV}}\mathbf{y}_{\text{DV}} \tag{24.4}$$

where

$$\underset{NT\times K}{\mathbf{X}_{\text{DV}}} \equiv \begin{bmatrix} \mathbf{X}_1 - \iota_T\bar{\mathbf{x}}'_1 \\ \vdots \\ \mathbf{X}_N - \iota_T\bar{\mathbf{x}}'_N \end{bmatrix}, \qquad \underset{NT\times 1}{\mathbf{y}_{\text{DV}}} \equiv \begin{bmatrix} \mathbf{y}_1 - \iota_T\bar{y}_1 \\ \vdots \\ \mathbf{y}_N - \iota_T\bar{y}_N \end{bmatrix} \tag{24.5}$$

$$\underset{T\times K}{\mathbf{X}_n} \equiv \begin{bmatrix} \mathbf{x}'_{n1} \\ \vdots \\ \mathbf{x}'_{nT} \end{bmatrix}, \qquad \underset{T\times 1}{\mathbf{y}_n} \equiv \begin{bmatrix} y_{n1} \\ \vdots \\ y_{nT} \end{bmatrix}$$

$$\underset{K\times 1}{\bar{\mathbf{x}}_n} \equiv \text{E}_T[\mathbf{x}_{nt}] \equiv \sum_{t=1}^{T} \mathbf{x}_{nt}\frac{1}{T}, \qquad \bar{y}_n \equiv \text{E}_T[y_{nt}] \equiv \sum_{t=1}^{T} y_{nt}\frac{1}{T} \tag{24.6}$$

ι_T is a column vector of T ones, and K denotes the number of elements in $\mathbf{x}_{nt}$ and $\boldsymbol{\beta}_0$. Rather than first differences, the relatively efficient estimator rests on deviations of each variable from the sample mean of each individual's time series.

This estimator is often called the *fixed-effects estimator*, alluding to the implicit estimation of the "fixed" α_n $(n = 1, \ldots, N)$. Another name is the *within-groups estimator*, which we explain below. Recently, the name *least-squares dummy variable* (LSDV) estimator has become a popular third alternative.

The implicit OLS estimator of each α_n can easily be computed with[2]

$$\hat{\alpha}_n = \bar{y}_n - \bar{\mathbf{x}}_n' \hat{\boldsymbol{\beta}}_{\mathrm{DV}}$$

Researchers occasionally use such estimates to make comparisons across the individuals of a data set. Power utility regulators, for example, can examine the fixed effects estimated for electricity production functions in a panel of public power utility firms. Their aim might be to identify relatively inefficient firms by large negative fixed effects. However, one should treat such interpretations cautiously. Because the fixed effects contain *all* time-invariant individual-specific effects, other unique characteristics of the firms are confounded with any persistent inefficiencies.

Moreover, the effects of time-invariant characteristics cannot be estimated separately in the fixed-effects framework. Even if some of the elements of $\mathbf{z}_n^*$ were observed, their coefficients would not be identified because every z_{nj}^* is linearly dependent on $\mathbf{d}_{nt}$: just as in (24.3),

$$z_{nj}^* = \underset{1\times N}{\mathbf{d}_{nt}'} \underset{N\times 1}{\left[\mathbf{z}_{nj}^*;\ n = 1, \ldots, N\right]'}$$

To see this another way, suppose that $\mathbf{z}_{1n}$ in the partition $\mathbf{z}_n^* = \left[\mathbf{z}_{1n}', \mathbf{z}_{2n}^{*\prime}\right]'$ were observed. Even knowing α_n is insufficient information to compute η_{01} from

$$\alpha_n = \mathbf{z}_n^{*\prime} \eta_0 = \mathbf{z}_{1n}' \eta_{01} + \mathbf{z}_{2n}^{*\prime} \eta_{02}, \qquad n = 1, \ldots, N$$

because $\mathbf{z}_{2n}^{*\prime} \eta_{02}$ remains as an unknown fixed effect for every n. If η_{01} is identified, there must be additional restrictions on the unknown α_n. We describe a leading example in the next section.

24.3 RANDOM INDIVIDUAL EFFECTS

In many cases, researchers extend the latent variables model to treat the α_n as random variables, or *random effects*. In addition to

$$\mathrm{E}[y_{nt} \mid \mathbf{X}, \boldsymbol{\alpha}] = \mathbf{x}_{nt}' \boldsymbol{\beta}_0 + \alpha_n, \qquad n = 1, \ldots, N, \quad t = 1, \ldots, T \tag{24.7}$$

they specify

$$\mathrm{E}[y_{nt} \mid \mathbf{X}] = \mathbf{x}_{nt}' \boldsymbol{\beta}_0 + \alpha_0 \tag{24.8}$$

assuming that the conditional mean of every α_n given $\mathbf{X} \equiv \left[\mathbf{X}_1', \ldots, \mathbf{X}_N'\right]'$ equals the same constant α_0. This assumption seems appropriate in situations in which adding individuals to a data set is like replicating a repeatable experiment. Without a priori ways to distinguish between the individuals, treating the α_n as random variables is a familiar expression of the researcher's ignorance.

If (24.8) holds, then we can estimate $\boldsymbol{\beta}_0$ with an OLS regression of y_{nt} on $\left[\mathbf{x}_{nt}', 1\right]'$. This estimator is equivalent to RLS for the LSDV estimator, restricting all of the individual effects to be equal.

---

[2] See Equation (3.22). If we denote $\mathbf{d}_n \equiv \left[\mathbf{d}_{n1}', \ldots, \mathbf{d}_{nT}'\right]'$, then we can apply that equation by setting $\mathbf{X}_2 = [\mathbf{d}_1, \ldots, \mathbf{d}_N]$, $\mathbf{X}_2'\mathbf{X}_2 = T \cdot \mathbf{I}_N$, $\mathbf{X}_2'\mathbf{y} = T \cdot [\bar{y}_1, \ldots, \bar{y}_N]'$, and $\mathbf{X}_2'\mathbf{X}_1 = T \cdot \left[\bar{\mathbf{x}}_1, \ldots, \bar{\mathbf{x}}_N\right]'$.

However, if the α_n are random variables then the OLS estimator is generally inefficient relative to a GLS estimator. Because every y_{nt} for $t = 1, \ldots, T$ contains the same α_n, there will be covariance among the observations for each individual that GLS will exploit. To formalize this, researchers often extend the second-moment assumptions (24.2) of the fixed-effects model as well. They consider the joint conditional behavior of the latent variables α_n and ε_{nt} in

$$y_{nt} = \mathbf{x}_{nt}'\boldsymbol{\beta}_0 + \alpha_n + \varepsilon_{nt} \tag{24.9}$$

where

$$\mathrm{E}[\alpha_n \mid \mathbf{X}] = \alpha_0 \qquad \text{and} \qquad \mathrm{E}[\varepsilon_{nt} \mid \mathbf{X}] = 0 \tag{24.10}$$

In the simplest case, one assumes that $\boldsymbol{\alpha}$ and $\boldsymbol{\varepsilon} \equiv \{[\varepsilon_{n1}, \ldots, \varepsilon_{nT}]\,;\, n = 1, \ldots, N\}'$ are mutually uncorrelated latent random components with scalar variance matrices:

$$\begin{aligned} \mathrm{Var}[\boldsymbol{\alpha} \mid \mathbf{X}] &= \sigma_{0\alpha}^2 \cdot \mathbf{I}_N, \qquad \mathrm{Cov}[\boldsymbol{\varepsilon}, \boldsymbol{\alpha} \mid \mathbf{X}] = \mathbf{0} \\ \mathrm{Var}[\boldsymbol{\varepsilon} \mid \mathbf{X}] &= \sigma_{0\varepsilon}^2 \cdot \mathbf{I}_{NT} \end{aligned} \tag{24.11}$$

As a result, *all* of the covariance among the observed y_{nt} for each individual comes through the variance of the shared latent α_n:

$$\begin{aligned} \mathrm{Var}[\mathbf{y}_n \mid \mathbf{X}] &= \mathrm{Var}[\boldsymbol{\iota}_T \alpha_n + \boldsymbol{\varepsilon}_n \mid \mathbf{X}] \\ &= \sigma_{0\alpha}^2 \cdot \boldsymbol{\iota}_T \boldsymbol{\iota}_T' + \sigma_{0\varepsilon}^2 \cdot \mathbf{I}_T, \qquad n = 1, \ldots, N \end{aligned} \tag{24.12}$$

where $\boldsymbol{\varepsilon}_n \equiv [\varepsilon_{n1}, \ldots, \varepsilon_{nT}]'$. More specifically, every covariance equals $\sigma_{0\alpha}^2$. Yet there is still no covariance among observations for different individuals so that

$$\mathrm{Var}[\mathbf{y} \mid \mathbf{X}] = \begin{bmatrix} \mathrm{Var}[\mathbf{y}_1 \mid \mathbf{X}] & \underset{T\times T}{\mathbf{0}} & \cdots & \underset{T\times T}{\mathbf{0}} \\ \underset{T\times T}{\mathbf{0}} & \mathrm{Var}[\mathbf{y}_2 \mid \mathbf{X}] & \cdots & \underset{T\times T}{\mathbf{0}} \\ \vdots & \vdots & \ddots & \vdots \\ \underset{T\times T}{\mathbf{0}} & \underset{T\times T}{\mathbf{0}} & \cdots & \mathrm{Var}[\mathbf{y}_N \mid \mathbf{X}] \end{bmatrix} \tag{24.13}$$

where $\mathbf{y} \equiv \left[\mathbf{y}_1', \ldots, \mathbf{y}_N'\right]'$ contains all of the y_{nt} ordered lexicographically by individual first and then (within the observations for one individual) by time period.

The GLS estimator corresponding to this *variance-components* structure has a special structure.[3] All of its reweighting occurs within the time series $\mathbf{y}_n$ of an individual. Therefore, to derive the GLS estimator we need focus only on the T-dimensional relationship

$$\underset{T\times 1}{\mathbf{y}_n} = \underset{T\times K}{\mathbf{X}_n} \underset{K\times 1}{\boldsymbol{\beta}_0} + \underset{T\times 1}{\boldsymbol{\iota}_T} \underset{1\times 1}{\alpha_n} + \underset{T\times 1}{\boldsymbol{\varepsilon}_n}, \qquad n = 1, \ldots, N$$

Furthermore, the conditional variance matrix of $\mathbf{y}_n$ given $\mathbf{X}_n$ depends on an orthogonal projector: we can rewrite (24.12) as

$$\begin{aligned} \mathrm{Var}[\mathbf{y}_n \mid \mathbf{X}] &= T\sigma_{0\alpha}^2 \cdot \boldsymbol{\iota}_T \left(\boldsymbol{\iota}_T'\boldsymbol{\iota}_T\right)^{-1} \boldsymbol{\iota}_T' + \sigma_{0\varepsilon}^2 \cdot \mathbf{I}_T \\ &= T\sigma_{0\alpha}^2 \cdot \mathbf{P}_{\iota_T} + \sigma_{0\varepsilon}^2 \cdot \mathbf{I}_T. \end{aligned} \tag{24.14}$$

[3] The term *variance components* generally refers to variance matrices whose elements are functions of variances of latent variables. The term *error components* is closely related, referring to the latent variables (or components) themselves.

Using (24.14), we show in Section 24.9 that the GLS estimator of $\left[\boldsymbol{\beta}_0', \alpha_0\right]'$ corresponds to OLS regression of the LHS variable

$$y_{*nt} \equiv y_{nt} - (1 - \omega_0)\,\bar{y}_n \tag{24.15}$$

on the RHS variables

$$\mathbf{x}_{*nt} \equiv \mathbf{x}_{nt} - (1 - \omega_0) \cdot \bar{\mathbf{x}}_n \tag{24.16}$$

and a constant, where

$$\omega_0 \equiv \frac{\sigma_{0\varepsilon}}{\sqrt{T\sigma_{0\alpha}^2 + \sigma_{0\varepsilon}^2}}$$

The $\bar{y}_n$ and $\bar{\mathbf{x}}_n$ terms arise in the orthogonal projections $\mathbf{P}_{\iota_T}\mathbf{y}_n = \iota_T \bar{y}_n$ and $\mathbf{P}_{\iota_T}\mathbf{X}_n = \iota_T \bar{\mathbf{x}}_n'$, respectively.

This GLS estimator is often called the *random-effects estimator*. It is reminiscent of the LSDV estimator (24.4). In fact, if $\omega_0 = 0$ then the random-effects GLS and LSDV estimators are identical. The parameter ω_0 can take any value between zero and one. It equals one when $\sigma_{0\alpha}^2 = 0$ and there is no covariance among the observations. In that case GLS reduces to OLS, as it should. As the $\sigma_{0\alpha}^2$ grows, or the length of the time series T grows, ω_0 falls toward zero and the GLS estimator puts more weight on the within-individual sample means. In the extreme with N fixed and $T \to \infty$, the GLS and LSDV estimators are asymptotically equivalent. In effect, the α_n become known constants because there is an infinite number of observations to estimate each one. Hence, the OLS estimator that conditions on the α_n is asymptotically relatively efficient.

The OLS regression of y_{*nt} on $\mathbf{x}_{*nt}$ reduces to two, more fundamental, OLS regressions. Because the conditional variance of $\mathbf{y}_n$ is also a weighted sum of two complementary orthogonal projectors,

$$\text{Var}[\mathbf{y}_n \,|\, \mathbf{X}] = \left(T\sigma_{0\alpha}^2 + \sigma_{0\varepsilon}^2\right) \cdot \mathbf{P}_{\iota_T} + \sigma_{0\varepsilon}^2 \cdot \left(\mathbf{I}_T - \mathbf{P}_{\iota_T}\right) \tag{24.17}$$

we can also express the random-effects (RE) estimator for $\boldsymbol{\beta}_0$ as the matrix-weighted average

$$\hat{\boldsymbol{\beta}}_{\text{RE}}(\omega_0) = \mathbf{A}(\omega_0)\,\hat{\boldsymbol{\beta}}_{\text{DV}} + \left[\mathbf{I}_K - \mathbf{A}(\omega_0)\right]\hat{\boldsymbol{\beta}}_{\text{B}} \tag{24.18}$$

where

$$\hat{\boldsymbol{\beta}}_{\text{B}} \equiv \left(\mathbf{X}_{\text{B}}'\mathbf{X}_{\text{B}}\right)^{-1}\mathbf{X}_{\text{B}}'\mathbf{y}_{\text{B}} \tag{24.19}$$

and

$$\underset{N\times K}{\mathbf{X}_{\text{B}}} \equiv \begin{bmatrix} \bar{\mathbf{x}}_1' - \bar{\bar{\mathbf{x}}}' \\ \vdots \\ \bar{\mathbf{x}}_N' - \bar{\bar{\mathbf{x}}}' \end{bmatrix}, \qquad \underset{N\times 1}{\mathbf{y}_{\text{B}}} \equiv \begin{bmatrix} \bar{y}_1 - \bar{\bar{y}} \\ \vdots \\ \bar{y}_N - \bar{\bar{y}} \end{bmatrix} \tag{24.20}$$

$$\underset{K\times 1}{\bar{\bar{\mathbf{x}}}} \equiv \text{E}_N[\bar{\mathbf{x}}_n] \equiv \sum_{n=1}^{N} \bar{\mathbf{x}}_n \frac{1}{N}, \qquad \bar{\bar{y}} \equiv \text{E}_N[\bar{y}_n] \equiv \sum_{n=1}^{N} \bar{y}_n \frac{1}{N} \tag{24.21}$$

$$\mathbf{A}(\omega_0) \equiv \left(\mathbf{X}_{\text{DV}}'\mathbf{X}_{\text{DV}} + T\omega_0^2 \cdot \mathbf{X}_{\text{B}}'\mathbf{X}_{\text{B}}\right)^{-1}\mathbf{X}_{\text{DV}}'\mathbf{X}_{\text{DV}} \tag{24.22}$$

The first RHS component of $\hat{\boldsymbol{\beta}}_{\text{RE}}(\omega_0)$ depends on $\hat{\boldsymbol{\beta}}_{\text{DV}}$, the LSDV estimator in (24.4). The second component contains $\hat{\boldsymbol{\beta}}_{\text{B}}$, the *between groups estimator*. The name "between-groups" refers to the property that no variation within the *group* (or time series) of observations for an individual appears in $\hat{\boldsymbol{\beta}}_{\text{B}}$.[4] Its data are all within-individual (or "within-group") sample means, which do not vary over the time dimension.

The origins of the decomposition of the random-effects estimator $\hat{\boldsymbol{\beta}}_{\text{RE}}(\omega_0)$ into $\hat{\boldsymbol{\beta}}_{\text{DV}}$ and $\hat{\boldsymbol{\beta}}_{\text{B}}$ appear in the variance decomposition (24.17). The orthogonal projection matrices $\mathbf{I} - \mathbf{P}_{\iota_T}$ and $\mathbf{P}_{\iota_T}$ project $\mathbf{y}_n$ into two uncorrelated components, $\left(\mathbf{I} - \mathbf{P}_{\iota_T}\right)\mathbf{y}_n$ and $\mathbf{P}_{\iota_T}\mathbf{y}_n$, with variances $\sigma_{0\varepsilon}^2 \cdot \left(\mathbf{I}_T - \mathbf{P}_{\iota_T}\right)$ and $\left(T\sigma_{0\alpha}^2 + \sigma_{0\varepsilon}^2\right) \cdot \mathbf{P}_{\iota_T}$, respectively.[5] Individually, these components yield the LSDV and between-groups estimators as GMM estimators. Moreover, $\hat{\boldsymbol{\beta}}_{\text{DV}}$ and $\hat{\boldsymbol{\beta}}_{\text{B}}$ are uncorrelated in turn:

$$\operatorname{Var}\left[\begin{bmatrix} \hat{\boldsymbol{\beta}}_{\text{DV}} - \boldsymbol{\beta}_0 \\ \hat{\boldsymbol{\beta}}_{\text{B}} - \boldsymbol{\beta}_0 \end{bmatrix}\right] = \begin{bmatrix} \sigma_{0\varepsilon}^2 \cdot \left(\mathbf{X}_{\text{DV}}'\mathbf{X}_{\text{DV}}\right)^{-1} & \underset{K\times K}{\mathbf{0}} \\ \underset{K\times K}{\mathbf{0}} & \frac{T\sigma_{0\alpha}^2 + \sigma_{0\varepsilon}^2}{T} \cdot \left(\mathbf{X}_{\text{B}}'\mathbf{X}_{\text{B}}\right)^{-1} \end{bmatrix}$$

As a result, the random effects estimator is also the minimum distance estimator

$$\hat{\boldsymbol{\beta}}_{\text{RE}}(\omega_0) = \underset{\boldsymbol{\beta}}{\operatorname{argmin}} \begin{bmatrix} \hat{\boldsymbol{\beta}}_{\text{DV}} - \boldsymbol{\beta} \\ \hat{\boldsymbol{\beta}}_{\text{B}} - \boldsymbol{\beta} \end{bmatrix}' \left\{ \operatorname{Var}\left[\begin{bmatrix} \hat{\boldsymbol{\beta}}_{\text{DV}} - \boldsymbol{\beta}_0 \\ \hat{\boldsymbol{\beta}}_{\text{B}} - \boldsymbol{\beta}_0 \end{bmatrix} |\mathbf{X}\right]\right\}^{-1} \begin{bmatrix} \hat{\boldsymbol{\beta}}_{\text{DV}} - \boldsymbol{\beta} \\ \hat{\boldsymbol{\beta}}_{\text{B}} - \boldsymbol{\beta} \end{bmatrix}$$

This minimum distance interpretation also justifies the matrix-weighted average in (24.18).

Feasible random-effects estimation requires an estimator of ω_0^2. Just as the random-effects GLS estimator is a weighted average of the LSDV and between-groups estimators, the feasible weighting depends on the estimated variances for these two estimators. The disturbance term of the fixed-effects model is ε_{nt} so that the OLS estimator of the variance from the LSDV estimator is an unbiased, consistent estimator of $\sigma_{0\varepsilon}^2$:[6]

$$\hat{\sigma}_\varepsilon^2 = \frac{\sum_{n=1}^{N}\sum_{t=1}^{T}\left[y_{nt} - \bar{y}_n - \left(\mathbf{x}_{nt} - \bar{\mathbf{x}}_n\right)'\hat{\boldsymbol{\beta}}_{\text{DV}}\right]^2}{NT - T - K} \tag{24.23}$$

The disturbance term of the between-groups regression is $\alpha_n + \bar{\varepsilon}_n$, which has a variance equal to $\left(T\sigma_\alpha^2 + \sigma_\varepsilon^2\right)/T$. Therefore, the OLS estimator of the variance from the between-groups estimator is an unbiased, consistent estimator of this term:

$$\left(\frac{\widehat{T\sigma_\alpha^2 + \sigma_\varepsilon^2}}{T}\right) = \frac{\sum_{n=1}^{N}\left[\bar{y}_n - \bar{\bar{y}} - \left(\bar{\mathbf{x}}_n - \bar{\bar{\mathbf{x}}}\right)'\hat{\boldsymbol{\beta}}_{\text{B}}\right]^2}{N - 1 - K} \tag{24.24}$$

---

[4] As we noted earlier, the LSDV estimator is also called the *within-groups estimator*. This term contrasts with the *between-groups estimator* and is a poetic carryover from analysis of covariance that is somewhat misleading in this context. Clearly, the fixed-effects estimator also exploits variation in the explanatory variables across individuals as well as "within" individuals.

[5] Recall the decomposition of $\mathbf{y}$ and $\operatorname{Var}[\mathbf{y}\,|\,\mathbf{X}]$ with $\mathbf{P}_{\mathbf{X}}$ and $\mathbf{I} - \mathbf{P}_{\mathbf{X}}$ in Proposition 5 (Variances of OLS, p. 157).

[6] In general, the OLS fitted residuals $(\mathbf{I} - \mathbf{P}_{\mathbf{X}})\,\mathbf{y}$ equal the partitioned OLS fitted residuals $\left(\mathbf{I} - \mathbf{P}_{\mathbf{X}_{1\perp 2}}\right)\mathbf{y}_{1\perp 2}$, where $\mathbf{X}_{1\perp 2} \equiv \left(\mathbf{I} - \mathbf{P}_{\mathbf{X}_2}\right)\mathbf{X}_1$ and $\mathbf{y}_{1\perp 2} \equiv \left(\mathbf{I} - \mathbf{P}_{X_2}\right)\mathbf{y}$. Therefore, this variance estimator can use the sum of squared residuals from the partitioned LSDV fit.

A consistent estimator of ω_0^2 combines these two estimators in the ratio

$$\hat{\omega}^2 = \frac{\hat{\sigma}_\varepsilon^2}{T \cdot \left[\widehat{\left(T\sigma_\alpha^2 + \sigma_\varepsilon^2\right)/T}\right]}$$

Plugging this estimator into $\hat{\boldsymbol{\beta}}_{\text{RE}}(\omega_0)$ gives the feasible random-effects estimator

$$\hat{\boldsymbol{\beta}}_{\text{RE}}(\hat{\omega}) = \mathbf{A}(\hat{\omega})\,\hat{\boldsymbol{\beta}}_{\text{DV}} + \left[\mathbf{I}_K - \mathbf{A}(\hat{\omega})\right]\hat{\boldsymbol{\beta}}_{\text{B}} \tag{24.25}$$

One can compute $\hat{\boldsymbol{\beta}}_{\text{RE}}(\hat{\omega})$ using the GLS transformation [(24.15)–(24.16)] and the OLS estimation procedure.

24.4 FIXED VERSUS RANDOM EFFECTS

The random-effects specification is a refinement of the fixed-effects specification. Thus, there are situations in which the latter is appropriate while the former is not. Having laid out the random-effects model, let us consider the exceptions that would lead a researcher away from this specification back toward fixed effects.

It is important to keep in mind that the decision concerns specification of conditional expectations, not necessarily whether the latent α_n $(n = 1, \ldots, N)$ are stochastic or nonstochastic. Occasionally, researchers describe the issue in this narrower sense. Indeed, the terms *fixed* and *random* suggest the contrast between stochastic and nonstochastic. Note however that we made no such distinction in our specification of the fixed-effects model.

Attention focuses on the conditional expectations $\text{E}[\mathbf{y}_n \mid \mathbf{X}, \alpha_n]$ and $\text{E}[\mathbf{y}_n \mid \mathbf{X}]$ where α_n contains the sum of all individual-specific effects. Provided that these functions are linear, their respective coefficient vectors for $\mathbf{x}_{nt}$ generally differ. If the conditional expectation of α_n given $\mathbf{X}$ is not constant as in (24.8), then the coefficient vector in $\text{E}[\mathbf{y}_n \mid \mathbf{X}]$ will reflect the covariance between α_n and $\mathbf{x}_{nt}$. More than this, the explanatory variables from other time periods ought to appear in this regression function. For example, Mundlak (1978) suggests the alternative specification[7]

$$\text{E}[\alpha_n \mid \mathbf{X}] = \sum_{t=1}^{T} \mathbf{x}_{nt}'\boldsymbol{\delta}_{0t} + \alpha_0 = \mathbf{x}_n'\boldsymbol{\delta}_0 + \alpha_0$$

where

$$\underset{TK\times 1}{\mathbf{x}_n} \equiv \begin{bmatrix}\mathbf{x}_{n1}' & \cdots & \mathbf{x}_{nT}'\end{bmatrix}'$$

and

$$\underset{TK\times 1}{\boldsymbol{\delta}_0} \equiv \begin{bmatrix}\boldsymbol{\delta}_{01}' & \cdots & \boldsymbol{\delta}_{0T}'\end{bmatrix}'$$

so that

[7] Notation for panel data models varies widely and we are following a particular approach. Here, with the introduction of $\mathbf{x}_n$, we run a risk of confusion between $\mathbf{x}_n$, $\bar{\mathbf{x}}_n$, and $\mathbf{X}_n$. The symbol $\mathbf{x}_n$ denotes the $1 \times TK$ row vector of $\mathbf{x}_{nt}$ row vectors for all t. The symbol $\bar{\mathbf{x}}_n$ denotes the $1 \times K$ row vector of the sample mean of the $\mathbf{x}_{nt}$ for all t. We omit the t subscript in both cases because both row vectors, $\mathbf{x}_n$ and $\bar{\mathbf{x}}_n$, exhibit no time variation. We indicate the reason for the lack of time variation by the absence or presence of the "bar" accent. Finally, $\mathbf{X}_n$ denotes the $T \times K$ matrix containing $\mathbf{x}_{nt}$ in its tth row. Upper case distinguishes this matrix from the two row vectors. There is no t subscript because the time dimension occurs within this matrix.

$$\begin{aligned}\mathrm{E}[y_{nt} \mid \mathbf{X}] &= \mathbf{x}_{nt}'\boldsymbol{\beta}_0 + \mathbf{x}_n'\boldsymbol{\delta}_0 + \alpha_0 \\ &= \mathbf{x}_{nt}'(\boldsymbol{\beta}_0 + \boldsymbol{\delta}_{0t}) + \sum_{\substack{v=1 \\ v\neq t}}^{T} \mathbf{x}_{nv}'\boldsymbol{\delta}_{0v} + \alpha_0 \end{aligned} \tag{24.26}$$

The OLS fitted coefficients from regressing y_{nt} on $\mathbf{x}_{nt}$ alone do not possess a marginal interpretation, except as estimators of the coefficients of the MMSE linear predictor of y_{nt} given only $\mathbf{x}_{nt}$.

In some settings, covariance between α_n and $\mathbf{x}_{nt}$ will seem likely. In his example of the wages of young American males, Griliches (1977) suggests that α_n includes the "spunk" of an individual. Spunky men receive high wages and they also obtain more schooling. Consequently, the explanatory variable schooling is a predictor of α_n. Hsiao (1986, p. 43) gives a similar example for the production function of firms, where α_n contains unobservable managerial skill. Firms with relatively efficient management tend to produce relatively more output and use relatively more inputs than other firms. As a result, the explanatory input levels are correlated with the omitted α_n. In such cases, $\mathrm{E}[\alpha_n \mid \mathbf{X}] \neq \alpha_0$ for all $n = 1, \ldots, N$ and the LSDV estimator is the only estimator that we have mentioned that provides a consistent estimator of $\boldsymbol{\beta}_0$.

On the other hand, given the additional restriction that $\mathrm{E}[\alpha_n \mid \mathbf{X}] = \alpha_0$, both $\mathrm{E}[\mathbf{y}_n \mid \mathbf{X}]$ and $\mathrm{E}[\mathbf{y}_n \mid \mathbf{X}, \boldsymbol{\alpha}]$ contain the same coefficient vector for $\mathbf{x}_{nt}$. Then LSDV, OLS, and FGLS estimators are all consistent for $\boldsymbol{\beta}_0$ under general conditions. If the variance-components structure in (24.11) also holds, then the random-effects FGLS estimator is asymptotically relatively efficient and becomes the estimator of choice.

The fixed-effects and random-effects models and the LSDV and random-effects estimators are useful starting points for introducing current approaches to panel data. We have just pointed out a fundamental issue in these approaches concerning $\mathrm{E}(\alpha_n \mid \mathbf{X})$. We will return to this issue in Sections 24.6–24.7, *Specification Tests* and *Linear Projection*. Before that, let us briefly describe several generalizations of the basic random-effects model with $\mathrm{E}(\alpha_n \mid \mathbf{X}) = \alpha_0$.

24.5 GENERALIZATIONS

The most fundamental generalization of the random-effects model includes explanatory variables that do not vary over time for an individual. This is not possible in the fixed-effects estimation framework because such individual-specific variables are collinear with the individual-specific dummy variables. But no such multicollinearity arises in OLS or GLS estimation of the random-effects models. After describing the impact of individual-specific variables on estimation, we go one step further and include time-specific variables as well.

In addition, we consider extending the specification of the random-effects model to include a lagged dependent explanatory variable. We have already seen that serial correlation in disturbances and a lagged dependent explanatory variable complicate estimation of regression models.[8] The situation is more severe in the random-effects model in which the regression parameters are not even identified. Researchers must assume additional moment restrictions in order to estimate such dynamic models.

[8] See (20.10)–(20.14).

We will not discuss models of conditional heteroskedasticity or autoregressive serial correlation. Such models do not raise any new issues and the methods that we have described in earlier chapters usually apply in predictable ways. For examples, we suggest consulting one of the general references, Baltagi (1995), Hsiao (1986), Maddala (1993), and Mátyás and Sevestre (1996).

24.5.1 Individual-Specific Explanatory Variables

We have restricted our treatment so far to cases for which all of the explanatory variables vary over time. This restriction is unnecessary when the α_n are random effects and so we introduce observable, time-invariant explanatory variables $\mathbf{z}_n$ and generalize (24.8) to

$$\mathrm{E}[y_{nt} \mid \mathbf{X}, \mathbf{Z}, \boldsymbol{\alpha}] = \mathbf{x}'_{nt}\boldsymbol{\beta}_0 + \mathbf{z}'_n\boldsymbol{\gamma}_0 + \alpha_n, \qquad n = 1, \ldots, N \quad t = 1, \ldots, T$$

where $\mathbf{Z} \equiv \left[\mathbf{z}'_1, \ldots, \mathbf{z}'_N\right]'$, $\mathbf{z}_n$ is a row vector of J additional explanatory variables, and $\boldsymbol{\gamma}_0$ is a column vector of J unknown coefficients. In wage equations for employed adults, such personal characteristics as race and sex are time invariant. In a panel data set describing electric power utilities, many characteristics of the regulatory environment differ across firms and remain constant over time. In both cases, $\boldsymbol{\gamma}_0$ contains parameters of interest. In addition, conditioning on observable $\mathbf{z}_n$ can potentially overcome situations in which $\mathrm{E}(\alpha_n \mid \mathbf{X}) \neq 0$.

Including $\mathbf{z}_n$ leaves much of the previous analysis unchanged. As mentioned at the end of Section 24.2, $\boldsymbol{\gamma}_0$ is not identified if the α_n are unknown fixed effects. Within the random-effects model, OLS and GLS estimators produce unbiased, consistent estimators. The variation in $\mathbf{z}_n$ across individuals identifies $\boldsymbol{\gamma}_0$ given that $\mathrm{E}[\alpha_n \mid \mathbf{X}, \mathbf{Z}] = \alpha_0$. If $\mathrm{Var}[\mathbf{y}_n \mid \mathbf{X}, \mathbf{Z}] = \sigma^2_{0\alpha} \cdot \boldsymbol{\iota}_T \boldsymbol{\iota}'_T + \sigma^2_{0\varepsilon} \cdot \mathbf{I}_T$, the GLS transformation in (24.15)–(24.16) produces the same $\mathbf{y}_*$ and the augmented RHS matrix

$$[\mathbf{X}_*, \ \mathbf{Z}_*] \equiv \left[\left[\mathbf{x}_{nt} - (1 - \omega_0) \cdot \bar{\mathbf{x}}_n\right]', \ \left[\omega_0 \cdot \mathbf{z}'_n\right]\right]$$

because $\bar{\mathbf{z}}_n = \mathbf{z}_n$. Both OLS and GLS remain matrix-weighted average of the LSDV and between-groups estimators. However, the LSDV estimator applies only to the estimation of $\boldsymbol{\beta}_0$ so that the GLS weighting matrix annihilates whatever (arbitrary) value is assigned to $\hat{\boldsymbol{\gamma}}_{\mathrm{DV}}$ for the LSDV estimator:

$$\begin{bmatrix} \hat{\boldsymbol{\beta}}_{\mathrm{RE}} \\ \hat{\boldsymbol{\gamma}}_{\mathrm{RE}} \end{bmatrix} = \mathbf{A}(\omega_0) \begin{bmatrix} \hat{\boldsymbol{\beta}}_{\mathrm{DV}} \\ \hat{\boldsymbol{\gamma}}_{\mathrm{DV}} \end{bmatrix} + [\mathbf{I}_K - \mathbf{A}(\omega_0)] \begin{bmatrix} \hat{\boldsymbol{\beta}}_{\mathrm{B}} \\ \hat{\boldsymbol{\gamma}}_{\mathrm{B}} \end{bmatrix}$$

As before, $\hat{\boldsymbol{\beta}}_{\mathrm{DV}}$ is defined in (24.4). On the other hand, we adjust $\hat{\boldsymbol{\beta}}_{\mathrm{B}}$ in (24.19) by augmenting $\mathbf{X}_{\mathrm{B}}$ to

$$\mathbf{W}_{\mathrm{B}} \equiv \left[\mathbf{X}_{\mathrm{B}}, \ \left[\mathbf{z}_n - \bar{\mathbf{z}}\right]'\right]$$

so that

$$\begin{bmatrix} \hat{\boldsymbol{\beta}}_{\mathrm{B}} \\ \hat{\boldsymbol{\gamma}}_{\mathrm{B}} \end{bmatrix} = \left(\mathbf{W}'_{\mathrm{B}}\mathbf{W}_{\mathrm{B}}\right)^{-1} \mathbf{W}'_{\mathrm{B}}\mathbf{y}$$

and extend $\mathbf{A}(\omega_0)$ correspondingly to

$$\mathbf{A}(\omega_0) \equiv \left\{ \begin{bmatrix} \mathbf{X}'_{\mathrm{DV}}\mathbf{X}_{\mathrm{DV}} & \underset{K \times J}{\mathbf{0}} \\ \underset{J \times K}{\mathbf{0}} & \underset{J \times J}{\mathbf{0}} \end{bmatrix} + T\omega_0^2 \cdot \mathbf{W}'_{\mathrm{B}}\mathbf{W}_{\mathrm{B}} \right\}^{-1} \begin{bmatrix} \mathbf{X}'_{\mathrm{DV}}\mathbf{X}_{\mathrm{DV}} & \underset{K \times J}{\mathbf{0}} \\ \underset{J \times K}{\mathbf{0}} & \underset{J \times J}{\mathbf{0}} \end{bmatrix}$$

Initial estimation of ω_0 for FGLS is essentially unchanged from when individual-specific explanatory variables are not present. The estimation of $\sigma_{0\varepsilon}^2$ with the LSDV variance estimator (24.23) is exactly the same. The estimator of $\sigma_{0\alpha}^2 + \sigma_{0\varepsilon}^2/T$ changes (24.24) to accommodate the presence of the $\mathbf{z}_n$ in the between-groups estimator:

$$\left(\frac{\widehat{T\sigma_\alpha^2 + \sigma_\varepsilon^2}}{T}\right) = \frac{\sum_{n=1}^N \left[\bar{y}_n - \bar{\bar{y}} - \left(\bar{\mathbf{x}}_n - \bar{\bar{\mathbf{x}}}\right)\hat{\boldsymbol{\beta}}_{\mathrm{B}} - (\mathbf{z}_n - \bar{\mathbf{z}})\,\hat{\boldsymbol{\gamma}}_{\mathrm{B}}\right]^2}{N - 1 - K - J}$$

Standard OLS software will calculate this statistic as the estimated variance parameter from the between-groups fit of $\bar{y}_n$ to $\bar{\mathbf{x}}_n$, $\mathbf{z}_n$, and a constant.

24.5.2 Time-Specific Effects

In many settings, researchers also include time-specific terms:

$$\mathrm{E}[y_{nt} \mid \mathbf{X}, \mathbf{Z}, \mathbf{R}, \boldsymbol{\alpha}, \boldsymbol{\lambda}] = \mathbf{x}_{nt}'\boldsymbol{\beta}_0 + \mathbf{z}_n'\boldsymbol{\gamma}_0 + \mathbf{r}_t'\boldsymbol{\rho}_0 + \alpha_n + \lambda_t, \qquad n = 1, \ldots, N \quad t = 1, \ldots, T$$

where $\boldsymbol{\lambda} \equiv [\lambda_t]$ and $\mathbf{R} \equiv [\mathbf{r}_1, \ldots, \mathbf{r}_T]'$, $\mathbf{r}_t$ is a column vector of L explanatory variables that are constant across individuals and vary over time, and $\boldsymbol{\rho}_0$ is a column vector of L additional parameters. For example, cross sections of individuals or firms may be subject to the same macroeconomic effects in each time period and one can model these with $\mathbf{r}_t'\boldsymbol{\rho}_0 + \lambda_t$.

LSDV estimation becomes somewhat more complicated, but the principles are the same. Of course, neither $\boldsymbol{\gamma}_0$ nor $\boldsymbol{\rho}_0$ is estimable if α_n and λ_t are fixed effects, owing to the multicollinearity between the dummy variables and $\left[\mathbf{z}_n', \mathbf{r}_t'\right]'$. Therefore, without loss of generality one removes $\mathbf{z}_n'\boldsymbol{\gamma}_0 + \mathbf{r}_t'\boldsymbol{\rho}_0$ from the RHS under the fixed-effects specification. Nor are all of the α_n and λ_t separately identified, because both individual-specific and time-specific dummy variables sum to one over all observations creating multicollinearity among the dummy variables.

The LSDV fitted coefficients for $\boldsymbol{\beta}_0$ are the OLS coefficients from fitting $y_{nt} - \bar{y}_n - \bar{y}_t + \bar{\bar{y}}$ to $\mathbf{x}_{nt} - \bar{\mathbf{x}}_n - \bar{\mathbf{x}}_t + \bar{\bar{\mathbf{x}}}$ where $\bar{y}_t$ is the sample mean of y_{nt} in period t and $\bar{\mathbf{x}}_t$ is the vector of sample means for the elements in $\mathbf{x}_{nt}$.[9] One can see by inspection that this transformation removes both time and individual fixed effects:

$$\mathrm{E}[\bar{y}_n \mid \mathbf{X}, \boldsymbol{\alpha}, \boldsymbol{\lambda}] = \bar{\mathbf{x}}_n'\boldsymbol{\beta}_0 + \alpha_n + \bar{\lambda}$$
$$\mathrm{E}[\bar{y}_t \mid \mathbf{X}, \boldsymbol{\alpha}, \boldsymbol{\lambda}] = \bar{\mathbf{x}}_t'\boldsymbol{\beta}_0 + \bar{\alpha} + \lambda_t$$
$$\mathrm{E}[\bar{\bar{y}} \mid \mathbf{X}, \boldsymbol{\alpha}, \boldsymbol{\lambda}] = \bar{\bar{\mathbf{x}}}'\boldsymbol{\beta}_0 + \bar{\alpha} + \bar{\lambda}$$

where $\bar{\alpha} \equiv \mathrm{E}_N[\alpha_n]$ and $\bar{\lambda} \equiv \mathrm{E}_T[\lambda_t]$. Although the α_n and λ_t are not identified, OLS estimates of the overall level $\bar{\alpha} + \bar{\lambda}$ and the deviations $\alpha_n - \bar{\alpha}$ and $\lambda_t - \bar{\lambda}$ are easily found:

$$\widehat{\bar{\alpha} + \bar{\lambda}} = \bar{\bar{y}} - \bar{\bar{\mathbf{x}}}'\hat{\boldsymbol{\beta}}_{\mathrm{DV}}$$
$$\widehat{\alpha_n - \bar{\alpha}} = \bar{y}_n - \bar{\bar{y}} - \left(\bar{\mathbf{x}}_n - \bar{\bar{\mathbf{x}}}\right)'\hat{\boldsymbol{\beta}}_{\mathrm{DV}}$$
$$\widehat{\lambda_t - \bar{\lambda}} = \bar{y}_t - \bar{\bar{y}} - \left(\bar{\mathbf{x}}_t - \bar{\bar{\mathbf{x}}}\right)'\hat{\boldsymbol{\beta}}_{\mathrm{DV}}$$

[9] We justify this transformation as part of Exercise 26.22.

Researchers also extend the random-effects model to include time-specific effects. There is a natural way to do this: one adopts the second-moment restrictions

$$\begin{aligned} \operatorname{Var}[\boldsymbol{\alpha} \mid \mathbf{X}, \mathbf{Z}, \mathbf{R}] &= \sigma_{0\alpha}^2 \cdot \mathbf{I}_N, & \operatorname{Cov}[\boldsymbol{\varepsilon}, \boldsymbol{\alpha} \mid \mathbf{X}, \mathbf{Z}, \mathbf{R}] &= \mathbf{0} \\ \operatorname{Var}[\boldsymbol{\lambda} \mid \mathbf{X}, \mathbf{Z}, \mathbf{R}] &= \sigma_{0\lambda}^2 \cdot \mathbf{I}_T, & \operatorname{Cov}[\boldsymbol{\varepsilon}, \boldsymbol{\lambda} \mid \mathbf{X}, \mathbf{Z}, \mathbf{R}] &= \mathbf{0} \\ \operatorname{Var}[\boldsymbol{\varepsilon} \mid \mathbf{X}, \mathbf{Z}, \mathbf{R}] &= \sigma_{0\varepsilon}^2 \cdot \mathbf{I}_{NT} & \operatorname{Cov}[\boldsymbol{\alpha}, \boldsymbol{\lambda} \mid \mathbf{X}, \mathbf{Z}, \mathbf{R}] &= \mathbf{0} \end{aligned}$$

GLS then follows lines similar to those that we described for pure individual-specific effects. The estimator can be calculated by OLS regression of $y_{nt} - \omega_{01}\bar{y}_n - \omega_{02}\bar{y}_t + \omega_{03}\bar{\bar{y}}$ on $\mathbf{x}_{nt} - \omega_{01}\bar{\mathbf{x}}_n - \omega_{02}\bar{\mathbf{x}}_t + \omega_{03}\bar{\bar{\mathbf{x}}}$ where the constants ω_{01}, ω_{02}, and ω_{03} are functions of N, T, $\sigma_{0\alpha}^2$, $\sigma_{0\lambda}^2$, and $\sigma_{0\varepsilon}^2$.[10]

24.5.3 Dynamic Models

Lagged dependent explanatory variables commonly appear in models for panel data for the same reasons that they appear in one-dimensional time-series models. Unfortunately, parameter identification fails in simple dynamic specifications, as we will now show.

Suppose that one also observes y_{n0}. It is natural to specify that

$$\mathrm{E}[y_{nt} \mid \mathbf{X}, \boldsymbol{\alpha}, y_{n,0}, \ldots, y_{n,t-1}] = \phi_0 y_{n,t-1} + \mathbf{x}_{nt}'\boldsymbol{\beta}_0 + \alpha_n, \qquad n = 1, \ldots, N, \quad t = 1, \ldots, T \tag{24.27}$$

and $|\phi_0| < 1$ by analogy with (24.7). But this restriction will not identify ϕ_0 and $\boldsymbol{\beta}_0$ because the dynamics prevent us from finding a moment restriction marginal of α_n. For example, we cannot escape our difficulty by first differencing:

$$\begin{aligned} \mathrm{E}[y_{nt} - y_{n,t-1} \mid \mathbf{X}, y_{n,0}, \ldots, y_{n,t-1}] = {} & (\phi_0 - 1)\, y_{n,t-1} + \mathbf{x}_{nt}'\boldsymbol{\beta}_0 \\ & + \mathrm{E}[\alpha_n \mid y_{n,0}, \ldots, y_{n,t-1}] \end{aligned}$$

still includes a term in α_n.

Consider also our faithful fallback, the LSDV estimator. This is the OLS fitted coefficients from regressing $y_{nt} - \bar{y}_n$ on $y_{n,t-1} - \bar{y}_{n,-1}$ and $\mathbf{x}_{nt} - \bar{\mathbf{x}}_n$, where

$$\bar{y}_{n,-1} \equiv \mathrm{E}_T[y_{n,t-1}] \equiv \sum_{t=1}^{T} y_{n,t-1}\frac{1}{T}$$

In this case, if $t < T$, the RHS variable $y_{n,t-1} - \bar{y}_{n,-1}$ is a function of the original LHS variable y_{nt} so that one should anticipate trouble. If we try to derive the conditional mean of $y_{nt} - \bar{y}_n$ given these RHS variables, we realize that (24.27) does not imply what this conditional mean is. Such conditioning sets, where future values of y_{nt} appear in a deviation from the sample mean, are not covered. We conclude that the LSDV estimator is generally inconsistent.

Until our specification asserts something about the joint distribution of the $\{y_{nt};\ t = 0, \ldots, T\}$ *marginal* of α_n, identification will elude us. Latent variable models play a key role in the way that researchers build such specifications. For an example, Ahn and Schmidt (1997) and Blundell and Bond (1998) start with the latent variable equation

[10] Exercise 26.23 describes the deriviation of the GLS transformation and its weights ω_{01}, ω_{02}, and ω_{03}.

$$y_{nt} = \phi_0 y_{n,t-1} + \mathbf{x}'_{nt}\boldsymbol{\beta}_0 + \alpha_n + \varepsilon_{nt} \tag{24.28}$$

and assume that $\left[\alpha_n, \boldsymbol{\varepsilon}'_n, y_{n0}\right]'$ are independently distributed over individuals with conditional first moments

$$\begin{aligned} \mathrm{E}[\alpha_n \mid \mathbf{X}] &= 0 \\ \mathrm{E}[\boldsymbol{\varepsilon}_n \mid \mathbf{X}] &= \mathbf{0} \\ \mathrm{E}[y_{n0} \mid \mathbf{X}] &= \mu_0 \end{aligned}$$

and conditional second moments

$$\begin{aligned} \mathrm{Var}[\alpha_n \mid \mathbf{X}] &= \sigma^2_{0\alpha}, & \mathrm{Cov}[\alpha_n, \boldsymbol{\varepsilon}_n \mid \mathbf{X}] &= \mathbf{0} \\ \mathrm{Var}[\boldsymbol{\varepsilon}_n \mid \mathbf{X}] &= \sigma^2_{0\varepsilon} \cdot \mathbf{I}_T, & \mathrm{Cov}[y_{n0}, \boldsymbol{\varepsilon}_n \mid \mathbf{X}] &= \mathbf{0} \\ \mathrm{Var}[y_{n0} \mid \mathbf{X}] &= \omega^2_0, & \mathrm{Cov}[y_{n0}, \alpha_n \mid \mathbf{X}] &= \rho_0 \end{aligned}$$

These assumptions imply first- and second-conditional moment restrictions on functions of observable data:

$$\mathrm{E}\left[\begin{bmatrix} y_{n0} - \mu_0 \\ \mathbf{y}_n - \phi_0 \cdot \mathbf{y}_{n[-1]} - \mathbf{x}'_{nt}\boldsymbol{\beta}_0 \end{bmatrix} \mid \mathbf{X}\right] = \begin{bmatrix} 0 \\ \underset{T\times 1}{\mathbf{0}} \end{bmatrix} \tag{24.29}$$

$$\mathrm{Var}\left[\begin{bmatrix} y_{n0} \\ \mathbf{y}_n - \phi_0 \cdot \mathbf{y}_{n[-1]} \end{bmatrix} \mid \mathbf{X}\right] = \begin{bmatrix} \omega^2_0 & \rho_0 \cdot \boldsymbol{\iota}'_T \\ \rho_0 \cdot \boldsymbol{\iota}_T & \sigma^2_{0\alpha} \cdot \boldsymbol{\iota}_T \boldsymbol{\iota}'_T + \sigma^2_{0\varepsilon} \cdot \mathbf{I}_T \end{bmatrix} \tag{24.30}$$

where $\mathbf{y}_{n[-1]} \equiv \left[y_{n0}, \ldots, y_{T-1}\right]'$. In this way, Ahn and Schmidt extend the random-effects variance matrix (24.12) to include the variance and covariances of the initial observation y_{n0}.[11] Although y_{n0} remains homoskedastic and equicorrelated with $y_{nt} - \phi_0 y_{n,t-1}$, these second moments involving y_{n0} have different parameters because y_{n0} cannot appear in a quasi first difference with $y_{n,-1}$.

The conditional moment restrictions in (24.29)–(24.30) identify all of the unknown parameters. The identification of ϕ_0 comes through the specification of the $(T+1)\times(T+1)$ conditional variance matrix, which depends on just four unknown parameters. Ahn and Schmidt (1997, equations 3a–3c) write the implicit $(T+1)(T+2)/2 - 4$ restrictions as

$$\mathrm{E}[u_{nt}u_{ns} \mid \mathbf{X}] = \mathrm{E}[u_{n1}u_{n2} \mid \mathbf{X}] = \sigma^2_{0\alpha}, \qquad t = 3, \ldots, T \quad s = 1, \ldots, t-1 \tag{24.31}$$

$$\mathrm{E}[y_{n0}u_{nt} \mid \mathbf{X}] = \mathrm{E}[y_{n0}u_{n,t-1} \mid \mathbf{X}] = \rho_0, \qquad t = 2, \ldots, T \tag{24.32}$$

$$\mathrm{E}[u^2_{nt} \mid \mathbf{X}] = \mathrm{E}[u^2_{n,t-1} \mid \mathbf{X}] = \sigma^2_{0\alpha} + \sigma^2_{0\varepsilon}, \qquad t = 2, \ldots, T \tag{24.33}$$

where $u_{nt} \equiv y_{nt} - \phi_0 y_{n,t-1} - \mathbf{x}'_{nt}\boldsymbol{\beta}_0$. These translate one to one into the $(T+1)(T+2)/2 - 4$ orthogonality conditions

$$\mathrm{E}[y_{ns}\Delta u_{nt} \mid \mathbf{X}] = 0, \qquad t = 2, \ldots, T \quad s = 0, \ldots, t-2 \tag{24.34}$$

11 See also (among others) Arellano and Bond (1991), Holtz-Eakin (1988), Holtz-Eakin et al. (1988).

$$\mathrm{E}[u_{nT}\Delta u_{nt}\,|\,\mathbf{X}] = 0, \qquad t = 2, \ldots, T-1 \tag{24.35}$$

$$\mathrm{E}[\bar{u}_{nt}\Delta u_{nt}\,|\,\mathbf{X}] = 0, \qquad t = 2, \ldots, T \tag{24.36}$$

where $\Delta u_{nt} \equiv u_{nt} - u_{n,t-1} = \varepsilon_{nt} - \varepsilon_{n,t-1}$. In (24.34), we can interpret y_{ns} $(s = 0, \ldots, t-2)$ as an instrumental variable for a differenced (24.28):

$$\Delta y_{nt} = \phi_0 \Delta y_{n,t-1} + \Delta \mathbf{x}'_{nt}\boldsymbol{\beta}_0 + \Delta\varepsilon_{nt}, \qquad t = 2, \ldots, T \tag{24.37}$$

Along with functions of the $\mathbf{x}_{nt}$ $(t = 1, \ldots, T)$, these instruments identify ϕ_0 and $\boldsymbol{\beta}_0$. The restrictions in (24.35) correspond to using the Δu_{ns} for $s = 2, \ldots, T-1$ as instrumental variables for the final time period in levels:

$$y_{nT} = \phi_0 y_{n,T-1} + \mathbf{x}'_{nT}\boldsymbol{\beta}_0 + u_{nT} \tag{24.38}$$

Together (24.37)–(24.38) are a simple linear transformation of expressions for $\mathbf{y}_n$.[12]

One can also construct a GMM estimator from these conditional moment restrictions, but it is not possible to derive efficient instrumental variables without still more assumptions. One can certainly find the conditional expectation of partial derivatives of the moment functions with respect to the unknown parameters because these are all quadratic in the observable variables. The moment restrictions in (24.29)–(24.30) specify all the necessary expected values. However, conditional fourth-order moments determine the best GLS transformation of these partial derivatives and such moments remain unspecified. These can depend on the $\mathbf{x}_{nt}$ so that nonlinear functions of these variables are optimal instruments. Not knowing these functions, one must be content with intuitive choices of the instrumental variables.

24.6 SPECIFICATION TESTS

The random-effects model restricts the conditional mean of the individual effects to be independent of the observed explanatory variables. As we mentioned at the close of Section 24.3, this restriction often seems dubious in applications to economic data. Hausman (1978) proposes a specification test of $\mathrm{E}[\alpha_n\,|\,\mathbf{X}] = \alpha_0$, based on a comparison of the LSDV and random-effects estimators of $\boldsymbol{\beta}_0$ in the regression function $\mathrm{E}[y_{nt}\,|\,\mathbf{X},\mathbf{Z}] = \mathbf{x}'_{nt}\boldsymbol{\beta}_0 + \mathbf{z}'_n\boldsymbol{\gamma}_0$. He applied (22.25) along with the relative efficiency of the FGLS estimator under the null hypothesis to obtain the test statistic

$$HS = \left(\hat{\boldsymbol{\beta}}_{\mathrm{DV}} - \hat{\boldsymbol{\beta}}_{\mathrm{RE}}\right)' \left\{\widehat{\mathrm{Var}[\hat{\boldsymbol{\beta}}_{\mathrm{DV}}] - \mathrm{Var}[\hat{\boldsymbol{\beta}}_{\mathrm{RE}}]}\right\}^{-1} \left(\hat{\boldsymbol{\beta}}_{\mathrm{DV}} - \hat{\boldsymbol{\beta}}_{\mathrm{RE}}\right) \tag{24.39}$$

Under the null hypothesis, HS has a χ^2_K distribution.

EXAMPLE 24.1

Hausman and Taylor (1981) collected a panel data set of 750 males aged 25–55 observed in 2 years, 1968 and 1972, in the Michigan panel study of income dynamics (PSID) to estimate a wage equation.[13] They estimated the wage equation with OLS, LSDV, and random-effects FGLS

[12] Some researchers do not use the additional moment restrictions in (24.36). These rest on the homoskedasticity restrictions in (24.33), whereas (24.34)–(24.35) depend only on the equicovariance restrictions in (24.31)–(24.32).

[13] These individuals were not in the "Survey of Economic Opportunity" portion of the PSID sample.

and their estimates are reproduced in Table 24.1. The explanatory variables experience, years of schooling, time effects (not shown), and indicator variables for unemployed in the previous year, nonwhite, union membership, and bad health.

The nonwhite, union, and education coefficients are not estimable by LSDV. Therefore, the Hausman specification test compares the coefficients for experience, health, and previously unemployed in the last two columns. There is a particularly marked difference between the LSDV and random-effects estimates for the experience coefficient. The statistic HS equals 20.2, which has a probability value on the order of 10^{-4} for a chi-square distribution with 3 degrees of freedom. Hausman and Taylor conclude, therefore, that the differences in Table 24.1 are statistically significant and reject the random-effects specification.

Table 24.1.
Hausman-Taylor Log-Wage Equations for Panel Data Set

Explanatory Variable	OLS	LSDV	Random Effects
Experience	0.0132 (0.0011)	0.0241 (0.0042)	0.0133 (0.0017)
Bad health	−0.0483 (0.0412)	−0.0388 (0.0460)	−0.0300 (0.0363)
Unemployed previous year	−0.0015 (0.0267)	−0.0560 (0.0295)	−0.0402 (0.0207)
Nonwhite	−0.0853 (0.0328)	n.a.[a]	−0.0878 (0.0518)
Union member	0.0450 (0.0191)	n.a.	0.0374 (0.0296)
Education	0.0669 (0.0033)	n.a.	0.0676 (0.0052)
$\sqrt{s^2}$	0.321	0.160	0.192

[a] not applicable

The between-groups estimator is also consistent under the null hypothesis and inconsistent under the alternative. It follows that one can construct another Hausman specification test from a contrast between the within-groups and LSDV estimators. The specification test statistic for this contrast is, in fact, equal to the test statistic suggested by Hausman (1978).[14] Using (24.25),

$$\hat{\boldsymbol{\beta}}_{\text{DV}} - \hat{\boldsymbol{\beta}}_{\text{RE}}(\hat{\omega}) = \left[\mathbf{I}_K - \mathbf{A}(\hat{\omega})\right]\left(\hat{\boldsymbol{\beta}}_{\text{DV}} - \hat{\boldsymbol{\beta}}_{\text{B}}\right)$$

and

$$\hat{\boldsymbol{\beta}}_{\text{B}} - \hat{\boldsymbol{\beta}}_{\text{RE}}(\hat{\omega}) = -\mathbf{A}(\hat{\omega})\left(\hat{\boldsymbol{\beta}}_{\text{DV}} - \hat{\boldsymbol{\beta}}_{\text{B}}\right)$$

so that $\hat{\boldsymbol{\beta}}_{\text{DV}} - \hat{\boldsymbol{\beta}}_{\text{RE}}(\hat{\omega})$, $\hat{\boldsymbol{\beta}}_{\text{B}} - \hat{\boldsymbol{\beta}}_{\text{RE}}(\hat{\omega})$, and $\hat{\boldsymbol{\beta}}_{\text{DV}} - \hat{\boldsymbol{\beta}}_{\text{B}}$ are all nonsingular linear transformations of each other. In a quadratic form normalized by estimators of their variance matrices, these linear transformations cancel out and leave the same test statistic.

Note that this specification test also has the power to detect misspecified second moments. If $\text{E}[\alpha_n \mid \mathbf{X}] = \alpha_0$ but the variance matrix of $\mathbf{y}$ is not given by (24.12) and (24.13), then $\mathcal{HS}$ will

[14] See (among others) Hausman and Taylor (1981, Proposition 2.2).

not have an asymptotic distribution that is χ^2_K because the quadratic form (24.39) is normalized by an inconsistent estimator of the variance matrix. For this reason, one should generally think of this test statistic as a test of the *joint* hypothesis that

$$\mathrm{E}[\iota_T\alpha_n + \varepsilon_n \mid \mathbf{X}] = \iota_T\alpha_0 \qquad \text{and} \qquad \mathrm{Var}[\mathbf{y}_n \mid \mathbf{X}] = \sigma^2_{0\alpha}\cdot \iota_T\iota_T' + \sigma^2_{0\varepsilon}\cdot \mathbf{I}_T$$

One can construct alternative test statistics that are asymptotically equivalent if the variance matrix has the homoskedastic, equicorrelated functional form and that are still χ^2_K random variables under the null hypothesis $\mathrm{E}[\iota_T\alpha_n + \varepsilon_n \mid \mathbf{X}] = \alpha_0$ otherwise. Perhaps the simplest example is a comparison of the LSDV and between-groups estimators assuming conditional heteroskedasticity with equicorrelation:

$$\mathrm{Var}[\mathbf{y}_n \mid \mathbf{X}] = \mathrm{Var}[\iota_T\alpha_n + \varepsilon_n \mid \mathbf{X}] = \sigma^2_{0\alpha}(\mathbf{x}_n)\cdot \iota_T\iota_T' + \sigma^2_{0\varepsilon}(\mathbf{x}_{nt})\cdot \mathbf{I}_T \tag{24.40}$$

Under this restriction, the $\hat{\boldsymbol{\beta}}_{\mathrm{DV}}$ and $\hat{\boldsymbol{\beta}}_{\mathrm{B}}$ remain conditionally uncorrelated so that the variance of their difference is the *sum* of their variances. Therefore, the alternative test statistic is

$$\mathcal{HS} = \left(\hat{\boldsymbol{\beta}}_{\mathrm{DV}} - \hat{\boldsymbol{\beta}}_{\mathrm{B}}\right)'\left(\hat{\mathbf{V}}_{\mathrm{DV}} + \hat{\mathbf{V}}_{\mathrm{B}}\right)^{-1}\left(\hat{\boldsymbol{\beta}}_{\mathrm{DV}} - \hat{\boldsymbol{\beta}}_{\mathrm{B}}\right)$$

where

$$\hat{\mathbf{V}}_{\mathrm{DV}} \equiv \left(\mathbf{X}_{\mathrm{DV}}'\mathbf{X}_{\mathrm{DV}}\right)^{-1}\mathrm{E}_N\left[\mathbf{X}_{\mathrm{DV},n}'\hat{\boldsymbol{\varepsilon}}_{\mathrm{DV},n}\hat{\boldsymbol{\varepsilon}}_{\mathrm{DV},n}'\mathbf{X}_{\mathrm{DV},n}\right]\left(\mathbf{X}_{\mathrm{DV}}'\mathbf{X}_{\mathrm{DV}}\right)^{-1}$$
$$\hat{\mathbf{V}}_{\mathrm{B}} \equiv \left(\mathbf{X}_{\mathrm{B}}'\mathbf{X}_{\mathrm{B}}\right)^{-1}\mathrm{E}_N\left[\mathbf{x}_{\mathrm{B}n}'\hat{u}^2_{\mathrm{B}n}\mathbf{x}_{\mathrm{B}n}\right]\left(\mathbf{X}_{\mathrm{B}}'\mathbf{X}_{\mathrm{B}}\right)^{-1}$$

and

$$\mathbf{X}_{\mathrm{DV},n} \equiv \mathbf{X}_n - \iota_T\bar{\mathbf{x}}_n, \qquad \mathbf{x}_{\mathrm{B}n} \equiv \bar{\mathbf{x}}_n$$
$$\hat{\boldsymbol{\varepsilon}}_{\mathrm{DV},n} \equiv \mathbf{y}_n - \iota_T\bar{y}_n - \mathbf{X}_{\mathrm{DV},n}\hat{\boldsymbol{\beta}}_{\mathrm{DV}}, \qquad \hat{u}_{\mathrm{B}n} \equiv \bar{y}_n - \bar{\mathbf{x}}_n'\hat{\boldsymbol{\beta}}_{\mathrm{B}}$$

These two variance estimators are Eicker–White estimators, with $\hat{\mathbf{V}}_{\mathrm{DV}}$ a multivariate extension accounting for covariance among the observations for an individual. Without the equicorrelation restriction (24.40), an appropriate variance estimator is $\hat{\mathbf{V}}_{\mathrm{DV}} + \hat{\mathbf{V}}_{\mathrm{B}} + \hat{\mathbf{C}} + \hat{\mathbf{C}}'$ where

$$\hat{\mathbf{C}} \equiv \left(\mathbf{X}_{\mathrm{DV}}'\mathbf{X}_{\mathrm{DV}}\right)^{-1}\mathrm{E}_N\left[\mathbf{X}_{\mathrm{DV},n}'\hat{\boldsymbol{\varepsilon}}_{\mathrm{DV},n}\hat{u}_{\mathrm{B}n}\bar{\mathbf{x}}_{\mathrm{B}n}'\right]\left(\mathbf{X}_{\mathrm{B}}'\mathbf{X}_{\mathrm{B}}\right)^{-1}$$

If such tests suggest that the first-moment restriction of the random-effects model is false, or if this restriction is not credible, then one desires estimation without it. The fixed-effects estimator is always available, but it is not the only possibility. In the next section, we describe a generalization of the random-effects model that leads to an attractive alternative.

24.7 LINEAR PROJECTION

The fixed-effects and random-effects models are two extreme settings for the panel data regression function

$$\mathrm{E}[y_{nt} \mid \mathbf{X}, \mathbf{Z}, \boldsymbol{\alpha}] = \mathbf{x}_{nt}'\boldsymbol{\beta}_0 + \mathbf{z}_n'\boldsymbol{\gamma}_0 + \alpha_n \tag{24.41}$$

On one hand the fixed-effects model sets no restrictions on the behavior of the latent α_n and on the other hand the random-effects model asserts a strong conditional homogeneity given

$[\mathbf{X}, \mathbf{Z}]$. Chamberlain (1982) proposes a generalization of the conditional random-effects model that permits $\mathrm{E}[\alpha_n \mid \mathbf{X}, \mathbf{Z}]$ to be an unknown nonlinear function. But his model preserves enough homogeneity to make the MMSE linear predictor (or projection), $\mathrm{E}^*[\alpha_n \mid \mathbf{X}, \mathbf{Z}]$, a constant function of $\mathbf{X}_n$ and $\mathbf{z}_n$. This property also identifies $\boldsymbol{\beta}_0$ and leads to a new estimator.

Assume that the $\{(\mathbf{y}_n, \mathbf{x}_n, \mathbf{z}_n, \alpha_n)\,;\, n = 1, \ldots, N\}$ are i.i.d. random variables from a joint multivariate distribution with finite fourth moments, nonsingular $\mathrm{E}[\mathbf{w}_n \mathbf{w}_n']$ where $\mathbf{w}_n \equiv \left[\mathbf{x}_n', \mathbf{z}_n'\right]'$, and the conditional mean (24.41).[15] Let the conditional moments $\mathrm{E}[\alpha_n \mid \mathbf{X}, \mathbf{Z}]$ and $\mathrm{Var}[\alpha_n \mid \mathbf{X}, \mathbf{Z}]$ exist, but they may depend on $\mathbf{X}_n$ and $\mathbf{z}_n$. Under these conditions, the MMSE linear predictor of α_n given $\mathbf{X}$ exists. If we denote this predictor by

$$\mathrm{E}^*[\alpha_n \mid \mathbf{X}, \mathbf{Z}] = \mathbf{x}_n' \boldsymbol{\delta}_{0x} + \mathbf{z}_n' \boldsymbol{\delta}_{0z} + \alpha_0 \tag{24.42}$$

where $\boldsymbol{\delta}_{0x} \in \mathbb{R}^{TK}$ and $\boldsymbol{\delta}_{0z} \in \mathbb{R}^{J}$, then the MMSE linear predictor of y_{nt} given $\mathbf{X}$ is

$$\mathrm{E}^*[y_{nt} \mid \mathbf{X}, \mathbf{Z}] = \mathbf{x}_{nt}' \boldsymbol{\beta}_0 + \mathbf{z}_n' \boldsymbol{\gamma}_0 + \mathrm{E}^*[\alpha_n \mid \mathbf{X}, \mathbf{Z}] \tag{24.43}$$

$$= \mathbf{x}_{nt}' \boldsymbol{\beta}_0 + \mathbf{x}_n' \boldsymbol{\delta}_{0x} + \mathbf{z}_n' (\boldsymbol{\gamma}_0 + \boldsymbol{\delta}_{0z}) + \alpha_0 \tag{24.44}$$

in contrast to (24.8).[16]

24.7.1 Identification and OLS

In this setting, the identification of $\boldsymbol{\beta}_0$ is apparent through a simple OLS estimator of $\boldsymbol{\theta}_0 \equiv \left[\boldsymbol{\beta}_0', \boldsymbol{\delta}_{0x}', (\boldsymbol{\gamma}_0 + \boldsymbol{\delta}_{0z})'\right]'$. One can simply combine all of the observations in a single OLS regression of y_{nt} on $\mathbf{x}_{nt}$, $\mathbf{x}_n$, $\mathbf{z}_n$ and a constant. Multicollinearity between $\mathbf{x}_{nt}$ and $\mathbf{x}_n$ may appear to be an obstacle to this regression: $\mathbf{x}_{nt}$ is always a subvector of $\mathbf{x}_n \equiv \left[\mathbf{x}_{n1}', \ldots, \mathbf{x}_{nT}'\right]'$. However, if $\mathbf{X}$ is full-column rank, multicollinearity among these explanatory variables does not occur. The columns of $\mathbf{x}_n'$ in which $\mathbf{x}_{nt}'$ appears vary with t, ruling out multicollinearity over all observations.

Thus, we obtain a simple alternative to the LSDV estimator that requires no assumptions about the functional form of $\mathrm{E}[\alpha_n \mid \mathbf{X}, \mathbf{Z}]$, though the α_n are random effects. When N is large relative to TK, we expect this alternative estimator to be efficient relative to the fixed LSDV estimator because there are fewer additional parameters to estimate besides $\boldsymbol{\beta}_0$. The vector $\boldsymbol{\delta}_0$ contains TK elements compared to the N fixed effects in $\boldsymbol{\alpha}$.

Like the LSDV estimator, this OLS estimator does not estimate $\boldsymbol{\gamma}_0$. Under these assumptions, that parameter vector is not identified, although the linear combination $\boldsymbol{\gamma}_0 + \boldsymbol{\delta}_{0z}$ is estimated by OLS. In fact, one can leave $\mathbf{z}_n$ completely out of the estimation and replace (24.42) with

$$\mathrm{E}^*[\mathbf{z}_n' \boldsymbol{\gamma}_0 + \alpha_n \mid \mathbf{X}] = \mathbf{x}_n \boldsymbol{\delta}_{0x} + \alpha_0 \tag{24.45}$$

It may be preferable to include $\mathbf{z}_n$ if it substantially reduces the variance of the residual term and, as a result, reduces the sampling variance of the estimator of $\boldsymbol{\beta}_0$ more than the added estimation of $\boldsymbol{\gamma}_0 + \boldsymbol{\delta}_{0z}$ increases it. For convenience, we will follow Chamberlain, drop $\mathbf{z}_n$ from our analysis, adopt (24.45) over (24.42), and restrict $\boldsymbol{\theta}_0 \equiv \left[\boldsymbol{\beta}_0', \boldsymbol{\delta}_{0x}'\right]$ in the remainder of this section.

Estimation of the variance matrix of this OLS estimator can take into account possible conditional covariance and heteroskedasticity among the prediction residuals $y_{nt} - \mathrm{E}^*[y_{nt} \mid \mathbf{x}_n]$.

---

[15] We alter some of the details, but not the spirit, of Chamberlain's (1982) analysis.

[16] See (24.26) also.

The Eicker–White approach does this when we apply it to the *vector* of T observations for each individual because these are uncorrelated across $n = 1, \ldots, N$. If we denote the complete explanatory variable matrix for $\mathbf{y}_n$ by

$$\mathbf{B}_n \equiv \begin{bmatrix} \mathbf{b}'_{n1} \\ \vdots \\ \mathbf{b}'_{nT} \end{bmatrix}$$

where

$$\mathbf{b}_{nt} \equiv \left[\mathbf{x}'_{nt}, \mathbf{x}'_{n}\right]', \ t = 1, \ldots, T$$

then the OLS estimator of $\boldsymbol{\theta}_0$ is

$$\hat{\boldsymbol{\theta}}_{\text{OLS}} = \left(\text{E}_N[\mathbf{B}'_n\mathbf{B}_n]\right)^{-1} \text{E}_N[\mathbf{B}'_n\mathbf{y}_n]$$

The $\mathbf{B}'_n\mathbf{B}_n$ and $\mathbf{B}'_n\mathbf{y}_n$ terms contain summation over the time index t. Denoting the OLS fitted residuals by $\hat{\mathbf{u}}_n \equiv \mathbf{y}_n - \mathbf{B}_n\hat{\boldsymbol{\theta}}_{\text{OLS}}$, the Eicker–White variance estimator for $\text{Var}(\sqrt{N}\hat{\boldsymbol{\theta}}_{\text{OLS}})$ is

$$\left(\text{E}_N[\mathbf{B}'_n\mathbf{B}_n]\right)^{-1} \text{E}_N[\mathbf{B}'_n\hat{\mathbf{u}}_n\hat{\mathbf{u}}'_n\mathbf{B}_n] \left(\text{E}_N[\mathbf{B}'_n\mathbf{B}_n]\right)^{-1}$$

which is a consistent estimator of the limiting variance of $\sqrt{N}\left(\hat{\boldsymbol{\theta}}_{\text{OLS}} - \boldsymbol{\theta}_0\right)$ as $N \to \infty$.[17]

24.7.2 Efficient Estimation

To construct a relatively efficient estimator, Chamberlain applies a two-step minimum distance procedure that exploits covariance among observations in different time periods.

Step 1: Estimate the coefficients of

$$\begin{aligned} \mathbf{x}'_{nt}\boldsymbol{\beta}_0 + \mathbf{x}'_n\boldsymbol{\delta}_{0x} + \alpha_0 &= \mathbf{x}'_{nt}\left(\boldsymbol{\beta}_0 + \boldsymbol{\delta}_{0t}\right) + \sum_{\substack{s=1 \\ s\neq t}}^{T} \mathbf{x}'_{ns}\boldsymbol{\delta}_{0s} + \alpha_0 \\ &= \mathbf{x}'_n\boldsymbol{\pi}_{0t} + \alpha_0 \end{aligned}$$

with the unconstrained OLS regression of y_{nt} on $\mathbf{x}_n$ $(n = 1, \ldots, N)$ and a constant for each time period t. Let $\hat{\boldsymbol{\pi}}_t$ $(t = 1, \ldots, T)$ denote the OLS fitted coefficients for $\boldsymbol{\pi}_{0t}$. Jointly, these $\hat{\boldsymbol{\pi}}_t$ are a GMM estimator for which the usual variance estimator is[18]

$$\underset{KT^2\times KT^2}{\widehat{\text{Var}[\hat{\boldsymbol{\pi}}]}} = \left[\frac{1}{N}\cdot\hat{\mathbf{G}}^{-1}\hat{\boldsymbol{\Lambda}}_{ts}\hat{\mathbf{G}}^{-1};\ t, s = 1, \ldots, T\right]$$

where

[17] One may also interpret this as the GMM variance estimator (21.32) corresponding to the GMM estimator

$$\hat{\boldsymbol{\theta}}_{\text{OLS}} = \underset{\boldsymbol{\theta}}{\text{argmin}} \left\{\text{E}_N[\mathbf{B}'_n(\mathbf{y}_n - \mathbf{B}_n\boldsymbol{\theta})]\right\}' \left\{\text{E}_N[\mathbf{B}'_n(\mathbf{y}_n - \mathbf{B}_n\boldsymbol{\theta})]\right\}$$

[18] There is another notational subtlety here: we refer to the empirical mean of the $\mathbf{x}_n$ as $\bar{\mathbf{x}}$. Recall that the empirical mean of the $\mathbf{x}_{nt}$ is $\bar{\bar{\mathbf{x}}}$ and the empirical mean of $\mathbf{x}_{nt}$ for a fixed n is $\bar{\mathbf{x}}_n$.

$$\underset{KT\times KT}{\hat{\mathbf{G}}} = \mathrm{E}_N[(\mathbf{x}_n - \bar{\mathbf{x}})(\mathbf{x}_n - \bar{\mathbf{x}})'] = \mathrm{Var}_N(\mathbf{x}_n)$$

$$\underset{KT\times KT}{\hat{\mathbf{\Lambda}}_{ts}} = \mathrm{E}_N[(\mathbf{x}_n - \bar{\mathbf{x}})\,\hat{u}_{nt}\hat{u}_{ns}\,(\mathbf{x}_n - \bar{\mathbf{x}})']$$

and

$$\hat{u}_{nt} \equiv y_{nt} - \bar{y}_t - (\mathbf{x}_n - \bar{\mathbf{x}})'\,\hat{\boldsymbol{\pi}}_t, \qquad \hat{\boldsymbol{\pi}} \equiv \left[\hat{\boldsymbol{\pi}}_t\right]$$

$$\bar{\mathbf{x}} \equiv \mathrm{E}_N[\mathbf{x}_n] = \left\{\mathrm{E}_N[\mathbf{x}'_{n1}], \ldots, \mathrm{E}_N[\mathbf{x}'_{nT}]\right\}', \qquad \bar{y}_t \equiv \mathrm{E}_N[y_{nt}]$$

Step 2: Estimate $\boldsymbol{\beta}_0$ with the minimum distance estimator

$$\hat{\boldsymbol{\theta}}_{\mathrm{MD}} = \begin{bmatrix} \hat{\boldsymbol{\beta}}_{\mathrm{MD}} \\ \hat{\boldsymbol{\delta}}_{\mathrm{MD}} \end{bmatrix} \equiv \underset{\boldsymbol{\beta},\boldsymbol{\delta}}{\mathrm{argmin}} \left[\hat{\boldsymbol{\pi}} - \boldsymbol{\pi}(\boldsymbol{\beta}, \boldsymbol{\delta})\right]' \left[\widehat{\mathrm{Var}(\hat{\boldsymbol{\pi}})}\right]^{-1} \left[\hat{\boldsymbol{\pi}} - \boldsymbol{\pi}(\boldsymbol{\beta}, \boldsymbol{\delta})\right]$$

where

$$\boldsymbol{\pi}(\boldsymbol{\beta}, \boldsymbol{\delta}) = \left[\boldsymbol{\pi}_t(\boldsymbol{\beta}, \boldsymbol{\delta})'\right]'$$
$$\boldsymbol{\pi}_t(\boldsymbol{\beta}, \boldsymbol{\delta}) = \left[(\mathbf{1}\{t = s\} \cdot \boldsymbol{\beta} + \boldsymbol{\delta}_s)';\ s = 1, \ldots, T\right]' \tag{24.46}$$

Then, according to Proposition 22 (Minimum Distance Estimation, p. 595),

$$\sqrt{N}\left(\hat{\boldsymbol{\theta}}_{\mathrm{MD}} - \boldsymbol{\theta}_0\right) \xrightarrow{d} \mathfrak{N}(\mathbf{0}, \mathbf{W}_0)$$

where $\mathbf{W}_0$ is estimated consistently by

$$\hat{\mathbf{W}} = \left(\frac{\partial \boldsymbol{\pi}(\hat{\boldsymbol{\beta}}_{\mathrm{MD}}, \hat{\boldsymbol{\delta}}_{\mathrm{MD}})'}{\partial \boldsymbol{\lambda}} \left[\widehat{\mathrm{Var}[\hat{\boldsymbol{\pi}}]}\right]^{-1} \frac{\partial \boldsymbol{\pi}(\hat{\boldsymbol{\beta}}_{\mathrm{MD}}, \hat{\boldsymbol{\delta}}_{\mathrm{MD}})}{\partial \boldsymbol{\lambda}'}\right)^{-1} \tag{24.47}$$

Minimum distance estimators are typically asymptotically equivalent to a GMM estimator (Proposition 23, p. 596). The GMM estimator corresponding to $\hat{\boldsymbol{\theta}}_{\mathrm{MD}}$ uses the $T\,(1 + K + TK)$ moment restrictions

$$\mathbf{0} = \mathrm{E}[(y_{nt} - \mathbf{x}'_{nt}\boldsymbol{\beta}_0 - \mathbf{x}'_n\boldsymbol{\delta}_{0x} - \alpha_0)]$$

and

$$\mathbf{0} = \mathrm{E}[\mathbf{b}_{nt}(y_{nt} - \mathbf{x}'_{nt}\boldsymbol{\beta}_0 - \mathbf{x}'_n\boldsymbol{\delta}_{0x} - \alpha_0)]$$
$$= \mathrm{E}[\mathbf{b}_{nt}(y_{nt} - \mathbf{b}'_{nt}\boldsymbol{\theta}_0)]$$

We can stack these by t to create a complete vector of all empirical moments:

$$\mathbf{g}(\boldsymbol{\theta}) = \left[(y_{nt} - \mathbf{b}'_{nt}\boldsymbol{\theta})[1, \mathbf{b}'_{nt}];\ t = 1, \ldots, T\right]'$$

Using an initial estimator like $\hat{\boldsymbol{\pi}}$ to compute fitted residuals $\hat{u}_{nt}$, we compute the empirical covariance matrices

$$\hat{\mathbf{\Lambda}}_{ts} = \mathrm{E}_N\left[[1, \mathbf{b}'_{nt}]'\hat{u}_{nt}\hat{u}_{ns}[1, \mathbf{b}'_{ns}]\right]$$

and

$$\begin{bmatrix} \hat{\boldsymbol{\theta}}_{\text{GMM}} \\ \hat{\alpha}_{\text{GMM}} \end{bmatrix} \equiv \underset{\boldsymbol{\theta},\alpha_0}{\operatorname{argmin}}\, \mathbf{g}_N(\boldsymbol{\theta})'\hat{\boldsymbol{\Lambda}}^{-1}\mathbf{g}_N(\boldsymbol{\theta})$$

where $\mathbf{g}_N(\boldsymbol{\theta}) \equiv \mathrm{E}_N[\mathbf{g}(\boldsymbol{\theta})]$ and $\hat{\boldsymbol{\Lambda}} \equiv \left[\hat{\boldsymbol{\Lambda}}_{ts}\right]$. Because the restrictions (24.46) are linear, this $\hat{\boldsymbol{\theta}}_{\text{GMM}}$ is identically equal to Chamberlain's MD estimator.

24.7.3 Diagnostic Tests

The projection model rests on the i.i.d. sampling assumption. The restrictions that this implies may be tested because the parameters are overidentified. The MD approach has a natural role in such diagnostic testing because estimation begins with the unrestricted estimator. One can proceed progressively from the unrestricted toward the most restricted model using a sequence of test statistics that is independently distributed under the null hypothesis.[19]

EXAMPLE 24.2

Chamberlain (1982) provides an example with log-wage regressions for a sample of 1454 men from the U.S. panel of Young Men in the National Longitudinal Survey (Parnes). He selected individuals who were not enrolled in school in 1969, 1970, or 1971 and whose data were complete for every dependent and explanatory variable. His unrestricted least-squares regression contains dummy variables for union-covered job, race, residence in the southern United States, and residence in a standard metropolitan statistical area (SMSA) as well as a constant, schooling, experience, and experience squared. He interacted the union dummy variables for all three years.

First, Chamberlain imposes the cross-year restrictions on the SMSA and region coefficients. The minimized GMM function equals 6.82, which is a random draw from the χ^2_{10} distribution under the null hypothesis. This is not a surprising value. Second, he imposes the restrictions on the union coefficients as well. The increase in the minimized GMM function equals $19.36 - 6.82 = 12.54$, which is an independent random draw from the χ^2_{13} distribution if the additional restrictions hold. This also is consistent with the comparison distribution and Chamberlain concludes that there is no evidence against the restrictions of the projection model.

We can also view $\hat{\boldsymbol{\beta}}_{\text{MD}}$ as an estimator that does not impose the restrictions that $\mathrm{E}[\alpha_n \mid \mathbf{X}] = 0$. When these hold, we have additional restrictions that $\boldsymbol{\delta}_{0t} = 0$ $(t = 1, \ldots, T)$. This suggests an MD counterpart to the random-effects estimator:

$$\hat{\boldsymbol{\beta}}_{\text{MD,R}} \equiv \underset{\boldsymbol{\beta}}{\operatorname{argmin}}\left[\hat{\boldsymbol{\pi}} - \boldsymbol{\pi}(\boldsymbol{\beta}, \mathbf{0})\right]'\left(\widehat{\mathrm{Var}[\hat{\boldsymbol{\pi}}]}\right)^{-1}\left[\hat{\boldsymbol{\pi}} - \boldsymbol{\pi}(\boldsymbol{\beta}, \mathbf{0})\right] \tag{24.48}$$

This estimator does not impose the second-moment restrictions (24.11) of the random-effects model and it will be efficient relative to the simple OLS estimator. One can construct a Hausman specification test for $\mathrm{E}[\alpha_n \mid \mathbf{X}] = 0$ comparing $\hat{\boldsymbol{\beta}}_{\text{MD}}$ and $\hat{\boldsymbol{\beta}}_{\text{MD,R}}$. Alternatively, one can test all of the overidentifying restrictions using the minimum chi-square test statistic

$$\mathcal{MC} = \left[\hat{\boldsymbol{\pi}} - \boldsymbol{\pi}(\hat{\boldsymbol{\beta}}_{\text{MD,R}}, \mathbf{0})\right]'\left(\widehat{\mathrm{Var}[\hat{\boldsymbol{\pi}}]}\right)^{-1}\left[\hat{\boldsymbol{\pi}} - \boldsymbol{\pi}(\hat{\boldsymbol{\beta}}_{\text{MD,R}}, \mathbf{0})\right]$$

[19] See Lemma 22.2 (Minimum Chi-Square II, p. 588) and Section 22.6.

Such a test will have a chi-square distribution with $KT^2 - K$ degrees of freedom under the null hypothesis that all of the moment restrictions hold.

24.8 ADDITIONAL MOMENT RESTRICTIONS

Researchers have proposed various additional moment restrictions that provide identification of γ_0 when $\mathrm{E}[\alpha_n \mid \mathbf{X}, \mathbf{Z}] \neq 0$. We will explain one example as restrictions on Chamberlain's model. Therefore we reintroduce γ_0 and $\mathbf{z}_n$, returning to the initial specification in (24.42) and (24.44):

$$\mathrm{E}^*[\alpha_n \mid \mathbf{X}, \mathbf{Z}] = \mathbf{x}_n' \delta_{0x} + \mathbf{z}_n' \delta_{0z} + \alpha_0 \tag{24.49}$$

$$\mathrm{E}^*[y_{nt} \mid \mathbf{X}, \mathbf{Z}] = \mathbf{x}_{nt}' \boldsymbol{\beta}_0 + \mathbf{x}_n' \delta_{0x} + \mathbf{z}_n' (\gamma_0 + \delta_{0z}) + \alpha_0 \tag{24.50}$$

Hausman and Taylor (1981) add the assumption that a subvector of the explanatory variables is uncorrelated with α_n. Let us partition

$$\mathbf{x}_{nt}' \boldsymbol{\beta}_0 = \mathbf{x}_{1nt}' \boldsymbol{\beta}_{01} + \mathbf{x}_{2nt}' \boldsymbol{\beta}_{02}$$

and

$$\mathbf{z}_n' \gamma_0 = \mathbf{z}_{1n}' \gamma_{01} + \mathbf{z}_{2n}' \gamma_{02}$$

where $\mathbf{x}_{1nt}$ contains K_1 variables and $\mathbf{z}_{1n}$ contains J_1 variables. Following these researchers, we will assume that $\mathbf{x}_{1nt}$ and $\mathbf{z}_{1n}$ are uncorrelated with α_n. In other words, these variables are valid instruments.

In the next section, we review the identification of γ_0 under these new assumptions. It turns out that the validity of $\mathbf{z}_{1n}$ as an instrumental variable is not enough to identify γ_{01}. Identification rests first on identifying γ_{02} through instrumental variables provided by $\mathbf{x}_{1nt}$. Following this, we briefly describe the extension of Chamberlain's estimator to this context and GMM alternatives based on conditional mean restrictions.

24.8.1 Identification

The zero correlations imply new restrictions on the parameters of (24.49). By integrating out the $\mathbf{x}_{2ns}$ $(s = 1, \ldots, T)$ and $\mathbf{z}_n$, we obtain

$$\begin{aligned}
\mathrm{E}^*[\alpha_n \mid \mathbf{X}_1, \mathbf{Z}_1] &= \alpha_0 \\
&= \mathbf{x}_{1n}' \delta_{0x_1} + \mathrm{E}^*[\mathbf{x}_{2n}' \mid \mathbf{X}_1, \mathbf{Z}_1] \delta_{0x_2} \\
&\quad + \mathbf{z}_{1n}' \delta_{0z_1} + \mathrm{E}^*[\mathbf{z}_{2n}' \mid \mathbf{X}_1, \mathbf{Z}_1] \delta_{0z_2} + \alpha_0
\end{aligned}$$

where $\mathbf{x}_{jn} \equiv \left[\mathbf{x}_{jn1}', \ldots, \mathbf{x}_{jnT}'\right]'$ $(j = 1, 2)$, $\delta_{0x} = \left[\delta_{0x_1}', \delta_{0x_2}'\right]'$ and $\delta_{0z} = \left[\delta_{0z_1}', \delta_{0z_2}'\right]'$. If we denote

$$\mathrm{E}^*[\mathbf{x}_{2n} \mid \mathbf{X}_1, \mathbf{Z}_1] = \underset{1 \times TK_1}{\mathbf{x}_{1n}'} \underset{TK_1 \times TK_2}{\xi_{0x}} + \underset{1 \times J_1}{\mathbf{z}_{1n}'} \underset{J_1 \times TK_2}{\xi_{0z}} \tag{24.51}$$

$$\mathrm{E}^*[\mathbf{z}_{2n} \mid \mathbf{X}_1, \mathbf{Z}_1] = \underset{1 \times TK_1}{\mathbf{x}_{1n}'} \underset{TK_1 \times J_2}{\zeta_{0x}} + \underset{1 \times J_1}{\mathbf{z}_{1n}'} \underset{J_1 \times J_2}{\zeta_{0z}} \tag{24.52}$$

then $E^*[\alpha_n \mid \mathbf{X}_1, \mathbf{Z}_1]$ will be constant if and only if the coefficients of $\mathbf{x}_{1n}$ and $\mathbf{z}_{1n}$ are zero. That is,

$$\mathbf{0} = \delta_{0x_1} + \xi_{0x}\delta_{0x_2} + \zeta_{0x}\delta_{0z_2} \tag{24.53}$$

$$\mathbf{0} = \delta_{0z_1} + \xi_{0z}\delta_{0x_2} + \zeta_{0z}\delta_{0z_2} \tag{24.54}$$

These restrictions can identify δ_{0z}. Because δ_{0x} is already identified (see Section 24.7.1), and ξ_{0x}, ξ_{0z}, ζ_{0x}, and ζ_{0z} are identified, (24.53)–(24.54) is a pair of linear equations in the unknown δ_{0z_2} and δ_{0z_1}. Moreover, these equations are recursive. Equation (24.53) identifies δ_{0z_2} if $TK_1 \geq J_2$ and $\text{rank}(\zeta_{0x}) = J_2$. The variables in $\mathbf{x}_{1n}$ are acting, in effect, as instrumental variables for $\mathbf{z}_{2n}$.[20] Equation (24.54) identifies δ_{0z_1} conditional on the identification of δ_{0z_2}. Because $\mathbf{z}_{1n}$ serves as its own instrumental variable, no additional instruments are required once δ_{0z_2} is identified.

The identification of δ_{0z} implies the identification of γ_0. We have already seen that $\gamma_0 + \delta_{0z}$ is identified in Chamberlain's projection model without the additional restrictions provided by assuming that $[\mathbf{x}_{1n}, \mathbf{z}_{1n}]$ are valid instrumental variables for α_n. Having established that δ_{0z} is identified, we see that the identification of γ_0 follows immediately.

24.8.2 Estimation

Chamberlain's two-step minimum distance estimator applies straightforwardly. In the first step, one also estimates the parameters in (24.51)–(24.52) and one includes these estimates in the distance function of the second step, which is minimized subject to (24.46) and (24.53)–(24.54). Alternatively, one can use GMM directly by including the additional moment restrictions

$$\mathbf{0} = E[\mathbf{w}_{1n}(\mathbf{x}_{2n} - \mathbf{x}_{1n}\xi_{0x} - z_{1n}\xi_{0z})]$$

$$\mathbf{0} = E[\mathbf{w}_{1n}(\mathbf{z}_{2n} - \mathbf{x}_{1n}\zeta_{0x} - z_{1n}\zeta_{0z})]$$

where $\mathbf{w}_{1n} \equiv [\mathbf{x}_{1n}, \mathbf{z}_{1n}]$.

Without the i.i.d. restriction of the projection model, one can still apply GMM to the moment restrictions. If the projection model is valid, such estimators will be inefficient relative to Chamberlain's estimator. But under certain conditions they remain consistent when the i.i.d. assumption fails and the projections are not constant across individuals.

All of the estimators that appear in the literature make efficient use of a chosen set of moments through GMM. The variety of estimators illustrates how the chosen moments can vary in the absence of sufficient structure to guide an optimal choice. Following Arellano and Bover (1995), suppose that we specify the conditional moment restrictions

$$E[\mathbf{y}_n \mid \mathbf{X}, \mathbf{Z}, \alpha_n] = \underset{T\times(K+J)}{\mathbf{W}_n} \underset{(K+J)\times 1}{\delta_0} + \iota_T\alpha_n$$

$$E[\alpha_n \mid \mathbf{X}_1, \mathbf{Z}_1] = \alpha_0$$

where $\mathbf{W}_n \equiv [\mathbf{w}_{n1}, \ldots, \mathbf{w}_{nT}]'$, $\mathbf{w}_{nt} \equiv \left[\mathbf{x}_{nt}', \mathbf{z}_n'\right]'$, and $\delta_0 \equiv \left[\beta_0', \gamma_0'\right]'$. Note that these are stronger restrictions than the marginal covariance restrictions of Hausman and Taylor (1981), but they have the same spirit. Written in terms of observable variables, these restrictions are

[20] See Amemiya and MaCurdy (1986).

$$\mathrm{E}[\mathbf{y}_n \mid \mathbf{X}, \mathbf{Z}] = \mathbf{W}_n \boldsymbol{\delta}_0 + \iota_T \, \mathrm{E}[\alpha_n \mid \mathbf{X}, \mathbf{Z}] \tag{24.55}$$

$$\mathrm{E}[\mathbf{y}_n \mid \mathbf{X}_1, \mathbf{Z}_1] = \mathbf{W}_{1n} \boldsymbol{\delta}_{01} + \mathrm{E}[\mathbf{W}_{2n} \mid \mathbf{X}_1, \mathbf{Z}_1] \boldsymbol{\delta}_{02} + \alpha_0 \tag{24.56}$$

which contain two nuisance parameters in addition to the elements of $\boldsymbol{\delta}_0$ that we seek to estimate. We are confronted, as usual, with $\mathrm{E}[\alpha_n \mid \mathbf{X}, \mathbf{Z}]$ and, in addition, with $\mathrm{E}[\mathbf{W}_{2n} \mid \mathbf{X}_1, \mathbf{Z}_1]$.

Given any transformation matrix $\mathbf{D}$ such that $\mathbf{D}\iota_T = \mathbf{0}$, we can eliminate the α_n term, obtaining the moments

$$\mathrm{E}[\mathbf{D}\mathbf{y}_n \mid \mathbf{X}, \mathbf{Z}] = \mathbf{D}\mathbf{W}_n \boldsymbol{\delta}_0 = \mathbf{D}\mathbf{X}_n \boldsymbol{\beta}_0$$

Two $\mathbf{D}$ matrices are particularly common. One is based on the orthogonal projector that takes deviations from the sample mean:

$$\mathbf{D}\mathbf{y}_n = [y_{nt} - \bar{y}_n; \; t = 1, \ldots, T]$$

Another takes first differences through time:

$$\mathbf{D}\mathbf{y}_n = \left[y_{nt} - y_{n,t-1}; \; t = 2, \ldots, T\right] = [\Delta y_{nt}]$$

The latter is convenient for considering models that involve predetermined variables. In general, $\mathbf{D}$ is a sort of difference operator that eliminates $\mathrm{E}[\alpha_n \mid \mathbf{x}_n]$ without losing moment restrictions. For the sake of concreteness, we will adopt the deviations from sample mean.

We cannot sweep away the $\mathrm{E}[\mathbf{W}_{2n} \mid \mathbf{X}_1, \mathbf{Z}_1]$ so easily. Researchers have generally left this part of the model unspecified. As a result, our statistical theorems provide no guidance toward an optimal estimator. This is not a deficiency in the model or in the theory. One should not make artificial assumptions merely for the sake of specifying an (artificial) optimal estimator. Nor should one expect optimal estimators to appear out of thin air. The assumptions may need to be a bit thicker.

The literature takes a conservative posture, assigning the same $\mathbf{w}_n \equiv \left[\mathbf{x}_n', \mathbf{z}_n'\right]'$ as instruments to each element of $\mathbf{D}(\mathbf{y}_n - \mathbf{W}_n \boldsymbol{\delta}_0)$ and the same $\mathbf{w}_{1n} \equiv \left[\mathbf{x}_{1n}', \mathbf{z}_{1n}', 1\right]'$ to each element of $\mathbf{y}_n - \mathbf{W}_n \boldsymbol{\delta}_0$. Thus, researchers replace (24.55)–(24.56) with the weaker restrictions

$$\mathbf{0} = \mathrm{E}\left[\mathbf{w}_n \left[y_{nt} - \bar{y}_n - (\mathbf{w}_{nt} - \bar{\mathbf{w}}_n)' \boldsymbol{\delta}_0\right]\right], \qquad t = 2, \ldots, T \tag{24.57}$$

$$\mathbf{0} = \mathrm{E}\left[\mathbf{w}_{1n} \left(y_{nt} - \mathbf{w}_{nt}' \boldsymbol{\delta}_0 - \alpha_0\right)\right], \qquad t = 1, \ldots, T \tag{24.58}$$

where $\bar{\mathbf{w}}_n \equiv \mathrm{E}_T[\mathbf{w}_{nt}]$. This reduction introduces linear dependence among these moment functions:[21] the deviation from sample mean of an element in (24.58) is a subvector of an element in (24.57). Therefore, we can reduce (24.58) further to a single linear combination that is linearly independent of (24.58).[22]

The particular linear combination is arbitrary without additional assumptions. If $\mathrm{Var}(\mathbf{y}_n | \mathbf{W}_n)$ has the equicorrelated structure of the random-effects model, for example, then we can anticipate

21 In general, different nonlinear functions of $\mathbf{w}_n$ and $\mathbf{w}_{1n}$ can serve as instrumental variables for each residual. Therefore, this linear dependence is an artifact of selecting these instrumental variables.

22 Arellano and Bover (1995, p. 34) show that the diagonal structure of the instrument matrix for $\mathbf{D}(\mathbf{y}_n - \mathbf{x}_n' \boldsymbol{\delta})$ implies that the efficient GMM estimator is invariant to the choice of $\mathbf{D}$. However, this is not so for the linear combination of $\mathbf{y}_n - \mathbf{x}_n' \boldsymbol{\delta}$ that removes the linear dependence among the moment functions. If the conditional variance of $\mathbf{y}_n$ were constant and known, then we could use that to make an optimal choice. Otherwise, the particular linear combination is arbitrary.

that the sample mean is the best choice. We know that the GLS estimator is a weighted average of within-groups and between-groups sample variation. We already have the within-groups component in the elements of (24.57). The sample mean of the elements of (24.58) provides the between-groups component.

Now, after all this reduction, we are down to

$$\mathbf{0} = \mathrm{E}[\mathbf{w}_n (y_{nt} - \bar{y}_n - (\mathbf{w}_{nt} - \bar{\mathbf{w}}_n)' \delta_0)], \qquad t = 2, \ldots, T$$
$$\mathbf{0} = \mathrm{E}\left[\mathbf{w}_{1n} \left(\bar{y}_n - \bar{\mathbf{w}}_n' \delta_0 - \alpha_0\right)\right]$$

which we can write in matrix form as $\mathrm{E}[\mathbf{C}_n' (\mathbf{y}_n - \mathbf{W}_n \delta_0 - \alpha_0)] = \mathbf{0}$. The feasible efficient GMM estimator for this vector of moment functions is, therefore,

$$\hat{\delta} = \left\{\mathrm{E}_N[\mathbf{W}_n' \mathbf{C}_n] \left(\mathrm{E}_N[\mathbf{C}_n' \hat{\mathbf{u}}_n \hat{\mathbf{u}}_n' \mathbf{C}_n]\right)^{-1} \mathrm{E}_N[\mathbf{C}_n' \mathbf{W}_n]\right\}^{-1}$$
$$\mathrm{E}_N[\mathbf{W}_n' \mathbf{C}_n] \left(\mathrm{E}_N[\mathbf{C}_n' \hat{\mathbf{u}}_n \hat{\mathbf{u}}_n' \mathbf{C}_n]\right)^{-1} \mathrm{E}_N[\mathbf{C}_n' \mathbf{y}_n]$$

where $\hat{\mathbf{u}}_n$ are the fitted residuals from an initial consistent estimator. This estimator is proposed by Arellano and Bover (1995) as a generalization of several other estimators. They show that $\hat{\delta}$ simplifies to Amemiya and MaCurdy's (1986) estimator if one restricts the estimation of the conditional variance of $\mathbf{y}_n$ to be homoskedastic and equicorrelated. If one also reduces the instruments $\mathbf{w}_{1n}$ to $\left[\bar{\mathbf{x}}_{1n}', \mathbf{z}_n', 1\right]'$, then the original Hausman and Taylor (1981) estimator results.

Researchers continue to experiment with the specification of moment restrictions and the choice of instrument matrix $\mathbf{C}_n$. Dynamic models, which we previously introduced, receive special attention. For additional information, one may consult the general references cited at the close of Section 24.5.

24.9 MATHEMATICAL NOTES

In these mathematical notes, we construct an OLS equivalent to GLS for the random-effects specification in Section 24.3. We find a matrix square root for the inverse of the variance matrix (24.12). Rewriting (24.17),

$$\mathrm{Var}[\mathbf{y}_n \mid \mathbf{X}] = \left(T\sigma_{0\alpha}^2 + \sigma_{0\varepsilon}^2\right) \cdot \mathbf{P}_{\iota T} + \sigma_{0\varepsilon}^2 \cdot \left(\mathbf{I}_T - \mathbf{P}_{\iota T}\right)$$

multiplication confirms that[23]

$$(\mathrm{Var}[\mathbf{y}_n \mid \mathbf{X}])^{-1} = \frac{1}{T\sigma_\alpha^2 + \sigma_\varepsilon^2} \cdot \mathbf{P}_{\iota T} + \frac{1}{\sigma_\varepsilon^2} \cdot \left(\mathbf{I}_T - \mathbf{P}_{\iota T}\right) \tag{24.59}$$

$$= \left[\frac{1}{\sqrt{T\sigma_{0\alpha}^2 + \sigma_{0\varepsilon}^2}} \cdot \mathbf{P}_{\iota T} + \frac{1}{\sigma_{0\varepsilon}} \cdot \left(\mathbf{I}_T - \mathbf{P}_{\iota T}\right)\right]^2 \tag{24.60}$$

$$= \sigma_{0\varepsilon}^{-2} \cdot \left[\mathbf{I}_T - (1 - \omega_0) \cdot \mathbf{P}_{\iota T}\right]^2$$

[23] This inverse follows from the more general observation that

$$[a \cdot (\mathbf{I} - \mathbf{P}_\iota) + b \cdot \mathbf{P}_\iota][c \cdot (\mathbf{I} - \mathbf{P}_\iota) + d \cdot \mathbf{P}_\iota] = ac \cdot (\mathbf{I} - \mathbf{P}_\iota) + bd \cdot \mathbf{P}_\iota$$

See Graybill (1969), Maddala (1971), Nerlove (1971), and Wallace and Hussain (1969).

where $\omega_0 \equiv \sigma_{0\varepsilon} / \sqrt{T\sigma_{0\alpha}^2 + \sigma_{0\varepsilon}^2}$. Therefore, given ω_0, for GLS we simply regress

$$\underset{NT\times 1}{\mathbf{y}_*} \equiv \left[\left[\mathbf{y}_n - (1-\omega_0)\cdot \mathbf{P}_{\iota_T}\mathbf{y}_n\right]';\ n = 1, \ldots, N\right]'$$
$$= [[y_{nt} - (1-\omega_0)\,\bar{y}_n;\ t = 1, \ldots, T];\ n = 1, \ldots, N]'$$

on the columns of the matrix

$$\underset{NT\times K}{\mathbf{X}_*} \equiv \left[\left[\mathbf{X}_n - (1-\omega_0)\cdot \mathbf{P}_{\iota_T}\mathbf{X}_n\right]';\ n = 1, \ldots, N\right]'$$
$$= \left[\left[\left[\mathbf{x}_{nt} - (1-\omega_0)\cdot \bar{\mathbf{x}}_n\right]';\ t = 1, \ldots, T\right];\ n = 1, \ldots, N\right]'$$

and a column of ones.[24] These are the transformed variables given in (24.15)–(24.16).

To derive the matrix-weighted average in (24.18), we must isolate the fitted coefficients for $\boldsymbol{\beta}$. According to the OLS partitioned regression formula, we can accomplish this by replacing the variables in $\mathbf{y}_*$ and $\mathbf{X}_*$ with deviations from their sample means.[25] Using (24.21), the sample mean of both y_{nt} and $\bar{y}_n$ is $\bar{\bar{y}}$ and the sample mean of both $\mathbf{x}_{nt}$ and $\bar{\mathbf{x}}_n$ is $\bar{\bar{\mathbf{x}}}$. Therefore, the sample mean of $\mathbf{y}_*$ is $\omega_0\bar{\bar{y}}$ and the random-effects estimator of $\boldsymbol{\beta}_0$ corresponds to OLS applied to the LHS vector

$$\begin{aligned}
\left(\mathbf{I}_{NT} - \mathbf{P}_{\iota_{NT}}\right)\mathbf{y}_* &= \mathbf{y}_* - \iota_{NT}\omega_0\bar{\bar{y}} \\
&= \left[\left[y_{nt} - \bar{\bar{y}} - (1-\omega_0)\left(\bar{y}_n - \bar{\bar{y}}\right)\right]\right]' \\
&= \left[\left[y_{nt} - \bar{y}_n + \omega_0\left(\bar{y}_n - \bar{\bar{y}}\right)\right]\right]' \\
&= \left[\left[\mathbf{y}_n - \iota_T\bar{y}_n + \omega_0\cdot\iota_T\left(\bar{y}_n - \bar{\bar{y}}\right)\right]'\right]' \\
&= \left[\left[\left(\mathbf{I}_T - \mathbf{P}_{\iota_T}\right)\mathbf{y}_n + \omega_0\cdot\mathbf{P}_{\iota_T}\left(\mathbf{y}_n - \iota_T\bar{\bar{y}}\right)\right]'\right]'
\end{aligned}$$

where the inner $[\cdot]$ gathers over $t = 1, \ldots, T$ as in $\mathbf{y}_*$ and $\mathbf{X}_*$ above. Similarly, the RHS matrix is

$$\left(\mathbf{I}_{NT} - \mathbf{P}_{\iota_{NT}}\right)\mathbf{X}_* = \left[\left[\left(\mathbf{I}_T - \mathbf{P}_{\iota_T}\right)\mathbf{X}_n + \omega_0\cdot\mathbf{P}_{\iota_T}\left(\mathbf{X}_n - \iota_T\bar{\bar{\mathbf{x}}}\right)\right]'\right]'$$

Now we will put these terms together to form $\hat{\boldsymbol{\beta}}_{\mathrm{RE}}$. Because $\mathbf{P}_{\iota_T}$ and $\mathbf{I}_T - \mathbf{P}_{\iota_T}$ are complementary orthogonal projectors,

$$\left[\left(\mathbf{I}_T - \mathbf{P}_{\iota_T}\right)\mathbf{X}_n\right]'\mathbf{P}_{\iota_T}\left(\mathbf{y}_n - \iota_T\bar{\bar{y}}\right) = \mathbf{0}$$

In addition, $\mathbf{P}_{\iota_T}$ and $\mathbf{I}_T - \mathbf{P}_{\iota_T}$ are idempotent so that

$$\begin{aligned}
\left[\mathbf{P}_{\iota_T}\left(\mathbf{X}_n - \iota_T\bar{\bar{\mathbf{x}}}\right)\right]'\mathbf{P}_{\iota_T}\left(\mathbf{y}_n - \iota_T\bar{\bar{y}}\right) &= \left(\mathbf{X}_n - \iota_T\bar{\bar{\mathbf{x}}}\right)'\mathbf{P}_{\iota_T}\left(\mathbf{y}_n - \iota_T\bar{\bar{y}}\right) \\
&= \left(\iota_T\bar{\mathbf{x}}_n - \iota_T\bar{\bar{\mathbf{x}}}\right)'\left(\iota_T\bar{y}_n - \iota_T\bar{\bar{y}}\right) \\
&= T\cdot\left(\bar{\mathbf{x}}_n - \bar{\bar{\mathbf{x}}}\right)'\left(\bar{y}_n - \bar{\bar{y}}\right)
\end{aligned}$$

and

[24] Actually, the constant 1 is transformed into the constant ω_0. But it is equivalent to use a column of ones or a column of ω_0s.

[25] See Proposition 2 (Partitioned Fit, p. 57) and Exercise 3.4.

$$\mathbf{X}_*' \left(\mathbf{I}_{NT} - \mathbf{P}_{\iota_{NT}}\right) \mathbf{y}_* = \sum_{n=1}^{N} \mathbf{X}_n' \left(\mathbf{I}_T - \mathbf{P}_{\iota_T}\right) \mathbf{y}_n + \omega_0^2 \cdot \left(\mathbf{X}_n - \iota_T \bar{\bar{\mathbf{x}}}\right) \mathbf{P}_{\iota_T} \left(\mathbf{y}_n - \iota_T \bar{\bar{y}}\right)$$
$$= \mathbf{X}_{\mathrm{DV}}' \mathbf{y}_{\mathrm{DV}} + T\omega_0^2 \cdot \mathbf{X}_{\mathrm{B}}' \mathbf{y}_{\mathrm{B}}$$

where

$$\mathbf{X}_{\mathrm{DV}} \equiv \left[\left[\left(\mathbf{I}_T - \mathbf{P}_{\iota_T}\right) \mathbf{X}_n\right]'\right]' = \left[\left[\mathbf{x}_{nt} - \bar{\mathbf{x}}_n\right]\right]'$$
$$\mathbf{y}_{\mathrm{DV}} \equiv \left[\left[\left(\mathbf{I}_T - \mathbf{P}_{\iota_T}\right) \mathbf{y}_n\right]'\right]' = \left[\left[y_{nt} - \bar{y}_n\right]\right]'$$

as in (24.5) and (24.20) defines $\mathbf{X}_{\mathrm{B}}$ and $\mathbf{y}_{\mathrm{B}}$. Similarly,

$$\mathbf{X}_*' \left(\mathbf{I}_{NT} - \mathbf{P}_{\iota_{NT}}\right) \mathbf{X}_* = \mathbf{X}_{\mathrm{DV}}' \mathbf{X}_{\mathrm{DV}} + T\omega_0^2 \cdot \mathbf{X}_{\mathrm{B}}' \mathbf{X}_{\mathrm{B}}$$

Therefore, we can write

$$\hat{\boldsymbol{\beta}}_{\mathrm{GLS}} = \left[\mathbf{X}_*' \left(\mathbf{I}_{NT} - \mathbf{P}_{\iota_{NT}}\right) \mathbf{X}_*\right]^{-1} \mathbf{X}_*' \left(\mathbf{I}_{NT} - \mathbf{P}_{\iota_{NT}}\right) \mathbf{y}_*$$
$$= \left(\mathbf{X}_{\mathrm{DV}}' \mathbf{X}_{\mathrm{DV}} + T\omega_0^2 \cdot \mathbf{X}_{\mathrm{B}}' \mathbf{X}_{\mathrm{B}}\right)^{-1} \left(\mathbf{X}_{\mathrm{DV}}' \mathbf{y}_{\mathrm{DV}} + T\omega_0^2 \cdot \mathbf{X}_{\mathrm{B}}' \mathbf{y}_{\mathrm{B}}\right)$$
$$= \mathbf{A}_0 \hat{\boldsymbol{\beta}}_{\mathrm{DV}} + \left(\mathbf{I}_K - \mathbf{A}_0\right) \hat{\boldsymbol{\beta}}_{\mathrm{B}}$$

where

$$\mathbf{A}_0 \equiv \left(\mathbf{X}_{\mathrm{DV}}' \mathbf{X}_{\mathrm{DV}} + T\omega_0^2 \cdot \mathbf{X}_{\mathrm{B}}' \mathbf{X}_{\mathrm{B}}\right)^{-1} \mathbf{X}_{\mathrm{DV}}' \mathbf{X}_{\mathrm{DV}}$$

as in (24.22).

24.10 OVERVIEW

1. Panel data contain (at least) two ways in which the observations are replicated, typically across individuals and time periods. Concern and interest focus on covariance among the observations across time periods, of which there are relatively few.
2. The basic regression function for models of panel data contains an individual-specific effect α_n:

$$\mathrm{E}[y_{nt} \mid \mathbf{X}, \boldsymbol{\alpha}] = \mathbf{x}_{nt}' \boldsymbol{\beta}_0 + \alpha_n, \qquad n = 1, \ldots, N \quad t = 1, \ldots, T$$

   Provided that the $\mathbf{x}_{nt}$ and the dummy variables $d_{ntk} \equiv \mathbf{1}\{n = k\}$, $k = 1, \ldots, N$ are linearly independent, one can estimate both $\boldsymbol{\beta}_0$ and $\boldsymbol{\alpha} \equiv [\alpha_n]'$ by OLS. This estimator is called the LSDV. Only $\boldsymbol{\beta}_0$ is estimated consistently.
3. If the α_n are i.i.d. random variables conditional on $\mathbf{X}$, then a GLS estimator is relatively efficient. This estimator is a matrix-weighted average of the LSDV estimator and the between estimator, which is the OLS fit of variables averaged over time for each individual.
4. One cannot estimate coefficients for time-invariant explanatory variables with LSDV. The random-effects specification does identify such parameters and GLS continues to provide consistent, relatively efficient estimators. The general approach also applies to time-specific effects and individual-invariant explanatory variables.

5. Lagged dependent explanatory variables require additional structure to identify the parameters of the conditional expectation

$$\mathrm{E}[y_{nt} \mid \mathbf{X}, \boldsymbol{\alpha}, y_{n,0}, \ldots, y_{n,t-1}] = \phi_0 y_{n,t-1} + \mathbf{x}_{nt}'\boldsymbol{\beta}_0 + \alpha_n, \qquad n = 1, \ldots, N \quad t = 1, \ldots, T$$

For example,

$$\mathrm{E}[\alpha_n \mid \mathbf{X}] = 0, \qquad \mathrm{E}[\boldsymbol{\varepsilon}_n \mid \mathbf{X}] = \mathbf{0}, \qquad \mathrm{E}[y_{n0} \mid \mathbf{X}] = \mu_0$$

and

$$\begin{aligned} \mathrm{Var}[\alpha_n \mid \mathbf{X}] &= \sigma_{0\alpha}^2, & \mathrm{Cov}[\alpha_n, \boldsymbol{\varepsilon}_n \mid \mathbf{X}] &= \mathbf{0} \\ \mathrm{Var}[\boldsymbol{\varepsilon}_n \mid \mathbf{X}] &= \sigma_{0\varepsilon}^2 \cdot \mathbf{I}_T, & \mathrm{Cov}[y_{n0}, \boldsymbol{\varepsilon}_n \mid \mathbf{X}] &= \mathbf{0} \\ \mathrm{Var}[y_{n0} \mid \mathbf{X}] &= \omega_0^2, & \mathrm{Cov}[y_{n0}, \alpha_n \mid \mathbf{X}] &= \rho_0 \end{aligned}$$

provide sufficient moment restrictions marginal of α_n to identify the regression coefficients $[\phi_0, \boldsymbol{\beta}_0']'$.

6. A principal concern with the random-effects specification is that the α_n may be correlated with some of the variables $\mathbf{x}_{nt}$. Hausman specification tests provide ways to detect this. Chamberlain's projection specification relaxes this assumption.

24.11 EXERCISES

24.11.1 Review

24.1 **(LSDV)** Show that when $T = 2$ the LSDV estimator of $\boldsymbol{\beta}_0$ in (24.1) is equivalent to OLS fitted coefficients from a regression of $y_{n2} - y_{n1}$ on $\mathbf{x}_{n2} - \mathbf{x}_{n1}$.

24.2 **(LSDV)** Show that, for $N \to \infty$ and T fixed, $\hat{\boldsymbol{\beta}}_{\mathrm{DV}}$ is a consistent estimator of $\boldsymbol{\beta}_0$ but the $\hat{\alpha}_n$, $n = 1, \ldots, N$, are not consistent estimators of the α_n.

24.3 **(LSDV)** Show that the OLS estimator is a matrix-weighted average of the LSDV and between-groups estimators, $\hat{\boldsymbol{\beta}}_{\mathrm{DV}}$ and $\hat{\boldsymbol{\beta}}_{\mathrm{B}}$, respectively.

24.4 **(OLS)** Consider the OLS estimator of $\mathrm{E}[y_{nt} \mid \mathbf{X}] = \mathbf{x}_{nt}'\boldsymbol{\beta}_0 + \alpha_0$ given that $y_{nt} = \mathbf{x}_{nt}'\boldsymbol{\beta}_0 + \alpha_n + \varepsilon_{nt}$ and (24.10)–(24.11) hold.

(a) What does the sample variance of the OLS fitted residuals estimate?

(b) Explain how to estimate the variance matrix of the OLS fitted coefficients.

24.5 **(Equicorrelation)** Consider estimation of the parameters of the equicorrelated variance matrix $\boldsymbol{\Omega}_0 = \sigma_{0\varepsilon}^2 \cdot \left[(1-\rho_0) \cdot \mathbf{I}_T + \rho_0 \cdot \boldsymbol{\iota}_T \boldsymbol{\iota}_T'\right]$ given an observed vector $\mathbf{y}$ with $\mathrm{E}[\mathbf{y}] = \mathbf{0}$ and $\mathrm{Var}[\mathbf{y}] = \boldsymbol{\Omega}_0$.

(a) Show that

$$\det \boldsymbol{\Omega}_0 = \sigma_{0\varepsilon}^{2T} \left[1 + (T-1)\rho_0\right](1-\rho_0)^{T-1}$$

(HINT: Use recursively the partitioned matrix determinant formula in Exercise 10.6.)

(b) What restrictions do positive definiteness of $\boldsymbol{\Omega}_0$ place on ρ_0? Does ρ_0 have to be positive?

24.6 (Feasible GLS) The estimators of variances in (24.23)–(24.24) contain an implicit estimator of $\sigma_{0\alpha}^2$.

(a) What is this estimator?

(b) Show that this estimator can be negative.

(c) What would a negative estimate of $\sigma_{0\alpha}^2$ suggest?

***24.7 (OLS versus GLS)** Let $\mathrm{E}[\mathbf{y} \mid \mathbf{X}] = \mathbf{X}\boldsymbol{\beta}_0$. If

$$\mathrm{Var}[\mathbf{y} \mid \mathbf{X}] = \sigma_{0\varepsilon}^2 \cdot \mathbf{I} + \sigma_{0\alpha}^2 \cdot \iota_T \iota_T'$$

the dependent data are conditionally equicorrelated. Show that if a constant is one of the explanatory variables then OLS and GLS are identical estimators. (HINT: Use Lemma 19.1.) Extend this equivalence to estimation of the random-effects model (24.9)–(24.11), normalizing $\alpha_0 = 0$.

24.8 Suggest a consistent estimator for the asymptotic variance of the LSDV estimator even if there is conditional heteroskedasticity and covariance across the observations of each individual over time.

24.9 (Hausman Test) Reconsider the Hausman specification test for the random-effects model (24.9)–(24.11).

(a) Construct a Hausman specification test statistic using the difference between the OLS and LSDV estimators.

(b) Show that this test statistic is identical to Hausman's test statistic under the random-effects specification (24.12) of the conditional variance of $\mathbf{y}_n$. [HINT: Show first that $\hat{\boldsymbol{\beta}}_{\mathrm{RE}}(1) = \hat{\boldsymbol{\beta}}_{\mathrm{OLS}} = \mathbf{A}(1)\hat{\boldsymbol{\beta}}_{\mathrm{DV}} + [\mathbf{I}_K - \mathbf{A}(1)]\,\hat{\boldsymbol{\beta}}_{\mathrm{B}}$ where $\mathbf{A}(\cdot)$ is defined in (24.22).]

(c) Generalize the test to cases in which the conditional variance of $\mathbf{y}_n$ is heteroskedastic and not equicorrelated.

(d) Derive an asymptotically equivalent gradient test statistic.

24.10 (Dynamic Models) The dynamic panel data model begins with (24.27), which is analogous to the static specification (24.7). We might also assume that

$$\mathrm{E}[\alpha_n \mid \mathbf{X}, y_{n,0}, \ldots, y_{n,t-1}] = \alpha_0 \tag{24.61}$$

by analogy with (24.8). Show that these two restrictions imply that α_n equals α_0 with probability one.

24.11 (Unbalanced Panel Data) In many panel data sets, the number of time periods available for each individual varies.

(a) Describe the LSDV estimator for such cases.

(b) Describe also the random-effects (GLS) estimator.

(c) Finally, describe a feasible random-effects estimator.

24.12 (MD) Reconsider the two-step restricted MD estimator in (24.48). Alternatively, one can reduce the dimension of the first step of estimation by imposing $\boldsymbol{\delta} = 0$ at that stage as well.

(a) Describe the two steps of this alternative restricted MD estimator.

(b) Explain why this alternative estimator is generally inefficient relative to (24.48).

(c) What sort of considerations in small samples might lead one to prefer this alternative estimator?

(d) Describe the Hausman specification test for $\boldsymbol{\delta}_0 = \mathbf{0}$ and compare this test with a test for the validity of the overidentifying moment restrictions.

24.13 (Hausman Test) Within the model of Chamberlain (1982) in Section 24.7, explain how to compute a Hausman specification test for $\mathrm{E}[\alpha_t \mid \mathbf{X}] = 0$ from the difference between the fitted coefficients from OLS regression of y_{nt} on $[\mathbf{x}_{nt}, 1]$ and the fitted coefficients of $\mathbf{x}_{nt}$ from OLS regression of y_{nt} on $[\mathbf{x}_{nt}, \mathbf{x}_n, 1]$.

24.14 (Linear Projection) The unrestricted estimation of the variance matrix (24.47) in Chamberlain's minimum distance estimator may be a liability in small samples if the population variance is conditionally homoskedastic. Suggest an alternative estimator that imposes the restrictions of homoskedasticity. Also explain how one might impose equicorrelation if this additional set of restrictions seemed appropriate.

24.15 (ML) Find the log-likelihood function for the random-effects panel data model, assuming that the latent variables are multivariate normal. Compare the MLE with the estimators discussed in this chapter.

24.16 (Heterogeneity) Suppose that $K < T$ and that the $y_{nt}, n = 1, \ldots, N, t = 1, \ldots, T$, are conditionally normally distributed in addition to the random-effects specification [(24.9)–(24.11)]. How could you test whether the slope coefficients are equal for all individuals against the alternative hypothesis that

$$y_{nt} = \mathbf{x}'_{nt}\boldsymbol{\beta}_{0n} + \alpha_n + \varepsilon_{nt}$$

How does your answer change if $K \geq T$?

24.11.2 Extensions

24.17 (Partitioned OLS) One can estimate the coefficients of the LSDV model with two steps: (1) take deviations from individual means and (2) fit these deviations with OLS. Extend this method to a model with a set of individual-specific slope coefficients:

$$\mathrm{E}[y_{nt} \mid \mathbf{x}_{nt}] = \mathbf{x}'_{1nt}\boldsymbol{\beta}_{10} + \mathbf{x}'_{2nt}\boldsymbol{\beta}_{n20}$$

Explain how to obtain the OLS fitted coefficients for both $\boldsymbol{\beta}_{10}$ and all of the $\boldsymbol{\beta}_{n20}$, $n = 1, \ldots, N$, given that all of the $\boldsymbol{\beta}$s are identified.

24.18 Derive the score test statistic

$$S = \frac{N}{2(T-1)} \left\{ \frac{\mathrm{Var}_N[T\,\mathrm{E}_T[\hat{\varepsilon}_{nt}]]}{\mathrm{Var}_{NT}[\hat{\varepsilon}_{nt}]} - 1 \right\}$$

for $\sigma^2_{0\alpha} = 0$ in the random-effects model [(24.9)–(24.11).[26] The log-likelihood function permits $\sigma^2_{0\alpha} < 0$ (Exercise 24.5). What are the implications for likelihood-ratio and Wald tests of this hypothesis?

24.19 Show that errors in variables can be overcome in a panel setting.[27]

24.20 (IV) Consider generalizing Chamberlain (1982) to instrumental variables estimation. Suppose that

$$y_{nt} = \mathbf{x}'_{nt}\boldsymbol{\beta}_0 + \alpha_n + \varepsilon_{nt}$$

and that $\mathbf{x}_{nt}$ contains elements that are correlated with ε_{nt} as well as α_n. Suppose also that there are instrumental variables $\mathbf{w}_{nt}$ that are correlated with $\mathbf{x}_{nt}$ but not ε_{nt} so that

$$\mathrm{E}^*[y_{nt} \mid \mathbf{w}_n] = \mathrm{E}^*[\mathbf{x}'_{nt} \mid \mathbf{w}_n]\boldsymbol{\beta}_0 + \mathrm{E}^*[\alpha_n \mid \mathbf{w}_n]$$

Give conditions so that $\boldsymbol{\beta}_0$ is identified and describe an estimation method.

---

26 See Breusch and Pagan (1980).

27 See Hsiao (1986, Section 3.9).

24.21 (Projection) Reconsider the panel data model in (24.42) and (24.44) with the additional moment restrictions in Section 24.8. Bhargava and Sargan (1983) and Breusch et al. (1989) suggest assuming also that $\mathrm{Cov}[\mathbf{x}_{2nt}, \alpha_n]$ is a constant vector of covariances.

(a) Show that this implies that $(T-1)\,K_2$ additional variables are uncorrelated with α_n and that one may take these variables to be $\Delta\mathbf{x}_{2nt} \equiv \mathbf{x}_{2nt} - \mathbf{x}_{2n,t-1}$ for $t = 2, \ldots, T$.

(b) How do these additional moment restrictions alter the estimation methods described in Section 24.8.2?

(c) Show that we may just as well take the additional instruments to be $\Delta\mathbf{X}_2 \equiv [\mathbf{x}_{2nt} - \bar{\mathbf{x}}_{2n}]'$ and use $\mathrm{E}^*[\bar{\mathbf{x}}_{2n} \mid \mathbf{X}_1, \mathbf{Z}_1, \Delta\mathbf{X}_2]$.

CHAPTER 25

AUTOREGRESSIVE MOVING-AVERAGE TIME SERIES MODELS

25.1 INTRODUCTION

For time-series data, latent-component models are central to parsimonious models of the autocorrelation. Stipulating that

$$y_t = \mathbf{x}_t'\boldsymbol{\beta}_0 + \varepsilon_t, \qquad \mathrm{E}[\varepsilon_t \mid \mathbf{x}_t] = 0 \tag{25.1}$$

a common approach models the latent disturbance ε_t in terms of uncorrelated, possibly independent, latent components whose variance captures covariance among observable variables. The random-effects panel data model is an example. The time series for an individual is autocorrelated by the presence of a latent random individual effect. Such specifications have the drawback that the covariances do not diminish over time, an observable phenomenon in lengthy time series. In addition, the covariance must be positive because it equals the variance of the random individual effect.

In this chapter, we describe another family of specifications for autocorrelation called *autoregressive moving-average* (ARMA) models. One can construct these models from linear combinations of the elements of a sequence of latent variables called *white noise*: let $\{u_t\} = \{\ldots, u_{-1}, u_0, u_1, \ldots\}$ be a sequence of random variables with

$$\mathrm{E}[u_t] = 0, \qquad \mathrm{Var}[u_t] = \sigma_{0u}^2 < \infty, \qquad \text{and } \mathrm{E}[u_t u_s] = 0,\ t \neq s$$

A *moving average* of the white noise phases out shared latent components:

$$\varepsilon_t = u_t + \psi_0 u_{t-1}, \qquad t = 1, \ldots, T$$

In this example, a particular u_s enters only ε_s and ε_{s+1}, rather than all ε_t as in panel data models. In addition, the second contribution of u_s in ε_{s+1} is altered by the coefficient ψ_0. The implied autocovariance structure of this moving-average specification is

$$\mathrm{Var}[\varepsilon_t] = \sigma_{0u}^2 + \psi_0^2\sigma_{0u}^2 = \sigma_{0u}^2\left(1 + \psi_0^2\right)$$
$$\mathrm{Cov}[\varepsilon_t, \varepsilon_{t-1}] = \sigma_{0u}^2\psi_0$$

$$\text{Cov}[\varepsilon_t, \varepsilon_{t-s}] = 0, \qquad s = 2, 3, \ldots, t-1$$

Thus, all autocovariances for the sequence $\{\varepsilon_t\}$ two or more periods apart are zero. Also, the sign of $\text{Cov}[\varepsilon_t, \varepsilon_{t-1}]$ depends on the sign of the parameter ψ_0.

Another possibility is to phase out the past less abruptly through an *autoregression*: in Chapter 19 we introduced the first-order autoregressive specification

$$\varepsilon_t = \phi_0 \varepsilon_{t-1} + u_t, \quad t = 1, \ldots, T$$

In this case, the autocovariances obey the difference equation

$$\text{Cov}[\varepsilon_t, \varepsilon_{t-s}] = \phi_0 \, \text{Cov}[\varepsilon_{t-1}, \varepsilon_{t-s}], \qquad s = 1, 2, \ldots, t-1$$

If and only if $|\phi_0| < 1$, this equation has the steady-state solution

$$\text{Cov}[\varepsilon_t, \varepsilon_{t-s}] = \phi_0^s \, \text{Var}[\varepsilon_t], \qquad s = 0, 1, 2, \ldots, t-1 \tag{25.2}$$

so that the autocovariances die out geometrically with the number of time periods between realizations. Furthermore, the autocovariances are all positive or alternate in sign, depending on whether ϕ_0 is positive or negative.

These specifications are not mutually exclusive. We can combine them into the *autoregressive moving-average* process

$$\varepsilon_t = \phi_0 \varepsilon_{t-1} + u_t + \psi_0 u_{t-1}$$

This yields a stochastic process $\{\varepsilon_t\}$ that has a mixture of the behavior of the autoregressive and moving-average processes provided that $\phi_0 \neq \psi_0$.[1] Given this, the *order* of the autocovariances is geometric $[O(\phi^s)]$, but their pattern is not strictly geometric.

All three examples are illustrated in Figure 25.1 using the values $\psi_0 = -0.4$, $\phi_0 = 0.6$, and $\sigma_{0u}^2 = 1$. The moving-average [MA(1)] example has a positive variance followed by a negative first-order autocovariance. Higher order autocovariances are zero. The autoregressive [AR(1)] example exhibits positive autocovariances that diminish 60% each period. The autoregressive moving-average [ARMA(1,1)] example shows a much lower first-order autocovariance because of its moving-average component, but additional autocovariances also diminish at the 60% rate.

As a brief empirical example, we return to the estimation of the Phillips curve by Staiger et al. (1996), which we introduced in Section 19.1. With experience, one might expect the first-order autoregressive model that we used to capture serial correlation to be inadequate. Monthly macroeconomic time series often exhibit more complex autocorrelation functions. Even without experience, there is evidence in our previous analysis that points toward possible model deficiency. First, the estimated autocorrelation function does not follow a pattern of geometric decay; the second- and third-order correlations have the same magnitude. Second, the OLS estimates appear to have smaller standard errors than the FGLS estimates [compare equations (19.4) and (19.28)]. The GLS estimator generally requires a correctly specified variance matrix to produce relatively efficient estimators.

We can produce an additional symptom with a higher-order OLS autoregression of the OLS fitted residuals of (19.2) on their lagged values; a score test for second-order autoregressive correlation applies to these fitted residuals as well. If a higher order AR specification is appropriate, this test has power to detect this. The OLS fit of the OLS residual $\hat{\varepsilon}_t$ to $\hat{\varepsilon}_{t-1}$ and $\hat{\varepsilon}_{t-2}$ is

[1] If these parameters are equal, then $\varepsilon_t = u_t$ is observationally equivalent and the parameters ϕ_0 and ψ_0 cannot be identified.

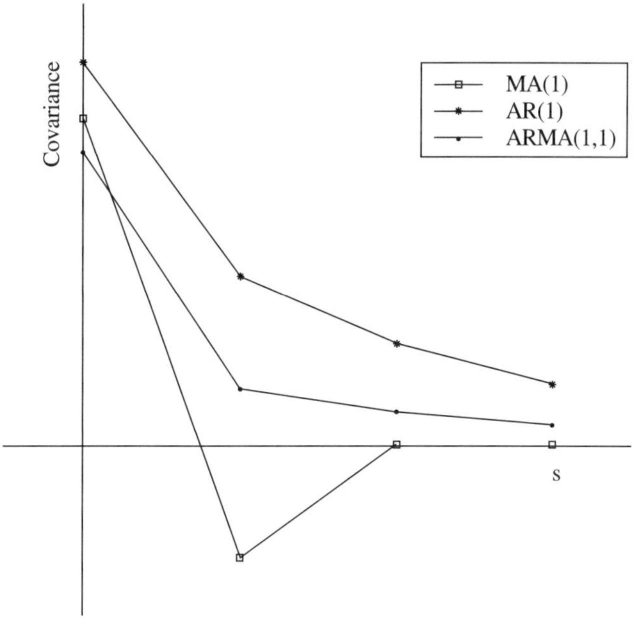

Figure 25.1 Cov$[\varepsilon_t, \varepsilon_{t+s}]$ for various ARMA models.

$$\hat{\varepsilon}_t = -\underset{(0.0449)}{0.601}\,\hat{\varepsilon}_{t-1} - \underset{(0.0449)}{0.206}\,\hat{\varepsilon}_{t-2} + \hat{v}_t$$

so that the second-order coefficient appears to be nonzero. Thus, there is strong evidence of serial correlation in the residuals of the quasi-first-differenced Phillips curve.

Staiger et al. (1996) specified an AR(15) process for the disturbance of their Phillips curve.[2] We will estimate this model with two-step FGLS. First, we expand the list of lagged $\hat{\varepsilon}_t$ to obtain the OLS fit

$$\begin{aligned}
\hat{\varepsilon}_t &= \sum_{s=1}^{15} \hat{\phi}_s \hat{\varepsilon}_{t-s} \\
&= -\underset{(0.047)}{0.736}\,\hat{\varepsilon}_{t-1} - \underset{(0.058)}{0.587}\,\hat{\varepsilon}_{t-2} - \underset{(0.064)}{0.579}\,\hat{\varepsilon}_{t-2} - \underset{(0.070)}{0.551}\,\hat{\varepsilon}_{t-4} - \underset{(0.074)}{0.442}\,\hat{\varepsilon}_{t-5} \\
&\quad - \underset{(0.077)}{0.409}\,\hat{\varepsilon}_{t-6} - \underset{(0.079)}{0.372}\,\hat{\varepsilon}_{t-7} - \underset{(0.081)}{0.307}\,\hat{\varepsilon}_{t-8} - \underset{(0.082)}{0.154}\,\hat{\varepsilon}_{t-9} - \underset{(0.082)}{0.101}\,\hat{\varepsilon}_{t-10} \\
&\quad - \underset{(0.081)}{0.050}\,\hat{\varepsilon}_{t-11} - \underset{(0.079)}{0.076}\,\hat{\varepsilon}_{t-12} - \underset{(0.076)}{0.065}\,\hat{\varepsilon}_{t-13} - \underset{(0.074)}{0.142}\,\hat{\varepsilon}_{t-14} - \underset{(0.069)}{0.028}\,\hat{\varepsilon}_{t-15} \\
&\quad - \underset{(0.064)}{0.024}\,\hat{\varepsilon}_{t-16} - \underset{(0.058)}{0.031}\,\hat{\varepsilon}_{t-17} - \underset{(0.045)}{0.002}\,\hat{\varepsilon}_{t-18} + \hat{v}'_t
\end{aligned}$$

By including three additional lags and fitting an AR(18) process, we can confirm that the last three slopes are small and insignificantly different from zero: the Wald test statistic for the hypothesis $H_0 : \phi_{16} = \phi_{17} = \phi_{18} = 0$ equals 0.420 and has a probability value of 0.936.

[2] Staiger et al. (1996) also permit the natural rate of unemployment to change over time. We simplify by restricting the natural rate to be constant.

We compare the fitted AR(1) and AR(18) specifications in Figure 25.2. This figure plots their implied autocorrelation functions. The AR(1) autocorrelation function exhibits its characteristic geometric approach to zero as the lag length grows. The autocorrelations alternate in sign. The AR(18) autocorrelation function also approaches zero asymptotically, but the approach is not monotonic. There appear to be relatively strong autocorrelations as far as 15 months back, long after the AR(1) autocorrelations have died out. This appears to be the failure of the AR(1) specification. We also plot the autocorrelations of the OLS fitted residuals, showing how the AR(18) autocorrelation function fits these over the shortest lags. We discount the apparent persistence of the residual autocorrelations because they are estimated imprecisely and the Wald test bears this out.

After reestimating an AR(15) process, we compute transformations of $y_t = \dot{p}_t - \dot{p}_{t-1}$ and the x_{tk} (n_{t-1}, pfe_t, and $nixon_t$) with these slopes by replacing $\hat{\varepsilon}_{t-j}$ with y_{t-j} or $x_{t-j,k}$ to obtain residuals analogous to the $\hat{v}'_t$. Labeling these y_{*t} and x_{*tk}, we fit a second OLS regression to replace (19.4):

$$y_{*t} = \underset{(0.095)}{0.190}\left(1 - \sum_{s=1}^{15}\hat{\phi}_s\right) - \underset{(0.015)}{0.031}\, n_{*t-1} + \underset{(0.0028)}{0.0092}\, pfe_{*t} + \underset{(0.168)}{0.311}\, nixon_{*t} + \hat{\varepsilon}_{*t} \qquad (25.3)$$

The estimated coefficients change very little, but the estimated standard errors are generally three to four times smaller. Furthermore, these standard errors are smaller than the adjusted standard errors for OLS in (19.28). The implied estimate of the natural rate of unemployment, 6.199%, also changes little but the approximate standard error falls to 6.152. Staiger et al. (1996) argue that in this instance confidence intervals based on the likelihood ratio are more reliable approximations than those using this estimate of the standard error.[3] The corresponding 90% confidence interval is [4.482, 8.718], which is considerably narrower than the delta-method interval.

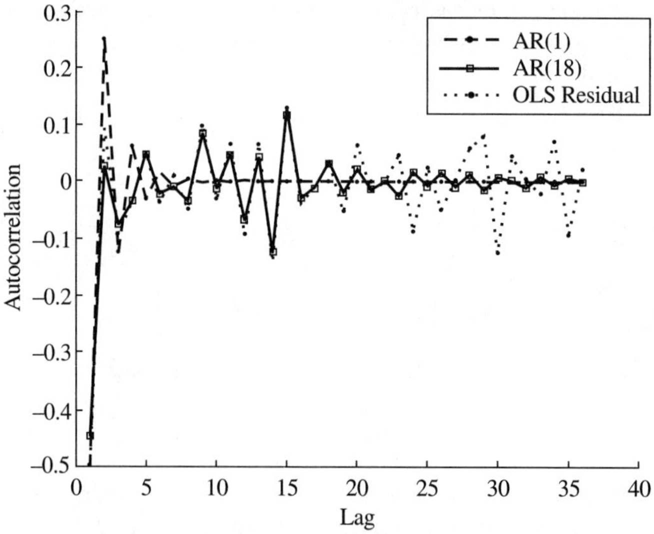

Figure 25.2 Estimates of the autocorrelation function.

[3] Strictly speaking, Staiger et al. (1996) use a slightly different method, replacing the log-likelihood ratio with an F statistic.

25.2 AUTOREGRESSIVE PROCESSES

We will begin our formal study of ARMA models with purely autoregressive specifications because these are analytically more tractable. The first-order process $\varepsilon_t = \phi_0\varepsilon_{t-1} + u_t$ generalizes to the pth-order autoregressive, or AR(p), process

$$\varepsilon_t = \phi_{01}\varepsilon_{t-1} + \cdots + \phi_{0p}\varepsilon_{t-p} + u_t, \qquad t = p+1, \ldots, T \tag{25.4}$$

where $\{u_t\}$ is white noise and uncorrelated with $\{\mathbf{x}_t\}$. Within this family, we studied the first-order autoregressive, or AR(1), model in Chapter 19. The AR(p) family has more flexible autocorrelation functions than (25.2) and part of their study concerns the nature of these functions. For example, there may be an AR(2) autocorrelation function such that the first-order autocorrelation is not the the largest autocorrelation. For another example, we anticipate that an AR(4) process might capture some seasonal correlation in quarterly data through the parameter ϕ_{04}.

The appeal of AR(p) models also comes from the direct way in which all of the econometric procedures that we have discussed generalize when $\{\varepsilon_t\}$ is covariance stationary with mean zero. First and fundamentally, we see from (25.4) that the conditional mean of y_t given the past is

$$\begin{aligned}
\mathrm{E}[y_t \mid t-1] &= \mathbf{x}_t'\boldsymbol{\beta}_0 + \phi_{01}\varepsilon_{t-1} + \cdots + \phi_{0p}\varepsilon_{t-p} \\
&= \mathbf{x}_t'\boldsymbol{\beta}_0 + \sum_{s=1}^{p} \phi_{0s}(y_{t-s} - \mathbf{x}_{t-s}'\boldsymbol{\beta}_0) \\
&= \sum_{s=1}^{p} \phi_{0s} y_{t-s} + \mathbf{x}_t'\boldsymbol{\beta}_0 + \sum_{s=1}^{p} \mathbf{x}_{t-s}' (\phi_{0s} \cdot \boldsymbol{\beta}_0)
\end{aligned}$$

This conditional mean is a finite distributed lag in past values of y_t and $\mathbf{x}_t$, where the coefficients obey a parsimonious set of restrictions: the ratios of the coefficients of $\mathbf{x}_{t-s}$ and $\mathbf{x}_t$ are equal to the coefficient of y_{t-s}.[4]

Second, this conditional mean also corresponds to a GLS transformation of the contemporaneous regression $\mathrm{E}[y_t \mid \mathbf{x}_t] = \mathbf{x}_t'\boldsymbol{\beta}_0$. The residual $y_t - \mathrm{E}[y_t \mid t-1]$ equals u_t and, by assumption, $\{u_t\}$ is homoskedastic and serially uncorrelated. Therefore, the variance matrix of $\left[y_t - \mathrm{E}[y_t \mid t-1]\right]'$ is a scalar matrix. Given $\boldsymbol{\phi}_0 \equiv [\phi_{01}, \ldots, \phi_{0p}]'$, the GLS estimator of $\boldsymbol{\beta}_0$ alone is the simple OLS estimator $\hat{\boldsymbol{\beta}}_{\mathrm{GLS}} = (\mathbf{X}_*'\mathbf{X}_*)^{-1}\mathbf{X}_*'\mathbf{y}_*$ applied to the pth-order quasidifferences

$$y_{*t} \equiv y_t - \sum_{j=1}^{p} \phi_{0j} y_{t-j} \qquad \text{and} \qquad \mathbf{x}_{*t} \equiv \mathbf{x}_t - \sum_{j=1}^{p} \phi_{0j} \cdot \mathbf{x}_{t-j} \tag{25.5}$$

$t = p+1, \ldots, T$.[5] A corresponding FGLS estimator of $\boldsymbol{\beta}_0$ that uses an initial consistent estimator $\check{\boldsymbol{\phi}}$ of $\boldsymbol{\phi}_0$ is asymptotically equivalent if there are no lagged y_t in $\mathbf{x}_t$. Joint estimation of $\boldsymbol{\beta}_0$ and $\boldsymbol{\phi}_0$ amounts to conditional NLS:[6]

---

[4] For comparative review, see equation (19.20).

[5] More precisely, this is an approximation to the GLS estimator because it conditions on the first p observations of y_t. We describe the exact GLS estimator at the end of Section 25.2.1.

[6] Previous, comparable, results for AR(1) serial correlation appear in Section 19.6. The asymptotic distribution theory of this NLS estimator is covered by Proposition 20 (GMM Asymptotics, p. 546). Also see Section 21.2.2, *Nonlinear Least Squares*, and Example 21.2 (Nonlinear Weighted Least Squares).

$$\begin{bmatrix} \hat{\boldsymbol{\beta}}_{\text{NLS}} \\ \hat{\boldsymbol{\phi}}_{\text{NLS}} \end{bmatrix} = \underset{\boldsymbol{\beta},\boldsymbol{\phi}}{\text{argmin}}\ Q_T(\boldsymbol{\beta}, \boldsymbol{\phi}) \tag{25.6}$$

where $\boldsymbol{\phi} \equiv [\phi_1, \ldots, \phi_p]'$ and

$$Q_T(\boldsymbol{\beta}, \boldsymbol{\phi}) \equiv \mathrm{E}_{T|p}\left[\frac{1}{2}\left(y_t - \mathbf{x}_t'\boldsymbol{\beta} - \sum_{s=1}^{p} \boldsymbol{\phi}_s\left(y_{t-s} - \mathbf{x}_{t-s}'\boldsymbol{\beta}\right)\right)^2\right] \tag{25.7}$$

If there are lagged dependent explanatory variables, then FGLS must be replaced with a generalization of Hatanaka's (1974) procedure. That is, given initial consistent estimators $\check{\boldsymbol{\beta}}$ and $\check{\boldsymbol{\phi}}$, the linearized NLS (Gauss–Newton) estimator for $\boldsymbol{\beta}_0$ is the OLS fitted coefficient vector of $\check{\mathbf{x}}_{*t}$ from fitting $\check{y}_{*t}$ to

$$\underset{1\times(K+p)}{\check{\mathbf{w}}_t} \equiv \begin{bmatrix} \check{\mathbf{x}}_{*t}' & \check{\varepsilon}_{t-1} & \cdots & \check{\varepsilon}_{t-p} \end{bmatrix}'$$

Third, one can compute a GMM diagnostic test statistic for an AR(p) disturbance process by regressing the OLS fitted residuals on the first p lags of the OLS fitted residuals and jointly testing whether the coefficients of the latter are zeros.[7] To see this, consider the gradient of the generalized sum of squares (25.7):

$$\begin{aligned} \mathbf{g}_T(\boldsymbol{\beta}, \boldsymbol{\phi}) &\equiv \frac{\partial Q_T(\boldsymbol{\beta}, \boldsymbol{\phi})}{\partial\,[\boldsymbol{\beta}', \boldsymbol{\phi}']'} \\ &= \mathrm{E}_{T|p}\left[\mathbf{w}_t(\boldsymbol{\beta})\left(y_t - \mathbf{x}_t'\boldsymbol{\beta} - \sum_{s=1}^{p} \phi_s \varepsilon_{t-s}(\boldsymbol{\beta})\right)\right] \end{aligned}$$

where

$$\mathbf{w}_t(\boldsymbol{\beta}, \boldsymbol{\phi}) \equiv \begin{bmatrix} \mathbf{x}_t' + \sum_{s=1}^{p} \phi_s \cdot \mathbf{x}_{t-s}' & \varepsilon_{t-1}(\boldsymbol{\beta}) & \cdots & \varepsilon_{t-p}(\boldsymbol{\beta}) \end{bmatrix}'$$

and $\varepsilon_t(\boldsymbol{\beta}) \equiv y_t - \mathbf{x}_t'\boldsymbol{\beta}$. The restricted GMM estimator is the OLS fitted coefficient vector $\hat{\boldsymbol{\beta}}_{\text{OLS}} = \left(\mathbf{X}'\mathbf{X}\right)^{-1}\mathbf{X}'\mathbf{y}$ and the associated s^2 is an estimator of σ_{0u}^2. Therefore, a gradient test statistic is[8]

$$\mathcal{G} = (T - p)\ \mathbf{g}_T(\hat{\boldsymbol{\beta}}_{\text{OLS}}, \mathbf{0})'\hat{\boldsymbol{\Lambda}}_T^{-1}\mathbf{g}_T(\hat{\boldsymbol{\beta}}_{\text{OLS}}, \mathbf{0})$$

where

$$\hat{\boldsymbol{\Lambda}}_T = s^2 \cdot \mathrm{E}_{T|p}[\mathbf{w}_t'(\hat{\boldsymbol{\beta}}_{\text{OLS}}, \mathbf{0})\,\mathbf{w}_t(\hat{\boldsymbol{\beta}}_{\text{OLS}}, \mathbf{0})]$$

One can compute this statistic as the regression sum of squares from the OLS fit of $\varepsilon_t(\hat{\boldsymbol{\beta}}_{\text{OLS}})/s$ to $s^{-1} \cdot \mathbf{w}_t(\hat{\boldsymbol{\beta}}_{\text{OLS}}, \mathbf{0})$. Under the null hypothesis $\boldsymbol{\phi}_0 = \mathbf{0}$, $\mathcal{G}$ will be approximately distributed as χ_p^2.

---

[7] See Section 19.4.1. This regression also yields an initial estimator of $\boldsymbol{\phi}_0$. If there are lagged y_t in $\mathbf{x}_t$, then this regression must also include $\mathbf{x}_t$ among the RHS variables for the hypothesis test. See Exercise 20.26. One can compute an estimator of $\boldsymbol{\phi}_0$ with a similar regression with IV fitted residuals.

[8] We are using the equivalent DD statistic here because under the alternative hypothesis the number of parameters equals the number of moment functions. See equation (22.18).

Fourth, if the $\{u_t\}$ are i.i.d. normal then the log-likelihood function continues to have a convenient prediction-error decomposition conditional on the first p observations:

$$L(\sigma_u^2; u_t) = -\frac{1}{2}\left[\log(2\pi\sigma_u^2) + \frac{u_t^2}{\sigma_u^2}\right]$$

so that

$$\begin{aligned}
\mathrm{E}_{T|p}[L(\boldsymbol{\theta} \mid y_1, \ldots, y_p)] &= -\frac{1}{2}\left\{\log(2\pi\sigma_u^2) + \frac{\mathrm{E}_{T|p}\left[\left(\varepsilon_t(\boldsymbol{\beta}) - \sum_{j=1}^{p}\phi_j\varepsilon_{t-j}(\boldsymbol{\beta})\right)^2\right]}{\sigma_u^2}\right\} \\
&= \frac{1}{T-p}\sum_{t=p+1}^{T} L(\boldsymbol{\theta}; y_t \mid y_{t-p}, \ldots, y_{t-1}) \\
&= -\frac{1}{2}\log(2\pi\sigma_u^2) + \frac{Q_T(\boldsymbol{\beta}, \boldsymbol{\phi})}{\sigma_u^2}
\end{aligned} \tag{25.8}$$

for $\boldsymbol{\theta} = \left[\boldsymbol{\beta}', \boldsymbol{\phi}', \sigma_u^2\right]'$.[9] Therefore, the conditional MLE given $\{y_1, \ldots, y_p\}$ is identical to the conditional NLS estimator above.

Finally, OLS calculations deliver convenient consistent estimators of the parameters. The OLS regression of y_t on $\mathbf{x}_t$ provides an initial estimator of $\boldsymbol{\beta}_0$ unless lagged values of y_t appear in $\mathbf{x}_t$.[10] In that case, one can use a 2SLS estimator based on lags of $\mathbf{x}_t$ as instrumental variables.[11] As just noted, the OLS regression of fitted residuals on p lags of the fitted residuals provides an initial estimator of $\boldsymbol{\phi}_0$.[12] This is the same regression that one uses to test the null hypothesis of no serial correlation against the alternative hypothesis that $\{\varepsilon_t\}$ is an AR(p) process.

In these five ways, we see that an analysis of the latent AR(p) model directly extends the AR(1) analysis. But if it is going to be useful, the AR(p) specification must be able to capture observable phenomena and we must be able to interpret its parameters. The AR(1) process is simple enough so that it can be motivated without a latent variable model and the properties of an AR(1) process relate to just one parameter. Now we will discuss the interpretation of the AR(p) specification.

25.2.1 Stationarity

The latent AR(p) model does not yield covariance-stationary time series in general. One must impose restrictions on $\boldsymbol{\phi}_0$, as in $|\phi_{01}| < 1$ for the AR(1) case. In this section, we show a general method for doing so. We begin by noting that the variance matrix $\boldsymbol{\Sigma}_0 \equiv \mathrm{Var}\left[[\varepsilon_{t-p}, \ldots, \varepsilon_{t-1}]'\right]$ is a critical factor in covariance stationarity: because the process is autoregressive, the variance of $\left[\varepsilon_{t-p+1}, \ldots, \varepsilon_t\right]'$ rests on that of $\left[\varepsilon_{t-p}, \ldots, \varepsilon_{t-1}\right]'$ and u_t. As a result, we can limit our attention to the implications of covariance stationarity for the variance matrix $\boldsymbol{\Sigma}_0$ of a sequence of length p.

---

[9] Compare with (19.11)–(19.19).

[10] See Section 19.3.

[11] See Example 20.7 and Section 20.5.

[12] See the various estimation methods for the AR(1) model described on p. 469.

EXAMPLE 25.1 [AR(1)]

We have already studied the case where $p = 1$ and noted that $|\phi_{01}| < 1$ is necessary for $[\varepsilon_1, \ldots, \varepsilon_T]'$ to have a nonsingular variance matrix.[13] We can relate this restriction to the way the autoregressive character of ε_t implies an autoregressive autocovariance function:

$$\varepsilon_t = \phi_{01}\varepsilon_{t-1} + u_t \qquad \Rightarrow \qquad \begin{cases} \operatorname{Var}[\varepsilon_t] = \phi_{01} \operatorname{Cov}[\varepsilon_t, \varepsilon_{t-1}] + \sigma_u^2 \\ \operatorname{Cov}[\varepsilon_t, \varepsilon_{t-1}] = \phi_{01} \operatorname{Var}[\varepsilon_{t-1}] \end{cases} \tag{25.9}$$

so that

$$\operatorname{Var}[\varepsilon_t] = \phi_{01}^2 \operatorname{Var}[\varepsilon_{t-1}] + \sigma_{0u}^2$$

If the sequence $\{\varepsilon_t\}$ is covariance stationary, then $\operatorname{Var}[\varepsilon_t] = \operatorname{Var}[\varepsilon_{t-1}] < \infty$. This equality holds if and only if

$$\operatorname{Var}[\varepsilon_{t-1}] = \frac{\sigma_{0u}^2}{1 - \phi_{01}^2} \tag{25.10}$$

This marginal variance is finite and positive if and only if $|\phi_{01}| < 1$.

To isolate this necessary and sufficient restriction for covariance stationarity of an AR(1) process we need find only what keeps $\operatorname{Var}[\varepsilon_{t-1}]$ positive and finite. The pth-order generalization for covariance stationarity is that the variance matrix of $\left[\varepsilon_{t-p}, \ldots, \varepsilon_{t-1}\right]'$ implied by stationarity is finite and positive definite. Lemma 7.7 (p. 142) provides a convenient characterization of nonsingular variance matrices that we will apply here: the variances of $\varepsilon_{t-p}, \varepsilon_{t-p+1} - \mathrm{E}^*[\varepsilon_{t-p+1} \mid \varepsilon_{t-p}], \ldots, \varepsilon_{t-1} - \mathrm{E}^*[\varepsilon_{t-1} \mid \varepsilon_{t-p}, \ldots, \varepsilon_{t-2}]$ must be strictly positive.

EXAMPLE 25.2 [AR(2)]

Consider the case in which $p = 2$. Then

$$\varepsilon_t = \phi_{01}\varepsilon_{t-1} + \phi_{02}\varepsilon_{t-2} + u_t \qquad \Rightarrow$$
$$\begin{cases} \operatorname{Var}[\varepsilon_t] = \phi_{01} \operatorname{Cov}[\varepsilon_t, \varepsilon_{t-1}] + \phi_{02} \operatorname{Cov}[\varepsilon_t, \varepsilon_{t-2}] + \sigma_u^2 \\ \operatorname{Cov}[\varepsilon_t, \varepsilon_{t-1}] = \phi_{01} \operatorname{Var}[\varepsilon_{t-1}] + \phi_{02} \operatorname{Cov}[\varepsilon_{t-1}, \varepsilon_{t-2}] \\ \operatorname{Cov}[\varepsilon_t, \varepsilon_{t-2}] = \phi_{01} \operatorname{Cov}[\varepsilon_{t-1}, \varepsilon_{t-2}] + \phi_{02} \operatorname{Var}[\varepsilon_{t-2}] \end{cases} \tag{25.11}$$

Covariance stationarity implies that

$$\begin{aligned} \gamma_0 &\equiv \operatorname{Var}[\varepsilon_t] = \operatorname{Var}[\varepsilon_{t-s}] \\ \gamma_1 &\equiv \operatorname{Cov}[\varepsilon_t, \varepsilon_{t-1}] = \operatorname{Cov}[\varepsilon_{t-s}, \varepsilon_{t-1-s}] \\ \gamma_2 &\equiv \operatorname{Cov}[\varepsilon_t, \varepsilon_{t-2}] = \operatorname{Cov}[\varepsilon_{t-s}, \varepsilon_{t-2-s}] \end{aligned}$$

Substituting these restrictions into (25.11) and solving the three linear equations for $(\gamma_0, \gamma_1, \gamma_2)$ gives

$$\gamma_0 = \sigma_{0u}^2 \frac{1 - \phi_{02}}{(\phi_{02} + 1)(\phi_{02} - 1 + \phi_{01})(\phi_{02} - 1 - \phi_{01})}$$

$$\gamma_1 = \sigma_{0u}^2 \frac{\phi_{01}}{(\phi_{02} + 1)(\phi_{02} - 1 + \phi_{01})(\phi_{02} - 1 - \phi_{01})}$$

[13] See equations (19.7)–(19.8).

$$\gamma_2 = \sigma_{0u}^2 \frac{\phi_{01}^2 + \phi_{02} - \phi_{02}^2}{(\phi_{02} + 1)(\phi_{02} - 1 + \phi_{01})(\phi_{02} - 1 - \phi_{01})}$$

Therefore, covariance stationarity requires that (Lemma 7.7)

$$\text{Var}[\varepsilon_{t-2}] = \gamma_0 = \sigma_{0u}^2 \frac{1}{\left(1 - \phi_{02}^2\right)\left(1 - \rho_1^2\right)} > 0$$

$$\text{Var}\left[\varepsilon_{t-1} - \text{E}^*[\varepsilon_{t-1} \,|\, \varepsilon_{t-2}]\right] = \gamma_0 - \frac{\gamma_1^2}{\gamma_0} = \gamma_0\left(1 - \rho_1^2\right) > 0$$

where $\rho_1 = \phi_{01}/(1 - \phi_{02})$. In terms of ϕ_{01} and ϕ_{02}, these two inequalities are equivalent to $\phi_{02}^2 < 1$ and $\rho_1^2 < 1$ or

$$\phi_{02} > -1$$

$$\phi_{02} + \phi_{01} < 1$$

and

$$\phi_{02} - \phi_{01} < 1$$

The inequality $\phi_{02} < 1$ is redundant, being implied by the last two.

For an AR(p) process, we can generalize this method of imposing covariance stationarity:

1. we solve a linear system for the *autocovariance function*

$$\gamma_s \equiv \text{Cov}[\varepsilon_t, \varepsilon_{t-s}], \quad s = 0, \pm 1, \pm 2, \ldots$$

   and the variance matrix of $\left[\varepsilon_{t-p}, \ldots, \varepsilon_{t-1}\right]'$ given stationarity and
2. we impose the restrictions that make this matrix finite and positive definite so that it is indeed a variance matrix.

Having done so, we have imposed necessary and sufficient conditions on the elements of $\boldsymbol{\phi}$ to make the AR(p) process stationary. The first step delivers the functional form that covariance stationarity imposes on the variance matrix in terms of $\boldsymbol{\phi}$ and σ_u^2. The second step is necessary (and sufficient) because a nonstationary process will not produce a constant, valid autocovariance function.

Thus, to impose covariance stationarity, we describe a derivation of the variance matrix of $\left[\varepsilon_{t-1}, \ldots, \varepsilon_{t-p}\right]'$. If $\{\varepsilon_t\}$ evolves according to the AR(p) process in (25.4), then multiplying (25.4) by ε_{t-j} and taking expectations, we obtain

$$\text{Cov}[\varepsilon_t, \varepsilon_{t-j}] = \phi_1 \text{Cov}[\varepsilon_{t-1}, \varepsilon_{t-j}] + \cdots + \phi_p \text{Cov}[\varepsilon_{t-p}, \varepsilon_{t-j}] + \text{Cov}[u_t \varepsilon_{t-j}] \tag{25.12}$$

Setting $j = 0$, the marginal variance of ε_t is

$$\gamma_0 = \phi_1\gamma_1 + \cdots + \phi_p\gamma_p + \sigma_u^2 \tag{25.13}$$

For $j > 1$, (25.12) simplifies to

$$\gamma_j = \phi_1\gamma_{j-1} + \phi_2\gamma_{j-2} + \cdots + \phi_p\gamma_{j-p}, \qquad j > 1 \tag{25.14}$$

because u_t is uncorrelated with past ε_{t-j}. Equations (25.13)–(25.14) comprise the *Yule–Walker equations*, a linear system of difference equations in the autocovariances γ_j.

The Yule–Walker equations break up conveniently into two sets of equations. The first set is indexed by $j = 0, 1, \ldots, p$. These equations contain only $\gamma_0, \gamma_1, \ldots, \gamma_p$ after we impose the symmetry of a stationary autocovariance function:

$$\gamma_s = \text{Cov}[\varepsilon_t, \varepsilon_{t-s}] = \text{Cov}[\varepsilon_{t+s}, \varepsilon_t] = \gamma_{-s}, \qquad s = 0, \pm 1, \pm 2, \ldots$$

This creates a linear system of $p + 1$ equations in $p + 1$ autocovariances. The second set of equations corresponds to $j > p$. In these cases, (25.14) gives γ_j as a recursive linear function of $\gamma_{j-1}, \ldots, \gamma_{j-p}$. Therefore, by solving the first $p + 1$ equations, one can ultimately derive the complete autocovariance function of a covariance-stationary AR(p) process.

For $p = 1$, Example 25.1 solves for γ_0 in (25.10). If we plug this back into the second part of (25.9), we obtain

$$\gamma_1 = \phi_1 \text{ Var}[\varepsilon_{t-1}] = \phi_1 \gamma_0$$

Furthermore, $\gamma_j = \phi_1 \gamma_{j-1}$ for $j > 1$. Example 25.2 solves the Yule–Walker equations for γ_0, γ_1, and γ_2 when $p = 2$. For higher-order autocovariances, $\gamma_j = \phi_1 \gamma_{j-1} + \phi_2 \gamma_{j-2}$, $j > 2$. For p greater than 2, the general solution to the Yule–Walker equations (25.13)–(25.14) appears in Section 25.7.1.[14] It has the functional form

$$\boldsymbol{\Sigma}(\sigma_u^2, \boldsymbol{\phi}) = \frac{\sigma_u^2}{1 - \boldsymbol{\phi}'\boldsymbol{\rho}(\boldsymbol{\phi})} \cdot \left[\rho_{|t-s|}(\boldsymbol{\phi}); \quad t, s = 1, \ldots, p\right] \tag{25.15}$$

where $\rho_{|t-s|}(\boldsymbol{\phi})$ denotes the autocorrelation of order $|t - s|$ and $\boldsymbol{\rho}(\boldsymbol{\phi}) \equiv \left[\rho_j(\boldsymbol{\phi}); \ j = 1, \ldots, p\right]'$.

Given the solution, one can rest covariance stationarity on the following result.

Lemma 25.1 [AR(p) Covariance Stationarity] *Let $\{\varepsilon_t\}$ be an AR(p) process $\varepsilon_t = \phi_1 \varepsilon_{t-1} + \cdots + \phi_p \varepsilon_{t-p} + u_t$ ($t = p+1, \ldots, T, T \geq 2p$), where $\{u_t\}$ is an i.i.d. sequence of random variables with mean zero and variance $\sigma_u^2 > 0$ and $\left[\varepsilon_1, \ldots, \varepsilon_p\right]'$ has mean zero and a finite variance matrix. Then $\{\varepsilon_t\}$ is covariance stationary if and only if $\boldsymbol{\Sigma}(\sigma_u^2, \boldsymbol{\phi})$ is positive definite and*

$$\text{Var}\left[\left[\varepsilon_{t-p}, \ldots, \varepsilon_{t-1}\right]'\right] = \boldsymbol{\Sigma}(\sigma_u^2, \boldsymbol{\phi})$$

Proof. **Necessity:** If $\{\varepsilon_t\}$ is covariance stationary, then the Yule–Walker equations yield $\boldsymbol{\Sigma}(\sigma_u^2, \boldsymbol{\phi})$ as the variance of $\left[\varepsilon_{t-p}, \ldots, \varepsilon_{t-1}\right]$ and it follows that $\boldsymbol{\Sigma}(\sigma_u^2, \boldsymbol{\phi})$ is positive semidefinite. If $\boldsymbol{\Sigma}(\sigma_u^2, \boldsymbol{\phi})$ were singular, then $\left[\varepsilon_{t-p}, \ldots, \varepsilon_{t-1}\right]\boldsymbol{\alpha} = 0$ with probability one for some $\boldsymbol{\alpha} \in \mathbb{R}^p$, $\boldsymbol{\alpha} \neq 0$.[15] But then for $t = 2p, \ldots, T$

$$\begin{aligned} 0 &= \left[\varepsilon_{t-p+1}, \ldots, \varepsilon_t\right]\boldsymbol{\alpha} \\ &= \phi_1 \left(\left[\varepsilon_{t-p}, \ldots, \varepsilon_{t-1}\right]\boldsymbol{\alpha}\right) + \cdots + \phi_p \left(\left[\varepsilon_{t-2p+1}, \ldots, \varepsilon_{t-p}\right]\boldsymbol{\alpha}\right) \\ &\quad + \left[u_{t-p+1}, \ldots, u_t\right]\boldsymbol{\alpha} \\ &= \left[u_{t-p+1}, \ldots, u_t\right]\boldsymbol{\alpha} \end{aligned}$$

[14] We use the solution of the Yule–Walker equations to compute the autocorrelation function of the AR(18) specification graphed in Figure 25.2.

[15] See Lemma 7.2 (Variance Column Space, p. 133).

with probability one, which contradicts that $\{u_t\}$ is an i.i.d. sequence with nonzero variance. Therefore $\boldsymbol{\Sigma}(\sigma_u^2, \boldsymbol{\phi})$ is positive semidefinite and *nonsingular*, or positive definite.

Sufficiency: If $\boldsymbol{\Sigma}(\sigma_u^2, \boldsymbol{\phi})$ is positive definite and equal to the variance matrix of $\left[\varepsilon_{t-p}, \ldots, \varepsilon_{t-1}\right]'$, then the Yule–Walker equations imply that the autocovariance function is constant. Therefore $\{\varepsilon_t\}$ is covariance stationary. □

There is an alternative characterization of stationarity that is also insightful.

LEMMA 25.2 (AR(p) COVARIANCE STATIONARITY) *The AR(p) process*

$$\varepsilon_t = \sum_{j=1}^{p} \phi_j \varepsilon_{t-j} + u_t$$

is stationary if and only if the roots of the pth-order polynomial equation

$$z^p - \sum_{j=1}^{p} \phi_j z^{p-j} = 0$$

lie strictly inside the complex unit circle.

For a proof of this result, see Anderson (1971, pp. 177–179).

Stationarity of an AR(1) process is a special case of this lemma: the root of $z - \phi_1 = 0$ is the real number ϕ_1 so that $|\phi_1| < 1$ is necessary and sufficient for stationarity. Insight comes from noting that the conditions of this lemma are also the necessary and sufficient conditions for the pth-order *deterministic* difference equation

$$z_t = \phi_1 z_{t-1} + \phi_2 z_{t-2} + \cdots + \phi_p z_{t-p}$$

to converge (as $t \to \infty$) to a steady state at 0 for all starting values.[16] Therefore, we can view AR(p) stationarity as a consequence of the dynamic stability of an associated deterministic process. The stability of the latter is sufficient to prevent disturbances u_t to the deterministic process from introducing explosive behavior.

The understanding of difference equations enhances one's understanding of both stationarity and other properties of AR(p) processes. Not only the processes, but also their autocovariance functions are governed by difference equations as in (25.14). We will not pursue the general study of difference equations in this book, but we recommend it for students who wish to study autoregressive processes more intensively.

As a byproduct of this analysis of stationarity, we have derived the conditional variance matrix $\boldsymbol{\Sigma}_0$ of $[y_{t-p}, \ldots, y_{t-1}]$ given $\mathbf{X}$, σ_{0u}^2, and $\boldsymbol{\phi}_0$. As a result, we can produce the exact GLS estimator that does not condition on $\{y_1, \ldots, y_p\}$. Given $\boldsymbol{\phi}_0$ we obtain the matrix

[16] For an introduction to the analysis of linear difference equations, see Fuller (1996, Section 2.4), Hamilton (1994, pp. 18–20, 730–731), and Simon and Blume (1994, Ch. 23). Also consult such linear algebra books as Lang (1971) and Nering (1970).

$$\mathbf{W}_0 \equiv \frac{1}{1 - \boldsymbol{\phi}_0' \boldsymbol{\rho}(\boldsymbol{\phi}_0)} \cdot \left[\rho_{|t-s|}(\boldsymbol{\phi}_0);\ t, s = 1, \ldots, p\right]$$

proportional to (25.15).[17] Denoting

$$\mathbf{y}_{*[p]} \equiv \mathbf{W}_0^{-1/2} \mathbf{y}_{[p]} \qquad \text{and} \qquad \mathbf{X}_{*[p]} \equiv \mathbf{W}_0^{-1/2} \mathbf{X}_{[p]}$$

where $\mathbf{y}_{[p]} \equiv \left[y_1, \ldots, y_p\right]'$ and $\mathbf{X}_{[p]} \equiv \left[\mathbf{x}_1, \ldots, \mathbf{x}_p\right]'$, then $\text{Var}[\mathbf{y}_{*[p]} \,|\, \mathbf{X}_{*[p]}] = \sigma_{0u}^2 \cdot \mathbf{I}_p$. Thus, one augments the quasidifferences in (25.5) with the elements of $\mathbf{y}_{*[p]}$ and $\mathbf{X}_{*[p]}$. The OLS fit of the transformed data is the exact GLS fit.

25.2.2 Restricted Estimation

The conditional NLS/ML estimator in (25.6) does not necessarily satisfy the constraints of covariance stationarity. However, just as in the AR(1) case, the MLE based on the complete data set and the assumption that the $\{u_t\}$ are normally distributed always obeys these constraints. We will show this next.

Like all segments of p consecutive observations, $\mathbf{y}_{[p]} \equiv \left[y_1, \ldots, y_p\right]'$ has the variance matrix $\boldsymbol{\Sigma}_0$ (conditional on $\mathbf{X}$) implied by covariance stationarity. As a result, the initial marginal log-likelihood for $\mathbf{y}_{[p]}$ conditional on $\mathbf{X}_{[p]} \equiv \left[\mathbf{x}_1, \ldots, \mathbf{x}_p\right]'$ has the prediction-error decomposition

$$\begin{aligned} L(\boldsymbol{\theta}; y_1, \ldots, y_p) = &-\frac{1}{2}\Big\{\log\det\left[2\pi \cdot \boldsymbol{\Sigma}(\sigma_u^2, \boldsymbol{\phi})\right] \\ &+ \left(\mathbf{y}_{[p]} - \mathbf{X}_{[p]}\boldsymbol{\beta}\right)' \boldsymbol{\Sigma}(\sigma_u^2, \boldsymbol{\phi})^{-1} \left(\mathbf{y}_{[p]} - \mathbf{X}_{[p]}\boldsymbol{\beta}\right)\Big\} \qquad (25.16) \\ = &-\frac{1}{2}\left[\sum_{t=1}^{p} \log(2\pi\omega_t^2) + \frac{v_t^2}{\omega_t^2}\right] \qquad (25.17) \end{aligned}$$

where

$$v_1 \equiv \varepsilon_1, \qquad v_t \equiv \varepsilon_t - \mathrm{E}^*[\varepsilon_t \,|\, \varepsilon_1, \ldots, \varepsilon_{t-1}]$$

$$\omega_1^2 \equiv \frac{\sigma_u^2}{1 - \boldsymbol{\phi}'\boldsymbol{\rho}(\boldsymbol{\phi})}, \qquad \omega_t^2 \equiv \text{Var}[v_t], \qquad t = 2, \ldots, p$$

As long as $v_t \neq 0$, $L(\boldsymbol{\theta}; y_1, \ldots, y_p)$ approaches negative infinity as ω_t^2 approaches zero. In this way maximum likelihood restricts each ω_t^2 $(t = 1, \ldots, p)$ to be strictly positive and, according to Lemma 7.7, $\boldsymbol{\Sigma}(\sigma_u^2, \boldsymbol{\phi})$ to be positive definite. Hence, including (25.17) in the log-likelihood function constrains the exact MLE of the AR(p) coefficients $\boldsymbol{\phi} \equiv \left[\phi_j;\ j = 1, \ldots, p\right]'$ to stationarity.

Note that it is insufficient to include (25.16) in the log-likelihood function. The log det $\boldsymbol{\Sigma}(\sigma_u^2, \boldsymbol{\phi})$ term in this expression will merely force the determinant of $\boldsymbol{\Sigma}(\sigma_u^2, \boldsymbol{\phi})$ to be positive so that it is possible to evaluate (25.16) at values of $\boldsymbol{\Sigma}(\sigma_u^2, \boldsymbol{\phi})$ that are not positive definite. The equality of (25.16) and (25.17) holds only when $\boldsymbol{\Sigma}(\sigma_u^2, \boldsymbol{\phi})$ is positive definite. Hence, the prediction-error decomposition (25.17) is necessary to imposing covariance stationarity.

Computing the exact MLE may be difficult. As a practical expedient, many researchers omit the initial log-likelihood term and check whether their unconstrained estimates satisfy the

[17] See Section 25.7.1 for complete details.

stationarity restrictions. Nevertheless, Harvey (1993, p. 69) reports evidence that in small samples the exact MLE generally performs at least as well and often better.

25.2.3 Sequential Testing for Order

As we mentioned, testing for an AR(p) covariance structure against no autocorrelation takes a familiar form in the score test. One regresses the OLS fitted residual $\hat{\varepsilon}_t$ on the p lagged residuals $\hat{\varepsilon}_{t-j}$, $j = 1, \ldots, p$ and (if there are lagged y_t in $\mathbf{x}_t$) $\mathbf{x}_t$. Under the null hypothesis of no autocorrelation, the squared length of the fitted vector converges in distribution to a χ^2_p random variable as the sample size approaches infinity.

In practice, one must also choose the order p of the AR process. One approach to this problem uses *sequential hypothesis tests* to find the p where the hypothesis $\phi_{0,p+1} = 0$ is not rejected. Within this approach there are two predominant strategies, testing from low order AR(p) toward higher order and testing from the highest order toward lower order. The first strategy usually employs a sequence of score tests, thereby avoiding the estimation of more complex models. The second strategy uses a sequence of Wald tests.[18]

The "bottom-up" strategy is appealing from a practical viewpoint because the score tests are so convenient and estimation is simplest. After estimating an AR(j) model by LML or ML, one can compute the score test as a t test for the coefficient of the $(j+1)$th lagged residual in the OLS regression of the ML fitted residual on $j+1$ lagged ML fitted residuals and, possibly, $\mathbf{x}_t$. If the null hypothesis is rejected, then one proceeds to estimate an AR($j+1$) model and test for an AR($j+2$) model.

The "top-down" testing strategy is appealing from a methodological viewpoint because one can easily compute the actual significance level of the sequence of tests. The jth null hypothesis is

$$H_{0j} : \phi_{0s} = 0, \qquad s \geq p - j + 1$$

and the jth test statistic is the univariate Wald statistic for

$$H'_{0j} : \phi_{0,p-j+1} = 0$$

restricting $\phi_{0s} = 0$, $s > p - j + 1$. Each Wald test is distributed independently of the preceding one under the null hypothesis. We discuss this as a general result in Section 22.6. Because of this independence, the signficance level of the jth test in the sequence is simply

$$\alpha_j = \begin{cases} \alpha_{0j} & \text{if j=1} \\ \alpha_{0j}(1-\alpha_{j-1}) + \alpha_{j-1} & \text{if j>1} \end{cases}$$

where α_{0j} is the nominal significance level of the test. In words, the probability of rejecting H_{0j} when it is true equals the probability of accepting $H_{0,j-1}$ and rejecting H_{0j} plus the probability of rejecting $H_{0,j-1}$. If one desires the signficance level α for the pth (and possibly final) test and if $\alpha_0 = \alpha_{0j}$ then choose α_0 so that

$$\alpha = 1 - (1 - \alpha_0)^p$$

For example, a 5% test of an AR(5) implies a significance level of 0.1%, a surprisingly low value to many practitioners.

[18] Note that both testing strategies result in pretest estimators for $\boldsymbol{\phi}$ that do not possess the distribution of a classical estimator.

The *choice* of p in an AR(p) specification is not really a hypothesis testing problem. One is *estimating* p, another parameter of the model. In such cases, both hypothesis testing strategies are *ad hoc* solutions to an estimation problem. Rather than formulating the estimation problem and deriving its solution, these methods apply tools at hand. However, this is more than a matter of mere convenience. Unfortunately, the extension of classical estimation methods to this estimation problem is not immediate.

The method of maximum likelihood, for example, does not provide a solution. Such estimation problems do not fit into the theory outlined in Chapter 14. Aimed as it is at fitting the data as well as possible, MLE provides no general protection against overfitting when the number of parameters is also unknown. The formulation of such estimation problems and their solution is an important and active research topic called *model selection* that we will not pursue here. For general reference, see Gourieroux and Monfort (1995, Ch. 22), Hendry (1995), and Poirier (1995, Chs. 7 and 10). Judge et al. (1980, Section 7.5.2) give an introduction specifically to the selection of p in AR(p) models.

25.3 MOVING-AVERAGE PROCESSES

Once we begin to model with such latent processes as the AR(p), other possibilities may come to mind as we think about the underlying causes of serial correlation. For example, we might conjecture that the current disturbance ε_t should depend directly on u_{t-1}, the "surprise" in the previous period, rather than on ε_{t-1}, which contains predictable components. The simplest example is the latent process

$$\varepsilon_t = u_t + \psi_1 u_{t-1} \tag{25.18}$$

where $\{u_t\}$ is a sequence of i.i.d. random variables with mean zero and variance $\sigma_u^2 > 0$. Rather than lagging ε_t as in an AR(1), this process contains the lagged value of u_t. Such processes are generally called *moving-average processes*. They are a natural parametric counterpart to autoregressive processes. The simplest moving average is the *first-order moving average* in (25.18) and it generalizes immediately to the *qth order moving-average*, or MA(q), process

$$\varepsilon_t = u_t + \psi_1 u_{t-1} + \psi_2 u_{t-2} + \cdots + \psi_q u_{t-q} \tag{25.19}$$

Given a new latent model, our first step is to understand what restrictions it places on observable behavior. The autocovariance function summarizes this information for time series.

EXAMPLE 25.3 [MA(1)]

Consider the MA(1) process (25.18). In contrast to an AR process, we can find its variance directly:

$$\begin{aligned}\gamma_0 &= \text{Var}[\varepsilon_t] \\ &= \text{Var}[u_t] + \text{Var}[\psi_1 u_{t-1}] \\ &= \sigma_u^2 \left(1 + \psi_1^2\right)\end{aligned} \tag{25.20}$$

More than this, there is no question that the MA(1) process is stationary. Regardless of what finite value ψ_1 takes, this variance exists because we do not have any covariance terms to analyze.

The first autocovariance is

$$\begin{aligned}\gamma_1 &= \mathrm{Cov}[\varepsilon_t, \varepsilon_{t-1}] \\ &= \mathrm{Cov}[u_t + \psi_1 u_{t-1}, u_{t-1} + \psi_1 u_{t-2}] \\ &= \psi_1 \sigma_u^2\end{aligned} \tag{25.21}$$

because both ε_t and ε_{t-1} are functions of u_{t-1}. But for $|j| \geq 2$,

$$\gamma_j = \mathrm{Cov}[\varepsilon_t, \varepsilon_{t-j}] = 0 \tag{25.22}$$

because the ε_t are functions of white noise u_t. Therefore, the autocorrelation function of the MA(1) process is

$$\rho_j = \frac{\psi_1 \cdot \mathbf{1}\{|j| = 1\}}{1 + \psi_1^2}, \quad j \neq 0 \tag{25.23}$$

In this example, we see the primary effect of the MA specification relative to the AR: MA processes have a qualitatively different autocorrelation function. The MA(1) autocorrelations are all zero for two time periods or more, whereas the AR(1) autocorrelations die out gradually. The truncation of nonzero autocovariances is a general property of MA(q) processes. For the specification in (25.19), the autocovariance function is qualitatively similar to the MA(1) case. If $0 \leq n \leq q$, then

$$\begin{aligned}\gamma_n &= \mathrm{E}\left[\left(\sum_{s=0}^{q} \psi_s u_{t-s}\right)\left(\sum_{s=0}^{q} \psi_s u_{t-n-s}\right)\right] \\ &= \mathrm{E}\left[\left(\sum_{s=-n}^{q-n} \psi_{s+n} u_{t-s-n}\right)\left(\sum_{s=0}^{q} \psi_s u_{t-n-s}\right)\right] \\ &= \mathrm{E}\left[\sum_{s=0}^{q-n} \psi_{n+s} \psi_s u_{t-s-n}^2\right] \\ &= \sigma_u^2 \sum_{s=0}^{q-n} \psi_{n+s} \psi_s\end{aligned} \tag{25.24}$$

For $-q \leq n < 0$ we use autocovariance stationarity to get $\gamma_n = \gamma_{-n}$. Otherwise, if $|n| > q$, then $\gamma_n = 0$. For convenience, we let $\psi_0 \equiv 1$.

The general covariance expression in (25.24) gives the variance

$$\mathrm{Var}[\varepsilon_t] = \sigma_u^2 \sum_{j=0}^{q} \psi_j^2 \tag{25.25}$$

when we set $n = 0$. Therefore, the autocorrelation function of the MA(q) process is

$$\rho_n = \begin{cases} \frac{\psi_{|n|} + \psi_1 \psi_{|n|+1} + \cdots + \psi_{q-|n|} \psi_q}{1 + \psi_1^2 + \cdots + \psi_q^2} & \text{if} \quad |n| \leq q \\ 0 & \text{if} \quad |n| > q \end{cases}$$

Like an AR(p) process, an MA(q) process can exhibit autocorrelations that die out. But after q time periods, all autocorrelations are identically zero.

This qualitative difference in autocovariances has an important implication for covariance stationarity of moving-average processes: an MA(q) process is *always* covariance stationary. In effect, the moving-average specification ensures that the dependence in the time series is limited to q periods. There is no possibility for the influence of a component u_t growing without bound as the process unfolds the way that the autoregressive specification allows. Thus, stationarity is guaranteed and solving for the autocovariance function is much simpler.

25.3.1 Identification

An identification issue arises in MA models that is not present in AR ones. In general, several distinct sets of parameter values correspond to one autocovariance function. Because the autocovariance function is identified and characterizes the second moments of the time series $\{\varepsilon_t\}$, the parameters of the MA(q) process are not globally identified.

EXAMPLE 25.4 [MA(1)]
Reconsider the MA(1) model in Example 25.3. If we suppose that

$$\text{Var}[u_t^*] = \sigma_u^2 \psi_1^2 \qquad \text{and} \qquad \varepsilon_t^* = u_t^* + \frac{1}{\psi_1} u_{t-1}^*$$

then, using (25.20)–(25.22), the autocovariance function of this alternative MA(1) process is

$$\gamma_0 = \sigma_u^2 \psi_1^2 \left(1 + \frac{1}{\psi_1^2}\right) = \sigma_u^2 \left(1 + \psi_1^2\right)$$

$$\gamma_1 = \frac{1}{\psi_1} \left(\sigma_u^2 \psi_1^2\right) = \psi_1 \sigma_u^2$$

$$\gamma_s = 0, \quad s > 1$$

Therefore $\{\varepsilon_t\}$ and $\{\varepsilon_t^*\}$ have the same autocovariance function. Provided that $\psi_1 \neq \pm 1$, two distinct latent MA(1) processes yield observationally equivalent distributions. In other words, the parameters σ_u^2 and ψ_1 are not globally identified.

To estimate these parameters, we must restrict the parameter space. This is not a substantive restriction, because our choice will preserve the observable properties of the model. Such identifying restrictions are often called *parameter normalizations*.

A convenient normalization for the MA(1) model is to restrict $|\psi_1| \leq 1$. Note that although this is formally comparable to the stationarity restriction for AR(1) processes, this is *not* a stationarity condition. MA(q) processes are *always* stationary. This is a restriction to the parameter space so that ψ_1 is globally identified within the smaller parameter space.

This identification problem illustrates the distinction between local and global identification. Although ψ_1 is not globally identified in $\mathbb{R}$, once we impose *inequality* constraints ψ_1 is globally identified. This contrasts with such failures of global identification as with exact multicollinearity among explanatory variables in a linear regression. To proceed, we must impose *equality* constraints. In effect, equality constraints are choices among an infinite set of observationally equivalent parameter values. But for σ_u^2 and ψ_1 in the MA(1) model we are choosing between only two distinct values.

The standard normalizations for MA(q) parameters require the (complex) roots of the *characteristic equation*

$$z^q \psi(z^{-1}) \equiv z^q + \psi_1 z^{q-1} + \psi_2 z^{q-2} + \cdots + \psi_q = 0 \tag{25.26}$$

to lie on or inside the complex unit circle. To explain this, we turn to a notation called the *lag operator.*

DEFINITION 43 (LAG OPERATOR) *Define the* lag operator L *by* $L^j u_t \equiv u_{t-j}$ *for* $j = 0, \pm 1, \pm 2, \ldots$.[19]

With this notation, we can rewrite an MA(q) process as

$$u_t + \sum_{j=1}^{q} \psi_j u_{t-j} = u_t + \sum_{j=1}^{q} \psi_j L^j u_t = \psi(L) u_t$$

where $\psi(L)$ is the qth-order polynomial defined in (25.26). We can transform the general MA(q) case into a composition of MA(1) transformations by factoring the MA polynomial into

$$z^q \psi(z^{-1}) = \prod_{j=1}^{q} (z - \lambda_j)$$

where λ_j, $j = 1, \ldots, q$ are the q (complex) roots of $z^q \psi(z^{-1}) = 0$.[20] Then we can write

$$\varepsilon_t = \prod_{j=1}^{q} (1 - \lambda_j L) u_t \tag{25.27}$$

EXAMPLE 25.5 [MA(2)]

Let

$$\varepsilon_t = \left(1 + \psi_1 L + \psi_2 L^2\right) u_t$$

where $\{u_t\}$ is a sequence of i.i.d. $\mathfrak{N}(0, \sigma_u^2)$ random variables. The roots

$$\lambda_1 = -\frac{1}{2}\left(\psi_1 - \sqrt{\psi_1^2 - 4\psi_2}\right) \quad \text{and} \quad \lambda_2 = -\frac{1}{2}\left(\psi_1 + \sqrt{\psi_1^2 - 4\psi_2}\right)$$

appear in the factored form

$$\varepsilon_t = (1 - \lambda_1 L)(1 - \lambda_2 L) u_t$$

---

[19] We also use the symbol L to denote log-likelihood functions. Both are traditional symbols and, because we do not mix them, no ambiguity should arise.

[20] In general, the *fundamental theorem of algebra* implies that a pth order polynomial with real coefficients has p (complex) roots. See Simon and Blume (1994, Section A3.2). There is a one-to-one relationship between a polynomial and its roots. Complex roots always occur in conjugate pairs, for example, $\lambda = a + ib$ and $\bar{\lambda} = a - ib$ where $i^2 = -1$. As is usual, we will denote the magnitude of a complex number with the absolute value notation:

$$|\lambda| = |a + ib| \equiv \sqrt{a^2 + b^2} = \sqrt{\lambda\bar{\lambda}} = |\bar{\lambda}|$$

$$= 1 + (-\lambda_1 - \lambda_2) L + \lambda_1\lambda_2 L^2$$

Even though λ_1 and λ_2 may be complex, the coefficients

$$\psi_1 = -\lambda_1 - \lambda_2 \qquad \text{and} \qquad \psi_2 = \lambda_1\lambda_2 \tag{25.28}$$

are real.

We can isolate the identication problems in MA(q) models with this factored representation (25.27), effectively working with a composition of MA(1) specifications. An MA(q) process with some roots that are reciprocals of those in (25.27) has the *same* autocovariance function.

EXAMPLE 25.6 [MA(2)]

Continuing Example 25.5, let

$$\begin{aligned}\varepsilon_t &= \left(1 + \psi_1 L + \psi_2 L^2\right) u_t \\ &= (1 - \lambda_1 L)(1 - \lambda_2 L) u_t\end{aligned}$$

denote an MA(2) process. Now consider the alternative MA(2) process

$$\begin{aligned}\varepsilon_t^* &= \left(1 - \frac{1}{\lambda_1} L\right)\left(1 - \frac{1}{\lambda_2} L\right) u_t^* \\ &= \left(1 - \frac{\lambda_1 + \lambda_2}{\lambda_1\lambda_2} L + \frac{1}{\lambda_1\lambda_2} L^2\right) u_t^*\end{aligned}$$

where u_t^* is i.i.d. with mean zero and variance $\lambda_1^2\lambda_2^2\sigma_u^2$. We will show that $\{\varepsilon_t\}$ and $\{\varepsilon_t^*\}$ have the same autocovariance functions.

Using (25.24) and (25.28), the MA(2) lag polynomial

$$\begin{aligned}(1 - \lambda_1 L)(1 - \lambda_2 L) &= 1 - (\lambda_1 + \lambda_2) L + \lambda_1\lambda_2 L^2 \\ &= 1 + \psi_1 L + \psi_2 L^2\end{aligned}$$

yields the autocovariance function

$$\gamma_n = \begin{cases} \sigma_u^2 \cdot \left[1 + (\lambda_1 + \lambda_2)^2 + \lambda_1^2\lambda_2^2\right] & \text{if} \quad n = 0 \\ \sigma_u^2 \cdot (\lambda_1 + \lambda_2)(1 + \lambda_1\lambda_2) & \text{if} \quad |n| = 1 \\ \sigma_u^2 \cdot \lambda_1\lambda_2 & \text{if} \quad |n| = 2 \\ 0 & \text{if} \quad |n| > 2 \end{cases}$$

But we can factor out $\lambda_1^2\lambda_2^2$ to obtain

$$\gamma_n = \begin{cases} \lambda_1^2\lambda_2^2\sigma_u^2 \cdot \left[1 + \left(\frac{\lambda_1+\lambda_2}{\lambda_1\lambda_2}\right)^2 + \left(\frac{1}{\lambda_1\lambda_2}\right)^2\right] & \text{if} \quad n = 0 \\ \lambda_1^2\lambda_2^2\sigma_u^2 \cdot \left(\frac{\lambda_1+\lambda_2}{\lambda_1\lambda_2}\right)\left(1 + \frac{1}{\lambda_1\lambda_2}\right) & \text{if} \quad |n| = 1 \\ \lambda_1^2\lambda_2^2\sigma_u^2 \cdot \left(\frac{1}{\lambda_1\lambda_2}\right) & \text{if} \quad |n| = 2 \\ 0 & \text{if} \quad |n| > 2 \end{cases}$$

which is the autocovariance function for $\{\varepsilon_t^*\}$.

This example shows that two *distinct* MA(2) polynomials can have the *same* autocovariance function.[21] It also suggests similar problems for MA(q) processes generally. A resolution of this identification failure is to choose a unique MA(q) representation for each autocovariance function. This is the effect of the requirement that the roots of $z^q\psi(z^{-1}) = 0$ lie inside the complex unit circle.

PROPOSITION 24 (MA(q) IDENTIFICATION) *Every MA(q) process $\varepsilon_t = \psi(L)u_t$ is observationally equivalent to a unique MA(q) process $\varepsilon_t^* = \psi_a(L)u_t$ for which all the roots of the characteristic equation $z^q\psi_a(z^{-1}) = 0$ lie on or inside the complex unit circle.*

We prove this proposition in Section 25.7.3. The essence of the proof is contained in Example 25.6: after factoring $\psi(L) = \prod_{j=1}^{q}(1 - \lambda_j L)$, one can replace the terms $(1 - \lambda_j L)$ that yield characteristic roots outside the unit circle ($|\lambda_j| > 1$) with terms $(1 - \lambda_j^{-1}L)\lambda_j$ that yield characteristic roots inside the unit circle without changing the autocovariance function of the resultant MA(q) process. This yields a unique reparameterization $\psi_a(L)$ because the roots of a polynomial are unique. This is the conventional normalization for MA specifications and we will use it from this point forward.

25.3.2 Kalman Filter

The relative ease with which one derives the autocovariance function of an MA(q) process contrasts with the relative difficulty in deriving a corresponding GLS transformation. Unlike the AR(p) case, this transformation depends on all the preceding observations and not just the most recent q.

EXAMPLE 25.7 [MA(1)]

The nature of the GLS transformation appears in the MA(1) specification. Given that the u_t are white noise, an immediate strategy is to transform the residuals ε_t into the u_t. This works for the AR(p) model for observations $t = p + 1, \ldots, T$; however, recursive substitution in the MA(1) equation gives

$$\begin{aligned} u_t &= \varepsilon_t - \psi_1 u_{t-1} \\ &= \varepsilon_t - \psi_1 \varepsilon_{t-1} + \psi_1^2 u_{t-2} \\ &\vdots \end{aligned}$$

[21] The MA(1) case in Example 25.4 is similar. In the notation of lag operators,

$$\varepsilon_t = u_t + \psi_1 u_{t-1} = (1 + \psi_1 L)\, u_t$$

is observationally equivalent to

$$\varepsilon_t^* = \left(1 + \frac{1}{\psi_1} L\right)(\psi_1 u_t)$$

We effectively noted the reciprocal root phenomenon without identifying it as such.

$$= \varepsilon_t - \sum_{s=1}^{t-1} (-\psi_1)^s \varepsilon_{t-s} + \psi_1^t u_0 \tag{25.29}$$

Every previous ε_t appears on the RHS. Moreover, we end up with a term involving the latent disturbance u_0 so that the transformation is infeasible.

For MA(q) specifications in general, one gets the same result: recursive substitution yields a distributed lag over all preceding residuals and terms containing the latent variables $u_0, \ldots, u_{-q+1}$. A successful strategy is to produce the standardized MMSE linear prediction-error sequence

$$\varepsilon_{*t} \equiv \frac{\varepsilon_t - \mathrm{E}^*[\varepsilon_t \mid \varepsilon_1, \ldots, \varepsilon_{t-1}]}{\sqrt{\mathrm{Var}\big[\varepsilon_t - \mathrm{E}^*[\varepsilon_t \mid \varepsilon_1, \ldots, \varepsilon_{t-1}]\big]}}, \qquad t = 1, \ldots, T$$

The $\{\varepsilon_{*t}\}$ is a Gram–Schmidt orthonormalization of the $\{\varepsilon_t\}$; $\{\varepsilon_{*t}\}$ has constant (unit) variance and is serially uncorrelated. Thus, it is a valid GLS transformation. Indeed, it amounts to using the Cholesky variance-matrix decomposition (Lemma 7.6, p. 140) to produce this transformation.

However, instead of applying the Cholesky decomposition directly to the variance matrix of $\varepsilon \equiv [\varepsilon_t]'$, we will use a convenient method called the *Kalman filter*.[22] In its simplest form, the Kalman filter is a direct application of Gram–Schmidt orthonormalization.

EXAMPLE 25.8 [MA(1)]

Let $\varepsilon_t = u_t + \psi_1 u_{t-1}$ $(t = 1, \ldots, T)$ where the u_t $(t = 0, 1, \ldots, T)$ are i.i.d. with mean zero and variance σ_u^2. To form an orthogonal basis for the ε_t, we begin by setting the first element to

$$\varepsilon_{*1} = \frac{\varepsilon_1}{\sqrt{1 + \psi_1^2}}$$

We will set the tth element of the basis to[23]

$$\varepsilon_{*t} = \frac{\varepsilon_t - \mathrm{E}^*[\varepsilon_t \mid \varepsilon_1, \ldots, \varepsilon_{t-1}]}{\sqrt{\mathrm{Var}\big[\varepsilon_t - \mathrm{E}^*[\varepsilon_t \mid \varepsilon_1, \ldots, \varepsilon_{t-1}]\big]}}$$

Noting that ε_t is correlated only with ε_{t-1}, we see that

$$\begin{aligned}
\mathrm{E}^*[\varepsilon_t \mid \varepsilon_1, \ldots, \varepsilon_{t-1}] &= \mathrm{E}^*[\varepsilon_t \mid \varepsilon_{*1}, \ldots, \varepsilon_{*t-1}] \\
&= \mathrm{E}^*[\varepsilon_t \mid \varepsilon_{*t-1}] \qquad (25.30) \\
&= \mathrm{Cov}[\varepsilon_t, \varepsilon_{*t-1}]\varepsilon_{*t-1} \\
&= \frac{\mathrm{Cov}[\varepsilon_t, \varepsilon_{t-1}]\,(\varepsilon_{t-1} - \mathrm{E}^*[\varepsilon_{t-1} \mid \varepsilon_1, \ldots, \varepsilon_{t-2}])}{\mathrm{Var}\big[\varepsilon_{t-1} - \mathrm{E}^*[\varepsilon_{t-1} \mid \varepsilon_1, \ldots, \varepsilon_{t-2}]\big]} \\
&= \frac{\sigma_u^2 \psi_1\,(\varepsilon_{t-1} - \mathrm{E}^*[\varepsilon_{t-1} \mid \varepsilon_1, \ldots, \varepsilon_{t-2}])}{\mathrm{Var}\big[\varepsilon_{t-1} - \mathrm{E}^*[\varepsilon_{t-1} \mid \varepsilon_1, \ldots, \varepsilon_{t-2}]\big]} \qquad (25.31)
\end{aligned}$$

We can calculate the variances in the denominator recursively with

[22] For reference, see Kalman (1960), Gardner et al. (1980), and Harvey (1989, 1993).

[23] Compare these basis elements with those in (7.12) and (7.14) of the Cholesky decomposition.

$$\begin{aligned}
\sigma_t^2 &\equiv \mathrm{Var}\big[\varepsilon_t - \mathrm{E}^*[\varepsilon_t \mid \varepsilon_1, \ldots, \varepsilon_{t-1}]\big] \\
&= \mathrm{Var}\big[\varepsilon_t - \mathrm{Cov}[\varepsilon_t, \varepsilon_{*t-1}]\varepsilon_{*t-1}\big] \\
&= \mathrm{Var}[\varepsilon_t] - (\mathrm{Cov}[\varepsilon_t, \varepsilon_{*t-1}])^2 \\
&= \sigma_u^2\left(1+\psi_1^2\right) - \frac{\sigma_u^4\psi_1^2}{\mathrm{Var}\big[\varepsilon_{t-1} - \mathrm{E}^*[\varepsilon_{t-1} \mid \varepsilon_1, \ldots, \varepsilon_{t-2}]\big]} \\
&= \sigma_u^2\left(1+\psi_1^2 - \frac{\psi_1^2}{\sigma_{t-1}^2/\sigma_u^2}\right)
\end{aligned} \tag{25.32}$$

These two equations permit us to calculate all ε_{*t} for $t > 1$.

If we expand this recursive system, we find that the $\varepsilon_t - \mathrm{E}^*[\varepsilon_t \mid \varepsilon_{*t-1}]$ are similar to the u_t in the previous example. Equation (25.31) expands to give

$$\varepsilon_t - \mathrm{E}^*[\varepsilon_t \mid \varepsilon_1, \ldots, \varepsilon_{t-1}] = \varepsilon_t + \sum_{s=1}^{t-1} \frac{(-\psi_1)^s\, \varepsilon_{t-s}}{\prod_{r=t-s}^{t-1} \sigma_r^2/\sigma_u^2} \tag{25.33}$$

and (25.32) expands to give

$$\sigma_t^2 = \sigma_u^2 \frac{1+\psi_1^2+\cdots+\psi_1^{2(t-1)}+\psi_1^{2t}}{1+\psi_1^2+\cdots+\psi_1^{2(t-1)}} > \sigma_u^2 \tag{25.34}$$

Compared to (25.29), one sees a similar accumulation of $\varepsilon_1, \ldots, \varepsilon_t$ with coefficients proportional to $(-\psi_1)^s$. However the sth coefficient above is divided by

$$\prod_{r=t-s}^{t-1} \frac{\sigma_r^2}{\sigma_u^2} = \frac{1+\psi_1^2+\cdots+\psi_1^{2(t-1)}}{1+\psi_1^2+\cdots+\psi_1^{2(t-s-1)}} > 1 \tag{25.35}$$

The MA(1) example is particularly simple because there is only one nonzero autocovariance. For MA(q) processes, it is convenient to employ a latent *multivariate* AR(1) representation of the univariate MA(q) process. This representation keeps track of the various autocovariances through first-order recursive equations for $\mathrm{E}^*[\varepsilon_t \mid \varepsilon_1, \ldots, \varepsilon_{t-1}]$ and $\mathrm{Var}\big[\varepsilon_t - \mathrm{E}^*[\varepsilon_t \mid \varepsilon_1, \ldots, \varepsilon_{t-1}]\big]$. One can always write the univariate latent MA(q) process in terms of a multivariate latent structure called a *state-space model*. Let us denote

$$\varepsilon_t = \boldsymbol{\delta}'\mathbf{z}_t \tag{25.36}$$

where $\boldsymbol{\delta} = \boldsymbol{\psi} \equiv [\psi_j;\ j = 0, \ldots, q]'$ and $\mathbf{z}_t \equiv [u_{t-j};\ j = 0, \ldots, q]'$.[24] We can artificially write $\mathbf{z}_t$ as a $(q+1)$-dimensional AR(1) process

$$\mathbf{z}_t = \mathbf{A}\mathbf{z}_{t-1} + \mathbf{w}_t$$

where $\mathbf{A}$ and $\mathbf{w}_t$ are laid out in

24 It *is* redundant at this point to introduce $\boldsymbol{\delta}$ as an additional parameter vector because it equals $\boldsymbol{\psi}$. However, we will also apply the Kalman filter to ARMA(p,q) models where $\boldsymbol{\delta}$ takes another form.

$$\mathbf{z}_t = \begin{bmatrix} u_t \\ u_{t-1} \\ u_{t-2} \\ \vdots \\ u_{t-q} \end{bmatrix} = \begin{bmatrix} 0 & 0 & \cdots & 0 & 0 \\ 1 & 0 & \cdots & 0 & 0 \\ 0 & 1 & \cdots & 0 & 0 \\ \vdots & \vdots & \ddots & 0 & 0 \\ 0 & 0 & \cdots & 1 & 0 \end{bmatrix} \begin{bmatrix} u_{t-1} \\ u_{t-2} \\ u_{t-3} \\ \vdots \\ u_{t-q-1} \end{bmatrix} + \begin{bmatrix} u_t \\ 0 \\ 0 \\ \vdots \\ 0 \end{bmatrix} \tag{25.37}$$

There is a $q \times q$ identity matrix in the lower left-hand corner of $\mathbf{A}$ that acts like a staircase, taking lagged values of u_{t-j} to a lower row, thereby producing a complete vector of q lags in $\mathbf{z}_t$. The variance matrix of $\mathbf{z}_t$ is simply $\sigma_u^2 \cdot \mathbf{I}_{q+1}$ and the variance of $\mathbf{w}_t$ is

$$\mathrm{Var}[\mathbf{w}_t] = \begin{bmatrix} \sigma_u^2 & \underset{1\times q}{\mathbf{0}} \\ \underset{q\times 1}{\mathbf{0}} & \underset{q\times q}{\mathbf{0}} \end{bmatrix}$$

Although the process for $\mathbf{z}_t$ in (25.37) may seem awkward, it greatly simplifies the derivation of the normalized prediction-error sequence $\{\varepsilon_{*t}\}$. Multivariate AR(1) processes share some of the analytical tractability of univariate ones.[25] In particular,

$$\mathrm{E}^*[\mathbf{z}_t \mid \varepsilon_1, \ldots, \varepsilon_{t-1}] = \mathbf{A}\,\mathrm{E}^*[\mathbf{z}_{t-1} \mid \varepsilon_1, \ldots, \varepsilon_{t-1}]$$

In Section 25.7.2, we combine this with an orthogonal projection just like (25.30) to obtain the recursive solution

$$\mathbf{m}_t = \mathbf{A}\left(\mathbf{m}_{t-1} + \mathbf{V}_{t-1}\boldsymbol{\delta}\frac{\varepsilon_{t-1} - \boldsymbol{\delta}'\mathbf{m}_{t-1}}{\boldsymbol{\delta}'\mathbf{V}_{t-1}\boldsymbol{\delta}}\right) \tag{25.38}$$

$$\mathbf{V}_t = \mathbf{A}\left(\mathbf{V}_{t-1} - \mathbf{V}_{t-1}\boldsymbol{\delta}\frac{1}{\boldsymbol{\delta}'\mathbf{V}_{t-1}\boldsymbol{\delta}}\boldsymbol{\delta}'\mathbf{V}_{t-1}\right)\mathbf{A}' + \mathrm{Var}[\mathbf{w}_t] \tag{25.39}$$

for $t = 2, \ldots, T$, where

$$\mathbf{m}_t \equiv \mathrm{E}^*[\mathbf{z}_t \mid \varepsilon_1, \ldots, \varepsilon_{t-1}] \qquad \text{and} \qquad \mathbf{V}_t \equiv \mathrm{Var}[\mathbf{z}_t - \mathbf{m}_t]$$

These equations comprise the Kalman filter for the state-space model (25.36)–(25.37). The starting conditions are simply the marginal moments

$$\mathbf{m}_1 \equiv \mathrm{E}[\mathbf{z}_1] = \mathbf{0} \qquad \text{and} \qquad \mathbf{V}_1 \equiv \mathrm{Var}[\mathbf{z}_1] = \sigma_u^2 \cdot \mathbf{I}_{q+1}$$

A new prediction $\mathbf{m}_t$ is a linear combination of the previous $\mathbf{m}_{t-1}$ and the latest realization of the MA(q) process, ε_{t-1}. Therefore, the Kalman filter continues to produce a distributed lag in all of the $\varepsilon_1, \ldots, \varepsilon_{t-1}$.

Equations (25.38)–(25.39) provide the general recursive relationships that deliver the terms

$$\mathrm{E}^*[\varepsilon_t \mid \varepsilon_1, \ldots, \varepsilon_{t-1}] = \boldsymbol{\delta}'\mathbf{m}_t$$

and

$$\mathrm{Var}\big[\varepsilon_t - \mathrm{E}^*[\varepsilon_t \mid \varepsilon_1, \ldots, \varepsilon_{t-1}]\big] = \boldsymbol{\delta}'\mathbf{V}_t\boldsymbol{\delta}$$

---

[25] In fact, pth-order difference equations such as

$$z_t = \phi_1 z_{t-1} + \phi_2 z_{t-2} + \cdots + \phi_p z_{t-p}$$

are generally analyzed in p-dimensional first-order difference form.

With them, we can produce a (nonlinear) GLS objective function. Before doing so, note that $\mathbf{V}_t = \sigma_u^2 \cdot \mathbf{C}_t$ where $\mathbf{C}_t$ depends only on $\boldsymbol{\delta} = \boldsymbol{\psi}$. Furthermore, $\mathbf{m}_t$ is not a function of σ_u^2.[26] Therefore, it is clearest to write the nonlinear weighted least-squares objective function as

$$Q_T(\boldsymbol{\beta}, \boldsymbol{\psi}) = \frac{1}{2} \mathrm{E}_T \left[\frac{\left(\varepsilon_t - \boldsymbol{\psi}'\mathbf{m}_t\right)^2}{\boldsymbol{\psi}'\mathbf{C}_t\boldsymbol{\psi}} \right] \tag{25.40}$$

where $\varepsilon_t = y_t - \mathbf{x}_t'\boldsymbol{\beta}$.

If we assume that the u_t are normally distributed, then the prediction-error decomposition yields the log-likelihood function

$$\mathrm{E}_T[L(\boldsymbol{\beta}, \boldsymbol{\psi}, \sigma_u^2)] = -\frac{1}{2} \log 2\pi\sigma_u^2 - \frac{1}{2} \mathrm{E}_T[\log(\boldsymbol{\psi}'\mathbf{C}_t\boldsymbol{\psi})] - \frac{Q_T(\boldsymbol{\beta}, \boldsymbol{\psi})}{\sigma_u^2} \tag{25.41}$$

Unlike the AR(p) version (25.8), this function exhibits a conditional heteroskedasticity that marks the difference between the moving-average and autoregressive models. Conditioning on a finite number of lagged values of ε_t yields an i.i.d. prediction error for the AR(p) but not for the MA(q).

25.3.3 Estimation

Using the Kalman filter (25.38)–(25.39), the GLS estimator is conceptually straightforward. For a given $\boldsymbol{\psi} = [\psi_j;\ j = 0, \ldots, q]$, one applies (25.38) to $\mathbf{y}$ and each of the columns of $\mathbf{X}$, $\mathbf{X}_k$ ($k = 1, \ldots, K$). If we denote the Kalman filter transformation of a variable $\mathbf{z} = \left[\mathbf{z}_t';\ t = 1, \ldots, T\right]'$ by

$$\mathbf{m}_t(\mathbf{z}) = \mathbf{A}\left(\mathbf{m}_{t-1}(\mathbf{z}) + \mathbf{C}_{t-1}\boldsymbol{\psi}\frac{\mathbf{z}_{t-1} - \boldsymbol{\psi}'\mathbf{m}_{t-1}}{\boldsymbol{\psi}'\mathbf{C}_{t-1}\boldsymbol{\psi}}\right), \qquad t = 2, \ldots, T$$

where $\mathbf{m}_1(\mathbf{z}) = \mathbf{0}$ and $\mathbf{V}_1 = \sigma_u^2 \cdot \mathbf{I}_{q+1}$, then a GLS transformation of y_t and $\mathbf{x}_t$ for an MA(q) is the quasidifference

$$y_{*t} = \frac{y_t - \boldsymbol{\psi}'\mathbf{m}_t(\mathbf{y})}{\sqrt{\boldsymbol{\psi}'\mathbf{C}_t\boldsymbol{\psi}}} \qquad \text{and} \qquad x_{*tk} = \frac{x_{tk} - \boldsymbol{\psi}'\mathbf{m}_t(\mathbf{X}_k)}{\sqrt{\boldsymbol{\psi}'\mathbf{C}_t\boldsymbol{\psi}}}$$

Thus, the GLS estimator is the standard OLS calculation $\hat{\boldsymbol{\beta}}_{\mathrm{GLS}} = (\mathbf{X}_*'\mathbf{X}_*)^{-1}\mathbf{X}_*'\mathbf{y}_*$. Under familiar conditions, this estimator is consistent, asymptotically normal so that

$$\sqrt{T}\left(\hat{\boldsymbol{\beta}}_{\mathrm{GLS}} - \boldsymbol{\beta}_0\right) \xrightarrow{d} \mathfrak{N}\left[\mathbf{0}, \operatorname{plim} \frac{\sigma_u^2}{T} \cdot (\mathbf{X}_*'\mathbf{X}_*)^{-1}\right]$$

and relatively efficient.

---

[26] Note that $\mathrm{Var}[\mathbf{w}_t]$, $\mathbf{V}_1$, and hence all $\mathbf{V}_t$ are proportional to σ_u^2. As a result, we can always rewrite (25.38)–(25.39) as

$$\mathbf{m}_t = \mathbf{A}\left(\mathbf{m}_{t-1} + \mathbf{C}_{t-1}\boldsymbol{\psi}\frac{\varepsilon_{t-1} - \boldsymbol{\psi}'\mathbf{m}_{t-1}}{\boldsymbol{\psi}'\mathbf{C}_{t-1}\boldsymbol{\psi}}\right)$$

$$\mathbf{C}_t = \mathbf{A}\left(\mathbf{C}_{t-1} - \mathbf{C}_{t-1}\boldsymbol{\psi}\frac{1}{\boldsymbol{\psi}'\mathbf{C}_{t-1}\boldsymbol{\psi}}\boldsymbol{\psi}'\mathbf{C}_{t-1}\right)\mathbf{A}' + \mathrm{Var}[\sigma_u^{-1} \cdot \mathbf{w}_t]$$

which does not depend on σ_u^2.

When the moving-average parameter vector $\boldsymbol{\psi}$ is unknown, researchers have proposed various approaches to estimation. All of them are more difficult than the simple OLS calculations for autoregressive models. The joint NLS estimator comparable to (25.6) is

$$\begin{bmatrix} \hat{\boldsymbol{\beta}}_{\text{NLS}} \\ \hat{\boldsymbol{\psi}}_{\text{NLS}} \end{bmatrix} = \underset{\boldsymbol{\beta},\boldsymbol{\psi}}{\text{argmin}}\ Q_T(\boldsymbol{\beta}, \boldsymbol{\psi})$$

where Q_T is given by (25.40). This requires the simultaneous calculation of estimators for $\boldsymbol{\beta}_0$ and $\boldsymbol{\psi}_0$ using a numerical algorithm such as Gauss–Newton regression.

Feasible GLS uses an initial consistent estimator of $\boldsymbol{\psi}_0$. One that uses the empirical autocovariances of the OLS (or IV, if $\mathbf{x}_t$ includes lagged y_t) fitted residuals $\check{\varepsilon}_t$ is the method-of-moments estimator $\left(\check{\boldsymbol{\psi}}, \check{\sigma}_u^2\right)$ that solves

$$\mathrm{E}_{T|s}(\check{\varepsilon}_t \check{\varepsilon}_{t-s}) = \check{\sigma}_u^2 \sum_{r=0}^{q-s} \check{\psi}_{s+r} \check{\psi}_r, \quad s = 0, 1, \ldots, q$$

This is a nonlinear system of equations, but rapid numerical solutions are available.

Alternatively, one can estimate $\boldsymbol{\psi}$ with NLS applied to the NLS objective function

$$Q_T^*(\boldsymbol{\beta}, \boldsymbol{\psi}) = \frac{1}{2}\,\mathrm{E}_T\left[\left(\varepsilon_t - \boldsymbol{\psi}'\mathbf{m}_t\right)^2\right] \tag{25.42}$$

This is the GLS sum of squares (25.40) after removing the conditional heteroskedasticity term $\boldsymbol{\psi}'\mathbf{C}_t\boldsymbol{\psi}$. Given the OLS (or IV) estimator $\check{\boldsymbol{\beta}}$ for $\boldsymbol{\beta}$, one can fix $\boldsymbol{\beta}$ at this value and minimize over $\boldsymbol{\psi}$ alone. Both of these methods yield an initial estimator $\check{\boldsymbol{\psi}}$ that one can use to compute the FGLS estimator for $\boldsymbol{\beta}_0$. Provided there are no lagged dependent explanatory variables, the FGLS estimator is asymptotically equivalent to GLS.

If the u_t are assumed to be normally distributed, the MLE for all of the parameters maximizes the log-likelihood function in (25.41). The computation of the MLE breaks up conveniently into the calculation of $\hat{\boldsymbol{\beta}}_{\text{ML}}$ and $\hat{\boldsymbol{\psi}}_{\text{ML}}$, followed by the calculation of $\hat{\sigma}_{\text{ML},u}^2$. Using (25.41), the MLE for σ_u^2 is

$$\hat{\sigma}_{\text{ML},u}^2 = \mathrm{E}_T\left[\frac{\left(\hat{\varepsilon}_t - \hat{\boldsymbol{\psi}}_{\text{ML}}'\hat{\mathbf{m}}_t\right)^2}{\hat{\boldsymbol{\psi}}_{\text{ML}}'\hat{\mathbf{C}}_t\hat{\boldsymbol{\psi}}_{\text{ML}}}\right]$$

where $\hat{\varepsilon}_t \equiv y_t - \mathbf{x}_t'\hat{\boldsymbol{\beta}}_{\text{ML}}$ and $\hat{\mathbf{m}}_t$ and $\hat{\mathbf{C}}_t$ are also evaluated at $\left[\hat{\boldsymbol{\beta}}_{\text{ML}}', \hat{\boldsymbol{\psi}}_{\text{ML}}'\right]$. Hence, the concentrated log-likelihood function is

$$\mathrm{E}_T[L(\boldsymbol{\beta}, \boldsymbol{\psi}, \sigma_u^2)] = -\frac{1}{2}\log 2\pi - \frac{1}{2}\log \mathrm{E}_T\left[\frac{\left(\varepsilon_t - \boldsymbol{\psi}'\mathbf{m}_t\right)^2}{\boldsymbol{\psi}'\mathbf{C}_t\boldsymbol{\psi}}\right] - \frac{1}{2}\mathrm{E}_T[\log(\boldsymbol{\psi}'\mathbf{C}_t\boldsymbol{\psi})]$$

For the MA(1) case, a grid search over ψ_1 is a simple algorithm for finding the MLE, comparable to the Hildreth–Lu algorithm for the AR(1) model. But this is not a general procedure. Maximization of the log-likelihood function for MA(q) models often requires care because quadratic approximations are poor. In addition, because of the identification issue accompanying moving averages, the MLE is not inherently constrained to satisfy the unit circle restrictions. It can be helpful to impose these restrictions and this requires additional work.

Researchers often use approximations to these estimators that are more convenient to compute. A common element of many of these approximations is treating the latent $u_0, \ldots, u_{1-q}$ as additional parameters. The conditional log-likelihood given these random variables is much simpler than the sample log-likelihood function. If we condition on $\mathbf{z}_0 \equiv [u_s;\ s = 1-q, \ldots, 0]'$, the Kalman filter simplifies to[27]

$$\mathbf{m}_t = \mathbf{z}_t = \left[u_{t-1}, \ldots, u_{t-q-1}\right]$$

$$\varepsilon_t - \boldsymbol{\psi}'\mathbf{m}_t = u_t = \varepsilon_t - \sum_{s=1}^{q} \psi_s u_{t-s}$$

and

$$\boldsymbol{\psi}'\mathbf{C}_t\boldsymbol{\psi} = 1, \qquad t = 1, \ldots, T$$

reducing ML computation to minimization of the NLS objective function

$$Q_T^{**}(\boldsymbol{\beta}, \boldsymbol{\psi}) = \frac{1}{2}\,\mathrm{E}_T[u_t^2] \tag{25.43}$$

The corresponding NLS estimator $\left[\hat{\boldsymbol{\beta}}'_{\mathrm{NLS}}, \hat{\boldsymbol{\psi}}'_{\mathrm{NLS}}\right]$ is asymptotically equivalent to the ML and GLS estimators. For a proof, see Fuller (1966, Theorem 8.3.1).

The Gauss–Newton regression (GNR) is a popular optimization method for these NLS problems. The necessary derivatives can be calculated recursively with

$$\frac{\partial u_t}{\partial \boldsymbol{\beta}} = -\mathbf{x}_t - \frac{\partial \mathbf{m}_t'}{\partial \boldsymbol{\beta}}\boldsymbol{\psi} = -\mathbf{x}_t - \sum_{s=1}^{q} \frac{\partial u_{t-s}}{\partial \boldsymbol{\beta}}\psi_j$$

$$\frac{\partial u_t}{\partial \boldsymbol{\psi}} = -\mathbf{m}_t - \frac{\partial \mathbf{m}_t'}{\partial \boldsymbol{\psi}}\boldsymbol{\psi} = -\mathbf{m}_t - \sum_{s=1}^{q} \frac{\partial u_{t-s}}{\partial \boldsymbol{\psi}}\psi_j$$

Because $\mathbf{m}_0 = [u_s;\ s = 1-q, \ldots, 0]'$ is fixed, the starting values for this recursion are all zeros:

$$\frac{\partial \boldsymbol{\psi}' u_{1-s}}{\partial \boldsymbol{\beta}} = \mathbf{0}, \qquad \frac{\partial \boldsymbol{\psi}' u_{1-s}}{\partial \boldsymbol{\psi}} = \mathbf{0}, \qquad s = 1, \ldots, q$$

The GNR is an OLS fit of y_t to these partial derivatives. This simple structure also makes the Newton–Raphson(NR) algorithm workable. In situations in which GNR does not converge quickly, NR is often worth the additional computation of the second derivatives.

The asymptotic distribution of estimators that maximizes (25.43) is identical to the MLE. This occurs because the initial $\mathbf{m}_0$ becomes irrelevant as $T \to \infty$. On the other hand, there are no general theoretical results for small T. The choice of $\mathbf{m}_0$ can be important. A common approach is to set $\mathbf{m}_0 = \mathbf{0}$, its marginal mean. Harvey (1993, Section 3.5) reviews Monte Carlo evidence for such approximate MLEs and concludes that the exact MLE has smaller MSE than the approximations when there is an appreciable difference between the estimators. Such differences are most pronounced near the unit root boundary of the MA(q) parameter space. Therefore, the general advice to use the exact MLE when possible continues to hold. The approximate estimators are good starting values for ML calculations.

---

27 When $u_0, u_{-1}, \ldots, u_{1-q}$ are known, $\mathbf{V}_1 = \mathrm{Var}(w_t)$ is the new starting point for the Kalman filter. Because the first row of $\mathbf{A}$ is all zeros, $\mathbf{V}_t = \mathbf{V}_1$ for all $t > 1$ and $\boldsymbol{\psi}'\mathbf{C}_t\boldsymbol{\psi} = 1$. Example 25.7 is the simplest case with $q = 1$.

One apparent difference between computing the MLE and its approximants is that the log-likelihood function may have an *unconstrained* maximum on the boundary of the parameter space while the approximants generally do not. This phenomenon relates to identification of moving-average models (Proposition 24): every MA(q) parameter vector with roots inside the complex unit circle has an observationally equivalent MA(q) parameter vector with roots outside the unit circle.

EXAMPLE 25.9 [MA(1)]

In Example 25.4, we noted that the MA(1) model has two, observationally equivalent, parameterizations. In particular, if we denote the average sample log-likelihood function for the standard parameterization in (25.18) as $\mathrm{E}_T[L(\boldsymbol{\beta}, \psi_1, \sigma_u^2)]$ then

$$\mathrm{E}_T[L(\boldsymbol{\beta}, 1/\psi_1, \psi_1^2\sigma_u^2)] = \mathrm{E}_T[L(\boldsymbol{\beta}, \psi_1, \sigma_u^2)]$$

Furthermore, if we concentrate the variance parameter out of the log-likelihood function then

$$\mathrm{E}_T[L^c(\boldsymbol{\beta}, 1/\psi_1)] = \mathrm{E}_T[L^c(\boldsymbol{\beta}, \psi_1)]$$

Differentiating this equality with respect to ψ_1,

$$-\frac{1}{\psi_1^2}\mathrm{E}_T[L_2^c(\boldsymbol{\beta}, 1/\psi_1)] = \mathrm{E}_T[L_2^c(\boldsymbol{\beta}, \psi_1)]$$

Evaluating this expression at $\psi_1 = \pm 1$ gives

$$-\mathrm{E}_T[L_2^c(\boldsymbol{\beta}, \pm 1)] = \mathrm{E}_T[L_2^c(\boldsymbol{\beta}, \pm 1)] \qquad \text{or} \qquad \mathrm{E}_T[L_2^c(\boldsymbol{\beta}, \pm 1)] = 0$$

In words, the concentrated log-likelihood always has a critical value at $\psi_1 = \pm 1$.

Occasionally one of these critical values is a global maximum of the sample log-likelihood function. Local maxima are more common. This example also underscores the point that the log-likelihood function does not constrain the parameters of an MA(q) to the region in which the characteristic roots lie within the unit circle. However, every local maximum outside this region has a counterpart within it yielding the same value of the log-likelihood function.

The approximating objective functions generally do not have this property. Instead, observationally equivalent parameter values yield different function values. This is contradictory and justified only by convenience. For this reason, it is sensible to constrain optimization in these cases also. Such constrained estimators also have a positive probability of falling on the parameter boundary.

25.3.4 Testing Serial Correlation

The MA(q) specification also offers an opportunity to construct a score test for serial correlation. As it turns out, the score test for whether the MA(q) coefficients are all zero is identical to the score test for whether the AR(q) coefficients are all zero. This is because the two tests have the same local alternatives.[28] We show the general equivalence in Section 25.7.4. Here we illustrate this with the MA(1) case.

[28] For other examples of identical local alternatives, see Examples 17.8 and 17.9.

EXAMPLE 25.10 [MA(1)]

Using the results of Example 25.8, we can write the exact sample average log-likelihood function as

$$\mathrm{E}_T[L(\psi_1)] = -\frac{1}{2}\,\mathrm{E}_T\left[\log 2\pi\sigma_t^2 + \frac{(\varepsilon_t - \mu_t)^2}{\sigma_t^2}\right]$$

where (25.31)–(25.32) give

$$\mu_t = \psi_1 \frac{\varepsilon_{t-1} - \mu_{t-1}}{\sigma_{t-1}^2/\sigma_u^2} \qquad \text{and} \qquad \sigma_t^2 = \sigma_u^2\left(1 + \psi_1^2 - \frac{\psi_1^2}{\sigma_{t-1}^2/\sigma_u^2}\right)$$

The score with respect to ψ_1 is

$$\mathrm{E}_T[L_{\psi_1}(\psi_1)] = -\frac{1}{2}\,\mathrm{E}_T\left[\frac{1}{\sigma_t^2}\frac{\partial\sigma_t^2}{\partial\psi_1} + 2\left(\frac{\varepsilon_t - \mu_t}{\sigma_t^2}\right)\left(-\frac{\partial\mu_t}{\partial\psi_1} - \frac{\varepsilon_t - \mu_t}{\sigma_t^2}\frac{\partial\sigma_t^2}{\partial\psi_1}\right)\right]$$

This score simplifies enormously at $\psi_1 = 0$: $\sigma_t^2 = \sigma_u^2$, $\mu_t = 0$,

$$\left.\frac{\partial\sigma_t^2}{\partial\psi_1}\right|_{\psi_1=0} = 0 \qquad \text{and} \qquad \left.\frac{\partial\mu_t}{\partial\psi_1}\right|_{\psi_1=0} = \varepsilon_{t-1}, \quad t > 1$$

so that

$$\mathrm{E}_T[L_{\psi_1}(\psi_1)] = \frac{1}{\sigma_u^2}\,\mathrm{E}_T[\varepsilon_t\varepsilon_{t-1}]$$

This is essentially the same score that we use to test for serial correlation in an AR(1) model.[29]

The general equivalence of the MA(q) and the AR(q) score tests is a symptom of a general duality between the two models. In the next section, we explore this duality as we consider the combination of AR and MA components in one specification for the serial correlation.

Let us take stock of what we have covered. We summarize the main points in Table 25.1, comparing the autoregressive and moving-average specifications for autocorrleation. They are like mirror images: one is a distributed lag in ε_t while the other is a distributed lag in u_t. The differences in their properties follow accordingly. First, the autocovariances of an AR(p) specification decline gradually as the distance between observations grows, whereas the MA(q) autocovariances collapse suddenly to zero. The variance-components character of the MA(q) specification also makes its autocovariances relatively easy to derive. The derivation of the AR(p) autocovariances requires the solution of a linear system called the Yule–Walker equations.

AR(p) models also require restrictions on the parameters to preserve the stationarity of the implied process. We wrote these restrictions in two ways, as restrictions on p conditional variances and as restrictions on the p roots of the characteristic polynomial associated with the distributed lag. MA(q) models are always stationary but analogous restrictions on the q roots of the characteristic polynomial provide the normalizations necessary to identify the parameters of the model.

Despite its awkward aspects, the AR(p) model also possesses an important advantage over the MA(q): the GLS estimator for AR(p) models of the disturbance term in the linear model

---

29 See equation (19.24). The difference in the scores is only a $T/(T-1)$ factor of proportionality.

Table 25.1
AR versus MA Specifications

Property	AR(p)	MA(q)
Specification	$\varepsilon_t = \phi_1\varepsilon_{t-1} + \cdots + \phi_p\varepsilon_{t-p} + u_t$ or $\phi(L)\varepsilon_t = u_t$	$\varepsilon_t = u_t + \psi_1 u_{t-1} + \cdots + \psi_q u_{t-q}$ or $\varepsilon_t = \psi(L)u_t$
Autocovariances	Decline geometrically, Yule–Walker equations	Zero after q lags, variance components
Restrictions	For stationarity: $\lambda^p\phi(\lambda^{-1}) = 0 \Rightarrow \lvert\lambda\rvert < 1$	For identification: $\lambda^q\psi(\lambda^{-1}) = 0 \Rightarrow \lvert\lambda\rvert \leq 1$
GLS	$\phi(L)y_t = \phi(L)\mathbf{x}_t'\boldsymbol{\beta}_0 + u_t$	Kalman filter

$y_t = \mathbf{x}_t'\boldsymbol{\beta}_0 + \varepsilon_t$ is simpler. A GLS transformation is the autoregressive distributed lag itself, making the latent i.i.d. u_t the disturbance terms in the transformed linear model. Furthermore, a consistent estimator of the AR(p) parameters is the OLS fitted coefficients from regressing OLS fitted residuals $\hat{\varepsilon}_t \equiv y_t - \mathbf{x}_t'\hat{\boldsymbol{\beta}}_{\text{OLS}}$ on p lagged values $\hat{\varepsilon}_{t-1}, \ldots, \hat{\varepsilon}_{t-p}$. In contrast, the transformation of the MA(q) model requires a method like the Kalman filter and initial parameter estimation requires numerical solution of nonlinear equations.

In closing this summary, we note another contrast that is dual to the differences in autocovariances. For an AR(p) process,

$$\mathrm{E}^*[\varepsilon_t \mid \varepsilon_{t-1}, \varepsilon_{t-2}, \ldots] = \phi_1\varepsilon_{t-1} + \cdots + \phi_p\varepsilon_{t-p}$$

On the other hand, MA(q) processes generally have MMSE linear predictors that are infinite series. Reconsider the MA(1), for example. We have already found its MMSE linear prediction function in (25.33)–(25.35):

$$\mathrm{E}^*[\varepsilon_t \mid \varepsilon_1, \ldots, \varepsilon_{t-1}] = -\sum_{s=1}^{t-1} \frac{1 + \psi_1^2 + \cdots + \psi_1^{2(t-s-1)}}{1 + \psi_1^2 + \cdots + \psi_1^{2(t-1)}} (-\psi_1)^s\, \varepsilon_{t-s}$$

No matter how large t is, the coefficient of ε_1 is nonzero. Even though its autocovariances become zero, the coefficients of MMSE linear predictors for an MA(q) process generally persist into the distant past.

The last coefficient in the distributed lag of an MMSE linear predictor is often called a *partial autocorrelation* because the coefficient of ε_{t-s} in

$$\mathrm{E}^*[\varepsilon_t \mid \varepsilon_{t-s}, \ldots, \varepsilon_{t-1}] \equiv \sum_{r=1}^{s} \phi_{sr}\varepsilon_{t-r}$$

is

$$\phi_{ss} = \frac{\mathrm{E}[(\varepsilon_t - \mu_t)(\varepsilon_{t-s} - \mu_{t-s})]}{\mathrm{E}[(\varepsilon_{t-s} - \mu_{t-s})^2]} = \frac{\mathrm{E}[(\varepsilon_t - \mu_t)(\varepsilon_{t-s} - \mu_{t-s})]}{\sqrt{\mathrm{E}[(\varepsilon_t - \mu_t)^2]\,\mathrm{E}[(\varepsilon_{t-s} - \mu_{t-s})^2]}}$$

where

$$\mu_t \equiv \mathrm{E}^*[\varepsilon_t \mid \varepsilon_{t-s+1}, \ldots, \varepsilon_{t-1}]$$

and

$$\mu_{t-s} \equiv \mathrm{E}^*[\varepsilon_{t-s} \mid \varepsilon_{t-s+1}, \ldots, \varepsilon_{t-1}]$$

Use the partitioned regression formula (7.25) and the stationarity of $\{\varepsilon_t\}$ to derive this expression.[30] In terms of the partial autocorrelation function, the final contrast between AR and MA processes is that the partial autocorrelations of an AR(p) process are zero after p lags whereas all the partial autocorrelations of an MA(q) process may be nonzero.

25.4 ARMA PROCESSES

One can combine the AR(p) and MA(q) specifications into *mixed* or *autoregressive moving-average* (ARMA) processes. These arise in econometric models when a time series is aggregated over time periods or several time series are added together.

EXAMPLE 25.11

Suppose that we observe data that are the bimonthly sum of a monthly time series

$$y_t = \mathbf{x}_t' \boldsymbol{\beta}_0 + \varepsilon_t$$

where the disturbance ε_t is a latent AR(1) process

$$\varepsilon_t = \phi_{01} \varepsilon_{t-1} + u_t$$

for $t = 1, 2, 3, \ldots$, where $\{u_t\}$ is a sequence of i.i.d. $\mathfrak{N}(0, \sigma_{0u}^2)$ latent disturbances. Observing only

$$y_{bt} = y_t + y_{t-1}, \qquad \mathbf{x}_{bt} = \mathbf{x}_t + \mathbf{x}_{t-1}$$

for $t = 2, 4, 6, \ldots$, we can only estimate the aggregated regression

$$y_{bt} = \mathbf{x}_{bt}' \boldsymbol{\beta}_0 + \varepsilon_{bt}$$

where

$$\varepsilon_{bt} = \varepsilon_t + \varepsilon_{t-1}$$

This disturbance has both AR(1) and MA(1) components.

To show this, we will rearrange the terms of the latent processes:

$$\begin{aligned} \varepsilon_{bt} &= (\phi_{01} \varepsilon_{t-1} + u_t) + (\phi_{01} \varepsilon_{t-2} + u_{t-1}) \\ &= \phi_{01} (\phi_{01} \varepsilon_{t-2} + u_{t-1}) + \phi_{01} (\phi_{01} \varepsilon_{t-3} + u_{t-2}) + u_t + u_{t-1} \\ &= \phi_{01}^2 (\varepsilon_{t-2} + \varepsilon_{t-3}) + u_t + (1 + \phi_{01}) u_{t-1} + \phi_{01} u_{t-2} \\ &= \phi_{01}^2 \varepsilon_{b,t-2} + u_t + u_{t-1} + \phi_{01} (u_{t-1} + u_{t-2}) \end{aligned} \tag{25.44}$$

The ε_{bt} enter this equation in an AR(1) form. The disturbance term

$$v_t \equiv u_t + u_{t-1} + \phi_{01} (u_{t-1} + u_{t-2}), \qquad t = 1, 2, 3, \ldots$$

[30] By analogy, we may call $\mathrm{E}[(\varepsilon_t - \mu_t)(\varepsilon_{t-s} - \mu_{t-s})] \equiv \mathrm{Cov}[\varepsilon_t, \varepsilon_{t-s} \mid \varepsilon_{t-s+1}, \ldots, \varepsilon_{t-1}]$ the partial autocovariance.

is an MA(1) process. It turns out that the subsequence $\{v_2, v_4, v_6, \ldots\}$ is also MA(1). To see this, note that its autocovariance function is

$$\begin{aligned}
\mathrm{Var}(v_t) &= \sigma_{0u}^2 \left[1 + (1+\phi_{01})^2 + \phi_{01}^2\right] \\
&= 2\sigma_{0u}^2 \left(1 + \phi_{01} + \phi_{01}^2\right) \\
\mathrm{Cov}(v_t, v_{t-2}) &= \mathrm{E}(\phi_{01} u_{t-2}^2) \\
&= \phi_{01}\sigma_{0u}^2 \\
\mathrm{Cov}(v_t, v_{t-j}) &= 0, \quad j = 4, 6, 8, \ldots
\end{aligned}$$

Therefore, we can just as well view v_t as the latent MA(1) process

$$v_t = \eta_t + \psi_1 \eta_{t-2} \tag{25.45}$$

where $\{\eta_t\}$ is a sequence of i.i.d. $\mathfrak{N}(0, \sigma_\eta^2)$ and, using the MA(1) autocovariance function in (25.20)–(25.21),

$$\begin{aligned}
\sigma_\eta^2 \left(1 + \psi_1^2\right) &= 2\sigma_{0u}^2 \left(1 + \phi_{01} + \phi_{01}^2\right) \\
\sigma_\eta^2 \psi_1 &= \phi_{01}\sigma_{0u}^2
\end{aligned}$$

That is,

$$\psi_1 = \phi_{01} + \frac{1+\phi_{01}}{\phi_{01}} \left(1 - \sqrt{1 + \phi_{01}^2}\right)$$

where we have chosen the MA(1) specification with the characteristic root inside the complex unit circle.

Taking (25.44) and (25.45) together, we can describe ε_{bt} as a bimonthly ARMA(1, 1) process that has the form

$$\varepsilon_{bt} = \phi_{01}^2 \varepsilon_{b,t-2} + v_t + \psi_1 v_{t-2}$$

We will write a general ARMA(p, q) process as

$$\varepsilon_t = \phi_1 \varepsilon_{t-1} + \cdots + \phi_p \varepsilon_{t-1} + u_t + \psi_1 u_{t-1} + \cdots + \psi_q u_{t-q}$$

or

$$\phi(L)\varepsilon_t = \psi(L) u_t$$

Such processes form a large family of serially correlated time series.[31] Through the ARMA mixture, one can specify autocovariance structures with the characteristics of both autoregressive and moving-average components. Autocovariances can die out slowly as the lag length grows and yet exhibit flexibility in the short run.

[31] There is a large literature on fitting these models to time series data. As starting points, one can consult Box and Jenkins (1976), Fuller (1996), and Hamilton (1994).

25.4.1 Identification and Invertibility

Identification of the ϕs and ψs requires restrictions on the polynomials $\phi(z)$ and $\psi(z)$. Because

$$(1-\alpha L)\phi(L)\varepsilon_t \equiv \phi^*(L)\varepsilon_t = \psi^*(L)u_t \equiv (1-\alpha L)\psi(L)u_t \quad (25.46)$$

is an observationally equivalent ARMA$(p+1, q+1)$ process, all of the coefficients in $\phi^*(z)$ and $\psi^*(z)$ are not identified. The term $(1-\alpha L)$ is called a *common factor*. In general, identification requires that the AR polynomial and the MA polynomial have no common factors.

There is no convenient method for imposing no-common-factors restrictions. As a result, computation of estimators of ARMA models is often awkward. In the vicinity of common factors in the parameter space, the Hessian of the estimation criterion function, whether GMM or log-likelihood, is nearly singular. Numerical imprecision creeps into the calculation of line-search directions and optimization algorithms perform poorly.

Near singularity of the Hessian also occurs frequently as the orders p and q are raised. Because the ϕ and ψ parameters both capture serial correlation, AR and MA components may produce similar autocovariances.

EXAMPLE 25.12 (AR vs. MA)

Consider the AR(2) process

$$\varepsilon_t = 0.7\varepsilon_{t-1} - 0.12\varepsilon_{t-2} + u_t$$

We can find the MA(2) process in u_t that gives the MMSE prediction of ε_t:

$$\varepsilon_t^* = u_t + 0.7u_{t-1} + 0.37u_{t-2}$$

The percentage of explained variation (or population R^2) is

$$\frac{\text{Var}[\varepsilon_t^*]}{\text{Var}[\varepsilon_t]} = 0.977$$

so that this MA(2) captures almost 98% of the AR(2) process. Thus, we anticipate that AR(2) and MA(2) specifications can be observationally similar.

A formal way to gain insight into such similarities is to see that stationary AR(p) models have MA representations. As a familiar example, consider a covariance-stationary first-order autoregressive process.

EXAMPLE 25.13 [AR(1)]

By recursive substitution, we can write the AR(1) process

$$\varepsilon_t = \phi_1\varepsilon_{t-1} + u_t$$

as

$$\varepsilon_t = \phi_1^r\varepsilon_{t-r} + \sum_{s=0}^{r-1}\phi_1^s u_{t-s}$$

If $\{u_t\}$ is serially uncorrelated and $|\phi_1| < 1$ then $\{\varepsilon_t\}$ is covariance stationary and $\text{Var}[\varepsilon_{t-r}] = \sigma_u^2/(1-\phi_1^2)$ for all r. Therefore,

$$\lim_{r\to\infty} \text{Var}[\phi_1^r \varepsilon_{t-v}] = \frac{\sigma_u^2}{1-\phi_1^2} \lim_{r\to\infty} \phi_1^{2r} = 0$$

or

$$\lim_{r\to\infty} \text{E}\left[\left(\varepsilon_t - \sum_{s=0}^{r-1} \phi_1^s u_{t-s}\right)^2\right] = 0$$

That is,

$$\varepsilon_t = \sum_{s=0}^{\infty} \phi_1^s u_{t-s} \tag{25.47}$$

in MSE.

There is an algebraic method for finding an MA representation of any stationary AR(p) process using the lag operator introduced in Section 25.3.1.

EXAMPLE 25.14 [AR(1)]

We can write an AR(1) process as

$$(1-\phi_1 L)\,\varepsilon_t = u_t \tag{25.48}$$

This notation is useful because we may think of L as a scalar with an absolute value less than one. If $|a| < 1$, then

$$\frac{1}{1-a} = 1 + a + a^2 + \cdots = \lim_{T\to\infty} \sum_{t=0}^{T} a^t \tag{25.49}$$

Similarly, if

$$z_t - z_{t-1} = (1-L)z_t = w_t$$

then

$$\begin{aligned} z_t &= w_t + w_{t-1} + w_{t-2} + \cdots \\ &= w_t + Lw_t + L^2 w_t + \cdots \\ &= \left(1 + L + L^2 + \cdots\right) w_t \\ &= \frac{1}{1-L} w_t \end{aligned}$$

is sensible if we just treat L like a.

Thus, we can rewrite (25.48) as

$$\varepsilon_t = \frac{1}{1-\phi_1 L} u_t$$

$$= \left(1 + \phi_1 L + \phi_1^2 L^2 + \ldots\right) u_t \tag{25.50}$$

$$= \sum_{j=0}^{\infty} \psi_j u_{t-j}$$

This is the expression we derived previously for the AR(1) as (25.47).

This transformation is called *inversion* of the AR process. We can transform the general AR(p) case into a sequence of AR(1) inversions like (25.50). To do this formally, we factor the AR polynomial into

$$\phi(z) = \prod_{j=1}^{p} \left(1 - \lambda_j z\right)$$

where λ_j^{-1}, $j = 1, \ldots, p$ are the p (complex) roots of $\phi(z) = 0$. Then we can write

$$\varepsilon_t = \frac{1}{\phi(L)} u_t = \left(\prod_{j=1}^{p} \frac{1}{1 - \lambda_j L}\right) u_t$$

making ε_t the composition of p successive AR(1) inversions.

We can find the MA coefficients using equations similar to the Yule–Walker equations (25.13)–(25.14): in general, $\psi_s \sigma_u^2 = \mathrm{E}[\varepsilon_t u_{t-s}]$ so that

$$\psi_s = \frac{\mathrm{E}[\varepsilon_t u_{t-s}]}{\sigma_u^2} = \frac{\sum_{j=1}^{p} \mathrm{E}[\phi_j \varepsilon_{t-j} u_{t-s}] + \mathrm{E}[u_t u_{t-s}]}{\sigma_u^2}$$

$$= \sum_{j=1}^{p} \phi_j \psi_{s-j} \mathbf{1}\{s \geq j\} + \mathbf{1}\{s = 0\} \tag{25.51}$$

$s = 0, 1, 2, \ldots$, is a recursive solution.

EXAMPLE 25.15

For the AR(2) calculations in Example 25.12, we found the MMSE MA(2) by truncating the infinite-order

$$\varepsilon_t = \sum_{s=0}^{\infty} \psi_s u_{t-s}$$

to three terms. Because $\{u_t\}$ is serially uncorrelated, the law of iterated projections (Lemma 20.2, p. 494) implies that

$$\mathrm{E}^*[\varepsilon_t \mid u_t, u_{t-1}, u_{t-2}] = \psi_0 u_t + \psi_1 u_{t-1} + \psi_2 u_{t-2} + \mathrm{E}^*\left[\sum_{s=3}^{\infty} \psi_s u_{t-s} \,\middle|\, u_t, u_{t-1}, u_{t-2}\right]$$

$$= \psi_0 u_t + \psi_1 u_{t-1} + \psi_2 u_{t-2}$$

Using (25.51), we obtain

$$\psi_0 = 1$$
$$\psi_1 = \phi_1 \psi_0$$

and

$$\psi_2 = \phi_1 \psi_1 + \phi_2 \psi_0$$

so that

$$\psi_1 = \phi_1 \qquad \text{and} \qquad \psi_2 = \phi_1^2 + \phi_2$$

The symmetry in AR and MA components suggests that an MA(q) process also possesses an autoregressive representation. This is true only under certain circumstances: it is necessary that all of the roots of the MA polynomial lie strictly inside the complex unit circle. With this restriction, the MA process is *invertible* to an AR(∞) representation.

EXAMPLE 25.16 [MA(1)]

In Example 25.7, (25.29) gives a partially autoregressive form for an MA(1) through recursive substitution:

$$\varepsilon_t = -\sum_{s=1}^{r-1} (-\psi_1)^s \varepsilon_{t-s} + u_t + \psi_1^r u_{t-r}$$

If we take r larger and larger and $|\psi_1| < 1$, the remainder term converges in mean square to zero because

$$\lim_{r\to\infty} \text{Var}[\psi_1^r u_{t-v}] = \sigma_u^2 \lim_{r\to\infty} \psi_1^{2r} = 0$$

In other words,

$$\lim_{r\to\infty} \text{E}\left[\left(\varepsilon_t + \sum_{s=1}^{r-1} (-\psi_1)^s \varepsilon_{t-s} - u_t\right)^2\right] = 0$$

That is, provided that $|\psi_1| < 1$ we can view the MA(1) process as an autoregression of infinite order (AR(∞)):

$$\varepsilon_t = -\sum_{s=0}^{\infty} (-\psi_1)^s \varepsilon_{t-s} + u_t$$

in MSE.

This example illustrates why there is no autoregressive counterpart to some moving-average processes. The MA specification is inherently covariance stationary so that roots on the unit circle are permissible. There is no stable AR representation of such MA processes.

Nevertheless, the ability to invert covariance-stationary AR(p) processes and certain MA(q) processes demonstrates that these two components bear similarities despite the qualitative differences in their autocorrelation and partial autocorrelation functions.

25.4.2 Kalman Filter and Estimation

To find GLS transformations of the latent disturbance term, we can extend the Kalman filter to ARMA(p,q) models. There are many state-space representations of ARMA models.[32] One well-known state-space specification that generalizes (25.37) sets $\varepsilon_t = z_{t1}$, $m = p + q + 1$,

$$\mathbf{A} = \begin{bmatrix} \begin{bmatrix} & \boldsymbol{\phi}' & \\ \mathbf{I}_{p-1} & & \underset{(p-1)\times 1}{\mathbf{0}} \\ \underset{(q+1)\times(p-1)}{\mathbf{0}} & & \underset{(q+1)\times 1}{\mathbf{0}} \end{bmatrix} & \begin{bmatrix} & \boldsymbol{\psi}' & \\ \underset{p\times q}{\mathbf{0}} & & \underset{p\times 1}{\mathbf{0}} \\ \mathbf{I}_q & & \underset{q\times 1}{\mathbf{0}} \end{bmatrix} \end{bmatrix}$$

$$\mathbf{w}_t = \begin{bmatrix} \underset{p\times 1}{\mathbf{0}} \\ u_{t+1} \\ \underset{q\times 1}{\mathbf{0}} \end{bmatrix}$$

and

$$\mathbf{z}_t = \begin{bmatrix} \varepsilon_t & \cdots & \varepsilon_{t-p+1} & u_{t+1} & u_t & \cdots & u_{t-q+1} \end{bmatrix}'$$

The initial conditions for such state-space models are more involved than the pure MA(q). Although the marginal mean is still $\mathbf{m}_1 \equiv \mathrm{E}[\mathbf{z}_1] = \mathbf{0}$, the marginal variance matrix includes the variance matrix of $[\varepsilon_{t-p+1}, \ldots, \varepsilon_t]$. This requires the first $p + 1$ autocovariances of the ARMA(p,q) process. We give a direct solution in Exercise 26.20, which depends on additional notation introduced in Chapter 26.

The Kalman filter in (25.38)–(25.39) applies directly. It delivers the prediction errors that make the GLS methods for MA(q) models (Section 25.3.3) work for ARMA(p,q) models.

Despite the similarities, there is an important practical difference in the distribution theory for ARMA(p,q) models. In practice, p and q are rarely known. As a result, a researcher may choose values that are too high, perhaps to avoid misspecification. Introducing additional terms for parameters that are actually zero usually preserves estimator consistency and generally leads to estimator inefficiency. However, when one specifies inflated values of p and q the GMM estimator of an ARMA model becomes inconsistent.

The lack of identification of an ARMA process with common factors is the source of this inconsistency. When p and q are artificially increased, it is as though a common factor $(1-0L) = 1$ multiplies both sides of the population ARMA(p,q) specification [see equation (25.46)]. Such common factors make an overparameterized model also an underidentified model.

This lack of identification and consequent estimator inconsistency do not necessarily prevent one from computing an estimator with an actual, finite, data set. In general, the GMM or likelihood estimation criterion function possesses a unique global optimum. As the sample size increases and this function approaches (in probability) its population counterpart, the criterion function becomes increasingly flat near its optimum and numerical optimization becomes difficult. Therefore, researchers often take such computational difficulty and extraordinarily large estimates of the standard errors of parameters as evidence of overparameterization.

25.4.3 Hypothesis Tests

The presence of common factors in overparameterized models also affects hypothesis tests for the orders of p and q in ARMA(p,q) models. Consider, for example, a Wald test of the null

[32] See Aoki (1987) for examples.

hypothesis that p and q in the unrestricted model can both be reduced by 1. Under the null hypothesis, the unrestricted estimator is inconsistent so that the usual distribution theory for the Wald test statistic fails. Thus, one cannot apply the Wald test method to this null hypothesis. In particular, examining various t statistics for the autoregressive and moving-average coefficients is futile when the model is overparameterized.

The likelihood ratio and score test methods are similarly invalidated. This is particularly obvious in the implementation of score tests. Under the null hypothesis, the overparameterized alternative model is not identified. This implies that the score vector of the constrained parameters contains linearly dependent elements when one imposes the restrictions of the null hypothesis. Thus, the value of the score test statistic is undefined.

EXAMPLE 25.17 [ARMA(1,1)]

Consider the score test of no autocorrelation in an ARMA(1,1) specification. Example 25.10 shows that the score for the moving-average parameter is proportional to the score for the autoregressive parameter. As a result, every estimator of the information matrix is singular and the estimated information matrix cannot be inverted to compute a score test statistic.

A consequence of this situation is that top-down sequential hypothesis testing is inappropriate for ARMA(p,q) specifications where both p and q are reduced. Nevertheless, given p, the sequential testing method applies to the reduction of q (and vice versa).

The difficulties with classical hypothesis testing have stimulated many approaches to estimation of p and q. Among the most influential is the three-step iterative procedure of Box and Jenkins (1976). In the first step, one chooses initial values for p and q based on estimates of autocorrelations and partial autocorrelations. The second step is estimation of $\boldsymbol{\phi}_0$ and $\boldsymbol{\psi}_0$ given p and q. The third step applies diagnostic hypothesis tests to check for misspecification. If the diagnostics suggest a misspecification, p and q are respecified and one returns to the second step. Ultimately, this approach is informal and the implicit estimator possesses no formal distribution theory. For an introduction to the *Box–Jenkins* approach and others, see Hamilton (1994, Section 4.8), Harvey (1993, Section 3.6), or Judge et al. (1980, Section 8.4).

25.5 WOLD DECOMPOSITION

A leading statistical justification for the ARMA(p,q) specification is that it provides a parsimonious parameterization of the autocovariance function of a covariance-stationary time series. As we will explain next, one can always represent such time series as pure moving-average processes provided that the order of the process is infinite. In many cases, a combination of low values of p and q is sufficient to approximate both AR(∞) and MA(∞) processes.

We have already shown how stationary AR(p) processes have MA(∞) representations. ARMA(p,q) processes have the same property for the same reasons. The result described in this section applies more generally to all covariance-stationary processes. Rather than specifying the ARMA(p, q) process as a transformation of a latent white noise process, one can construct a white noise process from a covariance-stationary process. As a result, one can make the assumption of covariance-stationarity part of a basis for the ARMA specification itself.

To do this, we must first distinguish ARMA processes from covariance-stationary processes that are *linearly deterministic*. The latter can be forecast perfectly as far into the future as desired, a property rarely possessed by economic time series. Second, we describe the *Wold decomposition*, which states that every covariance-stationary process can be represented as the sum of a moving-average process and a linearly deterministic process. Therefore, one can focus modeling effort on these two components. The moving average generally has an infinite order. As shown above, an AR process has such a moving-average representation. Thus, casting an MA(∞) process as an ARMA(p, q) is a parsimonious approximation to a general covariance-stationary process.

25.5.1 Linearly Deterministic Processes

Given the sequence of random variables $\{\varepsilon_t\}$, the sequence $\{z_t\}$ is *linearly deterministic* if

$$\mathrm{E}\big[(z_{t+s} - \mathrm{E}^*[z_{t+s} \mid \varepsilon_t, \varepsilon_{t-1}, \ldots])^2\big] = 0$$

for $s = 1, 2, \ldots$. In words, z_t can be predicted perfectly (*deterministic* in the MSE sense) arbitrarily far into the future with a *linear* function of past εs. Having focused on covariance-stationary processes with AR or MA specifications, it may seem odd at first that a mean-zero covariance-stationary time series can be linearly deterministic. But a simple example makes the possibility clear immediately: the sequence $\varepsilon_t = \alpha$, where α is a random variable with $\mathrm{E}[\alpha] = 0$ and $\mathrm{Var}[\alpha] = \sigma_\alpha^2 < \infty$. Such a sequence is covariance stationary because $\mathrm{Cov}[\varepsilon_t, \varepsilon_{t-s}] = \sigma_\alpha^2$ for all integers t and s; and it is linearly deterministic because $\mathrm{E}[\varepsilon_t \mid \varepsilon_{t-1}] = \varepsilon_{t-1} = \varepsilon_t$.

The time-series specification of the random-effects model for panel data is a slightly more interesting example. If $\varepsilon_t = \alpha + u_t$, where $\{u_t\}$ is a sequence of i.i.d. random variables with $\mathrm{E}[u_t] = 0$ and finite variance σ_u^2, then $\{\varepsilon_t\}$ is covariance stationary. Moreover

$$\lim_{T\to\infty} \mathrm{E}\left[\left(\alpha - \sum_{s=1}^{T} \frac{\varepsilon_{t-s+1}}{T}\right)^2\right] = 0$$

so that α is a linearly deterministic component of ε_t.

A more general example would be to replace α with a stochastic harmonic function of time:

$$\varepsilon_t = \sum_{i=1}^{n} (v_{1i} \cos \lambda_i t + v_{2i} \sin \lambda_i t) + u_t$$

where the vs are uncorrelated random variables with $\mathrm{E}[v_{ji}] = 0$ and $\mathrm{Var}[v_{ji}] = \sigma_i^2 < \infty$. Harmonic functions can capture such periodic trends as seasonal effects and business cycles. For fixed n and λ_i, this $\{\varepsilon_t\}$ is also mean zero and covariance stationary:[33]

$$\begin{aligned}\mathrm{Cov}[\varepsilon_t, \varepsilon_{t-s}] &= \sum_{i=1}^{n} \sigma_i^2\big[\cos \lambda_i t \cos \lambda_i (t-s) + \sin \lambda_i t \sin \lambda_i (t-s)\big] \\ &= \sum_{i=1}^{n} \sigma_i^2 \cos \lambda_i s\end{aligned}$$

[33] To derive this autocovariance function, one uses the trigonometric identity

$$\cos(\theta - \gamma) = \cos\theta \cos\gamma + \sin\theta \sin\gamma$$

And the sequence $\alpha_t \equiv \sum_{i=1}^{n} (v_{1i} \cos \lambda_i t + v_{2i} \sin \lambda_i t)$ is also linearly deterministic. With an infinite sequence of past εs, one can estimate the vs and λs consistently with NLS. Given these, one can forecast α_t without error into the indefinite future.

Like $\{\varepsilon_t\}$ in these examples, AR(p) and MA(q) processes are not linearly deterministic. The contemporaneous white noise term u_t prevents this. Together, however, linearly deterministic and moving-average specifications can represent *any* mean-zero covariance-stationary process. This is the essence of a theoretical result called the *Wold decomposition.*

25.5.2 Wold Decomposition Theorem

The Wold decomposition is an orthogonal decomposition of a sequence of covariance-stationary random variables into predictable and unpredictable components.[34] The unpredictable component is further broken down into a sequence of orthogonal subcomponents.

Theorem 16 (Wold Decomposition) *If $\{\varepsilon_t\}$ is a covariance-stationary sequence of random variables with* $E[\varepsilon_t] = 0$, *then ε_t has the decomposition*

$$\varepsilon_t = \mu_t + \sum_{s=0}^{\infty} \psi_s v_{t-s}$$

where

1. *μ_t is linearly deterministic,*
2. *$\{v_t\}$ is a unique sequence of serially uncorrelated random variables such that* $E[v_t] = 0$ *and* $\mathrm{Var}[v_t] < \infty$,
3. $E[\mu_t v_s] = 0$ *for all t and s, and*
4. *$\{\psi_t\}$ is a unique sequence of* square-summable $\left(\sum_{s=0}^{\infty} \psi_s^2 < \infty\right)$ *constants.*

For proofs of the Wold decomposition theorem (Theorem 16), see Anderson (1971, Theorem 7.6.7) and Fuller (1996, pp. 97–98). The projection theorem (Theorem 6, p. 119) is at the core of these proofs. We will follow parts of Sargent's (1987, Section XI.13) description of its application here.

A key element is the construction of the v_t as MMSE fitted residuals:[35]

$$v_t \equiv \varepsilon_t - E^*[\varepsilon_t \mid \varepsilon_{t-1}, \varepsilon_{t-2}, \ldots]$$

Given that they are well defined, these forecast errors are mutually orthogonal (uncorrelated) because v_t is orthogonal to the elements of $\mathbb{S}_{t-1}$, the subspace spanned by $\{\varepsilon_{t-1}, \varepsilon_{t-2}, \ldots\}$, and v_{t-s}

[34] Wold (1938).

[35] Given that the vector space $\mathbb{V}$ spanned by $\{\ldots, \varepsilon_{t-1}, \varepsilon_t, \varepsilon_{t+1}, \ldots\}$ with the inner product $\langle u_1, u_2 \rangle \equiv E[u_1 u_2], u_1, u_2 \in \mathbb{V}$, is complete, the unique orthogonal projection $E^*[u_1 \mid u_2, u_3, \ldots]$ exists by the projection theorem. This is the one place in this book where the existence of the projection is established, not directly assumed. See Anderson (1971, Theorem 7.6.1).

is a linear combination of the elements of $\mathbb{S}_{t-s} \subseteq \mathbb{S}_{t-1}$, the subspace spanned by $\{\varepsilon_{t-s}, \varepsilon_{t-s-1}, \ldots\}$. Also, given that $\{\varepsilon_t\}$ is covariance stationary, the $\{v_t\}$ are homoskedastic.

As a result, the MMSE prediction of ε_t given $\{v_t, v_{t-1}, \ldots\}$ has the form

$$\mathrm{E}^*[\varepsilon_t \mid v_t, v_{t-1}, \ldots] = \sum_{s=0}^{\infty} \psi_s v_{t-s}$$

where

$$\psi_s = \frac{\mathrm{Cov}[\varepsilon_t v_{t-s}]}{\mathrm{Var}[v_t]}$$

Furthermore,

$$\begin{aligned}\mathrm{Var}[v_t] \sum_{s=0}^{\infty} \psi_s^2 &= \mathrm{E}\big[(\mathrm{E}^*[\varepsilon_t \mid v_t, v_{t-1}, \ldots])^2\big] \\ &\le \mathrm{E}[\varepsilon_t^2]\end{aligned}$$

so that $\{\psi_t\}$ is square summable.

Thus, one can construct the v_t as the prediction errors $\varepsilon_t - \mathrm{E}^*[\varepsilon_t \mid \varepsilon_{t-1}, \varepsilon_{t-2}, \ldots]$ of MMSE linear forecasts of ε_t given past values. In effect, $\{v_t, v_{t-1}, v_{t-2}, \ldots\}$ is an orthogonal basis for the subspace $\mathbb{S}_t$ spanned by $\{\varepsilon_t, \varepsilon_{t-1}, \varepsilon_{t-2}, \ldots\}$ derived from Gram–Schmidt orthogonalization.

Finally, one defines the linearly deterministic component as the MMSE residual

$$\mu_t \equiv \varepsilon_t - \mathrm{E}^*[\varepsilon_t \mid v_t, v_{t-1}, \ldots]$$

One might expect this component to be identically zero, but we have already given counter-examples that demonstrate other possibilities. We can say that $\mu_t \perp \{v_t, v_{t-1}, \ldots\}$. Also $v_t \perp \mathbb{S}_{t-1}$ so that

$$\mathbb{S}_t = \{\alpha v_t \mid \alpha \in \mathbb{R}\} \oplus \mathbb{S}_{t-1}$$

Now $\mu_t, v_t \in \mathbb{S}_t$ and it follows that $\mu_t \in \mathbb{S}_{t-1}$ and, therefore, $\mu_t = \mathrm{E}^*[\mu_t \mid \varepsilon_{t-1}, \varepsilon_{t-2}, \ldots]$. More generally, $\{v_t, \ldots, v_{t-s}\} \perp \mathbb{S}_{t-s-1}$ for $s = 1, 2, \ldots$ and the same argument implies $\mu_t \in \mathbb{S}_{t-s-1}$, or $\mu_t = \mathrm{E}^*[\mu_t \mid \varepsilon_{t-s-1}, \varepsilon_{t-s-2}, \ldots]$. This completes our sketch of the proof.

The Wold decomposition theorem motivates the ARMA(p, q) specification in the following way. Every covariance-stationary process can be represented as the sum of two components: a linearly deterministic process and an infinite-order moving-average process. One assumes that for such latent disturbances as those of a linear regression model the linearly deterministic component is the constant zero. One further casts the MA(∞) component as an ARMA(p, q) to reduce an infinite number of parameters to a parsimonious approximation.

More specifically, if we denote the MA(∞) lag polynomial by

$$\psi(L) = \sum_{s=0}^{\infty} \psi_s L^s, \ \ \psi_0 = 1$$

then the ARMA(p, q) specification is

$$\psi(L) = \frac{\theta(L)}{\phi(L)} = \frac{1 + \theta_1 L + \theta_2 L^2 + \cdots + \theta_q L^q}{1 - \phi_1 L - \phi_2 L^2 - \cdots - \phi_p L^p}$$

restricted by

$$z^p - \phi_1 z^{p-1} - \phi_2 z^{p-2} - \cdots - \phi_p = 0 \Rightarrow |z| < 1$$

The restriction is necessary and sufficient for covariance stationarity. The rational lag polynomial is a more flexible family than the simple MA(q) family. In addition, a great many autoregressive parameters may be necessary to approximate a covariance-stationary process so that to achieve parsimony both AR and MA terms are included.

25.6 METHODOLOGICAL NOTES

Casual observation suggests that researchers tend to use pure autoregressive specifications in practice. Given the identification problems inherent in ARMA specifications, it is expedient to opt for either a pure AR or MA parameterization. AR(p) may be preferable because the computation of estimates for AR(p) models is typically much easier. Also, the AR(p) specification models time series dynamics directly in terms of observable, rather than latent, variables. On the other hand, the Wold decomposition theorem justifies the MA specification.

One can also apply the ARMA functional form directly to the observable $\{y_t\}$, as in

$$y_t = \phi_1 y_{t-1} + \mathbf{x}_t'\boldsymbol{\beta}_1 + \mathbf{x}_{t-1}'\boldsymbol{\beta}_2 + u_t + \psi_1 u_{t-1} \tag{25.52}$$

where $\{u_t\}$ is white noise. By including lagged explanatory variables, (25.52) is a generalization of the ARMA(1, 1) specification for the latent disturbance term $\varepsilon_t = y_t - \mathbf{x}_t'\boldsymbol{\beta}$ so that

$$y_t = \phi_1 y_{t-1} + \mathbf{x}_t'\boldsymbol{\beta} + \mathbf{x}_{t-1}'(-\phi_1 \cdot \boldsymbol{\beta}) + u_t + \psi_1 u_{t-1}$$

This is parsimonious, but its restrictions on $\boldsymbol{\beta}_1$ and $\boldsymbol{\beta}_2$ may not be supported by the data. Here again, researchers often ignore MA components and try to use sufficient AR terms to capture any serial correlation.

For example, Staiger et al. (1997) estimate unrestricted versions of the autoregressive specification of the Phillips curve, which we describe in the introduction. When we test (under the assumption of normally distributed disturbances) the restrictions that the AR(15) specification places on (25.3), a likelihood ratio test soundly rejects the null hypothesis. Thus, akin to Staiger et al. (1997), we prefer the Phillips curve specification

$$\mathrm{E}[y_t \mid t-1] = \sum_{s=1}^{15} \alpha_{0s} y_{t-s} + \sum_{s=0}^{15} \mathbf{x}_{t-s}'\boldsymbol{\beta}_{0s}$$

Nevertheless, the estimate of the natural rate of unemployment for this version continues to be around 6.2%.[36]

A further extension of ARMA models takes a multivariate form, for example,

$$\mathbf{y}_t' = \mathbf{y}_{t-1}'\boldsymbol{\Phi}_1 + \mathbf{x}_t'\mathbf{B}_1 + \mathbf{x}_{t-1}'\mathbf{B}_2 + \mathbf{u}_t'$$

where $\mathbf{y}_t$ is a *vector* of jointly distributed time series. The terms $\boldsymbol{\Phi}_1$, $\mathbf{B}_1$, and $\mathbf{B}_2$ are matrices of coefficients and $\mathbf{u}_t$ is a vector of jointly distributed white noise processes. Such multivariate

[36] The actual estimate is 6.231% with an estimated standard error of only 0.507. The 95% (log-likelihood ratio) confidence interval is [4.551, 7.592]. In this case, this interval is wider than the corresponding delta-method confidence interval.

models are called *vector autoregressions* (VARs) and they share the advantages and challenges of univariate AR models. Vector moving averages are conceptually straightforward, but neither these nor their autoregressive moving-average counterparts are commonly estimated.

25.7 MATHEMATICAL NOTES

Following our usual pattern, we provide some mathematical details for previous sections in the following. First, we outline the solution to the Yule–Walker equations that yields the autocovariance function of an AR(p) from its coefficients. Second, we derive the Kalman filter that provides a convenient method for prediction-error decomposition of an MA(q). Third, we prove Proposition 24 [MA(q) Identification], which motivates restricting MA(q) specifications to those with roots inside the complex unit circle. Finally, we show the equivalence of the score tests for no serial correlation in MA(q) and AR(q) specifications.

25.7.1 Yule–Walker Equations

To solve the Yule–Walker equations, we rewrite (25.13)–(25.14) in terms of correlations $\rho_j = \gamma_j / \gamma_0$ as

$$\gamma_0 \left[1 - \left(\phi_1 \rho_1 + \cdots + \phi_p \rho_p\right)\right] = \sigma_u^2 \tag{25.53}$$

$$\rho_j = \phi_1 \rho_{j-1} + \phi_2 \rho_{|j-2|} + \cdots + \phi_p \rho_{|j-p|}, \qquad j > 1 \tag{25.54}$$

Restricting $j = 1, \ldots, p$, we can rewrite (25.54) as

$$\begin{aligned}
\rho_j &= \sum_{i=1}^{p} \phi_i \rho_{|j-i|} \\
&= \sum_{i=1}^{j-1} \phi_i \rho_{j-i} + \phi_j + \sum_{i=j+1}^{p} \phi_i \rho_{i-j} \\
&= \sum_{k=1}^{j-1} \phi_{j-k} \rho_k + \phi_j + \sum_{k=1}^{p-j} \phi_{j+k} \rho_k
\end{aligned}$$

or

$$\rho_j - \sum_{k=1}^{j-1} \phi_{j-k} \rho_k - \sum_{k=1}^{p-j} \phi_{j+k} \rho_k = \phi_j \tag{25.55}$$

Therefore, the Yule–Walker equations for the first p autocorrelations are

$$\mathbf{W}(\boldsymbol{\phi}) \boldsymbol{\rho} = \boldsymbol{\phi} \tag{25.56}$$

where $\boldsymbol{\rho} \equiv \left[\rho_j;\ j = 1, \ldots, p\right]'$, $\boldsymbol{\phi} \equiv \left[\phi_j;\ j = 1, \ldots, p\right]'$, and

$$\mathbf{W}(\boldsymbol{\phi}) = \mathbf{I}_p - \mathbf{B}_1(\boldsymbol{\phi}) - \mathbf{B}_2(\boldsymbol{\phi}) \tag{25.57}$$

where

$$\mathbf{B}_1(\boldsymbol{\phi}) = \begin{bmatrix} 0 & 0 & \cdots & 0 & 0 & 0 \\ \phi_1 & 0 & \cdots & 0 & 0 & 0 \\ \phi_2 & \phi_1 & \cdots & 0 & 0 & 0 \\ \vdots & \vdots & \ddots & \vdots & \vdots & \vdots \\ \phi_{p-2} & \phi_{p-3} & \cdots & \phi_1 & 0 & 0 \\ \phi_{p-1} & \phi_{p-2} & \cdots & \phi_2 & \phi_1 & 0 \end{bmatrix} \tag{25.58}$$

$$\mathbf{B}_2(\boldsymbol{\phi}) = \begin{bmatrix} \phi_2 & \phi_3 & \cdots & \phi_{p-1} & \phi_p & 0 \\ \phi_3 & \phi_4 & \cdots & \phi_p & 0 & 0 \\ \vdots & \vdots & \cdots & \vdots & \vdots & \vdots \\ \phi_{p-1} & \phi_p & \cdots & 0 & 0 & 0 \\ \phi_p & 0 & \cdots & 0 & 0 & 0 \\ 0 & 0 & \cdots & 0 & 0 & 0 \end{bmatrix} \tag{25.59}$$

The coefficients in $\mathbf{B}_1(\boldsymbol{\phi})$ correspond to the coefficients in the first sum of (25.55), the coefficients in $\mathbf{B}_2(\boldsymbol{\phi})$ to the second sum.

Clearly, for some $\boldsymbol{\phi}$ the matrix $\mathbf{W}(\boldsymbol{\phi})$ is nonsingular and then $\boldsymbol{\rho} = \mathbf{W}(\boldsymbol{\phi})^{-1}\boldsymbol{\phi}$. Furthermore, we obtain $\gamma_0 = \sigma_u^2/(1 - \boldsymbol{\phi}'\boldsymbol{\rho})$ from (25.53) and $\gamma_j = \gamma_0\rho_j$.

25.7.2 Kalman Filter

In this section, we derive the Kalman filter [(25.38)–(25.39)] for the state-space model[37]

$$\mathbf{z}_t = \mathbf{A}\mathbf{z}_{t-1} + \mathbf{w}_t \tag{25.60}$$

$$\varepsilon_t = \boldsymbol{\delta}'\mathbf{z}_t \tag{25.61}$$

where $\mathbf{w}_t$ are i.i.d. with mean zero and finite variance matrix and $\mathbf{z}_t$ is covariance stationary so that

$$\begin{aligned} \mathrm{E}[\mathbf{z}_t] &= \mathbf{0} \\ \mathrm{Var}[\mathbf{z}_t] &= \mathbf{A}\,\mathrm{Cov}[\mathbf{z}_{t-1}, \mathbf{z}_t] + \mathrm{Var}[\mathbf{w}_t] \\ \mathrm{Cov}[\mathbf{z}_t, \mathbf{z}_{t-1}] &= \mathbf{A}\,\mathrm{Var}[\mathbf{z}_t] \end{aligned}$$

Therefore, $\mathrm{Var}[\mathbf{z}_t]$ solves the linear system of equations

$$\mathrm{Var}[\mathbf{z}_t] - \mathbf{A}\,\mathrm{Var}[\mathbf{z}_t]\mathbf{A}' = \mathrm{Var}[\mathbf{w}_t] \tag{25.62}$$

We shall take the solution for $\mathrm{Var}[\mathbf{z}_t]$ in terms of $\mathbf{A}$ and $\mathrm{Var}[\mathbf{w}_t]$ as given.[38]

Using the autoregressive structure and the orthogonal basis from the Gram–Schmidt process, we derive a linear, recursive system of equations for the MMSE linear predictor $\mathrm{E}^*[\varepsilon_t \mid \varepsilon_1, \ldots, \varepsilon_{t-1}]$ and its prediction variance. We begin by taking

---

[37] Equation (25.60) is often called the *transition equation* and equation (25.61) is called the *measurement equation*.

[38] For one solution, see Exercise 26.20.

$$\mathbf{m}_t \equiv \mathrm{E}^*[\mathbf{z}_t \mid \varepsilon_1, \ldots, \varepsilon_{t-1}]$$

and

$$\mathbf{V}_t \equiv \mathrm{Var}[\mathbf{z}_t - \mathbf{m}_t]$$

as given and seek $\mathbf{m}_{t+1}$ and $\mathbf{V}_{t+1}$. Initially, for $t = 1$, $\mathbf{m}_1 = \mathrm{E}[\mathbf{z}_1] = \mathbf{0}$ and $\mathbf{V}_1 = \mathrm{Var}[\mathbf{z}_1]$, the marginal moments of all $\mathbf{z}_t$. In this notation, the Gram–Schmidt orthonormalization of $\{\varepsilon_1, \ldots, \varepsilon_T\}$ depends on

$$\mathrm{E}^*[\varepsilon_t \mid \varepsilon_1, \ldots, \varepsilon_{t-1}] = \boldsymbol{\delta}'\mathbf{m}_t$$

and

$$\mathrm{Var}\{\varepsilon_t - \mathrm{E}^*[\varepsilon_t \mid \varepsilon_1, \ldots, \varepsilon_{t-1}]\} = \mathrm{Var}[\varepsilon_t - \boldsymbol{\delta}'\mathbf{m}_t] = \boldsymbol{\delta}'\mathbf{V}_t\boldsymbol{\delta}$$

for $t = 1, \ldots, T$. That is, $\{(\varepsilon_t - \boldsymbol{\delta}'\mathbf{m}_t) / \sqrt{\boldsymbol{\delta}'\mathbf{V}_t\boldsymbol{\delta}}\}$ is a sequence of uncorrelated and constant (unit) variance random variables. These are a simple byproduct of iterative calculation of $\mathbf{m}_t$ and $\mathbf{V}_t$ $(t = 1, \ldots, T)$.

In the first step, we use *partitioned projection*, an analogue to the partitioned OLS projection (Exercise 3.16).

Lemma 25.3 (Partitioned Projection) *Let the second moments of y_n and $\mathbf{x}_n$ be finite and* Var$[\mathbf{x}_n]$ *be nonsingular. If we partition $\mathbf{x}_n = [\mathbf{x}'_{1n}, \mathbf{x}'_{2n}]'$, then*

$$\mathrm{E}^*[y_n \mid \mathbf{x}_n] = \mathrm{E}^*[y_n \mid \mathbf{x}_{1n}] + \mathrm{E}^*\Big[y_n - \mathrm{E}^*[y_n \mid \mathbf{x}_{1n}] \,\Big|\, \mathbf{x}_{2n} - \mathrm{E}^*[y_n \mid \mathbf{x}_{1n}]\Big]$$

Proof. We can always write

$$y_n = \mathrm{E}^*[y_n \mid \mathbf{x}_{1n}] + y_n - \mathrm{E}^*[y_n \mid \mathbf{x}_{1n}]$$

and, taking the population projection onto $\mathbf{x}_n$ on both sides,

$$\mathrm{E}^*[y_n \mid \mathbf{x}_n] = \mathrm{E}^*[y_n \mid \mathbf{x}_{1n}] + \mathrm{E}^*\big[y_n - \mathrm{E}^*[y_n \mid \mathbf{x}_{1n}] \mid \mathbf{x}_n\big]$$

by the law of iterated projections (Lemma 7.9, p. 150). By construction, $y_n - \mathrm{E}^*[y_n | \mathbf{x}_{1n}]$ and $\mathbf{x}_{2n} - \mathrm{E}^*[y_n \mid \mathbf{x}_{1n}]$ are orthogonal to $\mathbf{x}_{1n}$ (Lemma 3.16, p. 71) so that we can rewrite the second term as

$$\begin{aligned}
\mathrm{E}^*\big[y_n - \mathrm{E}^*[y_n \mid \mathbf{x}_{1n}] \mid \mathbf{x}_n\big] &= \mathrm{E}^*\Big[y_n - \mathrm{E}^*[y_n \mid \mathbf{x}_{1n}] \,\Big|\, \mathbf{x}_{1n}, \mathbf{x}_{2n}\Big] \\
&= \mathrm{E}^*\Big[y_n - \mathrm{E}^*[y_n \mid \mathbf{x}_{1n}] \,\Big|\, \mathbf{x}_{1n}, \mathbf{x}_{2n} - \mathrm{E}^*[y_n \mid \mathbf{x}_{1n}]\Big] \\
&= \mathrm{E}^*\Big[y_n - \mathrm{E}^*[y_n \mid \mathbf{x}_{1n}] \,\Big|\, \mathbf{x}_{2n} - \mathrm{E}^*[y_n \mid \mathbf{x}_{1n}]\Big]
\end{aligned}$$

This gives the result. □

We use this lemma to obtain

$$\begin{aligned}\mathrm{E}^*[\mathbf{z}_t \mid \varepsilon_1, \ldots, \varepsilon_t] &= \mathrm{E}^*[\mathbf{z}_t \mid \varepsilon_1, \ldots, \varepsilon_{t-1}] \\ &\quad + \mathrm{E}^*\Big[\mathbf{z}_t - \mathrm{E}^*[\mathbf{z}_t \mid \varepsilon_1, \ldots, \varepsilon_{t-1}] \,\Big|\, \varepsilon_t - \mathrm{E}^*[\varepsilon_t \mid \varepsilon_1, \ldots, \varepsilon_{t-1}]\Big] \\ &= \mathbf{m}_t + \mathrm{E}^*[\mathbf{z}_t - \mathbf{m}_t \mid \varepsilon_t - \boldsymbol{\delta}'\mathbf{m}_t]\end{aligned}$$

Applying Lemma 7.4 (MMSE Linear Predictor, p. 135) and

$$\begin{aligned}\mathrm{Var}[\varepsilon_t - \boldsymbol{\delta}'\mathbf{m}_t] &= \mathrm{Var}[\boldsymbol{\delta}'(\mathbf{z}_t - \mathbf{m}_t)] = \boldsymbol{\delta}'\mathbf{V}_t\boldsymbol{\delta} \\ \mathrm{Cov}[\mathbf{z}_t - \mathbf{m}_t, \varepsilon_t - \boldsymbol{\delta}'\mathbf{m}_t] &= \mathrm{Cov}[\mathbf{z}_t - \mathbf{m}_t, \boldsymbol{\delta}'(\mathbf{z}_t - \mathbf{m}_t)] = \mathbf{V}_t\boldsymbol{\delta}\end{aligned}$$

gives

$$\mathrm{E}^*[\mathbf{z}_t \mid \varepsilon_1, \ldots, \varepsilon_t] = \mathbf{m}_t + \mathbf{V}_t\boldsymbol{\delta}\frac{\varepsilon_t - \boldsymbol{\delta}'\mathbf{m}_t}{\boldsymbol{\delta}'\mathbf{V}_t\boldsymbol{\delta}} \tag{25.63}$$

Furthermore,[39]

$$\mathrm{Var}\Big[\mathbf{z}_t - \mathrm{E}^*[\mathbf{z}_t \mid \varepsilon_1, \ldots, \varepsilon_t]\Big] = \mathbf{V}_t - \mathbf{V}_t\boldsymbol{\delta}\frac{1}{\boldsymbol{\delta}'\mathbf{V}_t\boldsymbol{\delta}}\boldsymbol{\delta}'\mathbf{V}_t \tag{25.64}$$

Equations (25.63)–(25.64) are often called the *updating equations* of the Kalman filter.

Now, using the AR structure, we can complete the process of finding predictors for $\mathbf{z}_{t+1}$ conditional on $\varepsilon_1, \ldots, \varepsilon_t$:

$$\begin{aligned}\mathbf{m}_{t+1} &= \mathbf{A}\,\mathrm{E}^*[\mathbf{z}_t \mid \varepsilon_1, \ldots, \varepsilon_t] \\ \mathbf{W}_{t+1} &= \mathbf{A}\,\mathrm{Var}\Big[\mathbf{z}_t - \mathrm{E}^*[\mathbf{z}_t \mid \varepsilon_1, \ldots, \varepsilon_t]\Big]\mathbf{A}' + \mathrm{Var}[\mathbf{w}_t]\end{aligned}$$

These are the *prediction equations* of the Kalman filter. By substituting (25.63)–(25.64) into the prediction equations, we obtain the iterative formulas

$$\begin{aligned}\mathbf{m}_{t+1} &= \mathbf{A}\left(\mathbf{m}_t + \mathbf{V}_t\boldsymbol{\delta}\frac{\varepsilon_t - \boldsymbol{\delta}'\mathbf{m}_t}{\boldsymbol{\delta}'\mathbf{V}_t\boldsymbol{\delta}}\right) \\ &= \mathbf{A}_t\mathbf{m}_t + A\mathbf{A}\mathbf{V}_t\boldsymbol{\delta}\frac{\varepsilon_t}{\boldsymbol{\delta}'\mathbf{V}_t\boldsymbol{\delta}} \end{aligned}\tag{25.65}$$

$$\begin{aligned}\mathbf{V}_{t+1} &= \mathbf{A}\left(\mathbf{V}_t - \mathbf{V}_t\boldsymbol{\delta}\frac{1}{\boldsymbol{\delta}'\mathbf{V}_t\boldsymbol{\delta}}\boldsymbol{\delta}'\mathbf{V}_t\right)\mathbf{A}' + \mathrm{Var}[\mathbf{w}_{t+1}] \\ &= \mathbf{A}_t\mathbf{V}_t\mathbf{A}' + \mathrm{Var}[\mathbf{w}_{t+1}]\end{aligned}\tag{25.66}$$

where

$$\mathbf{A}_t \equiv \mathbf{A}\left(\mathbf{I}_{q+1} - \mathbf{V}_t\boldsymbol{\delta}\frac{1}{\boldsymbol{\delta}'\mathbf{V}_t\boldsymbol{\delta}}\boldsymbol{\delta}'\right)$$

---

[39] This variance follows from

$$\begin{aligned}\mathbf{z}_t - \mathrm{E}^*[\mathbf{z}_t \mid \varepsilon_1, \ldots, \varepsilon_t] &= \mathbf{z}_t - \mathbf{m}_t - \mathbf{V}_t\boldsymbol{\psi}\frac{\varepsilon_t - \boldsymbol{\psi}'\mathbf{m}_t}{\boldsymbol{\psi}'\mathbf{V}_t\boldsymbol{\psi}} \\ &= \left(\mathbf{I} - \frac{1}{\boldsymbol{\psi}'\mathbf{V}_t\boldsymbol{\psi}}\mathbf{V}_t A\psi\psi'\right)(\mathbf{z}_t - \mathbf{m}_t)\end{aligned}$$

These two equations are equivalent to (25.38)–(25.39). The variance matrix recursion (25.66) is called the *Ricatti equation.*

25.7.3 MA(q) Identification

Proof of Proposition 24. An algebraic characterization of the MA(q) autocovariance function is that the coefficient of z^n in the polynomial

$$\sigma_u^2 \sum_{j=-q}^{q} \gamma_j z^j \equiv \sigma_u^2 \left(1 + \psi_1 z + \cdots + \psi_q z^q\right)\left(1 + \psi_1 z^{-1} + \cdots + \psi_q z^{-q}\right) \tag{25.67}$$

is the nth autocovariance. For $n > 0$, the z^n term is the sum of products of the form $\psi_{n+j} z^{n+j} \psi_j z^{-j}$. Therefore, the coefficient of z^n is $\sigma_u^2 \sum_{j=0}^{q-n} \psi_{n+j}\psi_j$. This equals the nth covariance as given by (25.24).

We can write the polynomial (25.67) in the factored form

$$\sigma_u^2 \sum_{j=-q}^{q} \gamma_j z^j = \sigma_u^2 \prod_{j=1}^{q} \left[\left(1 - \lambda_j z\right)\left(1 - \lambda_j z^{-1}\right)\right]$$

Because z and z^{-1} appear in pairs, we can change the roots of all these factors to their reciprocals:

$$\begin{aligned}\sigma_u^2 \sum_{j=-q}^{q} \gamma_j z^j &= \sigma_u^2 \prod_{j=1}^{q} \left\{\lambda_j z \lambda_j z^{-1}\left[\left(-\lambda_j z\right)^{-1} + 1\right]\left[\left(-\lambda_j z^{-1}\right)^{-1} + 1\right]\right\} \\ &= \sigma_u^2 \prod_{j=1}^{q} \left[\lambda_j^2 \left(1 - \lambda_j^{-1} z^{-1}\right)\left(1 - \lambda_j^{-1} z\right)\right] \\ &= \prod_{k=1}^{q} \left[\lambda_k^2\right] \cdot \sigma_u^2 \cdot \prod_{j=1}^{q} \left[\left(1 - \lambda_j^{-1} z^{-1}\right)\left(1 - \lambda_j^{-1} z\right)\right]\end{aligned}$$

This delivers a different MA(q) representation with the same autocovariances:

$$\varepsilon_t = \prod_{j=1}^{q} \left(1 - \lambda_j^{-1} L\right) v_t$$

where $\{v_t\}$ is a sequence of i.i.d. $\mathfrak{N}(0, \sigma_u^2 \prod_{j=1}^{q} \lambda_j^2)$ random variables. Even though the λ_j may be complex, they always come in conjugate pairs so that $\prod_{j=1}^{q} \lambda_j^2$ is real and the coefficients of $\prod_{j=1}^{q}\left(1 - \lambda_j^{-1} L\right)$ are real.

Of course, we can change the roots selectively also, preserving some and taking reciprocals of others. Let us order the λ_j so that $\lambda_1, \ldots, \lambda_n$ ($n \le q$) have magnitudes that exceed one. The characteristic roots corresponding to factors 1 through n all lie outside the complex unit circle. The rest are all on or inside. Then

$$\sigma_u^2 \sum_{j=-q}^{q} \gamma_j z^j = \left[\prod_{k=1}^{n} \lambda_k^2\right] \cdot \sigma_u^2 \cdot \left[\prod_{j=1}^{n} \left(1 - \lambda_j^{-1} z^{-1}\right)\left(1 - \lambda_j^{-1} z\right)\right]$$

$$\cdot \left[\prod_{m=n+1}^{q} (1 - \lambda_m z) \left(1 - \lambda_m z^{-1}\right) \right]$$

and

$$\varepsilon_t = \psi_a(L) v_t$$

where

$$\psi_a(L) = \prod_{j=1}^{n} \left(1 - \lambda_j^{-1} L\right) \cdot \prod_{m=n+1}^{q} (1 - \lambda_m L)$$

and v_t is i.i.d. $\mathfrak{N}(0, \sigma_u^2 \prod_{k=1}^{n} \lambda_k^2)$ is the required MA(q) representation. □

25.7.4 Score Test Equivalence

This section shows the equivalence of the score tests for no serial correlation in MA(q) and AR(q) specifications. We need the score for the parameters in the covariance parameters. Let $\boldsymbol{\gamma}(\boldsymbol{\theta}) \equiv \left[\mathrm{Cov}[\varepsilon_t, \varepsilon_{t-j}];\ j = 1, \ldots, T-1\right]'$ be the vector of the first $T-1$ autocovariances. Suppose that the estimation objective function $Q_N(\boldsymbol{\theta})$ depends on $\boldsymbol{\theta}$ only through $\boldsymbol{\gamma}(\boldsymbol{\theta})$. In general,

$$L_{\boldsymbol{\theta}}(\boldsymbol{\theta}) = \frac{\partial \boldsymbol{\gamma}(\boldsymbol{\theta})'}{\partial \boldsymbol{\theta}} \frac{\partial L(\boldsymbol{\theta})}{\partial \boldsymbol{\gamma}} \bigg|_{\boldsymbol{\gamma}=\boldsymbol{\gamma}(\boldsymbol{\theta})}$$

Using the autocovariance function of the MA(q) in (25.24),

$$\frac{\partial \gamma_j(\boldsymbol{\psi})}{\partial \psi_k} = \sigma_u^2 \left(\psi_{k-|j|} \mathbf{1}\{k \geq |j|\} + \psi_{k+|j|} \mathbf{1}\{q \geq k + |j|\}\right)$$

$k = 1, \ldots, q$. Note that $\psi_0 \equiv 1$. Evaluating these under the null hypothesis $H_0 : \psi_j = 0$, $j = 1, \ldots, q$ of no serial correlation, we obtain

$$\frac{\partial \gamma_j(\boldsymbol{\psi})}{\partial \psi_k} \bigg|_{\psi_1=\cdots=\psi_q=0} = \sigma_u^2 \cdot \mathbf{1}\{k = |j|\} \tag{25.68}$$

We will find comparable derivatives for an AR(p) process by implicit differentiation. Starting with the first p autocovariances given by (25.56)–(25.59),

$$\mathbf{W}(\boldsymbol{\phi}) \left[\gamma_j(\boldsymbol{\phi});\ j = 1, \ldots, p\right] = \sigma_u^2 \cdot \boldsymbol{\phi}$$

and by differentiating,[40]

$$\mathbf{W}(\boldsymbol{\phi}) \frac{\partial \left[\gamma_j(\phi);\ j = 1, \ldots, p\right]}{\partial \phi_k} + \frac{\partial \mathbf{W}(\boldsymbol{\phi})}{\partial \phi_k} \left[\gamma_j(\boldsymbol{\phi});\ j = 1, \ldots, p\right] = \sigma_u^2 \cdot e_k$$

we obtain

$$\frac{\partial \left[\gamma_j(\boldsymbol{\phi});\ j = 1, \ldots, p\right]}{\partial \phi_k} \bigg|_{\phi_1=\cdots=\phi_p=0} = \sigma_u^2 \cdot e_k \tag{25.69}$$

[40] The vector e_k denotes the kth elementary vector, with all elements equal to zero except the kth, which is one.

because $\mathbf{W}(\mathbf{0}) = \mathbf{I}_p$ and $\gamma_j(\mathbf{0}) = 0$, $j \neq 0$. For $\gamma_j(\boldsymbol{\phi})$, $j > p$, we use the difference equation (25.14) to get

$$\frac{\partial \gamma_j(\boldsymbol{\phi})}{\partial \phi_k} = \phi_1 \frac{\partial \gamma_{j-1}(\boldsymbol{\phi})}{\partial \phi_k} + \phi_2 \frac{\partial \gamma_{j-2}(\boldsymbol{\phi})}{\partial \phi_k} + \cdots + \phi_p \frac{\partial \gamma_{j-p}(\boldsymbol{\phi})}{\partial \phi_k}$$

so that

$$\left. \frac{\partial \gamma_j(\boldsymbol{\phi})}{\partial \phi_k} \right|_{\phi_1 = \cdots = \phi_p = 0} = 0, \quad j > p \tag{25.70}$$

Equations (25.69)–(25.70) combine into

$$\frac{\partial \gamma_j(\boldsymbol{\phi})}{\partial \phi_k} = \sigma_u^2 \cdot \mathbf{1}\{k = |j|\} \tag{25.71}$$

Finally, combining (25.68) and (25.71) when $p = q$, we have shown that

$$\left. \frac{\partial \gamma(\boldsymbol{\phi})}{\partial \phi_k} \right|_{\phi_1 = \cdots = \phi_p = 0} = \sigma_u^2 \cdot [\mathbf{1}\{k = |j|\}] = \left. \frac{\partial \gamma(\boldsymbol{\psi})}{\partial \psi_k} \right|_{\psi_1 = \cdots = \psi_q = 0}, \qquad k = 1, \ldots, p$$

We conclude that the score functions are identical when they are evaluated at the same parameter values that satisfy the null hypothesis of no serial correlation.

25.8 OVERVIEW

1. Researchers motivate autoregressive moving-average (ARMA) models of serial correlation with latent variable models or the Wold decomposition theorem.
   (a) Latent variable models specify shared, unobserved, white noise as the source of correlation among the observations in a time series.
   (b) The Wold decomposition theorem says a covariance-stationary process has an infinite-order moving-average representation in terms of the residuals from MMSE linear predictions.
2. The AR(p) specification is a pth-order distributed lag plus white noise:

$$\varepsilon_t = \phi_1 \varepsilon_{t-1} + \cdots + \phi_p \varepsilon_{t-p} + u_t \qquad \text{or} \qquad \phi(L)\varepsilon_t = u_t$$

   where $\phi(L) \equiv 1 + \phi_1 L + \cdots + \phi_p L^p$ is a polynomial in the lag operator L. The implied autocovariances are the solution to the equations generated by

$$\mathrm{E}[\varepsilon_t \varepsilon_{t-s}] = \phi_1 \mathrm{E}[\varepsilon_{t-1}\varepsilon_{t-s}] + \cdots + \phi_p \mathrm{E}[\varepsilon_{t-p}\varepsilon_{t-s}] + \mathrm{E}[u_t \varepsilon_{t-s}]$$

   These autocovariances are constant if and only if the roots of the characteristic equation

$$\lambda^p \phi(\lambda^{-1}) = 0$$

   lie strictly inside the complex unit circle. If so, then the autocovariances die out geometrically. On the other hand, the partial autocovariances $\mathrm{Cov}[\varepsilon_t, \varepsilon_{t-s} \mid \varepsilon_{t-1}, \ldots, \varepsilon_{t-s+1}]$ equal zero for $s > p$.
3. The MA(q) specification is a distributed lag of order $q + 1$ in a white noise sequence:

$$\varepsilon_t = u_t + \psi_1 u_{t-1} + \psi_2 u_{t-2} + \cdots + \psi_q u_{t-q} \qquad \text{or} \qquad \varepsilon_t = \psi(L) u_t$$

   where $\psi(L) \equiv 1 + \psi_1 L + \cdots + \psi_q L^q$. The implied autocovariance function is

$$\text{Cov}[\varepsilon_t, \varepsilon_{t-s}] = \begin{cases} \sigma_u^2 \sum_{n=0}^{q-|s|} \psi_{|s|+n}\psi_n & \text{if } |s| \le q \\ 0 & \text{if } |s| > q \end{cases}$$

where $\psi_0 \equiv 1$. In constrast, the partial autocovariances do not die out as the number of periods between realizations grows. Such moving averages are always covariance stationary but the ψ_ss are not globally identified. A unique parameterization is the representation with roots of the characteristic equation

$$\lambda^q \psi(\lambda^{-1}) = 0$$

on or inside the complex unit circle. The MA(q) parameterization is also invertible to an AR(∞) representation only if the roots lie strictly inside the unit circle.

4. As a special case of the Wold decomposition theorem, all stationary AR(p) processes possess an MA(∞) representation.

5. The ARMA(p, q) specification mixes the AR(p) and the MA(q):

$$\varepsilon_t = \phi_1\varepsilon_{t-1} + \cdots + \phi_p\varepsilon_{t-1} + u_t + \psi_1 u_{t-1} + \cdots + \psi_q u_{t-q}$$

or

$$\phi(L)\varepsilon_t = \psi(L)u_t$$

If the characteristic roots of the $\phi(\cdot)$ are strictly inside the complex unit circle, then the implied process is covariance stationary and its MA(∞) representation is

$$\varepsilon_t = \frac{\psi(L)}{\phi(L)} u_t$$

The family of rational polynomials provides parsimonious approximations to general covariance stationary moving averages. On the other hand, this family also contains observationally similar members so that application may be awkward.

6. The score test for AR(r) autocorrelation is identically equal to the score test for MA(r) autocorrelation. By association, Wald and likelihood ratio tests are also asymptotically equivalent under local alternatives to no autocorrelation. Furthermore, these testing methods break down when one applies them to both the autoregressive and moving-average components of the ARMA(p,q) specification. One implication is that t statistics for the ϕs and the ψs are meaningless for an overparameterized model.

7. On the other hand, sequential tests for lower order in either p or q given that the other order is correct are asymptotically independent. Thus, the overall size (or level of significance) of such a sequence of tests is easily found as the product of the sizes of the individual tests.

8. The Kalman filter is a recursive algorithm for computing the prediction errors of the GLS transformation:

$$\varepsilon_{*t} \equiv \frac{\varepsilon_t - \text{E}^*[\varepsilon_t \mid \varepsilon_{t-1}, \ldots, \varepsilon_1]}{\sqrt{\text{Var}\left[\varepsilon_t - \text{E}^*[\varepsilon_t \mid \varepsilon_{t-1}, \ldots, \varepsilon_1]\right]}}$$

so that $\{\varepsilon_{*t}\}$ is homoskedastic and serially uncorrelated. The Kalman filter is based on representing an ARMA(p,q) process as a partial observation, $\varepsilon_t = \boldsymbol{\delta}'\mathbf{z}_t$, of a latent, multivariate $\mathbf{z}_t \equiv [z_{t1}, \ldots, z_{tm}]'$ that follows a multivariate AR(1) process

$$\mathbf{z}_t = \mathbf{A}\mathbf{z}_{t-1} + \mathbf{w}_t$$

Given that $\varepsilon_t = z_{t1}$,

$$\mathbf{m}_t = \mathbf{A}\left(\mathbf{m}_{t-1} + \mathbf{V}_{t-1}\boldsymbol{\delta}\frac{\varepsilon_{t-1} - \boldsymbol{\delta}'\mathbf{m}_{t-1}}{\boldsymbol{\delta}'\mathbf{V}_{t-1}\boldsymbol{\delta}}\right)$$

$$\mathbf{V}_t = \mathbf{A}\left(\mathbf{V}_{t-1} - \mathbf{V}_{t-1}\boldsymbol{\delta}\frac{1}{\boldsymbol{\delta}'\mathbf{V}_{t-1}\boldsymbol{\delta}}\boldsymbol{\delta}'\mathbf{V}_{t-1}\right)\mathbf{A}' + \text{Var}[\mathbf{w}_t]$$

for $t = 2, \ldots, T$, where

$$\mathbf{m}_1 \equiv \text{E}[\mathbf{z}_1] \quad \text{and} \quad \mathbf{V}_1 \equiv \text{Var}[\mathbf{z}_1]$$

and

$$\mathbf{m}_t \equiv \text{E}^*[\mathbf{z}_t \mid \varepsilon_1, \ldots, \varepsilon_{t-1}] \quad \text{and} \quad \mathbf{V}_t \equiv \text{Var}[\mathbf{z}_t - \mathbf{m}_t], \qquad t = 2, \ldots, T$$

This process is essentially Gram–Schmidt orthonormalization.

25.9 EXERCISES

25.9.1 Review

25.1 (Kalman Filter) Reconsider the linear regression equation

$$y_t = \mathbf{x}_t'\boldsymbol{\beta}_0 + u_t$$

where the $\mathbf{x}_t$ are fixed $K \times 1$ vectors and the u_t are white noise ($t = 1, \ldots, T$). One can cast this relationship as a state-space model like (25.60)–(25.61) by taking the latent $\mathbf{z}_t$ to be $[\boldsymbol{\beta}_0', u_t]'$ and writing

$$y_t = \begin{bmatrix}\mathbf{x}_t' & 1\end{bmatrix}\begin{bmatrix}\boldsymbol{\beta}_0 \\ u_t\end{bmatrix}$$

$$\begin{bmatrix}\boldsymbol{\beta}_0 \\ u_t\end{bmatrix} = \begin{bmatrix}\mathbf{I}_K & \mathbf{0} \\ \mathbf{0} & 0\end{bmatrix}\begin{bmatrix}\boldsymbol{\beta}_0 \\ u_{t-1}\end{bmatrix} + \begin{bmatrix}\mathbf{0} \\ u_t\end{bmatrix}$$

According to the Gauss–Markov theorem (Theorem 7, p. 187), at $t = K$ the MMSE linear predictor of $\boldsymbol{\beta}_0$ is $\mathbf{X}_{[K]}^{-1}\mathbf{y}_{[K]}$ and of u_K is 0, where $\mathbf{X}_{[K]} \equiv [\mathbf{x}_1, \ldots, \mathbf{x}_K]'$ and $\mathbf{y}_{[K]} \equiv [y_1, \ldots, y_K]'$.

(a) Rederive the recursive updating formula for the OLS fitted coefficients given in Exercise 4.16 using the Kalman filter. [HINT: Apply the updating equation (25.63).]

(b) Also, interpret the recursive residuals in Exercise 8.15 in terms of the output of the Kalman filter.

25.2 [AR(p) Score Test] Consider the pth-order autoregressive model with the conditional log-likelihood function (25.8) and the null hypothesis of no serial correlation, $\boldsymbol{\phi}_0 = \mathbf{0}$. Show that one score test statistic is equal to the sample size times the R^2 from a regression of $\hat{\varepsilon}_t$ on $\hat{\varepsilon}_{t-1}, \ldots, \hat{\varepsilon}_{t-p}$.

25.3 (NLS) Consider the NLS estimator described in (25.6)–(25.7). Show that $\hat{\boldsymbol{\beta}}_{\text{NLS}}$ and $\hat{\boldsymbol{\phi}}_{\text{NLS}}$ are asymptotically independently distributed provided that $\mathbf{x}_t$ does not include lagged dependent explanatory variables. What significance does this finding have?

25.4 (Score Test) In Section 25.7.4 of the *Mathematical Notes*, we show that the score tests for no autocorrelation in normally distributed disturbance terms are identical in the AR(p) and MA(p) specifications. In this exercise, we focus on the special case $p = 1$. For any T-variate $\mathbf{y} \sim \mathfrak{N}[\boldsymbol{\mu}, \boldsymbol{\Omega}(\rho)]$, a score test about a parameter ρ rests on a derivative that has the chain-rule form

$$\left.\frac{\partial L(\boldsymbol{\mu}, \boldsymbol{\Omega}(\rho); \mathbf{y})}{\partial \rho}\right|_{\rho=0} = \sum_{t,s=1}^{T} \left.\frac{\partial L(\boldsymbol{\mu}, \boldsymbol{\Omega}; \mathbf{y})}{\partial \omega_{ts}}\right|_{\boldsymbol{\Omega}=\sigma_\varepsilon^2 \cdot \mathbf{I}_T} \left.\frac{\partial \omega_{ts}(\rho)}{\partial \rho}\right|_{\rho=0}$$

where $\boldsymbol{\Omega}(\rho) = [\omega_{ts}(\rho)]$ and $\boldsymbol{\Omega}(0) = \sigma_\varepsilon^2 \cdot \mathbf{I}_T$.

(a) For the MA(1) model, the variance matrix is tridiagonal:

$$\boldsymbol{\Omega}(\rho) = \sigma_u^2 \cdot \begin{bmatrix} 1+\rho^2 & \rho & 0 & \cdots & 0 \\ \rho & 1+\rho^2 & \rho & \cdots & 0 \\ 0 & \rho & 1+\rho^2 & \ddots & \vdots \\ \vdots & \vdots & \ddots & \ddots & \rho \\ 0 & 0 & \cdots & \rho & 1+\rho^2 \end{bmatrix}$$

Find $\partial \omega_{ts}(\rho)/\partial \rho|_{\rho=0}$.

(b) For the AR(1) model, the variance matrix is a Toeplitz matrix:

$$\boldsymbol{\Omega}(\rho) = \frac{\sigma_u^2}{1-\rho^2} \cdot \begin{bmatrix} 1 & \rho & \rho^2 & \cdots & \rho^{T-1} \\ \rho & 1 & \rho & \cdots & \rho^{T-2} \\ \rho^2 & \rho & 1 & \ddots & \vdots \\ \vdots & \vdots & \ddots & \ddots & \rho \\ \rho^{T-1} & \rho^{T-2} & \cdots & \rho & 1 \end{bmatrix}$$

Show that this yields the same $\partial \omega_{ts}(\rho)/\partial \rho|_{\rho=0}$, $t, s = 1, \ldots, T$.

(c) Why do these equalities prove that the score tests are identical?

25.5 [AR(2)] In the AR(p) log-likelihood function, the marginal term (25.17) contains

$$\sum_{t=1}^{p} \log(2\pi\omega_t^2)$$

which constrains the MLE of the autoregressive parameters $\boldsymbol{\phi}$ to stationary values.

(a) Find an analytical expression for this sum when $p = 2$ and show that it constrains the MLE to stationarity.

(b) Also show that the log-likelihood function of an AR(2) model does not constrain the MLE to stationary values if one collapses this sum to

$$\log\left(\prod_{t=1}^{p} 2\pi\omega_t^2\right)$$

as in (25.16).

25.6 [MA(1)] For an MA(1) model find an analytical expression for the term

$$\mathrm{E}_T[\log 2\pi\sigma_t^2] = \mathrm{E}_T[\log \boldsymbol{\psi}'\mathbf{V}_t\boldsymbol{\psi}] = \log 2\pi\sigma_u^2 + \mathrm{E}_T[\log(\boldsymbol{\psi}'\mathbf{C}_t\boldsymbol{\psi})]$$

that appears in the log-likelihood function (25.41). Confirm that this term does not constrain the MLE for the moving-average parameter ψ_1 to be less than one in absolute value. Also confirm that for large T the contribution of this term to the log-likelihood function is negligible if $|\psi_1| < 1$.

25.7 [MA(q)] Suppose that you numerically maximize the log-likelihood function of an MA(q) process for a data set and find that the values of the coefficients $\boldsymbol{\psi}$ yield roots of the characteristic equation outside the unit circle. Could this be evidence of misspecification? Why or why not?

25.8 **[MA(q)]** The Kalman filter provides one method for computing the GLS estimator. Pagan and Nicholls (1976) offer another. Let

$$\varepsilon_t = u_t + \psi_1 u_{t-1} + \cdots + \psi_q u_{t-q}, \qquad t = 1, \ldots, T$$

where the u_t are a sequence of i.i.d. random variables with mean zero and variance $\sigma_u^2 > 0$.

(a) Show that $\boldsymbol{\varepsilon} \equiv [\varepsilon_t;\ t = 1, \ldots, T]'$ can be written as

$$\underset{T\times 1}{\boldsymbol{\varepsilon}} = \underset{T\times T}{\mathbf{A}}\ \underset{T\times 1}{\mathbf{u}} + \underset{T\times q}{\mathbf{B}}\ \underset{q\times 1}{\mathbf{v}}$$

where $\mathbf{u} \equiv [u_t;\ t = 1, \ldots, T]'$ and $\mathbf{v} \equiv [u_t;\ t = 1 - q, \ldots, 0]$.

(b) Show that the transformation from $\left[\mathbf{u}', \mathbf{v}'\right]'$ to $\left[\boldsymbol{\varepsilon}', \mathbf{v}'\right]'$ is linear and one to one. Use this fact to argue that

$$\mathbf{u}'\mathbf{u} + \mathbf{v}'\mathbf{v} = \left[\boldsymbol{\varepsilon}', \mathbf{v}'\right]\left(\mathrm{Var}\left[\left[\boldsymbol{\varepsilon}', \mathbf{v}'\right]'\right]\right)^{-1}\left[\boldsymbol{\varepsilon}', \mathbf{v}'\right]'$$

(c) In addition, show that

$$\begin{aligned}&\left[\boldsymbol{\varepsilon}'\ \ \mathbf{v}'\right]\left(\mathrm{Var}\left[\left[\boldsymbol{\varepsilon}', \mathbf{v}'\right]'\right]\right)^{-1}\left[\boldsymbol{\varepsilon}', \mathbf{v}'\right]' \\ &\quad = \boldsymbol{\varepsilon}'\left(\mathrm{Var}[\boldsymbol{\varepsilon}]\right)^{-1}\boldsymbol{\varepsilon} + \left(\mathbf{v} - \mathrm{E}^*[\mathbf{v}\,|\,\boldsymbol{\varepsilon}]\right)'\left(\mathrm{Var}[\left(\mathbf{v} - \mathrm{E}^*[\mathbf{v}\,|\,\boldsymbol{\varepsilon}]\right)]\right)^{-1}\left(\mathbf{v} - \mathrm{E}^*[\mathbf{v}\,|\,\boldsymbol{\varepsilon}]\right)\end{aligned}$$

so that

$$\min_{\mathbf{v}} \mathbf{u}'\mathbf{u} + \mathbf{v}'\mathbf{v} = \boldsymbol{\varepsilon}'\left(\mathrm{Var}[\boldsymbol{\varepsilon}]\right)^{-1}\boldsymbol{\varepsilon}$$

(d) Given $\boldsymbol{\psi}$, explain how to use this result to compute the GLS estimator for $\boldsymbol{\beta}$ with observations on $\mathbf{x}_t$ and y_t in the data-generating process $y_t = \mathbf{x}_t'\boldsymbol{\beta} + \varepsilon_t$.

25.9 **[MA(q)]** Suggest a reparameterization of the MA(q) specification that provides a way to constrain the roots of the associated characteristic equation to the unit circle. (HINT: $\cos\theta \pm i \sin\theta$ are conjugate elements of the unit circle.)

25.10 **[MA(1)]** Apply the Kalman filter to an MA(1) process. Confirm your results with Example 25.8.

25.11 **[MA(1)]** Suppose that $\{\varepsilon_t\}$ is an MA(1) process. Show that the correlation between ε_t and ε_{t-1} is bounded in absolute value by one-half.

25.12 **(Inversion)** Show that the coefficients of the MA inversion of the AR(p) process $\phi(L)\varepsilon_t = u_t$ can be found by the Taylor series formula (Theorem D.18):

$$\psi_s = \frac{1}{s!}\frac{d^s}{dz^s}\frac{1}{\phi(z)}\bigg|_{z=0}$$

Find the MA(∞) representation of the AR(2) process

$$\varepsilon_t = \phi_1\varepsilon_{t-1} + \phi_2\varepsilon_{t-2} + u_t$$

25.13 **(ARMA)** Show that the sum of two AR(1) time series has an ARMA(2, 1) representation.

25.14 **[MA(1)]** Show that $\mathrm{E}^*[\varepsilon_t\,|\,\varepsilon_{t-1}, \varepsilon_{t-2}, \ldots]$ does not have a convergent set of coefficients for an MA(1) with a unit root.

25.15 **(Common Factor Test)** Consider the regression model

$$\mathrm{E}[y_t \mid t-1] = \beta_1 y_{t-1} + \mathbf{x}_t'\boldsymbol{\beta}_2 + \mathbf{x}_{t-1}'\boldsymbol{\beta}_3$$

and its restricted form

$$\mathrm{E}[y_t \mid t-1] = \rho y_{t-1} + (\mathbf{x}_t - \rho\mathbf{x}_{t-1})'\boldsymbol{\beta}_2$$

The latter has a common factor, as in

$$\mathrm{E}[(1-\rho L)y_t \mid t-1] = (1-\rho L)\mathbf{x}_t'\boldsymbol{\beta}_2$$

Describe a hypothesis test for the common factor restriction.

25.16 **[ARMA(p, q)]** Try to generalize the Breusch–Pagan score test (Section 19.4.1) for serial correlation to the ARMA(p, q) alternative hypothesis. What problems do you encounter? Why?

25.9.2 Extensions

25.17 **(Kalman Filter)** Generalize the the state-space model (25.36)–(25.37) to

$$\varepsilon_t = \boldsymbol{\delta}'\mathbf{z}_t + v_t$$
$$\mathbf{z}_t = \mathbf{A}\mathbf{z}_{t-1} + \mathbf{w}_t$$

where

$$\mathrm{E}\left[\begin{bmatrix} v_t \\ \mathbf{w}_t \end{bmatrix}\right] = \begin{bmatrix} 0 \\ \mathbf{0} \end{bmatrix}$$

and

$$\mathrm{Var}\left[\begin{bmatrix} v_t \\ \mathbf{w}_t \end{bmatrix}\right] = \begin{bmatrix} \sigma_v^2 & \mathbf{0} \\ \mathbf{0} & \mathrm{Var}[\mathbf{w}_t] \end{bmatrix}$$

and find the Kalman filter for this generalization.

25.18 **(Unit Circle)** In Example 25.2 we find the conditions for AR(2) stationarity. Lemma 25.2 [AR(p) Covariance Stationarity, p. 655] gives an alternative approach: the roots of

$$z^2 - \phi_1 z - \phi_2 = 0$$

must lie strictly inside the complex unit circle. Derive the stationarity restrictions on ϕ_1 and ϕ_2 from this characterization.

25.19 **[MA(1)]** Find an analogue to Hatanaka's estimator (p. 512) for $\boldsymbol{\beta}_0$ in $y_t = \mathbf{x}_t'\boldsymbol{\beta}_0 + \varepsilon_t$ when, conditional on $\{\mathbf{x}_t\}$, $\{\varepsilon_t\}$ is an MA(1) process instead of an AR(1) process.

25.20 **(Lagged Dependent Variable)** Generalize the score test for autocorrelation in Exercise 20.26 to the alternative hypothesis that $\{\varepsilon_t\}$ is an AR(p) process instead of an AR(1).

CHAPTER 26

Simultaneous Equations

26.1 INTRODUCTION

There are two ways in which systems of regression equations commonly arise in econometrics, economic models based on an equilibrium of some kind and economic models based on optimization. Models that specify the outcome of several variables as the result of an equilibrium typically predict that each of the endogenous variables will be determined simultaneously by a set of common factors. In an economy with many markets, for example, an exogenous change in the demand for one commodity will have an effect on prices and quantities throughout the economy. Here is a very simple example from macroeconomics to illustrate: let

$$\begin{aligned} C_t &= \alpha_0 + \alpha_1 Y_t + \alpha_2 r_t + \varepsilon_{Ct} \\ I_t &= \gamma_0 + \gamma_1 r_t + \varepsilon_{It} \\ Y_t &= C_t + I_t + G_t \end{aligned} \tag{26.1}$$

$(t = 1, \ldots, T)$, where C, I, and Y are the endogenous variables consumption, investment, and income, respectively, and exogenous r and G are policy instruments, the interest rate and government spending, respectively. Solving for the equilibrium gives three linear functions

$$\begin{aligned} C_t &= \beta_{0C1} + \beta_{0C2} G_t + \beta_{0C3} r_t + v_{Ct} \\ I_t &= \beta_{0I1} + \beta_{0I2} G_t + \beta_{0I3} r_t + v_{It} \\ Y_t &= \beta_{0Y1} + \beta_{0I2} G_t + \beta_{0Y3} r_t + v_{Yt} \end{aligned} \tag{26.2}$$

where

$$\begin{aligned} &\beta_{0C1} = \frac{\alpha_0 + \alpha_1\gamma_0}{1-\alpha_1}, &&\beta_{0C2} = \frac{\alpha_1}{1-\alpha_1}, &&\beta_{0C3} = \frac{\alpha_1\gamma_1 + \alpha_2}{1-\alpha_1} \\ &\beta_{0I1} = \gamma_0, &&\beta_{0I2} = 0, &&\beta_{0I3} = \gamma_1 \\ &\beta_{0Y1} = \frac{\alpha_0 + \gamma_0}{1-\alpha_1}, &&\beta_{0Y2} = \frac{1}{1-\alpha_1}, &&\beta_{0Y3} = \frac{\alpha_2 + \gamma_1}{1-\alpha_1} \end{aligned} \tag{26.3}$$

and the vs are linear functions of the εs. These equations are useful because they contain the multipliers for the policy instruments. From an econometric perspective, these equations have an interesting structure: they share the explanatory variables r_t and G_t and the parameters of the consumption and investment equations.

Our econometric specification of this model includes latent disturbance terms in these equations, the εs and the vs. Given the nature of simultaneity, we expect these disturbances to be correlated. Correlation describes the way in which the dependent variables also share a set of unobserved determinants.

Models based on optimizing behavior lead to a similar situation when there are several variables for the economic agent to adjust. Econometric models of the behavior of firms, for example, can lead to specifications formally like (26.2). A multiproduct firm generally will set its production levels in response to the prices of all the goods that are outputs and inputs and to its production technology. The simultaneous determination of outputs and inputs by the firm creates a situation analogous to models of equilibrium: these variables share a set of determinants. Thus, econometric analysis of observed levels of outputs and inputs examines covariance among these variables due to both the observed explanatory variables and the unobserved determinants that are represented by latent disturbance terms.

When the econometric model specifies an interdependent system of relationships like the simple macroeconomic model in (26.1), the model is called a *system of simultaneous equations*. In such systems, all of the equations are required to determine the outcome of at least one dependent variable. Specifications like the equilibrium in (26.2) are called *seemingly unrelated regressions*. Although there seems to be no relationship among the equations, the inclusion of correlated latent disturbance terms implies that the LHS variables are dependently distributed. This chapter covers the econometric analysis of both kinds of systems.

We begin with seemingly unrelated regressions, ignoring restrictions like (26.3) and treating the βs as the primitive parameters. Such seemingly unrelated regressions are a special case of simultaneous equations. The econometric significance of seemingly unrelated regressions is that the GLS estimator for the coefficients in all of the equations is more efficient than the OLS estimator applied to each equation separately. The bulk of the work in this part of the chapter involves developing a convenient notation for the GLS estimator.

Given this notation, the primary issue in systems of simultaneous equations is identification of parameters. Because estimation of a seemingly unrelated system like (26.2) can be fairly straightforward, identification of a simultaneous system like (26.1) is manifested as the conversion of such coefficients as the βs into the αs and γs through equations like (26.3). Efficient estimation in turn concerns optimal use of such equations.

26.2 SEEMINGLY UNRELATED REGRESSIONS

We will begin our study of seemingly unrelated regressions (SUR) with an empirical example of estimating a cost function for firms that minimize the costs of production, comparing OLS and GLS estimates. Then we formalize the SUR estimation problem with a notation and assumptions that generalize the case of a single equation. These provide the foundation for comparing the sampling distributions of the OLS and GLS estimators and constructing a feasible GLS estimator based on initial estimation by OLS. We also describe the MLE under the additional assumption that the dependent variables share a conditional multivariate normal distribution. As one might expect in this case, the MLE and FGLS estimators are asymptotically equivalent.

26.2.1 Estimation of a Cost Function

Let us recount a model of firms minimizing costs as an empirical example of SUR. If the firm is a price-taker in the factor markets and if the firm chooses factor input levels to minimize costs, then economic theory gives further guidance about the relationships among all of the variables. However, even though the firms in an industry have access to the same technology, there will be idiosyncracies among firms that will account for deviations in each firm's input levels from the predictions of an economic model.

Christensen and Greene (1976) published a classic study that we will revisit. They modeled the single output, kilowatt hours of electricity generated per year, as the product of a process requiring three inputs, labor, fuel, and capital. The logarithm of total costs and the cost shares of the inputs, as functions of the prices of inputs and the level of output, are correlated dependent variables that form a system of seemingly unrelated regressions. The translog cost function specification holds that

$$\begin{aligned}\log\frac{C}{p_{\mathrm{F}}} &= \alpha+\beta_{\mathrm{L}}\log\frac{p_{\mathrm{L}}}{p_{\mathrm{F}}}+\beta_{\mathrm{K}}\log\frac{p_{\mathrm{K}}}{p_{\mathrm{F}}}+\beta_{\mathrm{Q}}\log Q\\ &+\frac{1}{2}\gamma_{\mathrm{LL}}\left(\log\frac{p_{\mathrm{L}}}{p_{\mathrm{F}}}\right)^2+\gamma_{\mathrm{LK}}\log\frac{p_{\mathrm{L}}}{p_{\mathrm{F}}}\log\frac{p_{\mathrm{K}}}{p_{\mathrm{F}}}+\frac{1}{2}\gamma_{\mathrm{LL}}\left(\log\frac{p_{\mathrm{K}}}{p_{\mathrm{F}}}\right)^2\\ &+\gamma_{\mathrm{LQ}}\log\frac{p_{\mathrm{L}}}{p_{\mathrm{F}}}\log Q+\gamma_{\mathrm{KQ}}\log\frac{p_{\mathrm{K}}}{p_{\mathrm{F}}}\log Q+\gamma_{\mathrm{QQ}}(\log Q)^2\end{aligned} \tag{26.4}$$

where we have imposed the theoretical restriction that cost functions are first-degree homogeneous in prices. Shephard's (1953) lemma yields the share equations[1]

$$s_{\mathrm{L}}\equiv\frac{p_{\mathrm{L}}L}{C}=\beta_{\mathrm{L}}+\gamma_{\mathrm{LL}}\log\frac{p_{\mathrm{L}}}{p_{\mathrm{F}}}+\gamma_{\mathrm{LK}}\log\frac{p_{\mathrm{K}}}{p_{\mathrm{F}}}+\gamma_{\mathrm{LQ}}\log Q \tag{26.5}$$

$$s_{\mathrm{K}}\equiv\frac{p_{\mathrm{K}}K}{C}=\beta_{\mathrm{K}}+\gamma_{\mathrm{LK}}\log\frac{p_{\mathrm{L}}}{p_{\mathrm{F}}}+\gamma_{\mathrm{KK}}\log\frac{p_{\mathrm{K}}}{p_{\mathrm{F}}}+\gamma_{\mathrm{KQ}}\log Q \tag{26.6}$$

where

$$s_{\mathrm{F}}\equiv\frac{p_{\mathrm{F}}F}{C}=1-s_{\mathrm{L}}-s_{\mathrm{K}}$$

The variables $\log C/p_{\mathrm{F}}$, s_{L}, and s_{K} correspond to y_1, y_2, and y_3 in a trivariate SUR system. The fourth variable, s_{F}, has an exact linear relationship with two others (s_{L} and s_{K}) so that the analysis ignores this redundant variable.

To make an econometric model, Christensen and Greene (1976) added latent disturbances onto each of the equations (26.4)–(26.6), assuming these to be independently and identically trivariate normal across firms. Although one can estimate each of the equations separately with OLS, they applied a relatively effecient GLS technique to the three equations: this method imposes cross-equation parameter restrictions and reweights the equations to improve estimator efficiency. They collected data on a cross section of 114 firms producing electricity in 1970 and estimated the three equations together. Because all of the parameters appear in the cost function, we display the estimate of that function alone:

---

[1] See Mas-Colell et al. (1995, p. 141) or Varian (1992, p. 75).

$$\log\frac{C}{p_{\mathrm{F}}} = \underset{(0.22)}{7.14} - \underset{(0.082)}{0.151}\log\frac{p_{\mathrm{L}}}{p_{\mathrm{F}}} + \underset{(0.071)}{0.208}\log\frac{p_{\mathrm{K}}}{p_{\mathrm{F}}} + \underset{(0.028)}{0.587}\log Q$$
$$+\frac{1}{2}\underset{(0.016)}{0.081}\left(\log\frac{p_{\mathrm{L}}}{p_{\mathrm{F}}}\right)^2 - \underset{(0.015)}{0.011}\log\frac{p_{\mathrm{L}}}{p_{\mathrm{F}}}\log\frac{p_{\mathrm{K}}}{p_{\mathrm{F}}} + \frac{1}{2}\underset{(0.019)}{0.118}\left(\log\frac{p_{\mathrm{K}}}{p_{\mathrm{F}}}\right)^2$$
$$-\underset{(0.002)}{0.018}\log\frac{p_{\mathrm{L}}}{p_{\mathrm{F}}}\log Q - \underset{(0.002)}{0.003}\log\frac{p_{\mathrm{K}}}{p_{\mathrm{F}}}\log Q + \frac{1}{2}\underset{(0.004)}{0.049}(\log Q)^2$$

In addition to linear homogeneity in prices, cost functions satisfy several other restrictions: monotonicity and convexity in factor prices and monotonicity in output.[2] Because the derivatives of the translog cost function depend on prices and output, these restrictions do not imply simple parametric hypotheses. Christensen and Greene found, however, that they were met at every observation for their estimated cost function. They also investigated economies of scale with this cost function, concluding that approximately half of the firms were not exploiting such economies.

26.2.2 Assumptions

Now let us formalize the multivariate structure of this example as an extension of previous regression analysis. In the univariate linear regression model

$$\mathrm{E}[y_t \mid \mathbf{X}] = \mathbf{x}_t'\boldsymbol{\beta}_0, \qquad t = 1, \ldots, T$$

y_t is a scalar dependent variable, $\mathbf{x}_t'$ is a (row) vector of K exogenous variables, $\boldsymbol{\beta}_0$ is a conformable vector of K unknown parameters, and y_t is homoskedastic and nonautocorrelated conditional on $\mathbf{X}$. We wrote this in vector form as

$$\mathrm{E}[\mathbf{y} \mid \mathbf{X}] = \mathbf{X}\boldsymbol{\beta}_0 \qquad \text{and} \qquad \mathrm{Var}[\mathbf{y} \mid \mathbf{X}] = \sigma_0^2 \cdot \mathbf{I}_T$$

in Assumptions 6.1 (First Moments, 110) and 7.1 (Second Moments, p. 130).

In this chapter we are considering several regression equations:

$$\mathrm{E}[y_{tj} \mid \mathbf{X}] = \mathbf{x}_t'\boldsymbol{\beta}_{0j}, \qquad t = 1, \ldots, T \qquad j = 1, \ldots, J \tag{26.7}$$

where the additional subscript j denotes the regression equation for the jth dependent variable. We make comparable assumptions for each y_{tj}. Each y_{tj} has a conditional expectation that is a linear function of the observed vector $\mathbf{x}_t'$ of K explanatory variables and the unknown vector $\boldsymbol{\beta}_{0j} \equiv \left[\beta_{0kj};\ k = 1, \ldots, K\right]'$ of K slope parameters. For each j, we assume that each dependent vector $\mathbf{y}_j \equiv [y_{tj};\ t = 1, \ldots, T]'$ also has a spherical distribution:

$$\mathrm{E}[\mathbf{y}_j \mid \mathbf{X}] = \mathbf{X}\boldsymbol{\beta}_{0j} \qquad \text{and} \qquad \mathrm{Var}[\mathbf{y}_j \mid \mathbf{X}] = \omega_{0jj} \cdot \mathbf{I}_T \tag{26.8}$$

where $\mathbf{X} \equiv [\mathbf{x}_t;\ t = 1, \ldots, T]'$. Thus, one can still estimate each $\boldsymbol{\beta}_{0j}$ with OLS if $\mathbf{X}$ is full rank:

$$\hat{\boldsymbol{\beta}}_{\mathrm{OLS},j} = (\mathbf{X}'\mathbf{X})^{-1}\mathbf{X}'\mathbf{y}_j. \tag{26.9}$$

[2] See Varian (1992, p. 72).

As usual, $\hat{\boldsymbol{\beta}}_{\text{OLS},j}$ is unbiased, its conditional variance is $\text{Var}[\hat{\boldsymbol{\beta}}_{\text{OLS},j} \mid \mathbf{X}] = \omega_{0jj} \cdot (\mathbf{X}'\mathbf{X})^{-1}$, and it is conditionally normally distributed if $\mathbf{y}_j$ is.

In addition, for every t we wish to allow the y_{tj} to be correlated among the different dependent variables, or across j. Therefore, we introduce the covariance parameters

$$\omega_{0ij} \equiv \text{Cov}[y_{ti}, y_{tj} \mid \mathbf{X}], \qquad i, j = 1, \ldots, J$$

and assume that

$$\text{Cov}[\mathbf{y}_i, \mathbf{y}_j \mid \mathbf{X}] \equiv \omega_{0ij} \cdot \mathbf{I}_T, \qquad i, j = 1, \ldots, J \tag{26.10}$$

Note that we have extended zero conditional covariance to y_{tj} and y_{si} whenever $t \neq s$. The dependent variables are conditionally uncorrelated if they come from different observations. But when we collect together the dependent variables for the tth observation, their joint variance matrix is the nonscalar $J \times J$ matrix $\boldsymbol{\Omega}_0 \equiv \left[\omega_{0ij}\right]$. If we collect together the various dependent variables for one observation in $\mathbf{y}_t \equiv [y_{t1}, \ldots, y_{tJ}]'$, then we can write

$$\text{Var}[\mathbf{y}_t \mid \mathbf{X}] = \boldsymbol{\Omega}_0$$

26.2.3 OLS versus GLS

This econometric specification is called seemingly unrelated regressions (SUR) because the individual regression equations have no structural relationship in the sense that a y_{tj} does not appear as an RHS variable in the ith ($j \neq i$) equation. However, a relationship does exist among the regression equations through the covariances. As a result one can generally estimate the equations together efficiently relative to OLS equation by equation. The OLS estimator fails to take into account cross-equation information that can be exploited to improve estimator efficiency.

To see this, note that we can artificially cast the SUR system as a large univariate general linear model. Let

$$\underset{JT \times 1}{\mathbf{y}_{\text{V}}} \equiv [\mathbf{y}_j'; \; j = 1, \ldots, J]' = \begin{bmatrix} \mathbf{y}_1 \\ \mathbf{y}_2 \\ \vdots \\ \mathbf{y}_J \end{bmatrix} \tag{26.11}$$

be a vector of the dependent data for *every* observation and *every* variable. In this vector, we are stacking the data for each distinct dependent variable together in subvectors of T observations. It follows directly that the vector $\mathbf{y}_{\text{V}}$ has a linear regression function:

$$\text{E}[\mathbf{y}_{\text{V}} \mid \mathbf{X}] = \begin{bmatrix} \mathbf{X}\boldsymbol{\beta}_{01} \\ \mathbf{X}\boldsymbol{\beta}_{02} \\ \vdots \\ \mathbf{X}\boldsymbol{\beta}_{0J} \end{bmatrix} = \mathbf{X}_{\text{V}}\boldsymbol{\beta}_0 \tag{26.12}$$

where

$$\underset{JT \times JK}{\mathbf{X}_{\text{V}}} \equiv \text{diag}(\mathbf{X}; \; j = 1, \ldots, J) = \begin{bmatrix} \mathbf{X} & \mathbf{0} & \cdots & \mathbf{0} \\ \mathbf{0} & \mathbf{X} & \cdots & \mathbf{0} \\ \vdots & \vdots & \ddots & \vdots \\ \mathbf{0} & \mathbf{0} & \cdots & \mathbf{X} \end{bmatrix} \tag{26.13}$$

$$\underset{JK\times 1}{\boldsymbol{\beta}_0} \equiv \left[\boldsymbol{\beta}_{0j}';\ j=1,\ldots,J\right]' = \begin{bmatrix} \boldsymbol{\beta}_{01} \\ \boldsymbol{\beta}_{02} \\ \vdots \\ \boldsymbol{\beta}_{0J} \end{bmatrix} \tag{26.14}$$

In this notation, the OLS estimator in (26.9) is simply

$$\begin{aligned} \hat{\boldsymbol{\beta}}_{\text{OLS}} &= (\mathbf{X}_{\text{V}}'\mathbf{X}_{\text{V}})^{-1}\mathbf{X}_{\text{V}}'\mathbf{y}_{\text{V}} \\ &= \left\{\text{diag}\left[(\mathbf{X}'\mathbf{X});\ j=1,\ldots,J)\right]\right\}^{-1}\left[(\mathbf{X}'\mathbf{y}_j)';\ j=1,\ldots,J\right]' \\ &= \text{diag}\left((\mathbf{X}'\mathbf{X})^{-1};\ j=1,\ldots,J)\right)\left[(\mathbf{X}'\mathbf{y}_j)';\ j=1,\ldots,J'\right]' \\ &= [\hat{\boldsymbol{\beta}}_{\text{OLS},j}';\ j=1,\ldots,J]' \end{aligned} \tag{26.15}$$

But the conditional variance matrix of $\mathbf{y}_{\text{V}}$ in (26.11) is not scalar: using (26.8) and (26.10),

$$\text{Var}(\mathbf{y}_{\text{V}} \mid \mathbf{X}) = \begin{bmatrix} \omega_{011}\cdot\mathbf{I}_T & \omega_{012}\cdot\mathbf{I}_T & \cdots & \omega_{01J}\cdot\mathbf{I}_T \\ \omega_{021}\cdot\mathbf{I}_T & \omega_{022}\cdot\mathbf{I}_T & \cdots & \omega_{02J}\cdot\mathbf{I}_T \\ \vdots & \vdots & \ddots & \vdots \\ \omega_{0J1}\cdot\mathbf{I}_T & \omega_{0J2}\cdot\mathbf{I}_T & \cdots & \omega_{0JJ}\cdot\mathbf{I}_T \end{bmatrix} \tag{26.16}$$

Let us introduce the Kronecker product as a convenient notation for abbreviating this large partitioned matrix with the expression

$$\text{Var}(\mathbf{y}_{\text{V}} \mid \mathbf{X}) = \boldsymbol{\Omega}_0 \otimes \mathbf{I}_T \tag{26.17}$$

The blocks of the partitioned matrix in (26.16) are the elements of the first matrix of the Kronecker product multiplied as scalars times the second matrix. We summarize the Kronecker product and some of its properties in Section G.2.

A GLS estimator is generally efficient relative to an OLS estimator when the conditional variance of the LHS variable is not scalar. For this reason, one prefers GLS for the system of equations to OLS equation by equation. Our notation makes it possible to express the GLS estimator for the general linear model in a familiar form:

$$\hat{\boldsymbol{\beta}}_{\text{GLS}} = \left[\mathbf{X}_{\text{V}}'\,(\boldsymbol{\Omega}_0 \otimes \mathbf{I}_T)^{-1}\,\mathbf{X}_{\text{V}}\right]^{-1}\mathbf{X}_{\text{V}}'\,(\boldsymbol{\Omega}_0 \otimes \mathbf{I}_T)^{-1}\,\mathbf{y}_{\text{V}} \tag{26.18}$$

using (26.12) and (26.16).

The current case, in which every regression function contains the same explanatory variables $\mathbf{x}_t$, happens to be special: GLS and OLS are identical. To see this, note that the matrix $\mathbf{X}_{\text{V}}$ also has a special form as a Kronecker product:

$$\mathbf{X}_{\text{V}} = \mathbf{I}_J \otimes \mathbf{X} \tag{26.19}$$

In contrast to (26.17), an identity matrix appears as the first matrix in this Kronecker product, creating a block-diagonal matrix like (26.13) with $\mathbf{X}$ in every diagonal block.

In addition, $\text{Var}(\mathbf{y}_{\text{V}} \mid \mathbf{X}_{\text{V}})$ and $\mathbf{X}_{\text{V}}$ are *conformable* Kronecker products. As a result, one can apply two properties of Kronecker products,[3]

$$(\mathbf{A} \otimes \mathbf{B})^{-1} = \mathbf{A}^{-1} \otimes \mathbf{B}^{-1} \tag{26.20}$$

[3] For (26.20) and (26.21) to hold, the right-hand side expressions must be well defined: (26.20) requires A and B to be nonsingular and (26.21) requires A to be conformable with C and B with D.

and

$$(\mathbf{A} \otimes \mathbf{B})(\mathbf{C} \otimes \mathbf{D}) = (\mathbf{AC} \otimes \mathbf{BD}) \tag{26.21}$$

to obtain

$$\begin{aligned}
(\boldsymbol{\Omega}_0 \otimes \mathbf{I}_T)^{-1}\mathbf{X}_V &= (\boldsymbol{\Omega}_0^{-1} \otimes \mathbf{I}_T)(\mathbf{I}_J \otimes \mathbf{X}) && \text{[by (26.20) and (26.19)]} \\
&= \boldsymbol{\Omega}_0^{-1} \otimes \mathbf{X} && \text{[by (26.21)]} \\
&= (\mathbf{I}_J \otimes \mathbf{X})(\boldsymbol{\Omega}_0^{-1} \otimes \mathbf{I}_K) && \text{[by (26.21)]} \\
&= \mathbf{X}_V(\boldsymbol{\Omega}_0 \otimes \mathbf{I}_K)^{-1} && \text{[by (26.19) and (26.20)]}
\end{aligned}$$

In words, the columns of the GLS instrument matrix $(\boldsymbol{\Omega}_0 \otimes \mathbf{I}_T)^{-1}\mathbf{X}_V$ are elements of the column space of $\mathbf{X}_V$. It follows that the GLS estimator (26.18) simplifies to the OLS estimator (26.15):

$$\begin{aligned}
\hat{\boldsymbol{\beta}}_{GLS} &= \left[(\boldsymbol{\Omega}_0 \otimes \mathbf{I}_K)^{-1}\mathbf{X}_V'\mathbf{X}_V\right]^{-1}(\boldsymbol{\Omega}_0 \otimes \mathbf{I}_K)^{-1}\mathbf{X}_V'\mathbf{y}_V \\
&= (\mathbf{X}_V'\mathbf{X}_V)^{-1}(\boldsymbol{\Omega}_0 \otimes \mathbf{I}_K)(\boldsymbol{\Omega}_0 \otimes \mathbf{I}_K)^{-1}\mathbf{X}_V'\mathbf{y}_V \\
&= \hat{\boldsymbol{\beta}}_{OLS}
\end{aligned} \tag{26.22}$$

This is another example of Lemma 19.1 (OLS/GLS Identity, p. 475).

But this equivalence has an important exception. One should also note that this equality does not hold up under linear restrictions on the coefficient vectors $\boldsymbol{\beta}_{0j}$. One might impose such restrictions as excluding an explanatory variable from a particular regression equation, as suggested by (26.3) for the I_t equation. We consider the general case in which $\boldsymbol{\delta}_0$ contains the M elements of $\boldsymbol{\beta}_0$ that must be estimated and $\mathbf{r} = [\mathbf{r}_j']'$ contains the $JK - M$ elements that are known. That is, we can write

$$\mathbf{R}_j'\boldsymbol{\beta}_{0j} = \mathbf{r}_j \qquad \text{and} \qquad \mathbf{S}_j'\boldsymbol{\beta}_{0j} = \boldsymbol{\delta}_{0j}$$

for each equation $(j = 1, \ldots, J)$. The matrices $\mathbf{R}_j$ and $\mathbf{S}_j$ are selection matrices containing zeros and ones and satisfy

$$\mathbf{R}_j\mathbf{R}_j' + \mathbf{S}_j\mathbf{S}_j' = \mathbf{I}_K$$

because each parameter is either known or unknown.

We will impose the restrictions in estimation by substituting

$$\boldsymbol{\beta}_{0j} = \left(\mathbf{R}_j\mathbf{R}_j' + \mathbf{S}_j\mathbf{S}_j'\right)\boldsymbol{\beta}_{0j} = \mathbf{R}_j\mathbf{r}_j + \mathbf{S}_j\boldsymbol{\delta}_{0j}$$

into each regression equation, obtaining[4]

$$\mathrm{E}[\mathbf{y}_j \mid \mathbf{X}] = \mathbf{X}\mathbf{R}_j\mathbf{r}_j + \mathbf{X}\mathbf{S}_j\boldsymbol{\delta}_{0j}$$

Thus, we define

$$\mathbf{y}_{VR} \equiv \left[(\mathbf{y}_j - \mathbf{X}\mathbf{R}_j\mathbf{r}_j)';\ j = 1, \ldots, J\right]' \tag{26.23}$$

and

[4] See Sections 4.2 and 4.3.

$$\underset{JT\times M}{\mathbf{X}_{\text{VR}}} \equiv \text{diag}(\mathbf{X}\mathbf{S}_j;\quad j=1,\ldots,J) = \mathbf{X}_{\text{V}}\mathbf{S}_{\delta} \tag{26.24}$$

where

$$\underset{JK\times M}{\mathbf{S}_{\delta}} \equiv \frac{\partial \boldsymbol{\beta}_0}{\partial \boldsymbol{\delta}_0'} = \text{diag}(\mathbf{S}_j;\quad j=1,\ldots,J) \tag{26.25}$$

so that we can write $\text{E}(\mathbf{y}_{\text{VR}}\,|\mathbf{X}_{\text{V}}) = \mathbf{X}_{\text{VR}}\boldsymbol{\delta}_0$ where $\boldsymbol{\delta}_0 \equiv \left[\delta_{0j}';\ j=1,\ldots,J\right]'$.

Now $\mathbf{X}_{\text{VR}}$ does not have the form of a Kronecker product. Instead, each regression equation has a different matrix of explanatory variables, denoted by $\mathbf{X}\mathbf{S}_j$, $j=1,\ldots,J$, respectively. The effect is that the restricted GLS estimator of $\boldsymbol{\delta}_0$,

$$\begin{aligned}\hat{\boldsymbol{\delta}}_{\text{GLS}} &= \left[\mathbf{X}_{\text{VR}}'\left(\boldsymbol{\Omega}_0\otimes\mathbf{I}_T\right)^{-1}\mathbf{X}_{\text{VR}}\right]^{-1}\mathbf{X}_{\text{VR}}'\left(\boldsymbol{\Omega}_0\otimes\mathbf{I}_T\right)^{-1}\mathbf{y}_{\text{VR}} \\ &= \left[\mathbf{S}_{\delta}'(\boldsymbol{\Omega}_0^{-1}\otimes\mathbf{X}'\mathbf{X})\mathbf{S}_{\delta}\right]^{-1}\mathbf{S}_{\delta}'(\boldsymbol{\Omega}_0^{-1}\otimes\mathbf{X}')\mathbf{y}_{\text{VR}}\end{aligned} \tag{26.26}$$

does not simplify to OLS equation by equation. In general, this GLS estimator will be relatively efficient.

26.2.4 Feasible GLS Estimation

To compute a feasible GLS (FGLS) estimator, we must replace $\boldsymbol{\Omega}_0$ with a consistent estimator. Estimation of the variance matrix $\boldsymbol{\Omega}_0$ is a straightforward extension of the OLS estimator of the univariate variance. In OLS, the sample variance of the OLS fitted residuals is the estimator of the conditional variance parameter. In SUR, the sample variance *matrix* of the OLS fitted residuals for all of the equations is an estimator for the conditional variance matrix $\boldsymbol{\Omega}_0$.

Because covariance works among the various equations, it is convenient to group together the data for each observation for estimation of $\boldsymbol{\Omega}_0$. Therefore, instead of stacking the SUR system in the vector form (26.12), let us define the $J\times 1$ vector $\mathbf{y}_t \equiv [y_{t1},\ldots,y_{tJ}]'$. Then the SUR system (26.7) can also be written as

$$\text{E}[\underset{1\times J}{\mathbf{y}_t'}\,|\mathbf{X}] = \underset{1\times K}{\mathbf{x}_t'}\ \underset{K\times J}{\mathbf{B}_0} \tag{26.27}$$

where $\mathbf{B}_0 \equiv \left[\beta_{0kj};\ k=1,\ldots,K,\ j=1,\ldots,J\right]$ is a $K\times J$ matrix containing all slope coefficients in the system, unrestricted and restricted.

In this row form, we will denote a row of fitted residuals for the tth observation by

$$\boldsymbol{\varepsilon}_t(\mathbf{B})' \equiv \mathbf{y}_t' - \mathbf{x}_t'\mathbf{B}$$

Then, after writing the OLS estimators in (26.9) as the matrix

$$\hat{\mathbf{B}}_{\text{OLS}} \equiv \left(\mathbf{X}'\mathbf{X}\right)^{-1}\mathbf{X}'\mathbf{Y}$$

where

$$\underset{T\times J}{\mathbf{Y}} = \left[\mathbf{y}_1,\ldots,\mathbf{y}_T\right]' = \left[y_{tj}\right]$$

an estimator of $\boldsymbol{\Omega}_0$ is

$$\hat{\boldsymbol{\Omega}}_{\text{OLS}} \equiv \text{E}_T[\boldsymbol{\varepsilon}_t(\hat{\mathbf{B}}_{\text{OLS}})\boldsymbol{\varepsilon}_t(\hat{\mathbf{B}}_{\text{OLS}})'] \tag{26.28}$$

the empirical second-moment matrix of the OLS fitted residual vectors. Under assumptions similar to those for a single equation in Chapter 13, $\hat{\boldsymbol{\Omega}}_{\text{OLS}}$ is a consistent estimator of $\boldsymbol{\Omega}_0$.

Thus, a popular restricted FGLS estimator is

$$\hat{\boldsymbol{\delta}}_{\text{FGLS}} = \left[\mathbf{X}'_{\text{VR}}(\hat{\boldsymbol{\Omega}}_{\text{OLS}} \otimes \mathbf{I}_T)^{-1}\mathbf{X}_{\text{VR}}\right]^{-1} \mathbf{X}'_{\text{VR}}(\hat{\boldsymbol{\Omega}}_{\text{OLS}} \otimes \mathbf{I}_T)^{-1}\mathbf{y}_{\text{R}} \tag{26.29}$$

Again under familiar assumptions,

$$\sqrt{T}\left(\hat{\boldsymbol{\delta}}_{\text{FGLS}} - \boldsymbol{\delta}_0\right) \xrightarrow{d} \mathfrak{N}(\mathbf{0}, \mathbf{V})$$

where

$$\begin{aligned}
\mathbf{V} &= \underset{T\to\infty}{\text{plim}}\; T \cdot \left[\mathbf{X}'_{\text{VR}}(\boldsymbol{\Omega}_0 \otimes \mathbf{I}_T)^{-1}\mathbf{X}_{\text{VR}}\right]^{-1} \\
&= \underset{T\to\infty}{\text{plim}} \left[\mathbf{S}'_\delta(\boldsymbol{\Omega}_0^{-1} \otimes \frac{1}{T} \cdot \mathbf{X}'\mathbf{X})\mathbf{S}_\delta\right]^{-1} \\
&= \left[\mathbf{S}'_\delta(\boldsymbol{\Omega}_0^{-1} \otimes \mathbf{D})\mathbf{S}_\delta\right]^{-1}
\end{aligned}$$

and $\text{E}_T[\mathbf{x}_t\mathbf{x}_t'] \equiv (1/T) \cdot \mathbf{X}'\mathbf{X} \xrightarrow{p} \mathbf{D}$, a nonsingular, finite matrix. This asymptotic distribution does not depend on the asymptotic distribution of a consistent estimator for $\boldsymbol{\Omega}_0$. Therefore, the estimator $\hat{\mathbf{B}}_{\text{OLS}}$ that enters $\hat{\boldsymbol{\Omega}}_{\text{OLS}}$ may be a restricted or an unrestricted estimator without affecting this result.

26.2.5 Maximum Likelihood Estimation

Under the assumption that $\mathbf{y}_t$ is conditionally normally distributed given $\mathbf{X}$, we can find the MLE for SUR. As you might expect, the MLE for $\boldsymbol{\beta}_0$ is a GLS estimator. The MLE for $\boldsymbol{\Omega}_0$ is reminiscent of the OLS variance estimator because it is based on simple second moments of fitted residuals. To derive these two estimators, we will give two forms of the log-likelihood function. These correspond to the two ways of collecting the y_{tj} in the vectors $\mathbf{y}_j \equiv [y_{1j}, \ldots, y_{Tj}]'$ and $\mathbf{y}_t \equiv [y_{t1}, \ldots, y_{tJ}]$.

First, we will work with the restricted stacked-vector form of $\mathbf{y}_j$ in (26.23). Given that $\mathbf{y}_{\text{VR}} \mid \mathbf{X} \sim \mathfrak{N}(\mathbf{X}_{\text{VR}}\boldsymbol{\delta}_0, \boldsymbol{\Omega}_0 \otimes \mathbf{I}_T)$, the log-likelihood function for $\boldsymbol{\delta}_0$ and $\boldsymbol{\Omega}_0$ is[5]

$$\begin{aligned}
L(\boldsymbol{\delta}, \boldsymbol{\Omega}; \mathbf{y} \mid \mathbf{X}) = &-\frac{1}{2}\big[\log\det(2\pi \cdot \boldsymbol{\Omega} \otimes \mathbf{I}_T) \\
&+ (\mathbf{y}_{\text{VR}} - \mathbf{X}_{\text{VR}}\boldsymbol{\delta})'(\boldsymbol{\Omega} \otimes \mathbf{I}_T)^{-1}(\mathbf{y}_{\text{VR}} - \mathbf{X}_{\text{VR}}\boldsymbol{\delta})\big]
\end{aligned} \tag{26.30}$$

according to Definition 17 (Multivariate Normal Distribution, p. 206). This yields the score for $\boldsymbol{\delta}$,

$$L_\delta(\boldsymbol{\delta}, \boldsymbol{\Omega}; \mathbf{y} \mid \mathbf{X}) = \mathbf{X}'_{\text{VR}}(\boldsymbol{\Omega} \otimes \mathbf{I}_T)^{-1}(\mathbf{y}_{\text{VR}} - \mathbf{X}_{\text{VR}}\boldsymbol{\delta}) \tag{26.31}$$

This vector of partial derivatives is a generalization of (14.8) to a nonscalar variance matrix.[6] Equating this vector to zero and solving for $\boldsymbol{\delta}$ gives the MLE for $\boldsymbol{\delta}_0$ as a function of $\boldsymbol{\Omega}$:

---

5 Without losing any generality, we let $\mathbf{r}_j = \mathbf{0}$, $j = 1, \ldots, J$.

6 We work out this derivative in Appendix G. See particularly (G.34). Alternatively, one can derive it from a GLS transformation as in the proof of Aitken's theorem (Theorem 12, p. 432).

$$\hat{\boldsymbol{\delta}}(\boldsymbol{\Omega}) = \left[\mathbf{X}_{\mathrm{VR}}'(\boldsymbol{\Omega} \otimes \mathbf{I}_T)^{-1}\mathbf{X}_{\mathrm{VR}}\right]^{-1} \mathbf{X}_{\mathrm{VR}}'(\boldsymbol{\Omega} \otimes \mathbf{I}_T)^{-1}\mathbf{y}_{\mathrm{VR}} \tag{26.32}$$

which corresponds to the usual GLS estimator (26.29).

To find the MLE for $\boldsymbol{\Omega}_0$ we rewrite the log-likelihood function in terms of the row vector notation of (26.27). Conditional on $\mathbf{X}$, the $\boldsymbol{\varepsilon}_t(\mathbf{B}_0) = \mathbf{y}_t - \mathbf{B}_0'\mathbf{x}_t$ are i.i.d. $\mathfrak{N}(\mathbf{0}, \boldsymbol{\Omega}_0)$ vectors. Therefore, the joint log-likelihood function is a sum of marginal log-likelihoods:

$$L(\boldsymbol{\delta}, \boldsymbol{\Omega}; \mathbf{y} \mid \mathbf{X}) = -\frac{T}{2}\,\mathrm{E}_T[\log\det(2\pi \cdot \boldsymbol{\Omega}) + \boldsymbol{\varepsilon}_t(\mathbf{B})'\boldsymbol{\Omega}^{-1}\boldsymbol{\varepsilon}_t(\mathbf{B})] \tag{26.33}$$

where the unknown elements of $\mathbf{B}$ are the elements of $\boldsymbol{\delta}$. In Appendix G, we derive the score vector

$$\begin{aligned} L_{\boldsymbol{\Omega}}(\boldsymbol{\delta}, \boldsymbol{\Omega}; \mathbf{y} \mid X) &\equiv \frac{\partial L(\boldsymbol{\delta}, \boldsymbol{\Omega}; \mathbf{y} \mid X)}{\partial\, \mathrm{vec}\, \boldsymbol{\Omega}} \\ &= -\frac{T}{2}\,\mathrm{vec}\{\boldsymbol{\Omega}^{-1} - \boldsymbol{\Omega}^{-1}\,\mathrm{E}_T[\boldsymbol{\varepsilon}_t(\mathbf{B})\boldsymbol{\varepsilon}_t(\mathbf{B})']\boldsymbol{\Omega}^{-1}\} \end{aligned} \tag{26.34}$$

where $\mathrm{vec}(\boldsymbol{\Omega})$ is the column vector created by stacking the successive columns of $\boldsymbol{\Omega}$, from first to last.[7] This derivative is a matrix generalization of the scalar version in (14.9). Given $\boldsymbol{\delta}$, this score equals zero at

$$\hat{\boldsymbol{\Omega}}(\boldsymbol{\delta}) \equiv \mathrm{E}_T[\boldsymbol{\varepsilon}_t(\mathbf{B})\boldsymbol{\varepsilon}_t(\mathbf{B})'] \tag{26.35}$$

which is the second-moment matrix of the fitted residuals.

Thus, the MLE $(\hat{\boldsymbol{\delta}}_{\mathrm{ML}}, \hat{\boldsymbol{\Omega}}_{\mathrm{ML}})$ is the solution to $\hat{\boldsymbol{\delta}}_{\mathrm{ML}} = \hat{\boldsymbol{\delta}}(\hat{\boldsymbol{\Omega}}_{\mathrm{ML}})$ and $\hat{\boldsymbol{\Omega}}_{\mathrm{ML}} = \hat{\boldsymbol{\Omega}}(\hat{\boldsymbol{\delta}}_{\mathrm{ML}})$. In practice, the MLE is sometimes computed by iterating between the two equations that implicitly determine it: (26.32) and (26.35). This iterative scheme is called *iterated Zellner* or *iterated SUR*.[8] It is another example of the Gauss–Seidel algorithm mentioned in Section 16.8 and applied as iterated FGLS in Sections 18.5.2 and 19.6.1.

Finally, the MLE $\hat{\boldsymbol{\delta}}_{\mathrm{ML}}$ is asymptotically equivalent to the FGLS estimator (26.29). In Section 26.7.2, we derive the information matrix:

$$\mathrm{E}_T[\Im(\theta_0 \mid \mathbf{X})] = \begin{bmatrix} \mathbf{S}_\delta'(\boldsymbol{\Omega}_0^{-1} \otimes \mathrm{E}_T[\mathbf{x}_t\mathbf{x}_t'])\mathbf{S}_\delta & \mathbf{0} \\ \mathbf{0} & \frac{1}{2} \cdot \mathbf{S}_\omega'(\boldsymbol{\Omega}_0^{-1} \otimes \boldsymbol{\Omega}_0^{-1})\mathbf{S}_\omega \end{bmatrix}$$

for $\boldsymbol{\delta}$ and the nonrepeating elements of $\boldsymbol{\Omega}$. The matrix $\mathbf{S}_\omega'$ is akin to $\mathbf{S}_\delta'$, selecting appropriate elements from $\mathrm{vec}\,\boldsymbol{\Omega}$. Because the information matrix is block-diagonal in the regression and variance parameters, we see that the FGLS estimator is an LMLE for $\boldsymbol{\delta}_0$ and is, therefore, asymptotically equivalent to the MLE.

26.3 SIMULTANEOUS EQUATIONS

A linear system of seemingly unrelated regressions is a special case of a linear system of simultaneous equations. There are several ways to describe this relationship. In terms of model specification, an SUR system specifies the conditional expectation of each y_{tj} given $\mathbf{x}_t$ whereas

[7] See equation (G.37) and Definition G.3 (vec, p. 924).

[8] See Zellner (1962).

a general simultaneous system specifies the conditional expectations of *linear combinations of the* y_{tj}. This implies that in general the specification of a complete system is necessary to the specification of the conditional expectation of each y_{tj} given $\mathbf{x}_t$.

EXAMPLE 26.1

One of the simplest examples of such a system is the simultaneous determination of price and quantity in a single market implied by the equality of supply and demand (Example 20.2). The supply function is the linear relationship involving price and quantity that gives the total amount suppliers will produce in response to a prevailing market price:

$$q_{st} = -\gamma_{0s} p_t - \mathbf{x}'_{st}\boldsymbol{\beta}_{0s} + \varepsilon_{st} \tag{26.36}$$

The demand function is the linear relationship that gives the maximum total amount consumers will purchase at a given price:

$$q_{dt} = -\gamma_{0d} p_t - \mathbf{x}'_{dt}\boldsymbol{\beta}_{0d} + \varepsilon_{dt} \tag{26.37}$$

Specifying that $\mathrm{E}[\varepsilon_{st} \mid \mathbf{x}_t] = \mathrm{E}[\varepsilon_{dt} \mid \mathbf{x}_t] = 0$ is equivalent to specifying conditional expectations for the linear combinations $q_{st} + \gamma_{0s} p_t$ and $q_{st} + \gamma_{0d} p_t$. Only when taken together with the equilibrium condition $q_{st} = q_{dt} = q_t$ do these conditional expectations yield

$$\mathrm{E}[q_t \mid \mathbf{x}_t]) = \frac{\gamma_{0d} \cdot \mathbf{x}'_{st}\boldsymbol{\beta}_{0s} - \gamma_{0s} \cdot \mathbf{x}'_{dt}\boldsymbol{\beta}_{0d}}{\gamma_{0s} - \gamma_{0d}}$$

$$\mathrm{E}[p_t \mid \mathbf{x}_t] = \frac{\mathbf{x}'_{dt}\boldsymbol{\beta}_{0d} - \mathbf{x}'_{st}\boldsymbol{\beta}_{0s}}{\gamma_{0s} - \gamma_{0d}}$$

Porter (1983) estimates such a market model for railway transportation by a cartel of railroads shipping from Chicago to the Atlantic seaboard in the 1880s. His quantity variable is the total tonnage of grain shipped by members of the cartel in a week. His price variable is an index of prices reported by member firms to the cartel. He is primarily interested in studying price wars that erupted among the members of the cartel as an enforcement mechanism for the cartel. His demand function is log-linear in price and quantity:

$$\log q_t = -\gamma_{0d} \log p_t - \mathbf{x}'_{dt}\boldsymbol{\beta}_{0d} + \varepsilon_{dt}$$

where $\mathbf{x}_{dt}$ contains a dummy variable equal to one if the Great Lakes were open to navigation by cargo steamships and 12 seasonal dummy variables. His supply function is also log-linear:[9]

$$\log q_t = -\gamma_{0s} \log p_t - \mathbf{x}'_{st}\boldsymbol{\beta}_{0s} + \varepsilon_{st}$$

The $\mathbf{x}_{st}$ also contains the seasonal dummy variables. In addition, it contains four dummy variables for structural changes in the market corresponding to the entry and exit of members from the cartel. Finally, $\mathbf{x}_{st}$ contains a dummy variable indicating when collusive behavior was reported by a trade magazine called the *Railway Review*. During periods of collusion, one expects price to be elevated.

Porter estimates both equations with two-stage least squares (2SLS) using all of the dummy variables as instrumental variables. Although the equations fit loosely, many of the fitted coefficients have acceptable values and relatively small standard errors. For example, the opening

[9] Porter actually expresses the supply relationship as an equation for price because price is a strategic variable in his model with collusive behavior among the railways. We renormalize to make quantity the LHS variable.

of the Great Lakes appears to lower the demand for railway shipments approximately 44% with an estimated standard error of 12%. The estimated demand curve has a negative price elasticity (−74.2% with a standard error of 12%) and the supply curve has a positive price elasticity (395% with a standard error of 271%). The supply curve is extremely elastic but the elasticity is estimated imprecisely. Finally, periods of collusion correspond to a statistically significant upward shift in the supply curve. Hence, the noncooperative periods appear to be consistent with price wars.

Had he estimated these equations with OLS, Porter would have encountered similar estimates of the demand function coefficients but dramatically different estimates of the supply equation. The OLS estimator of the supply elasticity has the wrong sign (−51% with a standard error of 11%) and the shift in the supply curve during collusion is one-fifteenth the 2SLS estimate. Thus, the 2SLS estimates give more sensible, although imprecise, inferences about the market model.

To accommodate such market models within econometric analysis, we will generalize the system of seemingly unrelated regressions

$$y_{tj} = \mathbf{x}_t'\boldsymbol{\beta}_{0j} + \varepsilon_{tj}$$

where

$$\mathrm{E}[\varepsilon_{tj} \mid \mathbf{X}] = 0$$
$$\mathrm{Cov}[\varepsilon_{ti}, \varepsilon_{tj} \mid \mathbf{X}] = \omega_{0ij}$$

$(j = 1, \ldots, J)$ to the linear system of simultaneous equations

$$\mathbf{y}_t'\boldsymbol{\gamma}_{0j} + \mathbf{x}_t'\boldsymbol{\beta}_{0j} = \varepsilon_{tj}$$

where

$$\mathrm{E}[\varepsilon_{tj} \mid \mathbf{X}] = 0,$$
$$\mathrm{Cov}[\varepsilon_{ti}, \varepsilon_{tj} \mid \mathbf{X}] = \sigma_{0ij} \tag{26.38}$$

and where $\mathbf{y}_t \equiv [y_{t1}, \ldots, y_{tJ}]'$ is a $J \times 1$ vector containing the tth observation of each of the J-dependent variables. Each vector $\boldsymbol{\gamma}_{0j} \equiv \left[\gamma_{0ij};\ i = 1, \ldots, J\right]'$ is a $J \times 1$ vector of additional coefficients. These coefficients allow more than one dependent variable to enter each equation in the system.

The notation of simultaneous equations treats the dependent and conditional variables symmetrically. Both $\mathbf{y}_t$ and $\mathbf{x}_t$ are vectors of variables that appear in inner products with coefficient vectors. Also, the conditional term $\mathbf{x}_t'\boldsymbol{\beta}_{0j}$ appears on the LHS of the equation with the dependent term $\mathbf{y}_t'\boldsymbol{\gamma}_{0j}$, rather than the RHS. This is not a substantive change, of course. Rather it is a different normalization from the convention of ordinary regression.

The latent ε_{tj} terms are an important component of the formulation of these models. The expression $\mathbf{y}'\boldsymbol{\gamma}_{0j} + \mathbf{x}'\beta_{0j} = 0$ is a structural relationship from which observed y_{tj} deviate randomly. The ε_{tj} represent these random deviations. Interest focuses on the structural relationships because one expects them to hold under new circumstances. For example, even though the supply of a product may be altered by government intervention fixing the price, the demand function for the product will be unchanged and the effect of the intervention can be correctly predicted.

Another way to appreciate the role of ε_{tj} is to note that the latent εs are not merely residual deviations between a dependent variable and its conditional expectation. Indeed, (26.38) is silent about the conditional expectation of any y_{tj} conditional on $\mathbf{x}_t$ and the other y_{ti} $(i \neq j)$ in any equation. Thus, the motivation of the restrictions $E(\varepsilon_{tj} \mid \mathbf{X}) = 0$, $j = 1, \ldots, J$, is not simply a statistical definition but a potentially stronger claim about the data-generating process. Certain linear combinations of $\mathbf{y}_t$ and $\mathbf{x}_t$ have conditional expectation zero.

As Example 20.2 shows, an OLS fit of a y_{tj} to $\mathbf{x}_t$ and other y_{ti} $(i \neq j)$ generally misestimates $\boldsymbol{\gamma}_{0j}$ and $\boldsymbol{\beta}_{0j}$. More than this, $\boldsymbol{\gamma}_{0j}$ and $\boldsymbol{\beta}_{0j}$ may not even be identified so that no estimation method is available. Before discussing identification and estimation, however, we present several definitions and assumptions that set the stage for our formal analysis.

26.3.1 Definitions

Additional terminology accompanies simultaneous systems of equations. The terms describe various types of variables, equations, and systems.

Endogenous variables are variables whose behavior is described by the model. We could also call these variables the *dependent* variables. One is interested in their behavior conditional on the rest of the model. The term "endogenous" reflects the simultaneous character of the system that determines these variables. In simultaneous systems, y_{tj} is the jth *endogenous* variable, but not the jth *dependent* variable, because equations are not necessarily associated one to one with endogenous variables. For example, it is unnatural to think of either the supply or the demand equation as a "price" equation in the simple market model.

The model for the entire data set of endogenous variables is conditional on the *exogenous* variables. In this sense, exogenous variables are causal, characterizing the environment in which endogenous variables are determined. Exogenous variables are a subset of the *predetermined* variables. The simultaneous equations system conditions the behavior of each observation of the endogenous variables on the predetermined variables. They may include, in particular, lagged values of the endogenous variables if the data are time series. Thus, the variables denoted by x_{tk} are the predetermined variables.

A system of simultaneous equations is a model that requires all of the equations in order to determine at least one endogenous variable. The equations of such a model are called *structural*. Structural equations are often divided into *identities*, which are definitions, and *behavioral equations*. The structural equations in the small macroeconomic model (26.1) contain one identity: total income equals the sum of its parts.

Reduced-form equations express each endogenous variable in terms of predetermined variables and disturbance terms only. This set of equations is not, therefore, simultaneous. As in (26.27), we can gather together the equations from (26.38) into the row-vector equation

$$\underset{1\times J}{\mathbf{y}_t'}\ \underset{J\times J}{\boldsymbol{\Gamma}_0} + \underset{1\times K}{\mathbf{x}_t'}\ \underset{K\times J}{\mathbf{B}_0} = \underset{1\times J}{\boldsymbol{\varepsilon}_t'} \tag{26.39}$$

where

$$\boldsymbol{\Gamma}_0 \equiv \left[\gamma_{0ij};\quad i, j = 1, \ldots, J\right]$$

and

$$\mathbf{B}_0 \equiv \left[\beta_{0kj};\quad k = 1, \ldots, K,\ j = 1, \ldots, J\right]$$

If $\boldsymbol{\Gamma}_0$ is nonsingular then one can solve the simultaneous system for $\mathbf{y}_t$ as a function of $\mathbf{x}_t$ and $\boldsymbol{\varepsilon}_t$:

$$\mathbf{y}_t' = \left(-\mathbf{x}_t'\mathbf{B}_0 + \boldsymbol{\varepsilon}_t'\right)\boldsymbol{\Gamma}_0^{-1} = \mathbf{x}_t'\boldsymbol{\Pi}_0 + \mathbf{v}_t' \tag{26.40}$$

where

$$\boldsymbol{\Pi}_0 \equiv -\mathbf{B}_0\boldsymbol{\Gamma}_0^{-1} \qquad \text{and} \qquad \mathbf{v}_t' \equiv \boldsymbol{\varepsilon}_t'\boldsymbol{\Gamma}_0^{-1} \tag{26.41}$$

This reduced form expresses the conditional expectations implicitly specified by the structural form (26.38): $\mathrm{E}[\mathbf{y}_t' \mid \mathbf{X}] = \mathbf{x}_t'\boldsymbol{\Pi}_0$. An example of a reduced form appears in (26.2).[10]

The reduced form of a simultaneous system of equations is central to an understanding of its identification and estimation. We may view the simultaneous equations system as an SUR system with regression coefficients that are nonlinear functions of the structural parameters. This is a second way in which simultaneous equations contain SUR as a special case. We will exploit this relationship under the assumptions given in the next section.

26.3.2 Assumptions

Because the $\mathbf{y}_t$ are determined simultaneously by $\mathbf{x}_t$ and $\boldsymbol{\varepsilon}_t$, the distributional assumptions of the simultaneous equations model concern $\mathbf{x}_t$ and $\boldsymbol{\varepsilon}_t$. For theoretical simplicity, we will suppose i.i.d. sampling:

Assumption 26.1 (I.I.D.) *The* $\{(\boldsymbol{\varepsilon}_t, \mathbf{x}_t)\,;\ t = 1, \ldots, T\}$ *are independently and identically distributed (i.i.d.) across t and their fourth moments exist.*

Assumption 26.2 (First Moments) $\mathrm{E}(\boldsymbol{\varepsilon}_t \mid \mathbf{x}_t) = \mathbf{0}$.

These two assumptions have counterparts in the theory we developed for single-equation estimation. The distribution of $\mathbf{y}_t$ follows from the joint distribution of $\mathbf{x}_t$ and $\boldsymbol{\varepsilon}_t$ and the parameters in the structural equations (26.39), provided that the structural equations constitute an implicit function for $\mathbf{y}_t$. Therefore, we add the following assumption.

Assumption 26.3 (Simultaneity) *The matrix* $\boldsymbol{\Gamma}_0$ *is nonsingular.*

To develop GMM estimators of the parameters, we will focus our attention on the JK linear orthogonality conditions

$$\mathrm{E}[\mathbf{x}_t\boldsymbol{\varepsilon}_t'] = \mathrm{E}\big[\mathbf{x}_t\,\mathrm{E}[\boldsymbol{\varepsilon}_t' \mid \mathbf{x}_t]\big] = \mathbf{0} \tag{26.42}$$

[10] There is an additional distinction made by *final-form equations*. These express each endogenous variable in terms of exogenous variables and disturbance terms only. If all the predetermined variables are exogenous, then the reduced form and the final form are equivalent. This is the case that we will cover.

implied by the conditional expectations in Assumption 26.2. We will treat the conditional variance matrix $\boldsymbol{\Sigma}_0 \equiv \left[\sigma_{0ij}\right]$ as unrestricted, except that it must be symmetric. Our choice of instrumental variables, $\mathbf{x}_t$, anticipates that nonlinear functions of these predetermined variables will be redundant. After all, the conditional expectation of $\mathbf{y}_t$ given $\mathbf{x}_t$ is a linear function of $\mathbf{x}_t$.[11]

These assumptions place this model within the general structure of GMM estimation given in Sections 21.3 and 21.4 and, more narrowly, within the structure of IV in Section 20.4. Here the $\mathbf{x}_t$ have the properties of instrumental variables as described by (26.42). According to Chebychev's LLN (Theorem 8, p. 262) and Assumptions 26.1 (I.I.D.) and 26.2 (First Moment),

$$\mathrm{E}_T[\mathbf{x}_t\boldsymbol{\varepsilon}_t'] \xrightarrow{p} \mathbf{0} \tag{26.43}$$

$$\mathrm{E}_T[\mathbf{x}_t\mathbf{x}_t'] \xrightarrow{p} \mathrm{E}[\mathbf{x}_t\mathbf{x}_t'] \equiv \mathbf{D} \tag{26.44}$$

Such limits occur in IV Assumption 20.2 (Instruments, p. 499).

Adding Assumption 26.3 (Simultaneity), we can generalize (26.43) to the empirical moment functions:

$$\begin{aligned}\mathrm{E}_T[\mathbf{x}_t(\mathbf{y}_t'\boldsymbol{\Gamma} + \mathbf{x}_t'\mathbf{B})] &= \mathrm{E}_T\left[\mathbf{x}_t\left((\boldsymbol{\varepsilon}_t' - \mathbf{x}_t'\mathbf{B}_0)\boldsymbol{\Gamma}_0^{-1}\boldsymbol{\Gamma} + \mathbf{x}_t'\mathbf{B}\right)\right]\\ &= \mathrm{E}_T[\mathbf{x}_t\boldsymbol{\varepsilon}_t']\boldsymbol{\Gamma}_0^{-1}\boldsymbol{\Gamma} + \mathrm{E}_T[\mathbf{x}_t\mathbf{x}_t'](\boldsymbol{\Pi}_0\boldsymbol{\Gamma} + \mathbf{B})\\ &\xrightarrow{p} \mathbf{D}(\boldsymbol{\Pi}_0\boldsymbol{\Gamma} + \mathbf{B})\end{aligned} \tag{26.45}$$

According to Definition 41 (Moment Identification, p. 543), the identification of $\mathbf{B}_0$ and $\boldsymbol{\Gamma}_0$ rests on the last expression. If the unique solution to $\mathbf{D}(\boldsymbol{\Pi}_0\boldsymbol{\Gamma} + \mathbf{B}) = \mathbf{0}$ is $\mathbf{B} = \mathbf{B}_0$ and $\boldsymbol{\Gamma} = \boldsymbol{\Gamma}_0$ then these parameters are globally identified by the orthogonality conditions (26.42). This characterization of the identification problem is a substantial simplification and we consider restrictions for this next.

26.4 IDENTIFICATION

We have just found that the identification of the slope parameters in a linear system of simultaneous equations concerns two terms: the population second-moment matrix $\mathbf{D} \equiv \mathrm{E}[\mathbf{x}_t\mathbf{x}_t']$ and the parametric expression $\boldsymbol{\Pi}_0\boldsymbol{\Gamma} + \mathbf{B}$. Of course, $\mathbf{B}_0$ cannot be identified if there is multicollinearity among the $\mathbf{x}_t$. Thus, we add a familiar assumption to the current analysis.

ASSUMPTION 26.4 (FULL RANK) $\mathbf{D}$ *is nonsingular.*

This focuses the determination of identification on $\boldsymbol{\Pi}_0\boldsymbol{\Gamma} + \mathbf{B}$, because if $\mathbf{D}$ is nonsingular then $\mathbf{D}(\boldsymbol{\Pi}_0\boldsymbol{\Gamma} + \mathbf{B}) = \mathbf{0}$ if and only if

$$\underset{K\times J}{\boldsymbol{\Pi}_0}\ \underset{J\times J}{\boldsymbol{\Gamma}}\ \underset{K\times J}{\mathbf{B}} = \mathbf{0} \tag{26.46}$$

This last system of linear equations does not necessarily comprise an implicit function for $\mathbf{B}$ and $\boldsymbol{\Gamma}$; and if it does not then some elements of $\mathbf{B}_0$ or $\boldsymbol{\Gamma}_0$ are not identified. Counting equations

[11] See Lemma 20.4 (Efficient Instrumental Variables, p. 510).

and unknowns, one finds that in general the system is underdetermined: there are JK equations but there are $JK + J^2$ parameters in $\mathbf{B}$ and $\boldsymbol{\Gamma}$. In particular, (26.46) implies that no matter what (nonsingular) $\boldsymbol{\Gamma}$ one might choose there is a corresponding $\mathbf{B}$ so that the pair yields $\boldsymbol{\Pi}_0$. It is necessary, therefore, to place restrictions on $\mathbf{B}$ and $\boldsymbol{\Gamma}$ satisfied by $\mathbf{B}_0$ and $\boldsymbol{\Gamma}_0$ for their identification. We shall entertain a set of linear restrictions in our study.

The SUR system is an example of a restricted model that is identified. In SUR, $\boldsymbol{\Gamma}_0 = \mathbf{I}_J$. Including these restrictions, so that $\boldsymbol{\Gamma} = \mathbf{I}_J$, gives additional J^2 equations and the unique solution

$$\left.\begin{array}{c} \boldsymbol{\Pi}_0\boldsymbol{\Gamma} + \mathbf{B} = \mathbf{0} \\ \boldsymbol{\Gamma} = \mathbf{I}_J \end{array}\right\} \quad \Leftrightarrow \quad \left\{\begin{array}{c} \mathbf{B} = -\boldsymbol{\Pi}_0 = \mathbf{B}_0 \\ \boldsymbol{\Gamma} = \mathbf{I}_J \end{array}\right.$$

In this simple case, all of the parameters in $\mathbf{B}_0$ are identified without any additional restrictions. Of course, this identification is fairly obvious because we know that OLS is an estimator for $\mathbf{B}_0$ in SUR.

In general, we can view identification as a question of recovering the structural parameters from the reduced form parameters. In (26.46), $\mathbf{B}$ and $\boldsymbol{\Gamma}$ are implicit functions of $\boldsymbol{\Pi}_0$. The reduced form (26.40) is, in fact, an SUR system. It follows that without any restrictions on $\mathbf{B}_0$ and $\boldsymbol{\Gamma}_0$ the reduced form coefficients $\boldsymbol{\Pi}_0$ are identified under Assumptions 26.1–26.4. For this reason identification of $\mathbf{B}_0$ and $\boldsymbol{\Gamma}_0$ reduces to the study of (26.46).

EXAMPLE 26.2

Reconsider Example 26.1, the simultaneous system of two equations for supply and demand in a single market. Let us simplify this system further by supposing that $x_{dt} = x_{st} = 1$. Then

$$\mathrm{E}[q_t \mid \mathbf{x}_t] = \mathrm{E}[q_t] = \frac{\gamma_{0d}\beta_{0s} - \gamma_{0s}\beta_{0d}}{\gamma_{0s} - \gamma_{0d}}$$

$$\mathrm{E}[p_t \mid \mathbf{x}_t] = \mathrm{E}[p_t] = \frac{\beta_{0d} - \beta_{0s}}{\gamma_{0s} - \gamma_{0d}}$$

The observed price and quantity data will have constant means and these are identified. However, there is insufficient information to learn about the slopes and intercepts of the supply and demand equations because all of the observations are centered on a single point of both structural equations, their "intersection."

An escape from this dilemma is suggested by a graphic contrast between this example and another. In Figure 26.1, we depict the situation of a constant bivariate mean at the intersection of supply and demand. Although one can estimate the point of intersection, it is impossible to infer the slope of either function. Put another way, many different supply and demand functions are observationally equivalent if they intersect at the same equilibrium point

Figure 26.2, on the other hand, shows a situation in which the demand equation contains an additional predetermined variable: $\mathbf{x}'_{dt}\boldsymbol{\beta}_{0d} = \beta_{01d} + \beta_{02d}x_{t2}$. As x_{t2} varies from observation to observation, the demand curve shifts and the market equilibrium moves to various points along the supply curve. The ability to estimate several points on a single supply curve suggests how the *restriction* $\beta_{02s} = 0$ that *excludes* x_{t2} from the supply equation assists in the identification of β_{01s} and γ_{0s}.

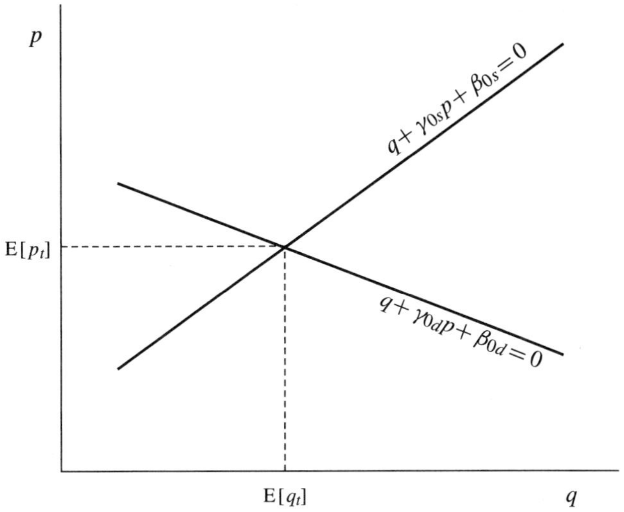

Figure 26.1 Fixed supply and demand functions.

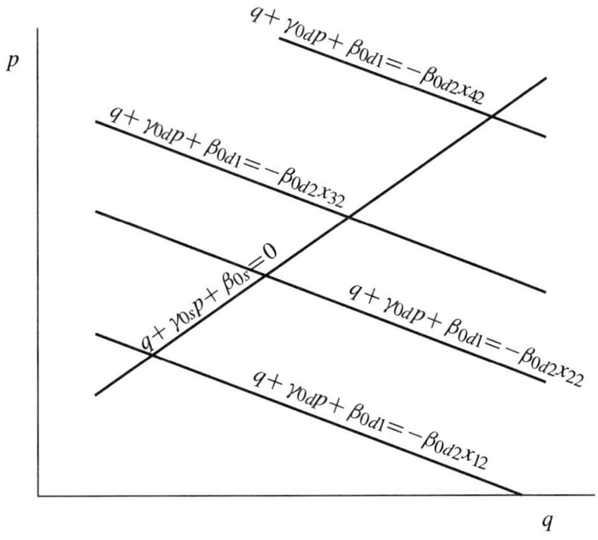

Figure 26.2 Fixed supply and shifting demand functions.

EXAMPLE 26.3

If $\mathbf{x}_{dt}\boldsymbol{\beta}_{0d} = \beta_{01d} + \beta_{02d}x_{t2}$ and $x_{st}\beta_{0s} = \beta_{01s}$, in contrast to the previous example, then

$$\mathrm{E}[q_t \mid \mathbf{x}_t] = \frac{\gamma_{0d}\beta_{01s} - \gamma_{0s}\beta_{01d} - \gamma_{0s}\beta_{02d}x_{t2}}{\gamma_{0s} - \gamma_{0d}}$$

$$\mathrm{E}[p_t \mid \mathbf{x}_t] = \frac{\beta_{01d} - \beta_{01s} + \beta_{02d}x_{t2}}{\gamma_{0s} - \gamma_{0d}}$$

and one can estimate

$$\boldsymbol{\Pi}_0 \equiv \begin{bmatrix} \pi_{01q} & \pi_{01p} \\ \pi_{02q} & \pi_{02p} \end{bmatrix} = \frac{1}{\gamma_{0s} - \gamma_{0d}} \cdot \begin{bmatrix} \gamma_{0d}\beta_{01s} - \gamma_{0s}\beta_{01d} & \beta_{01d} - \beta_{01s} \\ -\gamma_{0s}\beta_{02d} & \beta_{02d} \end{bmatrix}$$

As a result, γ_{0s} and β_{01s} are identified:

$$\gamma_{0s} = -\frac{\pi_{02q}}{\pi_{02p}} \quad \text{and} \quad \beta_{01s} = -\left(\pi_{01q} - \frac{\pi_{02q}}{\pi_{02p}}\pi_{01p}\right)$$

On the other hand, the parameters in the demand equation are unidentified. For example, many demand functions can intersect the same set of points on the supply curve in Figure 26.2 and they are all observationally equivalent.

In this example, an exclusion restriction in the supply equation participates in the identification of the unknown parameters in that equation. Without a similar restriction in the demand equation, its parameters are obscured. In general, the solutions to parameter identification problems provide guidelines about which parameters (or functions of parameters) are identified and which are not. We will develop such guidelines for simultaneous equations in two steps. In the first step, we consider identification of the parameters in a single structural equation and in the second step we focus on the identification of all of the parameters in the system. The notation for one equation is simpler and the strategy is the same in both steps.

26.4.1 Equation Identification

As Example 26.3 shows, the parameters of one structural equation may be identified while others are not. We will now characterize the identification of a single equation in isolation from the others. This is possible when the restrictions involve coefficients from that equation alone. Exclusion restrictions are a primary example; they concern only one parameter. Another instance is a normalization: typically one normalizes one of the γ_{ij} in the jth equation to 1. This takes into account that multiplying all the coefficients in an equation by a constant α does not change the distribution of the endogenous variables if the latent disturbance term ε_{tj} is replaced by a proportional disturbance term $\alpha\varepsilon_{tj}$.

Let the restrictions on the coefficients of the jth equation be

$$\underset{(K+J-M_j)\times J}{\mathbf{R}_{\gamma j}} \quad \boldsymbol{\gamma}_j + \underset{(K+J-M_j)\times K}{\mathbf{R}_{\beta j}} \quad \boldsymbol{\beta}_j = \underset{(K+J-M_j)\times 1}{\mathbf{r}_j} \tag{26.47}$$

where M_j is the number of unrestricted parameters. The number of restrictions is $K + J - M_j$. The part of (26.46) that involves these parameters is the jth column:

$$\underset{K\times J}{\boldsymbol{\Pi}_0}\ \underset{J\times 1}{\boldsymbol{\gamma}_j} + \underset{K\times 1}{\boldsymbol{\beta}_j} = \underset{K\times 1}{\mathbf{0}} \tag{26.48}$$

where $\boldsymbol{\beta}_j$ contains the coefficients of $\mathbf{x}_t$ and $\boldsymbol{\gamma}_j$ contains the coefficients of $\mathbf{y}_t$ in the jth structural equation. These combine in the linear system of equations

$$\underset{(2K+J-M_j)\times(K+J)}{\begin{bmatrix} \boldsymbol{\Pi}_0 & \mathbf{I}_K \\ \mathbf{R}_{\gamma j} & \mathbf{R}_{\beta j} \end{bmatrix}} \underset{(K+J)\times 1}{\begin{bmatrix} \boldsymbol{\gamma}_j \\ \boldsymbol{\beta}_j \end{bmatrix}} = \underset{(2K+J-M_j)\times 1}{\begin{bmatrix} \mathbf{0} \\ \mathbf{r}_j \end{bmatrix}} \tag{26.49}$$

that determines the identification of $\boldsymbol{\beta}_j$ and $\boldsymbol{\gamma}_j$. Mathematically then, this identification problem is a basic one from linear algebra. When does a system of linear equations have a unique solution?

A necessary condition for (26.49) to yield an implicit function for $\left[\boldsymbol{\gamma}_j', \boldsymbol{\beta}_j'\right]$ is that there are at least J (linearly independent) restrictions: there are $K+J$ unknown parameters and (26.48) provides K equations. Equivalently, if

$$2K + J - M_j \geq K + J \qquad \Leftrightarrow \qquad K \geq M_j$$

then there are at least as many equations as unknown parameters. This observation is the *order condition* for identification.[12] For a particular kind of restrictions, the order condition has a well-known form. We take the normalization $\gamma_{ij} = 1$ for some i as one restriction. When all of the remaining restrictions are exclusion restrictions, then the order condition can be stated as follows:

Proposition 25 (Equation Order Conditon) *If we normalize $\gamma_{ij} = 1$ for some i and the other unknown elements of $\left[\boldsymbol{\gamma}_j', \boldsymbol{\beta}_j'\right]$ are identified, the number of variables included in the jth equation minus one must be no greater than the number of predetermined variables in the system.*

When we discuss estimation below, we will explain how this condition relates to an IV interpretation of the 2SLS estimator for a single equation. One can interpret the order condition as a requirement that there are at least as many instrumental variables as there are RHS variables in the structural equation, a basic requirement for IV estimation.

The order condition is only necessary for identification. Because (26.49) is linear in the unknown parameters, a rank condition for single equation identification is necessary and sufficient.

Proposition 26 (Equation Rank Condition) *Under Assumptions 26.2–26.4 and the restrictions*

$$[\,\mathbf{R}_{\gamma j} \quad \mathbf{R}_{\beta j}\,]\begin{bmatrix} \gamma_{0j} \\ \beta_{0j} \end{bmatrix} = \mathbf{r}_j$$

the jth structural equation is identified if and only if

$$\operatorname{rank}\left(\mathbf{R}_{\gamma_j}\boldsymbol{\Gamma}_0 + \mathbf{R}_{\beta_j}\mathbf{B}_0\right) = J$$

[12] See also the order condition for GMM (Lemma 21.1, p. 543).

Proof. If the leading matrix in (26.49) has rank $K+J$ then $[\boldsymbol{\gamma}_j', \boldsymbol{\beta}_j']'$ is a nonsingular transformation of $[0, \mathbf{r}_j']$.[13] This matrix can be written as

$$\begin{bmatrix} \boldsymbol{\Pi}_0 & \mathbf{I}_K \\ \mathbf{R}_{\gamma j} & \mathbf{R}_{\beta j} \end{bmatrix} = \begin{bmatrix} \mathbf{I}_K & \mathbf{0} \\ \mathbf{R}_{\beta j} & -\mathbf{I}_J \end{bmatrix} \begin{bmatrix} \mathbf{B}_0 & \mathbf{I}_K \\ \mathbf{R}_{\gamma j}\boldsymbol{\Gamma}_0 + \mathbf{R}_{\beta j}\mathbf{B}_0 & \mathbf{0} \end{bmatrix} \begin{bmatrix} -\boldsymbol{\Gamma}_0^{-1} & \mathbf{0} \\ \mathbf{0} & \mathbf{I}_K \end{bmatrix}$$

The first RHS matrix is clearly nonsingular and so is the last RHS matrix under Assumption 26.3 (Simultaneity). Therefore, the rank of the LHS matrix equals the rank of the second RHS matrix. Its last K columns have rank K and its first J columns add J linearly independent vectors if and only if $\text{rank}(\mathbf{R}_{\gamma j}\boldsymbol{\Gamma}_0 + \mathbf{R}_{\beta j}\mathbf{B}_0) = J$. This is the required condition. □

Note how the rank condition involves coefficients from all of the other equations in the system. Furthermore, this condition uses the unknown values of these coefficients. As a result, identification is always an additional assumption. Nevertheless, the assumption is often quite reasonable.

EXAMPLE 26.4

Let us apply the order condition to Example 26.3. If we write the system of equations as

$$\mathbf{y}_t = \begin{bmatrix} q_t \\ p_t \end{bmatrix}, \qquad \boldsymbol{\Gamma}_0 = \begin{bmatrix} 1 & 1 \\ \gamma_{0d} & \gamma_{0s} \end{bmatrix}$$

$$\mathbf{x}_t = \begin{bmatrix} 1 \\ x_{t2} \end{bmatrix}, \qquad \mathbf{B}_0 = \begin{bmatrix} \beta_{01d} & \beta_{01s} \\ \beta_{02d} & 0 \end{bmatrix}$$

then the restrictions on the supply equation ($j = 2$) set

$$\mathbf{R}_{\beta 2} = \begin{bmatrix} 0 & 0 \\ 0 & 1 \end{bmatrix} \quad \text{and} \quad \mathbf{R}_{\gamma 2} = \begin{bmatrix} 1 & 0 \\ 0 & 0 \end{bmatrix}$$

Therefore, the rank condition requires that

$$\mathbf{R}_{\gamma j}\boldsymbol{\Gamma}_0 + \mathbf{R}_{\beta j}\mathbf{B}_0 = \begin{bmatrix} 1 & 1 \\ \beta_{02d} & 0 \end{bmatrix}$$

have a rank equal to $J = 2$. This will be true if and only if $\beta_{02d} \neq 0$. In other words, x_{t2} must be a determinant of demand. Otherwise, x_{t2} is not a predetermined variable in this simultaneous system and the system reduces to the unidentified model in Example 26.2.

When the number of restrictions equals J and the rank condition is met, the structural equation is said to be *exactly identified*. In that case, (26.49) has the same number of equations as unknowns. When the number of restrictions exceeds J, the parameters are *overidentified*. One could ignore some of the equations in (26.49) and still solve the implicit function for $\boldsymbol{\beta}_j$ and $\boldsymbol{\gamma}_j$.

The other (unrestricted) structural equations in the system are *underidentified* when the restrictions apply only to one structural equation. If one actually knew $\boldsymbol{\beta}_{0j}$ and $\boldsymbol{\gamma}_{0j}$ this would restrict the other parameters only through the requirement that $\boldsymbol{\Gamma}$ must be nonsingular. This still leaves enough room for a whole vector space of observationally equivalent parameter values for

[13] See Theorem C.9 (Rank Condition, p. 851).

the rest of the system. Thus, single-equation restrictions alone do not assist in the identification of other equations' parameters.

26.4.2 System Identification

We can carry out a similar analysis for an entire system of equations. First, we expand (26.48) to include all of the structural parameters in a single vector of equalities: by stacking over $j = 1, \ldots, J$, we can write

$$(\mathbf{I}_J \otimes \mathbf{\Pi}_0) \operatorname{vec} \mathbf{\Gamma} + \operatorname{vec} \mathbf{B} = \mathbf{0} \tag{26.50}$$

Similarly, the restrictions for the entire system have the form

$$\mathbf{R}_\gamma \operatorname{vec} \mathbf{\Gamma} + \mathbf{R}_\beta \operatorname{vec} \mathbf{B} = \mathbf{r} \tag{26.51}$$

For these two sets of equations to yield an implicit solution for the $J^2 + JK$ parameters in $\mathbf{\Gamma}$ and $\mathbf{B}$ there must be at least J^2 restrictions in addition to the JK equations in (26.50). This is the order condition for system identification.

The rank condition is an analogous replication of the single-equation analysis.

Proposition 27 (System Rank Condition) *Under Assumptions 26.2–26.4 and the restrictions (26.51), the structural parameters are locally identified if and only if*

$$\operatorname{rank}\big(\mathbf{R}_\gamma(\mathbf{I}_J \otimes \mathbf{\Gamma}_0) + \mathbf{R}_\beta(\mathbf{I}_J \otimes \mathbf{B}_0)\big) = J^2$$

The proof of this result is quite similar to that for Proposition 26 and we leave it as an exercise.

When there are only single-equation restrictions, the system rank condition breaks up into J single-equation rank conditions. The matrix $\mathbf{R}_\gamma(\mathbf{I}_J \otimes \mathbf{\Gamma}_0) + \mathbf{R}_\beta(\mathbf{I}_J \otimes \mathbf{B}_0)$ is block-diagonal with J blocks, one for each equation. The entire system is identified if and only if each equation is identified. However, if there are cross-equation restrictions the identification of one equation may rest on the identification of another.

EXAMPLE 26.5

Let us extend Example 26.4 to cover identification of the demand equation when we include the additional restriction that $\gamma_{02d} + 2\gamma_{02s} = 0$.[14] This is an artificial example of a cross-equation restriction in which we require the demand function to have a slope twice as large as and the opposite sign of the slope of the supply function. We also apply the normalization that the coefficient of $q_t = y_{t1}$ equals 1. Then

$$\operatorname{vec} \mathbf{B} = \begin{bmatrix} \beta_{01d} \\ \beta_{02d} \\ \beta_{01s} \\ \beta_{02s} \end{bmatrix} \quad \text{and} \quad \operatorname{vec} \mathbf{\Gamma} = \begin{bmatrix} \gamma_{01d} \\ \gamma_{02d} \\ \gamma_{01s} \\ \gamma_{02s} \end{bmatrix}$$

[14] Previously the normalizations allowed us to denote γ_{02d} by γ_{0d} and γ_{02s} by γ_{0s}. Here we must distinguish them and we will make the normalizations explicit.

In this market model we normalize $\gamma_{01d} = \gamma_{01s} = 1$ and restrict $\beta_{02s} = 0$. Thus, we may write

$$\mathbf{R}_\beta = \begin{bmatrix} 0 & 0 & 0 & 0 \\ 0 & 0 & 0 & 0 \\ 0 & 0 & 0 & 0 \\ 0 & 0 & 0 & 1 \end{bmatrix} \quad \text{and} \quad \mathbf{R}_\gamma = \begin{bmatrix} 1 & 0 & 0 & 0 \\ 0 & 1 & 0 & 2 \\ 0 & 0 & 1 & 0 \\ 0 & 0 & 0 & 0 \end{bmatrix}$$

where the first two rows correspond to the restrictions on the supply equation and the last two rows correspond to the restrictions on the demand equation that we considered earlier.

According to Proposition 27 we examine the rank of

$$\mathbf{R}_\gamma(\mathbf{I}_J \otimes \mathbf{\Gamma}_0) + \mathbf{R}_\beta(\mathbf{I}_J \otimes \mathbf{B}_0) = \begin{bmatrix} 1 & 1 & 0 & 0 \\ -2\gamma_{02s} & \gamma_{02s} & -4\gamma_{02s} & 2\gamma_{02s} \\ 0 & 0 & 1 & 1 \\ 0 & 0 & \beta_{02d} & 0 \end{bmatrix}$$

where we have substituted $\gamma_{02d} = -2\gamma_{02s}$. Unless $\gamma_{02s} = 0$ or $\beta_{02d} = 0$, this matrix has a rank of 4. Therefore, both supply and demand equations are identified even though the demand equation does not satisfy the order condition for single-equation identification.

Having presented necessary and sufficient conditions for identification of the regression parameters, we turn to their estimation. Identification concerns whether there are enough restrictions. Restrictions beyond a sufficient number do not affect identification. However, such "extra" restrictions will affect estimation methods. In general, exploiting the overidentifying restrictions can increase the efficiency of an optimal estimator. Now taking identification as given, we discuss relatively efficient estimation methods in the next section.

26.5 ESTIMATION

When a system of simultaneous equations is exactly identified, the number of unrestricted reduced-form coefficients equals the number of structural coefficients. In that special case, estimation of the structural coefficients is straightforward because the reduced form and the structural form are merely alternative parameterizations. Estimation is most convenient in the reduced-form parameterization, where OLS equation by equation is efficient. For the single-equation setting, the corresponding estimates of the structural-form parameters are solutions to the set of linear equations in (26.49). For system estimation, one solves (26.50)–(26.51). Such estimators are called *indirect least-squares* (ILS) estimators.

When a system of simultaneous equations is overidentified, such transformation of the unrestricted reduced-form estimator is ambiguous. Although the population coefficients $\mathbf{\Pi}_0$, $\mathbf{\Gamma}_0$, and $\mathbf{B}_0$ satisfy all the equations exactly, unrestricted estimates $\hat{\mathbf{\Pi}}$ do not. One can solve a subset of equations that identifies the structural coefficient exactly, but this procedure throws useful information away. Efficient estimation combines all of the restrictions.

To develop a theory of relatively efficient estimation, we must be able to find the variance matrix of an estimator. The basic simultaneous equation model specifies the same variance–covariance structure as that of the SUR specification (26.17).

ASSUMPTION 26.5 (SECOND MOMENTS) *Conditional on* $\mathbf{x}_t$, $\mathrm{Var}[\boldsymbol{\varepsilon}_t \mid \mathbf{x}_t] = \boldsymbol{\Sigma}_0$ *is finite and nonsingular.*

That is, there is neither conditional heteroskedasticity nor autocorrelation over observations $t = 1, \ldots, T$. On the other hand, the latent disturbances are correlated across structural equations. Also, this assumption requires that all of the structural equations that are identities have been substituted out of the system.

Given this additional assumption and the identification of the structural parameters, estimation theory fits within the generalized method of moments (GMM). The resulting estimators have IV interpretations and the relatively efficient estimators combine the principles of GLS and efficient instrumental variables in recognizable ways.

26.5.1 Limited Information

Estimation of a single structural equation with identifying restrictions for that equation alone is often called *limited-information* estimation because the rest of the system is left unrestricted. We will begin with limited-information estimation because we have discussed it previously in connection with the two-stage least-squares (2SLS) estimator.[15]

Let us write the restricted form of the first structural equation as

$$y_{t1} = [\mathbf{y}_t' \quad \mathbf{x}_t'] \begin{bmatrix} \mathbf{S}_{\gamma 1} & \mathbf{0} \\ \mathbf{0} & \mathbf{S}_{\beta 1} \end{bmatrix} \boldsymbol{\delta}_{01} + \varepsilon_{t1} \tag{26.52}$$

where

$$\begin{bmatrix} -\boldsymbol{\gamma}_{01} \\ -\boldsymbol{\beta}_{01} \end{bmatrix} = \begin{bmatrix} \mathbf{S}_{\gamma 1} & \mathbf{0} \\ \mathbf{0} & \mathbf{S}_{\beta 1} \end{bmatrix} \boldsymbol{\delta}_{01}$$

expresses the complete vector of $J + K$ coefficients in terms of M_1 unknown parameters only. The normalization restriction sets the first element of the endogenous variables' coefficient vector to 1. The elements in $\mathbf{y}_t'\mathbf{S}_{\gamma 1}$ are the other included endogenous variables; and $\mathbf{x}_t'\mathbf{S}_{\beta 1}$ contains the included predetermined variables. We will simplify this notation to

$$y_{t1} = \mathbf{z}_{1t}'\boldsymbol{\delta}_{01} + \varepsilon_{t1} \tag{26.53}$$

where $\mathbf{z}_{1t} \equiv \left[\mathbf{y}_t'\mathbf{S}_{\gamma 1}, \mathbf{x}_t'\mathbf{S}_{\beta 1}\right]$ and $\boldsymbol{\delta}_{01}$ is a vector of the unknown coefficients in $\boldsymbol{\gamma}_{01}$ and $\boldsymbol{\beta}_{01}$.[16]

For such circumstances, we have already discussed the two-stage least-squares (2SLS) estimator. The explanatory variables in $\mathbf{z}_{1t}$ contain elements $\mathbf{y}_t'\mathbf{S}_{\gamma 1}$ that are correlated with the latent disturbance ε_{t1} because the system of equations is simultaneous:

$$\mathrm{Cov}[\boldsymbol{\varepsilon}_t, \mathbf{y}_t' \mid \mathbf{x}_t] = \mathrm{Cov}[\boldsymbol{\varepsilon}_t, \boldsymbol{\varepsilon}_t'\boldsymbol{\Gamma}_0'^{-1} \mid \mathbf{x}_t] = \boldsymbol{\Sigma}_0\boldsymbol{\Gamma}_0'^{-1} \tag{26.54}$$

[15] See Sections 20.5, 20.7.1, and 21.2.3.

[16] Note that this notation is different from that in Chapter 20 where instrumental variables are denoted by z. Here z contains the RHS variables, both endogenous and predetermined.

Therefore, the OLS fit of y_{t1} on the RHS variables $\mathbf{z}_{1t}$ yields inconsistent estimators of $[\boldsymbol{\gamma}'_{01}, \boldsymbol{\beta}'_{01}]'$. According to the conditional expectation $\mathrm{E}[\boldsymbol{\varepsilon}_t \mid \mathbf{x}_t] = \mathbf{0}$, the vector $\mathbf{x}_t$ holds all of the variables that we can use to construct instruments. Thus, the corresponding 2SLS estimator for $\boldsymbol{\delta}_{01}$ is

$$\hat{\boldsymbol{\delta}}_{2\mathrm{SLS},1} = \left(\mathbf{Z}'_1 \mathbf{P}_{\mathbf{X}} \mathbf{Z}_1\right)^{-1} \mathbf{Z}'_1 \mathbf{P}_{\mathbf{X}} \mathbf{y}_1$$

where $\mathbf{y}_1 \equiv [y_{t1};\ t = 1, \ldots, T]'$ and $\mathbf{Z}_1 \equiv [\mathbf{z}_{1t};\ t = 1, \ldots, T]'$.

This estimator is well defined only if $\mathbf{x}_t$ contains at least as many variables as $\mathbf{z}_{1t}$, otherwise $\mathbf{Z}'_1 \mathbf{P}_{\mathbf{X}} \mathbf{Z}_1$ is singular and the inverse in $\hat{\boldsymbol{\delta}}_{2\mathrm{SLS},1}$ does not exist. This requirement is the order condition for identification (Proposition 25) of a single structural equation: the number of potential instrumental variables K in $\mathbf{x}_t$ must be greater than or equal to the number of RHS variables in $\mathbf{z}_{1t}$. That this requirement is merely necessary, and not sufficient, appears in the possibility that $\mathbf{Z}'_1 \mathbf{P}_{\mathbf{X}} \mathbf{Z}_1$ may be nonsingular while $\operatorname{plim} T^{-1} \cdot \mathbf{Z}'_1 \mathbf{P}_{\mathbf{X}} \mathbf{Z}_1$ is not. The rank condition (Proposition 26), which must be an assumption, guarantees the nonsingularity of the latter.

We showed in Section 21.2.3 that, under the assumptions above, this is the optimal GMM estimator for the orthogonality conditions $\mathrm{E}(\mathbf{x}_t \varepsilon_{t1}) = \mathbf{0}$.[17] An estimator of the asymptotic variance of $\sigma_{011}^{-1} \cdot \mathrm{E}_T[\mathbf{x}_t \varepsilon_{t1}]$ is $\mathrm{E}_T[\mathbf{x}_t \mathbf{x}'_t]$ so that an optimal feasible GMM estimator is

$$\begin{aligned}
&\operatorname*{argmin}_{\boldsymbol{\delta}_1} \frac{1}{\sigma_{011}^2} \cdot \left\{\mathrm{E}_T[\mathbf{x}_t(y_{t1} - \mathbf{z}'_{1t}\boldsymbol{\delta}_1)]\right\}' \left(\mathrm{E}_T[\mathbf{x}_t \mathbf{x}'_t]\right)^{-1} \mathrm{E}_T[\mathbf{x}_t(y_{t1} - \mathbf{z}'_{1t}\boldsymbol{\delta}_1)] \\
&= \operatorname*{argmin}_{\boldsymbol{\delta}_1} (\mathbf{y}_1 - \mathbf{Z}_1\boldsymbol{\delta}_1)' \mathbf{P}_{\mathbf{X}} (\mathbf{y}_1 - \mathbf{Z}_1\boldsymbol{\delta}_1) \qquad (26.55) \\
&= \hat{\boldsymbol{\delta}}_{2\mathrm{SLS},1}
\end{aligned}$$

In Section 20.7.1 we also showed that the 2SLS estimator is an optimal feasible IV estimator. There is no efficiency gain in alternative orthogonality conditions.[18] According to (26.40), the conditional expectation of the RHS endogenous variables, $\mathbf{y}'_t \mathbf{S}_{\gamma 1}$, given $\mathbf{X}$ is the linear function $\mathbf{x}'_t \boldsymbol{\Pi}_0 \mathbf{S}_{\gamma 1}$. This is an optimal IV matrix because it also contains the minimum MSE predictions of $\mathbf{y}'_t \mathbf{S}_{\gamma 1}$ given $\mathbf{X}$. However, $\boldsymbol{\Pi}_0$ is unknown and the corresponding IV estimator is infeasible. Nevertheless $\hat{\boldsymbol{\Pi}}_{\mathrm{OLS}} = (\mathbf{X}'\mathbf{X})^{-1}\mathbf{X}'\mathbf{Y}$ is a feasible and asymptotically equivalent substitute. In other words, $\mathbf{x}_t$ contains all of the variables necessary for efficient IV estimation. Including additional nonlinear transformations of the elements of $\mathbf{x}_t$ as instrumental variables would be redundant.

Also redundant are moment equations based on other disturbances besides ε_{t1}. Because the structural parameters of the rest of the system of simultaneous equations are not identified, we parameterize everything else in terms of identified reduced form coefficients:

$$[\, y_{t2} \quad \cdots \quad y_{tJ} \,] = \mathbf{x}'_t [\, \boldsymbol{\pi}_{02} \quad \cdots \quad \boldsymbol{\pi}_{0J} \,] + [\, v_{t2} \quad \cdots \quad v_{tJ} \,] \qquad (26.56)$$

which is (26.40)–(26.41) after removing the first column in each of $\mathbf{y}_t$, $\boldsymbol{\Pi}_0$, and $\mathbf{v}_t$. In addition to $\mathrm{E}[\mathbf{x}_t \varepsilon_{t1}] = \mathbf{0}$, the orthogonality conditions at our disposal are $\mathrm{E}[\mathbf{x}_t v_{tj}]$ $(j = 2, \ldots, J)$. Noting the relative efficiency of GLS applied to a system of SUR, one might expect to find a similar efficiency gain from exploiting these additional moments through GMM.

---

[17] See also Proposition 21 (GMM Efficiency, p. 551) and Example 21.2 (Nonlinear Weighted IV, p. 551).

[18] See especially Lemma 20.4 (Efficient Instrumental Variables, p. 510). Also see Example 21.3 (Nonlinear Weighted IV, p. 553).

In fact there is no such gain because the reduced-form coefficients in (26.56) are *exactly* identified. As a result, GMM estimation of the $\boldsymbol{\pi}_{0j}$ $(j = 2, \ldots, J)$ solves the empirical moment equations

$$\mathrm{E}_T[\mathbf{x}_t \hat{v}_{tj}] = \frac{1}{T} \cdot \mathbf{X}'\left(\mathbf{y}_j - \mathbf{X}\hat{\boldsymbol{\pi}}_j\right) = \mathbf{0} \qquad \Leftrightarrow \qquad \hat{\boldsymbol{\pi}}_j = \left(\mathbf{X}'\mathbf{X}\right)^{-1}\mathbf{X}'\mathbf{y}_j$$

Therefore, when we concentrate $\boldsymbol{\pi}_j$ $(j = 2, \ldots, J)$ out, we obtain the GMM criterion function based on $\mathrm{E}[\mathbf{x}_t \varepsilon_{t1}] = \mathbf{0}$ alone.[19]

Econometricians originally constructed the 2SLS estimator under the assumptions of conditional homoskedasticity and nonautocorrelation. Within the GMM estimation framework, it is natural to relax these assumptions. For example, if we replace Assumption 26.5 with $\mathrm{Var}(\boldsymbol{\varepsilon}_t \mid \mathbf{x}_t) = \boldsymbol{\Sigma}_t$ such that $\mathrm{E}_T[\boldsymbol{\Sigma}_t \otimes \mathbf{x}_t\mathbf{x}_t'] \xrightarrow{p} \boldsymbol{\Lambda}_0$, then a relatively efficient estimator is

$$\begin{aligned}\hat{\boldsymbol{\delta}}_{\mathrm{GMM},1} &= \underset{\boldsymbol{\delta}_1}{\operatorname{argmin}} \left\{\mathrm{E}_T[\mathbf{x}_t(y_{t1} - \mathbf{z}_{1t}'\boldsymbol{\delta}_1)]\right\}' \boldsymbol{\Lambda}_{011}^{-1}\, \mathrm{E}_T[\mathbf{x}_t(y_{t1} - \mathbf{z}_{1t}'\boldsymbol{\delta}_1)] \\ &= \left(\mathbf{Z}'\mathbf{X}\boldsymbol{\Lambda}_{011}^{-1}\mathbf{X}'\mathbf{Z}\right)^{-1}\mathbf{Z}'\mathbf{X}\boldsymbol{\Lambda}_{011}^{-1}\mathbf{X}'\mathbf{y}_1\end{aligned}$$

where $\boldsymbol{\Lambda}_{011}$ is the upper left-hand $K \times K$ block of $\boldsymbol{\Lambda}_0$. A feasible version of this estimator replaces $\boldsymbol{\Lambda}_{011}$ with the estimator

$$\hat{\boldsymbol{\Lambda}}_{11} = \mathrm{E}_T[\mathbf{x}_t(y_{t1} - \mathbf{z}_{1t}'\check{\boldsymbol{\delta}}_1)^2\mathbf{x}_t']$$

where $\check{\boldsymbol{\delta}}_1$ is such an initial consistent estimator of $\boldsymbol{\delta}_{01}$ as $\hat{\boldsymbol{\delta}}_{2\mathrm{SLS},1}$. Chamberlain (1982) first proposed this generalization of 2SLS.

In closing our discussion of limited-information estimation, we note that such estimation possesses a robustness to some forms of misspecification of the complete system of simultaneous equations. If the restrictions for a single equation are correct, so that the GMM estimator uses valid moment restrictions, then a limited-information estimator will be consistent even though some of the restrictions for other equations fail to hold. In the next section, we describe *full-information* estimation that uses the restrictions of the entire system at once. If all the restrictions hold, then these estimators will be efficient relative to limited-information estimators. On the other hand, if some of the restrictions fail then generally the full-information estimators will be inconsistent.

26.5.2 Full Information

For full-information estimation of a linear simultaneous system, it is convenient to recast the system (26.39) in a vector form that generalizes (26.11)–(26.14). We will associate each of the J equations with one of the J endogenous variables through the normalization that $\gamma_{0jj} = 1$ $(j = 1, \ldots, J)$. That is, the jth endogenous variable is "the LHS variable" of the jth equation. Imposing normalization and exclusion restrictions for each equation as we just did for the first in (26.52)–(26.53), we will write

$$y_{tj} = \mathbf{z}_{jt}'\boldsymbol{\delta}_{0j} + \varepsilon_{tj}, \qquad j = 1, \ldots, J \tag{26.57}$$

[19] For a general example, review (22.23) and the surrounding discussion.

where $\mathbf{z}_{jt} \equiv \left[\mathbf{y}_t'\mathbf{S}_{\gamma j}, \mathbf{x}_t'\mathbf{S}_{\beta j}\right]$ contains the included endogenous and predetermined RHS variables in the jth structural equation. Stacking (26.57) over $t = 1, \ldots, T$ and $j = 1, \ldots, J$, we will write the entire system as

$$\mathbf{y}_{\mathrm{V}} = \mathbf{Z}_{\mathrm{VR}}\boldsymbol{\delta}_0 + \boldsymbol{\varepsilon}$$

where

$$\mathbf{Z}_{\mathrm{VR}} \equiv \mathrm{diag}(\mathbf{Z}_j;\ j = 1, \ldots, J) \tag{26.58}$$

$$\mathbf{Z}_j \equiv \left[\mathbf{z}_{jt};\ t = 1, \ldots, T\right]'$$

and

$$\boldsymbol{\delta}_0 \equiv \left[\delta_{0j}';\ j = 1, \ldots, J\right]'$$

The JK empirical moments

$$\mathrm{E}_T[\mathbf{x}_t(y_{tj} - \mathbf{z}_{jt}'\boldsymbol{\delta}_j)] = T^{-1} \cdot \mathbf{X}'(\mathbf{y}_j - \mathbf{Z}_j\boldsymbol{\delta}_j), \qquad j = 1, \ldots, J$$

have the stacked form

$$\frac{1}{T} \cdot (\mathbf{I}_J \otimes \mathbf{X})'\,(\mathbf{y}_{\mathrm{V}} - \mathbf{Z}_{\mathrm{VR}}\boldsymbol{\delta})$$

Given our second-moments assumption, $\mathrm{Var}(\boldsymbol{\varepsilon}\,|\,\mathbf{X}) = \boldsymbol{\Sigma}_0 \otimes \mathbf{I}_T$ and

$$\begin{aligned}\mathrm{Var}[(\mathbf{I}_J \otimes \mathbf{X})'\,(\mathbf{y} - \mathbf{Z}_{\mathrm{V}}\boldsymbol{\delta}_0)\,|\,\mathbf{X}] &= (\mathbf{I}_J \otimes \mathbf{X})'\,(\boldsymbol{\Sigma}_0 \otimes \mathbf{I}_T)\,(\mathbf{I}_J \otimes \mathbf{X}) \\ &= \boldsymbol{\Sigma}_0 \otimes \mathbf{X}'\mathbf{X}\end{aligned}$$

Therefore,

$$\frac{1}{\sqrt{T}} \cdot (\mathbf{I}_J \otimes \mathbf{X})'\,(\mathbf{y}_{\mathrm{V}} - \mathbf{Z}_{\mathrm{VR}}\boldsymbol{\delta}_0) \xrightarrow{d} \mathfrak{N}(\mathbf{0}, \boldsymbol{\Sigma}_0 \otimes \mathbf{D})$$

Using the 2SLS fitted residuals, we can compute the consistent estimator

$$\hat{\boldsymbol{\Sigma}}_{2\mathrm{SLS}} = \mathrm{E}_T[\boldsymbol{\varepsilon}_t(\hat{\boldsymbol{\delta}}_{2\mathrm{SLS}})\boldsymbol{\varepsilon}_t(\hat{\boldsymbol{\delta}}_{2\mathrm{SLS}})'] \tag{26.59}$$

where

$$\hat{\boldsymbol{\delta}}_{2\mathrm{SLS}} \equiv [\hat{\boldsymbol{\delta}}_{2\mathrm{SLS},j}';\ j = 1, \ldots, J]'$$

and

$$\boldsymbol{\varepsilon}_t(\boldsymbol{\delta})' \equiv \mathbf{y}_t'\boldsymbol{\Gamma} - \mathbf{x}_t'\mathbf{B}$$

This is analogous to using OLS fitted residuals to estimate a variance matrix for FGLS estimation of SUR.[20] Thus, a feasible optimal GMM criterion function is

$$\begin{aligned}&(\mathbf{y}_{\mathrm{V}} - \mathbf{Z}_{\mathrm{VR}}\boldsymbol{\delta})'\,(\mathbf{I}_J \otimes \mathbf{X})\,(\hat{\boldsymbol{\Sigma}}_{2\mathrm{SLS}} \otimes \mathbf{X}'\mathbf{X})^{-1}\,(\mathbf{I}_J \otimes \mathbf{X})'\,(\mathbf{y}_{\mathrm{V}} - \mathbf{Z}_{\mathrm{VR}}\boldsymbol{\delta}) \\ &= (\mathbf{y}_{\mathrm{V}} - \mathbf{Z}_{\mathrm{VR}}\boldsymbol{\delta})'\,(\hat{\boldsymbol{\Sigma}}_{2\mathrm{SLS}}^{-1} \otimes \mathbf{P}_{\mathbf{X}})\,(\mathbf{y}_{\mathrm{V}} - \mathbf{Z}_{\mathrm{VR}}\boldsymbol{\delta})\end{aligned}$$

[20] See (26.28)–(26.29).

This is an expanded version of the criterion function in (26.55). The corresponding GMM estimator is

$$\hat{\boldsymbol{\delta}}_{3SLS} = \left[\mathbf{Z}_{VR}'(\hat{\boldsymbol{\Sigma}}_{2SLS}^{-1} \otimes \mathbf{P}_{\mathbf{X}})\mathbf{Z}_{VR}\right]^{-1} \mathbf{Z}_{VR}'(\hat{\boldsymbol{\Sigma}}_{2SLS}^{-1} \otimes \mathbf{P}_{\mathbf{X}})\mathbf{y}_{V}$$

and is called a *three-stage least-squares* (3SLS) estimator. This is an IV estimator that combines the 2SLS instrument matrices in $(\mathbf{I}_J \otimes \mathbf{P}_{\mathbf{X}})\,\mathbf{Z}_{VR} = \text{diag}(\mathbf{P}_{\mathbf{X}}\mathbf{Z}_j;\ j = 1, \ldots, J)$ with the feasible GLS weighting matrix $\hat{\boldsymbol{\Sigma}}_{2SLS}^{-1} \otimes \mathbf{I}_T$. Thus 3SLS provides an efficiency gain over 2SLS in the same way that system FGLS improves efficiency over equation-by-equation OLS in SUR.[21]

If there is conditional heteroskedasticity, then Chamberlain's (1982) generalization of the weighting matrix applies just as it does in 2SLS. Letting

$$\check{\boldsymbol{\Lambda}} = \text{E}_T[\boldsymbol{\varepsilon}_t(\check{\boldsymbol{\delta}})\boldsymbol{\varepsilon}_t(\check{\boldsymbol{\delta}})' \otimes \mathbf{x}_t\mathbf{x}_t']$$

where $\check{\boldsymbol{\delta}}$ is an initial consistent estimator of $\boldsymbol{\delta}_0$, this feasible GMM (FGMM) estimator is

$$\hat{\boldsymbol{\delta}}_{FGMM} = \left(\mathbf{Z}_{VR}'\mathbf{X}_V\check{\boldsymbol{\Lambda}}^{-1}\mathbf{X}_V'\mathbf{Z}_{VR}\right)^{-1} \mathbf{Z}_{VR}'\mathbf{X}_V\check{\boldsymbol{\Lambda}}^{-1}\mathbf{X}_V'\mathbf{y}_V$$

To obtain asymptotic relative efficiency, it is necessary to use such an estimator.

26.5.3 Maximum Likelihood

We complete our presentation of estimation of simultaneous equations models with maximum likelihood under a normality assumption. We add:

Assumption 26.6 (Normality) *The $\boldsymbol{\varepsilon}_t$ are multivariate normal random variables conditional on $\mathbf{x}_t$.*

Combined with our previous assumptions, we derive a *full-information maximum-likelihood* (FIML) estimator.

As before, it is convenient to begin with the implied reduced form. The reduced form disturbances $\mathbf{v}_t'$ are the linear transformation $\boldsymbol{\varepsilon}_t'\boldsymbol{\Gamma}_0^{-1}$. Therefore, the $\mathbf{v}_t$ are i.i.d. $\mathfrak{N}(\mathbf{0}, \boldsymbol{\Omega}_0)$, where $\boldsymbol{\Omega}_0 = \boldsymbol{\Gamma}_0^{-1\prime}\boldsymbol{\Sigma}_0\boldsymbol{\Gamma}_0^{-1}$. The log-likelihood for the $\mathbf{v}_t$s can be written in the SUR form (26.33) as

$$\text{E}_T[L(\boldsymbol{\Omega}; \mathbf{v}_t)] = -\frac{1}{2}\,\text{E}_T[\log\det(2\pi \cdot \boldsymbol{\Omega}) + \mathbf{v}_t'\boldsymbol{\Omega}^{-1}\mathbf{v}_t]$$

Because the Jacobian of the transformation from $\mathbf{v}_t$ to $\mathbf{y}_t$ equals 1, the sample mean log-likelihood of $\mathbf{y}_t' = \mathbf{x}_t'\boldsymbol{\Pi}_0 + \mathbf{v}_t'$ follows from substitution for $\mathbf{v}_t$, $\boldsymbol{\Pi} = -\mathbf{B}\boldsymbol{\Gamma}^{-1}$, and $\boldsymbol{\Omega} = \boldsymbol{\Gamma}'^{-1}\boldsymbol{\Sigma}\boldsymbol{\Gamma}^{-1}$:[22]

21 In fact, 3SLS and 2SLS reduce to these two SUR estimators when there is no simultaneity.

22 The second equality (26.61) uses a result in Lemma C.4 (p. 861): the determinant of a matrix product is the product of the matrix determinants. Therefore,

$$\begin{aligned}\det(2\pi \cdot \boldsymbol{\Omega}) &= \det(2\pi \cdot \boldsymbol{\Gamma}'^{-1}\boldsymbol{\Sigma}\boldsymbol{\Gamma}^{-1}) \\ &= \det(2\pi \cdot \boldsymbol{\Sigma})[\det(\boldsymbol{\Gamma})]^{-2}\end{aligned}$$

$$\begin{aligned}\mathrm{E}_T[L(\boldsymbol{\theta};\mathbf{y}_t\,|\,\mathbf{x}_t)] =& -\frac{1}{2}\log\det(2\pi\cdot\boldsymbol{\Omega}) && (26.60)\\ &-\frac{1}{2}\mathrm{E}_T[(\mathbf{y}_t'-\mathbf{x}_t'\boldsymbol{\Pi})\,\boldsymbol{\Omega}^{-1}\,(\mathbf{y}_t'-\mathbf{x}_t'\boldsymbol{\Pi})']\\ =& -\frac{1}{2}\log\det(2\pi\cdot\boldsymbol{\Sigma})+\log|\det\boldsymbol{\Gamma}| && (26.61)\\ &-\frac{1}{2}\mathrm{E}_T[(\mathbf{y}_t'\boldsymbol{\Gamma}+\mathbf{x}_t'\mathbf{B})\,\boldsymbol{\Sigma}^{-1}\,(\mathbf{y}_t'\boldsymbol{\Gamma}+\mathbf{x}_t'\mathbf{B})']\end{aligned}$$

We see once again in the log-likelihood function that the simultaneous equations model is a nonlinear restricted version of the linear SUR model.

Compared to SUR, simultaneous equations has a log-likelihood function with a novel feature: the slope coefficients in the matrix $\boldsymbol{\Gamma}$ appear in a log-determinant term as well as the residual quadratic form. Covariance among the elements of $\mathbf{y}_t$ is explained *both* by the simultaneity in $\boldsymbol{\Gamma}$ and the covariances among the disturbances in $\boldsymbol{\Sigma}$. As a result, the parameters in $\boldsymbol{\Gamma}$ appear not only as slope coefficients, but also (in effect) as covariance parameters.

Two consequences follow for the MLE of the simultaneous equations system. First, the MLE does not possess a familiar GLS form when $\boldsymbol{\Sigma}_0$ is known. Second, the information matrix is not block-diagonal in the slope coefficients in $\mathbf{B}$ and $\boldsymbol{\Gamma}$ versus the covariance parameters in $\boldsymbol{\Sigma}$. Both of these outcomes reflect the presence of $\log|\det\boldsymbol{\Gamma}|$ in the log-likelihood function. The derivatives of this term appear in the score for $\boldsymbol{\Gamma}$, making this score nonlinear in $\boldsymbol{\Gamma}$ and its covariance with the score for $\boldsymbol{\Sigma}$ nonzero.

However, it is still possible to derive a helpful expression for the MLE. To that end, we differentiate (26.60) with respect to the structural parameters $\boldsymbol{\delta}$ and $\boldsymbol{\Sigma}$, using (26.31) and the chain rule of differentiation:

$$\mathrm{E}_T[L_{\boldsymbol{\delta}}(\boldsymbol{\theta})] = \boldsymbol{\Omega}_{\boldsymbol{\delta}}'\,\mathrm{E}_T[L_{\boldsymbol{\Omega}}(\boldsymbol{\theta})]+\boldsymbol{\Pi}_{\boldsymbol{\delta}}'\,\mathrm{E}_T[L_{\boldsymbol{\pi}}(\boldsymbol{\theta})] \tag{26.62}$$

$$\mathrm{E}_T[L_{\boldsymbol{\Sigma}}(\boldsymbol{\theta})] = \boldsymbol{\Omega}_{\Sigma}'\,\mathrm{E}_T[L_{\boldsymbol{\Omega}}(\boldsymbol{\theta})] \tag{26.63}$$

where we define $\boldsymbol{\pi}\equiv\mathrm{vec}\,\boldsymbol{\Pi}$, $\boldsymbol{\Omega}_{\boldsymbol{\delta}}\equiv\partial\,\mathrm{vec}\,\boldsymbol{\Omega}/\partial\boldsymbol{\delta}'$, $\boldsymbol{\Pi}_{\boldsymbol{\delta}}\equiv\partial\,\mathrm{vec}\,\boldsymbol{\Pi}/\partial\boldsymbol{\delta}'$, and $\boldsymbol{\Omega}_{\boldsymbol{\Sigma}}\equiv\partial\,\mathrm{vec}\,\boldsymbol{\Omega}/\partial\,(\mathrm{vec}\,\boldsymbol{\Sigma})'$. Expressions for $\mathrm{E}_T[L_{\boldsymbol{\pi}}(\boldsymbol{\theta})]$ and $\mathrm{E}_T[L_{\boldsymbol{\Omega}}(\boldsymbol{\theta})]$ appear in (26.31) and (26.34), respectively. We derive expressions for $\boldsymbol{\Omega}_{\boldsymbol{\delta}}$, $\boldsymbol{\Pi}_{\boldsymbol{\delta}}$, and $\boldsymbol{\Omega}_{\Sigma}$ in Section 26.7.1.

Despite the appearance of $\mathrm{E}_T[L_{\boldsymbol{\Omega}}(\boldsymbol{\theta})]$ in both scores, there is a key simplification when we evaluate them at the MLE $\hat{\boldsymbol{\theta}}_{\mathrm{FI}}=\left[\hat{\boldsymbol{\delta}}_{\mathrm{FI}},\,\mathrm{vec}\,\hat{\boldsymbol{\Sigma}}_{\mathrm{FI}}\right]$. Because $\mathrm{E}_T[L_{\boldsymbol{\delta}}(\hat{\boldsymbol{\theta}}_{\mathrm{FI}})]=\mathbf{0}$ and $\mathrm{E}_T[L_{\boldsymbol{\Sigma}}(\hat{\boldsymbol{\theta}}_{\mathrm{FI}})]=\mathbf{0}=\mathrm{E}_T[L_{\boldsymbol{\Omega}}(\hat{\boldsymbol{\theta}}_{\mathrm{FI}})]$, (26.62)–(26.63) imply that[23]

$$\begin{aligned}\mathbf{0} &= \hat{\boldsymbol{\Pi}}_{\boldsymbol{\delta},\mathrm{FI}}'\,\mathrm{E}_T[L_{\boldsymbol{\pi}}(\hat{\boldsymbol{\theta}}_{\mathrm{FI}})]\\ &= \frac{1}{T}\cdot\hat{\boldsymbol{\Pi}}_{\boldsymbol{\delta},\mathrm{FI}}'\mathbf{X}_{\mathrm{V}}'\left(\hat{\boldsymbol{\Omega}}_{\mathrm{FI}}\otimes\mathbf{I}_T\right)^{-1}(\mathbf{y}_{\mathrm{V}}-\mathbf{X}_{\mathrm{V}}\hat{\boldsymbol{\pi}}_{\mathrm{FI}})\end{aligned}$$

This normal equation is recognizable as the orthogonality condition for GLS with nonlinear regression.[24] The inverse variance matrix $(\hat{\boldsymbol{\Omega}}_{\mathrm{FI}}\otimes\mathbf{I}_T)^{-1}$ normalizes the inner product of the residual

[23] There is a one-to-one relationship between $\mathrm{E}_T[L_{\Omega}(\boldsymbol{\theta})]$ and $\mathrm{E}_T[L_{\Sigma}(\boldsymbol{\theta})]$. See (26.81).

[24] The same structure appears in Example 21.3, which discusses univariate nonlinear regression with conditional heteroskedasticity. That example discusses the relative efficiency of such instrumental variables.

$\mathbf{y}_{\mathrm{V}} - \mathbf{X}_{\mathrm{V}}\hat{\boldsymbol{\pi}}_{\mathrm{FI}}$ with the derivative of the nonlinear regression function $\partial \mathbf{X}_{\mathrm{V}}\boldsymbol{\pi}/\partial\boldsymbol{\delta}' = \mathbf{X}_{\mathrm{V}}\boldsymbol{\Pi}_{\delta}$. In addition, rewritten in terms of the fitted structural residuals this orthogonality condition is

$$\bar{\mathbf{Z}}_{\mathrm{VR}}(\hat{\boldsymbol{\delta}}_{\mathrm{FI}})'\left(\hat{\boldsymbol{\Sigma}}_{\mathrm{FI}} \otimes \mathbf{I}_T\right)^{-1}\left(\mathbf{y}_{\mathrm{V}} - \mathbf{Z}_{\mathrm{VR}}\hat{\boldsymbol{\delta}}_{\mathrm{FI}}\right) = \mathbf{0} \tag{26.64}$$

where

$$\bar{\mathbf{Z}}_{\mathrm{VR}}(\boldsymbol{\delta}) = \mathbf{X}_{\mathrm{V}}\left(\boldsymbol{\Gamma}' \otimes \mathbf{I}_T\right)\boldsymbol{\Pi}_{\delta}$$

depends only on the **x**s and parameters. Provided that the necessary matrix inverse exists, this yields an IV representation for the FIML estimator derived by Durbin (1988), Hausman (1975), and Hendry (1976):

$$\hat{\boldsymbol{\delta}}_{\mathrm{FI}} = \hat{\boldsymbol{\delta}}(\hat{\boldsymbol{\delta}}_{\mathrm{FI}}, \hat{\boldsymbol{\Sigma}}_{\mathrm{FI}})$$

where

$$\hat{\boldsymbol{\delta}}(\boldsymbol{\delta}, \boldsymbol{\Sigma}) \equiv \left[\bar{\mathbf{Z}}_{\mathrm{VR}}(\boldsymbol{\delta})'\left(\boldsymbol{\Sigma} \otimes \mathbf{I}_T\right]^{-1}\mathbf{Z}_{\mathrm{VR}}\right)^{-1}\bar{\mathbf{Z}}_{\mathrm{VR}}(\boldsymbol{\delta})'\left(\boldsymbol{\Sigma}_{\mathrm{V}} \otimes \mathbf{I}_T\right)^{-1}\mathbf{y}_{\mathrm{V}} \tag{26.65}$$

The instrumental variables $\bar{\mathbf{Z}}_{\mathrm{VR}}(\hat{\boldsymbol{\delta}}_{\mathrm{FI}})$ have a useful interpretation. We show in 26.7.1 that $\bar{\mathbf{Z}}_{\mathrm{VR}}(\boldsymbol{\delta})$ is the explanatory variable matrix $\mathbf{Z}_{\mathrm{VR}}$ after the endogenous $\mathbf{y}_t'$ have been replaced by their fitted values $\mathbf{x}_t'\mathbf{B}\boldsymbol{\Gamma}^{-1}$. Such a replacement makes sense because simultaneity implies that $\mathbf{y}_t'$ is not orthogonal to $\boldsymbol{\varepsilon}_t'$. Furthermore, the variables in $\mathbf{x}_t'\mathbf{B}_0\boldsymbol{\Gamma}_0^{-1}$ appear to be the ideal instrumental variables for $\mathbf{y}_t'$ because those are the MMSE predictors of $\mathbf{y}_t'$ given $\mathbf{x}_t'$. Of course $\mathbf{x}_t'\mathbf{B}_0\boldsymbol{\Gamma}_0^{-1}$ is not a feasible instrument matrix. Thus, it appears that the FIML estimator replaces this matrix with a feasible and relatively efficient alternative, $\mathbf{x}_t'\hat{\mathbf{B}}_{\mathrm{FI}}\hat{\boldsymbol{\Gamma}}_{\mathrm{FI}}^{-1}$.

Unfortunately, these instruments are functions of the MLE that we seek; (26.65) does not provide an explicit solution for the MLE, just as in the GLS setting. However, the 3SLS and FIML estimators are asymptotically equivalent. Although these estimators bear similarities, one might anticipate that FIML is strictly efficient relative to 3SLS. On one hand, both use estimates of $\boldsymbol{\Pi}_0$ to form substitutes for the instrumental variables $\mathbf{x}_t'\boldsymbol{\Pi}_0$. The 3SLS estimator uses the OLS estimator of the unrestricted reduced form $\hat{\boldsymbol{\Pi}}_{\mathrm{OLS}}$ and FIML uses $\hat{\boldsymbol{\Pi}}_{\mathrm{FI}} \equiv -\hat{\mathbf{B}}_{\mathrm{FI}}\hat{\boldsymbol{\Gamma}}_{\mathrm{FI}}^{-1}$. On the other hand, the instrumental variables in FIML impose the restrictions of the structural model on the estimated $\boldsymbol{\Pi}$ and use efficient estimates of $\mathbf{B}$ and $\boldsymbol{\Gamma}$ besides. These were concerns in the early research into simultaneous equations models.

The difference in estimators for $\boldsymbol{\Sigma}$ in the 3SLS and FIML estimators could also make a difference. Although the estimator has the familiar functional form[25]

$$\hat{\boldsymbol{\Sigma}}_{\mathrm{FI}}(\boldsymbol{\delta}) = \mathrm{E}_T[\boldsymbol{\varepsilon}_t(\boldsymbol{\delta})\boldsymbol{\varepsilon}_t(\boldsymbol{\delta})']$$

the information matrix is not block-diagonal in the coefficients versus the covariance parameters in the simultaneous equations model. This is apparent in (26.62)–(26.63). Although $L_\pi(\boldsymbol{\theta})$ and $L_\Omega(\boldsymbol{\theta})$ are uncorrelated (as in univariate linear regression), the conditional information matrix for the structural parameters has the functional form

$$\Im(\boldsymbol{\theta}_0 \mid \mathbf{X}) = \begin{bmatrix} \boldsymbol{\Pi}_\delta' \operatorname{Var}[L_\pi(\boldsymbol{\theta}_0)]\boldsymbol{\Pi}_\delta + \boldsymbol{\Omega}_\delta' \operatorname{Var}[L_\Omega(\boldsymbol{\theta}_0)]\boldsymbol{\Omega}_\delta & \boldsymbol{\Omega}_\delta' \operatorname{Var}[L_\Omega(\boldsymbol{\theta}_0)]\boldsymbol{\Omega}_\Sigma \\ \boldsymbol{\Omega}_\Sigma' \operatorname{Var}[L_\Omega(\boldsymbol{\theta}_0)]\boldsymbol{\Omega}_\delta & \boldsymbol{\Omega}_\Sigma' \operatorname{Var}[L_\Omega(\boldsymbol{\theta}_0)]\boldsymbol{\Omega}_\Sigma \end{bmatrix} \tag{26.66}$$

[25] See equation (26.84).

This information matrix is not block-diagonal in $\boldsymbol{\delta}$ versus $\boldsymbol{\Sigma}$.[26] We saw in the dynamic regression model with serial correlation (see Sections 20.7.2 and 20.10.3) that a feasible GLS estimator is generally inefficient when the scores for regression and variance parameters are correlated.

Fortunately, matters are simpler than this. In the current case, inspection of the FIML IV estimator $\hat{\boldsymbol{\delta}}(\boldsymbol{\delta}, \boldsymbol{\Sigma})$ reveals that it is consistent for *any* $\boldsymbol{\delta}$ and $\boldsymbol{\Sigma}$ given that the necessary probability limits exist. For fixed $\boldsymbol{\delta}$, the matrix $\bar{\mathbf{Z}}_{\mathrm{VR}}(\boldsymbol{\delta})$ is a function of $\mathbf{x}_t$ alone so that the instrumental variables are orthogonal to the $\boldsymbol{\varepsilon}_t$. It follows from Newey's rule for two-step estimators that all estimators $\hat{\boldsymbol{\delta}}(\check{\boldsymbol{\delta}}, \check{\boldsymbol{\Sigma}})$ based on $\sqrt{T}$-consistent estimators $\check{\boldsymbol{\delta}}$ and $\check{\boldsymbol{\Sigma}}$ are asymptotically equivalent.[27] The FIML estimator is one member of this family. So is 3SLS, even though it uses an unrestricted estimator of $\boldsymbol{\Pi}_0$.[28]

There is an important special case of simultaneous equations where the MLE is a GLS estimator. Whenever $\boldsymbol{\Gamma}$ is restricted so that its determinant is a known constant, the log $|\det \boldsymbol{\Gamma}|$ term in the log-likelihood function plays no role in estimation. This occurs in *recursive* systems where $\boldsymbol{\Gamma}$ is a triangular matrix. When the diagonal elements are all normalized to one, then $\det \boldsymbol{\Gamma} = 1$ and the simultaneous equations log-likelihood function (26.61) has the functional form of the SUR log-likelihood function (26.60) where we substitute $[\mathbf{I} - \boldsymbol{\Gamma}, -\mathbf{B}]$ for $\boldsymbol{\Pi}$ and $\boldsymbol{\Sigma}$ for $\boldsymbol{\Omega}$. As a result, the FIML estimation function for $\boldsymbol{\delta}$ given $\boldsymbol{\Sigma}$ simplifies to GLS,

$$\hat{\boldsymbol{\delta}}(\boldsymbol{\Sigma}) = \left[\mathbf{Z}'_{\mathrm{VR}}(\boldsymbol{\Sigma} \otimes \mathbf{I}_T)^{-1}\mathbf{Z}_{\mathrm{VR}}\right]^{-1} \mathbf{Z}'_{\mathrm{VR}}(\boldsymbol{\Sigma} \otimes \mathbf{I}_T)^{-1}\mathbf{y}_{\mathrm{V}}$$

and recursive simultaneous systems can be estimated with software for SUR systems.

Note, however, that this GLS estimator *requires* a consistent estimator of $\boldsymbol{\Sigma}_0$. Even though the log-likelihood function simplifies for recursive systems, simultaneity is still present and (26.54) still holds. The endogenous explanatory variables are correlated with the disturbances so that if we replace $\boldsymbol{\Sigma}$ with $\mathbf{I}_J$ then $\hat{\boldsymbol{\delta}}(\mathbf{I}_J)$ is an inconsistent estimator. In this case, $(\boldsymbol{\Sigma}_0 \otimes \mathbf{I}_T)^{-1}\, \mathbf{Z}_{\mathrm{VR}}$ is a *particular* linear combination of the elements of $\mathbf{Z}_{\mathrm{VR}}$ that are orthogonal to the disturbance vector $\boldsymbol{\varepsilon}$.

As a result, an efficient estimator of $\boldsymbol{\Sigma}_0$ is required to construct an FGLS estimator for recursive systems that is asymptotically equivalent to $\hat{\boldsymbol{\delta}}_{\mathrm{FI}} = \hat{\boldsymbol{\delta}}(\hat{\boldsymbol{\Sigma}}_{\mathrm{FI}})$. In general, replacing $\boldsymbol{\Sigma}$ with such an estimator as $\hat{\boldsymbol{\Sigma}}_{\mathrm{2SLS}}$ in (26.59) produces a consistent, but inefficient, estimator and one must correct the estimated variance of the two-step FGLS estimator as in Proposition 19 (Two-Step Asymptotic Variance, p. 507). Alternatively, iterated SUR converges to the FIML estimator.

A leading case of a recursive simultaneous system is the limited-information specification in (26.53) and (26.56). In the limited-information framework, $\boldsymbol{\Gamma}$ partitions into

$$\boldsymbol{\Gamma} = \begin{bmatrix} 1 & \mathbf{0}_{1\times(J-1)} \\ \boldsymbol{\phi}_{(J-1)\times 1} & \mathbf{I}_{J-1} \end{bmatrix}$$

where we denote the coefficients of the endogenous variables in the first (structural) equation by $\boldsymbol{\phi}$. In general, some of the endogenous variables in the system do not appear in the structural equation so that we partition $\boldsymbol{\phi} = \left[\boldsymbol{\phi}'_1, \boldsymbol{\phi}'_2\right]'$ so that $\boldsymbol{\phi}_2 = \mathbf{0}$ captures all of these exclusion restrictions.

---

[26] Regarding the orthogonality of $L_\pi(\boldsymbol{\theta}_0)$ and $L_\Omega(\boldsymbol{\theta}_0)$, see Example 14.20 (OLS), equation (18.25) (heteroskedasticity), and equation (19.39) (serial correlation).

[27] See Proposition 19 (Two-Step Asymptotic Variance, p. 507) and Lemma 20.3 (p. 508).

[28] Implicitly, there are many consistent estimators of the structural coefficients corresponding to $\hat{\boldsymbol{\Pi}}_{\mathrm{OLS}}$ when the structural parameters are overidentified. By solving $\hat{\boldsymbol{\Pi}}_{\mathrm{OLS}}\hat{\boldsymbol{\Gamma}}_{\mathrm{ILS}} + \hat{\mathbf{B}}_{\mathrm{ILS}} = \mathbf{0}$ and a *subset* of restrictions that identify $\boldsymbol{\Gamma}$ and $\mathbf{B}$ *exactly*, one can always find such a $\check{\boldsymbol{\delta}}$ by ILS. Although such $\hat{\mathbf{B}}_{\mathrm{ILS}}$ and $\hat{\boldsymbol{\Gamma}}_{\mathrm{ILS}}$ are not unique, the fitted values $\mathbf{x}'_t\hat{\boldsymbol{\Pi}}_{\mathrm{OLS}}$ are, making this interpretation of 3SLS unambiguous.

The MLE for this case is called the *limited-information maximum-likelihood* (LIML) estimator. This estimator is the ML counterpart to the 2SLS estimator and the two are asymptotically equivalent. We can still apply the IV form of FIML (26.65) to LIML and, using

$$\mathbf{Z}_{\mathrm{VR}} = \begin{bmatrix} \mathbf{Z}_1 & \mathbf{0} \\ \mathbf{0} & \mathbf{I}_{J-1} \otimes \mathbf{X} \end{bmatrix} \quad \text{and} \quad \bar{\mathbf{Z}}_{\mathrm{VR}}(\boldsymbol{\delta}) = \begin{bmatrix} \bar{\mathbf{Z}}_1(\boldsymbol{\Pi}_1) & \mathbf{0} \\ \mathbf{0} & \mathbf{I}_{J-1} \otimes \mathbf{X} \end{bmatrix}$$

a partitioned inverse yields the LIML estimation function for $\boldsymbol{\delta}_1$

$$\hat{\boldsymbol{\delta}}_1(\boldsymbol{\Pi}_1) = \left[\bar{\mathbf{Z}}_1(\boldsymbol{\Pi}_1)'\mathbf{Z}_1\right]^{-1} \bar{\mathbf{Z}}_1(\boldsymbol{\Pi}_1)'\mathbf{y}_1$$

where $\boldsymbol{\Pi}_1$ denotes the reduced form coefficients for the regressions of the included endogenous variables. The LIML estimator uses the ML estimator for $\boldsymbol{\Pi}_1$ but all $\sqrt{T}$-consistent estimators deliver asymptotically equivalent estimators. In particular, the 2SLS estimator uses OLS estimators for $\boldsymbol{\Pi}_1$.[29]

26.6 HYPOTHESIS TESTS

Simultaneous equations models, especially those with many endogenous and predetermined variables, typically involve a large number of exclusion restrictions. For simplicity or statistical precision, researchers frequently specify parsimonious models so that their specifications are overidentified. As a result, it is natural to apply tests of overidentifying restrictions. Researchers may fear that they have been overzealous in their parsimony and they seek assurance that there is no clear evidence that they have excluded too much. Simultaneous equations systems have been a primary motivation for hypothesis tests of overidentifying restrictions.

In addition, simultaneous equations models risk classifying truly endogenous as predetermined. One can often argue for an expanded simultaneous system that reclassifies some predetermined variables as endogenous. Some simultaneous macroeconomic models, for example, treat monetary and fiscal policies as predetermined but over such horizons as a year many policies may be endogenous. Models of earnings, for another example, occasionally treat education as predetermined, but many labor economists argue that earnings and education are both under the influence of the individual who obtains them. In that case, education is not predetermined.

Hypothesis tests for simultaneous equations tend to focus on these two issues. Tests of overidentifying restrictions are direct applications of the standard Wald, likelihood ratio (LR), and score (or Lagrange multiplier) methods. Tests of whether variables are predetermined, which are sometimes called *exogeneity tests*, are Hausman specification tests. In this section we briefly detail these tests as they apply to these models.

Because the normally distributed case was the focus of the early literature, the LR test is the original test of overidentifying restrictions.[30] The restricted estimator is, of course, FIML. An unrestricted, exactly identified, specification is the reduced form $\mathbf{y}_t' = \mathbf{x}_t'\boldsymbol{\Pi}_0 + \mathbf{v}_t'$ treated as an unrestricted SUR model. Therefore, the equation-by-equation OLS fit of y_{tj} on $\mathbf{x}_t$ ($j =$

[29] Because $\boldsymbol{\Pi}_1$ only is required, researchers generally restrict the log-likelihood function to the joint distribution of the endogenous variables included in the structural equation. However, it is not apparent that one obtains the same estimator when the other endogenous variables in the system are included. For a proof that this is so, see Koopmans and Hood (1953, Appendix E) and Exercise 26.29.

[30] Among others, see Koopmans and Hood (1953).

$1, \ldots, J$) produces an unrestricted MLE. The LR test statistic equals twice the difference in the log-likelihood functions evaluated at these two points in the parameter space.

This test statistic simplifies somewhat when we concentrate the reduced-form variance matrix out of log-likelihood function. Because the variance matrix is unrestricted, the MLE of $\mathbf{\Omega}_0$ as a function of the regression parameters is given by (26.35): $\hat{\mathbf{\Omega}}(\mathbf{\Pi}) = \mathrm{E}_T[\mathbf{v}_t(\mathbf{\Pi})\mathbf{v}_t(\mathbf{\Pi})']$ where $\mathbf{v}_t(\mathbf{\Pi})' \equiv \mathbf{y}_t' - \mathbf{x}_t'\mathbf{\Pi}$. Substituting this expression into (26.33) gives the concentrated log-likelihood function[31]

$$L^{c}(\mathbf{\Pi}) = -\frac{T}{2}\left[J \log 2\pi + \log\det \hat{\mathbf{\Omega}}(\mathbf{\Pi}) + J\right] \tag{26.67}$$

A simple expression for the LR test statistic (17.13) is, therefore,

$$\mathcal{LR} = T \log \frac{\det \hat{\mathbf{\Omega}}(\hat{\mathbf{\Pi}}_{\mathrm{OLS}})}{\det \hat{\mathbf{\Omega}}(\hat{\mathbf{\Pi}}_{\mathrm{FI}})}$$

where $\hat{\mathbf{\Pi}}_{\mathrm{OLS}} \equiv (\mathbf{X}'\mathbf{X})^{-1}\mathbf{X}'\mathbf{Y}$ and $\hat{\mathbf{\Pi}}_{\mathrm{FI}} \equiv -\hat{\mathbf{B}}_{\mathrm{FI}}\hat{\mathbf{\Gamma}}_{\mathrm{FI}}^{-1}$ are the unrestricted SUR and restricted FIML estimators of the reduced-form regression parameters, respectively.

In the limited-information case in which GLS plays no role it is possible to concentrate the coefficients $\boldsymbol{\beta}_1$ of the predetermined variables out of the log-likelihood function as well. Koopmans and Hood (1953, Appendix E) show that[32]

$$L^{c}(\boldsymbol{\gamma}_1) = -\frac{T}{2}\left[J \log 2\pi + \log\det \hat{\mathbf{\Omega}}(\hat{\mathbf{\Pi}}_{\mathrm{OLS}}) + \frac{T}{2}\log \frac{\boldsymbol{\gamma}_1'\mathbf{Y}'\left(\mathbf{I}_J - \mathbf{P}_{\mathbf{X}_1}\right)\mathbf{Y}\boldsymbol{\gamma}_1}{\boldsymbol{\gamma}_1'\mathbf{Y}'\left(\mathbf{I} - \mathbf{P}_{\mathbf{X}}\right)\mathbf{Y}\boldsymbol{\gamma}_1} + J\right] \tag{26.68}$$

Therefore, the limited-information LR test for the overidentifying restrictions of a single structural equation is

$$\mathcal{LR} = T \log \frac{\hat{\boldsymbol{\gamma}}_{\mathrm{LIML},1}'\mathbf{Y}'\left(\mathbf{I} - \mathbf{P}_{\mathbf{X}_1}\right)\mathbf{Y}\hat{\boldsymbol{\gamma}}_{\mathrm{LIML},1}}{\hat{\boldsymbol{\gamma}}_{\mathrm{LIML},1}'\mathbf{Y}'\left(\mathbf{I} - \mathbf{P}_{\mathbf{X}}\right)\mathbf{Y}\hat{\boldsymbol{\gamma}}_{\mathrm{LIML},1}}$$

where $\hat{\boldsymbol{\gamma}}_{\mathrm{LIML},1}$ is the LIML estimator for the coefficients $\boldsymbol{\gamma}_1$ of the included endogenous variables.[33]

When both restricted and unrestricted estimators are available, one can compute the feasible minimum chi-square (MC) test statistic (17.23) instead of the LR:

$$\begin{aligned} \mathcal{MC} &= \left[\mathrm{vec}(\hat{\mathbf{\Pi}}_{\mathrm{OLS}} - \hat{\mathbf{\Pi}}_{\mathrm{ML}})\right]'\left(\hat{\mathbf{\Omega}}^{-1} \otimes \mathbf{X}'\mathbf{X}\right)\mathrm{vec}(\hat{\mathbf{\Pi}}_{\mathrm{OLS}} - \hat{\mathbf{\Pi}}_{\mathrm{ML}}) \\ &= \left[\mathrm{vec}(\mathbf{X}\hat{\mathbf{\Pi}}_{\mathrm{OLS}} - \mathbf{X}\hat{\mathbf{\Pi}}_{\mathrm{ML}})\right]'\left(\hat{\mathbf{\Omega}}^{-1} \otimes \mathbf{I}_T\right)\mathrm{vec}(\mathbf{X}\hat{\mathbf{\Pi}}_{\mathrm{OLS}} - \mathbf{X}\hat{\mathbf{\Pi}}_{\mathrm{ML}}) \end{aligned} \tag{26.69}$$

---

[31] The trace of a matrix is the sum of its diagonal elements. Therefore, tr $\mathbf{AB}$ = tr $\mathbf{BA}$. See also Exercise 8.8. As a result, $\mathrm{E}_T[\mathbf{v}_t(\mathbf{\Pi})'\hat{\mathbf{\Omega}}(\mathbf{\Pi})^{-1}\mathbf{v}_t(\Pi)] = \mathrm{E}_T\left[\mathrm{tr}\left(\hat{\mathbf{\Omega}}(\mathbf{\Pi})^{-1}\mathbf{v}_t(\mathbf{\Pi})\mathbf{v}_t(\mathbf{\Pi})'\right)\right] = \mathrm{tr}\left\{\hat{\mathbf{\Omega}}(\mathbf{\Pi})^{-1}\mathrm{E}_T[\mathbf{v}_t(\mathbf{\Pi})\mathbf{v}_t(\mathbf{\Pi})']\right\} = \mathrm{tr}\,\hat{\mathbf{\Omega}}(\mathbf{\Pi})^{-1}\hat{\mathbf{\Omega}}(\mathbf{\Pi}) = \mathrm{tr}\,\mathbf{I}_J = \mathbf{J}$. Also, det $\mathbf{AB}$ = det $\mathbf{A}$ · det $\mathbf{B}$ when $\mathbf{A}$ and $\mathbf{B}$ are square matrices. Therefore, $\log\det\left[2\pi \cdot \hat{\mathbf{\Omega}}(\mathbf{\Pi})\right] = \log\det(2\pi \cdot \mathbf{I}_J) + \log\det \hat{\mathbf{\Omega}}(\mathbf{\Pi}) = J \cdot \log 2\pi + \log\det \hat{\mathbf{\Omega}}(\mathbf{\Pi})$.

[32] See Exercise 26.29.

[33] Incidentally, note that the concentrated log-likelihood function (26.68) is a useful simplification for computing the LIML estimator. For a textbook presentation, see Davidson and MacKinnon (1993, Section 18.5), who also explain related k-class estimators.

where $\hat{\boldsymbol{\Omega}}$ is any consistent estimator of $\boldsymbol{\Omega}_0$.[34] Either the FIML or LIML estimator takes the place of $\hat{\boldsymbol{\Pi}}_{\text{ML}}$ depending on whether the test is for all overidentifying restrictions or only for those of a single structural equation. This test statistic is reminiscent of OLS test statistics that compare unrestricted and restricted fitted values.

Either $\hat{\boldsymbol{\Omega}}(\hat{\boldsymbol{\Pi}}_{\text{OLS}})$ or $\hat{\boldsymbol{\Omega}}(\hat{\boldsymbol{\Pi}}_{\text{ML}})$ will do; when $\hat{\boldsymbol{\Omega}}(\hat{\boldsymbol{\Pi}}_{\text{ML}})$, this statistic is identically equal to the score test statistic for overidentifying restrictions. This occurs because the unrestricted log-likelihood function is quadratic in the reduced-form regression coefficients. Because one usually computes restricted ML in terms of the structural equations, it is convenient to reexpress the statistic in terms of the structural residuals:[35]

$$S = \mathcal{MC} = \hat{\boldsymbol{\varepsilon}}(\hat{\boldsymbol{\delta}}_{\text{ML}})' \left(\hat{\boldsymbol{\Sigma}}_{\text{ML}}^{-1} \otimes \mathbf{P_X}\right) \hat{\boldsymbol{\varepsilon}}(\hat{\boldsymbol{\delta}}_{\text{ML}}) \tag{26.70}$$

Thus, the score test examines whether the ML fitted structural residuals are orthogonal to every predetermined variable, as opposed to particular linear combinations.

Byron (1974) notes that the Wald testing method is computationally convenient because one need not calculate the restricted (FIML) estimator. To apply this method, one finds restrictions $\mathbf{r}(\boldsymbol{\Pi}_0) = \mathbf{0}$ on the reduced-form regression parameters implied by the restricted structural form in the relationship $\boldsymbol{\Pi}_0\boldsymbol{\Gamma}_0 + \mathbf{B}_0 = \mathbf{0}$. The vector of nonlinear of restrictions can be tested with the Wald statistic in (17.28) and the unrestricted MLE $\hat{\boldsymbol{\Pi}}_{\text{OLS}}$:

$$\mathcal{W} = N \cdot \mathbf{r}(\hat{\boldsymbol{\Pi}}_{\text{OLS}})' \left[\hat{\mathbf{R}}' \Im_{\pi\pi}(\hat{\boldsymbol{\theta}})^{-1} \hat{\mathbf{R}}\right]^{-1} \mathbf{r}(\hat{\boldsymbol{\Pi}}_{\text{OLS}})$$

where

$$\hat{\mathbf{R}} \equiv \left. \frac{\partial \mathbf{r}(\boldsymbol{\Pi})}{\partial (\text{vec } \boldsymbol{\Pi})'} \right|_{\boldsymbol{\Pi} = \hat{\boldsymbol{\Pi}}_{\text{OLS}}}$$

and

$$\Im_{\pi\pi}(\hat{\theta}) = \hat{\boldsymbol{\Omega}}_{\text{OLS}} \otimes (\mathbf{X}'\mathbf{X})^{-1}$$

However, one can substitute asymptotically equivalent estimators (3SLS for FIML, 2SLS for LIML) into the LR and score test statistics and obtain asymptotically equivalent test statistics. This substantially simplifies the computation of such test statistics. A leading example is the limited-information score test. Substituting the 2SLS estimator for the LIML estimator in (26.70) leads to

$$S = T \cdot \frac{\boldsymbol{\varepsilon}_1(\hat{\boldsymbol{\delta}}_{2\text{SLS},1})' \mathbf{P_X} \boldsymbol{\varepsilon}_1(\hat{\boldsymbol{\delta}}_{2\text{SLS},1})}{\boldsymbol{\varepsilon}_1(\hat{\boldsymbol{\delta}}_{2\text{SLS},1})' \boldsymbol{\varepsilon}_1(\hat{\boldsymbol{\delta}}_{2\text{SLS},1})} \tag{26.71}$$

which equals the sample size times the uncentered R^2 from the OLS fit of the 2SLS fitted structural residual $\boldsymbol{\varepsilon}_1(\hat{\boldsymbol{\delta}}_{2\text{SLS},1})' \equiv \mathbf{y}_t'\hat{\boldsymbol{\gamma}}_{2\text{SLS},1} - \mathbf{x}_t'\hat{\boldsymbol{\beta}}_{2\text{SLS},1}$ on all the predetermined variables in the system.

Note also that the normality assumption (Assumption 26.6) is incidental to these tests of the overidentifying restrictions. The standard GMM test statistics are closely related to those we have just summarized. The Wald test statistic is identical in the GMM framework and the MC and gradient test statistics differ from the score test statistic only in their substitution of 3SLS or 2SLS for FIML or LIML and in their estimator of the parameters of the variance matrix. In addition,

[34] Malinvaud (1970) and Silvey (1959), among others, suggest this statistic.

[35] See Exercise 26.27.

because these are tests of overidentifying restrictions and the moment conditions are linear in the reduced-form coefficients, the MC, gradient, and distance difference (DD) statistics are all equal GMM test statistics. Thus, the GMM and likelihood tests are intimately related.

Hausman (1978) argues that researchers naturally compare the 3SLS and 2SLS estimators when they look for evidence of misspecification. If some of the moment restrictions are incorrect, then these two estimators generally converge to different probability limits. For example, the 2SLS estimator of a structural equation will be consistent even though there is a misspecification in another structural equation that makes the 3SLS estimator inconsistent for every equation. The formalization of such comparisons is a Hausman specification test, described in Section 22.3. Alternatively, one may use a test of moment restrictions to test whether particular variables are not predetermined. See Section 22.2 and Example 22.8.

26.7 MATHEMATICAL NOTES

These mathematical notes cover two topics. First, we confirm that the simultaneous system of equations specified in this chapter satisfies the conditions for GMM estimation laid out in Chapter 21. Second, we derive analytical expressions for the score and information matrix.

In the terms of GMM, Assumption 21.1.1 (Moments, p. 542) corresponds (in part) to a generalization of (26.43). Because the moment equations are linear in the unknown parameters $(\mathbf{B}_0, \mathbf{\Gamma}_0)$, the empirical moments are continuously differentiable and so is their probability limit. Furthermore, linearity implies that this convergence is uniform in the elements of $(\mathbf{B}, \mathbf{\Gamma})$ within the parameter space $\mathbf{\Theta}$.

This moment assumption also covers the first component of GMM Assumption 21.3 (Asymptotic Limits, p. 545). Again because of linearity, differentiation within the expectation is permissible and the derivatives of the empirical moment functions converge to constants that depend on the elements of $\mathbf{D}$ and $\mathbf{\Pi}_0$. Therefore, this convergence is also uniform in the parameters and the limit is continuous and constant rank in the parameters. We give an expression for these derivatives below.

26.7.1 Score Functions

In this section, we provide a derivation of the scores of the log-likelihood function for the coefficient parameters and covariance parameters of the linear simultaneous equations system. Our derivation makes use of the relationships between matrices, their vectorization, and Kronecker products. We list these in Section G.2 and the most useful here is equation (G.15), which states that

$$\operatorname{vec}(\mathbf{AB}) = (\mathbf{I}_J \otimes \mathbf{A}) \operatorname{vec} \mathbf{B} = (\mathbf{B}' \otimes \mathbf{I}_K) \operatorname{vec} \mathbf{A} \tag{26.72}$$

for a $K \times M$ matrix $\mathbf{A}$ and an $N \times J$ matrix $\mathbf{B}$.

Applying (26.72) to $\mathbf{\Pi} = \mathbf{B\Gamma}^{-1}$,

$$\begin{aligned} \operatorname{vec} \mathbf{\Pi} &= -\operatorname{vec} \mathbf{B\Gamma}^{-1} \\ &= -(\mathbf{\Gamma}^{-1\prime} \otimes \mathbf{I}_K) \operatorname{vec} \mathbf{B} \\ &= -(\mathbf{I}_J \otimes \mathbf{B}) \operatorname{vec} \mathbf{\Gamma}^{-1} \end{aligned}$$

Differentiating this equation with[36]

$$\frac{\partial \operatorname{vec} \boldsymbol{\Gamma}^{-1}}{\partial (\operatorname{vec} \boldsymbol{\Gamma})'} = -\left(\boldsymbol{\Gamma}^{-1\prime} \otimes \boldsymbol{\Gamma}^{-1}\right) \tag{26.73}$$

gives

$$\begin{aligned} \boldsymbol{\Pi}_{\delta} \equiv \frac{\partial \operatorname{vec} \boldsymbol{\Pi}}{\partial \boldsymbol{\delta}'} &= -\left(\mathbf{I}_J \otimes \mathbf{B}\right) \frac{\partial \operatorname{vec} \boldsymbol{\Gamma}^{-1}}{\partial (\operatorname{vec} \boldsymbol{\Gamma})'} \frac{\partial \operatorname{vec} \boldsymbol{\Gamma}}{\partial \boldsymbol{\delta}'} - (\boldsymbol{\Gamma}^{-1\prime} \otimes \mathbf{I}_K) \frac{\partial \operatorname{vec} \mathbf{B}}{\partial \boldsymbol{\delta}'} \\ &= -\left(\mathbf{I}_J \otimes \mathbf{B}\right) (\boldsymbol{\Gamma}^{-1\prime} \otimes \boldsymbol{\Gamma}^{-1}) \mathbf{S}_{\gamma} + (\boldsymbol{\Gamma}^{-1\prime} \otimes \mathbf{I}_K) \mathbf{S}_{\beta} \\ &= (\boldsymbol{\Gamma}^{-1\prime} \otimes \mathbf{I}_K) \left[(\mathbf{I}_J \otimes \boldsymbol{\Pi}) \mathbf{S}_{\gamma} + \mathbf{S}_{\beta} \right] \end{aligned} \tag{26.74}$$

where $\mathbf{S}_{\gamma} \equiv -\partial \operatorname{vec} \boldsymbol{\Gamma} / \partial \boldsymbol{\delta}'$ and $\mathbf{S}_{\beta} \equiv -\partial \operatorname{vec} \mathbf{B} / \partial \boldsymbol{\delta}'$.[37] Therefore,

$$\begin{aligned} \mathbf{X}_{\mathrm{V}} \boldsymbol{\Pi}_{\delta} &= (\mathbf{I}_J \otimes \mathbf{X}) (\boldsymbol{\Gamma}^{-1\prime} \otimes \mathbf{I}_K) \left[(\mathbf{I}_J \otimes \boldsymbol{\Pi}) \mathbf{S}_{\gamma} + \mathbf{S}_{\beta} \right] \\ &= (\boldsymbol{\Gamma}^{-1\prime} \otimes \mathbf{I}_T) \left[(\mathbf{I}_J \otimes \mathbf{X}\boldsymbol{\Pi}) \mathbf{S}_{\gamma} + (\mathbf{I}_J \otimes \mathbf{X}) \mathbf{S}_{\beta} \right] \end{aligned} \tag{26.75}$$

Applying (26.72) again,

$$\mathbf{y}_{\mathrm{V}} - \mathbf{Z}_{\mathrm{VR}} \boldsymbol{\delta} = \operatorname{vec}(\mathbf{Y}\boldsymbol{\Gamma} + \mathbf{X}\mathbf{B}) = (\mathbf{I}_J \otimes \mathbf{Y}) \operatorname{vec} \boldsymbol{\Gamma} + (\mathbf{I}_J \otimes \mathbf{X}) \operatorname{vec} \mathbf{B} \tag{26.76}$$

where $\mathbf{Y} \equiv \left[\mathbf{y}_t;\ t = 1, \ldots .T\right]'$. Differentiating (26.76), we derive a relationship between $\mathbf{Z}_{\mathrm{VR}}$ in (26.58), $\mathbf{Y}$, and $\mathbf{X}$:

$$\mathbf{Z}_{\mathrm{VR}} = -\frac{\partial (\mathbf{y}_{\mathrm{V}} - \mathbf{Z}_{\mathrm{VR}} \boldsymbol{\delta})}{\partial \boldsymbol{\delta}'} = (\mathbf{I}_J \otimes \mathbf{Y}) \mathbf{S}_{\gamma} + (\mathbf{I}_J \otimes \mathbf{X}) \mathbf{S}_{\beta}$$

Therefore,

$$\bar{\mathbf{Z}}_{\mathrm{VR}}(\boldsymbol{\delta}) \equiv (\mathbf{I}_J \otimes \mathbf{X}\boldsymbol{\Pi}) \mathbf{S}_{\gamma} + (\mathbf{I}_J \otimes \mathbf{X}) \mathbf{S}_{\beta} \tag{26.77}$$

is $\mathbf{Z}_{\mathrm{V}}$ with the elements containing y_{tj} replaced by its reduced-form regression function $\mathbf{x}_t' \boldsymbol{\pi}_j$ where $\boldsymbol{\pi}_j$ is the jth column of $\boldsymbol{\Pi}$. Furthermore, (26.75) is equivalent to

$$\mathbf{X}_{\mathrm{V}} \boldsymbol{\Pi}_{\delta} = (\boldsymbol{\Gamma}^{-1\prime} \otimes \mathbf{I}_T) \bar{\mathbf{Z}}_{\mathrm{VR}}(\boldsymbol{\delta}) \tag{26.78}$$

confirming our interpretation of the FIML instrumental variables in (26.65).

Applying (26.72) a third time,

$$\begin{aligned} (\boldsymbol{\Omega}^{-1} \otimes \mathbf{I}_T) (\mathbf{y}_{\mathrm{V}} - \mathbf{X}_{\mathrm{V}} \boldsymbol{\pi}) &= \operatorname{vec}\left[(\mathbf{Y} - \mathbf{X}\boldsymbol{\Pi}) \boldsymbol{\Omega}^{-1} \right] \\ &= \operatorname{vec}\left[(\mathbf{Y}\boldsymbol{\Gamma} - \mathbf{X}\mathbf{B}) \boldsymbol{\Sigma}^{-1} \boldsymbol{\Gamma}' \right] \\ &= \left(\boldsymbol{\Gamma} \boldsymbol{\Sigma}^{-1} \otimes \mathbf{I}_T \right) (\mathbf{y}_{\mathrm{V}} - \mathbf{Z}_{\mathrm{VR}} \boldsymbol{\delta}) \end{aligned} \tag{26.79}$$

Substituting (26.79) and (26.78) into (26.62) gives

$$\mathrm{E}_T[L_{\delta}(\boldsymbol{\theta})] = \boldsymbol{\Omega}_{\delta}' \, \mathrm{E}_T[L_{\Omega}(\boldsymbol{\theta})] + \bar{\mathbf{Z}}_{\mathrm{VR}}(\boldsymbol{\delta})' \, (\boldsymbol{\Sigma} \otimes \mathbf{I}_T)^{-1} \, (\mathbf{y}_{\mathrm{V}} - \mathbf{Z}_{\mathrm{VR}} \boldsymbol{\delta})$$

which yields (26.64) in turn.

---

[36] See (G.22).

[37] The matrices $\mathbf{S}_{\gamma}$ and $\mathbf{S}_{\beta}$ are selection matrices containing zeros and ones. They are made up of blocks of the $\mathbf{S}_{\gamma j}$ and $\mathbf{S}_{\beta j}$, $j = 1, \ldots, J$, respectively: $\mathbf{S}_{\gamma} = \operatorname{diag}(\mathbf{S}_{\gamma j})$ and $\mathbf{S}_{\beta} = \operatorname{diag}(\mathbf{S}_{\beta j})$.

To find $\boldsymbol{\Omega}_\delta$, we use (G.24) to write

$$\boldsymbol{\Omega}_\delta \equiv \frac{\partial \operatorname{vec} \boldsymbol{\Omega}}{\partial \boldsymbol{\delta}'} = (\mathbf{I}_{J^2} + \mathbf{T}) \left(\mathbf{I}_J \otimes \boldsymbol{\Gamma}^{-1\prime}\boldsymbol{\Sigma}\right) \frac{\partial \operatorname{vec} \boldsymbol{\Gamma}^{-1}}{\partial \boldsymbol{\delta}'}$$

where the matrix $\mathbf{T}$ is defined in (G.17) as the nonsingular matrix that sets $\mathbf{T} \operatorname{vec} \boldsymbol{\Gamma} = \operatorname{vec}\left(\boldsymbol{\Gamma}'\right)$. Using (26.73),

$$\frac{\partial \operatorname{vec} \boldsymbol{\Gamma}^{-1}}{\partial \boldsymbol{\delta}'} = \left(\boldsymbol{\Gamma}^{-1\prime} \otimes \boldsymbol{\Gamma}^{-1}\right) \mathbf{S}_\gamma$$

Combining these expressions,

$$\begin{aligned} \boldsymbol{\Omega}_\delta &= (\mathbf{I}_{J^2} + \mathbf{T}) \left(\mathbf{I}_J \otimes \boldsymbol{\Gamma}^{-1\prime}\boldsymbol{\Sigma}\right) \left(\boldsymbol{\Gamma}^{-1\prime} \otimes \boldsymbol{\Gamma}^{-1}\right) \mathbf{S}_\gamma \\ &= (\mathbf{I}_{J^2} + \mathbf{T}) \left(\boldsymbol{\Gamma}^{-1\prime} \otimes \boldsymbol{\Omega}\right) \mathbf{S}_\gamma \end{aligned} \tag{26.80}$$

The score for $\boldsymbol{\Sigma}$ in simultaneous equations has the same functional form as the score for $\boldsymbol{\Omega}$ in SUR. This is because $\boldsymbol{\Sigma}$ enters the log-likelihood function (26.61) in the same way that $\boldsymbol{\Omega}$ enters (26.60). Using the chain rule and (26.72),

$$\begin{aligned} \mathrm{E}_T[L_{\boldsymbol{\Sigma}}(\boldsymbol{\theta})] &= \boldsymbol{\Omega}_{\boldsymbol{\Sigma}}' \, \mathrm{E}_T[L_{\boldsymbol{\Omega}}(\boldsymbol{\theta})] \\ &= \left(\boldsymbol{\Gamma}^{-1} \otimes \boldsymbol{\Gamma}^{-1}\right) \left[-\frac{1}{2} \operatorname{vec}\left(\boldsymbol{\Omega}^{-1} - \boldsymbol{\Omega}^{-1} \mathrm{E}_T[\mathbf{v}_t(\boldsymbol{\Pi})\mathbf{v}_t(\boldsymbol{\Pi})']\boldsymbol{\Omega}^{-1}\right)\right] \qquad (26.81) \\ &= -\frac{1}{2} \operatorname{vec}\left\{\boldsymbol{\Gamma}^{-1}\boldsymbol{\Omega}^{-1}\boldsymbol{\Gamma}^{-1\prime}\right. \\ &\quad \left. - \boldsymbol{\Gamma}^{-1}\boldsymbol{\Omega}^{-1}\boldsymbol{\Gamma}^{-1\prime} \mathrm{E}_T[\boldsymbol{\varepsilon}_t(\boldsymbol{\delta})\boldsymbol{\varepsilon}_t(\boldsymbol{\delta})']\boldsymbol{\Gamma}^{-1}\boldsymbol{\Omega}^{-1}\boldsymbol{\Gamma}^{-1\prime}\right\} \\ &= -\frac{1}{2} \operatorname{vec}\left\{\boldsymbol{\Sigma}^{-1} - \boldsymbol{\Sigma}^{-1} \mathrm{E}_T[\boldsymbol{\varepsilon}_t(\boldsymbol{\delta})\boldsymbol{\varepsilon}_t(\boldsymbol{\delta})']\boldsymbol{\Sigma}^{-1}\right\} \qquad (26.82) \end{aligned}$$

where $\mathbf{v}_t(\boldsymbol{\Pi})' \equiv \mathbf{y}_t' - \mathbf{x}_t'\boldsymbol{\Pi}$, because

$$\operatorname{vec} \boldsymbol{\Omega} = \operatorname{vec}(\boldsymbol{\Gamma}^{-1\prime}\boldsymbol{\Sigma}\boldsymbol{\Gamma}^{-1}) = \left(\boldsymbol{\Gamma}^{-1\prime} \otimes \boldsymbol{\Gamma}^{-1\prime}\right) \operatorname{vec} \boldsymbol{\Sigma}$$

so that

$$\boldsymbol{\Omega}_{\boldsymbol{\Sigma}} \equiv \frac{\partial \operatorname{vec} \boldsymbol{\Omega}}{\partial \left(\operatorname{vec} \boldsymbol{\Sigma}\right)'} = \left(\boldsymbol{\Gamma}^{-1\prime} \otimes \boldsymbol{\Gamma}^{-1\prime}\right) \tag{26.83}$$

Thus, this score function is a nonsingular linear transformation of $\mathrm{E}_T[L_{\boldsymbol{\Omega}}(\boldsymbol{\theta})]$ and has the same functional form given the fitted residuals. We also see from (26.82) that

$$\hat{\boldsymbol{\Sigma}}_{\mathrm{FI}}(\boldsymbol{\delta}) = \mathrm{E}_T[\boldsymbol{\varepsilon}_t(\boldsymbol{\delta})\boldsymbol{\varepsilon}_t(\boldsymbol{\delta})'] \tag{26.84}$$

26.7.2 Information Matrix

To derive the information matrix of the normally distributed linear simultaneous-equations model, we begin with the unrestricted linear SUR specification given by the log-likelihood function in (26.60) for which

$$\mathrm{E}_T[L_{\boldsymbol{\pi}}(\boldsymbol{\pi}, \boldsymbol{\Omega})] = \frac{1}{T} \cdot \mathbf{X}_{\mathrm{V}}'(\boldsymbol{\Omega}^{-1} \otimes \mathbf{I}_T) (\mathbf{y}_{\mathrm{V}} - \mathbf{X}_{\mathrm{V}}\boldsymbol{\pi})$$

$$\mathrm{E}_T[L_{\mathbf{\Omega}}(\boldsymbol{\pi}, \mathbf{\Omega})] = \operatorname{vec}\{\mathbf{\Omega}^{-1} - \mathbf{\Omega}^{-1}\,\mathrm{E}_T[\mathbf{v}_t(\mathbf{\Pi})\mathbf{v}_t(\mathbf{\Pi})']\mathbf{\Omega}^{-1}\}$$

According to (26.16), $\mathrm{Var}[\mathbf{y}_\mathrm{V} \mid \mathbf{X}] = \mathbf{\Omega}_0 \otimes \mathbf{I}_T$ so that

$$\begin{aligned}\mathrm{Var}\big[\sqrt{T}\,\mathrm{E}_T[L_\pi(\boldsymbol{\pi}_0, \mathbf{\Omega}_0)] \mid \mathbf{X}\big] &= \frac{1}{T}\cdot \mathbf{X}_\mathrm{V}'(\mathbf{\Omega}_0^{-1} \otimes \mathbf{I}_T)\,\mathrm{Var}[\mathbf{y}_\mathrm{V} \mid \mathbf{X}](\mathbf{\Omega}_0^{-1} \otimes \mathbf{I}_T)\mathbf{X}_\mathrm{V} \\ &= \mathbf{\Omega}_0^{-1} \otimes \mathrm{E}_T[\mathbf{x}_t\mathbf{x}_t'] \end{aligned} \tag{26.85}$$

Also, $\mathrm{E}_T[L_\pi(\boldsymbol{\pi}_0, \mathbf{\Omega}_0)]$ is a linear function of $\mathbf{y}_t' - \mathbf{x}_t'\mathbf{\Pi}_0$ whereas $\mathrm{E}_T[L_{\mathbf{\Omega}}(\boldsymbol{\pi}, \mathbf{\Omega})]$ is a linear function of $\left(\mathbf{y}_t' - \mathbf{x}_t'\mathbf{\Pi}_0\right)\left(\mathbf{y}_t' - \mathbf{x}_t'\mathbf{\Pi}_0\right)'$. Therefore, by the symmetry of the normal distribution and the existence of its moments

$$\mathrm{Cov}\big[\mathrm{E}_T[L_\pi(\boldsymbol{\pi}_0, \mathbf{\Omega}_0)],\ \mathrm{E}_T[L_{\mathbf{\Omega}}(\boldsymbol{\pi}_0, \mathbf{\Omega}_0)] \mid \mathbf{X}\big] = \mathbf{0}$$

We will find the conditional variance of $\sqrt{T}\,\mathrm{E}_T[L_{\mathbf{\Omega}}(\boldsymbol{\pi}_0, \mathbf{\Omega}_0)]$ by taking the expectation of the Hessian term $L_{\mathbf{\Omega}\mathbf{\Omega}}(\boldsymbol{\pi}_0, \mathbf{\Omega}_0)$. In Appendix G, we show that

$$\begin{aligned}\mathrm{E}_T[L_{\mathbf{\Omega}\mathbf{\Omega}}(\boldsymbol{\pi}, \mathbf{\Omega})] = \frac{1}{4}\big\{&(\mathbf{\Omega}^{-1} \otimes \mathbf{\Omega}^{-1}) - (\mathbf{\Omega}^{-1} \otimes \mathbf{\Omega}^{-1}\,\mathrm{E}_T[\mathbf{v}_t(\mathbf{\Pi})\mathbf{v}_t(\mathbf{\Pi})']\mathbf{\Omega}^{-1}) \\ &- (\mathbf{\Omega}^{-1}\,\mathrm{E}_T[\mathbf{v}_t(\mathbf{\Pi})\mathbf{v}_t(\mathbf{\Pi})']\mathbf{\Omega}^{-1} \otimes \mathbf{\Omega}^{-1})\big\}(\mathbf{I}_{J^2} + \mathbf{T})\end{aligned}$$

Therefore, the information identity (Lemma 14.4, p. 302) implies that

$$\mathrm{Var}\big[\sqrt{T}\,\mathrm{E}_T[L_{\mathbf{\Omega}}(\boldsymbol{\pi}_0, \mathbf{\Omega}_0)] \mid \mathbf{X}\big] = \frac{1}{4}\cdot(\mathbf{\Omega}_0^{-1} \otimes \mathbf{\Omega}_0^{-1})(\mathbf{I}_{J^2} + \mathbf{T}) \tag{26.86}$$

If we reduce the parameter vector to a vector $\boldsymbol{\omega}$ of distinct elements of $\mathbf{\Omega}$, then

$$\mathrm{Var}\big[\sqrt{T}\,\mathrm{E}_T[L_\omega(\boldsymbol{\theta}_0)]\big] = \mathrm{Var}\big[\sqrt{T}\,\mathrm{E}_T[\mathbf{S}_\omega' L_{\mathbf{\Omega}}(\boldsymbol{\theta}_0)]\big] = \frac{1}{2}\cdot \mathbf{S}_\omega'(\mathbf{\Omega}_0^{-1} \otimes \mathbf{\Omega}_0^{-1})\mathbf{S}_\omega$$

because the symmetry of $\mathbf{\Omega}$ implies that

$$\mathbf{S}_\omega \equiv \frac{\partial \operatorname{vec}\mathbf{\Omega}}{\partial \boldsymbol{\omega}'} = \frac{\partial \operatorname{vec}\mathbf{\Omega}'}{\partial \boldsymbol{\omega}'} = \mathbf{T}\frac{\partial \operatorname{vec}\mathbf{\Omega}}{\partial \boldsymbol{\omega}'} = \mathbf{T}\mathbf{S}_\omega$$

We apply these results to find the information matrix of the restricted linear simultaneous equations model given by (26.66). Using (26.80), (26.86), and (G.18)–(G.20),

$$\begin{aligned}\mathbf{\Omega}_\delta'\,\mathrm{Var}[\sqrt{T}L_{\mathbf{\Omega}}(\boldsymbol{\theta}_0)]\mathbf{\Omega}_\delta &= \mathbf{S}_\gamma'\left[(\mathbf{\Sigma}_0 \otimes \mathbf{\Omega}_0)^{-1} + (\mathbf{\Gamma}_0^{-1} \otimes \mathbf{I}_\mathrm{K})\mathbf{T}(\mathbf{\Gamma}_0^{-1\prime} \otimes \mathbf{I}_\mathrm{K})\right]\mathbf{S}_\gamma \\ &= \mathbf{S}_\gamma'\left[(\mathbf{\Sigma}_0 \otimes \mathbf{\Omega}_0)^{-1} + (\mathbf{\Gamma}_0^{-1} \otimes \mathbf{\Gamma}_0^{-1\prime})\mathbf{T}\right]\mathbf{S}_\gamma\end{aligned}$$

If we also reduce the parameter vector for covariance parameters to a vector $\boldsymbol{\sigma}$ of distinct elements of $\mathbf{\Sigma}$, then

$$\mathbf{\Omega}_\delta'\,\mathrm{Var}[\sqrt{T}L_{\mathbf{\Omega}}(\boldsymbol{\theta}_0)]\mathbf{\Omega}_\Sigma\mathbf{S}_\sigma = \mathbf{S}_\gamma'\left(\mathbf{\Sigma}_0^{-1} \otimes \mathbf{\Gamma}_0^{-1\prime}\right)\mathbf{S}_\sigma$$

by (26.80) and

$$\mathbf{S}_\sigma'\mathbf{\Omega}_\Sigma'\,\mathrm{Var}[\sqrt{T}L_{\mathbf{\Omega}}(\boldsymbol{\theta})]\mathbf{\Omega}_\Sigma\mathbf{S}_\sigma = \frac{1}{2}\cdot \mathbf{S}_\sigma'(\mathbf{\Sigma}_0^{-1} \otimes \mathbf{\Sigma}_0^{-1})\mathbf{S}_\sigma$$

using (26.83) also. Finally, (26.74) and (26.85) lead to

$$\mathbf{\Pi}_\delta'\,\mathrm{Var}[L_\pi(\boldsymbol{\theta}_0)]\mathbf{\Pi}_\delta = \mathbf{S}_\delta'\{\mathbf{\Sigma}_0^{-1} \otimes \mathrm{E}_T[\bar{\mathbf{z}}_t(\mathbf{\Pi}_0)\bar{\mathbf{z}}_t(\mathbf{\Pi}_0)']\}\mathbf{S}_\delta$$

where

$$\mathbf{S}_{\delta} \equiv \frac{\partial \operatorname{vec}[\boldsymbol{\Gamma}', \mathbf{B}']'}{\partial \boldsymbol{\delta}'} = \operatorname{diag}([\mathbf{S}_{\gamma j}', \mathbf{S}_{\beta j}']'; \quad j = 1, \ldots, J)$$

and $\bar{\mathbf{z}}_t(\boldsymbol{\Pi}_0)' \equiv \left[\mathbf{x}_t'\boldsymbol{\Pi}_0, \mathbf{x}_t'\right]$. Therefore,

$$\mathrm{E}_T[\Im(\boldsymbol{\theta}_0 \,|\, \mathbf{X})] = \begin{bmatrix} \begin{array}{c} \mathbf{S}_\delta'\{\boldsymbol{\Sigma}_0^{-1} \otimes \mathrm{E}_T[\bar{\mathbf{z}}_t(\boldsymbol{\Pi}_0)\bar{\mathbf{z}}_t(\boldsymbol{\Pi}_0)']\}\mathbf{S}_\delta + \\ \mathbf{S}_\gamma'[(\boldsymbol{\Sigma}_0 \otimes \boldsymbol{\Omega}_0')^{-1} + (\boldsymbol{\Gamma}_0^{-1} \otimes \boldsymbol{\Gamma}_0^{-1\prime})\mathbf{T}]\mathbf{S}_\gamma \end{array} & \mathbf{S}_\gamma'[(\boldsymbol{\Sigma}_0 \otimes \boldsymbol{\Gamma}_0')^{-1}\mathbf{S}_\sigma \\ \mathbf{S}_\sigma'(\boldsymbol{\Sigma}_0 \otimes \boldsymbol{\Gamma}_0)^{-1}\mathbf{S}_\gamma & \frac{1}{2} \cdot \mathbf{S}_\sigma'(\boldsymbol{\Sigma}_0^{-1} \otimes \boldsymbol{\Sigma}_0^{-1})\mathbf{S}_\sigma \end{bmatrix}$$

is the sample mean of the conditional information matrix for the linear simultaneous equations model.

26.8 OVERVIEW

1. Seemingly unrelated regressions (SUR) are a set of regression equations with contemporaneous correlation:

$$\mathrm{E}[y_{tj} \,|\, \mathbf{X}] = \mathbf{x}_t'\boldsymbol{\beta}_{0j} \quad \text{and} \quad \mathrm{Cov}[y_{ti}, y_{tj} \,|\, \mathbf{X}] = \omega_{0ij}, \qquad t = 1, \ldots, T \quad j = 1, \ldots, J$$

   Such sets of regression equations arise in econometric models motivated by economic models that specify the simultaneous determination of several endogenous variables through equilibrium or optimization.
2. The SUR system can be estimated using OLS equation by equation provided that $\mathbf{X} \equiv [\mathbf{x}_1, \ldots, \mathbf{x}_T]'$ is full-column rank, but there is a GLS estimator that is generally strictly more efficient. The leading exception is unrestricted models in which every regression includes all of the explanatory variables in $\mathbf{x}_t$. In this case, OLS and GLS are identical.
3. There is some new notation for the analysis of the SUR system: Kronecker products and the vectorization of matrices. We use two ways to write the SUR system: stacked (vectorized) form and matrix form. The former is convenient for studying the estimation of the $\boldsymbol{\beta}_{0j}$ and the latter for $\boldsymbol{\Omega}_0 \equiv [\omega_{0ij}]$.
4. There are several analytical similarities between estimation of the SUR system and estimation of the linear model: estimation of the variance matrix with OLS fitted residuals, feasible GLS, and the likelihood function under a normality assumption.
5. Linear simultaneous equations systems are a generalization of SUR that specifies the conditional expectation of certain linear combinations of the dependent variables:

$$\mathbf{y}_t'\boldsymbol{\gamma}_{0j} + \mathbf{x}_t'\boldsymbol{\beta}_{0j} = \varepsilon_{tj}$$

   where

$$\mathrm{E}[\varepsilon_{tj} \,|\, \mathbf{X}] = 0,$$
$$\mathrm{Cov}[\varepsilon_{ti}, \varepsilon_{tj} \,|\, \mathbf{X}] = \sigma_{0ij}$$

   where $\mathbf{y}_t \equiv [y_{t1}, \ldots, y_{tJ}]'$. If $\boldsymbol{\Gamma}_0 \equiv [\boldsymbol{\gamma}_{01}, \ldots, \boldsymbol{\gamma}_{0J}]$ is nonsingular, we can always transform the structural form of a linear simultaneous system into a linear seemingly unrelated system called the reduced form:

$$\mathbf{y}_t' = \left(-\mathbf{x}_t'\mathbf{B}_0 + \boldsymbol{\varepsilon}_t'\right)\boldsymbol{\Gamma}_0^{-1} = \mathbf{x}_t'\boldsymbol{\Pi}_0 + \mathbf{v}_t'$$

   where

$$\boldsymbol{\Pi}_0 \equiv -\mathbf{B}_0\boldsymbol{\Gamma}_0^{-1} \quad \text{and} \quad \mathbf{v}_t' \equiv \boldsymbol{\varepsilon}_t'\boldsymbol{\Gamma}_0^{-1}$$

6. Identification of simultaneous equations coefficients is a question of recovering the structural parameters from the reduced-form parameters $\mathbf{\Pi}_0$ because they are identified. If there are no restrictions on the structural form then there are many $\mathbf{B}$ and $\mathbf{\Gamma}$ such that $\mathbf{B} + \mathbf{\Pi}_0\mathbf{\Gamma} = \mathbf{0}$ and $\mathbf{B}_0$ and $\mathbf{\Gamma}_0$ are not identified. With normalization and exclusion restrictions, some of the $\boldsymbol{\beta}_{0j}$ and $\boldsymbol{\gamma}_{0j}$ may be identified.
   (a) It is necessary to satisfy the order condition: the number of variables included in the jth equation minus one must be no greater than the number of predetermined variables in the system. This ensures that there are enough variables to estimate the equation with instrumental variables (IV).
   (b) It is necessary and sufficient to satisfy the rank condition: under the restrictions

$$[\,\mathbf{R}_{\gamma j} \quad \mathbf{R}_{\beta j}\,]\begin{bmatrix}\boldsymbol{\gamma}_{0j}\\ \boldsymbol{\beta}_{0j}\end{bmatrix} = \mathbf{r}_j$$

the jth structural equation is identified if and only if

$$\operatorname{rank}\left(\mathbf{R}_{\gamma_j}\mathbf{\Gamma}_0 + \mathbf{R}_{\beta_j}\mathbf{B}_0\right) = J$$

and the system is identified under the restrictions

$$\mathbf{R}_\gamma \operatorname{vec}\mathbf{\Gamma} + \mathbf{R}_\beta \operatorname{vec}\mathbf{B} = \mathbf{r}$$

if and only if

$$\operatorname{rank}\left[\mathbf{R}_\gamma(\mathbf{I}_J \otimes \mathbf{\Gamma}_0) + \mathbf{R}_\beta(\mathbf{I}_J \otimes \mathbf{B}_0)\right] = J^2$$

7. Limited-information estimation uses restrictions on the parameters of one structural equation. The limited-information GMM estimator of a single structural equation is the two-stage least-squares (2SLS) estimator. Full-information estimation uses restrictions on the entire simultaneous system efficiently. If we write the restricted system as

$$\mathbf{y} = \mathbf{Z}_{\text{VR}}\boldsymbol{\delta}_0 + \boldsymbol{\varepsilon}$$

where

$$\text{E}[\boldsymbol{\varepsilon} \mid \mathbf{X}] = \mathbf{0}$$
$$\text{Var}[\boldsymbol{\varepsilon} \mid \mathbf{X}] = \mathbf{\Sigma} \otimes \mathbf{I}_T$$

then the full-information GMM estimator is the three-stage least-squares (3SLS) estimator

$$\hat{\boldsymbol{\delta}}_{3\text{SLS}} = \left[\mathbf{Z}_{\text{VR}}'(\hat{\mathbf{\Sigma}}_{2\text{SLS}}^{-1} \otimes \mathbf{P}_{\mathbf{X}})\mathbf{Z}_{\text{VR}}\right]^{-1} \mathbf{Z}_{\text{VR}}'(\hat{\mathbf{\Sigma}}_{2\text{SLS}}^{-1} \otimes \mathbf{P}_{\mathbf{X}})\mathbf{y}_{\text{V}}$$

where

$$\hat{\mathbf{\Sigma}}_{2\text{SLS}} \equiv \hat{\mathbf{\Sigma}}(\hat{\boldsymbol{\delta}}_{2\text{SLS}})$$
$$\hat{\mathbf{\Sigma}}(\boldsymbol{\delta}) \equiv \text{E}_T[\boldsymbol{\varepsilon}_t(\boldsymbol{\delta})\boldsymbol{\varepsilon}_t(\boldsymbol{\delta})']$$

and

$$\boldsymbol{\varepsilon}_t(\boldsymbol{\delta}) \equiv \mathbf{\Gamma}'\mathbf{y}_t + \mathbf{B}'\mathbf{x}_t$$

8. Under the additional assumption of conditionally normally distributed $\boldsymbol{\varepsilon}_t$, the full-information maximum-likelihood (FIML) estimator is the implicit function

$$\hat{\boldsymbol{\delta}}_{\text{FI}} = \hat{\boldsymbol{\delta}}(\hat{\boldsymbol{\delta}}_{\text{FI}}, \hat{\mathbf{\Sigma}}_{\text{FI}}) \qquad \text{and} \qquad \hat{\mathbf{\Sigma}}_{\text{FI}} \equiv \hat{\mathbf{\Sigma}}(\hat{\boldsymbol{\delta}}_{\text{FI}})$$

where

$$\hat{\delta}(\delta, \Sigma) \equiv \left[\bar{\mathbf{Z}}_{\mathrm{VR}}(\delta)' (\Sigma \otimes \mathbf{I}_T]^{-1} \mathbf{Z}_{\mathrm{VR}}\right)^{-1} \bar{\mathbf{Z}}_{\mathrm{VR}}(\delta)' (\Sigma_{\mathrm{V}} \otimes \mathbf{I}_T)^{-1} \mathbf{y}_{\mathrm{V}}$$

and $\bar{\mathbf{Z}}_{\mathrm{VR}}(\delta)$ is the explanatory variable matrix $\mathbf{Z}_{\mathrm{VR}}$ after the endogenous $\mathbf{y}_t'$ have been replaced by their fitted values $\mathbf{x}_t'\mathbf{B}\Gamma^{-1}$. The FIML estimator has the functional form of an IV estimator so that plugging $\sqrt{T}$-consistent estimators of δ_0 and Σ_0 into $\hat{\delta}(\delta, \Sigma)$ produces asymptotically equivalent estimators. The GMM estimator is one example.

9. One can test all of the overidentifying restrictions of the simultaneous system of equations with the Wald, LR, or score test statistics. It is also natural to test in the limited-information setting whether subsets of variables are valid instruments. Alternatively, Hausman specification tests provide a formal way to compare 2SLS and 3SLS estimators for structural parameters. One may expect the 2SLS estimator to be robust to misspecifications of the system that cause inconsistency in the 3SLS estimator.

26.9 EXERCISES

26.9.1 Review

26.1 (Demand Systems) Reconsider the variance matrix of the translog equations (26.4)–(26.6). As a starting point, suppose that the shares have a constant variance matrix:

$$\mathrm{Var}\left[\begin{bmatrix} s_{\mathrm{L}} \\ s_{\mathrm{K}} \end{bmatrix} \middle| \frac{p_{\mathrm{L}}}{p_{\mathrm{F}}}, \frac{p_{\mathrm{K}}}{p_{\mathrm{F}}}, Q\right] = \begin{bmatrix} \omega_{\mathrm{LL}} & \omega_{\mathrm{LK}} \\ \omega_{\mathrm{LK}} & \omega_{\mathrm{KK}} \end{bmatrix}$$

(a) Given that $s_{\mathrm{L}} + s_{\mathrm{K}} + s_{\mathrm{F}} = 1$, find the variance matrix of a vector of all the shares: $\mathbf{s} \equiv [s_{\mathrm{L}}, s_{\mathrm{K}}, s_{\mathrm{F}}]'$. Show that SUR/GLS can drop any one share from the system without affecting the estimators of linear regression coefficients. [HINT: Recall Lemma 10.7 (p. 213), which states that quadratic forms $\mathbf{z}'\mathbf{A}^{-}\mathbf{z}$ are invariant to the choice of generalized inverse $\mathbf{A}^{-}$.]

(b) Let

$$\mathrm{E}[s_{\mathrm{L}} \mid \frac{p_{\mathrm{L}}}{p_{\mathrm{F}}}, \frac{p_{\mathrm{K}}}{p_{\mathrm{F}}}, Q] = \beta_{\mathrm{L}} + \gamma_{\mathrm{LL}} \log \frac{p_{\mathrm{L}}}{p_{\mathrm{F}}} + \gamma_{\mathrm{LK}} \log \frac{p_{\mathrm{K}}}{p_{\mathrm{F}}} + \gamma_{\mathrm{LQ}} \log Q$$

$$\mathrm{E}[s_{\mathrm{K}} \mid \frac{p_{\mathrm{L}}}{p_{\mathrm{F}}}, \frac{p_{\mathrm{K}}}{p_{\mathrm{F}}}, Q] = \beta_{\mathrm{K}} + \gamma_{\mathrm{LK}} \log \frac{p_{\mathrm{L}}}{p_{\mathrm{F}}} + \gamma_{\mathrm{KK}} \log \frac{p_{\mathrm{K}}}{p_{\mathrm{F}}} + \gamma_{\mathrm{KQ}} \log Q$$

so that

$$\begin{aligned}\mathrm{E}[s_{\mathrm{F}} \mid \frac{p_{\mathrm{L}}}{p_{\mathrm{F}}}, \frac{p_{\mathrm{K}}}{p_{\mathrm{F}}}, Q] &= \beta_{\mathrm{F}} + \gamma_{\mathrm{FK}} \log \frac{p_{\mathrm{L}}}{p_{\mathrm{F}}} + \gamma_{\mathrm{FK}} \log \frac{p_{\mathrm{K}}}{p_{\mathrm{F}}} + \gamma_{\mathrm{FQ}} \log Q \\ &= (1 - \beta_{\mathrm{L}} - \beta_{\mathrm{K}}) - (\gamma_{\mathrm{LL}} + \gamma_{\mathrm{LK}}) \log \frac{p_{\mathrm{L}}}{p_{\mathrm{F}}} \\ &\quad - (\gamma_{\mathrm{LK}} + \gamma_{\mathrm{KK}}) \log \frac{p_{\mathrm{K}}}{p_{\mathrm{F}}} - (\gamma_{\mathrm{LQ}} + \gamma_{\mathrm{KQ}}) \log Q\end{aligned}$$

Show that the OLS fitted coefficients from fitting each of the shares to the explanatory variables satisfy these restrictions: the intercepts sum to one and the other coefficients sum to zero.

(c) Give the share equations a latent variable specification:

$$s_{\mathrm{L}} = \beta_{\mathrm{L}} + \gamma_{\mathrm{LL}} \log \frac{p_{\mathrm{L}}}{p_{\mathrm{F}}} + \gamma_{\mathrm{LK}} \log \frac{p_{\mathrm{K}}}{p_{\mathrm{F}}} + \gamma_{\mathrm{LQ}} \log Q + \varepsilon_{\mathrm{L}}$$

$$s_{\mathrm{K}} = \beta_{\mathrm{K}} + \gamma_{\mathrm{LK}} \log \frac{p_{\mathrm{L}}}{p_{\mathrm{F}}} + \gamma_{\mathrm{KK}} \log \frac{p_{\mathrm{K}}}{p_{\mathrm{F}}} + \gamma_{\mathrm{KQ}} \log Q + \varepsilon_{\mathrm{K}}$$

where

$$\mathrm{E}\left[\begin{bmatrix}\varepsilon_{\mathrm{L}}\\ \varepsilon_{\mathrm{K}}\end{bmatrix}\middle|\frac{p_{\mathrm{L}}}{p_{\mathrm{F}}},\frac{p_{\mathrm{K}}}{p_{\mathrm{F}}},Q\right]=\begin{bmatrix}0\\0\end{bmatrix}$$

and

$$\mathrm{Var}\left[\begin{bmatrix}\varepsilon_{\mathrm{L}}\\ \varepsilon_{\mathrm{K}}\end{bmatrix}\middle|\frac{p_{\mathrm{L}}}{p_{\mathrm{F}}},\frac{p_{\mathrm{K}}}{p_{\mathrm{F}}},Q\right]=\begin{bmatrix}\omega_{\mathrm{LL}} & \omega_{\mathrm{LK}}\\ \omega_{\mathrm{LK}} & \omega_{\mathrm{KK}}\end{bmatrix}$$

Use Shephard's (1953) lemma to motivate an error-components specification for the latent disturbance u in the log-cost equation

$$\begin{aligned}\log\frac{C}{p_{\mathrm{F}}} &= \alpha+\beta_{\mathrm{L}}\log\frac{p_{\mathrm{L}}}{p_{\mathrm{F}}}+\beta_{\mathrm{K}}\log\frac{p_{\mathrm{K}}}{p_{\mathrm{F}}}+\beta_{\mathrm{Q}}\log Q\\ &\quad+\frac{1}{2}\gamma_{\mathrm{LL}}\left(\log\frac{p_{\mathrm{L}}}{p_{\mathrm{F}}}\right)^2+\gamma_{\mathrm{LK}}\log\frac{p_{\mathrm{L}}}{p_{\mathrm{F}}}\log\frac{p_{\mathrm{K}}}{p_{\mathrm{F}}}+\frac{1}{2}\gamma_{\mathrm{LL}}\left(\log\frac{p_{\mathrm{K}}}{p_{\mathrm{F}}}\right)^2\\ &\quad+\gamma_{\mathrm{LQ}}\log\frac{p_{\mathrm{L}}}{p_{\mathrm{F}}}\log Q+\gamma_{\mathrm{KQ}}\log\frac{p_{\mathrm{K}}}{p_{\mathrm{F}}}\log Q+\gamma_{\mathrm{QQ}}(\log Q)^2+u\end{aligned}$$

Show how this yields a variance-components model of conditional heteroskedasticity.

(d) Describe a consistent estimator of the conditional variance matrix of $[u, \varepsilon_{\mathrm{L}}, \varepsilon_{\mathrm{K}}]'$ based on OLS fitted residuals.

26.2 (OLS versus GLS) Consider a two-equation SUR system in which the first equation contains all of the explanatory variables in the second, and some additional explanatory variables as well. Let

$$\begin{aligned}y_{t1} &= \mathbf{z}_t'\boldsymbol{\alpha}_1+\mathbf{w}_t'\boldsymbol{\alpha}_2+\varepsilon_{t1}\\ y_{t2} &= \mathbf{z}_t'\boldsymbol{\beta}_2+\varepsilon_{t2}\end{aligned}$$

so that $\mathbf{X}_1 = [\mathbf{Z}, \mathbf{W}]$ and $\mathbf{X}_2 = \mathbf{Z}$. Suppose that the conditional variance matrix of $(\varepsilon_{t1}, \varepsilon_{t2})$, given $\mathbf{Z}$ and $\mathbf{W}$, is known.

(a) Using Gram–Schmidt orthogonalization, transform this SUR system into

$$\begin{aligned}y_{t1}-\gamma_0 y_{t2} &= \mathbf{z}_t'\boldsymbol{\delta}_1+\mathbf{w}_t'\boldsymbol{\alpha}_2+u_{t1}\\ y_{t2} &= \mathbf{z}_t'\boldsymbol{\beta}_2+u_{t2}\end{aligned}$$

where $\boldsymbol{\delta}_1 = \boldsymbol{\alpha}_1-\gamma_0\cdot\boldsymbol{\beta}_2$, such that $\mathrm{Cov}(u_{t1}, u_{t2}|\mathbf{z}_t, \mathbf{w}_t) = 0$ and $\mathrm{Var}(u_{t1}|\mathbf{z}_t, \mathbf{w}_t) \le \mathrm{Var}(\varepsilon_{t1}|\mathbf{z}_t, \mathbf{w}_t)$.

(b) Show directly that the OLS estimator of $\boldsymbol{\alpha}_2$ in the first equation of the transformed system has a smaller variance matrix than OLS applied to the first equation of the original system.

26.3 (Kronecker Product) Using Definition G.4 (Kronecker Product, p. 925), show that

$$(\mathbf{A}\otimes\mathbf{B})(\mathbf{C}\otimes\mathbf{D}) = \mathbf{AC}\otimes A\mathbf{BD}, \tag{26.87}$$

$$(\mathbf{A}\otimes\mathbf{B})^{-1} = \mathbf{A}^{-1}\otimes\mathbf{B}^{-1}, \tag{26.88}$$

$$(\mathbf{A}\otimes\mathbf{B})' = \mathbf{A}'\otimes\mathbf{B}', \tag{26.89}$$

$$\mathbf{A}\otimes(\mathbf{B}+\mathbf{C}) = (\mathbf{A}\otimes\mathbf{B})+(\mathbf{A}\otimes\mathbf{C}) \tag{26.90}$$

26.4 (SUR Sufficient Statistics) Show that the SUR log-likelihood function, (26.30) or (26.33), depends on the data only through the (sufficient) statistics $\mathbf{Y}'\mathbf{Y}$, $\mathbf{X}'\mathbf{Y}$, and $\mathbf{X}'\mathbf{X}$. [Hint: Recall from Exercise 8.8 that $\boldsymbol{\varepsilon}'\boldsymbol{\Omega}^{-1}\boldsymbol{\varepsilon} = \mathrm{tr}(\boldsymbol{\varepsilon}'\boldsymbol{\Omega}^{-1}\boldsymbol{\varepsilon}) = \mathrm{tr}(\boldsymbol{\Omega}^{-1}\boldsymbol{\varepsilon}\boldsymbol{\varepsilon}')$.]

26.5 **(Kronecker Products)** Given (26.17), show that the conditional variance matrix of $[\mathbf{y}_t';\ t = 1, \ldots, T]'$, where $\mathbf{y}_t = [y_{tj};\ j = 1, \ldots, J]'$, is $\mathbf{I}_T \otimes \mathbf{\Omega}$.

26.6 **(SUR)** Consider the special restricted SUR system where $\mathbf{X}_j = [\mathbf{X}_{j-1}, \mathbf{x}_j]$ and $\mathbf{x}_j$ is the jth explanatory variable in an unrestricted system. Show that under the assumption of conditional normality the MLE of $\boldsymbol{\beta}_0$ can be computed recursively by OLS, beginning with the OLS regression of $\mathbf{y}_1$ on $\mathbf{X}_1$ to compute $\hat{\boldsymbol{\beta}}_1$, followed by regressing y_j on $\mathbf{X}_j$ and $\hat{\boldsymbol{\varepsilon}}_1, \ldots, \hat{\boldsymbol{\varepsilon}}_{j-1}$ to obtain $\hat{\boldsymbol{\beta}}_j$ for $j = 2, 3, \ldots, J$, where $\hat{\boldsymbol{\varepsilon}}_j$ denotes the residual vector $\mathbf{y}_j - \mathbf{X}_j\hat{\boldsymbol{\beta}}_j$. How can you compute the MLE of $\mathbf{\Omega}_0$ from the coefficients on the residuals and the estimated variances for each regression?

26.7 **(SUR)** For the SUR system, find the expectation of the elements of $\mathrm{E}_T[\boldsymbol{\varepsilon}_t(\hat{\mathbf{B}}_{\mathrm{OLS}})\boldsymbol{\varepsilon}_t(\hat{\mathbf{B}}_{\mathrm{OLS}})']$. How can one compute an unbiased estimator of ω_{0ij}?

26.8 **(SUR Concentration)** Concentrate the variance matrix $\mathbf{\Omega}$ out of the SUR log-likelihood function, (26.30) or (26.33).

26.9 **(OLS versus GLS)** We have seen in (26.22) that OLS and GLS are identical for the SUR system if every regression equation contains the same explanatory variables. Show more generally that OLS equals GLS in SUR if

$$\mathrm{Col}(\mathbf{XS}_1) = \mathrm{Col}(\mathbf{XS}_2) = \cdots = \mathrm{Col}(\mathbf{XS}_J)$$

where $\mathbf{XS}_j$ contains the explanatory variables in the jth regression.

26.10 **(R^2)** In a study of a market model, the researcher reports the R^2 goodness of fit for the demand and supply equations, 0.312 and 0.320, respectively, estimated by 2SLS. He comments that these "fits" are not particularly good. Discuss the merits of the R^2 as a goodness-of-fit meausure. (HINT: When the LHS variable of the supply equation is changed by renormalization from the market price to the market quantity, the R^2 becomes -3.06.)

26.11 **(Recursive System)** A *recursive* simultaneous system has a triangular $\mathbf{\Gamma}$ and diagonal $\mathbf{\Sigma}$.

(a) Show that every simultaneous system can be written as a recursive system.

(b) Prove that a recursive simultaneous system can be estimated efficiently by applying OLS to each structural equation. (HINT: Show that

$$\mathbf{S}_\gamma \ \mathrm{vec}\, \mathbf{\Gamma}'^{-1}\mathbf{\Sigma} = \mathbf{0}$$

in this case.)

(c) Can every simultaneous system be estimated efficiently by OLS using these two results? Explain your answer.

26.12 **(Rank Condition)** Consider the case of two linear simultaneous equations ($J = 2$) with two exogenous variables ($K = 2$):

$$y_1\gamma_{11} + y_2\gamma_{21} + x_1\beta_{11} + x_2\beta_{21} = u_1$$

$$y_1\gamma_{12} + y_2\gamma_{22} + x_1\beta_{12} + x_2\beta_{22} = u_2$$

where

$$u = \begin{bmatrix} u_1 \\ u_2 \end{bmatrix} \sim \mathfrak{N}\left(\begin{bmatrix} 0 \\ 0 \end{bmatrix}, \begin{bmatrix} \sigma_{11} & \sigma_{12} \\ \sigma_{12} & \sigma_{22} \end{bmatrix}\right)$$

(a) Write this system in matrix notation.

(b) Write this system in stacked-vector notation.
Show how to use the rank condition for system identification (Proposition 27, p. 717) when there is a set of restrictions $\mathbf{R}_\gamma \operatorname{vec} \mathbf{\Gamma} + \mathbf{R}_\beta \operatorname{vec} \mathbf{B} = \mathbf{r}$.

(c) Let the restrictions be

$$\gamma_{11} = \gamma_{22} = 1$$
$$\gamma_{12} = \gamma_{21} = 0$$

which correspond to the SUR specification.

(d) Let the restrictions be

$$\gamma_{11} = \gamma_{22} = 1$$
$$\beta_{12} = \beta_{21} = 0$$

so that a different exogenous variable is omitted from each structural equation.

(e) Let the restrictions be

$$\gamma_{11} = \gamma_{22} = 1$$
$$\beta_{21} = \beta_{22} = 0$$

so that x_2 does not actually appear in the system.

(f) Let the restrictions be

$$\gamma_{11} = \gamma_{22} = 1$$
$$\beta_{11} = \beta_{21} = 0$$

so that neither x_1 nor x_2 appears in the first equation.

(g) Let the restrictions be

$$\gamma_{11} = \gamma_{22} = 1$$
$$\gamma_{12} = \gamma_{21}$$
$$\beta_{11} = \beta_{12}$$

so that $\mathbf{\Gamma}$ is constrained to be symmetric and the coefficient of x_1 is the same in both equations. These are cross-equation restrictions.

26.13 (Rank Condition) Let us denote a general set of linear restrictions on the coefficients of a simultaneous system by

$$\begin{bmatrix} \underset{(JK+J^2-M)\times JK}{\mathbf{R}_\beta} & \underset{(JK+J^2-M)\times J^2}{\mathbf{R}_\gamma} \end{bmatrix} \begin{bmatrix} \underset{JK\times 1}{\boldsymbol{\beta}} \\ \underset{J^2\times 1}{\boldsymbol{\gamma}} \end{bmatrix} = \underset{(JK+J^2-M)\times 1}{\mathbf{r}}, \tag{26.91}$$

where $\boldsymbol{\beta} \equiv \operatorname{vec} \mathbf{B}$ and $\gamma \equiv \operatorname{vec} \mathbf{\Gamma}$ are vectors formed by stacking the successive columns of their matrix counterparts, so that there are M unknown slope parameters in the restricted model, or $JK + J^2 - M$ restrictions.

(a) Show that one may rewrite (26.46) in the stacked-vector form

$$\boldsymbol{\beta} - \underset{JK\times J^2}{(\mathbf{I}_J \otimes \mathbf{\Pi}_0)}\, \boldsymbol{\gamma} = [\, \mathbf{I}_{JK} \quad -\mathbf{I}_J \otimes \mathbf{\Pi}_0 \,] \begin{bmatrix} \boldsymbol{\beta} \\ \boldsymbol{\gamma} \end{bmatrix} = \mathbf{0} \tag{26.92}$$

Combine (26.91) and (26.92) into one system of linear equations for $\boldsymbol{\beta}$ and $\boldsymbol{\gamma}$.

(b) Using this system of linear equations for $\boldsymbol{\beta}$ and $\boldsymbol{\gamma}$, show that the order condition for system identification requires at least J^2 restrictions for all of the parameters in the system to be identified.

(c) Prove Proposition 27 (System Rank Condition, p. 717).

26.14 (Rank Condition) In the case of linear exclusion restrictions on the simultaneous-equations structural coefficient vector $\boldsymbol{\delta}$, show that the rank condition for system identification implies that $\mathrm{E}[\bar{\mathbf{Z}}_{\mathrm{VR}}(\boldsymbol{\delta}_0)' (\boldsymbol{\Sigma}_0 \otimes \mathbf{I}_T)^{-1}\mathbf{Z}_{\mathrm{VR}}]$ is full rank.

26.15 (3SLS) Show how to compute the 3SLS estimator with software for SUR. Would the resultant estimator for the sampling variance of 3SLS be consistent?

26.16 (3SLS) Show that the 3SLS estimator is an LMLE.

26.17 (ILS) Suppose that a system of linear simultaneous equations is exactly identified by normalization and exclusion restrictions.

(a) Show that the ILS and FIML estimators are identical.

(b) Also, explain the equivalence of the LIML estimator applied equation by equation.

(c) Finally, show that ILS and 2SLS equation by equation are identical.

(d) How would your answers change if there were restrictions that involved parameters from several structural equations?

26.18 (Adaptive Estimation) Consider FIML estimation of a linear simultaneous system with normally distributed disturbances. Suppose that identification rests on linear restrictions on the structural coefficients. Show that the information matrix is not block-diagonal in the coefficients and the covariance parameters in $\boldsymbol{\Sigma}$. Also resolve the following paradox: the relatively efficient 3SLS estimator $\hat{\boldsymbol{\delta}}_{3\mathrm{SLS}}$ can employ the inefficient estimator $\hat{\boldsymbol{\Sigma}}_{2\mathrm{SLS}}$ of $\boldsymbol{\Sigma}_0$. Explain this paradox.

26.19 (Exogeneity Test) Consider Hausman's (1978) exogeneity test comparing 2SLS with 3SLS. Suppose that $\mathbf{X}_2$ is a matrix of questionable instrumental variables, where $\mathbf{X} = [\mathbf{X}_1, \mathbf{X}_2]$ is the matrix of all predetermined variables in the simultaneous equations system.

(a) Confirm that one can write the 2SLS estimators for the entire system in stacked form as

$$\begin{aligned}\hat{\boldsymbol{\delta}}_{2SLS} &= \left[\mathbf{S}_\delta' \left(\mathbf{I}_J \otimes \mathbf{Z}'\mathbf{P}_\mathbf{X}\mathbf{Z}\right)\mathbf{S}_\delta\right]^{-1} \mathbf{S}_\delta' \left(\mathbf{I}_J \otimes \mathbf{Z}'\mathbf{P}_\mathbf{X}\right)\mathbf{y}_\mathrm{V} \\ &= \left(\hat{\mathbf{Z}}_{\mathrm{VR}}'\hat{\mathbf{Z}}_{\mathrm{VR}}\right)^{-1}\hat{\mathbf{Z}}_{\mathrm{VR}}'\mathbf{y}_\mathrm{V}\end{aligned}$$

where $\mathbf{Z} \equiv [\mathbf{Y}, \mathbf{X}]$, $\hat{\mathbf{Z}} \equiv \mathbf{P}_\mathbf{X}\mathbf{Z}$, and $\hat{\mathbf{Z}}_{\mathrm{VR}} \equiv \left(\mathbf{I}_J \otimes \hat{\mathbf{Z}}\right)\mathbf{S}_\delta$.

(b) What is the 2SLS estimator if one omits $\mathbf{X}_2$ from the list of predetermined variables? Are there any potential problems with this estimator?

(c) Is it necessary to compare estimates in an equation that excludes $\mathbf{X}_2$ as an explanatory variable? Explain your answer.

26.20 (VAR) Solve (25.62) for the stationary variance matrix of the transition equation of a state-space model

$$\mathbf{z}_t = \mathbf{A}\mathbf{z}_{t-1} + \mathbf{w}_t$$

to show that

$$\mathrm{vec}(\mathrm{Var}[\mathbf{z}_t]) = \left[\mathbf{I} - (\mathbf{A} \otimes \mathbf{A})\right]^{-1} \mathrm{vec}(\mathrm{Var}[\mathbf{w}_t])$$

26.21 (Panel Data) Using Kronecker products, find an expression for the variance matrix $\text{Var}[\mathbf{y} \mid \mathbf{X}]$ in (24.13).

26.22 (LSDV) Reconsider the panel data model in Section 24.5.2 containing both fixed effects for all time periods and all individuals. Using the following steps, show that the LSDV fitted coefficients for $\boldsymbol{\beta}_0$ are the OLS coefficients from fitting $y_{nt} - \bar{y}_n - \bar{y}_t + \bar{\bar{y}}$ to $\mathbf{x}_{nt} - \bar{\mathbf{x}}_n - \bar{\mathbf{x}}_t + \bar{\bar{\mathbf{x}}}$ where $\bar{y}_n$ denotes the sample mean of y_{nt} for individual n, and $\bar{\bar{y}}$ denotes the sample mean of y_{nt} over all observations $n = 1, \ldots, N,\ t = 1, \ldots, T$.

(a) Show that the column space of the fixed effects is spanned by the columns of $[\iota_T \otimes \mathbf{I}_N,\ \mathbf{I}_T \otimes \iota_N]$.

(b) Let $\mathbf{Z}_1 = \iota_T \otimes \mathbf{I}_N$, $\mathbf{Z}_2 = \mathbf{I}_T \otimes \iota_N$, and $\mathbf{Z} = [\mathbf{Z}_1, \mathbf{Z}_2]$ and find the orthogonal projection matrix $\mathbf{P}_\mathbf{Z}$ with the partitioned projection formula (3.25)[38]

$$\mathbf{P}_\mathbf{Z} = \mathbf{P}_{\mathbf{Z}_2} - \mathbf{P}_{(\mathbf{I}-\mathbf{P}_{\mathbf{Z}_2})\mathbf{Z}_1}$$

i. Show that $\mathbf{P}_{\mathbf{Z}_2} = \mathbf{I}_T \otimes \mathbf{P}_{\iota_N}$.

ii. Show that $\left(\mathbf{I} - \mathbf{P}_{\mathbf{Z}_2}\right)\mathbf{Z}_1 = \iota_T \otimes \left(\mathbf{I}_N - \mathbf{P}_{\iota_N}\right)$.

iii. Show that generally $\mathbf{P}_{\mathbf{A}_1 \otimes \mathbf{A}_2} = \mathbf{P}_{\mathbf{A}_1} \otimes \mathbf{P}_{\mathbf{A}_2}$.

iv. Use the previous result to show that $\mathbf{P}_{\iota_T \otimes (\mathbf{I}_N - \mathbf{P}_{\iota_N})} = \left(\mathbf{P}_{\iota_T} \otimes \mathbf{I}_N\right) - \mathbf{P}_{\iota_T} \otimes \mathbf{P}_{\iota_N}$.

(c) Finally, show that an element of $(\mathbf{I} - \mathbf{P}_\mathbf{Z})\,\mathbf{y}$ is $y_{nt} - \bar{y}_n - \bar{y}_t + \bar{\bar{y}}$.

26.23 (Random-Effects GLS) Reconsider the panel data model in Section 25.4.2 containing both random effects for all time periods and all individuals. Use the following steps and the example in Section 24.9 to confirm the GLS transformation $y_{nt*} = y_{nt} - \omega_{01}\bar{y}_n - \omega_{02}\bar{y}_t + \omega_{03}\bar{\bar{y}}$ and to find the ωs.

(a) Show that

$$\text{Var}[\mathbf{y} \mid \mathbf{X}, \mathbf{Z}, \mathbf{R}] = \sigma_{0\alpha}^2 \cdot \left(\iota_T \iota_T' \otimes \mathbf{I}_N\right) + \sigma_{0\lambda}^2 \cdot \left(\mathbf{I}_T \otimes \iota_N \iota_N'\right) + \sigma_{0\varepsilon}^2 \cdot \mathbf{I}_{NT}$$

(b) Let

$$\mathbf{J}_T = \iota_T \iota_T' \otimes \mathbf{I}_N, \qquad \mathbf{J}_N = \mathbf{I}_T \otimes \iota_N \iota_N'$$
$$\mathbf{J}_{NT} = \iota_T \iota_T' \otimes \iota_N \iota_N' = \iota_{NT} \iota_{NT}'$$

Confirm that

$$\begin{aligned}
&[a_1 \cdot \mathbf{J}_{NT} + a_2 \cdot (\mathbf{J}_T \otimes \mathbf{I}_N) + a_3 \cdot (\mathbf{I}_T \otimes \mathbf{J}_N) + a_4 \cdot \mathbf{I}_{NT}] \\
&\quad \times [b_1 \cdot \mathbf{J}_{NT} + b_2 \cdot (\mathbf{J}_T \otimes \mathbf{I}_N) + b_3 \cdot (\mathbf{I}_T \otimes \mathbf{J}_N) + b_4 \cdot \mathbf{I}_{NT}] \\
&= c_1 \cdot \mathbf{J}_{NT} + c_2 \cdot (\mathbf{J}_T \otimes \mathbf{I}_N) + c_3 \cdot (\mathbf{J}_T \otimes \mathbf{I}_N) + c_4 \cdot \mathbf{I}_{NT}
\end{aligned}$$

and find the cs in terms of the as and bs.

(c) Use this intermediate result to find

$$[a_1 \cdot \mathbf{J}_{NT} + a_2 \cdot (\mathbf{J}_T \otimes \mathbf{I}_N) + a_3 \cdot (\mathbf{I}_T \otimes \mathbf{J}_N) + a_4 \cdot \mathbf{I}_{NT}]^{-1}$$

and

$$[b_1 \cdot J_{NT} + b_2 \cdot (\mathbf{J}_T \otimes \mathbf{I}_N) + b_3 \cdot (\mathbf{I}_T \otimes \mathbf{J}_N) + b_4 \cdot \mathbf{I}_{NT}]^2$$

(d) Find the ωs using these expressions.

(e) Show that if $N = cT$, $c > 0$, and $N \to \infty$, then the GLS estimator is asymptotically equivalent to the LSDV estimator.[39]

---

[38] See Exercises 3.16 and 3.17.

[39] See Wallace and Hussain (1969).

(f) How could you consistently estimate the ωs for FGLS estimation?

26.24 (Equation Identification) Consider the identification of the coefficients in the first equation of a simultaneous system partitioned as follows:

$$\mathbf{y}_t' \begin{bmatrix} \underset{G_1\times 1}{\boldsymbol{\gamma}_{011}} & \underset{G_1\times(J-1)}{\boldsymbol{\Gamma}_{012}} \\ \underset{(J-G_1)\times 1}{\boldsymbol{\gamma}_{021}} & \underset{(J-G_1)\times(J-1)}{\boldsymbol{\Gamma}_{022}} \end{bmatrix} + \mathbf{x}_t' \begin{bmatrix} \underset{K_1\times 1}{\boldsymbol{\beta}_{011}} & \underset{K_1\times(J-1)}{\mathbf{B}_{012}} \\ \underset{(K-K_1)\times 1}{\boldsymbol{\beta}_{021}} & \underset{(K-K_1)\times(J-1)}{\mathbf{B}_{022}} \end{bmatrix} = \boldsymbol{\varepsilon}_t'$$

Let the restrictions on the first equation be the exclusion restrictions that $\boldsymbol{\gamma}_{021} = \mathbf{0}$ and $\boldsymbol{\beta}_{021} = \mathbf{0}$ and the normalization that the first element of $\boldsymbol{\gamma}_{011}$ equals 1. Show that the rank condition (Proposition 26) for identification is equivalent to the condition that

$$\text{rank}\left(\begin{bmatrix} \boldsymbol{\Gamma}_{022} \\ \mathbf{B}_{022} \end{bmatrix}\right) = J - 1$$

Why does this condition for identification of the *first* equation involve the parameters of the *other* structural equations in the system?

26.9.2 Extensions

26.25 (Jacobian) Econometricians often refer to the terms

$$-\frac{1}{2}\log\det(2\pi \cdot \boldsymbol{\Sigma}) + \log|\det \boldsymbol{\Gamma}|$$

in the log-likelihood function (26.61) of the simultaneous equations system as the *Jacobian* terms. Using the change-of-variables formula for $\mathbf{y}_t$ as a function of $\boldsymbol{\varepsilon}_t$, show how these terms arise from the Jacobian of the transformation.

26.26 (MD) Consider the minimum distance estimator

$$\hat{\boldsymbol{\gamma}}_{\text{MD}} = \underset{\boldsymbol{\gamma}}{\text{argmin}} \left[\hat{\boldsymbol{\theta}} - \mathbf{s}(\boldsymbol{\gamma})\right]' \hat{\mathbf{V}}_\theta \left[\hat{\boldsymbol{\theta}} - \mathbf{s}(\boldsymbol{\gamma})\right]$$

where $\hat{\mathbf{V}}_\theta$ is a consistent estimator of the asymptotic variance of $\hat{\boldsymbol{\theta}}$. We may generalize this estimator by considering a one-to-one differentiable transformation of the statistic $\hat{\boldsymbol{\theta}}$: $\boldsymbol{\tau}(\hat{\boldsymbol{\theta}}, \boldsymbol{\gamma})$ such that

$$\boldsymbol{\tau}(\hat{\boldsymbol{\theta}}, \boldsymbol{\gamma}_0) \xrightarrow{p} \mathbf{0}$$

and

$$\sqrt{N}\boldsymbol{\tau}(\hat{\boldsymbol{\theta}}, \boldsymbol{\gamma}_0) \xrightarrow{d} \mathfrak{N}(\mathbf{0}, \mathbf{V}_\tau)$$

Let $\hat{\mathbf{V}}_\tau$ be a consistent estimator of $\mathbf{V}_\tau$ and

$$\hat{\boldsymbol{\gamma}} = \underset{\boldsymbol{\gamma}}{\text{argmin}}\, \boldsymbol{\tau}(\hat{\boldsymbol{\theta}}, \boldsymbol{\gamma})'\hat{\mathbf{V}}_\tau \boldsymbol{\tau}(\hat{\boldsymbol{\theta}}, \boldsymbol{\gamma})$$

and show when this estimator is asymptotically equivalent to the MD estimator $\hat{\boldsymbol{\gamma}}_{\text{MD}}$.

26.27 (MD) The OLS estimator of the unrestricted reduced form,

$$\hat{\boldsymbol{\Pi}}_{\text{OLS}} = \left[\mathbf{I}_J \otimes (\mathbf{X}'\mathbf{X})^{-1}\mathbf{X}'\right]\mathbf{y}_V$$

is relatively efficient. The variance matrix of $\hat{\boldsymbol{\pi}}_{\text{OLS}} \equiv \text{vec}\, \hat{\boldsymbol{\Pi}}_{\text{OLS}}$ is also conveniently estimated by $\hat{\boldsymbol{\Omega}}_{\text{OLS}} \otimes (\mathbf{X}'\mathbf{X})^{-1}$ where

$$\hat{\mathbf{\Omega}}_{\text{OLS}} = \text{E}_T[\hat{\mathbf{v}}_t\hat{\mathbf{v}}_t'] \qquad \text{and} \qquad \hat{\mathbf{v}}_t \equiv \mathbf{y}_t - \mathbf{x}_t'\hat{\mathbf{\Pi}}_{\text{OLS}}$$

Therefore, a minimum distance counterpart to the GMM (3SLS) estimator is

$$\hat{\boldsymbol{\delta}}_{\text{MD}} = \underset{\boldsymbol{\delta}}{\text{argmin}}\ \text{vec}(\hat{\mathbf{\Pi}}_{\text{OLS}} - \mathbf{B}\mathbf{\Gamma}^{-1})'\left(\hat{\mathbf{\Omega}}_{\text{OLS}}^{-1} \otimes \mathbf{X}'\mathbf{X}\right)\text{vec}(\hat{\mathbf{\Pi}}_{\text{OLS}} - \mathbf{B}\mathbf{\Gamma}^{-1}).$$

However, although it is easy to formulate the MD estimator, the nonlinear function $\mathbf{B}\mathbf{\Gamma}^{-1}$ of $\boldsymbol{\delta}$ makes $\hat{\boldsymbol{\delta}}_{\text{MD}}$ more complicated than $\hat{\boldsymbol{\delta}}_{\text{3SLS}}$.

Instead apply the minimum distance method to the one-to-one transformation $\text{vec}(\hat{\mathbf{\Pi}}\mathbf{\Gamma} + \mathbf{B})$, which is linear in $\boldsymbol{\delta}$, as described generally in Exercise 26.26.

(a) Show that

$$\text{Var}[\text{vec}(\hat{\mathbf{\Pi}}\mathbf{\Gamma}_0 + \mathbf{B}_0)\ \mathbf{X}] = \mathbf{\Sigma}_0 \otimes (\mathbf{X}'\mathbf{X})^{-1}$$

(b) Also show that

$$\hat{\boldsymbol{\delta}} = \underset{\boldsymbol{\delta}}{\text{argmin}}\ \text{vec}(\hat{\mathbf{\Pi}}_{\text{OLS}}\mathbf{\Gamma} - \mathbf{B})'\left(\hat{\mathbf{\Sigma}}_{\text{2SLS}}^{-1} \otimes \mathbf{X}'\mathbf{X}\right)\text{vec}(\hat{\mathbf{\Pi}}_{\text{OLS}}\mathbf{\Gamma} - \mathbf{B})$$

equals the GMM estimator.

26.28 (Identification) Consider the limited-information system

$$[\,\mathbf{y}_t' \quad \mathbf{x}_t'\,]\begin{bmatrix} \mathbf{\Gamma}_{01} & \mathbf{\Gamma}_{02} \\ \mathbf{B}_{01} & \mathbf{B}_{02} \end{bmatrix} = [\,\boldsymbol{\varepsilon}_{1t}' \quad \boldsymbol{\varepsilon}_{2t}'\,]$$

where $\mathbf{\Gamma}_{01}$ is $J \times J_1$ and $\mathbf{\Gamma}_{02}$ is $J \times (J - J_1)$. Suppose that $\mathbf{\Gamma}_{01}$ and $\mathbf{B}_{01}$ are identified through restrictions but $\mathbf{\Gamma}_{02}$ and $\mathbf{B}_{02}$ are unrestricted and, therefore, unidentified.

(a) Show that one may treat $\text{Cov}[\boldsymbol{\varepsilon}_{1t}, \boldsymbol{\varepsilon}_{2t} \mid \mathbf{x}_t] = \mathbf{0}$ without restricting the conditional distribution of $\mathbf{y}_t$ given $\mathbf{x}_t$.

(b) Show also that setting $\text{Var}[\boldsymbol{\varepsilon}_{2t} \mid \mathbf{x}_t] = \mathbf{I}_{J-J_1}$ does not restrict the conditional distribution of $\mathbf{y}_t$ given $\mathbf{x}_t$.

(c) Given these normalizations, are $\mathbf{\Gamma}_{02}$ and $\mathbf{B}_{02}$ identified?

26.29 (LIML) In LIML estimation, one may omit from the reduced-form part of the system regressions for endogenous variables that do not appear in the structural equation. This exercise develops a proof of this by Koopmans and Hood (1953).

Consider the limited-information system

$$[\,\mathbf{y}_t' \quad \mathbf{x}_t'\,]\,\mathbf{A}_0 = [\,\boldsymbol{\varepsilon}_{1t}' \quad \boldsymbol{\varepsilon}_{2t}'\,]$$

$$\mathbf{A}_0 \equiv \begin{bmatrix} \mathbf{\Gamma}_{01} & \mathbf{\Gamma}_{02} \\ \mathbf{B}_{01} & \mathbf{B}_{02} \end{bmatrix}$$

where $\mathbf{\Gamma}_{01}$ is $J \times J_1$ and $\mathbf{\Gamma}_{02}$ is $J \times (J - J_1)$. Suppose that $\mathbf{\Gamma}_{01}$ and $\mathbf{B}_{01}$ are identified through restrictions but $\mathbf{\Gamma}_{02}$ and $\mathbf{B}_{02}$ are unrestricted and, therefore, unidentified. Let $\boldsymbol{\varepsilon}_t \sim \mathfrak{N}(\mathbf{0}, \mathbf{\Sigma}_0)$ conditional on $\mathbf{x}_t$. Given the normalizations in Exercise 26.28, one may write the sample average log-likelihood function

$$\begin{aligned}\text{E}_T[L(\mathbf{A}, \mathbf{\Sigma})] = & -\frac{1}{2}\log\det(2\pi \cdot \mathbf{\Sigma}_{11}) - \frac{J - J_1}{2}\log 2\pi + \log|\det \mathbf{\Gamma}| \\ & -\frac{1}{2}\,\text{tr}\,\mathbf{\Sigma}_{11}^{-1}\mathbf{A}_1'\mathbf{M}\mathbf{A}_1 - \frac{1}{2}\,\text{tr}\,\mathbf{A}_2'\mathbf{M}\mathbf{A}_2\end{aligned}$$

where

$$\mathbf{M} = \begin{bmatrix} \mathbf{M}_{yy} & \mathbf{M}_{yx} \\ \mathbf{M}_{xy} & \mathbf{M}_{xx} \end{bmatrix} = \begin{bmatrix} \text{E}_T[y_t y_t'] & \text{E}_T[y_t x_t'] \\ \text{E}_T[x_t y_t'] & \text{E}_T[x_t x_t'] \end{bmatrix}$$

$$\mathbf{A} = [\mathbf{A}_1 \quad \mathbf{A}_2] = \begin{bmatrix} \boldsymbol{\Gamma}_1 & \boldsymbol{\Gamma}_2 \\ \mathbf{B}_1 & \mathbf{B}_2 \end{bmatrix}$$

and

$$\boldsymbol{\Sigma} = \begin{bmatrix} \boldsymbol{\Sigma}_{11} & \boldsymbol{\Sigma}_{12} \\ \boldsymbol{\Sigma}_{21} & \boldsymbol{\Sigma}_{22} \end{bmatrix} = \begin{bmatrix} \boldsymbol{\Sigma}_{11} & \mathbf{0} \\ \mathbf{0} & \mathbf{I}_{J_2} \end{bmatrix}$$

(a) Let $\hat{\mathbf{A}}_2 \equiv \hat{\mathbf{A}}_2(\mathbf{A}_1, \boldsymbol{\Sigma}_{11})$ denote a concentration function for $\mathbf{A}_2$. Show that this function is not unique.

(b) Show that $\hat{\mathbf{A}}_2'\mathbf{M}\hat{\mathbf{A}}_2 = \mathbf{I}_{J-J_1}$ using[40]

$$\frac{\partial L}{\partial \mathbf{A}_2} = \begin{bmatrix} [\boldsymbol{\Gamma}^{-1\prime}]_2 \\ \mathbf{0} \end{bmatrix} - \mathbf{M}\mathbf{A}_2 = \mathbf{0} \tag{26.93}$$

where we partition

$$\boldsymbol{\Gamma}^{-1\prime} = \left[[\boldsymbol{\Gamma}^{-1\prime}]_1 \quad [\boldsymbol{\Gamma}^{-1\prime}]_2 \right]$$

conformably with the partition of

$$\boldsymbol{\Gamma} = [\boldsymbol{\Gamma}_1 \quad \boldsymbol{\Gamma}_2]$$

(c) Also use (26.93) to show that

$$\hat{\mathbf{B}}_2(\mathbf{A}_1, \boldsymbol{\Sigma}_{11}) = -\mathbf{M}_{xx}^{-1}\mathbf{M}_{xy}\hat{\boldsymbol{\Gamma}}_2(\mathbf{A}_1, \boldsymbol{\Sigma}_{11})$$

$$\left[\hat{\boldsymbol{\Gamma}}(\mathbf{A}_1, \boldsymbol{\Sigma}_{11})^{-1\prime}\right]_2 = \left(\mathbf{M}_{yy} - \mathbf{M}_{yx}\mathbf{M}_{xx}^{-1}\mathbf{M}_{xy}\right)\hat{\boldsymbol{\Gamma}}_2(\mathbf{A}_1, \boldsymbol{\Sigma}_{11})$$

where

$$\hat{\boldsymbol{\Gamma}}(\mathbf{A}_1, \boldsymbol{\Sigma}_{11}) \equiv [\boldsymbol{\Gamma}_1 \quad \hat{\boldsymbol{\Gamma}}_2(\mathbf{A}_1, \boldsymbol{\Sigma}_{11})]$$

(d) Given Part (c), show that

$$\log\left|\det \hat{\boldsymbol{\Gamma}}(\mathbf{A}_1, \boldsymbol{\Sigma}_{11})\right| = \frac{1}{2}\log\det \boldsymbol{\Gamma}_1'\mathbf{W}\boldsymbol{\Gamma}_1 - \frac{1}{2}\log\det \mathbf{W}$$

where $\mathbf{W} = \mathbf{M}_{yy} - \mathbf{M}_{yx}\mathbf{M}_{xx}^{-1}\mathbf{M}_{xy} = (1/T)\cdot \mathbf{Y}'(\mathbf{I} - \mathbf{P}_{\mathbf{X}})\mathbf{Y}$. [Hint: Use $\det \mathbf{AB} = \det \mathbf{A} \cdot \det \mathbf{B}$ (Lemma C.4, p. 861) to write $\log|\det \boldsymbol{\Gamma}| = \frac{1}{2}\log\det \boldsymbol{\Gamma}'\mathbf{W}\boldsymbol{\Gamma} - \frac{1}{2}\log\det \mathbf{W}$.]

(e) Concentrate $\mathbf{A}_2$ and $\boldsymbol{\Sigma}_{11}$ out of $L(\mathbf{A}, \boldsymbol{\Sigma})$ to obtain

$$\begin{aligned} &\mathrm{E}_T[L^{\mathrm{c}}(\mathbf{A}_1)] \\ &= -\frac{1}{2}\left(J\log 2\pi + \log\det \mathbf{W} - \log\det \boldsymbol{\Gamma}_1'\mathbf{W}\boldsymbol{\Gamma}_1 + \log\det \mathbf{A}_1'\mathbf{M}\mathbf{A}_1 + J\right) \end{aligned}$$

[Hint: Recall equation (26.67).]

(f) Let $J_1 = 1$. Concentrate $\mathbf{B}_1$ out of $\mathrm{E}_T[L^{\mathrm{c}}(\mathbf{A}_1)]$ to obtain

$$\begin{aligned} \mathrm{E}_T[L^{\mathrm{c}}(\boldsymbol{\Gamma}_1)] = &-\frac{1}{2}[J\log 2\pi + \log\det \mathbf{W} - \log\det \boldsymbol{\Gamma}_1'\mathbf{W}\boldsymbol{\Gamma}_1 \\ &+ \log\det \boldsymbol{\Gamma}_1'\mathbf{Y}'\left(\mathbf{I}_T - \mathbf{P}_{\mathbf{X}_1}\right)\mathbf{Y}\boldsymbol{\Gamma}_1 + J] \\ = &-\frac{1}{2}\left\{J\log 2\pi + \log\det\left[\frac{1}{T}\cdot \mathbf{Y}'(\mathbf{I}_T - \mathbf{P}_{\mathbf{X}})\mathbf{Y}\right]\right. \end{aligned}$$

[40] This matrix of derivatives follows directly from (G.30)–(G.31).

$$+ \log \frac{\boldsymbol{\Gamma}_1' \mathbf{Y}' \left(\mathbf{I}_{T} - \mathbf{P}_{\mathbf{X}}\right) \mathbf{Y} \boldsymbol{\Gamma}_1}{\boldsymbol{\Gamma}_1' \mathbf{Y}' \left(\mathbf{I}_T - \mathbf{P}_{\mathbf{X}_1}\right) \mathbf{Y} \boldsymbol{\Gamma}_1} + J \Bigg\}$$

where $\mathbf{X}_1$ contains the predetermined variables included in the first structural equations.

(g) Show that the omitted endogenous variables can be excluded from the log-likelihood function for LIML.

26.30 (Identification) One way to think about identification of simultaneous equations is in terms of linear transformations to the system:

$$\mathbf{y}_t' \boldsymbol{\Gamma}_0 \mathbf{A} + \mathbf{x}_t' \mathbf{B}_0 \mathbf{A} = \boldsymbol{\varepsilon}_t' \mathbf{A}$$

Show that the system is identified by a set of linear restrictions on $\mathbf{B}_0$ and $\boldsymbol{\Gamma}_0$ if and only if $\mathbf{A} = \mathbf{I}_J$ is the only linear transformation that yields an observationally equivalent system.

26.31 (Recursive Systems) Consider the identification of the simultaneous system of equations for two special cases: triangular and recursive systems.

(a) When $\boldsymbol{\Gamma}$ is triangular, the system of equations is called a *triangular* system. The significance of triangularity is that one can solve the system recursively. Show that a triangular system is not identified by the triangular restrictions on $\boldsymbol{\Gamma}$ alone.

(b) If $\boldsymbol{\Sigma}$ is a diagonal matrix and $\boldsymbol{\Gamma}$ is triangular, then the system is called a recursive system. Show that a recursive system is exactly identified.

26.32 (Covariance Restrictions) Generalize the restrictions in (26.51) to include parameters in the variance matrix $\boldsymbol{\Sigma}$:

$$\mathbf{R}_\gamma \operatorname{vec} \boldsymbol{\Gamma} + \mathbf{R}_\beta \operatorname{vec} \mathbf{B} + \mathbf{R}_\sigma \operatorname{vec} \boldsymbol{\Sigma} = \mathbf{r}$$

Prove that the rank condition

$$\operatorname{rank} \left[\mathbf{R}_\gamma \left(\mathbf{I}_J \otimes \boldsymbol{\Gamma}_0\right) + \mathbf{R}_\beta \left(\mathbf{I}_J \otimes \mathbf{B}_0\right) + \mathbf{R}_\sigma \left(\mathbf{I}_J \otimes \boldsymbol{\Sigma}_0\right)\right] = J^2$$

is necessary and sufficient for local identification, generalizing Proposition 27 (System Rank Condition, p. 717).

26.33 (Covariance Restrictions) Consider the case of two linear simultaneous equations outlined in Exercise 26.12. Show how to use the rank condition for system identification in Exercise 26.32 when there is a set of restrictions $\mathbf{R}_\gamma \operatorname{vec} \boldsymbol{\Gamma} + \mathbf{R}_\beta \operatorname{vec} \mathbf{B} + \mathbf{R}_\sigma \operatorname{vec} \boldsymbol{\Sigma} = \mathbf{r}$ that includes covariance parameters.

(a) Let the restrictions be

$$\gamma_{11} = \gamma_{22} = 1$$

$$\gamma_{12} = 0$$

$$\sigma_{12} = \sigma_{21} = 0$$

so that the system is recursive.

(b) Show that a restriction to symmetry for $\boldsymbol{\Sigma}$, $\sigma_{12} = \sigma_{21}$, does not add to the rank of the test matrix.

26.34 (Nonlinear Restrictions) Generalize the restrictions in Exercise 26.32 to be nonlinear:

$$\mathbf{R}(\boldsymbol{\Gamma}, \mathbf{B}, \boldsymbol{\Sigma}) = \mathbf{0}$$

Let

$$\mathbf{R}_\gamma \equiv \left.\frac{\partial \mathbf{R}(\boldsymbol{\Gamma}, \mathbf{B}, \boldsymbol{\Sigma})}{\partial \operatorname{vec} \boldsymbol{\Gamma}}\right|_{\boldsymbol{\Gamma}_0, \mathbf{B}_0, \boldsymbol{\Sigma}_0}$$

$$\mathbf{R}_\beta \equiv \left.\frac{\partial \mathbf{R}(\boldsymbol{\Gamma}, \mathbf{B}, \boldsymbol{\Sigma})}{\partial \operatorname{vec} \mathbf{B}}\right|_{\boldsymbol{\Gamma}_0, \mathbf{B}_0, \boldsymbol{\Sigma}_0}$$

$$\mathbf{R}_\sigma \equiv \left.\frac{\partial \mathbf{R}(\boldsymbol{\Gamma}, \mathbf{B}, \boldsymbol{\Sigma})}{\partial \operatorname{vec} \boldsymbol{\Sigma}}\right|_{\boldsymbol{\Gamma}_0, \mathbf{B}_0, \boldsymbol{\Sigma}_0}$$

Prove that the same rank condition,

$$\operatorname{rank}\left[\mathbf{R}_\gamma \left(\mathbf{I}_J \otimes \boldsymbol{\Gamma}_0\right) + \mathbf{R}_\beta \left(\mathbf{I}_J \otimes \mathbf{B}_0\right) + \mathbf{R}_\sigma \left(\mathbf{I}_J \otimes \boldsymbol{\Sigma}_0\right)\right] = J^2$$

is necessary and sufficient for local identification.

26.35 (Nonlinear Restrictions) Consider the case of two linear simultaneous equations outlined in Exercise 26.12. Let one of the restrictions be nonlinear:

$$\begin{aligned} \gamma_{11} &= 1 \\ \gamma_{12} &= 0 \\ \beta_{12} - \beta_{21} &= 0 \\ \beta_{11}\beta_{22} - \beta_{12}\beta_{21} &= 1 \end{aligned}$$

so that **B** is symmetric and nonsingular. Apply the rank condition in Exercise 26.34 to show that the system is identified.

26.36 (2SLS and LIML) Show that 2SLS equation by equation is relatively efficient when all of the structural equations are exactly identified, except for one overidentified equation. Relate this to limited information estimation of a single equation where the reduced form is exactly identified.

CHAPTER 27

Discrete Dependent Variables

Many phenomena that economists study are inherently discrete. Binary dependent variables are the simplest case: the dependent variable has only two observable outcomes. If, for example, one seeks to explain the labor force participation of individuals then there are two possible outcomes of the dependent variable: in and out of the labor force. Multiple discrete outcomes also occur, as in the selection of a mode of transportation to work: car, bus, or bicycle. In some instances, the multiple outcomes are ordinal: many surveys request the respondent's income in ordinal categories to encourage response to a question about income that many respondents find uncomfortable to answer. Economists also study such discrete count data as individual years of education or the number of children in a household. These are some of the ways in which discrete dependent data appear.

The linear regression model is inappropriate for modeling the conditional mean of such data. Consider labor force participation. It is convenient to code the dependent variable as a dummy variable:

$$y_n = \begin{cases} 0 & \text{if individual } n \text{ is out of the labor force} \\ 1 & \text{if individual } n \text{ is in the labor force} \end{cases} \tag{27.1}$$

A scatter diagram of this dependent variable against net nonlabor income might look something like Figure 27.1. We also plot the simple OLS fit. Even though all of the observed values of y_n lie between 0 and 1, the OLS fitted values exceed one for the lowest values of nonlabor income. Because the dependent variable takes only two values, its mean lies between those values. The mean cannot possibly be lower than the lowest possible value that y_n can take or higher than the highest value.

Given the binomial convention (27.1), the conditional mean of binary dependent data has a simple interpretation that captures these restrictions: the conditional mean of y_n given $\mathbf{x}_n$ is the conditional probability that y_n will equal one,

$$\begin{aligned} \mathrm{E}[y_n \mid \mathbf{x}_n] &= 0 \cdot \Pr\{y_n = 0 \mid \mathbf{x}_n\} + 1 \cdot \Pr\{y_n = 1 \mid \mathbf{x}_n\} \\ &= \Pr\{y_n = 1 \mid \mathbf{x}_n\} \end{aligned}$$

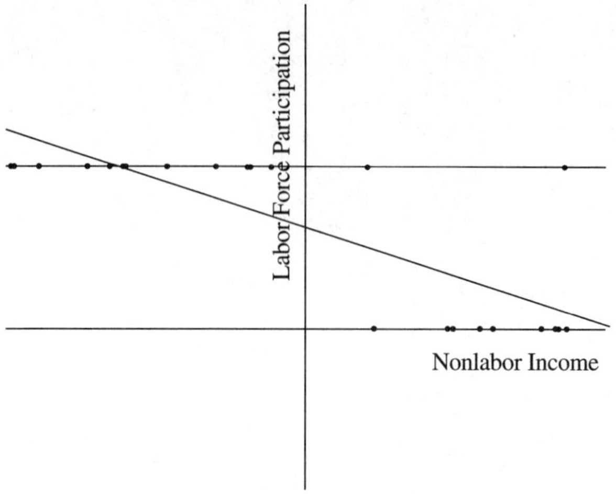

Figure 27.1 Binomial dependent variable.

Obviously, a probability function must lie in the unit interval. If we reexamine the specification of the linear regression model,

$$\mathrm{E}[y_n \mid \mathbf{x}_n] = \mathbf{x}_n' \boldsymbol{\beta}_0 \tag{27.2}$$

it is clear that this functional form will not satisfy the restrictions inherent in the binary nature of y_n: the linear regression function is unbounded in $\mathbf{x}_n$.

This chapter surveys important examples of discrete dependent data, starting with this binary case. We use this case to introduce the basic strategies for specifying econometric models for such data. These strategies are (1) direct nonlinear transformation of $\mathbf{x}_n' \boldsymbol{\beta}_0$ to capture the basic features of the nonlinear regression function and (2) latent variable models that generate such transformations indirectly. In cases more complicated than binary dependent data, latent variable models are especially helpful and we use them to develop econometric specifications for ordered data, count data, and multiple-choice data. Toward the end of the chapter, we discuss latent variable models for discrete data in more detail and point out the special uses of such models in the computation of maximum likelihood estimators and their approximations.

27.1 BERNOULLI DEPENDENT VARIABLES

Random variables with two discrete outcomes have a Bernoulli distribution, the simplest possible distribution. What makes their specification difficult here is that interest focuses on the conditional distribution given explanatory variables $\mathbf{x}_n$. How can we make the probability of each outcome depend on these variables in a simple and appropriate way?

27.1.1 Bernoulli Regression

Viewing the conditional mean of y_n as a probability function suggests a family of simple transformations to the specification of the linear model (27.2) that yields satisfactory multiple regression functions for a binary dependent variable. We can transform the unbounded $\mathbf{x}_n'\boldsymbol{\beta}_0$ to the unit interval with a cumulative distribution function (c.d.f.). Let $F(\cdot)$ denote a specific univariate c.d.f. whose domain is the real line and let

$$\mathrm{E}[y_n \mid \mathbf{x}_n] = F(\mathbf{x}_n'\boldsymbol{\beta}_0) \tag{27.3}$$

be the Bernoulli regression function. Then the linear index $\mathbf{x}_n'\boldsymbol{\beta}_0$, and hence the parameter vector $\boldsymbol{\beta}_0$, can take any real values and the conditional mean function remains in the unit interval. Furthermore, the conditional expectation of y_n remains a monotonic function of each x_{nk}.

For example, a simple and popular choice for $F(z)$ is the logistic c.d.f.,

$$F_L(z) \equiv \frac{1}{1+e^{-z}} \tag{27.4}$$

because this function is differentiable everywhere and it can be computed quickly and accurately. This Bernoulli regression specification is often called the *binomial logit* model.[1]

Another obvious choice for $F(z)$ is the univariate standard normal c.d.f., $\Phi(z)$, where[2]

$$\Phi(z) \equiv \int_{-\infty}^{z} \phi(w)\,dw = \int_{-\infty}^{z} \frac{1}{\sqrt{2\pi}} e^{-\frac{1}{2}w^2}\,dw \tag{27.5}$$

Although this function does not have an explicit form, there are simple, quick numerical approximations such as those used for exponentials and logarithms that make this *binomial probit* specification just as practical as the logistic.

The third and last choice that we will mention is the c.d.f. of the uniform (or rectangular) distribution,

$$F_U(z) \equiv \begin{cases} 0 & \text{if } z < 0 \\ z & \text{if } 0 \le z < 1 \\ 1 & \text{if } 1 \le z \end{cases} \tag{27.6}$$

This specification deserves special mention because it yields the linear regression model for the $\mathbf{x}_n'\boldsymbol{\beta}_0$ that lies within the unit interval. However, outside this interval, the uniform c.d.f. replaces $\mathbf{x}_n'\boldsymbol{\beta}_0$ with zero or one thereby meeting the restrictions of a probability. Without these constraints, this specification is called the *linear probability* model.

Figure 27.2 gives a graphic comparison of the three c.d.f.s. To show how qualitatively similar the distributions can be, we translated and scaled the logistic and the uniform c.d.f.s to have mean zero and variance one.[3] The normal and logistic c.d.f.s are quite close. We have compared these two distributions before and we have noted the differences in their tails, a difference that

[1] The word *logit* is usually pronounced *lō'jit*. The adjective *binomial* refers to the *binary* nature of the dependent variable. Econometricians rarely apply the binomial generalization (Definition D.20, p. 885) of the Bernoulli model.

[2] See Definition D.27 (Normal Distribution, p. 887) and equation (D.11).

[3] The logistic c.d.f. shown is actually

$$\frac{1}{1+e^{-\pi z/\sqrt{3}}} \tag{27.7}$$

and the uniform c.d.f. is

$$\begin{cases} 0 & \text{if } z < -\sqrt{3} \\ z/\sqrt{12}+0.5 & \text{if } -\sqrt{3} \le z < \sqrt{3} \\ 1 & \text{if } \sqrt{3} \le z \end{cases} \tag{27.8}$$

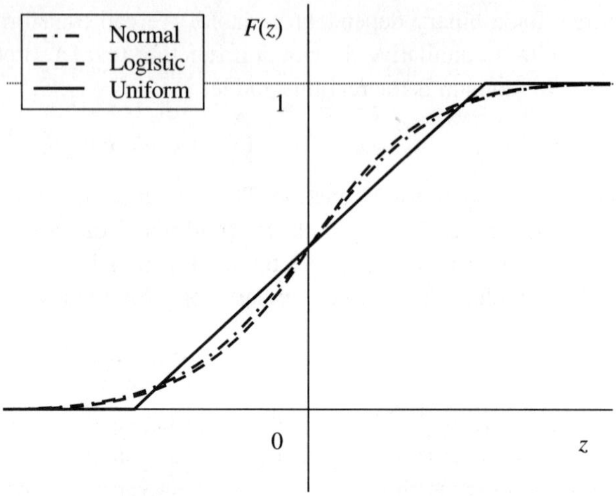

Figure 27.2 Alternative c.d.f.s

is not apparent in Figure 27.2.[4] Empirical researchers actually choose among these functions by convenience and convention. Once they became computationally attractive, the normal and logistic functions became the standard choices.

Note how the interpretation of the slope parameters changes when we introduce the nonlinear transformation $F(\cdot)$ to the regression function. For a linear mean, each β_{0k} is the partial derivative of $\mathrm{E}[y_n \mid \mathbf{x}_n]$ with respect to an x_{nk}. In the binomial regression model,

$$\frac{\partial\, \mathrm{E}[y_n \mid \mathbf{x}_n]}{\partial \mathbf{x}_n} = \frac{\partial F(\mathbf{x}_n' \boldsymbol{\beta}_0)}{\partial \mathbf{x}_n} = f(\mathbf{x}_n' \boldsymbol{\beta}_0) \cdot \boldsymbol{\beta}_0 \tag{27.9}$$

where $f(\cdot)$ is the p.d.f. corresponding to $F(\cdot)$. Thus, the kth partial derivative of the conditional mean is proportional to β_{0k}, where the positive factor of proportionality depends on $\mathbf{x}_n' \boldsymbol{\beta}_0$. The factor of proportionality is the slope of the c.d.f. at $\mathbf{x}_n' \boldsymbol{\beta}_0$, which is, of course, the p.d.f. at $\mathbf{x}_n' \boldsymbol{\beta}_0$. For such symmetric, unimodal distributions as the logistic and the normal, this factor is greatest for small $\left|\mathbf{x}_n' \boldsymbol{\beta}_0\right|$. But as the linear index increases in absolute value and the probability that $y_n = 1$ approaches zero or one, the marginal impact of x_{nk} on the probability diminishes. The logistic and normal curves in Figure 27.2 exhibit the diminution in their horizontal asymptotes at zero and one. This is the desired effect of the nonlinear transformation: when an outcome becomes virtually certain, there is little room left for change in its probability.

27.1.2 Estimation

Given the specification of F, we can estimate $\boldsymbol{\beta}_0$ with maximum likelihood (ML) or nonlinear least squares (NLS). Both will deliver $\sqrt{N}$-consistent, asymptotically normal estimators under suitable regularity conditions.

---

[4] See Figures 13.1 and 13.2 (pp. 249–251).

NONLINEAR LEAST SQUARES

Replacing OLS with NLS is a natural consequence of the nonlinear transformation of the linear index:

$$\hat{\boldsymbol{\beta}}_{\text{NLS}} = \underset{\boldsymbol{\beta}}{\operatorname{argmin}}\, \mathrm{E}_N\left[\left(y_n - F(\mathbf{x}_n'\boldsymbol{\beta})\right)^2\right] \tag{27.10}$$

The previous graphic comparison suggests that there are unlikely to be large differences between the NLS fitted values for the logistic, normal, and uniform c.d.f.s.

The most obvious difference will be in the *scale* of the fitted parameter values. As noted, we obtain similar c.d.f.s only after scaling and translating the distributions. Based on matching first and second moments to those of the standard normal, one should expect to see NLS fitted logit coefficients that are approximately $\pi/\sqrt{3} \approx 1.8$ times NLS fitted probit coefficients. The NLS fitted linear probability coefficients will be approximately $1/\sqrt{12} \approx 0.3$ times the probit coefficients, except the intercept, which is additionally increased by 0.5 after the rescaling.

But such differences are generally cosmetic. The fitted values will often be quite similar and so will the fitted partial derivatives, except near the kinks in the uniform c.d.f. In these ways the models are observationally close. The density factor of proportionality in (27.9) will remove most of the differences in scale present in the fitted coefficients. One generally finds close agreement in such summary measures as the partial derivatives evaluated at the sample average of the explanatory variables or the sample average of the partial derivatives. The latter measure may be particularly useful. When the sample of explanatory variables is representative of a population of interest, the sample average of a partial derivative is an estimator of the marginal change in the fraction of ones in the population associated with a marginal change in an explanatory variable.

To estimate the asymptotic variance of the NLS estimator, we apply results for GMM in (21.32). In NLS, the moment conditions are the first-order conditions for (27.10)

$$\mathbf{0} = \mathrm{E}_N\left[\mathbf{x}_n f(\mathbf{x}_n'\hat{\boldsymbol{\beta}}_{\text{NLS}})\left(y_n - F(\mathbf{x}_n'\hat{\boldsymbol{\beta}}_{\text{NLS}})\right)\right] \tag{27.11}$$

In this case, the GMM weighting matrix $\mathbf{C}_N$ equals the identity matrix.

Because the conditional variance of y_n is

$$\begin{aligned}\operatorname{Var}[y_n \mid \mathbf{x}_n] &= 0^2 \cdot \Pr\{y_n = 0 \mid \mathbf{x}_n\} + 1^2 \cdot \Pr\{y_n = 1 \mid \mathbf{x}_n\} \\ &\quad - (\Pr\{y_n = 1 \mid \mathbf{x}_n\})^2 \\ &= F(\mathbf{x}_n'\boldsymbol{\beta}_0)\left[1 - F(\mathbf{x}_n'\boldsymbol{\beta}_0)\right]\end{aligned}$$

we may set[5]

$$\hat{\boldsymbol{\Lambda}}_N = \mathrm{E}_N[\mathbf{x}_n \hat{f}_n^2 \hat{F}_n (1 - \hat{F}_n)\mathbf{x}_n']$$

where

$$\hat{f}_n \equiv f(\mathbf{x}_n'\hat{\boldsymbol{\beta}}_{\text{NLS}}) \qquad \text{and} \qquad \hat{F}_n \equiv F(\mathbf{x}_n'\hat{\boldsymbol{\beta}}_{\text{NLS}})$$

The binomial data exhibit conditional heteroskedasticity around their nonlinear conditional mean. As the probability of a zero or a one increases, y_n behaves more like a constant and its variance falls.

Finally, differentiating (27.11) gives

[5] Note that in $\boldsymbol{\Lambda}_N$ we have replaced the squared residual $(y_n - \hat{F}_n)^2$ that appears in the general GMM variance estimator with the known parametric form of the conditional heteroskedasticity, $\hat{F}_n(1 - \hat{F}_n)$.

$$\hat{\mathbf{G}}_N = \mathrm{E}_N[\mathbf{x}_n \hat{f}_n^2 \mathbf{x}_n']$$

Applying (21.32) for the asymptotic variance of a GMM estimator, we obtain an estimator of the asymptotic variance of $\hat{\boldsymbol{\beta}}_{\text{NLS}}$ in

$$\hat{\mathbf{V}}_{\text{NLS}} = \hat{\mathbf{G}}_N^{-1} \hat{\boldsymbol{\Lambda}}_N \hat{\mathbf{G}}_N^{-1}$$

Knowing the parameterization of the conditional heteroskedasticity of y_n also makes a weighted NLS (WNLS) estimator feasible. Weighting by the estimated variance offers an improvement in asymptotic efficiency relative to the NLS estimator. A feasible (two-step) WNLS estimator that accounts for this heteroskedasticity is

$$\hat{\boldsymbol{\beta}}_{\text{WNLS}} = \underset{\boldsymbol{\beta}}{\operatorname{argmin}}\, \mathrm{E}_N \left[\frac{\left[y_n - F(\mathbf{x}_n'\boldsymbol{\beta})\right]^2}{\hat{F}_n\left(1 - \hat{F}_n\right)} \right] \tag{27.12}$$

where $\hat{F}_n \equiv F(\mathbf{x}_n'\hat{\boldsymbol{\beta}}_{\text{NLS}})$ exploits $\hat{\boldsymbol{\beta}}_{\text{NLS}}$ as the first-step estimator. If we follow the same procedure as for deriving $\hat{\mathbf{V}}_{\text{NLS}}$, we obtain

$$\hat{\mathbf{V}}_{\text{WNLS}} = \left\{ \mathrm{E}_N \left[\mathbf{x}_n \frac{\hat{f}_n^2}{\hat{F}_n\left(1 - \hat{F}_n\right)} \mathbf{x}_n' \right] \right\}^{-1} \tag{27.13}$$

as an estimator of the asymptotic variance matrix of $\hat{\boldsymbol{\beta}}_{\text{WNLS}}$.[6]

Note that it is not necessary to account for the estimation of the weights. As in many GLS estimators, the correct weights are not necessary for this WNLS estimator to be consistent. So we can apply Lemma 20.3 to conclude that we should treat the estimated weights as known weights.

This WNLS estimator may not be workable for the linear probability model because some of the fitted variances may be zeros. This is all right for observations whose NLS fitted residual is also zero. They can be dropped from the sample as observations that have no information about $\boldsymbol{\beta}_0$. But if there are observations with nonzero fitted residuals and zero fitted variances, it seems likely that the binomial regression model is badly misspecified in some way, either in the explanatory variables, in the selection of the uniform c.d.f., or in miscoding in the data.

MAXIMUM LIKELIHOOD

Alternatively to NLS, one can estimate $\boldsymbol{\beta}_0$ with ML. The log-likelihood function of $\boldsymbol{\beta}$ given $(\mathbf{x}_n, y_n)$ is

$$\begin{aligned} L(\boldsymbol{\beta}; y_n, \mathbf{x}_n) &= \begin{cases} \log\left[1 - F(\mathbf{x}_n'\boldsymbol{\beta})\right] & \text{if } y_n = 0 \\ \log F(\mathbf{x}_n'\boldsymbol{\beta}) & \text{if } y_n = 1 \end{cases} \\ &= y_n \log F(\mathbf{x}_n'\boldsymbol{\beta}) + (1 - y_n) \log\left[1 - F(\mathbf{x}_n'\boldsymbol{\beta})\right] \end{aligned} \tag{27.14}$$

[6] The WNLS estimator is a relatively efficient GMM estimator and

$$\boldsymbol{\Lambda}_N(\boldsymbol{\beta}) = \mathbf{G}_N(\boldsymbol{\beta}) = \mathrm{E}_N\left[\mathbf{x}_n \frac{f(\mathbf{x}_n'\boldsymbol{\beta})^2}{F(\mathbf{x}_n'\boldsymbol{\beta})\left[1 - F(\mathbf{x}_n'\boldsymbol{\beta})\right]} \mathbf{x}_n'\right]$$

As noted on p. 773, if $\log f(\cdot)$ is concave, as for the normal, logistic, and uniform distributions, then $L(\boldsymbol{\beta}; y_n, \mathbf{x}_n)$ is also concave in $\boldsymbol{\beta}$ and the MLE is unique.[7] The MLE solves the normal equations

$$\begin{aligned} \mathbf{0} &= \left.\frac{\partial\, \mathrm{E}_N[L(\boldsymbol{\beta})]}{\partial \boldsymbol{\beta}}\right|_{\hat{\boldsymbol{\beta}}_{\mathrm{ML}}} \\ &= \mathrm{E}_N\left[y_n \cdot \mathbf{x}_n \frac{\hat{f}_n}{\hat{F}_n} - (1-y_n)\cdot \mathbf{x}_n \frac{\hat{f}_n}{1-\hat{F}_n}\right] \\ &= \mathrm{E}_N\left[\mathbf{x}_n \frac{\hat{f}_n}{\hat{F}_n\left(1-\hat{F}_n\right)}\left(y_n - \hat{F}_n\right)\right] \end{aligned} \tag{27.15}$$

where $\hat{f}_n \equiv f(\mathbf{x}_n'\hat{\boldsymbol{\beta}}_{\mathrm{ML}})$ and $\hat{F}_n \equiv F(\mathbf{x}_n'\hat{\boldsymbol{\beta}}_{\mathrm{ML}})$. These equations are similar to the first-order conditions for the WNLS estimator (27.12). The only difference is that $\hat{\boldsymbol{\beta}}_{\mathrm{ML}}$ takes the places of *both* $\hat{\boldsymbol{\beta}}_{\mathrm{NLS}}$ in the variance weights and $\hat{\boldsymbol{\beta}}_{\mathrm{WNLS}}$ in the nonlinear regression function. As just mentioned, all consistent $\hat{\boldsymbol{\beta}}_N$ in the variance weights produce the same asymptotic distribution of the WNLS estimator. And this includes the use of the MLE. Hence, the similarity of first-order conditions implies that $\hat{\boldsymbol{\beta}}_{\mathrm{WNLS}}$ and $\hat{\boldsymbol{\beta}}_{\mathrm{ML}}$ are asymptotically equivalent estimators. Indeed, one can easily confirm that (27.13) contains an estimator of the information matrix inside the inverse.

In a way, this asymptotic equivalence of the WNLS and ML estimators is surprising. One might anticipate that because the mean and variance depend on the same parameters it follows that an efficient estimator of the parameters is necessary for a weighted least-squares procedure to be efficient. After all, that is the situation for the linear regression model. If the parameters in the first conditional moment also appear in the second, then an efficient GMM estimator generally combines both moments. So does the MLE for normal linear regression, because the score would combine derivatives with respect to both moments.[8]

Yet the score in (27.15) exploits only the first conditional moment [through the difference $y_n - F(\mathbf{x}_n'\boldsymbol{\beta})$]. The reason is that the Bernoulli random variable y_n is equal to y_n^j for all $j = 1, 2, 3, \ldots$. Squaring zero or one gives, well, zero or one. As a result, higher moments contain no additional information and restricting the mean and variance to have the same coefficients provides no improvements in efficiency. If, on the other hand, the data were normally distributed then such restrictions can improve efficiency. First and second moments provide independent information about the parameters of the normal distribution.[9] But not so for the Bernoulli distribution.

PERFECT CLASSIFICATION

The MLE for $\boldsymbol{\beta}_0$ will permit a fitted probability to equal zero or one whenever this corresponds to a correct prediction of the actual data. Such prediction is called *perfect classification*. But the MLE does not allow contradictory predictions.

Consider, for example, the linear probability model, which has the average log-likelihood function

---

[7] This uniqueness also requires, of course, that $\mathbf{X} = [\mathbf{x}_n]'$ is full-column rank.

[8] See Exercise 18.13 for an example.

[9] See Section 18.5.3 for a discussion of this point. Exercise 18.13 provides an example in which the first and second moments must be combined to obtain an efficient estimator for the normal linear regression model.

$$L(\boldsymbol{\beta}) = \mathrm{E}_N[y_n \log(\mathbf{x}_n'\boldsymbol{\beta}) + (1 - y_n)\log(1 - \mathbf{x}_n'\boldsymbol{\beta})] \tag{27.16}$$

for all $\mathbf{y}$ provided that all $\mathbf{x}_n'\boldsymbol{\beta}$ are strictly between zero and one. If a $y_m = 1$ then its $\mathbf{x}_m'\boldsymbol{\beta}$ may also equal one. Similarly, if a $y_m = 0$ then its $\mathbf{x}_m'\boldsymbol{\beta}$ may equal zero. These are cases of perfect classification. On the other hand, if $y_m = 1$ and $\mathbf{x}_m'\boldsymbol{\beta} < 0$ or if $y_m = 0$ and $1 < \mathbf{x}_m'\boldsymbol{\beta}$ then $L(\boldsymbol{\beta})$ is undefined. Even if $0 < \mathbf{x}_n'\boldsymbol{\beta} < 1$ for all $n = 1, \ldots, N$, $L(\boldsymbol{\beta})$ approaches negative infinity if $y_m = 1$ and $\mathbf{x}_m'\boldsymbol{\beta} \to 0$ or if $y_m = 0$ and $\mathbf{x}_m'\boldsymbol{\beta} \to 1$ for any $n = 1, \ldots, N$. Therefore, the MLE never occurs on such boundaries where predictions contradict observations.

Even though the probit and logit probability functions constrain the fitted probabilities to lie between zero and one, there are also situations in which some of the ML fitted probabilities equal one for these models. Because an $|\mathbf{x}_n'\hat{\boldsymbol{\beta}}_{\mathrm{ML}}|$ must be infinite for this to occur, such situations cause numerical difficulties for many computer programs and researchers must be able to recognize the phenomenon.

To give an example, suppose that the kth explanatory variable x_{mk} is a dummy variable with the property that if its value is one in the sample the value of y_m is one. That is, for some k

$$\begin{aligned} x_{mk} = 1 \quad &\Rightarrow \quad y_m = 1 \\ x_{mk} = 0 \quad &\Rightarrow \quad y_m = 0 \text{ or } 1 \end{aligned}$$

Such a variable is called a *perfect classifier* even though it does not classify *all* observations perfectly. Only observations with $x_{mk} = 1$ have fitted probabilities that are affected by β_k. Furthermore, those fitted probabilities are always increased by increasing β_k. As a result, the unconstrained MLE of β_{0k} equals infinity and perfect classification occurs for the subsample $\{m \mid x_{mk} = 1\}$.

This phenomenon can occur with more than one explanatory variable, and not just with dummy variables. If $x_{mk} \geq c$ and

$$\begin{aligned} x_{mk} > c \quad &\Rightarrow \quad y_m = 1 \\ x_{mk} = c \quad &\Rightarrow \quad y_m = 0 \text{ or } 1 \end{aligned}$$

then a combination of the intercept (say β_1) and this variable ($k > 1$) creates perfect classification. If we keep

$$\beta_1 = -c\beta_k$$

then β_k can become infinitely large without causing $|\mathbf{x}_n'\boldsymbol{\beta}|$ to become infinite for all observations.

Less subtle are samples in which there is a $\boldsymbol{\beta}_1 \in \mathbb{R}^K$ such that

$$\mathbf{1}\{\mathbf{x}_n'\boldsymbol{\beta}_1 > 0\} = y_n \quad \text{and} \quad \mathbf{x}_n'\boldsymbol{\beta}_1 \neq 0, \qquad n = 1, \ldots, N$$

Then every observation in the sample is perfectly classified for $\boldsymbol{\beta} = c \cdot \boldsymbol{\beta}_1$ as c approaches infinity. This will always happen if the number of explanatory variables is greater than the number of observations, but such samples also occur more generally.

When a subsample is perfectly classified, general purpose estimation software often will increase the magnitudes of the coefficients involved in the perfect classification until a numerical problem occurs. To find the MLE for the other coefficients, one should remove the perfectly classified observations from the estimation sample, remove the associated explanatory variables from $\mathbf{x}_n$, and recompute the MLE for the remaining coefficients. This has the same effect as concentrating the perfectly classifying coefficients out of the likelihood function. Once their fitted probabilities reach one, the perfectly classified observations have no influence on the log-likelihood function as the finite coefficient values change.

MEASURING EFFECTS

Reporting the results of any nonlinear regression model can be challenging because the fitted regression function is poorly described by its parameters alone. As we noted in (27.9), the partial derivatives of the regression function depend on the value of the explanatory variables. One practical solution is to report the sample mean of these derivatives,

$$\mathrm{E}_N\left[\frac{\partial F(\mathbf{x}_n'\hat{\boldsymbol{\beta}})}{\partial \mathbf{x}_n}\right] = \hat{\boldsymbol{\beta}}\ \mathrm{E}_N[f(\mathbf{x}_n'\hat{\boldsymbol{\beta}})] \tag{27.17}$$

or the sample mean of the elasticities,

$$\mathrm{E}_N\left[\frac{x_{nk}}{F(\mathbf{x}_n'\hat{\boldsymbol{\beta}})}\ \frac{\partial F(\mathbf{x}_n'\hat{\boldsymbol{\beta}})}{\partial x_{nk}}\right] = \hat{\boldsymbol{\beta}}\ \mathrm{E}_N\left[\frac{x_{nk} f(\mathbf{x}_n'\hat{\boldsymbol{\beta}})}{F(\mathbf{x}_n'\hat{\boldsymbol{\beta}})}\right]$$

One may add such additional summary statistics as standard deviation and quartiles to give the reader an idea of how much these derivatives vary around their central value. If the sample does not represent the population of interest, then one can compute the mean of the partial derivatives with respect to a more representative distribution for $\mathbf{x}_n$.

Occasionally one sees reports of the partial derivatives evaluated at the sample mean of the explanatory variables:

$$\left.\frac{\partial\, \mathrm{E}[y \mid \mathbf{x}'\hat{\boldsymbol{\beta}}]}{\partial \mathbf{x}}\right|_{\mathbf{x}=\bar{\mathbf{x}}} = \hat{\boldsymbol{\beta}}\ f(\bar{\mathbf{x}}'\hat{\boldsymbol{\beta}}) \tag{27.18}$$

where $\bar{\mathbf{x}} = \mathrm{E}_N[\mathbf{x}_n]$. This measure can be misleading. There may not be any actual observations near $\bar{\mathbf{x}}$. Consider an extreme situation pictured in Figure 27.3. With the actual $\mathbf{x}_n'\hat{\boldsymbol{\beta}}$ in the tails of the distribution, the average derivative is much smaller than the derivative at the average. In many data sets the two derivative measures are quite similar, but unless there is specific interest in (27.18) one will report (27.17) to describe the fitted probability regression.

Note that partial derivatives and elasticities are unnatural for dummy explanatory variables, which change discretely from zero to one. To summarize the effect of a dummy variable, it is sensible to report the mean difference $\mathrm{E}_N[F(\mathbf{x}_n^{1\prime}\hat{\boldsymbol{\beta}}) - F(\mathbf{x}_n^{0\prime}\hat{\boldsymbol{\beta}})]$, where $\mathbf{x}_n^i$ is $\mathbf{x}_n$ with the dummy variable set equal to $i = 0, 1$.

27.1.3 A Latent Variable Interpretation

Economists often motivate the Bernoulli dependent variable as the partial observation of an unobserved, or *latent*, variable. We will describe other discrete data models in this way because several insights emerge from this approach. In many applications of Bernoulli regression, for example, researchers view the discrete binary outcome as the result of utility maximization. Consider an individual consumer with personal characteristics **w** faced with two choices: bundle

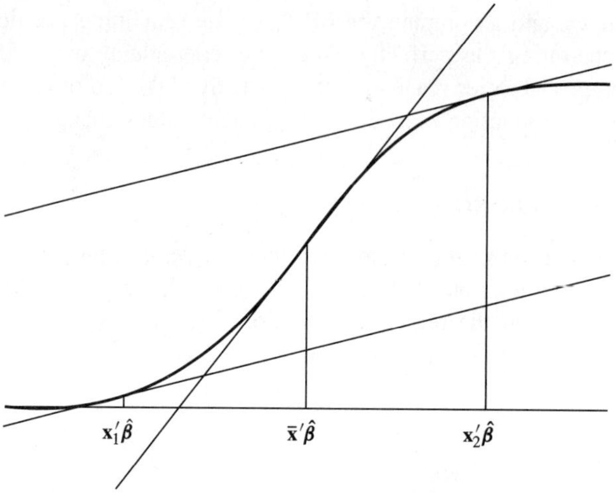

Figure 27.3 Average derivative versus derivative at average.

$\mathbf{z}_1$ or bundle $\mathbf{z}_2$ where $\mathbf{z}$ is a vector of the consumption levels of a list of goods. According to the textbook theory of the consumer, the individual will choose the alternative with the highest utility $U(\mathbf{z}, \mathbf{w})$. The two possible outcomes define a Bernoulli random variable

$$y = \begin{cases} 0 & \text{if } \{U(\mathbf{z}_1, \mathbf{w}) < U(\mathbf{z}_2, \mathbf{w})\} \Leftrightarrow \{\text{bundle 2 chosen}\} \\ 1 & \text{if } \{U(\mathbf{z}_1, \mathbf{w}) \geq U(\mathbf{z}_2, \mathbf{w})\} \Leftrightarrow \{\text{bundle 1 chosen}\} \end{cases} \tag{27.19}$$
$$= \mathbf{1}\{0 \leq U(\mathbf{z}_1, \mathbf{w}) - U(\mathbf{z}_2, \mathbf{w})\}$$

that is a partial observation of $U(\mathbf{z}_1, \mathbf{w}) - U(\mathbf{z}_2, \mathbf{w})$.[10] All that we observe is the sign of this variable.

The latent utility model and the partial observation rule (27.19) can lead to the Bernoulli regression (27.3). Let the utility function of all individuals equal the linear location-scale specification

$$U(\mathbf{z}, \mathbf{w}) = \mathbf{x}(\mathbf{z}, \mathbf{w})'\boldsymbol{\beta}_0 + \sigma_0 \varepsilon(\mathbf{z}, \mathbf{w}) \tag{27.20}$$

where $\mathbf{x}(\mathbf{z}, \mathbf{w})'\boldsymbol{\beta}_0$ is a systematic component of utility exhibiting the preferences of a representative consumer with characteristics $\mathbf{w}$. The second term $\sigma_0 \varepsilon(\mathbf{z}, \mathbf{w})$ is a random component that captures individual variations in tastes and unobserved characteristics of the consumption bundles. Then the probability that an individual chooses consumption bundle 1 is

$$\begin{aligned} \Pr\{y = 1 \mid \mathbf{z}_1, \mathbf{z}_2, \mathbf{w}\} &= \Pr\{U(\mathbf{z}_1, \mathbf{w}) > U(\mathbf{z}_2, \mathbf{w})\} \\ &= \Pr\left\{\varepsilon(\mathbf{z}_2, \mathbf{w}) - \varepsilon(\mathbf{z}_1, \mathbf{w}) < \frac{[\mathbf{x}(\mathbf{z}_1, \mathbf{w}) - \mathbf{x}(\mathbf{z}_2, \mathbf{w})]\,\boldsymbol{\beta}_0}{\sigma_0}\right\} \\ &= F\left(\frac{\mathbf{x}'\boldsymbol{\beta}_0}{\sigma_0}\right) \end{aligned} \tag{27.21}$$

[10] We will assume that $U(\mathbf{z}_1, \mathbf{w}) = U(\mathbf{z}_2, \mathbf{w})$ with a probability of zero.

where $\mathbf{x} \equiv \mathbf{x}(\mathbf{z}_1, \mathbf{w}) - \mathbf{x}(\mathbf{z}_2, \mathbf{w})$ and $F(\cdot)$ is the c.d.f. of $\varepsilon(\mathbf{z}_2, \mathbf{w}) - \varepsilon(\mathbf{z}_1, \mathbf{w})$,

$$F(c) \equiv \Pr\{\varepsilon(\mathbf{z}_2, \mathbf{w}) - \varepsilon(\mathbf{z}_1, \mathbf{w}) \leq c \mid \mathbf{z}_1, \mathbf{z}_2, \mathbf{w}\} \tag{27.22}$$

The probability (27.21) is the Bernoulli regression function that we have already discussed.

This simple model of choice establishes a connection between linear regression and Bernoulli probability. Several points concerning identification of the parameters in the latent regression equation emerge immediately. Note first that the scale parameter σ_0 is not identified separately from the coefficient vector $\boldsymbol{\beta}_0$. There are two ways to see this. The probability (27.21) is unchanged if we multiply both $\boldsymbol{\beta}_0$ and σ_0 by the same positive constant. All that we can hope to estimate is the scaled slope coefficient vector $\sigma_0^{-1} \cdot \boldsymbol{\beta}_0$. Alternatively, note that because we observe only the sign of $U(\mathbf{z}_1, \mathbf{w}) - U(\mathbf{z}_2, \mathbf{w})$ it is not possible to learn about its scale. If we multiply $U(\mathbf{z}_1, \mathbf{w}) - U(\mathbf{z}_2, \mathbf{w})$ by a positive scalar, we will not change the data that we observe through the observation rule (27.19).

We can also see that some of the slope parameters in the utility function may not be identified. The vector of explanatory variables is the difference $\mathbf{x}(\mathbf{z}_1, \mathbf{w}) - \mathbf{x}(\mathbf{z}_2, \mathbf{w})$ and any common variables in the $\mathbf{x}(\mathbf{z}_i, \mathbf{w})$, $i = 1, 2$, will produce explanatory variables that are always zero. This occurs, for example, if an element of $\mathbf{x}(\mathbf{z}, \mathbf{w})$ is a constant, a characteristic of the consumer, or a consumption level that is always the same in both consumption bundles.

From the perspective of modeling the consumer's choice, both identification issues make sense. Utility functions are purely ordinal concepts so that notions of their "scale" and "level" are inherently meaningless. Changes in scale or level do not affect the predictions of the model and, therefore, are not identified.

27.2 ADDITIONAL UNIVARIATE MODELS

The Bernoulli regression model is not necessarily the result of an observation rule and a latent regression model like equations (27.19)–(27.22). But there are many models in econometrics in which these elements are a natural or convenient motivation. In this section, we introduce two additional discrete probability models that researchers also base on the linear location-scale model

$$y_n^* = \mathbf{x}_n' \boldsymbol{\beta}_0 + \sigma_0 \varepsilon_n \tag{27.23}$$

One views y_n^* as a latent, continuous, dependent variable and ε_n as a random disturbance term with the c.d.f. $F(\cdot)$. The latent data are transformed into observed, discrete data through an observation rule

$$y_n = \tau(y_n^*) \tag{27.24}$$

that is many to one. As a result, the value of y_n^* is obscured, or partially observed.

This is often a natural framework for thinking about how discrete data are generated. In addition, such structure generates p.m.f.s, and hence moment functions, which are consistent with the particular discrete nature of y_n. In the next section we will continue this approach, extending the latent process y_n^* to be multivariate. In this section, we advance from binary dependent data to dependent data with several discrete outcomes.

27.2.1 Ordered Data

In the *ordered probability* model, the observable dependent variable is an ordinal measure of the latent y_n^*. Rather than two categories, y_n has several ordinal categorical values. In economics and other social sciences, categorical responses to survey questions are common. Income data from surveys are often collected as interval data. Survey respondents answer such questions as

Which interval below contains your total annual earnings before income taxes?

1. *$0–$10,000*
2. *$10,001–$20,000*
3. *$20,001–$50,000*
4. *$50,001–$100,000*
5. *$100,001 or more*

more frequently than

What are your total annual earnings before income taxes?

The survey categories are not always quantitative. We are familiar with a teaching evaluation questionnaire that asks

On a 7-point scale, where a 1 stands for "Among the Worst," a 4 stands for "About Average," and a 7 stands for "Among the Best," how do you rate the overall teaching quality of the professor in this course?

1	2	3	4	5	6	7
Among the Worst			About Average			Among the Best

In such cases, one may regard the qualitative responses as ordinal categorical measures of an underlying continuous variable. For teaching evaluations, the latent variable is an unobservable index of relative teaching quality that takes into account the organization of the course, the clarity of the lectures, and many other characteristics of the course material and the lecturer.

Note that in both cases, quantitative and qualitative, the categories are ordered according to the magnitude of a univariate latent variable, as in income or teaching quality. In the next section, we consider sets of discrete outcomes that are not ordered. For example, a selection of transportation modes {car, bus, train, bicycle} does not possess a general, unique ordering. Such categorical phenomena as transportation mode choice are usually modeled with multivariate latent variables.

The ordered probability model asserts an observation rule of the form

$$\tau(y_n^*) = \begin{cases} 0 & \text{if } y_n^* < \alpha_1 \\ 1 & \text{if } \alpha_1 \le y_n^* < \alpha_2 \\ \vdots & \vdots \\ J & \text{if } \alpha_J \le y_n^* \end{cases} \tag{27.25}$$

where $J+1$ denotes the number of ordered outcomes.[11] The α_js are boundary values, like the income brackets above, where τ steps up by one. One can describe this step-function quality formally with

$$\tau(y_n^*) = \sum_{j=1}^{J} \mathbf{1}\{\alpha_j \leq y_n^*\}$$

where $\alpha_0 \equiv -\infty$. Thus, $y_n = \tau(y_n^*)$ is a sum of binary variables.

Figure 27.4 pictures the observation rule in its top panel. Note that the vertical axis is not necessarily located at $y_n^* = 0$. In the middle panel, we plot the p.d.f. of y_n^*. The probability that $y_n = j$ is the probability that y_n^* falls into the $(j+1)$th interval, which equals the area under this p.d.f. within the interval. The c.d.f. of y_n appears in the bottom panel, making discrete steps at each interval boundary. The height of each step is the probability that y_n will equal the value at that point.

Specifying that ε_n has the c.d.f. $F(\cdot)$, these probabilities are

$$\begin{aligned} \Pr\{y_n = j \mid \mathbf{x}_n\} &= \Pr\{\alpha_j \leq y_n^* < \alpha_{j+1}\} \\ &= \Pr\left\{\frac{\alpha_j - \mathbf{x}_n'\boldsymbol{\beta}_0}{\sigma_0} \leq \varepsilon_n < \frac{\alpha_{j+1} - \mathbf{x}_n'\boldsymbol{\beta}_0}{\sigma_0}\right\} \\ &= F\left(\frac{\alpha_{j+1} - \mathbf{x}_n'\boldsymbol{\beta}_0}{\sigma_0}\right) - F\left(\frac{\alpha_j - \mathbf{x}_n'\boldsymbol{\beta}_0}{\sigma_0}\right) \end{aligned} \tag{27.26}$$

$(j = 0, 1, \ldots, J)$ where $\alpha_{J+1} = \infty$.[12] Therefore, the average log-likelihood function equals

$$\mathrm{E}_N\left[\sum_{j=0}^{J} \mathbf{1}\{y_n = j\} \log\left[F\left(\frac{\alpha_{j+1} - \mathbf{x}_n'\boldsymbol{\beta}}{\sigma}\right) - F\left(\frac{\alpha_j - \mathbf{x}_n'\boldsymbol{\beta}}{\sigma}\right)\right]\right]$$

Identification of the parameters in this log-likelihood function depends on whether the interval boundaries, the α_js, are data or parameters. Either treatment is possible. In our example of an income survey, the researcher chooses the intervals for the survey question so that the α_js are conditional data like the explanatory variables in $\mathbf{x}_n$. On the other hand, the survey of teaching quality contains no intervals for the latent quality index. The index itself is merely a convenient working concept and so are such interval boundaries. Hence, the α_js are parameters that implement a simplified description of the responses to the survey.

If the α_j are data, then both $\boldsymbol{\beta}_0$ and σ_0 are identified. One way to explain this identification is to view α_j as an additional explanatory variable in $F(\cdot)$:

$$\frac{\alpha_j - \mathbf{x}_n'\boldsymbol{\beta}_0}{\sigma_0} = \frac{1}{\sigma_0}\alpha_j - \mathbf{x}_n'\left(\frac{1}{\sigma_0} \cdot \boldsymbol{\beta}_0\right)$$

As in a Bernoulli likelihood function, the "coefficients" $1/\sigma_0$ and $(1/\sigma_0) \cdot \boldsymbol{\beta}_0$ are identified. So, then, are $\boldsymbol{\beta}_0$ and σ_0. In effect, the α_j provide information about the scale of the latent y_n^*.

When the α_js are parameters, the ordinal probability model does not identify σ_0 separately from the α_js and $\boldsymbol{\beta}_0$. The ratio α_j/σ_0 is like an intercept for each probability term in the likelihood function. Because of this, an intercept in $\mathbf{x}_n'\boldsymbol{\beta}_0$ is also not identified. If

[11] Unlike the examples above, we label the first ordered outcome 0, rather than 1, for notational convenience.

[12] We have defined α_0 and α_{J+1} so that $F(\alpha_0) = 0$ and $F(\alpha_{J+1}) = 1$.

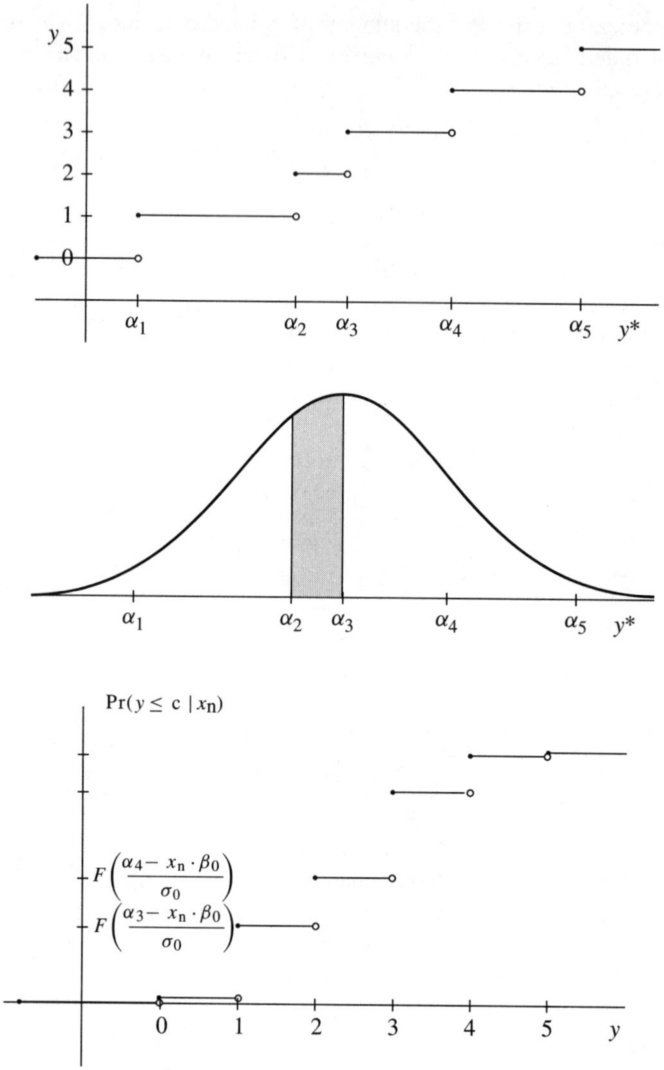

Figure 27.4 Ordered probability model.

$$\mathbf{x}_n'\boldsymbol{\beta}_0 = \beta_1 + \beta_2 x_{n2} + \cdots + \beta_K x_{nK}$$

then

$$\frac{\alpha_j - \mathbf{x}_n'\boldsymbol{\beta}_0}{\sigma_0} = \frac{\alpha_j - \beta_1}{\sigma_0} - \frac{\beta_2}{\sigma_0} x_{n2} - \cdots - \frac{\beta_K}{\sigma_0} x_{nK}$$

and the RHS coefficients are the identified functions of the parameters. Thus, one omits a constant from the list of explanatory variables in such ordered probability models.

Researchers generally estimate the ordered probability model with the MLE. By convention, one typically specifies F to be the standard normal c.d.f. although the logistic c.d.f. will usually produce similar inferences. These models are called *ordered probit* and *ordered logit*, respectively. NLS and WNLS for the mean of y_n are certainly feasible estimation methods, but they suffer from relative inefficiency. Unlike the simpler binomial case, higher moments of ordered data contain additional information about the parameters. NLS and WNLS rely exclusively on the first moment for moment restrictions.[13]

27.2.2 Count Data

Count data are distinct from general ordered discrete data in this very respect. The counts have *cardinal* meaning and their conditional mean holds interest. Such data as the number of spells of unemployment experienced by an individual in a year, the number of accidents at nuclear power stations in a month, and the number of children in a family are examples of count data studied by economists. In each case the probability of small counts is high so that the discreteness of the probability distribution is an important feature.

The statistical analysis of count data has a long history that significantly predates ordered probability models. The basic count-data probability model is the Poisson

$$f_P(y;\lambda) = \begin{cases} e^{-\lambda}\frac{\lambda^y}{y!} & y \in \mathbb{N} \\ 0 & y \notin \mathbb{N} \end{cases} \tag{27.27}$$

$\lambda > 0$, which, despite its simplicity, has successfully described many count phenomena.[14] Authors usually motivate this p.m.f. as a limit of the binomial p.m.f. (Definition D.20, p. 885) rather than from a latent regression model such as the ordered probability model. The Poisson is the approximate distribution of the number of ones from a large number of Bernoulli trials, each with a small probability of a one.

The mean of the Poisson distribution equals its one parameter λ and the variance also equals λ. To allow for the presence of explanatory variables in a conditional mean function, researchers generally appeal to an exponential transformation of the linear model:

$$\mathrm{E}[y_n \mid \mathbf{x}_n] = \lambda_n = \exp(\mathbf{x}_n'\boldsymbol{\beta}_0) \tag{27.28}$$

which restricts $\lambda_n > 0$ for all $\boldsymbol{\beta}$. Application of the Poisson regression model has also revealed a persistent weakness: researchers repeatedly find evidence that $\mathrm{Var}[y_n \mid \mathbf{x}_n] > \mathrm{E}[y_n \mid \mathbf{x}_n]$ in actual data. Because these moments are equal in the Poisson distribution, researchers call this phenomenon *overdispersion*.

Among the alternative distributions that permit overdispersion, the negative binomial (NB) is a leading substitute for the Poisson.[15] One expression for the negative binomial p.m.f. is

$$f_{\mathrm{NB}}(y \mid \alpha, p) = \begin{cases} \frac{\Gamma(y+\alpha)}{\Gamma(y+1)\Gamma(\alpha)} p^{\alpha}(1-p)^{y} & \text{if } y \in \mathbb{N} \\ 0 & \text{if } y \notin \mathbb{N} \end{cases} \tag{27.29}$$

---

13 For futher comment, see Exercise 27.8.

14 Hoel et al. (1971, pp. 56–57) mention these examples of phenomena that are approximately Poisson distributed:

> the number of atoms of a radioactive substance that disintegrate in a unit time interval, the number of calls that come into a telephone exchange in a unit time interval, the number of misprints on a page of a book, and the number of bacterial colonies that grow on a petri dish that has been smeared with a bacterial suspension.

15 Greenwood and Yule (1920) made early use of this specification.

where α is a positive real number and $0 \leq p \leq 1$ and $\Gamma(\cdot)$ is the gamma function (Definition D.28, p. 888).[16] The first two moments of the negative binomial distribution are $\alpha(1-p)/p$ and $\alpha(1-p)/p^2$ so that its variance always exceeds its mean.

Examples of both distributions appear in Figure 27.5. Both distributions have a mean value of three in this graph. The negative binomial p.m.f. has a fatter right tail, giving it a higher variance than the Poisson p.m.f. The fatter tail is balanced by placing the mode of this distribution to the left of the Poisson mode.

Part of the appeal of the negative binomial distribution is that the Poisson is a special case: the Poisson corresponds to the limiting distribution as p approaches 1 while restricting $\alpha = \lambda/(1-p)$.[17] Thus, setting

$$\alpha_n = \exp[\mathbf{x}_n'(\boldsymbol{\beta}_0 - \boldsymbol{\gamma}_0)] \quad \text{and} \quad p_n = \frac{\exp(-\mathbf{x}_n'\boldsymbol{\gamma}_0)}{1+\exp(-\mathbf{x}_n'\boldsymbol{\gamma}_0)} \tag{27.30}$$

extends the Poisson regression model (27.27)–(27.28) to the negative binomial framework. The first two conditional moments of the negative binomial p.m.f. are then

$$\mathrm{E}[y_n \mid \mathbf{x}_n] = \exp(\mathbf{x}_n'\boldsymbol{\beta}_0)$$
$$\mathrm{Var}[y_n \mid \mathbf{x}_n] = \exp(\mathbf{x}_n'\boldsymbol{\beta}_0)\left[1+\exp(\mathbf{x}_n'\boldsymbol{\gamma}_0)\right] > \mathrm{E}[y_n \mid \mathbf{x}_n]$$

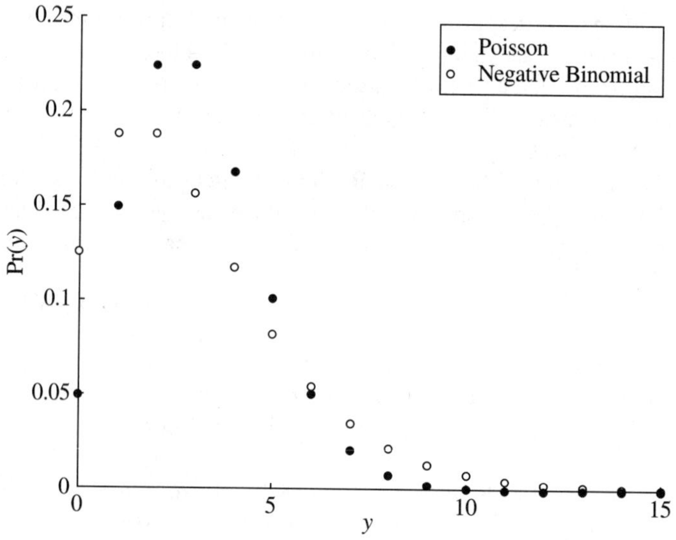

Figure 27.5 Count distributions.

[16] Introductory probability texts often describe the negative binomial probability function as

$$\Pr\{Y=n\} = \frac{(n-1)!}{(n-\alpha)!\,(\alpha-1)!}p^{\alpha}(1-p)^{n-\alpha}, \quad n = \alpha, \alpha+1, \alpha+2, \ldots$$

where α is a positive integer. See Definition D.22 (Negative Binomial Distribution, p. 885). With the properties of the gamma function, one can show that $Y = y + \alpha$ for this case. We confirm that α can be any positive real number in the *Mathematical Notes*, Section 27.6.1.

[17] See Section 27.6.1.

Estimation and inference within the maximum likelihood framework are straightforward in these models with two notable exceptions. First, if the distribution of the data is actually Poisson then the parameter vector $\boldsymbol{\gamma}_0$ in the negative binomial model is not identified. For this reason, researchers often focus on restricted models when the Poisson distribution is likely to be appropriate: the leading examples are

$$\text{Var}[y_n \mid \mathbf{x}_n] = \exp(\mathbf{x}_n'\boldsymbol{\beta}_0)\left[1 + \delta_0 \exp\left(j \cdot \mathbf{x}_n'\boldsymbol{\beta}_0\right)\right] \tag{27.31}$$

for $j = 0, 1$, or 2. These are convenient, restricted versions of (27.30), where

$$\mathbf{x}_n'\boldsymbol{\gamma}_0 = (\log \delta_0) + j \cdot \mathbf{x}_n'\boldsymbol{\beta}_0 \quad \text{and} \quad p_n = \frac{\exp\left(-j \cdot \mathbf{x}_n'\boldsymbol{\beta}_0\right)}{\delta_0 + \exp\left(-j \cdot \mathbf{x}_n'\boldsymbol{\beta}_0\right)}$$

respectively. Note that if the second RHS exponential term in (27.31) contained $\boldsymbol{\gamma}_0$ instead of $\boldsymbol{\beta}_0$, then $\delta_0 = 0$ would make $\boldsymbol{\gamma}_0$ redundant or unidentified.

Second, among the general methods of hypothesis testing that we have described, only the score version applies to testing the null hypothesis that $\delta_0 = 0$ in (27.31). This is because the null hypothesis lies on the boundary of the parameter space for the negative binomial distribution. In (27.31), $\delta_0 = 0$ corresponds to the limiting distribution of (27.29) as

$$p_n = \frac{\delta_0 \exp\left(-j \cdot \mathbf{x}_n'\boldsymbol{\beta}_0\right)}{1 + \delta_0 \exp\left(-j \cdot \mathbf{x}_n'\boldsymbol{\beta}_0\right)} \to 1$$

As a result, there is a positive probability under the null hypothesis that the unrestricted MLE will equal the restricted estimator and the LR and Wald test statistics will collapse to zero. The distribution of these statistics will not be chi-square.[18] The score test statistic, on the other hand, implicitly does not obey the negative binomial restriction that $\delta_0 > 0$ when it forecasts the unrestricted estimator. Hence, no such difficulty arises for that test.

The score test statistic (Cameron and Trivedi, 1986; Lee, 1986) equals one-half the explained sum of squares from the WLS fit of $\left(y_n - \hat{\mu}_n\right)^2 - y_n$ on $\hat{\mu}_n^j$ with weights $\hat{\mu}_n^{-1}$, where $\hat{\mu}_n = \exp(\mathbf{x}_n'\hat{\boldsymbol{\beta}})$ is the fitted mean value of the nth observation for the MLE of the Poisson model. We outline the derivation of this test statistic in Exercise 27.10. Under the null hypothesis, this statistic has an asymptotic chi-square distribution with one degree of freedom. One can accommodate all three $(j = 0, 1, 2)$ possibilities for the alternative hypothesis by extending (27.31) to

$$\text{Var}[y_n \mid \mathbf{x}_n] = \mu_n \left(1 + \delta_0 + \delta_1 \mu_n + \delta_2 \mu_n^2\right)$$

where $\mu_n \equiv \exp(\mathbf{x}_n'\boldsymbol{\beta}_0)$. The corresponding score test uses three explanatory variables (a constant, $\hat{\mu}_n$, and $\hat{\mu}_n^2$) in the WLS regression and its comparison distribution is χ_3^2.

Like the ordered-probability model, one can motivate models of count data with a latent variable model (27.23) and an observation rule (27.24). After all, count data are actually ordered data. The only important difference between the ordered data described above and count data is that J, the number of possible outcomes, is infinite for count data. Therefore, one can interpret count data within an extended ordered-data framework by allowing the intervals $\left(\alpha_{j-1}, \alpha_j\right)$ to be a sequence of intervals for $j = 1, 2, 3, \ldots$. Furthermore, any count-

[18] For another example of a test on the parameter space boundary, see Exercise 17.21. That example describes a test of one distribution (the normal) against a mixture of the distribution (the Student t). One can interpret the current test this way also (see Exercise 27.15).

data model (including the Poisson and the negative binomial) is equivalent to such an ordered-probability model.[19]

Latent models are a powerful modeling tool. This is particularly true in the next section in which we describe additional probability models for multiple discrete outcomes that rest on a latent *multivariate* structure.

27.3 MULTIVARIATE MODELS

We can view the ordered data described above as a transformation of a single latent variable. The magnitude of the observed variable can have a sensible monotonic relationship with the magnitude of a univariate latent variable. When the possible discrete outcomes do not possess a fundamental order then several latent variables may underlie the observed data. In place of (27.23), we now let $\mathbf{y}_n^* \equiv [y_{nj}^*; j = 1, \ldots, J]'$ be a column vector of J latent dependent variables whose joint conditional distribution follows an SUR system

$$\mathbf{y}_n^{*\prime} = \mathbf{x}_n' \mathbf{B}_0 + \boldsymbol{\varepsilon}_n' \tag{27.32}$$

where the $\boldsymbol{\varepsilon}_n$ are $J \times 1$ vectors of i.i.d. latent random components with mean zero and constant variance matrix $\boldsymbol{\Omega}_0$ conditional on $\mathbf{x}_n$. The unknown parameters are the slope coefficients in the matrix $\mathbf{B}_0 = [\boldsymbol{\beta}_{01}, \ldots, \boldsymbol{\beta}_{0J}]$ and the covariance parameters in the $J \times J$ matrix $\boldsymbol{\Omega}_0 = [\omega_{0ij}]$. For the moment, we leave $\mathbf{B}_0$ and $\boldsymbol{\Omega}_0$ unrestricted.

27.3.1 Multiple Choice

The leading example of unordered outcomes is multiple-choice data, where the alternative choices have no intrinsic ordering. Transportation mode choice by consumers is a classic application because of early work by McFadden (1974a, 1974b), among others. As part of planning for the installation of the Bay Area Rapid Transit (BART) system in the area surrounding Berkeley, California in the 1970s, McFadden and his co-researchers studied the demands for various modes of public transportation as well as private cars.[20] They modeled the demands of individual consumers as discrete choices that maximize their utility. Each transportation mode was described as a bundle of such generic mode characteristics as speed, convenience, and cost and the utility of each choice was an element of the latent $\mathbf{y}_n^*$. The characteristics of the mode choices and the individual consumers appear in $\mathbf{x}_n$, $\mathbf{B}_0$ contains the parameters capturing the common features of all consumers' preferences, and $\boldsymbol{\varepsilon}_n$ represents omitted characteristics and the variation in preferences across consumers.

According to the hypothesis of utility maximization, the observed choice each consumer makes is the transportation mode with the highest utility.[21] We will record the choice with J dummy variables according to the observation rule

---

[19] See Exercise 27.14.

[20] Originally the acronym BART stood for *Berkeley* Area Rapid Transit. The planners focused on the east-bay community, deeming the southern peninsula region too rural for service.

[21] Choice sets can differ across individuals.

$$y_{nj} = \mathbf{1}\left\{ y_{nj}^* = \max_{i \in \{1,\ldots,J\}} y_{ni}^* \right\} \tag{27.33}$$

The jth element of $\mathbf{y}_n = [y_{nj};\ j = 1, \ldots, J]'$ equals one if the jth mode is selected. Otherwise, y_{nj} equals zero.[22] Thus, we may write the sample average log-likelihood function in the general form

$$L(\boldsymbol{\theta}) = \mathrm{E}_N \left[\sum_{j=1}^{J} y_{nj} \log p_{nj} \right] \tag{27.34}$$

where

$$p_{nj} \equiv \Pr\left\{ y_{nj} = 1 \mid \mathbf{x}_n \right\}$$

For each observation, the y_{nj} that equals one enters the log probability for that outcome while the other y_{nj} zero out the remaining log probabilities. In that limited sense, this log-likelihood is a simple generalization of the Bernoulli log-likelihood in (27.14).

IDENTIFICATION

Identification of the parameters in $\mathbf{B}_0$ and $\boldsymbol{\Omega}_0$ requires somewhat more care than the Bernoulli model, although the insights are essentially the same. These are, first, that the *scale* of the distribution of $\mathbf{y}_n^*$ is not identified and, second, that only *differences* in the elements of $\mathbf{y}_n^*$ affect $\mathbf{y}_n$. Written in terms of the observation rule (27.33),

$$\begin{aligned} y_{nj} &= \mathbf{1}\left\{ y_{nj}^* = \max_{i \in \{1,\ldots,J\}} y_{ni}^* \right\} \\ &= \mathbf{1}\left\{ \sigma y_{nj}^* + \mu = \max_{i \in \{1,\ldots,J\}} \left(\sigma y_{ni}^* + \mu \right) \right\} \\ &= \mathbf{1}\left\{ 0 = \max_{i \in \{1,\ldots,J\}} \sigma \left(y_{ni}^* - y_{nj}^* \right) \right\} \end{aligned}$$

for all μ and all $\sigma > 0$. In addition, the differences that determine y_{nm} are one to one with the differences that determine y_{nj}:

$$y_{ni}^* - y_{nm}^* = \left(y_{ni}^* - y_{nj}^* \right) - \left(y_{nm}^* - y_{nj}^* \right)$$

Therefore, we may focus on the identification of the parameters through the distribution of one set of differences, say $\{y_{nj}^* - y_{n1}^*;\ \forall j \neq 1\}$.

Let us first consider the identification of the unrestricted variance–covariance matrix $\boldsymbol{\Omega}_0$. Because only differences matter in $\mathbf{y}$,

$$\begin{aligned} \mathbf{y}_n^{*\prime} &= \mathbf{x}_n' \mathbf{B}_0 + \boldsymbol{\varepsilon}_n' \\ &= \left[\mathbf{x}_n' \boldsymbol{\beta}_{0j} + \varepsilon_{nj};\quad j = 1, \ldots, J \right] \end{aligned}$$

and

[22] One could also record the index of the chosen mode, so that $\mathbf{y}_n$ would be a scalar, categorical variable. The indicator notation is more convenient.

$$y^*_{n1} = \mathbf{x}'_n \boldsymbol{\beta}_{01}$$
$$y^*_{nj} = \mathbf{x}'_n \boldsymbol{\beta}_{0j} + \varepsilon_{nj} - \varepsilon_{n1}, \qquad j = 2, \ldots, J \tag{27.35}$$

are different, but observationally equivalent, latent specifications. Therefore, we can set $\varepsilon_{n1} = 0$ and the first row and column of $\boldsymbol{\Omega}_0$ to zeros without restricting the log-likelihood function and we adopt this as a parameter normalization.

Because the scale is not identified,

$$y^*_{nj} = \mathbf{x}'_n \boldsymbol{\beta}_{0j} + \varepsilon_{nj}, \qquad j = 2, \ldots, J$$

and

$$\frac{1}{\sqrt{\sum_{i=2}^{J} \omega_{0ii}^2}} y^*_{nj} = \frac{1}{\sqrt{\sum_{i=2}^{J} \omega_{0ii}^2}} \left(\mathbf{x}'_{nj} \boldsymbol{\beta}_0 + \boldsymbol{\varepsilon}_{nj}\right), \qquad j = 2, \ldots, J$$

are also observationally equivalent. Therefore, we can also set $\sum_{i=2}^{J} \omega_{0ii}^2 = 1$ without restricting the log-likelihood function.[23] With these parameter normalizations, the elements of $\boldsymbol{\Omega}_0$ are locally identified.

Having addressed the matter of scale, we can focus on the implications of differencing the y^*_{ni} for the identification of $\mathbf{B}_0$. We can take the latent specification in (27.35) a step further and write another observationally equivalent latent model:

$$y^*_{n1} = 0$$
$$y^*_{nj} = \mathbf{x}'_n (\boldsymbol{\beta}_{0j} - \boldsymbol{\beta}_{01}) + \varepsilon_{nj} - \varepsilon_{n1}, \qquad j = 2, \ldots, J \tag{27.36}$$

The y_{nj} depend on $\mathbf{B}_0$ through $\mathbf{x}'_n(\boldsymbol{\beta}_{0j} - \boldsymbol{\beta}_{01})$ so that we must normalize $\mathbf{B}_0$. Two normalizations are common. First, we can simply set $\boldsymbol{\beta}_{01} = 0$. This is appropriate when there are no other restrictions and $\mathbf{X} \equiv [\mathbf{x}_1, \ldots, \mathbf{x}_N]'$ is full-column rank. Such specifications occur outside economic multiple-choice modeling.

However, in multiple-choice settings researchers restrict

$$\mathbf{B}_0 = \operatorname{diag}(\boldsymbol{\delta}_0;\ j = 1, \ldots, J)$$

so that $\mathbf{x}'_n \boldsymbol{\beta}_{0j} = \mathbf{x}'_{nj} \boldsymbol{\delta}_0$ where $\mathbf{x}'_n = \left[\mathbf{x}'_{n1}, \ldots, \mathbf{x}'_{nJ}\right]$. The $\mathbf{x}_{nj}$s are vectors of K characteristic values for the jth alternative and $\boldsymbol{\delta}_0$ is a vector of K unknown parameters that appear in every $\boldsymbol{\beta}_{0j}$. For example, transportation modes might be characterized by

$$\mathbf{x}'_{nj} \boldsymbol{\delta}_0 = (\text{trip time})_j\, \delta_{01} + (\text{seat availability})_j\, \delta_{02} + (\text{reliability})_j\, \delta_{03} \tag{27.37}$$

and the δs are the marginal utilities of each characteristic in the utility of a transportation mode. Under these restrictions,

$$\mathbf{x}'_n (\boldsymbol{\beta}_{0j} - \boldsymbol{\beta}_{01}) = \left(\mathbf{x}_{nj} - \mathbf{x}_{n1}\right)' \boldsymbol{\delta}_0$$

and the identification of $\boldsymbol{\delta}_0$ requires the matrix

[23] It is not equivalent to normalize by setting $\omega_{0ii} = 1$ for some i. The log-likelihood function permits the variance matrix $\boldsymbol{\Omega}_0$ to be singular so that a diagonal element may equal zero. Setting a particular element to any nonzero constant will, therefore, restrict the likelihood function.

$$\left[\mathbf{x}_{nj} - \mathbf{x}_{n1};\ j = 2, \ldots, J,\ n = 1, \ldots, N\right]' \tag{27.38}$$

to be full-column rank.

Subsets of *alternative-specific* coefficients also appear alongside such constrained coefficients. The simplest and most common example is the alternative-specific intercept so that (27.37) becomes

$$\mathbf{x}_n' \boldsymbol{\beta}_{0j} = \beta_{01j} + (\text{trip time})_j\, \delta_{01} + (\text{seat availability})_j\, \delta_{02} + (\text{reliability})_j\, \delta_{03} \tag{27.39}$$

The β_{01j} represents the effects of unique features of the jth alternative that are not captured by the characteristics in $\mathbf{x}_{nj}$. One normalizes one of the alternative-specific coefficients to equal zero, as above $\beta_{011} = 0$.

To analyze identification generally for such mixed cases, it is convenient to place the alternative-specific coefficients into $\boldsymbol{\delta}_0$ through alternative-specific variables in the $\mathbf{x}_{nj}$. For example, we can rewrite (27.39) as

$$\begin{aligned} \mathbf{x}_{nj}' \boldsymbol{\delta}_0 = {} & (\text{trip time})_j\, \delta_{01} + (\text{seat availability})_j\, \delta_{02} + (\text{reliability})_j\, \delta_{03} \\ & + \sum_{i=2}^{J} \delta_{0,3+i} \mathbf{1}\{i = j\} \end{aligned}$$

with alternative-specific dummy variables, where $\delta_{0,3+j} = \beta_{01j}$. The full-column rank condition on the matrix in (27.38) then requires dropping one dummy variable to avoid the dummy variable trap. This is equivalent to normalizing $\beta_{011} = 0$.

As another practical example, consider the inclusion of the characteristics of the decision maker in a multiple-choice model. Such variables are constant across the choices and must appear through interactions with characteristics of the alternatives. For example, one might specify

$$\begin{aligned} \mathbf{x}_{ni}' \boldsymbol{\delta}_0 = {} & (\text{trip time})_i\, \delta_{01} + (\text{trip time})_i \times (\text{wage})_n\, \delta_{02} \\ & + (\text{seat availability})_i\, \delta_{03} + (\text{reliability})_i\, \delta_{04} \end{aligned}$$

when the coefficient for *trip time* varies with the individual's wage, as in

$$\beta_{01n} = \gamma_{01} + (\text{wage})_n\, \gamma_{02}$$

Without such interaction with *trip time*, the *wage* variable would disappear in differences and its coefficient would not be identified.

LOG-LIKELIHOOD

To complete the derivation of the log-likelihood function, we must find expressions for the probabilities $\Pr\left\{y_{nj} = 1 \mid \mathbf{X}_n\right\}$. This turns out to be much more difficult than for the probabilities that we have faced so far. We begin with

$$\begin{aligned} p_{nj} & \equiv \Pr\left\{y_{nj} = 1 \mid \mathbf{X}_n\right\} \\ & = \Pr\{y_{ni}^* \le y_{nj}^*,\ \forall i \ne j \mid \mathbf{X}_n\} \\ & = \Pr\{\varepsilon_{ni} - \varepsilon_{nj} \le (\mathbf{x}_{nj} - \mathbf{x}_{ni})' \boldsymbol{\delta}_0,\ \forall i \ne j \mid \mathbf{X}_n\} \end{aligned} \tag{27.40}$$

From this expression we observe that evaluating the log-likelihood function involves multivariate integration over $J-1$ dimensions.

We might manage this integration easily if the $\varepsilon_{ni} - \varepsilon_{nj}$ were independently distributed over the index i, because the joint probability would be the product of $J-1$ marginal probabilities. But this does not generally occur for all possible choices j. Let $J = 3$ for example. Then the probability that $y_{n1} = 1$ will be a bivariate integral over the joint distribution of $\varepsilon_{n2} - \varepsilon_{n1}$ and $\varepsilon_{n3} - \varepsilon_{n1}$ and the probability that $y_{n2} = 1$ will be a bivariate integral over the joint distribution of

$$\varepsilon_{n1} - \varepsilon_{n2} = -(\varepsilon_{n2} - \varepsilon_{n1})$$

$$\varepsilon_{n3} - \varepsilon_{n2} = (\varepsilon_{n3} - \varepsilon_{n1}) - (\varepsilon_{n2} - \varepsilon_{n1})$$

So even if $\varepsilon_{n2} - \varepsilon_{n1}$ and $\varepsilon_{n3} - \varepsilon_{n1}$ are independent, $\varepsilon_{n1} - \varepsilon_{n2}$ and $\varepsilon_{n3} - \varepsilon_{n2}$ will be dependent unless $\varepsilon_{n2} - \varepsilon_{n1}$ is a constant (zero).

A workable approach is to restrict the ε_{nj} to be independently distributed over $j = 1, \ldots, J$. Denoting the c.d.f. of ε_{nj} by $F_j(\cdot)$, one can condition part of the integration on ε_{nj} to obtain

$$\begin{aligned} p_{nj} &= \Pr\{\varepsilon_{ni} \le \varepsilon_{nj} + (\mathbf{x}_{nj} - \mathbf{x}_{ni})'\boldsymbol{\beta}_0,\ i \ne j\} \\ &= \mathrm{E}\left[\prod_{i \ne j} F_i\left(\varepsilon_{nj} + (\mathbf{x}_{nj} - \mathbf{x}_{ni})'\boldsymbol{\beta}_0\right)\right] \end{aligned} \tag{27.41}$$

In general, this is as far as formal manipulation can take us. Implementation of the MLE involves computing this last univariate expectation with such numerical integration methods as quadrature. Researchers who use this specification sometimes specify the normal c.d.f. for F_j. However, there is also an important case in which the p_{nj}s have simple closed-form expressions.

LOGIT

If the ε_{nj} are i.i.d. random variables from the Weibull distribution, then the choice probabilities in (27.41) simplify to[24]

$$\begin{aligned} p_{nj} &= \Pr\{\varepsilon_{ni} - \varepsilon_{nj} \le \left(\mathbf{x}_{nj} - \mathbf{x}_{ni}\right)' \boldsymbol{\delta}_0, \quad i \ne j\} \\ &= \frac{\exp(\mathbf{x}_{nj}'\boldsymbol{\delta}_0)}{\sum_{i=1}^{J}\exp(\mathbf{x}_{ni}'\boldsymbol{\delta}_0)} \end{aligned} \tag{27.42}$$

One can see by inspection that these probabilities are positive, less than one, and sum over j to one. It is also clear that the choice with the highest $\mathbf{x}_{nj}'\boldsymbol{\delta}_0$ has the highest probability.

The multinomial logit MLE is also easy to compute because the log-likelihood function is globally concave. Substituting (27.42) into (27.34), we obtain the logit log-likelihood function

$$L(\boldsymbol{\theta}) = \mathrm{E}_N\left[\left(\sum_{j=1}^{J}\mathbf{x}_{nj}'\boldsymbol{\delta}\, y_{nj}\right) - \log\left(\sum_{i=1}^{J}\exp(\mathbf{x}_{ni}'\boldsymbol{\delta})\right)\right]$$

Differentiating with respect to $\boldsymbol{\delta}$ and simplifying gives the score function

[24] The c.d.f. of the Weibull distribution is $F(z) = \exp(-e^{-z})$. Also note that $\boldsymbol{\Omega}_0$ is restricted and normalized to be $\pi^2/6 \cdot \mathbf{I}_J$.

$$L_{\theta}(\theta) = \mathrm{E}_N\left[\sum_{j=1}^{J} \mathbf{x}'_{nj}\left(y_{nj} - p_{nj}\right)\right]$$

As in Bernoulli logit, the score depends on the dependent data through a simple statistic, $\mathrm{E}_N[\sum_j \mathbf{x}'_{nj} y_{nj}]$. This term disappears after further differentiation. As a result the Hessian does not depend on $\mathbf{y}_n$ and must *equal* the negative conditional information matrix. But the latter is negative definite so we conclude that the multinomial logit log-likelihood function is globally concave.

The multinomial logit specification also makes a clear restriction on the predicted behavior of the decision makers. The odds of choosing the jth alternative over the ith depend only on the characteristics of those two alternatives:

$$\frac{\Pr\{y_{nj} = 1 \mid \mathbf{X}_n\}}{\Pr\{y_{ni} = 1 \mid \mathbf{X}_n\}} = \frac{\exp(\mathbf{x}'_{nj}\boldsymbol{\delta}_0)}{\exp(\mathbf{x}'_{ni}\boldsymbol{\delta}_0)} = \exp[(\mathbf{x}_{nj} - \mathbf{x}_{ni})'\boldsymbol{\delta}_0]$$

In other words, the characteristics of any other alternative in the choice set have no influence on this ratio. This feature is called the *independence from irrelevant alternatives* (IIA) property.

A classic example called "the red-bus–blue-bus problem" illustrates the nature of the difficulty effectively. Consider an initial transportation mode choice between driving and taking a red bus. For simplicity, suppose that consumers are split fifty–fifty between driving and taking the red bus. London, England was once full of red double-decker buses, so let us make that fair city the setting for our story. Now suppose that public transportation is privatized and a new, rival bus company is formed. In the spirit of perfect competition, this company introduces a blue bus that is otherwise indistinguishable from the red bus, two decks and all. The English bus riders, caring nought about the color of the bus, would split their trips evenly between the two buses.[25] And if their choice probabilities obey the IIA property, the relative odds of taking the red bus over driving would continue to equal one.

Now here is the kicker. Because the choice probabilities must sum to one, the probabilities of driving, taking the red bus, and taking the blue bus must all equal one-third. But then English travelers would be taking the bus twice as often as driving without any change in their actual choice set. Because of the IIA property, the multinomial logit model cannot account adequately for the presence of an equivalent alternative in the choice set.

The IIA property does not render the multinomial logit model useless. In applications in which the choices are dissimilar, the fitted probabilities often pass diagnostic tests for the IIA property. A leading diagnostic test, proposed by Hausman and McFadden (1984), exploits a simple implication of IIA: one can omit alternatives that were not chosen from the observed choice sets and the associated conditional MLE will also be a consistent, albeit inefficient, estimator. In other words, the consistency of the MLE is impervious to omitting "irrelevant alternatives." With this in mind, Hausman and McFadden suggest a Hausman specification test comparing the MLEs based on complete and incomplete choice sets to detect departures from IIA.[26] The researcher must decide which alternatives to omit from the choice sets and it is difficult to anticipate which omissions will produce the most powerful test.

Should the IIA property appear to fail such tests or to be not credible, there are several workable alternatives to the multinomial logit specification for discrete choice models. Closest

---

[25] We admit some lack of realism here. Assume there are no tourists.

[26] For a further description of this specification test, see Exercise 27.13.

to the multinomial logit specification is the family of nested logit models.[27] In Section 27.4.4, we introduce estimation methods that use simulation to implement such otherwise intractable specifications as a multinomial probit model.

FORECASTING

Researchers frequently use these models to forecast the share of a new alternative. This will require extending the variance specification to the new alternative. Logit restricts the variance matrix to be a scalar matrix, which is easily extended. More generally, researchers use variance-component models.

27.3.2 Rank-Ordered Multiple Choice

In some cases, one observes the preference ordering for all or some of the alternatives in the choice set. This occurs mostly with survey data, where it is feasible to ask respondents directly to rank the alternatives. When the ranking process is relatively easy, so that respondents can give sensible answers, the researcher learns more about preferences than from a question soliciting only the most preferred alternative.

The likelihood for such data is quite similar to that for multiple choice. Suppose that alternatives are preferred in the order of the index j, with alternative J the most preferred and alternative 1 the least preferred. This implies that

$$y_{n1}^* < y_{n2}^* < \cdots < y_{n,J-1}^* < y_{nJ}^*$$

These $J - 1$ inequalities also imply such other inequalities as $y_{n1}^* < y_{n3}^*$, but this is redundant information that one can ignore. The probability of this rank ordering is, therefore,

$$\begin{aligned} &\Pr\{y_{n,j-1}^* \le y_{nj}^*,\ j = 2, \ldots, J \mid \mathbf{x}_n\} \\ &\quad = \Pr\{\varepsilon_{n,j-1} - \varepsilon_{n,j} \le (\mathbf{x}_{nj} - \mathbf{x}_{n,j-1})'\boldsymbol{\delta}_0,\ j > 2 \mid \mathbf{x}_n\} \end{aligned} \tag{27.43}$$

Compared to the multiple choice probability (27.40), the rank ordering probability requires the same order of integration and MLE is equally problematic.

If the ε_{nj} are Weibull random variables as in the latent multinomial logit model, then the rank ordering probabilities continue to be tractable. As Beggs et al. (1981) observe, the probability is simply a product of multinomial logit probabilities:

$$\Pr\{y_{n,j-1}^* \le y_{nj}^*,\ j = 2, \ldots, J \mid \mathbf{X}_n\} = \prod_{j=2}^{J} \frac{\exp(\mathbf{x}_{nj}'\boldsymbol{\delta}_0)}{\sum_{i=1}^{j} \exp(\mathbf{x}_{ni}'\boldsymbol{\delta}_0)} \tag{27.44}$$

In words, each multinomial logit probability equals the probability that a particular alternative is most preferred among a choice set that omits all of the alternatives ranked higher.

This result is additionally convenient because one can compute the MLE with ordinary multinomial logit estimation software. One replicates each observation $J - 1$ times as choices among progressively smaller choice sets, omitting alternatives in the rank order from most

[27] See McFadden (1978).

preferred to least. The observed "choice" for each replication is the alternative with the highest observed rank in the choice set.

Ruud and Wald (1999) note that the *complete* rank ordering of the alternatives permits estimation of specifications that are intractable as multiple choice models. The redundant inequalities just mentioned enable us to estimate parameters from the marginal likelihood functions of the indicator variables $\mathbf{1}\{y_{ni}^* < y_{nj}^*\}$, $i \neq j$. In multiple choice, researchers do not observe these indicator variables. But in complete rank ordering, they do. As a result, Bernoulli regression methods apply.

Suppose, for example, that the ε_{nj} are multivariate normal random variables. For each pair (i, j), the log-likelihood function is

$$L_{ij}(\boldsymbol{\theta}) = \mathrm{E}_N\left[\mathbf{1}\{y_{ni}^* < y_{nj}^*\}\log\Phi\left(\frac{(\mathbf{x}_{nj} - \mathbf{x}_{ni})'\boldsymbol{\delta}}{\sigma_{ij}}\right)\right.$$
$$\left. + \mathbf{1}\{y_{ni}^* \geq y_{nj}^*\}\log\Phi\left(\frac{(\mathbf{x}_{ni} - \mathbf{x}_{nj})'\boldsymbol{\delta}}{\sigma_{ij}}\right)\right]$$

where

$$\sigma_{ij}^2 = \mathrm{Var}[\varepsilon_{nj} - \varepsilon_{ni} \mid \mathbf{X}_n] = \omega_{jj} - 2\omega_{ij} + \omega_{ii}$$

The MLE $(\widehat{\omega_{ij}^{-1} \cdot \boldsymbol{\delta}})$ provides a scaled estimate of $\boldsymbol{\delta}_0$.[28] One can combine the $J(J-1)/2$ different pairs of estimators with the method of minimum distance (MD) to estimate $\boldsymbol{\delta}_0$ and the variance–covariance parameters in $\boldsymbol{\Omega}_0$.

A latent system of seemingly unrelated regressions and an observation rule can generate the econometric specification for each of the discrete dependent variable models that we have studied in this chapter. The structure of the latent variables and the observation rule has additional uses. In particular, it can provide insight about computation as well. In the next section, we describe some of these uses. Afterward we close this chapter with methodological and mathematical notes.

27.4 LATENT VARIABLES AND COMPUTATION

We will relate latent variables to three aspects of estimation: concavity of the log-likelihood function, numerical optimization, and numerical approximation. Each aspect is quite distinct from the others and this shows the analytical power of latent variable models.

First, we present some basic relationships between the score, Hessian, and information matrices of the latent- and observable-variable models. We note a useful result for establishing the global concavity of a log-likelihood function in terms of the p.d.f. of a latent probability model.

Second, we describe a new numerical technique for maximizing a log-likelihood function. One can attack that optimization problem directly with such numerical methods as those described in Chapter 16. There is another method, called the *EM algorithm*, that exploits the latent-variable structure to construct iterative numerical procedures. For many models, the algorithms consist of simple OLS calculations.

[28] Note that some of the slopes may not be identified in some of these log-likelihood functions. The $\mathbf{x}_{jn} - \mathbf{x}_{in}$ may exhibit multicollinearity. In such circumstances, normalizations will be required.

Finally, we consider situations in which the calculation of the log-likelihood function is an obstacle to computing the MLE. We discussed an example in Section 27.3.1 for multiple-choice models. Latent variables can also play a role in overcoming this difficulty. Frequently, one can simulate the latent variable process easily. Using the observation rule, simulation of the observable data process follows easily. Such simulation can support GMM estimation when ML is not feasible.

27.4.1 Score Functions

There is a simple relationship between the score functions of the latent-data model and the observable-data model.

Lemma 27.1 *The score of the log-likelihood function for* $\mathbf{y}$ *equals the conditional mean of the score of the log-likelihood function for* $\mathbf{y}^*$ *given* $\mathbf{y}$ *and* $\boldsymbol{\beta}_0 = \boldsymbol{\beta}$*:*

$$L_{\boldsymbol{\theta}}(\boldsymbol{\beta}; \mathbf{y}) = \mathrm{E}\left[L_{\boldsymbol{\theta}}(\boldsymbol{\theta}; \mathbf{y}^*) \mid \tau(\mathbf{y}^*) = \mathbf{y},\ \boldsymbol{\beta}_0 = \boldsymbol{\beta}\right] \tag{27.45}$$

Proof. If differentiation under the integral sign is appropriate, then

$$\begin{aligned}
\frac{\partial \log f_y(\boldsymbol{\beta}; \mathbf{y})}{\partial \boldsymbol{\beta}} &= \frac{1}{\Pr\{\boldsymbol{\tau}(\mathbf{y}^*) = \mathbf{y}; \boldsymbol{\beta}\}} \frac{\partial \Pr\{\boldsymbol{\tau}(\mathbf{y}^*) = \mathbf{y}; \boldsymbol{\beta}\}}{\partial \boldsymbol{\beta}} \\
&= \frac{1}{\Pr\{\boldsymbol{\tau}(\mathbf{y}^*) = \mathbf{y}; \boldsymbol{\beta}\}} \int_{\{\mathbf{y}^* \mid \boldsymbol{\tau}(\mathbf{y}^*) = \mathbf{y}\}} \frac{\partial f_{y^*}(\mathbf{y}^*; \boldsymbol{\beta})}{\partial \boldsymbol{\beta}} d\mathbf{y}^* \\
&= \int_{\{\mathbf{y}^* \mid \boldsymbol{\tau}(\mathbf{y}^*) = \mathbf{y}\}} \frac{\partial \log f_{y^*}(\mathbf{y}^*; \boldsymbol{\beta})}{\partial \boldsymbol{\beta}} \frac{f_{y^*}(\mathbf{y}^*; \boldsymbol{\beta})}{\Pr\{\boldsymbol{\tau}(\mathbf{y}^*) = \mathbf{y}; \boldsymbol{\beta}\}} d\mathbf{y}^* \\
&= \mathrm{E}\left[\frac{\partial \log f_{y^*}(\mathbf{y}^*; \boldsymbol{\beta})}{\partial \boldsymbol{\beta}} \middle| \boldsymbol{\tau}(\mathbf{y}^*) = \mathbf{y},\ \boldsymbol{\beta}_0 = \boldsymbol{\beta}\right]
\end{aligned}$$

Exchanging log p.f.s for the log-likelihood function notation gives the result. □

The actual use of this result is largely restricted to such exponential p.d.f.s as the normal that have simple score functions. For the normal,

$$\frac{\partial \log \phi(y_n^* - \mathbf{x}_n' \boldsymbol{\beta})}{\partial \boldsymbol{\beta}} = \mathbf{x}_n' \left(y_n^* - \mathbf{x}_n' \boldsymbol{\beta}\right)$$

so that the probit score is

$$\begin{aligned}
L_{\boldsymbol{\beta}}(\boldsymbol{\beta}; y_n, \mathbf{x}_n) &= \mathrm{E}[\mathbf{x}_n \left(y_n^* - \mathbf{x}_n' \boldsymbol{\beta}\right) \mid \tau(y_n^*) = y_n,\ \mathbf{x}_n,\ \boldsymbol{\beta}_0 = \boldsymbol{\beta}] \\
&= \mathbf{x}_n' \left\{\mu^*(\mathbf{x}_n' \boldsymbol{\beta}) - \mathbf{x}_n' \boldsymbol{\beta}\right\}
\end{aligned} \tag{27.46}$$

where

$$\mu^*(\mathbf{x}_n' \boldsymbol{\beta}) \equiv \mathrm{E}[y_n^* \mid \tau(y_n^*) = y_n,\ \mathbf{x}_n,\ \boldsymbol{\beta}_0 = \boldsymbol{\beta}]$$

In effect, the probit score is the OLS orthogonality condition after replacing the unknown y_n^* with its mean conditional on $\mathbf{x}_n$ *and* y_n and assuming that the population $\boldsymbol{\beta}_0$ equals $\boldsymbol{\beta}$, the argument of the score function.

The logistic p.d.f., on the other hand, does not yield such a simple score function. However, the logit score does have a simple functional form:

$$L_{\beta}(\boldsymbol{\beta}; y_n, \mathbf{x}_n) = \mathbf{x}_n \left[y_n - F_L(\mathbf{x}_n' \boldsymbol{\beta}) \right] \tag{27.47}$$

because

$$\frac{f_L(z)}{F_L(z)\,[1 - F_L(z)]} = 1$$

Like OLS, the logit MLE sets the residuals $y_n - F_L(\mathbf{x}_n'\boldsymbol{\beta})$ orthogonal to the explanatory variables. This reveals that the logit MLE depends on the y_n only through the sufficient statistic $\mathrm{E}_N[\mathbf{x}_n y_n]$. Furthermore, this MLE is a simple method of moments (MM) estimator.

27.4.2 Hessian and Information Functions

Differentiating (27.45), we obtain the Hessian

$$\begin{aligned} L_{\beta\beta}(\boldsymbol{\beta}; \mathbf{y}_n, \mathbf{x}_n) = {} & \mathrm{E}[L_{\beta\beta}(\boldsymbol{\beta}; \mathbf{y}_n^*, \mathbf{x}_n) \mid \boldsymbol{\tau}(\mathbf{y}_n^*) = \mathbf{y}_n,\ \boldsymbol{\beta}_0 = \boldsymbol{\beta}] \\ & + \mathrm{Var}[L_{\beta}(\boldsymbol{\beta}; \mathbf{y}_n^*, \mathbf{x}_n) \mid \boldsymbol{\tau}(\mathbf{y}_n^*) = \mathbf{y}_n,\ \boldsymbol{\beta}_0 = \boldsymbol{\beta}] \end{aligned} \tag{27.48}$$

This is not simply the conditional expectation of the Hessian given $\mathbf{y}_n^*$. One must add to this the conditional variance matrix of the score given $\mathbf{y}_n^*$.

Our primary interest in the Hessian is to check whether our log-likelihood functions are globally concave. If so, then the MLE is the unique local maximum and numerical optimization will probably be quick and easy. Unfortunately, we learn from (27.48) that even if the log-likelihood given $\mathbf{y}_n^*$ is globally concave the $L(\boldsymbol{\beta}; \mathbf{y}_n, \mathbf{x}_n)$ may not be. The variance term adds a positive semidefinite matrix onto the expected Hessian that makes the properties of the sum ambiguous.

Pratt (1981) pointed out the following:[29]

Lemma 27.2 (Pratt) *Let $F(\mathbf{z})$ be a multivariate c.d.f. and $f(\mathbf{z})$ the corresponding p.d.f. If $\log f(\mathbf{x})$ is (strictly) concave, then $\log[F(\mathbf{v}) - F(\mathbf{w})]$ is a (strictly) concave function of $(\mathbf{v}, \mathbf{w})$ for $\mathbf{v} \geq \mathbf{w}$.*

This lemma applies to both the probit and logit models. The normal and logistic p.d.f.s are log-concave.[30] Therefore, whenever we find a solution to the normal equations we have found the MLE.

We can also use (27.48) to derive the information matrix in terms of the latent data-generating process. After taking expectations with respect to the observed data,

[29] See also Karlin (1968, pp. 11–32).

[30] See Goldberger (1983) and Exercise 16.8.

$$\Im_y(\boldsymbol{\beta}_0) = \Im_{y^*}(\boldsymbol{\beta}_0) - \mathrm{E}\big[\mathrm{Var}[L_{\beta}(\boldsymbol{\beta};\, y_n^*, \mathbf{x}_n) \mid \boldsymbol{\tau}(\mathbf{y}_n^*) = \mathbf{y}_n]\big] \tag{27.49}$$

Alternatively, we could have derived this relationship from (27.45) and the variance decomposition[31]

$$\mathrm{Var}[U] = \mathrm{E}\big[\mathrm{Var}[U \mid V]\big] + \mathrm{Var}\big[\mathrm{E}[U \mid V]\big]$$

The interpretation of (27.49) is straightforward: the information in the latent data exceeds that in the observed data by the expectation of this variance term. There is an efficiency loss in the MLE given $\mathbf{y}_n$ relative to the MLE given $\mathbf{y}_n^*$. The actual expression is useful in survey design for observing the gain in statistical precision that collecting the latent data would yield.

27.4.3 EM Algorithm

If one can easily maximize

$$Q(\boldsymbol{\beta}, \boldsymbol{\beta}_0;\, \mathbf{y}, \mathbf{X}) \equiv \mathrm{E}[L(\boldsymbol{\beta};\, \mathbf{y}^*, \mathbf{X}) \mid \mathbf{y}]$$

over $\boldsymbol{\beta}$, then we can use the latent process to construct an iterative method for computing the MLE generally called an *EM algorithm.* Dempster et al. (1977) proposed such algorithms and gave them the name EM to describe the *expectation* and *maximization* steps of each iteration. The expectation step is finding $Q(\boldsymbol{\beta}, \boldsymbol{\beta}_0;\, y_n, \mathbf{x}_n)$ above and the maximization step is maximizing this function over $\boldsymbol{\beta}$.

An EM algorithm for probit is a helpful introductory example. First, we will describe the implementation of the algorithm. Second, we will use the expectation and maximization steps to show how this implementation arises.

Given an initial value $\boldsymbol{\beta}_1$ for the algorithm, one computes the conditional expectation of y_n^* given y_n and treating $\boldsymbol{\beta}_1$ as though it were the population value $\boldsymbol{\beta}_0$. Combining (27.46) with (27.15), we see that

$$\begin{aligned}
\mu^*(y_n, \boldsymbol{\beta}_1) &\equiv \mathrm{E}\big[y_n^* \mid \tau(y_n^*) = y_n,\ \mathbf{x}_n\,,\ \boldsymbol{\beta}_0 = \boldsymbol{\beta}_1\big] \\
&= \mathbf{x}_n'\boldsymbol{\beta}_1 + \frac{\phi(\mathbf{x}_n'\boldsymbol{\beta}_1)}{\Phi(\mathbf{x}_n'\boldsymbol{\beta}_1)\big[1 - \Phi(\mathbf{x}_n'\boldsymbol{\beta}_1)\big]}\big[y_n - \Phi(\mathbf{x}_n'\boldsymbol{\beta}_1)\big] \\
&= \begin{cases} \mathbf{x}_n'\boldsymbol{\beta}_1 - \frac{\phi(\mathbf{x}_n'\boldsymbol{\beta}_1)}{[1-\Phi(\mathbf{x}_n'\boldsymbol{\beta}_1)]} & \text{if } y_n = 0 \\ \mathbf{x}_n'\boldsymbol{\beta}_1 + \frac{\phi(\mathbf{x}_n'\boldsymbol{\beta}_1)}{\Phi(\mathbf{x}_n'\boldsymbol{\beta}_1)} & \text{if } y_n = 1 \end{cases}
\end{aligned} \tag{27.50}$$

One obtains a new value for $\boldsymbol{\beta}$ by regressing $\mu^*(y_n, \boldsymbol{\beta}_1)$ onto $\mathbf{x}_n$:

$$\boldsymbol{\beta}_2 = \left(\mathbf{X}'\mathbf{X}\right)^{-1}\mathbf{X}'\boldsymbol{\mu}^*(\mathbf{y}, \boldsymbol{\beta}_1)$$

where $\boldsymbol{\mu}^*(\mathbf{y}, \boldsymbol{\beta}_1) \equiv [\mu^*(y_n, \boldsymbol{\beta}_1)]'$. This new $\boldsymbol{\beta}_2$ gives a higher value of the probit log-likelihood than the old $\boldsymbol{\beta}_1$ gives. One repeats the process, starting from the new value, until one reaches the fixed point. That point is the probit MLE.

---

[31] We take $U = L_{\beta}(\beta;\, y_n^*, x_n)$ and $V = y_n$. Regarding the variance decomposition, see also Exercise 6.6.

This is sometimes called *data augmentation*, which aptly highlights the intriguing feature of the algorithm. It is as though one augments the data set by substituting for the latent y_n^* the prediction $\mu^*(y_n, \boldsymbol{\beta}_1)$. Then one simply maximizes the log-likelihood function for $\mathbf{y}^*$ as though it were actually observed.

EM algorithms do not always work out quite that neatly, but it is a good starting point for their understanding. Let us now work through the expectation and maximization steps to see how they yield this algorithm. The log-likelihood for $\boldsymbol{\beta}$ given y_n^* is

$$\begin{aligned}\log \phi(y_n^* - \mathbf{x}_n'\boldsymbol{\beta}) &= -\frac{1}{2}\log 2\pi - \frac{1}{2}\left(y_n^* - \mathbf{x}_n'\boldsymbol{\beta}\right)^2 \\ &= -\frac{1}{2}\log 2\pi - \frac{1}{2}\left(y_n^*\right)^2 + y_n^*\mathbf{x}_n'\boldsymbol{\beta} - \frac{1}{2}\left(\mathbf{x}_n'\boldsymbol{\beta}\right)^2\end{aligned}$$

We take the expectation of this over y_n^* conditional on y_n and supposing that $\boldsymbol{\beta}_0 = \boldsymbol{\beta}_1$: using (27.50),

$$\begin{aligned}Q(\boldsymbol{\beta}, \boldsymbol{\beta}_1; y_n, \mathbf{x}_n) =& -\frac{1}{2}\log 2\pi - \frac{1}{2}\mathrm{E}[\left(y_n^*\right)^2 \mid y_n, \boldsymbol{\beta}_0 = \boldsymbol{\beta}_1] \\ &+ \mathrm{E}[y_n^* \mid y_n, \boldsymbol{\beta}_0 = \boldsymbol{\beta}_1]\mathbf{x}_n'\boldsymbol{\beta} - \frac{1}{2}\left(\mathbf{x}_n'\boldsymbol{\beta}\right)^2 \\ &= c(y_n, \mathbf{x}_n, \boldsymbol{\beta}_1) + \mu^*(y_n, \boldsymbol{\beta}_1)\mathbf{x}_n'\boldsymbol{\beta} - \frac{1}{2}\boldsymbol{\beta}'\mathbf{x}_n'\mathbf{x}_n'\boldsymbol{\beta}\end{aligned}$$

We will be able to ignore the terms that do not depend on $\boldsymbol{\beta}$ because we are interested only in the maximum of the sample average over $\boldsymbol{\beta}$:

$$\begin{aligned}\boldsymbol{\beta}_2 &= \underset{\boldsymbol{\beta}}{\operatorname{argmax}}\, \mathrm{E}_N[Q(\boldsymbol{\beta}, \boldsymbol{\beta}_1; y_n, \mathbf{x}_n)] \\ &= \underset{\boldsymbol{\beta}}{\operatorname{argmax}}\, \mathrm{E}_N[\mu^*(y_n, \boldsymbol{\beta}_1)\mathbf{x}_n'\boldsymbol{\beta} - \frac{1}{2}\boldsymbol{\beta}'\mathbf{x}_n\mathbf{x}_n'\boldsymbol{\beta}] \\ &= \underset{\boldsymbol{\beta}}{\operatorname{argzero}}\, \mathrm{E}_N[\mathbf{x}_n\mu^*(y_n, \boldsymbol{\beta}_1) - \boldsymbol{\beta}'\mathbf{x}_n\mathbf{x}_n'] \\ &= \left(\mathbf{X}'\mathbf{X}\right)^{-1}\mathbf{X}'\boldsymbol{\mu}^*(\mathbf{y}, \boldsymbol{\beta}_1)\end{aligned}$$

Each new value of $\boldsymbol{\beta}$ gives a higher value of the probit log-likelihood function. We give a formal justification of this in the Mathematical Notes. We also explain how to interpret the EM algorithm as a quadratic approximation method like those in Section 16.4.3.

27.4.4 Simulation

Another estimation method associated with the latent model uses simulation to overcome difficulties in computing probabilities or expectations for the log-likelihood and score functions. For the sake of illustration, suppose that quick and accurate approximations to the univariate normal c.d.f. were not available. We will show how to use computer simulation of random variables from the normal distribution to construct a consistent, asymptotically normal estimator of the probit model.

Let us begin supposing that pseudorandom draws from the standard normal distribution are available.[32] Then for any value of the slope coefficients $\boldsymbol{\beta}$ we can simulate draws from the distribution of y_n^* and y_n with

$$\tilde{y}_n^*(\boldsymbol{\beta}, \tilde{z}) = \mathbf{x}_n'\boldsymbol{\beta} + \tilde{z}_n \tag{27.51}$$

$$\tilde{y}_n(\boldsymbol{\beta}, \tilde{z}) \equiv \mathbf{1}\{\tilde{y}_n^*(\boldsymbol{\beta}, \tilde{z}_n) \geq 0\} \tag{27.52}$$

where $\tilde{z}_n$ denotes a pseudorandom normal draw. It follows that for any $\boldsymbol{\beta}$

$$\mathrm{E}[\tilde{y}_n(\boldsymbol{\beta}, \tilde{z}_n) \mid \mathbf{x}_n] = \Phi(\mathbf{x}_n'\boldsymbol{\beta})$$

In addition,

$$\mathrm{E}[y_n - \tilde{y}_n(\boldsymbol{\beta}_0, \tilde{z}_n) \mid \mathbf{x}_n] = \mathbf{0}$$

providing us with a conditional moment restriction on y_n.

McFadden (1989) uses this insight to suggest feasible method of *simulated* moments (MSM) estimators.[33] First, generate an independent normal random variable for each observation: $\{\tilde{z}_n; n = 1, \ldots, N\}$. Second, construct a feasible sample moment vector that will identify $\boldsymbol{\beta}_0$. For this illustration, we will use

$$\mathrm{E}\big[\mathbf{x}_n\big(y_n - \tilde{y}_n(\boldsymbol{\beta}_0, \tilde{z}_n)\big)\big] = \mathbf{0} \tag{27.53}$$

as in OLS and the logit score function (27.47). Third, compute the corresponding method of moments estimator. Because $\boldsymbol{\beta}_0$ is exactly identified by (27.53), our estimator satisfies the orthogonality conditions

$$\mathrm{E}_N\big[\mathbf{x}_n\big(y_n - \tilde{y}_n(\hat{\boldsymbol{\beta}}_{\mathrm{MSM}}, \tilde{z}_n)\big)\big] = \mathbf{0} \tag{27.54}$$

This particular implicit function has a unique solution that one can compute with standard LAD software. For more detail, see *Mathematical Notes,* Section 27.6.

McFadden (1989) also notes that averaging replications of the simulations produces a more precise simulation of the mean of y_n. To generalize along these lines, suppose there are R independent replications of $\tilde{z}$ for each observation and denote the entire collection by $\{\tilde{z}_{nr}; n = 1, \ldots, N, r = 1, \ldots, R\}$. We let the simulation of $\mathrm{E}[y_n \mid \mathbf{x}_n]$ be

$$\mathrm{E}_R[\tilde{y}_n(\boldsymbol{\beta}_0, \tilde{z}_{nr})] \equiv \sum_{r=1}^{R} \tilde{y}_n(\boldsymbol{\beta}_0, \tilde{z}_{nr})\frac{1}{R}$$

and generalize (27.54) to

$$0 = \mathrm{E}_N\big[\mathbf{x}_n\big(y_n - \mathrm{E}_R[\tilde{y}_n(\hat{\boldsymbol{\beta}}_{\mathrm{MSM}}, \tilde{z}_{nr})]\big)\big]$$

[32] Most statistical software provides this capability. Occasionally, only the pseudorandom uniformly distributed draws are available. The Box and Muller (1958) method delivers two independent standard normal random variables from two independent uniform random variables u_1 and u_2:

$$z_1 = \sqrt{-2\log u_1}\cos(2\pi u_2)$$

$$z_2 = \sqrt{-2\log u_1}\sin(2\pi u_2)$$

[33] See also Pakes and Pollard (1989).

$$= \mathrm{E}_N\, \mathrm{E}_R\big[\mathbf{x}_n\big(y_n - \tilde{y}_n(\hat{\boldsymbol{\beta}}_{\mathrm{MSM}}, \tilde{z}_{nr})\big)\big]$$

Using the results of Pakes and Pollard (1989), one can show that

$$\hat{\boldsymbol{\beta}}_{\mathrm{MSM}} \xrightarrow{p} \boldsymbol{\beta}_0$$

$$\sqrt{N}\left(\hat{\boldsymbol{\beta}}_{\mathrm{MSM}} - \boldsymbol{\beta}_0\right) \xrightarrow{d} \mathfrak{N}\left(\mathbf{0}, \frac{R+1}{R} \cdot \mathbf{G}_0^{-1}\boldsymbol{\Lambda}_0\mathbf{G}_0\right)$$

where

$$\mathbf{G}_0 = \mathrm{E}[\mathbf{x}_n \phi(\mathbf{x}_n'\boldsymbol{\beta}_0)\mathbf{x}_n']$$
$$\boldsymbol{\Lambda}_0 = \mathrm{E}\big[\mathbf{x}_n \Phi(\mathbf{x}_n'\boldsymbol{\beta}_0)\big(1 - \Phi(\mathbf{x}_n'\boldsymbol{\beta}_0)\big)\mathbf{x}_n'\big]$$

$\mathbf{G}_0^{-1}\boldsymbol{\Lambda}_0\mathbf{G}_0$ is the asymptotic variance of the ordinary MM estimator based on $\Phi(\cdot)$: $\hat{\boldsymbol{\beta}}_{\mathrm{MM}}$ such that

$$\mathrm{E}_N\big[\mathbf{x}_n\big(y_n - \Phi(\mathbf{x}_n'\hat{\boldsymbol{\beta}}_{\mathrm{MM}})\big)\big] = \mathbf{0}$$

The matrix $\boldsymbol{\Lambda}_0$ is the variance of the moment function,

$$\boldsymbol{\Lambda}_0 = \mathrm{Var}\big[\mathbf{x}_n\big(y_n - \Phi(\mathbf{x}_n'\boldsymbol{\beta}_0)\big)\big]$$

and $\mathbf{G}_0$ is the expectation of the partial derivative matrix

$$\mathbf{G}_0 = \mathrm{E}\left[\frac{\partial}{\partial \boldsymbol{\beta}'}\mathbf{x}_n\big(y_n - \Phi(\mathbf{x}_n'\boldsymbol{\beta}_0)\big)\right]$$

Because the $\tilde{y}_n(\boldsymbol{\beta}_0, \tilde{z}_{nr})$ are independent simulations of y_n, they have the same distribution and contribute the same variance to the simulated moment function:

$$\begin{aligned}
&\mathrm{Var}\big[\mathbf{x}_n'\big(y_n - \mathrm{E}_R[\tilde{y}_n(\hat{\boldsymbol{\beta}}_{\mathrm{MSM}}, \tilde{z}_{nr})]\big)\big] \\
&\quad = \mathrm{Var}\big[\mathbf{x}_n'\big(y_n - \Phi(\mathbf{x}_n'\boldsymbol{\beta}_0)\big)\big] \\
&\qquad + \mathrm{E}_R\,\mathrm{Var}\big[\mathbf{x}_n'\big(\tilde{y}_n(\hat{\boldsymbol{\beta}}_{\mathrm{MSM}}, \tilde{z}_{nr}) - \Phi(\mathbf{x}_n'\boldsymbol{\beta}_0)\big)\big] \\
&\quad = \boldsymbol{\Lambda}_0 + \frac{1}{R} \cdot \boldsymbol{\Lambda}_0 \\
&\quad = \frac{R+1}{R} \cdot \boldsymbol{\Lambda}_0
\end{aligned}$$

Therefore, as McFadden (1989, p. 1006) noted, this MSM estimator has a variance that is a scalar multiple of the MM estimator. With one replication ($R = 1$), the MSM estimator has twice the variance. With 10 replications ($R = 10$), there is an efficiency loss of only 10%.

This illustration of MSM is stylized and we intend it to be an introduction to the ideas behind the estimation method. It shows a second way in which the latent model has relevance to estimation. Research in this approach is ongoing and such models as multinomial probit models are yielding to estimation with this sort of simulation.

27.5 METHODOLOGICAL NOTES

A fundamental issue in these models for discrete dependent variables is the specification of the distribution of the latent variables. In Bernoulli models, researchers generally prefer the logistic and normal distributions over the uniform distribution because their smoothness seems more natural and they are analytically and numerically more convenient. In general, the uniform distribution predicts that some of the outcomes of y_n are zero or one with certainty, whereas the logistic and the normal always hold out a small chance of another outcome. Many economists are uncomfortable making such certain predictions. Therefore the uniform distribution is rarely applied.

In multivariate settings, the logistic distribution dominates applications because of its tractability. The multivariate normal distribution has broader appeal because of its covariance parameterization and the property that sums of multivariate normal random variables are also normally distributed. But use of the normal distribution has been limited to low-dimensional problems by computational power. This limitation is becoming less severe as simulation methods become widespread.

Despite its familiarity, the normal distribution is a questionable specification and when it is questioned important issues of identification arise. For example, we noted that the scale of the latent regression model is not identified in Bernoulli models. The Bernoulli identification problems generalize when the latent distribution is unknown: any monotonic increasing function can be used to transform the latent model. Let g be any strictly increasing function, so that

$$y_n = \begin{cases} 0 & \text{if } g(\varepsilon_n) > g(\mathbf{x}_n'\boldsymbol{\beta}_0) \\ 1 & \text{if } g(\varepsilon_n) \le g(\mathbf{x}_n'\boldsymbol{\beta}_0) \end{cases}$$

and

$$\Pr\{y = 1\} = F\{g^{-1}[g(\mathbf{x}_n'\boldsymbol{\beta}_0)]\} = H\left[g(\mathbf{x}_n'\boldsymbol{\beta}_0)\right]$$

The function $H \equiv F[g^{-1}(\cdot)]$ is also a c.d.f. and the binomial regression model is nonlinear in $\mathbf{x}$. This points to a more fundamental issue: if the latent regression function is not known to be exactly $\mathbf{x}_n'\boldsymbol{\beta}_0$, then it will not be possible to distinguish misspecification of $\mathbf{x}_n'\boldsymbol{\beta}$ from misspecification of the distribution function F. Evidence that nonlinear transformations of $\mathbf{x}_n$ should be included as additional explanatory variables may indicate that the distribution function is misspecified.

In recognition of such issues, one may choose to avoid latent variable interpretations altogether. It is not necessary, for example, to motivate the multinomial specifications in Section 27.3 with a choice model. Researchers often interpret the $\mathbf{x}_n'\boldsymbol{\beta}_{0j}$ as reduced-form indices that increase the probability of the outcomes to which they are assigned. Such multinomial models as the multinomial logit model are then applied to nonchoice discrete data like type of government found in a cross section of countries.

27.6 MATHEMATICAL NOTES

These mathematical notes provide details about four topics covered above. First, we describe the Katz family of distributions for count-data models underlying the score test in Section 27.2.2. Second, we derive the multinomial logit probabilities in (27.42) from a latent Weibull distribution. We also derive the probabilities for rank-ordered data given in (27.44). Third, we prove that the EM algorithm described in Section 27.4.3 increases the log-likelihood function at each iteration. Finally, we show how to cast the simulation estimator in Section 27.4.4 as a calculation of least absolute deviations (LAD) regression.

27.6.1 Katz Family of Distributions

Cameron and Trivedi (1986) and Lee (1986) noted the usefulness of the Katz (1945, 1965) family of distributions. The difference equation

$$f(y+1) = \frac{\lambda + \gamma y}{y+1} f(y), \qquad y = 0, 1, 2, \ldots \tag{27.55}$$

and the probability restrictions

$$f(y) \geq 0$$

$$\sum_{y=0}^{\infty} f(y) = 1$$

characterize this family. Rewriting the difference equation as

$$f(y+1) = \gamma \frac{\alpha + y}{y+1} f(y)$$

where $\alpha = \lambda/\gamma$, recursive substitution shows that

$$f(y) = \gamma^y \frac{\alpha(\alpha+1)\cdots(\alpha+y-1)}{1 \cdot 2 \cdot \cdots \cdot y} f(0) = \gamma^y \frac{\Gamma(y+\alpha)}{\Gamma(y+1)\,\Gamma(\alpha)} f(0)$$

Because the Taylor series of $(1-c)^{-a}$ around $c = 0$ for $-1 < c < 1$ and $a > 0$ is[34]

$$(1-c)^{-a} = \sum_{t=0}^{\infty} \frac{\Gamma(a+t)}{\Gamma(t+1)\Gamma(a)} c^t$$

we see that for $0 < \gamma < 1$

$$\sum_{t=0}^{\infty} f(y) = (1-\gamma)^{-\alpha} f(0)$$

Therefore, if $0 < \gamma < 1$ and $\lambda > 0$ then $f(y) \geq 0$ for $y = 0, 1, 2, \ldots$ and

$$f(0) = (1-\gamma)^{\alpha} \tag{27.56}$$

These parameter values yield the negative binomial p.m.f. in (27.29).

The Katz family contains the binomial distribution (Definition D.20, p. 885) as a special case for $\gamma < 0$ and $\lambda > 0$. In this case, one must take care of potentially negative probabilities by restricting

$$f(y) = 0 \quad \text{if} \quad \lambda + \gamma(y-1) < 0$$

If $-\alpha = -\lambda/\gamma$ is a strictly positive integer, then

$$f(y+1) = -\gamma \frac{-\alpha - y}{y+1} f(y), \qquad y = 0, 1, 2, \ldots, -\alpha$$

yielding

[34] Incidentally, this Taylor series is also called the *negative binomial series* because the exponent of the binomial $1 + c$ is negative. This is the source of the name of the negative binomial distribution.

$$f(y) = (-\gamma)^y \frac{-\alpha\,(-\alpha-1)\cdots(-\alpha-y+1)}{1\cdot 2\cdot\cdots\cdot y} f(0) = (-\gamma)^y \frac{\Gamma(-\alpha+1)}{\Gamma(y+1)\,\Gamma(-\alpha-y+1)} f(0)$$

The binomial theorem states that[35]

$$(1-\gamma)^{-\alpha} = \sum_{y=0}^{-\alpha} (-\gamma)^y \frac{\Gamma(-\alpha+1)}{\Gamma(y+1)\,\Gamma(-\alpha-y+1)}$$

so that once again $f(0) = (1-\gamma)^{\alpha}$. Distributions are also defined for noninteger values of $-\alpha$.

The moments of Katz distributions follow relatively easily from the difference equation. Because

$$\sum_{y=0}^{\infty} y\, f(y) = \sum_{y=0}^{\infty} (y+1)\, f(y+1) = \sum_{y=0}^{\infty} \gamma\,(\alpha+y)\, f(y)$$

we obtain

$$\mathrm{E}[Y] = \gamma\alpha + \gamma\,\mathrm{E}[Y] \qquad \Leftrightarrow \qquad \mathrm{E}[Y] = \frac{\gamma\alpha}{1-\gamma}$$

Similarly,

$$\sum_{y=0}^{\infty} y^2 f(y) = \sum_{y=0}^{\infty} (y+1)^2 f(y+1) = \sum_{y=0}^{\infty} \gamma\,(y+1)\,(\alpha+y)\, f(y)$$

leads to

$$\mathrm{E}[Y^2] = \gamma\alpha + \gamma\,(1+\alpha)\,\mathrm{E}[Y] + \gamma\,\mathrm{E}[Y^2] \qquad \Leftrightarrow$$
$$\mathrm{E}[Y^2] = \frac{\gamma\alpha\,(1+\gamma\alpha)}{(1-\gamma)^2}$$

and

$$\mathrm{Var}[Y] = \frac{\gamma\alpha}{(1-\gamma)^2}$$

27.6.2 Logit Probabilities

Let us drop the observation subscript n and denote $\mathbf{x}_j'\boldsymbol{\beta}_0 = \mu_j$. The c.d.f. of the Weibull distribution is

$$F(z) = e^{-e^{-z}}$$

[35] Equivalently,

$$(a+b)^n = \binom{n}{0}a^n + \binom{n}{1}a^{n-1}b + \binom{n}{2}a^{n-2}b^2 + \cdots + \binom{n}{n-1}ab^{n-1} + \binom{n}{n}b^n$$
$$= \sum_{i=0}^{n} \frac{n!}{(n-i)!\,i!} a^{n-i} b^i$$

so that the p.d.f. is

$$f(z) = \frac{dF(z)}{dz} = e^{-z-e^{-z}}$$

It will be helpful to note that

$$\int e^{-z-ce^{-z}}\,dz = \frac{e^{-ce^{-z}}}{c} \tag{27.57}$$

Using (27.41), we write

$$\begin{aligned}
\Pr\left\{y_j = 1 \mid \mathbf{X}\right\} &= \mathrm{E}\left[\prod_{i \neq j} F[\varepsilon_j + \mu_j - \mu_i]\right] \\
&= \int_{-\infty}^{\infty} \exp\left\{-\sum_{i \neq j} e^{-z-\mu_j+\mu_i}\right\} e^{-z-e^{-z}}\,dz
\end{aligned} \tag{27.58}$$

because the product of exponentials is the exponential of the sum. Denoting

$$c \equiv 1 + \sum_{i \neq j} \exp(-\mu_j + \mu_i)$$

we gather terms and use (27.57) to obtain

$$\begin{aligned}
\Pr\left\{y_j = 1 \mid \mathbf{X}\right\} &= \int_{-\infty}^{\infty} \exp\left[-z - c\exp(-z)\right] dz \\
&= \left[\frac{e^{-ce^{-z}}}{c}\right]_{-\infty}^{\infty} \\
&= \frac{1}{1 + \sum_{i \neq j} \exp\left[-\mu_j + (\mu_i)\right]} \\
&= \frac{\exp(\mu_j)}{\sum_{i=1}^{J} \exp(\mu_i)}
\end{aligned} \tag{27.59}$$

For rank ordering probabilities, consider

$$\begin{aligned}
&\Pr\{\max_{i<j} y_i^* < y_j^* < y_{j+1}^* < \cdots < y_J^* \mid \mathbf{X}\} \\
&= \mathrm{E}\left[\prod_{i<j} F(\varepsilon_j + \mu_j - \mu_i) \,\middle|\, y_j^* < y_{j+1}^* < \cdots < y_J^*,\ \mathbf{X}\right] \\
&= \mathrm{E}\left[\mathrm{E}\left[\prod_{i<j} F(\varepsilon_j + \mu_j - \mu_i) \,\middle|\, y_j^* < y_{j+1}^*,\ y_{j+1}^*\right] \,\middle|\, y_{j+1}^* < \cdots < y_J^*,\ \mathbf{X}\right]
\end{aligned}$$

The inner conditional expectation has a closed-form expression:

$$\begin{aligned}
&\mathrm{E}\left[\prod_{i<j} F(\varepsilon_j + \mu_j - \mu_i) \,\middle|\, y_j^* < y_{j+1}^*,\ y_{j+1}^*\right] \\
&= \int_{-\infty}^{\varepsilon_{j+1}+\mu_{j+1}-\mu_j} \prod_{i<j} F(\varepsilon_j + \mu_j - \mu_i) f(\varepsilon_j)\, d\varepsilon_j \\
&= \left[\frac{e^{-c_j e^{-z}}}{c_j}\right]_{-\infty}^{\varepsilon_{j+1}+\mu_{j+1}-\mu_j} \\
&= \frac{e^{-c_j e^{-(\varepsilon_{j+1}+\mu_{j+1}-\mu_j)}}}{c_j} \\
&= \Pr\{\max_{i<j} y_i^* < y_j^*\} \cdot \prod_{i<j+1} F(\varepsilon_{n,j+1} + \mu_{j+1} - \mu_i)
\end{aligned}$$

using the equality of (27.58) and (27.59) and the indefinite integral (27.57), where

$$c_j \equiv 1 + \sum_{i<j} \exp(-\mu_j + \mu_i) = \frac{1}{\Pr\{\max_{i<j} y_i^* < y_j^* \mid \mathbf{X}\}}$$

Thus,

$$\begin{aligned}
&\Pr\{\max_{i<j} y_i^* < y_j^* < y_{j+1}^* < \cdots < y_J^* \mid \mathbf{X}\} \\
&\quad = \Pr\{\max_{i<j} y_i^* < y_j^* \mid \mathbf{X}\} \\
&\qquad \cdot \mathrm{E}\left[\prod_{i<j+1} F(\varepsilon_{n,j+1} + \mu_{j+1} - \mu_i) \,\middle|\, y_{j+1}^* < y_{j+1}^* < \cdots < y_J^*,\ \mathbf{X}\right] \\
&\quad = \Pr\{\max_{i<j} y_i^* < y_j^* \mid \mathbf{X}\} \cdot \Pr\{\max_{i<j+1} y_i^* < y_{j+1}^* < y_{j+1}^* < \cdots < y_J^* \mid \mathbf{X}\}
\end{aligned}$$

establishing a recursive relationship among the probabilities $\Pr\{\max_{i<j} y_i^* < y_j^* < y_{j+1}^* < \cdots < y_J^* \mid \mathbf{X}\}$ for various j. Expanding that relationship yields

$$\begin{aligned}
\Pr\{\max_{i<j} y_i^* < y_j^* < y_{j+1}^* < \cdots < y_J^* \mid \mathbf{X}\} &= \prod_{k=j}^{J} \Pr\{\max_{i<k} y_i^* < y_k^*\} \\
&= \prod_{k=j}^{J} \frac{\exp(\mu_k)}{\sum_{j=1}^{k} \exp(\mu_j)}
\end{aligned}$$

which is (27.44).

27.6.3 EM Algorithm

The EM algorithm rests on the following result, due to Dempster et al. (1977).

Lemma 27.3 *Let $Y = \tau(Y^*)$ be a transformation of the random variable Y^* with p.f. $f_{Y^*}(y^*; \boldsymbol{\theta}_0)$. Let $L(\boldsymbol{\theta}; y^*) \equiv \log f_{Y^*}(y^*; \boldsymbol{\theta})$ and*

$$Q(\boldsymbol{\theta}, \boldsymbol{\theta}_0; y) \equiv \mathrm{E}[L(\boldsymbol{\theta}; Y^*) | Y = y]$$

Then

$$Q(\boldsymbol{\theta}, \boldsymbol{\theta}_0; y) > Q(\boldsymbol{\theta}_0, \boldsymbol{\theta}_0; y) \quad \Rightarrow \quad L(\boldsymbol{\theta}; y) > L(\boldsymbol{\theta}_0; y).$$

Proof. Note that the p.f. of Y conditional on Y^* is

$$f_{Y \mid Y^*}(y \mid y^*) = \mathbf{1}\{y = \tau(y^*)\} = \begin{cases} 1 & \text{if } y = \tau(y^*) \\ 0 & \text{if } y \neq \tau(y^*) \end{cases}$$

The joint p.f. of Y and Y^* is the product of the marginal and the conditional p.f.s

$$f_{Y^*}(y^*; \boldsymbol{\theta}_0)\, \mathbf{1}\{y = \tau(y^*)\} = \begin{cases} f_{Y^*}(y^*; \boldsymbol{\theta}_0) & \text{if } y = \tau(y^*) \\ 0 & \text{if } y \neq \tau(y^*) \end{cases}$$

and the conditional p.f. of Y^* given Y is

$$f_{Y^* \mid Y}(y^* \mid y; \boldsymbol{\theta}_0) = \begin{cases} \frac{f_{Y^*}(y^*; \boldsymbol{\theta}_0)}{f_Y(y; \boldsymbol{\theta}_0)} & \text{if } y = \tau(y^*) \\ 0 & \text{if } y \neq \tau(y^*) \end{cases} \tag{27.60}$$

where $f_Y(y; \boldsymbol{\theta}_0)$ is the marginal p.f. of Y.

Thus, the log-likelihood function for $\boldsymbol{\theta}$ given Y^* drawn conditionally on $Y = y$ is

$$\begin{aligned} L(\boldsymbol{\theta}; y^* \mid y) &\equiv \log f_{Y^* \mid Y}(y^* \mid y; \boldsymbol{\theta}) \\ &= \log \frac{f_{Y^*}(y^*; \boldsymbol{\theta})}{f_Y(y; \boldsymbol{\theta})} && \text{[by (27.60)]} \\ &= \log f_{Y^*}(y^*; \boldsymbol{\theta}) - \log f_Y(y; \boldsymbol{\theta}) \\ &= L(\boldsymbol{\theta}; y^*) - L(\boldsymbol{\theta}; y) && \text{[by definition]} \end{aligned} \tag{27.61}$$

Let

$$\begin{aligned} H(\boldsymbol{\theta}, \boldsymbol{\theta}_0; y) &\equiv Q(\boldsymbol{\theta}, \boldsymbol{\theta}_0; y) - L(\boldsymbol{\theta}; y) \\ &= \mathrm{E}[L(\boldsymbol{\theta}; Y^*) | Y = y] - L(\boldsymbol{\theta}; y) && \text{[by definition]} \\ &= \mathrm{E}[L(\boldsymbol{\theta}; Y^*) - L(\boldsymbol{\theta}; y) | Y = y] && \text{[by conditioning]} \\ &= \mathrm{E}[L(\boldsymbol{\theta}; Y^* | y) \mid y] && \text{[by (27.61)]} \end{aligned} \tag{27.62}$$

According to the log-likelihood inequality (Lemma 14.1, p. 290), $H(\boldsymbol{\theta}, \boldsymbol{\theta}_0; y)$ is maximized at $\boldsymbol{\theta} = \boldsymbol{\theta}_0$. Therefore,

$$\begin{aligned} 0 &\geq H(\boldsymbol{\theta}, \boldsymbol{\theta}_0; y) - H(\boldsymbol{\theta}, \boldsymbol{\theta}_0; y) \\ &= Q(\boldsymbol{\theta}, \boldsymbol{\theta}_0; y) - Q(\boldsymbol{\theta}_0, \boldsymbol{\theta}_0; y) - [L(\boldsymbol{\theta}; y) - L(\boldsymbol{\theta}_0; y)] && \text{[by (27.62)]} \end{aligned}$$

or

$$L(\boldsymbol{\theta}; y) - L(\boldsymbol{\theta}_0; y) \geq Q(\boldsymbol{\theta}, \boldsymbol{\theta}_0; y) - Q(\boldsymbol{\theta}_0, \boldsymbol{\theta}_0; y)$$

□

The application of this lemma is usually to the maximization

$$\boldsymbol{\theta}_2 = \underset{\boldsymbol{\theta}}{\text{argmax}}\, Q(\boldsymbol{\theta}, \boldsymbol{\theta}_1; y)$$

which guarantees that $Q(\boldsymbol{\theta}_2, \boldsymbol{\theta}_1; y) > Q(\boldsymbol{\theta}_1, \boldsymbol{\theta}_1; y)$ so that each iteration of the EM algorithm increases $L(\boldsymbol{\theta}; y)$.

27.6.4 Simulation

Here we prove the claim above that the example simulation estimator in Section 27.4.4 that solves (27.54) can be computed as an LAD regression. We can rewrite the simulated moment equations as

$$\begin{aligned}
\sum_{n=1}^{N} \mathbf{x}_n \left[y_n - \tilde{y}_n(\boldsymbol{\beta})\right] &= \sum_{n=1}^{N} \mathbf{x}_n \left\{ y_n - \frac{1}{2}\left[\operatorname{sgn}(\mathbf{x}_n'\boldsymbol{\beta} + \varepsilon_n) + 1\right]\right\} \\
&= \frac{1}{2}\sum_{n=1}^{N}\left[\mathbf{x}_n(2y_n - 1) - \mathbf{x}_n \operatorname{sgn}(\mathbf{x}_n'\boldsymbol{\beta} + \varepsilon_n)\right] \\
&\equiv \frac{1}{2}\left[\breve{\mathbf{x}} - \sum_{n=1}^{N} \mathbf{x}_n \operatorname{sgn}(\mathbf{x}_n'\boldsymbol{\beta} + \varepsilon_n)\right] \\
&= \frac{1}{2}\left[-\breve{\mathbf{x}} \operatorname{sgn}(\breve{\mathbf{x}}'\boldsymbol{\beta} + \varepsilon^*) - \sum_{n=1}^{N} \mathbf{x}_n \operatorname{sgn}(\mathbf{x}_n'\boldsymbol{\beta} + \varepsilon_n)\right]
\end{aligned}$$

where $\breve{\mathbf{x}} \equiv \sum_{n=1}^{N} \mathbf{x}_n(2y_n - 1)$ and $\varepsilon^* \ll 0$ so that $\breve{\mathbf{x}}'\boldsymbol{\beta} + \varepsilon^* < 0$ for all conceivable $\boldsymbol{\beta}$. We can therefore integrate back to get

$$\min_{\boldsymbol{\beta}} \frac{1}{2}\left[\left|\breve{\mathbf{x}}'\boldsymbol{\beta} + \varepsilon^*\right| + \sum_{n=1}^{N}\left|\mathbf{x}_n'\boldsymbol{\beta} + \varepsilon_n\right|\right]$$

so that we merely add an artificial observation $(\breve{\mathbf{x}}, \varepsilon^*)$ to the data set $\{(\mathbf{x}_n, \varepsilon_n\}; n = 1, \ldots, N\}$ and fit the εs to the $\mathbf{x}$s.

27.7 OVERVIEW

1. Conditional expectations for discrete dependent data are generally nonlinear functions of explanatory variables. Otherwise the function has a range that extends beyond the support of the distribution of the dependent data.
2. For dependent variables with a Bernoulli distribution, transforming the linear function $\mathbf{x}_n'\boldsymbol{\beta}_0$ with a c.d.f. $F(\cdot)$ imposes the necessary constraints in a simple way. The conditional expectation is a monotonic function of each x_{nk}.
3. However, the interpretation of the slope coefficients is more complicated than for linear regression. The nonlinear specification causes the partial derivatives $\partial\, \mathrm{E}[y_n \mid \mathbf{x}_n]/\partial \mathbf{x}$ to be proportional to $\boldsymbol{\beta}_0$ where the factor of proportionality depends on $\mathbf{x}_n'\boldsymbol{\beta}_0$.

4. Latent-variable models provide a method for transforming linear regression models into nonlinear regression models for discrete data. The distribution of the latent variables and the observation rule that transforms latent variables into observable variables imply the probability of each outcome.

5. Ordinal- and count-data models are univariate generalizations of the Bernoulli model for multinomial data. In terms of the latent variable model

$$y_n^* = \mathbf{x}_n' \boldsymbol{\beta}_0 + \varepsilon_n$$

the Bernoulli outcome is generated by

$$y_n = \mathbf{1}\{0 \leq y_n^*\}$$

the ordinal-data model by

$$y_n = \sum_{j=0}^{J} \mathbf{1}\{\alpha_j \leq y_n^*\}$$

6. Multiple-choice models rest on a multivariate generalization of the Bernoulli model. Like ordinal models, multiple-choice models permit more than two discrete outcomes, but, unlike ordinal models, the outcomes do not bear an ordinal relationship to one another. The latent-variable model is a restricted system of seemingly unrelated regressions,

$$y_{nj}^* = \mathbf{x}_{nj}' \boldsymbol{\delta}_0 + \varepsilon_{nj}, \qquad j = 1, \ldots, J$$

and the observed data indicate the largest y_{nj}^*, as in

$$y_{nj} = \mathbf{1}\left\{ y_{nj}^* = \max_{i \in \{1,\ldots,J\}} y_{ni}^* \right\}, \qquad j = 1, \ldots, J$$

Rank-ordered data are a more informative transformation of the latent y_{nj}^*, which we can write as

$$y_{nj} = \sum_{i=1}^{J} \mathbf{1}\{y_{ni}^* \leq y_{nj}^*\}, \qquad j = 1, \ldots, J$$

Implicitly this observation rule reveals every $\mathbf{1}\{y_{ni}^* \leq y_{nj}^*\}$.

7. Multiple-choice data depend only on the differences $\varepsilon_{ni} - \varepsilon_{nj}$ and $(\mathbf{x}_{ni} - \mathbf{x}_{nj})'\boldsymbol{\delta}_0$. As a result, $\text{Var}[\boldsymbol{\varepsilon}_n \mid \mathbf{x}_n] = \boldsymbol{\Omega}_0$ is not identified. One can normalize $\text{Var}[\varepsilon_{n1} \mid \mathbf{x}_n] = 0$ and $\sum_{j=2}^{J} \text{Var}[\varepsilon_{nj} \mid \mathbf{x}_n] = 1$. The identification of $\boldsymbol{\delta}_0$ then rests on the matrix $[\mathbf{x}_{ni} - \mathbf{x}_{nj}]'$ having full-column rank. The p.f. of the observed data is a multivariate integral over $J-1$ dimensions. Multinomial logit models have relatively simple expressions for these integrals. For example,

$$\Pr\{y_{nj} = 1\} = \frac{1}{\sum_{i=1}^{J} \exp\left[(\mathbf{x}_{ni} - \mathbf{x}_{nj})'\boldsymbol{\delta}_0\right]}$$

8. Latent variable models also provide numerical solutions to estimating discrete data models.
   (a) If the latent p.d.f. is log-concave, then the log-likelihood function may be concave.
   (b) The EM algorithm generates iterative OLS calculations of the MLE.
   (c) One can combine estimation with simulation to compute feasible GMM estimators for problems in which the MLE is infeasible.

27.8 EXERCISES

27.8.1 Review

27.1 **(MMSE)** Show that the linear probability model estimates a MMSE linear approximation of a Bernoulli regression function $F(\mathbf{x}'\boldsymbol{\beta}_0)$.

27.2 **(Laplace)** Suppose that $y_n^* = \mathbf{x}_n'\boldsymbol{\beta}_0 + \varepsilon_n$, $y_n = \mathbf{1}\{y_n^* > 0\}$, and ε_n has the Laplace p.d.f. conditional on $\mathbf{x}_n$.

(a) Find the log-likelihood function for $\boldsymbol{\beta}$ given y_n and $\mathbf{x}_n$.

(b) Suppose that probit estimates of the regression slopes are roughly proportional to the MLE based on your answer to Part a. What is an approximate value for the ratio of the probit coefficients relative to their Laplacean counterparts?

(c) Argue that the log-likelihood function in Part a is globally concave in $\boldsymbol{\beta}$.

27.3 **(Global Concavity)** Derive the Hessian of the logit log-likelihood function by differentiation. Show that the Hessian also equals the negative of the information matrix. Confirm that this log-likelihood function is globally concave by showing that the Hessian is negative definite.

27.4 **(Global Concavity)** Suppose that $y_n^* \mid \mathbf{x}_n \sim \mathfrak{N}(\mathbf{x}_n'\boldsymbol{\beta}_0, 1)$ so that $y_n = \mathbf{1}\{y_n^* > 0\}$, $n = 1, \ldots, N$, are probit binomial random variables.

(a) Show that

$$\mathrm{E}[y^* \mid y^* > 0,\ \mathbf{x}_n] = \mathbf{x}_n'\boldsymbol{\beta}_0 + \frac{\phi(\mathbf{x}_n'\boldsymbol{\beta}_0)}{\Phi(\mathbf{x}_n'\boldsymbol{\beta}_0)}$$

Why does this imply that

$$\mathbf{x}_n'\boldsymbol{\beta}_0 + \frac{\phi(\mathbf{x}_n'\boldsymbol{\beta}_0)}{\Phi(\mathbf{x}_n'\boldsymbol{\beta}_0)} > 0$$

(b) Similarly, find $\mathrm{E}[y^* \mid y^* < 0,\ \mathbf{x}_n]$. (HINT: A quick method uses $\mathrm{E}[-y^* \mid -y^* > 0,\ \mathbf{x}_n]$.)

(c) Derive the Hessian of the probit log-likelihood function. Confirm that this log-likelihood function is globally concave by showing that the Hessian is negative definite. (HINT: Use the inequalities implied by the previous parts of this exercise.)

27.5 **(Logit)** The OLS fit of a linear regression model has the property that the average fitted value equals the average value of the LHS variable if one of the RHS variables is a constant. The logit estimator has a similar property. Show that the logit MLE sets the sample fraction of ones equal to the average fitted probability of ones if an explanatory variable is a constant. That is,

$$\bar{y} = \mathrm{E}_N[y_n] = \mathrm{E}_N[F_L(\mathbf{x}_n'\hat{\boldsymbol{\beta}}_{\mathrm{ML}})]$$

where

$$\hat{\boldsymbol{\beta}}_{\mathrm{ML}} = \underset{\boldsymbol{\beta}}{\operatorname{argmax}}\, \mathrm{E}_N\Big[y_n \log F_L(\mathbf{x}_n'\boldsymbol{\beta}) + (1 - y_n)\log\Big(1 - F_L(\mathbf{x}_n'\boldsymbol{\beta})\Big)\Big]$$

27.6 **(Perfect Classifier)** Suppose that one explanatory variable in a regression function is an indicator variable that equals one for the nth observation and zero for all other observations. The OLS fit of a linear regression will set the nth fitted residual to zero and the remaining coefficients will be the OLS fit based on the data set without the nth observation.[36] Show that a similar outcome occurs in fitting such Bernoulli regression models as logit and probit.

27.7 (Ordered Data) Comment: "Ordered probability model estimates of the boundary parameters show that those who receive a 4 are roughly one-third as good teachers as those who receive a 7. Those who receive a 1 or a 2 have negative teaching quality and are doing more harm than good. They should be removed from their classrooms immediately." (HINT: Confine your answer to the *econometric* issues.)

27.8 (Ordered Data) For ordered data, the values of y_n are *ordinal* labels, chosen for convenience. One could just as well replace the outcomes $j = 1, \ldots, J$ with $2, 2^2, \ldots, 2^J$, as the ordered values.

(a) Show that such replacement does not affect the MLE.

(b) Show how such replacement affects the NLS estimator.

27.9 (Errors in Variables) Consider a Bernoulli regression model with errors in the explanatory variables:

$$\mathrm{E}[y_n \mid \mathbf{x}_n^*] = F(\mathbf{x}_n^{*\prime}\boldsymbol{\beta}_0) \qquad \text{and} \qquad \mathbf{x}_n = \mathbf{x}_n^* + \mathbf{v}_n$$

where $\mathbf{v}_n$ is measurement error in $\mathbf{x}_n$. Suppose that $\mathbf{z}_n$ are instrumental variables in the sense that $\mathrm{E}[\mathbf{v}_n \mid \mathbf{z}_n] = \mathbf{0}$ and $\mathrm{E}[\mathbf{z}_n \mathbf{x}_n']$ is full rank.[37]

(a) Argue that a consistent IV estimator is not available for the Bernoulli model, in contrast to the linear regression model.

(b) Argue that if there are no errors in the explanatory variables ($\mathbf{v}_n = 0$) then the moment equations $\mathrm{E}_N\left[\mathbf{z}_n\left(y_n - F(\mathbf{x}_n'\boldsymbol{\beta})\right)\right] = \mathbf{0}$ provide a consistent GMM estimator.

(c) Suggest a GMM test for the hypothesis that there are no errors in variables.

27.10 (Poisson Score Test) Rederive the score test of Cameron and Trivedi (1990) for overdispersion in the Poisson model of count data using the following steps:[38]

(a) Consider the general reparameterization of the Katz distributions (27.55)–(27.56) in terms of dispersion given by

$$\mu = \frac{\lambda}{1-\gamma} \qquad \text{and} \qquad \mu + \sigma = \frac{\lambda}{(1-\gamma)^2}$$

Show that

$$\left.\frac{\partial \log f(y+1)}{\partial \sigma}\right|_{\sigma=0} - \left.\frac{\partial \log f(y)}{\partial \sigma}\right|_{\sigma=0} = \frac{y-\mu}{\mu^2}$$

$$\left.\frac{\partial \log f(0)}{\partial \sigma}\right|_{\sigma=0} = \frac{1}{2}$$

and, therefore,

$$\left.\frac{\partial \log f(y+1)}{\partial \sigma}\right|_{\sigma=0} = \frac{1}{2\mu^2}\left[(y-\mu)^2 - y\right]$$

(b) Confirm that the information matrix is block-diagonal in μ and σ and that

$$\mathrm{Var}\left[(Y-\mu)^2 - Y\right] = 2\mu^2$$

[36] This was the subject of Exercise 3.2.

[37] See Newey (1985).

[38] See also Cameron and Trivedi (1986) and Lee (1986).

if Y has a Poisson distribution with $\lambda = \mu$.

(c) Let the alternative hypothesis be $\sigma = \alpha\, g(\mu)$ where $g(\cdot)$ is a function from $\mathbf{R}_+$ to $\mathbf{R}_+$. Combine the previous expressions to obtain the score test statistic as one-half the explained sum of squares from the OLS fit of $\hat{\mu}_n^{-1}\left[\left(y_n - \hat{\mu}_n\right)^2 - y_n\right]$ on $\hat{\mu}_n^{-1} g(\hat{\mu}_n)$, where $\hat{\mu}_n$ is the fitted mean value of the nth observation for the Poisson model.[39]

(d) Cameron and Trivedi (1990) note that previous tests in the literature set $g(\mu)$ to either 1, μ, or μ^2.[40] Modify the score test to accommodate all three possibilities simultaneously. (HINT: The null distribution of the test statistic has *three* degrees of freedom.)

(e) Cameron and Trivedi (1990) suggest an alternative test based on the conditional moment restriction

$$\mathrm{E}[(Y - \mu)^2 - \mu \mid \mu] = \alpha\, g(\mu)$$

Show how to make such a test asymptotically equivalent to the score test given that there is an intercept in the linear index of $\mu_n = \exp(\mathbf{x}_n' \boldsymbol{\beta})$. (HINT: Write the moment function as a linear combination of the scores for $\boldsymbol{\beta}$ and α.)

27.8.2 Extensions

27.11 **(Hausman Test)** Ruud (1984) points out that many Hausman specification tests share a common basis in a likelihood factorization into conditional and marginal components. Such factorizations are popular in discrete-data and time-series settings. The factorizations give the Hausman specification tests interpretations as generalizations of the simple Chow test.[41] This exercise develops this framework.

Let $\mathrm{E}_N[L(\boldsymbol{\theta}; \mathbf{u})]$ be the average log-likelihood function for the parameter vector $\boldsymbol{\theta} \in \mathbb{R}^K$ given a random sample $\{\mathbf{u}_1, \ldots, \mathbf{u}_N\}$ of the random variable $\mathbf{U}$. Consider the partition of $\mathbf{U}$ into $[\mathbf{U}_1', \mathbf{U}_2']'$ and the factorization of their joint distribution into the conditional distribution of $\mathbf{U}_1$ given $\mathbf{U}_2$ and the marginal distribution of $\mathbf{U}_2$ so that

$$\mathrm{E}_N[L(\boldsymbol{\theta}; \mathbf{u})] = \mathrm{E}_N[L(\boldsymbol{\theta}; \mathbf{u}_1 \mid \mathbf{u}_2)] + \mathrm{E}_N[L(\boldsymbol{\theta}; \mathbf{u}_2)]$$

(a) Suppose that $\boldsymbol{\theta}$ is identified in all three log-likelihood functions. Show that

$$\hat{\boldsymbol{\theta}}_{(0)} = \operatorname*{argmax}_{\boldsymbol{\theta}} \mathrm{E}_N[L(\boldsymbol{\theta}; \mathbf{u})]$$

is efficient relative to

$$\hat{\boldsymbol{\theta}}_{(1)} = \operatorname*{argmax}_{\boldsymbol{\theta}} \mathrm{E}_N[L(\boldsymbol{\theta}; \mathbf{u}_1 \mid \mathbf{u}_2)] \qquad \text{and} \qquad \hat{\boldsymbol{\theta}}_{(2)} = \operatorname*{argmax}_{\boldsymbol{\theta}} \mathrm{E}_N[L(\boldsymbol{\theta}; \mathbf{u}_2)]$$

Suggest a Hausman specification test based on the comparison of $\hat{\boldsymbol{\theta}}_{(0)}$ with either $\hat{\boldsymbol{\theta}}_{(1)}$ or $\hat{\boldsymbol{\theta}}_{(2)}$.

(b) Show that $\hat{\boldsymbol{\theta}}_{(1)}$ and $\hat{\boldsymbol{\theta}}_{(2)}$ are asymptotically independently distributed and that asymptotically $\hat{\boldsymbol{\theta}}_{(0)}$ is a matrix-weighted average of $\hat{\boldsymbol{\theta}}_{(1)}$ and $\hat{\boldsymbol{\theta}}_{(2)}$.

(c) Use the previous result to show that specification test statistics based on the differences $\hat{\boldsymbol{\theta}}_{(1)} - \hat{\boldsymbol{\theta}}_{(0)}$, $\hat{\boldsymbol{\theta}}_{(2)} - \hat{\boldsymbol{\theta}}_{(0)}$, and $\hat{\boldsymbol{\theta}}_{(2)} - \hat{\boldsymbol{\theta}}_{(1)}$ are all asymptotically equivalent.

---

[39] We describe this as WLS with weight $\hat{\mu}_n^{-1}$ above.

[40] See the references Cameron and Trivedi (1990, p. 355) cite.

[41] See Examples 11.1 and 11.2 and Exercise 11.1.

(d) How is the specification test statistic based on $\hat{\boldsymbol{\theta}}_{(2)} - \hat{\boldsymbol{\theta}}_{(1)}$ a generalization of the Chow test?
(e) What are LR and score versions of these Hausman specification tests?

27.12 (Fixed and Random Effects) Show that the Hausman specification test statistic (24.39) is an example of the family of tests described in Exercise 27.11. This statistic compares the LSDV and random-effects estimators for panel data regression.

Suppose that

$$y_{nt} = \mathbf{x}_{nt}'\boldsymbol{\beta}_0 + \alpha_n + \varepsilon_{nt}, \qquad n = 1, \ldots, N$$
$$t = 1, \ldots, T$$

where α_n and ε_{nt} are jointly normally distributed, independent, and

$$\mathrm{E}[\alpha_n \mid \mathbf{X}] = 0, \qquad \mathrm{Var}[\alpha_n \mid \mathbf{X}] = \sigma_\alpha^2$$
$$\mathrm{E}[\varepsilon_{nt}] = 0, \qquad \mathrm{Var}[\varepsilon_{nt} \mid \mathbf{X}] = \sigma_\varepsilon^2$$

(a) Show that y_{nt} can be split into two independently, normally distributed random variables $y_{nt} - \bar{y}_n$ and $\bar{y}_n$.
(b) Use the general results of Exercise 27.11 to argue that the random-effects estimator $\hat{\boldsymbol{\beta}}_{\mathrm{RE}}$ is a matrix-weighted average of the LSDV and between estimators, $\hat{\boldsymbol{\beta}}_{\mathrm{DV}}$ and $\hat{\boldsymbol{\beta}}_{\mathrm{B}}$.[42]
(c) Describe two other, asymptotically equivalent, test statistics as alternatives to (24.39).
(d) Describe how to generalize the likelihood factorization in Exercise 27.11 to a GMM factorization, using this specification as an illustration. Show that the exogeneity test in Example 22.6 is another example of such GMM factorizations.

27.13 (Hausman Test of IIA) Hausman and McFadden (1984) propose a Hausman specification test of the multinomial logit model (27.42) based on its IIA property (p. 769). This exercise outlines various versions of the test.

Let the conditional probability that the jth alternative is chosen be

$$p_{nj} = \frac{\exp(\mathbf{x}_{nj}'\boldsymbol{\delta}_0)}{\sum_{i=1}^{J}\exp(\mathbf{x}_{ni}'\boldsymbol{\delta}_0)}, \qquad j = 1, \ldots, J$$

(a) Using the IIA property, show that one can estimate consistently $\boldsymbol{\delta}_0$ using the MLE for a subsample of observations that selected an alternative from the subset indexed $j = 1, \ldots, J_1 < J$. (HINT: What is the probability of choosing alternative $m < J_1$ given that the chosen alternative is in the subset of alternatives indexed $j = 1, \ldots, J_1$?)
(b) Suggest a Hausman specification test based on a comparison of the efficient MLE based on the complete sample and an inefficient MLE based on the subsample that selected an alternative from the subset indexed $j = 1, \ldots, J_1$.
(c) Put this comparison into the likelihood-factorization framework of Exercise 27.11 and suggest LR and score versions of the Hausman–McFadden specification test.[43]

27.14 (Ordered and Count Data) Ordered-probability and count-data models are closely related. Let us denote a count-data probability function by $p(y \mid \mu)$, $y = 0, 1, 2, \ldots$. This could be the Poisson or the negative binomial, for example. Show that one can always construct an equivalent normal ordered-probability model. In particular, show that there is a sequence of boundary point functions $\alpha_j(\cdot)$ $(j = 0, 1, 2, \ldots)$ such that

---

[42] See equations (24.4), (24.18), and (24.19).

[43] See Ruud (1984). McFadden (1987, Section 3) finds a convenient way to compute one of these score tests with OLS methods. He is also able to provide an omitted-explanatory-variables interpretation of the test.

$$p(0\,|\,\mu) = \Phi\Big[\alpha_1(\mu) - \mu\Big]$$
$$p(1\,|\,\mu) = \Phi\Big[\alpha_2(\mu) - \mu\Big] - \Phi\Big[\alpha_1(\mu) - \mu\Big]$$
$$\vdots$$
$$p(j\,|\,\mu) = \Phi\Big[\alpha_{j+1}(\mu) - \mu\Big] - \Phi\Big[\alpha_j(\mu) - \mu\Big]$$

Give a latent-variable model and an observation rule that could underlie a count-data model.

27.15 **(Poisson Mixture)** One approach to generalizing the Poisson p.m.f. (27.27) is to create a mixture after the fashion of creating the Student t distribution as a mixture of normal distributions.[44] One specifies that $f_P(y;\lambda)$ is the conditional distribution of y given λ and that λ is a latent random variable. Various mixing distributions for λ are workable, but researchers have probably given the gamma distribution the most attention.[45] The p.d.f. of the gamma distribution is usually written

$$f_G(\lambda;\alpha) = \begin{cases} \frac{1}{\Gamma(\alpha_1)}\alpha_2^{\alpha_1}\lambda^{\alpha_1-1}e^{-\alpha_2\lambda} & \text{if } \lambda > 0 \\ 0 & \text{if } \lambda \le 0 \end{cases}, \quad \alpha > 0 \tag{27.63}$$

Confirm that the distribution for y marginal of λ is the negative binomial p.m.f.

$$\begin{aligned} f(y) &= \int_0^\infty f_P(y;\lambda)\, f_G(\lambda;\alpha)\, d\lambda \\ &= \frac{\Gamma(y+\alpha_1)}{\Gamma(y+1)\Gamma(\alpha_1)}\left(\frac{1}{1+\alpha_2}\right)^y\left(\frac{\alpha_2}{1+\alpha_2}\right)^{\alpha_1} \end{aligned} \tag{27.64}$$

$y \in \mathbb{N}$ and $\alpha_1, \alpha_2 > 0$.

27.16 **(Panel Data)** Outside of regression linear models, it is often challenging to include individual effects in panel data models. Chamberlain (1984) shows that the binomial logit model is an exception. Let

$$\Pr\{y_{nt} = 1\,|\,\mathbf{x}_1,\ldots,\mathbf{x}_T,\alpha_n\} = F_L(\mathbf{x}'_{nt}\boldsymbol{\delta}_0 + \alpha_n), \qquad n = 1,\ldots,N$$
$$t = 1,\ldots,T$$

where $y_1,\ldots,y_T$ are independent conditional on $\{\mathbf{x}_{n1},\ldots,\mathbf{x}_{nT},\alpha_n\}$ and $F_L(z) = \left(1+e^{-z}\right)^{-1}$ as in (27.4).

(a) Suppose that $T = 2$. Show that

$$\Pr\{y_2 = 1\,|\,\mathbf{x}_{n1},\ldots,\mathbf{x}_{nT},\alpha_n, y_1 + y_2 = 1\} = F_L\Big[(\mathbf{x}_{n1} - \mathbf{x}_{n2})'\boldsymbol{\delta}_0\Big]$$

(b) How could one use this result to estimate $\boldsymbol{\delta}_0$ without making distributional assumptions about the α_n?

(c) Extend the result for general T by conditioning on $\sum_{t=1}^T y_{nt}$. Show that observations for which $\sum_{t=1}^T y_{nt} = 0$ or T contribute zero to the sample log-likelihood function.

27.17 **(Heteroskedasticity)** Show how to estimate the latent-variable model of conditional heteroskedasticty given in the introduction to Part IV using the EM algorithm.

---

[44] See the discussion of the Student t distribution on page 248.

[45] For example, see Hausman et al. (1984). Johnson et al. (1992) give an extensive summary of Poisson mixtures.

C H A P T E R 28

CENSORED AND TRUNCATED VARIABLES

Many observed economic variables assume a set of values that is limited but not necessarily discrete. Measured prices and quantities of goods often take positive values only. Official foreign currency exchange rates sometimes fall only within a range of values permitted by government policy. The linear regression model may describe the behavior of such economic variables poorly.

Consider, for example, the moments of such a dependent variable as an individual's hours of paid work per week, which is always positive. Two basic issues arise. First, the conditional mean of this dependent variable must be strictly positive.[1] But if we specify a linear conditional mean then our specification will permit negative values because the range of a linear function consists of all real values. Second, a dependent variable such as hours of work has a nonzero probability that it equals zero. Thus, it shares features of the purely discrete variables that we studied in Chapter 27. The ordinary linear regression model does not predict discrete outcomes with nonzero probability.

A dependent variable that is limited in these ways, whether discrete, continuous, or both, is generally called a *limited dependent variable* (LDV). In this chapter, we continue the development of econometric models for LDVs that we began with discrete dependent variables. The use of latent variables continues to play a key role.

28.1 LABOR SUPPLY

To introduce the modeling of general limited dependent variables, we will outline a labor supply model in which individuals behave as utility maximizers and obtain any desired hours of employment $h_n \leq 0$ at an observable predetermined market wage $w_n > 0$ (net of any taxes).[2] In this

[1] The only way that a positive random variable can have a mean equal to zero is for the random variable to equal zero with a probability of one.

[2] Generally, net wages are not actually observable. Wages before taxes are observable only for those individuals who are employed and even for these individuals taxes are rarely known. These issues lead to additional complications in current econometric models of labor supply.

model, leisure is a good and the market wage is the (positive) price of leisure. This leads to treating hours of work as negative. Those who choose $h_n = 0$ consume leisure or work outside the official labor market without wage compensation. An individual consumes c_n of a generic consumption good. Purchases of the consumption good are constrained by individual total income, the sum of wage income $-w_n h_n$ and observable nonwage income r_n:[3]

$$w_n h_n + c_n = r_n$$

This model is static, with a single, lifetime decision about hours and consumption levels.[4]

Following Hausman (1985), consider a linear (Marshallian) labor supply function

$$h_n^* = \alpha_n + \gamma_0 w_n + \delta_0 r_n \tag{28.1}$$

for nonzero amounts of employment given the market wage w_n and the nonwage income r_n. We expect $\gamma_0 > 0$ and $\delta_0 < 0$. To capture observable and unobservable differences in other factors determining individuals' labor supply, we specify that $\alpha_n \sim \mathfrak{N}(\mathbf{z}_n'\boldsymbol{\eta}_0, \sigma_\alpha^2)$ conditional on $\mathbf{z}_n$, w_n, and r_n.[5] $\mathbf{z}_n$ is a column vector of explanatory variables and $\boldsymbol{\eta}_0$ is a column vector of unknown coefficients. Thus, if all individuals were observed working one might estimate the parameters of the model with OLS, regressing h_n on z_n, w_n, and r_n.

However, many distinguishable groups of potential wage earners contain large fractions of individuals who are not employed. Women, for example, have a much lower labor force participation rate than men. The normal linear regression model fails to capture this phenomenon. To begin with, this statistical model states that hours are continuously distributed so that the probability that hours are exactly equal to zero should be infinitesimal. Moreover, the normal linear regression model states that hours can be negative as well as positive. The support of the normal distribution is the entire real line and the mean of h_n^* will even be *positive* for a sufficiently large nonwage income. Yet all observed h_n^* will be negative.

Within the economic model of utility maximization, individuals who do not work maximize utility on a boundary of the orthant containing feasible consumption bundles. Figure 28.1 illustrates both nonzero and zero labor supply with an indifference map. The tangent point **a** between the budget line **A** and the indifference curve is nonzero labor supply. If the wage is low enough, or the nonwage income is high enough, no indifference curve is tangent to the budget frontier and the preferred bundle of hours and consumption has hours equal to zero. The budget line **B** illustrates this case so that **b** is the preferred consumption bundle.

Let us rephrase these graphic ideas in economic terms. If the marginal rate of substitution of hours for income (or "reservation wage") exceeds the market wage rate for all $h \leq 0$, then zero hours is the most preferred point in the budget set. That is, desired hours of work h_n equal zero if

$$\forall h \leq 0 \qquad w^*(h, r_n) \equiv -\frac{h + \alpha_n + \delta_0 r_n}{\gamma_0} \geq w_n$$

or

$$h_n^* = \alpha_n + \gamma_0 w_n + \delta_0 r_n \leq 0 \tag{28.2}$$

[3] Nonwage income is also quite difficult to measure.

[4] See Blundell and MaCurdy (forthcoming) for dynamic models, including uncertainty.

[5] One can also permit γ and δ to exhibit such variation as in Hausman. This would substantially complicate our example.

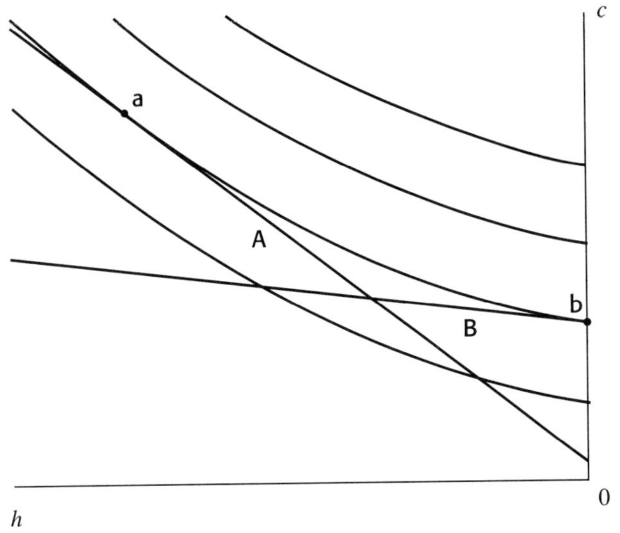

Figure 28.1 Labor supply.

where $w^*(h, r_n)$ denotes the reservation wage at hours h and nonwage income r_n. In other words, when the latent "labor supply" function becomes positive the actual labor supply is zero.

Therefore, we can meaningfully describe the observed (positive) hours of labor supply in terms of a latent normal linear regression model and an observation rule:

$$y_n^* \mid \mathbf{x}_n \sim \mathfrak{N}(\mathbf{x}_n'\boldsymbol{\beta}_0, \sigma_0^2) \tag{28.3}$$

$$y_n = \begin{cases} 0 & \text{if } y_n^* \leq 0 \\ y_n^* & \text{if } y_n^* > 0 \end{cases} \tag{28.4}$$

where

$$y_n^* \equiv -h_n^*, \qquad y_n \equiv -h_n$$

$$\mathbf{x}_n'\boldsymbol{\beta}_0 \equiv -\left(\mathbf{z}_n'\boldsymbol{\eta}_0 + \gamma_0 w_n + \delta_0 r_n\right), \quad \text{and} \quad \sigma_0^2 \equiv \sigma_\alpha^2$$

Although preferences are defined formally only for positive y_n^*, the model of the data-generating process behaves nevertheless as though negative y_n^* are censored and replaced with zeros. This LDV model is called *censored regression*.

Such models of partially observed latent variables are useful in several ways. They are a useful modeling tool for describing what we observe in terms of simple abstract descriptions of the world. When they are analytically tractable, these models also provide a motivation for an econometric specification. Given a latent model and an observation rule, we can in principle derive the likelihood of the observed variables. Having done this, one can examine the result to see whether it succeeds in capturing the actual behavior or fails in some observable way.

We can do all this informally with a scatter plot of latent and observed data from a simple regression model. Figure 28.2 shows a simulated example. The latent y_n^* are open circles and the censored y_n are solid dots so that when the positive y_n^* are observed the figure shows a dot within a circle. On the other hand, the negative y_n^* appear as circles with a set of y_n dots on the x-axis

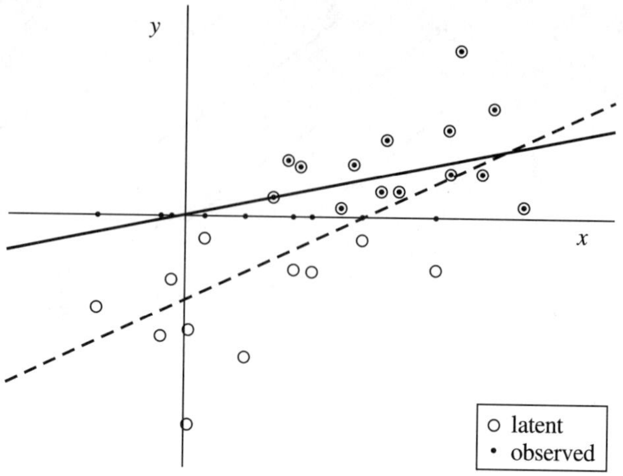

Figure 28.2 Censored regression.

above them. The dashed line is the conditional mean of y_n^* given x_n and the solid line is the OLS fit for the (x_n, y_n).

Several features of the simulated data in this figure are general characteristics of censored data that we will derive in this chapter. Perhaps the most noticeable feature is the increase in the fitted intercept and decrease in the fitted slope induced by censoring. In general, inference with OLS about the parameters of the latent regression is misleading, underestimating the slope coefficients of explanatory variables. Somehow one must take the censoring into account.

In addition, some of the OLS fitted values are actually negative even though every y_n is positive. Thus, the linear regression model is inadequate to describe the conditional mean of the observed data. That function is clearly nonlinear, bending up toward the left in order to remain positive. The variance of the y_n also appears to vary with x_n. As x_n decreases and the frequency of zeros increases, the conditional variance of y_n appears to fall. Therefore, neither the first nor the second moment assumption of the linear regression model appears to be satisfactory for the observed data.

In the next two sections, we will confirm that these simulated features correspond to properties of censored moments. First, we will derive the likelihood for y_n given the structure above. Second, we will examine what we have constructed, looking particularly at the implied moments of y_n. Third, we will describe estimation and prediction with NLS and ML. Then, in the remainder of the chapter, we introduce two LDV models that are closely related to censored regression, we discuss the role of distributional assumptions in these models, and we provide supporting mathematical material.

28.2 MIXED PROBABILITY FUNCTIONS

The random variable y_n in (28.2) is neither continuously nor discretely distributed. Its distribution contains elements of both types and is therefore called *mixed*. Estimation by ML and GMM is still feasible. But to use these methods, one must derive the likelihood function and the conditional moments of y_n. In this section, we offer a systematic, general procedure to find the likelihood function.

We will follow basic probability theory, first constructing the c.d.f. of y_n. There are two reasons for this. First, the c.d.f. is well defined for discrete, continuous, and mixed probability functions. The c.d.f. equals the probability of an *interval* of possible values so that no awkward issues of infinitesimal versus discrete probabilities arise. Second, it is natural to build the c.d.f. up from lowest to highest values of random variables. This approach systematically covers the support of the random variable, helping to avoid oversights.

Armed with the c.d.f., we find the probability function (p.f.) by differencing or differentiation, whichever is appropriate. To find the probability mass function (p.m.f.) of a discrete random variable, one locates the points where the c.d.f. is discontinuous and takes a positive step. The height of each step, or the *difference* in the c.d.f. at adjacent points, is the discrete probability of the associated random variable taking the value at that point.[6] On the other hand, to find the probability density function (p.d.f.) of a continuous random variable, one *differentiates* the c.d.f. The p.f. of a mixed distribution is a mixture of these two transformations of the c.d.f.

We begin with a location-scale specification: suppose that

$$y_n^* = \mathbf{x}_n'\boldsymbol{\beta}_0 + \sigma_0\varepsilon_n \tag{28.5}$$

$$y_n = \mathbf{1}\{y_n^* > 0\} \cdot y_n^* \tag{28.6}$$

where $\sigma_0 > 0$ and the ε_n are i.i.d. with a known, differentiable c.d.f. $F_\varepsilon(\cdot)$. In this notation, the c.d.f. of y_n^* is

$$\begin{aligned} F_{y_n^*}(c \mid \mathbf{x}_n) &\equiv \Pr\{y_n^* \le c \mid \mathbf{x}_n\} \\ &= \Pr\{\mu_0 + \sigma_0\varepsilon \le c \mid \mathbf{x}_n\} \\ &= \Pr\left\{ \varepsilon \le \frac{c - \mathbf{x}_n'\boldsymbol{\beta}_0}{\sigma_0} \,\middle|\, \mathbf{x}_n \right\} \\ &= F_\varepsilon\left(\frac{c - \mathbf{x}_n'\boldsymbol{\beta}_0}{\sigma_0}\right) \end{aligned}$$

The c.d.f. of $y_n = \mathbf{1}\{y_n^* > 0\} \cdot y_n^*$ follows directly from this function. Starting with the lowest values, consider $F_{y_n}(c)$ for a strictly negative c.

- According to the observation rule (28.6), negative values of y_n never occur and therefore the c.d.f. is zero for all $c < 0$.
- Consider next $c = 0$. This is a special point because many values of y_n^* yield $y_n = 0$. Using our previous results, we have

$$\Pr\{y_n \le 0 \mid \mathbf{x}_n\} = \Pr\{y_n^* \le 0 \mid \mathbf{x}_n\} = F_\varepsilon\left(\frac{-\mathbf{x}_n'\boldsymbol{\beta}_0}{\sigma_0}\right)$$

- Finally, take c to be strictly positive. Now $y_n \le c$ if and only if $y_n^* \le c$ according to (28.6) and

$$\Pr\{y_n \le c \mid \mathbf{x}_n\} = \Pr\{y_n^* \le c \mid \mathbf{x}_n\} = F_\varepsilon\left(\frac{c - \mathbf{x}_n'\boldsymbol{\beta}_0}{\sigma_0}\right)$$

[6] For example, see the ordered probability model, especially equation (27.26) and Figure 27.4.

Putting these results together,

$$F_{y_n}(c \mid \mathbf{x}_n) = \begin{cases} 0 & \text{if} \quad c < 0 \\ F_\varepsilon\left(\frac{c - \mathbf{x}_n' \boldsymbol{\beta}_0}{\sigma_0}\right) & \text{if} \quad c \geq 0 \end{cases} \tag{28.7}$$

Figure 28.3 graphs an example of this function when $F_\varepsilon(\cdot)$ is the standard normal c.d.f. The dashed line depicts the underlying c.d.f. of the latent y_n^*. This is replaced with a horizontal segment at zero for all strictly negative values of c with the missing probability recovered suddenly at $c = 0$. Thereafter, the c.d.f.s of y_n^* and y_n coincide.

Given the c.d.f. $F_{y_n}(c \mid \mathbf{x}_n)$, we derive the corresponding p.f. by differentiating wherever $F_{y_n}(c \mid \mathbf{x}_n)$ is differentiable and differencing wherever $F_{y_n}(c \mid \mathbf{x}_n)$ jumps discretely.[7] Thus,

$$f_{y_n}(c \mid \mathbf{x}_n) = \begin{cases} 0 & \text{if} \quad c < 0 \\ F_\varepsilon\left(\frac{-\mathbf{x}_n' \boldsymbol{\beta}_0}{\sigma_0}\right) & \text{if} \quad c = 0 \\ \frac{1}{\sigma_0} f_\varepsilon\left(\frac{c - \mathbf{x}_n' \boldsymbol{\beta}_0}{\sigma_0}\right) & \text{if} \quad c > 0 \end{cases} \tag{28.8}$$

where $f_\varepsilon(\cdot)$ is the p.d.f. of ε. The p.f. corresponding to the c.d.f. in Figure 28.3 appears in Figure 28.4. Like the c.d.f., the p.f. equals zero for strictly negative values because there is no probability of observing $y_n < 0$. At $c = 0$, there is a mass point, which we graph with a large dot. For strictly positive c, the p.f. is continuous.

The difference between the probability $F_\varepsilon(-\mathbf{x}_n' \boldsymbol{\beta}_0/\sigma_0)$ and $(1/\sigma_0) f_\varepsilon\left[(c - \mathbf{x}_n' \boldsymbol{\beta}_0)/\sigma_0\right]$ may seem small in Figure 28.4. But one should keep in mind that this difference changes with $\mathbf{x}_n' \boldsymbol{\beta}_0$. Figure 28.5 shows what happens when the latent mean is much smaller and the probability of a zero is greater. The change in the latent mean shifts the entire latent p.d.f. to the left and all

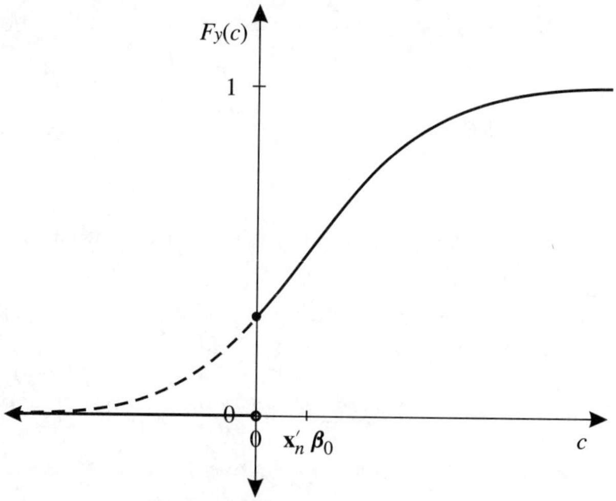

Figure 28.3 Censored c.d.f.

[7] For further discussion, see Section D.2.1, particularly Definition D.13 (Stieltjes Integral, p. 875) and its discussion.

of the area under the censored portion goes into the probability mass, raising it far above the continuous p.d.f.

With the p.f. of the observed y_n in hand, we can turn to the MLE for an estimator of $\boldsymbol{\theta}_0 = [\boldsymbol{\beta}_0', \sigma_0^2]'$. But before discussing such estimation, we consider the implications of the censored regression model for observable behavior. One can confirm analytically some of the properties suggested above. Knowledge of the first two moments is helpful for understanding what we ought to observe and, therefore, for judging whether the model is really appropriate.

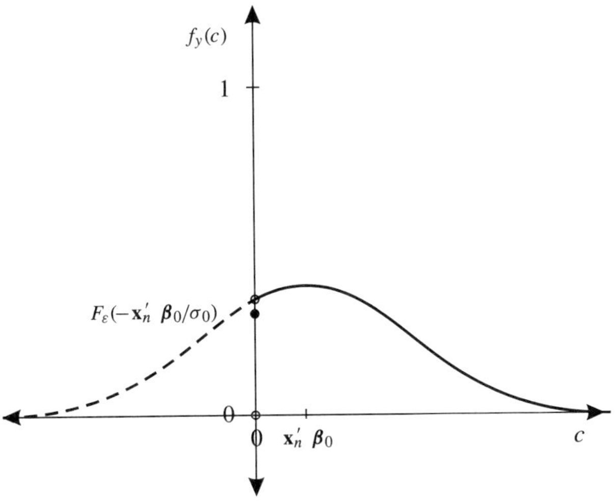

Figure 28.4 Censored p.f.

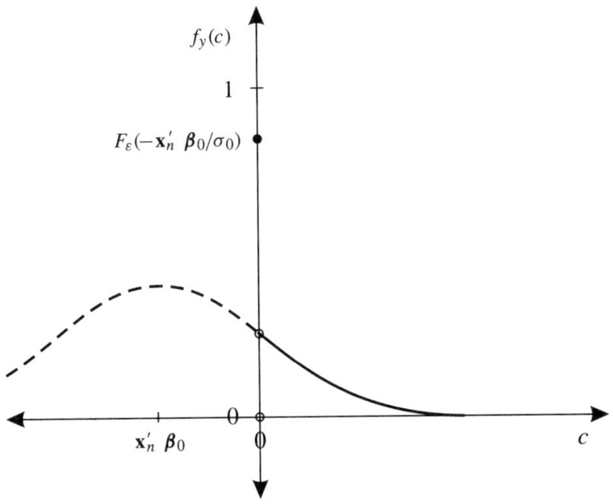

Figure 28.5 Censored p.f. with high censoring probability.

28.3 CENSORED MOMENTS

Expectations with respect to mixed p.f.s are defined as a combination of discrete and continuous expectation terms. In the case of the p.f. in (28.8),

$$\mathrm{E}[g(y_n)\,|\,\mathbf{x}_n] = g(0)\, F_\varepsilon\left(\frac{-\mathbf{x}_n'\boldsymbol{\beta}_0}{\sigma_0}\right) + \int_0^\infty g(z)\frac{1}{\sigma_0}\, f_\varepsilon\left(\frac{z-\mathbf{x}_n'\boldsymbol{\beta}_0}{\sigma_0}\right)\, dz$$

The first RHS expression is the sort of term one sums up in the expectation of a discrete random variable: the value of an outcome times the probability of that outcome. The second RHS is the analogous expression for the expectation of a continuous random variable. Rather than sum discrete terms, one integrates. But the integrand is still the product of an outcome and its probability density. The mean of y_n, for example, equals

$$\mathrm{E}[y_n\,|\,\mathbf{x}_n] = \frac{1}{\sigma_0}\int_0^\infty z\, f_\varepsilon\left(\frac{z-\mathbf{x}_n'\boldsymbol{\beta}_0}{\sigma_0}\right)\, dz \tag{28.9}$$

Of course, one does not need the p.f. of y_n to derive its mean. We can just as well use the p.d.f. of y_n^* [implied by (28.5)] and the observation rule (28.6):

$$\begin{aligned}\mathrm{E}[y_n\,|\,\mathbf{x}_n] &= \mathrm{E}[\mathbf{1}\{y_n^* > 0\}\cdot y_n^*\,|\,\mathbf{x}_n]\\ &= \int_{-\infty}^{\infty} \mathbf{1}\{z>0\}\, z\, f_{y^*}(z)\, dz\\ &= \int_{-\infty}^{0} 0\cdot f_{y^*}(z)\, dz + \int_0^\infty z\, f_{y^*}(z)\, dz\end{aligned}$$

which amounts to the same expression as (28.9). When $f_\varepsilon(\cdot)$ is the standard normal p.d.f. then this censored mean function has the particular functional form

$$m(\mathbf{x}_n'\boldsymbol{\beta}_0, \sigma_0) \equiv \mathrm{E}[y_n\,|\,\mathbf{x}_n] = \mathbf{x}_n'\boldsymbol{\beta}_0\, \Phi\left(\frac{\mathbf{x}_n'\boldsymbol{\beta}_0}{\sigma_0}, 1\right) + \sigma_0\, \phi\left(\frac{\mathbf{x}_n'\boldsymbol{\beta}_0}{\sigma_0}, 1\right) \tag{28.10}$$

We derive this equation in Section 28.9.1.[8]

In Figure 28.6, we plot (28.10) as a function of $\mu = \mathbf{x}_n'\boldsymbol{\beta}_0$, setting $\sigma_0 = 1$. We also plot the transformation $\mathbf{1}\{\mu > 0\}\cdot\mu$ to show how the expectation $\mathrm{E}[\mathbf{1}\{y^* > 0\}\cdot y^*]$ effectively smooths this function, retaining its properties of positiveness, monotonicity, and convexity.[9] Two asymptotes are also apparent. The left one shows the effects of severe censoring that makes almost all outcomes zero. The right asymptote exhibits the diminishing effect of censoring as the probability of a zero becomes negligible and the mean of the latent data becomes the mean of the observed data.

These functional properties of the censored normal mean correspond to the informal observations we made about Figure 28.2 and suggest that the fitted OLS slope coefficients from a regression of y_n on $\mathbf{x}_n$ are biased toward zero. By differentiating (28.10), we find that

$$\frac{\partial m(\mathbf{x}_n'\boldsymbol{\beta}_0, \sigma_0)}{\partial \mathbf{x}_n} = \frac{\partial\, \mathrm{E}[y_n\,|\,\mathbf{x}_n]}{\partial \mathbf{x}_n} = \boldsymbol{\beta}_0\, \Phi\left(\frac{\mathbf{x}_n'\boldsymbol{\beta}_0}{\sigma_0}, 1\right) \tag{28.11}$$

[8] See particularly (28.33) and (28.37).

[9] We give a more formal statement of these properties in Lemma 28.1 (Censored Mean, p. 811).

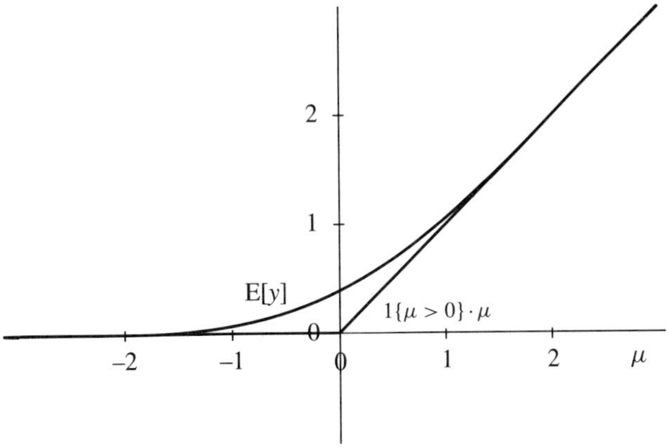

Figure 28.6 Censored mean for the normal distribution.

which equals $\boldsymbol{\beta}_0$ discounted by the probability that y_n^* is not censored. This derivative property translates into the observed bias in simple OLS regression. If $x_{n1} = 1$ and x_{n2} is variable, then

$$\begin{aligned}\mathrm{E}[\hat{\beta}_2 \mid \mathbf{X}] &= \frac{\sum_{n=1}^{N} (x_{n2} - \bar{x}_2)\, m(\mathbf{x}_n' \boldsymbol{\beta}_0, \sigma_0)}{\sum_{n=1}^{N} (x_{n2} - \bar{x}_2)^2} \\ &= \beta_{02} \frac{\sum_{n=1}^{N} (x_{n2} - \bar{x}_2)^2\, \Phi\big(\mathbf{x}_n^{*\prime} \beta_0/\sigma_0\big)}{\sum_{n=1}^{N} (x_{n2} - \bar{x}_2)^2}\end{aligned}$$

where $\bar{x}_2$ is the sample average of x_{n2}, $\bar{x} \equiv [1, \bar{x}_2]$, and $\Phi\big(\mathbf{x}_n^{*\prime} \boldsymbol{\beta}_0/\sigma_0\big)$ is part of the Taylor series expansion

$$m(\mathbf{x}_n' \boldsymbol{\beta}_0, \sigma_0) = m(\bar{x} \boldsymbol{\beta}_0, \sigma_0) + \Phi\left(\frac{\mathbf{x}_n^{*\prime} \boldsymbol{\beta}_0}{\sigma_0}\right) (x_{n2} - \bar{x}_2)\, \beta_{02}$$

$(n = 1, \ldots, N)$. Because $0 \le \Phi\big(\mathbf{x}_n^{*\prime} \boldsymbol{\beta}_0/\sigma_0\big) \le 1$,

$$0 \le \frac{\sum_{n=1}^{N} (x_{n2} - \bar{x}_2)^2\, \Phi\big(\mathbf{x}_n^{*\prime} \boldsymbol{\beta}_0/\sigma_0\big)}{\sum_{n=1}^{N} (x_{n2} - \bar{x}_2)^2} \le 1$$

implying that $\hat{\beta}_2$ is biased toward zero.

One cannot make this claim for all of the slope coefficients in multivariate regressions. But this special case is compelling evidence that such bias will occur as a general rule.

Like the conditional censored mean, the conditional censored variance changes with the location $\mathbf{x}_n' \boldsymbol{\beta}_0$ of the latent random variable. For the normal specification, this variance is[10]

$$\begin{aligned}\mathrm{Var}[y_n \mid \mathbf{x}_n] =& \Phi\left(\frac{\mathbf{x}_n' \boldsymbol{\beta}_0}{\sigma_0}, 1\right) \left[1 - \Phi\left(\frac{\mathbf{x}_n' \boldsymbol{\beta}_0}{\sigma_0}, 1\right)\right] (\mathbf{x}_n' \boldsymbol{\beta}_0)^2 \\ &+ \phi\left(\frac{\mathbf{x}_n' \boldsymbol{\beta}_0}{\sigma_0}, 1\right) \left[3 - 2\Phi\left(\frac{\mathbf{x}_n' \boldsymbol{\beta}_0}{\sigma_0}, 1\right)\right] \sigma_0 \mathbf{x}_n' \boldsymbol{\beta}_0 \qquad (28.12)\end{aligned}$$

[10] We also provide the elements of this formula in Section 28.9.1. See particularly (28.34) and (28.38).

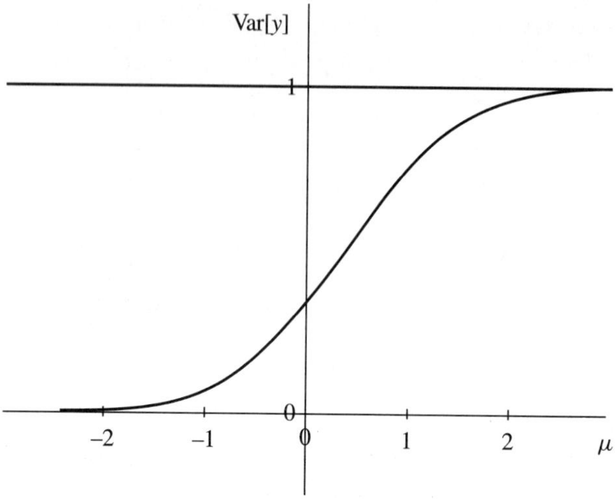

Figure 28.7 Censored variance for the normal distribution.

$$+\left[1-\Phi\left(\frac{\mathbf{x}_n'\boldsymbol{\beta}_0}{\sigma_0},1\right)-\phi^2\left(\frac{\mathbf{x}_n'\boldsymbol{\beta}_0}{\sigma_0},1\right)\right]\sigma_0^2$$

In Figure 28.7, we plot this censored variance as a function of $\mu = \mathbf{x}_n'\boldsymbol{\beta}_0$, setting $\sigma_0 = 1$. Like the mean, the variance shows the difference in censoring at the extremes. As μ approaches negative infinity and the censoring becomes severe, the variance approaches zero. On the other hand, as μ approaches infinity and the censoring virtually disappears, the variance approaches σ_0^2 (which we have set equal to 1), the variance of y_n^*. For moderate values of μ, the variance is increasing in μ, giving an overall shape to the variance function that looks like a c.d.f.

Relative to the latent homoskedastic regression equation (28.5), (28.12) and Figure 28.7 show how censored data will be conditionally heteroskedastic. At low values of $\mathbf{x}_n'\boldsymbol{\beta}_0$ the conditional variance is near zero whereas large values of $\mathbf{x}_n'\boldsymbol{\beta}_0$ correspond to a conditional variance near σ_0^2.

These properties of the conditional mean and variance of censored data help to describe the effects of censoring. They are reasonably simple and predictable. When the probability of censoring is high, the data behave almost like the constant zero. When the probability of censoring is low, the data behave almost like the uncensored data. And in between there is a smooth transition so that the conditional mean becomes more responsive to the explanatory variables and the conditional variance grows as the probability of censoring diminishes. Equipped with these properties, we now consider estimation of the parameters $(\boldsymbol{\beta}_0, \sigma_0^2)$ given a sample $\{(\mathbf{x}_n, y_n)\,;\, n = 1, \ldots, N\}$ and $f_\varepsilon(\cdot)$.

28.4 ESTIMATION

Researchers probably estimate censored regression models most often with the MLE based on the assumption that ε_n has the standard normal distribution. In economics, Tobin (1958) originally applied this approach to analyzing consumers' purchases of durables. For this reason, econometricians often refer to this estimator as *Tobit*. Following the pattern of our treatment of the Bernoulli model, we begin our discussion of estimation with the NLS estimator and then make a comparison with the MLE.

The NLS estimator of $\boldsymbol{\beta}_0$ is

$$\hat{\boldsymbol{\beta}}_{\mathrm{NLS}} = \underset{\boldsymbol{\beta},\sigma}{\operatorname{argmin}}\ \mathrm{E}_N\left[\left(y_n - m(\mathbf{x}_n'\boldsymbol{\beta},\sigma)\right)^2\right]$$

where

$$m(\mathbf{x}_n'\boldsymbol{\beta},\sigma) \equiv \mathbf{x}_n'\boldsymbol{\beta}\ \Phi\left(\frac{\mathbf{x}_n'\boldsymbol{\beta}}{\sigma},1\right) + \sigma\ \phi\left(\frac{\mathbf{x}_n'\boldsymbol{\beta}}{\sigma},1\right)$$

based on (28.10). Because $m(\mathbf{x}_n'\boldsymbol{\beta},\sigma)$ is nonlinear, σ is estimable here even though only the first moment of y_n appears in the NLS objective function.

The conditional heteroskedasticity in (28.12) suggests feasible WNLS (FWNLS) estimation as a two-step estimator. The observations with a high censoring probability have low variances so that weighting will improve asymptotic efficiency of estimation. Having discussed such estimation before, we do not elaborate further here. Our purpose is to make a comparison with the MLE.

Given the p.d.f. $f_\varepsilon(\cdot)$, the most efficient estimator of $\boldsymbol{\beta}_0$ and $\boldsymbol{\sigma}_0$ is the MLE. Using (28.8), we find the average log-likelihood function for censored regression to be

$$\begin{aligned}\mathrm{E}_N[L(\boldsymbol{\theta})] = \mathrm{E}_N\Bigg[&\mathbf{1}\{y_n=0\}\ \log F_\varepsilon\left(\frac{-\mathbf{x}_n'\boldsymbol{\beta}}{\sigma}\right)\\ &+(1-\mathbf{1}\{y_n=0\})\left[-\log\sigma + \log f_\varepsilon\left(\frac{y_n-\mathbf{x}_n'\boldsymbol{\beta}}{\sigma}\right)\right]\Bigg]\end{aligned} \tag{28.13}$$

For the Tobit model with standard normal $f_\varepsilon(\cdot)$,

$$\begin{aligned}\mathrm{E}_N[L(\boldsymbol{\theta})] = \mathrm{E}_N\Bigg[&\mathbf{1}\{y_n=0\}\ \log \Phi\left(\frac{-\mathbf{x}_n'\boldsymbol{\beta}}{\sigma},1\right)\\ &+(1-\mathbf{1}\{y_n=0\})\left[-\log\sigma - \frac{1}{2}\left(\frac{y_n-\mathbf{x}_n'\boldsymbol{\beta}}{\sigma}\right)^2\right]\Bigg]\end{aligned} \tag{28.14}$$

Note that this log-likelihood function depends on both the $\{y_n\}$ and the Bernoulli random variables $\{\mathbf{1}\{y_n=0\}\}$, reflecting the mixed nature of the p.f. It follows that the WNLS and MLE are not asymptotically equivalent, in contrast to the Bernoulli case.[11] WNLS fits the nonlinear regression function only to the $\{y_n\}$. The MLE, on the other hand, clearly depends on the $\{\mathbf{1}\{y_n=0\}\}$ as well. Knowing that it must be relatively efficient, we can infer that the MLE obtains additional gains in efficiency over reweighting the NLS estimator through a combination of $\{\mathbf{1}\{y_n=0\}\}$ and y_n.

The Tobit MLE is relatively easy to compute because (28.14) has a globally concave parameterization.[12] Hence, the MLE is unique and quadratic optimization methods work well. As a result, most econometric software will compute the Tobit MLE and researchers apply it widely.

---

11 See the discussion starting on p. 752 under *Maximum Likelihood*.

12 See Olsen (1978). We give a more general result in Lemma 28.3 (Global Concavity, p. 813).

28.5 PREDICTION AND TRUNCATED MEANS

When interpreting estimates of the slope coefficients of censored regression models, one should report the sample average of the derivative in (28.32) just as one does for purely discrete models. However, because the scale of the latent y_n^* is identifiable with censored data, the coefficients in $\boldsymbol{\beta}_0$ may also hold direct interest, particularly if $y_n^* \leq 0$ is a potentially actual outcome. $\boldsymbol{\beta}_0$ contains the regression coefficients of the conditional mean of the latent dependent variable y_n^* given $\mathbf{x}_n$. Foreign exchange rates constrained by government intervention are an example. The removal of the constraints is possible and the behavior of an exchange rate without constraints holds interest.

Furthermore, one can predict y_n^* for censored observations. The conditional mean $\mathbf{x}_n'\boldsymbol{\beta}_0$ given $\mathbf{x}_n$ is a simple prediction, but it does not use all of the available information. Because one also knows that $y_n^* \leq 0$ for these observations, $\mathrm{E}[y_n^* \mid \mathbf{x}_n, y_n^* \leq 0]$ is a smaller MSE prediction function.

To derive $\mathrm{E}[y_n^* \mid \mathbf{x}_n, y_n^* \leq 0]$ we require the conditional p.f. of y_n^* given that $y_n^* \leq 0$. Using the definition of conditional probability (Definition D.15, p. 879), the c.d.f. is

$$\begin{aligned} F_{y_n}(c \mid \mathbf{x}_n) &= \Pr\{y_n^* \leq c \mid \mathbf{x}_n, y^* \leq 0\} \\ &= \begin{cases} \frac{\Pr\{y_n^* \leq c \mid \mathbf{x}_n\}}{\Pr\{y_n^* \leq 0 \mid \mathbf{x}_n\}} & \text{if } c \leq 0 \\ 1 & \text{if } c > 0 \end{cases} \\ &= \begin{cases} \frac{F_\varepsilon\left[(c - \mathbf{x}_n'\boldsymbol{\beta}_0)/\sigma_0\right]}{F_\varepsilon\left(-\mathbf{x}_n'\boldsymbol{\beta}_0/\sigma_0\right)} & \text{if } c \leq 0 \\ 1 & \text{if } c > 0 \end{cases} \end{aligned}$$

This is a continuous function, differentiable everywhere except $c = 1$. It follows that the p.d.f. is

$$f_{y_n}(c \mid \mathbf{x}_n) = \frac{dF_{y_n}(c \mid \mathbf{x}_n)}{dc} = \begin{cases} \frac{\frac{1}{\sigma_0} f_\varepsilon\left[(c - \mathbf{x}_n'\boldsymbol{\beta}_0)/\sigma_0\right]}{F_\varepsilon\left(-\mathbf{x}_n'\boldsymbol{\beta}_0/\sigma_0\right)} & \text{if } c \leq 0 \\ 0 & \text{if } c > 0 \end{cases} \tag{28.15}$$

In effect, the ordinary p.d.f. for y_n^* is inflated by the factor $[F_\varepsilon(-\mathbf{x}_n'\boldsymbol{\beta}_0/\sigma_0)]^{-1}$ so that the truncated p.d.f. integrates to one over the limited range $(-\infty, 0]$, as a proper p.d.f. should. This is called a *truncated* p.d.f. because a tail of the distribution has been cut off. Figure 28.8 is an illustration where the right-hand tail of the dashed p.d.f. is truncated and the remainder of the p.d.f. is inflated to yield the black p.d.f. The two shaded regions have equal areas.

Using this p.d.f. we can find the conditional mean of y_n^* given $\mathbf{x}_n$ and $y_n^* \leq 0$. When $f_\varepsilon(\cdot)$ is the standard normal p.d.f., the truncated mean is

$$\mathrm{E}[y_n^* \mid \mathbf{x}_n, y_n^* \leq 0] = \mathbf{x}_n'\boldsymbol{\beta}_0 - \sigma_0 \frac{\phi(-\mathbf{x}_n'\boldsymbol{\beta}_0/\sigma_0, 1)}{\Phi(-\mathbf{x}_n'\boldsymbol{\beta}_0/\sigma_0, 1)} \tag{28.16}$$

This expression is like the censored normal mean (28.10) after division by the probability of observing y_n^*. However, because we are dealing with $y_n^* \leq 0$ the limits of integration have changed and the probability term is the probability of censoring, $\Phi(-\mathbf{x}_n'\boldsymbol{\beta}_0/\sigma_0, 1)$, instead of $\Phi(\mathbf{x}_n'\boldsymbol{\beta}_0/\sigma_0, 1)$.

One uses (28.16) to predict the value of y_n^* conditional on $\mathbf{x}_n$ and $y_n = 0$. This refined prediction function is always lower than the simple conditional mean $\mathbf{x}_n'\boldsymbol{\beta}_0$. The downward adjustment depends on the ratio of the p.d.f. over the c.d.f. Such ratios are generally called

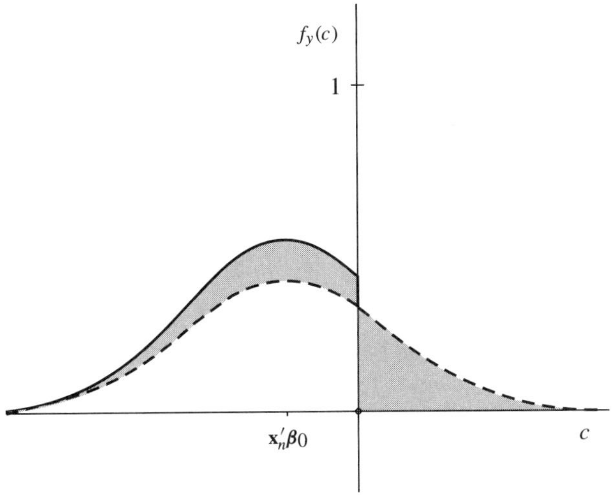

Figure 28.8 Truncated p.d.f.

hazard rates.[13] This term makes the prediction function negative for all values of $\mathbf{x}_n'\boldsymbol{\beta}_0$. Its effect is greatest for large positive $\mathbf{x}_n'\boldsymbol{\beta}_0$ and it diminishes as $\mathbf{x}_n'\boldsymbol{\beta}_0$ becomes large and negative where truncation is negligible. We examine this function more closely in the next section.

Censoring is one way that LDV models extend the linear regression framework. In the next section, we introduce truncation as another way. We will follow the same outline for discussing truncation that we just used for censoring, except that we condense somewhat. First, we derive the p.f. for the observed data given the latent data-generating process and an observation rule. Second, we discuss the moments of the observed data and, third, we describe NLS and ML estimators.

28.6 TRUNCATED REGRESSION

Truncation also occurs in some sampling methods. In many data sets, the censored observations are missing entirely. That is, there is no record of their occurrence let alone the values of the explanatory variables. This often happens because sampling is conditional on a positive y_n^*. For example, purchases of a good at a store record only the demands of those consumers who desire a positive amount of the good. Other consumers are missing entirely from the data set of store receipts. In this section we give a treatment parallel to censored data for such cases.

When some of the observations are missing, rather than merely censored, the data are said to be *truncated* and the expected value function of the remaining sample is a *truncated regression*. This is, of course, the regression function that we have just discussed regarding prediction of the censored observations. Here, however, in keeping with the censored data model (28.5)–(28.6), we will analyze

[13] The reciprocal is often called *Mills ratio*.

$$y_n^* = \mathbf{x}_n'\boldsymbol{\beta}_0 + \sigma_0\varepsilon_n$$

$$y_n = \begin{cases} y_n^* & \text{if } y_n^* \geq 0 \\ \text{no observation} & \text{if } y_n^* < 0 \end{cases}$$

where ε_n is a random draw from the p.d.f. $f_\varepsilon(z)$. Therefore, using the same steps as in the previous section, we obtain the truncated p.d.f. for y_n,

$$f_{y_n}(c \mid \mathbf{x}_n) = \begin{cases} 0 & \text{if } c < 0 \\ \dfrac{\frac{1}{\sigma_0} f_\varepsilon[(c - \mathbf{x}_n'\boldsymbol{\beta}_0)/\sigma_0]}{1 - F_\varepsilon(-\mathbf{x}_n'\boldsymbol{\beta}_0/\sigma_0)} & \text{if } c \geq 0 \end{cases} \tag{28.17}$$

and the truncated mean function

$$\mathrm{E}[y_n \mid \mathbf{x}_n] = \mathbf{x}_n'\boldsymbol{\beta}_0 + \sigma_0 \frac{\int_{-\mathbf{x}_n'\boldsymbol{\beta}_0/\sigma_0}^{\infty} z\, f_\varepsilon(z)\, dz}{1 - F_\varepsilon\big(-\mathbf{x}_n'\boldsymbol{\beta}_0/\sigma_0\big)}$$

For the standard normal distribution,

$$\mathrm{E}[y_n \mid \mathbf{x}_n] = \mathbf{x}_n'\boldsymbol{\beta}_0 + \sigma_0 \frac{\phi(\mathbf{x}_n'\boldsymbol{\beta}_0/\sigma_0, 1)}{\Phi(\mathbf{x}_n'\boldsymbol{\beta}_0/\sigma_0, 1)} \tag{28.18}$$

Figure 28.9 shows this function for various values of $\mathbf{x}_n'\boldsymbol{\beta}_0 = \mu$. It behaves essentially like the normal censored mean in Figure 28.6, except that it approaches the horizontal axis more slowly on the left. This reflects the absence of the zeros for censored observations which pull the mean down. Nevertheless, the truncated mean function does approach zero as $\mathbf{x}_n'\boldsymbol{\beta}_0$ approaches negative infinity.[14] As the truncation becomes more severe, the truncated normal p.d.f. places more and more of the probability in small neighborhoods of the truncation point.

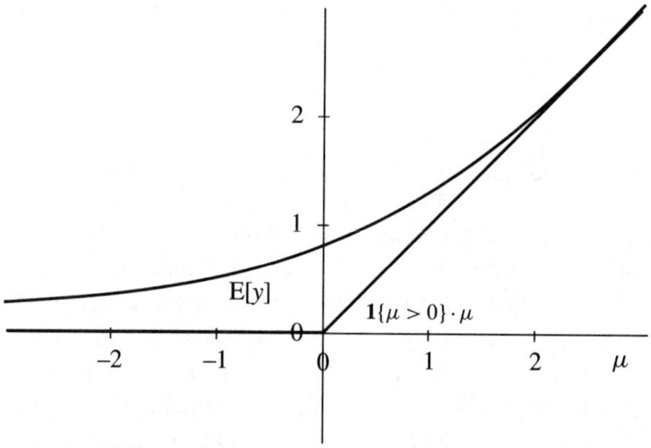

Figure 28.9 Truncated mean for the normal distribution.

[14] Using l'Hôpital's rule,

$$\lim_{\mu \to -\infty} \frac{\mu\Phi(\mu) + \phi(\mu)}{\Phi(\mu)} = \lim_{\mu \to -\infty} \frac{\Phi(\mu)}{\phi(\mu)} = \lim_{\mu \to -\infty} \frac{\phi(\mu)}{-\mu\phi(\mu)} = 0$$

The hazard rate in (28.18) is often called a *sample selectivity regressor* and it is frequently denoted by

$$\lambda\left(\frac{\mathbf{x}_n'\boldsymbol{\beta}_0}{\sigma_0}\right) \equiv \frac{\phi(\mathbf{x}_n'\boldsymbol{\beta}_0/\sigma_0, 1)}{\Phi(\mathbf{x}_n'\boldsymbol{\beta}_0/\sigma_0, 1)} \tag{28.19}$$

One can view the sample selectivity regressor as an omitted explanatory variable in OLS regressions of the truncated y_n on $\mathbf{x}_n$ alone. The likely effect of this omission on the OLS fitted coefficients (except the intercept) is bias toward zero. This follows from an argument similar to that for censored regression.[15]

Estimation of the truncated normal regression model is also similar to censored regression. One can apply NLS to (28.18) to estimate both $\boldsymbol{\beta}_0$ and σ_0. One can also apply FWNLS in a second step using the truncated normal variance formula

$$\text{Var}[y_n \mid \mathbf{x}_n] = \sigma_0^2\left[1 - \frac{\mathbf{x}_n'\boldsymbol{\beta}_0}{\sigma_0}\lambda\left(\frac{\mathbf{x}_n'\boldsymbol{\beta}_0}{\sigma_0}\right) - \lambda^2\left(\frac{\mathbf{x}_n'\boldsymbol{\beta}_0}{\sigma_0}\right)\right] \tag{28.20}$$

Using (28.17), one can write the average log-likelihood function for any $f_\varepsilon(\cdot)$ as

$$\text{E}_N[L(\boldsymbol{\theta})] = \text{E}_N\left[-\log\left[1 - F_\varepsilon\left(\frac{-\mathbf{x}_n'\boldsymbol{\beta}}{\sigma}\right)\right] - \log\sigma + \log f_\varepsilon\left(\frac{y_n - \mathbf{x}_n'\boldsymbol{\beta}}{\sigma}\right)\right] \tag{28.21}$$

This simplifies slightly in the standard normal case to

$$\text{E}_N[L(\boldsymbol{\theta})] = \text{E}_N\left[-\log\left[\Phi\left(\frac{\mathbf{x}_n'\boldsymbol{\beta}}{\sigma}, 1\right)\right] - \log\sigma - \frac{1}{2}\left(\frac{y_n - \mathbf{x}_n'\boldsymbol{\beta}}{\sigma}\right)^2\right] \tag{28.22}$$

Like censored regression, the FWNLS estimator based on the truncated mean does not produce an estimator of $\boldsymbol{\beta}_0$ that is asymptotically equivalent to the MLE. The reason in this case is that estimation of $\boldsymbol{\beta}_0$ and σ_0 is inseparable. One can see by inspection of (28.18) and (28.20) that the first and second moments of y_n depend nonlinearly on both parameters. In addition, the score for σ^2 depends on both y_n and y_n^2. The MLE for $\boldsymbol{\beta}_0$, therefore, is a nonlinear function of first and second moments. FWNLS estimates $(\boldsymbol{\beta}_0, \sigma_0)$ through the first moment restriction alone and, therefore, cannot be efficient.[16]

We cannot show that the log-likelihood function (28.22) has a globally concave parameterization like the probit and Tobit cases. Nevertheless, Orme and Ruud (1998) prove that there is a unique MLE. This substantially simplifies the computation of the estimator because the first local maximum that numerical optimization locates is the global maximum. In practice, numerical optimization of the truncated normal log-likelihood function is typically straightforward.

Censored, Bernoulli, and truncated variables are intimately related: given the censored variable $y_n^* \mathbf{1}\{y_n^* \geq 0\}$, one also observes the Bernoulli variable $\mathbf{1}\{y_n^* \geq 0\}$ and the truncated variable $y_n^* \geq 0$. One can estimate the parameters of the distribution of the latent y_n^* using any one of these variables and one expects to find the estimated coefficients from the Bernoulli variable model roughly proportional to those from the truncated variable model. The factor of proportionality should approximately equal the reciprocal of the estimated value for σ_0.

[15] The derivative of the truncated normal mean with respect to $\mathbf{x}_n$ also equals $\boldsymbol{\beta}_0$ times a scalar between zero and one. See Section 28.8.2.

[16] See Exercise 28.8.

The relationship between the process governing observation of y_n^* and the process generating y_n^* need not be so intimate. In the next section, we introduce an alternative to the censored regression model that is motivated by such a distinction between the latent sampling process and the process of selection into the actual sample.

28.7 NONRANDOM SAMPLE SELECTION

By way of introduction, let us return to the labor supply model that introduces this chapter and combine it with estimation of log-wage equations.[17] Labor supply and the analysis of wages are connected by the practical restriction that wages are observed only for those people who earn income. This raises the statistical concern that a sample of working individuals' wages is not representative of the population of interest. If one wishes to study the determinants of wages for all individuals who potentially supply labor then those who actually do supply labor are likely to be a biased sample.

Heckman (1974) formalized the issue by describing the labor supply decision in terms of the market wage and the reservation wage of an individual. According to his model, individuals choose not to take a job when their reservation wage $w_n^*(0, r_n)$ exceeds their market wage w_n for all hours of work as described by (28.2). We can rewrite this inequality as

$$y_{n1}^* \equiv \log w_n - \log w_n^*(0, r_n) \leq 0 \tag{28.23}$$

Combined with the usual log-wage equation for the market wage, we have two latent dependent variables for each individual in our model: the logarithm of the latent market wage, $y_{n2}^* \equiv \log w_n$, and its difference with the logarithm of the latent reservation wage, y_{n1}^*.

Heckman completes the model by specifying

$$\begin{bmatrix} y_{n1}^* \\ y_{n2}^* \end{bmatrix} \sim \mathfrak{N}\left(\begin{bmatrix} \mathbf{x}_{n1}'\boldsymbol{\beta}_{01} \\ \mathbf{x}_{n2}'\boldsymbol{\beta}_{02} \end{bmatrix}, \begin{bmatrix} \omega_{01}^2 & \rho_0\omega_{01}\omega_{02} \\ \rho_0\omega_{01}\omega_{02} & \omega_{02}^2 \end{bmatrix}\right) \tag{28.24}$$

conditional on $[\mathbf{x}_{n1}, \mathbf{x}_{n2}]$. The explanatory variables in $\mathbf{x}_{n1}$ include the determinants of both the latent market wage and the latent reservation wage, whereas $\mathbf{x}_{n2}$ contains only the former. Because the latent market wage is a component of both y_{n1}^* and y_{n2}^*, one expects ρ_0 to be nonzero.

The observation rule for the observable data describes (1) whether or not an individual is earning an income and (2) the income level when an individual is working:

$$\mathbf{y}_n = \begin{bmatrix} y_{n1} \\ y_{n2} \end{bmatrix} = \begin{bmatrix} \mathbf{1}\{y_{n1}^* \geq 0\} \\ \mathbf{1}\{y_{n1}^* \geq 0\} \cdot y_{n2}^* \end{bmatrix} \tag{28.25}$$

This is a clear generalization of the censoring observation rule: if the bivariate distribution is singular ($y_{n1}^* = y_{n2}^*$) the entire model collapses into the censored regression specification.[18] In its more general form, the observability of y_{n2}^* depends on another, correlated, latent variable y_{n1}^* and not just y_{n2}^*. In addition, the values of y_{n2} are not necessarily positive. One must augment the structure of this model if that feature is also required.[19] Alternatively, y_{n2} may be a transformation of an observed variable: the log-wage model implies positive wages.

[17] Heckman (1974, 1976) uses this motivation in his early work on nonrandom sample selection. Gronau (1974) also suggested the sample selectivity issue in observed wages.

[18] This singular distribution is well defined only if $\mathbf{x}_{1n}'\boldsymbol{\beta}_{01} = \mathbf{x}_{2n}'\boldsymbol{\beta}_{02}$, $\rho_0 = 1$, and $\omega_{01} = \omega_{02}$.

[19] Cragg's (1971) original generalization of the Tobit model delivers positive y_{2n}.

28.7.1 Log-Likelihood

Given the latent data-generating process (28.24) and the observation rule (28.25), we can derive the likelihood, check identification, examine moments, and discuss estimation methods as before. Section 28.9.3 contains a detailed derivation of the p.f. (28.40) that gives

$$\begin{aligned} \mathrm{E}_N[L(\boldsymbol{\theta})] = \mathrm{E}_N\Bigg[& (1-y_{n1}) \log \Phi(-\frac{1}{\omega_1}\mathbf{x}'_{n1}\boldsymbol{\beta}_1, 1) \\ & + y_{n1} \log \Phi\left[\frac{(1/\omega_1)\mathbf{x}'_{n1}\boldsymbol{\beta}_1 + (\rho/\omega_2)\left(y_{n2} - \mathbf{x}'_{n2}\boldsymbol{\beta}_2\right)}{\sqrt{1-\rho^2}}, 1\right] \\ & - \frac{y_{n1}}{2}\left[\log \omega_2^2 + \frac{\left(y_{n2} - \mathbf{x}'_{n2}\boldsymbol{\beta}_2\right)^2}{\omega_2^2}\right]\Bigg] \end{aligned} \tag{28.26}$$

Despite the awkward probability term in the middle, this log-likelihood function has several familiar features.

First, the two leading log-probability terms are reminiscent of the probit log-likelihood function (27.14). Because $\boldsymbol{\beta}_1$ and ω_1 always appear as $(1/\omega_1)\cdot\boldsymbol{\beta}_1$ it is apparent that both parameters are not separately identified. We can see also from the observation rule that the scale of y^*_{n1} is not identified. For analytical convenience, we will simply normalize $\omega_1 = 1$ and treat $\boldsymbol{\beta}_1$ as identified.

The remaining differences with a probit log-likelihood function are that (1) the residual $y_{n2} - \mathbf{x}'_{n2}\boldsymbol{\beta}_2$ appears as an additional explanatory variable in the probability for $y_{n1} = 1$ and (2) the entire argument is scaled by $\sqrt{1-\rho^2}$. These terms are present because this probability is conditional on y_{n2}. The second and third lines of the log-likelihood function are the joint log p.f. at $(y_{n1} = 1, y_{n2})$ factored into a conditional term for y_{n1} given y_{n2} and a marginal term for y_{n2}. This marginal term is the familiar log-likelihood function of the normal linear regression model.

If we ignore the conditional probability term, then this log-likelihood is similar to the censored log-likelihood (28.13). However, the leading log-probability term contains a different regression function than the trailing log-density term, reflecting the divorce between the observation/selection process and the dependent variable y_{n2}. This feature is a basic goal of the model. It enables the probability of censoring and the conditional mean of y_{n2} to be high simultaneously. It also means that the probability of censoring can be high yet the shape of the conditional distribution of y_{n2} can place relatively little probability in the neighborhood of zero.

Figure 28.10 shows examples of marginal p.d.f.s for y_{n2} for various values of ρ_0. These can be compared with Figure 28.5 for the censored regression p.d.f., which has the same censoring probability. As a result, the areas under the continuous parts of all the distributions are also equal. Note how the mode of the continuous portions no longer places the greatest probability just above zero. Also note the effect of positive correlation between y^*_{n1} and y^*_{n2}: the continuous portion has a higher mode and becomes positively skewed. Even for extremely high values ($\rho = 0.99$), the p.d.f. is well behaved.

To complete an analysis of identification, consider first $(\boldsymbol{\beta}_1, \boldsymbol{\beta}_2, \omega_2)$ given ρ (and $\omega_1 = 1$). The log-likelihood function is globally concave in the transformed parameterization $[\boldsymbol{\beta}_1, (1/\omega_2)\cdot\boldsymbol{\beta}_2, (1/\omega_2)]$ for the same reasons as the probit and censored log-likelihood functions. The concavity is strict provided that the $\mathbf{x}_{n1}$ and $\mathbf{x}_{n2}$ contain no multicollinearity. Hence, all of these parameters are identified given ρ. Furthermore, it is impossible to alter ρ and keep the coefficients of $\mathbf{x}_{n1}$, y_{n2}, and $\mathbf{x}_{n2}$ constant in the two log-probability terms. Therefore, all of the parameters are identified.

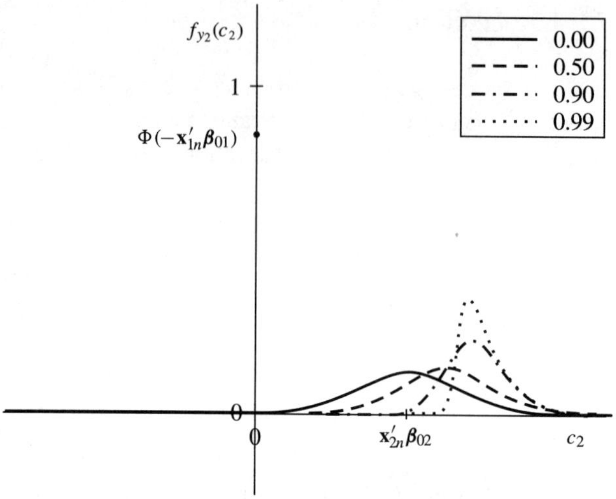

Figure 28.10 Sample selection p.d.f. for various ρ_0.

28.7.2 Moments

A key feature of Heckman's sample-selection model appears in the conditional mean of the observed, nonzero y_{n2} given $\mathbf{x}_n = \left[\mathbf{x}'_{n1}, \mathbf{x}'_{n2}\right]'$:[20]

$$\begin{aligned}
\mathrm{E}[y_{n2} \mid \mathbf{x}_n, y_{n1} = 1] &= \mathrm{E}\big[\mathrm{E}[y^*_{n2} \mid y^*_{n1}, \mathbf{x}_n] \mid \mathbf{x}_n, y_{n1} = 1\big] \\
&= \mathrm{E}\left[\mathbf{x}'_{n2}\boldsymbol{\beta}_{02} + \rho_0\omega_{02}(y^*_{n1} - \mathbf{x}'_{n1}\boldsymbol{\beta}_{01}) \mid \mathbf{x}_n, y_{n1} = 1\right] \\
&= \mathbf{x}'_{n2}\boldsymbol{\beta}_{02} + \rho_0\omega_{02}\,\mathrm{E}[y^*_{n1} - \mathbf{x}'_{n1}\boldsymbol{\beta}_{01} \mid y^*_{n1} \geq 0, \mathbf{x}_n] \\
&= \mathbf{x}'_{n2}\boldsymbol{\beta}_{02} + \rho_0\omega_{02}\lambda(\mathbf{x}'_{n1}\boldsymbol{\beta}_{01})
\end{aligned} \tag{28.27}$$

The significance of this conditional mean is that it depends on $\mathbf{x}_{n1}$ as well as $\mathbf{x}_{n2}$. Using Heckman's (1976) example, a married woman's reservation wage will depend on the number of children she has so that $\mathbf{x}_{n1}$ includes family size. As a result of the nonrandom sample selection, the incomes of married women who take jobs will appear to depend on the size of their families even when their latent market wages bear no relationship to the family-size variable.

We can predict the direction of this effect as well. Suppose that $\rho_0 > 0$, as we might expect from the way that $\log w_n$ enters y^*_{n1} and y^*_{n2}. Presumably, a woman's reservation wage rises with the number of children she has. This means that the number of children will enter $\mathbf{x}'_{n1}\boldsymbol{\beta}_{01}$ with a negative coefficient [see equation (28.23)]. The derivative of $\lambda(z)$ is also negative.[21] Therefore, the derivative of the conditional mean of a married woman's wage given that she has chosen

[20] In the first equality, we rewrite the mean in iterated form. The second equality uses the conditional mean of a multivariate normal distribution (Lemma 10.4, p. 208) for the inner conditional expectation. It also imposes the normalization $\omega_{01} = 1$. The third equality merely arranges terms and the fourth applies the definition of $\lambda(\cdot)$ given in (28.19).

[21] Equation (28.18) states that

$$\mathrm{E}(\mu + \sigma\varepsilon \mid \mu + \sigma\varepsilon \geq 0) = \mu + \sigma\lambda\left(\frac{\mu}{\sigma}\right) \geq 0$$

Differentiating $\lambda(\mu/\sigma)$, we find that

to take a job will be positive. On average, therefore, observed wages will tend to be higher for women with more children. This occurs because these women tend to have such unusually high market wages that these market wages exceed their systematically high reservation wages and the women choose to supply labor.

The expression for the conditional mean in (28.27) also leads researchers to prefer that the explanatory variables for selection $\mathbf{x}_{n1}$ include variables that do not appear in $\mathbf{x}_{n2}$. If $\mathbf{x}_{n1} = \mathbf{x}_{n2}$ then there is a danger that nonrandom sample selection may be mistaken for omitted nonlinearity in $\mathbf{x}_{n2}'\boldsymbol{\beta}_{02}$. For this reason, researchers consider estimation of the sample-selection model more convincing when the model dictates variables unique to $\mathbf{x}_{n1}$.

28.7.3 Estimation

Estimation of $(\boldsymbol{\beta}_{01}, \boldsymbol{\beta}_{02}, \omega_{02}^2)$ by application of NLS or FWNLS to (28.27) is obviously possible, but researchers tend to use ML or Heckman's (1976) two-step procedure.[22] The latter is analogous to the 2SLS estimator in (20.50).

1. In the first step, one estimates the parameters of the sample selectivity regressor $\lambda(\mathbf{x}_{n1}'\boldsymbol{\beta}_{01})$ using the probit estimator (call it $\hat{\boldsymbol{\beta}}_1$) for y_{n1}. This is the MLE based on the marginal distribution of y_{n1}. One also computes the fitted values $\lambda(\mathbf{x}_{n1}'\hat{\boldsymbol{\beta}}_1)$.

   The 2SLS analogues are OLS estimation of the coefficients of the reduced form and the fitted values of the reduced form residuals.

2. In the second step, one fits y_{n2} to $\mathbf{x}_{n2}$ and $\lambda(\mathbf{x}_{n1}'\hat{\boldsymbol{\beta}}_1)$ with OLS, estimating $\boldsymbol{\beta}_{02}$ and the product $\rho_0\omega_{02}$. This corresponds to OLS estimation of the structural equation, including the OLS fitted reduced-form residuals as additional explanatory variables.

Although it is very convenient, the Heckman two-step estimator is asymptotically inefficient relative to the MLE. In addition, the variance matrix of the estimated coefficients from the second step must be adjusted for the estimation of $\boldsymbol{\beta}_{01}$ in the first step.[23]

The MLE can be awkward to compute. A reliable approach is to initially compute the constrained MLE for a grid of values of ρ over the interval $[-1, 1]$ in order to identify the neighborhood of the unrestricted global maximum of the log-likelihood function. This method exploits the uniqueness of this restricted MLE. Additionally, one may reparameterize so that the restricted log-likelihood function is globally concave.[24]

Occasionally, unconstrained numerical optimization algorithms stray toward $\rho = \pm 1$ and fail to converge to a satisfactory local maximum. This can occur with any data set. The term

---

$$\begin{aligned}\frac{d\lambda(\mu/\sigma)}{d\mu} &= \frac{-(\mu/\sigma^2)\phi(\mu/\sigma)\Phi(\mu/\sigma) - (1/\sigma)\phi^2(\mu/\sigma)}{\Phi^2(\mu/\sigma)} \\ &= -\frac{1}{\sigma^2}\lambda\left(\frac{\mu}{\sigma}\right)\left[\mu + \sigma\lambda\left(\frac{\mu}{\sigma}\right)\right] \\ &\leq 0\end{aligned}$$

[22] Heckman's two-step procedure is also called *Heckit* or the Heckman–Lee procedure. See Heckman (1976, 1979) and Lee (1979).

[23] See Exercise 28.14.

[24] See the remarks on identification at the end of Section 28.7.1.

$$y_{n1} \log \Phi\left(\frac{\mathbf{x}_{n1}'\boldsymbol{\beta}_1 + (\rho/\omega_2)\left(y_{n2} - \mathbf{x}_{n2}'\boldsymbol{\beta}_2\right)}{\sqrt{1-\rho^2}}, 1\right) \tag{28.28}$$

is the source of this behavior. For example, if $\mathbf{x}_{n1}'\boldsymbol{\beta}_1 + (1/\omega_2)\left(y_{n2} - \mathbf{x}_{n2}'\boldsymbol{\beta}_2\right)$ is positive for all of the observations then this combination of variables acts as a perfect classifier. Maximization of the log-likelihood over ρ sets this parameter to its upper bound 1 and the fitted probabilities in (28.28) to 1. Thus, the log-likelihood function simplifies to

$$\mathrm{E}_N\left[(1-y_{n1})\log\Phi(-\mathbf{x}_{n1}'\boldsymbol{\beta}_1, 1) - \frac{y_{n1}}{2}\left[\log\omega_2^2 + \frac{\left(y_{n2} - \mathbf{x}_{n2}'\boldsymbol{\beta}_2\right)^2}{\omega_2^2}\right]\right] \tag{28.29}$$

on the boundary $\rho = 1$ provided that

$$\mathbf{x}_{n1}'\boldsymbol{\beta}_1 + \frac{1}{\omega_2}\left(y_{n2} - \mathbf{x}_{n2}'\boldsymbol{\beta}_2\right) > 0 \qquad \forall n : y_{n1} = 1 \tag{28.30}$$

This log-likelihood looks very much like the censored normal regression log-likelihood function (28.13).

However, unless $\mathbf{x}_{n1}'\boldsymbol{\beta}_1 = \mathbf{x}_{n2}'\boldsymbol{\beta}_2$ for all observations, what appears to be a local maximum on this boundary is actually not well defined. Because $\boldsymbol{\beta}_1$ appears only in one log-probability term in (28.29), further maximization over $\boldsymbol{\beta}_1$, $\boldsymbol{\beta}_2$, and ω_2 takes us toward values of $\boldsymbol{\beta}_1$ that make $-\mathbf{x}_{n1}'\boldsymbol{\beta}_1$ positive and as large as possible. Typically, this will eventually lead to a parameter vector value that violates (28.30) for some observation and at such a point the log-likelihood function suddenly plunges to negative infinity as a fitted probability changes from 1 to 0. Understandably, numerical optimization algorithms flounder in this region of the parameter space. The grid search over ρ will identify regions of interior local maxima where this problem can be avoided.

28.8 SPECIFICATION OF DISTRIBUTION

The normal distribution is the leading specification for the distribution of the latent disturbances in these LDV models. The popularity of the normal distribution reflects in part the historical development of regression analysis and the convenient multivariate form of this distribution. The bivariate normal distribution, for example, is central to Heckman's model of sample selection.

Researchers generally appreciate, however, that a parametric specification of the latent distributions in LDV models is a potential weakness in these econometric models. Unlike the normal linear regression model, the moment restrictions of censored and truncated normal specifications are specific to the normal distribution. These restrictions are false if the distribution is not normal. This implies in turn that all of the NLS and ML estimators are inconsistent.

In this section, we follow Goldberger's (1983) example and investigate the effects of alternative specifications of distribution. Focusing on the censored and truncated regressions, we describe which results for the normal specification carry over to other distributions.

28.8.1 Censored Regression

Section 28.9.1 gives analytical expressions for the censored mean corresponding to various parametric distributions that we have considered in other chapters. Perusal of these formulas reveals the wide range of expression $\mathrm{E}[y_n \mid \mathbf{x}_n]$ can take across different distributional specifications. In

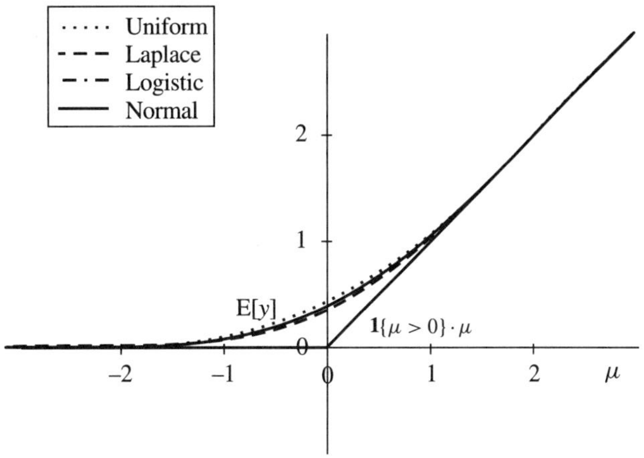

Figure 28.11 Censored mean.

Figure 28.11, we plot the mean for $y = \mathbf{1}\{\mu + \varepsilon \geq 0\} \cdot (\mu + \varepsilon)$ as a function of μ when $f_\varepsilon(\cdot)$ equals the standardized uniform, Laplace, logistic, and normal p.d.f.s.[25] This figure shows that these expressions conceal a basic similarity. This implies that for many data sets the NLS fitted values will differ little, even contrasting the uniform and Laplace specifications. There will be differences in the intercept and the overall scale of the slope coefficients that help the functions fit the same data even more closely than Figure 28.11 suggests. In that figure, we have constrained the means and variances of the underlying p.d.f.s to be equal. But the NLS estimator does not obey such location and scale constraints.

The graphic similarity of these censored mean functions reflects several properties that the functions all share.

LEMMA 28.1 (CENSORED MEAN) *Let $y^* = \mu + \sigma\varepsilon$ where ε is a random variable with mean zero and variance one. If $y = \mathbf{1}\{y^* > 0\} \cdot y^*$ then*

$$\mathrm{E}[y] = \mu\Big[1 - F_\varepsilon\Big(-\frac{\mu}{\sigma}\Big)\Big] + \sigma \int_{-\mu/\sigma}^{\infty} z\, f_\varepsilon(z)\, dz \tag{28.31}$$

which is

1. *positive,*
2. *greater than μ,*
3. *monotonically increasing in μ and σ,*
4. *convex in μ and σ,*
5. $\lim_{\mu\to\infty} \mathrm{E}[y] - \mu = 0$, *and*
6. $\lim_{\mu\to-\infty} \mathrm{E}[y] = 0$.

[25] All of the p.d.f.s are standardized to have mean zero and variance one. These p.d.f.s (except for the uniform) appear in Figure 13.1 (p.).

We give a proof in Section 28.9.2. An implication of the lemma is that the derivative of the conditional mean with respect to the index lies between zero and one. Indeed, if $\mu = \mathbf{x}_n'\boldsymbol{\beta}_0$ then generally

$$\frac{\partial\, \mathrm{E}[y_n \mid \mathbf{x}_n]}{\partial \mathbf{x}_n} = \boldsymbol{\beta}_0 \left[1 - F_\varepsilon\left(\frac{-\mathbf{x}_n'\boldsymbol{\beta}_0}{\sigma_0}\right)\right] \tag{28.32}$$

Thus, for several quite different distributions the normal specification yields a censored mean function satisfactory for NLS estimation.[26] However, differences between the chosen latent distributions are much more obvious in censored variance functions. In Figure 28.12, we plot the censored variance as a function of μ when $f_\varepsilon(\cdot)$ equals the Laplace, logistic, and standard normal p.d.f. These differences are even more marked in the corresponding weight function that one would use for WNLS estimation. Figure 28.13 plots the corresponding weight functions. The Laplace and uniform distributions are at the extremes, showing the difference that the tails of a p.d.f. can make. The tails of the Laplace p.d.f. are fattest and the relative weighting is least pronounced for this distribution. The uniform distribution has no tails because its support is bounded. As a result, the uniform distribution assigns infinite weight to some values of μ. Thus, we see that the distributional specification plays a more critical role in the relatively efficient WNLS estimator.

Despite the differences, the censored variance functions also share certain characteristics.

Lemma 28.2 (Censored Variance) *Let $y^* = \mu + \sigma\varepsilon$ where ε is a random variable with mean zero and variance one. If $y = \mathbf{1}\{y^* > 0\} \cdot y^*$ then* $\mathrm{Var}[y]$ *is*

1. *less than or equal to σ^2,*
2. *monotonically increasing in μ,*
3. $\lim_{\mu\to-\infty} \mathrm{Var}[y] = \sigma^2$, *and*
4. *if in addition* $\mathrm{E}[|\varepsilon|^{2+\delta}]$ *exists for some* $\delta > 0$, *then* $\lim_{\mu\to-\infty} \mathrm{Var}[y] = 0$.

We give a proof in Section 28.9.2.

The MLE is also sensitive to the differences in distributional assumptions. But because the log-likelihood function depends on $\mathbf{1}\{y_n^* > 0\}$ and $y_n = \mathbf{1}\{y_n^* > 0\} \cdot y_n^*$, an understanding of this sensitivity in terms of moment restrictions is subtler. We will return to this analysis shortly along with our discussion of truncated regression.

The global concavity of the censored log-likelihood function is another property of the Tobit model that rests on the normal specification.[27] We have already seen that the Bernoulli regression log-likelihood function has this property for a wider family of distributions: those for which $\log f_\varepsilon(z)$ is concave. This property continues to hold for a reparameterized form of the censored regression log-likelihood function.

[26] One can find, however, symmetric distributions with distinctly different censored mean functions. The Student t distribution, for example, can produce censored mean functions arbitrarily close to the lower bound $\mathbf{1}\{\mu > 0\} \cdot \mu$. See Exercise 28.24. For an example of an upper bound on the conditional mean of censored data, see Exercise 28.23. Other bounds are a subject for research.

[27] See Olsen (1978).

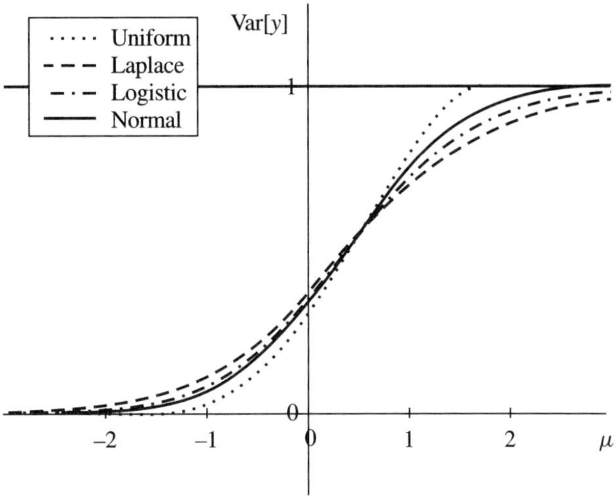

Figure 28.12 Censored variance.

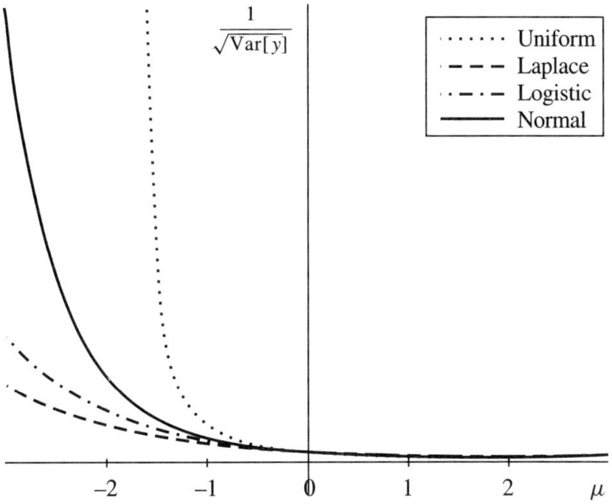

Figure 28.13 Censored weight.

LEMMA 28.3 (GLOBAL CONCAVITY) *If* $\log f_\varepsilon(z)$ *is concave, then the censored log-likelihood function is concave in* $\left[\boldsymbol{\delta} = (1/\sigma) \cdot \boldsymbol{\beta}, \gamma = 1/\sigma\right]$.

Proof. Rewriting (28.13) in terms of $\boldsymbol{\delta}$ and γ,

$$L(\boldsymbol{\delta}, \gamma; y_n) \equiv \mathbf{1}\{y_n = 0\} \log F_\varepsilon(-\mathbf{x}_n'\boldsymbol{\delta}) \\ + (1 - \mathbf{1}\{y_n = 0\}) \left[\log \gamma + \log f_\varepsilon\left(\gamma y_n - \mathbf{x}_n'\boldsymbol{\delta}\right)\right]$$

Obviously, $\log \gamma$ and, by assumption, $\log f_\varepsilon\left(\gamma y_n - \mathbf{x}_n'\boldsymbol{\delta}\right)$ are concave in $(\boldsymbol{\delta}, \gamma)$. In addition, we have already mentioned (pp. 753 and 773) that $\log F_\varepsilon(-\mathbf{x}_n'\boldsymbol{\delta})$ is concave in $\boldsymbol{\delta}$ if $\log f_\varepsilon(z)$ is concave. Therefore, because sums of concave functions are concave, $L(\boldsymbol{\delta}, \gamma; y_n)$ is concave. □

The condition that the p.d.f. be log-concave is restrictive, but many of the parametric p.d.f.s that we have discussed are log-concave. So are some that we have not. Karlin (1982) gives the following list:

> The class of log-concave densities includes the normal density, all Gamma densities . . . , the double exponential, all Pólya frequency densities, all B-spline densities, all the classical range densities and related order statistics (e.g., uniform, triangular, Beta family), the one and two sided Kolmogorov-Smirnov distributions, and all finite and infinite convolutions of the above. The Binomial, Poisson, geometric, negative Binomial, hypergeometric are all discrete log-concave analogues.

To this list we can add the Weibull and logistic distributions.

Therefore, although it is not widely available, the censored regression MLE based on the uniform, Laplace, or logistic distributions has the same concavity properties as Tobit. Of these specifications, the logistic p.d.f. is the only one that is continuously differentiable. Though it is not widely available in econometric software, the censored regression MLE for the logistic specification is just as easy to compute and offers a practical, relatively platykurtic, alternative to the normal specification.

28.8.2 Truncated Regression

Truncated regression problems are not so well behaved as the censored ones. In general, the truncated mean and variance functions vary much more over the distributions that we examined above. In addition, the log-likelihood function does not seem to have a globally concave parameterization within the family of log-concave p.d.f.s.

For some distributions, the truncated mean function has many similar properties to those of the censored mean function, but not generally. Figure 28.14 shows the truncated mean function for various distributions, including a standardized Student t with 3 degrees of freedom. Note that the left-hand asymptote of this function is not necessarily zero. One can see strictly positive asymptotes for the fat-tailed p.d.f.s, the Laplace and the logistic. The truncated mean function for the standardized Student t distribution is not even monotonic. Its tail is fat enough to cause severe truncation to *increase* the mean. The truncated mean of the uniform distribution has a piecewise linear shape symptomatic of its c.d.f. This is an extreme example of the behavior of thin-tailed distributions.

Given these examples of wide variation, it is not surprising that the we can establish far fewer general properties for the truncated mean function than for the censored mean function.

Lemma 28.4 (Truncated Mean) *Let $y^* = \mu + \sigma\varepsilon$ where ε is a random variable with mean zero, variance one, and p.d.f. $f_\varepsilon(\cdot)$. If $y = y^*$ when $y^* \geq 0$ but y is unobserved otherwise, then*

$$\mathrm{E}[y] = \mu + \sigma \frac{\int_{-\mu}^{\infty} z\, f_\varepsilon(z)\, dz}{1 - F_\varepsilon(-\mu/\sigma)}$$

is

1. *positive,*
2. *greater than or equal to* μ*,*
3. $\lim_{\mu\to\infty} \mathrm{E}[y] - \mu = 0$*, and*
4. $\frac{\partial\, \mathrm{E}[\mu+\varepsilon\,|\,0\le\mu+\varepsilon]}{\partial\mu} \le 1$.

If in addition $\log f_\varepsilon(z)$ *is concave, then*

5. $0 \le \frac{\partial\, \mathrm{E}[\mu+\varepsilon\,|\,0\le\mu+\varepsilon]}{\partial\mu}$.[28]

We leave the proof as Exercise 28.22.

The Student t p.d.f. is not log-concave and provides an example of a truncated mean function with negatively sloped regions. All of the other functions in Figure 28.14 correspond to log-concave densities and obey both derivative bounds. Despite the similarity of the normal truncated mean to the normal censored mean seen in Section 28.26, such behavior of the truncated mean is plainly specific. For negative values of $\mathbf{x}_n'\boldsymbol{\beta}_0$, where realizations come only from one tail of $f_\varepsilon(\cdot)$, a wide variety of functions is possible.

Given this variety in the mean function, we do not pursue the truncated variance function for which we anticipate the same sensitivity to distribution. Nevertheless it is interesting to note that the log-concave family of p.d.f.s also places a restriction on this moment. Goldberger (1983) cites the following result due to Karlin (1982, Theorem 2, p. 377):

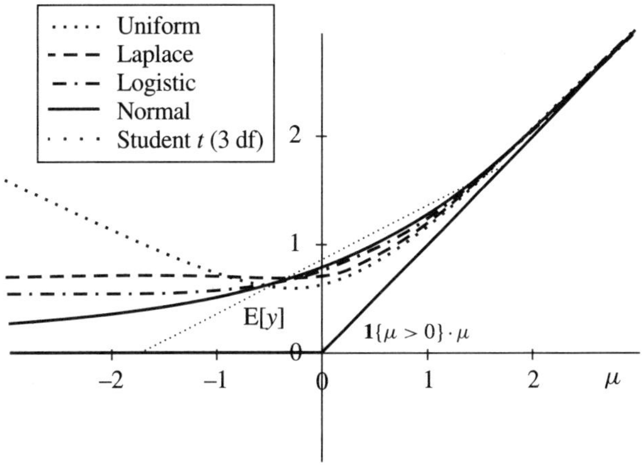

Figure 28.14 Truncated mean functions.

[28] See Goldberger (1983, pp. 80–82), who credits Gary Chamberlain with this result.

LEMMA 28.5 (TRUNCATED VARIANCE) *Let $y^* = \mu + \sigma\varepsilon$ where ε is a random variable with mean zero, variance one, and p.d.f. $f_\varepsilon(\cdot)$. Also let $y = y^*$ when $y^* \geq 0$ but y is unobserved otherwise. If $\log f_\varepsilon(\cdot)$ is concave, then the truncated variance,* $\text{Var}[y]$, *is monotonically increasing in μ such that* $\lim_{\mu\to\infty} \text{Var}[y] = \sigma^2$.

This variety in truncated moment functions has implications for the application of both the censored and the truncated normal regression models. Starting with the latter, one can see from Figure 28.14 that diagnostic checks for misspecification of the truncated mean function are appropriate. A method-of-moments test for whether $\alpha_1 = \alpha_2 = 0$ in

$$\text{E}[y_n \,|\, \mathbf{x}_n] = \alpha_1 + \mathbf{x}_n'\boldsymbol{\beta}_0 + \alpha_2 \left(\mathbf{x}_n'\boldsymbol{\beta}_0\right)^2 + \sigma_0\lambda(\mathbf{x}_n'\boldsymbol{\beta}_0/\sigma_0)$$

is a direct and practical approach that would catch the deviations observed in the figure. One could also extend the score test in Exercise 17.21 based on the Student t distribution to the truncated regression problem. Such Hausman specification tests as those suggested by Newey (1987) for censored regression are also possible.

The variety in truncated moments also leads us to rethink application of the censored normal regression model. First, prediction of the latent y_n^* is clearly sensitive to the choice of a normal $f_\varepsilon(\cdot)$ because $\text{E}[y_n^* \,|\, \mathbf{x}_n, y_n = 0]$ is a truncated mean function. In a sense, this is not surprising because such prediction is akin to out-of-sample forecasting. One is trying to predict outcomes for negative realizations of y_n^* that are never observed.[29]

Second, we can show how the truncated mean function directly influences the MLE for censored normal regression. If we factor the log-likelihood function for censored y_n into the marginal distribution for $d_n \equiv \mathbf{1}\{y_n = 0\}$ and the conditional distribution for y_n given $d_n = 0$ (or $y_n = y_n^* > 0$), then the log-likelihood function equals the sum of Bernoulli and truncated log-likelihoods. By adding and subtracting the term $(1 - d_n)\log[1 - F_\varepsilon(-\mathbf{x}_n'\sigma)]$, (28.13) becomes

$$\begin{aligned}\text{E}_N[L(\theta)] = {} & \text{E}_N\left[d_n \log F_\varepsilon\left(\frac{-\mathbf{x}_n'\boldsymbol{\beta}}{\sigma}\right) + (1 - d_n)\log\left[1 - F_\varepsilon\left(\frac{-\mathbf{x}_n'\boldsymbol{\beta}}{\sigma}\right)\right]\right] \\ & + \text{E}_N\left[(1 - d_n)\left(-\log\sigma + \log\frac{f_\varepsilon\left[(y_n - \mathbf{x}_n'\boldsymbol{\beta})/\sigma\right]}{1 - F_\varepsilon\left(-\mathbf{x}_n'\boldsymbol{\beta}/\sigma\right)}\right)\right]\end{aligned}$$

This factorization implies that the censored normal regression MLE is asymptotically equal to a weighted average of the probit and truncated normal regression MLEs that are asymptotically independent. Therefore, even though the probit estimator may be relatively robust to nonnormal latent distributions, the sensitivity of the truncated normal MLE is inherited by the censored normal MLE. Thus, a Hausman specification test that compares two of these estimators also serves as a practical check for misspecification of distribution.[30]

Concerns about the specificity of the normal distribution, or any parametric distribution, have led researchers to generalize the parametric distribution or to develop estimators that are

[29] Exercise 9.2 illustrates the sensitivity of out-of-sample forecasts to the functional form of the regression function.

[30] See Exercise 28.21.

distribution free. Lee (1983) is one example of the parametric generalization strategy. Powell (1984, 1986) and Honore and Powell (1994), among others, offer estimators that rest upon objective functions that are not distribution specific. Ahn and Powell (1993), Duncan (1986), Ichimura (1993), Klein and Spady (1993), and Lee (1992), among others, develop *semiparametric* methods that employ flexible estimators of the distribution function. For an introduction and additional references, see Powell (1994).

These issues surrounding the distribution of the latent variables in LDV models also compound the problems that potential heteroskedasticity, omitted explanatory variables, and nonlinear regression cause in the linear regression model. If the latent regression model exhibits any of these specification errors, then the validity of the LDV estimators becomes questionable. We have seen, for example, that the residual variance of the latent regression model enters the first moment of the observed dependent variable. We expect, therefore, that unspecified heteroskedasticity will influence estimates of the first-moment regression coefficients and diagnostic tests of normality. Unspecified nonlinear effects in the conditional expectation of the latent dependent variable will do the same.

Autocorrelation does not necessarily produce inconsistent estimators.[31] The general validity of the quasimaximum likelihood estimator that ignores the autocorrelation and treats the observations as independent may still apply.[32]

28.9 MATHEMATICAL NOTES

28.9.1 Integrals

In this section, we provide analytical expressions of the censored and truncated moments of common parametric distributions for ε, the latent disturbance term. We have expressed all of the p.d.f.s $f_\varepsilon(\cdot)$ in a "natural" form that has a mean of zero, but the variance differs from case to case. To reproduce figures such as 28.11 and 28.12, where the variance is normalized to unity, one must rescale the functions. We use the following relationships:

$$\begin{aligned} \mathrm{E}[(\mu+\gamma\varepsilon)\ \mathbf{1}\{\mu+\gamma\varepsilon\geq 0\}] &= \int_{-\frac{\mu}{\gamma}}^{\infty}(\mu+\gamma x)\ f_\varepsilon(x)\,dx \\ &= \mu\left[1-F_\varepsilon\left(-\frac{\mu}{\gamma}\right)\right]+\gamma\int_{-\frac{\mu}{\gamma}}^{\infty}x\ f_\varepsilon(x)\,dx \end{aligned} \tag{28.33}$$

$$\begin{aligned} \mathrm{E}[(\mu+\gamma\varepsilon)^2\ \mathbf{1}\{\mu+\gamma\varepsilon\geq 0\}] &= \int_{-\frac{\mu}{\gamma}}^{\infty}(\mu+\gamma x)^2\ f_\varepsilon(x)\,dx \\ &= \mu^2\left[1-F_\varepsilon\left(-\frac{\mu}{\gamma}\right)\right]+2\mu\gamma\int_{-\frac{\mu}{\gamma}}^{\infty}x\ f_\varepsilon(x)\,dx \\ &\quad+\gamma^2\int_{-\frac{\mu}{\gamma}}^{\infty}x^2\ f_\varepsilon(x)\,dx \end{aligned} \tag{28.34}$$

---

31 See, for example, Robinson (1982) and Poirier and Ruud (1988).

32 See the summary of Levine (1983) on p. 480.

and set γ equal to the reciprocal of the standard deviation for the natural form. The first two truncated moments are then

$$\mathrm{E}[\mu + \gamma\varepsilon \mid \mu + \gamma\varepsilon \geq 0] = \frac{\mathrm{E}[(\mu + \gamma\varepsilon)\ \mathbf{1}\{\mu + \gamma\varepsilon \geq 0\}]}{1 - F_\varepsilon\left(-\frac{\mu}{\gamma}\right)} \tag{28.35}$$

and

$$\mathrm{E}[(\mu + \gamma\varepsilon)^2 \mid \mu + \gamma\varepsilon \geq 0] = \frac{\mathrm{E}[(\mu + \gamma\varepsilon)^2\ \mathbf{1}\{\mu + \gamma\varepsilon \geq 0\}]}{1 - F_\varepsilon\left(-\frac{\mu}{\gamma}\right)} \tag{28.36}$$

Please note the following comments about the subsequent formulas:

1. Because all of the p.d.f.s are symmetric, $f_\varepsilon(-z)$ simplifies to $f_\varepsilon(z)$ and $1 - F_\varepsilon(-z)$ simplifies to $F_\varepsilon(z)$.
2. The entries marked "n.a." do not have closed-form expressions and must be numerically approximated.
3. Some entries for the Laplace distribution are undefined at zero. These entries equal their limits at zero.
4. The dilog function is defined by the integral $\mathrm{dilog}(x) = \int_1^x [\log(z)/(1-x)]\,dz$. It is also related to the limit of the series $\sum_{n=1}^{\infty}(x^n/n^2) = \mathrm{dilog}(1-x)$.

LAPLACE

$$f_\varepsilon(z) = \frac{1}{2}e^{-|z|}, \qquad \mathrm{E}[\varepsilon^2] = 2$$

$$F_\varepsilon(z) = \mathbf{1}\{z > 0\} - \frac{z}{|z|}\, f_\varepsilon(z), \qquad \gamma = \frac{1}{\sqrt{2}}$$

$$\int_{-z}^{\infty} x\, f_\varepsilon(x)\,dx = (1 + |z|)\, f_\varepsilon(z)$$

$$\int_{-z}^{\infty} x^2\, f_\varepsilon(x)\,dx = 2\left[\mathbf{1}\{z > 0\} - \frac{z}{|z|}\left(1 + |z| + \frac{1}{2}z^2\right) f_\varepsilon(z)\right]$$

LOGISTIC

$$f_\varepsilon(z) = \frac{e^{-z}}{(1 + e^{-z})^2}, \qquad \mathrm{E}[\varepsilon^2] = \frac{\pi^2}{3}$$

$$F_\varepsilon(z) = \frac{1}{1 + e^{-z}}, \qquad \gamma = \frac{\sqrt{3}}{\pi}$$

$$\int_{-z}^{\infty} x\, f_\varepsilon(x)\,dx = -\log F_\varepsilon(-z) - zF_\varepsilon(z)$$

$$\int_{-z}^{\infty} x^2\, f_\varepsilon(x)\,dx = z^2 F_\varepsilon(z) - 2\,\{\mathrm{dilog}\,[1/F_\varepsilon(-z)] - z\log F_\varepsilon(-z)\}$$

NORMAL

$$f_\varepsilon(z) = \frac{1}{\sqrt{2\pi}} e^{-\frac{1}{2}z^2}, \qquad \mathrm{E}[\varepsilon^2] = 1$$

$$F_\varepsilon(z) = \text{n.a.}, \qquad \gamma = 1$$

$$\int_{-z}^{\infty} x\, f_\varepsilon(x)\, dx = f_\varepsilon(z) \tag{28.37}$$

$$\int_{-z}^{\infty} x^2\, f_\varepsilon(x)\, dx = -z f_\varepsilon(z) + F_\varepsilon(z) \tag{28.38}$$

STUDENT t

$$f_\varepsilon(z) = \frac{\Gamma[(\nu+1)/2]}{\sqrt{\nu}\Gamma(\nu/2)\Gamma(1/2)} \left(1 + \frac{z^2}{\nu}\right)^{-\frac{\nu+1}{2}}, \qquad \mathrm{E}[\varepsilon^2] = \frac{\nu}{\nu-2}$$

$$F_\varepsilon(z) = \text{n.a.}, \qquad \gamma = \sqrt{\frac{\nu-2}{\nu}}$$

$$\int_{-z}^{\infty} x\, f_\varepsilon(x)\, dx = \frac{1}{\nu-1}\left(\nu + z^2\right) f_\varepsilon(z)$$

$$\int_{-z}^{\infty} x^2\, f_\varepsilon(x)\, dx = \frac{1}{\nu-2}\left[-z\left(\nu + z^2\right) f_\varepsilon(z) + \nu\, F_\varepsilon(z)\right]$$

UNIFORM

$$f_\varepsilon(z) = \frac{1}{2}\mathbf{1}\{|z| \leq 1\}, \qquad \mathrm{E}[\varepsilon^2] = \frac{1}{3}$$

$$F_\varepsilon(z) = (1+z)\, f_\varepsilon(z) + \mathbf{1}\{z > 1\}, \qquad \gamma = \sqrt{3}$$

$$\int_{-z}^{\infty} x\, f_\varepsilon(x)\, dx = \frac{1}{2}\left(1 - z^2\right) f_\varepsilon(z)$$

$$\int_{-z}^{\infty} x^2\, f_\varepsilon(x)\, dx = \frac{1}{6}\left(\mathbf{1}\{z > -1\} + \mathbf{1}\{z > 1\}\right) + \frac{1}{3} z^3 f(z)$$

28.9.2 Censored Moments

Proof of Lemma 28.1. The transformation

$$y = \mathbf{1}\{\mu + \sigma\varepsilon > 0\} \cdot (\mu + \sigma\varepsilon)$$

is monotonically increasing and convex in μ and σ and its value is positive. The mean inherits these properties because each property is preserved under addition of such functions. For example, the sum of two convex functions is also convex.

Because $y \geq y^*$, $\mathrm{E}[y] \geq \mathrm{E}[y^*] = \mu$.

We gave the expression for $\mathrm{E}[y]$ in (28.33). For $\mu > 0$,

$$
\begin{aligned}
0 \le \mu F_\varepsilon\Big(-\frac{\mu}{\sigma}\Big) &= \mu \Pr\Big\{\varepsilon \le -\frac{\mu}{\sigma}\Big\} \\
&\le \mu \Pr\Big\{|\varepsilon| \ge \frac{\mu}{\sigma}\Big\} \\
&\le \mu \frac{\sigma^2}{(\mu/\sigma)^2} \\
&= \frac{\sigma^4}{\mu} \\
&\to 0 \qquad \text{as } \mu \to \infty
\end{aligned}
$$

using Chebychev's inequality (Lemma D.3, p. 875). Because $\mathrm{E}[\varepsilon] = 0$,

$$
\lim_{\mu\to-\infty} \mathrm{E}[y] - \mu = -\lim_{\mu\to-\infty} \mu F_\varepsilon\Big(-\frac{\mu}{\sigma}\Big) + \sigma \lim_{\mu\to-\infty} \int_{-\mu/\sigma}^{\infty} w\, f_\varepsilon(w)\, dw = 0
$$

which proves Part 5. Furthermore, Chebychev's inequality also implies that for $\mu < 0$

$$
\begin{aligned}
|\mathrm{E}[y]| &= \left|\mu \Pr\Big\{\varepsilon \ge -\frac{\mu}{\sigma}\Big\} + \sigma \int_{-\mu/\sigma}^{\infty} w\, f_\varepsilon(w)\, dw\right| \\
&\le \left|\mu \Pr\Big\{|\varepsilon| \ge -\frac{\mu}{\sigma}\Big\}\right| + \sigma \left|\int_{-\mu/\sigma}^{\infty} w\, f_\varepsilon(w)\, dw\right| \\
&\le \left|\frac{\sigma^4}{\mu}\right| + \sigma \left|\int_{-\mu/\sigma}^{\infty} w\, f_\varepsilon(w)\, dw\right| \\
&\to 0 \quad \text{as } \mu \to -\infty
\end{aligned}
$$

proving Part 6. □

The following is an example of the existence of a moment implying a Chebychev inequality.

Lemma 28.6 *For any random variable W with finite* $\mathrm{E}[|W|^c]$, $c > 0$,

$$
\int_{|w|>a} |w|^z\, f_W(w)\, dw \le \frac{1}{a^{c-z}} \mathrm{E}[|W|^c]
$$

for all $0 \le z \le c$.

Proof. Because

$$
\begin{aligned}
a < |w| \Leftrightarrow 1 &< \left|\frac{w}{a}\right| \\
\Rightarrow 1 &< \left|\frac{w}{a}\right|^{c-z} \\
\Rightarrow |w|^z &< \frac{1}{a^{c-z}} |w|^c
\end{aligned}
$$

it follows that

$$\int_{|w|>a} |w|^z \, f_W(w)\, dw \le \int_{|w|>a} |w|^c \, f_W(w)\, dw \le \frac{1}{a^{c-z}} \, \mathrm{E}[|W|^c] \qquad \square$$

Note that if $\mathrm{E}[|W|^c]$ exists, then so does $\mathrm{E}[|W|^z]$ for all $0 \le z \le c$. This is because every absolute moment can be decomposed into

$$\mathrm{E}[|W|^z] = \int_{|W|\le a} |w|^z \, f_W(w)\, dw + \int_{|W|>a} |w|^z \, f_W(w)\, dw$$

for some $a > 0$. The first integral always exists. The second integral is bounded by the lemma and the existence of $\mathrm{E}[|W|^c]$. Hence, the second term also has a finite value and the overall absolute moment exists.

In the following proof, we make repeated use of Lemma 28.6 in the form

$$\int_{|w|>a} |w|^j \, f_\varepsilon(w)\, dw \le \frac{1}{a^{2+\delta-j}} \, \mathrm{E}[|\varepsilon|^{2+\delta}]$$

for $a > 0$ and $j = 0, 1, 2$.

Proof of Lemma 28.2.

Using (28.34),

$$\mathrm{E}[y^2] = \int_{-\mu/\sigma}^{\infty} (\mu + \sigma w)^2 \, f_\varepsilon(w)\, dw \le E[y^{*2}] = \mu^2 + \sigma^2$$

so that the variance of y is well defined. Differentiating with respect to μ, we obtain

$$\begin{aligned} \frac{\partial\, \mathrm{E}[y^2]}{\partial \mu} &= 2 \int_{-\mu/\sigma}^{\infty} (\mu + \sigma w)\, f_\varepsilon(w)\, dw + \frac{1}{\sigma} \left[(\mu + \sigma w)^2 \, f_\varepsilon(w)\right]_{w=-\mu/\sigma} \\ &= 2\,\mathrm{E}[y] \end{aligned}$$

Differentiating (28.33) with respect to μ, we obtain

$$\frac{\partial\, \mathrm{E}[y]}{\partial \mu} = 1 - F_\varepsilon\!\left(-\frac{\mu}{\sigma}\right)$$

Therefore,

$$\begin{aligned} \frac{\partial\, \mathrm{Var}[y]}{\partial \mu} &= 2\,\mathrm{E}[y] - 2\,\mathrm{E}[y] \frac{\partial\, \mathrm{E}[y]}{\partial \mu} \\ &= 2\,\mathrm{E}[y] F_\varepsilon\!\left(-\frac{\mu}{\sigma}\right) \end{aligned}$$

which is positive because $E[y] \ge 0$ by Lemma 28.1.

Because (1) $\mathrm{Var}[y]$ is continuously differentiable and monotonically increasing in μ and (2) $\mathrm{Var}[y] = \mathrm{Var}[y^*]$ at $\mu = \infty$, it follows that $\mathrm{Var}[y] \le \mathrm{Var}[y^*]$ and

$$\lim_{\mu \to -\infty} \mathrm{Var}[y] = \mathrm{Var}[y^*] = \sigma^2$$

Because $\mathrm{Var}[y] \ge 0$, it follows that $\mathrm{Var}[y]$ also has a lower limit as $\mu \to -\infty$.

Expanding,

$$\mathrm{E}[y^2] = \mu^2\left[1 - F_\varepsilon\left(-\frac{\mu}{\sigma}\right)\right] + 2\mu\sigma \int_{-\mu/\sigma}^{\infty} w\, f_\varepsilon(w)\, dw + \sigma^2 \int_{-\mu/\sigma}^{\infty} w^2 f_\varepsilon(w)\, dw \qquad (28.39)$$

We consider each term in (28.39) separately for $\mu < 0$. Starting with the first,

$$0 \le \mu^2\left[1 - F_\varepsilon\left(-\frac{\mu}{\sigma}\right)\right] \le \mu^2 \Pr\left\{|\varepsilon| > \left|\frac{\mu}{\sigma}\right|\right\} \le \frac{\sigma^{2+\delta}}{|\mu|^\delta} \mathrm{E}[|\varepsilon|^{2+\delta}]$$

Because $\mathrm{E}[\varepsilon] = 0$,

$$0 \le \mu \int_{-\mu/\sigma}^{\infty} w\, f_\varepsilon(w)\, dw = \mu \int_{|\mu/\sigma|}^{\infty} |w|\, f_\varepsilon(w)\, dw \le \frac{\sigma^{1+\delta}}{|\mu|^\delta} \mathrm{E}[|\varepsilon|^{2+\delta}]$$

Finally,

$$0 \le \int_{-\mu/\sigma}^{\infty} w^2 f_\varepsilon(w)\, dw = \int_{|\mu/\sigma|}^{\infty} |w|^2 f_\varepsilon(w)\, dw \le \frac{\sigma^\delta}{|\mu|^\delta} \mathrm{E}[|\varepsilon|^{2+\delta}]$$

Therefore, because each term is $O(|\mu|^{-\delta})$ we have the desired result:

$$\lim_{\mu\to\infty} \mathrm{E}[y^2] = 0 = \lim_{\mu\to\infty} \mathrm{Var}[y^2] \qquad \square$$

28.9.3 Nonrandom Sample Selection

This section derives the likelihood function for Heckman's model of nonrandom sample selection. The bivariate c.d.f. for y_n, $F_{y_n}(c_1, c_2) = \Pr\{y_{n1} \le c_1,\ y_{n2} \le c_2\}$, is given in the following table:[33]

	$c_2 < 0$	$0 \le c_2$
$c_1 < 0$	0	0
$0 \le c_1 < 1$	0	$\Pr\{y^*_{n1} < 0\}$
$1 \le c_1$	$\Pr\{y^*_{n1} \ge 0,\ y^*_{n2} \le c_2\}$	$\Pr\{y^*_{n1} \ge 0,\ y^*_{n2} \le c_2\} + \Pr\{y^*_{n1} < 0\}$

Along the left side we list the three regions required for the c.d.f. of a Bernoulli random variable such as y_{n1} that takes only the values 0 and 1. Across the top, we distinguish strictly negative c_2 from positive c_2 because the censoring of y^*_{n2} makes $c_2 = 0$ a special point for the c.d.f. of y_{n2}.

The first row of the table contains zeros because y_{n1} is never less than zero. The second row has a zero in the first column because $y_{n2} = 0$ whenever $y_{n1} = 0$. The entry in the second column equals the probability that both y_{n1} and y_{n2} equal zero. The third row adds in the probability that y_{n2} is less than a negative c_2. This occurs only when $y_{n1} = 1$ so that this probability concerns the joint event that y^*_{n1} is positive and y^*_{n2} is less than c_2.

[33] Let it be understood that these probabilities are conditional on $(\mathbf{x}_{1n}, \mathbf{x}_{2n})$.

The overall table clearly meets the monotonicity requirements of a bivariate c.d.f.: as one moves down a column or across a row from left to right the function is never decreasing. In addition, we confirm that

$$\begin{aligned}
\lim_{c_1 \to -\infty} F_{y_n}(c_1, c_2) &= 0 \\
\lim_{c_2 \to -\infty} F_{y_n}(c_1, c_2) &= \lim_{c_2 \to -\infty} \Pr\{y^*_{n1} \geq 0,\ y^*_{n2} \leq c_2\} = 0 \\
\lim_{c_1, c_2 \to \infty} F_{y_n}(c_1, c_2) &= \lim_{c_2 \to \infty} \Pr\{y^*_{n1} \geq 0,\ y^*_{n2} \leq c_2\} + \Pr\{y^*_{n1} < 0\} \\
&= \Pr\{y^*_{n1} \geq 0\} + \Pr\{y^*_{n1} < 0\} \\
&= 1
\end{aligned}$$

We can derive the p.f. once we replace these general probability expressions with integrals. We require only two:

$$\begin{aligned}
\Pr\{y^*_{n1} \leq 0\} &= \Phi(-\mathbf{x}'_{n1}\boldsymbol{\beta}_{01}, \omega^2_{01}) \\
\Pr\{y^*_{n1} \geq 0,\ y^*_{n2} \leq c_2\} &= \int_{-\infty}^{c_2 - \mathbf{x}'_{n2}\boldsymbol{\beta}_{02}} \int_{-\mathbf{x}'_{n1}\boldsymbol{\beta}_{01}}^{\infty} \phi(\mathbf{z}, \boldsymbol{\Omega})\, d\mathbf{z}
\end{aligned}$$

The second probability is a bivariate normal integral with variance matrix $\boldsymbol{\Omega}_0 = \text{Var}[y^*_n \mid \mathbf{x}_{n1}, \mathbf{x}_{n2}]$ given in (28.24).

We obtain the p.f. by differencing the c.d.f. as we change the values of c_1. There are no discontinuities with respect to c_2 alone and so we differentiate in that direction:[34]

$$\begin{aligned}
&\frac{\partial}{\partial c_2} \Pr\{-y^*_{n1} \leq 0,\ y^*_{n2} \leq c_2\} \\
&= \frac{\partial}{\partial c_2} \int_{-\infty}^{c_2 - \mathbf{x}'_{n2}\boldsymbol{\beta}_{02}} \int_{-\mathbf{x}'_{n1}\boldsymbol{\beta}_{01}}^{\infty} \phi(\mathbf{z}, \boldsymbol{\Omega})\, d\mathbf{z} \\
&= \int_{-\mathbf{x}'_{n1}\boldsymbol{\beta}_{01}}^{\infty} \phi\left(\begin{bmatrix} z_1 \\ c_2 - \mathbf{x}'_{n2}\boldsymbol{\beta}_{02} \end{bmatrix}, \begin{bmatrix} \omega^2_{01} & \rho_0\omega_{01}\omega_{02} \\ \rho_0\omega_{01}\omega_{02} & \omega^2_{02} \end{bmatrix} \right) dz_1 \\
&= \phi(c_2 - \mathbf{x}'_{n2}\boldsymbol{\beta}_{02}, \omega^2_{02}) \\
&\quad \int_{-\mathbf{x}'_{n1}\boldsymbol{\beta}_{01}}^{\infty} \phi\left[z_1 - \frac{\rho_0\omega_{01}}{\omega_{02}}(c_2 - x_{n2}\beta_{02}),\ \omega^2_{01}(1 - \rho^2_0) \right] dz_1 \\
&= \phi(c_2 - \mathbf{x}'_{n2}\boldsymbol{\beta}_{02}, \omega^2_{02})\, \Phi\left[\frac{(1/\omega_{01})\mathbf{x}'_{n1}\boldsymbol{\beta}_{01} + (\rho_0/\omega_{02})\left(c_2 - \mathbf{x}'_{n2}\boldsymbol{\beta}_{02}\right)}{\sqrt{1 - \rho^2_0}},\ 1 \right]
\end{aligned}$$

The resulting p.f. is

34 The second equality uses Leibniz rule. The third equality factors the bivariate normal p.d.f. into marginal and conditional terms using Lemma 10.4 (Multivariate Normal Factorization, p. 208). The fourth equality uses the definition of the univariate normal c.d.f. in (27.5).

$$f_{y_n}(c_1, c_2) = \begin{cases} \Phi(-\frac{1}{\omega_{01}}\mathbf{x}'_{n1}\boldsymbol{\beta}_{01}, 1) & \text{if } c_1 = c_2 = 0 \\ \Phi\left[\frac{(1/\omega_{01})\mathbf{x}'_{n1}\boldsymbol{\beta}_{01}+(\rho_0/\omega_{02})(c_2-\mathbf{x}'_{n2}\boldsymbol{\beta}_{02})}{\sqrt{1-\rho_0^2}}, 1\right]\phi(c_2 - \mathbf{x}'_{n2}\boldsymbol{\beta}_{02}, \omega_{02}^2) & \text{if } c_1 = 1 \\ 0 & \text{if otherwise} \end{cases} \tag{28.40}$$

28.10 OVERVIEW

1. Limited dependent variable (LDV) models describe dependent variables with mixed p.f.s. Discrete dependent variables are a special case. Other examples include censored, truncated, and nonrandomly selected, dependent variables.
2. Researchers frequently motivate LDV models with latent variable specifications. Given the latent location-scale relationship

$$y_n^* = \mathbf{x}'_n\boldsymbol{\beta}_0 + \sigma_0\varepsilon_n$$

a censored observation rule is

$$y_n = \mathbf{1}\{y_n^* \geq 0\} \cdot y_n^*$$

and a truncated observation rule is

$$y_n = \begin{cases} y_n^* & \text{if } y_n^* \geq 0 \\ \text{unobserved} & \text{if } y_n^* < 0 \end{cases}$$

Such models imply conditional expectation functions that are positive and conditional heteroskedasticity, given $\mathbf{x}_n$.
3. One can estimate $\boldsymbol{\beta}_0$ and σ_0^2 with nonlinear least-squares (NLS) and feasible weighted NLS estimators, but MLE is generally more efficient.
4. The nonrandom sample-selection model describes biased sampling. Its formulation consists of two latent dependent variables

$$y_{n1}^* = \mathbf{x}'_{n1}\boldsymbol{\beta}_{01} + \varepsilon_{n1} \qquad \text{and} \qquad y_{n2}^* = \mathbf{x}'_{n2}\boldsymbol{\beta}_{01} + \varepsilon_{n2}$$

where $\mathrm{E}[\varepsilon_{nj} \mid \mathbf{x}_{n1}, \mathbf{x}_{n2}] = 0$ and the observation rule

$$\mathbf{y}_n = \begin{bmatrix} y_{n1} \\ y_{n2} \end{bmatrix} = \begin{bmatrix} \mathbf{1}\{y_{n1}^* \geq 0\} \\ \mathbf{1}\{y_{n1}^* \geq 0\} \cdot y_{n2}^* \end{bmatrix}$$

The implied conditional expectation of y_{n2} depends on $\mathbf{x}_{n1}$ as well as $\mathbf{x}_{n2}$.
5. The normal distribution is the leading specification for the distribution of the latent disturbances in these LDV models. Researchers generally appreciate, however, that a parametric specification of the latent distributions in LDV models is a potential weakness in these econometric models. Moment functions depend on particular features of the normal distribution.

28.11 EXERCISES

28.11.1 Review

28.1 **(Logistic)** Suppose that $y^* = \mu_0 + \sigma_0\varepsilon$ where ε is a random draw from a logistic distribution with c.d.f.

$$F_L(z) = \frac{1}{1+e^{-z}}$$

Find the mean of $y = \mathbf{1}\{y^* > 0\} \cdot y^*$ and $\mathrm{E}[y^* \mid y^* > 0]$.

28.2 (Normal) Derive the normal censored moments in (28.10) and (28.12).

28.3 (Attenuation) For the case of the normal distribution, (28.11) shows that the partial derivative of the censored regression is attenuated relative to the latent linear regression. Show that for general F_ε the attenuation is

$$\frac{\partial\, \mathrm{E}[y_n \mid \mathbf{x}_n]}{\partial \mathbf{x}_n} = \left[1 - F_\varepsilon\left(\frac{-\mathbf{x}_n'\boldsymbol{\beta}_0}{\sigma_0}\right)\right] \cdot \boldsymbol{\beta}_0$$

28.4 (Censor Point) For censored regression data, the value of y_n when $y_n^* \le 0$ may be arbitrary or inappropriate. Instead of zero, one might assign $y_n = c$, where c is some real constant:

$$y_n = \begin{cases} c & \text{if } y_n^* \le 0 \\ y_n^* & \text{if } y_n^* > 0 \end{cases}$$

(a) Given that $y_n^* = \mathbf{x}_n'\boldsymbol{\beta}_0 + \sigma_0\varepsilon_n$ and ε_n is i.i.d. with mean zero and variance one ($n = 1, \ldots, N$), find the c.d.f. and conditional mean of y_n given $\mathbf{x}_n$ and c.
(b) How does the NLS estimator of $\boldsymbol{\beta}_0$ change with c?
(c) How does the MLE change with c?

28.5 (Double Censoring) Extend the Tobit model to truncation above and below. Let $y^* = \mathbf{x}'\boldsymbol{\beta}_0 + \sigma_0\varepsilon$ be a latent random variable and y be observed according to the rule

$$y = \begin{cases} \alpha_1 & \text{if } y^* \le \alpha_1 \\ y^* & \text{if } \alpha_1 < y^* \le \alpha_2 \\ \alpha_2 & \text{if } \alpha_2 < y^* \end{cases}$$

(a) Derive the c.d.f. of y conditional on $\mathbf{x}$ given that ε has the conditional p.d.f. $f_\varepsilon(z)$.
(b) Derive the conditional log-likelihood function for $\boldsymbol{\beta}_0$ and σ_0 given a random sample $\{(\mathbf{x}_1, y_1), \ldots, (\mathbf{x}_N, y_N)\}$.
(c) Find $\partial\, \mathrm{E}[y \mid \mathbf{x}]/\partial \mathbf{x}$. Compare this derivative to single truncation, either above or below a constant.

28.6 (Global Concavity) Confirm directly using calculus that the Tobit log-likelihood function is globally concave using the following steps.[35] To begin, consider the log-likelihood function (28.14):

$$L(\mu, \sigma; y) = \mathbf{1}\{y_n = 0\} \log \Phi\left(\frac{-\mu}{\sigma}, 1\right) + (1 - \mathbf{1}\{y_n = 0\})\left[-\log\sigma - \frac{1}{2}\left(\frac{y_n - \mu}{\sigma}\right)^2\right]$$

[35] Olsen (1978) uses this approach.

(a) Show that the Tobit log-likelihood function can take the form

$$L(\delta, \gamma; y) = \mathbf{1}\{y = 0\} \log \Phi(-\delta) + (1 - \mathbf{1}\{y = 0\}) \left[\log \gamma - \frac{1}{2} (\gamma y - \delta)^2 \right]$$

(b) Show that the sample average Hessian is the sum of three terms: for $\boldsymbol{\theta} \equiv [\delta, \gamma]'$,

$$\begin{aligned} \frac{\partial^2 \mathrm{E}_N[L(\delta, \gamma; y)]}{\partial \boldsymbol{\theta} \partial \boldsymbol{\theta}'} &= -\mathrm{E}_N\left[\mathbf{1}\{y_n > 0\} \cdot \begin{bmatrix} 1 \\ -y_n \end{bmatrix} [1 \quad -y_n] \right] \\ &\quad - \mathrm{E}_N\left[\mathbf{1}\{y_n > 0\} \cdot \begin{bmatrix} 0 & 0 \\ 0 & 1/\gamma^2 \end{bmatrix} \right] \\ &\quad - \mathrm{E}_N\left[\mathbf{1}\{y_n = 0\} \cdot \begin{bmatrix} \frac{-\mu\phi(-\mu)\Phi(-\mu)+\phi^2(-\mu)}{\Phi^2(-\mu)} & 0 \\ 0 & 0 \end{bmatrix} \right] \end{aligned}$$

(c) Show that each term is negative semidefinite. [Hint: Recall that (28.10) implies

$$\mathrm{E}[\mathbf{1}\{-\mu + \varepsilon \geq 0\} (\mu + \varepsilon)] = -\mu\Phi(-\mu) + \phi(-\mu) \geq 0]$$

(d) Why does this imply that the log-likelihood function is globally concave?

28.7 (Upper Truncation) Let $y^* \sim \mathfrak{N}(\mu_0, \sigma_0^2)$. Find the c.d.f. and p.d.f. for the truncated variable

$$y = \begin{cases} y^* & \text{if } y^* \geq c \\ \text{not observed} & \text{if } y^* < c \end{cases}$$

Given a random sample of y, is c identified? If so, how would you estimate c?

28.8 (Truncated Regression) Consider truncated normal regression, where the mean function is (28.18) and the log-likelihood function is (28.22).

(a) Show that, given σ_0, NLS and ML for $\boldsymbol{\beta}$ use different instrumental variables for the same regression.
(b) Argue that, given σ_0, WNLS and ML yield the same estimator.
(c) Explain why WNLS and ML do not yield asymptotically equivalent estimators when both $\boldsymbol{\beta}_0$ and σ_0 must be estimated.

28.9 (Truncated Regression) Using the reparameterization of Lemma 28.3, we can write the log-likelihood function for the truncated normal regression model (28.21) as

$$L(\boldsymbol{\theta}) = \mathrm{E}_N\left[-\log \Phi(-\mathbf{x}_n'\boldsymbol{\delta}, 1) + \log \gamma - \frac{1}{2} \left(\gamma y_n - \mathbf{x}_n'\boldsymbol{\delta}\right)^2 \right]$$

(a) Find the score function and use it to find the first two (uncentered) conditional moments of y_n given $\mathbf{x}_n$.
(b) Find the Hessian and use the conditional moments from the previous part to find the conditional information matrix as well.
(c) Show that if the Hessian is evaluated at a root of the normal equations then the Hessian equals the negative of the information matrix evaluated at the same point in the parameter space.[36] What does this imply about the concavity of the log-likelihood function?

28.10 (Sample Selection) Explain why the sample-selection model involves censoring of the latent data, not truncation.

[36] This is an alternative proof of part of Orme's (1989) demonstration that the MLE of the truncated normal regression model is unique.

28.11 (Sample Selection) Show that the log-likelihood function (28.26) of the nonrandom sample-selection model approaches the log-likelihood of the Tobit model as $\rho \to 1$ if $\mathbf{x}_{n1}'\boldsymbol{\beta}_1 = \mathbf{x}_{n2}'\boldsymbol{\beta}_2$, $n = 1, \ldots, N$, and $\omega_1 = \omega_2$.

28.12 (Sample Selection) Consider the nonrandom sample-selection model (28.24)–(28.25).

(a) Find the conditional mean and variance of y_{n2} given $\mathbf{x}_{n1}$ and $\mathbf{x}_{n2}$.

(b) Show that if $\rho_0 = 0$ then one can estimate $\boldsymbol{\beta}_{02}$ with OLS.

(c) Derive the score test for $\rho_0 = 0$ against the alternative hypothesis that $\rho_0 \neq 0$. Find a way to compute a score test with OLS.[37] (HINT: Review Heckman's two-step estimator in Section 28.7.3.)

28.13 (Diagnostic Tests) Consider the censored normal regression model described by (28.5)–(28.6) and the assumption that the ε_n are i.i.d. standard normal random variables conditional on $\{\mathbf{x}_n\}$. Develop score tests for

(a) homoskedasticity ($\boldsymbol{\gamma}_0 = 0$ in $\sigma_{0n}^2 = \sigma_0^2 + \mathbf{x}_n'\boldsymbol{\gamma}_0$) and

(b) no serial correlation ($\rho_0 = 0$ where $\varepsilon_n = \rho_0\varepsilon_{n-1} + u_n$, u_n i.i.d. normal).

28.14 (Two-Step Estimation) Using Proposition 19 (Two-Step Asymptotic Variance, p. 507) and the following steps, derive the asymptotic variance matrix for Heckman's two-step estimator (Section 28.7.3) of the normal nonrandom sample-selection model.[38]

(a) Write out the asymptotic variance of the first-step probit estimator $\hat{\boldsymbol{\beta}}_1$. Denote this matrix $\boldsymbol{\Omega}_{\gamma\gamma}$ (in keeping with the notation of the lemma).

(b) Use the approach in (28.27) to find $\mathrm{Var}[y_{n2} \mid \mathbf{x}_n, y_{n1} = 1]$.

(c) Write out the asymptotic variance for the second-step OLS estimator for $\boldsymbol{\beta}_{02}$ and $\rho_0\omega_{02}$ when $\boldsymbol{\beta}_{01}$ is known. Denote this matrix $\boldsymbol{\Omega}_{\theta\theta}$.

(d) Explain why there is no covariance ($\boldsymbol{\Omega}_{\gamma\theta} = \mathbf{0}$) in the limiting joint distribution of the probit estimator and the second-step estimator given $\boldsymbol{\beta}_{01}$. (HINT: y_{n2} is observed conditional on $y_{n1} = 1$).

(e) Finally, describe the matrix of partial derivatives of the second-step OLS estmator with respect to the first-step probit estimator.

28.11.2 Extensions

28.15 (Latent Score) Show that the score of the log-likelihood function for $y = \mathbf{1}\{y^* > 0\}\, y^*$ equals the conditional expectation of the score of the log-likelihood function for y^* given y. (HINT: Use Lemma 27.1.)

28.16 (EM and Tobit) Derive an EM algorithm for computing the MLE of the Tobit log-likelihood function (28.14). Why is it not possible to do the same for the truncated normal regression log-likelihood function (28.22)?

28.17 (EM and Sample Selection) Derive an EM algorithm for computing the MLE of the sample-selection log-likelihood function (28.26). Compare an iteration of this algorithm with Heckman's two-step estimator.

28.18 (Probit) Consider the multivariate latent-variable model

---

[37] See Melino (1982).

[38] See Lee et al. (1980).

$$y_{n1}^* = \mathbf{x}_{n1}'\boldsymbol{\beta}_0 + \mathbf{y}_{n2}'\boldsymbol{\gamma}_0 + \varepsilon_{n1}$$
$$\mathbf{y}_{n2}' = \mathbf{x}_n'\boldsymbol{\Pi}_0 + \boldsymbol{\varepsilon}_{n2}'$$

corresponding to a simultaneous system of linear equations.[39] Let $\mathbf{x}_n = [\mathbf{x}_{n1}', \mathbf{x}_{n2}']'$. If y_{n1}^* were observable, one could estimate $\boldsymbol{\beta}_0$ and $\boldsymbol{\gamma}_0$ with a limited-information estimator (Sec. 26.5.1). Suppose that one observes the indicator $y_{n1} = \mathbf{1}\{y_{n1}^* \geq 0\}$ instead.

(a) Assume that $\boldsymbol{\varepsilon}_n \equiv [\varepsilon_{n1}, \boldsymbol{\varepsilon}_{n2}']'$ possesses an $\mathfrak{N}(\mathbf{0}, \boldsymbol{\Sigma}_0)$ distribution conditional on $\mathbf{x}_n$. Write out the log-likelihood function for $\boldsymbol{\beta}_0$, $\boldsymbol{\gamma}_0$, $\boldsymbol{\Pi}_0$, and $\boldsymbol{\Sigma}_0$. Discuss identification.

(b) Show that the OLS estimator of $\boldsymbol{\Pi}_0$, $\hat{\boldsymbol{\Pi}} = (\mathbf{X}'\mathbf{X})^{-1}\mathbf{X}'\mathbf{Y}_2$ where $\mathbf{X} \equiv [\mathbf{x}_n]'$ and $\mathbf{Y}_2 \equiv [\mathbf{y}_{n2}]'$, is consistent. Discuss the relative efficiency of this estimator versus the MLE.

(c) Given any normalizations necessary for identification, work out a two-step estimator for $\boldsymbol{\beta}_0$ and $\boldsymbol{\gamma}_0$ based on the OLS estimator of $\boldsymbol{\Pi}_0$. Consider two approaches, one using the conditional distribution of y_{n1} given $\mathbf{x}_n$ and $\mathbf{y}_{n2}$ and another using the conditional distribution of y_{n1} given only $\mathbf{x}_n$.

28.19 (Labor Supply) In the labor supply model, positive hours of work are related to the market wage by utility maximization through the marginal condition

$$w_n^*(h_n, r_n) = w_n$$

Describe the benefits and difficulties of including hours in the sample-selection model for wages.

28.20 (Tobit and Sample Selection) The Tobit log-likelihood (28.14) is a special case of the sample-selection log-likelihood (28.26) in two cases. Thus, one might construct diagnostic tests for Tobit based on the sample-selection model as the alternative hypothesis.

(a) The sample-selection model collapses to the Tobit when $\rho_0 = 1$, as described in Exercise 28.11. Derive a score test for this restriction, conditional on $\mathbf{x}_{n1} = \mathbf{x}_{n2} = \mathbf{x}_n$, $\boldsymbol{\beta}_{01} = \boldsymbol{\beta}_{02}$ under the alternative hypothesis. Can one use the score test for the restrictions $\boldsymbol{\beta}_{01} = \boldsymbol{\beta}_{02}$ as well?

(b) Describe a (somewhat contrived) sample-selection model with the Tobit log-likelihood function when $\rho_0 = 0$. (Hint: Let the marginal distribution of y_{n2} be the truncated normal.) Consider score tests of $\rho_0 = 0$ and $\{\rho_0 = 0, \boldsymbol{\beta}_{01} = \boldsymbol{\beta}_{02}\}$ for this case as well.

28.21 (Censored Regression) Consider censored normal regression where the mean function is (28.10) and the log-likelihood function is (28.14).

(a) Show that the log-likelihood function is the sum of the truncated normal log-likelihood function and the probit log-likelihood function. Explain.

(b) Suggest a specification test for the normal distribution using this log-likelihood decomposition.[40] (Hint: See Exercise 27.11.)

(c) Also, show that given σ_0, the MLE for $\boldsymbol{\beta}_0$ is a weighted, nonlinear, restricted, SUR estimator. (Hint: See Exercise 28.8.)

28.22 (Truncated Mean) Prove Lemma 28.4 (Truncated Mean, p. 814). For Part 5, use the following steps:

(a) Show that

$$\frac{\partial\, \mathrm{E}[y]}{\partial \mu} = \mathrm{Cov}[y, s(y; \mu, \sigma)]$$

where

[39] See Lee (1981).

[40] See Ruud (1984).

$$s(y;\mu,\sigma) = \frac{\partial}{\partial\mu}\log\left[\frac{f_\varepsilon[(y-\mu/\sigma]}{1-F_\varepsilon(-\mu/\sigma)}\right]$$

(b) Show that this is equivalent to

$$\frac{\partial\, \mathrm{E}[y]}{\partial\mu} = \mathrm{Cov}[y,\ r(y;\mu,\sigma)]$$

where

$$r(y;\mu,\sigma) = \frac{\partial \log f_\varepsilon[(y-\mu)/\sigma]}{\partial\mu} = -\frac{\partial \log f_\varepsilon[(y-\mu)/\sigma]}{\partial y}$$

(c) Argue that if $\log f_\varepsilon(\cdot)$ is concave then $\mathrm{Cov}[y,\ r(y;\mu,\sigma)]$ is positive.

28.23 (Censored Mean Bound) At $\mu = 0$, the censored mean function for the uniform distribution is an upper bound on such functions over all symmetric, unimodal, continuous p.d.f.s with mean zero and variance one. Show this with the following steps.

(a) Symmetric, unimodal, continuous p.d.f.s can be approximated arbitrarily well with infinite mixtures of symmetric uniform p.d.f.s. Let

$$f(\varepsilon) = \sum_{n=1}^{\infty} p_n \cdot \mathbf{1}\{|\varepsilon| \le a_n\}$$

where $0 < a_1 < a_2 < \cdots$, $p_n > 0$ $(n = 1, 2, \ldots)$,

$$\sum_{n=1}^{\infty} p_n = 1$$

Find an additional constraint on the $\{p_n, a_n\}$ based on restricting the variance of $f(\varepsilon)$ to one.

(b) Show that the censored mean function is

$$\int_0^{\infty} \varepsilon\, f(\varepsilon)\, d\varepsilon = \frac{1}{4\,(a_1+a_2)}\left[a_1a_2 + 3 - \sum_{n=3}^{\infty}(a_n - a_2)\,(a_n - a_1)\,p_n\right]$$

What can you conclude about the values of p_n for $n \ge 3$ that maximize this censored mean?

(c) Now consider a mixture of just two uniform p.d.f.s and show that the largest possible censored mean function is attained at $p_1 = 1$, $p_2 = 0$, and $a_1 = \sqrt{3}$.

28.24 (Censored Mean Bound) Although the various $m(\mu, \gamma)$ depicted in Figure 28.11 represent a wide range of p.d.f.s., they do not reveal the full range of possible conditional means for y_n. In fact, the lower bound on such mean functions is the piecewise linear function $\mathbf{1}\{\mu > 0\} \cdot \mu$. Prove this using the Student t distribution and the following steps.

(a) Find the p.d.f. for ε where $\varepsilon \sim \sqrt{[(\nu-2)/\nu]} \cdot t_\nu$. What are the mean and variance of ε?

(b) Show that the c.d.f. for ε approaches $\mathbf{1}\{\mu \ge 0\}$, the c.d.f. of the constant 0, as ν approaches 2 from above. [HINT: Show first that (1) the p.d.f.

$$f(z) = \frac{\Gamma(3/2)}{\Gamma(1)\,\Gamma(1/2)}\,\frac{\{1 + [z^2/(\nu-2)]\}^{-3/2}}{\sqrt{(\nu-2)}}$$

exceeds the p.d.f. of ε for all z such that

$$(\nu-2)\left\{\left[\frac{2\,\Gamma[(\nu+1)/2]}{\Gamma(\nu/2)\Gamma(1/2)}\right]^{2/(\nu-2)} - 1\right\} \le z^2$$

and (2) the c.d.f. for $f(z)$ is

$$F(z) = \frac{1}{2}\left(1 + \frac{z\sqrt{\nu - 2 + z^2}}{\nu - 2 + z^2}\right)$$

which approaches $\mathbf{1}\{z \geq 0\}$ for all $z \neq 0$.]

(c) Show also that $\mathrm{E}[\varepsilon \cdot \mathbf{1}\{\mu + \varepsilon\}]$ approaches zero as ν approaches 2 from above.

(d) Use the previous two parts to show that $\mathrm{E}[(\mu + \gamma\varepsilon) \cdot \mathbf{1}\{\mu + \gamma\varepsilon\}]$ approaches $\mathbf{1}\{\mu > 0\} \cdot \mu$ as ν approaches 2 from above. What does this imply about the lower bound for $\mathrm{E}[(\mu + \gamma\varepsilon) \cdot \mathbf{1}\{\mu + \gamma\varepsilon\}]$ across all distributions for ε that have mean zero and variance one?

(e) Plot $m(\mu, \nu) = \mathrm{E}[(\mu + \varepsilon) \cdot \mathbf{1}\{\mu + \varepsilon\}]$ as a function of μ for various values of $\nu > 2$ and compare your plot with Figure 28.11.

CHAPTER 29

OVERVIEW

Part IV describes several important econometric models and applies the general tools from Part III to these models. The models themselves grow out of particular empirical situations and latent-variable models that describe simply key features. The econometric analysis capitalizes upon the latent-variable models to identify, estimate, and test parameters of interest.

1. Panel data replicate observations in several ways, typically across individuals and time periods. To account for covariance among the observations for an individual across time periods, a basic regression function contains a latent individual-specific effect α_n:

$$\mathrm{E}[y_{nt} \mid \mathbf{X}, \boldsymbol{\alpha}] = \mathbf{x}'_{nt}\boldsymbol{\beta}_0 + \alpha_n, \quad n = 1, \ldots, N \quad t = 1, \ldots, T$$

Depending upon the assumptions about the α_n, one may be able to estimate $\boldsymbol{\beta}_0$ with an IV or FGLS estimator.

2. Time series data produce a need for flexible models of autocovariance. As in panel-data models, autoregressive-moving-average (ARMA) models use shared latent variables to produce a large class of autocovariance functions: if we decompose the dependent variable y_t into its regression $\mathbf{x}'_t\boldsymbol{\beta}_0$ function and a latent disturance term ε_t,

$$y_t = \mathbf{x}'_t\boldsymbol{\beta}_0 + \varepsilon_t$$

then

$$\phi(L)\varepsilon_t = \psi(L)u_t$$

makes $\{\varepsilon_t\}$ an ARMA(p,q) sequence where $\phi(L)$ is a pth-order polynomial, $\psi(L)$ is a qth order polynomial, and $\{u_t\}$ is a white noise sequence. For $\{\varepsilon_t\}$ to be covariance stationary, the characteristic roots of $z^p\phi(z) = 0$ must lie strictly inside the complex unit circle. GLS estimation usually exploits a prediction-error decomposition constructed with the recursive structure of the ARMA specification.

3. Multivariate dependent data presents the difficulty of separating simultaneous structural dependence from other sources of covariance. In a simple market model, quantity transacted and price are codetermined by equilibrium in supply and demand; covariance between quantity and price results from equilibrium and shared, latent, determinants. This is captured by the simultaneous system of linear equations

$$\mathbf{y}'_t\boldsymbol{\gamma}_{0j} + \mathbf{x}'_t\boldsymbol{\beta}_{0j} = \varepsilon_{tj}, \quad j = 1, \ldots, J \quad t = 1, \ldots, T$$

where the ε_{tj} are latent, correlated variables. One builds relatively efficient IV estimators, when $\boldsymbol{\gamma}_{0j}$ and $\boldsymbol{\beta}_{0j}$ are identified, out of the $\mathbf{x}_t$.

4. Limited dependent variables generally possess nonlinear conditional expectations; their expected values are restricted by the limits of the supports of their distributions. If a limited dependent variable y_n is a many-to-one transformation of a latent dependent variable y_t^* with a linear conditional expectation, one can derive the implied, nonlinear, conditional expectation for y_n. For example, if $y_n \in \{0, 1\}$ then

$$y_n^* \mid \mathbf{x}_n \sim \mathfrak{N}(\mathbf{x}_n' \boldsymbol{\beta}_0, \sigma_0^2)$$

and $y_n = \mathbf{1}\{y_n^* \geq 0\}$ implies that

$$\mathrm{E}[y_n \mid \mathbf{x}_n] = \mathrm{E}[\mathbf{1}\{y_n^* \geq 0\} \mid \mathbf{x}_n] = \Phi(\mathbf{x}_n' \boldsymbol{\beta}_0 / \sigma_0)$$

Estimation proceeds with NLS or ML, because the conditional distribution of y_n follows from the conditional distribution of y_n^*.

PART V

APPENDICES

APPENDIX A

ABBREVIATIONS AND ACRONYMS

The page number accompanying each abbreviation and acronym refers to the location we use the acronym first.

2SLS two-stage least squares (p. 503)
3SLS three-stage least squares (p. 723)
AR autoregressive (p. 461)
ARMA autoregressive moving-average (p. 645)
BEA Bureau of Economic Analysis (p. 562)
BHHH Berndt, Hall, Hall, and Hausman (p. 358)
c.d.f. cumulative distribution function (p. 214)
c.f. characteristic function (p. 873)
CLT central limit theorem (p. 265)
CPS Current Population Survey (p. 3)
CUAN consistent uniformly asympotically normal (p. 320)
DD distance difference (p. 567)
DES Data Extraction System (p. 17)
DV dummy variables (p. 617)
DW Durbin–Watson (p. 466)
FGLS feasible generalized least squares (p. 435)
FGMM feasible generalized method of moments (p. 723)
FIML full-information maximum likelihood (p. 723)
FWLS feasible weighted least squares (p. 439)
FWNLS feasible weighted nonlinear least squares (p. 801)
GLS generalized least squares (p. 432)
GMM generalized method of moments (p. 531)
GNP gross national product (p. 615)
GNR Gauss–Newton regression (p. 359)
IIA independence from irrelevant alternatives (p. 769)
i.i.d. independent and identically distributed (p. 207)
ILS indirect least squares (p. 718)
i.n.i.d. independent but not identically distributed (p. 218)
IV instrumental variables (p. 486)
LAD least absolute deviations (p. 45)

LDV	limited dependent variable (p. 791)
LHS	left-hand side (p. 8)
LIML	limited-information maximum likelihood (p. 727)
LLN	law of large numbers (p. 262)
LM	Lagrange multiplier (p. 409)
LML	linearized maximum likelihood (p. 441)
LMLE	linearized maximum likelihood estimator (p. 333)
LP	linear programming (p. 295)
LR	likelihood ratio (p. 381)
LSDV	least-squares dummy variable (p. 617)
MA	moving average (p. 645)
MAE	mean absolute error (p. 124)
m.g.f.	moment-generating function (p. 477)
MC	minimum chi-square (p. 394)
MD	minimum distance (p. 594)
ML	maximum likelihood (p. 320)
MLE	maximum likelihood estimator (p. 205)
MM	method of moments (p. 536)
MME	method of moments estimator (p. 912)
MMSE	minimum mean squared error (p. 113)
MSE	mean squared error (p. 113)
MSM	method of simulated moments (p. 776)
NB	negative binomial (p. 761)
NIPA	national income and product accounts (p. 562)
NLS	nonlinear least squares (p. 359)
NR	Newton–Raphson (p. 357)
OLS	ordinary least squares (p. 7)
p.f.	probability function (p. 284)
p.d.f.	probability density function (p. 105)
p.m.f.	probability mass function (p. 284)
PSID	panel study of income dynamics (p. 628)
QMLE	quasimaximum likelihood estimator (p. 480)
RE	random effects (p. 620)
RHS	right-hand side (p. 8)
RLS	restricted least squares (p. 74)
SAR	sum of absolute value of the fitted residuals (p. 246)
SSR	sum of squared residuals (p. 11)
SUR	seemingly unrelated regressions (p. 698)
WLS	weighted least squares (p. 420)
WNLS	weighted nonlinear least squares (p. 752)

APPENDIX B

Notation

This appendix serves as a quick guide to our notation.

$\sum\limits_{n=1}^{N}$ $\sum_{n=1}^{N}$ $\sum_n$ are various forms of the same *summation* notation, the latter appearing when the range of the summation index is clear from the context:

$$\sum_{n=1}^{N} x_n = x_1 + x_2 + x_3 + \cdots + x_N$$

$\prod\limits_{n=1}^{N}$ $\prod_{n=1}^{N}$ $\prod_n$ are various forms of the analogous *multiplication* notation:

$$\prod_{n=1}^{N} x_n = x_1 \times x_2 \times x_3 \times \cdots \times x_N$$

B.1 LIMITS

A sequence $x_1, x_2, x_3, \ldots$ is denoted $\{x_n; n = 1, 2, 3, \ldots\}$ or simply $\{x_n\}$.

There is a common notation for order of magnitude, $o(n^r)$ and $O(n^r)$. An element of the sequence $\{x_n\}$ is "little 'o' of n^r," or $x_n = o(n^r)$, if

$$\lim_{n\to\infty} \frac{x_n}{n^r} = 0$$

An element of the sequence $\{x_n\}$ is "big 'O' of n^r," or $x_n = O(n^r)$, if there is a finite bound C and an integer $n^*(C)$ such that

$$n > n^*(C) \qquad \Rightarrow \qquad \left|\frac{x_n}{n^r}\right| < C$$

Limits from above: $\lim_{\epsilon\to 0^+}$ refers to a seqence of strictly positive values monotonically approaching zero. We occasionally denote

$$\lim_{\epsilon\to 0^+} f(x+\epsilon) = f(x+0)$$
$$\lim_{\epsilon\to 0^+} f(x-\epsilon) = f(x-0)$$

B.2 SETS

The empty, or null set, is denoted $\emptyset$. The complement of a set $\mathbb{A}$ is $\mathbb{A}^c$. If $\mathbb{B}$ is a subset of $\mathbb{A}$ then $\mathbb{B} \subseteq \mathbb{A}$ and if a proper subset then $\mathbb{B} \subset \mathbb{A}$. The *indicator function* $\mathbf{1}\{\cdot\}$ is a function of sets:

$$\mathbf{1}\{x \in \mathbb{A}\} = \begin{cases} 1 & \text{if } x \in \mathbb{A} \\ 0 & \text{if } x \notin \mathbb{A} \end{cases}$$

Intersection is $\cap$ and union is $\cup$. For $\mathbb{B} \subseteq \mathbb{A}$, subtraction is $\mathbb{A} \setminus \mathbb{B} \equiv \{v \in \mathbb{A} \mid v \notin \mathbb{B}\}$ where $\mid$ is an abbreviation for "such that."

$\mathbb{N}$ is the set of natural numbers: $\mathbb{N} = \{0, 1, 2, 3, \ldots\}$. $\mathbb{R}$ is the set of real numbers.

B.3 FUNCTIONS

Let $x \in \mathbb{R}$.

Notation	Page[1]	Description
$\exp(x)$	10	Exponential of x, e^x
$\phi(\boldsymbol{\mu}, \boldsymbol{\Omega})$	196	Multivariate normal p.d.f.
$\Phi(\boldsymbol{\mu}, \boldsymbol{\Omega})$	281	Multivariate normal c.d.f.
$\Gamma(x)$	248	Gamma function
$\log(x)$	10	Natural logarithm of $x > 0$
$\text{sgn}(x)$	45	Sign of x
$\psi(x)$	888	Psi function

B.4 LINEAR VECTOR SPACES

Let $\mathbb{S}$ a linear vector space. Let $\mathbf{x}, \mathbf{y} \in \mathbb{S}$.

Notation	Page	Description
$\dim \mathbb{S}$	24	Dimension of linear space/subspace $\mathbb{S}$
$\oplus$	62	Direct sum
$\langle \mathbf{x}, \mathbf{y} \rangle$	89	Inner product
$\mathbf{x} \perp \mathbf{y}$	28	$\langle \mathbf{x}, \mathbf{y} \rangle = 0$, orthogonality
$\mathbb{S}^{\perp}$	32	Orthogonal complement of $\mathbb{S}$
$\lVert \mathbf{x} \rVert$	22	Length
$\mathbb{R}^n$	23	Space of real n-tuples
$\mathbb{E}^n$	89	n-dimensional Euclidean space
$\mathbb{C}^n$	865	Space of complex n-tuples

[1] The page column lists the page number of the first appearance.

B.5 MATRICES

Let $\mathbf{z}$ be a row vector of N real-valued elements:

$$\mathbf{z} \equiv [x_1 \quad x_2 \quad \cdots \quad x_N]$$

or $\mathbf{z} = [x_n; n = 1, \ldots, N] = [x_n]$. Let $\mathbf{x}$ be the column vector $\mathbf{z}'$ or

$$\mathbf{x} = \begin{bmatrix} x_1 \\ x_2 \\ \vdots \\ x_N \end{bmatrix}$$

Let $\mathbf{y}$ be a column vector of M elements, $\mathbf{y} \equiv [y_m; m = 1, \ldots, M]'$. Let $\mathbf{A}$ be a matrix of real-valued elements with M rows and N columns:

$$\mathbf{A} = \begin{bmatrix} a_{11} & a_{12} & \cdots & a_{1N} \\ a_{21} & a_{22} & \cdots & a_{2N} \\ \vdots & \vdots & \ddots & \vdots \\ a_{M1} & a_{M2} & \cdots & a_{MN} \end{bmatrix}$$

or $\mathbf{A} = [a_{mn}; m = 1, \ldots, M,\ n = 1, \ldots, N]$. The mth row of $\mathbf{A}$ is $\mathbf{a}'_m \equiv [a_{m1}, \cdots, a_{mN}]$ and the nth column of $\mathbf{A}$ is $\mathbf{A}_n \equiv [a_{mn}; m = 1, \ldots, M]'$.

Notation	Page	Description
$\mathbf{A}'$	14	$[[a_{mn}; n = 1, \ldots, N];\ m = 1, \ldots, M]$, matrix (or vector) transpose
$\mathbf{x}'\mathbf{y}$	14	$\sum_n x_n y_n$ if $M = N$, vector inner product in $\mathbb{R}^N$
$\lVert\mathbf{x}\rVert$	22	$\sqrt{\mathbf{x}'\mathbf{x}}$, Euclidean length
$\lVert\mathbf{x}\rVert_\mathbf{A}$	86	$\sqrt{\mathbf{x}'\mathbf{A}\mathbf{x}}$, generalized Euclidean length for $\mathbf{x} \in \mathrm{Col}(\mathbf{A})$
$\mathrm{Col}(\mathbf{A})$	23	$\{\mathbf{x} \in \mathbb{R}^M \mid \mathbf{x} = \mathbf{A}\mathbf{b},\ \mathbf{b} \in \mathbb{R}^N\}$, column space
$\mathrm{tr}(\mathbf{A})$	169	$\sum_i a_{ii}$, trace of a square matrix
$\mathrm{vec}(\mathbf{A})$	441	$[\mathbf{A}'_n; n = 1, \ldots, N]'$, vectorized matrix
$\mathrm{rank}(\mathbf{A})$	30	Matrix rank, number of linearly independent rows/columns
$\mathrm{diag}(a_n)$	117	Diagonal matrix, a_n is the nth diagonal element
$\mathbf{P}_\mathbf{A}$	31	Orthogonal projector onto $\mathrm{Col}(\mathbf{A})$
$\mathbf{P}_{\mathbf{A}\perp\mathbf{B}}$	63	Projector onto $\mathrm{Col}(\mathbf{A})$ along $\mathrm{Col}(\mathbf{B})$
$\det(\mathbf{A})$	206	Determinant of a square matrix
$\otimes$	702	Kronecker (or tensor) product
$\mathbf{A}^{-1}$	24	Matrix inverse, for nonsingular $\mathbf{A}$
$\mathbf{A}^{-}$	44	Matrix generalized inverse
$\mathbf{A}^{+}$	212	Moore–Penrose generalized inverse

B.6 RANDOM VARIABLES

Notation	Page	Description
$\sim$	196	Distributed as
$\mathfrak{N}(\boldsymbol{\mu}, \boldsymbol{\Omega})$	196	Multivariate normal distribution, mean vector $\boldsymbol{\mu}$ and variance matrix $\boldsymbol{\Omega}$
$\mathrm{E}[\mathbf{z}]$	111	Expected value or expectation
$\mathrm{E}[\mathbf{z} \mid \mathbf{w}]$	110	Expected value of $\mathbf{z}$ condtional on $\mathbf{w}$
$\mathrm{E}[z_t \mid t-1]$	649	Expected value of z_t given all variables indexed $v \leq t-1$
$\mathrm{E}^*[\mathbf{z} \mid \mathbf{w}]$	138	Minimum mean squared error linear predictor
$\mathrm{Var}[\mathbf{z}]$	123	Variance
$\mathrm{Var}[\mathbf{z} \mid \mathbf{w}]$	123	Variance of $\mathbf{z}$ conditional on $\mathbf{w}$
$\mathrm{Cov}[\mathbf{z}, \mathbf{w}]$	129	Covariance between $\mathbf{z}$ and $\mathbf{w}$
$\mathrm{Cov}[\mathbf{z}, \mathbf{w} \mid \mathbf{y}]$	157	Covariance between $\mathbf{z}$ and $\mathbf{w}$ conditional on $\mathbf{y}$
$\phi(\mathbf{z} - \boldsymbol{\mu}, \boldsymbol{\Omega})$	196	p.d.f. of the multivariate normal distribution
$\Phi(\mathbf{z} - \boldsymbol{\mu}, \boldsymbol{\Omega})$	281	c.d.f. of the multivariate normal distribution
χ^2_ν	197	Chi-square distribution, ν degrees of freedom
t_ν	225	Student t distribution, ν degrees of freedom
F_{ν_1,ν_2}	203	Snedecor F distribution, ν_1 and ν_2 degrees of freedom
$\xrightarrow{p}$	256	Convergence in probability
$\xrightarrow{d}$	256	Convergence in distribution
plim	260	Probability limit
$\overset{p}{=}$	393	Asymptotically equal with proability one

B.7 OPTIMA AND ROOTS

We will denote the maximum of a real function $f : \mathbb{R}^K \to \mathbb{R}$ over a subset of its domain $\mathbb{A} \subseteq \mathbb{R}^K$ by

$$\max_{\mathbf{x} \in \mathbb{A}} f(\mathbf{x})$$

We will denote the set of values that achieves this maximum by

$$\operatorname*{argmax}_{\mathbf{x} \in \mathbb{A}} f(\mathbf{x}) \equiv \left\{ \mathbf{w} \in \mathbb{A} \mid f(\mathbf{w}) = \max_{\mathbf{x} \in \mathbb{A}} f(\mathbf{x}) \right\}$$

Similarly, we denote the set of roots of an homogeneous system of equations $\mathbf{g}(\mathbf{x}) = \mathbf{0}$ within the subset $\mathbb{A} \subseteq \mathbb{R}^K$, where $\mathbf{g} : \mathbb{R}^K \to \mathbb{R}^K$, by

$$\operatorname*{argzero}_{\mathbf{x} \in \mathbb{A}} \mathbf{g}(\mathbf{x}) \equiv \{\mathbf{w} \in \mathbb{A} \mid \mathbf{g}(\mathbf{w}) = \mathbf{0}\}$$

APPENDIX C

Linear Algebra and Matrix Theory

We describe linear algebra in its abstract form, using matrix theory to illustrate.[1] In the process, we describe many of the details of matrix manipulation.

C.1 LINEAR VECTOR SPACES

DEFINITION C.1 (VECTOR SPACE) *A vector space $\mathbb{V}$ is a nonempty set of elements called* vectors *with two laws of combination,* vector addition *and* scalar multiplication, *satisfying the following axioms: If $\mathbf{u}, \mathbf{v}, \mathbf{w} \in \mathbb{V}$ and a, b are scalars, then*

1. *$\mathbb{V}$ is closed under vector addition: $\mathbf{u} + \mathbf{v} \in \mathbb{V}$;*
2. *vector addition is commutative: $\mathbf{u} + \mathbf{v} = \mathbf{v} + \mathbf{u}$;*
3. *vector addition is associative: $(\mathbf{u} + \mathbf{v}) + \mathbf{w} = \mathbf{u} + (\mathbf{v} + \mathbf{w})$;*
4. *there is a zero vector, $\mathbf{0} \in \mathbb{V}$, such that $\mathbf{v} + \mathbf{0} = \mathbf{v}$;*
5. *$\mathbb{V}$ is closed under scalar multiplication: $a \cdot \mathbf{v} \in \mathbb{V}$;*
6. *scalar multiplication is distributive with respect to vector addition: $a \cdot (\mathbf{u} + \mathbf{v}) = a \cdot \mathbf{u} + a \cdot \mathbf{v}$;*
7. *scalar multiplication is distributive with respect to scalar addition: $(a + b) \cdot \mathbf{v} = a \cdot \mathbf{v} + b \cdot \mathbf{v}$;*
8. *scalar multiplication is associative: $(ab) \cdot \mathbf{v} = a \cdot (b \cdot \mathbf{v})$;*
9. $0 \cdot \mathbf{v} = \mathbf{0}$, $1 \cdot \mathbf{v} = \mathbf{v}$.

[1] Texts that contain proofs of the results in this appendix are Lang (1971) and Nering (1970). Simon and Blume (1994) give an introductory treatment.

In abstract vector spaces, the scalars a and b are elements of an algebraic *field*, but we will restrict ourselves to the set of real numbers where addition and multiplication and their associated properties are second nature to all students.

We will focus on a particular vector space, N-tuples of real numbers, for which we will use matrix notation. We denote an N-dimensional (column) vector by

$$\mathbf{v} = \begin{bmatrix} v_1 \\ \vdots \\ v_N \end{bmatrix}$$

The set of all such vectors of real numbers will be denoted $\mathbb{R}^N$. The N-tuple of zeros is the *zero vector*, which we will simply denote by $\mathbf{0}$ or $\underset{N\times 1}{\mathbf{0}}$. We depict vectors geometrically in two and three dimensions by arrows with tails at the origin, or *zero vector*, and tips at the point $(v_1, \ldots, v_N)$. Figure C.1 illustrates the two-dimensional case. The *vector sum* of two N-dimensional vectors equals the sum of their corresponding elements:

$$\mathbf{u} + \mathbf{v} = \begin{bmatrix} u_1 + v_1 \\ \vdots \\ u_N + v_N \end{bmatrix}$$

The sum of two vectors has a simple geometric representation in which one translates one vector from the origin to the tip of the other, the vector sum resting at the final tip. See Figure C.2.

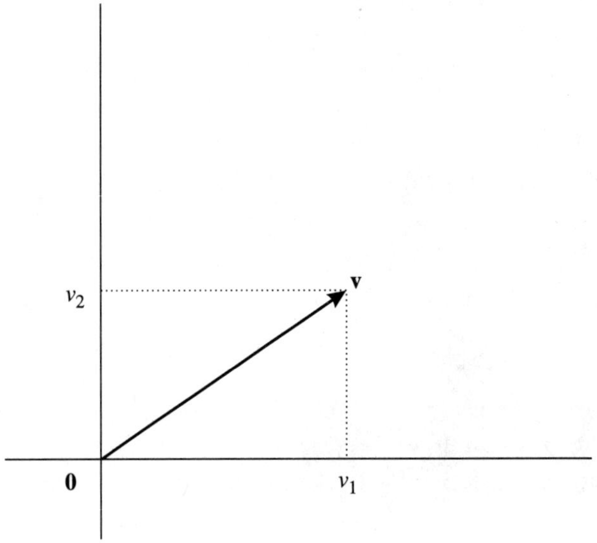

Figure C.1 A vector in two dimensions.

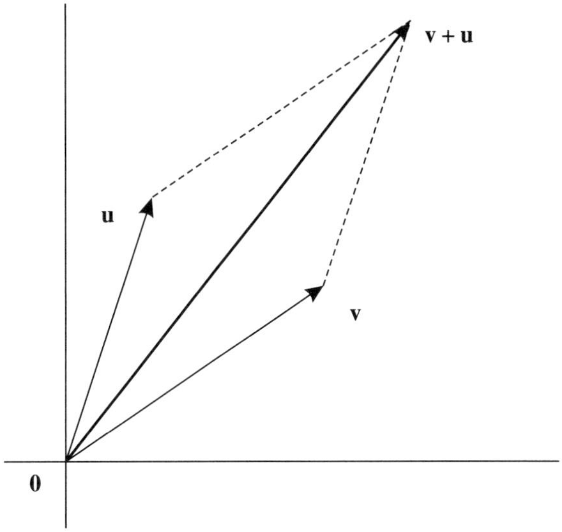

Figure C.2 A vector sum in two dimensions.

The *scalar product* of a vector **x** and a real number a is the product of each element with the scalar a:

$$a \cdot \mathbf{v} = \begin{bmatrix} av_1 \\ \vdots \\ av_N \end{bmatrix}$$

Figure C.3 depicts $\frac{1}{2} \cdot \mathbf{v}$ and $2 \cdot \mathbf{v}$. In general, we draw a vector in the original direction a times as long. We can mix vector addition and scalar multiplication to obtain a new vector or *linear combination*: if **u** and **v** are N-dimensional vectors and a and b are real scalars then $\mathbf{w} = a \cdot \mathbf{u} + b \cdot \mathbf{v}$ is also a member of $\mathbb{R}^N$. Under these specifications, $\mathbb{R}^N$ is a vector space according to Definition C.1.

Definition C.2 (Subspace) *A nonempty subset $\mathbb{S}$ of a vector space $\mathbb{V}$ is called a* subspace *of $\mathbb{V}$ if, for all* $\mathbf{u}, \mathbf{v} \in \mathbb{S}$ *and all scalars* a, b, $a \cdot \mathbf{u} + b \cdot \mathbf{v} \in \mathbb{S}$.

Subspaces are also vector spaces. The smallest subspace is the zero vector and the largest is the vector space itself. We will often generate subspaces from a subset of vectors in a vector space.

Definition C.3 (Spanned Subspace) *Let $\mathbb{W}$ be a subset of a vector space $\mathbb{V}$. The* subspace spanned by $\mathbb{W}$ *is the set consisting of all linear combinations of vectors in $\mathbb{W}$.*

Consider a set of K vectors from $\mathbb{R}^N$:

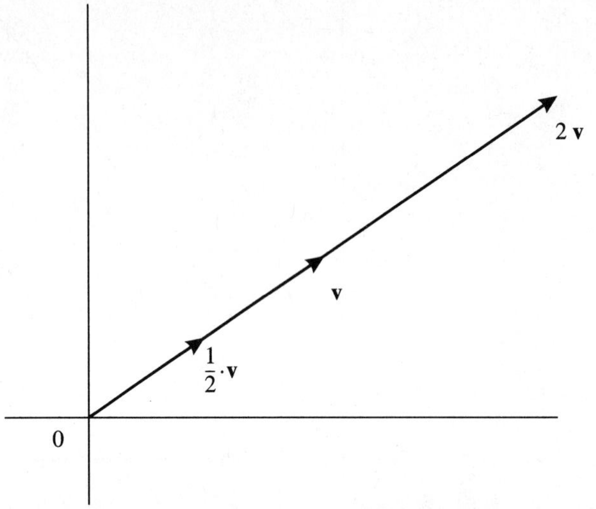

Figure C.3 A scalar product in two dimensions.

$$\mathbf{x}_k = \begin{bmatrix} x_{1k} \\ \vdots \\ x_{Nk} \end{bmatrix} = [x_{nk};\ n = 1, \ldots, N]', \qquad (k = 1, \ldots, K)$$

We combine such vectors into a *matrix* by placing each vector in its own column of a table or array:

$$\begin{aligned} \mathbf{X} &= [\mathbf{x}_1 \quad \cdots \quad \mathbf{x}_K] \\ &= \begin{bmatrix} x_{11} & \cdots & x_{1K} \\ \vdots & & \vdots \\ x_{N1} & \cdots & x_{NK} \end{bmatrix} \\ &= [x_{nk};\ n = 1, \ldots, N,\ k = 1, \ldots, K] \end{aligned}$$

When the ranges of the subscripts are clear, we may simply abbreviate $\mathbf{X} = [x_{nk}]$.

Incidentally, note that the matrix operator called the *transpose* turns a column vector into a row vector,

$$\mathbf{x}'_k = [x_{1k} \quad \cdots \quad x_{Nk}]$$

and the columns of a matrix into the rows of another matrix, as in

$$\begin{aligned} \mathbf{X}' &\equiv \begin{bmatrix} x_{11} & \cdots & x_{N1} \\ \vdots & & \vdots \\ x_{1K} & \cdots & x_{NK} \end{bmatrix} \\ &= \begin{bmatrix} \mathbf{x}'_1 \\ \vdots \\ \mathbf{x}'_K \end{bmatrix} \end{aligned} \tag{C.1}$$

where we drop the index ranges for brevity when these are clear. If $\mathbf{X} = \mathbf{X}'$ then $\mathbf{X}$ is said to be *symmetric*. Because ordinary text is horizontal, a row vector is easily written in text as $[v_1, \ldots, v_N] = [v_n]$. We use the transpose to denote a column vector in text, as in $\mathbf{v} = [v_n]'$.

We will usually distinguish vectors and matrices by assigning capital letters to matrices. Just as vectors are representations of N-tuples, matrices will often be representations of sets of vectors and we will use the same notation for both.

A linear combination of the K column vectors is

$$\mathbf{X}\mathbf{a} = \sum_{k=1}^{K} a_k \cdot \mathbf{x}_k = \left[\sum_{k=1}^{K} a_k x_{nk};\ n = 1, \ldots, N \right]' \tag{C.2}$$

where $\mathbf{a}$ denotes the K-dimensional vector $[a_k;\ k = 1, \ldots, K]'$ and $a_k \cdot \mathbf{x}_k$ is the scalar product of a_k and $\mathbf{x}_k$. We call the subspace spanned by the columns of $\mathbf{X}$ the *column space* of $\mathbf{X}$ and write

$$\mathrm{Col}(\mathbf{X}) = \left\{ \mathbf{z} \in \mathbb{R}^N \mid \mathbf{z} = \mathbf{X}\mathbf{a} \text{ for some } \mathbf{a} \in \mathbb{R}^K \right\}$$

We will also generate further subspaces from subspaces. We can do this by linear combination, as described below, or by intersection.

Theorem C.1 (Intersection of Subspaces) *Let $\mathbb{S}_1$ and $\mathbb{S}_2$ be subspaces of a vector space $\mathbb{V}$. Then the intersection $\mathbb{S}_1 \cap \mathbb{S}_2$ is a subspace of $\mathbb{V}$.*

In addition, vector spaces can be combined to produce other vector spaces.

Definition C.4 (Sum of Subspaces) *Let $\mathbb{S}_1$ and $\mathbb{S}_2$ be subspaces of a vector space $\mathbb{V}$. Then the sum of the subspaces, denoted $\mathbb{S}_1 + \mathbb{S}_2$, is defined to be the set of all vectors of the form $\mathbf{v}_1 + \mathbf{v}_2$ where $\mathbf{v}_1 \in \mathbb{S}_1$ and $\mathbf{v}_2 \in \mathbb{S}_2$.*

Theorem C.2 (Direct Sum) *If $\mathbb{S}_1 \cap \mathbb{S}_2 = \{\mathbf{0}\}$, then for every $\mathbf{v} \in \mathbb{S}_1 + \mathbb{S}_2$ there exist unique $\mathbf{v}_1 \in \mathbb{S}_1$ and $\mathbf{v}_2 \in \mathbb{S}_2$ such that $\mathbf{v} = \mathbf{v}_1 + \mathbf{v}_2$.*

Proof. If $\mathbf{v} = \mathbf{v}_3 + \mathbf{v}_4$, where $\mathbf{v}_3 \in \mathbb{S}_1$ and $\mathbf{v}_4 \in \mathbb{S}_2$ then $\mathbf{v}_1 - \mathbf{v}_3 = \mathbf{v}_2 - \mathbf{v}_4$. Because the left side is in $\mathbb{S}_1$ and the right side is in $\mathbb{S}_2$, both are in $\mathbb{S}_1 \cap \mathbb{S}_2$ and $\mathbf{v}_1 - \mathbf{v}_3 = \mathbf{v}_2 - \mathbf{v}_4 = \mathbf{0}$. □

This situation is distinguished by a special term.

Definition C.5 (Direct Sum) *If $\mathbb{S}_1 \cap \mathbb{S}_2 = \{\mathbf{0}\}$, then $\mathbb{S}_1 + \mathbb{S}_2$ is called the* direct sum *of $\mathbb{S}_1$ and $\mathbb{S}_2$, denoted $\mathbb{S}_1 \oplus \mathbb{S}_2$.*

Finally, one can combine vector spaces by creating a new vector through "joining" two given vectors together.

DEFINITION C.6 (CARTESIAN PRODUCT) *Let $\mathbb{V}_1$ and $\mathbb{V}_2$ be vector spaces over the same field of scalars. The* Cartesian product *of $\mathbb{V}_1$ and $\mathbb{V}_2$, denoted $\mathbb{V}_1 \times \mathbb{V}_2$, consists of the collection of ordered pairs $(\mathbf{v}_1, \mathbf{v}_2)$ such that $\mathbf{v}_1 \in \mathbb{V}_1$ and $\mathbf{v}_2 \in \mathbb{V}_2$. Vector addition is defined by $(\mathbf{u}_1, \mathbf{u}_2) + (\mathbf{v}_1, \mathbf{v}_2) = (\mathbf{u}_1 + \mathbf{v}_1, \mathbf{u}_2 + \mathbf{v}_2)$ and scalar multiplication by $a \cdot (\mathbf{v}_1, \mathbf{v}_2) = (a \cdot \mathbf{v}_1, a \cdot \mathbf{v}_2)$.*

Perhaps the first example of a Cartesian product that one meets is $\mathbb{R}^2 = \mathbb{R}^1 \times \mathbb{R}^1$. With n-dimensional real spaces, the Cartesian product leads to higher dimensional spaces, where vector addition and scalar multiplication still work in the same way. Cartesian products often arise when a function has two or more (vector) arguments so that the domain of the function is the Cartesian product of the vector spaces of the individual arguments.

All vector subspaces include the zero vector. Geometrically, subspaces must pass through the origin. Sometimes one studies hyperplanes that do not include the origin. These are called *affine subspaces*.

DEFINITION C.7 (AFFINE SUBSPACE) *The translation of a subspace is called an* affine subspace. *If $\mathbb{S}$ is a subspace of the vector space $\mathbb{V}$ and $\mathbf{v} \in \mathbb{V}$ then the subset*

$$\mathbb{A} = \{\mathbf{u} \in \mathbb{V} \mid \mathbf{u} = \mathbf{v} + \mathbf{w},\ \mathbf{w} \in \mathbb{S}\}$$

is an affine subspace. We will denote $\mathbb{A} = \mathbb{S} + \mathbf{v}$.

In $\mathbb{R}^3$, a line or a plane that does not contain the origin is an affine subspace. Of course, every subspace is an affine subspace (translated by the zero vector).

Vectors are related by linear combination and vector subspaces contain all linear combinations of a subset of vectors. Thus, it is often natural to ask whether a particular vector is or is not a linear combination of a subset of other vectors.

DEFINITION C.8 (LINEAR DEPENDENCE) *A vector $\mathbf{x}$ is* linearly dependent *on a set of vectors $\mathbb{W}$ if $\mathbf{x}$ can be expressed as a linear combination of the vectors in $\mathbb{W}$.*

The vector $\mathbf{x} \in \mathbb{R}^N$ is linearly dependent on the vectors in $\mathbf{X}$ if $\mathbf{x} \in \mathrm{Col}(\mathbf{X})$. If $\mathbf{x} \notin \mathrm{Col}(\mathbf{X})$, then $\mathbf{x}$ is *linearly independent* of the set of vectors in $\mathbf{X}$.

Linear independence is fundamental to the study of vector spaces. With this concept it is possible to define the basis and the dimension of a finite-dimensional vector space.

DEFINITION C.9 (BASIS) *A finite set $\mathbb{W}$ of linearly independent vectors is a* basis *for the vector space $\mathbb{V}$ if $\mathbb{W}$ spans $\mathbb{V}$.*

A familiar basis of $\mathbb{R}^N$ is the *natural basis* $\{\mathbf{e}_j;\ j = 1, \ldots, N\}$ where e_j is a vector of zeros except for a one in the jth element: $\mathbf{e}_j = [\mathbf{1}\{n = j\};\ n = 1, \ldots, N]'$. Any vector $\mathbf{x}$ can obviously be written as a linear combination of this basis: $\mathbf{x} = \sum_{j=1}^{N} x_j \cdot \mathbf{e}_j$. In addition, the elementary vectors are obviously linearly independent. When we collect the $\{\mathbf{e}_j\}$ into a matrix, we form the *identity* matrix

$$\mathbf{I}_N = [\mathbf{e}_1 \quad \cdots \quad \mathbf{e}_N] = \begin{bmatrix} 1 & 0 & \cdots & 0 \\ 0 & 1 & \ddots & \vdots \\ \vdots & \ddots & \ddots & 0 \\ 0 & \cdots & 0 & 1 \end{bmatrix}$$

and we can also write $\mathbf{x} = \mathbf{I}_N \mathbf{x}$. This basis is natural to us because it is obviously linearly independent and we graph $\mathbf{x}$ with this basis in the Cartesian plane for $\mathbb{R}^2$.

A vector space possessing a basis with a finite number of vectors is *finite dimensional*. A vector space generally possesses more than one basis. We speak unambiguously about the *dimension* of a finite-dimensional vector space $\mathbb{V}$, denoted $\dim(\mathbb{V})$, because of the fundamental uniqueness of the dimension of bases.

THEOREM C.3 (DIMENSION OF A VECTOR SPACE) *Any two bases for a finite-dimensional vector space contain the same number of vectors.*

The dimension of $\mathbb{R}^N$ seems obvious to us: the natural basis consists of N vectors.

Besides its relationship to dimension, the basis has another fundamental property: every element of the vector space is a unique linear combination of the vectors of a basis. This property follows from Theorem C.2 (Direct Sum).

C.2 LINEAR TRANSFORMATIONS

Linear transformations and the choice of basis are the central focus of matrix theory.

DEFINITION C.10 (LINEAR TRANSFORMATION) A linear transformation *f of the real vector space $\mathbb{U}$ into the real vector space $\mathbb{V}$ is a single-valued mapping that assigns to each vector $\mathbf{u} \in \mathbb{U}$ a unique vector $f(\mathbf{u}) \in \mathbb{V}$ such that*

$$f(a \cdot \mathbf{u} + b \cdot \mathbf{w}) = a \cdot f(\mathbf{u}) + b \cdot f(\mathbf{w})$$

for all $\mathbf{u}, \mathbf{w} \in \mathbb{U}$. The space $\mathbb{U}$ is called the domain *and the space $\mathbb{V}$ is called the* codomain.

Here are several terms and results associated with linear transformations.

DEFINITION C.11 *The* image *of f is the set $f(\mathbb{U}) \equiv \{\mathbf{v} \in \mathbb{V} \mid \mathbf{v} = f(\mathbf{u}),\ \mathbf{u} \in \mathbb{U}\}$.*

THEOREM C.4 *The image of f is a subspace of $\mathbb{V}$.*

DEFINITION C.12 *The* rank *of f is the dimension of the image of f.*

THEOREM C.5 *The rank of f is less than or equal to* $\min\{\dim(\mathbb{U}), \dim(\mathbb{V})\}$.

THEOREM C.6 *If $\mathbb{S}$ is a subspace of $\mathbb{V}$, then the set $f^{-1}(\mathbb{S}) \equiv \{\mathbf{u} \in \mathbb{U} \mid f(\mathbf{u}) \in \mathbb{S}\}$ is a subspace of $\mathbb{U}$.*

DEFINITION C.13 *The* kernel *of a linear transformation f is the subspace $f^{-1}(\{\mathbf{0}\})$.*

THEOREM C.7 *The rank of a linear transformation plus the dimension of its kernel equals the dimension of its domain.*

We will prove these theorems using the notation of matrices and vectors.

Matrices can represent sets of vectors or linear transformations. Therein lies the source of much confusion and delight in matrix algebra. Let $\{\mathbf{u}_1, \ldots, \mathbf{u}_K\}$ be any basis of the K-dimensional vector space $\mathbb{U}$ and $\{\mathbf{v}_1, \ldots, \mathbf{v}_N\}$ be any basis of the N-dimensional space $\mathbb{V}$. Then $f(\mathbf{u}_k)$ is an element of $\mathbb{V}$ so that it can be expressed as a linear combination of the basis:

$$f(\mathbf{u}_k) = \sum_{n=1}^{N} x_{nk} \cdot \mathbf{v}_n, \qquad k = 1, \ldots, K$$

where the x_{nk} are unique. The matrix $\mathbf{X} = [x_{nk}]$ corresponds one to one with the linear transformation f. Let $\sum_{k=1}^{K} a_k \cdot \mathbf{u}_k$ be a member of $\mathbb{U}$. Now

$$\begin{aligned} f\left(\sum_{k=1}^{K} a_k \cdot \mathbf{u}_k\right) &= \sum_{k=1}^{K} a_k \cdot f(\mathbf{u}_k) \\ &= \sum_{k=1}^{K} a_k \cdot \sum_{n=1}^{N} x_{nk}\mathbf{v}_n \\ &= \sum_{n=1}^{N}\left(\sum_{k=1}^{K} x_{nk}a_k\right) \cdot \mathbf{v}_n \\ &= \sum_{n=1}^{N} y_n \cdot \mathbf{v}_n \end{aligned} \tag{C.3}$$

where

$$y_n \equiv \sum_{k=1}^{K} x_{nk}a_k$$

Even though $\mathbb{U}$ is not the vector space $\mathbb{R}^K$, we can *represent* its vectors uniquely by elements of $\mathbb{R}^K$, as in $\mathbf{a} = [a_k]'$. Similarly, $\mathbf{y} = [y_n]' \in \mathbb{R}^N$ represents the vector $\sum_{n=1}^{N} y_n \cdot \mathbf{v}_n$ and we can uniquely represent (C.3) by the matrix equation $\mathbf{y} = \mathbf{Xa}$.

Above in (C.2), we interpreted the term $\mathbf{Xa}$ as a linear combination of K column vectors of $\mathbf{X}$, where the elements of $\mathbf{a}$ are the *scalar coefficients*. In contrast, we are now interpreting $\mathbf{Xa}$ as a linear transformation of the vector $\mathbf{a}$. Then we view $\mathbf{a}$ as a *vector* in a K-dimensional domain and $\mathbf{X}$ as a linear transformation from that space to a subspace in an N-dimensional image. One must be able to use both interpretations.

We will use some additional matrix notation. Because $f(c \cdot \mathbf{u}) = c \cdot f(\mathbf{u})$, *scalar multiplication for matrices* is given by

$$c \cdot \mathbf{X} = [c\, x_{nk}] \tag{C.4}$$

so that $\mathbf{X}(c \cdot \mathbf{a}) = (c \cdot \mathbf{X})\,\mathbf{a}$. The multiplication of two matrices is a direct extension of the multiplication of a matrix and a column vector given in (C.2): let $\mathbf{Z}$ be a $K \times M$ matrix of real numbers and

$$\mathbf{XZ} = \left[\sum_{k=1}^{K} x_{nk}z_{km};\ n = 1, \ldots, N,\ m = 1, \ldots, M\right] \tag{C.5}$$

is the $N \times M$ matrix product. The matrices must be *conformable*, which means that $\mathbf{X}$ has the same number of columns as $\mathbf{Z}$ has rows. Note that $(\mathbf{XZ})' = \mathbf{Z}'\mathbf{X}'$.

With this notation in hand, we now prove Theorems C.4–C.7. Let the $N \times K$ matrix $\mathbf{X} = [x_{nk}]$ represent a linear transformation. It follows that $\mathbb{R}^K$ represents the domain and $\mathbb{R}^N$ represents the codomain of the linear transformation. Without any loss of generality, we will simply refer to $\mathbf{X}$ as the linear transformation, $\mathbb{R}^K$ as the domain, and $\mathbb{R}^N$ as the codomain.

The image of the linear transformation is a subspace because it is the set spanned by the columns of $\mathbf{X}$, a subspace of $\mathbb{R}^N$. This observation confirms Theorem C.4. Furthermore, the dimension of this subspace cannot exceed the number of column vectors in $\mathbf{X}$. Therefore, the rank of the linear transformation is less than or equal to both K and N, confirming Theorem C.5.

Now consider a subspace $\mathbb{S}$ of $\mathbb{R}^N$ and the set $\{\mathbf{b} \in \mathbb{R}^K \mid \mathbf{Xb} \in \mathbb{S}\}$. This set is a subspace because if $\mathbf{Xb}_1, \mathbf{Xb}_2 \in \mathbb{S}$ then

$$\mathbf{X}(a_1 \cdot \mathbf{b}_1 + a_2 \cdot \mathbf{b}_2) = a_1 \cdot \mathbf{Xb}_1 + a_2 \cdot \mathbf{Xb}_2 \in \mathbb{S}$$

This proves Theorem C.6.

The kernel of the linear transformation is the special case $\{\mathbf{b} \in \mathbb{R}^K \mid \mathbf{Xb} = \mathbf{0}\}$. If we let $\mathbf{Z}_1$ be a $K \times P$ matrix whose columns are a basis for this set and $\mathbf{Z}_2$ be a $K \times (K - P)$ matrix such that the columns of $\mathbf{Z} = [\mathbf{Z}_1, \mathbf{Z}_2]$ are a basis for $\mathbb{R}^K$, then every $\mathbf{b} \in \mathbb{R}^K$ can be written

$$\mathbf{b} = \mathbf{Zc} = \mathbf{Z}_1\mathbf{c}_1 + \mathbf{Z}_2\mathbf{c}_2$$

and

$$\mathbf{Xb} = \mathbf{XZc} = \mathbf{XZ}_2\mathbf{c}_2$$

because the columns of $\mathbf{Z}_1$ belong to the kernel. Therefore, the columns of the $N \times (K - P)$ matrix $\mathbf{XZ}_2$ span the image of $\mathbf{X}$. If these columns are linearly dependent then there is a $\mathbf{d}$ such that $\mathbf{XZ}_2\mathbf{d} = \mathbf{0}$. But that would imply that $\mathbf{Z}_2\mathbf{d}$ is a member of the kernel, which is a contradiction. So the columns of $\mathbf{XZ}_2$ are a basis of the image of $\mathbf{X}$. Therefore, as Theorem C.7 states, the dimension of the image is $K - P$, and the sum of the dimension of the image and the dimension of the kernel equals the dimension of the domain. For matrices, we can restate this result in another useful form.

THEOREM C.8 *Let $\mathbf{X}$ be an $N \times K$ real matrix. The domain of $\mathbf{X}$, $\mathbb{R}^K$, is the direct sum of the column space of $\mathbf{X}'$ and the kernel of $\mathbf{X}$.*

The rank of a matrix is the rank of the linear transformation it represents. By definition then, the rank is the dimension of the column space of the matrix.

DEFINITION C.14 (MATRIX RANK) *The* rank *of a real $N \times K$ matrix $\mathbf{X}$ is* $\text{rank}(\mathbf{X}) \equiv \dim[\text{Col}(\mathbf{X})]$.

Finally, consider the special cases in which the elements of the domain and the image are one to one.

DEFINITION C.15 (NONSINGULAR) *A linear transformation is called* invertible *or* nonsingular *if f has an inverse. Otherwise the linear transformation is* singular.

The inverse of a nonsingular linear transformation is also linear. To see this, observe that if $f(\mathbf{u}_1) = \mathbf{v}_1$ and $f(\mathbf{u}_2) = \mathbf{v}_2$ so that

$$f(a_1 \cdot \mathbf{u}_1 + a_2 \cdot \mathbf{u}_2) = a_1 \cdot f(\mathbf{u}_1) + a_2 \cdot f(\mathbf{u}_2)$$

(by Definition C.10) then

$$\begin{aligned} f^{-1}[a_1 \cdot \mathbf{v}_1 + a_2 \cdot \mathbf{v}_2] &= f^{-1}[a_1 \cdot f(\mathbf{u}_1) + a_2 \cdot f(\mathbf{u}_2)] \\ &= f^{-1}[f(a_1 \cdot \mathbf{u}_1 + a_2 \cdot \mathbf{u}_2)] \\ &= a_1 \cdot \mathbf{u}_1 + a_2 \cdot \mathbf{u}_2 \\ &= a_1 \cdot f^{-1}(\mathbf{v}_1) + a_2 \cdot f^{-1}(\mathbf{v}_2) \end{aligned}$$

There is a rank condition that is necessary and sufficient to establish that a linear transformation is nonsingular.

THEOREM C.9 (RANK CONDITION) *A linear transformation is nonsingular if and only if its rank equals the dimension of its domain.*

Proof. **Sufficiency:** If a linear transformation is nonsingular, then Definition C.15 implies that the zero vector is the only vector in the domain transformed into the zero vector in the image. In other words, the kernel contains only the zero vector. According to Theorem C.7, this implies that its rank equals the dimension of its domain. **Necessity:** Conversely, if the rank of a linear transformation equals the dimension of its domain, then the kernel contains only the zero vector. If the linear transformation does not have an inverse, then there are two distinct vectors in the domain, $\mathbf{u}_1 \neq \mathbf{u}_2$, that are transformed into the same vector in the image. But then $\mathbf{u}_1 - \mathbf{u}_2 \neq \mathbf{0}$ is a member of the kernel also, which is a contradiction. □

The terms *rank*, *invertible*, *nonsingular*, and *singular* apply just as well to the matrices that represent linear transformations. Let $\mathbf{A}$ be the matrix of a linear transformation f that has an inverse. Obviously, the domain and the image of f must have the same dimension and the kernel must be the zero vector. Therefore, let $\mathbf{A}$ map from $\mathbb{R}^N$ to $\mathbb{R}^N$ so that $\mathbf{A}$ must be square: $N \times N$. The rank of $\mathbf{A}$ equals N. We denote the matrix of the inverse linear transformation by $\mathbf{A}^{-1}$. Then for all $\mathbf{u} \in \mathbb{R}^N$,

$$\mathbf{A}\mathbf{A}^{-1}\mathbf{u} = \mathbf{A}^{-1}\mathbf{A}\mathbf{u} = \mathbf{u}$$

and, by taking $\mathbf{u}$ to be each of the columns of $\mathbf{I}_N$,

$$\mathbf{A}\mathbf{A}^{-1} = \mathbf{A}^{-1}\mathbf{A} = \mathbf{I}_N$$

For any equation of the form $\mathbf{A}\mathbf{u} = \mathbf{v}$, we can always write $\mathbf{u} = \mathbf{A}^{-1}\mathbf{v}$.

C.3 INNER PRODUCTS AND ORTHOGONALITY

Vector spaces can be given additional features besides those described in Definition C.1. Two that are critical to this book are the *inner product* and the *norm*.

DEFINITION C.16 (INNER PRODUCT) *Let $\mathbb{V}$ be a real vector space. An* inner product *is a scalar function defined on $\mathbb{V} \times \mathbb{V}$. For every $\mathbf{u}, \mathbf{v} \in \mathbb{V}$ the inner product $\langle \mathbf{u}, \mathbf{v} \rangle$ has four properties:*

1. $\langle \mathbf{u}, \mathbf{v} \rangle = \langle \mathbf{v}, \mathbf{u} \rangle$;
2. $\langle \mathbf{u} + \mathbf{w}, \mathbf{v} \rangle = \langle \mathbf{u}, \mathbf{v} \rangle + \langle \mathbf{w}, \mathbf{v} \rangle$;
3. $\langle a \cdot \mathbf{u}, \mathbf{v} \rangle = a \cdot \langle \mathbf{u}, \mathbf{v} \rangle$; *and*
4. $\langle \mathbf{v}, \mathbf{v} \rangle \geq 0$ *and* $\langle \mathbf{v}, \mathbf{v} \rangle = 0 \Leftrightarrow \mathbf{v} = \mathbf{0}$.

The inner product commonly associated with vectors from $\mathbb{R}^N$ is

$$\langle \mathbf{u}, \mathbf{v} \rangle = \sum_{n=1}^{N} u_n v_n$$

This sum can be represented as the matrix product of a *row vector* with a column vector. Thus, the inner product of $\mathbf{u}, \mathbf{v} \in \mathbb{R}^N$ is usually expressed as

$$\langle \mathbf{u}, \mathbf{v} \rangle = \mathbf{u}'\mathbf{v} = \mathbf{v}'\mathbf{u}$$

LEMMA C.1 (CAUCHY–SCHWARZ INEQUALITY) *For every $\mathbf{u}, \mathbf{v}$ in a real inner product space*

$$\langle \mathbf{u}, \mathbf{v} \rangle^2 \leq \langle \mathbf{u}, \mathbf{u} \rangle \cdot \langle \mathbf{v}, \mathbf{v} \rangle$$

Equality holds if and only if $\mathbf{u} = a \cdot \mathbf{v}$ or $\mathbf{v} = \mathbf{0}$.

Proof. If $\mathbf{v} = \mathbf{0}$, then the result holds. Consider the cases where $\mathbf{v} \neq \mathbf{0}$. For any scalar a,

$$\begin{aligned} 0 &\leq \langle \mathbf{u} - a \cdot \mathbf{v},\ \mathbf{u} - a \cdot \mathbf{v} \rangle \\ &= \langle \mathbf{u}, \mathbf{u} \rangle - 2a \cdot \langle \mathbf{u}, \mathbf{v} \rangle + a^2 \cdot \langle \mathbf{v}, \mathbf{v} \rangle \end{aligned}$$

using the properties of inner products. Setting

$$a = \frac{\langle \mathbf{u}, \mathbf{v} \rangle}{\langle \mathbf{v}, \mathbf{v} \rangle}$$

this inequality becomes

$$0 \leq \langle \mathbf{u}, \mathbf{u} \rangle - \frac{\langle \mathbf{u}, \mathbf{v} \rangle^2}{\langle \mathbf{v}, \mathbf{v} \rangle}$$

which is equivalent to the inequality stated in the lemma. □

DEFINITION C.17 (ORTHOGONAL) *Let* $\mathbf{u}$ *and* $\mathbf{v}$ *be vectors in* $\mathbb{V}$. *If* $\langle \mathbf{u}, \mathbf{v} \rangle = 0$, *then* $\mathbf{u}$ *and* $\mathbf{v}$ *are said to be* orthogonal.

A common notation for orthogonality is to write $\mathbf{u} \perp \mathbf{v}$ if $\langle \mathbf{u}, \mathbf{v} \rangle = 0$.[2] If $\mathbf{v}$ is orthogonal to every member of the set $\mathbb{S}$ then we will write $\mathbf{v} \perp \mathbb{S}$.

DEFINITION C.18 (ORTHOGONAL BASIS) *An orthogonal basis is a basis with mutually orthogonal vectors.*

THEOREM C.10 (GRAM–SCHMIDT) *We can always construct an orthogonal basis from a basis.*

Proof. Let $\{\mathbf{u}_1, \ldots, \mathbf{u}_K\}$ be the basis of a subspace. Because $\mathbf{u}_1$ is a member of a linearly independent set, $\mathbf{u}_1 \neq \mathbf{0}$ and $\langle \mathbf{u}_1, \mathbf{u}_1 \rangle > 0$. Let

$$\mathbf{z}_1 = \frac{1}{\sqrt{\langle \mathbf{u}_1, \mathbf{u}_1 \rangle}} \mathbf{u}_1$$

and note that $\langle \mathbf{z}_1, \mathbf{z}_1 \rangle = 1$. For $k = 2, \ldots, K$, let

$$\mathbf{w}_k = \mathbf{u}_k - \sum_{j=1}^{k-1} \langle \mathbf{z}_j, \mathbf{u}_k \rangle \, \mathbf{z}_j$$

$$\mathbf{z}_k = \frac{1}{\sqrt{\langle \mathbf{w}_k, \mathbf{w}_k \rangle}} \mathbf{w}_k$$

The zs are linearly independent because the $\mathbf{u}$s are and $\langle \mathbf{z}_k, \mathbf{z}_k \rangle = 1$. Also, let $i < k$ and find that

$$\begin{aligned}
\langle \mathbf{z}_i, \mathbf{z}_k \rangle &= \frac{1}{\sqrt{\langle \mathbf{w}_k, \mathbf{w}_k \rangle}} \left\langle \mathbf{z}_i, \mathbf{u}_k - \sum_{j=1}^{k-1} \langle \mathbf{z}_j, \mathbf{u}_k \rangle \, \mathbf{z}_j \right\rangle \\
&= \frac{1}{\sqrt{\langle \mathbf{w}_k, \mathbf{w}_k \rangle}} \left(\langle \mathbf{z}_i, \mathbf{u}_k \rangle - \langle \mathbf{z}_i, \mathbf{u}_k \rangle \right) \\
&= 0
\end{aligned}$$

so that the $\mathbf{z}$s are orthogonal. This process for constructing the $\mathbf{z}$s is called *Gram–Schmidt orthonormalization.*

[2] The symbol $\perp$ depicts two perpendicular lines and it is often called "perp" for short.

DEFINITION C.19 (ORTHOGONAL COMPLEMENT) *We will denote the linear subspace of vectors orthogonal to the K-dimensional subspace $\mathbb{S}$ of the N-dimensional vector space $\mathbb{V}$ by*

$$\mathbb{S}^{\perp} \equiv \{\mathbf{v} \in \mathbb{V} \mid \langle \mathbf{u}, \mathbf{v} \rangle = 0 \; \forall \mathbf{u} \in \mathbb{S}\}$$

$\mathbb{S}^{\perp}$ *is called the* orthogonal complement *of* $\mathbb{S}$.

It is equivalent to write $\mathbf{v} \in \mathbb{S}^{\perp}$ as $\mathbf{v} \perp \mathbb{S}$. Note that if $\mathbf{v} \in \mathbb{S} \cap \mathbb{S}^{\perp}$ then $\langle \mathbf{v}, \mathbf{v} \rangle = 0$ so that $\mathbf{v}$ must be the zero vector. In other words, $\mathbb{S} \cap \mathbb{S}^{\perp} = \{\mathbf{0}\}$.

EXAMPLE C.1

The kernel of the matrix $\mathbf{X}'$ is the orthogonal complement $\mathrm{Col}^{\perp}(\mathbf{X})$.

THEOREM C.11 (ORTHOGONAL COMPLEMENT)

$$\mathbb{S} \oplus \mathbb{S}^{\perp} = \mathbb{V} \qquad \textit{and} \qquad \dim(\mathbb{S}) + \dim\left(\mathbb{S}^{\perp}\right) = \dim(\mathbb{V})$$

Proof. Because $\mathbb{S} \oplus \mathbb{S}^{\perp}$ is a subspace of $\mathbb{V}$, let $\{\mathbf{u}_1, \ldots, \mathbf{u}_K, \mathbf{v}_1, \ldots, \mathbf{v}_{N-K}\}$ be a basis for $\mathbb{V}$ such that $\{\mathbf{u}_1, \ldots, \mathbf{u}_K\}$ is a basis for $\mathbb{S}$. Using Gram–Schmidt orthonormalization, starting with the $\mathbf{u}$s, we can construct an orthonormal basis such that the last $N - K$ vectors of the process are all members of $\mathbb{S}^{\perp}$. Therefore, $\dim(\mathbb{S}^{\perp}) = N - K$ and $\dim(\mathbb{S} \oplus \mathbb{S}^{\perp}) = N = \dim(\mathbb{V})$. That is, a basis for $\mathbb{S} \oplus \mathbb{S}^{\perp}$ is a basis for $\mathbb{V}$ and we conclude that $\mathbb{S} \oplus \mathbb{S}^{\perp} = \mathbb{V}$. □

An implication of this theorem for matrices follows.

THEOREM C.12 *The dimension of the column space of a matrix and the dimension of its row space are equal.*

Proof. Theorem C.11 states that

$$N = \dim[\mathrm{Col}(\mathbf{X})] + \dim[\mathrm{Col}^{\perp}(\mathbf{X})]$$

Theorem C.7 and Example C.1 imply that

$$N = \dim[\mathrm{Col}(\mathbf{X}')] + \dim[\mathrm{Col}^{\perp}(\mathbf{X})]$$

It follows that $\dim[\mathrm{Col}(\mathbf{X})] = \dim[\mathrm{Col}(\mathbf{X}')]$. □

The result of this theorem is that we do not need to restrict the rank of a matrix to the dimension of its column space. Therefore we can amend Definition C.14 as follows.

Definition C.20 (Matrix Rank) *The rank of a matrix is the number of linearly independent rows or columns.*

Given this definition for the rank of a matrix, we obtain another useful matrix result.

Theorem C.13 *The rank of a matrix equals the rank of its product with a nonsingular matrix.*

Proof. Let $\mathbf{A}$ be nonsingular and consider the matrix product $\mathbf{AB}$ as the composition of two linear transformations. The image of $\mathbf{B}$ is one to one with the image of $\mathbf{AB}$ so that the ranks of $\mathbf{B}$ and $\mathbf{AB}$ are equal. Alternatively, consider a matrix product $\mathbf{CA}$. This can be recast as the first case by noting that the rank of a matrix equals the rank of its transpose. □

A consequence of this theorem is that the product $\mathbf{AB}$ of a full-column rank matrix $\mathbf{A}$ and a full-column rank matrix $\mathbf{B}$ is full rank. To see this, let $[\mathbf{B}, \mathbf{C}]$ be a nonsingular matrix so that $[\mathbf{AB}, \mathbf{AC}]$ is full-column rank like $\mathbf{A}$. If $\mathbf{AB}$ is not full-(column) rank, then we have a contradiction.

C.4 NORMED LINEAR VECTOR SPACES

Definition C.21 (Normed Linear Vector Space) A normed linear vector space *is a vector space $\mathbb{V}$ and a real-valued scalar function on all the vectors $\mathbf{v} \in \mathbb{V}$, denoted $\|\mathbf{v}\|$ and called the* norm of $\mathbf{v}$, *such that*

1. $\|a \cdot \mathbf{v}\| = |a| \cdot \|\mathbf{v}\|$ *for every scalar a;*
2. $\|\mathbf{v}\| \geq 0$ *and* $\|\mathbf{v}\| = 0$ *if and only if* $\mathbf{v} = \mathbf{0}$;
3. $\|\mathbf{u} + \mathbf{v}\| \leq \|\mathbf{u}\| + \|\mathbf{v}\|$ *for every* $\mathbf{u}, \mathbf{v} \in \mathbb{V}$.

The norm is intuitively a measure of distance or length. The vector space $\mathbb{R}^N$ becomes the *Euclidean* N-space, $\mathbb{E}^N$, when we define

$$\|\mathbf{v}\| = \sqrt{\sum_{n=1}^{N} v_n^2}$$

for $\mathbf{v} \in \mathbb{R}^N$. This is often written in matrix notation using the transpose of a matrix. Often, vector spaces have inner products and norms, where the norm is induced by the inner product according to

$$\|\mathbf{v}\| = \sqrt{\langle \mathbf{v}, \mathbf{v} \rangle}$$

This is the case for $\mathbb{E}^N$.

That $\sqrt{\langle \mathbf{v}, \mathbf{v} \rangle}$ has the properties of a norm follows from Definition C.16 and Lemma C.1 (Cauchy–Schwarz inequality). Because $\langle \mathbf{u}, \mathbf{v} \rangle = \langle \mathbf{v}, \mathbf{u} \rangle$ and $\langle a \cdot \mathbf{u}, \mathbf{v} \rangle = a \cdot \langle \mathbf{u}, \mathbf{v} \rangle$, it follows that

$$\begin{aligned} \|a \cdot \mathbf{v}\| &\equiv \sqrt{\langle a \cdot \mathbf{v}, a \cdot \mathbf{v} \rangle} = \sqrt{a \cdot \langle \mathbf{v}, a \cdot \mathbf{v} \rangle} = \sqrt{a \cdot \langle a \cdot \mathbf{v}, \mathbf{v} \rangle} \\ &= \sqrt{a^2 \cdot \langle \mathbf{v}, \mathbf{v} \rangle} = |a| \sqrt{\langle \mathbf{v}, \mathbf{v} \rangle} = |a| \cdot \|\mathbf{v}\| \end{aligned}$$

Because $\langle \mathbf{v}, \mathbf{v} \rangle \geq 0$ and $\langle \mathbf{v}, \mathbf{v} \rangle = 0$ if and only if $\mathbf{v} = \mathbf{0}$, it follows that $\|\mathbf{v}\| \geq 0$ and $\|\mathbf{v}\| = 0$ if and only if $\mathbf{v} = \mathbf{0}$. Finally, because $\langle \mathbf{u}, \mathbf{v} \rangle^2 \leq \langle \mathbf{u}, \mathbf{u} \rangle \cdot \langle \mathbf{v}, \mathbf{v} \rangle$, we obtain the so-called *triangle inequality*:

$$\begin{aligned} \|\mathbf{u} + \mathbf{v}\| &= \sqrt{\langle \mathbf{u} + \mathbf{v}, \mathbf{u} + \mathbf{v} \rangle} = \sqrt{\langle \mathbf{u}, \mathbf{u} \rangle + \langle \mathbf{v}, \mathbf{v} \rangle + 2 \cdot \langle \mathbf{u}, \mathbf{v} \rangle} \\ &\leq \sqrt{\langle \mathbf{u}, \mathbf{u} \rangle + \langle \mathbf{v}, \mathbf{v} \rangle + 2\sqrt{\langle \mathbf{u}, \mathbf{u} \rangle \cdot \langle \mathbf{v}, \mathbf{v} \rangle}} \\ &= \sqrt{\|\mathbf{u}\|^2 + \|\mathbf{v}\|^2 + 2 \cdot \|\mathbf{u}\| \cdot \|\mathbf{v}\|} \\ &= \sqrt{(\|\mathbf{u}\| + \|\mathbf{v}\|)^2} = \|\mathbf{u}\| + \|\mathbf{v}\| \end{aligned} \tag{C.6}$$

DEFINITION C.22 (ORTHOGONAL MATRIX) *An $N \times N$ matrix $\mathbf{A}$ is called* orthogonal *if $\mathbf{A}'\mathbf{A} = \mathbf{I}_N$.*

In this case, the columns of $\mathbf{A}$ are mutually orthogonal vectors, each with unit length. As a result, an orthogonal matrix is nonsingular and $\mathbf{A}^{-1} = \mathbf{A}'$. If $\mathbf{A}$ is $N \times N$, the columns (or rows) comprise an orthonormal basis of $\mathbb{E}^N$.

C.5 DETERMINANTS

The matrix determinant is an arcane matrix function, and its description varies from book to book. We will give a constructive description, shaped by our uses of the matrix determinant. First, we explain that the absolute value of the matrix determinant is a scalar measure of the magnitude of a matrix: it is the volume of an N-dimensional parallelogram. Second, we derive an expression for determinants called the *cofactor expansion*.

We will denote the determinant of an $N \times N$ matrix $\mathbf{A}$ by $\det(\mathbf{A})$, the absolute value of the determinant by $|\det(\mathbf{A})|$. The latter equals the volume of an N-dimensional parallelogram constructed from the column vectors of $\mathbf{A}$. This is a useful interpretation and so we will now describe its implementation.

C.5.1 Volume of a Parallelogram

Let $\mathbf{A} = [a_{ij}]$ be the $N \times N$ matrix whose columns are $\mathbf{a}_j$. Consider the N-dimensional many-sided volume consisting of all the points that are linear combinations of the column vectors of $\mathbf{A}$ where the scalar coefficients are bounded to the unit interval:

$$\mathbb{P}(\mathbf{A}) \equiv \left\{ \mathbf{v} \in \mathbb{R}^N \mid \mathbf{v} = \sum_{n=1}^{N} b_n \cdot \mathbf{a}_n, \quad 0 \le b_n \le 1, \quad n = 1, \ldots, N \right\}$$

This is the N-dimensional version of the two-dimensional parallelogram and its interior. See Figure C.4.

If $\mathbf{A} = \mathbf{I}_N$, then $\mathbb{P}(\mathbf{I}_N)$ is a unit cube with one vertex at the origin and all points within the positive orthant. The volume of $\mathbb{P}(\mathbf{I}_N)$ is 1. Let us use the notation $\text{Vol}(\mathbf{I}_N) = 1$.

We can compute the volume of general $\mathbb{P}(\mathbf{A})$ by considering two basic transformations of $\mathbb{P}(\mathbf{A})$ through transformations of $\mathbf{A}$ and their effect on volume. We will apply these transformations to the unit cube. The two elementary operations are

1. the vector addition of a scalar multiple of one column vector to another column vector of $\mathbf{A}$;
2. and the scalar multiplication of a column vector of $\mathbf{A}$.

With these two operations, we can relate $\mathbf{I}_N$ to any matrix $\mathbf{A}$, as we will explain below.

Suppose for the moment that we know that the volume of $\mathbb{P}(\mathbf{A})$ is $v_{\mathbf{A}} \ge 0$. If we replace an edge, $\mathbf{a}_n$, by the sum of the edge and a multiple of another edge, say $\mathbf{a}_m$, $m \ne n$, the volume of the new parallelogram equals the volume of the original. That is, if we replace $\mathbf{A}$ instead by

$$\mathbf{B} = \begin{bmatrix} \mathbf{a}_1 & \cdots & \mathbf{a}_{n-1} & \mathbf{a}_n + c \cdot \mathbf{a}_m & \mathbf{a}_{n+1} & \cdots & \mathbf{a}_N \end{bmatrix}$$

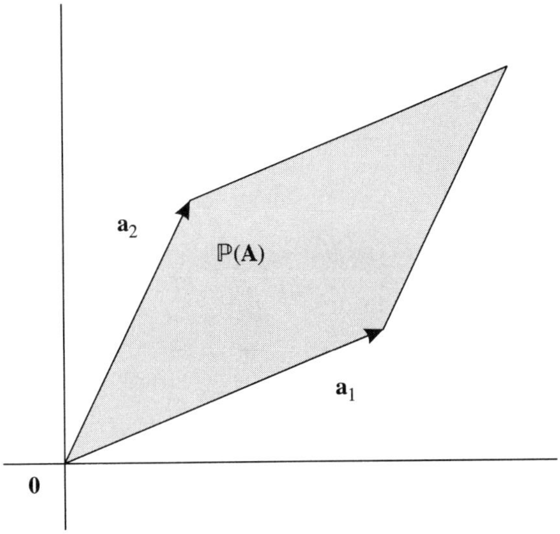

Figure C.4 A matrix as a parallelogram.

then the volume of $\mathbb{P}(\mathbf{B})$ is also $v_{\mathbf{A}}$. In effect, whatever is lost of the original parallelogram is tacked on at the other end. A two-dimensional example of this transformation to the unit cube is pictured in Figure C.5. Applying the same transformation to the other face yields the parallelogram in Figure C.4. On the other hand, if we change the length of one edge, $\mathbf{a}_n$, by a multiplicative factor then we must change the volume of the resultant parallelogram by the same multiplicative factor. That is, if we replace $\mathbf{A}$ by

$$\mathbf{B} = \begin{bmatrix} \mathbf{a}_1 & \cdots & \mathbf{a}_{n-1} & c \cdot \mathbf{a}_n & \mathbf{a}_{n+1} & \cdots & \mathbf{a}_N \end{bmatrix}$$

for some scalar $c \in \mathbb{R}$, then the volume of $\mathbb{P}(\mathbf{B})$ is $\text{Vol}(\mathbf{B}) = |c|\, v_{\mathbf{A}}$. See Figure C.6 for a two-dimensional illustration. These examples suggest how the elementary operations can be combined to construct any parallelogram.

We will represent these elementary operations by elementary matrices $\mathbf{E}_i$ with two functional forms:

1. for vector addition of a column vector with a scalar multiple of another column vector, $\mathbf{E}_i$ is $\mathbf{I}_N$ with an off-diagonal zero replaced by a scalar c;
2. for scalar multiplication of a column vector, $\mathbf{E}_i$ is $\mathbf{I}_N$ with a diagonal one replaced by a scalar $c \in \mathbb{R}$.

These elementary operations are merely scalar multiplication and vector addition, the building blocks of all linear transformations. Therefore, the column vectors of $\mathbf{A}$ can be written as a sequence of such matrix operations applied to the columns of $\mathbf{I}_N$:

$$\mathbf{A} = \mathbf{I}_N \left(\prod_i \mathbf{E}_i\right) = \prod_i \mathbf{E}_i$$

Furthermore, we understand the effect of each operation on the volume of the result: for scalar multiplication, we multiply the volume by the absolute value of the scalar. For vector addition,

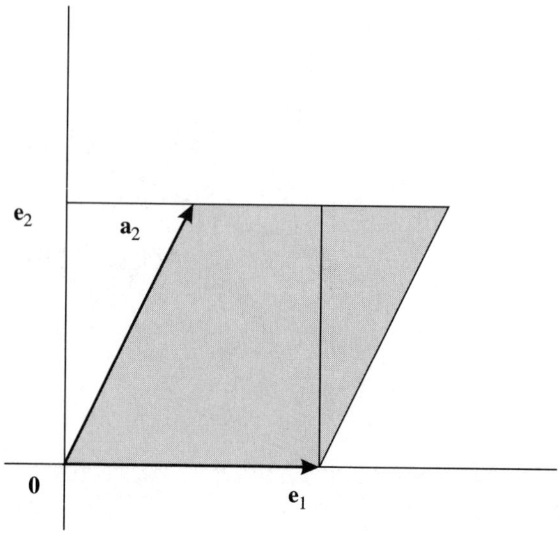

Figure C.5 Vector addition of a scalar multiple of another column vector.

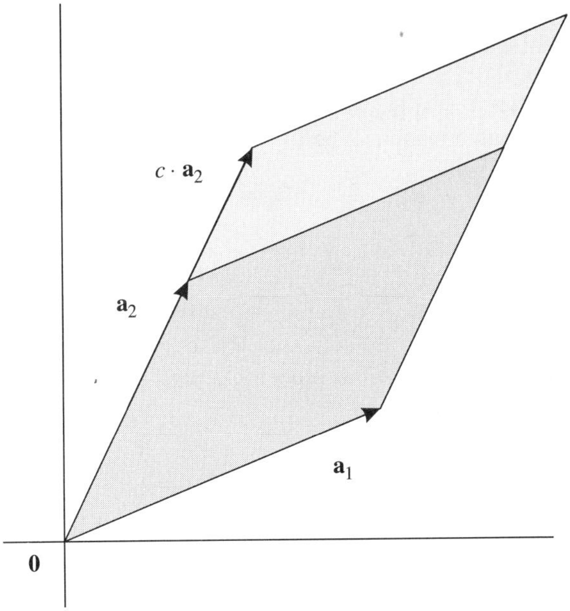

Figure C.6 Scalar multiplication of a column vector.

we keep the same volume (or multiply by 1). Therefore, the volume of $\mathbb{P}(\mathbf{A})$ is the product of the volumes of the $\mathbb{P}(\mathbf{E}_i)$:

$$\operatorname{Vol}(\mathbf{A}) = \operatorname{Vol}\left(\prod_i \mathbf{E}_i\right) = \prod_i \operatorname{Vol}(\mathbf{E}_i)$$

Several properties of this volume function follow directly.

Lemma C.2 *Let* $\mathbf{A}$ *and* $\mathbf{B}$ *be* $N \times N$ *matrices. Then*

1. $\operatorname{Vol}(\mathbf{A}) = \operatorname{Vol}(\mathbf{A}')$;
2. $\operatorname{Vol}(\mathbf{AB}) = \operatorname{Vol}(\mathbf{A}) \operatorname{Vol}(\mathbf{B})$;
3. *if* $\mathbf{A}$ *is nonsingular,* $\operatorname{Vol}(\mathbf{A}) \neq 0$ *and* $\operatorname{Vol}(\mathbf{A}^{-1}) = 1/\operatorname{Vol}(\mathbf{A})$; *and*
4. $\operatorname{Vol}(\mathbf{A}) = 0 \quad \Leftrightarrow \quad \operatorname{rank}(\mathbf{A}) < N$.

Proof.

1. Consider first the special cases of the elementary matrix transformations $\mathbf{E}_i$. For vector addition, $\operatorname{Vol}(\mathbf{E}_i) = 1 = \operatorname{Vol}(\mathbf{E}_i')$. For scalar multiplication, $\mathbf{E}_i = \mathbf{E}_i'$ so that $\operatorname{Vol}(\mathbf{E}_i) = \operatorname{Vol}(\mathbf{E}_i')$. Now, let there be J terms in the matrix product $\mathbf{A} = \prod_{i=1}^{J} \mathbf{E}_i$. Because $\mathbf{A}' = \prod_{i=1}^{J} \mathbf{E}_{J+1-i}'$,

$$\mathrm{Vol}(\mathbf{A}') = \prod_{i=1}^{J} \mathrm{Vol}(\mathbf{E}'_{J+1-i}) = \prod_{i=1}^{J} \mathrm{Vol}(\mathbf{E}_{J+1-i}) = \mathrm{Vol}(\mathbf{A})$$

2. Let $\mathbf{A} = \prod_{j=1}^{J} \mathbf{E}_j$ and $\mathbf{B} = \prod_{k=1}^{K} \mathbf{F}_k$ where the $\mathbf{F}_k$ are also elementary matrix transformations. Then

$$\begin{aligned}\mathrm{Vol}(\mathbf{AB}) &= \mathrm{Vol}\left(\prod_{j=1}^{J}\mathbf{E}_j \prod_{k=1}^{K}\mathbf{F}_k\right) \\ &= \left[\prod_{j=1}^{J} \mathrm{Vol}(\mathbf{E}_i)\right]\left[\prod_{k=1}^{K} \mathrm{Vol}(\mathbf{F}_j)\right] \\ &= \mathrm{Vol}(\mathbf{A})\,\mathrm{Vol}(\mathbf{B})\end{aligned}$$

3. Apply the previous property, setting $\mathbf{B} = \mathbf{A}^{-1}$, and obtain

$$\mathrm{Vol}(\mathbf{A})\,\mathrm{Vol}(\mathbf{A}^{-1}) = \mathrm{Vol}(\mathbf{I}_N) = 1$$

so that $\mathrm{Vol}(\mathbf{A}) \neq 0$ and $\mathrm{Vol}(\mathbf{A}^{-1}) = 1/\mathrm{Vol}(\mathbf{A})$.

4. If $\mathbf{A}$ is singular, then there is a $\mathbf{b} \neq \mathbf{0}$, $\mathbf{b} \in \mathbb{R}^N$ such that $\mathbf{Ab} = \mathbf{0}$. Let $\mathbf{B}$ be a nonsingular matrix containing $\mathbf{b}$ among its columns so that $\mathrm{Vol}(\mathbf{AB}) = 0$. Applying the previous property, $\mathrm{Vol}(\mathbf{A}) = 0/\mathrm{Vol}(\mathbf{B}) = 0$. □

The definition of volume implies that the volume of a diagonal matrix is the absolute value of the product of the diagonal elements. A handy extension of this simple result is the following.

LEMMA C.3 (TRIANGULAR MATRIX VOLUME) *The volume of a triangular matrix is the absolute value of the product of its diagonal elements.*

Proof. Let us denote the upper-right triangular matrix $\mathbf{A} = [a_{ij}]$ where $a_{ij} = 0$ if $j < i$. Let $\mathbf{B}$ be the diagonal matrix with the same diagonal elements as $\mathbf{A}$. Then $\mathrm{Vol}(\mathbf{B}) = \left|\prod_{j=1}^{J} a_{jj}\right|$. But $\mathbf{A}$ can be obtained from $\mathbf{B}$ by a series of vector sums of a scalar multiple of one column vector and another column vector. Therefore, $\mathrm{Vol}(\mathbf{A}) = \mathrm{Vol}(\mathbf{B})$. If $\mathbf{A}$ is lower-left triangular, $\mathrm{Vol}(\mathbf{A}) = \mathrm{Vol}(\mathbf{A}') = \mathrm{Vol}(\mathbf{B})$ so that the result still holds. □

C.5.2 Determinant of a Matrix

Now we will generalize matrix volume to matrix determinants, denoted $\det(\mathbf{A})$. A determinant is a signed version of a volume. Scalar multiplication of a column vector multiplies the determinant by the value of the scalar, instead of its absolute value. Vector addition still preserves the determinant (multiplication by 1). Thus, the absolute value of the determinant is the volume function,

$$|\det(\mathbf{A})| = \mathrm{Vol}(\mathbf{A})$$

and determinants have analogous properties to volumes.

LEMMA C.4 *Let* $\mathbf{A}$ *and* $\mathbf{B}$ *be* $N \times N$ *matrices. Then*

1. $\det(\mathbf{A}) = \det(\mathbf{A}')$;
2. $\det(\mathbf{AB}) = \det(\mathbf{A})\det(\mathbf{B})$;
3. *if* $\mathbf{A}$ *is nonsingular then* $\det(\mathbf{A}^{-1}) = 1/\det(\mathbf{A})$; *and*
4. $\det(\mathbf{A}) = 0 \quad \Leftrightarrow \quad \operatorname{rank}(\mathbf{A}) < N$.

The consequence of signing volumes is an additive property of determinants.[3]

LEMMA C.5 *Consider an* $N \times N$ *matrix* $\mathbf{A} = [\mathbf{a}_n;\ n = 1, \dots, N]$. *Let the* j*th column of* $\mathbf{A}$ *be written*

$$\mathbf{a}_j = (\mathbf{a}_j - \mathbf{u}) + \mathbf{u} = \mathbf{v} + \mathbf{u}$$

where $\mathbf{u} \in \mathbb{R}^N$ *and denote*

$$\begin{aligned} \mathbf{B}_u &= \begin{bmatrix} \mathbf{a}_1 & \cdots & \mathbf{a}_{j-1} & \mathbf{u} & \mathbf{a}_{j+1} & \cdots & \mathbf{a}_N \end{bmatrix} \\ \mathbf{B}_v &= \begin{bmatrix} \mathbf{a}_1 & \cdots & \mathbf{a}_{j-1} & \mathbf{v} & \mathbf{a}_{j+1} & \cdots & \mathbf{a}_N \end{bmatrix} \end{aligned} \tag{C.7}$$

Then

$$\det(\mathbf{A}) = \det(\mathbf{B}_v) + \det(\mathbf{B}_u)$$

Proof. We consider two cases. In the first case, suppose all three matrices are singular. Then all three determinants are zero and the lemma holds. In the second case, suppose that $\mathbf{A}$ is nonsingular so that $\mathbf{u} = \mathbf{A}\boldsymbol{\beta}$, $\boldsymbol{\beta} \in \mathbb{R}^N$. Then, following the rules of scalar multiplication and vector addition for determinants,

$$\begin{aligned} \det(\mathbf{B}_u) &= \det\left(\begin{bmatrix} \mathbf{a}_1 & \cdots & \mathbf{a}_{j-1} & \sum_{i=1}^{N} \beta_i \cdot \mathbf{a}_i & \mathbf{a}_{j+1} & \cdots & \mathbf{a}_N \end{bmatrix}\right) \\ &= \det\left(\begin{bmatrix} \mathbf{a}_1 & \cdots & \mathbf{a}_{j-1} & \beta_j \cdot \mathbf{a}_j & \mathbf{a}_{j+1} & \cdots & \mathbf{a}_N \end{bmatrix}\right) \\ &= \beta_j \det(\mathbf{A}) \end{aligned}$$

Similarly, $\det(\mathbf{B}_v) = (1 - \beta_j)\det(\mathbf{A})$ so that

$$\det(\mathbf{B}_v) + \det(\mathbf{B}_u) = (1 - \beta_j)\det(\mathbf{A}) + \beta_j \det(\mathbf{A}) = \det(\mathbf{A})$$

establishing the lemma for nonsingular $\mathbf{A}$. Similar arguments hold for the cases in which $\mathbf{B}_u$ or $\mathbf{B}_v$ are nonsingular. If, for example, $\mathbf{B}_u$ is nonsingular then

$$\mathbf{a}_j = \mathbf{B}_u\boldsymbol{\beta} = \sum_{i \neq j} \beta_i \cdot \mathbf{a}_i + \beta_j \cdot \mathbf{u}, \quad \boldsymbol{\beta} \in \mathbb{R}^N$$

[3] Davidson and MacKinnon (1993, pp. 785–786) inspired this lemma.

and

$$\mathbf{v} = \mathbf{a}_j - \mathbf{u} = \sum_{i \neq j} \beta_i \cdot \mathbf{a}_i + (\beta_j - 1) \cdot \mathbf{u}$$

so that

$$\begin{aligned} \det(\mathbf{A}) &= \beta_j \det(\mathbf{B}_u) \\ \det(\mathbf{B}_v) &= (\beta_j - 1) \det(\mathbf{B}_u) \\ \det(\mathbf{A}) - \det(\mathbf{B}_v) &= \det(\mathbf{B}_u) \end{aligned}$$

□

The signs of determinants are critical to this result because they correctly account for the net effects of vector addition on volumes. Figures C.7 and C.8 give an illustration. In Figure C.7, adding volumes would work just as well as adding determinants. However, in Figure C.8, this is not so. The $\mathrm{Vol}(\mathbf{B}_v)$ must be *subtracted* from $\mathrm{Vol}(\mathbf{B}_u)$ to obtain the $\mathrm{Vol}(\mathbf{A})$. Determinants make the correct calculation.

C.5.3 The Cofactor Expansion

Lemma C.5 is a stepping stone to a useful expression for determinants called the *cofactor expansion*. Using the natural basis (p. 847), we can always write a column vector as the sum

$$\mathbf{a}_j = \sum_{i=1}^{N} a_{ij} \mathbf{e}_i$$

so that

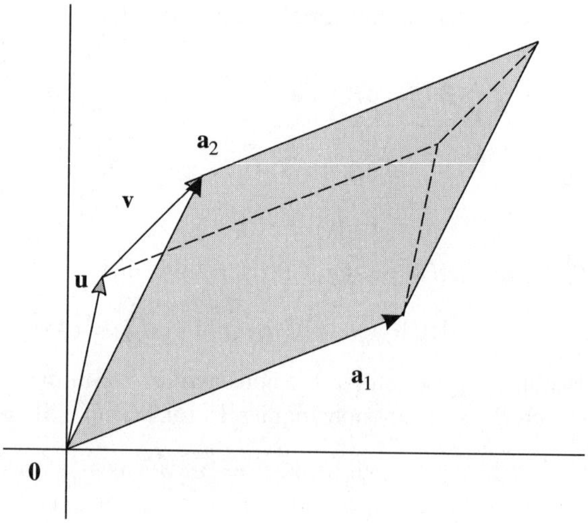

Figure C.7 Sum of positive determinants.

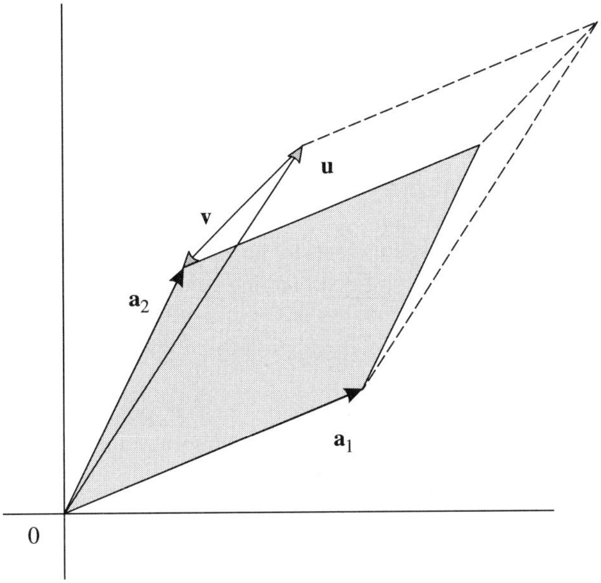

Figure C.8 Sum of positive and negative determinants.

$$\det(\mathbf{A}) = \sum_{i=1}^{N} a_{ij} A_{ij}$$

where

$$A_{ij} \equiv \det\left(\begin{bmatrix} \mathbf{a}_1 & \cdots & \mathbf{a}_{j-1} & \mathbf{e}_i & \mathbf{a}_{j+1} & \cdots & \mathbf{a}_N \end{bmatrix}\right)$$

The A_{in} can be simplified further by exploiting vector addition: if one adds $-a_{in} \cdot \mathbf{e}_i$ to the nth column, for every $n \neq j$, then

$$A_{ij} = \det\left(\begin{bmatrix} a_{11} & \cdots & a_{1,j-1} & 0 & a_{1,j+1} & \cdots & a_{1N} \\ \vdots & & \vdots & \vdots & \vdots & & \vdots \\ a_{i-1,1} & \cdots & a_{i-1,j-1} & 0 & a_{i-1,j+1} & \cdots & a_{i-1,N} \\ 0 & \cdots & 0 & 1 & 0 & \cdots & 0 \\ a_{i+1,1} & \cdots & a_{i+1,j-1} & 0 & a_{i+1,j+1} & \cdots & a_{i+1,N} \\ \vdots & & \vdots & \vdots & \vdots & & \vdots \\ a_{N1} & \cdots & a_{N,j-1} & 0 & a_{N,j+1} & \cdots & a_{NN} \end{bmatrix}\right)$$

For further simplification, we define a third elementary matrix operation (in addition to vector addition and scalar multiplication) and note its effect on determinants. We can interchange two columns of a matrix, say columns i and j, with the following sequence of vector additions and scalar multiplications:

1. add column i to column j;
2. multiply column i by -1;
3. add column j to column i;
4. add -1 times column i to column j.

The determinant of the result is -1 times the original determinant, because the second step is the only scalar multiplication.

We can apply the same logic to the row vectors, by applying the same elementary operation to the transpose of a matrix. Interchanging the rows of the matrix is equivalent to interchanging the columns of the transpose of a matrix because the determinant of a matrix equals the determinant of its transpose. Therefore, interchanging the rows or columns of a matrix multiplies the determinant by -1.

Using this rule for interchanging rows or columns, we can reorder the elements in A_{ij} by interchanging $i-1$ rows and $j-1$ columns to obtain

$$A_{ij} = (-1)^{i+j} \det\left(\begin{bmatrix} 1 & 0 & \cdots & 0 & 0 & \cdots & 0 \\ 0 & a_{11} & \cdots & a_{1,j-1} & a_{1,j+1} & \cdots & a_{1N} \\ \vdots & \vdots & & \vdots & \vdots & & \vdots \\ 0 & a_{i-1,1} & \cdots & a_{i-1,j-1} & a_{i-1,j+1} & \cdots & a_{i-1,N} \\ 0 & a_{i+1,1} & \cdots & a_{i+1,j-1} & a_{i+1,j+1} & \cdots & a_{i+1,N} \\ \vdots & \vdots & & \vdots & \vdots & & \vdots \\ 0 & a_{N1} & \cdots & a_{N,j-1} & a_{N,j+1} & \cdots & a_{NN} \end{bmatrix}\right)$$

The determinant on the RHS of this expression is the determinant of the $(N-1)\times(N-1)$ matrix created by deleting the ith row and jth column of $\mathbf{A}$. The orthogonality of the first column vector with all of the remaining column vectors implies that the volume will be the $(N-1)$-dimensional volume of the lower right-hand corner multiplied by 1, the "depth" of the N-dimensional volume. The significance of A_{ij} earns it a special label.

DEFINITION C.23 (MATRIX COFACTOR) *The (i, j)th* cofactor *of the matrix $\mathbf{A}$, denoted A_{ij}, is $(-1)^{i+j}$ times the determinant of the $(N-1)\times(N-1)$ matrix created by deleting the ith row and jth column of $\mathbf{A}$.*

Here is a formal statement summarizing our discussion.

THEOREM C.14 (COFACTOR EXPANSION) *The* cofactor expansion *of the determinant of an $N \times N$ matrix $\mathbf{A}$ is*

$$\det(\mathbf{A}) = \sum_{n=1}^{N} a_{in} A_{in} = \sum_{n=1}^{N} a_{nj} A_{nj}$$

for any row i and column j, where A_{ij} denotes the (i, j)th cofactor *of the matrix $\mathbf{A}$.*

C.6 EIGENVALUES AND EIGENVECTORS

DEFINITION C.24 (CHARACTERISTIC EQUATION) *Given the $N \times N$ real matrix* **A**, *the determinantal equation*

$$\det(\mathbf{A} - \lambda \cdot \mathbf{I}) = 0$$

is called the characteristic equation *of* **A**.

The characteristic equation is a polynomial equation of degree N. If **A** is a real matrix then the coefficients of this polynomial are all real. According to the *fundamental theorem of algebra*, every real polynomial factors into linear and quadratic real polynomials.[4] Therefore, there are N (complex) roots of the characteristic equation and complex roots occur in conjugate pairs. We will denote these roots by $\lambda_1, \ldots, \lambda_N$. According to the cofactor expansion, we can write

$$\det(\mathbf{A} - \lambda \cdot \mathbf{I}) = \prod_{n=1}^{N} (\lambda - \lambda_n)$$

because the coefficient of λ^N must be one. The roots are not necessarily distinct. If we reduce the roots to $K \leq N$ distinct λ_k^* $(k = 1, \ldots, K)$ and denote the multiplicity of the kth distinct root by m_k, then

$$\det(\mathbf{A} - \lambda \cdot \mathbf{I}) = \prod_{k=1}^{K} (\lambda - \lambda_k^*)^{m_k}$$

DEFINITION C.25 (EIGENVALUE) *A root λ of the characteristic equation of* **A** *is an* eigenvalue *of* **A**.

If λ is an eigenvalue of **A**, then $\mathbf{A} - \lambda \cdot \mathbf{I}$ is a singular matrix and there is a nonzero vector $\mathbf{x} \in \mathbb{C}^N$ such that

$$0 = (\mathbf{A} - \lambda \cdot \mathbf{I})\,\mathbf{x} \qquad \Leftrightarrow \qquad \mathbf{A}\mathbf{x} = \lambda \cdot \mathbf{x}$$

DEFINITION C.26 (EIGENVECTOR) *A vector $\mathbf{x} \in \mathbb{C}^N$ for which there is a scalar λ such that $\mathbf{A}\mathbf{x} = \lambda \cdot \mathbf{x}$ is an* eigenvector *of* **A**.

Eigenvalues and eigenvectors are also called *characteristic* or *latent* values and vectors.

---

[4] See Spivak (1967, pp. 317, 455) for a discussion of the fundamental theorem of algebra.

THEOREM C.15 *Let* $\mathbf{x}_k$ *and* λ_k, $k = 1, \ldots, K$, *be eigenvectors and eigenvalues of* $\mathbf{A}$ *such that all the eigenvalues are distinct. Then the eigenvectors* $\{\mathbf{x}_1, \ldots, \mathbf{x}_K\}$ *are linearly independent.*

See Rao (1973, pp. 38–40) for proofs of the following results.

THEOREM C.16 (EIGENVALUE DECOMPOSITION) *If* $\mathbf{A}$ *is a real symmetric* $N \times N$ *matrix, then*

1. *if* $\text{rank}(\mathbf{A}) = K$, *the characteristic equation has zero as a root of multiplicity* $N - K$;
2. *all the eigenvalues are real and the eigenvectors can be chosen to be real;*
3. *the eigenvectors corresponding to distinct eigenvalues are orthogonal; and*
4. *there exists an orthogonal matrix* $\mathbf{X}$ *such that* $\mathbf{X}'\mathbf{A}\mathbf{X} = \mathbf{\Lambda}$ *or* $\mathbf{A} = \mathbf{X}\mathbf{\Lambda}\mathbf{X}'$ *where* $\mathbf{\Lambda}$ *is a diagonal matrix composed of the eigenvalues of* $\mathbf{A}$.

The columns of the matrix $\mathbf{X}$ in this theorem are composed of the eigenvectors of $\mathbf{A}$.

APPENDIX D

Probability

The mathematical concept of probability is a description of uncertain events. The analysis begins with an observable process, called an *experiment*, that has an unpredictable outcome.[1] Rather than a deterministic outcome, all of the potential outcomes of the so-called experiment can be described in advance.

D.1 FUNDAMENTAL CONCEPTS

DEFINITION D.1 (SAMPLE SPACE) *The* sample space *of the experiment is the set S of all distinct, possible outcomes.*

A conventional example of an experiment is the toss of a coin. One can observe the face of the coin that is visible when the coin comes to rest. The sample space is often described as the set {heads, tails}. For clarity, the sample space cannot be {heads, heads, tails}.[2] In this appendix, we will denote a sample space by S.

DEFINITION D.2 (PROBABILITY) *A probability measure* $\Pr\{\cdot\}$ *is a real-valued function of subsets of a sample space S that satisfies certain axioms: if $\mathcal{E}$ denotes a subset of S ($\mathcal{E} \subseteq S$), then*

$$0 \leq \Pr\{\mathcal{E}\} \leq 1 \qquad \text{and} \qquad \Pr\{S\} = 1 \tag{D.1}$$

If $\mathcal{E}_1, \mathcal{E}_2 \subseteq S$ are disjoint subsets ($\mathcal{E}_1 \cap \mathcal{E}_2 = \emptyset$), then

$$\Pr\{\mathcal{E}_1 \cup \mathcal{E}_2\} = \Pr\{\mathcal{E}_1\} + \Pr\{\mathcal{E}_2\} \tag{D.2}$$

[1] This summary of probability theory is written at the level of an introductory undergraduate mathematical statistics book. We recommend Hoel et al. (1971) for a more advanced treatment. If a proof is not given, one can be found in Larsen and Marx (1986) and many similar texts. Simon and Blume (1944) provide basic mathematical material.

[2] Unless, of course, one is writing for such British comedies as Monty Python.

Such subsets $\mathcal{E}_1$ and $\mathcal{E}_2$ are often called *events*. An event "occurs" when one of the elements of the subset is the outcome of the experiment. Intuitively speaking, mathematical probability describes the relative likelihood of events. If the experiment can be repeated, then the limiting relative frequency of an event among a number of repetitions approaching infinity is a probability. But mathematical probability is often applied to unique experiments as well. For example, some of our feelings about the closing state of the San Francisco stock exchange tomorrow can be described with probability.

The coin toss experiment contains rather simple events. Rolling pairs of dice and observing which faces are up when they come to rest offer more possibilities: for example, a crap shooter would be interested in the event that exactly seven spots total are on the faces of the two dice.

D.2 RANDOM VARIABLES

DEFINITION D.3 (RANDOM VARIABLE) *A random variable is a real-valued function $Y(s)$, $s \in S$ such that $\{s \in S \mid Y(s) \leq y\}$ is an event for every $y \in \mathbb{R}$.*

Random variables provide a convenient way to describe the outcomes of experiments. For a coin toss, it is common to assign the real values 1 to {heads} and 0 to {tails}. This assignment is arbitrary, of course. For a dice roll, the number of spots on the top faces is a random variable. In this appendix, we denote random variables by uppercase Roman letters: Y. We denote particular real numbers with lowercase: y.

DEFINITION D.4 (CUMULATIVE DISTRIBUTION FUNCTION) *The* cumulative distribution function *(c.d.f.) of the random variable $Y = Y(s)$, denoted $F_Y(\cdot)$, is the probability*

$$F_Y(y) = \Pr\{Y \leq y\}$$

The c.d.f. is always a nondecreasing function of its argument Y: if $y_1 < y_2$, then (D.1) and (D.2) imply that

$$\begin{aligned}\Pr\{Y \leq y_1\} &\leq \Pr\{Y \leq y_1\} + \Pr\{y_1 < Y \leq y_2\} \\ &= \Pr\{Y \leq y_2\}\end{aligned}$$

The c.d.f. is continuous from above:

$$\begin{aligned}\lim_{\epsilon \to 0^+} \Pr\{Y \leq y_1 + \epsilon\} &\equiv \Pr\{Y \leq y_1 + 0\} \\ &= \Pr\{Y \leq y_1\} + \lim_{\epsilon \to 0^+} \Pr\{y_1 < Y \leq y_1 + \epsilon\} \\ &= \Pr\{Y \leq y_1\}\end{aligned}$$

Two polar types of c.d.f.s are step functions and differentiable functions. *Discrete* random variables have c.d.f.s that are step functions; the image of their sample space can be reduced to a countable set $\mathbb{S}_Y = \{\ldots, y_{-1}, y_0, y_1, \ldots\}$ because

$$\Pr\{\mathbb{S}_Y\} = \sum_{i=-\infty}^{\infty} \Pr\{Y = y_i\} = 1$$

Then

$$F_Y(y) = \sum_{i=-\infty}^{\infty} \mathbf{1}\{y_i \leq y\} \Pr\{Y = y_i\}$$

which makes a discrete jump at each element $y_i \in \mathbb{S}_Y$ with height

$$\Pr\{Y = y_i\} \equiv \Pr\{Y \leq y_i\} - \Pr\{Y \leq y_i - 0\}$$

The elements of $\mathbb{S}_Y$ with strictly positive probability are called *mass points* or *atoms* of the distribution. The set of mass points is called the *support* of the distribution. This is a subset of the range of the function that defines the random variable.

An important special case of a discrete random variable is a constant. The support of a constant has one element.

DEFINITION D.5 (DEGENERATE DISTRIBUTION) *The random variable Y has a* degenerate *distribution if* $\Pr\{Y = y_1\} = 1$, *so that Y is a constant equal to* y_1 *with probability equal to* 1.

Continuous random variables possess continuous c.d.f.s. It is always possible to find *subintervals* $(y_1, y_2]$ (where $y_1 < y_2$) of the range of the random variable that have strictly positive probability, so that

$$\Pr\{Y \in (y_1, y_2]\} = F_Y(y_2) - F_Y(y_1) > 0$$

But, in contrast to discrete random variables, the probability of any single value y_1 is assigned the value zero: because $F_Y(\cdot)$ is continuous,

$$\lim_{\varepsilon \to 0} F_Y(y_1 + \epsilon) \equiv F_Y(y_1 \pm 0) = F_Y(y_1)$$

and

$$\begin{aligned} \Pr\{Y = y_1\} &= \lim_{\varepsilon \to 0^+} \Pr\{|Y - y_1| \leq \varepsilon\} \\ &= F_Y(y_1 + 0) - F_Y(y_1 - 0) \\ &= 0 \end{aligned}$$

The support of the distribution of a continuous random variable is the union of the intervals on which $F_Y(\cdot)$ is strictly increasing. It is possible, then, for subsets of the support of a continuous random variable to have probabilities of zero. The subset $\{y_1\}$ is one example. This example generalizes directly to the observation that any countable subset $\{y_1, y_2, y_3, \ldots\}$ has probability zero.

The relationship between random variables and probability can be subtle and there are two complementary concepts, "with probability zero" and "with probability one," that reflect this subtlety. We have just seen that a continuous random variable equals a particular real number with probability (equal to) zero. As a result, one can make a mathematical distinction between a constant and a random variable equal to that constant with probability (equal to) one. For example, if Y is continuously distributed with the support $\mathbb{R}$ then, for $y_0, y_1 \in \mathbb{R}$,

$$g(Y) = \begin{cases} y_0 & \text{if} \quad Y \neq y_1 \\ y_1 & \text{if} \quad Y = y_1 \end{cases}$$

is a random variable that is equal to y_0 with probability one, but is not constant provided that $y_0 \neq y_1$. One generally views $g(Y)$ and y_0 as observationally equivalent so that no distinction between them is necessary. However, correct mathematical statements require the additional care to note properties that occur only with probability one.

The c.d.f. provides a complete description of a random variable, discrete or continuous. Analytically it is convenient to transform the c.d.f. into a probability function that measures the relative likelihood of different regions of the support directly. For discrete random variables, the probabilities of the mass points serve this purpose.

Definition D.6 (Probability Mass Function) *The* probability mass function *(p.m.f.) of the discrete random variable Y with support $\mathbb{S}_Y = \{\ldots, y_{-1}, y_0, y_1, \ldots\}$ is*

$$f_Y(y) = \begin{cases} \Pr\{Y = y\} & \text{if} \quad y \in \mathbb{S}_Y \\ 0 & \text{if} \quad y \notin \mathbb{S}_Y \end{cases}$$

for all $y \in \mathbb{R}$.

The p.m.f. is nonzero at the points at which the c.d.f. increases.

Definition D.7 (Probability Density Function) *The* probability density function *(p.d.f.) of the continuous random variable Y is the function $f_Y(\cdot)$ that satisfies*

$$F_Y(y) = \int_{-\infty}^{y} f_Y(x)\, dx$$

for all $y \in \mathbb{R}$.

For our purposes, continuous $F_Y(\cdot)$ will be differentiable everywhere so that

$$f_Y(y) = \frac{dF_Y(y)}{dy}$$

Thus, the p.d.f. is zero in regions in which the c.d.f. is constant (not increasing), just like the p.m.f. for discrete random variables. These probability functions are both derived from the c.d.f., and the process is reversible: we can always find the original c.d.f. given either a p.m.f. or a p.d.f. using

$$F_Y(y) = \begin{cases} \sum_{i:y_i \le y} f_Y(y_i) & \text{if } Y \text{ is discrete} \\ \int_{-\infty}^{y} f_Y(x)\,dx & \text{if } Y \text{ is continuous} \end{cases}$$

$$= \begin{cases} \sum_{i=-\infty}^{\infty} \mathbf{1}\{y_i \le y\}\, f_Y(y_i) & \text{if } Y \text{ is discrete} \\ \int_{-\infty}^{\infty} \mathbf{1}\{x \le y\}\, f_Y(x)\,dx & \text{if } Y \text{ is continuous} \end{cases}$$

The p.m.f. and p.d.f. also characterize a random variable completely.

One of the most important features of a random variable is its central tendency. The arithmetic average is a common notion of central tendency in a set of numbers and this familiar concept has its general form in the next definition.

DEFINITION D.8 (EXPECTATION) *The* expectation, *or* expected value, *of a function $g(\cdot)$ of a random variable Y is*

$$\mathrm{E}[g(Y)] = \begin{cases} \sum_{i=-\infty}^{\infty} g(y_i)\, f_Y(y_i) & \textit{if } Y \textit{ is discrete} \\ \int_{-\infty}^{\infty} g(y)\, f_Y(y)\,dy & \textit{if } Y \textit{ is continuous} \end{cases}$$

Probabilities can always be written as expectations:

$$\Pr\{Y \in \mathbb{A}\} = \mathrm{E}[\mathbf{1}\{Y \in \mathbb{A}\}]$$

THEOREM D.1 (LINEARITY OF EXPECTATIONS) *Let $g_1(\cdot)$ and $g_2(\cdot)$ be two real functions and Y be a random variable. Then*

$$\mathrm{E}[g_1(Y) + g_2(Y)] = \mathrm{E}[g_1(Y)] + \mathrm{E}[g_2(Y)]$$

There is a class of expectations called *moments* that summarizes salient features of the p.d.f. of a random variable.

DEFINITION D.9 (MOMENTS) *The* moments *of a random variable Y are the expectations $\mu'_r \equiv \mathrm{E}[Y^r]$ for $r = 0, 1, 2, 3, \ldots$.*[3] *The* centered moments *are the expectations $\mu_r \equiv \mathrm{E}[(Y - \mu'_1)^r]$.*

Moments are useful as descriptors of the shape of p.d.f.s. The term $\mu'_0 \equiv 1$ is defined for convenience. The *first moment* μ'_1 is the ordinary expectation and it is often denoted simply μ. The first moment is a measure of the *center* of the p.d.f. For comparisons across distributions, *higher* moments are standardized. The second centered moment of Y is called the *variance*:

[3] The prime on μ'_r merely distinguishes this symbol from μ_r. This is a common notation and we use it within this appendix. Throughout the rest of this book the prime is notation for *matrix transposition*.

$$\text{Var}[Y] \equiv \mu_2 \equiv \text{E}[(Y - \mu)^2]$$

The variance measures the *spread* of the p.d.f. around the first moment. The variance is often denoted by σ^2 (rather than μ_2) and the square root of the variance, σ, is called the *standard deviation*. Random variables are often *standardized* by the first and second moments:

$$W = \frac{Y - \mu}{\sigma}$$

so that the mean and variance of the transformed random variable W are 0 and 1, respectively, and are unit free. The standardized third moment is the third moment of W and is called the *skewness*:

$$\gamma_1 \equiv \text{E}\left[\left(\frac{Y - \mu}{\sigma}\right)^3\right]$$

Skewness is sensitive to the *asymmetry* of a p.d.f.: if the p.d.f. of Y is symmetric about μ then $\gamma_1 = 0$. Finally, the standardized fourth moment is

$$\gamma_2 \equiv \text{E}\left[\left(\frac{Y - \mu}{\sigma}\right)^4\right] - 3$$

This is a measure of *peakedness* (an admittedly aesthetic notion) and it is called *kurtosis*.

THEOREM D.2 (QUADRATICITY OF VARIANCE) *Let α be a real constant and Y be a random variable. Then*

$$\text{E}[Y^2] = \text{Var}[Y] + (\text{E}[Y])^2$$
$$\text{Var}[\alpha Y] = \alpha^2 \text{Var}[Y]$$

Two other important expectations are the *moment-generating function* and the *characteristic function*.

DEFINITION D.10 (MOMENT-GENERATING FUNCTION) *The* moment-generating function *(m.g.f.) of the random variable Y, denoted $M_Y(\cdot)$, is*

$$M_Y(t) \equiv \text{E}[e^{tY}]$$

This function derives its name from the following property: if the rth derivative of $M_Y(t)$ exists at $t = 0$ then

$$\left.\frac{d^r M_Y(t)}{dt^r}\right|_{t=0} = \text{E}\left[\left.\frac{d^r e^{tY}}{dt^r}\right|_{t=0}\right] = \text{E}[Y^r] \equiv \mu'_r$$

Like moments themselves, the m.g.f. does not always exist for $t \neq 0$. As a result, neither the sequence of moments $\{\mu'_r\}$ nor the m.g.f. generally characterizes distributions. There are sufficient conditions under which they do. Here is one.

THEOREM D.3 (MOMENT-GENERATING FUNCTION) *Let $\{\mu'_r\}$ be a sequence of moments of a distribution. There is only one c.d.f. with this sequence of moments if*

$$\sum_{r=1}^{\infty} \left| \frac{\mu'_r}{r!} \right| t^r$$

is convergent for some $t > 0$.

We will not prove this theorem.[4] We note, however, that we can interpret the condition in terms of the m.g.f. Under this condition, the m.g.f. has Taylor polynomial approximations in a neighborhood of $t = 0$:[5]

$$M_Y(t) = \sum_{r=0}^{R} \frac{\mu'_r}{r!} t^r + o(t^R)$$

For situations in which the m.g.f. does not exist there is an analogous function, called the *characteristic function* (c.f.), that takes its place.

DEFINITION D.11 (CHARACTERISTIC FUNCTION) *The* characteristic function *of the random variable Y, denoted $\varphi_Y(\cdot)$, is*

$$\varphi_Y(t) \equiv \mathrm{E}[e^{itY}] \equiv \mathrm{E}[\cos(tY) + i \sin(tY)]$$

where $i^2 \equiv -1$.

When the m.g.f. exists, $\varphi_Y(t) = M_Y(it)$. Even when the m.g.f. does not exist, the c.f. does and there is a one-to-one correspondence between c.f.s and c.d.f.s.[6] The universal existence of the c.f. rests on the fact that the cosine and sine functions are bounded. We describe this function more completely in Appendix H.

We do not need the p.d.f. of a random variable $g(Y)$ to find its expectation, but in some cases we do need the p.d.f. of such transformations.

THEOREM D.4 (TRANSFORMATION OF VARIABLE) Let Y be a continuous random variable and $g(\cdot)$ be a one-to-one differentiable real function on the support of Y, $\mathbb{S}_Y$. Then the p.d.f. of the random variable $Z = g(Y)$ is

$$f_Z(z) = \begin{cases} \left| \frac{dh(z)}{dz} \right| f_Y[h(z)] & \text{if} \quad z \in \mathbb{S}_Z \\ 0 & \text{if} \quad z \notin \mathbb{S}_Z \end{cases}$$

where $h(\cdot) \equiv g^{-1}(\cdot)$ is the inverse function of $g(\cdot)$ and $\mathbb{S}_Z$ is the image of $\mathbb{S}_Y$ under $g(\cdot)$.

[4] Rao (1973, p. 106) cites original sources. Alternatively, see Feller (1971).

[5] We describe Taylor polynomials in Section D.18 (p. 898).

[6] Rao (1973, p. 99).

The derivative term can be found using implicit differentiation:

$$z = g[h(z)] \Rightarrow 1 = g'[h(z)]\frac{dh(z)}{dz}$$
$$\Leftrightarrow \frac{dh(z)}{dz} = \frac{1}{g'[h(z)]}$$

where

$$g'(x) = \frac{dg(x)}{dx}$$

The multiplication of the original p.d.f. f_Y by the absolute value of $dh(z)/dz$ reflects the change in units from units of Y to units of Z.

If the transformation $g(\cdot)$ is not differentiable at a countable set of points $\{y_1, y_2, y_3, \ldots\}$ then, because that set has probability zero, the transformation-of-variable formula still applies everywhere else in the support of Y.

Moments do not always exist. An alternative set of descriptors of a distribution is *quantiles.*

DEFINITION D.12 (QUANTILES) *The qth* quantile ($0 \le q \le 1$) *of the c.d.f.* $F_Y(\cdot)$ *is the set* $\{y \mid q = F_Y(y)\}$.

If F_Y is one to one, then $F_Y^{-1}(q)$ is the unique qth quantile. Quantiles have an attractive invariance property. If one takes a monotonic transformation $h(Y)$ of a random variable Y, then the image of the qth quantile of Y is the qth quantile of $h(Y)$. Moments do not have this property: in general, $\mathrm{E}[h(Y)] \ne h(\mathrm{E}[Y])$. The general exception occurs when $h(\cdot)$ is a linear transformation. However, if $h(\cdot)$ is convex, there is a useful relationship between $\mathrm{E}[h(Y)]$ and $h(\mathrm{E}[Y])$.

LEMMA D.1 (JENSEN'S INEQUALITY) *If* $h(\cdot)$ *is a convex function and* $\mathrm{E}[Y]$ *exists, then*

$$h(\mathrm{E}[Y]) \le \mathrm{E}[h(Y)]$$

If $h(\cdot)$ *is strictly convex anywhere in* $\mathbb{S}_Y$, *then the inequality is strict unless* Y *equals a constant with probability one.*

One example of Jensen's inequality is

$$\mathrm{Var}[Y] = \mathrm{E}[Y^2] - (\mathrm{E}[Y])^2 \ge 0$$

because the quadratic function is convex.[7] Here is another:

[7] The proof of Jensen's inequality is on p. 878.

LEMMA D.2 (INFORMATION THEORY INEQUALITY) *Let $F_Y(y)$ and $F_Z(z)$ be two c.d.f.s and let $f_Y(y)$ and $f_Z(z)$ be their respective p.f.s. Then*

$$\mathrm{E}\left[\log\left(\frac{f_Y(Y)}{f_Z(Y)}\right)\right] = \int_{\mathbb{S}_Y} \log\left(\frac{f_Y(y)}{f_Z(y)}\right) dF_Y(y) \geq 0$$

where $\mathbb{S}_Y$ is the support of $f_Y(y)$. The inequality is strict if $\Pr\{f_Y(Y) \neq f_Z(Y)\} > 0$.

We will review the importance of this inequality with maximum likelihood estimation. In words, the information theory inequality states that the expectation of the logarithm of a p.f. evaluated at a random variable Y is highest when the p.f. is the p.f. of Y, $f_Y(y)$.

We state one final inequality, which bounds the probability of a random variable falling outside a closed interval centered on the expectation.

LEMMA D.3 (CHEBYCHEV'S INEQUALITY) *For any random variable Y with finite second moment,*

$$\Pr\{|Y - b| > a\} \leq \frac{\mathrm{E}[(Y - b)^2]}{a^2}$$

for any b and any $a > 0$. The proof of this lemma appears on *p. 878.*

D.2.1 Mathematical Notes

The two forms for the expectation given in Definition D.8, one for discrete and one for continuous random variables, have unified expression in the *Stieltjes integral.*

DEFINITION D.13 (STIELTJES INTEGRAL) *The* Stieltjes integral *of $g(y)$ with respect to the c.d.f. $F_Y(y)$ is the limit, if it exists,*

$$\int_{-\infty}^{\infty} g(y)\, dF_Y(y) \equiv \lim_{\epsilon \to 0^+} \sum_n g(\bar{y}_n) \left[F_Y(y_n) - F_Y(y_{n-1})\right] \tag{D.3}$$

where

$$\epsilon \equiv \sup_n y_n - y_{n-1}$$
$$y_{n-1} \leq \bar{y}_n \leq y_n \tag{D.4}$$

$\{y_n;\ n = \ldots, -1, 0, 1, \ldots\}$ *is any sequence of real numbers such that*

$$y_{n-1} < y_n$$
$$\lim_{n\to\infty} F_Y(y_{-n}) = 0 \tag{D.5}$$
$$\lim_{n\to\infty} F_Y(y_n) = 1$$

and

$$g(\bar{y}_n)\left[F_Y(y_n) - F_Y(y_{n-1})\right] = 0$$

whenever $F_Y(y_n) - F_Y(y_{n-1}) = 0$, *even if* $|g(\bar{y}_n)| = \infty$.

Rather than the p.m.f. or the p.d.f., the c.d.f. of Y appears in the Stieltjes integral. This is a generalization of the discrete sum and the Riemann integral for both discrete and continuous random variables. For discrete random variables, this limit takes the familiar form of the weighted sum given in the definition, because

$$f_Y(y) = [F_Y(y) - F_Y(y-0)]$$

where

$$F_Y(y-0) \equiv \lim_{\epsilon \to 0^+} F_Y(y-\epsilon)$$

For continuous random variables with differentiable c.d.f.s,

$$F_Y(y_i) - F_Y(y_{i-1}) \approx f_Y(\bar{y}_i)\,\epsilon$$

where $f_Y(\cdot)$ is the derivative of $F_Y(\cdot)$. Then the integral takes the more familiar Riemann form

$$\lim_{\varepsilon \to 0^+} \sum g(\bar{y}_i)\, f_Y(\bar{y}_i)\,\epsilon = \int_{-\infty}^{\infty} g(y)\, f_Y(y)\, dy$$

In either case, discrete or continuous, we may write

$$\mathrm{E}[g(Y)] = \int_{-\infty}^{\infty} g(y)\, dF_Y(y)$$

Although unfamiliar to many students, the Stieltjes integral involves familiar concepts and appears regularly in mathematical probability so that we introduce it here.

The Stieltjes integral circumvents the p.f., which is an awkward concept for *mixed distributions*, which are distributions with discrete and continuous components. We identify such distributions by their c.d.f.s, which are differentiable everywhere except at a countable set of points. In the situations we consider, we can always decompose a c.d.f. $F_Y(y)$ into $\alpha F_{Y_1}(y) + (1-\alpha)\, F_{Y_2}(y)$ where $0 \leq \alpha \leq 1$, $F_{Y_1}(y)$ is the c.d.f. of a discrete random variable (a step function) and $F_{Y_2}(y)$ is the c.d.f. of a continuous random variable (a differentiable function). In these cases, we define the p.f. to be the function

$$f_Y(y) = \begin{cases} \alpha\left[F_{Y_1}(y) - F_{Y_1}(y-0)\right] & \text{if} \quad F_{Y_1}(y) > F_{Y_1}(y-0) \\ (1-\alpha)\; f_{Y_2}(y) & \text{if} \quad F_{Y_1}(y) = F_{Y_1}(y-0) \end{cases}$$

Taking the points of discontinuity to be $\{y_1, y_2, \ldots\}$, the expectation with respect to the p.f. is defined as

$$\begin{aligned} \mathrm{E}[g(y)] &= \alpha \sum_{n=1}^{\infty} g(y_n)\left[F_{Y_1}(y_n) - F_{Y_1}(y_n - 0)\right] + (1-\alpha) \int g(y)\, f_{Y_2}(y)\, dy \\ &= \alpha \int g(y)\, dF_{Y_1}(y) + (1-\alpha) \int g(y)\, dF_{Y_2}(y) \\ &= \int g(y) dF_Y(y) \end{aligned}$$

so that an expectation with respect to the p.f. agrees with the Stieltjes integral.

The mixed distribution is called a *mixture* because the distribution is generated by the following experiment: flip a coin with probability α of "heads" and if "heads" then set Y to a draw of Y_1. Otherwise, set Y to a draw of Y_2.

Now we will give a proof of Jensen's inequality. This inequality is very similar to the definition of a convex function. Understanding the latter is the kernel of understanding the inequality. The definition of convex function states:

DEFINITION D.14 (CONVEX/CONCAVE FUNCTION) *A real-valued function $h(\cdot)$ defined on a convex subset $\mathbb{S}$ of $\mathbb{R}^K$ is* convex *if, for all y_1, y_2 in $\mathbb{S}$, and for all α, $0 < \alpha < 1$,*

$$h(\alpha y_1 + (1-\alpha)y_2) \le \alpha h(y_1) + (1-\alpha)\,h(y_2)$$

If the inequality is strict for all such y_1, y_2, and α then $h(\cdot)$ is strictly convex. *The function $h(\cdot)$ is* concave *if for all y_1, y_2 in $\mathbb{S}$, and for all α, $0 < \alpha < 1$,*

$$h(\alpha y_1 + (1-\alpha)y_2) \ge \alpha h(y_1) + (1-\alpha)\,h(y_2)$$

and strictly concave *if the inequality is strict.*

The inequality in this definition looks like an example of Jensen's inequality, the case of a binomial random variable Y with support $\{y_1, y_2\}$ and $\Pr\{Y = y_1\} = \alpha$. But it holds for *all* y_1, y_2. As a result, we can prove

LEMMA D.4 *If the real-valued function $h(\cdot)$ is* convex *on its domain $\mathbb{S}$ then at every point y_0 in $\mathbb{S}$ there is a b such that*

$$h(y_0) + b(y - y_0) \le h(y)$$

for every y in the domain of $h(\cdot)$. If $h(\cdot)$ is strictly convex, then the inequality is strict except at $y = y_0$.

Proof. Consider $y_0 < y_1 < y_2$. If we set α so that $y_1 = \alpha y_0 + (1-\alpha)y_2$, then convexity implies that $h(y_1) \le \alpha h(y_0) + (1-\alpha)\,h(y_2)$ so that

$$\frac{h(y_1) - h(y_0)}{y_1 - y_0} \le \frac{h(y_2) - h(y_0)}{y_2 - y_0}$$

Therefore, the slope of a chord from $(y_0, h(y_0))$ to $(y, h(y))$,

$$g(y) = \frac{h(y) - h(y_0)}{y - y_0} \tag{D.6}$$

is decreasing as y approaches y_0 from above. Similarly, $g(y)$ is increasing as y approaches y_0 from below.

Furthermore, consider $y_0 - \epsilon < y_0 < y_0 + \epsilon$ for $\epsilon > 0$. Then convexity implies that $h(y_0) \le [h(y_0 - \epsilon) + h(y_0 + \epsilon)]/2$ so that

$$\frac{h(y_0) - h(y_0 - \epsilon)}{\epsilon} \leq \frac{h(y_0 + \epsilon) - h(y_0)}{\epsilon} \tag{D.7}$$

Therefore, $g(y_0 - \epsilon) \leq g(y_0 + \epsilon)$ and there is a b such that

$$\lim_{y \uparrow y_0} g(y) \leq b \leq \lim_{y \downarrow y_0} g(y) \tag{D.8}$$

Therefore, combining (D.6) and (D.8),

$$h(y_0) + b(y - y_0) \leq h(y) \tag{D.9}$$

for all y. If $h(\cdot)$ is strictly convex, then (D.7) is a strict inequality so that (D.9) is also for all $y \neq y_0$. □

We will use this lemma to prove Jensen's inequality.

Proof of Lemma D.1. Applying Lemma D.4, let $y_0 = \mathrm{E}[Y]$ and b be any real number such that

$$h(\mathrm{E}[Y]) + b(Y - \mathrm{E}[Y]) \leq h(Y)$$

Taking expectations of both sides gives Jensen's inequality. If $h(\cdot)$ is strictly convex, then Jensen's inequality is strict unless $Y = \mathrm{E}[Y]$ (or Y is constant) with probability one. □

The information theory inequality is such an important example of Jensen's inequality that we use the proof of the former to illustrate the latter.

Proof of Lemma D.2. See the proof of the expected log-likelihood inequality (Lemma 14.1, p. 290). □

Finally, we prove Chebychev's inequality.

Proof of Lemma D.3. Let

$$\mathbf{A} \equiv \{y \mid |Y - b| > a\} = \{y \mid (Y - b)^2 > a^2\}$$

and write

$$\begin{aligned} \mathrm{E}[(Y-b)^2] &= \int (y-b)^2 \, dF_Y(y) \\ &= \int_{\mathbf{A}} (y-b)^2 \, dF_Y(y) + \int_{\mathbf{A}^c} (y-b)^2 \, dF_Y(y) \end{aligned}$$

Dropping the second term and replacing $(y - b)^2$ with a^2, we obtain

$$\mathrm{E}[(Y-b)^2] \geq a^2 \int_{\mathbf{A}} dF_Y(y) = a^2 \Pr\{Y \in \mathbf{A}\}$$

which is the result, after dividing both sides by a^2. □

D.3 JOINT AND CONDITIONAL PROBABILITY

We often consider several events that may occur at the same time. We view the events as outcomes of a common experiment and specify that $\mathcal{E}_1$ and $\mathcal{E}_2$ both occur when common elements of the sample space are realized. Formally,

$$\Pr\{\mathcal{E}_1 \text{ and } \mathcal{E}_2\} = \Pr\{\mathcal{E}_1 \cap \mathcal{E}_2\}$$

Such probability is usually called *joint* probability, as in the joint probability of $\mathcal{E}_1$ and $\mathcal{E}_2$. An important joint probability is the *joint c.d.f.* of a finite set of random variables $\{Y_1, \ldots, Y_N\}$:

$$F_Y(y_1, \ldots, y_N) = \Pr\{Y_1 \leq y_1, \ldots, Y_N \leq y_N\}$$

There is a corresponding *joint p.m.f.* if Y is discrete,

$$f_Y(y) = \Pr\{Y_1 = y_1, \ldots, Y_N = y_N\}$$

or *joint p.d.f.* if Y is continuous,

$$f_Y(y) = \frac{\partial^N F_Y(y)}{\partial y_1 \cdots \partial y_N}$$

For a subset of the random variables, $Z = \{Y_1, \ldots, Y_K\}$, $K < N$, we will speak of the *marginal c.d.f.*

$$F_Z(z) = \Pr\{Y_1 \leq y_1, \ldots, Y_K \leq y_K\} = F_Y(y_1, \ldots, y_K, \infty, \ldots, \infty)$$

and the corresponding *marginal p.m.f.* or *marginal p.d.f.* $f_Z(z)$. We discuss mixed cases in Chapter 28.

DEFINITION D.15 (CONDITIONAL PROBABILITY) *The* conditional probability *of* $\mathcal{E}_1$ *given the occurrence of* $\mathcal{E}_2$, *denoted* $\Pr\{\mathcal{E}_1 \mid \mathcal{E}_2\}$, *is*

$$\Pr\{\mathcal{E}_1 \mid \mathcal{E}_2\} = \frac{\Pr\{\mathcal{E}_1 \cap \mathcal{E}_2\}}{\Pr\{\mathcal{E}_2\}}$$

This definition yields a probability assignment that satisfies the axioms of Definition D.2: $\Pr\{\mathcal{E}_1 \mid \mathcal{E}_2\}$ is clearly positive and

$$\begin{aligned}\Pr\{\mathcal{E}_1 \mid \mathcal{E}_2\} + \Pr\{\mathcal{E}_1^c \mid \mathcal{E}_2\} &= \frac{\Pr\{\mathcal{E}_1 \cap \mathcal{E}_2\} + \Pr\{\mathcal{E}_1^c \cap \mathcal{E}_2\}}{\Pr\{\mathcal{E}_2\}} \\ &= \frac{\Pr\{(\mathcal{E}_1 \cap \mathcal{E}_2) \cup (\mathcal{E}_1^c \cap \mathcal{E}_2)\}}{\Pr\{\mathcal{E}_2\}} \\ &= 1\end{aligned}$$

where we denote the complement of the subset $\mathcal{E}_1$ by $\mathcal{E}_1^c$.

We distinguish such probabilities as $\Pr\{\mathcal{E}_2\}$ from conditional probabilities by calling the former *marginal* probabilities. The fundamental relationship between conditional and marginal probabilities is described by Bayes theorem.

THEOREM D.5 (BAYES) *Let $\{\mathcal{E}_i, i = 1, 2, \ldots\}$ be a countable collection of disjoint events such that $\bigcup_i \mathcal{E}_i = S$. Then*

$$\Pr\{\mathcal{E}_i \mid \mathcal{A}\} = \frac{\Pr\{\mathcal{A} \mid \mathcal{E}_i\} \Pr\{\mathcal{E}_i\}}{\sum_j \Pr\{\mathcal{A} \mid \mathcal{E}_j\} \Pr\{\mathcal{E}_j\}} = \frac{\Pr\{\mathcal{A} \mid \mathcal{E}_i\} \Pr\{\mathcal{E}_i\}}{\Pr\{\mathcal{A}\}}$$

for any $\mathcal{A} \subseteq S$ such that $\Pr\{\mathcal{A}\} > 0$.

If conditional probabilities for one random variable given another do not actually depend on the latter, then we have a special situation.

DEFINITION D.16 (INDEPENDENCE) *Two events $\mathcal{E}_1$ and $\mathcal{E}_2$ are* independent *if*

$$\Pr\{\mathcal{E}_1 \cap \mathcal{E}_2\} = \Pr\{\mathcal{E}_1\} \Pr\{\mathcal{E}_2\}$$

Definition D.15 yields an equivalent condition for independence when $\Pr\{\mathcal{E}_2\} > 0$: $\Pr\{\mathcal{E}_1 \mid \mathcal{E}_2\} = \Pr\{\mathcal{E}_1\}$.

Using these definitions, we can construct conditional c.d.f.s, p.m.f.s, and p.d.f.s for random variables. Let the joint c.d.f. be denoted by

$$F_{ZY}(z, y) = \Pr\{Z \le z,\ Y \le y\}$$

For all random variables Z and Y, discrete or continuous,

$$\begin{aligned} \Pr\{Z \le z \mid y_a < Y \le y_b\} &= \frac{\Pr\{Z \le z,\ y_a < Y \le y_b\}}{\Pr\{y_a < Y \le y_b\}} \\ &= \frac{F_{ZY}(z, y_b) - F_{ZY}(z, y_a)}{F_Y(y_b) - F_Y(y_a)} \end{aligned}$$

is well defined, provided $F_Y(y_b) - F_Y(y_a) > 0$. The conditional c.d.f. for two discrete random variables is a special case, where $y_a = y_b = y$ and $\Pr\{Y = y\} > 0$. For a countable support $\mathbb{S}_{ZY} = \{(z_i, y_i); i = 1, 2, \ldots\}$, the conditional p.m.f. of Z given that $Y = y$ is

$$\Pr\{Z = z \mid Y = y\} = \frac{\Pr\{Z = z,\ Y = y\}}{\Pr\{Y = y\}}$$

For continuous Z and Y, we find the conditional c.d.f. as

$$\begin{aligned} F_{Z|Y}(z \mid y) &= \Pr\{Z \le z \mid Y = y\} \\ &= \lim_{\varepsilon \to 0^+} \frac{F_{ZY}(z, y) - F_{ZY}(z, y - \varepsilon)}{F_Y(y) - F_Y(y - \varepsilon)} \\ &= \frac{\partial F(z, y)/\partial y}{f_Y(y)} \end{aligned}$$

provided that $f_Y(y) > 0$. Therefore, the conditional p.d.f. is

$$f_{Z|Y}(z \mid y) = \frac{\partial F_{Z|Y}(z \mid y)}{\partial z} = \frac{f_{ZY}(z, y)}{f_Y(y)}$$

which has a form analogous to the discrete conditional p.m.f.

It is possible for a conditional distribution to be degenerate.

DEFINITION D.17 (SINGULAR DISTRIBUTION) *Let Y and Z be jointly distributed random variables. If the conditional distribution of Y given Z is degenerate, then their joint distribution is called* singular.

Expectations taken with respect to conditional distributions are called *conditional expectations*. Such expectations have a notation similar to conditional distributions:

$$\mathrm{E}[Z \mid y] \equiv \int_{-\infty}^{\infty} z \, dF_{Z|Y}(z \mid y)$$

Note that the marginal expectation of a random variable can generally be written as an expectation of a conditional expectation. That is,

$$\begin{aligned} \mathrm{E}[Z] &= \int_{-\infty}^{\infty} \int_{-\infty}^{\infty} z \, dF_{ZY}(z, y) \\ &= \int_{-\infty}^{\infty} \int_{-\infty}^{\infty} z \, dF_{Z|Y}(z \mid y) \, dF_Y(y) \\ &= \int_{-\infty}^{\infty} \mathrm{E}[Z \mid y] \, dF_Y(y) \\ &= \mathrm{E}\big[\mathrm{E}[Z \mid Y]\big] \end{aligned}$$

This equality is called *the law of iterated expectations*. Such expectations are a useful analytical tool.

Another important second moment, called *covariance*, appears in the analysis of jointly distributed random variables. The covariance between Z and Y is

$$\mathrm{Cov}[Z, Y] \equiv \mathrm{E}[(Z - \mu_Z)(Y - \mu_Y)]$$

where $\mu_Z \equiv \mathrm{E}[Z]$ and $\mu_Y \equiv \mathrm{E}[Y]$. The symbol σ_{ZY} denotes this moment. Often, the covariance is standardized by the standard deviations of Z and Y to obtain a unit-free measure of association called the *correlation*:

$$\rho_{ZY} \equiv \frac{\sigma_{ZY}}{\sigma_Z \sigma_Y}$$

where $\sigma_Z \equiv \sqrt{\mathrm{Var}[Z]}$ and $\sigma_Y \equiv \sqrt{\mathrm{Var}[Y]}$.

Here is the generalization of the univariate transformation of variables theorem (Theorem D.4) to the multivariate case. Note that the matrix of partial derivatives $\partial h(z)/\partial z'$ is defined in Appendix G.

Theorem D.6 (Transformation of Variables) *Let $Y = (Y_1, \ldots, Y_N)$ be an N-tuple of real continuous random variables with support $\mathbb{S}_Y \subseteq \mathbb{R}^N$ and let $g(\cdot) = [g_1(\cdot), \ldots, g_N(\cdot)]$ be a one-to-one differentiable transformation from $\mathbb{S}_Y$ to $\mathbb{S}_Z \subseteq \mathbb{R}^N$. Then the p.d.f. of the random variable $Z = g(Y)$ is*

$$f_Z(z) = \begin{cases} \left|\det\left[\frac{\partial h(z)}{\partial z'}\right]\right| f_Y[h(z)], & \text{if } z \in \mathbb{S}_Z \\ 0, & \text{if } z \notin \mathbb{S}_Z \end{cases}$$

where $h(\cdot) \equiv g^{-1}(\cdot)$ is the inverse function of $g(\cdot)$.

An important application of transformation of variables is the derivation of the distribution of the sum of two independent random variables. This plays a role in deriving special distributions as well as the distribution of the average of a random sample.

Theorem D.7 (Convolution) *Let Z and Y be independent random variables. Then the c.d.f. of $X = Z + Y$ is*

$$F_X(x) = \int_{-\infty}^{\infty} F_Y(x - z)\, dF_Z(z)$$

and the p.d.f. is

$$f_X(x) = \begin{cases} \sum_z f_Y(x - z)\, f_Z(z), & \text{if } Z, Y \text{ are discrete} \\ \int_{-\infty}^{\infty} f_Y(x - z)\, f_Z(z)\, dz, & \text{if } Z, Y \text{ are continuous} \end{cases}$$

The proof of this theorem appears on p. 884.

We close this section on multivariate random variables with an extension of the definition of c.f.s to that case.

Definition D.18 (Multivariate Characteristic Function) *The c.f. of a K-variate random vector Y is*

$$\varphi_Y(\mathbf{t}) \equiv \mathrm{E}\left[\exp\left(i \sum_{k=1}^{K} t_k Y_k\right)\right]$$

Under this definition the c.f. retains all of its univariate properties in multivariate form. In particular, the c.f. is one to one with the c.d.f. and we can generate the finite moments of the distribution with the partial derivatives

$$\mathrm{E}[Y_1^{r_1} Y_2^{r_2} \cdots Y_K^{r_K}] = i^{-R} \left.\frac{\partial^R \varphi_Y(\mathbf{t})}{\partial t_1^{r_1} \partial t_2^{r_2} \cdots \partial t_K^{r_K}}\right|_{t=0}$$

where $R = \sum_{k=1}^{K} r_k$.

D.3.1 Mathematical Notes

TRANSFORMATION OF VARIABLES

The multivariate version of Theorem D.4 replaces a univariate derivative term with a term called the *Jacobian*, the determinant of the matrix of cross-partial derivatives

$$\frac{\partial h(z)}{\partial z} \equiv \begin{bmatrix} \frac{\partial h_1}{\partial z_1} & \frac{\partial h_1}{\partial z_2} & \cdots & \frac{\partial h_1}{\partial z_N} \\ \frac{\partial h_2}{\partial z_1} & \frac{\partial h_2}{\partial z_2} & \cdots & \frac{\partial h_2}{\partial z_N} \\ \vdots & \vdots & \ddots & \vdots \\ \frac{\partial h_N}{\partial z_1} & \frac{\partial h_N}{\partial z_2} & \cdots & \frac{\partial h_N}{\partial z_N} \end{bmatrix}$$

This determinant also reflects the change of units going from Y to Z and we will use the interpretation of determinants in terms of volume to explain this informally.

The p.d.f. $f_Y(y)$ is the probability of an infinitesimal N-dimensional cube of Y's support. The Riemann integral of the p.d.f. is effectively adding up the probability per cube at a point y, the term $f_Y(y)$, times the volume of each cube, represented by $dy \equiv dy_1 \cdots dy_N$. We will now show that if we translate this volume into the units of Z, then we add up the probability at a point z, now written as $f_Y[h(z)]$, times the volume of the infinitesimal Y-cube expressed in units of an infinitesimal Z-cube, written as $|\partial h(z)/\partial z|$.

In Section C.5, we described the absolute value of the determinant of an $N \times N$ matrix as the volume of a parallelogram constructed from a linear transformation of a unit cube. We can use that interpretation to find the volume of the Y-cube in units of the Z-cube. If $\mathbf{Y} = \mathbf{AZ}$ then Lemma C.2 (p. 859) states that

$$\mathrm{Vol}(\mathbf{Y}) = \mathrm{Vol}(\mathbf{A})\,\mathrm{Vol}(\mathbf{Z}) = |\det \mathbf{A}|\,\mathrm{Vol}(\mathbf{Z})$$

so that

$$dy_1 \cdots dy_N = |\det \mathbf{A}|\; dz_1 \cdots dz_N.$$

The Riemann integral can use linear approximations for such nonlinear transformations as $Y = h(Z)$. The mean value theorem implies that local to any z where $h(z)$ is continuously differentiable, small changes in Z transform linearly into small changes in Y, as in

$$\begin{bmatrix} dy_1 \\ \vdots \\ dy_N \end{bmatrix} = \frac{\partial h(z)}{\partial z'} \begin{bmatrix} dz_1 \\ \vdots \\ dz_N \end{bmatrix}$$

Therefore,

$$dy_1 \cdots dy_N = \left|\det\left(\frac{\partial h(z)}{\partial z}\right)\right| dz_1 \cdots dz_N$$

on the infinitesimally small scale and

$$\begin{aligned} \Pr\{Y \in h(\mathbb{A})\} &= \int_{h(\mathbf{A})} f_Y(y)\,dy \\ &= \int_{\mathbb{A}} \left|\det\left(\frac{\partial h(z)}{\partial z}\right)\right| f_Y[h(z)]\,dz \\ &= \Pr\{Z \in \mathbb{A}\} \end{aligned}$$

Theorem D.6 follows.

The proof of the convolution theorem illustrates the power of iterated expectations. Note also how the p.d.f. derives from the c.d.f. once again.

Proof of Theorem D.7. Beginning with the c.d.f.,

$$\begin{aligned} F_X(x) &= \Pr\{Z + Y \leq x\} = \mathrm{E}\big[\mathrm{E}[\mathbf{1}\{Z + Y \leq x\} \mid Z]\big] \\ &= \mathrm{E}\big[\mathrm{E}[\mathbf{1}\{Y \leq x - Z\} \mid Z]\big] = \mathrm{E}[\Pr\{Y \leq x - Z \mid Z\}] \\ &= \int_{-\infty}^{\infty} F_Y(x - z)\, dF_Z(z) \end{aligned}$$

For the discrete Z and Y,

$$\int_{-\infty}^{\infty} F_Y(x - z)\, dF_Z(z) = \sum_z \sum_{y \leq x - z} f_Y(y)\, f_Z(z) \quad \Rightarrow$$

$$f_X(x) = \sum_z f_Y(x - z)\, f_Z(z)$$

and for continuous Z and Y,

$$\int_{-\infty}^{\infty} F_Y(x - z)\, dF_Z(z) = \int_{-\infty}^{\infty} F_Y(x - z)\, f_Z(z)\, dz \quad \Rightarrow$$

$$\begin{aligned} f_X(x) &= \frac{d}{dx} \int_{-\infty}^{\infty} F_Y(x - z)\, f_Z(z)\, dz \\ &= \int_{-\infty}^{\infty} \frac{d}{dx} F_Y(x - z)\, f_Z(z)\, dz \\ &= \int_{-\infty}^{\infty} f_Y(x - z)\, f_Z(z)\, dz \end{aligned}$$

□

D.4 SPECIAL DISTRIBUTIONS

There are several distributions that are relatively tractable and arise commonly. We briefly describe univariate discrete distributions first, followed by univariate continuous distributions. The simplest nondegenerate distribution of all is the *Bernoulli* distribution.

DEFINITION D.19 (BERNOULLI DISTRIBUTION) *If the discrete random variable Y has the p.m.f.*

$$f_Y(y; \theta) = \begin{cases} \theta & \text{if } \ y = 1 \\ 1 - \theta & \text{if } \ y = 0 \\ 0 & \text{if } \ \text{otherwise} \end{cases}$$

where $0 \leq \theta \leq 1$, then Y has the Bernoulli *distribution.*

The outcome $Y = 1$ is euphemistically called a "success" in this setting. The θ parameter of the Bernoulli distribution is simply $\Pr\{Y = 1\}$, or the probability of a success. The discrete *binomial* distribution is closely related to the Bernoulli.

DEFINITION D.20 (BINOMIAL DISTRIBUTION) *If the discrete random variable Y has the p.m.f.*

$$f_Y(y;\theta) = \begin{cases} \binom{N}{y}\theta^y(1-\theta)^{N-y} & \text{if } y \in \{0, 1, \ldots, N\} \\ 0 & \text{if } y \notin \{0, 1, \ldots, N\} \end{cases}$$

where $0 \le \theta \le 1$ *and* $N \in \mathbb{N}$, *then Y has the* binomial *distribution.*

The binomial distribution appears most frequently as the distribution of the number of "successes" among N independent Bernoulli random variables. One can generate additional univariate discrete distributions from such repeated sampling of Bernoulli random variables. The *geometric* distribution is one.

DEFINITION D.21 (GEOMETRIC DISTRIBUTION) *If the discrete random variable Y has the p.m.f.*

$$f_Y(y;\theta) = \begin{cases} \theta(1-\theta)^y & \text{if } y \in \mathbb{N} \\ 0 & \text{if } y \notin \mathbb{N} \end{cases}$$

where $0 \le \theta \le 1$, *then Y has the* geometric *distribution.*

The geometric distribution is the distribution of the number of Bernoulli experiments that occurs before a success is realized. The *negative binomial* distribution generalizes this to the number of experiments that occurs before the Mth success:

DEFINITION D.22 (NEGATIVE BINOMIAL DISTRIBUTION) *If the discrete random variable Y has the p.m.f.*

$$f_Y(y;\theta) = \begin{cases} \binom{y-1}{M-1}\theta^M(1-\theta)^{y-M} & \text{if } y \ge M,\ y \in \mathbb{N} \\ 0 & \text{if } y \notin \mathbb{N} \end{cases}$$

where $0 \le \theta \le 1$, *then Y has the* negative binomial *distribution.*

The negative binomial distribution and the geometric distribution are often called *waiting-time* distributions. The *Poisson* distribution is the limit of the binomial distribution as $N \to \infty$ when θ is replaced with θ/N.

DEFINITION D.23 (POISSON DISTRIBUTION) *If the discrete random variable Y has the p.m.f.*

$$f_Y(y;\theta) = \begin{cases} \frac{\theta^y e^{-\theta}}{y!} & \textit{if} \quad y \in \mathbb{N} \\ 0 & \textit{if} \quad y \notin \mathbb{N} \end{cases}$$

where $0 < \theta$, *then Y has the* Poisson *distribution.*

The *multinomial* distribution is a multivariate generalization of the binomial.

DEFINITION D.24 (MULTINOMIAL DISTRIBUTION) *If the discrete random variable* $Y = (Y_1, \ldots, Y_J)$ *has the p.m.f.*

$$f_Y(y) = \begin{cases} \frac{N!}{\prod_{j=1}^{J} y_j!} \prod_{j=1}^{J} \theta_j^{y_j} & \textit{if} \quad y_j \in \{0, 1, \ldots, N\}, \ \sum_{j=1}^{J} y_j = N \\ 0 & \textit{if} \quad \textit{otherwise} \end{cases}$$

where $0 \leq \theta_j \leq 1$, $\sum_{j=1}^{J} \theta_j = 1$, *then Y has the* multinomial *distribution.*

The multinomial distribution is the distribution of the number of occurrences of each of J possible outcomes among N independent experiments, where the probability of the jth outcome is identically θ_j in each experiment.

Perhaps the simplest continuous distribution is the uniform.

DEFINITION D.25 (UNIFORM DISTRIBUTION) *If the continuous random variable Y has the p.d.f.*

$$f_Y(y) = \begin{cases} 1 & \textit{if} \quad y \in [0, 1] \\ 0 & \textit{if} \quad y \notin [0, 1] \end{cases}$$

then Y has the standard uniform *distribution.*

Almost as simple is the *exponential* distribution.

DEFINITION D.26 (EXPONENTIAL DISTRIBUTION) *If the continuous random variable Y has the p.d.f.*

$$f_Y(y) = \begin{cases} e^{-y} & \textit{if} \quad y \geq 0 \\ 0 & \textit{if} \quad y < 0 \end{cases}$$

then Y has the standard exponential *distribution.*

One can generate an exponential random variable by taking the logarithm of a uniform random variable. The *normal* distribution may be the most heavily studied continuous distribution.

DEFINITION D.27 (NORMAL DISTRIBUTION) *If the continuous random variable Y has the p.d.f.*

$$f_Y(y) = \frac{1}{\sqrt{2\pi}} e^{-\frac{1}{2}y^2} \equiv \phi(y) \tag{D.10}$$

then Y has the standard normal *distribution. As indicated, this p.d.f. will be denoted $\phi(y)$ and the corresponding c.d.f. by $\Phi(y)$.*

One can work out the m.g.f. or characteristic function for all of these special distributions. The m.g.f. and characteristic function of the normal play a special role in asymptotic distribution theory (below).

THEOREM D.8 (NORMAL DISTRIBUTION) *If the random variable Y has the standard normal distribution, then*

$$M_Y(t) = \exp\left(\frac{1}{2}t^2\right)$$

$$\varphi_Y(t) = M_Y(it) = \exp\left(-\frac{1}{2}t^2\right)$$

and the first four centered moments of Y are $\mu = 0$, $\sigma^2 = 1$, $\mu_3 = 0$, and $\mu_4 = 3$. The skewness and kurtosis are both zero. In general, $\mu_{2r} = \prod_{n=1}^{r} (2n-1)$ and $\mu_{2r-1} = 0$ $(r = 1, 2, 3, \ldots)$.

Note that kurtosis measures the peakedness of p.d.f.s relative to the normal p.d.f., for which $\mu_4 = 3$. By considering the transformation $Z = \mu + \sigma Y$, one finds the p.d.f. for the normal distribution as it is defined for unrestricted μ and σ^2:

$$f_Z(z; \mu, \sigma^2) = \frac{1}{\sqrt{2\pi\sigma^2}} \exp\left[-\frac{1}{2}\frac{(z-\mu)^2}{\sigma^2}\right] = \frac{1}{\sigma}\phi\left(\frac{z-\mu}{\sigma}\right) \tag{D.11}$$

This distribution for Z is denoted by $Z \sim \mathfrak{N}(\mu, \sigma^2)$. One of the most important analytical features of the normal distribution concerns the sum of two normal random variables.

THEOREM D.9 (SUMS OF INDEPENDENT NORMALS) *Let $Y_1 \sim \mathfrak{N}(\mu_1, \sigma_1^2)$ and $Y_2 \sim \mathfrak{N}(\mu_2, \sigma_2^2)$ be independently distributed. Then $Y_1 + Y_2 \sim \mathfrak{N}(\mu_1 + \mu_2, \sigma_1^2 + \sigma_2^2)$.*

Such other distributions as the uniform and the exponential do not possess this property. The sum of two independent standard uniform random variables has a tent-shaped p.d.f. with support on the interval [0, 2]. In effect, there are "more" pairs of numbers from the unit interval that sum to one than there are pairs summing to values near 0 or 2. A similar effect appears near zero in the p.d.f. of the sum of two independent standard exponential random variables, which is ye^{-y}.

DEFINITION D.28 (GAMMA FUNCTION) *The* gamma function, *denoted* $\Gamma(\cdot)$, *is*

$$\Gamma(y) \equiv \int_0^\infty x^{y-1} e^{-x}\, dx$$

The gamma function does not have a simpler algebraic form, except in such special cases as

$$\begin{aligned}\Gamma(1/2) &= \sqrt{\pi} \\ \Gamma(1) &= 1 \\ \Gamma(n+1) &= n\,\Gamma(n) \\ &= n! \text{ if } n \in \mathbb{N}\end{aligned}$$

A useful property of the gamma function is

$$\frac{\Gamma(z)\,\Gamma(y)}{\Gamma(z+y)} = \int_0^\infty x^{z-1}\,(1-x)^{y-1}\, dx \tag{D.12}$$

DEFINITION D.29 (PSI FUNCTION) *The* psi function, *denoted* $\psi(\cdot)$, *is*

$$\psi(y) \equiv \frac{d \log \Gamma(y)}{dy}$$

This function is also called the *digamma function*. Like the gamma it does not have a simple form, however

$$\begin{aligned}\psi(1/2) &= -\gamma - 2\log 2 \\ \psi(1) &= -\gamma \\ \psi(n+1) &= \psi(n) + \frac{1}{n} \\ &= 1 + \sum_{k=1}^{n} \frac{1}{k} \text{ if } n \in \mathbb{N}\end{aligned}$$

where $\gamma \approx 0.57722$ is Euler's constant.

DEFINITION D.30 (CHI-SQUARE DISTRIBUTION) *If the continuous random variable Y has the p.d.f.*

$$f_Y(y) = \begin{cases} \frac{1}{2^{\nu/2}\Gamma(\nu/2)} y^{(\nu/2)-1} e^{-\frac{1}{2}y} & \text{if } \; y > 0 \\ 0 & \text{if } \; y \le 0 \end{cases} \tag{D.13}$$

then Y possesses the chi-square distribution with degrees of freedom parameter ν. This is denoted by $Y \sim \chi^2_\nu$.

THEOREM D.10 (CHI-SQUARE DISTRIBUTION) *If the random variable Y has the chi-square distribution with ν degrees of freedom, then $\mu = \nu$, $\sigma^2 = 2\nu$.*

The degrees of freedom parameter ν can be any real number greater than zero, but when it is a positive integer the chi-square p.d.f. is the p.d.f. of the sum of ν squared i.i.d. standard normal random variables.

THEOREM D.11 (SUMS OF SQUARED STANDARD NORMALS) *Let Z_n $(n = 1, \ldots, N)$ be N i.i.d. $\mathfrak{N}(0, 1)$ random variables. Then $\sum_{n=1}^{N} Z_n^2 \sim \chi_N^2$.*

We also define a distribution closely related to the standard normal.

DEFINITION D.31 (STUDENT t DISTRIBUTION) *If the continuous random variable Y has the p.d.f.*

$$f_Y(y) = \frac{\Gamma[(\nu+1)/2]}{\nu^{1/2}\Gamma(1/2)\,\Gamma(\nu/2)}\left(1+\frac{y^2}{\nu}\right)^{-(\nu+1)/2}$$

then Y has the Student t distribution with degrees of freedom parameter ν. This is denoted by $Y \sim t_\nu$.

THEOREM D.12 (STUDENT t DISTRIBUTION) *The moments of the t_1 distribution (also called the* Cauchy *distribution) do not exist. For $\nu > 1$, μ_r is finite only if $r < \nu$. Odd-order moments that exist are zero. Finite even moments are*

$$\begin{aligned}\mu_r &= \nu^{r/2}\frac{\Gamma[(r+1)/2]\,\Gamma[(\nu-r)/2]}{\Gamma(1/2)\,\Gamma(\nu/2)}\\ &= \nu^{r/2}\frac{1\cdot 3\cdot\cdots\cdot(r-1)}{(\nu-r)(\nu-r+2)\cdots(\nu-2)}\end{aligned}$$

$(r = 2, 4, 6, \ldots)$ so that $\mu_2 = \nu/(\nu-2)$ and $\mu_4 = 3\nu^2/(\nu-4)(\nu-2)$.

The nonexistence of the mean of a symmetric p.d.f. like that of the t_1 distribution may seem puzzling. After all,

$$\int_{-a}^{a} u\, f_U(u)\, du = 0$$

for every a if $f_U(u) = f_U(-u)$. But the mean exists only if

$$\int_{-\infty}^{\infty} u\, f_U(u)\, du \equiv \lim_{a,b\to\infty} \int_{-a}^{b} u\, f_U(u)\, du$$

is the same finite outcome no matter what relative speeds a and b grow. That way this integral is always well defined.

The Cauchy p.d.f. is

$$f_Y(y) = \frac{1}{\pi} \frac{1}{1+y^2}$$

and the definite integral that we use to determine the mean is

$$\int_{-a}^{b} y\, f_Y(y)\, dy = \frac{1}{2\pi} \log\left(\frac{1+b^2}{1+a^2}\right)$$

If $b = a$, then this integral is always zero and so is the limit as $a \to \infty$. But we can set $b = a^2$, so that $\left(1+b^2\right) / \left(1+a^2\right) \to \infty$ and the definite integral approaches infinity. And we can also set $a = b^2$ so that the definite integral approaches negative infinity. In this way, the Cauchy distribution fails to have a mean.

The Student t distribution arises in statistics as the distribution of the ratio of a standard normal random variable and a chi-square random variable with ν degrees of freedom, where the two random variables are independent.

THEOREM D.13 (STUDENT t RATIO) *Let $Y_1 \sim \mathfrak{N}(0, 1)$ be independent of $Y_2 \sim \chi^2_\nu$. Then $Y_1/\sqrt{Y_2/\nu} \sim t_\nu$.*

The p.d.f. of the t distribution is qualitatively similar to the standard normal p.d.f. Both are symmetric about zero and have bell shapes. The t p.d.f. always has fatter tails; this is illustrated in Figure D.1. As the degrees of freedom parameter ν approaches infinity, however, the t p.d.f. approaches the standard normal p.d.f. One can prove this using the results described in the next section.

DEFINITION D.32 (SNEDECOR F DISTRIBUTION) *If the continuous random variable Y has the p.d.f.*

$$f_Y(y) = \begin{cases} \frac{\nu_1}{\nu_2} \frac{\Gamma[(\nu_1+\nu_2)/2]}{\Gamma(\nu_1/2)\,\Gamma(\nu_2/2)} \left(\frac{\nu_1}{\nu_2} y\right)^{(\nu_1/2)-1} \left(1 + \frac{\nu_1}{\nu_2} y\right)^{-(\nu_1+\nu_2)/2} & \text{if } y \geq 0 \\ 0 & \text{if } y < 0 \end{cases}$$

then Y has the Snedecor F distribution with degrees of freedom parameters ν_1 and ν_2. This is denoted by $Y \sim F_{\nu_1,\nu_2}$.

THEOREM D.14 (SNEDECOR F DISTRIBUTION) *If $Y \sim F_{\nu_1,\nu_2}$, then*

$$\mathrm{E}[Y] = \frac{\nu_2}{\nu_2 - 2}$$

if $\nu_2 > 2$. Otherwise, Y has no finite moments.

Like the t distribution, the F distribution arises in statistics as the distribution of a ratio: in this case, the ratio of two independent chi-square random variables.

THEOREM D.15 (SNEDECOR F RATIO) *Let $Y_1 \sim \chi^2_{\nu_1}$ be independent of $Y_2 \sim \chi^2_{\nu_2}$. Then*

$$\frac{Y_1/\nu_1}{Y_2/\nu_2} \sim F_{\nu_1,\nu_2}$$

One can see that Theorems D.13 and D.15 imply that $(t_\nu)^2 \sim F_{1,\nu}$. In the same way the t_ν distribution approaches the standard normal as $\nu \to \infty$, the F_{ν_1,ν_2} distribution approaches the $\chi^2_{\nu_1}/\nu_1$ distribution as $\nu_2 \to \infty$.

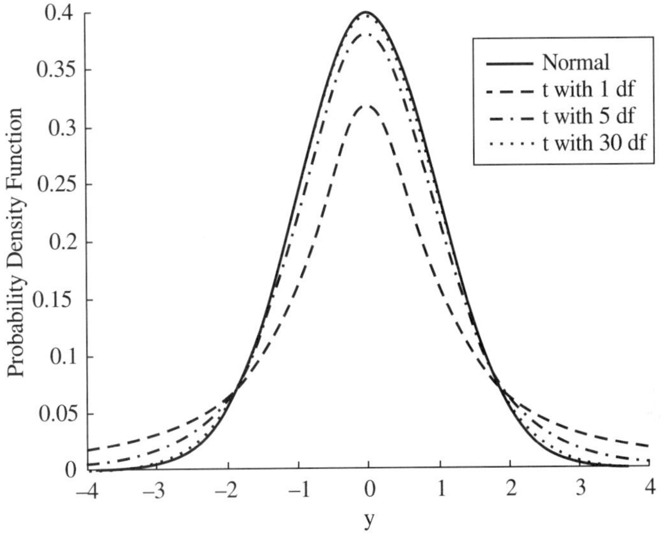

Figure D.1 The normal and student t distributions.

D.5 LIMITING APPROXIMATIONS

There are several cases in which a sequence of distribution functions converges in the limit to another distribution function.[8] Often, the limiting distribution is a useful approximation to elements of the sequence of distributions. We have already mentioned two examples: the *Poisson* distribution is a limit of a sequence of binomial distributions and the standard normal distribution

[8] This section of this appendix contains material that many students have not studied. It is extensive for this reason, and because some instructors prefer to take the central limit theorems as given.

is the limit of a sequence of t distributions. There are many other examples. The leading example is the normal distribution as the limiting distribution of a standardized sum of random variables.

First, we introduce a new term.

DEFINITION D.33 (CONVERGENCE IN DISTRIBUTION) *If the c.d.f.s F_{Z_N} of the sequence of random variables $\{Z_N\}$ converge to the c.d.f. F_Z as $N \to \infty$ at all points z where $F_Z(z)$ is continuous, then $\{Z_N\}$* converges in distribution *to Z. This will be denoted $Z_N \xrightarrow{d} Z$.*

This is an awkward phrase. Although the convergence concerns c.d.f.s, not random variables, it sounds as though there is some random variable out there to which the Z_N are getting closer. But this is not what is meant. The convergence refers only to the sequence of c.d.f.s, $\{F_{Z_N}\}$, which is a *deterministic* sequence.

One of the most important examples of convergence in distribution concerns the behavior of a sum of i.i.d. random variables:

THEOREM D.16 (LINDBERG–LEVY CENTRAL LIMIT THEOREM) *Let $\{Y_n\}$ be a sequence of independent and identically distributed (i.i.d.) random variables. If the variance σ^2 of Y_n is strictly positive and finite and μ denotes* $\mathrm{E}[Y_n]$, *then the distribution of*

$$Z_N \equiv \frac{\sum_{n=1}^{N} Y_n - \mu N}{\sigma \sqrt{N}}$$

converges to the $\mathfrak{N}(0, 1)$ distribution as N approaches infinity. That is, $Z_N \xrightarrow{d} Z \sim \mathfrak{N}(0, 1)$.

The random variable Z_N has the special properties that its first two moments do not change with N. The sum $\sum_{n=1}^{N} Y_n$ has been standardized by its mean, μN, and its standard deviation $\sigma\sqrt{N}$. As a result, $\mathrm{E}[Z_N] = 0$ and $\mathrm{Var}[Z_N] = 1$ for all N. The random variable $\sum_{n=1}^{N} Y_n$ has moments that explode with N. On the other hand, the average $\sum_{n=1}^{N} Y_n/N$ has a variance that collapses to zero. The standardization in Z_N provides a sequence of distributions with some stability over different values of N.

Because the c.d.f. of the normal distribution does not have a closed-form expression, proofs of this theorem and its generalizations do not actually demonstrate the convergence of a sequence of c.d.f.s. Less direct methods are used. In special cases, one can show that the sequence of p.d.f.s converges to the standard normal p.d.f., but the algebra is often convoluted. More general arguments examine the sequence of characteristic functions, which also characterize the sequence of distributions. When all of the moments of the sequence of distributions exist, an analogous analysis works with the sequence of m.g.f.s. This analysis is equivalent to studying the asymptotic behavior of all of the moments. In the remainder of this section, we illustrate each of these approaches.

D.5.1 A Sequence of Densities

A graph of the p.d.f. of Z_N for various values of N when $\{Y_n\}$ is a sequence of i.i.d. standard uniform random variables is given in Figure D.2. This figure shows how quickly the central limit can take effect.[9]

For an analytical example of a sequence of p.d.f.s converging to the standard normal p.d.f., suppose that the Y_n are exponential random variables:

$$f_{Y_n}(y) = e^{-y}, \qquad y \geq 0$$

$$F_{Y_n}(y) = 1 - e^{-y}, \qquad y \geq 0$$

We will find the p.d.f. for $S_N \equiv \sum_{n=1}^{N} Y_n$. First, $S_1 = Y_1$ has the p.d.f.

$$f_{S_1}(s) = e^{-s}, \qquad s \geq 0$$

We will use induction to show that this is the starting point for the p.d.f. $s^{N-1}e^{-s}/\,(N-1)!$ of any S_N. Theorem D.7 (Convolution, p. 882) implies that

$$f_{S_N}(s) = e^{-s} \int_0^s e^x \, f_{S_{N-1}}(x)\, dx, \; s \geq 0$$

so that if

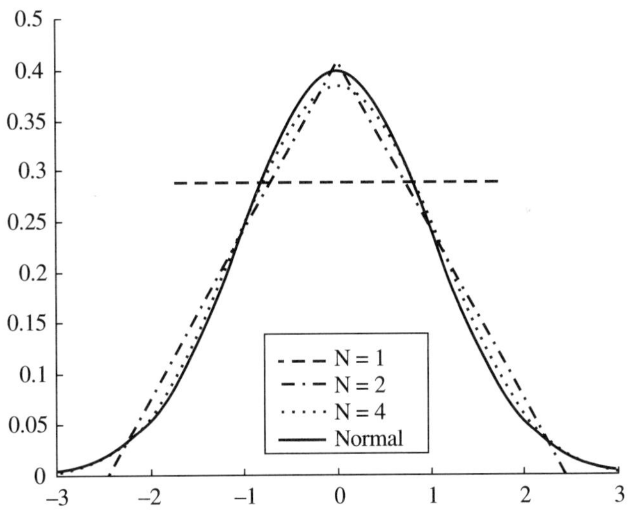

Figure D.2 Sequence of densities for average of uniforms.

[9] For those who are interested, we used the result that

$$f_{S_N}(s) = N\,\mathbf{1}\{s \leq N\} \sum_{k=0}^{N-1} \frac{1}{k!\,(N-k)!} (-1)^k\,(s-k)^{N-1}\,\mathbf{1}\{s \geq k\}$$

is the p.d.f. of the sum S_N of N i.i.d. uniform random variables to make Figure D.2. Only the lonely should attempt to prove this result with pencil and paper, although Theorem D.7 and induction do work. We did not use paper and pencil: we used symbolic mathematics software.

$$f_{N-1}(s) = \frac{s^{N-2}e^{-s}}{(N-2)!}$$

then

$$f_{S_N}(s) = e^{-s}\int_0^s e^x \frac{x^{N-2}e^{-x}}{(N-2)!}\,dx = \frac{s^{N-1}e^{-s}}{(N-1)!} \tag{D.14}$$

for $s \geq 0$.

Now we will find the p.d.f. for the standardized Z_N. The first two moments of the exponential distribution are

$$\begin{aligned}
\mathrm{E}[Y_n] &= \int_0^\infty x e^{-x}\,dx = 1 \\
\mathrm{E}[Y_n^2] &= \int_0^\infty x^2 e^{-x}\,dx = 2 \\
\mathrm{Var}[Y_n] &= 1
\end{aligned}$$

Therefore, the standardized sum is $Z_N = (S_N - N)/\sqrt{N}$ and

$$\begin{aligned}
f_{Z_N}(z) &= \sqrt{N} f_{S_N}(N + \sqrt{N}z) \\
&= \frac{N^{\frac{3}{2}}}{N!}\left(N + \sqrt{N}z\right)^{N-1} e^{-N-\sqrt{N}z} \\
&= \frac{N^{N+\frac{1}{2}}e^{-N}}{N!}\left(1 + \frac{z}{\sqrt{N}}\right)^{N-1} e^{-\sqrt{N}z}
\end{aligned} \tag{D.15}$$

for $z \geq -\sqrt{N}$. For $z < -\sqrt{N}$, $f_{Z_N}(z) = 0$. Using a Taylor polynomial approximation of the natural logarithm, we show (Section D.5.4, *Mathematical Notes*) that the terms involving z converge as N gets large to a simpler expression:

$$\lim_{N\to\infty}\left(1 + \frac{z}{\sqrt{N}}\right)^{N-1} e^{-\sqrt{N}z} = e^{-\frac{1}{2}z^2} \tag{D.16}$$

which is proportional to the standard normal p.d.f. in Definition D.27. We also show [see equation (D.20)] that

$$\lim_{N\to\infty}\frac{N^{N+\frac{1}{2}}e^{-N}}{N!}$$

exists. Therefore, because all $f_{Z_N}(z)$ integrate to one,

$$\lim_{N\to\infty} f_{Z_N}(z) = \frac{1}{\sqrt{2\pi}}e^{-\frac{1}{2}z^2} \tag{D.17}$$

Graphs of the $f_{Z_N}(z)$ in (D.15) are shown in Figure D.3, along with the standard normal p.d.f. for comparison. The asymmetry of the p.d.f.s for the exponential case seems to make convergence to the normal limit much slower than for the uniform case.

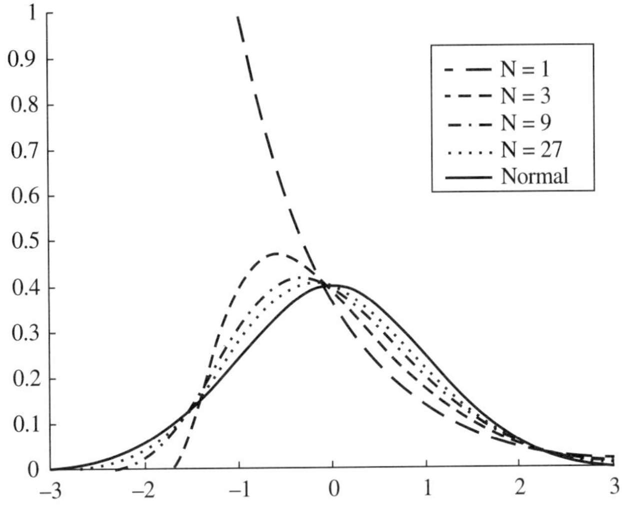

Figure D.3 Sequence of densities for average of exponentials.

D.5.2 Sequences of Moments

We can take another route if, as in the cases just described, the moments of the c.d.f.s uniquely determine the c.d.f.s.[10] Denote the first four moments of Y_n by μ_1', μ_2', μ_3', and μ_4', respectively, and let $W_n \equiv Y_n - \mu_1'$ be the centered Y_n and let $\sigma^2 \equiv \mu_2' - \left(\mu_1'\right)^2$. We can write $Z_N = \sum_{n=1}^{N} W_n / \sqrt{\sigma^2 N}$. We will find that the limits of the moments of Z_N depend only on second moments of W_n/σ, and do so in the same way as the higher moments of the $\mathfrak{N}(0, 1)$ distribution.

For example, consider the third moment of Z_N. First, expand

$$\left(\sum_{n=1}^{N} W_n\right)^3 = \frac{3!}{3!\,0!\,0!}\sum_{n=1}^{N} W_n^3 + \frac{3!}{2!\,1!}\sum_{n=1}^{N}\sum_{j>n}^{N} W_n^2 W_j + \frac{3!}{1!\,1!\,1!}\sum_{n=1}^{N}\sum_{j>n}^{N}\sum_{k>j}^{N} W_n W_j W_k$$

$$= \sum_{n=1}^{N} W_n^3 + 3\sum_{n=1}^{N}\sum_{j>n}^{N} W_n^2 W_j + 6\sum_{n=1}^{N}\sum_{j>n}^{N}\sum_{k>j}^{N} W_n W_j W_k$$

The coefficients of the sums compute the number of ways of obtaining the particular product term.[11] Only the leading sum has a nonzero expectation so that

[10] Davidson and MacKinnon (1993, pp. 126–127) inspired this section.

[11] A general expression for $\left(\sum_{n=1}^{N} W_n\right)^K$ is the *multinomial expansion*

$$\sum_{\substack{r_n \in \mathbb{N}: \\ r_1 + \cdots + r_N = K}} \frac{K!}{r_1!\, r_2! \cdots r_N!} W_1^{r_1} W_2^{r_2} \cdots W_N^{r_N}$$

A well-known special case is the *binomial expansion*

$$\mathrm{E}[Z_N^3] = \frac{N\mu_3}{\left(\sigma^2 N\right)^{3/2}} = \frac{\mu_3}{\sigma^3} N^{-1/2}$$

where μ_3 is the third *centered* moment of Y_n. For the fourth moment,

$$\left(\sum_{n=1}^{N} W_n\right)^4 = \sum_{n=1}^{N} W_n^4 + 4\sum_{n=1}^{N}\sum_{j>n}^{N}(W_n^3 W_j + W_n W_j^3) + \frac{4!}{2!\,2!}\sum_{n=1}^{N}\sum_{j>n}^{N} W_n^2 W_j^2$$

$$+\frac{4!}{2!}\sum_{n=1}^{N}\sum_{j>n}^{N}\sum_{k>j}^{N}(W_n^2 W_j W_k + W_n W_j^2 W_k + W_n W_j W_k^2)$$

$$+4!\sum_{n=1}^{N}\sum_{j>n}^{N}\sum_{k>j}^{N}\sum_{m>k}^{N} W_n W_j W_k W_m \quad \Rightarrow$$

$$\mathrm{E}[Z_N^4] = \frac{1}{\left(\sigma^2 N\right)^2}\left[N\mu_4 + 6\binom{N}{2}\left(\sigma^2\right)^2\right] = \frac{\mu_4}{\sigma^4}N^{-1} + 3\left(1 - N^{-1}\right)$$

where μ_4 is the fourth centered moment of Y_n. As N approaches infinity, the third moment vanishes and the fourth moment approaches 3, which does not depend on μ_4. These limiting moments are the third and fourth moments of the $\mathfrak{N}(0, 1)$ distribution.

For still higher moments, the influence of all moments but the second vanishes similarly. There are never enough terms to preserve them, because there are too few combinations of the necessary products within the expectation.

D.5.3 Sequences of c.f.s

Working with the moments themselves is cumbersome compared to an analysis of the c.f.s. All the moments are conveniently summarized in the c.f., and there is a simple relationship between the c.f.s of independently distributed X and Y, and their linear transformation $S = aX + bY + c$:

$$\begin{aligned}\varphi_S(t) &\equiv \mathrm{E}\big[\exp[it(aX + bY + c)]\big] \\ &= \mathrm{E}[\exp(itaX)\exp(itbY)\exp(ict)] \\ &= \varphi_X(at)\,\varphi_Y(bt)\,\exp(ict)\end{aligned}$$

To illustrate the convenience, we return to the exponential distribution and suppose the Y_n are i.i.d. exponential random variables. The exponential c.f. is

---

$$(W_1 + W_2)^K = \sum_{k=0}^{K}\binom{K}{k} W_1^{K-k} W_2^k$$

$$\begin{aligned}\varphi_Y(t) &\equiv \mathrm{E}[e^{itY}] \\ &= \int_0^\infty e^{ity} e^{-y}\, dy \\ &= \frac{1}{it-1} \lim_{y\to\infty} \left(e^{y(it-1)} - 1\right) \\ &= \frac{1}{1-it}, \qquad \text{if } t < 1\end{aligned}$$

so that the c.f. of the standardized $Z_N \equiv \sum_{n=1}^{N} (Y_N - 1) / \sqrt{N}$ is

$$\begin{aligned}\varphi_{Z_N}(t) &= \left[\varphi_Y\left(\frac{t}{\sqrt{N}}\right)\right]^N \exp(-it\sqrt{N}) \\ &= \left(1 - \frac{it}{\sqrt{N}}\right)^{-N} e^{-it\sqrt{N}}\end{aligned}$$

We used the limit of a similar expression in (D.16). A derivation is given below. In this case,

$$\lim_{N\to\infty} \varphi_{Z_N}(t) = \exp\left(-\frac{1}{2}t^2\right)$$

which is the c.f. of the standard normal distribution. This demonstrates that *all* moments, not only the third and fourth, converge to the moments of the standard normal distribution.

One can make similar algebraic demonstrations for other distributions with finite moments. The student may confirm this with the c.f.s of most distributions defined above. However, there is a general argument supporting the central limit theorem for all distributions with finite second moments. Although we do not know the functional form of the c.f. for general distributions, we do know that the c.f. of $W_n = (Y_n - \mu)/\sigma$ has the Taylor polynomial approximation

$$\varphi_W\left(\frac{t}{\sqrt{N}}\right) = 1 - \frac{1}{2}\frac{t^2}{N} + o\left(N^{-1}\right) \tag{D.18}$$

for some $t > 0$, because the first two moments of W_n are 0 and 1, respectively. Here we emphasize order in terms of N, which will grow, and not t, which remains fixed. We can apply our previous approach to this expression.

In effect, we have already seen that the c.f. of Z_N can be expressed as a function of the c.f. of the standardized Y_n:

$$\varphi_{Z_N}(t) = \mathrm{E}\left[\exp\left(it\frac{\sum_{n=1}^{N} W_n}{\sqrt{N}}\right)\right] = \left[\varphi_W\left(\frac{it}{\sqrt{N}}\right)\right]^N$$

Into this expression, we insert (D.18) and take the limit (see the next section):

$$\lim_{N\to\infty} \varphi_{Z_N}(t) = \left[1 - \frac{1}{2}\frac{t^2}{N} + o\left(N^{-1}\right)\right]^N = \exp\left(-\frac{1}{2}t^2\right) \tag{D.19}$$

obtaining the c.f. of the standard normal distribution. With one additional theorem, we have obtained a general result.

THEOREM D.17 *Suppose that Z_N has the c.f. $\varphi_{Z_N}(t)$. If $\varphi_{Z_N}(t) \to \varphi_Z(t)$, the c.f. of a random variable Z, for all t in a neighborhood of the origin, then $\{Z_N\}$ converges in distribution to the distribution of Z.*

For a proof of this theorem, see Feller (1971). We can apply this theorem to our proof of Theorem D.16, because we have just shown that the c.f. of $\{Z_N\}$ converges to the c.f. of the standard normal distribution.

D.5.4 Mathematical Notes

We often approximate functions with polynomial functions. The Kth order *Taylor polynomial* of $g(x)$ at $x = a$ is

$$\sum_{k=0}^{K} \frac{1}{k!} g^{(k)}(a)\, \epsilon^k$$

provided that $g(x)$ is K times continuously differentiable at a. The term $g^{(k)}(a)$ denotes the kth derivative of $g(x)$ at $x = a$. The Taylor polynomial is an approximation in the following sense.

THEOREM D.18 (TAYLOR'S APPROXIMATION) *Let $g(x)$ be a function defined on a closed interval $\mathbb{A}$ of $\mathbb{R}$. If g is K times continuously differentiable, then for any points $a,\ a + \epsilon \in \mathbb{A}$*

$$g(a+\epsilon) = \sum_{k=0}^{K} \frac{1}{k!} g^{(k)}(a)\, \epsilon^k + o\left(\epsilon^K\right)$$

If g is $K + 1$ times continuously differentiable, then the residual term can be expressed as

$$\frac{1}{(K+1)!} g^{(K+1)}(\bar{a})\, \epsilon^{K+1}$$

for some $\bar{a}$ between a and $a + \epsilon$.

The theorem gives an exact relationship with a residual term that is omitted or negligible in an approximation. We use the Taylor polynomial approximation of the natural logarithm: For small x

$$\log(1+x) = x - \frac{1}{2}x^2 + o\left(x^2\right)$$

so that

$$1 + x = \exp\left[x - \frac{1}{2}x^2 + o\left(x^2\right)\right]$$

We apply this approximation to

$$\begin{aligned}\left(1+\frac{z}{\sqrt{N}}\right)^{N-1} e^{-\sqrt{N}z} &= \exp\left\{(N-1)\left[\tfrac{z}{\sqrt{N}} - \tfrac{1}{2}\left(\tfrac{z}{\sqrt{N}}\right)^2 + o\left(N^{-1}\right)\right]\right\} \\ &\quad \times \exp\left(-\sqrt{N}z\right) \\ &= \exp\left[-\tfrac{z}{\sqrt{N}} - \tfrac{1}{2}\tfrac{N-1}{N}z^2 + o\left(N^{-1}\right)\right] \\ &\to e^{-\frac{1}{2}z^2} \quad \text{as } N \to \infty\end{aligned} \tag{D.20}$$

thereby confirming (D.16).

We can analyze (D.19) with the same tools:

$$N \log\left[1 - \frac{1}{2}\frac{t^2}{N} + o\left(N^{-1}\right)\right] = N\left[-\frac{1}{2}\frac{t^2}{N} + o\left(N^{-1}\right)\right] = -\frac{1}{2}t^2 + o(1)$$

so that

$$\lim_{N\to\infty}\left[1 - \frac{1}{2}\frac{t^2}{N} + o\left(N^{-1}\right)\right]^N = \exp\left(-\frac{1}{2}t^2\right)$$

Lemma D.5 (Stirling's Approximation) *For $N \in \mathbb{N}$,*

$$\lim_{N\to\infty} \frac{N^{N+\frac{1}{2}}e^{-N}}{N!}$$

exists.

Proof. This proof combines elements of the proofs by Billingsley (1968, Exercise 18.16, p. 206) and Feller (1968, p. 26). First, we derive a series of inequalities based on the facts that $\log(x)$ is positive for $x \geq 1$ and strictly concave:

$$\frac{1}{2}\left[\log(n+1) + \log(n)\right] < \int_n^{n+1} \log(x)\,dx \tag{D.21}$$

and[12]

$$\begin{aligned}\int_n^{n+1} \log(x)\,dx &< \int_n^{n+1}\left[\log(n+1) + \frac{x-(n+1)}{n+1}\right]dx \\ &= \log(n+1) - \frac{1}{2(n+1)}\end{aligned} \tag{D.22}$$

for $n > 1,\ n \in \mathbb{N}$. Because

$$\int_n^{n+1} \log(x)\,dx = (n+1)\log(n+1) - n\log(n) - 1$$

(D.21) and (D.22) can be restated as

[12] The second integrand is the first-order Taylor polynomial of $\log(x)$ at $x = n+1$.

$$\begin{aligned}
0 &< \int_{n}^{n+1} \log(x)\,dx - \frac{1}{2}\left[\log(n+1) + \log(n)\right] \\
&= \left(n + \frac{1}{2}\right)\left[\log(n+1) - \log(n)\right] - 1 \\
&\equiv a_n
\end{aligned}$$

and

$$\begin{aligned}
a_n &< \log(n+1) - \frac{1}{2\,(n+1)} - \frac{1}{2}\left[\log(n+1) + \log(n)\right] \\
&= \frac{1}{2}\left[\log\left(\frac{n+1}{n}\right) - \frac{1}{(n+1)}\right] \\
&\equiv b_n
\end{aligned}$$

The concavity of $\log(x)$ also implies that

$$\log(n+2) - \log(n+1) < \frac{1}{n+1}$$

so that

$$0 < \frac{1}{2}\left[\frac{1}{n+1} - \log\left(\frac{n+2}{n+1}\right)\right] \equiv c_n$$

Second, we combine these inequalities:

$$\begin{aligned}
b_n + c_n &= \frac{1}{2}\left[\log\left(\frac{n+1}{n}\right) - \log\left(\frac{n+2}{n+1}\right)\right] \\
\sum_{n=1}^{N-1} b_n + c_n &= \frac{1}{2}\left[\log(2) - \log\left(\frac{N+1}{N}\right)\right] < \frac{1}{2}\log(2)
\end{aligned}$$

and

$$\begin{aligned}
d_N &\equiv \sum_{n=1}^{N-1} a_n \\
&= \left(N + \frac{1}{2}\right)\log(N) - N + 1 - \log(N!) \\
&< \sum_{n=1}^{N-1} b_n \\
&< \frac{1}{2}\log(2)
\end{aligned}$$

The sequence $\{d_N\}$ is strictly increasing in N and bounded above by $\frac{1}{2}\log 2$. Therefore, $\{d_N\}$ has a limit and

$$\lim_{N\to\infty} \frac{N^{N+\frac{1}{2}}e^{-N}}{N!} = \lim_{N\to\infty} \exp(1 - d_N)$$

exists. □

Stirling's approximation actually includes that the limit above equals $1/\sqrt{2\pi}$. This follows from the argument leading to (D.17). If we merely assert the existence of the limit, then (D.17) would state only that the limiting p.d.f. is a function *proportional* to the standard normal p.d.f. It follows that the unknown limit is the constant that makes this limit a proper p.d.f. (integrating to one). That constant value is $1/\sqrt{2\pi}$.

APPENDIX E

Classical Statistics

We divide classical statistics in a conventional manner: sampling, estimation, and hypothesis testing.[1] We include separate sections on methods of estimation, maximum likelihood and the method of moments, and basic asymptotic approximations to distributions.

E.1 SAMPLING

The fundamental building block of classical statistics is repeated sampling, a process that permits the observer to learn about an experiment that generates a random variable.

DEFINITION E.1 (RANDOM SAMPLE) *Let* $(Y_1, \ldots, Y_N)$ *be random variables such that the* y_n *are mutually independent realizations of the random variable* Y *with c.d.f.,* $F_Y(y)$. *Then* $(Y_1, \ldots, Y_N)$ *is called a* random sample *of* N *from a population with c.d.f.* $F_Y(y)$.

There are several ways in which the random sample is transformed for classical statistical inference.

DEFINITION E.2 (ORDER STATISTICS) *The* order statistics *of a random sample* $(Y_1, \ldots, Y_N)$ *are the ordered values* $Y_{(n)}$ $(n = 1, \ldots, N)$ *where* $Y_{(1)} \le Y_{(2)} \le \cdots \le Y_{(N)}$.

DEFINITION E.3 (EMPIRICAL DISTRIBUTION) *Let* $(Y_1, \ldots, Y_N)$ *be a random sample. The* empirical distribution *is the multinomial distribution that assigns probability* $1/N$ *to each* Y_n $(n = 1, \ldots, N)$.

[1] This summary of statistical theory is written at the level of an introductory undergraduate mathematical statistics book. If a proof is not given, one can be found in Larsen and Marx (1986) and many similar texts.

Both the order statistics and the empirical distribution completely describe the sample. The moments of $f_Y(y)$ are often called *population moments*.

DEFINITION E.4 (SAMPLE MOMENT) *The moments of the empirical distribution are called the* sample moments: *for any transformation $h(Y)$, its sample moment is*

$$\mathrm{E}_N[h(Y)] \equiv \sum_{n=1}^{N} h(Y_n)\frac{1}{N}$$

Note that we use $\mathrm{E}_N[\cdot]$ to distinguish sample moments from the population moments determined by $\mathrm{E}[\cdot]$. The most heavily used sample moments are the sample mean (or expectation),

$$\mathrm{E}_N[Y] = \sum_{n=1}^{N} \frac{Y_n}{N} \equiv \bar{Y}$$

and the sample variance,

$$\mathrm{Var}_N[Y] \equiv \mathrm{E}_N[(Y - \mathrm{E}_N(Y))^2] = \sum_{n=1}^{N} \frac{(Y_n - \bar{Y})^2}{N}$$

There are other interesting features of the empirical distribution corresponding to such population characteristics as probabilities and quantiles.

DEFINITION E.5 (SAMPLE FREQUENCY) A sample frequency *is the observed frequency of an event $Y \in \mathbb{A}$.*

Sample frequencies are analogous to population probabilities:

$$\Pr\{Y \in \mathbb{A}\} = \mathrm{E}[\mathbf{1}\{Y \in \mathbb{A}\}]$$

and

$$\mathrm{E}_N[\mathbf{1}\{Y \in \mathbb{A}\}] = \sum_{n=1}^{N} \frac{\mathbf{1}\{Y_n \in \mathbb{A}\}}{N} = \sum_{\{n:Y_n \in \mathbb{A}\}} \frac{1}{N}$$

The empirical distribution is discrete, so sample quantiles are generally sets, not unique values.

DEFINITION E.6 (SAMPLE QUANTILE) *The qth sample quantile $(0 \leq q \leq 1)$ is the set*

$$\{y \mid \mathrm{E}_N[\mathbf{1}\{Y \leq y\}] \geq q,\ \mathrm{E}_N[\mathbf{1}\{Y \geq y\}] \geq 1 - q\}$$

A popular sample quantile is the *sample median*. It is the set of values that exceeds or equals at least half the sample and is exceeded by or equals at least half the sample. When the sample size N is odd, then this number is unique. But when N is even, and $Y_{(N/2)} < Y_{(N/2+1)}$, then the median is the interval $\left[Y_{(N/2)}, Y_{(N/2+1)}\right]$. Analysts frequently select the midpoint of this interval as the sample median, but this choice is arbitrary and, therefore, merely a convention.

E.2 CLASSICAL STATISTICAL INFERENCE

Statistical inference is the application of models of probability to the analysis of data and its interpretation. Classical inference posits a probability model for potential samples of data, derives a probability model for functions (or *statistics*) of the data, and infers unspecified features (or *parameters*) of the posited probability model from observed statistics.

E.2.1 Estimation

Presentations of classical statistical inference almost always begin with estimation of the first moment of a distribution. Consider a random sample $(Y_1, \ldots, Y_N)$ from the population with c.d.f. F_Y, the first sample moment $\bar{Y} \equiv \mathrm{E}_N[Y]$ is an estimator of $\mu = \mathrm{E}[Y]$ in the sense that $\mathrm{E}[\bar{Y}] = \mu$.

DEFINITION E.7 (UNBIASED ESTIMATOR) *Let θ be a real function of the c.d.f. F_Y and let $(Y_1, \ldots, Y_N)$ be a random sample from the population with c.d.f. F_Y. The random variable $Z = h(Y_1, \ldots, Y_N)$ is an* unbiased estimator *for θ if $\mathrm{E}[Z] = \theta$.*

Many methods of classical statistical inference focus on unbiased estimators, or similar concepts. Often one can construct several unbiased estimators and one chooses among the unbiased estimators based on a comparison of their variances.

DEFINITION E.8 (RELATIVELY EFFICIENT ESTIMATOR) *If Y_A and Y_B are unbiased estimators of θ and $\mathrm{Var}[Y_A] < \mathrm{Var}[Y_B]$ then Y_A is* efficient relative *to Y_B.*

We will use the first sample moment to illustrate most concepts in this section. Let $Y_A = \bar{Y}$ be one estimator of μ and consider some weighted sample average

$$Y_B = \frac{\sum_{n=1}^{N} w_n Y_n}{\sum_{n=1}^{N} w_n}$$

as an alternative unbiased estimator. We suppose that not all w_n are equal. If the variance of Y, σ^2, exists then we can derive the variances of these estimators:

$$\mathrm{Var}[Y_A] = \sigma^2 \frac{1}{N}, \qquad \mathrm{Var}[Y_B] = \sigma^2 \frac{\sum_{n=1}^{N} w_n^2}{\left(\sum_{n=1}^{N} w_n\right)^2}$$

The Cauchy–Schwarz inequality (Lemma C.1, p. 852) implies that

$$\left(\mathbf{w}'\boldsymbol{\iota}\right)^2 < \left(\mathbf{w}'\mathbf{w}\right)\left(\boldsymbol{\iota}'\boldsymbol{\iota}\right)$$

where $\mathbf{w} \equiv [w_n]'$ and $\boldsymbol{\iota}$ is a vector of N ones. In summation notation,

$$\left(\sum_{n=1}^{N} w_n\right)^2 < N \sum_{n=1}^{N} w_n^2 \qquad \Leftrightarrow \qquad \frac{1}{N} < \frac{\sum_{n=1}^{N} w_n^2}{\left(\sum_{n=1}^{N} w_n\right)^2}$$

so that $\mathrm{Var}[Y_A] < \mathrm{Var}[Y_B]$ and Y_A is efficient relative to Y_B.

To assess the statistical precision of an estimator, one estimates its variance. We know intuitively that small variances imply that a random variable is likely to occur near its mean. Chebychev's inequality (Lemma D.3) provides a lower bound on the probability that a random variable is within ε standard deviations of its mean:

$$\Pr\left\{|Y - \mu| \leq \varepsilon\sigma\right\} \geq 1 - \frac{1}{\varepsilon^2}$$

If the variance of Y, σ^2, exists then a correction of the sample variance yields an unbiased estimator of the variance of Y: if

$$s^2 \equiv \frac{N}{N-1} \mathrm{E}_N\left[(Y - \mathrm{E}_N[Y])^2\right] = \frac{\sum_{n=1}^{N}\left(Y_n - \bar{Y}\right)^2}{N-1} \tag{E.1}$$

then[2]

$$\begin{aligned} \mathrm{E}\left[\mathrm{E}_N[(Y - \mathrm{E}_N[Y])^2]\right] &= \mathrm{E}\left[\mathrm{E}_N[Y^2]\right] - \mathrm{E}\left[(\mathrm{E}_N[Y])^2\right] \\ &= \sigma^2 + \mu^2 - \left(\frac{\sigma^2}{N} + \mu^2\right) = \frac{N-1}{N}\sigma^2 \end{aligned}$$

so that

$$\mathrm{E}[s^2] = \sigma^2$$

Dividing s^2 by N gives an unbiased estimator of $\mathrm{E}[\bar{Y}]$.

So far in our example, the probability model for Y states only that the first two moments of Y are finite. If Y is normally distributed, then one can make more refined statements about the precision of $\bar{Y}$. According to Theorem D.2,

$$\bar{Y} \sim \mathfrak{N}(\mu, \sigma^2/N) \tag{E.2}$$

because $\bar{Y}$ is proportional to the sum of N i.i.d. normally distributed random variables. Most books on introductory statistics also state (and some prove) that s^2 is independent of $\bar{Y}$ and that[3]

$$\frac{s^2}{\sigma^2} \sim \frac{\chi^2_{N-1}}{N-1} \tag{E.3}$$

---

[2] This algebra makes heavy use of the moment identity

$$\mathrm{Var}[W] = \mathrm{E}[(W - \mathrm{E}[W])^2] = \mathrm{E}[W^2] - (\mathrm{E}[W])^2$$

[3] We prove this result in Chapter 10.

Then Theorem D.13 implies that

$$\left(\frac{\bar{Y}-\mu}{\sqrt{\sigma^2/N}}\right)\Bigg/\sqrt{\frac{s^2}{\sigma^2}}=\frac{\bar{Y}-\mu}{s/\sqrt{N}}\sim t_{N-1} \tag{E.4}$$

For this reason, this statistic is often called the *t statistic*.

This ratio is a *pivotal statistic* in the sense that its distribution does not depend on either unknown parameter, μ or σ^2. As a result, one can make the probability statement

$$\Pr\left\{\left|\frac{\bar{Y}-\mu}{s/\sqrt{N}}\right|\le t_{N-1;\alpha/2}\right\}=1-\alpha$$

where $t_{N-1;\alpha}$ is the $1-\alpha$ quantile $(0<\alpha<1)$ of the t_{N-1} distribution:

$$\Pr\{t_{N-1}\le t_{N-1;\alpha}\}=1-\alpha$$

This probability statement is equivalent to

$$\Pr\left\{\mu\in\left[\bar{Y}\pm t_{N-1;\alpha/2}\frac{s}{\sqrt{N}}\right]\right\}=1-\alpha \tag{E.5}$$

In words, the interval $[\bar{Y}\pm t_{N-1;\alpha/2}(s/\sqrt{N})]$ will contain μ with probability $1-\alpha$. The boundaries of this interval are random variables, because $\bar{Y}$ and s^2 are random variables in repeated samples.

This is an example of an *interval estimator*. It is a *set* of likely values and this set is usually called a *confidence interval*. In contrast, $\bar{Y}$ is a *point estimator* for μ. In this case, the interval estimator is centered on an unbiased point estimator and its width is proportional to the square root of an estimator of $\mathrm{E}(\bar{Y})$, the measure of statistical precision. Using (E.3), an analogous interval estimator for σ^2 is described by

$$\Pr\left\{\sigma^2\in\left[s^2\frac{\chi^2_{N-1;1-\alpha/2}}{N-1},\ s^2\frac{\chi^2_{N-1;\alpha/2}}{N-1}\right]\right\}=1-\alpha \tag{E.6}$$

where $\chi^2_{N-1;\alpha}$ is the $1-\alpha$ quantile of the χ^2_{N-1}distribution. Because the chi-square distribution is asymmetric, this confidence interval is not centered on the unbiased estimator s^2.

E.2.2 Hypothesis Tests

Statisticians also use such probability statements as (E.5) and (E.6) for hypothesis tests. In classical hypothesis testing, one chooses between two competing hypotheses. One hypothesis, called the *null hypothesis* (denoted H_0), is favored in the sense that the null hypothesis will be "accepted" unless there is strong evidence against it. The other hypothesis, called the *alternative hypothesis* (denoted H_1), specifies the violations of the null hypothesis that pose concern. Given a statistic with a known distribution under H_0, the test procedure is to choose a *significance level* α, defined as the probability of mistakenly "rejecting" H_0 when it is true. Lower significance levels might be assigned to null hypotheses in which there is high confidence. Based on the distribution of the test statistic and the significance level, one finds a *critical (or rejection) region* in the support of the test statistic that has probability α of containing the test statistic under H_0. Finally, if the test statistic falls in the critical region then this event is interpreted as strong evidence against H_0, and it is rejected in favor of H_1.

As an example, consider $H_0 : \mu = \mu_0$, the hypothesis that the mean of Y equals the specific value μ_0, versus $H_1 : \mu > \mu_0$. This H_1 is called a *one-sided* alternative hypothesis. The t-ratio (E.4) evaluated at $\mu = \mu_0$ is the test statistic and

$$H_0 \quad \Rightarrow \quad \frac{\bar{Y} - \mu_0}{s/\sqrt{N}} \sim t_{N-1}$$

Because μ is larger than μ_0 under H_1, one chooses a critical region of large negative values. Such values of the test statistic are consistent with H_1 and unlikely for H_0. Thus, the critical region is the one-sided interval $\left(-\infty, t_{N-1;1-\alpha}\right)$. Under H_0, the test statistic falls in this region with probability α:

$$\Pr\left\{\frac{\bar{Y} - \mu_0}{s/\sqrt{N}} \leq t_{N-1;1-\alpha}\right\} = \alpha$$

Further justification of this critical region comes from considering the *power* of the hypothesis test, the probability of rejecting H_0 when H_1 is true. Because H_1 does not specify a particular value of μ, one computes the *power function*

$$\gamma = \Pr\left\{\frac{\bar{Y} - \mu_0}{s/\sqrt{N}} \leq t_{N-1;1-\alpha}\right\}$$

as it varies with μ and σ. Under H_1, the test statistic has a *noncentral t* distribution with ν degrees of freedom and *noncentrality parameter* $(\sqrt{N}/\sigma)(\mu - \mu_0)$ and the c.d.f. of this distribution can be computed.[4] One discovers that any other critical region will have a power function that falls below the significance level of the test for some parameter values, whereas power always exceeds the significance level for the one-sided critical region. This is highly desirable; otherwise the hypothesis test may be more likely to reject the null hypothesis when it is true than when it is false.

When the alternative hypothesis is *two sided*, $H_1 : \mu \neq \mu_0$, there is a close relationship between interval estimators and hypothesis tests. Using the same test statistic (E.4), the critical region of the most powerful hypothesis test is $\{w \mid |w| > t_{N-1;\alpha/2}\}$. It is equivalent for the test statistic to fall in this region and for μ_0 to fall outside the $1 - \alpha$ level confidence interval $[\bar{Y} \pm t_{N-1;\alpha/2}(s/\sqrt{N})]$. Therefore, the evidence favors the null hypothesis at the significance level α if and only if the null hypothesis agrees with the $1 - \alpha$ confidence interval.

A classical hypothesis test for equal variances in two normal populations gives another example of a pivotal statistic and motivates the F distribution. Given a random sample of N_1 observations from the $\Re(\mu_1, \sigma_1^2)$ and another independent random sample of N_2 observations from the $\Re(\mu_2, \sigma_2^2)$ distribution, the ratio $s_1^2/s_2^2 \sim F_{N_1-1,N_2-1}$ if $H_0 : \sigma_1^2 = \sigma_2^2$ is true. An α-level test against $H_1 : \sigma_1^2 \neq \sigma_2^2$ accepts H_0 if s_1^2/s_2^2 falls within the acceptance interval $[F_{\nu_1,\nu_2;\alpha/2}, F_{\nu_1,\nu_2;1-\alpha/2}]$.

E.2.3 Estimation Methods

A random sample $(Y_1, \ldots Y_N)$ is drawn for the random variable Y with c.d.f. $F_Y(y; \boldsymbol{\theta}_0)$. The functional form of F_Y is completely known but the value of the parameter vector $\boldsymbol{\theta}_0$ is unknown. The parameter vector $\boldsymbol{\theta}_0$ is finite dimensional; $\boldsymbol{\theta}_0$ has K elements so that $\boldsymbol{\theta}_0 \in \mathbb{R}^K$. Let $f_Y(y; \boldsymbol{\theta})$

[4] See Johnson and Kotz (1970b) regarding the noncentral Student t distribution.

denote the p.m.f. or p.d.f. corresponding to $F_Y(y;\boldsymbol{\theta})$. Let the support of the distribution be denoted $\mathbf{S}_Y(\boldsymbol{\theta})$ so that $\int_{\mathbf{S}_Y(\boldsymbol{\theta})} f(y;\boldsymbol{\theta})\,dy = 1$.

In general, the p.d.f. is not defined over all possible values of the parameter vector $\boldsymbol{\theta}$. For example, a variance parameter must be positive. We will denote the parameter space of permissible values of $\boldsymbol{\theta}$ by $\boldsymbol{\Theta}$. From this point on, $\boldsymbol{\theta}$ will always be a member of $\boldsymbol{\Theta}$. In particular, $\boldsymbol{\theta}_0 \in \boldsymbol{\Theta}$.

EXAMPLE E.1 (Bernoulli Distribution)

If Y has the Bernoulli distribution then its support is $\mathbf{S}_Y(\theta) = \{0, 1\}$ and its p.m.f. is

$$f_Y(y;\theta) = \begin{cases} \theta^y (1-\theta)^{1-y}, & \text{if } \ y \in \{0,1\} \\ 0, & \text{if } \ y \notin \{0,1\} \end{cases}$$

where $\theta = \Pr\{Y = 1\}$ is a probability. Therefore, the parameter space is the unit interval: $\boldsymbol{\Theta} = [0, 1]$.

EXAMPLE E.2 (Uniform Distribution)

If Y has the *uniform* (or *rectangular*) distribution then its support is an interval $\mathbf{S}_Y(\theta) = [0, \theta]$ that depends on the parameter θ and its p.d.f. is

$$f_Y(y;\theta) = \left\{ \begin{matrix} 1/\theta, & \text{if } \ y \in \mathbf{S}_Y(\theta) \\ 0, & \text{if } \ y \notin \mathbf{S}_Y(\theta) \end{matrix} \right\} = \frac{\mathbf{1}\{y \in [0,\theta]\}}{\theta}$$

The parameter space is the positive real line excluding the boundaries 0 and ∞: $\boldsymbol{\Theta} = (0, \infty)$.

EXAMPLE E.3 (Normal Distribution)

If Y has a normal distribution such that $\mathrm{E}(Y) = \mu$ and $\mathrm{Var}(Y) = \sigma^2$ then $\mathbf{S}_Y(\boldsymbol{\theta}) = \mathbb{R} = (-\infty, \infty)$ and

$$f_Y(y,\theta) = \frac{1}{\sqrt{2\pi\sigma^2}} \exp\left[-\frac{(y-\mu)^2}{2\sigma^2}\right]$$

The parameter vector is $\boldsymbol{\theta} = [\mu, \sigma]'$. The parameter space is $\boldsymbol{\Theta} = (-\infty, \infty) \times (0, \infty)$, which excludes infinite moments and negative standard deviations.

MAXIMUM LIKELIHOOD

Let $y = (y_1, \ldots, y_N)$ denote a realization of the random sample $(Y_1, \ldots, Y_N)$. The expectation operator E_N denotes an expectation over Y with respect to the empirical distribution of y. The empirical distribution is the discrete distribution that assigns probability $1/N$ to each point in the sample, and no probability everywhere else. We will draw analogies between sample moments, which depend on the empirical distribution, and population moments, which depend on the distribution of the population.

DEFINITION E.9 (LIKELIHOOD FUNCTION) *The likelihood function of $\boldsymbol{\theta}$ given* $\mathbf{y}$ *is defined to be*

$$\ell(\boldsymbol{\theta}; \mathbf{y}) = \ell(\boldsymbol{\theta}; y_1, \ldots, y_N) \equiv f_{Y_1,\ldots,Y_N}(y_n; \boldsymbol{\theta})$$

We will denote the logarithm of the sample likelihood function by L:

$$L(\boldsymbol{\theta}; \mathbf{y}) \equiv \log[\ell(\boldsymbol{\theta}, \mathbf{y})]$$

Under the assumption of random sampling,

$$\ell(\boldsymbol{\theta}; \mathbf{y}) = \prod_{n=1}^{N} f_Y(y_n; \boldsymbol{\theta})$$

$$L(\boldsymbol{\theta}; \mathbf{y}) = \sum_{n=1}^{N} \log[f_Y(y_n; \boldsymbol{\theta})]$$

It will be convenient to denote the sample *average* log-likelihood function by

$$\mathrm{E}_N\left[L(\boldsymbol{\theta}; Y)\right] \equiv \sum_{n=1}^{N} L(\boldsymbol{\theta}; Y_n)\frac{1}{N}$$

The log-likelihood function is viewed as a function of the parameter vector $\boldsymbol{\theta}$ (for which the true value is unknown) given that the sample vector y has been observed. This is opposite to the way we usually think about the p.d.f. in which the parameter vector $\boldsymbol{\theta}$ is fixed and we examine the relative probability of different values for Y.

EXAMPLE E.4 (Bernoulli Distribution)

The sample average log-likelihood function of the Bernoulli distribution is

$$\mathrm{E}_N\left[L(\theta; Y)\right] = \sum_{n=1}^{N} \left[Y_n \log(\theta) + (1 - Y_n)\log(1 - \theta)\right]$$

EXAMPLE E.5 (Uniform Distribution)

A sample of N observations $(Y_1, \ldots Y_N)$ from the uniform distribution has the sample average log-likelihood function

$$\mathrm{E}_N\left[L(\theta; Y)\right] = \frac{1}{N}\sum_{n=1}^{N} \left[\log \mathbf{1}\{Y_n \in [0, \theta]\} - \log(\theta)\right]$$

EXAMPLE E.6 (Normal Distribution)

The sample average log-likelihood function of the normal location model with N observations is

$$\mathrm{E}_N\left[L(\theta; Y)\right] = \frac{1}{N}\sum_{n=1}^{N}\left[-\frac{1}{2}\log(2\pi\sigma^2) - \frac{(Y_n-\mu)^2}{2\sigma^2}\right]$$

The likelihood function (or p.f.) completely characterizes the behavior of the random variable Y and so it is through the sample log-likelihood function that information from the realized sample $\mathbf{y}$ about the unknown parameter vector $\boldsymbol{\theta}_0$ is completely described. A special feature of the log-likelihood function is that its expectation is maximized at the parameter value $\boldsymbol{\theta}_0$.

THEOREM E.1 (LOG-LIKELIHOOD INEQUALITY) *Let $L(\boldsymbol{\theta}_0; y) \equiv \log f_Y(y; \boldsymbol{\theta}_0)$ be the log-likelihood function for the random variable Y. Then*

$$\mathrm{E}[L(\boldsymbol{\theta}; Y)] \leq \mathrm{E}[L(\boldsymbol{\theta}_0; Y)]$$

for all $\boldsymbol{\theta} \in \boldsymbol{\Theta}$.

For a proof, see the discussion of this result in Chapter 14.

EXAMPLE E.7 (Bernoulli Distribution)

The expectation of the log-likelihood function of the Bernoulli random variable is

$$\mathrm{E}\left[L(\theta; Y)\right] = \theta_0\log(\theta) + (1-\theta_0)\log(1-\theta)$$

Ordinary univariate calculus shows that this function is uniquely maximized at $\theta = \theta_0$.

EXAMPLE E.8 (Uniform Distribution)

The expectation of the log-likelihood function of the uniform random variable given the true value θ_0 is

$$\mathrm{E}[L(\theta; Y)] = \begin{cases} -\infty, & \text{if } \theta < \theta_0 \\ -\log(\theta), & \text{if } \theta \geq \theta_0 \end{cases}$$

which is maximized at θ_0 because $-\log(\theta)$ is a strictly decreasing function of θ.

EXAMPLE E.9 (Normal Distribution)

The expected log-likelihood function of $Y \sim \mathfrak{N}(\mu_0, \sigma_0^2)$ is

$$\begin{aligned}\mathrm{E}\left[L(\boldsymbol{\theta}; Y)\right] &= -\frac{1}{2}\log(2\pi\sigma^2) - \frac{\mathrm{E}[(Y-\mu)^2]}{2\sigma^2} \\ &= -\frac{1}{2}\log(2\pi\sigma^2) - \frac{1}{2}\frac{\sigma_0^2 + (\mu-\mu_0)^2}{\sigma^2}\end{aligned}$$

For all values of σ^2, the quadratic term involving μ is uniquely maximized at $\mu = \mu_0$ where the quadratic equals zero. Setting $\mu = \mu_0$, we can show that $\sigma^2 = \sigma_0^2$ is the location of the unique maximum in σ^2: setting $\sigma^2 = x$,

$$\frac{d}{dx}\left[-\frac{1}{2}\log(2\pi x) - \frac{1}{2}\frac{\sigma_0^2}{x}\right] = -\frac{1}{2}\left(\frac{1}{x} - \frac{\sigma_0^2}{x^2}\right)$$

which equals zero at $x = \sigma_0^2$ and approaches zero as $x \to \pm\infty$. But negative values are not in the parameter space of σ^2 and

$$\lim_{x\to\infty} -\frac{1}{2}\log(2\pi x) - \frac{1}{2}\frac{\sigma_0^2}{x} = \lim_{x\to\infty} -\frac{1}{2}\log(2\pi x) = -\infty$$

leaving $x = \sigma^2 = \sigma_0^2$ as the maximizer.

Because the true parameter value $\boldsymbol{\theta}_0$ maximizes the expectation of the log-likelihood function, it is analogous to construct an estimator of $\boldsymbol{\theta}_0$ as the value of $\boldsymbol{\theta}$ that maximizes the empirical expectation (sample average) log-likelihood function. An intuitive motivation for estimating $\boldsymbol{\theta}$ by the method of maximizing the sample likelihood function is that one is finding a value for $\boldsymbol{\theta}$ that would have been "most likely" to yield the observed sample $(y_1, \ldots y_N)$.

DEFINITION E.10 (MAXIMUM LIKELIHOOD ESTIMATOR) *The* maximum likelihood estimator *(MLE) is a value of the parameter vector that maximizes the sample average log-likelihood function. We will denote this estimator by $\hat{\boldsymbol{\theta}}_N$:*

$$\hat{\boldsymbol{\theta}}_N \equiv \operatorname*{argmax}_{\boldsymbol{\theta}\in\boldsymbol{\Theta}} \mathrm{E}_N\left[L(\boldsymbol{\theta}; Y)\right]$$

Maximizing the sample average log-likelihood function is obviously equivalent to maximizing the sample likelihood because the logarithmic function is continuously increasing.

EXAMPLE E.10 (Bernoulli Distribution)

The sample average log-likelihood function of the Bernoulli distribution can be rewritten

$$\mathrm{E}_N\left[L(\theta; Y)\right] = \mathrm{E}_N[Y]\log(\theta) + (1 - \mathrm{E}_N[Y])\log(1 - \theta)$$

where $\mathrm{E}_N[Y] = \sum_{n=1}^{N} Y_n/N$. This function is maximized at $\hat{\theta}_N = \mathrm{E}_N[Y]$.

EXAMPLE E.11 (Uniform Distribution)

The average log-likelihood function of a uniformly distributed sample,

$$\begin{aligned}\mathrm{E}_N\left[L(\theta; Y)\right] &= \frac{1}{N}\sum_{n=1}^{N}\log \mathbf{1}\{Y_n \in [0, \theta]\} - \log(\theta) \\ &= \begin{cases} -\infty, & \text{if } \theta < \max_n y_n \\ -\log(\theta), & \text{if } \theta \geq \max_n y_n \end{cases}\end{aligned}$$

is not differentiable everywhere and cannot be maximized by ordinary calculus. Nevertheless, one can see by inspection that this function is maximized at $\hat{\theta}_N = \max_n Y_n = Y_{(N)}$.

EXAMPLE E.12 (Normal Distribution)

The sample average log-likelihood function of a normally distributed sample can be rewritten

$$\begin{aligned}\mathrm{E}_N\left[L(\theta; Y)\right] &= -\frac{1}{2}\log(2\pi\sigma^2) - \frac{1}{2}\frac{\mathrm{E}_N[Y_n - \mu]^2}{\sigma^2} \\ &= -\frac{1}{2}\log(2\pi\sigma^2) - \frac{1}{2}\frac{\mathrm{Var}_N[Y] + (\mathrm{E}_N[Y] - \mu)^2}{\sigma^2}\end{aligned}$$

where $\mathrm{Var}_N[Y] \equiv \mathrm{E}_N[(Y - \mathrm{E}_N[Y])^2]$ is the empirical variance of the sample. As in both previous examples, maximizing the empirical expectation of the log-likelihood is analogous to maximizing the population expectation: thus, $\hat{\boldsymbol{\theta}}_N = [\hat{\mu}_N, \hat{\sigma}_N^2]' = [\mathrm{E}_N[Y], \mathrm{Var}_N[Y]]'$.

METHOD OF MOMENTS

The *method of moments* is another method for finding estimators by analogy. In addition, this method may yield estimators that are more tractable than the method of maximum likelihood. The method of moments chooses estimators that equate sample moments with population moments evaluated at the estimator. Using the notation in Definition D.9 (p. 871),

$$\mu_k'(\boldsymbol{\theta}) \equiv \mathrm{E}\left[Y^k\right] = \int y^k \, dF_Y(y; \boldsymbol{\theta}), \qquad (k = 1, \ldots, K)$$

are the first K population moments of Y.

DEFINITION E.11 (METHOD OF MOMENTS ESTIMATOR) *If the first K moments exist, then the* method of moments estimator *(MME), denoted $\tilde{\theta}_N$, is the solution to the system of K simultaneous equations*

$$\mu_k'(\tilde{\theta}_N) = \mathrm{E}_N[Y^k], \qquad (k = 1, \ldots, K)$$

provided that a unique solution exists.

EXAMPLE E.13 (Bernoulli Distribution)

There is only one parameter in the Bernoulli distribution and so only one moment equation is required:

$$\tilde{\theta}_N = \mathrm{E}_N[Y]$$

The solution of the moment equations is immediate and we find that the MME and the MLE coincide.

EXAMPLE E.14 (Uniform Distribution)

Again, there is only one parameter:

$$\frac{1}{2}\tilde{\theta}_N = \mathrm{E}_N[Y]$$

so that $\tilde{\theta}_N = 2\ \mathrm{E}_N[Y]$. This estimator does not coincide with the MLE. But whereas the MLE is clearly biased,

$$\mathrm{E}[\hat{\theta}_N] = \mathrm{E}[Y_{(N)}] < \theta_0$$

the MME is unbiased,

$$\mathrm{E}[\tilde{\theta}_N] = 2\ \mathrm{E}\big[\mathrm{E}_N[Y]\big] = 2\left(\frac{1}{2}\theta_0\right) = \theta_0$$

This unbiasedness occurs because sample moments are unbiased estimators of population moments *and* this MME is a *linear function* of the sample moments.

EXAMPLE E.15 (Normal Distribution)

We require two moment equations for the two-parameter normal distribution:

$$\begin{aligned} \tilde{\mu}_N &= \mathrm{E}_N[Y] \\ \tilde{\sigma}_N^2 + \tilde{\mu}_N^2 &= \mathrm{E}_N[Y^2] \end{aligned}$$

Solving the second equations for the estimator of the σ^2,

$$\tilde{\sigma}_N^2 = \mathrm{E}_N[Y^2] - (\mathrm{E}_N[Y])^2 = \mathrm{Var}_N[Y]$$

Once again, the MME and the MLE coincide. In this case, $\tilde{\mu}_N = \hat{\mu}_N$ is unbiased but $\tilde{\sigma}_N^2 = \hat{\sigma}_N^2$ is biased because the variance estimator is a nonlinear function of the first sample moment.

E.2.4 Asymptotic Distribution Theory

Asymptotic distribution theory provides approximations to the distributions of estimators for large sample sizes. There are two basic results. First, estimators may converge to the parameters that they estimate as the sample size approaches infinity. This seems only sensible, and estimators that do not have this property are generally abandoned. Second, estimators may have an approximately normal distribution when N is large. If this approximation is reliable, the normal distribution provides a general simplification of distribution theory for estimators, resting on just the first two moments of the approximate distribution.

The first kind of result usually rests on the convergence of sample moments to population moments.

THEOREM E.2 (LAW OF LARGE NUMBERS) *Let $(Y_1, \ldots, Y_N)$ be a random sample of the random variable Y and denote* $\mathrm{E}[Y] = \mu$, $\mathrm{Var}[Y] = \sigma^2$. *If σ^2 exists then for any $\epsilon > 0$*

$$\lim_{N\to\infty} \Pr\{|\mathrm{E}_N[Y] - \mu| > \epsilon\} = 0$$

Proof. The variance of the first sample moment is

$$\mathrm{Var}[\mathrm{E}_N(Y)] = \frac{\sigma^2}{N}$$

According to Lemma D.3 (Chebychev's inequality, p. 875),

$$\Pr\{|\mathrm{E}_N[Y] - \mu| > \epsilon\} < \frac{\mathrm{Var}\big[\mathrm{E}_N[Y]\big]}{\epsilon^2} = \frac{\sigma^2}{N\epsilon^2}$$

which approaches zero as N approaches infinity. □

The interpretation of this law of large numbers is important. Literally, it states the probability the $\mathrm{E}_N[Y]$ is not arbitrarily close to μ approaches zero. If we think in terms of the limit of the c.d.f. of $\bar{Y} \equiv \mathrm{E}_N[Y]$, this theorem states that if σ^2 is finite then for any $y \neq \mu$

$$\lim_{N\to\infty} F_{\bar{Y}}(y) = \begin{cases} 0, & \text{if} \quad y < \mu \\ 1, & \text{if} \quad y > \mu \end{cases}$$

This limiting c.d.f. is the c.d.f. of a constant equal to μ. In this sense, the sequence of random variables $\mathrm{E}_N[Y]$ indexed by N is converging *in distribution* to a constant. The formal terms for "convergence in distribution to a constant" are *convergence in probability* and *weak convergence*.

We can apply this law of large numbers directly to such estimators as the MME/MLE of the Bernoulli parameter or the MLE of the mean of a normal distribution. Both of these estimators are first sample moments and both distributions have finite second moments. We show in Chapter 13 that such estimators as the MME/MLE for the variance of the normal distribution also converge in probability to their population values. Intuitively, MME estimators converge in probability because they are functions of sample moments that converge in probability to population moments. There are conditions on the cases in which this occurs of course, but these conditions are not very restrictive.

The law of large numbers does not apply directly to estimators like the MLE for the parameter of the uniform distribution either. That estimator is not a function of a sample moment. Rather, we can think of the estimator as a sample quantile. However, all MLEs are functions of the first sample moment of the log-likelihood function. It is also possible to apply the law of large numbers to this function in a way that establishes the convergence in probability of many MLEs. As a result, the MLE for the uniform distribution possesses a desirable asymptotic property even though it is a biased estimator. We discuss MLEs in Chapter 14.

The approximation of the distribution of estimators with the normal distribution rests on the central limit theorem (Theorem D.16, p. 892). We repeat it here for convenience:

Let $\{Y_n\}$ be a sequence of independent and identically distributed (i.i.d.) random variables and denote $\mu = \mathrm{E}[Y]$, $\sigma^2 = \mathrm{Var}[Y]$. If the σ^2 is strictly positive and finite, then the distribution of

$$Z_N \equiv \sqrt{N}\frac{\mathrm{E}_N[Y_n] - \mu}{\sigma} \xrightarrow{d} Z \sim \mathfrak{N}(0, 1)$$

as $N \to \infty$.

Among our examples, the most interesting application is the MME/MLE of the Bernoulli parameter. For finite N, the MLE is proportional to a random variable with a binomial distribution: $\hat{\theta}_N$ is the sum of N i.i.d. Bernoulli random variables (a binomial) divided by N. Thus, the central limit theorem implies that if Y is a binomial random variable and the probability of success is θ then

$$\lim_{N\to\infty} \Pr\left\{\frac{Y - N\theta}{\sqrt{N\theta\,(1-\theta)}} < c\right\} = \Phi(c)$$

For large N, it is often impractical to compute the exact probabilities of the binomial distribution. This approximation is widely used instead:

$$\Pr\{Y < c\} \approx \Phi\left[\frac{c - N\theta}{\sqrt{N\theta\,(1-\theta)}}\right]$$

Another application is the MME/MLE of the variance of the normal distribution. We noted in (E.3) that

$$\frac{s^2}{\sigma^2} \sim \frac{\chi^2_{N-1}}{N-1}$$

and in (E.1) that

$$s^2 = \frac{N}{N-1}\,\mathrm{E}_N\big[(Y - \mathrm{E}_N[Y])^2\big]$$

Therefore, the MME/MLE of σ^2 has the distribution

$$\hat{\sigma}^2_N \sim \frac{\sigma^2}{N}\,\chi^2_{N-1}$$

We also noted that the sum of ν squared i.i.d. $\mathfrak{N}(0, 1)$ random variables has the χ^2_ν distribution. Therefore, we can apply the central limit theorem and Theorem D.10 (p. 889) to claim that

$$\frac{\chi^2_{N-1} - (N-1)}{\sqrt{2\,(N-1)}} \xrightarrow{d} Z \sim \mathfrak{N}(0, 1)$$

Putting these results together, we have shown that

$$\sqrt{\frac{N}{2}}\left(\frac{\hat{\sigma}^2_N}{\sigma^2} - 1\right) \xrightarrow{d} Z \sim \mathfrak{N}(0, 1)$$

Therefore, we approximate the distribution of $\hat{\sigma}^2_N$ with the $\mathfrak{N}(\sigma^2,\ 2\sigma^4/N)$ distribution for large N.

APPENDIX F

Noncentral Distributions

In this appendix, we derive the standard expressions for the p.d.f. of the noncentral chi-square and F distributions. In addition, we prove Lemma 11.1 (Power Functions, p. 233) concerning the power functions of classical hypothesis tests. We take the material in Chapters 10 and 11 as given.

There is a simple relationship between the chi-square distribution and its noncentral generalization.

Lemma F.1 (Noncentral Chi-Square Decomposition) *Let $\chi^2_{\nu_j}(\lambda_j)$, $\nu_j \in \mathbb{N}$, $\lambda_j \geq 0$ $(j = 1, \ldots, J)$ denote J independently noncentral chi-square random variables. Then $\sum_{j=1}^{J} \chi^2_{\nu_j}(\lambda_j) \sim \chi^2_\nu(\lambda)$ where $\nu \equiv \sum_{j=1}^{J} \nu_j$ and $\lambda \equiv \sum_{j=1}^{J} \lambda_j$.*

Proof. Let $\mathbf{z} \sim \mathfrak{N}(\boldsymbol{\mu}, \mathbf{I}_\nu)$ where $\boldsymbol{\mu} \in \mathbb{R}^\nu$ so that by definition $z_i^2 \sim \chi_1^2(\mu_i^2)$ $(i = 1, \ldots, \nu)$ and $\sum_{i=1}^{\nu} z_i^2 = \mathbf{z}'\mathbf{z} \sim \chi^2_\nu(\lambda)$ where $\lambda = \boldsymbol{\mu}'\boldsymbol{\mu} = \sum_{i=1}^{\nu} \mu_i^2$. Therefore, for each $j = 1, \ldots, J$, we can choose a μ_j so that $\lambda_j = \mu_j'\mu_j = \sum_{i=1}^{\nu_j} \mu_{ij}^2$ and for independently distributed $\mathbf{z}_j \sim \mathfrak{N}(\boldsymbol{\mu}_j, \mathbf{I}_{\nu_j})$,

$$\sum_{i=1}^{\nu_j} z_{ij}^2(\mu_{ij}^2) \sim \sum_{i=1}^{\nu_j} \chi_1^2(\mu_{ij}^2) \sim \chi^2_{\nu_j}(\lambda_j)$$

where the $\chi_1^2(\mu_{ij}^2)$ are independently distributed. But then

$$\sum_{j=1}^{J} \chi^2_{\nu_j}(\lambda_j) \sim \sum_{j=1}^{J}\sum_{i=1}^{\nu_j} z_{ij}^2 \sim \chi^2_\nu(\lambda)$$ □

Special cases of this result are that $\chi^2_{\nu-1}(\lambda) + \chi_1^2 \sim \chi^2_\nu(\lambda)$ and $\chi^2_{\nu-1} + \chi_1^2(\lambda) \sim \chi^2_\nu(\lambda)$. This last relationship provides a convenient route to deriving the p.d.f. of the noncentral chi-square distribution.[1]

[1] Johnson et al. (1970b, p. 132) describe this approach and cite references.

Lemma F.2 (Noncentral Chi-Square Density) *If $Y \sim \chi^2_\nu(\lambda)$ then its p.d.f. is the mixture*

$$f_Y(y) = \sum_{j=0}^{\infty}\left[\frac{\left(\frac{1}{2}\lambda\right)^j}{j!}e^{-\frac{1}{2}\lambda}\right]\left[\frac{1}{2^{\nu/2+j}\Gamma(\nu/2+j)}y^{\nu/2+j-1}e^{-\frac{1}{2}y}\right]$$

$$= \sum_{j=0}^{\infty} f_{Po(\lambda/2)}(j)\cdot f_{\chi^2_{\nu+2j}}(y)$$

where $f_{Po(\lambda/2)}(j)$ is the p.m.f. of the Poisson distribution with parameter $\lambda/2$ and $f_{\chi^2_{\nu+2j}}(y)$ is the p.d.f. of the central chi-square distribution with $\nu + 2j$ degrees of freedom.[2]

Proof. We will use the process of induction starting with the $\chi^2_1(\lambda)$ p.d.f. and then applying the Convolution theorem (Theorem D.7, p. 882). Now let $Y \sim \chi^2_1(\lambda)$ so that

$$\begin{aligned}\Pr\{Y \le y\} &= \Pr\left\{-\sqrt{y} \le z + \sqrt{\lambda} \le \sqrt{y}\right\}\\ &= \Pr\left\{-\sqrt{y} - \sqrt{\lambda} \le z \le \sqrt{y} - \sqrt{\lambda}\right\} \qquad \text{(F.1)}\\ &= \int_{-\sqrt{y}-\sqrt{\lambda}}^{\sqrt{y}-\sqrt{\lambda}} \phi(z)\,dz\end{aligned}$$

where $z \sim \mathfrak{N}(0, 1)$.[3] Differentiating with respect to y, we obtain the p.d.f.

$$\begin{aligned}f_Y(y) &= \frac{1}{2}\frac{1}{\sqrt{2\pi y}}\left\{\exp\left[-\frac{1}{2}\left(\sqrt{y}+\sqrt{\lambda}\right)^2\right] + \exp\left[-\frac{1}{2}\left(\sqrt{y}-\sqrt{\lambda}\right)^2\right]\right\}\\ &= \frac{1}{\sqrt{2\pi y}}\exp\left(-\frac{y+\lambda}{2}\right)\frac{\exp\left(-\sqrt{\lambda y}\right)+\exp\left(\sqrt{\lambda y}\right)}{2}\end{aligned}$$

Expanding the sum of exponential functions in a Taylor series around $z = \sqrt{\lambda y} = 0$ gives[4]

$$\begin{aligned}\frac{\exp\left(-\sqrt{\lambda y}\right)+\exp\left(\sqrt{\lambda y}\right)}{2} &= \frac{e^{-z}+e^{z}}{2}\\ &= \sum_{j=0}^{\infty}\frac{1}{(2j)!}z^{2j}\end{aligned}$$

[2] See Definition D.23 (Poisson Distribution, p. 886) and Definition D.30 (Chi-Square distribution, p. 888).

[3] See Definition D.27 (Normal Distribution, p. 887).

[4] We are actually dealing with the hyperbolic cosine function

$$\cosh(x) \equiv \frac{e^x + e^{-x}}{2}$$

$$= \sum_{j=0}^{\infty} \frac{1}{(2j)!} (\lambda y)^j$$

Therefore, reordering terms gives

$$f_Y(y) = \sum_{j=0}^{\infty} \frac{\lambda^j}{j!} e^{-\frac{1}{2}\lambda} \frac{j!}{\sqrt{2\pi}\,(2j)!} y^{j-\frac{1}{2}} e^{-\frac{1}{2}y}$$

This is the required result for $\nu = 1$ because

$$\frac{(2j)!}{2^j \cdot j!} = (2j-1) \cdot \dots \cdot 3 \cdot 1$$

so that

$$\begin{aligned}
\Gamma\left(j+\frac{1}{2}\right) &= \left(j-\frac{1}{2}\right)\Gamma\left(j-\frac{1}{2}\right) \\
&= 2^{-1}(2j-1)\,\Gamma\left(j-\frac{1}{2}\right) \\
&= 2^{-j}(2j-1) \cdot \dots \cdot 3 \cdot 1 \cdot \Gamma\left(\frac{1}{2}\right) \\
&= \frac{(2j)!}{2^{2j} \cdot j!}\sqrt{\pi}
\end{aligned}$$

This gives

$$f_Y(y) = \sum_{j=0}^{\infty} \frac{\left(\frac{1}{2}\lambda\right)^j}{j!} e^{-\frac{1}{2}\lambda} \frac{1}{2^{\frac{1}{2}+j}\,\Gamma\left(\frac{1}{2}+j\right)} y^{j-\frac{1}{2}} e^{-\frac{1}{2}y}$$

Finally, we apply induction using convolution. According to Lemma F.1, $\chi^2_\nu(\lambda) \sim \chi^2_{\nu-1}(\lambda) + \chi^2_1$ where $\chi^2_{\nu-1}(\lambda)$ and χ^2_1 are independent. Therefore,

$$f_{\chi^2_\nu(\lambda)}(y) = \int_0^y f_{\chi^2_{\nu-1}(\lambda)}(y-x)\, f_{\chi^2_1}(x)\, dx$$

Now given the p.d.f. of the $\chi^2_{\nu-1}(\lambda)$ distribution, we have

$$\begin{aligned}
f_{\chi^2_\nu(\lambda)}(y) &= \sum_{j=0}^{\infty} f_{Po(\lambda/2)}(j) \int_0^y f_{\chi^2_{\nu-1+2j}}(y-x)\, f_{\chi^2_1}(x)\, dx \\
&= \sum_{j=0}^{\infty} f_{Po(\lambda/2)}(j)\, f_{\chi^2_{\nu+2j}}(y)
\end{aligned}$$

which is the required result. □

The following result for the noncentral F distribution is an immediate consequence of the noncentral chi-square p.d.f.

Lemma F.3 (Noncentral F Density) *If $Y \sim F_{\nu_1,\nu_2}(\lambda)$ then its p.d.f. is the mixture*

$$f_Y(y) = \nu_1 \sum_{j=0}^{\infty} f_{Po(\lambda/2)}(j) \cdot \frac{\nu_1}{\nu_1+2j} \cdot f_{F_{\nu_1+2j,\nu_2}}\left(\frac{\nu_1}{\nu_1+2j}y\right)$$

where $f_{Po(\lambda/2)}(j)$ is the p.m.f. of the Poisson distribution with parameter $\lambda/2$.

Proof. Using Definition 22 (Noncentral F Distribution, p. 233), the noncentral F p.d.f. is given by[5]

$$\begin{aligned}
f_{F_{\nu_1,\nu_2}(\lambda)}(y) &= \int_{(\nu_1/\nu_2)y=x_1/x_2} f_{\chi^2_{\nu_1}(\lambda)}(x_1)\; f_{\chi^2_{\nu_2}}(x_2)\, dx_1\, dx_2 \\
&= \int_{(\nu_1/\nu_2)y=x_1/x_2} \sum_{j=0}^{\infty} f_{Po(\lambda/2)}(j)\; f_{\chi^2_{\nu+2j}(\lambda)}(x_1)\; f_{\chi^2_{\nu_2}}(x_2)\, dx_1\, dx_2 \\
&= \sum_{j=0}^{\infty} f_{Po(\lambda/2)}(j) \int_{(\nu_1/\nu_2)y=x_1/x_2} f_{\chi^2_{\nu+2j}(\lambda)}(x_1)\; f_{\chi^2_{\nu_2}}(x_2)\, dx_1\, dx_2 \\
&= \frac{\nu_1}{\nu_2} \sum_{j=0}^{\infty} f_{Po(\lambda/2)}(j)\, \frac{\nu_2}{\nu_1+2j} \cdot f_{F_{\nu_1+2j,\nu_2}}\left[\frac{\nu_2}{\nu_1+2j}\left(\frac{\nu_1}{\nu_2}y\right)\right] \\
&= \sum_{j=0}^{\infty} f_{Po(\lambda/2)}(j) \cdot \frac{\nu_1}{\nu_1+2j} \cdot f_{F_{\nu_1+2j,\nu_2}}\left(\frac{\nu_1}{\nu_1+2j}y\right)
\end{aligned}$$

where the second to the last equality follows Definition D.32 (Snedecor F Distribution, p. 890). □

We use these functional forms for the p.d.f.s of the noncentral chi-square and F distributions to prove the basic proposition about statistical power of classical hypothesis tests. The simplest elements of Lemma 11.1 to prove are the following:

Lemma F.4 *The power functions $\Pr\{\chi^2_M(\lambda) \geq \chi^2_{M;1-\alpha}\}$ and $\Pr\{F_{M,N-K}(\lambda) \geq F_{M,N-K;1-\alpha}\}$ are increasing in the noncentrality parameter λ.*

Proof. To prove this, we focus on the $\chi^2_1(\lambda)$ component of the lemma: using (F.1), let

$$G(x;\lambda) = \Pr\{\chi^2_1(\lambda) \leq x\} = \Pr\{w^2 \leq x\} = \Pr\{-x \leq w \leq x\}$$

[5] We use the notation

$$\int_{y=(x_1/x_2)(\nu_2/\nu_2)} f_{\chi^2_{\nu_1}(\lambda)}(x_1)\, f_{\chi^2_{\nu_2}}(x_2)\, dx_1\, dx_2$$

as an abbreviation for the transformation and integration that one follows to convert the joint distribution of independent $\chi^2_{\nu_1}(\lambda)$ and $\chi^2_{\nu_2}$ random variables into the marginal distribution for $[\chi^2_{\nu_1}(\lambda)/\chi^2_{\nu_2}](\nu_2/\nu_1)$.

where $w \sim \mathfrak{N}(\sqrt{\lambda}, 1)$ and $x \geq 0$. This probability $G(x; \lambda)$ falls as λ grows. To see this formally, note that

$$\begin{aligned} G(x; \lambda) &= \Pr\left\{-\sqrt{x} \leq z + \sqrt{\lambda} \leq \sqrt{x}\right\} \\ &= \Pr\left\{-\sqrt{x} - \sqrt{\lambda} \leq z \leq \sqrt{x} - \sqrt{\lambda}\right\} \\ &= \int_{-\sqrt{x}-\sqrt{\lambda}}^{\sqrt{x}-\sqrt{\lambda}} \phi(z)\, dz \end{aligned}$$

where $z \sim \mathfrak{N}(0, 1)$. Differentiating with respect to λ,

$$\frac{\partial G(x; \lambda)}{\partial \lambda} = \frac{1}{2\sqrt{\lambda}}\left[\phi(\sqrt{x} + \sqrt{\lambda}) - \phi(\sqrt{x} - \sqrt{\lambda})\right] < 0$$

for all $x, \lambda > 0$ because the standard normal p.d.f. ϕ is unimodal and symmetric around the origin. The implication for any noncentral chi-square distribution is the same: using Lemma F.1 (p. 916),

$$\begin{aligned} \Pr\{\chi^2_M(\lambda) \leq x\} &= \Pr\{\chi^2_{M-1} + \chi^2_1(\lambda) \leq x\} \\ &= \mathrm{E}[\Pr\{\chi^2_1(\lambda) \leq x - \chi^2_{M-1} \mid \chi^2_{M-1}\}] \\ &= \mathrm{E}[G(x - \chi^2_{M-1}; \lambda)] \end{aligned}$$

because χ^2_{M-1} and $\chi^2_1(\lambda)$ are independent. Therefore,

$$\frac{\partial \Pr\{\chi^2_M(\lambda) \leq x\}}{\partial \lambda} = \mathrm{E}\left[\frac{\partial G(x - \chi^2_{M-1}; \lambda)}{\partial \lambda}\right] < 0$$

The same logic holds for the F ratio, which is now the ratio of independent noncentral chi-square and central chi-square random variables:

$$\Pr\left\{\frac{\chi^2_M(\lambda)/M}{\chi^2_{N-K}/(N-K)} \leq x\right\} = \mathrm{E}[G(x\, M\, \chi^2_{N-K}/(N-K) - \chi^2_{M-1}; \lambda)]$$

is decreasing in λ. □

Now we turn to studying the degrees of freedom. We use the proof technique of Gupta and Perlman (1974), which rests on the Neyman–Pearson Lemma (Theorem 11, p. 406). This result states that the likelihood ratio critical region, defined by c_α such that

$$\Pr\{Y \mid f_1(Y)/f_0(Y) \geq c_\alpha\} = \alpha$$

is the most powerful critical region for testing $H_0 : Y \sim f_0(y)$ against $H_1 : Y \sim f_1(y)$. Consider the case of

$$H_0 : Y \sim \chi^2_{\nu_0} \qquad \text{versus} \qquad H_1 : Y \sim \chi^2_{\nu_1}$$

where $\nu_0 < \nu_1$. The likelihood ratio is

$$\frac{f_1(y)}{f_0(y)} = \frac{\Gamma\left(\frac{1}{2}\nu_0\right)}{\Gamma\left(\frac{1}{2}\nu_1\right)}\left(\frac{y}{2}\right)^{\frac{1}{2}(\nu_1-\nu_0)}$$

which is strictly increasing in y. Therefore, the likelihood ratio critical region is $\{Y \mid Y \geq \chi^2_{\nu_0;1-\alpha}\}$. We can use this fact to demonstrate the method of proof most simply for another element of Lemma 11.1.

LEMMA F.5 *The power function* $\Pr\{\chi^2_M(\lambda) \geq \chi^2_{M;1-\alpha}\}$ *is decreasing in the degrees of freedom parameter* M.

Proof. Consider an alternative critical region with significance level α,

$$\left\{Y \mid Y + Z \geq \chi^2_{\nu_0+\xi;1-\alpha}\right\}$$

where $Z \sim \chi^2_\xi$ and independent of Y. Comparing the power of this critical region against the likelihood ratio region under the alternative, we have

$$\begin{aligned}\Pr\left\{\chi^2_{\nu_1} \geq \chi^2_{\nu_0;1-\alpha}\right\} &> \Pr\left\{\chi^2_{\nu_1} + \chi^2_\xi \geq \chi^2_{\nu_0+\xi;1-\alpha}\right\} \\ &= \Pr\left\{\chi^2_{\nu_1+\xi} \geq \chi^2_{\nu_0+\xi;1-\alpha}\right\}\end{aligned}$$

Therefore, after setting $\nu + \theta = \nu_1$ and $\nu = \nu_0$,

$$\Pr\left\{\chi^2_{\nu+\theta} \geq \chi^2_{\nu;1-\alpha}\right\}$$

is decreasing in ν (for $\nu, \theta > 0$).

Now we apply this result to the $\chi^2_\nu(\lambda)$ case. According to Lemma F.2

$$\Pr\{\chi^2_\nu(\lambda) \geq \chi^2_{\nu;1-\alpha}\} = \sum_{j=0}^{\infty} f_{Po(\lambda/2)}(j) \cdot \Pr\{\chi^2_{\nu+2j} \geq \chi^2_{\nu;1-\alpha}\}$$

where all the probabilities on the RHS are decreasing in ν. This gives the result. □

The essence of the proof is the observation that adding chi-square noise to the test statistic, and adjusting the critical value to maintain a level-α test, yields a less powerful test. The proof of the following lemma exploits the same insight.

LEMMA F.6 *The power function* $\Pr\{F_{M,N-K}(\lambda) \geq F_{M,N-K;1-\alpha}\}$ *is decreasing in the degrees of freedom parameter* M *and increasing in the degrees of freedom* $N - K$.

Proof. See Gupta and Perlman (1974).

Lemmas F.4–F.6 together constitute Lemma 11.1.

APPENDIX G

Multivariate Differentiation

This appendix develops a set of derivatives of functions of matrices. We use these derivatives for quadratic forms and log-likelihood functions. We do not recommend memorizing these results. They are the sort of thing of which you convince yourself once, and look up thereafter. It is often helpful as one studies this section to remember the scalar counterparts. All of the equations should hold when scalars are substituted for matrices.

G.1 BASIC NOTATION

Because differentiation is a linear operator, it is helpful to think of differentiation as a linear transformation. As long as we are differentiating scalars or row vectors, the following notation for differentiation with respect to a vector will suffice.

Definition G.1 (Vector Derivative) *Denote the vector operator for differentiation by*

$$\frac{\partial}{\partial \mathbf{x}} = \left[\frac{\partial}{\partial x_m};\ m = 1, \ldots, M\right] = \begin{bmatrix} \frac{\partial}{\partial x_1} \\ \vdots \\ \frac{\partial}{\partial x_M} \end{bmatrix}$$

where $\mathbf{x} = [x_m;\ m = 1, \ldots, M]'$ *is a column vector of M elements, and define* $(\partial/\partial\mathbf{x})\mathbf{y}'$ *to be the* $M \times N$ *matrix of partial derivatives*

$$\frac{\partial}{\partial \mathbf{x}}\mathbf{y}' \equiv \left[\frac{\partial y_n}{\partial x_m};\ m = 1, \ldots, M,\ n = 1, \ldots, N\right] \equiv \frac{\partial \mathbf{y}'}{\partial \mathbf{x}} \tag{G.1}$$

where $\mathbf{y} = [y_n;\ n = 1, \ldots, N]'$.

This notation is analogous to the usual matrix product

$$\mathbf{x}\mathbf{y}' = [x_m y_n]$$

The following results are immediate consequences of this definition:

$$\left[\frac{\partial \mathbf{y}'}{\partial \mathbf{x}}\right]' = \mathbf{y}\left(\frac{\partial}{\partial \mathbf{x}}\right)' = \mathbf{y}\left(\frac{\partial}{\partial \mathbf{x}'}\right) \equiv \frac{\partial \mathbf{y}}{\partial \mathbf{x}'} \tag{G.2}$$

and

$$\frac{\partial \mathbf{x}'}{\partial \mathbf{x}} = \frac{\partial \mathbf{x}}{\partial \mathbf{x}'} = \mathbf{I}_N \tag{G.3}$$

If $\mathbf{A}$ is a $K \times N$ matrix of constants, then

$$\frac{\partial}{\partial \mathbf{x}}(\mathbf{A}\mathbf{y})' = \frac{\partial}{\partial \mathbf{x}}\mathbf{y}'\mathbf{A}' = \frac{\partial \mathbf{y}'}{\partial \mathbf{x}}\mathbf{A}' \tag{G.4}$$

and

$$\frac{\partial}{\partial \mathbf{x}}\mathbf{z}'\mathbf{A}\mathbf{y} = \frac{\partial}{\partial \mathbf{x}}\mathbf{y}'\mathbf{A}'\mathbf{z} = \frac{\partial \mathbf{z}'}{\partial \mathbf{x}}\mathbf{A}\mathbf{y} + \frac{\partial \mathbf{y}'}{\partial \mathbf{x}}\mathbf{A}'\mathbf{z} \tag{G.5}$$

where $\mathbf{z} = [z_k;\ k = 1, \ldots, K]'$. If $K = N$ and $\mathbf{z} = \mathbf{y}$, then

$$\frac{\partial}{\partial \mathbf{x}}\mathbf{y}'\mathbf{A}\mathbf{y} = \frac{\partial \mathbf{y}'}{\partial \mathbf{x}}(\mathbf{A} + \mathbf{A}')\mathbf{y} \tag{G.6}$$

We will extend our notation along the lines of (G.2), for denoting matrices of second-order partial derivatives: given a multivariate function $f(\mathbf{x})$,

$$\frac{\partial^2}{\partial \mathbf{x}\,\partial \mathbf{x}'} f(\mathbf{x}) = \left[\frac{\partial^2 f(\mathbf{x})}{\partial x_i\,\partial x_j}\right]$$

It may be helpful to think of this matrix as the result of postmultiplication of the vector of first-order partial derivatives by a row of partial derivative operators:

$$\frac{\partial^2}{\partial \mathbf{x}\,\partial \mathbf{x}'} f(\mathbf{x}) = \left(\frac{\partial}{\partial \mathbf{x}} f(\mathbf{x})\right)\left(\frac{\partial}{\partial \mathbf{x}}\right)'$$

DEFINITION G.2 (SECOND PARTIAL DERIVATIVE MATRIX) *We will denote the* matrix of second partial derivatives *of the single-valued function y with respect to the elements of the vector x by*

$$\frac{\partial^2 y}{\partial \mathbf{x}\,\partial \mathbf{x}'} = \left[\frac{\partial^2 y}{\partial x_i \partial x_j};\ i = 1, \ldots, N,\ j = 1, \ldots, N\right]$$

This is consistent with our previous definition for the vector derivative operator, as the last equality shows.

This notation provides neat expressions of Taylor's first- and second-order approximations for a twice continuously differentiable function. If $f(x)$ is continuously differentiable, then we can apply Taylor's approximation (Theorem D.18, p. 898) to $f(\mathbf{x}_0 + \epsilon \cdot \boldsymbol{\delta})$ for $\mathbf{x}_0, \boldsymbol{\delta} \in \mathbb{R}^K$ and $\epsilon \in \mathbb{R}$ so that

$$f(\mathbf{x}_0 + \epsilon \cdot \boldsymbol{\delta}) = f(\mathbf{x}_0) + \frac{\partial f(\mathbf{x}_0 + \epsilon \cdot \boldsymbol{\delta})}{\partial \epsilon} \epsilon$$
$$= f(\mathbf{x}_0) + \sum_{i=1}^{N} f_i(\bar{\mathbf{x}})\, \delta_i\, \epsilon$$

where $\bar{\mathbf{x}} = \mathbf{x}_0 + \bar{\epsilon} \cdot \boldsymbol{\delta}$ for some $\bar{\epsilon}$ between 0 and ϵ. That is, $\bar{\mathbf{x}}$ is somewhere on the line segment joining $\mathbf{x}_0$ and $\mathbf{x}_0 + \epsilon \cdot \boldsymbol{\delta}$. If $f(\mathbf{x})$ is two times continuously differentiable, then

$$f(\mathbf{x}_0 + \epsilon \cdot \boldsymbol{\delta}) = f(\mathbf{x}_0) + \sum_{i=1}^{N} f_i(\mathbf{x}_0)\, \delta_i\, \epsilon + \frac{1}{2} \sum_{i=1}^{N} \sum_{j=1}^{N} f_{ij}(\bar{\bar{\mathbf{x}}})\, \delta_i\, \delta_j\, \epsilon^2$$

where $\bar{\bar{\mathbf{x}}} = \mathbf{x}_0 + \bar{\bar{\epsilon}} \cdot \boldsymbol{\delta}$ for some $\bar{\bar{\epsilon}}$ between 0 and ϵ. Written in the notation above, these approximations are

$$f(\mathbf{x}_1) = f(\mathbf{x}_0) + \left.\frac{\partial f(\mathbf{x})}{\partial \mathbf{x}'}\right|_{\mathbf{x}=\bar{\bar{\mathbf{x}}}} (\mathbf{x}_1 - \mathbf{x}_0) \tag{G.7}$$

and

$$f(\mathbf{x}_1) = f(\mathbf{x}_0) + \left.\frac{\partial f(\mathbf{x})}{\partial \mathbf{x}'}\right|_{\mathbf{x}=\mathbf{x}_0} (\mathbf{x}_1 - \mathbf{x}_0) + \frac{1}{2} (\mathbf{x}_1 - \mathbf{x}_0)' \left[\left.\frac{\partial^2 f(\mathbf{x})}{\partial \mathbf{x}\, \partial \mathbf{x}'}\right|_{\mathbf{x}=\bar{\mathbf{x}}} \right] (\mathbf{x}_1 - \mathbf{x}_0) \tag{G.8}$$

where $\mathbf{x}_1 = \mathbf{x}_0 + \epsilon \cdot \boldsymbol{\delta}$.

G.2 VECTORIZATION AND KRONECKER PRODUCTS

Sometimes we wish to differentiate with respect to the elements of a matrix. To do this, we use the notation just developed for differentiation with respect to vectors by introducing a transformation of a matrix into a vector.

DEFINITION G.3 (VEC) *Let* $\mathbf{A} = [a_{mn}]$ *be an* $M \times N$ *matrix. The* vectorized matrix $\mathbf{A}$, *denoted vec*$\mathbf{A}$, *is defined as*

$$\text{vec}\,\mathbf{A} \equiv \begin{bmatrix} \mathbf{a}_1 \\ \mathbf{a}_2 \\ \vdots \\ \mathbf{a}_N \end{bmatrix}$$

where $a_n \equiv [a_{mn};\ m = 1, \ldots, M]'$. *That is, vec*$\mathbf{A}$ *is a vector created by stacking the columns of the matrix* $\mathbf{A}$, *beginning with the first column and ending with the last.*

G.2.1 Kronecker Products

DEFINITION G.4 (KRONECKER PRODUCT) *Let* $\mathbf{A}$ *be an* $M \times N$ *matrix and* $\mathbf{B}$ *be a* $J \times K$ *matrix. The Kronecker product of* $\mathbf{A}$ *and* $\mathbf{B}$ *(the order is important) is defined as the* $MJ \times NK$ *matrix, which can be partitioned as*

$$\mathbf{A} \otimes \mathbf{B} \equiv \begin{bmatrix} a_{11}\mathbf{B} & a_{12}\mathbf{B} & \cdots & a_{1N}\mathbf{B} \\ a_{21}\mathbf{B} & a_{22}\mathbf{B} & \cdots & a_{2N}\mathbf{B} \\ \vdots & \vdots & \ddots & \vdots \\ a_{M1}\mathbf{B} & a_{M2}\mathbf{B} & \cdots & a_{MN}\mathbf{B} \end{bmatrix}$$

Kronecker products have several properties that follow directly from their definition. Provided that the matrices are conformable where necessary,

$$(\mathbf{A} \otimes \mathbf{B})(\mathbf{C} \otimes \mathbf{D}) = \mathbf{AC} \otimes \mathbf{BD} \tag{G.9}$$

$$(\mathbf{A} \otimes \mathbf{B})^{-1} = \mathbf{A}^{-1} \otimes \mathbf{B}^{-1} \tag{G.10}$$

$$(\mathbf{A} \otimes \mathbf{B})' = \mathbf{A}' \otimes \mathbf{B}' \tag{G.11}$$

$$\mathbf{A} \otimes (\mathbf{B} + \mathbf{C}) = (\mathbf{A} \otimes \mathbf{B}) + (\mathbf{A} \otimes \mathbf{C}) \tag{G.12}$$

If $M = N$ and $J = K$, then

$$\det(\mathbf{A} \otimes \mathbf{B}) = (\det \mathbf{A})^J (\det \mathbf{B})^M \tag{G.13}$$

$$\operatorname{tr}(\mathbf{A} \otimes \mathbf{B}) = (\operatorname{tr} \mathbf{A})(\operatorname{tr} \mathbf{B}) \tag{G.14}$$

There are several useful relationships between vectorized matrices and Kronecker products: if $N = J$ then

$$\operatorname{vec}(\mathbf{AB}) = (\mathbf{I}_K \otimes \mathbf{A}) \operatorname{vec} \mathbf{B} = (\mathbf{B}' \otimes \mathbf{I}_M) \operatorname{vec} \mathbf{A} \tag{G.15}$$

and

$$\operatorname{tr}(\mathbf{AB}) = [\operatorname{vec}(\mathbf{A}')]' \operatorname{vec} \mathbf{B} \tag{G.16}$$

One can confirm these by expanding terms.

There is a useful matrix that we will denote by $\mathbf{T}$ that transforms a vectorized matrix into its vectorized transpose:

$$\mathbf{T} \operatorname{vec} \mathbf{A} = \operatorname{vec}(\mathbf{A}') \tag{G.17}$$

Pollock (1979) calls this matrix the *tensor commutator*. It has the following properties:

$$\mathbf{T}^{-1} = \mathbf{T} \tag{G.18}$$

$$\mathbf{T}(\mathbf{A} \otimes \mathbf{B}) = (\mathbf{B} \otimes \mathbf{A})\mathbf{T} \tag{G.19}$$

$$\mathbf{T}' = \mathbf{T} \tag{G.20}$$

The first property, (G.18), follows from the definition: $\mathbf{T}\,\mathrm{vec}(\mathbf{A}') = \mathbf{T}^2\,\mathrm{vec}\,\mathbf{A} = \mathrm{vec}\,(\mathbf{A})$. So does (G.19): for all $\mathbf{x} \equiv \mathrm{vec}\,\mathbf{C}$,

$$\begin{aligned}\mathbf{T}(\mathbf{A}\otimes\mathbf{B})\mathbf{x} &= \mathbf{T}\,\mathrm{vec}(\mathbf{BCA}') \\ &= \mathrm{vec}(\mathbf{AC}'\mathbf{B}') \\ &= (\mathbf{B}\otimes\mathbf{A})\mathbf{Tx}\end{aligned}$$

For property (G.20), we use the fact that $\mathrm{tr}\,\mathbf{AB} = \mathrm{tr}\,\mathbf{BA}$ when $\mathbf{A}$ and $\mathbf{B}$ are right and left conformable: for all $\mathbf{x} = \mathrm{vec}\,\mathbf{A}'$, $\mathbf{y} = \mathrm{vec}\,\mathbf{B}$ such that $\mathrm{tr}\,\mathbf{AB} = \mathrm{tr}\,\mathbf{BA}$,

$$\begin{aligned}\mathbf{x}'\mathbf{y} &= \mathrm{tr}\,\mathbf{AB} \\ &= \mathrm{tr}\,\mathbf{BA} \\ &= [\mathrm{vec}(\mathbf{B}')]'\,\mathrm{vec}\,\mathbf{A} \\ &= [\mathrm{vec}(\mathbf{A}')]'\mathbf{T}'\mathbf{T}\,\mathrm{vec}\,\mathbf{B} \\ &= \mathbf{x}'\mathbf{T}'\mathbf{Ty}\end{aligned}$$

so that $\mathbf{T}'\mathbf{T} = \mathbf{I}$ and, using (G.18), $\mathbf{T}' = \mathbf{T}$.

G.3 DERIVATIVE VECTORS

Now combining these results with vector differentiation yields (when $N = K$)

$$\frac{\partial}{\partial \mathbf{x}}[\mathrm{vec}(\mathbf{AB})]' = \left[\frac{\partial}{\partial \mathbf{x}}(\mathrm{vec}\,\mathbf{B})'\right](\mathbf{I}_K\otimes\mathbf{A}') + \left[\frac{\partial}{\partial \mathbf{x}}(\mathrm{vec}\,\mathbf{A})'\right](\mathbf{B}\otimes\mathbf{I}_M) \tag{G.21}$$

using (G.15) with (G.21). In the special case that $\mathbf{x} = \mathrm{vec}\,\mathbf{A}$ and $\mathbf{B} = \mathbf{A}^{-1}$, (G.21) becomes

$$\begin{aligned}\frac{\partial}{\partial\,\mathrm{vec}\,\mathbf{A}}(\mathrm{vec}\,\mathbf{I})' &= \left[\frac{\partial}{\partial\,\mathrm{vec}\,\mathbf{A}}(\mathrm{vec}\,\mathbf{A}^{-1})'\right](\mathbf{I}_M\otimes\mathbf{A}') + \left[\frac{\partial}{\partial\,\mathrm{vec}\,\mathbf{A}}(\mathrm{vec}\,\mathbf{A})'\right](\mathbf{A}^{-1}\otimes\mathbf{I}_M) \\ &= \left[\frac{\partial}{\partial\,\mathrm{vec}\,\mathbf{A}}(\mathrm{vec}\,\mathbf{A}^{-1})'\right](\mathbf{I}_M\otimes\mathbf{A}') + (\mathbf{A}^{-1}\otimes\mathbf{I}_M)\end{aligned}$$

using (G.3). But the left-hand side holds derivatives of constants that equal zero. Rearranging terms gives the derivative of a matrix inverse with respect to itself:

$$\frac{\partial(\mathrm{vec}\,\mathbf{A}^{-1})'}{\partial\,\mathrm{vec}\,\mathbf{A}} = -(\mathbf{A}^{-1}\otimes\mathbf{A}^{-1\prime}) = -(\mathbf{A}\otimes\mathbf{A}')^{-1} \tag{G.22}$$

It follows from (G.22) and (G.15) that

$$\begin{aligned}\frac{\partial}{\partial\,\mathrm{vec}\,\mathbf{A}}(\mathbf{z}'\mathbf{A}^{-1}\mathbf{y}) &= \frac{\partial}{\partial\,\mathrm{vec}\,\mathbf{A}}\left[(\mathbf{I}\otimes\mathbf{z}')\,\mathrm{vec}(\mathbf{A}^{-1}\mathbf{y})\right]' \\ &= \frac{\partial}{\partial\,\mathrm{vec}\,\mathbf{A}}\left[(\mathbf{y}'\otimes\mathbf{z}')\,\mathrm{vec}(\mathbf{A}^{-1})\right]' \\ &= -(\mathbf{A}^{-1}\otimes\mathbf{A}^{-1\prime})\left[(\mathbf{y}'\otimes\mathbf{z}')\right]' \\ &= -\,\mathrm{vec}(\mathbf{A}^{-1\prime}\mathbf{z}\,\mathbf{y}'\mathbf{A}^{-1\prime})\end{aligned} \tag{G.23}$$

Also, for symmetric $\mathbf{B}$ ($J = K$) and $M = K$,

$$\begin{aligned}\operatorname{vec} \mathbf{A}'\mathbf{B}\mathbf{A} &= \left(\mathbf{I}_J \otimes \mathbf{A}'\mathbf{B}\right) \operatorname{vec} \mathbf{A} \\ &= \left(\mathbf{A}'\mathbf{B} \otimes \mathbf{I}_J\right) \operatorname{vec}(\mathbf{A}')\end{aligned}$$

so that

$$\begin{aligned}\frac{\partial}{\partial \operatorname{vec} \mathbf{A}} (\operatorname{vec} \mathbf{A}'\mathbf{B}\mathbf{A})' &= (\mathbf{I}_J \otimes \mathbf{B}\mathbf{A}) + \mathbf{T}\,(\mathbf{B}\mathbf{A} \otimes \mathbf{I}_J) \\ &= (\mathbf{I}_J \otimes \mathbf{B}\mathbf{A})\,(\mathbf{I}_{J^2} + \mathbf{T})\end{aligned} \tag{G.24}$$

Another useful matrix derivative is the derivative of a determinant. Recall that a matrix determinant has the cofactor expansion (Theorem C.14, p. 864)

$$\det \mathbf{A} = \sum_{i=1}^{N} a_{ij} A_{ij}$$

It follows immediately that

$$\frac{\partial}{\partial a_{ij}} \det \mathbf{A} = A_{ij}$$

Recall also the expression for a matrix inverse in terms of cofactors:

$$\mathbf{A}^{-1} = (\det \mathbf{A})^{-1} [A_{ij}]'$$

so that

$$\frac{\partial}{\partial \operatorname{vec} \mathbf{A}} \det \mathbf{A} = \operatorname{vec}[A_{ij}] = (\det \mathbf{A}) \operatorname{vec} \mathbf{A}^{-1\prime} \tag{G.25}$$

and

$$\frac{\partial}{\partial \operatorname{vec} \mathbf{A}} \log(\det \mathbf{A}) = \operatorname{vec} \mathbf{A}^{-1\prime} \tag{G.26}$$

Finally, we note that

$$\frac{\partial}{\partial \operatorname{vec} \mathbf{A}} \operatorname{tr} \mathbf{A} = \operatorname{vec} \mathbf{I}_M \tag{G.27}$$

which leads to

$$\frac{\partial}{\partial \operatorname{vec} \mathbf{A}} \operatorname{tr} \mathbf{A}\mathbf{B} = \operatorname{vec} \mathbf{B}' \tag{G.28}$$

G.4 DERIVATIVE MATRICES

Note that several matrix derivative results can be usefully written in matrix, rather than vector, form if the function differentiated is single valued.

DEFINITION G.5 (MATRIX DERIVATIVE) *Define the matrix operator for differentiation as*

$$\frac{\partial}{\partial \mathbf{A}} = \left[\frac{\partial}{\partial a_{ij}}\right]$$

where $\mathbf{A} = [a_{ij}]$, *so that*

$$\frac{\partial}{\partial \mathbf{A}} y = \left[\frac{\partial y}{\partial a_{ij}}\right]$$

where y *is a function onto* $\mathbb{R}$.

According to this definition, several results given above can be rewritten:

$$\frac{\partial}{\partial \mathbf{A}} \mathbf{z}'\mathbf{A}^{-1}\mathbf{y} = -\mathbf{A}^{-1\prime}\mathbf{z}\mathbf{y}'\mathbf{A}^{-1\prime} \tag{G.29}$$

$$\frac{\partial}{\partial \mathbf{A}} \log \det \mathbf{A} = \mathbf{A}^{-1\prime} \tag{G.30}$$

$$\frac{\partial}{\partial \mathbf{A}} \operatorname{tr} \mathbf{AB} = \mathbf{B}' \tag{G.31}$$

Equation (G.22) cannot be written in this way because $\operatorname{vec}(\mathbf{A}^{-1})$ is not a one-dimensional function of $\mathbf{A}$. One would need a three-dimensional object to handle all of the derivatives.

G.5 THE NORMAL LOG-LIKELIHOOD FUNCTION

Differentiation of the log-likelihood function of the multivariate normal distribution is our leading application of these results. If we denote this function by

$$L(\boldsymbol{\mu}, \boldsymbol{\Omega}) = -\frac{J}{2}\log 2\pi - \frac{1}{2}\left[\log \det \boldsymbol{\Omega} + (\mathbf{y} - \boldsymbol{\mu})'\boldsymbol{\Omega}^{-1}(\mathbf{y} - \boldsymbol{\mu})\right]$$

where J is the dimension of $\mathbf{y}$, then using (G.6)

$$\frac{\partial L(\boldsymbol{\mu}, \boldsymbol{\Omega})}{\partial \boldsymbol{\mu}} = \boldsymbol{\Omega}^{-1}(\mathbf{y} - \boldsymbol{\mu}) \tag{G.32}$$

and using (G.2)

$$\frac{\partial^2 L(\boldsymbol{\mu}, \boldsymbol{\Omega})}{\partial \boldsymbol{\mu}\, \partial \boldsymbol{\mu}'} = -\boldsymbol{\Omega}^{-1} \tag{G.33}$$

For the linear regression model, $\boldsymbol{\mu} = \mathbf{X}\boldsymbol{\beta}$,

$$\frac{\partial L(\boldsymbol{\mu}, \boldsymbol{\Omega})}{\partial \boldsymbol{\beta}} = \frac{\partial \boldsymbol{\mu}'}{\partial \boldsymbol{\beta}} \frac{\partial L(\boldsymbol{\mu}, \boldsymbol{\Omega})}{\partial \boldsymbol{\mu}} = \mathbf{X}'\boldsymbol{\Omega}^{-1}(\mathbf{y} - \boldsymbol{\mu}) \tag{G.34}$$

and, because $\partial \boldsymbol{\mu}'/\partial \boldsymbol{\beta}$ is not a function of $\boldsymbol{\beta}$,

$$\frac{\partial^2 L(\boldsymbol{\mu}, \boldsymbol{\Omega})}{\partial \boldsymbol{\beta}\, \partial \boldsymbol{\beta}'} = \frac{\partial \boldsymbol{\mu}'}{\partial \boldsymbol{\beta}} \frac{\partial^2 L(\boldsymbol{\mu}, \boldsymbol{\Omega})}{\partial \boldsymbol{\mu}\, \partial \boldsymbol{\mu}'} \frac{\partial \boldsymbol{\mu}}{\partial \boldsymbol{\beta}'} = -\mathbf{X}'\boldsymbol{\Omega}^{-1}\mathbf{X} \tag{G.35}$$

The derivatives for $\mathbf{\Omega}$ require some care. To take into account the symmetry of $\mathbf{\Omega}$ we will replace it with $\mathbf{\Omega} = \frac{1}{2}(\mathbf{A} + \mathbf{A}')$ and use

$$\frac{\partial(\text{vec}\,\mathbf{\Omega})'}{\partial\,\text{vec}\,\mathbf{A}} = \frac{\partial\left(\text{vec}\left(\mathbf{A} + \mathbf{A}'\right)/2\right)'}{\partial\,\text{vec}\,\mathbf{A}} = \frac{1}{2}(\mathbf{I}_{J^2} + \mathbf{T}) \tag{G.36}$$

along with the chain rule of differentiation. Using (G.23) and (G.26) and the symmetry of $\mathbf{\Omega}$,[1]

$$\begin{aligned}\frac{\partial L(\boldsymbol{\mu}, \mathbf{\Omega})}{\partial\,\text{vec}\,\mathbf{A}} &= -\frac{1}{4}(\mathbf{I}_{J^2} + \mathbf{T})\left\{\text{vec}\,\mathbf{\Omega}^{-1\prime} - \text{vec}\left[\mathbf{\Omega}^{-1\prime}(\mathbf{y} - \boldsymbol{\mu})(\mathbf{y} - \boldsymbol{\mu})'\mathbf{\Omega}^{-1\prime}\right]\right\} \\ &= -\frac{1}{2}\,\text{vec}\left(\mathbf{\Omega}^{-1} - \mathbf{\Omega}^{-1}\mathbf{W}\mathbf{\Omega}^{-1}\right)\end{aligned} \tag{G.37}$$

where $\mathbf{W} \equiv (\mathbf{y} - \boldsymbol{\mu})(\mathbf{y} - \boldsymbol{\mu})'$. The remaining Hessian terms are

$$\begin{aligned}\frac{\partial^2 L(\boldsymbol{\mu}, \mathbf{\Omega})}{\partial\boldsymbol{\mu}\,\partial(\text{vec}\,\mathbf{A})'} &= -\left[(\mathbf{y} - \boldsymbol{\mu})' \otimes \mathbf{I}_J\right](\mathbf{\Omega}^{-1\prime} \otimes \mathbf{\Omega}^{-1})\left[\frac{1}{2}(\mathbf{I}_{J^2} + \mathbf{T})\right] \\ &= -\frac{1}{2}\left[(\mathbf{y} - \boldsymbol{\mu})'\mathbf{\Omega}^{-1} \otimes \mathbf{\Omega}^{-1}\right](\mathbf{I}_{J^2} + \mathbf{T})\end{aligned} \tag{G.38}$$

using (G.22) and (G.32), and

$$\begin{aligned}\frac{\partial^2 L(\boldsymbol{\mu}, \mathbf{\Omega})}{\partial\,\text{vec}\,\mathbf{A}\,\partial(\text{vec}\,\mathbf{A})'} &= \frac{1}{2}\big[(\mathbf{\Omega}^{-1\prime} \otimes \mathbf{\Omega}^{-1}) - (\mathbf{I}_J \otimes \mathbf{\Omega}^{-1}\mathbf{W})(\mathbf{\Omega}^{-1\prime} \otimes \mathbf{\Omega}^{-1}) \\ &\quad -(\mathbf{\Omega}^{-1\prime}\mathbf{W} \otimes \mathbf{I}_J)(\mathbf{\Omega}^{-1\prime} \otimes \mathbf{\Omega}^{-1})\big]\left[\frac{1}{2}(\mathbf{I}_{J^2} + \mathbf{T})\right] \\ &= \frac{1}{4}\big[(\mathbf{\Omega}^{-1} \otimes \mathbf{\Omega}^{-1}) - (\mathbf{\Omega}^{-1} \otimes \mathbf{\Omega}^{-1}\mathbf{W}\mathbf{\Omega}^{-1}) \\ &\quad -(\mathbf{\Omega}^{-1}\mathbf{W}\mathbf{\Omega}^{-1} \otimes \mathbf{\Omega}^{-1})\big](\mathbf{I}_{J^2} + \mathbf{T})\end{aligned} \tag{G.39}$$

using (G.15), (G.22), and (G.37). Note that the Hessian for $\mathbf{\Omega}$ alone is singular because $\mathbf{I}_{J^2} + \mathbf{T}$ is singular.[2] Although it is not written symmetrically, the Hessian for $\mathbf{\Omega}$ is also symmetric. To confirm this, use the properties of $\mathbf{T}$ in (G.18–G.20).

Alternatively, one can impose symmetry by restricting the parameter vector to the unique elements of $\mathbf{\Omega}$. To do this, many authors restrict the parameter vector to the lower triangle of $\mathbf{\Omega}$.

DEFINITION G.6 (VECH) *Let* $\mathbf{\Omega} = \left[\omega_{ij};\ i, j = 1, \ldots, J\right]$. *Then*

$$\text{vech}\mathbf{\Omega} \equiv \left[[\omega_{ij};\ i = j, \ldots, J]';\ j = 1, \ldots, J\right]'$$

The full vec$\mathbf{\Omega}$ is a linear function of vech$\mathbf{\Omega}$ because symmetry makes elements in the upper triangle of $\mathbf{\Omega}$ equal to elements in vech$\mathbf{\Omega}$:

---

[1] By definition of $\mathbf{T}$ and symmetry of $\mathbf{\Omega}$, $\mathbf{T}\,\text{vec}\,\mathbf{\Omega} = \text{vec}\,\mathbf{\Omega}$.

[2] Note that $(\mathbf{I}_{J^2} + \mathbf{T})(\mathbf{I}_{J^2} - \mathbf{T}) = \mathbf{0}$
Therefore, $\mathbf{I}_{J^2} + \mathbf{T}$ is singular.

$$\text{vec}\boldsymbol{\Omega} = \mathbf{S}_\omega \text{ vech } \boldsymbol{\Omega}$$

where $\mathbf{S}_\omega$ is the matrix of zeros and ones

$$\mathbf{S}_\omega \equiv \frac{\partial \text{ vec } \boldsymbol{\Omega}}{\partial(\text{vech } \boldsymbol{\Omega})'}$$

Note that we can also write

$$(\mathbf{S}_\omega'\mathbf{S}_\omega)^{-1} \mathbf{S}_\omega' \text{ vec } \boldsymbol{\Omega} = (\mathbf{S}_\omega'\mathbf{S}_\omega)^{-1} \mathbf{S}_\omega'\mathbf{S}_\omega \text{ vech } \boldsymbol{\Omega} = \text{vech } \boldsymbol{\Omega}$$

and

$$\mathbf{S}_\omega \equiv \frac{\partial \text{ vec } \boldsymbol{\Omega}}{\partial(\text{vech } \boldsymbol{\Omega})'} = \frac{\partial \text{ vec } \boldsymbol{\Omega}'}{\partial(\text{vech } \boldsymbol{\Omega})'} = \mathbf{T}\frac{\partial \text{ vec } \boldsymbol{\Omega}}{\partial(\text{vech } \boldsymbol{\Omega})'} = \mathbf{T}\mathbf{S}_\omega$$

Let $\boldsymbol{\omega} \equiv \text{vech } \boldsymbol{\Omega}$. Applying the chain rule to (G.37), we obtain

$$\begin{aligned}
\frac{\partial L(\boldsymbol{\mu}, \boldsymbol{\Omega})}{\partial \boldsymbol{\omega}} &= -\frac{1}{2}\mathbf{S}_\omega' \text{ vec}(\boldsymbol{\Omega}^{-1} - \boldsymbol{\Omega}^{-1}\mathbf{W}\boldsymbol{\Omega}^{-1}) \\
&= -\frac{1}{2} \text{ vech}(\boldsymbol{\Omega}^{-1} - \boldsymbol{\Omega}^{-1}\mathbf{W}\boldsymbol{\Omega}^{-1})
\end{aligned}$$

Similarly, (G.38) becomes

$$\begin{aligned}
\frac{\partial^2 L(\boldsymbol{\mu}, \boldsymbol{\Omega})}{\partial \boldsymbol{\mu}\, \partial \boldsymbol{\omega}'} &= -\frac{1}{2}\left[(\mathbf{y} - \boldsymbol{\mu})'\boldsymbol{\Omega}^{-1} \otimes \boldsymbol{\Omega}^{-1}\right](\mathbf{I}_{J^2} + \mathbf{T})\mathbf{S}_\omega \\
&= -\left[(\mathbf{y} - \boldsymbol{\mu})'\boldsymbol{\Omega}^{-1} \otimes \boldsymbol{\Omega}^{-1}\right]\mathbf{S}_\omega
\end{aligned}$$

and (G.39) becomes

$$\begin{aligned}
\frac{\partial^2 L(\boldsymbol{\mu}, \boldsymbol{\Omega})}{\partial \boldsymbol{\omega}\, \partial \boldsymbol{\omega}'} &= \frac{1}{2}\mathbf{S}_\omega'\big[(\boldsymbol{\Omega}^{-1} \otimes \boldsymbol{\Omega}^{-1}) - (\boldsymbol{\Omega}^{-1} \otimes \boldsymbol{\Omega}^{-1}\mathbf{W}\boldsymbol{\Omega}^{-1}) \\
&\quad -(\boldsymbol{\Omega}^{-1}\mathbf{W}\boldsymbol{\Omega}^{-1} \otimes \boldsymbol{\Omega}^{-1})\big]\mathbf{S}_\omega
\end{aligned}$$

APPENDIX H

Characteristic Functions

1. Moment-generating functions do not always exist. The function e^{tY} is unbounded for $tY > 0$ and the p.d.f. or p.m.f. may not die out slowly enough as $|Y| \to \infty$.
2. The trigonometric functions sine and cosine are bounded, so that the expectations of $\sin tY$ and $\cos tY$ always exist. In addition, we can create a function like the m.g.f. that generates moments, when they exist, in a similar way. Recalling that

$$\frac{d}{dy}\cos y = -\sin y, \qquad \frac{d}{dy}\sin y = \cos y$$

we see that these functions reproduce themselves in a way similar to the exponential function, for which

$$\frac{d}{dy}e^y = e^y \tag{H.1}$$

More generally,

$$\frac{d^{2n-1}}{dy^{2n-1}}\cos y = (-1)^n \sin y, \qquad \frac{d^{2n}}{dy^{2n}}\cos y = (-1)^n \cos y$$

$$\frac{d^{2n-1}}{dy^{2n-1}}\sin y = (-1)^{n-1} \cos y, \qquad \frac{d^{2n}}{dy^{2n}}\sin y = (-1)^n \sin y$$

If we define

$$\varphi_1(t) \equiv \mathrm{E}[\cos tY], \qquad \varphi_2(t) \equiv \mathrm{E}[\sin tY]$$

then

$$\frac{d}{dt}\varphi_1(t) = \mathrm{E}[d(\cos tY)/dt] = -\,\mathrm{E}[Y \sin tY]$$

$$\frac{d}{dt}\varphi_2(t) = \mathrm{E}[d(\sin tY)/dt] = \mathrm{E}[Y \cos tY]$$

Recalling that $\cos(0) = 1$ and $\sin(0) = 0$, we have

$$\varphi_1^{(1)}(0) + \varphi_2^{(1)}(0) = \mathrm{E}[Y]$$

More generally, we have

$$\frac{d^n}{dt^n}\varphi_1(t) = \mathrm{E}[d^n(\cos tY)/dt^n] = \mathrm{E}\left[Y^n \left.\frac{d^n \sin z}{dz^n}\right|_{z=tY}\right]$$

$$\frac{d^n}{dt^n}\varphi_2(t) = \mathrm{E}[d^n(\sin tY)/dt^n] = \mathrm{E}\left[Y^n \left.\frac{d^n \cos z}{dz^n}\right|_{z=tY}\right]$$

so that

$$\mathrm{E}\left[Y^{2n-1}\right] = (-1)^{-n}\,\varphi_1^{(2n-1)}(0) + (-1)^{-n+1}\,\varphi_2^{(2n-1)}(0) \tag{H.2}$$

$$\mathrm{E}\left[Y^{2n}\right] = (-1)^{-n}\,\varphi_1^{(2n)}(0) + (-1)^{-n}\,\varphi_2^{(2n)}(0) \tag{H.3}$$

3. An algebraically neat way to keep track of these two functions is to create a "two-dimensional" function using complex numbers. Recall that if one denotes $i = \sqrt{-1}$, then complex numbers have the general representation

$$y = a + ib$$

and that one can think of the complex number as the pair of real numbers (a, b). We can create the complex-valued function

$$\begin{aligned}\varphi(t) &\equiv \varphi_1(t) + i\,\varphi_2(t)\\ &\equiv \mathrm{E}[\cos tY + i\sin tY]\end{aligned}$$

as equivalent to the pair of real functions $[\varphi_1(t),\ \varphi_2(t)]$. Now the derivatives follow a simpler pattern: the first derivative is

$$\begin{aligned}\frac{d}{dt}(\cos tY + i\sin tY) &= -\,(\sin tY)\,Y + i\,(\cos tY)\,Y\\ &= iY\,(\cos tY + i\sin tY)\end{aligned}$$

and, by induction,

$$\frac{d^n}{dt^n}(\cos tY + i\sin tY) = i^n Y^n\,(\cos tY + i\sin tY) \tag{H.4}$$

We therefore have

$$\mathrm{E}\left[\varphi^{(n)}(0)\right] = i^n\,\mathrm{E}\left[Y^n\right]$$

4. There is one additional algebraic convenience. Notice that (H.1) implies that

$$\frac{d^n}{dt^n}e^{at} = a^n e^{at}$$

for any real a. This is quite similar to (H.4). If we define the same derivative for $a = iY$ to be

$$\frac{d^n}{dt^n}e^{itY} \equiv (iY)^n\,e^{itY} = i^n Y^n e^{itY}$$

then we reproduce the pattern in (H.4) exactly. Furthermore,

$$t = 0 \qquad \Rightarrow \qquad \cos tY + i\sin tY = e^{itY}$$

As a result, the Taylor series expansions for these two functions around $z = 0$ are identical:

$$e^{iz} = \sum_{n=0}^{\infty} \frac{1}{n!} i^n z^n$$

Because neighborhoods of $t = 0$ are the only regions we care about, it is algebraically simpler to define

$$e^{itY} \equiv \cos tY + i \sin tY$$

This identity is called *Euler's equation*. Trigonometric functions are much more difficult to manipulate than exponential ones and we can make this substitution for algebraic purposes, even though we would never have known what to do with e^{itY} had we encountered it out of this context.

DEFINITION H.1 (CHARACTERISTIC FUNCTION) *The* characteristic function $\varphi_Y(t)$ *of a random variable Y is*

$$\varphi_Y(t) \equiv \mathrm{E}\left[e^{itY}\right] \equiv \mathrm{E}\left[\cos tY + i \sin tY\right]$$

As we have already pointed out, this (complex-valued) integral always exists. The absolute values of $\cos tY$ and $\sin tY$ are less than or equal to one. Therefore,

$$|\mathrm{E}[\cos tY]| \le \mathrm{E}[|\cos(tY)|] \le 1$$
$$|\mathrm{E}[\sin tY]| \le \mathrm{E}[|\sin(tY)|] \le 1$$

so that $\varphi_Y(t)$ exists. In addition to this important property, the characteristic function is unique for each distribution and it is always possible to recover the c.d.f. $F_Y(y)$ of a random variable Y from its characteristic function. Fortunately, we never need to do this.[1] Our exclusive use of the c.f. is for proving a central limit theorems. For this, we require only the c.f. of the normal distribution.

LEMMA H.1 *If* $\mathrm{E}[Y^r] = \mu'_r$ *exists for* $r = 1, \ldots, R$, *then* $\varphi_Y(t)$ *has the Taylor series approximation around* $t = 0$,

$$\varphi_Y(t) = \sum_{r=0}^{R} \frac{\mu'_r}{r!} (it)^r + o(t^R)$$

[1] In the continuous case, the c.f. is the Fourier transform of the p.d.f. As a result, the p.d.f. is the inverse Fourier transform. See Rao (1973, pp. 104–106).

BIBLIOGRAPHY

Ahn, H. & Powell, J. L. (1993). Semiparametric estimation of censored selection models with a nonparametric selection mechanism. *Journal of Econometrics* **58**(1–2), 3–29.

Ahn, S. & Schmidt, P. (1997). Efficient estimation of dynamic panel data models: Alternative assumptions and simplified estimation. *Journal of Econometrics* **76**(1–2), 309–321.

Aigner, D. J., Hsiao, C., Kapteyn, A. & Wansbeek, T. (1984). Latent variable models in econometrics. *In* Z. Griliches & M. D. Intriligator, eds., *Handbook of Econometrics,* Vol. II, Chapter 23. North-Holland, Amsterdam.

Aitchison, J. & Silvey, S. D. (1958). Maximum-likelihood estimation of parameters subject to restraints. *Annals of Mathematical Statistics* **29**(3), 813–828.

Aitken, A. C. (1935). On least squares and linear combination of observations. *Proceedings of the Royal Society of Edinburgh* **55**, 42–48.

Amemiya, T. (1973). Regression analysis when the dependent variable is truncated normal. *Econometrica* **41**(6), 997–1016.

Amemiya, T. (1985). *Advanced Econometrics*. Harvard University Press, Cambridge, MA.

Amemiya, T. & MaCurdy, T. E. (1986). Instrumental-variable estimation of an error-components model. *Econometrica* **54**(4), 869–880.

Andersen, P. K. & Gill, R. D. (1982). Cox's regression model for counting processes: A large sample study. *Annals of Statistics* **10**(4), 1100–1120.

Anderson, T. W. (1971). *The Statistical Analysis of Time Series*. Wiley, New York.

Andrews, D. W. K. (1991). Heteroskedasticity and autocorrelation consistent covariance matrix estimation. *Econometrica* **59**(3), 817–858.

Angrist, J. D. & Krueger, A. B. (1992). The effect of age at school entry on educational attainment: An application of instrumental variables with moments from two samples. *Journal of the American Statistical Association* **87**(418), 328–336.

Aoki, M. (1987). *State Space Modeling of Time Series*. Springer, New York.

Arellano, M. & Bond, S. (1991). Some tests of specification for panel data: Monte Carlo evidence and an application to employment equations. *Review of Economic Studies* **58**(2), 277–297.

Arellano, M. & Bover, O. (1995). Another look at the instrumental variable estimation of error-components models. *Journal of Econometrics* **68**(1), 29–51.

Azzalini, A. (1985). A class of distribution which includes the normal ones. *Scandinavian Journal of Statistics* **12**, 171–178.

Azzalini, A. (1986). Further results on a class of distribution which includes the normal ones. *Statistica* **46**, 199–208.

Bahadur, R. R. (1957). On unbiased estimates of uniformly minimum variance. *Sankhya* **18**(3–4), 211–224.

Baltagi, B. H. (1995). *Econometric Analysis of Panel Data*. Wiley, New York.

Barankin, E. W. (1949). Locally best unbiased estimates. *Annals of Mathematical Statistics* **20**(4), 477–501.

Basmann, R. L. (1957). A generalized classical method of linear estimation of coefficients in a structural equation. *Econometrica* **25**(1), 77–83.

Beach, C. M. & MacKinnon, J. G. (1978). A maximum likelihood procedure for regression with autocorrelated errors. *Econometrica* **46**(1), 51–58.

Beggs, S., Cardell, S. & Hausman, J. (1981). Assessing the potential demand for electric cars. *Journal of Econometrics* **17**(1), 1–19.

Bentler, P. M. (1982). Linear systems with multiple levels and types of latent variables. *In* K. G. Jöreskog & H. Wold, eds., *Systems Under Indirect Observations: Causality, Structure, Prediction*, Vol. I, Chapter 5, pp. 101–130. North-Holland, Amsterdam.

Berndt, E. R. & Savin, N. E. (1977). Conflict among criteria for testing hypotheses in the multivariate linear regression model. *Econometrica* **45**(5), 1263–1278.

Berndt, E. R., Hall, B. H., Hall, R. E. & Hausman, J. A. (1974). Estimation and inference in nonlinear structural models. *Annals of Economic and Social Measurement* **3**, 653–665.

Bhargava, A. & Sargan, J. D. (1983). Estimating dynamic random effects models from panel data covering short time periods. *Econometrica* **51**(6), 1635–1659.

Billingsley, P. (1968). *Convergence of Probability Measures*. Wiley, New York.

Bloomfield, P. & Steiger, W. L. (1983). *Least Absolute Deviations: Theory, Applications, and Algorithms*. Birkhäuser, Boston.

Blundell, R. & Bond, S. (1998). Initial conditions and moment restrictions in dynamic panel data models. *Journal of Econometrics* **87**(1), 115–143.

Blundell, R. & MaCurdy, T. (forthcoming). Labor supply: A review of alternative approaches. *In* O. Ashenfelter & D. Card, eds. *Handbook of Labor Economics*, Vol. 3. North-Holland, Amsterdam.

Bound, J., Jaeger, D. A. & Baker, R. M. (1995). Problems with instrumental variables estimation when the correlation between the instruments and the endogenous explanatory variable is weak. *Journal of the American Statistical Association* **90**(430), 443–450.

Bowman, K. O. & Shenton, L. R. (1975). Omnibus test contours for departures from normality based on $\sqrt{b_1}$ and b_2. *Biometrika* **62**(2), 243–250.

Box, G. E. P. & Cox, D. R. (1964). An analysis of transformations. *Journal of the Royal Statistical Society, Series B* **26**, 211–252.

Box, G. E. P. & Jenkins, G. M. (1976). *Time Series Analysis: Forecasting and Control*. Holden-Day, San Francisco.

Box, G. E. P. & Muller, M. E. (1958). A note on the generation of random normal deviates. *Annals of Mathematical Statistics* **29**(2), 610–611.

Breusch, T. S. (1978). Testing for autocorrelation in dynamic linear models. *Australian Economic Papers* **17**(31), 334–355.

Breusch, T. S. (1979). Conflict among criteria for testing hypotheses: Extensions and comments. *Econometrica* **47**(1), 203–207.

Breusch, T. S., Mizon, G. E. & Schmidt, P. (1989). Efficient estimation using panel data. *Econometrica* **57**(3), 695–700.

Breusch, T. S. & Pagan, A. R. (1979). A simple test for heteroskedasticity and random coefficient variation. *Econometrica* **47**(5), 1287–1294.

Breusch, T. S. & Pagan, A. R. (1980). The Lagrange multiplier test and its applications to model specification in econometrics. *Review of Economic Studies* **47**(1), 239–253.

Burguete, J. F., Gallant, A. R. & Souza, G. (1982). On the unification of the asymptotic theory of nonlinear econometric models. *Econometric Reviews* **1**(2), 151–190.

Byron, R. P. (1974). Testing structural specification using the unrestricted reduced form. *Econometrica* **42**(5), 869–883.

Cameron, C. A. & Trivedi, P. K. (1986). Econometric models based on count data: Comparisons and applications of some estimators and tests. *Journal of Applied Econometrics* **1**(1), 29–53.

Cameron, C. A. & Trivedi, P. K. (1990). Regression-based tests for overdispersion in the Poisson model. *Journal of Econometrics* **46**(3), 347–364.

Campbell, J. Y. & Mankiw, N. G. (1989). Consumption, income, and interest rates: Reinterpreting the time series evidence. *NBER Macroeconomics Annual* **4**, 185–216.

Card, D. (1992). Using regional variation in wages to measure the effects of the federal minimum wage. *Industrial and Labor Relations Review* **46**(1), 22–37.

Card, D. & Krueger, A. B. (1992a). Does school quality matter? Returns to education and the characteristics of public schools in the United States. *Journal of Political Economy* **100**(1), 1–40.

Card, D. & Krueger, A. B. (1992b). School quality and black-white relative earnings: A direct assessment. *Quarterly Journal of Economics* **107**(1), 151–200.

Chamberlain, G. (1982). Multivariate regression models for panel data. *Journal of Econometrics* **18**(1), 5–46.

Chamberlain, G. (1984). Panel data. *In* Z. Griliches & M. D. Intriligator, eds. *Handbook of Econometrics*, Vol. II, Chapter 22. North-Holland, Amsterdam.

Chamberlain, G. (1987). Asymptotic efficiency in estimation with conditional moment restrictions. *Journal of Econometrics* **34**(3), 305–334.

Chamberlain, G. (1990). Arthur S. Goldberger and latent variables in econometrics: Distinguished fellow. *Journal of Economic Perspectives* **4**(4), 125–152.

Chesher, A. (1984). Testing for neglected heterogeneity. *Econometrica* **52**(4), 865–872.

Chow, G. C. (1960). Tests of equality between sets of coefficients in two linear regressions. *Econometrica* **28**(3), 591–605.

Christensen, L. & Greene, W. (1976). Economies of scale in U. S. electric power generation. *Journal of Political Economy* **84**(4), 655–676.

Chung, K. L. (1974). *A Course in Probability Theory*, 2nd ed. Academic Press, New York.

Cochrane, D. & Orcutt, G. H. (1949). Application of least squares regression to relationships containing autocorrelated error terms. *Journal of the American Statistical Association* **44**(245), 32–61.

Copas, J. B. (1975). On the unimodality of the likelihood for the Cauchy distribution. *Biometrika* **62**(3), 701–704.

Cox, D. R. & Hinkley, D. V. (1974). *Theoretical Statistics*. Chapman and Hall, London.

Cragg, J. G. (1971). Some statistical models for limited dependent variables with application to the demand for durable goods. *Econometrica* **39**(5), 829–844.

Cragg, J. G. (1983). More efficient estimation in the presence of heteroskedasticity of unknown form. *Econometrica* **51**(3), 751–763.

Cramér, H. (1946). *Mathematical Methods of Statistics*. Princeton University Press, Princeton, NJ.

Crisp, A. & Burridge, J. (1994). A note on nonregular likelihood functions in heteroskedastic regression models. *Biometrika* **81**(3), 585–587.

Cumby, R. E., Huizinga, J. & Obstfeld, M. (1983). Two-step two-stage least squares estimation in models with rational expectations. *Journal of Econometrics* **21**(3), 333–355.

Darmois, G. (1945). Sur les limites de dispersion de certaines lois. *Revues de L'Institut International de Statistique* **13**, 288–293.

Davidson, R. & MacKinnon, J. G. (1993). *Estimation and Inference in Econometrics*. Oxford University Press, New York.

Dempster, A., Laird, N. & Rubin, D. (1977). Maximum likelihood estimation from incomplete data via the EM algorithm. *Journal of the Royal Statistical Society, Series B* **39**, 1–38.

Duncan, G. M. (1986). A semiparametric censored regression estimator. *Journal of Econometrics* **32**(1), 5–34.

Durbin, J. (1954). Errors in variables. *Review of the International Statistical Institute* **22**, 23–32.

Durbin, J. (1960). Estimation of parameters in time-series regression models. *Journal of the Royal Statistical Society, Series B* **22**, 139–153.

Durbin, J. (1970). Testing for serial correlation in least-squares regression when some of the regressors are lagged dependent variables. *Econometrica* **38**(3), 410–421.

Durbin, J. (1988). Maximum likelihood estimation of the parameters of a system of simultaneous regression equations. *Econometric Theory* **4**(1), 159–170.

Durbin, J. & Watson, G. S. (1950). Testing for serial correlation in least squares regression, I. *Biometrika* **37**(3–4), 409–428.

Durbin, J. & Watson, G. S. (1951). Testing for serial correlation in least squares regression, II. *Biometrika* **38**(1–2), 159–178.

Eicker, F. (1967). Limit theorems for regressions with unequal and dependent errors. *In* L. M. L. Cam & J. Neyman, eds., *Fifth Berkeley Symposium on Mathematical Statistics and Probability*, Vol. 1, pp. 59–82. University of California, Berkeley.

Eissa, N. (1995). Taxation and labor supply of married women: The tax reform act of 1986 as a natural experiment. National Bureau of Economic Research Working Paper No. 5023, Cambridge, MA.

Engle, R. F. (1984). Wald, likelihood ratio and Lagrange multiplier tests in econometrics. *In* Z. Griliches & M. D. Intriligator, eds. *Handbook of Econometrics*, Vol. II, Chapter 13. North-Holland, Amsterdam.

Farebrother, R. W. (1980). Pan's procedure for the tail probabilities of the Durbin-Watson statistic. *Applied Statistics* **29**(2), 224–227.

Farebrother, R. W. (1990). The distribution of a quadratic form in normal variables. *Applied Statistics* **39**(2), 294–309.

Feller, W. (1968). *An Introduction to Probability Theory and Its Applications*. Vol. I, 3d ed. Wiley, New York.

Feller, W. (1971). *An Introduction to Probability Theory and Its Applications*. Vol. II, 2d ed. Wiley, New York.

Fisher, R. A. (1922). On the mathematical foundations of theoretical statistics. *Philosophical Transactions of the Royal Society* **A**(222), 309–368.

Fisher, R. A. (1925). The theory of statistical estimation. *Proceedings of the Cambridge Philosophical Society* **22**, 700–725.

Friedman, M. (1968). The role of monetary policy. *American Economic Review* **58**(1), 1–17.

Fuller, W. A. (1996). *Introduction to Statistical Time Series*, 2nd ed. Wiley, New York.

Gabrielsen, G. (1982). On the unimodality of the likelihood for the Cauchy distribution: Some comments. *Biometrika* **69**(3), 677–678.

Gardner, G., Harvey, A. C. & Phillips, G. D. A. (1980). An algorithm for exact maximum likelihood estimation of autoregressive-moving average models by means of the Kalman filter. *Applied Statistics* **29**, 311–322.

Geweke, J. (1993). Bayesian treatment of the independent Student-t linear model. *Journal of Applied Econometrics* **8**, S19–40 (Supplement).

Godfrey, L. G. (1978a). Testing against general autoregressive and moving average error models when the regressors include lagged dependent variables. *Econometrica* **46**(6), 1293–1301.

Godfrey, L. G. (1978b). Testing for higher order serial correlation in regression equations when the regressors include lagged dependent variables. *Econometrica* **46**(6), 1303–1310.

Godfrey, L. G. (1978c). Testing for multiplicative heteroskedasticity. *Journal of Econometrics* **8**(2), 227–236.

Goldberger, A. S. (1983). Abnormal selection bias. *In* S. Karlin, T. Amemiya & L. A. Goodman, eds. *Studies in Econometrics, Time Series, and Multivariate Statistics*, pp. 67–84. Academic Press, New York.

Goldberger, A. S. (1991). *A Course in Econometrics*. Harvard University Press, Cambridge, MA.

Goldfeld, S. M. & Quandt, R. E. (1965). Some tests for homoskedasticity. *Journal of the American Statistical Association* **60**(310), 539–547.

Goldfeld, S. M., Quandt, R. E. & Trotter, H. (1966). Maximization by quadratic hill climbing. *Econometrica* **3**(3), 541–541.

Gordon, R. J. (1990). What is new-Keynesian economics? *Journal of Economic Literature* **28**(3), 1115–1171.

Gourieroux, C. & Monfort, A. (1995). *Statistics and Econometric Models*, Vol. 2, Q. Voung, trans. Cambridge University Press, Cambridge, U.K.

Gourieroux, C., Monfort, A. & Trognon, A. (1984). Pseudo maximum likelihood methods: Theory. *Econometrica* **52**(3), 681–700.

Graybill, F. A. (1969). *Introduction to Matrices with Applications in Statistics*. Wadsworth, Belmont, CA.

Greene, W. H. (1990). *Econometric Analysis*, 2nd ed. Macmillan, New York.

Greene, W. H. (1997). *Econometric Analysis*, 3rd ed. Prentice-Hall, Upper Saddle River, NJ.

Greenstadt, J. (1967). On the relative efficiencies of gradient methods. *Mathematics of Computation* **21**, 360–367.

Greenwood, M. & Yule, G. U. (1920). An enquiry into the nature of frequency distributions and multiple happenings, with particular reference to the occurrence of multiple attacks of disease or repeated accidents. *Journal of the Royal Statistical Society, Series A* **83**, 255–279.

Gregory, A. W. & Veall, M. R. (1985). Formulating Wald tests of nonlinear restrictions. *Econometrica* **53**(6), 1465–1468.

Griliches, Z. (1977). Estimating the returns to schooling: Some econometric problems. *Econometrica* **45**(1), 1–22.

Gronau, R. (1974). Wage comparisons—a selectivity bias. *Journal of Political Economy* **82**(6), 1119–1143.

Gupta, S. D. & Perlman, M. D. (1974). Power of the noncentral F-test: Effect of additional variates on Hotelling's T^2-test. *Journal of the American Statistical Association* **69**(345), 174–180.

Hall, R. E. (1978). Stochastic implications of the life cycle-permanent income hypothesis: Theory and evidence. *Journal of Political Economy* **86**(6), 971–987.

Hamilton, J. D. (1994). *Time Series Analysis*. Princeton University Press, Princeton, NJ.

Hansen, L. P. (1982). Large sample properties of generalized method of moments estimators. *Econometrica* **50**(4), 1029–1054.

Hansen, L. P. & Singleton, K. J. (1982). Generalized instrumental variables estimation of nonlinear rational expectations models. *Econometrica* **50**(5), 1269–1286.

Harvey, A. C. (1976). Estimating regression models with multiplicative heteroskedasticity. *Econometrica* **44**(3), 461–465.

Harvey, A. C. (1989). *Forecasting, Structural Time Series Models and the Kalman Filter*. Cambridge University Press, Cambridge.

Harvey, A. C. (1993). *Time Series Models*, 2nd ed. Harvester Wheatsheaf, New York.

Hatanaka, M. (1974). An efficient two-step estimator for the dynamic adjustment model with autoregressive errors. *Journal of Econometrics* **2**(3), 199–220.

Hausman, J. A. (1975). An instrumental variable approach to full information estimators for linear and certain nonlinear econometric models. *Econometrica* **43**(4), 727–738.

Hausman, J. A. (1978). Specification tests in econometrics. *Econometrica* **46**(6), 1251–1272.

Hausman, J. A. (1985). Taxes and labor supply. *In* A. J. Auerbach & M. Feldstein, eds. *Handbook of Public Economics*, Vol. 1, pp. 213–263. North-Holland, New York.

Hausman, J. A. & McFadden, D. (1984). Specification tests for the multinomial logit model. *Econometrica* **52**(5), 1219–1240.

Hausman, J. A. & Taylor, W. E. (1981). Panel data and unobservable individual effects. *Econometrica* **49**(6), 1377–1398.

Hausman, J., Hall, B. H. & Griliches, Z. (1984). Econometric models for count data with an application to the patents–r&d relationship. *Econometrica* **52**(4), 909–938.

Heckman, J. J. (1974). Shadow prices, market wages, and labor supply. *Econometrica* **42**(4), 679–694.

Heckman, J. J. (1976). The common structure of statistical models of truncation, sample selection and limited dependent variables and a simple estimator for such models. *Annals of Economic and Social Measurement* **5**(4), 475–492.

Heckman, J. J. (1979). Sample selection bias as a specification error. *Econometrica* **47**(1), 153–161.

Hendry, D. F. (1976). The structure of simultaneous equations estimators. *Journal of Econometrics* **4**(1), 51–88.

Hendry, D. F. (1995). *Dynamic Econometrics*. Oxford University Press, Oxford.

Hendry, D. F. & Morgan, M. S. (1995). *The Foundations of Econometrics Analysis*. Cambridge University Press, Cambridge, UK.

Hildreth, C. & Houck, J. P. (1968). Some estimators for a linear model with random coefficients. *Journal of the American Statistical Association* **63**(322), 584–595.

Hildreth, C. & Lu, J. Y. (1960). Demand relations with autocorrelated disturbances. Michigan State University Agricultural Experiment Station Technical Bulletin 276.

Hoel, P. G., Port, S. C. & Stone, C. J. (1971). *Introduction to Probability Theory*. Houghton-Mifflin, Boston.

Holtz-Eakin, D. (1988). Testing for individual effects in autoregressive models. *Journal of Econometrics* **39**(3), 297–307.

Holtz-Eakin, D., Newey, W. & Rosen, H. S. (1988). Estimating vector autoregressions with panel data. *Econometrica* **56**(6), 1371–1395.

Honore, B. E. & Powell, J. L. (1994). Pairwise difference estimators of censored and truncated regression models. *Journal of Econometrics* **64**(1–2), 241–278.

Hsiao, C. (1986). *Analysis of Panel Data*. Cambridge University Press, Cambridge, U.K.

Huber, P. J. (1967). The behavior of maximum likelihood estimates under nonstandard conditions. *In* L. M. LeCam & J. Neyman, eds. *Proceedings of the Fifth Berkeley Symposium on Mathematical Statistics and Probability*, Vol. I, pp. 221-233. University of California, Berkeley.

Ichimura, H. (1993). Semiparametric least squares (sls) and weighted sls estimation of single-index models. *Journal of Econometrics* **58**(1–2), 71–120.

Imhof, J. P. (1980). Computing the distribution of quadratic forms in normal variables. *Biometrika* **48**(3–4), 419–426.

Jarque, C. M. & Bera, A. K. (1980). Efficient tests for normality, heteroskedasticity and serial independence of regression residuals. *Economics Letters* **6**, 255–259.

Johnson, N. L., & Kotz, S. (1970a). *Continuous Univariate Distributions—1*. Houghton-Mifflin, Boston.

Johnson, N. L., & Kotz, S. (1970b). *Continuous Univariate Distributions—2*. Houghton-Mifflin, Boston.

Johnson, N. L., , Kotz, S. & Kemp, A. W. (1992). *Univariate Discrete Distributions*, 2nd ed. Wiley, Boston.

Judge, G. G., Griffiths, W. E., Hill, R. C., Lütkepohl, H. & Lee, T.-C. (1980). *The Theory and Practice of Econometrics*. Wiley, New York.

Kalman, R. E. (1960). A new approach to linear filtering and prediction problems. *Transactions ASME Journal of Basic Engineering* **82**, 35–45.

Karlin, S. P. (1968). *Total Positivity*, Vol. I. Stanford University Press, Stanford, CA.

Karlin, S. P. (1982). Some results on optimal partitioning of variance and monotonicity with truncation level. *In* G. Kallianpur, P. R. Krishnaiah & J. K. Ghosh, eds. *Statistics and Probability: Essays in Honor of C. R. Rao*, pp. 375–382. North-Holland, Amsterdam.

Katz, L. (1945). Characteristics of frequency functions defined by first order difference equations. Ph.D. thesis, University of Michigan, Ann Arbor.

Katz, L. (1965). Unified treatment of a broad class of discrete probability distributions. *In* G. P. Patil, ed. *Classical and Contagious Discrete Distributions*, pp. 175–182. Calcutta Statistical Publishing Society, Pergamon, Oxford.

Klein, R. W. & Spady, R. H. (1993). An efficient semiparametric estimator for binary response models. *Econometrica* **61**(2), 387–421.

Koenker, R. (1981). A note on Studentizing a test for heteroskedasticity. *Journal of Econometrics* **17**(1), 107–112.

Koenker, R. W. & Bassett, G., Jr. (1978). Regression quantiles. *Econometrica* **46**(1), 33–50.

Koenker, R. W. & Bassett, G., Jr. (1982). Robust tests for heteroscedasticity based on regression quantiles. *Econometrica* **50**(1), 43–61.

Koopmans, T. C. (1937). *Linear Regression Analysis of Economic Time Series*. Netherlands Economic Institute, Haarlem.

Koopmans, T. C. & Hood, W. C. (1953). The estimation of simultaneous linear economic relationships. *In* W. C. Hood & T. C. Koopmans, eds. *Studies in Econometric Method*, Chapter VI, pp. 112–199. Cowles Foundation Monograph, Yale University Press, New Haven, CT.

Landefeld, J. S. & Parker, R. P. (1997). BEA's chain indexes, time series, and measures of long-term economic growth. *Survey of Current Business*, pp. 58–68. Bureau of Economic Analysis, U.S. Department of Commerce.

Lang, S. (1971). *Linear Algebra*, 2nd ed. Addison-Wesley, Reading, MA.

Lange, K. L., Little, R. J. A. & Taylor, J. M. G. (1989). Robust statistical modelling using the t distribution. *Journal of the American Statistical Association* **84**(408), 881–896.

Larsen, R. J. & Marx, M. L. (1986). *An Introduction to Mathematical Statistics and Its Applications*. Prentice-Hall, Englewood Cliffs, NJ.

LeCam, L. (1953). On some asymptotic properties of maximum likelihood estimates and related Bayes estimates. *University of California Publications in Statistics* **1**, 277–330.

Lee, L.-F. (1979). Identification and estimation in binary choice models with limited (censored) dependent variables. *Econometrica* **47**(4), 977–996.

Lee, L.-F. (1981). Simultaneous equations models with discrete and censored variables. *In* C. F. Manski & D. McFadden, eds. *Structural Analysis of Discrete Data with Econometric Applications*, Chapter 9. MIT Press, Cambridge, MA.

Lee, L.-F. (1983). Generalized econometric models with selectivity. *Econometrica* **51**(2), 507–512.

Lee, L.-F. (1986). Specification test for Poisson regression models. *International Economic Review* **27**(3), 689–706.

Lee, L.-F. (1992). Semiparametric nonlinear least-squares estimation of truncated regression models. *Econometric Theory* **8**(1), 52–94.

Lee, L.-F., Maddala, G. S. & Trost, R. P. (1980). Asymptotic covariance matrices of two-stage probit and two-stage Tobit methods for simultaneous equations models with selectivity. *Econometrica* **48**(2), 491–503.

Lehmann, E. L. (1983). *Theory of Point Estimation*. Wiley, New York.

Lehmann, E. L. (1986). *Testing Statistical Hypotheses*, 2nd ed. Wiley, New York.

Levine, D. K. (1983). A remark on serial correlation in maximum likelihood. *Journal of Econometrics* **23**(3), 337–342.

Lipsey, R. G. & Parkin, M. (1970). Incomes policy: A reappraisal. *Economica* **37**(146), 115–138.

Lovell, M. C. (1963). Seasonal adjustment of economic time series. *Journal of the American Statistical Association* **58**(304), 993–1010.

Luenberger, D. G. (1969). *Optimization by Vector Space Methods*. Wiley, New York.

Maddala, G. S. (1971). The use of variance components models in pooling cross section and time series data. *Econometrica* **39**(2), 341–358.

Maddala, G. S. (1993). *The Econometrics of Panel Data*, Vols. 1 and 2. Elgar, Brookfield, VT.

Mäkeläinen, T., Schmidt, K. & Styan, G. P. H. (1981). On the existence and uniqueness of the maximum likelihood estimate of a vector-valued parameter in fixed-size samples. *Annals of Statistics* **9**(4), 758–767.

Malinvaud, E. (1970). *Statistical Methods of Econometrics*, 2nd rev. ed. North-Holland, Amsterdam.

Mas-Collell, A., Whinston, M. D. & Green, J. R. (1995). *Microeconomic Theory*. Oxford University Press, New York.

Mátyás, L. & Sevestre, P., eds. (1996). *The Econometrics of Panel Data: Handbook of Theory and Applications*, 2nd ed. Kluwer-Nijoff, Dordrecht.

McFadden, D. (1974*a*). Conditional logit analysis of qualitative choice behavior. *In* P. Zarembka, ed. *Frontiers in Econometrics*. Academic Press, New York.

McFadden, D. (1974*b*). The measurement of urban travel demand. *Journal of Public Economics* **3**(4), 303–328.

McFadden, D. (1978). Modelling the choice of residential location. *In* A. Karqvist *et al*, ed. *Spatial Interaction Theory and Planning Models*. North-Holland, Amsterdam.

McFadden, D. (1987). Regression-based specification tests for the multinomial logit model. *Journal of Econometrics* **34**(1–2), 63–82.

McFadden, D. (1989). A method of simulated moments for estimation of discrete response models without numerical integration. *Econometrica* **57**(5), 995–1026.

Melino, A. (1982). Testing for sample selection bias. *Review of Economic Studies* **49**(1), 151–153.

Milliken, G. A. & Albohali, M. (1984). On necessary and sufficient conditions for ordinary least squares to be best linear unbiased estimators. *The American Statistician* **38**(4), 298–299.

Mincer, J. (1974). *Schooling, Experience and Earnings*. University Press for the National Bureau of Economic Research, New York.

Mundlak, Y. (1978). On the pooling of time series and cross section data. *Econometrica* **46**(1), 69–85.

Murphy, K. M. & Topel, R. H. (1985). Estimation and inference in two-step econometric models. *Journal of Business and Economic Statistics* **3**(4), 370–379.

Nering, E. D. (1970). *Linear Algebra and Matrix Theory*, 2nd ed. Wiley, New York.

Nerlove, M. (1971). A note on error components models. *Econometrica* **39**(2), 383–396.

Newey, W. K. (1985). Maximum likelihood specification testing and conditional moment tests. *Econometrica* **53**(5), 1047–1072.

Newey, W. K. (1987*a*). Asymptotic properties of one-step estimator obtained from an optimal step size. *Econometric Theory* **3**(2), 305–306.

Newey, W. K. (1987*b*). Specification tests for distributional assumptions in the Tobit model. *Journal of Econometrics* **34**(1/2), 125–145.

Newey, W. K. (1988). Adaptive estimation of regression models via moment restrictions. *Journal of Econometrics* **38**(3), 301–339.

Newey, W. K. (1990). Efficient instrumental variables estimation of nonlinear models. *Econometrica* **58**(4), 809–837.

Newey, W. K. & McFadden, D. L. (1994). Large sample estimation and hypothesis testing. *In* R. F. Engle & D. L. McFadden, eds. *Handbook of Econometrics*, Vol. IV, Chapter 36, pp. 2111–2245. Elsevier Science B.V., Amsterdam.

Newey, W. K. & Powell, J. L. (1987). Asymmetric least squares estimation and testing. *Econometrica* **55**(4), 819–847.

Newey, W. K. & West, K. D. (1987a). Hypothesis testing with efficient method of moments estimation. *International Economic Review* **28**(3), 777–787.

Newey, W. K. & West, K. D. (1987b). A simple, positive semi-definite, heteroskedasticity and autocorrelation consistent covariance matrix. *Econometrica* **55**(3), 703–708.

Neyman, J. (1959). Optimal asymptotic tests of composite statistical hypotheses. *In* U. Grenander, ed. *Probability and Statistics*, Vol. 4, Wiley, New York.

Neyman, J. & Pearson, E. S. (1928). On the use and interpretation of certain test criteria for purposes of statistical inference. *Biometrika A* **20**, 175–240 and 263–294.

Okun, A. M. (1980). Postwar macroeconomic performance. *In* M. S. Feldstein, ed. *The American Economy in Transition,* pp. 162–169. University of Chicago Press, Chicago.

Olsen, R. J. (1978). Note on the uniqueness of the maximum likelihood estimator for the Tobit model. *Econometrica* **46**(5), 1211–1215.

Orme, C. (1989). On the uniqueness of the maximum likelihood estimator in truncated regression models. *Econometric Reviews* **8**(2), 217–222.

Orme, C. & Ruud, P. A. (1998). On the uniqueness of the maximum likelihood estimator for the truncated regression model. Technical report, University of California, Berkeley.

Pagan, A. R. & Nicholls, D. F. (1976). Exact maximum likelihood estimation of regression models with finite order moving average errors. *Review of Economic Studies* **43**(3), 383–387.

Pakes, A. & Pollard, D. (1989). Simulation and the asymptotics of optimization estimators. *Econometrica* **57**(5), 1027–1057.

Pearson, K. (1895). Contributions to the mathematical theory of evolution, I. Skew distribution in homogeneous material. *Philosophical Transactions of the Royal Society of London, Series A* **86**, 343–414.

Phelps, E. S. (1968). Money wage dynamics and labor market equilibrium. *Journal of Political Economy* **76**(4), 678–711.

Phillips, A. W. (1958). The relationship between unemployment and the rate of change in money wages in the United Kingdom, 1861–1957. *Economica* **25**(100), 283–299.

Phillips, P. C. B. (1983). Exact small sample theory in the simultaneous equations model. *In* Z. Griliches & M. D. Intriligator, eds. *Handbook of Econometrics*, Vol. I, Chapter 8. North-Holland, Amsterdam.

Pitman, E. J. G. (1949). Notes on non-parametric statistical inference. Mimeo, Columbia University.

Poirier, D. J., ed. (1994). *The Methodology of Econometrics*. Elgar, Aldershot, U.K.

Poirier, D. J. (1995). *Intermediate Statistics and Econometrics: A Comparative Approach*. MIT Press, Cambridge, MA.

Poirier, D. J. & Ruud, P. A. (1988). Probit with dependent observations. *Review of Economic Studies* **55**(4), 593–614.

Poirier, D. J., Tello, M. & Zin, S. (1986). A diagnostic test for normality within the power exponential family. *Journal of Business and Economic Statistics* **4**(3), 359–373.

Pollock, D. S. G. (1979). *The Algebra of Econometrics*. Wiley, New York.

Porter, R. H. (1983). A study of cartel stability: The Joint Executive Committee, 1880–1886. *Bell Journal of Economics* **14**(2), 301–314.

Powell, J. L. (1984). Least absolute deviations estimation for the censored regression model. *Journal of Econometrics* **25**(3), 303–325.

Powell, J. L. (1986). Symmetrically trimmed least squares estimation for Tobit models. *Econometrica* **54**(6), 1435–1460.

Powell, J. L. (1994). Estimation of semiparametric models. In *Handbook of Econometrics*, Vol. IV, pp. 2443–2521. North-Holland, Amsterdam.

Prais, S. J. & Winsten, C. B. (1954). Trend estimators and serial correlation. Cowles Commission Discussion Paper No. 373, Chicago.

Pratt, J. W. (1981). Concavity of the log likelihood. *Journal of the American Statistical Association* **76**(373), 103–106.

Quandt, R. E. (1983). Computational problems and methods. *In* Z. Griliches & M. D. Intriligator, eds. *Handbook of Econometrics*, Vol. I, Chapter 12. North-Holland, Amsterdam.

Rao, C. R. (1945). Information and accuracy attainable in estimation of statistical parameters. *Bulletin of the Calcutta Mathematical Society* **37**, 81–91.

Rao, C. R. (1947). Large sample tests of statistical hypotheses concerning several parameters with applications to problems of estimation. *Proceedings of the Cambridge Philosophical Society* **44**, 50–57.

Rao, C. R. (1963). Criteria of estimation in large samples. *Sankhyā A* **25**(2), 189–206.

Rao, C. R. (1973). *Linear Statistical Inference and Its Applications*, 2nd ed. Wiley, New York.

Reiersøl, O. (1941). Confluence analysis by means of lag moments and other methods of confluence analysis. *Econometrica* **9**(1), 1–24.

Robinson, P. M. (1982). On the asymptotic properties of estimators of models containing limited dependent variables. *Econometrica* **50**(1), 27–41.

Romer, D. (1996). *Advanced Macroeconomics*. McGraw-Hill, New York.

Rothenberg, T. J. (1971). Identification in parametric models. *Econometrica* **39**(3), 577–591.

Rothenberg, T. J. (1984a). Approximate normality of generalized least squares estimates. *Econometrica* **52**(4), 811–825.

Rothenberg, T. J. (1984b). Approximating the distributions of econometric estimators and test statistics. *In* Z. Griliches & M. D. Intriligator, eds. *Handbook of Econometrics*, Vol. II, Chapter 15. North-Holland, Amsterdam.

Rothenberg, T. J. & Leenders, C. T. (1964). Efficient estimation of simultaneous equation systems. *Econometrica* **32**(1–2), 57–76.

Ruud, P. A. (1984). Tests of specification in econometrics. *Econometric Reviews* **3**(2), 211–242.

Ruud, P. A., & Wald, J. (1999). Rank-ordered multinomial probit. Technical report, University of California, Berkeley.

Samuelson, P. A. & Solow, R. M. (1960). Analytical aspects of anti-inflation policy. *American Economic Review* **50**(2), 177–194.

Sargent, T. J. (1979). *Macroeconomic Theory*. Academic Press, New York.

Sargent, T. J. (1987). *Dynamic Macroeconomic Theory*, 2nd ed. Harvard University Press, Cambridge, MA.

Scheffé, H. (1959). *The Analysis of Variance*. Wiley, New York.

Shephard, R. W. (1953). *Cost and Production Functions*. Princeton University Press, Princeton, NJ.

Silvey, S. D. (1959). The Lagrangian multiplier test. *Annals of Mathematical Statistics* **30**(2), 389–407.

Simon, C. P. & Blume, L. (1994). *Mathematics for Economists*. Norton, New York.

Spencer, D. E. & Berk, K. N. (1981). A limited information specification test. *Econometrica* **49**(4), 1079–1086.

Spivak, M. (1967). *Calculus*. W. A. Benjamin, Menlo Park.

Staiger, D. & Stock, J. H. (1997). Instrumental variables regression with weak instruments. *Econometrica* **65**(3), 557–586.

Staiger, D., Stock, J. H. & Watson, M. W. (1996). How precise are estimates of the natural rate of unemployment? National Bureau of Economic Research Working Paper Series No. 5477, Cambridge, MA.

Staiger, D., Stock, J. H. & Watson, M. W. (1997). The time varying NAIRU and its implications for economic policy. *Journal of Economic Perspectives* **11**(1), 33–49.

Stein, C. (1950). Unbiased estimates of minimum variance. *Annals of Mathematical Statistics* **21**(3), 406–415.

Theil, H. (1953). Repeated least squares applied to complete equation systems. Central Planning Bureau mimeograph, The Hague.

Tobin, J. (1958). Estimation of relationships for limited dependent variables. *Econometrica* **26**(1), 24–36.

Varian, H. R. (1992). *Microeconomic Analysis*, 3rd ed. W. W. Norton, New York.

Wald, A. (1943). Tests of statistical hypotheses concerning several parameters when the number of observations is large. *Transactions of the American Mathematical Society* **54**(3), 426–482.

Wallace, T. D. & Hussain, A. (1969). The use of error components models in combining cross-section with time series data. *Econometrica* **37**(1), 55–72.

White, H. (1980). A heteroskedasticity-consistent covariance matrix estimator and a direct test for heteroskedasticity. *Econometrica* **48**(4), 817–838.

White, H. (1982). Maximum likelihood estimation of misspecified models. *Econometrica* **50**(1), 1–26.

White, H. (1984). *Asymptotic Theory for Econometricians*. Academic Press, Orlando, FL.

Wilks, S. S. (1938). The large-sample distribution of the likelihood ratio for testing composite hypotheses. *Annals of Mathematical Statistics* **9**(1), 60–62.

Wold, H. (1938). *The Analysis of Stationary Time Series*, 1st ed. Almqvist and Wiksell, Uppsala, Sweden.

Wu, D.-M. (1973). Alternative tests of independence between stochastic regressors and disturbances. *Econometrica* **41**(4), 733–750.

Zellner, A. (1962). An efficient method of estimating seemingly unrelated regressions and tests for aggregation bias. *Journal of the American Statistical Association* **57**(298), 348–368.

Index